H...

SPANISH
PAPERBACK
DICTIONARY

English-Spanish Spanish-English

Editor/Redacción
Liam Rodger

with/con
Jane Blanco
Lynda Carey
José A. Gálvez

Latin American Spanish/Español de América
Talia Bugel

Publishing Manager/Dirección editorial
Patrick White

Prepress/Preimpresión
David Reid

HARRAP

First published in Great Britain 2001
by Chambers Harrap Publishers Ltd
7 Hopetoun Crescent, Edinburgh EH7 4AY

© Chambers Harrap Publishers Ltd 2001
Reprinted 2001

ISBN 0245 60692 0

Designed and typeset by Chambers Harrap Publishers Ltd
Printed and bound in Great Britain by
Omnia Books Ltd, Glasgow

Contents/Contenido

Preface

This new edition has been revised and expanded to ensure it remains the most comprehensive and up-to-date dictionary of its size available.

Content has kept pace with changes in language and in the world. In particular, there is excellent coverage of computing terms (including e-mail and the Internet), and improved treatment of Latin American Spanish and US English.

In addition, a number of completely new features add to the effectiveness of the dictionary as a learning tool. We have added false friend boxes to help the user avoid common translation pitfalls, and grammar notes to indicate correct usage. The pronunciation guides have also been rewritten, with special attention given to the problems Spanish speakers encounter in pronouncing English.

Presentation has been improved as well as content. Adverbs and phrasal verbs now have separate entries, and each part of speech within an entry starts on a new line. This makes for a clearer layout of the text, so the book is now even easier to consult.

Prefacio

Esta nueva edición ha sido revisada y ampliada para convertirlo en el diccionario de su tamaño más completo y actualizado que existe.

El contenido refleja los cambios en el lenguaje y en el mundo. En particular, contiene una excelente selección de términos de informática (abarcando el correo electrónico e Internet) y un tratamiento mejorado del español de América y el inglés de Norteamérica.

Además, la utilidad del diccionario como herramienta de aprendizaje ha sido potenciada con varias características nuevas. Hemos añadido cuadros sobre falsos amigos para evitar trampas en las traducciones y notas gramaticales que indican el uso correcto de las palabras. Las guías sobre la pronunciación han sido escritas de nuevo, prestando especial atención a los problemas que los hablantes nativos de español tienen al pronunciar el inglés.

Tanto la presentación como el contenido han sido mejorados. Los adverbios y los phrasal verbs tienen ahora entradas individuales, y cada categoría gramatical comienza en una nueva línea. Esto hace que la presentación del texto sea más clara y que el libro sea todavía más fácil de consultar.

Structure of Entries

> **ceviche** *nm* ▦ raw fish marinated in lemon and garlic

- The equals sign = introduces an explanation when there is no direct translation.

> **inocentada** *nf Fam* ≃ April Fool's joke; **hacer una i. a algn** to play an April Fool's joke on sb

- The sign ≃ introduces a word that has a roughly equivalent status but is not identical.

> **aflojar 1** *vt* to loosen
> **2** *vi (viento etc)* to weaken, to grow weak
> **3 aflojarse** *vpr* to come o work loose; *(rueda)* to go down

- The different grammatical categories are cleary indicated, introduced by a bold Arabic numeral.

> **abrir²** (*pp* **abierto**) **1** *vi* to open
> **2** *vt* (**a**) to open; *(cremallera)* to undo (**b**) *(gas, grifo)* to turn on (**c**) *Jur* **a. (un) expediente** to start proceedings
> **3 abrirse** *vpr* (**a**) to open; *Fig* **a. paso** to make one's way (**b**) *Fam* **¡me abro!** I'm off!

- Usage and field labels are clearly shown.

> **reconocer** [34] *vt* (**a**) to recognize (**b**) *(admitir)* to recognize, to admit (**c**) *Med (paciente)* to examine

- A number before an irregular Spanish verb refers the user to the verb tables in the middle of the book for information on how to conjugate it.

> **bland** [blænd] *adj (food)* soso(a)
>
> 𝄐 Note that the Spanish word **blando** is a false friend and is never a translation for the English word **bland**. In Spanish, **blando** means "soft".

- Usage notes warn the user when a word is a false friend.

> **acodarse** *vpr* to lean (**en on**)

- The most common prepositions used are given after the translation.

> **acústica** *nf* acoustics *sing*

- The number of a translation is indicated where this is ambiguous.

Estructura de las Entradas

> **ceviche** *nm* = raw fish marinated in lemon and garlic

● Cuando no es posible dar una traducción se ofrece una explicación precedida por el signo igual (=).

> **inocentada** *nf Fam* ≃ April Fool's joke; **hacer una i. a algn** to play an April Fool's joke on sb

● El signo ≃ precede a una traducción que tiene un significado aproximado pero no idéntico.

> **aflojar 1** *vt* to loosen
> **2** *vi (viento etc)* to weaken, to grow weak
> **3 aflojarse** *vpr* to come *o* work loose; *(rueda)* to go down

● Las diferentes categorías gramaticales están separadas por un número en negrita.

> **abrir²** *(pp* **abierto)** **1** *vi* to open
> **2** *vt* (**a**) to open; *(cremallera)* to undo (**b**) *(gas, grifo)* to turn on (**c**) *Jur* **a. (un) expediente** to start proceedings
> **3 abrirse** *vpr* (**a**) to open; *Fig* **a. paso** to make one's way (**b**) *Fam* **¡me abro!** I'm off!

● Las marcas de uso y de campo semántico están claramente indicadas.

> **reconocer** [34] *vt o* (**a**) to recognize (**b**) *(admitir)* to recognize, to admit (**c**) *Med (paciente)* to examine

● Los números que aparecen detrás de los verbos irregulares remiten a las tablas verbales que se encuentran en el medio del diccionario.

> **blando,-a** *adj* soft
>
> ✏ Observa que la palabra inglesa **bland** es un falso amigo y no es la traducción de la palabra española **blando**. En inglés, **bland** significa "soso".

● Las notas de uso informan sobre los falsos amigos.

> **acodarse** *vpr* to lean (**en** on)

● Las preposiciones más comunes aparecen después de las traducciones.

> **acústica** *nf* acoustics *sing*

● El número de la traducción aparece en los casos en los que éste es ambiguo.

Abbreviations used in this dictionary
Abreviaturas usadas en este diccionario

abbreviation	*abbr, abr*	abreviatura
adjective	*adj*	adjetivo
adverb	*adv*	adverbio
agriculture	*Agr*	agricultura
somebody, someone	*algn*	alguien
Latin American Spanish	*Am*	español de América
anatomy	*Anat*	anatomía
Andean Spanish (Bolivia, Chile, Colombia, Ecuador, Peru)	*Andes*	español andino (Bolivia, Chile, Colombia, Ecuador, Perú)
approximately	*aprox*	aproximadamente
architecture	*Archit*	arquitectura
Argentinian Spanish	*Arg*	español de Argentina
architecture	*Arquit*	arquitectura
article	*art*	artículo
astronomy	*Astron*	astronomía
Australian	*Austral*	australiano
motoring	*Aut*	automóviles
auxiliary	*aux*	auxiliar
aviation	*Av*	aviación
biology	*Biol*	biología
Bolivian Spanish	*Bol*	español de Bolivia
botany	*Bot*	botánica
British English	*Br*	inglés británico
Central American Spanish	*CAm*	español centroamericano
Canary Islands Spanish	*Can*	español de Canarias
Caribbean Spanish (Cuba, Puerto Rico, Dominican Republic, Venezuela)	*Carib*	español caribeño (Cuba, Puerto Rico, República Dominicana, Venezuela)
chemistry	*Chem*	químico
Chilean Spanish	*Chile*	español de Chile
cinema	*Cin*	cine
Colombian Spanish	*Col*	español de Colombia
commerce	*Com*	comercio
comparative	*comp*	comparativo
computers	*Comput*	informática
conditional	*cond*	condicional
conjunction	*conj*	conjunción
building industry	*Constr*	construcción
sewing	*Cost*	costura
Costa Rican Spanish	*CRica*	español de Costa Rica
Spanish from the Southern Cone region (Argentina, Uruguay, Paraguay, Chile)	*CSur*	español del Cono Sur (Argentina, Uruguay, Paraguay, Chile)
Cuban Spanish	*Cuba*	español de Cuba
cookery	*Culin*	cocina
definite	*def*	definido
defective	*defect*	defectivo
demonstrative	*dem*	demostrativo
sport	*Dep*	deporte
economics	*Econ*	economía
Ecuadorian Spanish	*Ecuad*	español de Ecuador
education	*Educ*	educación
electricity	*Elec*	electricidad
especially	*esp*	especialmente
Peninsular Spanish	*Esp*	español de España
etcetera	*etc*	etcétera
euphemism	*Euph, Euf*	eufemismo
feminine	*f*	femenino
familiar	*Fam*	familiar
pharmacy	*Farm*	farmacia
railways	*Ferroc*	ferrocarriles
figurative use	*Fig*	uso figurado
finance	*Fin*	finanzas

physics	*Fís*	física
formal use	*Fml*	uso formal
photography	*Fot*	fotografía
feminine plural	*fpl*	plural femenino
football	*Ftb*	fútbol
future	*fut*	futuro
geography	*Geog*	geografía
geology	*Geol*	geología
geometry	*Geom*	geometría
present participle	*ger*	gerundio
Guatemalan Spanish	*Guat*	español de Guatemala
history	*Hist*	historia
humorous	*Hum*	humorístico
imperative	*imperat*	imperativo
imperfect	*imperf*	imperfecto
impersonal	*impers*	impersonal
printing	*Impr*	imprenta
industry	*Ind*	industria
indefinite	*indef*	indefinido
indeterminate	*indet*	indeterminado
indicative	*indic*	indicativo
infinitive	*infin*	infinitivo
computers	*Informát*	informática
insurance	*Ins*	seguros
interjection	*interj*	interjección
interrogative	*interr*	interrogativo
invariable	*inv*	invariable
ironic	*Irón*	irónico
law	*Jur*	derecho
linguistics	*Ling*	lingüística
literature	*Lit*	literatura
phrase	*loc*	locución
masculine	*m*	masculino
mathematics	*Math, Mat*	matemáticas
medicine	*Med*	medicina
meteorology	*Met*	meteorología
Mexican Spanish	*Méx*	español de México
military	*Mil*	militar
mining	*Min*	minas
masculine plural	*mpl*	plural masculino
music	*Mus, Mús*	música
noun	*n*	nombre
nautical	*Naut, Náut*	náutica
neuter	*neut*	neutro
feminine noun	*nf*	nombre femenino
plural feminine noun	*nfpl*	nombre femenino plural
masculine noun	*nm*	nombre masculino
masculine and feminine noun	*nmf/nm,f*	nombre masculino y femenino
plural masculine noun	*nmpl*	nombre masculino plural
plural noun	*npl*	nombre plural
optics	*Opt*	óptica
ornithology	*Orn*	ornitología
Panamanian Spanish	*Pan*	español de Panamá
Paraguayan Spanish	*Par*	español de Paraguay
pejorative	*Pej*	peyorativo
personal	*pers*	personal
Peruvian Spanish	*Perú*	español de Perú
pejorative	*Pey*	peyorativo
pharmacy	*Pharm*	farmacia
photography	*Phot*	fotografía
physics	*Phys*	física
plural	*pl*	plural
politics	*Pol*	política
possessive	*pos, poss*	posesivo
past participle	*pp*	participio pasado
prefix	*pref*	prefijo
preposition	*prep*	preposición
present	*pres*	presente
present participle	*pres p*	gerundio

Abbreviations/Abreviaturas

Puerto Rican Spanish	*PRico*	español de Puerto Rico
pronoun	*pron*	pronombre
psychology	*Psi, Psy*	psicología
past tense	*pt*	pretérito
chemistry	*Quím*	químico
radio	*Rad*	radio
railways	*Rail*	ferrocarriles
relative	*rel*	relativo
religion	*Rel*	religión
Spanish from the River Plate region (Argentina, Uruguay, Paraguay)	*RP*	español de los países ribereños del Río de la Plata
somebody, someone	*sb*	alguien
Scottish	*Scot*	escocés
insurance	*Seg*	seguros
singular	*sing*	singular
something	*sth*	algo
subjunctive	*subj*	subjuntivo
superlative	*superl*	superlativo
bullfighting	*Taurom*	tauromaquia
technical	*Tech, Téc*	técnica
telephones	*Tel*	teléfonos
textiles	*Tex*	textiles
theatre	*Th*	teatro
television	*TV*	televisión
typography	*Typ*	tipografía
university	*Univ*	universidad
Uruguayan Spanish	*Urug*	español de Uruguay
American English	*US*	inglés norteamericano
usually	*usu*	usualmente
verb	*v*	verbo
auxiliary verb	*v aux*	verbo auxiliar
Venezuelan Spanish	*Ven*	español de Venezuela
intransitive verb	*vi*	verbo intransitivo
impersonal verb	*v impers*	verbo impersonal
reflexive verb	*vpr*	verbo pronominal
transitive verb	*vt*	verbo transitivo
vulgar	*Vulg*	vulgar
zoology	*Zool*	zoología
cultural equivalent	≃	equivalente cultural
registered trademark	®	marca registrada

Spanish Pronunciation Guide

The pronunciation of most Spanish words is predictable as there is a close match between spelling and pronunciation. The table below gives an explanation of that pronunciation. In the dictionary text therefore, pronunciation is only given when the word does not follow these rules, usually because it is a word of foreign origin. In these cases, the IPA (International Phonetic Alphabet) is used (see column 2 of the table below).

Letter in Spanish	IPA Symbol	Example in Spanish	Pronunciation (example in English)
Vowels			
Note that all vowel sounds in Spanish are shorter than in English			
a	a	**a**la	Similar to the sound in "f**a**ther" but more central
e	e	**e**có	Similar to the sound in "m**e**t"
i	i	**i**ris	Like the vowel sound in "m**ea**t" but much shorter
o	o	**o**so	**o**ff, **o**n
u	u	**u**va	Like the vowel sound in "s**oo**n" but much shorter
Semiconsonants			
"i" in the diphthongs: ia, ie, io, iu	j	h**i**ato, h**i**elo, av**i**ón, v**i**uda	**y**es
"u" in the diphthongs: ua, ue, ui, uo	w	s**u**ave, f**u**ego, h**u**ida	**w**in
Consonants			
b	b	**b**om**b**a (at beginning of word or after m)	**b**oom
	β	a**b**ajo (all other contexts)	A "**b**" pronounced without quite closing the lips completely
c	θ (in Spain)	**c**eña (before e) **c**inco (before i)	**th**anks (in Spain)
	s (in Latin America and southern Spain)		**s**un (in Latin America and southern Spain)
	k	**c**asa (all other contexts)	**c**at
ch	tʃ	cau**ch**o	ar**ch**

Spanish Pronunciation Guide

Letter in Spanish	IPA Symbol	Example in Spanish	Pronunciation (example in English)
d	d	**d**onde (at beginning of word or after n) al**d**ea (after l)	**d**ay
	ð	a**d**orno (all other contexts)	Similar to the sound in "mo**th**er" but less strong
f	f	**f**uria	**f**ire
g	χ	**g**ema (before e) **g**irasol (before i)	Like an "**h**" but pronounced at the back of the throat (similar to Scottish "lo**ch**")
	g	**g**ato (at beginning of word) len**g**ua (after n)	**g**oose
	ɣ	a**g**ua (all other contexts)	Like a "**w**" pronounced while trying to say "**g**"
j	χ	**j**abalí	Like an "**h**" but pronounced at the back of the throat (similar to Scottish "lo**ch**")
l	l	**l**ado	**l**ake
ll	j	**ll**uvia	mi**lli**on
	ʒ		In some regions (eg the Rio de la Plata area of South America) it is pronounced like the "**s**" in "plea**s**ure"
m	m	**m**ano	**m**an
n	n	**n**ulo	**n**o
	ŋ	ma**n**co, fa**n**go (before c and g)	parki**ng**
ñ	ŋ	a**ñ**o	onio**n**
p	p	**p**a**p**a	**p**ool
r	r	do**r**ado (in between vowels) habla**r** (at end of syllable or word)	A rolled "**r**" sound (similar to Scottish "**r**")
	ɾ	**r**osa (at beginning of word) al**r**ededor (after l) en**r**edo (after n)	A much longer rolled "**r**" sound (similar to Scottish "**r**")
rr	ɾ	a**rr**oyo	A much longer rolled "**r**" sound (similar to Scottish "**r**")
s	s	**s**aco	**s**ound
sh	ʃ	**sh**ow	**sh**ow
t	t	**t**ela	**t**ea

Letter in Spanish	IPA Symbol	Example in Spanish	Pronunciation (example in English)
v	b	invierno (after "n")	**b**oom
	β	a**v**e (all other contexts)	A "**b**" pronounced without quite closing the lips completely
x	ks	e**x**amen	e**x**tra
y	j	a**y**er	**y**
	ʒ		In some regions (eg the Rio de la Plata area of South America) it is pronounced like the "**s**" in "plea**s**ure"
z	θ (in Spain)	**z**apato	**th**anks (in Spain)
	s (in Latin America and southern Spain)		**s**un (in Latin America and southern Spain)

Pronunciación del Inglés

Para ilustrar la pronunciación inglesa, en este diccionario utilizamos los símbolos del AFI (Alfabeto Fonético Internacional). En el siguiente cuadro, para cada sonido del inglés hay ejemplos de palabras en inglés y palabras en español donde aparece un sonido similar. En los casos en los que no hay sonido similar en español, ofrecemos una explicación de cómo pronunciar.

Carácter AFI	Ejemplo en inglés	Ejemplo en español
Consonantes		
[b]	**b**abb**l**e	**b**ebé
[d]	**d**ig	**d**edo
[dʒ]	**g**iant, **j**ig	se pronuncia como [ʒ] en "plea**s**ure" pero con una "**d**" adelante, o como "**gi**" en italiano - **Gi**ovanna
[f]	**f**it, **ph**ysics	**f**aro
[g]	**g**rey, bi**g**	**g**ris
[h]	**h**appy	"**h**" aspirada
[j]	**y**ellow	se pronuncia como "**y**" o "**ll**" en España - **y**o, **ll**uvia
[k]	**c**lay, **k**ick	**c**asa
[l]	**l**ip	**l**abio
	pi**ll**	pape**l**
[m]	**m**u**mm**y	**m**a**m**á
[n]	**n**ip, pi**n**	**n**ada
[ŋ]	si**ng**	se pronuncia como "**n**" antes de "**c**" - ba**n**co
[p]	**p**i**p**	**p**a**p**á
[r]	**r**ig, w**r**ite	sonido entre "**r**" y "**rr**"
[s]	**s**ick, **sc**ience	**s**apo
[ʃ]	**sh**ip, na**ti**on	**sh**ow
[t]	**t**ip, bu**tt**	**t**ela
[tʃ]	**ch**ip, ba**tch**	cau**ch**o
[θ]	**th**ick	**z**apato (como se pronuncia en España)
[ð]	**th**is	se pronuncia como la "**d**" de "ha**d**a" pero más fuerte
[v]	**v**ague, gi**v**e	se pronuncia como "**v**" de **v**ida, con los dientes apoyados sobre el labio inferior

Carácter AFI	Ejemplo en inglés	Ejemplo en español
[w]	**w**it, **w**hy	**wh**isky
[z]	**z**ip, phy**s**ics	"**s**" con sonido zumbante
[ʒ]	plea**s**ure	se pronuncia como "**y**" o "**ll**" en el Río de la Plata - **y**o, **ll**uvia
[χ]	lo**ch**	**j**ota

Vocales

En inglés, las vocales marcadas con dos puntos son mucho más alargadas

[æ]	r**a**g	se pronuncia "**a**" con posición bucal para "**e**"
[ɑː]	l**a**rge, b**a**th	"**a**" muy alargada
[ʌ]	c**u**p	"**a**" breve y cerrada
[e]	s**e**t	se pronuncia como "**e**" de **e**lefante pero más corta
[ɜː]	c**ur**tain, w**e**re	se pronuncia como una "**e**" larga con posición bucal entre "**o**" y "**e**"
[ə]	**u**tter	se pronuncia como "**e**" con posición bucal para "**o**"
[ɪ]	b**i**g, w**o**men	"**i**" breve, a medio camino entre "**e**" e "**i**"
[iː]	l**ea**k, w**ee**	"**i**" muy alargada
[ɒ]	l**o**ck	"**o**" abierta
[ɔː]	w**a**ll, c**o**rk	"**o**" cerrada y alargada
[ʊ]	p**u**t, l**oo**k	"**u**" breve
[uː]	m**oo**n	"**u**" muy alargada

Diptongos

[aɪ]	wh**y**, h**igh**, l**ie**	**ai**re
[aʊ]	h**ow**	**au**ra
[eə]	b**ear**	"**ea**" pronunciado muy brevemente y con sonido de "**e**" más marcado que el de "**a**"
[eɪ]	d**ay**, m**a**ke, m**ai**n	r**ei**na
[əʊ]	sh**ow**, g**o**	"**ou**" como en COU
[ɪə]	h**ere**, g**ear**	h**ie**lo pronunciedo con el sonido de "**i**" más marcado y alargado que el de "**e**"
[ɔɪ]	b**oy**, s**oi**l	v**oy**
[ʊə]	p**oor**	c**ue**rno pronunciado con el sonido de "**u**" más marcado y alargado que el de "**e**"

Spanish – English

Español – Inglés

A, a [a] *nf (la letra)* A, a

a *(abr* **área***)* area

a *prep*

> **a** combines with the article **el** to form the contraction **al** (e.g. **al centro** to the centre).

(**a**) *(dirección)* to; **ir a Colombia** to go to Colombia; **llegar a Valencia** to arrive in Valencia; **subir al tren** to get on the train; **ir al cine** to go to the cinema; **vete a casa** go home

(**b**) *(lugar)* at, on; **a la derecha** on the right; **a la entrada** at the entrance; **a lo lejos** in the distance; **a mi lado** at *o* by my side, next to me; **al sol** in the sun; **a la mesa** at (the) table

(**c**) *(tiempo)* at; **a las doce** at twelve o'clock; **a los sesenta años** at the age of sixty; **a los tres meses/la media hora** three months/half an hour later; **al final** in the end; **al principio** at first

(**d**) *(distancia)* away; **a 100 km de aquí** 100 km from here

(**e**) *(manera)* **a la inglesa** (in the) English fashion *o* manner *o* style; **escrito a máquina** typed, typewritten; **a mano** by hand

(**f**) *(proporción)* **a 90 km por hora** at 90 km an hour; **a 300 pesetas el kilo** 300 pesetas a kilo; **tres veces a la semana** three times a week

(**g**) *Dep* **ganar cuatro a dos** to win four (to) two

(**h**) *(complemento indirecto)* to; *(procedencia)* from; **díselo a Javier** tell Javier; **te lo di a ti** I gave it to you; **comprarle algo a algn** to buy sth from sb; *(para algn)* to buy sth for sb; *(complemento directo de persona)* **saludé a tu tía** I said hello to your aunt

(**i**) *Fam* **ir a por algn/algo** to go and fetch sb/ sth

(**j**) *(verbo + a + infin)* to; **aprender a nadar** to learn (how) to swim; **fueron a ayudarle** they went to help him

(**k**) *(nombre + a + infin)* **distancia a recorrer** distance to be covered

(**l**) **a decir verdad** to tell (you) the truth; **a no ser por ...** if it were not for ...; **a no ser que** unless; **a ver** let's see; **¡a comer!** lunch/dinner/ *etc* is ready!; **¡a dormir!** bedtime!; **¿a que no lo haces?** *(desafío)* I bet you don't do it!

abad *nm* abbot

abadía *nf* abbey

abajeño,-a *nm,f Am* lowlander

abajo 1 *adv* (**a**) *(en una casa)* downstairs; **el piso de a.** the downstairs flat (**b**) *(dirección)* down, downwards; **ahí/aquí a.** down there/ here; **la parte de a.** the bottom (part); **más a.** further down; **hacia a.** down, downwards; **calle a.** down the street; **echar algo a.** to knock sth down; **venirse a.** *(edificio)* to fall down; *Fig (proyecto)* to fall through

2 *interj* **¡a. la censura!** down with censorship!

abalanzarse [40] *vpr* **a. sobre/contra** to rush towards

abalear *vt Andes, CAm, Ven* to shoot at

abalorio *nm* (**a**) *(cuenta)* glass bead (**b**) *(baratija)* trinket

abanderado,-a *nm,f* standard bearer

abandonado,-a *adj* (**a**) abandoned; **tiene a su familia muy abandonada** he takes absolutely no interest in his family (**b**) *(desaseado)* untidy, unkempt

abandonar 1 *vt* (**a**) *(lugar)* to leave, to quit; *(persona, cosa)* to abandon; *(proyecto, plan)* to give up (**b**) *Dep (carrera)* to drop out of

2 abandonarse *vpr* to let oneself go

abandono *nm* (**a**) *(acción)* abandoning, desertion (**b**) *(de proyecto, idea)* giving up (**c**) *(descuido)* neglect

abanicarse *vpr* to fan oneself

abanico *nm* (**a**) fan (**b**) *(gama)* range; **un amplio a. de posibilidades** a wide range of possibilities

abaratar 1 *vt* to cut *o* reduce the price of

2 abaratarse *vpr (artículos)* to become cheaper, to come down in price; *(precios)* to come down

abarcar [44] *vt (incluir)* to cover

abarrotado,-a *adj* packed, crammed (**de** with)

abarrotar *vt* to pack, to cram (**de** with); **el público abarrotaba la sala** the room was packed (with people)

abarrote *nm Andes, CAm, Méx* grocer's (shop), grocery store; **abarrotes** groceries; **tienda de abarrotes** grocer's (shop), grocery store

abarrotería *nf Andes, CAm, Méx* grocer's (shop), grocery store

abarrotero,-a *nm,f Andes, CAm, Méx* grocer

abastecedor,-a *nm,f* supplier

abastecer [33] **1** *vt* to supply

2 abastecerse *vpr* **a. de** to be supplied with

abastecimiento *nm* supplying; **a. de agua** water supply

abasto *nm* (a) *Fam* **no doy a.** I can't cope, I can't keep up (b) **mercado de abastos** wholesale food market

abatible *adj* folding, collapsible; **asiento a.** reclining seat

abatido,-a *adj* downcast

abatir 1 *vt* (a) *(derribar)* to knock down, to pull down (b) *(matar)* to kill; **a. a tiros** to shoot down (c) *(desanimar)* to depress, to dishearten

2 abatirse *upr (desanimarse)* to lose heart, to become depressed

abdicación *nf* abdication

abdicar [44] *vt & vi* to abdicate

abdomen *nm* abdomen

abdominales *nmpl* sit-ups

abecedario *nm* alphabet

abedul *nm* birch

abeja *nf* bee; **a. reina** queen bee

abejorro *nm* bumblebee

aberración *nf* aberration

aberrante *adj* deviant

abertura *nf (hueco)* opening, gap; *(grieta)* crack, slit

abertzale *adj & nmf* Basque nationalist

abeto *nm Bot* fir (tree); **a. rojo** spruce

abierto,-a *adj* (a) open; *(grifo)* (turned) on; **a. de par en par** wide open (b) *(persona)* open-minded

abigarrado,-a *adj (mezclado)* jumbled, mixed up

abismal *adj* abysmal; *Fig* **una diferencia a.** a world of a difference

abismo *nm* abyss; *Fig* **al borde del a.** on the brink of ruin; *Fig* **entre ellos media un a.** they are worlds apart

ablandar 1 *vt* to soften

2 ablandarse *upr* (a) to soften, to go soft (b) *Fig (persona)* to mellow

abnegación *nf* abnegation, self-denial

abnegado,-a *adj* selfless, self-sacrificing

abocado,-a *adj* (a) **está a. al fracaso** it is doomed to failure (b) *(vino)* medium dry

abochornar *vt* to shame, to embarrass

abofetear *vt* to slap

abogacía *nf* legal profession

abogado,-a *nm,f* lawyer, solicitor; *(en tribunal supremo)* lawyer, *Br* barrister; **a. de oficio** legal aid lawyer; **a. defensor** counsel for the defense; **a. del diablo** devil's advocate; **a. laboralista** union lawyer

abogar [42] *vt* to plead; **a. a favor de** to plead for, to defend; **a. por algo** to advocate *o* champion sth

abolengo *nm* ancestry, lineage

abolición *nf* abolition

abolir *vt defect* to abolish

abolladura *nf* dent

abollar *vt* to dent

abominable *adj* abominable

abominar *vt & vi* **a. (de)** to abominate, to loathe

abonado,-a 1 *nm,f* subscriber

2 *adj Fin (pagado)* paid; **a. en cuenta** credited

abonar 1 *vt* (a) *Agr* to fertilize (b) *(pagar)* to pay (for) (c) *(subscribir)* to subscribe

2 abonarse *upr* to subscribe (**a** to)

abonero,-a *nm,f Méx* hawker, street trader

abono *nm* (a) *Agr (producto)* fertilizer; *(estiércol)* manure (b) *(pago)* payment (c) *(a revista etc)* subscription; *(billete)* season ticket (d) *Méx (plazo)* instalment; **pagar en abonos** to pay by instalments

abordar *vt (persona)* to approach; *(barco)* to board; **a. un asunto** to tackle a subject

aborigen *(pl* **aborígenes) 1** *adj* native, indigenous; *esp Austral* aboriginal

2 *nmf* native; *esp Austral* aborigine

aborrecer [33] *vt* to detest, to loathe

abortar 1 *vi (involuntariamente)* to miscarry, to have a miscarriage; *(intencionadamente)* to abort, to have an abortion

2 *vt* to abort

abortista *nmf* abortionist

aborto *nm* miscarriage; *(provocado)* abortion

abotargado,-a *adj* swollen

abotonar *vt (ropa)* to button (up)

abovedado,-a *adj* vaulted, arched

abracadabra *nm* abracadabra

abrasador,-a *adj* scorching

abrasar 1 *vt & vi* to scorch

2 abrasarse *upr* to burn

abrazadera *nf* clamp

abrazar [40] **1** *vt* to embrace, to hug; *Fig (doctrina)* to embrace

2 abrazarse *upr* **a. a algn** to embrace sb; **se abrazaron** they embraced each other

abrazo *nm* embrace, hug; **un a., abrazos** *(en carta)* best wishes

abrecartas *nm inv* letter-opener, paperknife

abrefácil *nm Com* **caja con a.** easy-open carton

abrelatas *nm inv* tin-opener, *US* can opener

abreviar [43] **1** (a) *vt (acortar)* to shorten; *(texto)* to abridge; *(palabra)* to abbreviate

2 *vi* to be quick *o* brief; **para a.** to cut a long story short

abreviatura *nf* abbreviation

abridor *nm (de latas, botellas)* opener

abrigado,-a *adj* wrapped-up; **ir muy a.** to be well wrapped-up

abrigar [42] *vt* (a) to keep warm; **esta chaqueta abriga mucho** this cardigan is very warm (b) *(proteger)* to protect, to shelter (c) *(esperanza)* to cherish; *(duda)* to have, to harbour

abrigo *nm* (a) *(prenda)* coat, overcoat; **ropa de a.** warm clothes (b) **al a. de** protected *o* sheltered from

abril *nm* April

abrillantador *nm* polish

abrillantar *vt* to polish

abrir¹ *nm* **en un a. y cerrar de ojos** in the twinkling of an eye

abrir² (*pp* **abierto**) **1** *vi* to open

2 *vt* (**a**) to open; (*cremallera*) to undo (**b**) (*gas, grifo*) to turn on (**c**) *Jur* **a. (un) expediente** to start proceedings

3 abrirse *vpr* (**a**) to open; *Fig* **a. paso** to make one's way (**b**) *Fam* **¡me abro!** I'm off!

abrochar *vt*, **abrocharse** *vpr* (*botones*) to do up; (*camisa*) to button (up); (*cinturón*) to fasten; (*zapatos*) to tie up; (*cremallera*) to do up

abrumado,-a *adj* overwhelmed

abrumador,-a *adj* overwhelming

abrumar *vt* to overwhelm, to crush; **tantos problemas me abruman** all these problems are getting on top of me

abrupto,-a *adj* (**a**) (*terreno*) steep, abrupt (**b**) *Fig* abrupt, sudden

absceso *nm* abscess

absentismo *nm* absenteeism; **a. laboral** absenteeism from work

absolución *nf* (**a**) *Rel* absolution (**b**) *Jur* acquittal

absolutamente *adv* absolutely, completely; **a. nada** nothing at all

absoluto,-a *adj* absolute; **en a.** not at all, by no means

absolutorio,-a *adj Jur* **sentencia absolutoria** verdict of not guilty

absolver [4] (*pp* **absuelto**) *vt* (**a**) *Rel* to absolve (**b**) *Jur* to acquit

absorbente *adj* (**a**) (*papel*) absorbent (**b**) *Fig* absorbing, engrossing

absorber *vt* to absorb

absorción *nf* absorption

absorto,-a *adj* absorbed, engrossed (**en** in)

abstemio,-a 1 *adj* teetotal, abstemious

2 *nm,f* teetotaller

abstención *nf* abstention

abstenerse [24] *vpr* to abstain (**de** from); (*privarse*) to refrain (**de** from)

abstinencia *nf* abstinence; **síndrome de a.** withdrawal symptoms

abstracción *nf* abstraction

abstracto,-a *adj* abstract

abstraer [25] **1** *vt* to abstract

2 abstraerse *vpr* to become lost in thought

abstraído,-a *adj* (*ensimismado*) absorbed, engrossed (**en** in); (*distraído*) absent-minded

absuelto,-a *pp de* **absolver**

absurdo,-a 1 *adj* absurd

2 *nm* absurdity, absurd thing

abuchear *vt* to boo, to jeer at

abucheo *nm* booing, jeering

abuela *nf* grandmother; *Fam* grandma, granny; *Fig* old woman

abuelo *nm* (**a**) grandfather; *Fam* grandad, grandpa; *Fig* old man (**b**) **abuelos** grandparents

abulense 1 *adj* of/from Avila

2 *nmf* person from Avila

abulia *nf* apathy, lack of willpower

abultado,-a *adj* bulky, big

abultar 1 *vi* to be bulky; **abulta mucho** it takes up a lot of space

2 *vt* to exaggerate

abundancia *nf* abundance, plenty; *Fig* **nadar en la a.** to be rolling in money

abundante *adj* abundant, plentiful

abundar *vi* to abound, to be plentiful

abur *interj Fam* cheerio!, see you!

aburrido,-a *adj* (**a**) **ser a.** to be boring (**b**) **estar a.** to be bored; **estar a. de** (*harto*) to be tired of

aburrimiento *nm* boredom; **¡qué a.!** how boring!, what a bore!

aburrir 1 *vt* to bore

2 aburrirse *vpr* to get bored; **a. como una ostra** to be bored stiff

abusado,-a *adj Méx* astute, shrewd

abusar *vi* (*propasarse*) to go too far (**b**) **a. de** (*situación, persona*) to take (unfair) advantage of; (*poder, amabilidad*) to abuse; **a. de la bebida/del tabaco** to drink/smoke too much *o* to excess; *Jur* **a. de un niño/una mujer** to abuse a child/woman

abusivo,-a *adj* (*precio*) exorbitant

abuso *nm* abuse

abyecto,-a *adj* abject

a. C. (*abr* **antes de Cristo**) BC

a/c *Com* (*abr* **a cuenta**) on account

acá *adv* (**a**) (*lugar*) here, over here; **más a.** nearer; **¡ven a.!** come here! (**b**) **de entonces a.** since then

acabado,-a 1 *adj* (**a**) (*terminado*) finished (**b**) *Fig* (*persona*) worn-out, spent

2 *nm* finish

acabar 1 *vt* to finish (off); (*completar*) to complete

2 *vi* (**a**) to finish, to end; **a. bien** to have a happy ending; **a. con algo** (*terminarlo*) to finish sth; (*romperlo*) to break sth (**b**) **a. de ...** to have just ...; **acaba de entrar** he has just come in; **no acaba de convencerme** I'm not quite convinced (**c**) **acabaron casándose** *o* **por casarse** they ended up getting married; **acabó en la cárcel** he ended up in jail

3 acabarse *vpr* to finish, to come to an end; **se nos acabó la gasolina** we ran out of *Br* petrol *o US* gas; *Fam* **¡se acabó!** that's that!

acabóse *nm Fam* **esto es el a.** this is the end

acacia *nf* acacia

academia *nf* academy; **a. de idiomas** language school

académico,-a *adj & nm,f* academic

acaecer [33] *v impers* to happen, to occur

acallar *vt* to silence

acalorado,-a *adj* (**a**) hot (**b**) *Fig* (*excitado*) worked up, excited; (*debate etc*) heated, angry

acalorarse *vpr* (**a**) to get warm *o* hot (**b**) *Fig* to get excited *o* worked up

acampada nf camping; **ir de a.** to go camping; **zona de a.** camp site, US campground

acampanado,-a adj bell-shaped; (prendas) flared

acampar vi to camp

acantilado nm cliff

acantonar vt (tropas) to billet, to quarter (en in)

acaparar vt (a) (productos) to hoard; (el mercado) to corner (b) Fig to monopolize

acápite nm Am (párrafo) paragraph

acaramelado,-a adj (a) (color) caramel-coloured (b) (pareja) lovey-dovey, starry-eyed

acariciar [43] vt to caress; (pelo, animal) to stroke; (esperanza) to cherish

acarrear vt (a) (transportar) to carry, to transport (b) Fig (conllevar) to entail

acaso adv perhaps, maybe; **¿a. no te lo dije?** did I not tell you, by any chance?; **por si a.** just in case; **si a. viene ...** if he should come ...

acatamiento nm respect; (de la ley) observance

acatar vt to observe, to comply with

acatarrado,-a adj **estar a.** to have a cold

acatarrarse upr to catch a cold

acaudalado,-a adj rich, wealthy

acaudalar vt to accumulate, to amass

acaudillar vt to lead

acceder vi **a. a** (consentir) to accede to, to consent to; (tener acceso) to gain admittance to; Informát to access

accesible adj accessible; (persona) approachable

acceso nm (a) (entrada) access, entry; Informát **a. al azar, a. directo** random access; Univ **prueba de a.** entrance examination; **a. a Internet** Internet access (b) (carretera) approach, access (c) Med & Fig fit

accesorio,-a adj & nm accessory

accidentado,-a 1 adj (terreno) uneven, hilly; (viaje, vida) eventful
2 nm,f casualty, accident victim

accidental adj accidental; **un encuentro a.** a chance meeting

accidente nm (a) accident; **por a.** by chance; **a. laboral** industrial accident (b) Geog **accidentes geográficos** geographical features

acción nf (a) action; (acto) act; **poner en a.** to put into action; **ponerse en a.** to go into action; **campo de a.** field of action; **película de a.** adventure film (b) Fin share

accionar vt to drive

accionista nmf shareholder

acebo nm (hoja) holly; (árbol) holly tree

acechar vt to lie in wait for; **un grave peligro nos acecha** great danger awaits us

acecho nm **estar al a. de** (esperar) to lie in wait for

acedía nf (pez) dab

aceite nm oil; **a. de girasol/maíz/oliva** sunflower/corn/olive oil

aceitera nf (a) Culin oil bottle; **aceiteras** oil and vinegar set (b) Aut oil can

aceitero,-a 1 adj oil
2 nm,f oil merchant

aceitoso,-a adj oily

aceituna nf olive; **a. rellena** stuffed olive

aceitunado,-a adj olive, olive-coloured

aceitunero,-a nm,f (a) (recolector) olive picker o harvester (b) (vendedor) olive seller

acelerado,-a adj accelerated, fast

acelerador nm Aut accelerator

acelerar vt to accelerate

acento nm (a) accent; (de palabra) stress (b) (énfasis) stress, emphasis

acentuar [30] **1** vt (a) to stress (b) Fig to emphasize, to stress
2 acentuarse upr Fig to become more pronounced o noticeable

aceña nf watermill

acepción nf meaning, sense

aceptable adj acceptable

aceptación nf (a) acceptance (b) **tener poca a.** to have little success, not to be popular

aceptar vt to accept

acequia nf irrigation ditch o channel

acera nf Br pavement, US sidewalk; Fam Pey **ser de la a. de enfrente** to be gay o queer

acerado nm pavement

acerbo,-a adj harsh, bitter

acerca adv **a. de** about

acercamiento nm bringing together, coming together; Pol rapprochement

acercar [44] **1** vt to bring near o nearer, to bring (over); Fig to bring together; **¿te acerco a casa?** can I give you a lift home?
2 acercarse upr (a) **acercarse (a)** to approach (b) (ir) to go; (venir) to come

acerico nm pincushion

acero nm steel; **a. inoxidable** stainless steel

acérrimo,-a adj (partidario) staunch; (enemigo) bitter

acertado,-a adj (a) (solución) right, correct; (decisión) wise (b) **no estuviste muy a. al decir eso** it wasn't very wise of you to say that

acertante 1 nmf winner
2 adj winning

acertar [1] **1** vt (pregunta) to get right; (adivinar) to guess correctly; **a. las quinielas** to win the pools
2 vi to be right; **acertó con la calle que buscaba** she found the street she was looking for

acertijo nm riddle

acervo nm **a. cultural** cultural tradition o heritage

achacar [44] vt (atribuir) to attribute

achacoso,-a adj ailing, unwell

achaque nm ailment, complaint

achicar [44] **1** vt (a) (amilanar) to intimidate (b) (encoger) to reduce, to make smaller (c) (barco) to bale out
2 achicarse upr (a) (amilanarse) to lose heart (b) (encogerse) to get smaller

achicharrar *vt* to burn to a crisp

achicoria *nf* chicory

achinado,-a *adj* (a) *(ojos)* slanting (b) *Am* Indian-looking

acholado,-a *adj Andes Pey* half-caste

achuchar *vt (empujar)* to shove

achuchón *nm (empujón)* push, shove

aciago,-a *adj* ill-fated, fateful

acicalado,-a *adj* well-dressed, smart

acicalarse *vpr* to dress up, to smarten up

acicate *nm Fig (aliciente)* spur, incentive

acidez *nf (de sabor)* sharpness, sourness; *Quím* acidity; *Med* **a. de estómago** heartburn

ácido,-a 1 *adj (sabor)* sharp, tart; *Quím* acidic; *Fig (tono)* harsh
  2 *nm Quím* acid

acierto *nm (buena decisión)* good choice *o* idea; **con gran a.** very wisely

aclamación *nf* acclamation, acclaim

aclamar *vt* to acclaim

aclaración *nf* explanation

aclarado *nm* rinsing, rinse

aclarar 1 *vt* (a) *(explicar)* to clarify, to explain; *(color)* to lighten, to make lighter (b) *(enjuagar)* to rinse
  2 *v impers Met* to clear (up)
  3 aclararse *vpr* (a) *(decidirse)* to make up one's mind; *(entender)* to understand (b) *Met* to clear (up)

aclaratorio,-a *adj* explanatory

aclimatación *nf Br* acclimatization, *US* acclimation

aclimatar 1 *vt Br* to acclimatize, *US* to acclimate (**a** to)
  2 aclimatarse *vpr Fig* **a. a algo** to get used to sth

acné *nf* acne

acobardar 1 *vt* to frighten
  2 acobardarse *vpr* to get frightened, to lose one's nerve

acodarse *vpr* to lean (**en** on)

acogedor,-a *adj* cosy, warm

acoger [53] **1** *vt* (a) *(recibir)* to receive; *(a invitado)* to welcome (b) *(persona desvalida)* to take in
  2 acogerse *vpr Fig* **a. a** to take refuge in; *(amnistía)* to avail oneself of; **a. a la ley** to have recourse to the law

acogida *nf* reception, welcome

acojonado,-a *adj muy Fam* shit-scared

acojonante *adj muy Fam* damn *o Br* bloody great *o* terrific

acojonarse *vpr muy Fam (acobardarse)* to shit oneself, to be shit-scared

acolchar *vt (rellenar)* to pad; *(prenda)* to quilt

acometer *vt* (a) *(emprender)* to undertake (b) *(atacar)* to attack

acometida *nf (ataque)* attack; *(de gas etc)* connection

acomodado,-a *adj* well-off, well-to-do

acomodador,-a *nm,f (hombre)* usher; *(mujer)* usherette

acomodar 1 *vt* (a) *(alojar)* to lodge, to accommodate (b) *(en cine etc)* to find a place for
  2 acomodarse *vpr* (a) to make oneself comfortable (b) *(adaptarse)* to adapt

acomodaticio,-a *adj* (a) accommodating, easy-going (b) *Pey* pliable

acompañante 1 *nmf* companion
  2 *adj* accompanying

acompañar *vt* (a) to accompany; **le acompañó hasta la puerta** she saw him to the door; **me acompañó al médico** he came with me to see the doctor; **¿te acompaño a casa?** can I walk you home?; *Fml* **le acompaño en el sentimiento** my condolences (b) *(adjuntar)* to enclose

acompasado,-a *adj (rítmico)* rhythmic

acomplejado,-a *adj* **estar a.** to have a complex (**por** about)

acomplejar 1 *vt* **a. alguien** to give sb a complex
  2 acomplejarse *vpr* **a. por** to develop a complex about

acondicionado,-a *adj* **aire a.** air conditioning

acondicionador *nm* conditioner

acondicionar *vt* to prepare, to set up; *(mejorar)* to improve; *(cabello)* to condition

acongojar *vt* to distress

aconsejable *adj* advisable

aconsejar *vt* to advise

acontecer [33] *v impers* to happen, to take place

acontecimiento *nm* event

acopio *nm* store, stock; **hacer a. de** to store

acoplar 1 *vt* (a) to fit (together), to join (b) *Téc* to couple, to connect
  2 acoplarse *vpr (nave espacial)* to dock

acorazado,-a 1 *adj* armoured, armour-plated
  2 *nm* battleship

acordado,-a *adj* agreed; **según lo a.** as agreed

acordar [2] **1** *vt* to agree; *(decidir)* to decide
  2 acordarse *vpr* to remember; **no me acuerdo (de Silvia)** I can't remember (Silvia)

acorde 1 *adj* in agreement
  2 *nm Mús* chord

acordeón *nm* (a) *(instrument)* accordion (b) *Col, Méx Fam (en examen)* crib

acordonado,-a *adj* cordoned off, sealed off

acordonar *vt* (a) *(zona)* to cordon off, to seal off (b) *(atar)* to lace up

acorralar *vt* to corner

acortar *vt* to shorten; **a. distancias** to cut down the distance

acosar *vt* to harass; *Fig* **a. algn a preguntas** to bombard sb with questions

acoso *nm* harassment; **a. sexual** sexual harassment

acostar [2] **1** *vt* to put to bed
  2 acostarse *vpr* (a) to go to bed (b) *Fam* **a.**

con algn to sleep with sb, to go to bed with sb
acostumbrado,-a adj (**a**) usual, customary; **es lo a.** it is the custom (**b**) **a. al frío/calor** used to the cold/heat
acostumbrar 1 vi **a. a** (soler) to be in the habit of
2 vt **a. a algn a algo** (habituar) to get sb used to sth
3 acostumbrarse vpr (habituarse) **a. a algo** to get used to sth

acotación nf (**a**) (en escrito) (marginal) note; Teatro stage direction (**b**) (en mapa) elevation mark
acotamiento nm Méx (arcén) verge; (de autopista) Br hard shoulder, US shoulder
acotar vt (**a**) (área) to enclose; Fig (tema) to delimit (**b**) (texto) to annotate (**c**) (mapa) to mark with elevations
ácrata adj & nmf anarchist
acre¹ adj (**a**) (sabor) sour, bitter; (olor) acrid (**b**) Fig (palabras) bitter, harsh; (crítica) biting
acre² nm (medida) acre
acrecentar [1] vt to increase
acreditación nf badge
acreditar vt (**a**) to be a credit to (**b**) (probar) to prove (**c**) (embajador) to accredit (**d**) Fin to credit
acreditativo,-a adj which proves, which gives proof
acreedor,-a nm,f Com creditor
acribillar vt to riddle, to pepper; **a. a algn a balazos** to riddle sb with bullets
acrílico,-a adj acrylic
acriollarse vpr Am to adopt native ways
acritud nf (mordacidad) acrimony
acrobacia nf acrobatics sing
acróbata nmf acrobat
acta nf (**a**) (de reunión) minutes, record (**b**) (certificado) certificate, official document; **a. notarial** affidavit; **A. Única (Europea)** Single European Act

> Takes the masculine articles **el** and **un**.

actitud nf attitude
activar vt (**a**) to activate (**b**) (avivar) to liven up
actividad nf activity
activista nmf activist
activo,-a 1 adj active; **en a.** on active service
2 nm Fin assets
acto nm (**a**) act, action; **a. sexual** sexual intercourse; **en el a.** at once; **a. seguido** immediately afterwards; Mil **en a. de servicio** in action; **hacer a. de presencia** to put in an appearance (**b**) (ceremonia) ceremony (**c**) Teatro act
actor nm actor
actriz nf actress
actuación nf (**a**) performance (**b**) (intervención) intervention, action
actual adj current, present; (al día) up-to-date; **un tema muy a.** a very topical subject

actualidad nf (**a**) present time; **en la a.** at present; **estar de a.** to be fashionable; **temas de a.** topical subjects (**b**) (hechos) current affairs
actualizar [40] vt to update, to bring up to date; Informát (software, hardware) to upgrade
actualmente adv (hoy en día) nowadays, these days; (ahora) at the moment, at present

> 🖉 Observa que las palabras inglesas **actual** y **actually** son falsos amigos y no son la traducción de las palabras españolas **actual** y **actualmente**. En inglés, **actual** significa "real, verdadero", y **actually** significa "en realidad".

actuar [30] vi (**a**) to act; **a. como o de** to act as (**b**) Cin & Teatro to perform, to act
acuarela nf watercolour
Acuario nm Aquarius
acuario nm aquarium
acuartelar vt to confine to barracks
acuático,-a adj aquatic; **esquí a.** water-skiing
acuchillar vt to knife, to stab
acuciante adj urgent, pressing
acuciar [43] vt to urge on
acudir vi (ir) to go; (venir) to come, to arrive; **nadie acudió en su ayuda** nobody came to help him; **no sé dónde a.** I don't know where to turn
acueducto nm aqueduct
acuerdo nm agreement; **¡de a.!** all right!, O.K.!; **de a. con** in accordance with; **de común a.** by common consent; **estar de a. en algo** to agree on sth; **ponerse de a.** to agree; **a. marco** framework agreement
acumular 1 vt to accumulate
2 acumularse vpr (**a**) to accumulate, to build up (**b**) (gente) to crowd
acunar vt to rock
acuñar vt (moneda) to mint; (frase) to coin
acuoso,-a adj watery; (jugoso) juicy
acupuntura nf acupuncture
acurrucarse [44] vpr to curl up, to snuggle up
acusación nf (**a**) accusation (**b**) Jur charge
acusado,-a 1 nm,f accused, defendant
2 adj (marcado) marked, noticeable
acusar 1 vt (**a**) to accuse (**de** of); Jur to charge (**de** with) (**b**) (golpe etc) to feel; Fig **su cara acusaba el cansancio** his face showed his exhaustion (**c**) Com **a. recibo** to acknowledge receipt
2 acusarse vpr (**a**) (acentuarse) to become more pronounced (**b**) Fig (notarse) to show
acuse nm **a. de recibo** acknowledgment of receipt
acusica adj & nmf Fam telltale
acústica nf acoustics sing
acústico,-a adj acoustic
adán nm Fam untidy o slovenly person
adaptable adj adaptable
adaptación nf adaptation

adaptador *nm* adapter
adaptar 1 *vt* (**a**) to adapt (**b**) *(ajustar)* to adjust
  2 adaptarse *vpr* to adapt oneself (**a** to)
adecentar *vt* to tidy (up), to clean (up)
adecuado,-a *adj* appropriate, suitable
adecuar [47] *vt* to adapt
adefesio *nm (persona)* freak; *(cosa)* monstrosity
a. de J.C. (*abr* **antes de Jesucristo**) BC
adelantado,-a *adj* (**a**) advanced; *(desarrollado)* developed; *(precoz)* precocious (**b**) *(reloj)* fast (**c**) **pagar por a.** to pay in advance
adelantamiento *nm* overtaking; **hacer un a.** to overtake
adelantar 1 *vt* (**a**) to move o bring forward; *(reloj)* to put forward; *Fig* to advance (**b**) *Aut* to overtake (**c**) *(fecha)* to bring forward; *Fig* **a. (los) acontecimientos** to get ahead of oneself
  2 *vi* (**a**) to advance (**b**) *(progresar)* to make progress (**c**) *(reloj)* to be fast
  3 adelantarse *vpr* (**a**) *(ir delante)* to go ahead (**b**) *(reloj)* to gain, to be fast (**c**) **el verano se ha adelantado** we are having an early summer
adelante 1 *adv* forward; **más a.** *(lugar)* further on; *(tiempo)* later; **seguir a.** to keep going, to carry on; **llevar a. un plan** to carry out a plan
  2 *interj* **¡a!** come in!
adelanto *nm* (**a**) advance; *(progreso)* progress (**b**) **el reloj lleva diez minutos de a.** the watch is ten minutes fast (**c**) *(de dinero)* advance payment
adelfa *nf* oleander, rosebay
adelgazamiento *nm* slimming
adelgazar [40] *vi* to slim, to lose weight
ademán *nm* (**a**) gesture (**b**) **ademanes** manners
además *adv* moreover, furthermore; **a., no lo he visto nunca** what's more, I've never seen him; **a. de él** besides him
adentrarse *vpr* **a. en** *(bosque)* to go deep into; *(asunto)* to study thoroughly
adentro 1 *adv (dentro)* inside; **mar a.** out to sea; **tierra a.** inland
  2 *nmpl* **decir algo para sus adentros** to say sth to oneself
adepto,-a *nm,f* follower, supporter

> *ℓ* Observa que la palabra inglesa **adept** es un falso amigo y no es la traducción de la palabra española **adepto**. En inglés, **adept** significa "experto".

aderezar [40] *vt (comida)* to season; *(ensalada)* to dress
aderezo *nm (de comida)* seasoning; *(de ensalada)* dressing
adeudar 1 *vt* to owe
  2 adeudarse *vpr* to get into debt
adherencia *nf* adherence; *Aut* roadholding

adherir [5] **1** *vt* to stick on
  2 adherirse *vpr* **a. a** to adhere to; *(partido)* to join
adhesión *nf* adhesion; *(a partido)* joining; *(a teoría)* adherence
adhesivo,-a *adj & nm* adhesive
adicción *nf* addiction; **crear a.** to be addictive
adición *nf* addition
adicional *adj* additional
adicto,-a 1 *nm,f* addict
  2 *adj* addicted (**a** to)
adiestrar *vt* to train
adinerado,-a 1 *adj* wealthy, rich
  2 *nm,f* rich person
adiós *(pl* **adioses**) **1** *interj* goodbye; *Fam* bye-bye; *(al cruzarse)* hello
  2 *nm* goodbye
aditivo,-a *adj & nm* additive
adivinanza *nf* riddle, puzzle
adivinar *vt* to guess; **a. el pensamiento de algn** to read sb's mind
adivino,-a *nm,f* fortune-teller
adjetivo,-a 1 *nm* adjective
  2 *adj* adjectival
adjudicación *nf* award; *(en subasta)* sale
adjudicar [44] **1** *vt* (**a**) *(premio, contrato)* to award (**b**) *(en subasta)* to sell
  2 adjudicarse *vpr* to appropriate, to take over
adjuntar *vt* to enclose
adjunto,-a 1 *adj* (**a**) enclosed, attached (**b**) *Educ* assistant
  2 *nm,f Educ* assistant teacher
adm., admón. (*abr* **administración**) admin.
administración *nf* (**a**) *(gobierno)* administration, authorities; *Pol* **a. central** central government; **a. pública** civil service (**b**) *(de empresa)* administration, management (**c**) *(oficina)* (branch) office
administrador,-a 1 *nm,f* administrator
  2 *adj* administrating
administrar 1 *vt* (**a**) to administer (**b**) *(dirigir)* to run, to manage
  2 administrarse *vpr* to manage one's own money
administrativo,-a 1 *adj* administrative
  2 *nm,f (funcionario)* official
admirable *adj* admirable
admiración *nf* (**a**) admiration; **causar a.** to impress (**b**) *Ling* exclamation mark
admirador,-a *nm,f* admirer
admirar 1 *vt* (**a**) to admire (**b**) *(sorprender)* to amaze, to astonish
  2 admirarse *vpr* to be amazed, to be astonished
admisible *adj* admissible, acceptable
admisión *nf* admission; **reservado el derecho de a.** *(en letrero)* the management reserves the right to refuse admission
admitir *vt* (**a**) to admit, to let in (**b**) *(aceptar)* to accept; **no se admiten cheques** *(en letrero)* no cheques accepted (**c**) *(tolerar)* to allow

(**d**) *(reconocer)* to admit, to acknowledge; **admito que mentí** I admit that I lied
admonición *nf* warning
ADN *nm* (*abr* **ácido desoxirribonucleico**) DNA
adobar *vt Culin* to marinate
adobe *nm* adobe
adobo *nm* marinade
adoctrinar *vt* to indoctrinate
adolecer [33] *vi* **a. de** *(carecer de)* to lack; *Fig Fml* to suffer from
adolescencia *nf* adolescence
adolescente *adj & nmf* adolescent
adonde *adv* where
adónde *adv interr* where (to)?
adondequiera *adv* wherever
adopción *nf* adoption
adoptar *vt* to adopt
adoptivo,-a *adj (hijo)* adopted; *(padres)* adoptive; *Fig* **país a.** country of adoption
adoquín *nm* cobble, paving stone
adorable *adj* adorable
adorar *vt* (**a**) *Rel* to worship (**b**) *Fig* to adore
adormecer [33] **1** *vt* to send to sleep, to make sleepy
  2 adormecerse *upr* (**a**) *(dormirse)* to doze off (**b**) *(brazo etc)* to go to sleep, to go numb
adormecido,-a *adj* sleepy, drowsy
adormilarse *upr* to doze, to drowse
adornar *vt* to adorn, to decorate
adorno *nm* decoration, adornment; **de a.** decorative
adosado,-a *adj* adjacent; *(casa)* semi-detached
adquirir [31] *vt* to acquire; *(comprar)* to purchase
adquisición *nf* acquisition; *(compra)* buy, purchase
adquisitivo,-a *adj* **poder a.** purchasing power
adrede *adv* deliberately, on purpose
adrenalina *nf* adrenalin
adriático,-a *nm* **el (Mar) A.** the Adriatic (Sea)
adscribir (*pp* **adscrito**) **1** *vt* (**a**) *(atribuir)* to ascribe to (**b**) *(a un trabajo)* to appoint to
  2 adscribirse *upr* to affiliate (**a** to)
adscrito,-a *pp de* **adscribir**
aduana *nf* customs
aduanero,-a **1** *adj* customs
  2 *nm,f* customs officer
aducir [10] *vt (motivo, pretexto)* to give
adueñarse *upr* **a. de** to take over; *(pánico etc)* to take hold of
aduje *pt indef de* **aducir**
adulación *nf* adulation
adular *vt* to adulate
adulterar *vt* to adulterate
adulterio *nm* adultery
adúltero,-a 1 *adj* adulterous
  2 *nm,f (hombre)* adulterer; *(mujer)* adulteress
adulto,-a *adj & nm,f* adult
adusto,-a *adj* harsh, severe

aduzco *indic pres de* **aducir**
advenedizo,-a *adj & nm,f* upstart
advenimiento *nm* advent, coming
adverbio *nm* adverb
adversario,-a 1 *nm,f* adversary, opponent
  2 *adj* opposing
adversidad *nf* adversity; *(revés)* setback
adverso,-a *adj* adverse
advertencia *nf* warning
advertido,-a *adj* warned; *(informado)* informed; **estás** o **quedas a.** you've been warned
advertir [5] *vt* (**a**) to warn; *(informar)* to inform, to advise; *Fam* **te advierto que yo tampoco lo vi** mind you, I didn't see it either (**b**) *(notar)* to realize, to notice
adviento *nm* Advent
adyacente *adj* adjacent
aéreo,-a *adj* (**a**) aerial (**b**) *Av* air; **tráfico a.** air traffic; *Com* **por vía aerea** by air
aero- *pref* aero-
aeróbic *nm* aerobics *sing*
aerodinámico,-a *adj* aerodynamic; **de línea aerodinámica** streamlined
aeródromo *nm* aerodrome
aeromodelismo *nm* aeroplane modelling
aeromoza *nf Am* air hostess
aeronáutica *nf* aeronautics *sing*
aeronáutico,-a *adj* **la industria aeronáutica** the aeronautics industry
aeronave *nf* airship
aeroplano *nm* light aeroplane
aeropuerto *nm* airport
aerosol *nm* aerosol
aerostático,-a *adj* **globo a.** hot-air balloon
a/f (*abr* **a favor**) in favour
afable *adj* affable
afamado,-a *adj* famous, well-known
afán *nm* (*pl* **afanes**) (**a**) *(esfuerzo)* effort (**b**) *(celo)* zeal
afanador,-a *nm,f Méx* cleaner
afanar 1 *vt Fam (robar)* to pinch
  2 afanarse *upr* **a. por conseguir algo** to do one's best to achieve sth
afanoso,-a *adj* (**a**) *(persona)* keen, eager (**b**) *(tarea)* hard, tough
afección *nf* disease
afectación *nf* affectation
afectado,-a *adj* affected
afectar *vt* **a. a** to affect; **le afectó mucho** she was deeply affected; **nos afecta a todos** it concerns all of us
afecto *nm* affection; **tomarle a. a algn** to become fond of sb
afectuoso,-a *adj* affectionate
afeitado *nm* shave
afeitar *vt*, **afeitarse** *upr* to shave
afeminado,-a *adj* effeminate
aferrado,-a *adj* **a.** clinging to
aferrar 1 *vt Náut* to anchor, to moor
  2 aferrarse *upr* to clutch, to cling; *Fig* **a. a una creencia** to cling to a belief

Afganistán n Afghanistan

afgano,-a adj & nm,f Afghan

afianzamiento nm strengthening, reinforcement

afianzar [40] **1** vt to strengthen, to reinforce
2 afianzarse vpr (persona) to become established

afiche nm Am poster

afición nf (a) liking; **tiene a. por la música** he is fond of music (b) Dep **la a.** the fans

aficionado,-a 1 nm,f (a) enthusiast; **un a. a la música** a music lover (b) (no profesional) amateur
2 adj (a) keen, fond; **ser a. a algo** to be fond of sth (b) (no profesional) amateur

aficionarse vpr to become fond (**a** of), to take a liking (**a** to)

afilado,-a nm,f sharp

afilar vt to sharpen

afiliación nf affiliation

afiliado,-a nm,f member

afiliarse [43] vpr to become a member

afín adj (semejante) kindred, similar; (relacionado) related

afinar vt (a) (puntería) to sharpen (b) (instrumento) to tune

afincarse [44] vpr to settle down

afinidad nf affinity

afirmación nf affirmation; **afirmaciones** (declaración) statement

afirmar (a) vt (aseverar) to state, to declare (b) (afianzar) to strengthen, to reinforce

afirmativo,-a adj affirmative; **en caso a. ...** if the answer is yes ...

aflicción nf affliction

afligir [57] **1** vt to afflict
2 afligirse vpr to grieve, to be distressed

aflojar 1 vt to loosen
2 vi (viento etc) to weaken, to grow weak
3 aflojarse vpr to come o work loose; (rueda) to go down

aflorar vi (río) to come to the surface; (sentimiento) to surface, to show

afluencia nf inflow, influx; **gran a. de público** great numbers of people

afluente nm tributary

afluir [37] vi to flow (**a** into)

afónico,-a adj estar **a.** to have lost one's voice

aforismo nm aphorism

aforo nm (capacidad) seating capacity

afortunado,-a adj fortunate; **las Islas Afortunadas** the Canaries

afrenta nf Fml affront

África n Africa

africano,-a adj & nm,f African

afrodisíaco,-a adj & nm aphrodisiac

afrontar vt to confront, to face; **a. las consecuencias** to face the consequences

afuera 1 adv outside; **la parte de a.** the outside; **más a.** further out; **salir a.** to come o go out
2 nfpl **afueras** outskirts

agachar 1 vt to lower
2 agacharse vpr to duck

agalla nf (a) (de pez) gill (b) **tiene agallas** she's got guts

agarraderas nfpl Fam **tener buenas a.** to be well-connected

agarrado,-a adj (a) Fam stingy, tight (b) **baile a.** cheek-to-cheek dancing

agarrar 1 vt (a) to grasp, to seize; **agárralo fuerte** hold it tight (b) Am (tomar) to take; **a. un taxi** to take a taxi (c) Fam (pillar) to catch; **a. una borrachera** to get drunk o pissed
2 agarrarse vpr (a) to hold on; **agarraos bien** hold tight

agarrotarse vpr (a) (músculo) to stiffen (b) (máquina) to seize up

agasajar vt to smother with attentions

ágata nf agate

Takes the masculine articles **el** and **un**.

agazaparse vpr to crouch (down)

agencia nf agency; (sucursal) branch; **a. de viajes** travel agency; **a. de seguros** insurance agency; **a. inmobiliaria** estate agency

agenciarse [43] vpr (a) to get oneself; **se agenció una moto** he got himself a motorbike (b) **agenciárselas** to manage

agenda nf diary

agente nmf agent; **a. de policía** (hombre) policeman; (mujer) policewoman; **a. de bolsa** stockbroker; **a. de seguros** insurance broker

agigantado,-a adj **a pasos agigantados** by leaps and bounds

ágil adj agile

agilidad nf agility

agilización nf speeding up

agilizar [40] vt (trámites) to speed up

agitación nf (intranquilidad) restlessness; (social, político) unrest

agitado,-a adj agitated; (persona) anxious; (mar) rough; **una vida muy agitada** a very hectic life

agitar 1 vt (botella) to shake; (multitud) to agitate
2 agitarse vpr (persona) to become agitated; (mar) to become rough

aglomeración nf agglomeration; (de gente) crowd

aglomerar 1 vt to bring together
2 aglomerarse vpr to mass o gather together

agnóstico,-a adj & nm,f agnostic

agobiado,-a adj Fig **a. de problemas** snowed under with problems; Fig **a. de trabajo** up to one's eyes in work

agobiante adj (trabajo) overwhelming; (lugar) claustrophobic; (calor) oppressive; (persona) tiresome, tiring

agobiar [43] **1** vt to overwhelm
2 agobiarse vpr (con problemas) to be over-anxious; (por el calor) to suffocate

agobio nm (a) (angustia) anxiety (b) (sofoco) suffocation

agolpamiento *nm* crowd, crush

agolparse *upr* to crowd, to throng

agonía *nf* dying breath, last gasp

agonizante *adj* dying

agonizar [40] *vi* to be dying

agosto *nm* August; *Fam* **hacer su a.** to make a packet

agotado,-a *adj* (**a**) *(cansado)* exhausted, worn out (**b**) *Com* sold out; *(existencias)* exhausted; *(libro)* out of print

agotador,-a *adj* exhausting

agotamiento *nm* exhaustion

agotar **1** *vt* (**a**) *(cansar)* to exhaust, to wear out (**b**) *(acabar)* to exhaust, to use up (completely)

2 agotarse *upr* (**a**) *(acabarse)* to run out, to be used up; *Com* to be sold out (**b**) *(persona)* to become exhausted *o* tired out

agraciado,-a *adj* (**a**) *(hermoso)* pretty (**b**) *(ganador)* winning; **ser a. con** to win

agradable *adj* pleasant

agradar *vi* to please; **no me agrada** I don't like it

agradecer [33] *vt* (**a**) *(dar las gracias)* to thank for; **les agradezco su atención** (I) thank you for your attention; **te lo agradezco mucho** thank you very much (**b**) *(estar agradecido)* to be grateful to; **te agradecería que vinieras** I'd be grateful if you'd come (**c**) *(uso impers)* **siempre se agradece un descanso** a rest is always welcome

agradecido,-a *adj* grateful; **le estoy muy a.** I am very grateful to you

agradecimiento *nm* gratitude

agrado *nm* pleasure; **no es de su a.** it isn't to his liking

agrandar **1** *vt* to enlarge, to make larger

2 agrandarse *upr* to enlarge, to become larger

agrario,-a *adj* agrarian; **política agraria** agricultural policy

agravamiento *nm* aggravation

agravante **1** *adj Jur* aggravating

2 *nm Jur* aggravating circumstance

agravar **1** *vt* to aggravate

2 agravarse *upr* to worsen, to get worse

agraviar [43] *vt* to offend, to insult

agravio *nm* offense, insult

agredir *vt defect* to assault

agregación *nf* aggregation

agregado,-a 1 *adj Educ* **profesor a.** *(escuela)* secondary school teacher; *Univ* assistant teacher

2 *nm,f Pol* attaché

agregar [42] **1** *vt* (**a**) *(añadir)* to add (**b**) *(destinar)* to appoint

2 agregarse *upr* **a. a** to join

agresión *nf* aggression

agresividad *nf* aggressiveness

agresivo,-a *adj* aggressive

agresor,-a 1 *nm,f* aggressor, attacker

2 *adj* attacking

agriarse *upr* to turn sour

agrícola *adj* agricultural

agricultor,-a *nm,f* farmer

agricultura *nf* agriculture; **a. biológica** *o* **ecológica** organic farming

agridulce *adj* bittersweet

agrietar **1** *vt* to crack; *(piel, labios)* to chap

2 agrietarse *upr* to crack; *(piel)* to get chapped

agringarse [42] *upr Am Pey* to behave like a gringo

agrio,-a 1 *adj* sour

2 *nmpl* **agrios** citrus fruits

agrónomo,-a *nm,f* **(ingeniero) a.** agronomist

agropecuario,-a *adj* farming, agricultural

agrupación *nf* association

agrupar **1** *vt* to group

2 agruparse *upr* (**a**) *(congregarse)* to group together, to form a group (**b**) *(asociarse)* to associate

agua *nf* water; **a. potable** drinking water; **a. corriente/del grifo** running/tap water; **a. dulce/salada** fresh/salt water; **a. mineral sin/con gas** still/fizzy *o* sparkling mineral water; **a. de colonia** (eau de) cologne; *Fig* **estar con el a. al cuello** to be up to one's neck in it; **aguas jurisdiccionales** territorial waters; **aguas residuales** sewage

> Takes the masculine articles **el** and **un**.

aguacate *nm* *(árbol)* avocado; *(fruto)* avocado (pear)

aguacero *nm* shower, downpour

aguado,-a *adj* watered down

aguafiestas *nmf inv* spoilsport, wet blanket

aguafuerte *nm* (**a**) *Arte* etching (**b**) *Quím* nitric acid

aguamala *nf Carib, Col, Ecuad, Méx* jellyfish

aguamarina *nf* aquamarine

aguamiel *nm* *o* *nf* (**a**) *Am (bebida)* = water mixed with honey or cane syrup (**b**) *Carib, Méx (jugo)* maguey juice

aguanieve *nf* sleet

aguantar **1** *vt* (**a**) *(soportar)* to tolerate; **no lo aguanto más** I can't stand it any longer (**b**) *(sostener)* to support, to hold; **aguanta esto** hold this (**c**) **aguanta la respiración** hold your breath

2 aguantarse *upr* (**a**) *(contenerse)* to keep back; *(lágrimas)* to hold back; **no pude aguantarme la risa** I couldn't help laughing (**b**) *(resignarse)* to resign oneself

aguante *nm* endurance; **tener mucho a.** *(ser paciente)* to be very patient; *(tener resistencia)* to be strong, to have a lot of stamina

aguar [45] *vt* to water down; *Fig* **a. la fiesta a algn** to spoil sb's fun

aguardar **1** *vt* to await

2 *vi* to wait

aguardiente *nm* liquor, brandy

aguarrás *nm* turpentine

aguatero,-a *nm,f Am* water seller

aguaviva *nf RP* jellyfish

agudeza *nf* (**a**) sharpness; *(del dolor)* acuteness (**b**) *Fig (ingenio)* witticism, witty saying

agudización *nf* (**a**) sharpening (**b**) *(empeoramiento)* worsening

agudizar [40] **1** *vt* to intensify, to make more acute

   2 agudizarse *vpr* to intensify, to become more acute

agudo,-a *adj (dolor)* acute; *(voz)* high-pitched; *(sonido)* treble, high; *Fig (ingenioso)* witty; *Fig (sentido)* sharp, keen

agüero *nm* omen

aguijón *nm* sting; *Fig (estímulo)* spur

águila *nf* eagle; **á. real** golden eagle; *Méx* ¿**á. o sol?** heads or tails?

> Takes the masculine articles **el** and **un**.

aguileño,-a *adj* aquiline; **nariz aguileña** aquiline nose

aguinaldo *nm* Christmas box; **pedir el a.** to go carol singing

agüita *nf Chile* (herbal) tea

aguja *nf* (**a**) needle; *(de reloj)* hand; *(de tocadiscos)* stylus (**b**) *Arquit* spire (**c**) *Ferroc* point, *US* switch

agujerear *vt* to make holes in

agujero *nm* (**a**) hole; **a. negro** black hole (**b**) *Econ* deficit, shortfall

agujetas *nfpl* stiffness; **tener a.** to be stiff

agur *interj Fam* bye!, see you!

aguzar [40] *vt* (**a**) *(afilar)* to sharpen (**b**) *Fig* **a. el oído** to prick up one's ears; **a. la vista** to look attentively; **aguzar el ingenio** to sharpen one's wits

ahí *adv* there; **a. está** there he/she/it is; **ve por a.** go that way; **está por a.** it's over there; **setenta o por a.** seventy or thereabouts; **de a.** hence

ahijado,-a *nm,f* godchild; *(niño)* godson; *(niña)* goddaughter; **ahijados** godchildren

ahínco *nm* eagerness; **con a.** eagerly

ahíto,-a *adj (de comida)* full, stuffed; *(harto)* fed up

ahogado,-a 1 *adj* (**a**) *(en líquido)* drowned; **morir a.** to drown (**b**) *(asfixiado)* suffocated

   2 *nm,f* drowned person

ahogar [42] **1** *vt* (**a**) *(en líquido)* to drown (**b**) *(asfixiar)* to suffocate

   2 ahogarse *vpr* (**a**) *(en líquido)* to drown, to be drowned; *Fig* **a. en un vaso de agua** to make a mountain out of a molehill (**b**) *(asfixiarse)* to suffocate (**c**) *(motor)* to be flooded

ahondar 1 *vt* to deepen

   2 *vi* to go deep; *Fig* **a. en un problema** to go into a problem in depth

ahora 1 *adv* (**a**) *(en este momento)* now; **a. mismo** right now; **de a. en adelante** from now on; **por a.** for the time being (**b**) **a. voy** I'm coming; **a. vuelvo** I'll be back in a minute (**c**)

hasta a. *(hasta el momento)* until now, so far; *(hasta luego)* see you later

   2 *conj* **a. bien** *(sin embargo)* however; *(y bueno)* well then

ahorcado,-a 1 *nm,f* hanged person

   2 *adj* hanged

ahorcar [44] **1** *vt* to hang

   2 ahorcarse *vpr* to hang oneself

ahorita, ahoritica *adv Andes, CAm, Carib, Méx Fam* (**a**) *(en el presente)* (right) now; **a. voy** I'm just coming (**b**) *(pronto)* in a second (**c**) *(hace poco)* just now, a few minutes ago

ahorrador,-a *adj* thrifty

ahorrar 1 *vt* to save

   2 ahorrarse *vpr* **ahórrate los comentarios** keep your comments to yourself

ahorrativo,-a *adj* thrifty

ahorro *nm* (**a**) saving; **a. energético** energy saving (**b**) **ahorros** savings; *Fin* **caja de ahorros** savings bank

ahuecar [44] *vt* (**a**) to hollow out; *Fam* **a. el ala** to clear off, to beat it (**b**) *(voz)* to deepen

ahuevado,-a *adj Andes, CAm Fam (tonto)* **estar a. con algo** to be bowled over by sth

ahumado,-a *adj (cristal, jamón)* smoked; *(bacon)* smoky; **salmón a.** smoked salmon

ahumar 1 *vt* to smoke

   2 *vi (echar humo)* to smoke, to give off smoke

ahuyentar *vt* to scare away

aindiado,-a *adj Am* Indian-like

airado,-a *adj* angry

airar 1 *vt* to anger

   2 airarse *vpr* to get angry

airbag ['erßaɣ, air'ßaɣ] *nm (pl* **airbags**) airbag

aire *nm* (**a**) air; **a. acondicionado** air conditioning; **al a.** *(hacia arriba)* into the air; *(al descubierto)* uncovered; **al a. libre** in the open air; **en el a.** *(pendiente)* in the air; *Rad* on the air; **hacerse a.** to fan oneself; **saltar por los aires** to blow up; **tomar el a.** to get some fresh air; **necesito un cambio de aires** I need a change of scene (**b**) *Aut* choke (**c**) *(viento)* wind; **hace a.** it's windy (**d**) *(aspecto)* air, appearance (**e**) **él va a su a.** he goes his own sweet way (**f**) **darse aires** to put on airs

airear *vt (ropa, lugar)* to air; *Fig (asunto)* to publicize

airoso,-a *adj* graceful, elegant; *Fig* **salir a. de una situación** to come out of a situation with flying colours

aislacionismo *nm* isolationism

aislado,-a *adj* (**a**) isolated (**b**) *Téc* insulated

aislamiento *nm* (**a**) isolation (**b**) *Téc* insulation

aislante 1 *adj* **cinta a.** insulating tape

   2 *nm* insulator

aislar *vt* (**a**) to isolate (**b**) *Téc* to insulate

ajar *vt* to wear out

ajedrez *nm* (**a**) *(juego)* chess (**b**) *(piezas y tablero)* chess set

ajeno,-a *adj* belonging to other people; **los**

bienes ajenos other peoples' goods; **por causas ajenas a nuestra voluntad** for reasons beyond our control

ajetreado,-a *adj* (very) busy, hectic

ajetreo *nm* activity, hard work, bustle

ají *nm* (a) *Andes, RP (pimiento)* chilli (pepper) (b) *Andes, RP (salsa)* = sauce made from oil, vinegar, garlic and chilli

ajiaco *nm* (a) *Andes, Carib (estofado)* = chilli-based stew (b) *Méx (estofado con ajo)* = tripe stew flavoured with garlic

ajillo *nm Culin* **al a.** fried with garlic

ajo *nm* garlic; **cabeza/diente de a.** head/clove of garlic; *Fam* **estar en el a.** to be in on it

ajonjolí *nm* sesame

ajorca *nf* bracelet; *(en el tobillo)* anklet

ajuar *nm (de novia)* trousseau

ajustado,-a *adj* tight

ajustador,-a *nm,f* fitter

ajustar *vt* (a) to adjust (b) *(apretar)* to tighten (c) *Fin (cuenta)* to settle; *Fig* **ajustarle las cuentas a algn** to settle a score with sb

ajuste *nm* (a) adjustment; *Téc* assembly; *TV* **carta de a.** test card (b) *(de precio)* fixing; *(de cuenta)* settlement; *Fig* **a. de cuentas** settling of scores

ajusticiar [43] *vt* to execute

al *(contracción de* **a** + **el**) (a) *ver* **a** (b) (**al** + *infin*) **al salir** on leaving; **está a caer** it's about to happen; **al parecer** apparently

ala 1 *nf* (a) wing; *Fig* **cortarle las alas a algn** to clip sb's wings (b) *(de sombrero)* brim

    2 *nmf Dep* winger

> Takes the masculine articles **el** and **un**.

alabanza *nf* praise

alabar *vt* to praise

alabastro *nm* alabaster

alacena *nf* (food) cupboard

alacrán *nm* scorpion

alambicado,-a *adj* intricate

alambique *nm* still

alambrada *nf,* **alambrado** *nm* wire fence

alambrar *vt* to fence with wire

alambre *nm* wire; **a. de púas** barbed wire

alambrista *nmf* tightrope walker

alameda *nf* (a) poplar grove (b) *(paseo)* avenue, boulevard

álamo *nm* poplar

alano,-a *nm,f (perro)* **a.** mastiff

alarde *nm (ostentación)* bragging, boasting; **hacer a. de** to show off

alardear *vi* to brag, to boast; **a. de rico** *o* **de riqueza** to flaunt one's wealth

alargadera *nf Elec* extension

alargado,-a *adj* elongated

alargar [42] **1** *vt* (a) to lengthen; *(estirar)* to stretch; **ella alargó la mano para cogerlo** she stretched out her hand to get it (b) *(prolongar)* to prolong, to extend (c) *(dar)* to pass, to hand over; **alárgame ese jersey** can you pass me that sweater?

2 alargarse *vpr* (a) to get longer (b) *(prolongarse)* to go on (c) **¿puedes a. a casa?** can you give me a lift home?

alarido *nm* screech, shriek; **dar un a.** to howl

alarma *nf* alarm; **la a. saltó** the alarm went off; **falsa a.** false alarm; **señal de a.** alarm (signal)

alarmado,-a *adj* alarmed

alarmante *adj* alarming

alarmar 1 *vt* to alarm

2 alarmarse *vpr* to be alarmed

alazán,-ana *adj & nm,f* **(caballo) a.** chestnut

alba *nf* dawn, daybreak

> Takes the masculine articles **el** and **un**.

albacea *nmf (hombre)* executor; *(mujer)* executrix

albahaca *nf* basil

albanés,-esa *adj & nm,f* Albanian

Albania *n* Albania

albañal *nm* sewer, drain

albañil *nm* bricklayer

albañilería *nf* bricklaying; **pared de a.** *(obra)* brick wall

albarán *nm Com* delivery note, despatch note

albaricoque *nm* apricot

albaricoquero *nm* apricot tree

albatros *nm inv* albatross

albedrío *nm* will; **libre a.** free will

alberca *nf* (a) *(depósito)* water tank (b) *Méx (piscina)* swimming pool

albergar [42] **1** *vt (alojar)* to house, to accommodate; *Fig (sentimientos)* to cherish, to harbour

2 albergarse *vpr* to stay

albergue *nm* hostel; **a. juvenil** youth hostel

albino,-a *adj & nm,f* albino

albóndiga *nf* meatball

albores *nmpl* beginning; **en los a. de ...** at the beginning of ...

albornoz *nm* bathrobe

alborotado,-a *adj* (a) worked up, agitated (b) *(desordenado)* untidy, messy (c) *(mar)* rough; *(tiempo)* stormy

alborotar 1 *vt* (a) *(agitar)* to agitate, to work up (b) *(desordenar)* to make untidy, to turn upside down

2 *vi* to kick up a racket

3 alborotarse *vpr* (a) to get excited *o* worked up (b) *(mar)* to get rough; *(tiempo)* to get stormy

alboroto *nm* (a) *(jaleo)* din, racket (b) *(desorden)* disturbance, uproar

alborozo *nm* merriment, gaiety

albufera *nf* lagoon

álbum *nm* album

alcachofa *nf* (a) *Bot* artichoke (b) *(de tubo, regadera)* rose, sprinkler

alcalde *nm* mayor

alcaldesa *nf* mayoress

alcaldía *nf* (a) *(cargo)* mayorship (b) *(oficina)* mayor's office

alcalino,-a adj alkaline
alcance nm (a) reach; **al a. de cualquiera** within everybody's reach; **dar a. a** to catch up with; **fuera del a. de los niños** out of the reach of children (b) Fig scope; (de noticia) importance
alcancía nf money box; (cerdito) piggy bank
alcanfor nm camphor
alcantarilla nf sewer; (boca) drain
alcantarillado nm sewer system
alcanzar [40] **1** vt (a) to reach; (persona) to catch up with; **la producción alcanza dos mil unidades** production is up to two thousand units (b) **alcánzame la sal** (pasar) pass me the salt (c) (conseguir) to attain, to achieve
2 vi (ser suficiente) to be sufficient; **con un kilo no alcanza para todos** one kilo won't be enough for all of us
alcaparra nf (fruto) caper; (planta) caper bush
alcatraz nm Orn gannet
alcaucil nm RP artichoke
alcayata nf hook
alcazaba nf fortress, citadel
alcázar nm (a) (fortaleza) fortress, citadel (b) (castillo) castle, palace
alcista **1** adj (bolsa) rising, bullish; **tendencia a.** upward tendency
2 nmf (bolsa) bull
alcoba nf bedroom

> *♪* Observa que la palabra inglesa **alcove** es un falso amigo y no es la traducción de la palabra española **alcoba**. En inglés, **alcove** significa "hueco".

alcohol nm alcohol
alcoholemia nf blood alcohol level; **prueba de a.** Breathalyser® test
alcohólico,-a adj & nm,f alcoholic
alcoholímetro nm Breathalyser®
alcoholismo nm alcoholism
alcoholizado,-a adj & nm,f alcoholic
alcornoque nm cork oak
alcurnia nf lineage, ancestry; **de alta a.** of noble lineage
alcuzcuz nm couscous
aldaba nf (llamador) door knocker
aldabonazo nm (a) loud knock (b) (advertencia) warning
aldea nf village
aldeano,-a 1 adj village
2 nm,f villager
aleación nf alloy
aleatorio,-a adj random
alebrestarse upr Col (ponerse nervioso) to get nervous o excited
aleccionador,-a adj (instructivo) instructive; (ejemplar) exemplary
aleccionar vt (instruir) to teach, to instruct; (adiestrar) to train
aledaño,-a 1 adj adjoining, adjacent

2 nmpl **aledaños** outskirts
alegar [42] vt (a) (aducir) to claim; Jur to allege (b) (presentar) to put forward
alegato nm argument
alegoría nf allegory
alegrar 1 vt (a) (complacer) to make happy o glad; **me alegra que se lo hayas dicho** I am glad you told her (b) Fig (avivar) to enliven, to brighten up
2 alegrarse upr to be glad, to be happy; **me alegro de verte** I am pleased to see you; **me alegro por ti** I am happy for you
alegre adj (a) (contento) happy, glad (b) (color) bright; (música) lively; (lugar) pleasant, cheerful (c) Fig (borracho) tipsy, merry
alegría nf joy, happiness
alejado,-a adj far away, remote
alejar 1 vt to move further away
2 alejarse upr to go away, to move away; **no te alejes de mí** keep close to me
aleluya nm o nf hallelujah, alleluia
alemán,-ana 1 adj & nm,f German
2 nm (idioma) German
Alemania n Germany; **A. del Este/Oeste** East/West Germany; **A. Occidental/Oriental** West/East Germany
alentador,-a adj encouraging; **un panorama poco a.** a rather bleak outlook
alentar [1] vt Fig to encourage
alergia nf allergy
alérgico,-a adj allergic
alero nm eaves
alerón nm Av aileron
alerta adj & adj alert; **estar en estado de a.** to be (on the) alert
alertar vt to alert (de to); **nos alertó del peligro** he alerted us to the danger
aleta nf (de pez) fin; (de foca, de nadador) flipper
aletargado,-a adj lethargic
aletargar [42] **1** vt to make lethargic
2 aletargarse upr to become lethargic
aletear vi to flutter o flap its wings
alevín nm (pescado) young fish; Fig (principiante) beginner
alevosía nf (traición) treachery; (premeditación) premeditation
alevoso,-a adj (persona) treacherous; (acto) premeditated
alfabético,-a adj alphabetic
alfabetización nf teaching to read and write; **campaña de a.** literacy campaign
alfabeto nm alphabet
alfajor nm CSur = large biscuit filled with toffee and coated with coconut
alfalfa nf lucerne, alfalfa
alfarería nf (a) (arte) pottery (b) (taller) potter's workshop; (tienda) pottery shop
alfarero,-a nm,f potter
alféizar nm sill, windowsill
alférez nm second lieutenant
alfil nm bishop

alfiler *nm* pin; *(broche)* pin, brooch; *(de corbata)* tiepin; *(para tender)* peg; *Andes, RP, Ven* **a. de gancho** *(imperdible)* safety pin
alfiletero *nm* pin box, pin case
alfombra *nf* rug; *(moqueta)* carpet
alfombrar *vt* to carpet
alfombrilla *nf* rug, mat
alforja *nf (para caballos)* saddlebag; *(para hombro)* knapsack
alga *nf* alga; *(marina)* seaweed

Takes the masculine articles **el** and **un**.

algarabía *nf* hubbub, hullabaloo
algarrobo *nm* carob tree
algazara *nf* din, row
álgebra *nf* algebra

Takes the masculine articles **el** and **un**.

álgido,-a *adj* culminating, critical; **el punto a.** the climax
algo 1 *pron indef* (a) *(afirmativo)* something; *(interrogativo)* anything; **a. así** something like that; **¿a. más?** anything else?; **por a. será** there must be a reason for it; *Fam* **a. es a.** it's better than nothing (b) *(cantidad indeterminada)* some; **¿queda a. de pastel?** is there any cake left?
2 *adv (un poco)* quite, somewhat; **se siente a. mejor** she's feeling a bit better
algodón *nm* cotton; **a. (hidrófilo)** *Br* cotton wool, *US* absorbent cotton; **a. de azúcar** *Br* candy floss, *US* cotton candy
algodonero,-a 1 *nm,f* cotton grower
2 *adj* cotton
alguacil *nm* bailiff
alguien *pron indef (afirmativo)* somebody, someone; *(interrogativo)* anybody, anyone
alguno,-a 1 *adj* (a) *(delante de nombre) (afirmativo)* some; *(interrogativo)* any; **algunos días** some days; **algunas veces** some times; **alguna que otra vez** now and then; **¿has tomado alguna medicina?** have you taken any medicine?; **¿le has visto alguna vez?** have you ever seen him? (b) *(después de nombre)* not at all; **no vino persona alguna** nobody came

algún is used instead of **alguno** before masculine singular nouns (e.g. **algún día** some day).

2 *pron indef* (a) someone, somebody; **a. dirá que ...** someone might say that ...; **a. que otro** some (b) **algunos,-as** some (people)
alhaja *nf* jewel
alhelí *nm (pl alhelíes)* wallflower, stock
aliado,-a 1 *adj* allied
2 *nm,f* **los Aliados** the Allies
alianza *nf* (a) *(pacto)* alliance (b) *(anillo)* wedding ring
aliarse [29] *vpr* to become allies, to form an alliance
alias *adv & nm inv* alias
alicaído,-a *adj* (a) *Fig (débil)* weak, feeble

(b) *Fig (deprimido)* down, depressed
alicatar *vt* to tile
alicates *nmpl* pliers
aliciente *nm* (a) *(atractivo)* lure, charm (b) *(incentivo)* incentive
alienación *nf* alienation
alienado,-a *adj* insane, deranged
alienar *vt* to alienate
alienígena *adj & nmf* alien
aliento *nm* (a) breath; **sin a.** breathless (b) *(ánimo)* encouragement
aligerar 1 *vt (acelerar)* to speed up; **a. el paso** to quicken one's pace
2 *vi Fam* **¡aligera!** hurry up!
alijo *nm* haul; **un a. de drogas** a consignment of drugs
alimaña *nf* vermin
alimentación *nf (comida)* food; *(acción)* feeding; *Téc* supply
alimentar 1 *vt* (a) *(dar alimento)* to feed; *(ser nutritivo)* to be nutritious (b) *Fig (sentimientos)* to nourish (c) *Informát* to feed; *Téc* to supply
2 alimentarse *vpr* **a. con** o **de** to live on
alimentario,-a *adj* food
alimenticio,-a *adj* nutritious; **productos alimenticios** food products, foodstuffs; **valor a.** nutritional value
alimento *nm* (a) *(comida)* food (b) *Fig* **tiene poco a.** it is not very nourishing
alimón *adv* **al a.** together
alineación *nf* (a) alignment (b) *Dep (equipo)* line-up
alineado,-a *adj* aligned, lined-up; **países no alineados** non-aligned countries
alineamiento *nm* alignment
alinear 1 *vt* to align, to line up
2 alinearse *vpr* to line up
aliñar *vt* to season, to flavour; *(ensalada)* to dress
aliño *nm* seasoning, dressing
alioli *nm* garlic mayonnaise
alisar *vt, alisarse* *vpr* to smooth
aliscafo, alíscafo *nm RP* hydrofoil
alistar 1 *vt Mil* to recruit, to enlist
2 alistarse *vpr* (a) *Mil* to enlist, to enrol (b) *Am (prepararse)* to get ready
aliviar [43] **1** *vt (dolor)* to soothe, to relieve; *(carga)* to lighten, to make lighter
2 aliviarse *vpr (dolor)* to diminish, to get better
alivio *nm* relief
aljibe *nm* cistern, tank
allá *adv* (a) *(lugar alejado)* there, over there; **a. abajo/arriba** down/up there; **¡a. voy!** here I go!; **más a.** further on; **más a. de** beyond; **el más a.** the beyond (b) *(tiempo)* **a. por los años veinte** back in the twenties (c) **a. tú** that's your problem
allanamiento *nm Jur* **a. de morada** breaking and entering
allanar *vt* (a) *(terreno)* to level, to flatten; *Fig*

(camino) to smooth (**b**)*Jur* to break into
allegado,-a 1 *adj* close
  2 *nm,f* close friend
allende *adv Fml* beyond; **a. los mares** overseas
allí *adv* there, over there; **a. abajo/arriba** down/up there; **de a. para acá** back and forth; **por a.** *(movimiento)* that way; *(posición)* over there
alma *nf* soul; **no había ni un a.** there was not a soul

> Takes the masculine articles **el** and **un**.

almacén *nm* (**a**) *(local)* warehouse; *(habitación)* storeroom (**b**) *Com* (**grandes**) **almacenes** department store (**c**) *Andes, RP (de alimentos)* grocer's (shop), grocery store
almacenaje *nm* storage, warehousing
almacenamiento *nm* storage, warehousing; *Informát* storage
almacenar *vt* to store
almacenista *nmf (vendedor)* wholesaler; *(propietario)* warehouse owner
almanaque *nm* calendar
almeja *nf* clam; *muy Fam* pussy
almena *nf* merlon
almendra *nf* almond; **a. garapiñada** sugared almond
almendro *nm* almond tree
almiar *nm* haystack
almíbar *nm* syrup
almidón *nm* starch
almidonar *vt* to starch
alminar *nm* minaret
almirante *nm* admiral
almizcle *nm* musk
almohada *nf* pillow; *Fam* **consultarlo con la a.** to sleep on it
almohadilla *nf* (small) cushion
almohadón *nm* large pillow, cushion
almorrana *nf Fam* pile
almorzar [2] **1** *vi* to have lunch
  2 *vt* to have for lunch
almuerzo *nm* lunch
aló *interj Andes, Carib (al teléfono)* hello!
alocado,-a *adj* thoughtless, rash
alocución *nf* speech, address
alojamiento *nm* accommodation; **dar a.** to accommodate
alojar 1 *vt* to accommodate
  2 *alojarse* *vpr* to stay
alondra *nf* lark; **a. común** skylark
alpaca *nf* alpaca
alpargata *nf* canvas sandal, espadrille
Alpes *npl* **los A.** the Alps
alpinismo *nm* mountaineering, climbing
alpinista *nmf* mountaineer, climber
alpino,-a *adj* Alpine; **esquí a.** downhill skiing
alquilar 1 *vt* to hire; *(pisos, casas)* to rent; **se alquila** *(en letrero)* to let
alquiler *nm* (**a**) *(de pisos, casas)* renting, letting; **a. de coches** car hire; **de a.** *(pisos,*

casas) to let, rented; *(coche)* for hire; *(televisión)* for rent (**b**) *(precio)* hire, rental; *(de pisos, casas)* rent
alquimia *nf* alchemy
alquitrán *nm* tar
alrededor 1 *adv (lugar)* round, around; **mira a.** look around; **a. de la mesa** round the table; **a. de las dos** around two o'clock; **a. de quince** about fifteen;
  2 *nmpl* **alrededores** surrounding area; **en los alrededores de Murcia** in the area round Murcia
alta *nf* **dar de** *o* **el a.** *(a un enfermo)* to discharge from hospital

> Takes the masculine articles **el** and **un**.

altamente *adv* highly, extremely
altanería *nf* arrogance
altanero,-a *adj* arrogant
altar *nm* altar
altavoz *nm* loudspeaker
alterable *adj* changeable
alteración *nf* (**a**) *(cambio)* alteration (**b**) *(alboroto)* quarrel, row; **a. del orden público** disturbance of the peace (**c**) *(excitación)* agitation
alterar 1 *vt* to alter, to change; **a. el orden público** to disturb the peace
  2 *alterarse* *vpr* (**a**) *(cambiar)* to change (**b**) *(inquietarse)* to be upset (**c**) *(alimentos)* to go off
altercado *nm* quarrel, argument
alternar 1 *vt* to alternate
  2 *vi (relacionarse)* to meet people, to socialize
  3 alternarse *vpr* to alternate
alternativa *nf* alternative
alternativo,-a *adj* alternative
alterno,-a *adj* alternate; **días alternos** alternate days
alteza *nf* Highness; **Su A. Real** His/Her Royal Highness
altibajos *nmpl Fig* ups and downs
altiplano *nm* high plateau
altísimo *nm* **el A.** the Almighty
altisonante *adj* grandiloquent
altitud *nf* altitude
altivez *nf* arrogance, haughtiness
altivo,-a *adj* arrogant, haughty
alto¹ *nm* (**a**) *(interrupción)* stop, break (**b**) *Mil* halt; **dar el a.** to order to halt; **un a. el fuego** a cease-fire
alto²,-a 1 *adj (persona, árbol, edificio)* tall; *(montaña, techo, presión)* high; *(sonido)* loud; *Fig (precio, tecnología)* high; *(tono)* high-pitched; **los pisos altos** the top floors; **en lo a.** at the top; **alta sociedad** high society; **clase alta** upper class; **en voz alta** aloud, in a loud voice; **a altas horas de la noche** late at night
  2 *adv* (**a**) high, high up (**b**) *(sonar, hablar etc)* loud, loudly; **pon la radio más alta** turn the radio up; **¡habla más a.!** speak up!

3 *nm* (**a**) *(altura)* height; **¿cuánto tiene de a.?** how tall/high is it?; *Fig* **por todo lo a.** in a grand way (**b**) *(elevación)* hill
altoparlante *nm Am* loudspeaker
altozano *nm* hillock, hill
altramuz *nm* lupin
altruista 1 *adj* altruistic
2 *nmf* altruist
altura *nf* (**a**) height; **de 10 m de a.** 10 m high (**b**) *(nivel)* level; **a la misma a.** on the same level; *Geog* on the same latitude; **a la a. del cine** by the cinema; *Fig* **estar a la a. de las circunstancias** to meet the challenge; *Fig* **no está a su a.** he does not measure up to him; *Fig* **a estas alturas** at this stage (**c**) *Rel* **alturas** heaven
alubia *nf* bean
alucinación *nf* hallucination
alucinado,-a *adj Fam* amazed
alucinante *adj Fam* brilliant, mind-blowing
alucinar 1 *vt* to hallucinate; *Fig (encantar)* to fascinate
2 *vi Fam* to be amazed, to be spaced out
alucinógeno,-a 1 *adj* hallucinogenic
2 *nm* hallucinogen
alud *nm* avalanche
aludido,-a *adj Fig* **darse por a.** to take it personally
aludir *vi* to allude to, to mention
alumbrado,-a 1 *adj* lit
2 *nm Elec* lighting; **a. público** street lighting
alumbrar 1 *vt (iluminar)* to light, to illuminate
2 *vi (parir)* to give birth
aluminio *nm* aluminium
alumnado *nm (de colegio)* pupils; *Univ* student body
alumno,-a *nm,f* (**a**) *(de colegio)* pupil; **a. externo** day pupil; **a. interno** boarder (**b**) *Univ* student
alusión *nf* allusion, mention
aluvión *nm* downpour; *Fig* **un a. de preguntas** a barrage of questions
alverja, alverjana *nf Am* pea
alza *nf* (**a**) rise; **en a.** rising; **jugar al a.** *(bolsa)* to bull the market (**b**) *Mil* sight

Takes the masculine articles **el** and **un**.

alzado,-a 1 *adj* raised, lifted; **votación a mano alzada** vote by a show of hands
2 *nm Arquit* elevation
alzamiento *nm (rebelión)* uprising
alzar [40] **1** *vt* to raise, to lift; **a. el vuelo** to take off; **a. los ojos/la vista** to look up; **álzate el cuello** turn your collar up
2 **alzarse** *vpr* (**a**) *(levantarse)* to get up, to rise (**b**) *(rebelarse)* to rise, to rebel (**c**) **a. con la victoria** to win, to be victorious
AM *nf (abr* **amplitude modulation**) AM
a.m. *adv* a.m.
ama *nf (señora)* lady of the house; *(dueña)* owner; **a. de casa** housewife; **a. de llaves** housekeeper

Takes the masculine articles **el** and **un**.

amabilidad *nf* kindness; *Fml* **tenga la a. de esperar** would you be so kind as to wait?
amable *adj* kind, nice; *Fml* **¿sería usted tan a. de ayudarme?** would you be so kind as to help me?
amado,-a 1 *adj* loved, beloved
2 *nm,f* sweetheart
amaestrar *vt* to train; *(domar)* to tame
amagar [42] *vt (amenazar)* to threaten; **amaga tormenta** a storm is threatening
amago *nm* (**a**) *(indicio)* first sign; **a. de infarto** onset of a heart attack (**b**) *(intento)* attempt (**c**) *Fig (amenaza)* threat
amainar *vi (viento etc)* to drop, to die down
amalgama *nf* amalgam
amalgamar *vt* to amalgamate
amamantar *vt* to breast-feed; *Zool* to suckle
amancay *nm Andes* amaryllis
amancebarse *vpr* to cohabit
amanecer [33] **1** *v impers* to dawn; **¿a qué hora amanece?** when does it get light?; **amaneció lluvioso** it was rainy at daybreak
2 *vi* **amanecimos en Finlandia** we were in Finland at daybreak; **amaneció muy enfermo** he woke up feeling very ill
3 *nm* dawn, daybreak; **al a.** at dawn
amanerado,-a *adj* mannered, affected
amansar *vt* (**a**) to tame (**b**) *Fig (apaciguar)* to tame, to calm
amante *nmf* lover; **a. del arte** art lover
amañar *vt* to fix, to fiddle; *(elecciones)* to rig
amapola *nf* poppy
amar 1 *vt* to love
2 **amarse** *vpr* to love each other
amaraje *nm Av* landing at sea
amargado,-a 1 *adj (rencoroso)* embittered, bitter; *Fam (agobiado)* pissed off; **estoy a. con los exámenes** I'm pissed off with the exams
2 *nm,f* bitter person
amargar [42] **1** *vt* to make bitter; *Fig* to embitter, to sour
2 **amargarse** *vpr Fig* to become embittered *o* bitter; **no te amargues por eso** don't let that make you bitter
amargo,-a *adj* bitter
amargor *nm*, **amargura** *nf* bitterness
amarillento,-a *adj* yellowish
amarillo,-a *adj & nm* yellow; **prensa amarilla** gutter press
amarilloso,-a *adj Ven* yellowish
amarra *nf* mooring rope; **soltar amarras** to cast off, to let go
amarradero *nm* mooring
amarrar *vt Náut* to moor, to tie up; *(atar)* to tie (up), to bind
amarrete,-a *adj Andes, RP Fam* mean, tight
amasar *vt* (**a**) *Culin* to knead (**b**) *Fig (fortuna)* to amass
amasiato *nm CAm, Méx* cohabitation, common-law marriage

amasijo *nm Fam* hotchpotch, jumble

amasio,-a *nm,f CAm, Méx* live-in lover, common-law partner

amateur *adj & nmf* amateur

amatista *nf* amethyst

amazona *nf* (a) *(jinete)* horsewoman (b) *(en mitología)* Amazon

Amazonas *n* el A. the Amazon

amazónico,-a *adj* Amazonian

ambages *nmpl* **hablar sin a.** to go straight to the point

ámbar *nm* amber

Amberes *n* Antwerp

ambición *nf* ambition

ambicionar *vt* to have as an ambition; **ambiciona ser presidente** his ambition is to become president

ambicioso,-a 1 *adj* ambitious

　2 *nm,f* ambitious person

ambidextro,-a *nm,f* ambidextrous person

ambientación *nf Cin & Teatro* setting

ambientado,-a *adj (bar etc)* lively

ambientador *nm* air freshener

ambiental *adj* environmental

ambientar 1 *vt* (a) *(bar etc)* to liven up (b) *Cin & Teatro* to set

　2 ambientarse *vpr (adaptarse)* to get used to

ambiente 1 *nm* (a) *(gen)* environment; *Fig (medio)* environment, milieu (b) *Andes, RP (habitación)* room

　2 *adj* environmental; **temperatura a.** room temperature

ambigüedad *nf* ambiguity

ambiguo,-a *adj* ambiguous

ámbito *nm* field, sphere; **empresa de a. nacional** nationwide company

ambos,-as *adj pl Fml* both; **por a. lados** on both sides

ambulancia *nf* ambulance

ambulante *adj* travelling, mobile; **biblioteca a.** mobile library

ambulatorio *nm* surgery, clinic

amedrentar *vt* to frighten, to scare

amén¹ *nm* amen

amén² *adv* a. de in addition to

amenaza *nf* threat

amenazador,-a, amenazante *adj* threatening, menacing

amenazar [40] *vt* to threaten; **a. de muerte a algn** to threaten to kill sb

amenizar [40] *vt* to liven up

ameno,-a *adj* entertaining

América *n* America; **A. Central/del Norte/del Sur** Central/North/South America

americana *nf (prenda)* jacket

americano,-a *adj & nm,f* American

amerindio,-a *adj & nm,f* Amerindian, American Indian

ameritar *vt Am* to deserve

amerizar [40] *vt* to land at sea

ametralladora *nf* machine gun

ametrallar *vt* to machine-gun

amianto *nm* asbestos

amigable *adj* friendly

amígdala *nf* tonsil

amigdalitis *nf* tonsillitis

amigo,-a 1 *nm,f* friend; **hacerse a. de** to make friends with; **hacerse amigos** to become friends; **son muy amigos** they are very good friends

　2 *adj (aficionado)* fond (**de** of)

amilanar 1 *vt* to frighten, to scare

　2 amilanarse *vpr* to be frightened o daunted

aminorar *vt* to reduce; **a. el paso** to slow down

amistad *nf* (a) friendship (b) **amistades** friends

amistoso,-a *adj* friendly

amnesia *nf* amnesia

amnistía *nf* amnesty

amo *nm* (a) *(dueño)* owner (b) *(señor)* master

amodorrarse *vpr* to become sleepy o drowsy

amoldar 1 *vt* to adapt, to adjust

　2 amoldarse *vpr* to adapt oneself

amonestación *nf* (a) rebuke, reprimand; *Dep* warning (b) *Rel* **amonestaciones** banns

amonestar *vt* (a) *(advertir)* to rebuke, to reprimand; *Dep* to warn (b) *Rel* to publish the banns of

amoniaco, amoníaco *nm* ammonia

amontonar 1 *vt* to pile up, to heap up

　2 amontonarse *vpr* to pile up, to heap up; *(gente)* to crowd together

amor *nm* love; **hacer el a.** to make love; **a. propio** self-esteem; **¡por el a. de Dios!** for God's sake!

amoral *adj* amoral

amoratado,-a *adj (de frío)* blue with cold; *(de un golpe)* black and blue

amordazar [40] *vt (perro)* to muzzle; *(persona)* to gag

amorfo,-a *adj* amorphous

amorío *nm* love affair, flirtation

amoroso,-a *adj* loving, affectionate

amortajar *vt* to shroud, to wrap in a shroud

amortiguador *nm Aut* shock absorber

amortiguar [45] *vt (golpe)* to cushion; *(ruido)* to muffle; *(luz)* to subdue

amortización *nf* repayment

amortizar [40] *vt* to pay off

amotinado,-a *nm,f* rioter; *Mil* mutineer

amotinamiento *nm* riot, rioting; *Mil* mutiny

amotinar *vt* to incite to riot; *Mil* to incite to mutiny

　2 amotinarse *vpr* to rise up; *Mil* to mutiny

amparar 1 *vt* to protect

　2 ampararse *vpr* to seek refuge

amparo *nm* protection, shelter; **al a. de la ley** under the protection of the law

amperio *nm* ampère, amp

ampliación *nf* enlargement; *(de plazo, casa)* extension

ampliar [29] *vt* to enlarge; *(casa, plazo)* to extend

amplificador *nm* amplifier

amplificar [44] *vt* to amplify

amplio,-a *adj* large, roomy; *(ancho)* wide, broad; **en el sentido más a. de la palabra** in the broadest sense of the word

amplitud *nf* (a) spaciousness; **a. de miras** broad-mindedness (b) *(de espacio)* room, space (c) *Fís* amplitude

ampolla *nf* (a) *Med* blister; *Fig* **levantar ampollas** to raise people's hackles (b) *(de medicina)* ampoule

ampuloso,-a *adj* pompous, bombastic

amputar *vt Med* to amputate; *Fig* to cut out

amueblar *vt* to furnish

amuermar *nf* (a) *(atontar)* to make feel dopey *o* groggy (b) *(aburrir)* to bore

amuleto *nm* amulet; **a. de la suerte** lucky charm

amurallar *vt* to wall, to fortify

anacronismo *nm* anachronism

ánade *nm* duck; **á. real** mallard

anales *nmpl* annals

analfabetismo *nm* illiteracy

analfabeto,-a *nm,f* illiterate

analgésico,-a *adj & nm* analgesic

análisis *nm inv* analysis; **a. de sangre** blood test

analista *nmf* analyst

analizar [40] *vt* to analyse

analogía *nf* analogy

analógico,-a *adj* analogue

análogo,-a *adj* analogous, similar

ananá *nm (pl* **ananaes**), **ananás** *nm (pl* **ananases**) pineapple

anaquel *nm* shelf

anaranjado,-a *adj & nm* orange

anarquía *nf* anarchy

anarquismo *nm* anarchism

anarquista *adj & nmf* anarchist

anatomía *nf* anatomy

anatómico,-a *adj* anatomical

anca *nf* haunch; **ancas de rana** frogs' legs

Takes the masculine articles **el** and **un**.

ancestral *adj* ancestral

ancho,-a 1 *adj* wide, broad; **a lo a.** breadthwise; **te está muy a.** it's too big for you
 2 *nm* (a) *(anchura)* width, breadth; **2 m de a.** 2 m wide; **¿qué a. tiene?** how wide is it? (b) *Cost* width
 3 *nfpl Fam* **a mis** *o* **tus anchas** at ease, comfortable

anchoa *nf* anchovy

anchura *nf* width, breadth

anciano,-a 1 *adj* very old
 2 *nm,f* old person; **los ancianos** old people

ancla *nf* anchor

Takes the masculine articles **el** and **un**.

anclar *vt & vi* to anchor

andadas *nfpl* **volver a las a.** to go back to one's old tricks

andaderas *nfpl* baby-walker

andadura *nf* walking

ándale *interj CAm, Méx Fam* come on!

Andalucía *n* Andalusia

andaluz,-a *adj & nm,f* Andalusian

andamiaje, andamio *nm* scaffolding

andanza *nf* adventure, happening

andar¹ *nm* **a.** *o* **andares** *nmpl* walk, gait

andar² [8] **1** *vi* (a) to walk (b) *(coche etc)* to move; **este coche anda despacio** this car goes very slowly (c) *(funcionar)* to work; **esto no anda** this doesn't work (d) *Fam* **anda por los cuarenta** he's about forty; **anda siempre diciendo que ...** he's always saying that ...; **¿cómo andamos de tiempo?** how are we off for time?; **tu bolso debe a. por ahí** your bag must be over there somewhere
 2 *vt (recorrer)* to walk

andariego,-a *adj* fond of walking

andén *nm* (a) *(en estación)* platform (b) *Andes, CAm (acera) Br* pavement, *US* sidewalk (c) *Andes (bancal de tierra)* terrace

Andes *nmpl* Andes

andinismo *nm Am* mountaineering

andinista *nmf Am* mountaineer

andino,-a *adj & nm,f* Andean

andrajo *nm* rag, tatter

andrajoso,-a *adj* ragged, tattered

androide *nm* android

andurriales *nmpl Fam* out-of-the-way place

anécdota *nf* anecdote

anecdótico,-a *adj* anecdotal

anegar [42] *vt*, **anegarse** *upr* to flood

anejo,-a 1 *adj* attached, joined (**a** to)
 2 *nm* appendix

anemia *nf* anaemia

anestesia *nf* anaesthesia

anestésico,-a *adj & nm* anaesthetic

anexar *vt* to annex

anexión *nf* annexation

anexionar *vt* to annex

anexo,-a 1 *adj* attached, joined (**a** to)
 2 *nm* appendix

anfetamina *nf* amphetamine

anfibio,-a 1 *adj* amphibious
 2 *nm* amphibian

anfiteatro *nm* (a) amphitheatre (b) *Cin & Teatro* gallery

anfitrión,-ona *nm,f* host, *f* hostess

ángel *nm* (a) angel; **á. de la guarda** guardian angel (b) *Am (micrófono)* hand-held microphone

angelical, angélico,-a *adj* angelic

angina *nf* angina; **tener anginas** to have tonsillitis; *Med* **a. de pecho** angina pectoris

anglófono,-a 1 *adj* English-speaking
 2 *nm,f* English speaker

anglosajón,-ona *adj & nm,f* Anglo-Saxon

Angola *n* Angola

angosto,-a *adj Fml* narrow

anguila *nf* eel; **a. de mar** conger eel

angula *nf* elver

angular *adj* angular; *Fot* **(objetivo) gran a.** wide-angle lens; **piedra a.** cornerstone

ángulo *nm* angle; *(rincón)* corner

angustia *nf* anguish

angustiar [43] *vt* to distress

angustioso,-a *adj* distressing

anhelar *vt* to long for, to yearn for

anhelo *nm* longing, yearning

anhídrido *nm* **a. carbónico** carbon dioxide

anidar *vi* to nest

anilla *nf* ring; **carpeta de anillas** ring-binder

anillo *nm* ring; **a. de boda** wedding ring

ánima *nf* soul

> Takes the masculine articles **el** and **un**.

animación *nf (diversión)* entertainment

animado,-a *adj (fiesta etc)* lively

animador,-a *nm,f* **(a)** entertainer; *TV* presenter; **a. cultural** cultural organizer **(b)** *Dep* cheerleader

animadversión *nf* ill feeling, animosity

animal 1 *nm* animal; *Fig (basto)* brute; *(necio)* dunce
  2 *adj* animal

animar 1 *vt* **(a)** *(alentar)* to encourage **(b)** *(alegrar) (persona)* to cheer up; *(fiesta, bar)* to liven up, to brighten up
  2 animarse *vpr* **(a)** *(persona)* to cheer up; *(fiesta, reunión)* to brighten up **(b)** ¿**te animas a venir?** do you fancy coming along?

anímico,-a *adj* **estado a.** frame o state of mind

ánimo *nm* **(a)** *(espíritu)* spirit; **estado de á.** frame o state of mind **(b)** **con á. de** *(intención)* with the intention of **(c)** *(valor, coraje)* courage; **dar ánimos a** to encourage; **¡á.!** cheer up!

animosidad *nf* animosity

animoso,-a *adj* cheerful

aniñado,-a *adj* childlike; *Pey* childish

aniquilación *nf* annihilation

aniquilar *vt* to annihilate

anís *nm* **(a)** *(bebida)* anisette **(b)** *(grano)* aniseed

anisete *nm* anisette

aniversario *nm* anniversary

ano *nm* anus

anoche *adv* last night; *(por la tarde)* yesterday evening; **antes de a.** the night before last

anochecer [33] **1** *v impers* to get dark; **cuando anochece** at nightfall, at dusk
  2 *vi* to be somewhere at dusk; **anochecimos en Cuenca** we were in Cuenca at dusk
  3 *nm* nightfall, dusk

anodino,-a *adj (insustancial)* insubstantial; *(soso)* insipid, dull

anomalía *nf* anomaly

anómalo,-a *adj* anomalous

anonadado,-a *adj* **me quedé/dejó a.** I was astonished

anonimato *nm* anonymity; **permanecer en el a.** to remain anonymous o nameless

anónimo,-a 1 *adj* **(a)** *(desconocido)* anonymous **(b)** *Com* **sociedad anónima** public liability company, *US* incorporated company
  2 *nm (carta)* anonymous letter

anorak *nm (pl* **anoraks***)* anorak

anorexia *nf* anorexia

anormal 1 *adj* **(a)** abnormal **(b)** *(inhabitual)* unusual; **una situación a.** an irregular situation **(c)** *Med* subnormal
  2 *nmf Med* subnormal person

anotación *nf* **(a)** annotation **(b)** *(apunte)* note

anotar 1 *vt* **(a)** to annotate **(b)** *(apuntar)* to take down, to make a note of
  2 anotarse *vpr RP (en curso)* to enrol

anquilosado,-a *adj Fig* fossilized; **a. en el pasado** locked in the past

anquilosarse *vpr Fig* to stagnate

ansia *nf* **(a)** *(deseo)* longing, yearning **(b)** *(ansiedad)* anxiety **(c)** *Med* sick feeling

> Takes the masculine articles **el** and **un**.

ansiar [29] *vt* to long for, to yearn for

ansiedad *nf* anxiety; **con a.** anxiously

ansioso,-a *adj* **(a)** *(deseoso)* eager **(por** for) **(b)** *(avaricioso)* greedy

antagónico,-a *adj* antagonistic

antagonismo *nm* antagonism

antagonista 1 *adj* antagonistic
  2 *nmf* antagonist

antaño *adv* in the past, formerly

antártico,-a 1 *adj* Antarctic
  2 *nm* **el A.** the Antarctic

Antártida *nf* Antarctica

ante¹ *nm* **(a)** *Zool* elk, moose **(b)** *(piel)* suede

ante² *prep* **(a)** before, in the presence of; *Jur* **a. notario** in the presence of a notary; **a. todo** most of all **(b)** *(en vista de)* faced with, in view of; **a. la crisis energética** faced with the energy crisis

anteanoche *adv* the night before last

anteayer *adv* the day before yesterday

antecedente 1 *adj* previous
  2 *nm* antecedent
  3 *nmpl* **(a)** **antecedentes** *(historial)* record; *Jur* **antecedentes penales** criminal record **(b)** *Fig* **poner en antecedentes** to put in the picture

anteceder *vt* to precede, to go before

antecesor,-a *nm,f* **(a)** *(en un cargo)* predecessor **(b)** *(antepasado)* ancestor

antedicho,-a *adj* above-mentioned

antelación *nf* notice; **con poca a.** at short notice; **con un mes de a.** a month beforehand, with a month's notice

antemano *adv* **de a.** beforehand, in advance

antena *nf* **(a)** *Rad & TV* aerial; **a. parabólica** satellite dish; **en a.** on the air **(b)** *Zool* antenna, feeler

anteojo *nm* **(a)** telescope **(b)** **anteojos** *(binoculares)* binoculars; *Am (gafas)* glasses, spectacles

antepasado,-a *nm,f* ancestor

antepecho *nm (de ventana)* sill; *(pretil)* parapet, guardrail

antepenúltimo,-a *adj* antepenultimate; **el capítulo a.** the last chapter but two

anteponer [19] *(pp* **antepuesto)** *vt Fig* to give preference to

anteproyecto *nm* preliminary plan, draft; *Pol* **a. de ley** draft bill

antepuesto,-a *pp de* anteponer

antepuse *pt indef de* anteponer

anterior *adj* (a) previous; **el día a.** the day before (b) *(delantero)* front; **parte a.** front part

anterioridad *nf* **con a.** before; **con a. a** prior to, before

anteriormente *adv* previously, before

antes *adv* (a) *(tiempo)* before; **a. de las tres** before three o'clock; **mucho a.** long before; **la noche a.** the night before; **cuanto a.** as soon as possible (b) *(antaño)* in the past; **a. llovía más** it used to rain more in the past (c) *(lugar)* before; **a. del semáforo** before the traffic lights (d) **a. prefiero hacerlo yo** I'd rather do it myself; **a. (bien)** on the contrary

antesala *nf* antechamber, anteroom; *Fig* **en la a. de** on the eve of

anti- *pref* anti-

antiadherente *adj* nonstick

antiaéreo,-a *adj* anti-aircraft

antibiótico,-a *adj & nm* antibiotic

anticaspa *adj* anti-dandruff

anticiclón *nm* anticyclone, high pressure area

anticipación *nf* bringing forward; **con a.** in advance

anticipadamente *adv* in advance

anticipado,-a *adj* brought forward; **elecciones anticipadas** early elections; **gracias anticipadas** thanks in advance; *Com* **por a.** in advance

anticipar 1 *vt (acontecimiento)* to bring forward; *(dinero)* to pay in advance; **no anticipemos acontecimientos** we'll cross that bridge when we come to it

2 anticiparse *upr* (a) *(adelantarse)* to beat to it; **iba a decírtelo, pero él se me anticipó** I was going to tell you, but he beat me to it (b) *(llegar pronto)* to arrive early; *Fig* **a. a su tiempo** to be ahead of one's time

anticipo *nm (adelanto)* advance; **pedir un a.** to ask for an advance (on one's wages)

anticonceptivo,-a *adj & nm* contraceptive

anticongelante *adj & nm (de radiador)* antifreeze; *(de parabrisas)* de-icer

anticonstitucional *adj* unconstitutional

anticuado,-a *adj* antiquated

anticuario,-a *nm,f* antique dealer

anticucho *nm Andes (brocheta)* kebab

anticuerpo *nm* antibody

antídoto *nm* antidote

antier *adv Am Fam* the day before yesterday

antiestético,-a *adj* ugly, unsightly

antifaz *nm* mask

antigás *adj* careta/mascarilla **a.** gas mask

antigualla *nf Pey* museum piece

antigüedad *nf* (a) *(período histórico)* antiquity; **en la a.** in olden days, in former times (b) *(en cargo)* seniority (c) **tienda de antigüedades** antique shop

antiguo,-a *adj* (a) old, ancient (b) *(pasado de moda)* old-fashioned (c) *(en cargo)* senior (d) *(anterior)* former

antihigiénico,-a *adj* unhygienic, unhealthy

antihistamínico,-a *adj & nm* antihistamine

Antillas *nfpl* **las A.** the West Indies, the Antilles

antinatural *adj* unnatural, contrary to nature

antiniebla *adj inv* **luces a.** foglights

antipatía *nf* antipathy, dislike; **tener a. a** to dislike

antipático,-a *adj* unpleasant; **Pedro me es a.** I don't like Pedro

antípodas *nfpl* **las A.** the Antipodes

antiquísimo,-a *(superl de* antiguo*) adj* very old, ancient

antirrobo 1 *adj inv* antitheft; **alarma a.** burglar alarm; *(para coche)* car alarm

2 *nm (para coche)* car alarm; *(para casa)* burglar alarm

antisemita 1 *adj* anti-Semitic

2 *nmf* anti-Semite

antiséptico,-a *adj & nm* antiseptic

antítesis *nf inv* antithesis

antivirus *nm inv Informát* antivirus system

antojadizo,-a *adj* capricious, unpredictable

antojarse *upr* (a) **cuando se me antoja** when I feel like it; **se le antojó un helado** he fancied an ice-cream (b) *(suponer)* **se me antoja que no lo sabe** I have the feeling that he doesn't know

antojitos *nmpl Méx* snacks, appetizers

antojo *nm* (a) *(capricho)* whim, caprice; *(de embarazada)* craving; **a su a.** in one's own way, as one pleases (b) *(en la piel)* birthmark

antología *nf* anthology

antonomasia *nf* **por a.** par excellence

antorcha *nf* torch

antro *nm* dump, hole; *Fig* **a. de perdición** den of vice

antropología *nf* anthropology

antropólogo,-a *nm,f* anthropologist

anual *adj* annual; **ingresos anuales** yearly income

anualidad *nf* annual payment, annuity

anuario *nm* yearbook

anudar *vt* (a) *(atar)* to knot, to tie (b) *Fig (unir)* to join, to bring together

anulación *nf* cancellation; *(de matrimonio)* annulment; *(de ley)* repeal

anular¹ *nm* ring finger

anular² *vt* (a) *Com (pedido)* to cancel; *Dep (gol)* to disallow; *(matrimonio)* to annul; *Jur* *(ley)* to repeal (**b**) *Informát* to delete

anunciador,-a *adj* empresa anunciadora advertising company

anunciante *nm* advertiser

anunciar [43] **1** *vt* (**a**) *(producto etc)* to advertise (**b**) *(avisar)* to announce
2 anunciarse *vpr* to advertise oneself; **a. en un periódico** to put an advert in a newspaper

anuncio *nm* (**a**) *(comercial)* advertisement, advert, ad (**b**) *(aviso)* announcement (**c**) *(cartel)* notice, poster

anzuelo *nm* (fish) hook

añadidura *nf* addition; **por a.** besides, on top of everything else

añadir *vt* to add (**a** to)

añejo,-a *adj* (**a**) *(vino, queso)* mature (**b**) *(estropeado)* stale

añicos *nmpl* smithereens; **hacer a.** to smash to smithereens

añil 1 *adj* indigo, blue
2 *nm* (**a**) *Bot* indigo plant (**b**) *(color)* indigo

año *nm* (**a**) year; **el a. pasado** last year; **el a. que viene** next year; **hace años** a long time ago, years ago; **los años noventa** the nineties; **todo el a.** all the year (round); **a. luz** light year (**b**) **¿cuántos años tienes?** how old are you?; **tiene seis años** he's six years old; **entrado en años** getting on

añoranza *nf* longing, yearning

añorar *vt (pasado)* to long for, to yearn for; *(país)* to feel homesick for, to miss

APA *nf* (*abr* **Asociación de Padres de Alumnos**) = Spanish association for parents of schoolchildren, ≃ PTA

Takes the masculine articles **el** and **un**.

apabullar *vt* to bewilder

apacentar [1] *vt* to put out to pasture, to graze

apacible *adj* mild, calm

apaciguar [45] **1** *vt (calmar)* to pacify, to appease
2 apaciguarse *vpr (persona)* to calm down; *(tormenta)* to abate

apadrinar *vt* (**a**) *(en bautizo)* to act as godfather to; *(en boda)* to be best man for (**b**) *(artista)* to sponsor

apagado,-a *adj* (**a**) *(luz, cigarro)* out (**b**) *(color)* dull; *(voz)* sad; *(mirada)* expressionless, lifeless; *(carácter, persona)* spiritless

apagar [42] *vt (fuego)* to put out; *(luz, tele etc)* to turn off, to switch off; *(color)* to soften; *(sed)* to quench

apagón *nm* power cut, blackout

apaisado,-a *adj* (**a**) oblong (**b**) *(papel)* landscape

apalabrar *vt (concertar)* to make a verbal agreement on

apalancar [44] **1** *vt* to lever up
2 apalancarse *vpr Fam* to ensconce oneself, to settle down

apalear¹ *vt* to beat, to thrash

apalear² *vt Agr (grano)* to winnow

apañar¹ *vt* to mend, to fix
2 apañarse *vpr Fam* **apañárselas** to manage

apaño *nm* mend, repair

apapachar *vt Méx Fam (mimar)* to cuddle; *(consentir)* to spoil

apapacho *nm Méx Fam (mimo)* cuddle

aparador *nm (mueble)* sideboard; *(de tienda)* shop window

aparato *nm* (**a**) (piece of) apparatus; *(dispositivo)* device; *(instrumento)* instrument; **a. de radio/televisión** radio/television set; **a. digestivo** digestive system; **a. eléctrico** thunder and lightning (**b**) *Tel* **¿quién está al a.?** who's speaking? (**c**) *(ostentación)* display

aparatoso,-a *adj* (**a**) *(pomposo)* ostentatious, showy (**b**) *(espectacular)* spectacular (**c**) *(grande)* bulky

aparcamiento *nm (en la calle)* parking place; *(parking)* Br car park, US parking lot

aparcar [44] *vt* to park

aparcería *nf Agr* sharecropping

apareamiento *nm* (**a**) *(de cosas)* pairing off (**b**) *(de animales)* mating

aparear *vt,* **aparearse** *vpr* to mate

aparecer [33] **1** *vi* (**a**) to appear; **no aparece en mi lista** he is not on my list (**b**) to turn up, to show up; **¿apareció el dinero?** did the money turn up?; **no apareció nadie** nobody turned up
2 aparecerse *vpr* to appear

aparejado,-a *adj* **llevar** *o* **traer a.** to entail

aparejador,-a *nm,f* quantity surveyor

aparejar *vt* (**a**) *(caballo)* to harness (**b**) *(emparejar)* to pair off

aparejo *nm* (**a**) *(equipo)* equipment (**b**) *(de caballo)* harness

aparentar 1 *vt* (**a**) *(fingir)* to affect (**b**) *(tener aspecto)* to look; **no aparenta esa edad** she doesn't look that age
2 *vi* to show off

aparente *adj* (**a**) apparent; **sin motivo a.** for no apparent reason (**b**) *Fam (conveniente)* suitable

aparición *nf* (**a**) appearance (**b**) *(visión)* apparition

apariencia *nf* appearance; **en a.** apparently; *Fig* **guardar las apariencias** to keep up appearances

apartado,-a 1 *adj (lugar)* remote, isolated; **mantente a. de él** keep away from him
2 *nm* (**a**) *(párrafo)* section, paragraph (**b**) **a. de correos** Post Office Box

apartamento *nm* (small) flat, apartment

apartar 1 *vt* (**a**) *(alejar)* to move away, to remove; **a. la mirada** to look away (**b**) *(guardar)* to put aside
2 *vi* **¡aparta!** move out of the way!
3 apartarse *vpr (alejarse)* to move over, to move away; **apártate de en medio** move out of the way

aparte 1 *adv* (**a**) aside; **ponlo a.** put it aside;

modestia/bromas a. modesty/joking apart (**b**) **eso hay que pagarlo a.** *(separadamente)* you have to pay for that separately (**c**) **a. de eso** *(además)* besides that; *(excepto)* apart from that (**d**) **eso es caso a.** that's completely different

2 *nm* (**a**) *Teatro* aside (**b**) *Ling* **punto y a.** full stop, new paragraph

apasionado,-a 1 *adj* passionate; **a. de la música** very fond of music

2 *nm,f* enthusiast

apasionante *adj* exciting

apasionar *vt* to excite, to thrill; **le apasiona el jazz** he is mad about jazz

apatía *nf* apathy

apático,-a 1 *adj* apathetic

2 *nm,f* apathetic person

apátrida 1 *adj* stateless

2 *nmf* stateless person

apdo. *(abr* **apartado***)* P.O. Box

apeadero *nm* halt

apearse *vpr (de un autobús, tren)* to get off, to alight; *(de un coche)* to get out; **se apeó en Jerez** he got off in Jerez

apechugar [42] *vi* **a. con** to shoulder

apedrear *vt* to throw stones at

apegado,-a *adj* devoted, attached (**a** to)

apegarse [42] *vpr* to become devoted *o* attached (**a** to)

apego *nm* love, affection; **tener a. a** to be attached to

apelación *nf* appeal; **interponer a.** to lodge an appeal

apelar *vi* (**a**) *Jur* to appeal (**b**) *(recurrir)* to resort (**a** to)

apellidarse *vpr* to have as a surname, to be called

apellido *nm* surname; **a. de soltera** maiden name

apelmazado,-a *adj* stodgy

apelotonar 1 *vt* to pile up, to put into a pile

2 apelotonarse *vpr (gente)* to crowd together

apenado,-a *adj* (**a**) *(entristecido)* sad (**b**) *Andes, CAm, Carib, Méx (avergonzado)* ashamed, embarrassed

apenar 1 *vt* to sadden

2 apenarse *vpr* (**a**) *(entristecerse)* to be saddened (**b**) *Andes, CAm, Carib, Méx (avergonzarse)* to be ashamed, to be embarrassed

apenas *adv* (**a**) *(casi no)* hardly, scarcely; **a. come** he hardly eats anything; **a. (si) hay nieve** there is hardly any snow (**b**) *(tan pronto como)* scarcely; **a. llegó, sonó el teléfono** no sooner had he arrived than the phone rang

apéndice *nm* appendix

apendicitis *nf* appendicitis

apercibir 1 *vt* to warn

2 apercibirse *vpr* **apercibirse (de)** to notice

aperitivo *nm (bebida)* apéritif; *(comida)* appetizer

apero *nm (usu pl)* equipment, tools; **aperos de labranza** farming implements

apertura *nf* (**a**) *(comienzo)* opening (**b**) *Pol* liberalization

apestar 1 *vi* to stink (**a** of)

2 *vt* to infect with the plague

apetecer [33] *vi* **¿qué te apetece para cenar?** what would you like for supper?; **¿te apetece ir al cine?** do you fancy going to the cinema?

apetecible *adj* tempting, inviting

apetito *nm* appetite; **tengo mucho a.** I'm really hungry

apetitoso,-a *adj* appetizing, tempting; *(comida)* delicious, tasty

apiadarse *vpr* to take pity (**de** on)

ápice *nm* (**a**) *(punta)* apex (**b**) *Fig* **ni un á.** not a bit

apicultura *nf* beekeeping, apiculture

apilar *vt,* **apilarse** *vpr* to pile up, to heap up

apiñarse *vpr* to crowd together

apio *nm* celery

apisonadora *nf* roadroller, steamroller

apisonar *vt* to roll

aplacar [44] **1** *vt* to placate, to calm

2 aplacarse *vpr* to calm down

aplanar *vt* to level

aplastante *adj* crushing; *Pol* **victoria a.** landslide victory

aplastar *vt* (**a**) to flatten, to squash (**b**) *Fig (vencer)* to crush

aplatanarse *vpr Fam* to become lethargic

aplaudir *vt* (**a**) to clap, to applaud (**b**) *Fig* to applaud

aplauso *nm* applause

aplazamiento *nm* postponement, adjournment; *(de un pago)* deferment

aplazar [40] *vt* to postpone, to adjourn; *Fin (pago)* to defer

aplicación *nf* application

aplicado,-a *adj* hard-working

aplicar [44] **1** *vt* to apply

2 aplicarse *vpr* (**a**) *(esforzarse)* to apply oneself, to work hard (**b**) *(norma, ley)* to apply, to be applicable

aplique *nm* wall light, wall lamp

aplomo *nm* aplomb

apocado,-a *adj* shy, timid

apocamiento *nm* timidity, lack of self-confidence

apocarse [44] *vpr* to become frightened

apodar *vt* to nickname

apoderado,-a *nm,f* (**a**) agent, representative (**b**) *(de torero, deportista)* manager

apoderarse *vpr* to take possession (**de** of), to seize; *Fig* **el miedo se apoderó de ella** she was seized by fear

apodo *nm* nickname

apogeo *nm* height; **estar en pleno a.** *(fama etc)* to be at its height

apolillarse *vpr* to get moth-eaten

apolítico,-a *adj* apolitical

apología *nf* apology, defence

apoltronarse *vpr Fam* to vegetate

apoplejía *nf* apoplexy

apoquinar *vt Fam* to cough up, to fork out
aporrear *vt* to beat, to hit, to thrash; *(puerta)* to bang; *Fam* **a. el piano** to bang (away) on the piano
aportación *nf* contribution
aportar 1 *vt* to contribute
2 *vi Náut* to reach port
aposentarse *upr* to stay, to lodge
aposento *nm* room
aposta *adv* on purpose, intentionally
apostar¹ [2] **1** *vt* to bet; **te apuesto una cena a que no viene** I bet you a dinner that he won't come
2 *vi* to bet (**por** on); **a. a los caballos** to bet on horses; **apuesto a que sí viene** I bet she will come
3 apostarse *upr* to bet; **me apuesto lo que quieras** I bet you anything
apostar² *vt (situar)* to post, to station
apostilla *nf* note
apóstol *nm* apostle
apóstrofo *nm* apostrophe
apostura *nf* good bearing
apoteósico,-a *adj* enormous, tremendous
apoyacabezas *nm Aut* headrest
apoyar 1 *vt* (**a**) to lean (**b**) *(causa)* to support
2 apoyarse *upr* (**a**) **a. en** to lean on; **apóyate en mi brazo** take my arm (**b**) **a. en** *(opinión)* to be based on, to rest on
apoyo *nm* support
apreciable *adj* appreciable, noticeable
apreciación *nf* appreciation
apreciar [43] **1** *vt* (**a**) to appreciate (**b**) *(percibir)* to notice, to see
2 apreciarse *upr* to be noticeable
aprecio *nm* regard, esteem; **tener a. a algn** to be fond of sb
aprehender *vt (alijo, botín)* to apprehend, to seize
aprehensión *nf* seizure
apremiante *adj* urgent, pressing
apremiar [43] *vi* to be urgent; **el tiempo apremia** time is at a premium
aprender *vt* to learn; **así aprenderás** that'll teach you
aprendiz,-a *nm,f* apprentice, trainee
aprendizaje *nm* (**a**) learning (**b**) *(instrucción)* apprenticeship, traineeship
aprensión *nf* apprehension
aprensivo,-a *adj* apprehensive
apresar *vt* to seize, to capture
aprestar 1 *vt* to prepare, to get ready
2 aprestarse *upr* to get ready
apresurado,-a *adj (persona)* in a hurry; *(cosa)* hurried
apresuramiento *nm* haste, hurry
apresurar 1 *vt (paso etc)* to speed up
2 apresurarse *upr* to hurry up
apretado,-a *adj* (**a**) *(ropa, cordón)* tight; **íbamos todos apretados en el coche** we were all squashed together in the car (**b**) *(día, agenda)* busy

apretar [1] **1** *vt (botón)* to press; *(nudo, tornillo)* to tighten; **a. el gatillo** to pull the trigger; **me aprietan las botas** these boots are too tight for me
2 *vi* **apretaba el calor** it was really hot
3 apretarse *upr* to squeeze together, to cram together; *Fig* **a. el cinturón** to tighten one's belt
apretón *nm* squeeze; **a. de manos** handshake
apretujar 1 *vt* to squeeze, to crush
2 apretujarse *upr* to squeeze together, to cram together
aprieto *nm* tight spot, fix, jam; **poner a algn en un a.** to put sb in an awkward position
aprisa *adv* quickly
aprisionar *vt (atrapar)* to trap
aprobación *nf* approval
aprobado *nm Educ* pass
aprobar [2] *vt* (**a**) *(autorizar)* to approve (**b**) *(estar de acuerdo con)* to approve of (**c**) *Educ* to pass (**d**) *Pol (ley)* to pass
aprontar 1 *vt (preparar)* to quickly prepare o get ready
2 aprontarse *upr RP (prepararse)* to get ready; **apróntate para cuando llegue tu papá!** just wait till your father gets back!
apropiado,-a *adj* suitable, appropriate
apropiarse [43] *upr* to appropriate
aprovechado,-a *adj* (**a**) **mal a.** *(recurso, tiempo)* wasted; **bien a.** put to good use (**b**) *(espacio)* well-planned (**c**) *(egoísta)* self-seeking
aprovechamiento *nm* use
aprovechar 1 *vt* (**a**) to make good use of, to make the most of; **aprovechamos bien la tarde** we've done lots of things this afternoon (**b**) *(recursos etc)* to take advantage of; **a. la ocasión** to seize the opportunity
2 *vi* **¡que aproveche!** enjoy your meal!, bon appétit!
3 aprovecharse *upr* to use to one's advantage, to take advantage; **a. de algn** to take advantage of sb; **a. de algo** to make the most of sth
aprovisionar *vt* to supply, to provide; **a. las tropas** to give supplies to the troops
aproximación *nf* (**a**) approximation (**b**) *(en lotería)* consolation prize
aproximadamente *adv* approximately, roughly
aproximado,-a *adj* approximate; **un cálculo a.** a rough estimate
aproximar 1 *vt* to bring o put nearer
2 aproximarse *upr* **aproximarse** (**a**) to approach
aproximativo,-a *adj* approximate, rough
aptitud *nf* aptitude; **prueba de a.** aptitude test
apto,-a *adj* (**a**) *(apropiado)* suitable, appropriate; *Cin* **a. para todos los públicos** *Br* U, *US* G (**b**) *(capacitado)* capable, able (**c**) *Educ* passed

apuesta *nf* bet, wager

apuesto,-a *adj* good-looking; *(hombre)* handsome

apunado,-a *adj Andes* **estar a.** to have altitude sickness

apunarse *upr Andes* to get altitude sickness

apuntador,-a *nm,f Teatro* prompter

apuntalar *vt* to prop up, to shore up, to underpin

apuntar 1 *vt* (a) *(con arma)* to aim (b) *(señalar)* to point out (c) *(anotar)* to note down, to make a note of (d) *(indicar)* to indicate, to suggest; **todo parece a. a ...** everything seems to point to ...

2 *vi* **cuando apunta el día** when day breaks

3 apuntarse *upr* (a) *(en una lista)* to put one's name down (b) *Fam* **¿te apuntas?** are you game?; **me apunto** count me in

apunte *nm (usu pl)* note; **tomar apuntes** to take notes

apuñalar *vt* to stab

apurado,-a 1 *adj* (a) *(necesitado)* in need; **a. de dinero** hard up for money; **a. de tiempo** in a hurry (b) *(preocupado)* worried; *(avergonzado)* embarrassed (c) *(situación)* awkward, difficult (d) *(afeitado)* close

2 *nm (afeitado)* close shave

apurar 1 *vt* (a) *(terminar)* to finish off, to end (b) *(preocupar)* to worry

2 apurarse *upr* (a) *(preocuparse)* to worry, to get worried; **no te apures** don't worry (b) *(darse prisa)* to rush, to hurry, to pester; **apúrate** get a move on

apuro *nm* (a) *(situación difícil)* tight spot, fix, jam; **estar en un a.** to be in a tight spot (b) *(escasez de dinero)* hardship; **pasar apuros** to be hard up (c) *(vergüenza)* embarrassment; **¡qué a.!** how embarrassing!

aquejado,-a *adj* suffering (**de** from)

aquel,-ella *adj dem* (a) that; **a. niño** that boy (b) **aquellos,-as** those; **aquellas niñas** those girls

aquél,-élla *pron dem m,f* (a) that one; *(el anterior)* the former; **aquél/aquélla ... éste/ésta** the former ... the latter (b) **todo a. que** anyone who, whoever (c) **aquéllos,-as** those; *(los anteriores)* the former

> Note that **aquél** and its various forms can be written without an accent when there is no risk of confusion with the adjective.

aquella *adj dem f ver* **aquel**

aquélla *pron dem f ver* **aquél**

aquello *pron neut f* that, it

aquellos,-as *adj dem pl ver* **aquel,-ella**

aquéllos,-as *pron dem m,f ver* **aquél,-élla**

aquí *adv* (a) *(lugar)* here; **a. arriba/fuera** up/out here; **a. está** here it is; **a. mismo** right here; **de a. para allá** up and down, to and fro; **hasta a.** this far; **por a., por favor** this way please; **está por a.** it's around here somewhere (b) *(tiempo)* **de a. en adelante** from now on; **de aquí a junio** between now and June; **hasta a.** up till now

aquietar *vt* to pacify, to calm down

ara *nf Fml* **en aras de** for the sake of

> Takes the masculine articles **el** and **un**.

árabe 1 *adj (de Arabia)* Arab

2 *nmf (persona)* Arab

3 *nm (idioma)* Arabic

Arabia *n* Arabia; **A. Saudita** Saudi Arabia

arado *nm* plough

Aragón *n* Aragon

aragonés,-esa *adj & nm,f* Aragonese

arancel *nm* tariff, customs duty

arancelario,-a *adj* tariff, duty; **derechos arancelarios** duties; **barreras arancelarias** customs barriers

arandela *nf Téc* washer; *(anilla)* ring

araña *nf* (a) spider (b) *(lámpara)* chandelier

arañar *vt* to scratch

arañazo *nm* scratch

arar *vt* to plough

araucaria *nf* araucaria, monkey puzzle tree

arbitraje *nm* (a) arbitration (b) *Dep* refereeing; *Ten* umpiring

arbitrar *vt* (a) to arbitrate (b) *Dep* to referee; *Ten* to umpire

arbitrariedad *nf* (a) arbitrariness (b) *(acto)* arbitrary action

arbitrario,-a *adj* arbitrary

arbitrio *nm (voluntad)* will; *(juicio)* judgement

árbitro,-a *nm,f* (a) *Dep* referee; *(de tenis)* umpire (b) *(mediador)* arbitrator

árbol *nm* (a) *Bot* tree (b) *Téc* shaft (c) *Náut* mast (d) *(gráfico)* tree (diagram); **á. genealógico** family o genealogical tree

arbolado,-a 1 *adj* wooded

2 *nm* woodland

arboleda *nf* grove

arbusto *nm* bush, shrub

arca *nf* (a) chest (b) *(para caudales)* strongbox, safe; **arcas públicas** Treasury

> Takes the masculine articles **el** and **un**.

arcada *nf* (a) arcade; *(de puente)* arch (b) *(náusea)* retching

arcaico,-a *adj* archaic

arcén *nm* verge; *(de autopista) Br* hard shoulder, *US* shoulder

archi- *pref* super-

archiconocido,-a *adj* extremely well-known

archipiélago *nm* archipelago

archivador *nm* filing cabinet

archivar *vt* (a) *(documento etc)* to file (away) (b) *(caso, asunto)* to shelve (c) *Informát* to save

archivo *nm* (a) file (b) *(archivador)* filing cabinet (c) **archivos** archives (d) *Informát* file; **a. adjunto** attachment

arcilla *nf* clay

arco *nm* (**a**) *Arquit* arch (**b**) *Mat & Elec* arc (**c**) *(de violín)* bow (**d**) *(para flechas)* bow; **tiro con a.** archery (**e**) **a. iris** rainbow (**f**) *Am Dep (portería)* goal, goalmouth

arder *vi* to burn; *Fam* **la conversación está que arde** the conversation is really heating up; **Juan está que arde** Juan is really fuming

ardid *nm* scheme, plot

ardiente *adj* (**a**) *(encendido)* burning; **capilla a.** chapel of rest (**b**) *Fig (fervoroso)* eager

ardilla *nf* squirrel

ardor *nm* (**a**) heat; *Med* **a. de estómago** heartburn (**b**) *Fig* ardour, fervour

ardoroso,-a *adj Fig* ardent, passionate

arduo,-a *adj* arduous

área *nf* (**a**) area; *Dep* penalty area (**b**) *(medida)* are *(100 square metres)*

Takes the masculine articles **el** and **un**.

arena *nf* (**a**) sand; **playa de a.** sandy beach (**b**) *Taurom* bullring

arengar [42] *vt* to harangue

arenisca *nf* sandstone

arenoso,-a *adj* sandy

arenque *nm* herring; *Culin* **a. ahumado** kipper

arepa *nf Carib, Col* = pancake made of maize flour

arete *nm Andes, Méx* earring

argamasa *nf* mortar

Argel *n* Algiers

Argelia *n* Algeria

argelino,-a *adj & nm,f* Algerian

Argentina *n* Argentina

argentino,-a *adj & nm,f* Argentinian, Argentine

argolla *nf* (**a**) *(aro)* (large) ring (**b**) *Col, Méx (alianza)* wedding ring

argot *nm (popular)* slang; *(técnico)* jargon

argucia *nf* ruse

argüende *nm Méx Fam* (**a**) *(alboroto)* rumpus, shindy; **armar (un) a.** to kick up a rumpus (**b**) *(enredo, confusión)* mess, trouble; **meterse en un a.** to get into a mess

argüir [62] *vt* (**a**) *(deducir)* to deduce, to conclude (**b**) *(argumentar)* to argue

argumentación *nf* argument

argumentar *vt* = argüir

argumento *nm* (**a**) *Lit & Teatro (trama)* plot (**b**) *(razonamiento)* argument

arguyo *indic pres de* argüir

aridez *nf* aridity; *Fig* dryness

árido,-a *adj* arid; *Fig* dry

Aries *nm* Aries

ariete *nm Mil* battering ram

ario,-a *adj & nm,f* Aryan

arisco,-a *adj (persona)* unfriendly, standoffish; *(animal)* unfriendly

arista *nf* edge

aristocracia *nf* aristocracy

aristócrata *nmf* aristocrat

aristocrático,-a *adj* aristocratic

aritmética *nf* arithmetic

arma *nf* weapon; **a. blanca** knife; **a. de fuego** firearm; **a. homicida** murder weapon; **a. nuclear** nuclear weapon; *Fig* **a. de doble filo** double-edged sword

Takes the masculine articles **el** and **un**.

armada *nf* navy

armado,-a *adj* armed; **ir a.** to be armed; **lucha armada** armed struggle

armador,-a *nm,f* shipowner

armadura *nf* (**a**) *(armazón)* frame (**b**) *Hist* suit of armour

armamentista *adj* arms; **la carrera a.** the arms race

armamento *nm* armaments; **a. nuclear** nuclear weapons

armar 1 *vt* (**a**) *(tropa, soldado)* to arm (**b**) *(piezas)* to fit o put together, to assemble (**c**) *Fam* **armaron un escándalo** they created a scandal

2 armarse *vpr* to arm oneself; *Fig* **a. de paciencia** to summon up one's patience; *Fig* **a. de valor** to pluck up courage; *Fam* **se armó la gorda** all hell broke loose

armario *nm (para ropa)* wardrobe; *(de cocina)* cupboard; **a. empotrado** built-in wardrobe o cupboard

armatoste *nm (cosa)* monstrosity

armazón *nm* frame; *(de madera)* timberwork; *Arquit* shell

Armenia *n* Armenia

armería *nf* gunsmith's (shop)

armiño *nm* ermine

armisticio *nm* armistice

armonía *nf* harmony

armonioso,-a *adj* harmonious

armonizar [40] *vt & vi* to harmonize

aro *nm* (**a**) *(gen)* hoop; *Fam* **pasar por el a.** to knuckle under (**b**) *Am (pendiente)* earring

aroma *nm* aroma; *(de vino)* bouquet

aromático,-a *adj* aromatic

arpa *nf* harp

Takes the masculine articles **el** and **un**.

arpía *nf (en mitología)* harpy; *Fig* harpy, old witch

arpón *nm* harpoon

arquear *vt,* **arquearse** *vpr* to bend, to curve

arqueología *nf* archaeology

arqueólogo,-a *nm,f* archaeologist

arquero,-a *nm,f* (**a**) *(tirador)* archer (**b**) *Am (portero de fútbol)* goalkeeper

arquetipo *nm* archetype

arquitecto,-a *nm,f* architect

arquitectónico,-a *adj* architectural

arquitectura *nf* architecture

arrabalero,-a *adj Pey* coarse

arrabales *nmpl* slums

arraigado,-a *adj* deeply rooted

arraigar [42] *vi* to take root

arraigo *nm Fig* roots; **una tradición con mucho a.** a deeply-rooted tradition

arrancar [44] **1** vt (a) (planta) to uproot, to pull up; **a. de raíz** to uproot (b) (extraer) to pull o tear off o out; (diente, pelo) to pull out; Fig (confesión etc) to extract; **arranca una hoja del cuaderno** tear a page out of the notebook (c) (coche, motor) to start; Informát to boot

2 vi (a) Aut & Téc to start; Informát to boot (up) (b) (empezar) to begin; **a. a llorar** to burst out crying

arranque nm (a) Aut & Téc starting (b) (comienzo) start (c) Fam (arrebato) outburst, fit

arrasar 1 vt to devastate, to destroy

2 vi (en elecciones etc) to win by a landslide

arrastrado,-a Fam **1** adj wretched

2 nm,f bad egg

arrastrar 1 vt to pull (along), to drag (along); **vas arrastrando el vestido** your dress is trailing on the ground; **lo arrastró la corriente** he was swept away by the current

2 arrastrarse vpr to drag oneself; Fig (humillarse) to crawl

arrastre nm (a) pulling, dragging; Fam **para el a.** (persona) on one's last legs; (cosa) done for (b) (pesca de) **a.** trawling (c) Am Fam **tener a.** to have a lot of influence

arrayán nm myrtle

arre interj gee up!, giddy up!

arrear vt (a) to spur on; (caballos) to urge on (b) Fam (bofetada) to give

arrebatador,-a adj Fig captivating, fascinating

arrebatar 1 vt (coger) to snatch, to seize; Fig (cautivar) to captivate, to fascinate

2 arrebatarse vpr (enfurecerse) to become furious; (exaltarse) to get carried away

arrebato nm outburst, fit

arreciar [43] vi (viento, tormenta) to get worse

arrecife nm reef

arreglado,-a adj (a) (reparado) repaired, fixed (b) (solucionado) settled (c) (habitación) tidy, neat (d) (persona) well-dressed, smart

arreglar 1 vt (a) to arrange; (problema) to sort out; (habitación) to tidy; (papeles) to put in order (b) (reparar) to repair, to fix (c) (vestir) to get ready

2 arreglarse vpr (a) (vestirse) to get ready (b) Fam **arreglárselas** to manage (c) (reconciliarse) to make up

arreglo nm (a) arrangement; (acuerdo) compromise (b) (reparación) repair; **no tiene a.** it is beyond repair; Fam **¡no tienes a.!** you're hopeless! (c) Fml **con a.** in accordance with

arrellanarse vpr to sit back

arremangarse [42] vpr to roll one's sleeves o trousers up

arremeter vi to attack

arremolinarse vpr to whirl about; Fig (gente) to crowd together, to cram together

arrendamiento nm (a) (alquiler) renting (b) (precio) rent

arrendar [1] vt (piso) to rent; (dar en arriendo) to let on lease; (tomar en arriendo) to take on lease

arrendatario,-a nm,f leaseholder, lessee; (inquilino) tenant

arreos nmpl (a) (de caballería) harness, trappings (b) (adornos) adornments

arrepentido,-a adj regretful

arrepentimiento nm regret

arrepentirse [5] vpr **a. de** to regret; Rel to repent

arrestar vt to arrest, to detain; (encarcelar) to put in prison

arresto nm arrest; Jur **a. domiciliario** house arrest

arriar [29] vt (bandera) to strike; (velas) to lower

arriba 1 adv up; (encima) on the top; **ahí a.** up there; **de a. abajo** from top to bottom; Fam **mirar a algn de a. abajo** to look sb up and down; **desde a.** from above; **hacia a.** upwards; **de un millón para a.** from one million upwards; **más a.** higher up, further up; **a. del todo** right on o at the top; **la parte de a.** the top (part); **vive a.** he lives upstairs; **véase más a.** see above

2 interj get up!, up you get!; **¡a. la República!** long live the Republic!; **¡a. las manos!** hands up!

3 prep Am **a. (de)** on top of

arribar vi to reach port, to arrive

arribeño,-a Am **1** adj highland

2 nm,f highlander

arribista nmf parvenu, social climber

arriendo nm lease; (de un piso) renting; **dar en a.** to let out on lease; **tomar en a.** to take on lease

arriesgado,-a adj (a) (peligroso) risky (b) (temerario) fearless, daring

arriesgar [42] **1** vt to risk

2 arriesgarse vpr to risk; **se arriesga demasiado** he's taking too many risks

arrimar 1 vt to move closer, to bring near o nearer; Fam **a. el hombro** to lend a hand

2 arrimarse vpr to move o get close, to come near o nearer

arrinconar vt (a) (poner en un rincón) to put in a corner (b) (abandonar) to put away, to lay aside (c) (acorralar) to corner

arrobo nm rapture, enthrallment

arrocero,-a adj **la industria arrocera** the rice industry

arrodillarse vpr to kneel down

arrogancia nf arrogance

arrogante adj arrogant

arrojadizo,-a adj **arma arrojadiza** missile

arrojado,-a adj (osado) bold, daring

arrojar 1 vt (a) (tirar) to throw, to fling (b) Com (saldo) to show

2 arrojarse vpr to throw oneself, to fling oneself

arrojo nm daring, courage

arrollador,-a adj Fig overwhelming; (éxito)

resounding; *(personalidad)* captivating

arrollar *vt* **1** *(atropellar)* to run over, to knock down

2 *vi Dep & Pol* to win easily

arropar 1 *vt* to wrap up; *(en la cama)* to tuck in

2 arroparse *upr* to wrap oneself up

arrostrar *vt* to face

arroyo *nm* brook, stream

arroz *nm* rice; **a. con leche** rice pudding

arruga *nf (en la piel)* wrinkle; *(en la ropa)* crease

arrugar [42] **1** *vt* *(piel)* to wrinkle; *(ropa)* to crease; *(papel)* to crumple (up)

2 arrugarse *upr (piel)* to wrinkle; *(ropa)* to crease

arruinado,-a *adj* bankrupt, ruined

arruinar 1 *vt* to ruin

2 arruinarse *upr* to be ruined

arrullar 1 *vt (bebé)* to lull

2 *vi (paloma)* to coo

arrullo *nm* (a) *(de paloma)* cooing (b) *(nana)* lullaby

arrumaco *nm Fam* kissing and hugging; *(halago)* flattery

arsenal *nm* arsenal

arsénico *nm* arsenic

arte *nm o nf* (a) art; **bellas artes** fine arts; *Fam* **por amor al a.** for the love of it (b) *(habilidad)* skill

> Takes the masculine articles **el** and **un**.

artefacto *nm* device; **a. explosivo** explosive device

arteria *nf* artery; *(carretera)* highway

artesanal *adj* handmade

artesanía *nf* (a) *(cualidad)* craftsmanship (b) *(objetos)* crafts, handicrafts

artesano,-a 1 *nm,f* craftsman, *f* craftswoman

2 *adj* handmade

ártico,-a 1 *adj* arctic; **el océano Á.** the Arctic Ocean

2 *nm* **el Á.** the Arctic

articulación *nf* (a) *Anat* joint, articulation (b) *Téc* joint

articulado,-a *adj (tren etc)* articulated

articular *vt* to articulate

artículo *nm* article; **a. de fondo** leader (article)

artífice *nmf* author; *Fig* **el a. del acuerdo** the architect of the agreement

artificial *adj* artificial; *Tex* man-made *o* synthetic

artificio *nm* (a) artifice; **fuego de a.** firework (b) *(artimaña)* ruse

artillería *nf* artillery; **a. antiaérea** anti-aircraft guns

artillero *nm* artilleryman

artilugio *nm* gadget, device

artimaña *nf* trick, ruse

artista *nmf* artist; **a. de cine** film star

artístico,-a *adj* artistic

artritis *nf* arthritis

arveja *nf Andes, Carib, RP* pea

arzobispo *nm* archbishop

as *nm* ace

asa *nf* handle

> Takes the masculine articles **el** and **un**.

asado,-a 1 *adj Culin* roast; **pollo a.** roast chicken; *Fig* **a. de calor** roasting, boiling hot

2 *nm Culin* roast; *Col, CSur (barbacoa)* barbecue

asaduras *nfpl* offal; *(de ave)* giblets

asalariado,-a 1 *adj* salaried

2 *nm,f* wage earner, salaried worker

asaltador,-a *nm,f*, **asaltante** *nmf* attacker; *(en un robo)* robber

asaltar *vt* to assault, to attack; *(banco)* to rob; *Fig* to assail

asalto *nm* (a) assault, attack; **a. a un banco** bank robbery (b) *(en boxeo)* round

asamblea *nf* meeting; **a. general** general meeting

asar 1 *vt* to roast

2 asarse *upr Fig* to be roasting, to be boiling hot

ascendencia *nf* ancestry, ancestors; **de a. escocesa** of Scottish descent

ascender [3] **1** *vt (en un cargo)* to promote

2 *vi* (a) to move upward; *(temperatura)* to rise; **la factura asciende a ...** the bill adds up to ... (b) *(al trono)* to ascend (c) *(de categoría)* to be promoted

ascendiente *nmf* ancestor

ascensión *nf* (a) climb (b) *(al trono)* accession

ascenso *nm* promotion; *(subida)* rise

ascensor *nm Br* lift, *US* elevator

asco *nm* disgust, repugnance; **me da a.** it makes me (feel) sick; **¡qué a.!** how disgusting *o* revolting!

ascua *nf* ember; *Fig* **en ascuas** on tenterhooks

> Takes the masculine articles **el** and **un**.

aseado,-a *adj* tidy, neat

asear 1 *vt* to clean, to tidy up

2 asearse *upr* to wash, to get washed

asediar [43] *vt* to besiege

asedio *nm* siege

asegurado,-a *adj* (a) insured (b) *(indudable)* secure

asegurador,-a 1 *adj* insurance

2 *nm,f* insurer

asegurar 1 *vt* (a) to insure (b) *(garantizar)* **me aseguró que ...** he assured me that ...; **a. el éxito de un proyecto** to ensure the success of a project (c) *(cuerda)* to fasten

2 asegurarse *upr* (a) to make sure; **a. de que ...** to make sure that ... (b) *Seg* to insure oneself

asemejarse *upr* **a. a** to look like

asentado,-a *adj (establecido)* established, settled

asentamiento *nm* settlement

asentar [1] **1** *vt* **a. la cabeza** to settle down

2 asentarse *vpr* (**a**) *(establecerse)* to settle down, to establish oneself (**b**) *(té, polvo)* to settle

asentimiento *nm* assent, consent

asentir [5] *vi* to assent, to agree; **a. con la cabeza** to nod

aseo *nm* (**a**) cleanliness, tidiness (**b**) **aseos** *o* **(cuarto de) a.** bathroom; *(retrete)* toilet

asequible *adj* affordable; *(comprensible)* easy to understand; *(alcanzable)* attainable

aserrín *nm* sawdust

asesinar *vt* to murder; *(rey, ministro)* to assassinate

asesinato *nm* murder; *(de rey, ministro)* assassination

asesino,-a 1 *adj* murderous

2 *nm,f* killer; *(hombre)* murderer; *(mujer)* murderess; *Pol* assassin

asesor,-a 1 *nm,f* adviser; **a. fiscal** tax adviser

2 *adj* advisory

asesoramiento *nm* (**a**) *(acción)* advising (**b**) *(consejo)* advice

asesorar 1 *vt* (**a**) to advise, to give (professional) advice to (**b**) *Com* to act as consultant to

2 asesorarse *vpr* to consult

asesoría *nf* consultant's office

asestar *vt* to deal; **a. un golpe a algn** to deal sb a blow

aseverar *vt* to assert

asfalto *nm* asphalt

asfixia *nf* asphyxiation, suffocation

asfixiante *adj* asphyxiating, suffocating; *Fam* **hace un calor a.** it's stifling

asfixiar [43] *vt,* **asfixiarse** *vpr* to asphyxiate, to suffocate

así *adv* (**a**) *(de esta manera)* like this *o* that, this way, thus; **ponlo a.** put it this way; **a. de grande/alto** this big/tall; **algo a.** something like this *o* that; **¿no es a.?** isn't that so *o* right?; **a. es la vida** such is life; **a. a.** so-so; **a. sin más,** *Am* **a. no más** *o* **nomás** just like that (**b**) **a las seis o a.** around six o'clock; **diez años o a.** ten years more or less (**c**) **a. como** as well as (**d**) **a. tenga que ...** *(aunque)* even if I have to ... (**e**) **aun a.** and despite that (**f**) **a. pues** so; **a. que ...** so ... (**g**) **a. que llegues** as soon as

Asia *n* Asia; **A. Menor** Asia Minor

asiático,-a *adj & nm,f* Asian

asidero *nm (asa)* handle; *Fig* pretext, excuse

asiduidad *nf* assiduity; **con a.** frequently, regularly

asiduo,-a 1 *adj* assiduous

2 *nm,f* regular customer

asiento *nm* (**a**) seat; **a. trasero/delantero** front/back seat; **tome a.** take a seat (**b**) *(poso)* sediment (**c**) *Fin* entry

asignación *nf* (**a**) *(de dinero)* assignment, allocation (**b**) *(de puesto)* appointment (**c**) *(paga)* allowance

asignar *vt* (**a**) to assign, to allocate (**b**) *(nombrar)* to appoint

asignatura *nf* subject; **a. pendiente** failed subject

asilado,-a *nm,f* refugee

asilar *vt* to grant *o* give political asylum to

asilo *nm* asylum; **a. de ancianos** old people's home; *Pol* **a. político** political asylum

asimilación *nf* assimilation

asimilar *vt* to assimilate

asimismo *adv* also, as well

asir [46] *vt* to grasp, to seize

asistencia *nf* (**a**) *(presencia)* attendance; **falta de a.** absence (**b**) **a. médica/técnica** medical/technical assistance (**c**) *(público)* audience, public

asistenta *nf* charlady, cleaning lady

asistente 1 *adj* attending; **el público a.** the audience

2 *nmf* (**a**) *(ayudante)* assistant; **a. social** social worker (**b**) **los asistentes** the public

asistido,-a *adj* assisted; **a. por ordenador** computer-assisted; *Aut* **dirección asistida** power steering

asistir 1 *vt* to assist, to help

2 *vi* **a.** (**a**) to attend, to be present (at)

asma *nf* asthma

> Takes the masculine articles **el** and **un**.

asno *nm* donkey, ass

asociación *nf* association

asociado,-a 1 *adj* associated

2 *nm,f* associate, partner

asociar [43] **1** *vt* to associate

2 asociarse *vpr* (**a**) to be associated (**b**) *Com* to become partners

asolar [2] *vt* to devastate, to destroy

asomar 1 *vt* to put out, to stick out; **asomó la cabeza por la ventana** he put his head out of the window

2 *vi* to appear

3 asomarse *vpr* (**a**) to lean out; **a. a la ventana** to lean out of the window (**b**) *(entrar)* to pop in; *(salir)* to pop out

asombrar 1 *vt* to amaze, to astonish

2 asombrarse *vpr* to be astonished; **a. de algo** to be amazed at sth

asombro *nm* amazement, astonishment

asombroso,-a *adj* amazing, astonishing

asomo *nm* trace, hint

asonada *nf* putsch, uprising

asorocharse *vpr Andes* to get altitude sickness

aspa *nf* (**a**) *(de molino)* arm; *(de ventilador)* blade (**b**) *(cruz)* cross

> Takes the masculine articles **el** and **un**.

aspaviento *nm* **hacer aspavientos** to wave one's arms about

aspecto *nm* (**a**) look, appearance (**b**) *(de un asunto)* aspect

aspereza *nf* roughness; *Fig* **limar asperezas** to smooth things over

áspero,-a *adj* rough; *Fig (carácter)* surly
aspersión *nf* sprinkling
aspersor *nm* sprinkler
aspiración *nf* (**a**) inhalation, breathing in (**b**) *(pretensión)* aspiration
aspiradora *nf* vacuum cleaner
aspirante *nmf* candidate, applicant
aspirar 1 *vt* (**a**) *(respirar)* to inhale, to breathe in (**b**) *(absorber)* to suck in, to draw in
  2 *vi Fig* **a. a algo** to aspire after sth
aspirina *nf* aspirin
asquear *vt* to disgust
asquerosidad *nf* filthy o revolting thing; **¡que a.!** how revolting!
asqueroso,-a 1 *adj (sucio)* filthy; *(desagradable)* revolting, disgusting
  2 *nm,f* filthy o revolting person
asta *nf* (**a**) *(de bandera)* staff, pole; **a media a.** at half-mast (**b**) *Zool (cuerno)* horn

Takes the masculine articles **el** and **un**.

asterisco *nm* asterisk
astilla *nf* splinter
astillero *nm* shipyard
astral *adj* astral; **carta a.** birth chart
astringente *adj & nm* astringent
astro *nm* star
astrología *nf* astrology
astrólogo,-a *nm,f* astrologer
astronauta *nmf* astronaut
astronave *nf* spaceship
astronomía *nf* astronomy
astronómico,-a *adj* astronomical
astrónomo,-a *nm,f* astronomer
astucia *nf* shrewdness; *(artimaña)* ruse
asturiano,-a *adj & nm,f* Asturian
Asturias *n* Asturias
astuto,-a *adj* astute, shrewd
asumir *vt* to assume
asunción *nf* assumption
asunto *nm* (**a**) subject; **no es a. tuyo** it's none of your business (**b**) **Asuntos Exteriores** Foreign Affairs
asustar 1 *vt* to frighten, to scare
  2 asustarse *vpr* to be frightened, to be scared
atacante *nmf* attacker, assailant
atacar [44] *vt* to attack, to assault; *Fig* **me ataca los nervios** he gets on my nerves
atado,-a *adj* tied; *(ocupado)* tied up
atadura *nf Fig* hindrance
atajar *vi* to take a shortcut (**por** across o through)
atajo *nm* (**a**) shortcut (**b**) *(grupo)* bunch
atalaya *nf* watchtower
atañer *v impers* to concern, to have to do with; **eso no te atañe** that has nothing to do with you
ataque *nm* (**a**) attack, assault; **a. aéreo** air raid (**b**) *Med* fit; **a. cardíaco** o **al corazón** heart attack; **a. de nervios/tos** fit of hysterics/coughing

atar 1 *vt* (**a**) to tie; *Fig* **a. cabos** to put two and two together; *Fam* **loco de a.** as mad as a hatter (**b**) *Fig* to tie down
  2 atarse *vpr Fig* to get tied up; **átate los zapatos** do your shoes up
atardecer [33] **1** *v impers* to get o grow dark
  2 *nm* evening, dusk
atareado,-a *adj* busy
atascado,-a *adj* stuck
atascar [44] **1** *vt (bloquear)* to block, to obstruct
  2 atascarse *vpr* (**a**) *(bloquearse)* to become obstructed, to become blocked (**b**) *Fig (estancarse)* to get bogged down
atasco *nm* traffic jam
ataúd *nm* coffin
ataviarse [29] *vpr* to dress oneself up
atavío *nm* dress, attire
ate *nm Méx* quince jelly
atemorizar [40] *vt* to frighten, to scare
atemperar *vt* to moderate, to temper
Atenas *n* Athens
atención 1 *nf* attention; **llamar la a.** to attract attention; **prestar/poner a.** to pay attention (**a** to)
  2 *interj* attention!
atender [3] **1** *vt* to attend to; *(petición)* to agree to
  2 *vi (alumno)* to pay attention (**a** to)
atenerse [24] *vpr* (**a**) *(a reglas etc)* to abide (**a** by); **a. a las consecuencias** to bear the consequences (**b**) *(remitirse)* to go by; **me atengo a sus palabras** I'm going by what he said; **no saber a qué a.** not to know what to expect
atentado *nm* attack; **a. terrorista** terrorist attack
atentamente *adv* **le saluda a.** *(en carta)* yours sincerely o faithfully
atentar *vi* **a. a** o **contra** to commit a crime against; **a. contra la vida de algn** to make an attempt on sb's life
atento,-a *adj* (**a**) attentive; **estar a. a** to be mindful o aware of (**b**) *(amable)* thoughtful, considerate; **atentos saludos de** *(en carta)* yours faithfully
atenuante 1 *adj* attenuating
  2 *nm Jur* extenuating circumstance
atenuar [30] *vt* (**a**) to attenuate; *Jur* to extenuate (**b**) *(importancia)* to lessen, to diminish
ateo,-a 1 *adj* atheistic
  2 *nm,f* atheist
aterciopelado,-a *adj* velvety; *(vino)* smooth
aterido,-a *adj* **a. de frío** stiff with cold, numb
aterrador,-a *adj* terrifying
aterrar 1 *vt* to terrify
  2 aterrarse *vpr* to be terrified
aterrizaje *nm Av* landing; **a. forzoso** forced landing
aterrizar [40] *vi* to land
aterrorizar [40] **1** *vt* to terrify; *Mil & Pol* to terrorize

2 aterrorizarse *upr* to be terrified
atesorar *vt* to accumulate; *(dinero)* to hoard
atestado¹ *nm Jur* affidavit, statement; **atestados** testimonials
atestado²,-a *adj* packed, crammed; **estaba a. de gente** it was full of people
atestar¹ *vt Jur* to testify
atestar² *vt (abarrotar)* to pack, to cram (**de** with)
atestiguar [45] *vt* (**a**) *Jur* to testify to (**b**) *Fig* to vouch for
atiborrar 1 *vt* to pack, to stuff (**de** with)
2 atiborrarse *upr Fam* to stuff oneself (**de** with)
ático *nm* attic
atinado,-a *adj (juicioso)* sensible; *(pertinente)* pertinent
atinar *vi* to get it right; **a. a hacer algo** to succeed in doing sth; **a. al blanco** to hit the target; **atinó con la solución** he found the solution
atingencia *nf Am* connection; *(observación)* comment
atípico,-a *adj* atypical
atisbar *vt* to make out
atisbo *nm Fig* slight sign, inkling
atizar [40] *vt* (**a**) *(fuego)* to poke, to stoke (**b**) *Fig (rebelión)* to stir up; *(pasión)* to rouse, to excite
atlántico,-a 1 *adj* Atlantic
2 *nm* **el (océano) A.** the Atlantic (Ocean)
atlas *nm inv* atlas
atleta *nmf* athlete
atlético,-a *adj* athletic
atletismo *nm* athletics *sing*
atmósfera *nf* atmosphere
atmosférico,-a *adj* atmospheric
atole, atol *nm CAm, Méx* = drink made of corn meal
atolladero *nm* fix, jam; **estar en un a.** to be in a jam
atolondrado,-a *adj* stunned, bewildered; *(atontado)* stupid
atolondrar 1 *vt* to confuse, to bewilder
2 atolondrarse *upr* to be confused, to be bewildered
atómico,-a *adj* atomic
átomo *nm* atom
atónito,-a *adj* amazed, astonished
atontado,-a *adj* (**a**) *(tonto)* silly, foolish (**b**) *(aturdido)* bewildered, amazed
atontar 1 *vt* to confuse, to bewilder
2 atontarse *upr* to be o get confused, to be bewildered
atorarse *upr* (**a**) *(atragantarse)* to choke (**con** on) (**b**) *Am (atascarse)* to get stuck
atormentar 1 *vt* to torment
2 atormentarse *upr* to torment oneself, to suffer agonies
atornillar *vt* to screw on
atorón *nm Méx* traffic jam
atorrante *adj CSur (holgazán)* lazy

atosigar [42] *vt* to harass
atracador,-a *nm,f (de banco)* (bank) robber; *(en la calle)* attacker, mugger
atracar [44] **1** *vt* to hold up; *(persona)* to rob
2 *vi Náut* to come alongside, to tie up
3 atracarse *upr (de comida)* to stuff oneself (**de** with), to gorge oneself (**de** on)
atracción *nf* attraction; **parque de atracciones** funfair
atraco *nm* hold-up, robbery; **a. a mano armada** armed robbery
atracón *nm Fam* binge, blowout; **darse un a. de comer** to make a pig of oneself
atractivo,-a 1 *adj* attractive, appealing
2 *nm* attraction, appeal
atraer [25] *vt* to attract
atragantarse *upr* to choke (**con** on), to swallow the wrong way; *Fig* **esa chica se me ha atragantado** I can't stand that girl
atraigo *indic pres de* **atraer**
atraje *pt indef de* **atraer**
atrancar [44] **1** *vt (puerta)* to bolt
2 atrancarse *upr* to get stuck; *(al hablar, leer)* to get bogged down
atrapar *vt* to catch
atrás *adv* (**a**) *(lugar)* at the back, behind; **hacia/para a.** backwards; **puerta de a.** back o rear door; *Fig* **echarse a.** to back out (**b**) *(tiempo)* previously, in the past, ago; **un año a.** a year ago; **venir de muy a.** to go o date back a long time
atrasado,-a *adj* late, slow; *(pago)* overdue; *(reloj)* slow; *(país)* backward; *Prensa* **número a.** back number
atrasar 1 *vt* to put back
2 *vi (reloj)* to be slow
3 atrasarse *upr* (**a**) to remain o stay behind, to lag behind (**b**) *(tren)* to be late
atraso *nm* (**a**) delay (**b**) *(de país)* backwardness (**c**) *Fin* **atrasos** arrears
atravesado,-a *adj (cruzado)* lying crosswise; *(persona)* difficult; **lo tengo a.** I can't stand him
atravesar [1] **1** *vt* (**a**) *(calle)* to cross (**b**) *(muro)* to pierce, to go through (**c**) *(poner a través)* to lay across, to put across, to put crosswise
2 atravesarse *upr* to get in the way; *Fig* **se me ha atravesado Luis** I can't stand Luis
atrayente *adj* attractive
atreverse *upr* to dare; **a. a hacer algo** to dare to do sth
atrevido,-a *adj* (**a**) *(osado)* daring, bold (**b**) *(insolente)* insolent, impudent (**c**) *(ropa etc)* daring, risqué
atrevimiento *nm* (**a**) *(osadía)* daring, audacity (**b**) *(insolencia)* insolence, impudence
atribuir [37] **1** *vt* to attribute, to ascribe
2 atribuirse *upr* to assume
atribular *vt* to afflict
atributo *nm* attribute
atril *nm* music stand

atrochar *vi* to take a short cut
atrocidad *nf* atrocity
atrofiar [43] *vt,* **atrofiarse** *upr* to atrophy
atropellado,-a *adj* hasty, impetuous
atropellar *vt* to knock down, to run over
atropello *nm* (**a**) *Aut* knocking down, running over (**b**) *(abuso)* abuse
atroz *adj* (**a**) *(bárbaro)* atrocious (**b**) *Fam (hambre, frío)* enormous, tremendous
ATS *nmf (abr* **ayudante técnico sanitario)** = qualified Spanish nurse
atuendo *nm* dress, attire
atún *nm* tuna, tunny
aturdido,-a *adj* stunned, dazed
aturdimiento *nm* confusion, bewilderment
aturdir *vt* (**a**) *(con un golpe)* to stun, to daze (**b**) *(confundir)* to bewilder, to confuse
aturrullar *vt* to confuse, to bewilder
atuve *pt indef de* **atenerse**
audacia *nf* audacity
audaz *adj* audacious, bold
audible *adj* audible
audición *nf* (**a**) hearing (**b**) *Teatro* audition
audiencia *nf* (**a**) *(público)* audience; *TV & Rad* **horas de máxima a.** prime time; **índice de a.** viewing figures, ratings (**b**) *(entrevista)* audience (**c**) *Jur* court hearing
audiovisual *adj* audio-visual
auditivo,-a 1 *adj* auditory; **comprensión auditiva** listening comprehension
   2 *nm* receiver
auditor *nm Fin* auditor
auditorio *nm* (**a**) *(público)* audience (**b**) *(sala)* auditorium, hall
auge *nm* peak; *Econ* boom; *Fig* **estar en a.** to be thriving *o* booming
augurar *vt* to augur
augurio *nm* omen
aula *nf (en colegio)* classroom; *Univ* lecture room; **a. magna** amphitheatre

Takes the masculine articles **el** and **un**.

aulaga *nf* gorse
aullar *vt* to howl, to yell
aullido *nm* howl, yell
aumentar 1 *vt* to increase; *(precios)* to put up; *(producción)* to step up; *Fot* to enlarge; *Opt* to magnify
   2 *vi (precios)* to go up, to rise; *(valor)* to appreciate
   3 aumentarse *upr* to increase, to be on the increase
aumento *nm* increase; *Opt* magnification; **a. de precios** rise in prices; **ir en a.** to be on the increase
aun *adv* even; **a. así** even so, even then; **a. más** even more
aún *adv* still; *(en negativas)* yet; **a. está aquí** he's still here; **ella no ha venido a.** she hasn't come yet
aunar *vt* to unite, to join
aunque *conj* although, though; *(enfático)* even if, even though; **a. no vengas** even if you don't come
aúpa *interj* up!, get up!
aura *nf* aura

Takes the masculine articles **el** and **un**.

aureola *nf* halo
auricular *nm* (**a**) *Tel* receiver (**b**) **auriculares** earphones, headphones
aurora *nf* daybreak, dawn
auscultar *vt* to sound (with a stethoscope)
ausencia *nf* absence
ausentarse *upr* to leave
ausente 1 *adj* absent
   2 *nmf* absentee
ausentismo *nm Am* absenteeism
austeridad *nf* austerity
austero,-a *adj* austere
austral 1 *adj* southern
   2 *nm Fin* = former standard monetary unit of Argentina
Australia *n* Australia
australiano,-a *adj & nm,f* Australian
Austria *n* Austria
austríaco,-a *adj & nm,f* Austrian
autenticidad *nf* authenticity
auténtico,-a *adj* authentic
autentificar [44] *vt* to authenticate
autismo *nm* autism
autista *adj* autistic
auto¹ *nm RP (coche)* car
auto² *nm Jur* decree, writ; **autos** *(pleito)* papers, documents
autoadhesivo,-a *adj* self-adhesive
autobiografía *nf* autobiography
autobiográfico,-a *adj* autobiographical
autobombo *nm Fam* self-praise, blowing one's own trumpet
autobús *nm* bus
autocar *nm* coach
autocrítica *nf* self-criticism
autóctono,-a *adj* indigenous
autodefensa *nf* self-defence
autodisciplina *nf* self-discipline
autoedición *nf Informát* desktop publishing
autoescuela *nf* driving school, school of motoring
autogobierno *nm* self-government
autógrafo *nm* autograph
autómata *nm* automaton
automático,-a *adj* automatic
automatización *nf* automation
automatizar [40] *vt* to automate
automotor,-a 1 *adj* self-propelled
   2 *nm Ferroc* diesel train
automóvil *nm* car
automovilismo *nm* motoring
automovilista *nmf* motorist
automovilístico,-a *adj* car; **accidente a.** car accident
autonomía *nf* (**a**) autonomy (**b**) *(región)* autonomous region

autonómico,-a *adj* autonomous, self-governing; **elecciones autonómicas** elections for the autonomous parliament; **televisión autonómica** regional television

autónomo,-a *adj* autonomous

autopista *nf* motorway; *Informát* **autopista de la información** information superhighway

autopsia *nf* autopsy, postmortem

autor,-a *nm,f (hombre)* author; *(mujer)* authoress; *(de crimen)* perpetrator

autoridad *nf* authority

autoritario,-a *adj* authoritarian

autorizado,-a *adj* authoritative, official

autorizar [40] *vt* to authorize

autorretrato *nm* self-portrait

autoservicio *nm* self-service; *(supermercado)* supermarket

autostop *nm* hitch-hiking; **hacer a.** to hitch-hike

autostopista *nmf* hitch-hiker

autosuficiencia *nf* self-sufficiency

autosuficiente *adj* self-sufficient

auxiliar [43] **1** *adj & nmf* auxiliary, assistant

2 *vt* to help, to assist

auxilio *nm* help, assistance; **primeros auxilios** first aid

auyama *nf Carib, Col* pumpkin

Av. *(abr* **Avenida)** Ave

aval *nm Com & Fin* endorsement

avalancha *nf* avalanche

avalar *vt* to guarantee, to endorse

avance *nm* **(a)** advance **(b)** *Fin* advance payment **(c)** *TV* **a. informativo** news summary, *US* news in brief

avanzado,-a *adj* advanced; **de avanzada edad** advanced in years

avanzar [40] *vt* to advance

avaricia *nf* avarice

avaricioso,-a *adj* greedy

avaro,-a 1 *adj* avaricious, miserly

2 *nm,f* miser

avasallar *vt* to subdue

avatares *nmpl* quirks

Avda. = **Av.**

AVE *nf (abr* **Alta Velocidad Española)** High Speed Train

ave *nf* bird; **aves de corral** poultry; **a. de rapiña** bird of prey

> Takes the masculine articles **el** and **un**.

avecinarse *upr* to approach, to come near

avellana *nf* hazelnut

avellano *nm* hazelnut tree

avena *nf* oats

avendré *indic fut de* **avenir**

avenencia *nf* compromise

avengo *indic pres de* **avenir**

avenida *nf* avenue

avenido,-a *adj* **bien/mal avenidos** on good/bad terms

avenir [27] **1** *vt* to reconcile

2 avenirse *upr* to be on good terms; *(consentir)* to agree **(en** to)

aventajado,-a *adj (destacado)* outstanding, exceptional; *(en cabeza)* in the lead

aventajar *vt* **(a)** to be ahead *o* in front of **(a** of) **(b)** *(superar)* to surpass, to outdo

aventar [1] **1** *vt* **(a)** *Agr* to winnow **(b)** *(el fuego)* to fan **(c)** *Andes, CAm, Méx (tirar)* to throw **(d)** *CAm, Méx, Perú (empujar)* to push, to shove

2 aventarse *upr Méx* **(a)** *(tirarse)* to throw oneself **(b)** *(atreverse)* **a. a hacer algo** to dare to do sth

aventón *nm Méx* **dar a. a algn** to give sb a ride; **pedir a.** to hitch a ride

aventura *nf* **(a)** adventure **(b)** *(amorosa)* (love) affair

aventurado,-a *adj* risky

aventurarse *upr* to venture

aventurero,-a *adj* adventurous

avergonzado,-a *adj* ashamed

avergonzar [63] **1** *vt* to shame

2 avergonzarse *upr* to be ashamed **(de** of)

avería *nf* breakdown

averiado,-a *adj* out of order; *(coche)* broken down

averiar [29] **1** *vt* to break

2 averiarse *upr (estropearse)* to malfunction, to go wrong; *(coche)* to break down

averiguación *nf* enquiry

averiguar [45] *vt* to ascertain

aversión *nf* aversion

avestruz *nm* ostrich

aviación *nf* **(a)** aviation; **accidente de a.** plane crash; **a. civil** civil aviation **(b)** *Mil* air force

aviador,-a *nm,f* aviator, flier; *Mil (piloto)* air force pilot

aviar [29] *vt (preparar)* to prepare, to get ready

avícola *adj* poultry

avicultura *nf* aviculture; *(de aves de corral)* poultry keeping

avidez *nf* avidity, eagerness

ávido,-a *adj* avid; **a. de** eager for

avinagrado,-a *adj* vinegary, sour; *Fig* sour

avinagrarse *upr* to turn sour; *Fig* to become sour *o* bitter

avión¹ *nm* aircraft, *Br* aeroplane, *US* airplane; **viajar en a.** to fly, to go by plane; **por a.** *(en carta)* airmail

avión² *nm Orn* martin

avioneta *nf* light aircraft *o* plane

avíos *nmpl Culin* ingredients

avisar *vt* **(a)** *(informar)* to inform; **avísame cuando hayas acabado** let me know when you finish **(b)** *(advertir)* to warn; **ya te avisé I** warned you **(c)** *(llamar)* to call for; **a. a la policía** to notify the police; **a. al médico** to send for the doctor

aviso *nm* **(a)** notice; *(advertencia)* warning; *(nota)* note; **hasta nuevo a.** until further notice; **sin previo a.** without notice **(b)** estar

sobre a. to know what's going on, to be in on it (**c**) *Am (anuncio)* advertisement; **a. clasificado** classified advertisement

avispa *nf* wasp

avispado,-a *adj Fam* quick-witted

avispero *nm (nido)* wasps' nest

avistar *vt* to see, to sight

avituallamiento *nm* provisioning

avivar *vt (fuego)* to stoke (up); *(pasión)* to intensify; *(paso)* to quicken

avizor,-a *adj* **estar ojo a.** to be on the alert *o* on the lookout

axila *nf* armpit, axilla

axioma *nm* axiom

ay *interj (dolor)* ouch!

aya *nf (niñera)* nanny

Takes the masculine articles **el** and **un**.

ayer 1 *adv* yesterday; **a. por la mañana/por la tarde** yesterday morning/afternoon; **a. por la noche** last night; **antes de a.** the day before yesterday

　2 *nm* **el a.** yesteryear

ayuda *nf* help, assistance; **ir en a. de algn** to come to sb's assistance; **a. al desarrollo** development aid

ayudante *nmf* assistant; *Med* **a. técnico-sanitario** nurse

ayudar 1 *vt* to help; **¿en qué puedo ayudarle?** (how) can I help you?

　2 ayudarse *vpr* (**a**) *(unos a otros)* to help (**b**) **a. de** to use, to make use of

ayunar *vi* to fast

ayunas *nfpl* **en a.** without having eaten breakfast

ayuno *nm* fasting; **guardar/hacer a.** to fast

ayuntamiento *nm (institución)* town council; *(edificio)* town hall

azabache *nm* jet; **negro a.** jet black

azada *nf* hoe

azafata *nf* (**a**) *Av* air hostess (**b**) *(de congresos)* stewardess; *(de concurso)* hostess

azafate *nm Andes (bandeja)* tray

azafrán *nm* saffron

azahar *nm (del naranjo)* orange blossom; *(del limonero)* lemon blossom

azar *nm* chance; **por a.** by chance; **al a.** at random; **juegos de a.** games of chance; **los azares de la vida** the ups and downs of life

azaroso,-a *adj* hazardous, dangerous

azogue *nm* mercury, quicksilver

azorado,-a *adj* embarrassed

azorar 1 *vt* to embarrass

　2 azorarse *vpr* to be embarrassed

Azores *nfpl* **las (Islas) A.** the Azores

azotar *vt* to beat; *(con látigo)* to whip, to flog; *Fig* to scourge

azote *nm* (**a**) *(golpe)* smacking; *(latigazo)* lash, stroke (of the whip) (**b**) *Fig* scourge

azotea *nf* flat roof

azteca *adj & nmf* Aztec

azúcar *nm o nf* sugar; **a. blanco** refined sugar; **a. moreno** brown sugar

azucarado,-a *adj* sweetened

azucarero,-a 1 *nm o nf* sugar bowl

　2 *adj* sugar

azucena *nf* white lily

azufre *nm* sulphur

azul *adj & nm* blue; **a. celeste** sky blue; **a. marino** navy blue; **a. turquesa** turquoise; **sangre a.** blue blood

azulado,-a *adj* bluish

azulejo *nm (glazed)* tile

azuzar [40] *vt* **a. los perros a algn** to set the dogs on sb

B, b [be] *nf (la letra)* B, b

baba *nf* dribble; *Fig* **se le caía la b.** he was delighted

babear *vi (niño)* to dribble; *(adulto, animal)* to slobber

babel *nm o nf* bedlam

babero *nm* bib

Babia *n Fig* **estar en B.** to be daydreaming

babor *nm Náut* port, port side

babosa *nf* slug

babosada *nf CAm, Méx Fam (disparate)* daft thing

baboso,-a 1 *adj* (a) *Fam (despreciable)* slimy (b) *Am Fam (tonto)* daft, stupid

   2 *nm,f Fam* (a) *(persona despreciable)* creep (b) *Am (tonto)* twit, idiot

babucha *nf* slipper

baca *nf Aut* roof rack

bacalao *nm (pez)* cod

bache *nm* (a) *(en carretera)* pot hole (b) *Av* air pocket (c) *Fig* bad patch; **pasar un b.** to go through a bad patch

bachillerato *nm* = academically orientated Spanish secondary school course for pupils aged 14-17

bacilo *nm* bacillus

bacon *nm* bacon

bacteria *nf* bacterium; **bacterias** bacteria

bacteriológico,-a *adj* bacteriological; **guerra bacteriológica** germ warfare

báculo *nm* walking stick; *(de obispo)* crosier

badén *nm Aut* bump

bádminton *nm* badminton

bafle *nm* loudspeaker

bagaje *nm* baggage

bagatela *nf (baratija)* knick-knack; *Fig* trifle

Bagdad *n* Baghdad

Bahamas *npl* **las (Islas) B.** the Bahamas

bahía *nf* bay

baila(d)or,-a *nm,f* flamenco dancer

bailar *vt & vi* to dance; *Fig* **b. al son que le tocan** to toe the line; *Fam* **¡que me quiten lo baila(d)o!** but at least I had a good time!

bailarín,-ina *nm,f* dancer; *(clásico)* ballet dancer

baile *nm* (a) *(danza)* dance (b) *(fiesta popular)* dance; *(formal)* ball; **b. de disfraces** fancy dress ball

baja *nf* (a) drop, fall; *Fin* **jugar a la b.** to bear (b) *Mil* loss, casualty (c) **dar de b. a algn** *(despedir)* to lay sb off; **darse de b.** *(por enfermedad)* to take sick leave; *(de un club)* to resign **(de** from), to drop out **(de** of)

bajada *nf* (a) *(descenso)* descent (b) *(cuesta)* slope (c) **b. de bandera** *(de taxi)* minimum fare

bajamar *nf* low tide

bajar 1 *vt* (a) to come/go down; **b. la escalera** to come/go downstairs (b) *(descender)* to bring/get/take down; *(volumen)* to turn down; *(voz, telón)* to lower; *(precios etc)* to reduce, to cut; *(persiana)* to let down; *(cabeza)* to bow *o* lower

   2 *vi* (a) to go/come down (b) *(apearse)* to get off; *(de un coche)* to get out **(de** of) (c) *(disminuir)* to fall, to drop

   3 bajarse *vpr* (a) to come/go down (b) *(apearse)* to get off; *(de un coche)* to get out **(de** of)

bajativo *nm Andes, RP (licor)* digestive liqueur; *(tisana)* herbal tea

bajeza *nf* despicable action

bajial *nm Perú* lowland

bajinis: por lo bajinis *loc adv Fam* on the sly

bajío *nm* (a) sandbank (b) *(terreno bajo)* lowland

bajista 1 *adj Fin* bearish; **tendencia b.** downward trend

   2 *nmf* (a) *Fin* bear (b) *Mús* bass guitarist

bajo,-a 1 *adj* (a) low; *(persona)* short; *(sonido)* faint, soft; **en voz baja** in a low voice; **planta baja** ground floor; **de baja calidad** of poor quality; **la clase baja** the lower class (b) *Fig (vil)* base, contemptible

   2 *nm* (a) *Mús* bass (b) *(planta baja)* ground floor

   3 *adv* low; **hablar b.** to speak quietly; *Fig* **por lo b.** on the sly

   4 *prep* (a) *(lugar)* under, underneath; **b. tierra** underground; **b. la lluvia** in the rain (b) *Pol & Hist* under the Republic; **b. la República** under the Republic (c) **b. cero** *(temperatura)* below zero (d) *Jur* under; **b. juramento** under oath; **b. pena de muerte** on pain of death; **b. fianza** on bail

bajón *nm* (a) *(bajada)* sharp fall, decline (b) *Com* slump (c) *(de salud)* relapse, deterioration

bajorrelieve *nm* bas-relief

bajura *nf* **pesca de b.** coastal fishing

bala *nf* bullet; *Fig* **como una b.** like a shot

balacear *vt Am (tirotear)* to shoot

balacera *nf Am* shootout

balada *nf* ballad

baladí *adj* (*pl* **baladíes**) trivial

balance *nm* (**a**) *Fin* balance; *(declaración)* balance sheet; *Fig* **hacer b. de una situación** to take stock of a situation (**b**) *(resultado)* outcome

balancear 1 *vt* to rock

2 balancearse *upr* (*en mecedora*) to rock; (*en columpio*) to swing

balanceo *nm* rocking, swinging; *(de barco, avión)* rolling; *Am Aut* wheel balance

balanza *nf* scales; *Fig* **estar en la b.** to be in the balance *o* in danger; **b. comercial** balance of trade; **b. de pagos** balance of payments

balar *vi* to bleat

balaustrada *nf* balustrade, railing

balazo *nm* (**a**) *(disparo)* shot; **matar a algn de un b.** to shoot sb dead (**b**) *(herida)* bullet wound

balboa *nm Fin* = standard monetary unit of Panama

balbucear *vi* *(adulto)* to stutter, stammer; *(niño)* to babble

balbuceo *nm* *(de adulto)* stuttering, stammering; *(de niño)* babbling

balbucir *vi defect* = **balbucear**

Balcanes *nmpl* **los B.** the Balkans

balcón *nm* balcony

baldado,-a *adj Fam* shattered

baldar *vt* to cripple, to maim

balde¹ *nm* pail, bucket

balde² *loc adv* (**a**) **de b.** *(gratis)* free (**b**) **en b.** (*en vano*) in vain

baldío,-a *adj* *(terreno)* uncultivated, waste; *(esfuerzo)* vain, useless

baldosa *nf* (ceramic) floor tile; *(para pavimentar)* flagstone, paving stone

balear¹ 1 *adj* Balearic

2 *nmf* person from the Balearic Islands

balear² *vt Am (disparar)* to shoot

Baleares *npl* **las (Islas) B.** the Balearic Islands

baleo *nm Am* shootout

balido *nm* bleating, bleat

balística *nf* ballistics *sing*

balístico,-a *adj* ballistic

baliza *nf* (**a**) *Náut* buoy (**b**) *Av* beacon

ballena *nf* whale

ballet *nm* ballet

balneario *nm* spa, health resort

balompié *nm* football

balón *nm* (**a**) *(pelota)* ball, football; *Fig* **b. de oxígeno** boost (**b**) *(bombona)* gas cylinder

baloncesto *nm* basketball

balonmano *nm* handball

balonvolea *nm* volleyball

balsa *nf* (**a**) *Náut* raft (**b**) *Fig* **como una b. de aceite** very quiet

bálsamo *nm* balsam, balm

balsero,-a *nm,f* *(de Cuba)* = refugee fleeing Cuba on a raft

Báltico *nm* **el (Mar) B.** the Baltic (Sea)

baluarte *nm Fig* stronghold

bambas® *nfpl* trainers

bambolear *vi,* **bambolearse** *upr* to swing; *(persona, árbol)* to sway; *(mesa, silla)* to wobble

bambú *nm* (*pl* **bambúes**) bamboo

banal *adj* banal, trivial

banalidad *nf* triviality, banality

banana *nf* banana

banano *nm* *(árbol)* banana tree; *Col (fruto)* banana

banca *nf* (**a**) *(asiento)* bench (**b**) *Com & Fin* (the) banks; *(actividad)* banking; **b. electrónica** electronic banking (**c**) *(en juegos)* bank

bancario,-a *adj* banking

bancarrota *nf Fin* bankruptcy; **estar en b.** to be bankrupt

banco *nm* (**a**) *(asiento)* bench (**b**) *Com & Fin* bank (**c**) **b. de arena** sandbank (**d**) *(de peces)* shoal, school (**e**) *Geol* layer

banda *nf* (**a**) *Mús* band (**b**) *Cin* **b. sonora** sound track (**c**) *(de pájaros)* flock (**d**) *(cinta)* sash (**e**) *(lado)* side; *Ftb* **línea de b.** touchline; **saque de b.** throw-in

bandada *nf* flock

bandazo *nm* **dar bandazos** to lurch

bandeja *nf* tray; *Fig* **servir algo a algn en b.** to hand sth to sb on a plate

bandera *nf* flag; **b. azul** *(en playa)* blue flag

banderín *nf* pennant, small flag

bandido *nm* bandit, outlaw

bando¹ *nm* (**a**) *Jur (edicto)* edict, proclamation (**b**) **bandos** banns

bando² *nm* faction, side; **pasarse al otro b.** to go over to the other side, to change allegiances

bandolero *nm* bandit, outlaw

banquero,-a *nm,f* banker

banqueta *nf* (**a**) *(asiento)* stool (**b**) *(para los pies)* footstool (**c**) *CAm, Méx (acera) Br* pavement, *US* sidewalk

banquete *nm* banquet, feast; **b. de bodas** wedding reception

banquillo *nm* (**a**) *Jur* dock (**b**) *Dep* bench

banquina *nf RP (arcén)* verge; *(de autopista) Br* hard shoulder, *US* shoulder

bañadera *nf* (**a**) *Arg (bañera)* bath (**b**) *RP (vehículo)* minibus

bañado *nm Bol, RP (terreno)* marshy area

bañador *nm* *(de mujer)* bathing *o* swimming costume; *(de hombre)* swimming trunks

bañar 1 *vt* (**a**) *(bebé)* to bath (**b**) *(cubrir)* to coat, to cover; **b. en oro** to goldplate

2 bañarse *upr* (*en baño*) to have *o* take a bath; (*en mar, piscina*) to go for a swim; *Am (ducharse)* to have a shower

bañera *nf* bath, bathtub

bañista *nmf* bather, swimmer

baño *nm* (**a**) bath; **tomar un b.** to have *o* take a bath; *Fig* **darse un b. de sol** to sunbathe; **b. de sangre** bloodbath (**b**) *(de oro etc)* coat; *(de chocolate etc)* coating, covering (**c**) *(cuarto de baño)* bathroom; *(lavabo)* toilet

bar *nm* bar, pub

barahúnda *nf* din, uproar

baraja *nf* pack, deck

barajar *vt (cartas)* to shuffle; *Fig (nombres, cifras)* to juggle with

baranda, barandilla *nf (de escalera)* handrail, banister; *(de balcón)* handrail

baratija *nf* trinket, knick-knack

baratillo *nm* flea market

barato,-a 1 *adj* cheap

2 *adv* cheaply

baraúnda *nf* din, uproar

barba *nf (a) Anat* chin (**b**) *(pelo)* beard; *Fig* **100 pesetas por b.** 100 pesetas a head

barbacoa *nf* barbecue

barbaridad *nf (a)* atrocity (**b**) *(disparate)* piece of nonsense; **no digas barbaridades** don't talk nonsense (**c**) **una b.** a lot; **costar una b.** to cost a fortune

barbarie *nf* savagery, cruelty

bárbaro,-a 1 *adj (a) Hist* barbarian (**b**) *(cruel)* barbaric, barbarous (**c**) *Fam (enorme)* massive (**d**) *RP Fam (estupendo)* tremendous, terrific

2 *nm,f Hist* barbarian

barbecho *nm* fallow land; **dejar en b.** to leave fallow

barbería *nf* barber's (shop)

barbero *nm* barber

barbilla *nf* chin

barbitúrico *nm* barbiturate

barbudo,-a *adj* with a heavy beard

barca *nf* small boat

barcaza *nf* lighter

barcelonés,-esa 1 *adj* of/from Barcelona

2 *nm,f* person from Barcelona

barco *nm* boat, ship; **b. de pasajeros** liner; **b. de vapor** steamer

baremo *nm* scale

barítono *nm* baritone

barlovento *nm* windward

barman *nm* barman

barniz *nm* (**a**) *(en madera)* varnish; *(en cerámica)* glaze (**b**) *Fig* veneer

barnizar [40] *vt (madera)* to varnish; *(cerámica)* to glaze

barómetro *nm* barometer

barón *nm* baron

baronesa *nf* baroness

barquero,-a *nm,f (hombre)* boatman; *(mujer)* boatwoman

barquillo *nm* wafer

barra *nf* (**a**) bar; **b. de pan** French loaf, baguette; **b. de labios** lipstick (**b**) *(mostrador)* bar; **b. americana** = bar where hostesses chat with clients (**c**) *Dep* **b. fija** horizontal bar; **barras paralelas** parallel bars (**d**) *Andes, RP Fam (grupo de amigos)* gang, group of friends; **b. brava** = group of violent soccer supporters

barraca *nf* (**a**) *(caseta)* shack, hut (**b**) *(en Valencia y Murcia)* thatched farmhouse

barracón *nm Mil* prefabricated hut

barranco *nm (despeñadero)* cliff, precipice; *(torrentera)* gully, ravine

barranquismo *nm Dep* canyoning

barrena *nf* twist drill

barrenar *vt Téc* to drill

barrendero,-a *nm,f* sweeper, street sweeper

barreno *nm* (**a**) *(taladro)* large drill (**b**) *Min* charge

barreño *nm* tub

barrer 1 *vt* to sweep

2 *vi (en elecciones)* to win by a landslide

barrera *nf* barrier

barriada *nf* (**a**) *(barrio popular)* neighbourhood, area (**b**) *Am (barrio de chabolas)* shanty town

barricada *nf* barricade

barrida *nf* landslide victory

barriga *nf* belly; *Fam* tummy

barrigón,-ona, barrigudo,-a *adj* pot-bellied

barril *nm* barrel; **cerveza de b.** draught beer

barrillo *nm* pimple, spot

barrio *nm* area, district; **del b.** local; **el B. Gótico** the Gothic Quarter; **b. chino** red-light district; **barrios bajos** slums

barrizal *nm* mire, quagmire

barro *nm* (**a**) *(lodo)* mud (**b**) *(arcilla)* clay; **objetos de b.** earthenware

barroco,-a *adj* baroque

barruntar *vt (sospechar)* to suspect; *(presentir)* to have a feeling

barrunto *nm (presentimiento)* feeling, presentiment; *(sospecha)* suspicion

bartola *nf* **a la bartola** *loc adv Fam* **tenderse** *o* **tumbarse a la b.** to laze around, to idle away one's time

bártulos *nmpl Fam* things, bits and pieces

barullo *nm (alboroto)* row, din; *(confusión)* confusion

basar 1 *vt* to base (**en** on)

2 basarse *vpr (teoría, película)* **b. en** to be based on; **¿en qué te basas para decir eso?** what grounds do you have for saying that?

basca *nf Fam* people, crowd

báscula *nf* scales; *(para camiones)* weighbridge

bascular *vi* to tilt

base *nf* (**a**) base; **sueldo b.** minimum wage; *Informát* **b. de datos** database (**b**) *(de argumento, teoría)* basis; **en b. a** on the basis of; **a b. de estudiar** by studying; **a b. de productos naturales** using natural products (**c**) *(de partido)* grass roots; **miembro de b.** rank and file member (**d**) *(nociones)* grounding

básico,-a *adj* basic

basílica *nf* basilica

básquet *nm* basketball

bastante 1 *adj* (**a**) *(suficiente)* enough; **b. tiempo/comida** enough time/food; **bastantes platos** enough plates (**b**) *(abundante)* quite a lot of; **hace b. calor/frío** it's quite hot/cold; **bastantes amigos** quite a lot of friends

2 *adv* (**a**) *(suficiente)* enough; **con esto hay b.** that is enough; **no soy lo b. rico (como) para ...** I am not rich enough to ... (**b**) *(considerablemente)* fairly, quite; **me gusta b.** I quite like it; **vamos b. al cine** we go to the cinema quite *o* fairly often

bastar 1 *vi* to be sufficient *o* enough, to suffice; **basta con tres** three will be enough; **¡basta de tonterías!** enough of this nonsense!; **basta con tocarlo para que se abra** you only have to touch it and it opens; **¡basta (ya)!** that's enough!, that will do!
2 bastarse *upr* **b. a sí mismo** to be self-sufficient, to rely only on oneself
bastardilla *nf Impr* italics
bastardo,-a *adj & nm,f* bastard
bastidor *nm* (**a**) frame (**b**) *Teatro* **bastidores** wings; *Fig* **entre bastidores** behind the scenes
bastión *nm* bastion
basto,-a *adj* *(cosa)* rough, coarse; *(persona)* coarse, uncouth
bastón *nm* stick, walking stick
bastos *nmpl Naipes* ≃ clubs
basura *nf Br* rubbish, *US* garbage, *US* trash
basurero *nm* (**a**) *(persona) Br* dustman, *US* garbage man (**b**) *(lugar) Br* rubbish tip *o* dump, *US* garbage dump
bata *nf (para casa)* dressing gown; *(de médico etc)* white coat; *(de científico)* lab coat
batacazo *nm* (**a**) crash, bang (**b**) *CSur Fam (triunfo inesperado)* surprise victory;
batalla *nf* battle; **librar b.** to do *o* join battle; **b. campal** pitched battle
batallar *vi* to fight, quarrel
batallón *nm* battalion
batata *nf* sweet potato
batatazo *nm Am* = **batacazo**
bate *nm Dep* bat; **b. de béisbol** baseball bat
batear 1 *vi* to bat
2 *vt* to hit
batería 1 *nf* (**a**) battery (**b**) *Mús* drums (**c**) **b. de cocina** pots and pans, set of pans
2 *nmf* drummer
batiburrillo *nm* jumble, mess
batida *nf* (**a**) *(de la policía)* raid (**b**) *(en caza)* beat
batido,-a 1 *adj* (**a**) *Culin* whipped (**b**) *Dep* **tierra batida** clay
2 *nm* milk shake
batidora *nf (eléctrica)* mixer
batiente *adj* **reírse a mandíbula b.** to laugh one's head off
batín *nm* short dressing gown
batir 1 *vt* (**a**) to beat (**b**) *(huevo)* to beat; *(nata)* to whip, to whisk (**c**) *(récord)* to break (**d**) *(en caza)* to beat
2 batirse *upr* to fight
batuta *nf Mús* baton; *Fig* **llevar la b.** to be in charge
baúl *nm* (**a**) *(cofre)* trunk (**b**) *RP (maletero) Br* boot, *US* trunk
bautismo *nm* baptism, christening

bautizar [40] *vt* to baptize, to christen; *(vino)* to water down
bautizo *nm* baptism, christening
Baviera *n* Bavaria
baya *nf* berry
bayeta *nf* floorcloth
bayo,-a *adj* whitish yellow
bayoneta *nf* bayonet
baza *nf* trick; *Fig* **meter b.** to butt in
bazar *nm* bazaar
bazo *nm* spleen
bazofia *nf* rubbish
be *nf (letra)* b; *Am* **be baja** *o* **corta** v *(to distinguish from "b")*; *Am* **be alta** *o* **grande** *o* **larga** b *(to distinguish from "v")*
beatería *nf* sanctimoniousness
beato,-a *adj (piadoso)* devout; *Pey* prudish, sanctimonious
bebe,-a *nm,f Andes, RP* baby
bebé *nm* baby; **b. probeta** test-tube baby
bebedero *nm* drinking trough, water trough
bebedor,-a *nm,f* (hard *o* heavy) drinker
beber *vt & vi* to drink
bebible *adj* drinkable
bebida *nf* drink; **darse a la b.** to take to drink
bebido,-a *adj* drunk
beca *nf* grant
becar [44] *vt* to award a grant to
becario,-a *nm,f* grant holder
becerro *nm* calf
bechamel *nf* bechamel; **salsa b.** bechamel sauce, white sauce
becuadro *nm Mús* natural sign
bedel *nm* beadle
begonia *nf* begonia
beige *adj & nm inv* beige
béisbol *nm* baseball
bejuco *nm (en América)* liana; *(en Asia)* rattan
Belén *n* Bethlehem
belén *nm* nativity scene, crib
belga *adj & nmf* Belgian
Bélgica *n* Belgium
Belgrado *n* Belgrade
Belice *n* Belize
bélico,-a *adj* warlike, bellicose; *(preparativos etc)* war; **material b.** armaments
belicoso,-a *adj* warlike, bellicose; *(agresivo)* aggressive
beligerancia *nf* belligerence
beligerante *adj* belligerent; **los países beligerantes** the countries at war
bellaco,-a 1 *adj* wicked, roguish
2 *nm,f* scoundrel, rogue
belleza *nf* beauty
bello,-a *adj* beautiful
bellota *nf Bot* acorn; *Fig* **animal de b.** block-head
bemol 1 *adj Mús* flat
2 *nm* **esto tiene bemoles** this is a tough one
bencina *nf Chile (gasolina) Br* petrol, *US* gas
bencinera *nf Chile Br* petrol station, *US* gas station

bendecir [12] *vt* to bless; **b. la mesa** to say grace; **¡Dios te bendiga!** God bless you!
bendición *nf* blessing
bendito,-a 1 *adj* blessed; *(maldito)* damned
 2 *nm (bonachón)* good sort, kind soul; *(tontorrón)* simple soul
beneficencia *nf* beneficence, charity
beneficiado,-a *adj* favoured; **salir b. de algo** to do well out of sth
beneficiar [43] **1** *vt* to benefit
 2 beneficiarse *upr* **b. de** *o* **con algo** to profit from *o* by sth
beneficiario,-a *nm,f* beneficiary; **margen b.** profit margin
beneficio *nm* (**a**) *Com & Fin* profit (**b**) *(bien)* benefit; **en b. propio** in one's own interest; **un concierto a b. de ...** a concert in aid of ...
beneficioso,-a *adj* beneficial
benéfico,-a *adj* charitable
benemérita *nf* **la B.** the Spanish Civil Guard
beneplácito *nm Fml* approval, consent
benevolencia *nf* benevolence
benevolente, benévolo,-a *adj* benevolent
bengala *nf* flare
benigno,-a *adj (persona)* gentle, benign; *(clima)* mild; *(tumor)* benign
benjamín,-ina *nm,f* youngest child
beodo,-a *adj* drunk
berberecho *nm* (common) cockle
berbiquí *nm Téc* drill
berenjena *nf Br* aubergine, *US* eggplant
Berlín *n* Berlin
berlina *nf (coche)* saloon; *(carruaje)* sedan
berlinés,-esa 1 *adj* of/from Berlin
 2 *nm,f* Berliner
berma *nf Andes (arcén)* verge; *(de autopista) Br* hard shoulder, *US* shoulder
bermejo,-a *adj* reddish
bermellón *nm* vermilion
Bermudas 1 *nfpl* **las (Islas) B.** Bermuda
 2 *nmpl* **bermudas** *(prenda)* Bermuda shorts
Berna *n* Bern
berrear *vi* to bellow, low
berrido *nm* bellowing, lowing
berrinche *nm Fam* rage, tantrum
berro *nm* cress, watercress
berza *nf* cabbage
besar 1 *vt* to kiss
 2 besarse *upr* to kiss
beso *nm* kiss
bestia 1 *nf* beast, animal; **b. de carga** beast of burden
 2 *nmf Fam Fig* brute, beast
 3 *adj Fig* brutish, boorish; **a lo b.** rudely
bestial *adj* bestial; *Fam (enorme)* huge, tremendous; *(extraordinario)* fantastic, terrific
bestialidad *nf* (**a**) *Fam (estupidez)* stupidity (**b**) *(crueldad)* act of cruelty (**c**) *Fam* **una b. de** tons of, stacks of
best-seller *nm* best-seller
besugo *nm* (**a**) *(pez)* sea bream (**b**) *(persona)* idiot, half-wit

besuquear *Fam* **1** *vt* to kiss, to cover with kisses
 2 besuquearse *upr* to smooch
betabel *nf Méx Br* beetroot, *US* beet
betarraga *nf Andes Br* beetroot, *US* beet
betún *nm (para el calzado)* shoe polish; *Quím* bitumen
biberón *nm* baby's bottle, feeding bottle
Biblia *nf* Bible
bíblico,-a *adj* biblical
bibliografía *nf* bibliography
bibliorato *nm RP* file
biblioteca *nf* (**a**) *(institución)* library; **b. ambulante** mobile library (**b**) *RP (mueble)* bookcase
bibliotecario,-a *nm,f* librarian
bicameral *adj Pol* bicameral, two-chamber
bicarbonato *nm* bicarbonate; **b. sódico** bicarbonate of soda
bicentenario *nm Br* bicentenary, *US* bicentennial
bíceps *nm inv* biceps
bicha *nf* snake
bicho *nm* (**a**) bug, insect; **¿qué b. te ha picado?** what's bugging you? (**b**) *Taurom* bull (**c**) *Fam* **todo b. viviente** every living soul; **un b. raro** a weirdo, an oddball
bici *nf Fam* bike
bicicleta *nf* bicycle; **montar en b.** to ride a bicycle
bicolor *adj* two-coloured; *Pol* **gobierno b.** two-party government
bidé *nm* bidet
bidón *nm* drum
biela *nf Aut* connecting rod
Bielorrusia *n* Belarus
bien¹ *adv* (**a**) *(correctamente)* well; **habla b. (el) inglés** he speaks English well; **responder b.** to answer correctly; **hiciste b. en decírmelo** you were right to tell me; **las cosas le van b.** things are going well for him; **¡b.!** good!, great!; **¡muy b.!** excellent, first class!; **¡qué b.!** great!, fantastic!
 (**b**) *(de salud)* well; **sentirse/encontrarse/estar b.** to feel well
 (**c**) **vivir b.** to be comfortably off; **¡está b.!** *(de acuerdo!)* fine!, all right!; **¡ya está b.!** that's (quite) enough!; **aquí se está muy b.** it's really nice here; **esta falda te sienta b.** this skirt suits you; *Fam* **ese libro está muy b.** that book is very good; *Fam* **su novia está muy b.** his girlfriend is very nice
 (**d**) *(intensificador)* very, quite; **b. temprano** very early, nice and early; **b. caliente** pretty hot; **b. es verdad que ...** it's quite clear that ...
 (**e**) **más b.** rather, a little
 (**f**) **b. podía haberme avisado** she might have let me know
 (**g**) *(de buena gana)* willingly, gladly; **b. me tomaría una cerveza** I'd really love a beer
 2 *conj* **ahora b.** now, now then; **o b.** or, or else; **b. ... o b. ...** either ... or ...; **no b.** as soon

as; **no b. llegó ...** no sooner had she arrived than ...; **si b.** although, even if

3 *adj* **la gente b.** the wealthy, the upper classes

bien² *nm* (**a**) *(bondad)* good; **el b. y el mal** good and evil; **un hombre/familia de b.** a good man/family (**b**) *(bienestar)* **por el b. de** for the good of; **lo hace por tu b.** he does it for your sake (**c**) **bienes** goods; **bienes de equipo** capital goods; **bienes gananciales** communal property; **bienes inmuebles** real estate; **bienes de consumo** consumer goods

bienal *nf* biennial exhibition

bienestar *nm (personal)* well-being, contentment; *(comodidad)* ease, comfort; **la sociedad del b.** the affluent society

bienhechor,-a *nm,f (hombre)* benefactor; *(mujer)* benefactress

bienintencionado,-a *adj* well-meaning, well-intentioned

bienio *nm* biennium, two-year period

bienvenida *nf* welcome; **dar la b. a algn** to welcome sb

bienvenido,-a *adj* welcome

bife *nm Andes, RP (bistec)* steak

bifocal *adj* bifocal; **gafas bifocales** bifocals

bifurcación *nf* bifurcation; *(de la carretera)* fork

bifurcarse [44] *vpr* to fork, to branch off

bigamia *nf* bigamy

bígamo,-a 1 *adj* bigamous

2 *nm,f* bigamist

bigote *nm (de persona)* moustache; *(de animal) (usu pl)* whiskers

> 🖉 Observa que la palabra inglesa **bigot** es un falso amigo y no es la traducción de la palabra española **bigote**. En inglés, **bigot** significa "intolerante".

bilateral *adj* bilateral; **acuerdo b.** bilateral agreement

bilbaíno,-a 1 *adj* of/from Bilbao

2 *nm,f* person from Bilbao

bilingüe *adj* bilingual

bilis *nf* bile

billar *nm* (**a**) *(juego)* billiards *sing*; **b. americano** pool; **b. ruso** snooker (**b**) *(mesa)* billiard table

billete *nm* (**a**) ticket; **b. de ida** *Br* single (ticket), *US* one-way ticket; **b. de ida y vuelta** *Br* return (ticket), *US* round-trip (ticket); (**b**) *(de banco) Br* note, *US* bill; **un b. de mil pesetas** a thousand peseta note

billetera *nf*, **billetero** *nm* wallet, *US* billfold

billón *nm* trillion

bimensual *adj* twice-monthly, bi-monthly

bimotor 1 *adj* twin-engined

2 *nm* twin-engined plane

binario,-a *adj* binary

bingo *nm* (**a**) *(juego)* bingo (**b**) *(sala)* bingo hall

binomio *nm* binomial

biodegradable *adj* biodegradable

biofísica *nf* biophysics *sing*

biografía *nf* biography

biográfico,-a *adj* biographical

biógrafo,-a *nm,f* biographer

biología *nf* biology

biológico,-a *adj* biological; *(agricultura, productos)* organic

biólogo,-a *nm,f* biologist

biomasa *nf* bio-mass

biombo *nm* (folding) screen

biopsia *nf* biopsy

bioquímica *nf* biochemistry

bioquímico,-a 1 *adj* biochemical

2 *nm,f* biochemist

bióxido *nm* dioxide; **b. de carbono** carbon dioxide

bipartidismo *nm* two-party system

biquini *nm* bikini

birlar *vt Fam* to pinch, to nick

Birmania *n* Burma

birmano,-a *adj & nm,f* Burmese

birome *nm RP* ballpoint pen, *Br* Biro®

birrete *nm* cap, beret; *Rel* biretta; *Univ* mortar-board

birria *nf Fam* rubbish

bis 1 *nm* encore

2 *adv* twice

bisabuela *nf* great-grandmother

bisabuelo *nm* great-grandfather; **bisabuelos** great-grandparents

bisagra *nf* hinge; **partido b.** party holding the balance of power

bisbisar, bisbisear *vt* to whisper

bisexual *adj & nmf* bisexual

bisiesto *adj* **año b.** leap year

bisnieto,-a *nm,f (niño)* great-grandson; *(niña)* great-granddaughter; **mis bisnietos** my great-grandchildren

bisonte *nm* bison, American buffalo

bisoño,-a *adj* inexperienced

bisté, bistec *nm* steak

bisturí *nm* scalpel

bisutería *nf* imitation jewellery

bit *nm Informát* bit

bíter *nm* bitters

bizantino,-a *adj Fig* **discusiones bizantinas** hair-splitting arguments

bizco,-a 1 *adj* cross-eyed

2 *nm,f* cross-eyed person

bizcocho *nm* sponge cake

biznieto,-a *nm,f* = **bisnieto,-a**

blanca *nf Fam* **estar sin b.** to be flat broke

blanco¹,-a 1 *adj* white; *(tez)* fair

2 *nm,f (hombre)* white man; *(mujer)* white woman; **los blancos** whites

blanco² *nm* (**a**) *(color)* white (**b**) *(hueco)* blank; **dejó la hoja en b.** he left the page blank; **votos en b.** blank votes; *Fig* **pasar la noche en b.** to have a sleepless night; **me quedé en b.** my mind went blank (**c**) *(diana)* target; **dar en el b.** to hit the target; *Fig* **ser el b. de todas las miradas** to be the centre of attention

blancura *nf* whiteness

blandengue *adj Pey* weak, soft

blandir *vt* to brandish

blando,-a *adj* soft

> Observa que la palabra inglesa **bland** es un falso amigo y no es la traducción de la palabra española **blando**. En inglés, **bland** significa "soso".

blanquear *vt* (a) to whiten (b) *(encalar)* to whitewash (c) *(dinero)* to launder

blanquecino,-a *adj* whitish

blanqueo *nm* (a) whitening (b) *(encalado)* whitewashing (c) *(de dinero)* laundering

blanquillo *nm CAm, Méx (huevo)* egg

blasfemar *vi* to blaspheme (**contra** against)

blasfemia *nf* blasphemy

blasón *nm* coat of arms

bledo *nm Fam* **me importa un b.** I couldn't give a damn

blindado,-a *adj Mil* armoured, armour-plated; *(antibalas)* bullet-proof; **coche b.** bullet-proof car; **puerta blindada** reinforced door, security door

blindaje *nm* armour; *(vehículo)* armour plating

bloc *nm* pad; **b. de notas** notepad

bloomer ['blumer], **blúmer** *nm CAm, Carib* panties, *Br* knickers

bloque *nm* (a) block; **en b.** en bloc; **b. de pisos** *BR* (block of) flats, *US* apartment block (b) *Pol* bloc; **el b. comunista** the Communist Bloc

bloquear *vt* (a) to block (b) *Mil* to blockade

bloqueo *nm* blockade; *Dep* block

blues *nm* blues

blusa *nf* blouse

blusón *nm* loose blouse, smock

bluyín *nm,* **bluyines** *nmpl Andes, Ven* jeans

boato *nm* show, ostentation

bobada *nf* nonsense; **decir bobadas** to talk nonsense

bobalicón,-ona *Fam* **1** *adj* simple, stupid
  2 *nm,f* simpleton, idiot

bobería *nf* = bobada

bobina *nf* (a) reel (b) *Elec* coil

bobo,-a **1** *adj (tonto)* stupid, silly; *(ingenuo)* naïve
  2 *nm,f* fool

boca *nf* (a) mouth; **b. abajo** face downward; **b. arriba** face upward; *Fig* **a pedir de b.** in accordance with one's wishes; *Fig* **andar de b. en b.** to be the talk of the town; *Fam* **¡cierra la b!** shut up!; *Fam* **con la b. abierta** open-mouthed; *Fam* **se le hizo la b. agua** his mouth watered; **el b. a b.** kiss of life, mouth-to-mouth resuscitation (b) **la b. del metro** the entrance to the *Br* underground *o US* subway

station; **b. de riego** hydrant

bocacalle *nf* entrance to a street

bocadillo *nm* (a) *(con pan)* sandwich; **un b. de jamón/tortilla** a ham/an omelette sandwich (b) *(de cómic)* balloon

bocado *nm* (a) *(mordedura)* bite (b) *(de caballo)* bit

bocajarro: a bocajarro *loc adv* point-blank

bocanada *nf* (a) *(de vino)* mouthful (b) *(de humo)* puff; **una b. de viento** a gust of wind

bocata *nm* sandwich

bocazas *nmf inv Fam* bigmouth, blabbermouth

boceto *nm Arte* sketch, outline; *(esquema)* outline, plan

bochinche *nm Fam* uproar; **armar un b.** to kick up a row

bochorno *nm* (a) *(tiempo)* sultry *o* close weather; *(calor sofocante)* stifling heat (b) *Fig (vergüenza)* shame, embarrassment

bochornoso,-a *adj* (a) *(tiempo)* sultry, close, muggy; *(calor)* stifling (b) *Fig (vergonzoso)* shameful, embarrassing

bocina *nf* horn; **tocar la b.** to blow *o* sound one's horn

bocinazo *nm* hoot, toot

bocón,-ona *nm,f Am Fam* bigmouth

boda *nf* wedding, marriage; **bodas de plata** silver wedding

bodega *nf* (a) wine cellar; *(tienda)* wine shop (b) *Náut* hold (c) *(almacén)* warehouse (d) *Am* grocery store, grocer's (shop)

bodegón *nm* still-life

bodrio *nm Fam* rubbish, trash

body *nm* bodystocking, leotard

BOE *nm (abr Boletín Oficial del Estado)* Official Gazette

bofetada *nf,* **bofetón** *nm* slap on the face; **dar una b./un b. a algn** to slap sb's face

boga *nf Fig* **estar en b.** to be in vogue

bogar [42] *vi* (a) *(remar)* to row (b) *(navegar)* to sail

bogavante *nm* lobster

bogotano,-a 1 *adj* of/from Bogotá
  2 *nm,f* person from Bogotá

bohío *nm Am* hut, cabin

boicot *nm (pl boicots)* boycott

boicotear *vt* to boycott

boicoteo *nm* boycott

bóiler *nm Méx* boiler

boina *nf* beret

bol *nm* bowl

bola *nf* (a) ball; *(canica)* marble; **b. de nieve** snowball; **no dar pie con b.** to be unable to do anything right (b) *Fam (mentira)* fib, lie; **meter bolas** to tell fibs (c) *(rumor)* rumour; **corre la b. por ahí de que te has echado novio** they say you've got yourself a boyfriend

bolchevique *adj & nmf* Bolshevik

bolear *vt Méx (sacar brillo)* to shine, to polish

bolera *nf* bowling alley

bolería *nf Méx* shoeshine store

boleta *nf* (**a**) *Méx, RP (para votar)* ballot, voting slip (**b**) *CSur (comprobante)* receipt (**c**) *CAm, CSur (multa)* parking ticket (**d**) *Méx (boletín)* (school) report card

boletería *nf Am (de cine, teatro)* box office; *(de estación)* ticket office

boletero,-a *nm,f Am* box office attendant

boletín *nm* bulletin; **B. Oficial del Estado** Official Gazette

boleto *nm* (**a**) *(de rifa)* ticket (**b**) *Am (de tren, metro)* ticket (**c**) *Méx (para espectáculo)* ticket

boli *nm Fam* pen, *Br* Biro®

boliche *nm* (**a**) *(juego)* bowling (**b**) *(bola)* jack (**c**) *(lugar)* bowling alley (**d**) *CSur Fam (bar)* small bar

bólido *nm Aut* racing car

bolígrafo *nm* ballpoint (pen), *Br* Biro®

bolita *nf CSur (bola)* marble; **jugar a las bolitas** to play marbles

bolívar *nm Fin* = standard monetary unit of Venezuela

Bolivia *n* Bolivia

boliviano,-a *adj & nm,f* Bolivian

bollar *vt* to blow up

bollo *nm* (**a**) *Culin* bun, bread roll (**b**) *(abolladura)* dent

bolo¹ *nm (pieza)* skittle, pin; **bolos** *(juego)* (ten-pin) bowling

bolo²,-a *nm,f CAm Fam (borracho)* drunk

bolsa¹ *nf* bag; *Méx (de mano) Br* handbag, *US* purse; *Av* **b. de aire** air pocket; **b. de deportes** sports bag; **b. de la compra** shopping bag; **b. de viaje** travel bag

bolsa² *nf Fin* Stock Exchange; **jugar a la b.** to play the market

bolsillo *nm (en prenda)* pocket; **de b.** pocket, pocket-size; **libro de b.** paperback; **lo pagó de su b.** he paid for it out of his own pocket

bolso *nm Br* handbag, *US* purse

boludear *vi RP Fam* (**a**) *(hacer tonterías)* to mess about (**b**) *(decir tonterías)* to talk rubbish (**c**) *(perder el tiempo)* to waste one's time

boludo,-a *nm,f RP Fam (estúpido)* idiot, twit

bomba¹ *nf* pump; *Andes, Ven (gasolinera) Br* petrol station, *US* gas station; **b. de aire** air pump; **b. de incendios** fire engine; *Andes, Ven* **b. (de gasolina)** *(surtidor) Br* petrol pump, *US* gas pump

bomba² *nf* bomb; **b. atómica/de hidrógeno/ de neutrones** atomic/hydrogen/neutron bomb; **b. de relojería** time bomb; **b. fétida** stink bomb; *Fam* **noticia b.** shattering piece of news; *Fam* **pasarlo b.** to have a whale of a time

bombacha *nf RP (braga)* panties, *Br* knickers; **bombachas** *(pantalones)* = loose-fitting trousers worn by cowboys

bombardear *vt* to bomb, to shell; **b. a algn a preguntas** to bombard sb with questions

bombardeo *nm* bombing, bombardment

bombardero *nm Av* bomber

bombazo *nm* bomb blast

bombear *vt* (**a**) *(agua etc)* to pump (**b**) *(pelota)* to blow up

bombeo *nm (de líquido)* pumping; **estación de b.** pumping station

bombero,-a *nm,f* (**a**) *(de incendios)* firefighter; *(hombre)* fireman; *(mujer)* firewoman; **cuerpo de bomberos** *Br* fire brigade, *US* fire department; **parque de bomberos** fire station (**b**) *Ven (de gasolinera) Br* petrolpump o *US* gas-pump attendant

bombilla *nf* (light) bulb

bombillo *nm CAm, Carib, Col, Méx* light bulb

bombín *nm* bowler hat

bombita *nf RP* light bulb

bombo *nm* (**a**) *Mús* bass drum; *Fig* **a b. y platillo(s)** with a great song and dance; *Fam* **darse b.** to blow one's own trumpet (**b**) *(de sorteo)* lottery drum

bombón *nm* chocolate

bombona *nf* cylinder; **b. de butano** butane gas cylinder

bombonera *nf* chocolate box

bonachón,-ona *adj* good-natured, easy-going

bonaerense 1 *adj* of/from Buenos Aires
2 *nmf* person from Buenos Aires

bonanza *nf* (**a**) *Náut (tiempo)* fair weather; *(mar)* calm at sea (**b**) *Fig (prosperidad)* prosperity

bondad *nf* goodness; *Fml* **tenga la b. de esperar** please be so kind as to wait

bondadoso,-a *adj* kind, good-natured

bonete *nm Rel* cap, biretta; *Univ* mortarboard

boniato *nm* sweet potato

bonificación *nf* bonus

bonificar [44] *vt Com* to give a bonus to

bonito¹,-a *adj* pretty, nice

bonito² *nm* tuna

bono *nm* (**a**) *(vale)* voucher (**b**) *Fin* bond, debenture; **bonos del tesoro** o **del Estado** Treasury bonds

bono-bus *nm* bus pass

boom *nm* boom

boomerang *nm* boomerang

boquerón *nm* anchovy

boquete *nm* hole

boquiabierto,-a *adj* open-mouthed; **se quedó b.** he was flabbergasted

boquilla *nf* (**a**) *(de cigarro)* tip; *(de pipa)* mouthpiece; **decir algo de b.** to pay lip service to sth (**b**) *Mús* mouthpiece (**c**) *(orificio)* opening

borbotar, borbotear *vi* to bubble

borbotón *nm* bubbling; *Fig* **salir a borbotones** to gush forth

borda *nf Náut* gunwale; **arrojar** o **echar por la b.** to throw overboard; **fuera b.** *(motor)* outboard motor

bordado,-a 1 *adj* embroidered; **el examen me salió b.** I made a good job of that exam
2 *nm* embroidery

bordar *vt* (a) to embroider (b) *Fig* to do excellently

borde¹ *nm* (de mesa, camino) edge; *Cost* hem, edge; (de vasija) rim, brim; **al b. de** on the brink of, on the verge of; **al b. del mar** at the seaside

borde² *Fam* **1** *adj* stroppy
   2 *nmf* stroppy person

bordear *vt* to go round the edge of, to skirt

bordillo *nm* Br kerb, US curb

bordo *nm* **a b.** on board; **subir a b.** to go on board

bordó *adj inv* RP maroon, burgundy

borla *nf* tassel

borne *nm* Elec terminal

borra *nf* (a) (pelusa) fluff (b) (poso) sediment, dregs

borrachera *nf* (embriaguez) drunkenness; **agarrarse** *o* **cogerse una b.** to get drunk;

borracho,-a 1 *adj* (a) (bebido) drunk; **estar b.** to be drunk (b) (bizcocho) with rum
   2 *nm,f* drunkard, drunk

borrador *nm* (a) (escrito) rough copy, first draft (b) (croquis) rough *o* preliminary sketch (c) (de pizarra) duster

borraja *nf* **quedar en agua de borrajas** to come to nothing, to fizzle *o* peter out

borrar *vt* (a) (con goma) to erase, to rub out; (pizarra) to clean (b) *Informát* to delete
   2 borrarse *vpr* (de un club etc) to drop out, to withdraw

borrasca *nf* area of low pressure

borrascoso,-a *adj* stormy

borrego,-a *nm,f* (a) yearling lamb (b) *Fam* (persona) sheep

borrico *nm* ass, donkey; *Fam Fig* ass, dimwit

borrón *nm* blot, smudge

borroso,-a *adj* blurred; **veo b.** I can't see clearly, everything's blurred

Bosnia *n* Bosnia; **B. y Herzegóvina** Bosnia-Herzegovina

bosnio,-a *adj & nm,f* Bosnian

bosque *nm* wood

bosquejar *vt* (dibujo) to sketch, outline; (plan) to draft, to outline

bosquejo *nm* (de dibujo) sketch, study; (de plan) draft, outline

bostezar [40] *vi* to yawn

bostezo *nm* yawn

bota *nf* (a) boot; *Fig* **ponerse las botas** to make a killing (b) (de vino) wineskin

botana *nf* Méx snack, appetizer

botánica *nf* botany

botánico,-a 1 *adj* botanic; **jardín b.** botanic gardens
   2 *nm,f* botanist

botar 1 *vi* (a) (saltar) to jump (b) (pelota) to bounce
   2 *vt* (a) (barco) to launch (b) (pelota) to bounce (c) *Am* (arrojar) to throw out

botarate *nmf* madcap, fool

bote¹ *nm* (a) jump, bound; **dar botes** to jump

up and down; **de un b.** with one leap (b) (de pelota) bounce, rebound

bote² *nm* (lata) can, tin; (para propinas) jar *o* box for tips; (en lotería) jackpot; *Fam* **chupar del b.** to scrounge

bote³ *nm* (lancha) boat; **b. salvavidas** lifeboat

bote⁴ *nm* **de b. en b.** packed, full to bursting

botella *nf* (a) bottle (b) *Cuba* (autoestop) **dar b. a algn** to give sb a lift; **hacer b.** to hitchhike

botellín *nm* small bottle

botepronto *nm* Fam **a b.** all of a sudden

botica *nf* pharmacy, *Br* chemist's (shop), US drugstore; *Fam* **hay de todo como en b.** there's everything under the sun

boticario,-a *nm,f* pharmacist, *Br* chemist, US druggist

botijo *nm* earthenware pitcher (with spout and handle)

botín¹ *nm* (de un robo) loot, booty

botín² *nm* (calzado) ankle boot

botiquín *nm* (a) medicine chest *o* cabinet; (portátil) first-aid kit (b) (enfermería) first-aid post

botón *nm* button; **pulsar el b.** to press the button; **b. de muestra** sample

botones *nm inv* (en hotel) bellboy, US bellhop; (recadero) messenger, errand boy

boutique *nf* boutique

bóveda *nf* vault

bovino,-a *adj* bovine; **ganado b.** cattle

box *nm* (pl boxes) (a) (de caballo) stall (b) (de coches) pit (c) Am (boxeo) boxing

boxeador *nm* boxer

boxear *vi* to box

boxeo *nm* boxing

boya *nf* (a) Náut buoy (b) (corcho) float

boyante *adj* buoyant

boy-scout *nm* boy scout

bozal *nm* (a) (para perro) muzzle (b) Am (cabestro) halter

bracero *nm* (day) labourer

bragas *nfpl* panties, *Br* knickers

bragueta *nf* (de pantalón etc) fly, flies

braguetazo *nm* Fam **dar el b.** to marry for money

braille *nm* braille

bramar *vi* to low, to bellow

bramido *nm* lowing, bellowing

brandy *nm* brandy

branquia *nf* gill

brasa *nf* ember, red-hot coal; **chuletas a la b.** barbecued chops

brasero *nm* brazier

brasier *nm* Carib, Col, Méx bra

Brasil *n* Brazil

brasileño,-a, *RP* **brasilero,-a** *adj & nm,f* Brazilian

bravata *nf* piece *o* act of bravado

bravo,-a 1 *adj* (a) (valiente) brave, courageous (b) (feroz) fierce, ferocious; **un toro b.** a fighting bull (c) (mar) rough, stormy
   2 *interj* **¡b.!** well done!, bravo!

bravucón,-ona *nm,f* boaster, braggart

bravura *nf* (**a**) *(de animal)* ferocity, fierceness (**b**) *(de persona)* courage, bravery (**c**) *(de toro)* fighting spirit

braza *nf* (**a**) *Náut* fathom (**b**) *(en natación)* breaststroke; **nadar a b.** to do the breaststroke

brazada *nf (en natación)* stroke

brazalete *nm* (**a**) *(insignia)* armband (**b**) *(pulsera)* bracelet

brazo *nm* arm; *(de animal)* foreleg; *(de sillón, tocadiscos)* arm; **en brazos** in one's arms; **ir del b.** to walk arm in arm; *Fig* **con los brazos abiertos** with open arms; *Fig* **no dar su b. a torcer** not to give in, stand firm; **b. de gitano** = type of Swiss roll containing cream

brea *nf* tar, pitch

brebaje *nm* concoction, brew

brecha *nf (en muro)* opening, gap; *Mil & Fig* breach; *Fig* **estar siempre en la b.** to be always in the thick of things

brécol *nm* broccoli

bregar [42] *vi* to fight

Bretaña *nf* (**a**) Brittany (**b**) **Gran B.** Great Britain

brete *nm Fig* **poner a algn en un b.** to put sb in a tight spot

bretel *nm CSur* strap; **un vestido sin breteles** a strapless dress

breva *nf* early fig; *Fam* **de higos a brevas** once in a blue moon; *Fam* **¡no caerá esa b.!** no such luck!

breve *adj* brief; **en b., en breves momentos** shortly, soon; **en breves palabras** in short

brevedad *nf* briefness; *(concision)* brevity; **con la mayor b. posible** as soon as possible

brevet *nm Chile (de avión)* pilot's licence; *Ecuad, Perú (de automóvil) Br* driving licence, *US* driver's license; *RP (de velero)* sailor's licence

brezo *nm* heather

bribón,-ona 1 *adj* roguish, dishonest
2 *nm,f* rogue, rascal

bricolaje *nm* do-it-yourself, DIY

brida *nf* (**a**) *(rienda)* rein, bridle (**b**) *Téc* flange

bridge *nm Naipes* bridge

brigada 1 *nf* (**a**) *Mil* brigade (**b**) *(de policías)* squad; **b. antiterrorista** anti-terrorist squad
2 *nm Mil* sergeant major

brigadier *nm* brigadier

brillante 1 *adj* brilliant
2 *nm* diamond

brillantez *nf* brilliance

brillantina *nf* brilliantine

brillar *vi (resplandecer)* to shine; *(ojos, joyas)* to sparkle; *(lentejuelas etc)* to glitter; **b. por su ausencia** to be conspicuous by one's absence

brillo *nm (resplandor)* shine; *(del sol, de la luna)* brightness; *(de lentejuelas etc)* glittering; *(del cabello, tela)* sheen; *(de color)* brilliance; *(de pantalla)* brightness; *(de zapatos)* shine; **sacar b. a** to shine, to polish

brilloso,-a *adj Am* shining

brincar [44] *vi* to skip

brinco *nm* skip

brindar 1 *vi* to drink a toast; **b. por algn/algo** to drink to sb/sth
2 *vt* (**a**) *(oportunidad)* to offer, to provide (**b**) *Taurom* to dedicate (**a** to)
3 brindarse *vpr* to offer (**a** to), to volunteer (**a** to)

brindis *nm* (**a**) toast (**b**) *Taurom* dedication (of the bull)

brío *nm* energy

brioso,-a *adj* energetic, vigorous

brisa *nf* breeze; **b. marina** sea breeze

británico,-a 1 *adj* British; **las Islas Británicas** the British Isles
2 *nm,f* Briton; **los británicos** the British

brizna *nf (de hierba)* blade; *(de carne)* string

broca *nf Téc* bit

brocha *nf (para pintar)* paintbrush; **b. de afeitar** shaving brush

broche *nm* (**a**) *(joya)* brooch; *Fig* **poner el b. de oro** to finish with a flourish (**b**) *(de vestido)* fastener

brócoli *nm* broccoli

broma *nf (chiste)* joke; **bromas aparte** joking apart; **en b.** as a joke; **¡ni en b.!** not on your life!; **b. pesada** practical joke; **gastar una b.** to play a joke

bromear *vi* to joke

bromista 1 *adj* fond of joking *o* playing jokes
2 *nmf* joker, prankster

bronca *nf* (**a**) *(riña)* quarrel, row (**b**) **echar una b. a algn** to bawl sb out (**c**) *RP Fam (rabia)* **me da b.** it hacks me off; **el jefe le tiene b.** the boss can't stand him

bronce *nm* bronze

bronceado,-a 1 *adj* suntanned, tanned
2 *nm* suntan, tan

bronceador,-a 1 *adj* **leche bronceadora** suntan cream
2 *nm* suntan cream *o* lotion

broncearse *vpr* to get a tan *o* a suntan

bronco,-a *adj* rough, coarse

bronquitis *nf inv* bronchitis

brotar *vi (planta)* to sprout; *(agua)* to spring, to gush; *(lágrimas)* to well up; *(epidemia)* to break out

brote *nm* (**a**) *Bot (renuevo)* bud, shoot; *(de agua)* gushing (**b**) *(de epidemia, violencia)* outbreak

bruces: de bruces *loc adv* face downwards; **se cayó de b.** he fell flat on his face

bruja *nf* witch, sorceress

brujería *nf* witchcraft, sorcery

brujo,-a 1 *nm* wizard, sorcerer
2 *adj Méx Fam* **estar b.** to be broke

brújula *nf* compass

bruma *nf* mist

brumoso,-a *adj* misty

bruñir *vt* to polish

brusco,-a *adj* (**a**) *(persona)* brusque, abrupt (**b**) *(repentino)* sudden, sharp

Bruselas *n* Brussels; **coles de B.** Brussels sprouts

brusquedad *nf* brusqueness, abruptness

brutal *adj* brutal

brutalidad *nf* brutality

bruto,-a 1 *adj* (**a**) *(necio)* stupid, thick; *(grosero)* coarse, uncouth (**b**) *Fin* gross; **peso b.** gross weight (**c**) **un diamante en b.** an uncut diamond

2 *nm,f* blockhead, brute

búcaro *nm* earthenware jug

bucear *vi* to swim under water

buche *nm* maw; *(de ave)* craw; *Fam (estómago)* belly, stomach

bucle *nm* curl, ringlet

budín *nm* pudding

budismo *nm* Buddhism

budista *adj & nmf* Buddhist

buen *adj (delante de un nombre masculino singular)* good; **¡b. viaje!** have a good trip!; *ver* **bueno,-a**

buenamente *adv* **haz lo que b. puedas** just do what you can; **si b. puedes** if you possibly can

buenaventura *nf* good fortune, good luck; **echar la b. a algn** to tell sb's fortune

bueno,-a 1 *adj* (**a**) good; **un alumno muy b.** a very good pupil; **una buena película** a good film; **lo b.** the good thing

(**b**) *(amable) (con* **ser***)* good, kind; **el b. de Carlos** good old Carlos; **es muy buena persona** he's a very kind soul

(**c**) *(sano) (con* **estar***)* well, in good health

(**d**) *(tiempo)* good; **hoy hace buen tiempo** it's fine today; **mañana hará b.** it will be fine *o* a nice day tomorrow

(**e**) *(conveniente)* good; **no es b. comer tanto** it's not good for you to eat so much; **sería b. que vinieras** it would be a good idea if you came

(**f**) *(considerable)* considerable; **un buen número de** a good number of; **una buena cantidad** a considerable amount

(**g**) *(grande)* good, big; **un buen trozo de pastel** a nice *o* good big piece of cake

(**h**) *Fam (atractivo)* gorgeous, sexy; **¡Rosa está muy buena!** Rosa's a bit of all right!; **una tía buena** a good-looking girl

(**i**) *Irón* fine, real, proper; **¡en buen lío te has metido!** that's a fine mess you've got yourself into!

(**j**) **¡buenas!** *(saludos)* hello!; **buenas tardes** *(desde mediodía hasta las cinco)* good afternoon; *(desde las cinco)* good evening; **buenas noches** *(al llegar)* good evening; *(al irse)* good night; **buenos días** good morning

(**k**) *(locuciones)* **de buenas a primeras** suddenly, all at once; **estar de buenas** to be in a good mood; **los buenos tiempos** the good old days; **por las buenas** willingly; **por las buenas o por las malas** willy-nilly; *Irón* **¡buena la has hecho!** that's done it!; **un susto de los buenos**

a real fright; *Irón* **¡estaría b.!** I should jolly well hope not!; *Irón* **librarse de una buena** to get off scot free

---

> **buen** is used instead of **bueno** before masculine singular nouns (e.g. **buen hombre** good man). The comparative form of **bueno** is **mejor** (better), and the superlative form is **el mejor** (masculine) or **la mejor** (feminine) (the best).

---

2 *interj* (**a**) *(vale)* all right, OK (**b**) *(expresa sorpresa)* hey! (**c**) *Col, Méx (al teléfono)* hello

buey *nm* ox, bullock

búfalo,-a *nm,f* buffalo

bufanda *nf* scarf

bufar *vi* (**a**) *(toro)* to snort; *(caballo)* to neigh (**b**) *(persona)* to be fuming

bufé *nm* buffet; **b. libre** self-service buffet meal

bufete *nm (despacho de abogado)* lawyer's office

buffet *nm (pl* **buffets***)* = **bufé**

bufido *nm (de toro)* snort; *(de caballo)* neigh

bufón,-ona *nm,f* clown, buffoon

buhardilla *nf* attic, garret

búho *nm* owl; **b. real** eagle owl

buhonero,-a *nm,f* pedlar, hawker

buitre *nm* vulture

bujía *nf* (**a**) *Aut* spark plug (**b**) *Fís* candlepower

bulbo *nm* bulb

buldog *nm* bulldog

bulevar *nm* boulevard

Bulgaria *n* Bulgaria

búlgaro,-a *adj & nm,f* Bulgarian

bulín *nm RP Fam* bachelor pad

bulla *nf* (**a**) *(muchedumbre)* crowd, mob (**b**) *(ruido)* din; **armar b.** to kick up a din

bullicio *nm* din, hubbub

bullir *vi* (**a**) *(hervir)* to boil, to bubble (up) (**b**) **b. de gente** to be teeming with people

bulto *nm* (**a**) *(cosa indistinta)* shape, form (**b**) *(maleta, caja)* piece of luggage (**c**) *Med* lump (**d**) **hacer mucho b.** to be very bulky; *Fam* **escurrir el b.** to pass the buck

bumerán, bumerang *nm* boomerang

bungalow *nm* bungalow

búnker *nm* bunker

buñuelo *nm* doughnut

BUP *nm (abr* **Bachillerato Unificado Polivalente***)* = academically orientated Spanish secondary school course for pupils aged 14-17

buque *nm* ship; **b. de guerra** warship; **b. de pasajeros** liner, passenger ship; **b. insignia** flagship

burbuja *nf* bubble; **hacer burbujas** to bubble, make bubbles

burbujear *vi* to bubble

burdel *nm* brothel

Burdeos *n* Bordeaux

burdo,-a *adj* coarse, rough

burgalés,-esa 1 *adj* of/from Burgos

2 *nm,f* person from Burgos

burgués,-esa *adj & nm,f* bourgeois

burguesía *nf* bourgeoisie

burla *nf* gibe, jeer; **hacer b. de algo/algn** to make fun of sth/sb; **hacer b. a algn** to stick one's tongue out at sb

burladero *nm Taurom* refuge in bullring

burlar 1 *vt* (**a**) *(engañar)* to deceive (**b**) *(eludir)* to dodge, to evade
    2 burlarse *upr* to make fun (**de** of), to laugh (**de** at)

burlón,-ona *adj* mocking

buró *nm* (**a**) *Pol* executive committee (**b**) *(escritorio)* bureau, desk (**c**) *Méx (mesa de noche)* bedside table

burocracia *nf* bureaucracy

burócrata *nmf* bureaucrat

burocrático,-a *adj* bureaucratic

buromática *nf* office automation

burrada *nf (comentario)* stupid *o* foolish remark; *(hecho)* stupid *o* foolish act

burro,-a 1 *nm,f* (**a**) donkey, ass; *Fam Fig* **bajarse del b.** to climb *o* back down (**b**) *Fam (estúpido)* dimwit, blockhead (**c**) **b. de carga** dogsbody, drudge
    2 *adj Fam* (**a**) *(necio)* stupid, dumb (**b**) *(obstinado)* stubborn

bursátil *adj* stock-market

bus *nm* bus

busca *nf* search; **ir en b. de** to go in search of

buscapersonas *nm* pager

buscapleitos *nmf inv* troublemaker

buscar [44] **1** *vt* (**a**) to look *o* search for; **b. una palabra en el diccionario** to look up a word in the dictionary (**b**) **ir a b. algo** to go and get sth, to fetch sth; **fue a buscarme a la estación** she picked me up at the station
    2 buscarse *upr Fam* **b. la vida** to try and earn one's living; *Fam* **te la estás buscando** you're asking for it; **se busca** *(en anuncios)* wanted

buseta *nf Col, CRica, Ecuad, Ven* minibus

búsqueda *nf* search, quest; *Informát* search

busto *nm* bust

butaca *nf* (**a**) *(sillón)* armchair, easy chair (**b**) *Cin & Teatro* seat; **b. de platea** *o* **patio** seat in the stalls

butano *nm* butane; **(gas) b.** butane gas

butifarra *nf* sausage

buzo *nm* (**a**) *(persona)* diver (**b**) *Arg, Col (sudadera)* sweatshirt (**c**) *Col, Urug (jersey)* sweater, *Br* jumper

buzón *nm Br* letter box, *US* mailbox; *Informát (de correo electrónico)* (electronic) mailbox; **echar una carta al b.** to *Br* post *o US* mail a letter; **b. de voz** voice mail

byte *nm Informát* byte

C, c [θe] *nf (la letra)* C, c

C (**a**) *(abr* **Celsius**) C (**b**) *(abr* **centígrado**) C

c/ (**a**) *(abr* **calle**) St; Rd (**b**) *(abr* **cargo**) cargo, freight (**c**) *(abr* **cuenta**) a/c

C., Ca *(abr* **compañía**) Co

cabal 1 *adj* (**a**) *(exacto)* exact, precise (**b**) *(honesto)* honest, upright

2 *nmpl Fam* **no está en sus cabales** he's not in his right mind

cábala *nf Fig* **hacer cábalas sobre algo** to speculate about sth

cabalgadura *nf* mount

cabalgar [42] *vt & vi* to ride

cabalgata *nf* cavalcade; **la c. de los Reyes Magos** the procession of the Three Wise Men

caballa *nf* mackerel

caballar *adj* **ganado c.** horses

caballería *nf* (**a**) *(cabalgadura)* mount, steed (**b**) *Mil* cavalry

caballeriza *nf* stable

caballero *nm* (**a**) gentleman; **¿qué desea, c.?** can I help you, sir?; **ropa de c.** menswear (**b**) *Hist* knight (**c**) **caballeros** *(en letrero)* gents

caballeroso,-a *adj* gentlemanly, chivalrous

caballete *nm* (**a**) *(de pintor)* easel (**b**) *Téc* trestle (**c**) *(de nariz)* bridge

caballito *nm* (**a**) **c. de mar** seahorse (**b**) **caballitos** merry-go-round, *US* carousel

caballo *nm* (**a**) horse; **a c.** on horseback; **montar a c.** to ride; *Fig* **a c. entre ...** halfway between ... (**b**) *Téc* **c. de vapor** horse power (**c**) *(pieza de ajedrez)* knight (**d**) *Naipes* queen (**e**) *Fam (heroína)* horse, smack

cabaña *nf* cabin

cabaret *nm (pl* **cabarets**) cabaret

cabecear *vi* to nod

2 *vt Dep* to head

cabecera *nf* (**a**) top, head (**b**) *Impr* headline

cabecilla *nmf* leader

cabellera *nf* head of hair

cabello *nm* (**a**) hair (**b**) *Culin* **c. de ángel** = sweet made of gourd and syrup

cabelludo,-a *adj* **cuero c.** scalp

caber [9] *vi* (**a**) to fit, to be (able to be) contained; **cabe en el maletero** it fits in the boot; **¿cabemos todos?** is there room for all of us?; **en este coche/jarro caben ...** this car/jug holds ...; **no cabe por la puerta** it won't go through the door; **no c.** **en sí de gozo** to be beside oneself with joy; **no me cabe en la cabeza** I can't understand it; **no cabe duda** there is no doubt; **cabe la posibilidad de** **que ...** there is a possibility *o* chance that ...; **no está mal dentro de lo que cabe** it isn't bad, under the circumstances

(**b**) **cabe señalar que ...** we should point out that ...

(**c**) *Mat* **doce entre cuatro caben a tres** four into twelve goes three (times)

cabestrillo *nm* sling

cabeza 1 *nf* head; **en c.** in the lead; **por c.** a head, per person; *Fig* **a la c. de** at the front *o* top of; *Fig* **estar mal de la c.** to be a mental case; **c. de turco** scapegoat; **el** *o* **la c. de** **familia** the head of the family

2 *nm* **c. rapada** skinhead

cabezada *nf* (**a**) *(golpe)* butt, blow on the head (**b**) *Fam* **echar una c.** to have a snooze; **dar cabezadas** to nod

cabezal *nm Téc* head; *(de tocadiscos)* pick-up

cabezota *Fam* **1** *adj* pigheaded

2 *nmf* pigheaded person

cabezudo *nm* = carnival figure with a huge head

cabida *nf* capacity; **dar c. a** to leave room for

cabildo *nm Rel* chapter

cabina *nf* cabin; **c. telefónica** telephone box, telephone booth

cabinera *nf Col* air hostess

cabizbajo,-a *adj* crestfallen

cable *nm* cable; *Fam* **echarle un c. a algn** to give sb a hand

cableoperador *nm* cable company, cable operator

cabo *nm* (**a**) *(extremo)* end; **al c. de** after; **de c.** **a rabo** from start to finish (**b**) *Mil* corporal; *(policía)* sergeant (**c**) *Náut* rope, cable; *Fig* **atar cabos** to put two and two together; *Fig* **no dejar ningún c. suelto** to leave no loose ends (**d**) *Geog* cape; **Ciudad del C.** Cape Town; **C. Verde** Cape Verde

cabra *nf* goat; *Fam* **estar como una c.** to be off one's head

cabré *indic fut de* **caber**

cabreado,-a *adj muy Fam* pissed off

cabrear *muy Fam* **1** *vt* to make angry, *Br* to piss off

2 **cabrearse** *vpr* to get *Br* pissed off *o* *US* pissed

cabreo *nm muy Fam* anger

cabrío,-a *adj* **macho c.** billy goat; **ganado c.** goats

cabriola *nf* skip

cabrito *nm Zool* kid

cabro,-a *nm,f Chile Fam* kid

cabrón,-ona *nm,f Vulg (hombre) Br* bastard, *US* asshole; *(woman)* bitch

cabronada *nf muy Fam* dirty trick

cabuya *nf* (**a**) *(planta)* agave (**b**) *(fibra)* fibre hemp (**c**) *CAm, Col, Ven (cuerda)* rope

caca *nf Fam* poopoo

cacahuete, *CAm, Méx* **cacahuate** *nm* peanut

cacao *nm* (**a**) *Bot* cacao (**b**) *(polvo, bebida)* cocoa (**c**) *Fam (lío)* mess

cacarear 1 *vi (gallina)* to cluck
  2 *vt Fig* to boast about

cacareo *nm* (**a**) *(de gallina)* clucking (**b**) *Fig* boasting, bragging

cacatúa *nf* cockatoo

cacereño,-a 1 *adj* of/from Cáceres
  2 *nm,f* person from Cáceres

cacería *nf* (**a**) *(actividad)* hunting, shooting (**b**) *(partida)* hunt, shoot

cacerola *nf* saucepan

cacha *nf Fam (muslo)* thigh; **estar cachas** to be really muscular

cachalote *nm* sperm whale

cacharro *nm* (**a**) earthenware pot *o* jar (**b**) *Fam (cosa)* thing, piece of junk (**c**) **cacharros** *(de cocina)* pots and pans

caché *nm Informát* (**memoria**) **c.** cache memory

cachear *vt* to frisk, to search

cachemir *nm,* **cachemira** *nf* cashmere

cacheo *nm* frisk, frisking

cachetada *nf Am* slap

cachete *nm* (**a**) *(bofetada)* slap (**b**) *Am (mejilla)* cheek

cachila *nf RP (automóvil)* vintage car

cachimba *nf* (**a**) *(pipa)* pipe (**b**) *RP (pozo)* well

cachiporra *nf* club, truncheon

cachivache *nm Fam* thing, knick-knack

cacho¹ *nm Fam (pedazo)* bit, piece; *Fig* **¡qué c. de animal!** what a nasty piece of work!

cacho² *nm Andes, Ven (cuerno)* horn

cachondearse *vpr Fam* **c. de** to take the mickey out of

cachondeo *nm Fam* laugh; **tomar algo a c.** to take sth as a joke

cachondo,-a *adj Fam* (**a**) *(sexualmente)* randy (**b**) *(divertido)* funny

cachorro,-a *nm,f (de perro)* pup, puppy; *(de gato)* kitten; *(de otros animales)* cub, baby

cacique *nm (jefe)* local boss

caco *nm Fam* thief

cacofonía *nf* cacophony

cacto *nm,* **cactus** *nm inv Bot* cactus

cada *adj (de dos)* each; *(de varios)* each, every; **c. día** every day; **c. dos días** every second day; **c. vez más** more and more; **¿c. cuánto?** how often?; **c. dos por tres** four out of (every) ten; **¡tienes c. cosa!** you come up with some fine ideas!

cadalso *nm* scaffold

cadáver *nm (de persona)* corpse, (dead) body; *(de animal)* body, carcass; **ingresar c.** to be dead on arrival

cadena *nf* (**a**) chain; *(correa de perro)* lead, leash (**b**) *TV* channel (**c**) *Ind* line; **c. de montaje** assembly line; **trabajo en c.** assembly line work (**d**) *Geog* **c. montañosa** mountain range (**e**) *Jur* **c. perpetua** life imprisonment (**f**) *Aut* **cadenas** tyre chains

cadencia *nf* rhythm; *Mús* cadenza

cadera *nf* hip

cadete *nm* cadet; *RP (chico de los recados)* errand boy, office junior

caducar [44] *vi* to expire

caducidad *nf* expiry; **fecha de c.** *(en alimentos)* ≃ sell-by date; *(en medicinas)* to be used before

caduco,-a *adj* (**a**) *Bot* deciduous (**b**) *(anticuado)* out-of-date

caer [39] **1** *vi* (**a**) to fall; **dejar c.** to drop; *Fig* **está al c.** *(llegar)* he'll arrive any minute now; *(ocurrir)* it's on the way
  (**b**) *(fecha)* to be; **su cumpleaños cae en sábado** his birthday falls on a Saturday
  (**c**) *(entender)* to understand, to see; **ya caigo** I get it; **no caí** I didn't twig
  (**d**) *(hallarse)* to be; **cae por Granada** it is somewhere near Granada
  (**e**) **me cae bien/mal** I like/don't like her
  (**f**) **al c. el día** in the evening; **al c. la noche** at nightfall
  2 caerse *vpr* to fall (down); **me caí de la moto** I fell off the motorbike; **se le ha cayó el pañuelo** she dropped her handkerchief

café *nm* (**a**) coffee; **c. solo/con leche** black/white coffee (**b**) *(cafetería)* café

cafeína *nf* caffeine

cafetal *nm* coffee plantation

cafetera *nf* coffee-maker

cafetería *nf* snack bar, coffee bar; *Ferroc* buffet car

cafetero,-a *adj* (**a**) coffee (**b**) *Fam* **es muy c.** *(persona)* he loves coffee

cafiche *nm Andes Fam (proxeneta)* pimp

cafre *nmf* savage, beast

cagado,-a *adj muy Fam (cobarde)* coward; **estar c. de miedo** to be shit-scared

cagar [42] *muy Fam* **1** *vi* (**a**) to (have a) shit (**b**) *(estropear)* to ruin, to spoil; **cagarla** to cock it up
  2 cagarse *vpr* to shit oneself; **c. de miedo** to be shit-scared; **¡me cago en diez!** *Br* bloody hell!, *US* goddamn it!

caída *nf* (**a**) fall; *(de pelo, diente)* loss (**b**) *(de precios)* drop (**c**) *Pol* downfall, collapse

caído,-a 1 *adj* fallen
  2 *nmpl* **los caídos** the fallen

caigo *indic pres de* **caer**

caimán *nm* alligator

Cairo *n* **El C.** Cairo

caja *nf* (**a**) box; **c. fuerte** safe; *Fam TV* **la c.**

tonta the idiot box (**b**) *(de leche etc)* carton (**c**) *(de embalaje)* crate, case; **una c. de cerveza** a crate of beer (**d**) *Fin (en tienda)* cash desk; *(en banco)* cashier's desk (**e**) *Aut* **c. de cambios** gearbox (**f**) *Com* **c. de ahorros** *o* **de pensiones** savings bank (**g**) *(féretro)* coffin

cajero,-a *nm,f* cashier; **c. automático** cash point, cash dispenser

cajetilla *nf* packet, pack

cajón *nm* (**a**) *(en un mueble)* drawer; *Fig* **c. de sastre** jumble; *Fam* **de c.** obvious, self-evident (**b**) *(caja grande)* crate, chest

cajuela *nf* *CAm, Méx (maletero)* *Br* boot, *US* trunk

cal¹ *nf* lime; *Fig* **a c. y canto** hermetically; *Fam* **una de c. y otra de arena** six of one and half a dozen of the other

cal² *(abr* **caloría(s))** cal

cala *nf* (**a**) *Geog* creek, cove (**b**) *Náut* hold

calabacín *nm Bot* (**a**) *(pequeño)* *Br* courgette, *US* zucchini (**b**) *(grande)* *Br* marrow, *US* squash

calabaza *nf* pumpkin, gourd

calabobos *nm inv Fam* drizzle

calabozo *nm* (**a**) *(prisión)* jail, prison (**b**) *(celda)* cell

calada *nf Fam (de cigarrillo)* drag, puff

calado,-a 1 *adj* soaked
2 *nm Náut* draught

calamar *nm* squid *inv*; *Culin* **calamares a la romana** squid fried in batter

calambre *nm* (**a**) *Elec (descarga)* electric shock; **ese cable da c.** that wire is live (**b**) *(en músculo)* cramp

calamidad *nf* calamity

calaña *nf* kind, sort; **una persona de mala c.** a bad sort

calar 1 *vt* (**a**) *(mojar)* to soak, to drench (**b**) *(agujerear)* to pierce, to penetrate (**c**) *Fam (a alguien)* to rumble; **¡te hemos calado!** we've got your number!
2 *vi* (**a**) *(prenda)* to let in water (**b**) *Náut* to draw
3 **calarse** *upr* (**a**) *(prenda, techo)* to let in water; *(mojarse)* to get soaked (**b**) *(el sombrero)* to pull down (**c**) *Aut* to stall

calavera 1 *nf* (**a**) *(cráneo)* skull (**b**) *Méx Aut* **calaveras** tail lights
2 *nm* tearaway

calcar [44] *vt* (**a**) *(un dibujo)* to trace (**b**) *Fig (imitar)* to copy, to imitate

calceta *nf* (**a**) *(prenda)* stocking (**b**) **hacer c.** to knit

calcetín *nm* sock

calcinar *vt* to burn

calcio *nm* calcium

calco *nm* tracing; **papel de c.** carbon paper

calcomanía *nf* transfer

calculadora *nf* calculator

calcular *vt* (**a**) *Mat* to calculate (**b**) *(evaluar)* to (make an) estimate (**c**) *(suponer)* to figure, to guess

cálculo *nm* (**a**) calculation; **según mis cálculos** by my reckoning (**b**) *Med* gallstone (**c**) *Mat* calculus

caldear *vt* to heat up

caldera *nf* (**a**) *(industrial)* boiler; *(olla)* cauldron (**b**) *Urug (hervidor)* kettle

caldereta *nf* stew

calderilla *nf* small change

caldo *nm* stock, broth; **c. de cultivo** culture medium; *Fig* breeding ground

calé *adj & nm* gypsy

calefacción *nf* heating; **c. central** central heating

calefaccionar *vt CSur (calentar)* to heat (up), to warm (up)

calefactor *nm* heater

calefón *nm CSur (calentador)* water heater

caleidoscopio *nm* kaleidoscope

calendario *nm* calendar

calentador *nm* heater

calentamiento *nm Dep* warm-up

calentar [1] 1 *vt* (**a**) *(agua, horno)* to heat; *(comida, habitación)* to warm up; *Fig* **no me calientes la cabeza** don't bug me (**b**) *Fam (pegar)* to smack (**c**) *Fam (excitar)* to arouse (sexually), to turn on
2 **calentarse** *upr* (**a**) to get hot *o* warm, to heat up (**b**) *Fig* **se calentaron los ánimos** people became very excited

calentón,-ona, calentorro,-a *adj Fam* randy

calentura *nf* fever, temperature

calesita *nf RP* merry-go-round, carousel

calibrar *vt* to gauge, to bore

calibre *nm* (**a**) *(de arma)* calibre (**b**) *Fig (importancia)* importance

calidad *nf* (**a**) quality; **de primera c.** first-class; **un vino de c.** good-quality wine (**b**) **en c. de** as

cálido,-a *adj* warm; **una cálida acogida** a warm welcome

calidoscopio *nm* = **caleidoscopio**

caliente *adj* (**a**) hot (**b**) *Fig (debate)* heated; **en c.** in the heat of the moment (**c**) *Fam (cachondo)* hot, randy

calificación *nf* (**a**) qualification (**b**) *Educ* mark

calificar [44] *vt* (**a**) to describe (**de** as); **le calificó de inmoral** he called him immoral (**b**) *(examen)* to mark, to grade

calificativo *nm* epithet

caligrafía *nf* calligraphy; *(modo de escribir)* handwriting

calima *nf* haze, mist

calimocho *nm* = drink made with wine and Coca-Cola®

calina *nf* = **calima**

cáliz *nm* chalice

caliza *nf* limestone

calizo,-a *adj* lime

callado,-a *adj* quiet; **te lo tenías muy c.** you were keeping that quiet

callar 1 *vi* (a) *(dejar de hablar)* to stop talking; **¡calla!** be quiet!, *Fam* shut up! (b) *(no hablar)* to keep quiet, to say nothing

2 *vt (noticia)* not to mention, to keep to oneself

3 callarse *vpr* to stop talking, to be quiet; **¡cállate!** shut up!

calle *nf* (a) street, road; **c. de dirección única** one-way street; **c. mayor** *Br* high street, *US* main street; **el hombre de la c.** the man in the street (b) *Dep* lane

calleja *nf* narrow street

callejero,-a 1 *nm (mapa)* street directory

2 *adj* street; **gato c.** alley cat

callejón *nm* back alley *o* street; **c. sin salida** cul-de-sac, dead end

callejuela *nf* narrow street, lane

callista *nmf* chiropodist

callo *nm* (a) *Med* callus, corn; *Fam* **dar el c.** to slog (b) *Culin* **callos** tripe

calma *nf* (a) calm; **¡c.!** calm down!; **en c.** calm; **tómatelo con c.** take it easy (b) *Met* calm weather; **c. chicha** dead calm

calmante *nm* painkiller

calmar 1 *vt (persona)* to calm (down); *(dolor)* to soothe, to relieve

2 calmarse *vpr* (a) *(persona)* to calm down (b) *(dolor, viento)* to ease off

caló *nm* gypsy dialect

calor *nm* (a) heat; **hace c.** it's hot; **tengo c.** I'm hot; **entrar en c.** to warm up (b) *Fig (afecto)* warmth

caloría *nf* calorie

calote *nm RP Fam* swindle

calumnia *nf* (a) calumny (b) *Jur* slander

calumniar [43] *vt* (a) to calumniate (b) *Jur* to slander

caluroso,-a *adj* hot; *(acogida etc)* warm

calva *nf* bald patch

calvicie *nf* baldness

calvinismo *nm* Calvinism

calvo,-a 1 *adj* bald; **ni tanto ni tan c.** neither one extreme nor the other

2 *nm* bald man

calza *nf* wedge

calzada *nf* road, carriageway

calzado *nm* shoes, footwear

calzador *nm* shoehorn

calzar [40] **1** *vt* (a) *(poner calzado)* to put shoes on; **¿qué número calzas?** what size do you take? (b) *(mueble)* to wedge

2 calzarse *vpr* **c. los zapatos** to put on one's shoes

calzón *nm* (a) *Dep* shorts (b) *Andes, RP* **calzones** *(bragas)* panties, *Br* knickers (c) *Méx* **calzones** *(calzoncillos)* underpants

calzonazos *nm inv Fam* henpecked husband

calzoncillos *nmpl* underpants, pants

calzoneta *nf CAm* swimming trunks

cama *nf* bed; **estar en** *o* **guardar c.** to be confined to bed; **hacer la c.** to make the bed; **irse a la c.** to go to bed; **c. doble/sencilla** double/single bed; **c. turca** couch

camada *nf* litter; *(de pájaros)* brood

camafeo *nm* cameo

camaleón *nm* chameleon

cámara 1 *nf* (a) *(aparato)* camera; **a c. lenta** in slow motion (b) *Pol* Chamber, House; **C. Alta/Baja** Upper/Lower House (c) *Aut* inner tube (d) *(habitación)* room, chamber; **c. de gas** gas chamber; **c. frigorífica** cold-storage room; **música de c.** chamber music

2 *nmf (hombre)* cameraman; *(mujer)* camerawoman

camarada *nmf* comrade

camaradería *nf* camaraderie

camarera *nf (de hotel)* chambermaid

camarero,-a *nm,f* (a) *(de restaurante)* (hombre) waiter; *(mujer)* waitress; *(tras la barra)* (hombre) barman; *(mujer)* barmaid (b) *(de avión)* (hombre) steward; *(mujer)* stewardess

camarilla *nf* clique

camarón *nm* (common) prawn

camarote *nm* cabin

camba *Bol Fam* **1** *adj* of/from the forested lowland region of Bolivia

2 *nmf* person from the forested lowland region of Bolivia

cambalache *nm RP (tienda)* junk shop

cambiante *adj* changing; *(carácter)* changeable

cambiar [43] **1** *vt* (a) to change; **c. algo de sitio** to move sth (b) *(intercambiar)* to swap, to exchange (c) *(dinero)* to change

2 *vi* to change; **c. de casa** to move (house); **c. de idea** to change one's mind; **c. de trabajo** to get another job; **c. de velocidad** to change gear

3 cambiarse *vpr* (a) *(de ropa)* to change (clothes) (b) *(de casa)* to move (house)

cambiazo *nm Fam* switch

cambio *nm* (a) change; *(de impresiones)* exchange; **c. de planes** change of plans; **un c. en la opinión pública** a shift in public opinion; *Fig* **a c. de** in exchange for; **en c.** on the other hand (b) *(dinero)* change; **¿tienes c. de mil pesetas?** have you got change for a thousand pesetas? (c) *Fin (de divisas)* exchange; *(de acciones)* price (d) *Aut* gear change; **c. automático** automatic transmission

cambista *nmf* moneychanger

Camboya *n* Cambodia

cambur *nm Ven (plátano)* banana

camelar *vt*, **camelarse** *vpr Fam* (a) to cajole (b) *(galantear)* to win over

camelia *nf* camellia

camello,-a 1 *nm,f* camel

2 *nm Fam (traficante de drogas)* (drug) pusher

camellón *nm Col, Méx (en avenida)* *Br* central reservation, *US* median (strip)

camelo *nm Fam* (a) *(engaño)* hoax (b) *(trola)* cock-and-bull story

camerino *nm* dressing room

Camerún n Cameroon

camilla nf (**a**) (ruta) stretcher (**b**) **mesa c.** = small round table under which a heater is placed

caminante nmf walker

caminar **1** vi to walk

2 vt to cover, to travel; **caminaron 10 km** they walked for 10 km

caminata nf long walk

camino nm (**a**) (ruta) route, way; **ir c. de** to be going to; **ponerse en c.** to set off; Fig **ir por buen/mal c.** to be on the right/wrong track; **abrirse c.** to break through; **a medio c.** halfway; **en el c. a** o **de c. a** on the way to; **estar en c.** to be on the way; **nos coge** o **pilla de c.** it is on the way (**b**) (vía) path, track (**c**) (modo) way

camión nm (**a**) truck, Br lorry; **c. cisterna** tanker; **c. de la basura** Br dustcart, US garbage truck; **c. frigorífico** refrigerated truck (**b**) CAm, Méx (autobús) bus

camionero,-a nm,f truck o Br lorry driver

camioneta nf van

camisa nf shirt; **en mangas de c.** in one's shirtsleeves; Fig **cambiar de c.** to change sides; **c. de fuerza** straightjacket

camiseta nf (**a**) (de uso interior) Br vest, US undershirt (**b**) (de uso exterior) T-shirt (**c**) Dep shirt; **sudar la c.** to run oneself into the ground

camisón nm nightdress, Fam nightie

camomila nf camomile

camorra nf Fam trouble

camorrista **1** adj quarrelsome, rowdy

2 nmf troublemaker

camote nm Andes, CAm, Méx (batata) sweet potato

campal adj **batalla c.** pitched battle

campamento nm camp

campana nf bell; **pantalones de campana** bell-bottom trousers

campanada nf peal o ring of a bell

campanario nm belfry, bell tower

campanilla nf (**a**) small bell (**b**) Anat uvula (**c**) Bot bell flower

campante adj Fam **se quedó tan c.** he didn't bat an eyelid

campaña nf (**a**) campaign; **c. electoral** election campaign; **c. publicitaria** advertising campaign (**b**) Mil campaign; **hospital/ambulancia de c.** field hospital/ambulance (**c**) RP (campo) countryside

campar vi Fam **c. por sus respetos** to do as one pleases

campechano,-a adj unpretentious

campeón,-ona nm,f champion; **c. mundial** world champion

campeonato nm championship; **un tonto de c.** an utter idiot

campera nf (**a**) **camperas** (botas) cowboy boots (**b**) RP (chaqueta) jacket

campero,-a adj country, rural; (botas) **camperas** leather boots

campesino,-a nm,f (hombre) countryman; (mujer) countrywoman

campestre adj rural

camping nm campsite; **hacer** o **ir de c.** to go camping

campiña nf open country

campista nmf camper

campo nm (**a**) country, countryside; **a c. traviesa** o **a través** cross-country; **trabaja (en) el c.** he works (on) the land; **trabajo de c.** fieldwork (**b**) (parcela) field (**c**) Fís & Fot field (**d**) (ámbito) field; **c. de acción** field of action; Mil **c. de batalla** battlefield; **c. de concentración** concentration camp; **c. de trabajo** work camp (**e**) Dep field; (de fútbol) pitch; (de golf) course (**f**) RP (hacienda) farm (**g**) Andes (sitio) room, space

camposanto nm cemetery

camuflaje nm camouflage

camuflar vt to camouflage

cana nf (gris) grey hair; (blanco) white hair; **tener canas** to have grey hair; Fam **echar una c. al aire** to let one's hair down

Canadá n Canada

canadiense adj & nmf Canadian

canal nf (**a**) (artificial) canal; (natural) channel; **C. de la Mancha** English Channel (**b**) TV, Elec & Informát channel

canalizar [40] vt to channel

canalla **1** nm swine, rotter

2 nf riffraff, mob

canallesco,-a adj rotten, despicable

canalón nm gutter

canapé nm (**a**) Culin canapé (**b**) (sofá) couch, sofa

canario,-a **1** adj & nm,f Canarian; **Islas Canarias** Canary Islands, Canaries

2 nm Orn canary

canasta nf basket

canastilla nf small basket; (de un bebé) layette

canasto nm big basket, hamper

cancán nm frilly petticoat; RP **cancanes** (leotardos) Br tights, US pantyhose

cancela nf wrought-iron gate

cancelación nf cancellation

cancelar vt (**a**) (acto etc) to cancel (**b**) (deuda) to pay off (**c**) Chile, Ven (compra) to pay for

cáncer nm cancer; **c. de pulmón/mama** lung/breast cancer

cancerbero,-a nm,f Ftb goalkeeper

cancerígeno,-a adj carcinogenic

canceroso,-a adj cancerous

cancha nf ground; Ten court

canchero,-a adj RP Fam (desenvuelto) streetwise, savvy

canciller nm chancellor

cancillería nf Am foreign ministry

canción nf song

candado nm padlock

candela nf fire

candelabro nm candelabrum

candelero *nm* candlestick; *Fig* **en el c.** at the top

candente *adj* red-hot; *Fig* **tema c.** topical issue

candidato,-a *nm,f* candidate; *(a un puesto)* applicant

candidatura *nf* (a) *(lista)* list of candidates (b) **presentar su c.** to submit one's application

candidez *nf* candour

cándido,-a *adj* ingenuous, naive

> ⚠ Observa que la palabra inglesa **candid** es un falso amigo y no es la traducción de la palabra española **cándido**. En inglés, **candid** significa "franco, sincero".

candil *nm* oil lamp; *Méx (candelabro)* chandelier

candilejas *nfpl Teatro* footlights

candor *nm* innocence, naivety

> ⚠ Observa que la palabra inglesa **candour** es un falso amigo y no es la traducción de la palabra española **candor**. En inglés, **candour** significa "sinceridad, franqueza".

candoroso,-a *adj* innocent, pure

canela *nf* cinnamon

canelones *nmpl* cannelloni

cangrejo *nm (de mar)* crab; *(de río)* freshwater crayfish

canguro 1 *nm* kangaroo
2 *nmf Fam* baby-sitter

caníbal *adj & nmf* cannibal

canica *nf* marble

caniche *nm* poodle

canícula *nf* dog days, midsummer heat

canijo,-a *adj Fam* puny, weak

canilla *nf* (a) *Fam (espinilla)* shinbone (b) *RP (grifo)* Br tap, US faucet

canillera *nf Am (cobardía)* cowardice; *(miedo)* fear

canillita *nm Andes, RP* newspaper vendor

canino,-a 1 *adj* canine; *Fam* **tener un hambre canina** to be starving
2 *nm (colmillo)* canine

canjear *vt* to exchange

cano,-a *adj (blanco)* white; *(gris)* grey

canoa *nf* canoe

canódromo *nm* dog *o* greyhound track

canon *nm* (a) canon, norm (b) *Mús & Rel* canon (c) *Com* royalty

canónigo *nm* canon

canonizar [40] *vt* to canonize

canoso,-a *adj (de pelo blanco)* white-haired; *(de pelo gris)* grey-haired; *(pelo)* white, grey

cansado,-a *adj* (a) *(agotado)* tired, weary; **estar c.** to be tired (b) **ser c.** *(pesado)* to be boring *o* tiresome

cansador,-a *adj Andes, RP (que cansa)* tiring; *(que aburre)* boring

cansancio *nm* tiredness, weariness; *Fam* **es-**

toy muerto de c. I'm on my last legs

cansar 1 *vt* to tire
2 *vi* to be tiring
3 cansarse *vpr* to get tired; **se cansó de esperar** he got fed up with (with) waiting

Cantabria *n* Cantabria

cantábrico,-a *adj* Cantabrian; **Mar C.** Bay of Biscay

cántabro,-a *adj & nm,f* Cantabrian

cantaleta *nf Am* **la misma c.** the same old story

cantante 1 *nmf* singer
2 *adj* singing; **llevar la voz c.** to rule the roost

cantaor,-a *nm,f* flamenco singer

cantar¹ *vt & vi* (a) *Mús* to sing; *Fig* **en menos que canta un gallo** in a flash (b) *Fam (confesar)* to sing, to spill the beans (c) *Fam (oler mal)* to hum

cantar² *nm Literario* song; *Fam* **¡eso es otro c.!** that's a totally different thing!

cantarín,-ina *adj (voz)* singsong

cántaro *nm* pitcher; *Fig* **llover a cántaros** to rain cats and dogs

cante *nm* (a) *(canto)* singing; **c. hondo, c. jondo** flamenco (b) *Fam* **dar el c.** to attract attention

cantegril *nm Urug* shanty town

cantera *nf* (a) *(de piedra)* quarry (b) *Fig Ftb* young players

cantero *nm* (a) *(masón)* stonemason (b) *Cuba, RP (parterre)* flowerbed

cantidad 1 *nf* quantity; *(de dinero)* amount, sum; **en c.** a lot; *Fam* **c. de gente** thousands of people
2 *adv Fam* a lot; **me gusta c.** I love it

cantimplora *nf* water bottle

cantina *nf* canteen

cantinero,-a *nm,f* bar attendant

canto¹ *nm* (a) *(arte)* singing (b) *(canción)* song

canto² *nm (borde)* edge; **de c.** on its side

canto³ *nm (guijarro)* pebble, stone; **c. rodado** *(grande)* boulder; *(pequeño)* pebble

cantor,-a 1 *adj* singing; **pájaro c.** songbird
2 *nm,f* singer

canturrear *vi* to hum, to croon

canutas *nfpl Fam* **pasarlas c.** to have a hard time

canuto *nm* (a) *(tubo)* tube (b) *Fam (porro)* joint

caña *nf* (a) *(vaso)* glass; *(de cerveza)* glass of beer (b) *Bot* reed; *(tallo)* cane, stem; **c. de azúcar** sugar cane (c) *(de pescar)* rod (d) *Fam* **darle c. al coche** to go at full speed (e) *Andes, Cuba, RP (aguardiente)* cane spirit, cheap rum

cañada *nf* gully, ravine

cáñamo *nm* hemp

cañería *nf (piece of)* piping; **cañerías** plumbing

cañero,-a *nm,f Am (trabajador)* = worker on sugar plantation

cañí *adj & nmf (pl* **cañís)** *Fam* gypsy
caño *nm (tubo)* tube; *(tubería)* pipe
cañón *nm* (**a**) cannon; *Fig* **estar siempre al pie del c.** to be always ready for a fight (**b**) *(de fusil)* barrel (**c**) *Geog* canyon
cañonazo *nm* gunshot
caoba *nf* mahogany
caos *nm* chaos
caótico,-a *adj* chaotic
cap. *(abr* **capítulo)** ch
capa *nf* (**a**) *(prenda)* cloak, cape; **de c. caída** low-spirited (**b**) *(de pintura)* layer, coat; *Culin* coating (**c**) *Geol* stratum, layer
capacidad *nf* (**a**) *(cabida)* capacity (**b**) *(aptitud)* capacity, ability
capacitación *nf* qualification
capacitar *vt (autorizar)* to authorize
capar *vt* to castrate
caparazón *nm* shell
capataz,-a *nm,f (hombre)* foreman; *(mujer)* forewoman
capaz *adj* (**a**) capable, able; **ser c. de hacer algo** *(tener la habilidad de)* to be able to do sth; *(atreverse a)* to dare to do sth; **si se entera es c. de despedirle** if he finds out, he could quite easily sack him (**b**) *Am* **es c. que** it is likely that
capcioso,-a *adj* captious; **pregunta capciosa** catch question
capea *nf* amateur bullfight
capear *vt (dificultad etc)* to dodge, to shirk; *Fig* **c. el temporal** to weather the storm
capellán *nm* chaplain
caperuza *nf* hood
capicúa *adj* **número c.** reversible number; **palabra c.** palindrome
capilar *adj* hair; **loción c.** hair lotion
capilla *nf* chapel; **c. ardiente** chapel of rest
capirote *nm Fam* **tonto de c.** silly idiot
capital 1 *nf* capital
 2 *nm Fin* capital; **c. activo** *o* **social** working *o* share capital
 3 *adj* capital, main; **de importancia c.** of capital importance; **pena c.** capital punishment
capitalismo *nm* capitalism
capitalista *adj & nmf* capitalist
capitalizar [40] *vt* to capitalize
capitán,-ana *nm,f* captain; **c. general** *Br* field marshal, *US* general of the army
capitanear *vt* (**a**) *Mil & Náut* to captain, to command (**b**) *(dirigir)* to lead; *Dep* to captain
capitulación *nf* agreement; *Mil* capitulation; **capitulaciones matrimoniales** marriage settlement
capitular *vi* (**a**) *Mil* to capitulate, to surrender (**b**) *(convenir)* to reach an agreement
capítulo *nm* (**a**) *(de libro)* chapter (**b**) *Fig* **dentro del c. de ...** *(tema)* under the heading of ...
capó *nm Aut Br* bonnet, *US* hood
capón *nm* rap on the head with the knuckles

capota *nf Aut* folding hood *o* top
capote *nm* (**a**) *Taurom* cape (**b**) *Mil* greatcoat
capricho *nm* (**a**) *(antojo)* whim, caprice (**b**) *Mús* caprice, capriccio
caprichoso,-a *adj* whimsical
Capricornio *nm* Capricorn
cápsula *nf* capsule
captar *vt* (**a**) *(ondas)* to receive, to pick up (**b**) *(comprender)* to understand, to grasp (**c**) *(interés etc)* to attract
captura *nf* capture
capturar *vt (criminal)* to capture; *(cazar, pescar)* to catch; *Mil* to seize
capucha *nf* hood
capuchino *nm (café)* cappuccino
capullo *nm* (**a**) *(de insecto)* cocoon (**b**) *Bot* bud (**c**) *Vulg (prepucio)* foreskin (**d**) *muy Fam (persona despreciable) Br* dickhead, *US* jerk
caqui 1 *adj (color)* khaki
 2 *nm (fruto)* persimmon
cara 1 *nf* (**a**) face; **c. a c.** face to face; **c. a la pared** facing the wall; **poner mala c.** to pull a long face; **tener buena/mala c.** to look good/ bad; *Fig* **c. de circunstancias** serious look; *Fig* **dar la c.** to face the consequences (of one's acts); *Fig* **dar la c. por algn** to stand up for sb; *Fig* **(de) c. a** with a view to; *Fig* **echarle a algn algo en c.** to reproach sb for sth; *Fig* **plantar c. a algn** to face up to sb
 (**b**) *(lado)* side; *(de moneda)* right side; **¿c. o cruz?** heads or tails?; **echar algo a c. o cruz** to toss (a coin) for sth
 (**c**) *Fam (desfachatez)* cheek, nerve; **¡qué c. (más dura) tienes!** what a cheek you've got!
 2 *nm Fam (desvergonzado)* cheeky person
carabela *nf* caravel
carabina *nf* (**a**) *(arma)* carbine, rifle (**b**) *(persona)* chaperon
carabinero *nm* (**a**) *(marisco)* scarlet shrimp, = type of large red prawn (**b**) *Chile (policía)* military policeman
caracense 1 *adj* of/from Guadalajara
 2 *nmf* person from Guadalajara
caracol 1 *nm* (**a**) *(de tierra)* snail; *Am* shell (**b**) *(rizo)* kiss-curl
 2 *interj* **¡caracoles!** good heavens!
caracola *nf* conch
carácter *nm (pl* **caracteres)** (**a**) *(temperamento)* character; **de mucho c.** with a strong character; **tener buen/mal c.** to be good-natured/bad-tempered (**b**) *Fig (índole)* nature; **con c. de invitado** as a guest (**c**) *Impr* character
característica *nf* characteristic
característico,-a *adj* characteristic
caracterizar [40] *vt* to characterize
caradura *nmf Fam* cheeky devil; **¡qué c. eres!** you're so cheeky!
carajillo *nm Fam* = coffee with a dash of brandy
carajo *interj Vulg* shit!; **¡vete al c.!** go to hell!
caramba *interj Fam (sorpresa)* good grief!; *(enfado)* damn it!

carámbano *nm* icicle

carambola *nf Br* cannon, *US* carom

caramelo *nm* (**a**) *(dulce) Br* (boiled) sweet, *US* candy (**b**) *(azúcar quemado)* caramel; *Culin* **a punto de c.** syrupy

carantoña *nf* caress

caraota *nf Ven* bean

caraqueño,-a **1** *adj* of/from Caracas

  2 *nm,f* person from Caracas

carátula *nf* (**a**) *(cubierta)* cover (**b**) *(máscara)* mask

caravana *nf* (**a**) *(vehículo)* caravan (**b**) *(de tráfico) Br* tailback, *US* backup (**c**) *Urug (aro, pendiente)* earring

caray *interj* God!, good heavens!

carbón *nm* coal; **c. vegetal** charcoal; **c. mineral** coal

carboncillo *nm* charcoal

carbonero *nm* coal merchant

carbónico,-a *adj* carbonic; **agua carbónica** mineral water

carbonilla *nf* coal dust

carbonizar [40] **1** *vt* to carbonize, to char; **morir carbonizado** to be burnt to death

  2 carbonizarse *upr* to carbonize, to char

carbono *nm* carbon

carburador *nm* carburettor

carburante *nm* fuel

carburar *vi Fam (funcionar)* to work properly

carca *adj & nmf Fam* old fogey; *Pol* reactionary

carcaj *nm* quiver

carcajada *nf* guffaw

carcamal *nm Fam* old fogey

cárcel *nf* prison, jail

carcelario,-a *adj* prison, jail

carcelero,-a *nm,f* jailer, warder

carcoma *nf* woodworm

carcomer 1 *vt* to eat away

  2 carcomerse *upr* to be consumed (**de** with)

cardar *vt* (**a**) *(lana, algodón)* to card (**b**) *(pelo)* to backcomb

cardenal *nm* (**a**) *Rel* cardinal (**b**) *Med* bruise

cárdeno,-a *adj* purple

cardiaco,-a, cardíaco,-a 1 *adj* cardiac, heart; **ataque c.** heart attack

  2 *nm,f* person with a heart condition

cardinal *adj* cardinal; **punto/número c.** cardinal point/number

cardiólogo,-a *nm,f* cardiologist

cardo *nm (con espinas)* thistle

carear *vt* (**a**) *Jur* to bring two people face to face (**b**) *(cotejar)* to compare

carecer [33] *vi* **c. de** to lack

carencia *nf* lack (**de** of)

carente *adj* lacking; **c. de interés** lacking interest

careo *nm Jur* confrontation

carestía *nf* (**a**) *(falta)* lack, shortage (**b**) *Fin* high price o cost

careta *nf* mask; **c. antigás** gas mask

carey *nm* tortoiseshell

carezco *indic pres de* **carecer**

carga *nf* (**a**) *(acción)* loading (**b**) *(cosa cargada)* load; *(de avión, barco)* cargo, freight; *Fig* **c. afectiva** emotional content (**c**) *Fin (gasto)* debit; **c. fiscal** tax charge (**d**) *Fig (obligación)* burden (**e**) *Mil & Elec* charge

cargado,-a *adj* (**a**) loaded (**b**) *(bebida)* strong; **un café c.** a strong coffee (**c**) *(ambiente)* heavy; **atmósfera cargada** stuffy atmosphere (**d**) *Fig* burdened; **c. de deudas** up to one's eyes in debt (**e**) *Elec* charged

cargamento *nm* (**a**) *(carga)* load (**b**) *(mercancías)* cargo, freight

cargante *adj Fam* annoying

cargar [42] **1** *vt* (**a**) to load; *(mechero, pluma)* to fill; *(batería)* to charge; *Fig* **c. las culpas a algn** to put the blame on sb (**b**) *Com* to charge; **cárguelo a mi cuenta** charge it to my account; *Fam Educ* **me han cargado las matemáticas** I failed maths

  2 *vi* (**a**) *con (llevar)* to carry; *Fig* **c. con la responsabilidad** to take the responsibility; *Fig* **c. con las consecuencias** to suffer the consequences (**b**) *Mil* **c. contra** to charge

  3 cargarse *upr* (**a**) *Fam* **te la vas a c.** you're asking for trouble and you're going to get it (**b**) *Fam (estropear)* to smash, to ruin (**c**) *Fam (matar)* to kill, to bump off

cargo *nm* (**a**) *(puesto)* post, position; **alto c.** *(puesto)* top job, high ranking position; *(persona)* top person **c. estar al c. de** to be in charge of; **correr a c. de** *(gastos)* to be met by; **hacerse c. de** to take charge of; **hazte c. de mi situación** please try to understand my situation; **c. de conciencia** weight on one's conscience (**c**) *Fin* charge, debit; **con c. a mi cuenta** charged to my account (**d**) *Jur* charge, accusation

cargosear *vt CSur* to annoy, to pester

cargoso,-a *adj CSur* annoying

carguero *nm* (**a**) *(avión)* transport plane (**b**) *(barco)* freighter

cariarse *upr* to decay

caribe *nm (idioma)* Carib; **el (mar) C.** the Caribbean Sea

caricatura *nf* caricature

caricaturizar [40] *vt* to caricature

caricia *nf* caress, stroke

caridad *nf* charity

caries *nf inv* decay, caries

carilla *nf* page, side of a piece of paper

cariño *nm* (**a**) *(amor)* affection; **coger/tener c. a algo/algn** to grow/to be fond of sth/sb; **con c.** *(en carta)* love (**b**) *(querido)* darling (**c**) *(abrazo)* cuddle

cariñoso,-a *adj* loving, affectionate

carisma *nm* charisma

carismático,-a *adj* charismatic

caritativo,-a *adj* charitable

cariz *nm* look

carmesí *adj & nm* crimson

carmín *nm* **(de color) c.** carmine; **c. (de labios)** lipstick

carnal *adj* (a) *(de carne)* carnal (b) *(pariente)* first; **primo c.** first cousin

carnaval *nm* carnival

carne *nf* (a) flesh; *Fam* **ser de c. y hueso** to be only human; *Fig* **c. de cañón** cannon fodder; **c. de gallina** goosepimples; **c. viva** raw flesh (b) *(alimento)* meat; **c. de cerdo/cordero/ternera/vaca** pork/lamb/veal/beef (c) *(de fruta)* pulp

carné *nm* card; **c. de conducir** *Br* driving licence, *US* driver's license; **c. de identidad** identity card

carnear *vt Andes, RP (sacrificar)* to slaughter, to butcher

carnero *nm* ram; *Culin* mutton

carnet *nm* = **carné**

carnicería *nf* (a) butcher's (shop) (b) *Fig (masacre)* slaughter

carnicero,-a *nm,f* butcher

cárnico,-a *adj* **productos cárnicos** meat products

carnitas *nfpl Méx* = small pieces of fried or grilled pork

carnívoro,-a 1 *adj* carnivorous
2 *nm,f* carnivore

carnoso,-a *adj* fleshy

caro,-a 1 *adj* expensive, dear
2 *adv* **salir c.** to cost a lot; **te costará c.** *(amenaza)* you'll pay dearly for this

carozo *nm RP (de fruta, aceituna)* stone, *US* pit

carpa *nf* (a) *(pez)* carp (b) *(de circo)* big top; *(en parque, la calle)* marquee (c) *Am (de camping)* tent

Cárpatos *nmpl* Carpathians

carpeta *nf* file, folder

> 🖉 Observa que la palabra inglesa **carpet** es un falso amigo y no es la traducción de la palabra española **carpeta**. En inglés, **carpet** significa "alfombra".

carpetazo *nm* **dar c. a un asunto** to shelve a matter

carpintería *nf* (a) *(oficio)* carpentry; **c. metálica** metalwork (b) *(taller)* carpenter's (shop)

carpintero,-a *nm,f* carpenter

carraca *nf* rattle

carraspear *vi* to clear one's throat

carraspeo *nm* clearing of the throat

carraspera *nf* hoarseness

carrera *nf* (a) run; *(de media)* run, ladder; **a la c.** in a hurry (b) *(competición)* race; **c. contra reloj** race against the clock; **c. de coches** rally, meeting; **echar una c. a algn** to race sb; **c. de armamentos** arms race (c) *(estudios)* university course; **hacer la c. de derecho/físicas** to study law/physics (at university) (d) *(profesión)* career, profession

carrerilla *nf* run; **tomar c.** to take a run; **de c.** parrot fashion

carreta *nf* cart

carrete *nm (de hilo)* reel; *(de película)* spool; *(de cable)* coil

carretera *nf* road; **c. de acceso** access road; *(en autopista)* slip road; **c. de circunvalación** *Br* ring road, *US* beltway; **c. comarcal** minor road; *Méx* **c. de cuota** toll road; **c. nacional** *Br* ≃ A road, *US* ≃ state highway

carretero,-a *adj Am* road; **un accidente c.** a road accident

carretilla *nf* wheelbarrow

carricoche *nm* caravan

carril *nm* (a) *Ferroc* rail (b) *Aut* lane

carrillo *nm* cheek; *Fam* **comer a dos carrillos** to devour, to gobble up

carriola *nf* (a) *(cama)* truckle bed (b) *Méx (coche de bebé)* *Br* pram, *US* baby carriage

carro *nm* (a) *(carreta)* cart; *RP Fam* **¡pará el c.!** hold your horses! (b) *Mil* **c. de combate** tank (c) *(de máquina de escribir)* carriage (d) *Andes, CAm, Carib, Méx* car (e) *Méx (vagón)* car; **c. comedor** dining car

carrocería *nf Aut* bodywork

carroña *nf* carrion

carroza 1 *nf* (a) *(coche de caballos)* coach, carriage (b) *(de carnaval)* float
2 *nmf Fam* old fogey

carruaje *nm* carriage, coach

carrusel *nm Andes* roundabout, merry-go-round

carta *nf* (a) letter; **c. certificada/urgente** registered/express letter (b) *(menú)* menu; **a la c.** à la carte; **c. de vinos** wine list (c) *Naipes* card; **echar las cartas a algn** to tell sb's fortune; *Fig* **poner las cartas sobre la mesa** to put *o* lay one's cards on the table, to come clean (d) *Geog (mapa)* chart (e) *Fig* **adquirir c. de naturaleza** to become widely accepted; **tomar cartas en un asunto** to take part in an affair

cartabón *nm* set square

cartearse *vpr* to correspond (**con** with), to exchange letters (**con** with)

cartel *nm* poster; **pegar/fijar carteles** to put *o* stick up bills

cartél *nm Com* cartel

cartelera *nf* billboard, *Br* hoarding; *Prensa* **c. de espectáculos** entertainments section *o* page

cartera *nf* (a) *(de bolsillo)* wallet, *US* billfold (b) *(de mano)* handbag; *(para documentos etc)* briefcase; *(de colegial)* satchel, schoolbag (c) *Pol (ministerio)* portfolio (d) *Com* portfolio; **c. de pedidos** order book

carterista *nm* pickpocket

cartero,-a *nm,f (hombre)* *Br* postman, *US* mailman; *(mujer)* *Br* postwoman, *US* mailwoman

cartilla *nf* (a) *(libreta)* book; **c. de ahorros** savings book (b) *(libro)* first reader; *Fam* **leerle la c. a algn** to tell sb off

cartografía *nf* cartography

cartón *nm* (**a**) *(material)* card, cardboard; **c. piedra** papier mâché (**b**) *(de cigarrillos)* carton

cartucho *nm* (**a**) *(de balas)* cartridge (**b**) *(de papel)* cone

cartulina *nf* card

casa *nf* (**a**) *(edificio)* house; **c. de huéspedes** boarding house; **c. de socorro** first-aid post (**b**) *(hogar)* home; **vete a c.** go home; **en c. de Daniel** at Daniel's; **de andar por c.** everyday (**c**) *(empresa)* company, firm; **c. matriz/principal** head/central office

casación *nf Jur* annulment

casadero,-a *adj* of marrying age

casado,-a 1 *adj* married
  2 *nm,f* married person; **los recién casados** the newlyweds

casamiento *nm* marriage; *(boda)* wedding

casar¹ *vt* to marry
  2 *vi* to match, to go *o* fit together
  3 casarse *upr* to marry, to get married; **c. por la iglesia/por lo civil** to get married in church/in a registry office

casar² *vt Jur* to annul, to quash

cascabel *nm* bell

cascada *nf* waterfall, cascade

cascanueces *nm inv* nutcracker

cascar [44] **1** *vt* (**a**) to crack (**b**) *Fam* **cascarla** to kick the bucket, to snuff it
  2 *vi Fam (charlar)* to chat away
  3 cascarse *upr* to crack

cáscara *nf* shell; *(de fruta)* skin, peel; *(de grano)* husk

cascarón *nm* eggshell

cascarrabias *nmf inv Fam* short-tempered person

casco *nm* (**a**) *(para la cabeza)* helmet (**b**) *(de caballo)* hoof (**c**) *(envase)* empty bottle (**d**) **c. urbano** city centre (**e**) *(de barco)* hull (**f**) **cascos** *(auriculares)* headphones

cascote *nm* piece of rubble *o* debris

caserío *nm* country house

casero,-a 1 *adj* (**a**) *(hecho en casa)* homemade (**b**) *(persona)* home-loving
  2 *nm,f (dueño) (hombre)* landlord; *(mujer)* landlady

caseta *nf* hut, booth; *(de feria, exposición)* stand, stall; *Méx* **c. de cobro** tollbooth; *Méx* **c. telefónica** phone box, phone booth

casete 1 *nm (magnetófono)* cassette player *o* recorder
  2 *nf (cinta)* cassette (tape)

casi *adv* almost, nearly; **c. mil personas** almost one thousand people; **c. ni me acuerdo** I can hardly remember it; **c. nunca** hardly ever; **c. nadie** hardly anyone; **c. me caigo** I almost fell

casilla *nf* (**a**) *(de casillero)* pigeonhole; *Andes, RP* **c. de correos** PO Box; *CAm, Carib, Méx* **c. postal** PO Box (**b**) *(recuadro)* box (**c**) *Fig* **sacar a algn de sus casillas** to drive sb mad

casillero *nm* pigeonholes

casino *nm* casino

caso *nm* case; **el c. es que ...** the fact *o* thing is that ...; **el c. Mattei** the Mattei affair; **(en) c. contrario** otherwise; **en c. de necesidad** if need be; **en cualquier c.** in any case; **en el mejor/peor de los casos** at best/worst; **en ese c.** in such a case; **en todo c.** in any case; **en un c. extremo, en último c.** as a last resort; **hacer c. a** *o* **de algn** to pay attention to sb; **hacer c. omiso de** to take no notice of; **no venir al c.** to be beside the point; **pongamos por c.** let's say

caspa *nf* dandruff

casquete *nm* (**a**) *(de bala)* case, shell (**b**) *Geog* **c. polar** polar cap

🔎 Observa que la palabra inglesa **casket** es un falso amigo y no es la traducción de la palabra española **casquete**. En inglés, **casket** significa "cofre, ataúd".

casquillo *nm (de bala)* case

cassette *nm & nf =* **casete**

casta *nf* (**a**) *(linaje)* lineage, descent (**b**) *(animales)* breed; **de c.** thoroughbred, purebred (**c**) *(división social)* caste

castaña *nf* chestnut; *Fig* **sacarle a algn las castañas del fuego** to save sb's bacon

castañetear *vi (dientes)* to chatter

castaño,-a 1 *adj* chestnut-brown; *(pelo, ojos)* brown, dark
  2 *nm Bot* chestnut

castañuela *nf* castanet

castellano,-a 1 *adj* Castilian
  2 *nm,f (persona)* Castilian
  3 *nm (idioma)* Spanish, Castilian

castidad *nf* chastity

castigar [42] *vt* (**a**) to punish (**b**) *(dañar)* to harm, to ruin (**c**) *Jur & Dep* to penalize

castigo *nm* punishment; *Jur* penalty; *Dep* **área de c.** penalty area

Castilla *n* Castile

castillo *nm* castle

castizo,-a *adj* pure, authentic

casto,-a *adj* chaste

castor *nm* beaver

castrar *vt* to castrate

castrense *adj* military

casual 1 *adj* accidental, chance
  2 *nm Fam* chance

casualidad *nf* chance, coincidence; **de** *o* **por c.** by chance; **dio la c. que ...** it so happened that ...; **¿tienes un lápiz, por c.?** do you happen to have a pencil?; **¡que c.!** what a coincidence!

🔎 Observa que la palabra inglesa **casualty** es un falso amigo y no es la traducción de la palabra española **casualidad**. En inglés, **casualty** significa "víctima".

casualmente *adv* by chance

cata *nf* tasting

cataclismo *nm* cataclysm

catador,-a *nm,f* taster
catalán,-ana 1 *adj & nm,f* Catalan
  2 *nm (idioma)* Catalan
catalejo *nm* telescope
catalepsia *nf* catalepsy
catalizador *nm* catalyst; *Aut* catalytic converter
catalizar [40] *vt Fig* to act as a catalyst for
catalogar [42] *vt* (**a**) to catalogue (**b**) *(clasificar)* to classify
catálogo *nm* catalogue
Cataluña *n* Catalonia
cataplasma *nf* (**a**) *Farm* cataplasm, poultice (**b**) *Fam (pelmazo)* bore
catapulta *nf* catapult; *Fig* springboard
catapultar *vt* to catapult
catar *vt* to taste
catarata *nf* (**a**) waterfall (**b**) *Med* cataract
catarro *nm* (common) cold
catastral *adj* **valor c.** rateable value
catastro *nm* land registry
catástrofe *nf* catastrophe
catastrófico,-a *adj* catastrophic
catear *vt* (**a**) *Fam (suspender)* to fail, *US* to flunk (**b**) *Am (casa)* to search
catecismo *nm* catechism
cátedra *nf* (professorial) chair; **le han dado la c.** they have appointed him professor
catedral *nf* cathedral
catedrático,-a *nm,f Educ* (**a**) *Univ* professor (**b**) *(de instituto)* head of department
categoría *nf* category; *Fig* class; **de c.** *(persona)* important; *(vino etc)* quality
categórico,-a *adj* categoric; **un no c.** a flat refusal
cateto,-a *nm,f Pey* yokel, bumpkin
catire,-a *adj Carib (rubio)* blond, blonde
catolicismo *nm* Catholicism
católico,-a *adj & nm,f* Catholic
catorce *adj & nm inv* fourteen
catre *nm Fam* bed
Cáucaso *n* Caucasus
cauce *nm* (**a**) *(de un río)* bed (**b**) *Fig (canal)* channel; **cauces oficiales** official channels
caucho *nm* (**a**) rubber (**b**) *Am (cubierta)* tyre
caudal *nm* (**a**) *(de un río)* flow (**b**) *(riqueza)* wealth, riches
caudaloso,-a *adj (río)* plentiful
caudillo *nm* leader, head
causa *nf* (**a**) cause; **a** *o* **por c. de** because of (**b**) *(ideal)* cause (**c**) *Jur (caso)* case; *(juicio)* trial
causante 1 *adj* causal, causing
  2 *nmf* **el c. del incendio** the person who caused the fire
causar *vt* to cause, to bring about; **me causa un gran placer** it gives me great pleasure; **c. buena/mala impresión** to make a good/bad impression
cáustico,-a *adj* caustic
cautela *nf* caution
cautivar *vt* (**a**) to capture, to take prisoner

(**b**) *Fig (fascinar)* to captivate
cautiverio *nm*, **cautividad** *nf* captivity
cautivo,-a *adj & nm,f* captive
cauto,-a *adj* cautious, wary
cava 1 *nf (bodega)* wine cellar
  2 *nm (vino espumoso)* cava, champagne
cavar *vt* to dig
caverna *nf* cave; **hombre de las cavernas** caveman
cavernícola *nmf* cave dweller
caviar *nm* caviar
cavidad *nf* cavity
cavilar *vt* to ponder
cayado *nm* (**a**) *(de pastor)* crook (**b**) *(de obispo)* crosier, crozier
cayuco *nm Am* small flat-bottomed canoe
caza 1 *nf* (**a**) hunting; **ir de c.** to go hunting; **c. furtiva** poaching (**b**) *(animales)* game; **c. mayor/menor** big/small game (**c**) *Fig (persecución)* hunt; **c. de brujas** witch hunt
  2 *nm Av* fighter, fighter plane
cazabe *nm Am* cassava bread
cazabombardero *nm Av* fighter bomber
cazador,-a *nm,f* hunter; **c. furtivo** poacher
cazadora *nf (waist-length)* jacket
cazar [40] *vt* to hunt; *Fam* **cazarlas al vuelo** to be quick on the uptake
cazatalentos *nmf inv* head-hunter
cazo *nm* (**a**) *(cacerola)* saucepan (**b**) *(cucharón)* ladle
cazuela *nf* saucepan; *(guiso)* casserole, stew; **a la c.** stewed
c/c *(abr* **cuenta corriente**) c/a
CC. OO. *nfpl (abr* **Comisiones Obreras**) = Spanish left-wing trade union
CD-ROM *nm* CD-ROM
cebada *nf* barley
cebar 1 *vt* (**a**) *(animal)* to fatten; *(persona)* to feed up (**b**) *(anzuelo)* to bait (**c**) *(fuego, caldera)* to stoke, to fuel; *(máquina, arma)* to prime (**d**) *RP (mate)* to prepare, to brew
  2 cebarse *vpr* **c. con** *(ensañarse)* to delight in tormenting
cebo *nm* bait
cebolla *nf* onion
cebolleta *nf* (**a**) *(especie)* chives (**b**) *(cebolla tierna)* spring onion
cebra *nf* zebra; **paso de c.** *Br* zebra crossing, *US* crosswalk
cecear *vi* to lisp
ceceo *nm* lisp
cedazo *nm* sieve
ceder 1 *vt* to give, to hand over; *Aut* **c. el paso** to give way
  2 *vi* (**a**) *(cuerda, cable)* to give way (**b**) *(lluvia, calor)* to diminish, to slacken (**c**) *(consentir)* to give in
cederrón *nm* CD-ROM
cedro *nm* cedar
cédula *nf* (**a**) document, certificate; *Am* **c. de identidad** identity card (**b**) *Com & Fin* bond, certificate, warrant

C(E)E *nf* (*abr* **Comunidad (Económica) Europea**) E(E)C

cegador,-a *adj* blinding

cegar [1] *vt* (**a**) to blind (**b**) (*puerta, ventana*) to wall up

ceguera *nf* blindness

CEI (*abr* **Comunidad de Estados Independientes**) CIS

Ceilán *n* Ceylon

ceja *nf* eyebrow

cejar *vi* **c. en el empeño** to give up

celada *nf* trap, ambush

celador,-a *nm,f* attendant; (*de una cárcel*) warder

celda *nf* cell; **c. de castigo** punishment cell

celebración *nf* (**a**) (*festejo*) celebration (**b**) (*de juicio etc*) holding

celebrar [1] *vt* (**a**) to celebrate; **celebro que todo saliera bien** I'm glad everything went well (**b**) (*reunión, juicio, elecciones*) to hold (**c**) (*triunfo*) to laud

   2 celebrarse *upr* to take place, to be held

célebre *adj* famous, well-known

celebridad *nf* (**a**) celebrity, fame (**b**) (*persona*) celebrity

celeste 1 *adj* (**a**) (*de cielo*) celestial (**b**) (*color*) sky-blue

   2 *nm* sky blue

celestial *adj* celestial, heavenly

celibato *nm* celibacy

célibe *adj & nmf* celibate

celo *nm* (**a**) zeal (**b**) **en c.** (*macho*) in rut; (*hembra*) on o in heat (**c**) **celos** jealousy; **tener celos (de algn)** to be jealous (of sb)

celo® *nm Fam Br* Sellotape®, *US* Scotch tape®

celofán *nm* cellophane®

celosía *nf* lattice

celoso,-a *adj* (**a**) jealous (**b**) (*cumplidor*) conscientious

celta 1 *adj* Celtic

   2 *nmf* Celt

   3 *nm* (*idioma*) Celtic

célula *nf* cell

celular 1 *adj* (**a**) cellular (**b**) **coche c.** police van (**c**) *Am* **teléfono c.** mobile phone, cellphone

   2 *nm Am* mobile, cellphone

celulitis *nf inv* cellulitis

celuloide *nm* celluloid

celulosa *nf* cellulose

cementerio *nm* cemetery, graveyard; **c. de coches** scrapyard

cemento *nm* cement; **c. armado** reinforced cement

cena *nf* evening meal; (*antes de acostarse*) supper; **la Ultima C.** the Last Supper

cenagal *nm* marsh, swamp

cenar 1 *vi* to have supper o dinner

   2 *vt* to have for supper o dinner

cencerro *nm* cowbell

cenefa *nf* (*de ropa*) edging, trimming; (*de suelo, techo*) ornamental border, frieze

cenetista 1 *adj* = of or related to the CNT (Confederación Nacional del Trabajo)

   2 *nmf* member of the CNT

cenicero *nm* ashtray

cenit *nm* zenith

ceniza *nf* ash

cenizo *nm Fam* (*gafe*) jinx

censo *nm* census; **c. electoral** electoral roll

censor *nm* censor

censura *nf* (**a**) censorship (**b**) *Pol* **moción de c.** vote of no confidence

censurar *vt* (**a**) (*libro, película*) to censor (**b**) (*criticar*) to censure, to criticize

centavo *nm Am Fin* cent, centavo

centella *nf* spark

centellear *vi* to flash, to sparkle

centelleo *nm* flashing, sparkling

centena *nf*, **centenar** *nm* hundred; **a centenares** in hundreds

centenario *nm* centenary, hundredth anniversary

centeno *nm* rye

centésimo,-a *adj & nm,f* hundredth

centígrado,-a *adj* centigrade

centilitro *nm* centilitre

centímetro *nm* centimetre

céntimo *nm* cent

centinela *nm* sentry

centollo *nm* spider crab

centrado,-a *adj* (**a**) centred (**b**) (*equilibrado*) balanced

central 1 *adj* central

   2 *nf* (**a**) *Elec* **c. nuclear/térmica** nuclear/coal-fired power station (**b**) (*oficina principal*) head office

centralismo *nm* centralism

centralita *nf Tel* switchboard

centralizar [40] *vt* to centralize

centrar 1 *vt* (**a**) to centre (**b**) (*esfuerzos, atención*) to concentrate, to centre (**en** on)

   2 centrarse *upr* (**a**) to be centred o based (**b**) **c. en** (*concentrarse*) to concentrate on

céntrico,-a *adj* centrally situated; **zona céntrica** centrally situated area

centrifugar [42] *vt* to centrifuge; (*ropa*) to spin-dry

centrista *Pol* **1** *adj* centre; **partido c.** centre party

   2 *nmf* centrist

centro *nm* (**a**) middle, centre; **c. de la ciudad** town o city centre (**b**) (*establecimiento*) institution, centre; **c. comercial** shopping centre

Centroamérica *n* Central America

centroamericano,-a *adj & nm,f* Central American

centrocampista *nmf Ftb* midfielder

centuria *nf* century

ceñido,-a *adj* tight-fitting, clinging

ceñirse [6] *upr* (**a**) (*atenerse, limitarse*) to limit oneself, to stick (**a** to); **c. al tema** to keep to the subject; **ciñéndonos a este caso en**

concreto coming down to this particular case (**b**) **c. a** (*prenda*) to cling to

ceño *nm* scowl, frown; **con el c. fruncido** frowning

CEOE *nf* (*abr* **Confederación Española de Organizaciones Empresariales**) = Spanish employers' organization, ≃ CBI

cepa *nf* (**a**) (*de vid*) vine (**b**) *Fig* **vasco de pura c.** (*origen*) Basque through and through

cepillar **1** *vt* (**a**) to brush (**b**) (*en carpintería*) to plane (down) (**c**) *Fam* (*robar*) to pinch

2 cepillarse *vpr* (**a**) (*con cepillo*) to brush (**b**) *Fam* (*matar*) to do in (**c**) *muy Fam* to lay

cepillo *nm* brush; (*en carpintería*) plane; **c. de dientes** toothbrush; **c. del pelo** hairbrush

cepo *nm* (**a**) (*para cazar*) trap (**b**) *Aut* clamp

CEPYME *nf* (*abr* **Confederación Española de la Pequeña y Mediana Empresa**) = Spanish confederation of small and medium-sized businesses

cera *nf* wax; (*de abeja*) beeswax

cerámica *nf* ceramics *sing*

cerca[1] *adv* (**a**) near, close; **ven más c.** come closer; **ya estamos c.** we are almost there (**b**) **c. de** (*al lado de*) near, close to; **el colegio está c. de mi casa** the school is near my house (**c**) **c. de** (*casi*) nearly, around; **c. de cien personas** about one hundred people (**d**) **de c.** closely; **lo vi muy de c.** I saw it close up

cerca[2] *nf* fence, wall

cercado *nm* (**a**) (*lugar cerrado*) enclosure (**b**) (*valla*) fence, wall

cercanía *nf* (**a**) proximity, nearness (**b**) **cercanías** outskirts, suburbs; (**tren de**) **cercanías** suburban train

cercano,-a *adj* nearby; **el C. Oriente** the Near East

cercar [44] *vt* (**a**) (*tapiar*) to fence, to enclose (**b**) (*rodear*) to surround

cercenar *vt* to cut off, to amputate

cerciorar **1** *vt* to assure

2 cerciorarse *vpr* to make sure

cerco *nm* (**a**) circle, ring (**b**) *Mil* (*sitio*) siege; **poner c. (a una ciudad)** to besiege (a town)

cerda *nf* (**a**) *Zool* sow (**b**) (*pelo*) bristle; **cepillo de c.** bristle brush

Cerdeña *n* Sardinia

cerdo *nm* (**a**) pig (**b**) (*carne*) pork (**c**) *Fam* pig, arsehole

cereal *nm* cereal

cerebral *adj* (**a**) cerebral (**b**) (*frío*) calculating

cerebro *nm* brain; *Fig* (*inteligencia*) brains

ceremonia *nf* ceremony

ceremonioso,-a *adj* ceremonious, formal; *Pey* pompous, stiff

cereza *nf* cherry

cerezo *nm* cherry tree

cerilla *nf* match

cerillo *nm* *CAm, Méx* match

cernerse [3] *vpr Fig* to loom (**sobre** above)

cernícalo *nm* kestrel

cernirse [54] *vpr* = **cernerse**

cero *nm* zero; *Dep* nil; *Fig* **partir de c.** to start from scratch; *Fig* **ser un c. a la izquierda** to be useless o a good-for-nothing

cerquillo *nm* *Am Br* fringe, *US* bangs

cerrado,-a *adj* (**a**) closed, shut; **a puerta cerrada** behind closed doors (**b**) (*reservado*) reserved; (*intransigente*) uncompromising, unyielding; *Fam* (*torpe*) thick; (*acento*) broad; (*curva*) tight, sharp (**c**) (*barba*) bushy

cerradura *nf* lock

cerrajero,-a *nm,f* locksmith

cerrar [1] **1** *vt* to shut, to close; (*grifo, gas*) to turn off; (*luz*) to turn off, to switch off; (*cremallera*) to do up; (*negocio*) to close down; (*cuenta*) to close; (*carta*) to seal; (*puños*) to clench; **c. con llave** to lock; **c. el paso a algn** to block sb's way; *Fam* **c. el pico** to shut one's trap

2 *vi* to close, to shut

3 cerrarse *vpr* to close, to shut; *Fam* **c. en banda** to stick to one's guns

cerro *nm* hill; *Fig* **irse por los cerros de Ubeda** to beat around the bush

cerrojo *nm* bolt; **echar el c. (de una puerta)** to bolt (a door)

certamen *nm* competition, contest

certero,-a *adj* accurate

certeza, certidumbre *nf* certainty; **saber (algo) con c.** to be certain (of sth); **tener la c. de que ...** to be sure o certain that ...

certificado,-a **1** *adj* (**a**) certified (**b**) (*correo*) registered

2 *nm* certificate

certificar [44] *vt* (**a**) to certify (**b**) (*carta*) to register

cervatillo *nm* fawn

cervecería *nf* (**a**) (*bar*) pub, bar (**b**) (*fábrica*) brewery

cerveza *nf* beer; **c. de barril** draught beer; **c. dorada** o **ligera** lager; **c. negra** stout

cervical *adj* cervical

cesante *adj* (*destituido*) dismissed, *Br* sacked; *CSur, Méx* (*parado*) unemployed

cesantear *vt CSur* to make redundant

cesar **1** *vi* **c. (de)** to stop, to cease; **sin c.** incessantly

2 *vt* (*empleado*) to dismiss, *Br* to sack

cesárea *nf* Caesarean (section)

cese *nm* (**a**) cessation, suspension (**b**) (*despido*) dismissal

Cesid *nm* (*abr* **Centro Superior de Investigación de la Defensa**) = Spanish military intelligence and espionage service

césped *nm* lawn, grass

cesta *nf* basket; **c. de Navidad** Christmas hamper

cesto *nm* basket

cetáceo *nm* cetacean, whale

cetrino,-a *adj* sallow

cetro *nm* sceptre

Ceuta *n* Ceuta

ceutí 1 adj of/from Ceuta
2 nmf person from Ceuta
ceviche nm = raw fish marinated in lemon and garlic
chabacano,-a 1 adj cheap
2 nm Méx (fruto) apricot; (árbol) apricot tree
chabola nf shack; **barrio de chabolas** shanty town
chacal nm jackal
chacarero,-a nm,f Andes, RP farmer
chacha nf maid
cháchara nf Fam small talk, chinwag; **estar de c.** to have a yap
chachi adj smashing
chacinados nmpl RP pork products
chacinería nf pork butcher's (shop)
chacra nf Andes, RP farm
chafar vt (a) Fam (plan etc) to ruin, to spoil (b) (aplastar) to squash, to flatten
chal nm shawl
chalado,-a adj Fam crazy, nuts (**por** about)
chalé nm (pl **chalés**) = chalet
chaleco nm Br waistcoat, US vest; (de punto) sleeveless pullover; **c. antibalas** bullet-proof vest; **c. salvavidas** life jacket
chalet nm villa
chalupa nf (a) (embarcación) boat, launch (b) Méx (torta) = small tortilla with a raised rim to contain a filling
chamaco,-a nm,f Méx Fam kid
chamarra nf sheepskin jacket
chamba nf CAm, Méx, Perú, Ven Fam (trabajo) job
chambelán nm chamberlain
chambergo nm heavy coat
chambón,-ona nm,f Am Fam sloppy o shoddy worker
chamizo nm thatched hut
champa nf CAm (tienda de campaña) tent
champán, champaña nm o nf champagne
champiñón nm mushroom
champú nm shampoo
chamuscar [44] vt to singe, to scorch
chamusquina nf singeing, scorching; Fam **esto me huele a c.** there's something fishy going on here
chancaca nf CAm (torta) syrup cake
chance 1 nm Am opportunity
2 adv Méx maybe
chancear vi Am to joke, to horse around
chanchada nf Am (a) (porquería) **no hagas chanchadas** stop that, don't be disgusting! (b) Fam (jugarreta) dirty trick
chancho,-a nm,f Am pig, hog, f sow
chanchullo nm Fam fiddle, wangle
chancla nf Br flip-flop, US thong
chanclo nm (zueco) clog; (de goma) over-shoe, galosh
chándal nm track o jogging suit
changa nf Bol, RP (trabajo temporal) odd job
changador nm RP (cargador) porter
changarro nm Méx small shop

chantaje nm blackmail; **hacer c. a algn** to blackmail sb
chantajear vt to blackmail
chantajista nmf blackmailer
chanza nf joke
chapa nf (a) (de metal) sheet (b) (de madera) panel-board (c) (tapón) bottle top, cap (d) (de adorno) badge (e) RP Br number plate, US license plate (f) Col (cerradura) lock
chapado,-a adj (metal) plated; **c. en oro** gold-plated; Fig **c. a la antigua** old-fashioned
chaparro nm Bot holm oak
chaparrón nm downpour, heavy shower
chapopote nm Carib, Méx bitumen, pitch
chapotear vi to splash about, to paddle
chapucero,-a adj (trabajo) slapdash, shoddy; (persona) bungling
chapulín nm CAm, Méx (saltamontes) grass-hopper
chapurrear vt to speak badly o with diffi-culty; **sólo chapurreaba el francés** he spoke only a few words of French
chapuza nf (a) (trabajo mal hecho) shoddy piece of work (b) (trabajo ocasional) odd job
chapuzón nm (baño corto) dip; **darse un c.** to have a dip
chaqué nm morning coat
chaqueta nf jacket; Pol **cambiar de c.** to change sides
chaquetero,-a nm,f Fam Pol turncoat
chaquetilla nf short jacket
charanga nf Mús brass band
charca nf pond, pool
charco nm puddle
charcutería nf delicatessen
charla nf (conversación) talk, chat; (conferen-cia) informal lecture o address; Informát chat
charlar vi to talk, to chat; Informát to chat
charlatán,-ana 1 adj (parlanchín) talkative; (chismoso) gossipy
2 nm,f (a) (parlanchín) chatterbox; (chismo-so) gossip; (bocazas) bigmouth (b) (embau-cador) trickster, charmer
charol nm (a) (piel) patent leather; **zapatos de c.** patent leather shoes (b) Andes (bande-ja) tray
charola nf CAm, Méx tray
charqui nm Andes, RP (carne) jerked o salted beef
chárter adj inv (vuelo) **c.** charter (flight)
chasca nf Andes (greña) mop of hair
chascar [44] vt (lengua) to click; (dedos) to snap; (látigo) to crack
chascarrillo nm shaggy dog story
chasco nm Fam disappointment; **llevarse un c.** to be disappointed
chasis nm inv chassis
chasquear vt (lengua) to click; (dedos) to snap; (látigo) to crack
chasqui nm = Inca messenger or courier
chasquido nm (de la lengua) click; (de los dedos) snap; (de látigo, madera) crack

chatarra *nf* scrap (metal), scrap iron; *Fam* junk

chato,-a 1 *adj* (a) *(nariz)* snub; *(persona)* snub-nosed (b) *(objeto)* flat, flattened (c) *PRico, RP Fam (sin ambiciones)* common-place; **una vida chata** a humdrum existence
2 *nm* (small) glass of wine

chau *interj Andes, RP Fam* bye!, see you!

chaucha 1 *adj RP Fam* dull, boring
2 *nf Bol, RP* green bean

chauvinista *adj & nmf* chauvinist

chaval,-a *nm,f Fam (chico)* boy, lad; *(chica)* girl

chaveta *nf* (a) *(clavija)* cotter pin (b) *Fam (cabeza)* nut, head; **perder la c.** *(volverse loco)* to go off one's rocker (c) *Andes (navaja)* penknife

chavo,-a *Fam* **1** *nm,f Méx (chico)* guy; *(chica)* girl
2 *nm (dinero)* **no tener un c.** to be broke

che *interj RP Fam* **¿qué hacés, c.?, ¿cómo andás, c.?** how are things o how's it going, then?; **c., ¡vení para acá!** over here, you!

checo,-a *adj* Czech

checoslovaco,-a 1 *adj* Czechoslovakian, Czech
2 *nm,f (persona)* Czechoslovakian, Czechoslovak, Czech

Checoslovaquia *n* Czechoslovakia

chele,-a *CAm* **1** *adj (rubio)* blond, blonde; *(de piel blanca)* fair-skinned
2 *nm,f (rubio)* blond(e) person; *(de piel blanca)* fair-skinned person

chelín *nm* shilling

chepa *nf Fam* hump

cheque *nm* cheque; **c. al portador** cheque payable to bearer; **c. de viaje** o **(de) viajero** traveller's cheque

chequeo *nm Med* checkup; *Aut* service

chévere *adj Andes, CAm, Carib, Méx Fam* great, fantastic

chic *adj inv* chic, elegant

chicano,-a *adj & nm,f* chicano

chicha¹ *nf Andes* = alcoholic drink made from fermented maize

chicha² *adj inv Náut* **calma c.** dead calm

chícharo *nm CAm, Méx* pea

chicharra *nf* (a) *(insecto)* cicada (b) *Méx, RP (timbre)* electric buzzer

chiche *nm* (a) *Andes, RP Fam (juguete)* toy (b) *Andes, RP (adorno)* delicate ornament (c) *CAm, Méx muy Fam (pecho)* tit

chichón *nm* bump, lump

chichonera *nf* helmet

chicle *nm* chewing gum

chico,-a 1 *nm,f (muchacho)* boy, lad; *(muchacha)* girl
2 *adj* small, little

chicoria *nf* chicory

chicote *nm Am (látigo)* whip

chiflado,-a *adj Fam* mad, crazy (**por** about)

chiflar *vt* (a) *(silbar)* to hiss (at), to boo (at)

(b) *Fam* **le chiflan las motos** he's really into motorbikes

chiflido *nm Am* whistle, whistling

chigüín,-ina *nm,f CAm Fam* kid

chiita *adj & nmf* Shiite

chilango,-a *Méx Fam* **1** *adj* of/from Mexico City
2 *nm,f* person from Mexico City

Chile *n* Chile

chile *nm* chilli (pepper)

chileno,-a *adj & nm,f* Chilean

chillar *vi (persona)* to scream, to shriek; *(ratón)* to squeak; *(frenos)* to screech, to squeal; *(puerta)* to creak, to squeak

chillido *nm (de persona)* scream, shriek; *(de ratón)* squeak; *(de frenos)* screech, squeal; *(de puerta)* creaking, squeaking

chillón,-ona *adj* (a) *(voz)* shrill, high-pitched; *(sonido)* harsh, strident (b) *(color)* loud, gaudy

chilpotle *nm Méx* = smoked or pickled jalapeño chilli

chimbo,-a *adj Col, Ven Fam* (a) *(de mala calidad)* crap, useless (b) *(complicado)* screwed-up

chimenea *nf* (a) *(hogar abierto)* fireplace, hearth (b) *(conducto)* chimney; *(de barco)* funnel, stack

chimichurri *nm RP* = barbecue sauce made from garlic, parsley, herbs and vinegar

China *n* China

china *nf* (a) *(piedra)* pebble, small stone; *Fam* **tocarle a uno la c.** to get the short straw (b) *Fam (droga)* deal

> ℐ Observa que la palabra inglesa **china** es un falso amigo y no es la traducción de la palabra española **china**. En inglés, **china** significa "loza, porcelana".

chinampa *nf Méx* = man-made island for growing flowers, fruit and vegetables, found in Xochimilco near Mexico City

chinche 1 *nf* bug, bedbug; *Fam* **caer como chinches** to fall like flies
2 *nmf Fam* nuisance, pest

chincheta *nf Br* drawing pin, *US* thumbtack

chinchín *interj* **¡c.!** cheers!, (to) your (good) health!

chinchulín *nm*, **chinchulines** *nmpl Andes, RP (plato)* = piece of sheep or cow intestine, plaited and then roasted

chinesco,-a *adj* **sombras chinescas** shadow theatre

chingado,-a *adj muy Fam (estropeado)* bust, *Br* knackered

chingana *nf Perú Fam* bar

chingar [42] *vt* (a) *(fastidiar)* to annoy (b) *muy Fam (estropear)* to bust, *Br* to knacker (c) *Vulg (joder)* to fuck, to screw

chino¹ *nm (piedrecita)* pebble, stone

chino²,-a *adj* (a) *(de la China)* Chinese; *Fam*

eso me suena a c. it's all Greek to me (**b**) *Am (mestizo)* of mixed ancestry

chip *nm (pl* **chips)** *Informát* chip

chipirón *nm* baby squid

Chipre *n* Cyprus

chipriota *adj & nmf* Cypriot

chiqueo *nm Méx* cuddle

chiquilín,-ina *nm,f RP* small boy, *f* small girl

chiquillo,-a *nm,f* kid

chiquito,-a *adj* tiny

chirimiri *nm* drizzle, fine misty rain

chirimoya *nf* custard apple

chiringuito *nm (en playa etc)* refreshment stall; *(en carretera)* roadside snack bar

chiripa *nf* fluke, lucky stroke; *Fam Fig* **de o por c.** by a fluke, by chance; **cogió el tren por c.** it was sheer luck that he caught the train

chiripá *nm (pl* **chiripaes)** *Bol, CSur* = garment worn by gauchos as trousers

chirla *nf* small clam

chirona *nf Fam* clink, nick

chirriar [29] *vi (puerta etc)* to creak; *(frenos)* to screech, to squeal

chirrido *nm (de puerta etc)* crack, cracking; *(de frenos)* screech, squeal

chisme *nm* (**a**) *(habladuría)* piece of gossip (**b**) *Fam (trasto)* knick-knack; *(cosa)* thing

chismorrear *vi Fam* to gossip

chismorreo *nm Fam* gossip, gossiping

chismoso,-a 1 *adj* gossipy

   2 *nm,f* gossip

chispa *nf* (**a**) spark; **echar chispas** to fume (**b**) *Fam (un poco)* bit, tiny amount (**c**) *Fam (agudeza)* wit, sparkle; *(viveza)* liveliness

chispear *vi* (**a**) to spark, to throw out sparks (**b**) *(lloviznar)* to spit

chiste *nm* joke; **contar un c.** to tell a joke; **c. verde** blue joke, dirty joke

chistera *nf* top hat

chistoso,-a *adj (persona)* funny, witty; *(anécdota)* funny, amusing

chivarse *vpr Fam* to tell tales

chivatazo *nm Fam* tip-off; **dar el c.** to squeal

chivato,-a 1 *nm,f Fam (delator) Br* grass, *US* rat; *(acusica)* telltale

   2 *nm* (**a**) *(luz)* warning light (**b**) *(alarma)* alarm bell (**c**) *Ven Fam (pez gordo)* big cheese

chivito *nm Urug* = steak sandwich *(containing cheese and salad)*

chivo,-a *nm,f Zool* kid, young goat; *Fig* **c. expiatorio** scapegoat

chocante *adj* (**a**) *(persona)* off-putting (**b**) *(sorprendente)* surprising, startling; *(raro)* strange

chocar [44] **1** *vi* (**a**) *(topar)* to crash, to collide; **c. con o contra** to run into, to collide with (**b**) *(en discusión)* to clash

   2 *vt* (**a**) *(copas)* to knock; *(la mano)* to shake; *Fam* **¡chócala!, ¡choca esos cinco!** shake (on it)!, put it there! (**b**) *(sorprender)* to surprise

chochear *vi* (**a**) to be senile *o* in one's dotage (**b**) **c. con algn** to dote on sb

chocho,-a 1 *adj* (**a**) *(senil)* senile; **viejo c.** old dodderer

   2 *nm* (**a**) *(altramuz)* lupin (**b**) *muy Fam Br* fanny, *US* beaver

choclo *nm Andes, RP (mazorca)* corncob, ear of maize *o US* corn; *(granos)* sweetcorn; *(cultivo)* maize, *US* corn

chocolate *nm* (**a**) chocolate; **c. con leche** milk chocolate (**b**) *Fam (droga)* dope

chocolatina *nf* bar of chocolate, chocolate bar

chófer *nm (pl* **chóferes),** *Am* **chofer** *nm (pl* **choferes)** driver; *(particular)* chauffeur

chollo *nm Fam (ganga)* bargain, snip

chomba *nf Arg* polo shirt

chompa *nf Andes* sweater, *Br* jumper

chompipe *nm CAm, Méx* turkey

chongo *nm Méx* (**a**) *(moño)* bun (**b**) **chongos zamoranos** *(dulce)* = Mexican dessert made from milk curds, served in syrup

chonta *nf Am* palm tree

chop *nm CSur* (**a**) *(jarra)* beer mug/glass (**b**) *(cerveza)* (glass of) beer

chopo *nm* poplar

chopp *nm CSur* = **chop**

choque *nm* (**a**) impact; *(de coches etc)* crash, collision; **c. frontal** head-on collision; **c. múltiple** pile-up (**b**) *Fig (contienda)* clash

choricear, chorizar *vt Fam* to pinch

chorizo *nm* (**a**) chorizo, highly-seasoned pork sausage (**b**) *Fam (ratero)* thief, pickpocket

chorlito *nm Orn* plover; *Fam Fig* **cabeza de c.** scatterbrain

choro *nm Andes* mussel

chorra *Fam* **1** *nmf (tonto)* idiot, fool

   2 *nf (suerte)* luck

chorrada *nf Fam* piece of nonsense

chorrear *vi* to drip, to trickle; *Fam* **c. de sudor** to pour with sweat; *Fam* **tengo el abrigo chorreando** my coat is dripping wet

chorro *nm* (**a**) *(de agua etc)* spurt; *(muy fino)* trickle; **salir a chorros** to gush forth (**b**) *Téc* jet (**c**) *Fig* stream, flood

chovinismo *nm* chauvinism

chovinista 1 *adj* chauvinistic

   2 *nmf* chauvinist

choza *nf* hut, shack

christmas *nm* Christmas card

chubasco *nm* heavy shower, downpour

chubasquero *nm* raincoat

chúcaro,-a *adj Andes, CAm, RP* (**a**) *(animal)* wild (**b**) *(persona)* unsociable

chuchería *nf Fam Br* sweet, *US* candy

chueco,-a 1 *adj Am (torcido)* twisted; *(patizambo)* bowlegged; *Méx, Ven Fam (cojo)* lame

   2 *nm,f Am (patizambo)* bowlegged person; *Méx, Ven Fam (cojo)* lame person

chufa *nf* groundnut

chulear *vi Fam* to strut around; **c. de** to go on about

chuleta *nf* (**a**) chop, cutlet; **c. de cerdo** pork chop (**b**) *Educ Fam* crib

chullo *nm Andes* woollen cap
chulo,-a *Fam* **1** *nm,f* show-off
2 *nm (proxeneta)* pimp
3 *adj (bonito)* smashing
chungo,-a *adj Fam* dodgy
chuño *nm Andes, RP* potato starch
chupa *nf Arg* short jacket
chupachups® *nm* lollipop
chupacirios *nmf inv Fam Pey* holy Joe
chupado,-a *adj* (a) *(flaco)* skinny, thin (b) *Fam* **está c.** it's dead easy
chupamedias *nmf Andes, RP, Ven Fam* toady, sycophant
chupar 1 *vt* (a) to suck (b) *(lamer)* to lick (c) *(absorber)* to soak up, to absorb
2 *vi* to suck
3 chuparse *vpr* (a) **está para c. los dedos** it's really mouthwatering (b) *Fam* to put up with; **nos chupamos toda la película** we sat through the whole film
chupatintas *nm inv Pey* penpusher
chupe *nm Andes, Arg* stew
chupete *nm Br* dummy, *US* pacifier
chupi *adj Fam* great, terrific, fantastic
chupón *nm* (a) lollipop (b) *(desatrancador)* plunger
churrasco *nm* barbecued meat
churrería *nf* fritter shop
churrete *nm* dirty mark, grease spot
churro *nm* (a) = dough formed into sticks or rings, fried in oil and covered in sugar (b) *Fam (chapuza)* mess
chusco *nm* chunk of stale bread; *Mil Fam* ration bread
chusma *nf* rabble, mob
chutar 1 *vi* (a) *Dep (a gol)* to shoot (b) *Fam* **¡y vas que chutas!** and then you're well away!
2 chutarse *vpr Fam (drogas)* to shoot up
chute *nm* (a) *Dep* shot (b) *Fam (drogas)* fix
CI *nm (abr* **coeficiente intelectual)** IQ
Cía., cía *(abr* **compañía)** Co
cianuro *nm* cyanide
cibercafé *nm Informát* Internet cafe, cybercafe
ciberespacio *nm Informát* cyberspace
cibernética *nf* cybernetics *sing*
cicatero,-a 1 *adj* stingy, mean
2 *nm,f* miser
cicatriz *nf* scar
cicatrizar [40] *vt & vi Med* to heal
cíclico,-a *adj* cyclical
ciclismo *nm* cycling
ciclista 1 *adj* cycling
2 *nmf* cyclist
ciclo *nm* cycle; *(de conferencias etc)* course, series
ciclocróss *nm* cyclo-cross
ciclomotor *nm* moped
ciclón *nm* cyclone
ciego,-a 1 *adj (persona)* blind; *Fam (borracho)* blind drunk; *(de droga)* stoned; **a ciegas** blindly

2 *nm,f* blind person; **los ciegos** the blind
cielo *nm* (a) sky (b) *Rel* heaven; *Fig* **caído del c.** *(oportuno)* heaven-sent; *(inesperado)* out of the blue; **¡c. santo!** good heavens! (c) *Arquit* **c. raso** ceiling (d) **c. de la boca** roof of the mouth
ciempiés *nm inv* centipede
cien *adj & nm inv* hundred; **c. libras** a o one hundred pounds; **c. por c.** one hundred percent
ciénaga *nf* marsh, bog
ciencia *nf* (a) science; *Fig* **saber algo a c. cierta** to know sth for certain; **c. ficción** science fiction; **c. infusa** intuition; **ciencias ocultas** the occult (b) *(conocimiento)* knowledge
cieno *nm* mud, mire
científico,-a 1 *adj* scientific
2 *nm,f* scientist
cientista *nmf CSur* **c. social** social scientist
ciento *adj & nm inv* hundred; **c. tres** one hundred and three; **por c.** percent
cierne *nm Fig* **en ciernes** budding
cierre *nm* (a) *(acción)* closing, shutting; *(de fábrica)* shutdown; *TV* close-down; **c. patronal** lockout (b) *(de bolso)* clasp; *(de puerta)* catch; *(prenda)* fastener; **c. de seguridad** safety lock; **c. centralizado** central locking; *Am* **c. relámpago** *Br* zip, *US* zipper
cierto,-a 1 *adj* (a) *(verdadero)* true; *(seguro)* certain; **estar en lo c.** to be right; **lo c. es que ...** the fact is that ...; **por c.** by the way (b) *(algún)* certain; **ciertas personas** certain o some people
2 *adv* certainly
ciervo,-a *nm,f* deer; *(macho)* stag; *(hembra)* doe, hind
cifra *nf* (a) *(número)* figure, number (b) *(código)* cipher, code
cifrar *vt* to express in figures
cigala *nf* Norway lobster, scampi
cigarra *nf* cicada
cigarrillo *nm* cigarette
cigarro *nm* (a) *(puro)* cigar (b) *(cigarrillo)* cigarette
cigüeña *nf* (a) *Orn* stork (b) *Téc* crank
cigüeñal *nm* crankshaft
cilindrada *nf Aut* cylinder capacity
cilíndrico,-a *adj* cylindrical
cilindro *nm* cylinder
cima *nf* summit
cimbrearse *vpr* to sway
cimentar *vt* to lay the foundations of; *Fig (amistad)* to strengthen
cimientos *nmpl* foundations; **echar** o **poner los c.** to lay the foundations
cinc *nm* zinc
cincel *nm* chisel
cincelar *vt* to chisel
cinco *adj & nm inv* five
cincuenta *adj & nm inv* fifty
cine *nm* (a) *(local)* cinema, *US* movie theater

(**b**) *(arte)* cinema; **c. mudo/sonoro** silent/ talking films

cineasta *nmf* movie director, movie maker

cinéfilo,-a *nm,f (que va al cine)* (keen) moviegoer *o Br* filmgoer; *(que entiende de cine)* movie *o Br* film buff

cinematográfico,-a *adj* cinematographic; **la industria cinematográfica** the movie *o Br* film industry

cíngaro,-a *adj & nm,f* gypsy

cínico,-a 1 *adj* shameless

  2 *nm,f* shameless person; **es un c.** he's shameless, he has no shame

🖉 Observa que la palabra inglesa **cynic** es un falso amigo y no es la traducción de la palabra española **cínico**. En inglés, **cynic** significa tanto "descreído, suspicaz" como "desaprensivo".

cinismo *nm* shamelessness

🖉 Observa que la palabra inglesa **cynicism** es un falso amigo y no es la traducción de la palabra española **cinismo**. En inglés, **cynicism** significa "descreimiento, suspicacia".

cinta *nf* (**a**) *(tira)* band, strip; *(para adornar)* ribbon; *Cost* braid, edging (**b**) *Téc & Mús* tape; **c. adhesiva/aislante** adhesive/insulating tape; **c. de vídeo** video tape; **c. transportadora** conveyor belt (**c**) *Cin* film

cinto *nm* belt

cintura *nf* waist

cinturón *nm* belt; *Fig* **apretarse el c.** to tighten one's belt; **c. de seguridad** safety belt; *Am* **c. de miseria** = slum or shanty town area round a large city

ciprés *nm* cypress

circense *adj* circus

circo *nm* circus

circuito *nm* circuit

circulación *nf* (**a**) circulation (**b**) *Aut (tráfico)* traffic

circular 1 *adj & nf* circular

  2 *vi (moverse)* to circulate; *(líquido)* to flow; *(tren, autobús)* to run; *Fig (rumor)* to go round; **circule por la izquierda** *(en letrero)* keep to the left

circulatorio,-a *adj* circulatory; *Aut* **un caos c.** traffic chaos

círculo *nm* circle; *Fig* **c. vicioso** vicious circle

circuncisión *nf* circumcision

circundante *adj* surrounding

circundar *vt* to surround, to encircle

circunferencia *nf* circumference

circunloquio *nm* circumlocution

circunscribirse *(pp circunscrito) vpr* **c. a** to confine *o* limit oneself to

circunscripción *nf* district; **c. electoral** constituency

circunscrito,-a *adj* circumscribed

circunspecto,-a *adj* circumspect

circunstancia *nf* circumstance; **en estas cir-** cunstancias ... under the circumstances ...

circunstancial *adj* circumstantial

cirio *nm* wax candle

cirrosis *nf* cirrhosis

ciruela *nf* plum; **c. claudia** greengage; **c. pasa** prune

ciruelo *nm* plum tree

cirugía *nf* surgery; **c. estética** *o* **plástica** plastic surgery

cirujano,-a *nm,f* surgeon

cisma *nm* (**a**) *Rel* schism (**b**) *Pol* split

cisne *nm* swan

cisterna *nf* cistern, tank

cistitis *nf inv* cystitis

cita *nf* (**a**) appointment; **darse c.** to come together (**b**) *(amorosa)* date (**c**) *(mención)* quotation

citación *nf Jur* citation, summons *sing*

citado,-a *adj* aforementioned

citar 1 *vt* (**a**) *(dar cita)* to arrange to meet, to make an appointment with (**b**) *(mencionar)* to quote (**c**) *Jur* to summons

  2 citarse *vpr* to arrange to meet, to make a date (**con** with)

cítrico,-a 1 *adj* citric, citrus

  2 *nmpl* **cítricos** citrus fruits

ciudad *nf* town; *(capital)* city; *Méx* **c. perdida** shanty town

ciudadanía *nf* citizenship

ciudadano,-a 1 *nm,f* citizen; **el c. de a pie** the man in the street

  2 *adj* civic

cívico,-a *adj* civic

civil 1 *adj* (**a**) civil; **matrimonio c.** civil marriage (**b**) *Mil* civilian

  2 *nm* member of the Guardia Civil

civilización *nf* civilization

civilizado,-a *adj* civilized

civilizar [40] *vt* to civilize

civismo *nm* (**a**) *(urbanidad)* public-spiritedness (**b**) *(cortesía)* civility

cizaña *nf Bot* bearded darnel; *Fig* **sembrar c.** to sow discord

cl *(abr* **centilitro(s)**) cl

clamar *vt* to cry out for, to clamour for

clamor *nm* clamour

clamoroso,-a *adj* resounding

clan *nm* clan

clandestinidad *nf* **en la c.** underground

clandestino,-a *adj* clandestine, underground; **aborto c.** backstreet abortion

clara *nf (de huevo)* white

claraboya *nf* skylight

clarear *vi* (**a**) *(amanecer)* to dawn (**b**) *(despejar)* to clear up (**c**) *(transparentar)* to wear thin, to become transparent

clarete *adj & nm* claret

claridad *nf* (**a**) *(luz)* light, brightness (**b**) *(inteligibilidad)* clarity; **con c.** clearly

clarificador,-a *adj* clarifying

clarificar [44] *vt* to clarify

clarín *nm* bugle

clarinete nm clarinet
clarividente 1 adj (a) far-sighted (b) (lúcido) lucid
2 nmf (persona) clairvoyant
claro,-a 1 adj (a) clear; **dejar algo c.** to make sth clear (b) (líquido, salsa) thin (c) (color) light
2 interj of course!; **¡c. que no!** of course not!; **¡c. que sí!** certainly!
3 nm (a) (espacio) gap, space; (en un bosque) clearing (b) Met bright spell
4 adv clearly
clase nf (a) (grupo) class; **c. alta/media** upper/middle class; **clases pasivas** pensioners; **primera/segunda c.** first/second class (b) (tipo) kind, sort; **toda c. de ...** all kinds of ... (c) Educ (curso) class; (aula) classroom; **c. particular** private class o lesson (d) (estilo) class; **tener c.** to have class
clásico,-a 1 adj classical; (típico) classic; (en el vestir) classic
2 nm classic
clasificación nf (a) classification; Dep league table (b) (para campeonato, concurso) qualification
clasificar [44] **1** vt to classify, to class
2 clasificarse upr Dep to qualify
claudicar [44] vi to give in
claustro nm (a) Arquit cloister (b) (reunión) staff meeting
claustrofobia nf claustrophobia
cláusula nf clause
clausura nf (a) (cierre) closure; **ceremonia de c.** closing ceremony (b) Rel enclosure
clausurar vt to close
clavadista nmf CAm, Méx diver
clavar 1 vt (a) to nail; (clavo) to bang o hammer in; (estaca) to drive in (b) Fam (timar) to sting o fleece
2 clavarse upr **c. una astilla** to get a splinter
clave 1 nf key; **la palabra c.** the key word
2 nm harpsichord
clavel nm carnation
clavícula nf collarbone
clavija nf Téc jack
clavo nm (a) nail; Fig **dar en el c.** to hit the nail on the head (b) Bot clove
claxon nm (pl cláxones) horn; **tocar el c.** to sound the horn
clemencia nf mercy, clemency
clementina nf clementine
cleptómano,-a adj & nm,f kleptomaniac
clerical adj clerical
clericó nm RP = drink made of white wine and fruit
clérigo nm priest
clero nm clergy
cliché nm (a) Fig (tópico) cliché (b) Fot negative (c) Impr plate
cliente nmf customer, client
clientela nf clientele
clima nm climate

climatizado,-a adj air-conditioned
climatizar [40] vt to air-condition
clímax nm inv climax
clínica nf clinic
clínico,-a adj clinical
clip nm clip
clítoris nm inv clitoris
cloaca nf sewer, drain
clorhídrico,-a adj hydrochloric
cloro nm chlorine
cloroformo nm chloroform
cloruro nm chloride; **c. sódico** sodium chloride
clóset nm (pl clósets) Am fitted cupboard
club nm (pl clubs o clubes) club; **c. náutico** yacht club
cm (abr centímetro(s)) cm
CNT nf (abr **Confederación Nacional del Trabajo**) = Spanish anarchist trade union federation
coacción nf coercion
coaccionar vt to coerce
coactivo,-a adj coercive
coadyuvar vt to assist
coagular vt & vi, **coagularse** upr to coagulate; (sangre) to clot; (leche) to curdle
coágulo nm coagulum, clot
coalición nf coalition
coartada nf alibi
coartar vt to restrict
coba nf Fam **dar c. a algn** to soft-soap sb
cobalto nm cobalt
cobarde 1 adj cowardly
2 nmf coward
cobardía nf cowardice
cobaya nf guinea pig
cobertizo nm shed, shack
cobertor nm bedspread
cobertura nf cover; (de noticia) coverage
cobija nf Am blanket
cobijar 1 vt to shelter
2 cobijarse upr to take shelter
cobijo nm shelter; Fig (protección) protection
cobra nf cobra
cobrador,-a nm,f (a) (de autobús) (hombre) conductor; (mujer) conductress (b) (de luz, agua etc) collector
cobrar 1 vt (a) (dinero) to charge; (cheque) to cash; (salario) to earn (b) Fig (fuerza) to gain, to get; **c. ánimos** to take courage o heart; **c. importancia** to become important
2 vi Fam to catch it
3 cobrarse upr **¿se cobra?** (al pagar) take it out of this, please
cobre nm (a) copper (b) Am (moneda) copper cent
cobrizo,-a adj copper, copper-coloured
cobro nm (pago) collecting; (de cheque) cashing; Tel **llamada a c. revertido** Br reverse-charge call, US collect call
coca nf (a) Bot coca (b) Fam (droga) cocaine, coke

cocaína *nf* cocaine

cocainómano,-a *nm,f* cocaine addict

cocalero,-a *Bol, Perú* **1** *adj* región cocalera coca-producing area; **productor c.** coca farmer *o* producer

2 *nm,f* coca farmer *o* producer

cocción *nf* cooking; *(en agua)* boiling; *(en horno)* baking

cocer [41] **1** *vt* to cook; *(hervir)* to boil; *(hornear)* to bake

2 *vi* *(hervir)* to boil

3 cocerse *vpr* **(a)** *(comida)* to cook; *(hervir)* to boil; *(hornear)* to bake **(b)** *(tramarse)* to be going on

cochambroso,-a *adj* squalid

coche *nm* **(a)** car; **en c.** by car; **c. de carreras** racing car; **c. de bomberos** fire engine; **c. fúnebre** hearse **(b)** *Ferroc* carriage, coach; **c. cama** sleeping car, sleeper **(c)** *(de caballos)* carriage, coach

cochecito *nm* *(de niño)* *Br* pram, *US* baby carriage

cochera *nf* **(a)** garage **(b)** *(de autobuses)* depot

cochinillo *nm* suckling pig

cochino,-a 1 *nm,f* **(a)** *(macho)* pig; *(hembra)* sow **(b)** *Fam (persona)* filthy person, pig

2 *adj (sucio)* filthy, disgusting

cocido *nm* stew

cociente *nm* quotient

cocina *nf* **(a)** kitchen **(b)** *(aparato)* cooker, stove; **c. eléctrica/de gas** electric/gas cooker **(c)** *(arte)* cooking; **c. casera** home cooking; **c. española** Spanish cooking *o* cuisine

cocinar *vt & vi* to cook

cocinero,-a *nm,f* cook

cocktail *nm* = **cóctel**

coco¹ *nm* coconut; *Fam (cabeza)* nut; **comerle el c. a algn** to brainwash sb; **comerse el c.** to get obsessed

coco² *nm Fam (fantasma)* bogeyman

cocodrilo *nm* crocodile

cocoliche *nm RP Fam* = pidgin Spanish spoken by Italian immigrants

cocotero *nm* coconut palm

cóctel *nm* cocktail; **c. Molotov** Molotov cocktail

coctelera *nf* cocktail shaker

codazo *nm* **(a)** *(señal)* nudge with one's elbow **(b)** *(golpe)* blow with one's elbow

codearse *vpr* to rub shoulders (**con** with), to hobnob (**con** with)

codeína *nf* codeine

codicia *nf* greed

codiciar [43] *vt* to covet

codicioso,-a *adj* covetous, greedy

codificar [44] *vt (ley)* to codify; *(mensajes)* to encode

código *nm* code; **c. de circulación** highway code; **c. postal** *Br* postcode, postal code, *US* zip code

codo *nm* elbow; *Fig* **c. con c.** side by side; *Fam*

hablar por los codos to talk nonstop

codorniz *nf* quail

coeficiente *nm* **(a)** coefficient **(b)** *(grado)* rate; **c. intelectual** intelligence quotient

coercitivo,-a *adj* coercive

coetáneo,-a *adj & nm,f* contemporary

coexistencia *nf* coexistence

coexistir *vi* to coexist

cofia *nf* bonnet

cofradía *nf (hermandad)* brotherhood; *(asociación)* association

cofre *nm (arca)* trunk, chest; *(para joyas)* box, casket

coger [53] **1** *vt* **(a)** to take; *(del suelo)* to pick (up); *(fruta, flores)* to pick; *(asir)* to seize, to take hold of; *(bus, tren)* to take, to catch; *(pelota, ladrón, resfriado)* to catch; *(entender)* to grasp; *(costumbre)* to pick up; *(velocidad, fuerza)* to gather; *(atropellar)* to run over, to knock down **(b)** *Am Vulg* to fuck

2 *vi Fam* **cogió y se fue** he upped and left

3 cogerse *vpr (agarrarse)* to hold on

cogida *nf* goring

cogollo *nm (de lechuga)* heart

cogotazo *nm Fam* blow on the back of the neck

cogote *nm* nape *o* back of the neck

cohabitación *nf* cohabitation

cohabitar *vi* to live together, to cohabit

cohecho *nm Jur* bribery

coherencia *nf* coherence

coherente *adj* coherent

cohesión *nf* cohesion

cohete *nm* rocket; **c. espacial** space rocket

cohibido,-a *adj* inhibited

cohibir 1 *vt* to inhibit

2 cohibirse *vpr* to feel inhibited

COI *nm Dep (abr* **Comité Olímpico Internacional***)* IOC

coima *nf (Andes, RP Fam)* bribe, *Br* backhander

coincidencia *nf* coincidence

coincidir *vi* **(a)** to coincide **(b)** *(concordar)* to agree; **todos coincidieron en señalar que** everyone agreed that **(c)** *(encontrarse)* to meet by chance

coito *nm* coitus, intercourse

cojear *vi (persona)* to limp, to hobble; *(mueble)* to wobble

cojera *nf* limp

cojín *nm* cushion

cojinete *nm Téc* bearing; **c. de agujas/bolas** needle/ball bearing

cojo,-a 1 *adj (persona)* lame; *(mueble)* rickety

2 *nm,f* lame person

cojón *nm Vulg* ball; **de cojones** *(estupendo)* fucking brilliant *o* good; *(pésimo)* fucking awful *o* bad

cojonudo,-a *adj muy Fam Br* bloody *o* *US* goddamn brilliant

cojudez *nf Andes muy Fam* ¡**qué c.!** *(acto)* what a *Br* bloody *o* *US* goddamn stupid thing to do!; *(dicho)* what a *Br* bloody *o* *US* goddamn stupid thing to say!

cojudo,-a *adj Andes muy Fam Br* bloody *o US* goddamn stupid

col *nf* cabbage; **c. de Bruselas** Brussels sprout

cola¹ *nf* (a) *(de animal)* tail; *(de vestido)* train; *(de pelo)* ponytail; *Am (de persona) Br* bum, *US* fanny; **a la c.** at the back *o* rear; *Fam* **traer c.** to have consequences (**b**) *(fila) Br* queue, *US* line; **hacer c.** *Br* to queue (up), *US* to stand in line

cola² *nf (pegamento)* glue

colaboración *nf* (a) collaboration (**b**) *Prensa* contribution

colaboracionismo *nm Pol* collaboration

colaborador,-a **1** *nm,f* (a) collaborator (**b**) *Prensa* contributor

2 *adj* collaborating

colaborar *vi* to collaborate, to cooperate

colación *nf* **sacar** *o* **traer (algo) a c.** to bring (sth) up

colada *nf* wash, laundry; **hacer la c.** to do the washing *o* laundry

colador *nm* colander, sieve; *(de té, café)* strainer

colapsar **1** *vt* to bring to a standstill

2 colapsarse *vpr* to come to a standstill

colapso *nm* (a) *Med* collapse (**b**) *Aut* **c. circulatorio** traffic jam, hold-up

colar [2] **1** *vt* (a) *(líquido)* to strain, to filter (**b**) *(por agujero)* to slip

2 *vi Fam* **esa mentira no cuela** that lie won't wash

3 colarse *vpr* (a) to slip in; *(a fiesta)* to gatecrash; *(en una cola)* to jump the queue (**b**) *Fam (pasarse)* to go too far

colateral *adj* collateral

colcha *nf* bedspread

colchón *nm* mattress

colchoneta *nf* air bed

colear *vi* (a) to wag its tail; *Fam* **vivito y coleando** alive and kicking (**b**) *Fam* **el asunto aún colea** we haven't heard the last of it yet

colección *nf* collection

coleccionable *adj & nm* collectable

coleccionar *vt* to collect

coleccionista *nmf* collector

colecta *nf* collection

colectividad *nf* community

colectivo,-a **1** *adj* collective

2 *nm* (a) *(asociación)* association (**b**) *Andes (taxi)* (collective) taxi (**c**) *Arg (autobús)* bus

colega *nmf* (a) colleague (**b**) *Fam (amigo)* pal, *Br* mate, *US* buddy

colegiado,-a *nm,f Dep* referee

colegial,-ala **1** *adj (escolar)* school

2 *nm,f (alumno)* schoolboy; *(alumna)* schoolgirl; **los colegiales** the schoolchildren

colegio *nm* (a) *(escuela)* school; **c. privado** private school, *Br* public *o* independent school (**b**) *(profesional)* association, college; **c. de abogados** the Bar; *Pol* **c. electoral** electoral college (**c**) *Univ* **c. mayor** *o* **universitario**

hall of residence

colegir [58] *vt* to infer, to deduce

cólera¹ *nf* anger, rage

cólera² *nm Med* cholera

colérico,-a *adj* furious

colesterol *nm* cholesterol

coleta *nf* pigtail, ponytail; *Fig* **cortarse la c.** to retire

coletazo *nm* **dar los últimos coletazos** to be on one's last legs

coletilla *nf* postcript

colgado,-a *adj* (a) *Fam* **dejar (a algn) c.** to leave (sb) in the lurch (**b**) *Fam* weird; *(drogado)* high

colgante **1** *nm (joya)* pendant

2 *adj* hanging

colgar [2] **1** *vt* (a) to hang (up); *(colada)* to hang (out) (**b**) *(ahorcar)* to hang

2 *vi* (a) to hang (**de** from); *Fig* **c. de un hilo** to hang by a thread (**b**) *Tel* to hang up

3 colgarse *vpr (ahorcarse)* to hang oneself

colibrí *nm* hummingbird

cólico *nm* colic

coliflor *nf* cauliflower

colijo *indic pres de* **colegir**

colilla *nf (cigarette)* end *o* butt

colimba *nf Arg Fam* military service

colina *nf* hill

colindante *adj* adjoining, adjacent

colindar *vi* to be adjacent (**con** to)

colirio *nm* eye-drops

colisión *nf* collision, crash; *(de ideas)* clash

colisionar *vi* to collide, to crash

colitis *nf* colitis

colla *Bol* **1** *adj* of/from the altiplano

2 *nmf* = indigenous person from the altiplano

collage *nm* collage

collar *nm* (a) *(adorno)* necklace (**b**) *(de perro)* collar

colmado,-a *adj* full, filled; *(cucharada)* heaped

colmar *vt* (a) to fill (right up); *(vaso, copa)* to fill to the brim; *Fig* to shower (**de** with) (**b**) *(ambiciones)* to fulfil, to satisfy

colmena *nf* beehive

colmillo *nm* eye *o* canine tooth; *Zool (de carnívoro)* fang; *(de jabalí, elefante)* tusk

colmo *nm* height; **el c. de** the height of; **¡eso es el c.!** that's the last straw!; **para c.** to top it all

colocación *nf* (a) *(acto)* positioning (**b**) *(disposición)* lay-out (**c**) *(empleo)* job, employment

colocado,-a *adj* (a) *(empleado)* employed (**b**) *Fam (drogado)* high

colocar [44] **1** *vt* (a) to place, to put (**b**) *Fin (invertir)* to invest (**c**) *(emplear)* to give work to (**d**) *Fam (drogar)* to stone

2 colocarse *vpr* (a) *(situarse)* to put oneself (**b**) *(emplearse)* to take a job (**de** as) (**c**) *Fam (drogarse)* to get high

colofón *nm* (**a**) *(apéndice)* colophon (**b**) *Fig* climax

Colombia *n* Colombia

colombiano,-a *adj & nm,f* Colombian

Colón *n* Columbus

colón *nm Fin* = standard monetary unit of Costa Rica and El Salvador

colonia[1] *nf* colony; *(campamento)* summer camp; *Méx (barrio)* district

colonia[2] *nf (perfume)* cologne

colonial *adj* colonial

colonialismo *nm* colonialism

colonización *nf* colonization

colonizar [40] *vt* to colonize

coloquial *adj* colloquial

coloquio *nm* discussion, colloquium

color *nm* colour; *Cin & Fot* **en c.** in colour; **de colores** multicoloured; **persona de c.** coloured person

colorado,-a **1** *adj* red; **ponerse c.** to blush

  2 *nm* red

> *Observa que la palabra inglesa* **coloured** *es un falso amigo y no es la traducción de la palabra española* **colorado**. *En inglés,* **coloured** *significa "coloreado".*

colorante *nm* colouring

colorear *vt* to colour

colorete *nm* rouge

colorido *nm* colour

colorín *nm* goldfinch

colosal *adj* colossal

columna *nf* column; *Anat* **c. vertebral** vertebral column, spinal column

columpiar [43] **1** *vt* to swing

  2 columpiarse *vpr* to swing

columpio *nm* swing

coma[1] *nf* (**a**) *Ling & Mús* comma (**b**) *Mat* point; **tres c. cinco** three point five

coma[2] *nm Med* coma

comadre *nf* (**a**) *(madrina)* = godmother of one's child, or mother of one's godchild (**b**) *Am Fam (amiga)* friend

comadreja *nf* weasel

comadreo *nm* gossip, gossiping

comadrona *nf* midwife

comal *nm CAm, Méx* = flat clay or metal dish used for baking "tortillas"

comandancia *nf* command

comandante *nm* (**a**) *Mil* commander, commanding officer (**b**) *Av* captain

comandar *vt* to command

comando *nm* (**a**) *Mil* commando (**b**) *Informát* command

comarca *nf* region

comarcal *adj* regional

comba *nf* (**a**) *(curvatura)* curve, bend (**b**) *(cuerda)* skipping rope; **saltar a la c.** to skip, *US* to jump rope

combar *vt* to bend

combate *nm* combat; *(en boxeo)* fight; *Mil* battle; **fuera de c.** out for the count; *(eliminado)* out of action

combatiente **1** *adj* fighting

  2 *nmf* combatant

combatir **1** *vt* to combat

  2 *vi* **c. contra** to fight against

combativo,-a *adj* spirited, aggressive

combinación *nf* (**a**) combination (**b**) *(prenda)* slip

combinado,-a **1** *adj* combined

  2 *nm* (**a**) *(cóctel)* cocktail (**b**) *Dep* line-up

combinar *vt,* **combinarse** *vpr* to combine

combustible **1** *nm* fuel

  2 *adj* combustible

combustión *nf* combustion

comedia *nf* comedy

comediante,-a *nm,f (hombre)* actor; *(mujer)* actress

comedido,-a *adj* self-restrained, reserved

comedor *nm* dining room

comensal *nmf* companion at table

comentar *vt* **c. algo con algn** to talk sth over with sb; **me han comentado que** I've been told that

comentario *nm* (**a**) comment, remark; *(crítica)* commentary; **sin c.** no comment (**b**) **comentarios** *(cotilleos)* gossip

comentarista *nmf* commentator

comenzar [51] *vt & vi* to begin, to start; **comenzó a llover** it started raining *o* to rain; **comenzó diciendo que ...** he started by saying that ...

comer **1** *vt* (**a**) to eat (**b**) *(en juegos)* to take, to capture

  2 *vi* to eat; **dar de c. a algn** to feed sb

  3 comerse *vpr* (**a**) to eat (**b**) *Fig (saltarse)* to skip

comercial *adj* commercial

comercialización *nf* marketing

comercializar [40] *vt* to market

comerciante *nmf* merchant

comerciar [43] *vi* to trade; **comercia con oro** he trades in gold

comercio *nm* (**a**) commerce, trade; **c. exterior** foreign trade; *Informát* **c. electrónico** e-commerce; **c. justo** fair trade (**b**) *(tienda)* shop

comestible **1** *adj* edible

  2 *nmpl* **comestibles** food, foodstuff(s); **tienda de comestibles** grocer's shop, *US* grocery store

cometa **1** *nm Astron* comet

  2 *nf (juguete)* kite

cometer *vt (error, falta)* to make; *(delito, crimen)* to commit

cometido *nm* (**a**) *(tarea)* task, assignment (**b**) *(deber)* duty; **cumplir su c.** to do one's duty

comezón *nm* itch

cómic *nm* comic

comicios *nmpl* elections

cómico,-a **1** *adj* (**a**) comical, funny (**b**) *Teatro* **actor c.** comedian

2 *nm,f* comic; *(hombre)* comedian; *(mujer)* comedienne

comida *nf* (a) *(alimento)* food (b) *(almuerzo, cena)* meal

comidilla *nf Fam* **la c. del pueblo** the talk of the town

comienzo *nm* beginning, start; **a comienzos de** at the beginning of; **dar c. (a algo)** to begin *o* start (sth)

comillas *nfpl* inverted commas; **entre c.** in inverted commas

comilón,-ona 1 *adj* greedy, gluttonous
2 *nm,f* big eater, glutton

comilona *nf Fam* big meal, feast

comino *nm* cumin, cummin; *Fam* **me importa un c.** I don't give a damn (about it)

comisaría *nf* police station

comisario *nm* (a) *(de policía)* police inspector (b) *(delegado)* commissioner; **c. europeo** European Commissioner

comisión *nf* (a) *Com (retribución)* commission; **a** *o* **con c.** on a commission basis (b) *(comité)* committee; **la C. Europea** the European Commission

comité *nm* committee

comitiva *nf* suite, retinue

como 1 *adv* (a) *(manera)* how; **me gusta c. cantas** I like the way you sing; **dilo c. quieras** say it however you like

(b) *(comparación)* as; **blanco c. la nieve** as white as snow; **habla c. su padre** he talks like his father

(c) *(según)* as; **c. decíamos ayer** as we were saying yesterday

(d) *(en calidad de)* as; **c. presidente** as president; **lo compré c. recuerdo** I bought it as a souvenir

(e) *(aproximadamente)* about; **c. a la mitad de camino** halfway; **c. unos diez** about ten

2 *conj* (a) *(+ subjunctive) (si)* if; **c. no estudies vas a suspender** if you don't study hard, you'll fail

(b) *(porque)* as, since; **c. no venías me marché** as you didn't come, I left

(c) **c. si** as if; **c. si nada** *o* **tal cosa** as if nothing had happened; *Fam* **c. si lo viera** I can imagine perfectly well

cómo 1 *adv* (a) **¿c.?** *(¿perdón?)* what?

(b) *(interrogativo)* how; **¿c. estás?** how are you?; **¿c. lo sabes?** how do you know?; **¿c. es de grande/ancho?** how big/wide is it?; **¿a c. están los tomates?** how much are the tomatoes?; **¿c. es que no viniste a la fiesta?** *(por qué)* how come you didn't come to the party?; *Fam* **¿c. es eso?** how come?

(c) *(exclamativo)* how; **¡c. has crecido!** you've really grown a lot!; **¡c. no!** but of course!

2 *nm* **el c. y el porqué** the whys and wherefores

cómoda *nf* chest of drawers

comodidad *nf* (a) comfort (b) *(conveniencia)* convenience

> 𝒫 Observa que la palabra inglesa **commodity** es un falso amigo y no es la traducción de la palabra española **comodidad**. En inglés, **commodity** significa "producto básico".

comodín *nm Naipes* joker

cómodo,-a *adj* (a) comfortable; **ponerse c.** to make oneself comfortable (b) *(útil)* handy, convenient

comoquiera *adv* (a) however, whatever way; **c. que sea** one way or another (b) **c. que no estaba enterado** *(puesto que)* as he didn't know

compa *nmf Fam* pal, *Br* mate, *US* buddy

compacto,-a *adj* compact; **disco c.** compact disc

compadecer [33] *vt* to feel sorry for, to pity
2 compadecerse *vpr* to have *o* take pity (**de** on)

compadre *nm* (a) *(padrino)* = godfather of one's child, or father of one's godchild (b) *Am Fam (amigo)* friend, mate

compadrear *vi RP* to brag, to boast

compaginar *vt* to combine

compañerismo *nm* companionship, comradeship

compañero,-a *nm,f* companion; **c. de colegio** school friend; **c. de piso** flat-mate

compañía *nf* company; **hacer c. (a algn)** to keep (sb) company; **c. de seguros/de teatro** insurance/theatre company

comparable *adj* comparable

comparación *nf* comparison; **en c.** comparatively; **en c. con** compared to; **sin c.** beyond compare

comparar *vt* to compare (**con** with)

comparativo,-a *adj & nm* comparative

comparecencia *nf* appearance

comparecer [33] *vi Jur* to appear (**ante** before)

comparsa *nf* band of revellers

compartimento, compartimiento *nm* compartment; **c. de primera/segunda clase** first-/second-class compartment

compartir *vt* to share

compás *nm* (a) *Téc* (pair of) compasses (b) *Náut* compass (c) *Mús (división)* time; *(intervalo)* beat; *(ritmo)* rhythm; **c. de espera** *Mús* bar rest; *Fig (pausa)* delay; **al c. de** in time to

compasión *nf* compassion, pity; **tener c. (de algn)** to feel sorry (for sb)

compasivo,-a *adj* compassionate

compatible *adj* compatible

compatriota *nmf* compatriot; *(hombre)* fellow countryman; *(mujer)* fellow countrywoman

compendiar [43] *vt* to abridge, to summarize

compendio *nm* compendium

compenetrarse *vpr* to understand each other *o* one another

compensación *nf* compensation

compensar 1 *vt (pérdida, error)* to make up for; *(indemnizar)* to compensate (for)
2 *vi* to be worthwhile; **este trabajo no compensa** this job's not worth my time
competencia *nf* (**a**) *(rivalidad, empresas rivales)* competition (**b**) *(capacidad)* competence (**c**) *(incumbencia)* field, province; **no es de mi c.** it's not up to me
competente *adj* competent
competición *nf* competition, contest
competido,-a *adj* hard-fought
competidor,-a 1 *nm,f* (**a**) *Com & Dep* competitor (**b**) *(participante)* contestant
2 *adj* competing
competir [6] *vi* to compete (**con** with *o* against; **en** in; **por** for)
competitividad *nf* competitivity
competitivo,-a *adj* competitive
compilar *vt* to compile
compinche *nmf* (**a**) *(compañero)* chum, pal (**b**) *(cómplice)* accomplice
complacencia *nf* (**a**) *(satisfacción)* satisfaction (**b**) *(indulgencia)* indulgence

> *Observa que la palabra inglesa **complacency** es un falso amigo y no es la traducción de la palabra española **complacencia**. En inglés, **complacency** significa "autocomplacencia".*

complacer [60] **1** *vt* to please; *Fml* **me complace presentarles a ...** it gives me great pleasure to introduce you ...
2 complacerse *upr* to delight (**en** in), to take pleasure (**en** in)
complaciente *adj* obliging
complejidad *nf* complexity
complejo,-a *adj & nm* complex
complementar 1 *vt* to complement
2 complementarse *upr* to complement (each other), to be complementary to (each other)
complementario,-a *adj* complementary
complemento *nm* complement; *Ling* object
completamente *adv* completely
completar *vt* to complete
completo,-a *adj* (**a**) *(terminado)* complete; **por c.** completely (**b**) *(lleno)* full; **al c.** full up to capacity
complexión *nf* build; **de c. fuerte** well-built

> *Observa que la palabra inglesa **complexion** es un falso amigo y no es la traducción de la palabra española **complexión**. En inglés, **complexion** significa "tez".*

complicación *nf* complication
complicado,-a *adj* (**a**) *(complejo)* complicated (**b**) *(implicado)* involved
complicar [44] **1** *vt* (**a**) to complicate (**b**) **c. en** *(involucrar)* to involve in
2 complicarse *upr* to get complicated; **c. la vida** to make life difficult for oneself
cómplice *nmf* accomplice
complot *nm* (*pl* **complots**) conspiracy, plot

componente 1 *adj* component
2 *nm* (**a**) *(pieza)* component; *(ingrediente)* ingredient (**b**) *(persona)* member
componer [19] (*pp* **compuesto**) **1** *vt* (**a**) *(formar)* to compose, to make up (**b**) *Mús & Lit* to compose (**c**) *(reparar)* to mend, to repair
2 componerse *upr* (**a**) **c. de** *(consistir)* to be made up of, to consist of (**b**) *(arreglarse)* to dress up (**c**) *Fam* **componérselas** to manage
comportamiento *nm* behaviour
comportar 1 *vt* to entail, to involve
2 comportarse *upr* to behave; **c. mal** to misbehave
composición *nf* composition
compositor,-a *nm,f* composer
compostelano,-a *adj* from Santiago de Compostela
compostura *nf* composure
compota *nf* compote
compra *nf (acción)* buying; *(cosa comprada)* purchase, buy; **ir de c.** to go shopping
comprador,-a *nm,f* purchaser, buyer
comprar *vt* (**a**) to buy (**b**) *Fig (sobornar)* to bribe, to buy off
compraventa *nf* buying and selling; **contrato de c.** contract of sale
comprender *vt* (**a**) *(entender)* to understand; **se comprende** it's understandable (**b**) *(contener)* to comprise, to include
comprensible *adj* understandable
comprensión *nf* understanding
comprensivo,-a *adj* understanding

> *Observa que la palabra inglesa **comprehensive** es un falso amigo y no es la traducción de la palabra española **comprensivo**. En inglés, **comprehensive** significa "amplio, detallado".*

compresa *nf* (**a**) *(para mujer)* sanitary towel (**b**) *Med* compress
comprimido,-a 1 *nm Farm* tablet
2 *adj* compressed; **escopeta de aire c.** air rifle
comprimir *vt* to compress
comprobante *nm (de compra etc)* voucher, receipt
comprobar [2] *vt* to check
comprometer 1 *vt* (**a**) *(arriesgar)* to compromise, to jeopardize (**b**) *(obligar)* to compel, to force
2 comprometerse *upr* (**a**) **c. a hacer algo** to undertake to do sth (**b**) *(novios)* to become engaged
comprometido,-a *adj* (**a**) *(situación)* difficult (**b**) *(para casarse)* engaged
compromiso *nm* (**a**) *(obligación)* obligation, commitment; **sin c.** without obligation; **por c.** out of a sense of duty (**b**) **poner (a algn) en un c.** to put (sb) in a difficult *o* embarrassing situation (**c**) *(acuerdo)* agreement; *Fml* **c. matrimonial** engagement; **soltero y sin c.** single and unattached

♪ Observa que la palabra inglesa **compromise** es un falso amigo y no es la traducción de la palabra española **compromiso**. En inglés, **compromise** significa "solución negociada".

compuesto,-a 1 adj (**a**) compound (**b**) **c. de** composed of
2 nm compound

compulsar vt to make a certified true copy of

compungido,-a adj (arrepentido) remorseful; (triste) sorrowful, sad

compuse pt indef de **componer**

computadora nf computer

cómputo nm calculation

comulgar [42] vi (**a**) to receive Holy Communion (**b**) Fig **no comulgo con sus ideas** I don't share his ideas

común 1 adj (**a**) common; **de c. acuerdo** by common consent; **hacer algo en c.** to do sth jointly; **poco c.** unusual; **por lo c.** generally (**b**) (compartido) shared, communal; **amigos comunes** mutual friends
2 nm Br Pol **los Comunes** the Commons

comuna nf Am (municipalidad) municipality

comunal adj communal

comunero,-a nm,f Perú, Méx (indígena) = member of an indigenous village community

comunicación nf (**a**) communication; **ponerse en c. (con algn)** to get in touch with sb (**b**) (comunicado) communication; **c. oficial** communiqué (**c**) Tel connection; **se nos cortó la c.** we were cut off (**d**) (unión) link, connection

comunicado,-a 1 adj **una zona bien comunicada** a well-served zone; **dos ciudades bien comunicadas** two towns with good connections (between them)
2 nm communiqué; **c. de prensa** press release

comunicar [44] **1** vt to communicate; **comuníquenoslo lo antes posible** let us know as soon as possible
2 vi (**a**) to communicate (**b**) Tel to be engaged; **está comunicando** it's engaged
3 comunicarse vpr to communicate

comunicativo,-a adj communicative

comunidad nf community; **C. Europea** European Community; **C. de Estados Independientes** Commonwealth of Independent States

comunión nf communion

comunismo nm communism

comunista adj & nmf communist

comunitario,-a adj (**a**) of o relating to the community (**b**) (de UE) of o relating to the EU; **la política agraria comunitaria** the common agricultural policy

con prep (**a**) with; **córtalo c. las tijeras** cut it with the scissors; **voy cómodo c. este jersey** I'm comfortable in this sweater
(**b**) (compañía) with; **vine c. mi hermana** I came with my sister
(**c**) **c. ese frío/niebla** in that cold/fog; **estar c. (la) gripe** to have the flu
(**d**) (contenido) with; **una bolsa c. dinero** a bag (full) of money
(**e**) (a) to; **habló c. todos** he spoke to everybody; **sé amable c. ella** be nice to her
(**f**) (con infinitivo) **c. llamar será suficiente** it will be enough just to phone
(**g**) (+ que + subjuntivo) **bastará c. que lo esboces** a general idea will do
(**h**) **c. tal (de) que ...** provided that ...; **c. todo (y eso)** even so

conato nm attempt; **c. de asesinato** attempted murder

concebible adj conceivable, imaginable

concebir [6] **1** vt (**a**) (plan, hijo) to conceive (**b**) (entender) to understand
2 vi (mujer) to become pregnant, to conceive

conceder vt to grant; (premio) to award

concejal,-a nm,f town councillor

concejo nm council

concentración nf concentration; (de manifestantes) gathering; (de coches, motos) rally; (de equipo) base

concentrado nm concentrate

concentrar 1 vt to concentrate
2 concentrarse vpr (**a**) to concentrate (**en** on) (**b**) (reunirse) to gather

concepción nf conception

concepto nm (**a**) (idea) concept; **tener buen/mal c. de** to have a good/a bad opinion of; **bajo/por ningún c.** under no circumstances (**b**) **en c. de** under the heading of (**c**) (en factura) item

concerniente adj **c.** (**a**) concerning, regarding; Fml **en lo c. a** with regard to

concernir [54] v impers (**a**) (afectar) to concern; **en lo que a mí concierne** as far as I am concerned; **en lo que concierne a** with regard/respect to (**b**) (corresponder) to be up to

concertación nf compromise, agreement

concertar [1] **1** vt (**a**) (cita) to arrange; (precio) to agree on; (acuerdo) to reach (**b**) (una acción etc) to plan, to co-ordinate
2 vi to agree, to tally

concesión nf (**a**) concession (**b**) (de un premio, contrato) awarding

concesionario,-a nm,f dealer

concha nf (**a**) Zool (caparazón) shell; (carey) tortoiseshell (**b**) Andes, RP Vulg Br fanny, US beaver (**c**) Ven (de árbol) bark; (de fruta) peel, rind; (del pan) crust; (de huevo) shell

conchabarse vpr to gang up

concheto,-a RP Fam **1** adj posh
2 nm,f rich kid

conchudo,-a nm,f Perú, RP Vulg prick, Br dickhead

conciencia nf (**a**) conscience; **tener la c. tranquila** with a clear conscience (**b**) (conocimiento) consciousness, awareness; **a c.**

conscientiously; **tener/tomar c. (de algo)** to be/to become aware (of sth)
concienciar [43], *Am* **concientizar** [40] **1** *vt*
c. de to make aware of
  2 concienciarse *vpr* to become aware (**de** of)
concienzudo,-a *adj* conscientious
concierto *nm* (**a**) *Mús* concert; *(composición)* concerto (**b**) *(acuerdo)* agreement
conciliar [43] *vt* to reconcile; **c. el sueño** to get to sleep
concilio *nm* council
conciso,-a *adj* concise
conciudadano,-a *nm,f* fellow citizen
concluir [37] *vt* to conclude
conclusión *nf* conclusion; **sacar una c.** to draw a conclusion
concluyente *adj* conclusive
concomerse *vpr* to be consumed; **c. de envidia** to be green with envy
concordar [2] **1** *vi* to agree; **esto no concuerda con lo que dijo ayer** this doesn't fit in with what he said yesterday
  2 *vt* to bring into agreement
concordia *nf* concord
concretamente *adv* specifically
concretar *vt (precisar)* to specify, to state explicitly; *(fecha, hora)* to fix
concreto,-a 1 *adj* (**a**) *(preciso, real)* concrete (**b**) *(particular)* specific; **en c.** specifically; **en el caso c. de ...** in the specific case of ...
  2 *nm Am* concrete
concurrencia *nf* (**a**) *(de dos cosas)* concurrence (**b**) *(público)* audience
concurrido,-a *adj* crowded, busy
concurrir *vi* (**a**) *(gente)* to converge (**en** on), to meet (**en** in) (**b**) *(coincidir)* to concur, to coincide (**c**) *(participar)* to compete; *(en elecciones)* to be a candidate
concursante *nmf* (**a**) *(competidor)* contestant, competitor (**b**) *(para un empleo)* candidate
concursar *vi* to compete, to take part
concurso *nm* (**a**) *(competición)* competition; *(de belleza etc)* contest; *TV* quiz show; **presentar (una obra) a c.** to invite tenders (for a piece of work) (**b**) *Fml (ayuda)* help

> 🔔 Observa que la palabra inglesa **concourse** es un falso amigo y no es la traducción de la palabra española **concurso**. En inglés, **concourse** significa "vestíbulo".

condal *adj* of o relating to a count; **la Ciudad C.** Barcelona
conde *nm* count
condecoración *nf* decoration
condecorar *vt* to decorate
condena *nf* (**a**) *Jur* sentence (**b**) *(desaprobación)* condemnation, disapproval
condenado,-a 1 *adj* (**a**) *Jur* convicted; **c. a muerte** condemned to death (**b**) *Rel & Fam* damned; **c. al fracaso** doomed to failure
  2 *nm,f* (**a**) *Jur* convicted person; *(a muerte)*

condemned person (**b**) *Rel* damned person
condenar 1 *vt* (**a**) *Jur* to convict, to find guilty; **c. a algn a muerte** to condemn sb to death (**b**) *(desaprobar)* to condemn
  2 condenarse *vpr Rel* to be damned
condensado,-a *adj* condensed; **leche condensada** condensed milk
condensador *nm* condenser
condensar *vt*, **condensarse** *vpr* to condense
condesa *nf* countess
condescender [3] *vi* (**a**) to condescend (**b**) *(ceder)* to comply (with), to consent (to)
condescendiente *adj* (**a**) *(displicente)* condescending (**b**) *(complaciente)* complacent
condición *nf* (**a**) condition; **en buenas/malas condiciones** in good/bad condition; **condiciones de trabajo** working conditions; **con la c. de que ...** on the condition that ... (**b**) *(manera de ser)* nature, character (**c**) **en su c. de director** *(calidad)* in his capacity as director
condicional *adj* conditional
condicionar *vt* (**a**) to condition (**b**) **una cosa condiciona la otra** one thing determines the other
condimentar *vt* to season, to flavour
condimento *nm* seasoning, flavouring
condolerse [4] *vpr* **c. de** to sympathize with
condominio *nm Am (edificio) Br* block of flats, *US* condominium
condón *nm* condom
condonar *vt (ofensa)* to condone; *(deuda)* to cancel
cóndor *nm* condor
conducir [10] **1** *vt (coche)* to drive; *(electricidad)* to conduct
  2 *vi* (**a**) *Aut* to drive; **permiso de c.** *Br* driving licence, *US* driver's license (**b**) *(camino, actitud)* to lead; **eso no conduce a nada** this leads nowhere
conducta *nf* behaviour, conduct; **mala c.** misbehaviour, misconduct
conducto *nm* (**a**) *(tubería)* pipe; *Fig* **por conductos oficiales** through official channels (**b**) *Anat* duct, canal
conductor,-a 1 *nm,f Aut* driver
  2 *nm Elec* conductor
conectar *vt* (**a**) to connect up (**b**) *Elec* to plug in, to switch on
coneja *nf* doe rabbit
conejillo *nm* **c. de Indias** guinea pig
conejo *nm* rabbit
conexión *nf* connection
confabularse *vpr* to conspire, to plot
confección *nf* (**a**) *Cost* dressmaking, tailoring; **la industria de la c.** the rag trade (**b**) *(de un plan etc)* making, making up
confeccionar *vt* to make (up)
confederación *nf* confederation
conferencia *nf* (**a**) lecture; **dar una c. (sobre algo)** to give a lecture (on sth) (**b**) **c. de prensa** press conference (**c**) *Tel* long-distance call

conferenciante *nmf* lecturer

conferir [5] *vt Fml (honor, privilegio)* to con-fer

confesar [1] **1** *vt* to confess, to admit; *(crimen)* to own up to; *Rel (pecados)* to confess

2 *vi Jur* to own up

3 confesarse *vpr* to confess; **c. culpable** to admit one's guilt; *Rel* to go to confession

confesión *nf* confession, admission; *Rel* con-fession

confesionario *nm Rel* confessional

confeti *nm (pl* confetis*)* confetti

confiado,-a *adj* (**a**) *(seguro)* self-confident (**b**) *(crédulo)* gullible, unsuspecting

confianza *nf* (**a**) *(seguridad)* confidence; **te-ner c. en uno mismo** to be self-confident (**b**) **de c.** reliable (**c**) **tener c. con algn** to be on intimate terms with sb; **con toda c.** in all confidence; **tomarse (demasiadas) confian-zas** to take liberties

confiar [29] **1** *vt (entregar)* to entrust; *(infor-mación, secreto)* to confide

2 *vi* **c. en** to trust; **confío en ella** I trust her; **no confíes en su ayuda** don't count on his help

3 confiarse *vpr* to confide (**en** *o* in); **c. demasiado** to be over-confident

confidencia *nf* confidence

confidencial *adj* confidential

confidente,-a *nm,f* (**a**) *(hombre)* confidant; *(mujer)* confidante (**b**) *(de la policía)* infor-mer

configuración *nf* configuration; *Informát* configuration

configurar *vt* to shape, to form

confín *nm* limit, boundary

confinar *vt Jur* to confine

confirmación *nf* confirmation

confirmar *vt* to confirm; *Prov* **la excepción confirma la regla** the exception proves the rule

confiscar [44] *vt* to confiscate

confite *nm Br* sweet, *US* candy

confitería *nf* (**a**) confectioner's (shop), *US* candy store (**b**) *CSur* café

confitura *nf* preserve, jam

conflagración *nf Fig* **c. mundial** world war

conflictividad *nf* **c. laboral** industrial unrest

conflictivo,-a *adj (asunto)* controversial; *(época)* unsettled; **niño c.** problem child

conflicto *nm* conflict; **c. laboral** industrial dispute

confluencia *nf* confluence

confluir [37] *vi* to converge; *(caminos, ríos)* to meet, to come together

conformar 1 *vt* to shape

2 conformarse *vpr* to resign oneself, to be content

conforme 1 *adj* (**a**) *(satisfecho)* satisfied; **c.** agreed, all right; **no estoy c.** I don't agree (**b**) **c. a** in accordance *o* keeping with

2 *conj* (**a**) *(según, como)* as; **c. lo vi/lo oí** as I saw/heard it (**b**) *(a medida que)* as; **la policía**

los detenía c. iban saliendo the police were arresting them as they came out

conformidad *nf* (**a**) approval, consent (**b**) **en c. con** in conformity with

conformismo *nm* conformity

conformista *adj & nmf* conformist

confort *nm (pl* conforts*)* comfort; **todo c. (en anuncio)** all mod cons

confortable *adj* comfortable

confortar *vt* to comfort

confraternizar [40] *vi* to fraternize

confrontación *nf* (**a**) *(enfrentamiento)* con-frontation (**b**) *(comparación)* contrast

confrontar *vt* (**a**) to confront (**b**) *(cotejar)* to compare, to collate

confundir 1 *vt* (**a**) to confuse (**con** with); **c. a una persona con otra** to mistake somebody for somebody else (**b**) *(persona)* to mislead (**c**) *(turbar)* to confound

2 confundirse *vpr* (**a**) *(equivocarse)* to be mistaken; *Tel* **se ha confundido** you've got the wrong number (**b**) *(mezclarse)* to mingle; **se confundió entre el gentío** he disappeared into the crowd

confusión *nf* confusion

confuso,-a *adj* (**a**) confused; *(formas, recuer-do)* blurred, vague (**b**) *(mezclado)* mixed up

congelación *nf* (**a**) freezing (**b**) *Fin* freeze; **c. salarial** wage freeze (**c**) *Med* frostbite

congelado,-a 1 *adj* frozen; *Med* frostbitten

2 *nmpl* **congelados** frozen food

congelador *nm* freezer

congelar 1 *vt* to freeze

2 congelarse *vpr* (**a**) to freeze; *Fam* **me estoy congelando** I'm freezing (**b**) *Med* to get *o* become frostbitten

congeniar [43] *vi* to get on (**con** with)

congénito,-a *adj* congenital

congestión *nf* congestion; *Med* **c. cerebral** stroke

congestionar *vt* to congest

conglomerado *nm* conglomerate

conglomerar *vt,* **conglomerarse** *vpr* to conglomerate

congoja *nf* sorrow, grief

congraciarse [43] *vpr* to ingratiate oneself (**con** with)

congratular *vt Fml* to congratulate (**por** on)

congregación *nf* congregation

congregar [42] *vt,* **congregarse** *vpr* to con-gregate, to assemble

congresista *nmf* member of a congress

congreso *nm* congress, conference; *Pol* **c. de los Diputados** *Br* ≃ Parliament, *US* ≃ Con-gress

congrio *nm* conger (eel)

congruente *adj* coherent, suitable

conjetura *nf* conjecture; **por c.** by guesswork

conjeturar *vt* to conjecture

conjugación *nf* conjugation

conjugar [42] *vt* to conjugate; *Fig (planes, opiniones)* to combine

conjunción *nf* conjunction

conjuntar *vt* to co-ordinate

conjuntivitis *nf* conjunctivitis

conjunto,-a 1 *nm* (**a**) *(grupo)* collection, group (**b**) *(todo)* whole; **de c.** overall; **en c.** on the whole (**c**) *Mús* (pop) group, band (**d**) *(prenda)* outfit, ensemble (**e**) *Mat* set (**f**) *Dep* team
  2 *adj* joint

conjurar 1 *vt* to exorcise; *(peligro)* to ward off
  2 conjurarse *vpr* to conspire, to plot

conjuro *nm* (**a**) *(exorcismo)* exorcism (**b**) *(encantamiento)* spell, incantation

conllevar *vt* to entail

conmemoración *nf* commemoration

conmemorar *vt* to commemorate

conmigo *pron pers* with me; **vino c.** he came with me; **él habló c.** he talked to me

conminar *vt* to threaten, to menace

conmoción *nf* commotion, shock; **c. cerebral** concussion

conmocionar *vt* to shock; *Med* to concuss

conmovedor,-a *adj* touching; **una película conmovedora** a moving film

conmover [4] *vt* to touch, to move

conmutador *nm* (**a**) *Elec* switch (**b**) *Am Tel* switchboard

conmutar *vt* to exchange; *Jur* to commute; *Elec* to commutate

connivencia *nf* connivance, collusion

connotación *nf* connotation

cono *nm* cone; **C. Sur** South America

conocedor,-a *adj & nm,f* expert; *(de vino, arte etc)* connoisseur

conocer [34] **1** *vt* (**a**) to know; **dar (algo/algn) a c.** to make (sth/sb) known (**b**) *(a una persona)* to meet (**c**) *(reconocer)* to recognize; **te conocí por la voz** I recognized you by your voice
  2 conocerse *vpr (dos personas)* to know each other; *(por primera vez)* to meet

conocido,-a 1 *adj* known; *(famoso)* well-known
  2 *nm,f* acquaintance

conocimiento *nm* (**a**) knowledge; **con c. de causa** with full knowledge of the facts (**b**) *(conciencia)* consciousness; **perder/recobrar el c.** to lose/regain consciousness (**c**) **conocimientos** knowledge

conque *conj* so

conquense 1 *adj* of/from Cuenca
  2 *nmf* person from Cuenca

conquista *nf* conquest

conquistador,-a *nm,f* conqueror

conquistar *vt (país, ciudad)* to conquer; *Fig (puesto, título)* to win; *(a una persona)* to win over

consabido,-a *adj* (**a**) *(bien conocido)* well-known (**b**) *(usual)* familiar, usual

consagración *nf* (**a**) *Rel* consecration (**b**) *(de un artista)* recognition

consagrar 1 *vt* (**a**) *Rel* to consecrate (**b**)

(artista) to confirm (**c**) *(tiempo, vida)* to devote
  2 consagrarse *vpr* (**a**) **c. a** *(dedicarse)* to devote oneself to, to dedicate oneself to (**b**) *(lograr fama)* to establish oneself

consciente *adj* (**a**) conscious, aware; **ser c. de algo** to be aware of sth (**b**) *Med* conscious

conscripto *nm Andes, Arg* conscript

consecución *nf* (**a**) *(de un objetivo)* achievement (**b**) *(obtención)* obtaining

consecuencia *nf* (**a**) consequence; **a o como c. de** as a consequence *o* result of; **en c.** therefore; **tener o traer (malas) consecuencias** to have (ill) effects; **sacar como o en c.** to come to a conclusion (**b**) *(coherencia)* consistency; **actuar en c.** to be consistent

consecuente *adj* consistent

consecutivo,-a *adj* consecutive; **tres días consecutivos** three days in a row

conseguir [6] *vt* (**a**) to get, to obtain; *(objetivo)* to achieve (**b**) **conseguí terminar** I managed to finish

consejero,-a *nm,f* (**a**) *(asesor)* adviser (**b**) *Pol* councillor (**c**) *Com* **c. delegado** managing director

consejo *nm* (**a**) *(recomendación)* advice; **un c.** a piece of advice (**b**) *(junta)* council; **c. de ministros** cabinet; *(reunión)* cabinet meeting; **c. de administración** board of directors; **c. de guerra** court martial

consenso *nm* consensus

consensuar *vt* to approve by consensus

consentido,-a *adj* spoiled

consentimiento *nm* consent

consentir [5] **1** *vt* (**a**) *(tolerar)* to allow, to permit; **no consientas que haga eso** don't allow him to do that (**b**) *(mimar)* to spoil
  2 *vi* to consent; **c. en** to agree to

conserje *nm* commissionaire; *(en escuela etc)* janitor

conserva *nf* tinned *o* canned food

conservación *nf* (**a**) preservation (**b**) *(mantenimiento)* maintenance, upkeep

conservador,-a 1 *adj & nm,f* conservative; *Pol* Conservative
  2 *nm (de museo)* curator

conservadurismo *nm* conservatism

conservante *nm* preservative

conservar 1 *vt* to conserve, to preserve; *(mantener)* to keep up, to maintain; *(alimentos)* to preserve
  2 conservarse *vpr* (**a**) *(tradición etc)* to survive (**b**) **c. bien** *(persona)* to age well

conservatorio *nm* conservatory

considerable *adj* considerable

consideración *nf* (**a**) consideration; **tomar algo en c.** to take sth into account (**b**) *(respeto)* regard (**c**) **de c.** important, considerable; **herido de c.** seriously injured

considerado,-a *adj* (**a**) *(atento)* considerate, thoughtful (**b**) **estar bien/mal c.** to be well/ badly thought of

considerar *vt* to consider; **lo considero imposible** I think it's impossible

consigna *nf* (a) *(para maletas) Br* left-luggage office, *US* checkroom (b) *Mil* orders, instructions

consignar *vt* (a) *(puesto)* to allocate; *(cantidad)* to assign (b) *(mercancía)* to ship, to dispatch

consigo[1] *pron pers* (a) *(tercera persona) (hombre)* with him; *(mujer)* with her; *(cosa, animal)* with it; *(plural)* with them; *(usted)* with you (b) **hablar c. mismo** to speak to oneself

consigo[2] *indic pres de* **conseguir**

consiguiente *adj* resulting, consequent; **por c.** therefore, consequently

consistencia *nf* (a) consistency (b) *(de argumento)* soundness

consistente *adj* (a) *(firme)* firm, solid (b) *(teoría)* sound (c) **c. en** consisting of

> *Observa que la palabra inglesa* **consistent** *es un falso amigo y no es la traducción de la palabra española* **consistente**. *En inglés,* **consistent** *significa "consecuente".*

consistir *vi* to consist (**en** of); **el secreto consiste en tener paciencia** the secret lies in being patient

consistorial *adj* **casa c.** town hall

consola *nf* console table; *Informát* console

consolación *nf* consolation; **premio de c.** consolation prize

consolador,-a **1** *adj* consoling, comforting **2** *nm* dildo

consolar [2] *vt* to console, to comfort **2 consolarse** *vpr* to console oneself, to take comfort (**con** from)

consolidar *vt*, **consolidarse** *vpr* to consolidate

consomé *nm* clear soup, consommé

consonancia *nf* **en c. con** in keeping with

consonante *adj & nf* consonant

consorcio *nm* consortium

consorte **1** *adj* **príncipe c.** prince consort **2** *nmf (cónyuge)* partner, spouse

conspicuo,-a *adj* prominent, outstanding

conspiración *nf* conspiracy, plot

conspirar *vi* to conspire, to plot

constancia *nf* (a) constancy, perseverance (b) *(testimonio)* proof, evidence; **dejar c. de algo** to put sth on record

constante **1** *adj* constant; *(persona)* steadfast **2** *nf* constant feature; *Mat* constant

constantemente *adv* constantly

constar *vi* (a) *(figurar)* to figure, to be included (**en** in); **en acta** to be on record (b) **me consta que ...** I am absolutely certain that ... (c) **c. de** to be made up of, to consist of

constatar *vt* to state; *(comprobar)* to check

constelación *nf* constellation

consternación *nf* consternation

consternar *vt* to dismay

constipado,-a **1** *adj* **estar c.** to have a cold *o* a chill **2** *nm* cold, chill

> *Observa que la palabra inglesa* **constipated** *es un falso amigo y no es la traducción de la palabra española* **constipado**. *En inglés,* **constipated** *significa "estreñido".*

constiparse *vpr* to catch a cold *o* a chill

constitución *nf* constitution

constitucional *adj* constitutional

constituir [37] **1** *vt* (a) *(formar)* to constitute; **estar constituido por** to consist of (b) *(suponer)* to represent (c) *(fundar)* to constitute, to set up **2 constituirse** *vpr* **c. en** to set oneself up as

constituyente *adj & nmf* constituent

constreñir [6] *vt* (a) *(forzar)* to compel, to force (b) *(oprimir)* to restrict (c) *Med* to constrict

construcción *nf* (a) construction; *(sector)* the building industry; **en c.** under construction (b) *(edificio)* building

constructivo,-a *adj* constructive

constructor,-a **1** *nm,f* builder **2** *adj* **empresa constructora** builders, construction company

construir [37] *vt* to build, to manufacture

> *Observa que el verbo inglés* **to construe** *es un falso amigo y no es la traducción del verbo español* **construir**. *En inglés,* **to construe** *significa "interpretar".*

consuelo *nm* consolation

cónsul *nmf* consul

consulado *nm* consulate

consulta *nf* (a) consultation; **obra de c.** reference book (b) *Med* surgery; *(despacho)* consulting room; **horas de c.** surgery hours

consultar *vt* to consult, to seek advice (**con** from); *(libro)* to look up

consultivo,-a *adj* consultative, advisory

consultorio *nm* (a) *Med* medical centre (b) *Prensa* problem page, advice column

consumado,-a *adj* (a) consummated; **hecho c.** fait accompli, accomplished fact (b) *Fig (artista)* consummate

consumar *vt* to complete, to carry out; *(crimen)* to commit

consumición *nf* (a) consumption (b) *(bebida)* drink

consumidor,-a **1** *nm,f* consumer **2** *adj* consuming

consumir **1** *vt* to consume **2 consumirse** *vpr (al hervir)* to boil away; *Fig (persona)* to waste away

consumismo *nm* consumerism

consumo *nm* consumption; **bienes de c.** consumer goods; **sociedad de c.** consumer society

contabilidad *nf Com* (**a**) *(profesión)* accountancy (**b**) *(de empresa, sociedad)* accounting, book-keeping

contabilizar [40] *vt Com* to enter in the books; *Dep* to score

contable *nmf* accountant

contactar *vi* **c. con** to contact, to get in touch with

contacto *nm* contact; *Aut* ignition; **perder el c.** to lose touch; **ponerse en c.** to get in touch

contado,-a 1 *adj* few and far between; **contadas veces** very seldom; **tiene los días contados** his days are numbered

 2 *nm* **pagar al c.** to pay cash

contador,-ora 1 *nm,f Am (persona)* accountant; **c. público** *Br* chartered accountant, *US* certified public accountant

 2 *nm (aparato)* meter; **c. de agua** water meter

contagiar [43] 1 *vt Med* to pass on

 2 **contagiarse** *vpr* (**a**) *(persona)* to get infected (**b**) *(enfermedad)* to be contagious

contagio *nm* contagion

contagioso,-a *adj* contagious; *Fam (risa)* infectious

contaminación *nf* contamination; *(del aire)* pollution

contaminar *vt* to contaminate; *(aire, agua)* to pollute

contante *adj* **dinero c. (y sonante)** hard *o* ready cash

contar [2] 1 *vt* (**a**) *(sumar)* to count (**b**) *(narrar)* to tell

 2 *vi* (**a**) to count (**b**) **c. con** *(confiar en)* to count on; *(tener)* to have

 3 **contarse** *vpr Fam* **¿qué te cuentas?** how's it going?

contemplación *nf* contemplation; *Fam* **no andarse con contemplaciones** to make no bones about it

contemplar *vt* to contemplate; *(considerar)* to consider; *(estipular)* to stipulate

contemporáneo,-a *adj & nm,f* contemporary

contención *nf* **muro de c.** retaining wall; **c. salarial** wage restraint

contencioso,-a 1 *adj* contentious; *Jur* litigious

 2 *nm Jur* legal dispute

contendiente *nmf* contender, contestant

contenedor *nm* container

contener [24] 1 *vt* (**a**) to contain (**b**) *(pasiones etc)* to restrain, to hold back

 2 **contenerse** *vpr* to control oneself, to hold (oneself) back

contenido *nm* content, contents

contentar 1 *vt* (**a**) *(satisfacer)* to please (**b**) *(alegrar)* to cheer up

 2 **contentarse** *vpr* (**a**) *(conformarse)* to make do (**con** with), to be satisfied (**con** with) (**b**) *(alegrarse)* to cheer up

contento,-a *adj* happy, pleased (**con** with)

contestación *nf* answer; **dar c.** to answer

contestador *nm* **c. automático** answering machine

contestar *vt* (**a**) to answer (**b**) *Fam (replicar)* to answer back

contestatario,-a *adj* anti-establishment

contexto *nm* context

contienda *nf* struggle

contigo *pron pers* with you

contiguo,-a *adj* contiguous (**a** to), adjoining

continente *nm* (**a**) *Geog* continent (**b**) *(compostura)* countenance

contingencia *nf* contingency

contingente *nm* contingent

continuación *nf* continuation; **a c.** next

continuamente *adv* continuously

continuar [30] *vt & vi* to continue, to carry on (with); **continúa en Francia** he's still in France; **continuará** to be continued

continuidad *nf* continuity

continuo,-a 1 *adj* (**a**) continuous; *Aut* **línea continua** solid white line (**b**) *(reiterado)* continual, constant

 2 *nm* continuum

contonearse *vpr* to swing one's hips

contorno *nm* (**a**) outline (**b**) **contornos** surroundings, environment

contorsión *nf* contortion

contorsionarse *vpr* to contort *o* twist oneself

contra 1 *prep* against; **en c. de** against

 2 *nm* **los pros y los contras** the pros and cons

contraataque *nm* counterattack

contrabajo *nm* double bass

contrabandista *nmf* smuggler; **c. de armas** gunrunner

contrabando *nm* smuggling; **c. de armas** gunrunning; **pasar algo de c.** to smuggle sth in

contracción *nf* contraction

contracepción *nf* contraception

contrachapado *nm* plywood

contracorriente 1 *nf* crosscurrent

 2 *adv* **ir (a) c.** to go against the tide

contradecir [12] *(pp* **contradicho***) vt* to contradict

contradicción *nf* contradiction

contradictorio,-a *adj* contradictory

contraer [25] 1 *vt* to contract; **c. matrimonio con algn** to marry sb

 2 **contraerse** *vpr* to contract

contraigo *indic pres de* **contraer**

contraindicación *nf* contraindication

contraje *pt indef de* **contraer**

contralor *nm Am* = inspector of public spending

contraloría *nf Am* = office controlling public spending

contraluz *nm* view against the light; **a c.** against the light

contramaestre *nm* (**a**) *(en buque)* boatswain (**b**) *(capataz)* foreman

contramano: a contramano *loc adv* the wrong way *o* direction

contrapartida *nf* **en c.** in return

contrapelo: a contrapelo *loc adv* the wrong way; *Fig* against the grain

contrapesar *vt* (**a**) to counterbalance, to counterpoise (**b**) *Fig (compensar)* to offset, to balance

contrapeso *nm* counterweight

contraportada *nf* back page

contraposición *nf* contrast

contraproducente *adj* counterproductive

contraprogramación *nf TV* competitive scheduling

contrapunto *nm* counterpoint

contrariamente *adv* **c. a ...** contrary to ...

contrariar [29] *vt* (**a**) *(oponerse a)* to oppose, to go against (**b**) *(disgustar)* to upset

contrariedad *nf* (**a**) *(contratiempo)* obstacle, setback (**b**) *(disgusto)* annoyance

contrario,-a 1 *adj* (**a**) opposite; **lo c. de** the opposite of; **en el lado/sentido c.** on the other side/in the other direction; **al c., por el c.** on the contrary; **de lo c.** otherwise; **todo lo c.** quite the opposite (**b**) *(perjudicial)* contrary (**a** to)

2 *nm,f* opponent, rival

3 *nf* **llevar la contraria** to be contrary

contrarrestar *vt* to offset, to counteract

contrasentido *nm* contradiction

contraseña *nf* password

contrastar *vt* to contrast (**con** with)

contraste *nm* (**a**) contrast (**b**) *(en oro, plata)* hallmark

contrata *nf* contract

contratar *vt* to hire, to engage

contratiempo *nm* setback, hitch

contratista *nmf* contractor

contrato *nm* contract; **c. de trabajo** work contract; **c. de alquiler** lease, leasing agreement; **c. basura** short-term contract with poor conditions

contravenir [27] *vt* to contravene, to infringe

contraventana *nf* shutter

contribución *nf* (**a**) contribution (**b**) *(impuesto)* tax

contribuir [37] **1** *vt* to contribute (**a** to)

2 *vi* (**a**) to contribute (**b**) *(pagar impuestos)* to pay taxes

contribuyente *nmf* taxpayer

contrincante *nmf* rival, opponent

control *nm* (**a**) control; **c. a distancia** remote control (**b**) *(inspección)* check; *(de policía etc)* checkpoint

controlador,-a *nm,f* **c. (aéreo)** air traffic controller

controlar 1 *vt* (**a**) to control (**b**) *(comprobar)* to check

2 controlarse *upr* to control oneself

controversia *nf* controversy

controvertido,-a *adj* controversial

contumaz *adj* obstinate

contundente *adj* (**a**) *(arma)* blunt (**b**) *(argumento)* forceful, convincing

contusión *nf* contusion, bruise

conuco *nm Carib, Col* small farm, *Br* smallholding

convalecencia *nf* convalescence

convaleciente *adj & nmf* convalescent

convalidar *vt* to validate; *(documento)* to ratify

convencer [49] *vt* to convince; **c. a algn de algo** to convince sb about sth

convencimiento *nm* conviction; **tener el c. de que ...** to be convinced that ...

convención *nf* convention

convencional *adj* conventional

convenido,-a *adj* agreed; **según lo c.** as agreed

conveniencia *nf* (**a**) *(provecho)* convenience (**b**) **conveniencias sociales** social proprieties

conveniente *adj* (**a**) *(oportuno)* convenient; *(aconsejable)* advisable (**b**) *(precio)* good, fair

convenio *nm* agreement; **c. laboral** agreement on salary and conditions

convenir [27] *vt & vi* (**a**) *(acordar)* to agree; **c. una fecha** to agree on a date; **sueldo a c.** salary negotiable; **c. en** to agree on (**b**) *(ser oportuno)* to suit, to be good for; **conviene recordar que ...** it's as well to remember that ...

convento *nm (de monjas)* convent; *(de monjes)* monastery

convergente *adj* convergent

converger [53] *vi* to converge

conversación *nf* conversation

conversada *nf Am Fam* chat

conversar *vi* to converse, to talk

conversión *nf* conversion

converso,-a *nm,f* convert

convertible *adj* convertible

convertir [54] **1** *vt* to change, to convert

2 convertirse *upr* (**a**) **c. en** to turn into, to become (**b**) *Rel* to be converted (**a** to)

convexo,-a *adj* convex

convicción *nf* conviction; **tengo la c. de que ...** I am convinced that ..

convicto,-a *adj* convicted

convidado,-a *adj & nm,f* guest

convidar *vt* to invite

convincente *adj* convincing

convite *nm* reception

convivencia *nf* life together; *Fig* coexistence

convivir *vi* to live together; *Fig* to coexist (**con** with)

convocar [44] *vt* to summon; *(reunión, elecciones)* to call

convocatoria *nf* (**a**) *(a huelga etc)* call (**b**) *Educ* diet

convulsión *nf Med* convulsion; *(agitación social)* upheaval

convulsivo,-a *adj* convulsive

conyugal *adj* conjugal; **vida c.** married life

cónyuge *nmf* spouse; **cónyuges** married couple, husband and wife

coña *nf muy Fam* **estar de c.** to be joking

coñac *nm* brandy, cognac

coñazo *nm muy Fam* pain, drag; **dar el c.** to be a real pain

coño 1 *nm Vulg* cunt

  2 *interj Vulg* for fuck's sake!

cooperación *nf* co-operation

cooperador,-a *nm,f* collaborator, co-operator

cooperante *nmf* aid worker

cooperar *vi* to co-operate (**con** with)

cooperativa *nf* co-operative

coordenada *nf* co-ordinate

coordinación *nf* co-ordination

coordinador,-a *nm,f* co-ordinator

coordinadora *nf* co-ordinating committee; **c. general** joint committee

coordinar *vt* to co-ordinate

copa *nf* (a) glass; **tomar una c.** to have a drink (**b**) *(de árbol)* top (**c**) *Dep* cup (**d**) *Naipes* **copas** hearts

copar *vt* to take up

copartícipe *adj & nmf (socio)* partner; *(colaborador)* collaborator; *(copropietario)* joint owner, co-owner

Copenhague *n* Copenhagen

copetín *nm RP* pre-lunch/pre-dinner drinks

copia *nf* copy; *Informát* **c. de seguridad** backup; *Informát* **hacer una c. de seguridad de algo** to back up sth

copiar [43] *vt* to copy

copiloto *nm Av* copilot; *Aut* co-driver

copioso,-a *adj* abundant, copious

copistería *nf* photocopying service

copla *nf* verse, couplet

copo *nm* flake; *(de nieve)* snowflake; **copos de maíz** cornflakes

coproducción *nf* co-production, joint production

cópula *nf* (a) *(coito)* copulation, intercourse (**b**) *Ling* conjunction

copular *vt* to copulate (**con** with)

coqueta *nf* dressing table

coquetear *vi* to flirt (**con** with)

coqueto,-a 1 *adj* coquettish

  2 *nm,f* flirt

coraje *nm* (a) *(valor)* courage (**b**) *(ira)* anger, annoyance; *Fig* **dar c. a algn** to infuriate sb; **¡qué c.!** how maddening!

coral¹ *nm Zool* coral

coral² *nf Mús* choral, chorale

Corán *nm* Koran

coraza *nf* armour; *Fig* protection

corazón *nm* (a) heart; *Fig* **de (todo) c.** in all sincerity; *Fig* **tener buen c.** to be kindhearted (**b**) *(parte central)* heart; *(de fruta)* core (**c**) *Naipes* **corazones** hearts

corazonada *nf* hunch, feeling

corbata *nf* tie, *US* necktie; **con c.** wearing a tie

Córcega *n* Corsica

corchete *nm* (a) *Impr* square bracket (**b**) *Cost* hook and eye, snap fastener

corcho *nm* cork; *(de pesca)* float

cordel *nm* rope, cord

cordero,-a *nm,f* lamb

cordial *adj* cordial, warm

cordialidad *nf* cordiality, warmth

cordillera *nf* mountain chain o range

córdoba *nm Fin* = monetary unit of Nicaragua

cordón *nm* string; *(de zapatos)* shoelace; *Anat* **c. umbilical** umbilical cord; **c. policial** police cordon; *CSur, Cuba (de la vereda)* *Br* kerb, *US* curb

cordura *nf* common sense

Corea *n* Korea; **C. del Norte/Sur** North/South Korea

coreano,-a *adj & nm,f* Korean

corear *vt* (a) *(cantar a coro)* to sing in chorus (**b**) *(aclamar)* to applaud

coreografía *nf* choreography

cornada *nf Taurom* goring

corneja *nf* crow

córner *nm Ftb* corner (kick); **sacar un c.** to take a corner

corneta *nf* bugle; **c. de llaves** cornet

cornisa *nf* cornice

cornudo *nm Fam (marido)* cuckold

coro *nm Mús* choir; *Teatro* chorus; *Fig* **a c.** all together

corona *nf* (a) crown (**b**) *(de flores etc)* wreath, garland; **c. funeraria** funeral wreath

coronación *nf* (a) coronation (**b**) *Fig (culminación)* crowning point

coronar *vt* to crown

coronel *nm* colonel

coronilla *nf* crown of the head; *Fam* **estar hasta la c. (de)** to be fed up (with)

corpiño *nm (vestido)* bodice; *Arg (sostén)* bra

corporación *nf* corporation

corporal *adj* corporal; **castigo c.** corporal punishment; **olor c.** body odour, BO

corporativo,-a *adj* corporative

corpulento,-a *adj* corpulent, stout

corpus *nm* corpus

corral *nm* farmyard, *US* corral; *(de casa)* courtyard

correa *nf* (a) *(tira)* strap; *(de reloj)* watchstrap; *(de pantalón)* belt; *(de perro)* lead, leash (**b**) *Téc* belt

corrección *nf* (a) *(rectificación)* correction (**b**) *(urbanidad)* courtesy, politeness

correcto,-a *adj* (a) *(sin errores)* correct (**b**) *(educado)* polite, courteous (**con** to); *(conducta)* proper

corredera *nf* **puerta/ventana de c.** sliding door/window

corredizo,-a *adj* sliding; **nudo c.** slipknot; **techo c.** sunroof

corredor,-a *nm,f* (a) *Dep* runner (**b**) *Fin* **c. de bolsa** stockbroker

corregir [58] 1 *vt* to correct

  2 **corregirse** *vpr* to mend one's ways

correo *nm* (a) post, mail; **echar al c.** to post;

por c. by post; **c. aéreo** airmail; **c. certificado** registered post; *Informát* **c. electrónico** electronic mail, e-mail; *Informát* **me envió un c. (electrónico)** *(un mensaje)* she e-mailed me, she sent me an e-mail; **(tren) c.** mail train (b) **correos** *(edificio)* post office

correr 1 *vi* (a) to run; *(coche)* to go fast; *(conductor)* to drive fast; *(viento)* to blow; *Fig* **no corras, habla más despacio** don't rush, speak slower; **c. prisa** to be urgent (b) **c. con los gastos** to foot the bill; **corre a mi cargo** I'll take care of it

2 *vt* (a) *(cortina)* to draw; *(cerrojo)* to close; *(aventura etc)* to have; **c. el riesgo o peligro** to run the risk (b) *(mover)* to pull up, to draw up

3 correrse *upr* (a) *(moverse)* to move over (b) *Fam* **c. una juerga** to go on a spree (c) *muy Fam (tener orgasmo)* to come

correspondencia *nf* (a) correspondence (b) *Ferroc* connection

corresponder 1 *vi* (a) to correspond (**a** to; **con** with) (b) *(incumbir)* to concern, to be incumbent upon; **esta tarea te corresponde a ti** it's your job to do this (c) *(pertenecer)* to belong; **me dieron lo que me correspondía** they gave me my share

2 corresponderse *upr* (a) *(ajustarse)* to correspond (b) *(dos cosas)* to tally; **no se corresponde con la descripción** it does not match the description (c) *(dos personas)* to love each other

correspondiente *adj* corresponding (**a** to)

corresponsal *nmf* correspondent

corrida *nf* **c. (de toros)** bullfight

corrido,-a *adj* (a) *(avergonzado)* abashed (b) **de c.** without stopping; **se lo sabe de c.** she knows it by heart

corriente 1 *adj* (a) *(común)* common (b) *(agua)* running (c) *(mes, año)* current, present; **el diez del c.** the tenth of this month (d) *Fin (cuenta)* current (e) **estar al c.** to be up to date

2 *nf* (a) current, stream; *Fig* **ir o navegar contra c.** to go against the tide; *Fam* **seguirle o llevarle la c. a algn** to humour sb; *Elec* **c. eléctrica** (electric) current (b) *(de aire)* draught (c) *(tendencia)* trend, current

corrijo *indic pres de* **corregir**

corrillo *nm* small group of people talking; *Fig* clique

corro *nm* (a) circle, ring (b) *(juego)* ring-a-ring-a-roses

corroborar *vt* to corroborate

corroer [38] *vt* to corrode; *Fig* **la envidia le corroe** envy eats away at him

corromper 1 *vt* (a) *(pudrir)* to turn bad, to rot (b) *(pervertir)* to corrupt, to pervert

2 corromperse *upr* (a) *(pudrirse)* to go bad, to rot (b) *(pervertirse)* to become corrupted

corrosivo,-a *adj* corrosive; *Fig (mordaz)* caustic

corrupción *nf* (a) *(putrefacción)* rot, decay

(b) *Fig* corruption; *Jur* **c. de menores** corruption of minors

corrupto,-a *adj* corrupt

corsé *nm* corset

cortacésped *nm o nf* lawnmower

cortado,-a 1 *adj* (a) cut (up) (b) *(leche)* sour (c) *(labios)* chapped (d) *Fam (tímido)* shy

2 *nm* small coffee with a dash of milk

cortafuego *nm* firebreak

cortapisa *nf Fig* restriction, limitation

cortar 1 *vt* (a) to cut; *(carne)* to carve; *(árbol)* to cut down; *Fam* **c. por lo sano** to take drastic measures; *Fam* **cortó con su novio** she split up with her boyfriend (b) *(piel)* to chap, to crack (c) *(luz, teléfono)* to cut off (d) *(paso, carretera)* to block

2 cortarse *upr* (a) *(herirse)* to cut oneself (b) **c. el pelo** to have one's hair cut (c) *(leche etc)* to curdle (d) *Tel* **se cortó la comunicación** we were cut off (e) *Fam (aturdirse)* to become all shy

cortaúñas *nm inv* nail clippers

corte¹ *nm* (a) cut; **c. de pelo** haircut; *TV* **c. publicitario** commercial break; **c. de mangas** ≃ V-sign (b) *(sección)* section; **c. transversal** cross section (c) *Fam* rebuff; **dar un c. a algn** to cut sb dead

corte² *nf* (a) *(real)* court (b) **Las Cortes** (Spanish) Parliament

cortejar *vt* to court

cortejo *nm* (a) *(galanteo)* courting (b) *(comitiva)* entourage, retinue; **c. fúnebre** funeral cortège

cortés *adj* courteous, polite

cortesía *nf* courtesy, politeness

corteza *nf (de árbol)* bark; *(de queso)* rind; *(de pan)* crust

cortijo *nm* Andalusian farm o farmhouse

cortina *nf* curtain; **c. de humo** smoke screen

corto,-a 1 *adj* (a) *(distancia, tiempo)* short; *Fam* **c. de luces** dim-witted; **c. de vista** shortsighted; *Aut* **luz corta** dipped headlights (b) *Fam* **quedarse c.** *(calcular mal)* to underestimate (c) *(apocado)* timid, shy

2 *nm Cin* short (film)

cortocircuito *nm* short circuit

cortometraje *nm* short (film)

corvo,-a *adj* curved, bent

cosa *nf* (a) thing; **no he visto c. igual** I've never seen anything like it; **no ser gran c.** not to be up to much (b) *(asunto)* matter, business; **eso es c. tuya** that's your business o affair; **eso es otra c.** that's different (c) **hace c. de una hora** about an hour ago

coscorrón *nm* knock o blow on the head

cosecha *nf* (a) *Agr* harvest, crop (b) *(año del vino)* vintage

cosechadora *nf* combine harvester

cosechar *vt* (a) to harvest, to gather (in)

coser *vt* (a) to sew; *Fam* **es c. y cantar** it's a piece of cake (b) *Med* to stitch up

cosmético,-a *adj & nm* cosmetic

cósmico,-a adj cosmic
cosmonauta nmf cosmonaut
cosmopolita adj & nmf cosmopolitan
cosmos nm inv cosmos
coso nm (a) Taurom bullring (b) CSur Fam (objeto) whatnot, thing
cosquillas nfpl tickling; **hacer c. a algn** to tickle sb; **tener c.** to be ticklish
cosquilleo nm tickling
costa¹ nf coast; (litoral) coastline; (playa) beach, seaside
costa² nf **a c. de** at the expense of; **a toda c.** at all costs, at any price; **vive a c. mía** he lives off me
costado nm side; **de c.** sideways; **es catalana por los cuatro costados** she's Catalan through and through
costal nm sack
costanera nf CSur seaside promenade
costar [2] vi (a) to cost; **¿cuánto cuesta?** how much is it?; **c. barato/caro** to be cheap/expensive (b) Fig **te va a c. caro** you'll pay dearly for this; **c. trabajo o mucho** to be hard; **me cuesta hablar francés** I find it difficult to speak French; **cueste lo que cueste** at any cost
costarricense adj & nmf, **costarriqueño,-a** adj & nm,f Costa Rican
coste nm cost; **a precio de c.** (at) cost price; **c. de la vida** cost of living
costear 1 vt to afford, to pay for; **c. los gastos** to foot the bill
2 costearse vpr to pay for
costero,-a 1 adj coastal; **ciudad costera** seaside town
2 nf Méx **costera** seaside promenade
costilla nf (a) Anat rib (b) Culin cutlet
costo¹ nm cost
costo² nm Fam (hachís) dope, shit, stuff
costoso,-a adj costly, expensive
costra nf crust; Med scab
costumbre nf (a) (hábito) habit; **como de c.** as usual; **tengo la c. de levantarme temprano** I usually get up early; **tenía la c. de ...** he used to ... (b) (tradición) custom
costura nf (a) sewing (b) (confección) dressmaking; **alta c.** haute couture (c) (línea de puntadas) seam
costurera nf seamstress
costurero nm sewing basket
cota nf Geog height above sea level; Fig rating
cotejar vt to compare
cotidiano,-a adj daily; **vida cotidiana** everyday life
cotilla nmf Fam busybody, gossip
cotillear vi Fam to gossip (**de** about)
cotilleo nm Fam gossip
cotización nf (a) Fin (market) price, quotation (b) (cuota) membership fees, subscription
cotizar [40] **1** vt Fin to quote
2 vi to pay national insurance

3 cotizarse vpr Fin **c. a** to sell at
coto nm (a) enclosure, reserve; **c. de caza** game reserve (b) **poner c. a** to put a stop to
cotorra nf parrot; Fig (persona) chatterbox
COU nm Educ (abr **Curso de Orientación Universitaria**) = one-year course which prepares students aged 17-18 for Spanish university entrance examinations
country ['kauntri] nm Arg = luxury suburban housing development
coyote nm coyote, prairie wolf
coyuntura nf (a) Anat articulation, joint (b) Fig (circunstancia) juncture; **la c. económica** the economic situation
coz nf kick; **dar una c.** to kick
C.P. (abr **código postal**) Br postcode, US zip code
crac(k) nm (a) Fin crash (b) (droga) crack
cráneo nm cranium, skull
cráter nm crater
creación nf creation
creador,-a nm,f creator
crear vt to create
creatividad nf creativity
creativo,-a adj creative
crecer [33] vi (a) to grow; **c. en importancia** to become more important (b) (al tricotar) to increase
creces nfpl **con c.** fully, in full; **devolver con c.** to return with interest
crecido,-a adj (persona) grown-up
creciente adj growing, increasing; **cuarto c.** crescent
crecimiento nm growth
credencial adj credential; (**cartas**) **credenciales** credentials
credibilidad nf credibility
crédito nm (a) Com & Fin credit (b) (confianza) belief; **dar c. a** to believe
credo nm creed
crédulo,-a adj credulous, gullible
creencia nf belief
creer [36] **1** vt (a) to believe (b) (pensar) to think; **creo que no** I don't think so; **creo que sí** I think so; **ya lo creo** I should think so
2 vi to believe; **c. en** to believe in
3 creerse vpr (a) to consider oneself to be; **¿qué te has creído?** what o who do you think you are? (b) **no me lo creo** I can't believe it
creíble adj credible, believable
creído,-a 1 adj arrogant, vain
2 nm,f big head
crema nf cream
cremallera nf Br zip (fastener), US zipper
crematorio nm (**horno**) **c.** crematorium
cremoso,-a adj creamy
crepe nm crêpe, pancake
crepería nf creperie
crepitar vi to crackle
crepúsculo nm twilight
crespo,-a adj frizzy
crespón nm crepe

cresta *nf* (**a**) crest; *(de gallo)* comb (**b**) *(de punk)* mohican
Creta *n* Crete
cretino,-a 1 *adj* stupid, cretinous
  2 *nm,f* cretin
creyente *nmf* believer
crezco *indic pres de* **crecer**
cría *nf* (**a**) *(cachorro)* young (**b**) *(crianza)* breeding, raising
criada *nf* maid
criadero *nm* nursery
criadilla *nf Culin* bull's testicle
criado,-a 1 *adj* **mal c.** spoilt
  2 *nm,f* servant
crianza *nf (de animales)* breeding; *Fig* **vinos de c.** vintage wines
criar [29] *vt* (**a**) *(animales)* to breed, to raise; *(niños)* to bring up, to rear (**b**) *(producir)* to have, to grow
criatura *nf* (**a**) *(living)* creature (**b**) *(crío)* baby, child
criba *nf* sieve
cribar *vt* to sieve, to sift
crimen *nm (pl* **crímenes**) murder; **c. de guerra** war crime
criminal *nmf & adj* criminal
crin *nf,* **crines** *nfpl* mane
crío,-a 1 *nm Fam* kid
  2 *adj* babyish
criollo,-a *adj & nm,f* Creole
críquet *nm* cricket
crisantemo *nm* chrysanthemum
crisis *nf inv* (**a**) crisis (**b**) *(ataque)* fit, attack; **c. nerviosa** nervous breakdown
crispación *nf* tension
crispar *vt* to make tense; *Fig* **eso me crispa los nervios** that sets my nerves on edge
cristal *nm* (**a**) crystal; **c. de roca** rock crystal (**b**) *(vidrio)* glass; *(de gafas)* lense; *(de ventana)* (window) pane
cristalera *nf* window
cristalería *nf (conjunto)* glassware; *(vasos)* glasses
cristalino,-a *adj* crystal clear
cristalizar [40] *vi* to crystallize
cristiandad *nf* Christendom
cristianismo *nm* Christianity
cristiano,-a *adj & nm,f* Christian
Cristo *nm* Christ
criterio *nm* (**a**) *(pauta)* criterion (**b**) *(opinión)* opinion (**c**) *(discernimiento)* discretion; **lo dejo a tu c.** I'll leave it up to you
crítica *nf* (**a**) criticism (**b**) *Prensa* review; **tener buena c.** to get good reviews (**c**) *(conjunto de críticos)* critics
criticar [44] **1** *vt* to criticize
  2 *vi (murmurar)* to gossip
crítico,-a 1 *adj* critical
  2 *nm,f* critic
criticón,-ona *nm,f Fam* fault-finder
Croacia *n* Croatia
croar *vi* to croak

croata 1 *adj* Croatian
  2 *nmf* Croat, Croatian
croché *nm* crochet
croissant *nm* croissant
crol *nm* crawl
cromo *nm* (**a**) *(metal)* chromium, chrome (**b** *(estampa)* picture card
cromosoma *nm* chromosome
crónica *nf* (**a**) account, chronicle (**b**) *Prens* feature, article
crónico,-a *adj* chronic
cronista *nmf Prensa* feature writer
cronología *nf* chronology
cronológico,-a *adj* chronological
cronometrar *vt* to time
cronómetro *nm* stopwatch
croqueta *nf* croquette
croquis *nm inv* sketch
cruce *nm* (**a**) crossing; *(de carreteras)* cross roads; *(de razas)* crossbreeding (**b**) *Te* crossed line
crucero *nm Náut* cruise; *(barco)* cruiser
crucial *adj* crucial
crucificar [44] *vt* to crucify
crucifijo *nm* crucifix
crucigrama *nm* crossword (puzzle)
crudeza *nf* crudeness, coarseness
crudo,-a 1 *adj* (**a**) raw; *(comida)* underdone *Fam Fig* **lo veo muy c.** it doesn't look too goo (**b**) *(clima)* harsh (**c**) *(color)* cream
  2 *nm (petróleo)* crude
cruel *adj* cruel
crueldad *nf* cruelty; *Fig (del clima)* severity
cruento,-a *adj* bloody
crujido *nm (de puerta)* creak, creaking; *(d dientes)* grinding
crujiente *adj* crunchy
crujir *vi (madera)* to creak; *(comida)* to crunch; *(dientes)* to grind
cruz *nf* (**a**) cross; **C. Roja** Red Cross; **c. gamad** swastika (**b**) **¿cara o c.?** ≃ heads or tails?
cruza *nf Am* cross, crossbreed
cruzada *nf* crusade
cruzado,-a 1 *adj* (**a**) crossed; **con los braz** **cruzados** arms folded (**b**) *Cost* doubl breasted (**c**) *(atravesado)* lying across (**** *(animal)* crossbred
  2 *nm Hist* crusader
cruzar [40] **1** *vt* (**a**) to cross (**b**) *(palabra miradas)* to exchange (**c**) *(animal, planta)* cross, to crossbreed
  2 *vi (atravesar)* to cross
  3 **cruzarse** *vpr* to cross; **c. con algn** to pass s
cta. *Com (abr* **cuenta**) a/c
cta. cte. *Com (abr* **cuenta corriente**) c/a
c/u *(abr* **cada uno**) ea
cuaderno *nm* notebook
cuadra *nf* (**a**) *(establo)* stable (**b**) *Am* block (houses)
cuadrado,-a 1 *adj* (**a**) *Geom* square (**b**) *(cor plexión física)* broad, stocky (**c**) *Fig (ment* rigid

2 *nm* (**a**) *Geom* square (**b**) *Mat* square; **elevar (un número) al c.** to square (a number)

uadrar 1 *vt* (**a**) *Mat* to square (**b**) *Andes (aparcar)* to park

2 *vi (coincidir)* to square, to agree (**con** with); *(sumas, cifras)* to tally

3 cuadrarse *vpr (soldado)* to stand to attention

uadriculado,-a *adj* **papel c.** square paper

uadrilátero,-a 1 *adj* quadrilateral

2 *nm (en boxeo)* ring

uadrilla *nf (equipo)* gang, team; *Mil* squad; *Taurom* bullfighter's team

uadro *nm* (**a**) *Geom* square; **tela a cuadros** checked cloth (**b**) *Arte* painting, picture (**c**) *Teatro* scene (**d**) *Elec & Téc* panel; **c. de mandos** control panel (**e**) *(gráfico)* chart, graph

uádruple *adj* quadruple, fourfold

uajada *nf* curd

uajar 1 *vt (leche)* to curdle; *(sangre)* to clot

2 *vi* (**a**) *(nieve)* to lie (**b**) *(moda)* to catch on; *(plan, esfuerzo)* to get off the ground

ual 1 *pron rel (precedido de artículo)* (**a**) *(persona) (sujeto)* who; *(objeto)* whom (**b**) *(cosa)* which

2 *pron* (**a**) **tal c.** exactly as (**b**) *Literario (comparativo)* such as, like

uál 1 *pron interr* which (one)?, what?; **¿c. quieres?** which one do you want?

2 *adj interr* which

3 *loc adv* **a c. más tonto** each more stupid than the other

ualidad *nf* quality

ualificado,-a *adj* qualified

ualquier *adj indef* any; **c. cosa** anything; **en c. momento** at any moment *o* time

ualquiera *(pl cualesquiera)* **1** *adj indef* (**a**) *(indefinido)* any; **un profesor c.** any teacher (**b**) *(corriente)* ordinary

Note that **cualquier** is used before singular nouns (e.g. **cualquier hombre** any man).

2 *pron indef* (**a**) *(persona)* anybody; **c. te lo puede decir** anybody can tell you (**b**) *(cosa, animal)* anyone (**c**) **c. que sea** whatever it is

3 *nmf Fig* **ser un c.** to be a nobody; **es una c.** she's a tart

uando 1 *adv (de tiempo)* when; **c. más** at the most; **c. menos** at least; **de c. en c., de vez en c.** from time to time

2 *conj* (**a**) *(temporal)* when; **c. quieras** whenever you want; **c. vengas** when you come (**b**) *(condicional) (si)* if (**c**) *(concesiva) (aunque)* **(aun) c.** even if

3 *prep* during, at the time of; **c. la guerra** during the war; **c. niño** as a child

uándo *adv interr* when?; **¿desde c.?** since when?; **¿para c. lo quieres?** when do you want it for?

uantía *nf* quantity, amount

uantioso,-a *adj* substantial, considerable

cuanto,-a 1 *adj* all; **gasta c. dinero gana** he spends all the money *o* as much as he earns; **unas cuantas niñas** a few girls

2 *pron rel* as much as; **coma c. quiera** eat as much as you want; **regala todo c. tiene** he gives away everything he's got

3 *pron indef pl* **unos cuantos** a few

4 *adv* (**a**) *(tiempo)* **c. antes** as soon as possible; **en c.** as soon as

(**b**) *(cantidad)* **c. más … más** the more … the more; **c. más lo miro, más me gusta** the more I look at it, the more I like it; **cuantas más personas (haya) mejor** the more the merrier

(**c**) **en c. a** with respect to, regarding; **en c. a Juan** as for Juan, as far as Juan is concerned

cuánto,-a 1 *adj & pron interr (sing)* how much?; *(pl)* how many?; **¿cuántas veces?** how many times?; **¿c. es?** how much is it?

2 *adv* how, how much; **¡cuánta gente hay!** what a lot of people there are!

cuarenta *adj & nm inv* forty; *Fam* **cantarle a algn las c.** to give sb a piece of one's mind

cuarentena *nf Med* quarantine

cuarentón,-ona *adj,nm,f* forty-year-old

cuaresma *nf* Lent

cuartear *vt* to quarter

cuartel *nm Mil* barracks; **c. general** headquarters; *Fig* **no dar c.** to give no quarter

cuartelada *nf*, **cuartelazo** *nm* putsch, military uprising

cuartelillo *nm Mil* post, station

cuarteto *nm* quartet

cuartilla *nf* sheet of paper

cuarto,-a 1 *nm* (**a**) *(habitación)* room; **c. de baño** bathroom; **c. de estar** living room (**b**) *(cuarta parte)* quarter; **c. de hora** quarter of an hour; *Dep* **cuartos de final** quarter finals (**c**) *Fam* **cuartos** *(dinero)* dough, money

2 *adj & nm,f* fourth

cuarzo *nm* quartz

cuate *nmf Méx Fam* pal, *Br* mate, *US* buddy

cuatro 1 *adj & nm inv* four

2 *nm Fam* a few; **cayeron c. gotas** it rained a little bit

cuatrocientos,-as *adj & nm* four hundred

Cuba *n* Cuba

cuba *nf* cask, barrel; *Fam* **como una c.** (as) drunk as a lord

cubalibre *nm* rum/gin and coke

cubano,-a *adj & nm,f* Cuban

cubata *nm Fam* = cubalibre

cubertería *nf* cutlery

cúbico,-a *adj* cubic; *Mat* **raíz cúbica** cube root

cubierta *nf* (**a**) cover (**b**) *(de rueda)* tyre (**c**) *Náut* deck (**d**) *(techo)* roof

cubierto,-a 1 *adj* (**a**) covered; *(piscina)* indoors; *(cielo)* overcast (**b**) *(trabajo, plaza)* filled

2 *nm* (**a**) *(en la mesa)* place setting (**b**) **cubiertos** cutlery

cubil *nm* lair

cubismo *nm* cubism

cubito *nm* little cube; **c. de hielo** ice cube
cubo *nm* (a) bucket; **c. de la basura** rubbish bin (b) *Mat* cube (c) *(de rueda)* hub
cubrecama *nm* bedspread
cubrir *(pp cubierto)* **1** *vt* to cover
   2 cubrirse *vpr (cielo)* to become overcast
cucaracha *nf* cockroach
cuchara *nf* spoon
cucharada *nf* spoonful; **c. rasa/colmada** level/heaped spoonful
cucharilla *nf* teaspoon; **c. de café** coffee spoon
cucharón *nm* ladle
cuchichear *vi* to whisper
cuchicheo *nm* whispering
cuchilla *nf* blade; **c. de afeitar** razor blade
cuchillada *nf,* **cuchillazo** *nm* stab
cuchillo *nm* knife
cuchitril *nm Fam* hovel, hole
cuclillas: en cuclillas *loc adv* **en c.** crouching; **ponerse en c.** to crouch down
cuco,-a **1** *nm* cuckoo
   2 *adj Fam (astuto)* shrewd, crafty
cucurucho *nm* (a) *(para helado)* cornet (b) *(de papel)* paper cone
cuello *nm* (a) neck (b) *(de camisa etc)* collar
cuenca *nf* (a) *Geog* basin (b) *(de los ojos)* socket
cuenco *nm* earthenware bowl
cuenta *nf* (a) *(factura)* bill (b) *Fin (de banco)* account; **c. corriente** current account (c) *(cálculo)* count; **hacer cuentas** to do sums; **c. atrás** countdown (d) *(de collar)* bead (e) *(locuciones)* **caer en la c., darse c.** to realize; **dar c.** to report; **tener en c.** to take into account; **traer c.** to be worthwhile; **más sillas de la c.** too many chairs; **en resumidas cuentas** in short; **pedir cuentas** to ask for an explanation; **trabajar por c. propia** to be self-employed
cuentagotas *nm inv* dropper
cuentakilómetros *nm inv (distancia)* mileometer; *(velocidad)* speedometer
cuento *nm* story; *Lit* short story; **contar un c.** to tell a story; *Fig* **eso no viene a c.** that's beside the point; **c. chino** tall story; **c. de hadas** fairy story
cuerda *nf* (a) *(cordel)* rope; *Fig* **bajo c.** dishonestly; **c. floja** tightrope; **cuerdas vocales** vocal chords (b) *(de instrumento)* string (c) *(del reloj)* spring; **dar c. al reloj** to wind up a watch
cuerdo,-a *adj* sane
cueriza *nf Andes Fam* beating, leathering
cuerno *nm* horn; *(de ciervo)* antler; *Fam* **¡vete al c.!** get lost!; *Fam* **ponerle cuernos a algn** to be unfaithful to sb
cuero *nm* (a) leather; **chaqueta de c.** leather jacket (b) **c. cabelludo** scalp; *Fam* **en cueros (vivos)** (stark) naked
cuerpo *nm* (a) body; **de c. entero** full-length; *Fig* **tomar c.** to take shape (b) *(cadáver)*

corpse; **de c. presente** lying in state (c) *(parte)* section, part (d) *(grupo)* corps, force; **c. de bomberos** fire brigade; **c. diplomático** diplomatic corps
cuervo *nm* raven
cuesta **1** *nf* slope; **c. abajo** downhill; **c. arriba** uphill
   2 *loc adv* **a cuestas** on one's back *o* shoulders
cuestión *nf* (a) *(asunto)* matter, question; **es c. de vida o muerte** it's a matter of life or death; **en c. de unas horas** in just a few hours (b) *(pregunta)* question
cuestionario *nm* questionnaire
cueva *nf* cave
cuezo *indic pres de* **cocer**
cuico,-a *nm,f Méx Fam* cop
cuidado **1** *nm* (a) care; **con c.** carefully; **tener c.** to be careful; **estar al c. de *(cosa)* to be in charge of; *(persona)* to look after; **me trae sin c.** I couldn't care less (b) *Med* **cuidados intensivos** intensive care
   2 *interj* **¡c.!** look out!, watch out!; **¡c. con lo que dices!** watch what you say!; **¡c. con el escalón!** mind the step!
cuidadoso,-a *adj* careful
cuidar **1** *vt* to care for, to look after; **c. de que todo salga bien** to make sure that everything goes all right; **c. los detalles** to pay attention to details
   2 cuidarse *vpr* **cuídate** look after yourself
cuitlacoche *nm CAm, Méx* corn smut, = edible fungus which grows on maize
culata *nf* (a) *(de arma)* butt (b) *Aut* cylinder head
culebra *nf* snake
culebrilla *nf Med* ringworm
culebrón *nm* soap opera
culinario,-a *adj* culinary
culminación *nf* culmination
culminante *adj (punto)* highest; *(momento)* culminating
culminar *vi* to culminate
culo *nm* (a) *Fam (trasero)* backside; *Vulg* **¡vete a tomar por c.!** fuck off! (b) *(de recipiente)* bottom
culpa *nf* (a) blame; **echar la c. a algn** to put the blame on sb; **fue c. mía** it was my fault; **por tu c.** because of you (b) *(culpabilidad)* guilt
culpabilidad *nf* guilt, culpability
culpable **1** *nmf* offender, culprit
   2 *adj* guilty; *Jur* **declararse c.** to plead guilty
culpar *vt* to blame; **c. a algn de un delito** to accuse sb of an offence
cultivado,-a *adj* (a) *Agr* cultivated (b) *(cultura)* cultured, refined
cultivar *vt* (a) to cultivate (b) *Biol* to culture
cultivo *nm* (a) cultivation; *(planta)* crop (b) *Biol* culture
culto,-a **1** *adj* educated; *(palabra)* learned
   2 *nm* cult; *Rel* worship
cultura *nf* culture

cultural adj cultural
culturismo nm body building
culturista nmf body builder
cumbre nf (a) (de montaña) summit, top; **(conferencia) c.** summit conference (b) Fig (culminación) pinnacle
cumple nm Fam birthday
cumpleaños nm inv birthday; **¡feliz c.!** happy birthday!
cumplido,-a 1 adj (a) completed; (plazo) expired; **misión cumplida** mission accomplished (b) (cortés) polite
  2 nm compliment
cumplidor,-a adj reliable, dependable
cumplimiento nm fulfilment; **c. de la ley** observance of the law
cumplir 1 vt (a) to carry out, to fulfil; (deseo) to fulfil; (promesa) to keep; (sentencia) to serve (b) **ayer cumplí veinte años** I was twenty (years old) yesterday
  2 vi (a) (plazo) to expire, to end (b) **c. con el deber** to do one's duty
  3 cumplirse vpr (a) (deseo, sueño) to be fulfilled, to come true (b) (plazo) to expire
cúmulo nm pile, load
cuna nf (a) cot (b) Fig (origen) cradle
cundir vi (a) **me cunde mucho el trabajo** o **el tiempo** I seem to get a lot done (b) (extenderse) to spread; **cundió el pánico** panic spread; **cundió la voz de que ...** rumour had it that ...
cuneta nf (de la carretera) gutter; **quedarse en la c.** to be left behind
cuña nf (a) (pieza) wedge; **c. publicitaria** commercial break (b) Andes, RP Fam (enchufe) **tener c.** to have friends in high places
cuñado,-a nm,f (hombre) brother-in-law; (mujer) sister-in-law
cuño nm **de nuevo c.** newly-coined
cuota nf (a) (de club etc) membership fees, dues (b) (porción) quota, share (c) Méx **carretera de c.** toll road
cupe pt indef de **caber**
cupiera subj imperf de **caber**
cupo nm ceiling; Mil **excedente de c.** exempt from military service
cupón nm coupon, voucher
cúpula nf dome, cupola; (líderes) leadership
cura 1 nm Rel priest
  2 nf Med cure; Fig **no tiene c.** there's no remedy
curación nf cure, treatment
curandero,-a nm,f quack
curar 1 vt (a) (sanar) to cure; (herida) to dress; (enfermedad) to treat (b) (carne, pescado) to cure

  2 vi (sanar) to recover, to get well; (herida) to heal up
  3 curarse vpr to recover, to get well; (herida) to heal up; **c. en salud** to make sure
curcuncho,-a adj Andes Fam hunchbacked
curiosear vi to pry
curiosidad nf curiosity; **tener c. de** to be curious about
curioso,-a 1 adj (a) (indiscreto) curious, inquisitive (b) (extraño) strange, odd; **lo c. es que ...** the strange thing is that ... (c) (limpio) neat, tidy
  2 nm,f (a) (mirón) onlooker (b) (chismoso) nosey-parker, busybody
curita nf Am Br sticking-plaster, US Band-aid®
currante nmf Fam worker
currar, currelar vi Fam to graft, to grind
currículum nm (pl curricula) **c. vitae** curriculum vitae
curro nm Fam job
cursar vt (estudiar) to study; (enviar) to send
cursi adj vulgar
cursillo nm short course; **c. de reciclaje** refresher course
cursivo,-a adj **letra cursiva** italics
curso nm (a) (año académico) year; (clase) class (b) Fig **año/mes en c.** current year/month; **en el c. de** during (c) (de acontecimientos, río) course (d) Fin **moneda de c. legal** legal tender
cursor nm cursor
curtido,-a adj (a) (piel) weatherbeaten; (cuero) tanned (b) Fig (persona) hardened
curtiembre nf Andes, RP tannery
curtir vt (a) (cuero) to tan (b) Fig (avezar) to harden, to toughen
curva nf (a) curve (b) (en carretera) bend; **c. cerrada** sharp bend
curvilíneo,-a adj curvaceous
curvo,-a adj curved
cuscús nm couscous
cúspide nf summit, peak; Fig peak
custodia nf custody
custodiar [43] vt to watch over
cutáneo,-a adj cutaneous, skin; Med **erupción cutánea** rash
cutícula nf cuticle
cutis nm complexion
cuyo,-a pron rel & pos (de persona) whose; (de cosa) of which; **en c. caso** in which case
cv (abr **caballos de vapor**) hp

D, d [de] *nf (la letra)* D, d
D. (*abr* **don**) Mr
Da. (*abr* **doña**) Mrs/Miss
dactilar *adj* **huellas dactilares** fingerprints
dádiva *nf (regalo)* gift, present; *(donativo)* donation
dadivoso,-a *adj* generous
dado¹,-a *adj* (**a**) given; **en un momento d.** at a certain point (**b**) **ser d. a** to be given to (**c**) **d. que** since, given that
dado² *nm* die, dice
daga *nf* dagger
dalia *nf* dahlia
dálmata *nm* Dalmatian (dog)
daltónico,-a *adj* colour-blind
dama *nf* (**a**) *(señora)* lady (**b**) *(en damas)* king (**c**) **damas** *(juego)* Br draughts, US checkers
damasco *nm* (**a**) *(tela)* damask (**b**) *Andes, CAm, Carib, RP (albaricoque)* apricot
damnificado,-a *nm,f* victim, injured person
danés,-esa 1 *adj* Danish
  2 *nm,f (persona)* Dane
  3 *nm* (**a**) *(idioma)* Danish (**b**) **gran d.** *(perro)* Great Dane
Danubio *nm* **el D.** the Danube
danza *nf* dancing; *(baile)* dance
danzar [40] *vt & vi* to dance
dañar *vt (cosa)* to damage; *(persona)* to hurt, to harm
dañino,-a *adj* harmful, damaging (**para** to)
daño *nm (a cosa)* damage; *(a persona) (físico)* hurt; *(perjuicio)* harm; **se hizo d. en la pierna** he hurt his leg; *Jur* **daños y perjuicios** (legal) damages
dar [11] **1** *vt* (**a**) *(dar)* to give; *(recado, recuerdos)* to pass on, to give; *(noticia)* to tell
  (**b**) *(mano de pintura, cera)* to apply, to put on
  (**c**) *(película)* to show, to screen; *(fiesta)* to throw, to give
  (**d**) *(cosecha)* to produce, to yield; *(fruto, flores)* to bear; *(beneficio, interés)* to give, to yield
  (**e**) *(bofetada etc)* to deal; **d. a algn en la cabeza** to hit sb on the head
  (**f**) **dale a la luz** switch the light on; **d. la mano a algn** to shake hands with sb; **d. los buenos días/las buenas noches a algn** to say good morning/good evening to sb; **me da lo mismo, me da igual** it's all the same to me; **¿qué más da?** what difference does it make?
  (**g**) *(hora)* to strike; **ya han dado las nueve** it's gone nine (o'clock)
  (**h**) **d. de comer a** to feed
  (**i**) **d. a conocer** *(noticia)* to release; **d. a entender a algn que ...** to give sb to understand that ...
  (**j**) **d. por** *(considerar)* to assume, to consider; **lo dieron por muerto** he was assumed dead, he was given up for dead; **d. por descontado/sabido** to take for granted, to assume
  2 *vi* (**a**) **me dio un ataque de tos/risa** I had a coughing fit/an attack of the giggles
  (**b**) **d. a** *(ventana, habitación)* to look out onto, to overlook; *(puerta)* to open onto, to lead to
  (**c**) **d. con** *(persona)* to come across; **d. con la solución** to hit upon the solution
  (**d**) **d. de sí** *(ropa)* to stretch, to give
  (**e**) **d. en** to hit; **el sol me daba en los ojos** the sun was (shining) in my eyes
  (**f**) **d. para** to be enough *o* sufficient for; **el presupuesto no da para más** the budget will not stretch any further
  (**g**) **le dio por nadar** he took it into his head to go swimming
  (**h**) **d. que hablar** to set people talking; **el suceso dio que pensar** the incident gave people food for thought
  3 darse *vpr* (**a**) **se dio un caso extraño** something strange happened
  (**b**) *(hallarse)* to be found, to exist
  (**c**) **d. a** to take to; **se dio a la bebida** he took to drink
  (**d**) **d. con** *o* **contra** to bump *o* crash into
  (**e**) **dárselas de** to consider oneself
  (**f**) **d. por satisfecho** to feel satisfied; **d. por vencido** to give in
  (**g**) **se le da bien/mal el francés** she's good/bad at French
dardo *nm* dart
dársena *nf* dock
datar 1 *vt* to date
  2 *vi* **d. de** to date back to *o* from
dátil *nm* date
dato *nm* (**a**) piece of information; **datos personales** personal details (**b**) *Informát* **datos** data
d.C. (*abr* **después de Cristo**) AD
dcha. (*abr* **derecha**) rt.
de *prep*

---

de combines with the article **el** to form the contraction **del** (e.g. **del hombre** of the man).

(**a**) *(pertenencia)* of; **el título de la novela** the title of the novel; **el coche/hermano de Sofía** Sofía's car/brother; **las bicicletas de los niños** the boys' bicycles

(**b**) *(procedencia)* from; **de Madrid a Valencia** from Madrid to Valencia; **soy de Palencia** I'm from o I come from Palencia

(**c**) *(descripción)* **el niño de ojos azules** the boy with blue eyes; **el señor de la chaqueta** the man in the jacket; **el bobo del niño** the silly boy; **un reloj de oro** a gold watch; **un joven de veinte años** a young man of twenty

(**d**) *(contenido)* of; **un saco de patatas** a sack of potatoes

(**e**) **gafas de sol** sunglasses; **goma de borrar** eraser, *Br* rubber

(**f**) *(oficio)* by, as; **es arquitecto de profesión** he's an architect by profession; **trabaja de secretaria** she's working as a secretary

(**g**) *(acerca de)* about; **curso de informática** computer course

(**h**) *(tiempo)* **a las tres de la tarde** at three in the afternoon; **de día** by day; **de noche** at night; **de lunes a jueves** from Monday to Thursday; **de pequeño** as a child; **de año en año** year in year out

(**i**) *(precio)* at; **patatas de 30 pesetas el kilo** potatoes at 30 pesetas a kilo

(**j**) **una avenida de 15 km** an avenue 15 km long; **una botella de litro** a litre bottle

(**k**) *(con superlativo)* in; **el más largo de España** the longest in Spain

(**l**) *(causa)* with, because of; **llorar de alegría** to cry with joy; **morir de hambre** to die of hunger

(**m**) *(condicional)* **de haber llegado antes** if he had arrived before; **de no ser así** if that wasn't o weren't the case; **de ser cierto** if it was o were true

(**n**) **lo mismo de siempre** the usual thing

(**o**) **de cuatro en cuatro** in fours, four at a time

deambular *vi* to saunter, to stroll

debajo *adv* underneath, below; **el mío es el de d.** mine is the one below; **está d. de la mesa** it's under the table; **por d. de lo normal** below normal; **salió por d. del coche** he came out from under the car

debate *nm* debate

debatir **1** *vt* to debate

2 debatirse *vpr* to struggle; **d. entre la vida y la muerte** to fight for one's life

debe *nm Com* debit, debit side

deber[1] *nm* (**a**) *(deuda)* duty; **cumplir con su d.** to do one's duty (**b**) *Educ* **deberes** homework

deber[2] **1** *vt (dinero, explicación)* to owe

2 *vi* (**a**) must, to have to; **debe (de) comer** he must eat; **debe (de) irse ahora** she has to leave now; **la factura debe pagarse mañana** the bill must be paid tomorrow; **el tren debe llegar a las dos** the train is expected to arrive at two

(**b**) *(consejo)* **deberías visitar a tus padres**

you ought to visit your parents; **debería haber ido ayer** I should have gone yesterday; **no debiste hacerlo** you shouldn't have done it

(**c**) *(suposición)* **deben de estar fuera** they must be out

3 deberse *vpr* **d. a** to be due to; **esto se debe a la falta de agua** this is due to lack of water

debidamente *adv* duly, properly

debido,-a *adj* (**a**) due; **a su d. tiempo** in due course; **con el d. respeto** with due respect (**b**) *(adecuado)* proper; **más de lo d.** too much; **tomaron las debidas precauciones** they took the proper precautions; **como es d.** properly (**c**) **d. a** because of, due to; **d. a que** because of the fact that

débil *adj* weak; *(luz)* dim; **punto d.** weak spot

debilidad *nf* weakness; *Fig* **tener d. por** *(persona)* to have a soft spot for; *(cosa)* to have a weakness for

debilitamiento *nm* weakening

debilitar **1** *vt* to weaken, to debilitate

2 debilitarse *vpr* to weaken, to grow weak

débito *nm* (**a**) *(deuda)* debt (**b**) *(debe)* debit

debut *nm* début, debut

debutar *vi* to make one's début o debut

década *nf* decade; **en la d. de los noventa** during the nineties

decadencia *nf* decadence

decadente *adj & nmf* decadent

decaer [39] *vi* to deteriorate

decaído,-a *adj* down

decaimiento *nm* (**a**) *(debilidad)* weakness (**b**) *(desaliento)* low spirits

decano,-a *nm,f Univ* dean

decantarse *vpr* to lean towards; **d. por** to come down on the side of

decapitar *vt* to behead, to decapitate

decena *nf* (about) ten; **una d. de veces** (about) ten times; **por decenas** in tens

decencia *nf* (**a**) *(decoro)* decency (**b**) *(honradez)* honesty

decenio *nm* decade

decente *adj* decent; *(decoroso)* modest

decepción *nf* disappointment

🖋 Observa que la palabra inglesa **deception** es un falso amigo y no es la traducción de la palabra española **decepción**. En inglés, **deception** significa "engaño".

decepcionante *adj* disappointing

decepcionar *vt* to disappoint

decididamente *adv* (**a**) *(resueltamente)* resolutely (**b**) *(definitivamente)* definitely

decidido,-a *adj* determined, resolute

decidir **1** *vt & vi* to decide

2 decidirse *vpr* to make up one's mind; **d. a hacer algo** to make up one's mind to do sth; **d. por algo** to decide on sth

décima *nf* tenth

decimal *adj & nm* decimal; **el sistema métrico d.** the decimal system

décimo,-a 1 *adj & nm,f* tenth

  2 nm (**a**) (*parte*) tenth (**b**) (*billete de lotería*) tenth part of a lottery ticket

decir¹ *nm* saying

decir² [12] (*pp* **dicho**) **1** *vt* (**a**) to say; **dice que no quiere venir** he says he doesn't want to come

  (**b**) **d. una mentira/la verdad** to tell a lie/the truth

  (**c**) *Tel* **dígame** hello

  (**d**) **¿qué me dices del nuevo jefe?** what do you think of the new boss?

  (**e**) (*mostrar*) to tell, to show; **su cara dice que está mintiendo** you can tell from his face that he's lying

  (**f**) (*sugerir*) to mean; **esta película no me dice nada** this film doesn't appeal to me; **¿qué te dice el cuadro?** what does the picture mean to you?

  (**g**) **querer d.** to mean

  (**h**) (*locuciones*) **es d.** that is (to say); **por así decirlo** as it were, so to speak; **digamos** let's say; **digo yo** in my opinion; **el qué dirán** what people say; **ni que d. tiene** needless to say; **¡no me digas!** really!; **¡y que lo digas!** you bet!

  2 decirse *vpr* **¿cómo se dice "mesa" en inglés?** how do you say "mesa" in English?; **se dice que ...** they say that ...; **sé lo que me digo** I know what I am saying

decisión *nf* (**a**) decision; **tomar una d.** to take *o* make a decision (**b**) (*resolución*) determination; **con d.** decisively

decisivo,-a *adj* decisive

decisorio,-a *adj* decision-making

declamar *vt & vi* to declaim, to recite

declaración *nf* (**a**) declaration; **d. de (la) renta** tax declaration *o* return (**b**) (*afirmación*) statement; **hacer declaraciones** to comment (**c**) *Jur* **prestar d.** to give evidence

declarante *nmf Jur* witness

declarar 1 *vt* (**a**) to declare; **d. la guerra a** to declare war on (**b**) (*afirmar*) to state (**c**) *Jur* **d. culpable/inocente a algn** to find sb guilty/not guilty

  2 *vi* (**a**) to declare (**b**) *Jur* to testify

  3 declararse *vpr* (**a**) **d. a favor/en contra de** to declare oneself in favour of/against; **d. en huelga** to go on strike; **d. a algn** to declare one's love for sb (**b**) (*guerra, incendio*) to start, to break out (**c**) *Jur* **d. culpable** to plead guilty

declinar *vt & vi* to decline

declive *nm* (**a**) (*del terreno*) incline, slope (**b**) (*de imperio etc*) decline

decolaje *nm Am* take-off

decolar *vi Am* to take off

decolorante *nm* bleaching agent

decolorar 1 *vt* to fade; (*pelo*) to bleach

  2 decolorarse *vpr* to fade

decomisar *vt* to confiscate, to seize

decoración *nf* decoration

decorado *nm* scenery, set

decorador,-a *nm,f* (**a**) decorator (**b**) *Teatro* set designer

decorar *vt* to decorate

decorativo,-a *adj* decorative

decoro *nm* (**a**) (*respeto*) dignity, decorum (**b**) (*pudor*) modesty, decency

decoroso,-a *adj* (**a**) (*correcto*) seemly, decorous (**b**) (*decente*) decent, modest

decrecer [33] *vi* to decrease, to diminish

decrépito,-a *adj* decrepit

decretar *vt* to decree

decreto *nm* decree; **d.-ley** decree

dedal *nm* thimble

dedicación *nf* dedication

dedicar [44] **1** *vt* to dedicate; (*tiempo, esfuerzos*) to devote (**a** to)

  2 dedicarse *vpr* **¿a qué se dedica Vd.?** what do you do for a living?; **los fines de semana ella se dedica a pescar** at weekends she spends her time fishing

dedicatoria *nf* dedication

dedillo *nm* **saber algo al d.** to have sth at one's fingertips, to know sth very well

dedo *nm* (*de la mano*) finger; (*del pie*) toe; **d. anular/corazón/índice/meñique** ring/middle/index/little finger; **d. pulgar, d. gordo** thumb; *RP* **hacer d.** to hitchhike; *Fig* **elegir a algn a d.** to hand-pick sb

deducción *nf* deduction

deducible *adj Com* deductible

deducir [10] **1** *vt* (**a**) to deduce, to infer (**b**) *Com* to deduct

  2 deducirse *vpr* **de aquí se deduce que ...** from this it follows that ...

deductivo,-a *adj* deductive

defecar [44] *vi* to defecate

defecto *nm* defect, fault; **d. físico** physical defect

defectuoso,-a *adj* defective, faulty

defender [3] **1** *vt* to defend (**de** from); **d. del frío/viento** to shelter from the cold/wind

  2 defenderse *vpr* (**a**) to defend oneself (**b**) *Fam* **se defiende en francés** he can get by in French

defendido,-a *adj Jur* defendant

defensa 1 *nf* defence; **en d. propia, en legítima d.** in self-defence; **salir en d. de algn** to come out in defence of sb

  2 nm *Dep* defender, back

defensiva *nf* defensive; **estar/ponerse a la d.** to be/go on the defensive

defensivo,-a *adj* defensive

defensor,-a *nm,f* defender; **abogado d.** counsel for the defence; **el defensor del pueblo** the ombudsman

deferencia *nf* deference; **en** *o* **por d. a** out of deference for

deficiencia *nf* deficiency, shortcoming; **d. mental** mental deficiency; **d. renal** kidney failure

deficiente 1 *adj* deficient

2 *nmf* **d. mental** mentally retarded person

3 *nm Educ* fail

déficit *nm (pl* **déficits)** deficit; *(carencia)* shortage

deficitario,-a *adj* showing a deficit

definición *nf* definition; **por d.** by definition

definido,-a *adj* clear; *Ling* definite

definir *vt* to define

definitivamente *adv* (a) *(para siempre)* for good, once and for all (b) *(con toda seguridad)* definitely

definitivo,-a *adj* definitive; **en definitiva** in short

deflación *nf Econ* deflation

deflacionista *adj Econ* deflationary

deformación *nf* deformation

deformar 1 *vt* to deform, to put out of shape; *(cara)* to disfigure; *Fig (la verdad, una imagen)* to distort

2 deformarse *vpr* to go out of shape, to become distorted

deforme *adj* deformed; *(objeto)* misshapen

defraudación *nf* fraud; **d. fiscal** tax evasion

defraudar *vt* (a) *(decepcionar)* to disappoint (b) *(al fisco)* to defraud, to cheat; **d. a Hacienda** to evade taxes

defunción *nf Fml* decease, demise

degeneración *nf* degeneration

degenerado,-a *adj & nm,f* degenerate

degenerar *vi* to degenerate

degollar [2] *vt* to behead

degradación *nf* degradation

degradante *adj* degrading

degradar *vt* to degrade

degustación *nf* tasting

degustar *vt* to taste, to sample

dehesa *nf* pasture, meadow

deificar [44] *vt* to deify

dejadez *nf* slovenliness

dejado,-a *adj* (a) *(descuidado)* untidy, slovenly (b) *(negligente)* negligent, careless (c) *Fam* **d. de la mano de Dios** godforsaken

dejar 1 *vt* (a) to leave; **déjame en paz** leave me alone; **d. dicho** to leave word *o* a message (b) *(prestar)* to lend

(c) *(abandonar)* to give up; **d. algo por imposible** to give sth up; **dejé el tabaco y la bebida** I gave up smoking and drinking

(d) *(permitir)* to let, to allow; **d. caer** to drop; **d. entrar/salir** to let in/out

(e) *(omitir)* to leave out, to omit

(f) *(ganancias)* to produce

(g) *(+ adj)* to make; **d. triste** to make sad; **d. preocupado/sorprendido** to worry/surprise (h) *(posponer)* **dejaron el viaje para el verano** they put the trip off until the summer

2 *v aux* **d. de** + *inf* to stop, to give up; **dejó de fumar el año pasado** he gave up smoking last year; **no deja de llamarme** she's always phoning me up

3 dejarse *vpr* (a) **me he dejado las llaves dentro** I've left the keys inside (b) *(locucio-*

nes) **d. barba** to grow a beard; **d. caer** to flop down; **d. llevar por** to be influenced by

del *(contracción de* **de** + **el)** *ver* **de**

delantal *nm* apron

delante *adv* (a) in front; **la entrada de d.** the front entrance (b) **d. de** in front of; *(en serie)* ahead of (c) **por d.** in front; **se lo lleva todo por d.** he destroys everything in his path; **tiene toda la vida por d.** he has his whole life ahead of him

delantera *nf* (a) *(ventaja)* lead; **tomar la d.** take the lead (b) *Ftb* forward line, forwards

delantero,-a 1 *adj* front

2 *nm Ftb* forward; **d. centro** centre forward

delatar *vt* (a) to inform against (b) *Fig* to give away

delator,-a *nm,f* informer

delegación *nf* (a) *(acto, delegados)* delegation (b) *(oficina)* local office, branch; **D. de Hacienda** Tax Office (c) *Méx (distrito municipal)* district; *(comisaría)* police station

delegado,-a *nm,f* (a) delegate; **d. de Hacienda** chief tax inspector (b) *Com* representative

delegar [42] *vt* to delegate (**en** to)

deleitar 1 *vt* to delight

2 deleitarse *vpr* to delight in, to take delight in

deleite *nm* delight

deletrear *vt* to spell (out)

deleznable *adj* brittle

delfín *nm* dolphin

delgadez *nf* slimness

delgado,-a *adj* slim; *(capa)* fine

deliberación *nf* deliberation

deliberado,-a *adj* deliberate

deliberar *vi* to deliberate (on), to consider

delicadeza *nf* (a) *(finura)* delicacy, daintiness (b) *(tacto)* tactfulness; **falta de d.** tactlessness

delicado,-a *adj* (a) delicate (b) *(exigente)* fussy, hard to please (c) *(sensible)* hypersensitive

delicia *nf* delight; **hacer las delicias de algn** to delight sb

delicioso,-a *adj (comida)* delicious; *(agradable)* delightful

delictivo,-a *adj* criminal, punishable

delimitar *vt* to delimit

delincuencia *nf* delinquency

delincuente *adj & nmf* delinquent; **d. juvenil** juvenile delinquent

delineante *nmf (hombre)* draughtsman; *(mujer)* draughtswoman

delinear *vt* to delineate, to outline

delinquir [48] *vi* to break the law, to commit an offence

delirante *adj* delirious

delirar *vi* to be delirious

delirio *nm* delirium; **delirios de grandeza** delusions of grandeur

delito *nm* crime, offence

delta *nm* delta; **ala d.** hang-glider
demacrado,-a *adj* emaciated
demagogia *nf* demagogy
demagogo,-a *nm,f* demagogue
demanda *nf* (**a**) *Jur* lawsuit (**b**) *Com* demand
demandado,-a 1 *nm,f* defendant
  2 *adj* in demand
demandante *nmf* claimant
demandar *vt* to sue
demarcar [44] *vt* to demarcate
demás 1 *adj* **los/las d.** the rest of; **la d. gente** the rest of the people
  2 *pron* **lo/los/las d.** the rest; **por lo d.** otherwise, apart from that; **y d.** etcetera
demasía *nf* **en d.** excessively
demasiado,-a 1 *adj* *(singular)* too much; *(plural)* too many; **hay demasiada comida** there is too much food; **quieres demasiadas cosas** you want too many things
  2 *adv* too (much); **es d. grande/caro** it is too big/dear; **fumas/trabajas d.** you smoke/work too much
demencia *nf* dementia, insanity
demente 1 *adj* insane, mad
  2 *nmf* mental patient
democracia *nf* democracy
demócrata 1 *adj* democratic
  2 *nmf* democrat
democrático,-a *adj* democratic
democratizar [40] *vt* to democratize
demografía *nf* demography
demográfico,-a *adj* demographic; **crecimiento d.** population growth
demoledor,-a *adj Fig* devastating
demoler [4] *vt* to demolish
demonio *nm* devil, demon; *Fam* **¿cómo/dónde de demonios ...?** how/where the hell ...?; *Fam* **¡demonio(s)!** hell!, damn!; *Fam* **¡d. de niño!** you little devil!
demora *nf* delay
demorar 1 *vt* (**a**) *(retrasar)* to delay, to hold up (**b**) *(tardar)* **demoraron tres días en pintar la casa** it took them three days to paint the house
  2 *vi Am (tardar)* **¡no demores!** don't be late!; **demorar en hacer algo** *(llevar tiempo)* to take one's time doing sth; *(retrasarse)* to take too long doing sth; **no demoraron en venir** they came immediately
  3 **demorarse** *vpr* (**a**) *(retrasarse)* to be delayed, to be held up (**b**) *(detenerse)* to dally
demostrable *adj* demonstrable
demostración *nf* demonstration; **una d. de fuerza/afecto** a show of strength
demostrar [2] *vt* (**a**) *(mostrar)* to show, to demonstrate (**b**) *(evidenciar)* to prove
demudado,-a *adj* pale
denegar [1] *vt* to refuse; *Jur* **d. una demanda** to dismiss a claim
denigrante *adj* humiliating
denigrar *vt* to humiliate
denominación *nf* denomination; **d. de origen** *(vinos)* = guarantee of region of origin

denominado,-a *adj* so-called
denominador *nm* denominator
denominar *vt* to name, to designate
denotar *vt* to denote
densidad *nf* density; **d. de población** population density
denso,-a *adj* dense
dentadura *nf* teeth, set of teeth; **d. postiza** false teeth, dentures
dental *adj* dental
dentera *nf* **me da d.** it sets my teeth on edge
dentífrico,-a 1 *adj* **pasta/crema dentífrica** toothpaste
  2 *nm* toothpaste
dentista *nmf* dentist
dentro *adv* (**a**) *(en el interior)* inside; **aquí d.** in here; **por d.** (on the) inside; **por d. está triste** deep down (inside) he feels sad (**b**) **d. de** *(lugar)* inside (**c**) **d. de poco** shortly, soon; **d. de un mes** in a month's time; **d. de lo que cabe** all things considered
denuncia *nf* (**a**) *Jur* report (**b**) *(crítica)* denunciation
denunciar [43] *vt* (**a**) *(delito)* to report (**a** to) (**b**) *(criticar)* to denounce
deparar *vt* to give; **no sabemos qué nos depara el destino** we don't know what fate has in store for us
departamento *nm* (**a**) department (**b**) *Ferroc* compartment (**c**) *(territorial)* province, district (**d**) *Arg (piso) Br* flat, *US* apartment
dependencia *nf* (**a**) dependence (**de** on) (**b**) **dependencias** premises
depender *vi* to depend (**de** on); *(económicamente)* to be dependent (**de** on)
dependienta *nf* shop assistant
dependiente 1 *adj* dependent (**de** on)
  2 *nm* shop assistant
depilación *nf* depilation; **d. a la cera** waxing
depilar *vt* to remove the hair from; *(cejas)* to pluck
depilatorio,-a *adj & nm* depilatory; **crema depilatoria** hair-remover, hair-removing cream
deplorable *adj* deplorable
deplorar *vt* to deplore
deponer [19] *(pp depuesto) vt* (**a**) *(destituir)* to remove from office; *(líder)* to depose (**b**) *(actitud)* to abandon
deportado,-a *nm,f* deportee, deported person
deportar *vt* to deport
deporte *nm* sport; **hacer d.** to practise sports; **d. de aventura** adventure sport
deportista 1 *nmf (hombre)* sportsman; *(mujer)* sportswoman
  2 *adj* sporty
deportividad *nf* sportsmanship
deportivo,-a 1 *adj* sports; **club/chaqueta d.** sports club/jacket
  2 *nm Aut* sports car

deposición *nf* removal from office; *(de un líder)* deposition

depositar 1 *vt* (**a**) *Fin* to deposit (**b**) *(colocar)* to place, to put
  2 **depositarse** *vpr* to settle

depósito *nm* (**a**) *Fin* deposit; **en d.** on deposit (**b**) *(de agua, gasolina)* tank (**c**) **d. de basuras** rubbish tip *o* dump; **d. de cadáveres** mortuary, morgue

depravación *nf* depravity

depravar *vt* to deprave

depre *nf Fam* downer, depression

depreciación *nf* depreciation

depreciar [43] 1 *vt* to reduce the value of
  2 **depreciarse** *vpr* to depreciate, to lose value

depredador,-a 1 *adj* predatory
  2 *nm,f* predator

depresión *nf* depression; **d. nerviosa** nervous breakdown

depresivo,-a *adj* depressive

deprimente *adj* depressing

deprimido,-a *adj* depressed

deprimir 1 *vt* to depress
  2 **deprimirse** *vpr* to get depressed

deprisa *adv* quickly

depuesto,-a *pp de* **deponer**

depuración *nf* (**a**) *(del agua)* purification (**b**) *(purga)* purge

depurador,-a *adj* **planta depuradora** purification plant

depuradora *nf* purifier

depurar *vt* (**a**) *(agua)* to purify (**b**) *(partido)* to purge (**c**) *(estilo)* to refine

derecha *nf* (**a**) *(mano)* right hand (**b**) *(lugar)* right, right-hand side; **a la d.** to *o* on the right, on the right-hand side (**c**) *Pol* **la d.** the right; **de derechas** right-wing

derechista *nmf* right-winger

derecho,-a 1 *adj* (**a**) *(de la derecha)* right (**b**) *(recto)* upright, straight
  2 *nm* (**a**) *(privilegio)* right; **derechos civiles/ humanos** civil/human rights; **tener d. a** to be entitled to, to have the right to; **estar en su d.** to be within one's rights; **no hay d.** it's not fair; **d. de admisión** right to refuse admission (**b**) *Jur* law; **d. penal/político** criminal/constitutional law (**c**) *Com* **derechos** duties; **derechos de autor** royalties; **derechos de matrícula** enrolment fees
  3 *adv* **siga todo d.** go straight ahead

deriva *nf* drift; **ir a la d.** to drift

derivado *nm* *(producto)* derivative, by-product

derivar 1 *vt* to divert; *(conversación)* to steer
  2 *vi* (**a**) to drift (**b**) **d. de** to derive from
  3 **derivarse** *vpr* (**a**) **d. de** *(proceder)* to result *o* stem from (**b**) **d. de** *Ling* to be derived from

dermatitis *nf inv* dermatitis

dermatólogo,-a *nm,f* dermatologist

derogar [42] *vt* to repeal

derramamiento *nm* spilling; **d. de sangre** bloodshed

derramar 1 *vt* to spill; *(lágrimas)* to shed
  2 **derramarse** *vpr* to spill

derrame *nm Med* discharge; **d. cerebral** brain haemorrhage

derrapar *vi* to skid

derredor *nm* **en d. de** round, around

derretir [6] *vt,* **derretirse** *vpr* to melt; *(hielo, nieve)* to thaw

derribar *vt* (**a**) *(edificio)* to pull down, to knock down (**b**) *(avión)* to shoot down (**c**) *(gobierno)* to bring down

derrocar [44] *vt* to bring down; *(violentamente)* to overthrow

derrochador,-a 1 *adj* wasteful
  2 *nm,f* wasteful person, squanderer

derrochar *vt* to waste, to squander

derroche *nm* (**a**) *(de dinero, energía)* waste, squandering (**b**) *(abundancia)* profusion, abundance

derrota *nf* (**a**) defeat (**b**) *Náut* (ship's) course

derrotar *vt* to defeat, to beat

derrotero *nm* (**a**) *Fig* path, course *o* plan of action (**b**) *Náut* sailing directions

derrotista *adj & nmf* defeatist

derruido,-a *adj* in ruins

derruir [37] *vt* to demolish

derrumbar 1 *vt* *(edificio)* to knock down, to pull down
  2 **derrumbarse** *vpr* to collapse, to fall down; *(techo)* to fall in, to cave in

desabastecido,-a *adj* **d. de** out of

desaborido,-a 1 *adj* (**a**) *(comida)* tasteless (**b**) *Fig (persona)* dull
  2 *nm,f Fam* dull person

desabrido,-a *adj* (**a**) *(comida)* tasteless (**b**) *(tiempo)* unpleasant (**c**) *Fig (tono)* harsh; *(persona)* moody, irritable

desabrigado,-a *adj* **ir/estar d.** to be lightly dressed

desabrochar 1 *vt* to undo
  2 **desabrocharse** *vpr* (**a**) **desabróchate la camisa** undo your shirt (**b**) *(prenda)* to come undone

desacatar *vt* to disobey

desacato *nm* lack of respect, disrespect (**a** for); *Jur* **d. al tribunal** contempt of court

desacertado,-a *adj* unwise

desacierto *nm* mistake, error

desaconsejar *vt* to advise against

desacorde *adj* **estar d. con** to be in disagreement with

desacreditar *vt* (**a**) *(desprestigiar)* to discredit, to bring into discredit (**b**) *(criticar)* to disparage

desactivador,-a *nm,f* bomb disposal expert

desactivar *vt* *(bomba)* to defuse

desacuerdo *nm* disagreement

desafiante *adj* defiant

desafiar [29] *vt* to challenge

desafinado,-a *adj* out of tune

desafinar 1 *vi* to sing out of tune; *(instrumento)* to play out of tune
2 *vt* to put out of tune
3 desafinarse *upr* to go out of tune
desafío *nm* challenge
desaforado,-a *adj* wild
desafortunado,-a *adj* unlucky, unfortunate
desagradable *adj* unpleasant, disagreeable
desagradar *vi* to displease
desagradecido,-a 1 *adj* ungrateful
2 *nm,f* ungrateful person
desagrado *nm* displeasure
desagraviar [43] *vt* to make amends for
desaguar [45] *vt* to drain
desagüe *nm (vaciado)* drain; *(cañería)* waste pipe, drainpipe
desaguisado *nm* mess
desahogado,-a *adj* (**a**) *(acomodado)* well-off, well-to-do (**b**) *(espacioso)* spacious, roomy
desahogarse [42] *upr* to let off steam; **se desahogó de su depresión** he got his depression out of his system
desahogo *nm* (**a**) *(alivio)* relief (**b**) **vivir con d.** to live comfortably
desahuciado,-a *adj* (**a**) *(enfermo)* hopeless (**b**) *(inquilino)* evicted
desahuciar [43] *vt* (**a**) *(desalojar)* to evict (**b**) *(enfermo)* to deprive of all hope
desahucio *nm* eviction
desairado,-a *adj* (**a**) *(humillado)* spurned (**b**) *(sin gracia)* awkward
desairar *vt* to slight, to snub
desaire *nm* slight, rebuff
desajustar 1 *vt* to upset
2 desajustarse *upr (piezas)* to come apart
desajuste *nm* upset; **d. económico** economic imbalance; **un d. de horarios** clashing timetables
desalentador,-a *adj* discouraging, disheartening
desalentar [1] **1** *vt* to discourage, to dishearten
2 desalentarse *upr* to get discouraged, to lose heart
desaliento *nm* discouragement
desaliñado,-a *adj* scruffy, untidy
desaliño *nm* scruffiness, untidiness
desalmado,-a *adj* cruel, heartless
desalojamiento *nm (de inquilino)* eviction; *(de público)* removal; *(de lugar)* evacuation
desalojar *vt* (**a**) *(inquilino)* to evict; *(público)* to move on; *(lugar)* to evacuate (**b**) *(abandonar)* to move out of, to abandon
desalojo *nm* = **desalojamiento**
desamor *nm* lack of affection
desamortizar [40] *vt* to alienate, to disentail
desamparado,-a 1 *adj (persona)* helpless, unprotected; *(lugar)* abandoned, forsaken
2 *nm,f* helpless o abandoned person
desamparar *vt* (**a**) to abandon, to desert (**b**) *Jur* to renounce, to relinquish

desamparo *nm* helplessness
desamueblado,-a *adj* unfurnished
desandar [8] *vt* **d. lo andado** to retrace one's steps
desangrarse *upr* to lose (a lot of) blood
desanimado,-a *adj* (**a**) *(persona)* downhearted, dejected (**b**) *(fiesta etc)* dull, lifeless
desanimar 1 *vt* to discourage, to dishearten
2 desanimarse *upr* to lose heart, to get discouraged
desánimo *nm* discouragement, dejection
desapacible *adj* unpleasant
desaparecer [33] *vi* to disappear
desaparecido,-a 1 *adj* missing
2 *nm,f* missing person
desaparición *nf* disappearance
desapego *nm* indifference, lack of affection
desapercibido,-a *adj* (**a**) *(inadvertido)* unnoticed; **pasar d.** to go unnoticed (**b**) *(desprevenido)* unprepared
desaprensivo,-a 1 *adj* unscrupulous
2 *nm,f* unscrupulous person
desaprobar [2] *vt* (**a**) *(no aprobar)* to disapprove of (**b**) *(rechazar)* to reject
desaprovechar *vt (dinero, tiempo)* to waste; **d. una ocasión** to fail to make the most of an opportunity
desarmable *adj* that can be taken to pieces
desarmador *nm Méx* screwdriver
desarmar *vt* (**a**) *(desmontar)* to dismantle, to take to pieces (**b**) *Mil* to disarm
desarme *nm* disarmament; **d. nuclear** nuclear disarmament
desarraigado,-a *adj* rootless, without roots
desarraigar [42] *vt* to uproot
desarraigo *nm* rootlessness
desarreglado,-a *adj* (**a**) *(lugar)* untidy (**b**) *(persona)* untidy, slovenly
desarreglar *vt* (**a**) *(desordenar)* to make untidy, to mess up (**b**) *(planes etc)* to spoil, to upset
desarreglo *nm* difference of opinion
desarrollado,-a *adj* developed; **país d.** developed country
desarrollar 1 *vt* to develop
2 desarrollarse *upr* (**a**) *(persona, enfermedad)* to develop (**b**) *(tener lugar)* to take place
desarrollo *nm* development; **países en vías de d.** developing countries
desarticular *vt* to dismantle; **d. un complot** to foil a plot
desaseado,-a *adj* unkempt
desasir [46] **1** *vt* to release
2 desasirse *upr* to get loose; **d. de** to free o rid oneself of
desasosegar [1] *vt* to make restless o uneasy
desasosiego *nm* restlessness, uneasiness
desastrado,-a 1 *adj* untidy, scruffy
2 *nm,f* scruffy person
desastre *nm* disaster; **eres un d.** you're just hopeless
desastroso,-a *adj* disastrous

desatar 1 *vt* to untie, to undo; *(provocar)* to unleash
  2 desatarse *vpr* (**a**) *(zapato, cordón)* to come undone (**b**) *(tormenta)* to break; *(pasión)* to run wild
desatascar [44] *vt* to unblock, to clear
desatender [3] *vt* to neglect, not to pay attention to
desatento,-a *adj* inattentive; *(descortés)* impolite, discourteous
desatinado,-a *adj* unwise
desatino *nm* blunder
desatornillar *vt* to unscrew
desatrancar [44] *vt* to unblock; *(puerta)* to unbolt
desautorizar [40] *vt* (**a**) to disallow (**b**) *(huelga etc)* to ban, to forbid (**c**) *(desmentir)* to deny
desavenencia *nf* disagreement
desaventajado,-a *adj* at a disadvantage
desayunar 1 *vi* to have breakfast; *Fml* to breakfast
  2 *vt* to have for breakfast
desayuno *nm* breakfast
desazón *nf* unease
desazonar *vt* to cause unease to, to worry
desbancar [44] *vt* to oust
desbandada *nf* scattering; **hubo una d. general** everyone scattered
desbandarse *vpr* to scatter, to disperse
desbarajuste *nm* confusion, disorder
desbaratar *vt* to ruin, to wreck; *(jersey)* to unravel
desbloquear *vt* (**a**) *(negociaciones)* to get going again (**b**) *(créditos, precios)* to unfreeze
desbocado,-a *adj (caballo)* runaway
desbocarse *vpr (caballo)* to bolt, to run away
desbolado,-a *RP Fam* **1** *adj* messy, untidy
  2 *nm,f* untidy person
desbolarse *vpr RP Fam* to undress, to strip
desbole *nm RP Fam* mess, chaos
desbordante *adj* overflowing, bursting
desbordar 1 *vt* to overflow; *Fig* to overwhelm
  2 *vi* to overflow (**de** with)
  2 desbordarse *vpr* to overflow, to flood
descabalgar [42] *vi* to dismount
descabellado,-a *adj* crazy, wild
descafeinado,-a *adj* (**a**) *(café)* decaffeinated (**b**) *Fig* watered-down, diluted
descalabrar *vt* (**a**) to wound in the head (**b**) *Fig* to damage, to harm
descalabro *nm* setback, misfortune
descalificar [44] *vt* to disqualify
descalzarse [40] *vpr* to take one's shoes off
descalzo,-a *adj* barefoot
descambiar [43] *vt* to exchange
descaminado,-a *adj Fig* **ir d.** to be on the wrong track
descampado *nm* waste ground
descansado,-a *adj* (**a**) *(persona)* rested (**b**) *(vida, trabajo)* restful

descansar *vi* (**a**) to rest, to have a rest; *(corto tiempo)* to take a break (**b**) *Euf* **que en paz descanse** may he/she rest in peace
descansillo *nm* landing
descanso *nm* (**a**) rest, break; **un día de d.** a day off (**b**) *Cin & Teatro* interval; *Dep* half-time, interval (**c**) *(alivio)* relief (**d**) *(rellano)* landing
descapotable *adj & nm* convertible
descarado,-a 1 *adj* (**a**) *(insolente)* cheeky, insolent; *(desvergonzado)* shameless (**b**) *Fam* **d. que sí/no** *(por supuesto)* of course/ course not
  2 *nm,f* cheeky person
descarga *nf* (**a**) unloading (**b**) *Elec & Mil* discharge
descargar [42] **1** *vt* (**a**) to unload (**b**) *Elec* to discharge (**c**) *(disparar)* to fire; *(golpe)* to deal
  2 *vi (tormenta)* to burst
  3 descargarse *vpr (batería)* to go flat
descargo *nm Jur* discharge; **testigo de d.** witness for the defence
descarnado,-a *adj* crude
descaro *nm* cheek, nerve; **¡qué d.!** what a cheek!
descarriar [29] **1** *vt* to lead astray, to put on the wrong road
  2 descarriarse *vpr* to go astray, to lose one's way
descarrilar *vi* to go off the rails, to be derailed
descartar 1 *vt* to rule out
  2 descartarse *vpr Naipes* to discard cards; **me descarté de un cinco** I got rid of a five
descascarillarse *vpr* to chip, to peel
descendencia *nf* descendants; **morir sin d.** to die without issue
descendente *adj* descending, downward
descender [3] **1** *vi* (**a**) *(temperatura, nivel)* to fall, to drop (**b**) **d. de** to descend from
  2 *vt* to lower
descendiente *nmf* descendant
descenso *nm* (**a**) descent; *(de temperatura)* fall, drop (**b**) *Dep* relegation
descentrado,-a *adj* off-centre
descentralizar [40] *vt* to decentralize
descifrar *vt* to decipher; *(mensaje)* to decode; *(misterio)* to solve; *(motivos, causas)* to figure out
descojonarse *vpr muy Fam (reírse)* to piss oneself laughing
descolgar [2] **1** *vt* *(el teléfono)* to pick up; *(cuadro, cortinas)* to take down
  2 descolgarse *vpr* to let oneself down, to slide down
descolorido,-a *adj* faded
descombros *nmpl* rubble, debris
descompasado,-a *adj* inconsistent
descomponer [19] *(pp* **descompuesto)** **1** *vt* (**a**) to break down (**b**) *(corromper)* to rot, to decompose
  2 descomponerse *vpr* (**a**) *(corromperse)* to

rot, to decompose (**b**) (*ponerse nervioso*) to lose one's cool (**c**) *Am* (*el tiempo*) to turn nasty

descomposición *nf* (**a**) (*de carne*) decomposition, rotting; (*de país*) disintegration (**b**) *Quím* breakdown

descompostura *nf* (**a**) *Am* (*malestar*) unpleasant turn (**b**) *Méx, RP* (*avería*) breakdown

descompuesto,-a *adj* (**a**) (*podrido*) rotten, decomposed (**b**) (*furioso*) furious

descompuse *pt indef de* **descomponer**

descomunal *adj* huge, massive

desconcertante *adj* disconcerting

desconcertar [1] **1** *vt* to disconcert
   2 desconcertarse *upr* to be bewildered, to be puzzled

desconchón *nm* bare patch

desconcierto *nm* chaos, confusion

desconectar *vt* to disconnect

desconexión *nf* disconnection

desconfiado,-a *adj* distrustful, wary

desconfianza *nf* distrust, mistrust

desconfiar [29] *vi* **d. (de)** to distrust, to mistrust

descongelar *vt* (*nevera*) to defrost; (*créditos*) to unfreeze

descongestionar *vt* to clear

desconocer [34] *vt* not to know, to be unaware of

desconocido,-a **1** *adj* unknown; (*irreconocible*) unrecognizable
   2 *nm* **lo d.** the unknown
   3 *nm,f* stranger

desconsiderado,-a **1** *adj* inconsiderate, thoughtless
   2 *nm,f* inconsiderate *o* thoughtless person

desconsolado,-a *adj* disconsolate, griefstricken

desconsuelo *nm* grief, sorrow

descontado,-a *adj Fam* **dar por d.** to take for granted; **por d.** needless to say, of course

descontar [2] *vt* (**a**) to deduct (**b**) *Dep* (*tiempo*) to add on

descontento,-a 1 *adj* unhappy
   2 *nm* dissatisfaction

descontrol *nm Fam* lack of control; **había un d. total** it was absolute chaos

descontrolarse *upr* to lose control

desconvocar *vt* to call off

descorchar *vt* to uncork

descornarse [2] *upr Fam* (*trabajar*) to slave (away)

descorrer *vt* to draw back

descortés *adj* impolite, discourteous

descortesía *nf* discourtesy, impoliteness

descoser *vt* to unstitch, to unpick

descosido *nm* (*en camisa etc*) open seam; *Fam* **como un d.** like mad, wildly

descoyuntar *vt* to dislocate

descrédito *nm* disrepute, discredit

descremado,-a *adj* skimmed

describir (*pp* **descrito**) *vt* to describe

descripción *nf* description

descriptivo,-a *adj* descriptive

descrito,-a *pp de* **describir**

descuajaringar [42] *vt Fam* to pull *o* take to pieces

descuartizar [40] *vt* to cut up, to cut into pieces

descubierto,-a 1 *adj* open, uncovered; **a cielo d.** in the open
   2 *nm* (**a**) *Fin* overdraft (**b**) **al d.** in the open; **poner al d.** to uncover, to bring out into the open

descubridor,-a *nm,f* discoverer

descubrimiento *nm* discovery

descubrir (*pp* **descubierto**) *vt* to discover; (*conspiración*) to uncover; (*placa*) to unveil

descuento *nm* discount

descuidado,-a *adj* (**a**) (*desaseado*) untidy, neglected (**b**) (*negligente*) careless, negligent (**c**) (*desprevenido*) off one's guard

descuidar 1 *vt* to neglect, to overlook
   2 *vi* **descuida, voy yo** don't worry, I'll go
   3 descuidarse *upr* (*despistarse*) to be careless; **como te descuides, llegarás tarde** if you don't watch out, you'll be late

descuido *nm* (**a**) oversight, mistake; **por d.** inadvertently, by mistake (**b**) (*negligencia*) negligence, carelessness

desde *adv* (**a**) (*tiempo*) since; **d. ahora** from now on; **d. el lunes/entonces** since Monday/then; **espero d. hace media hora** I've been waiting for half an hour; **no lo he visto d. hace un año** I haven't seen him for a year; **¿d. cuándo?** since when?; **d. siempre** always
   (**b**) (*lugar*) from; **d. aquí** from here; **d. arriba/abajo** from above/below
   (**c**) **d. luego** of course
   (**d**) **d. que** ever since; **d. que lo conozca** ever since I've known him

desdecir [12] (*pp* **desdicho**) **1** *vi* **d. de** not to live up to
   2 desdecirse *upr* to go back on one's word

desdén *nm* disdain

desdentado,-a *adj* toothless

desdeñar *vt* to disdain

desdeñoso,-a *adj* disdainful

desdibujarse *upr* to become blurred *o* faint

desdicha *nf* misfortune; **por d.** unfortunately

desdichado,-a 1 *adj* unfortunate
   2 *nm,f* poor devil, wretch

desdigo *indic pres de* **desdecir**

desdiré *indic fut de* **desdecir**

desdoblar *vt* to unfold

deseable *adj* desirable

desear *vt* (**a**) to desire; **deja mucho que d.** it leaves a lot to be desired (**b**) (*querer*) to want; **¿qué desea?** can I help you?; **estoy deseando que vengas** I'm looking forward to your coming (**c**) **te deseo buena suerte/feliz Navidad** I wish you good luck/a merry Christmas

desecar [44] *vt* to dry up

desechable *adj* disposable, throw-away

desechar *vt* (**a**) *(tirar)* to discard, to throw out *o* away (**b**) *(oferta)* to turn down, to refuse; *(idea, proyecto)* to drop, to discard

desechos *nmpl* waste

desembalar *vt* to unpack

desembarcar [44] **1** *vt (mercancías)* to unload; *(personas)* to disembark
  2 *vi* to disembark

desembarco, desembarque *nm (de mercancías)* unloading; *(de personas)* disembarkation

desembocadura *nf* mouth

desembocar [44] *vi* **d. en** *(río)* to flow into; *(calle, situación)* to lead to

desembolsar *vt* to pay out

desembolso *nm* expenditure

desembragar [42] *vt Aut* to declutch

desembrollar *vt Fam* (**a**) *(aclarar)* to clarify, to clear up (**b**) *(desenredar)* to disentangle

desembuchar *vt Fig* to blurt out; *Fam* ¡**desembucha!** out with it!

desempañar *vt* to wipe the condensation from; *Aut* to demist

desempaquetar *vt* to unpack, to unwrap

desempatar *vi Dep* to break the deadlock

desempate *nm* play-off; **partido de d.** play-off, deciding match

desempeñar *vt* (**a**) *(cargo)* to hold, to occupy; *(función)* to fulfil; *(papel)* to play (**b**) *(recuperar)* to redeem

desempleado,-a 1 *adj* unemployed, out of work
  2 *nm,f* unemployed person; **los desempleados** the unemployed

desempleo *nm* unemployment; **cobrar el d.** to be on the dole

desempolvar *vt* (**a**) to dust (**b**) *Fig (pasado)* to revive

desencadenar 1 *vt* (**a**) to unchain (**b**) *(provocar)* to unleash
  2 desencadenarse *vpr* (**a**) *(prisionero)* to break loose; *(viento, pasión)* to rage (**b**) *(conflicto)* to start, to break out

desencajar 1 *vt (pieza)* to knock out; *(hueso)* to dislocate
  2 desencajarse *vpr* (**a**) *(pieza)* to come out; *(hueso)* to become dislocated (**b**) *(cara)* to become distorted

desencaminado,-a *adj* = **descaminado,-a**

desencanto *nm* disenchantment

desenchufar *vt* to unplug

desenfadado,-a *adj* carefree, free and easy

desenfado *nm* ease

desenfocado,-a *adj* out of focus

desenfoque *nm* incorrect focusing; *Fig (de asunto)* wrong approach

desenfrenado,-a *adj* frantic, uncontrolled; *(vicio, pasión)* unbridled

desenfreno *nm* debauchery

desenganchar *vt* to unhook; *(vagón)* to uncouple

desengañar 1 *vt* **d. a algn** to open sb's eyes
  2 desengañarse *vpr* (**a**) to be disappointed (**b**) *Fam* ¡**desengáñate!** get real!

desengaño *nm* disappointment; **llevarse** *o* **sufrir un d. con algo** to be disappointed in sth

desengrasar *vt* to degrease, to remove the grease from

desenlace *nm* (**a**) result, outcome; **un feliz d.** a happy end (**b**) *Cin & Teatro* ending, dénouement

desenmarañar *vt (pelo)* to untangle; *(problema)* to unravel; *(asunto)* to sort out

desenmascarar *vt* to unmask

desenredar *vt* to untangle, to disentangle

desenrollar *vt* to unroll; *(cable)* to unwind

desenroscar [44] *vt* to unscrew

desentenderse [3] *vpr* **se desentendió de mi problema** he didn't want to have anything to do with my problem

desenterrar [1] *vt* (**a**) *(cadáver)* to exhume, to disinter; *(tesoro etc)* to dig up (**b**) *(recuerdo)* to revive

desentonar *vi* (**a**) *Mús* to sing out of tune, to be out of tune (**b**) *(colores etc)* not to match (**c**) *(persona, comentario)* to be out of place

desentrañar *vt (misterio)* to unravel, to get to the bottom of

desentrenado,-a *adj* out of training *o* shape

desentumecer [33] *vt* to put the feeling back into

desenvoltura *nf* ease

desenvolver [4] (*pp* **desenvuelto**) **1** *vt* to unwrap
  2 desenvolverse *vpr* (**a**) *(persona)* to manage, to cope (**b**) *(hecho)* to develop

desenvuelto,-a *adj* relaxed

deseo *nm* wish; *(sexual)* desire; **formular un d.** to make a wish

deseoso,-a *adj* eager; **estar d. de** be eager to

desequilibrado,-a 1 *adj* unbalanced
  2 *nm,f* unbalanced person

desequilibrar 1 *vt* to unbalance, to throw off balance
  2 desequilibrarse *vpr* to become mentally disturbed

desequilibrio *nm* imbalance; **d. mental** mental disorder

deserción *nf* desertion

desertar *vi* to desert

desértico,-a *adj* desert

desertización *nf* desertification

desertor,-a *nm,f* deserter

desesperación *nf (desesperanza)* despair; *(exasperación)* desperation

desesperado,-a *adj* (**a**) *(sin esperanza)* desperate, hopeless (**b**) *(exasperado)* exasperated, infuriated

desesperante *adj* exasperating

desesperar 1 *vt* to drive to despair; *(exasperar)* to exasperate
  2 desesperarse *vpr* to despair

desestabilizar [40] *vt* to destabilize
desestatización *nf Am* privatization
desestatizar *vt Am* to privatize
desestimar *vt* to reject
desfachatez *nf* cheek, nerve
desfalco *nm* embezzlement, misappropriation
desfallecer [33] *vi* (a) *(debilitarse)* to feel faint; *(desmayarse)* to faint (b) *(desanimarse)* to lose heart
desfasado,-a *adj* (a) outdated (b) *(persona)* old-fashioned, behind the times (c) *Téc* out of phase
desfase *nm* gap; **d. horario** time lag
desfavorable *adj* unfavourable
desfigurar *vt (cara)* to disfigure; *(verdad)* to distort
desfiladero *nm* narrow pass
desfilar *vi* (a) to march in single file (b) *Mil* to march past, to parade
desfile *nm Mil* parade, march past; **d. de modas** fashion show
desfogar [42] **1** *vt* to give vent to
2 desfogarse *vpr* to let off steam
desgajar 1 *vt (arrancar)* to rip *o* tear out; *(rama)* to tear off
2 desgajarse *vpr* to come off
desgana *nf* (a) *(inapetencia)* lack of appetite (b) *(apatía)* apathy, indifference; **con d.** reluctantly, unwillingly
desganado,-a *adj* (a) **estar d.** *(inapetente)* to have no appetite (b) *(apático)* apathetic
desgañitarse *vpr Fam* to shout oneself hoarse
desgarbado,-a *adj* ungraceful, ungainly
desgarrador,-a *adj* harrowing
desgarrar *vt* to tear
desgarrón *nm* big tear, rip
desgastar 1 *vt* to wear out
2 desgastarse *vpr (consumirse)* to wear out; *(persona)* to wear oneself out
desgaste *nm* wear; **d. del poder** wear and tear of power
desgracia *nf* (a) misfortune; **por d.** unfortunately (b) *(deshonor)* disgrace (c) **desgracias personales** loss of life
desgraciadamente *adv* unfortunately
desgraciado,-a 1 *adj* unfortunate; *(infeliz)* unhappy
2 *nm,f* unfortunate person; **un pobre d.** a poor devil
desgravable *adj* tax-deductible
desgravación *nf* deduction; **d. fiscal** tax deduction
desgravar *vt* to deduct
desguazar [40] *vt (un barco)* to break up; *Aut* to scrap
deshabitado,-a *adj* uninhabited, unoccupied
deshabitar *vt* to abandon, to vacate
deshacer [15] *(pp* **deshecho)** **1** *vt* (a) *(paquete)* to undo; *(maleta)* to unpack (b) *(plan)* to

destroy, to ruin (c) *(acuerdo)* to break off (d) *(disolver)* to dissolve; *(derretir)* to melt
2 deshacerse *vpr* (a) to come undone *o* untied (b) **d. de algn/algo** to get rid of sb/sth (c) *(afligirse)* to go to pieces; **d. en lágrimas** to cry one's eyes out (d) *(disolverse)* to dissolve; *(derretirse)* to melt (e) *(niebla)* to fade away, to disappear
deshecho,-a *adj* (a) *(cama)* unmade; *(maleta)* unpacked; *(paquete)* unwrapped (b) *(roto)* broken, smashed (c) *(disuelto)* dissolved; *(derretido)* melted (d) *(abatido)* devastated, shattered (e) *(cansado)* exhausted, tired out
desheredar *vt* to disinherit
deshidratar *vt* to dehydrate
deshielo *nm* thaw
deshilachar *vt* to fray
deshilvanado,-a *adj Fig (inconexo)* disjointed
deshonesto,-a *adj* (a) dishonest (b) *(indecente)* indecent, improper
deshonor *nm*, **deshonra** *nf* dishonour
deshonrar *vt* (a) to dishonour (b) *(a la familia)* to bring disgrace on
deshora: a deshora *loc adv* at an inconvenient time; **comer a d.** to eat at odd times
deshuesar *vt (carne)* to bone; *(fruta)* to stone
deshumanizar [40] *vt* to dehumanize
desidia *nf* apathy
desierto,-a 1 *nm* desert
2 *adj* (a) *(deshabitado)* uninhabited (b) *(vacío)* empty, deserted (c) *(premio)* void
designación *nf* designation
designar *vt* (a) to designate (b) *(fecha, lugar)* to fix
designio *nm* intention, plan
desigual *adj* (a) uneven (b) *(lucha)* unequal (c) *(carácter)* changeable
desigualdad *nf* (a) inequality (b) *(del terreno)* unevenness
desilusión *nf* disappointment, disillusionment
desilusionar *vt* to disappoint, to disillusion
desinfectante *adj & nm* disinfectant
desinfectar *vt* to disinfect
desinflar 1 *vt* to deflate; *(rueda)* to let down
2 desinflarse *vpr* to go flat
desintegración *nf* disintegration
desintegrar *vt*, **desintegrarse** *vpr* to disintegrate
desinterés *nm* (a) *(indiferencia)* lack of interest, apathy (b) *(generosidad)* unselfishness
desinteresado,-a *adj* selfless, unselfish
desintoxicar [44] **1** *vt* to detoxicate; *(de alcohol)* to dry out
2 desintoxicarse *vpr Med* to detoxicate oneself; *(de alcohol)* to dry out
desistir *vi* to desist
deslavazado,-a *adj* disjointed
deslave *nm Am* landslide *(caused by flooding or rain)*

esleal *adj* disloyal; *(competencia)* unfair

eslealtad *nf* disloyalty

eslenguado,-a *adj (insolente)* insolent, cheeky; *(grosero)* coarse, foul-mouthed

esliar [29] *vt* to unwrap

esligar [42] **1** *vt* (**a**) *(separar)* to separate (**b**) *(desatar)* to untie, to unfasten

2 desligarse *upr* **d. de** to disassociate oneself from

esliz *nm* mistake, slip; **cometer** *o* **tener un d.** to slip up

eslizar [40] **1** *vi* to slide

2 deslizarse *upr* (**a**) *(patinar)* to slide (**b**) *(fluir)* to flow

eslucir [35] *vt* (**a**) *(espectáculo)* to spoil (**b**) *(metal)* to make dull

eslumbrador,-a, deslumbrante *adj* dazzling; *Fig* stunning

eslumbrar *vt* to dazzle

esmadrarse *upr Fam* to go wild

esmadre *nm Fam* hullabaloo

esmandarse *upr* to get out of hand, to run wild; *(caballo)* to bolt

esmano: a desmano *loc adv* out of the way; **me coge a d.** it is out of my way

esmantelar *vt* (**a**) to dismantle (**b**) *Náut* to dismast, to unrig

esmaquillador,-a 1 *nm* make-up remover

2 *adj* **leche desmaquilladora** cleansing cream

esmaquillarse *upr* to remove one's make-up

esmarcarse [44] *upr Dep* to lose one's marker

esmayado,-a *adj* unconscious; **caer d.** to faint

esmayarse *upr* to faint

esmayo *nm* faint, fainting fit; **tener un d.** to faint

esmedido,-a *adj* disproportionate, out of all proportion; *(ambición)* unbounded

esmejorar *vi*, **desmejorarse** *upr* to deteriorate, to go downhill

esmelenarse *upr Fam* to let one's hair down

esmembración *nf*, **desmembramiento** *nm* dismemberment

esmemoriado,-a *adj* forgetful, absent-minded

esmentir [5] *vt* to deny

esmenuzar [40] *vt* (**a**) *(deshacer)* to break into little pieces, to crumble; *(carne)* to cut into little pieces (**b**) *(asunto)* to examine in detail

esmerecer [33] *vi* to lose value

esmesura *nf* excess

esmesurado,-a *adj* excessive

esmilitarizar [40] *vt* to demilitarize

esmontable *adj* that can be taken to pieces

esmontar 1 *vt* (**a**) *(desarmar)* to take to pieces, to dismantle (**b**) *(allanar)* to level

2 *vi* **d. (de)** to dismount, to get off

esmoralizar [40] *vt* to demoralize

desmoronarse *upr* to crumble, to fall to pieces

desnatado,-a *adj (leche)* skimmed

desnivel *nm (en el terreno)* drop, difference in height

desnivelar *vt* to throw out of balance

desnucarse [44] *upr* to break one's neck

desnuclearizar *vt* to denuclearize

desnudar 1 *vt* to undress

2 desnudarse *upr* to get undressed

desnudismo *nm* nudism

desnudista *adj & nmf* nudist

desnudo,-a 1 *adj* naked, nude

2 *nm Arte* nude

desnutrición *nf* malnutrition

desnutrido,-a *adj* undernourished

desobedecer [33] *vt* to disobey

desobediencia *nf* disobedience

desobediente 1 *adj* disobedient

2 *nmf* disobedient person

desocupado,-a *adj* (**a**) *(vacío)* empty, vacant (**b**) *(ocioso)* free, not busy (**c**) *(sin empleo)* unemployed

desocupar *vt* to empty, to vacate

desodorante *adj & nm* deodorant

desolación *nf* desolation

desolar *vt* to devastate

desollar [2] **1** *vt* to skin

2 desollarse *upr* to scrape; **me desollé el brazo** I scraped my arm

desorbitado,-a *adj (precio)* exorbitant

desorden *nm* untidiness, mess; **¡qué d.!** what a mess!; **d. público** civil disorder

desordenado,-a *adj* messy, untidy

desordenar *vt* to make untidy, to mess up

desorganizar [40] *vt* to disorganize, to disrupt

desorientación *nf* disorientation

desorientar 1 *vt* to disorientate

2 desorientarse *upr* to lose one's sense of direction, to lose one's bearings; *Fig* to become disoriented

despabilado,-a *adj* (**a**) *(sin sueño)* wide awake (**b**) *(listo)* quick, smart

despachar *vt* (**a**) *(asunto)* to get through (**b**) *(correo)* to send, to dispatch (**c**) *(en tienda)* to serve (**d**) *Fam (despedir)* to send packing, to sack (**e**) *Am (facturar)* to check in

despacho *nm* (**a**) *(oficina)* office; *(en casa)* study (**b**) *(venta)* sale (**c**) *(comunicación)* dispatch

despachurrar *vt Fam* to squash, to flatten

despacio *adv* (**a**) *(lentamente)* slowly (**b**) *(en voz baja)* quietly

despampanante *adj Fam* stunning

desparpajo *nm* self-assurance; **con d.** in a carefree manner

desparramar *vt*, **desparramarse** *upr* to spread, to scatter; *(líquido)* to spill

despavorido,-a *adj* terrified

despecho *nm* spite; **por d.** out of spite

despectivo,-a *adj* derogatory, disparaging

despedazar [40] *vt* to cut *o* tear to pieces
despedida *nf* farewell, goodbye; **d. de soltera/soltero** hen/stag party
despedido,-a *adj* **salir d.** to be off like a shot
despedir [6] **1** *vt* (**a**) *(empleado)* to fire, *Br* to sack (**b**) *(decir adiós)* to see off, to say goodbye to (**c**) *(olor, humo etc)* to give off
2 despedirse *vpr* (**a**) *(decir adiós)* to say goodbye (**de** to) (**b**) *Fig* to forget, to give up; **ya puedes despedirte del coche** you can say goodbye to the car
despegado,-a *adj* (**a**) unstuck (**b**) *(persona)* couldn't-care-less
despegar [42] **1** *vt* to take off, to detach
2 *vi Av* to take off
3 despegarse *vpr* to come unstuck
despego *nm* detachment
despegue *nm* take-off
despeinado,-a *adj* dishevelled, with untidy hair
despejado,-a *adj* clear; *(cielo)* cloudless
despejar 1 *vt* to clear; *(misterio, dudas)* to clear up
2 despejarse *vpr* (**a**) *(cielo)* to clear (**b**) *(persona)* to clear one's head
despeje *nm Dep* clearance
despellejar *vt* to skin
despelotarse *vpr Fam* (**a**) *(desnudarse)* to strip (**b**) **d. de risa** to laugh one's head off
despensa *nf* pantry, larder
despeñadero *nm* cliff, precipice
despeñarse *vpr* to go over a cliff
desperdiciar [43] *vt* to waste; *(oportunidad)* to throw away
desperdicio *nm* (**a**) *(acto)* waste (**b**) **desperdicios** *(basura)* rubbish; *(desechos)* scraps, leftovers
desperdigar [42] *vt*, **desperdigarse** *vpr* to scatter, to separate
desperezarse [40] *vpr* to stretch (oneself)
desperfecto *nm* (**a**) *(defecto)* flaw, imperfection (**b**) *(daño)* damage
despertador *nm* alarm clock
despertar [1] **1** *vt* to wake (up), to awaken; *Fig (sentimiento etc)* to arouse
2 despertarse *vpr* to wake (up)
despiadado,-a *adj* merciless
despido *nm* dismissal, sacking
despierto,-a *adj* (**a**) *(desvelado)* awake (**b**) *(vivo)* quick, sharp
despilfarrar *vt* to waste, to squander
despilfarro *nm* wasting, squandering
despintar *vi*, **despintarse** *vpr (ropa)* to fade
despiole *nm RP Fam* rumpus, shindy
despistado,-a 1 *adj* (**a**) *(olvidadizo)* scatter-brained (**b**) *(confuso)* confused
2 *nm,f* scatterbrain
despistar 1 *vt* (**a**) *(hacer perder la pista a)* to lose, to throw off one's scent (**b**) *Fig* to mislead
2 despistarse *vpr* (**a**) *(perderse)* to get lost (**b**) *(distraerse)* to switch off

despiste *nm* (**a**) *(cualidad)* absent mindedness (**b**) *(error)* slip-up
desplazamiento *nm (viaje)* trip, journey; **dietas de d.** travelling expenses
desplazar [40] **1** *vt* to displace
2 desplazarse *vpr* to travel
desplegar [1] **1** *vt* (**a**) to open (out), to spread (out) (**b**) *(energías etc)* to use, to deploy
2 desplegarse *vpr* (**a**) *(abrirse)* to open (out) to spread (out) (**b**) *Mil* to deploy
despliegue *nm* (**a**) *Mil* deployment (**b**) *(de medios etc)* display
desplomarse *vpr* to collapse; *(precios)* to slump, to fall sharply
desplumar *vt* to pluck
despoblar [2] *vt* to depopulate
despojar *vt* (**a**) to strip (**de** of) (**b**) *Fig* to divest, to deprive (**de** of)
despojo *nm* (**a**) stripping (**b**) **despojos** leftovers, scraps
desposado,-a *adj Fml* newly-wed
desposar *vt Fml* to marry
desposeer [36] *vt* **d. de** to dispossess of *(autoridad)* to strip of
desposeído *nm* **los desposeídos** the have nots
déspota *nmf* despot
despótico,-a *adj* despotic
despotismo *nm* despotism
despotricar [44] *vi* to rant and rave (**contra** about)
despreciable *adj* despicable, contemptible *(cantidad)* negligible
despreciar [43] *vt* (**a**) *(desdeñar)* to scorn, to despise (**b**) *(rechazar)* to reject, to spurn
desprecio *nm* (**a**) *(desdén)* scorn, disdain (**b**) *(desaire)* slight, snub
desprender 1 *vt* (**a**) *(separar)* to remove, to detach (**b**) *(olor, humo etc)* to give off
2 desprenderse *vpr* (**a**) *(soltarse)* to come off *o* away (**b**) **d. de** to rid oneself of, to free oneself from (**c**) **de aquí se desprende que ..** it can be deduced from this that ...
desprendido,-a *adj Fig* generous, unselfish
desprendimiento *nm* (**a**) loosening, detachment; **d. de tierras** landslide (**b**) *Fig (generosidad)* generosity, unselfishness
despreocupado,-a *adj* (**a**) *(tranquilo)* unconcerned (**b**) *(descuidado)* careless; *(estilo)* casual
despreocuparse *vpr* (**a**) *(tranquilizarse)* to stop worrying (**b**) *(desentenderse)* to be unconcerned, to be indifferent (**de** to)
desprestigiar [43] *vt* to discredit, to run down
desprestigio *nm* discredit, loss of reputation; **campaña de d.** smear campaign
desprevenido,-a *adj* unprepared; **coger** *o* **pillar a algn d.** to catch sb unawares
desprolijo,-a *adj Am (casa)* messy, untidy *(cuaderno)* untidy; *(persona)* unkempt dishevelled

desproporción *nf* disproportion, lack of proportion

desproporcionado,-a *adj* disproportionate

desprovisto,-a *adj* **d. (de)** lacking, without, devoid (of)

después *adv* (**a**) afterwards, later; *(entonces)* then; *(seguidamente)* next; **una semana d.** a week later; **poco d.** soon after (**b**) *(lugar)* next (**c**) **d. de** after; **d. de la guerra** after the war; **mi calle está d. de la tuya** my street is the one after yours; **d. de cenar** after eating; **d. de todo** after all (**d**) **d. de que** after; **d. de que viniera** after he came

despuntar 1 *vt* to blunt, to make blunt
  2 *vi* (**a**) *(día)* to dawn (**b**) *(destacar)* to excel, to stand out

desquiciar [43] **1** *vt (persona)* to unhinge
  2 desquiciarse *vpr (persona)* to go crazy

desquitarse *vpr* to take revenge (**de** for)

desquite *nm* revenge

destacado,-a *adj* outstanding

destacamento *nm* detachment

destacar [44] **1** *vt Fig* to emphasize, to stress
  2 *vi* to stand out
  3 destacarse *vpr* to stand out

destajo *nm* piecework; **trabajar a d.** to do piecework

destapador *nm Am* bottle opener

destapar 1 *vt* to take the lid off; *(botella)* to open; *Fig (asunto)* to uncover; *RP (caño)* to unblock
  2 destaparse *vpr* to get uncovered

destartalado,-a *adj* rambling; *(desvencijado)* ramshackle

destello *nm* flash, sparkle

destemplado,-a *adj* (**a**) *(voz, gesto)* sharp, snappy; **con cajas destempladas** rudely, brusquely (**b**) *(tiempo)* unpleasant (**c**) *(enfermo)* indisposed, out of sorts (**d**) *Mús* out of tune, discordant

desteñir [6] **1** *vt & vi* to discolour
  2 desteñirse *vpr* to lose colour, to fade

desternillarse *vpr* **d. (de risa)** to split one's sides laughing

desterrar [1] *vt* to exile

destiempo: a destiempo *loc adv* at the wrong time o moment

destierro *nm* exile

destilado,-a *adj* distilled; **agua destilada** distilled water

destilar *vt* to distil

destilería *nf* distillery

destinado,-a *adj* destined, bound; *Fig* **d. al fracaso** doomed to failure

destinar *vt* (**a**) *(dinero etc)* to set aside, to assign (**b**) *(empleado)* to appoint

destinatario,-a *nm,f* (**a**) *(de carta)* addressee (**b**) *(de mercancías)* consignee

destino *nm* (**a**) *(rumbo)* destination; **el avión con d. a Bilbao** the plane to Bilbao (**b**) *(sino)* fate, fortune (**c**) *(de empleo)* post

destitución *nf* dismissal from office

destituir [37] *vt* to dismiss o remove from office

destornillador *nm* screwdriver

destornillar *vt* to unscrew

destreza *nf* skill

destrozado,-a *adj* (**a**) *(roto)* torn-up, smashed (**b**) *(cansado)* worn-out, exhausted (**c**) *(abatido)* shattered

destrozar [40] *vt* (**a**) *(destruir)* to destroy; *(rasgar)* to tear to shreds o pieces (**b**) *(afligir)* to shatter; *(vida, reputación)* to ruin

destrozo *nm* (**a**) destruction (**b**) **destrozos** damage

destrucción *nf* destruction

destructivo,-a *adj* destructive

destructor,-a 1 *adj* destructive
  2 *nm Náut* destroyer

destruir [37] *vt* to destroy

desubicado,-a *nm,f Andes, RP* **ser un d.** to have no idea how to behave, to be clueless

desusado,-a *adj* old-fashioned, outdated

desuso *nm* disuse; **caer en d.** to fall into disuse; **en d.** obsolete, outdated

desvalido,-a *adj* defenceless

desvalijar *vt (robar)* to clean out, to rob; *(casa, tienda)* to burgle

desvalorizar [40] *vt* to devalue

desván *nm* attic, loft

desvanecerse [33] *vpr* (**a**) *(disiparse)* to vanish, to fade away (**b**) *(desmayarse)* to faint

desvariar [29] *vi* to talk nonsense

desvarío *nm* (**a**) *(delirio)* raving, delirium (**b**) *(disparate)* nonsense

desvelado,-a *adj* awake, wide awake

desvelar 1 *vt* to keep awake
  2 desvelarse *vpr* (**a**) *(despabilarse)* to stay awake (**b**) *(desvivirse)* to devote oneself (**por** to) (**c**) *CAm, Méx (quedarse despierto)* to stay up o awake

desvencijar 1 *vt* to take apart
  2 desvencijarse *vpr* to fall apart

desventaja *nf* (**a**) disadvantage; **estar en d.** to be at a disadvantage (**b**) *(inconveniente)* drawback

desventura *nf* misfortune, bad luck

desvergonzado,-a 1 *adj* (**a**) *(indecente)* shameless (**b**) *(descarado)* insolent
  2 *nm,f* (**a**) *(sinvergüenza)* shameless person (**b**) *(fresco)* insolent o cheeky person

desvergüenza *nf* (**a**) *(indecencia)* shamelessness (**b**) *(atrevimiento)* insolence; **tuvo la d. de negarlo** he had the cheek to deny it (**c**) *(impertinencia)* insolent o rude remark

desvestir [6] **1** *vt* to undress
  2 desvestirse *vpr* to undress, to get undressed

desviación *nf* deviation; *(de carretera)* diversion, detour; *Med* **d. de columna** slipped disc

desviar [29] **1** *vt (río, carretera)* to divert; *(golpe, conversación)* to deflect; **d. la mirada** to look away
  2 desviarse *vpr* to go off course; *(coche)* to

turn off; *Fig* **d. del tema** to digress
desvincular 1 *vt* to separate
  2 desvincularse *vpr* to separate, to cut oneself off
desvío *nm* diversion, detour
desvirgar [42] *vt* to deflower
desvirtuar [30] *vt* to distort
desvivirse *vpr* to bend over backwards
detalladamente *adv* in (great) detail
detallado,-a *adj* detailed, thorough
detallar *vt* to give the details of
detalle *nm* (a) detail; **entrar en detalles** to go into details (b) *(delicadeza)* nice thought, nicely; **¡qué d.!** how nice!, how sweet! (c) *(toque decorativo)* touch, ornament
detallista 1 *adj* perfectionist
  2 *nmf Com* retailer
detectar *vt* to detect
detective *nmf* detective; **d. privado** private detective o eye
detector,-a *nm,f* detector; **d. de incendios** fire detector
detención *nf* (a) *Jur* detention, arrest (b) **con d.** carefully, thoroughly
detener [24] **1** *vt* (a) to stop, to halt (b) *Jur (arrestar)* to arrest, to detain
  2 detenerse *vpr* to stop
detenidamente *adv* carefully, thoroughly
detenido,-a 1 *adj* (a) *(parado)* standing still, stopped (b) *(arrestado)* detained (c) *(minucioso)* detailed, thorough
  2 *nm,f* detainee, person under arrest
detenimiento *nm* **con d.** carefully, thoroughly
detentar *vt* to hold
detergente *adj & nm* detergent
deteriorar 1 *vt* to spoil, to damage
  2 deteriorarse *vpr* (a) *(estropearse)* to get damaged (b) *(empeorar)* to get worse
deterioro *nm* (a) *(empeoramiento)* deterioration, worsening (b) *(daño)* damage; **ir en d. de** to be to the detriment of
determinación *nf* (a) determination; **con d.** determinedly (b) *(decisión)* decision
determinado,-a *adj* (a) *(preciso)* definite, precise (b) *(resuelto)* decisive, resolute (c) *Ling* definite
determinante *adj* decisive
determinar 1 *vt* (a) *(fecha etc)* to fix, to set (b) *(decidir)* to decide on (c) *(condicionar)* to determine (d) *(ocasionar)* to bring about
  2 determinarse *vpr* to make up one's mind to
detestable *adj* detestable, repulsive
detestar *vt* to detest, to hate
detonante *nm* detonator; *Fig* trigger
detonar *vt* to detonate
detractor,-a *nm,f* detractor
detrás *adv* (a) behind, on o at the back (**de** of) (b) **d. de** behind
detrimento *nm* detriment; **en d. de** to the detriment of
detuve *pt indef de* **detener**

deuda *nf* debt; **estoy en d. contigo** *(monetaria)* I am in debt to you; *(moral)* I am indebted to you; **d. del Estado** public debt; **d. pública** national debt
deudor,-a 1 *adj* indebted
  2 *nm,f* debtor
devaluación *nf* devaluation
devaluar [30] *vt* to devalue
devanar 1 *vt (hilo)* to wind; *(alambre)* to coil
  2 devanarse *vpr Fam* **d. los sesos** to rack one's brains
devaneo *nm* dabbling
devastador,-a *adj* devastating
devastar *vt* to devastate, to ravage
devengar [42] *vt Com* to earn, to accrue
devenir [27] *vi* to become
devoción *nf* (a) *Rel* devoutness (b) *(al trabajo etc)* devotion; *Fam* **Juan no es santo de m** **d.** Juan isn't really my cup of tea
devolución *nf* (a) giving back, return; *Com* refund, repayment (b) *Jur* devolution
devolver [4] *(pp* **devuelto)** **1** *vt* to give back, to return; *(dinero)* to refund
  2 *vi (vomitar)* to vomit, to throw o bring up
  3 devolverse *vpr Am* to go o come back, to return
devorar *vt* to devour
devoto,-a 1 *adj* pious, devout
  2 *nm,f* (a) *Rel* pious person (b) *(seguidor* devotee
devuelto,-a *pp de* **devolver**
DF *nm (abr* **Distrito Federal)** *(en México* Mexico City
DGI *nf RP (abr* **Dirección General Impositiva** *Br* ≃ Inland Revenue, *US* ≃ IRS
DGT *nf (abr* **Dirección General de Tráfico)** = government department responsible fo road transport
di (a) *pt indef de* **dar** (b) *imperat de* **decir**
día *nm* day; **¿qué d. es hoy?** what's the date today?; **d. a d.** day by day; **de d.** by day; **durante el d.** during the daytime; **de un d** **para otro** overnight; **un d. sí y otro no** every other day; **pan del d.** fresh bread; **hoy (en) d** nowadays; **el d. de mañana** in the future; *Fig* **estar al d.** to be up to date; *Fig* **poner al d. t** bring up to date; **d. festivo** holiday; **d. labora** **ble** working day; **d. libre** free day, day off; **es** **de d.** it is daylight; **hace buen/mal d.** it's a nice/bad day, the weather is nice/bad today
diabetes *nf* diabetes
diabético,-a *adj & nm,f* diabetic
diablo *nm* devil; *Fam* **¡al d. con ...!** to hell with ...!; *Fam* **vete al d.** get lost; *Fam* **¿qué/cóm** **diablos ...?** what/how the hell ...?
diablura *nf* mischief
diácono *nm* deacon
diadema *nf* tiara
diáfano,-a *adj* clear
diafragma *nm* diaphragm; *Fot* aperture; *Med* cap
diagnosis *nf inv* diagnosis

diagnosticar [44] *vt* to diagnose
diagnóstico *nm* diagnosis
diagonal *adj & nf* diagonal; **en d.** diagonally
diagrama *nm* diagram; *Informát* **d. de flujo** flowchart
dial *nm* dial
dialecto *nm* dialect
dialogar [42] *vi* to have a conversation; *(para negociar)* to talk
diálogo *nm* dialogue
diamante *nm* diamond
diámetro *nm* diameter
diana *nf* (a) *Mil* reveille (b) *(blanco)* bull's eye
diapositiva *nf* slide
diariamente *adv* daily, every day
diariero,-a *nm,f Andes, RP* newspaper seller
diario,-a 1 *nm* (a) *Prensa* (daily) newspaper (b) *(memorias)* diary; *Náut* **d. de a bordo, d. de navegación** logbook
 2 *adj* daily; **a d.** daily, every day
diarrea *nf* diarrhoea
diatriba *nf* diatribe
dibujante *nmf* (a) drawer (b) *(de cómic)* cartoonist (c) *(hombre)* draughtsman; *(mujer)* draughtswoman
dibujar *vt* to draw
dibujo *nm* (a) drawing; **dibujos animados** cartoons (b) *(arte)* drawing; **d. artístico** artistic drawing; **d. lineal** draughtsmanship
diccionario *nm* dictionary; **buscar/mirar una palabra en el d.** to look up a word in the dictionary
dicha *nf* happiness
dicharachero,-a *adj* talkative and witty
dicho,-a *adj* (a) said; **mejor d.** or rather; **d. de otro modo** to put it another way; **d. sea de paso** let it be said in passing; **d. y hecho** no sooner said than done (b) **dicha persona** *(mencionado)* the above-mentioned person
dichoso,-a *adj* (a) *(feliz)* happy (b) *Fam* damned; **¡este d. trabajo!** this damned job!
diciembre *nm* December
dictado *nm* dictation; *Fig* **dictados** dictates
dictador,-a *nm,f* dictator
dictadura *nf* dictatorship
dictáfono® *nm* Dictaphone®
dictamen *nm (juicio)* ruling; *(informe)* report
dictaminar *vi* to rule (**sobre** on)
dictar *vt* (a) to dictate (b) *(ley)* to enact; *(sentencia)* to pass
dictatorial *adj* dictatorial
didáctico,-a *adj* didactic
diecinueve *adj & nm inv* nineteen
dieciocho *adj & nm inv* eighteen
dieciséis *adj & nm inv* sixteen
diecisiete *adj & nm inv* seventeen
diente *nm* tooth; *Téc* cog; *(de ajo)* clove; **d. de leche** milk tooth; **dientes postizos** false teeth; *Fig* **hablar entre dientes** to mumble; *Fig* **poner los dientes largos a algn** to make sb green with envy
diera *subj imperf de* **dar**

diéresis *nf inv* diaeresis
diesel *adj & nm* diesel
diestra *nf* right hand
diestro,-a 1 *adj* (a) *(hábil)* skilful, clever (b) **a d. y siniestro** right, left and centre
 2 *nm Taurom* bullfighter, matador
dieta *nf* (a) diet; **estar a d.** to be on a diet (b) **dietas** expenses *o* subsistence allowance
dietética *nf* dietetics *sing*
dietista *nmf* dietician
diez *adj & nm inv* ten
difamación *nf* defamation, slander; *(escrita)* libel
difamar *vt* to defame, to slander; *(por escrito)* to libel
diferencia *nf* difference; **a d. de** unlike
diferencial 1 *adj* distinguishing
 2 *nm* differential
diferenciar [43] **1** *vt* to differentiate, to distinguish (**entre** between)
 2 diferenciarse *vpr* to differ (**de** from), to be different (**de** from)
diferente 1 *adj* different (**de** from *o US* than)
 2 *adv* differently
diferido,-a *adj TV* **en d.** recorded
difícil *adj* difficult, hard; **d. de creer/hacer** difficult to believe/do; **es d. que venga** it is unlikely that she'll come
dificultad *nf* difficulty; *(aprieto)* trouble, problem
dificultar *vt* to make difficult
dificultoso,-a *adj* difficult, hard
difuminar *vt* to blur
difundir *vt,* **difundirse** *vpr* to spread
difunto,-a 1 *adj* late, deceased
 2 *nm,f* deceased
difusión *nf* (a) *(de noticia)* spreading; **tener gran d.** to be widely broadcast (b) *Rad & TV* broadcasting
difuso,-a *adj* diffuse
digerir [5] *vt* to digest; *Fig* to assimilate
digestión *nf* digestion; **corte de d.** sudden indigestion
digestivo,-a *adj* easy to digest
digitador,-a *nm,f Am* keyboarder
digital *adj* digital; **huellas digitales** fingerprints; **tocadiscos d.** CD player
digitalizar *vt* digitize
digitar *vt Am* to key
dígito *nm* digit
dignarse *vpr* **d. (a)** to deign to, to condescend to
dignidad *nf* dignity
digno,-a *adj* (a) *(merecedor)* worthy; **d. de admiración** worthy of admiration; **d. de mención/verse** worth mentioning/seeing (b) *(decoroso)* decent, good
digo *indic pres de* **decir**
dije *pt indef de* **decir**
dilación *nf* delay, hold-up; **sin d.** without delay
dilatado,-a *adj* (a) *(agrandado)* dilated (b) *(vasto)* vast, extensive

dilatar 1 vt (a) (agrandar) to expand (b) (pupila) to dilate
2 dilatarse vpr (a) (agrandarse) to expand (b) (pupila) to dilate
dilema nm dilemma
diligencia nf (a) diligence; **con d.** diligently (b) **diligencias** formalities
diligente adj diligent
dilucidar vt to elucidate, to clarify
diluir [37] **1** vt to dilute
2 diluirse vpr to dilute
diluviar [43] v impers to pour with rain
diluvio nm flood; **el D. (Universal)** the Flood
diluyo indic pres de **diluir**
dimensión nf (a) dimension, size; **de gran d.** very large (b) Fig (importancia) importance
diminutivo,-a adj & nm diminutive
diminuto,-a adj minute, tiny
dimisión nf resignation; **presentar la d.** to hand in one's resignation
dimitir vi to resign (**de** from); **d. de un cargo** to give in o tender one's resignation
Dinamarca n Denmark
dinámica nf dynamics sing
dinámico,-a adj dynamic
dinamita nf dynamite
dinamitar vt to dynamite
dinamo, dínamo nf dynamo
dinar nm Fin dinar
dinastía nf dynasty
dineral nm Fam fortune
dinero nm money; **d. contante (y sonante)** cash; **d. efectivo** o **en metálico** cash; **gente de d.** wealthy people
dinosaurio nm dinosaur
diócesis nf inv diocese
dios nm god; **¡D. mío!** my God!; **¡por D.!** for goodness sake!; **a la buena de D.** any old how; **hacer algo como D. manda** to do sth properly; Fam **ni d.** nobody; Fam **todo d.** everybody
diosa nf goddess
diploma nm diploma
diplomacia nf diplomacy
diplomarse vpr to graduate
diplomático,-a 1 adj diplomatic; **cuerpo d.** diplomatic corps
2 nm,f diplomat
diptongo nm diphthong
diputación nf **d. provincial** ≃ county council
diputado,-a nm,f Br ≃ Member of Parliament, MP; US (hombre) Congressman; (mujer) Congresswoman; **Congreso de Diputados** Br ≃ House of Commons, US ≃ Congress; **d. provincial** ≃ county councillor
dique nm dike
diré fut de **decir**
dirección nf (a) direction; Aut (en letrero) **d. prohibida** no entry; **calle de d. única** one-way street (b) (señas) address; Informát **d. de correo electrónico** e-mail address (c) Cin &

Teatro direction (d) (destino) destination (e) Aut & Téc steering (f) (dirigentes) management; (cargo) directorship; (de un partido) leadership; (de un colegio) headship
direccional nm Col, Méx Aut Br indicator, US turn signal
directa nf Aut top gear
directamente adv directly, straight away
directiva nf board of directors, management
directivo,-a adj directive; **junta directiva** board of directors
directo,-a adj direct; TV & Rad **en d.** live
director,-a nm,f director; (de colegio) (hombre) headmaster; (mujer) headmistress; (de periódico) editor; **d. de cine** (film) director; **d. de orquesta** conductor; **d. gerente** managing director
directorio nm Informát directory; Andes, Méx **d. telefónico** telephone directory
directriz nf directive; Mat directrix
dirigente 1 adj leading; **clase d.** ruling class
2 nmf leader
dirigir [57] **1** vt to direct; (empresa) to manage; (negocio, colegio) to run; (orquesta) to conduct; (partido) to lead; (periódico) to edit; (coche, barco) to steer; **d. la palabra a algn** to speak to sb
2 dirigirse vpr (a) **d. a** o **hacia** to go to, to make one's way towards (b) (escribir) to write; **diríjase al apartado de correos 42** write to PO Box 42 (c) (hablar) to speak
discapacidad nf disability
discar vt Andes, RP to dial
discernir [54] vt to discern
disciplina nf discipline
disciplinado,-a adj disciplined
discípulo,-a nm,f disciple
disco nm (a) disc; **d. de freno** brake disc (b) Mús record; **d. compacto** compact disc (c) Informát disk; **d. duro** o **fijo/flexible** hard/floppy disk (d) Dep discus (e) Tel dial
discográfico,-a adj **casa/compañía discográfica** record company
disconforme adj **estar d. con** to disagree with
discontinuo,-a adj discontinuous; Aut **línea discontinua** broken line
discordante adj discordant; **ser la nota d.** to be the odd man out
discordia nf discord; **la manzana de la d.** the bone of contention; **sembrar d.** to sow discord
discoteca nf (a) (lugar) discotheque (b) (colección) record collection
discreción nf (a) discretion (b) **a d.** at will
discrecional adj optional; **servicio d.** special service
discrepancia nf (desacuerdo) disagreement; (diferencia) discrepancy
discrepar vi (disentir) to disagree (**de** with; **en** on); (diferenciarse) to be different (**de** from)

discreto,-a *adj* (**a**) discreet (**b**) *(mediocre)* average

discriminación *nf* discrimination

discriminar *vt* (**a**) to discriminate against (**b**) *Fml (diferenciar)* to discriminate between, to distinguish

disculpa *nf* excuse; **dar disculpas** to make excuses; **pedir disculpas a algn** to apologize to sb

disculpar 1 *vt* to excuse

2 disculparse *vpr* to apologize (**por** for)

discurrir *vi* (**a**) *(reflexionar)* to think (**b**) *Fig (transcurrir)* to pass, to go by (**c**) *Fml (río)* to wander

discurso *nm* speech; **dar** *o* **pronunciar un d.** to make a speech

discusión *nf* argument

discutir 1 *vi* to argue (**de** about)

2 *vt* to discuss, to talk about

disecar [44] *vt* (**a**) *(animal)* to stuff (**b**) *(planta)* to dry

diseminar *vt* to disseminate, to spread

disentir [54] *vi* to dissent, to disagree (**de** with)

diseñar *vt* to design

diseño *nm* design; **d. de interiores** interior design

disertar *vi* to expound (**sobre** on *o* upon)

disfraz *nm* disguise; *(para fiesta)* fancy dress; **fiesta de disfraces** fancy dress party

disfrazar [40] **1** *vt* to disguise

2 disfrazarse *vpr* to disguise oneself; **d. de pirata** to dress up as a pirate

disfrutar 1 *vi* (**a**) *(gozar)* to enjoy oneself (**b**) *(poseer)* **d. (de)** to enjoy

2 *vt* to enjoy

disgregar [42] *vt* (**a**) to disintegrate, to break up (**b**) *(dispersar)* to disperse

disgustado,-a *adj* upset, displeased

disgustar 1 *vt* to upset

2 disgustarse *vpr* (**a**) *(molestarse)* to get upset (**b**) *(dos amigos)* to quarrel

⚠ Observa que el verbo inglés **to disgust** es un falso amigo y no es la traducción del verbo español **disgustar**. En inglés, **to disgust** significa "repugnar, indignar".

disgusto *nm* (**a**) *(preocupación)* annoyance; **llevarse un d.** to get upset; **dar un d. a algn** to upset sb (**b**) *(desgracia)* trouble; **a d.** unwillingly; **sentirse** *o* **estar a d.** to feel ill at ease (**c**) *(desavenencia)* fall-out, disagreement

⚠ Observa que la palabra inglesa **disgust** es un falso amigo y no es la traducción de la palabra española **disgusto**. En inglés, **disgust** significa "repugnancia, asco".

disidente *adj & nmf* dissident

disimuladamente *adv* surreptitiously

disimulado,-a *adj* (**a**) *(persona)* sly, crafty

(**b**) *(oculto)* hidden, concealed

disimular *vt* to conceal, to hide

disimulo *nm* pretence

disipar 1 *vt* *(niebla)* to drive away; *(temor, duda)* to dispel

2 disiparse *vpr* *(gaseosa)* to go flat; *(niebla, temor etc)* to disappear

disketera *nf Informát* disk drive

dislexia *nf* dyslexia

dislocar [44] *vt* to dislocate

disminución *nf* decrease

disminuir [37] **1** *vt* to reduce

2 *vi* to diminish

disolución *nf* dissolution

disolvente *adj & nm* solvent

disolver [4] *(pp disuelto)* *vt* to dissolve

disparar 1 *vt* *(pistola etc)* to fire; *(flecha, balón)* to shoot; **d. a algn** to shoot at sb

2 dispararse *vpr* (**a**) *(arma)* to go off, to fire (**b**) *(precios)* to rocket

disparatado,-a *adj* absurd

disparate *nm* (**a**) *(dicho)* nonsense; **decir disparates** to talk nonsense (**b**) *(acto)* foolish act

disparidad *nf* disparity

disparo *nm* shot; *Dep* **d. a puerta** shot

dispensar *vt* (**a**) *(disculpar)* to pardon, to forgive (**b**) *(eximir)* to exempt

dispersar 1 *vt* to disperse; *(esparcir)* to scatter

2 dispersarse *vpr* to disperse

disperso,-a *adj (separado)* dispersed; *(esparcido)* scattered

displicencia *nf* condescension, disdain

displicente *adj* condescending, disdainful

disponer [19] *(pp dispuesto)* **1** *vt* (**a**) *(arreglar)* to arrange, to set out (**b**) *(ordenar)* to order

2 *vi* **d. de** to have at one's disposal

3 disponerse *vpr* to prepare, to get ready

disponible *adj* available

disposición *nf* (**a**) *(uso)* disposal; **a su d.** at your disposal *o* service (**b**) *(colocación)* arrangement, layout (**c**) **no estar en d. de** not to be prepared to (**d**) *(orden)* order, law

dispositivo *nm* device

dispuesto,-a *adj* (**a**) *(ordenado)* arranged (**b**) *(a punto)* ready (**c**) *(decidido)* determined; **no estar d. a** not to be prepared to (**d**) **según lo d. por la ley** in accordance with what the law stipulates

disputa *nf* *(discusión)* argument; *(contienda)* contest

disputar 1 *vt* (**a**) *(premio)* to compete for (**b**) *Dep (partido)* to play

2 disputarse *vpr (premio)* to compete for

disquete *nm Informát* diskette, floppy disk

disquetera *nf Informát* disk drive

distancia *nf* distance; **a d.** from a distance

distanciamiento *nm* distancing

distanciar [43] **1** *vt* to separate

2 distanciarse *vpr* to become separated; *(de otra persona)* to distance oneself

distante *adj* distant, far-off

distar *vi* to be distant o away; *Fig* to be far from; **dista mucho de ser perfecto** it's far from (being) perfect

distender [3] *vt Fig* to ease, to relax

distensión *nf Pol* détente

distinción *nf* distinction; **a d. de** unlike; **sin d. de** irrespective of

distinguido,-a *adj* distinguished

distinguir [59] **1** *vt* (a) *(diferenciar)* to distinguish (b) *(reconocer)* to recognize (c) *(honrar)* to honour

2 *vi (diferenciar)* to discriminate

3 distinguirse *upr* to distinguish oneself

distintivo,-a 1 *adj* distinctive, distinguishing

2 *nm* distinctive sign o mark

distinto,-a *adj* different

distorsión *nf* (a) distortion (b) *Med* sprain

distracción *nf* (a) entertainment; *(pasatiempo)* pastime, hobby (b) *(descuido)* distraction, absent-mindedness

distraer [25] **1** *vt* (a) *(atención)* to distract (b) *(divertir)* to entertain, to amuse

2 distraerse *upr* (a) *(divertirse)* to amuse oneself (b) *(abstraerse)* to let one's mind wander

distraído,-a *adj* (a) *(divertido)* entertaining (b) *(abstraido)* absent-minded

distribución *nf* (a) distribution (b) *(disposición)* layout

distribuidor,-a 1 *adj* distributing

2 *nm,f* (a) distributor (b) *Com* wholesaler

distribuir [37] *vt* to distribute; *(trabajo)* to share out

distrito *nm* district; **d. postal** postal district

disturbio *nm* riot, disturbance

disuadir *vt* to dissuade

disuasión *nf* dissuasion

disuelto,-a *pp de* disolver

DIU *nm (abr* dispositivo intrauterino) IUD

diurético,-a *adj & nm* diuretic

diurno,-a *adj* daytime

divagar [42] *vi* to digress, to wander

diván *nm* divan, couch

divergencia *nf* divergence

divergente *adj* diverging

diversidad *nf* diversity

diversificar [44] **1** *vt* to diversify

2 diversificarse *upr* to be diversified o varied; *(empresa)* to diversify

diversión *nf* fun

diverso,-a *adj* different; **diversos** several, various

divertido,-a *adj* amusing, funny

divertir [5] **1** *vt* to amuse, to entertain

2 divertirse *upr* to enjoy oneself, to have a good time; **¡que te diviertas!** enjoy yourself!, have fun!

dividendo *nm* dividend

dividir 1 *vt* to divide (**en** into); *Mat* **15 dividido entre 3** 15 divided by 3

2 dividirse *upr* to divide, to split up

divinidad *nf* divinity

divino,-a *adj* divine

divisa *nf* (a) *(emblema)* symbol, emblem (b) *Com* **divisas** foreign currency

divisar *vt* to make out, to discern

división *nf* division

divisorio,-a *adj* dividing

divorciado,-a 1 *adj* divorced

2 *nm,f (hombre)* divorcé; *(mujer)* divorcée

divorciar [43] **1** *vt* to divorce

2 divorciarse *upr* to get divorced; **se divorció de él** she divorced him, she got a divorce from him

divorcio *nm* divorce

divulgación *nf* disclosure

divulgar [42] *vt* to disclose; *Rad & TV* to broadcast

dizque *adv Andes, Carib, Méx* apparently

DNI *nm (abr* Documento Nacional de Identidad) Identity Card, ID card

do *nm Mús (de solfa)* doh, do; *(de escala diatónica)* C; **do de pecho** high C

doberman *nm* Doberman (pinscher)

dobladillo *nm* hem

doblaje *nm Cin* dubbing

doblar 1 *vt* (a) to double; **me dobla la edad** he is twice as old as I am (b) *(plegar)* to fold o turn up (c) *(torcer)* to bend (d) *(la esquina)* to go round (e) *(película)* to dub

2 *vi* (a) *(girar)* to turn; **d. a la derecha/ izquierda** to turn right/left (b) *(campanas)* to toll

3 doblarse *upr* (a) *(plegarse)* to fold (b) *(torcerse)* to bend

doble 1 *adj* double; **arma de d. filo** double-edged weapon

2 *nm* (a) double; **gana el d. que tú** she earns twice as much as you do (b) *Dep* **dobles** doubles

doblegar [42] **1** *vt* to bend

2 doblegarse *upr* to give in

doblez 1 *nm (pliegue)* fold

2 *nm o nf Fig* two-facedness, hypocrisy

doce *adj & nm inv* twelve

docena *nf* dozen

docencia *nf* teaching

docente *adj* teaching; **centro d.** educational centre

dócil *adj* docile

doctor,-a *nm,f* doctor

doctorado *nm Univ* doctorate, PhD

doctrina *nf* doctrine

documentación *nf* documentation; *(DNI, de conducir etc)* papers

documental *adj & nm* documentary

documentar *vt* to document

2 documentarse *upr* **d. (sobre)** to research, to get information (about o on)

documento *nm* document; **d. nacional de identidad** identity card

dogma *nm* dogma

dogmático,-a *adj & nm,f* dogmatic

dogo *nm* bulldog

dólar *nm* dollar

dolarización *nf* dollarization

dolencia *nf* ailment

doler [4] *vi* to hurt, to ache; **me duele la cabeza** I've got a headache; **me duele la mano** my hand is sore

  2 dolerse *vpr* to be sorry *o* sad

dolido,-a *adj* **estar d.** to be hurt

dolor *nm* (a) *Med* pain; **d. de cabeza** headache; **d. de muelas** toothache (b) *(pena)* grief, sorrow

dolorido,-a *adj* (a) *(dañado)* sore, aching (b) *(apenado)* hurt

doloroso,-a *adj* painful

domar *vt* to tame; *(caballo)* to break in

domesticar [44] *vt* to domesticate; *(animal)* to tame

doméstico,-a *adj* domestic; **animal d.** pet

domiciliación *nf* payment by standing order

domiciliar [43] *vt* (a) to house (b) *Fin* to pay by standing order

domiciliario,-a *adj* **arresto d.** house arrest

domicilio *nm* home, residence; *(señas)* address; **sin d. fijo** of no fixed abode; **d. fiscal** registered office

dominación *nf* domination

dominante *adj* (a) dominant (b) *(déspota)* domineering

dominar 1 *vt* (a) to dominate, to rule (b) *(situación)* to control; *(idioma)* to speak very well; *(asunto)* to master; *(paisaje etc)* to overlook

  2 *vi* (a) to dominate (b) *(resaltar)* to stand out

  3 dominarse *vpr* to control oneself

domingo *nm inv* Sunday; **D. de Resurrección** *o* **Pascua** Easter Sunday

dominguero,-a *nm,f Fam (excursionista)* weekend tripper; *(conductor)* weekend driver

dominical 1 *adj* Sunday

  2 *nm (suplemento)* Sunday supplement

dominicano,-a *adj & nm,f* Dominican; **República Dominicana** Dominican Republic

dominio *nm* (a) *(poder)* control; *(de un idioma)* command; **d. de sí mismo** self-control (b) *(ámbito)* scope, sphere; **ser del d. público** to be public knowledge (c) *(territorio)* dominion (d) *Informát* domain

dominó, dómino *nm* dominoes

don¹ *nm* (a) *(habilidad)* gift, talent; **tener el d. de** to have a knack for; **tener d. de gentes** to get on well with people (b) *(regalo)* present, gift

don² *nm* Señor D. José García Mr José García; **D. Fulano de Tal** Mr So-and-So; **un d. nadie** a nobody

donaire *nm* grace, elegance

donante *nmf* donor; *Med* **d. de sangre** blood donor

donar *vt Fml* to donate; *(sangre)* to give

donativo *nm* donation

doncella *nf Literario* (a) *(joven)* maid, maiden (b) *(criada)* maid, housemaid

donde *adv rel* where; **a** *o* **en d.** where; **de** *o* **desde d.** from where; **está d. lo dejaste** it is where you left it; *Fam* **está d. su tía** he's at his aunt's

> **donde** combines with the preposition **a** to form **adonde** when following a noun, a pronoun or an adverb expressing location (e.g. **el sitio adonde vamos** the place where we're going; **es allí adonde iban** that's where they were going).

dónde *adv interr* where?; **¿de d. eres?** where are you from?; **¿por d. se va a la playa?** which way is it to the beach?

> **dónde** can combine with the preposition **a** to form **adónde** (e.g. **¿adónde vamos?** where are we going?).

dondequiera *adv* everywhere; **d. que vaya** wherever I go

donostiarra 1 *adj* of/from San Sebastián

  2 *nmf* person from San Sebastián

doña *nf* **(Señora) D. Leonor Benítez** Mrs Leonor Benítez

dopaje *nm Dep* drug-taking

dopar 1 *vt (caballo etc)* to dope

  2 doparse *vpr* to take drugs

doping *nm Dep* drug-taking

doquier, doquiera *adv Literario* **por d.** everywhere

dorada *nf (pez)* gilthead bream

dorado,-a 1 *adj* golden

  2 *nm Téc* gilding

dorar *vt* (a) to gild (b) *Culin* to brown

dormido,-a *adj* (a) asleep; **quedarse d.** to fall asleep; *(no despertarse)* to oversleep, to sleep in (b) *(pierna, brazo)* numb

dormilón,-ona 1 *adj Fam* sleepyheaded

  2 *nm,f* sleepyhead

  3 *nf Ven* **dormilona** nightdress

dormir [7] **1** *vi* to sleep; **tener ganas de d.** to feel sleepy;

  2 *vt* **d. la siesta** to have an afternoon nap

  3 dormirse *vpr* to fall asleep; **se me ha dormido el brazo** my arm has gone to sleep

dormitar *vi* to doze, to snooze

dormitorio *nm* (a) *(de una casa)* bedroom (b) *(de colegio, residencia)* dormitory; **ciudad d.** dormitory town

dorsal 1 *adj* **espina d.** spine

  2 *nm Dep* number

dorso *nm* back; **instrucciones al d.** instructions over; **véase al d.** see overleaf

dos *adj & nm inv* two; **los d.** both; **nosotros/vosotros d.** both of us/you; *Fam* **cada d. por tres** every other minute; *Fam* **en un d. por tres** in a flash

doscientos,-as *adj & nm* two hundred

dosel *nm* canopy

dosificación *nf* dosage

dosificar [44] *vt* (**a**) to dose (**b**) *(esfuerzos, energías)* to measure
dosis *nf inv* dose
dossier *nm* dossier
dotación *nf (dinero)* grant; *(personal)* personnel, staff; *(de barco)* crew
dotado,-a *adj* (**a**) *(persona)* gifted (**b**) *(equipado)* equipped; **d. de** provided with
dotar *vt* **d. de** to provide with
dote *nf* (**a**) *(de novia)* dowry (**b**) **dotes** *(talento)* gift, talent
doy *indic pres de* **dar**
dpto. *(abr* **departamento**) Dept
Dr. *(abr* **doctor**) Dr
Dra. *(abr* **doctora**) Dr
dragar [42] *vt* to dredge
dragón *nm* dragon
drama *nm* drama
dramático,-a *adj* dramatic
dramatismo *nm* drama, dramatic quality
dramaturgo,-a *nm,f* playwright, dramatist
drástico,-a *adj* drastic
drenar *vt* to drain
driblar *vi* to dribble
droga *nf* drug; **d. blanda/dura** soft/hard drug
drogadicto,-a *nm,f* drug addict
drogar [42] **1** *vt* to drug
2 drogarse *vpr* to drug oneself, to take drugs
droguería *nf* hardware and household goods shop
dto. *(abr* **descuento**) discount
dual *adj* dual
dualidad *nf* duality
dubitativo,-a *adj* doubtful
Dublín *n* Dublin
dublinés,-esa 1 *adj* of/from Dublin
2 *nm,f* Dubliner
ducha *nf* shower; **darse/tomar una d.** to take/have a shower
ducharse *vpr* to shower, to have *o* take a shower
ducho,-a *adj* expert; **ser d. en** to be well versed in
duda *nf* doubt; **sin d.** without a doubt; **no cabe d.** (there is) no doubt; **poner algo en d.** to question sth; **sacar a algn de dudas** to dispel sb's doubts
dudar 1 *vi* (**a**) to doubt (**b**) *(vacilar)* to hesitate (**en** to); **dudaba entre ir o quedarme** I hesitated whether to go *o* to stay (**c**) **d. de algn** *(desconfiar)* to suspect sb
2 *vt* to doubt
dudoso,-a *adj* (**a**) **ser d.** *(incierto)* to be uncertain *o* doubtful (**b**) **estar d.** *(indeciso)* to be undecided (**c**) *(poco honrado)* dubious

duelo¹ *nm (combate)* duel
duelo² *nm (luto)* mourning
duende *nm* (**a**) *(espíritu)* goblin, elf (**b**) *(encanto)* magic, charm
dueña *nf* owner; *(de pensión)* landlady
dueño *nm* owner; *(de casa etc)* landlord; *Fig* **ser d. de sí mismo** to be self-possessed
Duero *n* el D. the Douro
dulce 1 *adj* (**a**) *(sabor)* sweet (**b**) *(carácter, voz)* gentle (**c**) *(metal)* soft (**d**) **agua d.** fresh water
2 *nm* (**a**) *Culin (pastel)* cake (**b**) *(caramelo)* *Br* sweet, *US* candy
dulzura *nf* (**a**) sweetness (**b**) *Fig* gentleness, softness
duna *nf* dune
dúo *nm* duet
duodécimo,-a *adj & nm,f* twelfth
dúplex *nm* (**a**) *(piso)* duplex, duplex apartment (**b**) *Tel* link-up
duplicado,-a 1 *adj* **por d.** in duplicate
2 *nm* duplicate, copy
duplicar [44] **1** *vt* to duplicate; *(cifras)* to double
2 duplicarse *vpr* to double
duplo,-a *adj & nm,f* double
duque *nm* duke
duquesa *nf* duchess
duración *nf* duration, length; **disco de larga d.** long-playing record
duradero,-a *adj* durable, lasting
durante *prep* during; **d. el día** during the day; **d. todo el día** all day long; **viví en La Coruña d. un año** I lived in La Coruña for a year
durar *vi* (**a**) to last (**b**) *(ropa, calzado)* to wear well, to last
durazno *nm (fruto)* peach; *(árbol)* peach tree
dúrex *nm Méx Br* Sellotape®, *US* Scotch tape®
dureza *nf* (**a**) hardness; *(severidad)* harshness, severity (**b**) *(callosidad)* corn

> *Observa que la palabra inglesa* **duress** *es un falso amigo y no es la traducción de la palabra española* **dureza**. *En inglés,* **duress** *significa "coacción".*

duro,-a 1 *adj* (**a**) hard; *Dep* **juego d.** rough play (**b**) *(resistente)* tough; *(severo)* hard (**c**) *(clima)* harsh
2 *nm (moneda)* 5-peseta coin
3 *adv* hard; **trabajar d.** to work hard
DVD *nm Informát (abr* **Disco Versátil Digital**) DVD

E, e [e] *nf (la letra)* E, e

E *(abr* **Este***)* E

e *conj* and

> **e** is used instead of **y** in front of words beginning with "i" or "hi" (e.g. **apoyo e interés** support and interest; **corazón e hígado** heart and liver).

ebanista *nm* cabinet-maker

ébano *nm* ebony

ebrio,-a *adj* inebriated; **e. de dicha** drunk with joy

ebullición *nf* boiling; **punto de e.** boiling point

eccema *nm* eczema

echar 1 *vt* (**a**) *(lanzar)* to throw; *Fig* **e. una mano** to give a hand; *Fig* **e. una mirada/una ojeada** to have a look/a quick look *o* glance

(**b**) *(carta)* to post; *(vino, agua)* to pour; **e. sal al estofado** to put salt in the stew; **e. gasolina al coche** to put *Br* petrol *o US* gas in the car

(**c**) *(expulsar)* to throw out; *(despedir)* to fire, *Br* to sack

(**d**) *(humo, olor etc)* to give off

(**e**) *Fam (película)* to show

(**f**) **le echó 37 años** he reckoned she was about 37

(**g**) **e. de menos** *o* **en falta** to miss

(**h**) **e. abajo** *(edificio)* to demolish

2 *vi* (+ **a** + *infin) (empezar)* to begin to; **echó a correr** he ran off

3 echarse *upr* (**a**) *(tumbarse)* to lie down; *(lanzarse)* to throw oneself; *Fig* **la noche se nos echó encima** it was night before we knew it

(**b**) **échate a un lado** stand aside; *Fig* **e. atrás** to get cold feet

(**c**) *Fam* **e. novio/novia** to get a boyfriend/girlfriend

(**d**) (+ **a** + *infin) (empezar)* to begin to; **e. a llorar** to burst into tears; **e. a reír** to burst out laughing; **e. a perder** *(comida)* to go bad

ecléctico,-a 1 *adj & nm,f* eclectic

eclesiástico,-a 1 *adj* ecclesiastical

2 *nm* clergyman

eclipsar *vt* to eclipse

eclipse *nm* eclipse

eco *nm* echo; *Fig* **hacerse e. de una noticia** to publish an item of news; **tener e.** to arouse interest

ecografía *nf* scan

ecología *nf* ecology

ecológico,-a *adj* ecological; *(alimentos)* organic; *(detergente)* environmentally-friendly

ecologista 1 *adj* ecological; *Pol* **partido e.** ecology party

2 *nmf* ecologist

economía *nf* (**a**) economy; **con e.** economically (**b**) *(ciencia)* economics *sing*

económico,-a *adj* (**a**) economic (**b**) *(barato)* economical, inexpensive (**c**) *(persona)* thrifty

economista *nmf* economist

economizar [40] *vt & vi* to economize

ecosistema *nm* ecosystem

ecotasa *nf* ecotax

ecoturismo *nm* ecotourism

ecuación *nf* equation

Ecuador *n* Ecuador

ecuador *nm Geog* equator

ecualizador *nm* **e. (gráfico)** graphic equalizer

ecuánime *adj* (**a**) *(temperamento)* equable, even-tempered (**b**) *(juicio)* impartial

ecuatorial *adj* equatorial; **Guinea E.** Equatorial Guinea

ecuatoriano,-a *adj & nm,f* Ecuadorian

ecuestre *adj* equestrian

ecuménico,-a *adj* ecumenical

eczema *nm* eczema

edad *nf* age; **¿qué e. tienes?** how old are you?; **la tercera e.** senior citizens; **E. Media** Middle Ages

edición *nf* (**a**) *(publicación)* publication; *(de sellos)* issue (**b**) *(conjunto de ejemplares)* edition

edicto *nm* edict, proclamation

edificante *adj* edifying

edificar [44] *vt* to build

edificio *nm* building

edil,-a *nm,f* town councillor

Edimburgo *n* Edinburgh

editar *vt* (**a**) *(libro, periódico)* to publish; *(disco)* to release (**b**) *Informát* to edit

editor,-a 1 *adj* publishing

2 *nm,f* publisher

editorial 1 *adj* publishing

2 *nf* publishers, publishing house

3 *nm Prensa* editorial, leader article

edredón *nm Br* duvet, *US* comforter

educación *nf* (**a**) education; **e. física** physical education (**b**) *(formación)* upbringing (**c**) **buena/mala e.** *(modales)* good/bad manners; **falta de e.** bad manners

educado,-a adj polite

educador,-a 1 adj educating

  2 nm,f educationalist

educar [44] vt (hijos) to raise; (alumnos) to educate; (la voz) to train

educativo,-a adj educational; **sistema e.** education system

edulcorante nm sweetener

EE.UU. (abr **Estados Unidos**) USA

efectista adj spectacular

efectivamente adv quite!, yes indeed!

efectividad nf effectiveness

efectivo,-a 1 adj effective; **hacer algo e.** to carry sth out; Fin **hacer e. un cheque** to cash a cheque

  2 nm (a) Fin **en e.** in cash (b) Mil **efectivos** forces

efecto nm (a) (resultado) effect; **efectos especiales/sonoros** special/sound effects; **efectos personales** personal belongings o effects; **a efectos de ...** for the purposes of ...; **en e.** quite!, yes indeed! (b) (impresión) impression; **causar** o **hacer e.** to make an impression (c) Dep spin

efectuar [30] vt to carry out; (viaje) to make; Com (pedido) to place

efeméride nf event

efervescente adj effervescent; **aspirina e.** soluble aspirin

eficacia nf (de persona) efficiency; (de remedio etc) effectiveness

eficaz adj (persona) efficient; (remedio, medida etc) effective

eficiencia nf efficiency

eficiente adj efficient

efigie nf effigy

efímero,-a adj ephemeral

efusivo,-a adj effusive

EGB nf Educ (abr **Enseñanza General Básica**) = formerly, stage of Spanish education system for pupils aged 6-14

Egeo n **el (Mar) E.** the Aegean Sea

egipcio,-a adj & nm,f Egyptian

Egipto n Egypt

egocéntrico,-a adj egocentric, self-centred

egoísmo nm egoism, selfishness

egoísta 1 adj ego(t)istic, selfish

  2 nmf ego(t)ist, selfish person

egregio,-a adj eminent, illustrious

egresar vi Am to leave school, US to graduate

Eire n Eire, Republic of Ireland

ej. (abr **ejemplo**) example

eje nm (a) Téc (de rueda) axle; (de máquina) shaft (b) Mat axis (c) Hist **El E.** the Axis

ejecución nf (a) (de orden) carrying out (b) (ajusticiamiento) execution (c) Mús performance

ejecutar vt (a) (orden) to carry out (b) (ajusticiar) to execute (c) Mús to perform, to play (d) Informát to run

ejecutiva nf Pol executive

ejecutivo,-a 1 adj executive; Pol **el poder e.** the government

  2 nm executive

ejecutor,-a nm,f (a) Jur executor (b) (verdugo) executioner

ejemplar 1 nm (a) (de libro) copy; (de revista, periódico) number, issue (b) (espécimen) specimen

  2 adj exemplary, model

ejemplificar [44] vt to exemplify

ejemplo nm example; **por e.** for example; **dar e.** to set an example

ejercer [49] **1** vt (a) (profesión etc) to practise (b) (influencia) to exert (c) **e. el derecho de/a ...** to exercise one's right to ...

  2 vi to practise (**de** as)

ejercicio nm (a) exercise; (de profesión) practice; **hacer e.** to take o do exercise (b) Fin tax year; **e. económico** financial o fiscal year

ejercitar vt to practise

ejército nm army

ejote nm CAm, Méx green bean

el 1 art def m (a) the (b) (no se traduce) **el Sr. García** Mr. García; **el hambre/destino** hunger/fate (c) (con partes del cuerpo, prendas de vestir) **me he cortado el dedo** I've cut my finger; **métetelo en el bolsillo** put it in your pocket (d) (con días de la semana) **el lunes** on Monday

> **el** is used instead of **la** before feminine nouns which are stressed on the first syllable and begin with "a" or "ha" (e.g. **el agua, el hacha**). Note that **el** combines with the prepositions **a** and **de** to produce the contracted forms **al** and **del.**

  2 pron (a) the one; **el de las once** the eleven o'clock one; **el que tienes en la mano** the one you've got in your hand; **el que quieras** whichever one you want (b) (no se traduce) **el de tu amigo** your friend's

él pron pers (a) (sujeto) (persona) he; (animal, cosa) it (b) (complemento) (persona) him; (animal, cosa) it

> Usually omitted in Spanish as a subject except for emphasis or contrast.

elaboración nf (a) (de un producto) manufacture, production (b) (de una idea) working out, development

elaborar vt (a) (producto) to manufacture, to produce (b) (teoría) to develop

elasticidad nf elasticity; Fig flexibility

elástico,-a adj & nm elastic

elección nf choice; Pol election

elector,-a nm,f elector

electorado nm electorate

electoral adj electoral; **campaña e.** election campaign; **colegio e.** polling station

electoralismo nm electioneering

electricidad nf electricity

electricista nmf electrician

eléctrico,-a *adj* electric
electrificar [44] *vt* to electrify
electrizar [40] *vt* to electrify
electrochoque *nm* electric shock therapy
electrocutar *vt* to electrocute
electrodo *nm* electrode
electrodoméstico *nm* (domestic) electrical appliance
electroimán *nm* electromagnet
electromagnético,-a *adj* electromagnetic
electrón *nm* electron
electrónica *nf* electronics *sing*
electrónico,-a *adj* electronic
elefante *nm* elephant
elegancia *nf* elegance
elegante *adj* elegant
elegía *nf* elegy
elegir [58] *vt* (a) to choose (b) *Pol* to elect
elemental *adj* (a) *(fundamental)* basic, fundamental (b) *(simple)* elementary
elemento *nm* (a) element (b) *(componente)* component, part (c) *(individuo)* type, individual (d) **elementos** elements; *(fundamentos)* rudiments
elepé *nm* LP (record)
elevación *nf* elevation; **e. de precios** rise in prices; **e. del terreno** rise in the ground
elevado,-a *adj* (a) high; *(edificio)* tall (b) *(pensamiento etc)* lofty, noble
elevalunas *nm inv Aut* **e. eléctrico** electric windows
elevar 1 *vt* to raise
  2 elevarse *vpr* (a) *(subir)* to rise; *(edificio)* to stand (b) **e.** *(cantidad)* to amount o come to
elijo *indic pres de* **elegir**
eliminación *nf* elimination
eliminar *vt* to eliminate
eliminatoria *nf Dep* heat, qualifying round
eliminatorio,-a *adj* qualifying, eliminatory
élite *nf* elite, élite
elitista *adj* elitist
elixir *nm (enjuague bucal)* mouthwash; *Literario* elixir
ella *pron pers f* (a) *(sujeto)* she; *(animal, cosa)* it, she (b) *(complemento)* her; *(animal, cosa)* it, her

Usually omitted in Spanish as a subject except for emphasis or contrast.

ellas *pron pers fpl ver* **ellos**
ello *pron pers neut* it; **por e.** for that reason
ellos *pron pers mpl*
(a) *(sujeto)* they (b) *(complemento)* them

Usually omitted in Spanish as a subject except for emphasis or contrast.

elocuencia *nf* eloquence
elocuente *adj* eloquent; **los hechos son elocuentes** the facts speak for themselves
elogiar [43] *vt* to praise
elogio *nm* praise
elote *nm CAm, Méx* corncob, ear of maize

El Salvador *n* El Salvador
elucidar *vt* to elucidate
eludir *vt* to avoid
emanar *vi* to emanate; *Fig* **e. de** *(derivar)* to derive o come from
emancipar 1 *vt* to emancipate
  2 emanciparse *vpr* to become emancipated
embadurnar *vt* to daub, to smear (**de** with)
embajada *nf* embassy
embajador,-a *nm,f* ambassador
embalaje *nm* packing, packaging
embalar *vt* to pack
embalarse *vpr* to speed up; *Fig* **no te embales** hold your horses
embalsamar *vt* to embalm
embalsar 1 *vt* to dam; *(problema)* to contain
  2 embalsarse *vpr* to form a pool
embalse *nm* dam, reservoir
embarazada 1 *adj* pregnant; **dejar e.** to get pregnant
  2 *nf* pregnant woman, expectant mother

> Observa que la palabra inglesa **embarrassed** es un falso amigo y no es la traducción de la palabra española **embarazada**. En inglés **embarrassed** significa "avergonzado".

embarazar [40] *vt Fig* to hinder
embarazo *nm* (a) *(preñez)* pregnancy (b) *(obstáculo)* obstacle (c) *(turbación)* embarrassment
embarazoso,-a *adj* awkward, embarrassing
embarcación *nf* (a) *(nave)* boat, craft (b) *(embarco)* embarkation
embarcadero *nm* quay
embarcar [44] **1** *vt* to ship
  2 *vi* to embark, to go on board
  3 embarcarse *vpr* (a) *Náut* **e. (en)** to go on board; *Av* to board (b) **e. en un proyecto** to embark on a project
embarco *nm* embarkation
embargar [42] *vt* (a) *Jur* to seize, to impound (b) *Fig* **le embarga la emoción** he's overwhelmed with joy
embargo *nm* (a) *Jur* seizure of property (b) *Com & Pol* embargo (c) **sin e.** however, nevertheless
embarque *nm (de persona)* boarding; *(de mercancías)* loading; **tarjeta de e.** boarding card
embarrancar [44] *vi*, **embarrancarse** *vpr Náut* to run aground
embaucador,-a 1 *adj* deceitful
  2 *nm,f* swindler, cheat
embaucar [44] *vt* to swindle, to cheat
embeber 1 *vt* to soak up
  2 embeberse *vpr* to become absorbed o engrossed
embelesar *vt* to fascinate
embellecer [33] *vt* to embellish
embestida *nf* (a) onslaught (b) *Taurom* charge

embestir [6] vt (a) Taurom to charge (b) (atacar) to attack

emblandecer [33] **1** vt to soften

2 emblandecerse upr Fig to relent

emblema nm emblem

embobado,-a adj fascinated

embobarse upr to be fascinated o besotted (con by)

embolia nf embolism

émbolo nm piston

embolsar vt, **embolsarse** upr to pocket

emborrachar vt, **emborracharse** upr to get drunk

emboscada nf ambush; **tender una e.** to lay an ambush

embotar vt to blunt; Fig (sentidos) to dull; (mente) to befuddle

embotellado nm bottling

embotellamiento nm Aut traffic jam

embotellar vt (a) to bottle (b) (tráfico) to block

embragar [42] vi Aut to engage the clutch

embrague nm clutch

embravecerse [33] upr (a) (enfadarse) to become enraged (b) (mar) to become rough

embriagador,-a adj intoxicating

embriagar [42] **1** vt to intoxicate; Fig to enrapture

2 embriagarse upr to get drunk; Fig to be enraptured

embriaguez nf intoxication

embridar vt to bridle

embrión nm embryo

embrollar 1 vt to confuse, to muddle

2 embrollarse upr to get muddled o confused

embrollo nm (a) (lío) muddle, confusion (b) (aprieto) fix, jam

embrujado,-a adj (persona) bewitched; (sitio) haunted

embrujo nm spell, charm; Fig attraction, fascination

embrutecer [33] vt to stultify

embuchar vt to stuff

embudo nm funnel

embuste nm lie, trick

embustero,-a nm,f cheater, liar

embutido nm sausage

embutir vt (a) (carne) to stuff (b) (meter) to stuff o cram o squeeze (en into) (c) (incrustar) to inlay

emergencia nf emergency; **salida de e.** emergency exit; **en caso de e.** in an emergency

emerger [53] vi to emerge

emigración nf emigration; (de pájaros) migration

emigrado,-a nm,f emigrant; Pol émigré

emigrante adj & nmf emigrant

emigrar vi to emigrate; (pájaros) to migrate

emilio nm Fam Informát e-mail (message)

eminencia nf eminence; (genio) genius

eminente adj eminent

emirato nm emirate

emisario,-a nm,f emissary

emisión nf (a) emission (b) (de bonos, sellos) issue (c) Rad & TV broadcasting

emisora nf radio o television station

emitir vt (a) to emit; (luz, calor) to give off (b) (opinión, juicio) to express (c) Rad & TV to transmit (d) (bonos, sellos) to issue

emoción nf (a) emotion (b) (excitación) excitement; **¡qué e.!** how exciting!

emocionado,-a adj deeply moved o touched

emocionante adj (a) (conmovedor) moving, touching (b) (excitante) exciting, thrilling

emocionar 1 vt (a) (conmover) to move, to touch (b) (excitar) to thrill

2 emocionarse upr (a) (conmoverse) to be moved (b) (excitarse) to get excited

emotivo,-a adj emotional

empacar [44] vt (a) (mercancías) to pack (b) Am to annoy

empachar vt to give indigestion to

empacho nm (de comida) indigestion, upset stomach; Fig surfeit

empadronar vt, **empadronarse** upr to register

empalagar [42] vi to pall

empalagoso,-a adj (a) (dulce) sickly sweet (b) Fig (persona) smarmy

empalizada nf fence

empalmar 1 vt (a) (unir) to join; (cuerdas, cables) to splice (b) Ftb to volley

2 vi to converge; Ferroc to connect

3 empalmarse upr Vulg to get a hard-on

empalme nm (a) connection (b) Ferroc junction; (en carretera) intersection, T-junction

empanada nf pie

empanadilla nf pasty

empanado,-a adj (filete etc) breaded, in breadcrumbs

empantanarse upr (a) (inundarse) to become flooded (b) Fig to be bogged down

empañar vt, **empañarse** upr (cristales) to steam up

empapado,-a adj soaked

empapar 1 vt (a) (mojar) to soak (b) (absorber) to soak up

2 empaparse upr (a) (persona) to get soaked (b) Fam Fig **empaparse (de)** to take in

empapelar vt to wallpaper

empaque nm bearing, presence

empaquetar vt to pack

emparedado nm sandwich

emparejar vt (cosas) to match; (personas) to pair off

empastar vt (diente) to fill

empaste nm (de diente) filling

empatado,-a adj drawn; **estar/ir empatados** to be drawing

empatar 1 vi Dep to tie, to draw

2 *vt* (**a**) *Dep* **e. el partido** to equalize (**b**) *Am* (*unir*) to join

empate *nm Dep* draw, tie

empecinarse *vpr* to dig one's heels in

empedernido,-a *adj* (*fumador, bebedor*) hardened

empedrado,-a 1 *adj* cobbled

2 *nm* (**a**) (*adoquines*) cobblestones (**b**) (*acción*) paving

empeine *nm* instep

empellón *nm* push, shove

empeñar 1 *vt* to pawn

2 empeñarse *vpr* (**a**) (*insistir*) to insist (**en** on), to be determined (**en** to) (**b**) (*endeudarse*) to get into debt

empeño *nm* (**a**) (*insistencia*) insistence; **poner e. en algo** to put a lot of effort into sth (**b**) (*deuda*) pledge; **casa de empeños** pawnshop

empeoramiento *nm* deterioration, worsening

empeorar 1 *vi* to deteriorate, to worsen

2 *vt* to make worse

3 empeorarse *vpr* to deteriorate, to worsen

empequeñecer [33] *vt Fig* to belittle

emperador *nm* emperor

emperatriz *nf* empress

emperifollarse *vpr Fam* to get dolled up

emperrarse *vpr* to dig one's heels in, to become stubborn

empezar [51] *vt & vi* (*a hacer algo*) to begin; (*algo*) to start, to commence

empinado,-a *adj* (*cuesta*) steep

empinar 1 *vt* to raise; *Fam* **e. el codo** to drink

2 empinarse *vpr* (*persona*) to stand on tiptoe

empírico,-a *adj* empirical

emplasto *nm* poultice

emplazamiento *nm* (**a**) (*colocación*) site, location (**b**) *Jur* summons *sing*

emplazar[1] [40] *vt* to locate, to situate

emplazar[2] [40] *vt* (**a**) *Jur* to summons (**b**) (*a una reunión etc*) to call

empleado,-a *nm,f* employee; (*de oficina, banco*) clerk; **empleada del hogar** servant, maid

emplear *vt* (**a**) (*usar*) to use; (*contratar*) to employ (**b**) (*dinero, tiempo*) to spend

empleo *nm* (**a**) (*oficio*) job; *Pol* employment (**b**) (*uso*) use; **modo de e.** instructions for use

emplomar *vt Am* (*diente*) to fill

empobrecer [33] **1** *vt* to impoverish

2 empobrecerse *vpr* to become impoverished *o* poor

empobrecimiento *nm* impoverishment

empollar *vt* (**a**) (*huevos*) to sit on (**b**) *Fam* (*estudiar*) to bone up on, *Br* to swot up

empollón,-ona *nm,f Br Fam* swot, *US* grind

empolvar 1 *vt* to cover in dust

2 empolvarse *vpr* (*la cara*) to powder

emponzoñar *vt* to poison

emporcar [44] *vt* to foul, to dirty

emporio *nm* (**a**) *Com* emporium, trading *o* commercial centre (**b**) *Am* department store

emporrarse *vpr Fam* to get high

empotrado,-a *adj* fitted

emprendedor,-a *adj* enterprising

emprender *vt* to undertake; *Fam* **emprenderla con algn** to pick on sb

empresa *nf* (**a**) *Com & Ind* firm, company; **e. punto com** dot com (company); **e. de trabajo temporal** temping agency (**b**) *Pol* **la libre e.** free enterprise (**c**) (*tarea*) undertaking

empresariado *nm* employers

empresarial *adj* (**a**) (*de empresa*) business; **(ciencias) empresariales** business studies (**b**) (*espíritu*) entrepreneurial; **organización e.** employers' organization

empresario,-a *nm,f* (**a**) (*hombre*) businessman; (*mujer*) businesswoman (**b**) (*patrón*) employer

empréstito *nm Fin* debenture loan

empujar *vt* to push, to shove

empuje *nm* push; *Fig* (*brío*) verve, get-up-and-go

empujón *nm* push, shove; **dar empujones** to push and shove

empuñadura *nf* (*de espada*) hilt

empuñar *vt* to grasp, to seize

emular *vt* to emulate

emulsión *nf* emulsion

en *prep* (**a**) (*posición*) in, on, at; **en Madrid/ Bolivia** in Madrid/Bolivia; **en la mesa** on the table; **en el bolso** in the bag; **en casa/el trabajo** at home/work

(**b**) (*movimiento*) into; **entró en el cuarto** he went into the room

(**c**) (*tiempo*) in, on, at; **en 1940** in 1940; **en verano** in summer; *Am* **en la mañana** in the morning; **cae en martes** it falls on a Tuesday; **en ese momento** at that moment

(**d**) (*transporte*) by, in; **en coche/tren** by car/ train; **en avión** by air

(**e**) (*modo*) in; **en español** in Spanish; **en broma** jokingly; **en serio** seriously

(**f**) (*reducción, aumento*) by; **los precios aumentaron en un diez por ciento** the prices went up by ten percent

(**g**) (*tema, materia*) at, in; **bueno en deportes** good at sports; **experto en política** expert in politics

(**h**) (*división, separación*) in; **lo dividió en tres partes** he divided it in three

(**i**) (*con infinitivo*) **fue rápido en responder** he was quick to answer; **la conocí en el andar** I recognized her by her walk; **ser sobrio en el vestir** to dress simply

enaguas *nfpl* underskirt, petticoat

enajenación *nf,* **enajenamiento** *nm* alienation; **e. mental** mental derangement, insanity

enajenar 1 *vt* (**a**) *Jur* to alienate (**b**) (*turbar*) to drive insane

2 enajenarse *vpr* (*enloquecer*) to go insane

enaltecer [33] *vt* (**a**) (*alabar*) to praise, to extol (**b**) (*ennoblecer*) to do credit to

enamorado,-a 1 *adj* in love

2 *nm,f* person in love

enamorar 1 *vt* to win the heart of

2 enamorarse *vpr* to fall in love (**de** with)

enano,-a *adj & nm,f* dwarf

enardecer [33] **1** *vt (sentimientos)* to rouse, to stir up; *(persona)* to fill with enthusiasm

2 enardecerse *vpr Fig* to become excited

encabezamiento *nm (de carta)* heading; *(de periódico)* headline; *(preámbulo)* foreword, preamble

encabezar [40] *vt* (**a**) *(carta, lista)* to head; *(periódico)* to lead (**b**) *(rebelión, carrera, movimiento)* to lead

encabritarse *vpr* (**a**) *(caballo)* to rear (up) (**b**) *Fig (persona)* to get cross

encadenar *vt* to chain

encajar 1 *vt* (**a**) *(ajustar)* to insert; **e. la puerta** to push the door to (**b**) *Fam (asimilar)* to take (**c**) *(comentario)* to get in; **e. un golpe a algn** to land sb a blow

2 *vi* (**a**) *(ajustarse)* to fit (**b**) *Fig* **e. con** to fit (in) with, to square with

encaje *nm* lace

encalar *vt* to whitewash

encallar *vi* (**a**) *Náut* to run aground (**b**) *Fig* to flounder, to fail

encaminado,-a *adj* **estar bien/mal e.** to be on the right/wrong track

encaminar 1 *vt* to direct

2 encaminarse *vpr* to head (**a** for; **hacia** towards)

encandilar *vt* to dazzle

encantado,-a *adj* (**a**) *(contento)* delighted; **e. de conocerle** pleased to meet you (**b**) *(embrujado)* enchanted

encantador,-a 1 *adj* charming, delightful

2 *nm,f* magician

encantamiento *nm* spell

encantar *vt (hechizar)* to bewitch, to cast a spell on; *Fig* **me encanta nadar** I love swimming

encanto *nm* (**a**) *(atractivo)* charm; **ser un e.** to be charming (**b**) *(hechizo)* spell

encapricharse *vpr* **e. con** to set one's mind on; *(encariñarse)* to take a fancy to; *(enamorarse)* to get a crush on

encapuchado,-a *adj* hooded

encaramarse *vpr* to climb up

encarar 1 *vt* to face, to confront

2 encararse *vpr* **e. con** to face up to

encarcelar *vt* to imprison, to jail

encarecer [33] **1** *vt* to put up the price of

2 encarecerse *vpr* to go up (in price)

encarecidamente *adv* earnestly, insistently; **le rogamos e. que ...** we would earnestly request you to ...

encarecimiento *nm* increase o rise in price

encargado,-a 1 *nm,f Com (hombre)* manager; *(mujer)* manager, manageress; *(responsable)* person in charge

2 *adj* in charge

encargar [42] **1** *vt* (**a**) to put in charge of, to entrust with (**b**) *Com (mercancías)* to order, to place an order for; *(encuesta)* to commission

2 encargarse *vpr* **e. de** to see to, to deal with

encargo *nm* (**a**) *Com* order; **hecho de e.** *(a petición)* made to order (**b**) *(recado)* errand (**c**) *(tarea)* job, assignment

encariñarse *vpr* **e. con** to become fond of, to get attached to

encarnación *nf* incarnation, embodiment

encarnado,-a *adj (rojo)* red

encarnar *vt* to personify, to embody

encarnizado,-a *adj* fierce

encarrilar *vt (coche, tren)* to put on the road o rails; *Fig* to put on the right track

encasillar *vt* to pigeonhole

encausar *vt* to prosecute

encauzar [40] *vt* to channel

encenagarse [42] *vpr* to get covered in mud

encendedor *nm* lighter

encender [3] **1** *vt* (**a**) *(luz, radio, tele)* to switch on, to put on; *(cigarro, vela, fuego)* to light; *(cerilla)* to strike, to light (**b**) *Fig* to inflame, to stir up

2 encenderse *vpr* (**a**) *(fuego)* to catch; *(luz)* to go o come on (**b**) *(cara)* to blush, to go red

encendido *nm* ignition

encerado *nm (pizarra)* blackboard

encerar *vt* to wax, polish

encerrar [1] **1** *vt* to shut in; *(con llave)* to lock in (**b**) *Fig (contener)* to contain, to include

2 encerrarse *vpr* to shut oneself up o in; *(con llave)* to lock oneself in

encestar *vi Dep* to score (a basket)

enchaquetado,-a *adj* smartly dressed

encharcar [44] **1** *vt* to flood, to swamp

2 encharcarse *vpr* to get flooded

enchilada *nf Culin* = stuffed corn tortilla seasoned with chilli

enchironar *vt Fam* to put away

enchufado,-a 1 *adj Fam* **estar e.** to have good connections o contacts

2 *nm,f Fam (favorito)* pet

enchufar *vt* (**a**) *Elec* to plug in (**b**) *(unir)* to join, to connect (**c**) *Fam (para un trabajo)* to pull strings for

enchufe *nm* (**a**) *Elec (hembra)* socket; *(macho)* plug (**b**) *Fam* contact

enchufismo *nm Fam* string-pulling

encía *nf* gum

enciclopedia *nf* encyclopedia

encierro *nm Pol (protesta)* sit-in

encima *adv* (**a**) on top; *(arriba)* above; *(en el aire)* overhead; **déjalo e.** put it on top; **¿llevas cambio e.?** do you have any change on you?; *Fig* **quitarse algo de e.** to get rid of sth; **ahí e.** up there (**b**) *(además)* besides (**c**) **e. de** *(sobre)* on; *(en el aire)* above; *Fig (además)* besides; **e. de la mesa** on the table (**d**) **por e.** above; *Fig* **por e. de sus posibilidades** beyond his abilities; **leer un libro por e.** to skip through a book

encimera *nf (de cocina)* worktop

encina *nf* holm oak

encinta *adj* pregnant

enclaustrarse *vpr* to shut oneself up

enclave *nm* enclave

enclenque *adj (débil)* puny; *(enfermizo)* sickly

encoger [53] **1** *vi (contraerse)* to contract; *(prenda)* to shrink

2 *vt* to contract; *(prenda)* to shrink

3 encogerse *vpr (contraerse)* to contract; *(prenda)* to shrink; **e. de hombros** to shrug (one's shoulders)

encolar *vt (papel)* to paste; *(madera)* to glue

encolerizar [40] **1** *vt* to infuriate, to anger

2 encolerizarse *vpr* to become furious

encomendar [1] **1** *vt* to entrust with, to put in charge of

2 encomendarse *vpr* **e. a** to entrust oneself

encomienda *nf* **(a)** assignment, mission **(b)** *(paquete postal)* parcel

encomio *nm* praise

enconado,-a *adj* **(a)** *(discusión)* bitter, fierce **(b)** *Med* inflamed, sore

enconarse *vpr* **(a)** *(exasperarse)* to get angry o irritated **(b)** *Med (herida)* to become inflamed o sore

encono *nm* spitefulness, ill feeling

encontrado,-a *adj (contrario)* conflicting

encontrar [2] **1** *vt* **(a)** *(hallar)* to find; **no lo encuentro** I can't find it; **lo encuentro muy agradable** I find it very pleasant **(b)** *(dar con)* to meet; *(problema)* to run into, to come up against

2 encontrarse *vpr* **(a)** *(persona)* to meet **(b)** *(sentirse)* to feel, to be; **e. a gusto** to feel comfortable **(c)** *(estar)* to be

encontronazo *nm* **(a)** *(choque)* collision, crash **(b)** *Fig (de ideas etc)* clash

encorvar 1 *vt* to bend

2 encorvarse *vpr* to stoop o bend (over)

encrespar 1 *vt* **(a)** *(pelo)* to curl **(b)** *(mar)* to make choppy o rough **(c)** *Fig (enfurecer)* to infuriate

2 encresparse *vpr* **(a)** *(mar)* to get rough **(b)** *Fig (enfurecerse)* to get cross o irritated

encrucijada *nf* crossroads

encrudecer [33] *vi*, **encrudecerse** *vpr* to get worse

encuadernación *nf* **(a)** *(oficio)* bookbinding **(b)** *(cubierta)* binding

encuadernador,-a *nm,f* bookbinder

encuadernar *vt* to bind

encuadrar *vt* **(a)** *(imagen etc)* to frame **(b)** *Fig (encajar)* to fit, to insert

encuadre *nm Cin & TV* framing

encubierto,-a *adj (secreto)* hidden; *(operación)* covert

encubridor,-a *nm,f Jur* accessory (after the fact), abettor

encubrir *vt* to conceal

encuentro *nm* **(a)** encounter, meeting **(b)** *Dep* meeting, match; **e. amistoso** friendly (match)

encuesta *nf* **(a)** *(sondeo)* (opinion) poll, survey **(b)** *(investigación)* investigation, inquiry

encuestador,-a *nm,f* pollster

encuestar *vt* to poll

encumbrar 1 *vt* to exalt

2 encumbrarse *vpr* to rise to a high (social) position

ende: por ende *loc adv* therefore

endeble *adj* weak, feeble

endeblez *nf* weakness, feebleness

endémico,-a *adj Med* endemic; *Fig* chronic

endemoniado,-a *adj* **(a)** *(poseso)* possessed **(b)** *Fig (travieso)* mischievous

enderezar [40] **1** *vt (poner derecho)* to straighten out; *(poner vertical)* to set upright

2 enderezarse *vpr* to straighten up

endeudarse *vpr* to get o fall into debt

endiablado,-a *adj* **(a)** *(poseso)* possessed **(b)** *(travieso)* mischievous, devilish

endibia *nf* endive

endiosar *vt* to deify

endomingarse [42] *vpr Fam* to put on one's Sunday best

endosar *vt* **(a)** *(cheque)* to endorse **(b)** *Fam* **e. algo a algn** *(tarea)* to lumber sb with sthg

endrina *nf Bot* sloe

endrogarse [42] *vpr Am* to take drugs, to use drugs

endulzar [40] *vt* to sweeten

endurecer [33] **1** *vt* to harden

2 endurecerse *vpr* to harden, to become hard

enebro *nm* juniper

enema *nm* enema

enemigo,-a 1 *adj* enemy; **soy e. de la bebida** I'm against drink

2 *nm,f* enemy

enemistad *nf* hostility, enmity

enemistar 1 *vt* to set at odds, to cause a rift between

2 enemistarse *vpr* to become enemies; **e. con algn** to fall out with sb

energético,-a *adj* energy

energía *nf* energy; **e. hidráulica/nuclear** hydro-electric/nuclear power; *Fig* **e. vital** vitality

enérgico,-a *adj* energetic; *(decisión)* firm; *(tono)* emphatic

energúmeno,-a *nm,f Fam (hombre)* madman; *(mujer)* mad woman; **ponerse como un e.** to go up the wall

enero *nm* January

enervante *adj* enervating

enervar *vt* to enervate

enésimo,-a *adj* **(a)** *Mat* nth **(b)** *Fam* umpteenth; **por enésima vez** for the umpteenth time

enfadado,-a *adj (enojado)* angry; *(molesto)* annoyed; **estamos enfadados** we've fallen out with each other

enfadar 1 *vt* to make angry *o* annoyed

2 enfadarse *upr* (**a**) to get angry (**con** with) (**b**) *(dos personas)* to fall out

enfado *nm* anger; *(desavenencia)* fall-out

enfangarse [42] *upr* to get muddy; *Fig* to get involved (in dirty business)

énfasis *nm inv* emphasis, stress; **poner e. en algo** to lay stress on sth

enfático,-a *adj* emphatic

enfatizar [40] *vt* to emphasize, to stress

enfermar *vi*, **enfermarse** *upr* to become *o* fall ill, to be taken ill

enfermedad *nf* illness; *(contagiosa)* disease

enfermería *nf* infirmary

enfermero,-a *nm,f (mujer)* nurse; *(hombre)* male nurse

enfermizo,-a *adj* unhealthy, sickly

enfermo,-a 1 *adj* ill; **caer e.** to be taken ill; *Fam* **esa gente me pone e.** those people make me sick

2 *nm,f* ill person; *(paciente)* patient

enfervorizar [40] *vt* to enthuse

enfilar *vi* **e. hacia** to make for

enflaquecer [33] *vt (adelgazar)* to make thin; *(debilitar)* to weaken

enfocado,-a *adj Fot* **bien/mal enfocado** in/out of focus

enfocar [44] *vt* (**a**) *(imagen)* to focus; *(persona)* to focus on (**b**) *(tema)* to approach (**c**) *(con linterna)* to shine a light on

enfoque *nm* (**a**) focus; *(acción)* focusing (**b**) *(de un tema)* approach

enfrentamiento *nm* clash

enfrentar 1 *vt* (**a**) *(situación, peligro)* to confront (**b**) *(enemistar)* to set at odds

2 enfrentarse *upr* (**a**) **e. con** *o* **a** to face up to, to confront (**b**) *Dep* **enfrentarse (a)** *(rival)* to meet

enfrente *adv* (**a**) opposite, facing; **la casa de e.** the house opposite *o* across the road (**b**) **e. de.** opposite (to), facing; **e. del colegio** opposite the school

enfriamiento *nm* (**a**) *(proceso)* cooling (**b**) *Med (catarro)* cold, chill

enfriar [29] **1** *vt* to cool (down), to chill

2 *vi* to cool down

3 enfriarse *upr* (**a**) to get *o* go cold (**b**) *(resfriarse)* to get *o* catch a cold (**c**) *Fig (pasión)* to cool down

enfurecer [33] **1** *vt* to enrage, to infuriate

2 enfurecerse *upr* to get furious, to lose one's temper

enfurruñarse *upr Fam* to sulk

engalanar 1 *vt* to deck out, to adorn

2 engalanarse *upr* to dress up, to get dressed up

enganchado,-a *adj Fam* **estar e. (a la droga)** to be hooked (on drugs)

enganchar 1 *vt* (**a**) to hook; *Ferroc* to couple (**b**) *Fam (pillar)* to nab

2 engancharse *upr* to get caught *o* hooked; *Fam (a la droga)* to get hooked

enganche *nm (gancho)* hook; *Ferroc* cou[pling]

engañabobos *nm inv (persona)* con ma[n], confidence trickster; *(truco)* con trick

engañar 1 *vt* to deceive, to mislead; *(estafa[r])* to cheat, to trick; *(mentir a)* to lie to; *([a] marido, mujer)* to be unfaithful to

2 engañarse *upr* to deceive oneself

engañifa *nf Fam* swindle

engaño *nm* (**a**) deceit; *(estafa)* fraud, swi[n]dle; *(mentira)* lie (**b**) *(error)* mistake, misu[n]derstanding

engañoso,-a *adj (palabras)* deceitful; *(ap[a]riencias)* deceptive; *(consejo)* misleading

engarzar [40] *vt* (**a**) *(unir)* to link (**b**) *(e[n]gastar)* to mount, to set

engastar *vt* to set, to mount

engatusar *vt Fam* to coax; **e. a algn para qu[e] haga algo** to coax sb into doing sth

engendrar *vt* (**a**) *Biol* to engender (**b**) *Fig* [to] give rise to, to cause

engendro *nm* freak

englobar *vt* to include

engomar *vt* to gum, to glue

engordar 1 *vt* to fatten (up), to make fat

2 *vi* (**a**) to put on weight, to get fat; **h[e] engordado 3 kilos** I've put on 3 kilos (**[b]** *(comida, bebida)* to be fattening

engorro *nm Fam* bother, nuisance

engorroso,-a *adj Fam* bothersome, tiresom[e]

engranaje *nm* (**a**) *Téc* gearing (**b**) *Fig* m[a]chinery

engranar *vt Téc* to engage

engrandecer [33] *vt* to exalt

engrasar *vt* (**a**) *(lubricar)* to lubricate, to [oil] (**b**) *(manchar)* to make greasy, to stain wi[th] grease

engrase *nm* lubrication

engreído,-a *adj* vain, conceited

engreírse [56] *upr* to become vain *o* conce[i]ted

engrosar [2] *vt (incrementar)* to enlarg[e]; *(cantidad)* to increase, to swell

engrudo *nm* paste

enguatar *vt* to pad

engullir *vt* to gobble up

enharinar *vt* to cover with flour

enhebrar *vt* to thread

enhorabuena *nf* congratulations; **dar la e.** [a] **algn** to congratulate sb

enigma *nm* enigma

enigmático,-a *adj* enigmatic

enjabonar *vt* to soap

enjalbegar [42] *vt* to whitewash

enjambre *nm* swarm

enjaular *vt* (**a**) *(animal)* to cage (**b**) *Fam* [to] put inside, to put in jail

enjuagar [42] *vt* to rinse

enjuague *nm* rinse; **e. bucal** mouthwash

enjugar [42] *vt*, **enjugarse** *upr* (**a**) *(secar)* [to] mop up; *(lágrimas)* to wipe away (**b**) *(deud[a], déficit)* to clear, to wipe out

enjuiciamiento *nm* (a) *(opinión)* judgement (b) *Jur (civil)* lawsuit; *(criminal)* trial, prosecution

enjuiciar [43] *vt* (a) *(juzgar)* to judge, to examine (b) *Jur (criminal)* to indict, to prosecute

enjundia *nf Fig (sustancia)* substance; *(importancia)* importance

enjuto,-a *adj* lean, skinny

enlace *nm* (a) *(unión)* link, connection; **e. químico** chemical bond (b) *Ferroc* connection (c) *(casamiento)* marriage (d) *(persona)* liaison officer; **e. sindical** shop steward

enlatado,-a *adj* canned, tinned

enlatar *vt* to can, to tin

enlazar [40] *vt & vi* to link, to connect (**con** with)

enlodar *vt* (a) *(enfangar)* to muddy, to cover with mud (b) *Fig (reputación)* to stain, to besmirch

enloquecedor,-a *adj* maddening

enloquecer [33] **1** *vi* to go mad

  2 *vt* (a) *(volver loco)* to drive mad (b) *Fam* **me enloquecen las motos** I'm mad about motorbikes

  3 enloquecerse *upr* to go mad, to go out of one's mind

enlosar *vt* to tile

enlucir [35] *vt (pared)* to plaster; *(plata, oro)* to polish

enlutado,-a *adj* in mourning

enmadrado,-a *adj* **estar e.** to be tied to one's mother's apron strings

enmarañar 1 *vt* (a) *(pelo)* to tangle (b) *Fig (complicar)* to complicate, confuse

  2 enmarañarse *upr* (a) *(pelo)* to get tangled (b) *Fig (situación)* to get confused, to get into a mess o a muddle

enmarcar [44] *vt* to frame

enmascarar 1 *vt* (a) to mask (b) *(problema, la verdad)* to mask, to disguise

  2 enmascararse *upr* to put on a mask

enmendar [1] **1** *vt (corregir)* to correct, to put right; *Jur* to amend

  2 enmendarse *upr (persona)* to reform, to mend one's ways

enmienda *nf* correction; *Jur & Pol* amendment

enmohecerse [33] *upr (metal)* to rust, to get rusty; *Bot* to go mouldy

enmoquetar *vt* to carpet

enmudecer [33] *vi (callar)* to fall silent; *Fig* to be dumbstruck

ennegrecer [33] *vt*, **ennegrecerse** *upr* to blacken, to turn black

ennoblecer *vt* to ennoble

enojadizo,-a *adj* irritable, touchy

enojado,-a *adj (enojado)* angry; *(molesto)* annoyed;

enojar 1 *vt* to anger, to annoy

  2 enojarse *upr* to get angry, to lose one's temper

enojo *nm* anger, annoyance

enorgullecer [33] **1** *vt* to fill with pride

  2 enorgullecerse *upr* to be o feel proud (**de** of)

enorme *adj* enormous

enormidad *nf* enormity; *Fam* **una e.** loads

enraizado,-a *adj* rooted

enraizar [40], **enraizarse** *upr (persona)* to put down roots; *(planta, costumbre)* to take root

enrarecerse [33] *upr (aire)* to become rarefied

enredadera *nf* climbing plant, creeper

enredar 1 *vt* (a) *(pelo)* to entangle, to tangle up (b) *Fig (asunto)* to confuse, to complicate (c) *Fig (implicar)* to involve (**en** in) (d) *(confundir)* to mix up

  2 enredarse *upr* (a) *(pelo)* to get entangled, to get tangled (up) o in a tangle (b) *Fig (asunto)* to get complicated o confused (c) *Fig* **e. con** *(involucrarse)* to get involved with (d) *(confundirse)* to get mixed up

enredo *nm* (a) *(maraña)* tangle (b) *Fig (lío)* muddle, mess

enrejado *nm (de ventana)* lattice

enrevesado,-a *adj* complicated, difficult

enriquecer [33] **1** *vt* to make rich; *Fig* to enrich

  2 enriquecerse *upr* to get o become rich, to prosper; *Fig* to become enriched

enrocar [44] *vi (en ajedrez)* to castle

enrojecer [33] **1** *vt* to redden, to turn red

  2 *vi (ruborizarse)* to blush

  3 enrojecerse *upr* to blush

enrolarse *upr* to enrol, to sign on; *Mil* to enlist, to join up

enrollado,-a *adj* (a) rolled up (b) *(persona)* great (c) *Fam* **estar e. con algn** *(estar saliendo con)* to go out with sb

enrollar 1 *vt* to roll up; *(cable)* to coil; *(hilo)* to wind up

  2 enrollarse *upr* (a) *Fam (hablar)* to chatter, to go on and on (b) *Fam* **e. con algn** *(tener relaciones)* to have an affair with sb

> 🖉 Observa que el verbo inglés **to enrol** es un falso amigo y no es la traducción del verbo español **enrollar**. En inglés, **to enrol** significa "matricular, inscribir".

enroque *nm (en ajedrez)* castling

enroscar [44] **1** *vt* (a) to coil (round), to wind (b) *(tornillo, tapón)* to screw in o on

  2 enroscarse *upr* to coil, to wind

ensaimada *nf* = kind of spiral pastry from Majorca

ensalada *nf* salad

ensaladera *nf* salad bowl

ensaladilla *nf* **e. rusa** Russian salad

ensalzar [40] *vt (enaltecer)* to exalt; *(elogiar)* to praise, to extol

ensamblador *nm Informát* assembler

ensamblaje *nm Téc* assembly

ensamblar *vt* to assemble

ensanchar 1 *vt* to enlarge, to widen; *Cost* to let out
2 ensancharse *upr* to get wider

ensanche *nm* enlargement, widening; *(de ciudad)* urban development

ensangrentado,-a *adj* bloodstained, covered in blood

ensangrentar [1] *vt* to stain with blood, to cover in blood

ensañarse *upr* **e. con** to be brutal with; *(cebarse)* to delight in tormenting

ensartar *vt* (a) *(perlas etc)* to string together (b) *(mentiras etc)* to reel off, to rattle off

ensayar *vt* to test, to try out; *Teatro* to rehearse; *Mús* to practise

ensayista *nmf* essayist

ensayo *nm* (a) *(prueba)* test, trial (b) *Teatro* rehearsal; **e. general** dress rehearsal (c) *(escrito)* essay

enseguida, en seguida *adv* *(inmediatamente)* at once, straight away; *(poco después)* in a minute, soon; **e. voy** I'll be right there

ensenada *nf* inlet, cove

enseña *nf* ensign, standard

enseñanza *nf* (a) *(educación)* education (b) *(de idioma etc)* teaching (c) **enseñanzas** teachings

enseñar *vt* (a) to teach; **e. a algn a hacer algo** to teach sb how to do sth (b) *(mostrar)* to show; *(señalar)* to point out

enseres *nmpl* *(bártulos)* belongings, goods; *(de trabajo)* tools

ensillar *vt* to saddle (up)

ensimismado,-a *adj* *(en la lectura etc)* engrossed; *(abstraído)* lost in thought

ensimismarse *upr* *(en la lectura etc)* to become engrossed; *(abstraerse)* to be lost in thought

ensombrecer [33] **1** *vt* to cast a shadow over
2 ensombrecerse *upr* to darken

ensopar *vt Am* to soak

ensordecedor,-a *adj* deafening

ensordecer [33] **1** *vt* to deafen
2 *vi* to go deaf

ensortijado,-a *adj* curly

ensuciar [43] **1** *vt* (a) to get dirty (b) *Fig (reputación)* to harm, to damage
2 ensuciarse *upr* to get dirty

ensueño *nm* dream; **una casa de e.** a dream house

entablado *nm* (a) *(entarimado)* planking, planks (b) *(suelo)* wooden floor

entablar *vt* (a) *(conversación)* to open, to begin; *(amistad)* to strike up; *(negocios)* to start (b) *(en juegos de tablero)* to set up (c) *(pleito)* to initiate

entablillar *vt Med* to splint

entallado,-a *adj* *(vestido)* close-fitting; *(camisa)* fitted

entallar 1 *vt* to take in at the waist

2 *vi* to fit at the waist

entarimado *nm* parquet floor

entarimar *vt* to cover with parquet

ente *nm* (a) *(institución)* organization, body, **e. público** public service organization (b) *(ser)* being

entendederas *nfpl Fam* brains; **ser duro d e.** to be slow on the uptake

entender [3] **1** *vt* *(comprender)* to under stand; **a mi e.** to my way of thinking; **dar algn a e. que ...** to give sb to understand tha ...
2 *vi* (a) *(comprender)* to understand (b) **de** *(saber)* to know about
3 entenderse *upr* (a) *(comprenderse)* to b understood, to be meant (b) *Fam* **e. (bien con** to get on (well) with

entendido,-a 1 *nm,f* expert
2 *adj* **tengo e. que ...** I understand that ...

entendimiento *nm* understanding

enterado,-a 1 *adj* knowledgeable, wel informed; **estar e.** to be in the know; **estar de ...** to be aware of ...
2 *nm,f (listillo)* know-all

enteramente *adv* entirely, completely

enterar 1 *vt* to inform (**de** about o of)
2 enterarse *upr* to find out; **me he enterad de que ...** I understand ...; **ni me enteré** didn't even realize it

entereza *nf* strength of character

enternecedor,-a *adj* moving, touching

enternecer [33] **1** *vt* to move, to touch
2 enternecerse *upr* to be moved o touched

entero,-a 1 *adj* (a) *(completo)* entire, whole **por e.** completely (b) *Fig (íntegro)* hones upright (c) *Fig (firme)* strong
2 *nm* (a) *Mat* whole number (b) *Fin* point

enterrador *nm* gravedigger

enterramiento *nm* burial

enterrar [1] *vt* to bury

entidad *nf* organization; **e. comercial** com pany, firm

entierro *nm* (a) burial (b) *(ceremonia)* fu neral

entomología *nf* entomology

entonación *nf* intonation

entonar 1 *vt* (a) *(canto)* to sing (b) *Med* t tone up
2 *vi* to be in harmony, to be in tune (**co** with)

entonces *adv* then; **por aquel e.** at that time **el e. ministro** the then minister

entornar *vt (ojos etc)* to half-close; *(puerta* to leave ajar

entorno *nm* environment

entorpecer [33] *vt (obstaculizar)* to hinder, t impede

entrada *nf* (a) entrance (b) *(billete)* ticke *(recaudación)* takings (c) **de e.** for a start *(d Culin* entrée (e) *Com* entry; *(pago inicia* down payment, deposit; **e. de capital** capita inflow (f) *Com* **entradas** *(ingresos)* receipts akings (**g**) *(en la frente)* receding hairline

ntrado,-a *adj* **e. en años** advanced in years; **asta bien entrada la noche** well into the night

ntramado *nm* framework; *(de sistema etc)* network

ntramparse *vpr Fam* to get into debt

ntrante **1** *adj* coming; **el mes e.** next month; **el ministro e.** the incoming minister

2 *Culin* starter

ntrañable *adj* (**a**) *(lugar)* intimate, close (**b**) *(persona)* affectionate, warm-hearted

ntrañar *vt* to entail

ntrañas *nfpl* bowels

ntrar 1 *vi* (**a**) to come in, to go in, to enter; *Fig* **no me entran las matemáticas** I can't get the hang of maths (**b**) *(encajar)* to fit (**c**) **el año que entra** next year, the coming year (**d**) *(venir)* to come over; **me entró dolor de cabeza** I got a headache; **me entraron ganas de reír** I felt like laughing

2 *vt* (**a**) to introduce (**b**) *Informát* to enter

ntre *prep* (**a**) *(dos)* between (**b**) *(más de dos)* among(st)

ntreabierto,-a *adj (ojos etc)* half-open; *(puerta)* ajar

ntreacto *nm* interval, intermission

ntrecejo *nm* space between the eyebrows; **fruncir el e.** to frown, to knit one's brow

ntrecortado,-a *adj (voz)* faltering, hesitant

ntrecot *nm* fillet steak

ntrecruzar [40] *vt,* **entrecruzarse** *vpr* to entwine

ntredicho *nm* (**a**) *Jur* injunction (**b**) **estar en e.** to be suspect; **poner algo en e.** to bring sth into question

ntrega *nf* (**a**) *(de productos)* delivery; *(de premios)* presentation (**b**) *(fascículo)* part, instalment (**c**) *(devoción)* selflessness

ntregar [42] **1** *vt* to hand over; *(deberes etc)* to give in, to hand in; *Com* to deliver

2 entregarse *vpr* (**a**) *(rendirse)* to give in, to surrender (**b**) **e. a** to devote oneself to; *Pey* to indulge in

ntreguismo *nm Pol* appeasement

ntrelazar [40] *vt,* **entrelazarse** *vpr* to entwine

ntremedias *adv* in between; *(mientras tanto)* meanwhile, in the meantime

ntremés *nm Culin* hors d'oeuvres

ntremeterse *vpr* = **entrometerse**

ntremezclarse *vpr* to mix, to mingle

ntrenador,-a *nm,f* trainer, coach

ntrenamiento *nm* training

ntrenar *vi,* **entrenarse** *vpr* to train

ntrepierna *nf* crotch, crutch

ntresacar [44] *vt* to pick out, to select

ntresijos *nmpl* nooks and crannies

ntresuelo *nm* mezzanine

ntretanto 1 *adv* meanwhile

2 *nm* **en el e.** in the meantime

ntretejer *vt* to interweave

entretención *nf Am* amusement, entertainment

entretener [24] **1** *vt* (**a**) *(divertir)* to entertain, to amuse (**b**) *(retrasar)* to delay; *(detener)* to hold up, to detain

2 entretenerse *vpr* (**a**) *(distraerse)* to amuse oneself, to while away the time (**b**) *(retrasarse)* to be delayed, to be held up

entretenido,-a *adj* enjoyable, entertaining

entretenimiento *nm* entertainment, amusement

entretiempo: de entretiempo *loc adj* **ropa de e.** lightweight clothing

entrever [28] *vt* to glimpse, to catch sight of; *Fig* **dejó e. que ...** she hinted that ...

entrevista *nf* interview

entrevistador,-a *nm,f* interviewer

entrevistar 1 *vt* to interview

2 entrevistarse *vpr* **e. con algn** to have an interview with sb

entristecer [33] **1** *vt* to sadden, to make sad

2 entristecerse *vpr* to be sad (**por** about)

entrometerse *vpr* to meddle, to interfere (**en** in)

entrometido,-a 1 *nm,f* meddler, busybody

2 *adj* interfering

entroncar *vi* to connect

entumecer [33] **1** *vt* to numb

2 entumecerse *vpr* to go numb

entumecido,-a *adj* numb

enturbiar [43] **1** *vt* (**a**) *(agua)* to make cloudy (**b**) *Fig (asunto)* to cloud, to obscure

2 enturbiarse *vpr* to become cloudy

entusiasmar 1 *vt* to fill with enthusiasm

2 entusiasmarse *vpr* to get excited *o* enthusiastic (**con** about)

entusiasmo *nm* enthusiasm; **con e.** enthusiastically

entusiasta 1 *adj* enthusiastic, keen (**de** on)

2 *nmf* enthusiast

enumerar *vt* to enumerate

enunciado *nm (de teoría, problema)* wording

envainar *vt* to sheathe

envalentonar *vt* to make proud *o* vain

2 envanecerse *vpr* to become conceited *o* proud, to give oneself airs

envasado,-a 1 *nm (en botella)* bottling; *(en paquete)* packing; *(en lata)* canning

2 *adj* **e. al vacío** vacuum-packed

envasar *vt (embotellar)* to bottle; *(empaquetar)* to pack; *(enlatar)* to can, to tin

envase *nm* (**a**) *(acto)* packing; *(de botella)* bottling; *(de lata)* canning (**b**) *(recipiente)* container (**c**) *(botella vacía)* empty

envejecer [33] **1** *vi* to grow old

2 *vt* to age

envejecimiento *nm* ageing

envenenar *vt* to poison

envergadura *nf* (**a**) *(importancia)* importance, scope; **de gran e.** large-scale (**b**) *(de pájaro, avión)* span, wingspan; *Náut* breadth (of sail)

envés nm other side
envestidura nf investiture
enviado,-a nm,f envoy; Prensa **e. especial** special correspondent
enviar [29] vt to send
enviciarse [43] upr to become addicted (**con** to)
envidia nf envy; **tener e. de algn** to envy sb
envidiable adj enviable
envidiar [43] vt to envy; **no tener nada que e.** to be in no way inferior (**a** to)
envidioso,-a adj envious

> ℓ Observa que la palabra inglesa **invidious** es un falso amigo y no es la traducción de la palabra española **envidioso**. En inglés, **invidious** significa "ingrato" o "injusto".

envilecer [33] vt to degrade, to debase
envío nm sending; (remesa) consignment; (paquete) parcel; **gastos de e.** postage and packing; **e. contra reembolso** cash on delivery
enviudar vi (hombre) to become a widower, to lose one's wife; (mujer) to become a widow, to lose one's husband
envoltorio nm, **envoltura** nf wrapper, wrapping
envolver [4] (pp envuelto) **1** vt (a) (con papel) to wrap (b) (cubrir) to envelop (c) (en complot etc) to involve (**en** in)
2 envolverse upr (a) to wrap oneself up (**en** in) (b) (implicarse) to become involved (**en** in)
enyesar vt to plaster; Med to put in plaster
enzima nf enzyme
épica nf epic poetry
epicentro nm epicentre
épico,-a adj epic
epidemia nf epidemic
epilepsia nf epilepsy
epílogo nm epilogue
episcopal adj episcopal
episodio nm episode
epístola nf epistle
epitafio nm epitaph
epíteto nm epithet
época nf time; Hist period, epoch; Agr season; **en esta é. del año** at this time of the year; **hacer é.** to be a landmark; **mueble de é.** period furniture
equidad nf equity
equilátero nm equilateral
equilibrar vt to balance
equilibrio nm balance
equilibrismo nm balancing act
equilibrista nmf (a) tightrope walker (b) Am Pol opportunist
equipaje nm luggage; **hacer el e.** to pack, do the packing
equipar vt to equip, to furnish (**con** o **de** with)
equiparable adj comparable (**a** to; **con** with)

equiparar vt to compare (**con** with), to like (**con** to)
equipo nm (a) (de expertos, jugadores) tea (b) (aparatos) equipment; **e. de alta fidelida** hi-fi stereo system (c) (ropas) outfit
equis nf = name of the letter X in Spanish
equitación nf horse o US horseback riding
equitativo,-a adj equitable, fair
equivalente adj equivalent
equivaler [26] vi to be equivalent (**a** to)
equivocación nf error, mistake
equivocado,-a adj mistaken, wrong
equivocar [44] **1** vt to mix up
2 equivocarse upr to make a mistake; Tel **s** equivocó de número he dialled the wror number; **se equivocó de fecha** he got th wrong date
equívoco,-a 1 adj equivocal, misleading
2 nm misunderstanding
era¹ nf (época) era, age
era² nf Agr threshing floor
era³ pt indef de ser
erario nm exchequer, treasury
eras pt indef de ser
erección nf erection
erecto,-a adj upright; (pene) erect
eres indic pres de ser
erguir [55] **1** vt to erect
2 erguirse upr to straighten up, to stand/s up straight
erial nm uncultivated land
erigir [57] **1** vt to erect
2 erigirse upr **e. en algo** to set oneself up sth
erizado,-a adj bristly, prickly
erizarse [40] upr to bristle, to stand on end
erizo nm hedgehog; **e. de mar** o **marino** se urchin
ermita nf hermitage

> ℓ Observa que la palabra inglesa **hermit** es u falso amigo y no es la traducción de la palabr española **ermita**. En inglés, **hermit** significa "ermitaño".

ermitaño,-a nm,f hermit
erosión nf erosion
erosionar vt to erode
erótico,-a adj erotic
erotismo nm eroticism
erradicar [44] vt to eradicate
errante adj wandering
errar [50] **1** vt to miss, to get wrong
2 vi (a) (vagar) to wander, to roam (b (fallar) to err
errata nf erratum, misprint
erre nf **e. que e.** stubbornly, pigheadedly
erróneo,-a adj erroneous, wrong
error nm error, mistake; Informát bug; **por e** by mistake, in error; Impr **e. de imprent** misprint; **caer en un e.** to make a mistake
Ertzaintza nf = Basque police force

ructar *vi* to belch, to burp

ructo *nm* belch, burp

rudición *nf* erudition

rudito,-a 1 *adj* erudite, learned
  2 *nm,f* scholar

rupción *nf* (**a**) *(de volcán)* eruption (**b**) *(en a piel)* rash

s *indic pres de* **ser**

sa *adj dem ver* **ese**

sa *pron dem ver* **ése**

sbelto,-a *adj* slender

sbirro *nm* henchman

sbozar [40] *vt* to sketch, to outline

sbozo *nm* sketch, outline, rough draft

scabeche *nm* brine

scabechina *nf* massacre

scabroso,-a *adj* (**a**) *(espinoso)* tricky (**b**) *(indecente)* crude

scabullirse *vpr* to slip away, to scuttle *o* curry off

scacharrar *vt Fam* to break

scafandra *nf* diving suit; **e. espacial** space-suit

scala *nf* (**a**) scale; *(de colores)* range; **e. musical** scale; **en gran e.** on a large scale (**b**) *(parada) Náut* port of call; *Av* stopover; **hacer e. en** to call in at, to stop over in (**c**) *(escalera)* adder, stepladder

scalada *nf* (**a**) climb (**b**) *Fig (de violencia)* escalation; *(de precios)* rise

scalador,-a *nm,f* climber, mountaineer

🔊 Observa que la palabra inglesa **escalator** es un falso amigo y no es la traducción de la palabra española **escalador**. En inglés, **escalator** significa "escalera mecánica".

scalafón *nm (graduación)* rank; *(de salarios)* salary *o* wage scale

scalar *vt* to climb, to scale

scaldar *vt* to scald

scalera *nf* (**a**) stair; **e. de incendios** fire escape; **e. mecánica** escalator; **e. de caracol** spiral staircase (**b**) *(escala)* ladder (**c**) *Naipes* run

scalerilla *nf (de piscina)* steps; *Náut* gangway; *Av* (boarding) ramp

scalfar *vt* to poach

scalinata *nf* stoop

scalofriante *adj* hair-raising, bloodcurdling

scalofrío *nm* shiver; **me dio un e.** it gave me he shivers

scalón *nm* step; **e. lateral** *(en letrero)* ramp

scalonar *vt* to place at intervals, to space out

scalope *nm* escalope

scalpelo *nm* scalpel

scama *nf Zool* scale; *(de jabón)* flake

scamarse *vpr* to smell a rat, to become suspicious

scamotear *vt Fam* to diddle out of, to do out of

escampar *vi* to stop raining, to clear up

escanciar [43] *vt (vino)* to pour out, to serve

escandalizar [40] **1** *vt* to scandalize, to shock
  2 escandalizarse *vpr* to be shocked (**de** at *o* by)

escándalo *nm* (**a**) *(alboroto)* racket, din; **armar un e.** to kick up a fuss (**b**) *(desvergüenza)* scandal

escandaloso,-a *adj* (**a**) *(ruidoso)* noisy, rowdy (**b**) *(ofensivo)* scandalous

Escandinavia *n* Scandinavia

escandinavo,-a *adj & nm,f* Scandinavian

escáner *nm Med & Informát* scanner

escaño *nm Parl* seat

escapada *nf* (**a**) *(de prisión)* escape; *(en ciclismo)* breakaway (**b**) *(viaje rápido)* flying visit, quick trip

🔊 Observa que la palabra inglesa **escapade** es un falso amigo y no es la traducción de la palabra española **escapada**. En inglés, **escapade** significa "aventura".

escapar 1 *vi* to escape, to run away
  2 escaparse *vpr* (**a**) to escape, to run away; **se me escapó de las manos** it slipped out of my hands; **se me escapó el tren** I missed the train (**b**) *(gas etc)* to leak, to escape

escaparate *nm* shop window

escapatoria *nf* escape; **no tener e.** to have no way out

escape *nm* (**a**) *(de gas etc)* leak, escape (**b**) *Téc* exhaust; **tubo de e.** exhaust (pipe) (**c**) *(huida)* escape; *(escapatoria)* way out

escaquearse *vpr Fam* to duck out; **e. de hacer algo** to worm one's way out of doing sth

escarabajo *nm* beetle

escaramuza *nf Mil* skirmish; *Fig (riña)* squabble, brush

escarbar *vt* (**a**) *(suelo)* to scratch; *(fuego)* to poke (**b**) *Fig* to inquire into, to investigate

escarceo *nm* attempt

escarcha *nf* hoarfrost, frost

escarchado,-a *adj (fruta)* crystallized, candied

escardar *vt* to hoe

escardillo *nm* weeding hoe

escarlata *adj* scarlet

escarlatina *nf* scarlet fever

escarmentar [1] *vi* to learn one's lesson

escarmiento *nm* punishment, lesson

escarnio *nm* derision, mockery

escarola *nf* curly endive

escarpado,-a *adj (paisaje)* craggy; *(pendiente)* steep

escasear *vi* to be scarce

escasez *nf* scarcity

escaso,-a *adj* scarce; *(dinero)* tight; *(conocimientos)* scant; **e. de dinero** short of money

escatimar *vt* to skimp on; **no escatimó esfuerzos para ...** he spared no efforts to ...

escayola nf (a) plaster of Paris, stucco (b) Med plaster

escayolar vt Med to put in plaster

escena nf (a) scene (b) (escenario) stage; **poner en e.** to stage

escenario nm (a) Teatro stage (b) (entorno) scenario; (de crimen) scene; (de película) setting

escénico,-a adj scenic

escenografía nf Cin set design; Teatro stage design

escepticismo nm scepticism

escéptico,-a adj & nm,f sceptic

escindirse vpr to split (off) (en into)

escisión nf split

esclarecer [33] vt to shed light on

esclava nf bangle

esclavitud nf slavery

esclavizar [40] vt to enslave

esclavo,-a adj & nm,f slave

esclusa nf lock, sluicegate

escoba nf brush, broom

escocer [41] **1** vi to sting, to smart
2 escocerse vpr (piel) to chafe

escocés,-esa 1 adj Scottish, Scots; **falda escocesa** kilt
2 nm,f (hombre) Scotsman; (mujer) Scotswoman

Escocia n Scotland

escoger [53] vt to choose

escogido,-a adj chosen, selected; (producto) choice, select; Lit **obras escogidas** selected works

escolar 1 adj (curso, año) school
2 nmf (niño) schoolboy; (niña) schoolgirl

escolaridad nf schooling

escollo nm reef; Fig pitfall

escolta nf escort

escoltar vt to escort

escombros nmpl rubbish, debris

esconder 1 vt to hide (de from), to conceal (de from)
2 esconderse vpr to hide (de from)

escondidas adv **a e.** secretly

escondite nm (a) (lugar) hiding place, hideout (b) (juego) hide-and-seek

escondrijo nm hiding place, hide-out

escopeta nf shotgun; **e. de aire comprimido** air gun; **e. de cañones recortados** sawn-off shotgun

escopetazo nm gunshot

escorbuto nm scurvy

escoria nf (a) (de metal) slag (b) Fig scum, dregs

Escorpio nm Scorpio

escorpión nm scorpion

escotado,-a adj low-cut

escote nm low neckline

escotilla nf hatch, hatchway

escozor nm stinging, smarting

escribiente nmf clerk

escribir (pp escrito) **1** vt to write; **e. a mano** to write in longhand; **e. a máquina** to type
2 escribirse vpr (a) (dos personas) to write to each other, to correspond (b) **se escribe con h** it is spelt with an h

escrito,-a 1 adj written; **e. a mano** handwritten, in longhand; **por e.** in writing
2 nm writing

escritor,-a nm,f writer

escritorio nm (a) (mueble) writing desk, bureau; (oficina) office (b) Informát desktop

escritura nf (a) Jur deed, document; **e. de propiedad** title deed (b) Rel **Sagradas Escrituras** Holy Scriptures

escrúpulo nm (a) scruple; **una persona sin escrúpulos** an unscrupulous person (b) (esmero) care (c) **me da e.** (asco) it makes me feel squeamish

escrupuloso,-a adj (a) (honesto) scrupulous (b) (meticuloso) painstaking (c) (delicado) squeamish

escrutar vt (a) to scrutinize (b) (votos) to count

escrutinio nm (a) scrutiny (b) (de votos) count

escuadra nf (a) (instrumento) square (b) Mil squad; Náut squadron; Dep team; (de coches) fleet

escuadrilla nf Náut squadron

escuadrón nm Av squadron

escuálido,-a adj emaciated

escucha nf listening; **escuchas telefónicas** phone tapping; **estar a la e. de** to be listening out for

escuchar 1 vt to listen to; (oír) to hear
2 vi to listen; (oír) to hear

escudarse vpr Fig **e. en algo** to hide behind sth

escudería nf motor racing team

escudilla nf bowl

escudo nm (a) (arma defensiva) shield (b) (blasón) coat of arms

escudriñar vt to scrutinize

escuela nf school; **e. de Bellas Artes** Art School; **e. de conducir/de idiomas** driving/language school

escueto,-a adj plain, unadorned

escuezo indic pres de escocer

esculcar [44] vt Am to search

esculpir vt to sculpt; (madera) to carve; (metal) to engrave

escultor,-a nm,f (hombre) sculptor; (mujer) sculptress; (de madera) woodcarver; (de metales) engraver

escultura nf sculpture

escultural adj sculptural; (persona) statuesque

escupidera nf (a) (recipiente) spittoon (b) (orinal) chamberpot

escupir 1 vi to spit
2 vt to spit out

escupitajo nm Fam spit

escurreplatos nm inv dish rack

scurridizo,-a adj (a) (resbaladizo) slippery (b) Fig (huidizo) elusive, slippery

curridor nm colander; (escurreplatos) dish ack

currir 1 vt (plato, vaso) to drain; (ropa) to wring out; **e. el bulto** to wriggle out
2 escurrirse upr (a) (platos etc) to drip (b) (escaparse) to run o slip away (c) (resbalarse) o slip

cúter nm (motor) scooter

e,-a adj dem (a) that (b) **esos,-as** those **e,-a** pron dem m,f (a) that one (b) **ésos,-as** hose (ones); Fam **¡ni por ésas!** no way!; Fam **no me vengas con ésas!** come off it!

Note that **ése** and its various forms can be written without an accent when there is no risk of confusion with the adjective.

sencia nf essence

encial adj essential; **lo e.** the main thing

encialmente adv essentially

fera nf (a) sphere; Fig sphere, field (b) (de loj de pulsera) dial; (de reloj de pared) face

férico,-a 1 adj spherical
2 nm (balón) ball

finge nf sphinx

forzarse [2] upr to make an effort (**por** to)

fuerzo nm effort

fumarse upr Fam to beat it

grima nf Dep fencing

grimir vt to wield

guince nm sprain

labón nm link

lavo,-a 1 adj Slav, Slavonic
2 nm,f (persona) Slav
3 nm (idioma) Slavonic

lip nm (pl eslips) men's briefs, underpants

logan nm (pl eslóganes) slogan; **e. publicitario** advertising slogan

lora nf Náut length

lovaco,-a 1 adj & nm,f Slovak, Slovakian
2 nm (idioma) Slovak

lovaquia n Slovakia

lovenia n Slovenia

loveno,-a 1 adj & nm,f Slovene
2 nm (idioma) Slovene

maltar vt to enamel

malte nm enamel; (de uñas) nail polish o arnish

merado,-a adj painstaking, careful

meralda nf emerald

merarse upr to be careful; (esforzarse) to o to great lengths

mero nm great care

moquin nm (pl esmóquines) dinner cket, US tuxedo

nifar vt Fam (drogas) to sniff

nob (pl esnobs) **1** adj (persona) snobbish; estaurante etc) posh
2 nmf snob

nobismo nm snobbery, snobbishness

O nf (abr **Enseñanza Secundaria Obligatoria**) = mainstream secondary education in Spain for pupils aged 12-16

eso pron neut that; **¡e. es!** that's it!; **por e.** that's why; Fam **a e. de las diez** around ten; Fam **e. de las Navidades sale muy caro** this whole Christmas thing costs a fortune

esófago nm oesophagus

esos,-as adj dem pl ver **ese,-a**

ésos,-as pron dem m,fpl ver **ése,-a**

esotérico,-a adj esoteric

espabilado,-a adj (a) (despierto) wide awake (b) (niño) bright

espabilar 1 vt to wake up
2 espabilarse upr to wake up, to waken up

espachurrar vt to squash

espacial adj spatial, spacial; **nave e.** space ship

espaciar [43] vt to space out

espacio nm (a) space; (de tiempo) length; **a doble e.** double-spaced (b) Rad & TV programme

espacioso,-a adj spacious, roomy

espada 1 nf (a) sword; **estar entre la e. y la pared** to be between the devil and the deep blue sea; **pez e.** swordfish (b) Naipes spade
2 nm Taurom matador

> Observa que la palabra inglesa **spade** es un falso amigo y no es la traducción de la palabra española **espada**. En inglés, **spade** significa "pala".

espadaña nf belfry

espaguetis nmpl spaghetti

espalda nf (a) Anat back; **espaldas** back; **a espaldas de algn** behind sb's back; **por la e.** from behind; **volver la e. a algn** to turn one's back on sb; Fam **e. mojada** wetback (b) (en natación) backstroke

espaldar nm (de silla) back

espaldilla nf shoulder blade

espantapájaros nm inv scarecrow

espantar 1 vt (a) (asustar) to frighten, to scare (b) (ahuyentar) to frighten away
2 espantarse upr to get o feel frightened (**de** of), to get o feel scared (**de** of)

espanto nm fright; Fam **de e.** dreadful, shocking

espantoso,-a adj dreadful

España n Spain

español,-a 1 adj Spanish
2 nm,f Spaniard; **los españoles** the Spanish
3 nm (idioma) Spanish

esparadrapo nm sticking plaster

esparcimiento nm (relajación) relaxation

esparcir [52] **1** vt (papeles, semillas) to scatter; Fig (rumor) to spread
2 esparcirse upr (a) to be scattered (b) (relajarse) to relax

espárrago nm asparagus

espartano,-a adj Fig spartan

espasmo nm spasm

espástico,-a *adj* spastic

espátula *nf Culin* spatula; *Arte* palette knife; *Téc* stripping knife; *(de albañil)* trowel

especia *nf* spice

especial *adj* special; **en e.** especially; **e. para ...** suitable for ...

especialidad *nf* speciality, *US* specialty; *Educ* main subject

especialista *nmf* specialist

especializarse [40] *vpr* to specialize (**en** in)

especialmente *adv (exclusivamente)* specially; *(muy)* especially

especie *nf* (a) *Biol* species *inv* (b) *(clase)* kind; **una e. de salsa** a kind of sauce (c) *Com* **en e.** in kind

específicamente *adv* specifically

especificar [44] *vt* to specify

específico,-a *adj* specific; **peso e.** specific gravity

espécimen *nm (pl* **especímenes)** specimen

espectacular *adj* spectacular

espectacularidad *nf* **de gran e.** really spectacular

espectáculo *nm* (a) *(escena)* spectacle, sight; *Fam* **dar un e.** to make a spectacle of oneself (b) *Teatro, Cin & TV* show; **montar un e.** to put on a show

espectador,-a *nm,f Dep* spectator; *(de accidente)* onlooker; *Teatro & Cin* member of the audience; **los espectadores** the audience; *TV* the viewers

espectro *nm* (a) *Fís* spectrum (b) *(fantasma)* spectre (c) *(gama)* range

especulación *nf* speculation; **e. del suelo** land speculation

especulador,-a *nm,f Fin* speculator

especular *vi* to speculate

especulativo,-a *adj* speculative

espejismo *nm* mirage

espejo *nm* mirror; *Aut* **e. retrovisor** rearview mirror

espeleología *nf* potholing, speleology

espeluznante *adj* hair-raising, horrifying

espera *nf* wait; **en e. de ...** waiting for ...; **a la e. de** expecting; **sala de e.** waiting room

esperanza *nf* hope; **tener la e. puesta en algo** to have one's hopes pinned on sth; **e. de vida** life expectancy; **en estado de buena e.** expecting, pregnant

esperanzador,-a *adj* encouraging

esperanzar *vt* to give hope to

esperar 1 *vi* (a) *(aguardar)* to wait (b) *(tener esperanza de)* to hope

2 *vt* (a) *(aguardar)* to wait for; **espero a mi hermano** I'm waiting for my brother (b) *(tener esperanza de)* to hope for; **espero que sí** I hope so; **espero que vengas** I hope you'll come (c) *(estar a la espera de)* to expect; **te esperábamos ayer** we were expecting you yesterday (d) *Fig (bebé)* to expect

esperma (a) *nm Biol* sperm (b) *Am (vela)* candle

espermaticida *nm* spermicide

espermatozoide *nm* spermatozoid

esperpéntico,-a *adj Fam* grotesque

espesar 1 *vt* to thicken

2 espesarse *vpr* to thicken, to get thicker

espeso,-a *adj (bosque, niebla)* dense; *(líqu-do)* thick; *(masa)* stiff

espesor *nm* thickness; **3 m de e.** 3 m thick

espesura *nf* denseness

espetar *vt Fig* to spit out

espía *nmf* spy

espiar [29] **1** *vi* to spy

2 *vt* to spy on

espichar *vi Fam* **espichar(la)** *(morir)* to kic the bucket

espiga *nf* (a) *(de trigo)* ear (b) *Téc* pin

espigado,-a *adj* slender

espina *nf* (a) *Bot* thorn (b) *(de pescado)* bon (c) *Anat* **e. dorsal** spinal column, spine (« *Fig* **ése me da mala e.** there's something fish about that one

espinaca *nf* spinach

espinal *adj* spinal; **médula e.** spinal marrov

espinazo *nm* spine, backbone

espinilla *nf* (a) *Anat* shin (b) *(en la piel)* sp

espinillera *nf Dep* shin pad

espino *nm* hawthorn; **alambre de e.** barbe wire

espionaje *nm* spying, espionage; **novela «** **e.** spy story

espiral *adj & nf* spiral

espirar *vi* to breathe out, to exhale

espiritismo *nm* spiritualism

espíritu *nm* (a) spirit; **e. deportivo** spor manship (b) *Rel (alma)* soul; **el E. Santo** t**l** Holy Ghost

espiritual *adj* spiritual

espléndido,-a *adj* (a) *(magnífico)* splend **(b)** *(generoso)* lavish, generous

esplendor *nm* splendour

esplendoroso,-a *adj* magnificent

espliego *nm* lavender

espolear *vt* to spur on

espolio *nm* = **expolio**

espolvorear *vt* to sprinkle (**de** with)

esponja *nf* sponge

esponjoso,-a *adj* spongy; *(bizcocho)* light

esponsales *nmpl* betrothal, engagement

espontaneidad *nf* spontaneity; **con e. n** urally

espontáneo,-a 1 *adj* spontaneous

2 *nm Taurom* = spectator who spont neously joins in the bullfight

esporádico,-a *adj* sporadic

esposado,-a *adj* (a) *(recién casado)* new married **(b)** *(con esposas)* handcuffed

esposar *vt* to handcuff

esposas *nfpl* handcuffs

esposo,-a *nm,f* spouse; *(hombre)* husban *(mujer)* wife

esprint *nm* sprint

esprintar *vi* to sprint

espuela *nf* spur

espuerta *nf* hod

espuma *nf* foam; *(de olas)* surf; *(de cerveza)* froth, head; *(de jabón)* lather; **e. de afeitar** shaving foam

espumoso,-a *adj* frothy; *(vino)* sparkling

esputo *nm* spit

esquela *nf* notice, announcement; **e. mortuoria** announcement of a death

esquelético,-a *adj* (a) *Anat* skeletal (b) *(flaco)* skinny

esqueleto *nm* (a) skeleton (b) *Constr* framework

esquema *nm* diagram

esquemático,-a *adj (escueto)* schematic; *(con diagramas)* diagrammatic

esquí *nm* (a) *(objeto)* ski (b) *(deporte)* skiing; **e. acuático** waterskiing

esquiador,-a *nm,f* skier

esquiar [29] *vi* to ski

esquilar *vt* to shear

esquimal *adj & nmf* Eskimo

esquina *nf* corner; *Dep* **saque de e.** corner kick)

esquinazo *nm* **dar e. a algn** to give sb the slip

esquirla *nf* splinter

esquirol *nm Ind* blackleg, scab

esquivar *vt (a una persona)* to avoid; *(un golpe)* to dodge

esquivo,-a *adj* cold, aloof

esquizofrenia *nf* schizophrenia

esquizofrénico,-a *adj & nm,f* schizophrenic

esta *adj dem ver* **este,-a**

esta *pron dem f ver* **éste,-a**

está *indic pres de* **estar**

estabilidad *nf* stability

estabilizar [40] *vt* to stabilize

estable *adj* stable

establecer [33] **1** *vt* to establish; *(fundar)* to set up, to found; *(récord)* to set

2 establecerse *upr* to settle

establecimiento *nm* establishment

establo *nm* cow shed

estaca *nf* stake, post; *(de tienda de campaña)* peg

estacada *nf* fence; *Fig* **dejar a algn en la e.** to leave sb in the lurch

estacazo *nm* blow with a stick

estación *nf* (a) station; **e. de servicio** service station; **e. de esquí** ski resort (b) *(del año)* season

estacional *adj* seasonal

estacionamiento *nm Aut (acción)* parking; *(lugar) Br* car park, *US* parking lot

estacionar *vt,* **estacionarse** *upr Aut* to park

estacionario,-a *adj* stationary

estada *nf,* **estadía** *nf Am* stay

estadio *nm* (a) *Dep* stadium (b) *(fase)* stage, phase

estadista *nmf Pol (hombre)* statesman; *(mujer)* stateswoman

estadística *nf* statistics *sing*; **una e.** a statistic

estado *nm* (a) *Pol* state (b) *(situación)* state, condition; **en buen e.** in good condition; **e. de salud** condition, state of health; **e. de excepción** state of emergency; **estar en e.** to be pregnant; **e. civil** marital status; *Com* **e. de cuentas** statement of accounts (c) *Mil* **e. mayor** general staff

Estados Unidos *npl* the United States

estadounidense 1 *adj* United States, American

2 *nmf* American

estafa *nf* swindle

estafador,-a *nm,f* swindler

estafar *vt* to swindle

estafeta *nf* **e. de Correos** sub-post office

estalactita *nf* stalactite

estalagmita *nf* stalagmite

estallar *vi* (a) to burst; *(bomba)* to explode, to go off; *(guerra)* to break out (b) *Fig (de cólera etc)* to explode; **e. en sollozos** to burst into tears

estallido *nm* explosion; *(de guerra)* outbreak

estambre *nm Bot* stamen

Estambul *n* Istanbul

estamento *nm Hist* estate; *Fig (grupo)* group

estampa *nf* print, image

> 🖉 Observa que la palabra inglesa **stamp** es un falso amigo y no es la traducción de la palabra española **estampa**. En inglés, **stamp** significa "sello, tampón".

estampado,-a 1 *adj (tela)* printed

2 *nm* (a) *(tela)* print (b) *(proceso)* printing

estampar *vt* (a) *(tela)* to print (b) *(dejar impreso)* to imprint (c) *Fig (bofetada, beso)* to plant, to place

estampida *nf* (a) *(estampido)* bang (b) *(carrera rápida)* stampede; **de e.** suddenly

estampido *nm* bang

estampilla *nf Am (postage)* stamp

estancado,-a *adj (agua)* stagnant; *Fig* static, at a standstill; **quedarse e.** to get stuck *o* bogged down

estancar [44] **1** *vt* (a) *(agua)* to hold back (b) *Fig (asunto)* to block; *(negociaciones)* to bring to a standstill

2 estancarse *upr* to stagnate; *Fig* to get bogged down

estancia *nf* (a) *(permanencia)* stay (b) *(habitación)* room (c) *Am (hacienda)* ranch, farm

estanco,-a 1 *nm* tobacconist's

2 *adj* watertight

estándar *(pl* **estándares)** *adj & nm* standard

estandarizar [40] *vt* to standardize

estandarte *nm* standard, banner

estanque *nm* pool, pond

estanquero,-a *nm,f* tobacconist

estante *nm* shelf; *(para libros)* bookcase

estantería *nf* shelves, shelving

estaño *nm* tin

estar [13] **1** *vi* (a) to be; **está en la playa** he is at the beach; **e. en casa** to be in, to be at home; **estamos en Caracas** we are in Caracas; **¿está tu madre?** is your mother in?; **¿cómo estás?** how are you?; **los precios están bajos** prices are low; **el problema está en el dinero** the problem is money; **e. en lo cierto** to be right; **e. en todo** not to miss a trick

(**b**) (+ *adj*) to be; **está cansado/enfermo** he's tired/ill; **está vacío** it's empty

(**c**) (+ *adv*) to be; **está bien/mal** it's all right/wrong; **e. mal de dinero** he's short of money; **estará enseguida** it'll be ready in a minute

(**d**) (+ *ger*) to be; **está escribiendo** she is writing; **estaba comiendo** he was eating

(**e**) (+ *a* + *fecha*) to be; **¿a cuántos estamos?** what's the date (today)?; **estamos a 2 de Noviembre** it is the 2nd of November

(**f**) (+ *precio*) to be at; **están a 100 pesetas el kilo** they're at 100 pesetas a kilo

(**g**) (*locuciones*) **e. al caer** to be just round the corner; **¿estamos?** OK?

(**h**) (+ *de*) **e. de más** not to be needed; **e. de paseo** to be out for a walk; **e. de vacaciones/viaje** to be (away) on holiday/a trip; **estoy de jefe hoy** I'm the boss today

(**i**) (+ *para*) to be; **estará para las seis** it will be finished by six; **hoy no estoy para bromas** I'm in no mood for jokes today; **el tren está para salir** the train is just about to leave

(**j**) (+ *por*) **está por hacer** it has still to be done; **eso está por ver** it remains to be seen; **estoy por esperar** (*a favor de*) I'm for waiting

(**k**) (+ *con*) to have; **e. con la gripe** to have the flu, to be down with flu; **estoy con Jaime** (*de acuerdo con*) I agree with Jaime

(**l**) (+ *sin*) to have no; **e. sin luz/agua** to have no light/water

(**m**) (+ *que*) **está que se duerme** he is nearly asleep; *Fam* **está que rabia** he's hopping mad

2 estarse *vpr* **¡estáte quieto!** keep still!, stop fidgeting!

estatal *adj* state; **enseñanza e.** state education

estático,-a *adj* static

estatua *nf* statue

estatura *nf* (a) height; **¿cuál es tu e.?** how tall are you? (b) (*renombre*) stature

estatus *nm* status; **e. quo** status quo

estatutario,-a *adj* statutory

estatuto *nm Jur* statute; (*de ciudad*) bylaw; (*de empresa etc*) rules

este¹ *adj* eastern; (*dirección*) easterly
  2 *nm* east; **al e. de** to the east of

este²,-a *adj dem* (a) this (b) **estos,-as** these

éste,-a *pron dem m,f* (a) this one; **aquél ... é.** the former ... the latter (b) **éstos,-as** these (ones); **aquéllos ... é.** the former ... the latter

Note that **éste** and its various forms can be written without an accent when there is no risk of confusion with the adjective.

esté *subj pres de* estar

estela *nf* (*de barco*) wake; (*de avión*) vapor trail; (*de cometa*) tail

estelar *adj* (a) *Astron* stellar (b) *Fig Cin Teatro* star

estentóreo,-a *adj* stentorian, thundering

estepa *nf* steppe

estera *nf* rush mat

estercolero *nm* dunghill; *Fig* pigsty

estéreo *nm & adj* stereo

estereofónico,-a *adj* stereophonic, stereo

estereotipar *vt* to stereotype

estereotipo *nm* stereotype

estéril *adj* (a) sterile (b) *Fig* (*esfuerzo*) futil

esterilidad *nf* (a) sterility (b) *Fig* futilit uselessness

esterilizar [40] *vt* to sterilize

esterilla *nf* small mat

esterlina *adj & nf* sterling; **libra e.** pour (sterling)

esternón *nm* sternum, breastbone

estero *nm Am* marsh, swamp

estertor *nm* death rattle

estética *nf* aesthetics *sing*

esteticienne, esteticista *nf* beautician

estético,-a *adj* aesthetic; **cirugía estéti** plastic surgery

estibador *nm* docker, stevedore

estiércol *nm* manure, dung

estigma *nm* stigma; *Rel* stigmata

estilarse *vpr* to be in vogue, to be fashionab

estilete *nm* (*punzón*) stylus; (*puñal*) stiletto

estilístico,-a *adj* stylistic

estilizar [40] *vt* to stylize

estilo *nm* (a) style; (*modo*) manner, fashio **algo por el e.** something like that; **e. de vi** way of life (b) (*en natación*) stroke (c) *Ling* **directo/indirecto** direct/indirect speech

estilográfica *nf* **(pluma) e.** fountain pen

estima *nf* esteem, respect

estimación *nf* (a) (*estima*) esteem, respe (b) (*valoración*) evaluation; (*cálculo aprox* mado) estimate

estimado,-a *adj* esteemed, respected; **Señor** (*en carta*) Dear Sir

estimar *vt* (a) (*apreciar*) to esteem (b) (*co siderar*) to consider, to think; **lo estimo co veniente** I think it appropriate (c) (*valorar*) value

estimativo,-a *adj* approximate, estimated

estimulante 1 *adj* stimulating
  2 *nm* stimulant

estimular *vt* (a) to stimulate (b) *Fig* to e courage

estímulo *nm Biol & Fís* stimulus; *Fig* e couragement

estío *nm* summer

estipendio *nm* stipend, fee

estipular *vt* to stipulate

estirado,-a *adj Fig* stiff

estirar 1 *vt* to stretch; *Fig* (*dinero*) to spin o
· *Fig* **e. la pata** to kick the bucket

2 estirarse *vpr* to stretch

estirón *nm* pull, jerk, tug; *Fam* **dar** *o* **pegar un e.** to shoot up *o* grow quickly

estirpe *nf* stock, pedigree

estival *adj* summer; **época e.** summertime

esto *pron neut* this, this thing, this matter; *Fam* **e. de la fiesta** this business about the party

estocada *nf Taurom* stab

Estocolmo *n* Stockholm

estofado *nm* stew

estoico,-a 1 *adj* stoical

   2 *nm,f* stoic

estómago *nm* stomach; **dolor de e.** stomach ache

Estonia *n* Estonia

estonio,-a 1 *adj & nm,f* Estonian

   2 *nm (lengua)* Estonian

estoque *nm Taurom* sword

estorbar 1 *vt* (**a**) *(dificultar)* to hinder, to get in the way of (**b**) *(molestar)* to disturb

   2 *vi* to be in the way

estorbo *nm* (**a**) *(obstáculo)* obstruction, obstacle (**b**) *(molestia)* nuisance

estornino *nm* starling

estornudar *vi* to sneeze

estornudo *nm* sneeze

estos,-as *adj dem pl ver* **este,-a**

éstos,-as *pron dem m,fpl ver* **éste,-a**

estoy *indic pres de* **estar**

estrabismo *nm* squint

estrado *nm* platform; *Mús* bandstand; *Jur* stand

estrafalario,-a *adj Fam* outlandish

estragos *nmpl* **hacer e. en** to wreak havoc with *o* on

estrambótico,-a *adj Fam* outlandish, eccentric

estrangulador,-a *nm,f* strangler

estrangular *vt* to strangle; *Med* to strangulate

estraperlo *nm* black market; **tabaco de e.** black market cigarettes

Estrasburgo *n* Strasbourg

estratagema *nf Mil* stratagem; *Fam* trick, ruse

estratega *nmf* strategist

estrategia *nf* strategy

estratégico,-a *adj* strategic

estratificar [44] *vt* to stratify

estrato *nm* stratum

estraza *nf* **papel de e.** brown paper

estrechamente *adv* *(íntimamente)* closely, intimately; **e. relacionados** closely related

estrechamiento *nm* (**a**) narrowing; **e. de calzada** *(en letrero)* road narrows (**b**) *(de amistad etc)* tightening

estrechar 1 *vt* (**a**) to make narrow (**b**) *(mano)* to shake; *(lazos de amistad)* to tighten; **me estrechó entre sus brazos** he hugged me

   2 estrecharse *vpr* to narrow, to become narrower

> 🔔 Observa que el verbo inglés **to stretch** es un falso amigo y no es la traducción del verbo español **estrechar**. En inglés, **to stretch** significa "estirar, desplegar".

estrechez *nf* (**a**) narrowness; *Fig* **e. de miras** narrow-mindedness (**b**) *Fig (dificultad económica)* want, need; **pasar estrecheces** to be hard up

estrecho,-a 1 *adj* (**a**) narrow; *(ropa, zapato)* tight; *(amistad, relación)* close, intimate (**b**) *Fig* **e. de miras** narrow-minded

   2 *nm Geog* strait, straits

estregar *vt* to scrub

estrella *nf* star; **e. de cine** film star; *Zool* **e. de mar** starfish; **e. fugaz** shooting star

estrellado,-a *adj* (**a**) *(en forma de estrella)* star-shaped (**b**) *(cielo)* starry (**c**) *(huevos)* scrambled

estrellar 1 *vt Fam* to smash

   2 estrellarse *vpr (morir)* to die in a car crash; *Aut & Av* **e. contra** *(chocar)* to crash into

estrellato *nm* stardom

estremecedor,-a *adj* bloodcurdling

estremecer [33] *vt*, **estremecerse** *vpr* to shake

estrenar *vt* (**a**) to use for the first time; *(ropa)* to wear for the first time (**b**) *Teatro & Cin* to premiere

estreno *nm Teatro* first performance; *Cin* premiere

estreñido,-a *adj* constipated

estreñimiento *nm* constipation

estrépito *nm* din, racket

estrepitoso,-a *adj* deafening; *Fig (fracaso)* spectacular

estrés *nm* stress

estresante *adj* stressful

estría *nf* (**a**) *(en la piel)* stretch mark (**b**) *Arquit* flute, fluting

estribar *vi* **e. en** to lie in, to be based on

estribillo *nm (en canción)* chorus; *(en poema)* refrain

estribo *nm* (**a**) stirrup; *Fig* **perder los estribos** to lose one's temper, to lose one's head (**b**) *Arquit* buttress; *(de puente)* pier, support

estribor *nm* starboard

estricto,-a *adj* strict

estridente *adj* strident

estrofa *nf* verse

estropajo *nm* scourer

estropear 1 *vt (máquina, cosecha)* to damage; *(fiesta, plan)* to spoil, to ruin; *(pelo, manos)* to ruin

   2 estropearse *vpr* to be ruined; *(máquina)* to break down

estropicio *nm Fam (destrozo)* damage; *(ruido)* crash, clatter

estructura *nf* structure; *(armazón)* frame, framework

estructurar *vt* to structure

estruendo *nm* roar

estrujar 1 *vt (limón etc)* to squeeze; *(ropa)* to wring; *(apretar)* to crush

  2 estrujarse *vpr Fam* **e. los sesos** *o* **el cerebro** to rack one's brains

estrujón *nm* tight squeeze, big hug

estuche *nm* case; *(para lápices)* pencil case

estuco *nm* stucco

estudiante *nmf* student

estudiantil *adj* student

estudiar [43] *vt & vi* to study

estudio *nm* (**a**) study; *(encuesta)* survey; *Com* **e. de mercado** market research (**b**) *(sala)* studio; **e. cinematográfico/de grabación** film/recording studio (**c**) *(apartamento)* studio (flat) (**d**) **estudios** studies

estudioso,-a 1 *adj* studious

  2 *nm,f* specialist

estufa *nf (calentador)* heater; *(de leña)* stove

estupefaciente *nm* drug, narcotic

estupefacto,-a *adj* astounded, flabbergasted

estupendamente *adv* marvellously, wonderfully

estupendo,-a *adj* super, marvellous; **¡e.!** great!

estupidez *nf* stupidity

estúpido,-a 1 *adj* stupid

  2 *nm,f* idiot

estupor *nm* amazement, astonishment

estuve *pt indef de* **estar**

esvástica *nf* swastika

ETA *nf (abr* **Euzkadi Ta Askatasuna** *(Patria Vasca y Libertad))* ETA

etapa *nf* stage; **por etapas** in stages

etarra *nmf* = member of ETA

etc. *(abr* **etcétera**) etc

etcétera *adv* etcetera

éter *nm* ether

etéreo,-a *adj* ethereal

eternidad *nf* eternity; *Fam* **una e.** ages

eterno,-a *adj* eternal

ética *nf* ethic; *(ciencia)* ethics *sing*

ético,-a *adj* ethical

etílico,-a *adj* ethylic; **alcohol e.** ethyl alcohol; **en estado e.** intoxicated; **intoxicación etílica** alcohol poisoning

etimología *nf* etymology

etimológico,-a *adj* etymological

etiope, etíope *adj & nmf* Ethiopian

Etiopía *nf* Ethiopia

etiqueta *nf* (**a**) *(de producto)* label (**b**) *(ceremonia)* etiquette; **de e.** formal

etiquetar *vt* to label

etnia *nf* ethnic group

étnico,-a *adj* ethnic

ETT *nf (abr* **Empresa de Trabajo Temporal**) temping agency

eucalipto *nm* eucalyptus

eucaristía *nf* eucharist

eufemismo *nm* euphemism

euforia *nf* euphoria

eufórico,-a *adj* euphoric

eureka *interj* eureka!

euro *nm (moneda)* euro

eurocomunismo *nm* Eurocommunism

eurodiputado,-a *nm,f* Euro MP

euromisil *nm* Euromissile

Europa *n* Europe

europeísmo *nm* Europeanism

europeizar [40] *vt* to europeanize

europeo,-a *adj & nm,f* European

euscalduna 1 *adj* Basque; *(que habla vasco)* Basque-speaking

  2 *nmf* Basque speaker

euskera *adj & nm* Basque

eutanasia *nf* euthanasia

evacuación *nf* evacuation

evacuar [47] *vt* to evacuate

evadir 1 *vt (respuesta, peligro, impuestos)* to avoid; *(responsabilidad)* to shirk

  2 evadirse *vpr* to escape

evaluación *nf* evaluation; *Educ* assessment; **e. continua** continuous assessment

evaluar [30] *vt* to evaluate, to assess

evangélico,-a *adj* evangelical

evangelio *nm* gospel

evangelista *nm* evangelist

evaporación *nf* evaporation

evaporar 1 *vt* to evaporate

  2 evaporarse *vpr* to evaporate; *Fig* to vanish

evasión *nf (fuga)* escape; *Fig* evasion; **e. fiscal** *o* **de impuestos** tax evasion

evasiva *nf* evasive answer

evasivo,-a *adj* evasive

evento *nm* (**a**) *(acontecimiento)* event (**b**) *(incidente)* contingency, unforeseen event

eventual *adj* (**a**) *(posible)* possible; *(gastos)* incidental (**b**) *(trabajo, obrero)* casual, temporary

eventualidad *nf* contingency

eventualmente *adv* by chance; **los problemas que e. surjan** such problems as may arise

> 🖉 Observa que las palabras inglesas **eventual** y **eventually** son falsos amigos y no son la traducción de las palabras españolas **eventual** y **eventualmente**. En inglés, **eventual** significa "final" o "consiguiente" y **eventually** "finalmente".

evidencia *nf* obviousness; **poner a algn en e.** to show sb up

evidenciar [43] *vt* to show, to demonstrate

evidente *adj* obvious

evidentemente *adv* obviously

evitar *vt* to avoid; *(prevenir)* to prevent; *(desastre)* to avert

evocador,-a *adj* evocative

evocar [44] *vt (traer a la memoria)* to evoke; *(acordarse de)* to recall

evolución *nf* evolution; *(desarrollo)* development

evolucionar *vi* to develop; *Biol* to evolve; **el**

enfermo evoluciona favorablemente the patient is improving

ex 1 *pref* former, ex-; **ex alumno** former pupil, ex-student; **ex combatiente** *Br* ex-serviceman, *f* ex-servicewoman, *US* (war) veteran; **ex marido** ex-husband

2 *nmf Fam* **mi ex** my ex

exabrupto *nm* sharp comment

exacerbar 1 *vt* (**a**) *(agravar)* to exacerbate, to aggravate (**b**) *(irritar)* to exasperate, to irritate

2 exacerbarse *upr* (**a**) *(agravarse)* to get worse (**b**) *(irritarse)* to feel exasperated

exactamente *adv* exactly, precisely

exactitud *nf* accuracy; **con e.** precisely

exacto,-a *adj* exact; **¡e.!** precisely!; **para ser e.** to be precise

exageración *nf* exaggeration

exagerado,-a *adj* exaggerated; *(excesivo)* excessive

exagerar 1 *vt* to exaggerate

2 *vi* to overdo it

exaltado,-a 1 *adj (persona)* excitable, hotheaded

2 *nm,f Fam* fanatic

exaltar 1 *vt (ensalzar)* to praise, to extol

2 exaltarse *upr (acalorarse)* to get overexcited, to get carried away

examen *nm* examination, exam; **e. de conducir** driving test; *Med* **e. médico** checkup

examinador,-a *nm,f* examiner

examinar 1 *vt* to examine

2 examinarse *upr* to take *o* sit an examination

exasperante *adj* exasperating

exasperar 1 *vt* to exasperate

2 exasperarse *upr* to become exasperated

Exc., Exca., Exc.ª (*abr* **Excelencia**) Excellency

excavación *nf* excavation; *(en arqueología)* dig

excavadora *nf* digger

excavar *vt* to excavate, to dig

excedencia *nf* leave (of absence)

excedente *adj & nm* excess, surplus

exceder 1 *vt* to exceed, to surpass

2 excederse *upr* to go too far

excelencia *nf* (**a**) excellence; **por e.** par excellence (**b**) *(título)* **Su E.** His/Her Excellency

excelente *adj* excellent

excelso,-a *adj* sublime, lofty

excentricidad *nf* eccentricity

excéntrico,-a *adj* eccentric

excepción *nf* exception; **a e. de** with the exception of, except for; **de e.** exceptional; *Pol* **estado de e.** state of emergency

excepcional *adj* exceptional

excepto *adv* except (for), apart from

exceptuar [30] *vt* to except, to exclude

excesivo,-a *adj* excessive

exceso *nm* excess; **en e.** in excess, excessively; **e. de equipaje** excess baggage; **e. de velocidad** speeding

excitable *adj* excitable

excitación *nf (sentimiento)* excitement

excitante 1 *adj* exciting; *Med* stimulating

2 *nm* stimulant

excitar 1 *vt* to excite

2 excitarse *upr* to get excited

exclamación *nf* exclamation

exclamar *vt & vi* to exclaim, to cry out

excluir [37] *vt* to exclude; *(rechazar)* to reject

exclusión *nf* exclusion

exclusiva *nf Prensa* exclusive; *Com* sole right

exclusive *adv (en fechas)* exclusive

exclusivo,-a *adj* exclusive

Excma. (*abr* **Excelentísima**) Most Excellent

Excmo. (*abr* **Excelentísimo**) Most Excellent

excomulgar [42] *vt Rel* to excommunicate

excomunión *nf* excommunication

excremento *nm* excrement

exculpar *vt* to exonerate

excursión *nf* excursion

excursionista *nmf* tripper; *(a pie)* hiker

excusa *nf (pretexto)* excuse; *(disculpa)* apology

excusado *nm (retrete)* toilet

excusar 1 *vt* (**a**) *(justificar)* to excuse (**b**) *(eximir)* to exempt (**de** from)

2 excusarse *upr (disculparse)* to apologize

execrar *vt* to execrate, to abhor

exención *nf* exemption; **e. de impuestos** tax exemption

exento,-a *adj* exempt, free (**de** from)

exequias *nfpl* funeral rites

exhalar *vt* to exhale, to breathe out; *(gas)* to give off, to emit; *(suspiro)* to heave

exhaustivo,-a *adj* exhaustive

exhausto,-a *adj* exhausted

exhibición *nf* exhibition

exhibicionista *nmf* exhibitionist

exhibir 1 *vt* (**a**) *(mostrar)* to exhibit, to display (**b**) *(lucir)* to show off

2 exhibirse *upr* to show off, to make an exhibition of oneself

exhortar *vt* to exhort

exhumar *vt* to exhume

exigencia *nf* (**a**) demand (**b**) *(requisito)* requirement

exigente *adj* demanding, exacting

exigir [57] *vt* to demand

exiguo,-a *adj* minute

exilado,-a 1 *adj* exiled, in exile

2 *nm,f* exile

exilar *vt* to exile, to send into exile

2 exilarse *upr* to go into exile

exiliado,-a *adj & nm,f* = **exilado,-a**

exiliar [43] *vt*, **exiliarse** *upr* = **exilar**

exilio *nm* exile

eximio,-a *adj* distinguished, eminent

eximir *vt* to exempt (**de** from)

existencia *nf* (**a**) *(vida)* existence (**b**) *Com* **existencias** stock, stocks

existente *adj* existing; *Com* in stock

existir *vi* to exist, to be (in existence)
éxito *nm* success; **con é.** successfully; **tener é.** to be successful

> *Observa que la palabra inglesa* **exit** *es un falso amigo y no es la traducción de la palabra española* **éxito**. *En inglés,* **exit** *significa "salida".*

exitoso,-a *adj* successful
éxodo *nm* exodus
exonerar *vt* to exonerate
exorbitante *adj* exorbitant, excessive
exorcista *nmf* exorcist
exorcizar [40] *vt* to exorcize
exótico,-a *adj* exotic
expandir 1 *vt* to expand
   2 expandirse *vpr (gas etc)* to expand; *(noticia)* to spread
expansión *nf* (a) expansion; *(de noticia)* spreading (b) *(diversión)* relaxation, recreation
expansionarse *vpr Fig (divertirse)* to relax, to let one's hair down
expatriado,-a *adj & nm,f* expatriate
expatriar [29] 1 *vt* to exile, to banish
   2 expatriarse *vpr* to leave one's country
expectación *nf* excitement
expectativa *nf* expectancy; **estar a la e. de** to be on the lookout for
expectorante *nm* expectorant
expedición *nf* expedition
expedientar *vt* to place under enquiry
expediente *nm* (a) *(informe)* dossier, record; *(ficha)* file; *Educ* **e. académico** student's record; **abrirle e. a algn** to place sb under enquiry (b) *Jur* proceedings, action
expedir [6] *vt* (a) *(carta)* to send, to dispatch (b) *(pasaporte etc)* to issue
expedito,-a *adj* free, clear
expendedor,-a 1 *nm,f* seller
   2 nm e. automático vending machine
expendeduría *nf* tobacconist's
expensas *nfpl* **a e. de** at the expense of
experiencia *nf* (a) experience; **por e.** from experience (b) *(experimento)* experiment
experimentado,-a *adj* experienced
experimental *adj* experimental
experimentar 1 *vi* to experiment
   2 *vt* to undergo; *(aumento)* to show; *(pérdida)* to suffer; *(sensación)* to experience, to feel; *Med* **e. una mejoría** to improve, to make progress
experimento *nm* experiment
experto,-a *nm,f* expert
expiar [29] *vt* to expiate, to atone for
expirar *vi* to expire
explanada *nf* esplanade
explayarse *vpr* to talk at length (about)
explicación *nf* explanation
explicar [44] 1 *vt* to explain
   2 explicarse *vpr (persona)* to explain (oneself); **no me lo explico** I can't understand it

explicativo,-a *adj* explanatory
explícito,-a *adj* explicit
exploración *nf* exploration; *Téc* scanning; *Med (interna)* exploration; *(externa)* examination; *Mil* reconnaissance
explorador,-a *nm,f* (a) *(persona)* explorer (b) *Med* probe; *Téc* scanner
explorar *vt* to explore; *Med (internamente)* to explore; *(externamente)* to examine; *Téc* to scan; *Mil* to reconnoitre
explosión *nf* explosion, blast; **hacer e.** to explode; **motor de e.** internal combustion engine; **e. demográfica** population explosion
explosionar *vt & vi* to explode, to blow up
explosivo,-a *adj & nm* explosive
explotación *nf* (a) *(abuso)* exploitation (b) *(uso)* exploitation, working; *Agr* cultivation (of land); *(granja)* farm
explotador,-a *nm,f* exploiter
explotar 1 *vi (bomba)* to explode, to go off
   2 *vt* (a) *(aprovechar)* to exploit; *(recursos)* to tap; *(tierra)* to cultivate (b) *(abusar de)* to exploit
expoliar [43] *vt* to plunder, to pillage
exponente *nmf* exponent
exponer [19] *(pp expuesto)* 1 *vt* (a) *(mostrar)* to exhibit, to display (b) *(explicar)* to expound, to put forward (c) *(arriesgar)* to expose
   2 exponerse *vpr* to expose oneself (**a** to); **te expones a perder el trabajo** you run the risk of losing your job
exportación *nf* export
exportador,-a 1 *adj* exporting
   2 nm,f exporter
exportar *vt* to export
exposición *nf* (a) *Arte* exhibition; **e. universal** world fair; **sala de exposiciones** gallery (b) *(de hechos, ideas)* exposé (c) *Fot* exposure
exprés *adj* express; **(olla) e.** pressure cooker **(café) e.** espresso (coffee)
expresamente *adv* specifically, expressly
expresar 1 *vt* to express; *(manifestar)* to state
   2 expresarse *vpr* to express oneself
expresión *nf* expression; **la mínima e.** the bare minimum
expresivo,-a *adj* expressive
expreso,-a 1 *adj* express; **con el fin e. de** with the express purpose of
   2 nm *Ferroc* express (train)
   3 *adv* on purpose, deliberately
exprimidor *nm* squeezer, juicer
exprimir *vt (limón)* to squeeze; *(zumo)* to squeeze out; *Fig (persona)* to exploit, to bleed dry
expropiar [43] *vt* to expropriate
expuesto,-a *adj* (a) *(sin protección)* exposed; **estar e. a** to be exposed to (b) *(peligroso)* risky, dangerous (c) *(exhibido)* on display, or show

expulsar *vt* (**a**) to expel, to throw out; *Dep (jugador)* to send off (**b**) *(gas etc)* to belch out
expulsión *nf* expulsion; *Dep* sending off
expurgar [42] *vt* to expurgate; *Fig* to purge
expuse *pt indef de* **exponer**
exquisito,-a *adj* exquisite; *(comida)* delicious; *(gusto)* refined
extasiado,-a *adj* ecstatic; **quedarse e.** to go into ecstasies o raptures
extasiarse [29] *vpr* to go into ecstasies o raptures
éxtasis *nm inv* ecstasy
extender [3] **1** *vt* (**a**) to extend; *(agrandar)* to enlarge (**b**) *(mantel, mapa)* to spread (out), to open (out); *(mano, brazo)* to stretch (out) (**c**) *(crema, mantequilla)* to spread (**d**) *(cheque)* to make out; *(documento)* to draw up; *(certificado)* to issue
2 extenderse *vpr* (**a**) *(en el tiempo)* to extend, to last (**b**) *(en el espacio)* to spread out, to stretch (**c**) *(rumor, noticia)* to spread, to extend (**d**) *Fig (hablar demasiado)* to go on
extendido,-a *adj* (**a**) extended; *(mapa, plano)* spread out, open; *(mano, brazo)* outstretched (**b**) *(costumbre, rumor)* widespread
extensible *adj* extending
extensión *nf (de libro etc)* length; *(de cuerpo)* size; *(de terreno)* area, expanse; *(edificio anexo)* extension; **en toda la e. de la palabra** in every sense of the word; **por e.** by extension
extensivo,-a *adj* **hacer e.** to extend; **ser e. a** to cover
extenso,-a *adj (terreno)* extensive; *(libro, película)* long
extenuar [30] **1** *vt* to exhaust
2 extenuarse *vpr* to exhaust oneself
exterior 1 *adj* (**a**) *(de fuera)* outer; *(puerta)* outside (**b**) *(política, deuda)* foreign; *Pol* **Ministerio de Asuntos Exteriores** Ministry of Foreign Affairs, *Br* ≃ Foreign Office, *US* ≃ State Department
2 *nm* (**a**) *(parte de fuera)* exterior, outside (**b**) *(extranjero)* abroad (**c**) **exteriores** *Cin* location
exteriorizar [40] *vt* to show
exteriormente *adv* outwardly
exterminar *vt* to exterminate
exterminio *nm* extermination
externalización *nf Com* outsourcing
externo,-a 1 *adj* external; *Farm* **de uso e.** for external use only
2 *nm,f Educ* day pupil
extinción *nf* extinction
extinguir [59] **1** *vt (fuego)* to extinguish, to put out; *(raza)* to wipe out
2 extinguirse *vpr (fuego)* to go out; *(especie)* to become extinct, to die out
extinto,-a *adj* extinct
extintor *nm* fire extinguisher
extirpar *vt* (**a**) *Med* to remove (**b**) *Fig* to eradicate, to stamp out
extorsión *nf* extortion

extorsionar *vt* to extort
extra 1 *adj* (**a**) *(suplementario)* extra; **horas e.** overtime; **paga e.** bonus (**b**) *(superior)* top-quality
2 *nm* extra
3 *nmf Cin & Teatro* extra
extra- *pref* extra-; **extramatrimonial** extramarital
extracción *nf* (**a**) extraction (**b**) *(en lotería)* draw
extracto *nm* (**a**) extract; **e. de fresa** strawberry extract; **e. de regaliz** liquorice; *Fin* **e. de cuenta** statement of account (**b**) *(resumen)* summary
extractor *nm* extractor
extradición *nf* extradition
extraer [25] *vt* to extract, to take out
extraescolar *adj (actividad etc)* extracurricular
extrafino,-a *adj* superfine
extralimitarse *vpr* to overstep the mark
extranjería *nf* **ley de e.** law on aliens
extranjero,-a 1 *adj* foreign
2 *nm,f* foreigner
3 *nm* abroad; **en el e.** abroad
extrañar 1 *vt* (**a**) *(sorprender)* to surprise; **no es de e.** it's hardly surprising (**b**) *Am (echar de menos)* to miss
2 extrañarse *vpr* **e. de** to be surprised at
extrañeza *nf* (**a**) *(sorpresa)* surprise, astonishment (**b**) *(singularidad)* strangeness
extraño,-a 1 *adj* strange; *Med* **cuerpo e.** foreign body
2 *nm,f* stranger
extraoficial *adj* unofficial
extraordinaria *nf (paga)* bonus
extraordinario,-a *adj* extraordinary; *Prensa* **edición extraordinaria** special edition
extrarradio *nm* outskirts, suburbs
extraterrestre *nmf* alien
extravagancia *nf* extravagance
extravagante *adj* odd, outlandish
extravertido,-a *adj* = **extrovertido,-a**
extraviado,-a *adj* lost, missing
extraviar [29] **1** *vt* to mislay, to lose
2 extraviarse *vpr* to be missing, to get mislaid
extremadamente *adv* extremely
extremado,-a *adj* extreme
Extremadura *n* Estremadura
extremar *vt* **e. la prudencia** to be extremely careful
2 extremarse *vpr* to take great pains, to do one's utmost
extremaunción *nf* extreme unction
extremeño,-a 1 *adj* of/from Estremadura
2 *nm,f* person from Estremadura
extremidad *nf* (**a**) *(extremo)* end, tip (**b**) *Anat (miembro)* limb, extremity
extremista *adj & nmf* extremist
extremo,-a 1 *nm (de calle, cable)* end; *(máximo)* extreme; **en e.** very much; **en último e.** as a last resort

2 *nm,f (en fútbol)* winger; **e. derecha/izquierda** outside right/left

3 *adj* extreme; **E. Oriente** Far East

extrovertido,-a *adj & nm,f* extrovert

exuberante *adj* exuberant; *(vegetación)* lush, abundant

eyaculación *nf* ejaculation; **e. precoz** premature ejaculation

eyacular *vi* to ejaculate

eyectable *adj* **asiento e.** ejector seat

F, f ['efe] *nf (la letra)* F, f

fa *nm Mús* F

fabada *nf* stew of beans, pork sausage and bacon

fábrica *nf* factory; **marca de f.** trademark; **precio de f.** factory *o* ex-works price

> *Observa que la palabra inglesa **fabric** es un falso amigo y no es la traducción de la palabra española **fábrica**. En inglés, **fabric** significa "tejido".*

fabricación *nf* manufacture; **de f. casera** home-made; **de f. propia** our own make; **f. en cadena** mass production

fabricante *nmf* manufacturer

fabricar [44] *vt* (**a**) *Ind* to manufacture (**b**) *Fig (mentiras etc)* to fabricate

fabril *adj* manufacturing

fábula *nf* fable

fabuloso,-a *adj* fabulous

faca *nf* large curved knife

facción *nf* (**a**) *Pol* faction (**b**) **facciones** *(rasgos)* features

faccioso,-a 1 *adj* seditious

  2 *nm,f* rebel

faceta *nf* facet

facha¹ *nf Fam* appearance, look

facha² *nmf Pey* fascist

fachada *nf* façade

facial *adj* facial

fácil *adj* (**a**) easy; **f. de comprender** easy to understand (**b**) *(probable)* likely, probable; **es f. que ...** it's (quite) likely that ...

facilidad *nf* (**a**) *(sencillez)* easiness (**b**) *(soltura)* ease (**c**) *(servicio)* facility; **dar facilidades** to make things easy; **Com facilidades de pago** easy terms (**d**) **f. para los idiomas** gift for languages

facilitar *vt (proporcionar)* to provide, to supply (**a** with)

fácilmente *adv* easily

facineroso,-a *adj* criminal

facsímil, facsímile *nm* facsimile

factible *adj* feasible

fáctico,-a *adj* **poderes fácticos** vested interests

factor *nm* (**a**) factor (**b**) *Ferroc* luggage clerk

factoría *nf (fábrica)* factory

factura *nf* (**a**) *Com* invoice (**b**) *Arg (bollo)* = rolls and pastries

facturación *nf* (**a**) *Com* invoicing (**b**) *(de equipajes) (en aeropuerto)* check-in; *(en estación)* registration

facturar *vt* (**a**) *Com* to invoice (**b**) *(en aeropuerto)* to check in; *(en estación)* to register

facultad *nf* faculty; **facultades mentales** faculties

facultativo,-a 1 *adj* optional

  2 *nm,f* doctor

faena *nf* (**a**) *(tarea)* task (**b**) *Fam (mala pasada)* dirty trick (**c**) *Taurom* performance

faenar *vi* to fish

fagot *nm Mús* bassoon

fainá *nf Urug (plato)* = baked dough made with chickpea flour and olive oil, served with pizza

faisán *nm* pheasant

faja *nf* (**a**) *(corsé)* girdle, corset (**b**) *(banda)* sash (**c**) *(de terreno)* strip

fajo *nm (de ropa etc)* bundle; *(de billetes)* wad

falacia *nf* fallacy

falaz *adj* (**a**) *(erróneo)* fallacious (**b**) *(engañoso)* deceitful

falda *nf* (**a**) *(prenda)* skirt; **f. pantalón** culottes (**b**) *(de montaña)* slope, hillside (**c**) *(de mesa)* cover (**d**) *(regazo)* lap

faldero,-a *adj* **perro f.** lapdog

falencia *nf* (**a**) *Am Com (bancarrota)* bankruptcy (**b**) *CSur (error)* fault

falla¹ *nf Am (defecto)* defect, fault

falla² *nf Geol* fault

fallar¹ 1 *vi Jur* to rule

  2 *vt (premio)* to award

fallar² 1 *vi* to fail; **le falló la puntería** he missed his aim; *Fig* **no me falles** don't let me down

  2 *vt* to miss

fallecer [33] *vi Fml* to pass away, to die

fallecido,-a *adj* deceased

fallecimiento *nm* demise

fallido,-a *adj* unsuccessful, vain

fallo¹ *nm* (**a**) *(error)* mistake; **f. humano** human error (**b**) *(del corazón, de los frenos)* failure

fallo² *nm* (**a**) *Jur* judgement, sentence (**b**) *(en concurso)* awarding

falluto,-a *RP Fam* **1** *adj* phoney, hypocritical

  2 *nm,f* hypocrite

falo *nm* phallus

falsear *vt* (**a**) *(informe etc)* to falsify; *(hechos, la verdad)* to distort (**b**) *(moneda)* to forge

falsedad *nf* (**a**) falseness, *(doblez)* hypocrisy (**b**) *(mentira)* falsehood

falsificar [44] *vt* to falsify; *(cuadro, firma, moneda)* to forge

falso,-a *adj* (a) false; **dar un paso en f.** *(tropezar)* to trip, to stumble; *Fig* to make a blunder; **jurar en f.** to commit perjury (b) *(persona)* insincere

falta *nf* (a) *(carencia)* lack; **por f. de** for want o lack of; **sin f.** without fail; **f. de educación** bad manners

(b) *(escasez)* shortage

(c) *(ausencia)* absence; **echar algo/a algn en f.** to miss sth/sb

(d) *(error)* mistake; *(defecto)* fault, defect; **f. de ortografía** spelling mistake; **sacar faltas a algo/a algn** to find fault with sth/sb

(e) *Jur* misdemeanour

(f) *(en fútbol)* foul; *(en tenis)* fault

(g) **hacer f.** to be necessary; **(nos) hace f. una escalera** we need a ladder; **harán f. dos personas para mover el piano** it'll take two people to move the piano; **no hace f. que ...** there is no need for ...

faltante *nm Am* deficit

faltar *vi* (a) *(no estar)* to be missing; **¿quién falta?** who is missing?

(b) *(escasear)* to be lacking o needed; **le falta confianza en sí mismo** he lacks confidence in himself; **¡lo que me faltaba!** that's all I needed!; **¡no faltaría o faltaba más!** *(por supuesto)* but) of course!

(c) *(quedar)* to be left; **¿cuántos kilómetros faltan para Managua?** how many kilometres is it to Managua?; **ya falta poco para las vacaciones** it won't be long now till the holidays; **faltó poco para que me cayera** I very nearly fell

(d) **f. a la verdad** not to tell the truth; **f. al deber** to fail in one's duty; **f. a su palabra/promesa** to break one's word/promise; **f. al respeto a algn** to treat sb with disrespect

falto,-a *adj* **f. de** lacking in

fama *nf* (a) fame, renown; **de f. mundial** world-famous (b) *(reputación)* reputation

famélico,-a *adj* starving, famished

familia *nf* family; **estar en f.** to be among friends; **f. numerosa** large family

familiar 1 *adj* (a) *(de la familia)* family; **empresa f.** family business (b) *(conocido)* familiar

2 *nmf* relation, relative

familiaridad *nf* familiarity

familiarizarse [40] *vpr* **f. con** to familiarize oneself with

famoso,-a 1 *adj* famous

2 *nm* famous person

fan *nmf* fan

fanático,-a 1 *adj* fanatical

2 *nm,f* fanatic

fanatismo *nm* fanaticism

fanfarrón,-ona *Fam* **1** *adj* boastful

2 *nm,f* show-off

fanfarronear *vi Fam (chulear)* to show off;

(bravear) to brag, to boast

fango *nm* (a) *(barro)* mud (b) *Fig* degradation

fantasear *vi* to daydream, to dream

fantasía *nf* fantasy; **joya de f.** imitation jewellery

fantasioso,-a *adj* imaginative

fantasma *nm* (a) *(espectro)* ghost (b) *Fam (fanfarrón)* braggart, show-off

fantasmal *adj* ghostly

fantástico,-a *adj* fantastic

fantoche *nm Pey* nincompoop, ninny

faraón *nm* Pharaoh

fardar *vi Fam* to show off

fardo *nm* bundle

farfullar *vt* to jabber

faringe *nf* pharynx

faringitis *nf* pharyngitis

fariseo,-a *nm,f (falso)* hypocrite

farmacéutico,-a 1 *adj* pharmaceutical

2 *nm,f* pharmacist, *Br* chemist, *US* druggist

farmacia *nf* (a) *(tienda)* Br chemist's (shop), *US* drugstore (b) *(ciencia)* pharmacology

fármaco *nm* medicine, medication

faro *nm* (a) *(torre)* lighthouse (b) *(de coche)* headlight, headlamp

farol *nm* (a) lantern; *(en la calle)* streetlight, streetlamp (b) *Fam (fanfarronada)* bragging; **tirarse un f.** to brag (c) *(en naipes)* bluff

farola *nf* streetlight, streetlamp

farolear *vi Fam* to brag

farolillo *nm Fig* **ser el f. rojo** to bring up the rear

farragoso,-a *adj* confused, rambling

farruco,-a *adj Fam* cocky

farsa *nf* farce

farsante *nmf* fake, impostor

fascículo *nm Impr* instalment

fascinador,-a, fascinante *adj* fascinating

fascinar *vt* to fascinate

fascismo *nm* fascism

fascista *adj & nmf* fascist

fase *nf* (a) *(etapa)* phase, stage (b) *Elec & Fís* phase

fastidiado,-a *adj Fam* (a) *(roto)* broken (b) *(enfermo)* sick; **tiene el estómago f.** he's got a bad stomach

fastidiar [43] **1** *vt* (a) *(molestar)* to annoy, to bother; *(dañar)* to hurt; *Fam* **¡no fastidies!** you're kidding! (b) *Fam (estropear)* to damage, to ruin; *(planes)* to spoil

2 fastidiarse *vpr* (a) *(aguantarse)* to put up with it, to resign oneself; **que se fastidie** that's his tough luck (b) *Fam (estropearse)* to get damaged, to break down (c) **me he fastidiado el tobillo** I've hurt my ankle

fastidio *nm* nuisance

fastuoso,-a *adj* (a) *(acto)* splendid, lavish (b) *(persona)* lavish, ostentatious

fatal 1 *adj* (a) *Fam (muy malo)* awful, dreadful (b) *(mortal)* deadly, fatal (c) *(inexorable)* fateful, inevitable

2 *adv Fam* awfully, terribly; **lo pasó f.** he had a rotten time

fatalidad *nf* (**a**) *(destino)* fate (**b**) *(desgracia)* misfortune

🖉 Observa que la palabra inglesa **fatality** es un falso amigo y no es la traducción de la palabra española **fatalidad**. En inglés, **fatality** significa "víctima mortal".

fatalista 1 *adj* fatalistic
  2 *nmf* fatalist

fatiga *nf* (**a**) *(cansancio)* fatigue (**b**) **fatigas** *(dificultades)* troubles, difficulties

fatigar [42] **1** *vt* to tire, to weary
  2 fatigarse *vpr* to tire, to become tired

fatigoso,-a *adj* tiring, exhausting

fatuo,-a *adj* (**a**) *(envanecido)* vain, conceited (**b**) *(necio)* fatuous, foolish

fauces *nfpl Fig* jaws

fauna *nf* fauna

favor *nm* favour; **por f.** please; **¿puedes hacerme un f.?** can you do me a favour?; **estar a f. de** to be in favour of; **haga el f. de sentarse** please sit down

favorable *adj* favourable; **f. a** in favour of

favorecedor,-a *adj* flattering

favorecer [33] *vt* (**a**) to favour (**b**) *(sentar bien)* to flatter

favoritismo *nm* favouritism

favorito,-a *adj & nm,f* favourite

faz *nf* (*pl* **faces**) *Literario (cara)* face

fe *nf* (**a**) faith; **de buena/mala fe** with good/ dishonest intentions (**b**) *(certificado)* certificate; **fe de bautismo/matrimonio** baptism/ marriage certificate (**c**) *Impr* **fe de erratas** errata

fealdad *nf* ugliness

febrero *nm* February

febril *adj* (**a**) *Med* feverish (**b**) *(actividad)* hectic

fecha *nf* (**a**) date; **f. límite** *o* **tope** deadline; **f. de caducidad** sell-by date; **hasta la f.** so far; **en f. próxima** at an early date (**b**) **fechas** *(época)* time; **el año pasado por estas fechas** this time last year

fechar *vt* to date

fechoría *nf (de niños)* mischief; *Literario* misdeed

fécula *nf* starch

fecundación *nf* fertilization; **f. in vitro** in vitro fertilization

fecundar *vt* to fertilize

fecundo,-a *adj* fertile

federación *nf* federation

federal *adj & nmf* federal

fehaciente *adj* (**a**) *Fml* authentic, reliable (**b**) *Jur* irrefutable; **documento** *o* **prueba f.** irrefutable proof

felicidad *nf* happiness; **(muchas) felicidades** *(en cumpleaños)* many happy returns

felicitación *nf* **tarjeta de f.** greetings card

felicitar *vt* to congratulate (**por** on); **¡te felicito!** congratulations!

feligrés,-esa *nm,f* parishioner

felino,-a *adj & nm* feline

feliz *adj* (**a**) *(contento)* happy; **¡felices Navidades!** Happy *o* Merry Christmas! (**b**) *(decisión etc)* fortunate

felonía *nf* treachery

felpa *nf* (**a**) *Tex* plush; **oso** *o* **osito de f.** teddy bear (**b**) *(para el pelo)* hairband

felpudo *nm* mat, doormat

femenino,-a *adj* feminine; *(equipo, ropa)* women's; **el sexo f.** the female sex, women

feminismo *nm* feminism

feminista *adj & nmf* feminist

fémur *nm* femur

fenecer [33] *vi Euf* to pass away, to die

fenomenal 1 *adj* (**a**) phenomenal (**b**) *Fam (fantástico)* great, terrific
  2 *adv Fam* wonderfully, marvellously; **lo pasamos f.** we had a fantastic time

fenómeno,-a 1 *nm* (**a**) phenomenon (**b**) *(prodigio)* genius (**c**) *(monstruo)* freak
  2 *adj Fam* fantastic, terrific
  3 *interj* fantastic!, terrific!

feo,-a 1 *adj* ugly; *(asunto etc)* nasty
  2 *nm Fam* **hacerle un f. a algn** to offend sb

féretro *nm* coffin

feria *nf* fair; **f. de muestras/del libro** trade/ book fair

feriado,-a *Am* **1** *adj* **día f.** (public) holiday
  2 *nm* (public) holiday

ferial *adj* **recinto f.** *(de exposiciones)* exhibition centre; *(de fiestas)* fairground

ferina *adj* **tos f.** whooping cough

fermentar *vi* to ferment

fermento *nm* ferment

ferocidad *nf* ferocity, fierceness

feroz *adj* fierce, ferocious; **el lobo f.** the big bad wolf

férreo,-a *adj* ferreous; *Fig* iron

ferretería *nf* ironmonger's (shop), hardware store

ferrocarril *nm Br* railway, *US* railroad

ferroviario,-a *adj* rail, *Br* railway

ferry *nm* ferry

fértil *adj* fertile

fertilidad *nf* fertility

fertilizante 1 *adj* fertilizing
  2 *nm* fertilizer

fertilizar [40] *vt* to fertilize

ferviente *adj* fervent

fervor *nm* fervour

fervoroso,-a *adj* fervent

festejar *vt* to celebrate

festejos *nmpl* festivities

festín *nm* feast, banquet

festival *nm* festival

festividad *nf* festivity

festivo,-a 1 *adj* (**a**) *(ambiente etc)* festive (**b**) **día f.** holiday
  2 *nm* holiday

feta *nf RP* slice
fetal *adj* foetal
fetiche *nm* fetish
fétido,-a *adj* stinking, fetid
feto *nm* foetus
feudalismo *nm* feudalism
feudo *nm* fief; *Pol* stronghold
FEVE *nm* (*abr* **Ferrocarriles de Vía Estrecha**) = Spanish narrow-gauge railways
FF.AA. *nfpl* (*abr* **Fuerzas Armadas**) Armed Forces
FF.CC. *nmpl* (*abr* **ferrocarriles**) railways
fiabilidad *nf* reliability, trustworthiness
fiable *adj* reliable, trustworthy
fiaca *nf Méx, CSur Fam* (*pereza*) laziness
fiador,-a *nm,f* guarantor; **salir** *o* **ser f. de algn** (*pagar fianza*) to stand bail for sb; (*avalar*) to vouch for sb
fiambre *nm* (**a**) *Culin* cold meat (**b**) *Fam* (*cadáver*) stiff, corpse
fiambrera *nf* lunch box
fianza *nf* (*depósito*) deposit; *Jur* bail; **en libertad bajo f.** on bail
fiar [29] **1** *vt* (**a**) (*avalar*) to guarantee (**b**) (*vender sin cobrar*) to sell on credit
 2 fiarse *vpr* **fiarse (de)** to trust
fiasco *nm* fiasco
fibra *nf* fibre; (*de madera*) grain; **f. de vidrio** fibreglass
ficción *nf* fiction
ficha *nf* (**a**) (*tarjeta*) filing card; **f. técnica** specifications, technical data; *Cin* credits (**b**) (*en juegos*) counter; (*de ajedrez*) piece, man; (*de dominó*) domino
fichado,-a *adj* **está f. por la policía** he has a police record
fichaje *nm Dep* signing
fichar 1 *vt* (**a**) to put on file (**b**) *Dep* to sign up
 2 *vi* (**a**) (*en el trabajo*) (*al entrar*) to clock in; (*al salir*) to clock out (**b**) *Dep* to sign
fichero *nm* card index
ficticio,-a *adj* fictitious
fidedigno,-a *adj* reliable, trustworthy; **fuentes fidedignas** reliable sources
fidelidad *nf* faithfulness; **alta f.** high fidelity, hi-fi
fideo *nm* noodle
fiebre *nf* fever; **tener f.** to have a temperature
fiel 1 *adj* (**a**) (*leal*) faithful, loyal (**b**) (*exacto*) accurate, exact
 2 *nm* (**a**) (*de balanza*) needle, pointer (**b**) *Rel* **los fieles** the congregation
fieltro *nm* felt
fiera *nf* (**a**) wild animal; *Fam* **estaba hecho una f.** he was hopping mad (**b**) *Taurom* bull
fiero,-a *adj* (*salvaje*) wild; (*feroz*) fierce, ferocious
fierro *nm Am* (*hierro*) iron
fiesta *nf* (**a**) (*entre amigos*) party (**b**) **día de f.** holiday (**c**) *Rel* feast; **f. de guardar** holy day of obligation (**d**) (*festividad*) celebration, festivity
figura *nf* figure

figurado,-a *adj* figurative; **en sentido f.** figuratively
figurar 1 *vi* (*en lista*) to figure
 2 figurarse *vpr* (**a**) to imagine, to suppose; **ya me lo figuraba** I thought as much (**b**) **¡figúrate!, ¡figúrese!** just imagine!
figurinista *nmf Teatro & Cin* costume designer
fijador *nm* (**a**) (*gomina*) gel (**b**) *Fot* fixative
fijamente *adv* **mirar f.** to stare
fijar 1 *vt* to fix; **prohibido f. carteles** (*en letrero*) post no bills
 2 fijarse *vpr* (**a**) (*darse cuenta*) to notice (**b**) (*poner atención*) to pay attention, to watch
fijo,-a *adj* (**a**) fixed; **sin domicilio f.** of no fixed abode (**b**) (*trabajo*) steady
fila *nf* (**a**) file; **en f. india** in single file; **poner en f.** to line up (**b**) (*de cine, teatro*) row (**c**) *Mil* **filas** ranks; **llamar a algn a filas** to call sb up; **¡rompan filas!** fall out!, dismiss!
filamento *nm* filament
filantropía *nf* philanthropy
filántropo,-a *nm,f* philanthropist
filarmónico,-a *adj* philharmonic
filatelia *nf* philately, stamp collecting
filete *nm* (*de carne, pescado*) fillet
filiación *nf Pol* affiliation
filial 1 *adj* (**a**) (*de hijos*) filial (**b**) *Com* subsidiary
 2 *nf Com* subsidiary
filigrana *nf* (**a**) filigree (**b**) *Fig* **filigranas** intricacy, intricate work
Filipinas *npl* (**las**) **F.** (the) Philippines
filipino,-a *adj & nm,f* Philippine, Filipino
film *nm* film
filmar *vt* to film, to shoot
filme *nm* film
fílmico,-a *adj* film
filmoteca *nf* (*archivo*) film library
filo *nm* (*cutting*) edge; **al f. de la medianoche** on the stroke of midnight; *Fig* **de doble f.** double-edged
filón *nm* (**a**) *Min* seam, vein (**b**) *Fig* (*buen negocio*) gold mine
filoso,-a *adj Am* sharp
filosofal *adj* **piedra f.** philosopher's stone
filosofía *nf* philosophy; *Fig* **con f.** philosophically
filosófico,-a *adj* philosophical
filósofo,-a *nm,f* philosopher
filtración *nf* filtration; (*de información*) leak
filtrar 1 *vt* (**a**) to filter (**b**) (*información*) to leak
 2 filtrarse *vpr* (**a**) (*líquido*) to seep (**b**) (*información*) to leak out
filtro *nm* filter
fin *nm* (**a**) (*final*) end; **dar** *o* **poner f. a** to put an end to; **llegar** *o* **tocar a su f.** to come to an end; **en f.** anyway; **¡por** *o* **al f.!** at last!; **f. de semana** weekend; **f. y al cabo** when all's said and done; **noche de F. de Año** New Year's Eve (**b**) (*objetivo*) purpose, aim; **a f. de** in

order to, so as to; **a f. de que** in order that, so that; **con el f. de** with the intention of
final 1 *adj* final
  2 *nm* end; **al f.** in the end; **f. de línea** terminal; **f. feliz** happy ending; **a finales de octubre** at the end of October
  3 *nf Dep* final
finalidad *nf* purpose, aim
finalista 1 *nmf* finalist
  2 *adj* in the final
finalizar [40] *vt & vi* to end, to finish
finalmente *adv* finally
financiación *nf* financing
financiar [43] *vt* to finance
financiero,-a 1 *adj* financial
  2 *nm,f* financier
financista *nmf Am* financier, financial expert
finanzas *nfpl* finances
finca *nf (inmueble)* property; *(de campo)* country house
finés,-esa *adj & nm,f* = **finlandés,-esa**
fingido,-a *adj* feigned, false; **nombre f.** assumed name
fingir [57] **1** *vt* to feign
  2 fingirse *vpr* to pretend to be
finlandés,-esa 1 *adj* Finnish
  2 *nm,f (persona)* Finn
  3 *nm (idioma)* Finnish
Finlandia *n* Finland
fino,-a 1 *adj* (a) *(hilo, capa)* fine (b) *(flaco)* thin (c) *(educado)* refined, polite (d) *(oído)* sharp, acute; *(olfato)* keen (e) *(humor, ironía)* subtle
  2 *nm (vino)* = type of dry sherry
finta *nf (en boxeo)* feint; *(en fútbol)* dummy
finura *nf* (a) *(refinamiento)* refinement, politeness (b) *(sutileza)* subtlety
firma *nf* (a) *(signature)* (b) *(empresa)* firm, company
firmamento *nm* firmament
firmante *adj & nmf* signatory; **el o la abajo f.** the undersigned
firmar *vt* to sign
firme 1 *adj* (a) firm; *Fig* **mantenerse f.** to hold one's ground; **tierra f.** terra firma (b) *Mil* **¡firmes!** attention!
  2 *nm (de carretera)* road surface
  3 *adv* hard
firmemente *adv* firmly
firmeza *nf* firmness
fiscal 1 *adj* fiscal, tax
  2 *nmf Jur* public prosecutor, *US* district attorney
fisco *nm* treasury, exchequer
fisgar [42] *vi Fam* to snoop, to pry
fisgón,-ona *nm,f* snooper
fisgonear *vi* to snoop, to pry
física *nf* physics *sing*
físico,-a 1 *adj* physical
  2 *nm,f (profesión)* physicist
  3 *nm* physique
fisión *nf* fission

fisioterapeuta *nmf* physiotherapist
fisioterapia *nf Med* physiotherapy
fisonomía *nf* physiognomy
fisonomista *nmf Fam* **ser buen/mal f.** to be good/no good at remembering faces
fisura *nf* fissure
flácido,-a *adj* flaccid, flabby
flaco,-a 1 *adj* (a) *(delgado)* skinny (b) *Fig* **punto f.** weak spot
  2 *nm,f Am Fam (como apelativo)* **¿cómo estás, flaca?** hey, how are you doing?
flagelar *vt* to flagellate
flagelo *nm (látigo)* whip; *Fig* scourge
flagrante *adj* flagrant; **en f. delito** red-handed
flamante *adj* (a) **nuevecito f.** *(nuevo)* brand-new (b) *(vistoso)* splendid, brilliant
flamenco,-a 1 *adj* (a) *Mús* flamenco (b) *(de Flandes)* Flemish
  2 *nm* (a) *Mús* flamenco (b) *Orn* flamingo (c) *(idioma)* Flemish
flan *nm* crème caramel

> *Observa que la palabra inglesa* **flan** *es un falso amigo y no es la traducción de la palabra española* **flan**. *En inglés,* **flan** *significa "tarta".*

---

flanco *nm* flank, side
flanquear *vt* to flank
flaquear *vi (fuerzas, piernas)* to weaken, to give way
flaqueza *nf* weakness
flash *nm Fot* flash
flato *nm* wind, flatulence
flatulencia *nf* flatulence
flauta *nf* flute; **f. dulce** recorder
flautín *nm (instrumento)* piccolo
flautista *nmf Mús* flute player, flautist, *US* flutist
flecha *nf* arrow
flechazo *nm Fig (enamoramiento)* love at first sight
fleco *nm* fringe
flema *nf* phlegm
flemático,-a *adj* phlegmatic
flemón *nm* gumboil, abscess
flequillo *nm Br* fringe, *US* bangs
fletar *vt* to charter
flete *nm* (a) *(alquiler)* charter (b) *(carga)* freight
flexibilidad *nf* flexibility
flexible *adj* flexible
flexión *nf* (a) *Gram* inflection (b) **flexiones** push-ups, *Br* press-ups
flexionar *vt* to bend; *(músculo)* to flex
flexo *nm* reading lamp
flipante *adj Fam* great, cool
flipar *vt Fam* **le flipan las motos** he's crazy about motorbikes
flirtear *vi* to flirt
flirteo *nm* flirting
flojear *vi (ventas etc)* to fall off, to go down;

(piernas) to weaken, to grow weak; *(memoria)* to fail; *Andes Fam (holgazanear)* to laze around o about
flojedad nf weakness
flojera nf Fam weakness, faintness
flojo,-a adj (a) *(tornillo, cuerda etc)* loose, slack (b) *(perezoso)* lazy, idle; *(exámen, trabajo, resultado)* poor
flor nf (a) flower; **en f.** in blossom; *Fig* **en la f. de la vida** in the prime of life; *Fig* **la f. y nata** the cream (of society) (b) **a f. de piel** skin-deep
flora nf flora
floreado,-a adj flowery
florecer [33] vi (a) *(plantas)* to flower (b) *Fig (negocio)* to flourish, to thrive
floreciente adj Fig flourishing, prosperous
Florencia n Florence
florero nm vase
floricultura nf flower growing, floriculture
florido,-a adj (a) *(con flores)* flowery (b) *(estilo)* florid
floripondio nm *Pey (adorno)* heavy ornamentation
florista nmf florist
floristería nf florist's (shop)
flota nf fleet
flotador nm (a) *(de pesca)* float (b) *(para nadar)* rubber ring
flotar vi to float
flote nm floating; **a f.** afloat; **sacar a f. un negocio** to put a business on a sound footing
flotilla nf flotilla
fluctuación nf fluctuation
fluctuar [30] vi to fluctuate
fluidez nf fluency
fluido,-a 1 adj fluid; *(estilo etc)* fluent
2 nm fluid; **f. eléctrico** current
fluir [37] vi to flow
flujo nm (a) flow (b) rising tide; **f. y reflujo** ebb and flow (c) *Fís* flux (d) *Med* discharge (e) *Informát* stream
flúor nm fluorine
fluorescente adj fluorescent
fluvial adj river
FM nf (abr **Frecuencia Modulada**) FM
FMI nm (abr **Fondo Monetario Internacional**) IMF
fobia nf phobia (a about)
foca nf seal
foco nm (a) *Elec* spotlight, floodlight (b) *(de ideas, revolución etc)* centre, focal point (c) *Am (de coche)* headlight; *(farola)* street light (d) *Col, Méx (bombilla)* light bulb
fofo,-a adj soft; *(persona)* flabby
fogata nf bonfire
fogón nm *(de cocina)* ring
fogonazo nm flash
fogosidad nf ardour, fire
fogoso,-a adj fiery, spirited
fogueo nm **cartucho de f.** blank cartridge
fólder nm *Andes, CAm, Méx (carpeta)* folder

folio nm sheet of paper
folklore nm folklore
folklórico,-a adj **música folklórica** folk music
follaje nm foliage
follar muy Fam **1** vi to screw, to shag
2 vt *(suspender)* to fail
3 follarse upr **f. a algn** to screw sb, to shag sb
folletín nm (a) *(relato)* newspaper serial (b) *Fig* melodrama
folleto nm leaflet; *(turístico)* brochure
follón nm *Fam* (a) *(alboroto)* rumpus, shindy; **armar (un) f.** to kick up a rumpus (b) *(enredo, confusión)* mess, trouble; **meterse en un f.** to get into a mess (c) **un f. de** *(montón)* a load of
follonero,-a nm,f troublemaker
fomentar vt to promote
fomento nm promotion
fonda nf inn
fondear vi to anchor
fondista nmf *Dep* long-distance runner
fondo¹ nm (a) *(parte más baja)* bottom; **a f.** thoroughly; **al f. de la calle** at the bottom of the street; **tocar f.** *Náut* to touch bottom; *Fig* to reach rock bottom; *Fig* **en el f. es bueno** deep down he's kind; **bajos fondos** dregs of society; **doble f.** false bottom
(b) *(de habitación)* back; *(de pasillo)* end
(c) *(segundo término)* background; **música de f.** background music
(d) *Prensa* **artículo de f.** leading article
(e) *Dep* **corredor de f.** long-distance runner; **esquí de f.** cross-country skiing
(f) *RP (patio)* back patio
(g) *Carib, Méx (prenda)* petticoat
fondo² nm *Fin* fund; **cheque sin fondos** bad cheque; *Fam* **f. común** kitty
fonendoscopio nm stethoscope
fonética nf phonetics *sing*
fonético,-a adj phonetic
fono nm *Am Fam* phone
fontanería nf plumbing
fontanero,-a nm,f plumber
footing nm jogging; **hacer f.** to go jogging
forajido,-a nm,f outlaw
foráneo,-a adj foreign
forastero,-a nm,f outsider, stranger
forcejear vi to wrestle, to struggle
forcejeo nm struggle
fórceps nm inv forceps
forense 1 adj forensic
2 nmf **(médico) f.** forensic surgeon
forestal adj forest; **repoblación f.** reafforestation
forjado,-a adj wrought
forjar vt *(metal)* to forge; *Fig* to create, to make
forma nf (a) form, shape; **en f. de L** L-shaped; **¿qué f. tiene?** what shape is it? (b) *(manera)* way; **de esta f.** in this way; **de f. que** so that; **de todas formas** anyway, in any case; **no hubo f. de convencerla** there was no way we could convince her; **f. de pago** method of

payment (**c**) *Dep* form; **estar en f.** to be on form; **estar en baja f.** to be off form (**d**) *Rel* **Sagrada F.** Host (**e**) **formas** *(modales)* manners

formación *nf* (**a**) formation (**b**) *(educación)* upbringing (**c**) *(enseñanza)* training; **f. profesional** vocational training

formal *adj* (**a**) formal (**b**) *(serio)* serious, serious-minded (**c**) *(fiable)* reliable, dependable

formalidad *nf* (**a**) formality (**b**) *(seriedad)* seriousness (**c**) *(fiabilidad)* reliability (**d**) **formalidades** *(trámites)* formalities

formalizar [40] **1** *vt* to formalize
2 formalizarse *vpr* to settle down

formar 1 *vt* (**a**) to form; **f. parte de algo** to be a part of sth (**b**) *(educar)* to bring up; *(enseñar)* to educate, to train
2 formarse *vpr* (**a**) to be formed, to form; **se formó un charco** a puddle formed; **f. una impresión de algo** to get an impression of sth (**b**) *(educarse)* to be educated *o* trained

formatear *vt Informát* to format

formato *nm* format; *(del papel)* size

formica® *nf* Formica®

formidable *adj* (**a**) *(estupendo)* wonderful, terrific (**b**) *(espantoso)* formidable

fórmula *nf* formula; *Aut* **f. uno** formula one

formular *vt* *(quejas, peticiones)* to make; *(deseo)* to express; *(pregunta)* to ask; *(una teoría)* to formulate

formulario *nm* form

fornicación *nf* fornication

fornicar [44] *vi* to fornicate

fornido,-a *adj* strapping, hefty

foro *nm* (**a**) forum (**b**) *(mesa redonda)* round table (**c**) *Teatro* back (of the stage) (**d**) *Jur* law court, court of justice

forofo,-a *nm,f Fam* fan, supporter

forrado,-a *adj* lined; *Fam* **estar f.** to be well-heeled, to be well-off

forraje *nm* fodder

forrar 1 *vt* *(por dentro)* to line; *(por fuera)* to cover
2 forrarse *vpr Fam (de dinero)* to make a packet

forro *nm* (**a**) *(por dentro)* lining; *(por fuera)* cover, case (**b**) *RP Fam (preservativo)* rubber, condom

fortalecer [33] *vt* to fortify, to strengthen

fortaleza *nf* (**a**) strength; *(de espíritu)* fortitude (**b**) *Mil* fortress, stronghold

fortificante 1 *adj* fortifying
2 *nm* tonic

fortificar [44] *vt* to fortify

fortísimo,-a *adj* very strong

fortuito,-a *adj* fortuitous

fortuna *nf* (**a**) *(destino)* fortune, fate (**b**) *(suerte)* luck; **por f.** fortunately (**c**) *(capital)* fortune

forzado,-a *adj* forced; **a marchas forzadas** at a brisk pace; **trabajos forzados** hard labour

forzar [2] *vt* (**a**) *(obligar)* to force; **f. a algn a hacer algo** to force sb to do sth (**b**) *(puerta, candado)* to force, to break open

forzosamente *adv* necessarily

forzoso,-a *adj* obligatory, compulsory; *Av* **aterrizaje f.** forced landing

fosa *nf* (**a**) *(sepultura)* grave (**b**) *(hoyo)* pit (**c**) *Anat* **fosas nasales** nostrils

fosforescente *adj* phosphorescent

fósforo *nm (cerilla)* match

fósil *adj & nm* fossil

fosilizarse [40] *vpr* to fossilize, to become fossilized

foso *nm* (**a**) *(hoyo)* pit (**b**) *(de fortificación)* moat (**c**) *(en garage)* inspection pit

foto *nf Fam* photo; **sacar/echar una f.** to take a photo

fotocopia *nf* photocopy

fotocopiadora *nf* photocopier

fotocopiar [43] *vt* to photocopy

fotogénico,-a *adj* photogenic

fotografía *nf* (**a**) photograph; **echar** *o* **hacer** *o* **sacar fotografías** to take photographs (**b**) *(arte)* photography

fotografiar [29] *vt* to photograph, to take a photograph of

fotográfico,-a *adj* photographic

fotógrafo,-a *nm,f* photographer

fotograma *nm* still, shot

fotomatón *nm* passport photo machine

fotómetro *nm* light meter, exposure meter

FP *nf Educ* (*abr* **Formación Profesional**) vocational training

frac *nm* (*pl* **fracs** *o* **fraques**) dress coat, tails

fracasado,-a 1 *adj* unsuccessful
2 *nm,f (persona)* failure

fracasar *vi* to fail

fracaso *nm* failure

📖 Observa que la palabra inglesa **fracas** es un falso amigo y no es la traducción de la palabra española **fracaso**. En inglés, **fracas** significa "gresca, refriega".

fracción *nf* (**a**) fraction (**b**) *Pol* faction

fraccionamiento *nm Méx (urbanización)* housing estate

fraccionar *vt*, **fraccionarse** *vpr* to break up, to split up

fraccionario,-a *adj* fractional; **moneda fraccionaria** small change

fractura *nf* fracture

fracturar *vt*, **fracturarse** *vpr* to fracture, to break

fragancia *nf* fragrance

fragata *nf* frigate

frágil *adj* (**a**) *(quebradizo)* fragile (**b**) *(débil)* frail

fragmentar 1 *vt* to fragment
2 fragmentarse *vpr* to break up

fragmento *nm* fragment; *(de novela etc)* passage

fragor nm din

fragua nf forge

fraguar [45] vt (a) (metal) to forge (b) (plan) to think up, to fabricate; (conspiración) to hatch

fraile nm friar, monk

frailecillo nm puffin

frambuesa nf raspberry

francamente adv frankly

francés,-esa 1 adj French; Culin **tortilla francesa** plain omelette

2 nm,f (hombre) Frenchman; (mujer) Frenchwoman

3 nm (idioma) French

Francfort, Francfurt n Frankfurt; Culin **salchicha estilo f.** frankfurter

Francia n France

francmasón,-ona nm,f freemason

franco¹,-a adj (a) (persona) frank (b) Com **f. a bordo** free on board; **f. fábrica** ex-works; **puerto f.** free port (c) CSur (día) **me dieron el día f.** they gave me the day off

franco² nm Fin (moneda) franc

francotirador,-a nm,f sniper

franela nf (a) (paño) flannel (b) Bol, Col, Ven (camiseta) T-shirt

franja nf (de terreno) strip; (de bandera) stripe; Cost fringe, border

franquear vt (a) (atravesar) to cross; Fig (dificultad, obstáculo) to overcome (b) (carta) to frank (c) (camino, paso) to free, to clear

franqueo nm postage

franqueza nf frankness

franquicia nf exemption; Com franchise

franquismo nm Hist (a) (ideología) Franco-ism (b) **el f.** (régimen) the Franco regime

franquista adj & nmf Francoist

frasco nm small bottle, flask

frase nf (oración) sentence; (expresión) phrase; **f. hecha** set phrase o expression

fraternidad nf brotherhood, fraternity

fraternizar [40] vi to fraternize

fraterno,-a adj fraternal, brotherly

fraude nm fraud; **f. fiscal** tax evasion

fraudulento,-a adj fraudulent

fray nm Rel brother

frazada nf Am blanket

frecuencia nf frequency; **con f.** frequently, often

frecuentar vt to frequent

frecuente adj frequent

frecuentemente adv frequently, often

fregadero nm (kitchen) sink

fregado¹ nm (a) (lavado) washing (b) Fam (follón) racket

fregado²,-a adj Am Fam (a) (persona) (difícil) tiresome, annoying (b) (objeto) (roto) broken

fregar [1] vt (a) (lavar) to wash; (suelo) to mop (b) Am Fam (molestar) to annoy, to irritate (c) Am Fam (romper) to bust, to break

fregón,-ona adj Am annoying

fregona nf mop

freidora nf (deep fat) fryer

freír [56] (pp frito) **1** vt to fry

2 freírse vpr to fry; Fig **f. de calor** to be roasting

frenar vt to brake; Fig (inflación etc) to slow down; (impulsos) to restrain

frenazo nm sudden braking; **dar un f.** to jam on the brakes

frenesí nm frenzy

frenético,-a adj frantic

freno nm (a) brake; **pisar/soltar el f.** to press/release the brake; **f. de disco/tambor** disc/drum brake; **f. de mano** handbrake (b) (de caballería) bit (c) Fig curb, check; **poner f. a algo** to curb sth

frente 1 nm front; **al f. de** at the head of; **chocar de f.** to crash head on; **hacer f. a algo** to face sth, to stand up to sth

2 nf Anat forehead; **f. a f.** face to face

3 adv **f. a** in front of, opposite

fresa nf (a) strawberry (b) Téc milling cutter

fresca nf Fam cheeky remark

fresco,-a 1 adj (a) (frío) cool (b) (comida, fruta) fresh (c) (reciente) fresh, new (d) (descarado) cheeky, shameless; **se quedó tan f.** he didn't bat an eyelid; **¡qué f.!** what a nerve!

2 nm (a) (frescor) fresh air, cool air; **al f.** in the cool; **hace f.** it's chilly (b) Arte fresco

frescor nm freshness

frescura nf (a) freshness (b) (desvergüenza) cheek, nerve

fresno nm ash tree

fresón nm (large) strawberry

frialdad nf coldness

fríamente adv coolly

fricción nf (a) friction (b) (masaje) massage

friega nf rub

friegaplatos nmf inv (persona) dishwasher

frigider nm Andes refrigerator, fridge

frígido,-a adj frigid

frigorífico,-a 1 nm refrigerator, fridge

2 adj **cámara frigorífica** cold store

frijol, fríjol nm Andes, CAm, Carib, Méx bean

frío,-a 1 adj (a) cold (b) (indiferente) cold, cool, indifferent; **su comentario me dejó f.** her remark left me cold

2 nm cold; **hace f.** it's cold

friolento,-a adj Am sensitive to the cold

friolera nf Fam **la f. de diez mil pesetas/dos horas** a mere ten thousand pesetas/two hours

friolero,-a adj sensitive to the cold

fritanga nf Fam fried food; Am greasy food

frito,-a 1 adj (a) Culin fried (b) Fam exasperated, fed up; **me tienes f.** I'm sick to death of you

2 nm **fritos** fried food

frívolo,-a adj frivolous

frondoso,-a adj leafy, luxuriant

frontera nf frontier

fronterizo,-a adj frontier, border; **países fronterizos** neighbouring countries

frontón *nm Dep* pelota

frotar 1 *vt* to rub

  2 frotarse *vpr* to rub; **f. las manos** to rub one's hands together

fructífero,-a *adj (árbol)* fruit-bearing; *(esfuerzo)* fruitful

frugal *adj* frugal

fruncir [52] *vt* (**a**) *Cost* to gather (**b**) *(labios)* to purse, to pucker; **f. el ceño** to frown, to knit one's brow

frustración *nf* frustration

frustrado,-a *adj* frustrated; **intento f.** unsuccessful attempt

frustrante *adj* frustrating

frustrar 1 *vt* to frustrate; *(defraudar)* to disappoint

  2 frustrarse *vpr* (**a**) *(esperanza)* to fail, to go awry (**b**) *(persona)* to be frustrated *o* disappointed

fruta *nf* fruit; **f. del tiempo** fresh fruit

frutería *nf* fruit shop

frutero,-a 1 *nm,f* fruiterer

  2 *nm* fruit dish *o* bowl

frutilla *nf Bol, CSur, Ecuad* strawberry

fruto *nm* fruit; **frutos secos** nuts; **dar f.** to bear fruit; *Fig (dar buen resultado)* to be fruitful; **sacar f. de algo** to profit from sth

fu *interj* **ni fu ni fa** so-so

fucsia *nf* fuchsia

fuego *nm* (**a**) fire; **fuegos artificiales** fireworks (**b**) *(lumbre)* light; **¿me da f., por favor?** have you got a light, please? (**c**) *Culin* **a f. lento** on a low flame; *(al horno)* in a slow oven

fuel, fuel-oil *nm* diesel

fuente *nf* (**a**) fountain; *Chile, Col, Méx, Ven* **f. de soda** *(cafetería)* cafe *(serving soft drinks and alcohol)* (**b**) *(recipiente)* dish, serving dish (**c**) *(de información)* source

fuera¹ *adv* (**a**) *(fuera, al)*; **quédate f.** stay outside; **sal f.** go out; **desde f.** from (the) outside; **por f.** on the outside; **la puerta de f.** the outer door (**b**) **f. de** out of; **f. de serie** extraordinary; *Fig* **estar f. de sí** to be beside oneself (**c**) *Dep* **el equipo de f.** the away team; **jugar f.** to play away; **f. de juego** offside

fuera² **1** *subj imperf de* **ir**

  2 *subj imperf de* **ser**

fuero *nm* (**a**) *Hist* code of laws (**b**) *Fig* **en tu f. interno** deep down, in your heart of hearts

fuerte 1 *adj* strong; *(dolor)* severe; *(sonido)* loud; *(comida)* heavy; **el plato f.** the main course; *Fig* the most important event

  2 *nm* (**a**) *(fortaleza)* fort (**b**) *(punto fuerte)* forte, strong point

  3 *adv* **¡abrázame f.!** hold me tight!; **comer f.** to eat a lot; **¡habla más f.!** speak up!; **¡pégale f.!** hit him hard!

fuerza *nf* (**a**) *(fortaleza)* strength; *Fig* **a f. de** by dint of (**b**) *(violencia)* force; **a la f.** *(por obligación)* of necessity; *(con violencia)* by force; **por f.** of necessity; **f. mayor** force majeure (**c**) *Fís* force (**d**) *(cuerpo)* force; **las fuerzas del orden** the forces of law and order; **f. aérea** air force; **fuerzas armadas** armed forces

fuese 1 *subj imperf de* **ir**

  2 *subj imperf de* **ser**

fuete *nm Am* whip

fuga *nf* (**a**) *(huida)* escape; **darse a la f.** to take flight (**b**) *(de gas etc)* leak

fugarse [42] *vpr* to escape; **f. de casa** to run away from home

fugaz *adj* fleeting, brief

fugitivo,-a *nm,f* fugitive

fui 1 *pt indef de* **ir**

  2 *pt indef de* **ser**

fulana *nf* whore, tart

fulano,-a *nm,f* so-and-so; *(hombre)* what's-his-name; *(mujer)* what's-her-name; **Doña Fulana de tal** Mrs So-and-so

fular *nm* headscarf

fulgor *nm Literario* brilliance, glow

fullería *nf* cheating; **hacer fullerías** to cheat

fullero,-a 1 *adj* cheating

  2 *nm,f* cheat

fulminante *adj (cese)* summary; *(muerte, enfermedad)* sudden; *(mirada)* withering

fulminar *vt Fig* to strike dead; **f. a algn con la mirada** to look daggers at sb

fumada *nf Am (calada)* pull, drag

fumado,-a *adj Fam (colocado)* stoned

fumador,-a *nm,f* smoker; **los no fumadores** nonsmokers

fumar 1 *vt & vi* to smoke; **no f.** *(en letrero)* no smoking

  2 fumarse *vpr* to smoke; **f. un cigarro** to smoke a cigarette

> 🖉 Observa que el verbo inglés **to fume** es un falso amigo y no es la traducción del verbo español **fumar**. En inglés, **to fume** significa "despedir humo".

fumigar [42] *vt* to fumigate

funambulista *nmf*, **funámbulo,-a** *nm,f* tightrope walker

función *nf* (**a**) function; **en f. de** according to (**b**) *(cargo)* duties; **entrar en funciones** to take up one's duties; **presidente en funciones** acting president (**c**) *Cin & Teatro* performance

funcionamiento *nm* operation; **poner/entrar en f.** to put/come into operation

funcionar *vi* to work; **no funciona** *(en letrero)* out of order

funcionario,-a *nm,f* civil servant; **f. público** public official

funda *nf* cover; *(de gafas etc)* case; *(de espada)* sheath; **f. de almohada** pillowcase

fundación *nf* foundation

fundador,-a *nm,f* founder

fundamental *adj* fundamental

fundamentar *vt* to base (**en** on)

fundamento *nm* basis, grounds; **sin f.** unfounded

fundar 1 *vt* (**a**) *(empresa)* to found (**b**) *(teoría)* to base, to found

2 fundarse *vpr* (**a**) *(empresa)* to be founded (**b**) *(teoría)* to be based (**en** on)

> Observa que el verbo inglés **to fund** es un falso amigo y no es la traducción del verbo español **fundar**. En inglés, **to fund** significa "financiar".

fundición *nf* (**a**) *(de metales)* smelting (**b**) *(fábrica)* foundry

fundir 1 *vt* (**a**) to melt; *(bombilla, plomos)* to blow (**b**) *(unir)* to unite, to join

2 fundirse *vpr* (**a**) *(derretirse)* to melt (**b**) *(bombilla, plomos)* to blow (**c**) *(unirse)* to merge (**d**) *RP Fam (arruinarse)* to go bust, to be ruined

fúnebre *adj* (**a**) *(mortuorio)* funeral; **coche f.** hearse (**b**) *(lúgubre)* mournful, lugubrious

funeral *nm* funeral

funeraria *nf* undertaker's, *US* funeral home

funesto,-a *adj* ill-fated, fatal; *(consecuencias)* disastrous

fungir [57] *vi Méx* to act (**de** *o* **como** as)

funicular *nm* funicular (railway)

furcia *nf Pey* whore, tart

furgón *nm Aut* van

furgoneta *nf* van

furia *nf* fury; **ponerse hecho una f.** to become

furious, to fly into a rage

furibundo,-a *adj* furious, enraged

furioso,-a *adj* furious; **ponerse f.** to get furious

furor *nm* fury, rage; *Fig* **hacer f.** to be all the rage

furtivo,-a *adj* furtive, stealthy; **caza/pesca furtiva** poaching; **cazador/pescador f.** poacher

furúnculo *nm Med* boil

fuselaje *nm* fuselage

fusible *nm* fuse

fusil *nm* gun, rifle

fusilamiento *nm* shooting, execution

fusilar *vt* to shoot, to execute

fusión *nf* (**a**) *(de metales)* fusion; *(del hielo)* thawing, melting; **punto de f.** melting point (**b**) *Com* merger

fusionar *vt*, **fusionarse** *vpr* (**a**) *Fís* to fuse (**b**) *Com* to merge

fustán *nm Am* petticoat

fútbol *nm* soccer, *Br* football

futbolín *nm Br* table football, *US* foosball

futbolista *nmf* soccer player, *Br* footballer

fútil *adj* futile, trivial

futilidad *nf* futility, triviality

futurista *adj* futuristic

futuro,-a 1 *adj* future

2 *nm* future; **en un f. próximo** in the near future; *CSur, Méx* **a f.** in the future

G, g [xe] *nf (la letra)* G, g
gabán *nm* overcoat
gabardina *nf (prenda)* raincoat
gabinete *nm* (**a**) *(despacho)* study; **g. de abogados** lawyers' office (**b**) *Pol* cabinet
gaceta *nf* gazette
gachas *nfpl* porridge
gacho,-a *adj* **con la cabeza gacha** hanging one's head
gaditano,-a 1 *adj* of/from Cadiz
   2 *nm,f* person from Cadiz
gafar *vt Fam* to put a jinx on, to bring bad luck to
gafas *nfpl* glasses, spectacles; **g. de sol** sunglasses
gafe *adj & nm Fam* **ser g.** to be a jinx

>   Observa que la palabra inglesa **gaffe** es un falso amigo y no es la traducción de la palabra española **gafe**. En inglés, **gaffe** significa "metedura de pata, desliz".

gafete *nm Méx* badge
gaita *nf* bagpipes
gajes *nmpl Fam Irón* **g. del oficio** occupational hazards
gajo *nm* (**a**) *(de naranja, pomelo etc)* segment (**b**) *(rama desprendida)* torn-off branch
gala *nf* (**a**) *(vestido)* full dress; **de g.** dressed up; *(ciudad)* decked out (**b**) *(espectáculo)* gala; **hacer g. de** to glory in (**c**) **galas** finery
galán *nm* (**a**) handsome young man; *Hum* ladies' man (**b**) *Teatro* leading man
galante *adj* gallant
galantear *vt* to court
galanteo *nm* courtship
galantería *nf* gallantry
galápago *nm* turtle
galardón *nm* prize
galardonado,-a 1 *adj nm,f* prizewinner
galardonar *vt* to award a prize to
galaxia *nf* galaxy
galeón *nm* galleon
galeote *nm* galley slave
galera *nf* (**a**) *Náut* galley (**b**) *(carro)* covered wagon (**c**) *Impr* galley proof
galería *nf* (**a**) *Arquit* covered balcony (**b**) *(museo)* art gallery (**c**) *Teatro* gallery, gods
Gales *n* (**el país de**) **G.** Wales
galés,-esa 1 *adj* Welsh
   2 *nm,f (hombre)* Welshman; *(mujer)* Welshwoman; **los galeses** the Welsh
   3 *nm (idioma)* Welsh

galgo *nm* greyhound
Galicia *n* Galicia
galimatías *nm inv Fam* gibberish
gallardo *adj* (**a**) *(apuesto)* smart (**b**) *(valeroso)* brave
gallego,-a 1 *adj* (**a**) Galician (**b**) *CSur, Cuba Pey* Spanish
   2 *nm,f* (**a**) Galician, person from Galicia (**b**) *CSur, Cuba Pey* Spaniard
   3 *nm (idioma)* Galician
galleta *nf* (**a**) *Culin Br* biscuit, *US* cookie (**b**) *Fam (cachete)* slap
gallina 1 *nf* hen
   2 *nmf Fam* coward, chicken
gallinero *nm* (**a**) hen run (**b**) *Teatro* **el g.** the gods
gallito *nm Fam (peleón)* bully
gallo *nm* (**a**) cock, rooster; *Fam Fig* **en menos que un canto de g.** before you could say Jack Robinson (**b**) *Fam Mús* off-key note
galón¹ *nm Mil* stripe
galón² *nm (medida)* gallon, *Br* = 4.55 l, *US* = 3.79 l
galopante *adj Fig (inflación etc)* galloping
galopar *vi* to gallop
galope *nm* gallop; **a g. tendido** flat out
galpón *nm Am* shed
gama *nf* range; *Mús* scale
gamba *nf* prawn
gamberrismo *nm* hooliganism
gamberro,-a 1 *nm,f* hooligan
   2 *adj* uncouth
gamo *nm* fallow deer
gamonal *nm Andes, CAm, Ven* local boss
gamuza *nf* (**a**) *Zool* chamois (**b**) *(trapo)* chamois *o* shammy leather
gana *nf* (**a**) *(deseo)* wish (**de** for); **de buena g.** willingly; **de mala g.** reluctantly; *Fam* **no me da la g.** I don't feel like it (**b**) **tener ganas de (hacer) algo** to feel like (doing) sth; **quedarse con las ganas** not to manage (**c**) *(apetito)* appetite; **comer con ganas** to eat heartily
ganadería *nf* (**a**) *(crianza)* livestock farming (**b**) *(conjunto de ganado)* livestock
ganadero,-a *nm,f* livestock farmer
ganado *nm* (**a**) livestock (**b**) *Fam Fig (gente)* crowd
ganador,-a 1 *adj* winning
   2 *nm,f* winner
ganancia *nf* profit
ganar 1 *vt* (**a**) *(sueldo)* to earn (**b**) *(victoria)* to

win (**c**) *(aventajar)* to beat (**d**) *(alcanzar)* to reach

2 ganarse *vpr* (**a**) to earn; **g. el pan** to earn one's daily bread (**b**) *(merecer)* to deserve; **se lo ha ganado** he deserves it

ganchillo *nm* crochet work

gancho *nm* (**a**) hook (**b**) *Fam Fig (gracia, atractivo)* charm (**c**) *Andes, CAm, Méx (horquilla)* hairpin (**d**) *Andes, CAm, Méx, Ven (percha)* hanger

gandul,-a *nm,f* loafer

ganga *nf* bargain

gangoso,-a *adj* nasal

gangrena *nf* gangrene

gansada *nf Fam* silly thing to say/do

ganso,-a 1 *nm,f* (**a**) goose; *(macho)* gander (**b**) *Fam* dolt

2 *adj Fam* ginormous; **pasta gansa** bread, dough

ganzúa *nf* picklock

gañán *nm (obrero)* farmhand; *Fam (bribón)* cheat

garabatear *vt & vi* to scribble

garabato *nm* scrawl

garaje *nm* garage

garante *nmf Fin* guarantor

garantía *nf* (**a**) *(cajón)* drawer (**b**) *Jur (fianza)* bond, security

garantizar [40] *vt* to guarantee

garbanzo *nm* chickpea

garbeo *nm Fam (paseo)* stroll; **darse un g.** to go for a stroll

garbo *nm* grace

garfio *nm* hook, grappling iron

gargajo *nm* spit

garganta *nf* (**a**) *(throat)* throat (**b**) *(desfiladero)* narrow pass

gargantilla *nf* short necklace

gárgaras *nfpl* (**a**) gargling; *Fam* ¡**vete a hacer g.!** get lost! (**b**) *Am (licor)* gargling solution

gárgola *nf* gargoyle

garita *nf (caseta)* hut; *Mil* sentry box

garito *nm Fam* joint

garra *nf* (**a**) *Zool* claw; *(de ave)* talon (**b**) *Fig (fuerza)* force; **tener g.** to be compelling

garrafa *nf* carafe

garrafal *adj* monumental

garrapata *nf* tick

garrote *nm* (**a**) *(porra)* club (**b**) *Jur* garrotte

garrucha *nf* pulley

gárrulo,-a *adj Fig* garrulous

garúa *nf Andes, RP, Ven* drizzle

garza *nf* heron

gas *nm* (**a**) gas; **g. ciudad** town gas; **gases (nocivos)** fumes; **g. de escape** exhaust fumes (**b**) *(en bebida)* fizz; **agua con g.** fizzy water (**c**) *Med* **gases** flatulence

gasa *nf* gauze

gaseosa *nf* lemonade

gasfitería *nf Chile, Ecuad, Perú* plumber's (shop)

gasfitero,-a *nm,f Chile, Ecuad, Perú* plumber

gasoducto *nm* gas pipeline

gasoil, gasóleo *nm* diesel oil

gasolina *nf Br* petrol, *US* gasoline

gasolinera, *Méx* **gasolinería** *nf Br* petrol *o US* gas station

gastado,-a *adj (zapatos etc)* worn-out; *Fig (frase)* hackneyed

gastar 1 *vt* (**a**) *(consumir) (dinero, tiempo)* to spend; *(gasolina, electricidad)* to consume (**b**) *Fig (malgastar)* to waste (**c**) *(ropa)* to wear; **¿qué número gastas?** what size do you take? (**d**) **g. una broma a algn** to play a practical joke on sb

2 gastarse *vpr* (**a**) *(zapatos etc)* to wear out (**b**) *(gasolina etc)* to run out

gasto *nm* expenditure; **gastos** expenses; **gastos de viaje** travelling expenses

gatas: a gatas *loc adv* on all fours

gatear *vi* (**a**) to crawl (**b**) *(trepar)* to climb

gatillo *nm (de armas)* trigger; **apretar el g.** to pull the trigger

gato *nm* (**a**) cat (**b**) *Aut & Téc* jack

gauchada *nf CSur* favour

gaucho,-a 1 *adj RP Fam (servicial)* helpful, obliging

2 *nm,f* gaucho

gaveta *nf* (**a**) *(cajón)* drawer (**b**) *Am Aut (guantera)* glove compartment

gavilán *nm Orn* sparrowhawk

gavilla *nf (de ramillas etc)* sheaf

gaviota *nf* seagull

gay *adj inv & nm (pl* gays*)* homosexual, gay

gazapo *nm* (**a**) *(error)* misprint (**b**) *Zool* young rabbit

gaznate *nm* gullet

gazpacho *nm Culin* gazpacho

gel *nm* gel; **g. (de ducha)** shower gel

gelatina *nf (ingrediente)* gelatin; *Culin* jelly

gema *nf* gem

gemelo,-a 1 *adj & nm,f* (identical) twin

2 *nmpl* **gemelos** (**a**) *(de camisa)* cufflinks (**b**) *(anteojos)* binoculars

gemido *nm* groan

Géminis *nm* Gemini

gemir [6] *vi* to groan

generación *nf* generation

general 1 *adj* general; **por lo** *o* **en g.** in general, generally;

2 *nm Mil & Rel* general

Generalitat *nf* Catalan/Valencian/Balearic parliament

generalización *nf* (**a**) generalization (**b**) *(extensión)* spread

generalizar [40] **1** *vt* (**a**) to generalize (**b**) *(extender)* to spread

2 generalizarse *vpr* to become widespread *o* common

generalmente *adv* generally

generar *vt* to generate

género *nm* (**a**) *(clase)* kind, sort (**b**) *Arte & Lit* genre (**c**) *(mercancía)* article (**d**) *Ling* gender (**e**) *Biol* genus; **el g. humano** mankind

generosidad *nf* generosity
generoso,-a *adj* (**a**) generous (**con** to) (**b**) *(vino)* full-bodied
Génesis *nm Rel* Genesis
genética *nf* genetics *sing*
genético,-a *adj* genetic
genial *adj* brilliant; *Fam* terrific

Observa que la palabra inglesa **genial** *es un falso amigo y no es la traducción de la palabra española* **genial**. *En inglés,* **genial** *significa "cordial, amable".*

genio *nm* (**a**) *(carácter)* temperament; *(mal carácter)* temper; **estar de mal g.** to be in a bad mood (**b**) *(facultad)* genius
genocidio *nm* genocide
Génova *n* Genoa
gente *nf* (**a**) *(personas)* people (**b**) *(familia)* folks (**c**) *Am* respectable people
gentil *adj* (**a**) *(amable)* kind (**b**) *(pagano)* pagan

Observa que la palabra inglesa **genteel** *es un falso amigo y no es la traducción de la palabra española* **gentil**. *En inglés,* **genteel** *significa "fino, distinguido".*

gentileza *nf* kindness; *Fml* **por g. de** by courtesy of
gentío *nm* crowd
gentuza *nf Pey* riffraff
genuino,-a *adj* *(puro)* genuine; *(verdadero)* authentic
geografía *nf* geography
geología *nf* geology
geometría *nf* geometry
geranio *nm* geranium
gerencia *nf* management
gerente *nmf* manager
germano,-a 1 *adj* German, Germanic
  2 *nm,f* German
gérmen *nm* (**a**) *Biol* germ (**b**) *Fig (inicio)* germ; *(fuente)* origin
germinar *vi* to germinate
gerundio *nm* gerund
gesta *nf* heroic exploit
gestación *nf* gestation
gestar *vt* to gestate
gesticular *vi* to gesticulate
gestión *nf* (**a**) *(administración)* management (**b**) **gestiones** *(negociaciones)* negotiations; *(trámites)* formalities
gestionar *vt* to take steps to acquire *o* obtain; *(negociar)* to negotiate
gesto *nm* (**a**) *(mueca)* face (**b**) *(con las manos)* gesture
gestor,-a *nm,f* ≃ solicitor
giba *nf* hump
gibar *vt Fam* to annoy
Gibraltar *n* Gibraltar; **el peñón de G.** the Rock of Gibraltar
gibraltareño,-a 1 *adj* of/from Gibraltar

  2 *nm,f* Gibraltarian
gigante,-a 1 *nm,f* giant
  2 *adj* giant, enormous
gigantesco,-a *adj* gigantic
gigoló *nm* gigolo
gil, gila *nm,f CSur Fam* twit, idiot
gili, gilí *nm muy Fam* = gilipollas
gilipollas *nmf muy Fam Br* prat, *US* dork
gimnasia *nf* gymnastics
gimnasio *nm* gymnasium
gimotear *vi* to whine
Ginebra *n* Geneva
ginebra *nf (bebida)* gin
ginecología *nf* gynaecology
ginecólogo,-a *nm,f* gynaecologist
gira *nf Teatro & Mús* tour
girar 1 *vi* (**a**) *(dar vueltas)* to spin (**b**) **g. a la derecha/izquierda** to turn right/left
  2 *vt Fin* (**a**) *(expedir)* to draw (**b**) *(dinero)* to transfer
girasol *nm* sunflower
giratorio,-a *adj* revolving
giro *nm* (**a**) *(vuelta)* turn (**b**) *(de acontecimientos)* direction (**c**) *(frase)* turn of phrase (**d**) *Fin* draft; **g. telegráfico** money order; **g. postal** postal *o* money order
gis *nm Andes, Méx* chalk
gitano,-a *adj & nm,f* gypsy, gipsy
glacial *adj* icy
glaciar *nm* glacier
glándula *nf* gland
glasear *vt Culin* to glaze
global *adj* comprehensive; **precio g.** all-inclusive price
globalmente *adv* as a whole
globo *nm* (**a**) *(balloon)* balloon (**b**) *(esfera)* globe (**c**) *(lámpara)* globe, glass lampshade
glóbulo *nm* globule
gloria *nf* (**a**) *(fama)* glory (**b**) *Rel* heaven; *Fam Fig* **estar en la g.** to be in seventh heaven (**c**) *Fam (delicia)* delight
glorieta *nf* (**a**) *(plazoleta)* small square (**b**) *(encrucijada de calles)* *Br* roundabout, *US* traffic circle (**c**) *(en un jardín)* arbour
glorificar [44] *vt* to glorify
glorioso,-a *adj* glorious
glosa *nf* (**a**) *(gloss)* gloss (**b**) *Lit (comentario)* notes, commentary
glosar *vt* (**a**) *(explicar)* to gloss; *(texto)* to interpret (**b**) *(comentar)* to comment on
glosario *nm* glossary
glotón,-ona 1 *adj* greedy
  2 *nm,f* glutton
glotonería *nf* gluttony
glucosa *nf Quím* glucose
gobernación *nf* government; *Pol & Hist* **Ministerio de la G.** *Br* ≃ Home Office, *US* ≃ Department of the Interior
gobernador,-a *nm,f* governor
gobernante *adj* ruling
gobernar [1] **1** *vt* to govern; *(un país)* to rule
  2 *vi Náut* to steer

gobiernista *Am* **1** *adj* government

2 *nmf* government supporter

gobierno *nm* (**a**) *Pol* government (**b**) *(mando)* running (**c**) *Náut* steering (**d**) *Náut (timón)* rudder

goce *nm* enjoyment

gofio *nm Am Can* roasted maize meal

gol *nm* goal

goleada *nf* lots of goals; **ganar por g.** to win by a barrowload

golear *vt* to hammer

golf *nm* golf; **palo de g.** golf club

golfista *nmf* golfer

golfo¹,-a **1** *nm,f* good-for-nothing

2 *nf* golfa *Fam Pey* tart

golfo² *nm Geog* gulf; **el g. Pérsico** the Persian Gulf

golondrina *nf* swallow

golosina *nf Br* sweet, *US* candy

goloso,-a *adj* sweet-toothed

golpe *nm* (**a**) blow; *(llamada)* knock; *(puñetazo)* punch; **de g.** all of a sudden; **g. de estado** coup d'état; **g. de suerte** stroke of luck; **no dar ni g.** not to lift a finger (**b**) *Aut* bump (**c**) *(desgracia)* blow; **un duro g.** a great blow (**d**) *(de humor)* witticism

golpear *vt* to hit; *(con el puño)* to punch; *(puerta, cabeza)* to bang

golpiza *nf Am* beating

goma *nf* (**a**) rubber; **g. de pegar** glue; **g. de borrar** eraser, *Br* rubber (**b**) *(elástica)* rubber band (**c**) *Cuba, CSur (neumático)* tyre (**d**) *Fam (preservativo)* rubber

gomaespuma *nf* foam rubber

gomal *nm Am Agr* rubber plantation

gomería *nf CSur* tyre centre

gomero *nm Am* (**a**) *Bot* gum tree (**b**) *(recolector)* rubber collector

gomina *nf* hair cream

góndola *nf* (**a**) *(embarcación)* gondola (**b**) *Bol, Chile (autobús)* (long distance) bus

gordo,-a **1** *adj* (**a**) *(carnoso)* fat (**b**) *(grueso)* thick (**c**) *(importante)* big; **me cae g.** I can't stand him; **de g.** in a big way

2 *nm,f* (**a**) fat person; *Fam* fatty (**b**) *Am Fam (como apelativo)* **¿cómo estás, gorda?** hey, how are you doing?

3 *nm* **el g.** *(de lotería)* the jackpot

gordura *nf* fatness

gorgorito *nm* trill

gorila *nm* (**a**) gorilla (**b**) *Fig (en discoteca etc)* bouncer

gorjear **1** *vi* to chirp

2 gorjearse *vpr Am* **g. de algn** to laugh at sb's expense

gorjeo *nm* chirping

gorra *nf* cap; *(con visera)* peaked cap; *Fam* **de g.** free

gorrión *nm* sparrow

gorro *nm* (**a**) cap (**b**) *Fam* **estar hasta el g. (de)** to be up to here (with)

gorrón,-ona *nm,f* sponger

gota *nf* (**a**) drop; *(de sudor)* bead; **g. a g.** drop by drop; **ni g.** not a bit (**b**) *Med* gout

gotear *v impers* to drip; **el techo gotea** there's a leak in the ceiling

gotera *nf* leak

gótico,-a *adj* Gothic

gozar [40] **1** *vt* to enjoy

2 *vi (disfrutar)* **g. (de)** to enjoy

gozne *nm* hinge

gozo *nm* pleasure

grabación *nf* recording

grabado *nm* (**a**) *(arte)* engraving (**b**) *(dibujo)* drawing

grabadora *nf* tape recorder

grabar *vt* (**a**) *(sonidos, imágenes)* to record (**b**) *Informát* to save (**c**) *Arte* to engrave

gracia *nf* (**a**) *(atractivo)* grace (**b**) *(chiste)* joke; **hacer** o **tener g.** to be funny (**c**) *(indulto)* pardon

gracias *nfpl (agradecimiento)* thanks; **g. a Dios** thank God, thank goodness; **g. a** thanks to; **muchas** o **muchísimas g.** thank you very much

gracioso,-a **1** *adj* (**a**) *(divertido)* funny (**b**) *(garboso)* graceful

2 *nm,f Teatro* comic character

grada *nf* (**a**) *(peldaño)* step (**b**) **gradas** *(en estadio)* terraces

gradación *nf* (**a**) gradation (**b**) *Mús* scale

graderío *nm* tiers of seats; *Dep* terraces, *US* bleachers

gradiente **1** *nm* gradient

2 *nf Am* slope

grado *nm* (**a**) degree (**b**) *Mil* rank (**c**) **de buen g.** willingly, gladly

graduable *adj* adjustable

graduación *nf* (**a**) gradation (**b**) *Mil* rank

graduado,-a *nm,f* graduate

gradual *adj* gradual

gradualmente *adv* gradually

graduar [30] **1** *vt* (**a**) *Educ & Mil* to confer degree o a rank on (**b**) *(regular)* to regulate

2 graduarse *vpr* (**a**) *Educ & Mil* to graduate (**b**) **g. la vista** to have one's eyes tested

gráfico,-a **1** *adj* graphic; **diseño g.** graphic design

2 *nm* graph

grafista *nmf* graphic designer

gragea *nf Med* pill

grajo,-a **1** *nm,f Orn* rook

2 *nm Am* body odour

gral. *(abr* **General)** gen

gramática *nf* grammar

gramo *nm* gram, gramme

gran *adj* = **grande**

grana *adj* scarlet

granada *nf* (**a**) *(fruto)* pomegranate (**b**) *Mil* grenade

granate **1** *adj inv (color)* maroon

2 *nm (color)* maroon

Gran Bretaña *n* Great Britain

grande *adj* (**a**) *(tamaño)* big, large; *Fig (persona)* great (**b**) *(cantidad)* large; **vivir a lo g.**

gran is used instead of **grande** before masculine singular nouns (e.g. **gran hombre** great man).

grandeza *nf* (a) *(importancia)* greatness (b) *(grandiosidad)* grandeur; **delirios de g.** delusions of grandeur

grandioso,-a *adj* grandiose

granel: a granel *loc adv* *(sin medir exactamente)* loose

granero *nm Agr* granary

granito *nm* granite

granizada *nf*, **granizado** *nm* iced drink

granizar [40] *v impers* to hail

granizo *nm* hail

granja *nf* farm

granjear *vt*, **granjearse** *vpr* to gain

granjero,-a *nm,f* farmer

grano *nm* (a) grain; *(de café)* bean; **ir al g.** to get to the point (b) *(espinilla)* spot

granuja *nf* (a) *(pilluelo)* ragamuffin (b) *(estafador)* con-man

grapa *nf* (a) staple (b) *Constr* cramp (c) *CSur (bebida)* grappa

grapadora *nf* stapler

grapar *vt* to staple

grasa *nf* grease

grasiento,-a *adj* greasy

graso,-a *adj (pelo)* greasy; *(materia)* fatty

gratificar [44] *vt* (a) *(satisfacer)* to gratify (b) *(recompensar)* to reward

gratinar *vt Culin* to cook in a sauce until golden brown

gratis *adj inv & adv* free

gratitud *nf* gratitude

grato,-a *adj* pleasant

gratuito,-a *adj* (a) *(de balde)* free (of charge) (b) *(arbitrario)* gratuitous

grava *nf (guijas)* gravel; *(en carretera)* chippings

gravamen *nm Jur* (a) *(carga)* burden (b) *(impuesto)* tax

gravar *vt Jur* (a) *(cargar)* to burden (b) *(impuestos)* to tax

grave *adj* (a) *(importante)* serious (b) *(muy enfermo)* seriously ill (c) *(voz, nota)* low

gravedad *nf* (a) *(seriedad, importancia)* seriousness (b) *Fís* gravity

gravilla *nf* chippings

gravitar *vi* (a) *Fís* to gravitate (b) **g. sobre** to rest on

gravoso,-a *adj* (a) *(costoso)* costly (b) *(molesto)* burdensome

graznar *vi* to squawk; *(de pato)* to quack; *(de cuervo)* to caw

graznido *nm (un sonido)* squawk; *(varios)* squawking; *(de pato)* quack; *(de cuervo)* caw

Grecia *n* Greece

gregario,-a *adj* gregarious; **instinto g.** herd instinct

gremio *nm* (a) *Hist* guild (b) *(profesión)* profession

greña *nf* lock of entangled hair; *Fam* **andar a la g.** to squabble

gres *nm* **artículos de g.** stoneware

gresca *nf* (a) *(bulla)* racket (b) *(riña)* row

griego,-a *adj & nm,f* Greek

grieta *nf* crack; *(en la piel)* chap

grifo *nm* (a) *(llave)* Br tap, US faucet (b) *Perú (gasolinera)* Br petrol station, US gas station

grillete *nm* shackle

grillo *nm* cricket

gringo,-a *Fam* **1** *adj* (a) *(estadounidense)* gringo, American (b) *Am (extranjero)* foreign **2** *nm,f* (a) *(estadounidense)* gringo, American (b) *Am (extranjero)* = non-Spanish-speaking foreigner

gripa *nf Col, Méx* flu

gripe *nf* flu

gris *adj & nm* grey

grisáceo,-a *adj* greyish

gritar *vt & vi* to shout

grito *nm* shout; **a voz en g.** at the top of one's voice

Groenlandia *n* Greenland

grosella *nf (fruto)* redcurrant; **g. negra** blackcurrant; **g. silvestre** gooseberry

grosería *nf* (a) *(ordinariez)* rude word *o* expression (b) *(rusticidad)* rudeness

grosero,-a *adj (tosco)* coarse; *(maleducado)* rude

grosor *nm* thickness

grotesco,-a *adj* grotesque

grúa *nf* (a) *Constr* crane (b) *Aut Br* breakdown van *o* truck, *US* tow truck

grueso,-a **1** *adj* thick; *(persona)* stout **2** *nm (parte principal)* bulk

grulla *nf Orn* crane

grumo *nm* lump; *(de leche)* curd

gruñido *nm* grunt

gruñir *vi* to grunt

gruñón,-ona *adj* grumpy

grupa *nf* hindquarters

grupo *nm* (a) group; *Informát* **g. de noticias** newsgroup (b) *Téc* unit, set

gruta *nf* cave

guaca *nf Am (sepultura)* = pre-Columbian Indian tomb

guacal *nm* (a) *CAm, Méx (calabaza)* calabash (b) *Carib, Col, Méx (jaula)* cage

guacamayo,-a *nm,f Orn* macaw

guacamol, guacamole *nm Culin* guacamole

guachafita *nf Am* uproar

guachimán *nm Am* night watchman

guacho,-a *adj & nm,f Andes, RP* (a) *muy Fam (persona huérfana)* orphan (b) *Fam (sinvergüenza)* bastard, swine

guaco *nm Am (cerámica)* = pottery object found in pre-Columbian Indian tomb

guadaña *nf* scythe

guagua[1] *nf Can, Cuba* bus

guagua² *nf Andes* baby

guajiro,-a *nm,f Cuba Fam (campesino)* peasant

guajolote *nm CAm, Méx* (a) *(pavo)* turkey (b) *(tonto)* fool, idiot

guampa *nf Bol, CSur* horn

guanajo *nm Carib* turkey

guantazo *nm* slap

guante *nm* glove

guantera *nf Aut* glove compartment

guapo,-a *adj* (a) *(hombre)* handsome, good-looking; *(mujer)* pretty, good-looking (b) *Am (matón)* bully

guaraca *nf Am* sling

guarache *nm Méx (sandalia)* sandal

guarangada *nf Bol, CSur* rude remark

guarango,-a *adj Bol, CSur* rude

guarda *nmf* guard; **g. jurado** security guard

guardabarros *nm inv Aut Br* mudguard, *US* fender

guardabosque *nmf* gamekeeper

guardacoches *nmf inv* parking attendant

guardacostas *nm inv (persona)* coastguard; *(embarcación)* coastguard vessel

guardaespaldas *nmf inv* bodyguard

guardafangos *nm inv Andes, CAm, Carib Aut Br* mudguard, *US* fender

guardameta *nmf Dep* goalkeeper

guardapolvo *nm* overalls

guardar [33] *vt* (a) *(conservar)* to keep (b) *(un secreto)* to keep; **g. silencio** to remain silent; **g. cama** to stay in bed (c) *(poner en un sitio)* to put away (d) *(reservar)* to keep (e) *Informát* to save

  2 **guardarse** *vpr* **g. de hacer algo** *(abstenerse)* to be careful not to do sth; **guardársela a algn** to have it in for sb

guardarropa *nm* (a) *(cuarto)* cloakroom (b) *(armario)* wardrobe

guardería *nf* **g. infantil** nursery (school)

guardia 1 *nf* (a) *(vigilancia)* watch (b) **la G. Civil** the civil guard (c) *(turno de servicio)* duty; *Mil* guard duty; **de g.** on duty; **farmacia de g.** duty chemist

  2 *nmf* policeman; *(mujer)* policewoman

guardián,-ana *nm,f* watchman

guarecer [33] 1 *vt* to shelter

  2 **guarecerse** *vpr* to take shelter o refuge (de from)

guarida *nf (de animal)* lair; *(refugio)* hide-out

guarismo *nm* digit

guarnecer [33] *vt* (a) *Culin* to garnish (b) *(dotar)* to provide (de with) (c) *Mil* to garrison

guarnición *nf* (a) *Culin* garnish (b) *Mil* garrison

guarro,-a 1 *adj* filthy

  2 *nm,f* pig

guarura *nm Méx Fam* bodyguard

guasa *nf* mockery

guasearse *vpr Fam* **g. de** to make fun of

guaso,-a *adj Am* peasant

guasón,-ona 1 *adj* humorous

  2 *nm,f* joker

guata *nf* (a) *(relleno)* padding (b) *Am (bar ga)* paunch

Guatemala *n* (a) *(país)* Guatemala (b) *(c dad)* Guatemala City

guatemalteco,-a *adj & nm,f* Guatemalan

guay *adj inv Fam* brilliant, terrific

guayabera *nf* short jacket

guayabo,-a *nm,f Am Fig (chica bonita)* pre young girl; *(chico guapo)* good-looking boy

guepardo *nm* cheetah

güero,-a *adj Méx Fam* blond, blonde

guerra *nf* war; **en g.** at war; **g. bacteriológi** germ warfare; **g. civil/fría/mundial/nucle** civil/cold/world/nuclear war; *Fam* **dar g.** be a real nuisance

guerrero,-a 1 *nm,f* warrior

  2 *adj* warlike

guerrilla *nf* (a) *(partida armada)* guerril force o band (b) *(lucha)* guerrilla warfare

güevón,-ona *nm,f Andes, Arg, Ven muy Fe (estúpido) Br* prat, *US* dork

guía 1 *nmf (persona)* guide

  2 *nf* (a) *(norma)* guideline (b) *(libro)* guid *(lista)* directory; **g. de teléfonos** telepho directory

guiar [29] 1 *vt* (a) *(indicar el camino)* to gui (b) *Aut* to drive; *Náut* to steer; *(caballo, bi* to ride

  2 **guiarse** *vpr* **g. por** to be guided by, to go l

guija *nf* pebble

guijarro *nm* pebble

guinda *nf (fruto)* morello (cherry)

guindilla *nf* chilli

guineo *nm Andes, CAm* banana

guiñapo *nm* (a) *(andrajo)* rag (b) *Fig (pers na)* wreck; **poner a algn como un g.** to tear to pieces

guiñar *vt* to wink

guiño *nm* wink

guión *nm* (a) *Cin & TV* script (b) *Lin* hyphen, dash (c) *(esquema)* sketch

guionista *nmf* scriptwriter

guiri *nmf Fam* foreigner

guirigay *nm* hubbub

guirnalda *nf* garland

guisa *nf* way, manner; **a g. de** as, by way of

guisado *nm Culin* stew

guisante *nm* pea

guisar *vt* to cook

guiso *nm* dish; *(guisado)* stew

guita *nf* (a) *(cuerda)* rope (b) *Fam* dough

guitarra 1 *nf* guitar

  2 *nmf* guitarist

guitarreada *nf CSur* singalong *(to guitars)*

guitarrista *nmf* guitarist

gula *nf* gluttony

gurí,-isa *nm,f RP Fam (niño)* kid, child; *(j ven)* (hombre) lad; *(mujer)* lass

gusano *nm* worm; *(oruga)* caterpillar; *Fa Pey (exiliado cubano)* = anti-Castro Cuba living in exile; **g. de seda** silkworm

gustar 1 *vt* (**a**) **me gusta el vino** I like wine; **me gustaban los caramelos** I used to like sweets; **me gusta nadar** I like swimming; **me gustaría** I would like to go (**b**) *Fml* **¿gustas?** would you like some?; **cuando gustes** whenever you like **2** *vi* **g. de** to enjoy

gusto *nm* (**a**) *(sentido)* taste (**b**) *(en fórmulas de cortesía)* pleasure; **con (mucho) g.** with (great) pleasure; **tanto g.** pleased to meet you (**c**) **estar a g.** to feel comfortable *o* at ease; **por g.** for the sake of it; **ser de buen/mal g.** to be in good/bad taste; **tener buen/mal g.** to have good/bad taste; **tenemos el gusto de comunicarle que ...** we are pleased to inform you that ...

gutural *adj* guttural

H, h [atʃe] *nf (la letra)* H,h; **bomba H** H-bomb
ha *indic pres de* **haber**
haba *nf* broad bean

Takes the masculine articles **el** and **un**.

Habana *nf* La H. Havana
habano *nm* Havana cigar
haber [14] **1** *v aux* (**a**) *(en tiempos compues-tos)* to have; **lo he visto** I have seen it; **ya lo había hecho** he had already done it
(**b**) **h. de** + *infin (obligación)* to have to; **has de ser bueno** you must be good
2 *v impers (special form of present tense:* **hay**) (**a**) *(existir, estar) (singular used also with plural nouns)* **hay** there is/are; **había** there was/were; **había un gato en el tejado** there was a cat on the roof; **había muchos libros** there were a lot of books; **hay 500 km entre Madrid y Granada** it's 500 km from Madrid to Granada
(**b**) **h. que** + *infin* it is necessary to; **hay que trabajar** you've got to *o* you must work; **habrá que comprobarlo** I/you/we/*etc* will have to check it
(**c**) *(tener lugar)* **habrá una fiesta** there will be a party; **hoy hay partido** there's a match today; **los accidentes habidos en esta carre-tera** the accidents which have happened on this road
(**d**) **había una vez …** once upon a time …; **no hay de qué** you're welcome, don't mention it; **¿qué hay?** how are things?
3 *nm* (**a**) *Fin* credit; **haberes** assets
(**b**) **en su h.** in his possession
habichuela *nf (judía)* kidney bean; *Carib, Col (judía verde)* green bean
hábil *adj* (**a**) *(diestro)* skilful (**b**) *(astuto)* smart (**c**) **días hábiles** working days
habilidad *nf* (**a**) *(destreza)* skill (**b**) *(astucia)* cleverness
habilitar *vt* (**a**) *(espacio)* to fit out (**b**) *(perso-na)* to entitle (**c**) *Fin (financiar)* to finance
habiloso,-a *adj Chile* shrewd, astute
habitación *nf (cuarto)* room; *(dormitorio)* bedroom; **h. individual/doble** single/double room
habitante *nmf* inhabitant
habitar 1 *vt* to live in, to inhabit
2 *vi* to live
hábitat *nm (pl* **hábitats**) habitat
hábito *nm* (**a**) *(costumbre)* habit (**b**) *Rel* habit
habitual *adj* usual, habitual; *(cliente, lector)* regular

habituar [30] **1** *vt* to accustom (**a** to)
2 habituarse *vpr* **habituarse a** to get used to *o* to become accustomed to
habla *nf* (**a**) *(idioma)* language; **países de ▸ española** Spanish-speaking countries (**b** *(facultad de hablar)* speech; **quedarse sin ▸** to be left speechless (**c**) *Tel* **¡al h.!** speaking▸

Takes the masculine articles **el** and **un**.

hablado,-a *adj* spoken; **el inglés h.** spoke▸ English; **mal h.** coarse, foul-mouthed
hablador,-a *adj (parlanchín)* talkative; *(chi moso)* gossipy
habladuría *nf (rumor)* rumour; *(chism* piece of gossip
hablante *nmf* speaker
hablar 1 *vi* (**a**) to speak, to talk; **h. con algn** speak to sb (**b**) **¡ni h.!** certainly not!; *Fa* **¡quién fue a h.!** look who's talking!
2 *vt* (**a**) *(idioma)* to speak; **habla alemán** h speaks German (**b**) *(tratar un asunto)* to tal over, to discuss
3 hablarse *vpr* (**a**) to speak *o* talk to on another (**b**) **se habla español** *(en letrer* Spanish spoken
habré *indic fut de* **haber**
hacendado,-a *nm,f Am* farmer
hacendoso,-a *adj* hardworking
hacer [15] **1** *vt* (**a**) *(crear, producir, fabricar)* t make; **h. una casa** to build a house
(**b**) *(obrar, ejecutar)* to do; **eso no se hace** isn't done; **hazme un favor** do me a favou **¿qué haces?** *(en este momento)* what are yo doing?; *(para vivir)* what do you do (for living)?; **tengo mucho que h.** I have a lot ▸ do; **h. deporte** to do sports; **h. una carrera medicina** to do a degree/medicine
(**c**) *(conseguir) (amigos, dinero)* to make
(**d**) *(obligar)* to make; **hazle callar/trabaja** make him shut up/work
(**e**) *(arreglar)* to make; **h. la cama** to mak the bed
(**f**) *Mat (sumar)* to make; **y con éste hace cien** and that makes a hundred
(**g**) *(dar aspecto)* to make look; **el negro** **hace más delgado** black makes him loo slimmer
(**h**) *(sustituyendo a otro verbo)* to do; **ya n puedo leer como solía hacerlo** I can't read a well as I used to
(**i**) *(representar)* to play; **h. el bueno** to pla

he (part of the) goody

(**j**) **¡bien hecho!** well done!

2 *vi* (**a**) *(actuar)* to play; **hizo de Desdémona** she played Desdemona

(**b**) **h. por** o **para** + *infin* to try to; **hice por venir** I tried to come

(**c**) *(fingir)* to pretend; **h. como si** to act as if

(**d**) *(convenir)* to be suitable; **a las ocho si te hace** will eight o'clock be all right for you?

3 *v impers* (**a**) **hace calor/frío** it's hot/cold

(**b**) *(tiempo transcurrido)* ago; **hace mucho tiempo)** a long time ago; **hace dos días que no le veo** I haven't seen him for two days; **hace dos años que vivo en Glasgow** I've been living in Glasgow for two years

4 hacerse *vpr* (**a**) *(volverse)* to become, to grow; **h. viejo** to grow old

(**b**) *(simular)* to pretend; **h. el dormido** to pretend to be sleeping

(**c**) **h. con** *(apropiarse)* to get hold of

(**d**) **h. a** *(habituarse)* to get used to; **enseguida me hago a todo** I soon get used to anything

acha *nf* (**a**) *(herramienta)* axe (**b**) *Fam* **ser un h. en algo** to be an ace o a wizard at sth

> Takes the masculine articles **el** and **un**.

achís *nm* hashish

acia *prep* (**a**) *(dirección)* towards, to; **h. abajo** down, downwards; **h. adelante** forwards; **h. arriba** up, upwards; **h. atrás** back, backwards (**b**) *(tiempo)* at about, at around; **h. las tres** at about three o'clock

acienda *nf* (**a**) *Am (finca agrícola)* estate, *US* ranch (**b**) *Fin* Treasury; **h. pública** public funds o finances; **Ministerio de H.** = Exchequer, Treasury

acinamiento *nm* (**a**) *Agr* stacking; *Fig (montón)* piling (**b**) *(de gente)* overcrowding

acinar 1 *vt Agr* to stack; *Fig (amontonar)* to pile up, to heap up

2 hacinarse *vpr* **h. en** *(gente)* to be packed into

ada *nf* fairy; **cuento de hadas** fairy tale; **h. madrina** fairy godmother

> Takes the masculine articles **el** and **un**.

ado *nm* destiny

ago *indic pres de* **hacer**

alagar [42] *vt* to flatter

alago *nm* flattery

alagüeño,-a *adj (noticia, impresión)* promising

alcón *nm* falcon; **h. peregrino** peregrine (falcon)

álito *nm* (**a**) *(aliento)* breath (**b**) *(vapor)* vapour

allar 1 *vt (encontrar)* to find; *(averiguar)* to find out; *(descubrir)* to discover

2 hallarse *vpr (estar)* to be, to find oneself; *(estar situado)* to be situated

allazgo *nm* (**a**) *(descubrimiento)* discovery

(**b**) *(cosa encontrada)* find

hamaca *nf* hammock; *(mecedora)* rocking chair

hambre *nf (apetito)* hunger; *(inanición)* starvation; *(catástrofe)* famine; **tener h.** to be hungry

> Takes the masculine articles **el** and **un**.

hambriento,-a *adj* starving

hamburguesa *nf* hamburger

hampa *nf* underworld

> Takes the masculine articles **el** and **un**.

han *indic pres de* **haber**

harapo *nm* rag; **hecho un h.** in tatters

haré *indic fut de* **hacer**

harén *nm (pl* **harenes**) harem

harina *nf* flour

hartar 1 *vt* (**a**) *(cansar, fastidiar)* to annoy (**b**) *(atiborrar)* to satiate; **el dulce harta enseguida** sweet things soon fill you up

2 hartarse *vpr* (**a**) *(saciar el apetito)* to eat one's fill (**b**) *(cansarse)* to get fed up (**de** with), to grow tired (**de** of)

harto,-a 1 *adj* (**a**) *(de comida)* full (**b**) *(cansado)* fed up; **¡me tienes h.!** I'm fed up with you!; **estoy h. de trabajar** I'm fed up working (**c**) *Andes, CAm, Carib, Méx (mucho)* lots of; **tiene h. dinero** he's got lots of money

2 *adv* (**a**) *Fml (muy)* very (**b**) *Andes, CAm, Carib, Méx (muy, mucho)* really

hartura *nf* bellyful; **¡qué h.!** what a drag!

has *indic pres de* **haber**

hasta 1 *prep* (**a**) *(lugar)* up to, as far as, down to (**b**) *(tiempo)* until, till, up to; **h. el domingo** until Sunday; **h. el final** right to the end; **h. la fecha** up to now; **h. luego** see you later (**c**) *(con cantidad)* up to, as many as (**d**) *(incluso)* even (**e**) *CAm, Col, Méx (no antes de)* **pintaremos la casa h. fin de mes** we won't paint the house till the end of the month

2 *conj* **h. que** until

hastiado,-a *adj* sick, tired (**de** of)

hastiar [29] *vt* to sicken

hastío *nm* weariness

hato *nm* bundle

hay *indic pres de* **haber**

Haya *nf* **La H.** The Hague

haya¹ *nf* (**a**) *Bot (árbol)* beech (**b**) *(madera)* beech (wood)

> Takes the masculine articles **el** and **un**.

haya² *subj pres de* **haber**

haz¹ *nm* (**a**) *Agr* sheaf (**b**) *(de luz)* shaft

haz² *nf (de hoja)* top side

haz³ *imperat de* **hacer**

hazaña *nf* deed, exploit

hazmerreír *nm* laughing stock

he¹ *adv* **he ahí/aquí ...** there/here you have ...

he² *indic pres de* **haber**

hebilla *nf* buckle

hebra *nf* thread; *(de carne)* sinew; *(de*

madera) grain; **pegar la h.** to chat
hebreo,-a 1 *adj* Hebrew
  2 *nm,f* Hebrew
hecatombe *nf* disaster
hechicería *nf* witchcraft
hechicero,-a 1 *adj* bewitching
  2 *nm,f (hombre)* wizard, sorcerer; *(mujer)* witch, sorceress
hechizar [40] *vt* (a) *(embrujar)* to cast a spell on (b) *Fig (fascinar)* to bewitch, to charm
hechizo,-a 1 *nm* (a) *(embrujo)* spell (b) *Fig (fascinación)* fascination, charm
hecho,-a 1 *adj* (a) made, done; **¡bien h.!** well done! (b) *(carne)* done (c) *(persona)* mature (d) *(frase)* set; *(ropa)* ready-made
  2 *nm* (a) *(realidad)* fact; **de h.** in fact; **el h. es que ...** the fact is that ... (b) *(acto)* act, deed (c) *(suceso)* event, incident
hechura *nf (forma)* shape; *Cost* cut
hectárea *nf* hectare
hectolitro *nm* hectolitre
heder [3] *vi* to stink, to smell foul
hediondo,-a *adj* foul-smelling
hedor *nm* stink, stench
hegemonía *nf* hegemony
helada *nf* frost
heladera *nf RP (nevera)* refrigerator, fridge
heladería *nf* ice-cream parlour
helado,-a 1 *nm* ice cream
  2 *adj* (a) *(muy frío)* frozen, freezing cold; **estoy h. (de frío)** I'm frozen (b) *Fig* **quedarse h.** *(atónito)* to be flabbergasted
helar [1] **1** *vt (congelar)* to freeze
  2 *v impers* to freeze; **anoche heló** there was a frost last night
  3 helarse *vpr (congelarse)* to freeze
helecho *nm Bot* fern
hélice *nf* (a) *Av & Náut* propeller (b) *Anat, Arquit & Mat* helix
helicóptero *nm Av* helicopter
helipuerto *nm Av* heliport
hematoma *nm Med* haematoma
hembra *nf* (a) *Bot & Zool* female (b) *(mujer)* woman (c) *Téc* female; *(de tornillo)* nut; *(de enchufe)* socket
hemiciclo *nm Fam* (Spanish) parliament
hemisferio *nm* hemisphere
hemorragia *nf Med* haemorrhage
hemos *indic pres de* haber
henchir [6] *vt* to stuff
hender [3] *vt (resquebrajar)* to crack, to split; *Fig (olas)* to cut
hendidura *nf* crack
hendir [5] *vt* = hender
heno *nm* hay
heráldica *nf* heraldry
herbicida *nm* weedkiller, herbicide
herbívoro,-a 1 *adj* herbivorous, grass-eating
  2 *nm,f Zool* herbivore
herbolario *nm* herbalist's (shop)
herboso,-a *adj* grassy
hercio *nm* Herz

heredad *nf* (a) *(finca)* country estate (b) *(conjunto de bienes)* private estate
heredar *vt* (a) *Jur* to inherit (b) **ha heredado la sonrisa de su madre** she's got her mother's smile
heredero,-a *nm,f (hombre)* heir; *(mujer)* heiress; **príncipe h.** crown prince
hereditario,-a *adj* hereditary
hereje *nmf Rel* heretic
herejía *nf Rel* heresy
herencia *nf* (a) *Jur* inheritance, legacy (b) *Biol* heredity
herida *nf (lesión)* injury; *(corte)* wound
herido,-a *nm,f* injured person; **no hubo heridos** there were no casualties
herir [5] **1** *vt* (a) *(físicamente) (lesionar)* to injure; *(cortar)* to wound (b) *(emocionalmente)* to hurt, to wound (c) *(vista)* to offend
  2 herirse *vpr* to injure o hurt oneself
hermana *nf* (a) sister (b) *Rel (monja)* sister
hermanado,-a *adj* twinned; **ciudad hermanada** twin town
hermanar 1 *vt* (a) *(personas)* to unite spiritually (b) *(ciudades)* to twin (c) *(unir)* to unite, to combine
  2 hermanarse *vpr* (a) *(ciudades)* to twin (b) *(combinar)* to combine
hermanastro,-a *nm,f (hombre)* stepbrother; *(mujer)* stepsister
hermandad *nf* (a) *(grupo)* fraternity, brotherhood, sisterhood (b) *(relación)* brotherhood, sisterhood
hermano *nm* (a) brother; **h. político** brother-in-law; **primo h.** first cousin (b) *Rel (fraile)* brother (c) **hermanos** brothers and sisters
herméticamente *adv* **h. cerrado** hermetically sealed
hermético,-a *adj* (a) *(cierre)* hermetic, airtight (b) *Fig (abstruso)* secretive
hermetismo *nm* airtightness; *Fig* impenetrability
hermoso,-a *adj* beautiful, lovely; *(grande)* fine
hermosura *nf* beauty
héroe *nm* hero
heroico,-a *adj* heroic
heroína *nf* (a) *(mujer)* heroine (b) *(droga)* heroin
heroinómano,-a *nm,f* heroin addict
heroísmo *nm* heroism
herrador *nm* blacksmith
herradura *nf* horseshoe
herramienta *nf Téc* tool; **caja de herramientas** toolbox
herrar [1] *vt* (a) *(caballo)* to shoe (b) *(ganado)* to brand
herrería *nf* forge, smithy
herrero *nm* blacksmith, smith
herrumbre *nf* rust
hervidero *nm Fig (lugar)* hotbed
hervir [5] **1** *vt (hacer bullir)* to boil
  2 *vi* (a) *Culin* to boil; **romper a h.** to come to

the boil (**b**) *(abundar)* to swarm, to seethe (**de** with)

heterodoxo,-a *adj* unorthodox

heterogéneo,-a *adj* heterogeneous

hez *nf* (**a**) *(usu pl) (poso)* sediment, dregs (**b**) **heces** faeces

hiato *nm Ling* hiatus

híbrido,-a *adj & nm,f* hybrid

hice *pt indef de* **hacer**

hiciste *pt indef de* **hacer**

hidalgo *nm Hist* nobleman, gentleman

hidalguía *nf* nobility; *Fig* chivalry, gentlemanliness

hidratación *nf* (**a**) *Quím* hydration (**b**) *(de la piel)* moisturizing

hidratante *adj* moisturizing; **crema/leche h.** moisturizing cream/lotion

hidráulico,-a *adj* hydraulic; **energía hidráulica** hydro-electric energy

hidroavión *nm* seaplane, *US* hydroplane

hidrocarburo *nm* hydrocarbon

hidrófilo,-a *adj* absorbent; **algodón h.** *Br* cotton wool, *Am* absorbent cotton

hidrógeno *nm Quím* hydrogen

hidroterapia *nf Med* hydrotherapy

hiedra *nf* ivy

hiel *nf* (**a**) *Anat* bile (**b**) *Fig* bitterness, gall

hielo *nm* ice; *Fig* **romper el h.** to break the ice

hiena *nf* hyena

hierba *nf* (**a**) grass; **mala h.** *Bot* weed; *Fig (persona)* bad lot; *Fam Hum* **y otras hierbas** among others (**b**) *Culin* herb; **h. luisa** lemon verbena (**c**) *Fam (marihuana)* grass

hierbabuena *nf* mint

hierro *nm* (**a**) *(metal)* iron; **h. forjado** wrought iron (**b**) *(punta de arma)* head, point (**c**) *(marca en el ganado)* brand

hígado *nm* (**a**) *Anat* liver (**b**) *Euf* guts

higiene *nf* hygiene

higiénico,-a *adj* hygienic; **papel h.** toilet paper

higo *nm Fam Fig* **hecho un h.** wizened, crumpled

higuera *nf Bot* fig tree

hija *nf* daughter

hijastro,-a *nm,f (hombre)* stepson; *(mujer)* stepdaughter

hijo *nm* (**a**) son, child; *Pey* **h. de papá** rich kid; *Vulg* **h. de puta** *o Méx* **de la chingada** bastard, *US* asshole (**b**) **hijos** children

hijoputa *nm Vulg* bastard, *US* asshole

hilacha *nf,* **hilacho** *nm* loose *o* hanging thread

hilandería *nf* mill; *(de algodón)* cotton mill

hilandero,-a *nm,f* spinner

hilar *vt & vi* (**a**) to spin (**b**) *Fig (idea, plan)* to work out; **h. muy fino** to split hairs

hilaridad *nf* hilarity, mirth

hilera *nf* line, row

hilo *nm* (**a**) *Cost* thread; *(grueso)* yarn (**b**) *Fig (de historia, discurso)* thread; *(de pensamiento)* train; **perder el h.** to lose the thread; **h.**

musical background music (**c**) *Tex* linen

hilvanar *vt* (**a**) *Cost* to tack, to baste (**b**) *Fig (ideas etc)* to outline

himno *nm* hymn; **h. nacional** national anthem

hincapié *nm* **hacer h. en** *(insistir)* to insist on; *(subrayar)* to emphasize, to stress

hincar [44] **1** *vt (clavar)* to drive (in); **h. el diente a** to sink one's teeth into

2 hincarse *vpr* **h. de rodillas** to kneel (down)

hincha *Fam* **1** *nmf Ftb* fan, supporter

2 *nf (antipatía)* grudge, dislike; **me tiene h.** he's got it in for me

hinchada *nf Ftb Fam* fans, supporters

hinchado,-a *adj* (**a**) inflated, blown up (**b**) *Med (cara etc)* swollen, puffed up; *(estómago)* bloated (**c**) *Fig (estilo)* bombastic, pompous

hinchar 1 *vt* (**a**) *(inflar)* to inflate, to blow up (**b**) *Fig (exagerar)* to inflate, to exaggerate

2 hincharse *vpr* (**a**) *Med* to swell (up) (**b**) *Fam* **me hinché de comida** I stuffed myself; **me hinché de llorar** I cried for all I was worth

hinchazón *nf Med* swelling

hindú *adj & nmf* Hindu

hipermercado *nm* hypermarket

hipertensión *nf* high blood pressure

hípica *nf* (horse) riding

hípico,-a *adj* horse; **club h.** riding club

hipnotizar [40] *vt* to hypnotize

hipo *nm* hiccups, hiccough; **me ha dado h.** it's given me the hiccups

hipocondríaco,-a *adj & nm,f* hypochondriac

hipocresía *nf* hypocrisy

hipócrita 1 *adj* hypocritical

2 *nmf* hypocrite

hipódromo *nm* racetrack, racecourse

hipopótamo *nm* hippopotamus

hipoteca *nf Fin* mortgage

hipotecar [44] *vt* (**a**) *Fin* to mortgage (**b**) *Fig* to jeopardize

hipótesis *nf inv* hypothesis

hipotético,-a *adj* hypothetical

hiriente *adj* offensive, wounding; *(palabras)* cutting

hirsuto,-a *adj* hirsute, hairy; *(cerdoso)* bristly

hispánico,-a *adj* Hispanic, Spanish

hispanidad *nf* **el Día de la H.** Columbus Day *(12 October)*

hispano,-a 1 *adj (español)* Spanish; *(español y sudamericano)* Hispanic; *(sudamericano)* Spanish American

2 *nm,f (hispanoamericano)* Spanish American; *(estadounidense)* Hispanic

Hispanoamérica *nf* Latin America

hispanoamericano,-a *adj & nm,f* Latin American

hispanohablante 1 *adj* Spanish-speaking

2 *nmf* Spanish speaker

histeria *nf* hysteria; **un ataque de h.** hysterics

histérico,-a *adj* hysterical; *Fam Fig* **me pones h.** you're driving me mad

historia nf (a) history; **esto pasará a la h.** this will go down in history (b) (narración) story, tale; Fam **¡déjate de historias!** don't give me that!

historiador,-a nm,f historian

historial nm (a) Med medical record, case history (b) (antecedentes) background

historiar [29] vt to recount

histórico,-a adj (a) historical (b) (auténtico) factual, true; **hechos históricos** true facts (c) (de gran importancia) historic, memorable

historieta nf (a) (cuento) short story, tale (b) (tira cómica) comic strip

hito nm milestone; **mirar de h. en h.** to stare at

hizo pt indef de **hacer**

hnos. (abr **Hermanos**) Bros

hocico nm (a) (de animal) snout (b) (de persona) mug, snout; Fam **meter los hocicos en algo** to stick o poke one's nose into sth

hogar nm (a) (casa) home (b) (de la chimenea) hearth, fireplace (c) Fig **formar** o **crear un h.** (familia) to start a family

hogareño,-a adj (vida) home, family; (persona) home-loving, stay-at-home

hoguera nf bonfire

hoja nf (a) Bot leaf (b) (pétalo) petal (c) (de papel) sheet, leaf; **h. de cálculo** spreadsheet (d) (de libro) leaf, page (e) (de metal) sheet (f) (de cuchillo, espada) blade (g) (impreso) hand-out, printed sheet (h) (de puerta o ventana) leaf

hojalata nf tin, tin plate

hojaldre nm Culin puff pastry

hojarasca nf fallen o dead leaves

hojear vt to leaf through, to flick through

hola interj hello!, hullo!, hi!

Holanda n Holland

holandés,-esa 1 adj Dutch

2 nm,f (hombre) Dutchman; (mujer) Dutchwoman

3 nm (idioma) Dutch

holding nm Fin holding company

holgado,-a adj (a) (ropa) loose, baggy (b) (económicamente) comfortable (c) (espacio) roomy; **andar h. de tiempo** to have plenty of time

holgar [2] vi (a) (no trabajar) to be idle (b) (sobrar) **huelga decir que ...** it goes without saying that ...

holgazán,-ana 1 adj lazy, idle

2 nm,f lazybones, layabout

holgura nf (a) (ropa) looseness (b) (espacio) space, roominess (c) Téc play, give (c) (bienestar económico) affluence, comfort; **vivir con h.** to be comfortably off, to be well-off

hollar [2] vt Fig to walk on; **terrenos jamás hollados** uncharted territory

hollín nm soot

hombre nm (a) man; **de h. a h.** man-to-man; **¡pobre h.!** poor chap!; **ser muy h.** to be every inch a man; **h. de estado** statesman; **h. de negocios** businessman (b) (especie)

mankind, man

2 interj (a) (saludo) hey!, hey there!; **¡h. Juan!** hey, Juan! (b) **¡sí h.!**, **¡h. claro!** (enfático) sure!, you bet!; **¡anda, h.!** (incredulidad) oh come on!

hombrera nf shoulder pad

hombría nf manliness, virility

hombrillo nm Ven (arcén) verge; (de auto pista) Br hard shoulder, US shoulder

hombro nm shoulder; **a hombros** on one' shoulders; **encogerse de hombros** to shru; one's shoulders; **mirar a algn por encima de h.** to look down one's nose at sb

hombruno,-a adj mannish, butch

homenaje nm homage, tribute; **rendir h.** algn to pay homage o tribute to sb

homenajear vt to pay tribute to

homicida 1 nmf (hombre) murderer; (mujer murderess

2 adj homicidal; **el arma h.** the murde weapon

homicidio nm homicide

homogéneo,-a adj homogeneous, uniform

homologable adj comparable (**con** with)

homologar [42] vt to give official approval recognition to

homólogo,-a 1 adj (equiparable) compar able

2 nm,f (persona con mismas condiciones counterpart

homosexual adj & nmf homosexual

homosexualidad nf homosexuality

honda nf (arma) sling

hondo,-a adj (a) (profundo) deep; **plato h** soup dish (b) Fig (pesar) profound, deep

hondonada nf Geog hollow, depression

hondura nf depth; Fig **meterse en hondura** (profundizar) to go into too much detail

Honduras n Honduras

hondureño,-a adj & nm,f Honduran

honestidad nf (a) (honradez) honesty uprightness (b) (decencia) modesty

honesto,-a adj (a) (honrado) honest upright (b) (decente) modest

hongo nm (a) Bot fungus; **h. venenoso** toad stool (b) (sombrero) Br bowler (hat), US derb

honor nm (a) (virtud) honour; **palabra de** word of honour (b) **en h. a la verdad ...** to be fair ...; **es un h. para mí** it's an honour for me (c) hacer h. a to live up to

honorable adj honourable; Pol **el h.** = head of the Catalan government

honorario,-a 1 adj honorary

2 nmpl **honorarios** fees, fee

honorífico,-a adj honorary

honra nf (a) (dignidad) dignity, self-esteem (b) (fama) reputation, good name (c) (honor) honour; **me cabe la h. de ...** I have the honou of ...; **¡a mucha h.!** and proud of it!

honradez nf honesty, integrity

honrado,-a adj (a) (de fiar) honest (b) (de cente) upright, respectable

honrar *vt* (**a**) *(respetar)* to honour (**b**) *(enaltecer)* to be a credit to

honrilla *nf* self-respect, pride

honroso,-a *adj (loable)* honourable

hora *nf* (**a**) *hour;* **media h.** half an hour; **a altas horas de la madrugada** in the small hours; **dar la h.** to strike the hour; **(trabajo) por horas** (work) paid by the hour; **h. punta,** *Am* **h. pico** *(de mucho tráfico)* rush hour; *(de agua, electricidad)* peak times; **horas extra** overtime (hours) (**b**) *Fig* time; **¿qué h. es?** what time is it?; **a su h.** at the proper time; **la última h.** at the last moment; **la h. de la verdad** the moment of truth (**c**) *(cita)* appointment; **pedir h.** *(al médico etc)* to ask for an appointment

horadar *vt (perforar)* to drill *o* bore a hole in

horario,-a 1 *nm* timetable, *US* schedule

2 *adj* time; *Rad* **señal horaria** pips

horca *nf* gallows *sing*

horcajada: a horcajadas *loc adv* astride

horchata *nf Culin* = sweet, milky drink made from chufa nuts or almonds

horda *nf* horde, mob

horizonte *nm* horizon

horma *nf (de zapato)* last

hormiga *nf* ant

hormigón *nm Constr* concrete; **h. armado** reinforced concrete

hormiguear *vi* to itch, to tingle; **me hormigueaba la pierna** I had pins and needles in my leg

hormigueo *nm* (**a**) pins and needles, tingling *o* itching sensation (**b**) *Fig* anxiety

hormiguero *nm* (**a**) anthill (**b**) *Fig* **ser un h.** *(lugar)* to be swarming (with people)

hormona *nf* hormone

hornada *nf* (**a**) *(pan)* batch (**b**) *Fig* set, batch

hornillo *nm (de cocinar)* stove; *(placa)* hotplate

horno *nm (cocina)* oven; *Téc* furnace; *(para cerámica, ladrillos)* kiln; *Culin* **pescado al h.** baked fish; *Fam Fig* **esta habitación es un h.** this room is boiling hot

Hornos *n* **Cabo de H.** Cape Horn

horóscopo *nm* horoscope

horquilla *nf* (**a**) *(del pelo)* hairpin, *Br* hairgrip, *US* bobby-pin (**b**) *(estadística)* chart (**c**) **h. de precios** price range

horrendo,-a *adj* horrifying, horrible

hórreo *nm Agr* granary

horrible *adj* horrible, dreadful, awful

horripilante *adj* hair-raising, scary

horror *nm* (**a**) horror, terror; **¡qué h.!** how awful!; *Fam* **tengo h. a las motos** I hate motorbikes (**b**) *Fam* **me gusta horrores** *(muchísimo)* I like it an awful lot

horrorizar [40] *vt* to horrify, to terrify

horroroso,-a *adj* (**a**) *(que da miedo)* horrifying, terrifying (**b**) *Fam (muy feo)* hideous, ghastly (**c**) *Fam (malísimo)* awful, dreadful

hortaliza *nf* vegetable

hortelano,-a *nm,f Br* market gardener, *US* truck farmer

hortensia *nf Bot* hydrangea

hortera *adj Fam (persona)* flashy; *(cosa)* tacky, kitsch

horterada *nf Fam* tacky thing *o* act

hosco,-a *adj* (**a**) *(poco sociable)* surly, sullen (**b**) *(tenebroso)* dark, gloomy (**c**) *(difícil)* tough

hospedaje *nm* lodgings, *Br* accommodation, *US* accommodations

hospedar 1 *vt* to put up, to lodge

2 hospedarse *vpr* to stay (**en** at)

hospicio *nm* orphanage

hospital *nm* hospital

hospitalario,-a *adj* (**a**) *(acogedor)* hospitable (**b**) *Med* hospital; **instalaciones hospitalarias** hospital facilities

hospitalidad *nf* hospitality

hospitalizar [40] *vt* to take *o* send into hospital, to hospitalize

hostal *nm* guest house

hostelería *nf (negocio)* catering business; *(estudios)* hotel management

hostelero,-a *nm,f (hombre)* landlord; *(mujer)* landlady

hostería *nf CSur* inn, lodging house

hostia 1 *nf* (**a**) *Rel* host (**b**) *Vulg (tortazo)* bash (**c**) *Vulg* **estar de mala h.** to be in a foul mood; **ser la h.** *(fantástico)* to be *Br* bloody *o US* goddamn amazing; *(penoso)* to be *Br* bloody *o US* goddamn awful

2 *interj Vulg* damn! *Br* bloody hell!

hostiar [29] *vt Vulg* to bash, to sock

hostigar [42] *vt* (**a**) to harass (**b**) *(caballerías)* to whip

hostil *adj* hostile

hostilidad *nf* hostility

hotel *nm* hotel

hotelero,-a 1 *adj* hotel; **el sector h.** the hotel sector

2 *nm,f* hotel-keeper, hotelier

hoy *adv* (**a**) *(día)* today (**b**) *Fig (presente)* now; **h. (en) día** nowadays; **h. por h.** at the present time

hoya *nf Geog* vale, valley

hoyo *nm* (**a**) *(agujero)* hole, pit (**b**) *(sepultura)* grave (**c**) *(de golf)* hole

hoyuelo *nm* dimple

hoz *nf Agr* sickle; **la h. y el martillo** the hammer and sickle

HR *nm* (*abr* **Hostal Residencia**) boarding house

huachafo,-a *adj Perú Fam* tacky

huasipungo *nm Andes* = plot of land given to Indian for his own use in exchange for work on the landowner's farm

huaso,-a *nm,f Chile Fam* farmer, peasant

hube *pt indef de* **haber**

hubiera *subj imperf de* **haber**

hucha *nf* piggy bank

hueco,-a 1 *adj* (**a**) *(vacío)* empty, hollow (**b**) *(sonido)* resonant

2 *nm* (a) *(cavidad)* hollow, hole (b) *(sitio no ocupado)* empty space (c) *(rato libre)* free time

huele *indic pres de* **oler**

huelga *nf* strike; **estar en** o **de h.** to be on strike; **h. de brazos caídos** go-slow; **h. de celo** work-to-rule

huelguista *nmf* striker

huella *nf* (a) *(del pie)* footprint; *(coche)* track; **h. dactilar** fingerprint (b) *Fig (vestigio)* trace, sign; **dejar h.** to leave one's mark

huérfano,-a *nm,f* orphan

huero,-a *adj Fig* empty

huerta *nf Agr* (a) *(parcela) Br* market garden, *US* truck farm (b) *(región)* = irrigated area used for cultivation

huerto *nm (de verduras)* vegetable garden, kitchen garden; *(de frutales)* orchard

hueso *nm* (a) *Anat* bone; **estar en los huesos** to be all skin and bone (b) *(de fruto)* stone, *US* pit (c) *Fig (difícil)* hard work; *(profesor)* hard nut (d) *Méx (enchufe)* contact

huésped,-a *nm,f (invitado)* guest; *(en hotel etc)* lodger, boarder; **casa de huéspedes** guesthouse

hueste *nf Mil* army, host

huesudo,-a *adj* bony

huevada *nf Andes, RP muy Fam (dicho)* garbage, bullshit, *Br* bollocks

huevera *nf (caja)* egg box

huevo *nm* (a) egg; **h. duro** hard-boiled egg; **h. escalfado** poached egg; **h. frito** fried egg; **h. pasado por agua**, *Am* **h. tibio** o **a la copa** soft-boiled egg; **huevos revueltos** scrambled eggs (b) *muy Fam (usu pl)* balls; **hacer algo por huevos** to do sth even if it kills you; **tener huevos** to have guts

huida *nf* flight, escape

huidizo,-a *adj* elusive

huipil *nm CAm, Méx* = traditional Indian woman's dress or blouse

huir [37] *vi* to run away (**de** from), to flee; **h. de la cárcel** to escape from prison; **h. de algn** to avoid sb

hule *nm* (a) *(tela impermeable)* oilcloth, oilskin (b) *(de mesa)* tablecloth (c) *Am* rubber

hulla *nf* soft coal

humanidad *nf* (a) *(género humano)* humanity, mankind (b) *(cualidad)* humanity, humaneness (c) *(bondad)* compassion, kindness

humanitario,-a *adj* humanitarian

humano,-a **1** *adj* (a) *(relativo al hombre)* human (b) *(compasivo)* humane

2 *nm* human (being); **ser h.** human being

humear *vi (echar humo)* to smoke; *(arrojar vapor)* to steam, to be steaming hot

humedad *nf (atmosférica)* humidity; *(de lu-*

gar) dampness; **a prueba de h.** damp-proof

humedecer [33] **1** *vt* to moisten, to dampen

2 **humedecerse** *upr* to become damp o wet o moist

húmedo,-a *adj (casa, ropa)* damp; *(clima)* humid, damp, moist

humildad *nf* humility; *(pobreza)* humbleness

humilde *adj* humble, modest; *(pobre)* poor

humillación *nf* humiliation

humillante *adj* humiliating, humbling

humillar **1** *vt (rebajar)* to humiliate, to humble

2 **humillarse** *upr* **humillarse ante algn** to humble oneself before sb

humita *nf Andes, Arg (pasta de maíz)* = paste made of mashed maize o *US* corn, used to make steamed dumplings

humo *nm* (a) smoke; *(gas)* fumes; *(vapor)* vapour, steam (b) **¡qué humos tiene!** she thinks a lot of herself!

humor *nm* (a) *(genio)* mood; **estar de buen/mal h.** to be in a good/bad mood (b) *(carácter)* temper; **es persona de mal h.** he's bad-tempered (c) *(gracia)* humour; **sentido del h.** sense of humour

humorismo *nm* humour

humorista *nmf* humorist; **h. gráfico** cartoonist

humorístico,-a *adj* humorous, funny

hundido,-a *adj* (a) *(barco)* sunken; *(ojos)* deep-set (b) *Fig (abatido)* down, demoralized

hundimiento *nm* (a) *(de edificio)* collapse (b) *(de barco)* sinking (c) *(de tierra)* subsidence (d) *Fig Fin* crash, slump; *(ruina)* downfall

hundir **1** *vt* (a) *(barco)* to sink (b) *(edificio)* to bring o knock down (c) *Fig (desmoralizar)* to demoralize

2 **hundirse** *upr* (a) *(barco)* to sink (b) *(edificio)* to collapse (c) *Fig (empresa)* to collapse, to crash

húngaro,-a 1 *adj* Hungarian

2 *nm,f (persona)* Hungarian

3 *nm (idioma)* Hungarian

Hungría *n* Hungary

huracán *nm* hurricane

huraño,-a *adj Pey* unsociable

hurgar [42] **1** *vi (fisgar)* to poke one's nose in

2 *vt (fuego etc)* to poke, to rake

3 **hurgarse** *upr* **h. las narices** to pick one's nose

hurón,-ona 1 *nm Zool* ferret

2 *nm,f Fam Fig (fisgón)* busybody, nosey-parker

hurraca *nf Orn* = **urraca**

hurtadillas *adv* **a h.** stealthily, on the sly

hurtar *vt* to steal, to pilfer

hurto *nm* petty theft, pilfering

husmear **1** *vt (olfatear)* to sniff out, to scent

2 *vi Fig (curiosear)* to snoop, to pry

huyo *indic pres de* **huir**

i [i] *nf (la letra)* I, i; **i griega** Y, y

B *nm Educ (abr* **Instituto de Bachillerato**) ≃
state secondary school

b. *(abr* **ibídem**) ibid.

bérico,-a *adj* Iberian

beroamérica *n* Latin America

beroamericano,-a *adj & nm,f* Latin American

ceberg *nm (pl* **icebergs**) iceberg

CONA *nm Antes (abr* **Instituto Nacional para
a Conservación de la Naturaleza**) = Spanish
national institute for conservation

cono *nm* icon; *Informát* icon

conoclasta 1 *adj* iconoclastic
2 *nmf* iconoclast

conografía *nf* iconography

ctericia *nf Med* jaundice

d. *(abr* **ídem**) id

+D *(abr* **Investigación más Desarrollo**) R&D

da *nf* **billete de i. y vuelta** *Br* return ticket, *US*
round-trip ticket; **idas y venidas** comings and
goings

dea *nf* (a) idea; **i. fija** fixed idea (b) *(noción)*
idea; **hacerse a la i. de** to get used to the idea
of; *Fam* **ni i.** no idea, not a clue (c) *(opinión)*
opinion; **cambiar de i.** to change one's mind
(d) *(intención)* intention; **a mala i.** on purpose

deal *adj & nm* ideal

dealismo *nm* idealism

dealista 1 *adj* idealistic
2 *nmf* idealist

dealizar [40] *vt* to idealize, to glorify

dear *vt* (a) *(inventar)* to devise, to invent (b)
(concebir) to think up, to conceive

dem *adv* idem, ditto; *Fam* **í. de í.** exactly the
same

déntico,-a *adj* identical

dentidad *nf* (a) identity; **carnet de i.** identity
card (b) *(semejanza)* identity, sameness

dentificación *nf* identification

dentificar [44] **1** *vt* to identify
2 identificarse *vpr* to identify oneself; *Fig* **i.
con** to identify with

deología *nf* ideology

deológico,-a *adj* ideological

dílico,-a *adj* idyllic

dilio *nm* (a) *Lit* idyll (b) *Fig (romance)*
romance, love affair

dioma *nm* language

diomático,-a *adj* idiomatic

diosincrasia *nf* idiosyncrasy

idiota 1 *adj* idiotic, stupid
2 *nmf* idiot, fool

idiotez *nf* idiocy, stupidity

ido,-a *adj* (a) *(distraído)* absent-minded (b)
Fam (chiflado) crazy, nuts

idólatra 1 *adj* idolatrous
2 *nmf (hombre)* idolater; *(mujer)* idolatress

idolatrar *vt* to worship; *Fig* to idolize

idolatría *nf* idolatry

ídolo *nm* idol

idóneo,-a *adj* suitable, fit

iglesia *nf* (a) *(edificio)* church (b) **la i.** *(institución)* the Church

ignominia *nf* ignominy

ignominioso,-a *adj* ignominious, shameful

ignorancia *nf* ignorance

ignorante 1 *adj* (a) *(sin instrucción)* ignorant
(b) *(no informado)* ignorant, unaware (**de** of)
2 *nmf* ignoramus

ignorar 1 *vt* (a) *(algo)* not to know (b) *(a algn)*
to ignore
2 ignorarse *vpr* to be unknown

ignoto,-a *adj* unknown

igual 1 *adj* (a) *(idéntico)* the same, alike; **son
todos iguales** they're all the same; **es i.** it
doesn't matter; **i. que** the same as (b) *(equivalente)* equal; **a partes iguales** fifty-fifty (c)
Dep (empatados) even; **treinta iguales** thirty
all (d) *Mat* equal; **tres más tres i. a seis** three
plus three equals six (e) **al i. que** just like (f)
por i. equally
2 *nm* equal; **de i. a i.** on an equal footing; **sin
i.** unique, unrivalled
3 *adv* (a) **lo haces i. que yo** you do it the
same way I do (b) *(probablemente)* probably;
i. vengo I'll probably come (c) *Andes, RP (aún
así)* anyway, still; **estaba nublado pero i.
fuimos a la playa** it was cloudy but we still
went to the beach *o* we went to the beach
anyway

igualar 1 *vt* (a) to make equal (b) *(nivelar)* to
level (c) *Dep* **i. el partido** to equalize, to
square the match
2 igualarse *vpr* (a) to be equal (b) **igualarse
con algn** to place oneself on an equal footing
with sb

igualdad *nf* (a) equality; **i. ante la ley** equality before the law (b) *(identidad)* sameness;
en i. de condiciones on equal terms

igualitario,-a *adj* egalitarian

igualmente *adv* equally; *(también)* also,
likewise; *Fam* **encantado de conocerlo – ¡i.!**

pleased to meet you – likewise!

ijada *nf*, **ijar** *nm Anat* flank

ikastola *nf* = primary school in the Basque Country where classes are given entirely in Basque

ikurriña *nf* = Basque national flag

ilegal *adj* illegal

ilegalidad *nf* illegality

ilegalmente *adv* illegally

ilegible *adj* illegible, unreadable

ilegítimo,-a *adj* illegitimate

ileso,-a *adj* unhurt, unharmed

ilícito,-a *adj* illicit, unlawful

ilimitado,-a *adj* unlimited, limitless

Ilmo. (*abr* **Ilustrísimo**) His Excellence *o* Excellency

ilógico,-a *adj* illogical

iluminación *nf* (*alumbrado*) illumination, lighting

iluminar *vt* (a) to illuminate, to light (up) (b) *Fig* (*a persona*) to enlighten; (*tema*) to throw light upon

ilusión *nf* (a) (*esperanza*) hope; (*esperanza vana*) illusion, delusion; **hacerse ilusiones** to build up one's hopes (b) (*sueño*) dream (c) (*emoción*) excitement, thrill; **me hace i. verla** I'm looking forward to seeing her; **¡qué i.!** how exciting!

ilusionar 1 *vt* (a) (*esperanzar*) to build up sb's hopes (b) (*entusiasmar*) to excite, to thrill
  2 ilusionarse *vpr* (a) (*esperanzarse*) to build up one's hopes (b) (*entusiasmarse*) to be excited *o* thrilled (**con** about)

iluso,-a *adj* easily deceived, gullible

ilusorio,-a *adj* illusory, unreal

ilustración *nf* (a) (*grabado*) illustration, picture; (*ejemplo*) illustration (b) (*erudición*) learning, erudition; *Hist* **la I.** the Enlightenment

ilustrado,-a *adj* (a) (*con dibujos, ejemplos*) illustrated (b) (*erudito*) learned, erudite

ilustrar 1 *vt* (a) to illustrate (b) (*aclarar*) to explain, to make clear
  2 ilustrarse *vpr* to acquire knowledge (**sobre** of), to learn (**sobre** about)

ilustrativo,-a *adj* illustrative

ilustre *adj* illustrious, distinguished

imagen *nf* (a) image; **ser la viva i. de algn** to be the spitting image of sb; **tener buena i.** to have a good image (b) *Rel* image, statue (c) *TV* picture

imaginación *nf* imagination; **eso son imaginaciones tuyas** you're imagining things

imaginar 1 *vt* to imagine
  2 imaginarse *vpr* to imagine; **me imagino que sí** I suppose so

imaginario,-a *adj* imaginary

imaginativo,-a *adj* imaginative

imán *nm* magnet

imbatible *adj* unbeatable

imbatido,-a *adj* unbeaten, undefeated

imbécil 1 *adj* stupid, silly
  2 *nmf* idiot, imbecile

imbecilidad *nf* stupidity, imbecility

imborrable *adj* indelible

imbuir [37] *vt Fml* to imbue

imitación *nf* imitation

imitar *vt* to imitate; (*gestos*) to mimic; **este collar imita al oro** this necklace is imitation gold

impaciencia *nf* impatience

impacientar 1 *vt* **i. a algn** to make sb lose patience, to exasperate sb
  2 impacientarse *vpr* to get *o* grow impatient (**por** at)

impaciente *adj* (*deseoso*) impatient; (*intranquilo*) anxious

impactante *adj* **una noticia i.** a sensational piece of news

impactar *vt* to shock, to stun

impacto *nm* impact; *Mil* hit

impar *adj Mat* odd; **número i.** odd number

imparable *adj Dep* unstoppable

imparcial *adj* impartial, unbiased

imparcialidad *nf* impartiality

impartir *vt* (*clases*) to give

impasible *adj* impassive

impávido,-a *adj* fearless

impecable *adj* impeccable

impedido,-a 1 *adj* disabled, handicapped
  2 *nm,f* disabled *o* handicapped person

impedimento *nm* impediment; (*obstáculo*) hindrance, obstacle

impedir [6] *vt* (*obstaculizar*) to impede, to hinder; (*imposibilitar*) to prevent, to stop; **i. el paso** to block the way

impeler *vt Téc* to drive, to propel; *Fig* to drive, to impel

impenetrable *adj* impenetrable

impenitente *adj Rel* impenitent, unrepentant

impensable *adj* unthinkable

impepinable *adj Fam* dead sure, certain

imperante *adj* (*gobernante*) ruling; (*predominante*) prevailing

imperar *vi* (*gobernar*) to rule; (*predominar*) to prevail

imperativo,-a 1 *adj* imperative
  2 *nm Ling* imperative

imperceptible *adj* imperceptible

imperdible *nm* safety pin

imperdonable *adj* unforgivable, inexcusable

imperecedero,-a *adj* imperishable; *Fig* enduring

imperfección *nf* (a) imperfection (b) (*defecto*) defect, fault

imperfecto,-a *adj* (a) imperfect, fallible (b) (*defectuoso*) defective, faulty (c) *Ling* imperfect

imperial *adj* imperial

imperialismo *nm* imperialism

impericia *nf* incompetence

imperio *nm* empire; **el i. de la ley** the rule of law

imperioso,-a *adj* (**a**) *(autoritario)* imperious (**b**) *(ineludible)* urgent, imperative; **una necesidad imperiosa** a pressing need

impermeable 1 *adj* impermeable, impervious; *(ropa)* waterproof
2 *nm* raincoat, mac

impersonal *adj* impersonal

impertérrito,-a *adj* undaunted, fearless

impertinencia *nf* impertinence

impertinente 1 *adj (insolente)* impertinent; *(inoportuno)* irrelevant
2 *nmpl* **impertinentes** lorgnette

imperturbable *adj* imperturbable, unruffled

ímpetu *nm* (**a**) *(impulso)* impetus, momentum (**b**) *(violencia)* violence (**c**) *(energía)* energy

impetuosidad *nf* (**a**) *(violencia)* violence (**b**) *(fogosidad)* impetuosity, impulsiveness

impetuoso,-a *adj* (**a**) *(violento)* violent (**b**) *(fogoso)* impetuous, impulsive

impío,-a *adj* ungodly, irreligious

implacable *adj* relentless, implacable

implantar *vt (costumbres)* to implant, to instil; *(reformas)* to introduce; *Med* to implant

implicación *nf (participación)* involvement; *(significado)* implication

implicancia *nf CSur* implication

implicar [44] *vt* (**a**) *(involucrar)* to involve, to implicate (**en** in) (**b**) *(conllevar)* to imply

implícito,-a *adj* implicit, implied

implorar *vt* to implore, to beg

impoluto,-a *adj* pure, spotless

imponente *adj* (**a**) *(impresionante)* imposing, impressive (**b**) *(sobrecogedor)* stunning (**c**) *Fam (atractivo)* terrific, tremendous, smashing

imponer [19] *(pp* **impuesto)** **1** *vt* (**a**) to impose (**b**) *(respeto)* to inspire (**c**) *Fin* to deposit
2 *vi (impresionar)* to be impressive;
3 imponerse *upr* (**a**) *(infundir respeto)* to command respect (**b**) *(prevalecer)* to prevail (**c**) *(ser necesario)* to be necessary

imponible *adj Fin* taxable

impopular *adj* unpopular, disliked

importación *nf (mercancía)* import; *(acción)* importing; **artículos de i.** imported goods

importancia *nf* importance, significance; **dar i. a** to attach importance to; **sin i.** unimportant

importante *adj* important, significant; **una suma i.** a considerable sum

importar¹ 1 *vi* (**a**) *(atañer)* **eso no te importa a tí** that doesn't concern you, that's none of your business (**b**) *(tener importancia)* to be important; **no importa** it doesn't matter; *Fam* **me importa un bledo** *o* **un pito** I couldn't care less (**c**) *(molestar)* **¿te importaría repetirlo?** would you mind repeating it?; **¿te importa si fumo?** do you mind if I smoke?
2 *vt (valer)* to amount to; **los libros importan 2.000 pesetas** the books come to 2,000 pesetas

importar² *vt* to import

importe *nm Com & Fin* amount, total

importunar *vt* to bother, to pester

imposibilidad *nf* impossibility

imposibilitar *vt* (**a**) *(impedir)* to make impossible, to prevent (**b**) *(incapacitar)* to disable, to cripple

imposible *adj* impossible; **me es i. hacerlo** I can't (possibly) do it

imposición *nf* (**a**) *(disciplina, condiciones)* imposing (**b**) *Fin* deposit; *(impuesto)* taxation

impostor,-a *nm,f (farsante)* impostor

impotencia *nf* powerlessness, helplessness; *Med* impotence

impotente *adj* powerless, helpless; *Med* impotent

impracticable *adj* (**a**) *(inviable)* impracticable, unviable (**b**) *(camino)* impassable

imprecar [44] *vt* to imprecate, to curse

imprecisión *nf* imprecision, vagueness

impreciso,-a *adj* imprecise, vague

impregnar 1 *vt* to impregnate (**de** with)
2 impregnarse *upr* to become impregnated

imprenta *nf* (**a**) *(taller)* printer's, print works (**b**) *(aparato)* printing press (**c**) **libertad de i.** freedom of the press

imprescindible *adj* essential, indispensable

impresentable *adj* unpresentable

impresión *nf* (**a**) *Fig (efecto)* impression; **causar i.** to make an impression (**b**) *Fig (opinión)* impression; **cambiar impresiones** to exchange impressions (**c**) *Impr (acto)* printing; *(edición)* edition (**d**) *(huella)* impression, imprint

impresionable *adj* impressionable

impresionante *adj* impressive, striking; *Fam* **un error i.** *(tremendo)* a terrible mistake

impresionar *vt* (**a**) *(causar admiración)* to impress; *(sorprender)* to stun, to shock (**b**) *Fot* to expose

impresionismo *nm Arte* impressionism

impresionista *adj & nmf* impressionist

impreso,-a 1 *adj* printed
2 *nm* (**a**) *(papel, folleto)* printed matter (**b**) *(formulario)* form; **i. de solicitud** application form (**c**) **impresos** *(de correos)* printed matter

impresora *nf Informát* printer; **i. láser** laser printer; **i. de chorro de tinta** inkjet printer

imprevisible *adj* unforeseeable, unpredictable

imprevisión *nf* lack of foresight

imprevisto,-a 1 *adj* unforeseen, unexpected
2 *nm (incidente)* unforeseen event

imprimir *(pp* **impreso)** *vt* (**a**) *Impr & Informát* to print (**b**) *(marcar)* to stamp

improbable *adj* improbable, unlikely

ímprobo,-a *adj (inmoral)* dishonest, corrupt

improcedente *adj* (**a**) *(inadecuado)* inappropriate, unsuitable (**b**) *Jur* inadmissible

improductivo,-a *adj* unproductive

improperio *nm* insult, offensive remark

improbio,-a *adj (inadecuado)* inappropriate, unsuitable; **i. de** uncharacteristic of

improvisación *nf* improvisation; *Mús* extemporization

improvisado,-a *adj (espontáneo)* improvised, impromptu, ad lib; *(provisional)* makeshift; **discurso i.** impromptu speech

improvisar *vt* to improvise; *Mús* to extemporize

improviso *adj* **de i.** unexpectedly, suddenly; *Fam* **coger** *o* **pillar a algn de i.** to catch sb unawares

imprudencia *nf* imprudence, rashness; *(indiscreción)* indiscretion

imprudente *adj* imprudent, unwise; *(indiscreto)* indiscreet

impudicia *nf (falta de pudor)* immodesty; *(desvergüenza)* shamelessness

impudor *nm* immodesty; *(desvergüenza)* shamelessness

impuesto,-a 1 *nm Fin* tax; **i. sobre la renta** income tax; **libre de impuestos** tax-free; **i. sobre el valor añadido** value-added tax

2 *adj* imposed

impugnar *vt (teoría)* to refute, to disprove; *(decisión)* to challenge, to contest

impulsar *vt* to impel, to drive

impulsivo,-a *adj* impulsive

impulso *nm* impulse, thrust; *Dep* **tomar i.** to take a run-up

impune *adj* unpunished

impunemente *adv* with impunity

impunidad *nf* impunity

impureza *nf* impurity

impuro,-a *adj* impure

impuse *pt indef de* **imponer**

imputar *vt* to impute, to attribute

inabarcable *adj* unfathomable

inabordable *adj* unapproachable, inaccessible

inacabable *adj* interminable, endless

inaccesible *adj* inaccessible

inaceptable *adj* unacceptable

inactividad *nf* inactivity; *Fin* lull, stagnation

inactivo,-a *adj* inactive

inadaptación *nf* maladjustment

inadaptado,-a 1 *adj* maladjusted

2 *nm,f* misfit

inadecuado,-a *adj* unsuitable, inappropriate

inadmisible *adj* inadmissible

inadvertido,-a *adj (desapercibido)* unnoticed, unseen; **pasar i.** to escape notice, to pass unnoticed

inagotable *adj* (**a**) *(recursos etc)* inexhaustible (**b**) *(persona)* tireless, indefatigable

inaguantable *adj* unbearable, intolerable

inalámbrico,-a 1 *adj* cordless

2 *nm* cordless telephone

inalcanzable *adj* unattainable, unachievable

inalterable *adj* (**a**) unalterable (**b**) *(persona)* impassive, imperturbable

inamovible *adj* immovable, fixed

inanición *nf* starvation; *Med* inanition

inanimado,-a *adj* inanimate

inapreciable *adj* (**a**) *(valioso)* invaluable, inestimable (**b**) *(insignificante)* insignificant, trivial

inasequible *adj* (**a**) *(producto)* unaffordable (**b**) *(meta)* unattainable, unachievable (**c**) *(persona)* unapproachable, inaccessible (**d**) *(cuestión)* incomprehensible

inaudito,-a *adj* (**a**) *(sin precedente)* unprecedented (**b**) *Fig (escandaloso)* outrageous

inauguración *nf* inauguration, opening

inaugural *adj* inaugural, opening; **ceremonia i.** inaugural ceremony

inaugurar *vt* to inaugurate, to open

inca *adj & nmf* Inca

incalculable *adj* incalculable, indeterminate

incandescente *adj* white-hot, incandescent

incansable *adj* tireless, indefatigable

incapacidad *nf* incapacity, inability; **i. física** physical disability (**b**) *(incompetencia)* incompetence, inefficiency

incapacitado,-a *adj (imposibilitado)* incapacitated, disabled; *(desautorizado)* incapacitated

incapacitar *vt* (**a**) to incapacitate, to disable (**b**) *(inhabilitar)* to disqualify, to make unfit (**para** for)

incapaz *adj* (**a**) unable (**de** to), incapable (**de** of); **soy i. de continuar** I can't go on (**b**) *Jur* unfit

incario *nm* = period of the Inca empire

incautación *nf Jur* seizure, confiscation

incautarse *vpr Jur* **i. de** to seize, to confiscate

incauto,-a *adj* (**a**) *(imprudente)* incautious, unwary (**b**) *(crédulo)* gullible

incendiar [43] **1** *vt* to set fire to, to set alight

2 incendiarse *vpr* to catch fire

incendiario,-a 1 *adj* incendiary; *Fig (discurso etc)* inflammatory

2 *nm,f (persona)* arsonist, fire-raiser

incendio *nm* fire; **i. forestal** forest fire

incentivar *vt* to give an incentive to

incentivo *nm* incentive

incertidumbre *nf* uncertainty, doubt

incesante *adj* incessant, never-ending

incesto *nm* incest

incestuoso,-a *adj* incestuous

incidencia *nf* (**a**) *(repercusión)* impact, effect; **la huelga tuvo escasa i.** the strike had little effect (**b**) *(hecho)* incident (**c**) *Fís* incidence

incidente *nm* incident

incidir *vi* (**a**) *(incurrir)* to fall (**en** into) (**b**) **i. en** *(afectar)* to affect, to influence

incienso *nm* incense

incierto,-a *adj (inseguro)* uncertain

incineración *nf (de basuras)* incineration;

(de cadáveres) cremation

incinerar *vt (basura)* to incinerate; *(cadáveres)* to cremate

incipiente *adj* incipient, budding

incisión *nf* incision, cut

incisivo,-a 1 *adj (mordaz)* incisive, cutting; *(cortante)* sharp

　　2 *nm Anat* incisor

inciso *nm (paréntesis)* digression; **a modo de i.** in passing, incidentally

incitación *nf* incitement

incitante *adj* (a) *(instigador)* inciting (b) *(provocativo)* provocative

incitar *vt* to incite, to urge

incivil *adj* uncivil, rude

inclemencia *nf* inclemency, harshness

inclemente *adj* inclement, harsh

inclinación *nf* (a) *(de terreno)* slope, incline; *(del cuerpo)* stoop (b) *(reverencia)* bow (c) *Fig (tendencia)* tendency, inclination, penchant

inclinado,-a *adj* inclined, slanting; *Fig* **me siento i. a creerle** I feel inclined to believe him

inclinar 1 *vt* (a) to incline, to bend; *(cabeza)* to nod (b) *Fig (persuadir)* to persuade, to induce

　　2 inclinarse *vpr* (a) to lean, to slope, to incline (b) *(al saludar)* to bow; **i. ante** to bow down to (c) *Fig (optar)* **i. a** to be o feel inclined to; **me inclino por éste** I'd rather have this one, I prefer this one

incluido,-a *adj* (a) *(después del sustantivo)* included; *(antes del sustantivo)* including; **servicio no i.** service not included; **i. I.V.A.** including VAT; **todos pagan, incluidos los niños** everyone has to pay, including children (b) *(adjunto)* enclosed

incluir [37] *vt* (a) to include (b) *(contener)* to contain, to comprise (c) *(adjuntar)* to enclose

inclusión *nf* inclusion

inclusive *adv* (a) *(incluido)* inclusive; **de martes a viernes i.** from Tuesday to Friday inclusive; **hasta la lección ocho i.** up to and including lesson eight (b) *(incluso)* even

incluso *adv* even; **i. mi madre** even my mother

incoar *vt* defect *Jur* to initiate

incógnita *nf* (a) *Mat* unknown quantity, unknown (b) *(misterio)* mystery

incógnito *nm* **de i.** incognito

incoherencia *nf* incoherence

incoherente *adj* incoherent

incoloro,-a *adj* colourless

incólume *adj Fml* unharmed; **salir i.** to escape unharmed

incombustible *adj* incombustible, fireproof

incomodar 1 *vt* (a) *(causar molestia)* to inconvenience, to put out (b) *(fastidiar)* to bother, to annoy

　　2 incomodarse *vpr* (a) *(tomarse molestias)* to put oneself out, to go out of one's way (b) *(disgustarse)* to get annoyed o angry

incomodidad *nf (falta de comodidad)* discomfort; *(molestia)* inconvenience

incómodo,-a *adj* uncomfortable; **sentirse i.** to feel uncomfortable o awkward

incompatibilidad *nf* incompatibility; *Jur* **i. de caracteres** mutual incompatibility

incompatible *adj* incompatible

incompetencia *nf* incompetence

incompetente *adj & nmf* incompetent

incompleto,-a *adj* incomplete; *(inacabado)* unfinished

incomprensible *adj* incomprehensible

incomprensión *nf* lack of understanding, failure to understand; *(indiferencia)* lack of sympathy

incomunicado,-a *adj* (a) *(aislado)* isolated; **el pueblo se quedó i.** the town was cut off (b) *(en la cárcel)* in solitary confinement

incomunicar [44] *vt* (a) *(ciudad)* to isolate, to cut off (b) *(recluso)* to place in solitary confinement

inconcebible *adj* inconceivable, unthinkable

inconcluso,-a *adj* unfinished

incondicional 1 *adj* unconditional; *(apoyo)* wholehearted; *(amigo)* faithful; *(partidario)* staunch

　　2 *nm* die-hard

inconexo,-a *adj (incoherente)* incoherent, confused

inconformismo *nm* nonconformity

inconformista *adj & nmf* nonconformist

inconfundible *adj* unmistakable, obvious

incongruencia *nf* incongruity

incongruente *adj* incongruous

inconmensurable *adj* immeasurable, vast

inconsciencia *nf Med* unconsciousness; *Fig (irreflexión)* thoughtlessness; *(irresponsabilidad)* irresponsibility

inconsciente *adj* (a) *(con estar) (desmayado)* unconscious (b) *(con ser) (despreocupado)* unaware (**de** of); *Fig (irreflexivo)* thoughtless, irresponsible

inconsecuente *adj* inconsistent

inconsistente *adj* flimsy; *(argumento)* weak

inconstancia *nf* inconstancy, fickleness

inconstante *adj* inconstant, fickle

incontable *adj* countless, innumerable

incontenible *adj* uncontrollable, irrepressible

incontestable *adj* indisputable, unquestionable

incontinencia *nf* incontinence

incontrolable *adj* uncontrollable

incontrolado,-a 1 *adj* uncontrolled

　　2 *nm,f* troublemaker

inconveniencia *nf* (a) inconvenience (b) *(impropiedad)* unsuitability

inconveniente 1 *adj* (a) inconvenient (b) *(inapropiado)* unsuitable

　　2 *nm* (a) *(objeción)* objection; **poner inconvenientes** to raise objections (b) *(desventaja)*

disadvantage, drawback; *(problema)* difficulty; **¿tienes i. en acompañarme?** would you mind coming with me?

incordiar [43] *vt Fam* to bother, to pester

incordio *nm Fam* nuisance, pain

incorporación *nf* incorporation

incorporar 1 *vt* (**a**) to incorporate (**en** into) (**b**) *(levantar)* to help to sit up
2 incorporarse *vpr* (**a**) **i. a** *(sociedad)* to join; *(trabajo)* to start; *Mil* **i. a filas** to join up (**b**) *(en la cama)* to sit up

incorrección *nf* (**a**) *(falta)* incorrectness, inaccuracy; *(gramatical)* mistake (**b**) *(descortesía)* discourtesy, impropriety

incorrecto,-a *adj* (**a**) *(equivocado)* incorrect, inaccurate (**b**) *(grosero)* impolite, discourteous

incorregible *adj* incorrigible

incrédulo,-a 1 *adj* (**a**) incredulous, disbelieving (**b**) *Rel* unbelieving
2 *nm,f* (**a**) disbeliever (**b**) *Rel* unbeliever

increíble *adj* incredible, unbelievable

incrementar 1 *vt* to increase
2 incrementarse *vpr* to increase

incremento *nm (aumento)* increase; *(crecimiento)* growth; **i. de la temperatura** rise in temperature

increpar *vt Fml* to rebuke, to reprimand

incruento,-a *adj* bloodless

incrustar *vt* (**a**) *(insertar)* to encrust *o* incrust (**b**) *(embutir)* to inlay; **incrustado con perlas** inlaid with pearls

incubadora *nf* incubator

incubar *vt* to incubate

incuestionable *adj* unquestionable, indisputable

inculcar [44] *vt (principios, ideas)* to instil (**en** into)

inculpado,-a *nm,f* **el i.** the accused

inculpar *vt* to accuse (**de** of), to blame (**de** for); *Jur* to charge (**de** with)

inculto,-a 1 *adj (ignorante)* uneducated, uncouth
2 *nm,f* ignoramus

incultura *nf (ignorancia)* ignorance, lack of culture

incumbencia *nf* **no es de mi i.** it doesn't come within my province, it isn't my concern

incumbir *vi* to be incumbent (**a** upon); **esto no te incumbe** this is none of your business

incumplimiento *nm (de un deber)* nonfulfilment; *(de una orden)* failure to execute; **i. de contrato** breach of contract

incumplir *vt* not to fulfil; *(deber)* to fail to fulfil; *(promesa, contrato)* to break; *(orden)* to fail to carry out

incurrir *vi (cometer)* to fall (**en** into); **i. en delito** to commit a crime; **i. en (un) error** to fall into error

incursión *nf* raid, incursion

incursionar *vi Am* (**a**) *(en ciudad, territorio)* to make an incursion (**b**) **i. en algo** *(tema,*

asunto) to dabble in sth

indagar [42] *vt* to investigate, to inquire into

indebido,-a *adj* (**a**) *(desconsiderado)* improper, undue (**b**) *(ilegal)* unlawful, illegal

indecencia *nf* indecency, obscenity

indecente *adj* (**a**) *(impúdico)* indecent (**b**) *(impresentable)* dreadful

indecible *adj* unspeakable; *(inefable)* indescribable; **sufrir lo i.** to suffer agonies

indecisión *nf* indecision, hesitation

indeciso,-a *adj* (**a**) *(vacilante)* hesitant, irresolute (**b**) *(resultados etc)* inconclusive

indefenso,-a *adj* defenceless, helpless

indefinidamente *adv* indefinitely

indefinido,-a *adj* (**a**) *(indeterminado)* indefinite; *(impreciso)* undefined, vague (**b**) *Ling* indefinite

indeleble *adj* indelible

indemne *adj (persona)* unharmed, unhurt; *(cosa)* undamaged

indemnización *nf* (**a**) *(acto)* indemnification (**b**) *Fin (compensación)* indemnity, compensation; **i. por despido** redundancy payment

indemnizar [40] *vt* to indemnify, to compensate (**por** for)

independencia *nf* independence

independiente *adj (libre)* independent; *(individualista)* self-reliant

independientemente *adv* (**a**) independently (**de** of) (**b**) *(aparte de)* regardless, irrespective (**de** of)

independizar [40] **1** *vt* to make independent, to grant independence to
2 independizarse *vpr* to become independent

indescifrable *adj* indecipherable

indescriptible *adj* indescribable

indeseable *adj & nmf* undesirable

indeterminación *nf* indecision, irresolution

indeterminado,-a *adj* (**a**) indefinite; *(impreciso)* vague (**b**) *(persona)* irresolute (**c**) *Ling* indefinite

India *nf* **(la) I.** India

Indias *nfpl* **(las) I.** the Indies; **las I. Orientales/Occidentales** the East/West Indies

indicación *nf* (**a**) *(señal)* indication, sign (**b**) *(instrucción)* instruction, direction; **por i. de algn** at sb's suggestion

indicado,-a *adj* right, suitable; **a la hora indicada** at the specified time; **en el momento menos i.** at the worst possible moment

indicador *nm* (**a**) indicator (**b**) *Téc* gauge, dial, meter; *Aut* **i. del nivel de aceite** (oil) dipstick; *Aut* **i. de velocidad** speedometer

indicar [44] *vt (señalar)* to indicate, to show, to point out; **¿me podría i. el camino?** could you show me the way?

indicativo,-a *adj* (**a**) indicative (**de** of) (**b**) *Ling* **(modo) i.** indicative (mood)

índice *nm* (**a**) *(de libro)* index, table of contents (**b**) *(relación)* rate; **í. de natalidad/**

mortalidad birth/death rate; *Fin* **í. de precios** price index (**c**) *Anat* (**dedo**) **í.** index finger, forefinger

indicio *nm* (**a**) *(señal)* indication, sign, token (**de** of) (**b**) *Jur* **indicios** *(prueba)* evidence

índico,-a *adj* Indian; **Océano Í.** Indian Ocean

indiferencia *nf* indifference, apathy

indiferente *adj* (**a**) *(no importante)* unimportant; **me es i.** it makes no difference to me (**b**) *(apático)* indifferent

indígena 1 *adj* indigenous, native (**de** to)
    2 *nmf* native (**de** of)

indigencia *nf Fml* poverty, indigence

indigente *adj Fml* needy, poverty-stricken

indigestarse *vpr* (**a**) **se le indigestó la comida** the meal gave her indigestion (**b**) *(sufrir indigestión)* to get indigestion

indigestión *nf* indigestion

indigesto,-a *adj (comida)* indigestible, difficult to digest; **me siento i.** I've got indigestion

indignación *nf* indignation

indignado,-a *adj* indignant (**por** at *o* about)

indignante *adj* outrageous, infuriating

indignar 1 *vt* to infuriate, to make angry
    2 indignarse *vpr* to be *o* feel indignant (**por** at *o* about)

indigno,-a *adj* (**a**) unworthy (**de** of) (**b**) *(despreciable)* wretched, dreadful

indio,-a *adj & nm,f* Indian; **en fila india** in single file; *Fam* **hacer el i.** to act the fool

indirecta *nf Fam (insinuación)* hint, insinuation; **tirar** *o* **lanzar una i.** to drop a hint; **coger la i.** to get the message

indirecto,-a *adj* indirect; *Ling* **estilo i.** indirect *o* reported speech

indisciplinado,-a *adj* undisciplined, unruly

indiscreción *nf* indiscretion; *(comentario)* tactless remark

indiscreto,-a *adj* indiscreet, tactless

indiscutible *adj* indisputable, unquestionable

indispensable *adj* indispensable, essential

indisponer [19] *(pp* **indispuesto**) **1** *vt* to upset, to make unwell
    2 indisponerse *vpr* (**a**) to fall ill, to become unwell (**b**) *Fig* **i. con algn** to fall out with sb

indispuesto,-a *adj* indisposed, unwell

indispuse *pt indef de* **indisponer**

indistintamente *adv* **pueden escribir en inglés o en español i.** you can write in English or in Spanish, it doesn't matter which

indistinto,-a *adj (indiferente)* immaterial, inconsequential

individual 1 *adj* individual; **habitación i.** single room
    2 *nmpl Dep* **individuales** singles

individualismo *nm* individualism

individualista 1 *adj* individualistic
    2 *nmf* individualist

individuo *nm* (**a**) individual (**b**) *(tío)* bloke, guy

índole *nf* (**a**) *(carácter)* character, nature (**b**)

(clase, tipo) kind, sort

indolencia *nf* indolence, laziness

indolente 1 *adj* indolent, lazy
    2 *nmf* idler

indomable *adj* (**a**) *(animal)* untamable (**b**) *(pueblo)* ungovernable, unruly; *(niño)* uncontrollable; *(pasión)* indomitable

indómito,-a *adj* (**a**) *(no domado)* untamed; *(indomable)* untamable (**b**) *(pueblo)* unruly; *(persona)* uncontrollable

Indonesia *n* Indonesia

inducir [10] *vt* (**a**) *(incitar, mover)* to lead, to induce; **i. a error** to lead into error, to mislead (**b**) *Elec (corriente)* to induce

inductivo,-a *adj* inductive

indudable *adj* indubitable, unquestionable; **es i. que** there is no doubt that

induje *pt indef de* **inducir**

indulgencia *nf* indulgence, leniency

indulgente *adj* indulgent (**con** towards), lenient (**con** with)

indultar *vt Jur* to pardon

indulto *nm Jur* pardon, amnesty

indumentaria *nf* clothing, clothes

industria *nf* industry

industrial 1 *adj* industrial
    2 *nmf* industrialist

industrialización *nf* industrialization

industrializar [40] *vt* to industrialize

induzco *indic pres de* **inducir**

INE *nm* (*abr* **Instituto Nacional de Estadística**) = organization that publishes official statistics about Spain

inédito,-a *adj* (**a**) *(libro, texto)* unpublished (**b**) *(nuevo)* completely new; *(desconocido)* unknown

inefable *adj* ineffable, indescribable

ineficacia *nf (ineptitud)* inefficiency; *(inutilidad)* ineffectiveness

ineficaz *adj (inepto)* inefficient; *(inefectivo)* ineffective

ineludible *adj* inescapable, unavoidable

INEM *nm* (*abr* **Instituto Nacional de Empleo**) = Spanish department of employment

ineptitud *nf* ineptitude, incompetence

inepto,-a 1 *adj* inept, incompetent
    2 *nm,f* incompetent person

inequívoco,-a *adj* unmistakable, unequivocal

inercia *nf* (**a**) *Fís* inertia (**b**) *Fig (pasividad)* inertia, passivity; **hacer algo por i.** to do sth out of habit

inerte *adj (inanimado)* inert; *(inmóvil)* motionless

inesperado,-a *adj (fortuito)* unexpected, unforeseen; *(imprevisto)* sudden

inestabilidad *nf* instability

inestable *adj* unstable, unsteady

inestimable *adj* inestimable, invaluable

inevitable *adj* inevitable, unavoidable

inexistente *adj* non-existent

inexorable *adj* inexorable

inexperiencia *nf* lack of experience

inexperto,-a *adj (inexperto)* inexpert; *(sin experiencia)* inexperienced

inexplicable *adj* inexplicable

inexpugnable *adj Mil* impregnable

infalible *adj* infallible

infamar *vt* to defame, to slander

infame *adj (vil)* infamous, vile; *(despreciable)* dreadful, awful

infamia *nf* disgrace, infamy

infancia *nf* childhood, infancy

infanta *nf* infanta, princess

infante *nm* (a) infante, prince (b) *Mil* infantryman

infantería *nf Mil* infantry; **la i. de marina** the marines

infantil *adj* (a) **literatura i.** *(para niños)* children's literature (b) *(aniñado)* childlike; *Pey* childish, infantile

infarto *nm Med* infarction, infarct; **i. (de miocardio)** heart attack, coronary thrombosis; *Fam* **de i.** thrilling, stunning

infatigable *adj* indefatigable, tireless

infección *nf* infection

infeccioso,-a *adj* infectious

infectar 1 *vt* to infect

2 infectarse *vpr* to become infected (**de** with)

infeliz 1 *adj* unhappy; *(desdichado)* unfortunate

2 *nmf Fam* simpleton; **es un pobre i.** he is a poor devil

inferior 1 *adj* (a) *(más bajo)* lower (b) *(calidad)* inferior; **de calidad i.** of inferior quality (c) *(cantidad)* lower, less; **i. a la media** below average

2 *nmf (persona)* subordinate, inferior

inferioridad *nf* inferiority; **estar en i. de condiciones** to be at a disadvantage; **complejo de i.** inferiority complex

inferir [5] *vt Literario (deducir)* to infer, to deduce (**de** from)

infernal *adj* infernal, hellish; *Fig* **había un ruido i.** there was a hell of a noise

infestar *vt* (a) **infestado de** *(parásitos)* infested with; *(plantas)* overgrown with (b) *Fig (llenar)* to overrun, to invade; **infestado de turistas** swarming with tourists (c) *(infectar)* to infect

infición *nf Méx* pollution

infidelidad *nf* infidelity, unfaithfulness

infiel 1 *adj (desleal)* unfaithful

2 *nmf Rel* infidel

infierno *nm* (a) *Rel* hell (b) *Fig (tormento)* hell; **su vida es un i.** his life is sheer hell (c) *(horno)* inferno; **en verano esto es un i.** in summer it's like an inferno here; *Fam* **¡vete al i.!** go to hell!, get lost!

infiltración *nf (de agua)* infiltration; *(de noticia)* leak

infiltrado,-a *nm,f* infiltrator

infiltrar 1 *vt* to infiltrate; *(noticia)* to leak

2 infiltrarse *vpr* to infiltrate (**en** into)

ínfimo,-a *adj Fml (mínimo)* extremely low; **detalle í.** smallest detail; **ínfima calidad** very poor quality

infinidad *nf* (a) infinity (b) *(sinfín)* great number; **en i. de ocasiones** on countless occasions

infinitivo,-a *adj & nm Ling* infinitive

infinito,-a 1 *adj* infinite, endless

2 *nm* infinity

3 *adv Fam (muchísimo)* infinitely, immensely

inflación *nf Econ* inflation

inflacionario,-a, inflacionista *adj Econ* inflationary

inflamable *adj* flammable

inflamación *nf Med* inflammation

inflamar 1 *vt* (a) *Med* to inflame (b) *(encender)* to set on fire, to ignite

2 inflamarse *vpr* (a) *Med* to become inflamed (b) *(incendiarse)* to catch fire

inflar 1 *vt* (a) *(hinchar)* to inflate, to blow up; *Náut (vela)* to swell (b) *Fig (exagerar)* to exaggerate

2 inflarse *vpr* (a) to inflate; *Náut (vela)* to swell (b) *Fam* **i. de** to overdo; **se inflaron de macarrones** they stuffed themselves with macaroni

inflexible *adj* inflexible

infligir [57] *vt* to inflict

influencia *nf* influence; **ejercer** *o* **tener i. sobre algn** to have an influence on *o* upon sb; **tener influencias** to be influential; **tráfico de influencias** Old-Boy network

influenciar [43] *vt* to influence

influir [37] **1** *vt* to influence

2 *vi* (a) to have influence (b) **i. en** *o* **sobre** to influence, to have an influence on

influjo *nm* influence

influyente *adj* influential

información *nf* (a) information; **oficina de i.** information bureau (b) **una i.** *(noticia)* a piece of news, news *sing* (c) *Tel Br* directory enquiries, *US* information (d) *(referencias)* references

informado,-a *adj* informed; **de fuentes bien informadas** from well-informed sources

informal *adj* (a) *(reunión, cena)* informal (b) *(comportamiento)* casual (c) *(persona)* unreliable, untrustworthy

informalidad *nf (incumplimiento)* unreliability; *(desenfado)* informality

informar 1 *vt* to inform (**de** of); *(dar informes)* to report

2 informarse *vpr (procurarse noticias)* to find out (**de** about); *(enterarse)* to inquire (**de** about)

informática *nf* computing, information technology

informático,-a 1 *adj* computer, computing

2 *nm,f* (computer) technician

informativo,-a 1 *adj* (a) *Rad & TV* news; **boletín i.** news (broadcast) (b) *(explicativo)*

informative, explanatory
  2 *nm Rad & TV* news bulletin
informe *nm* (**a**) report (**b**) **informes** references; **pedir informes sobre algn** to make inquiries about sb
infracción *nf* (*de ley*) infringement, breach (**de** of)
infractor,-a *nm,f* offender
infraestructura *nf* infrastructure
in fraganti *loc adv* in the act; **coger** *o* **pillar a algn i.** to catch sb redhanded
infrahumano,-a *adj* subhuman
infranqueable *adj* impassable; *Fig* insurmountable
infrarrojo,-a *adj* infrared
infrautilizar *vt* to underutilize
infringir [57] *vt* to infringe, to contravene; **i. una ley** to break a law
infructuoso,-a *adj* fruitless, unsuccessful
infundado,-a *adj* unfounded, groundless
infundir *vt* to infuse; *Fig* to instil; **i. dudas** to give rise to doubt; **i. respeto** to command respect
infusión *nf* infusion
infuso,-a *adj Fam Irón* **ciencia infusa** sheer genius
ingeniar [43] **1** *vt* to invent, to devise
  2 ingeniarse *vpr* **ingeniárselas para hacer algo** to manage to do sth
ingeniería *nf* engineering
ingeniero,-a *nm,f* engineer; **i. agrónomo** agricultural engineer; **i. de caminos** civil engineer; **i. de minas/montes** mining/forestry engineer; **i. de telecomunicaciones** telecommunications engineer; **i. técnico** technician
ingenio *nm* (**a**) (*talento*) talent; (*inventiva*) inventiveness, creativeness; (*agudeza*) wit (**b**) (*aparato*) device
ingenioso,-a *adj* ingenious, clever; (*vivaz*) witty
ingente *adj* huge, enormous
ingenuidad *nf* ingenuousness, naïveté
ingenuo,-a 1 *adj* ingenuous, naïve
  2 *nm,f* naïve person
ingerir [5] *vt* (*comida*) to ingest, to consume; (*líquidos, alcohol*) to drink, to consume
Inglaterra *n* England
ingle *nf Anat* groin
inglés,-esa 1 *adj* English
  2 *nm,f* (*hombre*) Englishman; (*mujer*) Englishwoman; **los ingleses** the English
  3 *nm* (*idioma*) English
ingratitud *nf* ingratitude, ungratefulness
ingrato,-a 1 *adj* (**a**) (*persona*) ungrateful (**b**) (*noticia*) unpleasant (**c**) (*trabajo*) thankless, unrewarding (**d**) (*tierra*) unproductive
  2 *nm,f* ungrateful person
ingrediente *nm* ingredient
ingresar 1 *vt* (**a**) *Fin* to deposit, to pay in (**b**) *Med* to admit; **la ingresaron en el hospital** she was admitted to hospital
  2 *vi* (**a**) to enter; **i. en el ejército** to enlist in

the army, to join the army; **i. en un club** to join a club (**b**) **i. cadáver** to be dead on arrival
ingreso *nm* (**a**) *Fin* deposit; **hacer un i. en una cuenta** to pay money into an account (**b**) (*entrada*) entry (**en** into); (*admisión*) admission (**en** to) (**c**) **ingresos** (*sueldo, renta*) income; (*beneficios*) revenue
inhábil *adj* (**a**) (*incapaz*) unfit; **i. para el trabajo** unfit for work (**b**) **día i.** non-working day
inhabilitación *nf* (**a**) *Fml* (*incapacidad*) disablement (**b**) *Jur* disqualification
inhabilitar *vt* (**a**) *Fml* (*incapacitar*) to disable; **inhabilitado para el trabajo** unfit for work (**b**) *Jur* to disqualify
inhabitable *adj* uninhabitable

> 🖋 Observa que la palabra inglesa **inhabitable** es un falso amigo y no es la traducción de la palabra española **inhabitable**. En inglés, **inhabitable** significa "habitable".

inhalación *nf* inhalation
inhalador *nm Med* inhaler
inhalar *vt* to inhale
inherente *adj* inherent (**a** in)
inhibición *nf* inhibition
inhibir 1 *vt* to inhibit
  2 inhibirse *vpr* (**a**) (*cohibirse*) to be *o* feel inhibited (**b**) (*abstenerse*) to refrain (**de** from)
inhóspito,-a *adj* inhospitable
inhumación *nf* burial
inhumano,-a *adj* inhumane; (*cruel*) inhuman
inhumar *vt* to bury
INI *nm Antes* (*abr* **Instituto Nacional de Industria**) = Spanish governmental organization that promotes industry
inicial *adj & nf* initial; **punto i.** starting point
iniciar [43] **1** *vt* (**a**) (*empezar*) to begin, to start; (*discusión*) to initiate; (*una cosa nueva*) to pioneer (**b**) (*introducir*) to initiate
  2 iniciarse *vpr* (**a**) **i. en algo** (*aprender*) to start to study sth (**b**) (*empezar*) to begin, to start
iniciativa *nf* initiative; **i. privada** private enterprise; **por i. propia** on one's own initiative
inicio *nm* beginning, start; **a inicios de** at the beginning of
inimitable *adj* inimitable
ininterrumpido,-a *adj* uninterrupted, continuous
iniquidad *nf* iniquity
injerencia *nf* interference, meddling (**en** in)
injerirse *vpr* to interfere, to meddle (**en** in)
injertar *vt Agr & Med* to graft
injerto *nm* graft
injuria *nf* (*insulto*) insult, affront; (*agravio*) outrage
injuriar [43] *vt* (*insultar*) to insult; (*ultrajar*) to outrage
injusticia *nf* injustice, unfairness

injustificado,-a adj unjustified

injusto,-a adj unjust, unfair

inmaculado,-a adj immaculate

inmadurez nf immaturity

inmaduro,-a adj immature

inmediaciones nfpl neighbourhood

inmediatamente adv immediately, at once

inmediato,-a adj (a) (en el tiempo) immediate; **de i.** at once (b) (en el espacio) next (a to), adjoining

inmejorable adj (trabajo) excellent; (precio) unbeatable

inmemorial adj immemorial; **desde tiempos inmemoriales** since time immemorial

inmensidad nf immensity, enormity

inmenso,-a adj immense, vast

inmerecido,-a adj undeserved, unmerited

inmersión nf immersion; (de submarino) dive

inmerso,-a adj immersed (en in)

inmigración nf immigration

inmigrante adj & nmf immigrant

inmigrar vi to immigrate

inminente adj imminent, impending

inmiscuirse [37] vpr to interfere, to meddle (en in)

inmobiliaria nf Br estate agent's, US real estate company

inmobiliario,-a adj property, US real-estate; **agente i.** Br estate agent, US realtor

inmolar vt Fml to immolate, to sacrifice

inmoral adj immoral

inmoralidad nf immorality

inmortal adj & nmf immortal

inmortalidad nf immortality

inmortalizar [40] vt to immortalize

inmóvil adj motionless, immobile

inmovilista adj ultra-conservative

inmovilizar [40] vt (a) (persona, cosa) to immobilize (b) Fin (capital) to immobilize, to tie up

inmueble 1 adj **bienes inmuebles** real estate

2 nm building

inmundicia nf (a) (suciedad) dirt, filth; Fig dirtiness (b) (basura) rubbish, refuse

inmundo,-a adj dirty, filthy; Fig nasty

inmune adj immune (a to), exempt (de from)

inmunidad nf immunity (contra against); **i. diplomática/parlamentaria** diplomatic/parliamentary immunity

inmunizar [40] vt to immunize (contra against)

inmutarse vpr to change countenance; **ni se inmutó** he didn't turn a hair

innato,-a adj innate, inborn

innecesario,-a adj unnecessary

innegable adj undeniable

innovación nf innovation

innovar vt & vi to innovate

innumerable adj innumerable, countless

inocencia nf (a) innocence (b) (ingenuidad) naïveté

inocentada nf Fam ≃ April Fool's joke; **hacer una i. a algn** to play an April Fool's joke on sb

inocente 1 adj innocent

2 nmf innocent; **día de los Inocentes** Holy Innocents' Day, 28 December, ≃ April Fools' Day

inocuo,-a adj innocuous

inodoro,-a 1 adj odourless

2 nm toilet, lavatory

inofensivo,-a adj harmless

inolvidable adj unforgettable

inoperante adj ineffective

inopia nf Fig **estar en la i.** to be in the clouds, to be miles away

inopinado,-a adj unexpected

inoportuno,-a adj inappropriate; **llegó en un momento muy i.** he turned up at a very awkward moment

inorgánico,-a adj inorganic

inoxidable adj **acero i.** stainless steel

inquebrantable adj Fig unshakable; (persona) unyielding

inquietante adj worrying

inquietar 1 vt to worry

2 inquietarse vpr to worry (por about)

inquieto,-a adj (a) (preocupado) worried (por about) (b) (intranquilo) restless (c) (emprendedor) eager

inquietud nf (a) (preocupación) worry (b) (agitación) restlessness (c) (anhelo) eagerness

inquilino,-a nm,f tenant

inquirir [31] vt to investigate

inquisitivo,-a adj inquisitive

inri nm Fam insult; **para más o mayor i.** to make matters worse

insaciable adj insatiable

insalubre adj unhealthy

INSALUD nm (abr **Instituto Nacional de la Salud**) = Spanish national health service, Br ≃ NHS, US ≃ Medicaid

insano,-a adj (a) (loco) insane, mad (b) (insalubre) unhealthy

insatisfecho,-a adj dissatisfied

inscribir (pp **inscrito**) **1** vt (a) (registrar) to register; **i. a un niño en el registro civil** to register a child's birth (b) (matricular) to enrol (c) (grabar) to inscribe

2 inscribirse vpr (a) (registrarse) to register; (hacerse miembro) to join (b) (matricularse) to enrol

inscripción nf (a) (matriculación) enrolment, registration (b) (escrito etc) inscription

insecticida nm insecticide

insecto nm insect

inseguridad nf (a) (falta de confianza) insecurity (b) (duda) uncertainty (c) (peligro) lack of safety; **la i. ciudadana** the breakdown of law and order

inseguro,-a adj (a) (poco confiado) insecure (b) (dubitativo) uncertain (c) (peligroso) unsafe

inseminar vt to inseminate

insensatez *nf* foolishness
insensato,-a 1 *adj* foolish
  2 *nm,f* fool
insensibilidad *nf* insensitivity
insensible *adj* (**a**) *(indiferente)* insensitive (**a** to), unfeeling (**b**) *(imperceptible)* imperceptible (**c**) *Med* numb
inseparable *adj* inseparable
insertar *vt* to insert
inservible *adj* useless
insidia *nf* (**a**) *(trampa)* malicious ploy (**b**) *(malicia)* maliciousness
insidioso,-a *adj* insidious
insigne *adj* distinguished
insignia *nf* (**a**) *(emblema)* badge (**b**) *(bandera)* flag
insignificancia *nf* (**a**) *(intrascendencia)* insignificance (**b**) *(nadería)* trifle
insignificante *adj* insignificant
insinuación *nf* insinuation
insinuante *adj* insinuating; *(atrevido)* forward
insinuar [30] **1** *vt* to insinuate
  2 insinuarse *vpr* **i. a algn** to make advances to sb
insípido,-a *adj* insipid; *Fig* dull, flat
insistencia *nf* insistence; **con i.** insistently
insistente *adj* insistent
insistir *vi* to insist (**en** on); **insistió en ese punto** he stressed that point
insociable *adj* unsociable
insolación *nf Med* sunstroke; **coger una i.** to get sunstroke
insolencia *nf* insolence
insolente *adj* insolent
insolidaridad *nf* unsupportive stance
insólito,-a *adj* (*poco usual*) unusual; *(extraño)* strange, odd
insoluble *adj* insoluble
insolvencia *nf Fin* insolvency
insolvente *adj Fin* insolvent
insomnio *nm* insomnia; **noche de i.** sleepless night
insondable *adj* unfathomable
insonorizado,-a *adj* soundproof
insonorizar [40] *vt* to soundproof
insoportable *adj* unbearable
insospechado,-a *adj* unsuspected
insostenible *adj* untenable
inspección *nf* inspection
inspeccionar *vt* to inspect
inspector,-a *nm,f* inspector; **i. de Hacienda** tax inspector
inspiración *nf* (**a**) inspiration (**b**) *(inhalación)* inhalation
inspirado,-a *adj* inspired
inspirar 1 *vt* (**a**) to inspire (**b**) *(inhalar)* to inhale, to breathe in
  2 inspirarse *vpr* **i. en** to be inspired by
instalación *nf* installation; **instalaciones deportivas** sports facilities
instalar 1 *vt* (**a**) to install (**b**) *(puesto, tienda)* to set up
  2 instalarse *vpr (persona)* to settle (down)
instancia *nf* (**a**) *(solicitud)* request; **a instancia(s) de** at the request of (**b**) *(escrito)* application form (**c**) *Jur* **tribunal de primera i.** court of first instance (**d**) **en primera i.** first of all; **en última i.** as a last resort

> *Observa que la palabra inglesa* **instance** *es un falso amigo y no es la traducción de la palabra española* **instancia**. *En inglés,* **instance** *significa "caso, ejemplo".*

instantánea *nf* snapshot
instantáneamente *adv* instantly
instantáneo,-a *adj* instantaneous; **café i.** instant coffee
instante *nm* instant, moment; **a cada i.** constantly; **al i.** immediately, right away; **por instantes** with every second; **¡un i.!** just a moment!
instar *vt* to urge
instauración *nf* founding
instaurar *vt* to found
instigador,-a *nm,f* instigator
instigar [42] *vt* to instigate; **i. a la rebelión** to incite a rebellion
instintivo,-a *adj* instinctive
instinto *nm* instinct; **por i.** instinctively; **i. de conservación** survival instinct
institución *nf* institution
instituir [37] *vt* to institute
instituto *nm* (**a**) institute (**b**) *Educ Br* state secondary school, *US* high school
institutriz *nf* governess
instituyo *indic pres de* **instituir**
instrucción *nf* (**a**) *(educación)* education (**b**) *(usu pl)* *(indicación)* instruction; **instrucciones para el o de uso** directions for use (**c**) *Jur* preliminary investigation; **la i. del sumario** proceedings; **juez de i.** examining magistrate (**d**) *Mil* drill
instructivo,-a *adj* instructive
instruido,-a *adj* educated, well-educated
instruir [37] *vt* (**a**) to instruct (**b**) *(enseñar)* to educate (**c**) *Mil* to drill (**d**) *Jur* to investigate
instrumental *adj* instrumental
instrumento *nm* instrument
insubordinación *nf* insubordination
insubordinado,-a *adj* insubordinate
insubordinarse *vpr (sublevarse)* to rebel (**contra** against)
insuficiencia *nf* insufficiency
insuficiente 1 *adj* insufficient
  2 *nm Educ (nota)* fail
insufrible *adj* insufferable
insular 1 *adj* insular, island
  2 *nmf* islander
insulso,-a *adj* insipid
insultante *adj* insulting
insultar *vt* to insult
insulto *nm* insult

insumisión *nf* = refusal to do military service

insumiso,-a 1 *adj* unsubmissive
  2 *nm* = person who refuses to do military service

insuperable *adj* (**a**) *(inmejorable)* unsurpassable (**b**) *(problema)* insurmountable

insurgente *adj & nmf* insurgent

insurrección *nf* insurrection

intachable *adj* irreproachable; **conducta i.** impeccable behaviour

intacto,-a *adj* intact

integral 1 *adj* integral; *Culin* **pan i.** wholemeal bread; **arroz i.** brown rice
  2 *nf Mat* integral

integrante 1 *adj* integral; **ser parte i. de** to be an integral part of
  2 *nm* member

integrar 1 *vt (formar)* to compose, to make up; **el equipo lo integran once jugadores** there are eleven players in the team
  2 integrarse *vpr* to integrate (**en** with)

integridad *nf* integrity

íntegro,-a *adj* (**a**) *(entero)* whole, entire; *Cin & Lit* **versión íntegra** unabridged version (**b**) *(honrado)* upright

intelecto *nm* intellect

intelectual *adj & nmf* intellectual

inteligencia *nf (intelecto)* intelligence; **coeficiente de i.** intelligence quotient, IQ

inteligente *adj* intelligent

inteligible *adj* intelligible

intemperie *nf* bad weather; **a la i.** in the open (air)

intempestivo,-a *adj* untimely

intención *nf* intention; **con i.** deliberately, on purpose; **con segunda o doble i.** with an ulterior motive; **tener la i. de hacer algo** to intend to do sth

intencionadamente *adv* on purpose

intencionado,-a *adj* deliberate

intencional *adj* intentional

intendencia *nf* (**a**) *RP (corporación municipal)* town council, *US* city council (**b**) *RP (edificio)* town hall, *US* city hall (**c**) *Chile (gobernación)* administrative region

intendente *nm* (**a**) *RP (alcalde)* mayor (**b**) *Chile (gobernador)* governor

intensidad *nf* intensity; *(del viento)* force

intensificar [44] *vt,* **intensificarse** *vpr* to intensify; *(amistad)* to strengthen

intensivo,-a *adj* intensive; *Agr* **cultivo i.** intensive farming; *Educ* **curso i.** crash course

intenso,-a *adj* intense

intentar *vt* to try, to attempt; *Fam* **¡inténtalo!** give it a go!

intento *nm* attempt; **i. de suicidio** attempted suicide

intentona *nf* putsch

inter- *pref* inter-

intercalar *vt* to insert

intercambiar [43] *vt* to exchange

intercambio *nm* exchange; **i. comercial** trade

interceder *vi* to intercede

interceptar *vt* (**a**) *(detener)* to intercept (**b**) *(carretera)* to block; *(tráfico)* to hold up

intercesión *nf* intercession

intercontinental *adj* intercontinental

interdicto *nm* prohibition

interés *nm* (**a**) interest; **poner i. en** to take an interest in; **tener i. en o por** to be interested in (**b**) *(provecho personal)* self-interest; **hacer algo (sólo) por i.** to do sth out of self-interest; **intereses creados** vested interests (**c**) *Fin* interest; **con un i. del 11 por ciento** at an interest of 11 percent; **tipos de i.** interest rates

interesado,-a 1 *adj* (**a**) interested (**en** in); **las partes interesadas** the interested parties (**b**) *(egoísta)* selfish
  2 *nm,f* interested person; **los interesados** those interested *o* concerned

interesante *adj* interesting

interesar 1 *vt* (**a**) *(tener interés)* to interest; **la poesía no me interesa nada** poetry doesn't interest me at all (**b**) *(concernir)* to concern
  2 *vi (ser importante)* to be of interest, to be important; **interesaría llegar pronto** it is important to get there early
  3 interesarse *vpr* **i. por** *o* **en** to be interested in; **se interesó por ti** he asked about *o* after you

interferencia *nf* interference; *Rad & TV* jamming

interferir [5] *vt* (**a**) to interfere with; *(plan)* to upset (**b**) *Rad & TV* to jam

interfono *nm Tel* intercom

interinidad *nf* (**a**) *(temporalidad)* temporariness (**b**) *(empleo)* temporary employment

interino,-a 1 *adj (persona)* acting
  2 *nm,f (trabajador temporal)* temporary worker

interior 1 *adj* (**a**) inner, inside, interior; **habitación i.** inner room; **ropa i.** underwear (**b**) *Pol* domestic, internal (**c**) *Geog* inland
  2 *nm* (**a**) inside, interior; *Fig* **en su i. no estaba de acuerdo** deep down she disagreed (**b**) *Geog* interior; *Pol* **Ministerio del I.** *Br* ≃ Home Office, *US* ≃ Department of the Interior

interiorizar [40] *vt* to internalize

interjección *nf Ling* interjection

interlocutor,-a *nm,f* speaker; *(negociador)* negotiator

intermediario *nm Com* middleman

intermedio,-a 1 *adj* intermediate
  2 *nm TV (intervalo)* break

interminable *adj* endless

intermitente 1 *adj* intermittent
  2 *nm Aut Br* indicator, *US* turn signal

internacional *adj* international

internado,-a 1 *nm,f* inmate
  2 *nm (colegio)* boarding-school

internar 1 *vt (en hospital)* to confine

internarse *vpr* (**a**) *(penetrar)* to advance (en into); (**b**) *Dep* to break through

ternauta *nmf Informát* Net user

ternet *nf Informát* Internet; **está en l.** it's on e Internet

terno,-a 1 *adj* (**a**) internal; **por vía interna** ternally (**b**) *Pol* domestic
· *nm,f (alumno)* boarder; *Med (enfermo)* atient; *(preso)* inmate

· *nm RP (extensión)* (telephone) extension; **28, por favor** extension 28, please

terponer [19] *(pp interpuesto)* **1** *vt* to insert; *Jur* **i. un recurso** to give notice of appeal **·** **interponerse** *vpr* to intervene

terpretación *nf* (**a**) interpretation (**b**) *Mús* *Teatro* performance

terpretar *vt* (**a**) to interpret (**b**) *Teatro* *·apel)* to play; *(obra)* to perform; *Mús (concerto)* to play, to perform; *(canción)* to sing

térprete *nmf* (**a**) *(traductor)* interpreter (**b**) *·atro* performer; *Mús (cantante)* singer; *(mú·co)* performer

terpuse *pt indef de* **interponer**

terrogación *nf* interrogation; *Ling* (signo **·**) **i.** question *o* interrogation mark

terrogante *nf Fig* question mark

terrogar [42] *vt* to question; *(testigo etc)* to terrogate

terrogatorio *nm* interrogation

terrumpir *vt* to interrupt; *(tráfico)* to block

terrupción *nf* interruption; **i. del embara·** termination of pregnancy

terruptor *nm Elec* switch

tersección *nf* intersection

terurbano,-a *adj* intercity; *Tel* **conferencia** **terurbana** long-distance call

tervalo *nm* interval; **habrá intervalos de** **uvia** there will be periods of rain

tervención *nf* (**a**) *(participación)* intervention, participation (**en** in); *(aportación)* con·bution (**en** to) (**b**) *Med* intervention

tervenir [27] **1** *vi (mediar)* to intervene (**en** ·); *(participar)* to take part (**en** in); *(contri·ir)* to contribute (**en** to)
· *vt* (**a**) *(confiscar)* to confiscate, to seize (**b**) ·l *(teléfono)* to tap (**c**) *Med* to operate on

terventor,-a *nm,f (supervisor)* inspector; *n* **i. (de cuentas)** auditor

terviú *nf (pl interviús)* interview

testino,-a 1 *adj (luchas)* internal
· *nm Anat* intestine

timar *vi* to become close (**con** to)

timidad *nf (amistad)* intimacy; *(vida priva·*) private life; *(privacidad)* privacy; **en la i.** ·ivately, in private

timidar *vt* to intimidate

timo,-a 1 *adj* (**a**) intimate (**b**) *(vida)* pri·ate; **una boda íntima** a quiet wedding (**c**) ·mistad) close
· *nm,f* close friend, intimate

tolerable *adj* intolerable

tolerancia *nf* intolerance

intolerante 1 *adj* intolerant
2 *nmf* intolerant person

intoxicación *nf* poisoning; **i. alimentaria** food poisoning

> *♪* Observa que la palabra inglesa **intoxication** es un falso amigo y no es la traducción de la palabra española **intoxicación**. En inglés, **intoxication** significa "embriaguez".

intoxicar [44] *vt* to poison

> *♪* Observa que el verbo inglés **to intoxicate** es un falso amigo y no es la traducción del verbo español **intoxicar**. En inglés, **to intoxicate** significa "embriagar, emborrachar".

intra- *pref* intra-

intranet *nf Informát* intranet

intranquilidad *nf* worry

intranquilizarse *vpr* to get worried

intranquilo,-a *adj (preocupado)* worried; *(agitado)* restless

intransigente *adj* intransigent

intransitable *adj* impassable

intransitivo,-a *adj Ling* intransitive

intratable *adj* (**a**) *(problema)* intractable (**b**) *(persona)* unsociable

intrépido,-a *adj* intrepid

intriga *nf* intrigue; *Cin & Teatro* plot

intrigante 1 *adj* (**a**) *(interesante)* intriguing, interesting (**b**) *(maquinador)* scheming
2 *nmf (persona)* schemer

intrigar [42] **1** *vt (interesar)* to intrigue, to interest
2 *vi (maquinar)* to plot

intrincado,-a *adj* (**a**) *(cuestión, problema)* intricate (**b**) *(bosque)* dense

intrínseco,-a *adj* intrinsic

introducción *nf* introduction

introducir [10] *vt* (**a**) to introduce (**b**) *(meter)* to insert, to put in

intromisión *nf (injerencia)* meddling; **per·dón por la i.** forgive the intrusion

introspectivo,-a *adj* introspective

introvertido,-a 1 *adj* introverted
2 *nm,f* introvert

intruso,-a 1 *adj* intrusive
2 *nm,f* intruder; *Jur* trespasser

intuición *nf* intuition

intuir [37] *vt* to know by intuition

intuitivo,-a *adj* intuitive

inundación *nf* flood

inundar *vt* to flood; *Fig (de trabajo etc)* to swamp

inusitado,-a *adj* unusual

inútil 1 *adj* (**a**) useless; *(esfuerzo, intento)* vain, pointless (**b**) *Mil* unfit (for service)
2 *nmf Fam* good-for-nothing

inutilidad *nf* uselessness

inutilizar [40] *vt* to make *o* render useless; *(máquina etc)* to put out of action

invadir *vt* to invade; *Fig* **los estudiantes**

invadieron la calle students poured out onto the street

invalidar *vt* to invalidate

invalidez *nf* (a) *Jur (nulidad)* invalidity (b) *Med (minusvalía)* disability

inválido,-a 1 *adj* (a) *Jur (nulo)* invalid (b) *Med (minusválido)* disabled, handicapped
2 *nm,f Med* disabled o handicapped person

invariable *adj* invariable

invasión *nf* invasion

invasor,-a 1 *adj* invading
2 *nm,f* invader

invencible *adj* (a) *(enemigo)* invincible (b) *(obstáculo)* insurmountable

invención *nf (invento)* invention; *(mentira)* fabrication

inventar *vt* to invent; *(excusa, mentira)* to make up, to concoct

inventario *nm* inventory

inventiva *nf* inventiveness; *(imaginación)* imagination

invento *nm* invention

inventor,-a *nm,f* inventor

invernadero *nm* greenhouse; **efecto i.** greenhouse effect

invernal *adj* winter, wintry

invernar [1] *vi* to hibernate

inverosímil *adj* unlikely, improbable

inversión *nf* (a) inversion (b) *Fin* investment

inverso,-a *adj* opposite; **en sentido i.** in the opposite direction; **en orden i.** in reverse order

inversor,-a *nm,f Fin* investor

invertebrado,-a *adj & nm Zool* invertebrate

invertido,-a 1 *adj* inverted, reversed
2 *nm,f* homosexual

invertir [5] *vt* (a) *(orden)* to invert, to reverse (b) *(dinero)* to invest (**en** in); *(tiempo)* to spend (**en** on)

investidura *nf* investiture; *Pol* vote of confidence

investigación *nf* (a) *(policial etc)* investigation (b) *(científica)* research

investigador,-a *nm,f* (a) *(detective)* investigator (b) *(científico)* researcher, research worker

investigar [42] *vt* to research; *(indagar)* to investigate

investir [6] *vt* to invest

invidente 1 *adj* unsighted
2 *nmf* unsighted person

invierno *nm* winter

invisible *adj* invisible

invitación *nf* invitation

invitado,-a 1 *adj* invited; **artista i.** guest artist
2 *nm,f* guest

invitar *vt* to invite; **hoy invito yo** it's on me today; **me invitó a una copa** he treated me to a drink

invocar [44] *vt* to invoke

involucrar 1 *vt* to involve (**en** in)
2 involucrarse *vpr* to get involved (**en** in)

involuntario,-a *adj* involuntary; *(imprem ditado)* unintentional

invulnerable *adj* invulnerable

inyección *nf* injection; **poner una i.** to give a injection

inyectar *vt* to inject (**en** into); **i. algo a algn** inject sb with sth

IPC *nm (abr* **Índice de Precios al Consumo)** R

ir [16] **1** *vi* (a) to go; **¡vamos!** let's go!; **voy** Lima I'm going to Lima; **¡ya voy!** (I'n coming!
(b) *(río, camino)* to lead; **esta carretera va** **la frontera** this road leads to the border
(c) *(funcionar)* to work (properly); **el ascen** **sor no va** the lift is out of order
(d) *(desenvolverse)* **¿cómo le va el nuev** **trabajo?** how is he getting on in his ne job?; **¿cómo te va?** how are things?, how ar you doing?
(e) *(sentar bien)* to suit; **el verde te va much** green really suits you
(f) *(combinar)* to match; **el rojo no va con** **verde** red doesn't go with green
(g) *(vestir)* to wear; **ir con falda** to wear skirt; **ir de blanco/de uniforme** to be dresse in white/in uniform
(h) *Fam (importar, concernir)* to concern **eso va por ti también** and the same goes fo you; **ni me va ni me viene** I don't care one wa or the other
(i) *Fam (comportarse)* to act; **ir de guapo po** **la vida** to be a flash Harry
(j) **va para abogado** he's studying to be lawyer
(k) *(ir + por)* **ir por la derecha** to keep (t the) right; *(ir a buscar)* **ve (a) por agua** go an fetch some water; *(haber llegado)* **voy por** **página 90** I've got as far as page 90
(l) *(locuciones)* **a eso iba** I was coming t that; **¡ahí va!** catch!; **en lo que va de año s** far this year; **ir a parar** to end up; **¡qué va!** course not!, nothing of the sort!; **va a lo suy** he looks after his own interests; **¡vamos** **ver!** let's see!; **¡vaya!** fancy that!; **¡vaya moto** what a bike!
2 *v aux* (a) *(ir + gerundio)* **ir andando** to g on foot; **va mejorando** she's improving
(b) *(ir + pp)* **ya van rotos tres** three (c them) have already been broken
(c) *(ir a + inf)* **iba a decir que** I was going t say that; **va a llover** it's going to rain; **vas** **caerte** you'll fall
3 irse *vpr* (a) *(marcharse)* to go away, t leave; **me voy** I'm off; **¡vámonos!** let's go **¡vete!** go away!; **vete a casa** go home
(b) *(líquido, gas) (escaparse)* to leak
(c) *(direcciones)* **¿por dónde se va a ...** which is the way to ...? **por aquí se va al rí** this is the way to the river

ira *nf* wrath, rage, anger

iracundo,-a *adj* (a) *(irascible)* irascible (b *(enfadado)* irate, angry

Irak *n* Iraq
Irán *n* Iran
iraní *adj & nmf (pl* **iraníes**) Iranian
Iraq *n* = **Irak**
iraquí *adj & nmf (pl* **iraquíes**) Iraqi
irascible *adj* irascible, irritable
iris *nm inv Anat* iris; **arco i.** rainbow
Irlanda *n* Ireland; **I. del Norte** Northern Ireland
irlandés,-esa 1 *adj* Irish
2 *nm,f (hombre)* Irishman; *(mujer)* Irishwoman; **los irlandeses** the Irish
3 *nm (idioma)* Irish
ironía *nf* irony
irónico,-a *adj* ironic
IRPF *nm Econ (abr* **impuesto sobre la renta de las personas físicas**) income tax
irracional *adj* irrational
irradiar [43] *vt* (**a**) *(emitir)* to radiate (**b**) *Am Fig (expulsar)* to expel
irreal *adj* unreal
irrealizable *adj* unattainable, unfeasible; *Fig* unreachable
irreconocible *adj* unrecognizable
irregular *adj* irregular
irregularidad *nf* irregularity
irremediable *adj* irremediable, incurable
irremplazable *adj* irreplaceable
irreparable *adj* irreparable
irreprochable *adj* irreproachable, blameless
irresistible *adj* (**a**) *(impulso, persona)* irresistible (**b**) *(insoportable)* unbearable
irresoluto,-a *adj* irresolute
irresponsable *adj* irresponsible
irrestricto,-a *adj Am* unconditional, complete
irreverente *adj* irreverent
irrigación *nf* irrigation
irrigar [42] *vt* to irrigate, to water
irrisorio,-a *adj* derisory, ridiculous
irritación *nf* irritation

irritante *adj* irritating
irritar 1 *vt* (**a**) *(enfadar)* to irritate, to exasperate (**b**) *Med* to irritate
2 irritarse *vpr* (**a**) *(enfadarse)* to lose one's temper, to get angry (**b**) *Med* to become irritated
irrompible *adj* unbreakable
irrumpir *vi* to burst (**en** into)
isla *nf* island, isle
islam *nm Rel* Islam
islámico,-a *adj* Islamic
islandés,-esa 1 *adj* Icelandic
2 *nm,f (persona)* Icelander
3 *nm (idioma)* Icelandic
Islandia *n* Iceland
isleño,-a 1 *adj* island
2 *nm,f* islander
islote *nm* small island
ismo *nm Fam* ism
Israel *n* Israel
israelí *adj & nmf (pl* **israelíes**) Israeli
istmo *nm Geog* isthmus
itacate *nm Méx* packed lunch
Italia *n* Italy
italiano,-a 1 *adj* Italian
2 *nm,f (persona)* Italian
3 *nm (idioma)* Italian
itinerante *adj* itinerant, itinerating
itinerario *nm* itinerary, route
IVA *nm Econ (abr* **impuesto sobre el valor añadido**) VAT
izar [40] *vt* to hoist, to raise
izqda., izqda *(abr* **izquierda**) left
izqdo., izqdo *(abr* **izquierdo**) left
izquierda *nf* (**a**) left; **a la i.** on the left; **girar a la i.** to turn left (**b**) *(mano)* left hand (**c**) *Pol* **la i.** the left; **de izquierdas** left-wing
izquierdista *Pol* **1** *adj* leftist, left-wing
2 *nmf* leftist, left-winger
izquierdo,-a *adj* (**a**) left; **brazo i.** left arm (**b**) *(zurdo)* left-handed
izquierdoso,-a *adj Fam* leftish

J, j ['xota] *nf (la letra)* J, j
jabalí *nm (pl jabalíes)* wild boar
jabalina *nf Dep* javelin
jabón *nm* soap; **j. de afeitar/tocador** shaving/toilet soap
jabonera *nf* soap dish
jaca *nf* gelding
jacal *nm Méx* hut
jacinto *nm Bot* hyacinth
jactancia *nf* boastfulness
jactancioso,-a 1 *adj* boastful
   2 *nm,f* braggart
jactarse *upr* to boast, to brag (**de** about)
jadeante *adj* panting, breathless
jadear *vi* to pant, to gasp
jadeo *nm* panting, gasping
jaez *nm Pey (ralea)* kind, sort
jaiba *nf Andes, CAm, Carib, Méx (cangrejo)* crayfish
jalar 1 *vt* (**a**) *Fam (comer)* to wolf down (**b**) *Andes, CAm, Carib, Méx (tirar)* to pull
   2 jalarse *upr Fam (comerse)* to wolf down, to scoff
jalbegar [42] *vt* to whitewash
jalea *nf* jelly; **j. real** royal jelly
jalear *vt (animar)* to cheer (on)
jaleo *nm (alboroto)* din, racket; *(riña)* row; *(confusión)* muddle; **armar j.** to make a racket
jalón¹ *nm (estaca)* stake; *Fig (hito)* milestone
jalón² *nm* (**a**) *(tirón)* pull, tug (**b**) *Am Aut* lift
jamaicano,-a *adj & nm,f* Jamaican
jamar *vt Fam* to scoff, to eat
jamás *adv* (**a**) never; **j. he estado allí** I have never been there (**b**) ever; **el mejor libro que j. se ha escrito** the best book ever written (**c**) **nunca j.** never again; **por siempre j.** for ever (and ever)
jamba *nf Arquit* jamb
jamón *nm* ham; **j. de York/serrano** boiled/cured ham
jamona *adj Fam* buxom
Japón *n* **(el) J.** Japan
japonés,-esa 1 *adj* Japanese
   2 *nm,f (persona)* Japanese; **los japoneses** the Japanese
   3 *nm (idioma)* Japanese
japuta *nf (pez)* Ray's bream
jaque *nm (en ajedrez)* check; **dar j. a** to check; **j. mate** checkmate; **j. al rey** check; *Fig* **estar en j.** to be stymied
jaqueca *nf* migraine
jara *nf Bot* rock rose

jarabe *nm* syrup; **j. para la tos** cough mixture
jarana *nf Fam* (**a**) *(juerga)* wild party, spree; **ir de j.** to go on a spree *o* a binge (**b**) *(jaleo)* racket, din
jaranero,-a 1 *adj* fun-loving, party-loving
   2 *nm,f* pleasure seeker, party-lover
jardín *nm* garden; **j. botánico** botanical garden; **j. de infancia** nursery school, kindergarten
jardinería *nf* gardening
jardinero *nm* gardener
jarra *nf* pitcher; **j. de cerveza** beer mug; *Fig* **de** *o* **en jarras** (with) arms akimbo, hands on hips
jarro *nm (recipiente)* jug; *(contenido)* jugful; *Fig* **echar un j. de agua fría a** to pour cold water on
jarrón *nm* vase; *(en arqueología)* urn
jaspe *nm* jasper; **como el j.** spotless, like a new pin
Jauja *nf Fig* promised land; **¡esto es J.!** this is the life!
jaula *nf (para animales)* cage
jauría *nf* pack of hounds
jazmín *nm Bot* jasmine
J.C. *(abr Jesucristo)* J.C.
jeba = **jeva**
jebo,-a = **jevo,-a**
jeep [jip] *nm Aut* jeep
jefa *nf* female boss, manageress
jefatura *nf* (**a**) *(cargo, dirección)* leadership (**b**) *(sede)* central office; **j. de policía** police headquarters
jefe *nm* (**a**) head, chief, boss; *Com* manager; **j. de estación** stationmaster; **j. de redacción** editor-in-chief; **j. de ventas** sales manager (**b**) *Pol* leader; **J. de Estado** Head of State (**c**) *Mil* officer in command; **comandante en j.** commander-in-chief
Jehová *nm* Jehovah; **testigos de J.** Jehovah's Witnesses
jején *nm Am* gnat
jengibre *nm Bot* ginger
jeque *nm* sheik, sheikh
jerarquía *nf* (**a**) hierarchy (**b**) *(categoría)* rank
jerárquico,-a *adj* hierarchical
jeremías *nmf inv* whiner, whinger
jerez *nm* sherry
jerga *nf (argot) (técnica)* jargon; *(vulgar)* slang; **la j. legal** legal jargon
jerigonza *nf* (**a**) *(extravagancia)* oddness (**b**) *(galimatías)* gibberish

eringa *nf* Med syringe; *Aut* **j. de engrase** grease gun

eringar [42] *vt Fam* (**a**) *(molestar)* to pester, to annoy (**b**) *(romper)* to break

eringuilla *nf* (hypodermic) syringe

eroglífico,-a 1 *adj* hieroglyphic
  2 *nm* (**a**) Ling hieroglyph, hieroglyphic (**b**) *(juego)* rebus

ersey *nm* (*pl* **jerseis**) sweater, *Br* jumper

Jerusalén *n* Jerusalem

Jesucristo *nm* Jesus Christ

esuita *adj & nmf* Jesuit

Jesús 1 *nm* Jesus
  2 *interj* (**a**) *(expresa sorpresa)* good heavens! (**b**) *(al estornudar)* bless you!

et *nf* jet set

eta *nf Fam* (**a**) *(descaro)* cheek; **tener j.** to be cheeky, to have a nerve (**b**) *(cara)* mug, face (**c**) *(hocico)* snout

et-set *nf* jet set

eva *nf Carib Fam (mujer)* chick, *Br* bird

evo,-a *nm,f Ven Fam (novio)* guy, boyfriend; *(novia)* girl, girlfriend

íbaro,-a *nm,f Am* peasant

ícama *nf* yam bean, jicama

ícara *nf CAm, Méx, Ven (bol)* small cup; *(calabaza)* gourd

ilguero *nm Orn* goldfinch

ilipollas *nmf inv muy Fam* = gilipollas

inete *nm* rider, horseman

inetera *nf Cuba Fam* prostitute

iñar *vi muy Fam* to shit

irafa *nf* (**a**) giraffe (**b**) *(de micrófono)* boom

irón *nm* (**a**) *(trozo desgarrado)* shred, strip; *(pedazo suelto)* bit, scrap; **hecho jirones** in shreds o tatters (**b**) *Perú (calle)* street

itomate *nm Méx* tomato

JOO *nmpl (abr Juegos Olímpicos)* Olympic Games

ocoso,-a *adj* funny, humorous

oda *nf RP muy Fam* (**a**) *(fastidio)* pain, drag (**b**) *(broma)* joke; **decir/hacer algo en j.** to say/do sth as a joke (**c**) *(juerga)* wild party

oder *Vulg* **1** *interj* shit!, *Br* bloody hell!
  2 *vt* (**a**) *(fastidiar)* to piss off; **¡no me jodas!** come on, don't give me that! (**b**) *(copular)* to fuck (**c**) *(echar a perder)* to screw up; **¡la jodiste!** you screwed it up! (**d**) *(romper)* to bugger
  3 joderse *vpr* (**a**) *(aguantarse)* to put up with it; **¡hay que j.!** you'll just have to grin and bear it! (**b**) *(echarse a perder)* to get screwed up; **¡se jodió el invento!** that's really screwed things up!; **¡que se joda!** to hell with him! (**c**) *(romperse)* to go bust

odido,-a *adj Vulg* (**a**) *(maldito)* damned, *Br* bloody (**b**) *(molesto)* annoying (**c**) *(enfermo)* in a bad way; *(cansado)* knackered, exhausted (**d**) *(estropeado, roto)* bust, kaput, buggered (**e**) *(difícil)* shitty

odienda *nf Vulg* (**a**) *(coito)* fuck (**b**) *(molestia)* pain in the arse

jofaina *nf* washbasin

jogging ['joɣin] *nm Urug (ropa)* track o jogging suit

jolgorio *nm Fam (juerga)* binge; *(algazara)* fun

jolín, jolines *interj Fam (sorpresa)* gosh!, good grief!; *(enfado)* blast!, damn!

Jordania *n* Jordan

jornada *nf* (**a**) **j. (laboral)** *(día de trabajo)* working day; **j. intensiva** continuous working day; **j. partida** working day with a lunch break; **trabajo de media j./j. completa** part-time/full-time work (**b**) **jornadas** conference

jornal *nm (paga)* day's wage; **trabajar a j.** to be paid by the day

---

🖉 Observa que la palabra inglesa **journal** es un falso amigo y no es la traducción de la palabra española **jornal**. En inglés, **journal** significa "revista, diario".

---

jornalero,-a *nm,f* day labourer

joroba 1 *nf (jiba)* hump
  2 *interj* drat!

jorobado,-a 1 *adj* hunchbacked
  2 *nm,f* hunchback

jorobar *Fam* **1** *vt* (**a**) *(fastidiar)* to annoy, to bother; **me joroba** it really gets up my nose; **¡no jorobes!** *(incredulidad)* pull the other one! (**b**) *(estropear)* to ruin, to wreck
  2 jorobarse *vpr* (**a**) *(fastidiarse)* to grin and bear it (**b**) *(estropearse)* to break

jorongo *nm Méx* (**a**) *(manta)* blanket (**b**) *(poncho)* poncho

jota¹ *nf* (**a**) = name of the letter J in Spanish (**b**) *(cantidad mínima)* jot, scrap; **ni j.** not an iota; **no entiendo ni j.** I don't understand a thing

jota² *nf Mús* = Spanish dance and music

joven 1 *adj* young; **de aspecto j.** young-looking
  2 *nmf (hombre)* youth, young man; *(mujer)* girl, young woman; **de j.** as a young man/woman; **los jóvenes** young people, youth

jovial *adj* jovial, good-humoured

joya *nf* (**a**) jewel, piece of jewellery; **joyas de imitación** imitation jewellery (**b**) *Fig* **ser una j.** *(persona)* to be a real treasure o gem

joyería *nf (tienda)* jewellery shop, jeweller's (shop)

joyero,-a 1 *nm,f* jeweller
  2 *nm* jewel case o box

juanete *nm (en el pie)* bunion

jubilación *nf* (**a**) *(acción)* retirement; **j. anticipada** early retirement (**b**) *(pensión)* pension

jubilado,-a 1 *adj* retired
  2 *nm,f* retired person, pensioner; **los jubilados** retired people

jubilar 1 *vt (retirar)* to retire, to pension off; *Fam Fig* to get rid of, to ditch

2 jubilarse *vpr (retirarse)* to retire, to go into retirement

júbilo *nm* jubilation, joy

jubón *nm* doublet, jerkin

judería *nf (barrio)* Jewish quarter

judía *nf* bean; **j. verde** French bean, green bean

judicial *adj* judicial; **vía j.** legal channels

judío,-a 1 *adj* Jewish

 2 *nm,f* Jew

judo *nm Dep* judo

juego *nm* (a) game; **j. de azar** game of chance; **j. de cartas** card game; *Fig* **j. de manos** sleight of hand; *Fig* **j. de palabras** play on words, pun; **j. de rol** fantasy role-playing game; *Fig* **j. limpio/sucio** fair/foul play (b) *Dep* game; **Juegos Olímpicos** Olympic Games; **terreno de j.** *Ten* court; *Ftb* field; **fuera de j.** offside (c) *(apuestas)* gambling; *Fig* **poner algo en j.** to put sth at stake (d) *(conjunto de piezas)* set; **j. de café/té** coffee/tea service; *Fig* **ir a j. con** to match

juerga *nf Fam* binge, rave-up; **ir de j.** to go on a binge

juerguista 1 *adj* fun-loving

 2 *nmf* fun-loving person, raver

jueves *nm inv* Thursday; **J. Santo** Maundy Thursday

juez *nmf* judge; **j. de instrucción** examining magistrate; **j. de paz** justice of the peace; *Dep* **j. de salida** starter; **j. de línea** linesman

jugada *nf* (a) move; *(en billar)* shot (b) *Fam* dirty trick

jugador,-a *nm,f* player; *(apostador)* gambler

jugar [32] **1** *vi* (a) to play; **j. a(l) fútbol/tenis** to play football/tennis; *Fig* **j. sucio** to play dirty (b) **j. con** *(no tomar en serio)* to toy with

 2 *vt* (a) to play (b) *(apostar)* to bet, to stake

 3 jugarse *vpr* (a) *(arriesgar)* to risk; *Fam* **j. el pellejo** to risk one's neck (b) *(apostar)* to bet, to stake

jugarreta *nf Fam* dirty trick

jugo *nm* juice; *Fig* **sacar el j. a** *(aprovechar)* to make the most of; *(explotar)* to squeeze dry

jugoso,-a *adj* (a) juicy; **un filete j.** a juicy steak (b) *Fig (sustancioso)* substantial, meaty; **un tema j.** a meaty topic

juguete *nm* toy; **pistola de j.** toy gun; *Fig* **ser el j. de algn** to be sb's plaything

juguetear *vi* to play

juguetón,-ona *adj* playful

juicio *nm* (a) *(facultad mental)* judgement, discernment; *(opinión)* opinion, judgement; **a j. de** in the opinion of; **a mi j.** in my opinion (b) *(sensatez)* reason, common sense; **en su sano j.** in one's right mind; **perder el j.** to go mad *o* insane (c) *Jur* trial, lawsuit; **llevar a algn a j.** to take legal action against sb, to sue sb

juicioso,-a *adj* judicious, wise

julepe *nm PRico, RP Fam (susto)* scare, fright; **dar un j. a algn** to give sb a scare

julio *nm* July

junco *nm Bot* rush

jungla *nf* jungle

junio *nm* June

júnior *adj Dep* junior; **campeonato j. de golf** junior golf championship

junta *nf* (a) *(reunión)* meeting, assembly; *Pol* **j. de gobierno** cabinet meeting (b) *(dirección)* board, committee; **j. directiva** board of directors (c) *Mil* junta; **j. militar** military junta (d) *(parlamento regional)* regional parliament (e) *Téc* joint

juntar 1 *vt* (a) *(unir)* to join, to put together; *(piezas)* to assemble (b) *(reunir) (sellos)* to collect; *(dinero)* to raise

 2 juntarse *vpr* (a) *(unirse)* to join; *(ríos, caminos)* to meet; *(personas)* to gather (b) *(amancebarse)* to live together

junto,-a 1 *adj* together; **dos mesas juntas** two tables side by side; **todos juntos** all together

 2 *adv* **j. con** together with; **j. a** next to

juntura *nf* (a) *Téc* joint, seam (b) *Anat* joint

jura *nf (acción)* oath; *(ceremonia)* swearing in; **j. de bandera** oath of allegiance to the flag

jurado *nm* (a) *(tribunal)* jury; *(en un concurso)* panel of judges, jury (b) *(miembro del tribunal)* juror, member of the jury

juramento *nm* (a) *Jur* oath; **bajo j.** under oath (b) *(blasfemia)* swearword, curse

jurar 1 *vi Jur & Rel* to swear, to take an oath

 2 *vt* to swear; **j. el cargo** to take the oath of office; **j. por Dios** to swear to God

 3 jurarse *vpr Fam* **jurársela(s) a algn** to have it in for sb

jurel *nm (pez)* scad, horse mackerel

jurídico,-a *adj* legal

jurisdicción *nf* jurisdiction

jurisdiccional *adj* jurisdictional; **aguas jurisdiccionales** territorial waters

jurista *nmf* jurist, lawyer

justamente *adv* **¡j.!** precisely!; **j. detrás de** right behind

justicia *nf* justice; **tomarse la j. por su mano** to take the law into one's own hands

justicialismo *nm Pol* = Argentinian nationalistic political movement founded by Juan Domingo Perón

justicialista *adj Pol* = belonging or related to "justicialismo"

justiciero,-a *adj* severe

justificable *adj* justifiable

justificación *nf* justification

justificado,-a *adj* justified, well-grounded

justificante *nm* written proof; **j. de pago** proof of payment

justificar [44] **1** *vt* to justify

 2 justificarse *vpr* to clear oneself, to justify oneself

justo,-a 1 *adj* (a) just, fair, right; **un trato j.** a fair deal (b) *(apretado) (ropa)* tight; **estamos justos de tiempo** we're pressed for time (c) *(exacto)* right, accurate; **la palabra justa** the right word (**d**) *(preciso)* **llegamos en el momento j. en que salían** we arrived just as they were leaving (**e**) **lo j.** just enough

   2 *nm,f* just *o* righteous person; **los justos** the just, the righteous

   3 *adv (exactamente)* exactly, precisely; **j. al lado** right beside

juvenil 1 *adj (aspecto)* youthful, young; **ropa j.** young people's clothes; **delincuencia j.** juvenile delinquency

   2 *nmf* **los juveniles** the juveniles

juventud *nf* (**a**) *(edad)* youth (**b**) *(jóvenes)* young people

juzgado *nm* court, tribunal; **j. de guardia** police court

juzgar [42] *vt* to judge; **a j. por ...** judging by ...

K, k [ka] *nf (la letra)* K, k
ka *nf* = name of the letter K in Spanish
kárate *nm Dep* karate
karateka *nmf Dep* person who does karate
Kenia *n* Kenya
kermés [ker'mes] (*pl* **kermeses**), **kermesse** [ker'mes] (*pl* **kermesses**) *nf* fair, kermesse
Kg, kg (*abr* **kilogramo(s)**) kg
kilo *nm* (**a**) *(medida)* kilo; *Fam* **pesa un k.** it weighs a ton (**b**) *Fam (millón)* a million pesetas
kilogramo *nm* kilogram, kilogramme
kilolitro *nm* kilolitre

kilometraje *nm* ≃ mileage
kilométrico,-a *adj* kilometric, kilometrical; **billete k.** multiple-journey ticket
kilómetro *nm* kilometre
kilovatio *nm* kilowatt; **k. hora** kilowatt-hour
kínder *nm Andes, Méx* kindergarten, nursery school
kiosco *nm* = **quiosco**
kiwi *nm* (**a**) *Orn* kiwi (**b**) *(fruto)* kiwi (fruit), Chinese gooseberry
Kleenex® *nm* Kleenex®, tissue
Km, km (*abr* **kilómetro(s)**) km
Kw, kw (*abr* **kilovatio(s)**) kW

L, l ['ele] *nf (la letra)* L, l

l *(abr* **litro(s))** l

la¹ 1 *art def f* the; **la mesa** the table

2 *pron dem* the one; **la del vestido azul** the one in the blue dress; **la que vino ayer** the one who came yesterday; *ver* **el**

la² *pron pers f (persona)* her; *(usted)* you; *(cosa)* it; **la invitaré** I'll invite her along; **no la dejes abierta** don't leave it open; **ya la avisaremos, señora** we'll let you know, madam; *ver* **le**

la³ *nm Mús* la, A

laberinto *nm* labyrinth

labia *nf Fam* loquacity; *Pey* glibness; **tener mucha l.** to have the gift of the gab

labio *nm* lip

labor *nf* (**a**) job, task; **l. de equipo** teamwork; **(de profesión) sus labores** housewife (**b**) *Agr* farmwork (**c**) *(de costura)* needlework, sewing

laborable *adj* (**a**) **día l.** *(no festivo)* working day (**b**) *Agr* arable

laboral *adj* industrial; **accidente l.** industrial accident; **conflictividad l.** industrial unrest; **jornada l.** working day; **Universidad L.** technical training college

laboratorio *nm* laboratory

laborioso,-a *adj* (**a**) *(persona)* hardworking (**b**) *(tarea)* laborious

laborista *Pol* **1** *adj* Labour; **partido l.** Labour Party

2 *nmf* Labour (Party) member/supporter

labrado,-a *adj Arte* carved

labrador,-a *nm,f (granjero)* farmer; *(trabajador)* farm worker

labranza *nf* farming

labrar 1 *vt* (**a**) *Agr* to till (**b**) *(madera)* to carve; *(piedra)* to cut; *(metal)* to work

2 labrarse *vpr Fig* **l. un porvenir** to build a future for oneself

laburar *vi RP Fam* to work

laburo *nm RP Fam* job

laca *nf* (**a**) *(hair)* lacquer, hairspray; **l. de uñas** nail polish *o* varnish (**b**) *Arte* lacquer

lacio,-a *adj* (**a**) *(pelo)* lank, limp (**b**) **qué l.!** *(soso)* what a weed!

lacónico,-a *adj* laconic; *(conciso)* terse

lacra *nf* evil, curse; **una l. social** a scourge of society

lacrar *vt* to seal with wax

lacre *nm* sealing wax

lacrimógeno,-a *adj* (**a**) **gas l.** tear gas (**b**) *Fig* una película lacrimógena a tear-jerker

lactar *vi* to breast-feed

lácteo,-a *adj* **productos lácteos** milk *o* dairy products; *Astron* **Vía Láctea** Milky Way

ladear 1 *vt (inclinar)* to tilt; *(cabeza)* to lean

2 ladearse *vpr* (**a**) *(inclinarse)* to lean, to tilt (**b**) *(desviarse)* to go off to one side

ladera *nf* slope

ladino,-a 1 *adj (astuto)* cunning, crafty

2 *nm,f CAm, Méx, Ven (no blanco)* = Spanish-speaking person of mixed race

lado *nm* (**a**) side; **a un l.** aside; **al l.** close by, nearby; **al l. de** next to, beside; **ponte de l.** stand sideways (**b**) *(en direcciones)* direction; **por todos lados** on/from all sides (**c**) *Fig* **dar de l. a algn** to cold-shoulder sb; **por otro l.** *(además)* moreover; **por un l. ..., por otro l. ...** on the one hand ..., on the other hand ...

ladrar *vi* to bark

ladrillo *nm* (**a**) *Constr* brick (**b**) *Fam (pesado)* bore, drag

ladrón,-ona 1 *nm,f* thief, robber; **¡al l.!** stop thief!

2 *nm Elec* multiple socket

lagartija *nf* small lizard

lagarto *nm* lizard

lago *nm* lake

lágrima *nf* (**a**) tear; **llorar a l. viva** to cry one's eyes out (**b**) *(en lámpara)* teardrop

lagrimoso,-a *adj* tearful

laguna *nf* (**a**) small lake (**b**) *Fig (hueco)* gap

La Haya *n* The Hague

laico,-a 1 *adj* lay

2 *nm,f* lay person; *(hombre)* layman; *(mujer)* laywoman

lameculos *nmf inv muy Fam* bootlicker, arse-licker

lamentable *adj* regrettable; *(infame)* lamentable

lamentar 1 *vt* to regret; **lo lamento** I'm sorry

2 lamentarse *vpr* to complain

lamento *nm* moan, wail

lamer *vt* to lick

lámina *nf* (**a**) sheet, plate; **l. de acero** steel sheet (**b**) *Impr* plate

laminado,-a 1 *adj* (**a**) laminated (**b**) *(metales)* rolled; **acero l.** rolled steel

2 *nm* lamination

laminar *vt (metal)* to roll

lámpara *nf* (**a**) lamp; **l. de pie** standard lamp (**b**) *Elec (bombilla)* bulb (**c**) *Rad* valve

lamparón *nm Fam* oil *o* grease stain

lana *nf* (a) *(de oveja)* wool; **pura l. virgen** pure new wool (b) *Andes, Méx Fam (dinero)* dough, cash

lanar *adj* **ganado l.** sheep

lance *nm Literario (episodio)* event, incident

📖 Observa que la palabra inglesa **lance** es un falso amigo y no es la traducción de la palabra española **lance**. En inglés, **lance** significa "lanza".

lanceta *nf Andes, Méx* sting

lancha *nf* motorboat, launch; **l. motora** speedboat; **l. neumática** rubber dinghy; **l. salvavidas** lifeboat

langosta *nf* (a) lobster (b) *(insecto)* locust

langostino *nm* king prawn

languidecer [33] *vi* to languish

lánguido,-a *adj* languid; *(sin vigor)* listless

lanudo,-a *adj* woolly, fleecy; *(peludo)* furry

lanza *nf* spear, lance; **punta de l.** spearhead; *Fig* **romper una l. en favor de algn/de algo** to defend sb/sth

lanzadera *nf* shuttle; **l. espacial** space shuttle

lanzado,-a *adj Fam* reckless; **ir l.** to tear along

lanzagranadas *nm inv Mil* grenade launcher

lanzamiento *nm* (a) throwing, hurling (b) *Dep (de disco, jabalina)* throw; *(de peso)* put (c) *Mil (de cohete etc)* launching (d) *Com* launch; **precio de l.** launch price (e) *Náut* launch

lanzar [40] **1** *vt* (a) *(arrojar)* to throw, to fling (b) *Fig (grito)* to let out (c) *Náut, Com & Mil* to launch

2 lanzarse *vpr* (a) *(arrojarse)* to throw o hurl oneself; **l. al suelo** to throw oneself to the ground (b) *(emprender)* **l. a** to embark on; **l. a los negocios** to go into business (c) *Fam (irse, largarse)* to scram

lapa *nf* (a) *Zool* limpet (b) **es una verdadera l.** he/she sticks to you like glue

lapicera *nf CSur* ballpoint (pen), *Br* Biro®; **l. fuente** fountain pen

lapicero *nm* (a) *(lápiz)* pencil (b) *CAm, Perú (bolígrafo)* ballpoint (pen), *Br* Biro®

lápida *nf* headstone

lapidario,-a *adj* lapidary

lápiz *nm* pencil; **l. labial** o **de labios** lipstick; **l. de ojos** eyeliner

lapso *nm* (a) *(periodo de tiempo)* period (b) *(error)* lapse, slip

lapsus *nm* slip; **l. linguae** slip of the tongue

largar [42] **1** *vt* (a) *Fam (golpe, discurso, dinero)* to give (b) *Náut* **l. amarras** to cast off

2 largarse *vpr Fam* to clear off, to split; **¡lárgate!** beat it!

largas *nfpl* **dar l. a algo** to put sth off

largavistas *nm inv Bol, CSur* binoculars

largo,-a **1** *adj* (a) *(espacio)* long; *(tiempo)* long, lengthy; **pasamos un mes l. allí** we spent a good month there; **a lo l. de** *(espacio)* along; *(tiempo)* through; **a la larga** in the long run (b) *(excesivo)* too long; **se hizo l. el día** the day dragged on (c) **largos años** many years

2 *nm* (a) *(longitud)* length; **¿cuánto tiene de l.?** how long is it? (b) *Mús* largo

3 *adv* **l. y tendido** at length; *Fam* **¡l. (de aquí)!** clear off!; **esto va para l.** this is going to last a long time

📖 Observa que la palabra inglesa **large** es un falso amigo y no es la traducción de la palabra española **largo**. En inglés, **large** significa "grande".

largometraje *nm* feature film, full-length film

laringe *nf* larynx

laringitis *nf* laryngitis

las¹ 1 *art def fpl* the; **l. sillas** the chairs; **lávate l. manos** wash your hands; *(no se traduce)* **me gustan l. flores** I like flowers

2 *pron* **l. que** *(personas)* the ones who, those who; *(objetos)* the ones that, those that; **toma l. que quieras** take whichever ones you want; *ver* **la** y **los**

las² *pron pers fpl (ellas)* them; *(ustedes)* you; **l. llamaré mañana (a ustedes)** I'll call you tomorrow; **no l. rompas** don't break them; **Pepa es de l. mías** Pepa thinks the way I do; *ver* **los**

lasaña *nf* lasagna, lasagne

lascivo,-a *adj* lewd, lecherous

láser *nm inv* laser; **impresora l.** laser printer

lástima *nf* pity; **¡qué l.!** what a pity!, what a shame!; **es una l. que ...** it's a pity (that) ...; **estar hecho una l.** to be a sorry sight; **tener l. a algn** to feel sorry for sb

lastimar *vt* to hurt, to injure

lastre *nm* (a) *(peso)* ballast (b) *Fig* dead weight

lata¹ *nf* (a) *(envase)* tin, can; **en l.** tinned, canned (b) *(hojalata)* tin(plate); **hecho de l.** made of tin

lata² *nf Fam* nuisance, drag; **dar la l.** to be a nuisance o a pest

latente *adj* latent

lateral **1** *adj* side, lateral; **salió por la puerta l.** he went out by the side door; **escalón l.** *(en letrero)* ramp

2 *nm* side passage; *Aut* **(carril) l.** side lane

latido *nm (del corazón)* beat

latifundio *nm* large landed estate

latigazo *nm* (a) lash (b) *Fam (trago)* drink, swig

látigo *nm* whip

latín *nm* Latin

latino,-a **1** *adj* Latin; **América Latina** Latin America

2 *nm,f* Latin American

Latinoamérica *nf* Latin America

latinomericano,-a *adj & nm,f* Latin American

latir *vi* to beat

latitud *nf* (**a**) *Geog* latitude (**b**) **latitudes** region, area

latón *nm* brass

latoso,-a *adj Fam* annoying

laucha *nf Am* mouse

laúd *nm* lute

laurel *nm Bot* laurel, (sweet) bay; *Culin* bay leaf; *Fig* **dormirse en los laureles** to rest on one's laurels

lava *nf* lava

lavable *adj* washable

lavabo *nm* (**a**) *(pila)* washbasin (**b**) *(cuarto de aseo)* washroom (**c**) *(retrete)* lavatory, toilet

lavadero *nm (de coches)* carwash

lavado *nm* wash, washing; *Fig* **l. de cerebro** brainwashing; **l. en seco** dry-cleaning

lavadora *nf* washing machine

lavanda *nf* lavender

lavandería *nf* (**a**) *(automática)* Br launderette, *US* Laundromat® (**b**) *(atendida por personal)* laundry

lavaplatos *nm inv* dishwasher

lavar *vt* to wash; **l. en seco** to dry-clean

lavativa *nf* enema

lavatorio *nm Andes, RP (lavabo)* Br washbasin, *US* washbowl

lavavajillas *nm inv* dishwasher

laxante *adj & nm* laxative

laxar *vt (vientre)* to loosen

laxitud *nf* laxity, laxness

lazada *nf (nudo)* bow

lazarillo *nm* **perro l.** guide dog, *US* seeing-eye dog

lazo *nm* (**a**) *(adorno)* bow (**b**) *(nudo)* knot; **l. corredizo** slipknot (**c**) *(para reses)* lasso (**d**) *Fig (usu pl) (vínculo)* tie, bond

le 1 *pron pers mf (objeto indirecto) (a él)* (to) him; *(a ella)* (to) her; *(a cosa)* (to) it; *(a usted)* (to) you; **lávale la cara** wash his face; **le compraré uno** I'll buy one for her; **¿qué le pasa a usted?** what's the matter with you?

2 *pron pers m (objeto directo) (él)* him; *(usted)* you; **no le oigo** I can't hear him; **no quiero molestarle** I don't wish to disturb you

leal 1 *adj* loyal, faithful

2 *nmf* loyalist

lealtad *nf* loyalty, faithfulness

lebrel *nm* greyhound

lección *nf* lesson; *Fig* **dar una l. a algn** to teach sb a lesson; *Fig* **te servirá de l.** let that be a lesson to you

leche *nf* (**a**) milk; *Anat* **dientes de l.** milk teeth; **l. descremada** *o* **desnatada** skim *o* skimmed milk (**b**) *Fam* **mala l.** badness (**c**) **¡l.!** damn! (**d**) *muy Fam (golpe)* knock; **dar** *o* **pegar una l. a algn** to clobber sb (**e**) *Vulg* semen

lechera *nf* (**a**) *(vasija)* churn (**b**) *muy Fam* police car

lechería *nf* dairy, creamery

lechero,-a 1 *adj* milk, dairy; **central lechera** dairy co-operative; **vaca lechera** milk cow

2 *nm* milkman

lecho *nm Lit* bed; **l. del río** river-bed; **l. mortuorio** death-bed

lechón *nm* sucking-pig

lechosa *nf Carib* papaya

lechoso,-a *adj* milky

lechuga *nf* lettuce

lechuza *nf* owl

lectivo,-a *adj* school; **horas lectivas** teaching hours

lector,-a 1 *nm,f* (**a**) *(persona)* reader (**b**) *Univ* lector, (language) assistant

2 *nm* **l. de microfichas** *(aparato)* microfiche reader

lectura *nf* reading

leer [36] *vt* to read; **léenos el menú** read out the menu for us; *Fig* **l. entre líneas** to read between the lines

legado *nm (herencia)* legacy

legajo *nm* bundle (of papers)

legal *adj* (**a**) *Jur* legal, lawful; **requisitos legales** legal formalities (**b**) *Fam (persona)* honest, trustworthy

legalidad *nf* legality, lawfulness

legalizar [40] *vt* to legalize; *(documento)* to authenticate

legaña *nf* sleep

legar [42] *vt (propiedad etc)* to bequeath; *Fig (tradiciones etc)* to hand down, to pass on

legendario,-a *adj* legendary

legión *nf* legion

legionella *nf* Legionnaire's Disease

legislación *nf* legislation

legislar *vi* to legislate

legislativo,-a *adj* legislative; **el poder l.** parliament

legislatura *nf* legislature

legitimar *vt* to legitimize; *(legalizar)* to legalize

legitimidad *nf Jur* legitimacy; *(licitud)* justice

legítimo,-a *adj* (**a**) *Jur* legitimate; **en legítima defensa** in self-defence (**b**) *(auténtico)* authentic, real; **oro l.** pure gold

lego,-a 1 *adj Rel* lay

2 *nm* (**a**) layman; **ser l. en la materia** to be a layman in the subject (**b**) *Rel* lay brother

legua *nf (medida)* league; *Fig* **se nota a la l.** it stands out a mile

legumbres *nfpl* pulses

lejanía *nf* distance

lejano,-a *adj* distant, far-off; **parientes lejanos** distant relatives; **el L. Oriente** the Far East

lejía *nf* bleach

lejos *adv* far (away); **a lo l.** in the distance; **de l.** from a distance; *Fig* **ir demasiado l.** to go too far; *Fig* **llegar l.** to go a long way; *Fig* **sin ir más l.** to take an obvious example

lelo,-a *Fam* **1** *adj* stupid, silly

2 *nm,f* ninny

lema *nm* (**a**) *(divisa)* motto, slogan (**b**) *(contraseña)* code name

lencería *nf* (**a**) *(prendas)* lingerie (**b**) *(ropa blanca)* linen (goods)

lendakari *nm* = head of the Basque government

lengua *nf* (**a**) tongue; *Fig* **malas lenguas** gossips; *Fam Fig* **irse de la l.** to spill the beans; *Fam Fig* **tirarle a algn de la l.** to draw sb out (**b**) *Ling* language; **l. materna** native *o* mother tongue

lenguado *nm (pez)* sole

lenguaje *nm* language; *Informát* language; **l. corporal** body language

lengüeta *nf* (**a**) *(de zapato)* tongue (**b**) *Mús* reed

lente 1 *nf* lens; **l. de contacto** contact lens
2 *nm Am* **lentes** *(gafas)* glasses, spectacles; **l. de contacto** contact lens

lenteja *nf* lentil

lentejuela *nf* sequin, spangle

lentilla *nf* contact lens

lentitud *nf* slowness; **con l.** slowly

lento,-a *adj* slow; **a fuego l.** on a low heat

leña *nf* (**a**) firewood; *Fig* **echar l. al fuego** to add fuel to the fire (**b**) *Fam (golpes)* knocks

leñazo *nm Fam (golpe)* blow, smash

leñe *interj Fam* damn it!

leño *nm* (**a**) log (**b**) *Fam (persona)* blockhead, halfwit

león *nm* lion

leona *nf* lioness

leonera *nf* lion's den; *Fig (habitación)* den

leopardo *nm* leopard

leotardos *nmpl* thick tights

lépero,-a *adj Fam* (**a**) *CAm, Méx (vulgar)* coarse, vulgar (**b**) *Cuba (ladino)* smart, crafty

lepra *nf* leprosy

leproso,-a 1 *adj* leprous
2 *nm,f* leper

les 1 *pron pers mfpl (objeto indirecto) (a ellos,-as)* them; *(a ustedes)* you; **dales el dinero** give them the money; **l. he comprado un regalo** I've bought you a present
2 *pron pers mpl (objeto directo) (ellos)* them; *(ustedes)* you; **l. esperaré** I shall wait for you; **no quiero molestarles** I don't wish to disturb you

lesbiana *nf* lesbian

leseras *nfpl Chile Fam (tonterías)* nonsense, *Br* rubbish

lesión *nf* (**a**) *(corporal)* injury (**b**) *Jur (perjuicio)* damage

lesionar *vt* to injure

leso,-a *adj Jur* **crimen de lesa humanidad** crime against humanity

letal *adj* lethal, deadly

letanía *nf* litany

letargo *nm* lethargy

letón,-ona 1 *adj* Latvian
2 *nm,f* Latvian
3 *nm (idioma)* Latvian, Lettish

Letonia *n* Latvia

letra *nf* (**a**) letter; **l. de imprenta** block cap-

itals; **l. mayúscula** capital letter; **l. minúscula** small letter; **l. pequeña** small print (**b**) *(escritura)* (hand)writing (**c**) *Mús (texto)* lyrics, words (**d**) *Fin* **l. (de cambio)** bill of exchange, draft (**e**) *Univ* **letras** arts

letrado,-a *nm,f* lawyer

letrero *nm (aviso)* notice, sign; *(cartel)* poster; **l. luminoso** neon sign

leucemia *nf* leukaemia

levadizo,-a *adj* **puente l.** drawbridge

levadura *nf* yeast; **l. en polvo** baking powder

levantamiento *nm* (**a**) raising, lifting; *Dep* **l. de pesos** weightlifting (**b**) *(insurrección)* uprising, insurrection

levantar 1 *vt* (**a**) to raise, to lift; *(mano, voz)* to raise; *(edificio)* to erect; *Fig (ánimos)* to raise; **l. los ojos** to look up (**b**) *(castigo)* to suspend
2 levantarse *vpr* (**a**) *(ponerse de pie)* to stand up, to rise (**b**) *(salir de la cama)* to get up (**c**) *(concluir)* to finish; **se levanta la sesión** the meeting is closed (**d**) *Pol* to rise, to revolt; **l. en armas** to rise up in arms (**e**) *(viento)* to come up; *(tormenta)* to gather

levante *nm* (**a**) **(el) L.** Levante, = the regions of Valencia and Murcia (**b**) *(viento)* east wind, Levanter

levar *vt* **l. ancla** to weigh anchor

leve *adj (ligero)* light; *Fig (de poca importancia)* slight

levedad *nf (ligereza)* lightness; *Fig* slightness; *Fig (de ánimo)* levity; **heridas de l.** minor injuries

levemente *adv* slightly

levitar *vi* to levitate

léxico,-a *Ling* **1** *nm (diccionario)* lexicon; *(vocabulario)* vocabulary, word list
2 *adj* lexical

ley *nf* (**a**) law; *Parl* bill, act; **aprobar una l.** to pass a bill (**b**) **oro de l.** pure gold; **plata de l.** sterling silver

leyenda *nf* (**a**) *(relato)* legend (**b**) *(en un mapa)* legend; *(en una moneda)* inscription; *(bajo ilustración)* caption

liar [29] **1** *vt* (**a**) *(envolver)* to wrap up; *(un cigarrillo)* to roll (**b**) *(enredar)* to muddle up; *(confundir)* to confuse
2 liarse *vpr* (**a**) *(embarullarse)* to get muddled up (**b**) *Fam (salir con)* to get involved (*besarse*) to neck (**c**) **l. a bofetadas** to come to blows

libanés,-esa *adj & nm,f* Lebanese

Líbano *n* **el L.** the Lebanon

libelo *nm (difamación)* lampoon, satire

libélula *nf* dragonfly

liberación *nf (de país)* liberation; *(de rehén)* release, freeing

liberal 1 *adj* (**a**) liberal; *(carácter)* open-minded; *Pol* **Partido L.** Liberal Party; **profesión l.** profession (**b**) *(generoso)* generous, liberal
2 *nmf* liberal

liberalizar [40] *vt* to liberalize

liberar vt (país) to liberate; (prisionero) to free, to release

libero nm Ftb sweeper

libertad nf freedom, liberty; **en l.** free; Jur **(en) l. bajo palabra/fianza** (on) parole/bail; Jur **(en) l. condicional** (on) parole; **l. de comercio** free trade; **l. de expresión** freedom of speech

libertador,-a nm,f liberator

libertar vt to set free, to release

libertinaje nm licentiousness

libertino,-a adj & nm,f libertine

Libia n Libya

libio,-a adj & nm,f Libyan

libra nf (moneda, peso) pound; **l. esterlina** pound sterling

librador,-a nm,f Fin drawer

librar 1 vt (a) to free; Jur to free, to release (b) Com (una letra) to draw (c) **l. batalla** to do o join battle

2 vi **libro los martes** (no ir a trabajar) I have Tuesdays off

3 librarse vpr to escape; **l. de algn** to get rid of sb

libre adj free; **entrada l.** (gratis) admission free; (sin restricción) open to the public; **l. cambio** free trade; **l. de impuestos** tax-free

librecambio, librecambismo nm free trade

librería nf (a) (tienda) bookshop, US bookstore (b) (estante) bookcase

> _Observa que la palabra inglesa **library** es un falso amigo y no es la traducción de la palabra española **librería**. En inglés, **library** significa "biblioteca"._

librero,-a 1 nm,f bookseller
2 nm CAm, Col, Méx (mueble) bookcase

> _Observa que la palabra inglesa **librarian** es un falso amigo y no es la traducción de la palabra española **librero**. En inglés, **librarian** significa "bibliotecario"._

libreta nf notebook; **l. (de ahorro)** savings book

libretista nmf Am Cin screenwriter, scriptwriter

libreto nm Am Cin script

libro nm book; **l. de texto** textbook; Com **l. de caja** cashbook; Fin **l. mayor** ledger

liceal nmf Urug Br secondary school o US high school pupil

liceano,-a nm,f Chile Br secondary school o US high school pupil

liceísta nmf Ven Br secondary school o US high school pupil

licencia nf (a) (permiso) permission; (documentos) permit, licence; **l. de armas/caza** gun/hunting licence (b) (libertad abusiva) licence, licentiousness (c) Am Aut Br driving licence, US driver's license

licenciado,-a nm,f (a) Univ graduate; **l. en Ciencias** Bachelor of Science (b) Am lawyer

licenciar [43] 1 vt (a) Mil to discharge (b) Univ to confer a degree on
2 licenciarse vpr Univ to graduate

licenciatura nf Univ (título) (bachelor's) degree (course); (carrera) degree (course)

liceo nm (a) (sociedad literaria) literary society (b) (escuela) Br secondary school, US high school

licitar vt Com (pujar) to bid for

lícito,-a adj (permisible) allowed; Jur lawful

licor nm liquor, spirits

licuadora nf liquidizer

licuar [30] vt to liquidize

lid nf (combate) contest

líder nmf leader

liderar vt to lead, to head

liderato, liderazgo nm leadership; Dep top o first position

lidia nf bullfight, bullfighting

lidiador nm bullfighter

lidiar [43] 1 vt Taurom to fight
2 vi to fight; **l. con** to contend with, to fight against

liebre nf (a) hare (b) Dep pacemaker

liendre nf nit

lienzo nm (a) Tex linen (b) Arte canvas

lifting nm face-lift

liga nf (a) Dep & Pol league; **hacer buena l.** to get on well together (b) (prenda) garter

ligamento nm ligament

ligar [42] 1 vt (a) to join; Fig (dos personas) to unite (b) Fam (coger) to get
2 vi Fam **l. con algn** (seducir) to Br get off o US make out with sb
3 ligarse vpr (vincularse) to become attached (a to)

ligazón nf bond, tie

ligeramente adv (a) (levemente) lightly (b) (un poco) slightly

ligereza nf (a) lightness; (de tela, argumento) flimsiness (b) (frivolidad) flippancy; (acto) indiscretion; (dicho) indiscreet remark (c) (rapidez) speed

ligero,-a 1 adj (a) (peso) light, lightweight; **l. de ropa** lightly clad (b) (ágil) light on one's feet; (veloz) swift, quick (c) (leve) slight; **brisa/comida ligera** light breeze/meal (d) **a la ligera** lightly
2 adv (rápido) fast, swiftly

light adj inv (tabaco) mild; Fig (persona) lightweight

ligón,-ona adj & nm,f Fam (hombre) ladies' man; **es muy ligona** she's hot stuff

ligue nm pick-up

liguero,-a 1 adj Dep league; **partido l.** league match
2 nm Br suspender belt, US garter belt

lija nf sandpaper; **papel de l.** sandpaper

lijar vt to sand o sandpaper (down)

lila¹ 1 nm (color) lilac

2 *nf (flor)* lilac
3 *adj inv* lilac
lila² *Fam* **1** *adj (tonto)* dumb, stupid
  2 *nmf (tonto)* twit
lima¹ *nf (fruto)* lime
lima² *nf (herramienta)* file; **l. de uñas** nail-file
limar *vt* to file; *Fig* **l. asperezas** to smooth things over
limbo *nm* limbo
limitación *nf* limitation; **l. de velocidad** speed limit
limitar 1 *vt* to limit, to restrict
  2 *vi* to border; **l. con** to border on
límite *nm* limit; *Geog & Pol* boundary, border; **caso l.** borderline case; **fecha l.** deadline; **velocidad l.** maximum speed
limítrofe *adj* neighbouring
limo *nm* slime
limón *nm* lemon
limonada *nf* lemon squash
limonero *nm* lemon tree
limosna *nf* alms; **pedir l.** to beg
limpiabotas *nm inv* bootblack, shoeshine
limpiacristales *nm inv* window cleaner
limpiador,-a 1 *adj* cleansing
  2 *nm,f (persona)* cleaner
  3 *nm (producto)* cleaner
limpiaparabrisas *nm inv Br* windscreen *o US* windshield wiper
limpiar [43] *vt* **(a)** to clean; *(con un trapo)* to wipe; *(zapatos)* to polish; *Fig* to cleanse **(b)** *Fam (hurtar)* to pinch, to nick
limpieza *nf (calidad)* cleanliness; *(acción)* cleaning; *Fig (integridad)* integrity; **con l.** cleanly
limpio,-a 1 *adj* **(a)** *(aseado)* clean **(b)** *Dep* **juego l.** fair play **(c)** *Fin (neto)* net; **beneficios en l.** net profit **(d)** *Fam* **pasar algo a l.** to produce a fair copy of sth
  2 *adv* fairly; **jugar l.** to play fair
linaje *nm* lineage
linaza *nf* **aceite de l.** linseed oil
lince *nm* lynx; **tiene ojos de l.** he's eagle-eyed
linchar *vt* to lynch; *Fam (pegar)* to beat up
lindante *adj* bordering
lindar *vi* **l. con** to border on
linde *nm o nf* boundary, limit
lindero,-a 1 *adj* bordering, adjoining
  2 *nm* boundary, limit
lindo,-a 1 *adj (bonito)* pretty, lovely; **de lo l.** a great deal
  2 *adv Am (bien)* nicely
línea *nf* **(a)** line; **l. aérea** airline; **en líneas generales** roughly speaking; *Informát* **fuera de l.** off-line; **en l.** on-line **(b)** **guardar la l.** to watch one's figure
lineal *adj* linear; **dibujo l.** line drawing
lingote *nm* ingot; *(de oro, plata)* bar
lingüista *nmf* linguist
lino *nm* **(a)** *Bot* flax **(b)** *Tex* linen
linterna *nf* torch
linyera *nmf CSur (vagabundo)* tramp, *US* bum

lío *nm* **(a)** *(paquete)* bundle **(b)** *Fam (embrollo)* mess, muddle; **hacerse un l.** to get mixed up; **meterse en líos** to get into trouble; **armar un l.** to kick up a fuss **(c)** *Fam (relación amorosa)* affair
lioso,-a *adj Fam (asunto)* confusing
lipotimia *nf* fainting fit
liquidación *nf* **(a)** *Com (saldo)* clearance sale **(b)** *Fin* liquidation
liquidar 1 *vt Com (deuda, cuenta)* to settle; *(mercancías)* to sell off
  2 liquidarse *vpr Fam* **(a)** *(gastar)* to spend **(b)** **l. a algn** *(matar)* to bump sb off
liquidez *nf Fin* liquidity
líquido,-a 1 *adj* **(a)** liquid **(b)** *Fin* net
  2 *nm* **(a)** *(fluido)* liquid **(b)** *Fin* liquid assets; **l. imponible** taxable income
lira *nf (moneda)* lira
lírico,-a *adj* lyrical
lirio *nm* iris
lirismo *nm* lyricism
lirón *nm* dormouse; *Fig* **dormir como un l.** to sleep like a log
Lisboa *n* Lisbon
lisiado,-a 1 *adj* crippled
  2 *nm,f* cripple
lisiar [43] *vt* to maim, to cripple
liso,-a 1 *adj* **(a)** *(superficie)* smooth, even; *Dep* **los cien metros lisos** the one hundred metres sprint **(b)** *(pelo, falda)* straight **(c)** *(tela)* self-coloured **(d)** *Am (desvergonzado)* rude **(e)** **lisa y llanamente** purely and simply
lisonjero,-a 1 *adj* flattering
  2 *nm,f* flatterer
lista *nf* **(a)** *(relación)* list; **l. de espera** waiting list; *(en avión)* standby; **pasar l.** to call the register *o* the roll; *Informát* **l. de correo** mailing list **(b)** *(franja)* stripe; **a listas** striped
listado,-a 1 *adj* striped
  2 *nm* list; *Informát* listing
listar *vt Am* to list
listín *nm* **l. telefónico** telephone directory
listo,-a *adj* **(a)** **ser l.** *(inteligente)* to be clever *o* smart **(b)** **estar l.** *(a punto)* to be ready
listón *nm Dep* bar; *Fig* **subir el l.** to raise the requirements level
litera *nf (cama)* bunk bed; *(en tren)* couchette
literal *adj* literal
literario,-a *adj* literary
literato,-a *nm,f* writer, author

> 🖉 Observa que la palabra inglesa **literate** es un falso amigo y no es la traducción de la palabra española **literato**. En inglés, **literate** significa "alfabetizado".

literatura *nf* literature
litigar [42] *vi Jur* to litigate
litigio *nm Jur* lawsuit; *Fig* dispute; **en l.** in dispute
litografía *nf* **(a)** *(técnica)* lithography **(b)** *(imagen)* lithograph

toral 1 nm coast, seaboard

2 adj coastal

tro nm litre

ituania n Lithuania

tuano,-a 1 adj & nm,f Lithuanian

2 nm (idioma) Lithuanian

turgia nf liturgy

viano,-a adj (de poco peso) lightweight

vido,-a adj livid

ving ['lißin] (pl **livings**) nm living room

za nf contest

aga nf sore; (herida) wound

ama nf flame; **en llamas** in flames, ablaze

amada nf call; Tel **l. interurbana** long-distance call; **señal de l.** ringing tone

amado,-a 1 adj so-called

2 nm Am (**a**) (en general) call; (a la puerta) knock; (con timbre) ring (**b**) (telefónico) call; **hacer un l.** to make a phone call (**c**) (apelación) appeal, call; **hacer un l. a algn para que aga algo** to call upon sb to do sth; **hacer un l. a la huelga** to call a strike

amamiento nm appeal

amar 1 vt (**a**) to call; **l. (por teléfono)** to ring up, to call (**b**) (atraer) to draw, to attract; **l. la atención** to attract attention

2 vi (a la puerta) to knock

3 llamarse upr to be called; **¿cómo te llamas?** what's your name?

amarada nf blaze

amativo,-a adj (**a**) (color, ropa) loud, flashy (**b**) (persona) striking

anero,-a nm,f (del llano) plainsman, f plainswoman

aneza nf (sencillez) simplicity

ano,-a 1 adj (**a**) (superficie) flat, level (**b**) (claro) clear (**c**) (sencillo) simple; **el pueblo l.** the common people

2 nm plain

anta nf (**a**) (de rueda) wheel rim (**b**) Am (neumático) tyre

anto nm crying, weeping

anura nf plain

ave nf (**a**) key; **cerrar con l.** to lock; **llaves en mano** (en anuncio) available for immediate occupation; Aut **l. de contacto** ignition key (**b**) Téc spanner; **l. inglesa** adjustable spanner (**c**) (interruptor) switch; **l. de paso** stopcock (**d**) (en lucha) lock (**e**) Impr brace (**f**) Chile, Méx (grifo) Br tap, US faucet

avero nm key-ring

egada nf arrival; Dep finish

egar [42] **1** vi (**a**) to arrive; **l. a Madrid** to arrive in Madrid (**b**) (ser bastante) to be enough (**c**) (alcanzar) **l. a** to reach; **¿llegas al techo?** can you reach the ceiling? (**d**) Fig **l. a las manos** to come to blows; **l. a presidente** to become president (**e**) **l. a** + inf to go so far as to (**f**) **l. a ser** to become

2 llegarse upr to stop by

enar 1 vt (**a**) to fill; (cubrir) to cover (**b**) (satisfacer) to satisfy

2 vi (comida) to be filling

3 llenarse upr to fill (up), to become full

lleno,-a 1 adj full (up); Fig **de l.** fully

2 nm Teatro full house

llevadero,-a adj bearable, tolerable

llevar 1 vt (**a**) to take; (hacia el oyente) to bring; **¿adónde llevas eso?** where are you taking that?; **te llevaré un regalo** I'll bring you a present

(**b**) (transportar) to carry; **dejarse l.** to get carried away

(**c**) (prenda) to wear; **llevaba falda** she was wearing a skirt

(**d**) (soportar) to bear; **¿cómo lleva lo de su enfermedad?** how's he bearing up?

(**e**) (tiempo) **llevo dos años aquí** I've been here for two years; **esto lleva mucho tiempo** this takes a long time

(**f**) (negocio) to be in charge of

2 v aux (**a**) **l.** + gerundio to have been + present participle; **llevo dos años estudiando español** I've been studying Spanish for two years

(**b**) **l.** + participio pasado to have + past participle; **llevaba escritas seis cartas** I had written six letters

3 llevarse upr (**a**) to take away; (premio) to win; (recibir) to get

(**b**) (arrastrar) to carry away

(**c**) (estar de moda) to be fashionable

(**d**) **l. bien con algn** to get on well with sb

llorar vi to cry; Lit to weep

llorica nmf Fam crybaby

lloriquear vi to whimper, to snivel

llorón,-ona adj **un bebé l.** a baby which cries a lot

lloroso,-a adj tearful

llover [4] v impers to rain

llovizna nf drizzle

lloviznar v impers to drizzle

lluvia nf rain; **una l. de** lots of; **l. radiactiva** fallout; **l. ácida** acid rain

lluvioso,-a adj rainy

lo¹ art neut the; **lo mejor** the best (part); **lo mismo** the same thing; **lo mío** mine; **lo tuyo** yours

lo² pron pers m & neut (**a**) (cosa) it; **debes hacerlo** you must do it; **no lo creo** I don't think so; (no se traduce) **no se lo dije** I didn't tell her; ver **le** (**b**) **lo que ...** what ...; **no sé lo que pasa** I don't know what's going on (**c**) **lo cual ...** which ... (**d**) **lo de ...** the business of ...; **cuéntame lo del juicio** tell me about the trial

loable adj praiseworthy, laudable

loar vt to praise

lobo nm wolf; **como boca de l.** pitch-dark; Fam **¡menos lobos!** pull the other one!

lóbrego,-a adj gloomy

lóbulo nm lobe

local 1 adj local

2 nm (recinto) premises, site

localidad nf (**a**) (pueblo) locality; (en impreso)

place of residence (**b**) *Cin & Teatro (asiento)* seat; *(entrada)* ticket

localizar [40] *vt* (**a**) *(encontrar)* to find (**b**) *(fuego, dolor)* to localize

loción *nf* lotion

loco,-a 1 *adj* mad, crazy; **a lo l.** crazily; **l. por** crazy about; **volverse l.** to go mad; *Fam* **¡ni l.!** I'd sooner die!

2 *nm,f* madman, *f* madwoman; **hacerse el l.** to act the fool

3 *nm Chile (molusco)* = type of abalone

locomotora *nf* locomotive

locomotriz *adj* locomotive

locuaz *adj* loquacious, talkative

locución *nf* phrase

locura *nf (enfermedad)* madness, insanity; **con l.** madly; *Fam* **esto es una l.** this is crazy

locutor,-a *nm,f TV & Rad* presenter

locutorio *nm* telephone booth

lodo *nm* mud

logaritmo *nm* logarithm

lógica *nf* logic; **no tiene l.** there's no logic to it

lógico,-a *adj* logical; **era l. que ocurriera** it was bound to happen

logística *nf* logistics *sing o pl*

logotipo *nm* logo

lograr *vt* (**a**) to get, to obtain; *(premio)* to win; *(ambición)* to achieve (**b**) **l. hacer algo** to manage to do sth

logro *nm* achievement

loma *nf* hillock, rise

lombriz *nf* worm, earthworm

lomo *nm* (**a**) back; **a lomo(s)** on the back (**b**) *Culin* loin (**c**) *(de libro)* spine

lona *nf* canvas

loncha *nf* slice; **l. de bacon** rasher of bacon

lonche *nm* (**a**) *Méx, Perú, Ven (merienda) (en escuela)* mid-morning snack; *(en casa)* (afternoon) tea (**b**) *Méx, Ven (comida rápida)* (mid-morning) snack, *Br* elevenses

lonchería *nf Méx* snack-bar

londinense 1 *adj* of/from London

2 *nmf* Londoner

Londres *n* London

longaniza *nf* spicy (pork) sausage

longevo,-a *adj* long-lived

longitud *nf* (**a**) length; **2 m de l.** 2 m long; **l. de onda** wavelength; *Dep* **salto de l.** long jump (**b**) *Geog* longitude

lonja¹ *nf (loncha)* slice; **l. de bacon** rasher of bacon

lonja² *nf* **l. de pescado** fish market

loquería *nf Am* mental asylum, mental hospital

lord *nm (pl* lores) lord; *Br Parl* **Cámara de los Lores** House of Lords

loro *nm* parrot

los¹ 1 *art def mpl* the; **l. libros** the books; **cierra l. ojos** close your eyes; **l. García** the Garcías; *ver* **el, las** *y* **lo**

2 *pron* **l. que** *(personas)* those who; *(cosas)* the ones (that); **toma l. que quieras** take

whichever ones you want; **esos son l. míos.** **tuyos** these are mine/yours; *ver* **les**

los² *pron pers mpl* them; **¿l. has visto?** have you seen them?

losa *nf (stone)* slab, flagstone

lote *nm* (**a**) set (**b**) *Com* lot (**c**) *Informát* batch (**d**) *Fam* **darse el l.** to pet (**e**) *Am (solar)* plot (of land)

loteamiento *nm Bol, Urug* parcelling out, division into plots

loteo *nm Chile, Col* = **loteamiento**

lotería *nf* lottery; **me tocó la l.** I won a prize in the lottery

lotización *nf Ecuad, Perú* = **loteamiento**

loto 1 *nm Bot* lotus

2 *nf (lotería)* lottery

loza *nf* (**a**) *(material)* earthenware (**b**) *(de cocina)* crockery

lozano,-a *adj* (**a**) *(persona)* healthy-looking (**b**) *(plantas)* lush, luxuriant

Ltda. *(abr* Limitada) Ltd

lubricante *nm* lubricant

lubricar [44] *vt* to lubricate

lucero *nm* (bright) star

lucha *nf* (**a**) fight, struggle; **l. de clases** class struggle (**b**) *Dep* wrestling; **l. libre** freestyle wrestling

luchador,-a *nm,f* (**a**) fighter (**b**) *Dep* wrestler

luchar *vi* (**a**) to fight, to struggle (**b**) *Dep* to wrestle

lucidez *nf* lucidity

lúcido,-a *adj* lucid, clear

luciérnaga *nf* glow-worm

lucir [35] **1** *vi* (**a**) *(brillar)* to shine (**b**) *Am (parecer)* to seem (**c**) *Fam (compensar)* **no le luce lo que estudia** his studies don't get him anywhere

2 *vt (ropas)* to sport; *(talento)* to display

3 lucirse *vpr* (**a**) *(hacer buen papel)* to do very well (**b**) *(pavonearse)* to show off

lucrativo,-a *adj* lucrative, profitable

lucro *nm* profit, gain; **afán de l.** greed for money

lúcuma *nf Andes* lucuma, = sweet, pearshaped fruit

lúdico,-a *adj* relating to games, recreational

luego 1 *adv* (**a**) *(después)* then, next, afterwards (**b**) *(más tarde)* later (on); **¡hasta l.!** so long!; **l. de** after (**c**) *desde* **l.** of course (**d**) *Chile, Ven (pronto)* soon; *Méx Fam* **l. l.** *o* **lueguito** right *o* straight away

2 *conj* therefore

lugar *nm* (**a**) place; **en primer l.** in the first place; **en l. de** instead of; **sin l. a dudas** without a doubt; **tener l.** to take place (**b**) **dar l. a** to cause, to give rise to

lugareño,-a *adj & nm,f* local

lugarteniente *nmf* lieutenant

lúgubre *adj* gloomy, lugubrious

lujo *nm* luxury; **productos de l.** luxury products; **no puedo permitirme ese l.** I can't afford that

lujoso,-a *adj* luxurious
lujuria *nf* lust

> 🖉 Observa que la palabra inglesa **luxury** es un
> *also amigo* y no es la traducción de la palabra
> española **lujuria**. En inglés, **luxury** significa
> "lujo".

lujurioso,-a *adj* lecherous, lustful
lumbre *nf* fire
lumbrera *nf* luminary
luminoso,-a *adj* luminous; *Fig* bright
luna *nf* (a) moon; *Fig* **estar en la l.** to have
one's head in the clouds; **l. creciente/llena**
crescent/full moon; *Fig* **l. de miel** honeymoon (b) *(de escaparate)* pane; *(espejo)* mirror
lunar 1 *adj* lunar
2 *nm (redondel)* dot; *(en la piel)* mole,
beauty spot; **vestido de lunares** spotted
dress
lunático,-a *nm,f* lunatic
lunes *nm inv* Monday; **vendré el l.** I'll come on
Monday

lupa *nf* magnifying glass
luso,-a *adj & nm,f* Portuguese
lustrabotas *nm inv*, **lustrador,-a** *nm,f*
Andes, RP bootblack
lustradora *nf Andes, RP* floor polisher
lustrar *vt* to polish; *(zapatos)* to shine
lustre *nm (brillo)* shine, lustre; *Fig (esplendor)*
splendour, glory; **dar** *o* **sacar l. a algo** to
polish sth
lustro *nm* five-year period
lustroso,-a *adj* shiny, glossy
luto *nm* mourning
Luxemburgo *n* Luxembourg
luz *nf* (a) light; **apagar la l.** to put out the light;
a la l. de in the light of; **a todas luces**
obviously; *Fig* **dar a l.** *(parir)* to give birth to;
Fig **dar l. verde a** to give the green light to (b)
Aut light; **luces de cruce** dipped headlights;
luces de posición sidelights; **l. larga** headlights (c) **luces** *(inteligencia)* intelligence;
corto de luces dim-witted (d) **traje de luces**
bullfighter's costume
luzco *indic pres de* **lucir**

M, m ['eme] *nf (la letra)* M, m

m (a) *(abr* **metro(s))** m (b) *(abr* **minuto(s))** min

macabro,-a *adj* macabre

macana *nf* (a) *Andes, Carib, Méx (palo)* club (b) *CSur, Perú, Ven Fam (fastidio)* pain, drag

macanear *vt CSur, Ven (hacer mal)* to botch, to do badly

macanudo,-a *adj Fam* great, terrific

macarra *nm Fam* yob

macarrón *nm* (a) macaroon (b) *Elec* sheath

macarrones *nmpl* macaroni

macedonia *nf* fruit salad

macerar *vt* to macerate

maceta *nf (tiesto)* plant-pot, flowerpot

machacar [44] **1** *vt* (a) to crush; *Dep* to smash (b) *Fam (estudiar con ahínco) Br* to swot up on, *US* to bone up on (c) *Fam (insistir en)* to harp on about, to go on about

2 *vi* (a) *Fam (insistir mucho)* to harp on, to go on (b) *Fam (estudiar con ahínco) Br* to swot, *US* to grind (c) *(en baloncesto)* to smash

machacón,-ona *Fam* **1** *adj (repetitivo)* repetitious; *(pesado)* boring, tiresome

2 *nm,f (muy estudioso) Br* swot, *US* grind

machamartillo: a machamartillo *loc adv (con firmeza)* firmly; *(con obstinación)* obstinately

machete *nm* (a) *(arma)* machete (b) *Arg Fam (chuleta)* crib

machismo *nm* machismo, male chauvinism

machista *adj & nm* male chauvinist

macho 1 *adj* (a) *(animal, planta)* male (b) *Fam (viril)* manly, virile, macho

2 *nm* (a) *(animal, planta)* male (b) *Téc (pieza)* male piece o part; *(de enchufe)* plug (c) *Fam (hombre viril)* macho, he-man, tough guy

machote *nm Am (borrador)* rough draft

macilento,-a *adj* gaunt

macizo,-a 1 *adj* (a) *(sólido)* solid; **de oro m.** of solid gold (b) *(robusto)* solid, robust; *Fam (atractivo)* well-built

2 *nm (masa sólida)* mass

macramé *nm* macramé

macro *nf Informát* macro

macro- *pref* macro-

macroeconomía *nf* macroeconomics *sing*

macuto *nm (morral)* knapsack, haversack

madeja *nf (de lana etc)* hank, skein

madera *nf* (a) wood; *(de construcción)* timber, *US* lumber; **de m.** wood, wooden (b) *Fig* **tiene m. de líder** he has all the makings of a leader

madero *nm* (a) *(de construcción)* timber *(leño)* log (b) *muy Fam (policía)* cop; **los maderos** the fuzz *pl*

madrastra *nf* stepmother

madre 1 *nf* (a) mother; **es m. de tres hijos** she is a mother of three (children); **m. adoptiva** adoptive mother; **m. alquilada** surrogate mother; **m. de familia** mother, housewife; **m. política** mother-in-law; **m. soltera** unmarried mother; *Fig* **la m. patria** one's motherland, *Méx muy Fam* **me vale m.** I couldn't give a damn o *Br* a toss (b) *(de río)* bed

2 *interj* **¡m. de Dios!, ¡m. mía!** good heavens!

madreperla *nf (nácar)* mother-of-pearl

madreselva *nf* honeysuckle

Madrid *n* Madrid

madriguera *nf* burrow, hole

madrileño,-a 1 *adj* of/from Madrid

2 *nm,f* person from Madrid

madrina *nf* (a) *(de bautizo)* godmother (b) *(de boda)* ≃ bridesmaid (c) *Fig (protectora)* protectress

madrugada *nf* (a) dawn; **de m.** in the wee small hours (b) early morning; **las tres de la m.** three o'clock in the morning

madrugador,-a 1 *adj* early-rising

2 *nm,f* early riser

madrugar [42] *vi* to get up early

madurar 1 *vt Fig (un plan)* to think out

2 *vi* (a) *(persona)* to mature (b) *(fruta)* to ripen

madurez *nf* (a) maturity (b) *(de la fruta)* ripeness

maduro,-a *adj* (a) mature; **de edad madura** middle-aged (b) *(fruta)* ripe

maestría *nf* mastery; **con m.** masterfully

maestro,-a 1 *nm,f* (a) *Educ* teacher; **m. de escuela** schoolteacher (b) *Méx (en universidad) Br* lecturer, *US* professor (c) *(especialista)* master; **m. de obras** foreman (d) *Mús* maestro

2 *adj* **obra maestra** masterpiece; **llave maestra** master key

mafia *nf* mafia

mafioso,-a 1 *adj* of/relating to the mafia

2 *nm,f* member of the mafia, mafioso

magdalena *nf* bun, cake

magia *nf* magic; **por arte de m.** as if by magic

mágico,-a *adj* (a) magic (b) *Fig (maravilloso)* magical, wonderful

magisterio *nm* teaching

magistrado,-a *nm,f* judge; *Am* **primer m.** prime minister

magistral *adj (excelente)* masterly; **una jugada m.** a master stroke

magistratura *nf* magistracy

magnánimo,-a *adj* magnanimous

magnate *nm* magnate, tycoon

magnesio *nm* magnesium

magnético,-a *adj* magnetic

magnetizar [40] *vt* (a) *(imantar)* to magnetize (b) *Fig (hipnotizar)* to hypnotize

magnetofón, magnetófono *nm* tape recorder

magnetofónico,-a *adj* magnetic

magnífico,-a *adj* magnificent, splendid

magnitud *nf* magnitude, dimension; **de primera m.** of the first order

magno,-a *adj Literario* great; **aula magna** main amphitheatre

mago,-a *nm,f* wizard, magician; **los tres Reyes Magos** the Three Wise Men, the Three Kings

magrear *vt muy Fam* to grope

magro,-a 1 *nm (de cerdo)* lean meat

2 *adj (sin grasa)* lean

magullar 1 *vt* to bruise, to damage

2 magullarse *vpr* to get bruised, to get damaged

mahometano,-a *adj & nm,f Rel* Mohammedan, Muslim

mahonesa *nf* mayonnaise

maillot *nm (malla)* leotard; *Dep* shirt

maíz *nm* maize, *US* corn

maizal *nm* field of maize o *US* corn

majadería *nf* silly thing, absurdity

majadero,-a *nm,f* fool, idiot

majara, majareta *adj Fam* loony, nutty

majestad *nf* majesty

majestuosidad *nf* majesty

majestuoso,-a *adj* majestic, stately

majo,-a *adj (bonito)* pretty, nice; *Fam (simpático)* nice; **tiene un hijo muy m.** she's got a lovely little boy; *Fam* **ven aquí, m.** come here, dear

mal 1 *nm* (a) *(evil, wrong)* (b) *(daño)* harm; **no le deseo ningún m.** I don't wish him any harm (c) *(enfermedad)* illness, disease; *Fam* **el m. de las vacas locas** mad cow disease

2 *adj* bad; **un m. año** a bad year; *ver* **malo,-a**

3 *adv* badly, wrong; **lo hizo muy m.** he did it very badly; **menos m. que ...** it's a good job (that) ...; **no está (nada) m.** it is not bad (at all); **te oigo/veo (muy) m.** I can hardly hear/see you; **tomar a m.** *(enfadarse)* to take badly

malabar *adj* **(juegos)** malabares juggling

malabarista *nmf* juggler

malapata *nf Fam (mala suerte)* bad luck

malaria *nf* malaria

malcriado,-a 1 *adj* ill-mannered, ill-bred

2 *nm,f* ill-mannered o uncivil person

malcriar [29] *vt* to spoil

maldad *nf* (a) badness, evil (b) *(acción perversa)* evil o wicked thing

maldecir [12] **1** *vt* to curse

2 *vi* (a) *(blasfemar)* to curse (b) *(criticar)* to speak ill (**de** of)

maldición 1 *nf* curse

2 *interj* damnation!

maldito,-a *adj* (a) *Fam (molesto)* damned, *Br* bloody (b) *(endemoniado)* damned, cursed; **¡maldita sea!** damn it!

maleante *adj & nmf* criminal

malear 1 *vt Fig* to corrupt, to pervert

2 malearse *vpr* to go bad

maleducado,-a 1 *adj* bad-mannered

2 *nm,f* bad-mannered person

maleficio *nm (hechizo)* curse, spell

maléfico,-a *adj* evil, harmful

malentendido *nm* misunderstanding

malestar *nm* (a) *(molestia)* discomfort (b) *Fig (inquietud)* uneasiness; **tengo m.** I feel uneasy

maleta 1 *nf* suitcase, case; **hacer la m.** to pack one's things o case

2 *nm Fam (persona)* bungler

maletero *nm Aut Br* boot, *US* trunk

maletín *nm* briefcase

malévolo,-a *adj* malevolent

maleza *nf* (a) *(arbustos)* thicket, undergrowth (b) *(malas hierbas)* weeds

malgastar *vt & vi* to waste, to squander

malhablado,-a 1 *adj* foul-mouthed

2 *nm,f* foul-mouthed person

malhechor,-a *nm,f* wrongdoer, criminal

malhumor *nm* bad temper o mood; **de m.** in a bad temper o mood

malicia *nf* (a) *(mala intención)* malice, maliciousness (b) *(astucia)* cunning, slyness (c) *(maldad)* badness, evil

malicioso,-a 1 *adj* malicious, spiteful

2 *nm,f* malicious o spiteful person

maligno,-a *adj* malignant

malintencionado,-a 1 *adj* ill-intentioned

2 *nm,f* ill-intentioned person

malla *nf* (a) *(prenda)* leotard (b) *(red)* mesh (c) *Perú, RP (bañador)* swimsuit, swimming costume

Mallorca *n* Majorca

mallorquín,-ina *adj & nm,f* Majorcan

malo,-a 1 *adj* (a) *(bad)* (b) *(bad)* bad; **un año m.** a bad year; **estar a malas** to be on bad terms; **por las malas** by force (b) *(persona) (malvado)* wicked, bad; *(travieso)* naughty (c) *(de poca calidad)* bad, poor; **una mala canción/comida** a poor song/meal (d) *(perjudicial)* harmful; **el tabaco es m.** tobacco is harmful (e) **lo m. es que ...** the problem is that ... (f) *(enfermo)* ill, sick

> **Mal** is used instead of **malo** before masculine singular nouns (e.g. **un mal ejemplo** a bad example). The comparative form of **malo** (= worse) is **peor**, the superlative forms (= worst) are **el peor** (masculine) and **la peor** (feminine).

2 *nm,f Fam* **el m.** the baddy o villain

malograr 1 *vt Andes (estropear)* to make a mess of, to ruin

2 malograrse *upr* (**a**) *(fracasar)* to fail, to fall through (**b**) *Andes (estropearse) (el tiempo)* to turn nasty; *(máquina)* to break down; *(alimento)* to go off, to spoil

maloliente *adj* foul-smelling

malparado,-a *adj* **salir m.** to end up in a sorry state

malpensado,-a 1 *adj* nasty-minded

2 *nm,f* nasty-minded person

malsonante *adj (grosero)* rude, offensive; **palabras malsonantes** foul language

malta *nf (cebada)* malt

maltratado,-a *adj* battered

maltratar *vt* to ill-treat, to mistreat

maltrecho,-a *adj* in a sorry state, wrecked

malva 1 *adj inv* mauve

2 *nm (color)* mauve

3 *nf Bot* mallow

malvado,-a 1 *adj* evil, wicked

2 *nm,f* villain, evil person

malvender *vt* to sell at a loss

malversar *vt* to misappropriate, to embezzle

Malvinas *npl* **las (Islas) M.** the Falkland Islands

malviviente *nmf CSur* criminal

malvivir *vi* to live very badly

mama *nf* (**a**) *(de mujer)* breast; *(de animal)* teat (**b**) *Fam (mamá)* mum, mummy

mamá *nf Fam* mum, mummy; *Col, Méx Fam* **m. grande** grandma

mamada *nf* (**a**) *(bebé)* feed (**b**) *Vulg (felatio)* blowjob

mamadera *nf Am* feeding bottle

mamar *vt (leche)* to suck; *Fig (adquirir)* to absorb

mamarracho,-a *nm,f Fam (persona)* ridiculous-looking person, mess, sight; *(cosa)* mess

mameluco *nm Fig* (**a**) fool, idiot, dimwit (**b**) *Am* boiler suit

mamey *nm* (**a**) *(árbol)* mamey, mammee (**b**) *(fruto)* mamey, mammee (apple)

mamífero,-a *nm,f* mammal

mamón *nm muy Fam Br* prat, *US* jerk

mampara *nf* screen

mamporro *nm Fam* wallop

mampostería *nf* masonry

mamut *nm* mammoth

manada *nf* (**a**) *Zool (de vacas, elefantes)* herd; *(de ovejas)* flock; *(de lobos, perros)* pack; *(de leones)* pride (**b**) *Fam (multitud)* crowd, mob; **en manada(s)** in crowds

manager *nmf Dep & Mús* manager

manantial *nm* spring

manar 1 *vi* to flow, to run (**de** from)

2 *vt* to run with, to flow with; **la herida manaba sangre** blood flowed from his wound

manazas *nmf inv Fam* ham-fisted person

mancebo *nm* (**a**) *(de farmacia)* assistant (**b**) *Literario (muchacho)* young man

Mancha *n* **el Canal de la M.** the English Channel

mancha *nf* stain, spot; **m. solar** sunspot; **m. de tinta/vino** ink/wine stain

manchado,-a *adj* dirty, stained; **leche manchada** milky coffee

manchar 1 *vt* to stain, to dirty; *Fig* to stain, to blemish

2 mancharse *upr* to get dirty

manchego,-a 1 *adj* of/from La Mancha

2 *nm,f* person from La Mancha

manco,-a 1 *adj* (**a**) *(de un brazo)* one-armed *(sin brazos)* armless (**b**) *(de una mano)* one-handed; *(sin manos)* handless

2 *nm,f* (**a**) *(de brazos)* one-armed/armless person (**b**) *(de manos)* one-handed/handless person

mancomunidad *nf* community, association

mancornas, mancuernas *nfpl CAm, Chile, Col, Méx, Ven* cufflinks

mandado *nm (recado)* order, errand; **hacer un m.** to run an errand

mandamás *nmf (pl* **mandamases)** *Fam* bigwig, boss

mandamiento *nm* (**a**) *(orden)* order, command (**b**) **los Diez Mandamientos** the Ten Commandments

mandar *vt* (**a**) to order; *Fam* **¿mande?** pardon? (**b**) *(grupo)* to lead, to be in charge *o* command of; *Mil* to command (**c**) *(enviar)* to send; **m. (a) por** to send for; **m. algo por correo** to post sth, to send sth by post; **m. recuerdos** to send regards

mandarina *nf* mandarin (orange), tangerine

mandatario,-a *nm,f Pol* president

mandato *nm* (**a**) *(orden)* order, command (**b**) *Jur* writ, warrant (**c**) *Pol (legislatura)* mandate, term of office

mandíbula *nf* jaw; *Fam* **reír a m. batiente** to laugh one's head off

mandil *nm* apron

Mandinga *nm Am* the Devil

mando *nm* (**a**) *(autoridad)* command, control (**b**) **los altos mandos del ejército** high-ranking army officers (**c**) *Téc (control)* controls; *Aut* **cuadro** *o* **tablero de mandos** dashboard; **m. a distancia** remote control; **palanca de m.** *Téc* control lever; *(de avión, videojuego)* joystick

mandón,-ona 1 *adj Fam* bossy, domineering

2 *nm,f Fam* bossy *o* domineering person

3 *nm Am (mine)* foreman

manecilla *nf (de reloj)* hand

manejable *adj* manageable; *(herramienta)* easy-to-use; *(coche)* manoeuvrable

manejar 1 *vt* (**a**) *(máquina)* to handle, to operate; *Fig (situación)* to handle (**b**) *(negocio)* to run, to manage (**c**) *Fig (a otra persona)* to domineer, to boss about (**d**) *Am (coche)* to drive

2 *vi Am (conducir)* to drive

3 manejarse *upr* to manage

manejo *nm* (a) *(uso)* handling, use; **de fácil m.** easy-to-use (b) *Fig (de un negocio)* management; *(de un coche)* driving (c) *Fig* tricks

manera *nf* (a) way, manner; **a mi/tu m.** (in) my/your way; **de cualquier m.** *(mal)* carelessly, any old how; *(en cualquier caso)* in any case; **de esta m.** in this way; **de ninguna m.** in no way, certainly not; **de todas maneras** anyway, at any rate, in any case; **es mi m. de ser** that's the way I am; **no hay m.** it's impossible (b) **de tal m. que** in such a way that (c) **maneras** manners; **de buenas maneras** politely

manga *nf* (a) *(uso)* sleeve; **de m. corta/larga** short-/long-sleeved; **sin mangas** sleeveless; *Fig* **hacer un corte de mangas a algn** ≃ to give sb the fingers; *Fig* **m. por hombro** messy and untidy; *Fig* **sacarse algo de la m.** to pull sth out of one's hat (b) *(de riego)* hose (c) *(del mar)* arm (d) *Dep* leg, round; *Ten* set

mangante *nmf Fam* thief

mangar [42] *vt Fam* to pinch, to nick, to swipe

mango *nm* (a) *(asa)* handle (b) *RP Fam (dinero)* **no tengo un m.** I haven't got a bean, I'm broke

mangonear *vi Fam* (a) *(entrometerse)* to meddle (b) *(dar órdenes)* to throw one's weight around

manguera *nf* hose

mangui *nmf Fam* thief

manguito *nm* (a) *(para las mangas)* oversleeve; *(para flotar)* armband (b) *Téc* sleeve

maní *nm (pl maníes)* peanut

manía *nf* (a) dislike, ill will; **me tiene m.** he has it in for me (b) *(costumbre)* habit; **tiene la m. de llegar tarde** he's always arriving late (c) *(afición exagerada)* craze; **la m. de las motos** the motorbike craze (d) *Med* mania

maniaco,-a, maníaco,-a *adj & nm,f Psi* manic; *Fam (obseso)* maniac

maniatar *vt* to tie the hands of

maniático,-a 1 *adj* fussy
2 *nm,f* fusspot

manicomio *nm* mental hospital

manicura *nf* manicure

manido,-a *adj (comida)* off (b) *(asunto)* trite, hackneyed

manifestación *nf* (a) demonstration (b) *(expresión)* manifestation, expression

manifestante *nmf* demonstrator

manifestar [1] **1** *vt* (a) *(declarar)* to state, to declare (b) *(mostrar)* to show, to display
2 manifestarse *vpr* (a) *(por la calle)* to demonstrate (b) *(declararse)* to declare oneself; **se manifestó contrario a ...** he spoke out against ...

manifiesto,-a 1 *adj* clear, obvious; **poner de m.** *(revelar)* to reveal, to show; *(hacer patente)* to make clear
2 *nm* manifesto

manigua *nf Am Geog* scrubland

manilla *nf* (a) *(de reloj)* hand (b) *Am (palanca)* lever

manillar *nm* handlebar

maniobra *nf* manoeuvre

maniobrar *vi* to manoeuvre

manipulación *nf* manipulation

manipular *vt* to manipulate; *(máquina)* to handle

maniquí *nm (muñeco)* dummy

manitas *nmf inv Fam* (a) **ser un m.** to be handy, to be very good with one's hands (b) **hacer m.** to hold hands

manito *nm Méx Fam* pal, *Br* mate, *US* buddy

manivela *nf Téc* crank

manjar *nm* dish, food

mano 1 *nf* (a) hand; **a m.** *(sin máquina)* by hand; *(asequible)* at hand; **escrito a m.** handwritten; **hecho a m.** hand-made; **m. armada** armed; **estrechar la m. a algn** to shake hands with sb; **de segunda m.** second-hand; **echar una m. a algn** to give sb a hand; **¡manos a la obra!** shoulders to the wheel!; **meter m. a** *(un problema)* to tackle; *Fam* to touch up; **traerse algo entre manos** to be up to sth; **equipaje de m.** hand luggage (b) *(lado)* side; **a m. derecha/izquierda** on the right/left(-hand side) (c) **m. de pintura** coat of paint (d) **m. de obra** labour (force) (e) *RP (dirección)* direction *(of traffic)*; **calle de una/doble m.** one-/two-way street
2 *nm Andes, CAm, Carib, Méx Fam* pal, *Br* mate, *US* buddy

manojo *nm* bunch; **ser un m. de nervios** to be a bundle of nerves

manopla *nf* mitten

manoseado,-a *adj (objeto)* worn(-out); *(tema)* hackneyed

manosear *vt* to touch repeatedly, to finger; *Fam* to paw

manotazo *nm* cuff, slap

mansalva: a mansalva *loc adv (en gran cantidad)* galore

mansedumbre *nf* (a) *(de persona)* meekness, gentleness (b) *(de animal)* tameness, docility

manso,-a *adj* (a) *(persona)* gentle, meek (b) *(animal)* tame, docile (c) *Chile (extraordinario)* great

manta 1 *nf* (a) blanket; **m. eléctrica** electric blanket (b) *(zurra)* beating, hiding (c) *Ven (vestido)* = traditional costume worn by women from Guajira
2 *nmf Fam* lazy person, idler

manteca *nf* (a) *(de animal)* fat; **m. de cacao/cacahuete** cocoa/peanut butter; **m. de cerdo** lard (b) *Am (mantequilla)* butter

mantecado *nm* shortcake

mantel *nm* tablecloth

📌 Observa que la palabra inglesa **mantle** es un falso amigo y no es la traducción de la palabra española **mantel**. En inglés, **mantle** significa "manto, capa".

mantener [24] **1** *vt* (**a**) *(conservar)* to keep; **mantén el fuego encendido** keep the fire burning; **m. la línea** to keep in trim (**b**) *(entrevista, reunión)* to have; **m. correspondencia con algn** to correspond with sb (**c**) *(ideas, opiniones)* to defend, to maintain (**d**) *(familia)* to support, to feed (**e**) *(peso)* to support, to hold up
2 mantenerse *vpr* (**a**) *(sostenerse)* to stand (**b**) **m. firme** *(perseverar)* to hold one's ground (**c**) *(sustentarse)* to live (**de** on)

mantenimiento *nm* (**a**) *Téc* maintenance, upkeep; **servicio de m.** maintenance service (**b**) *(alimento)* sustenance, support (**c**) **gimnasia y m.** keep fit

mantequilla *nf* butter

manto *nm* cloak

mantón *nm* shawl

mantuve *pt indef de* **mantener**

manual 1 *adj* manual; **trabajo m.** manual labour; *Educ* **trabajos manuales** handicrafts
2 *nm* manual, handbook

manubrio *nm Am (manillar)* handlebars

manufactura *nf* (**a**) *(fabricación)* manufacture (**b**) *(fábrica)* factory

manufacturar *vt* to manufacture

manuscrito *nm* manuscript

manutención *nf* maintenance

manzana *nf* (**a**) apple (**b**) *(de edificios)* block

manzanilla *nf* (**a**) *Bot* camomile (**b**) *(infusión)* camomile tea (**c**) *(vino)* manzanilla

maña *nf* (**a**) *(astucia)* cunning (**b**) *(habilidad)* skill

mañana 1 *nf* morning; **a las dos de la m.** at two in the morning; **de m.** early in the morning; **por la m.** in the morning
2 *nm* tomorrow, the future
3 *adv* tomorrow; **¡hasta m.!** see you tomorrow! **m. por la m.** tomorrow morning; **pasado m.** the day after tomorrow

mañanitas *nfpl Méx* birthday song

mañoco *nm Ven* tapioca

mañoso,-a *adj* skilful

mapa *nm* map; **m. mudo** blank map; *Fam* **borrar del m.** to wipe out

maqueta *nf* (**a**) *(miniatura)* scale model, maquette (**b**) *Mús* demo (tape)

maquiavélico,-a *adj* Machiavellian

maquila *nf Méx (of machines)* assembly

maquiladora *nf Méx* assembly plant

maquillaje *nm* make-up

maquillar 1 *vt* to make up
2 maquillarse *vpr* (**a**) *(ponerse maquillaje)* to put one's make-up on, to make (oneself) up (**b**) *(usar maquillaje)* to wear make-up

máquina *nf* (**a**) machine; **escrito a m.** typewritten; **hecho a m.** machine-made; *Fam* **a toda m.** at full speed **m. de afeitar (eléctrica)** (electric) razor *o* shaver; **m. de coser** sewing machine; **m. de escribir** typewriter; **m. fotográfica** *o* **de fotos** camera; **m. tragaperras** *o Am* **tragamonedas** slot machine, one-armed

bandit (**b**) *CAm, Cuba (coche)* car

maquinar *vt* to machinate, to plot

maquinaria *nf* (**a**) machinery, machines (**b**) *(de reloj etc) (mecanismo)* mechanism, works

maquinilla *nf* **m. de afeitar** safety razor

maquinista *nmf (de tren)* engine driver

mar 1 *nm o nf* (**a**) sea; **en alta m.** on the high seas; **m. adentro** out to sea; **por m.** by sea; **m. gruesa** heavy sea; **m. picada** rough sea (**b**) *Fam* **está la m. de guapa** she's looking really beautiful; **llover a mares** to rain cats and dogs

> Note that the feminine is used in literary language, by people such as fishermen with a close connection with the sea, and in some idiomatic expressions.

2 *nm* sea; **M. del Norte** North Sea; **M. Muerto/Negro** Dead/Black Sea

maracuyá *nf* passion fruit

maraña *nf* tangle

maratón *nm* marathon

maratoniano,-a *adj* marathon

maravilla *nf* marvel, wonder; **de m.** wonderfully; **¡qué m. de película!** what a wonderful film!; *Fam* **a las mil maravillas** marvellously

maravillar 1 *vt* to amaze, to astonish
2 maravillarse *vpr* to marvel (**con** at), to wonder (**con** at)

maravilloso,-a *adj* wonderful, marvellous

marca *nf* (**a**) mark, sign (**b**) *Com* brand, make; **ropa de m.** brand-name clothes; **m. de fábrica** trademark; **m. registrada** registered trademark (**c**) *Dep (récord)* record; **batir la m. mundial** to break the world record

marcador *nm* (**a**) marker (**b**) *Dep (tablero)* scoreboard; *(persona)* scorer (**c**) *Am (rotulador)* felt-tip pen; *Méx (fluorescente)* highlighter pen

marcaje *nm Dep* marking

marcapasos *nm inv Med* pacemaker

marcar [44] **1** *vt* (**a**) to mark (**b**) *Tel* to dial (**c**) *(indicar)* to indicate, to show; **el contador marca 1.327** the meter reads 1,327 (**d**) *Dep (gol, puntos)* to score; *(a jugador)* to mark (**e**) *(cabello)* to set
2 marcarse *vpr Fam* **m. un farol** to show off, to boast

marcha *nf* (**a**) march; **hacer algo sobre la m.** to do sth as one goes along; **a marchas forzadas** against the clock (**b**) **estar en m.** *(vehículo)* to be in motion; *(máquina)* to be working; *(proyecto etc)* to be under way; **poner en m.** to start (**c**) *Aut* gear; **m. atrás** reverse (gear) (**d**) *Mús* march (**e**) *Fam (juerga)* **hay mucha m.** there's lots going on; **ella tiene mucha m.** she likes a good time

marchante,-a *nm,f* (**a**) *(de arte)* dealer (**b**) *CAm, Méx, Ven Fam (cliente)* customer, patron

marchar 1 *vi* (**a**) *(ir)* to go, to walk; *Fam* **¡marchando!** on your way!; **¡una cerveza! – ¡marchando!** a beer, please! – coming right up! (**b**) *(aparato)* to be on; **m. bien** *(negocio)* to be going well (**c**) *Mil* to march

2 marcharse *vpr (irse)* to leave, to go away

marchitar *vt*, **marchitarse** *vpr* to shrivel, to wither

marchito,-a *adj* shrivelled, withered

marchoso,-a *Fam* **1** *adj (persona)* fun-loving, wild

2 *nm,f* raver, fun-lover

marcial *adj* martial; **artes marciales** martial arts

marcianitos *nmpl (juego)* space invaders

marciano,-a *adj & nm,f* Martian

marco *nm* (**a**) *(de cuadro etc)* frame (**b**) *Fig (ámbito)* framework; **acuerdo m.** framework agreement (**c**) *Fin (moneda)* mark

marea *nf* (**a**) tide; **m. alta/baja** high/low tide; **m. negra** oil slick (**b**) *Fig (multitud)* crowd, mob

mareado,-a *adj* (**a**) sick; *(en un avión)* air-sick; *(en un coche)* car-sick, travel-sick; *(en el mar)* seasick (**b**) *Euf (bebido)* tipsy (**c**) *(aturdido)* dizzy

marear 1 *vt* (**a**) to make sick; *(en el mar)* to make seasick; *(en un avión)* to make airsick; *(en un coche)* to make car-sick *o* travel-sick (**b**) *(aturdir)* to make dizzy (**c**) *Fam (fastidiar)* to annoy, to pester (**d**) *Culin* to stir

2 marearse *vpr* (**a**) to get sick/seasick/air-sick/car-sick *o* travel-sick (**b**) *(quedar aturdido)* to get dizzy (**c**) *Euf (emborracharse)* to get tipsy

mareo *nm* (**a**) *(náusea)* sickness; *(en el mar)* seasickness; *(en un avión)* airsickness; *(en un coche)* car-sickness, travel-sickness (**b**) *(aturdimiento)* dizziness, light-headedness

marfil *nm* ivory

margarina *nf* margarine

margarita *nf* daisy

margen 1 *nm* (**a**) border, edge; *Fig* **dejar algn/algo al m.** to leave sb/sth out; *Fig* **mantenerse al m.** not to get involved; **al m. de** leaving aside (**b**) *(del papel)* margin (**c**) *Com* **m. beneficiario** profit margin

2 *nf (de río)* bank

marginación *nf (exclusión)* exclusion

marginado,-a 1 *adj* excluded

2 *nm,f* dropout

marginal *adj* (**a**) marginal (**b**) *Pol* fringe

marginar *vt (de un grupo, sociedad)* to leave out, to exclude

maría *nf Fam* (**a**) *(droga)* marijuana, pot (**b**) *Educ (asignatura fácil)* easy subject (**c**) *(ama de casa)* housewife

marica *nm Fam* queer, *Br* poof, *US* fag

maricón *nm muy Fam* queer, *Br* poof, *US* fag

marido *nm* husband

mariguana, marihuana, marijuana *nf* marijuana

marimacho *nm Fam* mannish woman, butch woman

marimandón,-ona *nm,f Fam* domineering person

marimorena *nf Fam* row, fuss; *Fam* **armar(se) la m.** to kick up a racket

marina *nf* (**a**) *Náut* seamanship (**b**) *Mil* navy; **m. de guerra** navy; **m. mercante** merchant navy (**c**) *Geog (zona costera)* seacoast

marinero,-a 1 *nm* sailor, seaman

2 *adj* seafaring

marino,-a 1 *adj* marine; **brisa marina** sea breeze

2 *nm* sailor

marioneta *nf* marionette, puppet

mariposa *nf* (**a**) *(insecto)* butterfly (**b**) *(lamparilla)* oil lamp (**c**) *(en natación)* butterfly

mariposear *vi Fig* (**a**) *(flirtear)* to flirt (**b**) *(ser inconstante)* to be fickle

mariposón *nm* (**a**) *(galanteador)* flirt (**b**) *Fam (marica)* fairy, pansy

mariquita 1 *nf (insecto) Br* ladybird, *US* ladybug

2 *nm Fam (marica)* queer, *Br* poof, *US* fag

mariscal *nm Mil* marshal; **m. de campo** *Br* field marshal, *US* general of the army

marisco *nm* shellfish; **mariscos** seafood

marisma *nf* marsh

marisquería *nf* seafood restaurant, shellfish bar

marítimo,-a *adj* maritime; sea; **ciudad marítima** coastal town; **paseo m.** promenade

mármol *nm* marble

marmóreo,-a *adj* marble

maroma *nf* (**a**) *Náut* cable (**b**) *(cuerda)* thick rope

marqués *nm* marquis

marquesa *nf* marchioness

marquesina *nf* canopy; **m. (del autobús)** bus shelter

marquetería *nf* marquetry, inlaid work

marrano,-a 1 *adj (sucio)* filthy, dirty

2 *nm,f* (**a**) *Fam (persona)* dirty pig, slob (**b**) *(animal)* pig

marras: de marras *loc adv* **el individuo de m.** the man in question

marrón 1 *adj (color)* brown

2 *nm* (**a**) *(color)* brown (**b**) *Fam (condena)* sentence

marroquí *adj & nmf* Moroccan

marroquinería *nf* leather goods

Marruecos *n* Morocco

marrullero,-a 1 *adj* cajoling, wheedling

2 *nm,f* cajoler, wheedler

Marte *n* Mars

martes *nm inv* Tuesday; **m. y trece** ≃ Friday the thirteenth

martillero *nm CSur* auctioneer

martillo *nm* hammer

mártir *nmf* martyr

martirio *nm* (**a**) martyrdom (**b**) *Fig (fastidio)* torment

martirizar [40] *vt* (**a**) to martyr (**b**) *Fig (fastidiar)* to torture, to torment

marxista *adj & nmf* Marxist

marzo *nm* March

mas *conj Literario* but

más 1 *adv* (**a**) *(adicional)* more; **no tengo m.** I haven't got any more

(**b**) *(comparativo)* more; **es m. alta/inteligente que yo** she's taller/more intelligent than me; **tengo m. dinero que tú** I've more money than you; **m. gente de la que esperas** more people than you're expecting; **m. de** *(con numerales, cantidad)* more than, over

(**c**) *(superlativo)* most; **es el m. bonito/caro** it's the prettiest/most expensive

(**d**) *interj* so ..., what a ...; **¡qué casa m. bonita!** what a lovely house! **¡está m. guapa!** she looks so beautiful!

(**e**) *(después de pron interr e indef)* else; **¿algo m.?** anything else?; **no, nada m.** no, nothing else; **¿quién m.?** who else?; **nadie/alguien m.** nobody/somebody else

(**f**) **cada día o vez m.** more and more; **estar de m.** to be unnecessary; **traje uno de m.** I brought a spare one; **es m.** what's more, furthermore; **lo m. posible** as much as possible; **m. bien** rather; **m. o menos** more or less; **m. aún** even more; **¿qué m. da?** what's the difference?; **todo lo m.** at the most

(**g**) **por m.** (+ *adj/adv*) + **que** (+ *subjunctive*) however (much), no matter how (much); **por m. fuerte que sea** however strong he may be; **por m. que grites no te oirá nadie** no matter how much you shout nobody will hear you

2 *nm inv* **los m.** the majority, most people; **sus m. y sus menos** its pros and cons

3 *prep Mat* plus; **dos m. dos** two plus o and two

masa *nf* (**a**) mass (**b**) *(de cosas)* bulk, volume; **m. salarial** total wage bill (**c**) *(gente)* mass; **en m.** en masse; **medios de comunicación de masas** mass media (**d**) *Culin* dough (**e**) *Constr* mortar (**f**) *RP (pastelito)* shortcake cookie

masacrar *vt* to massacre

masacre *nf* massacre

masaje *nm* massage; **dar masaje(s) (a)** to massage

masajista *nmf (hombre)* masseur; *(mujer)* masseuse

mascar [44] *vt & vi* to chew, to masticate

máscara *nf* mask; **m. de gas** gas mask; **traje de m.** fancy dress

> Observa que la palabra inglesa **mascara** es un falso amigo y no es la traducción de la palabra española **máscara**. En inglés, **mascara** significa "rímel".

mascarilla *nf* (**a**) mask; **m. de oxígeno** oxygen mask (**b**) *Med* face mask (**c**) *(cosmética)* face pack

mascota *nf* mascot

masculino,-a *adj* (**a**) *Zool & Bot* male (**b**) *(de hombre)* male, manly; **una voz masculina** a manly voice (**c**) *(para hombre)* men's; **ropa masculina** men's clothes, menswear (**d**) *Ling* masculine

mascullar *vt* to mumble

masificación *nf* overcrowding

masificado,-a *adj* overcrowded

masilla *nf* putty

masivo,-a *adj* massive

masón *nm* freemason, mason

masonería *nf* freemasonry, masonry

masoquista 1 *adj* masochistic

2 *nmf* masochist

máster *nm* master's degree

masticar [44] *vt* to chew

mástil *nm* (**a**) *(asta)* mast, pole (**b**) *Náut* mast (**c**) *(de guitarra)* neck

mastín *nm* mastiff

masturbación *nf* masturbation

masturbar *vt*, **masturbarse** *vpr* to masturbate

mata *nf* (**a**) *(matorral)* bush, shrub; **m. de pelo** head of hair (**b**) *(ramita)* sprig

matadero *nm* slaughterhouse, abattoir

matador *nm* matador, bullfighter

matadura *nf* sore

matambre *nm Andes, RP* = flank steak rolled with boiled egg, olives and red pepper, which is cooked, then sliced and served cold

matamoscas *nm inv (pala)* fly swat

matanza *nf* slaughter

matar *vt* (**a**) to kill; *Fam* **m. el hambre/el tiempo** to kill one's hunger/the time; *Fam* **que me maten si ...** I'll be damned if ... (**b**) *(cigarro, bebida)* to finish off (**c**) *(sello)* to frank

matasellos *nm inv* postmark

matasuegras *nm inv* party blower

mate¹ *adj (sin brillo)* matt

mate² *nm (en ajedrez)* mate; **jaque m.** checkmate

mate³ *nm (infusión)* maté

matemática *nf*, **matemáticas** *nfpl* mathematics *sing*

matemático,-a 1 *adj* mathematical

2 *nm,f* mathematician

materia *nf* (**a**) matter; **m. prima** raw material (**b**) *(tema)* matter, question; **índice de materias** table of contents (**c**) *Educ (asignatura)* subject

material 1 *adj* material, physical; **daños materiales** damage to property

2 *nm* (**a**) material; **m. escolar/de construcción** teaching/building material o materials (**b**) *(equipo)* equipment; **m. de oficina** office equipment

materialista *adj & nmf* materialist

materialmente *adv* physically

maternal *adj* maternal, motherly

maternidad *nf* maternity, motherhood

materno,-a *adj* maternal; **abuelo m.** maternal grandfather; **lengua materna** native o mother tongue

mates *nfpl Fam Br* maths *sing*, *US* math

matinal *adj* morning; **televisión m.** breakfast television

matiz *nm* (**a**) *(de color)* shade (**b**) *(de palabra)* shade of meaning, nuance; **un m. irónico** a touch of irony

matización *nf* hacer una m. to add a rider

matizar [40] *vt* (**a**) *Fig (precisar)* to be more precise *o* explicit about (**b**) *Arte* to blend, to harmonize (**c**) *Fig (palabras, discurso)* to tinge; *(voz)* to vary, to modulate

matón,-ona *nm,f Fam* thug, bully

matorral *nm* brushwood, thicket

matraca *nf (ruido)* rattle; *Fam* **dar la m. a algn** to pester *o* bother sb

matrero,-a *nm,f Am (bandolero)* bandit, brigand

matriarcado *nm* matriarchy

matrícula *nf* (**a**) registration; **derechos de m.** registration fee; **m. de honor** distinction; **plazo de m.** registration period (**b**) *Aut (número)* Br registration number, US license number; *(placa)* Br number plate, US license plate

matriculación *nf* registration

matricular *vt*, **matricularse** *vpr* to register

matrimonial *adj* matrimonial; **agencia m.** marriage bureau; **enlace m.** wedding; **vida m.** married life

matrimonio *nm* (**a**) marriage; **m. civil/religioso** registry office/church wedding; **contraer m.** to marry; **cama de m.** double bed (**b**) *(pareja casada)* married couple; **el m. y los niños** the couple and their children; **el m. Romero** Mr and Mrs Romero, the Romeros

matriz *nf* (**a**) *Anat* womb, uterus (**b**) *Mat* matrix (**c**) *(de documento) (original)* original, master copy (**d**) *Téc* mould (**e**) **casa m.** parent company

matrona *nf* midwife

matutino,-a *adj* morning; **prensa matutina** morning papers

maullar *vi* to miaow

maullido *nm* miaowing, miaow

maxilar *nm* jaw, jawbone

máxima *nf* (**a**) *Met* maximum temperature (**b**) *(aforismo)* maxim

máxime *adv* especially, all the more so

máximo,-a 1 *adj* maximum, highest; **la máxima puntuación** the highest score

   2 *nm* maximum; **al m.** to the utmost; **como m.** *(como mucho)* at the most; *(lo más tarde)* at the latest

mayo *nm* May

mayonesa *nf* mayonnaise

mayor 1 *adj* (**a**) *(comparativo) (tamaño)* larger, bigger (**que** than); *(edad)* older, elder; **m. que yo** older than me (**b**) *(superlativo) (tamaño)* largest, biggest; *(edad)* oldest, eldest; **la m. parte** the majority; **la m. parte de las veces** most often (**c**) *(adulto)* grown-up; **ser m. de edad** to be of age (**d**) *(maduro)* elderly, mature (**e**) *(principal)* major, main; *Educ* **colegio** **m.** hall of residence (**f**) *Mús* major (**g**) *Com* **al por m.** wholesale; *Fig (en abundancia)* by the score, galore

   2 *nm* (**a**) *Mil* major (**b**) **mayores** *(adultos)* grown-ups, adults

mayordomo *nm* butler

mayoreo *nm Andes, Méx Com* wholesale

mayoría *nf* majority; **en su m.** in the main; **la m. de los niños** most children; **m. absoluta/relativa** absolute/relative majority; **m. de edad** majority

mayorista 1 *adj* wholesale

   2 *nmf* wholesaler; **precios de m.** wholesale prices

mayoritario,-a *adj* majority; **un gobierno m.** a majority government

mayúscula *nf* capital letter

mayúsculo,-a *adj* (**a**) *Ling (letra)* capital (**b**) *(error)* very big, enormous

mazacote *nm* (**a**) *Culin* solid mass, stodge (**b**) *(mezcla confusa)* hotchpotch

mazapán *nm* marzipan

mazmorra *nf* dungeon

mazo *nm* mallet

mazorca *nf Agr* cob

me *pron pers* (**a**) *(objeto directo)* me; **no me mires** don't look at me (**b**) *(objeto indirecto)* me, to me, for me; **¿me das un caramelo?** will you give me a sweet?; **me lo dio** he gave it to me; **me es difícil hacerlo** it is difficult for me to do it (**c**) *(pron reflexivo)* myself; **me he cortado** I've cut myself; **me voy/muero** *(no se traduce)* I'm off/dying

meada *nf Fam* piss; **echar una m.** to have a piss

meadero *nm Fam Br* bog, *US* john

meandro *nm* meander

mear *Fam* **1** *vi* to (have a) piss

   2 mearse *vpr* to wet oneself; *Fig* **m. de risa** to piss oneself (laughing)

MEC *nm (abr* **Ministerio de Educación y Ciencia**) = Spanish ministry of education and science

mecachis *interj Fam* darn it!, damn it!

mecánica *nf* (**a**) *(ciencia)* mechanics *sing* (**b**) *(mecanismo)* mechanism, works

mecánico,-a 1 *adj* mechanical

   2 *nm,f* mechanic

mecanismo *nm* mechanism

mecanizar [40] *vt* to mechanize

mecanografía *nf* typewriting, typing

mecanografiar [29] *vt* to type

mecanógrafo,-a *nm,f* typist

mecapal *nm CAm, Méx* = porter's leather harness

mecedora *nf* rocking-chair

mecenas *nmf inv* patron

mecer [49] **1** *vt* to rock

   2 mecerse *vpr* to swing, to rock

mecha *nf* (**a**) *(de vela)* wick (**b**) *Mil & Min* fuse; *Fam* **aguantar m.** to grin and bear it (**c**) *(de pelo)* streak; **hacerse mechas** to have one's hair streaked

mechar vt (carne) to lard

mechero nm (cigarette) lighter

mechón nm (a) (de pelo) lock (b) (de lana) tuft

medalla 1 nf medal

2 nmf Dep (campeón) medallist

medallón nm medallion

media nf (a) stocking; Am (calcetín) sock (b) (promedio) average; Mat mean; **m. aritmética/geométrica** arithmetic/geometric mean (c) **a medias** (incompleto) unfinished; (entre dos) half and half; **ir a medias** to go halves

⎯⎯⎯⎯⎯⎯⎯⎯⎯⎯⎯⎯⎯⎯⎯⎯
📖 Observa que la palabra inglesa **media** es un falso amigo y no es la traducción de la palabra española **media**. En inglés, **media** significa "medios de comunicación".
⎯⎯⎯⎯⎯⎯⎯⎯⎯⎯⎯⎯⎯⎯⎯⎯

mediación nf mediation, intervention; **por m. de un amigo** through a friend

mediado,-a adj half-full, half-empty; **a mediados de mes/semana** about the middle of the month/week

mediador,-a nm,f mediator

medialuna nf (a) (símbolo musulmán) crescent (b) Am Culin (pasta) croissant

mediano,-a adj (a) middling, average (b) (tamaño) medium-sized

medianoche nf midnight

mediante prep by means of, with the help of, using; **Dios m.** God willing

mediar [43] vi (a) (intervenir) to mediate, to intervene; **m. en favor de** o **por algn** to intercede on behalf of sb (b) (tiempo) to pass; **mediaron tres semanas** three weeks passed

mediático,-a adj media

medicación nf medication, medical treatment

medicamento nm medicine, medicament

medicina nf medicine; **estudiante de m.** medical student, medic

médico,-a 1 nm,f doctor; **m. de cabecera** family doctor, general practitioner, GP

2 adj medical

medida nf (a) measure; **a (la) m.** (ropa) made-to-measure; **a m. que avanzaba** as he advanced; **en gran m.** to a great extent (b) (dimensión) measurement (c) (disposición) measure; **adoptar** o **tomar medidas** to take steps; **m. represiva** deterrent

medidor nm Am (contador) meter

medieval adj medieval

medievo nm Middle Ages

medio,-a 1 adj (a) half; **a m. camino** halfway; **m. kilo** half a kilo; **una hora y media** one and a half hours, an hour and a half (b) (intermedio) middle; **a media mañana/tarde** in the middle of the morning/afternoon; **clase media** middle class; **punto m.** middle ground (c) (normal) average; **salario m.** average wage

2 adv half; **está m. muerta** she is half dead

3 nm (a) (mitad) half (b) (centro) middle; **en**

m. (de) (en el centro) in the middle (of); (entre dos) in between (c) **medios de transporte** means of transport; **por m. de ...** by means of ...; **medios económicos** means; **medios de comunicación** (mass) media (d) **m. ambiente** environment (e) Dep (jugador) half back

medioambiental adj environmental

medioambientalista nmf environmentalist

mediocre adj mediocre

mediocridad nf mediocrity

mediodía nm (a) (hora exacta) midday, noon (b) (período aproximado) early afternoon, lunch-time (c) (sur) south

medir [6] **1** vt (a) (distancia, superficie, temperatura) to measure (b) (moderar) to weigh; **mide tus palabras** weigh your words

2 vi to measure, to be; **¿cuánto mides?** how tall are you?; **mide 2 m** he is 2 m tall; **mide 2 m de alto/ancho/largo** it is 2 m high/wide/long

meditar vt & vi to meditate, to ponder; **m. sobre algo** to ponder over sth

mediterráneo,-a 1 adj Mediterranean

2 nm el M. the Mediterranean

medrar vi to climb the social ladder

medroso,-a adj (a) (temeroso) fearful, faint-hearted (b) (que causa miedo) frightening

médula nf (a) marrow; **m. ósea** bone marrow (b) Fig (lo más profundo) marrow, pith; **hasta la m.** to the marrow

medusa nf jellyfish

megafonía nf public-address system, PA system

megáfono nm megaphone

megalito nm megalith

megalómano,-a adj megalomaniac

mejicano,-a adj & nm,f Mexican

Méjico n Mexico; **ciudad de M.** Mexico City; **Nuevo M.** New Mexico

mejilla nf cheek

mejillón nm mussel

mejor 1 adj (a) (comparativo) better (que than); **es m. no decírselo** it's better not to tell her; **es m. que vayas** you'd better go (b) (superlativo) best; **el m. de los tres** the best of the three; **tu m. amiga** your best friend; **lo m.** the best thing

2 adv (a) (comparativo) better (que than); **cada vez m.** better and better; **ella conduce m.** she drives better; **m. dicho** or rather; **¡mucho** o **tanto m.!** so much the better! (b) (superlativo) best; **es el que m. canta** he is the one who sings the best; **a lo m.** (quizás) perhaps; (ojalá) hopefully

mejora nf improvement

mejorar 1 vt to improve; **m. la red vial** to improve the road system; **m. una marca** o **un récord** to break a record

2 vi to improve, to get better

3 mejorarse vpr to get better; **¡que te mejores!** get well soon!

mejoría nf improvement

melancolía nf melancholy

melancólico,-a *adj* melancholic, melancholy

melé *nf Dep* scrum

melena *nf* (head of) hair; *(de león)* mane

Melilla *n* Melilla

melindroso,-a 1 *adj* affected, fussy, finicky

   2 *nm,f* affected *o* finicky person

mella *nf* (a) *(hendedura)* nick, notch; *(en plato, taza etc)* chip (b) *(en dentadura)* gap (c) *Fig* impression; **hacer m. en algn** to make an impression on sb

mellado,-a *adj* (sin dientes) gap-toothed

mellizo,-a *adj & nm,f* twin

melocotón *nm* peach

melodía *nf* melody, tune

melodrama *nm* melodrama

melón *nm* (a) *(fruto)* melon (b) *(tonto)* ninny (c) *muy Fam* **melones** *(tetas)* boobs

melopea *nf Fam* **coger** *o* **agarrar/llevar una m.** to get/be drunk *o* pissed

meloso,-a *adj* sweet, honeyed

membrana *nf* membrane

membresía *nf Am* membership

membrete *nm* letterhead

membrillo *nm* (a) *Bot* quince; *(árbol)* quince tree; *(dulce)* quince preserve *o* jelly (b) *Fam (tonto)* dimwit

memela *nf Méx* = thick corn tortilla

memo,-a *Fam* **1** *adj* silly, stupid

   2 *nm,f* nincompoop, ninny

memorable *adj* memorable

memorándum *nm* (*pl* **memorándums**) memorandum

memoria *nf* (a) memory; **aprender/saber algo de m.** to learn/know sth by heart; **irse de la m.** to slip one's mind (b) *(informe)* report, statement; **m. anual** annual report (c) *(recuerdo)* memory, recollection (d) **memorias** *(biografía)* memoirs

memorístico,-a *adj* acquired by memory

memorizar [40] *vt* to memorize

menaje *nm* furniture and furnishing; **m. de cocina** kitchen equipment *o* utensils

mención *nf* mention; **m. honorífica** honourable mention

mencionar *vt* to mention

mendicidad *nf* begging

mendigar [42] *vt & vi* to beg

mendigo,-a *nm,f* beggar

mendrugo *nm* (a) crust *o* chunk (of stale bread) (b) *(tonto)* dimwit

mene *nm Ven* = deposit of oil at surface level

menear 1 *vt* to shake, to move; *(cola)* to wag, to waggle; *Fam (culo)* to wiggle

   2 menearse *vpr* to move, to shake; *Fam* **una tormenta de no te menees** a hell of a storm; *Vulg* **meneársela** to wank

meneo *nm* shake; *(de cola)* wag, waggle; *(de culo)* wiggle

menester *nm* (a) **es m.** it is necessary (b) **menesteres** *(deberes)* jobs

menestra *nf* vegetable stew

mengano,-a *nm,f Fam* so-and-so, what's-his-o her-name

menguante *adj* waning, on the wane; **cuarto m.** last quarter

menguar [45] **1** *vt* (a) to diminish, to reduce (b) *(en labor de punto)* to decrease

   2 *vi* (a) to diminish, to decrease (b) *(la luna)* to wane

menopausia *nf Med* menopause

menor 1 *adj* (a) *(comparativo)* *(de tamaño)* smaller (**que** than); *(de edad)* younger (**que** than); **mal m.** the lesser of two evils; **el m. de los dos** the smaller of the two; **ser m. de edad** to be a minor *o* under age (b) *(superlativo)* *(de tamaño)* smallest; *(de intensidad)* least, slightest; *(de edad)* youngest; **al m. ruido** at the slightest noise; **el m. de los tres** the youngest of the three; **es la m.** she's the youngest child (c) *Mús* minor (d) *Com* **al por m.** retail

   2 *nmf* minor; *Jur* **tribunal de menores** juvenile court

menos 1 *adj* (a) *(comparativo)* *(con singular)* less; *(con plural)* fewer; **m. dinero/leche/tiempo que** less money/milk/time than; **m. libros/pisos que** fewer books/flats than; *(con cláusula)* **tiene m. años de lo que parece** he's younger than he looks

   (b) *(superlativo)* **fui el que perdí m. dinero** I lost the least money

   2 *adv* (a) **m. de** *(con singular)* less than; *(con plural)* fewer than, less than; **m. de media hora** less than half an hour

   (b) *(superlativo)* *(con singular)* least; *(con plural)* the fewest; *(con cantidad)* the least; **el m. inteligente de la clase** the least intelligent boy in the class; **ayer fue cuando vinieron m. personas** yesterday was when the fewest people came

   3 *(locuciones)* **a m. que** (+ *subjunctive*) unless; **al** *o* **por lo m.** at least; **echar a algn de m.** to miss sb; **eso es lo de m.** that's the least of it; **¡m. mal!** just as well!; **nada m. que** no less *o* no fewer than; **ni mucho m.** far from it

   4 *prep* (a) but, except; **todo m. eso** anything but that

   (b) *Mat* minus; **tres m. uno** three minus one

menoscabar *vt* (a) *(perjudicar)* to damage (b) *Fig (desacreditar)* to discredit

menoscabo *nm* harm, damage; **ir en m. de algo** to be to the detriment of sth

menospreciar [43] *vt* to scorn, to disdain

menosprecio *nm* contempt, scorn, disdain

mensáfono *nm* pager

mensaje *nm* message

mensajero,-a *nm,f* messenger, courier

menso,-a *adj Méx Fam* foolish, stupid

menstruación *nf* menstruation

mensual *adj* monthly; **dos visitas mensuales** two visits a month

mensualidad *nf* *(pago)* monthly payment; *(sueldo)* monthly salary *o* wage

menta *nf* (**a**) *Bot* mint (**b**) *(licor)* crème de menthe

mental *adj* mental

mentalidad *nf* mentality; **de m. abierta/cerrada** open-/narrow-minded

mentalizar [40] **1** *vt (concienciar)* to make aware

2 mentalizarse *vpr* (**a**) *(concienciarse)* to become aware (**b**) *(hacerse a la idea)* to come to terms (**a** with)

mentar [1] *vt* to mention, to name

mente *nf* mind; **se me quedó la m. en blanco** my mind went blank; **m. abierta/tolerante/cerrada** open/broad/closed mind

mentecato,-a *nm,f* fool, idiot

mentir [5] *vi* to lie, to tell lies

mentira *nf* lie; **aunque parezca m.** strange as it may seem; **parece m.** it is unbelievable

mentiroso,-a 1 *adj* lying

2 *nm,f* liar

mentís *nm* denial

mentón *nm Anat* chin

menú *nm* menu

menudeo *nm Andes, Méx Com* retailing

menudillos *nmpl* giblets

menudo,-a 1 *adj* minute, tiny; *(irónico)* tremendous; **la gente menuda** the little ones; **¡m. lío/susto!** what a mess/fright!

2 *adv* **a m.** often

meñique *adj & nm* (**dedo**) **m.** little finger

meollo *nm* (**a**) *Fig (quid)* essence (**b**) *(miga)* crumb

mercado *nm* market; **M. Común** Common Market; **m. negro** black market; **m. único** single market; **sacar algo al m.** to put sth on the market

mercadotecnia *nf* marketing

mercancía *nf* commodity, goods

mercante *adj* merchant; **barco/marina m.** merchant ship/navy

mercantil *adj* mercantile, commercial

merced *nf Fml* favour, grace; **a m. de** at the mercy of

mercenario,-a *adj & nm,f* mercenary

mercería *nf Br* haberdasher's (shop), *US* notions store

MERCOSUR *nm* (*abr* **Mercado Común del Sur**) = South American economic community consisting of Argentina, Brazil, Paraguay and Uruguay

mercurio *nm* (**a**) *Quím* mercury, quicksilver (**b**) **M.** Mercury

merecer [33] **1** *vt* (**a**) to deserve (**b**) *(uso impers)* **no merece la pena hacerlo** it's not worth while doing it

2 merecerse *vpr* to deserve

merecido,-a 1 *adj* deserved; **ella lo tiene m.** *(recompensa)* she deserves it; *(castigo)* it serves her right

2 *nm* just deserts

merendar [1] **1** *vt* to have as an afternoon snack, to have for tea

2 *vi* to have an afternoon snack, to have tea

merendero *nm (establecimiento)* tea room, snack-bar; *(en el campo)* picnic spot

merengue *nm Culin* meringue

merezco *indic pres de* **merecer**

meridiano *nm* meridian

meridional 1 *adj* southern

2 *nmf* southerner

merienda *nf* afternoon snack, tea

mérito *nm* merit, worth; **hacer méritos para algo** to strive to deserve sth

merluza *nf (pez)* hake

merma *nf* decrease, reduction

mermar 1 *vt* to cause to decrease *o* diminish

2 *vi* to decrease, to diminish

3 mermarse *vpr* to decrease, to diminish

mermelada *nf* (**a**) jam; **m. de fresa** strawberry jam (**b**) *(de agrios)* marmalade; **m. de naranja** orange marmalade

mero,-a *adj* mere, pure; **por el m. hecho de** through the mere fact of

merodear *vi* to prowl

mes *nm* (**a**) month; **el m. pasado/que viene** last/next month (**b**) *(cobro)* monthly salary *o* wages; *(pago)* monthly payment (**c**) *Fam (menstruación)* period

mesa *nf* (**a**) table; **poner/recoger la m.** to set/clear the table; *(de despacho etc)* desk; **m. redonda** round table (**b**) *(junta directiva)* board, executive; **el presidente de la m.** the chairman; **m. electoral** electoral college

mesada *nf* (**a**) *Am (dinero)* monthly payment (**b**) *RP (para adolescentes)* (monthly) pocket money, *US* (monthly) allowance (**c**) *RP (encimera)* worktop

mesero,-a *nm,f CAm, Col, Méx* waiter, *f* waitress

meseta *nf* plateau, tableland, meseta; **la M.** the plateau of Castile

mesilla *nf* **m. de noche** bedside table

mesón *nm* = old-style tavern

mesonero,-a *nm,f* (**a**) *(en mesón)* innkeeper (**b**) *Chile, Ven (camarero)* waiter, *f* waitress

mestizo,-a *adj & nm,f* half-breed, half-caste, mestizo

mesura *nf Fml* moderation, restraint

📖 Observa que la palabra inglesa **measure** es un falso amigo y no es la traducción de la palabra española **mesura**. En inglés, **measure** significa "medida".

---

meta *nf* (**a**) *(objetivo)* goal, aim, objective (**b**) *(de carrera)* finish, finishing line (**c**) *Ftb (portería)* goal

metafísica *nf* metaphysics *sing*

metáfora *nf* metaphor

metal *nm* (**a**) metal; **metales preciosos** precious metals (**b**) *(timbre de la voz)* timbre (**c**) *Mús* brass

metálico,-a 1 *adj* metallic

2 *nm* cash; **pagar en m.** to pay (in) cash

metalizado,-a *adj* metallic

metalúrgico,-a 1 *adj* metallurgical
  2 *nm,f* metallurgist
metate *nm Guat, Méx* grinding stone
metedura *nf Fam* **m. de pata** blunder
meteorito *nm* meteorite
meteorología *nf* meteorology
meteorológico,-a *adj* meteorological; **parte m.** weather report *o* forecast
meter 1 *vt* (**a**) *(poner)* to put (**en** in); *Fig* **m. las narices en algo** to poke one's nose into sth (**b**) *(comprometer)* to involve (**en** in), to get mixed up (**en** in) (**c**) *Fam Fig (dar)* to give; **m. un rollo** to go on and on; **m. prisa a algn** to hurry sb up (**d**) *(hacer)* to make; **m. ruido** to make a noise
  2 meterse *vpr* (**a**) *(entrar)* to go *o* come in, to get into (**b**) *(estar)* to be; **¿dónde te habías metido?** where have you been (all this time)? (**c**) *(entrometerse)* to meddle (**d**) **m. con algn** *(en broma)* to get at sb
meterete *nmf RP Fam* meddler
metete *nmf Andes, CAm Fam* meddler, busybody
metiche *nmf Méx, Ven Fam* meddler
meticuloso,-a *adj* meticulous
metido,-a *adj Fam* **estar muy m. en algo** to be deeply involved in sth; **m. en años** getting on (in years)
metódico,-a *adj* methodical
método *nm* (**a**) method (**b**) *Educ* course
metodología *nf* methodology
metomentodo *nmf inv Fam* busybody
metralleta *nf* submachine-gun
métrico,-a *adj* metric; **sistema m.** metric system
metro *nm* (**a**) *(medida)* metre (**b**) *(tren) Br* underground, *Br* tube, *US* subway
metrópoli *nf* metropolis
metropolitano,-a 1 *adj* metropolitan
  2 *nm Fml Br* underground, *Br* tube, *US* subway
mexicano,-a *adj & nm,f* Mexican
México *n* Mexico
mezcla *nf* (**a**) *(acción)* mixing, blending; *Rad & Cin* mixing (**b**) *(producto)* mixture, blend
mezclar 1 *vt* (**a**) *(dos o más cosas)* to mix, to blend (**b**) *(desordenar)* to mix up (**c**) *(involucrar)* to involve, to mix up
  2 mezclarse *vpr* (**a**) *(cosas)* to get mixed up; *(gente)* to mingle (**b**) *(relacionarse)* to get involved (**con** with)
mezcolanza *nf Fml* strange mixture, hotchpotch
mezquino,-a *adj* (**a**) *(persona)* mean, stingy (**b**) *(sueldo)* miserable
mezquita *nf* mosque
m/g *(abr* **miligramo***)* mg
mi¹ *adj* my; **mi casa/trabajo** my house/job; **mis cosas/libros** my things/books
mi² *nm Mús* E; **mi menor** E minor
mí *pron pers* me; **a mí me dio tres** he gave me three; **compra otro para mí** buy one for me too; **por mí mismo** just by myself

mía *adj & pron pos f ver* **mío**
miaja *nf* crumb; *Fig* bit
miche *nm Ven (aguardiente)* = cane spirit flavoured with herbs and spices
michelín *nm Fam* spare tyre
mico *nm* (**a**) *Zool* long-tailed monkey (**b**) *Fam (pequeñajo)* little kid
micra *nf (medida)* micron
micro 1 *nm Fam* mike, microphone
  2 *nm o nf Arg, Chile (microbús)* minibus
microbio *nm* microbe
microbús *nm* (**a**) *(autobús)* minibus (**b**) *Méx (taxi)* (collective) taxi
microchip *nm* (*pl* **microchips**) *Informát* microchip
microficha *nf* microfiche
micrófono *nm* microphone
microonda *nf* **un (horno) microondas** a microwave (oven)
microscopio *nm* microscope
miedica *nmf Fam* scaredy-cat
miedo *nm (pavor)* fear; *(temor)* apprehension; **una película de m.** a horror film; **tener m. de algn/algo** to be afraid of sb/sth; *Fam* **lo pasamos de m.** we had a fantastic time; **un calor de m.** sizzling heat
miedoso,-a *adj* fearful
miel *nf* honey; **luna de m.** honeymoon
miembro *nm* (**a**) *(socio)* member; **estado m.** member state (**b**) *Anat* limb; **m. viril** penis
mientras 1 *conj* (**a**) *(al mismo tiempo que)* while (**b**) *(durante el tiempo que)* when, while; **m. viví en Barcelona** when I lived in Barcelona (**c**) **m. que** *(por el contrario)* whereas (**d**) *Fam (cuanto más)* **m. más/ menos ...** the more/less ...
  2 *adv* **m. (tanto)** meanwhile, in the meantime
miércoles *nm inv* Wednesday; **M. de Ceniza** Ash Wednesday
mierda *nf Vulg* (**a**) shit; **ese libro es una m.** that book is crap; **¡vete a la m.!** piss off! (**b**) *Fig (porquería)* dirt, filth (**c**) *(borrachera)* bender
miga *nf (de pan etc)* crumb; *Fig* **hacer buenas migas con algn** to get on well with sb
migaja *nf* (**a**) *(de pan)* crumb (**b**) *Fig* bit, scrap (**c**) **migajas** *(del pan)* crumbs; *Fig* leftovers
migra *nf Méx Fam Pey* = US police border patrol
migraña *nf Med* migraine
mil *adj & nm* thousand; **m. pesetas** a *o* one thousand pesetas
milagro *nm* miracle
milagroso,-a *adj* miraculous
milanesa *nf (de ternera)* Wiener schnitzel, breaded veal escalope
milano *nm Orn* kite; **m. real** red kite
milenario,-a 1 *adj* millenarian, millennial
  2 *nm* millennium
milenio *nm* millennium

milésimo,-a *adj & nm,f* thousandth
mili *nf Fam* military o national service; **hacer la m.** to do one's military service
milicia *nf (ejército)* militia; *(servicio militar)* military service
milico *nm Andes, RP Fam Pey (militar)* soldier; **los milicos tomaron el poder** the military took power
milímetro *nm* millimetre
militar 1 *adj* military
  2 *nm* military man, soldier
  3 *vi Pol (en un partido)* to be a member
milla *nf* mile
millar *nm* thousand
millón *nm* million
millonario,-a *adj & nm,f* millionaire
milpa *nf CAm, Méx* cornfield
mimar *vt* to spoil, to pamper

> 🖉 Observa que el verbo inglés **to mime** es un falso amigo y no es la traducción del verbo español **mimar**. En inglés, **to mime** significa "representar con gestos".

mimbre *nm* wicker
mimetismo *nm* mimicry
mímica *nf* mimicry
mimo *nm* (a) *(delicadeza)* care (b) *Fig (zalamería)* pampering (c) *Teatro (actor)* mime
mina *nf* (a) *(mine);* **ingeniero de minas** mining engineer (b) *(explosivo)* mine; **campo de minas** minefield (c) *(de lápiz)* lead; **lápiz de m.** propelling pencil (d) *Fig (ganga)* gold mine
minar *vt* (a) *Mil & Min* to mine (b) *Fig (desgastar)* to undermine
mineral 1 *adj* mineral
  2 *nm* ore
minería *nf* (a) *Min* mining (b) *Ind* mining industry
minero,-a 1 *nm,f* miner
  2 *adj* mining
miniatura *nf* miniature
minifalda *nf* miniskirt
minifundio *nm* smallholding
mínima *nf* minimum temperature
minimizar *vt* to minimize
mínimo,-a 1 *adj* (a) *(muy pequeño)* minute, tiny (b) *Mat & Téc* minimum, lowest; **m. común múltiplo** lowest common denominator
  2 *nm* minimum; **como m.** at least; **ni lo más m.** not in the least
minipimer® *nm o nf* liquidizer, blender
ministerio *nm* (a) *Pol Br* ministry, *US* department (b) *Rel* ministry
ministro,-a *nm,f* (a) *Pol* minister; **primer m.** Prime Minister (b) *Rel* minister
minoría *nf* minority; *Jur* **m. de edad** minority
minoritario,-a *adj* minority
minucioso,-a *adj* (a) *(persona)* meticulous (b) *(informe, trabajo etc)* minute, detailed

minúsculo,-a *adj* minuscule, minute; **letra minúscula** lower-case o small letter
minusválido,-a 1 *adj* handicapped, disabled
  2 *nm,f* handicapped person, disabled person
minuta *nf* (a) *(cuenta)* lawyer's bill (b) *(menú)* menu (c) *RP (comida)* one-plate meal
minutero *nm* minute hand
minuto *nm* minute
mío,-a 1 *adj pos* of mine; **un amigo m.** a friend of mine; **no es asunto m.** it is none of my business
  2 *pron pos* mine; **ese libro es m.** that book is mine; **lo m. es el tenis** tennis is my strong point; *Fam* **los míos** my people o folks
miope *nmf* myopic o short-sighted person
miopía *nf* myopia, short-sightedness
mira *nf* (a) *(Téc* sight (b) *Fig (objetivo)* aim, target; **con miras a** with a view to; **amplitud de miras** broad-mindedness
mirada *nf* look; **lanzar** o **echar una m. a** to glance at; **levantar la m.** to raise one's eyes; **m. fija** stare
mirador *nm* (a) *(lugar con vista)* viewpoint (b) *(balcón)* bay window, windowed balcony
mirar 1 *vt* (a) to look at (b) *(observar)* to watch (c) **m. por algn/algo** *(cuidar)* to look after sb/sth (d) *(procurar)* to see; **mira que no le pase nada** see that nothing happens to him
  2 *vi (dar a)* to look, to face; **la casa mira al sur** the house faces south
mirilla *nf* spyhole, peephole
mirlo *nm* blackbird
misa *nf* mass
misántropo,-a 1 *adj* misanthropic
  2 *nm,f* misanthrope, misanthropist
miscelánea *nf Méx (tienda)* = small general store
miserable 1 *adj* (a) *(mezquino) (persona)* despicable; *(sueldo etc)* miserable (b) *(pobre)* wretched, poor; **una vida m.** a wretched life
  2 *nmf* (a) *(mezquino)* miser (b) *(canalla)* wretch
miseria *nf* (a) *(pobreza extrema)* extreme poverty (b) *(insignificancia)* pittance; **ganar una m.** to earn next to nothing (c) *(tacañería)* miserliness, meanness
misericordia *nf* mercy, compassion
mísero,-a *adj* miserable, wretched
misil *nm* missile; **m. tierra-aire** surface-to-air missile
misión *nf* mission; **m. cumplida** mission accomplished
misionero,-a *nm,f* missionary
mismísimo,-a *adj superl Fam* (a) *(preciso)* very; **en el m. centro** right in the centre (b) *(en persona)* in person
mismo,-a 1 *adj* (a) same (b) *(uso enfático)* **yo m.** I myself; **aquí m.** right here
  2 *pron* same; **es el m. de ayer** it's the same one as yesterday; **estamos en las mismas**

we're back to square one; **lo m.** the same thing); **dar** *o* **ser lo m.** to make no difference; **por eso m.** that is why; **por uno** *o* **sí m.** by oneself

3 *adv* (**a**) *(por ejemplo)* for instance; **que venga algn, Juan m.** ask one of them to come, Juan, for instance (**b**) **así m.** likewise

misógino,-a 1 *adj* misogynous

2 *nm,f* misogynist

miss *nf* beauty queen

míster *nm Ftb* coach, trainer

misterio *nm* mystery

misterioso,-a *adj* mysterious

mitad *nf* (**a**) half; **a m. de camino** halfway there; **a m. de precio** half-price (**b**) *(centro)* middle; **en la m. del primer acto** halfway through the first act; *Fam* **eso me parte por la m.** that really screws things up for me

mítico,-a *adj* mythical

mitigar [42] *vt Fml* to mitigate, to palliate; *(luz)* to reduce

mitin *nm Pol* meeting, rally

mito *nm* myth

mitología *nf* mythology

mitote *nm Méx Fam (alboroto)* racket

mixto,-a *adj* mixed

moai *nm* = statue of giant head found on Easter Island

mobiliario *nm* furniture

moca *nm* mocha

mochila *nf* rucksack, backpack

mochuelo *nm Zool* little owl

moción *nf* motion; **m. de censura** vote of censure

moco *nm* snot; **sonarse los mocos** to blow one's nose

mocoso,-a *nm,f Fam* brat

moda *nf* (**a**) fashion; **a la m., de m.** in fashion; **pasado de m.** old-fashioned (**b**) *(furor pasajero)* craze

modales *nmpl* manners

modalidad *nf* form, category; *Com* **m. de pago** method of payment; *Dep* **m. deportiva** sport

modelar *vt* to model, to shape

modélico,-a *adj* model

modelo 1 *adj inv & nm* model

2 *nmf* (fashion) model; **desfile de modelos** fashion show

módem *nm Informát* modem; **m. fax** fax modem

moderación *nf* moderation

moderado,-a *adj* moderate; **un m. aumento de temperatura** a mild increase in temperature

moderador,-a *nm,f* chairperson; *(hombre)* chairman; *(mujer)* chairwoman

moderar 1 *vt* (**a**) to moderate; *(velocidad)* to reduce (**b**) *(debate)* to chair

2 moderarse *vpr* to be moderate

modernizar [40] *vt*, **modernizarse** *vpr* to modernize

moderno,-a *adj* modern

modestia *nf* modesty; **m. aparte** without wishing to be immodest

modesto,-a *adj* modest

módico,-a *adj* moderate; **una módica suma** a modest *o* small sum

modificar [44] *vt* to modify

modismo *nm* idiom

modisto,-a *nm,f* (**a**) *(diseñador)* fashion designer (**b**) *(sastre) (hombre)* couturier; *(mujer)* couturière

modo *nm* (**a**) *(manera)* way, manner; **m. de empleo** instructions for use; **= manera** (**b**) **modos** manners (**c**) *Ling* mood

modorra *nf (somnolencia)* drowsiness

modoso,-a *adj* (**a**) *(educado)* well-behaved (**b**) *(recatado)* modest

modulación *nf* modulation

modular *vt* to modulate

módulo *nm* module

mofa *nf* mockery; **en tono de m.** in a gibing tone

mofarse *vpr* to laugh (**de** at), to make fun (**de** of)

moflete *nm* chubby cheek

mogollón *nm Fam* (**a**) **m. de** loads of; **me gusta un m.** I like it loads (**b**) *(confusión)* commotion; *(ruido)* racket

moho *nm* (**a**) *Bot* mould (**b**) *(de metales)* rust

mohoso,-a *adj* (**a**) mouldy (**b**) *(oxidado)* rusty

mojado,-a *adj (empapado)* wet; *(húmedo)* damp

mojar 1 *vt* (**a**) to wet; *(humedecer)* to damp; **m. pan en la leche** to dip *o* dunk bread in one's milk (**b**) *muy Fam* **mojarla** to have it off

2 mojarse *vpr* to get wet

mojón *nm* (**a**) **m. kilométrico** ≃ milestone (**b**) *muy Fam (mierda)* shit

moka *nm* mocha

molar 1 *vi Fam* **me mola cantidad** I really love it, it's brilliant

2 *adj & nm Anat* molar

molcajete *nm Méx* mortar

molde *nm* mould; **letras de m.** printed letters; **pan de m.** ≃ sliced bread

moldeador *nm (del pelo)* wave

moldear *vt* to mould

mole 1 *nf* mass, bulk

2 *nm Méx* (**a**) *(salsa)* = thick, cooked chilli sauce (**b**) *(guiso)* = dish served in "mole" sauce

molécula *nf* molecule

moler [4] *vt* (**a**) *(triturar)* to grind (**b**) **m. a algn a golpes** to beat sb up

molestar 1 *vt* (**a**) *(incomodar)* to disturb, to bother (**b**) *Fml* to bother; **¿le molestaría esperar fuera?** would you mind waiting outside? (**c**) *(causar malestar a)* to hurt

2 molestarse *vpr* (**a**) *(tomarse la molestia)* to bother (**b**) *(ofenderse)* to take offence, to get upset

molestia *nf* (a) bother; **no es ninguna m.** it is no trouble at all; **perdone las molestias** forgive the inconvenience (b) *Med (dolor)* trouble, slight pain

molesto,-a *adj* (a) *(irritante)* annoying, upsetting (b) **estar m. con algn** *(enfadado)* to be annoyed o upset with sb

molinillo *nm* grinder

molino *nm* mill; **m. de agua** watermill; **m. de viento** windmill

mollera *nf* Fam brains; **duro de m.** *(tonto)* dense, thick; *(testarudo)* pigheaded

molón,-ona *adj Fam* flashy, showy

momentáneo,-a *adj* momentary

momento *nm* (a) *(instante)* moment; **al m.** at once; **por momentos** by the minute (b) *(periodo)* time; **de m.** for the time being; **en cualquier m.** at any time

momia *nf* mummy

mona *nf Fam* **coger una m.** to get drunk; **dormir la m.** to sleep it off

Mónaco *n* Monaco

monada *nf Fam* **¡qué m.!** how cute!

monaguillo *nm Rel* altar boy

monarca *nmf* monarch

monarquía *nf* monarchy

monasterio *nm Rel* monastery

monda *nf* (a) *(piel)* peel, skin (b) *Fam* **ser la m.** *(divertido)* to be a scream

mondadientes *nm inv* toothpick

mondar 1 *vt* to peel

2 mondarse *upr Fam* **m. (de risa)** to laugh one's head off

moneda *nf* (a) *(pieza)* coin; **m. suelta** small change; **acuñar m.** to mint money (b) *Fin* currency; **m. única** single currency

monedero *nm* purse

monería *nf Fam* = **monada**

monetario,-a *adj* monetary

mongol 1 *adj* Mongolian

2 *nmf (persona)* Mongolian

3 *nm (idioma)* Mongolian

mongólico,-a *Med* **1** *adj* Down's syndrome

2 *nm,f* **ser m.** to have Down's syndrome

monigote *nm* (a) *Pey (persona)* wimp (b) *(dibujo)* rough drawing o sketch (of a person)

monitor,-a *nm,f* monitor; *(profesor)* instructor

monja *nf* nun

monje *nm* monk

mono,-a 1 *nm* (a) monkey (b) *(prenda) (de trabajo)* boiler suit, overalls; *(de vestir)* catsuit; *Ven (de deporte)* track o jogging suit (c) *Fam (droga)* cold turkey

2 *adj Fam (bonito)* pretty, cute

monobloque *nm Arg* tower block

monográfico,-a 1 *adj* monographic

2 *nm* monograph

monólogo *nm* monologue

monopolio *nm* monopoly

monopolizar [40] *vt* to monopolize

monótono,-a *adj* monotonous

monserga *nf Fam* drag

monstruo *nm* (a) monster (b) *(genio)* geniu[...]

monstruoso,-a *adj* (a) *(repugnante)* mon[...] strous (b) *(enorme)* massive, huge

monta *nf Fig* **de poca m.** of little importance

montacargas *nm inv Br* service lift, *US* freight elevator

montado,-a 1 *adj (nata)* whipped

2 *nm* sandwich

montador,-a *nm,f* (a) *(operario)* fitter (b) *Cin & TV* film editor (c) *Teatro* producer

montaje *nm* (a) *Téc (instalación)* fitting; *(ensamblaje)* assembling; **cadena de m.** assembly line (b) *Cin* editing and mounting (c) *Teatro* staging (d) *Fot* montage (e) *Fam (farsa)* farce

montante *nm* (a) *Fin* amount (b) *(de puerta)* post

montaña *nf* mountain; **m. rusa** big dipper

montañismo *nm* mountaineering

montañoso,-a *adj* mountainous

montar 1 *vi* (a) *(subirse)* to get in; *(en bici, a caballo)* to ride (b) *Fin (ascender)* **m. a t[...]** amount to, to come to

2 *vt* (a) *(colocar)* to put on (b) *(máquina etc)* to assemble, *(negocio)* to set up, to start (c) *Culin* to whip (d) *Cin & Fot (película)* to edit[...] to mount; *(fotografía)* to mount (e) *Teatro (obra)* to stage, to mount (f) *Zool (cubrir)* t[...] mount

3 montarse *upr* (a) *(subirse)* to get on; *(en coche)* to get in (**en** to) (b) *Fam (armarse)* t[...] break out; *Fam* **montárselo bien** to have things (nicely) worked out o set up

monte *nm* (a) *(montaña)* mountain; *(con nombre propio)* mount; **de m.** wild (b) **el m[...]** *(zona)* the hills

montés *adj (animal)* wild

monto *nm* total

montón *nm* heap, pile; **un m. de** a load of[...] *Fam* **me gusta un m.** I really love it; *Fam* **del m[...]** run-of-the-mill, nothing special

montura *nf* (a) *(cabalgadura)* mount (b) *(de gafas)* frame

monumento *nm* monument

monzón *nm* monsoon

moño *nm* (a) *(de pelo)* bun (b) *Am (lazo)* bow

MOPU *nm (abr* **Ministerio de Obras Públicas y Urbanismo)** = Spanish ministry of public works and town planning

moquear *vi* to have a runny nose

moqueta *nf* fitted carpet

mora *nf (zarzamora)* blackberry

morado,-a 1 *adj* purple; *Fam* **pasarlas mora[...] das** to have a tough time; **ponerse m.** to stuff[...] oneself

2 *nm* purple

moral 1 *adj* moral

2 *nf* (a) *(ética)* morals (b) *(ánimo)* morale[...] spirits; **levantar la m. a algn** to raise sb's[...] spirits

moraleja *nf* moral

moralista 1 *adj* moralistic
  2 *nmf* moralist

moratoria *nf* moratorium

morbo *nm Fam (interés malsano)* morbid curiosity

morboso,-a *adj (malsano)* morbid

morcilla *nf Br* black pudding, *US* blood sausage; *Fam* **que le den m.** he can drop dead for all I care

mordaz *adj* biting

mordaza *nf* gag

mordedura *nf* bite

morder [4] *vt* to bite; **me ha mordido** it has bitten me; *Fig* **m. el anzuelo** to take the bait

mordida *nf CAm, Méx (soborno)* bribe

mordisco *nm* bite

mordisquear *vt* to nibble (at)

moreno,-a 1 *adj* (a) *(pelo)* dark-haired; *(piel)* dark-skinned (b) *(bronceado)* tanned; **ponerse m.** to get a suntan; **pan/azúcar m.** brown bread/sugar
  2 *nm,f* (a) *(persona) (de pelo)* dark-haired person; *(de piel)* dark-skinned person

morera *nf Bot* white mulberry

moretón *nm Fam* bruise

morfina *nf* morphine

morfinómano,-a 1 *nm,f* morphine addict
  2 *adj* addicted to morphine

morgue *nf Am* morgue

moribundo,-a *adj & nm,f* moribund

morir [7] **1** *vi* to die; **m. de frío/hambre/cáncer** to die of cold/hunger/cancer; **m. de amor o pena** to die from a broken heart
  2 morirse *vpr* to die; **m. de hambre** to starve to death; *Fig* to be starving; **m. de aburrimiento** to be bored to death; **m. de ganas (de hacer algo)** to be dying (to do sth); **m. de risa** to die laughing

mormón,-ona *adj & nm,f* Mormon

moro,-a *nm,f* (a) *Hist* Moor; *Fam* **no hay moros en la costa** the coast is clear (b) *Pey (musulmán)* Muslim; *(árabe)* Arab

morocho,-a 1 *adj* (a) *Andes, RP (moreno)* dark-haired (b) *Ven (gemelo)* twin
  2 *nm,f* (a) *Andes, RP (moreno)* dark-haired person (b) *Ven (gemelo)* twin

moronga *nf CAm, Méx Br* black pudding, *US* blood sausage

moroso,-a *nm,f* bad debtor

🖉 Observa que la palabra inglesa **morose** es un falso amigo y no es la traducción de la palabra española **moroso**. En inglés, **morose** significa "hosco, huraño".

morral *nm* (a) *(para pienso)* nosebag (b) *Mil* haversack; *(de cazador)* game bag

morralla *nf* (a) *(cosas sin valor)* rubbish, junk (b) *(chusma)* scum

morrear *vt*, **morrearse** *vpr Fam* to snog

morreo *nm Fam* snog

morro *nm* (a) *(de animal) (hocico)* snout (b) *Fam (de persona)* mouth, (thick) lips; **caerse de m.** to fall flat on one's face; **por los morros** without so much as a by-your-leave; *Fam* **¡vaya m.!** what a cheek! (c) *(de coche)* nose

morrón *adj* **pimiento m.** (fleshy) red pepper

morsa *nf* walrus

morse *nm* Morse

mortadela *nf* mortadella

mortaja *nf* shroud

mortal 1 *adj* (a) mortal (b) *(mortífero)* fatal; **un accidente m.** a fatal accident
  2 *nmf* mortal

mortalidad *nf* mortality; **índice de m.** death rate

mortandad *nf* death toll

mortecino,-a *adj* colourless

mortero *nm Culin & Mil* mortar

mortífero,-a *adj* deadly, lethal

mortificar [44] *vt* to mortify

mortuorio,-a *adj* death; **lecho m.** death-bed

moruno,-a *adj* Moorish; *Culin* **pincho m.** ≃ kebab

mosaico *nm* mosaic

mosca *nf* fly; **peso m.** flyweight; *Fam* **estar m.** *(suspicaz)* to be suspicious; *(borracho)* to be pissed; *Fam* **por si las moscas** just in case; *Fam* **¿qué m. te ha picado?** what's biting you?

moscada *adj* **nuez m.** nutmeg

moscardón *nm* (a) *(insecto)* blowfly (b) *Fam (pesado)* pest

moscovita *adj & nmf* Muscovite

Moscú *n* Moscow

mosquearse *vpr Fam* (a) *(enfadarse)* to get cross (b) *(sospechar)* to smell a rat

mosquetero *nm Hist* musketeer

mosquitero *nm (red)* mosquito net

mosquito *nm* mosquito

mostaza *nf Bot & Culin* mustard

mosto *nm (bebida)* grape juice; *(del vino)* must

mostrador *nm* (a) *(de tienda)* counter (b) *(de bar)* bar

mostrar 1 *vt* to show; **muéstramelo** show it to me
  2 mostrarse *vpr* to be; **se mostró muy comprensiva** she was very understanding

mostrenco,-a 1 *nm,f* (a) *(ignorante)* blockhead (b) *(gordo)* very fat person
  2 *adj (sin dueño)* ownerless; **bienes mostrencos** ownerless property

mota *nf* speck

mote¹ *nm (apodo)* nickname; **poner m. a algn** to give sb a nickname

mote² *nm Andes* stewed maize *o US* corn

moteado,-a *adj* dotted

motín *nm (amotinamiento)* mutiny; *(disturbio)* riot

motivación *nf* motivation

motivar *vt* (a) *(causar)* to cause, to give rise to (b) *(inducir)* to motivate

motivo *nm* (a) *(causa)* reason; *(usu pl)* grounds; **con este** *o* **tal m.** for this reason;

con m. de on the occasion of; **sin m.** for no reason at all; **bajo ningún m.** under no circumstances (**b**) *Arte & Mús* motif, leitmotiv

moto *nf Aut* motorbike; **m. náutica** *o* **acuática** jet ski

motocicleta *nf* motorbike

motociclismo *nm* motorcycling

motociclista *nmf* motorcyclist

motocross *nm* motocross

motoneta *nf Am* (motor) scooter

motonetista *nmf Am* scooter rider

motor,-a 1 *nm* (*grande*) engine; (*pequeño*) motor; **m. de reacción** jet engine; **m. de explosión** internal combustion engine; **m. eléctrico** electric motor; *Informát* **m. de busca** search engine

2 *adj Téc* motive

motora *nf* motorboat

motorista *nmf* motorcyclist

motorizar [40] **1** *vt* to motorize

2 motorizarse *vpr Fam* to get oneself a car *o* motorbike

motosierra *nf* power saw

motriz *adj* **fuerza m.** motive power

movedizo,-a *adj* **arenas movedizas** quicksand

mover [4] **1** *vt* (**a**) to move; **m. algo de su sitio** to move sth out of its place (**b**) (*hacer funcionar*) to drive; **el motor mueve el coche** the engine drives the car

2 moverse *vpr* (**a**) to move (**b**) *Fam* (*gestionar*) to do everything possible (**c**) (*darse prisa*) to hurry up; **¡muévete!** get a move on!

movida *nf Fam* **hay mucha m.** there's a lot going on

movido,-a *adj* (**a**) *Fot* blurred (**b**) (*ocupado*) busy

móvil 1 *adj* mobile; **teléfono m.** mobile phone; *TV & Rad* **unidad m.** outside broadcast unit

2 *nm* (**a**) (*de delito*) motive (**b**) (*teléfono*) mobile

movilización *nf* mobilization

movilizar [40] *vt* to mobilize

movimiento *nm* (**a**) (*gen*) movement; *Fís & Téc* motion; (**poner algo**) **en m.** (to set sth) in motion; **m. sísmico** earth tremor (**b**) (*actividad*) activity (**c**) *Com & Fin* (*entradas y salidas*) operations (**d**) *Hist* **el M.** the Falangist Movement

moviola *nf Cin & TV* (**a**) (*cámara*) editing projector (**b**) (*repetición*) action replay

moza *nf* lass, young girl

mozo,-a *nm,f* (**a**) (*niño*) young boy, young lad; (*niña*) young girl (**b**) (*de estación*) porter (**c**) *Mil* conscript (**d**) *Perú, RP* (*camarero*) waiter, *f* waitress

mucamo,-a *nm,f Andes, RP* (*en hotel*) chamberperson, *f* chambermaid

muchacha *nf* girl

muchachada *nf Am* group of youngsters

muchacho *nm* boy

muchedumbre *nf* (*de gente*) crowd

mucho,-a 1 *adj* (*usu en frases afirmativas*) a lot of, lots of; (*usu en frases negativas*) much; **m. tiempo** a long time; **tengo m. sueño/mucha sed** I am very sleepy/thirsty; **hay m. tonto suelto** there are lots of idiots around; **¿bebes m. café?** – **no, no m.** do you drink a lot of coffee? – no, not much

(**b**) (*demasiado*) **es m. coche para mí** this car is a bit too much for me

(**c**) **muchos,-as** (*usu en frases afirmativas*) a lot of, lots of; (*usu en frases neg*) many; **tiene muchos años** he is very old

2 *pron* (**a**) a lot, a great deal; **¿cuánta leche queda?** – **mucha** how much milk is there left? – a lot

(**b**) **muchos,-as** a lot, lots, many; **¿cuántos libros tienes?** – **muchos** how many books have you got? – lots *o* a lot; **muchos creemos que ...** many of us believe that ...

3 *adv* (**a**) a lot, very much; **lo siento m.** I'm very sorry; **como m.** at the most; **con m.** by far; **m. antes/después** long before/after; **¡ni m. menos!** no way!; **por m. (que)** (+ subjunctive) however much

(**b**) (*tiempo*) **hace m. que no viene por aquí** he has not been to see us for a long time

(**c**) (*a menudo*) often; **vamos m. al cine** we go to the cinema quite often

muda *nf* (*de ropa*) change of clothes

mudanza *nf* move; **estar de m.** to be moving; **camión de m.** removal van

mudar 1 *vt* (**a**) (*ropa*) to change (**b**) (*plumas, pelo*) to moult; (*piel*) to shed, to slough

2 mudarse *vpr* **m. de casa/ropa** to move house/to change one's clothes

mudo,-a 1 *adj* (**a**) (*que no habla*) dumb; *cine* **m. silent films** (**b**) *Fig* (*callado*) speechless

2 *nm,f* mute

mueble 1 *nm* piece of furniture; **muebles** furniture; **con/sin muebles** furnished/unfurnished; **m. bar** cocktail cabinet

2 *adj* movable

mueca *nf* (**a**) (*de burla*) mocking face; **hacer muecas** to pull faces (**b**) (*de dolor, asco*) grimace

muela *nf* (**a**) *Anat* molar; **dolor de muelas** toothache; **m. del juicio** wisdom tooth (**b**) *Téc* (*de molino*) millstone

muelle¹ *nm* spring

muelle² *nm Náut* dock

muermo *nm Fam* (*tedio*) boredom; (*rollo*) drag

muerte *nf* death; **m. natural** natural death; **dar m. a algn** to kill sb; **odiar a algn a m.** to loathe sb; *Fam* **de mala m.** lousy, rotten; *Fam* **un susto de m.** the fright of one's life

muerto,-a 1 *adj* dead; **caer m.** to drop dead; **m. de hambre** starving; **m. de frío** frozen to death; **m. de miedo** scared stiff; **m. de risa** laughing one's head off; **horas muertas** spare time; *Aut* **(en) punto m.** (in) neutral

2 *nm,f* (**a**) *(difunto)* dead person; **hacerse el m.** to pretend to be dead; *Fam* **cargar con el m.** to do the dirty work (**b**) *(víctima)* fatality; **hubo dos muertos** two (people) died

muesca *nf* notch

muestra *nf* (**a**) *(espécimen)* sample, specimen (**b**) *(modelo a copiar)* model (**c**) *(prueba, señal)* sign; **dar muestras de** to show signs of; **m. de cariño/respeto** token of affection/respect; **una m. más de ...** yet another example of ...

muestral *adj* **error m.** margin of error

muestreo *nm* sampling

mugido *nm (de vaca)* moo; *(de toro)* bellow

mugir [57] *vi (vaca)* to moo, to low; *(toro)* to bellow

mugre *nf* filth

mugriento,-a *adj* filthy

mujer *nf* (**a**) woman; **dos mujeres** two women; **m. de la limpieza** cleaner; **m. de su casa** houseproud woman (**b**) *(esposa)* wife; **su futura m.** his bride-to-be

mujeriego 1 *adj* woman-chasing
2 *nm* womanizer, woman chaser

muleta *nf* (**a**) *(prótesis)* crutch (**b**) *Taurom* muleta

muletilla *nf* pet word o phrase

mullido,-a *adj* soft

mulo *nm* mule

multa *nf* fine; *Aut* ticket

multar *vt* to fine

multi- *pref* multi-

multicolor *adj* multicoloured

multicopista *nf* duplicator

multilateral *adj* multilateral

multinacional *adj & nf* multinational

múltiple *adj* (**a**) multiple; **accidente m.** pile-up (**b**) **múltiples** *(muchos)* many

multiplicación *nf Mat* multiplication

multiplicar [44] **1** *vt & vi* to multiply (**por** by)
2 multiplicarse *vpr (reproducirse, aumentar)* to multiply

múltiplo,-a *adj & nm* multiple

multirriesgo *adj inv* **póliza m.** multiple risk policy

multitud *nf* (**a**) *(de personas)* crowd (**b**) *(de cosas)* multitude

mundano,-a *adj* worldly

📖 Observa que la palabra inglesa **mundane** es un falso amigo y no es la traducción de la palabra española **mundano**. En inglés, **mundane** significa "prosaico".

mundial 1 *adj* worldwide; **campeón m.** world champion; **de fama m.** world-famous
2 *nm* world championship

mundialmente *adv* **m. famoso** world-famous, famous worldwide

mundo *nm* world; **todo el m.** everyone; **correr** o **ver m.** to travel widely; **nada del otro m.** nothing special; **el otro m.** the hereafter

munición *nf* ammunition

municipal 1 *adj* municipal
2 *nm (municipal)* policeman

municipio *nm* (**a**) *(territorio)* municipality (**b**) *(ayuntamiento)* town council

muñeca *nf* (**a**) wrist (**b**) *(juguete, muchacha)* doll (**c**) *Andes, RP Fam* **tener m.** *(enchufe)* to have friends in high places; *(habilidad)* to have the knack

muñeco *nm (juguete)* (little) boy doll; **m. de trapo** rag doll; **m. de nieve** snowman

muñequera *nf* wristband

muñón *nm Anat* stump

muralla *nf* wall

Murcia *n* Murcia

murciélago *nm Zool* bat

murmullo *nm* murmur

murmuración *nf* gossip

murmurar *vi* (**a**) *(criticar)* to gossip (**b**) *(susurrar)* to whisper; *(refunfuñar)* to grumble (**c**) *Fig (río)* to murmur

muro *nm* wall

murrio,-a *adj Fam* sad, blue

musa *nf* muse

musaraña *nf Fam* **estar mirando a** o **pensando en las musarañas** to be daydreaming o in the clouds

musculatura *nf* musculature; **desarrollar la m.** to develop one's muscles

músculo *nm* muscle

musculoso,-a *adj* muscular

museo *nm* museum; **m. de arte** o **pintura** art gallery

musgo *nm* moss

música *nf* music; **m. clásica** classical music; **m. de fondo** background music

musical 1 *adj* musical
2 *nm* musical

músico,-a 1 *adj* musical
2 *nm,f* musician

muslo *nm* thigh

mustio,-a *adj* (**a**) *(plantas)* wilted, withered (**b**) *(persona)* sad, gloomy

musulmán,-ana *adj & nm,f* Muslim, Moslem

mutación *nf Biol* mutation

mutilación *nf* mutilation

mutilado,-a *nm,f* disabled person; **m. de guerra** disabled serviceman

mutilar *vt* to mutilate

mutis *nm Teatro* exit

mutua *nf* mutual benefit society

mutual *nf Arg, Chile, Perú* mutual benefit society

mutualidad *nf* (**a**) *(reciprocidad)* mutuality (**b**) *(asociación)* mutual benefit society

mutuo,-a *adj* mutual

muy *adv* very; **m. bueno/malo** very good/bad; **¡m. bien!** very good!; *Fam* **m. mucho** very much; **M. señor mío** Dear Sir; **m. de los andaluces** typically Andalusian; **m. de mañana/noche** very early/late

N, n ['ene] *nf (la letra)* N, n

N *(abr Norte)* N

n/ *(abr nuestro,-a)* our

nabo *nm* (a) *Bot* turnip (b) *Vulg (pene)* prick

nácar *nm* mother-of-pearl

nacer [60] *vi* (a) to be born; **al n.** at birth; **nací en Montoro** I was born in Montoro; *Fam Fig* **n. de pie** to be born under a lucky star (b) *(pájaro)* to hatch (out) (c) *(pelo)* to begin to grow (d) *(río)* to rise

nacido,-a *adj* born; **n. de padre español** born of a Spanish father; **recién n.** newborn; *Fig* **mal n.** despicable, mean

naciente *adj (nuevo)* new, recent; *(sol)* rising

nacimiento *nm* (a) birth; **sordo de n.** deaf from birth; **lugar de n.** birthplace, place of birth (b) *Fig (principio)* origin, beginning; *(de río)* source (c) *(belén)* Nativity scene, crib

nación *nf* nation; **las Naciones Unidas** the United Nations

nacional 1 *adj* (a) national (b) *(producto, mercado)* domestic; **vuelos nacionales** domestic flights

2 *nmf* national; *Hist* **los nacionales** the Francoist forces

nacionalidad *nf* nationality

nacionalismo *nm* nationalism

nacionalista *adj & nmf* nationalist

nacionalizar [40] **1** *vt* (a) *Econ (banca, industria)* to nationalize (b) *(naturalizar)* to naturalize

2 nacionalizarse *vpr* to become naturalized; **n. español** to take up Spanish citizenship

nada 1 *pron* (a) *(como respuesta)* nothing; **¿qué quieres? – n.** what do you want? – nothing

(b) *(con verbo)* not ... anything; *(enfático)* nothing; **no sé n.** I don't know anything; **yo no digo n.** I'm saying nothing

(c) *(con otro negativo)* anything; **no hace nunca n.** he never does anything; **nadie sabía n.** nobody knew anything

(d) *(en ciertas construcciones)* anything; **más que n.** more than anything; **sin decir n.** without saying anything; **casi n.** hardly anything

(e) **gracias – de n.** thanks – don't mention it; *Fam* **para n.** not at all; **casi n.** almost nothing; **como si n.** just like that; **un rasguño de n.** an insignificant little scratch; **n. de eso** nothing of the kind; **n. de n.** nothing at all; **n. más verla** as soon as he saw her

2 *adv* not at all; **no me gusta n.** I don't like it at all; **no lo encuentro n. interesante** I don't find it remotely interesting

3 *nf* nothingness; **salir de la n.** to come out of nowhere

nadador,-a *nm,f* swimmer

nadar *vi* (a) *Dep* to swim; **n. a braza** to do the breaststroke (b) *(flotar)* to float

nadie 1 *pron* (a) *(como respuesta)* no one, nobody; **¿quién vino? – n.** who came? – no one (b) *(con verbo)* not ... anyone, not ... anybody; *(enfático)* no one, nobody; **no conozco a n.** I don't know anyone o anybody; **no vi a n.** I saw no one (c) *(con otro negativo)* anyone, anybody; **nunca habla con n.** he never speaks to anybody (d) *(en ciertas construcciones)* anybody, anyone; **más que n.** more than anyone; **sin decírselo a n.** without telling anyone; **casi n.** hardly anyone

2 *nm* nobody; **ser un don n.** to be a nobody

nado: a nado *loc adv* swimming; **cruzar** o **pasar a n.** to swim across

NAFTA *nm (abr North American Free Trade Agreement)* NAFTA

nafta *nf RP (gasolina) Br* petrol, *US* gas(oline)

nahua, náhuatl 1 *adj* Nahuatl

2 *nm (individuo)* Nahuatl (Indian)

nailon *nm* nylon

naipe *nm* playing card

nalga *nf* buttock; **nalgas** bottom, buttocks

nana *nf* (a) *(canción)* lullaby (b) *Col, Méx (niñera)* nanny

napalm *nm* napalm

napias *nfpl Fam* snout

Nápoles *n* Naples

napolitano,-a *adj & nm,f* Neapolitan

naranja 1 *nf* orange; *Fig* **mi media n.** my better half

2 *adj & nm (color)* orange

naranjada *nf* orangeade

naranjo *nm* orange tree

narciso *nm* (a) *(blanco)* narcissus; *(amarillo)* daffodil (b) *Fig (hombre)* narcissist

narcótico *nm* narcotic; *(droga)* drug

narcotizar [40] *vt (drogar)* to drug

narcotraficante *nmf* drug trafficker

narcotráfico *nm* drug trafficking

nariz *nf* (a) nose; *Fam* **me da en la n. que ...** I've got this feeling that ... (b) *Fam* **narices** nose; *Fam* **en mis (propias) narices** right under my very nose; *Fam* **estar hasta las narices de** to be totally fed up with; *Fam* meter **las narices en algo** to poke one's nose into sth; *Fam* **por narices** because I say so; *Fam* **tocarle a algn las narices** to get on sb's wick

narración *nf* narration

narrar *vt* to narrate, to tell

narrativo,-a *adj & nf* narrative

nata *nf* (a) cream; n. **batida** *o* **montada** whipped cream (b) *(de leche hervida)* skin (c) *Fig* cream, best

natación *nf Dep* swimming

natal *adj* **mi país n.** my native country; **su pueblo n.** his home town

natalicio *nm Fml* birthday

natalidad *nf* birth rate; **control de n.** birth control

natillas *nfpl Culin* custard

natividad *nf* Nativity

nativo,-a *adj & nm,f* native

nato,-a *adj* born

natura *nf Literario* nature; **contra n.** against nature

natural 1 *adj* natural; *(fruta, flor)* fresh; **de tamaño n.** life-size; **en estado n.** in its natural state; *Jur* **hijo n.** illegitimate child
2 *nmf* native

naturaleza *nf* (a) nature; **en plena n.** in the wild, in unspoilt countryside; *Arte* **n. muerta** still life (b) *(complexión)* physical constitution

naturalidad *nf (sencillez)* naturalness; **con n.** naturally, straightforwardly

naturalismo *nm* naturalism

naturalista 1 *adj* naturalistic
2 *nmf* naturalist

naturalización *nf* naturalization

naturalizar [40] **1** *vt* to naturalize
2 naturalizarse *upr* to become naturalized

naturalmente *adv* naturally; **¡n.!** of course!

naturismo *nm* naturism

naturista *nmf* naturist

naufragar [42] *vi (barco)* to sink, to be wrecked; *(persona)* to be shipwrecked

naufragio *nm Náut* shipwreck

náufrago,-a *nm,f* shipwrecked person, castaway

náusea *nf (usu pl)* nausea, sickness; **me da n.** it makes me sick; **sentir náuseas** to feel sick

nauseabundo,-a *adj* nauseating, sickening

náutico,-a *adj* nautical

navaja *nf* (a) *(cuchillo)* penknife, pocketknife; **n. de afeitar** razor (b) *(molusco)* razor-shell

navajada *nf,* **navajazo** *nm* stab, gash

navajero *nm Fam* thug

naval *adj* naval

Navarra *n* Navarre

navarro,-a 1 *adj* Navarrese, of/from Navarre
2 *nm,f* person from Navarre

nave *nf* (a) ship; **n. (espacial)** spaceship, spacecraft (b) *Ind* plant, building (c) *(de iglesia)* nave; **n. lateral** aisle

navegable *adj* navigable

navegación *nf* navigation; **n. costera** coastal shipping

navegador *nm Informát* browser

navegar [42] *vi* (a) to navigate, to sail (b) *Av* to navigate, to fly (c) **n. por Internet** to surf the Net

Navidad(es) *nf(pl)* Christmas; **árbol de Navidad** Christmas tree; **Feliz Navidad, Felices Navidades** Merry Christmas

navideño,-a *adj* Christmas

navío *nm* ship

nazi *adj & nmf* Nazi

nazismo *nm* Nazism

n/c., n/cta. *(abr nuestra cuenta)* our account, our acct

neblina *nf* mist, thin fog

nebulosa *nf Astron* nebula

nebuloso,-a *adj* (a) *Met* cloudy, hazy (b) *Fig* nebulous, vague

necedad *nf* (a) *(estupidez)* stupidity, foolishness (b) *(tontería)* stupid thing to say o to do

necesario,-a *adj* necessary; **es n. hacerlo** it has to be done; **es n. que vayas** you must go; **no es n. que vayas** there is no need for you to go; **si fuera n.** if need be

neceser *nm (de aseo)* toilet bag; *(de maquillaje)* make-up bag

necesidad *nf* (a) necessity, need; **artículos de primera n.** essentials; **por n.** of necessity; **tener n. de** to need (b) *(pobreza)* poverty, hardship (c) **hacer sus necesidades** to relieve oneself

necesitado,-a 1 *adj (pobre)* needy, poor; **n. de** in need of
2 *nmpl* **los necesitados** the needy

necesitar *vt* to need; **se necesita chico** *(en anuncios)* boy wanted

necio,-a 1 *adj* (a) *(tonto)* silly, stupid (b) *Méx (pesado)* boring
2 *nm,f* (a) *(tonto)* fool, idiot (b) *Méx (pesado)* bore

necrología *nf* obituary

néctar *nm* nectar

nectarina *nf* nectarine

neerlandés,-esa 1 *adj* Dutch, of/from the Netherlands
2 *nm,f (persona) (hombre)* Dutchman; *(mujer)* Dutchwoman; **los neerlandeses** the Dutch
3 *nm (idioma)* Dutch

nefasto,-a *adj* (a) *(perjudicial)* harmful (b) *(funesto)* unlucky, ill-fated (c) *(inútil)* hopeless

negación *nf* (a) negation (b) *(negativa)* denial; *(rechazo)* refusal (c) *Ling* negative

negado,-a 1 *adj* **ser n. para algo** to be hopeless *o* useless at sth
2 *nm,f* no-hoper

negar [1] **1** *vt* (a) to deny; **negó haberlo robado** he denied stealing it (b) *(rechazar)* to refuse, to deny; **le negaron la beca** they

refused him the grant
2 negarse *vpr* to refuse (**a** to)
negativa *nf* denial
negativo,-a *adj & nm* negative
negligencia *nf* negligence
negociación *nf* negotiation
negociado *nm Andes, RP (chanchullo)* shady deal
negociador,-a *adj* negotiating; **comité n.** negotiating committee
negociante *nmf* dealer; *(hombre)* businessman; *(mujer)* businesswoman
negociar [43] **1** *vt Fin & Pol* to negotiate
2 *vi (comerciar)* to do business, to deal
negocio *nm Com & Fin* business; *(transacción)* deal, transaction; *(asunto)* affair; **hombre de negocios** businessman; **mujer de negocios** businesswoman
negra *nf* (**a**) *Fig (mala suerte)* bad luck; **tener la n.** to be very unlucky (**b**) *Mús Br* crotchet, *US* quarter note
negrilla, negrita *adj & nf Impr* bold (face)
negro,-a 1 *adj* (**a**) black; **estar n.** *(bronceado)* to be suntanned (**b**) *Fig (suerte)* awful; *(desesperado)* desperate; *(furioso)* furious; **verlo todo n.** to be very pessimistic; **vérselas negras para hacer algo** to have a tough time doing sth
2 *nm,f (hombre)* black; *(mujer)* black (woman)
3 *nm (color)* black
nene,-a *nm,f (niño)* baby boy; *(niña)* baby girl
nenúfar *nm Bot* waterlily
neocelandés,-esa, neozelandés,-esa 1 *adj* of/from New Zealand
2 *nm,f* New Zealander
neoclásico,-a *adj Arte & Lit* neoclassic, neoclassical
neologismo *nm* neologism
neón *nm* neon
neoyorquino,-a 1 *adj* of/from New York
2 *nm,f* New Yorker
neozelandés,-esa *adj & nm,f =* **neocelandés,-esa**
nepotismo *nm* nepotism
Neptuno *n* Neptune
nervio *nm* (**a**) *Anat & Bot* nerve; *(de la carne)* sinew (**b**) *Fig (fuerza, vigor)* nerve, courage (**c**) **nervios** nerves; **ataque de nervios** fit of hysterics; **ser un manojo de nervios** to be a bundle of nerves; **tener los nervios de acero** to have nerves of steel
nerviosismo *nm* nerves
nervioso,-a *adj* (**a**) nervous; **poner n. a algn** to get on sb's nerves (**b**) *(inquieto)* fidgety
neto,-a *adj* (**a**) *(peso, cantidad)* net (**b**) *(nítido)* neat, clear
neumático,-a 1 *adj* pneumatic
2 *nm* tyre; **n. de recambio** spare tyre
neumonía *nf* pneumonia
neurálgico,-a *adj* neuralgic; *Fig* **punto n.** nerve centre

neurólogo,-a *nm,f* neurologist
neurosis *nf* neurosis
neurótico,-a *adj & nm,f* neurotic
neutral *adj* neutral
neutralidad *nf* neutrality
neutralizar [40] *vt* to neutralize
neutro,-a *adj* (**a**) *(imparcial)* neutral (**b**) *Ling* neuter
neutrón *nm Fís* neutron; **bomba de neutrones** neutron bomb
nevada *nf* snowfall
nevar [1] *v impers* to snow
nevera *nf* (**a**) *(frigorífico)* refrigerator, fridge (**b**) *(portátil)* cool box
nexo *nm* connection, link
ni *conj* (**a**) **no ... ni, ni ... ni** neither ... nor, not ... or; **no tengo tiempo ni dinero** I have got neither time nor money; **ni ha venido ni ha llamado** he hasn't come or phoned; **no vengas ni hoy ni mañana** don't come today or tomorrow (**b**) *(ni siquiera)* not even; **ni por dinero** not even for money; **ni se te ocurra** don't even think about it; **¡ni hablar!** no way!
Nicaragua *n* Nicaragua
nicaragüense *adj & nmf* Nicaraguan
nicho *nm* niche
nicotina *nf* nicotine
nido *nm* nest
niebla *nf* fog; **hay mucha n.** it is very foggy
nieto,-a *nm,f (niño)* grandson; *(niña)* granddaughter; **mis nietos** my grandchildren
nieve *nf* (**a**) *Met* snow; *Culin* **a punto de n.** (beaten) stiff (**b**) *Fam (cocaína)* snow (**c**) *Carib, Méx (granizado)* = drink of flavoured crushed ice
nigeriano,-a *adj & nm,f* Nigerian
Nilo *n* **el N.** the Nile
nilón *nm Tex* nylon
nimio,-a *adj (insignificante)* insignificant, petty
ninfómana *nf* nymphomaniac
ninguno,-a 1 *adj* (**a**) *(con verbo)* not ... any; **no leí ninguna revista** I didn't read any magazines; **no tiene ninguna gracia** it is not funny at all (**b**) **en ninguna parte** nowhere; **de ningún modo** no way

> **Ningún** is used instead of **ninguno** before masculine singular nouns (e.g. **ningún hombre** no man).

2 *pron* (**a**) *(persona)* nobody, no one; **n. lo vio** no one saw it; **n. de los dos** neither of the two; **n. de ellos** none of them (**b**) *(cosa)* not ... any of them; *(enfático)* none of them; **me gusta n.** I don't like any of them; **no vi n.** I saw none of them
niña *nf* (**a**) girl; *ver* **niño,-a** (**b**) *Anat* pupil; *Fig* **es la n. de sus ojos** she's the apple of his eye
niñera *nf* nursemaid, nanny
niñez *nf* infancy; *(a partir de los cuatro años)* childhood
niño,-a *nm,f* (**a**) child; *(muchacho)* (small)

oy; *(muchacha)* (little) girl; **de n.** as a child;
. **prodigio** child prodigy; *Pey* **n. bien** *o* **de
apá** rich boy, rich kid; *Pey* **n. bonito** *o*
nimado mummy's/daddy's boy (**b**) *(bebé)*
aby (**c**) **niños** children; *Fig* **juego de niños**
child's play (**d**) *Met* **el N.** el Niño

ipón,-ona *adj & nm,f* Japanese; **los nipones**
the Japanese

iquel *nm* nickel

iqui *nm* T-shirt

íspero *nm (fruto)* medlar; *(árbol)* medlar
ree

ítido,-a *adj (claro)* clear; *(imagen)* sharp

itrógeno *nm* nitrogen

itroglicerina *nf* nitroglycerine

ivel *nm* (**a**) *(altura)* level; **a n. del mar** at sea
evel (**b**) *(categoría)* standard; **n. de vida**
standard of living (**c**) *(instrumento)* level; **n.
de aire** spirit level (**d**) *Ferroc* **paso a n.** *Br* level
crossing, *US* grade crossing

ivelar *vt* (**a**) to level out *o* off (**b**) *(equilibrar)*
o balance out

⁰ *(abr número)* no

o 1 *adv* (**a**) *(como respuesta)* no; **¿te gusta? –
o** do you like it? – no (**b**) *(en otros contextos)*
not; **no vi a nadie** I didn't see anyone; **aún no**
not yet; **ya no** no longer, not any more; **no sin
antes …** not without first …; **¿por qué no?**
why not? (**c**) **no fumar/aparcar** *(en letrero)* no
smoking/parking (**d**) **no sea que** (+ *subjunct-
ve)* in case (**e**) **si no es rubia, ¿no?** she's blonde,
isn't she?; **llegaron anoche, ¿no?** they arrived
yesterday, didn't they? (**f**) *(como prefijo negativo)* non; **la no violencia** non-violence
  2 *nm* no; **un no rotundo** a definite no

oble 1 *adj* noble
  2 *nmf (hombre)* nobleman; *(mujer)* noblewoman; **los nobles** the nobility

obleza *nf* nobility

oche *nf* evening; *(después de las diez)* night,
night-time; **de n., por la n.** at night; **esta n.**
tonight; **mañana por la n.** tomorrow night *o*
evening; **buenas noches** *(saludo)* good
evening; *(despedida)* good night; **son las nueve de la n.** it's nine p.m.

ochebuena *nf* Christmas Eve

ochero *nm CSur (vigilante)* night-watchman

ochevieja *nf* New Year's Eve

oción *nf* (**a**) notion, idea (**b**) **nociones** smattering, basic knowledge; **nociones de es-
pañol** a smattering of Spanish

ocivo,-a *adj* noxious, harmful

octámbulo,-a *nm,f* sleepwalker; *Fam*
nightbird

octurno,-a *adj* (**a**) night; **vida nocturna**
night life; **clases nocturnas** evening classes
(**b**) *Bot & Zool* nocturnal

odriza *nf* (**a**) *(ama)* wet nurse (**b**) **buque n.**
supply ship

ogal *nm Bot* walnut (tree)

ómada 1 *adj* nomadic
  2 *nmf* nomad

nombrado,-a *adj (célebre)* famous, well-
known

nombramiento *nm* appointment

nombrar *vt* (**a**) *(designar)* to name, to appoint; **n. a algn director** to appoint sb director (**b**) *(mencionar)* to name, to mention

nombre *nm* (**a**) name; **n. de pila** Christian
name; **n. y apellidos** full name; *Informát* **n. de
dominio** domain name; **a n. de** addressed to;
en n. de on behalf of (**b**) *Ling* noun; **n. propio**
proper noun

nómina *nf* (**a**) *(de sueldo)* pay slip (**b**) *(plantilla)* payroll

nominar *vt* to nominate

nominativo,-a *adj* **cheque n. a** cheque made
out to

non *nm* (**a**) *Mat* odd number; **pares y nones**
odds and evens (**b**) *Fam* **nones** *(negación)* no;
decir (que) nones to refuse

nono,-a *adj* = **noveno,-a**

norcoreano,-a *adj & nm,f* North Korean

nordeste *nm* = **noreste**

nórdico,-a 1 *adj* (**a**) *(del norte)* northern (**b**)
(escandinavo) Nordic
  2 *nm,f* Nordic person

noreste *nm* northeast

noria *nf* (**a**) *(de feria)* big wheel (**b**) *(para
agua)* water wheel

norirlandés,-esa 1 *adj* Northern Irish
  2 *nm,f (persona) (hombre)* Northern Irishman; *(mujer)* Northern Irishwoman; **los norir-
landeses** the Northern Irish

norma *nf* norm; **n. de seguridad** safety standard

normal *adj* normal, usual; **lo n.** the normal
thing, what usually happens

normalidad *nf* normality; **volver a la n.** to
return to normal

normalizar [40] **1** *vt* to normalize, to restore
to normal
  2 normalizarse *upr* to return to normal

normativa *nf* rules

noroeste *nm* northwest

norte *nm* (**a**) north; **al n. de** to the north of (**b**)
Fig aim, goal

norteafricano,-a *adj & nm,f* North African

Norteamérica *n* North America

norteamericano,-a *adj & nm,f* (North)
American

norteño,-a 1 *adj* northern
  2 *nm,f* Northerner

Noruega *n* Norway

noruego,-a 1 *adj* Norwegian
  2 *nm,f* Norwegian
  3 *nm (idioma)* Norwegian

nos 1 *pron pers (directo)* us; *(indirecto)* (to) us;
n. ha visto he has seen us; **n. trajo un regalo**
he brought us a present; **n. lo dio** he gave it to
us
  2 *pron (reflexivo)* ourselves; *(recíproco)*
each other; **n. hemos divertido mucho** we
enjoyed ourselves a lot; **n. queremos mucho**

we love each other very much

nosotros,-as *pron pers pl* (a) *(sujeto)* we; **n. lo vimos** we saw it; **somos n.** it is us (b) *(complemento)* us; **con n.** with us

> Usually omitted in Spanish except for emphasis or contrast.

nostalgia *nf* nostalgia; *(morriña)* homesickness

nostálgico,-a *adj* nostalgic; *(con morriña)* homesick

nota *nf* (a) *(anotación)* note (b) *Educ* mark, grade; **sacar buenas notas** to get good marks (c) *Fig (detalle)* element, quality; **la n. dominante** the prevailing quality (d) *Mús* note; *Fam* **dar la n.** to make oneself noticed

notable 1 *adj (apreciable)* noticeable; *(destacado)* outstanding, remarkable
2 *nm (nota)* very good

notar 1 *vt (percibir)* to notice, to note
2 notarse *vpr* to be noticeable o evident, to show; **no se nota** it doesn't show; **se nota que ...** one can see that ...

notaría *nf (despacho)* notary's office

notarial *adj* notarial; **acta n.** affidavit

notario,-a *nm,f* notary (public), solicitor

noticia *nf* news *sing*; **una n.** a piece of news; **una buena n.** good news; **no tengo n. de esto** I don't know anything about it

> ⚠ Observa que la palabra inglesa **notice** es un falso amigo y no es la traducción de la palabra española **noticia**. En inglés, **notice** significa "aviso, anuncio".

noticiario, *Am* **noticiero** *nm* (a) *Cin* newsreel (b) *Rad & TV* television news *sing*

notificación *nf* notification; **sin n. previa** without (previous) notice; *Jur* **n. judicial** summons *sing*

notificar [44] *vt* to notify

notorio,-a *adj* (a) *(evidente)* obvious, evident (b) *(famoso)* famous, well-known

> ⚠ Observa que la palabra inglesa **notorious** es un falso amigo y no es la traducción de la palabra española **notorio**. En inglés, **notorious** significa "tristemente célebre".

novatada *nf* (a) *(broma)* rough joke, rag (b) **pagar la n.** to learn the hard way

novato,-a 1 *adj (persona)* inexperienced; *Fam* green
2 *nm,f* (a) *(principiante)* novice, beginner (b) *Univ* fresher

novecientos,-as *adj & nm* nine hundred

novedad *nf* (a) *(cosa nueva)* novelty; **últimas novedades** latest arrivals (b) *(cambio)* change, development (c) *(cualidad)* newness

novedoso,-a *adj* (a) *(nuevo)* new, full of novelties (b) *(innovador)* innovative

novel 1 *adj* new, inexperienced

2 *nmf* beginner, novice

novela *nf Lit* novel; **n. corta** short story; **r policíaca** detective story

novelero,-a *adj* (a) fond of new things (b *(fantasioso)* highly imaginative

novelesco,-a *adj* (a) *(de novela)* novelistic fictional (b) *(extraordinario)* bizarre, fantas tic

novelista *nmf* novelist

noveno,-a *adj & nm* ninth; **novena part** ninth

noventa *adj & nm inv* ninety

novia *nf* (a) *(amiga)* girlfriend (b) *(promet* da) fiancée (c) *(en boda)* bride

noviar *vi CSur, Méx* **n. con algn** to go out wit sb; **novian hace tiempo** they've been goin out together for a while

noviazgo *nm* engagement

noviembre *nm* November

novillada *nf Taurom* = bullfight with youn bulls

novillero,-a *nm,f Taurom* apprentice ma ador

novillo,-a *nm,f* (a) *(toro)* young bull; *(vaca* young cow (b) *Fam Educ* **hacer novillos** t play *Br* truant o *US* hooky

novio *nm* (a) *(amigo)* boyfriend (b) *(prome tido)* fiancé (c) *(en boda)* bridegroom; **lo novios** the bride and groom

nubarrón *nm Fam* storm cloud

nube *nf* cloud; *Fig* **vivir en las nubes** to hav one's head in the clouds; *Fig* **poner a algn po las nubes** to praise sb to the skies

nublado,-a *adj* cloudy, overcast

nublarse *vpr* to become cloudy, to clou over; *Fig* **se le nubló la vista** his eyes cloude over

nuboso,-a *adj* cloudy

nuca *nf* nape, back of the neck

nuclear *adj* nuclear; **central n.** nuclear powe station

núcleo *nm* nucleus; *(parte central)* core; **r urbano** city centre

nudillo *nm (usu pl)* knuckle

nudista *adj & nmf* nudist

nudo *nm* (a) knot; **hacer un n.** to tie a knot *Fig* **se me hizo un n. en la garganta** I got lump in my throat (b) *(punto principal)* crux core (c) *(de comunicaciones)* centre

nuera *nf* daughter-in-law

nuestro,-a 1 *adj pos* (a) our; **nuestra famili** our family (b) *(después del sustantivo)* o ours; **un amigo n.** a friend of ours
2 *pron pos* ours; **este libro es n.** this book i ours

nuevamente *adv* again

Nueva Zelanda *n* New Zealand

nueve *adj & nm inv* nine

nuevo,-a 1 *adj* (a) new; *Fam* **¿qué hay de n.** what's new?; **de n.** again; **Nueva York** Nev York; **Nueva Zelanda** New Zealand (b) *(adi cional)* further

2 *nm,f* newcomer; *(principiante)* beginner

uez *nf* (a) walnut; **n. moscada** nutmeg (b) *nat* **n. (de Adán)** Adam's apple

ulidad *nf* (a) *(ineptitud)* incompetence (b) *ur* nullity

ulo,-a *adj* (a) *(inepto)* useless, totally incapable (b) *(sin valor)* null and void, invalid; **oto n.** invalid vote (c) **crecimiento n.** zero rowth

úm. (*abr* **número**) no

umeral *adj & nm* numeral

umerar *vt* to number

umerario,-a 1 *adj* **profesor no n.** teacher on temporary contract

2 *nm* (a) *(miembro)* full member (b) *(dinero)* ash

umérico,-a *adj* numerical

úmero *nm* (a) number; **n. de matrícula** *Br* egistration number, *US* license number; **n. e serie** serial number; *Fig* **sin n.** countless b) *Prensa* number, issue; **n. atrasado** back umber (c) *(de zapatos)* size (d) *(en espec-*

táculo) sketch, act; *Fam* **montar un n.** to make a scene

numeroso,-a *adj* numerous

nunca *adv* (a) *(como respuesta)* never; ¿**cuándo volverás? – n.** when will you come back? – never (b) *(con verbo)* never; *(enfático)* not ... ever; **no he estado n. en España** I've never been to Spain; **yo no haría n. eso** I wouldn't ever do that (c) *(en ciertas construcciones)* ever; **casi n.** hardly ever; **más que n.** more than ever (d) **n. jamás** never ever; *(futuro)* never again

nupcial *adj* wedding, nuptial; **marcha n.** wedding march

nupcias *nfpl Fml* wedding, nuptials; **casarse en segundas n.** to marry again

nutrición *nf* nutrition

nutricionista *nmf* nutritionist

nutrir 1 *vt* to nourish, to feed

2 nutrirse *vpr* to feed (**de** *o* **con** on)

nutritivo,-a *adj* nutritious, nourishing; **valor n.** nutritional value

andutí *nm Par* fine lace

apa *nf Ven Fam* bonus, extra

ñato,-a *adj Andes, RP* snub-nosed

O, o [o] *nf (la letra)* O, o

o *conj* or; **jueves o viernes** Thursday or Friday; **o ... o** either ... or; **o sea** that is (to say), in other words

> **u** is used instead of **o** in front of words beginning with "o" or "ho" (e.g. **mujer u hombre** woman or man). Note that **ó** (with acute accent) is used between figures.

O. *(abr* **Oeste)**W

oasis *nm inv* oasis

obcecado,-a *adj Fig* stubborn

obcecar [44] **1** *vt Fig* to blind; **la ira lo obceca** he is blinded by anger

2 obcecarse *vpr Fig* to refuse to budge; *(obsesionarse)* to become obsessed

obedecer [33] **1** *vt* to obey

2 *vi* **o. a** *(provenir)* to be due to; **¿a qué obedece esa actitud?** what's the reason behind this attitude?

obediencia *nf* obedience

obediente *adj* obedient

obertura *nf* overture

obesidad *nf* obesity

obeso,-a *adj* obese

óbice *nm* obstacle; **eso no es ó. para que yo no lo haga** it won't prevent me from doing it

obispo *nm* bishop

objeción *nf* objection; **poner una o.** to raise an objection, to object

objetar 1 *vt* **no tengo nada que o.** I've got no objections

2 *vi Mil* to be a conscientious objector

objetividad *nf* objectivity

objetivo,-a 1 *nm* **(a)** *(fin, meta)* objective, aim **(b)** *Mil* target **(c)** *Cin & Fot* lens; **o. zoom** zoom lens

2 *adj* objective

objeto *nm* **(a)** object; **objetos perdidos** lost property; **mujer o.** sex object **(b)** *(fin)* aim, purpose; **con o. de ...** in order to ...; **tiene por o. ...** it is designed to ... **(c)** *Ling* object

objetor,-a 1 *nm,f* objector; **o. de conciencia** conscientious objector

2 *adj* objecting, dissenting

obligación *nf* **(a)** *(deber)* obligation; **por o.** out of a sense of duty; **tengo o. de ...** I have to ... **(b)** *Fin* bond, debenture

obligado,-a *adj* obliged; **verse o estar o. a** to be obliged to

obligar [42] *vt* to compel, to force

obligatorio,-a *adj* compulsory, obligatory

obra *nf* **(a)** *(trabajo)* (piece of) work; **por o. d** thanks to **(b)** *Arte* work; **o. maestra** master piece **(c)** *(acto)* deed **(d)** *Constr* building sit **(e) obras** *(arreglos)* repairs; **carretera e obras** *(en letrero)* roadworks; **cerrado po obras** *(en letrero)* closed for repairs

obrar 1 *vi* **(a)** *(proceder)* to act, to behave; **bien/mal** to do the right/wrong thing **(b)** *Fn* **obra en nuestro poder ...** we are in receip of ...

2 *vt (milagro)* to work

obrero,-a 1 *nm,f* worker, labourer

2 *adj* working; **clase obrera** working class **movimiento o.** labour movement

obscenidad *nf* obscenity

obsceno,-a *adj* obscene

obscurecer [33] **1** *v impers* to get dark

2 *vt* to darken

3 obscurecerse *vpr (nublarse)* to becom cloudy

obscuridad *nf* darkness; *Fig* obscurity

obscuro,-a *adj* **(a)** dark **(b)** *Fig (origen, idec* obscure; *(futuro)* uncertain, gloomy; *(asur to)* shady; *(nublado)* overcast

obsequiar [43] *vt* to give away

obsequio *nm* gift, present

observación *nf* observation

observador,-a 1 *nm,f* observer

2 *adj* observant

observancia *nf* observance

observar *vt* **(a)** *(mirar)* to observe, to watch **(b)** *(notar)* to notice **(c)** *(cumplir)* to observe

observatorio *nm* observatory

obsesión *nf* obsession

obsesionar 1 *vt* to obsess; **estoy obsesionad con eso** I can't get it out of my mind

2 obsesionarse *vpr* to get obsessed

obsesivo,-a *adj* obsessive

obseso,-a *nm,f* obsessed person; **un o sexual** a sex maniac

obsoleto,-a *adj* obsolete

obstaculizar [40] *vt* to obstruct, to get in th way of

obstáculo *nm* obstacle

obstante: no obstante 1 *loc adv* neverthe less

2 *prep* notwithstanding

obstetricia *nf* obstetrics *sing*

obstinación *nf* obstinacy

obstinado,-a *adj* obstinate

obstinarse *vpr* to persist **(en** in)

obstrucción *nf* obstruction; *Med* blockage

bstruir [37] **1** *vt* (**a**) *(salida, paso)* to block, o obstruct (**b**) *(progreso)* to impede, to block

2 obstruirse *vpr* to get blocked up

btención *nf* obtaining

btener [24] **1** *vt (alcanzar)* to obtain, to get

2 obtenerse *vpr* **o. de** *(provenir)* to come rom

bturador *nm Fot* shutter

btuso,-a *adj* obtuse

bús *nm* shell

bviar [43] *vt (problema)* to get round

bvio,-a *adj* obvious

ca *nf* goose

casión *nf* (**a**) *(momento)* occasion; **con o. e ...** on the occasion of ...; **en cierta o.** once (**b**) *(oportunidad)* opportunity, chance; **aprovechar una o.** to make the most of an opportunity (**c**) *Com* bargain; **de o.** cheap; **precios e o.** bargain prices

casional *adj* (**a**) *(eventual)* occasional; **trajo o.** casual work; **de forma o.** occasionally (**b**) *(fortuito)* accidental, chance

casionar *vt* to cause, to bring about

caso *nm (anochecer)* sunset; *Fig (declive)* all, decline

ccidental *adj* western, occidental

ccidente *nm* west; **el O.** the West

CDE *nf (abr* **Organización para la Cooperaión y el Desarrollo Económico)** OECD

ceanía *n* Oceania

ceánico,-a *adj* oceanic

céano *nm* ocean

chenta *adj & nm inv* eighty

cho *adj & nm inv* eight

chocientos,-as *adj & nm* eight hundred

cio *nm* leisure; **en mis ratos de o.** in my pare o leisure time

cioso,-a *adj* (**a**) *(inactivo)* idle (**b**) *(inútil)* ointless

cre *nm* ochre

ctavilla *nf (panfleto)* handout, leaflet

ctavo,-a *adj & nm,f* eighth

ctogenario,-a *adj & nm,f* octogenarian

ctogésimo,-a *adj & nm,f* eightieth

ctubre *nm* October

cular *adj* **testigo o.** eye witness

culista *nmf* ophthalmologist

cultar 1 *vt* to conceal, to hide; **o. algo a algn** hide sth from sb

2 ocultarse *vpr* to hide

culto,-a *adj* concealed, hidden

cupación *nf* occupation

cupado,-a *adj (persona)* busy; *(asiento)* aken; *(aseos, teléfono)* engaged; *(puesto e abajo)* filled

cupante *nmf (de casa)* occupant, occuier; *(ilegal)* squatter; *(de vehículo)* occuant

cupar 1 *vt* (**a**) to occupy (**b**) *(espacio, tiem-o)* to take up; *(cargo)* to hold, to fill (**c**) *CAm, léx (usar, emplear)* to use

2 ocuparse *vpr* **o. de** *(cuidar)* to look after; *(encargarse)* to see to

ocurrencia *nf (agudeza)* witty remark, wise-crack; *(idea)* bright idea

> Observa que la palabra inglesa **occurrence** es un falso amigo y no es la traducción de la palabra española **ocurrencia**. En inglés, **occurrence** significa "suceso, incidencia".

ocurrente *adj* witty

ocurrir 1 *v impers* to happen, to occur; **¿qué ocurre?** what's going on?; **¿qué te ocurre?** what's the matter with you?

2 ocurrirse *vpr* **no se me ocurre nada** I can't think of anything; **se me ocurre que ...** it occurs to me that ...

odiar [43] *vt* to detest, to hate; **odio tener que ...** I hate having to ...

odio *nm* hatred, loathing; **mirada de o.** hateful look

odioso,-a *adj* hateful

odontología *nf* dentistry, odontology

odontólogo,-a *nm,f* dental surgeon, odontologist

odre *nm* wineskin

OEA *nf (abr* **Organización de Estados Americanos)** OAS

oeste *nm* west

ofender 1 *vt* to offend

2 ofenderse *vpr* to get offended (**por** by), to take offence (**por** at)

ofensa *nf* offence

ofensiva *nf* offensive

ofensivo,-a *adj* offensive

oferta *nf* offer; *Fin & Ind* bid, tender, proposal; *Com* **de o en o.** on (special) offer; **o. y demanda** supply and demand

ofertar *vt* to offer

off *adj* **voz en o.** *Cin & TV* voice-over; *Teatro* voice offstage

offset *nm Impr* offset

oficial 1 *adj* official

2 *nmf* (**a**) *Mil & Náut* officer (**b**) *(empleado)* clerk (**c**) *(obrero)* skilled worker

oficialismo *nm Am* (**a**) **el o.** *(gobierno)* the Government (**b**) **el o.** *(partidarios del gobierno)* government supporters

oficialista *Am* **1** *adj* pro-government

2 *nmf* government supporter

oficina *nf* office; **o. de empleo** *Br* job centre, *US* job office; **o. de turismo** tourist office; **o. de correos** post office; **horas/horario de o.** business hours

oficinista *nmf* office worker, clerk

oficio *nm* (**a**) *(ocupación)* job, occupation; *(profesión)* trade; **ser del o.** to be in the trade (**b**) *(comunicación oficial)* official letter o note; **de o.** ex-officio; **abogado de o.** state-appointed lawyer (**c**) *Rel* service

oficioso,-a *adj (noticia, fuente)* unofficial

---

*Observa que la palabra inglesa **officious** es un falso amigo y no es la traducción de la palabra española **oficioso**. En inglés, **officious** significa "excesivamente celoso o diligente".*

---

ofimática *nf* office automation

ofimático,-a *adj Informát* **paquete o.** business package

ofrecer [33] **1** *vt* (**a**) to offer (**b**) *(aspecto)* to present

2 ofrecerse *vpr* (**a**) *(prestarse)* to offer, to volunteer (**b**) *(situación)* to present itself (**c**) *Fml* **¿qué se le ofrece?** what can I do for you?

ofrecimiento *nm* offering

ofrendar *vt Rel* to offer up

ofrezco *indic pres de* **ofrecer**

oftalmología *nf* ophthalmology

oftalmólogo,-a *nm,f* ophthalmologist

ofuscación *nf,* **ofuscamiento** *nm* blinding, dazzling

ofuscar [44] *vt* (**a**) *Fig (confundir)* to blind (**b**) *(deslumbrar)* to dazzle

oídas: de oídas *loc adv* by hearsay

oído *nm* (**a**) *(sentido)* hearing (**b**) *(órgano)* ear; **aprender de o.** to learn by ear; *Fig* **hacer oídos sordos** to turn a deaf ear

oír [17] *vt* to hear; **¡oye!** hey!; **¡oiga!** excuse me!; *Fam* **como lo oyes** believe it or not

OIT *nf* (*abr* **Organización Internacional del Trabajo**) ILO

ojal *nm* buttonhole

ojalá 1 *interj* let's hope so!, I hope so!

2 *conj* (+ *subjunctive*) **¡o. sea cierto!** I hope it's true!

ojeada *nf* **echar una o.** to have a quick look

ojeras *nfpl* rings *o* bags under the eyes

ojeriza *nf* dislike

ojo 1 *nm* (**a**) eye; **o. morado** black eye; **ojos saltones** bulging eyes; *Fig* **a ojos vista** clearly, openly; *Fig* **calcular a o.** to guess; *Fam* **no pegué o.** I didn't sleep a wink (**b**) *(de aguja)* eye; *(de cerradura)* keyhole (**c**) *(de un puente)* span

2 *interj* careful!, look out!

ojota *nf* (**a**) *Méx (sandalia)* sandal (**b**) *RP (chancletas) Br* flip-flop, *US* thong

okupa *nmf* squatter

ola *nf* wave; **o. de calor** heat wave

ole, olé *interj* bravo!

oleada *nf* wave; *Fig* **o. de turistas** influx of tourists

oleaje *nm* swell

óleo *nm Arte* oil; **pintura** *o* **cuadro al ó.** oil painting

oleoducto *nm* pipeline

oler [65] **1** *vt* (**a**) *(percibir olor)* to smell (**b**) *Fig (adivinar)* to smell, to feel

2 *vi* (**a**) *(exhalar)* to smell; **o. a** to smell of; **o. bien/mal** to smell good/bad (**b**) *Fig (parecer)* to smack (**a** of)

3 olerse *vpr Fig (adivinar)* to feel, to sense;

me lo olía I thought as much

olfatear *vt* (**a**) *(oler)* to sniff (**b**) *Fig (indaga* to pry into

olfato *nm* sense of smell; *Fig* good nos instinct

oligarquía *nf* oligarchy

olimpiada *nf Dep* Olympiad, Olymp Games; **las olimpiadas** the Olympic Games

olímpicamente *adv* **paso o. de estudiar** couldn't give a damn about studying

olímpico,-a *adj* Olympic; **Juegos Olímpico** Olympic Games

oliva *nf* olive; **aceite de o.** olive oil

olivar *nm* olive grove

olivo *nm* olive (tree)

olla *nf* saucepan, pot; **o. exprés** *o* **a presió** pressure cooker

olmo *nm* smooth-leaved elm

olor *nm* smell; **o. corporal** body odour

oloroso,-a *adj* fragrant, sweet-smelling

OLP *nf* (*abr* **Organización para la Liberació de Palestina**) PLO

olvidadizo,-a *adj* forgetful

olvidar 1 *vt* (**a**) to forget; *Fam* **¡olvídam** leave me alone! (**b**) **olvidé el paraguas all** left my umbrella there

2 olvidarse *vpr* to forget; **se me ha olvidad hacerlo** I forgot to do it

olvido *nm* (**a**) *(desmemoria)* oblivion (**b** *(lapsus)* oversight

ombligo *nm* navel

ominoso,-a *adj* shameful

omisión *nf* omission

omiso,-a *adj* **hacer caso o. de** to take n notice of

omitir *vt* to omit, to leave out

ómnibus *nm* (*pl* **ómnibus** *o* **omnibuse** *Cuba, Urug* bus

omnipotente *adj* omnipotent, almighty

omnipresente *adj* omnipresent

omnisciente *adj* omniscient, all-knowing

omnívoro,-a 1 *adj* omnivorous

2 *nm,f* omnivore

omóplato, omoplato *nm* shoulder blade

OMS *nf* (*abr* **Organización Mundial de Salud**) WHO

ONCE *nf* (*abr* **Organización Nacional de Cie gos Españoles**) ≃ RNIB

once 1 *adj inv* eleven

2 *nm inv* eleven; *Ftb* eleven, team

onda *nf* (**a**) *Fís* wave; *Fam Fig* **estar en la o.** be with it; **o. expansiva** shock wave; *Rad* **larga/media/corta** long/medium/short wav (**b**) *(en el agua)* ripple (**c**) *(de pelo)* wave (* *Méx, RP* **¿qué o.?** *(¿qué tal?)* how's it going how are things?

ondear *vi* (**a**) *(bandera)* to flutter (**b**) *(agua)* to ripple

ondulación *nf* undulation; *(de agua)* ripple

ondulado,-a *adj* (pelo) wavy; *(paisaje)* ro ing

ondulante *adj* undulating

ondular 1 vt (el pelo) to wave
2 vi (moverse) to undulate
oneroso,-a adj (impuesto) heavy
ONG nf inv (abr **Organización no Gubernamental**) NGO
onomástica nf saint's day
onomatopeya nf onomatopoeia
ONU nf (abr **Organización de las Naciones Unidas**) UN(O)
onubense 1 adj of/from Huelva
2 nmf person from Huelva
onza nf (medida) ounce
OPA nf (abr **Oferta Pública de Adquisición**) takeover bid
opaco,-a adj opaque
ópalo nm opal
opción nf (a) (elección) option, choice; (alternativa) alternative (b) (posibilidad) opportunity, chance
opcional adj optional
open nm Dep open
OPEP nf (abr **Organización de los Países Exportadores de Petróleo**) OPEC
ópera nf Mús opera
operación nf (a) Med operation; **o. quirúrgica** surgical operation (b) Fin transaction, deal; **operaciones bursátiles** stock exchange transactions (c) Mat operation
operador,-a nm,f (a) (técnico) operator (b) Cin (de cámara) (hombre) cameraman; (mujer) camerawoman; (del proyector) projectionist (c) Tel operator
operante adj operative
operar 1 vt (a) Med **o. a algn (de algo)** to operate on sb (for sth) (b) (cambio etc) to bring about
2 vi Fin to deal, to do business (**con** with)
3 operarse upr (a) Med to have an operation (**de** for) (b) (producirse) to occur, to come about
operario,-a nm,f operator; (obrero) worker
operativo,-a 1 adj operative
2 nm Am operation
opereta nf operetta
opinar vi (a) (pensar) to think (b) (declarar) to give one's opinion, to be of the opinion
opinión nf (juicio) opinion; **cambiar de o.** to change one's mind
opio nm opium
oponente nmf opponent
oponer [19] (pp **opuesto**) **1** vt (resistencia) to offer
2 oponerse upr (estar en contra) to be opposed; **se opone a aceptarlo** he refuses to accept it
oporto nm (vino) port
oportunidad nf opportunity, chance
oportunista adj & nmf opportunist
oportuno,-a adj (a) (adecuado) timely; **¡qué o.!** what good timing! (b) (conveniente) appropriate; **si te parece o.** if you think it appropriate

oposición nf (a) opposition (b) (examen) competitive examination
opositar vi = to sit a competitive examination
opositor,-a nm,f (a) (candidato) = candidate for a competitive examination (b) Am Pol opponent
opresión nf oppression; **o. en el pecho** tightness of the chest
opresivo,-a adj oppressive
opresor,-a 1 nm,f oppressor
2 adj oppressive, oppressing
oprimir vt (a) (pulsar) to press (b) (subyugar) to oppress
oprobio nm ignominy, opprobrium
optar vi (a) (elegir) to choose (**entre** between); **opté por ir yo mismo** I decided to go myself (b) (aspirar) to apply (**a** for); **puede o. a medalla** he's in with a chance of winning a medal
optativo,-a adj optional
óptica nf (a) (tienda) optician's (shop) (b) (punto de vista) angle
óptico,-a 1 adj optical
2 nm,f optician
optimismo nm optimism
optimista 1 adj optimistic
2 nmf optimist
óptimo,-a adj optimum, excellent
opuesto,-a adj (a) (contrario) contrary; **en direcciones opuestas** in opposite directions; **gustos opuestos** conflicting tastes (b) (de enfrente) opposite; **el extremo o.** the other end
opulencia nf opulence
opulento,-a adj opulent
opuse pt indef de **oponer**
oración nf (a) Rel prayer (b) Ling clause, sentence
oráculo nm oracle
orador,-a nm,f speaker, orator
oral adj oral; Med **por vía o.** to be taken orally
órale interj Méx Fam (a) (venga) come on! (b) (de acuerdo) right!, sure!
orangután nm orang-outang, orang-utan
orar vi Rel to pray
oratoria nf oratory
órbita nf (a) orbit (b) Anat eye socket
orden 1 nm order; **o. público** law and order; **por o. alfabético** in alphabetical order; **de primer o.** first-rate; **o. del día** agenda; **del o. de** approximately
2 nf (a) (mandato) order; Mil **¡a la o.!** sir! (b) Jur warrant, order; **o. de registro** search warrant; **o. judicial** court order
ordenado,-a adj tidy
ordenador nm computer; **o. personal** personal computer
ordenamiento nm ordering
ordenanza 1 nm (empleado) office boy
2 nf regulations; **o. municipal** bylaw
ordenar 1 vt (a) (organizar) to put in order;

(habitación) to tidy up (**b**) *(mandar)* to order (**c**) *Am (pedir)* to order
  2 ordenarse *upr Rel* to be ordained (**de** as), to take holy orders

ordeñar *vt* to milk

ordinario,-a *adj* (**a**) *(corriente)* ordinary, common (**b**) *(grosero)* vulgar, common

orégano *nm* oregano, marjoram

oreja *nf* ear; *(de sillón)* wing

orejero,-a *nm,f Am (soplón)* grass

orfanato *nm* orphanage

orfebre *nm (del oro)* goldsmith; *(de la plata)* silversmith

orfebrería *nf* gold/silver work

orfelinato *nm* orphanage

orgánico,-a *adj* organic

organigrama *nm* organization chart; *Informát* flow chart

organismo *nm* (**a**) *(ser vivo)* organism (**b**) *(institución)* organization, body

organista *nmf* organist

organización *nf* organization

organizado,-a *adj* organized; **viaje o.** package tour

organizador,-a 1 *adj* organizing
  2 *nm,f* organizer

organizar [40] **1** *vt* to organize
  2 organizarse *upr Fig (armarse)* to happen

órgano *nm* organ

orgasmo *nm* orgasm

orgía *nf* orgy

orgullo *nm* (**a**) *(propia estima)* pride (**b**) *(arrogancia)* arrogance

orgulloso,-a *adj* (**a**) **estar o.** *(satisfecho)* to be proud (**b**) **ser o.** *(arrogante)* to be arrogant *o* haughty

orientación *nf* (**a**) *(dirección)* orientation, direction (**b**) *(guía)* guidance; **curso de o.** induction course

oriental 1 *adj* (**a**) *(del este)* eastern, oriental; *(del Lejano Oriente)* oriental (**b**) *Am (uruguayo)* Uruguayan
  2 *nmf* (**a**) *(del Lejano Oriente)* oriental (**b**) *Am (uruguayo)* Uruguayan

orientar 1 *vt* (**a**) *(enfocar)* to aim (**a** at), to intend (**a** for); **orientado al consumo** intended for consumption (**b**) *(indicar camino)* to give directions to; *Fig (aconsejar)* to advise (**c**) **una casa orientada al sur** a house facing south (**d**) *(esfuerzo)* to direct
  2 orientarse *upr (encontrar el camino)* to get one's bearings, to find one's way about

oriente *nm* East, Orient; **el Extremo** *o* **Lejano/Medio/Próximo O.** the Far/Middle/Near East

orificio *nm* hole, opening; *Anat & Téc* orifice; **o. de entrada** inlet; **o. de salida** outlet

origen *nm* origin; **país de o.** country of origin; **dar o. a** to give rise to

original *adj & nm* original

originalidad *nf* originality

originar 1 *vt* to cause, to give rise to

2 originarse *upr* to originate

originariamente *adv* originally

originario,-a *adj* native

orilla *nf (borde)* edge; *(del río)* bank; *(del mar)* shore

orillero,-a *adj Am (persona)* suburban

orín¹ *nm (herrumbre)* rust

orín² *nm (usu pl) (orina)* urine

orina *nf* urine

orinal *nm* chamberpot; *Fam* potty

orinar 1 *vi* to urinate
  2 orinarse *upr* to wet oneself

oriundo,-a *adj* **ser o. de** to come from

orla *nf Univ* graduation photograph

ornamentar *vt* to adorn, to embellish

ornamento *nm* ornament

ornar *vt* to adorn, to embellish

ornato *nm (atavío)* finery; *(adorno)* decoration

ornitología *nf* ornithology

ornitólogo,-a *nm,f* ornithologist

oro *nm* (**a**) gold; **de o.** gold, golden; **o. de ley** fine gold (**b**) *Naipes* **oros** *(baraja española)* ≃ diamonds

orquesta *nf* orchestra; *(de verbena)* dance band

orquestar *vt* to orchestrate

orquídea *nf* orchid

ortiga *nf (stinging)* nettle

ortodoxia *nf* orthodoxy

ortodoxo,-a *adj* orthodox

ortografía *nf* orthography, spelling; **faltas de o.** spelling mistakes

ortográfico,-a *adj* orthographic, orthographical; **signos ortográficos** punctuation

ortopédico,-a *adj* orthopaedic; **pierna ortopédica** artificial leg

oruga *nf* caterpillar

orzuelo *nm Med* sty, stye

os *pron pers pl* (**a**) *(complemento directo)* you; **os veo mañana** I'll see you tomorrow (**b**) *(complemento indirecto)* you, to you; **os daré el dinero** I'll give you the money; **os escribiré** I'll write to you (**c**) *(con verbo reflexivo)* yourselves (**d**) *(con verbo recíproco)* each other; **os queréis mucho** you love each other very much

osa *nf* **O. Mayor** *Br* Great Bear, *US* Big Dipper; **O. Menor** *Br* Little Bear, *US* Little Dipper

osadía *nf* (**a**) *(audacia)* daring (**b**) *(desvergüenza)* impudence

osado,-a *adj* (**a**) *(audaz)* daring (**b**) *(desvergonzado)* shameless

osar *vi* to dare

osario *nm* ossuary

Óscar *nm Cin* Oscar

oscilación *nf* (**a**) oscillation (**b**) *(de precios)* fluctuation

oscilante *adj* (**a**) oscillating (**b**) *(precios)* fluctuating

oscilar *vi* (**a**) *Fís* to oscillate (**b**) *(variar)* to vary, to fluctuate

oscuras: a oscuras *loc adv* in the dark; **nos quedamos a o.** we were left in darkness

oscurecer [33] *v impers, vt & vpr* = **obscurecer**

oscuridad *nf* = **obscuridad**

oscuro,-a *adj* = **obscuro,-a**

óseo,-a *adj* osseous, bony; **tejido ó.** bone tissue

osito *nm Fam* **o. (de peluche)** teddy bear

osmosis, ósmosis *nf inv* osmosis

oso *nm* bear; **o. polar** polar bear; **o. hormiguero** anteater; **o. marino** fur seal; *Fam Fig* **hacer el o.** to play the fool

ostensible *adj* ostensible

ostentación *nf* ostentation; **hacer o. de algo** to show sth off

ostentar *vt* (**a**) *(lucir)* to flaunt (**b**) *(cargo)* to hold

ostentoso,-a *adj* ostentatious

osteópata *nmf* osteopath

osteopatía *nf* osteopathy

ostión *nm* (**a**) *Méx (ostra)* large oyster (**b**) *Chile (vieira)* scallop

ostra *nf* oyster; *Fig* **aburrirse como una o.** to be bored stiff; *Fam* **¡ostras!** *Br* crikey!, *US* gee!

ostracismo *nm* ostracism

OTAN *nf* (*abr* **Organización del Tratado del Atlántico Norte**) NATO

otear *vt (horizonte)* to scan, to search

OTI *nf* (*abr* **Organización de Televisiones Iberoamericanas**) = association of all Spanish-speaking television networks

otitis *nf inv* infection and inflammation of the ear, otitis

otoñal *adj* autumn, *US* fall

otoño *nm* autumn, *US* fall

otorgamiento *nm (concesión)* granting; *(de un premio)* award

otorgar [42] *vt* (**a**) *(premio)* to award (**a** to); **o. un indulto** to grant pardon (**b**) *(permiso)* to grant (**a** to)

otorrinolaringólogo,-a *nm,f* ear, nose and throat specialist

otro,-a 1 *adj indef* (**a**) *(sin artículo)* (sing) another; *(pl)* other; **o. coche** another car; **otras personas** other people (**b**) *(con artículo definido)* other; **el o. coche** the other car (**c**) **otra cosa** something else; **otra vez** again

2 *pron indef* (**a**) *(sin artículo)* (sing) another (one); *(pl) (personas)* others; *(cosas)* other ones; **dame o.** give me another (one); **no es mío, es de o.** it's not mine, it's somebody else's (**b**) *(con artículo definido)* (sing) **el o./la otra** the other (one); *(pl) (personas)* **los otros/las otras** the others; *(cosas)* the other ones (**c**) **hacer o. tanto** to do likewise

ovación *nf* ovation

ovacionar *vt* to give an ovation to, to applaud

oval, ovalado,-a *adj* oval

óvalo *nm* oval

ovario *nm* ovary

oveja *nf* sheep; *(hembra)* ewe; *Fig* **la o. negra** the black sheep

overol *nm Am* overalls

ovillo *nm* ball (of wool); *Fig* **hacerse un o.** to curl up into a ball

ovino,-a *adj* ovine; **ganado o.** sheep *pl*

OVNI *nm* (*abr* **objeto volador no identificado**) UFO

ovular 1 *adj* ovular

2 *vi* to ovulate

óvulo *nm* ovule

oxidación *nf (metal)* rusting

oxidado,-a *adj (metal)* rusty; *Fig* **su inglés está un poco o.** her English is a bit rusty

oxidar 1 *vt Quím* to oxidize; *(metales)* to rust

2 oxidarse *vpr Quím* to oxidize; *(metales)* to rust, to go rusty

óxido *nm* (**a**) oxide; **ó. de carbono** carbon monoxide (**b**) *(orín)* rust

oxigenado,-a *adj* oxygenated; **agua oxigenada** (hydrogen) peroxide

oxígeno *nm* oxygen; **bomba de o.** oxygen cylinder *o* tank

oye *indic pres & imperat de* **oír**

oyente *nmf* (**a**) *Rad* listener (**b**) *Univ* occasional student

ozono *nm* ozone; **capa de o.** ozone layer

P, p [pe] *nf (la letra)* P, p
pabellón *nm* **(a)** **p. de deportes** sports centre **(b)** *(en feria)* stand **(c)** *(bloque)* wing **(d)** *(bandera)* flag
pábulo *nm Fml Fig* fuel; **dar p. a** to encourage
pacer [60] *vt & vi* to graze, to pasture
pachá *nm Fam Fig* **vivir como un p.** to live like a king
Pachamama *n* Mother Earth
pachanguero,-a *adj Fam Pey (música)* catchy
pachón,-ona *nm,f (perro)* pointer
pachorra *nf Fam* sluggishness; **tener p.** to be phlegmatic
paciencia *nf* patience; **armarse de p.** to grin and bear it
paciente *adj & nmf* patient
pacificación *nf* pacification
pacificador,-a 1 *adj* pacifying
   2 *nm,f* peacemaker
pacificar [44] **1** *vt* to pacify; *Fig (apaciguar)* to appease, to calm
   2 pacificarse *vpr* to calm down
Pacífico *nm* **el (océano) P.** the Pacific (Ocean)
pacífico,-a *adj* peaceful
pacifismo *nm* pacifism
pacifista *adj & nmf* pacifist
paco *nm Andes, Pan Fam (policía)* cop
pacotilla *nf Fam* **de p.** second-rate
pactar *vt* to agree to
pacto *nm* pact; **el P. de Varsovia** the Warsaw Pact; **p. de caballeros** gentlemen's agreement
padecer [33] *vt & vi* to suffer; **padece del corazón** he suffers from heart trouble
padecimiento *nm* suffering
padrastro *nm* **(a)** stepfather **(b)** *(pellejo)* hangnail
padrazo *nm* easy-going *o* indulgent father
padre **1** *nm* **(a)** father; **p. de familia** family man **(b)** **padres** parents
   2 *adj inv Fam* **(a)** *(tremendo)* huge; **pegarse la vida p.** to live like a king **(b)** *Méx (genial)* great
padrenuestro *nm* Lord's Prayer
padrino *nm* **(a)** *(de bautizo)* godfather; *(de boda)* best man; **padrinos** godparents **(b)** *(espónsor)* sponsor
padrísimo,-a *adj Méx Fam* fantastic, great
padrón *nm* census
padrote *nm Méx Fam (proxeneta)* pimp
paella *nf* paella, = rice dish made with ve-

getables, meat and/or seafood
paellera *nf* paella pan
pág *(abr página)* p
paga *nf (salario)* wage; *(de niños)* pocket money; **p. extra** bonus
pagadero,-a *adj* payable; *Fin* **cheque p. al portador** cheque payable to bearer
pagador,-a *nm,f* payer
pagano,-a *adj & nm,f* pagan, heathen
pagar [42] *vt* **(a)** to pay; **p. en metálico** *o* **al contado** to pay cash; **p. por** *(producto, mala acción)* to pay for; *Fig* **(ella) lo ha pagado caro** she's paid dearly for it **(b)** *(recompensar)* to repay
pagaré *nm Fin* promissory note, IOU; **p. del tesoro** treasury note
página *nf* page; **en la p. 3** on page 3; *Fig* **una p. importante de la historia** an important chapter in history; *Informát* **p. personal** home page; *Informát* **p. web** web page
pago *nm* payment; **p. adelantado** *o* **anticipado** advance payment; **p. contra reembolso** cash on delivery; **p. inicial** down payment; **p. por visión** pay-per-view
paila *nf Andes, CAm, Carib (frying)* pan
paipái, paipay *nm (pl* **paipáis)** = large palm fan
país *nm* country, land; **vino del p.** local wine; **P. Vasco** Basque Country; **P. Valenciano** Valencia
paisaje *nm* landscape, scenery
paisano,-a 1 *adj* of the same country
   2 *nm,f (compatriota)* fellow countryman/countrywoman, compatriot; **en traje de p.** in plain clothes
Países Bajos *npl* **(los) P.** the Netherlands, the Low Countries
paja *nf* **(a)** straw **(b)** *Fam Fig (bazofia)* padding, waffle **(c)** *Vulg* **hacerse una p.** to wank
pajar *nm (almacén)* straw loft; *(en el exterior)* straw rick
pajarita *nf* **(a)** bow tie **(b)** *(de papel)* paper bird
pájaro *nm* **(a)** bird; **Madrid a vista de p.** a bird's-eye view of Madrid; **p. carpintero** woodpecker **(b)** *Fam* **tener pájaros** to have daft ideas
pajita, pajilla *nf* (drinking) straw
Pakistán *n* Pakistan
pakistaní *adj & nmf* Pakistani
pala *nf* **(a)** shovel; *(de jardinero)* spade; *(de cocina)* slice **(b)** *Dep (de ping-pong, frontón)*

bat, US paddle; *(de remo)* blade

palabra nf (a) word; **de p.** by word of mouth; **dirigir la p. a algn** to address sb; **juego de palabras** pun (b) *(promesa)* word; **p. de honor** word of honour (c) *(turno para hablar)* right to speak; **tener la p.** to have the floor

palabrería nf palaver

palabrota nf swearword

palacio nm *(grande)* palace; *(pequeño)* mansion; **P. de Justicia** Law Courts

paladar nm (a) palate (b) *(sabor)* taste

paladear vt to savour, to relish

palanca nf (a) lever (b) *(manecilla)* handle, stick; *Aut* **p. de cambio** *Br* gear-stick, *US* gearshift; **p. de mando** control lever (c) *Dep (trampolín)* diving board

palangana nf washbasin

palco nm box

paleolítico,-a adj palaeolithic, paleolithic

paleontología nf palaeontology, paleontology

Palestina n Palestine

palestino,-a adj & nm,f Palestinian

palestra nf arena; *Fig* **salir** o **saltar a la p.** to enter the fray, to take the field

paleta nf (a) *(espátula)* slice (b) *(de pintor)* palette; *(de albañil)* trowel (c) *Dep (de ping-pong)* bat (d) *CAm, Méx (pirulí)* lollipop; *(polo) Br* ice lolly, *US* Popsicle®

paletilla nf (a) shoulder blade (b) *Culin* shoulder

paleto,-a *Fam Pey* **1** adj unsophisticated, boorish

2 nm,f country bumpkin, yokel

paliar [43] vt to alleviate, to palliate

paliativo,-a adj & nm palliative

palidecer [33] vi (a) *(persona)* to turn pale (b) *Fig (disminuir)* to diminish, to be on the wane

palidez nf paleness, pallor

pálido,-a adj pale

palillero nm toothpick case

palillo nm (a) *(mondadientes)* toothpick; **palillos chinos** chopsticks (b) *Mús* drumstick

palio nm (a) canopy (b) *Rel* pallium

palique nm *Fam* chat, small talk

paliza nf (a) *(zurra)* thrashing, beating; **darle algn una p.** to beat sb up (b) *(derrota)* beating (c) *Fam (pesadez)* bore, pain (in the neck)

palma nf (a) *Anat* palm (b) *Bot* palm tree (c) **hacer palmas** to applaud

palmada nf (a) *(golpe)* slap (b) **palmadas** applause, clapping

palmar vt *Fam* **palmarla** to snuff it, to kick the bucket

palmarés nm (a) *(historial)* service record (b) *(vencedores)* list of winners

palmatoria nf candlestick

palmera nf palm tree

palmo nm *(medida)* span; *Fig* **p. a p.** inch by inch

palo nm (a) stick; *(vara)* rod; *(de escoba)* broomstick; *Fig* **a p. seco** on its own (b) *(golpe)* blow; *Fig* **dar un p. a algn** to let sb down (c) **de p.** wooden (d) *Dep (de portería)* woodwork (e) *(de golf)* club (f) *Naipes* suit

paloma nf pigeon; *Lit* dove; **p. mensajera** homing o carrier pigeon

palomar nm pigeon house, dovecot

palomilla nf (a) grain moth (b) *(tuerca)* wing o butterfly nut

palomitas (de maíz) nfpl popcorn

palpable adj palpable

palpar vt to touch, to feel; *Med* to palpate

palpitación nf palpitation, throbbing

palpitante adj palpitating, throbbing; *(asunto)* burning

palpitar vi to palpitate, to throb

palta nf *Andes, RP (fruto)* avocado

palúdico,-a adj malarial

paludismo nm malaria

palurdo,-a adj uncouth, boorish

pamela nf broad-brimmed hat

pampa nf pampa, pampas

pamplina nf *Fam* nonsense

pan nm bread; **p. de molde** loaf of bread; **p. integral** wholemeal o wholewheat bread; **p. rallado** breadcrumbs; **p. dulce** *Méx* cake; *RP* = type of fruitcake eaten at Christmas; *Arg* **p. lactal** sliced bread; *Fam Fig* **más bueno que el p.** as good as gold; *Fam Fig* **es p. comido** it's a piece of cake

pana nf corduroy

panacea nf panacea

panadería nf baker's (shop), bakery

panadero,-a nm,f baker

panal nm honeycomb

Panamá n Panama

panamá nm *(sombrero)* Panama hat

panameño,-a adj & nm,f Panamanian

pancarta nf placard; *(en manifestación)* banner

pancho nm *RP (perrito caliente)* hot dog

páncreas nm inv pancreas

panda¹ nm panda

panda² nf gang

pandereta nf tambourine

pandilla nf *Fam* gang

panecillo nm bread roll

panel nm panel

panera nf bread-basket

pánfilo,-a adj *Fam (bobo)* silly, stupid; *(crédulo)* gullible

panfleto nm lampoon, political pamphlet

pánico nm panic; **sembrar el p.** to cause panic

panocha nf *Bot* corn cob; *(de trigo etc)* ear

panoli nmf *Fam* idiot

panorama nm *(vista)* panorama, view; *Fig* panorama

panorámico,-a adj panoramic

panqueque nm *Am* pancake

pantaleta nf, **pantaletas** nfpl *Carib, Méx*

(bragas) panties, *Br* knickers

pantalla *nf* (a) *Cin, TV & Informát* screen (b) *(de lámpara)* shade (c) *Fig* **servir de p.** to act as a decoy

pantalón *nm (usu pl)* trousers, *US* pants; **p. vaquero** jeans

pantano *nm Geog* (a) *(natural)* marsh, bog (b) *(artificial)* reservoir

panteón *nm* pantheon, mausoleum; **p. familiar** family vault

pantera *nf* panther

pantimedias *nfpl Méx Br* tights, *US* pantyhose

pantomima *nf Teatro* pantomime, mime; *Pey (farsa)* farce

pantorrilla *nf Anat* calf

pantry *nm Ven (comedor diario)* = family dining area off kitchen

pants *nmpl Méx* track o jogging suit

pantufla *nf* slipper

panty *nm* (pair of) *Br* tights, *US* pantyhose

> ⚠ Observa que la palabra inglesa **panties** es un falso amigo y no es la traducción de la palabra española **panty**. En inglés, **panties** significa "bragas".

panza *nf Fam* belly, paunch

panzada *nf Fam* bellyful

panzudo,-a, panzón,-ona *adj* pot-bellied, paunchy

pañal *nm Br* nappy, *US* diaper; *Fig* **estar en pañales** to be in one's infancy

paño *nm* (a) cloth material; *(de lana)* woollen cloth; *(para polvo)* duster, rag; *(de cocina)* dishcloth; *Fig* **paños calientes** half-measures (b) **paños** *(ropa)* clothes; **en paños menores** in one's underclothes

pañoleta *nf* (a) shawl (b) *Taurom* bullfighter's tie

pañuelo *nm* handkerchief; *(pañoleta)* shawl

Papa *nm* **el P.** the Pope

papa *nf* potato; *Fam* **no saber ni p. (de algo)** not to have the faintest idea (about sth); *Am* **papas fritas** *Br* chips, *US* (French) fries; *(de bolsa) Br* crisps, *US* (potato) chips

papá *nm Fam* dad, daddy

papada *nf* double chin

papagayo *nm* (a) *(animal)* parrot (b) *Carib, Méx (cometa)* kite

papalote *nm CAm, Méx* kite

papamoscas *nm inv* flycatcher

papanatas *nmf inv* sucker, twit

paparrucha(da) *nf* (piece of) nonsense

papaya *nf* papaya o pawpaw fruit

papear *vi Fam* to eat

papel *nm* (a) paper; *(hoja)* piece o sheet of paper; **papeles** *(documentos)* documents, identification papers; **p. higiénico** toilet paper; **p. carbón** carbon paper; **p. de carta** writing paper, stationery; *Chile* **p. confort** toilet paper; **p. de aluminio/de estraza** alu-

minium foil/brown paper; **p. de fumar** cigarette paper; **p. de lija** sandpaper; *Fin* **p. moneda** paper money, banknotes; **p. pintad**o wallpaper; *Cuba* **p. sanitario** toilet paper; **p.** **secante** blotting paper; *Guat, Ven* **p. toilette** o **tualé** toilet paper (b) *Cin & Teatro* role, part

papeleo *nm Fam* paperwork

papelera *nf (en despacho)* wastepaper basket; *(en calle)* litter bin

papelería *nf (tienda)* stationer's (shop)

papeleta *nf* (a) *(de rifa)* ticket; *(de votación)* ballot paper; *(de resultados)* report (b) *Fam (dificultad)* tricky problem, difficult job

papeo *nm Fam* grub

paperas *nfpl Med* mumps *sing*

papilla *nf* pap, mush; *(de niños)* baby food

papista *nmf* papist

Papúa Nueva Guinea *n* Papua New Guinea

paquete *nm* (a) *(de cigarrillos etc)* packet *(postal)* parcel, package (b) *(conjunto)* set package; **p. de acciones** share package (c) *Informát* software package (d) *Fam (castigo)* punishment (e) *muy Fam (genitales)* packet, bulge

Paquistán *n* Pakistan

paquistaní *adj & nmf* Pakistani

par **1** *adj Mat* even

2 *nm* (a) *(pareja)* pair; *(dos)* couple (b) *Mat* even number; **pares y nones** odds and evens (c) *(noble)* peer (d) *(locuciones)* **a la p.** *(a la vez)* at the same time; **de p. en p.** wide open; *Fig* **sin p.** matchless

para *prep* (a) for; **bueno p. la salud** good for your health; **¿p. qué?** what for?; **p. ser inglés** **habla muy bien español** for an Englishman he speaks very good Spanish (b) *(finalidad)* to, in order to; **p. terminar antes** to o in order to finish earlier; **p. que lo disfrutes** for you to enjoy (c) *(tiempo)* by; **p. entonces** by then (d) *(a punto de)* **está p. salir** it's about to leave (e) *(locuciones)* **decir p. sí** to say to oneself; **ir p. viejo** to be getting old; **no es p. tanto** it's not as bad as all that; **p. mí** in my opinion

parábola *nf* (a) *Geom* parabola (b) *Rel* parable

parabólico,-a *adj* parabolic; *TV* **antena parabólica** satellite dish

parabrisas *nm inv Aut Br* windscreen, *US* windshield

paraca *nm Fam* para(chutist)

paracaídas *nm inv* parachute

paracaidista *nmf Dep* parachutist; *Mil* para-trooper

parachoques *nm inv Br* bumper, *US* fender

parada *nf* (a) stop; **p. de autobús** bus stop; **p.** **de taxis** taxi stand o rank (b) *Ftb* save, stop

paradero *nm* (a) *(lugar)* whereabouts *sing* (b) *Méx, Perú (apeadero)* stop

parado,-a **1** *adj* (a) stopped, stationary *(quieto)* still; *(fábrica)* at a standstill; *Fig* **sali** **bien/mal p.** to come off well/badly (b) *(desempleado)* unemployed, out of work (c) *Fig*

(lento) slow (**d**) *Am (de pie)* standing
   2 *nm,f* unemployed person
paradoja *nf* paradox
paradójico,-a *adj* paradoxical
parador *nm* roadside inn; **p. nacional** *o* **de turismo** state-run hotel
parafernalia *nf* paraphernalia *pl*
parafrasear *vt* to paraphrase
paráfrasis *nf inv* paraphrase
paragolpes *nm inv RP (de automóvil) Br* bumper, *US* fender
paraguas *nm inv* umbrella
Paraguay *n* Paraguay
paragüero *nm* umbrella stand
paraíso *nm* (**a**) paradise; **p. terrenal** heaven on earth; *Fin* **p. fiscal** tax haven (**b**) *Teatro* gods, gallery
paraje *nm* spot, place
paralelo,-a *adj & nm* parallel
parálisis *nf inv* paralysis; **p. infantil** poliomyelitis
paralítico,-a *adj & nm,f* paralytic
paralización *nf* (**a**) *Med* paralysis (**b**) *(detención)* halting, stopping
paralizar [40] **1** *vt* to paralyse; *(circulación)* to stop
   2 paralizarse *vpr Fig* to come to a standstill
parámetro *nm* parameter
paramilitar *adj* paramilitary
páramo *nm* bleak plain *o* plateau, moor
parangón *nm Fml* comparison; **sin p.** incomparable
paranoia *nf* paranoia
paranoico,-a *adj & nm,f* paranoiac, paranoid
parapente *nm (desde montaña)* paragliding, parapenting
parapeto *nm* (**a**) parapet (**b**) *(de defensa)* barricade
parapléjico,-a *adj & nm,f* paraplegic
parar 1 *vt* (**a**) to stop (**b**) *Dep* to save (**c**) *Am (levantar)* to raise
   2 *vi* (**a**) to stop; **p. de hacer algo** to stop doing sth; **sin p.** non-stop, without stopping; *Fam* **no p.** to be always on the go (**b**) *(alojarse)* to stay (**c**) *(acabar)* **fue a p. a la cárcel** he ended up in jail
   3 pararse *vpr* (**a**) to stop; **p. a pensar** to stop to think (**b**) *Am (ponerse en pie)* to stand up
pararrayos *nm inv* lightning rod *o* conductor
parásito,-a 1 *adj* parasitic
   2 *nm* parasite
parasol *nm* sunshade, parasol
parcela *nf* plot
parche *nm* (**a**) patch (**b**) *(emplasto)* plaster (**c**) *Pey (chapuza)* botched-up job *o* slapdash job
parchís *nm Br* ludo, *US* Parcheesi®
parcial 1 *adj* (**a**) *(partidario)* biased (**b**) *(no completo)* partial; **a tiempo p.** part-time
   2 *nm (examen)* **p.** class examination
parcialmente *adv* partially, partly
parco,-a *adj (moderado)* sparing; *(frugal)* scant

pardillo,-a 1 *nm,f Pey* yokel, bumpkin
   2 *nm Orn* linnet
pardo,-a *adj (marrón)* brown; *(gris)* dark grey
parecer¹ *nm* (**a**) *(opinión)* opinion (**b**) *(aspecto)* appearance
parecer² [33] **1** *vi* to seem, to look (like); **parece difícil** it seems *o* looks difficult; **parecía (de) cera** it looked like wax; *(uso impers)* **parece que no arranca** it looks as if it won't start; **como te parezca** whatever you like; **¿te parece?** is that okay with you?; **parece que sí/ no** I think/don't think so; **¿qué te parece?** what do you think of it?
   2 parecerse (**a**) to be alike; **no se parecen** they're not alike (**b**) **p. a** to look like, to resemble; **se parecen a su madre** they look like their mother
parecido,-a 1 *adj* (**a**) alike, similar (**b**) **bien p.** good-looking
   2 *nm* likeness, resemblance; **tener p. con algn** to bear a resemblance to sb
pared *nf* wall
paredón *nm* (**a**) thick wall (**b**) *Fam* **le llevaron al p.** he was shot by firing squad
pareja *nf* (**a**) pair; **por parejas** in pairs (**b**) *(hombre y mujer)* couple; *(hijo e hija)* boy and girl; **hacen buena p.** they make a nice couple, they're well matched; **p. de hecho** = common-law heterosexual or homosexual relationship (**c**) *(en naipes)* pair; **doble p.** two pairs (**d**) *(de baile, juego)* partner
parejo,-a *adj* (**a**) *(parecido)* similar, alike (**b**) **ir parejos** to be neck and neck
parentela *nf Fam* relations, relatives
parentesco *nm* relationship, kinship
paréntesis *nm inv* (**a**) parenthesis, bracket; **entre p.** in parentheses *o* brackets (**b**) *(descanso)* break, interruption; *(digresión)* digression
parezco *indic pres de* **parecer**
paria *nmf* pariah
parida *nf Fam* silly thing
pariente *nmf* relative, relation

🖉 Observa que la palabra inglesa **parent** es un falso amigo y no es la traducción de la palabra española **pariente**. En inglés, **parent** significa tanto "padre" como "madre".

parir *vt & vi* to give birth (to)
París *n* Paris
parking *nm Br* car park, *US* parking lot
parlamentario,-a 1 *adj* parliamentary
   2 *nm,f Br* Member of Parliament, MP, *US* Congressman, *f* Congresswoman
parlamento *nm* parliament
parlanchín,-ina *adj Fam* talkative, chatty
parné *nm Fam* dough, cash
paro *nm* (**a**) *(huelga)* strike, stoppage (**b**) *(desempleo)* unemployment; **estar en p.** to be unemployed; **cobrar el p.** *Br* to be on the dole

parodia *nf* parody

parodiar [43] *vt* to parody

parpadear *vi (ojos)* to blink; *Fig (luz)* to flicker

parpadeo *nm (de ojos)* blinking; *Fig (de luz)* flickering

párpado *nm* eyelid

parque *nm* (**a**) park; **p. de atracciones** funfair; **p. zoológico** zoo; **p. nacional/natural** national park/nature reserve; **p. eólico** wind farm (**b**) *(de niños)* playpen (**c**) **p. móvil** total number of cars

parqué *nm* parquet

parqueadero *nm Carib, Col, Pan Br* car park, *US* parking lot

parquear *vt Carib, Col, Pan* to park

parquet *nm* = **parqué**

parquímetro *nm Aut* parking meter

parra *nf* grapevine

párrafo *nm* paragraph

parranda *nf Fam* spree

parricidio *nm* parricide

parrilla *nf* (**a**) *Culin* grill; **pescado a la p.** grilled fish (**b**) *Téc* grate (**c**) *Aut & Dep* starting grid

párroco *nm* parish priest

parronal *nm Chile* vineyard

parroquia *nf* parish; *(iglesia)* parish church

parroquiano,-a *nm,f (regular)* customer

parsimonia *nf* phlegm, calmness

parte 1 *nf* (**a**) *(sección)* part (**b**) *(en una repartición)* share (**c**) *(lugar)* place, spot; **en o por todas partes** everywhere; **se fue por otra p.** he went another way (**d**) *Jur* party (**e**) *(bando)* side; **estoy de tu p.** I'm on your side (**f**) *Euf* **partes** *(genitales)* private parts (**g**) *(locuciones)* **por mi p.** as far as I am concerned; **de p. de ...** on behalf of ...; *Tel* **¿de p. de quién?** who's calling?; **en gran p.** to a large extent; **en p.** partly; **la mayor p.** the majority; **por otra p.** on the other hand; **tomar p. en** to take part in

  2 *nm (informe)* report

partición *nf (reparto)* division, sharing out; *(de herencia)* partition; *(de territorio)* partition

participación *nf* (**a**) participation (**b**) *Fin (acción)* share; **p. en los beneficios** profit-sharing (**c**) *(en lotería)* part of a lottery ticket (**d**) *(notificación)* notice, notification

participante 1 *adj* participating

  2 *nmf* participant

participar 1 *vi* (**a**) to take part, to participate (**en** in) (**b**) *Fin* to have a share (**en** in) (**c**) *Fig* **p. de** to share

  2 *vt (notificar)* to notify

partícipe *nmf* (**a**) participant; **hacer p. de algo** *(notificar)* to inform about sth (**b**) *Com & Fin* partner

participio *nm Ling* participle

partícula *nf* particle

particular 1 *adj* (**a**) *(concreto)* particular (**b**) *(privado)* private, personal (**c**) *(raro)* peculiar

  2 *nmf (individuo)* private individual

  3 *nm (asunto)* subject, matter

particularidad *nf* special feature

partida *nf* (**a**) *(salida)* departure (**b**) *Com (remesa)* batch, consignment (**c**) *(juego)* game (**d**) *Fin (entrada)* item (**e**) *Jur (certificado)* certificate; **p. de nacimiento** birth certificate

partidario,-a 1 *adj* **ser/no ser p. de algo** to be for/against sth

  2 *nm,f* supporter, follower; **es p. del aborto** he is in favour of abortion

partidista *adj* biased, partisan

partido *nm* (**a**) *Pol* party (**b**) *Dep* match, game; **p. amistoso** friendly game; **p. de vuelta** return match (**c**) *(provecho)* advantage; **sacar p. de** to profit from (**d**) *Jur (distrito)* district (**e**) **tomar p. por** to side with (**f**) **ser un buen p.** to be a good catch

partir 1 *vt* to break; *(dividir)* to split, to divide; *(cortar)* to cut; **p. a algn por la mitad** to mess things up for sb

  2 *vi* (**a**) *(marcharse)* to leave, to set out o off (**b**) **a p. de** from

  3 partirse *vpr* to split (up), to break (up); *Fam* **p. de risa** to split one's sides laughing

partisano,-a *nm,f* partisan

partitura *nf Mús* score

parto *nm* childbirth, labour; **estar de p.** to be in labour

parvulario *nm* nursery school, kindergarten

párvulo,-a *nm,f* infant

pasa *nf* raisin; **p. de Corinto** currant

pasable *adj* passable, tolerable

pasaboca *nm Col* snack, appetizer

pasacalle *nm Col, Urug* banner *(hung across street)*

pasada *nf* (**a**) **de p.** in passing (**b**) *(jugarreta)* dirty trick (**c**) *Fam* **¡eso es una p.!** it's too much!

pasadizo *nm* corridor, passage

pasado,-a 1 *adj* (**a**) *(último)* last; **el año/lunes p.** last year/Monday (**b**) *(anticuado)* dated, old-fashioned; **p. (de moda)** out of date o fashion (**c**) *(alimento)* bad (**d**) *Culin* cooked; **lo quiero muy p.** I want it well done (**e**) **p. mañana** the day after tomorrow

  2 *nm* past

pasador *nm* (**a**) *(prenda)* pin, clasp; *(para el pelo)* (hair) slide (**b**) *(pestillo)* bolt, fastener

pasaje *nm* (**a**) passage (**b**) *(calle)* alley (**c**) *(pasajeros)* passengers (**d**) *(billete)* ticket

pasajero,-a 1 *adj* passing, temporary; **aventura pasajera** fling

  2 *nm,f* passenger

pasamanos *nm inv (barra)* handrail; *(de escalera)* banister, bannister

pasamontañas *nm inv* balaclava

pasapalo *nm Ven* snack, appetizer

pasaporte *nm* passport

pasapurés *nm inv Culin* potato masher
pasar 1 *vt* (a) to pass; *(objeto)* to pass, to give; *(mensaje)* to give; *(página)* to turn; *(trasladar)* to move; **p. algo a limpio** to make a clean copy of sth
(b) *(tiempo)* to spend, to pass; **p. el rato** to kill time
(c) *(padecer)* to suffer, to endure; **p. hambre** to go hungry
(d) *(río, calle)* to cross; *(barrera)* to pass through *o* over; *(límite)* to go beyond
(e) *(perdonar)* to forgive, to tolerate; **p. algo (por alto)** to overlook sth
(f) *(introducir)* to insert, to put through
(g) *(examen)* to pass
(h) *Cin* to run, to show
2 *vi* (a) to happen; **¿ha pasado el autobús?** has the bus gone by?; **ha pasado un hombre** a man has gone past; **p. de largo** to go by (without stopping); **el tren pasa por Burgos** the train goes via Burgos; **pasa por casa mañana** come round to my house tomorrow
(b) **p. a** *(continuar)* to go on to; **p. a ser** to become
(c) *(entrar)* to come in
(d) *(tiempo)* to pass, to go by
(e) **p. sin** to do without; *Fam* **paso de tí** I couldn't care less about you; *Fam* **yo paso** count me out
3 *v impers (suceder)* to happen; **¿qué pasa aquí?** what's going on here?; **¿qué te pasa?** what's the matter?; *Fam* **¿qué pasa?** *(saludo)* how are you?; **pase lo que pase** whatever happens, come what may
4 pasarse *upr* (a) **se me pasó la ocasión** I missed my chance; **se le pasó llamarme** he forgot to phone me
(b) *(gastar tiempo)* to spend *o* pass time; **pasárselo bien/mal** to have a good/bad time
(c) *(comida)* to go off
(d) *Fam (excederse)* to go too far; **no te pases** don't overdo it
(e) **pásate por mi casa** call round at my place
pasarela *nf (puente)* footbridge; *(de barco)* gangway; *(de moda)* catwalk
pasatiempo *nm* pastime, hobby
pascua *nf* (a) Easter (b) **pascuas** *(Navidad)* Christmas; **¡felices Pascuas!** Merry Christmas!
pascualina *nf RP, Ven* = pie made with spinach and hard-boiled egg
pase *nm* (a) pass, permit (b) *Cin* showing
pasear 1 *vi* to go for a walk, to take a walk
2 *vt* (a) *(persona)* to take for a walk; *(perro)* to walk (b) *Fig (exhibir)* to show off
3 pasearse *upr* to go for a walk
paseíllo *nm Taurom* opening parade
paseo *nm* (a) walk; *(en bicicleta, caballo)* ride; *(en coche)* drive; **dar un p.** to go for a walk/a ride (b) *(avenida)* avenue
pasillo *nm* corridor; *Av* **p. aéreo** air corridor

pasión *nf* passion
pasional *adj* passionate; **crimen p.** crime of passion
pasividad *nf* passivity, passiveness
pasivo,-a 1 *adj* passive; *(inactivo)* inactive
2 *nm Com* liabilities
pasmado,-a *adj (asombrado)* astounded, amazed; *(atontado)* flabbergasted; **dejar p.** to astonish; **quedarse p.** to be amazed
pasmo *nm* astonishment, amazement
paso¹,-a *adj* **ciruela pasa** prune; **uva pasa** raisin
paso² *nm* (a) step; *(modo de andar)* gait, walk; *(ruido al andar)* footstep; *Mil* **llevar el p.** to keep in step; *Fig* **a dos pasos** a short distance away; *Fig* **seguir los pasos de algn** to follow in sb's footsteps
(b) *(camino)* passage, way; **abrirse p.** to force one's way through; *Aut* **ceda el p.** *(en letrero)* give way; **prohibido el p.** *(en letrero)* no entry; **p. a nivel** *Br* level crossing, *US* grade crossing; **p. de cebra** zebra crossing; **p. de peatones** *Br* pedestrian crossing, *US* crosswalk; **p. elevado** *Br* flyover, *US* overpass; **p. subterráneo** *(para peatones)* subway; *(para coches)* underpass
(c) *(acción)* passage, passing; **a su p. por la ciudad** when he was in town; **el p. del tiempo** the passage of time; **estar de p.** to be just passing through
(d) **p. de montaña** mountain pass
pasodoble *nm* paso doble
pasota *nmf Fam* waster
pasta *nf* (a) paste; **p. de dientes** *o* **dentífrica** toothpaste (b) *(de pan, pasteles)* dough; *(italiana)* pasta (c) *(galleta)* *Br* biscuit, *US* cookie (d) *Fam (dinero)* dough, bread
pastar *vt & vi* to graze, to pasture
pastel *nm* (a) cake; *(de carne, fruta)* pie (b) *Arte* pastel (c) *Fam* **descubrir el p.** to spill the beans
pastelería *nf* (a) *(tienda)* confectioner's (shop) (b) *(dulces)* confectionery
pastelero,-a *nm,f* pastry cook, confectioner
pastiche *nm* (a) pastiche (b) *Fam (chapuza)* botch(-up)
pastilla *nf* (a) tablet, pill; **pastillas para la tos** cough drops (b) *(de jabón)* bar (c) *Fam* **a toda p.** at full speed
pastizal *nm* grazing land, pasture
pasto *nm* (a) *(hierba)* grass (b) *(alimento)* fodder; **ser p. de** to fall prey to (c) *Am (césped)* lawn, grass
pastor,-a 1 *nm,f* shepherd; *(mujer)* shepherdess; **perro p.** sheepdog
2 *nm* (a) *Rel* pastor, minister (b) *(perro)* **p. alemán** Alsatian
pastoreo *nm* shepherding
pastoso,-a *adj* pasty; *(lengua)* furry
pata 1 *nf* leg; *Fig* **patas arriba** upside down; **estirar la p.** to kick the bucket; **mala p.** bad luck; **meter la p.** to put one's foot in it; **p. de**

gallo crow's foot

2 *nm Perú Fam (amigo)* pal, *Br* mate, *US* buddy

patada *nf (puntapié)* kick, stamp

patalear *vi* to stamp one's feet (with rage)

pataleo *nm* kicking; *(de rabia)* stamping

patán *nm* bumpkin, yokel

patata *nf* potato; **patatas fritas** *Br* chips, *US* (French) fries; *(de bolsa) Br* crisps, *US* (potato) chips

patatús *nm inv Fam* dizzy spell, queer turn

paté *nm* pâté

patear 1 *vt (pelota)* to kick; *(pisotear)* to stamp on

2 *vi (patalear)* to stamp (one's foot with rage)

patentar *vt* to patent

patente 1 *nf* (a) *(autorización)* licence; *(de invención)* patent (b) *CSur (matrícula) Br* number plate, *US* license plate

2 *adj (evidente)* patent, obvious

pateo *nm* stamping; *(abucheo)* boo(ing), jeer(ing)

paternal *adj* paternal, fatherly

paternalista *adj* paternalistic

paternidad *nf* paternity, fatherhood

paterno,-a *adj* paternal

patético,-a *adj* moving

patíbulo *nm* scaffold, gallows *sing*

patidifuso,-a *adj Fam* dumbfounded, flabbergasted

patilla *nf* (a) *(de gafas)* leg (b) **patillas** *(pelo)* sideburns

patín *nm* (a) skate; *(patinete)* scooter; **p. de ruedas/de hielo** roller-/ice-skate; **p. en línea** rollerblade (b) *Náut* pedal boat

patinaje *nm* skating; **p. artístico** figure skating; **p. sobre hielo/ruedas** ice-/roller-skating

patinar *vi* (a) to skate; *(sobre ruedas)* to roller-skate; *(sobre hielo)* to ice-skate (b) *(deslizarse)* to slide; *(resbalar)* to slip; *(vehículo)* to skid (c) *Fam (equivocarse)* to put one's foot in it, to slip up

patinazo *nm* (a) skid (b) *Fam (equivocación)* blunder, boob

patinete *nm* scooter

patio *nm* (a) *(de una casa)* yard, patio; *(de recreo)* playground (b) *Teatro & Cin* **p. de butacas** stalls

pato *nm* duck; *Fam* **pagar el p.** to carry the can

patochada *nf* blunder, boob

patógeno,-a *adj* pathogenic

patología *nf* pathology

patológico,-a *adj* pathological

patoso,-a *adj* clumsy, awkward

patota *nf Perú, RP (de gamberros)* street gang

patraña *nf* nonsense

patria *nf* fatherland, native country; **madre p.** motherland; **p. chica** one's home town/region

patriarca *nm* patriarch

patrimonio *nm (bienes)* wealth; *(herencia)* inheritance

patriota *nmf* patriot

patriótico,-a *adj* patriotic

patriotismo *nm* patriotism

patrocinador,-a 1 *adj* sponsoring

2 *nm,f* sponsor

patrocinar *vt* to sponsor

patrocinio *nm* sponsorship, patronage

patrón,-ona 1 *nm,f* (a) *(jefe)* boss (b) *(de pensión) (hombre)* landlord; *(mujer)* landlady (c) *Rel* patron saint

2 *nm* (a) *(patrón)* pattern (b) *(medida)* standard

patronal 1 *adj* employers'; **cierre p.** lockout; **clase p.** managerial class

2 *nf (dirección)* management

patronato, patronazgo *nm* (a) *(institución benéfica)* foundation (b) *(protección)* patronage

patrono,-a *nm,f* (a) *(jefe)* boss; *(empresario)* employer (b) *Rel* patron saint

patrulla *nf* (a) patrol; **estar de p.** to be on patrol; **coche p.** patrol car (b) *(grupo)* group, band; **p. de rescate** rescue party; **p. ciudadana** vigilante group

patrullar 1 *vt* to patrol

2 *vi* to be on patrol

patrullero *nm CSur (auto)* police (patrol) car

paulatino,-a *adj* gradual

paupérrimo,-a *adj* extremely poor, poverty-stricken

pausa *nf* pause, break; *Mús* rest

pausado,-a *adj* unhurried, calm

pauta *nf* guidelines

pava *nf* (a) *Fam* **pelar la p.** to chat (b) *Arg (tetera)* kettle

pavada *nf RP (tontería)* stupid thing

pavesa *nf* ash

pavimentar *vt* to pave

pavimento *nm (de carretera)* road (surface), *US* pavement; *(de acera)* paving; *(de habitación)* flooring

pavo *nm* (a) turkey; *Fam* **no ser moco de p.** to be nothing to scoff at (b) *Fam (tonto)* twit; *Fam* **estar en la edad del p.** to be growing up

pavonearse *vpr Fam* to show off, to strut

pavoneo *nm Fam* showing off, strutting

pavor *nm* terror, dread

pay *nm Chile, Méx, Ven* pie

payaso *nm* clown; **hacer el p.** to act the clown

payés,-esa *nm,f* = Catalan or Balearic peasant

payo,-a *nm,f* non-gipsy person

paz *nf* peace; *(sosiego)* peacefulness; *Fam* **¡déjame en p.!** leave me alone!, **hacer las paces** to make (it) up

pazguato,-a *adj* (a) *(estúpido)* silly, stupid (b) *(mojigato)* prudish

PC *nm (abr personal computer)* PC

PCE *nm Pol (abr Partido Comunista de España)* = Spanish Communist party

pe *nf Fam* **de pe a pa** from A to Z

peaje *nm* toll; **autopista de p.** *Br* toll motorway, *US* turnpike

peatón *nm* pedestrian

peca *nf* freckle

pecado *nm Rel* sin; **p. capital** *o* **mortal** deadly sin

pecador,-a *nm,f* sinner

pecaminoso,-a *adj* sinful

pecar [44] *vi* to sin; *Fig* **p. por defecto** to fall short of the mark

pecera *nf* fish bowl, fish tank

pecho *nm* (**a**) *(de hombre)* chest; *(de mujer)* breast, bust; *(de animal)* breast; **dar el p. (a un bebé)** to breast-feed (a baby); *Fig* **tomar(se) (algo) a p.** to take (sth) to heart (**b**) *Am (en natación)* breaststroke; **nadar p.** to do the breaststroke

pechuga *nf* (**a**) *(de ave)* breast (**b**) *Fam (de mujer)* boob

pectoral *adj* pectoral, chest

peculiar *adj (raro)* peculiar; *(característico)* characteristic

peculiaridad *nf* peculiarity

pedagogía *nf* pedagogy

pedagógico,-a *adj* pedagogical

pedal *nm* pedal

pedalear *vi* to pedal

pedante 1 *adj* pedantic

2 *nmf* pedant

pedantería *nf* pedantry

pedazo *nm* piece, bit; **a pedazos** in pieces; **caerse a pedazos** to fall apart *o* to pieces; **hacer pedazos** to break *o* tear to pieces, to smash (up); *Fam* **¡qué p. de coche!** what a terrific car!

pederasta *nm* pederast

pedernal *nm* flint

pedestal *nm* pedestal

pediatra *nmf* paediatrician

pediatría *nf* paediatrics *sing*

pedicuro,-a *nm,f* chiropodist, *US* podiatrist

pedido *nm* (**a**) *Com* order; **hacer un p. a** to place an order with (**b**) *(petición)* request

pedigrí *nm* pedigree

pedir [6] *vt* (**a**) to ask (for); **p. algo a algn** to ask sb for sth; **te pido que te quedes** I'm asking you to stay; **p. prestado** to borrow; *Fig* **p. cuentas** to ask for an explanation (**b**) *Com & (en bar etc)* to order (**c**) *(mendigar)* to beg

pedo *nm Fam* (**a**) fart; **tirarse un p.** to fart (**b**) *(borrachera)* bender

pedrada *nf (golpe)* blow from a stone; *(lanzamiento)* throw of a stone

pedrea *nf (en lotería)* small prizes

pedregoso,-a *adj* stony, rocky

pedrería *nf* precious stones, gems

pedrisco *nm* hailstorm

pega *nf* (**a**) *Fam (objeción)* objection; **poner pegas** to find fault (**b**) **de p.** *(falso)* sham

pegadizo,-a *adj* catchy

pegado,-a *adj* (**a**) *(adherido)* stuck (**b**) *(quemado)* burnt

pegajoso,-a *adj (pegadizo)* sticky; *Fig (persona)* tiresome, hard to get rid of

pegamento *nm* glue

pegar [42] **1** *vt* (**a**) *(adherir)* to stick; *(con pegamento)* to glue; *(coser)* to sew on; *Fam* **no pegó ojo** he didn't sleep a wink; **p. fuego a** to set fire to

(**b**) *(golpear)* to hit

(**c**) **p. un grito** to shout; **p. un salto** to jump

(**d**) *Fam (contagiar)* to give; **me ha pegado sus manías** I've caught his bad habits

(**e**) *(arrimar)* **p. algo a** *o* **contra algo** to put *o* place sth against sth

2 *vi* (**a**) *(adherirse)* to stick

(**b**) *(armonizar)* to match, to go; **el azul no pega con el verde** blue and green don't go together *o* don't match; *Fig* **ella no pegaría aquí** she wouldn't fit in here

(**c**) *(sol)* to beat down

3 pegarse *vpr* (**a**) *(adherirse)* to stick; *(pelearse)* to fight

(**b**) *Fam (darse)* to have, to get; **p. un tiro** to shoot oneself

(**c**) *(comida)* to get burnt; **se me ha pegado el sol** I've got a touch of the sun

(**d**) *Fam* **pegársela a algn** to trick *o* deceive sb

(**e**) *(arrimarse)* to get close

(**f**) *Fam Fig* to stick

(**g**) *Med (enfermedad)* to be catching *o* contagious; *Fig (melodía)* to be catchy

pegatina *nf* sticker

peinado *nm* hairstyle, *Fam* hairdo

peinar 1 *vt* (**a**) *(pelo)* to comb (**b**) *(registrar)* to comb

2 peinarse *vpr* to comb one's hair

peine *nm* comb

peineta *nf* = ornamental comb worn in hair

pela *nf Fam* peseta

pelado,-a 1 *adj* (**a**) *(cabeza)* shorn; *(piel, fruta)* peeled; *(terreno)* bare (**b**) *Fam* **saqué un cinco p.** *(en escuela)* I just scraped a pass; **a grito p.** shouting and bawling (**c**) *Fam (arruinado)* broke, penniless (**d**) *(desvergonzado)* impudent, insolent

2 *nm Fam* haircut

3 *nm,f* (**a**) *Andes Fam (niño, adolescente)* kid (**b**) *CAm, Méx Fam (pobre)* poor person

peladura *nf* peeling

pelagatos *nmf inv Fam* poor devil, nobody

pelaje *nm* (**a**) fur, hair (**b**) *Pey (apariencia)* looks, appearance

pelambrera *nf Fam* mop (of hair), long/thick hair

pelapatatas *nm inv* potato peeler

pelar 1 *vt (cortar el pelo a)* to cut the hair of; *(fruta, patata)* to peel; *Fam* **hace un frío que pela** it's brass monkey weather

2 *vi (despellejar)* to peel

3 pelarse *vpr* (**a**) *(cortarse el pelo)* to get one's hair cut (**b**) *Fam* **corre que se las pela** she runs like the wind

peldaño nm step; (de escalera de mano) rung
pelea nf fight; (riña) row, quarrel; **buscar p.** to look for trouble
peleado,-a adj **estar p. (con algn)** not to be on speaking terms (with sb)
pelear 1 vi to fight; (reñir) to quarrel
2 pelearse vpr (a) to fight; (reñir) to quarrel (b) (enemistarse) to fall out
pelele nm (muñeco) straw puppet; Fig puppet
peleón,-ona adj (a) quarrelsome, aggressive (b) (vino) cheap
peletería nf furrier's; (tienda) fur shop
peletero,-a nm,f furrier
peliagudo,-a adj difficult, tricky
pelícano nm pelican
película nf (a) Cin movie, Br film; **p. de miedo** o **terror** horror film; **p. del Oeste** Western; Fam **de p.** fabulous (b) Fot film
peligrar vi to be in danger, to be threatened; **hacer p.** to endanger, to jeopardize
peligro nm danger; (riesgo) risk; **con p. de ...** at the risk of ...; **correr (el) p. de ...** to run the risk of ...; **poner en p.** to endanger
peligroso,-a adj dangerous, risky
pelirrojo,-a 1 adj red-haired; (anaranjado) ginger-haired
2 nm,f redhead
pellejo nm (a) (piel) skin (b) (odre) wineskin (c) Fam **arriesgar** o **jugarse el p.** to risk one's neck
pelliza nf fur jacket
pellizcar [44] vt to pinch, to nip
pellizco nm pinch, nip
pelma nmf, **pelmazo,-a** nm,f (persona) bore, drag
pelo nm (a) hair; **cortarse el p.** (uno mismo) to cut one's hair; (en la peluquería) to have one's hair cut; Fig **no tiene ni un p. de tonto** he's no fool; Fig **no tener pelos en la lengua** to be very outspoken; Fig **tomar el p. a algn** to pull sb's leg, to take the mickey out of sb; Fam **con pelos y señales** in full detail; Fam **por los pelos** by the skin of one's teeth; Fam **me puso el p. de punta** it gave me the creeps (b) (de animal) fur, coat, hair (c) Tex (de una tela) nap, pile (d) (cerda) bristle
pelón,-ona adj (sin pelo) bald
pelota 1 nf (a) ball; Fam **devolver la p.** to give tit for tat (b) Dep pelota (c) Fam (cabeza) nut (d) **hacer la p. a algn** to toady to sb, to butter sb up (e) muy Fam **pelotas** (testículos) balls; **en pelotas** Br starkers, US butt-naked
2 nmf Fam (pelotillero) crawler
pelotari nm pelota player
pelotear vi Dep to kick a ball around; Ten to knock up
peloteo nm Ten knock-up
pelotilla nf Fam **hacer la p. (a algn)** to fawn (on sb)
pelotillero,-a nm,f Fam crawler
pelotón nm (a) Mil squad (b) Fam (grupo) small crowd, bunch; (en ciclismo) pack (c) (amasijo) bundle

pelotudo,-a adj RP Fam (a) (estúpido) stupid (b) (grande) great big, massive
peluca nf wig
peluche nm **osito de p.** teddy bear
peludo,-a adj hairy, furry
peluquería nf hairdresser's (shop)
peluquero,-a nm,f hairdresser
peluquín nm toupee
pelusa, pelusilla nf (a) fluff; (de planta) down (b) Fam jealousy
pelvis nf inv pelvis
pena nf (a) (tristeza) grief, sorrow; Fig **me da p. de ella** I feel sorry for her; **¡qué p.!** what a pity! (b) (dificultad) hardships, trouble; **no merece** o **vale la p. (ir)** it's not worth while (going); **a duras penas** with great difficulty (c) (castigo) punishment, penalty; **p. de muerte** o **capital** death penalty (d) CAm, Carib, Col, Méx (vergüenza) shame, embarrassment; **me da p.** I'm ashamed of it
penacho nm (a) (de ave) crest, tuft (b) Mil (de plumas) plume
penal 1 adj penal; Jur **código p.** penal code
2 nm prison, jail
penalidad nf (usu pl) hardships, troubles
penalización nf penalization; Dep penalty
penalizar [40] vt to penalize
penalti nm Dep (pl **penaltis**) penalty; Fam **casarse de p.** to have a shotgun wedding
penar 1 vt to punish
2 vi to be in torment, to suffer
pendejo,-a nm,f muy Fam (a) Am (tonto) jerk, idiot (b) RP Pey (adolescente) kid
pendenciero,-a adj quarrelsome, argumentative
pendiente 1 adj (a) (por resolver) pending; Educ **asignatura p.** failed subject; Com **p. de pago** unpaid (b) **estar p. de** (esperar) to be waiting for; (vigilar) to be on the lookout for (c) (colgante) hanging (**de** from)
2 nm (joya) earring
3 nf slope; (de tejado) pitch
pendón nm (a) (bandera) banner (b) Pey (mujer) slut, whore; (hombre) playboy
péndulo nm pendulum
pene nm penis
penetración nf penetration; (perspicacia) insight, perception
penetrante adj penetrating; (frío, voz, mirada) piercing; Fig (inteligencia) sharp, acute
penetrar 1 vt to penetrate; **p. un misterio** to get to the bottom of a mystery
2 vi (entrar) to go o get (**en** in)
penicilina nf penicillin
península nf peninsula
penique nm penny, pl pence
penitencia nf penance
penitenciaría nf prison
penitenciario,-a adj penitentiary, prison
penoso,-a adj (a) (lamentable) sorry, distressing (b) (laborioso) laborious, difficult

(**c**) *CAm, Carib, Col, Méx (vergonzoso)* shy

pensado,-a *adj* (**a**) thought out; **bien p., ...** on reflection, ...; **en el momento menos p.** when least expected; **mal p.** twisted; **tener algo p.** to have sth planned, to have sth in mind; **tengo p. ir** I intend to go (**b**) *(concebido)* designed

pensamiento *nm* (**a**) thought (**b**) *(máxima)* saying, motto (**c**) *Bot* pansy

pensar [1] **1** *vi* to think (**en** of o about; **sobre** about o over); *Fig* **sin p.** *(con precipitación)* without thinking; *(involuntariamente)* involuntarily

2 *vt* (**a**) to think (**de** of); *(considerar)* to think over o about; **piénsalo bien** think it over; *Fam* **¡ni pensarlo!** not on your life! (**b**) *(proponerse)* to intend; **pienso quedarme** I plan to stay (**c**) *(concebir)* to make; **p. un plan** to make a plan; **p. una solución** to find a solution

pensativo,-a *adj* pensive, thoughtful

pensión *nf* (**a**) *(residencia)* boarding house; *(hotel)* guesthouse; **media p.** half board; **p. completa** full board (**b**) *(paga)* pension, allowance; **p. vitalicia** life annuity

pensionista *nmf* pensioner

pentágono *nm* pentagon

pentagrama *nm* staff, stave

penthouse [pent'χaus] *nm CSur, Ven* penthouse

penúltimo,-a *adj & nm,f* next to the last, penultimate

penumbra *nf* penumbra, half-light

penuria *nf* scarcity, shortage

peña *nf* (**a**) rock, crag (**b**) *(de amigos)* club (**c**) *Fam (gente)* people

peñasco *nm* rock, crag

peñón *nm* rock; **el P. de Gibraltar** the Rock of Gibraltar

peón *nm* (**a**) unskilled labourer; **p. agrícola** farmhand (**b**) *(en ajedrez)* pawn

peonada *nf* day's work

peonza *nf (spinning)* top

peor 1 *adj* (**a**) *(comparativo)* worse (**b**) *(superlativo)* worst; **en el p. de los casos** if the worst comes to the worst; **lo p. es que** the worst of it is that

2 *adv* (**a**) *(comparativo)* worse; **¡p. para mí/ti/etc.!** too bad! (**b**) *(superlativo)* worst

pepa *nf Col, Ven (carozo)* stone, *US* pit *(of fruit)*

pepenador,-a *nm,f CAm, Méx* scavenger *(on rubbish tip)*

pepián *nm CAm, Méx* = sauce thickened with ground nuts or seeds

pepinillo *nm* gherkin

pepino *nm* cucumber; *Fam* **me importa un p.** I don't give a hoot

pepita *nf (de fruta)* pip, seed; *(de metal)* nugget

pepitoria *nf* fricassee; **pollo en p.** fricassee of chicken

peque *nm Fam (niño)* kid

pequeño,-a 1 *adj* small, little; *(bajo)* short

2 *nm,f* child; **de p.** as a child

Pequín *n* Peking

pera *nf* (**a**) *Bot* pear; **p. de agua** juicy pear (**b**) *CSur Fam (mentón)* chin

peral *nm* pear tree

percance *nm* mishap, setback

percatarse *vpr* **p. de** to realize

percepción *nf* perception

perceptible *adj* (**a**) perceptible (**b**) *Fin* receivable, payable

percha *nf (colgador)* (coat) hanger; *(de gallina)* perch

perchero *nm* clothes rack

percibir *vt* (**a**) *(notar)* to perceive, to notice (**b**) *(cobrar)* to receive

percusión *nf* percussion

perdedor,-a 1 *adj* losing

2 *nm,f* loser

perder [3] **1** *vt* (**a**) to lose (**b**) *(tren, autobús)* to miss; *(tiempo)* to waste; *(oportunidad)* to miss (**c**) *(pervertir)* to be the ruin o downfall of

2 *vi* to lose; **echar (algo) a p.** to spoil (sth); **echarse a p.** to be spoilt; **salir perdiendo** to come off worst

3 perderse *vpr* (**a**) *(extraviarse) (persona)* to get lost; **se me ha perdido la llave** I've lost my key; **no te lo pierdas** don't miss it (**b**) *(pervertirse)* to go to rack and ruin

perdición *nf* undoing, downfall

pérdida *nf* (**a**) loss; **no tiene p.** you can't miss it (**b**) *(de tiempo, esfuerzos)* waste (**c**) *Mil* **pérdidas** losses

perdido,-a *adj* (**a**) *(extraviado)* lost (**b**) *Fam (sucio)* filthy (**c**) *Fam* **loco p.** mad as a hatter (**d**) **estar p. por algn** *(enamorado)* to be crazy about sb (**e**) *(acabado)* finished; **¡estoy p.!** I'm a goner!

perdigón *nm* pellet

perdiguero,-a *adj* partridge-hunting; **perro p.** setter

perdiz *nf* partridge

perdón *nm* pardon, forgiveness; **¡p.!** sorry!; **pedir p.** to apologize

perdonar *vt* (**a**) *(remitir)* to forgive (**b**) **¡perdone!** sorry!; **perdone que le moleste** sorry for bothering you (**c**) *(eximir)* to pardon; **perdonarle la vida a algn** to spare sb's life; **p. una deuda** to write off a debt

perdurable *adj* (**a**) *(eterno)* everlasting (**b**) *(duradero)* durable, long-lasting

perdurar *vi* (**a**) *(durar)* to endure, to last (**b**) *(persistir)* to persist, to continue to exist

perecedero,-a *adj* perishable; **artículos perecederos** perishables

perecer [33] *vi* to perish, to die

peregrinación *nf*, **peregrinaje** *nm* pilgrimage

peregrino,-a 1 *nm,f* pilgrim

2 *adj* **ideas peregrinas** crazy ideas

perejil *nm* parsley

perenne *adj* perennial, everlasting

perentorio,-a *adj* peremptory, urgent

pereza nf laziness, idleness
perezoso,-a adj (vago) lazy, idle
perfección nf perfection; **a la p.** to perfection
perfeccionamiento nm (a) (acción) perfecting (b) (mejora) improvement
perfeccionar vt to perfect; (mejorar) to improve, to make better
perfeccionista adj & nmf perfectionist
perfectamente adv perfectly; **¡p.!** (de acuerdo) agreed!, all right!
perfecto,-a adj perfect
perfidia nf perfidy, treachery
perfil nm (a) profile; (contorno) outline, contour; **de p.** in profile (b) Geom cross-section
perfilar 1 vt (dar forma a) to shape, to outline
2 perfilarse vpr (tomar forma) to take shape
perforación nf, **perforado** nm perforation; Min drilling, boring; Informát (de tarjetas) punching
perforadora nf punch; Min drill; Informát **p. de teclado** keypunch
perforar vt to perforate; Min to drill, to bore; Informát to punch
perfumar 1 vt to perfume
2 perfumarse vpr to put on perfume
perfume nm perfume, scent
pergamino nm parchment
pericia nf expertise, skill
periferia nf periphery; (alrededores) outskirts
periférico,-a 1 adj peripheral
2 nm (a) Informát peripheral (b) CAm, Méx (carretera) Br ring road, US beltway
perífrasis nf inv periphrasis, long-winded explanation
perilla nf (barba) goatee; Fam **de perilla(s)** (oportuno) at the right moment; (útil) very handy
perímetro nm perimeter
periódico,-a 1 nm newspaper
2 adj periodic(al); Quím **tabla periódica** periodic table
periodismo nm journalism
periodista nmf journalist, reporter
periodo, período nm period
peripecia nf sudden change, vicissitude
periplo nm voyage, tour
periquete nm Fam **en un p.** in a jiffy
periquito nm budgerigar, Fam budgie
periscopio nm periscope
peritaje nm (estudios) technical studies
perito,-a nm,f technician, expert; **p. industrial/agrónomo** ≃ industrial/agricultural expert
peritonitis nf peritonitis
perjudicar [44] vt to harm, to injure; (intereses) to prejudice
perjudicial adj prejudicial, harmful
perjuicio nm harm, damage; **en p. de** to the detriment of; **sin p. de** without prejudice to
perjurar vi to commit perjury
perjurio nm perjury

perla nf pearl; Fig (persona) gem, jewel; Fam **me viene de perlas** it's just the ticket
permanecer [33] vi to remain, to stay
permanencia nf (a) (inmutabilidad) permanence (b) (estancia) stay
permanente 1 adj permanent
2 nf (de pelo) permanent wave, perm; **hacerse la p.** to have one's hair permed
permisivo,-a adj permissive
permiso nm (a) (autorización) permission (b) (licencia) licence, permit; **p. de conducir** Br driving licence, US driver's license; **p. de residencia/trabajo** residence/work permit (c) Mil leave; **estar de p.** to be on leave
permitir 1 vt to permit, to allow; **¿me permite?** may I?
2 permitirse vpr (a) to permit o allow oneself; **me permito recordarle que** let me remind you that (b) **no se permite fumar** (en letrero) no smoking
permutar vt to exchange
pernicioso,-a adj pernicious
pernil nm (de pantalón) leg; (jamón) leg of pork
pernocta nf Mil **(pase de) p.** overnight pass
pero 1 conj but; **p., ¿qué pasa aquí?** now, what's going on here?
2 nm objection
perogrullada nf truism, platitude
perol nm large saucepan, pot
perorata nf boring speech
perpendicular adj & nf perpendicular
perpetrar vt to perpetrate, to commit
perpetuar [30] vt to perpetuate
perpetuo,-a adj perpetual, everlasting; Jur **cadena perpetua** life imprisonment
perplejidad nf perplexity, bewilderment
perplejo,-a adj perplexed, bewildered
perra nf (a) bitch (b) Fam (moneda) penny; **estar sin una p.** to be broke
perrera nf kennel, kennels
perrería nf Fam dirty trick
perro,-a 1 nm dog; Fam **un día de perros** a lousy day; Fam **vida de perros** dog's life; Culin **p. caliente** hot dog
2 adj Fam (vago) lazy
persecución nf (a) pursuit (b) Pol (represión) persecution
perseguir [6] vt (a) to pursue, to chase; (correr trás) to run after, to follow (b) (reprimir) to persecute
perseverante adj persevering
perseverar vi (a) to persevere, to persist (b) (durar) to last
persiana nf blinds
pérsico,-a adj Persian; **golfo P.** Persian Gulf
persignarse vpr to cross oneself
persistencia nf persistence
persistente adj persistent
persistir vi to persist
persona nf person; **algunas personas** some people; Fam **p. mayor** grown-up

personaje nm (a) *Cin, Lit & Teatro* character (b) *(celebridad)* celebrity, important person

personal 1 adj personal, private

  2 nm (a) *(plantilla)* staff, personnel (b) *Fam (gente)* people

personalidad nf personality

personarse vpr to present oneself, to appear in person

personero,-a nm,f Am representative

personificar [44] vt to personify

perspectiva nf (a) perspective (b) *(futuro)* prospect

perspicacia nf insight, perspicacity

perspicaz adj sharp, perspicacious

persuadir vt to persuade; **estar persuadido de que** to be convinced that

persuasión nf persuasion

persuasivo,-a adj persuasive, convincing

pertenecer [33] vi to belong (**a** to)

perteneciente adj belonging

pertenencia nf (a) possessions, property (b) *(a un partido etc)* affiliation, membership

pértiga nf pole; *Dep* **salto con p.** pole vault

pertinaz adj (a) persistent (b) *(obstinado)* obstinate, stubborn

pertinente adj (a) pertinent, relevant (b) *(apropiado)* appropriate

perturbación nf disturbance; **p. del orden público** breach of the peace; *Med* **p. mental** mental disorder

perturbado,-a adj (mentally) deranged o unbalanced

perturbador,-a 1 adj disturbing

  2 nm,f unruly person

perturbar vt *(el orden)* to disturb

Perú n Peru

peruano,-a adj & nm,f Peruvian

perversión nf perversion

perverso,-a adj perverse, evil

pervertir [5] vt to pervert, to corrupt

pervivir vi to survive

pesa nf weight; **levantamiento de pesas** weightlifting

pesadez nf (a) heaviness; *(de estómago)* fullness (b) *Fam (fastidio)* drag, nuisance

pesadilla nf nightmare; **de p.** nightmarish

pesado,-a 1 adj (a) heavy (b) *(aburrido)* tedious, dull; **¡qué p.!** what a drag!

  2 nm,f bore

pesadumbre nf grief, affliction

pésame nm condolences, sympathy; **dar el p.** to offer one's condolences; **mi más sentido p.** my deepest sympathy

pesar 1 vt to weigh; *Fig (entristecer)* to grieve

  2 vi (a) to weigh; **¿cuánto pesas?** how much do you weigh? (b) *(ser pesado)* to be heavy (c) *Fig (tener importancia)* **este factor pesa mucho** this is a very important factor

  3 nm (a) *(pena)* sorrow, grief (b) *(arrepentimiento)* regret; **a su p.** to his regret (c) **a p. de** in spite of

pesaroso,-a adj (a) *(triste)* sorrowful, sad

pesca nf fishing; *Fam* **y toda la p.** and all that

pescadería nf fish shop, fishmonger's (shop)

pescadero,-a nm,f fishmonger

pescadilla nf young hake

pescado nm fish

pescador,-a 1 adj fishing

  2 nm,f *(hombre)* fisherman; *(mujer)* fisherwoman

pescante nm (a) *(de carruaje)* coachman's seat (b) *Constr* jib, boom (c) *Náut* davit

pescar [44] **1** vi to fish

  2 vt (a) to fish (b) *Fam (coger)* to catch

pescozada nf, **pescozón** nm slap on the neck/head

pescuezo nm *Fam* neck

pese a (que) loc adv in spite of (the fact that)

pesebre nm manger, stall

pesero nm *CAm, Méx* fixed-rate taxi service

peseta nf peseta

pesetero,-a nm,f skinflint

pesimismo nm pessimism

pesimista 1 adj pessimistic

  2 nmf pessimist

pésimo,-a adj very bad, awful, terrible

peso nm (a) weight; **al p.** by weight; **p. bruto/neto** gross/net weight; *Fig* **me quité un p. de encima** it took a load off my mind; **p. mosca/pesado** *(en boxeo)* flyweight/heavyweight (b) *(importancia)* importance; **de p.** *(persona)* influential; *(razón)* convincing

pespunte nm backstitch

pesquero,-a 1 adj fishing

  2 nm fishing boat

pesquisa nf inquiry

pestaña nf (a) eyelash, lash (b) *Téc* flange; *(de neumático)* rim

pestañear vi to blink; **sin p.** without batting an eyelid

peste nf (a) *(hedor)* stench, stink (b) *Med* plague; *Hist* **la p. negra** the Black Death (c) **decir** o **echar pestes** to curse

pesticida nm pesticide

pestilencia nf stench, stink

pestilente adj stinking, foul

pestillo nm bolt, latch

petaca nf (a) *(para cigarrillos)* cigarette case; *(para bebidas)* flask (b) *Méx (maleta)* suitcase (c) *Méx* **petacas** *(nalgas)* buttocks

petaco nm *(de juego)* flipper; **máquina de petacos** pinball machine

pétalo nm petal

petardo nm (a) firecracker, firework; *Mil* petard (b) *Fam (persona aburrida)* bore (c) *(droga)* joint

petate nm *Mil* luggage

petición nf request; *Jur* petition, plea

petiso,-a adj *Andes, RP Fam* short

peto nm **pantalón de p.** dungarees

petrificar [44] vt, **petrificarse** vpr to petrify

petróleo nm petroleum, oil

> Observa que en el inglés británico **petrol** es un falso amigo y no es la traducción de la palabra española **petróleo**. En inglés británico, **petrol** significa "gasolina".

petrolero nm oil tanker

petulante adj arrogant, vain

> Observa que la palabra inglesa **petulant** es un falso amigo y no es la traducción de la palabra española **petulante**. En inglés, **petulant** significa "caprichoso".

petunia nf petunia
peyorativo,-a adj pejorative, derogatory
pez¹ nm fish; **ella está como p. en el agua** she's in her element; **p. gordo** big shot
pez² nf pitch, tar
pezón nm nipple
pezuña nf hoof
piadoso,-a adj (a) (devoto) pious (b) (compasivo) compassionate; **mentira piadosa** white lie
pianista nmf pianist, piano player
piano nm piano
piar [29] vi to chirp, to tweet
piara nf herd of pigs
PIB nm Fin (abr **producto interior bruto**) GDP
pibe,-a nm,f Fam (a) (hombre) guy; (mujer) girl (b) RP (niño) kid, boy; (niña) kid, girl
picada nf RP (tapas) appetizers, snacks
picadero nm riding school
picadillo nm (a) (de carne) Br minced o US ground meat; (de verduras) vegetable salad (b) Chile (tapas) appetizers, snacks
picado,-a 1 adj (a) (carne) Br minced, US ground (b) (fruta) bad; (diente) decayed (c) (mar) choppy (d) Fam (enfadado) narked (e) **estar p. con** (en competición) to be at loggerheads with
2 nm Av dive; **caer en p.** to plummet
picador nm Taurom mounted bullfighter, picador
picadora nf Br mincer, US grinder
picadura nf (a) (mordedura) bite; (de avispa, abeja) sting (b) (en fruta) spot; Med (de viruela) pockmark; (en diente) decay, caries sing; (en metalurgia) pitting
picajoso,-a 1 adj touchy
2 nm,f touchy person
picante adj (a) Culin hot, spicy (b) Fig (chiste etc) risqué, spicy
picantería nf Andes cheap restaurant
picapica nm (polvos de) **p.** itching powder
picaporte nm (aldaba) door knocker; (pomo) door handle
picar [44] **1** vt (a) (de insecto, serpiente) to bite; (de avispas, abejas) to sting; (barba) to prick (b) (comer) (aves) to peck (at); (persona) to nibble, to pick at (c) (de pez) to bite (d) (perforar) to prick, to puncture (e) Culin

(carne) Br to mince, US to grind (f) (incita to incite, to goad; **p. la curiosidad (de algn)** arouse (sb's) curiosity
2 vi (a) (escocer) to itch; (herida) to smart; (sol) to burn (b) Culin to be hot (c) (pez) to bi (d) Fig (dejarse engañar) to swallow it
3 picarse vpr (a) (hacerse rivales) to be loggerheads (b) (fruta) to spot, to rot; (rop to become moth-eaten; (dientes) to decay (enfadarse) to get cross (d) (drogadicto) shoot up
picardía nf (a) (astucia) craftiness (b) (pal brota) swearword (c) (prenda) baby-do pyjamas
pícaro,-a 1 adj (a) (travieso) naughty, mi chievous; (astuto) sly, crafty (b) (procaz) risqu
2 nm,f rascal, rogue
picatoste nm crouton
pichi nm Br pinafore dress, US jumper
pichincha nf RP Fam snip, bargain
pichón nm young pigeon; **tiro al o de** pigeon shooting
pickles ['pikles] nmpl RP pickles
pico nm (a) (de ave) beak, bill; Fam (boc mouth; **tener un p. de oro** to have the gift the gab (b) (punta) corner (c) Geog peak (c (herramienta) pick, pickaxe (e) (cantida odd amount; **cincuenta y p.** fifty odd; **las do y p.** just after two (f) (drogas) fix
picoleto nm Fam civil guard
picor nm itch, tingling
picoso,-a adj Méx spicy, hot
picotazo nm peck
picotear vt & vi (a) (pájaro) to peck (b (comer) to nibble
pictórico,-a adj pictorial
pídola nf leapfrog
pie nm (a) foot; **pies** feet; **a p.** on foot; **de** standing up; **de pies a cabeza** from head foot; **en p.** standing; **el acuerdo sigue en** the agreement still stands; **hacer p.** to touc the bottom; **perder p.** to get out of one depth; Fig **a pies juntillas** blindly; Fig **al p. d la letra** to the letter, word for word; Fig **co buen/mal p.** on the right/wrong footing; F **con pies de plomo** gingerly, cautiously; F **dar p. a** to give cause for (b) (de instrumente stand; (de copa) stem (c) (de página) foot; (c una ilustración) caption; **p. de página** foot the page (d) (medida) foot (e) Teatro cue (Lit foot
piedad nf (a) devoutness, piety (b) (compc sión) compassion, pity
piedra nf stone; (de mechero) flint; **poner primera p.** to lay the foundation stone; Far Fig **me dejó o me quedé de p.** I was flabbe gasted
piel nf (a) skin; **p. de gallina** goose pimple (b) (de fruta, de patata) skin, peel (c) (cuerc leather; (con pelo) fur
pienso nm fodder, feed; **piensos compuesto** mixed feed

pierna *nf* leg

pieza *nf* (a) piece, part; **p. de recambio** spare part; *Fig* **me dejó** o **me quedé de una p.** I was speechless o dumbfounded o flabbergasted (b) *(habitación)* room (c) *Teatro* play

pigmento *nm* pigment

pigmeo,-a 1 *adj* pigmy; *Fig* pygmean
2 *nm,f* Pygmy, Pigmy; *Fig* pygmy, pigmy

pijama *nm* pyjamas

pijo,-a *Fam* **1** *adj* posh; **un barrio p.** a posh area
2 *nm,f (chico)* poor little rich boy; *(chica)* poor little rich girl
3 *nm (pene)* willy

pila *nf* (a) *Elec* battery (b) *(montón)* pile, heap; *Fig* **una p. de** *(muchos)* piles o heaps o loads of (c) *(lavadero)* basin (d) *Fig* **nombre de p.** Christian name

pilar *nm* (a) *Arquit* pillar (b) *(fuente)* waterhole

píldora *nf* pill; **p. abortiva** morning-after pill; *Fig* **dorar la p. a algn** to butter sb up

pileta *nf* (a) *(pila)* sink (b) *Am (piscina)* swimming pool

pililí *nf Fam Br* willy, *US* peter

pillaje *nm* looting, pillage

pillar 1 *vt* (a) *(robar)* to plunder, to loot (b) *(coger)* to catch; *(alcanzar)* to catch up with; **o pilló un coche** he was run over by a car (c) *Fam* to be; **me pilla un poco lejos** it's a bit far o from me
2 pillarse *vpr* to catch; **p. un dedo/una mano** to catch one's finger/hand

pillo,-a 1 *adj* (a) *(travieso)* naughty (b) *(astuto)* sly, cunning
2 *nm,f* rogue

pilotar *vt Av* to pilot, to fly; *Aut* to drive; *Náut* to pilot, to steer

piloto *nm* (a) *Av & Náut* pilot; *Aut* driver; **piso p.** show flat; **programa p.** pilot programme (b) *(luz)* pilot lamp o light

piltrafa *nf* (a) *Fam* weakling; **estar hecho una p.** to be on one's last legs (b) *(desecho)* scraps

pimentón *nm* paprika, red pepper

pimienta *nf* pepper

pimiento *nm (fruto)* pepper; *(planta)* pimiento; **p. morrón** sweet pepper; *Fam* **me importa un p.** I don't give a damn, I couldn't care less

pimpollo *nm* (a) *Bot* shoot (b) *Fam (hombre)* handsome young man; *(mujer)* elegant young woman

pinacoteca *nf* art gallery

pináculo *nm* pinnacle

pinar *nm* pine grove, pine wood

pincel *nm* brush, paintbrush

pincelada *nf* brushstroke, stroke of a brush

pinchadiscos *nmf inv Fam* disc jockey, DJ

pinchar 1 *vt* (a) *(punzar)* to prick; *(balón, globo)* to burst; *(rueda)* to puncture (b) *Fam (incitar)* to prod; *(molestar)* to get at, to nag (c) *Med* to inject, to give an injection

to (d) *Tel* to bug
2 *vi* (a) *Aut* to get a puncture (b) *Fam* **ni pincha ni corta** he cuts no ice

> 🖉 Observa que el verbo inglés **to pinch** es un falso amigo y no es la traducción del verbo español **pinchar**. En inglés, **to pinch** significa "pellizcar".

pinchazo *nm* (a) *(punzadura)* prick; *Aut* puncture, blowout (b) *(de dolor)* sudden o sharp pain

pinche *nm* (a) **p. de cocina** kitchen assistant (b) *Am (bribón)* rogue

pinchito *nm (de carne)* = type of kebab

pincho *nm* (a) *(púa)* barb (b) **p. moruno** ≃ shish kebab; **p. de tortilla** = small portion of omelette

ping-pong® *nm* table tennis, ping-pong

pingüe *adj* abundant, plentiful; **pingües beneficios** fat profits

pingüino *nm* penguin

pino *nm* pine; *Fig* **hacer el p.** to do a handstand; *Fam* **en el quinto p.** in the back of beyond

pinole *nm Am* maize o *US* corn drink

pinta 1 *nf* (a) *Fam (aspecto)* look; **tiene p. de ser interesante** it looks interesting (b) *(mota)* dot; *(lunar)* spot (c) *(medida)* pint
2 *nmf Fam* shameless person

pintada *nf* graffiti

pintado,-a *adj* recién p. *(en letrero)* wet paint; *Fam Fig* **nos viene que ni p.** it is just the ticket; *Fam Fig* **te está que ni p.** it suits you to a tee

pintar 1 *vt* (a) *(dar color)* to paint (b) *(dibujar)* to draw, to sketch
2 *vi (importar)* to count; *Fig* **yo aquí no pinto nada** I am out of place here
3 pintarse *vpr* (a) *(maquillarse)* to put makeup on (b) *Fam* **pintárselas** to manage

pintarraj(e)ar *vt* to daub

pintor,-a *nm,f* painter

pintoresco,-a *adj* (a) *(lugar)* picturesque (b) *(raro)* eccentric, bizarre

pintura *nf* (a) painting; **p. rupestre** cave painting; *Fam Fig* **no la puedo ver ni en p.** I can't stand the sight of her (b) *(materia)* paint

pinza *nf (para depilar)* tweezers; *(para tender)* Br clothes peg, *US* clothespin; *(de animal)* pincer, nipper; *Téc* tongs

piña *nf* (a) *(de pino)* pine cone; *(ananás)* pineapple (b) *Fig (grupo)* clan, clique (c) *Fam (golpe)* thump

piñón *nm* (a) pine seed o nut (b) *Téc* pinion

pío¹ *nm Fam* **no dijo ni p.** there wasn't a cheep out of him

pío²,-a *adj* pious

piojo *nm* louse

piola *adj RP Fam* (a) *(simpático)* fun (b) *Irón (listo)* smart, clever (c) *(lugar)* cosy

piolín *nm Am* cord

pionero,-a *nm,f* pioneer

pipa *nf* (a) *(de fumar)* pipe; **fumar en p.** to smoke a pipe (b) *(de fruta)* pip; *(de girasol)* sunflower seed

pipí *nm Fam* pee, *Br* wee-wee; **hacer p.** to pee, *Br* to wee-wee

pique *nm* (a) resentment (b) *(rivalidad)* needle (c) **a p. de** on the point of (d) **irse a p.** *Náut* to sink; *(un plan)* to fall through; *(un negocio)* to go bust

piqueta *nf* pickaxe

piquete *nm* (a) *(de huelga)* picket (b) *Mil* **p. de ejecución** firing squad

pira *nf* pyre

pirado,-a *adj Fam* crazy

piragua *nf* canoe

piragüismo *nm* canoeing

piragüista *nmf* canoeist

pirámide *nf* pyramid

piraña *nf* piranha

pirarse, pirárselas *vpr Fam* to clear off, to hop it

pirata *adj & nmf* pirate

piratear *vt Fig* to pirate

Pirineo(s) *nm(pl)* Pyrenees

pirita *nf* pyrite

pirómano,-a *nm,f Med* pyromaniac; *Jur* arsonist

piropo *nm* **echar un p.** to pay a compliment

pirueta *nf* pirouette; *Fig Pol* **hacer una p.** to do a U-turn

pirulí *nm* lollipop; *TV* television tower

pis *nm Fam* pee, *Br* wee-wee; **hacer p.** to have a pee, *Br* to wee-wee

pisada *nf* step, footstep; *(huella)* footprint

pisapapeles *nm inv* paperweight

pisar *vt* to tread on, to step on

piscifactoría *nf* fish farm

piscina *nf* swimming pool

pisco *nm* pisco, = Andean grape brandy

piscolabis *nm inv Fam* snack

piso *nm* (a) apartment, *Br* flat; *Pol* **p. franco** safe house (b) *(planta)* floor; *(de carretera)* surface

pisotear *vt (aplastar)* to stamp on; *(pisar)* to trample on

pisotón *nm* **me dio un p.** he stood on my foot

pista *nf* (a) track; **p. de baile** dance floor; *Dep* **p. de esquí** ski run *o* slope; *Dep* **p. de patinaje** ice rink; *Dep* **p. de tenis** tennis court; **p. de aterrizaje** landing strip; **p. de despegue** runway (b) *(rastro)* trail, track (c) **dame una p.** give me a clue

pistacho *nm* pistachio nut

pisto *nm Culin* ≃ ratatouille

pistola *nf* (a) gun, pistol (b) *(para pintar)* spray gun

pistolero *nm* gunman, gangster

pistón *nm* (a) *Téc (émbolo)* piston (b) *(de arma)* cartridge cap (c) *Mús* key

pita *nf* agave

pitada *nf* (a) *(silbidos de protesta)* booing,
whistling (b) *Am Fam (calada)* drag, puff

pitar **1** *vt* (a) *(silbato)* to blow (b) *Dep* **árbitro pitó un penalti** the referee awarde a penalty
2 *vi* (a) to whistle (b) *Aut* to toot one's hor (c) *Dep* to referee (d) *Fam* **salir pitando** to fl off

pitido *nm* whistle

pitillera *nf* cigarette case

pitillo *nm* (a) *(cigarrillo)* cigarette (b) *Ce (paja)* drinking straw

pito *nm* (a) *(silbato)* whistle; *Aut* horn; *Fam* **me impo ta un p.** I don't give a hoot (b) *Fam (cigarrille* fag (c) *Fam (pene)* prick, willie

pitón *nm* (a) *(serpiente)* python (b) *(de tor* horn

pitorreo *nm Fam* scoffing, teasing; **hace algo de p.** to do sth for a laugh

pivot, pivote *nmf* pivot

pizarra *nf* (a) *(encerado)* blackboard (b *(roca, material)* slate

pizarrón *nm Am (encerado)* blackboard

pizca *nf* little bit, tiny piece; **ni p.** not a bit; **un p. de sal** a pinch of salt

placa *nf* (a) plate (b) *(conmemorativ* plaque

placaje *nm Dep* tackle

placentero,-a *adj* pleasant, agreeable

placer [33] **1** *vt* to please
2 *nm* pleasure; **ha sido un p. (conocerle)** it been a pleasure (meeting you); *Fml* **tengo** **p. de** it gives me great pleasure to; **un viaje d p.** a holiday trip

placidez *nf* placidity

plácido,-a *adj* placid, easy-going

plaga *nf* (a) plague (b) *Agr* pest, blight

plagar [42] *vt* to fill

plagiar [43] *vt* (a) *(copiar)* to plagiarize (b *Andes, CAm, Méx (secuestrar)* to kidnap

plagiario,-a *nm,f Andes, CAm, Méx (secue. trador)* kidnapper

plagio *nm* plagiarism

plan *nm* (a) *(proyecto)* plan (b) *(programe* scheme, programme; *Educ* **p. de estudio** syllabus; **estar a p.** to be on a diet (c) *Fam* **e p. de broma** for a laugh; **si te pones en ese p** if you're going to be like that (about it); **en p barato** cheaply (d) *Fam (cita)* date

plana *nf* (a) page; **a toda p.** full page; **primer p.** front page (b) *Mil* **p. mayor** staff

plancha *nf* (a) iron; *(de metal)* plate (b) *Culi* hotplate; **sardinas a la p.** grilled sardines (c *Impr* plate

planchado *nm* ironing

planchar *vt* to iron

planchazo *nm Fam* blunder, boob

planeador *nm* glider

planear 1 *vt* to plan
2 *vi* to glide

planeta *nm* planet

planetario,-a 1 *adj* planetary
2 *nm* planetarium

planicie *nf* plain
planificación *nf* planning; **p. familiar** family planning
planificar [44] *vt* to plan
planilla *nf Am* application form
plano,-a 1 *nm* (**a**) *(de ciudad)* map; *Arquit* plan, draft (**b**) *Cin* shot; **un primer p.** a close-up; *Fig* **estar en primer/segundo p.** to be in the limelight/in the background (**c**) *Mat* plane
  2 *adj* flat, even
planta *nf* (**a**) plant (**b**) *(del pie)* sole (**c**) *(piso)* floor, storey; **p. baja** *Br* ground floor, *US* first floor
plantación *nf* (**a**) plantation (**b**) *(acción)* planting
plantado,-a *adj Fam* **dejar a algn p.** to stand sb up
plantar 1 *vt* (**a**) *(árboles, campo)* to plant (**b**) *(poner)* to place; **p. cara a algn** to stand up to sb (**c**) *Fam* **p. a algn en la calle** to throw sb out; **le ha plantado su novia** his girlfriend has ditched him
  2 plantarse *upr* (**a**) *(considerar)* to stand (**b**) *(llegar)* to arrive; **en cinco minutos se plantó aquí** he got here in five minutes flat
planteamiento *nm (enfoque)* approach
plantear 1 *vt* (**a**) *(problema)* to pose, to raise (**b**) *(planear)* to plan (**c**) *(proponer)* to put forward (**d**) *(exponer)* to present
  2 plantearse *upr* (**a**) *(considerar)* to consider (**b**) *(problema)* to arise
plantel *nm Fig* cadre, clique
plantilla *nf* (**a**) *(personal)* staff, personnel (**b**) *(de zapato)* insole (**c**) *(patrón)* model, pattern
plantón *nm Fam* **dar un p. a algn** to stand sb up
plañir *vi* to mourn
plasmar 1 *vt* (**a**) *(reproducir)* to capture (**b**) *(expresar)* to express
  2 plasmarse *upr* **p. en** to take the shape of
plasta *nmf Fam* bore
plástico,-a 1 *adj* plastic
  2 *nm* (**a**) plastic (**b**) *(disco)* record
plastificar [44] *vt* to coat o cover with plastic
plastilina® *nf* Plasticine®
plata *nf* (**a**) silver; *(objetos de plata)* silverware; *Fam* **hablar en p.** to lay (it) on the line; **p. de ley** sterling silver (**b**) *Am* money
plataforma *nf* platform
plátano *nm* (**a**) *(fruta)* banana (**b**) *(árbol)* plane tree; **falso p.** sycamore
platea *nf Cin & Teatro Br* stalls, *US* orchestra
platear *vt* to silver-plate
platense 1 *adj* of/from the River Plate
  2 *nmf* person from the River Plate
plática *nf CAm, Méx* chat, talk
platicar [44] *vi CAm, Méx* to chat, to talk
platillo *nm* (**a**) saucer; **p. volante** flying saucer (**b**) *Mús* cymbal
platina *nf (de tocadiscos)* deck; **doble p.**

double deck
platino *nm* (**a**) platinum (**b**) *Aut* **platinos** contact breaker, points
plato *nm* (**a**) plate, dish (**b**) *(parte de una comida)* course; **de primer p.** for starters; **p. fuerte** main course; **p. combinado** one-course meal (**c**) *(guiso)* dish (**d**) *(de balanza)* pan, tray (**e**) *(de tocadiscos)* turntable
plató *nm Cin & TV* (film) set
platudo,-a *adj Am Fam* loaded, rolling in it
plausible *adj* (**a**) *(admisible)* plausible, acceptable (**b**) *(loable)* commendable
playa *nf* (**a**) beach; *(costa)* seaside (**b**) *Am* **p. de estacionamiento** *Br* car park, *US* parking lot
playera *nf* (**a**) *(zapatilla)* *Br* sandshoe, *US* sneaker (**b**) *Méx (camiseta)* teeshirt
plaza *nf* (**a**) square (**b**) *(mercado)* market, marketplace (**c**) *Aut* seat (**d**) *(laboral)* post, position (**e**) **p. de toros** bullring
plazo *nm* (**a**) *(periodo)* time, period; *(término)* deadline; **a corto/largo p.** in the short term/in the long run; **el p. termina el viernes** Friday is the deadline (**b**) *Fin* **comprar a plazos** to buy on *Br* hire purchase *o US* an installment plan; **en seis plazos** in six instalments
pleamar *nf* high tide
plebe *nf* masses, plebs
plebeyo,-a 1 *adj* plebeian
  2 *nm,f* plebeian, pleb
plebiscito *nm* plebiscite
plegable *adj* folding, collapsible
plegar [1] **1** *vt* to fold
  2 plegarse *upr* to give way, to bow
plegaria *nf* prayer
pleitear *vi* to conduct a lawsuit, to plead
pleito *nm* (**a**) *Jur* lawsuit, litigation; **poner un p. (a algn)** to sue (sb) (**b**) *Am (discusión)* argument
plenilunio *nm* full moon
plenitud *nf* plenitude, fullness; **en la p. de la vida** in the prime of life
pleno,-a 1 *adj* full; **en plena noche** in the middle of the night; **los empleados en p.** the entire staff
  2 *nm* plenary meeting
pletórico,-a *adj* abundant
plexiglás® *nm (plástico)* Perspex®, *US* Plexiglass®
pliego *nm* (**a**) *(hoja)* sheet o piece of paper; **p. de condiciones** bidding specifications (**b**) *(carta)* sealed letter
pliegue *nm* (**a**) fold (**b**) *(de vestido)* pleat
plinto *nm Dep* horse
plisar *vt* to pleat
plomería *nf Méx, RP, Ven* plumber's
plomero *nm Méx, RP, Ven* plumber
plomizo,-a *adj* lead, leaden; *(color)* lead-coloured
plomo *nm* (**a**) *(en metalurgia)* lead (**b**) *Elec (fusible)* fuse (**c**) *(bala)* slug, pellet

pluma *nf* (a) feather (b) *(estilográfica)* fountain pen (c) *Carib, Méx (bolígrafo)* (ballpoint) pen

plumaje *nm* plumage

plumazo *nm* **de un p.** at a stroke

plumero *nm* (a) *(para el polvo)* feather duster (b) *Fam* **se te ve el p.** I can see through you

plumier *nm* pencil box

plural *adj & nm* plural

pluralismo *nm* pluralism

pluriempleo *nm* moonlighting

plus *nm* bonus, bonus payment

plusmarca *nf* record

plusmarquista *nmf* record breaker

plusvalía *nf* capital gain

Plza. (*abr* **Plaza**) Sq

población *nf* (a) *(ciudad)* town; *(pueblo)* village (b) *(habitantes)* population (c) *Chile (barrio)* **p. (callampa)** shanty town

poblado,-a *adj* (a) populated; *Fig* **p. de** full of (b) *(barba)* bushy, thick

poblador,-a *nm,f* settler

poblar [2] *vt* (a) *(con gente)* to settle, to people; *(con plantas)* to plant (b) *(vivir)* to inhabit

pobre 1 *adj* poor; **¡p.!** poor thing!; **un hombre p.** a poor man; **un p. hombre** a poor devil
2 *nmf* poor person; **los pobres** the poor

pobreza *nf* poverty; *Fig (de medios, recursos)* lack

pocho,-a *adj* (a) *(fruta)* bad, overripe (b) *Fig (persona) (débil)* off-colour; *(triste)* depressed, down (c) *Méx Fam (americanizado)* Americanized

pochoclo *nm Arg* popcorn

pocilga *nf* pigsty

pocillo *nm RP* (a) *(pequeño)* small cup (b) *Méx, Ven (grande)* enamel mug

pócima, poción *nf* potion; *Pey* concoction, brew

poco,-a 1 *nm* (a) **un p.** *(con adj o adv)* a little; **un p. tarde/frío** a little late/cold
(b) **un p.** *(con sustantivo)* a little; **un p. de azúcar** a little sugar
2 *adj* (a) not much, little; **p. sitio/tiempo** not much o little space/time; **poca cosa** not much
(b) **pocos,-as** not many, few; **pocas personas** not many o few people
(c) **unos,-as pocos,-as** a few
3 *pron* (a) *(escasa cantidad)* not much; **queda p.** there isn't much left
(b) *(breve tiempo)* **p. antes/después** shortly o a little before/afterwards; **a p. de** shortly o a little after; **dentro de p.** soon
(c) **pocos,-as** *(cosas)* few, not many; **tengo muy pocos** I have very few, I don't have very many
(d) **pocos,-as** *(personas)* few people, not many people; **vinieron pocos** few people came, not many people came
4 *adv* (a) *(con verbo)* not (very) much; little;

ella come p. she doesn't eat much, she eats little
(b) *(con adj)* not very; **es p. probable** it's not very likely
(c) *(en frases)* **p. a p.** little by little, gradually; **por p.** almost

podadera, *Am* **podadora** *nf* garden shears

podar *vt* to prune

poder¹ *nm* power; *Econ* **p. adquisitivo** purchasing power

poder² [18] **1** *vi* (a) *(capacidad)* to be able to; **no puede hablar** she can't speak; **no podré llamarte** I won't be able to phone; **no puedo más** I can't take any more; **guapa a más no p.** unbelievably pretty
(b) *(permiso)* may, might; **¿puedo pasar?** can o may I come in?; **¿se puede (entrar)?** may I (come in)?; **aquí no se puede fumar** you can't smoke here
(c) *(uso impers) (posibilidad)* may, might; **puede que no lo sepan** they may o might not know; **no puede ser** that's impossible; **puede (ser) (que sí)** maybe, perhaps
(d) *(deber)* **podrías haberme advertido** you might have warned me
(e) to cope (**con** with); **no puede con tanto trabajo** he can't cope with so much work
2 *vt (batir)* to be stronger than; **les puede a todos** he can take on anybody

poderoso,-a *adj* powerful

podio, pódium *nm Dep* podium

podré *indic fut de* **poder**

podrido,-a *adj* (a) *(putrefacto)* rotten, putrid (b) *(corrupto)* corrupt; *Fam* **p. de dinero** *o Am* **en plata** stinking rich (c) *RP Fam (harto)* fed up, sick

podrir *vt defect* = **pudrir**

poema *nm* poem

poesía *nf* (a) *(género)* poetry (b) *(poema)* poem

poeta *nmf* poet

poético,-a *adj* poetic

póker *nm* poker

polaco,-a 1 *adj* Polish
2 *nm,f* Pole
3 *nm (idioma)* Polish

polaridad *nf* polarity

polarizar [40] *vt* (a) *Fís* to polarize (b) *Fig (ánimo, atención)* to concentrate

polea *nf* pulley

polémica *nf* controversy

polémico,-a *adj* controversial

polemizar [40] *vi* to argue, to debate

polen *nm* pollen

polera *nf RP* polo shirt

poli *Fam* **1** *nmf* cop
2 *nf* **la p.** the fuzz *pl*

poli- *pref* poly-

policía 1 *nf* police (force)
2 *nmf (hombre)* policeman; *(mujer)* policewoman

policíaco,-a, policiaco,-a, policial *adj*

lice; **novela/película policíaca** detective
ry/film
·lideportivo nm sports centre
·liéster nm polyester
·lietileno nm Br polythene, US polyethy-
ne
·lifacético,-a adj versatile, many-sided; **es
 hombre muy p.** he's a man of many talents
·ligamia nf polygamy
·líglota adj & nmf polyglot
·lígono nm polygon; **p. industrial** indus-
al estate
·lilla nf moth
·liomielitis nf polio, poliomyelitis
·litécnico,-a adj & nm polytechnic
·lítica nf (a) politics sing (b) (estrategia)
licy
·líticamente adv **p. correcto** politically
rrect
·lítico,-a 1 adj (a) political (b) (pariente) in-
w; **hermano p.** brother-in-law; **su familia
lítica** her in-laws
 nm,f politician
·liza nf (a) (sello) stamp (b) **p. de seguros**
surance policy
·lizón nm stowaway
·lla nf (a) Vulg (pene) prick (b) Orn **p. de
ua** moorhen
·llera nf (a) RP (occidental) skirt (b) Andes
ndígena) = long skirt worn by Indian
omen
·llo nm (a) chicken (b) Fam (joven) lad
·lo nm (a) Elec & Geog pole; **P. Norte/Sur**
rth/South Pole (b) (helado) Br ice lolly, US
psicle® (c) (prenda) sports shirt, polo neck
weater) (d) Dep poncho
·lolear vi Chile Fam to go out (together)
·lolo,-a nm,f Chile Fam boyfriend, f girl-
iend
·lonia n Poland
·ltrona nf easy chair
·lución nf pollution
·lvareda nf cloud of dust
·lvera nf powder compact
·lvo nm (a) dust; **limpiar** o **quitar el p.** to
ust; **en p.** powdered; **polvo(s) de talco** tal-
m powder (b) Fam **estar hecho p.** (cansa-
) to be Br knackered o US bushed;
eprimido) to be depressed (c) muy Fam
har un p. to have a screw
·lvora nf gunpowder
·lvoriento,-a adj dusty
·lvorín nm gunpowder arsenal; Fig powder
eg
·lvorón nm sweet pastry
·mada nf ointment
·melo nm (fruto) grapefruit; (árbol) grape-
uit tree
·mez adj inv **piedra p.** pumice (stone)
·mo nm (de puerta) knob
·mpa nf (a) bubble (b) (ostentación) pomp
) Méx Fam **pompas** botty

pompis nm inv Fam botty
pomposo,-a adj pompous
pómulo nm cheekbone
ponchar 1 vt (a) CAm, Carib, Méx (rueda) to
puncture (b) Am (en béisbol) to strike out
  2 poncharse upr (a) CAm, Carib, Méx (rueda)
to get a puncture (b) Am (en béisbol) to strike
out
ponche nm punch
poncho nm poncho
ponderar vt (a) (asunto) to weigh up o consider (b) (alabar) to praise
pondré indic fut de **poner**
ponencia nf paper
poner [19] (pp puesto) **1** vt (a) to put; (mesa,
huevo) to lay; (gesto) to make; (multa) to
impose; (telegrama) to send; (negocio) to set
up
  (b) (tele, radio etc) to turn o switch on
  (c) (+ adj) to make; **p. triste a algn** to make
sb sad; **p. colorado a algn** to make sb blush
  (d) **¿qué llevaba puesto?** what was he
wearing?
  (e) (decir) **¿qué pone aquí?** what does it say
here?
  (f) (suponer) to suppose; **pongamos que
Ana no viene** supposing Ana doesn't turn up
  (g) TV & Cin to put on, to show; **¿qué ponen
en la tele?** what's on the telly?
  (h) Tel **ponme con Manuel** put me through to
Manuel
  (i) (nombrar) **le pondremos (de nombre)
Pilar** we are going to call her Pilar
  2 v impers Am Fam (parecer) **se me pone
que ...** it seems to me that ...
  3 ponerse upr (a) to put oneself; **ponte en mi
lugar** put yourself in my place; **ponte más
cerca** come closer
  (b) (vestirse) to put on; **ella se puso el jersey**
she put her sweater on
  (c) (+ adj) to become; **p. furioso/malo** to
become furious/ill
  (d) (sol) to set
  (e) Tel **p. al teléfono** to answer the phone
  (f) **p. a** to start to; **p. a trabajar** to get down to
work
poney nm pony
pongo indic pres de **poner**
poniente nm (a) (occidente) West (b) (viento) westerly (wind)
ponqué nm Col, Ven = large sponge cake,
filled with cream and/or fruit, and covered in
icing or chocolate
pontífice nm Pontiff; **el Sumo P.** His Holiness
the Pope
ponzoña nf (a) venom, poison (b) **tener p.**
(tristeza) to be down in the dumps
ponzoñoso,-a adj (a) venomous, poisonous
  (b) (triste) down in the dumps
popa nf stern; Fig **ir viento en p.** to go full
speed ahead
popote nm Méx drinking straw

populacho *nm Pey* plebs, masses
popular *adj* (a) folk; **arte/música p.** folk art/ music (b) *(medida)* popular (c) *(actor)* well-known
popularidad *nf* popularity
popularizar [40] *vt* to popularize
populoso,-a *adj* densely populated
popurrí *nm Mús* medley
póquer *nm* poker
por *prep* (a) *(agente)* by; **pintado p. Picasso** painted by Picasso
(b) **p. qué** why
(c) *(causa)* because of; **p. sus ideas** because of her ideas; **p. necesidad/amor** out of need/ love; **suspendió p. no estudiar** he failed because he didn't study
(d) *(tiempo)* **p. la mañana/noche** in the morning/at night; **p. ahora** for the time being; **p. entonces** at that time
(e) *(en favor de)* for; **lo hago p. mi hermano** I'm doing it for my brother('s sake)
(f) *(lugar)* **pasamos p. Córdoba** we went through Córdoba; **p. ahí** over there; **¿p. dónde vamos?** which way are we taking o going?; **p. la calle** in the street; **mirar p. la ventana** to look out the window; **entrar p. la ventana** to get in through the window
(g) *(medio)* by; **p. avión/correo** by plane/ post
(h) *(a cambio de)* for; **cambiar algo p. otra cosa** to exchange sth for something else
(i) *(distributivo)* **p. cabeza** a head, per person; **p. hora/mes** per hour/month
(j) *Mat* **dos p. tres, seis** two times three is six; **un 10 p. ciento** 10 percent
(k) *(con infinitivo)* in order to, so as to; **hablar p. hablar** to talk for the sake of it
(l) *(locuciones)* **p. así decirlo** so to speak; **p. más o muy ... que sea** no matter how... he/she is; **p. mí** as far as I'm concerned
porcelana *nf* porcelain
porcentaje *nm* percentage
porche *nm* porch
porcino,-a *adj* **ganado p.** pigs
porción *nf* portion, part
pordiosero,-a *nm,f* tramp, *US* bum
porfía *nf* *(obstinación)* obstinacy, stubbornness
porfolio *nm* portfolio
pormenor *nm* detail; **venta al p.** retail
porno *adj inv Fam* porn
pornografía *nf* pornography
pornográfico,-a *adj* pornographic
poro *nm* pore
poroso,-a *adj* porous
poroto *nm RP* *(judía)* kidney bean
porque *conj* (a) *(causal)* because; **¡p. no!** just because! (b) *(final)* (+ *subjunctive*) so that, in order that
porqué *nm* reason
porquería *nf* (a) *(suciedad)* dirt, filth (b) *(birria)* *Br* rubbish, *US* garbage (c) *Fam* *(chu-*

chería) junk food, *Br* rubbish
porra *nf* (a) *(de policía)* truncheon, baton (	 *Fam* *(locuciones)* **¡una p.!** *Br* rubbish!, garbage!; **¡vete a la p.!** get lost!
porrazo *nm* thump
porro *nm* (a) *Fam* *(de droga)* joint (b) *A (puerro)* leek
porrón *nm* = glass bottle with a spo coming out of its base, used for drinking wi
portaaviones *nm inv* aircraft carrier
portada *nf* (a) *(de libro etc)* cover; *(de per dico)* front page; *(de disco)* sleeve (b) *(fach da)* front, facade
portador,-a *nm,f Com* bearer; *Med* carrier
portaequipajes *nm inv* (a) *Aut* *(maletero)* boot, *US* trunk; *(baca)* roof rack (b) *(carri* luggage trolley
portafolios *nm inv* briefcase
portal *nm* (a) *(zaguán)* porch, entrance h (b) *(puerta de la calle)* main door (c) **p. Belén** Nativity scene (d) *Informát* portal
portamaletas *nm inv* = **portaequipajes**
portaminas *nm inv* propelling pencil
portamonedas *nm inv* purse
portarse *vpr* to behave; **p. mal** to misbeha
portátil *adj* portable
portaviones *nm inv* = **portaaviones**
portavoz *nmf* spokesperson; *(hombr* spokesman; *(mujer)* spokeswoman
portazo *nm* **oímos un p.** we heard a slam bang; **dar un p.** to slam the door
porte *nm* (a) *(aspecto)* bearing (b) *(transpo te)* carriage
portento *nm* (a) *(cosa)* wonder, marvel (*(persona)* genius
portentoso,-a *adj* extraordinary, prodigio
porteño,-a **1** *adj* of/from Buenos Aires
2 *nm,f* person from Buenos Aires
portería *nf* (a) porter's lodge (b) *Dep* goal
portero,-a *nm,f* (a) *(de vivienda)* porte caretaker; **p. automático** Entryphone® (*Dep* goalkeeper
pórtico *nm* (a) *(portal)* portico, porch (*(con arcadas)* arcade
portorriqueño,-a *adj & nm,f* Puerto Rican
portuario,-a *adj* harbour, port
Portugal *n* Portugal
portugués,-esa **1** *adj* Portuguese
2 *nm* *(idioma)* Portuguese
porvenir *nm* future; **sin p.** with no prospec
pos *adv* **en p. de** after
pos- *pref* post-
posada *nf* inn
posaderas *nfpl Fam* buttocks
posadero,-a *nm,f* innkeeper
posar **1** *vi* *(para retrato etc)* to pose
2 *vt* to put o lay down
3 posarse *vpr* to settle, to alight
posdata *nf* postscript
pose *nf* (a) *(postura)* pose (b) *(afectació* posing
poseedor,-a *nm,f* possessor

poseer [36] *vt* to possess, to own

poseído,-a *adj* possessed

posesión *nf* possession; **estar en p. de** to have; **tomar p. (de un cargo)** to take up (a post)

posesivo,-a *adj* possessive

poseso,-a *adj & nm,f* possessed

posguerra *nf* postwar period

posibilidad *nf* possibility; *(oportunidad)* chance

posibilitar *vt* to make possible

posible 1 *adj* possible; **de ser p.** if possible; **en (la medida de) lo p.** as far as possible; **haré todo lo p.** I'll do everything I can; **lo antes p.** as soon as possible; **es p. que venga** he might come

  2 *nmpl* **posibles** means

posición *nf* position

positivo,-a *adj* positive

posmoderno,-a *adj* postmodern

poso *nm* dregs, sediment

posponer [19] *vt* (a) *(aplazar)* to postpone, to put off (b) *(relegar)* to put in second place *o* behind, to relegate

post- *pref* post-

posta *nf* **a p.** on purpose

postal 1 *adj* postal

  2 *nf* postcard

poste *nm* pole; *Dep (de portería)* post

póster *nm* poster

postergar [42] *vt* (a) *(relegar)* to relegate (b) *(retrasar)* to delay; *(aplazar)* to postpone

posteridad *nf* posterity; **pasar a la p.** to go down in history

posterior *adj* (a) *(lugar)* posterior, rear (b) *(tiempo)* later (**a** than), subsequent (**a** to)

posterioridad *nf* posteriority; **con p.** later

posteriormente *adv* subsequently, later

postgraduado,-a *adj & nm,f* postgraduate

postigo *nm (de puerta)* wicket; *(de ventana)* shutter

postín *nm Fam* boasting, showing off; **darse p.** to show off, to swank; **de p.** posh, swanky

postizo,-a 1 *adj* false, artificial; **dentadura postiza** false teeth, dentures

  2 *nm* hairpiece

postor *nm* bidder

postrarse *upr* to prostrate oneself, to kneel down

postre *nm* dessert, sweet

postrero,-a *adj* last

> **Postrer** is used instead of **postrero** before masculine singular nouns (e.g. **el postrer día** the last day).

postrimería *nf (usu pl)* last part *o* period

postular 1 *vt* (a) *(defender)* to call for (b) *Am (candidatar)* to propose, to nominate

  2 *vi (en colecta)* to collect

  3 postularse *upr Am* (a) *Pol (para cargo)* to stand, to run (b) *(para trabajo)* to apply (**para** for)

póstumo,-a *adj* posthumous

postura *nf* (a) position, posture (b) *Fig (actitud)* attitude

pos(t)venta *adj* **servicio p.** after-sales service

potable *adj* drinkable; **agua p./no p.** drinking water/not drinking water

potaje *nm* hotpot, stew

pote *nm* pot; *(jarra)* jug

potencia *nf* power; **en p.** potential

potencial 1 *adj* potential

  2 *nm* (a) potential; **p. eléctrico** voltage; **p. humano** manpower (b) *Ling* conditional (tense)

potenciar [43] *vt* to promote, to strengthen

potente *adj* powerful, strong

potestad *nf* power, authority

potingue *nm Fam Pey* (a) *(bebida)* concoction (b) *(maquillaje)* make-up, face cream/lotion

potra *nf Fam* luck

potrero *nm Am* field, pasture

potro *nm Zool* colt; *(de gimnasia)* horse

poyo *nm* stone bench

pozo *nm* well; *Min* shaft, pit

pozole *nm CAm, Carib, Méx (guiso)* = stew made with maize kernels, pork or chicken and vegetables

PP *nm (abr* **Partido Popular**) = Spanish political party to the right of the political spectrum

práctica *nf* (a) practice; **en la p.** in practice (b) *(formación)* placement; **período de prácticas** practical training period

practicante 1 *adj Rel* practising

  2 *nmf Med* medical assistant

practicar [44] **1** *vt* to practise; *(operación)* to carry out

  2 *vi* to practise

práctico,-a *adj* practical; *(útil)* handy, useful

pradera *nf* meadow

prado *nm* meadow, field

Praga *n* Prague

pragmático,-a 1 *adj* pragmatic

  2 *nm,f* pragmatist

pre- *pref* pre-

preámbulo *nm* (a) *(introducción)* preamble (b) *(rodeo)* circumlocution

preaviso *nm* previous warning, notice

precalentamiento *nm* warm-up

precalentar [1] *vt* to preheat

precario,-a *adj* precarious

precaución *nf* (a) *(cautela)* caution; **con p.** cautiously (b) *(medida)* precaution

precaver 1 *vt* to guard against

  2 precaverse *upr* to take precautions (**de** *o* **contra** against)

precavido,-a *adj* cautious, prudent

precedencia *nf* precedence, priority

precedente 1 *adj* preceding

  2 *nmf* predecessor

  3 *nm* precedent; **sin p.** unprecedented

preceder *vt* to precede

precepto nm precept
preciarse [43] upr to fancy oneself (**de** as)
precintar vt to seal
precinto nm seal

> 🖉 Observa que la palabra inglesa **precinct** es un falso amigo y no es la traducción de la palabra española **precinto**. En inglés, **precinct** significa "recinto" o "distrito".

precio nm price; **p. de coste** cost price; **a cualquier p.** at any price
preciosidad nf (**a**) (hermosura) (cosa) lovely thing; (persona) darling (**b**) Fml (cualidad) preciousness
precioso,-a adj (**a**) (hermoso) lovely, beautiful (**b**) (valioso) precious, valuable
precipicio nm precipice
precipitación nf (**a**) (prisa) haste (**b**) (lluvia) rainfall
precipitado,-a adj (apresurado) hasty, hurried; (irreflexivo) rash
precipitar 1 vt (**a**) (acelerar) to hurry, to rush (**b**) (arrojar) to throw, to hurl down
  2 precipitarse upr (**a**) (persona) to hurl oneself; (acontecimientos) to gather speed (**b**) (actuar irreflexivamente) to hurry, to rush
precisamente adv (con precisión) precisely; (exactamente) exactly; **p. por eso** for that very reason
precisar vt (**a**) (determinar) to determine, to give full details of; (especificar) to specify (**b**) (necesitar) to require, to need
precisión nf (**a**) (exactitud) precision, accuracy; **con p.** precisely, accurately (**b**) (aclaración) clarification
preciso,-a adj (**a**) (necesario) necessary, essential (**b**) (exacto) accurate, exact; **en este p. momento** at this very moment (**c**) (claro) concise, clear
preconizar [40] vt to advocate
precoz adj (**a**) (persona) precocious (**b**) (fruta) early
precursor,-a nm,f precursor
predecesor,-a nm,f predecessor
predecir [12] (pp predicho) vt to foretell, to predict
predestinado,-a adj predestined
predeterminar vt to predetermine
predicado nm predicate
predicador,-a nm,f preacher
predicar [44] vt to preach
predicción nf prediction, forecast
predice indic pres de **predecir**
predije pt indef de **predecir**
predilección nf predilection
predilecto,-a adj favourite, preferred
predisponer [19] (pp predispuesto) vt to predispose
predisposición nf predisposition
predominante adj predominant
predominar vi to predominate

predominio nm predominance
preescolar adj preschool; **en p.** in the nursery school
prefabricado,-a adj prefabricated
prefacio nm preface
preferencia nf preference
preferente adj preferable, preferential
preferible adj preferable; **es p. que no vengas** you'd better not come
preferido,-a nm,f favourite
preferir [5] vt to prefer
prefijo nm (**a**) Tel Br dialling code, US area code (**b**) Ling prefix
pregonar vt (anunciar) to announce publicly; Fig (divulgar) to reveal, to disclose
pregunta nf question; **hacer una p.** to ask a question
preguntar 1 vt to ask; **p. algo a algn** to ask sb sth; **p. por algn** to ask after o about sb
  2 preguntarse upr to wonder; **me pregunto si ...** I wonder whether ...
preguntón,-ona nm,f Fam busybody
prehistoria nf prehistory
prehistórico,-a adj prehistoric
prejuicio nm prejudice; **tener prejuicios** to be prejudiced, to be biased
preliminar adj & nm preliminary
preludio nm prelude
prematrimonial adj premarital
prematuro,-a adj premature
premeditación nf premeditation; **con p.** deliberately
premeditado,-a adj premeditated, deliberate
premiado,-a adj prize-winning
premiar [43] vt (**a**) to award a prize to (**b**) (recompensar) to reward
premio nm prize, award; (recompensa) reward
premisa nf premise
premonición nf premonition
premura nf (urgencia) urgency; **p. de tiempo** haste
prenatal adj antenatal, prenatal
prenda nf (**a**) (prenda) garment (**b**) (garantía) token, pledge
prendar 1 vt to captivate, to delight
  2 prendarse upr (enamorarse) to fall in love (**de** with)
prendedor nm brooch, pin
prender 1 vt (**a**) (sujetar) to fasten, to attach; (con alfileres) to pin (**b**) **p. fuego a** to set fire to (**c**) (arrestar) to arrest
  2 vi (fuego) to catch; (madera) to catch fire; (planta) to take root
  3 prenderse upr to catch fire
prensa nf press; Fig **tener buena/mala p.** to have a good/bad press
prensar vt to press
preñada,-a adj (**a**) pregnant (**b**) Fig (lleno) pregnant (**de** with), full (**de** of)
preñar vt (mujer) to make pregnant; (animal) to impregnate

preocupación nf worry, concern

preocupado,-a adj worried, concerned

preocupar 1 vt to worry; **me preocupa que llegue tan tarde** I'm worried about him arriving so late

2 preocuparse vpr to worry, to get worried (**por** about); **no te preocupes** don't worry; **p. de algn** to look after sb; **p. de algo** to see to sth

reparación nf preparation; (formación) training

reparado,-a 1 adj (**a**) (dispuesto) ready, prepared; **comidas preparadas** ready-cooked meals (**b**) (capacitado) trained, qualified

2 nm Farm preparation

reparador,-a nm,f coach, trainer

reparar 1 vt (**a**) to prepare, to get ready; **p. un examen** to prepare for an exam (**b**) Dep (entrenar) to train, to coach

2 prepararse vpr (**a**) to prepare oneself, to get ready (**b**) Dep (entrenarse) to train

reparativo nm preparation

reparatorio,-a adj preparatory

reponderante adj preponderant

reposición nf Ling preposition

repotente adj domineering; (arrogante) overbearing

rerrogativa nf prerogative

resa nf (**a**) prey; Fig **ser p. de** to be a victim of; **p. del pánico** panic-stricken (**b**) (embalse) dam

resagiar [43] vt to predict, to foretell

resagio nm (**a**) (señal) omen; **buen/mal p.** good/bad omen (**b**) (premonición) premonition

resbiteriano,-a adj & nm,f Presbyterian

resbítero nm priest

rescindir vi **p. de** to do without

rescribir (pp prescrito) vt to prescribe

rescripción nf prescription; **p. facultativa** medical prescription

resencia nf presence; **hacer acto de p.** to put in an appearance; **p. de ánimo** presence of mind

resencial adj **testigo p.** eyewitness

resenciar [43] vt (ver) to witness

resentable adj presentable; **no estoy p.** I'm not dressed for the occasion

resentación nf presentation; (aspecto) appearance; (de personas) introduction

resentador,-a nm,f Rad & TV presenter, host, f hostess

resentar 1 vt (**a**) to present; (mostrar) to show, to display; (ofrecer) to offer (**b**) (una persona a otra) to introduce; **le presento al doctor Ruiz** may I introduce you to Dr Ruiz

2 presentarse vpr (**a**) (comparecer) to present oneself; (inesperadamente) to turn o come up (**b**) (ocasión, oportunidad) to present itself, to arise (**c**) (candidato) to stand; **p. a unas elecciones** to stand for election, US to run for office; **p. a un examen** to sit an examination (**d**) (darse a conocer) to introduce oneself (**a** to)

presente 1 adj present; **la p. (carta)** this letter; **hacer p.** to declare, to state; **tener p.** (tener en cuenta) to bear in mind; (recordar) to remember

2 nm present

presentimiento nm presentiment, premonition; **tengo el p. de que ...** I have the feeling that ...

presentir [5] vt to have a presentiment o premonition of; **presiento que lloverá** I've got the feeling that it's going to rain

preservación nf preservation, protection

preservar vt to preserve, to protect (**de** from; **contra** against)

preservativo nm sheath, condom

presidencia nf (**a**) Pol presidency (**b**) (de una reunión) (hombre) chairmanship; (mujer) chairwomanship

presidenciable nmf Am potential president

presidencial adj presidential

presidente,-a nm,f (**a**) Pol president; **p. del gobierno** Prime Minister, Premier (**b**) (de una reunión) chairperson

presidiario,-a nm,f prisoner, convict

presidio nm prison, penitentiary

presidir vt (**a**) Pol to rule, to head (**b**) (reunión) to chair, to preside over

presión nf pressure; **a** o **bajo p.** under pressure; **grupo de p.** pressure group, lobby; **p. arterial** o **sanguínea** blood pressure; **p. atmosférica** atmospheric pressure

presionar vt to press; Fig to pressurize, to put pressure on

preso,-a 1 adj imprisoned

2 nm,f prisoner

prestación nf (**a**) service (**b**) **prestaciones** (de coche etc) performance

prestado,-a adj **dejar p.** to lend; **pedir p.** to borrow; **vivir de p.** to scrounge

prestamista nmf moneylender

préstamo nm loan

prestar 1 vt (**a**) to lend, to loan; **¿me prestas tu pluma?** can I borrow your pen? (**b**) (atención) to pay; (ayuda) to give; (servicio) to do

2 prestarse vpr (**a**) (ofrecerse) to offer oneself (**a** to) (**b**) **p. a** (dar motivo) to cause; **se presta a (crear) malentendidos** it makes for misunderstandings

presteza nf promptness; **con p.** promptly

prestidigitador,-a nm,f conjuror, magician

prestigiar [43] vt to give prestige to

prestigio nm prestige

prestigioso,-a adj prestigious

presto,-a adj Fml (**a**) (dispuesto) ready, prepared (**b**) (rápido) swift, prompt

presumible adj probable, likely

presumido,-a 1 adj vain, conceited

2 nm,f vain person

presumir 1 vt (suponer) to presume, to suppose

2 *vi* (**a**) (*ser vanidoso*) to show off (**b**) **presume de guapo** he thinks he's good-looking

presunción *nf* (**a**) (*suposición*) presumption, supposition (**b**) (*vanidad*) vanity, conceit

presunto,-a *adj* supposed; *Jur* alleged

presuntuoso,-a *adj* (**a**) (*vanidoso*) vain, conceited (**b**) (*pretencioso*) pretentious, showy

⚠ Observa que la palabra inglesa **presumptuous** es un falso amigo y no es la traducción de la palabra española **presuntuoso**. En inglés, **presumptuous** significa "impertinente".

presuponer [19] (*pp* **presupuesto**) *vt* to presuppose

presupuestar *vt* to budget for; (*importe*) to estimate for

presupuestario,-a *adj* budgetary

presupuesto *nm* (**a**) *Fin* budget; (*cálculo*) estimate (**b**) (*supuesto*) supposition, assumption

presuroso,-a *adj* (*rápido*) quick; (*con prisa*) in a hurry

pretencioso,-a *adj* pretentious

pretender *vt* (**a**) (*intentar*) to try; **¿qué pretendes insinuar?** what are you getting at? (**b**) (*afirmar*) to claim (**c**) (*aspirar a*) to try for (**d**) (*cortejar*) to court, to woo

pretendiente,-a *nm,f* (**a**) (*al trono*) pretender (**b**) (*a un cargo*) applicant, candidate (**c**) (*amante*) suitor

pretensión *nf* (**a**) (*aspiración*) aim, aspiration (**b**) (*presunción*) pretentiousness

pretérito,-a 1 *adj* past, former

2 *nm* Ling preterite, simple past tense

pretextar *vt* to plead, to allege

pretexto *nm* pretext, excuse

pretil *nm* parapet

prevalecer [33] *vi* to prevail

prevaler [26] *vi* = **prevalecer**

prevención *nf* (**a**) (*precaución*) prevention; **en p. de** as a prevention against (**b**) (*medida*) precaution

prevenir [27] *vt* (**a**) (*preparar*) to prepare, to get ready (**b**) (*prever*) to prevent, to forestall; (*evitar*) to avoid; **para p. la gripe** to prevent flu; *Prov* **más vale p. que curar** prevention is better than cure (**c**) (*advertir*) to warn

preventivo,-a *adj* preventive; (*medidas*) precautionary; *Jur* **detención** *o* **prisión preventiva** remand in custody

prever [28] (*pp* **previsto**) *vt* (**a**) (*prevenir*) to foresee, to forecast (**b**) (*preparar de antemano*) to cater for

previo,-a *adj* previous, prior; **p. pago de su importe** only on payment; **sin p. aviso** without prior notice

previsible *adj* predictable

previsión *nf* (**a**) (*predicción*) forecast; **p. del tiempo** weather forecast (**b**) (*precaución*) precaution; **en p. de** as a precaution against

(**c**) *Andes, RP* **p. social** social security

previsor,-a *adj* careful, far-sighted

previsto,-a *adj* foreseen, forecast; **según lo p.** as expected

prieto,-a *adj* (**a**) (*ceñido*) tight; **íbamos muy prietos en el coche** we were really squashed together in the car (**b**) *Méx Fam* (*moreno*) dark-skinned

prima *nf* (**a**) (*gratificación*) bonus; **p. de seguro** insurance premium (**b**) (*persona*) *ver* **primo,-a**

primacía *nf* primacy

primar 1 *vi* to have priority, to prevail

2 *vt* to give a bonus to

primario,-a *adj* primary

primavera *nf* spring

primer *adj* (*delante de nm*) *ver* **primero,-a**

primera *nf* (**a**) (*en tren*) first class (**b**) *Aut* (*marcha*) first gear (**c**) **a la p.** at the first attempt; *Fam* **de p.** great, first-class

primero,-a 1 *adj* first; **a primera hora de la mañana** first thing in the morning; **primera página** *o* **plana** front page; **de primera necesidad** basic

> **Primer** is used instead of **primero** before masculine singular nouns (e.g. **el primer hombre** the first man).

2 *nm,f* first; **a primero(s) de mes** at the beginning of the month

3 *adv* (**a**) first (**b**) (*más bien*) rather, sooner

ver **primera**

primicia *nf* novelty; **p. informativa** scoop; **p. mundial** world premiere

primitivo,-a *adj* (**a**) primitive (**b**) (*tosco*) coarse, rough

primo,-a 1 *nm,f* (**a**) cousin; **p. hermano** first cousin (**b**) *Fam* (*tonto*) fool, drip, dunce

2 *adj* (**a**) **materia prima** raw material (**b**) (*número*) prime

primogénito,-a *adj* & *nm,f* first-born

primor *nm* (**a**) (*delicadeza*) delicacy (**b**) (*belleza*) beauty

primordial *adj* essential, fundamental

primoroso,-a *adj* delicate, exquisite

princesa *nf* princess

principado *nm* principality

principal *adj* main, principal; **lo p. es que …** the main thing is that …; **puerta p.** front door

príncipe *nm* prince

principiante 1 *adj* novice

2 *nmf* beginner, novice

principio *nm* (**a**) beginning, start; **a principio(s) de** at the beginning of; **al p., en un p.** at first, in the beginning (**b**) (*fundamento*) principle; **en p.** in principle (**c**) **principios** rudiments, basics

pringar [42] **1** *vt* (*ensuciar*) to make greasy, dirty

2 *vi Fam* (*trabajar*) to work hard

3 pringarse *upr* (**a**) (*ensuciarse*) to get greasy, dirty (**b**) *Fam* (*meterse de lleno*) to get involved

pringoso,-a adj (grasiento) greasy; (sucio) dirty

pringue nm (grasa) grease

prior,-a nm,f (hombre) prior; (mujer) prioress

priori: a priori loc adv a priori

prioridad nf priority

prioritario,-a adj priority

prisa nf (a) (rapidez) hurry; **date p.** hurry up; **tener p.** to be in a hurry; **de/a p.** in a hurry (b) **correr p.** to be urgent; **me corre mucha p.** I need it right away

prisión nf prison, jail

prisionero,-a nm,f prisoner

prisma nm prism

prismáticos nmpl binoculars, field glasses

priva nf Fam booze

privación nf deprivation

privado,-a adj private

privar 1 vt (despojar) to deprive (**de** of)

  2 vi (a) Fam (gustar) to like; (estar de moda) to be fashionable o popular (b) Fam (beber) to booze

  3 privarse vpr (abstenerse) to deprive oneself (**de** of), to go without

privativo,-a adj exclusive (**de** of)

privilegiado,-a 1 adj privileged

  2 nm,f privileged person

privilegio nm privilege

pro 1 nm advantage; **los pros y los contras** the pros and cons; **en p. de** in favour of

  2 prep in favour of; **campaña p. desarme** campaign for disarmament, disarmament campaign

pro- pref pro-

proa nf prow, bows

probabilidad nf probability, likelihood; **tiene pocas probabilidades** he stands little chance

probable adj probable, likely; **es p. que llueva** it'll probably rain

probador nm fitting room

probar [2] **1** vt (a) (comida, bebida) to try (b) (comprobar) to test, to check (c) (intentar) to try (d) (demostrar) to prove, to show

  2 vi to try; **p. a** to attempt o try to

  3 probarse vpr (ropa) to try on

probeta nf test tube; **niño p.** test-tube baby

problema nm problem

problemático,-a adj problematic

procedencia nf origin, source

procedente adj (a) (originario) coming (**de** from) (b) (adecuado) appropriate; Jur proper

proceder 1 vi (a) **p. de** (provenir) to come from (b) (actuar) to act (c) (ser oportuno) to be advisable o appropriate; Jur **la protesta no procede** objection overruled (d) **p. a** (continuar) to go on to

  2 nm (comportamiento) behaviour

procedimiento nm (a) (método) procedure (b) Jur (trámites) proceedings

procesado,-a 1 nm,f accused

  2 nm Informát processing

procesador nm processor; **p. de textos** word processor

procesamiento nm (a) Jur prosecution (b) Informát **p. de datos/textos** data/word processing

procesar vt (a) Jur to prosecute (b) (elaborar, transformar) to process; Informát to process

procesión nf procession

proceso nm (a) process; Informát **p. de datos** data processing (b) Jur trial

proclamación nf proclamation

proclamar vt to proclaim

proclive adj prone, inclined

procreación nf procreation

procrear vt to procreate

procurador,-a nm,f Jur attorney

procuraduría nf Méx **p. general** Ministry of Justice

procurar vt (a) (intentar) to try, to attempt; **procura que no te vean** make sure they don't see you (b) (proporcionar) (to manage) to get

prodigar [42] Fml **1** vt (dar generosamente) to lavish

  2 prodigarse vpr **p. en** to be lavish in

prodigio nm prodigy, miracle; **hacer prodigios** to work wonders; **niño p.** child prodigy

prodigioso,-a adj (sobrenatural) prodigious; (maravilloso) wonderful, marvellous

pródigo,-a adj generous, lavish; **ella es pródiga en regalos** she's very generous with presents

producción nf (acción) production; (producto) product; Cin production; **p. en cadena/serie** assembly-line/mass production

producir [10] **1** vt (a) to produce; (fruto, cosecha) to yield, to bear; (ganancias) to yield (b) Fig (originar) to cause, to bring about

  2 producirse vpr to take place, to happen

productividad nf productivity

productivo,-a adj productive; (beneficioso) profitable

producto nm product; Agr (producción) produce

productor,-a 1 adj producing

  2 nm,f producer

proeza nf heroic deed, exploit

profanación nf desecration, profanation

profanar vt to desecrate, to profane

profano,-a 1 adj profane, secular

  2 nm,f (hombre) layman; (mujer) laywoman

profecía nf prophecy

proferir [31] vt to utter; **p. insultos** to hurl insults

profesar vt to profess

profesión nf profession; **de p.** by profession

profesional adj & nmf professional

profesionista adj & nmf Méx professional

profeso adj **ex p.** intentionally

profesor,-a nm,f teacher; Univ lecturer

profesorado nm (profesión) teaching; (grupo de profesores) staff

profeta nm prophet
profetizar [40] vt to prophesy, to foretell
profiláctico,-a 1 adj prophylactic
2 nm condom
prófugo,-a 1 adj & nm,f fugitive
2 nm Mil deserter
profundidad nf depth; **un metro de p.** one metre deep o in depth; Fig (de ideas etc) profundity, depth
profundizar [40] vt & vi (cavar) to deepen; Fig (examinar) to study in depth
profundo,-a adj deep; Fig (idea, sentimiento) profound
profusión nf profusion
progenitor,-a nm,f (antepasado) ancestor, progenitor; **progenitores** (padres) parents
programa nm programme; Informát program; Educ syllabus
programación nf Rad & TV programme planning
programador,-a nm,f Informát programmer
programar vt to programme; Informát to program
progre adj & nmf Fam trendy, lefty
progresar vi to progress, to make progress
progresista adj & nmf progressive
progresivo,-a adj progressive
progreso nm progress; **hace grandes progresos** he's making great progress
prohibición nf prohibition, ban
prohibido,-a adj forbidden, prohibited; **prohibida la entrada** (en letrero) no admittance; **p. aparcar/fumar** (en letrero) no parking/smoking
prohibir vt to forbid, to prohibit; **se prohíbe pasar** (en letrero) no admittance o entry
prohibitivo,-a, prohibitorio,-a adj prohibitive
prójimo,-a nm,f one's fellow man, one's neighbour
proletariado nm proletariat
proletario,-a adj & nm,f proletarian
proliferar vi to proliferate
prolífico,-a adj prolific
prolijo,-a adj verbose, long-winded
prólogo nm prologue
prolongación nf prolonging, extension, prolongation
prolongado,-a adj long
prolongar [42] **1** vt (alargar) to prolong, to extend
2 prolongarse vpr (continuar) to carry on
promedio nm average; **como p.** on average
promesa nf promise; Fig **la joven p. de la música** the promising young musician
prometedor,-a adj promising
prometer 1 vt to promise; **te lo prometo** I promise
2 vi to be promising
3 prometerse vpr (pareja) to get engaged
prometido,-a 1 adj promised
2 nm,f (hombre) fiancé; (mujer) fiancée

prominente adj (elevado) protruding, projecting; (importante) prominent
promiscuo,-a adj promiscuous
promoción nf promotion; Educ **p. universitaria** class, year
promocionar vt (cosas) to promote; (personas) to give promotion to
promotor,-a 1 adj promoting
2 nm,f promoter
promover [4] vt (a) (cosas, personas) to promote; (juicio, querella) to initiate (b) (causar) to cause, to give rise to
promulgar [42] vt to promulgate
pronombre nm pronoun
pronosticar [44] vt to predict, to forecast; Med to make a prognosis of
pronóstico nm (del tiempo) forecast; Med prognosis
pronto,-a 1 adj quick, prompt; Fml (dispuesto) prepared
2 nm (impulso) sudden impulse
3 adv (a) (deprisa) quickly, rapidly; **al p.** at first; **de p.** suddenly; **por de** o **lo p.** (para empezar) to start with (b) (temprano) soon, early; **¡hasta p.!** see you soon!
pronunciación nf pronunciation
pronunciamiento nm (a) Mil uprising, insurrection (b) Jur pronouncement
pronunciar [43] **1** vt to pronounce; (discurso) to deliver
2 pronunciarse vpr (a) (opinar) to declare oneself (b) (sublevarse) to rise up
propagación nf propagation, spreading
propagador,-a nm,f propagator
propaganda nf (política) propaganda; (comercial) advertising, publicity
propagar [42] **1** vt to propagate, to spread
2 propagarse vpr to spread
propano nm propane
propasarse vpr to go too far
propensión nf tendency, inclination
propenso,-a adj (a) (inclinado) prone, inclined (b) Med susceptible
propiamente adv **p. dicho** strictly speaking
propiciar [43] vt (a) (causar) to cause (b) Am (patrocinar) to sponsor
propicio,-a adj propitious, suitable; **ser p. a** to be inclined to
propiedad nf (a) (posesión) ownership; (cosa poseída) property (b) (cualidad) property, quality; Fig **con p.** properly, appropriately
propietario,-a nm,f owner
propina nf tip; **dar p. (a algn)** to tip (sb)
propinar vt to give
propio,-a adj (a) (de uno) own; **en su propia casa** in his own house (b) (correcto) suitable, appropriate; **juegos propios para su edad** games suitable for their age (c) (característico) typical, peculiar (d) (mismo) (hombre) himself; (mujer) herself; (animal, cosa) itself; **el p. autor** the author himself (e) **propios,-as** themselves; **los propios inquilinos** the

tenants themselves (**f**) *Ling* proper
proponer [19] (*pp* **propuesto**) **1** *vt* to propose, to suggest
  2 proponerse *vpr* to intend
proporción *nf* (**a**) proportion; **en p. con** in proportion to (**b**) **proporciones** *(tamaño)* size
proporcionado,-a *adj (mesurado)* proportionate, in proportion
proporcional *adj* proportional
proporcionar *vt (dar)* to give, to supply, to provide
proposición *nf* (**a**) *(propuesta)* proposal (**b**) *(oración)* clause
propósito *nm* (**a**) *(intención)* intention (**b**) **a p.** *(por cierto)* by the way; *(adrede)* on purpose, intentionally; **a p. de viajes ...** speaking of travelling ...
propuesta *nf* suggestion, proposal
propuesto,-a *pp de* **proponer**
propugnar *vt* to advocate
propulsar *vt (vehículo)* to drive; *Fig (idea)* to promote
propulsión *nf* propulsion
propulsor,-a *nm,f Fig (persona)* promoter
propuse *pt indef de* **proponer**
prórroga *nf* (**a**) *(prolongación)* extension; *Dep Br* extra time, *US* overtime (**b**) *(aplazamiento)* postponement; *Mil* deferment
prorrogar [42] *vt* (**a**) *(prolongar)* to extend (**b**) *(aplazar)* to postpone; *Mil* to defer
prorrumpir *vi* to burst (**en** into)
prosa *nf* prose
proscrito,-a 1 *adj (persona)* exiled, banished; *(cosa)* banned
  2 *nm,f* exile, outlaw
proseguir [6] *vt & vi* to carry on, to continue
prospección *nf* (**a**) *Min* prospect (**b**) *Com* survey
prospecto *nm* leaflet, prospectus
prosperar *vi (negocio, país)* to prosper, to thrive; *(propuesta)* to be accepted
prosperidad *nf* prosperity
próspero,-a *adj* prosperous, thriving; **¡p. año nuevo!** Happy New Year!
prostíbulo *nm* brothel
prostitución *nf* prostitution
prostituir [37] **1** *vt* to prostitute
  2 prostituirse *vpr* to prostitute oneself
prostituta *nf* prostitute
protagonista *nmf* (**a**) main character, leading role; **¿quién es el p.?** who plays the lead? (**b**) *Fig (centro)* centre of attraction
protagonizar [40] *vt* to play the lead in, to star in
protección *nf* protection
proteccionismo *nm* protectionism
protector,-a 1 *adj* protecting, protective
  2 *nm,f* protector
proteger [53] *vt* to protect, to defend
protegido,-a *nm,f (hombre)* protégé; *(mujer)* protégée
proteína *nf* protein

prótesis *nf inv* prosthesis
protesta *nf* protest; *Jur* objection
protestante *adj & nmf Rel* Protestant
protestar *vi* (**a**) to protest; *Jur* to object (**b**) *Fam (quejarse)* to complain
protestón,-ona *nm,f* moaner, grumbler
protocolo *nm* protocol
protón *nm* proton
prototipo *nm* prototype
protuberancia *nf* protuberance
protuberante *adj* protuberant, bulging
prov. (*abr* **provincia**) prov
provecho *nm* profit, benefit; **¡buen p.!** enjoy your meal!; **sacar p. de algo** to benefit from sth
provechoso,-a *adj* beneficial
proveedor,-a *nm,f* supplier, purveyor; *Informát* **p. de acceso (a Internet)** Internet access provider
proveer [36] (*pp* **provisto**) *vt* to supply, to provide
proveniente *adj (procedente)* coming; *(resultante)* arising, resulting
provenir [27] *vi* **p. de** to come from
proverbio *nm* proverb
providencia *nf* providence
provincia *nf* province
provincial *adj* provincial
provinciano,-a *adj & nm,f Pey* provincial
provisión *nf* provision
provisional, *Am* **provisorio,-a** *adj* provisional
provisto,-a *adj* **p. de** equipped with
provocación *nf* provocation
provocado,-a *adj* provoked, caused; **incendio p.** arson
provocador,-a 1 *nm,f* instigator, agent provocateur
  2 *adj* provocative
provocar [44] *vt* (**a**) *(causar)* to cause; **p. un incendio** to start a fire (**b**) *(instigar)* to provoke (**c**) *Carib, Col, Méx Fam (apetecer)* **¿te provoca ir al cine?** would you like to go to the movies?, *Br* do you fancy going to the cinema?; **¿qué te provoca?** what would you like to do?, *Br* what do you fancy doing?
provocativo,-a *adj* provocative
proxeneta *nmf* procurer, pimp
próximamente *adv (pronto)* soon; *Cin & Teatro (en letrero)* coming soon
proximidad *nf* proximity, closeness; **en las proximidades de** close to, in the vicinity of
próximo,-a *adj* (**a**) *(cercano)* near, close (**b**) *(siguiente)* next
proyección *nf* (**a**) projection (**b**) *Cin* showing
proyectar *vt* (**a**) *(luz)* to project (**b**) *(planear)* to plan (**c**) *Cin* to show
proyectil *nm* projectile
proyecto *nm (plan)* project, plan; **tener algo en p.** to be planning sth; **p. de ley** bill
proyector *nm Cin* projector

prudencia *nf* prudence, discretion; *(moderación)* care

prudente *adj* prudent, sensible; *(conductor)* careful; **a una hora p.** at a reasonable time

prueba *nf* (a) *(de)* proof; **en p. de** as a sign of (b) *(examen etc)* test; **a p.** on trial; **a p. de agua/balas** waterproof/bullet-proof; **haz la p.** try it (c) *Dep* event

pseudo *adj* pseud, pseudo

psicoanálisis *nm inv* psychoanalysis

psicodélico,-a *adj* psychedelic

psicología *nf* psychology

psicológico,-a *adj* psychological

psicólogo,-a *nm,f* psychologist

psicópata *nmf* psychopath

psicosis *nf inv* psychosis

psicotécnico,-a *adj* psychometric

psicoterapeuta 1 *nmf* psychotherapist
2 *adj* psychotherapeutic

psicoterapia *nf* psychotherapy

psicótico,-a *adj & nm,f* psychotic

psique *nf* psyche

psiquiatra *nmf* psychiatrist

psiquiatría *nf* psychiatry

psiquiátrico,-a 1 *adj* psychiatric; **hospital p.** psychiatric hospital
2 *nm* psychiatric hospital

psíquico,-a *adj* psychic

PSOE *nm Pol* (*abr* **Partido Socialista Obrero Español**) = Spanish political party to the centre-left of the political spectrum

pta(s). (*abr* **peseta(s)**) peseta(s)

púa *nf* (a) *(de planta)* thorn; *(de animal)* quill, spine; *(de peine)* tooth; **alambre de púas** barbed wire (b) *Mús* plectrum

pub *nm* (*pl* **pubs, pubes**) pub

pubertad *nf* puberty

publicación *nf* publication

publicar [44] *vt* (a) *(libro etc)* to publish (b) *(secreto)* to publicize

publicidad *nf* (a) *Com* advertising (b) *(conocimiento público)* publicity

publicitario,-a *adj* advertising

público,-a 1 *adj* public
2 *nm* public; *Teatro* audience; *Dep* spectators

pucha *interj Andes, RP Fam Euf* (a) *(lamento)* Br sugar!, US shoot!; **¡p. digo, ya son las doce!** oh, Br sugar o US shoot! it's twelve o'clock already! (b) *(sorpresa)* wow!; **¿cincuenta años? ¡la p.!** fifty years old? get away! o never! (c) *(enojo)* Br sugar!, US shoot!; **¡la p.!, perdí las llaves** Br sugar o US shoot! I've lost my keys!

pucherazo *nm* rigging of an election

puchero *nm* (a) *(olla)* cooking pot; *(cocido)* stew (b) **hacer pucheros** to pout

pucho *nm CSur* dog-end

pude *pt indef de* **poder**

pudendo,-a *adj* **partes pudendas** private parts

púdico,-a *adj* modest

pudiente *adj* rich, wealthy

pudor *nm* modesty

pudoroso,-a *adj* modest

pudrir *vt* defect, **pudrirse** *vpr* to rot, to decay

pueblerino,-a *adj Pey (provinciano)* countrified, provincial

pueblo *nm* (a) *(población)* *(pequeña)* village; *(grande)* town (b) *(gente)* people; **el p. español** the Spanish people

puente *nm* (a) *(de río)* bridge; *Av* **p. aéreo** *(civil)* air shuttle service; *Mil* airlift; **p. colgante** suspension bridge; **p. levadizo** drawbridge (b) *(entre dos fiestas)* ≃ long weekend

puerco,-a 1 *adj* filthy
2 *nm,f* pig
3 *nm* **p. espín** porcupine

puericultura *nf* paediatrics *sing*

pueril *adj* childish, puerile

puerro *nm* leek

puerta *nf* door; *(verja, en aeropuerto)* gate; *Dep* goal; **p. corredera/giratoria** sliding/revolving door; *Fig* **a las puertas, en puertas** imminent; *Fig* **a p. cerrada** behind closed doors

puerto *nm* (a) *(de mar)* port, harbour; **p. deportivo** marina (b) *(de montaña)* (mountain) pass

Puerto Rico *n* Puerto Rico

puertorriqueño,-a *adj & nm,f* Puerto Rican

pues *conj* (a) *(puesto que)* as, since (b) *(por lo tanto)* therefore (c) *(entonces)* then (d) *(para reforzar)* **¡p. claro que sí!** but of course!; **p. como iba diciendo** well, as I was saying; **¡p. mejor!** so much the better!; **¡p. no!** certainly not! (e) *(como pregunta)* **¿p.?** why?

puesta *nf* (a) **p. de sol** sunset (b) *Fig* **p. a punto** tuning, adjusting; *Fig* **p. al día** updating; *Teatro* **p. en escena** staging; **p. en marcha** starting-up, start-up; *ver* **puesto,-a**

puestero,-a *nm,f Am* stallholder

puesto,-a 1 *conj* **p. que** since, as
2 *nm* (a) *(lugar)* place; *(asiento)* seat (b) *(empleo)* position, post, job; **p. de trabajo** job, post (c) *(tienda)* stall (d) *Mil* post
3 *adj* (a) *(colocado)* set, put (b) **llevar p.** *(ropa)* to have on; *Fam* **ir muy p.** to be all dressed up (c) *Fam (borracho)* drunk (d) *Fam* **estar p. en una materia** to be well up in a subject

púgil *nm* boxer

pugilato *nm* boxing

pugna *nf* battle, fight

pugnar *vi* to fight, to struggle (**por** for)

puja *nf (acción)* bidding; *(cantidad)* bid

pujante *adj* thriving, prosperous

pujanza *nf* strength, vigour

pujar *vi* (a) *(pugnar)* to struggle (b) *(en una subasta)* to bid higher

pulcro,-a *adj (extremely)* neat

pulga *nf* flea; *Fam* **tener malas pulgas** to be nasty, to have a nasty streak

pulgada *nf* inch

pulgar *nm* thumb

pulimentar *vt* to polish

pulir *vt* (a) *(metal, madera)* to polish (b) *(mejorar)* to polish up

pulla *nf* dig

pulmón *nm* lung

pulmonía *nf* pneumonia

pulóver *nm* pullover

pulpa *nf* pulp

pulpería *nf Am* store

púlpito *nm* pulpit

pulpo *nm* octopus

pulque *nm CAm, Méx* pulque, = fermented maguey juice

pulquería *nf CAm, Méx* "pulque" bar

pulsación *nf* pulsation; *(en mecanografía)* stroke, tap; **pulsaciones por minuto** $\simeq$ keystrokes per minute

pulsar *vt (timbre, botón)* to press; *(tecla)* to hit, to strike

pulsera *nf (aro)* bracelet; *(de reloj)* watchstrap; **reloj de p.** wristwatch

pulso *nm* (a) pulse; *Fig* **tomar el p. a la opinión pública** to sound out opinion (b) *(mano firme)* steady hand; **a p.** freehand; **ganarse algo a p.** to deserve sth (c) *Fig* trial of strength; **echarse un p.** to arm-wrestle

pulverizador *nm* spray, atomizer

pulverizar [40] *vt (sólidos)* to pulverize; *(líquidos)* to spray; *(un récord)* to smash

puma *nm* puma

puna *nf Andes* (a) high moor (b) *(mal)* mountain *o* altitude sickness

pundonor *nm* self-respect, self-esteem

punta *nf* (a) *(extremo)* tip; *(extremo afilado)* point; *(de cabello)* end; **sacar p. a un lápiz** to sharpen a pencil; **tecnología p.** state-of-the-art technology; **me pone los nervios de p.** he makes me very nervous (b) *(periodo)* peak; **hora p.** rush hour (c) *(pequeña cantidad)* bit; **una p. de sal** a pinch of salt (d) *(clavo)* nail

puntada *nf Am (dolor)* stabbing pain

puntaje *nm Am (calificación)* Br mark, US grade; *(en concursos, competiciones)* score

puntal *nm* prop; *(travesaño)* beam; *Fig (soporte)* pillar, support

puntapié *nm* kick

puntear *vt* (a) *(dibujar)* to dot (b) *Mús (guitarra)* to pluck

punteo *nm* plucking

puntería *nf* aim; **tener buena/mala p.** to be a good/bad shot

puntero,-a 1 *adj* leading

  2 *nm,f CSur Dep* back

puntiagudo,-a *adj* pointed, sharp

puntilla *nf* (a) *(encaje)* lace (b) **dar la p.** *Taurom* to finish (the bull) off; *Fig (liquidar)* to finish off (c) **de puntillas** on tiptoe

puntilloso,-a *adj* touchy

punto *nm* (a) point; **a p.** ready; *Culin* **en su p.** just right; **a p. de** on the point of; **hasta cierto p.** to a certain *o* some extent; **p. muerto** *Aut* neutral; *Fig (impase)* deadlock; **p. de vista** point of view (b) *(marca)* dot; **línea de puntos** dotted line (c) *(lugar)* place, point (d) **p. y seguido** full stop; **p. y coma** semicolon; **dos puntos** colon; **p. y aparte** full stop, new paragraph (e) *(tiempo)* **en p.** sharp, on the dot (f) *Dep (tanto)* point (g) *Cost & Med* stitch; **hacer p.** to knit

puntuable *adj Dep* **una prueba p. para** a race counting towards

puntuación *nf* (a) *Ling* punctuation (b) *Dep* score (c) *Educ* mark

puntual 1 *adj* (a) punctual (b) *(exacto)* accurate, precise (c) *(caso)* specific

  2 *adv* punctually

puntualidad *nf* punctuality

puntualizar [40] *vt* to specify, to clarify

puntuar [30] **1** *vt* (a) *(al escribir)* to punctuate (b) *Educ (calificar)* to mark

  2 *vi Dep* (a) *(marcar)* to score (b) *(ser puntuable)* to count

punzada *nf (de dolor)* sudden sharp pain

punzante *adj (objeto)* sharp; *(dolor)* acute, piercing

punzar [40] *vt Téc* to punch

puñado *nm* handful; *Fam* **a puñados** by the score, galore

puñal *nm* dagger

puñalada *nf* stab; *Fig* **p. trapera** stab in the back

puñeta *nf Fam* **hacer la p. a algn** to pester sb, to annoy sb; **¡puñetas!** damn!; **¡vete a hacer puñetas!** go to hell!

puñetazo *nm* punch

puño *nm* (a) fist (b) *(de camisa etc)* cuff (c) *(de herramienta)* handle

pupa *nf* (a) *(herida)* cold sore (b) *Fam (daño)* pain

pupila *nf (de ojo)* pupil

pupilo,-a *nm,f* pupil

pupitre *nm* desk

purasangre *adj & nm* thoroughbred

puré *nm* purée; **p. de patata** mashed potatoes; **p. de verduras** thick vegetable soup

pureta *nmf* old fogey

pureza *nf* (a) purity (b) *(castidad)* chastity

purga *nf Med* purgative; *Fig* purge

purgante *adj & nm* purgative

purgar [42] *vt Med & Fig* to purge

purgatorio *nm* purgatory

purificación *nf* purification

purificar [44] *vt* to purify

purista *nmf* purist

puritano,-a 1 *adj* puritanical

  2 *nm,f* puritan, Puritan

puro,-a 1 *adj* (a) *(sin mezclas)* pure; **aire p.** fresh air; **la pura verdad** the plain truth; *Pol* **p. y duro** hardline (b) *(mero)* sheer, mere; **por pura curiosidad** out of sheer curiosity (c) *(casto)* chaste, pure

  2 *nm (cigarro)* cigar

púrpura *adj inv* purple

purpúreo,-a *adj* purple

pus *nm* pus

puse *pt indef de* **poner**

pusilánime *adj* faint-hearted

pústula *nf* sore, pustule

puta *nf Vulg* whore; **de p. madre** great, terrific; **de p. pena** *Br* bloody *o US* goddamn awful; **no tengo ni p. idea** I haven't (got) a *Br* bloody *o US* goddamn clue; **pasarlas putas** to go through hell, to have a rotten time

putada *nf Vulg* dirty trick

puteada *nf RP muy Fam (insulto)* swearword

putear *vt* (**a**) *Vulg (fastidiar)* to fuck *o* piss around (**b**) *RP muy Fam (insultar)* **p. a algn** to call sb for everything, to call sb every name under the sun

puticlub *nm Fam* brothel

puto,-a 1 *adj Vulg* fucking
2 *nm* male prostitute, stud

putrefacto,-a, pútrido,-a *adj* putrefied, rotten

puzzle *nm* jigsaw puzzle

PVC *nm* (*abr* **cloruro de polivinilo**) PVC

PVP *nm* (*abr* **precio de venta al público**) RRP

PYME *nf* (*abr* **Pequeña y Mediana Empresa**) SME

Pza. (*abr* **Plaza**) Sq

Q, q [ku] *nf (la letra)* Q, q

que¹ *pron rel* (a) *(sujeto) (persona)* who; *(cosa)* that, which; **el hombre q. vino** the man who came; **la bomba q. estalló** the bomb that *o* which went off (b) *(complemento) (persona)* no se traduce *o* that *o* who *o Fml* whom; *(cosa)* no se traduce *o* that *o* which; **la chica q. conocí** the girl (that *o* who *o* whom) I met; **el coche q. compré** the car (that *o* which) I bought (c) **lo q.** what; **lo q. más me gusta** what I like best (d) *(con infinitivo) no se traduce*; **hay mucho q. hacer** there's a lot to do

que² *conj* (a) *no se traduce o* that; **dijo q. llamaría** he said (that) he would call; **quiero q. vengas** I want you to come

(b) *(consecutivo) no se traduce o* that; *(en comparativas)* than; **habla tan bajo q. no se le oye** he speaks so quietly (that) he can't be heard; **más alto q. yo** taller than me

(c) *(causal) no se traduce* date deprisa **q. no tenemos mucho tiempo** hurry up, we haven't got much time

(d) *(enfático) no se traduce* ¡q. no! no!; ¡q. te calles! I said be quiet!

(e) *(deseo, mandato)* (+ *subjunctive) no se traduce*; ¡q. te diviertas! enjoy yourself!

(f) *(final)* so that; **ven q. te dé un beso** come and let me give you a kiss

(g) *(disyuntivo)* whether; **me da igual q. suba o no** it doesn't matter to me whether he comes up or not

(h) *(locuciones)* ¿a **q. no ...?** I bet you can't ...!; **q. yo sepa** as far as I know; **yo q. tú** if I were you

qué 1 *pron interr* (a) what; ¿**q. quieres?** what do you want?; *Fam* ¿**y q.?** so what? (b) *(exclamativo)* (+ *adj)* how; ¡**q. bonito!** how pretty! (c) (+ *n)* what a; ¡**q. lástima!** what a pity! (d) *Fam* ¡**q. de ...!** what a lot of ...!

2 *adj interr* which; ¿**q. libro quieres?** which book do you want?

quebrada *nf Am* stream

quebradero *nm Fig* **q. de cabeza** headache

quebradizo,-a *adj (débil)* fragile; *(cabello, hielo)* brittle

quebrado *nm Mat* fraction

quebradura *nf* (a) *(grieta)* crack (b) *Med* hernia, rupture

quebrantamiento *nm (de una ley)* violation, infringement

quebrantar 1 *vt (promesa, ley)* to break
2 quebrantarse *vpr* to break down

quebrar [1] **1** *vt (romper)* to break
2 *vi Fin* to go bankrupt
3 quebrarse *vpr* to break; *Med* to rupture oneself

queda *nf* **toque de q.** curfew

quedar 1 *vi* (a) *(restar)* to be left, to remain; **quedan dos** there are two left

(b) *(en un lugar)* to arrange to meet; **quedamos en el bar** I'll meet you in the bar

(c) **me queda corta** *(ropa)* it is too short for me; **quedaría muy bien allí** *(objeto)* it would look very nice there

(d) *(acordar)* to agree (**en** to); ¿**en qué quedamos?** so what's it to be?

(e) *(estar situado)* to be; ¿**dónde queda la estación?** where's the station?

(f) *(terminar)* to end; ¿**en qué quedó la película?** how did the film end?

(g) *(locuciones)* **q. en ridículo** to make a fool of oneself; **q. bien/mal** to make a good/bad impression

2 quedarse *vpr* (a) *(permanecer)* to stay; **se quedó en casa** she stayed (at) home; **q. sin dinero/pan** to run out of money/bread; **q. con hambre** to still be hungry

(b) **q. (con)** *(retener)* to keep; **quédese (con) el cambio** keep the change

(c) *Fam* **q. con algn** to make a fool of sb

quedo *adv* softly, quietly

quehacer *nm* task, chore

queja *nf* complaint; *(de dolor)* groan, moan

quejarse *vpr* to complain (**de** about)

quejica *Fam* **1** *adj* grumpy
2 *nmf* moaner

quejido *nm* groan, cry

quemado,-a *adj* (a) burnt, burned; *(del sol)* sunburnt (b) *Fig (agotado)* burnt-out

quemador *nm (de cocina etc)* burner

quemadura *nf* burn

quemar 1 *vt* to burn; *Fig (agotar)* to burn out
2 *vi* to be burning hot; **este café quema** this coffee's boiling hot
3 quemarse *vpr Fig* to burn oneself out

quemarropa: a quemarropa *loc adv* point-blank

quemazón *nf* smarting

quena *nf* Andean flute

quepo *indic pres de* **caber**

queque *nm Andes, CAm, Méx* sponge (cake)

querella *nf Jur* lawsuit

querer [20] **1** *vt* (a) *(amar)* to love (b) *(desear)* to want; ¿**cuánto quiere por la casa?** how much does he want for the house?; **sin q.** without meaning to; **queriendo** on purpose; **¡por lo que más quieras!** for heaven's sake!; **¿quiere pasarme el pan?** would you pass me the bread? (**c**) **q. decir** to mean (**d**) **no quiso darme permiso** he refused me permission

2 quererse *vpr* to love each other

3 *nm* love, affection

querido,-a 1 *adj* dear, beloved; **q. amigo** *(en carta)* dear friend

2 *nm,f (amante)* lover; *(mujer)* mistress

queroseno *nm* kerosene, kerosine

querré *indic fut de* **querer**

quesadilla *nf CAm, Méx* = filled fried tortilla

queso *nm* cheese; **q. rallado** grated cheese; **q. de cerdo** *Br* brawn, *US* headcheese

quetzal *nm (moneda)* = standard monetary unit of Guatemala

quiché *adj & nm* Quiché

quicio *nm* (**a**) *(de puerta)* doorpost (**b**) *Fig* **fuera de q.** beside oneself; **sacar de q.** *(a algn)* to infuriate; *(algo)* to take too far

quid *nm* crux; **has dado en el q.** you've hit the nail on the head

quiebra *nf Fin (bancarrota)* bankruptcy; *(crack)* crash

quiebro *nm (con el cuerpo)* dodge; *Ftb* dribbling

quien *pron rel* (**a**) *(con prep)* no se traduce o *Fml* whom; **el hombre con q. vino** the man she came with; *Fml* the man with whom she came (**b**) *(indefinido)* whoever, anyone who; **q. quiera venir que venga** whoever wants to can come; **hay q. dice lo contrario** some people say the opposite; *Fig* **q. más q. menos** everybody

quién *pron interr* (**a**) *(sujeto)* who?; **¿q. es?** who is it? (**b**) *(complemento)* who, *Fml* whom; **¿para q. es?** who is it for?; **¿de q. es esa bici?** whose bike is that?

quienquiera *pron indef (pl* **quienesquiera)** whoever

quieto,-a *adj* still; *(mar)* calm; **¡estáte q.!** keep still!, don't move!

quietud *nf* stillness; *(calma)* calm

quijada *nf* jawbone

quilate *nm* carat

quilla *nf* keel

quillango *nm Arg, Chile* hide blanket

quilo *nm* = kilo

quilombo *nm RP muy Fam* (**a**) *(burdel)* whorehouse (**b**) *(lío, desorden)* god-awful ruckus o rumpus

quimera *nf Fig* fantasy, pipe dream

química *nf* chemistry

químico,-a 1 *adj* chemical

2 *nm,f* chemist

quimioterapia *nf* chemotherapy

quimono *nm* kimono

quincalla *nf* metal pots and pans, tinware

quince *adj & nm inv* fifteen

quinceañero,-a *adj & nm,f* fifteen-year-old

quincena *nf* fortnight, two weeks

quincenal *adj* fortnightly

quincho *nm CSur* (**a**) *(techo)* thatched roof (**b**) *(refugio)* thatched shelter

quiniela *nf* football pools

quinientos,-as *adj & nm* five hundred

quinina *nf* quinine

quinqué *nm* oil lamp

quinquenal *adj* quinquennial, five-year

quinqui *nm Fam* delinquent, petty criminal

quinta *nf* (**a**) *(casa)* country house (**b**) *Mil* call-up year

quintaesencia *nf* quintessence

quintal *nm (medida)* = 46 kg; **q. métrico** ≃ 100 kg

quinteto *nm* quintet

quinto,-a 1 *adj & nm,f* fifth

2 *nm Mil* conscript, recruit

quiosco *nm* kiosk; **q. de periódicos** newspaper stand

quirófano *nm* operating theatre

quiromancia *nf* palmistry

quirúrgico,-a *adj* surgical

quise *indic fut de* **querer**

quisque, quisqui *pron Fam* **todo** o **cada q.** everyone, everybody

quisquilloso,-a 1 *adj* fussy, finicky

2 *nm,f* fusspot

quiste *nm* cyst

quitaesmalte(s) *nm inv* nail varnish o polish remover

quitamanchas *nm inv* stain remover

quitanieves *nm (máquina)* **q.** snowplough

quitar 1 *vt* (**a**) to remove; *(ropa)* to take off; *(la mesa)* to clear; *(mancha)* to remove; *(dolor)* to relieve; *(hipo)* to stop; *(sed)* to quench; *(hambre)* to take away

(**b**) *(apartar)* to take away, to take off; *Fig* **q. importancia a algo** to play sth down; *Fig* **q. las ganas a algn** to put sb off

(**c**) *(robar)* to steal, to take; *Fig (tiempo)* to take up; *(sitio)* to take

(**d**) *(descontar)* to take off

(**e**) *Fam (apagar)* to turn off

(**f**) **eso no quita para que ...** that's no reason not to be ...

(**g**) **¡quita!** go away!

2 quitarse *vpr* (**a**) *(apartarse)* to move away

(**b**) *(mancha)* to come out; *(dolor)* to go away; **se me han quitado las ganas** I don't feel like it any more

(**c**) *(ropa, gafas)* to take off

(**d**) **q. de beber/fumar** to give up drinking/smoking

(**e**) **q. a algn de encima** to get rid of sb

> Observa que el verbo inglés **to quit** es un falso amigo y no es la traducción del verbo español **quitar**. En inglés, **to quit** significa "dejar, abandonar".

quizá(s) *adv* perhaps, maybe

r ['erre] *nf (la letra)* R, r

ábano *nm* radish; *Fam* **me importa un r.** I couldn't care less

abia *nf* (**a**) *Fig (ira)* fury, rage; **¡qué r.!** how annoying!; **me da r.** it gets up my nose; **me tiene r.** he's got it in for me (**b**) *Med* rabies *sing*

abiar [43] *vi* (**a**) *Fig (sufrir)* to be in great pain (**b**) *Fig (enfadar)* to rage; **hacer r. a algn** to make sb see red (**c**) *Med* to have rabies

abieta *nf Fam* tantrum; **coger una r.** to throw a tantrum

abillo *nm (del ojo)* corner

abino *nm* rabbi

abioso,-a *adj* (**a**) *Med* rabid; **perro r.** rabid dog (**b**) *Fig (enfadado)* furious (**c**) **de rabiosa actualidad** up-to-the-minute

acanear *vi Fam (ser tacaño)* to be stingy

ácano,-a *adj Fam (tacaño)* stingy, mean

acha *nf (de viento)* gust, squall; *Fam (período)* spell, patch; **a rachas** in fits and starts

acial *adj* **discriminación r.** racial discrimination; **disturbios raciales** race riots

acimo *nm* bunch, cluster

aciocinio *nm* reason

ación *nf* portion

acional *adj* rational

acionalizar [40] *vt* to rationalize

acionamiento *nm* rationing; **cartilla de r.** ration book

acionar *vt (limitar)* to ration; *(repartir)* to ration out

acismo *nm* racism

acista *adj & nmf* racist

adar *nm (pl* **radares**) *Téc* radar

adiación *nf* radiation

adiactividad *nf* radioactivity

adiactivo,-a *adj* radioactive

adiador *nm* radiator

adial *adj* (**a**) *(en forma de estrella)* radial (**b**) *Am (de la radio)* radio

adiante *adj* radiant (**de** with)

adiar [43] *vt* to broadcast, to transmit

adical *adj* radical

adicalizar [40] *vt,* **radicalizarse** *vpr (conflicto)* to intensify; *(postura)* to harden

adicar [44] *vi (estar)* to be (situated) (**en** in), to be rooted (**en** in)

adio 1 *nf* radio; *(aparato)* radio (set)

2 *nm* (**a**) radius; **r. de acción** field of action, scope (**b**) *(de rueda)* spoke

adioactividad *nf* radioactivity

radioactivo,-a *adj* radioactive

radioaficionado,-a *nm,f* radio ham

radiocasete *nm (pl* **radiocasetes**) radio cassette

radioescucha *nmf* listener

radiograbador *nm,* **radiograbadora** *nf CSur* radio cassette

radiografía *nf (imagen)* X-ray

radioyente *nmf* listener

ráfaga *nf (de viento)* gust, squall; *(de disparos)* burst

raído,-a *adj* (**a**) *(gastado)* worn (**b**) *Fam (desvergonzado)* insolent

raigambre *nf* roots

raíl *nm* rail

raíz *nf (pl* **raíces**) root; **r. cuadrada** square root; *Fig* **a r. de** as a result of

raja *nf (corte)* cut, slit; *(hendidura)* crack, split

rajar 1 *vt (hender)* to crack, to split; *Fam (acuchillar)* to cut up

2 *vi Fam* to backbite

3 rajarse *vpr* (**a**) *(partirse)* to crack, to split (**b**) *Fam (echarse atrás)* to back out (**c**) *Am (acobardarse)* to chicken out

rajatabla: a rajatabla *loc adv* strictly

ralea *nf Pey* type, sort

ralentí *nm* neutral; **estar al r.** to be ticking over

ralentizar *vt* to slow down

rallado,-a *adj* **queso r.** grated cheese; **pan r.** breadcrumbs

rallador *nm* grater

ralladura *nf* gratings

rallar *vt* to grate

ralo,-a *adj* sparse, thin

rama *nf* branch; *Fam* **andarse *o* irse por las ramas** to beat about the bush

ramaje *nm* branches

ramalazo *nm Fam (toque)* touch

rambla *nf (avenida)* boulevard, avenue

ramera *nf* prostitute, whore

ramificación *nf* ramification

ramificarse [44] *vpr* to ramify, to branch (out)

ramillete *nm (de flores)* posy

ramo *nm* (**a**) *(de flores)* bunch, bouquet (**b**) *(sector)* branch

rampa *nf* ramp; **r. de lanzamiento** launch pad

ramplón,-ona *adj* coarse, vulgar

rana *nf* frog; *Fam* **salir r.** to be a disappointment

ranchero,-a *nm,f (granjero)* rancher, farmer

rancho *nm* (**a**) *(granja)* ranch (**b**) *Mil (comida)* mess (**c**) *RP (en la playa)* = thatched beachside building (**d**) *CSur, Ven (en la ciudad)* shack, shanty

rancio,-a *adj* (**a**) *(comida)* stale (**b**) *(antiguo)* ancient

rango *nm* rank; *(jerarquía elevada)* high social standing

ranura *nf* slot

rapar *vt (afeitar)* to shave; *(pelo)* to crop

rapaz¹ *adj* predatory; **ave de r.** bird of prey

rapaz²,-aza *nm,f* youngster; *(muchacho)* lad; *(muchacha)* lass

rape *nm* (**a**) *(pez)* angler fish (**b**) *Fam* **cortado al r.** close-cropped

rapidez *nf* speed, rapidity

rápido,-a 1 *adj* quick, fast, rapid
  2 *adv* quickly
  3 *nm* (**a**) *(tren)* fast train (**b**) **rápidos** *(de un río)* rapids

rapiña *nf* robbery, theft; **ave de r.** bird of prey

raptar *vt* to kidnap, to abduct

rapto *nm* (**a**) *(secuestro)* kidnapping, abduction (**b**) *Fig (arrebato)* outburst, fit

raqueta *nf* (**a**) *(de tenis)* racket; *(de pingpong)* Br bat, US paddle (**b**) *(de nieve)* snowshoe

raquítico,-a *adj Fam (escaso)* small, meagre; *(delgado)* emaciated

raquitismo *nm* rickets *sing*

rareza *nf* (**a**) rarity, rareness (**b**) *(extravagancia)* eccentricity

raro,-a *adj* (**a**) rare; **rara vez** seldom (**b**) *(extraño)* odd, strange

ras *nm* level; **a r. de** (on a) level with; **a r. de tierra** at ground level

rasante *1 nf Aut* **cambio de r.** brow of a hill
  2 *adj (vuelo)* low

rasar *vt (nivelar)* to level

rasca *nf Fam (frío)* cold

rascacielos *nm inv* skyscraper

rascar [44] **1** *vt (con las uñas)* to scratch; *(guitarra)* to strum
  2 *vi* to chafe

rasero *nm Fig* **medir con el mismo r.** to treat impartially

rasgado,-a *adj (ojos)* slit, almond-shaped

rasgar [42] *vt* to tear, to rip

rasgo *nm (característica)* characteristic, feature; *(de la cara)* feature; *Fig* **a grandes rasgos** broadly speaking

rasgón *nm* tear, rip

rasguñar *vt* to scratch, to scrape

rasguño *nm* scratch, scrape

rasilla *nf (ladrillo)* tile

raso,-a 1 *adj (llano)* flat, level; *(vuelo)* low; *(cielo)* clear, cloudless; **soldado r.** private
  2 *nm* satin

raspa *nf (de pescado)* bone, backbone

raspador *nm* scraper

raspadura *nf (ralladura)* scraping, scrapings

raspar 1 *vt (limar)* to scrape (off)

2 *vi (ropa etc)* to chafe

rasposo,-a *adj* rough, sharp

rastra *nf Agr* harrow; **a la r., a rastras** dragging; *Fig (de mal grado)* grudgingly

rastreador *nm* tracker

rastrear *vt (zona)* to comb

rastreo *nm* search

rastrero,-a *adj* creeping; *Fig (despreciable)* vile, base

rastrillo *nm* (**a**) rake (**b**) *Fam (mercadillo)* flea market

rastro *nm* (**a**) trace, sign; *(en el suelo)* track, trail (**b**) **el R.** = the Madrid flea market

rastrojo *nm* stubble

rasurar *vt*, **rasurarse** *vpr* to shave

rata 1 *nf* rat
  2 *nm Fam (tacaño)* mean o stingy person

ratero,-a *nm,f* pickpocket

raticida *nm* rat poison

ratificar [44] *vt* to ratify

rato *nm* (**a**) *(momento)* while, time; **a ratos** a times; **al poco r.** shortly after; **hay para r.** it'l take a while; **pasar un buen/mal r.** to have a good/bad time; **ratos libres** free time (**b**) *Fam* **un r. (mucho)** very, a lot

ratón *nm* mouse; *Informát* mouse

ratonera *nf* mousetrap

raudal *nm* torrent, flood; *Fig* **a raudales** in abundance

raya *nf* (**a**) *(línea)* line; *(del pantalón)* crease *(del pelo)* parting; **camisa a rayas** striped shir (**b**) *Fig* **tener a r.** to keep at bay; **pasarse de la r.** to go over the score (**c**) *(de droga)* fix, dose

rayano,-a *adj* bordering (**en** on)

rayar 1 *vt (arañar)* to scratch
  2 *vi* **r. en** o **con** to border on

rayo *nm* (**a**) ray, beam; **rayos X** X-rays (**b** *(relámpago)* (flash of) lightning; **¡mal r. l parta!** to hell with her!

rayón *nm* rayon

rayuela *nf* hopscotch

raza *nf* (**a**) *(humana)* race (**b**) *(de animal* breed (**c**) *Perú (descaro)* cheek, nerve

razón *nf* (**a**) *(facultad)* reason; **uso de r** power of reasoning (**b**) *(motivo)* reason; **r de más para** all the more reason to (**c**) *(justi cia)* rightness, justice; **dar la r. a algn** to say that sb is right; **tienes r.** you're right (**d** *(proporción)* ratio, rate; **a r. de** at the rate o (**e**) **r. aquí** *(en letrero)* enquire within, appl within

razonable *adj* reasonable

razonado,-a *adj* reasoned, well-reasoned

razonamiento *nm* reasoning

razonar 1 *vt (argumentar)* to reason out
  2 *vi (discurrir)* to reason

RDA *nf Hist (abr* **República Democrática Ale mana** o **de Alemania**) GDR

re- *pref* re-

reacción *nf* reaction; **avión de r.** jet (plane); **en cadena** chain reaction

reaccionar *vi* to react

reaccionario,-a *adj & nm,f* reactionary

reacio,-a *adj* reluctant, unwilling

reactor *nm* reactor; *(avión)* jet (plane)

readaptación *nf* rehabilitation; **r. profesional** industrial retraining

reafirmar *vt* to reaffirm, to reassert

reagrupar *vt*, **reagruparse** *upr* to regroup

reajuste *nm* readjustment; *Com* **r. de plantillas** downsizing; **r. ministerial** cabinet reshuffle

real¹ *adj (efectivo, verdadero)* real; **en la vida r.** in real life

real² *adj (regio)* royal

realce *nm (relieve)* relief; *Fig (esplendor)* splendour

realeza *nf* royalty

realidad *nf* reality; **en r.** in fact, actually; **la r. es que ...** the fact of the matter is that ...

realismo *nm* realism

realista 1 *adj* realistic
2 *nmf* realist

realizable *adj* feasible

realización *nf (ejecución)* carrying out; *Cin & TV* production

realizador,-a *nm,f Cin & TV* producer

realizar [40] **1** *vt* **a** *(hacer)* to carry out; *(ambición)* to achieve, to fulfil **b** *Cin & TV* to produce **c** *Fin* to realize
2 realizarse *upr (persona)* to fulfil oneself; *(sueño)* to come true

realmente *adv* really; *(en realidad)* actually, in fact

realzar [40] *vt (recalcar)* to highlight; *Fig (belleza, importancia)* to enhance, to heighten

reanimación *nf* revival

reanimar *vt*, **reanimarse** *upr* to revive

reanudación *nf* renewal, resumption, reestablishment; **r. de las clases** return to school

reanudar 1 *vt* to renew, to resume; **r. el paso** *o* **la marcha** to set off again; **r. las clases** to go back to school
2 reanudarse *upr* to start again, to resume

reaparición *nf* reappearance, recurrence; *(de artista etc)* comeback

reapertura *nf* reopening

rearme *nm* rearmament

reaseguro *nm* reinsurance

reavivar *vt* to revive

rebaja *nf (descuento)* reduction, discount; **rebajas** sales; **precio de r.** sale price

rebajar 1 *vt* **a** *(precio)* to cut, to reduce; *(cantidad)* to take off **b** *(color)* to tone down, to soften; *(intensidad)* to diminish **c** *(trabajador)* to excuse, to exempt **(de** from) **d** *(humillar)* to humiliate
2 rebajarse *upr (humillarse)* to humble oneself

rebanada *nf* slice

rebanar *vt* to slice, to cut into slices

rebañar *vt (plato etc)* to finish off

rebaño *nm (de ovejas)* flock; *(de otros animales)* herd

rebasar *vt* **a** *(exceder)* to exceed, to go beyond **b** *Aut* to overtake

rebatir *vt* to refute

🔎 Observa que la palabra inglesa **rebate** es un falso amigo y no es la traducción del verbo español **rebatir**. En inglés, **rebate** significa "devolución".

rebeca *nf* cardigan

rebelarse *upr* to rebel, to revolt

rebelde 1 *nmf* rebel
2 *adj* rebellious; *Fig* **una tos r.** a persistent cough

rebeldía *nf* **a** rebelliousness **b** *Jur* default

rebelión *nf* rebellion, revolt

rebenque *nm RP* whip

reblandecer [33] *vt* to soften

rebobinar *vt* to rewind

rebosante *adj* overflowing **(de** with), brimming **(de** with)

rebosar 1 *vi* to overflow, to brim over; *Fig* **r. de** to be overflowing *o* brimming with
2 *vt (irradiar)* to radiate

rebotar *vi (pelota)* to bounce, to rebound; *(bala)* to ricochet

rebote *nm (de pelota)* bounce, rebound; *(de bala)* ricochet; **de r.** on the rebound

rebozar [40] *vt* to coat in breadcrumbs/batter

rebozo *nm Am* wrap, shawl

rebullir *vi*, **rebullirse** *upr* to stir

rebuscado,-a *adj* recherché

rebuznar *vi* to bray

recabar *vt (información)* to obtain, to manage to get

recado *nm (mandado)* errand; *(mensaje)* message; **dejar un r.** to leave a message

recaer [39] *vi* **a** *Med* to relapse **b** *(culpa, responsabilidad)* to fall **(sobre** on)

recaída *nf* relapse

recalcar [44] *vt* to stress, to emphasize

recalcitrante *adj* recalcitrant

recalentar [1] *vt (comida)* to reheat, to warm up; *(calentar demasiado)* to overheat

recámara *nf* **a** *(de rueda)* tube **b** *(habitación)* dressing room **c** *CAm, Col, Méx (dormitorio)* bedroom

recamarera *nf CAm, Col, Méx* chambermaid

recambiar [43] *vt* to change (over)

recambio *nm* **a** *(repuesto)* spare (part); **rueda de r.** spare wheel **b** *(de pluma etc)* refill

recapacitar *vi* to reflect, to think

recargable *adj (pluma)* refillable; *(mechero)* rechargeable

recargado,-a *adj* overloaded; *Fig (estilo)* overelaborate, affected

recargar [42] **1** *vt* **a** *Elec* to recharge **b** *(sobrecargar)* to overload; *(adornar mucho)* to

overelaborate (**c**) *Fin* to increase
2 recargarse *vpr Méx (apoyarse)* to lean (**contra** against)
recargo *nm* extra charge, surcharge
recatado,-a *adj (prudente)* prudent, cautious; *(modesto)* modest, decent
recato *nm (cautela)* caution, prudence; *(pudor)* modesty
recaudación *nf (cobro)* collection; *(cantidad recaudada)* takings; *Dep* gate
recaudador,-a *nm,f* tax collector
recaudar *vt* to collect
recaudo *nm* **estar a buen r.** to be in safekeeping
recelar *vi* **r. de** to distrust
recelo *nm* suspicion, distrust
receloso,-a *adj* suspicious, distrustful
recepción *nf* reception; *(en hotel)* reception (desk)
recepcionista *nmf* receptionist
receptivo,-a *adj* receptive
receptor,-a 1 *nm,f (persona)* recipient
2 *nm Rad & TV* receiver
recesión *nf* recession
receta *nf* recipe; *Med* prescription
recetar *vt Med* to prescribe
rechace *nm Dep* clearance
rechazar [40] *vt* to reject, to turn down; *Mil* to repel, to drive back
rechazo *nm* rejection
rechiflar *vt* (**a**) *(silbar)* to hiss, to boo (**b**) *(mofarse)* to mock, to jeer at
rechinar *vi (madera)* to creak; *(metal)* to squeak, to screech; *(dientes)* to chatter
rechistar *vi* **sin r.** that's final
rechoncho,-a *adj Fam* chubby, tubby
rechupete: de rechupete *loc Fam* **me sé el tema de r.** I know the subject inside out; **la comida estaba de r.** the food was mouthwateringly good
recibidor *nm* entrance hall
recibimiento *nm* reception, welcome
recibir 1 *vt* to receive; *(en casa)* to welcome; *(en la estación etc)* to meet
2 recibirse *vpr Am (graduarse)* to graduate, to qualify (**de** as)
recibo *nm* (**a**) *(factura)* invoice, bill; *(resguardo)* receipt; **r. de la luz** electricity bill (**b**) **acusar r. de** to acknowledge receipt of
reciclado,-a 1 *adj* recycled
2 *nm (reciclaje)* recycling
reciclaje *nm (de residuos)* recycling; *Fig (renovación)* retraining; **curso de r.** refresher course
reciclar *vt (residuos)* to recycle; *Fig (profesores etc)* to retrain
recién *adv* (**a**) *(recientemente) (antes de pp)* recently, newly; **café r. hecho** freshly made coffee; **r. casados** newlyweds; **r. nacido** newborn baby (**b**) *Am (hace poco)* recently
reciente *adj* recent
recientemente *adv* recently, lately

recinto *nm (cercado)* enclosure; **r. comercial** shopping precinct
recio,-a 1 *adj (robusto)* strong, sturdy; *(grueso)* thick; *(voz)* loud
2 *adv* hard
recipiente *nm* receptacle, container

> *ℓ* Observa que la palabra inglesa **recipient** es un falso amigo y no es la traducción de la palabra española **recipiente**. En inglés, **recipient** significa "receptor, destinatario".

recíproco,-a *adj* reciprocal
recital *nm Mús* recital; *Lit* reading
recitar *vt* to recite
reclamación *nf* (**a**) *(demanda)* claim, demand (**b**) *(queja)* complaint
reclamar 1 *vt* to claim, to demand
2 *vi* (**a**) to protest (**contra** against) (**b**) *Jur* to appeal
reclamo *nm* (**a**) *(publicitario)* appeal (**b**) *(en caza)* decoy bird, lure; *Fig* inducement (**c**) *Am (queja)* complaint (**d**) *Am (reivindicación)* claim
reclinar 1 *vt* to lean (**sobre** on)
2 reclinarse *vpr* to lean back, to recline
recluir [37] *vt* to shut away, to lock away; *(encarcelar)* to imprison, to intern
reclusión *nf* seclusion; *(encarcelamiento)* imprisonment, internment
recluso,-a *nm,f* prisoner

> *ℓ* Observa que la palabra inglesa **recluse** es un falso amigo y no es la traducción de la palabra española **recluso**. En inglés, **recluse** significa "solitario".

recluta *nmf* recruit
reclutamiento *nm (voluntario)* recruitment *(obligatorio)* conscription
recobrar 1 *vt* to recover, to retrieve; *(conocimiento)* to regain; **r. el aliento** to get one's breath back
2 recobrarse *vpr* to recover, to recuperate
recochineo *nm Fam* mockery
recodo *nm (de río)* twist, turn; *(de camino)* bend
recogedor *nm* dustpan
recoger [53] **1** *vt* (**a**) *(del suelo etc)* to pick up (**b**) *(datos etc)* to gather, to collect (**c**) *(ordenar, limpiar)* to clean; **r. la mesa** to clear the table (**d**) *(ir a buscar)* to pick up, to fetch (**e**) *(cosecha)* to gather, to pick
2 recogerse *vpr* (**a**) *(irse a casa)* to go home (**b**) *(pelo)* to lift up
recogida *nf* collection; *Agr (cosecha)* harvest, harvesting
recolección *nf Agr* harvest, harvesting; *(recogida)* collection, gathering

> *ℓ* Observa que la palabra inglesa **recollection** es un falso amigo y no es la traducción de la palabra española **recolección**. En inglés, **recollection** significa "recuerdo".

recomendable *adj* recommendable

recomendación *nf* recommendation, reference

recomendado,-a *adj Am (carta, paquete)* registered

recomendar [1] *vt* to recommend

recompensa *nf* reward

recompensar *vt* to reward

recomponer [19] (*pp* **recompuesto**) *vt* to repair, to mend

reconciliación *nf* reconciliation

reconciliar [43] **1** *vt* to reconcile
2 reconciliarse *upr* to be reconciled

recóndito,-a *adj* hidden, secret

reconfortante *adj* comforting

reconfortar *vt* to comfort

reconocer [34] *vt* (a) to recognize (b) *(admitir)* to recognize, to admit (c) *Med (paciente)* o examine

reconocimiento *nm* (a) recognition (b) *Med* examination, checkup

reconquista *nf* reconquest

reconstituyente *nm* tonic

reconstruir [37] *vt* to reconstruct

reconversión *nf* reconversion; **r. industrial** industrial redeployment

reconvertir [5] *vt* to reconvert; *Ind* to modernize

recopilación *nf* (a) *(resumen)* summary, résumé (b) *(compendio)* compilation, collection

recopilar *vt* to compile, to collect

récord *nm* record

recordar [2] **1** *vt* (a) *(rememorar)* to remember (b) **r. algo a algn** to remind sb of sth
2 *vi* to remember

recordatorio *nm (aviso)* reminder; *(de defunción)* notice of death

recordman *nm* record holder

recorrer *vt (distancia)* to cover, to travel; *(país)* to tour, to travel through o round; *(ciudad)* to visit, to walk round

recorrido *nm, Am* **recorrida** *nf (distancia)* distance travelled; *(trayecto)* trip, journey; *(itinerario)* itinerary, route

recortable *adj & nm* cutout

recortar *vt* to cut out

recorte *nm (acción, de periódico)* cutting; *(de pelo)* trim, cut; *Fig (de salarios etc)* cut

recostado,-a *adj* reclining, leaning

recostar [2] **1** *vt* to lean
2 recostarse *upr (tumbarse)* to lie down

recoveco *nm (curva)* turn, bend; *(rincón)* nook, corner

recreación *nf* recreation

recrear 1 *vt* (a) *(divertir)* to amuse, to entertain (b) *(crear de nuevo)* to recreate
2 recrearse *upr* to amuse oneself, to enjoy oneself; **r. con** to take pleasure o delight in

recreativo,-a *adj* recreational

recreo *nm* (a) *(diversión)* recreation (b) *(en el colegio)* break, recreation

recriminar *vt* to recriminate; *(reprochar)* to reproach

recrudecer [33] *vt*, **recrudecerse** *upr* to worsen

recrudecimiento *nm* worsening

recta *nf Geom* straight line; *(de carretera)* straight stretch; *Dep* **la r. final** the home straight

rectangular *adj* rectangular

rectángulo *nm* rectangle

rectificación *nf* rectification; *(corrección)* correction

rectificar [44] *vt* to rectify; *(corregir)* to correct, to remedy

rectilíneo,-a *adj* straight

rectitud *nf* straightness; *Fig* uprightness, rectitude

recto,-a 1 *adj* (a) *(derecho)* straight (b) *(honesto)* upright, honest (c) *Geom* right
2 *nm Anat* rectum
3 *adv* straight (on)

rector,-a 1 *adj (principio)* guiding, ruling
2 *nm,f* rector

recua *nf Fig* string, series

recuadro *nm Prensa* box

recubrir (*pp* **recubierto**) *vt* to cover

recuento *nm* count; **hacer (el) r. de** to count

recuerdo *nm* (a) *(memoria)* memory (b) *(regalo etc)* souvenir (c) **recuerdos** regards

recuperación *nf* recovery; *(examen)* resit

recuperar 1 *vt (salud)* to recover; *(conocimiento)* to regain; *(tiempo, clases)* to make up
2 recuperarse *upr* to recover

recurrir *vi* (a) *Jur* to appeal (b) **r. a** *(a algn)* to turn to; *(a algo)* to make use of, to resort to

> Observa que el verbo inglés **to recur** es un falso amigo y no es la traducción del verbo español **recurrir**. En inglés, **to recur** significa "repetirse".

recurso *nm* (a) resource; **recursos naturales** natural resources; **como último r.** as a last resort (b) *Jur* appeal

recusar *vt* to challenge, to object to

red *nf* net; *(sistema)* network; *Com (cadena)* chain of supermarkets; *Fig (trampa)* trap; **la R.** *(Internet)* the Net

redacción *nf (escrito)* composition, essay; *(acción)* writing; *Prensa* editing; *(redactores)* editorial staff

redactar *vt* to draft; *Prensa* to edit

redactor,-a *nm,f Prensa* editor

redada *nf* **r. policial** *(en un solo sitio)* raid; *(en varios lugares a la vez)* round-up

redentor,-a *nm,f* redeemer

redicho,-a *adj Fam* affected, pretentious

redil *nm* fold, sheepfold

redimir *vt* to redeem

rédito *nm* yield, interest

redituable *adj* interest-yielding

redoblar 1 *vt* to redouble

2 *vi (tambor)* to roll
redoble *nm* roll; *(de campanas)* peal
redomado,-a *adj* utter, out-and-out
redonda *nf* **a la r.** around
redondear *vt (objeto)* to round, to make round; *(cantidad)* to round up
redondel *nm Fam (círculo)* circle, ring; *Taurom* ring, arena
redondo,-a *adj* **(a)** round; *Fig* **caer r.** to collapse **(b)** *(rotundo)* categorical; *(perfecto)* perfect
reducción *nf* reduction
reducido,-a *adj (disminuido)* reduced, decreased; *(pequeño)* limited, small
reducir [10] **1** *vt (disminuir)* to reduce
2 reducirse *vpr* **(a)** *(disminuirse)* to be reduced, to diminish **(b)** *(limitarse)* to confine oneself
redundancia *nf* redundancy, superfluousness; **valga la r.** if I may say so again
redundante *adj* redundant
redundar *vi* **r. en** *(resultar)* to result in, to lead to
reduplicar [44] *vt* to redouble
reembolsar *vt* to reimburse; *(deuda)* to repay; *(importe)* to refund
reembolso *nm* reimbursement; *(de deuda)* repayment; *(devolución)* refund; **contra r.** cash on delivery
reemplazar [40] *vt* to replace (**con** with)
reemplazo *nm* replacement; *Mil* call-up
reestructuración *nf* restructuring
reestructurar *vt* to restructure
ref. *(abr* **referencia)** ref
refacción *nf* **(a)** *Andes, CAm, RP, Ven (reparación)* repair **(b)** *Méx (recambio)* spare part
refaccionar *vt Am* to repair, to do up
refectorio *nm* refectory, canteen
referencia *nf* reference; **con r. a** with reference to
referéndum *nm (pl* **referéndums)** referendum
referente *adj* **r. a** concerning, regarding
referir [5] **1** *vt* to tell, to relate
2 referirse *vpr (aludir)* to refer (**a** to); **¿a qué te refieres?** what do you mean?
refilón: de refilón *loc adv (de pasada)* briefly
refinado,-a *adj* refined
refinamiento *nm* refinement
refinar *vt* to refine
refinería *nf* refinery
reflector,-a 1 *adj* reflecting
2 *nm Elec* spotlight, searchlight
reflejar 1 *vt* to reflect
2 reflejarse *vpr* to be reflected (**en** in)
reflejo,-a 1 *nm* **(a)** *(imagen)* reflection **(b)** *(destello)* gleam, glint **(c)** *Anat* reflex **(d)** **reflejos** *(en el cabello)* streaks, highlights
2 *adj (movimiento)* reflex
reflexión *nf* reflection
reflexionar *vi* to reflect (**sobre** on), to think (**sobre** about)
reflexivo,-a *adj* **(a)** *(persona)* thoughtful **(b)**

Ling reflexive
reflujo *nm* ebb (tide)
reforma *nf* **(a)** reform; **r. fiscal** tax reform **(b)** *(reparación)* repair
reformador,-a *nm,f* reformer
reformar 1 *vt* to reform; *(edificio)* to renovate
2 reformarse *vpr* to reform
reformatorio *nm* reformatory, reform school
reforzar [2] *vt* to reinforce, to strengthen
refractario,-a *adj* **(a)** *Téc* heat-resistant **(b)** *(persona)* unwilling, reluctant
refrán *nm* proverb, saying
refregar [1] *vt* to rub vigorously; *Fig* **no me lo refriegues** don't rub it in
refrenar 1 *vt (contener)* to restrain, to curb
2 refrenarse *vpr* to restrain oneself
refrendar *vt (firmar)* to endorse, to countersign; *(aprobar)* to approve
refrescante *adj* refreshing
refrescar [44] **1** *vt* to refresh
2 *vi* **(a)** *(tiempo)* to turn cool **(b)** *(bebida)* to be refreshing
3 refrescarse *vpr* to cool down
refresco *nm* soft drink, refreshments
refriega *nf (lucha)* scuffle, brawl; *(escaramuza)* skirmish
refrigeración *nf (enfriamiento)* refrigeration; *(aire acondicionado)* air conditioning
refrigerado,-a *adj* air-conditioned
refrigerador *nm* refrigerator, fridge
refrigerar *vt* to refrigerate; *(habitación)* to air-condition
refrigerio *nm* snack, refreshments
refuerzo *nm* reinforcement, strengthening
refugiado,-a *adj & nm,f* refugee
refugiarse [43] *vpr* to shelter, to take refuge
refugio *nm* refuge
refulgente *adj* radiant, brilliant
refulgir [57] *vi (brillar)* to shine; *(resplandecer)* to glitter, to sparkle
refunfuñar *vi* to grumble, to moan
refutar *vt* to refute
regadera *nf* **(a)** *(para regar)* watering can *Fam* **estar como una r.** to be as mad as a hatter **(b)** *Col, Méx, Ven (ducha)* shower
regadío *nm (tierra)* irrigated land
regalado,-a *adj* **(a)** *(gratis)* free; *(muy barato)* dirt-cheap **(b)** **una vida regalada** an easy life
regalar *vt* **(a)** *(dar)* to give (as a present); *(en ofertas etc)* to give away **(b)** **r. el oído a algn** to flatter sb
regaliz *nm* liquorice
regalo *nm* **(a)** gift, present; **de r.** as a present **(b)** *(comodidad)* pleasure, comfort
regalón,-ona *adj CSur Fam (niño)* spoilt
regañadientes: a regañadientes *loc adv* reluctantly, unwillingly
regañar 1 *vt Fam* to scold, to tell off
2 *vi* to nag
regañina *nf* scolding, telling-off
regañón,-ona *nm,f Fam* nag

regar [1] *vt* to water

regata *nf* boat race

regatear 1 *vi* (**a**) to haggle, to bargain (**b**) *Dep* to dribble

  2 *vt* **no r. esfuerzos** to spare no effort

regateo *nm* (**a**) (*de precios*) haggling (**b**) *Dep* dribbling

regazo *nm* lap

regeneración *nf* regeneration

regenerar *vt* to regenerate

regentar *vt* to rule, to govern; (*cargo*) to hold

regente *nmf* (**a**) *Pol* regent (**b**) (*director*) manager (**c**) *Méx* (*alcalde*) mayor, *f* mayoress

régimen *nm* (*pl* **regímenes**) (**a**) *Pol* regime (**b**) *Med* diet; **estar a r.** to be on a diet

regimiento *nm* regiment

regio,-a *adj* (**a**) (*real*) royal, regal (**b**) (*suntuoso*) sumptuous, luxurious; *Am* (*magnífico*) splendid, majestic

región *nf* region

regional *adj* regional

regionalista *adj & nmf* regionalist

regir [58] **1** *vt* to govern

  2 *vi* to be in force

  3 regirse *upr* to be guided, to go (**por** by)

registrado,-a *adj* (**a**) (*patentado, inscrito*) registered; **marca registrada** registered trademark (**b**) *Am* (*certificado*) registered

registrador,-a *adj* **caja registradora** cash register

registradora *nf Am* cash register

registrar 1 *vt* (**a**) (*examinar*) to inspect; (*cachear*) to frisk (**b**) (*inscribir*) to register (**c**) (*grabar*) to record

  2 registrarse *upr* (**a**) (*inscribirse*) to register, o enrol (**b**) (*detectarse*) to be recorded

registro *nm* (**a**) inspection (**b**) (*inscripción*) registration, recording; (*oficina*) registry office (**c**) *Mús* register

regla *nf* (**a**) (*norma*) rule; **en r.** in order; **por r. general** as a (general) rule; **r. de oro** golden rule (**b**) (*instrumento*) ruler (**c**) *Mat* rule (**d**) *Med* (*periodo*) period

reglamentación *nf* (**a**) (*acción*) regulation (**b**) (*reglamento*) regulations, rules

reglamentar *vt* to regulate

reglamentario,-a *adj* statutory; *Mil* **arma reglamentaria** regulation gun

reglamento *nm* regulations, rules

reglar *vt* to regulate

regocijar 1 *vt* to delight, to amuse

  2 regocijarse *upr* to be delighted, to rejoice

regocijo *nm* (*placer*) delight, joy; (*alborozo*) rejoicing, merriment

regodearse *upr Fam* to delight (**con** in)

regodeo *nm Fam* delight

regordete,-a *adj Fam* plump, chubby

regresar 1 *vi* to return

  2 *vt Andes, CAm, Carib, Méx* (*devolver*) to give back

  3 regresarse *upr Andes, CAm, Carib, Méx* (*yendo*) to go back, to return; (*viniendo*) to come back, to return

regresión *nf* regression; (*decaimiento*) deterioration, decline

regreso *nm* return

reguero *nm* (*corriente*) trickle; (*de humo*) trail

regulable *adj* adjustable

regular 1 *vt* (**a**) to regulate, to control (**b**) (*ajustar*) to adjust

  2 *adj* (**a**) regular; **por lo r.** as a rule; **vuelo r.** scheduled flight (**b**) *Fam* (*mediano*) average, so-so

  3 *adv* so-so

regularidad *nf* regularity; **con r.** regularly

regularizar [40] *vt* to regularize

regusto *nm* aftertaste

rehabilitar *vt* to rehabilitate; (*edificio*) to convert

rehacer [15] (*pp* **rehecho**) **1** *vt* to redo

  2 rehacerse *upr* (*recuperarse*) to recover, to recuperate

rehén *nm* hostage

rehogar [42] *vt* to brown

rehuir [37] *vt* to shun, to avoid

rehusar *vt* to refuse

reina *nf* queen

reinado *nm* reign

reinante *adj* (*que reina*) reigning, ruling; (*prevaleciente*) prevailing

reinar *vi* to reign

reincidente *nmf/Jur* recidivist

reincidir *vi* to relapse, to fall back (**en** into)

reincorporarse *upr* **r. al trabajo** to return to work

reino *nm* kingdom; **el R. Unido** the United Kingdom

reinserción *nf* reintegration

reinsertar *vt*, **reinsertarse** *upr* to reintegrate

reintegrar *vt* (**a**) (*trabajador*) to reinstate (**b**) (*dinero*) to reimburse, to refund

reintegro *nm* (*en lotería*) winning of one's stake

reír [56] **1** *vi* to laugh

  2 reírse *upr* (**a**) to laugh (**b**) (*mofarse*) to laugh (**de** at), to make fun (**de** of)

reiterar *vt* to reiterate, to repeat

reivindicación *nf* claim, demand

reivindicar [44] *vt* to claim, to demand; **el atentado fue reivindicado por los terroristas** the terrorists claimed responsibility for the attack

reivindicativo,-a *adj* protest

reja *nf* (**a**) (*de ventana*) grill, grating; *Fam* **estar entre rejas** to be behind bars (**b**) *Agr* ploughshare

rejilla *nf* (*de ventana, ventilador, radiador*) grill; (*de horno*) gridiron; (*para equipaje*) luggage rack

rejoneador,-a *nm,f Taurom* = bullfighter on horseback

rejonear *vt Taurom* to fight on horseback

rejuvenecer [33] *vt* to rejuvenate

relación *nf* (**a**) relationship; *(conexión)* connection, link; **con** *o* **en r. a** with regard to; **relaciones públicas** public relations (**b**) *(lista)* list (**c**) *(relato)* account (**d**) *Mat & Téc* ratio

relacionado,-a *adj* related (**con** to), connected (**con** with)

relacionar 1 *vt* to relate (**con** to), to connect (**con** with)

2 relacionarse *vpr* (**a**) to be related, to be connected (**b**) *(alternar)* to mix, to get acquainted

relajación *nf* relaxation

relajante *adj* relaxing

relajar 1 *vt* to relax

2 relajarse *vpr* to relax; *(moral)* to deteriorate

relajo *nm Am Fam (alboroto)* racket, din

relamerse *vpr* to lick one's lips

relamido,-a *adj (afectado)* affected; *(pulcro)* prim and proper

relámpago *nm* flash of lightning; *Fig* **pasó como un r.** he flashed past; *Fig* **visita r.** flying visit

relampaguear *v impers* to flash

relanzar *vt* to relaunch

relatar *vt* to narrate, to relate

relatividad *nf* relativity

relativo,-a *adj* relative (**a** to); **en lo r. a** with regard to, concerning

relato *nm (cuento)* tale, story

relax *nm Fam* relaxation

relegar [42] *vt* to relegate

relente *nm* dew

relevancia *nf* importance

> 🖉 Observa que la palabra inglesa **relevance** es un falso amigo y no es la traducción de la palabra española **relevancia**. En inglés, **relevance** significa "pertinencia".

relevante *adj* important

relevar 1 *vt* to relieve, to take over from; **fue relevado del cargo** he was relieved of his duties

2 relevarse *vpr (turnarse)* to relieve one another

relevo *nm* relief; *Dep* relay

relieve *nm Arte* relief; *Fig* **poner de r.** to emphasize

religión *nf* religion

religioso,-a 1 *adj* religious

2 *nm,f (hombre)* monk; *(mujer)* nun

relinchar *vi* to neigh, to whinny

relincho *nm* neigh, whinny

reliquia *nf* relic

rellamada *nf Tel* redial

rellano *nm* landing

rellenar *vt* (**a**) *(impreso etc)* to fill in (**b**) *(un ave)* to stuff; *(un pastel)* to fill

relleno,-a 1 *nm (de aves)* stuffing; *(de pasteles)* filling

2 *adj* stuffed

reloj *nm* clock; *(de pulsera)* watch; **r. de aren** hourglass; **r. de sol** sundial; **r. despertado** alarm clock

relojería *nf (tienda)* watchmaker's, clock maker's; **bomba de r.** time bomb

relojero,-a *nm,f* watchmaker, clockmaker

reluciente *adj* shining, gleaming

relucir [35] *vi (brillar)* to shine, to gleam **sacar a r. un tema** to bring up a subject

relumbrar *vi* to shine, to gleam

reluzco *indic pres de* **relucir**

remachar *vt* to drive home, to hammer home

remache *nm* rivet

remanente *nm (restos)* remainder; *(extra* surplus

remangar [42] *vt*, **remangarse** *vpr (mangas pantalones)* to roll up; *(camisa)* to tuck up

remanso *nm* pool; *(lugar tranquilo)* quie place

remar *vi* to row

remarcar [44] *vt* to stress, to underline

> 🖉 Observa que el verbo inglés **to remark** es ur falso amigo y no es la traducción del verbo español **remarcar**. En inglés, **to remark** significa "comentar, observar".

rematadamente *adv* **r. loco** as mad as hatter

rematar *vt* (**a**) to finish off, to put the fir ishing touches to (**b**) *Com* to sell off cheapl (**c**) *Dep* to shoot

remate *nm* (**a**) *(final)* end, finish; **para r. t** crown it all (**b**) *Dep* shot at goal (**c**) **de r.** utte utterly

rembolsar *vt* = **reembolsar**

rembolso *nm* = **reembolso**

remedar *vt* to imitate, to copy

remediar [43] *vt* (**a**) to remedy; *(enmenda* to repair, to make good (**b**) *(evitar)* to avoic to prevent; **no pude remediarlo** I couldn help it

remedio *nm (cura)* remedy, cure; *(solución* solution; **¡qué r.!** what else can I do?; **no ha más r.** there's no choice; **sin r.** without fai *Fam* **¡no tienes r.!** you're hopeless!

remedo *nm (imitación)* imitation, copy; *(pc rodia)* parody

rememorar *vt* to remember, to recall

remendar [1] *vt (ropa)* to patch

remera *nf RP (prenda)* T-shirt

remero,-a *nm,f* rower

remesa *nf (de mercancías)* consignmen shipment; *(de dinero)* remittance

remiendo *nm (parche)* patch

remilgado,-a *adj (afectado)* affected; *(melir droso)* fussy, finicky; *(gazmoño)* prudish

remilgo *nm* affectation; *(gazmoñería)* pre dishness

reminiscencia *nf* reminiscence

remise *nm RP* taxi *(in private car witho. meter)*

remisero,-a *nm,f RP* taxi driver *(of private car without meter)*

remiso,-a *adj* reluctant

remite *nm (en carta)* = sender's name and address

remitente *nmf* sender

remitir 1 *vt* (**a**) *(enviar)* to send (**b**) *(referir)* to refer

2 *vi (fiebre, temporal)* to subside

3 remitirse *upr* **si nos remitimos a los hechos** if we look at the facts; **remítase a la página 10** see page 10

remo *nm* oar; *(deporte)* rowing

remoción *nf Andes, RP (de objetos)* transport, removal; *(de heridos)* transport

remodelación *nf (modificación)* reshaping; *(reorganización)* reorganization; *Pol* **r. ministerial** *o* **del gobierno** cabinet reshuffle

remodelar *vt* to reshape; *(reorganizar)* to reorganize

remojar *vt* to soak (**en** in)

remojo *nm* **dejar** *o* **poner en r.** to soak, to leave to soak

remojón *nm Fam* **darse un r.** to go for a dip

remolacha *nf Br* beetroot, *US* beet

remolcador *nm* (**a**) *Náut* tug, tugboat (**b**) *Aut Br* breakdown van *o* truck, *US* tow truck

remolcar [44] *vt* to tow

remolino *nm (de agua)* whirlpool, eddy; *(de aire)* whirlwind

remolón,-ona 1 *adj* lazy

2 *nm,f* **hacerse el r.** to shirk, to slack

remolonear *vi* to shirk, to slack

remolque *nm (acción)* towing; *(vehículo)* trailer; *Fig* **ir a r. de algn** to trundle along behind sb

remontar 1 *vt* (**a**) *(subir)* to go up (**b**) *(superar)* to overcome

2 remontarse *upr* (**a**) *(pájaros, aviones)* to soar (**b**) *(datar)* to go back, to date back (**a** to)

remorder [4] *vt* (**a**) *(trasladar)* **me remuerde la conciencia por ...** I've got a bad conscience about ...

remordimiento *nm* remorse

remoto,-a *adj* remote, faraway; **no tengo la más remota idea** I haven't got the faintest idea

remover [4] *vt* (**a**) *(trasladar)* to move over (**b**) *(tierra)* to turn over; *(líquido)* to shake up; *(comida etc)* to stir; *(asunto)* to stir up

> 🖉 Observa que el verbo inglés **to remove** es un falso amigo y no es la traducción del verbo español **remover**. En inglés, **to remove** significa "quitar, despedir".

remozar [40] *vt* to modernize

remplazar [40] *vt* = **reemplazar**

remplazo *nm* = **reemplazo**

remuneración *nf* remuneration

remunerar *vt* to remunerate

renacentista *adj* Renaissance

renacer [60] *vi* to be reborn; *Fig (revivir)* to revive, to come back to life

renacimiento *nm* **el R.** the Renaissance

renacuajo *nm* tadpole; *Fam (niño pequeño)* shrimp

renal *adj* kidney; **insuficiencia r.** kidney failure

rencilla *nf* quarrel

rencor *nm* rancour; *(resentimiento)* resentment; **guardar r. a algn** to have a grudge against sb

rencoroso,-a *adj (hostil)* rancorous; *(resentido)* resentful

rendición *nf* surrender

rendido,-a *a adj (muy cansado)* exhausted, worn out

rendija *nf* crack, split

rendimiento *nm (producción)* yield, output; *(de máquina, motor)* efficiency, performance

rendir [6] **1** *vt* (**a**) *(fruto, beneficios)* to yield, to produce (**b**) *(cansar)* to exhaust, to wear out (**c**) **r. culto a** to worship; **r. homenaje a** to pay homage to

2 *vi (dar beneficios)* to pay, to be profitable

3 rendirse *upr* (**a**) to surrender, to give in; **¡me rindo!** I give up! (**b**) *(cansarse)* to wear oneself out

renegado,-a *adj & nm,f* renegade

renegar [1] *vt* **r. de** to renounce, to disown

renegrido,-a *adj* blackened

RENFE *nf (abr* **Red Nacional de los Ferrocarriles Españoles)** = Spanish state railway company

renglón *nm* line; **a r. seguido** immediately afterwards

rengo,-a *adj Andes, RP* lame

renguear *vi Andes, RP* to limp, to hobble

reno *nm* reindeer

renombrado,-a *adj* renowned, famous

renombre *nm* renown, fame

renovable *adj* renewable

renovación *nf (de contrato, pasaporte)* renewal; *(de una casa)* renovation

renovar [2] *vt* to renew; *(edificio)* to renovate

renta *nf* (**a**) *Fin (ingresos)* income; *(beneficio)* interest, return; **r. per cápita** per capita income; **r. fija** fixed-interest security (**b**) *(alquiler)* rent

rentable *adj* profitable

rentar 1 *vt (rendir)* to produce, to yield; *Méx (alquilar)* to rent

2 *vi* to be profitable

renuncia *nf* (**a**) renunciation (**b**) *(dimisión)* resignation

renunciar [43] *vi* (**a**) **r. a** to renounce, to give up; *(no aceptar)* to decline (**b**) *(dimitir)* to resign

reñido,-a *adj (disputado)* tough, hard-fought

reñir [6] **1** *vt (regañar)* to scold, to tell off

2 *vi (discutir)* to quarrel, to argue; *(pelear)* to fight; **r. con algn** to fall out with sb

reo *nmf (acusado)* defendant, accused; *(culpable)* culprit

reojo: de reojo *loc adv* **mirar algo de r.** to look at sth out of the corner of one's eye

reparación *nf* repair; *(compensación)* reparation, amends

reparar 1 *vt* to repair; *(ofensa, injuria)* to make amends for; *(daño)* to make good

2 *vi* **r. en** *(darse cuenta de)* to notice; *(reflexionar sobre)* to think about

reparo *nm* **no tener reparos en** not to hesitate to; **me da r.** I feel embarrassed

repartidor,-a *nm,f* distributor

repartir *vt* (a) *(dividir)* to distribute, to share out (b) *(regalo, premio)* to give out, to hand out; *(correo)* to deliver; *Naipes* to deal

reparto *nm* (a) distribution, sharing out (b) *(distribución)* handing out; *(de mercancías)* delivery (c) *Cin & Teatro* cast

repasador *nm RP (trapo)* tea towel

repasar *vt* (a) to revise, to go over (b) *(ropa)* to mend

repaso *nm* revision

repatear *vt Fam* to annoy, to turn off

repatriar [29] *vt* to repatriate

repecho *nm* short steep slope

repelente *adj* repulsive, repellent; *Fam* **niño r.** little know-all

repeler *vt (rechazar)* to repel, to repulse; *(repugnar)* to disgust

repente *nm Fam (arrebato)* fit, outburst; **de r.** suddenly, all of a sudden

repentino,-a *adj* sudden

repercusión *nf* repercussion

repercutir *vi* (a) *(sonido)* to resound, to reverberate; *(objeto)* to rebound (b) *Fig* **r. en** to have repercussions on, to affect

repertorio *nm* repertoire, repertory

repesca *nf Fam* second chance; *(examen)* resit

repetición *nf* repetition; **r. de la jugada** action replay

repetido,-a *adj* **repetidas veces** repeatedly

repetidor,-a 1 *adj* repeating

2 *nm,f Fam Educ* = student who is repeating a year

repetir [6] **1** *vt* (a) to repeat (b) *(plato)* to have a second helping

2 *vi Educ* to repeat a year

3 repetirse *vpr* (a) *(persona)* to repeat oneself (b) *(hecho)* to recur (c) **el pepino se repite** cucumber repeats (on me/you/him/ *etc*)

repicar [44] *vt (las campanas)* to peal, to ring out

repipi *adj Fam* **niño r.** little know-all

repique *nm (de campanas)* peal, ringing

repiquetear *vt & vi (campanas)* to ring; *(tambor)* to beat

repisa *nf* shelf, ledge

replantear *vt*, **replantearse** *vpr* to reconsider, to rethink

replegarse [1] *vpr* to fall back, to retreat

repleto,-a *adj* full (up), jam-packed; **r. de** packed with, crammed with

réplica *nf* (a) answer, reply (b) *(copia)* replica

replicar [44] **1** *vt* to answer back

2 *vi* (a) to reply, to retort (b) *(objetar)* to argue (c) *Jur* to answer

repliegue *nm Mil* withdrawal, retreat

repoblación *nf* repopulation; **r. forestal** reafforestation

repoblar [2] *vt* to repopulate; *(bosque)* to reafforest

repollo *nm* cabbage

reponer [19] **1** *vt* (a) to put back, to replace (b) *Teatro (obra)* to put on again; *Cin (película)* to rerun; *TV (programa)* to repeat

2 reponerse *vpr* **r. de** to recover from, to get over

reportaje *nm Prensa & Rad* report; *(noticias)* article, news item

reportar 1 *vt (beneficios etc)* to bring; *Am (informar)* to report

2 reportarse *vpr Am (presentarse)* to report (a to)

reporte *nm Méx (informe)* report; *(noticia)* news item o report; **recibí reportes de mi hermano** I was sent news by my brother; **el r. del tiempo** the weather report o forecast

reportero,-a *nm,f* reporter

reposar 1 *vt* to rest (**en** on)

2 *vi (descansar)* to rest, to take a rest; *(té)* to infuse; *(comida)* to stand

reposera *nf RP Br* sun-lounger, *US* beach recliner

reposición *nf TV* repeat; *Cin* rerun, reshowing

reposo *nm* rest; **en r.** at rest

repostar *vt (provisiones)* to stock up with; *Aut (gasolina)* to fill up with

repostería *nf* confectionery; *(tienda)* confectioner's (shop)

repostero,-a *nm,f* confectioner

reprender *vt* to reprimand, to scold

represalia *nf (usu pl)* reprisals, retaliation

representación *nf* (a) representation (b) *Teatro* performance

representante *nmf* representative

representar *vt* (a) to represent (b) *(significar)* to mean, to represent (c) *Teatro (obra)* to perform

representativo,-a *adj* representative

represión *nf* repression

represivo,-a *adj* repressive

reprimenda *nf* reprimand

reprimir *vt* to repress

reprobar [2] *vt (cosa)* to condemn; *(a persona)* to reproach, to reprove; *Am (estudiante, examen)* to fail

réprobo,-a *adj & nm,f* reprobate

reprochable *adj* reproachable

reprochar *vt* to reproach; **r. algo a algn** to reproach sb for sth

reproche *nm* reproach

reproducción *nf* reproduction

reproducir [10] **1** *vt* to reproduce

2 reproducirse *vpr* (**a**) to reproduce, to breed (**b**) *(repetirse)* to recur, to happen again

reproductor,-a *adj* reproductive

reptar *vi* to slither

reptil *nm* reptile

república *nf* republic; **la R. Checa** the Czech Republic

republicano,-a *adj & nm,f* republican

repudiar [43] *vt* to repudiate

repuesto *nm (recambio)* spare part, spare; **Aut rueda de r.** spare wheel

repugnancia *nf* loathing, disgust

repugnante *adj* disgusting, revolting

repugnar *vt* to disgust, to revolt

repujar *vt* to emboss

repulsa *nf* rebuff

repulsión *nf* repulsion, repugnance

repulsivo,-a *adj* repulsive, revolting

repuntar *vi Am (mejorar)* to improve

repunte *nm Am (recuperación)* recovery; *(aumento)* rise, increase; **un r. en las ventas** n improvement o increase in sales

repuse *pt indef de* **reponer**

reputación *nf* reputation

reputar *vt* to consider, to deem

requemar *vt* to scorch

requerimiento *nm* (**a**) *(súplica)* request (**b**) *Jur (aviso)* summons *sing*

🖉 Observa que la palabra inglesa **requirement** es un falso amigo y no es la traducción de la palabra española **requerimiento**. En inglés, **requirement** significa "requisito".

requerir [5] *vt* (**a**) to require (**b**) *(solicitar)* to request (**c**) *Jur (avisar)* to summon

requesón *nm* cottage cheese

requete- *pref Fam* really, very, incredibly; **requetebueno** brilliant

réquiem *nm (pl* **réquiems***)* requiem

requisa *nf* (**a**) *(inspección)* inspection (**b**) *Mil* requisition

requisar *vt* to requisition

requisito *nm* requirement, requisite

res *nf* animal

resabiado,-a *adj Pey* pedantic

resabio *nm* (**a**) *(mal sabor)* unpleasant o bad aftertaste (**b**) *(vicio)* bad habit

resaca *nf* (**a**) hangover (**b**) *Náut* undertow, undercurrent

resaltar *vi* (**a**) *(sobresalir)* to project, to jut out (**b**) *Fig* to stand out

resarcir [52] *vt* to compensate

resbalada *nf Am Fam* slip

resbaladizo,-a *adj* slippery

resbalar *vi,* **resbalarse** *vpr* to slip; *Aut* to skid

resbalón *nm* slip

rescatar *vt (persona)* to rescue; *(objeto)* to recover

rescate *nm* (**a**) *(salvamento)* rescue; *(recupe-*

ración) recovery (**b**) *(suma)* ransom

rescindir *vt* to rescind, to annul; *(contrato)* to cancel

rescisión *nf* rescission, annulment

rescoldo *nm* (**a**) embers (**b**) *Fig (recelo)* lingering doubt

resecarse [44] *vpr* to dry up, to become parched

reseco,-a *adj* very dry, parched

resentido,-a *adj* resentful

resentimiento *nm* resentment

resentirse [5] *vpr* (**a**) **r. de** to suffer from, to feel the effects of (**b**) *(ofenderse)* to feel offended; **r. por algo** to take offence at sth, to feel bitter about sth

reseña *nf* review; *Prensa* write-up

reserva 1 *nf* (**a**) *(de entradas etc)* reservation, booking (**b**) *(provisión)* reserve, stock; **un vino de r.** a vintage wine (**c**) *Mil* reserve, reserves (**d**) *(duda)* reservation

2 *nmf Dep* reserve, substitute

reservado,-a 1 *adj (persona)* reserved, quiet

2 *nm* private room

reservar 1 *vt* (**a**) *(billetes etc)* to reserve, to book (**b**) *(dinero, tiempo etc)* to keep, to save

2 reservarse *vpr* (**a**) to save oneself (**para** for) (**b**) *(sentimientos)* to keep to oneself (**c**) **r. el derecho de** to reserve the right to

resfriado,-a 1 *nm (catarro)* cold; **coger un r.** to catch (a) cold

2 *adj* **estar r.** to have a cold

resfriarse *vpr* to catch (a) cold

resfrío *nm Andes, RP* cold

resguardar *vt (proteger)* to protect, to shelter (**de** from)

resguardo *nm* (**a**) *(recibo)* receipt (**b**) *(protección)* protection, shelter

residencia *nf* residence; **r. de ancianos** old people's home

residencial *adj* residential

residente *adj & nmf* resident

residir *vi* to reside, to live (**en** in); *Fig* to lie (**en** in)

residuo *nm* (**a**) residue (**b**) **residuos** waste

resignación *nf* resignation

resignado,-a *adj* resigned

resignarse *vpr* to resign oneself (**a** to)

resina *nf* resin

resistencia *nf* (**a**) resistance (**b**) *(aguante)* endurance, stamina (**c**) *Elec* element

resistente *adj* (**a**) resistant (**a** to) (**b**) *(fuerte)* tough, hardy

resistir 1 *vi* (**a**) to resist (**b**) *(aguantar)* to hold (out)

2 *vt (situación, persona)* to put up with; *(tentación)* to resist

3 resistirse *vpr* to resist; *(oponerse)* to offer resistance; *(negarse)* to refuse

resollar [2] *vi* to breathe heavily; *(con silbido)* to wheeze

resolución *nf* (**a**) *(solución)* solution (**b**) *(decisión)* resolution

resolver [4] (*pp* **resuelto**) **1** *vt* (*problema*) to solve; (*asunto*) to settle

2 *vi* (*decidir*) to resolve, to decide

3 resolverse *vpr* (**a**) (*solucionarse*) to be solved (**b**) (*decidirse*) to resolve, to make up one's mind (**a** to)

resonancia *nf* (**a**) (*sonora*) resonance (**b**) (*repercusión*) repercussions

resonar [2] *vi* to resound; (*tener eco*) to echo

resoplar *vi* (*respirar*) to breathe heavily; (*de cansancio*) to puff and pant; (*de enfado*) to huff and puff

resoplido *nm* (*silbido*) wheezing; (*de cansancio*) panting; (*de enfado*) snort

resorte *nm* (**a**) (*muelle*) spring (**b**) *Fig* means

🖉 Observa que la palabra inglesa **resort** es un falso amigo y no es la traducción de la palabra española **resorte**. En inglés, **resort** significa "recurso" o "lugar de vacaciones".

respaldar *vt* to support, to back (up)

respaldo *nm* (*de silla etc*) back; *Fig* (*apoyo*) support, backing

respectar *vt* to concern, to regard; **por lo que a mí respecta** as far as I'm concerned

respectivo,-a *adj* respective; **en lo r. a** with regard to, regarding

respecto *nm* **al r., a este r.** in this respect; **con r. a, r. a, r. de** with regard to; **r. a mí** as for me, as far as I am concerned

respetable 1 *adj* respectable

2 *nm Fam* **el r.** the audience

respetar *vt* to respect; **hacerse r. de todos** to command everyone's respect

respeto *nm* (**a**) respect; **por r.** out of consideration (**b**) (*recelo*) fear

respetuoso,-a *adj* respectful

respingar [42] *vi* to shy

respingo *nm* start, jump

respingón,-ona *adj* (*nariz*) snub, upturned

respiración *nf* (*acción*) breathing, respiration; (*aliento*) breath; **r. artificial** artificial resuscitation

respirar *vi* to breathe; **¡por fin respiro!** well, that's a relief!

respiratorio,-a *adj* respiratory

respiro *nm* (**a**) breathing (**b**) (*descanso*) breather, break

resplandecer [33] *vi* to shine

resplandeciente *adj* (*brillante*) shining; (*esplendoroso*) resplendent, radiant

resplandor *nm* (*brillo*) brightness; (*muy intenso*) brilliance; (*de fuego*) glow, blaze

responder 1 *vt* to answer

2 *vi* (**a**) (*una carta*) to reply (**b**) (*reaccionar*) to respond (**c**) (*protestar*) to answer back (**d**) **r. de algn** to be responsible for sb; **r. por algn** to vouch for sb

respondón,-ona *adj Fam* argumentative, cheeky

responsabilidad *nf* responsibility

responsabilizar [40] **1** *vt* to make *o* hold responsible (**de** for)

2 responsabilizarse *vpr* to assume *o* claim responsibility (**de** for)

responsable 1 *adj* responsible

2 *nmf* **el/la r.** (*encargado*) the person in charge; (*de robo etc*) the perpetrator

respuesta *nf* answer, reply; (*reacción*) response

resquebrajarse *vpr* to crack

resquemor *nm* resentment, ill feeling

resquicio *nm* crack, chink

resta *nf* subtraction

restablecer [33] **1** *vt* to re-establish; (*el orden*) to restore

2 restablecerse *vpr Med* to recover

restablecimiento *nm* (**a**) re-establishment; (*del orden etc*) restoration (**b**) *Med* recovery

restante *adj* remaining; **lo r.** the rest, the remainder

restar 1 *vt* (**a**) *Mat* to subtract, to take away (**b**) **r. importancia a algo** to play sth down

2 *vi* (*quedar*) to be left, to remain

restauración *nf* restoration

restaurador,-a 1 *nm,f* restorer

2 *adj* restoring

restaurante *nm* restaurant

restaurar *vt* to restore

restitución *nf* restitution

restituir [37] *vt* (*restablecer*) to restore; (*devolver*) to return, to give back

resto *nm* (**a**) rest, remainder; *Mat* remainder (**b**) **restos** remains; (*de comida*) leftovers

restregar [1] *vt* to rub hard, to scrub

restricción *nf* restriction

restrictivo,-a *adj* restrictive

restringir [57] *vt* to restrict, to limit

resucitar *vt* & *vi* to resuscitate

resuello *nm* breath, gasp

resuelto,-a *adj* (*decidido*) resolute, determined

resultado *nm* result; (*consecuencia*) outcome; **dar buen r.** to work, to give results

resultante *adj* resulting

resultar *vi* (**a**) (*ser*) to turn *o* work out; **así resulta más barato** it works out cheaper this way; **me resultó fácil** it turned out to be easy for me (**b**) (*ocurrir*) **resulta que ...** the thing is ...; **y ahora resulta que no puede venir** and now it turns out that she can't come (**c**) (*tener éxito*) to be successful; **la fiesta no resultó** the party wasn't a success

resultas *nfpl* **a r. de** as a result of

resumen *nm* summary; **en r.** in short, to sum up

resumir 1 *vt* to sum up; (*recapitular*) to summarize

2 resumirse *vpr* (**a**) (*abreviarse*) **se resume en pocas palabras** it can be summed up in a few words (**b**) **r. en** (*saldarse con*) to result in

∅ Observa que la palabra inglesa **resume** es un falso amigo y no es la traducción de la palabra española **resumir**. En inglés, **resume** significa "reanudar".

resurgir [57] *vi* to reappear
resurrección *nf* resurrection
retablo *nm* altarpiece
retaguardia *nf* rearguard
retahíla *nf* series *sing*, string
retal *nm (pedazo)* scrap
retar *vt* to challenge
retardarse *upr* to be delayed
retardo *nm* delay
retazo *nm (pedazo)* scrap; *(fragmento)* fragment, piece
rete- *pref Méx Fam* very
retén *nm* (a) **r. (de bomberos)** squad (of firefighters) (b) *Am (prisión)* reformatory, reform school
retención *nf* retention; *Fin* withholding; **r. de tráfico** (traffic) hold-up, traffic jam
retener [24] *vt* (a) *(conservar)* to retain (b) *Fin (descontar)* to deduct (c) *(detener)* to detain
reticencia *nf* reticence, reserve
reticente *adj* reticent, reserved
retina *nf* retina
retintín *nm (tono irónico)* innuendo, sarcastic tone
retirada *nf* retreat, withdrawal
retirado,-a **1** *adj* (a) *(alejado)* remote (b) *(jubilado)* retired
2 *nm,f* retired person, *US* retiree
retirar **1** *vt* to take away, to remove; *(dinero)* to withdraw; *(ofensa)* to take back
2 retirarse *upr* (a) *(apartarse)* to withdraw, to draw back; *(irse)* to retire (b) *(jubilarse)* to retire (c) *Mil* to retreat, to withdraw
retiro *nm* (a) *(jubilación)* retirement; *(pensión)* pension (b) *(lugar tranquilo)* retreat (c) *Rel* retreat
reto *nm* challenge
retocar [44] *vt* to touch up
retoño *nm (rebrote)* shoot, sprout; *Fig (niño)* kid
retoque *nm* retouching, touching up; **los últimos retoques** the finishing touches
retorcer [41] **1** *vt (cuerda, hilo)* to twist; *(ropa)* to wring (out)
2 retorcerse *upr* to twist, to become twisted; **r. de dolor** to writhe in pain
retorcido,-a *adj Fig* twisted
retórica *nf* rhetoric
retórico,-a *adj* rhetorical
retornable *adj* returnable; **envase no r.** non-deposit bottle
retornar **1** *vt* to return, to give back
2 *vi* to return, to come back, to go back
retorno *nm* return
retortijón *nm (dolor)* stomach cramp

retozar [40] *vi* to frolic, to romp
retracción *nf* retraction
retractar **1** *vt* to retract
2 retractarse *upr* **r. (de)** to retract, to take back
retraerse *upr (retirarse)* to withdraw; *(por miedo)* to shy away
retraído,-a *adj* shy, reserved
retraimiento *nm (timidez)* shyness
retransmisión *nf* broadcast, transmission
retransmitir *vt* to broadcast
retrasado,-a **1** *adj* (a) *(tren)* late; *(reloj)* slow; **voy r.** I'm behind schedule (b) *(país)* backward, underdeveloped (c) *(mental)* retarded, backward
2 *nm,f* **r. (mental)** mentally retarded person
retrasar **1** *vt* (a) *(retardar)* to slow down (b) *(atrasar)* to delay, to postpone (c) *(reloj)* to put back
2 retrasarse *upr* to be late, to be delayed; *(reloj)* to be slow
retraso *nm* delay; **con r.** late; **una hora de r.** an hour behind schedule; **r. mental** mental deficiency
retratar **1** *vt (pintar)* to paint a portrait of; *Fot* to take a photograph of; *Fig (describir)* to describe, to depict
2 retratarse *upr Fot* to have one's photograph taken
retrato *nm (pintura)* portrait; *Fot* photograph; **r. robot** identikit picture, Photofit® picture; **ser el vivo r. de** to be the spitting image of
retreta *nf* retreat
retrete *nm* lavatory, toilet
retribución *nf (pago)* payment; *(recompensa)* reward

∅ Observa que la palabra inglesa **retribution** es un falso amigo y no es la traducción de la palabra española **retribución**. En inglés, **retribution** significa "represalias".

retribuir *vt (pagar)* to pay; *(recompensar)* to reward
retro *adj inv Fam (retrógrado)* reactionary; *(antiguo)* old-fashioned
retroactivo,-a *adj* retroactive; **con efecto r.** retrospectively
retroceder *vi* to move back, to back away
retroceso *nm* (a) *(movimiento)* backward movement (b) *Med* deterioration, worsening (c) *Econ* recession
retrógrado,-a *adj & nm,f (reaccionario)* reactionary
retropropulsión *nf Av* jet propulsion
retrospectivo,-a *adj & nf* retrospective
retrovisor *nm Aut* rear-view mirror
retumbar *vi (resonar)* to resound, to echo; *(tronar)* to thunder, to boom
retuve *pt indef de* **retener**
reúma *nm* rheumatism

reumático,-a *adj & nm,f* rheumatic

reumatismo *nm* rheumatism

reunión *nf* meeting; *(reencuentro)* reunion

reunir 1 *vt* to gather together; *(dinero)* to raise; *(cualidades)* to have, to possess; *(requisitos)* to fulfil

2 reunirse *vpr* to meet, to gather; **r. con algn** to meet sb

revalidar *vt* to ratify, to confirm; *Dep (título)* to retain

revalorizar [40] *vt*, **revalorizarse** *vpr (moneda)* to revalue

revancha *nf* revenge; *Dep* return match

revanchista *adj* vengeful, vindictive

revelación *nf* revelation

revelado *nm Fot* developing

revelar *vt* (a) to reveal, to disclose (b) *Fot (película)* to develop

revender *vt (entradas)* to tout

reventa *nf (de entradas)* touting

reventado,-a *adj Fam (cansado)* knackered

reventar [1] **1** *vt* (a) to burst (b) *(romper)* to break, to smash (c) *(fastidiar)* to annoy, to bother

2 *vi (estallar)* to burst; **r. de ganas de hacer algo** to be dying to do sth; **está que revienta** he's bursting at the seams

3 reventarse *vpr (estallar)* to burst, to explode

reventón *nm (de neumático)* blowout, puncture, flat tyre

reverberación *nf* reverberation

reverberar *vi* to reverberate

reverencia *nf* (a) *(respeto)* reverence (b) *(inclinación) (de hombre)* bow; *(de mujer)* curtsy

reverenciar [43] *vt* to revere, to venerate

reverendo,-a *adj & nm,f* reverend

reversa *nf Méx* reverse

reversible *adj* reversible

reverso *nm* reverse, back

revertido,-a *adj* **llamada a cobro r.** *Br* reverse-charge call, *US* collect call

revertir [5] *vi* to result (**en** in)

revés *nm* (a) *(reverso)* reverse; **al** o **del r.** *(al contrario)* the other way round; *(la parte interior en el exterior)* inside out; *(boca abajo)* upside down; *(la parte de detrás delante)* back to front; **al r. de lo que dicen** contrary to what they say (b) *(bofetada)* slap; *Ten* backhand (stroke) (c) *Fig (contrariedad)* setback, reverse; **los reveses de la vida** life's misfortunes; **reveses de fortuna** setbacks, blows of fate

revestimiento *nm Téc* covering, coating

revestir [6] *vt* (a) *(recubrir)* to cover (**de** with), to coat (**de** with), to line (**de** with) (b) *Fig* **la herida no reviste importancia** the wound is not serious

revisar *vt* to check; *(coche)* to service

revisión *nf* checking; *(de coche)* service, overhaul; **r. médica** checkup

revisor,-a *nm,f* ticket inspector

revista *nf* (a) magazine (b) **pasar r. a** to inspect, to review (c) *Teatro* revue

revitalizar [40] *vt* to revitalize

revivido,-a *adj* revived

revivir *vt & vi* to revive

revocar [44] *vt* to revoke, to repeal

revolcar [2] **1** *vt Fam (oponente)* to floor, to crush

2 revolcarse *vpr* to roll about

revolcón *nm* fall, tumble; *Fam (sexual)* romp

revolotear *vi* to fly about, to flutter about

revoltijo, revoltillo *nm* mess, jumble

revoltoso,-a *adj (travieso)* mischievous, naughty

revolución *nf* revolution

revolucionar *vt* to revolutionize

revolucionario,-a *adj & nm,f* revolutionary

revolver [4] *(pp* revuelto) **1** *vt (mezclar)* to stir, to mix; *(desordenar)* to mess up; **me revuelve el estómago** it turns my stomach

2 revolverse *vpr* (a) *(agitarse)* to roll (b) *Fig* **r. contra algn** to turn against sb (c) *(el tiempo)* to turn stormy; *(el mar)* to become rough

> ⚠ Observa que el verbo inglés **to revolve** es un falso amigo y no es la traducción del verbo español **revolver**. En inglés, **to revolve** significa "girar".

revólver *nm (pl* revólveres) revolver

revuelo *nm Fig* stir, commotion

revuelta *nf* (a) *(insurrección)* revolt (b) *(curva)* bend, turn

revuelto,-a *adj* (a) *(desordenado)* jumbled, in a mess (b) *(tiempo)* stormy, unsettled; *(mar)* rough (c) *(agitado)* excited

revulsivo,-a *adj & nm* revulsive

rey *nm* king; *Rel* **(el día de) Reyes** (the) Epiphany, 6 January

reyerta *nf* quarrel, dispute

rezagado,-a *nm,f* straggler, latecomer

rezagarse *vpr* to lag o fall behind

rezar [40] **1** *vi* (a) *(orar)* to pray (b) *(decir)* to say, to read

2 *vt (oración)* to say

rezo *nm* prayer

rezumar *vt* to ooze; *Fig* to exude

RFA *nf Hist (abr* **República Federal de Alemania)** FRG

ría *nf* estuary

riada *nf* flood

ribera *nf (de río)* bank; *(zona)* riverside, waterfront

ribete *nm* edging, border

ribetear *vt* to edge, to border

ricamente *adv Fam* **tan r.** very well

rico,-a 1 *adj* (a) **ser r.** *(adinerado)* to be rich o wealthy; *(abundante)* to be rich; *(bonito)* to be lovely o adorable; *(fértil)* to be rich o fertile (b) **estar r.** *(delicioso)* to be delicious

2 *nm,f* rich person

rictus *nm inv* grin

ridiculez *nf* ridiculous thing; *(cualidad)* ridiculousness

ridiculizar [40] *vt* to ridicule

ridículo,-a 1 *adj* ridiculous

2 *nm* ridicule; **hacer el r., quedar en r.** to make a fool of oneself; **poner a algn en r.** to make a fool of sb

riego *nm* watering, irrigation; **r. sanguíneo** blood circulation

riel *nm* rail

rienda *nf* rein; *Fig* **dar r. suelta a** to give free rein to; *Fig* **llevar las riendas** to hold the reins, to be in control

riesgo *nm* risk; **correr el r. de** to run the risk of; **seguro a todo r.** fully comprehensive insurance

riesgoso,-a *adj Am* risky

rifa *nf* raffle

rifar *vt* to raffle (off)

rifle *nm* rifle

rigidez *nf* rigidity, stiffness; *Fig (severidad)* strictness, inflexibility

rígido,-a *adj* rigid, stiff; *Fig (severo)* strict, inflexible

rigor *nm* rigour; *(severidad)* severity; **con r.** rigorously; **de r.** indispensable

rigurosamente *adv* rigorously; *(meticulosamente)* meticulously; *(severamente)* severely; **r. cierto** absolutely true

riguroso,-a *adj* rigorous; *(severo)* severe, strict

rijo *indic pres de* **regir**

rima *nf* rhyme

rimar *vt & vi* to rhyme (**con** with)

rimbombante *adj (lenguaje)* pompous, pretentious

rímel *nm* mascara

Rin *n* **el R.** the Rhine

rincón *nm* corner; *Fam (lugar remoto)* nook

rinoceronte *nm* rhinoceros

riña *nf (pelea)* fight; *(discusión)* row, quarrel

riñón *nm* kidney; *Fam* **costar un r.** to cost an arm and a leg; *Med* **r. artificial** kidney machine

río *nm* river; **r. abajo** downstream; **r. arriba** upstream

rioja *nm* Rioja (wine)

rioplatense *adj* of/from the River Plate region

ripio *nm (palabras de relleno)* waffle; *Fam* **no perder r.** not to miss a trick

riqueza *nf* (a) wealth (b) *(cualidad)* wealthiness

risa *nf* laugh; *(carcajadas)* laughter; **es (cosa) de r.** it's laughable; **me da r.** it makes me laugh; **tomarse algo a r.** to laugh sth off; *Fig* **morirse** o **mondarse de r.** to die o fall about laughing; *Fam* **mi hermano es una r.** my brother is a laugh; *Fam Fig* **tener algo muerto de r.** to leave sth lying around

risco *nm* crag, cliff

risible *adj* laughable

risilla, risita *nf* giggle, titter; *(risa falsa)* false laugh

risotada *nf* guffaw

ristra *nf* string

ristre *nm* **en r.** at the ready

risueño,-a *adj* smiling

rítmico,-a *adj* rhythmic; **gimnasia rítmica** eurhythmics *sing*

ritmo *nm* (a) rhythm (b) *(paso)* rate; **llevar un buen r. de trabajo** to work at a good pace

rito *nm* (a) rite (b) *(ritual)* ritual

ritual *adj & nm* ritual

rival *adj & nmf* rival

rivalidad *nf* rivalry

rivalizar [40] *vi* to rival (**en** in)

rizado,-a *adj* (a) *(pelo)* curly (b) *(mar)* choppy

rizar [40] **1** *vt (pelo)* to curl; *(tela, papel)* to crease; *Fig* **r. el rizo** to make things even more complicated

2 rizarse *vpr (pelo)* to curl, to go curly

rizo *nm* (a) *(de pelo)* curl (b) *(en el agua)* ripple

RNE *nf (abr* **Radio Nacional de España***)* = Spanish state radio station

robalo *nm (pez)* bass

robar *vt* (a) *(objeto)* to steal; *(banco, persona)* to rob; *(casa)* to burgle; *Fig* **en aquel supermercado te roban** they really rip you off in that supermarket (b) *Naipes* to draw

roble *nm* oak (tree)

robledal, robledo *nm* oak grove o wood

robo *nm* robbery, theft; *(en casa)* burglary; *Fam (timo)* rip-off

robot *nm (pl* **robots***)* robot; **r. de cocina** food processor

robótica *nf* robotics *sing*

robustecer [33] *vt* to strengthen

robusto,-a *adj* robust, sturdy

roca *nf* rock

rocalla *nf* pebbles, stone chippings

rocambolesco,-a *adj* incredible, far-fetched

roce *nm* (a) *(fricción)* rubbing; *(en la piel)* chafing (b) *(marca) (en la pared etc)* scuff mark; *(en la piel)* chafing mark, graze (c) *(contacto ligero)* brush, light touch (d) *Fam (trato entre personas)* contact (e) *Fam (discusión)* brush

rociar [29] *vt (salpicar)* to spray, to sprinkle

rocín *nm* nag, hack

rocío *nm* dew

Rocosas *nfpl* **las R.** the Rockies

rocoso,-a *adj* rocky, stony

rodaballo *nm (pez)* turbot

rodado,-a *adj* (a) *(piedra)* smooth, rounded; **canto r.** boulder (b) **tráfico r.** road traffic, vehicular traffic

rodaja *nf* slice; **en rodajas** sliced

rodaje *nm* (a) *(filmación)* filming, shooting (b) *Aut* running in

Ródano *n* **el R.** the Rhone

rodante *adj* rolling

rodar [2] **1** *vt (película etc)* to film, to shoot
2 *vi* to roll, to turn

rodear 1 *vt* to surround, to encircle
2 rodearse *vpr* to surround oneself (**de** with)

rodeo *nm* (**a**) *(desvío)* detour (**b**) *(al hablar)* evasiveness; **andarse con rodeos** to beat about the bush; **no andarse con rodeos** to get straight to the point (**c**) *Am* rodeo

rodilla *nf* knee; **de rodillas** *(arrodillado)* kneeling; **hincarse** *o* **ponerse de rodillas** to kneel down, to go down on one's knees

rodillera *nf (de pantalón)* knee patch; *Dep* knee pad

rodillo *nm* roller; **r. de cocina** rolling pin

rododendro *nm* rhododendron

roedor *nm* rodent

roer [38] *vt (hueso)* to gnaw; *(galleta)* to nibble at; *Fig (conciencia)* to gnaw at, to nag at; *Fig* **un hueso duro de r.** a hard nut to crack

rogar [2] *vt (pedir)* to request, to ask; *(implorar)* to beg; **hacerse de r.** to play hard to get; **se ruega silencio** *(en letrero)* silence please; **rogamos disculpen la molestia** please forgive the inconvenience

roído,-a *adj* gnawed, eaten away

rojizo,-a *adj* reddish

rojo,-a 1 *adj* (**a**) red; *Fin* **estar en números rojos** to be in the red (**b**) *Pol (comunista)* red
2 *nm (color)* red; **al r. vivo** *(caliente)* red-hot; *Fig (tenso)* very tense
3 *nm,f Pol (comunista)* red

rol *nm* role; **juego de r.** role play

rollizo,-a *adj* chubby, plump

rollo *nm* (**a**) *(de papel etc)* roll (**b**) *Fam (pesadez)* drag, bore; **es el mismo r. de siempre** it's the same old story; **un r. de libro** a boring book (**c**) *Fam (amorío)* affair

Roma *n* Rome

romana *nf* **calamares a la r.** = squid in batter

romance *nm* (**a**) *(aventura amorosa)* romance (**b**) *(idioma)* Romance; *Fig* **hablar en r.** to speak plainly (**c**) *Lit* narrative poem, ballad

románico,-a *adj & nm* Romanesque

romanticismo *nm* romanticism

romántico,-a *adj & nm,f* romantic

rombo *nm* rhombus

romería *nf Rel* pilgrimage

romero *nm Bot* rosemary

romo,-a *adj* (**a**) blunt (**b**) *(nariz)* snub

rompecabezas *nm inv (juego)* (jigsaw) puzzle; *Fig (problema)* riddle, puzzle

rompeolas *nm inv* breakwater, jetty

romper *(pp* roto*)* **1** *vt* (**a**) to break; *(papel, tela)* to tear; *(vajilla, cristal)* to smash, to shatter (**b**) *(relaciones)* to break off
2 *vi* (**a**) *(olas, día)* to break (**b**) *(acabar)* to break (**con** with); **rompió con su novio** she broke it off with her boyfriend (**c**) **r. a llorar** to burst out crying; **r. en llanto** to burst into tears

3 romperse *vpr* to break; *(papel, tela)* to tear; **se rompió por la mitad** it broke *o* split in half; *Fig* **r. la cabeza** to rack one's brains

rompevientos *nm RP (jersey)* polo neck jersey; *(anorak)* anorak

rompimiento *nm Am* breaking off

ron *nm* rum

roncar [44] *vi* to snore

roncha *nf (en la piel)* swelling, lump

ronco,-a *adj* hoarse; **quedarse r.** to lose one's voice

ronda *nf* (**a**) round; *(patrulla)* patrol (**b**) *(carretera)* ring road; *(paseo)* avenue (**c**) **pagar una r.** to pay for a round of drinks

rondar 1 *vt* (**a**) *(vigilar)* to patrol, to do the rounds of (**b**) *Pey (merodear)* to prowl around, to hang about (**c**) *(estar cerca de)* to be about *o* approximately; **ronda los cuarenta** she is about forty
2 *vi* (**a**) *(vigilar)* to patrol (**b**) *(merodear)* to prowl around, to roam around

ronquera *nf* hoarseness

ronquido *nm* snore

ronronear *vi* to purr

ronroneo *nm* purring

roña *nf* (**a**) *(mugre)* filth, dirt (**b**) *(sarna)* mange

roñica *Fam* **1** *adj* mean, stingy
2 *nmf* scrooge, miser

roñoso,-a *adj* (**a**) *(mugriento)* filthy, dirty (**b**) *(sarnoso)* mangy (**c**) *Fam (tacaño)* mean, stingy

ropa *nf* clothes, clothing; *Fig* **a quema r.** point-blank; **r. blanca** (household) linen; **r. interior** underwear

> Observa que la palabra inglesa **rope** es un falso amigo y no es la traducción de la palabra española **ropa**. En inglés, **rope** significa "cuerda, soga".

ropaje *nm* clothes

ropero *nm (armario)* **r.** wardrobe

roque *nm* (**a**) *(en ajedrez)* rook (**b**) *Fam* **quedarse r.** to fall fast asleep

rosa 1 *adj inv (color)* pink; **novela r.** romantic novel
2 *nf Bot* rose; *(en la piel)* birthmark; **r. de los vientos** compass (rose)
3 *nm (color)* pink

rosáceo,-a *adj* rose-coloured, rosy

rosado,-a 1 *adj (color)* pink, rosy; *(vino)* rosé
2 *nm (vino)* rosé

rosal *nm* rosebush

rosaleda *nf* rose garden

rosario *nm Rel* rosary; *(sarta)* string, series sing

rosbif *nm* roast beef

rosca *nf* (**a**) *(de tornillo)* thread; **tapón de r.** screw top; *Fig* **pasarse de r.** to go too far (**b**) *(espiral)* spiral, coil

rosco *nm (pastel)* = ring-shaped roll or

pastry; *Fam* **no comerse un r.** not to get one's oats

rosetón *nm* rose window

rosquilla *nf* ring-shaped pastry; *Fam Fig* **venderse como rosquillas** to sell like hot cakes

rosticería *nf Chile, Méx* = shop selling roast chicken

rostro *nm* face; *Fam* **tener mucho r.** to have a lot of nerve; *Fam* **¡vaya r.!** what a cheek!

> 🖉 Observa que la palabra inglesa **rostrum** es un falso amigo y no es la traducción de la palabra española **rostro**. En inglés, **rostrum** significa "estrado".

rotación *nf* rotation

rotativo,-a 1 *adj* rotary, revolving
  2 *nm* newspaper

roto,-a 1 *adj* broken; *(papel)* torn; *(ropa)* in tatters, tattered
  2 *nm (agujero)* hole, tear
  3 *nm,f Chile Fam (trabajador)* worker

rotoso,-a *adj Andes, RP* ragged, in tatters

rótula *nf* (a) *Anat* kneecap (b) *Téc* ball-and-socket joint

rotulador *nm* felt-tip pen

rotular *vt* to letter, to label

rótulo *nm (letrero)* sign, notice; *(titular)* title, heading

rotundo,-a *adj* categorical; **éxito r.** resounding success; **un no r.** a flat refusal

rotura *nf (ruptura)* breaking; *Med* fracture

roturar *vt* to plough

roulotte *nf Br* caravan, *US* trailer

rozadura *nf* scratch, abrasion

rozamiento *nm* rubbing, friction

rozar [40] **1** *vt* to touch, to rub against, to brush against
  2 *vi* to rub
  3 rozarse *vpr* to rub, to brush (**con** against)

Rte. (*abr* **remite, remitente**) sender

RTVE *nf* (*abr* **Radiotelevisión Española**) = Spanish state broadcasting company

ruana *nf Andes* poncho

rubéola *nf* German measles *sing*, rubella

rubí *nm* (*pl* **rubíes**) ruby

rubicundo,-a *adj* rosy, reddish

rubio,-a 1 *adj (pelo, persona)* fair, blond, *f* blonde; **r. de bote** peroxide blonde; **tabaco r.** Virginia tobacco
  2 *nm,f* blond, *f* blonde

rublo *nm* rouble

rubor *nm* blush, flush

ruborizarse [40] *vpr* to blush, to go red

ruboroso,-a *adj* blushing, bashful

rúbrica *nf* (a) *(de firma)* = flourish added to a signature (b) *(título)* title, heading

rubricar [44] *vt* (a) *(firmar)* to sign with a flourish (b) *(respaldar)* to endorse, to ratify

rudeza *nf* roughness, coarseness

rudimentario,-a *adj* rudimentary

rudimento *nm* rudiment

rudo,-a *adj* rough, coarse

rueda *nf* (a) wheel; *Aut* **r. de recambio** spare wheel; *Aut* **r. delantera/trasera** front/rear wheel; **r. de prensa** press conference; *Fam* **ir sobre ruedas** to go very smoothly (b) *(rodaja)* round slice

ruedo *nm* (a) *Taurom* bullring, arena (b) *(de falda)* hem

ruego *nm* request

rufián *nm* villain, scoundrel

rugby *nm* rugby

rugido *nm (de animal)* roar; *(del viento)* howl; *(de tripas)* rumbling

rugir [57] *vi* to roar; *(viento)* to howl

rugoso,-a *adj* rough

ruibarbo *nm* rhubarb

ruido *nm* noise; *(sonido)* sound; *(jaleo)* din, row; *Fig* stir, commotion; **hacer r.** to make a noise

ruidoso,-a *adj* noisy, loud

ruin *adj* (a) *(vil)* vile, despicable (b) *(tacaño)* mean, stingy

ruina *nf* ruin; *(derrumbamiento)* collapse; *(de persona)* downfall

ruindad *nf* vileness, meanness; *(acto)* mean act, low trick

ruinoso,-a *adj* dilapidated, tumbledown

ruiseñor *nm* nightingale

ruleta *nf* roulette

ruletear *vi CAm, Méx Fam (en taxi)* to drive a taxi

ruletero *nm CAm, Méx Fam (de taxi)* taxi driver

rulo *nm* (a) *(para el pelo)* curler, roller (b) *Culin* rolling pin

rulot(a) *nf* (*pl* **rulots**) *Br* caravan, *US* trailer

ruma *nf Andes, Ven* heap, pile

Rumanía, Rumania *n* Romania

rumba *nf* rhumba, rumba

rumbo *nm* direction, course; **(con) r. a** bound for, heading for

rumiante *nm* ruminant

rumiar [43] **1** *vt* (a) *(mascar)* to chew (b) *Fig (pensar)* to ruminate, to reflect on, to chew over
  2 *vi* to ruminate, to chew the cud

rumor *nm* (a) rumour (b) *(murmullo)* murmur

rumorearse *v impers* to be rumoured

runrún, runruneo *nm* buzz, noise

rupestre *adj* **pintura r.** cave painting

ruptura *nf* breaking; *(de relaciones)* breaking off

rural *adj* rural, country

Rusia *n* Russia

ruso,-a *adj & nm,f* Russian

rústico,-a *adj* rustic, rural

ruta *nf* route, road

rutilar *vi* to sparkle

rutina *nf* routine; **por r.** as a matter of course

rutinario,-a *adj* routine

S, s ['ese] *nf (la letra)* S, s
S (*abr* **Sur**) S
S. (*abr* **San, Santo**) St
s. (*abr* **siglo**) c
S.A. (*abr* **Sociedad Anónima**) *Br* ≃ PLC, *US* ≃ Inc
sábado *nm* Saturday
sabana *nf* savannah
sábana *nf* sheet; *Fam* **se me pegaron las sábanas** I overslept
sabandija *nf (insecto)* creepy-crawly; *(persona)* creep
sabañón *nm* chilblain
sabático,-a *adj* sabbatical
sabelotodo *nmf inv* know-all
saber¹ *nm* knowledge
saber² [21] **1** *vt* (**a**) to know; **hacer s.** to inform; **para que lo sepas** for your information; **que yo sepa** as far as I know; **vete tú a s.** goodness knows; **¡y yo qué sé!** how should I know!; *Fig* **a s.** namely (**b**) *(tener habilidad)* to be able to; **¿sabes cocinar?** can you cook?; **¿sabes hablar inglés?** can you speak English? (**c**) *(enterarse)* to learn, to find out; **lo supe ayer** I found this out yesterday
2 *vi* (**a**) *(tener sabor)* to taste (**a** of); **sabe a fresa** it tastes of strawberries; *Fig* **me sabe mal** I feel guilty *o* bad about that (**b**) *Am (soler)* to be accustomed to
sabido,-a *adj* known; **como es s.** as everyone knows
sabiduría *nf* wisdom
sabiendas: a sabiendas *loc adv* **lo hizo a s.** he did it in the full knowledge of what he was doing; **a s. de que ...** knowing full well that ...
sabihondo,-a *nm,f Fam (sabelotodo)* know-all; *(pedante)* pedant
sabio,-a 1 *adj (prudente)* wise
2 *nm,f* scholar
sabiondo,-a *nm,f Fam* = sabihondo,-a
sable *nm* sabre
sabor *nm (gusto)* taste, flavour; **con s. a limón** lemon-flavoured; **sin s.** tasteless; **me deja mal s. de boca** it leaves a bad taste in my mouth
saborear *vt (degustar)* to taste; *Fig (apreciar)* to savour
sabotaje *nm* sabotage
saboteador,-a *nm,f* saboteur
sabotear *vt* to sabotage
sabré *indic fut de* saber
sabroso,-a *adj* (**a**) tasty; *(delicioso)* delicious

(**b**) *(agradable)* delightful
sabueso *nm* bloodhound
sacacorchos *nm inv* corkscrew
sacamuelas *nmf inv Fam* dentist
sacapuntas *nm inv* pencil sharpener
sacar [44] *vt* (**a**) to take out; *(con más fuerza)* to pull out; **s. dinero del banco** to withdraw money from the bank; **s. la lengua** to stick one's tongue out; *Fig* **s. faltas a algo** to find fault with sth; *Fig* **s. adelante** to help to get on; **s. provecho de algo** to benefit from sth; **s. algo en claro** *o* **en limpio** to make sense of sth (**b**) *(obtener)* to get; *(dinero)* to get, to make; *(conclusiones)* to draw, to reach; *(entrada)* to get, to buy (**c**) *(producto, libro, disco)* to bring out; *(nueva moda)* to bring in (**d**) *(fotografía)* to take; *(fotocopia)* to make (**e**) *Ten* to serve; *Ftb* to kick off
sacarina *nf* saccharin
sacerdotal *adj* priestly
sacerdote *nm* priest; **sumo s.** high priest
saciar [43] *vt* to satiate; *(sed)* to quench; *(deseos, hambre)* to satisfy; *(ambiciones)* to fulfil
saciedad *nf* satiety; **repetir algo hasta la s.** to repeat sth ad nauseam
saco *nm* (**a**) sack; **s. de dormir** sleeping bag (**b**) *Mil* **entrar a s. en una ciudad** to pillage a town (**c**) *Am (chaqueta)* jacket
sacralizar [40] *vt* to consecrate
sacramento *nm* sacrament
sacrificar [44] **1** *vt* to sacrifice
2 **sacrificarse** *vpr* to make a sacrifice *o* sacrifices
sacrificio *nm* sacrifice
sacrilegio *nm* sacrilege
sacrílego,-a *adj* sacrilegious
sacristán *nm* verger, sexton
sacristía *nf* vestry, sacristy
sacro,-a *adj* sacred
sacudida *nf* (**a**) shake; *(espasmo)* jolt, jerk; **s. eléctrica** electric shock (**b**) *(de terremoto)* tremor
sacudir *vt* (**a**) *(agitar)* to shake; *(alfombra, sábana)* to shake out; *(arena, polvo)* to shake off (**b**) *(golpear)* to beat (**c**) *(conmover)* to shock, to stun
sádico,-a 1 *adj* sadistic
2 *nm,f* sadist
sadismo *nm* sadism
sadomasoquista 1 *adj* sadomasochistic
2 *nmf* sadomasochist

saeta *nf* (a) *(dardo)* dart (b) *(canción)* = popular religious song

safari *nm (cacería)* safari; *(parque)* safari park

sagacidad *nf Fml (listeza)* cleverness; *(astucia)* astuteness, shrewdness

sagaz *adj (listo)* clever; *(astuto)* astute, shrewd

Sagitario *nm* Sagittarius

sagrado,-a *adj* sacred

sagrario *nm* tabernacle

Sáhara *n* Sahara

saharaui *adj & nmf* Saharan

sahariana *nf* safari jacket

sainete *nm Teatro* comic sketch, one-act farce

sajón,-ona *adj & nm,f* Saxon

sal¹ *nf* (a) salt; **s. fina** table salt; **s. gema** salt crystals; **s. gorda** cooking salt (b) *Fig (gracia)* wit

sal² *imperat de* salir

sala *nf* room; *(en un hospital)* ward; *Jur* courtroom; **s. de estar** lounge, living room; **s. de espera** waiting room; **s. de exposiciones** exhibition hall; **s. de fiestas** nightclub, discotheque; **s. de lectura** reading room

saladito *nm RP* savoury snack *o* appetizer

salado,-a *adj* (a) *(con sal)* salted; *(con exceso de sal)* salty; **agua salada** salt water (b) *Fig (encantador)* charming (c) *Am (infortunado)* unlucky

salamandra *nf* salamander

salamanquesa *nf* gecko

salame, salami *nm* salami

salar *vt* to salt, to add salt to

salarial *adj* salary, wage

salario *nm* salary, wages; **s. mínimo** minimum wage

salazones *nfpl* salted meat *o* fish

salchicha *nf* sausage

salchichón *nm* = salami-type sausage

salchichonería *nf Méx* delicatessen

saldar *vt* (a) *Fin (cuenta)* to settle; *(deuda)* to pay off (b) *Com (vender barato)* to sell off (c) *Fig (diferencias)* to settle, to resolve

saldo *nm* (a) **saldos** sales; **a precio de s.** at bargain prices (b) *Fin* balance (c) *(de una deuda)* liquidation, settlement (d) *(resto de mercancía)* remainder, leftover

saldré *indic fut de* salir

saledizo,-a *adj* projecting

salero *nm* (a) *(recipiente)* saltcellar (b) *Fig (gracia)* charm

salgo *indic pres de* salir

salida *nf* (a) *(partida)* departure; *(puerta etc)* exit, way out; **callejón sin s.** dead end; **s. de emergencia** emergency exit (b) *Dep* start; **línea de s.** starting line; **s. nula** false start (c) **te vi a la s. del cine** I saw you leaving the cinema (d) *(de un astro)* rising; **s. del sol** sunrise (e) *(profesional)* opening; *Com* outlet (f) *(recurso)* solution, way out; **no tengo otra s.** I have no other option (g) *Fam (ocu-*

rrencia) witty remark, witticism (h) *Informát* output

salido,-a *adj* (a) prominent, projecting (b) *muy Fam (persona)* horny

saliente *adj* (a) projecting, prominent; *Fig* outstanding (b) *(cesante)* outgoing

salina *nf* salt mine

salino,-a *adj* saline

salir [22] **1** *vi* (a) *(de un sitio)* to go out, to leave; *(venir de dentro)* to come out; **salió de la habitación** she left the room; **s. de la carretera** to turn off the road

(b) *(tren etc)* to depart

(c) *(novios)* to go out (**con** with)

(d) *(aparecer)* to appear; *(revista, disco)* to come out; *(ley)* to come in; *(trabajo, vacante)* to come up

(e) *(resultar)* to turn out, to turn out to be; **el pequeño les ha salido muy listo** their son has turned out to be very clever; **¿cómo te salió el examen?** how did your exam go?; **s. ganando** to come out ahead *o* on top; **salió presidente** he was elected president

(f) **s. a** *(precio)* to come to, to work out at; **s. barato/caro** to work out cheap/expensive

(g) **ha salido al abuelo** she takes after her grandfather

(h) *(problema)* to work out; **esta cuenta no me sale** I can't work this sum out

(i) **¡con qué cosas sales!** the things you come out with!

2 salirse *vpr* (a) *(líquido, gas)* to leak (out); *Fig* **s. de lo normal** to be out of the ordinary; **se salió de la carretera** he went off the road

(b) *Fam* **s. con la suya** to get one's own way

saliva *nf* saliva

salivar *vi* to salivate

salivazo *nm* spit

salmantino,-a 1 *adj* of/from Salamanca

2 *nm,f* person from Salamanca

salmo *nm* psalm

salmón 1 *nm (pescado)* salmon

2 *adj inv (color)* salmon pink, salmon

salmonete *nm (pescado)* red mullet

salmorejo *nm (salsa)* = sauce made from vinegar, water, pepper and salt

salmuera *nf* brine

salobre *adj (agua)* brackish; *(gusto)* salty, briny

salón *nm* (a) *(en una casa)* lounge, sitting room (b) **s. de actos** assembly hall; **s. de baile** dance hall (c) **s. de belleza** beauty salon; **s. de té** tearoom, teashop (d) **s. del automóvil** motor show

salpicadera *nf Méx Br* mudguard, *US* fender

salpicadura *nf* splashing

salpicar [44] *vt* (a) *(rociar)* to splash; **me salpicó el abrigo de barro** he splashed mud on my coat (b) *Fig (esparcir)* to sprinkle

salpicón *nm* (a) splash (b) *Culin* cocktail

salpimentar [1] *vt* to season

salpullido *nm* rash

salsa *nf* sauce; *(de carne)* gravy; *Fig* **en su (propia) s.** in one's element

saltador,-a *nm,f Dep* jumper

saltamontes *nm inv* grasshopper

saltar 1 *vt (obstáculo, valla)* to jump (over)

2 *vi* (a) to jump; *Fig* **s. a la vista** to be obvious (b) *(cristal etc)* to break, to shatter; *(plomos)* to go, to blow (c) *(desprenderse)* to come off (d) *(encolerizarse)* to explode, to blow up; **por menos de nada salta** the smallest thing makes him explode

3 saltarse *vpr* (a) *(omitir)* to skip, to miss out; **s. el semáforo/turno** to jump the lights/the queue (b) *(botón)* to come off; **se me saltaron las lágrimas** tears came to my eyes

salteado,-a *adj* (a) *(espaciado)* spaced out (b) *Culin* sauté, sautéed

saltear *vt Culin* to sauté

saltimbanqui *nmf* acrobat, tumbler

salto *nm* (a) *(acción)* jump, leap; *Fig (paso adelante)* leap forward; **a saltos** in leaps and bounds; **dar o pegar un s.** to jump, to leap; **de un s.** in a flash; *Fig* **a s. de mata** every now and then; **s. de agua** waterfall; **s. de cama** negligée (b) *Dep* jump; **s. de altura** high jump; **s. de longitud** long jump; **s. mortal** somersault

saltón,-ona *adj* prominent; **ojos saltones** bulging eyes

salubre *adj* salubrious

salubridad *nf* healthiness; **por razones de s.** for health reasons

salud *nf* health; **beber a la s. de algn** to drink to sb's health; *Fam* **¡s.!** cheers!

saludable *adj* (a) *(sano)* healthy, wholesome (b) *Fig (beneficioso)* good, beneficial

saludar *vt* (a) *(decir hola a)* to say hello to, to greet; **saluda de mi parte a** give my regards to; **le saluda atentamente** *(en una carta)* yours faithfully (b) *Mil* to salute

saludo *nm* (a) greeting; **un s. de** best wishes from (b) *Mil* salute

salva *nf Mil* salvo, volley

salvación *nf* salvation

salvado *nm* bran

salvador,-a 1 *nm,f* saviour; *(rescatador)* rescuer

2 *nm* **El S.** El Salvador

salvadoreño,-a *adj & nm,f* Salvadoran, Salvadorian

salvaguarda *nf (defensa)* protection

salvaguardar *vt* to safeguard (**de** from), to protect (**de** from)

salvaguardia *nf* = **salvaguarda**

salvajada *nf* brutal act

salvaje *adj* (a) *Bot* wild, uncultivated; *Zool* wild; *(pueblo, tribu)* savage, uncivilized (b) *Fam (violento)* savage, wild

salvajismo *nm* savagery

salvamento, salvamiento *nm* rescue

salvar 1 *vt* (a) to save, to rescue (**de** from) (b) *(obstáculo)* to clear; *(dificultad)* to get round,

to overcome (c) *(exceptuar)* to exclude, to except; **salvando ciertos errores** except for a few mistakes

2 salvarse *vpr* (a) *(sobrevivir)* to survive, to come out alive; *Fam (escaparse)* to escape (**de** from); **¡sálvese quien pueda!** every man for himself!; *Fam* **s. por los pelos** to have a narrow escape (b) *Rel* to be saved, to save one's soul

salvavidas *nm inv* life belt

salvedad *nf* (a) *(excepción)* exception (b) *(reserva)* proviso

salvia *nf Bot* sage

salvo,-a 1 *adj* unharmed, safe; **a s.** safe

2 *adv (exceptuando)* except (for); **s. que** unless

salvoconducto *nm* safe-conduct

san *adj* saint

sanar 1 *vt (curar)* to cure, to heal

2 *vi* (a) *(persona)* to recover, to get better (b) *(herida)* to heal

sanatorio *nm* sanatorium

sanción *nf* (a) sanction (b) *(aprobación)* sanction, approval (c) *Jur* penalty

sancionar *vt* (a) *(castigar)* to penalize (b) *(aprobar)* to sanction

sancochar *vt* to parboil; *Am* = to boil in water and salt

sancocho *nm Andes, Ven (comida)* = stew of beef, chicken or fish, vegetables and green bananas

sandalia *nf* sandal

sándalo *nm* sandalwood

sandez *nf* piece of nonsense

sandía *nf* watermelon

sándwich *nm* sandwich

sandwichera *nf* toasted sandwich maker

saneamiento *nm (de terreno)* drainage, draining; *(de una empresa)* reorganization

sanear *vt (terrenos)* to drain; *(empresa)* to reorganize

sangrar 1 *vt* (a) to bleed (b) *Fam (sacar dinero)* to bleed dry

2 *vi* to bleed

sangre *nf* blood; **donar s.** to give blood; **s. fría** sangfroid; **a s. fría** in cold blood

sangría *nf* (a) *Med* bleeding, bloodletting; *Fig* drain (b) *(timo)* rip-off (c) *(bebida)* sangria

sangriento,-a *adj (guerra etc)* bloody

sanguijuela *nf* leech, bloodsucker

sanguinario,-a *adj* bloodthirsty

sanguíneo,-a *adj* blood; **grupo s.** blood group

sanidad *nf* health; **Ministerio de S.** Department of Health

> *Observa que la palabra inglesa* **sanity** *es un falso amigo y no es la traducción de la palabra española* **sanidad**. *En inglés,* **sanity** *significa "cordura, sensatez".*

sanitario,-a 1 *adj* health

2 *nm* toilet

sano,-a adj (a) (bien de salud) healthy; **s. y salvo** safe and sound (b) (comida) healthy, wholesome (c) **en su s. juicio** in one's right mind

🔎 Observa que la palabra inglesa **sane** es un falso amigo y no es la traducción de la palabra española **sano**. En inglés, **sane** significa "cuerdo, sensato".

Santa Claus, Méx, Ven **Santa Clos** n Santa Claus

santería nf (a) (religión) santería, = form of religion common in the Caribbean, in which people allegedly have contact with the spirit world (b) Am (tienda) = shop selling religious mementos such as statues of saints

santero,-a nm,f (curandero) = faith healer who calls on the saints to assist with the healing process

santiamén nm Fam **en un s.** in a flash, in no time at all

santidad nf saintliness, holiness

santificar [44] vt to sanctify

santiguarse [45] vpr to cross oneself

santo,-a 1 adj (a) holy, sacred (b) (bueno) saintly; **un s. varón** a saint

2 nm,f (a) saint; Fam **¡por todos los santos!** for heaven's sake!; Fig **se me fue el s. al cielo** I clean forgot (b) (día onomástico) saint's day; Fig **¿a s. de qué?** why on earth?

santuario nm sanctuary, shrine

saña nf fury; **con s.** furiously

sapo nm toad; Fam **echar sapos y culebras** to rant and rave

saque nm (a) Ftb **s. inicial** kick-off; **s. de banda** throw-in; **s. de esquina** corner kick (b)Ten service

saquear vt (ciudad) to sack, to plunder; (casas, tiendas) to loot

saqueo nm (de ciudades) sacking, plundering; (de casa, tienda) looting

S.A.R. (abr Su Alteza Real) H.R.H.

sarampión nm measles sing

sarao nm knees-up

sarcasmo nm sarcasm

sarcástico,-a adj sarcastic

sarcófago nm sarcophagus

sardana nf sardana, = Catalan dance and music

sardina nf sardine

sardónico,-a adj sardonic

sargento nm sergeant

sarmiento nm vine shoot

sarna nf Med scabies sing; Zool mange

sarpullido nm rash

sarracina nf massacre

sarro nm (sedimento) deposit; (en los dientes) tartar; (en la lengua) fur

sarta nf string

sartén nf frying pan, US fry-pan; Fig **tener la s. por el mango** to have the upper hand

sastre nm tailor

Satanás n Satan

satánico,-a adj satanic

satélite nm satellite; Fig **país s.** satellite state; **televisión vía s.** satellite TV

satén nm satin

satinar vt to gloss, to make glossy

sátira nf satire

satírico,-a adj satirical

satirizar [40] vt to satirize

satisfacción nf satisfaction; **s. de un deseo** fulfilment of a desire

satisfacer [15] (pp **satisfecho**) vt (a) (deseos, necesidades) to satisfy (b) (requisitos) to meet, to satisfy (c) (deuda) to pay

satisfactorio,-a adj satisfactory

satisfecho,-a adj satisfied; **me doy por s.** that's good enough for me; **s. de sí mismo** self-satisfied, smug

saturar vt to saturate

Saturno n Saturn

sauce nm willow; **s. llorón** weeping willow

saudí, saudita adj & nmf Saudi; **Arabia Saudita** Saudi Arabia

sauna nf sauna

savia nf sap

saxo nm Fam Mús sax

saxofón nm saxophone

saxofonista nmf saxophonist

sayo nm cassock, smock

sazonar vt to season, to flavour

s/c. (abr su cuenta) your account

Sdad. (abr sociedad) Soc.

se¹ pron (a) (reflexivo) (objeto directo) (a él mismo) himself; (animal) itself; (a ella misma) herself; (animal) itself; (a usted mismo) yourself; (a ellos mismos) themselves; (a ustedes mismos) yourselves

(b) (objeto indirecto) (a él mismo) (to/for) himself; (animal) (to/for) itself; (a ella misma) (to/for) herself; (animal) (to/for) itself; (a usted mismo) (to/for) yourself; (a ellos mismos) (to/for) themselves; (a ustedes mismos) (to/for) yourselves; **se compró un nuevo coche** he bought himself a new car; **todos los días se lava el pelo** she washes her hair every day

(c) (recíproco) one another, each other

(d) (voz pasiva) **el vino se guarda en cubas** wine is kept in casks

(e) (impersonal) **nunca se sabe** you never know; **se habla inglés** (en letrero) English spoken here; **se dice que ...** it is said that ...

se² pron pers (a él) (to/for) him; (a ella) (to/for) her; (a usted o ustedes) (to/for) you; (a ellos) (to/for) them; **se lo diré en cuanto les vea** I'll tell them as soon as I see them; **¿se lo explico?** shall I explain it to you?; **¿se lo has dado ya?** have you given it to him yet?

sé¹ indic pres de saber

sé² imperat de ser

S.E. (abr Su Excelencia) HE

sea *subj pres de* **ser**
sebo *nm (grasa)* fat
secado *nm* drying
secador *nm* dryer; **s. de pelo** hairdryer
secadora *nf* tumble dryer
secano *nm* dry land
secante *adj* **papel s.** blotting paper
secar [44] **1** *vt* to dry
  2 secarse *vpr* (**a**) to dry; **sécate** dry yourself; **s. las manos** to dry one's hands (**b**) *(marchitarse)* to dry up, to wither
sección *nf* section
seco,-a *adj* (**a**) dry; **frutos secos** dried fruit; **limpieza en s.** dry-cleaning; **a palo s.** on its own; *Fig* **a secas** just, only (**b**) *(tono)* curt, sharp; *(golpe, ruido)* sharp; *Fig* **frenar en s.** to pull up sharply; *Fig* **parar en s.** to stop dead (**c**) *(delgado)* skinny
secreción *nf* secretion
secretaría *nf (oficina)* secretary's office; **S. de Estado** *(en España)* = government department under the control of a *Br* junior minister *o US* under-secretary; *(en Latinoamérica)* department, *Br* ministry; *(en Estados Unidos)* State Department
secretariado *nm* (**a**) *(oficina)* secretariat (**b**) *Educ* secretarial course
secretario,-a *nm,f* secretary; **s. de dirección** secretary to the director; **s. de Estado** *(en España) Br* junior minister, *US* under-secretary; *(en Latinoamérica)* minister; *(en Estados Unidos)* Secretary of State
secreto,-a 1 *adj* secret; **en s.** in secret, secretly
  2 *nm* secret; **guardar un s.** to keep a secret; **con mucho s.** in great secrecy
secta *nf* sect
sectario,-a *adj* sectarian
sector *nm* (**a**) sector (**b**) *(zona)* area; **un s. de la ciudad** an area of the city
sectorial *adj* sectoral
secuela *nf* consequence
secuencia *nf* sequence
secuestrador,-a *nm,f* (**a**) *(de persona)* kidnapper; *(de un avión)* hijacker (**b**) *Jur* sequestrator
secuestrar *vt* (**a**) *(persona)* to kidnap; *(aviones)* to hijack (**b**) *Jur* to confiscate
secuestro *nm* (**a**) *(de persona)* kidnapping; *(de un avión)* hijacking (**b**) *Jur* confiscation
secular *adj* (**a**) *Rel* secular, lay (**b**) *(antiquísimo)* ancient, age-old
secundar *vt* to back
secundario,-a *adj* secondary
secuoya *nf Bot* redwood, sequoia; **s. gigante** giant sequoia
sed *nf* thirst; **tener s.** to be thirsty
seda *nf* silk
sedal *nm* fishing line
sedante *adj & nm* sedative
sede *nf* (**a**) headquarters, head office; *(de gobierno)* seat (**b**) **la Santa S.** the Holy See

sedentario,-a *adj* sedentary
sedición *nf* sedition
sedicioso,-a 1 *adj* rebellious
  2 *nm,f* rebel
sediento,-a *adj* thirsty; *Fig* **s. de poder** hungry for power
sedimentario,-a *adj* sedimentary
sedimentarse *vpr* to settle
sedimento *nm* sediment, deposit
sedoso,-a *adj* silky, silken
seducción *nf* seduction
seducir [10] *vt* to seduce; *(persuadir)* to tempt
seductor,-a 1 *adj* seductive; *(persuasivo)* tempting
  2 *nm,f* seducer
segadora *nf (máquina)* reaper, harvester
segar [1] *vt* to reap, to cut
seglar 1 *adj* secular, lay
  2 *nmf* lay person; *(hombre)* layman; *(mujer)* laywoman
segmento *nm* segment
segregación *nf* (**a**) *(separación)* segregation (**b**) *(secreción)* secretion
segregar [42] *vt* (**a**) *(separar)* to segregate (**b**) *(secretar)* to secrete
seguida *nf* **en s.** immediately, straight away
seguido,-a 1 *adj* (**a**) *(continuo)* continuous (**b**) *(consecutivo)* consecutive, successive; **tres veces seguidas** on three consecutive occasions; **tres lunes seguidos** three Mondays in a row
  2 *adv* (**a**) *(en línea recta)* straight on; **todo s.** straight on *o* ahead (**b**) *Am (a menudo)* often
seguidor,-a *nm,f* follower
seguimiento *nm* (**a**) pursuit (**b**) *Prensa* in-depth coverage (**c**) **estación de s. (espacial)** tracking station
seguir [6] **1** *vt* (**a**) to follow (**b**) *(camino)* to continue (**c**) *(perseguir)* to chase
  2 *vi* (**a**) to follow (**b**) **s.** + *ger (continuar)* to continue, to go on, to keep on; **siguió hablando** he continued *o* went on *o* kept on speaking (**c**) **s.** + *adj/pp* to continue to be, to be still; **sigo resfriado** I've still got the cold; **sigue con vida** he's still alive
  3 seguirse *vpr* to follow, to ensue
según 1 *prep* (**a**) according to; **s. la Biblia** according to the Bible (**b**) *(en función de)* depending on; **varía s. el tiempo (que haga)** it varies depending on the weather
  2 *adv* (**a**) depending on; **s. estén las cosas** depending on how things stand; **¿vendrás mañana? – s.** will you come tomorrow? – it depends (**b**) *(tal como)* just as; **estaba s. lo dejé** it was just as I had left it (**c**) *(a medida que)* as; **s. iba leyendo ...** as I read on ...
segundero *nm* second hand
segundo¹,-a 1 *adj* second; *Fig* **decir algo con segundas (intenciones)** to say sth with a double meaning
  2 *nm,f (de una serie)* second (one)

segundo² *nm (tiempo)* second; **sesenta segundos** sixty seconds

seguramente *adv* (**a**) *(seguro)* surely (**b**) *(probablemente)* most probably; **s. no lloverá** it isn't likely to rain

seguridad *nf* (**a**) security; **cerradura de s.** security lock (**b**) *(física)* safety; **s. en carretera** road safety; **para mayor s.** to be on the safe side (**c**) *(confianza)* confidence; **s. en sí mismo** self-confidence (**d**) *(certeza)* sureness; **con toda s.** most probably; **tener la s. de que ...** to be certain that ... (**e**) **S. Social** ≃ Social Security, *Br* ≃ National Health Service (**f**) *(fiabilidad)* reliability

seguro,-a **1** *adj* (**a**) *(cierto)* sure; **estoy s. de que ...** I am sure that ...; **dar algo por s.** to take sth for granted (**b**) *(libre de peligro)* safe; *Fig* **ir sobre s.** to play safe (**c**) *(protegido)* secure (**d**) *(fiable)* reliable (**e**) **está segura de ella misma** she has self-confidence (**f**) *(firme)* steady, firm

  2 *nm* (**a**) *Seg* insurance; **s. a todo riesgo** fully comprehensive insurance; **s. contra terceros** third-party insurance; **s. de vida** life insurance (**b**) *(dispositivo)* safety catch *o* device (**c**) *CAm, Méx (imperdible)* safety pin

  3 *adv* for sure, definitely

seis *adj & nm inv* six

seiscientos,-as *adj & nm* six hundred

seísmo *nm (terremoto)* earthquake; *(temblor de tierra)* earth tremor

selección *nf* (**a**) selection (**b**) *Dep* team

seleccionador,-a *nm,f* (**a**) selector (**b**) *Dep* manager

seleccionar *vt* to select

selectividad *nf* selectivity; *Univ* **(prueba de) s.** entrance examination

selectivo,-a *adj* selective

selecto,-a *adj* select; **ambiente s.** exclusive atmosphere

self-service *nm* self-service cafeteria

sellar *vt (documento)* to seal; *(carta)* to stamp

sello *nm* (**a**) *(de correos)* stamp; *(para documentos)* seal (**b**) *(precinto)* seal

selva *nf* jungle

semáforo *nm* traffic lights

semana *nf* week; **entre s.** during the week; **S. Santa** Holy Week

semanada *nf Am Br* (weekly) pocket money, *US* (weekly) allowance

semanal *adj & nm* weekly

semanario *nm* weekly magazine

semblante *nm Literario (cara)* face; *Fig (aspecto)* look

sembrado *nm* sown field

sembrar [1] *vt* (**a**) *Agr* to sow (**b**) *Fig* **s. el pánico** to spread panic

semejante **1** *adj* (**a**) *(parecido)* similar; **nunca he visto nada s.** I've never seen anything like it (**b**) *Pey (comparativo)* such; **s. desvergüenza** such insolence

  2 *nm (prójimo)* fellow being

semejanza *nf* similarity, likeness

semen *nm* semen

semental *nm* stud

semestral *adj* half-yearly

semestre *nm* six-month period, semester

semicírculo *nm* semicircle

semifinal *nf* semifinal

semifinalista *nmf* semifinalist

semilla *nf* seed

semillero *nm* seedbed

seminario *nm* (**a**) *Educ* seminar (**b**) *Rel* seminary

sémola *nf* semolina

Sena *n* **el S.** the Seine

senado *nm* senate

senador,-a *nm,f* senator

sencillez *nf* simplicity

sencillo,-a **1** *adj* (**a**) *(fácil)* simple, easy (**b**) *(natural)* natural, unaffected (**c**) *(billete)* single (**d**) *(sin adornos)* simple, plain

  2 *nm Andes, CAm, Méx Fam (cambio)* loose change

senda *nf*, **sendero** *nm* path

sendos,-as *adj pl* one each; **con sendas carteras** each carrying a briefcase

senil *adj* senile

seno *nm* (**a**) *(pecho)* breast (**b**) *Fig* bosom, heart; **en el s. de** within (**c**) *Mat* sine

sensación *nf* (**a**) sensation, feeling; **tengo la s. de que ...** I have a feeling that ... (**b**) *(impresión)* sensation; **causar s.** to cause a sensation

sensacional *adj* sensational

sensacionalista *adj* sensationalist; **prensa s.** gutter press

sensato,-a *adj* sensible

sensibilizar [40] *vt* to make aware; **s. a la opinión pública** to increase public awareness

sensible *adj* (**a**) sensitive (**b**) *(perceptible)* perceptible

sensiblemente *adv* noticeably, considerably

> 🖉 Observa que la palabra inglesa **sensible** es un falso amigo y no es la traducción de la palabra española **sensible**. En inglés, **sensible** significa tanto "sensato" como "práctico".

sensiblero,-a *adj* over-sentimental, mawkish

sensitivo,-a *adj* sense; **órgano s.** sense organ

sensorial, sensorio,-a *adj* sensory

sensual *adj* sensual

sensualidad *nf* sensuality

sentada *nf* (**a**) sitting (**b**) *Fam (protesta)* sit-in (demonstration)

sentado,-a *adj (establecido)* established, settled; **dar algo por s.** to take sth for granted; **dejar s. que ...** to make it clear that ...

sentar [1] **1** *vt* (**a**) to sit (**b**) *(establecer)* to establish; **s. las bases** to lay the foundations

2 *vi* (**a**) *(color, ropa etc)* to suit; **el pelo corto te sienta mal** short hair doesn't suit you (**b**) **s. bien/mal a** *(comida)* to agree/disagree with; **la sopa se sentará bien** the soup will do you good (**c**) **le sentó mal la broma** she didn't like the joke

3 sentarse *vpr* to sit, to sit down

sentencia *nf* (**a**) sentence; **visto para s.** ready for judgement (**b**) *(aforismo)* maxim, saying

sentenciar [43] *vt Jur* to sentence (**a** to)

sentido,-a 1 *nm* (**a**) sense; **los cinco sentidos** the five senses; **s. común** common sense; **s. del humor** sense of humour *(significado)* meaning; **doble s.** double meaning; **no tiene s.** it doesn't make sense (**c**) *(dirección)* direction; **(de) s. único** one-way (**d**) *(conciencia)* consciousness; **perder el s.** to faint

2 *adj* deeply felt; *Fml* **mi más s. pésame** my deepest sympathy

sentimental 1 *adj* sentimental; **vida s.** love life

2 *nmf* sentimental person

sentimiento *nm* (**a**) feeling (**b**) *(pesar)* sorrow, grief; *Fml* **le acompaño en el s.** my deepest sympathy

sentir¹ *nm* (**a**) *(sentimiento)* feeling (**b**) *(opinión)* opinion, view

sentir² [5] **1** *vt* (**a**) to feel; **s. hambre/calor** to feel hungry/hot (**b**) *(lamentar)* to regret, to be sorry about; **lo siento (mucho)** I'm (very) sorry; **siento molestarle** I'm sorry to bother you

2 sentirse *vpr* to feel; **me siento mal** I feel ill; **s. con ánimos de hacer algo** to feel like doing sth

senyera *nf* Catalan flag

seña *nf* (**a**) mark (**b**) *(gesto)* sign; **hacer señas a algn** to signal to sb (**c**) *(indicio)* sign (**d**) **señas** *(dirección)* address

señal *nf* (**a**) *(indicio)* sign, indication; **en s. de** as a sign of, as a token of (**b**) *(placa)* sign; **s. de tráfico** road sign (**c**) *(gesto etc)* signal, sign (**d**) *(marca)* mark; *(vestigio)* trace (**e**) *Tel* tone; **s. de llamada** *Br* dialling tone, *US* dial tone (**f**) *Com* deposit

señalado,-a *adj* *(importante)* important; **un día s.** a red-letter day

señalar *vt* (**a**) *(indicar)* to mark, to indicate; **s. con el dedo** to point at (**b**) *(resaltar)* to point out (**c**) *(precio, fecha)* to fix, to arrange

señalero *nm* *Urug* *Br* indicator, *US* turn signal

señor *nm* (**a**) *(hombre)* man; *(caballero)* gentleman (**b**) *Rel* **El S.** the Lord (**c**) *(con apellido)* Mr; *(tratamiento de respeto)* sir; **el Sr. Gutiérrez** Mr Gutiérrez; **muy s. mío** *(en carta)* Dear Sir (**d**) *(con título) (no se traduce)* **el s.** ministro the Minister

señora *nf* (**a**) *(mujer)* woman, *Fml* lady; **¡señoras y señores!** ladies and gentlemen! (**b**) *Rel* **Nuestra S.** Our Lady (**c**) *(con apellido)* Mrs; *(tratamiento de respeto)* madam; **la Sra. Sali-**

nas Mrs Salinas; **muy s. mía** *(en carta)* Dear Madam (**d**) *(con título) (no se traduce)* **la s. ministra** the Minister (**e**) *(esposa)* wife

señoría *nf* (**a**) *Jur (hombre)* lordship; *(mujer)* ladyship (**b**) *Pol* **sus señorías** the honourable gentlemen

señorita *nf* (**a**) *(joven)* young woman, *Fml* young lady (**b**) *(tratamiento de respeto)* Miss; **S. Padilla** Miss Padilla (**c**) *Educ* **la s.** the teacher, Miss

señuelo *nm* *(en caza)* decoy

sepa *subj pres de* **saber**

separación *nf* (**a**) separation; *Jur* **s. conyugal** legal separation (**b**) *(espacio)* space, gap

separado,-a *adj* (**a**) separate; **por s.** separately, individually (**b**) *(divorciado)* separated

separar 1 *vt* (**a**) to separate (**b**) *(desunir)* to detach, to remove (**c**) *(dividir)* to divide, to separate (**d**) *(apartar)* to move away

2 separarse *vpr* (**a**) to separate, to part company (**b**) *(matrimonio)* to separate (**c**) *(apartarse)* to move away (**d** from)

separata *nf* offprint

separatismo *nm* separatism

separatista *adj & nmf* separatist

separo *nm* *Méx* (prison) cell

sepia 1 *nf (pez)* cuttlefish

2 *adj & nm (color)* sepia

septentrional *adj* northern

septiembre *nm* September; **el 5 de s.** the 5th of September; **en s.** in September

séptimo,-a *adj & nm,f* seventh; **la** *o* **una séptima parte** a seventh

sepulcral *adj (silencio)* deathly

sepulcro *nm* tomb

sepultura *nf* grave

sepulturero,-a *nm,f* gravedigger

sequía *nf* drought

séquito *nm* entourage, retinue

ser¹ *nm* being; **s. humano** human being; **s. vivo** living being

ser² [23] *vi* (**a**) *(+ adj)* to be; **es alto y rubio** he is tall and fair; **el edificio es gris** the building is grey

(**b**) *(+ profesión)* to be a(n); **Rafael es músico** Rafael is a musician

(**c**) **s. de** *(procedencia)* to be *o* come from; **¿de dónde eres?** where are you from?, where do you come from?

(**d**) **s. de** *(+ material)* to be made of

(**e**) **s. de** *(+ poseedor)* to belong to; **el perro es de Miguel** the dog belongs to Miguel; **¿de quién es este abrigo?** whose coat is this?

(**f**) **s. para** *(finalidad)* to be for; **esta agua es para lavar** this water is for washing

(**g**) *(+ día, hora)* to be; **hoy es 2 de noviembre** today is the 2nd of November; **son las cinco de la tarde** it's five o'clock

(**h**) *(+ cantidad)* **¿cuántos estaremos en la fiesta?** how many of us will there be at the party?

(**i**) *(costar)* to be, to cost; **¿cuánto es?**

how much is it?

(**j**) *(tener lugar)* to be; **el estreno será maña-na** tomorrow is the opening night

(**k**) **¿qué es de Gonzalo?** what has become of Gonzalo?

(**l**) *(auxiliar en pasiva)* to be; **fue asesinado** he was murdered

(**m**) *(locuciones)* **¿cómo es eso?, ¿cómo puede s.?** how can that be?; **es más** furthermore; **es que ...** it's just that ...; **como sea** anyhow; **lo que sea** whatever; **o sea** that is (to say); **por si fuera poco** to top it all; **sea como sea** in any case, be that as it may; **a no s. que** unless; **de no s. por ...** had it not been for ...; **eso era de esperar** it was to be expected

> The auxiliary verb **ser** is used with the past participle of a verb to form the passive (e.g. **la película fue criticada** the film was criticized).

serenarse *vpr* to calm down
serenidad *nf* serenity
sereno¹ *nm (vigilante)* nightwatchman
sereno²,-a *adj* (a) calm (b) *Fam* **estar s.** *(sobrio)* to be sober
serial *nm Rad & TV* serial
serie *nf* (a) series *sing*; **fabricación en s.** mass production; **lleva ABS de s.** it has ABS fitted as standard; **fuera de s.** out of the ordinary (b) *Rad & TV* series *sing*
seriedad *nf* (a) seriousness (b) *(formalidad)* reliability, dependability; **falta de s.** irresponsibility
serio,-a *adj* (a) *(severo)* serious; **en s.** seriously (b) *(formal)* reliable, responsible
sermón *nm* sermon
sermonear *vt & vi Fam* to lecture
seropositivo,-a *adj* HIV-positive
serpentear *vi (zigzaguear)* to wind one's way, to meander
serpentina *nf (de papel)* streamer
serpiente *nf* snake; **s. de cascabel** rattlesnake; **s. pitón** python
serranía *nf* mountainous area/country
serrar [1] *vt* to saw
serrín *nm* sawdust
serrucho *nm* handsaw
servicial *adj* helpful, obliging
servicio *nm* (a) service; **s. a domicilio** delivery service (b) *Mil* service; **s. militar** military service; **estar de s.** to be on duty (c) **servicios** *(retrete)* toilet, *US* rest room
servidor,-a *nm,f* servant; *Fam* **un s.** yours truly
servil *adj* servile
servilleta *nf* serviette, napkin
servilletero *nm* serviette ring, napkin ring
servio,-a *adj & nm,f* Serbian
servir [6] **1** *vt* to serve; **¿en qué puedo servirle?** what can I do for you?, may I help you?; **¿te sirvo una copa?** will I pour you a drink?

2 *vi* (a) to serve (b) *(valer)* to be useful, to be suitable; **no sirve de nada llorar** it's no use

crying; **ya no sirve** it's no use; **¿para qué sirve esto?** what is this (used) for? (c) **s. de** to serve as, to act as

3 servirse *vpr* (a) *(comida etc)* to help oneself (b) *Fml* **sírvase comunicarnos su decisión** please inform us of your decision
sésamo *nm* sesame
sesenta *adj & nm inv* sixty
sesgar [42] *vt* (a) *(cortar)* to cut diagonally (b) *(torcer)* to slant
sesgo *nm Fig* slant, turn; **tomar un s. favorable** to take a turn for the better
sesión *nf* (a) *(reunión)* meeting, session; *Jur* session, sitting (b) *Cin* showing
seso *nm* brain
set *nm Ten* set
seta *nf (comestible)* mushroom; **s. venenosa** toadstool
setecientos,-as *adj & nm* seven hundred
setenta *adj & nm inv* seventy
setiembre *nm* September
seto *nm* hedge
seudónimo *nm* pseudonym; *(de escritores)* pen name
severidad *nf* severity
severo,-a *adj* severe
Sevilla *n* Seville
sexismo *nm* sexism
sexista *adj* sexist
sexo *nm* (a) sex (b) *(órgano)* genitals
sexólogo,-a *nm,f* sexologist
sexto,-a *adj & nm,f* sixth
sexual *adj* sexual; **vida s.** sex life
sexualidad *nf* sexuality
sexy *adj* sexy
s/f. *(abr* **su favor)** your favour
shock *nm* shock
short *nm RP* swimming trunks
show *nm* show
si¹ *conj* (a) *(condicional)* if; **como si** as if; **si no** if not; **si quieres** if you like, if you wish (b) *(pregunta indirecta)* whether, if; **me preguntó si me gustaba** he asked me if I liked it; **no sé si ir o no** *(disyuntivo)* I don't know whether to go or not (c) *(sorpresa)* **¡si está llorando!** but she's crying!
si² *nm (pl* **sis)** *Mús* B; *(en solfeo)* ti
sí¹ *pron pers* (a) *(singular) (él)* himself; *(ella)* herself; *(cosa)* itself; *(plural)* themselves; **de por sí, en sí** in itself; **hablaban entre sí** they were talking between themselves *o* to each other; **por sí mismo** by himself (b) *(uno mismo)* oneself; **decir para sí** to say to oneself
sí² **1** *adv* (a) yes; **dije que sí** I said yes, I accepted, I agreed; **porque sí** just because; **¡que sí!** yes, I tell you!; **un día sí y otro no** every other day (b) *(uso enfático) (no se traduce)* **sí que me gusta** of course I like it; **¡eso sí que no!** certainly not!

2 *nm (pl* **síes)** yes; **los síes** *(en parlamento)* the ayes
siamés,-esa *nm,f* Siamese twin

sibarita *nmf* sybarite

sicario *nm* hired gunman; *Fam* hitman

Sicilia *n* Sicily

sico- = psico-

sicómoro *nm* sycamore

sida *nm* (*abr* **síndrome de inmunodeficiencia adquirida**) AIDS

sidecar *nm* sidecar

siderurgia *nf* iron and steel industry

siderúrgico,-a *adj* iron and steel; **la industria siderúrgica** the iron and steel industry

sidra *nf Br* cider, *US* hard cider

siempre *adv* (**a**) always; **s. pasa lo mismo** it's always the same; **como s.** as usual; **a la hora de s.** at the usual time; **eso es así desde s.** it has always been like that; **para s.** for ever; **s. que** (*cada vez que*) whenever; (*a condición de que*) provided, as long as; **s. y cuando** provided, as long as (**b**) *Am* (*todavía*) still; **s. viven allí** they still live there (**c**) *Méx Fam* (*enfático*) still; **s. sí quiero ir** I still want to go; **s. no me marcho** I'm still not leaving

sien *nf* temple

sierra *nf* (**a**) saw; **s. mecánica** power saw (**b**) *Geog* mountain range, sierra

siervo,-a *nm,f* slave

siesta *nf* siesta, nap; **dormir la s.** to have a siesta *o* an afternoon nap

siete 1 *adj* seven

2 *nm inv* seven

3 *nf RP Fam Euf* **¡la gran s.!** *Br* sugar!, *US* shoot!

sietemesino,-a *nm,f* seven-month baby, premature baby

sífilis *nf inv* syphilis

sifón *nm* siphon; **whisky con s.** whisky and soda

sig. (*abr* **siguiente**) following

sigilo *nm* secrecy; **entrar con mucho s.** to tiptoe in

sigilosamente *adv* (*secretamente*) secretly; **entró s. en la habitación** she crept *o* slipped into the room

sigiloso,-a *adj* secretive

sigla *nf* acronym

siglo *nm* century; **el s. veintiuno** the twenty-first century; *Fam* **hace siglos que no le veo** I haven't seen him for ages

signatario,-a *adj & nm,f* signatory

significación *nf* (**a**) (*sentido*) meaning (**b**) (*importancia*) significance

significado *nm* meaning

significar [44] *vt* to mean

significativo,-a *adj* significant; (*expresivo*) meaningful

signo *nm* (**a**) sign; **s. del zodiaco** zodiac sign (**b**) *Ling* mark; **s. de interrogación** question mark

sigo *indic pres de* **seguir**

siguiente *adj* following, next; **¡el s.!** next, please!; **al día s.** the following day

sílaba *nf* syllable

silbar *vi* to whistle; (*abuchear*) to hiss, to boo

silbato *nm* whistle

silbido *nm* whistle, whistling; (*agudo*) hiss

silenciador *nm* (*de arma*) silencer; (*de coche, moto*) *Br* silencer, *US* muffler

silenciar [43] *vt* (**a**) (*un sonido*) to muffle (**b**) (*noticia*) to hush up

silencio *nm* silence; **imponer s. a algn** to make sb be quiet

silencioso,-a *adj* (*persona*) quiet; (*motor etc*) silent

silicio *nm* silicon

silicona *nf* silicone

silla *nf* (**a**) chair; **s. de ruedas** wheelchair; **s. giratoria** swivel chair (**b**) (*de montura*) saddle

sillín *nm* saddle

sillón *nm* armchair

silo *nm* silo

silueta *nf* silhouette; (*de cuerpo*) figure

silvestre *adj* wild

simbólico,-a *adj* symbolic; **precio s.** token price

simbolizar [40] *vt* to symbolize

símbolo *nm* symbol

simetría *nf* symmetry

simétrico,-a *adj* symmetrical

simiente *nf* seed

similar *adj* similar

similitud *nf* similarity

simio *nm* monkey

simpatía *nf* liking, affection; **le tengo mucha s.** I am very fond of him

> 🔎 Observa que la palabra inglesa **sympathy** es un falso amigo y no es la traducción de la palabra española **simpatía**. En inglés, **sympathy** significa tanto "compasión" como "comprensión".

simpático,-a *adj* (*amable*) nice, likeable; **me cae s.** I like him

> 🔎 Observa que la palabra inglesa **sympathetic** es un falso amigo y no es la traducción de la palabra española **simpático**. En inglés, **sympathetic** significa tanto "comprensivo" como "compasivo".

simpatizante *nmf* sympathizer

simpatizar [40] *vi* (**a**) to sympathize (**con** with) (**b**) (*llevarse bien*) to hit it off (**con** with)

simple 1 *adj* (**a**) simple (**b**) (*fácil*) simple, easy (**c**) (*mero*) mere (**d**) (*persona*) simple, simple-minded

2 *nm* (*persona*) simpleton

simpleza *nf* simple-mindedness; (*tontería*) nonsense

simplificar [44] *vt* to simplify

simposio *nm* symposium

simulacro *nm* sham, pretence; **un s. de ataque** a mock attack

simular *vt* to simulate

simultanear *vt* to combine; **simultanea el**

trabajo y los estudios he's working and studying at the same time

simultáneo,-a *adj* simultaneous

sin *prep* (**a**) without; **s. dinero/tí** without money/you; **estamos s. pan** we're out of bread; **s. hacer nada** without doing anything; **cerveza s.** alcohol-free beer; **s. más ni más** without further ado (**b**) (*+ inf*) **está s. secar** it hasn't been dried

sinagoga *nf* synagogue

sincerarse *vpr* to open one's heart (**con** to)

sinceridad *nf* sincerity; **con toda s.** in all sincerity

sincero,-a *adj* sincere

sincronizar [40] *vt* to synchronize

sindical *adj* (*Br* trade *o US* labor) union

sindicalista *nmf* union member, *Br* trade unionist

sindicar *vt Andes, RP, Ven* to accuse

sindicato *nm* union, trade union

síndrome *nm* syndrome

sinfín *nm* endless number; **un s. de** lots of

sinfonía *nf* symphony

singani *nm Bol* grape brandy

single *nm* (**a**) (*disco*) single, 7-inch (**b**) *CSur* (*habitación*) single room

singular 1 *adj* (**a**) singular (**b**) (*excepcional*) exceptional, unique (**c**) (*raro*) peculiar, odd
    2 *nm Ling* singular; **en s.** in the singular

siniestrado,-a *adj* stricken

siniestro,-a 1 *adj* sinister, ominous
    2 *nm* disaster, catastrophe

sino¹ *nm Fml* fate, destiny

sino² *conj* (**a**) but; **no fui a Madrid, s. a Barcelona** I didn't go to Madrid but to Barcelona (**b**) (*excepto*) **nadie s. él** no one but him; **no quiero s. que me oigan** I only want them to listen (to me)

sinónimo,-a 1 *adj* synonymous
    2 *nm* synonym

sinóptico,-a *adj* **cuadro s.** diagram, chart

sinsabor *nm* (*usu pl*) trouble, worry

sintético,-a *adj* synthetic

sintetizador *nm* synthesizer

sintetizar [40] *vt* to synthesize

síntoma *nm* symptom

sintonía *nf* (**a**) *Elec & Rad* tuning (**b**) *Más & Rad* (*de programa*) signature tune (**c**) *Fig* harmony

sintonizador *nm Rad* tuning knob

sintonizar [40] *vt* (**a**) *Rad* to tune in to (**b**) (*simpatizar*) **sintonizaron muy bien** they clicked straight away

sinuoso,-a *adj* (*camino*) winding

sinvergüenza 1 *adj* (*desvergonzado*) shameless; (*descarado*) cheeky
    2 *nmf* (*desvergonzado*) rogue; (*caradura*) cheeky devil

sionismo *nm* Zionism

siquiera 1 *adv* (*por lo menos*) at least; **ni s.** not even
    2 *conj Fml* (*aunque*) although, even though

sirena *nf* (**a**) siren, mermaid (**b**) (*señal acústica*) siren

Siria *n* Syria

sirimiri *nm* fine drizzle

sirio,-a *adj & nm,f* Syrian

sirviente,-a *nm,f* servant

sisar *vt* (*hurtar*) to pilfer, to filch

sisear *vi* to hiss

sísmico,-a *adj* seismic

sismógrafo *nm* seismograph

sistema *nm* system; **por s.** as a rule; **s. nervioso** nervous system; **s. montañoso** mountain chain

sistemático,-a *adj* systematic

sitiar [43] *vt* to besiege

sitio¹ *nm* (**a**) (*lugar*) place; **en cualquier s.** anywhere; **en todos los sitios** everywhere; *Fig* **quedarse en el s.** to die (**b**) (*espacio*) room; **hacer s.** to make room (**c**) *Méx* (*parada de taxis*) taxi stand *o Br* rank

sitio² *nm* siege; **estado de s.** state of emergency

sito,-a *adj Fml* situated, located

situación *nf* (**a**) situation; **su s. económica es buena** his financial position is good (**b**) (*ubicación*) situation, location

situado,-a *adj* situated; *Fig* **estar bien s.** to have a good position

situar [30] **1** *vt* to locate
    2 situarse *vpr* to be situated *o* located

sketch *nm Cin & Teatro* sketch

S.L. (*abr* **Sociedad Limitada**) *Br* ≃ Ltd, *US* ≃ Inc

slip *nm* underpants

slogan *nm* slogan

S.M. (*abr* **Su Majestad**) (*rey*) His Majesty; (*reina*) Her Majesty

smoking *nm* dinner jacket, *US* tuxedo

s/n. (*abr* **sin número**) = abbreviation used in addresses after the street name, where the building has no number

snob *adj & nmf* = esnob

snobismo *nm* = esnobismo

so¹ *prep* (*bajo*) under; **so pena de** under penalty of

so² *nm Fam* **¡so imbécil!** you damned idiot!

sobaco *nm* armpit

sobar *Fam* **1** *vt* (*manosear*) to fondle, to paw
    2 *vi* (*dormir*) to sleep

soberanía *nf* sovereignty

soberano,-a 1 *adj* (**a**) sovereign (**b**) *Fam* huge, great
    2 *nm,f* (*monarca*) sovereign

soberbia *nf* pride

soberbio,-a *adj* (**a**) proud (**b**) (*magnífico*) splendid, magnificent

sobón,-ona *nm,f Fam* **ser un s.** to be fresh *o* all hands

sobornar *vt* to bribe

soborno *nm* (*acción*) bribery; (*dinero etc*) bribe

sobra *nf* (**a**) **de s.** (*no necesario*) superfluous;

tener de s. to have plenty; **estar de s.** not to be needed; **saber algo de s.** to know sth only too well (**b**) **sobras** *(restos)* leftovers

sobradamente *adv* only too well

sobrado,-a *adj (que sobra)* abundant, more than enough; **sobradas veces** repeatedly; **andar s. de tiempo/dinero** to have plenty of time/money

sobrante 1 *adj* remaining, spare
2 *nm* surplus, excess

sobrar *vi* (**a**) to be more than enough, *(sing)* to be too much, *(pl)* to be too many; **sobran tres sillas** there are three chairs too many; **sobran comentarios** I've nothing further to add; *Fam* **tú sobras aquí** you are not wanted here (**b**) *(quedar)* to be left over; **ha sobrado carne** there's still some meat left

sobrasada *nf* sausage spread

sobre¹ *nm* (**a**) *(para carta)* envelope (**b**) *(de sopa etc)* packet

sobre² *prep* (**a**) *(encima de)* on, upon, on top of (**b**) *(por encima de)* over, above (**c**) *(acerca de)* about, on (**d**) *(aproximadamente)* about; **vendré s. las ocho** I'll come at about eight o'clock (**e**) **s. todo** especially, above all

sobre- *pref* super-, over-

sobrealimentado,-a *adj* overfed

sobrecarga *nf* overload

sobrecargar [42] *vt* to overload

sobrecogedor,-a *adj* dramatic, awesome

sobrecoger [53] *vt (conmover)* to shock

sobredosis *nf inv* overdose

sobreentenderse *upr* **se sobreentiende** that goes without saying

sobregiro *nm* overdraft

sobrehumano,-a *adj* superhuman

sobreimpresión *nf Fot & Cin* superimposing

sobrellevar *vt* to endure, to bear

sobremesa¹ *nf* afternoon

sobremesa² *nf* **ordenador de s.** desktop computer

sobrenatural *adj* supernatural

sobrenombre *nm* nickname

sobrepasar 1 *vt* to exceed, to surpass; *(rival)* to beat
2 sobrepasarse *upr* to go too far

sobrepeso *nm (de carga)* overload, excess weight; *(de persona)* excess weight

sobreponerse *upr* (**a**) **s. a** *(superar)* to overcome; **s. al dolor** to overcome pain (**b**) *(animarse)* to pull oneself together

sobreproducción *nf* overproduction

sobresaliente 1 *nm (nota)* ≃ A
2 *adj (que destaca)* outstanding, excellent

sobresalir [22] *vi* to stick out, to protrude; *Fig (destacar)* to stand out, to excel

sobresaltar 1 *vt* to startle
2 sobresaltarse *upr* to be startled, to start

sobresalto *nm (movimiento)* start; *(susto)* fright

sobreseer [36] *vt Jur* to stay; **s. una causa** to stay proceedings

sobretiempo *nm Andes* (**a**) *(en trabajo)* overtime (**b**) *(en deporte) Br* extra time, *US* overtime

sobretodo *nm (abrigo)* overcoat; *(guardapolvo)* overalls

sobrevalorar *vt* to overestimate

sobrevenir [27] *vi* to happen unexpectedly

sobreviviente 1 *adj* surviving
2 *nmf* survivor

sobrevivir *vi* to survive

sobrevolar [2] *vt* to fly over

sobriedad *nf* sobriety; *(en la bebida)* soberness

sobrina *nf* niece

sobrino *nm* nephew

sobrio,-a *adj* sober

socarrón,-ona *adj* (**a**) *(sarcástico)* sarcastic (**b**) *(astuto)* sly, cunning

socavar *vt Fig* to undermine

socavón *nm (bache)* pothole

sociable *adj* sociable, friendly

social *adj* social

socialdemócrata 1 *adj* social democratic
2 *nmf* social democrat

socialismo *nm* socialism

socialista *adj & nmf* socialist

socializar [40] *vt* to socialize

sociedad *nf* (**a**) society; **s. de consumo** consumer society (**b**) *(asociación)* association, society (**c**) *Com* company; **s. anónima** *Br* public (limited) company, *US* incorporated company; **s. limitada** private limited company

socio,-a *nm,f* (**a**) *(miembro)* member; **hacerse s. de un club** to become a member of a club, to join a club (**b**) *Com (asociado)* partner

sociología *nf* sociology

sociológico,-a *adj* sociological

sociólogo,-a *nm,f* sociologist

socorrer *vt* to help, to assist

socorrido,-a *adj* handy, useful

socorrista *nmf* life-saver, lifeguard

socorro *nm* help, assistance; **¡s.!** help!; **puesto de s.** first-aid post

soda *nf* soda water

soez *adj* vulgar, crude

sofá *nm (pl* **sofás)** sofa, settee; **s. cama** sofa bed, studio couch

Sofía *n* Sofia

sofisticado,-a *adj* sophisticated

sofocado,-a *adj* suffocated

sofocante *adj* suffocating, stifling; **hacía un calor s.** it was unbearably hot

sofocar [44] **1** *vt* (**a**) *(ahogar)* to suffocate, to smother (**b**) *(incendio)* to extinguish, to put out
2 sofocarse *upr* (**a**) *(ahogarse)* to suffocate, to stifle (**b**) *Fam (irritarse)* to get upset

sofoco *nm Fig (vergüenza)* embarrassment; **le dio un s.** *(disgusto)* it gave her quite a turn

sofocón *nm Fam* shock; **llevarse un s.** to get upset

sofreír [56] vt to fry lightly, to brown

sofrito nm = fried tomato and onion sauce

software nm software

soga nf rope; Fig **estar con la s. al cuello** to be in dire straits

soja nf (**a**) (planta, fruto) Br soya bean, US soy bean (**b**) (proteína) soya

sojuzgar [42] vt to subjugate

sol¹ nm (**a**) sun (**b**) (luz) sunlight; (luz y calor) sunshine; **hace s.** it's sunny, the sun is shining; **tomar el s.** to sunbathe; **al o bajo el s.** in the sun; **de s. a s.** from sunrise to sunset (**c**) 'in = standard monetary unit of Peru

sol² nm Mús G; (solfeo) so

solamente adv only; **no s.** not only; **s. con mirarte lo sé** I know just by looking at you; **s. que …** except that …

solapa nf (de chaqueta) lapel; (de sobre, bolsillo, libro) flap

solapadamente adv stealthily, in an underhand way

solapado,-a adj (persona) sly

solapamiento nm overlap

solapar 1 vt Fig to conceal, to cover up
  2 vi to overlap

solar¹ adj solar; **luz s.** sunlight

solar² nm (terreno) plot; (en obras) building site

solario, solárium nm sunbed

solaz nm Fml (descanso) rest, relaxation; (esparcimiento) recreation, entertainment

solazarse [40] vpr (relajar) to relax; (divertir) to entertain oneself, to amuse oneself

soldado nm soldier; **s. raso** private

soldador,-a 1 nm,f welder
  2 nm soldering iron

soldar [2] vt (cable) to solder; (chapa) to weld

soleado,-a adj sunny

soledad nf (estado) solitude; (sentimiento) loneliness

solemne adj (**a**) (majestuoso) solemn (**b**) Pey downright

solemnidad nf solemnity

soler [4] vi defect (**a**) (en presente) to be in the habit of; **solemos ir en coche** we usually go by car; **sueles equivocarte** you are usually wrong (**b**) (en pasado) **solía pasear por aquí** he used to walk round here

solera nf Fig tradition; **de s.** old-established; **vino de s.** vintage wine

solfa nf (**a**) Mús solfa; Fam **poner en s.** to ridicule (**b**) Fam (paliza) thrashing, beating

solicitar vt (información etc) to request, to ask for; (trabajo) to apply for

solícito,-a adj obliging, attentive

solicitud nf (petición) request; (de trabajo) application

solidaridad nf solidarity

solidario,-a adj (**a**) supportive; **una sociedad solidaria** a caring society (**b**) Jur jointly responsible

solidarizarse vpr to show one's solidarity (**con** with)

solidez nf solidity, strength

sólido,-a adj solid, strong

soliloquio nm soliloquy

solista nmf soloist

solitario,-a 1 adj (que está solo) solitary, lone; (que se siente solo) lonely
  2 nm (**a**) (diamante) solitaire (**b**) Naipes solitaire, patience

soliviantar vt (irritar) to irritate

sollozar [40] vi to sob

sollozo nm sob

solo,-a 1 adj (**a**) only, single; **ni un s. día** not a single day; **una sola vez** only once, just once (**b**) (solitario) lonely (**c**) **hablar s.** to talk to oneself; **se enciende s.** it switches itself on automatically; **a solas** alone, by oneself
  2 nm Mús solo

sólo adv only; **tan s.** only; **no s. … sino (también)** not only … but (also); **con s., (tan) s. con** just by

> Note that the adverb **sólo** can be written without an accent when there is no risk of confusion with the adjective.

solomillo nm sirloin

soltar [2] **1** vt (**a**) (desasir) to let go of; **¡suéltame!** let me go! (**b**) (prisionero) to release (**c**) (humo, olor) to give off (**d**) (bofetada) to deal; (carcajada) to let out; **me soltó un rollo** he bored me to tears
  2 soltarse vpr (**a**) (desatarse) to come loose (**b**) (perro etc) to get loose, to break loose (**c**) (desprenderse) to come off

soltero,-a 1 adj single, unmarried
  2 nm (hombre) bachelor, single man
  3 nf **soltera** (mujer) single woman, spinster

solterón, -ona nm,f old bachelor, f old maid

soltura nf (agilidad) agility; (seguridad) confidence, assurance; **habla italiano con s.** he speaks Italian fluently

soluble adj soluble; **café s.** instant coffee

solución nf solution

solucionar vt (resolver; arreglar) to settle

solvencia nf (**a**) Fin solvency (**b**) (fiabilidad) reliability; **fuentes de toda s.** completely reliable sources

solventar vt (problema) to solve, to resolve; (deuda, asunto) to settle

solvente adj (**a**) Fin solvent (**b**) (fiable) reliable

sombra nf (**a**) shade (**b**) (silueta proyectada) shadow; **s. de ojos** eyeshadow; **sin s. de duda** beyond a shadow of doubt (**c**) **tener buena s.** (tener suerte) to be lucky

sombrero nm hat; **s. de copa** top hat; **s. hongo** bowler hat

sombrilla nf parasol, sunshade

sombrío,-a adj (oscuro) dark; (tenebroso) sombre, gloomy; Fig (persona) gloomy, sullen

somero,-a adj superficial, shallow

someter 1 vt (**a**) to subject; **s. a prueba** to put

to the test; **s. algo a votación** to put sth to the vote (**b**) *(rebeldes)* to subdue, to put down

   2 someterse *vpr* (**a**) *(subordinarse)* to submit (**b**) *(rendirse)* to surrender, to yield (**c**) **s. a un tratamiento** to undergo treatment

somier *nm* (*pl* **somieres**) spring mattress

somnífero *nm* sleeping pill

somnoliento,-a *adj* sleepy, drowsy

son *nm* sound; **al s. del tambor** to the sound of the drum; **venir en s. de paz** to come in peace

sonado,-a *adj* (**a**) much talked of (**b**) *(trastocado)* mad, crazy

sonajero *nm* baby's rattle

sonámbulo,-a *nm,f* somnambulist, sleep-walker

sonar [2] **1** *vi* (**a**) to sound; **s. a** to sound like; **suena bien** it sounds good (**b**) *(timbre, teléfono)* to ring; **sonaron las cinco** the clock struck five (**c**) **tu nombre/cara me suena** your name/face rings a bell

   2 sonarse *vpr* **s. (la nariz)** to blow one's nose

sonda *nf* (**a**) *Med* sound, probe (**b**) **s. espacial** space probe

sondear *vt* (**a**) *(opinión)* to test, to sound out (**b**) *Med* to sound, to probe (**c**) *Náut* to sound

sondeo *nm* (**a**) *(encuesta)* poll (**b**) *Med* sounding, probing (**c**) *Náut* sounding

soneto *nm Lit* sonnet

sonido *nm* sound

sonoro,-a *adj* (**a**) *Cin* sound; **banda sonora** soundtrack (**b**) *(resonante)* loud, resounding (**c**) *Ling* voiced

sonreír [56] *vi*, **sonreírse** *vpr* to smile; **me sonrió** he smiled at me

sonriente *adj* smiling

sonrisa *nf* smile

sonrojarse *vpr* to blush

sonrojo *nm* blush

sonsacar [44] *vt* to wheedle; *(secreto)* to worm out

sonso,-a *adj Am* foolish, silly

soñador,-a *nm,f* dreamer

soñar [2] *vt & vi* (**a**) to dream; **s. con** to dream of *o* about; *Fig* **¡ni soñarlo!** not on your life! (**b**) *(fantasear)* to daydream, to dream

soñoliento,-a *adj* sleepy, drowsy

sopa *nf* soup; **s. juliana** spring vegetable soup; *Fig* **quedar hecho una s.** to get soaked to the skin

sope *nm Méx* = fried corn tortilla, with beans and cheese or other toppings

sopera *nf* soup tureen

sopero,-a *adj* **cucharada sopera** soup spoon

sopesar *vt* to try the weight of; *Fig* to weigh up

sopetón *nm Fam* slap; **de s.** all of a sudden

soplado *nm* glass-blowing

soplagaitas *nmf inv Fam (estúpido, pesado)* jerk, *Br* prat

soplar 1 *vi (viento)* to blow

   2 *vt* (**a**) *(polvo etc)* to blow away; *(para enfriar)* to blow on (**b**) *(para apagar)* to blow

out (**c**) *(para inflar)* to blow up (**d**) *(en exame etc)* **me sopló las respuestas** he whispere the answers to me

soplete *nm* blowlamp, blowtorch

soplido *nm* blow, puff

soplillo *nm* fan; *Fam* **orejas de s.** sticky-o ears

soplo *nm* (**a**) *(acción)* blow, puff; *(de vient* gust (**b**) *Med* murmur

soplón,-ona *nm,f Fam (niño)* telltale, snea *(delator) Br* grass, *US* rat

soporífero,-a *adj* (**a**) *(que adormece)* so orific, sleep-inducing (**b**) *(aburrido)* borin dull

soportable *adj* bearable

soportal *nm* porch; **soportales** arcade

soportar *vt* (**a**) *(peso)* to support, to bear (**|** *Fig (calor, ruido)* to bear, to endure; *(situ ción)* to put up with, to bear; **no te soporte** can't stand you

soporte *nm* support; **s. publicitario** adver sing medium

soprano *nmf* soprano

sorber *vt* (**a**) *(beber)* to sip (**b**) *(absorber)* soak up, to absorb

sorbete *nm* sorbet, sherbet

sorbo *nm* sip; *(trago)* gulp; **de un s.** in o gulp

sordera *nf* deafness

sórdido,-a *adj* squalid, sordid

sordo,-a 1 *adj (a) (persona)* deaf; **s. como ur tapia** stone-deaf (**b**) *(golpe, ruido, dolor)* du

   2 *nm,f* deaf person; **los sordos** the deaf *p Fam Fig* **hacerse el s.** to turn a deaf ear

sordomudez *nf* deaf-muteness

sordomudo,-a 1 *adj* deaf and dumb, dea mute

   2 *nm,f* deaf and dumb person, deaf-mute

soroche *nm Andes, Arg (mal de altura)* al tude sickness

sorprendente *adj* surprising

sorprender *vt* (**a**) *(extrañar)* to surprise (**|** *(coger desprevenido)* to catch unawares, take by surprise

sorpresa *nf* surprise; **coger de** *o* **por s.** to tal by surprise

sorpresivo,-a *adj Am* unexpected, surprisi

sortear *vt* (**a**) to draw *o* cast lots for; *(rifar)* raffle (off) (**b**) *(evitar)* to avoid, to get roun

sorteo *nm* draw; *(rifa)* raffle

sortija *nf* ring

sortilegio *nm* spell

S.O.S. *nm* SOS

sosa *nf* soda; **s. cáustica** caustic soda

sosegado,-a *adj (tranquilo)* calm, quiet; *(p cífico)* peaceful

sosegar [1] **1** *vt* to calm, to quieten

   2 sosegarse *vpr* to calm down

sosiego *nm (calma)* calmness; *(paz)* peac tranquillity

soslayo: de soslayo *loc adv* **mirar de s.** to loc sideways (at)

soso,-a *adj* lacking in salt; *Fig (persona)* insipid, dull

sospecha *nf* suspicion

sospechar 1 *vi (desconfiar)* to suspect; **s. de algn** to suspect sb
  2 *vt (pensar)* to suspect

sospechoso,-a 1 *adj* suspicious; **s. de** suspected of
  2 *nm,f* suspect

sostén *nm* (a) *(apoyo)* support (b) *(sustento)* sustenance (c) *(prenda)* bra, brassière

sostener [24] **1** *vt* (a) *(sujetar)* to support, to hold up (b) *(con la mano)* to hold (c) *Fig (teoría etc)* to defend, to uphold; **s. que ...** to maintain that ... (d) *(conversación)* to hold, to sustain (e) *(familia)* to support
  2 sostenerse *vpr* (a) *(mantenerse)* to support oneself (b) *(permanecer)* to stay, to remain

sostenido,-a *adj* (a) *(continuado)* sustained (b) *Mús* sharp

sostuve *pt indef de* **sostener**

sota *nf Naipes* jack, knave

sotana *nf* cassock, soutane

sótano *nm* basement, cellar

soto *nm* grove

soviético,-a *adj & nm,f* Soviet; *Hist* **la Unión Soviética** the Soviet Union

soy *indic pres de* **ser**

soya *nf* = **soja**

SP *(abr servicio público)* = sign indicating public transport vehicle

sport: de sport *loc adj* casual, sports; **chaqueta de s.** sports jacket

spot *nm (pl spots) TV* commercial, advert, ad

spray *nm (pl sprays)* spray

sprint *nm* sprint

Sr. *(abr Señor)* Mr

Sra. *(abr Señora)* Mrs

S.R.C., s.r.c. *(abr se ruega contestación)* please reply, R.S.V.P.

Srta. *(abr Señorita)* Miss

SS *nf (abr Seguridad Social)* Social Security

SS.AA. *(abr Sus Altezas)* Their Royal Highnesses

Sta., sta. *(abr Santa)* St

stand *nm Com* stand

standard *adj & nm* standard

status *nm inv* status

Sto., sto. *(abr Santo)* St

su *adj pos (de él)* his; *(de ella)* her; *(de usted, ustedes)* your; *(de animales o cosas)* its; *(impersonal)* one's; *(de ellos)* their; **su coche** his/her/your/their car; **su pata** its leg; **sus libros** his/her/your/their books; **sus patas** its legs

suave *adj* (a) smooth; *(luz, voz etc)* soft (b) *Met (templado)* mild

⌐ Observa que la palabra inglesa **suave** es un ‎falso amigo y no es la traducción de la palabra ‎española **suave**. En inglés, **suave** significa "fino, ‎cortés".

suavidad *nf* (a) smoothness; *(dulzura)* softness (b) *Met* mildness

suavizante *nm (para el pelo)* (hair) conditioner; *(para la ropa)* fabric softener

suavizar [40] **1** *vt* to smooth (out)
  2 suavizarse *vpr (temperatura)* to get milder; *(persona)* to calm down

subacuático,-a *adj* underwater

subalimentado,-a *adj* undernourished, underfed

subalterno,-a *adj & nm,f* subordinate, subaltern

subarrendar [1] *vt Com* to sublet, to sublease

subasta *nf* auction

subastar *vt* to auction (off), to sell at auction

subcampeón *nm Dep* runner-up

subconsciente *adj & nm* subconscious

subcontratación *nf Com* outsourcing

subdesarrollado,-a *adj* underdeveloped

subdesarrollo *nm* underdevelopment

subdirector,-a *nm,f* assistant director/manager

súbdito,-a *nm,f* subject, citizen; **s. francés** French citizen

subdividir *vt* to subdivide

subestimar *vt* to underestimate

subida *nf* (a) *(de temperatura)* rise; *(de precios, salarios)* rise, increase (b) *(ascenso)* ascent, climb (c) *(pendiente)* slope, hill (d) *Fam (drogas)* high

subido,-a *adj* **s. de tono** daring, risqué

subir 1 *vt* (a) to go up (b) *(llevar arriba)* to take up, to bring up (c) *(cabeza, mano)* to lift, to raise (d) *(precio, salario)* to raise, to put up (e) *(volumen)* to turn up; *(voz)* to raise
  2 *vi* (a) *(ir arriba)* to go up, to come up (b) **s. a** *(un coche)* to get into; *(un autobús)* to get on; *(un barco, avión, tren)* to board, to get on (c) *(aumentar)* to rise, to go up
  3 subirse *vpr* (a) to climb up; *Fig* **el vino se le subió a la cabeza** the wine went to his head (b) **s. a** *(un coche)* to get into; *(un autobús, avión, tren)* to get on, to board; *(caballo, bici)* to get on (c) *(cremallera)* to do up; *(mangas)* to roll up

súbitamente *adv* suddenly

súbito,-a *adj* sudden

subjetivo,-a *adj* subjective

sublevación *nf* rising, rebellion

sublevar 1 *vt Fig (indignar)* to infuriate, to enrage
  2 sublevarse *vpr* to rebel, to revolt

sublime *adj* sublime

submarinismo *nm* skin-diving

submarino,-a 1 *adj* submarine, underwater
  2 *nm* submarine

subnormal 1 *adj* mentally handicapped
  2 *nmf* mentally handicapped person

suboficial *nm* (a) *Mil* noncommissioned officer (b) *Náut* petty officer

subordinado,-a *adj & nm,f* subordinate

subordinar *vt* to subordinate

subproducto *nm* by-product

subrayar *vt* to underline; *Fig (recalcar)* to emphasize, to stress

subrepticio,-a *adj* surreptitious

subrutina *vi* subroutine

subsanar *vt (error)* to rectify, to put right; *(daño)* to make up for

subscribir (*pp* **subscrito**) *vt* = **suscribir**

subscripción *nf* subscription

subsecretario,-a *nm,f* undersecretary

subsidiario,-a *adj* subsidiary

subsidio *nm* allowance, benefit; **s. de desempleo** unemployment benefit

subsistencia *nf* subsistence

subsistir *vi* to subsist, to remain; *(vivir)* to live on, to survive

subsuelo *nm* subsoil

subte *nm RP Br* underground, *Br* tube, *US* subway

subterráneo,-a 1 *adj* underground
2 *nm (túnel)* tunnel, underground passage

subtítulo *nm* subtitle

suburbano,-a *adj* suburban

suburbio *nm (barrio pobre)* slums; *(barrio periférico)* suburb

subvención *nf* subsidy

subvencionar *vt* to subsidize

subversión *nf* subversion

subversivo,-a *adj* subversive

subyacente *adj* underlying

subyugar [42] *vt* to subjugate

succionar *vt* to suck (in)

sucedáneo,-a *adj & nm* substitute

suceder 1 *vi* (**a**) *(ocurrir) (uso impers)* to happen, to occur; **¿qué sucede?** what's going on?, what's the matter? (**b**) *(seguir)* to follow, to succeed
2 sucederse *upr* to follow one another, to come one after the other

sucesión *nf* (**a**) *(serie)* series *sing*, succession (**b**) *(al trono)* succession (**c**) *(descendencia)* issue, heirs

sucesivamente *adv* **y así s.** and so on

sucesivo,-a *adj* following, successive; **en lo s.** from now on

suceso *nm (hecho)* event, occurrence; *(incidente)* incident; *Prensa* **sección de sucesos** accident and crime reports

> Observa que la palabra inglesa **success** es un falso amigo y no es la traducción de la palabra española **suceso**. En inglés, **success** significa "éxito".

sucesor,-a *nm,f* successor

suciedad *nf* (**a**) dirt (**b**) *(calidad)* dirtiness

sucinto,-a *adj* concise, succinct

sucio,-a 1 *adj* dirty; **en s.** in rough; *Fig* **juego s.** foul play; *Fig* **negocio s.** shady business
2 *adv* **jugar s.** to play dirty

sucre *nm Fin* = standard monetary unit of Ecuador

suculento,-a *adj* succulent, juicy

sucumbir *vi* to succumb, to yield

sucursal *nf Com & Fin* branch, branch office

sudaca *nmf Pey* South American

sudadera *nf* sweatshirt

Sudáfrica *n* South Africa

sudafricano,-a *adj & nm,f* South African

Sudamérica *n* South America

sudamericano,-a *adj & nm,f* South American

sudar *vt & vi* to sweat; *Fam Fig* **s. la gota gorda** to sweat blood

sudeste *nm* southeast

sudoeste *nm* southwest

sudor *nm* sweat; *Fig* **con el s. de mi frente** by the sweat of my brow

sudoroso,-a *adj* sweaty

Suecia *n* Sweden

sueco,-a 1 *adj* Swedish
2 *nm,f (persona)* Swede
3 *nm (idioma)* Swedish

suegra *nf* mother-in-law

suegro *nm* father-in-law; **mis suegros** my in-laws

suela *nf (de zapato)* sole

sueldo *nm* salary, wages

suelo *nm* (**a**) *(superficie)* ground; *(de interior)* floor; *Fig* **estar por los suelos** *(precios)* to be rock-bottom (**b**) *(territorio)* soil, land (**c**) *(campo, terreno)* land; **s. cultivable** arable land (**d**) *(de carretera)* surface

suelto,-a 1 *adj* (**a**) loose; *(desatado)* undone (**b**) *Fig* **dinero s.** loose change; **hojas sueltas** loose sheets (of paper); **se venden sueltos** they are sold singly *o* separately *o* loose (**c**) *(en libertad)* free; *(huido)* at large (**d**) *(vestido, camisa)* loose, loose-fitting
2 *nm (dinero)* (loose) change

sueño *nm* (**a**) sleep; *(ganas de dormir)* sleepiness; **tener s.** to feel *o* be sleepy (**b**) *(cosa soñada)* dream

suero *nm Med* serum; *(de la leche)* whey

suerte *nf* (**a**) *(fortuna)* luck; **por s.** fortunately; **probar s.** to try one's luck; **tener s.** to be lucky; **¡que tengas s.!** good luck! (**b**) **echar algo a suertes** to draw lots for sth (**c**) *(destino)* fate, destiny (**d**) *Fml (género)* kind, sort, type

suéter *nm* sweater

suficiencia *nf* (**a**) *(engreimiento)* smugness, complacency (**b**) *Educ* **prueba de s.** final exam

suficiente 1 *adj (bastante)* sufficient, enough
2 *nm Educ* pass

suficientemente *adv* sufficiently; **no es lo s. rico como para ...** he isn't rich enough to ...

sufijo *nm* suffix

sufragar [42] **1** *vt (gastos)* to pay, to defray
2 *vi Am* to vote (**por** for)

sufragio *nm Pol* suffrage; *(voto)* vote

sufrido,-a *adj (persona)* long-suffering

sufrimiento *nm* suffering

sufrir 1 *vi* to suffer; **s. del corazón** to have a heart condition
  2 *vt* (**a**) *(accidente)* to have; *(operación)* to undergo; *(dificultades, cambios)* to experience; **s. dolores de cabeza** to suffer from headaches (**b**) *(aguantar)* to bear, to put up with
sugerencia *nf* suggestion
sugerente *adj* suggestive
sugerir [5] *vt* to suggest
sugestión *nf* suggestion
sugestionar *vt* to influence, to persuade
sugestivo,-a *adj* suggestive; *(atractivo)* alluring
suiche *nm Andes, Ven* switch
suicida 1 *nmf (persona)* suicide
  2 *adj* suicidal
suicidarse *vpr* to commit suicide, to kill oneself
suicidio *nm* suicide
suite *nf* suite
Suiza *n* Switzerland
suizo,-a 1 *adj* Swiss
  2 *nm,f (persona)* Swiss
  3 *nm Culin* éclair
sujetador *nm (prenda)* bra, brassière
sujetar 1 *vt* (**a**) *(agarrar)* to hold (**b**) *(fijar)* to hold down, to hold in place (**c**) *Fig (someter)* to restrain
  2 **sujetarse** *vpr (agarrarse)* to hold on
sujeto,-a 1 *nm* subject; *(individuo)* fellow, individual
  2 *adj (atado)* fastened, secure; **s. a** *(sometido)* subject to, liable to
sulfato *nm* sulphate
sulfurar 1 *vt Fam (exasperar)* to exasperate, to infuriate
  2 **sulfurarse** *vpr Fam* to lose one's temper, to blow one's top
sultán *nm* sultan
suma *nf* (**a**) *(cantidad)* sum, amount (**b**) *Mat* sum, addition; **s. total** sum total (**c**) **en s.** in short
sumamente *adv* extremely, highly
sumar 1 *vt Mat* to add, to add up
  2 **sumarse** *vpr* **s. a** *(huelga)* to join; *(propuesta)* to support
sumario,-a 1 *adj* summary, brief; *Jur* **juicio s.** summary proceedings
  2 *nm Jur* summary
sumarísimo,-a *adj Jur* swift, expeditious
sumergible *adj & nm* submersible
sumergir [57] **1** *vt* to submerge, to submerse; *(hundir)* to sink, to plunge
  2 **sumergirse** *vpr* to submerge, to go underwater; *(hundirse)* to sink
sumidero *nm* drain, sewer
suministrar *vt* to supply, to provide; **s. algo a algn** to supply sb with sth
suministro *nm* supply
sumir *vt (hundir)* to sink, to plunge; *Fig* to plunge
sumiso,-a *adj* submissive, obedient

sumo,-a *adj (supremo)* supreme; **con s. cuidado** with extreme care; **a lo s.** at (the) most
suntuoso,-a *adj* sumptuous, magnificent
supe *pt indef de* **saber**
supeditar *vt* to subject (**a** to)
super- *pref* super-
súper *Fam* **1** *adj* super, great
  2 *nm* (**a**) *(supermercado)* supermarket (**b**) *(gasolina)* 4-star
superado,-a *adj* outdated, obsolete
superar 1 *vt* (**a**) *(obstáculo etc)* to overcome, to surmount; *(prueba)* to pass (**b**) *(aventajar)* to surpass, to excel
  2 **superarse** *vpr* to improve o better oneself
superávit *nm* surplus
superdotado,-a 1 *adj* exceptionally gifted
  2 *nm,f* genius
superficial *adj* superficial
superficialidad *nf* superficiality
superficie *nf* surface; *(área)* area; *Com* **grandes superficies** hypermarkets
superfluo,-a *adj* superfluous
superhombre *nm* superman
superior 1 *adj* (**a**) *(posición)* top, upper (**b**) *(cantidad)* greater, higher, larger (**a** than) (**c**) *(calidad)* superior; **calidad s.** top quality (**d**) *Educ* higher
  2 *nm (jefe)* superior
superioridad *nf* superiority
supermán *nm (pl* **supermanes***)* superman
supermercado *nm* supermarket
superpoblación *nf* overpopulation
superponer [19] *vt* to superimpose
superpotencia *nf* superpower
superproducción *nf* (**a**) *Ind* overproduction (**b**) *Cin* mammoth production
supersónico,-a *adj* supersonic
superstición *nf* superstition
supersticioso,-a *adj* superstitious
supervisar *vt* to supervise
supervisor,-a *nm,f* supervisor
supervivencia *nf* survival
supino,-a *adj* (**a**) *(boca arriba)* supine, face up (**b**) *Fig (absoluto)* total absolute
súpito,-a *adj Am* sudden
suplantar *vt* to supplant, to take the place of
suplementario,-a *adj* supplementary, additional
suplemento *nm* supplement; **sin s.** without extra charge
suplente *adj & nmf (sustituto)* substitute, deputy; *Dep* substitute
supletorio,-a *adj* supplementary, additional; **cama supletoria** extra bed; **teléfono s.** extension
súplica *nf* entreaty, plea
suplicar [44] *vt* to beseech, to beg
suplicio *nm (tortura)* torture; *Fig (tormento)* torment
suplir *vt* (**a**) *(reemplazar)* to replace, to substitute (**b**) *(compensar)* to make up for
suponer [19] *(pp* **supuesto***) vt* (**a**) *(significar)*

to mean (**b**) *(implicar)* to entail (**c**) *(representar)* to account for (**d**) *(pensar)* to suppose; **supongo que sí** I suppose so; **supongamos que ...** let's assume that ... (**e**) *(adivinar)* to guess; **(me) lo suponía** I guessed as much

suposición *nf* supposition

supositorio *nm* suppository

supremacía *nf* supremacy

supremo,-a *adj* supreme

supresión *nf (de una ley etc)* abolition; *(de restricciones)* lifting; *(de una palabra)* deletion; *(de una rebelión)* suppression; *(omisión)* omission

suprimir *vt* (**a**) *(ley, impuesto)* to abolish; *(restricción)* to lift; *(palabra)* to delete, to take/leave out; *(rebelión)* to suppress (**b**) *(omitir)* to omit

supuesto,-a 1 *adj* (**a**) *(asumido)* supposed, assumed; **¡por s.!** of course!; **dar algo por s.** to take sth for granted (**b**) *(presunto)* alleged
  2 *nm* assumption; **en el s. de que** on the assumption that

supurar *vi* to suppurate, to fester

supuse *pt indef de* **suponer**

sur *nm* south

Suramérica *n* South America

suramericano,-a *adj & nm,f* South American

surcar [44] *vt Agr* to plough; *Fig (olas)* to cut through

surco *nm Agr* furrow; *(en un disco)* groove

sureño,-a 1 *adj* southern
  2 *nm,f* southerner

sureste *nm* = **sudeste**

surf(ing) *nm Dep* surfing

surfista *nmf* surfer

surgir [57] *vi (aparecer)* to arise, to emerge, to appear; *(problema, dificultad)* to crop up

suroeste *nm* = **sudoeste**

surrealista *adj & nmf* surrealist

surtido,-a 1 *adj* (**a**) *(variado)* assorted (**b**) **bien s.** well-stocked
  2 *nm* selection, assortment

surtidor *nm* spout; **s. de gasolina** *Br* petrol pump, *US* gas pump

surtir *vt* (**a**) to supply, to provide (**b**) **s. efecto** to have the desired effect

susceptible *adj* susceptible; *(quisquilloso)* oversensitive, touchy

suscitar *vt (provocar)* to cause, to provoke; *(rebelión)* to stir up, to arouse; *(interés etc)* to arouse

suscribir *(pp* **suscrito)** **1** *vt* (**a**) to subscribe to, to endorse (**b**) *Fml (firmar)* to sign
  2 suscribirse *vpr* to subscribe (**a** to)

suscripción *nf* subscription

susodicho,-a *adj* above-mentioned, aforesaid

suspender 1 *vt* (**a**) *(ley)* to suspend; *(reunión)* to adjourn (**b**) *(examen)* to fail; **me han suspendido** I've failed (the exam) (**c**) *(colgar)* to hang, to suspend
  2 *vi Educ* **he suspendido** I've failed

suspense *nm* suspense; **novela/película de s.** thriller

suspensión *nf* (**a**) hanging (up), suspension (**b**) *Aut* suspension (**c**) *Fin & Jur* **s. de pagos** suspension of payments

suspensivo,-a *adj* **puntos suspensivos** suspension points

suspenso *nm* (**a**) *Educ* fail (**b**) **en s.** *(asunto, trabajo)* pending; **estar en s.** to be pending

suspicacia *nf* suspiciousness

suspicaz *adj* suspicious; *(desconfiado)* distrustful

suspirar *vi* to sigh

suspiro *nm* sigh

sustancia *nf* substance

sustancial *adj* (**a**) substantial (**b**) *(fundamental)* essential, fundamental

sustantivo,-a 1 *adj* substantive
  2 *nm Ling* noun

sustentar *vt* (**a**) *(peso)* to support (**b**) *(familia)* to maintain, to support (**c**) *(teoría)* to support, to defend

sustento *nm* (**a**) *(alimento)* sustenance, food (**b**) *(apoyo)* support

sustitución *nf* substitution, replacement

sustituir [37] *vt* to substitute, to replace

sustituto,-a *nm,f* substitute, stand-in

susto *nm* fright, scare; **llevarse** *o* **darse un s.** to get a fright

sustraer [25] *vt* (**a**) *Mat* to subtract (**b**) *(robar)* to steal, to remove

sustrato *nm* substratum

susurrar *vt* to whisper

susurro *nm* whisper

sutil *adj* (**a**) *(diferencia, pregunta)* subtle (**b**) *(delgado)* thin, fine (**c**) *(aroma)* delicate

sutileza *nf* (**a**) *(dicho)* subtlety (**b**) *(finura)* fineness

suyo,-a *adj & pron pos (de él)* his; *(de ella)* hers; *(de usted, ustedes)* yours; *(de animal o cosa)* its; *(de ellos, ellas)* theirs; **los zapatos no son suyos** the shoes aren't hers; **varios amigos suyos** several friends of his/hers/yours/theirs; *Fam* **es muy s.** he's very aloof; *Fam* **hacer de las suyas** to be up to one's tricks; *Fam* **ir (cada uno) a lo s.** to mind one's own business; *Fam* **salirse con la suya** to get one's (own) way

svástica *nf* swastika

T, t [te] *nf (la letra)* T, t

t (*abr* **tonelada(s)**) t

tabacalero,-a 1 *nm,f (vendedor)* tobacco trader

  2 *nf* **La Tabacalera** = Spanish state tobacco monopoly

tabaco *nm* (**a**) *(planta, hoja)* tobacco; **t. rubio** Virginia tobacco (**b**) *(cigarrillos)* cigarettes

tábano *nm* horsefly

tabaquismo *nm* nicotine poisoning

tabarra *nf Fam* nuisance, bore; **dar la t.** to go on and on

tabasco® *nm* Tabasco® sauce

taberna *nf* pub, bar; *(antiguamente)* tavern

tabernero,-a *nm,f* publican; *(hombre)* landlord; *(mujer)* landlady

tabique *nm* (**a**) *(pared)* partition (wall) (**b**) *Anat* **t. nasal** nasal wall

tabla *nf* (**a**) board; *Dep* **t. de surf** surfboard; *Dep* **t. de windsurf** sailboard (**b**) *(de vestido)* pleat (**c**) *Mat* table (**d**) **tablas** *(en ajedrez)* stalemate, draw; **quedar en tablas** *(juego)* to end in a draw (**e**) *Taurom* **tablas** fence (**f**) *Teatro* **las tablas** the stage; *Fig* **tener (muchas) tablas** to be an old hand

tablado *nm* (**a**) *(plataforma)* wooden platform (**b**) *Teatro* stage

tablao *nm Fam* = flamenco bar or show

tablero *nm* (**a**) *(tablón)* panel, board; **t. de mandos** *(de coche)* dash(board) (**b**) *(en juegos)* board; **t. de ajedrez** chessboard

tableta *nf (de chocolate)* bar

tablón *nm* plank; *(en construcción)* beam; **t. de anuncios** *Br* noticeboard, *US* bulletin board

tabú *adj & nm (pl* **tabúes**) taboo

tabular *vt* to tabulate

taburete *nm* stool

tacaño,-a 1 *adj* mean, stingy

  2 *nm,f* miser

tacatá, tacataca *nm* baby-walker

tacha *nf (defecto)* flaw, defect; **sin t.** flawless, without blemish

tachar *vt* (**a**) to cross out (**b**) *Fig* **t. de** to accuse of

tachero *nm RP Fam (de taxi)* taxi driver

tacho *nm Am* bucket

tachón *nm (borrón)* crossing out

tachuela *nf* tack, stud

tácito,-a *adj* tacit

taciturno,-a *adj* (**a**) *(callado)* taciturn (**b**) *(triste)* sullen

taco *nm* (**a**) plug; *(de billetes)* wad; *(de bota de fútbol)* stud; *(en billar)* cue (**b**) *(cubo) (de jamón, queso)* cube, piece (**c**) *Culin (tortilla de maíz)* taco, = rolled-up tortilla pancake (**d**) *Fam (palabrota)* swearword (**e**) *Fam (lío)* mess, muddle; **armarse** *o* **hacerse un t.** to get all mixed up (**f**) **me gusta un t.** I like it a lot (**g**) *Fam* **tacos** *(años)* years

tacón *nm* heel; **zapatos de t.** high-heeled shoes

taconeo *nm (pisada)* heel-tapping; *(golpe)* stamping with the heels

táctica *nf* tactics

táctico,-a *adj* tactical

táctil *adj* tactile; **pantalla t.** touch screen

tacto *nm* (**a**) *(sentido)* touch (**b**) *Fig (delicadeza)* tact; **tener t.** to be tactful

taekwondo *nm* tae kwon do

tafetán *nm* taffeta

tahur *nm* cardsharp

tailandés,-esa 1 *adj* Thai

  2 *nm,f (persona)* Thai; **los tailandeses** the Thai *o* Thais

  3 *nm (idioma)* Thai

Tailandia *n* Thailand

taimado,-a *adj* sly, crafty

tajada *nf* (**a**) *(de carne)* slice; *Fig* **sacar** *o* **llevarse t.** to take one's share (**b**) *Fam (borrachera)* drunkenness

tajante *adj* incisive

Tajo *n* **el T.** the Tagus

tal 1 *adj* (**a**) *(semejante)* such; *(más sustantivo singular contable)* such a; **en tales condiciones** in such conditions; **nunca dije t. cosa** I never said such a thing

  (**b**) *(indeterminado)* such and such; **t. día y a t. hora** such and such a day and at such and such a time

  (**c**) *(persona)* person called ...; **te llamó una t. Amelia** someone called Amelia phoned you

  (**d**) *(locuciones)* **t. vez** perhaps, maybe; **como si t. cosa** as if nothing had happened

  2 *adv* (**a**) *(así)* just; **t. cual** just as it is; **t. (y) como** just as

  (**b**) **¿qué t.?** how are things?; **¿qué t. ese vino?** how do you find this wine?

  3 *conj* as; **con t. (de) que** (+ *subjunctive*) so long as, provided

  4 *pron (cosa)* something; *(persona)* someone, somebody; **t. para cual** two of a kind; **y t. y cual** and so on

tala *nf* tree felling

taladradora *nf* drill

taladrar *vt* to drill; *(pared)* to bore through; *(papeles)* to punch

taladro *nm* (**a**) *(herramienta)* drill (**b**) *(agujero)* hole

talante *nm* (**a**) *(carácter)* disposition (**b**) *(voluntad)* **de buen t.** willingly; **de mal t.** unwillingly, reluctantly

talar *vt* *(árboles)* to fell, to cut down

talco *nm* talc; **polvos de t.** talcum powder

talega *nf* bag, sack

talego *nm* (**a**) long bag, long sack (**b**) *Fam (cárcel)* clink, hole (**c**) *Fam (mil pesetas)* = 1,000 peseta note

talento *nm* talent

Talgo *nm* = fast passenger train

talismán *nm* talisman, lucky charm

talla *nf* (**a**) *(de prenda)* size; **¿qué t. usas?** what size are you? (**b**) *(estatura)* height; *Fig* stature; *Fig* **dar la t.** to make the grade (**c**) *(escultura)* carving, sculpture (**d**) *(tallado)* cutting, carving

tallado *nm* *(de madera)* carving; *(de piedras preciosas)* cutting; *(de metales)* engraving

tallar *vt* (**a**) *(madera, piedra)* to carve, to shape; *(piedras preciosas)* to cut; *(metales)* to engrave (**b**) *(medir)* to measure the height of

tallarines *nmpl* tagliatelle

talle *nm* (**a**) *(cintura)* waist (**b**) *(cuerpo) (de hombre)* build, physique; *(de mujer)* figure, shape

taller *nm* (**a**) *(obrador)* workshop; *Aut* **t. de reparaciones** garage (**b**) *Ind* factory, mill

tallo *nm* stem, stalk

talón *nm* (**a**) *(del pie)* heel (**b**) *(cheque)* cheque

> ⚠ Observa que la palabra inglesa **talon** es un falso amigo y no es la traducción de la palabra española **talón**. En inglés, **talon** significa "garra".

talonario *nm* *(de cheques)* cheque book; *(de billetes)* book of tickets

tamal *nm* *(comida)* tamale, = steamed maize dumpling with savoury or sweet filling, wrapped in maize husks or a banana leaf

tamaño,-a 1 *adj* such a big, so big a
2 *nm* size; **de gran t.** large; **del t. de** as large as, as big as

tamarindo *nm* tamarind

tambalearse *upr* *(persona)* to stagger; *(mesa)* to wobble; *Fig* to teeter

tambero *nm* *RP (granja)* dairy farm

también *adv* *(igualmente)* too, also, as well; **tú t. puedes venir** you can come too; **¿lo harás? yo t.** are you going to do it? so am I

tambo *nm* *RP (granja)* dairy farm

tambor *nm* (**a**) *(Mús, de lavadora, de freno)* drum (**b**) *Anat* eardrum

Támesis *n* **el T.** the Thames

tamiz *nm* sieve

tamizar [40] *vt* to sieve

tampoco *adv* (**a**) *(en afirmativas)* nor, neither; **Juan no vendrá y María t.** Juan won't come and neither will María; **no lo sé – yo t.** I don't know – neither do I (**b**) *(en negativas)* either, not ... either; **la Bolsa no sube, pero t. baja** the stock market isn't going up, but it's not going down either

tampón *nm* tampon

tan *adv* (**a**) such; *(más sustantivo singular contable)* such a; **es t. listo** he's such a clever fellow; **no me gusta t. dulce** I don't like it so sweet; **¡qué gente t. agradable!** such nice people!; **¡qué vestido t. bonito!** what a beautiful dress! (**b**) *(comparativo)* **t. ... como** as ... as; **t. alto como tú** as tall as you (are) (**c**) *(consecutivo)* so ... (that); **iba t. deprisa que no lo ví** he was going so fast that I couldn't see him (**d**) **t. siquiera** at least; **t. sólo** only

tanda *nf (conjunto)* batch, lot; *(serie)* series *sing*; **por tandas** in groups

tándem *nm* tandem

tanga *nm* tanga

tangente *nf* tangent; *Fig* **salirse** *o* **escaparse por la t.** to go off at a tangent

Tánger *n* Tangier

tangible *adj* tangible

tango *nm* tango

tanguería *nf* = nightclub for tango dancing

tanguero,-a *nm,f (aficionado)* tango enthusiast

tanque *nm* tank

tantear 1 *vt* (**a**) *Fig* **t. a algn** to sound sb out; **t. el terreno** to see how the land lies (**b**) *(calcular)* to estimate, to guess
2 *vi Dep* to (keep) score

tanteo *nm* (**a**) *(cálculo)* estimate, guess (**b**) *Dep* score

tanto,-a 1 *nm* (**a**) *(punto)* point
(**b**) *(cantidad imprecisa)* so much, a certain amount; **t. por ciento** percentage
(**c**) **un t.** a bit; **la casa es un t. pequeña** the house is rather *o* somewhat small
(**d**) **estar al t.** *(informado)* to be informed; *(pendiente)* to be on the lookout
2 *adj* (**a**) *(+ singular)* so much; **no le des t. dinero** don't give him so much money; **¡ha pasado t. tiempo!** it's been so long!; **no comas tantas manzanas** don't eat so many apples
(**b**) **cincuenta y tantas personas** fifty odd people; **en el año sesenta y tantos** in nineteen sixty something
(**c**) **t. como** as much as; **tantos,-as como** as many as
3 *pron* (**a**) *(+ singular)* so much; **otro t.** as much again, the same again; **no es** *o* **hay para t.** it's not that bad
(**b**) *(+ plural)* so many; **otros tantos** as many again; **uno de tantos** run-of-the-mill; *Fam* **a las tantas** very late, at an unearthly hour

4 *adv* (**a**) *(cantidad)* so much; **t. mejor/peor** so much the better/worse; **t. más cuanto que** all the more so because

(**b**) *(tiempo)* so long

(**c**) *(frecuencia)* so often

(**d**) **t. ... como** both ... and; **t. tú como yo** both you and I; **t. si vienes como si no** whether you come or not

(**e**) *(locuciones)* **por lo t.** therefore; **¡y t.!** oh yes!, and how!

tañer *vt* to play

tapa *nf* (**a**) *(cubierta)* lid; *Andes, RP (de botella)* top; *(de libro)* cover; *(de zapato)* heel-plate; *Aut (de cilindro)* head (**b**) *(aperitivo)* appetizer, snack

tapadera *nf (tapa)* cover, lid; *Fig* cover, front

tapadillo *nm* **hacer algo de t.** to do sth secretly

tapado *nm CSur (abrigo)* overcoat

tapar 1 *vt* (**a**) to cover; *(botella etc)* to put the lid/top on; *(con ropas o mantas)* to wrap up (**b**) *(ocultar)* to hide; *(vista)* to block (**c**) *(encubrir)* to cover up

2 taparse *vpr (cubrirse)* to cover oneself; *(abrigarse)* to wrap up

taparrabos *nm inv* loincloth

tapete *nm* (table) cover; *Fig* **poner algo sobre el t.** to table sth

tapia *nf* garden wall

tapiar [43] *vt* (**a**) *(área)* to wall off (**b**) *(puerta, ventana etc)* to wall, to close up

tapicería *nf* (**a**) tapestry; *(de muebles, coche)* upholstery (**b**) *(tienda)* upholsterer's shop/workshop

tapioca *nf* tapioca

tapiz *nm* tapestry

tapizar [40] *vt* to upholster

tapón *nm* (**a**) *(de lavabo etc)* stopper, plug; *(de botella)* cap, cork; **t. de rosca** screw-on cap (**b**) *(de oídos)* earplug (**c**) *(en baloncesto)* block (**d**) *Aut* traffic jam (**e**) *Am (plomo)* fuse

taponar 1 *vt* (**a**) *(tubería, hueco)* to plug (**b**) *Med (herida)* to tampon

2 taponarse *vpr* **se me han taponado los oídos** my ears are blocked up

taquería *nf Méx (quiosco)* taco stall; *(restaurante)* taco restaurant

taquigrafía *nf* shorthand

taquígrafo,-a *nm,f* shorthand writer

taquilla *nf* (**a**) ticket office, booking office; *Cin & Teatro* box-office; **un éxito de t.** a box-office success (**b**) *(recaudación)* takings (**c**) *(armario)* locker

taquillero,-a 1 *adj* popular; **película taquillera** box-office hit

2 *nm,f* booking *o* ticket clerk

tara *nf* (**a**) *(peso)* tare (**b**) *(defecto)* defect, fault

tarántula *nf* tarantula

tararear *vt* to hum

tardanza *nf* delay

tardar 1 *vt (llevar tiempo)* to take; **¿cuánto va**

a t.? how long will it take?; **tardé dos horas en venir** it took me two hours to get here

2 *vi (demorar)* to take long; **si tarda mucho, me voy** if it takes much longer, I'm going; **no tardes** don't be long; **a más t.** at the latest

3 tardarse *vpr* **¿cuánto se tarda en llegar?** how long does it take to get there?

tarde 1 *nf* (**a**) *(hasta las cinco)* afternoon (**b**) *(después de las cinco)* evening (**c**) **la t. noche** late evening

2 *adv* (**a**) late; **siento llegar t.** sorry I'm late (**b**) *(locuciones)* **de t. en t.** very rarely, not very often; **(más) t. o (más) temprano** sooner or later

tardío,-a *adj* late, belated

tardo,-a *adj* slow

tarea *nf* job, task; **tareas** *(de ama de casa)* housework; *(de estudiante)* homework

tarifa *nf* (**a**) *(precio)* tariff, rate; *(en transportes)* fare (**b**) *(lista de precios)* price list

tarima *nf* platform, dais

tarjeta *nf* card; **t. postal** postcard; **t. de crédito** credit card; **t. de visita** *Br* visiting card, *US* calling card; *Informát* **t. perforada** punch *o* punched card

tarraconense 1 *adj* of/from Tarragona

2 *nmf* person from Tarragona

tarro *nm* (**a**) *(vasija)* jar, pot, tub (**b**) *Fam (cabeza)* bonce (**c**) *Am (lata)* tin, can

tarta *nf* tart, pie

tartamudear *vi* to stutter, to stammer

tartamudo,-a 1 *adj* stuttering, stammering

2 *nm,f* stutterer, stammerer

tartana *nf Fam (coche viejo)* banger, heap

tártaro,-a *adj* **salsa tártara** tartar sauce

tartera *nf* (**a**) *(fiambrera)* lunch box (**b**) *(cazuela)* baking tin

tarugo *nm* (**a**) *(de madera)* lump of wood (**b**) *Fam (persona)* blockhead

tarumba *adj Fam* crazy, mad; **estar t.** to be bonkers

tasa *nf* (**a**) *(precio)* fee; **tasas académicas** course fees (**b**) *(impuesto)* tax; **tasas de aeropuerto** airport tax (**c**) *(índice)* rate; **t. de natalidad/mortalidad** birth/death rate (**d**) *(valoración)* valuation, appraisal

tasación *nf* valuation

tasador,-a *nm,f* valuer

tasar *vt* (**a**) *(valorar)* to value; **t. una casa en 10 millones de pesetas** to value a house at 10 million pesetas (**b**) *(poner precio)* to set *o* fix the price of

tasca *nf Fam* bar, pub

tata 1 *nf (niñera)* nanny

2 *nm Am Fam (papá)* dad, daddy, *US* pop

tatarabuelo,-a *nm,f* great-great-grandfather, *f* great-great-grandmother; **tatarabuelos** great-great-grandparents

tataranieto,-a *nm,f* great-great-grandson, *f* great-great-granddaughter; **tataranietos** great-great-grandchildren

tatuaje *nm* tattoo

tatuar [30] *vt* to tattoo
taurino,-a *adj* bullfighting
Tauro *nm* Taurus
tauromaquia *nf* tauromachy, (art of) bull-fighting
taxativo,-a *adj* categorical
taxi *nm* taxi
taxímetro *nm* taximeter, clock
taxista *nmf* taxi driver
taza *nf* (**a**) (*complemento directo*) cup; **una t. de café** (*recipiente*) coffee cup; (*contenido*) a cup of coffee (**b**) (*de retrete*) bowl
tazón *nm* bowl
te *pron pers* (**a**) (*complemento directo*) you; (*complemento indirecto*) (to/for) you; **no quiero verte** I don't want to see you; **te compraré uno** I'll buy one for you, I'll buy you one; **te lo dije** I told you so (**b**) (*reflexivo*) yourself; **lávate** wash yourself; (*sin traducción*) **bébetelo todo** drink it up; **no te vayas** don't go
té *nm* (*pl* **tés**) tea; **té con limón** lemon tea
tea *nf* torch
teatral *adj* (**a**) **grupo t.** theatre company; **obra t.** play (**b**) *Fig* (*teatrero*) theatrical
teatrero,-a *adj* theatrical
teatro *nm* (**a**) theatre; **obra de t.** play; **autor de t.** playwright (**b**) *Lit* drama
tebeo *nm* children's comic
techar *vt* to roof
techo *nm* (*de habitación*) ceiling; (*tejado*) roof; *Aut* **t. corredizo** sun roof
tecla *nf* key; *Fig* **dar en la t.** to get it right
teclado *nm* keyboard; *Informát* **t. expandido** expanded keyboard
teclear 1 *vt* to key in
2 *vi* to drum with one's fingers
técnica *nf* (**a**) (*tecnología*) technology (**b**) (*método*) technique (**c**) (*habilidad*) skill
técnico,-a 1 *adj* technical
2 *nm,f* technician, technical expert
tecnicolor® *nm* Technicolor®
tecno- *pref* techno-
tecnócrata *nmf* technocrat
tecnología *nf* technology
tecnológico,-a *adj* technological
tecolote *nm CAm, Méx* (*búho*) owl
tedio *nm* tedium, boredom
tedioso,-a *adj* tedious, boring
teja *nf Constr* tile; *Fam Fig* **a toca t.** on the nail
tejado *nm* roof
tejanos *nmpl* jeans
tejemaneje *nm Fam* (**a**) (*actividad*) bustle, fuss (**b**) (*maquinación*) intrigue, scheming
tejer *vt* (*en el telar*) to weave; (*hacer punto*) to knit; (*telaraña*) to spin; *Fig* (*plan*) to plot, to scheme
tejido *nm* (**a**) fabric; **t. de punto** knitted fabric (**b**) *Anat* tissue
tejo *nm Fam* **tirar los tejos a algn** to make a play for sb
tejón *nm* badger
tel. (*abr* **teléfono**) tel.

tela *nf* (**a**) *Tex* material, fabric, cloth; (*de la leche*) skin; **t. de araña** cobweb; **t. metálica** gauze (**b**) *Fam* (*dinero*) dough (**c**) *Arte* canvas (**d**) *Fig* **poner en t. de juicio** to question; *Fig* **tiene mucha t.** it's not an easy thing
telar *nm Tex* loom
telaraña *nf* cobweb, spider's web
tele *nf Fam* telly, TV
telearrastre *nm* ski lift
telebanca *nf* telephone banking, home banking
telebasura *nf Fam* junk TV
telecabina *nf* cable car
telecomunicaciones *nfpl* telecommunications
telediario *nm TV* television news bulletin
teledirigido,-a *adj* remote-controlled
telefax *nm* telefax, fax
teleférico *nm* cable car/railway
telefilm, telefilme *nm* TV film
telefonazo *nm* **dar un t. (a algn)** to give (sb) a ring
telefonear *vt & vi* to telephone, to phone
telefonía *nf* **t. móvil** mobile phones
telefónica *nf* **Compañía T.** ≃ British Telecom
telefónico,-a *adj* telephone; **llamada telefónica** telephone call
telefonista *nmf* (telephone) operator
teléfono *nm* telephone, phone; **t. portátil** portable telephone; **t. móvil** car phone; **está hablando por t.** she's on the phone; **te llamó por t.** she phoned you
telegrafiar [29] *vt* to telegraph, to wire
telegráfico,-a *adj* telegraphic; **giro t.** giro, money order
telégrafo *nm* (**a**) telegraph (**b**) **telégrafos** post office
telegrama *nm* telegram, cable
teleimpresor *nm*, **teleimpresora** *nf* teleprinter
telele *nm Fam* **darle a uno un t.** to have a fit
telemando *nm* remote control (unit)
telenovela *nf* television serial
teleobjetivo *nm* telephoto lens *sing*
telepático,-a *adj* telepathic
telescopio *nm* telescope
teleserie *nf* television series *sing*
telesilla *nm* chair lift
telespectador,-a *nm,f* TV viewer
telesquí *nm* ski lift
teletexto *nm* teletext
teletienda *nf* home shopping programme
teletipo *nm* teleprinter
teletrabajador,-a *nm,f* teleworker
teletrabajo *nm* teleworking
televidente *nmf* TV viewer
televisar *vt* to televise
televisión *nf* (**a**) (*sistema*) television (**b**) *Fam* (*aparato*) television set; **t. en color/en blanco y negro** colour/black-and-white television; **t. digital** digital television; **t. por cable** cable television; **ver la t.** to watch television

televisivo,-a *adj* television; **espacio t.** television programme
televisor *nm* television set
télex *nm inv* telex
telón *nm Teatro* curtain; *Pol & Hist* **t. de acero** Iron Curtain; **t. de fondo** *Teatro* backdrop; *Fig* background
telonero,-a *adj* **(grupo) t.** support band
tema *nm* (**a**) *(asunto)* topic, subject; *(de examen)* subject; **temas de actualidad** current affairs (**b**) *Mús* theme
temario *nm (de examen)* programme
temática *nf* subject matter
temático,-a *adj* thematic
temblar [1] *vi (de frío)* to shiver; *(de miedo)* to tremble (**de** with); *(voz)* to quiver; *(pulso)* to shake
tembleque *nm Fam* shaking fit
temblón,-ona *adj Fam* trembling, shaky
temblor *nm* tremor, shudder; **t. de tierra** earth tremor
tembloroso,-a, tembloso,-a *adj* shaking; *(voz)* quivering; *(de frío)* shivering; *(de miedo)* trembling; **manos temblorosas** shaky hands
temer 1 *vt* to fear, to be afraid of; **temo que esté muerto** I fear he's dead; **temo que no podrá recibirte** I'm afraid (that) he won't be able to see you
 2 *vi* to be afraid
 3 temerse *vpr* to fear, to be afraid; **¡me lo temía!** I was afraid this would happen!
temerario,-a *adj* reckless, rash
temeridad *nf* (**a**) *(actitud)* temerity, rashness (**b**) *(acto temerario)* reckless act
temeroso,-a *adj* (**a**) fearful, timid (**b**) *(temible)* frightful
temible *adj* fearful, frightful
temor *nm* (**a**) fear (**b**) *(recelo)* worry, apprehension
témpano *nm* ice floe
temperamental *adj* temperamental
temperamento *nm* temperament; **tener t.** to have a strong character
temperatura *nf* temperature
tempestad *nf* storm; *Fig* turmoil, uproar
tempestuoso,-a *adj* stormy, tempestuous
templado,-a *adj* (**a**) *(agua)* lukewarm; *(clima)* mild, temperate (**b**) *Mús (afinado)* tuned
templanza *nf* moderation, restraint
templar *vt* (**a**) to moderate (**b**) *(algo frío)* to warm up; *(algo caliente)* to cool down (**c**) *Mús (instrumento)* to tune (**d**) *Téc (metal)* to temper
temple *nm* (**a**) *(fortaleza)* boldness, courage (**b**) *Arte* tempera
templete *nm* bandstand
templo *nm* temple
temporada *nf* (**a**) season; **t. alta** high *o* peak season; **t. baja** low *o* off season (**b**) *(período)* period, time; **por temporadas** on and off
temporal 1 *adj* temporary, provisional
 2 *nm* storm

temporario,-a *adj Am* temporary
temporero,-a *nm,f* seasonal *o* temporary worker
tempranero,-a *adj* (**a**) *(persona)* early-rising (**b**) *(cosecha)* early
temprano,-a *adj & adv* early
tenacidad *nf* (**a**) *(perseverancia)* tenacity, perseverance (**b**) *(de metal)* tensile strength
tenacillas *nfpl (para pelo)* curling tongs
tenaz *adj* tenacious
tenaza *nf*, **tenazas** *nfpl (herramienta)* pliers, pincers; *(para el fuego)* tongs
tendedero *nm* clothes line, drying place
tendencia *nf* tendency
tendencioso,-a *adj* tendentious, biased
tender [3] **1** *vt* (**a**) *(mantel etc)* to spread out; *(para secar)* to hang out (**b**) *Am (cama)* to make; *(mesa)* to set, to lay (**c**) *(red)* to cast; *(puente)* to build; *(vía, cable)* to lay; *(trampa)* to lay, to set (**d**) *(mano)* to stretch *o* hold out (**e**) *(tumbar)* to lay
 2 *vi* to tend (**a** to), to have a tendency (**a** to)
 3 tenderse *vpr* to lie down, to stretch out
tenderete *nm (puesto)* market stall
tendero,-a *nm,f* shopkeeper
tendido *nm* (**a**) *(de vía, cable)* laying; *(de puente)* construction; **t. eléctrico** electrical installation (**b**) *Taurom (asientos)* = front tiers of seats
tendón *nm* tendon, sinew
tenebroso,-a *adj (sombrío)* dark, gloomy; *(siniestro)* sinister, shady
tenedor *nm* fork
teneduría *nf* **t. de libros** bookkeeping
tenencia *nf Jur* **t. ilícita de armas** illegal possession of arms
tener [24] **1** *vt* (**a**) to have, to have got; **tenemos un examen** we've got *o* we have an exam; **va a t. un niño** she's going to have a baby, she's expecting; **¡ahí (lo) tienes!** here you are!
 (**b**) *(poseer)* to own, to possess
 (**c**) *(sostener)* to hold; **tenme el bolso un momento** hold my bag a minute; **ten, es para ti** take this *o* here you are, it's for you
 (**d**) **t. calor/frío** to be hot/cold; **t. cariño a algn** to be fond of sb; **t. miedo** to be frightened
 (**e**) *(edad)* to be; **tiene dieciocho (años)** he's eighteen (years old)
 (**f**) *Am (llevar)* **tengo tres años aquí** I've been here for three years
 (**g**) *(medida)* **la casa tiene 100 metros cuadrados** the house is 100 square metres
 (**h**) *(contener)* to hold, to contain
 (**i**) *(mantener)* to keep; **me tuvo despierto toda la noche** he kept me up all night
 (**j**) **t. por** *(considerar)* to consider, to think; **me tienen por estúpido** they think I'm a fool; **ten por seguro que lloverá** you can be sure it'll rain
 (**k**) **t. que** to have (got) to; **tengo que irme** I

must leave; **tienes/tendrías que verlo** you must/should see it

2 tenerse *upr* (**a**) **t. en pie** to stand (up)

(**b**) **t. por** *(considerarse)* to think *o* consider oneself; **se tiene por muy inteligente** he thinks he's very intelligent

tenga *subj pres de* **tener**

tengo *indic pres de* **tener**

teniente *nm* (**a**) *Mil* lieutenant (**b**) **t. (de) alcalde** deputy mayor

tenis *nm* tennis

tenista *nmf* tennis player

tenor¹ *nm Mús* tenor

tenor² *nm* **a t. de** according to

tensar *vt (cable etc)* to tighten; *(arco)* to draw

tensión *nf* (**a**) tension; **en t.** tense (**b**) *Elec* tension, voltage (**c**) *Med* **t. arterial** blood pressure; **t. nerviosa** nervous strain (**d**) *Téc* stress

tenso,-a *adj* (**a**) *(cuerda, cable)* tense, taut (**b**) *(persona)* tense; *(relaciones)* strained

tentación *nf* temptation

tentáculo *nm* tentacle

tentador,-a *adj* tempting

tentar [1] *vt* (**a**) *(palpar)* to feel, to touch (**b**) *(incitar)* to tempt

tentativa *nf* attempt; *Jur* **t. de asesinato** attempted murder

tentempié *nm Fam (pl* **tentempiés***)* (**a**) *(comida)* snack, bite (**b**) *(juguete)* tumbler

tenue *adj* (**a**) *(luz, sonido)* subdued, faint (**b**) *(delgado)* thin, light

teñir [6] **1** *vt* (**a**) *(pelo etc)* to dye (**b**) *Fig* to tinge with

2 teñirse *upr* **t. el pelo** to dye one's hair

teocalli *nm Hist* = Mexican pyramid

teología *nf* theology

teorema *nm* theorem

teoría *nf* theory; **en t.** theoretically

teórico,-a *adj* theoretical

teorizar [40] *vi* to theorize (**sobre** on)

tepache *nm* = mildly alcoholic Mexican drink made from fermented pineapple peelings and unrefined sugar

tequila *nm* tequila

terapeuta *nmf* therapist

terapia *nf* therapy

tercer *adj* third; **el t. mundo** the third world

tercerización *nf Am Com* outsourcing

tercermundista *adj* third-world

tercero,-a 1 *adj* third

Tercer is used instead of tercero before masculine singular nouns (e.g. **el tercer piso** the third floor).

---

2 *nm,f (de una serie)* third; **a la tercera va la vencida** third time lucky

3 *nm (mediador)* mediator; *Jur* third party

terceto *nm Mús* trio

terciar [43] **1** *vi* (**a**) *(mediar)* to mediate, to arbitrate (**b**) *(participar)* to take part, to participate

2 terciarse *upr* **si se tercia** should the occasion arise

terciario,-a *adj* tertiary

tercio *nm* (**a**) *(parte)* (one) third (**b**) *(de cerveza)* = medium-sized bottle of beer (**c**) *Taurom* stage, part *(of a bullfight)*

terciopelo *nm* velvet

terco,-a *adj* stubborn, obstinate

tereré *nm Arg, Par (mate)* = refreshing drink made from maté in cold water with lemon juice

tergiversar *vt (verdad)* to distort; *(palabras)* to twist

termal *adj* thermal

termas *nfpl (baños)* spa, hot baths *o* springs

térmico,-a *adj* thermal; **central térmica** coal-fired power station

terminación *nf* completion

terminal 1 *adj* terminal

2 *nf* (**a**) *(de aeropuerto)* terminal; *(de autobús)* terminus (**b**) *Elec & Informát* terminal

terminante *adj* (**a**) *(categórico)* categorical, final (**b**) *(dato, resultado)* conclusive

terminantemente *adv* categorically; **t. prohibido** strictly forbidden

terminar 1 *vt (acabar)* to finish, to complete; *(completamente)* to finish off

2 *vi* (**a**) *(acabarse)* to finish, to end; **termina en seis** it ends with a six; **no termina de convencerse** he still isn't quite convinced (**b**) *(ir a parar)* to end up (**en** in); **terminó por comprarlo** he ended up buying it (**c**) **t. con** *(eliminar)* to put an end to

3 terminarse *upr* (**a**) to finish, to end, to be over (**b**) *(vino, dinero etc)* to run out

término *nm* (**a**) *(final)* end, finish (**b**) *(palabra)* term, word; **en otros términos** in other words; **en términos generales** generally speaking (**c**) **t. municipal** district (**d**) **por t. medio** on average (**e**) *Fig* **en último t.** as a last resort

terminología *nf* terminology

termo *nm* Thermos® (flask), flask

termodinámico,-a *adj* thermodynamic

termómetro *nm* thermometer

termonuclear *adj* thermonuclear

termostato *nm* thermostat

ternera *nf* calf; *(carne)* veal

ternero *nm* calf

terno *nm Andes, Méx (traje)* three-piece suit

ternura *nf* tenderness

terquedad *nf* stubbornness, obstinacy

terracota *nf* terracotta

terraja *adj RP Fam (persona)* flashy; *(cosa)* tacky, kitsch

terrajada *nf RP Fam* tacky thing/act

terral *nm Am (polvareda)* dust cloud

Terranova *n* Newfoundland

terraplén *nm* embankment

terráqueo,-a *adj* **globo t.** *(tierra)* (the) earth; *(esfera)* globe

terrateniente *nmf* landowner

terremoto *nm* earthquake
terrenal *adj* **un paraíso t.** a heaven on earth
terreno *nm* (**a**) *(tierra)* (piece of) land, ground; *Geol* terrain; *(campo)* field; **ganar/perder t.** to gain/lose ground (**b**) *Dep* field, ground (**c**) *Fig* field, sphere
terrestre *adj* (**a**) *(de la tierra)* terrestrial, earthly (**b**) *(por tierra)* by land; **por vía t.** by land
terrible *adj* terrible, awful
terrícola *nmf* *(en ciencia ficción)* earthling
terrier *nm* terrier
territorio *nm* territory
terrón *nm* *(de azúcar)* lump; *(de tierra)* clod
terror *nm* terror; *Cin* horror
terrorífico,-a *adj* terrifying, frightening
terrorismo *nm* terrorism
terrorista *adj & nmf* terrorist
terroso,-a *adj (color)* earth-coloured
terruño *nm (terreno)* piece of land; *(patria chica)* homeland, native land
terso,-a *adj* smooth
tersura *nf* smoothness
tertulia *nf* get-together; **t. literaria** literary gathering
tesina *nf* first degree dissertation
tesis *nf inv* thesis; *(opinión)* view, theory
tesón *nm* tenacity, firmness
tesorero,-a *nm,f* treasurer
tesoro *nm* (**a**) treasure (**b**) *(erario)* exchequer; **T. Público** Treasury
test *nm* test
testaferro *nm* front man
testamentario,-a *Jur* **1** *adj* testamentary
2 *nm,f* executor
testamento *nm* (**a**) *Jur* will; **hacer** *o* **otorgar t.** to make *o* draw up one's will (**b**) *Rel* Testament
testar *vi* to make *o* draw up one's will
testarudo,-a *adj* stubborn, obstinate
testear *vt CSur* to test
testículo *nm* testicle
testificar [44] *vt* to testify
testigo 1 *nmf* witness; *Jur* **t. de cargo/descargo** witness for the prosecution/defence; *Jur* **t. ocular/presencial** eyewitness; *Rel* **Testigos de Jehová** Jehovah's Witnesses
2 *nm Dep* baton
testimoniar [43] *vt* (**a**) *(dar testimonio)* to testify to, to attest to (**b**) *(mostrar)* to show
testimonio *nm Jur* testimony; *(prueba)* evidence, proof
teta *nf Fam* (**a**) tit, boob; **niño de t.** breast-feeding baby (**b**) *(de vaca)* udder
tétanos *nm* tetanus
tetera *nf* teapot
tetero *nm Col, Ven (biberón)* baby's bottle
tetilla *nf* (**a**) *Anat* man's nipple (**b**) *(de biberón)* (rubber) teat
tetina *nf* (rubber) teat
tétrico,-a *adj* gloomy, dull
textil *adj & nm* textile

texto *nm* text; **libro de t.** textbook
textual *adj* textual; *(exacto)* literal; **en palabras textuales** literally
textura *nf Tex* texture; *(en minerales)* structure
tez *nf* complexion
ti *pron pers* you; **es para ti** it's for you; **hazlo por ti** do it for your own sake; **piensas demasiado en ti mismo** you think too much about yourself
tía *nf* (**a**) *(pariente)* aunt (**b**) *Fam (mujer)* girl, woman
tianguis *nm inv CAm, Méx* open-air market
tibieza *nf* tepidity; *Fig* lack of enthusiasm
tibio,-a *adj* tepid, lukewarm; *Fam* **ponerse t. de cerveza** to get pissed
tiburón *nm* shark
tic *nm (pl* **tiques)** tic, twitch; **t. nervioso** nervous tic *o* twitch
ticket *nm (pl* **tickets)** *(billete)* ticket; *(recibo)* receipt
tictac *nm* tick-tock, ticking
tiempo *nm* (**a**) time; **a t.** in time; **a su (debido) t.** in due course; **a un t., al mismo t.** at the same time; **al poco t.** soon afterwards; **antes de t.** (too) early *o* soon; **con el t.** in the course of time, with time; **con t.** in advance; **¿cuánto t.?** how long?; **¿cuánto t. hace?** how long ago?; **demasiado t.** too long; **estar a t. de** to still have time to; **hacer t.** to kill time; **¿nos da t. de llegar?** have we got (enough) time to get there?; **t. libre** free time; *Fig* **dar t. al t.** to let matters take their course
(**b**) *(meteorológico)* weather; **¿qué t. hace?** what's the weather like?; **hace buen/mal t.** the weather is good/bad
(**c**) *(edad)* age; **¿cuánto** *o* **qué t. tiene tu niño?** how old is your baby/child?
(**d**) *Mús* movement
(**e**) *Dep* half
(**f**) *Ling* tense
tienda *nf* (**a**) shop, store; **ir de tiendas** to go shopping (**b**) **t. (de campaña)** tent
tienta *nf* **a tientas** by touch; **andar a tientas** to feel one's way; **buscar (algo) a tientas** to grope (for sth)
tiento *nm* tact; **con t.** tactfully
tierno,-a *adj* (**a**) *(blando)* tender, soft (**b**) *(reciente)* fresh
tierra *nf* (**a**) *(planeta)* earth (**b**) *Agr* land, soil (**c**) *(continente)* land; **tocar t.** to land (**d**) *(país)* country; **t. de nadie** no-man's-land (**e**) *(suelo)* ground; *Fig* **echar** *o* **tirar por t.** to spoil (**f**) *Elec* **(toma de) t.** *Br* earth, *US* ground
tierral *nm Am* cloud of dust
tieso,-a *adj (rígido)* stiff, rigid; *(erguido)* upright, erect
tiesto *nm* flowerpot
tifoidea *nf* **(fiebre) t.** typhoid (fever)
tifón *nm* typhoon
tifus *nm inv* typhus (fever)
tigre *nm* tiger; *Am* jaguar

tijeras *nfpl* (pair of) scissors

tijereta *nf* (**a**) *(insecto)* earwig (**b**) *Dep* scissors

tila *nf (flor)* lime *o* linden blossom; *(infusión)* lime *o* linden blossom tea

tildar *vt* to call, to brand; **me tildó de ladrón** he called me a thief

tilde *nf* written accent

tilín *nm (sonido)* ting-a-ling; *Fig* **José le hace t.** she fancies José

tilma *nf Méx* woollen blanket

tilo *nm* lime tree

timar *vt* to swindle; **me han timado** they did me

timbal *nm* kettledrum

timbrar *vt (carta)* to stamp; *(documento)* to seal

timbre *nm* (**a**) *(de la puerta)* bell (**b**) *(sello)* stamp, seal; *Fin* fiscal *o* revenue stamp (**c**) *Mús (sonido)* timbre

timidez *nf* shyness, timidity

tímido,-a *adj* shy, timid; *Fig (mejoría)* light; *(intento)* cautious

timo *nm* swindle, fiddle; **es un t.** it's a rip-off

timón *nm* (**a**) *Náut & Av* rudder; **golpe de t.** U-turn (**b**) *Andes Aut* steering wheel

timonel *nm* helmsman

tímpano *nm Anat* eardrum

tina *nf* (**a**) *(tinaja)* pitcher (**b**) *(gran cuba)* vat (**c**) *CAm, Col, Méx (bañera)* bathtub

tinaja *nf* large earthenware jar

tinerfeño,-a 1 *adj* of/from Tenerife

2 *nm,f* person from Tenerife

tinglado *nm* (**a**) *(intriga)* intrigue (**b**) *(cobertizo)* shed

tinieblas *nfpl* darkness

tino *nm* (**a**) *(puntería)* (good) aim; **tener buen t.** to be a good shot (**b**) *(tacto)* (common) sense, good judgement

tinta *nf* (**a**) ink; **t. china** Indian ink; **t. simpática** invisible ink (**b**) *Fig* **medias tintas** ambiguities, half measures

tintar *vt* to dye

tinte *nm* (**a**) dye (**b**) *Fig (matiz)* shade, overtone

tintero *nm* inkpot, inkwell; *Fig* **se quedó en el t.** it wasn't said

tintinear *vi (vidrio)* to clink; *(campana)* to jingle, to tinkle

tintineo *nm (de vidrio)* clinking; *(de campana)* jingling

tinto,-a 1 *adj (vino)* red

2 *nm* (**a**) *(vino)* red wine (**b**) *Col, Ven (café)* black coffee

tintorería *nf* dry-cleaner's

tintura *nf* (**a**) *(colorante)* dye (**b**) *Quím* tincture; **t. de yodo** iodine

tío *nm* (**a**) *(pariente)* uncle; **mis tíos** my uncle and aunt (**b**) *Fam* guy, *Br* bloke

tiovivo *nm* roundabout, merry-go-round

tipazo *nm Fam* good figure

tipear *vt & vi Am* to type

típico,-a *adj* (**a**) typical; **eso es t. de Antonio** that's just like Antonio (**b**) *(baile, traje)* traditional

tipificar [44] *vt* (**a**) *(normalizar)* to standardize (**b**) *(caracterizar)* to typify

tipismo *nm* local colour

tipo *nm* (**a**) *(clase)* type, kind (**b**) *Fam (persona)* guy, *Br* bloke; **t. raro** weirdo (**c**) *Anat (de hombre)* build, physique; *(de mujer)* figure; *Fig* **jugarse el t.** to risk one's neck; **aguantar el t.** to keep one's cool *o* head (**d**) *Fin* rate; **t. bancario** *o* **de descuento** bank rate; **t. de cambio/interés** rate of exchange/interest (**e**) **el político t. de la izquierda** the typical left-wing politician

tipografía *nf* typography

tipográfico,-a *adj* typographic; **error t.** printing error

tipógrafo,-a *nm,f* typographer

tiquismiquis *Fam* **1** *nmf inv* fusspot

2 *nmpl* (**a**) *(escrúpulos)* silly scruples (**b**) *(rencillas)* bickering

tira *nf* (**a**) *(banda, cinta)* strip (**b**) *(de dibujos)* comic strip (**c**) *Fam* **la t. de gente** a lot *o* loads of people (**d**) *Méx Fam* **la t.** *(la policía)* the cops (**e**) **t. y afloja** tug of war

tirabuzón *nm* ringlet

tirachinas *nm inv Br* catapult, *US* slingshot

tirada *nf* (**a**) *(lanzamiento)* throw (**b**) *(impresión)* print run

tirado,-a *adj Fam* (**a**) *(precio)* dirt-cheap (**b**) *(examen)* dead easy (**c**) *Fam* **dejar t. (a algn)** to let (sb) down

tirador *nm* (**a**) *(persona)* marksman (**b**) *(pomo)* knob, handle; *(cordón)* bell pull (**c**) *(tirachinas)* *Br* catapult, *US* slingshot

tiraje *nm Am* print run

tiralíneas *nm inv* tracer, drawing *o* ruling pen

tiranía *nf* tyranny

tiránico,-a *adj* tyrannical

tiranizar [40] *vt* to tyrannize

tirano,-a *nm,f* tyrant

tirante 1 *adj (cable etc)* tight, taut; *(situación, relación)* tense

2 *nm* (**a**) *(de vestido etc)* strap; **tirantes** *Br* braces, *US* suspenders (**b**) *Téc* brace, stay

tirar 1 *vt* (**a**) *(echar)* to throw (**b**) *(dejar caer)* to drop (**c**) *(desechar)* to throw away; *Fig (dinero)* to squander (**d**) *(derribar)* to knock down; **t. la puerta (abajo)** to smash the door in (**e**) *(foto)* to take (**f**) *Impr* to print (**g**) *(beso)* to blow

2 *vi* (**a**) **t. de** *(cuerda, puerta)* to pull (**b**) *(chimenea, estufa)* to draw (**c**) *(funcionar)* to work, to run (**d**) **ir tirando** to get by (**e**) **t. a** to tend towards; **tira a rojo** it's reddish (**f**) **tira a la izquierda** turn left; **¡venga, tira**

ya! come on, get going!
　(**g**) *(disparar)* to shoot, to fire; *Ftb* **t. a puerta** to shoot at goal
　3 tirarse *vpr* (**a**) *(lanzarse)* to throw o hurl oneself; **t. de cabeza al agua** to dive into the water
　(**b**) *(tumbarse)* to lie down
　(**c**) *Fam (tiempo)* to spend; **me tiré una hora esperando** I waited (for) a good hour
　(**d**) *Vulg* **t. a algn** to lay sb
tirita® *nf* Elastoplast®, Band-aid®, plaster
tiritar *vi* to shiver, to shake
tiro *nm* (**a**) *(lanzamiento)* throw (**b**) *(disparo, ruido)* shot; *Ftb* **t. a gol** shot at goal; **t. al blanco** target shooting; **t. al plato** clay pigeon shooting; **t. con arco** archery (**c**) *(de vestido)* shoulder width (**d**) *(de chimenea)* draught; **animal de t.** draught animal
tirón *nm* pull, tug; *(del bolso)* snatch; *Fam* **de un t.** in one go
tirotear *vt* to shoot at, to snipe at
tiroteo *nm* shooting, firing to and fro
tirria *nf Fam* dislike; **le tengo t.** I dislike him, I can't stand him
tísico,-a *adj* tubercular, consumptive
tisis *nf inv* tuberculosis, consumption
tisú *nm* tissue, paper hankie
títere *nm (marioneta)* puppet; **no dejar t. con cabeza** to spare no one
titilar *vi (luz)* to flicker; *(estrella)* to twinkle
titiritero,-a *nm,f* (**a**) puppeteer (**b**) *(acróbata)* travelling acrobat
titubeante *adj (indeciso)* hesitant; *(al hablar)* stammering
titubear *vi* (**a**) *(dudar)* to hesitate, to waver (**b**) *(al hablar)* to stammer
titubeo *nm* (**a**) *(duda)* hesitation (**b**) *(al hablar)* stammering
titulación *nf* qualifications
titulado,-a *adj (licenciado)* graduate; *(diplomado)* qualified
titular¹ 1 *nmf (persona)* holder
　2 *nm Prensa* headline
　3 *adj* appointed, official
titular² **1** *vt (poner título)* to call
　2 titularse *vpr* (**a**) *(película etc)* to be called; **¿cómo se titula?** what is it called? (**b**) *Educ* to graduate (**en** in)
titularidad *nf Educ* tenure
titulitis **1** *nf* obsession with qualifications
　2 *nm Fam* certificate
título *nm* (**a**) title (**b**) *Educ* degree; *(diploma)* diploma (**c**) *Prensa (titular)* headline (**d**) **a t. de ejemplo** by way of example
tiza *nf* chalk; **una t.** a piece of chalk
tiznada *nf Am* **hijo de la t.** son of a bitch
tiznar *vt* to blacken (with soot)
tizne *nm* soot
tizón *nm* half-burnt stick, brand
tlapalería *nf Méx* ironmonger's (shop)
toalla *nf* towel; **tirar la t.** to throw in the towel
toallero *nm* towel Br rail o US bar

tobera *nf* nozzle
tobillo *nm* ankle
tobogán *nm* slide, chute
toca *nf (sombrero)* headdress; *(de monja)* wimple
tocadiscos *nm inv* record player; **t. digital** o **compacto** CD player
tocado¹ *nm* (**a**) *(peinado)* coiffure, hairdo (**b**) *(prenda)* headdress
tocado²,-a *adj Fam* crazy, touched
tocador *nm* (**a**) *(mueble)* dressing table (**b**) *(habitación)* dressing room; **t. de señoras** powder room
tocante a *loc adv* **en lo t. a ...** with reference to ...
tocar [44] **1** *vt* (**a**) to touch; *Fam Fig* **toca madera** touch wood (**b**) *(instrumento, canción)* to play; *(timbre, campana)* to ring; *(bocina)* to blow (**c**) *(tema, asunto)* to touch on (**d**) *(afectar)* to concern; **por lo que a mí me toca** as far as I am concerned
　2 *vi* (**a**) **¿a quién le toca?** *(en juegos)* whose turn is it? (**b**) **me tocó el gordo** *(en rifa)* I won the jackpot (**c**) **t. con** to be next to; *Fig* **t. a su fin** to be coming to an end (**d**) *(llamar)* **t. a la puerta** to knock on the door
　3 tocarse *vpr (una cosa con otra)* to touch each other; **¿os tocáis algo?** *(ser parientes)* are you related?
tocarse *vpr (cubrirse)* to cover one's head
tocata 1 *nf Mús* toccata
　2 *nm Fam* record player
tocateja: a tocateja *loc adv* **pagar a t.** to pay on the nail
tocayo,-a *nm,f* namesake
tocho *nm Fam (libro grande)* tome
tocino *nm* lard; **t. ahumado** smoked bacon; **t. de cielo** = sweet made with egg yolk
tocólogo,-a *nm,f* obstetrician
tocuyo *nm Am* coarse cotton cloth
todavía *adv* (**a**) *(aún)* still; *(en negativas)* yet; **t. la quiere** he still loves her; **t. no** not yet; **no mires t.** don't look yet (**b**) *(para reforzar)* even, still; **t. más/menos** even more/less
todo,-a 1 *adj* (**a**) all; **t. el pan** all the bread; **t. el mundo** (absolutely) everybody; **t. el día** all day, the whole o entire day; *Fam* **t. quisqui** every Tom, Dick and Harry
　(**b**) *(cada)* every; **t. ciudadano de más de dieciocho años** every citizen over eighteen years of age
　(**c**) *(entero)* complete, thorough; **es toda una mujer** she is every inch a woman
　(**d**) **todos,-as** all; *(con expresiones de tiempo)* every; **todos los niños** all the children; **todos los martes** every Tuesday
　2 *nm (totalidad)* whole
　3 *pron* (**a**) *(sin excluir nada)* all, everything; **ante t.** first of all; **con t.** in spite of everything; **del t.** completely; **después de t.** after all; **eso es t.** that's all, that's it; **estar en t.** to be really

with it; **hay de t.** there are all sorts; **lo sé t.** I know all about it; **t. lo contrario** quite the contrary *o* opposite; **t. lo más** at the most

 (**b**) *(cualquiera)* anybody; **t. aquél** *o* **el que quiera** anybody who wants (to)

 (**c**) *(cada uno)* **todos aprobamos** we all passed; **todos fueron** they all went

 4 *adv* completely, totally; **volvió t. sucio** he was all dirty when he got back

todopoderoso,-a *adj* all-powerful, almighty

todoterreno *nm* all-terrain vehicle

toga *nf* (**a**) gown, robe (**b**) *Hist* toga

Tokio *n* Tokyo

toldo *nm* (**a**) *(cubierta)* awning (**b**) *Am (cabaña)* tent, teepee

tolerancia *nf* tolerance

tolerante *adj* tolerant

tolerar *vt* to tolerate; *(situación)* to stand; *(gente)* to put up with

toma *nf* (**a**) *(acción)* taking; *Elec* **t. de corriente** plug, socket (**b**) *Med* dose (**c**) *Mil* capture (**d**) *Cin* take, shot (**e**) **t. de posesión** swearing in (**f**) *Fam* **Fig t. y daca** give and take

tomado,-a *adj* (**a**) *(voz)* hoarse (**b**) *Am (borracho)* drunk (**c**) **tenerla tomada con algn** to have it in for sb

tomadura *nf Fam* **t. de pelo** leg-pull; *(timo)* rip-off

tomar 1 *vt* (**a**) *(coger)* to take; *(autobús, tren)* to catch; *(decisión)* to make, to take; **toma** here (you are); **t. el sol** to sunbathe; *Av* **t. tierra** to land; *Fam* **tomarla con algn** to have it in for sb (**b**) *(comer, beber)* to have (**c**) **t. algo a mal** to take sth badly; **t. en serio/broma** to take seriously/as a joke (**d**) *(confundir)* to take (**por** por) (**e**) *Mil* to storm

 2 *vi Am (beber alcohol)* to drink

 3 tomarse *vpr* (**a**) *(comer)* to eat; *(beber)* to drink (**b**) *Fam* **no te lo tomes así** don't take it like that

tomate *nm* tomato; **salsa de t.** *(de lata)* tomato sauce; *(de botella)* ketchup

tomavistas *nm inv* cine *o* movie camera

tómbola *nf* tombola

tomillo *nm* thyme

tomo *nm* volume; *Fam* **de t. y lomo** utter, out-and-out

ton *sin* **t. ni son** without rhyme or reason

tonada *nf* (**a**) *Mús* tune, song (**b**) *Am (acento)* accent

tonalidad *nf* tonality

tonel *nm* barrel, cask

tonelada *nf* ton; **t. métrica** tonne

tonelaje *nm* tonnage

tonelero,-a *nm,f* cooper

tongo *nm* fix

tónico,-a 1 *nm Med* tonic; *(cosmético)* skin tonic

 2 *nf* **tónica** (**a**) *(tendencia)* tendency, trend; **tónica general** overall trend (**b**) *(bebida)* tonic (water) (**c**) *Mús* tonic

 3 *adj* (**a**) *Ling* tonic, stressed (**b**) *Mús & Med* tonic

tonificante *adj* invigorating

tonificar [44] *vt* to tone up, to invigorate

tono *nm* tone; **a t. con** in tune *o* harmony with; **subir de t.** *o* **el t.** to speak louder; **un t. alto/bajo** a high/low pitch; *Fig* **darse t.** to put on airs; *Fig* **fuera de t.** inappropriate, out of place; **dar el t.** to set the tone

tontear *vi* (**a**) to act the clown, to fool about (**b**) *(galantear)* to flirt

tontería *nf* (**a**) stupidity, silliness (**b**) *(dicho, hecho)* silly *o* stupid thing (**c**) *(insignificancia)* trifle

tonto,-a 1 *adj* silly, dumb

 2 *nm,f* fool, idiot; **t. de remate** *o* **de capirote** prize idiot

topacio *nm* topaz

topadora *nf RP* bulldozer

toparse *vpr* **t. con** to bump into; *(dificultades)* to run up against, to encounter; **t. con algo** to come across sth

tope 1 *nm* (**a**) *(límite)* limit, end; *Fam* **a t.** *(al máximo)* flat out; *Fig* **estar hasta los topes** to be full up; **fecha t.** deadline (**b**) *Téc* stop, check (**c**) *Ferroc* buffer

 2 *adv Fam* incredibly; **t. difícil** really difficult

tópico,-a 1 *nm* cliché

 2 *adj Med & Farm* for external use

📕 Observa que la palabra inglesa **topic** es un falso amigo y no es la traducción de la palabra española **tópico**. En inglés, **topic** significa "tema".

---

topo *nm* mole

topografía *nf* topography

topónimo *nm* place name

toque *nm* (**a**) touch; *Fam* **dar un t. a algn** *(avisar)* to let sb know; *(advertir)* to warn sb (**b**) *(de campanas)* peal; *Fig* warning; **t. de queda** curfew

toquetear *vt* to fiddle with, to finger

toquilla *nf* (knitted) shawl

tórax *nm* thorax

torbellino *nm* (**a**) *(de viento)* whirlwind (**b**) *Fig (confusión)* whirl, turmoil

torcedura *nf (acción)* twist, twisting; *Med* sprain

torcer [41] **1** *vt* (**a**) *(metal)* to bend; *(cuerda, hilo)* to twist; *Med* to sprain; *Fig (esquina)* to turn (**b**) *(inclinar)* to slant

 2 *vi* to turn (left *o* right)

 3 torcerse *vpr* (**a**) *(doblarse)* to twist, to bend (**b**) *Med* **se me torció el tobillo** I sprained my ankle (**c**) *(plan)* to fall through (**d**) *(desviarse)* to go off to the side

torcido,-a *adj* twisted; *(ladeado)* slanted, lopsided; *(corbata)* crooked

tordo,-a 1 *adj* dapple-grey

 2 *nm Orn* thrush

torear 1 *vt* to fight; *Fam* **t. a algn** to tease *o* onfuse sb; *Fam* **t. un asunto** to tackle a matter skilfully

2 *vi* to fight

oreo *nm* bullfighting

orero,-a *nm,f* bullfighter

ormenta *nf* storm

ormento *nm* (*tortura*) torture; (*padecimiento*) torment

ormentoso,-a *adj* stormy

ornado *nm* tornado

ornar *Fml* **1** *vt* (*convertir*) to transform, to turn (**en** into)

2 *vi* (*regresar*) to return, to go back; **t. en sí** to regain consciousness

3 tornarse *vpr* to become, to turn

ornasolado,-a *adj* iridescent

orneo *nm* (a) *Dep* tournament (b) *Hist* tourney, joust

ornillo *nm* screw

orniquete *nm* (a) turnstile (b) *Med* tourniquet

orno *nm* (a) *Téc* lathe; (*de alfarero*) wheel (b) **en t. a** (*alrededor de*) around; (*acerca de*) about

oro *nm* bull; **¿te gustan los toros?** do you like bullfighting?

oronja *nf* grapefruit

orpe *adj* (a) (*sin habilidad*) clumsy (b) (*tonto*) dim, thick (c) (*movimiento*) slow, awkward

orpedear *vt* to torpedo

orpedo *nm* torpedo

orpeza *nf* (a) (*física*) clumsiness; (*mental*) dimness, stupidity (b) (*lentitud*) slowness, heaviness (c) (*error*) blunder

orre *nf* (a) tower (b) *Mil & Náut* turret (c) (*en ajedrez*) rook, castle

orrefacto,-a *adj* roasted; **café t.** high roast coffee

orrencial *adj* torrential

orrente *nm* (a) (*de agua*) torrent (b) *Fig* **t. de voz** strong o powerful voice

orrezno *nm* = rasher of fried bacon

órrido,-a *adj* torrid

orrija *nf* French toast

orsión *nf* (a) (*torcedura*) twist, twisting (b) *Téc* torsion

orso *nm* (a) *Anat* torso (b) *Arte* bust

orta *nf* (a) *Culin* cake (b) *Fam* (*golpe*) slap, punch

ortazo *nm Fam* (a) (*bofetada*) slap, punch (b) (*golpe*) whack, thump

ortícolis *nf inv* crick in the neck

ortilla *nf* (a) (*egg*) omelette; **t. francesa/española** (plain)/potato omelette (b) *Am* tortilla

ortillera *nf muy Fam* dyke, lesbian

órtola *nf* dove

ortuga *nf* (*de tierra*) tortoise, *US* turtle; (*de mar*) turtle

ortuoso,-a *adj* tortuous

ortura *nf* torture

torturar *vt* to torture

tos *nf* cough; **t. ferina** whooping cough

tosco,-a *adj* (*basto*) rustic, rough; (*persona*) uncouth

toser *vi* to cough

tosquedad *nf* roughness

tostada *nf* (slice of) toast

tostado,-a *adj* (a) (*pan*) toasted (b) (*moreno*) tanned, brown

tostador *nm* toaster

tostar [2] *vt* (*pan*) to toast; (*café*) to roast; (*carne, pescado*) to brown; *Fig* (*la piel*) to tan

tostón *nm* (a) *Culin* (*pan frito*) crouton (b) *Fam* (*tabarra*) bore, drag

total 1 *adj* (*completo*) total

2 *nm* (a) (*todo*) whole; **en t.** in all (b) *Mat* total

3 *adv* so, in short; **¿t. para qué?** what's the point anyhow?; *Fam* **t. que ...** so ...; **t., tampoco te hará caso** he won't listen to you anyway

totalidad *nf* whole, totality; **la t. de** all of; **en su t.** as a whole

totalitario,-a *adj* totalitarian

totalizar [40] **1** *vt* to total

2 *vi* to amount to

tóxico,-a 1 *adj* toxic, poisonous

2 *nm* poison

toxicología *nf* toxicology

toxicólogo,-a *nm,f* toxicologist

toxicomanía *nf* drug addiction

toxicómano,-a *Med* **1** *adj* addicted to drugs

2 *nm,f* drug addict

tozudo,-a *adj* obstinate, stubborn

traba *nf* (a) (*de rueda*) chock; (*enlace*) bond, tie (b) *Fig* (*obstáculo*) hindrance, obstacle

trabajador,-a 1 *nm,f* worker, labourer

2 *adj* hard-working

trabajar 1 *vi* to work; **trabaja mucho** he works hard; **t. de camarera** to work as a waitress

2 *vt* (a) to work (on); (*la tierra*) to till (b) (*asignatura etc*) to work on (c) *Fam* (*convencer*) to (try to) persuade

trabajo *nm* (a) (*ocupación*) work; **t. a destajo** piecework; **t. eventual** casual labour; **trabajos manuales** arts and crafts (b) (*empleo*) employment, job (c) (*tarea*) task, job (d) *Educ* (*redacción*) report, paper (e) (*esfuerzo*) effort; **cuesta t. creerlo** it's hard to believe

trabajoadicto,-a *nm,f* workaholic

trabajoso,-a *adj* (*laborioso*) hard, laborious; (*difícil*) difficult

trabalenguas *nm inv* tongue twister

trabar 1 *vt* (a) (*sujetar*) to lock, to fasten; (*un plan*) to obstruct (b) (*conversación, amistad*) to start, to strike up (c) *Culin* to thicken

2 trabarse *vpr* (a) (*cuerdas*) to get tangled up (b) *Fig* **se le trabó la lengua** he got tongue-tied

trabazón *nf* (*de ideas*) link

trabilla *nf* (*de pantalón*) belt loop

trabuco *nm* blunderbuss

tracción *nf* traction; *Aut* **t. delantera/trasera**

front-/rear-wheel drive; *Aut* **t. en las cuatro ruedas** four-wheel drive
tractor *nm* tractor
tradición *nf* tradition
tradicional *adj* traditional
traducción *nf* translation; **t. directa/inversa** translation from/into a foreign language
traducir [10] **1** *vt* to translate (**a** into)
2 traducirse *vpr Fig* to result (**en** in)
traductor,-a *nm,f* translator
traer [25] **1** *vt* (**a**) to bring; **trae** give it to me (**b**) *(llevar puesto)* to wear (**c**) *(llevar consigo)* to carry (**d**) *(problemas)* to cause; **traerá como consecuencia ...** it will result in ...
2 traerse *vpr (llevar consigo)* to bring along; *Fig* **¿qué se trae entre manos?** what is he up to?
traficante *nmf (de drogas etc)* trafficker, pusher
traficar [44] *vi (ilegalmente)* to traffic (**con** in)
tráfico *nm* (**a**) *Aut* traffic; **t. rodado** road traffic (**b**) *Com* traffic, trade; **t. de drogas** drug traffic
tragaluz *nm* skylight
tragaperras *nf inv (máquina)* **t.** slot machine
tragar [42] **1** *vt* (**a**) *(ingerir)* to swallow (**b**) *Fam (engullir)* to gobble up, to tuck away (**c**) *Fig (a una persona)* to stand, to stomach (**d**) *Fig (creer)* to believe, to swallow
2 tragarse *vpr* (**a**) *(ingerir)* to swallow (**b**) *Fig (creer)* to believe, to swallow
tragedia *nf* tragedy
trágico,-a *adj* tragic
trago *nm* (**a**) *(bebida)* swig; **de un t.** in one go (**b**) *Fig* **pasar un mal t.** to have a bad time of it
tragón,-ona *nm,f* glutton, big eater
traición *nf* treason, betrayal; **a t.** treacherously; **alta t.** high treason
traicionar *vt* to betray; *(delatar)* to give away, to betray
traicionero,-a *adj* treacherous
traidor,-a **1** *adj* treacherous
2 *nm,f* traitor
traigo *indic pres de* **traer**
tráiler *nm (pl* **tráilers)** (**a**) *Cin* trailer, *US* preview (**b**) *Aut Br* articulated lorry, *US* semi-trailer (**c**) *Méx (casa rodante) Br* caravan, *US* trailer
traje¹ *nm* (**a**) *(de hombre)* suit; **t. de baño** bathing suit *o* costume, swimsuit; **t. de paisano** civilian clothes; **t. de luces** bullfighter's costume (**b**) *(de mujer)* dress; **t. de chaqueta** two-piece suit; **t. de novia** wedding dress
traje² *pt indef de* **traer**
trajeado,-a *adj Fam* sharp, dapper
trajearse *vpr* to dress up
trajín *nm Fam* comings and goings, hustle and bustle
trajinar *vi* to run *o* bustle about
trama *nf* (**a**) *Tex* weft, woof (**b**) *Lit* plot
tramar *vt* to plot, to cook up; **¿qué tramas?** what are you up to?

tramitar *vt* (**a**) *(gestionar)* to take the necesary (legal) steps to obtain (**b**) *Fml (despechar)* to convey, to transmit (**c**) *Com, Jur & Fi[n]* to carry out, to process
trámite *nm (paso)* step; *(formalidad)* forma[l]ity; *Com, Jur & Fin* procedures, proceedings
tramo *nm (de carretera)* section, stretch; *(de escalera)* flight
tramoya *nf (maquinaria)* stage machiner[y]; *(trama)* plot, scheme
trampa *nf* (**a**) *(de caza)* trap, snare (**b**) *(pue[r]ta)* trapdoor (**c**) *(engaño)* fiddle; **hacer trampa(s)** to cheat (**d**) *(truco)* trick

> *Observa que la palabra inglesa* **tramp** *es un falso amigo y no es la traducción de la palabr[a] española* **trampa**. *En inglés,* **tramp** *significa "vagabundo".*

trampilla *nf* trapdoor, hatch
trampolín *nm* (**a**) *(de piscina)* diving boar[d] (**b**) *(de esquí)* ski jump

> *Observa que la palabra inglesa* **trampolin[e]** *es un falso amigo y no es la traducción de la pa[]labra española* **trampolín**. *En inglés,* **trampoline** *significa "cama elástica".*

tramposo,-a **1** *adj* deceitful
2 *nm,f* cheat; *Naipes* cardsharp
tranca *nf* (**a**) *(garrote)* cudgel; *Fam* **a trancas barrancas** with great difficulty (**b**) *(en puert[a,] ventana)* bar
trancar **1** *vt (asegurar) (con cerrojo)* to bol[t] *(con tranca)* to bar
2 trancarse *vpr Am (atorarse)* to get stuck; **[l]a llave se trancó en la cerradura** the key go[t] stuck in the lock
trance *nm* (**a**) *(coyuntura)* (critical) momen[t;] **estar en t. de ...** to be on the point of ... (**b**) *(éxtasis)* trance
tranquilidad *nf* calmness, tranquillity; **con [t.]** calmly; **pídemelo con toda t.** don't hesitate t[o] ask me
tranquilizante *nm* tranquillizer
tranquilizar [40] **1** *vt* to calm down; **lo dij[o] para tranquilizarme** he said it to reassure m[e]
2 tranquilizarse *vpr (calmarse)* to calm dow[n]
tranquillo *nm Fig* knack; **coger el t. a algo t[o]** get the knack of sth
tranquilo,-a *adj* (**a**) *(persona, lugar)* calm[,] *(agua)* still; *(conciencia)* clear; *Fam* **tú t.** don['t] you worry (**b**) *(despreocupado)* placid, eas[y] going
transacción *nf* transaction, deal
transar *vi Am Fam* (**a**) *(transigir)* to compro[]mise, to give in (**b**) *(negociar)* to negotiate
transatlántico,-a **1** *adj* transatlantic
2 *nm Náut* (ocean) liner
transbordador *nm* (car) ferry; **t. espacia[l]** space shuttle
transbordar **1** *vt* to transfer; *Náut (mercancías)* to tranship

2 vi Ferroc to change trains, US to transfer

ransbordo nm (**a**) Ferroc change, US transer; **hacer t.** to change, US to transfer (**b**) Náut ranshipment

ranscurrir vi (**a**) (tiempo) to pass, to go by (**b**) (acontecer) to take place

ranscurso nm course o passing (of time); **en el t. de** in the course of, during

ranseúnte nmf (**a**) (peatón) passer-by (**b**) (residente temporal) temporary resident

ansferencia nf transference; Fin transfer; **t. bancaria** banker's order

ransferible adj transferable

ransferir [5] vt to transfer; Informát to download

ransformación nf transformation

ransformador nm Elec transformer

ransformar 1 vt to transform, to change

2 transformarse upr to change, to turn (**en** nto); (algo plegable) to convert

ránsfuga nmf (**a**) Mil deserter (**b**) Pol turncoat

ransfusión nf transfusion

ransgénico,-a 1 adj transgenic

2 nmpl **transgénicos** GM foods

ransgredir vt defect to transgress, to break

ransgresor,-a nm,f transgressor, lawbreaker

ransición nf transition

ransido,-a adj Fml **t. de angustia** overcome by anxiety; **t. de dolor** racked with pain

ransigente adj tolerant

ransigir [57] vi to compromise

ransistor nm transistor

ransitable adj passable

ransitado,-a adj (carretera) busy

ransitar vi to pass

ransitivo,-a adj transitive

ránsito nm (**a**) Aut traffic (**b**) (movimiento) movement, passage; **pasajeros en t.** passengers in transit

ransitorio,-a adj transitory

ranslucirse [35] upr = traslucirse

ransmisión nf (**a**) transmission (**b**) Téc drive; **t. delantera/trasera** front-/rear-wheel drive (**c**) Rad & TV transmission, broadcast

ransmisor nm transmitter

ransmitir vt (**a**) to transmit, to pass on (**b**) Rad & TV to transmit, to broadcast (**c**) Jur to transfer, to hand down

ransparencia nf (**a**) transparency; Pol openness (**b**) Fot slide

ransparentarse upr to be transparent; **esta tela se transparenta** this is see-through material; **se le transparentaban las bragas** you could see her panties

ransparente 1 adj transparent; Pol open

2 nm (**a**) (visillo) net curtain (**b**) (pantalla) shade, blind

ranspiración nf perspiration

ranspirar vi to perspire

ransplante nm transplant; Med **t. de cora-** **zón/córnea** heart/eye transplant

transponer [19] **1** vt (mudar de sitio) to transpose, to move about

2 transponerse upr (desmayarse) to faint

transportar vt to transport; (pasajeros) to carry; (mercancías) to ship

transporte nm (**a**) transport (**b**) Com freight; **t. de mercancías** freight transport; **t. marítimo** shipment

transportista nmf carrier

transvase nm (**a**) (de líquidos) decanting (**b**) (de ríos) transfer

transversal adj transverse, cross

tranvía nm Br tram, tramcar, US streetcar

trapecio nm trapeze

trapecista nmf trapeze artist

trapero,-a 1 nm Br rag-and-bone man, US junkman

2 adj **puñalada trapera** stab in the back

trapichear vi to be up to something

trapicheo nm jiggery-pokery

trapo nm (**a**) (viejo, roto) rag (**b**) (bayeta) cloth; **t. de cocina** dishcloth; **t. del polvo** duster; Fam **poner (a algn) como un t.** (sucio) to tear (sb) apart

tráquea nf trachea, windpipe

traqueteo nm rattle, clatter

tras prep (**a**) (después de) after; **uno t. otro** one after the other (**b**) (detrás) behind; **sentados uno t. otro** sitting one behind the other (**c**) andar/ir **t.** to be after; **la policía iba t. ella** the police were after her

trasatlántico,-a adj & nm = transatlántico,-a

trasbordador nm = transbordador

trasbordar vt & vi = transbordar

trasbordo nm = transbordo

trascendencia nf (**a**) (importancia) importance, significance (**b**) (en filosofía) transcendence

trascendental, trascendente adj (**a**) significant, far-reaching (**b**) (en filosofía) transcendental

trascender [3] vi (**a**) (noticia) to become known, to leak out (**b**) (tener consecuencias) to have far-reaching consequences (**c**) **t. de** to go beyond

trascurrir vi = transcurrir

trascurso nm = transcurso

trasero,-a 1 adj back, rear; **en la parte trasera** at the back

2 nm Euf backside

trasferencia nf = transferencia

trasferible adj = transferible

trasferir [5] vt = transferir

trasfondo nm background

trasformación nf = transformación

trasformador nm = transformador

trasformar vt = transformar

trásfuga nmf = tránsfuga

trasfusión nf = transfusión

trasgredir vt = transgredir

trasgresor,-a nm,f = transgresor,-a

trashumancia *nf* = seasonal movement of livestock

trasiego *nm* comings and goings, hustle and bustle

trasladar 1 *vt* (*cosa*) to move; (*persona*) to move, to transfer

2 trasladarse *upr* to go, to move

traslado *nm* (*de casa*) move, removal; (*de personal*) transfer; *Educ* **t. de expediente** transfer of student record

traslucirse [35] *upr* to show (through)

trasluz *nm* **mirar algo al t.** to hold sth against the light

trasmano *nm* **a t.** out of reach; **(me) coge a t.** it's out of my way

trasmisión *nf* = transmisión

trasmisor *nm* = transmisor

trasmitir *vt* = transmitir

trasnochado,-a *adj* (*desfasado*) old, hackneyed

trasnochador,-a 1 *adj* given to staying up late

2 *nm,f* night bird, nighthawk

trasnochar *vi* to stay up (very) late

traspapelarse *upr* to get mislaid o misplaced

trasparencia *nf* = transparencia

trasparentarse *upr* = transparentarse

trasparente *adj & nm* = transparente

traspasar *vt* (a) (*atravesar*) to go through; (*río*) to cross (b) (*negocio, local*) to transfer; **se traspasa** (*en letrero*) for sale (c) *Fig* (*exceder*) to exceed, to go beyond

📖 Observa que el verbo inglés **to trespass** es un falso amigo y no es la traducción del verbo español **traspasar**. En inglés, **to trespass** significa "entrar sin autorización".

traspaso *nm* (a) (*de propiedad etc*) transfer (b) *Com* (*venta*) sale

traspié *nm* (*pl* **traspiés**) stumble, trip; **dar un t.** to trip; *Fig* to slip up

traspiración *nf* = transpiración

traspirar *vi* = transpirar

trasplante *nm* = transplante

trasponer [19] *vt* = transponer

trasportar *vt* = transportar

trasporte *nm* = transporte

traspuesto,-a *adj* **quedarse t.** to faint

trasquilar *vt* (*oveja*) to shear; (*pelo*) to crop

trastabillar *vi* (*tambalearse*) to stagger, to totter

trastada *nf* *Fam* **hacer trastadas** to be up to mischief

trastazo *nm* *Fam* wallop, thump

traste¹ *nm* *Mús* fret

traste² *nm* (a) (*trasto*) piece of junk (b) *Andes, CAm, Carib, Méx* **trastes** dirty dishes; **fregar los trastes** to wash the dishes, *US* to do the washing-up (c) *CSur Fam* (*trasero*) bottom (d) *Fig* **dar al t. con un plan** to spoil a plan; **irse al t.** to fall through

trastear *vi* (*revolver*) to rummage about

trastero *nm* **(cuarto) t.** junk room

trastienda *nf* back shop

trasto *nm* (*objeto cualquiera*) thing; (*cos‌ inservible*) piece of junk

trastocar [44] *vt* = trastornar

trastornado,-a *adj* (*loco*) mad, unhinged

trastornar 1 *vt* (a) (*planes*) to disrupt (b) *F‌ (persona*) to unhinge

2 trastornarse *upr* (*enloquecer*) to go out ‌ one's mind, to go mad

trastorno *nm* (*molestia*) trouble, inconven‌ ence; **t. mental** mental disorder o disturbanc‌

trasvase *nm* = transvase

trasversal *adj* = transversal

trata *nf* slave trade o traffic; **t. de blanca** white slave trade

tratable *adj* easy to get along with, co‌ genial

tratado *nm* (a) (*pacto*) treaty (b) (*estudi‌ treatise

tratamiento *nm* (a) treatment (b) *Téc* pr‌ cessing, treatment (c) *Informát* processing; **de textos** word processing

tratar 1 *vt* (a) (*atender*) to treat; **t. bien/mal** treat well/badly (b) *Med* to treat (c) (*asunt‌ to discuss (d) *Informát & Téc* to process (‌ **me trata de tú** he addresses me as "tu"

2 *vi* (a) **t. de** (*intentar*) to try (b) **t. de** o **sobr‌ o acerca** to be about; **¿de qué trata?** what is ‌ about? (c) **t. con** (*tener tratos*) to deal wit‌ (*negociar*) to negotiate with; (*relacionarse*) ‌ move among (d) *Com* **t. en** to deal in

3 tratarse *upr* (a) (*relacionarse*) to be o‌ speaking terms (b) **se trata de** (*es cuestió‌ de*) it's a question of; **se trata de un cas‌ excepcional** it's an exceptional case

tratativas *nfpl* *CSur* negotiation

trato *nm* (a) (*de personas*) manner; (*contact‌ contact; **malos tratos** ill-treatment (‌ (*acuerdo*) agreement; **¡t. hecho!** it's a dea‌ (c) *Com* deal

trauma *nm* trauma

traumático,-a *adj* traumatic

traumatizar *vt* *Med* to traumatize; *Fam* t‌ shock

través 1 *prep* (a) **a t. de** (*superficie*) across‌ over; (*agujero etc*) through; **a t. del río** acros‌ the river; **a t. del agujero** through the hole (b‌ *Fig* **a t. de** through; **a t. del periódico** throug‌ the newspaper

2 *adv* **de t.** (*transversalmente*) crosswise; (d‌ *lado*) sideways

3 *nm* (*pl* **traveses**) *Fig* (*desgracia*) misfortun‌

travesaño *nm* *Ftb* crossbar

travesía *nf* (*viaje*) crossing

travesti, travestí *nmf* transvestite

📖 Observa que la palabra inglesa **travesty** es‌ un falso amigo y no es la traducción de la palabra‌ española **travesti**. En inglés, **travesty** significa‌ "parodia burda".

291

travesura ▶ trivializar

travesura *nf* mischief, childish prank
travieso,-a *adj* mischievous
trayecto *nm* (a) *(distancia)* distance; *(recorrido)* route; *(trecho)* stretch (b) *(viaje)* journey
trayectoria *nf* (a) *(de proyectil, geométrica)* trajectory (b) *Fig (orientación)* line, course
traza *nf* (a) *(apariencia)* looks, appearance; **no lleva trazas de curarse** it doesn't look as if he's going to get better (b) *Arquit* plan, design
trazado *nm* (a) *(plano)* layout, plan (b) *(de carretera, ferrocarril)* route
trazar [40] *vt (línea)* to draw; *(plano)* to design; *Fig (plan)* to sketch out
trazo *nm* (a) *(línea)* line (b) *(de letra)* stroke
trébol *nm* (a) trefoil (b) *Naipes* club
trece 1 *adj inv* thirteen
  2 *nm inv* thirteen; *Fig* **estar** *o* **mantenerse** *o* **seguir en sus t.** to stick to one's guns
trecho *nm* distance, way; *(tramo)* stretch; **de t. en t.** from time to time
tregua *nf Mil* truce; *Fig* respite
treinta *adj & nm inv* thirty
treintavo,-a *adj & nm* thirtieth
treintena *nf* **una t. de** (about) thirty
tremendista *adj* over the top
tremendo,-a *adj* (a) *(terrible)* terrible, dreadful (b) *(muy grande)* enormous; *Fig* tremendous
trementina *nf* turpentine
trémulo,-a *adj Literario (vacilante)* quivering, tremulous; *(luz)* flickering
tren *nm* (a) train (b) *Av* **t. de aterrizaje** undercarriage; **t. de lavado** car wash (c) **t. de vida** lifestyle
trenca *nf* duffle coat
trenza *nf (de pelo)* plait, *esp US* braid
trepador,-a *adj* climbing
trepar *vt & vi* to climb
trepidante *adj* vibrating, shaking; *Fig* **lleva un ritmo de vida t.** he leads a hectic *o* frantic life
trepidar *vi* to vibrate, to shake
tres 1 *adj inv (cardinal)* three; *(ordinal)* third; *Fam* **de t. al cuarto** cheap, of little value
  2 *nm (pl treses)* three; **t. en raya** *Br* noughts and crosses, *US* tick-tack-toe
trescientos,-as *adj & nm* three hundred
tresillo *nm* (a) *(mueble)* (three-piece) suite (b) *Mús* triplet
treta *nf* trick, ruse
triángulo *nm* triangle; *Fig* **t. amoroso** eternal triangle
tribal *adj* tribal
tribu *nf* tribe
tribuna *nf* (a) *(plataforma)* rostrum, dais; **t. de (la) prensa** press box (b) *Dep* stand
tribunal *nm* (a) *Jur* court; **t. de apelación** court of appeal; **T. Supremo** *Br* High Court, *US* Supreme Court; **t. (tutelar) de menores** juvenile court (b) *(de examen)* board of examiners

tributar *vt* to pay
tributario,-a *adj* **sistema t.** tax system
tributo *nm* (a) *Com* tax (b) **pagar t. a** *(homenaje)* to pay tribute to
triciclo *nm* tricycle
tricornio *nm* three-cornered hat
tridimensional *adj* three-dimensional
trienio *nm* three-year period
trifásico,-a 1 *adj Elec* three-phase
  2 *nm* adapter
trigésimo,-a *adj & nm,f* thirtieth; **t. primero** thirty-first
trigo *nm* wheat
trigueño,-a *adj Am (pelo)* dark brown; *(persona)* olive-skinned
trilla *nf* threshing
trillado,-a *adj Fig* well-worn
trilladora *nf* threshing machine; **t. segadora** combine harvester
trillar *vt* to thresh
trilogía *nf* trilogy
trimestral *adj* quarterly, three-monthly
trimestre *nm* quarter; *Educ* term
trinar *vi* (a) to warble (b) *Fam* to rage, to fume; **Santiago está que trina** Santiago is really fuming
trincar¹ [44] *vt Fam (capturar)* to catch
trincar² *vt Fam* to drink
trinchar *vt (carne)* to carve, to slice (up)
trinchera *nf* trench
trineo *nm* sledge, sleigh
Trinidad *nf* **la Santísima T.** the Holy Trinity
trino *nm* (a) warble, trill (b) *Mús* trill
trío *nm* trio
tripa *nf* (a) *(intestino)* gut, intestine; *Fam* tummy; **dolor de t.** stomach ache (b) **tripas** innards
triple *adj & nm* triple
triplicado,-a *adj* triplicate; **por t.** in triplicate
triplicar [44] *vt* to triple, to treble
trípode *nm* tripod
tríptico *nm* (a) *(cuadro)* triptych (b) *(folleto)* leaflet
tripulación *nf* crew
tripulante *nmf* crew member
tripular *vt* to man
triquiñuela *nf Fam* trick, dodge
tris *nm* **estar en un t. de** to be on the verge of
triste *adj* (a) *(persona, situación)* sad (b) *(lugar)* gloomy
tristeza *nf* sadness
triturar *vt (machacar)* to grind (up)
triunfador,-a 1 *adj* winning
  2 *nm,f* winner
triunfal *adj* triumphant
triunfar *vi* to triumph
triunfo *nm* (a) *(victoria)* triumph, victory; *Dep* win (b) *(éxito)* success
trivial *adj* trivial
trivialidad *nf* triviality
trivializar *vt* to trivialize, to minimize

triza *nf* bit, fragment; **hacer trizas** to tear to shreds

trocar [64] *vt* to barter

trocear *vt* to cut up (into bits *o* pieces)

trochemoche: a trochemoche *loc adv Fam* haphazardly

trofeo *nm* trophy

trola *nf Fam* fib

trolebús *nm* trolleybus

tromba *nf* **t. de agua** violent downpour

trombón *nm* trombone

trombosis *nf inv* thrombosis

trompa *nf* (a) *Mús* horn (b) *(de elefante)* trunk (c) *Anat* tube (d) *Fam* **estar t.** to be sloshed *o* plastered

trompazo *nm Fam* bump; **darse** *o* **pegarse un t.** to have a bump

trompeta *nf* trumpet

trompetista *nmf* trumpet player, trumpeter

trompicón *nm* trip, stumble; **hacer algo a trompicones** to do sth in fits and starts

trompo *nm* spinning top

tronar [2] **1** *vi* to thunder
2 *vt Méx Fam* (a) *(destruir, acabar con)* to destroy; **este remedio es para t. anginas** this remedy will clear up tonsillitis (b) *(reprobar)* to fail

tronchar 1 *vt (rama, tronco)* to cut down, to fell; *Fig (esperanzas etc)* to destroy
2 troncharse *upr* **t. de risa** to split one's sides with laughter

troncho *nm* stem, stalk

tronco *nm* (a) *Anat* trunk, torso (b) *Bot (de árbol)* trunk; *(leño)* log; *Fam Fig* **dormir como un t.** to sleep like a log

tronera *nf* (a) *(de billar)* pocket (b) *(ventana)* small window; *(de fortificación)* loophole; *Náut* porthole

trono *nm* throne

tropa *nf* (a) squad (b) **tropas** troops

tropel *nm* throng, mob; **en t.** in a mad rush

tropezar [1] *vi* (a) to trip, to stumble (**con** on) (b) **t. con algo** to come across sth; **t. con algn/dificultades** to run into sb/difficulties

tropezón *nm* (a) *(traspié)* trip, stumble; **dar un t.** to trip (b) *(error)* slip-up, faux pas (c) *(de comida)* chunk of meat

tropical *adj* tropical

trópico *nm* tropic

tropiezo 1 *nm* (a) *(obstáculo)* trip (b) *Fig (error)* blunder, faux pas
2 *indic pres de* **tropezar**

trotamundos *nmf inv* globetrotter

trotar *vi* to trot

trote *nm* (a) trot; **al t.** at a trot (b) *Fam* **ya no está para esos trotes** he cannot keep up the pace any more

trovador *nm* troubadour

trozar *vt Am (carne)* to cut up; *(res, tronco)* to butcher, to cut up

trozo *nm* piece

trucar [44] *vt* to doctor, to alter

trucha *nf* trout

truco *nm* (a) *(ardid)* trick; **aquí hay t.** there's something fishy going on here (b) **coger el t. (a algo)** to get the knack *o* hang (of sth)

truculento,-a *adj* horrifying, terrifying

> 🖉 Observa que la palabra inglesa **truculent** es un falso amigo y no es la traducción de la palabra española **truculento**. En inglés, **truculent** significa "agresivo, airado".

trueno *nm* thunder; **un t.** a thunderclap

trueque *nm* barter

trufa *nf* truffle

truhán,-ana *nm,f* rogue, crook

truncar [44] *vt* to truncate; *Fig (vida etc)* to cut short; *Fig (esperanzas)* to shatter

trusa *nf Méx (calzoncillo)* underpants; *(braga)* panties, *Br* knickers

trust *nm (pl* **trusts)** trust, cartel

tu *adj pos* your; **tu libro** your book; **tus libros** your books

tú *pron* you; **de tú a tú** on equal terms

> Usually omitted in Spanish except for emphasis or contrast.

tuba *nf* tuba

tubérculo *nm* (a) *Bot* tuber (b) *Med* tubercle

tuberculosis *nf inv* tuberculosis

tubería *nf* (a) *(de agua)* piping, pipes (b) *(de gas)* pipeline

tubo *nm* (a) tube; **t. de ensayo** test tube (b) *(tubería)* pipe; *Aut* **t. de escape** exhaust (pipe)

tucán *nm* toucan

tuerca *nf* nut

tuerto,-a 1 *adj* one-eyed, blind in one eye
2 *nm,f* one-eyed person

tuerzo *indic pres de* **torcer**

tuétano *nm* marrow; **hasta el t.** to one's fingertips

tufo *nm* foul odour *o* smell

tugurio *nm* hovel

tul *nm* tulle

tulipa *nf* small tulip

tulipán *nm* tulip

tullido,-a *adj* crippled, disabled

tullir *vt* to cripple

tumba *nf* grave, tomb

tumbar 1 *vt* to knock down *o* over
2 tumbarse *vpr (acostarse)* to lie down, to stretch out

tumbo *nm* **dar tumbos** to reel

tumbona *nf Br* sun-lounger, *US* beach recliner

tumor *nm* tumour

tumulto *nm* tumult, commotion

tumultuoso,-a *adj* tumultuous, riotous

tuna *nf* (a) *(agrupación musical)* = group of student minstrels (b) *Am (higo chumbo)* prickly pear

🖉 Observa que la palabra inglesa **tuna** es un falso amigo y no es la traducción de la palabra española **tuna**. En inglés, **tuna** significa "atún, bonito".

tunante,-a *nm,f* rogue, crook

túnel *nm* tunnel; **el t. del Canal de la Mancha** the Channel Tunnel

Túnez *n* (**a**) *(país)* Tunisia (**b**) *(ciudad)* Tunis

túnica *nf* tunic

tuno,-a 1 *nm,f (bribón)* rogue, crook

2 *nm* = member of a "tuna"

tuntún: al tuntún *loc adv* haphazardly, any old how

tupé *nm* (*pl* **tupés**) *(flequillo)* quiff

tupido,-a *adj* thick, dense

turba¹ *nf (combustible)* peat

turba² *nf (muchedumbre)* mob, crowd

turbado,-a *adj* (**a**) *(alterado)* disturbed (**b**) *(preocupado)* worried, anxious (**c**) *(desconcertado)* confused

turbante *nm* turban

turbar 1 *vt* (**a**) *(alterar)* to unsettle (**b**) *(preocupar)* to upset *o* worry (**c**) *(desconcertar)* to baffle, to put off

2 turbarse *vpr* (**a**) *(preocuparse)* to be *o* become upset (**b**) *(desconcertarse)* to be *o* become confused *o* baffled

turbina *nf* turbine

turbio,-a *adj (agua)* cloudy; *(negocio etc)* shady, dubious

turborreactor *nm* turbojet (engine)

turbulencia *nf* turbulence

turbulento,-a *adj* turbulent

turco,-a 1 *adj* Turkish

2 *nm,f (persona)* Turk; *Fig* **cabeza de t.** scapegoat

3 *nm (idioma)* Turkish

turismo *nm* (**a**) tourism; **ir de t.** to go touring; **t. rural** rural tourism (**b**) *Aut* car

turista *nmf* tourist

turístico,-a *adj* tourist; **de interés t.** of interest to tourists

turnarse *vpr* to take turns

turno *nm* (**a**) *(en juegos etc)* turn, go (**b**) *(de trabajo)* shift; **estar de t.** to be on duty; **t. de día/noche** day/night shift

turquesa *adj inv & nf* turquoise

Turquía *n* Turkey

turrón *nm* nougat

tute *nm Fam* **darse un t. de algo** to go to town doing sth

tutear 1 *vt* = to address as "tú"

2 tutearse *vpr* = to address each other as "tú"

tutela *nf* (**a**) *Jur* guardianship, tutelage (**b**) *Fig (protección)* protection, guidance

tuteo *nm* = use of the "tú" form of address

tutor *nm* (**a**) *Jur* guardian (**b**) *Educ* tutor

tuve *pt indef de* **tener**

tuyo,-a 1 *adj pos (con personas)* of yours; *(con objetos)* one of your; **¿es amigo t.?** is he a friend of yours?; **unas amigas tuyas** some friends of yours; **un libro t.** one of your books

2 *pron pos* yours; **éste es t.** this one is yours; *Fam* **los tuyos** *(familiares)* your family

TV *nf (abr* **televisión***)* TV

TVE *nf (abr* **Televisión Española***)* = Spanish state television network

U, u [u] *nf (la letra)* U, u

u *conj (delante de palabras que empiecen por* **o** *o* **ho**) or; **siete u ocho** seven or eight; **ayer u hoy** yesterday or today

ubicación *nf* location, position

ubicar [44] **1** *vt Am (situar)* to locate, to situate **2 ubicarse** *vpr* to be situated *o* located

ubicuo,-a *adj* ubiquitous

ubre *nf* udder

Ucrania *n* Ukraine

ucraniano,-a *adj & nm,f* Ukrainian

Ud. *(abr* **usted***)* you

Uds. *(abr* **ustedes***)* you

UE *nf (abr* **Unión Europea***)* EU

UEM *nf (abr* **unión económica y monetaria***)* EMU

ufanarse *vpr* to boast (**de** of)

ufano,-a *adj* conceited

ugetista *adj* = relating to the UGT

UGT *nf (abr* **Unión General de los Trabajadores***)* = major socialist trade union in Spain

ujier *nm* usher

úlcera *nf* ulcer

ulcerar *vt,* **ulcerarse** *vpr* to ulcerate

ulterior *adj (siguiente)* subsequent

últimamente *adv* lately, recently

ultimar *vt* (**a**) *(terminar)* to finalize (**b**) *Am (matar)* to kill, to finish off

ultimátum *nm (pl* **ultimátums***)* ultimatum

último,-a 1 *adj* (**a**) *(último)* last; **el ú. día** the last day; **por ú.** finally (**b**) *(más reciente)* latest; **últimas noticias** latest news (**c**) *(más alto)* top; **el ú. piso** the top flat (**d**) *(más bajo)* lowest (**e**) *(más lejano)* back, last; **la última fila** the back row (**f**) *(definitivo)* final

2 *nm,f* **llegar el ú.** to arrive last; **a últimos de mes** at the end of the month; **en las últimas** on one's last legs; *Fam* **a la última** up to the minute; **el ú. de la lista** the lowest in the list

ultra *nmf* extreme right-winger; **los ultras** the extreme right

ultra- *pref* ultra-

ultraderecha *nf Pol* extreme right

ultraderechista *Pol* **1** *adj* extreme right-wing **2** *nmf* extreme right-winger

ultraizquierda *nf* extreme left

ultrajar *vt* to outrage, to offend

ultraje *nm* outrage, offence

ultramar *nm* overseas (countries), abroad; **del** *o* **en u.** overseas

ultramarinos *nmpl* groceries; **tienda de u.** greengrocer's (shop)

ultranza: a ultranza *loc adv* (**a**) *(a todc trance)* at all costs, at any price; **defende algo a u.** to defend sth to the death (**b** *(acérrimo)* out-and-out, extreme

ultrasónico,-a *adj* ultrasonic

ultratumba *nf* afterlife

ultravioleta *adj inv* ultraviolet

ulular *vi (viento)* to howl; *(búho)* to hoot

umbral *nm* threshold

umbrío,-a, umbroso,-a *adj* shady

un, una 1 *art indet* (**a**) a; *(antes de vocal)* an **un coche** a car; **un huevo** an egg; **una flor** ¿ flower (**b**) **unos,-as** some; **unas flores** some flowers

2 *adj (delante de nm sing)* one; **un chico y do: chicas** one boy and two girls; *ver tambiér* **uno,-a**

unánime *adj* unanimous

unanimidad *nf* unanimity; **por u.** unan imously

unción *nf* unction

undécimo,-a *adj* eleventh

UNED *nf (abr* **Universidad Nacional de Educa ción a Distancia***)* = Spanish open university

ungir [57] *vt Rel* to anoint

ungüento *nm* ointment

únicamente *adv* only, solely

único,-a *adj* (**a**) *(solo)* only; **es el ú. que teng** it's the only one I've got; **hijo ú.** only child; **l ú. que quiero** the only thing I want; **el Merca do Ú.** the Single Market; **el Acta Única** th Single European Act (**b**) *(extraordinario* unique

unidad *nf* (**a**) unit (**b**) *(cohesión)* unity

unido,-a *adj* united; **están muy unidos** the are very attached to one another; **una famili muy unida** a very close family

unifamiliar *adj* **vivienda u.** detached house

unificación *nf* unification

unificar [44] *vt* to unify

uniformar *vt* (**a**) *(igualar)* to make uniform to standardize (**b**) *(poner un uniforme a)* t put into uniform, to give a uniform to

uniforme 1 *nm (prenda)* uniform

2 *adj* (**a**) *(igual)* uniform (**b**) *(superficie* even

uniformidad *nf* (**a**) *(igualdad)* uniformit (**b**) *(de superficie)* evenness

unilateral *adj* unilateral

unión *nf* union

Unión Soviética *n* Soviet Union

unir 1 *vt (juntar)* to unite, to join (together

esta carretera une las dos comarcas this road links both districts

2 unirse *vpr (juntarse)* to unite, to join

unisex *adj inv* unisex

unísono *nm* unison; **al u.** in unison

unitario,-a *adj* unitary; **precio u.** unit price

universal *adj* universal; **historia u.** world history

universidad *nf* university; **u. a distancia** ≃ Open University; **u. laboral** technical college

universitario,-a 1 *adj* university

2 *nm,f* university student

universo *nm* universe

uno,-a 1 *nm inv* one; **el u.** (number) one; **el u. de mayo** the first of May

2 *nf* **es la una** *(hora)* it's one o'clock

3 *adj* **unos,-as** some; **unas cajas** some boxes; **habrá unos** o **unas veinte** there must be around twenty

4 *pron* (**a**) one; **u. (de ellos), una (de ellas)** one of them; **unos cuantos** a few; **se miraron el u. al otro** they looked at each other; **de u. en u.** one by one; **un trás otro** one after the other; **una de dos** one of the two

(**b**) *(persona)* someone, somebody; **u. que pasaba por allí** some passer-by; **vive con u.** she's living with some man; **unos ... otros** some people ... others

(**c**) *(impers)* you, one; **u. tiene que ...** you have to ...

untar *vt* to grease, to smear; *(mantequilla)* to spread

untura *nf* ointment

uña *nf* (**a**) nail; **morderse** o **comerse las uñas** to bite one's fingernails; *Fig* **ser u. y carne** to be hand in glove (**b**) *Zool (garra)* claw; *(pezuña)* hoof

uperizado,-a *adj* **leche uperizada** UHT milk

Urales *nmpl* **los U.** the Urals

uranio *nm* uranium

Urano *nm* Uranus

urbanidad *nf* urbanity, politeness

urbanismo *nm* town planning

urbanístico,-a *adj* town-planning

urbanización *nf* (**a**) *(barrio)* housing development o estate (**b**) *(proceso)* urbanization

urbanizar *vt* to build up

urbano,-a *adj* urban, city; **guardia u.** (traffic) policeman

urbe *nf* large city

urdimbre *nf* (**a**) *Tex* warp (**b**) *(trama)* intrigue

urdir *vt* (**a**) *Tex* to warp (**b**) *(tramar)* to plot, to scheme

urgencia *nf* (**a**) urgency (**b**) *(emergencia)* emergency

urgente *adj* urgent; **correo u.** express mail

urgir [57] *vi* to be urgent o pressing; **me urge (tenerlo)** I need it urgently

urinario *nm* urinal

urna *nf* (**a**) *Pol* ballot box (**b**) *(vasija)* urn

urólogo,-a *nm,f Med* urologist

urraca *nf* magpie

URSS *nf Hist (abr* **Unión de Repúblicas Socialistas Soviéticas**) USSR

urticaria *nf Med* hives

Uruguay *n* Uruguay

uruguayo,-a *adj & nm,f* Uruguayan

usado,-a *adj (ropa)* second-hand, used

usanza *nf Literario* **a la antigua u.** in the old style

usar 1 *vt* (**a**) to use (**b**) *(prenda)* to wear

2 usarse *vpr* to be used o in fashion

usina *nf Am (central eléctrica)* power station; **u. nuclear** nuclear power station

uso *nm* (**a**) use; *Farm* **u. externo/tópico** external/local application (**b**) *(de poder, privilegio)* exercise (**c**) *(de prenda)* wearing; **haga u. del casco** wear a helmet (**d**) *(costumbre)* usage, custom; **al u.** conventional

usted *(pl* **ustedes**) *pron pers Fml* you; **¿quién es u.?, ¿quiénes son ustedes?** who are you?

> Usually omitted in Spanish except for emphasis or contrast. Although formal in peninsular Spanish, it is not necessarily so in Latin American Spanish.

usual *adj* usual, common

usuario,-a *nm,f* user

usura *nf* usury

usurero,-a *nm,f* usurer

usurpar *vt* to usurp

utensilio *nm* utensil; *(herramienta)* tool

útero *nm* uterus, womb

útil 1 *adj* useful; *(día)* working

2 *nm (herramienta)* tool, instrument

utilidad *nf* usefulness, utility; *(beneficio)* profit

utilitario,-a 1 *nm (coche)* utility vehicle

2 *adj* utilitarian

utilización *nf* use, utilization

utilizar [40] *vt* to use, to utilize

utopía *nf* utopia

utópico,-a *adj & nm,f* utopian

uva *nf* grape; **u. blanca** green grape

UVI *nf (abr* **unidad de vigilancia intensiva**) ICU

úvula *nf* uvula

V, v ['uße] *nf (la letra)* V, v
V *Elec (abr* **voltio(s))** V
vaca *nf* (**a**) *(carne)* cow (**b**) *(carne)* beef
vacaciones *nfpl Br* holidays, *US* vacation; *(viaje)* holiday; **durante las v.** during the holidays; **estar/irse de v.** to be/go on holiday
vacacionista *nmf Am Br* holidaymaker, *US* vacationer
vacante 1 *adj* vacant
   2 *nf* vacancy
vaciar [29] **1** *vt* (**a**) *(recipiente)* to empty; *(contenido)* to empty out (**b**) *(terreno)* to hollow out (**c**) *Arte* to cast, to mould
   2 vaciarse *upr* to empty
vacilación *nf* hesitation
vacilante *adj* (**a**) *(persona)* hesitant, irresolute (**b**) *(voz)* hesitant, faltering (**c**) *(luz)* flickering
vacilar *vi* (**a**) *(dudar)* to hesitate; **sin v.** without hesitation (**b**) *(voz)* to falter (**c**) *(luz)* to flicker (**d**) *Fam (jactarse)* to show off
vacilón,-ona *Fam* **1** *adj* (**a**) *(fanfarrón)* swanky (**b**) *(bromista)* jokey, teasing (**c**) *CAm, Méx Fam (juerguista)* fond of partying
   2 *nm,f* (**a**) *(fanfarrón)* show-off (**b**) *(bromista)* tease
   3 *nm Carib (fiesta)* party
vacío,-a 1 *adj* (**a**) empty; *(hueco)* hollow (**b**) *(sin ocupar)* vacant, unoccupied
   2 *nm* (**a**) emptiness, void (**b**) *(hueco)* gap; *(espacio)* (empty) space (**c**) *Fís* vacuum; **envasado al v.** vacuum-packed
vacuna *nf* vaccine
vacunación *nf* vaccination
vacunar 1 *vt* to vaccinate (**contra** against); *Fig* to inure
   2 vacunarse *upr* to get oneself vaccinated
vacuno,-a *adj* bovine; **ganado v.** cattle
vacuo,-a *adj* vacuous, empty
vadear *vt (río)* to ford; *Fig (dificultad)* to overcome
vado *nm* (**a**) *(de un río)* ford (**b**) *Aut* **v. permanente** *(en letrero)* keep clear
vagabundear *vi* to wander, to roam
vagabundo,-a 1 *adj (errante)* wandering; *Pey* vagrant; **perro v.** stray dog
   2 *nm,f* wanderer; *(sin casa)* tramp, *US* hobo; *Pey* vagrant, tramp
vagancia *nf* idleness, laziness
vagar [42] *vi* to wander about, to roam about
vagido *nm* cry *(of a newborn baby)*
vagina *nf* vagina

vago,-a 1 *adj* (**a**) *(perezoso)* lazy (**b**) *(indefinido)* vague
   2 *nm,f* (**a**) *(holgazán)* layabout (**b**) *Jur* vagrant
vagón *nm (para pasajeros)* carriage, coach, *US* car; *(para mercancías)* truck, wagon, *US* freight car, *US* boxcar
vaguedad *nf* vagueness
vaho *nm (de aliento)* breath; *(vapor)* vapour
vaina 1 *nf* (**a**) *(de espada)* sheath, scabbard (**b**) *Bot* pod (**c**) *Col, Perú, Ven muy Fam (molestia)* bother, pain (in the neck); **¡qué v.!** what a pain!
   2 *nmf (persona)* dimwit
vainilla *nf* vanilla
vaivén *nm* (**a**) *(oscilación)* swinging, to-and-fro movement (**b**) *(de gente)* coming and going, bustle; *Fig* **vaivenes** ups and downs
vajilla *nf* crockery, dishes; **una v.** a set of dishes, a dinner service
valdré *indic fut de* **valer**
vale¹ *interj* all right!, O.K.!
vale² *nm* (**a**) *(comprobante)* voucher (**b**) *(pagaré)* promissory note, IOU (**c**) *Méx, Ven Fam (amigo)* pal, *Br* mate, *US* buddy
valedero,-a *adj* valid
valenciano,-a *adj* Valencian
valentía *nf* courage, bravery
valentón,-ona *Pey* **1** *adj* bragging, boastful
   2 *nm,f* braggart
valer [26] **1** *vt* (**a**) to be worth; **no vale nada** it is worthless; **vale una fortuna** it is worth a fortune; **no vale la pena (ir)** it's not worth while (going) (**b**) *(costar)* to cost; **¿cuánto vale?** how much is it? (**c**) *(proporcionar)* to earn
   2 *vi* (**a**) *(servir)* to be useful, to be of use (**b**) *(ser válido)* to be valid, to count; **no vale hacer trampa** cheating isn't on (**c**) **más vale** it is better; **más vale que te vayas ya** you had better leave now
   3 valerse *upr* **v. de** to use, to make use of; **v. por sí mismo** to be able to manage on one's own
valeroso,-a *adj* brave, courageous
valgo *indic pres de* **valer**
valía *nf* value, worth
validez *nf* validity
válido,-a *adj* valid
valiente *adj* (**a**) *(valeroso)* brave, courageous (**b**) *Irón* **¡v. amigo eres tú!** a fine friend you are!

valija nf (a) (maleta) case, suitcase; **v. diplomática** diplomatic bag (b) (de correos) mailbag

valioso,-a adj valuable

valla nf (a) (cerca) fence; (muro) wall; **v. publicitaria** billboard, Br hoarding (b) Dep hurdle; **los 100 metros vallas** the 100 metres hurdle race

vallado nm fence

vallar vt to fence (in)

valle nm valley

vallisoletano,-a 1 adj of/from Valladolid
2 nm,f person from Valladolid

valor nm (a) (valía) value, worth; (precio) price; **objetos de v.** valuables; **sin v.** worthless; **v. alimenticio** food value (b) (valentía) courage (c) Fin **valores** securities, bonds

valoración nf valuation

valorar vt to value, to calculate the value of

valorización nf (a) (tasación) valuation (b) (revalorización) appreciation

valorizar [40] vt (a) (tasar) to value (b) (revalorizar) to raise the value of

vals nm waltz; **bailar el v.** to waltz

válvula nf valve; **v. de seguridad** safety valve

vampiro nm vampire

vanagloriarse [43] vpr to boast (**de** of)

vandalismo nm vandalism

vándalo,-a nm,f vandal

vanguardia nf (a) avant-garde, vanguard; Fig **ir a la v. de** to be at the forefront of (b) Mil vanguard, van

vanguardista 1 adj avant-garde
2 nmf avant-gardist

vanidad nf vanity

vanidoso,-a adj vain, conceited

vano,-a adj (a) (vanidoso) vain, conceited (b) (esfuerzo, esperanza) vain, futile; **en v.** in vain

vapor nm (a) (de agua hirviendo) steam; Culin **al v.** steamed (b) (gas) vapour; **v. de agua** water vapour

vaporizador nm vaporizer, spray

vaporizar [40] **1** vt to vaporize
2 vaporizarse vpr to vaporize, to evaporate

vaporoso,-a adj vaporous

vapulear vt (físicamente) to shake; (con palabras) to slate

vaqueriza nf cowshed

vaquero,-a 1 nm cowherd, cowboy
2 adj **pantalón v.** jeans, pair of jeans
3 nmpl **vaqueros** (prenda) jeans, pair of jeans

vara nf pole, rod

varar 1 vt to beach, to dock
2 vi to run aground

variable adj & nf variable

variación nf variation

variado,-a adj varied; **galletas variadas** assorted Br biscuits o US cookies

variante nf variant; Aut detour

variar [29] **1** vt to vary, to change

2 vi to vary, to change; Irón **para v.** as usual, just for a change

varice, várice nf = **variz**

varicela nf chickenpox

variedad nf (a) variety (b) Teatro **variedades** variety show

varilla nf (vara) rod, stick; (de abanico, paraguas) rib

variopinto,-a adj diverse, assorted; **un público v.** a varied audience

varios,-as adj several

varita nf **v. mágica** magic wand

variz nf varicose vein

varón nm (hombre) man; (chico) boy; **hijo v.** male child; **sexo v.** male sex

varonil adj manly, virile

Varsovia n Warsaw

vas indic pres de **ir**

vasallo,-a nm,f Hist vassal

vasco,-a adj Basque; **el País V.** the Basque Country

vascuence nm (idioma) Basque

vasectomía nf vasectomy

vaselina nf Vaseline®

vasija nf pot

vaso nm (a) (para beber) glass (b) Anat vessel

> Observa que la palabra inglesa **vase** es un falso amigo y no es la traducción de la palabra española **vaso**. En inglés, **vase** significa "jarrón".

vástago nm (a) Bot shoot (b) Fig (hijo) offspring (c) Téc rod, stem

vasto,-a adj vast

Vaticano nm **el V.** the Vatican

vaticinar vt to prophesy, to predict

vaticinio nm prophecy, prediction

vatio nm watt

vaya¹ interj **¡v. lío!** what a mess!

vaya² subj pres de **ir**

Vd., Vds. (abr **usted, ustedes**) you

ve 1 imperat de **ir**
2 indic pres de **ver**

vecinal adj local

vecindad nf, **vecindario** nm (a) (área) neighbourhood, vicinity (b) (vecinos) community, residents (c) Méx (inquilinato) tenement house

vecino,-a 1 nm,f (a) (persona) neighbour; **el v. de al lado** the next-door neighbour (b) (residente) resident
2 adj neighbouring, nearby

veda nf (de caza) closed season; **levantar la v.** to open the season

vedado,-a adj **coto v. de caza** private hunting ground

vedar vt to forbid, to prohibit

vega nf fertile plain o lowland

vegetación nf (a) Bot vegetation (b) Med **vegetaciones** adenoids

vegetal nm vegetable

vegetar vi Fig to vegetate

vegetariano,-a *adj & nm,f* vegetarian
vehemencia *nf* vehemence
vehemente *adj* vehement
vehículo *nm* vehicle
veinte *adj & nm inv* twenty
veintena *nf (veinte)* twenty; **una v. de** about twenty
vejación *nf* humiliation
vejar *vt* to humiliate
vejatorio,-a *adj* humiliating
vejez *nf* old age
vejiga *nf* bladder
vela¹ *nf* (a) candle (b) *Fam* **quedarse a dos velas** to be in the dark (c) **pasar la noche en v.** to have a sleepless night
vela² *nf Náut* sail
velada *nf* evening (party)
velado,-a *adj* (a) *(oculto)* veiled, hidden (b) *Fot* blurred
velador 1 *nm* (a) *(mesa)* table (b) *Andes, Méx (mesilla de noche)* bedside table (c) *Méx, RP (lámpara)* bedside lamp
 2 *nm Méx (sereno)* nightwatchman
velar¹ *vi* (a) **v.** to watch over (b) *(hacer guardia)* to keep watch
velar² *Fot* **1** *vt* to blur
 2 velarse *vpr* to become blurred
velatorio *nm* vigil, wake
veleidad *nf* fickleness
veleidoso,-a *adj* fickle
velero *nm* sailing boat *o* ship
veleta 1 *nf* weather vane, weathercock
 2 *nmf Fam* fickle *o* changeable person
veliz *nf Méx* suitcase, case
vello *nm* hair
vellón *nm* fleece
velloso,-a, velludo,-a *adj* downy
velo *nm* veil
velocidad *nf* (a) *(rapidez)* speed; *(de proyectil etc)* velocity; *Aut* **v. máxima** speed limit; *Informát* **v. de transmisión** bit rate; *Informát* **v. operativa** operating speed (b) *Aut (marcha)* gear
velocímetro *nm* speedometer
velocista *nmf* sprinter
velódromo *nm* cycle track, velodrome
veloz 1 *adj* swift, rapid
 2 *adv* quickly, fast
vena *nf* vein
venado *nm* deer, stag; *Culin* venison
vencedor,-a 1 *nm,f* winner
 2 *adj* winning
vencejo *nm Orn* swift
vencer [49] **1** *vt* (a) *(al enemigo)* to defeat; *(al contrincante)* to beat (b) *(dificultad)* to overcome, to surmount
 2 *vi* (a) *(pago, deuda)* to fall due, to be payable (b) *(plazo)* to expire
 3 vencerse *vpr (torcerse)* to warp
vencido,-a *adj* (a) *Mil (derrotado)* defeated; *Dep* beaten; *Fig* **darse por v.** to give up, to accept defeat (b) *(pago, deuda)* due, payable

(c) *(plazo)* expired (d) *Fam* **a la tercera va la vencida** third time lucky
vencimiento *nm* (a) *Com* maturity (b) *(de un plazo)* expiry
venda *nf* bandage
vendaje *nm* dressing
vendar *vt* to bandage; *Fig* **v. los ojos a algn** to blindfold sb
vendaval *nm* gale
vendedor,-a *nm,f* seller; *(hombre)* salesman; *(mujer)* saleswoman
vender 1 *vt* to sell; **v. a plazos/al contado** to sell on credit/for cash; **v. al por mayor/menor** to (sell) wholesale/retail
 2 venderse *vpr* (a) to sell; **este disco se vende bien** this record is selling well; **se vende** *(en letrero)* for sale (b) *(claudicar)* to sell out
vendimia *nf* grape harvest
vendré *indic fut de* venir
Venecia *n* Venice
veneno *nm* poison; *(de serpiente)* venom
venenoso,-a *adj* poisonous
venerable *adj* venerable
veneración *nf* veneration
venerar *vt* to venerate, to revere
venéreo,-a *adj* venereal
venero *nm* spring
venezolano,-a *adj & nm,f* Venezuelan
Venezuela *n* Venezuela
venga *subj pres de* venir
venganza *nf* vengeance, revenge
vengar [42] **1** *vt* to avenge
 2 vengarse *vpr* to avenge oneself; **v. de algn** to take revenge on sb
vengativo,-a *adj* vengeful, vindictive
vengo *indic pres de* venir
venia *nf* (a) *Fml (permiso)* permission (b) *(perdón)* pardon
venial *adj* venial
venida *nf* coming, arrival
venidero,-a *adj* future, coming
venir [27] **1** *vi* (a) to come; *Fig* **v. a menos** to come down in the world; *Fig* **v. al mundo** to be born; **el año que viene** next year; *Fig* **me viene a la memoria** I remember; *Fam* **¡venga ya!** *(vamos)* come on!; *(expresa incredulidad)* come off it! (b) **v. grande/pequeño** *(ropa)* to be too big/small; **v. mal/bien** to be inconvenient/convenient; **el metro me viene muy bien** I find the *Br* underground *o US* subway very handy (c) *(en pasivas)* **esto vino provocado por ...** this was brought about by ... (d) **esto viene ocurriendo desde hace mucho tiempo** this has been going on for a long time now
 2 venirse *vpr* **v. abajo** to collapse
venta *nf* (a) sale; **en v.** for sale; **a la v.** on sale; **v. a plazos/al contado** credit/cash sale; **v. al por mayor/al por menor** wholesale/retail (b) *(posada)* country inn
ventaja *nf* advantage; **llevar v. a** to have the

advantage over; **le sacó 2 m de v.** he beat him by 2 m

ventajoso,-a *adj* advantageous

ventana *nf* (**a**) window (**b**) *(de la nariz)* nostril

ventanal *nm* large window

ventanilla *nf* (**a**) window (**b**) *(de la nariz)* nostril

ventanuco *nm* small window

ventilación *nf* ventilation; **sin v.** unventilated

ventilador *nm* ventilator; *(de coche)* fan

ventilar 1 *vt* (**a**) *(habitación)* to ventilate, to air (**b**) *Fig (opinión)* to air

2 ventilarse *vpr Fam (terminar)* to finish off

ventisca *nf* blizzard; *(de nieve)* snowstorm

ventosa *nf* sucker; *Med* cupping glass

ventosear *vi* to break wind

ventoso,-a *adj* windy

ventrílocuo,-a *nm,f* ventriloquist

ventura *nf* (**a**) *(felicidad)* happiness (**b**) *(suerte)* luck; *(casualidad)* chance

venturoso,-a *adj* lucky, fortunate

Venus *nm* Venus

veo-veo *nm Fam* **el (juego del) v.** I-spy

ver¹ *nm* **de buen v.** good-looking

ver² [28] **1** *vt* (**a**) to see; *(televisión)* to watch; **a v. si escribes** I hope you'll write; **(ya) veremos** we'll see; *Fam* **había un jaleo que no veas** you should have seen the fuss that was made; **no veo por qué** I can't see why; **a mi modo de v.** as I see it (**b**) **no tener nada que v. con** to have nothing to do with

2 verse *vpr* (**a**) *(imagen etc)* to be seen (**b**) *(encontrarse con algn)* to meet, to see each other; **¡nos vemos!** see you later! (**c**) **no se pueden ni v.** *(soportarse)* they can't stand (the sight of) each other (**d**) *Am* **te ves divina** you look divine

vera *nf* edge, border; **a la v. de** beside, next to

veracidad *nf* veracity, truthfulness

veraneante *nmf Br* holidaymaker, *US* (summer) vacationer

veranear *vi* to spend one's summer *Br* holiday *o US* vacation

veraneo *nm* summer *Br* holiday *o US* vacation

veraniego,-a *adj* summer

veranillo *nm* Indian summer; **el v. de San Juan** *(en el hemisferio sur)* = warm spell around 24 June; **el v. de San Martín** *(en el hemisferio norte)* = warm spell around 11 November

verano *nm* summer

veras *nfpl* **de v.** really, seriously

veraz *adj* veracious, truthful

verbal *adj* verbal

verbena *nf* street party

verbo *nm* verb

verborrea *nf Fam* verbosity, verbal diarrhoea

verdad *nf* (**a**) truth; **es v.** it is true; **a decir v.** to tell the truth; **¡de v!** really!, truly!; **un amigo de v.** a real friend (**b**) *(en frase afirmativa)* **está muy bien, ¿(no es) v.?** it is very good, isn't it?; *(en frase negativa)* **no te gusta, ¿v.?** you don't like it, do you?

verdaderamente *adv* truly, really

verdadero,-a *adj* true, real

verde 1 *adj* (**a**) green (**b**) *(fruta)* unripe (**c**) *Fam (chiste, película)* blue; **viejo v.** dirty old man (**d**) *Fam Fig* **poner v. a algn** to call sb every name under the sun

2 *nm* (**a**) *(color)* green (**b**) *Pol* **los verdes** the Greens

verdear *vi* to turn green

verdor *nm* *(color)* greenness; *(de plantas)* verdure

verdoso,-a *adj* greenish

verdugo,-a 1 *nm* executioner

2 *nm,f Fig* tyrant

verdulería *nf* greengrocer's (shop)

verdulero,-a *nm,f* greengrocer

verdura *nf* vegetables, greens

vereda *nf* (**a**) *(camino)* path, lane (**b**) *CSur, Perú (acera) Br* pavement, *US* sidewalk

veredicto *nm* verdict

verga *nf* penis

vergonzoso,-a *adj* (**a**) *(penoso)* shameful, disgraceful (**b**) *(tímido)* shy, bashful

vergüenza *nf* (**a**) shame; **¿no te da v.?** aren't you ashamed?, have you no shame?; **¡es una v.!** it's a disgrace! (**b**) *(timidez)* shyness, bashfulness; **tener v.** to be shy; **me da v.** I'm too embarrassed

vericueto *nm* winding path; *Fig* **los vericuetos** the ins and outs

verídico,-a *adj* truthful, true

verificar [44] **1** *vt (comprobar)* to check

2 verificarse *vpr* to take place, to occur

verja *nf (reja)* grating; *(cerca)* railing, railings; *(puerta)* iron gate

vermut, vermú *nm* (*pl* **vermús**) (**a**) *(licor)* vermouth (**b**) *(aperitivo)* aperitif (**c**) *Andes, RP (en cine)* early evening showing; *(en teatro)* early evening performance

verosímil *adj* probable, likely; *(creíble)* credible

verruga *nf* wart

versado,-a *adj* well-versed (**en** in)

versar *vi* **v. sobre** to be about, to deal with

versátil *adj* (**a**) versatile (**b**) *(voluble)* changeable, inconstant

versatilidad *nf* (**a**) versatility (**b**) *(volubilidad)* changeableness, inconstancy

versículo *nm* verse

versión *nf* version; **película en v. original** film in the original language

verso *nm* (**a**) *(poesía)* verse (**b**) *(línea)* line

vértebra *nf* vertebra

vertebrado,-a *adj & nm* vertebrate

vertedero *nm (de basura) Br* rubbish tip *o* dump, *US* garbage dump

verter [3] **1** *vt* (**a**) to pour (out) (**b**) *(basura)* to dump

2 *vi (río)* to flow, to run (**a** into)
vertical *adj* vertical
vértice *nm* vertex
vertiente *nf* (**a**) *(de una montaña, un tejado)* slope; *Fig* aspect (**b**) *Am (manantial)* spring
vertiginoso,-a *adj* dizzy, giddy; *Fig (velocidad)* breakneck
vértigo *nm* vertigo; **me da v.** it makes me dizzy
vesícula *nf* vesicle; **v. biliar** gall bladder
vespa® *nf* (motor) scooter
vespertino,-a 1 *adj* evening
2 *nm Prensa* evening newspaper
vespino® *nm* moped
vestíbulo *nm (de casa)* hall; *(de edificio público)* foyer
vestido,-a 1 *nm (ropa)* clothes; *(de mujer)* dress
2 *adj* dressed; **policía v. de paisano** plainclothes policeman
vestidura *nf* clothing, clothes
vestigio *nm* vestige, trace
vestimenta *nf* clothes, garments
vestir [6] **1** *vt* (**a**) *(a algn)* to dress (**b**) *(llevar puesto)* to wear
2 *vi* (**a**) to dress; **ropa de (mucho) v.** formal dress (**b**) *Fam* **la seda viste mucho** silk always looks very elegant
3 vestirse *vpr* (**a**) to get dressed, to dress (**b**) **v. de** to wear, to dress in; *(disfrazarse)* to disguise oneself as, to dress up as
vestuario *nm* (**a**) *(conjunto de vestidos)* clothes, wardrobe; *Teatro* wardrobe, costumes (**b**) *(camerino)* dressing room (**c**) *Dep* changing room
veta *nf Min* vein, seam; *(de carne)* streak
vetar *vt* to veto
veterano,-a *adj & nm,f* veteran
veterinario,-a 1 *nm,f* vet, *Br* veterinary surgeon, *US* veterinarian
2 *nf* **veterinaria** veterinary medicine *o* science
veto *nm* veto; **derecho a v.** power *o* right of veto
vetusto,-a *adj Fml* ancient
vez *nf* (**a**) time; **una v.** once; **dos veces** twice; **cinco veces** five times; **a** *o* **algunas veces** sometimes; **cada v.** each *o* every time; **cada v. más** more and more; **de v. en cuando** now and again, every now and then; **¿le has visto alguna v.?** have you ever seen him?; **otra v.** again; **a la v.** at the same time; **tal v.** perhaps, maybe; **de una v.** in one go; **de una v. para siempre** once and for all; **en v. de** instead of; **érase** *o* **había una v.** *(en cuentos etc)* once upon a time (**b**) *(turno)* turn (**c**) **hacer las veces de** to do duty as
v.g(r). *(abr verbigracia)* eg
vía 1 *nf* (**a**) *Ferroc* track, line (**b**) *(camino)* road; **v. pública** public thoroughfare; **V. Láctea** Milky Way (**c**) *Anat* passage, tract; *Farm* **(por) v. oral** to be taken orally (**d**) *Fig* **por v.**

oficial through official channels; **por v. aérea/marítima** by air/sea (**e**) **en vías de** in the process of; **países en vías de desarrollo** developing countries
2 *prep (a través de)* via, through; **v. París** via Paris; **transmisión v. satélite** satellite transmission
viable *adj* viable
viaducto *nm* viaduct
viajante *nmf* commercial traveller, travelling salesman, *f* saleswoman
viajar *vi* to travel
viaje *nm (recorrido)* journey, trip; *(largo, en barco)* voyage; **¡buen v.!** bon voyage!, have a good trip!; **estar de v.** to be away (on a trip); **irse** *o* **marcharse de v.** to go on a journey *o* trip; **v. de negocios** business trip; **v. de novios** honeymoon
viajero,-a 1 *nm,f* (**a**) traveller (**b**) *(en transporte público)* passenger
2 *adj* **cheque v.** traveller's cheque
vianda *nf RP* (**a**) *(tentempié)* packed lunch (**b**) *(fiambrera)* lunchbox
viandante *nmf* passer-by
viario,-a *adj* road, highway; **red viaria** road network
víbora *nf* viper
vibración *nf* vibration
vibrador *nm* vibrator
vibrar *vt & vi* to vibrate
vicario,-a *nm,f* vicar
vicepresidente,-a *nm,f* (**a**) *Pol* vice-president (**b**) *(de compañía, comité)* vice-chairperson; *(hombre)* vice-chairman; *(mujer)* vice-chairwoman
vicesecretario,-a *nm,f* assistant secretary
viceversa *adv* vice versa
viciado,-a *adj* (**a**) *(corrompido)* corrupt (**b**) *(aire)* foul
viciar [43] **1** *vt* (**a**) *(corromper)* to corrupt (**b**) *(estropear)* to waste
2 viciarse *vpr* (**a**) *(deformarse)* to go out of shape (**b**) *(corromperse)* to become corrupted
vicio *nm* (**a**) vice (**b**) *(mala costumbre)* bad habit (**c**) *Fam (destreza)* skill
vicioso,-a 1 *adj* (**a**) *(persona)* depraved, perverted (**b**) **círculo v.** vicious circle
2 *nm,f* depraved person; **v. del trabajo** workaholic
vicisitud *nf (usu pl)* vicissitude
víctima *nf* victim
victimar *vt Am* to kill, to murder
victimario,-a *nm,f Am* killer, murderer
victoria *nf* victory
victorioso,-a *adj* victorious
vicuña *nf* vicuña
vid *nf* vine, grapevine
vida *nf* life; *(período)* lifetime; **de toda la v.** lifelong; **en mi v.** never in my life; **de por v.** for life; **ganarse la v.** to earn one's living; **¿qué es de tu v.?** how's life?; **estar con/sin v.** to be alive/dead

vidente *nmf* clairvoyant
vídeo *nm* video; **grabar en v.** to videotape
videocámara *nf* video camera
videoclub *nm* video club
videoconferencia *nf* videoconferencing; *(sesión)* videoconference
videojuego *nm* video game
vidriera *nf* (a) stained-glass window (b) *Am (escaparate)* shop window
vidrio *nm* glass
viejo,-a 1 *adj* old; **hacerse v.** to grow old; **un v. amigo** an old friend
　　2 *nm,f* (a) *(hombre, padre)* old man; *(mujer, madre)* old woman; **los viejos** old people; *Fam* **mis viejos** my parents (b) *RP Fam* **¡mi v.!** *(apelativo cariñoso)* young man *o* fellow!; **¡mi vieja!** *(apelativo cariñoso)* my dear! (c) *Chile* **el V. de Pascua** *o* **Pascuero** Father Christmas
　　3 *nf* **vieja** *Col, Méx, Ven Fam (mujer, chica)* chick, *Br* bird, *US* broad
Viena *n* Vienna
vienés,-esa *adj & nm,f* Viennese
viento *nm* wind; **hace** *o* **sopla mucho v.** it is very windy; *Fam Fig* **¡vete a tomar v.!** get lost!
vientre *nm* (a) belly; **hacer de v.** to have a bowel movement (b) *(útero)* womb
viernes *nm inv* Friday; **V. Santo** Good Friday
Vietnam *n* Vietnam
vietnamita *adj & nmf* Vietnamese
viga *nf* (de madera) beam; *(de hierro)* girder
vigencia *nf* validity; **entrar en v.** to come into force *o* effect
vigente *adj* in force
vigésimo,-a *adj & nm,f* twentieth
vigía 1 *nf* watchtower, lookout post
　　2 lookout; *(hombre)* watchman; *(mujer)* watchwoman
vigilancia *nf* vigilance, watchfulness; *Med* **unidad de v. intensiva** intensive care unit
vigilante *nm* watchman; *(de banco)* guard
vigilar 1 *vt* to watch; *(un lugar)* to guard; **vigila que no entren** make sure they don't get in
　　2 *vi (gen)* to keep watch
vigilia *nf* (a) vigil (b) *(víspera)* eve (c) *Rel (abstinencia)* abstinence
vigor *nm* (a) vigour; *(fuerza)* strength (b) **en v.** in force
vigoroso,-a *adj* vigorous
VIH *nm* (*abr* **Virus de la Inmunodeficiencia Humana**) HIV
vikingo,-a *adj & nm* Viking
vil *adj Fml* vile, base
vileza *nf* (a) vileness, baseness (b) *(acto)* vile act, despicable deed
vilipendiar [43] *vt Fml* to vilify, to revile
villa *nf* (a) *(población)* town (b) *(casa)* villa, country house (c) *Arg* **v. miseria** shanty town
villancico *nm* (Christmas) carol
vilo: en vilo *loc adv (persona)* on tenterhooks; *(cosa)* up in the air
vinagre *nm* vinegar

vinagrera *nf* **vinagreras** oil and vinegar cruets, cruet (stand)
vinagreta *nf* vinaigrette sauce
vinajeras *nfpl* cruets
vincha *nf Am* headband
vinculante *adj* binding
vincular *vt* to link, to bind; *(relacionar)* to relate, to connect
vínculo *nm* link
vine *pt indef de* **venir**
vinícola *adj* wine-producing
vinicultor,-a *nm,f* wine producer
vinicultura *nf* wine production *o* growing
vinilo *nm* vinyl
vino *nm* wine; **tomar un v.** to have a glass of wine; **v. blanco/tinto/dulce/seco** white/red/ sweet/dry wine; **v. rosado** rosé
viña *nf* vineyard
viñedo *nm* vineyard
viñeta *nf* illustration
viola *nf* viola
violación *nf* (a) *(de una persona)* rape (b) *(de ley, derecho)* violation, infringement
violador *nm* rapist
violar *vt* (a) *(persona)* to rape (b) *(ley, derecho)* to violate, to infringe
violencia *nf* (a) violence; **la no v.** non-violence (b) *(incomodidad)* embarrassment
violentar *vt* (a) *(forzar)* to force, to break open; *(sitio)* to break into, to enter by force (b) *(enojar)* to infuriate
violento,-a *adj* (a) violent (b) *(situación)* embarrassing, awkward (c) **sentirse v.** *(incómodo)* to feel embarrassed *o* awkward
violeta 1 *adj & nm (color)* violet
　　2 *nf (flor)* violet
violín *nm* violin; *Fam* fiddle
violinista *nmf* violinist
violón *nm* double bass
violoncelista, violonchelista *nmf* cellist
violoncelo, violonchelo *nm* violoncello, cello
viraje *nm* (a) turn (b) *Fig* about-face, U-turn
virar *vi* (a) *(girar)* to turn round (b) *Fig* to change
virgen 1 *adj* (a) *(persona, selva)* virgin (b) *(aceite, lana)* pure; *(cinta)* blank
　　2 *nmf* virgin; *Fam* **ser un viva la v.** to be a devil-may-care person
virginidad *nf* virginity
Virgo *nm* Virgo
virgo *nm* hymen
virguería *nf Fam* gem, marvel; **hacer virguerías** to work wonders, to be a dab hand
virguero,-a *adj Fam* smart, great; **esta camisa es muy virguera** that shirt is the business
vírico,-a *adj* viral
viril *adj* virile, manly; **miembro v.** penis
virilidad *nf* virility
virtual *adj* virtual
virtud *nf* (a) virtue; *Fig* **en v. de** by virtue of (b) *(propiedad)* property, quality

virtuoso,-a 1 *adj* virtuous

2 *nm,f* (**a**) virtuous person (**b**) *(músico)* virtuoso

viruela *nf* smallpox; **viruelas** pockmarks

virulé: a la virulé *loc adj Fam* (**a**) *(torcido)* crooked, twisted (**b**) **un ojo a la v.** a black eye

virulencia *nf* virulence

virulento,-a *adj* virulent

virus *nm inv* virus

visado *nm, Am* **visa** *nf* visa

víscera *nf* (**a**) internal organ (**b**) **vísceras** viscera, entrails

visceral *adj* (**a**) *Anat* visceral (**b**) *Fig* profound, deep-rooted

viscoso,-a *adj* viscous

visera *nf (de gorra)* peak; *(de casco)* visor

visibilidad *nf* visibility; **curva con mala v.** blind corner

visible *adj* visible; *(evidente)* evident

visillo *nm* small lace *o* net curtain

visión *nf* (**a**) vision (**b**) *(vista)* sight; *Fig* **v. de conjunto** overall view; **con v. de futuro** forward-looking (**c**) *(aparición)* vision

visionario,-a *nm,f* visionary; *(iluso)* person who imagines things

visita *nf* (**a**) *(acción)* visit; **hacer una v.** to pay a visit; **estar de v.** to be visiting (**b**) *(invitado)* visitor, guest

visitador,-a *nm,f Farm* pharmaceutical salesman, *f* saleswoman

visitante 1 *nmf* visitor

2 *adj (equipo)* away

visitar *vt* to visit

vislumbrar *vt* to glimpse

viso *nm* (**a**) *(reflejo)* sheen (**b**) *Fig* **tener visos de** to seem, to appear

visón *nm* mink

visor *nm Fot* viewfinder

> *Observa que la palabra inglesa* **visor** *es un falso amigo y no es la traducción de la palabra española* **visor**. *En inglés,* **visor** *significa "visera".*

víspera *nf (día anterior)* day before; *(de festivo)* eve; **en vísperas de** in the period leading up to

vista *nf* (**a**) sight; **a la v.** visible; **a primera** *o* **simple v.** at first sight, on the face of it; **con vistas a** with a view to; **en v. de** in view of, considering; **corto de v.** short-sighted; **conocer a algn de v.** to know sb by sight; **perder de v. a** to lose sight of; **quítalo de mi v.** take it away; *Fig* **tener mucha v. para** to have a good eye for; *Fig* **volver la v. atrás** to look back; *Fam* **¡hasta la v.!** goodbye!, see you!; *Fam* **hacer la v. gorda** to turn a blind eye (**b**) *(panorama)* view; **con vista(s) al mar** overlooking the sea (**c**) *Jur* trial, hearing

vistazo *nm* glance; **echar un v. a algo** *(ojear)* to have a (quick) look at sth; *(tener cuidado de)* to keep an eye on sth

visto,-a 1 *adj* (**a**) **está v. que ...** it is obvious that ...; **por lo v.** evidently, apparently; **v. que** in view of the fact that, seeing *o* given that (**b**) **estar bien v.** to be well looked upon, to be considered acceptable; **estar mal v.** to be frowned upon (**c**) **estar muy v.** to be old hat

2 *nm* **v. bueno** approval, O.K.

vistoso,-a *adj* eye-catching

visual *adj* visual; **campo v.** field of vision

visualizar [40] *vt* to visualize; *(película)* to view

vital *adj* (**a**) vital (**b**) *(persona)* full of vitality

vitalicio,-a *adj* life, for life; **pensión/cargo v.** life pension/permanent post

vitalidad *nf* vitality

vitamina *nf* vitamin

vitamínico,-a *adj* vitamin; **complejo v.** multivitamins

viticultor,-a *nm,f* wine grower

viticultura *nf* wine growing

vitorear *vt* to cheer

vítreo,-a *adj* vitreous

vitrina *nf (aparador)* glass *o* display cabinet; *(de exposición)* glass case, showcase; *Am (escaparate)* shop window

vituallas *nfpl* provisions

vituperar *vt* to condemn

vituperio *nm* condemnation

viudo,-a *nm,f (hombre)* widower; *(mujer)* widow

viva *interj* **¡v.!** hurrah!

vivacidad *nf* vivacity

vivaracho,-a *adj Fam* lively, sprightly

vivaz *adj* (**a**) lively, vivacious (**b**) *(perspicaz)* sharp, quick-witted

vivencias *nfpl* personal experience

víveres *nmpl* provisions, supplies

vivero *nm (de plantas)* nursery; *(de peces)* fish farm *o* hatchery; *Fig* breeding ground, hotbed

viveza *nf* (**a**) liveliness, vivacity; *(en los ojos)* sparkle (**b**) *(agudeza)* sharpness, quickwittedness

vividor,-a *nm,f Pey* sponger, scrounger

vivienda *nf* (**a**) housing (**b**) *(casa)* house; *(piso)* flat

vivir 1 *vi* to live; **vive de sus ahorros** she lives off her savings; **viven de la pesca** they make their living by fishing

2 *vt* to live through

3 *nm* life

vivito,-a *adj Fam* **v. y coleando** alive and kicking

vivo,-a 1 *adj* (**a**) alive; **de viva voz** verbally, by word of mouth; **en v.** *(programa)* live; *Fam* **es el v. retrato** *o* **la viva imagen de** she is the spitting image of (**b**) **al rojo v.** red-hot (**c**) *(vivaz)* lively, vivacious (**d**) *(listo)* sharp, clever (**e**) *(color)* vivid, bright (**f**) *(descripción)* lively, graphic

2 *nm,f* **los vivos** the living

Vizcaya *n* **el golfo de V.** the Bay of Biscay

..º B.º (*abr* **visto bueno**) (*en documento*) pproved

ocablo *nm* word, term

ocabulario *nm* vocabulary

ocación *nf* vocation, calling; **con v. europea** with leanings towards Europe

ocacional *adj* vocational

ocal 1 *nf Ling* vowel

2 *nmf* member

ocalista *nmf Mús* vocalist, singer

ocalizar [40] *vt & vi* to vocalize

oceador,-a *nm,f Am* vendor

ocerío *nm* shouting

ocero,-a *nm,f Am* spokesperson; *(hombre)* pokesman; *(mujer)* spokeswoman

ociferante *adj* vociferous

ociferar *vt & vi* to vociferate

odka *nm* vodka

ol. (*abr* **volumen**) vol

olado,-a *adj Fam* **estar v.** to have a screw oose

olador,-a *adj* flying

olandas: en volandas *loc adv (por el aire)* in he air, flying through the air

olante 1 *nm* (**a**) *Aut* steering wheel; **ir al v.** ›e driving; **un as del v.** a motor-racing cham-›ion (**b**) *Cost* frill, ruffle (**c**) *Med* note

2 *adj* flying; **platillo v.** flying saucer

olantín *nm Am (cometa)* small kite

olar [2] **1** *vi* (**a**) to fly; *Fig* **lo hizo volando** he ›id it in a flash (**b**) *Fam (desaparecer)* to ›isappear, to vanish

2 *vt (edificios)* to blow up; *(caja fuerte)* to ›low open; *Min* to blast

3 *volarse* *vpr (papel etc)* to be blown away

olátil *adj* volatile

olatinero,-a *nm,f* acrobat

olcán *nm* volcano

olcánico,-a *adj* volcanic

olcar [2] **1** *vt* (**a**) *(cubo etc)* to knock over; *(barco, bote)* to capsize (**b**) *(vaciar)* to empty ›ut (**c**) *(tiempo)* to invest

2 *vi (coche)* to turn over; *(barco)* to capsize

3 *volcarse* *vpr* (**a**) *(vaso, jarra)* to fall over, to ›p over; *(coche)* to turn over; *(barco)* to ›apsize (**b**) *Fig* **v. con** to do one's utmost for

oleibol *nm* volleyball

oleo *nm Fig* **a(l) v.** at random, haphazardly

oltaje *nm* voltage

oltear 1 *vt* (**a**) *(dar la vuelta a)* to turn upside ›own (**b**) *CSur (derribar)* to knock over (**c**) ›*ndes, CAm, Carib, Méx (cabeza)* to turn; **v. la** ›**spalda a algn** to turn one's back on sb

2 *vi* (**a**) to turn o roll over (**b**) *Méx (doblar la* ›*squina)* to go round

3 *voltearse* *vpr* (**a**) *Andes, CAm, Carib, Méx* ›*volverse)* to turn around (**b**) *Méx (vehículo)* ›o turn over

oltereta *nf* somersault

oltio *nm* volt

›luble *adj* fickle, changeable

---

volumen *nm* volume

voluminoso,-a *adj* voluminous; *(enorme)* massive, bulky

voluntad *nf* will; **fuerza de v.** willpower; **tiene mucha v.** he is very strong-willed; **a v.** at will

voluntario,-a 1 *adj* voluntary

2 *nm,f* volunteer; **ofrecerse v.** to volunteer

voluntarioso,-a *adj* willing

voluptuoso,-a *adj* voluptuous

volver [4] *(pp vuelto)* **1** *vi* (**a**) to return; *(venir)* to come back; *(ir)* to go back; **v. en sí** to come round, to recover consciousness (**b**) **v. a hacer algo** to do sth again

2 *vt* (**a**) *(convertir)* to turn, to make; **me vas a v. loco** you are driving me mad (**b**) *(dar vuelta a)* to turn; *(boca abajo)* to turn upside down; *(de fuera adentro)* to turn inside out; *(de atrás adelante)* to turn back to front; *(dar la vuelta a)* to turn over; **volverle la espalda a algn** to turn one's back on sb; *Fig* **v. la vista atrás** to look back; **al v. la esquina** on turning the corner

3 *volverse* *vpr* (**a**) to turn (**b**) *(regresar)* *(venir)* to come back; *(ir)* to go back (**c**) *(convertirse)* to become; **v. loco,-a** to go mad

vomitar 1 *vi* to vomit, to be sick; **tengo ganas de v.** I feel sick, I want to be sick

2 *vt* to vomit, to bring up

vómito *nm (lo vomitado)* vomit; *(acción)* vomiting

vomitona *nf Fam* vomit

voracidad *nf* voracity, voraciousness

vorágine *nf* whirlpool; *Fig* maelstrom

voraz *adj* voracious; *Fig* raging, fierce

vórtice *nm* vortex

vos *pron pers Am (tú)* you

The **vos** form is used alongside **tú** in many Latin American countries, and in some countries (Argentina, Paraguay and Uruguay) is the preferred form.

vosotros,-as *pron pers pl* (**a**) *(sujeto)* you (**b**) *(con prep)* you; **entre v.** among yourselves; **sin vosotras** without you

Usually omitted in Spanish except for emphasis or contrast. In Latin America, **vosotros** is not used. Instead, **ustedes** is used as the second person plural in all contexts, without necessarily suggesting formality.

votación *nf* (**a**) *(voto)* vote, ballot (**b**) *(acción)* voting

votante *nmf* voter

votar *vi* to vote; **v. a algn** to vote (for) sb

voto *nm* (**a**) vote; **tener v.** to have the right to vote; **v. secreto** secret ballot (**b**) *Rel* vow

vox *nf* **esto es v. populi** this is common knowledge

voy *indic pres de* **ir**

voz *nf* (**a**) voice; **en v. alta** aloud; **en v. baja** in a low voice; **a media v.** in a low voice, softly; **de viva v.** verbally (**b**) *(grito)* shout; **a voces** shouting; **dar voces** to shout; *Fig* **estar pidiendo algo a voces** to be crying out for sth; *Fig* **secreto a voces** open secret; **a v. en grito** at the top of one's voice (**c**) **no tener ni v. ni voto** to have no say in the matter; *Fig* **llevar la v. cantante** to rule the roost (**d**) *Gram* **v. pasiva** passive voice

vudú *nm* voodoo

vuelco *nm* upset, tumble; **dar un v.** *(coche)* to overturn; *Fig* **me dio un v. el corazón** my heart missed a beat

vuelo *nm* (**a**) flight; **v. chárter/regular** charter/scheduled flight; **v. sin motor** gliding; *Fig* **cazarlas** *o* **cogerlas al v.** to be quick on the uptake (**b**) *Cost* **una falda de v.** a full skirt

vuelta *nf* (**a**) *(regreso)* return; *(viaje)* return journey; **a v. de correo** by return of post; **estar de v.** to be back; *Dep* **partido de v.** return match (**b**) *(giro)* turn; *(en carreras)* lap; *Dep (ciclista)* tour; **dar media v.** to turn round; *Fig* **la cabeza me da vueltas** my head is spinning;

Fig **no le des más vueltas** stop worryin about it; **v. de campana** somersault (**c**) *(a nero)* change (**d**) **dar una v.** *(a pie)* to go for walk *o* stroll; *(en coche)* to go for a drive *o* spin (in the car) (**e**) *Fig* **no tiene v. de ho** there's no doubt about it

vuelto,-a 1 *adj* **jersey de cuello v.** rollnec sweater

2 *nm Am* change

vuestro,-a 1 *adj pos (antes del sustantivo* your; *(después del sustantivo)* of yours; **libro** your book; **un amigo v.** a friend of you

2 *pron pos* yours; **éstos son los vuestro** these are yours; **lo v.** what is yours, wh belongs to you

vulgar *adj* (**a**) vulgar (**b**) **el término v.** th everyday term

vulgaridad *nf* vulgarity

vulgarizar [40] *vt (popularizar)* to popula ize

vulgarmente *adv* **v. llamado** common known as

vulgo *nm* **el v.** the common people; *Pey* th masses

vulnerable *adj* vulnerable

vulnerar *vt (ley, acuerdo)* to violate

vulva *nf* vulva

W, w [uße'ðoßle] *nf (la letra)* W, w

W *(abr* vatio**(s)***)* W

walkie-talkie *nm* walkie-talkie

Walkman® *nm* Walkman®

wáter *nm (pl* wáteres*) Fam* toilet

waterpolo *nm* water polo

Web, web [web] *Informát* **1** *nf (World Wide Web)* **la W.** the Web

2 *nm o nf (página web)* web site

whisky *nm (escocés)* whisky; *(irlandés, US)* whiskey

windsurf, windsurfing *nm* windsurfing

windsurfista *nmf* windsurfer

xenofobia *nf* xenophobia

xenófobo,-a **1** *adj* xenophobic

2 *nm,f* xenophobe

Y, y [iɣri'eɣa] *nf (la letra)* Y, y

conj (**a**) and; **una chica alta y morena** a tall, dark-haired girl; **son las tres y cuarto** it's a quarter past three (**b**) **¿y qué?** so what?; **¿y si no llega a tiempo?** what if he doesn't arrive in time?; **¿y tú?** what about you?; **¿y eso?** how come?; **y eso que** although, even though; **¡y tanto!** you bet!, and how!; *ver* **e**

ya **1** *adv* (**a**) already; **ya lo sabía** I already knew; **ya en la Edad Media** as far back as the Middle Ages (**b**) *(ahora mismo)* now; **es preciso actuar ya** it is vital that we act now; **hazlo ya!** do it at once!; **ya mismo** right away (**c**) *(en el futuro)* **ya hablaremos luego** we'll talk about it later; **ya nos veremos** see you!; **ya verás** you'll see (**d**) **ya no** no longer; **ya no viene por aquí** he doesn't come round here any more (**e**) *(refuerza el verbo)* **ya era hora** about time too; **ya lo creo** of course, I should think so; **¡ya voy!** coming!; **¡ya está!** that's it!

2 *conj* **ya que** since

yacaré *nm* cayman

yacer [61] *vi* to lie, to be lying

yacimiento *nm* bed, deposit; **yacimientos petrolíferos** oilfields

yaguar *nm* jaguar

yanqui *Pey* **1** *adj* Yankee

2 *nmf* Yankee, Yank

yarará *nf Am* = large poisonous snake

yaraví *nm Am* = Quechuan song

yarda *nf* yard

yate *nm* yacht

yaya *nf Am Bot* lance-wood; *Fam (abuela)* granny

yedra *nf* = hiedra

yegua *nf* mare

yema *nf* (**a**) *(de huevo)* yolk (**b**) *Bot* bud (**c**) **y. del dedo** fingertip (**d**) *Culin* = sweet made from sugar and egg yolk

Yemen *n* Yemen

yen *nm (moneda)* yen

yendo *ger de* **ir**

yerba *nf* (**a**) = hierba (**b**) *RP* maté; **y. mate** yerba maté

yerbatero,-a *Am* **1** *nm,f (curandero)* = witch doctor who uses herbs

2 *adj* maté

yermo,-a *adj* (**a**) *(baldío)* barren, uncultivated (**b**) *(despoblado)* deserted, uninhabited

yerno *nm* son-in-law

yerro *indic pres de* **errar**

yeso *nm* (**a**) *Geol* gypsum (**b**) *Constr* plaster

Yibuti *n* Djibouti

yiu-yitsu *nm* ju-jitsu

yo *pron pers* I; **entre tú y yo** between you and me; **¿quién es? – soy yo** who is it? – it's me; **yo no** not me; **yo que tú** if I were you; **yo mismo** I myself

> Usually omitted as a personal pronoun in Spanish except for emphasis or contrast.

yodo *nm* iodine

yoga *nm* yoga

yogur *nm* yogurt, yoghurt

yogurtera *nf* yoghurt maker

yonqui *nmf Fam* junkie, drug addict

yoyo, yoyó *nm* yo-yo

yuca *nf* yucca

Yucatán *n* Yucatan

yudo *nm* judo

yudoka *nmf* judoka

yugo *nm* yoke

Yugoslavia *n* Yugoslavia

yugoslavo,-a, yugoeslavo,-a *adj & nm,f* Yugoslav, Yugoslavian

yugular *nf* jugular

yunque *nm* anvil

yunta *nf* yoke *o* team of oxen

yuxtaponer [19] *(pp* yuxtapuesto*) vt* to juxtapose

yuxtaposición *nf* juxtaposition

yuyo *nm* (**a**) *CSur (mala hierba)* weed; *(hierba medicinal)* medicinal herb (**b**) *Andes (hierba silvestre)* wild herb

Z

Z, z ['θeta] *nf (la letra)* Z, z
zacate *nm CAm, Méx* fodder
zafarse *upr (librarse)* to get away (**de** from), to escape (**de** from)
zafio,-a *adj* uncouth
zafiro *nm* sapphire
zaga *nf* **a la z.** behind, at the rear
zaguán *nm* hall, hallway
zaherir *vt* to hurt
zahúrda *nf* pigsty
zaino,-a *adj (caballo)* chestnut; *(toro)* black
Zaire *n* Zaire
zalamería *nf* flattery
zalamero,-a 1 *nm,f* flatterer, fawner
   2 *adj* flattering, fawning
zamarra *nf (prenda)* sheepskin jacket
Zambia *n* Zambia
zambo,-a *adj* (a) *(patizambo)* knock-kneed (**b**) *Am (persona)* half Indian and half Negro
   2 *nm,f Am (persona)* = person who is half Indian and half Negro
zambomba *nf* = kind of primitive drum
zambullida *nf* plunge
zambullirse *upr* to plunge
zamparse *upr Fam* to gobble down
zanahoria *nf* carrot
zancada *nf* stride
zancadilla *nf* **ponerle la z. a algn** to trip sb up
zanco *nm* stilt
zancudo,-a 1 *adj* (a) long-legged (**b**) *Orn* wading; **ave zancuda** wading bird, wader
   2 *nm Am* mosquito
zángano,-a 1 *nm (insecto)* drone
   2 *nm,f Fam (persona)* idler, lazybones *inv*
zanja *nf* ditch, trench
zanjar *vt (asunto)* to settle
zapallito *nm CSur Br* courgette, *US* zucchini
zapallo *nm Andes, RP* sweet pumpkin
zapata *nf* (a) *(cuña)* wedge (**b**) *Téc* shoe
zapatear *vi* to tap one's feet
zapatería *nf* shoe shop
zapatero,-a *nm,f (vendedor)* shoe dealer; *(fabricante)* shoemaker, cobbler
zapatilla *nf* slipper; **zapatillas de deporte** trainers
zapato *nm* shoe; **zapatos de tacón** high-heeled shoes
zar *nm* czar, tsar
Zaragoza *n* Saragossa
zaragozano,-a 1 *adj* of/from Saragossa
   2 *nm,f* person from Saragossa
zarandear *vt* to shake

zarandeo *nm* shaking
zarcillo *nm* (a) *(pendiente)* earring (**b**) *B* tendril
zarina *nf* czarina, tsarina
zarpa *nf* claw
zarpar *vi* to weigh anchor, to set sail
zarpazo *nm* clawing; **dar** o **pegar un z. a** claw
zarza *nf* bramble, blackberry bush
zarzal *nm* bramble patch
zarzamora *nf (zarza)* blackberry bush; *(fruto)* blackberry
zarzuela *nf* (a) = Spanish operetta (**b**) **la Z.** royal residence in Madrid (**c**) *Culin* = fish ste
zenit *nm* zenith
zigzag *nm (pl zigzags o zigzagues)* zigzag
zigzaguear *vi* to zigzag
Zimbabwe *n* Zimbabwe
zinc *nm* zinc
zíper *nm CAm, Méx Br* zip, *US* zipper
zócalo *nm* (a) *(de pared)* skirting board (*(pedestal)* plinth
zodiaco, zodíaco *nm* zodiac; **signo del** sign of the zodiac
zona *nf* zone; *(región)* region; **z. euro** eu zone; **z. verde** park
zoo *nm* zoo
zoología *nf* zoology
zoológico,-a 1 *adj* zoological; **parque z.** zo
   2 *nm* zoo
zoom *nm Cin & Fot* zoom
zopenco,-a *nm,f Fam* dope, halfwit
zopilote *nm Am* buzzard
zoquete 1 *nmf Fam* blockhead
   2 *nm CSur (calcetín)* ankle sock
zorra *nf* (a) vixen (**b**) *Fam* slut
zorro,-a 1 *nm* fox
   2 *adj* (a) *(astuto)* cunning, sly (**b**) *muy Fa* **no tengo ni zorra (idea)** I haven't got a bloody o *US* goddamn clue
zorzal *nm Orn* thrush
zozobrar *vi* to be in danger of going under
zueco *nm* clog
zumbado,-a *adj Fam* crazy, mad
zumbar 1 *vi* to buzz, to hum; **me zumban l** **oídos** my ears are buzzing; *Fam* **salir zu** **bando** to zoom off
   2 *vt Fam* to thrash
zumbido *nm* buzzing, humming
zumo *nm* juice
zurcir [52] *vt Cost* to darn; *Fam* **¡que** **zurzan!** go to hell!

zurda *nf (mano)* left hand
zurdo,-a 1 *nm,f (persona)* left-handed person
2 *adj* left-handed

zurrar *vt (pegar)* to beat, to flog
zutano,-a *nm,f Fam* so-and-so; *(hombre)* what's-his-name; *(mujer)* what's-her-name

Spanish Verbs

◆

Regular Spelling Changes

The rules of spelling in Spanish cause a number of verbs to have regular spelling changes. These are listed below.

Spanish verbs fall into three groups depending on whether their infinitive ends in **-ar, -er** or **-ir**. The stem of the verb is the part which is left when the **-ar, -er** or **-ir** is removed from the infinitive. For example, the stem of **tomar** is **tom**, the stem of **beber** is **beb**, and the stem of **salir** is **sal**.

In the examples given below, the following indicators are used:

(**1**) = first person singular present indicative
(**2**) = present subjunctive, all persons
(**3**) = first person singular preterite

Verbs ending in -ar

Verbs with a stem ending in **c**, for example **buscar**

The **c** changes to **qu** in:

(**2**) busque, busques, busque, busquemos, busquéis, busquen
(**3**) busqué

Verbs with a stem ending in **g**, for example **cargar**

The **g** changes to **gu** in:

(**2**) cargue, cargues, cargue, carguemos, carguéis, carguen
(**3**) cargué

Verbs with a stem ending in **gu**, for example **averiguar**

The **gu** changes to **gü** in:

(**2**) averigüe, averigües, averigüe, averigüemos, averigüéis, averigüen
(**3**) averigüé

Verbs with a stem ending in **z**, for example **realizar**

The **z** changes to **c** in:

(**2**) realice, realices, realice, realicemos, realicéis, realicen
(**3**) realicé

Verbs ending in -er *or* -ir

Verbs with a stem ending in **c**, for example **esparcir**

The **c** changes to **z** in:

(**1**) esparzo
(**2**) esparza, esparzas, esparza, esparzamos, esparzáis, esparzan

Verbs with a stem ending in **g**, for example **coger**

The **g** changes to **j** in:

(**1**) cojo
(**2**) coja, cojas, coja, cojamos, cojáis, cojan

Verbs with a stem ending in **qu**, for example **delinquir**

The **qu** changes to **c** in:

(**1**) delinco
(**2**) delinca, delincas, delinca, delincamos, delincáis, delincan

Verbs with a stem ending in **gu**, for example **distinguir**

The **gu** changes to **g** in:

(**1**) distingo
(**2**) distinga, distingas, distinga, distingamos, distingáis, distingan

Models for Regular Conjugation

TOMAR to take

INDICATIVE

PRESENT	**FUTURE**	**CONDITIONAL**
1. tomo	tomaré	tomaría
2. tomas	tomarás	tomarías
3. toma	tomará	tomaría
1. tomamos	tomaremos	tomaríamos
2. tomáis	tomaréis	tomaríais
3. toman	tomarán	tomarían

IMPERFECT	**PRETERITE**	**PERFECT**
1. tomaba	tomé	he tomado
2. tomabas	tomaste	has tomado
3. tomaba	tomó	ha tomado
1. tomábamos	tomamos	hemos tomado
2. tomabais	tomasteis	habéis tomado
3. tomaban	tomaron	han tomado

FUTURE PERFECT	**CONDITIONAL PERFECT**	**PLUPERFECT**
1. habré tomado	habría tomado	había tomado
2. habrás tomado	habrías tomado	habías tomado
3. habrá tomado	habría tomado	había tomado
1. habremos tomado	habríamos tomado	habíamos tomado
2. habréis tomado	habríais tomado	habíais tomado
3. habrán tomado	habrían tomado	habían tomado

SUBJUNCTIVE

PRESENT	**IMPERFECT**	**PERFECT/PLUPERFECT**
1. tome	tom-ara/ase	haya/hubiera* tomado
2. tomes	tom-aras/ases	hayas/hubieras tomado
3. tome	tom-ara/ase	haya/hubiera tomado
1. tomemos	tom-áramos/ásemos	hayamos/hubiéramos tomado
2. toméis	tom-arais/aseis	hayáis/hubierais tomado
3. tomen	tom-aran/asen	hayan/hubieran tomado

IMPERATIVE / INFINITIVE / PARTICIPLE

IMPERATIVE	INFINITIVE	PARTICIPLE
(tú) toma	**PRESENT**	**PRESENT**
(Vd) tome	tomar	tomando
(nosotros) tomemos		
(vosotros) tomad	**PERFECT**	**PAST**
(Vds) tomen	haber tomado	tomado

* the alternative form 'hubiese' etc is also possible

COMER to eat

INDICATIVE

PRESENT	**FUTURE**	**CONDITIONAL**
1. como	comeré	comería
2. comes	comerás	comerías
3. come	comerá	comería
1. comemos	comeremos	comeríamos
2. coméis	comeréis	comeríais
3. comen	comerán	comerían

IMPERFECT	**PRETERITE**	**PERFECT**
1. comía	comí	he comido
2. comías	comiste	has comido
3. comía	comió	ha comido
1. comíamos	comimos	hemos comido
2. comíais	comisteis	habéis comido
3. comían	comieron	han comido

FUTURE PERFECT	**CONDITIONAL PERFECT**	**PLUPERFECT**
1. habré comido	habría comido	había comido
2. habrás comido	habrías comido	habías comido
3. habrá comido	habría comido	había comido
1. habremos comido	habríamos comido	habíamos comido
2. habréis comido	habríais comido	habías comido
3. habrán comido	habrían comido	habían comido

SUBJUNCTIVE

PRESENT	**IMPERFECT**	**PERFECT/PLUPERFECT**
1. coma	com-iera/iese	haya/hubiera* comido
2. comas	com-ieras/ieses	hayas/hubieras comido
3. coma	com-iera/iese	haya/hubiera comido
1. comamos	com-iéramos/iésemos	hayamos/hubiéramos comido
2. comáis	com-ierais/ieseis	hayáis/hubierais comido
3. coman	com-ieran/iesen	hayan/hubieran comido

IMPERATIVE   INFINITIVE   PARTICIPLE

IMPERATIVE	**INFINITIVE**	**PARTICIPLE**
(tú) come	**PRESENT**	**PRESENT**
(Vd) coma	comer	comiendo
(nosotros) comamos		
(vosotros) comed	**PERFECT**	**PAST**
(Vds) coman	haber comido	comido

* the alternative form 'hubiese' etc is also possible

PARTIR to leave

INDICATIVE

PRESENT	FUTURE	CONDITIONAL
1. parto	partiré	partiría
2. partes	partirás	partirías
3. parte	partirá	partiría
1. partimos	partiremos	partiríamos
2. partís	partiréis	partiríais
3. parten	partirán	partirían

IMPERFECT	PRETERITE	PERFECT
1. partía	partí	he partido
2. partías	partiste	has partido
3. partía	partió	ha partido
1. partíamos	partimos	hemos partido
2. partíais	partisteis	habéis partido
3. partían	partieron	han partido

FUTURE PERFECT	CONDITIONAL PERFECT	PLUPERFECT
1. habré partido	habría partido	había partido
2. habrás partido	habrías partido	habías partido
3. habrá partido	habría partido	había partido
1. habremos partido	habríamos partido	habíamos partido
2. habréis partido	habríais partido	habíais partido
3. habrán partido	habían partido	habían partido

SUBJUNCTIVE

PRESENT	IMPERFECT	PERFECT/PLUPERFECT
parta	parti-era/ese	haya/hubiera* partido
partas	parti-eras/eses	hayas/hubieras partido
parta	parti-era/ese	haya/hubiera partido
partamos	parti-éramos/ésemos	hayamos/hubiéramos partido
partáis	parti-erais/eseis	hayáis/hubierais partido
partan	parti-eran/esen	hayan/hubieran partido

IMPERATIVE	INFINITIVE	PARTICIPLE
(tú) parte	**PRESENT**	**PRESENT**
(Vd) parta	partir	partiendo
(nosotros) partamos		
(vosotros) partid	**PERFECT**	**PAST**
(Vds) partan	haber partido	partido

* the alternative form 'hubiese' etc is also possible

Models for Irregular Conjugation

[1] **pensar PRES** pienso, piensas, piensa, pensamos, pensáis, piensan; **PRES SUBJ** piense, pienses, piense, pensemos, penséis, piensen; **IMPERAT** piensa, piense, pensemos, pensad, piensen

[2] **contar PRES** cuento, cuentas, cuenta, contamos, contáis, cuentan; **PRES SUBJ** cuente, cuentes, cuente, contemos, contéis, cuenten; **IMPERAT** cuenta, cuente, contemos, contad, cuenten

[3] **perder PRES** pierdo, pierdes, pierde, perdemos, perdéis, pierden; **PRES SUBJ** pierda, pierdas, pierda, perdamos, perdáis, pierdan; **IMPERAT** pierde, pierda, perdamos, perded, pierdan

[4] **morder PRES** muerdo, muerdes, muerde, mordemos, mordéis, muerden; **PRES SUBJ** muerda, muerdas, muerda, mordamos, mordáis, muerdan; **IMPERAT** muerde, muerda, mordamos, morded, muerdan

[5] **sentir PRES** siento, sientes, siente, sentimos, sentís, sienten; **PRES SUBJ** sienta, sientas, sienta, sintamos, sintáis, sientan; **PRES P** sintiendo; **IMPERAT** siente, sienta, sintamos, sentid, sientan

[6] **vestir PRES** visto, vistes, viste, vestimos, vestís, visten; **PRES SUBJ** vista, vistas, vista, vistamos, vistáis, vistan; **PRES P** vistiendo; **IMPERAT** viste, vista, vistamos, vestid, vistan

[7] **dormir PRES** duermo, duermes, duerme, dormimos, dormís, duermen; **PRES SUBJ** duerma, duermas, duerma, durmamos, durmáis, duerman; **PRES P** durmiendo; **IMPERAT** duerme, duerma, durmamos, dormid, duerman

[8] **andar PRET** anduve, anduviste, anduvo, anduvimos, anduvisteis, anduvieron; **IMPERF SUBJ** anduviera/anduviese

[9] **caber PRES** quepo, cabes, cabe, cabemos, cabéis, caben; **PRES SUBJ** quepa, quepas, quepa, quepamos, quepáis, quepan; **FUT** cabré; **COND** cabría; **PRET** cupe, cupiste, cupo, cupimos, cupisteis, cupieron; **IMPERF SUBJ** cupiera/cupiese; **IMPERAT** cabe, quepa, quepamos, cabed, quepan

[10] **conducir PRES** conduzco, conduces, conduce, conducimos, conducís, conducen; **PRES SUBJ** conduzca, conduzcas, conduzca, conduzcamos, conduzcáis, conduzcan; **PRET** conduje, condujiste, condujo, condujimos, condujisteis, condujeron; **IMPERF SUBJ** condujera/condujese; **IMPERAT** conduce, conduzca, conduzcamos, conducid, conduzcan

[11] **dar PRES** doy, das, da, damos, dais, dan; **PRES SUBJ** dé, des, dé, demos, deis, den; **PRET** di, diste, dio, dimos, disteis, dieron; **IMPERF SUBJ** diera/diese; **IMPERAT** da, dé, demos, dad, den

[12] **decir PRES** digo, dices, dice, decimos, decís, dicen; **PRES SUBJ** diga, digas, diga, digamos, digáis, digan; **FUT** diré; **COND** diría; **PRET** dije, dijiste, dijo, dijimos, dijisteis, dijeron; **IMPERF SUBJ** dijera/dijese; **PRES P** diciendo; **PP** dicho; **IMPERAT** di, diga, digamos, decid, digan

[13] **ESTAR** to be

INDICATIVE

PRESENT	FUTURE	CONDITIONAL
1. estoy	estaré	estaría
2. estás	estarás	estarías
3. está	estará	estaría
1. estamos	estaremos	estaríamos
2. estáis	estaréis	estaríais
3. están	estarán	estarían

IMPERFECT	PRETERITE	PERFECT
1. estaba	estuve	he estado
2. estabas	estuviste	has estado
3. estaba	estuvo	ha estado
1. estábamos	estuvimos	hemos estado
2. estabais	estuvisteis	habéis estado
3. estaban	estuvieron	han estado

FUTURE PERFECT	CONDITIONAL PERFECT	PLUPERFECT
1. habré estado	habría estado	había estado
2. habrás estado	habrías estado	habías estado
3. habrá estado	habría estado	había estado
1. habremos estado	habríamos estado	habíamos estado
2. habréis estado	habríais estado	habíais estado
3. habrán estado	habrían estado	habían estado

SUBJUNCTIVE

PRESENT	IMPERFECT	PERFECT/PLUPERFECT
1. esté	estuv-iera/iese	haya/hubiera* estado
2. estés	estuv-ieras/ieses	hayas/hubieras estado
3. esté	estuv-iera/iese	haya/hubiera estado
1. estemos	esuv-iéramos/iésemos	hayamos/hubiéramos estado
2. estéis	estuv-ierais/ieseis	hayáis/hubierais estado
3. estén	estuv-ieran/iesen	hayan/hubieran estado

IMPERATIVE	INFINITIVE	PARTICIPLE
(tú) está	**PRESENT**	**PRESENT**
(Vd) esté	estar	estando
(nosotros) estemos		
(vosotros) estad	**PERFECT**	**PAST**
(Vds) estén	haber estado	estado

* the alternative form 'hubiese' etc is also possible

[14] **HABER** to have (*auxiliary*)

INDICATIVE

PRESENT	FUTURE	CONDITIONAL
1. he	habré	habría
2. has	habrás	habrías
3. ha/hay*	habrá	habría
1. hemos	habremos	habríamos
2. habéis	habréis	habríais
3. han	habrán	habrían

IMPERFECT	PRETERITE	PERFECT
1. había	hube	
2. habías	hubiste	
3. había	hubo	ha habido*
1. habíamos	hubimos	
2. habíais	hubisteis	
3. habían	hubieron	

FUTURE PERFECT	CONDITIONAL PERFECT	PLUPERFECT
1.		
2.		
3. habrá habido*	habría habido*	había habido*
1.		
2.		
3.		

SUBJUNCTIVE

PRESENT	IMPERFECT	PERFECT/PLUPERFECT
1. haya	hub-iera/iese	
2. hayas	hub-ieras/ieses	
3. haya	hub-iera/iese	haya/hubiera** habido*
1. hayamos	hub-iéramos/iésemos	
2. hayáis	hub-ierais/ieseis	
3. hayan	hub-ieran/iesen	

INFINITIVE   PARTICIPLE

PRESENT	PRESENT
haber	habiendo
PERFECT	**PAST**
haber habido*	habido

* 'haber' is an auxiliary verb used with the participle of another verb to form compound tenses (eg he bebido - I have drunk). 'hay' means 'there is/are' and all third person singular forms in their respective tenses have this meaning. The forms highlighted with an asterisk are used only for this latter construction.

** the alternative form 'hubiese' is also possible.

[15] **hacer PRES** hago, haces, hace, hacemos, hacéis, hacen; **PRES SUBJ** haga, hagas, haga hagamos, hagáis, hagan; **FUT** haré; **COND** haría; **PRET** hice, hiciste, hizo, hicimos, hicisteis, hicieron; **IMPERF SUBJ** hiciera/hiciese; **PP** hecho; **IMPERAT** haz, haga, hagamos, haced, hagan

[16] **ir PRES** voy, vas, va, vamos, vais, van; **PRES SUBJ** vaya, vayas, vaya, vayamos, vayáis, vayan; **IMPERF** iba, ibas, iba, íbamos, ibais, iban; **PRET** fui, fuiste, fue, fuimos, fuisteis, fueron; **IMPERF SUBJ** fuera/fuese; **PRES P** yendo; **IMPERAT** ve, vaya, vamos, id, vayan

[17] **oir PRES** oigo, oyes, oye, oímos, oís, oyen; **PRES SUBJ** oiga, oigas, oiga, oigamos, oigáis, oigan; **PRET** oí, oíste, oyó, oímos, oísteis, oyeron; **IMPERF SUBJ** oyera/oyese; **PRES P** oyendo; **PP** oído; **IMPERAT** oye, oiga, oigamos, oíd, oigan

[18] **poder PRES** puedo, puedes, puede, podemos, podéis, pueden; **PRES SUBJ** pueda, puedas, pueda, podamos, podáis, puedan; **FUT** podré; **COND** podría; **PRET** pude, pudiste, pudo, pudimos, pudisteis, pudieron; **IMPERF SUBJ** pudiera/pudiese; **PRES P** pudiendo; **IMPERAT** puede, pueda, podamos, poded, puedan

[19] **poner PRES** pongo, pones, pone, ponemos, ponéis, ponen; **PRES SUBJ** ponga, pongas, ponga, pongamos, pongáis, pongan; **FUT** pondré; **PRET** puse, pusiste, puso, pusimos, pusisteis, pusieron; **IMPERF SUBJ** pusiera/pusiese; **PP** puesto; **IMPERAT** pon, ponga, pongamos, poned, pongan

[20] **querer PRES** quiero, quieres, quiere, queremos, queréis, quieren; **PRES SUBJ** quiera, quieras, quiera, queramos, queráis, quieran; **FUT** querré; **COND** querría; **PRET** quise, quisiste, quiso, quisimos, quisisteis, quisieron; **IMPERF SUBJ** quisiera/quisiese; **IMPERAT** quiere, quiera, queramos, quered, quieran

[21] **saber PRES** sé, sabes, sabe, sabemos, sabéis, saben; **PRES SUBJ** sepa, sepas, sepa, sepamos, sepáis, sepan; **FUT** sabré; **COND** sabría; **PRET** supe, supiste, supo, supimos, supisteis, supieron; **IMPERF SUBJ** supiera/supiese; **IMPERAT** sabe, sepa, sepamos, sabed, sepan

[22] **salir PRES** salgo, sales, sale, salimos, salís, salen; **PRES SUBJ** salga, salgas, salga, salgamos, salgáis, salgan; **FUT** saldré; **COND** saldría; **IMPERAT** sal, salga salgamos, salid, salgan

[23] **ser PRES** soy, eres, es, somos, sois, son; **PRES SUBJ** sea, seas, sea, seamos, seáis, sean; **IMPERF** era, eras, era, éramos, erais, eran; **PRET** fui, fuiste, fue, fuimos, fuisteis, fueron; **IMPERF SUBJ** fuera/fuese; **IMPERAT** sé, sea, seamos, sed, sean

[24] **tener PRES** tengo, tienes, tiene, tenemos, tenéis, tienen; **PRES SUBJ** tenga, tengas, tenga, tengamos, tengáis, tengan; **FUT** tendré; **COND** tendría; **PRET** tuve, tuviste, tuvo, tuvimos, tuvisteis, tuvieron; **IMPERF SUBJ** tuviera/tuviese; **IMPERAT** ten, tenga, tengamos, tened tengan

[25] **traer PRES** traigo, traes, trae, traemos, traéis, traen; **PRES SUBJ** traiga, traigas, traiga, traigamos, traigáis, traigan; **PRET** traje, trajiste, trajo, trajimos, trajisteis, trajeron; **IMPERF SUBJ** trajera/trajese; **IMPERAT** trae, traiga, traigamos, traed, traigan

[26] **valer PRES** valgo, vales, vale, valemos, valéis, valen; **PRES SUBJ** valga, valgas, valga, valgamos, valgáis, valgan; **FUT** valdré; **COND** valdría; **IMPERAT** vale, valga, valemos, valed, valgan

[27] **venir PRES** vengo, vienes, viene, venimos, venís, vienen; **PRES SUBJ** venga, vengas, venga, vengamos, vengáis, vengan; **FUT** vendré; **COND** vendría; **PRET** vine, viniste, vino, vinimos, vinisteis, vinieron; **IMPERF SUBJ** viniera/viniese; **PRES P** viniendo; **IMPERAT** ven, venga, vengamos, venid, vengan

[28] **ver PRES** veo, ves, ve, vemos, veis, ven; **PRES SUBJ** vea, veas, vea, veamos, veáis, vean; **IMPERF** veía, veías, veía, veíamos, veíais, veían; **PRET** vi, viste, vio, vimos, visteis, vieron; **IMPERF SUBJ** viera/viese; **IMPERAT** ve, vea, veamos, ved, vean

[29] **desviar PRES** desvío, desvías, desvía, desviamos, desviáis, desvían; **PRES SUBJ** desvíe, desvíes, desvíe, desviemos, desviéis, desvíen; **IMPERAT** desvía, desvíe, desviemos, desviéis, desvíen

[30] **continuar PRES** continúo, continúas, continúa, continuamos, continuáis, continúan; **PRES SUBJ** continúe, continúes, continúe, continuemos, continuéis, continúen; **IMPERAT** continúa, continúe, continuemos, continuad, continúen

[31] **adquirir PRES** adquiero, adquieres, adquiere, adquirimos, adquirís, adquieren; **PRES SUBJ** adquiera, adquiras, adquiera, adquiramos, adquiráis, adquieran; **IMPERAT** adquiere, adquiera, adquiramos, adquirid, adquieran

[32] **jugar PRES** juego, juegas, juega, jugamos, jugáis, juegan; **PRES SUBJ** juegue, juegues, juegue, juguemos, juguéis, jueguen; **IMPERAT** juega, juegue, juguemos, jugad, jueguen

[33] **agradecer PRES** agradezco, agradeces, agradece, agradecemos, agradecéis, agradecen; **PRES SUBJ** agradezca, agradezcas, agradezca, agradezcamos, agradezcáis, agradezcan; **IMPERAT** agradece, agradezca, agradezcamos, agradeced, agradezcan

[34] **conocer PRES** conozco, conoces, conoce, conocemos, conocéis, conocen; **PRES SUBJ** conozca, conozcas, conozca, conozcamos, conozcáis, conozcan; **IMPERAT** conoce, conozca, conozcamos, conoced, conozcan

[35] **lucir PRES** luzco, luces, luce, lucimos, lucís, lucen; **PRES SUBJ** luzca, luzcas, luzca, luzcamos, luzcáis, luzcan; **IMPERAT** luce, luzca, luzcamos, lucid, luzcan

[36] **leer PRET** leí, leíste, leyó, leímos, leísteis, leyeron; **IMPERF SUBJ** leyera/leyese; **PRES P** leyendo; **PP** leído; **IMPERAT** lee, lea, leamos, leed, lean

[37] **huir PRES** huyo, huyes, huye, huimos, huís, huyen; **PRES SUBJ** huya, huyas, huya, huyamos, huyáis, huyan; **PRET** huí, huiste, huyó, huimos, huisteis, huyeron; **IMPERF SUBJ** huyera/huyese; **PRES P** huyendo; **PP** huido; **IMPERAT** huye, huya, huyamos, huid, huyan

[38] **roer PRES** roo/roigo/royo, roes, roe, roemos, roéis, roen; **PRES SUBJ** roa/roiga/roya, roas, roa, roamos, roáis, roan; **PRET** roí, roíste, royó, roímos, roísteis, royeron; **IMPERF SUBJ** royera/royese; **PRES P** royendo; **PP** roído; **IMPERAT** roe, roa, roamos, roed, roan

[39] **caer PRES** caigo, caes, cae, caemos, caéis, caen; **PRES SUBJ** caiga, caigas, caiga, caigamos, caigáis, caigan; **PRES P** cayendo; **PP** caído; **IMPERAT** cae, caiga caigamos, caed, caigan

[40] **cazar PRET** cacé, cazaste, cazó, cazamos, cazasteis, cazaron; **PRES SUBJ** cace, caces, cacen, cacemos, cacéis, cacen

[41] **cocer PRES** cuezo, cueces, cuece, cocemos, cocéis, cuecen; **PRES SUBJ** cueza, cueza, cueza, cozamos, cozáis, cuezan; **IMPERAT** cuece, cueza, cozamos, cozed, cuezan

[42] **llegar PRET** llegué, llegaste, llegó, llegamos, llegasteis, llegaron; **PRES SUBJ** llegue, llegues, llegue, lleguemos, lleguéis, lleguen

[43] **cambiar PRES** cambio, cambias, cambia, cambiamos, cambiáis, cambian; **PRES SUBJ** cambie, cambies, cambie, cambiemos, cambiéis, cambien; **IMPERAT** cambia, cambie, cambiemos, cambiad, cambien

[44] **sacar PRET** saqué, sacaste, sacó, sacamos, sacasteis, sacaron; **PRES SUBJ** saque, saques, saque, saquemos, saquéis, saquen; **IMPERAT** saca, saque, saquemos, sacad, saquen

[45] **averiguar PRET** averigüé, averiguaste, averiguó, averiguamos, averiguasteis, averiguaron; **PRES SUBJ** averigüe, averigües, averigüe, averigüemos, averigüéis, averigüen; **IMPERAT** averigua, averigüe, averigüemos, averiguad, averigüen

[46] **asir PRES** asgo, ases, ase, asimos, asís, asen; **PRES SUBJ** asga, asgas, asga, asgamos, asgáis, asgan; **IMPERAT** ase, asga, asgamos, asid, asgan

[47] **adecuar PRES** adecuo, adecuas, adecua, adecuamos, adecuáis, adecuan; **PRES SUBJ** adecue, adecues, adecue, adecuemos, adecuéis, adecuen; **IMPERAT** adecua, adecuen, adecuemos, adecuad, adecuen

[48] **delinquir PRES** delinco, delinques, delinque, delinquimos, delinquís, delinquen; **PRES SUBJ** delinca, delincas, delinca, delincamos, delincáis, delincan; **IMPERAT** delinque, delinca, delincamos, delinquid, delincan

[49] **mecer PRES** mezo, meces, mece, mecemos, mecéis, mecen; **PRES SUBJ** meza, mezas, meza, mezamos, mezáis, mezan; **IMPERAT** mece, meza, mezamos, meced, mezan

[50] **errar PRES** yerro, yerras, yerra, erramos, erráis, yerran; **PRES SUBJ** yerre, yerres, yerre, erremos, erréis, yerren; **IMPERAT** yerra, yerre, erremos, errad, yerren

[51] **comenzar PRES** comienzo, comienzas, comienza, comenzamos, comenzáis, comienzan; **PRES SUBJ** comience, comiences, comience, comencemos, comencéis, comiencen; **IMPERAT** comienza, comience, comencemos, comenzad, comiencen

[52] **zurcir PRES** zurzo, zurces, zurce, zurcimos, zurcís, zurcen; **PRES SUBJ** zurza, zurzas, zurza, zurzamos, zurzáis, zurzan; **IMPERAT** zurce, zurza, zurzamos, zurcid, zurzan

[53] **proteger PRES** protejo, proteges, protege, protegemos, protegéis, protegen; **PRES SUBJ** proteja, protejas, proteja, protejamos, protejáis, protejan; **IMPERAT** protege, proteja, protejamos, proteged, protejan

[54] **discernir PRES** discierno, disciernes, discierne, discernimos, discernís, disciernen; **PRES SUBJ** discierna, disciernas, discierna, discernamos, discernáis, disciernan; **IMPERAT** discierne, discierna, discernamos, discernid, disciernan

[55] **erguir PRES** irgo/yergo, irgues/yergues, irgue/yergue, erguimos, erguís, irguen/yerguen; **PRET** erguí, erguiste, irguió, erguimos, erguisteis, irguieron; **PRES SUBJ** irga/yerga, irgas/yergas, irga/yerga, irgamos/yergamos, irgáis/yergáis, irgan/yergan; **IMPERF SUBJ** irguiera/irguiese; **IMPERAT** irgue/yergue, irga/yerga, irgamos/yergamos, erguid, irgan/yergan

[56] **reír PRES** río, ríes, ríe, reímos, reís, ríen; **PRET** reí, reíste, rió, reímos, reísteis, rieron; **PRES SUBJ** ría, rías, ría, riamos, riáis, rían; **IMPERF SUBJ** riera/riese; **IMPERAT** ríe, ría, riamos, reíd, rían

[57] **dirigir PRES** dirijo, diriges, dirige, dirigimos, dirigís, dirigen; **PRES SUBJ** dirija, dirijas, dirija, dirijamos, dirijáis, dirijan; **IMPERAT** dirige, dirija, dirijamos, dirigid, dirijan

[58] **regir** PRES rijo, riges, rige, regimos, regís, rigen; PRES SUBJ rija, rijas, rija, rijamos, rijáis, rijan; IMPERAT rige, rija, rijamos, regid, rijan

[59] **distinguir** PRES distingo, distingues, distingue, distinguimos, distinguís, distinguen; PRES SUBJ distinga, distingas, distinga, distingamos, distingáis, distingan; IMPERAT distingue, distinga, distingamos, distinguid, distingan

[60] **nacer** PRES nazco, naces, nace, nacemos, nacéis, nacen; PRES SUBJ nazca, nazcas, nazca, nazcamos, nazcáis, nazcan; IMPERAT nace, nazca, nazcamos, naced, nazcan

[61] **yacer** PRES yazco/yazgo/yago, yaces, yace, yacemos, yacéis, yacen; PRES SUBJ yazca/yazga/yaga, yace/yaz, yazca/yazga/yaga, yazcamos/yazgamos/yagamos, yaced, yazcan/yazgan/yagan

[62] **argüir** PRES arguyo, arguyes, arguye, argüimos, argüís, arguyen; PRET argüí, argüiste, arguyó, argüimos, argüisteis, arguyeron; PRES SUBJ arguya, arguyas, arguya, arguyamos, arguyáis, arguyan; IMPERF SUBJ arguyera/arguyese; IMPERAT arguye, arguya, arguyamos, argüid, arguyan

[63] **avergonzar** PRES avergüenzo, avergüenzas, avergüenza, avergonzamos, avergonzáis, avergüenzan; PRET avergoncé, avergonzaste, avergonzó, avergonzamos, avergonzasteis, avergonzaron; PRES SUBJ avergüence, avergüences, avergüence, avergoncemos, avergoncéis, avergüencen; IMPERAT avergüenza, avergüence, avergoncemos, avergonzad, avergüencen

[64] **trocar** PRES trueco, truecas, trueca, trocamos, trocáis, truecan; PRET troqué, trocaste, trocó, trocamos, trocasteis, trocaron; PRES SUBJ trueque, trueques, trueque, troquemos, troquéis, truequen; IMPERAT trueca, trueque, troquemos, trocad, truequen

[65] **oler** PRES huelo, hueles, huele, olemos, oléis, huelen; PRES SUBJ huela, huelas, huela, olamos, oláis, huelan; IMPERAT huele, huela, olamos, oled, huelan

Verbos Irregulares Ingleses

INFINITIVO	PRETÉRITO	PARTICIPIO
arise	arose	arisen
awake	awoke	awoken
awaken	awoke, awakened	awakened, awoken
be	were/was	been
bear	bore	borne
beat	beat	beaten
become	became	become
begin	began	begun
bend	bent	bent
beseech	besought, beseeched	besought, beseeched
bet	bet, betted	bet, betted
bid	bade, bid	bidden, bid
bind	bound	bound
bite	bit	bitten
bleed	bled	bled
blow	blew	blown
break	broke	broken
breed	bred	bred
bring	brought	brought
build	built	built
burn	burnt, burned	burnt, burned
burst	burst	burst
buy	bought	bought
cast	cast	cast
catch	caught	caught
choose	chose	chosen
cling	clung	clung
clothe	clad, clothed	clad, clothed
come	came	come
cost	cost	cost
creep	crept	crept
cut	cut	cut
deal	dealt	dealt
dig	dug	dug
do	did	done
draw	drew	drawn
dream	dreamt, dreamed	dreamt, dreamed
drink	drank	drunk
drive	drove	driven
dwell	dwelt	dwelt
eat	ate	eaten
fall	fell	fallen
feed	fed	fed
feel	felt	felt
fight	fought	fought
find	found	found

INFINITIVO	PRETÉRITO	PARTICIPIO
flee	fled	fled
fling	flung	flung
fly	flew	flown
forget	forgot	forgotten
forgive	forgave	forgiven
forsake	forsook	forsaken
freeze	froze	frozen
get	got	got, *US* gotten
give	gave	given
go	went	gone
grind	ground	ground
grow	grew	grown
hang	hung/hanged	hung/hanged
have	had	had
hear	heard	heard
hide	hid	hidden
hit	hit	hit
hold	held	held
hurt	hurt	hurt
keep	kept	kept
kneel	knelt	knelt
knit	knitted, knit	knitted, knit
know	knew	known
lay	laid	laid
lead	led	led
lean	leant, leaned	leant, leaned
leap	leapt, leaped	leapt, leaped
learn	learnt, learned	learnt, learned
leave	left	left
lend	lent	lent
let	let	let
lie	lay	lain
light	lit	lit
lose	lost	lost
make	made	made
mean	meant	meant
meet	met	met
mow	mowed	mown, mowed
pay	paid	paid
put	put	put
quit	quit	quit
read	read	read
rend	rent	rent
rid	rid	rid
ride	rode	ridden
ring	rang	rung
rise	rose	risen
run	ran	run
saw	sawed	sawn, sawed
say	said	said
see	saw	seen
seek	sought	sought
sell	sold	sold
send	sent	sent

INFINITIVO	PRETÉRITO	PARTICIPIO
set	set	set
sew	sewed	sewn
shake	shook	shaken
shear	sheared	shorn, sheared
shed	shed	shed
shine	shone	shone
shoe	shod	shod
shoot	shot	shot
show	showed	shown
shrink	shrank	shrunk
shut	shut	shut
sing	sang	sung
sink	sank	sunk
sit	sat	sat
slay	slew	slain
sleep	slept	slept
slide	slid	slid
sling	slung	slung
slink	slunk	slunk
slit	slit	slit
smell	smelled, smelt	smelled, smelt
sow	sowed	sown, sowed
speak	spoke	spoken
speed	sped, speeded	sped, speeded
spell	spelt, spelled	spelt, spelled
spend	spent	spent
spill	spilt, spilled	spilt, spilled
spin	span	spun
spit	spat	spat
split	split	split
spoil	spoilt, spoiled	spoilt, spoiled
spread	spread	spread
spring	sprang	sprung
stand	stood	stood
steal	stole	stolen
stick	stuck	stuck
sting	stung	stung
stink	stank, stunk	stunk
strew	strewed	strewed, strewn
stride	strode	stridden
strike	struck	struck
string	strung	strung
strive	strove	striven
swear	swore	sworn
sweep	swept	swept
swell	swelled	swollen
swing	swung	swung
swim	swam	swum
take	took	taken
teach	taught	taught
tear	tore	torn
tell	told	told
think	thought	thought
thrive	thrived, throve	thrived, thriven

INFINITIVO	PRETÉRITO	PARTICIPIO
throw	threw	thrown
thrust	thrust	thrust
tread	trod	trodden
wake	woke	woken
wear	wore	worn
weave	wove	woven
weep	wept	wept
wet	wet	wet
win	won	won
wind	wound	wound
wring	wrung	wrung
write	wrote	written

English – Spanish

Inglés – Español

A, a [eɪ] *n* (**a**) *(the letter)* A, a *f* (**b**) *Mus* A la *m* (**c**) *Br* **A road** ≃ carretera *f* nacional

a [eɪ, *unstressed* ə] *indef art (before vowel or silent h* **an**) (**a**) un, una; **a man/a woman** un hombre/una mujer; **he has a big nose** tiene la nariz grande (**b**) *(omitted in Spanish)* **half a litre/an hour** medio litro/media hora; **a hundred/thousand people** cien/mil personas; **let's have a drink** vamos a beber algo; **he's a teacher** es profesor; **what a pity** qué pena (**c**) *(each)* **60 pence a kilo** 60 peniques el kilo; **to eat grapes two at a time** comer las uvas de dos en dos; **three times a week** tres veces a la semana (**d**) *(a certain)* un/una tal; **a Mr Rees phoned** llamó un tal Sr. Rees

AA [eɪˈeɪ] *n* (**a**) *(abbr* **Alcoholics Anonymous**) AA, alcohólicos *mpl* anónimos (**b**) *(abbr* **Automobile Association**) ≃ AC

AAA [eɪeɪˈeɪ] *n* (**a**) *Br (abbr* **Amateur Athletic Association**) = federación británica de atletismo aficionado (**b**) *US (abbr* **American Automobile Association**) ≃ AC

aback [əˈbæk] *adv* **to be taken a.** quedarse de una pieza (**by** por)

abandon [əˈbændən] **1** *n* desenfreno *m*; **with reckless a.** desenfrenadamente

2 *vt (child)* abandonar; *(job)* dejar; *(project)* renunciar a

abase [əˈbeɪs] *vt* **to a. oneself** humillarse

abashed [əˈbæʃt] *adj* desconcertado(a)

abate [əˈbeɪt] *vi (anger)* apaciguarse; *(storm)* amainar

abattoir [ˈæbətwɑː(r)] *n* matadero *m*

abbey [ˈæbɪ] *n* abadía *f*

abbot [ˈæbət] *n* abad *m*

abbreviate [əˈbriːvɪeɪt] *vt* abreviar

abbreviation [əbriːvɪˈeɪʃən] *n* abreviatura *f*

abdicate [ˈæbdɪkeɪt] *vt & vi* abdicar

abdication [æbdɪˈkeɪʃən] *n* abdicación *f*

abdomen [ˈæbdəmən] *n* abdomen *m*

abduct [æbˈdʌkt] *vt* raptar, secuestrar

aberration [æbəˈreɪʃən] *n* aberración *f*

abet [əˈbet] *vt* **to aid and a. sb** ser cómplice de algn

abeyance [əˈbeɪəns] *n* **to be in a.** estar en desuso

abhor [əbˈhɔː(r)] *vt* aborrecer

abhorrent [əbˈhɒrənt] *adj* aborrecible

abide [əˈbaɪd] *vt* aguantar; **I can't a. it** no lo aguanto

▸ **abide by** *vt insep (promise)* cumplir con; *(rules)* atenerse a

ability [əˈbɪlɪtɪ] *n (capability)* capacidad *f*, aptitud *f*; *(talent)* talento *m*

abject [ˈæbdʒekt] *adj (state)* miserable; *(apology)* rastrero(a)

ablaze [əˈbleɪz] *adj & adv* en llamas, ardiendo

able [ˈeɪbəl] *adj (capable)* capaz; **will you be a. to come on Tuesday?** ¿podrás venir el martes?

able-bodied [eɪbəlˈbɒdɪd] *adj* sano(a); **a. seaman** marinero *m* de primera

abnormal [æbˈnɔːməl] *adj* anormal

abnormally [æbˈnɔːməlɪ] *adv* anormalmente; *(large)* extraordinariamente

aboard [əˈbɔːd] **1** *adv* a bordo; **to go a.** *(ship)* embarcarse; *(train)* subir

2 *prep* a bordo de

abode [əˈbəʊd] *n Jur* **of no fixed a.** sin domicilio fijo

abolish [əˈbɒlɪʃ] *vt* abolir

abolition [æbəˈlɪʃən] *n* abolición *f*

abominable [əˈbɒmɪnəbəl] *adj* abominable; *(dreadful)* terrible

aborigine [æbəˈrɪdʒɪnɪ] *n* aborigen *mf* australiano(a)

abort [əˈbɔːt] **1** *vt Med* hacer abortar; *Fig (plan etc)* archivar

2 *vi Med* abortar

abortion [əˈbɔːʃən] *n Med* aborto *m*; **a. law** ley *f* del aborto; **to have an a.** abortar

abortive [əˈbɔːtɪv] *adj (plan)* fracasado(a); *(attempt)* frustrado(a)

abound [əˈbaʊnd] *vi* **to a. in** *or* **with** abundar en

about [əˈbaʊt] *adv & prep* (**a**) *(concerning)* acerca de, sobre; **a programme a. Paris** un programa sobre París; **to be worried a. sth** estar preocupado(a) por algo; **to speak a. sth** hablar de algo; **what's it all a.?** *(what's happening?)* ¿qué pasa?; *(story etc)* ¿de qué se trata?; *Fam* **how a. a game of tennis?** ¿qué te parece un partido de tenis?

(**b**) *(around)* por todas partes; **don't leave things lying a.** no dejes las cosas por medio; **there's nobody a.** no hay nadie; **to look a.** mirar alrededor; **to rush a.** correr de un lado para otro; **we went for a walk a. the town** dimos una vuelta por el pueblo

(**c**) *(approximately)* más o menos; **it's a. three o'clock** son más o menos las tres; **it's a. time you got up** ya es hora de que te levantes; **it's just a. finished** está casi terminado; **she's**

a. forty tiene unos cuarenta años
(**d**) **it's a. to start** está a punto de empezar; **not to be a. to do sth** no estar dispuesto(a) a hacer algo

about-turn [əbaʊt'tɜːn], *US* **about-face** [əbaʊt'feɪs] *n* media vuelta *f*; **to do an a.** dar media vuelta; *Fig* cambiar de idea por completo

above [ə'bʌv] *adv & prep* (**a**) *(higher than)* encima de, sobre, arriba; **100 m a. sea level** 100 m sobre el nivel del mar; **it's a. the door** está encima de la puerta; **the flat a.** el piso de arriba (**b**) *(greater than)* superior (a); **amounts a. £10** cantidades superiores a las 10 libras; *Fig* **a policy imposed from a.** una política impuesta desde arriba (**c**) **a. all** sobre todo; **he's not a. stealing** es capaz incluso de robar (**d**) *(in book etc)* más arriba

above-board [ə'bʌv'bɔːd] *adj (scheme)* legítimo(a)

above-mentioned [ə'bʌvmenʃənd] *adj* susodicho(a)

abrasive [ə'breɪsɪv] **1** *adj (substance)* abrasivo(a); *Fig (voice, wit etc)* cáustico(a)
2 *n* abrasivo *m*

abreast [ə'brest] *adv* **to walk three a.** ir de tres en fondo; *Fig* **to keep a. of things** mantenerse al día

abridged [ə'brɪdʒd] *adj (book)* abreviado(a)

abroad [ə'brɔːd] *adv* **to be a.** estar en el extranjero; **to go a.** irse al extranjero

abrupt [ə'brʌpt] *adj (manner)* brusco(a); *(tone)* áspero(a); *(change)* súbito(a)

abruptly [ə'brʌptlɪ] *adv (act)* bruscamente; *(speak)* con aspereza; *(change)* repentinamente

abscess ['æbses] *n* absceso *m*; *(on gum)* flemón *m*

abscond [əb'skɒnd] *vi* huir

absence ['æbsəns] *n (of person)* ausencia *f*; *(of thing)* falta *f*

absent ['æbsənt] *adj* ausente; *Fig* **an a. look** una mirada distraída

absentee [æbsən'tiː] *n* ausente *mf*

absenteeism [æbsən'tiːɪzəm] *n* absentismo *m*

absently ['æbsəntlɪ] *adv* distraídamente

absent-minded [æbsənt'maɪndɪd] *adj* distraído(a)

absolute ['æbsəluːt] *adj* absoluto(a); *(failure)* total; *(truth)* puro(a); **it's an a. disgrace** es una auténtica vergüenza

absolutely [æbsə'luːtlɪ] **1** *adv (completely)* completamente; **a. wrong** totalmente equivocado(a); **a. not** en absoluto; **you're a. right** tienes toda la razón
2 *interj* **a.!** ¡desde luego!

absolve [əb'zɒlv] *vt* absolver (**from** de)

absorb [əb'zɔːb] *vt (liquid)* absorber; *(sound, blow)* amortiguar; *Fig* **to be absorbed in sth** estar absorto(a) en algo

absorbing [əb'zɔːbɪŋ] *adj (book, work)* absorbente

abstain [əb'steɪn] *vi* abstenerse (**from** de)

abstemious [əb'stiːmɪəs] *adj* abstemio(a)

abstention [əb'stenʃən] *n* abstención *f*

abstinence ['æbstɪnəns] *n* abstinencia *f*

abstract ['æbstrækt] **1** *adj* abstracto(a)
2 *n (of thesis etc)* resumen *m*

abstruse [əb'struːs] *adj* abstruso(a)

absurd [əb'sɜːd] *adj* absurdo(a)

abundance [ə'bʌndəns] *n* abundancia *f*

abundant [ə'bʌndənt] *adj* abundante, rico(a) (**in** en)

abuse 1 *n* [ə'bjuːs] (**a**) *(ill-treatment)* malos tratos; *(misuse)* abuso *m* (**b**) *(insults)* injurias *fpl*
2 *vt* [ə'bjuːz] (**a**) *(ill-treat)* maltratar; *(misuse)* abusar de (**b**) *(insult)* injuriar

abusive [ə'bjuːsɪv] *adj (insulting)* insultante

abysmal [ə'bɪzməl] *adj (conditions)* extremo(a); *Fam (very bad)* fatal, pésimo(a)

abyss [ə'bɪs] *n* abismo *m*; *Fig* extremo *m*

AC [eɪ'siː] *n (abbr alternating current)* CA

academic [ækə'demɪk] **1** *adj* académico(a); *(career)* universitario(a); *(discussion)* teórico(a); **a. year** año *m* escolar
2 *n* académico(a) *m,f*

academy [ə'kædəmɪ] *n (society)* academia *f*; *Educ* instituto *m* de enseñanza media; **a. of music** conservatorio *m*

accede [æk'siːd] *vi* acceder (**to** a)

accelerate [æk'seləreɪt] **1** *vt (engine)* acelerar; *(step)* aligerar
2 *vi (car, engine)* acelerar

acceleration [ækselə'reɪʃən] *n* aceleración *f*

accelerator [æk'seləreɪtə(r)] *n* acelerador *m*

accent ['æksənt] *n* acento *m*

accentuate [æk'sentjʊeɪt] *vt* subrayar

accept [ək'sept] *vt & vi* aceptar; *(theory)* admitir; **do you a. that ...?** ¿estás de acuerdo en que ...?

acceptable [ək'septəbəl] *adj (satisfactory)* aceptable; *(tolerable)* admisible

acceptance [ək'septəns] *n (act of accepting)* aceptación *f*; *(good reception)* aprobación *f*

access ['ækses] *n* acceso *m*; *Comput* **a. provider** proveedor *m* de acceso (a Internet); **a. road** carretera *f* de acceso; **to have a. to sth** tener libre acceso a algo

accessible [ək'sesəbəl] *adj (place, position)* accesible; *(person)* asequible

accession [ək'seʃən] *n* subida *f* (al trono)

accessory [ək'sesərɪ] *n* (**a**) *Jur* cómplice *mf* (**b**) **accessories** accesorios *mpl*; *(for outfit)* complementos *mpl*

accident ['æksɪdənt] *n* accidente *m*; *(coincidence)* casualidad *f*; **it was an a. on my part** lo hice sin querer; **car a.** accidente *m* de carretera; **by a.** por casualidad

accidental [æksɪ'dentəl] *adj* fortuito(a); *(unintended)* imprevisto(a)

accidentally [æksɪ'dentəlɪ] *adv (by chance)* por casualidad; **he did it a.** lo hizo sin querer

accident-prone ['æksɪdəntprəʊn] *adj* propenso(a) a los accidentes
acclaim [ə'kleɪm] **1** *n* aclamación *f*
2 *vt* aclamar
acclimatization [əklaɪmətaɪ'zeɪʃən], *US* **acclimation** [æklɪ'meɪʃən] *n* aclimatación *f*
acclimatize [ə'klaɪmətaɪz], *US* **acclimate** ['æklɪmeɪt] *vt* aclimatar
acclimatized [ə'klaɪmətaɪzd] *adj* aclimatado(a); **to become a.** aclimatarse
accolade ['ækəleɪd] *n* elogio *m*
accommodate [ə'kɒmədeɪt] *vt* (**a**) (*guests*) alojar (**b**) **to a. sb's wishes** complacer a algn
accommodating [ə'kɒmədeɪtɪŋ] *adj* (*obliging*) complaciente; (*understanding*) comprensivo(a)
accommodation [əkɒmə'deɪʃən] *n* (*US also* **accommodations**) (*lodgings*) alojamiento *m*
accompany [ə'kʌmpənɪ] *vt* acompañar
accomplice [ə'kʌmplɪs] *n* cómplice *mf*
accomplish [ə'kʌmplɪʃ] *vt* (*aim*) conseguir; (*task, mission*) llevar a cabo
accomplished [ə'kʌmplɪʃt] *adj* dotado(a), experto(a)
accomplishment [ə'kʌmplɪʃmənt] *n* (**a**) (*of task*) realización *f*; (*of duty*) cumplimiento *m* (**b**) **accomplishments** (*talents*) dotes *fpl*
accord [ə'kɔːd] **1** *n* (*agreement*) acuerdo *m*; **of her/his own a.** espontáneamente
2 *vt* (*honour etc*) conceder
accordance [ə'kɔːdəns] *n* **in a. with** de acuerdo con
according [ə'kɔːdɪŋ] *prep* **a. to** según; **everything went a. to plan** todo salió conforme a los planes
accordingly [ə'kɔːdɪŋlɪ] *adv* (**a**) **to act a.** (*appropriately*) obrar según y conforme (**b**) (*therefore*) así pues
accordion [ə'kɔːdɪən] *n* acordeón *m*
account [ə'kaʊnt] *n* (**a**) (*report*) informe *m*; **by all accounts** al decir de todos (**b**) **I was fearful on her a.** sufría por ella; **it's of no a.** no tiene importancia; **on a. of** a causa de; **on no a.** bajo ningún concepto; **to take a. of, to take into a.** tener en cuenta (**c**) *Com* cuenta *f*; **to keep the accounts** llevar las cuentas; **accounts department** servicio *m* de contabilidad; **to open/close an a.** abrir/cancelar una cuenta; **current a.** cuenta corriente; **a. number** número *m* de cuenta
▸ **account for** *vt insep* (*explain*) explicar
accountable [ə'kaʊntəbəl] *adj* **to be a. to sb for sth** ser responsable ante algn de algo
accountancy [ə'kaʊntənsɪ] *n* contabilidad *f*
accountant [ə'kaʊntənt] *n* contable *mf*
accredited [ə'kredɪtɪd] *adj* acreditado(a)
accrue [ə'kruː] *vi* (*interest*) acumularse
accumulate [ə'kjuːmjʊleɪt] **1** *vt* acumular; (*fortune*) amasar
2 *vi* acumularse
accuracy ['ækjʊrəsɪ] *n* (*of number etc*) exactitud *f*; (*of shot, criticism*) certeza *f*

accurate ['ækjʊrət] *adj* (*number*) exacto(a); (*shot, criticism*) certero(a); (*answer*) correcto(a); (*observation*) acertado(a); (*instrument*) de precisión; (*translation*) fiel
accusation [ækjʊ'zeɪʃən] *n* acusación *f*
accuse [ə'kjuːz] *vt* acusar
accused [ə'kjuːzd] *n* **the a.** el/la acusado(a)
accustom [ə'kʌstəm] *vt* acostumbrar; **to be accustomed to doing sth** estar acostumbrado(a) a hacer algo
ace [eɪs] *n* (**a**) *Cards & Fig* as *m* (**b**) (*in tennis*) ace *m*
acetate ['æsɪteɪt] *n* acetato *m*
acetone ['æsɪtəʊn] *n* acetona *f*
ache [eɪk] **1** *n* dolor *m*; **aches and pains** achaques *mpl*
2 *vi* doler; **my back aches** me duele la espalda
achieve [ə'tʃiːv] *vt* (*attain*) conseguir, alcanzar; (*accomplish*) llevar a cabo, realizar
achievement [ə'tʃiːvmənt] *n* (*attainment*) logro *m*; (*completion*) realización *f*; (*feat*) hazaña *f*
acid ['æsɪd] **1** *adj* ácido(a); (*taste*) agrio(a); (*remark*) mordaz; **a. rain** lluvia ácida; *Fig* **a. test** prueba decisiva
2 *n* ácido *m*
acknowledge [ək'nɒlɪdʒ] *vt* (**a**) (*recognize*) reconocer; (*claim, defeat*) admitir; (*present*) agradecer; (*letter*) acusar recibo de (**b**) (*greet*) saludar
acknowledgement [ək'nɒlɪdʒmənt] *n* (**a**) (*recognition*) reconocimiento *m*; (*of letter*) acuse *m* de recibo (**b**) **acknowledgements** (*in preface*) menciones *fpl*
acne ['æknɪ] *n* acné *m*
acorn ['eɪkɔːn] *n* bellota *f*
acoustic [ə'kuːstɪk] **1** *adj* acústico(a)
2 *npl* **acoustics** acústica *f*
acquaint [ə'kweɪnt] *vt* **to a. sb with the facts** informar a algn de los detalles; **to be acquainted with the procedure** estar al corriente de como se procede; **to be acquainted with sb** conocer a algn
acquaintance [ə'kweɪntəns] *n* (**a**) conocimiento *m*; **to make sb's a.** conocer a algn (**b**) (*person*) conocido(a) *m,f*
acquiesce [ækwɪ'es] *vi* consentir (**in** en)
acquiescent [ækwɪ'esənt] *adj* conforme
acquire [ə'kwaɪə(r)] *vt* adquirir
acquisition [ækwɪ'zɪʃən] *n* adquisición *f*
acquisitive [ə'kwɪzɪtɪv] *adj* codicioso(a)
acquit [ə'kwɪt] *vt* (**a**) *Jur* **to a. sb of sth** absolver a algn de algo (**b**) **to a. oneself well** defenderse bien
acquittal [ə'kwɪtəl] *n* absolución *f*
acre ['eɪkə(r)] *n* acre *m* (= *aprox 40,47 áreas*)
acrid ['ækrɪd] *adj* (*smell, taste*) acre
acrimonious [ækrɪ'məʊnɪəs] *adj* (*remark*) cáustico(a); (*dispute*) enconado(a)
acrobat ['ækrəbæt] *n* acróbata *mf*
across [ə'krɒs] **1** *adv* a través; **the river is**

30 m a. el río mide 30 m de ancho; **to go a.** atravesar; **to run a.** atravesar corriendo

2 *prep* (**a**) a través de; **they live a. the road** viven enfrente; **to go a. the street** cruzar la calle (**b**) *(at the other side of)* al otro lado de

acrylic [ə'krɪlɪk] *adj* acrílico(a)

act [ækt] **1** *n* (**a**) *(action)* acto *m*, acción *f*; **a. of God** caso *m* de fuerza mayor (**b**) *(in parliament)* ley *f*, decreto *m* (**c**) *Th* acto *m*; *(turn in show)* número *m*

2 *vt Th (part)* interpretar; *(character)* representar; *Fig* **to a. the fool** hacer el tonto

3 *vi* (**a**) *Th* hacer teatro; *Cin* hacer cine; *Fig (pretend)* fingir (**b**) *(behave)* comportarse (**c**) *(take action)* actuar, obrar; **to a. on sb's advice** seguir el consejo de algn (**d**) *(work)* funcionar; *(drug etc)* actuar; **to a. as a deterrent** servir de disuasivo (**e**) **to a. as director** hacer de director

▸ **act out** *vt sep* exteriorizar

▸ **act up** *vi Fam (machine)* funcionar mal; *(child)* dar guerra

acting ['æktɪŋ] **1** *adj* interino(a)

2 *n (profession)* teatro *m*; **he's done some a.** ha hecho algo de teatro

action ['ækʃən] *n* (**a**) *(deed)* acción *f*; *Mil* acción de combate; **to be out of a.** *(person)* estar fuera de servicio; *(machine)* estar estropeado(a); **to take a.** tomar medidas (**b**) *Jur* demanda *f* (**c**) *TV* **a. replay** repetición *f*

activate ['æktɪveɪt] *vt* activar

active ['æktɪv] *adj* activo(a); *(energetic)* vigoroso(a); *(interest)* vivo(a); *Ling* **a. voice** voz activa

activist ['æktɪvɪst] *n* activista *mf*

activity [æk'tɪvɪtɪ] *n (of person)* actividad *f*; *(on street etc)* bullicio *m*

actor ['æktə(r)] *n* actor *m*

actress ['æktrɪs] *n* actriz *f*

actual ['æktʃʊəl] *adj* real, verdadero(a)

> 🔗 Note that the Spanish word **actual** is a false friend and is never a translation for the English word **actual**. In Spanish, **actual** means "current, up-to-date, topical".

actually ['æktʃʊəlɪ] *adv (really)* en efecto, realmente; *(even)* incluso, hasta; *(in fact)* de hecho

> 🔗 Note that the Spanish word **actualmente** is a false friend and is never a translation for the English word **actually**. In Spanish, **actualmente** means "nowadays, at the moment".

acumen ['ækjʊmən] *n* perspicacia *f*

acupuncture ['ækjʊpʌŋktʃə(r)] *n* acupuntura *f*

acute [ə'kju:t] *adj* agudo(a); *(pain)* intenso(a); *(hearing)* muy fino(a); *(shortage)* grave; *(mind)* perspicaz

AD [eɪ'di:] *(abbr* **Anno Domini)** d.J.C., d.C.

ad [æd] *n Fam* anuncio *m*

adamant ['ædəmənt] *adj* firme, inflexible

adapt [ə'dæpt] **1** *vt* adaptar (**to** a); **to a. oneself to sth** adaptarse a algo

2 *vi* adaptarse

adaptable [ə'dæptəbəl] *adj (instrument)* ajustable; **he's very a.** se amolda fácilmente a las circunstancias

adaptation [ædəp'teɪʃən] *n* adaptación *f*

adapter, adaptor [ə'dæptə(r)] *n Elec* ladrón *m*

add [æd] **1** *vt (numbers)* sumar; *(one thing to another)* añadir

2 *vi (count)* sumar

▸ **add to** *vt insep* aumentar

▸ **add up 1** *vt sep* sumar

2 *vi (numbers)* sumar; *Fig* **it doesn't a. up** no tiene sentido; **it doesn't a. up to much** no es gran cosa

added ['ædɪd] *adj* adicional

adder ['ædə(r)] *n* víbora *f*

addict ['ædɪkt] *n* adicto(a) *m,f*; *Fam* **television a.** teleadicto(a) *m,f*

addicted [ə'dɪktɪd] *adj* adicto(a); **to become a. to sth** enviciarse con algo

addiction [ə'dɪkʃən] *n (to gambling etc)* vicio *m*; *(to drugs)* adicción *f*

addictive [ə'dɪktɪv] *adj* que crea adicción

addition [ə'dɪʃən] *n Math* adición *f*; *(increase)* aumento *m*; **an a. to the family** un nuevo miembro de la familia; **in a. to** además de

additional [ə'dɪʃənəl] *adj* adicional

additive ['ædɪtɪv] *n* aditivo *m*

address [ə'dres] **1** *n* (**a**) *(on letter)* dirección *f*, señas *fpl* (**b**) *(speech)* discurso *m*

2 *vt* (**a**) *(letter)* dirigir (**b**) *(speak to)* dirigirse (**to** a); **to a. the floor** tomar la palabra (**c**) *(use form of address to)* tratar de

adenoids ['ædɪnɔɪdz] *npl* vegetaciones *fpl* (adenoideas)

adept [ə'dept] **1** *adj* experto(a) (**at** en)

2 *n* experto(a) *m,f*

> 🔗 Note that the Spanish word **adepto** is a false friend and is never a translation for the English word **adept**. In Spanish, **adepto** means "follower, supporter".

adequate ['ædɪkwɪt] *adj (enough)* suficiente; *(satisfactory)* adecuado(a)

adhere [əd'hɪə(r)] *vi (stick)* pegarse (**to** a)

▸ **adhere to** *vt insep (policy)* adherirse a; *(contract)* cumplir con

adherent [əd'hɪərənt] *n* partidario(a) *m,f*

adhesive [əd'hi:sɪv] **1** *adj* adhesivo(a); *(sticky)* pegajoso(a); **a. tape** cinta adhesiva

2 *n* adhesivo *m*

ad hoc [æd'hɒk] *adj (remark)* improvisado(a); **an a. committee** un comité especial

ad infinitum [ædɪnfɪ'naɪtəm] *adv* hasta el infinito

adjacent [ə'dʒeɪsənt] *adj (building)* contiguo(a); *(land)* colindante; **a. to** contiguo(a) a

adjective ['ædʒɪktɪv] *n* adjetivo *m*

adjoining [ə'dʒɔɪnɪŋ] *adj* contiguo(a); *(land)* colindante; **the a. room** la habitación de al lado

adjourn [ə'dʒɜːn] **1** *vt (postpone)* aplazar; *(court)* levantar
  2 *vi* aplazarse (**until** hasta)

adjudicate [ə'dʒuːdɪkeɪt] *vt* juzgar

adjudicator [ə'dʒuːdɪkeɪtə(r)] *n* juez(a) *m,f*

adjust [ə'dʒʌst] **1** *vt (machine etc)* ajustar; *Fig (methods)* variar
  2 *vi (person)* adaptarse (**to** a)

adjustable [ə'dʒʌstəbəl] *adj* ajustable

adjustment [ə'dʒʌstmənt] *n* (**a**) *(to machine etc)* ajuste *m*; *(by person)* adaptación *f* (**b**) *(change)* modificación *f*

ad lib [æd'lɪb] **1** *adv (speak)* sin preparación; *(continue)* a voluntad
  2 *adj (speech)* improvisado(a)
  3 ad-lib *vi* improvisar

administer [əd'mɪnɪstə(r)] *vt (country)* gobernar; *(justice)* administrar

administration [ədmɪnɪ'streɪʃən] *n (of country)* gobierno *m*; *(of justice)* administración *f*; *(governing body)* dirección *f*

administrative [əd'mɪnɪstrətɪv] *adj* administrativo(a)

admirable [æd'mərəbəl] *adj* admirable

admiral ['ædmərəl] *n* almirante *m*

admiration [ædmə'reɪʃən] *n* admiración *f*

admire [əd'maɪə(r)] *vt* admirar

admirer [əd'maɪərə(r)] *n* admirador(a) *m,f*

admissible [əd'mɪsəbəl] *adj* admisible

admission [əd'mɪʃən] *n* (**a**) *(to school etc)* ingreso *m*; *(price)* entrada *f* (**b**) *(of fact)* reconocimiento *m*; *(confession)* confesión *f*

admit [əd'mɪt] *vt* (**a**) *(person)* dejar entrar; **to be admitted to hospital** ser ingresado(a) en el hospital (**b**) *(acknowledge)* reconocer; *(crime, guilt)* confesar

admittance [əd'mɪtəns] *n (entry)* entrada *f*

admittedly [əd'mɪtɪdlɪ] *adv* la verdad es que ...

admonish [əd'mɒnɪʃ] *vt* amonestar

ad nauseam [æd'nɔːzɪæm] *adv* hasta la saciedad

ado [ə'duː] *n* **without further a.** sin más

adolescence [ædə'lesəns] *n* adolescencia *f*

adolescent [ædə'lesənt] *n* adolescente *mf*

adopt [ə'dɒpt] *vt* adoptar; *(suggestion)* aceptar

adopted [ə'dɒptɪd] *adj* **a. child** hijo(a) *m,f* adoptivo(a)

adoption [ə'dɒpʃən] *n* adopción *f*; **country of a.** país adoptivo

adore [ə'dɔː(r)] *vt* adorar

adorn [ə'dɔːn] *vt* adornar

adornment [ə'dɔːnmənt] *n* adorno *m*

adrenalin [ə'drenəlɪn] *n* adrenalina *f*

Adriatic [eɪdrɪ'ætɪk] *adj* **the A. (Sea)** el (mar) Adriático

adrift [ə'drɪft] *adv* **to come a.** *(boat)* irse a la deriva; *(rope)* soltarse; *Fig* **to go a.** *(plans)* ir a la deriva

adult ['ædʌlt] **1** *adj (person)* adulto(a), mayor; *(film, education)* para adultos
  2 *n* adulto(a) *m,f*

adulterate [ə'dʌltəreɪt] *vt* adulterar

adulterer [ə'dʌltərə(r)] *n* adúltero *m*

adulteress [ə'dʌltrɪs] *n* adúltera *f*

adultery [ə'dʌltərɪ] *n* adulterio *m*

advance [əd'vɑːns] **1** *n* (**a**) *(movement)* avance *m*; *Fig (progress)* progreso *m*; **to have sth ready in a.** tener algo preparado de antemano; **to make advances (to)** *(person)* insinuarse a (**b**) *(loan)* anticipo *m*
  2 *adj (before time)* adelantado(a); *Cin & Th* **a. bookings** reservas *fpl* por adelantado
  3 *vt* (**a**) *(troops)* avanzar; *(time, date)* adelantar (**b**) *(idea)* proponer; *(opinion)* dar (**c**) *Fin (sum of money)* anticipar
  4 *vi (move forward)* avanzar, adelantarse; *(make progress)* hacer progresos; *(gain promotion)* ascender

advanced [əd'vɑːnst] *adj (developed)* avanzado(a); *(student)* adelantado(a); *(course)* superior; *Educ* **A. level** examen *m* superior de segunda enseñanza, ≃ COU *m*

advancement [əd'vɑːnsmənt] *n (progress)* adelanto *m*; *(promotion)* ascenso *m*

advantage [əd'vɑːntɪdʒ] *n* ventaja *f*; *(in tennis)* **a. Velasco** ventaja para Velasco; **to take a. of sb/sth** abusar de algn/aprovechar algo

advantageous [ædvən'teɪdʒəs] *adj* ventajoso(a)

advent ['ædvent] *n (arrival)* llegada *f*; *(of Christ)* advenimiento *m*; **A.** Adviento *m*

adventure [əd'ventʃə(r)] *n* aventura *f*; **a. sport** deporte *m* de aventura

adventurous [əd'ventʃərəs] *adj* aventurero(a)

adverb ['ædvɜːb] *n* adverbio *m*

adversary ['ædvəsərɪ] *n* adversario(a) *m,f*

adverse ['ædvɜːs] *adj (effect)* desfavorable; *(conditions)* adverso(a); *(winds)* contrario(a)

adversity [əd'vɜːsɪtɪ] *n* adversidad *f*

advert ['ædvɜːt] *n Fam* anuncio *m*

advertise ['ædvətaɪz] **1** *vt* anunciar
  2 *vi* hacer publicidad; *(in newspaper)* poner un anuncio; **to a. for sth/sb** buscar algo/a algn mediante un anuncio

advertisement [əd'vɜːtɪsmənt] *n* anuncio *m*; **advertisements** publicidad *f*

advertiser ['ædvətaɪzə(r)] *n* anunciante *mf*

advertising ['ædvətaɪzɪŋ] **1** *n* publicidad *f*, propaganda *f*; *(in newspaper)* anuncios *mpl*
  2 *adj* publicitario(a); **a. agency** agencia *f* de publicidad

advice [əd'vaɪs] *n* consejos *mpl*; **a piece of a.** un consejo; **to take legal a. on a matter** consultar el caso con un abogado; **to take sb's a.** seguir los consejos de algn

advisable [əd'vaɪzəbəl] *adj* aconsejable

advise [əd'vaɪz] *vt* aconsejar; *(on business etc)* asesorar; **I a. you to do it** te aconsejo que lo hagas

adviser [əd'vaɪzə(r)] *n* consejero(a) *m,f*; *(in business etc)* asesor(a) *m,f*

advisory [əd'vaɪzərɪ] *adj* asesor(a)

advocate 1 *n* ['ædvəkɪt] *Scot Jur* abogado(a) *m,f*; *(supporter)* defensor(a) *m,f*
2 *vt* ['ædvəkeɪt] *(reform)* abogar por; *(plan)* apoyar

aerial ['eərɪəl] **1** *adj* aéreo(a)
2 *n* antena *f*

aerobics [eə'rəʊbɪks] *n sing* aerobic *m*

aerodrome ['eərədrəʊm] *n Br* aeródromo *m*

aerodynamics [eərəʊdaɪ'næmɪks] *n sing* aerodinámica *f*

aeroplane ['eərəpleɪn] *n Br* avión *m*

aerosol ['eərəsɒl] *n* aerosol *m*

aerospace ['eərəʊspeɪs] *adj* aeroespacial

aesthetic [iːs'θetɪk] *adj* estético(a)

afar [ə'fɑː(r)] *adv* lejos; **from a.** desde lejos

affair [ə'feə(r)] *n (matter)* asunto *m*; *(event)* acontecimiento *m*; **that's my a.** eso es asunto mío; **business affairs** negocios *mpl*; **foreign affairs** asuntos exteriores; **love a.** aventura amorosa

affect [ə'fekt] *vt (person, health)* afectar; *(prices, future)* influir en; *(touch emotionally)* conmover

affected [ə'fektɪd] *adj* (**a**) *(unnatural)* afectado(a) (**b**) *(influenced)* influido(a) (**c**) *(touched emotionally)* conmovido(a) (**d**) *(pretended)* fingido(a)

affection [ə'fekʃən] *n* afecto *m*, cariño *m*

affectionate [ə'fekʃənɪt] *adj* cariñoso(a)

affidavit [æfɪ'deɪvɪt] *n* declaración escrita y jurada

affiliated [ə'fɪlɪeɪtɪd] *adj* afiliado(a); **to be/become a. (to** *or* **with)** afiliarse

affinity [ə'fɪnɪtɪ] *n* afinidad *f*; *(liking)* simpatía *f*

affirm [ə'fɜːm] *vt* afirmar, sostener

affirmation [æfə'meɪʃən] *n* afirmación *f*

affirmative [ə'fɜːmətɪv] **1** *adj* afirmativo(a)
2 *n* **he answered in the a.** contestó que sí

affix [ə'fɪks] *vt (stamp)* pegar

afflict [ə'flɪkt] *vt* afligir

affluence ['æflʊəns] *n* opulencia *f*

affluent ['æflʊənt] *adj (society)* opulento(a); *(person)* rico(a)

afford [ə'fɔːd] *vt* (**a**) *(be able to buy)* permitirse el lujo de; **I can't a. a new car** no puedo pagar un coche nuevo (**b**) *(be able to do)* permitirse; **you can't a. to miss the opportunity** no puedes perderte la ocasión

affront [ə'frʌnt] **1** *n* afrenta *f*
2 *vt* afrentar

afield [ə'fiːld] *adv* **far a.** muy lejos

afloat [ə'fləʊt] *adv* **to keep a.** mantenerse a flote

afoot [ə'fʊt] *adv* **there's a plan a.** hay un proyecto en marcha; **there's something strange a.** se está tramando algo

aforementioned [ə'fɔːmenʃənd], **aforesaid** [ə'fɔːsed] *adj* susodicho(a)

afraid [ə'freɪd] *adj* (**a**) **to be a.** tener miedo (**of sb** a algo; **of sth** de algo); **I'm a. of the** miedo (**b**) **I'm a. not** me temo que no; **I'm a. so** me temo que sí; **I'm a. you're wrong** me temo que estás equivocado(a)

afresh [ə'freʃ] *adv* de nuevo

Africa ['æfrɪkə] *n* Africa

African ['æfrɪkən] *adj & n* africano(a) *(m,f)*

Afro ['æfrəʊ] *adj & n Fam (hairstyle)* afro *(m)*

aft [ɑːft] *adv* en popa; **to go a.** ir en popa

after [ɑːftə(r)] **1** *adv* después; **soon a.** poco después; **the day a.** el día siguiente
2 *prep* (**a**) *(later)* después de; *US* **it's ten a. five** son las cinco y diez; **soon a. arriving** al poco rato de llegar; **the day a. tomorrow** pasado mañana
(**b**) *(behind)* detrás de, tras; **a. you!** ¡pase usted!; **they went in one a. the other** entraron uno tras otro; **the police are a. them** la policía anda tras ellos
(**c**) *(about)* por; **they asked a. you** preguntaron por ti; **what's he a.?** ¿qué pretende?
(**d**) **he takes a. his uncle** se parece a su tío; **she was named a. her grandmother** le llamaron como su abuela
3 *conj* después (de) que; **a. it happened** después de que ocurriera

after-effect [ɑːftərɪfekt] *n* efecto secundario

afterlife ['ɑːftəlaɪf] *n* vida *f* después de la muerte

aftermath ['ɑːftəmæθ] *n* secuelas *fpl*

afternoon [ɑːftə'nuːn] *n* tarde *f*; **good a.!** ¡buenas tardes!; **in the a.** por la tarde

afternoons [ɑːftə'nuːnz] *adv US* por las tardes

afters ['ɑːftəz] *npl Fam* postre *m*

after-sales service [ɑːftəseɪlz'sɜːvɪs] *n Com* servicio *m* posventa

aftershave (lotion) ['ɑːftəʃeɪv('ləʊʃən)] *n* loción *f* para después del afeitado

afterthought ['ɑːftəθɔːt] *n* ocurrencia *f* tardía

afterwards ['ɑːftəwədz] *adv* después, más tarde

again [ə'gen] *adv* (**a**) otra vez, de nuevo; **I tried a. and a.** lo intenté una y otra vez; **to do sth a.** volver a hacer algo; **never a.!** ¡nunca más!; **now and a.** de vez en cuando; **once a.** otra vez (**b**) *(besides)* además; **then a.** por otra parte

against [ə'genst] *prep* (**a**) *(touching)* contra (**b**) *(opposing)* contra, en contra (**c**); **a. the grain** a contrapelo; **it's a. the law** es ilegal (**c**) **as a.** en contraste con, comparado con

age [eɪdʒ] **1** *n* (**a**) edad *f*; **she's eighteen years of a.** tiene dieciocho años; **to be under a.** ser menor de edad; **to come of a.** llegar a la mayoría de edad; **a. limit** límite *m* de edad;

old a. vejez f (**b**) (period) época f; **the Iron A.** la Edad de Hierro (**c**) Fam (long time) eternidad f; **it's ages since I last saw her** hace siglos que no la veo
2 vt & vi envejecer

aged¹ [ˈeɪdʒd] adj de o a la edad de

aged² [ˈeɪdʒɪd] npl **the a.** los ancianos

agency [ˈeɪdʒənsɪ] n (**a**) Com agencia f (**b**) **by the a. of** por medio de

agenda [əˈdʒendə] n orden m del día

agent [ˈeɪdʒənt] n agente mf; (representative) representante mf

aggravate [ˈægrəveɪt] vt (worsen) agravar; (annoy) molestar

aggregate [ˈægrɪgɪt] n conjunto m; **on a.** en conjunto

aggression [əˈgreʃən] n agresión f

aggressive [əˈgresɪv] adj (violent) agresivo(a), violento(a); (dynamic) dinámico(a)

aggrieved [əˈgriːvd] adj apenado(a)

aghast [əˈgɑːst] adj espantado(a)

agile [ˈædʒaɪl] adj ágil

agitate [ˈædʒɪteɪt] **1** vt (shake) agitar; Fig (worry) perturbar
2 vi Pol **to a. against sth** hacer campaña en contra de algo

agitator [ˈædʒɪteɪtə(r)] n Pol agitador(a) m,f

AGM [eɪdʒiːˈem] n (abbr **annual general meeting**) junta f general anual

agnostic [ægˈnɒstɪk] n agnóstico(a) m,f

ago [əˈgəʊ] adv **a long time a.** hace mucho tiempo; **as long a. as 1910** ya en 1910; **a week a.** hace una semana; **how long a.?** ¿hace cuánto tiempo?

agog [əˈgɒg] adj ansioso(a)

agonizing [ˈægənaɪzɪŋ] adj (pain) atroz; (decision) desesperante

agony [ˈægənɪ] n dolor m muy fuerte; (anguish) angustia f; **he was in a. with his back** tenía un dolor insoportable de espalda

agree [əˈgriː] **1** vi (**a**) (be in agreement) estar de acuerdo; (reach agreement) ponerse de acuerdo; (consent) consentir; **to a. to do sth** consentir en hacer algo; **to a. with sb** estar de acuerdo con algn (**b**) (harmonize) (things) concordar, (people) congeniar; **onions don't a. with me** la cebolla no me sienta bien
2 vt acordar

agreeable [əˈgriːəbl] adj (pleasant) agradable; (person) simpático(a); (in agreement) de acuerdo

agreement [əˈgriːmənt] n (arrangement) acuerdo m; Com contrato m; **to reach an a.** llegar a un acuerdo

agricultural [ægrɪˈkʌltʃərəl] adj agrícola; (college) de agricultura

agriculture [ˈægrɪkʌltʃə(r)] n agricultura f

aground [əˈgraʊnd] adv **to run a.** encallar, varar

ahead [əˈhed] adv delante; (early) antes; **go a.!** ¡adelante!; **to be a.** llevar la ventaja; **to go a.** ir adelante; Fig **to go a. with sth** llevar algo

adelante; (start) comenzar algo; **to get a.** triunfar; **to look a.** pensar en el futuro

aid [eɪd] **1** n ayuda f; (rescue) auxilio m; **in a. of** a beneficio de; **to come to the a. of sb** acudir en ayuda de algn; **a. worker** cooperante mf
2 vt ayudar; **to a. and abet sb** ser cómplice de algn

aide [eɪd] n ayudante mf

AIDS [eɪdz] n (abbr **Acquired Immune Deficiency Syndrome**) sida m

ailing [ˈeɪlɪŋ] adj achacoso(a)

ailment [ˈeɪlmənt] n enfermedad f (leve), achaque m

aim [eɪm] **1** n (with weapon) puntería f; (target) propósito m
2 vt (gun) apuntar (**at** a or hacia); (attack, action) dirigir (**at** a or hacia)
▸ **aim at** vt insep (target) tirar para; **to a. at doing sth** tener pensado hacer algo
▸ **aim to** vt insep **to a. to do sth** tener la intención de hacer algo

aimless [ˈeɪmlɪs] adj sin objeto, sin propósito

aimlessly [ˈeɪmlɪslɪ] adv (wander) sin rumbo fijo

air [eə(r)] **1** n (**a**) aire m; **to travel by a.** viajar en avión; **to throw sth up in the a.** lanzar algo al aire; Fig **it's still in the a.** todavía queda por resolver; Aut **a. bag** airbag m; **a. base** base aérea; **a. bed** colchón m hinchable; **a. conditioning** aire acondicionado; **A. Force** Fuerzas Aéreas; **a. freshener** ambientador m; **a. gun** pistola f de aire comprimido; **a. hostess** azafata f; **a. letter** carta aérea; **a. pocket** bache m; **a. pressure** presión atmosférica; **a. raid** ataque aéreo; **a. terminal** terminal aérea; **a. traffic control** control m de tráfico aéreo; **a. traffic controller** controlador(a) m,f aéreo(a)
(**b**) Rad TV **to be on the a.** (programme) estar emitiendo; (person) estar transmitiendo
(**c**) (appearance) aspecto m
2 vt (bed, clothes) airear; (room) ventilar; Fig (grievance) airear; (knowledge) hacer alarde de

airborne [ˈeəbɔːn] adj (aircraft) en vuelo; (troops) aerotransportado(a)

air-conditioned [ˈeəkɒndɪʃənd] adj climatizado(a)

aircraft [ˈeəkrɑːft] n (pl **aircraft**) avión m; **a. carrier** portaviones m inv

airfield [ˈeəfiːld] n campo m de aviación

airlift [ˈeəlɪft] n puente aéreo

airline [ˈeəlaɪn] n línea aérea

airlock [ˈeəlɒk] n (in pipe) bolsa f de aire; (in spacecraft) esclusa f de aire

airmail [ˈeəmeɪl] n correo aéreo; **by a.** por avión

airplane [ˈeəpleɪn] n US avión m

airport [ˈeəpɔːt] n aeropuerto m; **a. tax** tasas fpl de aeropuerto

airsick [ˈeəsɪk] adj **to be a.** marearse en avión

airstrip ['eəstrɪp] *n* pista *f* de aterrizaje

airtight ['eətaɪt] *adj* hermético(a)

airy ['eəri] *adj* (**airier, airiest**) *(well-ventilated)* bien ventilado(a); *(vague, carefree)* ligero(a)

aisle [aɪl] *n (in church)* nave *f; (in theatre)* pasillo *m*

ajar [ə'dʒɑː(r)] *adj & adv* entreabierto(a)

akin [ə'kɪn] *adj* semejante

alacrity [ə'lækrɪti] *n* with a. con presteza

à la mode [ælə'məʊd] *adj US (dessert)* con helado

alarm [ə'lɑːm] **1** *n* (**a**) alarma *f;* **a. clock** despertador *m* (**b**) *(fear)* inquietud *f;* **to cause a.** provocar temor
　　2 *vt* alarmar

alas [ə'læs] *interj* ¡ay!, ¡ay de mí!

albatross ['ælbətrɒs] *n* albatros *m*

albeit [ɔːl'biːɪt] *conj* aunque, no obstante

album ['ælbəm] *n* álbum *m*

alcohol ['ælkəhɒl] *n* alcohol *m*

alcoholic [ælkə'hɒlɪk] *adj & n* alcohólico(a) *(m,f)*

alcopop ['ælkəʊpɒp] *n Br* refresco *m* con alcohol

alcove ['ælkəʊv] *n* hueco *m*

📖 Note that the Spanish word **alcoba** is a false friend and is never a translation for the English word **alcove**. In Spanish, **alcoba** means "bedroom".

---

ale [eɪl] *n* cerveza *f;* **brown/pale a.** cerveza negra/rubia

alert [ə'lɜːt] **1** *adj* alerta; *(lively)* despabilado(a)
　　2 *n* alerta *m;* **to be on the a.** estar alerta
　　3 *vt* **to a. sb to sth** avisar a algn de algo

A-level ['eɪlevəl] *n Br Educ (abbr Advanced level)* = examen final o diploma en una asignatura de los estudios preuniversitarios

algae ['ældʒiː] *npl* algas *fpl*

algebra ['ældʒɪbrə] *n* álgebra *f*

Algeria [æl'dʒɪərɪə] *n* Argelia

Algerian [æl'dʒɪərɪən] *adj & n* argelino(a) *(m,f)*

Algiers [æl'dʒɪəz] *n* Argel

alias ['eɪlɪəs] **1** *n* alias *m*
　　2 *adv* alias

alibi ['ælɪbaɪ] *n* coartada *f*

alien ['eɪlɪən] **1** *adj (foreign)* extranjero(a); *(from space)* extraterrestre; **a. to** ajeno(a) a
　　2 *n (foreigner)* extranjero(a) *m,f; (from space)* extraterrestre *mf*

alienate ['eɪlɪəneɪt] *vt* (**a**) **to a. sb** ofender a algn; **to a. oneself from sb** alejarse de algn (**b**) *Jur* enajenar

alight¹ [ə'laɪt] *adj (on fire)* ardiendo(a)

alight² [ə'laɪt] *vi (get off)* apearse (**from** de)

align [ə'laɪn] *vt* alinear

alike [ə'laɪk] **1** *adj (similar)* parecidos(as); *(the same)* iguales

---

　　2 *adv (in the same way)* de la misma manera, igualmente; **dressed a.** vestidos(as) iguales

alimony ['ælɪmənɪ] *n Jur* pensión alimenticia

alive [ə'laɪv] *adj* vivo(a); *Fig (teeming)* lleno(a) (**with** de); **to be a.** estar vivo(a)

alkaline ['ælkəlaɪn] *adj* alcalino(a)

all [ɔːl] **1** *adj* todo(a), todos(as); **a. year** *(durante)* todo el año; **a. kinds of things** todo tipo de cosas; **at a. hours** a todas horas; **at a. times** siempre; **she works a. the time** siempre está trabajando; **a. six of us were there** los seis estábamos allí
　　2 *pron* todo(a), todos(as); **after a.** al fin y al cabo; **a. of his work** toda su obra; **a. of us** todos(as) nosotros(as); **a. who saw it** todos los que lo vieron; **a. you can do is wait** lo único que puedes hacer es esperar; **I don't like it at a.** no me gusta en absoluto; **is that a.?** ¿eso es todo?; **most of** *or* **above a.** sobre todo; **once and for a.** de una vez por todas; **thanks – not at a.** gracias – de nada; **a. in a.** en conjunto; **that's a.** ya está; **the score was one a.** empataron a uno
　　3 *adv* **a. by myself** completamente solo(a); **a. at once** *(suddenly)* de repente; *(altogether)* de una vez; **a. the better** tanto mejor; **a. the same** de todos modos; **he knew a. along** lo sabía desde el principio; **if it's a. the same to you** si no te importa; **it's a. but impossible** es casi imposible; **I'm not a. that tired** no estoy tan cansado(a) como eso
　　4 *n* **to give one's a.** darse por completo

Allah ['ælə] *n* Alá *m*

allay [ə'leɪ] *vt (fears, doubts)* apaciguar

allegation [ælɪ'geɪʃən] *n* alegato *m*

allege [ə'ledʒ] *vt* sostener, pretender (**that** que)

allegedly [ə'ledʒɪdlɪ] *adv* supuestamente

allegiance [ə'liːdʒəns] *n* lealtad *f*

allergic [ə'lɜːdʒɪk] *adj* alérgico(a) (**to** a)

allergy ['ælədʒɪ] *n* alergia *f*

alleviate [ə'liːvɪeɪt] *vt (pain)* aliviar

alley ['ælɪ] *n* callejón *m*

alliance [ə'laɪəns] *n* alianza *f*

allied ['ælaɪd] *adj* aliado(a)

alligator ['ælɪgeɪtə(r)] *n* caimán *m*

all-in ['ɔːlɪn] *adj (price)* todo incluido; *Sport* **a. wrestling** lucha *f* libre

alliteration [əlɪtə'reɪʃən] *n* aliteración *f*

all-night ['ɔːlnaɪt] *adj (café etc)* abierto(a) toda la noche; *(vigil)* que dura toda la noche

allocate ['æləkeɪt] *vt* destinar (**to** para)

allocation [ælə'keɪʃən] *n* (**a**) *(distribution)* asignación *f* (**b**) *(amount allocated)* cuota *f*

allot [ə'lɒt] *vt* asignar

allotment [ə'lɒtmənt] *n* (**a**) *(distribution)* asignación *f* (**b**) *(land)* parcela *f*

all-out ['ɔːlaʊt] **1** *adj* (**a**) *(effort)* supremo(a); *(attack)* concentrado(a)
　　2 **all out** *adv* **to go all out to do sth** emplearse a fondo para hacer algo

allow [əˈlaʊ] *vt* (**a**) *(permit)* permitir; *(a request)* acceder a; **to a. sb to do sth** permitir que algn haga algo (**b**) *(allot) (time)* dejar; *(money)* destinar
▸ **allow for** *vt insep* tener en cuenta

allowance [əˈlaʊəns] *n (payment)* pensión *f*, subvención *f*; *(discount)* descuento *m*; **to make allowances for sb/sth** disculpar a algn/tener algo en cuenta; **tax a.** desgravación *f* fiscal; **travel a.** dietas *fpl* de viaje

alloy [ˈælɔɪ] *n* aleación *f*

all right [ɔːlˈraɪt] **1** *adj (okay)* bien; **thank you very much – that's a.** muchas gracias – de nada
   2 *adv* (**a**) *(well)* bien (**b**) *(definitely)* sin duda (**c**) *(okay)* de acuerdo, vale

all-round [ˈɔːlraʊnd] *adj (athlete etc)* completo(a)

all-terrain [ɔːltəˈreɪn] *adj* **a. vehicle** todoterreno *m*

all-time [ˈɔːltaɪm] *adj* **an a. low** una baja sin antecedente; **the a. greats** los grandes de siempre

allude [əˈluːd] *vi* **to a. to** aludir a

alluring [əˈljʊərɪŋ] *adj* atractivo(a)

allusion [əˈluːʒən] *n* alusión *f*

ally [ˈælaɪ] **1** *n* aliado(a) *m,f*
   2 *vt* **to a. oneself to/with sb** aliarse a/con algn

almighty [ɔːlˈmaɪtɪ] **1** *adj (all-powerful)* todopoderoso(a)
   2 *n* **the A.** El Todopoderoso

almond [ˈɑːmənd] *n* almendra *f*

almost [ˈɔːlməʊst] *adv* casi

alms [ɑːmz] *npl* limosna *f*

aloft [əˈlɒft] *adv* arriba

alone [əˈləʊn] **1** *adj* solo(a); **can I speak to you a.?** ¿puedo hablar contigo a solas?; **let a.** ni mucho menos; **leave it a.!** ¡no lo toques!; **leave me a.** déjame en paz; **to be a.** estar solo(a)
   2 *adv* solamente, sólo

along [əˈlɒŋ] **1** *adv* **come a.!** ¡anda, ven!; **he'll be a. in ten minutes** llegará dentro de diez minutos; **a. with** junto con
   2 *prep (the length of)* a lo largo de; **to walk a. the street** andar por la calle; **it's just a. the street** está un poco más abajo

alongside [əˈlɒŋsaɪd] **1** *adv Naut* de costado
   2 *prep* al lado de

aloof [əˈluːf] **1** *adj (person)* distante
   2 *adv* **to keep oneself a. (from)** mantenerse a distancia (de)

aloud [əˈlaʊd] *adv* en voz alta

alphabet [ˈælfəbet] *n* alfabeto *m*

alphabetical [ælfəˈbetɪkəl] *adj* alfabético(a)

alphabetically [ælfəˈbetɪkəlɪ] *adv* por orden alfabético

alpine [ˈælpaɪn] *adj* alpino(a)

Alps [ælps] *npl* **the A.** los Alpes

already [ɔːlˈredɪ] *adv* ya

alright [ɔːlˈraɪt] *adj & adv* = **all right**

Alsatian [ælˈseɪʃən] *n* pastor *m* alemán

also [ˈɔːlsəʊ] *adv* también, además

also-ran [ˈɔːlsəʊræn] *n Fam (person)* segundón(ona) *m,f*

altar [ˈɔːltə(r)] *n* altar *m*

alter [ˈɔːltə(r)] **1** *vt (plan)* cambiar, retocar; *(project)* modificar; *(clothing)* arreglar; *(timetable)* revisar
   2 *vi* cambiar, cambiarse

alteration [ɔːltəˈreɪʃən] *n (to plan)* cambio *m*; *(to project)* modificación *f*; *(to clothing)* arreglo *m*; *(to timetable)* revisión *f*; **alterations** *(to building)* reformas *fpl*

alternate 1 *adj* [ɔːlˈtɜːnɪt] alterno(a); **on a. days** cada dos días
   2 *vt* [ˈɔːltəneɪt] alternar

alternately [ɔːlˈtɜːnɪtlɪ] *adv* **a. hot and cold** ahora caliente, ahora frío

alternative [ɔːlˈtɜːnətɪv] **1** *adj* alternativo(a)
   2 *n* alternativa *f*; **I have no a. but to accept** no tengo más remedio que aceptar

alternatively [ɔːlˈtɜːnətɪvlɪ] *adv* o bien; **a., you could walk** o bien podrías ir andando

alternator [ˈɔːltəneɪtə(r)] *n Aut* alternador *m*

although [ɔːlˈðəʊ] *conj* aunque

altitude [ˈæltɪtjuːd] *n* altitud *f*

alto [ˈæltəʊ] *adj & n (male singer, instrument)* alto *(m)*; *(female singer)* contralto *(f)*

altogether [ɔːltəˈgeðə(r)] *adv (in total)* en conjunto, en total; *(completely)* completamente, del todo

altruism [ˈæltruːɪzəm] *n* altruismo *m*

aluminium [æljʊˈmɪnɪəm], *US* **aluminum** [əˈluːmɪnəm] *n* aluminio *m*

alumnus [əˈlʌmnəs] *n (pl* **alumni** [əˈlʌmnaɪ]) *US* antiguo alumno

always [ˈɔːlweɪz] *adv* siempre

AM [eɪˈem] *Rad (abbr* **amplitude modulation**) AM

am [æm] *1st person sing pres of* **be**

a.m. [eɪˈem] *(abbr* **ante meridiem**) a.m., de la mañana

amalgamate [əˈmælgəmeɪt] **1** *vt (metals)* amalgamar
   2 *vi (metals)* amalgamarse; *(companies)* fusionarse

amalgamation [əmælgəˈmeɪʃən] *n* fusión *f*

amass [əˈmæs] *vt (money)* amontonar; *(information)* acumular

amateur [ˈæmətə(r)] **1** *n* amateur *mf*, aficionado(a) *m,f*
   2 *adj* aficionado(a); *Pej (work etc)* chapucero(a)

amateurish [ˈæmətərɪʃ] *adj* chapucero(a)

amaze [əˈmeɪz] *vt* asombrar, pasmar; **to be amazed at sth** quedarse pasmado(a) de algo

amazement [əˈmeɪzmənt] *n* asombro *m*, sorpresa *f*

amazing [əˈmeɪzɪŋ] *adj* asombroso(a), increíble

ambassador [æmˈbæsədə(r)] *n* embajador(a) *m,f*

amber ['æmbə(r)] **1** n ámbar m
2 adj ambarino(a); (traffic light) amarillo(a)
ambiguity [æmbɪ'gjuːɪtɪ] n ambigüedad f
ambiguous [æm'bɪgjʊəs] adj ambiguo(a)
ambition [æm'bɪʃən] n ambición f
ambitious [æm'bɪʃəs] adj ambicioso(a)
ambivalent [æm'bɪvələnt] adj ambivalente
amble ['æmbəl] vi deambular
ambulance ['æmbjʊləns] n ambulancia f; **a. man** ambulanciero m
ambush ['æmbʊʃ] **1** n emboscada f
2 vt tender una emboscada a; Fig atacar por sorpresa
amen [ɑː'men] interj amén
amenable [ə'miːnəbəl] adj **I'd be quite a. to doing that** no me importaría nada hacer eso; **a. to reason** razonable
amend [ə'mend] vt (law) enmendar; (error) subsanar
amendment [ə'mendmənt] n enmienda f
amends [ə'mendz] npl **to make a. to sb for sth** compensar a algn por algo
amenities [ə'miːnɪtɪz] npl comodidades fpl
America [ə'merɪkə] n (continent) América f; (USA) (los) Estados Unidos; **South A.** América del Sur, Sudamérica f
American [ə'merɪkən] adj & n americano(a) (m,f); (of USA) norteamericano(a) (m,f), estadounidense (mf)
amiable ['eɪmɪəbəl] adj amable, afable
amicable ['æmɪkəbəl] adj amistoso(a)
amid(st) ['æmɪd(st)] prep entre, en medio de
amiss [ə'mɪs] adj & adv mal; **there's sth a.** algo anda mal; **to take sth a.** tomar algo a mal
ammonia [ə'məʊnɪə] n amoníaco m
ammunition [æmjʊ'nɪʃən] n municiones fpl
amnesia [æm'niːʒə] n amnesia f
amnesty ['æmnɪstɪ] n amnistía f
amok [ə'mɒk] adv Fig **to run a.** (child) desmadrarse; (inflation etc) dispararse
among(st) [ə'mʌŋ(st)] prep entre
amoral [eɪ'mɒrəl] adj amoral
amorous ['æmərəs] adj cariñoso(a)
amorphous [ə'mɔːfəs] adj amorfo(a)
amount [ə'maʊnt] n cantidad f; (of money) suma f; (of bill) importe m
▶ **amount to** vt insep ascender a; Fig equivaler a
amp [æmp], **ampère** ['æmpeə(r)] n amperio m
amphetamine [æm'fetəmiːn] n anfetamina f
amphibian [æm'fɪbɪən] adj & n anfibio(a) (m)
amphibious [æm'fɪbɪəs] adj anfibio(a)
amphitheatre ['æmfɪθɪətə(r)] n anfiteatro m
ample ['æmpəl] adj (enough) bastante; (more than enough) abundante; (large) amplio(a)
amplifier ['æmplɪfaɪə(r)] n amplificador m
amputate ['æmpjʊteɪt] vt amputar
amuck [ə'mʌk] adv = amok
amuse [ə'mjuːz] vt divertir, entretener

amusement [ə'mjuːzmənt] n (enjoyment) diversión f; (laughter) risa f; (pastime) pasatiempo m; **a. arcade** salón m de juegos; **a. park** parque m de atracciones
amusing [ə'mjuːzɪŋ] adj divertido(a)
an [æn, unstressed ən] see **a**
anabolic steroid [ænəbɒlɪk'stɪərɔɪd] n esteroide m anabolizante
anaemia [ə'niːmɪə] n anemia f
anaemic [ə'niːmɪk] adj anémico(a); Fig (weak) débil
anaesthetic [ænɪs'θetɪk] n anestesia f
anaesthetist [ə'niːsθətɪst] n anestesista mf
analog(ue) ['ænəlɒg] n análogo m; **a computer** ordenador analógico, Am computadora analógica; **a. watch** reloj m de agujas
analogy [ə'nælədʒɪ] n analogía f
analyse ['ænəlaɪz] vt analizar
analysis [ə'nælɪsɪs] n (pl **analyses** [ə'nælɪsiːz]) análisis m inv
analyst ['ænəlɪst] n analista mf; (psychoanalyst) psicoanalista mf
analytic(al) [ænə'lɪtɪk(əl)] adj analítico(a)
analyze ['ænəlaɪz] vt US = **analyse**
anarchist ['ænəkɪst] n anarquista mf
anarchy ['ænəkɪ] n anarquía f
anathema [ə'næθəmə] n **the very idea was a. to him** le repugnaba sólo de pensarlo
anatomy [ə'nætəmɪ] n anatomía f
ancestor ['ænsestə(r)] n antepasado m
anchor ['æŋkə(r)] **1** n Naut ancla f; Fig áncora f; **to drop a.** echar el ancla; **to weigh a.** zarpar
2 vt Naut anclar; Fig (fix securely) sujetar
3 vi anclar
anchovy ['æntʃəvɪ] n anchoa f
ancient ['eɪnʃənt] adj antiguo(a)
ancillary [æn'sɪlərɪ] adj & n auxiliar (mf)
and [ænd, unstressed ənd, ən] conj y; (before i-, hi-) e; **a hundred a. one** ciento uno; **a. so on** etcétera; **Bill a. Pat** Bill y Pat; **Chinese a. Indian** chino e indio; **come a. see us** ven a vernos; **four a. a half** cuatro y medio; **she cried a. cried** no paró de llorar; **try a. help me** trata de ayudarme; **wait a. see** espera a ver; **worse a. worse** cada vez peor
Andalusia [ændə'luːzɪə] n Andalucía
Andalusian [ændə'luːzɪən] adj andaluz(a)
Andes ['ændiːz] npl **the A.** los Andes
Andorra [æn'dɔːrə] n Andorra
anecdote ['ænɪkdəʊt] n anécdota f
anemia [ə'niːmɪə] n US = **anaemia**
anesthetic [ænɪs'θetɪk] n US = **anaesthetic**
angel ['eɪndʒəl] n ángel m
anger ['æŋgə(r)] **1** n cólera f
2 vt enojar
angina [æn'dʒaɪnə] n angina f (de pecho)
angle ['æŋgəl] n ángulo m; Fig punto m de vista
angler ['æŋglə(r)] n pescador(a) m,f de caña
Anglican ['æŋglɪkən] adj & n anglicano(a) (m,f)
Anglo-Saxon [æŋgləʊ'sæksən] adj & n

anglosajón(ona) *(m,f)*
Angola [ænˈɡəʊlə] *n* Angola
angrily [ˈæŋɡrɪlɪ] *adv* furiosamente
angry [ˈæŋɡrɪ] *adj* (**angrier, angriest**) *(person etc)* enfadado(a); *(voice)* airado(a); **to get a. with sb about sth** enfadarse con algn por algo
anguish [ˈæŋɡwɪʃ] *n* angustia *f*
angular [ˈæŋɡjʊlə(r)] *adj (shape)* angular; *(face)* anguloso(a)
animal [ˈænɪməl] **1** *adj* animal
     2 *n* animal *m*; *Fig* bestia *f*
animate 1 *adj* [ˈænɪmɪt] vivo(a)
     2 *vt* [ˈænɪmeɪt] animar; *Fig* estimular
animated [ˈænɪmeɪtɪd] *adj (lively)* animado(a)
animosity [ænɪˈmɒsɪtɪ] *n* animosidad *f*
aniseed [ˈænɪsiːd] *n* anís *m*
ankle [ˈæŋkəl] *n* tobillo *m*; **a. boots** botines *mpl*; **a. socks** calcetines cortos
annex [əˈneks] *vt (territory)* anexionar
annexe, US annex [ˈæneks] *n (building)* (edificio *m*) anexo *m*
annihilate [əˈnaɪəleɪt] *vt* aniquilar
anniversary [ænɪˈvɜːsərɪ] *n* aniversario *m*; **wedding a.** aniversario de bodas
announce [əˈnaʊns] *vt* anunciar; *(news)* comunicar; *(fact)* hacer saber
announcement [əˈnaʊnsmənt] *n* anuncio *m*; *(news)* comunicación *f*; *(statement)* declaración *f*
announcer [əˈnaʊnsə(r)] *n TV & Rad* locutor(a) *m,f*
annoy [əˈnɔɪ] *vt* molestar, fastidiar; **to get annoyed** enfadarse, molestarse
annoyance [əˈnɔɪəns] *n (feeling)* enojo *m*; *(thing)* molestia *f*, fastidio *m*
annoying [əˈnɔɪɪŋ] *adj* molesto(a), fastidioso(a)
annual [ˈænjʊəl] **1** *adj* anual
     2 *n (book)* anuario *m*; *(plant)* anual *m*
annually [ˈænjʊəlɪ] *adv* anualmente
annul [əˈnʌl] *vt* anular
annulment [əˈnʌlmənt] *n* anulación *f*
anomaly [əˈnɒməlɪ] *n* anomalía *f*
anonymity [ænəˈnɪmɪtɪ] *n* anonimato *m*
anonymous [əˈnɒnɪməs] *adj* anónimo(a)
anorak [ˈænəræk] *n* anorak *m*
anorexia [ænəˈreksɪə] *n* anorexia *f*
another [əˈnʌðə(r)] **1** *adj* otro(a); **a. one** otro(a); **without a. word** sin más
     2 *pron* otro(a); **have a.** toma otro(a); **to love one a.** quererse el uno al otro
Ansaphone® [ˈɑːnsəfəʊn] *n* mensáfono *m*
answer [ˈɑːnsə(r)] **1** *n (to letter etc)* contestación *f*; *(to question)* respuesta *f*; *(to problem)* solución *f*; **in a. to your letter** contestando a su carta; **there's no a.** *(on telephone)* no contestan; *(at door)* no abren
     2 *vt* contestar a; *(problem)* resolver; *(door)* abrir; *(phone)* contestar
     3 *vi* contestar, responder

▸ **answer back** *vi* replicar; **don't a. back!** ¡no seas respondón!
▸ **answer for** *vt insep* responder de; **he's got a lot to a. for** es responsable de muchas cosas
▸ **answer to** *vt insep (name)* responder a; *(description)* corresponder a
answerable [ˈɑːnsərəbəl] *adj* **to be a. to sb for sth** ser responsable ante algn de algo
answering machine [ˈɑːnsərɪŋməʃiːn] *n* contestador automático
ant [ænt] *n* hormiga *f*; **a. hill** hormiguero *m*
antagonism [ænˈtæɡənɪzəm] *n* antagonismo *m* (**between** entre), hostilidad *f* (**towards** hacia)
antagonize [ænˈtæɡənaɪz] *vt* enemistar, malquistar
Antarctic [ænˈtɑːktɪk] **1** *adj* antártico(a); **A. Ocean** océano Antártico
     2 *n* **the A.** la Antártida
Antarctica [ænˈtɑːktɪkə] *n* Antártida
antecedent [æntɪˈsiːdənt] *n* antecedente *m*
antelope [ˈæntɪləʊp] *n* antílope *m*
antenatal [æntɪˈneɪtəl] *adj* antenatal; *(clinic)* prenatal
antenna [ænˈtenə] *n* (**a**) *(pl* antennae [ænˈteniː]) *(of animal, insect)* antena *f* (**b**) *(pl* antennas) *TV & Rad* antena *f*
anthem [ˈænθəm] *n* motete *m*; **national a.** himno *m* nacional
anthology [ænˈθɒlədʒɪ] *n* antología *f*
anthracite [ˈænθrəsaɪt] *n* antracita *f*
anthropology [ænθrəˈpɒlədʒɪ] *n* antropología *f*
anti-aircraft [æntɪˈeəkrɑːft] *adj* antiaéreo(a)
antibiotic [æntɪbaɪˈɒtɪk] *n* antibiótico *m*
antibody [ˈæntɪbɒdɪ] *n* anticuerpo *m*
anticipate [ænˈtɪsɪpeɪt] *vt* (**a**) *(expect)* esperar (**b**) *(predict)* prever; *(get ahead of)* anticiparse a, adelantarse a
anticipation [æntɪsɪˈpeɪʃən] *n (expectation)* esperanza *f*; *(expectancy)* ilusión *f*
anticlimax [æntɪˈklaɪmæks] *n (disappointment)* decepción *f*
anticlockwise [æntɪˈklɒkwaɪz] *adv Br* en sentido opuesto al de las agujas del reloj
antics [ˈæntɪks] *npl* payasadas *fpl*; *(naughtiness)* travesuras *fpl*
anticyclone [æntɪˈsaɪkləʊn] *n* anticiclón *m*
antidote [ˈæntɪdəʊt] *n* antídoto *m*
antifreeze [ˈæntɪfriːz] *n* anticongelante *m*
antihistamine [æntɪˈhɪstəmɪn] *n* antihistamínico *m*
antinuclear [æntɪˈnjuːklɪə(r)] *adj* antinuclear
antipathy [ænˈtɪpəθɪ] *n* antipatía *f* (**to** a)
antiquated [ˈæntɪkweɪtɪd] *adj* anticuado(a)
antique [ænˈtiːk] **1** *adj* antiguo(a)
     2 *n* antigüedad *f*; **a. dealer** anticuario(a) *m,f*; **a. shop** tienda *f* de antigüedades
antiquity [ænˈtɪkwɪtɪ] *n* antigüedad *f*
anti-Semitism [æntɪˈsemɪtɪzəm] *n* antisemitismo *m*

antiseptic [æntɪ'septɪk] *adj & n* antisépti-co(a) *(m)*

antisocial [æntɪ'sɔʊʃəl] *adj (delinquent)* anti-social; *(unsociable)* insociable

antithesis [æn'tɪθɪsɪs] *n* antítesis *f*

antivirus ['æntɪ'vaɪrəs] *adj* Comput *(pro-gram, software)* antivirus

antler ['æntlə(r)] *n* cuerna *f*; **antlers** corna-menta *f*

Antwerp ['æntwɜ:p] *n* Amberes

anus ['eɪnəs] *n* ano *m*

anvil ['ænvɪl] *n* yunque *m*

anxiety [æŋ'zaɪtɪ] *n (concern)* inquietud *f*; *(worry)* preocupación *f*; *(fear)* angustia *f*; *(eagerness)* ansia *f*

anxious ['æŋkʃəs] *adj (concerned)* inquie-to(a); *(worried)* preocupado(a); *(fearful)* an-gustiado(a); *(eager)* ansioso(a); **to be a. about sth** estar preocupado(a) por algo

any ['enɪ] **1** *adj (in questions, conditionals)* al-gún(una); *(in negative clauses)* ningún(una); *(no matter which)* cualquier(a); *(every)* todo(a); **a. doctor will say the same** cual-quier médico te dirá lo mismo; **are there a. seats left?** ¿quedan plazas?; **at a. moment** en cualquier momento; **have you a. apples?** ¿tie-nes manzanas?; **have you a. money?** ¿tienes (algo de) dinero?; **I don't have a. time** no tengo tiempo; **in a. case** de todas formas

2 *pron (in questions)* alguno(a); *(in negative clauses)* ninguno(a); *(no matter which)* cual-quiera; **do they have a.?** ¿tienen alguno?; **I don't want a.** no quiero ninguno(a); **I need some paper, have you a.?** necesito papel, ¿tienes?; **you can have a. (one)** coge el/la que quieras

3 *adv* **is there a. more?** ¿hay más?; **I used to like it, but not a. more/longer** antes me gustaba pero ya no; **is he a. better?** ¿está mejor?

anybody ['enɪbɒdɪ] *pron (in questions, con-ditionals)* alguien, alguno(a); *(in negative clauses)* nadie, ninguno(a); *(no matter who)* cualquiera; **a. but me** cualquiera menos yo; **bring a. you like** trae a quien quieras; **do you see a. over there?** ¿ves a alguien allí?; **I can't find a.** no encuentro a nadie

anyhow ['enɪhaʊ] *adv* **(a)** *(in spite of that)* en todo caso, de todas formas; *(changing the subject)* bueno, pues **(b)** *(carelessly)* desor-denadamente, de cualquier modo *or* forma

anyone ['enɪwʌn] *pron* = **anybody**

anyplace ['enɪpleɪs] *adv US* = **anywhere**

anything ['enɪθɪŋ] **1** *pron (in questions, con-ditionals)* algo, alguna cosa; *(in negative clauses)* nada; *(no matter what)* cualquier cosa; **a. but that** cualquier cosa menos eso; **a. else?** ¿algo más?; **can I do a. for you?** ¿puedo ayudarte en algo?; **hardly a.** casi nada; **if a., I'd buy the big one** de comprar uno compraría el grande; **to run/work like a.** correr/trabajar a más no poder

2 *adv* **is this a. like what you wanted?** ¿viene a ser éste lo que querías?

anyway ['enɪweɪ] *adv* = **anyhow** (**a**)

anywhere ['enɪweə(r)] *adv* (**a**) *(in questions, conditionals)* *(situation)* en alguna parte; *(movement)* a alguna parte; **could it be a. else?** ¿podría estar en otro sitio? (**b**) *(in negative clauses)* *(situation)* en ninguna par-te; *(movement)* a ninguna parte; *(no matter where)* dondequiera, en cualquier parte; **go a. you like** ve a donde quieras; **we aren't a. near finished** no hemos terminado ni mucho menos

apart [ə'pɑ:t] *adv* (**a**) aparte; **to fall a.** desha-cerse; **to take sth a.** desmontar algo (**b**) *(distant)* alejado(a); *(separate)* separado(a); **to be poles a.** ser polos opuestos; **you can't tell the twins a.** no se puede distinguir los mellizos el uno del otro (**c**) **a. from** aparte de

apartheid [ə'pɑ:theɪt] *n* apartheid *m*

apartment [ə'pɑ:tmənt] *n (large room)* salón *m*; *US (flat)* piso *m*, apartamento *m*; **a. block** bloque *m* de pisos

apathetic [æpə'θetɪk] *adj* apático(a)

apathy ['æpəθɪ] *n* apatía *f*

ape [eɪp] **1** *n* mono *m*

2 *vt* imitar, copiar

apéritif [ə'perɪti:f] *n* aperitivo *m*

aperture ['æpətʃə(r)] *n (hole, crack)* resqui-cio *m*, rendija *f*; Phot abertura *f*

apex ['eɪpeks] *n (of triangle)* vértice *m*; Fig cumbre *f*

aphrodisiac [æfrə'dɪzɪæk] *n* afrodisíaco *m*

apiece [ə'pi:s] *adv* cada uno(a)

aplomb [ə'plɒm] *n* aplomo *m*

apocalypse [ə'pɒkəlɪps] *n* apocalipsis *m inv*

apolitical [eɪpə'lɪtɪkəl] *adj* apolítico(a)

apologetic [əpɒlə'dʒetɪk] *adj (remorseful)* de disculpa; **he was very a.** pidió mil perdo-nes

apologetically [əpɒlə'dʒetɪklɪ] *adv* discul-pándose, pidiendo perdón

apologize [ə'pɒlədʒaɪz] *vi (say sorry)* discul-parse; **they apologized to us for the delay** se disculparon con nosotros por el retraso

apology [ə'pɒlədʒɪ] *n* disculpa *f*, excusa *f*; Fam **what an a. for a meal!** ¡vaya birria de comida!

apoplectic [æpə'plektɪk] *adj* Med apopléc-ti-co(a); Fam **to be a. with rage** estar furioso(a)

apostle [ə'pɒsəl] *n* apóstol *m*

apostrophe [ə'pɒstrəfɪ] *n* apóstrofo *m*

appal, *US* **appall** [ə'pɔ:l] *vt* horrorizar; **to be appalled by sth** quedar horrorizado(a) por algo

appalling [ə'pɔ:lɪŋ] *adj (horrifying)* horroro-so(a); Fam *(very bad)* pésimo(a), fatal

apparatus [æpə'reɪtəs] *n* aparato *m*; *(equip-ment)* equipo *m*

apparent [ə'pærənt] *adj (obvious)* evidente; *(seeming)* aparente; **to become a.** ponerse de manifiesto

apparently [ə'pærəntlɪ] *adv (seemingly)* por lo visto

apparition [æpə'rɪʃən] *n* aparición *f*

appeal [ə'piːl] **1** *n* (**a**) *(request)* solicitud *f*; *(plea)* súplica *f* (**b**) *(attraction)* atractivo *m*; *(interest)* interés *m* (**c**) *Jur* apelación *f*

2 *vi* (**a**) *(plead)* rogar, suplicar (**to** a); **to a. for help** solicitar ayuda (**b**) *(attract)* atraer; *(interest)* interesar; **it doesn't a. to me** no me dice nada (**c**) *Jur* apelar

appealing [ə'piːlɪŋ] *adj (moving)* conmovedor(a); *(attractive)* atractivo(a); *(tempting)* atrayente

appear [ə'pɪə(r)] *vi* (**a**) *(become visible)* aparecer; *(publicly)* presentarse; *(on stage)* actuar; **to a. before a court** comparecer ante un tribunal; **to a. on television** salir en la televisión (**b**) *(seem)* parecer; **he appears relaxed** parece relajado; **so it appears** según parece

appearance [ə'pɪərəns] *n* (**a**) *(becoming visible)* aparición *f*; *(publicly)* presentación *f*; *(on stage)* actuación *f*; *(before court)* comparecencia *f*; *(of book etc)* publicación *f*; **to put in an a.** hacer acto de presencia (**b**) *(look)* apariencia *f*, aspecto *m*; **to all appearances** al parecer

appease [ə'piːz] *vt* apaciguar; *(curiosity)* satisfacer

appeasement [ə'piːzmənt] *n Pol* entreguismo *m*

appendices [ə'pendɪsiːz] *pl of* **appendix**

appendicitis [əpendɪ'saɪtɪs] *n* apendicitis *f*

appendix [ə'pendɪks] *n (pl* **appendices***)* apéndice *m*

appetite ['æpɪtaɪt] *n* apetito *m*; *Fig* deseo *m*

appetizer [ə'pɪtaɪzə(r)] *n (drink)* aperitivo *m*; *(snack)* tapa *f*, pincho *m*

applaud [ə'plɔːd] *vt & vi* aplaudir

applause [ə'plɔːz] *n* aplausos *mpl*

apple ['æpəl] *n* manzana *f*; **a. tree** manzano *m*

appliance [ə'plaɪəns] *n* dispositivo *m*

applicable [ə'plɪkəbəl] *adj* aplicable

applicant ['æplɪkənt] *n (for post)* candidato(a) *m,f*; *(to court, for tickets)* solicitante *mf*

application [æplɪ'keɪʃən] *n* (**a**) *(of cream)* aplicación *f* (**b**) *(for post etc)* solicitud *f*; **a. form** solicitud; **job a.** solicitud de empleo (**c**) *(effort)* aplicación *f*; **she lacks a.** no se aplica

applied [ə'plaɪd] *adj* aplicado(a)

apply [ə'plaɪ] **1** *vt* aplicar; *(brake)* echar; *(law)* recurrir a; *(force)* usar; **to a. oneself to** dedicarse a

2 *vi* (**a**) *(refer)* aplicarse (**to** a) (**b**) *(for job)* presentar una solicitud; *(for information, to court)* presentar una petición

▸ **apply for** *vt insep (post, information)* solicitar; *(tickets)* pedir

appoint [ə'pɔɪnt] *vt (person)* nombrar; *(time, place etc)* fijar, señalar

appointment [ə'pɔɪntmənt] *n* (**a**) *(to post)* nombramiento *m*; *(post)* cargo *m* (**b**) *(meeting)* cita *f*; **to make an a. with** citarse con; *(at doctor's)* pedir hora a

apportion [ə'pɔːʃən] *vt Fig (blame)* echar

appraisal [ə'preɪzəl] *n* evaluación *f*

appreciable [ə'priːʃəbəl] *adj (difference)* apreciable; *(sum)* importante

appreciate [ə'priːʃɪeɪt] **1** *vt* (**a**) *(be thankful for)* agradecer (**b**) *(understand)* entender (**c**) *(value)* apreciar, valorar

2 *vi (increase in value)* apreciarse

appreciation [əpriːʃɪ'eɪʃən] *n* (**a**) *(of help, advice)* agradecimiento *m*; *(of difficulty)* comprensión *f*; *(of wine etc)* aprecio *m*; *(appraisal)* evaluación *f* (**b**) *(increase in value)* apreciación *f*

appreciative [ə'priːʃɪətɪv] *adj (thankful)* agradecido(a); *(responsive)* apreciativo(a)

apprehend [æprɪ'hend] *vt (arrest)* detener

apprehension [æprɪ'henʃən] *n* (**a**) *(arrest)* detención *f* (**b**) *(fear)* aprensión *f*

apprehensive [æprɪ'hensɪv] *adj (fearful)* aprensivo(a)

apprentice [ə'prentɪs] *n* aprendiz(a) *m,f*

apprenticeship [ə'prentɪsʃɪp] *n* aprendizaje *m*

approach [ə'prəʊtʃ] **1** *n* (**a**) *(coming near)* acercamiento *m*; *(to town)* acceso *m*; **a. road** vía *f* de acceso (**b**) *(to problem)* enfoque *m*

2 *vt (come near to)* acercarse a; *(be similar to)* aproximarse a; *Fig (problem)* abordar; *(person)* dirigirse a; **to a. sb about sth** dirigirse a algn a propósito de algo

3 *vi* acercarse

approachable [ə'prəʊtʃəbəl] *adj (person)* accesible

appropriate¹ [ə'prəʊprɪət] *adj (suitable)* apropiado(a), adecuado(a); *(convenient)* oportuno(a)

appropriate² [ə'prəʊprɪeɪt] *vt (allocate)* asignar; *(steal)* apropiarse de

approval [ə'pruːvəl] *n* aprobación *f*, visto bueno; *Com* **to get sth on a.** adquirir algo sin compromiso de compra

approve [ə'pruːv] *vt* aprobar; **approved school** reformatorio *m*

▸ **approve of** *vt insep* aprobar

approving [ə'pruːvɪŋ] *adj (look etc)* aprobatorio(a)

approx [ə'prɒks] *(abbr* **approximately***)* aprox.

approximate 1 *adj* [ə'prɒksɪmɪt] aproximado(a)

2 *vt* [ə'prɒksɪmeɪt] aproximarse a

approximately [ə'prɒksɪmɪtlɪ] *adv* aproximadamente

apricot ['eɪprɪkɒt] *n* albaricoque *m*, *Am* damasco *m*, *Méx* chabacano *m*

April ['eɪprəl] *n* abril *m*; **A. Fools' Day** día *m* uno de abril, ≃ día de los Inocentes (28 de diciembre)

apron ['eɪprən] *n* delantal *m*; *(for workman)* mandil *m*

apt [æpt] *adj* (**a**) *(suitable)* apropiado(a); *(remark)* acertado(a), oportuno(a); *(name)* justo(a); *(description)* exacto(a) (**b**) **to be a. to do sth** ser propenso(a) a hacer algo

aptitude ['æptɪtjuːd] *n* capacidad *f*; **a. test** prueba *f* de aptitud

aptly ['æptlɪ] *adv* acertadamente

aqualung ['ækwəlʌŋ] *n* botella *f* de oxígeno

aquamarine [ækwəmə'riːn] **1** *n (gem)* aguamarina *f*
2 *adj* de color de aguamarina

aquarium [ə'kweərɪəm] *n* acuario *m*

Aquarius [ə'kweərɪəs] *n* Acuario *m*

aquatic [ə'kwætɪk] *adj* acuático(a)

aqueduct ['ækwɪdʌkt] *n* acueducto *m*

Arab ['ærəb] *adj & n* árabe *(mf)*

Arabian [ə'reɪbɪən] *adj* árabe

Arabic ['ærəbɪk] **1** *adj* árabe, arábigo(a); **A. numerals** numeración arábiga
2 *n (language)* árabe *m*

arable ['ærəbəl] *adj* cultivable

Aragon ['ærəgən] *n* Aragón

arbitrary ['ɑːbɪtrərɪ] *adj* arbitrario(a)

arbitrate ['ɑːbɪtreɪt] *vt & vi* arbitrar

arbitration [ɑːbɪ'treɪʃən] *n* arbitraje *m*

arc [ɑːk] *n* arco *m*; **a. lamp** arco voltaico

arcade [ɑː'keɪd] *n* arcada *f*; *(passageway)* pasaje *m*; **shopping a.** galerías *fpl* (comerciales)

arch [ɑːtʃ] **1** *n* (**a**) *Archit* arco *m*; *(vault)* bóveda *f* (**b**) *Anat* empeine *m*
2 *vt (back)* arquear

archaeologist [ɑːkɪ'ɒlədʒɪst] *n* arqueólogo(a) *m,f*

archaeology [ɑːkɪ'ɒlədʒɪ] *n* arqueología *f*

archaic [ɑː'keɪɪk] *adj* arcaico(a)

archbishop [ɑːtʃ'bɪʃəp] *n* arzobispo *m*

arched [ɑːtʃt] *adj* arqueado(a)

archeologist [ɑːkɪ'ɒlədʒɪst] *n US* = **archaeologist**

archeology [ɑːkɪ'ɒlədʒɪ] *n US* = **archaeology**

archer ['ɑːtʃə(r)] *n* arquero(a) *m,f*

archery ['ɑːtʃərɪ] *n* tiro *m* con arco

archetypal ['ɑːkɪtaɪpəl] *adj* arquetípico(a)

archipelago [ɑːkɪ'peligəʊ] *n* archipiélago *m*

architect ['ɑːkɪtekt] *n* arquitecto(a) *m,f*

architectural [ɑːkɪ'tektʃərəl] *adj* arquitectónico(a)

architecture ['ɑːkɪtektʃə(r)] *n* arquitectura *f*

archives ['ɑːkaɪvz] *npl* archivos *mpl*

archway ['ɑːtʃweɪ] *n (arch)* arco *m*; *(vault)* bóveda *f*; *(in church)* atrio *m*; *(passage)* pasaje *m*

arctic ['ɑːktɪk] **1** *adj* ártico(a); **A. Circle** círculo *m* polar Ártico
2 *n* **the A.** el Ártico

ardent ['ɑːdənt] *adj (supporter etc)* apasionado(a); *(desire)* ardiente

ardour, *US* **ardor** ['ɑːdə(r)] *n* pasión *f*, ardor *m*

arduous ['ɑːdjʊəs] *adj* arduo(a), penoso(a)

are [ɑː(r)] *2nd person sing pres, 1st, 2nd, 3rd person pl pres of* **be**

area ['eərɪə] *n (surface)* área *f*, superficie *f*; *(space)* extensión *f*; *(region)* región *f*; *(of town)* zona *f*; *Fig (field)* campo *m*; *US Tel* **a. code** prefijo *m* local

arena [ə'riːnə] *n (stadium)* estadio *m*; *(bullring)* plaza *f*; *(circus)* pista *f*; *Fig (stage)* campo *m* de batalla

Argentina [ɑːdʒən'tiːnə] *n* Argentina

Argentinian [ɑːdʒən'tɪnɪən] *adj & n* argentino(a) *(m,f)*

arguable ['ɑːgjʊəbəl] *adj* discutible

arguably ['ɑːgjʊəblɪ] *adv* **it's a. the best** hay quienes dicen que es el mejor

argue ['ɑːgjuː] **1** *vt (reason)* discutir; *(point of view)* mantener
2 *vi (quarrel)* discutir; *(reason)* argumentar, razonar; **to a. for** abogar por; **to a. against sth** ponerse en contra de algo

argument ['ɑːgjʊmənt] *n (reason)* argumento *m* (**for** a favor de; **against** en contra de); *(quarrel)* discusión *f*, disputa *f*; **for the sake of a.** por decir algo

argumentative [ɑːgjʊ'mentətɪv] *adj* **she's very a.** le gusta discutir por todo

aria ['ɑːrɪə] *n* aria *f*

arid ['ærɪd] *adj* árido(a)

Aries ['eəriːz] *n* Aries *m*

arise [ə'raɪz] *vi (pt* **arose**; *pp* **arisen** [ə'rɪzən]) *(get up)* levantarse; *(happen)* surgir; **should the occasion a.** si se presenta la ocasión

aristocracy [ærɪ'stɒkrəsɪ] *n* aristocracia *f*

aristocrat ['ærɪstəkræt] *n* aristócrata *mf*

arithmetic [ə'rɪθmətɪk] *n* aritmética *f*

ark [ɑːk] *n* arca *f*; **Noah's A.** el arca de Noé

arm [ɑːm] **1** *n* (**a**) *(of body)* brazo *m*; *(of garment)* manga *f*; **to walk a. in a.** ir cogidos(as) del brazo (**b**) *Mil* **arms** armas *fpl*; **arms race** carrera armamentística; **coat of arms** escudo *m*
2 *vt* armar; **to a. oneself against sth** armarse contra algo

armaments ['ɑːməmənts] *npl* armamentos *mpl*

armchair ['ɑːmtʃeə(r)] *n* sillón *m*

armed ['ɑːmd] *adj* armado(a); **a. forces** fuerzas armadas; **a. robbery** robo *m* a mano armada

Armenia [ɑː'miːnɪə] *n* Armenia

armistice ['ɑːmɪstɪs] *n* armisticio *m*

armour, *US* **armor** ['ɑːmə(r)] *n (on vehicle)* blindaje *m*; **(suit of) a.** armadura *f*

armoured car, *US* **armored car** [ɑːməd'kɑː(r)] *n* coche *m* blindado

armour-plated ['ɑːmə'pleɪtɪd] *adj* acorazado(a)

armoury, *US* **armory** ['ɑːmərɪ] *n* arsenal *m*

armpit ['ɑːmpɪt] *n* axila *f*, sobaco *m*

army ['ɑːmɪ] *n* ejército *m*

aroma [ə'rəʊmə] *n* aroma *m*

arose [əˈrəʊz] *pt of* **arise**

around [əˈraʊnd] **1** *adv* alrededor; **all a.** por todos los lados; **are the children a.?** ¿están los niños por aquí?; **he looked a.** miró (a su) alrededor

2 *prep* (**a**) alrededor de; **a. the corner** a la vuelta de la esquina; **a. here** por aquí (**b**) *(approximately)* aproximadamente

arouse [əˈraʊz] *vt* despertar; *(sexually)* excitar

arrange [əˈreɪndʒ] **1** *vt* (**a**) *(order)* ordenar; *(hair, flowers)* arreglar; *Mus* adaptar (**b**) *(plan)* organizar; *(agree on)* quedar en; **to a. a time** fijar una hora; **arranged marriage** boda arreglada

2 *vi* **I shall a. for him to be there** lo arreglaré para que pueda asistir

arrangement [əˈreɪndʒmənt] *n* (**a**) *(display)* colocación *f*; *Mus* adaptación *f* (**b**) *(agreement)* acuerdo *m* (**c**) **arrangements** *(plans)* planes *mpl*; *(preparations)* preparativos *mpl*

array [əˈreɪ] *n* colección *f*; **a great a. of goods** un gran surtido de productos

arrears [əˈrɪəz] *npl* atrasos *mpl*; **to be in a. with the rent** estar atrasado(a) con el alquiler; **to be paid in a.** cobrar con retraso

arrest [əˈrest] **1** *n* detención *f*; **to be under a.** estar detenido(a)

2 *vt* *(criminal)* detener; *Fig (progress)* frenar

arresting [əˈrestɪŋ] *adj* llamativo(a)

arrival [əˈraɪvəl] *n* llegada *f*; **a new a.** un(a) recién llegado(a)

arrive [əˈraɪv] *vi* llegar (**at/in** a)

arrogance [ˈærəgəns] *n* arrogancia *f*

arrogant [ˈærəgənt] *adj* arrogante

arrow [ˈærəʊ] *n* flecha *f*

arse [ɑːs] *n Vulg* culo *m*

arsenal [ˈɑːsənəl] *n* arsenal *m*

arsenic [ˈɑːsənɪk] *n* arsénico *m*

arson [ˈɑːsən] *n* incendio *m* provocado

art [ɑːt] *n* (**a**) arte *m*; *(drawing)* dibujo *m*; **the arts** las bellas artes; **arts and crafts** artes *f pl* y oficios *mpl*; **a. gallery** galería *f* de arte (**b**) **arts** *(branch of knowledge)* letras *fpl*

artefact [ˈɑːtɪfækt] *n* artefacto *m*; *(in archaeology)* objeto *m* de arte

artery [ˈɑːtərɪ] *n* arteria *f*

artful [ˈɑːtfʊl] *adj (cunning)* ladino(a)

arthritis [ɑːˈθraɪtɪs] *n* artritis *f*

artichoke [ˈɑːtɪtʃəʊk] *n* alcachofa *f*, *RP* alcaucil *m*

article [ˈɑːtɪkəl] *n* (**a**) artículo *m*; *Press* artículo; **a. of clothing** prenda *f* de vestir (**b**) *Jur* **articles** contrato *m* de aprendizaje

articulate¹ [ɑːˈtɪkjʊlɪt] *adj (speech)* claro(a); *(person)* que se expresa bien

articulate² [ɑːˈtɪkjʊleɪt] *vt & vi* articular; *(words)* pronunciar; *Br* **articulated lorry** camión articulado

artificial [ɑːtɪˈfɪʃəl] *adj* artificial; *(limb)* postizo(a); **a. intelligence** inteligencia *f* artificial

artillery [ɑːˈtɪlərɪ] *n* artillería *f*

artisan [ˈɑːtɪzæn] *n* artesano(a) *m,f*

artist [ˈɑːtɪst] *n* artista *mf*; *(painter)* pintor(a) *m,f*

artistic [ɑːˈtɪstɪk] *adj* artístico(a)

artistry [ˈɑːtɪstrɪ] *n* arte *m*, talento artístico

as [æz, *unstressed* əz] **1** *adv & conj* (**a**) *(comparison)* **as ... as ...** tan ... como ...; **as far as** hasta; *Fig* **as far as I'm concerned** por lo que a mi respecta; **as many as** tantos(as) como; **as much as** tanto(a) como; **as tall as me** tan alto(a) como yo; **as opposed to** a diferencia de; **as little as £5** tan sólos 5 libras; **as soon as they arrive** en cuanto lleguen; **I'll stay as long as I can** quedaré todo el tiempo que pueda; **just as big** igual de grande; **three times as fast** tres veces más rápido; **the same as** igual que

(**b**) *(manner)* como; **as a rule** por regla general; **as you know** como ya sabéis; **as you like** como quieras; **do as I say** haz lo que yo te digo; **he's working as a doctor** está trabajando de médico; **I thought as much** ya me lo suponía; **it serves as a table** sirve de mesa; **leave it as it is** déjalo tal como está; **he was dressed as a pirate** iba vestido de pirata

(**c**) *(while, when)* mientras (que); **as a child** de niño(a); **as I was eating** mientras comía; **as we were leaving, we saw Pat** al salir vimos a Pat

(**d**) *(though)* aunque; **be that as it may** por mucho que así sea; **young as he is** aunque es joven

(**e**) *(because)* como, ya que

(**f**) *(and so)* igual que; **as do I** igual que yo; **as well** también

(**g**) *(purpose)* para; **so as to do sth** para hacer algo

(**h**) **as for my brother** en cuanto a mi hermano

(**i**) **as from, as of** a partir de

(**j**) **to act as if** actuar como si *(+ subj)*; **it looks as if the concert is off** parece ser que no habrá concierto

(**k**) **it's late enough as it is** ya es muy tarde; **as it were** por así decirlo

(**l**) **as long as** *(only if)* siempre que, con tal de que

(**m**) **as regards** en cuanto a, por lo que se refiere a; **as usual** como siempre; **as yet** aún, todavía

2 *rel pron* **such as** tal(es) como

asbestos [æzˈbestəs] *n* amianto *m*, asbesto *m*

ascend [əˈsend] *vi* subir, ascender

ascendancy [əˈsendənsɪ] *n* dominio *m*, influencia *f*

ascendant [əˈsendənt] *n* **to be in the a.** estar en auge

ascent [əˈsent] *n* subida *f*

ascertain [æsəˈteɪn] *vt* averiguar, enterarse de

ascribe [əˈskraɪb] *vt* **to a. sth to sb/sth** imputar algo a alguien/algo

aseptic [ə'septɪk] *adj* aséptico(a)

ash¹ [æʃ] *n Bot* fresno *m*

ash² [æʃ] *n* ceniza *f*; **a. bin**, *US* **a. can** cubo *m* de la basura; *Rel* **A. Wednesday** miércoles *m inv* de ceniza

ashamed [ə'ʃeɪmd] *adj* avergonzado(a); **you ought to be a. of yourself!** ¡te debería dar vergüenza!

ashen ['æʃən] *adj (face)* pálido(a)

ashore [ə'ʃɔː(r)] *adv (position)* en tierra; **to go a.** desembarcar; **to swim a.** nadar hacia tierra

ashtray ['æʃtreɪ] *n* cenicero *m*

Asia ['eɪʒə] *n* Asia; **A. Minor** Asia Menor

Asian ['eɪʒən] *adj & n* asiático(a) *(m,f)*

aside [ə'saɪd] **1** *adv* al lado, aparte; **to cast a.** echar a un lado; **to stand a.** apartarse
  2 *prep* **a. from** *(apart from)* aparte de; *(as well as)* además de
  3 *n Th* aparte *m*

ask [ɑːsk] **1** *vt* **(a)** preguntar; **to a. sb a question** hacer una pregunta a algn **(b)** *(request)* pedir, solicitar; **she asked me to post it** me pidió que lo echara al buzón **(c)** *(invite)* invitar
  2 *vi (inquire)* preguntar; *(request)* pedir
  ▶ **ask after** *vt insep* **to a. after sb** preguntar por algn
  ▶ **ask for** *vt insep (help)* pedir, solicitar; *(person)* preguntar por
  ▶ **ask out** *vt sep* **to a. sb out** invitar a algn a salir

askance [ə'skæns] *adv* **to look a. at sb** mirar a algn con recelo

askew [ə'skjuː] **1** *adj* ladeado(a)
  2 *adv* de lado

asleep [ə'sliːp] *adj (person)* dormido(a); *(limb)* adormecido(a); **to fall a.** quedarse dormido(a)

asparagus [ə'spærəgəs] *n inv* espárragos *mpl*

aspect ['æspekt] *n* **(a)** *(of question)* aspecto *m* **(b)** *(of building)* orientación *f*

aspersions [ə'spɜːʃənz] *npl* **to cast a. on sb** difamar a algn

asphalt ['æsfælt] *n* asfalto *m*

asphyxiation [æsfɪksɪ'eɪʃən] *n* asfixia *f*

aspiration [æspə'reɪʃən] *n* aspiración *f*

aspire [ə'spaɪə(r)] *vi* **to a. to** aspirar a

aspirin ['æsprɪn] *n* aspirina *f*

ass¹ [æs] *n Zool* asno(a) *m,f*, burro(a) *m,f*; *Fam Fig* burro(a)

ass² [æs] *n US Vulg* culo *m*

assailant [ə'seɪlənt] *n* agresor(a) *m,f*, atacante *mf*

assassin [ə'sæsɪn] *n* asesino(a) *m,f*

assassinate [ə'sæsɪneɪt] *vt* asesinar

assassination [əsæsɪ'neɪʃən] *n* asesinato *m*

assault [ə'sɔːlt] **1** *n Mil* ataque *m* **(on** a); *Jur* agresión *f*
  2 *vt Mil* asaltar, atacar; *Jur* agredir; *(sexually)* violar

assemble [ə'sembəl] **1** *vt (people)* reunir, juntar; *(furniture)* montar
  2 *vi (people)* reunirse, juntarse

assembly [ə'semblɪ] *n* reunión *f*, asamblea *f*; *Tech* montaje *m*; *Ind* **a. line** cadena *f* de montaje; *Educ* **morning a.** servicio *m* matinal

assent [ə'sent] **1** *n (agreement)* asentimiento *m*; *(consent)* consentimiento *m*; *(approval)* aprobación *f*
  2 *vi* asentir, consentir (**to** en)

assert [ə'sɜːt] *vt* afirmar; **to a. oneself** imponerse; **to a. one's rights** hacer valer sus derechos

assertive [ə'sɜːtɪv] *adj* enérgico(a)

assess [ə'ses] *vt (estimate value)* valorar; *(damages, price)* calcular; *(tax)* gravar; *Fig (effect)* evaluar

assessment [ə'sesmənt] *n (of value)* valoración *f*; *(of damages etc)* cálculo *m*; *(of taxes)* gravamen *m*; *Fig* juicio *m*

assessor [ə'sesə(r)] *n* asesor(a) *m,f*

asset ['æset] *n* **(a)** ventaja *f*; **to be an a.** *(person)* ser de gran valor **(b)** *Fin* **assets** bienes *mpl*; **fixed assets** bienes raíces

asshole ['æʃhəʊl] *n US Vulg (unpleasant person)* hijo(a) *m,f* de puta, cabrón(ona) *m,f*

assiduous [ə'sɪdjʊəs] *adj* asiduo(a)

assign [ə'saɪn] *vt (task)* asignar; *(property etc)* ceder; **to a. sb to a job** designar a algn para un trabajo

assignment [ə'saɪnmənt] *n (allocation)* asignación *f*; *(task)* tarea *f*; *(mission)* misión *f*; *(appointment)* cita *f*

assimilate [ə'sɪmɪleɪt] *vt* asimilar

assist [ə'sɪst] *vt & vi* ayudar

assistance [ə'sɪstəns] *n* ayuda *f*, auxilio *m*

assistant [ə'sɪstənt] *n* ayudante *mf*; **a. manager** subdirector(a) *m,f*; **shop a.** dependiente(a) *m,f*; **(language) a.** lector(a) *m,f*

associate¹ [ə'səʊʃɪeɪt] *vt (ideas)* relacionar; *(companies)* asociar; **to be associated with sth** estar relacionado(a) con algo
  2 *vi* **a. with** tratar con

associate² [ə'səʊʃɪt] **1** *adj* asociado(a)
  2 *n (colleague)* colega *mf*; *(partner)* socio(a) *m,f*; *(accomplice)* cómplice *mf*

association [əsəʊsɪ'eɪʃən] *n* asociación *f*; *(company)* sociedad *f*

assorted [ə'sɔːtɪd] *adj* surtido(a), variado(a)

assortment [ə'sɔːtmənt] *n* surtido *m*, variedad *f*

assume [ə'sjuːm] **1** *vt (power)* asumir; *(attitude, name)* adoptar; **an assumed name** un nombre falso
  2 *vi (suppose)* suponer

assumption [ə'sʌmpʃən] *n* **(a)** *(of power)* toma *f*; **a. of office** toma de posesión **(b)** *(supposition)* suposición *f*

assurance [ə'ʃʊərəns] *n* **(a)** *(guarantee)* garantía *f* **(b)** *(confidence)* confianza *f* **(c)** *(insurance)* seguro *m*

assure [ə'ʃʊə(r)] *vt* asegurar

asterisk ['æstərɪsk] n asterisco m

astern [ə'stɜːn] adv a popa

asthma ['æsmə] n asma f

astonish [ə'stɒnɪʃ] vt asombrar, pasmar; **I was astonished** me quedé pasmado(a)

astonishing [ə'stɒnɪʃɪŋ] adj asombroso(a), pasmoso(a)

astonishment [ə'stɒnɪʃmənt] n asombro m; **to my a.** para gran sorpresa mía

astound [ə'staʊnd] vt asombrar, pasmar

astray [ə'streɪ] adv **to go a.** extraviarse; Fig equivocarse; **to lead sb a.** llevar a algn por mal camino

astride [ə'straɪd] prep a horcajadas sobre

astrology [ə'strɒlədʒɪ] n astrología f

astronaut ['æstrənɔːt] n astronauta mf

astronomer [ə'strɒnəmə(r)] n astrónomo(a) m,f

astronomical [æstrə'nɒmɪkəl] adj astronómico(a)

astronomy [ə'strɒnəmɪ] n astronomía f

Asturias [æ'stʊərɪæs] n Asturias

astute [ə'stjuːt] adj astuto(a)

asylum [ə'saɪləm] n (a) (protection) asilo m; **to seek political a.** pedir asilo político (b) **mental a.** manicomio m

at [æt, unstressed ət] prep (a) (position) a, en; **at school/work** en el colegio/trabajo; **at the window** a la ventana; **at the top** en lo alto
(b) (direction) a; **to be angry at sb/sth** enfadarse con algn/por algo; **to laugh at sb** reírse de algn; **to look at sth/sb** mirar algo/a algn; **to shout at sb** gritarle a algn
(c) (time) a; **at Easter/Christmas** en Semana Santa/Navidad; **at six o'clock** a las seis; **at first** al principio; **at last** por fin; **at once** enseguida; **at that time** entonces; **at the moment** ahora
(d) (manner) a, en; **at best/worst** en el mejor/peor de los casos; **at hand** a mano; **at least** por lo menos; **not at all** en absoluto; (don't mention it) de nada
(e) (rate) a; **they retail at 100 pesetas each** se venden a 100 pesetas la unidad; **two at a time** de dos en dos

ate [et, eɪt] pt of **eat**

atheist ['eɪθɪɪst] n ateo(a) m,f

Athens ['æθɪnz] n Atenas

athlete ['æθliːt] n atleta mf

athletic [æθ'letɪk] **1** adj atlético(a); (sporty) deportista
2 npl **athletics** atletismo m

Atlantic [ət'læntɪk] adj **the A. (Ocean)** el (océano) Atlántico

atlas ['ætləs] n atlas m

atmosphere ['ætməsfɪə(r)] n atmósfera f; Fig (ambience) ambiente m

atmospheric [ætməs'ferɪk] adj atmosférico(a)

atom ['ætəm] n átomo m; **a. bomb** bomba atómica

atomic [ə'tɒmɪk] adj atómico(a)

atone [ə'təʊn] vi **to a. for** expiar

atrocious [ə'trəʊʃəs] adj atroz

attach [ə'tætʃ] vt (stick) pegar; (fasten) sujetar; (document) adjuntar; **to a. importance to sth** dar importancia a algo; Fig **to be attached to** (be fond of) tener cariño a

attaché [ə'tæʃeɪ] n agregado(a) m,f; **a. case** maletín m

attachment [ə'tætʃmənt] n (a) Tech accesorio m; (action) acoplamiento m (b) (fondness) apego m (**to** por) (c) Comput (to e-mail) archivo adjunto, anexo m

attack [ə'tæk] **1** n (a) (assault) ataque m, asalto m; **an a. on sb's life** un atentado contra la vida de algn (b) Med ataque m
2 vt (assault) atacar, asaltar; Fig (problem) abordar; (job) emprender; Fig (criticize) atacar

attacker [ə'tækə(r)] n asaltante mf, agresor(a) m,f

attain [ə'teɪn] vt (aim) lograr; (rank, age) llegar a

attainment [ə'teɪnmənt] n (achievement) logro m; (skill) talento m

attempt [ə'tempt] **1** n intento m, tentativa f; **at the second a.** a la segunda; **an a. on sb's life** un atentado contra la vida de algn
2 vt intentar; **to a. to do sth** tratar de or intentar hacer algo; Jur **attempted murder/rape** intento m de asesinato/violación

attend [ə'tend] **1** vt (be present at) asistir a; (care for, wait on) atender
2 vi (be present) asistir; (pay attention) prestar atención
▸ **attend to** vt insep (business) ocuparse de; (in shop) atender a

attendance [ə'tendəns] n asistencia f

attendant [ə'tendənt] n (in cinema etc) acomodador(a) m,f; (in museum) guía mf; (in car park) vigilante(a) m,f

attention [ə'tenʃən] n (a) atención f; **for the a. of Miss Jones** a la atención de la Srta. Jones; **pay a.!** ¡atiende!; **to pay a. to sb/sth** prestar atención a algn/algo (b) Mil **a.!** ¡firmes!; **to stand to a.** estar firmes

attentive [ə'tentɪv] adj (listener) atento(a); (helpful) solícito(a)

attest [ə'test] vi **to a. to** dar testimonio a

attic ['ætɪk] n ático m

attire [ə'taɪə(r)] n Fml traje m

attitude ['ætɪtjuːd] n actitud f; (position of body) postura f; **an a. of mind** un estado de ánimo

attorney [ə'tɜːnɪ] n (a) US (lawyer) abogado(a) m,f; **A. General** ≃ Ministro(a) m,f de Justicia; **district a.** fiscal mf (b) Jur **power of a.** poderes mpl

attract [ə'trækt] vt atraer; **to a. attention** llamar la atención; **to a. a waiter's attention** llamar a un camarero

attraction [ə'trækʃən] n (a) (power) atracción f (b) (attractive thing) atractivo m;

(charm) encanto *m*; *(incentive)* aliciente *m*;
the main a. el número fuerte
attractive [ə'træktɪv] *adj* atractivo(a); *(good-looking)* guapo(a); *(idea, proposition)* atrayente
attribute¹ ['ætrɪbjuːt] *n (quality)* atributo *m*
attribute² [ə'trɪbjuːt] *vt* atribuir
attrition [ə'trɪʃən] *n* **war of a.** guerra *f* de desgaste
aubergine ['əʊbəʒiːn] *n Br* berenjena *f*
auburn ['ɔːbən] *adj* castaño rojizo *inv*
auction ['ɔːkʃən] **1** *n* subasta *f*
2 *vt* subastar
auctioneer [ɔːkʃə'nɪə(r)] *n* subastador(a) *m,f*
audacious [ɔː'deɪʃəs] *adj (daring)* audaz; *(bold)* atrevido(a); *(impudent)* descarado(a)
audible ['ɔːdɪbəl] *adj* audible
audience ['ɔːdɪəns] *n* (**a**) *(spectators)* público *m*; *(at concert, conference)* auditorio *m*; *(television)* telespectadores *mpl* (**b**) *(meeting)* audiencia *f*
audio-visual [ɔːdɪəʊ'vɪzjʊəl] *adj* audiovisual; **a. aids** apoyo *m* audiovisual
audit ['ɔːdɪt] **1** *n* revisión *f* de cuentas
2 *vt* revisar, intervenir
audition [ɔː'dɪʃən] **1** *n* prueba *f*
2 *vt* **to a. sb for a part** probar a algn para un papel
auditor ['ɔːdɪtə(r)] *n* revisor(a) *m,f* de cuentas
auditorium [ɔːdɪ'tɔːrɪəm] *n* auditorio *m*
augment [ɔːg'ment] *vt* aumentar
augur ['ɔːgə(r)] *vi* **to a. well** ser de buen agüero
August ['ɔːgəst] *n* agosto *m*
aunt [ɑːnt] *n (also Fam* **auntie, aunty** ['ɑːntɪ]) tía *f*
au pair [əʊ'peə(r)] *n* **a. (girl)** au pair *f*
aura ['ɔːrə] *n* aura *f*; *Rel* aureola *f*
aural ['ɔːrəl] *adj* auditivo(a), del oído
auspices ['ɔːspɪsɪz] *npl* **under the a. of** bajo los auspicios de
auspicious [ɔː'spɪʃəs] *adj* de buen augurio
austere [ɒ'stɪə(r)] *adj* austero(a)
austerity [ɒ'sterɪtɪ] *n* austeridad *f*
Australia [ɒ'streɪlɪə] *n* Australia
Australian [ɒ'streɪlɪən] *adj & n* australiano(a) *(m,f)*
Austria ['ɒstrɪə] *n* Austria
Austrian ['ɒstrɪən] *adj & n* austríaco(a) *(m,f)*
authentic [ɔː'θentɪk] *adj* auténtico(a)
author ['ɔːθə(r)] *n* autor(a) *m,f*
authoritarian [ɔːθɒrɪ'teərɪən] *adj* autoritario(a)
authoritative [ɔː'θɒrɪtətɪv] *adj (reliable)* autorizado(a); *(authoritarian)* autoritario(a)
authority [ɔː'θɒrɪtɪ] *n* autoridad *f*; **local a.** ayuntamiento *m*
authorize ['ɔːθəraɪz] *vt* autorizar; *(payment etc)* aprobar; **to a. sb to do sth** autorizar a algn a hacer algo

auto ['ɔːtəʊ] *n US* coche *m*, *Andes, CAm, Carib, Méx* carro *m*
autobiography [ɔːtəʊbaɪ'ɒgrəfɪ] *n* autobiografía *f*
autograph ['ɔːtəgrɑːf] **1** *n* autógrafo *m*
2 *vt (sign)* firmar; *(book, photo)* dedicar
automata [ɔː'tɒmətə] *pl of* **automaton**
automatic [ɔːtə'mætɪk] **1** *adj* automático(a)
2 *n (car)* coche automático; *(gun)* pistola automática
automatically [ɔːtə'mætɪklɪ] *adv* automáticamente
automation [ɔːtə'meɪʃən] *n* automatización *f*; **office a.** ofimática *f*
automaton [ɔː'tɒmətɒn] *n (pl* **automata** autómata *m*
automobile ['ɔːtəməbiːl] *n US* coche *m* automóvil *m*, *Andes, CAm, Carib, Méx* carro *m*
autonomous [ɔː'tɒnəməs] *adj* autónomo(a)
autonomy [ɔː'tɒnəmɪ] *n* autonomía *f*
autopsy ['ɔːtɒpsɪ] *n* autopsia *f*
autumn ['ɔːtəm] *n* otoño *m*
auxiliary [ɔːg'zɪljərɪ] *adj* auxiliar
Av., av. *(abbr* **Avenue**) Av., Avda.
avail [ə'veɪl] **1** *n* **to no a.** en vano
2 *vt* **to a. oneself of sth** aprovecharse de algo
available [ə'veɪləbəl] *adj (thing)* disponible *(person)* libre
avalanche ['ævəlɑːnʃ] *n* avalancha *f*
avarice ['ævərɪs] *n* avaricia *f*
Ave *(abbr* **Avenue**) Av., Avda.
avenge [ə'vendʒ] *vt* vengar
avenue ['ævɪnjuː] *n* avenida *f*; *Fig* vía *f*
average ['ævərɪdʒ] **1** *n* promedio *m*, media *f* **on a.** por término medio
2 *adj* medio(a); *(condition)* regular
3 *vt* sacar la media de; **he averages eight hours' work a day** trabaja una media de ocho horas al día
▸ **average out at** *vt insep* salir a una media de
averse [ə'vɜːs] *adj* **to be a. to sth** ser reacio(a) a algo
aversion [ə'vɜːʃən] *n (feeling)* aversión *f (thing)* bestia negra
avert [ə'vɜːt] *vt (eyes, thoughts)* apartar (**from** de); *(accident)* impedir; *(danger)* evitar
avid ['ævɪd] *adj (reader)* voraz
avidly ['ævɪdlɪ] *adv* vorazmente
avocado [ævə'kɑːdəʊ] *n* **a. (pear)** aguacate *m*, *Andes, RP* palta *f*
avoid [ə'vɔɪd] *vt* evitar; *(question)* eludir
avoidable [ə'vɔɪdəbəl] *adj* evitable
await [ə'weɪt] *vt* esperar, aguardar
awake [ə'weɪk] **1** *adj* despierto(a); **to be a** estar despierto(a)
2 *vt (pt* **awoke, awaked**; *pp* **awoken, awaked**) despertar
awaken [ə'weɪkən] *vt & vi (pt* **awakened**; *pp, awoken)* = awake 2
awakening [ə'weɪkənɪŋ] *n* despertar *m*
award [ə'wɔːd] **1** *n (prize)* premio *m*; *(medal*

condecoración *f*; *Jur* indemnización *f*; *(grant)* beca *f*

2 *vt (prize)* conceder, otorgar; *(medal)* dar; *(damages)* adjudicar

aware [ə'weə(r)] *adj (informed)* enterado(a); **not that I'm a.** que yo sepa no; **to be a. of sth** ser consciente de algo; **to become a. of sth** darse cuenta de algo

awareness [ə'weənɪs] *n* conciencia *f* (**of** de)

awash [ə'wɒʃ] *adj* inundado(a) (**with** de)

away [ə'weɪ] *adv* **far a.** lejos; **go a.!** ¡lárgate!; **it's 3 miles a.** está a 3 millas (de distancia); **keep a. from the fire!** ¡no te acerques al fuego!; **right a.** en seguida; **to be a.** *(absent)* estar ausente; *(out)* estar fuera; **to die a.** desvanecerse; **to give sth a.** regalar algo; *(secret)* revelar algo; **to go a.** irse; *Sport* **to play a.** jugar fuera; **to turn a.** volver la cara; **to work a.** trabajar

awe [ɔː] *n (fear)* temor *m*; *(amazement)* asombro *m*; **he was in a. of his father** le intimidaba su padre

awe-inspiring ['ɔːɪnspaɪərɪŋ] *adj* impresionante, imponente

awesome ['ɔːsəm] *adj* impresionante

awful ['ɔːfʊl] *adj Fam* espantoso(a); **an a. lot of work** muchísimo trabajo

awfully ['ɔːfʊlɪ] *adv Fam* terriblemente

awkward ['ɔːkwəd] *adj (clumsy)* torpe; *(difficult)* pesado(a); *(object)* incómodo(a); *(moment)* inoportuno(a); *(situation)* embarazoso(a); *(problem)* difícil

awning ['ɔːnɪŋ] *n (on ship)* toldo *m*; *(on shop)* marquesina *f*

awoke [ə'wəʊk] *pt of* **awake**

awoken [ə'wəʊkən] *pp of* **awake, awaken**

axe, *US* **ax** [æks] **1** *n* hacha *f*

2 *vt Fig (jobs)* eliminar; *(costs)* reducir; *(plan)* cancelar; *(person)* despedir

axis ['æksɪs] *n (pl* **axes** ['æksiːz]) eje *m*

axle ['æksəl] *n* eje *m*; *Tech* árbol *m*

ayatollah [aɪə'tɒlə] *n* ayatolá *m*

Aztec ['æztek] *adj & n* azteca *(mf)*

B

B, b [biː] *n* (**a**) *(the letter)* B, b *f*; *Br Aut* **B road** carretera secundaria (**b**) *Mus* **B** si *m*; **B flat** si bemol

BA [biːˈeɪ] *n* *(abbr* **Bachelor of Arts)** *(person)* licenciado(a) *m,f* en Filosofía y Letras

babble [ˈbæbəl] *vi (baby)* balbucear; *(brook)* murmurar

babe [beɪb] *n* (**a**) *(baby)* bebé *m* (**b**) *US Fam* **hi, b.!** ¡hola, guapa!

baboon [bəˈbuːn] *n* zambo *m*

baby [ˈbeɪbɪ] *n* (**a**) bebé *m*; *(young child)* niño(a) *m,f*; *Br* **B. Buggy**® sillita *f* de paseo *or* de niño; *US* **b. buggy** *or* **carriage** cochecito *m* de niño; **b. face** cara *f* de niño (**b**) *(animal)* cría *f* (**c**) *Fam (darling)* querido(a) *m,f*

baby-sit [ˈbeɪbɪsɪt] *vi* hacer de canguro

baby-sitter [ˈbeɪbɪsɪtə(r)] *n* canguro *mf*

baby-walker [ˈbeɪbɪwɔːkə(r)] *n* tacataca *m*

bachelor [ˈbætʃələ(r)] *n* (**a**) soltero *m* (**b**) *Univ* licenciado(a) *m,f*; **B. of Arts/Science** licenciado(a) *m,f* en Filosofía y Letras/Ciencias

back [bæk] **1** *n* (**a**) *(of person)* espalda *f*; *(of animal)* lomo *m*; **b. to front** al revés; *Fig* **to get sb's b. up** poner negro a algn; *Fig* **to have one's b. to the wall** estar en un aprieto

(**b**) *(of book)* lomo *m*; *(of chair)* respaldo *m*; *(of coin)* reverso *m*; *(of hand)* dorso *m*; *(of house, car)* parte *f* de atrás; *Fig* **he knows Leeds like the b. of his hand** se conoce Leeds como la palma de la mano

(**c**) *(of stage, cupboard)* fondo *m*; *Fam* **at the b. of beyond** en el quinto pino

(**d**) *Ftb* defensa *mf*

(**e**) *US* **in b. (of)** *(behind)* en la parte de atrás (de), detrás (de); *(to the rear of)* al fondo (de)

2 *adj* (**a**) trasero(a), de atrás; **b. door** puerta *f* de atrás; **b. seat** asiento *m* de detrás; *Fig* **to take a b. seat** pasar al segundo plano; *Aut* **b. wheel** rueda trasera

(**b**) **b. rent** alquiler atrasado; **b. pay** atrasos *mpl*; *Press* **b. number** número *m* atrasado

3 *adv* (**a**) *(to the rear)* atrás; *(towards the rear)* hacia atrás; **b. and forth** de acá para allá

(**b**) **some years b.** hace unos años

4 *vt* (**a**) *(support)* apoyar, respaldar

(**b**) *Fin* financiar

(**c**) *(bet on)* apostar por

(**d**) *(car etc)* dar marcha atrás a

5 *vi* (**a**) *(move backwards)* retroceder

(**b**) *(car etc)* dar marcha atrás

▸ **back away** *vi* retirarse

▸ **back down** *vi* echarse atrás

▸ **back off** *vi* desistir

▸ **back out** *vi (withdraw)* retractarse, volverse atrás

▸ **back up 1** *vt sep* (**a**) *(support)* apoyar (**b**) *Comput (file)* hacer una copia de seguridad de

2 *vi Aut* ir marcha atrás

backache [ˈbækeɪk] *n* dolor *m* de espalda

backbencher [bækˈbentʃə(r)] *n* diputado(a) *m,f* que no es ministro

backbiting [ˈbækbaɪtɪŋ] *n* murmuración *f*

backbone [ˈbækbəʊn] *n Anat* columna *f*

backcloth [ˈbækklɒθ] *n* telón *m* de fondo

backdate [bækˈdeɪt] *vt* antedatar

backdated [bækˈdeɪtɪd] *adj* con efecto retroactivo

backdrop [ˈbækdrɒp] *n* telón *m* de fondo

backer [ˈbækə(r)] *n* (**a**) *Fin* promotor(a) *m,* (**b**) *Pol* partidario(a) *m,f* (**c**) *(person who bets)* apostante *mf*

backfire [bækˈfaɪə(r)] *vi* (**a**) *Aut* petardear (**b**) *Fig* **our plan backfired** nos salió el tiro por la culata

background [ˈbækgraʊnd] *n* (**a**) fondo *m*; **to stay in the b.** quedarse en segundo plano; **b. music** música *f* de fondo (**b**) *(origin)* origen *m* *(past)* pasado *m*; *(education)* formación *f* (**c**) *(circumstances)* antecedentes *mpl* (**d**) *(atmosphere)* ambiente *m*

backhand [ˈbækhænd] *n Sport* revés *m*

backhanded [ˈbækhændɪd] *adj* equívoco(a), ambiguo(a)

backhander [ˈbækhændə(r)] *n Fam (bribe)* soborno *m*

backing [ˈbækɪŋ] *n* (**a**) *(support)* apoyo *m,* *Com & Fin* respaldo financiero (**b**) *Mus* acompañamiento *m*

backlash [ˈbæklæʃ] *n* reacción violenta y repentina

backlog [ˈbæklɒg] *n* **to have a b. of work** tener un montón de trabajo atrasado

backpack [ˈbækpæk] *n* mochila *f*

backpedal [bækˈpedəl] *vi Fam* dar marcha atrás

backside [bækˈsaɪd] *n Fam* trasero *m*, culo *m*

backstage [bækˈsteɪdʒ] *adv* entre bastidores

backstroke [ˈbækstrəʊk] *n* espalda *f*

backtrack [ˈbæktræk] *vi Fig* volverse atrás

backup [ˈbækʌp] *n* (**a**) *(support)* apoyo *m* respaldo *m*; *Comput* **b. (file)** fichero *m* de apoyo (**b**) *US* *(of traffic)* caravana *f*

backward ['bækwəd] **1** *adj* (**a**) *(movement)* hacia atrás (**b**) *(country)* subdesarrollado(a); *(child)* retrasado(a)

2 *adv esp US* hacia atrás

backwards ['bækwədz] *adv* hacia atrás; **to walk b.** andar de espaldas

backyard [bæk'jɑːd] *n* patio trasero; *US* jardín trasero

bacon ['beɪkən] *n* tocino *m*, beicon *m*

bacteria [bæk'tɪərɪə] *npl* bacterias *fpl*

bad [bæd] **1** *adj* (**worse, worst**) (**a**) *(poor)* malo(a); **to go from b. to worse** ir de mal en peor (**b**) *(decayed)* podrido(a); **to go b.** echarse a perder (**c**) *(wicked)* malo(a); **to use b. language** ser mal hablado(a) (**e**) *(accident)* grave; *(headache)* fuerte (**f**) *(ill)* enfermo(a) (**g**) **b. debt** deuda *f* incobrable

2 *n* lo malo

bade [beɪd] *pt of* **bid**

badge [bædʒ] *n* insignia *f*; *(metal disc)* chapa *f*

badger ['bædʒə(r)] **1** *n* tejón *m*

2 *vt* acosar

badly ['bædlɪ] *adv* (**a**) *mal*; **he did b. in the exam** le salió mal el examen; **to be b. off** andar mal de dinero (**b**) *(seriously)* gravemente (**c**) *(very much)* mucho; **to miss sb b.** echar mucho de menos a algn; **we need it b.** nos hace mucha falta

badminton ['bædmɪntən] *n* bádminton *m*

bad-tempered [bæd'tempəd] *adj* **to be b.** *(temperament)* tener mal genio; *(temporarily)* estar de mal humor

baffle ['bæfəl] **1** *vt* desconcertar

2 *n Tech* pantalla acústica

baffling ['bæflɪŋ] *adj* incomprensible, enigmático(a)

bag [bæg] **1** *n* (**a**) *(large)* bolsa *f*; *(handbag)* bolso *m*, cartera *f*, *Méx* bolsa; *Fam* **bags of** montones de; **travel b.** bolsa de viaje (**b**) *(hunting)* caza *f*; *Fam* **it's in the b.** es cosa hecha (**c**) *Pej* **old b.** *(woman)* bruja *f* (**d**) **bags** *(under eyes)* ojeras *fpl*

2 *vt* (**a**) *(put into sacks)* meter en sacos (**b**) *Fam* coger

baggage ['bægɪdʒ] *n* (**a**) equipaje *m* (**b**) *Mil* bagaje *m*

baggy ['bægɪ] *adj* (**baggier, baggiest**) holgado(a); **b. trousers** pantalones anchos

bagpipes ['bægpaɪps] *npl* gaita *f*

Bahamas [bə'hɑːməz] *npl* **the B.** las Bahamas

bail¹ [beɪl] *n Jur* fianza *f*; **on b.** bajo fianza; **to stand b. for sb** salir fiador por algn

► **bail out** *vt sep Fig (person)* sacar de un apuro

bail² [beɪl] *vi Naut* **to b. (out)** achicar

bailiff ['beɪlɪf] *n* (**a**) *Jur* alguacil *m* (**b**) *(steward)* administrador *m*

bait [beɪt] **1** *n* cebo *m*; **to rise to the b.** tragar el anzuelo, picar

2 *vt* (**a**) *(for fishing)* cebar (**b**) *(torment)* hostigar

baize [beɪz] *n* bayeta *f*; **green b.** tapete *m* verde

bake [beɪk] **1** *vt* (**a**) cocer al horno (**b**) *(harden)* endurecer

2 *vi Fam* hacer mucho calor

baked [beɪkt] *adj* al horno; **b. potato** patata *f* *or Am* papa *f* al horno

baker ['beɪkə(r)] *n* panadero(a) *m,f*

bakery ['beɪkərɪ] *n* panadería *f*

baking ['beɪkɪŋ] *n* cocción *f*; **b. dish** fuente *f* para horno; **b. powder** levadura *f* en polvo; **b. tin** molde *m*

balaclava [bælə'klɑːvə] *n* pasamontañas *m inv*

balance ['bæləns] **1** *n* (**a**) *(scales)* balanza *f*; *Fig* **to hang in the b.** estar en juego (**b**) *(equilibrium)* equilibrio *m*; *Pol* **b. of power** equilibrio de fuerzas (**c**) *Fin* saldo *m*; **b. of payments** balanza *f* de pagos; **b. sheet** balance *m*; **credit b.** saldo acreedor (**d**) *(remainder)* resto *m*

2 *vt* (**a**) poner en equilibrio (**on** en) (**b**) *(budget)* equilibrar; **to b. the books** hacer el balance (**c**) *(weigh up)* sopesar

3 *vi* guardar el equilibrio

► **balance out** *vi (figures)* corresponderse

balanced ['bælənst] *adj* equilibrado(a)

balcony ['bælkənɪ] *n* balcón *m*; *Th* anfiteatro *m*

bald [bɔːld] *adj* (**a**) *(person)* calvo(a) (**b**) *(tyre)* desgastado(a) (**c**) *(style)* escueto(a)

baldness ['bɔːldnɪs] *n* (**a**) *(of person)* calvicie *f* (**b**) *(of tyre)* desgaste *m* (**c**) *(of style)* sencillez *f*

bale¹ [beɪl] **1** *n (of cloth)* fardo *m*

2 *vt* embalar

bale² [beɪl] *vt* = **bail²**

► **bale out** **1** *vi Av* saltar en paracaídas de un avión

2 *vt sep Fig (person)* sacar de apuros a

Balearic [bælɪ'ærɪk] *adj* **the B. Islands** las Islas Baleares

baleful ['beɪlfʊl] *adj* funesto(a), siniestro(a)

Balkan ['bɔːlkən] *adj* **the Balkans** los Balcanes

ball¹ [bɔːl] *n* (**a**) *(in cricket, tennis etc)* pelota *f*; *Ftb* balón *m*; *(in billiards, golf etc)* bola *f*; *Fig* **the b. is in your court** ahora te toca a ti; *Fig* **to play b. with sb** cooperar con algn; *Fam* **to be on the b.** ser un espabilado; *Tech* **b. bearing** rodamiento *m* de bolas (**b**) *(of paper)* bola *f*, *(of wool)* ovillo *m* (**c**) *US* béisbol *m*; *Fig* **it's a whole new b. game** es otra historia (**d**) *very Fam* **balls** cojones *mpl*

ball² [bɔːl] *n (dance)* baile *m*

ballad ['bæləd] *n* balada *f*

ballast ['bæləst] *n Naut* lastre *m*

ballerina [bælə'riːnə] *n* bailarina *f*

ballet ['bæleɪ] *n* ballet *m*; **b. dancer** bailarín(ina) *m,f*

ballistic [bə'lɪstɪk] *adj* balístico(a)

ballistics [bə'lɪstɪks] *n sing* balística *f*

balloon [bə'luːn] 1 *n* (a) globo *m* (b) *(in cartoon)* bocadillo *m*
2 *vi* hincharse; *Fig* aumentar rápidamente

ballot ['bælət] 1 *n* votación *f*; **b. box** urna *f*; **b. paper** papeleta *f*
2 *vt* someter a votación

ballpoint (pen) ['bɔːlpɔɪnt('pen)] *n* bolígrafo *m*, *CSur* lapicera *f*

ballroom ['bɔːlruːm] *n* salón *m* de baile

ballyhoo [bælɪ'huː] *n Fam (fuss)* jaleo *m*

balm [bɑːm] *n* bálsamo *m*

balmy ['bɑːmɪ] *adj* (**balmier, balmiest**) *(weather)* suave

Baltic ['bɔːltɪk] *adj* báltico(a); **the B. (Sea)** el (mar) Báltico

balustrade ['bæləstreɪd] *n* barandilla *f*

bamboo [bæm'buː] *n* bambú *m*

bamboozle [bæm'buːzəl] *vt Fam* (a) *(puzzle)* dejar perplejo (b) *(trick)* engañar, embaucar

ban [bæn] 1 *n* prohibición *f*
2 *vt* (a) *(prohibit)* prohibir (b) *(exclude)* excluir

banal [bə'nɑːl] *adj* banal, trivial

banana [bə'nɑːnə] *n* plátano *m*, banana *f*, *Col* banano *m*, *Ven* cambur *m*; *Fam* **to go bananas** volverse loco(a)

band [bænd] 1 *n* (a) *(strip)* tira *f*; *(ribbon)* cinta *f* (b) *(stripe)* raya *f* (c) *Rad* banda *f* (d) *(group)* grupo *m*; *(of youths)* pandilla *f*; *(of thieves)* banda *f* (e) *Mus* banda *f*
2 *vi* **to b. together** unirse, juntarse

bandage ['bændɪdʒ] 1 *n* venda *f*
2 *vt* vendar

Band-Aid® ['bændeɪd] *n US* tirita® *f*, *Am* curita *f*

B & B [biːn'biː] *n (abbr* **bed and breakfast)** *(hotel)* = hostal familiar en el que el desayuno está incluido en el precio de la habitación

bandit ['bændɪt] *n* bandido *m*

bandstand ['bændstænd] *n* quiosco *m* de música

bandwagon ['bændwægən] *n Fig* **to jump on the b.** subirse al tren

bandy ['bændɪ] 1 *vt (words, ideas)* intercambiar
2 *adj* (**bandier, bandiest**) torcido(a) hacia fuera
▸ **bandy about** *vt sep (ideas)* propagar, difundir

bandy-legged ['bændɪ'leg(ɪ)d] *adj* patizambo(a)

bang [bæŋ] 1 *n* (a) *(blow)* golpe *m* (b) *(noise)* ruido *m*; *(explosion)* estallido *m*; *(of gun)* estampido *m*; **to shut the door with a b.** dar un portazo
2 *npl US* **bangs** flequillo *m*, *Am* cerquillo *m (corto)*
3 *vt* golpear; **to b. sth shut** cerrar algo de golpe
4 *vi* golpear; **to b. shut** cerrarse de golpe

5 *interj (blow)* ¡zas!; **b., b.!** *(of gun)* ¡pum, pum!
6 *adv Fam* justo

banger ['bæŋə(r)] *n* (a) *(firework)* petardo *m* (b) *Fam (sausage)* salchicha *f* (c) *Fam* **old b.** *(car)* tartana *f*

bangle ['bæŋgəl] *n* brazalete *m*

banish ['bænɪʃ] *vt* desterrar

banister ['bænɪstə(r)] *n* pasamanos *m inv*

bank¹ [bæŋk] 1 *n* (a) *Com & Fin* banco *m*; **b. account** cuenta bancaria; **b. card** tarjeta *f* de banca; **b. clerk** empleado(a) *m,f* de banca; **b. draft** letra bancaria; **b. holiday** fiesta *f* nacional; **b. statement** extracto *m* de cuenta (b) *(in gambling)* banca *f* (c) *(store)* banco *m*
2 *vt Com & Fin* depositar, ingresar
3 *vi Com & Fin* **to b. with** tener una cuenta en
▸ **bank on** *vt insep* contar con

bank² [bæŋk] 1 *n* (a) *(mound)* loma *f*; *(embankment)* terraplén *m* (b) *(of river)* ribera *f*, *(edge)* orilla *f*
2 *vt Av* ladear
3 *vi Av* ladearse

bankbook ['bæŋkbʊk] *n* libreta *f* de ahorros

banker ['bæŋkə(r)] *n* banquero(a) *m,f*

banking ['bæŋkɪŋ] *n* banca *f*

banknote ['bæŋknəʊt] *n* billete *m* de banco

bankrupt ['bæŋkrʌpt] 1 *adj* en quiebra; **to go b.** quebrar
2 *vt* llevar a la bancarrota

bankruptcy ['bæŋkrʌptsɪ] *n* quiebra *f*, bancarrota *f*

banner ['bænə(r)] *n (in demonstration)* pancarta *f*; *(flag)* bandera *f*

banns [bænz] *npl* amonestaciones *fpl*

banquet ['bæŋkwɪt] *n* banquete *m*

banter ['bæntə(r)] 1 *n* bromas *fpl*
2 *vi* bromear

bap [bæp] *n* bollo *m*, panecillo *m*

baptism ['bæptɪzəm] *n* bautismo *m*

baptize [bæp'taɪz] *vt* bautizar

bar [bɑː(r)] 1 *n* (a) *(of gold)* barra *f*; *(of chocolate)* tableta *f*; *(of soap)* pastilla *f*; *Com* **b. code** código *m* de barras (b) *(of cage)* barrote *m*; *Fam* **to be behind bars** estar en la cárcel (c) *(obstacle)* obstáculo *m* (d) *Jur (dock)* banquillo *m*; *(court)* tribunal *m* (e) *Jur* **the B.** *(profession)* abogacía *f*; *(body of lawyers)* colegio *m* de abogados (f) *(pub)* bar *m*; *(counter)* barra *f* (g) *Mus* compás *m*
2 *vt* (a) *(door)* atrancar; *(road)* cortar (b) *(exclude)* excluir (**from** de) (c) *(prohibit)* prohibir
3 *prep* salvo; **b. none** sin excepción

barbarian [bɑː'beərɪən] *adj & n* bárbaro(a) *(m,f)*

barbaric [bɑː'bærɪk] *adj* bárbaro(a)

barbecue ['bɑːbɪkjuː] 1 *n* barbacoa *f*
2 *vt* asar a la parrilla

barbed [bɑːbd] *adj* (a) **b. wire** alambre *m* de púas (b) *Fig (remark)* mordaz

barber ['bɑːbə(r)] *n* barbero(a) *m,f*; **b.'s (shop)** barbería *f*

arbiturate [bɑː'bɪtjʊrɪt] *n* barbitúrico *m*

bare [beə(r)] **1** *adj* (**a**) desnudo(a); *(head)* descubierto(a); *(foot)* descalzo(a); *(room)* sin muebles; **to lay b.** poner al descubierto; **with his b. hands** sólo con las manos (**b**) *(basic)* mero(a); **the b. minimum** lo mínimo
2 *vt* desnudar; *(uncover)* descubrir

bareback(ed) ['beə'bæk(t)] *adv* **to ride b.** montar un caballo a pelo

barefaced ['beəfeɪst] *adj* desvergonzado(a)

barefoot ['beə'fʊt] *adj & adv* descalzo(a)

barely ['beəlɪ] *adv* apenas

bargain ['bɑːgɪn] **1** *n* (**a**) *(agreement)* pacto *m*; *(deal)* negocio *m*; **into the b.** por añadidura, además; **to drive a hard b.** imponer condiciones duras; **to strike a b.** cerrar un trato (**b**) *(cheap purchase)* ganga *f*; **b. price** precio *m* de oferta
2 *vi* (**a**) negociar (**b**) *(haggle)* regatear
▸ **bargain for** *vt insep* esperar, contar con

barge [bɑːdʒ] **1** *n* gabarra *f*
2 *vt Fam* **to b. into** *(room)* irrumpir en; *(person)* tropezar con
▸ **barge in** *vi Fam* (**a**) *(go in)* entrar sin permiso (**b**) *(interfere)* entrometerse

baritone ['bærɪtəʊn] *adj & n* barítono (*m*)

bark¹ [bɑːk] **1** *n* ladrido *m*
2 *vi (dog)* ladrar

bark² [bɑːk] *n Bot* corteza *f*

barley ['bɑːlɪ] *n* cebada *f*; **b. sugar** azúcar *m* cande

barmaid ['bɑːmeɪd] *n* camarera *f*

barman ['bɑːmən] *n* camarero *m*, barman *m*

barn [bɑːn] *n* granero *m*; **b. dance** baile *m* popular

barnacle ['bɑːnəkəl] *n* percebe *m*

barometer [bə'rɒmɪtə(r)] *n* barómetro *m*

baron ['bærən] *n* barón *m*

baroness ['bærənɪs] *n* baronesa *f*

baroque [bə'rɒk] *adj* barroco(a)

barrack ['bærək] *vt* abuchear

barracks ['bærəks] *n Mil* cuartel *m*

barrage ['bærɑːdʒ] *n* (**a**) *(dam)* presa *f* (**b**) *Mil* barrera *f* de fuego (**c**) *Fig (of questions)* lluvia *f*

barrel ['bærəl] *n* (**a**) *(of wine)* tonel *m*; *(of beer, oil)* barril *m* (**b**) *(of firearm)* cañón *m*

barren ['bærən] *adj* estéril; *(land)* yermo(a)

barricade [bærɪ'keɪd] **1** *n* barricada *f*
2 *vt* levantar barricadas; **to b. oneself in** parapetarse

barrier ['bærɪə(r)] *n* barrera *f*

barrister ['bærɪstə(r)] *n Br* abogado(a) *m,f (capacitado(a) para ejercer ante tribunales superiores)*

barrow ['bærəʊ] *n* carretilla *f*

bartender ['bɑːtendə(r)] *n US* camarero *m*, barman *m*

barter ['bɑːtə(r)] *vt* trocar (**for** por)

base [beɪs] **1** *n* base *f*; *(foot)* pie *m*; *(of column)* basa *f*; *Sport (of team)* concentración *f*; **air/naval b.** base *f* aérea/naval
2 *vt* (**a**) basar, fundar (**on** en) (**b**) *(troops)* estacionar
3 *adj* (**a**) *(despicable)* bajo(a), despreciable (**b**) *(metals)* común

baseball ['beɪsbɔːl] *n* béisbol *m*

baseline ['beɪslaɪn] *n (in tennis)* línea *f* de saque

basement ['beɪsmənt] *n* sótano *m*

bases ['beɪsiːz] *pl of* **basis**

bash [bæʃ] **1** *n (heavy blow)* golpetazo *m*; *(dent)* bollo *m*; *Fam (attempt)* intento *m*
2 *vt* golpear

bashful ['bæʃfʊl] *adj* tímido(a)

basic ['beɪsɪk] **1** *adj* básico(a); **b. pay** sueldo *m* base
2 *npl* **basics** lo fundamental

basically ['beɪsɪklɪ] *adv* fundamentalmente

basil ['bæzəl] *n* albahaca *f*

basin ['beɪsən] *n* (**a**) *(washbowl)* palangana *f*; *(for washing up)* barreño *m*; *(in bathroom)* lavabo *m*; *(dish)* cuenco *m* (**b**) *(of river)* cuenca *f*

basis ['beɪsɪs] *n (pl* **bases**) base *f*; **on the b. of** en base a

bask [bɑːsk] *vi* tostarse; **to b. in the sun** tomar el sol

basket ['bɑːskɪt] *n* cesta *f*, cesto *m*

basketball ['bɑːskɪtbɔːl] *n* baloncesto *m*

Basque [bæsk, bɑːsk] **1** *adj* vasco(a); **B. Country** País Vasco, Euskadi; **B. flag** ikurriña *f*; **B. nationalist** abertzale *mf*
2 *n* (**a**) *(person)* vasco(a) *m,f* (**b**) *(language)* vasco *m*, euskera *m*

bass¹ [bæs] *n inv (seawater)* lubina *f*; *(freshwater)* perca *f*

bass² [beɪs] **1** *n* (**a**) *(singer)* bajo *m* (**b**) *(notes)* graves *mpl*; **b. drum** bombo *m*; **b. guitar** bajo *m*
2 *adj* bajo(a)

bassoon [bə'suːn] *n* fagot *m*

bastard ['bɑːstəd, 'bæstəd] **1** *n* (**a**) bastardo(a) *m,f* (**b**) *Pej* cabrón *m*, hijo *m* de puta; **poor b.!** ¡el pobre!
2 *adj* bastardo(a)

baste [beɪst] *vt Culin* untar

bastion ['bæstɪən] *n* baluarte *m*, bastión *m*

bat¹ [bæt] **1** *n (in cricket, baseball)* bate *m*; *(in table tennis)* pala *f*; *Fig* **to do sth off one's own b.** hacer algo por cuenta propia
2 *vi (in cricket, baseball)* batear

bat² [bæt] *n Zool* murciélago *m*

bat³ [bæt] *vt Fam* **without batting an eyelid** sin pestañear

batch [bætʃ] *n (of bread)* hornada *f*; *(of goods)* lote *m*; *Comput* **b. processing** procesamiento *m* por lotes

bated ['beɪtɪd] *adj* **with b. breath** sin respirar

bath [bɑːθ] **1** *n* (**a**) baño *m*; **to have a b.** bañarse; **b. towel** toalla *f* de baño (**b**) *(tub)* bañera *f* (**c**) **baths** piscina *f* municipal
2 *vt* bañar

bathe [beɪð] **1** *vi* bañarse
2 *vt* (**a**) *(wound)* lavar (**b**) **he was bathed in sweat** *(covered)* estaba empapado de sudor
bather ['beɪðə(r)] *n* bañista *mf*
bathing ['beɪðɪŋ] *n* baño *m*; **b. cap** gorro *m* de baño; **b. costume** traje *m* de baño; **b. trunks** bañador *m* de hombre
bathrobe ['bɑːθrəʊb] *n* albornoz *m*
bathroom ['bɑːθruːm] *n* cuarto *m* de baño
bathtub ['bɑːθtʌb] *n* bañera *f*
baton ['bætən, 'bætɒn] *n* (**a**) *Mus* batuta *f* (**b**) *(truncheon)* porra *f* (**c**) *Sport* testigo *m*
battalion [bə'tæljən] *n* batallón *m*
batter¹ ['bætə(r)] *vt* aporrear, apalear
batter² ['bætə(r)] *n* (*in cricket, baseball*) bateador(a) *m,f*
batter³ ['bætə(r)] *Culin* **1** *n* pasta *f* (para rebozar); **fish in b.** pescado rebozado
2 *vt* rebozar
battered ['bætəd] *adj* (*car*) abollado(a); *(person)* maltratado(a)
battering ['bætərɪŋ] *n* paliza *f*; **to take a b.** recibir una paliza; *Mil* **b. ram** ariete *m*
battery ['bætərɪ] *n* (**a**) *(for torch, radio)* pila *f*; *Aut* batería *f* (**b**) *Jur* **assault and b.** lesiones *fpl*
battle ['bætəl] **1** *n* batalla *f*; *Fig* lucha *f*; **to do b.** librar batalla; *Fig* **b. cry** lema *m*
2 *vi* luchar
battlefield ['bætəlfiːld] *n* campo *m* de batalla
battleship ['bætəlʃɪp] *n* acorazado *m*
bauble ['bɔːbəl] *n* chuchería *f*
bawdy ['bɔːdɪ] *adj* (*joke etc*) verde
bawl [bɔːl] *vi* gritar, chillar
bay¹ [beɪ] *n Geog* bahía *f*; *(large)* golfo *m*; **B. of Biscay** golfo de Vizcaya; **B. of Bengal** golfo de Bengala
bay² [beɪ] *n* (**a**) *(recess)* hueco *m*; **b. window** ventana salediza (**b**) *(in factory)* nave *f*; **cargo b.** bodega *f* de carga
bay³ [beɪ] *n* laurel *m*
bay⁴ [beɪ] **1** *vi* (*dog*) aullar
2 *n* ladrido *m*; *Fig* **at b.** acorralado(a); *Fig* **to keep sb at b.** mantener a algn a raya
bayonet ['beɪənɪt] *n* bayoneta *f*
bazaar [bə'zɑː(r)] *n* (**a**) *(market)* bazar *m* (**b**) *(church)* (*charity sale*) rastrillo benéfico
BBC [biːbiːˈsiː] *n* (*abbr* **British Broadcasting Corporation**) BBC *f*
BC [biːˈsiː] (*abbr* **before Christ**) a.d.C.
be [biː, *unstressed* bɪ]

> En el inglés hablado, y en el escrito en estilo coloquial, el verbo **be** se contrae de forma que **I am** se transforma en **I'm**, **he/she/it is** se transforman en **he's/she's/it's** y **you/we/they are** se transforman en **you're/we're/they're**. Las formas negativas **is not**, **are not**, **was not** y **were not** se transforman en **isn't**, **aren't**, **wasn't** y **weren't**.

1 *vi* (*pres* 1st person sing **am**; 3rd person sing **is**; 2nd person sing & all persons pl **are**; *pt* 1st

& 3rd persons sing **was**; 2nd person sing & all persons pl **were**; *pp* **been**) (**a**) ser; **he is very tall** es muy alto; **Madrid is the capital** Madrid es la capital; **sugar is sweet** el azúcar es dulce
(**b**) *(nationality, occupation)* ser; **he's Italian** es italiano
(**c**) *(origin, ownership)* ser; **the car is Domingo's** el coche es de Domingo; **this painting is by Goya** este cuadro es de Goya
(**d**) *(price)* costar; *(total)* ser; **a return ticket is £24** un billete de ida y vuelta cuesta £24; **how much is a kilo of cod?** ¿a cuánto está el kilo de bacalao?; **how much is it?** ¿cuánto es?
(**e**) *(temporary state)* estar; **how are you? – I'm very well** ¿cómo estás? – estoy muy bien; **this soup is cold** esta sopa está fría; **to be cold/afraid/hungry** tener frío/miedo/hambre; **to be lucky** tener suerte
(**f**) *(location)* estar; **Aberdeen is in Scotland** Aberdeen está en Escocia; **Birmingham is 200 miles from London** Birmingham está a 200 millas de Londres
(**g**) *(age)* tener; **she is thirty (years old)** tiene treinta años
2 *v aux* (**a**) *(with pres p)* estar; **he is writing a letter** está escribiendo una carta; **she was singing** estaba cantando; **they are leaving next week** se van la semana que viene; **we have been waiting for a long time** hace mucho que estamos esperando; **he is coming** *(emphatic)* es seguro que viene
(**b**) *(passive)* ser; **he was murdered** fue asesinado; **she is allowed to smoke** se le permite fumar
(**c**) *(obligation)* **I am to see him this afternoon** debo verle esta tarde; **you are not to smoke here** no se puede fumar aquí
3 *v impers* (**a**) *(with* there) haber; **there is, there are** hay; **there was, there were** había; **there will be** habrá; **there would be** habría; **there have been a lot of complaints** ha habido muchas quejas; **there were ten of us** éramos diez
(**b**) *(with* it) **it's late** es tarde; **it is said that** se dice que; **who is it? – it's me** ¿quién es? – soy yo; **what is it?** ¿qué pasa?
(**c**) *(weather)* **it's foggy** hay niebla; **it's cold/hot** hace frío/calor
(**d**) *(time)* ser; **it's one o'clock** es la una; **it's four o'clock** son las cuatro
(**e**) *(date)* **it's the 11th/Tuesday today** hoy es 11/martes
(**f**) *(in tag questions)* **it's lovely, isn't it?** es bonito, ¿no?; **you're happy, aren't you?** estás contento, ¿verdad?; **he's not very clever, is he?** no es muy listo, ¿verdad?
(**g**) *(unreal conditions)* **if I was/were you ...** yo en tu lugar ...; **if you were a millionaire ...** si fueras millonario ...
(**h**) *pres & past perfect (visit, go)* estar, ir; **I've been to Paris** he estado en París

beach [biːtʃ] **1** n playa f
 2 vt varar
beacon ['biːkən] n (**a**) Av & Naut baliza f (**b**) (lighthouse) faro m
bead [biːd] n (**a**) (of necklace etc) cuenta f; **glass b.** abalorio m (**b**) (of liquid) gota f
beady ['biːdɪ] adj (**beadier, beadiest**) (eyes) pequeños y brillantes
beagle ['biːgəl] n beagle m
beak [biːk] n (**a**) (of bird) pico m (**b**) Fam (nose) nariz ganchuda
beaker ['biːkə(r)] n (tumbler) taza alta, jarra f
beam [biːm] **1** n (**a**) Archit viga f (**b**) (of light) rayo m; Phys haz m (**c**) (in gymnastics) barra fija (**d**) (smile) sonrisa f radiante
 2 vi (**a**) (sun) brillar (**b**) (smile) sonreír
 3 vt (**a**) (broadcast) difundir, emitir (**b**) (transmit) transmitir
beaming ['biːmɪŋ] adj (smiling) radiante
bean [biːn] n alubia f, judía f, Andes, CAm, Carib, Méx frijol m, RP poroto m; Fam **to spill the beans** descubrir el pastel; **baked beans** = alubias cocidas en salsa de tomate; **broad b.** haba f; **butter b.** judía blanca, Andes, CAm, Carib, Méx frijol blanco, RP poroto de manteca; **coffee b.** grano m de café; **green/runner b.** judía verde, Bol, RP chaucha f, CAm ejote m, Col, Cuba habichuela f, Chile poroto verde, Ven vainita f; **haricot b.** alubia; **kidney b.** frijol
beansprout ['biːnspraʊt] n brote m de soja
bear¹ [beə(r)] (pt bore; pp borne) **1** vt (**a**) (carry) llevar
 (**b**) (support) sostener
 (**c**) (endure) soportar, aguantar; **I can't b. him** no lo soporto
 (**d**) (fruit) dar; Fin (interest) devengar
 (**e**) **to b. a resemblance to** parecerse a
 (**f**) **to b. a grudge against sb** guardar rencor a algn; **to b. in mind** tener presente
 (**g**) **to b. witness** atestiguar
 (**h**) (pt **born** passive only, not followed by **by**) (give birth to) dar a luz; **he was born in Wakefield** nació en Wakefield
 2 vi (turn) girar, torcer; **to b. left** girar a la izquierda
 ▸ **bear down** vi (approach) correr (**on** sobre)
 ▸ **bear out** vt sep (confirm) confirmar
 ▸ **bear up** vi (endure) resistir
 ▸ **bear with** vt insep tener paciencia con
bear² [beə(r)] n (**a**) oso m; **b. cub** osezno m; Astron **Great B.** Osa f Mayor; **Little B.** Osa Menor (**b**) Fin bajista mf
beard [bɪəd] n barba f
bearer ['beərə(r)] n portador(a) m,f; (of passport, office) titular mf
bearing ['beərɪŋ] n (**a**) (posture) porte m (**b**) (relevance) relación f; **to have a b. on** estar relacionado(a) con (**c**) (bearing m (**d**) Naut **bearings** posición f, orientación f; **to get one's bearings** orientarse; **to lose one's bearings** desorientarse

beast [biːst] n (**a**) bestia f; **b. of burden** bestia de carga (**b**) Fig bestia f, bruto m (**c**) **beasts** (cattle) reses fpl
beastly ['biːstlɪ] adj (**beastlier, beastliest**) Fam asqueroso(a)
beat [biːt] **1** vt (pt beat; pp beaten ['biːtən]) (**a**) (hit) pegar, golpear; (clothes) sacudir; (drum) tocar; **off the beaten track** en un lugar muy apartado; Fam **b. it!** ¡lárgate!
 (**b**) Culin batir
 (**c**) (defeat) batir, vencer; **we b. them 5-2** les ganamos 5 a 2
 (**d**) **to b. a retreat** batirse en retirada
 (**e**) Mus (time) marcar
 (**f**) **to b. the traffic** evitar los embotellamientos de tráfico
 (**g**) Fam (puzzle) extrañar; **it beats me** no lo entiendo
 2 vi (**a**) (heart) latir
 (**b**) (strike) dar golpes; Fig **to b. about the bush** andarse por las ramas
 3 n (**a**) (of heart) latido m
 (**b**) Mus ritmo m, compás m
 (**c**) (of policeman) ronda f
 4 adj Fam (exhausted) agotado(a)
 ▸ **beat down** vi (sun) apretar
 ▸ **beat off** vt sep rechazar
 ▸ **beat up** vt sep Fam dar una paliza a
beating ['biːtɪŋ] n (**a**) (thrashing) paliza f (**b**) (defeat) derrota f (**c**) (of drum) toque m (**d**) (of heart) latido m
beautician [bjuːˈtɪʃən] n esteticista mf
beautiful ['bjuːtɪfʊl] adj hermoso(a), bello(a); (delicious) delicioso(a); **b. people** gente guapa
beauty ['bjuːtɪ] n belleza f, hermosura f; **b. contest** concurso m de belleza; **b. queen** miss f; **b. salon** salón m de belleza; **b. spot** (on face) lunar m; (place) lugar pintoresco
beaver ['biːvə(r)] **1** n castor m
 2 vi **to b. away at sth** meterse de lleno en algo
became [bɪˈkeɪm] pt of **become**
because [bɪˈkɒz] **1** conj porque
 2 prep **b. of** a causa de, debido a
beckon ['bekən] vt & vi llamar (con la mano); **to b. to sb** llamar a algn con señas
become [bɪˈkʌm] **1** vi (pt became; pp become) (a teacher, doctor) hacerse; (boring, jealous, suspicious) volverse; (old, difficult, stronger) hacerse; (happy, sad, thin) ponerse; **to b. angry/interested** enfadarse/interesarse; **what will b. of him?** ¿qué va a ser de él?
 2 vt Fml (of clothes, colour) sentar bien a
becoming [bɪˈkʌmɪŋ] adj (**a**) (dress) favorecedor(a) (**b**) (behaviour) conveniente, apropiado(a)
bed [bed] n (**a**) cama f; **to get out of b.** levantarse de la cama; **to go to b.** acostarse; **to make the b.** hacer la cama; Br **b. and breakfast** (service) cama y desayuno m; (sign) pensión f; **b. linen** ropa f de cama (**b**) (of river)

lecho m; (of sea) fondo m (c) Geol capa f (d) (flower) b. arriate m

bedbug ['bedbʌg] n chinche f

bedclothes ['bedkləʊðz] npl, **bedding** ['bedɪŋ] n ropa f de cama

bedlam ['bedləm] n algarabía f, alboroto m

bedraggled [bɪ'dræɡəld] adj (wet) mojado(a); (dirty) ensuciado(a)

bedridden ['bedrɪdən] adj postrado(a) en cama

bedroom ['bedru:m] n dormitorio m

bedside ['bedsaɪd] n **at sb's b.** junto a la cama de algn; **b. table** mesilla f de noche

bedsit ['bedsɪt] n Fam, **bedsitter** [bed'sɪtə(r)] n estudio m

bedspread ['bedspred] n colcha f

bedtime ['bedtaɪm] n hora f de acostarse

bee [bi:] n abeja f

beech [bi:tʃ] n haya f

beef [bi:f] n carne f de vaca, Méx carne de res; **roast b.** rosbif m
  ▸ **beef up** vt sep Fam reforzar

beefburger ['bi:fbɜːɡə(r)] n hamburguesa f

beefsteak ['bi:fsteɪk] n bistec m

beehive ['bi:haɪv] n colmena f

beeline ['bi:laɪn] n Fam **to make a b. for sth** ir directo hacia algo

been [bi:n, bɪn] pp of **be**

beep [bi:p] n (of apparatus) pitido m; (of horn) pito m

beer [bɪə(r)] n cerveza f; **a glass of b.** una caña

beet [bi:t] n US remolacha f, Andes betarraga f, Méx betabel f; US **red b.** remolacha

beetle ['bi:təl] n escarabajo m

beetroot ['bi:tru:t] n Br remolacha f, Andes betarraga f, Méx betabel f

befit [bɪ'fɪt] vt convenir a, corresponder a

before [bɪ'fɔ:(r)] **1** conj (a) (earlier than) antes de que (+ subj), antes de (+ infin); **b. she goes** antes de que se vaya; **b. leaving** antes de salir (b) (rather than) antes que (+ infin)
  2 prep (a) (place) delante de; (in the presence of) ante (b) (order, time) antes de; **b. Christ** antes de Cristo; **b. long** dentro de poco; **b. 1950** antes de 1950; **I saw it b. you** lo vi antes que tú
  3 adv (a) (time) antes; **I have met him b.** ya lo conozco; **not long b.** poco antes; **the night b.** la noche anterior (b) (place) delante, por delante

beforehand [bɪ'fɔ:hænd] adv (a) (earlier) antes (b) (in advance) de antemano, con anticipación

befriend [bɪ'frend] vt trabar amistad con

beg [beg] **1** vt (a) (money etc) pedir (b) (beseech) rogar, suplicar; **I b. your pardon!** ¡perdone usted!; **I b. your pardon?** ¿cómo ha dicho usted?
  2 vi (a) (solicit) mendigar; (dog) pedir; **to b. for money** pedir limosna (b) **to b. for help/**

mercy (beseech) implorar ayuda/compasión

began [bɪ'gæn] pt of **begin**

beggar ['begə(r)] n (a) mendigo(a) m,f (b) Fam Euph (chap) tío m

begin [bɪ'gɪn] vt & vi (pt **began**; pp **begun**) empezar, comenzar; **to b. again** volver a empezar; **to b. at the beginning** empezar por el principio; **to b. doing** or **to do sth** empezar a hacer algo; **to b. with ...** (initially) para empezar ...

beginner [bɪ'gɪnə(r)] n principiante mf

beginning [bɪ'gɪnɪŋ] n (a) principio m, comienzo m; **at the b. of May** a principios de mayo; **from the b.** desde el principio; **in the b.** al principio (b) (origin) origen m

begonia [bɪ'gəʊnɪə] n begonia f

begrudge [bɪ'grʌdʒ] vt dar de mala gana; (envy) envidiar

beguile [bɪ'gaɪl] vt (charm) seducir

begun [bɪ'gʌn] pp of **begin**

behalf [bɪ'hɑ:f] n **on b. of, US in b. of** en nombre de, de parte de; **don't worry on my b.** no te preocupes por mí

behave [bɪ'heɪv] vi (a) (person) portarse, comportarse; **b. yourself!** ¡pórtate bien!; **to b. well/badly** portarse bien/mal (b) (machine) funcionar

behaviour, US **behavior** [bɪ'heɪvjə(r)] n (a) (of person) comportamiento m, conducta f (b) (of machine) funcionamiento m

behead [bɪ'hed] vt decapitar

beheld [bɪ'held] pt & pp of **behold**

behind [bɪ'haɪnd] **1** prep (a) detrás de; **b. sb's back** a espaldas de algn; **b. the scenes** entre bastidores; **to be b. sb** apoyar a algn; **what motive was there b. the crime?** ¿cuál fue el móvil del crimen? (b) **b. the times** (less advanced than) anticuado(a)
  2 adv (a) (in the rear) detrás, atrás; **I've left my umbrella b.** se me ha olvidado el paraguas (b) **to be b. with one's payments** (late) estar atrasado(a) en los pagos
  3 n Fam trasero m

behold [bɪ'həʊld] vt (pt & pp **beheld**) Literary contemplar

beige [beɪʒ] adj & n beige (m)

being ['bi:ɪŋ] n (a) ser m (b) (existence) existencia f; **to come into b.** nacer

Belarus [belə'ru:s] n Bielorrusia

belated [bɪ'leɪtɪd] adj tardío(a)

belch [beltʃ] **1** vi (person) eructar
  2 vt (smoke, flames) vomitar, arrojar
  3 n eructo m

beleaguered [bɪ'li:gəd] adj asediado(a)

belfry ['belfrɪ] n campanario m

Belgian ['beldʒən] adj & n belga (mf)

Belgium ['beldʒəm] n Bélgica

Belgrade [bel'greɪd] n Belgrado

belie [bɪ'laɪ] vt desmentir

belief [bɪ'li:f] n (a) creencia f; **beyond b.** increíble (b) (opinion) opinión f (c) (faith) fe f (d) (confidence) confianza f (**in** en)

believe [bɪˈliːv] **1** vi (a) (have faith) creer (b) **to b. in** (be in favour of) ser partidario(a) de (c) (think) creer; **I b. so** creo que sí
2 vt creer

believer [bɪˈliːvə(r)] n (a) Rel creyente mf (b) partidario(a) m,f (**in** de)

belittle [bɪˈlɪtəl] vt (person) menospreciar; (problem) minimizar

bell [bel] n (of church) campana f; (small) campanilla f; (of school, door, bicycle etc) timbre m; (on cat) cascabel m; (on cow) cencerro m; Fig **that rings a b.** eso me suena; **b. jar** campana; **b. tower** campanario m

bell-bottoms [ˈbelbɒtəmz] npl pantalones mpl de campana

bellboy [ˈbelbɔɪ], US **bellhop** [ˈbelhɒp] n botones m inv

belligerent [bɪˈlɪdʒərənt] adj agresivo(a)

bellow [ˈbeləʊ] vi (bull) bramar; (person) rugir

bellows [ˈbeləʊz] npl **(pair of) b.** fuelle m

belly [ˈbelɪ] n (a) (of person) barriga f; **b. flop** panzazo m (b) (of animal) panza f

bellyache [ˈbelɪeɪk] n Fam dolor m de vientre

belong [bɪˈlɒŋ] vi (a) pertenecer (**to** a) (b) (be a member) ser socio(a) (**to** de); Pol **to b. to a party** ser miembro de un partido (c) (have a proper place) corresponder; **this chair belongs here** esta silla va aquí

belongings [bɪˈlɒŋɪŋz] npl efectos mpl personales

beloved [bɪˈlʌvɪd, bɪˈlʌvd] **1** adj amado(a), querido(a)
2 n amado(a) m,f

below [bɪˈləʊ] **1** prep debajo de; **b. average** por debajo de la media; **10 degrees b. zero** 10 grados bajo cero
2 adv abajo; **above and b.** arriba y abajo; **see b.** véase más abajo

belt [belt] **1** n (a) cinturón m; **blow below the b.** golpe bajo (b) Tech correa f, cinta f (c) (area) zona f
2 vt Fam pegar una paliza a
▸ **belt along** vi Fam ir a todo gas
▸ **belt out** vt sep Fam (song) cantar a voz en grito
▸ **belt up** vi Fam callarse

beltway [ˈbeltweɪ] n US carretera f de circunvalación

bemused [bɪˈmjuːzd] adj perplejo(a)

bench [bentʃ] n (a) (seat) banco m (b) (in parliament) escaño m (c) Jur **the b.** (judges) la magistratura (d) Sport banquillo m (e) **b. mark** Geol cota f de referencia; Fig punto m de referencia

bend [bend] **1** vt (pt & pp bent) doblar; (back) encorvar; (head) inclinar; Fam **to b. the rules** hacer una excepción
2 vi (a) doblarse; (road) torcerse (b) **to b. (over)** inclinarse; Fam **he bends over backwards to please her** hace lo imposible por complacerla

3 n (in river, road) curva f; (in pipe) recodo m; Br Fam **round the b.** loco(a) perdido(a)
▸ **bend down** vi inclinarse

beneath [bɪˈniːθ] **1** prep (below) bajo, debajo de; Fig **it's b. him** es indigno de él
2 adv debajo

benefactor [ˈbenɪfæktə(r)] n bienhechor(a) m,f

beneficial [benɪˈfɪʃəl] adj (a) (doing good) benéfico(a) (b) (advantageous) beneficioso(a)

beneficiary [benɪˈfɪʃərɪ] n beneficiario(a) m,f

benefit [ˈbenɪfɪt] **1** vt beneficiar
2 vi sacar provecho (**from** or **by** de)
3 n (a) (advantage) beneficio m, provecho m; **for the b. of** en beneficio de; **I did it for your b.** lo hice por tu bien (b) (allowance) subsidio m; **unemployment b.** subsidio de desempleo (c) (event) función benéfica

benevolent [bɪˈnevələnt] adj benévolo(a)

Bengal [beŋˈɡɔːl] n Bengala

benign [bɪˈnaɪn] adj benigno(a)

bent [bent] **1** adj (a) (curved) curvado(a) (b) **to be b. on doing sth** (determined) estar empeñado(a) en hacer algo (c) Fam (corrupt) deshonesto(a) (d) very Fam (homosexual) gay (e) pt & pp of **bend**
2 n (inclination) inclinación f (**towards** hacia)

benzine [ˈbenziːn] n Chem bencina f

bequeath [bɪˈkwiːð] vt Jur legar

bequest [bɪˈkwest] n Jur legado m

bereaved [bɪˈriːvd] npl **the b.** los familiares del/de un difunto

bereavement [bɪˈriːvmənt] n (mourning) duelo m

bereft [bɪˈreft] adj **b. of** privado(a) de

beret [ˈbereɪ] n boina f

Berlin [bɜːˈlɪn] n Berlín

Bermuda [bəˈmjuːdə] n las (Islas) Bermudas; **B. shorts** bermudas fpl

Bern [bɜːn] n Berna

berry [ˈberɪ] n baya f

berserk [bəˈsɜːk, bəˈzɜːk] adj **to go b.** volverse loco(a)

berth [bɜːθ] Naut **1** n (a) (mooring) amarradero m; Fig **to give sb a wide b.** evitar a algn (b) (bed) litera f
2 vi atracar

beseech [bɪˈsiːtʃ] vt (pt & pp besought or beseeched) suplicar, implorar

beset [bɪˈset] vt (pt & pp beset) acosar; **it is b. with dangers** está plagado de peligros

beside [bɪˈsaɪd] prep (a) (next to) al lado de, junto a (b) (compared with) comparado con (c) **he was b. himself with joy** estaba loco de alegría; **that's b. the point** eso no viene al caso; **to be b. oneself** estar fuera de sí

besides [bɪˈsaɪdz] **1** prep (a) (in addition to) además de (b) (except) excepto, menos; **no one b. me** nadie más que yo
2 adv además

besiege [bɪˈsiːdʒ] vt (city) sitiar; Fig asediar

besought [bɪˈsɔːt] pt & pp of beseech

best [best] **1** adj (superl of good) mejor; **b. man** ≃ padrino m de boda; **her b. friend** su mejor amiga; **the b. thing would be to phone them** lo mejor sería llamarles; **we had to wait the b. part of a year** tuvimos que esperar casi un año; **with b. wishes from Mary** (in letter) con mis mejores deseos, Mary

2 adv (superl of well) mejor; **as b. I can** lo mejor que pueda; **I like this one b.** éste es el que más me gusta; **the world's b. dressed man** el hombre mejor vestido del mundo

3 n **the b.** el/la/lo mejor; **all the b.!** ¡que te vaya bien!; **at b.** a lo más; **to be at one's b.** estar en plena forma; **to do one's b.** hacer todo lo posible; **to make the b. of sth** sacar el mejor partido de algo; **to the b. of my knowledge** que yo sepa

bestiality [bestɪˈælɪtɪ] n bestialidad f

bestow [bɪˈstəʊ] vt (favour etc) conceder; (honours, power) otorgar (**on** a); (title etc) conferir (**on** a)

best-seller [best'selə(r)] n best-seller m

best-selling ['bestselɪŋ] adj **a b. author** un autor de superventas

bet [bet] **1** n apuesta f

2 vt (pt bet or betted) apostar

3 vi apostar (**on** por); Fam **you b.!** ¡y tanto!

Bethlehem ['beθlɪhem] n Belén

betray [bɪˈtreɪ] vt (a) traicionar (b) (be unfaithful to) engañar (c) (reveal) revelar

betrayal [bɪˈtreɪəl] n traición f

better ['betə(r)] **1** adj (a) (comp of good) mejor; **that's b.!** ¡así está mejor!; **the weather is b. than last week** hace mejor tiempo que la semana pasada; **to be no b. than ...** no ser más que ...; **to get b.** mejorar

(**b**) (healthier) mejor (de salud)

(**c**) **b. off** (better) mejor; (richer) más rico(a); **you'd be b. off going home** lo mejor es que te vayas a casa

(**d**) **the b. part of the day** la mayor parte del día

2 adv (comp of well) (a) mejor; **all the b., so much the b.** tanto mejor; **b. and b.** cada vez mejor; Prov **b. late than never** más vale tarde que nunca

(**b**) **we had b. leave** más vale que nos vayamos

(**c**) **to think b. of** (plan) cambiar de

3 n mejor; **a change for the b.** una mejora; **to get the b. of sb** vencer a algn

4 vt (a) (improve) mejorar

(**b**) (surpass) superar

betting ['betɪŋ] n apuestas fpl; Br **b. shop** quiosco m de apuestas

between [bɪˈtwiːn] **1** prep entre; **b. you and me** entre nosotros; **closed b. one and two** cerrado de una a dos

2 adv **in b.** (position) en medio; (time) entretanto, mientras (tanto)

beverage ['bevərɪdʒ] n bebida f

bevy ['bevɪ] n bandada f

beware [bɪˈweə(r)] vi tener cuidado (**of** con); **b.!** ¡cuidado!; **b. of the dog** (sign) cuidado con el perro

bewildered [bɪˈwɪldəd] adj desconcertado(a)

bewilderment [bɪˈwɪldəmənt] n desconcierto m

bewitching [bɪˈwɪtʃɪŋ] adj fascinador(a)

beyond [bɪˈjɒnd] **1** prep más allá de; **b. belief** increíble; **b. doubt** sin lugar a dudas; **it is b. me why ...** no comprendo por qué ...; **it's b. a joke** eso ya no tiene gracia; **she is b. caring** ya no le importa; **this task is b. me** no puedo con esta tarea

2 adv más allá, más lejos

bias ['baɪəs] n (tendency) tendencia f (**towards** hacia); (prejudice) prejuicio m

bias(s)ed ['baɪəst] adj parcial; **to be b. against sth/sb** tener prejuicio en contra de algo/algn

bib [bɪb] n (for baby) babero m; (of apron) peto m

Bible ['baɪbəl] n Biblia f; Fam **B. basher, B. thumper** evangelista mf

bibliography [bɪblɪˈɒgrəfɪ] n bibliografía f

bicarbonate [baɪˈkɑːbənɪt] n bicarbonato m; **b. of soda** bicarbonato sódico

bicentenary [baɪsenˈtiːnərɪ], US **bicentennial** [baɪsenˈtenɪəl] n bicentenario m

biceps ['baɪseps] n bíceps m

bicker ['bɪkə(r)] vi reñir

bicycle ['baɪsɪkəl] n bicicleta f; **b. pump** bomba f (de aire); **to go by b.** ir en bicicleta

bid [bɪd] **1** vt (pt bid or bade; pp bid or bidden ['bɪdən]) (a) (say) decir; **to b. sb farewell** despedirse de algn (b) (command) mandar, ordenar; **she bade him be quiet** le mandó que se callase (c) (invite) invitar; **he bade me sit down** me invitó a sentarme (d) (at auction) (pt & pp bid) pujar

2 vi (pt & pp bid) (at auction) pujar (**for** por)

3 n (a) (offer) oferta f (b) (at auction) puja f (c) (attempt) intento m, tentativa f

bidder ['bɪdə(r)] n **the highest b.** el mejor postor

bidding ['bɪdɪŋ] n (a) (at auction) puja f (b) (order) orden f; **to do sb's b.** cumplir la orden de algn

bide [baɪd] vt (pt bided or bode; pp bided) esperar; **to b. one's time** esperar el momento oportuno

bidet ['biːdeɪ] n bidé m

bifocal [baɪˈfəʊkəl] **1** adj bifocal

2 npl **bifocals** lentes fpl bifocales

big [bɪg] **1** adj grande (gran before singular noun); **a b. clock** un reloj grande; **a b. surprise** una gran sorpresa; **my b. brother** mi hermano mayor; Fam Ironic **b. deal!** ¿y qué?; **b. business** los grandes negocios; **b. dipper** montaña rusa; US Astron **B. Dipper** Osa f

Mayor; **b. toe** dedo gordo del pie; *Fam* **b. gun, b. shot** pez gordo; *Fam* **to make the b. time** tener éxito; *Fam* **b. top** carpa *f*

2 *adv* (**a**) *(on a grand scale)* a lo grande (**b**) *(well)* de manera excepcional

bigamy ['bɪɡəmɪ] *n* bigamia *f*

bighead ['bɪɡhed] *n Fam* creído(a) *m,f*, engreído(a) *m,f*

bigheaded [bɪɡ'hedɪd] *adj* creído(a), engreído(a)

bigot ['bɪɡət] *n* intolerante *mf*

🖉 Note that the Spanish word **bigote** is a false friend and is never a translation for the English word **bigot**. In Spanish, **bigote** means "moustache".

bigoted ['bɪɡətɪd] *adj* intolerante

bigotry ['bɪɡətrɪ] *n* intolerancia *f*

bigwig ['bɪɡwɪɡ] *n Fam* pez gordo

bike [baɪk] *n Fam (abbr* **bicycle** *or* **motorbike**) *(bicycle)* bici *f*; *(motorcycle)* moto *f*; **on your b.!** ¡vete de aquí!

bikini [bɪ'kiːnɪ] *n* bikini *m*

bilateral [baɪ'lætərəl] *adj* bilateral

bile [baɪl] *n* bilis *f*

bilingual [baɪ'lɪŋɡwəl] *adj* bilingüe

Bill [bɪl] *n Br Fam* **the Old B.** la poli

bill¹ [bɪl] **1** *n* (**a**) *(for gas etc)* factura *f*, recibo *m* (**b**) *esp Br (in restaurant)* cuenta *f* (**c**) *Parl* proyecto *m* de ley (**d**) *US (banknote)* billete *m* de banco (**e**) *(poster)* cartel *m*; **on the b.** en cartel; **post no bills** *(sign)* prohibido fijar carteles; *Th* **to top the b.** encabezar el reparto; **b. of exchange** letra *f* de cambio; *Pol* **B. of Rights** declaración *f* de derechos

2 *vt* (**a**) *(send bill to)* facturar (**b**) *Th* programar

bill² [bɪl] *n (of bird)* pico *m*

billboard ['bɪlbɔːd] *n (hoarding)* cartelera *f*

billet ['bɪlɪt] **1** *n* alojamiento *m*

2 *vt* alojar

billfold ['bɪlfəʊld] *n US* cartera *f*, billetero *m*

billiards ['bɪljədz] *n sing* billar *m*

billion ['bɪljən] *n US* mil millones *mpl; Br Old-fashioned* billón *m*

billionaire [bɪljə'neə(r)] *n* multimillonario(a) *m,f*

billow ['bɪləʊ] **1** *n (of water)* ola *f; (of smoke)* nube *f*

2 *vi (sea)* ondear; *(sail)* hincharse

billy goat ['bɪlɪɡəʊt] *n* macho cabrío

bin [bɪn] *n (for storage)* cajón *m*; **bread b.** panera *f*; **(rubbish) b.** cubo *m* de la basura

binary ['baɪnərɪ] *adj* **b. number** número binario

bind [baɪnd] *vt (pt & pp bound)* (**a**) *(tie up)* atar (**b**) *Med (bandage)* vendar (**c**) *(book)* encuadernar (**d**) *(require)* obligar (**e**) *(join etc)* unir

▸ **bind over** *vt sep Jur* obligar legalmente

binder ['baɪndə(r)] *n (file)* carpeta *f*

binding ['baɪndɪŋ] *adj (promise)* comprometedor(a); *(contract)* vinculante

binge [bɪndʒ] *n Fam* borrachera *f*; **to go on a b.** irse de juerga

bingo ['bɪŋɡəʊ] *n* bingo *m*

binoculars [bɪ'nɒkjʊləz] *npl* prismáticos *mpl*, gemelos *mpl*

biochemistry [baɪəʊ'kemɪstrɪ] *n* bioquímica *f*

biodegradable [baɪəʊdɪ'greɪdəbəl] *adj* biodegradable

biography [baɪ'ɒɡrəfɪ] *n* biografía *f*

biological [baɪə'lɒdʒɪkəl] *adj* biológico(a); **b. warfare** guerra biológica

biologist [baɪ'ɒlədʒɪst] *n* biólogo(a) *m,f*

biology [baɪ'ɒlədʒɪ] *n* biología *f*

biorhythm ['baɪəʊrɪðəm] *n* biorritmo *m*

biosphere ['baɪəsfɪə(r)] *n* biosfera *f*

birch [bɜːtʃ] **1** *n* (**a**) *Bot* abedul *m* (**b**) *(rod)* vara *f* (de abedul)

2 *vt* azotar

bird [bɜːd] *n* (**a**) pájaro *m*, ave *f; Fig* **to kill two birds with one stone** matar dos pájaros de un tiro; **they're birds of a feather** son tal para cual; **b. of prey** ave de rapiña (**b**) *Br Fam (girl)* tía *f*, chica *f*

birdcage ['bɜːdkeɪdʒ] *n* jaula *f*

birdie ['bɜːdɪ] *n (in golf)* birdie *m*

bird's-eye view [bɜːdzaɪ'vjuː] *n* vista *f* de pájaro

bird-watcher ['bɜːdwɒtʃə(r)] *n* ornitólogo(a) *m,f*

Biro® ['baɪrəʊ] *n Fam* boli *m*

birth [bɜːθ] *n* (**a**) nacimiento *m*; *(childbirth)* parto *m*; **by b.** de nacimiento; **to give b. to a child** dar a luz a un niño; **b. certificate** partida *f* de nacimiento; **b. control** *(family planning)* control *m* de la natalidad; *(contraception)* métodos anticonceptivos; **b. rate** índice *m* de natalidad (**b**) **of noble b.** *(parentage)* de noble linaje

birthday ['bɜːθdeɪ] *n* cumpleaños *m inv*

birthmark ['bɜːθmɑːk] *n* antojo *m*

birthplace ['bɜːθpleɪs] *n* lugar *m* de nacimiento

Biscay ['bɪskeɪ] *n* Vizcaya; **the Bay of B.** el golfo de Vizcaya

biscuit ['bɪskɪt] *n* (**a**) *Br (sweet, salted)* galleta *f; Fam* **that really takes the b.!** ¡eso ya es el colmo! (**b**) *US (savoury)* bollo *m*, bizcocho *m*

bisect [baɪ'sekt] *vt* bisegmentar; *Geom* bisecar

bisexual [baɪ'seksjʊəl] *adj* bisexual

bishop ['bɪʃəp] *n* (**a**) *Rel* obispo *m* (**b**) *(in chess)* alfil *m*

bison ['baɪsən] *n inv* bisonte *m*

bit¹ [bɪt] *n* (**a**) *(small piece)* trozo *m*, pedazo *m*; **to smash sth to bits** hacer añicos algo; *Fig* **thrilled to bits** muy emocionado(a); *Fig* **to do one's b.** poner de su parte (**b**) *(small quantity)* poco *m*; **a b. of sugar** un poco de azúcar; **a b.**

of advice un consejo; **a b. of news** una noticia; **bits and pieces** trastos *mpl*; *Fig* **b. by b.** poco a poco (**c**) *(slightly)* un poco; **a b. longer** un ratito más; **a b. worried** un poco preocupado (**d**) *(coin)* moneda *f*

bit² [bɪt] *n (of tool)* broca *f*

bit³ [bɪt] *n Comput* bit *m*

bit⁴ [bɪt] *pt of* **bite**

bitch [bɪtʃ] **1** *n* (**a**) *Zool (female)* hembra *f*; *(dog)* perra *f* (**b**) *Fam (spiteful woman)* bruja *f*
2 *vi Fam* **to b.** *(criticize)* criticar

bitchy ['bɪtʃɪ] *adj Fam (spiteful)* maldiciente; *(malicious)* malicioso(a); *(malevolent)* malintencionado(a)

bite [baɪt] **1** *n* (**a**) *(act)* mordisco *m* (**b**) *(wound)* mordedura *f*; **(insect) b.** picadura *f* (**c**) *(mouthful)* bocado *m* (**d**) *Fam (snack)* bocado *m*
2 *vt (pt* **bit**; *pp* **bitten**) morder; *(insect)* picar; **to b. one's nails** morderse las uñas; *Fig* **to b. the dust** *(suffer defeat)* morder el polvo; *(die)* palmarla; *Fam* **to b. sb's head off** echarle una bronca a algn
3 *vi* (**a**) morder; *(insect)* picar (**b**) *Fig (take effect)* surtir efecto (**c**) *(fish)* picar

biting ['baɪtɪŋ] *adj (wind)* cortante; *Fig (criticism)* mordaz

bitten ['bɪtən] *pp of* **bite**

bitter ['bɪtə(r)] **1** *adj* (**a**) amargo(a) (**b**) *(weather)* glacial; *(wind)* cortante (**c**) *(person)* amargado(a) (**d**) *(struggle)* enconado(a); *(hatred)* implacable
2 *n* (**a**) *(beer)* cerveza amarga (**b**) **bitters** bíter *m*

bitterly ['bɪtəlɪ] *adv* **she was b. disappointed** sufrió una terrible decepción

bitterness ['bɪtənɪs] *n* (**a**) amargura *f* (**b**) *(of weather)* crudeza *f* (**c**) *(of person)* rencor *m*

bittersweet [bɪtə'swiːt] *adj* agridulce

bitumen ['bɪtjʊmɪn] *n* betún *m*

bizarre [bɪ'zɑː(r)] *adj (odd)* extraño(a); *(eccentric)* estrafalario(a)

blab [blæb] *vi Fam* parlotear; *(let out a secret)* chivarse

black [blæk] **1** *adj* (**a**) *(colour)* negro(a); **a b. and white television** un televisor en blanco y negro; *Fig* **b. and blue** amoratado(a); **to put sth down in b. and white** poner algo por escrito; *Av* **b. box** caja negra; **b. coffee** café solo; **b. eye** ojo morado; **b. hole** agujero negro; **b. humour** humor negro; **b. magic** magia negra; **b. market** mercado negro; *Br* **b. pudding** morcilla *f*; **the B. Sea** el Mar Negro; *Aut* **b. spot** punto negro; *Br* **the B. Country =** la región de los Midlands; *Fig* **b. sheep** oveja negra
(**b**) *(gloomy)* negro(a); *Fig* **a b. day** un día aciago
2 *n* (**a**) *(colour)* negro *m*
(**b**) *(person)* negro(a) *m,f*
3 *vt* (**a**) *(make black)* ennegrecer
(**b**) *(polish)* lustrar

(**c**) *(boycott)* boicotear

▸ **black out 1** *vt sep* (**a**) *(extinguish lights in)* apagar las luces de (**b**) *(censor)* censurar
2 *vi (faint)* desmayarse

blackberry ['blækbərɪ] *n* zarzamora *f*

blackbird ['blækbɜːd] *n* mirlo *m*

blackboard ['blækbɔːd] *n* pizarra *f*, encerado *m*

blackcurrant [blæk'kʌrənt] *n* grosella negra

blacken ['blækən] *vt* (**a**) *(make black)* ennegrecer (**b**) *Fig (defame)* manchar

blackhead ['blækhed] *n* espinilla *f*

blackjack ['blækdʒæk] *n Cards* veintiuna *f*

blackleg ['blækleg] *n* esquirol *m*

blacklist ['blæklɪst] *n* lista negra

blackmail ['blækmeɪl] **1** *n* chantaje *m*
2 *vt* chantajear

blackout ['blækaʊt] *n* (**a**) *(of lights)* apagón *m* (**b**) *Rad & TV* censura *f* (**c**) *(fainting)* pérdida *f* de conocimiento

blacksmith ['blæksmɪθ] *n* herrero *m*

bladder ['blædə(r)] *n* vejiga *f*; **gall b.** vesícula *f* biliar

blade [bleɪd] *n* (**a**) *(of grass)* brizna *f* (**b**) *(of knife etc)* hoja *f* (**c**) *(of propeller, oar)* pala *f*

blame [bleɪm] **1** *n* culpa *f*; **to take the b. for sth** asumir la responsabilidad de algo
2 *vt* echar la culpa a; **he is to b.** él tiene la culpa

blameless ['bleɪmlɪs] *adj (person)* inocente; *(conduct)* intachable

blancmange [blə'mɒnʒ] *n =* tipo de budín dulce

bland [blænd] *adj (food)* soso(a)

---

*Note that the Spanish word **blando** is a false friend and is never a translation for the English word **bland**. In Spanish, **blando** means "soft".*

---

blank [blæŋk] **1** *adj* (**a**) *(without writing)* en blanco; *Fin* **b. cheque** cheque *m* en blanco (**b**) *(empty)* vacío(a); **a. b. look** una mirada inexpresiva (**c**) **a b. refusal** *(absolute)* una negativa rotunda
2 *n* (**a**) *(space)* espacio *m* en blanco; **to draw a b.** no tener éxito (**b**) *Mil* cartucho *m* de fogueo (**c**) *US (form)* impreso *m*

blanket ['blæŋkɪt] **1** *n* manta *f*, *Am* frazada *f*, cobija *f*; *Fig* capa *f*
2 *adj* general

blare [bleə(r)] *vi* resonar
▸ **blare out** *vt sep* pregonar

blasé ['blɑːzeɪ] *adj* de vuelta (de todo)

blasphemous ['blæsfəməs] *adj* blasfemo(a)

blasphemy ['blæsfəmɪ] *n* blasfemia *f*

blast [blɑːst] **1** *n* (**a**) *(of wind)* ráfaga *f* (**b**) *(of horn etc)* toque *m*; **at full b.** a toda marcha (**c**) *(explosion)* explosión *f*; **b. furnace** alto horno (**d**) *(shock wave)* onda *f* de choque
2 *vt (blow up)* volar; *Fam* **b. (it)!** ¡maldito sea! (**b**) *Fig (destroy)* arruinar (**c**) *Fig (criticize)* criticar

blasted ['blɑːstɪd] *adj* maldito(a)

blast-off ['blɑ:stɒf] *n* despegue *m*

blatant ['bleɪtənt] *adj (very obvious)* evidente; *(shameless)* descarado(a); **a b. lie** una mentira patente

blaze¹ [bleɪz] **1** *n* (a) *(burst of flame)* llamarada *f* (b) *(fierce fire)* incendio *m* (c) *(of sun)* resplandor *m* (d) *Fig (of anger)* arranque *m*
2 *vi* (a) *(fire)* arder (b) *(sun etc)* brillar

blaze² [bleɪz] *vt* **to b. a trail** abrir un camino

blazer ['bleɪzə(r)] *n* chaqueta *f* sport

bleach [bli:tʃ] **1** *n (household)* lejía *f*
2 *vt* (a) *(whiten)* blanquear; *(fade)* descolorir (b) *(hair)* decolorar

bleachers ['bli:tʃəz] *npl US Sport (seats)* gradas *fpl*

bleak [bli:k] *adj* (a) *(countryside)* desolado(a) (b) *(weather)* desapacible (c) *(future)* poco prometedor(a)

bleary ['blɪərɪ] *adj (blearier, bleariest) (eyes) (due to tears)* lloroso(a); *(due to tiredness)* cansado(a)

bleary-eyed [blɪərɪ'aɪd] *adj* con los ojos llorosos/cansados

bleat [bli:t] **1** *n* balido *m*
2 *vi (animal)* balar

bleed [bli:d] **1** *vi (pt & pp* **bled** [bled]) sangrar
2 *vt Med* sangrar; *Fam* **to b. sb dry** sacarle a algn hasta el último céntimo

bleeding ['bli:dɪŋ] **1** *n (loss of blood)* pérdida *f* de sangre
2 *adj* (a) *Med* sangrante (b) *Fam Pej* puñetero(a)

bleep [bli:p] **1** *n* bip *m*, pitido *m*
2 *vi* pitar

bleeper ['bli:pə(r)] *n Fam* busca *m*, buscapersonas *m inv*

blemish ['blemɪʃ] *n (flaw)* defecto *m*; *(on fruit)* maca *f*; *Fig* mancha *f*; *Fig* **without b.** sin tacha

blend [blend] **1** *n* mezcla *f*
2 *vt (mix)* mezclar; *(colours)* armonizar
3 *vi (mix)* mezclarse; *(colours)* armonizar

blender ['blendə(r)] *n* licuadora *f*

bless [bles] *vt (pt & pp* **blessed** *or* **blest**) (a) bendecir; *Fam* **b. you!** *(after a sneeze)* ¡Jesús! (b) **blessed with good eyesight** dotado(a) de buena vista

blessing ['blesɪŋ] *n* bendición *f*; *(advantage)* ventaja *f*; **a mixed b.** una ventaja relativa

blest [blest] *pt & pp of* **bless**

blew [blu:] *pt of* **blow**

blight [blaɪt] **1** *n* plaga *f*
2 *vt Fig (spoil)* arruinar; *(frustrate)* frustrar

blimey ['blaɪmɪ] *interj Fam* ¡caramba!, ¡caray!

blind [blaɪnd] **1** *adj* ciego(a); **a b. man** un ciego; **a b. woman** una ciega; *Fig* **b. faith** fe ciega; *Fig* **to turn a b. eye** hacer la vista gorda; **b. alley** callejón *m* sin salida; *Aut* **b. corner** curva *f* sin visibilidad; **b. spot** ángulo muerto; *Fam* **b. date** cita *f* a ciegas
2 *adv* a ciegas; *Fam* **to get b. drunk** agarrar

una curda
3 *n* (a) *(on window)* persiana *f* (b) **the b.** los ciegos
4 *vt* (a) cegar, dejar ciego; *Fig* **blinded by ambition** cegado por la ambición (b) *(dazzle)* deslumbrar

blinders ['blaɪndəz] *npl US* anteojeras *fpl*

blindfold ['blaɪndfəʊld] **1** *n* venda *f*
2 *vt* vendar los ojos a

blinding ['blaɪndɪŋ] *adj* cegador(a), deslumbrante

blindly ['blaɪndlɪ] *adv* a ciegas, ciegamente

blindness ['blaɪndnɪs] *n* ceguera *f*

blink [blɪŋk] *vi (eyes)* pestañear; *(lights)* parpadear

blinkered ['blɪŋkəd] *adj Fig* de miras estrechas

blinkers ['blɪŋkəz] *npl (on horse)* anteojeras *fpl*

bliss [blɪs] *n* felicidad *f*; **it was b.!** ¡fue maravilloso!

blissful ['blɪsfʊl] *adj (happy)* feliz; *(marvellous)* maravilloso(a)

blister ['blɪstə(r)] **1** *n (on skin)* ampolla *f*; *(on paint)* burbuja *f*
2 *vi* ampollarse

blithe [blaɪð] *adj* alegre

blithely ['blaɪðlɪ] *adv* alegremente

blitz [blɪts] **1** *n* bombardeo aéreo
2 *vt* bombardear

blizzard ['blɪzəd] *n* ventisca *f*

bloated ['bləʊtɪd] *adj* hinchado(a)

blob [blɒb] *n (drop)* gota *f*; *(spot)* mancha *f*

bloc [blɒk] *n Pol* bloque *m*

block [blɒk] **1** *n* (a) bloque *m*; *(of wood)* taco *m*; **in b. capitals** en mayúsculas (b) **a b. of flats** un bloque de pisos (c) *(group of buildings)* manzana *f* (d) *(obstruction)* bloqueo *m* (e) *Fin* **a b. of shares** un paquete de acciones (f) *Fam (head)* coco *m*
2 *vt* (a) *(obstruct)* obstruir; *Aut* **road blocked** *(sign)* carretera cortada; **to b. the way** cerrar el paso (b) *Sport (player)* obstaculizar (c) *Fin* bloquear
► **block up** *vt sep* bloquear, obstruir; **to get blocked up** *(pipe)* obstruirse

blockade [blɒ'keɪd] *n* bloqueo *m*

blockage ['blɒkɪdʒ] *n* bloqueo *m*, obstrucción *f*; *(traffic jam)* atasco *m*

blockbuster ['blɒkbʌstə(r)] *n Fam* exitazo *m*; *Cin & TV* gran éxito *m* de taquilla; *(book)* éxito de ventas

bloke [bləʊk] *n Fam* tío *m*, tipo *m*

blond [blɒnd] *adj & n* rubio *(m)*

blonde [blɒnd] *adj & n* rubia *(f)*

blood [blʌd] *n* (a) sangre *f*; **b. bank** banco *m* de sangre; **b. cell** glóbulo *m*; **b. donor** donante *mf* de sangre; **b. group** grupo sanguíneo; **b. pressure** tensión *f* arterial; *US* **b. sausage** morcilla *f*; **b. test** análisis *m* de sangre; **b. transfusion** transfusión *f* de sangre; **b. vessel** vaso sanguíneo; **blue b.** sangre azul; **high/**

low **b. pressure** hipertensión *f*/hipotensión *f* (**b**) *(race)* sangre *f*, raza *f*

bloodbath ['blʌdbɑ:θ] *n Fig* baño *m* de sangre

bloodhound ['blʌdhaʊnd] *n* sabueso *m*

bloodshed ['blʌdʃed] *n* derramamiento *m* de sangre

bloodshot ['blʌdʃɒt] *adj* inyectado(a) de sangre

bloodstream ['blʌdstri:m] *n* corriente sanguínea

bloodthirsty ['blʌdθɜ:stɪ] *adj* sanguinario(a)

bloody ['blʌdɪ] **1** *adj* (**bloodier, bloodiest**) (**a**) *(battle)* sangriento(a) (**b**) *(bloodstained)* manchado(a) de sangre (**c**) *Br very Fam (damned)* condenado(a), puñetero(a), *Andes* cojudo(a), *Méx* pinche
2 *adv Br very Fam* **it's b. difficult!** ¡joder, qué difícil!; **not b. likely!** ¡ni de coña!

bloody-minded [blʌdɪ'maɪndɪd] *adj Fam* terco(a)

bloom [blu:m] **1** *n* (**a**) *(flower)* flor *f*; **in full b.** en flor (**b**) *(on fruit)* vello *m*
2 *vi (blossom)* florecer

blooming ['blu:mɪŋ] *adj* (**a**) *(blossoming)* floreciente (**b**) *Fam Euph (damned)* maldito(a), condenado(a)

blossom ['blɒsəm] **1** *n (flower)* flor *f*
2 *vi* florecer; *Fig* **to b. out** alcanzar la plenitud

blot [blɒt] **1** *n (of ink)* borrón *m*; *Fig* mancha *f*
2 *vt* (**a**) *(with ink)* emborronar (**b**) *(dry)* secar
3 *vi (ink)* correrse
▶ **blot out** *vt sep (memories)* borrar; *(view)* ocultar

blotchy ['blɒtʃɪ] *adj* (**blotchier, blotchiest**) *(skin etc)* enrojecido(a); *(paint etc)* cubierto(a) de manchas

blotting-paper ['blɒtɪŋpeɪpə(r)] *n* papel *m* secante

blouse [blaʊz] *n* blusa *f*

blow¹ [bləʊ] *n* golpe *m*; **to come to blows** llegar a las manos; **it came as a terrible b.** fue un duro golpe

blow² [bləʊ] **1** *vi (pt blew; pp blown)* (**a**) *(wind)* soplar; **to b. shut** cerrarse de golpe (**b**) *(fuse)* fundirse (**c**) *(tyre)* reventar
2 *vt* (**a**) *(kiss)* mandar (**b**) *(trumpet etc)* tocar; *Fig* **to b. one's own trumpet** darse bombo (**c**) *(one's nose)* sonarse (**d**) *(fuse)* fundir (**e**) *Fam (waste)* despilfarrar (**f**) *Fam (chances)* dar al traste con (**g**) *(explode)* volar; *Fig* **to b. sb's cover** descubrir la tapadera de algn; *Fam* **to b. one's top** salirse de sus casillas
▶ **blow away** *vt sep & vi* = **blow off**
▶ **blow down** *vt sep* derribar
▶ **blow off 1** *vt sep (by wind)* llevarse
2 *vi (hat)* salir volando
▶ **blow out** *vt sep* apagar

2 *vi* apagarse
▶ **blow over** *vi (storm)* calmarse; *(scandal)* olvidarse
▶ **blow up 1** *vt sep* (**a**) *(building)* volar (**b**) *(inflate)* inflar (**c**) *Phot* ampliar
2 *vi (explode)* explotar

blowlamp ['bləʊlæmp] *n* soplete *m*

blown [bləʊn] *pp of* **blow**

blowout ['bləʊaʊt] *n Aut* reventón *m*; *Fam (meal)* comilona *f*

blowtorch ['bləʊtɔ:tʃ] *n US* soplete *m*

blow-up ['bləʊʌp] *n Phot* ampliación *f*

blubber ['blʌbə(r)] **1** *n* grasa *f* de ballena
2 *vi Fam* llorar a moco tendido

bludgeon ['blʌdʒən] *vt* aporrear; *Fig* **to b. sb into doing sth** forzar a algn a hacer algo

blue [blu:] **1** *adj* (**a**) *(colour)* azul; *Fig* **once in a b. moon** de higos a brevas; *Fam* **to scream b. murder** gritar como un loco; **b. jeans** vaqueros *mpl*, tejanos *mpl* (**b**) *(sad)* triste; **to feel b.** sentirse deprimido (**c**) *(obscene)* verde; **b. joke** chiste *m* verde
2 *n* (**a**) *(colour)* azul *m*; *Fam* **the boys in b.** los maderos (**b**) **out of the b.** *(suddenly)* de repente; *(unexpectedly)* como llovido del cielo

bluebell ['blu:bel] *n* campanilla *f*

blueberry ['blu:bərɪ] *n* arándano *m*

bluebottle ['blu:bɒtəl] *n* moscarda *f*, mosca *f* azul

blue-collar ['blu:kɒlə(r)] *adj* **b. worker** obrero(a) *m,f*

blueprint ['blu:prɪnt] *n* anteproyecto *m*

blues [blu:z] *n* (**a**) *Mus* **the b.** el blues (**b**) *Fam (sadness)* tristeza *f*, melancolía *f*; **to have the b.** sentirse deprimido

bluetit ['blu:tɪt] *n* herrerillo *m* común

bluff [blʌf] **1** *n (trick)* farol *m*; **to call sb's b.** hacer que algn ponga sus cartas encima de la mesa
2 *adj (abrupt)* brusco(a); *(forthright)* francote(a)
3 *vi* tirarse un farol; **to b. one's way through sth** hacer colar algo

blunder ['blʌndə(r)] **1** *n* metedura *f* de pata; *Fam* patinazo *m*
2 *vi* meter la pata, pegar un patinazo

blunt [blʌnt] **1** *adj* (**a**) *(knife)* desafilado(a); *(pencil)* despuntado(a); **b. instrument** instrumento *m* contundente (**b**) *(frank)* directo(a), francote(a); *(statement)* tajante
2 *vt (pencil)* despuntar; *(knife)* desafilar

bluntly ['blʌntlɪ] *adv* francamente

blur [blɜ:(r)] **1** *n* aspecto borroso
2 *vt (windows)* empañar; *(shape)* desdibujar; *(memory)* enturbiar

blurb [blɜ:b] *n (in book)* resumen *m*

blurred [blɜ:d] *adj* borroso(a)

blurt [blɜ:t] *vt* **to b. out** dejar escapar

blush [blʌʃ] **1** *n* rubor *m*
2 *vi* ruborizarse

blusher ['blʌʃə(r)] *n* colorete *m*

blustery ['blʌstərɪ] *adj* borrascoso(a)

boar [bɔː(r)] *n* verraco *m*; **wild b.** jabalí *m*

board [bɔːd] **1** *n* (**a**) *(plank)* tabla *f* (**b**) *(work surface)* mesa *f*; *(blackboard)* pizarra *f*; *(for games)* tablero *m* (**c**) *(meals)* pensión *f*; **full b.** pensión completa; **b. and lodging** casa *f* y comida (**d**) *(committee)* junta *f*, consejo *m*; **b. of directors** consejo de administración; **b. room** sala *f* del consejo (**e**) *Naut* **on b.** a bordo (**f**) *Fig* **above b.** en regla; **across-the-b.** general; **to let sth go by the b.** abandonar algo

2 *vt (ship, plane etc)* embarcarse en, subir a

3 *vi* (**a**) *(lodge)* alojarse (**b**) *(at school)* estar interno(a)

► **board up** *vt sep* tapar

boarder ['bɔːdə(r)] *n* (**a**) *(in boarding house)* huésped *mf* (**b**) *(at school)* interno(a) *m,f*

boarding ['bɔːdɪŋ] *n* (**a**) *(embarkation)* embarque *m*; **b. card, b. pass** tarjeta *f* de embarque (**b**) *(lodging)* alojamiento *m*, pensión *f*; **b. house** pensión; **b. school** internado *m*

boardwalk ['bɔːdwɔːk] *n US* paseo marítimo entarimado

boast [bəʊst] **1** *n* jactancia *f*, alarde *m*

2 *vi* jactarse, alardear (**about** de)

3 *vt* presumir de, alardear de; **the town boasts an Olympic swimming pool** la ciudad disfruta de una piscina olímpica

boat [bəʊt] *n* barco *m*; *(small)* barca *f*, bote *m*; *(launch)* lancha *f*; *(large)* buque *m*; *Fig* **we're all in the same b.** todos estamos en el mismo barco; **fishing b.** barco de pesca

boater ['bəʊtə(r)] *n* canotié *m*, canotier *m*

boatswain ['bəʊsən] *n* contramaestre *m*

boatyard ['bəʊtjɑːd] *n* astillero *m*

bob [bɒb] **1** *n* (**a**) *(haircut)* pelo *m* a lo chico (**b**) *Fam (pl* **bob)** *(shilling)* chelín *m*

2 *vi* **to b. up and down** subir y bajar

bobbin ['bɒbɪn] *n* (*of sewing machine)* canilla *f*; *(for lace-making)* bolillo *m*

bobby ['bɒbɪ] *n Br Fam (policeman)* poli *m*

bobby-pin ['bɒbɪpɪn] *n US (hairgrip)* horquilla *f*

bobsleigh ['bɒbsleɪ] *n* bobsleigh *m*

bode¹ [bəʊd] *pt of* **bide**

bode² [bəʊd] *vt & vi* presagiar; **to b. well/ill** ser de buen/mal agüero

bodice ['bɒdɪs] *n* (**a**) *(sleeveless undergarment)* corpiño *m* (**b**) *(of dress)* cuerpo *m*

bodily ['bɒdɪlɪ] **1** *adj* físico(a); **b. harm** daños *mpl* corporales

2 *adv* **to carry sb b.** llevar a algn en brazos

body ['bɒdɪ] *n* (**a**) *(of person)* cuerpo *m*; **b. language** expresión *f* corporal; **b. odour** olor *m* corporal; **b. piercing** perforaciones *fpl* en el cuerpo, piercing *m* (**b**) *(corpse)* cadáver *m* (**c**) *(main part)* parte *f* principal (**d**) *Aut* carrocería *f*; *Naut* casco *m* (**e**) *(organization)* organismo *m*; *(profession)* cuerpo *m*; **the b. politic** el estado (**f**) *(group of people)* conjunto *m*, grupo *m*

body-blow ['bɒdɪbləʊ] *n Fig* duro golpe

body-builder ['bɒdɪbɪldə(r)] *n* culturista *mf*

body-building ['bɒdɪbɪldɪŋ] *n* culturismo *m*

bodyguard ['bɒdɪgɑːd] *n* guardaespaldas *mf inv*

bodywork ['bɒdɪwɜːk] *n Aut* carrocería *f*

Boer ['bəʊə(r)] *adj* **the B. War** la guerra del Transvaal

bog [bɒg] *n* (**a**) ciénaga *f* (**b**) *Br very Fam (lavatory)* meódromo *m*

► **bog down** *vt sep* **to get bogged down** atascarse

bogey ['bəʊgɪ] *n* (**a**) *(spectre)* espectro *m*, fantasma *m* (**b**) *(bugbear)* pesadilla *f* (**c**) *(in golf)* bogey *m* (**d**) *Fam (mucus)* moco *m*

boggle ['bɒgəl] *vi Fam* **the mind boggles!** ¡es alucinante!

bogus ['bəʊgəs] *adj* falso(a); **b. company** compañía *f* fantasma

boil¹ [bɔɪl] **1** *n* **to come to the b.** empezar a hervir

2 *vt (water)* hervir; *(food)* cocer; *(egg)* cocer, pasar por agua

3 *vi* hervir; *Fig* **to b. with rage** estar furioso(a)

► **boil down** *vi* reducirse (**to** a)

► **boil over** *vi (milk)* salirse

boil² [bɔɪl] *n Med* furúnculo *m*

boiled [bɔɪld] *adj* **b. egg** huevo cocido *or* pasado por agua

boiler ['bɔɪlə(r)] *n* caldera *f*; *Br* **b. suit** mono *m*

boiling ['bɔɪlɪŋ] *adj* **b. water** agua hirviendo; **it's b. hot** *(food)* quema; *(weather)* hace un calor agobiante; **b. point** punto *m* de ebullición

boisterous ['bɔɪstərəs] *adj* (**a**) *(person, party)* bullicioso(a) (**b**) *(weather)* borrascoso(a)

bold [bəʊld] *adj* (**a**) *(brave)* valiente (**b**) *(daring)* audaz (**c**) *(features)* marcado(a); *Typ* **b. type** negrita *f* (**d**) *(impudent)* descarado(a)

Bolivia [bə'lɪvɪə] *n* Bolivia

Bolivian [bə'lɪvɪən] *adj & n* boliviano(a) *(m,f)*

bollard ['bɒlɑːd] *n Aut* baliza *f*

bollocks ['bɒləks] *npl Br very Fam* cojones *mpl*; **b.!** *(disagreement)* ¡y un huevo!

Bolshevik ['bɒlʃəvɪk] *adj & n* bolchevique *(mf)*

bolster ['bəʊlstə(r)] **1** *n (pillow)* cabezal *m*, travesaño *m*

2 *vt (strengthen)* reforzar; *(support)* apoyar

bolt [bəʊlt] **1** *n* (**a**) *(on door)* cerrojo *m*; *(small)* pestillo *m* (**b**) *Tech* perno *m*, tornillo *m* (**c**) *(of lightning)* rayo *m* (**d**) *(crossbow)* flecha *f*

2 *vt* (**a**) *(lock)* cerrar con cerrojo (**b**) *Tech* sujetar con pernos (**c**) *Fam (food)* engullir

3 *vi (person)* largarse; *(horse)* desbocarse

4 *adv* **b. upright** derecho

bomb [bɒm] **1** *n* bomba *f*; *Br Fam* **to cost a b.** costar un ojo de la cara; **b. disposal squad**

brigada *f* de artificieros; **b. scare** amenaza *f* de bomba; **car b.** coche-bomba *m*; **letter b.** carta-bomba *f*

2 *vt* (*city etc*) bombardear; (*by terrorists*) volar

3 *vi Fam* **to b. (along)** (*car*) ir a toda pastilla

bombard [bɒm'bɑːd] *vt* bombardear

bombardment [bɒm'bɑːdmənt] *n* bombardeo *m*

bombastic [bɒm'bæstɪk] *adj* rimbombante

bomber ['bɒmə(r)] *n* (**a**) *Av* bombardero *m*; **b. jacket** cazadora *f* (**b**) terrorista *mf* que coloca bombas

bombshell ['bɒmʃel] *n* (**a**) *Mil* obús *m* (**b**) *Fig* (*surprise*) bomba *f* (**c**) *Fam* **a blonde b.** una rubia explosiva

bona fide ['bəʊnə'faɪdɪ] *adj* (**a**) (*genuine*) auténtico(a) (**b**) (*in good faith*) bienintencionado(a)

bond [bɒnd] **1** *n* (**a**) (*link*) lazo *m*, vínculo *m* (**b**) *Fin* bono *m* (**c**) *Jur* (*bail*) fianza *f* (**d**) (*binding agreement*) acuerdo *m* (**e**) (*warehouse*) depósito *m*; **in b.** en depósito (**f**) *US* (*guarantee*) garantía *f* (**g**) **bonds** (*shackles*) cadenas *fpl*

2 *vt* (**a**) (*join*) pegar (**b**) (*merchandise*) poner en depósito

bondage ['bɒndɪdʒ] *n* esclavitud *f*

bone [bəʊn] **1** *n* (**a**) hueso *m*; (*in fish*) espina *f*; *Fig* **b. of contention** manzana *f* de la discordia; *Fig* **he made no bones about it** no trató de disimularlo; **b. china** porcelana fina (**b**) **bones** (*remains*) restos *mpl*; **the bare bones** lo esencial

2 *vt* (*meat*) deshuesar; (*fish*) quitar las espinas a

▸ **bone up on** *vt insep Fam* empollar

bone-dry ['bəʊn'draɪ] *adj* completamente seco(a)

bone-idle ['bəʊn'aɪdəl] *adj* gandul(a)

bonfire ['bɒnfaɪə(r)] *n* hoguera *f*, fogata *f*; *Br* **B. Night** = fiesta del 5 de noviembre en que de noche se hacen hogueras y hay fuegos artificiales

bonkers ['bɒŋkəz] *adj Br Fam* chalado(a)

bonnet ['bɒnɪt] *n* (**a**) (*child's*) gorra *f* (**b**) *Br Aut* capó *m*

bonus ['bəʊnəs] *n* (**a**) (*on wages*) prima *f* (**b**) *Fin* (*on shares*) dividendo *m* extraordinario (**c**) *Br Ins* beneficio *m*

bony ['bəʊnɪ] *adj* (**bonier, boniest**) (*person*) huesudo(a); (*fish*) lleno(a) de espinas

boo [buː] **1** *interj* ¡bu!

2 *n* abucheo *m*

3 *vt* abuchear

boob [buːb] *n Br Fam* (**a**) (*silly mistake*) patinazo *m* (**b**) **boobs** (*breasts*) tetas *fpl*

booby ['buːbɪ] *n* **b. prize** premio *m* de consolación; **b. trap** trampa *f*; *Mil* trampa explosiva

boogie ['buːgɪ] *vi Fam* bailar

book [bʊk] **1** *n* (**a**) libro *m*; *Fig* **in my b.** según

mi punto de vista; *Fig* **by the b.** según las reglas; **b. end** sujetalibros *m inv*; *Br* **b. token** vale *m* para comprar libros; **savings b.** libreta *f* de ahorros (**b**) (*of stamps*) carpeta *f*; (*of matches*) cajetilla *f* (**c**) *Com* **books** cuentas *fpl*; **to keep the books** llevar las cuentas

2 *vt* (**a**) (*reserve*) reservar; (*return flight*) cerrar (**b**) (*engage*) contratar (**c**) (*by police*) poner una multa a (**d**) *Ftb* amonestar

▸ **book into** *vt insep* (*hotel*) reservar una habitación en

▸ **book out** *vi* (*of hotel*) marcharse

▸ **book up** *vt sep* **booked up** (*sign*) completo

booking ['bʊkɪŋ] *n esp Br* (*reservation*) reserva *f*; **b. office** taquilla *f*

bookmaker ['bʊkmeɪkə(r)] *n* corredor(a) *m* de apuestas

bookseller ['bʊkselə(r)] *n* librero(a) *m,f*

bookshelf ['bʊkʃelf] *n* **bookshelves** estantería *f*

bookshop ['bʊkʃɒp] *n* librería *f*

bookstall ['bʊkstɔːl] *n* quiosco *m*

bookstore ['bʊkstɔː(r)] *n US* librería *f*

bookworm ['bʊkwɜːm] *n Fam* ratón *m* de biblioteca

boom¹ [buːm] **1** *n* (**a**) (*noise*) estampido *m*, trueno *m* (**b**) (*sudden prosperity*) boom *m*, auge *m*

2 *vi* (**a**) (*thunder*) retumbar; (*cannon*) tronar (**b**) (*prosper*) estar en auge

boom² [buːm] *n* (*of microphone*) jirafa *f*

boomerang ['buːməræŋ] *n* bumerang *m*, bumerán *m*

booming ['buːmɪŋ] *adj* (**a**) (*voice, thunder*) que retumba (**b**) (*prosperous*) en auge

boon [buːn] *n* (*blessing*) bendición *f*

boost [buːst] **1** *n* estímulo *m*, empujón *m*

2 *vt* (**a**) (*increase*) aumentar (**b**) **to b. sb's confidence** subirle la moral a algn (**c**) (*tourism, exports*) fomentar (**d**) (*voltage*) elevar

booster ['buːstə(r)] *n* (**a**) *Elec* elevador *m* de voltaje (**b**) *Rad & TV* (*amplifier*) amplificador *m* (**c**) *Med* **b. (shot)** revacunación *f*

boot¹ [buːt] **1** *n* (**a**) bota *f*; (*short*) botín *m*; *Fig* **he's too big for his boots** es muy creído; *Fam* **to put the b. in** pisotear; *Fam* **she got the b.** la echaron (del trabajo); **b. polish** betún *m* (**b**) *Br Aut* maletero *m*, *CAm, Méx* cajuela *f*, *RP* baúl *m*

2 *vt Fam* (**a**) *Ftb* (*ball*) chutar (**b**) **to b. (out)** echar a patadas (**c**) *Comput* arrancar

3 *vi Comput* **to b. (up)** arrancar

boot² [buːt] *n* **to b.** además

bootblack ['buːtblæk] *n esp US* limpiabotas *mf inv*

booth [buːð, buːθ] *n* (**a**) (*in language lab etc*) cabina *f*; **telephone b.** cabina telefónica (**b**) (*at fair*) puesto *m*

bootleg ['buːtleg] *adj* de contrabando

bootlegger ['buːtlegə(r)] *n* contrabandista *m*

booty ['buːtɪ] *n* botín *m*

ooze [buːz] *Fam* **1** *n* priva *f*
2 *vi* privar

op [bɒp] **1** *n* (**a**) *Mus* be-bop *m* (**b**) *Fam (dance)* baile *m*
2 *vi Fam (dance)* bailar

ordeaux [bɔːˈdəʊ] *n* (**a**) *(city)* Burdeos (**b**) *(wine)* burdeos *m*

order [ˈbɔːdə(r)] **1** *n* (**a**) borde *m*, margen *m* (**b**) *Sewing* ribete *m* (**c**) *(frontier)* frontera *f*; **b. town** pueblo fronterizo (**d**) *(flowerbed)* arriate *m*
2 *vt Sewing* ribetear
► border on *vt insep* (**a**) *Geog* lindar con (**b**) *Fig* rayar en

orderline [ˈbɔːdəlaɪn] **1** *n* (**a**) *(border)* frontera *f* (**b**) *(dividing line)* línea divisoria
2 *adj* (**a**) *(on the border)* fronterizo(a) (**b**) *Fig (case etc)* dudoso(a)

ore¹ [bɔː(r)] **1** *vt Tech* taladrar, perforar
2 *n* (**a**) *Tech (hole)* taladro *m* (**b**) *(of gun)* calibre *m*

ore² [bɔː(r)] **1** *vt* aburrir
2 *n (person)* pesado(a) *m,f*, pelma *mf*; *(thing)* lata *f*, rollo *m*; **what a b.!** ¡qué rollo!

ore³ [bɔː(r)] *pt of* **bear**

ored [bɔːd] *adj* aburrido(a); **to be b. stiff** *or* **to tears** estar aburrido(a) como una ostra

oredom [ˈbɔːdəm] *n* aburrimiento *m*

oring [ˈbɔːrɪŋ] *adj (uninteresting)* aburrido(a); *(tedious)* pesado(a), latoso(a)

orn [bɔːn] **1** *pp of* **bear**; **to be b.** nacer; **I wasn't b. yesterday** no nací ayer
2 *adj (having natural ability)* nato(a); **b. poet** poeta nato

orn-again [ˈbɔːnəgen] *adj Rel* converso(a)

orne [bɔːn] *pp of* **bear**

orough [ˈbʌrə] *n* (**a**) *(town)* ciudad *f*; *US (municipality)* municipio *m* (**b**) *esp Br (constituency)* distrito *m* electoral

orrow [ˈbɒrəʊ] **1** *vt* (**a**) pedir *or* tomar prestado; **can I b. your pen?** ¿me dejas tu bolígrafo? (**b**) *(ideas etc)* apropiarse
2 *vi* pedir *or* tomar prestado

orstal [ˈbɔːstəl] *n Br Fam* reformatorio *m*

Bosnia [ˈbɒznɪə] *n* Bosnia

Bosnia-Herzegovina [ˈbɒznɪəhəˈtsəgə-ˈviːnə] *n* Bosnia y Hercegovina

Bosnian [ˈbɒznɪən] *adj & n* bosnio(a) *(m,f)*

osom [ˈbʊzəm] *n* (**a**) *(breast)* pecho *m*; *(breasts)* pechos *mpl*; **b. friend** amigo(a) *m,f* del alma (**b**) *Fig* seno *m*

oss [bɒs] **1** *n* (**a**) *(head)* jefe(a) *m,f*; *(factory owner etc)* patrón(ona) *m,f* (**b**) *esp US Pol* jefe *m*; *Pej* cacique *m*
2 *vt* **to b. sb about** *or* **around** mandar sobre algn

ossy [ˈbɒsɪ] *adj (bossier, bossiest) Fam* mandón(ona)

osun [ˈbəʊsən] *n* contramaestre *m*

otanic(al) [bəˈtænɪk(əl)] *adj* botánico(a); **b. garden** jardín botánico

otany [ˈbɒtənɪ] *n* botánica *f*

botch [bɒtʃ] **1** *vt* chapucear; **a botched job** una chapuza
2 *n* chapuza *f*

both [bəʊθ] **1** *adj* ambos(as), los dos/las dos; **b. men are teachers** ambos son profesores; **hold it with b. hands** sujétalo con las dos manos
2 *pron* (**a**) ambos(as), los dos/las dos; **b. of them** ambos(as), los dos/las dos; **b. of you** vosotros dos
3 *conj* a la vez; **b. England and Spain are in Europe** tanto Inglaterra como España están en Europa

bother [ˈbɒðə(r)] **1** *vt* (**a**) *(disturb)* molestar; *(be a nuisance to)* dar la lata a (**b**) *(worry)* preocupar; *Fam* **I can't be bothered** no tengo ganas
2 *vi* molestarse; **don't b. about me** no te preocupes por mí; **he didn't b. shaving** no se molestó en afeitarse
3 *n* (**a**) *(disturbance)* molestia *f*; *(nuisance)* lata *f* (**b**) *(trouble)* problemas *mpl*
4 *interj Br* ¡maldito sea!

bothersome [ˈbɒðəsəm] *adj* molesto(a)

bottle [ˈbɒtəl] **1** *n* (**a**) botella *f*; *(of perfume, ink)* frasco *m*; *Fam* **to hit the b.** darle a la bebida; **baby's b.** biberón *m*; **b. opener** abrebotellas *m inv* (**b**) *Br Fam* **to have a lot of b.** *(nerve)* tener muchas agallas
2 *vt (wine)* embotellar; *(fruit)* enfrascar
► bottle out *vi Br Fam* encogerse
► bottle up *vt sep* reprimir

bottle-bank [ˈbɒtəlbæŋk] *n* contenedor *m* de vidrio

bottled [ˈbɒtəld] *adj (beer, wine)* en botella, embotellado(a); *(fruit)* envasado(a)

bottle-green [ˈbɒtəlgriːn] *adj* verde botella

bottleneck [ˈbɒtəlnek] *n Aut* embotellamiento *m*, atasco *m*

bottom [ˈbɒtəm] **1** *adj* (**a**) *(lowest)* más bajo(a); *(drawer, shelf)* de abajo; *Aut* **b. gear** primera *f* (**b**) *(last)* último(a); **b. line** saldo *m* final; *Fig* resultado *m* final
2 *n* (**a**) *(of sea, garden, street, box)* fondo *m*; *(of bottle)* culo *m*; *(of page, hill)* pie *m*; *Educ* **to be (at) the b. of the class** ser el último/la última de la clase; **to touch b.** tocar fondo; *Fam* **bottoms up!** ¡salud! (**b**) **to get to the b. of a matter** llegar al meollo de una cuestión; **who is at the b. of all this?** ¿quién está detrás de todo esto? (**c**) *(buttocks)* trasero *m*
► bottom out *vi Fin* tocar fondo

bottomless [ˈbɒtəmlɪs] *adj (pit)* sin fondo; *(mystery)* insondable

boudoir [ˈbuːdwɑː(r)] *n* tocador *m*

bough [baʊ] *n* rama *f*

bought [bɔːt] *pt & pp of* **buy**

bouillon [ˈbuːjɒn] *n* caldo *m*

boulder [ˈbəʊldə(r)] *n* canto rodado *m*

boulevard [ˈbuːləvɑː(r)] *n* bulevar *m*

bounce [baʊns] **1** *vi* (**a**) *(ball)* rebotar (**b**) *(jump)* saltar (**c**) *Fam (cheque)* ser rechazado

(por el banco)

2 vt (ball) botar

3 n (**a**) (of ball) bote m (**b**) (jump) salto m (**c**) (energy) vitalidad f

▸ **bounce back** vi (recover health) recuperarse, recobrarse

bouncer ['baʊnsə(r)] n Fam gorila m

bound¹ [baʊnd] adj (**a**) (tied up) atado(a) (**b**) (book) encuadernado(a) (**c**) (obliged) obligado(a) (**d**) **b. (up)** (linked) vinculado(a) (**with** a) (**e**) **it's b. to happen** sucederá con toda seguridad; **it was b. to fail** estaba destinado al fracaso

bound² [baʊnd] **1** vi saltar

2 n salto m

bound³ [baʊnd] pt & pp of **bind**

bound⁴ [baʊnd] adj **b. for** con destino a, rumbo a; **to be b. for** dirigirse a

boundary ['baʊndərɪ] n límite m

boundless ['baʊndlɪs] adj ilimitado(a), sin límites

bounds [baʊndz] npl **beyond the b. of reality** más allá de la realidad; **her ambition knows no b.** su ambición no conoce límites; **the river is out of b.** está prohibido bajar al río

bounty ['baʊntɪ] n prima f, gratificación f

bouquet n (**a**) [bu:'keɪ, baʊ'keɪ] (of flowers) ramillete m (**b**) [bu:'keɪ] (of wine) aroma m, buqué m

bourbon ['bɜːbən] n US (whiskey) whisky americano, bourbon m

bourgeois ['bʊəʒwɑː] adj & n burgués(esa) (m,f)

bourgeoisie [bʊəʒwɑː'ziː] n burguesía f

bout [baʊt] n (**a**) (of work) turno m; (of illness) ataque m (**b**) (in boxing) combate m

boutique [bu:'tiːk] n boutique f, tienda f

bow¹ [baʊ] **1** vi (**a**) hacer una reverencia (**b**) (give in) ceder

2 n (with head, body) reverencia f

▸ **bow out** vi retirarse (**of** de)

bow² [bəʊ] n (**a**) Sport & Mus arco m; Fig **to have more than one string to one's b.** ser una persona de recursos (**b**) (knot) lazo m; **b. tie** pajarita f

bow³ [baʊ] n esp Naut proa f

bowel ['baʊəl] n (**a**) intestino m (**b**) **bowels** entrañas fpl

bowl¹ [bəʊl] n (**a**) (dish) cuenco m; (for soup) tazón m; (for washing hands) palangana f; (for washing clothes, dishes) barreño m; (of toilet) taza f (**b**) Geol cuenca f

bowl² [bəʊl] **1** n bola f

2 vt (in cricket) lanzar

3 vi (**a**) (play bowls) jugar a los bolos (**b**) (in cricket) lanzar la pelota

▸ **bowl along** vi Fam (car) ir volando

▸ **bowl out** vt sep (in cricket) eliminar

▸ **bowl over** vt sep (**a**) (knock down) derribar (**b**) Fig (astonish) desconcertar

bow-legged ['bəʊleg(ɪ)d] adj patizambo(a)

bowler¹ ['bəʊlə(r)] n (in cricket) lanzador(a m,f

bowler² ['bəʊlə(r)] n (hat) bombín m

bowling ['bəʊlɪŋ] n (game) bolos mpl; **b. alle** bolera f; **b. ball** bola f (de jugar a los bolos)

bowls [bəʊlz] npl Sport bolos mpl

box¹ [bɒks] **1** n (**a**) caja f; (large) cajón m; (c matches) cajetilla f; (jewellery) joyero m; T **b. office** taquilla f; **b. office success** éxit taquillero (**b**) Press recuadro m (**c**) Th palc m (**d**) Br Fam (television) caja tonta

2 vt (pack) embalar

box² [bɒks] Sport **1** vi boxear

2 vt (hit) pegar; **to b. sb's ears** dar un cachet a algn

boxcar ['bɒkskɑː(r)] n US vagón m de mer cancías, furgón m (de mercancías)

boxer ['bɒksə(r)] n (**a**) boxeador m (**b**) (dog bóxer m

boxing ['bɒksɪŋ] n boxeo m; **b. ring** cuadr látero m

Boxing Day ['bɒksɪŋdeɪ] n Br = el día de Sa Esteban (26 de diciembre)

boxroom ['bɒksruːm] n trastero m

boy [bɔɪ] n (**a**) (child) niño m, chico m (youth) joven m; **b. band** = grupo musica juvenil compuesto por adolescentes varo nes; Fam **oh b.!** ¡vaya! (**b**) (son) hijo m

boycott ['bɔɪkɒt] **1** n boicot m

2 vt boicotear

boyfriend ['bɔɪfrend] n novio m; (live-in compañero m

boyhood ['bɔɪhʊd] n niñez f, juventud f

boyish ['bɔɪʃ] adj juvenil, de muchacho

bra [brɑː] n sostén m, Esp sujetador m, Carib Col, Méx brasier m, RP corpiño m

brace [breɪs] **1** n (**a**) (clamp) abrazadera f; (c drill) berbiquí m; (for teeth) aparato m (**b**) (c wood) puntal m (**c**) (pair) par m (**d**) Br **brace** tirantes mpl

2 vt (**a**) (wall) apuntalar (**b**) (strengther reforzar (**c**) **to b. oneself** prepararse (**fo** para)

▸ **brace up** vi cobrar ánimo

bracelet ['breɪslɪt] n pulsera f

bracing ['breɪsɪŋ] adj (wind) fresco(a); (sti mulating) tonificante

bracken ['brækən] n helecho m

bracket ['brækɪt] **1** n (**a**) Typ (round) parénte sis m; (square) corchete m; (curly) llave f; i **brackets** entre paréntesis (**b**) (support) so porte m; (for lamp) brazo m; (shelf) repisa f (c (for tax) sector m

2 vt Ling (phrase etc) poner entre parén tesis (**b**) (group together) agrupar, juntar

brag [bræg] vi jactarse (**about** de)

braggart ['brægət] n fanfarrón(ona) m,f

braid [breɪd] **1** vt trenzar

2 n (**a**) Sewing galón m (**b**) esp US (plai trenza f

Braille [breɪl] n braille m

brain [breɪn] n (**a**) cerebro m; **she's got car**

on the b. está obsesionada por los coches; *Med* **b. death** muerte *f* cerebral; *Fig* **b. drain** fuga *f* de cerebros; **b. wave** idea *f* genial (**b**) *Fam* **brains** inteligencia *f*; **to have brains** ser inteligente; *Br* **brains** or *US* **b. trust** grupo *m* de expertos (**c**) *Culin* **brains** sesos *mpl*

brainchild ['breɪntʃaɪld] *n* invento *m*, idea *f* genial

brainpower ['breɪnpaʊə(r)] *n* capacidad *f* intelectual

brainstorm ['breɪnstɔːm] *n* (**a**) *(outburst)* arranque *m* (**b**) *(brainwave)* genialidad *f*, lluvia *f* de ideas

brainwash ['breɪnwɒʃ] *vt* lavar el cerebro a

brainy ['breɪnɪ] *adj* (**brainier, brainiest**) *Fam* listo(a)

braise [breɪz] *vt* cocer a fuego lento

brake [breɪk] **1** *n Aut (also pl)* freno *m*; **b. drum** tambor *m* del freno; **b. fluid** líquido *m* de frenos; **b. light** luz *f* de freno
2 *vi* frenar, echar el freno

bramble ['bræmbəl] *n* zarza *f*, zarzamora *f*

bran [bræn] *n* salvado *m*

branch [brɑːntʃ] **1** *n* *(of tree)* rama *f*; *(of road)* bifurcación *f*; *(of science etc)* ramo *m*; *Com* **b. (office)** sucursal *f*
2 *vi (road)* bifurcarse
► **branch off** *vi* desviarse
► **branch out** *vi* diversificarse

brand [brænd] **1** *n* (**a**) *Com* marca *f*; **b. name** marca de fábrica (**b**) *(type)* clase *f* (**c**) *(on cattle)* hierro *m*
2 *vt* (**a**) *(animal)* marcar con hierro candente (**b**) *(label)* tildar

brandish ['brændɪʃ] *vt* blandir

brand-new ['bræd'njuː] *adj* flamante

brandy ['brændɪ] *n* coñac *m*, brandy *m*

brash [bræʃ] *adj* (**a**) *(impudent)* descarado(a) (**b**) *(reckless)* temerario(a) (**c**) *(loud, showy)* chillón(ona)

brass [brɑːs] *n* latón *m*; *Fam (money)* pasta *f*; *Mus* instrumentos *mpl* de metal; **b. band** banda *f* de metal

brassiere ['bræzɪə(r)] *n* sostén *m*, sujetador *m*

brat [bræt] *n Fam* mocoso(a) *m,f*

bravado [brə'vɑːdəʊ] *n* bravuconería *f*

brave [breɪv] **1** *adj* valiente, valeroso(a)
2 *n US (Indian)* **b.** guerrero *m* indio
3 *vt* (**a**) *(face)* hacer frente a (**b**) *(defy)* desafiar

bravely ['breɪvlɪ] *adv* valientemente

bravery ['breɪvərɪ] *n* valentía *f*, valor *m*

bravo [brɑː'vəʊ] *interj* ¡bravo!

brawl [brɔːl] **1** *n* reyerta *f*
2 *vi* pelearse

brawn [brɔːn] *n* (**a**) *(strength)* fuerza física (**b**) *Br Culin* queso *m* de cerdo

bray [breɪ] **1** *n* *(of donkey)* rebuzno *m*
2 *vi* rebuznar

brazen ['breɪzən] *adj* descarado(a)

Brazil [brə'zɪl] *n* (el) Brasil

brazil [brə'zɪl] *n* **b. nut** nuez *f* del Brasil

Brazilian [brə'zɪlɪən] *adj & n* brasileño(a) *(m,f)*

breach [briːtʃ] **1** *n* (**a**) *(in wall)* brecha *f* (**b**) *(violation)* incumplimiento *m*; **b. of confidence** abuso *m* de confianza; **b. of contract** incumplimiento de contrato; **b. of the law** violación *f* de la ley; **b. of the peace** alteración *f* del orden público (**c**) *(in relations)* ruptura *f*
2 *vt* violar

bread [bred] *n* (**a**) pan *m*; **b. and butter** pan con mantequilla, *Am* pan con manteca; *Fig* **our daily b.** el pan nuestro de cada día (**b**) *Fam (money)* pasta *f*, *Am* plata *f*

breadboard ['bredbɔːd] *n* tabla *f* (para cortar el pan)

breadcrumb ['bredkrʌm] *n* miga *f* de pan; **breadcrumbs** pan rallado

breadline ['bredlaɪn] *n Fam* miseria *f*; **to be on the b.** vivir en la miseria

breadth [bredθ] *n* (**a**) *(width)* anchura *f*; **it is 2 m in b.** tiene 2 m de ancho (**b**) *(extent)* amplitud *f*

breadwinner ['bredwɪnə(r)] *n* cabeza *mf* de familia

break [breɪk] **1** *vt* (*pt* **broke**; *pp* **broken**) (**a**) romper; **to b. a leg** romperse la pierna; **to b. a record** batir un récord; **to b. even** no tener ni ganancias ni pérdidas; *Fig* **to b. one's back** matarse a trabajar; *Fig* **to b. sb's heart** partirle el corazón a algn; *Fig* **to b. the ice** romper el hielo
(**b**) *(fail to keep)* faltar a; **to b. a contract** romper un contrato; **to b. the law** violar la ley
(**c**) *(destroy)* destrozar; *Fin* arruinar
(**d**) *(interrupt)* interrumpir
(**e**) *(code)* descifrar
(**f**) *(fall)* amortiguar
(**g**) **she broke the news to him** le comunicó la noticia
2 *vi* (**a**) romperse; *(clouds)* dispersarse; *(waves)* romper
(**b**) *(storm)* estallar
(**c**) *(voice)* cambiar
(**d**) *(health)* resentirse
(**e**) **when day breaks** al rayar el alba
(**f**) *(story)* divulgarse
3 *n* (**a**) *(fracture)* rotura *f*; *(crack)* grieta *f*; *(opening)* abertura *f*
(**b**) *(in relationship)* ruptura *f*
(**c**) *(pause)* pausa *f*, descanso *m*; *(at school)* recreo *m*; **to take a b.** descansar un rato; *(holiday)* tomar unos días libres; **without a b.** sin parar
(**d**) *Fam (chance)* oportunidad *f*; **a lucky b.** un golpe de suerte
► **break away** *vi* (**a**) *(become separate)* desprenderse *(from do)* (**b**) *(escape)* escaparse
► **break down 1** *vt sep* (**a**) *(door)* derribar (**b**) *(resistance)* acabar con (**c**) *(costs)* desglosar
2 *vi* (**a**) *Aut* tener una avería (**b**) *(resistance)*

ceder (**c**) *(health)* debilitarse (**d**) *(weep)* ponerse a llorar
► **break in** *vt sep* acostumbrar; **to b. in a pair of shoes** cogerle la forma a los zapatos
2 *vi (burglar)* entrar por la fuerza
► **break into** *vt insep* (**a**) *(burgle) (house)* allanar; *(safe)* forzar (**b**) **to b. into song** empezar a cantar
► **break off** *vt sep* partir
2 *vi* (**a**) *(become detached)* desprenderse (**b**) *(talks)* interrumpirse (**c**) *(stop)* pararse
► **break out** *vi* (**a**) *(prisoners)* escaparse (**b**) *(war etc)* estallar; **she broke out in a rash** le salió un sarpullido
► **break through 1** *vt insep* (**a**) *(crowd)* abrirse paso por; *(cordon)* romper (**b**) *(clouds)* atravesar
2 *vi* (**a**) *(crowd)* abrirse paso (**b**) *(sun)* salir
► **break up 1** *vt sep (object)* romper; *(car)* desguazar; *(crowd)* disolver
2 *vi* (**a**) *(object)* romperse (**b**) *(crowd)* disolverse; *(meeting)* levantarse (**c**) *(relationship)* fracasar; *(couple)* separarse (**d**) *Educ* terminar
► **break with** *vt insep (past)* romper con
breakable ['breɪkəbəl] *adj* frágil
breakage ['breɪkɪdʒ] *n (breaking)* rotura *f*
breakaway ['breɪkəweɪ] *adj* disidente
breakdown ['breɪkdaʊn] *n* (**a**) *Aut* avería *f*; *Br* **b. truck** *or* **van** grúa *f* (**b**) **(nervous) b. crisis** nerviosa (**c**) *(in communications)* ruptura *f* (**d**) *(analysis)* análisis *m*; *Fin* desglose *m*
breaker ['breɪkə(r)] *n* (**a**) *(wave)* ola *f* grande (**b**) *Tech* trituradora *f* (**c**) *(switch)* interruptor automático
breakfast ['brekfəst] **1** *n* desayuno *m*; **to have b.** desayunar
2 *vi* desayunar
break-in ['breɪkɪn] *n* robo *m (con allanamiento de morada)*
breaking ['breɪkɪŋ] *n* (**a**) *rotura f*; **b. point** punto *m* de ruptura (**b**) *Jur* **b. and entering** allanamiento *m* de morada
breakthrough ['breɪkθruː] *n* paso *m* adelante, avance *m*
breakwater ['breɪkwɔːtə(r)] *n* rompeolas *m inv*
breast [brest] *n (chest)* pecho *m*; *(of woman)* pecho, seno *m*; *(of chicken etc)* pechuga *f*; *Fig* **to make a clean b. of it** dar la cara
breast-feed ['brestfiːd] *vt* dar el pecho a, amamantar a
breaststroke ['breststrəʊk] *n* braza *f*
breath [breθ] *n* (**a**) aliento *m*; *(breathing)* respiración *f*; **in the same b.** al mismo tiempo; **out of b.** sin aliento; **to catch one's b.** recobrar el aliento; **to draw b.** respirar; **under one's b.** en voz baja; *Fig* **to take sb's b. away** dejar pasmado a algn; *Aut* **b. test** alcoholemia *f* (**b**) **to go out for a b. of fresh air** salir a tomar el aire
Breathalyser®, *US* **Breathalyzer®** ['breθəlaɪzə(r)] *n Br* Alcoholímetro *m*

breathe [briːð] **1** *vt* respirar; **to b. a sigh of relief** dar un suspiro de alivio
2 *vi* respirar; **to b. in** aspirar; **to b. out** espirar; **to b. heavily** resoplar
breather ['briːðə(r)] *n Fam (rest)* descanso *m*
breathing ['briːðɪŋ] *n* respiración *f*; **b. space** pausa *f*, respiro *m*
breathless ['breθlɪs] *adj* sin aliento, jadeante
breathtaking ['breθteɪkɪŋ] *adj* impresionante
bred [bred] *pt & pp of* **breed**
breeches ['brɪtʃɪz, 'briːtʃɪz] *npl* bombachos *mpl*; **knee b., riding b.** pantalones *mpl* de montar
breed [briːd] **1** *n (of animal)* raza *f*; *Fig (class)* clase *f*
2 *vt (pt & pp* **bred)** *(animals)* criar; *Fig (ideas)* engendrar
3 *vi (animals)* reproducirse
breeder ['briːdə(r)] *n* (**a**) *(person)* criador(a) *m,f* (**b**) **(fast) b. reactor** reactor *m* generador
breeding ['briːdɪŋ] *n* (**a**) *(of animals)* cría *f*; *Fig* **b. ground** caldo *m* de cultivo (**b**) *(of person)* educación *f*
breeze [briːz] **1** *n* brisa *f*; *Constr* **b. block** bloque *m* de cemento
2 *vi* **to b. in/out** entrar/salir despreocupadamente
breezy ['briːzɪ] *adj* **(breezier, breeziest)** (**a**) *(weather)* ventoso(a) (**b**) *(person)* despreocupado(a)
brevity ['brevɪtɪ] *n* brevedad *f*
brew [bruː] **1** *vt (beer)* elaborar; *(hot drink)* preparar
2 *vi (tea)* reposar; *Fig* **a storm is brewing** se prepara una tormenta; *Fam* **something's brewing** algo se está cociendo
3 *n* (**a**) *(of tea)* infusión *f*; *Fam (of beer)* birra *f* (**b**) *(magic potion)* brebaje *m*
brewer ['bruːə(r)] *n* cervecero(a) *m,f*
brewery ['bruːərɪ] *n* cervecería *f*
brewing ['bruːɪŋ] **1** *adj* cervecero(a)
2 *n (of beer)* elaboración *f* de la cerveza
briar ['braɪə(r)] *n* brezo *m*
bribe [braɪb] **1** *vt* sobornar
2 *n* soborno *m*
bribery ['braɪbərɪ] *n* soborno *m*
bric-a-brac ['brɪkəbræk] *n* baratijas *fpl*
brick [brɪk] *n* ladrillo *m*; *Fam (reliable person)* persona *f* de confianza
bricklayer ['brɪkleɪə(r)] *n* albañil *m*
brickwork ['brɪkwɜːk] *n* ladrillos *mpl*
bridal ['braɪdəl] *adj* nupcial
bride [braɪd] *n* novia *f*; **the b. and groom** los novios
bridegroom ['braɪdgruːm] *n* novio *m*
bridesmaid ['braɪdzmeɪd] *n* dama *f* de honor
bridge¹ [brɪdʒ] **1** *n* puente *m*; *(of nose)* caballete *m*; *(of ship)* puente de mando
2 *vt* (**a**) *(river)* tender un puente sobre (**b**) *(gap)* llenar; *Fin* **bridging loan** crédito *m* a corto plazo

bridge² [brɪdʒ] n Cards bridge m
bridle ['braɪdəl] **1** n brida f; (bit) freno m; **b. path** camino m de herradura
2 vt (horse) embridar
brief [briːf] **1** adj (a) (short) breve (b) (concise) conciso(a)
2 n (a) (report) informe m; **in b.** en resumen (b) Jur expediente m (c) Mil instrucciones fpl (d) **briefs** (for men) calzoncillos mpl; (for women) bragas fpl
3 vt (a) (inform) informar (b) (instruct) dar instrucciones a
briefcase ['briːfkeɪs] n cartera f, portafolios m inv
briefing ['briːfɪŋ] n (meeting) reunión informativa
briefly ['briːflɪ] adv brevemente; **as b. as possible** con la mayor brevedad (posible)
brigade [brɪ'geɪd] n brigada f
brigadier [brɪgə'dɪə(r)] n general m de brigada
bright [braɪt] adj (a) (light, sun, eyes) brillante; (colour) vivo(a); (day) claro(a) (b) (cheerful) alegre; **to look on the b. side** mirar el lado bueno (c) (clever) listo(a), espabilado(a) (d) (promising) prometedor(a)
brighten ['braɪtən] vi (prospects) mejorarse; (face) iluminarse
▸ **brighten up 1** vt sep (room etc) alegrar
2 vi (weather) despejarse; (person) animarse
brightly ['braɪtlɪ] adv brillantemente
brightness ['braɪtnɪs] n (a) (of sun) resplandor m; (of day) claridad f; (of colour) viveza f (b) (cleverness) inteligencia f
brilliance ['brɪljəns] n (a) (of light) brillo m; (of colour) viveza f (b) (of person) brillantez f
brilliant ['brɪljənt] **1** adj brillante; (idea) genial; Fam (very good) estupendo(a)
2 n brillante m
brim [brɪm] **1** n borde m; (of hat) ala f; **full to the b.** lleno hasta el borde
2 vi rebosar (with de)
▸ **brim over** vi rebosar
brine [braɪn] n salmuera f
bring [brɪŋ] vt (pt & pp brought) (a) (carry, take) traer; **could you b. that book?** ¿podrías traerme el libro?
(b) (take to a different position) llevar; **the war brought hunger to many homes** la guerra llevó el hambre a muchos hogares
(c) (cause) provocar; **he brought it upon himself** se lo buscó
(d) (persuade) convencer; **how did they b. themselves to do it?** ¿cómo llegaron a hacerlo?
(e) (lead) llevar
(f) **to b. an action against** acusar
▸ **bring about** vt sep provocar
▸ **bring along** vt sep traer
▸ **bring back** vt sep (a) (return) devolver (b) (reintroduce) volver a introducir (c) (make

one remember) traerle a la memoria
▸ **bring down** vt sep (a) (from upstairs) bajar (b) (government) derribar; Th **to b. the house down** echar el teatro abajo con los aplausos (c) (reduce) rebajar
▸ **bring forward** vt sep (a) (meeting etc) adelantar (b) (present) presentar (c) Fin **brought forward** suma y sigue
▸ **bring in** vt sep (a) (yield) dar (b) (show in) hacer entrar (c) (law etc) introducir; (fashion) lanzar
▸ **bring off** vt sep lograr, conseguir
▸ **bring on** vt sep provocar
▸ **bring out** vt sep (a) (publish) publicar (b) (reveal) recalcar; **he brings out the worst in me** despierta lo peor que hay en mí
▸ **bring round** vt sep (a) (revive) hacer volver en sí (b) (persuade) convencer
▸ **bring to** vt sep reanimar
▸ **bring up** vt sep (a) (educate) criar, educar (b) (subject) plantear (c) (vomit) devolver
brink [brɪŋk] n (edge) borde m; Fig **on the b. of ruin** al borde de la ruina; **on the b. of tears** a punto de llorar
brisk [brɪsk] adj enérgico(a); (pace) rápido(a); (trade) activo(a); (weather) fresco(a)
bristle ['brɪsəl] **1** n cerda f
2 vi (a) erizarse (b) (show anger) enfurecer (at con)
▸ **bristle with** vt insep (be full of) estar lleno(a) de
Brit [brɪt] n Fam británico(a) m,f
Britain ['brɪtən] n **(Great) B.** Gran Bretaña
British ['brɪtɪʃ] **1** adj británico(a); **the B. Isles** las Islas Británicas
2 npl **the B.** los británicos
brittle ['brɪtəl] adj quebradizo(a), frágil
broach [brəʊtʃ] vt (subject) abordar
broad [brɔːd] **1** adj (a) (wide) ancho(a); (large) extenso(a) (b) **a b. hint** (clear) una indirecta clara (c) (daylight) pleno(a) (d) (not detailed) general (e) (accent) marcado(a), cerrado(a)
2 n US Fam (woman) tía f, chica f
broadcast ['brɔːdkɑːst] Rad & TV **1** n emisión f
2 vt (pt & pp broadcast) emitir, transmitir
broadcaster ['brɔːdkɑːstə(r)] n locutor(a) m,f
broadcasting ['brɔːdkɑːstɪŋ] n Rad radiodifusión f; TV transmisión f; Rad **b. station** emisora f
broaden ['brɔːdən] vt ensanchar
broadly ['brɔːdlɪ] adv en términos generales
broad-minded [brɔːd'maɪndɪd] adj liberal, tolerante
broadsheet ['brɔːdʃiːt] n folleto m
broccoli ['brɒkəlɪ] n brécol m
brochure ['brəʊʃə(r), 'brəʊʃjʊə(r)] n folleto m
broil [brɔɪl] vt US asar a la parrilla
broiler ['brɔɪlə(r)] n (a) (chicken) pollo m (tomatero) (b) US (grill) parrilla f

broke [brəʊk] **1** *adj Fam* **to be (flat) b.** estar sin blanca
2 *pt of* **break**
broken ['brəʊkən] **1** *adj* (**a**) roto(a); *(machinery)* averiado(a); *(leg)* fracturado(a) (**b**) *(home)* deshecho(a); *(person)* destrozado(a); *(ground)* accidentado(a); **to speak b. English** chapurrear el inglés
2 *pp of* **break**
broken-hearted [brəʊkən'hɑ:tɪd] *adj Fig* con el corazón destrozado
broker ['brəʊkə(r)] *n* corredor *m*, agente *mf* de Bolsa
brolly ['brɒlɪ] *n Fam* paraguas *m inv*
bronchitis [brɒŋ'kaɪtɪs] *n* bronquitis *f*
bronze [brɒnz] **1** *n* bronce *m*
2 *adj (material)* de bronce; *(colour)* bronceado(a)
bronzed [brɒnzd] *adj (suntanned)* bronceado(a)
brooch [brəʊtʃ] *n* broche *m*
brood [bru:d] **1** *n (birds)* cría *f*, *Hum (children)* prole *m*
2 *vi (hen)* empollar; *Fig (ponder)* rumiar; *Fig* **to b. over a problem** darle vueltas a un problema
broody ['bru:dɪ] *adj* (**a**) *Fam (woman)* con ganas de tener hijos (**b**) *(pensive)* pensativo(a) (**c**) *(moody)* melancólico(a)
brook¹ [brʊk] *n* arroyo *m*
brook² [brʊk] *vt (usu in negative)* soportar, aguantar
broom [bru:m] *n* (**a**) escoba *f* (**b**) *Bot* retama *f*
broomstick ['bru:mstɪk] *n* palo *m* de escoba
Bros *Com (abbr* **Brothers)** Hnos
broth [brɒθ] *n* caldo *m*
brothel ['brɒθəl] *n* burdel *m*
brother ['brʌðə(r)] *n* hermano *m*; **brothers and sisters** hermanos
brotherhood ['brʌðəhʊd] *n* hermandad *f*
brother-in-law ['brʌðərɪnlɔ:] *n* cuñado *m*
brotherly ['brʌðəlɪ] *adj* fraternal
brought [brɔ:t] *pt & pp of* **bring**
brow [braʊ] *n* (**a**) *(forehead)* frente *f* (**b**) *(eyebrow)* ceja *f* (**c**) *(of hill)* cima *f*
brown [braʊn] **1** *adj* (**a**) marrón; *(hair, eyes)* castaño(a); **b. bread** pan *m* integral; **b. paper** papel *m* de estraza; **b. sugar** azúcar moreno (**b**) *(tanned)* moreno(a)
2 *n* marrón *m*
3 *vt Culin* dorar; *(tan)* broncear
Brownie ['braʊnɪ] *n* niña exploradora
brownish ['braʊnɪʃ] *adj* pardusco(a)
browse [braʊz] **1** *vi (in shop)* mirar; *(through book)* hojear
2 *vt Comput* **to b. the Web** navegar por la Web
3 *n* **to have a b. (in)** dar un vistazo (a)
browser ['braʊzə(r)] *n Comput* navegador *m*
bruise [bru:z] *n* morado *m*, cardenal *m*
2 *vt (body)* contusionar; *(fruit)* estropear
3 *vi (body)* magullarse; *(fruit)* estropearse

brunch [brʌntʃ] *n* = combinación de desayuno y almuerzo
brunette [bru:'net] *adj & n* morena *(f)*
brunt [brʌnt] *n* **the b.** lo peor; **to bear the b.** llevar el peso
brush¹ [brʌʃ] **1** *n* (**a**) *(for hair, teeth)* cepillo *m* *Art* pincel *m*; *(for house-painting)* brocha *f* (**b**) *(with the law)* roce *m*
2 *vt* (**a**) cepillar; **to b. one's hair** cepillarse el pelo; **to b. one's teeth** cepillarse los dientes (**b**) *(touch lightly)* rozar
3 *vi* **to b. against** rozar al pasar
▸ **brush aside** *vt sep* dejar de lado
▸ **brush off** *vt sep* ignorar
▸ **brush up** *vt sep* repasar
brush² [brʌʃ] *n (undergrowth)* broza *f*, maleza *f*
brushwood ['brʌʃwʊd] *n* maleza *f*
brusque [bru:sk, brʊsk] *adj* brusco(a); *(words)* áspero(a)
Brussels ['brʌsəlz] *n* Bruselas
brutal ['bru:təl] *adj* brutal, cruel
brute [bru:t] **1** *adj* bruto(a); **b. force** fuerza bruta
2 *n (animal)* bruto *m*; *(person)* bestia *f*
BSc [bi:es'si:] *n (abbr* **Bachelor of Science)** *(person)* licenciado(a) *m,f* en Ciencias
bubble ['bʌbəl] **1** *n* burbuja *f*; **b. bath** espuma *f* de baño; **b. gum** chicle *m*; **soap b.** pompa de jabón
2 *vi* burbujear; *Culin* borbotear
bubbly ['bʌblɪ] **1** *adj* (**bubblier, bubbliest)** efervescente
2 *n* champán *m*, cava *m*
buck¹ [bʌk] **1** *n Zool* macho *m*; *(male deer)* ciervo *m*; *(male goat)* macho cabrío; *Fam* **to pass the b. to sb** echarle el muerto a algn
2 *vi (horse)* corcovear
▸ **buck up 1** *vt sep Fam* **b. your ideas up!** ¡espabílate!
2 *vi (cheer up)* animarse
buck² [bʌk] *n US Fam* dólar *m*
bucket ['bʌkɪt] **1** *n* cubo *m*; *Fam* **it rained buckets** llovía a cántaros
2 *vi Fam (rain)* llover a cántaros
buckle ['bʌkəl] **1** *n* hebilla *f*
2 *vt* abrochar con hebilla
3 *vi* (**a**) *(wall, metal)* combarse (**b**) *(knees)* doblarse
bud [bʌd] **1** *n (shoot)* brote *m*; *(flower)* capullo *m*
2 *vi* brotar; *Fig* florecer
Buddhism ['bʊdɪzəm] *n* budismo *m*
budding ['bʌdɪŋ] *adj* en ciernes
buddy ['bʌdɪ] *n US Fam* amigote *m*, compinche *m*
budge [bʌdʒ] *vi* (**a**) *(move)* moverse (**b**) *(yield)* ceder
budgerigar ['bʌdʒərɪga:(r)] *n* periquito *m*
budget ['bʌdʒɪt] **1** *n* presupuesto *m*; *Br Pol* **the B.** ≃ los Presupuestos Generales del Estado

2 *vi* hacer un presupuesto (**for** para)

budgie ['bʌdʒɪ] *n Fam* = budgerigar

buff¹ [bʌf] **1** *adj & n (colour)* color (*m*) de ante **2** *vt* dar brillo a

buff² [bʌf] *n Fam (enthusiast)* aficionado(a) *m,f*

buffalo ['bʌfələʊ] *n (pl* buffaloes *or* buffalo*)* búfalo *m*

buffer ['bʌfə(r)] **1** *n* (**a**) *(device)* amortiguador *m*; *Rail* tope *m*; **b. zone** zona *f* de seguridad (**b**) *Comput* memoria intermedia **2** *vt* amortiguar

buffet¹ ['bʊfeɪ] *n* (**a**) *(snack bar)* bar *m*; *(at railway station)* cantina *f*; *Rail* **b. car** coche *m* restaurante (**b**) *(self-service meal)* bufet *m* libre (**c**) *(item of furniture)* aparador *m*

buffet² ['bʌfɪt] *vt* golpear

buffoon [bə'fu:n] *n* bufón *m*, payaso *m*

bug [bʌg] **1** *n* (**a**) *(insect)* bicho *m* (**b**) *Fam (microbe)* microbio *m*; **the flu b.** el virus de la gripe (**c**) *(hidden microphone)* micrófono oculto (**d**) *Comput* error *m* **2** *vt Fam* (**a**) **to b. a room** ocultar micrófonos en una habitación; **to b. a phone** pinchar un teléfono (**b**) *(annoy)* fastidiar, molestar

bugger ['bʌgə(r)] **1** *n* (**a**) sodomita *m* (**b**) *very Fam Pej (person)* gilipollas *mf inv*; *(thing)* coñazo *m*; **poor b.!** ¡el pobre! **2** *interj very Fam Pej* ¡joder! **3** *vt* sodomizar ▸ **bugger about** *very Fam* **1** *vi* hacer chorradas **2** *vt sep* **they really buggered him about** se las hicieron pasar canutas ▸ **bugger off** *vi very Fam Pej* pirarse; **b. off!** ¡vete a la mierda! ▸ **bugger up** *vt sep very Fam* jorobar

buggy ['bʌgɪ] *n* (**a**) *Br (baby's pushchair)* cochecito *m* de niño (**b**) *US (pram)* cochecito *m* (de niño)

bugle ['bju:gəl] *n* bugle *m*

build [bɪld] **1** *vt (pt & pp* built*)* construir **2** *n (physique)* tipo *m*, físico *m* ▸ **build up** *vt sep (accumulate)* acumular; **to b. up a reputation** labrarse una buena reputación

builder ['bɪldə(r)] *n* constructor(a) *m,f*, *(contractor)* contratista *mf*

building ['bɪldɪŋ] *n* edificio *m*, construcción *f*; **b. site** obra *f*; **b. society** sociedad hipotecaria

build-up ['bɪldʌp] *n* (**a**) *(accumulation)* aumento *m*; *(of gas)* acumulación *f* (**b**) *(publicity)* propaganda *f*

built [bɪlt] *pt & pp of* build

built-in ['bɪlt'ɪn] *adj* (**a**) *(cupboard)* empotrado(a) (**b**) *(incorporated)* incorporado(a)

built-up ['bɪlt'ʌp] *adj* urbanizado(a)

bulb [bʌlb] *n* (**a**) *Bot* bulbo *m* (**b**) *(light bulb)* bombilla *f*

Bulgaria [bʌl'geərɪə] *n* Bulgaria

Bulgarian [bʌl'geərɪən] **1** *adj* búlgaro(a) **2** *n* (**a**) *(person)* búlgaro(a) *m,f* (**b**) *(language)* búlgaro *m*

bulge [bʌldʒ] **1** *n* protuberancia *f*; *(in pocket)* bulto *m* **2** *vi (swell)* hincharse; *(be full)* estar repleto(a)

bulk [bʌlk] *n* (**a**) *(mass)* masa *f*, volumen *m*; *Com* **in b.** a granel; **to buy sth in b.** comprar algo al por mayor (**b**) *(greater part)* mayor parte *f*

bulky ['bʌlkɪ] *adj* (**bulkier, bulkiest**) (**a**) *(large)* voluminoso(a) (**b**) **this crate is rather b.** esta caja es un armatoste

bull [bʊl] *n* (**a**) toro *m*; *Fig* **to take the b. by the horns** coger al toro por los cuernos (**b**) *Fin* **b. market** mercado *m* al alza

bulldog ['bʊldɒg] *n* buldog *m*

bulldoze ['bʊldəʊz] *vt (land)* nivelar; *(building)* derribar

bulldozer ['bʊldəʊzə(r)] *n* bulldozer *m*

bullet ['bʊlɪt] *n* bala *f*; **b. wound** balazo *m*

bulletin ['bʊlɪtɪn] *n* boletín *m*; *Rad & TV* **news b.** boletín de noticias; *US* **b. board** tablón *m* de anuncios

bullet-proof ['bʊlɪtpru:f] *adj* a prueba de balas; **b. vest** chaleco *m* antibalas

bullfight ['bʊlfaɪt] *n* corrida *f* de toros

bullfighter ['bʊlfaɪtə(r)] *n* torero(a) *m,f*

bullfighting ['bʊlfaɪtɪŋ] *n* los toros *mpl*; *(art)* tauromaquia *f*

bullion ['bʊljən] *n (gold, silver)* lingote *m*

bullish ['bʊlɪʃ] *adj Fin (market)* en alza

bullock ['bʊlək] *n* buey *m*

bullring ['bʊlrɪŋ] *n* plaza *f* de toros

bull's-eye ['bʊlzaɪ] *n (of target)* blanco *m*

bully ['bʊlɪ] **1** *n* matón *m* **2** *vt (terrorize)* intimidar; *(bulldoze)* tiranizar **3** *interj Ironic* **b. for you!** ¡bravo!

bulwark ['bʊlwək] *n* baluarte *m*

bum¹ [bʌm] *n Fam (bottom)* culo *m*

bum² [bʌm] *Fam* **1** *n* (**a**) *US (tramp)* vagabundo *m* (**b**) *(idler)* holgazán(ana) *m,f* **2** *vi* gorronear ▸ **bum around** *vi Fam* vaguear

bumblebee ['bʌmbəlbi:] *n* abejorro *m*

bumbling ['bʌmblɪŋ] *adj* torpe

bump [bʌmp] **1** *n* (**a**) *(swelling)* chichón *m*; *(lump)* abolladura *f*; *(on road)* bache *m* (**b**) *(blow)* choque *m*, golpe *m* (**c**) *(jolt)* sacudida *f* **2** *vt* golpear; **to b. one's head** darse un golpe en la cabeza **3** *vi* chocar (**into** contra) ▸ **bump into** *vt insep (meet)* tropezar con ▸ **bump off** *vt sep Fam* liquidar

bumper ['bʌmpə(r)] **1** *adj* abundante; **b. edition** edición *f* especial **2** *n Aut* parachoques *m inv*

bumptious ['bʌmpʃəs] *adj* presuntuoso(a), engreído(a)

bumpy ['bʌmpɪ] *adj* (**bumpier, bumpiest**) con muchos baches

bun [bʌn] *n* (**a**) *(bread)* panecillo *m*; *(sweet)* bollo *m*; *Fig Euph* **she's got a b. in the oven**

está preñada (**b**) *(of hair)* moño *m*

bunch [bʌntʃ] **1** *n (of keys)* manojo *m; (of flowers)* ramo *m; (of grapes)* racimo *m; (of people)* grupo *m; (gang)* pandilla *f*

2 *vi* **to b. together** juntarse, agruparse

bundle ['bʌndəl] **1** *n (of clothes)* bulto *m,* fardo *m; (of papers)* fajo *m; (of wood)* haz *m*

2 *vt* (**a**) *(make a bundle of)* liar, atar (**b**) *(push)* empujar

bung [bʌŋ] **1** *n* tapón *m*

2 *vt Fam* (**a**) *(throw)* arrojar (**b**) *(put)* meter

▸ **bung up** *vt sep Fam* atascar

bungalow ['bʌŋgələʊ] *n* chalé *m,* bungalow *m*

bungle ['bʌŋgəl] *vt* chapucear

bunion ['bʌnjən] *n* juanete *m*

bunk [bʌŋk] *n (bed)* litera *f*

bunker ['bʌŋkə(r)] *n* (**a**) *(coal)* carbonera *f* (**b**) *Mil* búnker *m* (**c**) *(in golf)* búnker *m*

bunny ['bʌnɪ] *n Fam (baby talk)* **b. (rabbit)** conejito *m*

bunting ['bʌntɪŋ] *n (material)* lanilla *f; (flags)* banderines *mpl; Naut* empavesada *f*

buoy [bɔɪ] *n* boya *f*

▸ **buoy up** *vt sep* (**a**) *(keep afloat)* mantener a flote (**b**) *(person, spirits)* alentar, animar

buoyancy ['bɔɪənsɪ] *n* (**a**) *(of object)* flotabilidad *f* (**b**) *Fin* tendencia *f* alcista (**c**) *(optimism)* optimismo *m*

buoyant ['bɔɪənt] *adj* (**a**) *(object)* flotante (**b**) *Fin* con tendencia alcista (**c**) *(optimistic)* optimista

burble ['bɜːbəl] *vi* (**a**) *(stream)* murmurar; *(baby)* balbucear (**b**) *(talk quickly)* farfullar

burden ['bɜːdən] **1** *n* carga *f, Fig* **to be a b. to sb** ser una carga para algn

2 *vt* cargar (**with** con)

bureau ['bjʊərəʊ] *n (pl* **bureaux**) (**a**) *(desk)* escritorio *m* (**b**) *(office)* agencia *f,* oficina *f* (**c**) *US (chest of drawers)* cómoda *f* (**d**) *US Pol* departamento *m* del Estado

bureaucracy [bjʊə'rɒkrəsɪ] *n* burocracia *f*

bureaucrat ['bjʊərəkræt] *n* burócrata *mf*

bureaucratic [bjʊərə'krætɪk] *adj* burocrático(a)

burgeon ['bɜːdʒən] *vi* florecer

burger ['bɜːgə(r)] *n Fam (hamburger)* hamburguesa *f*

burglar ['bɜːglə(r)] *n* ladrón(ona) *n,f,* **b. alarm** alarma *f* antirrobo

burglarize ['bɜːgləraɪz] *vt US* robar, desvalijar

burglary ['bɜːglərɪ] *n* robo *m* con allanamiento de morada

burgle ['bɜːgəl] *vt* robar, desvalijar

burial ['berɪəl] *n* entierro *m*

burly ['bɜːlɪ] *adj* (**burlier, burliest**) fornido(a), fuerte

Burma ['bɜːmə] *n* Birmania

Burmese [bɜː'miːz] **1** *adj* birmano(a)

2 *n* (**a**) *(person)* birmano(a) *m,f* (**b**) *(language)* birmano *m*

burn [bɜːn] **1** *n* quemadura *f*

2 *vt (pt & pp* **burnt** *or* **burned**) quemar

3 *vi* (**a**) *(fire)* arder; *(building, food)* quemarse (**b**) *(lamp)* estar encendido(a) (**c**) *(sore)* escocer

▸ **burn down 1** *vt sep* incendiar

2 *vi* incendiarse

▸ **burn out** *vi (people)* quemarse

▸ **burn up** *vt sep (energy, calories)* quemar

burner ['bɜːnə(r)] *n* quemador *m*

burning ['bɜːnɪŋ] *adj* (**a**) *(on fire)* incendiado(a); *(hot)* abrasador(a) (**b**) *(passionate)* ardiente (**c**) **a b. question** una cuestión candente

burnt [bɜːnt] **1** *adj* quemado(a); **b. almonds** almendras tostadas

2 *pt & pp of* **burn**

burp [bɜːp] **1** *n* eructo *m*

2 *vi* eructar

burrow ['bʌrəʊ] **1** *n* madriguera *f; (for rabbits)* conejera *f*

2 *vi* (**a**) hacer una madriguera (**b**) *(search)* hurgar

bursar ['bɜːsə(r)] *n* tesorero(a) *m,f*

bursary ['bɜːsərɪ] *n* beca *f*

burst [bɜːst] **1** *n* (**a**) *(explosion)* estallido *m; (of tyre)* reventón *m* (**b**) *(of applause)* arranque *m; (rage)* arrebato *m;* **b. of gunfire** ráfaga *f* de tiros; **b. of laughter** carcajadas *fpl*

2 *vt (pt & pp* **burst**) *(balloon)* reventar; *Fig* **the river b. its banks** el río se salió de madre

3 *vi* (**a**) reventarse; *(shell)* estallar (**b**) *(enter suddenly)* irrumpir (**into** en)

▸ **burst into** *vt insep* **to b. into laughter/tears** echarse a reír/allorar

▸ **burst open** *vi* abrirse violentamente

▸ **burst out** *vi* **to b. out laughing** echarse a reír

bursting ['bɜːstɪŋ] *adj* **the bar was b. with people** el bar estaba atestado de gente; *Fam* **to be b. to do sth** reventar por hacer algo

bury ['berɪ] *vt* (**a**) enterrar; **to be buried in thought** estar absorto en pensamientos (**b**) *(hide)* ocultar

bus [bʌs] *n (pl* **buses,** *US* **busses**) autobús *m, Andes, CAm,* Ven bus *m, Arg* colectivo *m, CAm, Méx* camión *m, Chile* micro *m, Cuba* guagua *f, Urug* ómnibus *m;* **b. conductor** revisor *m;* **b. driver** conductor(a) *m,f;* **b. stop** parada *f* de autobús

bush [bʊʃ] *n* (**a**) *(shrub)* arbusto *m* (**b**) *Austral* **the b.** el monte; *Fam* **b. telegraph** radio *f* macuto

bushy ['bʊʃɪ] *adj* espeso(a), tupido(a)

business ['bɪznɪs] *n* (**a**) *(commerce)* negocios *mpl;* **how's b.?** ¿cómo andan los negocios?; **to be away on b.** estar en viaje de negocios; **b. deal** negocio *m;* **b. hours** horas *fpl* de oficina; **b. trip** viaje *m* de negocios (**b**) *(firm)* empresa *f* (**c**) *(matter)* asunto *m;* **I mean b.** estoy hablando en serio; **it's no b. of mine** no es asunto mío; **to make it one's b. to …**

encargarse de ...; **to get down to b.** ir al grano; **to go about one's b.** ocuparse de sus asuntos

businesslike ['bɪznɪslaɪk] *adj (practical)* eficiente; *(methodical)* metódico(a); *(serious)* serio(a)

businessman ['bɪznɪsmən] *n* hombre *m* de negocios

businesswoman ['bɪznɪswʊmən] *n* mujer *f* de negocios

busker ['bʌskə(r)] *n Fam* músico(a) *m,f* callejero(a)

bust¹ [bʌst] *n* (a) *(of woman)* pecho *m* (b) *Art* busto *m*

bust² [bʌst] *Fam* 1 *vt* (a) estropear (b) *(person)* trincar; *(place)* hacer una redada en

2 *adj* (a) *(damaged)* estropeado(a) (b) **to go b.** *(bankrupt)* quebrar

bustle ['bʌsəl] 1 *n (activity, noise)* bullicio *m*

2 *vi* to b. about ir y venir

bustling ['bʌslɪŋ] *adj* bullicioso(a)

bust-up ['bʌstʌp] *n Fam* riña *f*, pelea *f*

busy ['bɪzɪ] 1 *adj* (a) ocupado(a), atareado(a); *(life)* ajetreado(a); *(street)* concurrido(a) (b) *esp US Tel* ocupado(a); **b. signal** señal *f* de comunicando

2 *vt* to b. oneself doing sth ocuparse haciendo algo

busybody ['bɪzɪbɒdɪ] *n* entrometido(a) *m,f*

but [bʌt] 1 *conj* (a) pero; **b. yet** a pesar de todo (b) *(after negative)* sino; **not three, b. three** no dos sino tres; **she's not Spanish b. Portuguese** no es española sino portuguesa

2 *adv* had we b. known de haberlo sabido; **we can b. try** al menos podemos intentarlo; **b. for her we would have drowned** si no hubiera sido por ella, nos habríamos ahogado

3 *prep* salvo, menos; **everyone b. her** todos menos ella; **he's anything b. handsome** es todo menos guapo

4 *npl* ifs and buts pegas *fpl*

butane ['bjuːteɪn] *n* butano *m*; **b. gas** gas butano

butcher ['bʊtʃə(r)] 1 *n* carnicero(a) *m,f*; **b.'s (shop)** carnicería *f*

2 *vt (animals)* matar; *(people)* masacrar

butler ['bʌtlə(r)] *n* mayordomo *m*

butt¹ [bʌt] *n* (a) *(end)* extremo *m*; *(of rifle)* culata *f*; *(of cigarette)* colilla *f* (b) **he was the b. of all the jokes** era el blanco de todas las bromas (c) *US Fam (bottom)* culo *m*

butt² [bʌt] 1 *n (with head)* cabezazo *m*

2 *vt (strike with head)* dar un cabezazo a

▸ **butt in** *vi* entrar en la conversación

butt³ [bʌt] *n (barrel)* tonel *m*

butter ['bʌtə(r)] 1 *n* mantequilla *f*, *Am* manteca *f*; **b. dish** mantequera *f*

2 *vt* untar con mantequilla *or Am* manteca

buttercup ['bʌtəkʌp] *n* ranúnculo *m*, botón *m* de oro

butterfingers ['bʌtəfɪŋgəz] *n sing Fam* ma-

nazas *mf inv*

butterfly ['bʌtəflaɪ] *n* mariposa *f*

buttock ['bʌtək] *n* nalga *f*; **buttocks** nalgas *fpl*

button ['bʌtən] 1 *n* (a) *(on clothes, machine)* botón *m* (b) *US (badge)* chapa *f*

2 *vt* to b. (up) abrochar(se), abotonar(se)

buttonhole ['bʌtənhəʊl] *n* ojal *m*

buttress ['bʌtrɪs] 1 *n* (a) contrafuerte *m* (b) *(support)* apoyo *m*

2 *vt* apuntalar; *Fig* reforzar, apoyar

buxom ['bʌksəm] *adj (woman)* pechugona

buy [baɪ] 1 *n* compra *f*; **a good b.** una ganga

2 *vt (pt & pp bought)* (a) comprar; **she bought that car from a neighbour** compró ese coche a un vecino (b) *Fam (believe)* tragar

▸ **buy off** *vt sep* sobornar

▸ **buy out** *vt sep* adquirir la parte de

▸ **buy up** *vt sep* comprar en grandes cantidades

buyer ['baɪə(r)] *n* comprador(a) *m,f*

buzz [bʌz] 1 *n* (a) *(of bee)* zumbido *m*; *(of conversation)* rumor *m* (b) *Fam (telephone call)* telefonazo *m*

2 *vi* zumbar

buzzer ['bʌzə(r)] *n* timbre *m*

by [baɪ] 1 *prep* (a) *(indicating agent)* por; **composed by Bach** compuesto(a) por Bach; **a film by Almodóvar** una película de Almodóvar

(b) *(via)* por; **he left by the back door** salió por la puerta trasera

(c) *(manner)* por; **by car/train** en coche/tren; **by credit card** con tarjeta de crédito; **by chance** por casualidad; **by oneself** solo(a); **made by hand** hecho(a) a mano; **you can obtain a ticket by filling in the coupon** puede conseguir una entrada llenando el cupón

(d) *(amount)* por; **little by little** poco a poco; **they are sold by the dozen** se venden por docenas; **to be paid by the hour** cobrar por horas

(e) **by far** con mucho; **he won by a foot** ganó por un pie

(f) *(beside)* al lado de, junto a; **side by side** juntos

(g) **to walk by a building** *(pass)* pasar por delante de un edificio

(h) *(time)* para; **by now** ya; **by then** para entonces; **we have to be there by nine** tenemos que estar allí para las nueve; **by the time we arrive** (para) cuando lleguemos; **by this time next year** el año que viene por estas fechas

(i) *(during)* de; **by day/night** de día/noche

(j) *(in an oath)* por; **by God!** ¡por Dios!

(k) *Math* por

(l) *(according to)* según; **is that O.K. by you?** ¿te viene bien?

(m) **he had two children by his first wife** tuvo dos hijos con su primera esposa (**n**) *(phrases)* **bit by bit** poco a poco; **day by day** día a día; **what do you mean by that?** ¿qué quieres decir con eso?; **by the way** a propósito

2 *adv* (**a**) **to go by** *(past)* pasar; **she just walked by** pasó de largo

(**b**) **by and by** con el tiempo; **by and large** en conjunto

bye [baɪ] **1** *n* **by the b.** por cierto

2 *interj Fam* ¡hasta luego!

bye-bye ['baɪ'baɪ] *interj Fam* ¡adiós!, ¡hasta luego!

by-election ['baɪɪlekʃən] *n* elección *f* parcial

bygone ['baɪgɒn] **1** *adj* pasado(a)

2 *npl* **let bygones be bygones** lo pasado

pasado está

by-law ['baɪlɔ:] *n* ley *f* municipal

bypass ['baɪpɑːs] **1** *n* (**a**) *(road)* carretera *f* de circunvalación (**b**) *Med* **b. surgery** cirugía de by-pass

2 *vt* evitar

by-product ['baɪprɒdʌkt] *n Chem & Ind* derivado *m*, subproducto *m*; *Fig* consecuencia

byroad ['baɪrəʊd] *n* carretera secundaria

bystander ['baɪstændə(r)] *n* testigo *mf*

byte [baɪt] *n Comput* byte *m*, octeto *m*

byword ['baɪwɜːd] *n* **it became a b. for modernity** se convirtió en sinónimo de modernidad

C

C, c [siː] *n* (**a**) *(the letter)* C, c *f* (**b**) *Mus* C do *m*

C (**a**) *(abbr* **Celsius***)* C (**b**) *(abbr* **centigrade***)* C

cab [kæb] *n US* taxi *m*; **c. driver** taxista *mf*

cabaret ['kæbəreɪ] *n* cabaret *m*

cabbage ['kæbɪdʒ] *n* col *f*, berza *f*; **red c.** (col) lombarda *f*

cabin ['kæbɪn] *n* (**a**) *(hut)* choza *f*; **log c.** cabaña *f* (**b**) *Naut* camarote *m* (**c**) *(of lorry, plane)* cabina *f*

cabinet ['kæbɪnɪt] *n* (**a**) *(item of furniture)* armario *m*; *(glass-fronted)* vitrina *f*; **c. maker** ebanista *mf* (**b**) *Pol* gabinete *m*, consejo *m* de ministros

cable ['keɪbəl] **1** *n* cable *m*; **c. car** teleférico *m*; **c. company** cableoperador(a) *m,f*; **c. TV** televisión *f* por cable
2 *vt & vi* cablegrafiar, telegrafiar

caboose [kə'buːs] *n US (on train)* furgón *m* de cola

cache [kæʃ] *n* (**a**) *(place)* alijo *m* (**b**) *Comput* caché *f*

cackle ['kækəl] *vi* cacarear

cactus ['kæktəs] *n (pl* **cacti** ['kæktaɪ]*)* cactus *m*

CAD [kæd] *n (abbr* **computer-aided** *or* **-assisted design***)* CAD *m*

cad [kæd] *n Br Fam* canalla *m*

caddie ['kædɪ] *n (in golf)* cadi *m*

cadet [kə'det] *n Mil* cadete *m*

cadge [kædʒ] *vt & vi Fam* gorronear

Caesarean [siː'zeərɪən] *n Med* **she had a c.** le hicieron una cesárea; **C. section** operación *f* cesárea

café ['kæfeɪ], **cafeteria** [kæfɪ'tɪərɪə] *n* cafetería *f*

caffeine ['kæfiːn] *n* cafeína *f*

cage [keɪdʒ] **1** *n* jaula *f*
2 *vt* enjaular

cagey ['keɪdʒɪ] *adj (***cagier, cagiest***) Fam* reservado(a)

cagoule [kə'guːl] *n (garment)* canguro *m*

Cairo ['kaɪrəʊ] *n* (el) Cairo

cajole [kə'dʒəʊl] *vt* engatusar

cake [keɪk] **1** *n* (**a**) pastel *m*, tarta *f*; *Fam Fig* **it's a piece of c.** está chupado; **birthday c.** pastel *m* de cumpleaños; **c. shop** pastelería *f* (**b**) *(of soap)* pastilla *f*
2 *vi (mud)* endurecerse
3 *vt* **caked with ...** cubierto(a) de ...

calamity [kə'læmɪtɪ] *n* calamidad *f*

calcium ['kælsɪəm] *n* calcio *m*

calculate ['kælkjʊleɪt] *vt* calcular

calculated ['kælkjʊleɪtɪd] *adj* intencionado(a)

calculating ['kælkjʊleɪtɪŋ] *adj* (**a**) **c. machine** calculadora *f* (**b**) *Pej (person)* calculador(a)

calculation [kælkjʊ'leɪʃən] *n* cálculo *m*

calculator ['kælkjʊleɪtə(r)] *n* calculadora *f*

calendar ['kælɪndə(r)] *n* calendario *m*; **c. year** año *m* civil

calf¹ [kɑːf] *n (pl* **calves***) (of cattle)* becerro(a) *m,f*, ternero(a) *m,f*; *(of other animals)* cría *f*

calf² [kɑːf] *n (pl* **calves***) Anat* pantorrilla *f*

calfskin ['kɑːfskɪn] *n* piel *f* de becerro

calibre, *US* **caliber** ['kælɪbə(r)] *n* calibre *m*

call [kɔːl] **1** *vt* (**a**) llamar; **to c. sb names** poner verde a algn; **what's he called?** ¿cómo se llama?
(**b**) *(meeting etc)* convocar; **to c. sth to mind** traer algo a la memoria
2 *vi* (**a**) llamar; *Tel* **who's calling?** ¿de parte de quién?
(**b**) *(visit)* visita *f*; **to c. at sb's (house)** pasar por casa de algn; **to c. for sth/sb** pasar a recoger algo/a algn
(**c**) *(trains)* parar
(**d**) **to c. for** *(require)* exigir; **that wasn't called for** eso no estaba justificado
3 *n* (**a**) llamada *f*, grito *m*
(**b**) *(visit)* visita *f*; **to pay a c. on sb** visitar a algn
(**c**) *Tel* **(phone) c.** llamada *f*, *Am* llamado *m*; **c. box** cabina telefónica; **c. centre** centro *m* de atención telefónica
(**d**) *Med* **to be on c.** estar de guardia
(**e**) **there's no c. for you to worry** no hay motivo para que te preocupes
▸ **call away** *vt sep* **to be called away on business** tener que ausentarse por motivos de trabajo
▸ **call back** *vi (phone again)* llamar otra vez; *(visit again)* volver
▸ **call in 1** *vt sep (doctor)* llamar
2 *vi* (**a**) **I'll c. in tomorrow** *(visit)* mañana me paso (**b**) *Naut* hacer escala (**at** en)
▸ **call off** *vt sep* suspender
▸ **call on** *vt insep* (**a**) visitar (**b**) **to c. on sb for support** recurrir a algn en busca de apoyo
▸ **call out 1** *vt sep* (**a**) *(shout)* gritar (**b**) *(doctor)* hacer venir; *(workers)* convocar a la huelga
2 *vi* gritar
▸ **call up** *vt sep* (**a**) *Tel* llamar (por teléfono) (**b**) *Mil* llamar a filas, reclutar

caller ['kɔːlə(r)] n visita mf; Tel persona f que llama

calling ['kɔːlɪŋ] n esp Rel llamada f, vocación f; US **c. card** tarjeta f de visita;

callous ['kæləs] adj insensible, duro(a)

call-up ['kɔːlʌp] n llamamiento m a filas

calm [kɑːm] **1** adj (a) (weather, sea) en calma (b) (relaxed) tranquilo(a); **keep c.!** ¡tranquilo(a)!
2 n (a) (of weather, sea) calma f (b) (tranquillity) tranquilidad f
3 vt calmar, tranquilizar
4 vi **to c. (down)** calmarse, tranquilizarse

Calor Gas® ['kælɒgæs] n (gas m) butano m

calorie, calory ['kælərɪ] n caloría f

calve [kɑːv] vi (cow) parir (un becerro)

calves [kɑːvz] pl of **calf¹**, **calf²**

Cambodia [kæm'bəʊdɪə] n Camboya

came [keɪm] pt of **come**

camel ['kæməl] n camello(a) m,f

cameo ['kæmɪəʊ] n camafeo m

camera ['kæmərə] n (a) cámara f or máquina f fotográfica; Cin & TV cámara (b) Jur **in c.** a puerta cerrada

cameraman ['kæmərəmən] n cámara m

Cameroon [kæmə'ruːn] n Camerún

camomile ['kæməmaɪl] n camomila f; **c. tea** (infusión f de) manzanilla f

camouflage ['kæməflɑːʒ] **1** n camuflaje m
2 vt camuflar

camp¹ [kæmp] **1** n campamento m; **c. bed** cama f plegable; **c. site** camping m
2 vi **to go camping** ir de camping

camp² [kæmp] adj Fam afeminado(a); (affected) amanerado(a)

campaign [kæm'peɪn] **1** n campaña f
2 vi **to c. for/against** hacer campaña a favor de/en contra de

campaigner [kæm'peɪnə(r)] n defensor(a) m,f (**for** de)

camper ['kæmpə(r)] n (a) (person) campista mf (b) US (vehicle) caravana f

camping ['kæmpɪŋ] n **c. ground, c. site** camping m

campus ['kæmpəs] n campus m, ciudad universitaria

can¹ [kæn, unstressed kən] v aux (pt **could**)

El verbo **can** carece de infinitivo, de gerundio y de participio. En infinitivo o en participio, se empleará la forma correspondiente de **be able to**, por ejemplo: **he wanted to be able to speak English; she has always been able to swim**. En el inglés hablado, y en el escrito en estilo coloquial, la forma negativa **cannot** se transforma en **can't** y la forma negativa **could not** se transforma en **couldn't**.

(a) (be able to) poder; **he could have come** podría haber venido; **I'll phone you as soon as I c.** te llamaré en cuanto pueda; **she can't do it** no puede hacerlo; **I can't understand why** no entiendo por qué (b) (know how to)

saber; **c. you ski?** ¿sabes esquiar?; **I can't speak English** no sé hablar inglés (c) (be permitted to) poder; **he can't go out tonight** no le dejan salir esta noche (d) (be possible) poder; **she could have forgotten** puede (ser) que lo haya olvidado; **they can't be very poor** no deben ser muy pobres; **what c. it be?** ¿qué será?

can² [kæn] **1** n (a) (of oil) bidón m (b) US (tin) lata f, bote m; **c. opener** abrelatas m inv
2 vt (a) (fish, fruit) envasar, enlatar (b) US Fam desestimar

Canada ['kænədə] n Canadá

Canadian [kə'neɪdɪən] adj & n canadiense (mf)

canal [kə'næl] n canal m

canary [kə'neərɪ] n canario m

Canary Islands [kə'neərɪaɪləndz] npl (Islas fpl) Canarias fpl

cancel ['kænsəl] vt (train, contract) cancelar Com anular; (permission) retirar; (decree) revocar

cancellation [kænsɪ'leɪʃən] n cancelación f Com anulación f

cancer ['kænsə(r)] n (a) Med cáncer m **breast c.** cáncer de mama; **c. research** cancerología f (b) **C.** (in astrology) Cáncer m

candelabra [kændɪ'lɑːbrə] n candelabro m

candid ['kændɪd] adj franco(a), sincero(a)

> 🖉 Note that the Spanish word **cándido** is a false friend and is never a translation for the English word **candid**. In Spanish, **cándido** means "ingenuous, naïve".

candidate ['kændɪdeɪt, 'kændɪdɪt] n candidato(a) m,f; (in exam) opositor(a) m,f

candle ['kændəl] n vela f; (in church) cirio m

candlelight ['kændəllaɪt] n luz f de vela; **by c.** a la luz de las velas

candlestick ['kændəlstɪk] n candelero m palmatoria f; (in church) cirial m

candour, US **candor** ['kændə(r)] n sinceridad f, ranqueza f

> 🖉 Note that the Spanish word **candor** is a false friend and is never a translation for the English word **candour**. In Spanish, **candor** means "innocence, naïvety".

candy ['kændɪ] n US caramelo m; **c. store** confitería f

candyfloss ['kændɪflɒs] n Br algodón m dulce

cane [keɪn] **1** n (a) Bot caña f; **c. sugar** azúcar m de caña (b) (wicker) mimbre m (c) (walking stick) bastón m; (for punishment) palmeta f
2 vt castigar con la palmeta

canine ['keɪnaɪn] adj Zool canino(a); **c. tooth** colmillo m

canister ['kænɪstə(r)] n bote m

canned [kænd] adj enlatado(a); **c. foods** conservas fpl

cannelloni [kænəˈləʊnɪ] *n* canelones *mpl*

cannibal [ˈkænɪbəl] *adj & n* caníbal *(mf)*

cannon [ˈkænən] **1** *n* (a) (*pl* **cannons** or **cannon**) cañón *m*; *Fig* **c. fodder** carne *f* de cañón (b) *Br (in billiards, snooker)* carambola *f*
  2 *vi* chocar (**into** contra)

cannonball [ˈkænənbɔːl] *n* bala *f* de cañón

cannot [ˈkænɒt, kæˈnɒt] = **can not**

canoe [kəˈnuː] *n* canoa *f*; *Sport* piragua *f*

canon [ˈkænən] *n Rel* canon *m*

canopy [ˈkænəpɪ] *n* (a) *(on throne)* dosel *m* (b) *(awning)* toldo *m*

can't [kɑːnt] = **can not**

Cantabria [kænˈtæbrɪə] *n* Cantabria

cantankerous [kænˈtæŋkərəs] *adj* intratable

canteen [kænˈtiːn] *n* (a) *(restaurant)* cantina *f* (b) *(set of cutlery)* juego *m* de cubiertos (c) *(flask)* cantimplora *f*

canter [ˈkæntə(r)] **1** *n* medio galope
  2 *vi* ir a medio galope

canvas [ˈkænvəs] *n* (a) *Tex* lona *f* (b) *(painting)* lienzo *m*

canvass [ˈkænvəs] *vi* (a) *Pol* hacer propaganda electoral (b) *Com* hacer promoción, buscar clientes

canvasser [ˈkænvəsə(r)] *n Pol* = persona que hace propaganda electoral de puerta en puerta

canyon [ˈkænjən] *n* cañón *m*; **the Grand C.** el Gran Cañón

canyoning [ˈkænjənɪŋ] *n Sport* barranquismo *m*

cap [kæp] **1** *n* (a) gorro *m*; *(soldier's)* gorra *f* (b) *Br Sport* **to win a c. for England** ser seleccionado(a) para el equipo de Inglaterra (c) *(of pen)* capuchón *m*; *(of bottle)* chapa *f*
  2 *vt* *(bottle)* poner la chapa a; *Fig* **to c. it all** para colmo (b) *Br Sport* seleccionar

capability [keɪpəˈbɪlɪtɪ] *n* habilidad *f*

capable [ˈkeɪpəbəl] *adj* (a) *(skilful)* hábil (b) *(able)* capaz (**of** de)

capacity [kəˈpæsɪtɪ] *n* (a) capacidad *f* (b) *(position)* puesto *m*; **in her c. as manageress** en calidad de gerente

cape¹ [keɪp] *n* *(garment)* capa *f*

cape² [keɪp] *n* *Geog* cabo *m*, promontorio *m*; **C. Horn** Cabo de Hornos; **C. Town** Ciudad del Cabo; **C. Verde** Cabo Verde

caper [ˈkeɪpə(r)] *n* *(prank)* travesura *f*

capital [ˈkæpɪtəl] **1** *n* (a) *(town)* capital *f* (b) *Fin* capital *m*; **c. expenditure** inversión *f* de capital (c) *(letter)* mayúscula *f*
  2 *adj* (a) *(city)* capital (b) **c. punishment** pena *f* capital (c) *(primary)* primordial (d) **c. letter** mayúscula *f*

capitalism [ˈkæpɪtəlɪzəm] *n* capitalismo *m*

capitalist [ˈkæpɪtəlɪst] *adj & n* capitalista *(mf)*

capitalize [ˈkæpɪtəlaɪz] *vi Fin* capitalizar; *Fig* **to c. on sth** sacar provecho or beneficio de algo

capitulate [kəˈpɪtjʊleɪt] *vi* capitular

cappuccino [kæpəˈtʃiːnəʊ] *n* (café *m*) capuchino *m*

Capricorn [ˈkæprɪkɔːn] *n* Capricornio *m*

capsicum [ˈkæpsɪkəm] *n* pimiento *m*

capsize [kæpˈsaɪz] **1** *vt* hacer zozobrar
  2 *vi* zozobrar

capsule [ˈkæpsjuːl] *n* cápsula *f*

captain [ˈkæptɪn] **1** *n* capitán *m*
  2 *vt* capitanear

caption [ˈkæpʃən] *n* *(under picture)* leyenda *f*; *Cin* subtítulo *m*

captivating [ˈkæptɪveɪtɪŋ] *adj* seductor(a)

captive [ˈkæptɪv] **1** *n* cautivo(a) *m,f*
  2 *adj* cautivo(a)

captivity [kæpˈtɪvɪtɪ] *n* cautiverio *m*

capture [ˈkæptʃə(r)] **1** *vt* (a) capturar, apresar; *Mil (town)* tomar (b) *(market)* acaparar (c) *Fig (mood)* captar
  2 *n* *(of fugitive)* captura *f*; *(of town)* toma *f*

car [kɑː(r)] *n* (a) coche *m*, *Andes*, *CAm*, *Carib*, *Méx* carro *m*, *RP* auto *m*; **c. ferry** transbordador *m* para coches; *Br* **c. park** parking *m*, aparcamiento *m*; **c. wash** túnel *m* de lavado (b) *US Rail* coche *m*

carafe [kəˈræf, kəˈrɑːf] *n* garrafa *f*

caramel [ˈkærəmel] *n* azúcar *m* quemado; *(sweet)* caramelo *m*

carat [ˈkærət] *n* quilate *m*

caravan [ˈkærəvæn] *n* (a) *(vehicle)* remolque *m*, caravana *f* (b) *(in desert)* caravana *f*

carbohydrate [kɑːbəʊˈhaɪdreɪt] *n* hidrato *m* de carbono, carbohidrato *m*

carbon [ˈkɑːbən] *n* carbono *m*; **c. copy** copia *f* al papel carbón; *Fig* copia exacta; **c. dioxide** dióxido *m* de carbono; **c. paper** papel *m* carbón

carburettor [kɑːbjʊˈretə(r)], *US* **carburetor** [ˈkɑːrbəreɪtər] *n* carburador *m*

carcass [ˈkɑːkəs] *n* res muerta

card [kɑːd] *n* (a) tarjeta *f*; *(of cardboard)* cartulina *f*; **birthday/Christmas c.** tarjeta *f* de cumpleaños/de Navidad (b) *(in file)* ficha *f*; *(identity)* carnet *m*; **c. index** fichero *m* (c) **pack of cards** baraja *f*, cartas *fpl*; **(playing) c.** naipe *m*, carta *f*; *Fig Br* **on** or *US* **in the cards** previsto

cardboard [ˈkɑːdbɔːd] *n* cartón *m*; **c. box** caja *f* de carton; **c. cutout** recortable *m*

cardiac [ˈkɑːdɪæk] *adj* cardíaco(a); **c. arrest** paro cardíaco

cardigan [ˈkɑːdɪgən] *n* rebeca *f*

cardinal [ˈkɑːdɪnəl] **1** *n Rel* cardenal *m*
  2 *adj* cardinal; **c. numbers** números *mpl* cardinales

care [keə(r)] **1** *vi* *(be concerned)* preocuparse (**about** por); **I don't c.** no me importa; *Fam* **for all I c.** me trae sin cuidado; *Fam* **he couldn't c. less** le importa un bledo
  2 *n* (a) *(attention, protection)* cuidado *m*, atención *f*; **c. of ...** *(on letter)* al cuidado de ...; **medical c.** asistencia *f* médica; **to take**

c. of cuidar; *(business)* ocuparse de (**b**) *(carefulness)* cuidado *m*; **take c.** ten cuidado; *(as farewell)* ¡cuídate! (**c**) *(worry)* preocupación *f*
▸ **care for** *vt insep* (**a**) *(look after)* cuidar (**b**) *(like)* gustar, interesar; **would you c. for a coffee?** ¿te apetece un café?
career [kə'rɪə(r)] **1** *n* carrera *f*
2 *vi* correr a toda velocidad
carefree ['keəfriː] *adj* despreocupado(a)
careful ['keəful] *adj* cuidadoso(a); *(cautious)* prudente; **be c.!** ¡ojo!; **to be c.** tener cuidado
carefully ['keəfulɪ] *adv (painstakingly)* cuidadosamente; *(cautiously)* con cuidado
careless ['keəlɪs] *adj* descuidado(a); *(about clothes)* desaliñado(a); *(driving)* negligente; **a c. mistake** un descuido
carelessly ['keəlɪslɪ] *adv* descuidadamente, a la ligera
carelessness ['keəlɪsnɪs] *n* descuido *m*
caress [kə'res] **1** *n* caricia *f*
2 *vt* acariciar
caretaker ['keəteɪkə(r)] *n (in school etc)* bedel *mf*; *(in block of flats)* portero(a) *m,f*
carfare ['kɑːrfeər] *n US* (precio *m* del) billete *m or Am* boleto *m*
cargo ['kɑːgəʊ] *n (pl* **cargoes** *or* **cargos)** carga *f*, cargamento *m; Naut* **c. boat** buque *m* de carga, carguero *m*
Caribbean [kærɪ'bɪən, *US* kə'rɪbɪən] *adj* caribe, caribeño(a); **the C. (Sea)** el (mar) Caribe
caricature ['kærɪkətjʊə(r)] *n* caricatura *f*
caring ['keərɪŋ] *adj* solidario(a)
carnage ['kɑːnɪdʒ] *n Fig* carnicería *f*
carnal ['kɑːnəl] *adj* carnal
carnation [kɑː'neɪʃən] *n* clavel *m*
carnival ['kɑːnɪvəl] *n* carnaval *m*
carnivorous [kɑː'nɪvərəs] *adj* carnívoro(a)
carol ['kærəl] *n* villancico *m*
carom ['kærəm] *n US (in billiards, pool)* carambola *f*
carousel [kærə'sel] *n US* tiovivo *m*
carp¹ [kɑːp] *n (fish)* carpa *f*
carp² [kɑːp] *vi* refunfuñar
carpenter ['kɑːpɪntə(r)] *n* carpintero(a) *m,f*
carpentry ['kɑːpɪntrɪ] *n* carpintería *f*
carpet ['kɑːpɪt] **1** *n* alfombra *f*
2 *vt Fig* **carpeted with** cubierto(a) de

> 🖉 Note that the Spanish word **carpeta** is a false friend and is never a translation for the English word **carpet**. In Spanish, **carpeta** means "file, folder".

carriage ['kærɪdʒ] *n* (**a**) *(horse-drawn)* carruaje *m; Rail* vagón *m*, coche *m; (of gun)* cureña *f; (of typewriter)* carro *m* (**b**) *(of goods)* porte *m*, transporte *m*
carriageway ['kærɪdʒweɪ] *n Br* carril *m*, autovía *f*; **dual c.** autovía
carrier ['kærɪə(r)] *n* (**a**) *(company)* transportista *mf; Br* **c. bag** bolsa *f* de plástico; **c. pigeon**

paloma mensajera (**b**) *Med* portador(a) *m,f*
carrot ['kærət] *n* zanahoria *f*
carry ['kærɪ] **1** *vt* (**a**) llevar; *(goods)* transportar (**b**) *(stock)* tener; *(responsibility, penalty)* conllevar, implicar (**c**) **the motion was carried** se aprobó la moción (**d**) *(disease)* ser portador(a) de
2 *vi (sound)* oírse
▸ **carry away** *vt sep* llevarse; **to get carried away** entusiasmarse
▸ **carry forward** *vt sep Fin* **carried forward** suma y sigue
▸ **carry off** *vt sep (prize)* llevarse; *Fam* **to c. it off** salir airoso(a)
▸ **carry on 1** *vt sep* continuar; *(conversation)* mantener
2 *vi* (**a**) continuar, seguir adelante; **c. on!** ¡adelante! (**b**) *Fam (make a fuss)* hacer una escena; **don't c. on about it!** ¡no te enrolles! (**c**) *Fam* **to c. on with sb** estar liado(a) con algn
▸ **carry out** *vt sep (plan)* llevar a cabo, realizar; *(test)* verificar
carryall ['kærɪɔːl] *n US* bolsa *f (de viaje o de deporte)*
carrycot ['kærɪkɒt] *n Br* cuna *f* portátil
carsick ['kɑːsɪk] *adj* mareado(a) (en el coche)
cart [kɑːt] **1** *n (horse-drawn)* carro *m; (hand-cart)* carretilla *f; US (in supermarket)* carrito *m*
2 *vt* carretear
cartel [kɑː'tel] *n* cártel *m*
carton ['kɑːtən] *n (of cream etc)* caja *f*
cartoon [kɑː'tuːn] *n (strip)* tira cómica, historieta *f; Art* cartón *m; (animated)* dibujos *mpl* animados
cartoonist [kɑː'tuːnɪst] *n* caricaturista *mf*
cartridge ['kɑːtrɪdʒ] *n* (**a**) cartucho *m* (**b**) *(for pen)* recambio *m;* **c. paper** papel guarro
carve [kɑːv] *vt* (**a**) *(wood)* tallar; *(stone, metal)* cincelar, esculpir (**b**) *(meat)* trinchar
cascade [kæ'skeɪd] *n* cascada *f*
case¹ [keɪs] *n* (**a**) caso *m*; **a c. in point** un buen ejemplo; **in any c.** en cualquier caso, de todas formas; **in c. of doubt** en caso de duda; **just in c.** por si acaso (**b**) *Med* caso *m;* **c. history** historial clínico (**c**) *Jur* causa *f*
case² [keɪs] *n* (**a**) *(suitcase)* maleta *f, Méx* petaca *f, RP* valija *f; (small)* estuche *m; (soft)* funda *f* (**b**) **a c. of wine** una caja de botellas de vino (**c**) *Typ* **lower c.** minúscula *f;* **upper c.** mayúscula *f*
cash [kæʃ] **1** *n* dinero efectivo; **to pay c.** pagar al contado *or* en efectivo; **c. desk** caja *f;* **c. on delivery** entrega *f* contra reembolso; **c. dispenser** cajero automático; **c. register** caja registradora
2 *vt (cheque)* cobrar
▸ **cash in 1** *vi Fam Fig* **to c. in on sth** sacar provecho de algo
2 *vt sep* hacer efectivo(a)

cash-and-carry [kæʃən'kærɪ] *adj & adv* = de venta al por mayor y pago al contado

cashew ['kæʃuː] *n* c. (nut) anacardo *m*

cashier [kæ'ʃɪə(r)] *n* cajero(a) *m,f*

cashmere [kæʃ'mɪə(r)] *n* cachemira *f*

casino [kə'siːnəʊ] *n* casino *m*

cask [kɑːsk] *n* tonel *m*, barril *m*

casket ['kɑːskɪt] *n (box)* cofre *m*; *US (coffin)* ataúd *m*

🖉 Note that the Spanish word **casquete** is a false friend and is never a translation for the English word **casket**. In Spanish, **casquete** means "shell case".

casserole ['kæsərəʊl] *n* (**a**) *(container)* cacerola *f* (**b**) *Culin* guisado *m*

cassette [kə'set] *n* cassette *f*; **c. recorder** cassette *m*

cast [kɑːst] **1** *vt (pt & pp* cast) (**a**) *(net, fishing line)* echar, arrojar; *(light)* proyectar; *(glance)* lanzar; *(anchor)* echar; *(vote)* emitir; *(skin)* mudar (**b**) *Fig* **to c. doubts on sth** poner algo en duda; **to c. suspicion on sb** levantar sospechas sobre algn (**c**) *(metal)* moldear; **c. iron** hierro fundido (**d**) *Th (play)* hacer el reparto de
2 *n* (**a**) *(mould)* molde *m*; *(product)* pieza *f* (**b**) *Med* **(plaster) c.** escayola *f* (**c**) *Th* reparto *m*
▸ **cast off** *vi Naut* soltar (las) amarras

castanets [kæstə'nets] *npl* castañuelas *fpl*

castaway ['kɑːstəweɪ] *n* náufrago(a) *m,f*

caste [kɑːst] *n* casta *f*

caster ['kɑːstə(r)] *n* **c. sugar** azúcar *m* or *f* extrafino(a)

castile [kæ'stiːl] *n* Castilla

Castilian [kæ'stɪlɪən] **1** *adj* castellano(a)
2 *n* C. (Spanish) *(language)* castellano *m*

casting ['kɑːstɪŋ] *n* **c. vote** voto *m* de calidad

cast-iron ['kɑːstaɪən] *adj* de hierro fundido

castle ['kɑːsəl] **1** *n* (**a**) *(castle)* castillo *m* (**b**) *(in chess)* torre *f*
2 *vi (in chess)* enrocar

castor¹ ['kɑːstə(r)] *n* **c. oil** aceite *m* de ricino

castor² ['kɑːstə(r)] *n (on furniture)* ruedecilla *f*

castrate [kæ'streɪt] *vt* castrar

casual ['kæʒjʊəl] *adj* (**a**) *(meeting etc)* fortuito(a) (**b**) *(worker)* eventual (**c**) *(clothes)* (de) sport (**d**) *(visit)* de paso (**e**) *(person, attitude)* despreocupado(a), informal

casualty ['kæʒjʊəltɪ] *n* (**a**) *Mil* baja *f*; **casualties** pérdidas *fpl* (**b**) *(injured)* herido(a) *m,f*

🖉 Note that the Spanish word **casualidad** is a false friend and is never a translation for the English word **casualty**. In Spanish, **casualidad** means "chance, coincidence".

cat [kæt] *n* gato(a) *m,f*; *Fig* **to let the c. out of the bag** descubrir el pastel

catalan ['kætəlæn] **1** *adj* catalán(ana)
2 *n* (**a**) *(person)* catalán(ana) *m,f* (**b**) *(language)* catalán *m*

catalogue, *US* **catalog** ['kætəlɒg] **1** *n* catálogo *m*
2 *vt* catalogar

Catalonia [kætə'ləʊnɪə] *n* Cataluña

catalyst ['kætəlɪst] *n* catalizador *m*

catapult ['kætəpʌlt] *n Br* tirachinas *m inv*

catarrh [kə'tɑː(r)] *n* catarro *m*

catastrophe [kə'tæstrəfɪ] *n* catástrofe *f*

catastrophic [kætə'strɒfɪk] *adj* catastrófico(a)

catch [kætʃ] **1** *vt (pt & pp* caught) (**a**) *(ball, thief)* coger; *(fish)* pescar; *(mouse etc)* atrapar; *(train, bus)* coger, *Am* agarrar; **to c. a cold** coger un resfriado; **to c. fire** *(log)* prenderse; *(building)* incendiarse; **to c. hold of** agarrar; **to c. sb's eye** captar la atención de algn; **to c. sight of** entrever
(**b**) *(surprise)* pillar, sorprender
(**c**) *(hear)* entender
(**d**) **to c. one's breath** *(hold)* sostener la respiración; *(recover)* recuperar el aliento
2 *vi (sleeve etc)* engancharse (**on** en); *(fire)* encenderse
3 *n* (**a**) *(of ball)* parada *f*; *(of fish)* presa *f*
(**b**) *(on door)* pestillo *m*
(**c**) *(drawback)* pega *f*; **c. question** pregunta *f* con pega
(**d**) **c. phrase** slogan *m*
▸ **catch on** *vi Fam* (**a**) *(become popular)* ganar popularidad (**b**) *(understand)* caer en la cuenta
▸ **catch out** *vt sep Fam* **to c. sb out** pillar a algn cometiendo una falta
▸ **catch up** *vi* (**a**) **to c. up with sb** *(reach)* alcanzar a algn (**b**) *(with news)* ponerse al corriente (**on** de); **to c. up on sleep** recuperar el sueño perdido; **to c. up with work** ponerse al día de trabajo

catching ['kætʃɪŋ] *adj (disease)* contagioso(a)

catchment ['kætʃmənt] *n* **c. area** zona *f* de captación

catchword ['kætʃwɜːd] *n* lema *m*

catchy ['kætʃɪ] *adj* (**catchier, catchiest**) *Fam (tune)* pegadizo(a)

categoric(al) [kætɪ'gɒrɪk(əl)] *adj* categórico(a)

categorize ['kætɪgəraɪz] *vt* clasificar

category ['kætɪgərɪ] *n* categoría *f*

cater ['keɪtə(r)] *vi* (**a**) **to c. for** *(wedding etc)* proveer comida para (**b**) **to c. for** *(taste)* atender a

caterer ['keɪtərə(r)] *n* proveedor(a) *m,f*

catering ['keɪtərɪŋ] *n* abastecimiento *m* (de comidas por encargo)

caterpillar ['kætəpɪlə(r)] *n* (**a**) oruga *f* (**b**) **c. (tractor)** tractor *m* de oruga

cathedral [kə'θiːdrəl] *n* catedral *f*

Catholic ['kæθəlɪk] *adj & n* católico(a) *(m,f)*

catholic ['kæθəlɪk] *adj* católico(a)

Catholicism [kəˈθɒlɪsɪzəm] n catolicismo m
cat's-eye® [ˈkætsaɪ] n Br captafaro m, = baliza reflectante en la calzada
cattle [ˈkætəl] npl ganado m (vacuno)
catty [ˈkætɪ] adj (**cattier, cattiest**) Fam (remark) malintencionado(a); (person) malicioso(a)
catwalk [ˈkætwɔːk] n pasarela f
Caucasian [kɔːˈkeɪzɪən] adj & n caucásico(a) (m,f), blanco(a) (m,f)
caucus [ˈkɔːkəs] n comité m central, ejecutiva f
caught [kɔːt] pt & pp of catch
cauliflower [ˈkɒlɪflaʊə(r)] n coliflor f
cause [kɔːz] 1 n (a) (origin) causa f (b) (reason) motivo m (c) for a good c. por una buena causa
 2 vt causar; to c. sb to do sth hacer que algn haga algo
caustic [ˈkɔːstɪk] adj cáustico(a); Fig mordaz
caution [ˈkɔːʃən] 1 n (a) (care) cautela f, prudencia f (b) (warning) aviso m, advertencia f (c) Br Jur reprensión f
 2 vt advertir, amonestar
cautious [ˈkɔːʃəs] adj cauteloso(a), prudente
cavalcade [kævəlˈkeɪd] n cabalgata f
cavalier [kævəˈlɪə(r)] 1 adj arrogante
 2 n caballero m
cavalry [ˈkævəlrɪ] n caballería f
cave [keɪv] n cueva f
 ▸ **cave in** vi (roof etc) derrumbarse, hundirse
caveman [ˈkeɪvmæn] n hombre m de las cavernas
cavern [ˈkævən] n caverna f
caviar(e) [ˈkævɪɑː(r)] n caviar m
cavity [ˈkævɪtɪ] n (a) (hole) cavidad f (b) (in tooth) caries f inv
cavort [kəˈvɔːt] vi retozar, brincar
CB [siːˈbiː] (abbr Citizens' Band) banda ciudadana
CBI [siːbiːˈaɪ] n Br (abbr Confederation of British Industry) ≃ CEOE f
cc [siːˈsiː] (abbr cubic centimetre(s)) cc
CD [siːˈdiː] n (abbr compact disc) CD m; CD player (lector m or reproductor m de) CD m
CD-ROM [siːdiːˈrɒm] n Comput (abbr compact disc read-only memory) CD-ROM m
cease [siːs] 1 vt cesar; to c. doing or to do sth dejar de hacer algo
 2 vi terminar
cease-fire [siːsˈfaɪə(r)] n alto m el fuego
ceaseless [ˈsiːslɪs] adj incesante
cedar [ˈsiːdə(r)] n cedro m
cede [siːd] vt ceder
ceiling [ˈsiːlɪŋ] n techo m
celebrate [ˈselɪbreɪt] 1 vt (occasion) celebrar
 2 vi divertirse
celebrated [ˈselɪbreɪtɪd] adj célebre
celebration [selɪˈbreɪʃən] n (a) celebración f (b) **celebrations** festividades fpl
celebrity [sɪˈlebrɪtɪ] n celebridad f

celery [ˈselərɪ] n apio m
celibate [ˈselɪbət] adj & n célibe (mf)
cell [sel] n (a) (in prison) celda f (b) Biol & P' célula f (c) Elec pila f
cellar [ˈselə(r)] n sótano m; (for wine) bodega
cello [ˈtʃeləʊ] n violoncelo m
cellophane® [ˈseləfeɪn] n Br celofán m
celluloid [ˈseljʊlɔɪd] n celuloide m
cellulose [ˈseljʊləʊs] n celulosa f
Celsius [ˈselsɪəs] adj Celsio
Celt [kelt, selt] n celta mf
Celtic [ˈkeltɪk, ˈseltɪk] 1 n (language) celta ʀ
 2 adj celta
cement [sɪˈment] 1 n cemento m; c. mixe hormigonera f
 2 vt Constr unir con cemento; Fig (frien ship) cimentar
cemetery [ˈsemɪtrɪ] n cementerio m
censor [ˈsensə(r)] 1 n censor(a) m,f
 2 vt censurar
censorship [ˈsensəʃɪp] n censura f
censure [ˈsenʃə(r)] 1 n censura f
 2 vt censurar
census [ˈsensəs] n censo m
cent [sent] n (a) centavo m, céntimo m (ʀ per c. por ciento
centenary [senˈtiːnərɪ] n centenario m
center [ˈsentər] n & vt US = centre
centigrade [ˈsentɪɡreɪd] adj centígrado(a)
centilitre, US **centiliter** [ˈsentɪliːtə(r)] n ce tilitro m
centimetre, US **centimeter** [ˈsentɪmiːtə(ɾ n centímetro m
centipede [ˈsentɪpiːd] n ciempiés m inv
central [ˈsentrəl] adj central; c. heating cal facción f central; C. America Centroaméric C. American centroamericano(a) m,f; Br reservation (on motorway) mediana f, Cc Méx camellón m
centralize [ˈsentrəlaɪz] vt centralizar
centrally [ˈsentrəlɪ] adv c. heated con cal facción central; c. situated céntrico(a)
centre [ˈsentə(r)] 1 n centro m; town c. cent de la ciudad; Ftb c. forward delantero centr Ftb c. half medio centro; Pol c. party partic m centrista; sports c. centro deportivo
 2 vt (attention etc) centrar (on en)
century [ˈsentʃərɪ] n siglo m; the nineteen c. el siglo diecinueve
ceramic [sɪˈræmɪk] 1 n cerámica f
 2 adj de cerámica
ceramics [sɪˈræmɪks] n sing cerámica f
cereal [ˈsɪərɪəl] n cereal m
cerebral [ˈserɪbrəl, sɪˈriːbrəl] adj cerebral; palsy parálisis f cerebral
ceremony [ˈserɪmənɪ] n ceremonia f
certain [ˈsɜːtən] 1 adj (a) (sure) seguro(a); be c. estar seguro(a); to make c. of s asegurarse de algo (b) to a c. extent has cierto punto (c) (not known) cierto(a); a Miss Ward una tal señorita Ward (d) (tru cierto(a)

2 adv **for c.** a ciencia cierta
certainly ['sɜːtənlɪ] adv desde luego; **c. not** de ninguna manera
certainty ['sɜːtntɪ] n certeza f; (assurance) seguridad f
certificate [sə'tɪfɪkɪt] n certificado m; Educ diploma m
certified ['sɜːtɪfaɪd] adj certificado(a); (copy) compulsado(a); US **c. public accountant** censor(a) m,f jurado(a) de cuentas, auditor(a) m,f, Am contador(a) m,f público(a)
certify ['sɜːtɪfaɪ] vt certificar
cervical ['sɜːvɪkəl, sə'vaɪkəl] adj **c. cancer** cáncer m del útero; **c. smear** frotis m cervical
cervix ['sɜːvɪks] n (a) (uterus) cuello m del útero (b) (neck) cerviz f, cuello m
cessation [se'seɪʃən] n cese m
cesspit ['sespɪt] n pozo negro
Ceylon [sɪ'lɒn] n Ceilán f
cf [siː'ef] (abbr confer, compare) cf., cfr.
chafe [tʃeɪf] **1** vt (make sore) rozar
2 vi (skin) irritarse; (item of clothing) rozar
chaffinch ['tʃæfɪntʃ] n pinzón m vulgar
chagrin ['ʃæɡrɪn] n disgusto m, desilusión f
chain [tʃeɪn] **1** n cadena f; Fig (of events) serie f; **c. of mountains** cordillera f; **c. reaction** reacción f en cadena; **c. saw** sierra mecánica
2 vt to **c. (up)** encadenar
chain-smoke ['tʃeɪnsməʊk] vi fumar un pitillo tras otro
chair [tʃeə(r)] **1** n (a) silla f; (with arms) sillón m; **c. lift** telesilla m (b) (position) presidencia f; Univ cátedra f
2 vt presidir
chairman ['tʃeəmən] n presidente m
chairperson ['tʃeəpɜːsən] n presidente(a) m,f
chalet ['ʃæleɪ] n chalet m, chalé m
chalk [tʃɔːk] n (for writing) tiza f
▸ **chalk up** vt sep Fam (victory etc) apuntarse
challenge ['tʃælɪndʒ] **1** vt (a) retar, desafiar; **to c. sb to do sth** retar a algn a que haga algo (b) (authority etc) poner a prueba; (statement) poner en duda (c) Mil dar el alto a
2 n (a) reto m, desafío m (b) Mil quién vive m
challenging ['tʃælɪndʒɪŋ] adj (idea) desafiante; (task) que presenta un desafío
chamber ['tʃeɪmbə(r)] n (a) (hall) cámara f; **C. of Commerce** Cámara de Comercio (b) Mus **c. music** música f de cámara (c) Br Jur **chambers** gabinete m
chambermaid ['tʃeɪmbəmeɪd] n camarera f
chameleon [kə'miːlɪən] n camaleón m
champagne [ʃæm'peɪn] n (French) champán m; (from Catalonia) cava m
champion ['tʃæmpɪən] n campeón(ona) m,f; Fig **c. of human rights** defensor(a) m,f de los derechos humanos
championship ['tʃæmpɪənʃɪp] n campeonato m
chance [tʃɑːns] **1** n (a) (fortune) casualidad f, azar m; **by c.** por casualidad; **to take a c.**

arriesgarse; **c. meeting** encuentro m casual (b) (likelihood) posibilidad f; **(the) chances are that ...** lo más posible es que ... (c) (opportunity) oportunidad f
2 vt arriesgar
▸ **chance upon** vt insep encontrar por casualidad
chancellor ['tʃɑːnsələ(r)] n (a) (head of state, in embassy) canciller m (b) Br Univ rector(a) m,f (c) Br **C. of the Exchequer** ≃ ministro(a) m,f de Hacienda
chandelier [ʃændɪ'lɪə(r)] n araña f (de luces)
change [tʃeɪndʒ] **1** vt cambiar; **to c. gear** cambiar de marcha; **to c. one's mind/the subject** cambiar de opinión/de tema; **to c. trains** hacer transbordo; **to get changed** cambiarse de ropa; Fig **to c. hands** cambiar de dueño(a)
2 vi cambiar, cambiarse; **to c. for the better/worse** mejorar/empeorar; **to c. into** convertirse en
3 n (a) cambio m; **for a c.** para variar; **c. of heart** cambio de parecer; **c. of scene** cambio de aires (b) (money) cambio m; (after purchase) vuelta f; **small c.** suelto m
▸ **change over** vi cambiarse
changeable ['tʃeɪndʒəbəl] adj (weather) variable; (person) inconstante
changeover ['tʃeɪndʒəʊvə(r)] n conversión f
changing ['tʃeɪndʒɪŋ] **1** n (a) **c. room** vestuario m (b) Mil relevo m (de la guardia)
2 adj cambiante
channel ['tʃænəl] **1** n (a) Geog canal m; (of river) cauce m; **the C. Islands** las Islas Anglonormandas; **the English C.** el Canal de la Mancha (b) (administrative) vía f (c) TV Rad canal m, cadena f
2 vt Fig (ideas etc) canalizar, encauzar
chant [tʃɑːnt] **1** n Rel cántico m; (of demonstrators) slogan m
2 vt & vi Rel cantar; (demonstrators) corear
chaos ['keɪɒs] n caos m
chaotic [keɪ'ɒtɪk] adj caótico(a)
chap [tʃæp] n Fam chico m, tío m
chapel ['tʃæpəl] n capilla f
chaperon(e) ['ʃæpərəʊn] n carabina f
chaplain ['tʃæplɪn] n capellán m
chapter ['tʃæptə(r)] n (a) capítulo m (b) Rel cabildo m
char [tʃɑː(r)] vt chamuscar, carbonizar
character ['kærɪktə(r)] n (a) carácter m (b) Fam (person) tipo m (c) Th personaje m
characteristic [kærɪktə'rɪstɪk] **1** n característica f
2 adj característico(a)
characterize ['kærɪktəraɪz] vt caracterizar
charcoal ['tʃɑːkəʊl] n carbón m vegetal; Art **c. drawing** carboncillo m; **c. grey** gris marengo or oscuro
charge [tʃɑːdʒ] **1** vt (a) cobrar; **c. it to my account** cárguelo en mi cuenta (b) **to c. sb with a crime** acusar a algn de un crimen (c)

Mil cargar contra (**d**) *Elec* cargar
  2 *vi Elec & Mil* cargar; **to c. about** andar a lo loco
  3 *n* (**a**) *(cost)* precio *m*; **bank charges** comisión *f*; **free of c.** gratis; **service c.** servicio *m*; **c. account** cuenta *f* corriente (**b**) **to be in c. of** estar a cargo de; **to take c. of** hacerse cargo de (**c**) *Jur* cargo *m*, acusación *f* (**d**) *(explosive)* carga explosiva (**e**) *Elec* carga *f*

charged [tʃɑːdʒd] *adj Fig* emotivo(a)

charismatic [kærɪz'mætɪk] *adj* carismático(a)

charitable ['tʃærɪtəbəl] *adj (person)* caritativo(a); *(organization)* benéfico(a)

charity ['tʃærɪtɪ] *n* caridad *f*; *(organization)* institución benéfica

charlady ['tʃɑːleɪdɪ] *n Br* mujer *f* de la limpieza

charlatan ['ʃɑːlətən] *n (doctor)* curandero(a) *m,f*

charm [tʃɑːm] **1** *n* (**a**) *(quality)* encanto *m* (**b**) *(spell)* hechizo *m*; **lucky c.** amuleto *m*
  2 *vt* encantar

charming ['tʃɑːmɪŋ] *adj* encantador(a)

chart [tʃɑːt] **1** *n* (**a**) *(giving information)* tabla *f*; *(graph)* gráfico *m* (**b**) *(map)* carta *f* de navegación (**c**) *Mus* **the charts** la lista de éxitos
  2 *vt Av & Naut (on map)* trazar

charter ['tʃɑːtə(r)] **1** *n* (**a**) *(of institution)* estatutos *mpl*; *(of rights)* carta *f* (**b**) **c. flight** vuelo *m* chárter
  2 *vt (plane, boat)* fletar

chartered accountant [tʃɑːtədə'kaʊntənt] *n Br* censor(a) *m,f* jurado/a de cuentas, *Am* contador(a) *m,f* público(a)

chase [tʃeɪs] **1** *vt (person); (hunt)* cazar
  2 *n* persecución *f*; *(hunt)* caza *f*

chasm ['kæzəm] *n Geog* sima *f*; *Fig* abismo *m*

chassis ['ʃæsɪ] *n* chasis *m inv*

chastise [tʃæs'taɪz] *vt* castigar

chastity ['tʃæstɪtɪ] *n* castidad *f*

chat [tʃæt] **1** *n* (**a**) *(informal conversation)* charla *f*; *Br* **c. show** coloquio *m* (**b**) *Comput* charla *f*; **c. room** sala *f* de conversación
  2 *vi* (**a**) *(talk informally)* charlar (**b**) *Comput* charlar (**to** *or* **with** con)
  ▸ **chat up** *vt sep Br Fam* **to chat sb up** *(intentar)* ligar con algn

chatter ['tʃætə(r)] **1** *vi (person)* parlotear; *(bird)* piar; *(teeth)* castañetear
  2 *n (of person)* parloteo *m*; *(of birds)* gorjeo *m*; *(of teeth)* castañeteo *m*

chatterbox ['tʃætəbɒks] *n Fam* parlanchín(ina) *m,f*

chatty ['tʃætɪ] *adj* (**chattier, chattiest**) hablador(a)

chauffeur ['ʃəʊfə(r), ʃəʊ'fɜː(r)] *n* chófer *m*

chauvinism ['ʃəʊvɪnɪzəm] *n* chovinismo *m*; **male c.** machismo *m*

chauvinist ['ʃəʊvɪnɪst] *adj & n* chovinista *(mf)*; **male c.** machista *m*

cheap [tʃiːp] **1** *adj* barato(a); *(fare)* económico(a); *(joke)* de mal gusto; *(contemptible)* bajo(a); *Fam* **dirt c.** tirado(a)
  2 *n Br Fam* **on the c.** en plan barato
  3 *adv* barato

cheapen ['tʃiːpən] *vt Fig* degradar

cheaply ['tʃiːplɪ] *adv* barato, en plan económico

cheat [tʃiːt] **1** *vt* engañar; **to c. sb out of sth** estafar algo a algn
  2 *vi* (**a**) *(at games)* hacer trampa; *(in exam etc)* copiar(se) (**b**) *Fam (husband, wife)* poner cuernos (**on** a)
  3 *n (trickster)* tramposo(a) *m,f*

check [tʃek] **1** *vt* (**a**) *(revise)* repasar; *(facts)* comprobar; *(tickets)* controlar; *(tyres, oil)* revisar (**b**) *(impulse)* refrenar; *(growth)* retardar (**c**) *(stop)* detener (**d**) *(in chess)* dar jaque a
  2 *vi* comprobar
  3 *n* (**a**) *(of documents etc)* revisión *f*; *(of facts)* comprobación *f* (**b**) *(in chess)* jaque *m* (**c**) *(pattern)* cuadro *m* (**d**) **to keep in c.** *(feelings)* contener; *(enemy)* mantener a raya (**e**) *US* = cheque
  ▸ **check in** *vi (at airport)* facturar; *(at hotel)* registrarse (**at** en)
  ▸ **check out** **1** *vi (of hotel)* dejar el hotel
  2 *vt sep (facts)* verificar
  ▸ **check up** *vi* **to c. up on sb** hacer averiguaciones sobre algn; **to c. up on sth** comprobar algo

checked [tʃekt] *adj* a cuadros

checker ['tʃekər] *n US (cashier)* cajero(a) *m,f*

checkered ['tʃekərd] *adj US* = chequered

checkers ['tʃekərz] *n sing US (game)* damas *fpl*

check-in ['tʃekɪn] *n* **c. desk** *(at airport)* mostrador *m* de facturación

checkmate ['tʃekmeɪt] **1** *n* jaque mate *m*
  2 *vt* dar (jaque) mate a; *Fig* poner en un callejón sin salida

checkout ['tʃekaʊt] *n (counter)* caja *f*

checkpoint ['tʃekpɔɪnt] *n* control *m*

checkroom ['tʃekruːm] *n US (for coats, hats)* guardarropa *m*; *(for luggage)* consigna *f*

checkup ['tʃekʌp] *n Med* chequeo *m*, examen médico

cheek [tʃiːk] *n* (**a**) mejilla *f* (**b**) *Fam (nerve)* cara *f*; **what c.!** ¡vaya jeta!

cheekbone ['tʃiːkbəʊn] *n* pómulo *m*

cheeky ['tʃiːkɪ] *adj* (**cheekier, cheekiest**) *Fam* fresco(a), descarado(a)

cheep [tʃiːp] **1** *n (of bird)* pío *m*
  2 *vi* piar

cheer [tʃɪə(r)] **1** *vi* aplaudir, aclamar
  2 *vt* (**a**) *(applaud)* vitorear, aclamar (**b**) *(make hopeful)* animar
  3 *n* viva *m*; **cheers** aplausos *mpl*; *Fam* **cheers!** *(thank you)* ¡gracias!; *(before drinking)* ¡salud!
  ▸ **cheer up 1** *vi* animarse
  2 *vt sep* **to c. sb up** alegrar *or* animar a algn

cheerful ['tʃɪəfʊl] *adj* alegre

cheerio [tʃɪərɪ'əʊ] *interj Br Fam* ¡hasta luego!

cheese [tʃiːz] *n* queso *m*

cheesecake ['tʃiːzkeɪk] *n* tarta *f* de queso

cheetah ['tʃiːtə] *n* guepardo *m*

chef [ʃef] *n* chef *m*

chemical ['kemɪkəl] **1** *n* sustancia química, producto químico
  2 *adj* químico(a)

chemist ['kemɪst] *n* (**a**) químico(a) *m,f* (**b**) *Br* **c.'s (shop)** farmacia *f*; **(dispensing) c.** farmacéutico(a) *m,f*

chemistry ['kemɪstrɪ] *n* química *f*

cheque [tʃek] *n* cheque *m*; **to pay by c.** pagar con (un) cheque; **c. book** talonario *m* (de cheques); **c. card** tarjeta *f* de identificación bancaria

chequered ['tʃekəd] *adj* a cuadros; *Fig* **a c. career** una carrera con altibajos

cherish ['tʃerɪʃ] *vt* (**a**) *(person)* tenerle mucho cariño a (**b**) *Fig (hopes etc)* abrigar

cherry ['tʃerɪ] *n* cereza *f*

chess [tʃes] *n* ajedrez *m*

chessboard ['tʃesbɔːd] *n* tablero *m* de ajedrez

chesspiece ['tʃespiːs] *n* pieza *f* de ajedrez

chest [tʃest] *n* (**a**) *Anat* pecho *m* (**b**) *(for linen)* arca *f*; *(for valuables)* cofre *m*; **c. of drawers** cómoda *f*

chestnut ['tʃesnʌt] *n (tree, colour)* castaño *m*; *(nut)* castaña *f*

chew [tʃuː] *vt* masticar, mascar

chewing gum ['tʃuːɪŋɡʌm] *n* chicle *m*

chic [ʃiːk] *adj* elegante

chick [tʃɪk] *n* (**a**) *(young chicken)* pollito *m* (**b**) *Fam (woman)* nena *f*, *Arg* piba *f*, *Méx* chava *f*

  2 *vi Fam* **to c. out** rajarse (por miedo)

chickenpox ['tʃɪkɪnpɒks] *n* varicela *f*

chickpea ['tʃɪkpiː] *n* garbanzo *m*

chicory ['tʃɪkərɪ] *n* achicoria *f*

chief [tʃiːf] **1** *n* jefe *m*
  2 *adj* principal

chiefly ['tʃiːflɪ] *adv (above all)* sobre todo; *(mainly)* principalmente

chiffon ['ʃɪfɒn] *n* gasa *f*

chilblain ['tʃɪlbleɪn] *n* sabañón *m*

child [tʃaɪld] *n (pl* **children)** niño(a) *m,f*; *(son)* hijo *m*; *(daughter)* hija *f*; **c. minder** = persona que cuida niños en su propia casa

childbirth ['tʃaɪldbɜːθ] *n* parto *m*

childhood ['tʃaɪldhʊd] *n* infancia *f*, niñez *f*

childish ['tʃaɪldɪʃ] *adj* pueril, aniñado(a)

childlike ['tʃaɪldlaɪk] *adj* infantil

children ['tʃɪldrən] *pl of* **child**

Chile ['tʃɪlɪ] *n* Chile

Chilean ['tʃɪlɪən] *adj & n* chileno(a) *(m,f)*

chili ['tʃɪlɪ] *n* = **chilli**

chill [tʃɪl] **1** *n* (**a**) *Med* resfriado *m* (**b**) *(coldness)* fresco *m*

  2 *adj* frío(a)
  3 *vt (meat)* refrigerar; *(wine)* enfriar

chilli ['tʃɪlɪ] *n* chile *m*

chilly ['tʃɪlɪ] *adj* (**chillier, chilliest**) frío(a)

chime [tʃaɪm] **1** *n (peal)* campanada *f*
  2 *vt* **to c. five o'clock** *(of clock)* dar las cinco
  3 *vi* sonar
  ► **chime in** *vi Fam* intervenir

chimney ['tʃɪmnɪ] *n* chimenea *f*; **c. sweep** deshollinador *m*

chimpanzee [tʃɪmpæn'ziː] *n* chimpancé *m*

chin [tʃɪn] *n* barbilla *f*, mentón *m*; **double c.** papada *f*

China ['tʃaɪnə] *n* China

china ['tʃaɪnə] *n* loza *f*, porcelana *f*

> Note that the Spanish word **china** is a false friend and is never a translation for the English word **china**. In Spanish, **china** means "pebble, small stone".

Chinese [tʃaɪ'niːz] **1** *adj* chino(a)
  2 *n* (**a**) *(person)* chino(a) *m,f* (**b**) *(language)* chino *m*

chink¹ [tʃɪŋk] *n (opening)* resquicio *m*; *(crack)* grieta *f*

chink² [tʃɪŋk] **1** *vi* tintinear
  2 *n* tintineo *m*

chip [tʃɪp] **1** *n* (**a**) *(of wood)* astilla *f*; *(of stone)* lasca *f*; *(in cup)* mella *f* (**b**) *Br Culin* **chips** patatas *or Am* papas fritas; *US* **(potato) chips** *(crisps)* patatas *or Am* papas fritas *(de bolsa)* (**c**) *Comput* chip *m* (**d**) *(in gambling)* ficha *f*
  2 *vt (wood)* astillar; *(stone)* resquebrajar; *(china, glass)* mellar
  3 *vi (wood)* astillarse; *(china, glass)* mellarse; *(paint)* desconcharse
  ► **chip in** *vi Fam* (**a**) meterse (**b**) *(with money)* poner algo (de dinero)

chiropodist [kɪ'rɒpədɪst] *n* pedicuro(a) *m,f*

chirp [tʃɜːp] *vi (birds)* gorjear

chisel ['tʃɪzəl] *n* cincel *m*

chit [tʃɪt] *n* nota *f*; *(small invoice)* vale *m*

chitchat ['tʃɪttʃæt] *n Fam* palique *m*

chivalry ['ʃɪvəlrɪ] *n* caballerosidad *f*

chives [tʃaɪvz] *npl* cebolleta *f*

chlorine ['klɔːriːn] *n* cloro *m*

chock-a-block [tʃɒkə'blɒk], **chock-full** [tʃɒk'fʊl] *adj Fam* (lleno(a)) hasta los topes

chocolate ['tʃɒkəlɪt] **1** *n* chocolate *m*; **chocolates** bombones *mpl*
  2 *adj* de chocolate

choice [tʃɔɪs] **1** *n* elección *f*; **a wide c.** un gran surtido; **by c.** por gusto
  2 *adj* selecto(a)

choir ['kwaɪə(r)] *n* coro *m*, coral *f*

choirboy ['kwaɪəbɔɪ] *n* niño *m* de coro

choke [tʃəʊk] **1** *vt* (**a**) *(person)* ahogar (**b**) *(obstruct)* obstruir
  2 *vi* ahogarse; **to c. on food** atragantarse con la comida
  3 *n Aut* estárter *m*

▸ **choke back** vt sep (emotions) tragarse
cholera [ˈkɒlərə] n cólera m
cholesterol [kəˈlestərɒl] n colesterol m
choose [tʃuːz] 1 vt (pt chose; pp chosen) escoger, elegir; (decide on) optar por
2 vi escoger, elegir
choos(e)y [ˈtʃuːzɪ] adj (choosier, choosiest) Fam exigente
chop [tʃɒp] 1 vt (a) (wood) cortar; (tree) talar (b) Culin cortar a pedacitos
2 n (a) (blow) tajo m; (with axe) hachazo m (b) Culin chuleta f
chopper [ˈtʃɒpə(r)] n Fam helicóptero m
choppy [ˈtʃɒpɪ] adj (choppier, choppiest) (sea) picado(a)
chopsticks [ˈtʃɒpstɪks] npl palillos mpl
chord [kɔːd] n Mus acorde m; Fig **it strikes a c.** (me) suena
chore [tʃɔː(r)] n quehacer m, tarea f
chortle [ˈtʃɔːtəl] vi reír con ganas
chorus [ˈkɔːrəs] n Mus & Th coro m; (in a song) estribillo m; **c. girl** corista f
chose [tʃəʊz] pt of **choose**
chosen [ˈtʃəʊzən] pp of **choose**
Christ [kraɪst] n Cristo m, Jesucristo m
christen [ˈkrɪsən] vt bautizar
christening [ˈkrɪsənɪŋ] n bautizo m
Christian [ˈkrɪstʃən] 1 adj cristiano(a); **c. name** nombre m de pila
2 n cristiano(a) m,f
Christianity [krɪstɪˈænɪtɪ] n cristianismo m
Christmas [ˈkrɪsməs] n Navidad f; **merry C.!** ¡feliz Navidad!; **C. carol** villancico m; **C. Day** día m de Navidad; **C. Eve** Nochebuena f
chrome [krəʊm] n cromo m
chromium [ˈkrəʊmɪəm] n cromo m; **c. plating** cromado m
chromosome [ˈkrəʊməsəʊm] n cromosoma m
chronic [ˈkrɒnɪk] adj crónico(a)
chronicle [ˈkrɒnɪkəl] 1 n crónica f
2 vt hacer la crónica de
chronological [krɒnəˈlɒdʒɪkəl] adj cronológico(a)
chrysanthemum [krɪˈsænθəməm] n crisantemo m
chubby [ˈtʃʌbɪ] adj (chubbier, chubbiest) rellenito(a)
chuck [tʃʌk] vt Fam tirar; **to c. one's job in** or **up** dejar el trabajo; **to c. sb out** echar a algn; **to c. sth away** or **out** tirar algo
chuckle [ˈtʃʌkəl] 1 vi reír entre dientes
2 n sonrisita f
chug [tʃʌg] vi traquetear
chum [tʃʌm] n compinche mf, compañero(a) m,f
chunk [tʃʌŋk] n Fam cacho m, pedazo m
church [tʃɜːtʃ] n iglesia f; **to go to c.** ir a misa; **C. of England** Iglesia Anglicana
churchyard [ˈtʃɜːtʃjɑːd] n cementerio m, campo santo
churlish [ˈtʃɜːlɪʃ] adj grosero(a)

churn [tʃɜːn] 1 n (for butter) mantequera f; B (for milk) lechera f
2 vt (butter) hacer
3 vi revolverse, agitarse
▸ **churn out** vt sep Fam producir en serie
chute [ʃuːt] n (channel) conducto m; (slide tobogán m
chutney [ˈtʃʌtnɪ] n conserva f (de frutas picante
CIA [siːaɪˈeɪ] n US (abbr **Central Intelligenc Agency**) CIA f
CID [siːaɪˈdiː] n Br (abbr **Criminal Investiga tion Department**) = policía judicial británic
cider [ˈsaɪdə(r)] n sidra f
cigar [sɪˈgɑː(r)] n puro m
cigarette [sɪgəˈret] n cigarrillo m; **c. cas** pitillera f; **c. end** colilla f; **c. holder** boquilla **c. lighter** mechero m
Cinderella [sɪndəˈrelə] n Cenicienta f
cine camera [ˈsɪnɪkæmərə] n Br cámara c nematográfica
cinema [ˈsɪnɪmə] n (a) Br (building) cine r (b) (art) cine m
cinnamon [ˈsɪnəmən] n canela f
cipher [ˈsaɪfə(r)] n (numeral) cifra f
circle [ˈsɜːkəl] 1 n (a) círculo m; (of people corro m; **in business circles** en el mundo d los negocios (b) Th anfiteatro m
2 vt (surround) rodear; (move round) dar l vuelta a
3 vi dar vueltas
circuit [ˈsɜːkɪt] n (a) (journey) recorrido r (b) Elec circuito m (c) Sport (events) liga f; B (track) circuito m (d) Br Jur **c. judge** juez mf d distrito
circular [ˈsɜːkjʊlə(r)] adj & n circular (f)
circulate [ˈsɜːkjʊleɪt] 1 vt (news) hacer circu lar
2 vi circular
circulation [sɜːkjʊˈleɪʃən] n (a) (of blooc circulación f (b) (of newspaper) tirada f
circumcise [ˈsɜːkəmsaɪz] vt circuncidar
circumference [səˈkʌmfərəns] n circunfe rencia f
circumspect [ˈsɜːkəmspekt] adj prudente
circumstance [ˈsɜːkəmstəns] n (usu pl) cir cunstancia f; **under no circumstances** e ningún caso; **economic circumstances** situa ción económica
circumvent [sɜːkəmˈvent] vt Fig burlar
circus [ˈsɜːkəs] n circo m
cirrhosis [sɪˈrəʊsɪs] n cirrosis f
CIS [siːaɪˈes] n (abbr **Commonwealth of Inde pendent States**) CEI f
cistern [ˈsɪstən] n cisterna f
cite [saɪt] vt (quote) citar
citizen [ˈsɪtɪzən] n ciudadano(a) m,f
citizenship [ˈsɪtɪzənʃɪp] n ciudadanía f
citrus [ˈsɪtrəs] adj **c. fruits** agrios mpl
city [ˈsɪtɪ] n (a) ciudad f; US **c. council** ayun tamiento m; US **c. hall** ayuntamiento (b) Fi the C. = el centro financiero de Londres

vic ['sɪvɪk] *adj* cívico(a); *Br* **c. centre** centro cívico; **c. duties** obligaciones cívicas

vil ['sɪvəl] *adj* (**a**) civil; **c. defence** defensa *f* civil; **c. rights** derechos *mpl* civiles; **c. servant** uncionario(a) *m,f*; *Pol* **c. service** administraión pública (**b**) *(polite)* cortés, educado(a)

vilian [sɪ'vɪljən] *adj & n* civil *(mf)*; **c. lothing** traje *m* de paisano

vilization [sɪvɪlaɪ'zeɪʃən] *n* civilización *f*

vilized ['sɪvɪlaɪzd] *adj* civilizado(a)

ad [klæd] **1** *adj Literary* vestido(a)
2 *pt & pp of* **clothe**

aim [kleɪm] **1** *vt* (**a**) *(benefits, rights)* reclamar; *Jur (compensation)* exigir (**b**) *(assert)* firmar
2 *n* (**a**) *(demand)* reclamación *f*; *Jur* demanda *f*; **to put in a c.** reclamar una indemnización (**b**) *(right)* derecho *m* (**c**) *(assertion)* retensión *f*

aimant ['kleɪmənt] *n Jur* demandante *mf*

airvoyant [kleə'vɔɪənt] *n* clarividente *mf*

am [klæm] *n* almeja *f*
clam up *vi Fam* callarse

amber ['klæmbə(r)] *vi* trepar (**over** por)

ammy ['klæmɪ] *adj* (**clammier, clammiest**) *weather)* bochornoso(a); *(hand)* pegajoso(a)

amour, *US* **clamor** ['klæmə(r)] **1** *n* clamor *n*
2 *vi* clamar; **to c. for** pedir a gritos

amp [klæmp] **1** *n (for carpentry)* tornillo *m* e banco; *Tech* abrazadera *f*; **wheel c.** cepo *m*
2 *vt* sujetar con abrazaderas
clamp down on *vt insep* aumentar los esuerzos contra

an [klæn] *n* clan *m*

andestine [klæn'destɪn] *adj* clandestio(a)

ang [klæŋ] **1** *vi* sonar
2 *n* sonido metálico

ap [klæp] **1** *vt* aplaudir
2 *n* (**a**) palmada *f* (**b**) **a c. of thunder** un rueno

apping ['klæpɪŋ] *n* aplausos *mpl*

aret ['klærət] *n Br (wine)* clarete *m*; *(colour)* urdeos *m*

arify ['klærɪfaɪ] *vt* aclarar

arinet [klærɪ'net] *n* clarinete *m*

arity ['klærɪtɪ] *n* claridad *f*

ash [klæʃ] **1** *vi* (**a**) *(cymbals)* sonar; *(swords)* hocar; *Fig (disagree)* estar en desacuerdo (**b**) *(colours)* desentonar (**c**) *(dates)* coincidir
2 *n* (**a**) *(sound)* sonido *m* (**b**) *(fight)* choque *n*; *Fig (conflict)* conflicto *m*

asp [klɑːsp] **1** *n* (**a**) *(on belt)* cierre *m*; *(on ecklace)* broche *m* (**b**) *(grasp)* apretón *m*; **c. nife** navaja *f*
2 *vt (object)* agarrar; **to c. hands** juntar las manos

ass [klɑːs] **1** *n* clase *f*; **c. struggle** lucha *f* de lases; *US Educ* **c. of '84** promoción *f* de 1984; *ail* **second c. ticket** billete *m* de segunda clase)

2 *vt* clasificar

classic ['klæsɪk] **1** *adj* clásico(a)
2 *n* (**a**) *(author)* autor clásico; *(work)* obra clásica (**b**) **the classics** *(literature)* las obras clásicas; **classics** *(languages)* clásicas *fpl*

classical ['klæsɪkəl] *adj* clásico(a)

classified ['klæsɪfaɪd] *adj (information)* secreto(a); **c. advertisements** anuncios *mpl* por palabras

classify ['klæsɪfaɪ] *vt* clasificar

classless ['klɑːslɪs] *adj* sin clases

classmate ['klɑːsmeɪt] *n* compañero(a) *m,f* de clase

classroom ['klɑːsruːm] *n* aula *f*, clase *f*

clatter ['klætə(r)] **1** *vi* hacer ruido; *(things falling)* hacer estrépito
2 *n* ruido *m*, estrépito *m*

clause [klɔːz] *n* (**a**) *Jur* cláusula *f* (**b**) *Ling* oración *f*

claw [klɔː] **1** *n (of bird, lion)* garra *f*; *(of cat)* uña *f*; *(of crab)* pinza *f*
2 *vt* agarrar, arañar; *(tear)* desgarrar
▸ **claw at** *vt insep* agarrar, arañar

clay [kleɪ] *n* arcilla *f*; **c. pigeon shooting** tiro *m* al plato

clean [kliːn] **1** *adj* (**a**) limpio(a) (**b**) *(unmarked, pure)* sin defecto; **a c. copy** una copia en limpio; **to have a c. record** no tener antecedentes (penales) (**c**) *(not obscene)* decente (**d**) *Fig* **to make a c. sweep of it** arrasar
2 *adv* (**a**) **to play c.** jugar limpio; *Fam* **to come c.** confesarlo todo (**b**) *Fam* por completo; **it went c. through the middle** pasó justo por el medio
3 *vt (room)* limpiar; **to c. one's teeth** lavarse los dientes
▸ **clean out** *vt sep (room)* limpiar a fondo
▸ **clean up** *vt sep & vi* limpiar

clean-cut ['kliːn'kʌt] *adj (person)* limpio(a), pulcro(a)

cleaner ['kliːnə(r)] *n* limpiador(a) *m,f*

cleaning ['kliːnɪŋ] *n* limpieza *f*

cleanliness ['klenlɪnɪs] *n* limpieza *f*

cleanse [klenz] *vt* limpiar

cleansing ['klenzɪŋ] *n* **c. lotion** leche limpiadora

clear [klɪə(r)] **1** *adj* (**a**) claro(a); *(road, day)* despejado(a); **c. conscience** conciencia tranquila (**b**) *(obvious)* claro(a); **to make sth c.** aclarar algo (**c**) *(majority)* absoluto(a); *(profit)* neto(a); **three c. days** tres días completos (**d**) *(free)* libre
2 *adv* (**a**) *Fig* **loud and c.** claramente (**b**) **stand c.!** ¡apártese!; **to stay c. of** evitar
3 *vt* (**a**) *(room)* vaciar; *Com* liquidar; **to c. one's throat** aclararse la garganta; **to c. the table** quitar la mesa (**b**) *(authorize)* autorizar (**c**) *(hurdle)* salvar (**d**) **to c. sb of a charge** exculpar a algn de un delito
4 *vi (sky)* despejarse
▸ **clear away** *vt sep* quitar
▸ **clear off** *vi Fam* largarse; **c. off!** ¡largo!

▸ **clear out** *vt sep (room)* limpiar a fondo; *(cupboard)* vaciar

▸ **clear up 1** *vt sep* (**a**) *(tidy)* recoger; *(arrange)* ordenar (**b**) *(mystery)* resolver; *(misunderstanding)* aclarar

2 *vi (weather)* despejarse; *(problem)* desaparecer

clearance ['klɪərəns] *n* (**a**) *(of area)* despeje *m*; *Com* **c. sale** liquidación *f* (de existencias) (**b**) *(space)* espacio *m* libre (**c**) *(authorization)* autorización *f*

clear-cut [klɪə'kʌt] *adj* claro(a)

clearing ['klɪərɪŋ] *n* (**a**) *(in wood)* claro *m* (**b**) *(of rubbish)* limpieza *f* (**c**) *(of cheque)* compensación *f*

clearly ['klɪəlɪ] *adv* (**a**) claramente (**b**) *(at start of sentence)* evidentemente

clearway ['klɪəweɪ] *n Br* = carretera donde está prohibido parar

cleaver ['kliːvə(r)] *n* cuchillo *m* de carnicero

clef [klef] *n* clave *f*; **bass/treble c.** clave de fa/de sol

cleft [kleft] *n* hendidura *f*, grieta *f*

clementine ['kleməntaɪn] *n* clementina *f*

clench [klentʃ] *vt (teeth, fist)* apretar

clergy ['klɜːdʒɪ] *n* clero *m*

clergyman ['klɜːdʒɪmən] *n* clérigo *m*

clerical ['klerɪkəl] *adj* (**a**) *Rel* clerical (**b**) *(staff, work)* de oficina

clerk [klɑːk, *US* klɜːrk] *n* (**a**) *(office worker)* oficinista *mf*; *(civil servant)* funcionario(a) *m,f* (**b**) *US Com* dependiente(a) *m,f*, vendedor(a) *m,f*

clever ['klevə(r)] *adj* (**a**) *(person)* inteligente, listo(a); **to be c. at sth** tener aptitud para algo; *Fam* **c. Dick** sabiondo(a) *m,f* (**b**) *(argument)* ingenioso(a)

cliché ['kliːʃeɪ] *n* cliché *m*

click [klɪk] **1** *n (sound)* clic *m*

2 *vt (tongue)* chasquear

3 *vi* **it didn't c.** *(I didn't realize)* no me dio cuenta

client ['klaɪənt] *n* cliente *mf*

clientele [kliːɒn'tel] *n* clientela *f*

cliff [klɪf] *n* acantilado *m*

climate ['klaɪmɪt] *n* clima *m*

climax ['klaɪmæks] *n* (**a**) *(peak)* clímax *m*, punto *m* culminante (**b**) *(sexual)* orgasmo *m*

climb [klaɪm] **1** *vt (ladder)* subir a; *(mountain)* escalar; *(tree)* trepar a

2 *vi (plants)* trepar; *Av* subir; *Fig (socially)* ascender

3 *n* subida *f*, ascensión *f*

▸ **climb down** *vi* bajar; *Fig* volverse atrás

climber ['klaɪmə(r)] *n* alpinista *mf*, *Am* andinista *mf*

climbing ['klaɪmɪŋ] *n Sport* montañismo *m*, alpinismo *m*, *Am* andinismo *m*

clinch [klɪntʃ] **1** *vt* resolver; *(deal)* cerrar

2 *n Fam* abrazo apasionado

cling [klɪŋ] *vi (pt & pp* **clung**) *(hang on)* agarrarse; *(clothes)* ajustarse; *(smell)* pegarse; **to c. together** unirse

clinic ['klɪnɪk] *n (in state hospital)* ambulato rio *m*; *(specialized)* clínica *f*

clinical ['klɪnɪkəl] *adj* (**a**) *Med* clínico(a) (**b** *(detached)* frío(a)

clink [klɪŋk] **1** *vi* tintinear

2 *n* tintineo *m*

clip¹ [klɪp] **1** *vt (cut)* cortar; *(ticket)* picar

2 *n* (**a**) *(of film)* extracto *m* (**b**) *(with scissors* tijeretada *f*

clip² [klɪp] **1** *n (for hair)* pasador *m*; *(for pape* clip *m*, sujetapapeles *m inv*; *(brooch)* clip

2 *vt* sujetar

clippers ['klɪpəz] *npl (for hair)* maquinilla para rapar; *(for nails)* cortauñas *m inv*; *(fc hedge)* tijeras *fpl* de podar

clipping ['klɪpɪŋ] *n* recorte *m*

clique [kliːk] *n Pej* camarilla *f*

cloak [kləʊk] **1** *n (garment)* capa *f*

2 *vt* encubrir

cloakroom ['kləʊkruːm] *n* guardarropa *n Euph (toilets)* servicios *mpl*

clock [klɒk] **1** *n* reloj *m*

2 *vt (race)* cronometrar

▸ **clock in, clock on** *vi* fichar

▸ **clock off, clock out** *vi* fichar a la salida

▸ **clock up** *vt sep (mileage)* hacer

clockwise ['klɒkwaɪz] *adj & adv* en el senti do de las agujas del reloj

clockwork ['klɒkwɜːk] *n* mecanismo *m*; **toy** juguete *m* de cuerda

clog [klɒg] **1** *vt* obstruir; *(pipe)* atascar; **to ge clogged up** atascarse

2 *n (footwear)* zueco *m*

cloister ['klɔɪstə(r)] *n* claustro *m*

close¹ [kləʊs] **1** *adj* (**a**) *(in space, time)* cerca no(a); *(print, weave)* compacto(a); *(encour ter)* cara a cara; *(contact)* directo(a); **c. te** cerca de; **c. together** juntos(as); *Fig* **we ha a c. shave** nos libramos por los pelos (**b** *(relationship)* estrecho(a); *(friend)* íntimo(a) (**c**) *(inspection)* detallado(a); *(watch)* aten to(a) (**d**) *(contest)* reñido(a); **a c. resemblanc** un gran parecido (**e**) *(air)* cargado(a *(weather)* bochornoso(a) (**f**) *(secretive)* rese vado(a) (**g**) **c. season** *(in hunting)* veda *f*

2 *adv* cerca; **they live c. by** or **c. at han** viven cerca; **to stand c. together** estar apre tados(as)

close² [kləʊz] **1** *vt* (**a**) cerrar; **closing tim** hora *f* de cierre (**b**) *(end)* concluir, terminar *(meeting)* levantar

2 *vi* (**a**) *(shut)* cerrar, cerrarse (**b**) *(end* concluirse, terminarse

3 *n* fin *m*, final *m*

▸ **close down** *vi (business)* cerrar para siem pre; *Rad & TV* cerrar

▸ **close in** *vi* **to c. in on sb** rodear a algn

closed [kləʊzd] *adj* cerrado(a); *Ind* **c. shop** empresa que emplea solamente a miembro de un sindicato

close-knit [kləʊs'nɪt] *adj Fig* unido(a)

closely ['kləʊslɪ] *adv* (a) *(tightly)* estrechamente, muy; **c. contested** muy reñido(a); **they are c. related** *(people)* son parientes próximos (b) *(attentively)* con atención; **to follow (events) c.** seguir de cerca (los acontecimientos)

closet ['klɒzɪt] *n US* armario *m*

close-up ['kləʊsʌp] *n* primer plano *m*

closure ['kləʊʒə(r)] *n* cierre *m*

clot [klɒt] **1** *n* (a) *(of blood)* coágulo *m*; *Med* **c. on the brain** embolia *f* cerebral (b) *Br Fam* tonto(a) *m,f*
2 *vi* coagularse

cloth [klɒθ] *n* tela *f*, paño *m*; *(rag)* trapo *m*; *(tablecloth)* mantel *m*

clothe [kləʊð] *vt* (*pt & pp* **clothed** *or* **clad**) vestir (**in** *or* **with** de); *Fig* revestir, cubrir (**in** *or* **with** de)

clothes [kləʊðz] *npl* ropa *f*, vestidos *mpl*; **c. brush** cepillo *m* de la ropa; **c. hanger** percha *f*; **c. horse** tendedero *m* plegable; **c. line** tendedero *m*; **c. peg** *or US* **pin** pinza *f*

clothing ['kləʊðɪŋ] *n* ropa *f*

cloud [klaʊd] **1** *n* nube *f*
2 *vt* nublar; *Fig* **to c. the issue** complicar el asunto
3 *vi* **to c. over** nublarse

cloudy ['klaʊdɪ] *adj* (**cloudier, cloudiest**) (a) *(sky)* nublado(a) (b) *(liquid)* turbio(a)

clout [klaʊt] *Fam* **1** *n* (a) *(blow)* tortazo *m* (b) *(influence)* influencia *f*
2 *vt* dar un tortazo a

clove[1] [kləʊv] *n (spice)* clavo *m*

clove[2] [kləʊv] *n (of garlic)* diente *m*

clover ['kləʊvə(r)] *n* trébol *m*

clown [klaʊn] **1** *n* payaso *m*
2 *vi* **to c. (about** *or* **around)** hacer el payaso

cloying ['klɔɪɪŋ] *adj* empalagoso(a)

club [klʌb] **1** *n* (a) *(society)* club *m*; **sports c.** club deportivo (b) *(heavy stick)* garrote *m*, porra *f*; *(in golf)* palo *m* (c) *Cards* trébol *m* (d) *Culin* **c. sandwich** sándwich *m* doble; *US* **c. soda** soda *f*
2 *vt* aporrear
3 *vi* **to c. together** pagar entre varios

clubhouse ['klʌbhaʊs] *n* sede *f* de un club

cluck [klʌk] **1** *n* cloqueo *m*
2 *vi* cloquear

clue [kluː] *n (sign)* indicio *m*; *(to mystery)* pista *f*; *(in crossword)* clave *f*; *Fam* **I haven't a c.** no tengo ni idea

clump [klʌmp] *n (of trees)* grupo *m*; *(of plants)* mata *f*

clumsy ['klʌmzɪ] *adj* (**clumsier, clumsiest**) desmañado(a), torpe; *(awkward)* tosco(a)

clung [klʌŋ] *pt & pp of* **cling**

cluster ['klʌstə(r)] **1** *n* grupo *m*; *(of grapes)* racimo *m*
2 *vi* agruparse

clutch [klʌtʃ] **1** *vt* agarrar
2 *vi* *Fig* **to c. at straws** aferrarse a cualquier cosa

3 *n* (a) *Aut* embrague *m* (b) *Fig* **to fall into sb's clutches** caer en las garras de algn

clutter ['klʌtə(r)] *vt* **to c. (up)** llenar, atestar

cm (*abbr* **centimetre(s)**) cm

CND [siːen'diː] *n Br* (*abbr* **Campaign for Nuclear Disarmament**) = organización británica en favor del desarme nuclear

Co (a) *Com* (*abbr* **Company**) Cía. (b) *abbr* **County**

c/o [siː'əʊ] (*abbr* **care of**) en el domicilio de

coach [kəʊtʃ] **1** *n* (a) *Aut* autocar *m*; *(carriage)* carruaje *m*; **c. tour** excursión *f* en autocar (b) *Rail* coche *m*, vagón *m* (c) *Sport* entrenador(a) *m,f*
2 *vt Sport* entrenar; *Educ* dar clases particulares a

coagulate [kəʊ'ægjʊleɪt] *vi* coagularse

coal [kəʊl] *n* carbón *m*, hulla *f*; **c. bunker** carbonera *f*; **c. merchant** carbonero *m*; **c. mine** mina *f* de carbón

coalfield ['kəʊlfiːld] *n* yacimiento *m* de carbón

coalition [kəʊə'lɪʃən] *n* coalición *f*

coarse [kɔːs] *adj (material)* basto(a); *(skin)* áspero(a); *(language)* grosero(a), ordinario(a)

coast [kəʊst] **1** *n* costa *f*, litoral *m*; *Fam Fig* **the c. is clear** no hay moros en la costa
2 *vi Aut* ir en punto muerto

coastal ['kəʊstəl] *adj* costero(a)

coaster ['kəʊstə(r)] *n (mat)* salvamanteles *m inv*

coastguard ['kəʊstɡɑːd] *n* guardacostas *m inv*

coastline ['kəʊstlaɪn] *n* litoral *m*, costa *f*

coat [kəʊt] **1** *n* (a) *(overcoat)* abrigo *m*; *(short)* chaquetón *m*; **c. hanger** percha *f* (b) *(of animal)* pelo *m* (c) *(of paint)* mano *f*, capa *f* (d) **c. of arms** escudo *m* de armas
2 *vt* cubrir (**with** de); *(with liquid)* bañar (**with** en)

coating ['kəʊtɪŋ] *n* capa *f*, baño *m*

coax [kəʊks] *vt* engatusar

cob [kɒb] *n* mazorca *f*

cobble ['kɒbəl] *n* adoquín *m*

cobbler ['kɒblə(r)] *n* zapatero *m*

cobweb ['kɒbweb] *n* telaraña *f*

cocaine [kə'keɪn] *n* cocaína *f*

cock [kɒk] **1** *n* (a) *Orn* gallo *m*; *(male bird)* macho *m* (b) *(on gun)* percutor *m* (c) *Vulg (penis)* polla *f*
2 *vt (gun)* amartillar; *(ears)* erguir
▸ **cock up** *vt sep Br very Fam* chapucear

cocker ['kɒkə(r)] *n* **c. spaniel** cocker *m*

cockerel ['kɒkərəl] *n* gallo *m* joven

cockeyed ['kɒkaɪd] *adj Fam (lopsided)* torcido(a); *(scheme)* disparatado(a)

cockle ['kɒkəl] *n* berberecho *m*

cockney ['kɒknɪ] **1** *adj* = del East End londinense
2 *n* = persona del East End londinense

cockpit ['kɒkpɪt] *n* cabina *f* del piloto

cockroach [ˈkɒkrəʊtʃ] *n* cucaracha *f*

cocktail [ˈkɒkteɪl] *n* cóctel *m*; **c. lounge** bar *m*; **c. party** cóctel; **prawn c.** cóctel de gambas; **Molotov c.** cóctel Molotov

cocky [ˈkɒkɪ] *adj* (**cockier, cockiest**) *Fam* creído(a)

cocoa [ˈkəʊkəʊ] *n* cacao *m*

coconut [ˈkəʊkənʌt] *n* coco *m*

cocoon [kəˈkuːn] *n* capullo *m*

COD [siːəʊˈdiː] *Br* (*abbr* **cash on delivery**) CAE

cod [kɒd] *n* bacalao *m*; **c. liver oil** aceite *m* de hígado de bacalao

code [kəʊd] **1** *n* código *m*; (*symbol*) clave *f*; *Tel* prefijo *m*
   2 *vt* (*message*) cifrar, poner en clave

co-ed [kəʊˈed] *Fam* **1** *adj* mixto(a)
   2 *n* colegio mixto

coerce [kəʊˈɜːs] *vt* coaccionar

coercion [kəʊˈɜːʃən] *n* coacción *f*

coexist [kəʊɪgˈzɪst] *vi* coexistir

coffee [ˈkɒfɪ] *n* café *m*; **c. bar/shop** cafetería *f*; **c. break** descanso *m*; **c. table** mesita *f* de café

coffeepot [ˈkɒfɪpɒt] *n* cafetera *f*

coffer [ˈkɒfə(r)] *n* arca *f*

coffin [ˈkɒfɪn] *n* ataúd *m*

cog [kɒg] *n* diente *m*

cognac [ˈkɒnjæk] *n* coñac *m*

coherent [kəʊˈhɪərənt] *adj* coherente

coil [kɔɪl] **1** *vt* **to c. (up)** enrollar
   2 *vi* enroscarse
   3 *n* (**a**) (*loop*) vuelta *f*; (*of rope*) rollo *m*; (*of hair*) rizo *m* (**b**) (*contraceptive*) espiral *f* (**c**) *Elec* carrete *m*, bobina *f*

coin [kɔɪn] **1** *n* moneda *f*
   2 *vt* (**a**) (*money*) acuñar (**b**) *Fig* **to c. a phrase** por así decirlo

coinage [ˈkɔɪnɪdʒ] *n* moneda *f*, sistema monetario

coincide [kəʊɪnˈsaɪd] *vi* coincidir (**with** con)

coincidence [kəʊˈɪnsɪdəns] *n* coincidencia *f*

coincidental [kəʊɪnsɪˈdentəl] *adj* casual

coincidentally [kəʊɪnsɪˈdentəlɪ] *adv* por casualidad *or* coincidencia

Coke® [kəʊk] *n Fam* Coca-Cola® *f*

coke [kəʊk] *n* (*coal*) coque *m*

colander [ˈkɒləndə(r)] *n* colador *m*

cold [kəʊld] **1** *adj* frío(a); **I'm c.** tengo frío; **it's c.** (*weather*) hace frío; (*thing*) está frío(a); *Fig* **to get c. feet** (**about doing sth**) entrarle miedo a algn (de hacer algo); **c. cream** crema *f* hidratante; *Fig* **it leaves me c.** no me dice nada; **c. war** guerra fría
   2 *n* (**a**) frío *m* (**b**) *Med* resfriado *m*; **to catch a c.** resfriarse, acatarrarse; **to have a c.** estar resfriado(a); **c. sore** herpes *m* (en el labio)

cold-blooded [kəʊldˈblʌdɪd] *adj* (**a**) (*animal*) de sangre fría (**b**) *Fig* (*person*) frío(a); (*crime*) a sangre fría

coleslaw [ˈkəʊlslɔː] *n* ensalada *f* de col

collaborate [kəˈlæbəreɪt] *vi* colaborar (**with** con)

collaborator [kəˈlæbəreɪtə(r)] *n Pol* colaboracionista *mf*

collapse [kəˈlæps] **1** *vi* (*break down*) derrumbarse; (*cave in*) hundirse; *Fig* (*prices*) caer en picado; *Med* sufrir un colapso
   2 *vt* (*table*) plegar
   3 *n* (*breaking down*) derrumbamiento *m*; (*caving in*) hundimiento *m*; *Med* colapso *m*

collapsible [kəˈlæpsəbəl] *adj* plegable

collar [ˈkɒlə(r)] **1** *n* (*of garment*) cuello *m*; (*for dog*) collar *m*
   2 *vt Fam* pescar, agarrar

collarbone [ˈkɒləbəʊn] *n* clavícula *f*

collateral [kɒˈlætərəl] **1** *n Fin* garantía subsidiaria
   2 *adj* colateral

colleague [ˈkɒliːg] *n* colega *mf*

collect [kəˈlekt] **1** *vt* (**a**) (*gather*) recoger (**b**) (*stamps etc*) coleccionar (**c**) (*taxes*) recaudar
   2 *vi* (**a**) (*people*) reunirse (**b**) (*for charity*) hacer una colecta (**for** para)
   3 *adj US* **c. call** llamada *f or Am* llamado *m* a cobro revertido
   4 *adv US Tel* **to call c.** llamar a cobro revertido

collection [kəˈlekʃən] *n* (**a**) (*of mail*) recogida *f*; (*of money*) colecta *f* (**b**) (*of stamps*) colección *f* (**c**) (*of taxes*) recaudación *f* (**d**) (*of people*) grupo *m*

collective [kəˈlektɪv] **1** *adj* colectivo(a); **c. bargaining** negociación colectiva
   2 *n* colectivo *m*

collector [kəˈlektə(r)] *n* (**a**) (*of stamps*) coleccionista *mf* (**b**) **tax c.** recaudador(a) *m,f* (de impuestos)

college [ˈkɒlɪdʒ] *n* colegio *m*; (*of university*) colegio mayor; *US* (*university*) universidad *f*

collide [kəˈlaɪd] *vi* chocar, colisionar

collie [ˈkɒlɪ] *n* perro *m* pastor escocés

colliery [ˈkɒljərɪ] *n Br* mina *f* de carbón

collision [kəˈlɪʒən] *n* choque *m*

colloquial [kəˈləʊkwɪəl] *adj* coloquial

collusion [kəˈluːʒən] *n* conspiración *f*

cologne [kəˈləʊn] *n* (*agua f* de) colonia *f*

Colombia [kəˈlɒmbɪə] *n* Colombia

Colombian [kəˈlɒmbɪən] *adj & n* colombiano(a) (*m,f*)

colon[1] [ˈkəʊlən] *n Typ* dos puntos *mpl*

colon[2] [ˈkəʊlən] *n Anat* colon *m*

colonel [ˈkɜːnəl] *n* coronel *m*

colonial [kəˈləʊnɪəl] *adj* colonial

colonize [ˈkɒlənaɪz] *vt* colonizar

colony [ˈkɒlənɪ] *n* colonia *f*

color [ˈkʌlər] *n, vt & vi US* = **colour**

colossal [kəˈlɒsəl] *adj* colosal

colour [ˈkʌlə(r)] **1** *n* (**a**) color *m*; **what c. is it?** ¿de qué color es?; **c. film/television** película *f*/televisión *f* en color; **c. scheme** combinación *f* de colores (**b**) (*race*) color *m*; **c. bar** discriminación *f* racial (**c**) **colours** *Br Sport* colores *mpl*; *Mil* (*flag*) bandera *f*
   2 *vt* colorear

3 *vi* **to c. (up)** ruborizarse

colour-blind ['kʌləblaɪnd] *adj* daltónico(a)

Coloured ['kʌləd] *adj* de color

coloured ['kʌləd] *adj (photograph)* en color

> 📖 Note that the Spanish word **colorado** is a false friend and is never a translation for the English word **coloured**. In Spanish, **colorado** means "red".

colourful ['kʌləfʊl] *adj* (a) con muchos colores (b) *Fig* lleno(a) de color; *(person)* pintoresco(a)

colouring ['kʌlərɪŋ] *n (colour)* colorido *m*

colourless ['kʌləlɪs] *adj* incoloro(a); *Fig* soso(a)

colt [kəʊlt] *n* potro *m*

column ['kɒləm] *n* columna *f*

columnist ['kɒləmnɪst] *n* columnista *mf*

coma ['kəʊmə] *n* coma *m*; **to go into a c.** entrar en coma

comb [kəʊm] **1** *n* peine *m*

2 *vt* peinar; **to c. one's hair** peinarse

combat ['kɒmbæt] **1** *n* combate *m*

2 *vt (enemy, disease)* combatir

3 *vi* combatir **(against** contra)

combination [kɒmbɪ'neɪʃən] *n* combinación *f*

combine [kəm'baɪn] **1** *vt* combinar

2 *vi* combinarse; *(companies)* asociarse

3 *n* ['kɒmbaɪn] (a) *Com* asociación *f* (b) **c. harvester** cosechadora *f*

combustion [kəm'bʌstʃən] *n* combustión *f*

come [kʌm] *vi (pt* came*; pp* come*)* (a) venir; *(arrive)* llegar; **coming!** ¡voy!; **to c. and go** ir y venir; *Fig* **in years to c.** en el futuro

(b) **to c. apart/undone** desatarse/soltarse

(c) *(happen)* suceder; **that's what comes of being too impatient** es lo que pasa por ser demasiado impaciente; *Fam* **c. how c.?** ¿y eso?

(d) **I came to believe that ...** llegué a creer que ...

(e) *Fig* **c. what may** pase lo que pase

(f) *very Fam (have orgasm)* correrse

▸ **come about** *vi* ocurrir, suceder

▸ **come across 1** *vt insep (thing)* encontrar por casualidad; **to c. across sb** tropezar con algn

2 *vi Fig* **to c. across well** causar buena impresión

▸ **come along** *vi* (a) *(arrive)* venir; **c. along!** ¡venga! (b) *(make progress)* progresar

▸ **come away** *vi (leave)* salir; *(part)* desprenderse **(from** de)

▸ **come back** *vi (return)* volver

▸ **come before** *vt insep* (a) preceder (b) *(court)* comparecer ante

▸ **come by** *vt insep* adquirir

▸ **come down** *vi* bajar; *(rain)* caer; *(building)* ser derribado(a); **to c. down with the flu** coger la gripe

▸ **come forward** *vi (advance)* avanzar; *(volunteer)* ofrecerse

▸ **come in** *vi* (a) *(enter)* entrar; **c. in!** ¡pase! (b) *(arrive) (train)* llegar; *(tide)* subir; *Fam Fig* **where do I c. in?** y yo ¿qué pinto? (c) **to c. in handy** venir bien (d) **to c. in for** ser objeto de

▸ **come into** *vt insep* (a) *(enter)* entrar en (b) *(inherit)* heredar

▸ **come off 1** *vt insep (fall from)* caerse de; *Fam* **c. off it!** ¡venga ya!

2 *vi* (a) *(fall)* caerse; *(stain)* quitarse; *(button)* caerse (b) *Fam (take place)* pasar; *(succeed)* salir bien; **to c. off badly** salir mal

▸ **come on** *vi* (a) **c. on!** *(hurry)* ¡venga! (b) *(make progress)* progresar (c) *(rain, illness)* comenzar

▸ **come out** *vi* (a) salir **(of** de); *(book)* aparecer; *(product)* estrenarse; *(facts)* revelarse (b) *(stain)* quitarse; *(colour)* desteñir (c) **to c. out against/in favour of sth** declararse en contra/a favor de algo; *Br Ind* **to c. out (on strike)** declararse en huelga (d) *(turn out)* salir

▸ **come over 1** *vi* venir

2 *vt insep* (a) *(hill)* aparecer en lo alto de (b) *Fam* **what's c. over you?** ¿qué te pasa?

▸ **come round 1** *vt insep (corner)* dar la vuelta a

2 *vi* (a) *(visit)* venir (b) *(regain consciousness)* volver en sí (c) **to c. round to sb's way of thinking** dejarse convencer por algn

▸ **come through 1** *vt insep* (a) *(cross)* cruzar (b) *(illness)* recuperarse de; *(accident)* sobrevivir

2 *vi (message)* llegar

▸ **come to 1** *vi (regain consciousness)* volver en sí

2 *vt insep* (a) *Fig* **to c. to one's senses** recobrar la razón (b) *(amount to)* costar (c) *(arrive at)* llegar a; **to c. to an end** terminar; *Fam* **c. to that** a propósito

▸ **come under** *vt insep Fig* **to c. under fire from sb** ser criticado(a) por algn

▸ **come up** *vi* (a) *(rise)* subir; *(approach)* acercarse **(to** a) (b) *(difficulty, question)* surgir; **to c. up with a solution** encontrar una solución; **to c. up against problems** encontrarse con problemas (c) *(sun)* salir (d) **to c. up to** igualar; **to c. up to sb's expectations** satisfacer a algn (e) *Fam* **three chips, coming up!** ¡van tres de patatas fritas!

▸ **come upon** *vt insep* = **come across**

comeback ['kʌmbæk] *n Fam* (a) *(of person)* reaparición *f*; **to make a c.** reaparecer (b) *(answer)* réplica *f*

comedian [kə'miːdɪən] *n* cómico *m*

comedienne [kəmiːdɪ'en] *n* cómica *f*

comedown ['kʌmdaʊn] *n Fam* desilusión *f*, revés *m*

comedy ['kɒmɪdɪ] *n* comedia *f*

comet ['kɒmɪt] *n* cometa *m*

comeuppance [kʌm'ʌpəns] *n Fam* **to get one's c.** llevarse su merecido

comfort ['kʌmfət] **1** *n* (a) comodidad *f*; *US* **c. station** servicios *mpl* (b) *(consolation)* consuelo *m*; **to take c. in** *or* **from sth** consolarse con algo

2 *vt* consolar

comfortable ['kʌmfətəbəl] *adj (chair, person, margin)* cómodo(a); *(temperature)* agradable

comfortably ['kʌmfətəblɪ] *adv (win)* con facilidad; **to be c. off** vivir cómodamente

comforter ['kʌmfətə(r)] *n* (**a**) *Br (scarf)* bufanda *f* (**b**) *(for baby)* chupete *m* (**c**) *US (quilt)* edredón *m*

comforting ['kʌmfətɪŋ] *adj* consolador(a)

comic ['kɒmɪk] **1** *adj* cómico(a); **c. strip** tira cómica, historieta *f*

2 *n* (**a**) *(person)* cómico(a) *m,f* (**b**) *Press* tebeo *m*, comic *m*

coming ['kʌmɪŋ] **1** *adj (year)* próximo(a); *(generation)* futuro(a)

2 *n* venida *f*, llegada *f*; **comings and goings** idas *fpl* y venidas; *Fig* **c. and going** ajetreo *m*

comma ['kɒmə] *n* coma *f*

command [kə'mɑːnd] **1** *vt* (**a**) mandar (**b**) *(respect)* infundir; *(sympathy)* merecer; *(money etc)* disponer de

2 *n* (**a**) *(order)* orden *f*; *(authority)* mando *m*; **to be at sb's c.** estar a las órdenes de algn (**b**) *(of language)* dominio *m* (**c**) *(disposal)* disposición *f* (**d**) *Comput* comando *m*, instrucción *f*

commandeer [kɒmən'dɪə(r)] *vt* requisar

commander [kə'mɑːndə(r)] *n* comandante *m*

commanding [kə'mɑːndɪŋ] *adj* dominante; *Mil* **c. officer** comandante *m*

commandment [kə'mɑːndmənt] *n* mandamiento *m*

commando [kə'mɑːndəʊ] *n* comando *m*

commemorate [kə'meməreɪt] *vt* conmemorar

commence [kə'mens] *vt & vi Fml* comenzar

commend [kə'mend] *vt* (**a**) *(praise)* alabar, elogiar (**b**) *(entrust)* encomendar (**c**) *(recommend)* recomendar

commensurate [kə'menʃərɪt] *adj* proporcional; **c. to** *or* **with** en proporción a

comment ['kɒment] **1** *n* comentario *m*; **no c.** sin comentario

2 *vi* hacer comentarios

commentary ['kɒməntərɪ] *n* comentario *m*

commentator ['kɒmənteɪtə(r)] *n* comentarista *mf*

commerce ['kɒmɜːs] *n* comercio *m*

commercial [kə'mɜːʃəl] **1** *adj* comercial; *TV* **c. break** corte publicitario

2 *n TV* anuncio *m*

commiserate [kə'mɪzəreɪt] *vi* compadecerse (**with** de)

commission [kə'mɪʃən] **1** *n* (**a**) *Mil* despacho *m* (de oficial); **out of c.** fuera de servicio (**b**) *(of inquiry)* comisión *f*; *(job)* encargo *m* (**c**) *(payment)* comisión *f*

2 *vt* (**a**) *Mil* nombrar (**b**) *(order)* encargar (**c**) *Naut* poner en servicio

commissionaire [kəmɪʃə'neə(r)] *n Br* portero *m*

commissioner [kə'mɪʃənə(r)] *n (official)* comisario *m*; **c. of police** comisario de policía

commit [kə'mɪt] *vt* (**a**) *(crime)* cometer; **to c. suicide** suicidarse (**b**) **to c. oneself (to do sth)** comprometerse (a hacer algo) (**c**) **to c. sth to sb's care** confiar algo a algn

commitment [kə'mɪtmənt] *n* compromiso *m*

committee [kə'mɪtɪ] *n* comisión *f*, comité *m*

commode [kə'məʊd] *n (chair)* silla *f* con orinal; *(chest of drawers)* cómoda *f*

commodity [kə'mɒdɪtɪ] *n* producto *m* básico

> Note that the Spanish word **comodidad** is a false friend and is never a translation for the English word **commodity**. In Spanish, **comodidad** means "comfort, convenience".

common ['kɒmən] **1** *adj* (**a**) común; **that's c. knowledge** eso lo sabe todo el mundo; **c. law** derecho consuetudinario; **C. Market** Mercado *m* Común; *Br* **c. room** sala *f* de profesores/ de estudiantes (**b**) *(ordinary)* corriente (**c**) *(vulgar)* ordinario(a), maleducado(a)

2 *n (land)* campo *m or* terreno *m* comunal

commonplace ['kɒmənpleɪs] *adj* corriente

Commons ['kɒmənz] *npl Br* **the (House of) C.** (la Cámara de) los Comunes

Commonwealth ['kɒmənwelθ] *n Br* **the C.** la Commonwealth; **C. of Independent States** Comunidad *f* de Estados Independientes

commotion [kə'məʊʃən] *n* alboroto *m*

commune¹ [kə'mjuːn] *vi (converse)* conversar íntimamente; *(with nature)* estar en comunión (**with** con)

commune² ['kɒmjuːn] *n* comuna *f*

communicate [kə'mjuːnɪkeɪt] **1** *vi* comunicarse (**with** con)

2 *vt* comunicar

communication [kəmjuːnɪ'keɪʃən] *n* (**a**) comunicación *f* (**b**) *Br Rail* **c. cord** timbre *m* de alarma

communion [kə'mjuːnɪən] *n* comunión *f*; **to take c.** comulgar

communiqué [kə'mjuːnɪkeɪ] *n* comunicado *m* oficial

communism ['kɒmjʊnɪzəm] *n* comunismo *m*

communist ['kɒmjʊnɪst] *adj & n* comunista *(mf)*

community [kə'mjuːnɪtɪ] *n* comunidad *f*; *(people)* colectividad *f*; **c. centre** centro *m* social

commute [kə'mjuːt] **1** *vi* = viajar diariamente al lugar de trabajo

2 *vt Jur* conmutar

commuter [kə'mjuːtə(r)] *n* = persona que viaja diariamente al lugar de trabajo

compact¹ **1** *adj* [kəm'pækt] compacto(a); *(style)* conciso(a)

2 *n* ['kɒmpækt] *(for powder)* polvera *f*

compact² ['kɒmpækt] *n Pol* pacto *m*

compact disc ['kɒmpækt'dɪsk] *n* disco compacto

companion [kəm'pænjən] *n* compañero(a) *m,f*

companionship [kəm'pænjənʃɪp] *n* compañerismo *m*

company ['kʌmpənɪ] *n* (**a**) compañía *f*; **to keep sb c.** hacer compañía a algn (**b**) *Com* empresa *f*, compañía *f*

comparable ['kɒmpərəbəl] *adj* comparable (**to** *or* **with** con)

comparative [kəm'pærətɪv] **1** *adj* comparativo(a); *(relative)* relativo(a)

    2 *n Ling* comparativo *m*

comparatively [kəm'pærətɪvlɪ] *adv* relativamente

compare [kəm'peə(r)] **1** *vt* comparar (**to** *or* **with** con); **(as) compared with** en comparación con

    2 *vi* compararse

comparison [kəm'pærɪsən] *n* comparación *f*; **by c.** en comparación; **there's no c.** no se puede comparar

compartment [kəm'pɑːtmənt] *n (section)* compartimiento *m*; *Rail* departamento *m*

compass ['kʌmpəs] *n* (**a**) brújula *f* (**b**) **(pair of) compasses** compás *m* (**c**) *Fig (range)* límites *mpl*

compassion [kəm'pæʃən] *n* compasión *f*

compassionate [kəm'pæʃənət] *adj* compasivo(a)

compatible [kəm'pætəbəl] *adj* compatible

compel [kəm'pel] *vt* (**a**) *(oblige)* obligar; **to c. sb to do sth** obligar a algn a hacer algo (**b**) *(admiration)* despertar

compelling [kəm'pelɪŋ] *adj* irresistible

compensate ['kɒmpənseɪt] **1** *vt* compensar; **to c. sb for sth** indemnizar a algn de algo

    2 *vi* compensar

compensation [kɒmpən'seɪʃən] *n* compensación *f*; *(for loss)* indemnización *f*

compere ['kɒmpeə(r)] *n Br* animador(a) *m,f*

compete [kəm'piːt] *vi* competir

competence ['kɒmpɪtəns] *n* (**a**) *(ability)* aptitud *f* (**b**) *(of court etc)* competencia *f*

competent ['kɒmpɪtənt] *adj* competente

competition [kɒmpɪ'tɪʃən] *n* (**a**) *(contest)* concurso *m* (**b**) *Com* competencia *f*

competitive [kəm'petɪtɪv] *adj* competitivo(a)

competitor [kəm'petɪtə(r)] *n* competidor(a) *m,f*

compilation [kɒmpɪ'leɪʃən] *n* recopilación *f*

compile [kəm'paɪl] *vt* compilar, recopilar

complacency [kəm'pleɪsənsɪ] *n* autocomplacencia *f*

    ⚠ Note that the Spanish word **complacencia** is a false friend and is never a translation for the English word **complacency**. In Spanish, **complacencia** means "satisfaction, indulgence".

complacent [kəm'pleɪsənt] *adj* autocomplaciente

complain [kəm'pleɪn] *vi* quejarse (**of/about** de)

complaint [kəm'pleɪnt] *n* (**a**) queja *f*; *Com* reclamación *f* (**b**) *Jur* demanda *f* (**c**) *Med* enfermedad *f*

complement ['kɒmplɪmənt] **1** *n* (**a**) complemento *m* (**b**) *Naut* dotación *f*

    2 *vt* complementar

complementary [kɒmplɪ'mentərɪ] *adj* complementario(a)

complete [kəm'pliːt] **1** *adj* (**a**) *(entire)* completo(a) (**b**) *(absolute)* total

    2 *vt* completar; **to c. a form** rellenar un formulario

completely [kəm'pliːtlɪ] *adv* completamente, por completo

completion [kəm'pliːʃən] *n* terminación *f*; **near c.** casi terminado(a); **on c.** en cuanto se termine

complex ['kɒmpleks] **1** *adj* complejo(a)

    2 *n* complejo *m*; **inferiority c.** complejo de inferioridad

complexion [kəm'plekʃən] *n* tez *f*; *Fig* aspecto *m*

    ⚠ Note that the Spanish word **complexión** is a false friend and is never a translation for the English word **complexion**. In Spanish, **complexión** means "build".

compliance [kəm'plaɪəns] *n* conformidad *f*; **in c. with** de acuerdo con

complicate ['kɒmplɪkeɪt] *vt* complicar

complicated ['kɒmplɪkeɪtɪd] *adj* complicado(a)

complication [kɒmplɪ'keɪʃən] *n* complicación *f*

complicity [kəm'plɪsɪtɪ] *n* complicidad *f*

compliment 1 *n* ['kɒmplɪmənt] (**a**) cumplido *m*; **to pay sb a c.** hacerle un cumplido a algn (**b**) **compliments** saludos *mpl*

    2 *vt* ['kɒmplɪment] felicitar; **to c. sb on sth** felicitar a algn por algo

complimentary [kɒmplɪ'mentərɪ] *adj* (**a**) *(praising)* elogioso(a) (**b**) *(free)* gratis

comply [kəm'plaɪ] *vi* obedecer; **to c. with** *(order)* cumplir con; *(request)* acceder a

component [kəm'pəʊnənt] **1** *n* componente *m*

    2 *adj* componente; **c. part** parte *f*

compose [kəm'pəʊz] *vt & vi* (**a**) componer; **to be composed of** componerse de (**b**) **to c. oneself** calmarse

composed [kəm'pəʊzd] *adj (calm)* sereno(a)

composer [kəm'pəʊzə(r)] *n* compositor(a) *m,f*

composite ['kɒmpəzɪt] *adj* compuesto(a)

composition [kɒmpə'zɪʃən] *n* composición *f*; *(essay)* redacción *f*

compost ['kɒmpɒst] *n* abono *m*

composure [kəm'pəʊʒə(r)] *n* calma *f*, serenidad *f*

compound¹ ['kɒmpaʊnd] **1** n compuesto m
2 adj compuesto(a); (fracture) complicado(a)
3 vt [kəm'paʊnd] (problem) agravar
compound² ['kɒmpaʊnd] n (enclosure) recinto m
comprehend [kɒmprɪ'hend] vt comprender
comprehensible [kɒmprɪ'hensəbəl] adj comprensible
comprehension [kɒmprɪ'henʃən] n comprensión f
comprehensive [kɒmprɪ'hensɪv] adj (a) (knowledge) amplio(a); (study) detallado(a) (b) Ins a todo riesgo (c) Br c. school ≃ instituto m de segunda enseñanza

> *Note that the Spanish word* **comprensivo** *is a false friend and is never a translation for the English word* **comprehensive**. *In Spanish,* **comprensivo** *means "understanding".*

compress 1 vt [kəm'pres] comprimir
2 n ['kɒmpres] compresa f
comprise [kəm'praɪz] vt comprender; (consist of) constar de
compromise ['kɒmprəmaɪz] **1** n solución f negociada; **to reach a c.** llegar a un acuerdo
2 vi (two people) llegar a un acuerdo; (individual) transigir
3 vt (person) comprometer

> *Note that the Spanish word* **compromiso** *is a false friend and is never a translation for the English word* **compromise**. *In Spanish,* **compromiso** *means "obligation, commitment, agreement".*

compulsion [kəm'pʌlʃən] n obligación f
compulsive [kəm'pʌlsɪv] adj compulsivo(a)
compulsory [kəm'pʌlsərɪ] adj obligatorio(a)
computer [kəm'pjuːtə(r)] n ordenador m, Am computadora f; **c. programmer** programador(a) m,f de ordenadores; **c. science** informática f; **personal c.** ordenador personal, Am computadora personal
computerize [kəm'pjuːtəraɪz] vt informatizar
computing [kəm'pjuːtɪŋ] n informática f
comrade ['kɒmreɪd] n (a) (companion) compañero(a) m,f (b) Pol camarada mf
comradeship ['kɒmreɪdʃɪp] n camaradería f
con [kɒn] Fam **1** vt estafar, timar
2 n estafa f, camelo m; **c. man** estafador m
concave ['kɒnkeɪv] adj cóncavo(a)
conceal [kən'siːl] vt ocultar; (emotions) disimular
concede [kən'siːd] vt conceder
conceit [kən'siːt] n presunción f, vanidad f
conceited [kən'siːtɪd] adj presuntuoso(a)
conceivable [kən'siːvəbəl] adj concebible
conceive [kən'siːv] vt & vi concebir
concentrate ['kɒnsəntreɪt] **1** vt concentrar
2 vi **to c. on sth** concentrarse en algo

concentration [kɒnsən'treɪʃən] n concentración f; **c. camp** campo m de concentración
concept ['kɒnsept] n concepto m
conception [kən'sepʃən] n Med concepción f; (understanding) concepto m, idea f
concern [kən'sɜːn] **1** vt (a) concernir, afectar; **as far as I'm concerned** por lo que a mí se refiere (b) (worry) preocupar
2 n (a) **it's no c. of mine** no es asunto mío (b) (worry) preocupación f (c) Com negocio m
concerned [kən'sɜːnd] adj (a) (affected) afectado(a) (b) (worried) preocupado(a) (**about** por)
concerning [kən'sɜːnɪŋ] prep con respecto a, en cuanto a
concert ['kɒnsət, 'kɒnsɜːt] n Mus concierto m; **c. hall** sala f de conciertos
concerted [kən'sɜːtɪd] adj concertado(a)
concertina [kɒnsə'tiːnə] n concertina f
concerto [kən'tʃɜːtəʊ] n concierto m
concession [kən'seʃən] n (a) concesión f; **tax c.** privilegio m fiscal (b) Com reducción f
concise [kən'saɪs] adj conciso(a)
conclude [kən'kluːd] vt & vi concluir
conclusion [kən'kluːʒən] n conclusión f; **to reach a c.** llegar a una conclusión
conclusive [kən'kluːsɪv] adj concluyente
concoct [kən'kɒkt] vt (dish) confeccionar; Fig (plan) fraguar; (excuse) inventar
concoction [kən'kɒkʃən] n (mixture) mezcolanza f; Pej (brew) brebaje m
concourse ['kɒŋkɔːs] n explanada f

> *Note that the Spanish word* **concurso** *is a false friend and is never a translation for the English word* **concourse**. *In Spanish,* **concurso** *means "competition, contest".*

concrete ['kɒnkriːt] **1** n hormigón m; **c. mixer** hormigonera f
2 adj (a) (definite) concreto(a) (b) (made of concrete) de hormigón
concur [kən'kɜː(r)] vi (a) **to c. with** (agree) estar de acuerdo con (b) (coincide) coincidir
concurrent [kən'kʌrənt] adj simultáneo(a)
concussion [kən'kʌʃən] n conmoción f cerebral
condemn [kən'dem] vt condenar
condemnation [kɒndem'neɪʃən] n condena f
condensation [kɒnden'seɪʃən] n condensación f
condense [kən'dens] **1** vt condensar
2 vi condensarse
condensed [kən'denst] adj **c. milk** leche condensada
condescending [kɒndɪ'sendɪŋ] adj condescendiente
condition [kən'dɪʃən] **1** n condición f; **to be in good c.** estar en buen estado; **on c. that ...** a condición de que ...; **on one c.** con una

condición; **heart c.** enfermedad cardíaca; **conditions** *(circumstances)* circunstancias *fpl*
   2 *vt* condicionar
conditional [kən'dɪʃənəl] *adj* condicional
conditioner [kən'dɪʃənə(r)] *n* acondicionador *m*
condolences [kən'dəʊlənsɪz] *npl* pésame *m*; **please accept my c.** le acompaño en el sentimiento
condom ['kɒndəm] *n* preservativo *m*
condominium [kɒndə'mɪnɪəm] *n* US *(building)* = bloque de apartamentos poseídos por diferentes propietarios; *(apartment)* apartamento *m*, piso *m* *(en propiedad)*
condone [kən'dəʊn] *vt* perdonar, consentir
condor ['kɒndɔ:(r)] *n* cóndor *m*
conducive [kən'dju:sɪv] *adj* conducente
conduct 1 *n* ['kɒndʌkt] *(behaviour)* conducta *f*, comportamiento *m*
   2 *vt* [kən'dʌkt] *(lead)* guiar; *(business, orchestra)* dirigir; **conducted tour** visita acompañada; **to c. oneself** comportarse
   3 *vi Mus* dirigir
conductor [kən'dʌktə(r)] *n* **(a)** *Br (on bus)* cobrador *m* **(b)** *US Rail* revisor(a) *m,f* **(c)** *Mus* director(a) *m,f* **(d)** *Phys* conductor *m*
conductress [kən'dʌktrɪs] *n* *(on bus)* cobradora *f*
cone [kəʊn] *n* **(a)** cono *m*; **ice-cream c.** cucurucho *m* **(b)** *Bot* piña *f*
confectioner [kən'fekʃənə(r)] *n* confitero(a) *m,f*; **c.'s (shop)** confitería *f*
confectionery [kən'fekʃənərɪ] *n* dulces *mpl*
confederate [kən'fedərɪt] **1** *adj* confederado(a)
   2 *n* confederado(a) *m,f*; *Jur* cómplice *mf*
confer [kən'fɜ:(r)] **1** *vt* **to c. a title on sb** conferir un título a algn
   2 *vi* consultar
conference ['kɒnfərəns] *n* conferencia *f*
confess [kən'fes] *vi* confesar; *Rel* confesarse
   2 *vt* confesar
confession [kən'feʃən] *n* confesión *f*
confessional [kən'feʃənəl] *n* confesionario *m*
confetti [kən'fetɪ] *n* confeti *m*
confide [kən'faɪd] *vi* **to c. in sb** confiar en algn
confidence ['kɒnfɪdəns] *n* **(a)** confianza *f*; **vote of c./no c.** voto *m* de confianza/de censura; **c. trick** camelo *m* **(b)** *(secret)* confidencia *f*; **in c.** en confianza
confident ['kɒnfɪdənt] *adj* seguro(a)
confidential [kɒnfɪ'denʃəl] *adj (secret)* confidencial; *(entrusted)* de confianza
confine [kən'faɪn] *vt* encerrar; *Fig* limitar
confinement [kən'faɪnmənt] *n* **(a)** *(prison)* prisión *f*; **to be in solitary c.** estar incomunicado(a) **(b)** *Med* parto *m*
confirm [kən'fɜ:m] *vt* confirmar
confirmation [kɒnfə'meɪʃən] *n* confirmación *f*

confirmed [kən'fɜ:md] *adj* empedernido(a)
confiscate ['kɒnfɪskeɪt] *vt* confiscar
conflict 1 *n* ['kɒnflɪkt] conflicto *m*
   2 *vi* [kən'flɪkt] chocar (**with** con)
conflicting [kən'flɪktɪŋ] *adj* contradictorio(a)
conform [kən'fɔ:m] *vi* conformarse; **to c. to** *or* **with** *(customs)* amoldarse a; *(rules)* someterse a
confound [kən'faʊnd] *vt* confundir, desconcertar
confront [kən'frʌnt] *vt* hacer frente a
confrontation [kɒnfrʌn'teɪʃən] *n* confrontación *f*
confuse [kən'fju:z] *vt* *(person)* despistar; *(thing)* confundir (**with** con); **to get confused** confundirse
confused [kən'fju:zd] *adj* *(person)* confundido(a); *(mind, ideas)* confuso(a)
confusing [kən'fju:zɪŋ] *adj* confuso(a)
confusion [kən'fju:ʒən] *n* confusión *f*
congeal [kən'dʒi:l] *vi* coagularse
congenial [kən'dʒi:nɪəl] *adj* agradable
congenital [kən'dʒenɪtəl] *adj* congénito(a)
congested [kən'dʒestɪd] *adj* **(a)** *(street)* repleto(a) de gente; *(city)* superpoblado(a) **(b)** *Med* congestionado(a)
congestion [kən'dʒestʃən] *n* congestión *f*
conglomeration [kənglɒmə'reɪʃən] *n* conglomeración *f*
congratulate [kən'grætjʊleɪt] *vt* felicitar
congratulations [kəngrætjʊ'leɪʃənz] *npl* felicitaciones *fpl*; **c.!** ¡enhorabuena!
congregate ['kɒngrɪgeɪt] *vi* congregarse
congregation [kɒngrɪ'geɪʃən] *n* *(group)* congregación *f*; *Rel* fieles *mpl*
congress ['kɒngres] *n* **(a)** *(conference)* congreso *m* **(b)** *US Pol* **C.** el Congreso *(de los Estados Unidos)*
Congressman ['kɒngresmən] *n* *US Pol* congresista *m*, *Am* congresal *m*
Congresswoman ['kɒngreswʊmən] *n* *US Pol* congresista *f*, *Am* congresal *f*
conifer ['kɒnɪfə(r)] *n* conífera *f*
conjecture [kən'dʒektʃə(r)] **1** *n* conjetura *f*
   2 *vt* conjeturar
   3 *vi* hacer conjeturas
conjugal ['kɒndʒʊgəl] *adj* conyugal
conjugate ['kɒndʒʊgeɪt] *vt* conjugar
conjunction [kən'dʒʌŋkʃən] *n* conjunción *f*; *Fig* **in c. with** conjuntamente con
conjunctivitis [kəndʒʌŋktɪ'vaɪtɪs] *n* conjuntivitis *f*
conjure ['kʌndʒə(r)] **1** *vt* **to c. (up)** *(magician)* hacer aparecer; *(memories)* evocar
   2 *vi* hacer juegos de manos
conjurer ['kʌndʒərə(r)] *n* prestidigitador(a) *m,f*
conker ['kɒŋkə(r)] *n Fam* castaña *f*
connect [kə'nekt] **1** *vt* **(a)** *(join)* juntar, unir; *(wires)* empalmar; *Fig* **to be connected by marriage** estar emparentado(a) por matri-

monio (**b**) *(install)* instalar; *Elec* conectar (**c**) *Tel (person)* poner (**d**) *Fig (associate)* asociar

2 *vi* unirse; *(rooms)* comunicarse; *(train, flight)* enlazar *or* empalmar (**with** con)

connected [kə'nektɪd] *adj* unido(a); *(events)* relacionado(a); *Fig* **to be well c.** *(person) (socially)* estar bien relacionado(a)

connection [kə'nekʃən] *n* (**a**) *(joint)* juntura *f*, unión *f*; *Elec* conexión *f*; *Tel* instalación *f* (**b**) *Rail* correspondencia *f* (**c**) *Fig (of ideas)* relación *f*; **in c. with** *(regarding)* con respecto a (**d**) *(person)* contacto *m*

connive [kə'naɪv] *vi* **to c. at** hacer la vista gorda con

connoisseur [kɒnɪ'sɜ:(r)] *n* conocedor(a) *m,f*

connotation [kɒnə'teɪʃən] *n* connotación *f*

conquer ['kɒŋkə(r)] *vt (enemy, bad habit)* vencer; *(country)* conquistar

conqueror ['kɒŋkərə(r)] *n* conquistador *m*

conquest ['kɒŋkwest] *n* conquista *f*

conscience ['kɒnʃəns] *n* conciencia *f*; **to have a clear c.** tener la conciencia tranquila; **to have a guilty c.** sentirse culpable

conscientious [kɒnʃɪ'enʃəs] *adj* concienzudo(a); **c. objector** objetor(a) *m,f* de conciencia

conscious ['kɒnʃəs] *adj (aware)* consciente; *(choice etc)* deliberado(a)

consciousness ['kɒnʃəsnɪs] *n* *Med* conocimiento *m*; *(awareness)* consciencia *f*

conscript ['kɒnskrɪpt] *n* recluta *m*

conscription [kən'skrɪpʃən] *n* servicio *m* militar obligatorio

consecrate ['kɒnsɪkreɪt] *vt* consagrar

consecutive [kən'sekjʊtɪv] *adj* consecutivo(a)

consensus [kən'sensəs] *n* consenso *m*

consent [kən'sent] **1** *n* consentimiento *m*; **by common c.** de común acuerdo

2 *vi* consentir (**to** en)

consequence ['kɒnsɪkwəns] *n* consecuencia *f*

consequent ['kɒnsɪkwənt] *adj* consiguiente

consequently ['kɒnsɪkwəntlɪ] *adv* por consiguiente

conservation [kɒnsə'veɪʃən] *n* conservación *f*

conservative [kən'sɜ:vətɪv] **1** *adj* cauteloso(a)

2 *adj & n* *Pol* **C.** conservador(a) *(m,f)*

conservatory [kən'sɜ:vətrɪ] *n* (**a**) *(greenhouse)* invernadero *m* (**b**) *Mus* conservatorio *m*

conserve 1 *vt* [kən'sɜ:v] conservar

2 *n* ['kɒnsɜ:v] conserva *f*

consider [kən'sɪdə(r)] *vt* (**a**) *(ponder on, regard)* considerar; **to c. doing sth** pensar hacer algo (**b**) *(keep in mind)* tener en cuenta

considerable [kən'sɪdərəbəl] *adj* considerable

considerably [kən'sɪdərəblɪ] *adv* bastante

considerate [kən'sɪdərɪt] *adj* considerado(a)

consideration [kənsɪdə'reɪʃən] *n* consideración *f*; **without due c.** sin reflexión

considering [kən'sɪdərɪŋ] *prep* teniendo en cuenta

consign [kən'saɪn] *vt* *Com* consignar; *Fig* entregar

consignment [kən'saɪnmənt] *n* envío *m*

consist [kən'sɪst] *vi* **to c. of** consistir en

consistency [kən'sɪstənsɪ] *n* (**a**) *(of actions)* consecuencia *f* (**b**) *(of mixture)* consistencia *f*

consistent [kən'sɪstənt] *adj* consecuente; **c. with** de acuerdo con

> *Note that the Spanish word **consistente** is a false friend and is never a translation for the English word **consistent**. In Spanish, **consistente** means "firm, solid, sound".*

consolation [kɒnsə'leɪʃən] *n* consuelo *m*; **c. prize** premio *m* de consolación

console¹ [kən'səʊl] *vt* consolar

console² ['kɒnsəʊl] *n* consola *f*

consolidate [kən'sɒlɪdeɪt] **1** *vt* consolidar

2 *vi* consolidarse

consonant ['kɒnsənənt] *n* consonante *f*

consortium [kən'sɔːtɪəm] *n* consorcio *m*

conspicuous [kən'spɪkjʊəs] *adj (striking)* llamativo(a); *(easily seen)* visible; *(mistake)* evidente

conspiracy [kən'spɪrəsɪ] *n* conjura *f*

conspire [kən'spaɪə(r)] *vi* conspirar

constable ['kʌnstəbəl] *n* policía *m*, guardia *m*; **chief c.** jefe *m* de policía

constabulary [kən'stæbjʊlərɪ] *n* *Br* comisaría *f*

constant ['kɒnstənt] **1** *adj* constante; *(continuous)* incesante; *(loyal)* fiel, leal

2 *n* constante *f*

constellation [kɒnstɪ'leɪʃən] *n* constelación *f*

consternation [kɒnstə'neɪʃən] *n* consternación *f*

constipated ['kɒnstɪpeɪtɪd] *adj* **to be c.** estar estreñido(a)

> *Note that the Spanish word **constipado** is a false friend and is never a translation for the English word **constipated**. In Spanish, **constipado** means both "cold, chill" and "suffering from a cold".*

constipation [kɒnstɪ'peɪʃən] *n* estreñimiento *m*

constituency [kən'stɪtjʊənsɪ] *n* circunscripción *f* electoral

constituent [kən'stɪtjʊənt] **1** *adj (component)* constituyente

2 *n* (**a**) *(part)* componente *m* (**b**) *Pol* votante *mf*

constitute ['kɒnstɪtjuːt] *vt* constituir

constitution [kɒnstɪ'tjuːʃən] *n* constitución *f*

constitutional [kɒnstɪ'tjuːʃənəl] *adj* constitucional

constrained [kən'streɪnd] *adj* **to feel c. to do sth** sentirse obligado(a) a hacer algo
constraint [kən'streɪnt] *n* coacción *f*; **to feel c. in sb's presence** sentirse cohibido(a) ante algn
construct [kən'strʌkt] *vt* construir
construction [kən'strʌkʃən] *n* construcción *f*
constructive [kən'strʌktɪv] *adj* constructivo(a)
construe [kən'stru:] *vt* interpretar

> ⚠ Note that the Spanish verb **construir** is a false friend and is never a translation for the English verb **to construe**. In Spanish, **construir** means "to build, to manufacture".

consul ['kɒnsəl] *n* cónsul *mf*
consulate ['kɒnsjʊlɪt] *n* consulado *m*
consult [kən'sʌlt] *vt & vi* consultar (**about** sobre)
consultant [kən'sʌltənt] *n* Med especialista *mf*; Com & Ind asesor(a) *m,f*
consultation [kɒnsəl'teɪʃən] *n* consulta *f*
consulting [kən'sʌltɪŋ] *adj* **c. room** consulta *f*
consume [kən'sju:m] *vt* consumir
consumer [kən'sju:mə(r)] *n* consumidor(a) *m,f*; **c. goods** bienes *mpl* de consumo
consummate 1 *vt* ['kɒnsəmeɪt] consumar
  2 *adj* ['kɒnsəmɪt] consumado(a)
consumption [kən'sʌmpʃən] *n* (**a**) *(of food)* consumo *m*; **fit for c.** apto(a) para el consumo (**b**) *Med* tisis *f*
cont. *(abbr continued)* sigue
contact ['kɒntækt] **1** *n* contacto *m*; **c. lenses** lentes *fpl* de contacto
  2 *vt* ponerse en contacto con
contagious [kən'teɪdʒəs] *adj* contagioso(a)
contain [kən'teɪn] *vt* contener; **to c. oneself** contenerse
container [kən'teɪnə(r)] *n* (**a**) *(box, package)* recipiente *m*; *(bottle)* envase *m* (**b**) *Naut* contenedor *m*
contaminate [kən'tæmɪneɪt] *vt* contaminar
contamination [kəntæmɪ'neɪʃən] *n* contaminación *f*
contd. *(abbr continued)* sigue
contemplate ['kɒntempleɪt] *vt* (**a**) *(consider)* considerar, pensar en (**b**) *(look at)* contemplar
contemporary [kən'tempərərɪ] *adj & n* contemporáneo(a) *(m,f)*
contempt [kən'tempt] *n* desprecio *m*; **to hold in c.** despreciar; **c. of court** desacato *m* a los tribunales
contemptible [kən'temptəbəl] *adj* despreciable
contemptuous [kən'temptjʊəs] *adj* despectivo(a)
contend [kən'tend] **1** *vi* competir; *Fig* **there are many problems to c. with** se han planteado muchos problemas
  2 *vt* afirmar

contender [kən'tendə(r)] *n* contendiente *mf*
content¹ ['kɒntent] *n* contenido *m*; **table of contents** índice *m* de materias
content² [kən'tent] **1** *adj* contento(a)
  2 *vt* contentar
  3 *n* contento *m*; **to one's heart's c.** todo lo que uno quiera
contented [kən'tentɪd] *adj* contento(a), satisfecho(a)
contention [kən'tenʃən] *n* (**a**) *(dispute)* controversia *f* (**b**) *(point)* punto *m* de vista
contentment [kən'tentmənt] *n* contento *m*
contest 1 *n* ['kɒntest] concurso *m*; *Sport* prueba *f*
  2 *vt* [kən'test] (**a**) *(matter)* rebatir; *(verdict)* impugnar; *Fig (will)* disputar (**b**) *Pol (seat)* luchar por
contestant [kən'testənt] *n* concursante *mf*
context ['kɒntekst] *n* contexto *m*
continent ['kɒntɪnənt] *n* continente *m*; **(on) the C.** (en) Europa
continental [kɒntɪ'nentəl] *adj* (**a**) continental; **c. shelf** plataforma *f* continental (**b**) *Br* **C. europeo(a)**; **c. quilt** edredón *m* de pluma
contingency [kən'tɪndʒənsɪ] *n* contingencia *f*; **c. plans** planes *mpl* para casos de emergencia
contingent [kən'tɪndʒənt] *adj & n* contingente *(m)*
continual [kən'tɪnjʊəl] *adj* continuo(a), constante
continuation [kəntɪnjʊ'eɪʃən] *n* *(sequel etc)* continuación *f*; *(extension)* prolongación *f*
continue [kən'tɪnju:] *vt & vi* continuar, seguir; **to c. to do sth** seguir *or* continuar haciendo algo
continuous [kən'tɪnjʊəs] *adj* continuo(a)
contort [kən'tɔːt] *vt* retorcer
contortion [kən'tɔːʃən] *n* contorsión *f*
contour ['kɒntʊə(r)] *n* contorno *m*; **c. line** línea *f* de nivel
contraband ['kɒntrəbænd] *n* contrabando *m*
contraception [kɒntrə'sepʃən] *n* anticoncepción *f*
contraceptive [kɒntrə'septɪv] *adj & n* anticonceptivo *(m)*
contract 1 *vi* [kən'trækt] *Phys* contraerse
  2 *vt* (**a**) contraer (**b**) **to c. to do sth** *(make agreement)* comprometerse por contrato a hacer algo
  3 *n* ['kɒntrækt] contrato *m*; **to enter into a c.** hacer un contrato
contraction [kən'trækʃən] *n* contracción *f*
contractor [kən'træktə(r)] *n* contratista *mf*
contradict [kɒntrə'dɪkt] *vt* contradecir
contradiction [kɒntrə'dɪkʃən] *n* contradicción *f*; **it's a c. in terms** no tiene lógica
contradictory [kɒntrə'dɪktərɪ] *adj* contradictorio(a)
contraption [kən'træpʃən] *n* *Fam* cacharro *m*
contrary ['kɒntrərɪ] **1** *adj* (**a**) *(opposite)* con-

trario(a) (**b**) [kən'treərɪ] *(awkward)* terco(a)
  2 *n* **on the c.** todo lo contrario; **unless I tell you to the c.** a menos que te diga lo contrario
  3 *adv* **c. to** en contra de
contrast 1 *vi* [kən'trɑ:st] contrastar
  2 *n* ['kɒntrɑ:st] contraste *m*
contrasting [kən'trɑ:stɪŋ] *adj* opuesto(a)
contravene [kɒntrə'vi:n] *vt* contravenir
contribute [kən'trɪbju:t] **1** *vt (money)* contribuir con; *(ideas, information)* aportar
  2 *vi* (**a**) contribuir; *(in discussion)* participar (**b**) *Press* colaborar (**to** en)
contribution [kɒntrɪ'bju:ʃən] *n* (**a**) *(of money)* contribución *f*; *(of ideas etc)* aportación *f* (**b**) *Press* colaboración *f*
contributor [kən'trɪbjʊtə(r)] *n (to newspaper)* colaborador(a) *m,f*
contrive [kən'traɪv] *vt* inventar, idear; **to c. to do sth** buscar la forma de hacer algo
contrived [kən'traɪvd] *adj* artificial, forzado(a)
control [kən'trəʊl] **1** *vt* controlar; *(person, animal)* dominar; *(vehicle)* manejar; **to c. one's temper** controlarse
  2 *n* (**a**) *(power)* control *m*, dominio *m*; *(authority)* autoridad *f*; **out of c.** fuera de control; **to be in c.** estar al mando; **to be under c.** *(situation)* estar bajo control; **to go out of c.** descontrolarse; **to lose c.** perder los estribos (**b**) *Aut Av (device)* mando *m*; *Rad & TV* botón *m* de control; **c. panel** tablero *m* de instrumentos; **c. room** sala *f* de control; *Av* **c. tower** torre *f* de control
controversial [kɒntrə'vɜ:ʃəl] *adj* controvertido(a), polémico(a)
controversy ['kɒntrəvɜ:sɪ, kən'trɒvəsɪ] *n* polémica *f*
conurbation [kɒnɜ:'beɪʃən] *n* conurbación *f*
convalesce [kɒnvə'les] *vi* convalecer
convalescence [kɒnvə'lesəns] *n* convalecencia *f*
convalescent [kɒnvə'lesənt] *adj* convaleciente; **c. home** clínica *f* de reposo
convene [kən'vi:n] **1** *vt* convocar
  2 *vi* reunirse
convenience [kən'vi:nɪəns] *n* conveniencia *f*, comodidad *f*; **all modern conveniences** todas las comodidades; **at your c.** cuando le convenga; **c. food** comida precocinada; *Br Euph* **public conveniences** aseos públicos
convenient [kən'vi:nɪənt] *adj (time, arrangement)* conveniente, oportuno(a); *(place)* bien situado(a)
convent ['kɒnvənt] *n* convento *m*
convention [kən'venʃən] *n* convención *f*
conventional [kən'venʃənəl] *adj* clásico(a); *(behaviour)* convencional
converge [kən'vɜ:dʒ] *vi* convergir
conversant [kən'vɜ:sənt] *adj Fml* **to be c. with a subject** ser versado(a) en una materia
conversation [kɒnvə'seɪʃən] *n* conversación *f*

conversational [kɒnvə'seɪʃənəl] *adj* coloquial
converse¹ [kən'vɜ:s] *vi* conversar
converse² ['kɒnvɜ:s] *n* **the c.** lo opuesto
conversely ['kɒnvɜ:slɪ] *adv* a la inversa
conversion [kən'vɜ:ʃən] *n Math & Rel* conversión *f* (**to** a; **into** en)
convert 1 *vt* [kən'vɜ:t] convertir
  2 *n* ['kɒnvɜ:t] converso(a) *m,f*
convertible [kən'vɜ:təbəl] **1** *adj* convertible
  2 *n Aut* descapotable *m*
convex ['kɒnveks, kən'veks] *adj* convexo(a)
convey [kən'veɪ] *vt* (**a**) *(carry)* transporta (**b**) *(sound)* transmitir; *(idea)* comunicar
conveyor [kən'veɪə(r)] *n* **c. belt** cinta trans portadora
convict 1 *vt* [kən'vɪkt] declarar culpable a condenar
  2 *n* ['kɒnvɪkt] presidiario(a) *m,f*
conviction [kən'vɪkʃən] *n* (**a**) *(belief)* creen cia *f*, convicción *f* (**b**) *Jur* condena *f*
convince [kən'vɪns] *vt* convencer
convincing [kən'vɪnsɪŋ] *adj* convincente
convoluted ['kɒnvəlu:tɪd] *adj* intrincado(a)
convoy ['kɒnvɔɪ] *n* convoy *m*
convulse [kən'vʌls] *vt* convulsionar; *Fam* t be convulsed with laughter** troncharse de risa
convulsion [kən'vʌlʃən] *n* convulsión *f*
coo [ku:] *vi (pigeon)* arrullar
cook [kʊk] **1** *vt* cocinar, guisar; *(dinner)* pre parar; *Fam* **to c. the books** falsificar las cuentas
  2 *vi (person)* cocinar, guisar; *(food)* cocerse
  3 *n* cocinero(a) *m,f*
cookbook ['kʊkbʊk] *n US* libro *m* de cocina
cooker ['kʊkə(r)] *n* cocina *f*
cookery ['kʊkərɪ] *n* cocina *f*; **c. book** libro *m* de cocina
cookie ['kʊkɪ] *n US* galleta *f*
cooking ['kʊkɪŋ] *n* cocina *f*
cool [ku:l] **1** *adj* (**a**) fresco(a); **it's c.** *(weather)* hace fresquito (**b**) *Fig (calm)* tranquilo(a) *(reserved)* frío(a)
  2 *n* (**a**) *(coolness)* fresco *m* (**b**) *Fam* **to lose one's c.** perder la calma
  3 *vt (air)* refrescar; *(drink)* enfriar
  4 *adv Fam* **to play it c.** hacer como si nada
  ▶**cool down, cool off** *vi Fig* calmarse; *(feelings)* enfriarse
coolness ['ku:lnɪs] *n* (**a**) *Fig (calmness)* calma *f*; *(composure)* aplomo *m* (**b**) *Fam (nerve, cheek)* frescura *f*
coop [ku:p] **1** *n* gallinero *m*
  2 *vt* **to c. (up)** encerrar
co-operate [kəʊ'ɒpəreɪt] *vi* cooperar
co-operation [kəʊɒpə'reɪʃən] *n* cooperación *f*
co-operative [kəʊ'ɒpərətɪv] **1** *adj (helpful)* cooperador(a)
  2 *n* cooperativa *f*
co-ordinate 1 *vt* [kəʊ'ɔ:dɪneɪt] coordinar

2 *n* [kəʊˈɔːdɪnɪt] (**a**) *Math* coordenada *f* (**b**)
co-ordinates *(clothes)* conjunto *m*
co-ordination [kəʊɔːdɪˈneɪʃən] *n* coordinación *f*
cop [kɒp] *Fam* **1** *n (policeman)* poli *m*
  2 *vt* **you'll c. it** te vas a ganar una buena
  ▸ **cop out** *vi* rajarse
cope [kəʊp] *vi* arreglárselas; **to c. with**
(person, work) poder con; *(problem)* hacer
frente a
Copenhagen [kəʊpənˈheɪɡən] *n* Copenhague
copious [ˈkəʊpɪəs] *adj* copioso(a), abundante
copper¹ [ˈkɒpə(r)] **1** *n (metal)* cobre *m*
  2 *adj (colour)* cobrizo(a)
copper² [ˈkɒpə(r)] *n Fam* poli *mf*
coppice [ˈkɒpɪs], **copse** [kɒps] *n* arboleda *f*,
bosquecillo *m*
copulate [ˈkɒpjʊleɪt] *vi* copular
copy [ˈkɒpɪ] **1** *n* (**a**) copia *f* (**b**) *(of book)*
ejemplar *m*
  2 *vt & vi* copiar
copycat [ˈkɒpɪkæt] *n Fam* copión(ona) *m,f*
copyright [ˈkɒpɪraɪt] *n* derechos *mpl* de
autor
coral [ˈkɒrəl] *n* coral *m*; **c. reef** arrecife *m* de
coral
cord [kɔːd] *n* (**a**) *(string)* cuerda *f*; *Elec* cordón
m (**b**) *Tex (corduroy)* pana *f*; **cords** pantalones
mpl de pana
cordial [ˈkɔːdɪəl] **1** *adj* cordial
  2 *n* licor *m*
cordon [ˈkɔːdən] **1** *n* cordón *m*
  2 *vt* **to c. off a street** acordonar una calle
corduroy [ˈkɔːdərɔɪ] *n* pana *f*
core [kɔː(r)] **1** *n (of fruit)* corazón *m*; *Elec*
núcleo *m*; *Fig* **the hard c.** los incondicionales
  2 *vt* quitarle el corazón a
coriander [kɒrɪˈændə(r)] *n* culantro *m*
cork [kɔːk] *n* corcho *m*; **c. oak** alcornoque
m
corkscrew [ˈkɔːkskruː] *n* sacacorchos *m inv*
corn¹ [kɔːn] *n* cereal *m*; *(grain)* granos *mpl*;
(maize) maíz *m*; **c. on the cob** mazorca *f* de
maíz *or Andes, RP* choclo, *Méx* elote *m*
corn² [kɔːn] *n Med* callo *m*
corncob [ˈkɔːnkɒb] *n* mazorca *f*
cornea [ˈkɔːnɪə] *n* córnea *f*
corner [ˈkɔːnə(r)] **1** *n* (**a**) *(of street)* esquina *f*;
(bend in road) curva *f*; **round the c.** a la vuelta
de la esquina; *Ftb* **c. kick** córner *m*; **c. shop**
tienda pequeña de barrio (**b**) *(of room)* rincón *m*
  2 *vt* (**a**) *(enemy)* arrinconar (**b**) *Com* acaparar
  3 *vi Aut* tomar una curva
cornerstone [ˈkɔːnəstəʊn] *n* piedra *f* angular
cornet [ˈkɔːnɪt] *n* (**a**) *Mus* corneta *f* (**b**) *Br (for
ice cream)* cucurucho *m*
cornflakes [ˈkɔːnfleɪks] *npl* copos *mpl* de
maíz, cornflakes *mpl*

cornflour [ˈkɔːnflaʊə(r)], *US* **cornstarch**
[ˈkɔːnstɑːtʃ] *n* harina *f* de maíz
Cornwall [ˈkɔːnwəl] *n* Cornualles
corny [ˈkɔːnɪ] *adj* (**cornier, corniest**) *Fam*
gastado(a)
corollary [kəˈrɒlərɪ] *n* corolario *m*
coronary [ˈkɒrənərɪ] *adj* coronario(a); **c.
thrombosis** trombosis coronaria
coronation [kɒrəˈneɪʃən] *n* coronación *f*
coroner [ˈkɒrənə(r)] *n* juez *mf* de instrucción
corporal¹ [ˈkɔːpərəl] *adj* corporal; **c. punishment** castigo *m* corporal
corporal² [ˈkɔːpərəl] *n Mil* cabo *m*
corporate [ˈkɔːpərɪt] *adj* corporativo(a)
corporation [kɔːpəˈreɪʃən] *n* (**a**) *(business)*
sociedad anónima (**b**) *(of city)* ayuntamiento
m
corps [kɔː(r)] *n (pl corps* [kɔːz]*)* cuerpo *m*
corpse [kɔːps] *n* cadáver *m*
corpulent [ˈkɔːpjʊlənt] *adj* corpulento(a)
corpuscle [ˈkɔːpʌsəl] *n* corpúsculo *m*
corral [kəˈrɑːl] *n US* corral *m*
correct [kəˈrekt] **1** *vt* (**a**) *(mistake)* corregir
(**b**) *(child)* reprender
  2 *adj* correcto(a), exacto(a); *(behaviour)*
formal
correction [kəˈrekʃən] *n* corrección *f*
correlation [kɒrəˈleɪʃən] *n* correlación *f*
correspond [kɒrɪˈspɒnd] *vi* (**a**) corresponder; **to c. to** equivaler a (**b**) *(by letter)* escribirse
correspondence [kɒrɪˈspɒndəns] *n* correspondencia *f*; **c. course** curso *m* por correspondencia
correspondent [kɒrɪˈspɒndənt] *n Press* corresponsal *mf*; **special c.** enviado(a) *m,f* especial
corridor [ˈkɒrɪdɔː(r)] *n* pasillo *m*
corroborate [kəˈrɒbəreɪt] *vt* corroborar
corrode [kəˈrəʊd] **1** *vt* corroer
  2 *vi* corroerse
corrosion [kəˈrəʊʒən] *n* corrosión *f*
corrugated [ˈkɒrʊɡeɪtɪd] *adj* **c. iron** hierro
ondulado
corrupt [kəˈrʌpt] **1** *adj (person)* corrompido(a), corrupto(a); *(actions)* deshonesto(a)
  2 *vt & vi* corromper
corruption [kəˈrʌpʃən] *n* corrupción *f*
corset [ˈkɔːsɪt] *n (garment)* faja *f*
Corsica [ˈkɔːsɪkə] *n* Córcega
cortège [kɔːˈteɪʒ] *n* cortejo *m*, comitiva *f*
cosh [kɒʃ] *n Br* porra *f*
cosmetic [kɒzˈmetɪk] **1** *n* cosmético *m*
  2 *adj* cosmético(a); **c. surgery** cirugía plástica
cosmic [ˈkɒzmɪk] *adj* cósmico(a)
cosmonaut [ˈkɒzmənɔːt] *n* cosmonauta *mf*
cosmopolitan [kɒzməˈpɒlɪtən] *adj* cosmopolita
cosset [ˈkɒsɪt] *vt* mimar
cost [kɒst] **1** *n (price)* precio *m*, coste *m*; **c.
of living** coste de la vida; **to count the c.**

considerar las desventajas; **at all costs** a toda costa

2 *vt & vi (pt & pp* **cost)** costar, valer; **how much does it c.?** ¿cuánto cuesta?; **whatever it costs** cueste lo que cueste

3 *vt (pt & pp* **costed)** *Com & Ind* calcular el coste de

co-star ['kəʊstɑː(r)] *n Cin & Th* coprotagonista *mf*

Costa Rica [kɒstə'riːkə] *n* Costa Rica

Costa Rican [kɒstə'riːkən] *adj & n* costarricense *(mf)*

cost-effective [kɒstɪ'fektɪv] *adj* rentable

costly ['kɒstlɪ] *adj* (**costlier, costliest**) costoso(a)

costume ['kɒstjuːm] *n* traje *m;* **swimming c.** bañador *m;* **c. jewellery** bisutería *f*

cosy ['kəʊzɪ] *adj* (**cosier, cosiest**) *(atmosphere)* acogedor(a); *(bed)* calentito(a); **it's c. in here** aquí se está bien

cot [kɒt] *n* (**a**) *Br (for child)* cuna *f* (**b**) *US (folding bed)* catre *m,* cama *f* plegable

cottage ['kɒtɪdʒ] *n* casa *f* de campo; **c. cheese** queso fresco; **c. industry** industria casera; *Br* **c. pie** = pastel de carne picada con puré de patatas *orAm* papas

cotton ['kɒtən] *n* (**a**) *Bot* algodonero *m; Tex* algodón *m; Br* **c. wool,** *US* **absorbent c.** algodón hidrófilo (**b**) *(thread)* hilo *m*
▸ **cotton on** *vi Fam* **to c. on to sth** caer en la cuenta de algo

couch [kaʊtʃ] *n* sofá *m; (in surgery)* camilla *f*

couchette [kuː'ʃet] *n Rail* litera *f*

cough [kɒf] **1** *vi* toser

2 *n* tos *f;* **c. drop** pastilla *f* para la tos; **c. mixture** jarabe *m* para la tos
▸ **cough up** *vt sep Fam* **to c. up the money** soltar la pasta

could [kʊd] *v aux see* **can¹**

council ['kaʊnsəl] *n* (**a**) *(body)* consejo *m; Br* **c. house** vivienda *f* de protección oficial; **town c.** consejo municipal, ayuntamiento *m*

councillor, *US* **councilor** ['kaʊnsələ(r)] *n* concejal *mf*

counsel ['kaʊnsəl] **1** *n* (**a**) *(advice)* consejo *m* (**b**) *Jur* abogado(a) *m,f*

2 *vt* aconsejar

counsellor, *US* **counselor** ['kaʊnsələ(r)] *n* (**a**) *(adviser)* asesor(a) *m,f* (**b**) *US Jur* abogado(a) *m,f*

count¹ [kaʊnt] **1** *vt* (**a**) contar (**b**) *Fig* **to c. oneself lucky** considerarse afortunado(a)

2 *vi* contar; **that doesn't c.** eso no vale; **to c. to ten** contar hasta diez

3 *n* (**a**) cuenta *f; (total)* recuento *m* (**b**) *Jur* cargo *m*
▸ **count on** *vt insep* contar con

count² [kaʊnt] *n (nobleman)* conde *m*

countdown ['kaʊntdaʊn] *n* cuenta *f* atrás

countenance ['kaʊntɪnəns] **1** *n* semblante *m,* rostro *m*

2 *vt* aprobar

counter¹ ['kaʊntə(r)] *n* (**a**) *(in shop)* mostrador *m; (in bank)* ventanilla *f* (**b**) *(in board games)* ficha *f*

counter² ['kaʊntə(r)] *n* contador *m*

counter³ ['kaʊntə(r)] **1** *adv* **c. to** en contra de

2 *vt (attack)* contestar a; *(trend)* contrarrestar

3 *vi* contestar

counteract [kaʊntər'ækt] *vt* contrarrestar

counterattack ['kaʊntərətæk] *n* contraataque *m*

counter-clockwise ['kaʊntə'klɒkwaɪz] *adv US* en sentido opuesto al de las agujas del reloj

counterfeit ['kaʊntəfɪt] **1** *adj* falsificado(a); **c. coin** moneda falsa

2 *n* falsificación *f*

3 *vt* falsificar

counterfoil ['kaʊntəfɔɪl] *n Br (of cheque)* matriz *f*

countermand [kaʊntə'mɑːnd] *vt (command)* revocar; *Com (order)* anular

counterpart ['kaʊntəpɑːt] *n* homólogo(a) *m,f*

counterproductive [kaʊntəprə'dʌktɪv] *adj* contraproducente

countersign ['kaʊntəsaɪn] *vt* refrendar

countess ['kaʊntɪs] *n* condesa *f*

countless ['kaʊntlɪs] *adj* innumerable, incontable

country ['kʌntrɪ] *n* (**a**) *(state)* país *m;* **native c.** patria *f* (**b**) *(rural area)* campo *m;* **c. dancing** baile *m* popular

countryman ['kʌntrɪmən] *n* (**a**) *(rural)* hombre *m* del campo (**b**) *(compatriot)* compatriota *m*

countryside ['kʌntrɪsaɪd] *n (area)* campo *m; (scenery)* paisaje *m*

county ['kaʊntɪ] *n* condado *m*

coup [kuː] *n (pl* **coups** [kuːz]) golpe *m;* **c. d'état** golpe de estado

couple ['kʌpəl] **1** *n* (**a**) *(of people)* pareja *f;* **a married c.** un matrimonio (**b**) *(of things)* par *m; Fam* **a c. of times** un par de veces

2 *vt (wagons)* enganchar

coupling ['kʌplɪŋ] *n Rail* enganche *m*

coupon ['kuːpɒn] *n* (**a**) cupón *m* (**b**) *Br Ftb* quiniela *f*

courage ['kʌrɪdʒ] *n* coraje *m,* valentía *f*

courageous [kə'reɪdʒəs] *adj* valeroso(a), valiente

courgette [kʊə'ʒet] *n Br* calabacín *m, CSur* zapallito *m*

courier ['kʊrɪə(r)] *n* (**a**) *(messenger)* mensajero(a) *m,f* (**b**) *(guide)* guía *mf* turístico(a)

course [kɔːs] *n* (**a**) *(of river)* curso *m; Naut & Av* rumbo *m* (**b**) *Fig* desarrollo *m;* **in the c. of construction** en vías de construcción; **in the c. of time** con el tiempo (**c**) *(series)* ciclo *m;* **a c. of treatment** un tratamiento (**d**) *Educ* curso *m; Univ* asignatura *f* (**e**) *(for golf)* campo *m; (for horse-racing)* hipódromo *m*

(f) *Culin* plato *m* (**g**) **of c.** claro, por supuesto;
of c. not! ¡claro que no!

court [kɔːt] **1** *n* (**a**) *Jur* tribunal *m*; **c. martial**
consejo *m* de guerra; **c. order** orden *f* judicial
(**b**) *(royal)* corte *f* (**c**) *Sport* pista *f*, cancha *f*
2 *vt (woman)* hacer la corte a; *Fig* **to c.
danger** buscar el peligro; *Fig* **to c. disaster**
exponerse al desastre
3 *vi (couple)* tener relaciones

courteous ['kɜːtɪəs] *adj* cortés

courtesy ['kɜːtɪsɪ] *n* (**a**) cortesía *f*, educación
f (**b**) **by c. of** por cortesía de

courthouse ['kɔːthaʊs] *n US* palacio *m* de
justicia

courtier ['kɔːtɪə(r)] *n* cortesano *m,f*

court-martial [kɔːt'mɑːʃəl] *vt* someter a
consejo de guerra

courtroom ['kɔːtruːm] *n* sala *f* de justicia

courtyard ['kɔːtjɑːd] *n* patio *m*

cousin ['kʌzən] *n* primo(a) *m,f*; **first c.** pri-
mo(a) hermano(a)

cove [kəʊv] *n* cala *f*, ensenada *f*

covenant ['kʌvənənt] *n* convenio *m*, pacto *m*

cover ['kʌvə(r)] **1** *vt* (**a**) cubrir (**with** de);
(furniture) revestir (**with** de); *(with lid)* tapar
(**b**) *(hide)* disimular
(**c**) *(protect)* abrigar
(**d**) *(distance)* recorrer
(**e**) *Press* investigar
(**f**) *(deal with)* abarcar
(**g**) *(include)* incluir
(**h**) *Sport* marcar
2 *vi* **to c. for sb** sustituir a algn
3 *n* (**a**) cubierta *f*; *(lid)* tapa *f*; *(on bed)* manta
f, *Am* frazada *f*, cobija *f*; *(of chair etc)* funda *f*
(**b**) *(of book)* tapa *f*; *(of magazine)* portada *f*;
c. girl modelo *f* de revista
(**c**) *(in restaurant)* cubierto *m*
(**d**) **under separate c.** por separado
(**e**) *Ins* **full c.** cobertura completa; *Br* **c. note**
seguro *m* provisional
(**f**) *(protection)* abrigo *m*; **to take c.** abrigarse; **under c.** al abrigo; *(indoors)* bajo techo
▸ **cover up 1** *vt sep* (**a**) cubrir (**b**) *(crime)*
encubrir
2 *vi* (**a**) *(person)* abrigarse (**b**) **to c. up for sb**
encubrir a algn

coverage ['kʌvərɪdʒ] *n* cobertura *f*

coveralls ['kʌvərɔːlz] *npl US* mono *m*

covering ['kʌvərɪŋ] **1** *n* cubierta *f*, envoltura *f*
2 *adj (letter)* explicatorio(a)

covert ['kʌvət] *adj* disimulado(a), secreto(a)

cover-up ['kʌvərʌp] *n* encubrimiento *m*

covet ['kʌvɪt] *vt* codiciar

cow¹ [kaʊ] *n* vaca *f*, *Pej (woman)* arpía *f*, bruja
f

cow² [kaʊ] *vt* intimidar

coward ['kaʊəd] *n* cobarde *mf*

cowardice ['kaʊədɪs] *n* cobardía *f*

cowardly ['kaʊədlɪ] *adj* cobarde

cowboy ['kaʊbɔɪ] *n* vaquero *m*

cower ['kaʊə(r)] *vi (with fear)* encogerse

cox [kɒks] *n* timonel *m*

coy [kɔɪ] *adj (shy)* tímido(a); *(demure)* coque-
tón(ona)

cozy ['kəʊzɪ] *adj US* = **cosy**

crab [kræb] *n* (**a**) cangrejo *m* (**b**) **c. apple**
manzana *f* silvestre

crack [kræk] **1** *vt* (**a**) *(cup)* partir; *(bone)*
fracturar; *(nut)* cascar; *(safe)* forzar (**b**)
(whip) hacer restallar (**c**) *Fig (problem)* dar
con la solución de; *(joke)* contar
2 *vi* (**a**) *(glass)* partirse; *(wall)* agrietarse (**b**)
(whip) restallar (**c**) *Fam* **to get cracking on sth**
ponerse a hacer algo
3 *n* (**a**) *(in cup)* raja *f*; *(in wall, ground)* grieta
f (**b**) *(of whip)* restallido *m*; *(of gun)* detonación *f* (**c**) *Fam (blow)* golpetazo *m* (**d**) *Fam* **to
have a c. at sth** *(attempt)* intentar hacer algo
(**e**) *Fam (wisecrack)* réplica aguda (**f**) *Fam
(drug)* crack *m*
4 *adj Fam* de primera
▸ **crack down on** *vt insep* atajar con mano
dura
▸ **crack up** *vi Fam Fig (go mad)* desquiciarse;
(with laughter) partirse de risa

cracker ['krækə(r)] *n* (**a**) *(biscuit)* galleta
salada (**b**) *(firework)* petardo *m*

crackle ['krækəl] *vi (cr017)* crepitar

cradle ['kreɪdəl] *n (baby's)* cuna *f*

craft [krɑːft] *n* (**a**) *(occupation)* oficio *m*; *(art)*
arte *m*; *(skill)* destreza *f* (**b**) *(cunning)* maña *f*
(**c**) *Naut* embarcación *f*

craftsman ['krɑːftsmən] *n* artesano *m*

craftsmanship ['krɑːftsmənʃɪp] *n* arte *f*

crafty ['krɑːftɪ] *adj* (**craftier, craftiest**) astu-
to(a)

crag [kræg] *n* peña *f*, peñasco *m*

cram [kræm] **1** *vt* atiborrar; **crammed with**
atestado(a) de
2 *vi Fam Educ* empollar

cramp¹ [kræmp] *n Med* calambre *m*; **cramps**
retortijones *mpl*

cramp² [kræmp] *vt (development etc)* poner
trabas a

cramped [kræmpt] *adj* atestado(a); *(writing)*
apretado(a)

cranberry ['krænbərɪ] *n* arándano *m*

crane [kreɪn] **1** *n* (**a**) *Zool* grulla *f* común (**b**)
(device) grúa *f*
2 *vt* estirar

crank [kræŋk] *n* (**a**) *Tech* manivela *f* (**b**) *Fam
(eccentric)* tío raro

crankshaft ['kræŋkʃɑːft] *n* árbol *m* del cigüeñal

cranny ['krænɪ] *n Fig* **in every nook and c.** en
todos los rincones

crap [kræp] *n Fam* mierda *f*

crash [kræʃ] **1** *vt* **to c. one's car** tener un
accidente con el coche
2 *vi* (**a**) *(car, plane)* estrellarse; *(collide)*
chocar; **to c. into** estrellarse contra (**b**) *Com*
quebrar
3 *n* (**a**) *(noise)* estrépito *m* (**b**) *(collision)*

choque *m*; **car/plane c.** accidente *m* de coche/avión; *Fig* **c. course** curso intensivo; **c. helmet** casco *m* protector (**c**) *Com* quiebra *f*

crash-land [kræʃ'lænd] *vi* hacer un aterrizaje forzoso

crass [kræs] *adj* (*person*) grosero(a); (*error*) garrafal

crate [kreɪt] *n* caja *f*, cajón *m* (*para embalaje*)

crater ['kreɪtə(r)] *n* cráter *m*

cravat [krə'væt] *n* pañuelo *m* (*de hombre*)

crave [kreɪv] *vi* **to c. for sth** ansiar algo

craving ['kreɪvɪŋ] *n* ansia *f*; (*in pregnancy*) antojo *m*

crawfish ['krɔːfɪʃ] *n* langosta *f*

crawl [krɔːl] **1** *vi* (*baby*) gatear; (*vehicle*) avanzar lentamente; *Fig* **to c. to sb** arrastrarse a los pies de algn
2 *n* (*swimming*) crol *m*

crayfish ['kreɪfɪʃ] *n* cangrejo *m* de río

crayon ['kreɪɒn] *n* cera *f*

craze [kreɪz] *n* manía *f*; (*fashion*) moda *f*; **it's the latest c.** es el último grito

crazy ['kreɪzɪ] *adj* (**crazier, craziest**) *Fam* loco(a), chalado(a); *Br* **c. paving** pavimento *m* en mosaico

creak [kriːk] *vi* (*floor*) crujir; (*hinge*) chirriar

cream [kriːm] **1** *n* (**a**) (*of milk*) nata *f*; **c.-coloured** color crema; *Fig* **the c.** la flor y nata; **c. cheese** queso *m* crema (**b**) (*cosmetic*) crema *f*
2 *vt* (**a**) (*milk*) desnatar (**b**) *Culin* batir; **creamed potatoes** puré *m* de patatas *or Am* papas

creamy ['kriːmɪ] *adj* (**creamier, creamiest**) cremoso(a)

crease [kriːs] **1** *n* (*wrinkle*) arruga *f*; (*fold*) pliegue *m*; (*on trousers*) raya *f*
2 *vt* (*clothes*) arrugar
3 *vi* arrugarse

create [kriː'eɪt] *vt* crear

creation [kriː'eɪʃən] *n* creación *f*

creative [kriː'eɪtɪv] *adj* (*person*) creativo(a)

creativity [kriːeɪ'tɪvɪtɪ] *n* creatividad *f*

creator [kriː'eɪtə(r)] *n* creador(a) *m,f*

creature ['kriːtʃə(r)] *n* (*animal*) criatura *f*

crèche [kreʃ, kreʃ] *n* guardería *f*

credence ['kriːdəns] *n* **to give c. to** dar crédito a

credentials [krɪ'denʃəlz] *npl* credenciales *fpl*

credible ['kredɪbəl] *adj* creíble

credit ['kredɪt] **1** *n* (**a**) *Com* crédito *m*; **on c.** a crédito; **c. card** tarjeta *f* de crédito (**b**) **to give c. to sb for sth** reconocer algo a algn (**c**) (*benefit*) honor *m*; **to be a c. to** hacer honor a (**d**) *Cin TV* **credits** créditos *mpl*
2 *vt* (**a**) *Com* abonar (**b**) (*believe*) creer (**c**) *Fig* atribuir; **he is credited with having** se le atribuye haber

creditor ['kredɪtə(r)] *n* acreedor(a) *m,f*

creed [kriːd] *n* credo *m*

creek [kriːk] *n* (**a**) *Br* cala *f* (**b**) *US & Austral*

riachuelo *m*

creep [kriːp] **1** *vi* (*pt & pp* **crept**) andar silenciosamente; (*insect*) arrastrarse; (*plant*) trepar; **to c. up on sb** sorprender a algn
2 *n Fam* (*person*) pelotillero(a) *m,f*

creeper ['kriːpə(r)] *n Bot* trepadora *f*

creepy ['kriːpɪ] *adj* (**creepier, creepiest**) *Fam* espeluznante

cremate [krɪ'meɪt] *vt* incinerar

crematorium [kremə'tɔːrɪəm] *n* crematorio *m*

crêpe [kreɪp] *n* (**a**) *Tex* crepé *m* (**b**) **c. paper** papel *m* crespón

crept [krept] *pt & pp of* **creep**

crescendo [krɪ'ʃendəʊ] *n* crescendo *m*

crescent ['kresənt] **1** *n* (*shape*) medialuna *f*; *Br* (*street*) calle *f* en medialuna
2 *adj* creciente

cress [kres] *n* berro *m*

crest [krest] *n* (**a**) (*of cock, wave*) cresta *f*; (*on helmet*) penacho *m*; (*of hill*) cima *f* (**b**) (*heraldic*) blasón *m*

crestfallen ['krestfɔːlən] *adj* abatido(a)

Crete [kriːt] *n* Creta

cretin ['kretɪn] *n* cretino(a) *m,f*

crevasse [krɪ'væs] *n* grieta *f*, fisura *f*

crevice ['krevɪs] *n* grieta *f*, hendedura *f*

crew [kruː] *n Av & Naut* tripulación *f*; **c. cut** corte *m* al rape; **c.-neck sweater** jersey *m* con cuello redondo

crib [krɪb] **1** *n* (**a**) (*manger*) pesebre *m* (**b**) (*for baby*) cuna *f* (**c**) *Fam* (*in exam*) chuleta *f*, *Arg* machete *m*, *Col, Méx* acordeón *m*
2 *vt Fam* (**a**) (*copy*) copiar (**b**) (*steal*) quitar

crick [krɪk] *n Fam* **a c. in the neck** una tortícolis

cricket¹ ['krɪkɪt] *n* (*insect*) grillo *m*

cricket² ['krɪkɪt] *n Sport* cricket *m*

crikey ['kraɪkɪ] *interj Fam* Old-fashioned ¡caramba!

crime [kraɪm] *n* delincuencia *f*; (*offence*) delito *m*

criminal ['krɪmɪnəl] *adj & n* criminal (*mf*); **c. law** derecho *m* penal; **c. record** antecedentes *mpl* penales

crimson ['krɪmzən] *adj & n* carmesí (*m*)

cringe [krɪndʒ] *vi* abatirse, encogerse

crinkle ['krɪŋkəl] *vt* fruncir, arrugar

cripple ['krɪpəl] **1** *n* lisiado(a) *m,f*, mutilado(a) *m,f*
2 *vt* mutilar, dejar cojo(a); *Fig* paralizar

crisis ['kraɪsɪs] *n* (*pl* **crises** ['kraɪsiːz]) crisis *f inv*

crisp [krɪsp] **1** *adj* crujiente; (*lettuce*) fresco(a); (*banknote*) nuevo(a); (*weather*) frío(a) y seco(a); (*style*) directo(a)
2 *n Br* (*potato*) **c.** patata *or Am* papa frita

crisscross ['krɪskrɒs] *n* líneas entrecruzadas

criterion [kraɪ'tɪərɪən] *n* (*pl* **criteria** [kraɪ'tɪərɪə]) criterio *m*

critic ['krɪtɪk] *n Art & Th* crítico(a) *m,f*

critical ['krɪtɪkəl] *adj* crítico(a)

critically ['krɪtɪkəlɪ] *adv* críticamente; **c. ill** gravemente enfermo(a)
criticism ['krɪtɪsɪzəm] *n* crítica *f*
criticize ['krɪtɪsaɪz] *vt* criticar
croak [krəʊk] *vi (frog)* croar; *(raven)* graznar; *(person)* hablar con voz ronca
Croat ['krəʊæt] **1** *adj* croata
  2 *n* (**a**) *(person)* croata *mf* (**b**) *(language)* croata *m*
Croatia [krəʊ'eɪʃə] *n* Croacia
Croatian [krəʊ'eɪʃən] *adj & n* = **Croat**
crochet ['krəʊʃeɪ] *n* ganchillo *m*
crockery ['krɒkərɪ] *n* loza *f*
crocodile ['krɒkədaɪl] *n* cocodrilo *m*
crocus ['krəʊkəs] *n* azafrán *m*
crony ['krəʊnɪ] *n* compinche *mf*
crook [krʊk] **1** *n* (**a**) *(of shepherd)* cayado *m* (**b**) *Fam* caco *m*
  2 *vt (arm)* doblar
crooked ['krʊkɪd] *adj* (**a**) *(stick, picture)* torcido(a); *(path)* tortuoso(a) (**b**) *Fam (dishonest)* deshonesto(a)
crop [krɒp] **1** *n* (**a**) cultivo *m*; *(harvest)* cosecha *f*; *(of hair)* mata *f*; *(whip)* fusta *f*
  2 *vt (hair)* rapar; *(grass)* cortar
  ▸ **crop up** *vi Fam* surgir, presentarse
croquet ['krəʊkeɪ] *n* croquet *m*
cross [krɒs] **1** *n* (**a**) cruz *f* (**b**) *(breeds)* cruce *m* (**c**) **c. section** sección *f* transversal
  2 *vt* (**a**) cruzar; *Rel* **to c. oneself** hacer la señal de la cruz; *Fam* **c. my heart!** ¡te lo juro! (**c**) *(thwart)* contrariar
  3 *vi* cruzar; *(roads)* cruzarse; **to c. over** cruzar
  4 *adj* (**a**) *Fig* **they are at c. purposes** hay un malentendido entre ellos (**b**) *(angry)* enfadado(a)
  ▸ **cross off, cross out** *vt sep* tachar, rayar
crossbar ['krɒsbɑː(r)] *n* travesaño *m*
cross-country 1 *adj* ['krɒskʌntrɪ] **c. race** cros *m*
  2 *adv* [krɒs'kʌntrɪ] campo través
cross-examine [krɒsɪg'zæmɪn] *vt* interrogar
cross-eyed ['krɒsaɪd] *adj* bizco(a)
crossfire ['krɒsfaɪə(r)] *n* fuego cruzado
crossing ['krɒsɪŋ] *n* cruce *m*; **pedestrian c.** paso *m* de peatones; **sea c.** travesía *f*
cross-legged [krɒs'leg(ɪ)d] *adj* con las piernas cruzadas
cross-reference [krɒs'refərəns] *n* remisión *f*
crossroads ['krɒsrəʊdz] *n* cruce *m*; *Fig* encrucijada *f*
crosswalk ['krɒswɔːk] *n US* paso *m* de peatones
crosswind ['krɒswɪnd] *n* viento *m* lateral
crossword ['krɒswɜːd] *n* **c. (puzzle)** crucigrama *m*
crotch [krɒtʃ] *n* entrepierna *f*
crotchet ['krɒtʃɪt] *n Br Mus* negra *f*
crotchety ['krɒtʃɪtɪ] *adj Fam* gruñón(ona)
crouch [kraʊtʃ] *vi* **to c. (down)** agacharse
crow¹ [krəʊ] *n* cuervo *m*; *Fig* **as the c. flies** en

línea recta; **c.'s-feet** patas *fpl* de gallo
crow² [krəʊ] **1** *vi* (**a**) *(cock)* cantar; *Fig* **to c. over sth** jactarse de algo (**b**) *(baby)* balbucir
  2 *n (of cock)* canto *m*
crowbar ['krəʊbɑː(r)] *n* palanca *f*
crowd [kraʊd] **1** *n* muchedumbre *f*; *Fam (gang)* pandilla *f*; **the c.** el populacho
  2 *vt (streets)* llenar
  3 *vi* apiñarse; **to c. in/out** entrar/salir en tropel
crowded ['kraʊdɪd] *adj* atestado(a), lleno(a)
crown [kraʊn] **1** *n* (**a**) corona *f*; *(garland)* guirnalda *f*; **the c. jewels** las joyas de la corona; *Br Jur* **c. court** tribunal *m* superior; **C. Prince** príncipe heredero (**b**) *Anat* coronilla *f*; *(of hat, tree)* copa *f*
  2 *vt* coronar; *Fam Fig* **to c. it all** y para más inri
crucial ['kruːʃəl] *adj* decisivo(a)
crucifix ['kruːsɪfɪks] *n* crucifijo *m*
crucifixion [kruːsɪ'fɪkʃən] *n* crucifixión *f*
crucify ['kruːsɪfaɪ] *vt* crucificar
crude [kruːd] *adj* (**a**) *(manners, style)* tosco(a), grosero(a); *(tool)* primitivo(a) (**b**) **c. oil** crudo *m*
cruel [kruːəl] *adj* cruel (**to con**)
cruelty ['kruːəltɪ] *n* crueldad *f* (**to hacia**)
cruet ['kruːɪt] *n* **c. set** vinagreras *fpl*
cruise [kruːz] **1** *vi* (**a**) *Naut* hacer un crucero (**b**) *Aut* viajar a velocidad constante; *Av* viajar a velocidad de crucero
  2 *n* (**a**) *Naut* crucero *m* (**b**) **c. missile** misil teledirigido
cruiser ['kruːzə(r)] *n (barco m)* crucero *m*
crumb [krʌm] *n* miga *f*, migaja *f*
crumble ['krʌmbəl] **1** *vt* desmigar
  2 *vi (wall)* desmoronarse; *Fig (hopes)* desvanecerse
crumbly ['krʌmblɪ] *adj* (**crumblier, crumbliest**) que se desmigaja
crumpet ['krʌmpɪt] *n Br* = clase de crepe grueso que se puede tostar
crumple ['krʌmpəl] *vt* arrugar
crunch [krʌntʃ] **1** *vt (food)* ronchar; *(with feet)* hacer crujir
  2 *n Fam* **when it comes to the c.** a la hora de la verdad
crunchy ['krʌntʃɪ] *adj* (**crunchier, crunchiest**) crujiente
crusade [kruː'seɪd] *n* cruzada *f*
crush [krʌʃ] **1** *vt* aplastar; *(wrinkle)* arrugar; *(grind)* moler; *(squeeze)* exprimir
  2 *n* (**a**) *(of people)* gentío *m* (**b**) **orange c.** naranjada *f*
crushing ['krʌʃɪŋ] *adj Fig (defeat, reply)* aplastante
crust [krʌst] *n* corteza *f*
crutch [krʌtʃ] *n Med* muleta *f*; *Fig* apoyo *m*
crux [krʌks] *n* **the c. of the matter** el quid de la cuestión
cry [kraɪ] **1** *vi* (*pt & pp* **cried**) (**a**) gritar (**b**) *(weep)* llorar

2 *vt* gritar; *Fig* **to c. wolf** dar una falsa alarma

3 *n* (**a**) grito *m* (**b**) *(weep)* llanto *m*

▸ **cry off** *vi Fam* rajarse

▸ **cry out** *vi* gritar; **to c. out for sth** pedir algo a gritos

crying ['kraɪɪŋ] *adj* **it's a c. shame** es una vergüenza

cryptic ['krɪptɪk] *adj* enigmático(a)

crystal ['krɪstəl] *n* cristal *m*

crystal-clear [krɪstəl'klɪə(r)] *adj* claro(a) como el agua

crystallize ['krɪstəlaɪz] **1** *vt* cristalizar

2 *vi* cristalizarse

cub [kʌb] *n* (**a**) *(animal)* cachorro *m* (**b**) *(junior scout)* niño *m* explorador

Cuba ['kju:bə] *n* Cuba

Cuban ['kju:bən] *adj & n* cubano(a) *(m,f)*

cubbyhole ['kʌbɪhəʊl] *n* cuchitril *m*

cube [kju:b] **1** *n* cubo *m*; *(of sugar)* terrón *m*; **c. root** raíz cúbica

2 *vt Math* elevar al cubo

cubic ['kju:bɪk] *adj* cúbico(a)

cubicle ['kju:bɪkəl] *n* cubículo *m*; *(at swimming pool)* caseta *f*

cuckoo ['kʊku:] **1** *n* cuco *m*; **c. clock** reloj *m* de cuco

2 *adj Fam* lelo(a)

cucumber ['kju:kʌmbə(r)] *n* pepino *m*

cuddle ['kʌdəl] **1** *vt* abrazar

2 *vi* abrazarse

cuddly ['kʌdlɪ] *adj* **c. toy** muñeco *m* de peluche

cue¹ [kju:] *n Th* pie *m*

cue² [kju:] *n* *(in billiards)* taco *m*; **c. ball** bola blanca

cuff¹ [kʌf] *n* *(of sleeve)* puño *m*; *US (of trousers)* dobladillo *m*; *Fig* **to do sth off the c.** improvisar algo

cuff² [kʌf] **1** *vt* abofetear

2 *n* bofetada *f*

cufflinks ['kʌflɪŋks] *npl* gemelos *mpl*

cul-de-sac ['kʌldəsæk] *n* callejón *m* sin salida

cull [kʌl] *vt* (**a**) *(choose)* escoger (**b**) *(animals)* eliminar

culminate ['kʌlmɪneɪt] *vi* **to c. in** terminar en

culmination [kʌlmɪ'neɪʃən] *n* culminación *f*, punto *m* culminante

culottes [kju:'lɒts] *npl* falda-pantalón *f*

culprit ['kʌlprɪt] *n* culpable *mf*

cult [kʌlt] *n* culto *m*; **c. figure** ídolo *m*

cultivate ['kʌltɪveɪt] *vt* cultivar

cultivated ['kʌltɪveɪtɪd] *adj (person)* culto(a)

cultivation [kʌltɪ'veɪʃən] *n* cultivo *m* (de la tierra)

cultural ['kʌltʃərəl] *adj* cultural

culture ['kʌltʃə(r)] *n* cultura *f*

cultured ['kʌltʃəd] *adj* = **cultivated**

cumbersome ['kʌmbəsəm] *adj (awkward)* incómodo(a); *(bulky)* voluminoso(a)

cum(m)in ['kʌmɪn] *n* comino *m*

cumulative ['kju:mjʊlətɪv] *adj* acumulativo(a)

cunning ['kʌnɪŋ] **1** *adj* astuto(a)

2 *n* astucia *f*

cup [kʌp] **1** *n* taza *f*; *Sport* copa *f*; **C. Final** final *f* de copa; **c. tie** partido *m* de copa

2 *vt (hands)* ahuecar

cupboard ['kʌbəd] *n* armario *m*; *(on wall)* alacena *f*

curate ['kjʊərɪt] *n* cura *m* coadjutor

curator [kjʊə'reɪtə(r)] *n* conservador(a) *m,f*

curb [kɜ:b] **1** *n* (**a**) *(limit)* freno *m* (**b**) *US (kerb)* bordillo *m*

2 *vt (horse)* refrenar; *Fig (public spending)* contener

curd [kɜ:d] *n* cuajada *f*

curdle ['kɜ:dəl] *vi* cuajarse

cure [kjʊə(r)] **1** *vt* curar

2 *n (remedy)* cura *f*, remedio *m*

curfew ['kɜ:fju:] *n* toque *m* de queda

curiosity [kjʊərɪ'ɒsɪtɪ] *n* curiosidad *f*

curious ['kjʊərɪəs] *adj* (**a**) *(inquisitive)* curioso(a) (**b**) *(odd)* extraño(a)

curl [kɜ:l] **1** *vt (hair)* rizar; *(lip)* fruncir

2 *vi* rizarse

3 *n (of hair)* rizo *m*; *(of smoke)* espiral *f*

▸ **curl up** *vi* enroscarse

curly ['kɜ:lɪ] *adj* (**curlier, curliest**) rizado(a)

currant ['kʌrənt] *n* pasa *f* (de Corinto)

currency ['kʌrənsɪ] *n* (**a**) moneda *f*; **foreign c.** divisa *f* (**b**) **to gain c.** cobrar fuerza

current ['kʌrənt] **1** *adj* (**a**) *(opinion)* general; *(word)* en uso; *(year)* en curso; **c. account** cuenta *f* corriente; **c. affairs** actualidad *f* (política); *Fin* **c. assets** activo *m* disponible (**b**) **the c. issue** *(of magazine, newspaper)* el último número

2 *n* corriente *f*

currently ['kʌrəntlɪ] *adv* actualmente

curriculum [kə'rɪkjʊləm] *n* (*pl* **curricula** [kə'rɪkjʊlə]) plan *m* de estudios; **c. vitae** curriculum *m* (vitae)

curry¹ ['kʌrɪ] *n* curry *m*; **chicken c.** pollo *m* al curry

curry² ['kʌrɪ] *vt* **to c. favour with** congraciarse con

curse [kɜ:s] **1** *n* maldición *f*; *(oath)* palabrota *f*; *Fig* azote *m*

2 *vt* maldecir

3 *vi* blasfemar

cursor ['kɜ:sə(r)] *n* cursor *m*

cursory ['kɜ:sərɪ] *adj* rápido(a)

curt [kɜ:t] *adj* brusco(a), seco(a)

curtail [kɜ:'teɪl] *vt (expenses)* reducir; *(text)* acortar

curtain ['kɜ:tən] *n* cortina *f*; *Th* telón *m*; *Fig* velo *m*

curts(e)y ['kɜ:tsɪ] **1** *n* reverencia *f*

2 *vi* hacer una reverencia (**to** a)

curve [kɜ:v] **1** *n* curva *f*

2 *vt* encorvar

3 *vi* torcerse, describir una curva

cushion ['kʊʃən] **1** n cojín m; (large) almohadón m; (of billiard table) banda f
2 vt Fig amortiguar; (person) proteger
cushy ['kʊʃɪ] adj (**cushier, cushiest**) Fam cómodo(a)
custard ['kʌstəd] n natillas fpl; **c. powder** polvos mpl para natillas
custodian [kʌ'stəʊdɪən] n conserje mf, guarda mf
custody ['kʌstədɪ] n custodia f; **to take into c.** detener
custom ['kʌstəm] n (**a**) (habit) costumbre f (**b**) Com clientela f
customary ['kʌstəmərɪ] adj habitual
customer ['kʌstəmə(r)] n cliente mf
customize ['kʌstəmaɪz] vt hacer por encargo
custom-made [kʌstəm'meɪd] adj hecho(a) a la medida
customs ['kʌstəmz] n sing or pl aduana f; **c. duty** derechos mpl de aduana; **c. officer** agente mf de aduana
cut [kʌt] **1** vt (pt & pp **cut**) (**a**) cortar; (stone) tallar; (record) grabar; **he's cutting a tooth** le está saliendo un diente; **to c. one's finger** cortarse el dedo; Fig **to c. a long story short** en resumidas cuentas; Fig **to c. corners** recortar presupuestos
(**b**) (reduce) reducir
(**c**) (divide up) dividir (**into** en)
2 n (**a**) corte m; (in skin) cortadura f; (wound) herida f; (with knife) cuchillada f
(**b**) (of meat) clase f de carne
(**c**) (reduction) reducción f
(**d**) Fig **to be a c. above sb** estar por encima de algn
3 adj cortado(a); (price) reducido(a); Fig **c. and dried** convenido(a) de antemano; **c. glass** cristal tallado
4 vi (**a**) cortar; Fam Fig **to c. loose** romper con todo
(**b**) Cin **c.!** ¡corten!
▶ **cut back** vt sep (expenses) reducir; (production) disminuir
▶ **cut down 1** vt sep (tree) talar
2 vt insep **to c. down on** reducir
▶ **cut in** vi (driver) adelantar bruscamente
▶ **cut off** vt sep (water etc) cortar; (place) aislar; (heir) excluir; Tel **I've been c. off** me han cortado (la comunicación)
▶ **cut out 1** vt sep (**a**) (from newspaper) recortar; (person) **to be c. out for sth** estar hecho(a) para algo (**b**) (delete) suprimir
2 vi (engine) calarse
▶ **cut up** vt sep cortar en pedazos
cutback ['kʌtbæk] n reducción f (**in** de)
cute [kjuːt] adj mono(a), lindo(a); US Fam Pej listillo(a)
cuticle ['kjuːtɪkəl] n cutícula f
cutlery ['kʌtlərɪ] n cubiertos mpl
cutlet ['kʌtlɪt] n chuleta f

cut-price [kʌt'praɪs] adj (article) a precio rebajado
cutthroat ['kʌtθrəʊt] **1** n asesino(a) m,f, matón m
2 adj (cruel) cruel; (competition) feroz
cutting ['kʌtɪŋ] **1** n (from newspaper) recorte m; Rail tajo m
2 adj cortante; (remark) mordaz
CV, cv [siː'viː] n (abbr **curriculum vitae**) CV m
cwt. (abbr **hundredweight**) (metric) 50 kg; (imperial) Br = 50,8 kg; US = 45,36 kg
cyanide ['saɪənaɪd] n cianuro m
cybercafe ['saɪbəkæfeɪ] n Comput cibercafé m
cyberspace ['saɪbəspeɪs] n Comput ciberespacio m
cycle ['saɪkəl] **1** n (**a**) ciclo m (**b**) (bicycle) bicicleta f; (motorcycle) moto f
2 vi ir en bicicleta
cycling ['saɪklɪŋ] n ciclismo m
cyclist ['saɪklɪst] n ciclista mf
cyclone ['saɪkləʊn] n ciclón m
cygnet ['sɪgnɪt] n pollo m de cisne
cylinder ['sɪlɪndə(r)] n (**a**) cilindro m (**b**) (for gas) bombona f
cymbal ['sɪmbəl] n címbalo m, platillo m
cynic ['sɪnɪk] n descreído(a) m,f, suspicaz mf

> 🖉 Note that the Spanish word **cínico** is a false friend and is never a translation for the English word **cynic**. In Spanish, **cínico** means "shameless person".

cynical ['sɪnɪkəl] adj (**a**) (sceptical) descreído(a), suspicaz (**b**) (unscrupulous) desaprensivo(a), sin escrúpulos

> 🖉 Note that the Spanish word **cínico** is a false friend and is never a translation for the English word **cynical**. In Spanish, **cínico** means "shameless".

cynicism ['sɪnɪsɪzəm] n descreimiento m, suspicacia f

> 🖉 Note that the Spanish word **cinismo** is a false friend and is never a translation for the English word **cynicism**. In Spanish, **cinismo** means "shamelessness".

cypress ['saɪprəs] n ciprés m
Cypriot ['sɪprɪət] adj & n chipriota (mf)
Cyprus ['saɪprəs] n Chipre
cyst [sɪst] n quiste m
cystitis [sɪ'staɪtɪs] n cistitis f
czar [zɑː(r)] n zar m
Czech [tʃek] **1** adj checo(a); **the C. Republic** la República Checa
2 n (**a**) (person) checo(a) m,f (**b**) (language) checo m
Czechoslovakia [tʃekəʊsləˈvækɪə] n Checoslovaquia

D, d [di:] *n* (a) *(the letter)* D, d *f* (b) *Mus* D re *m*
D.A. [di:'eɪ] *n US (abbr* **district attorney)** fiscal *mf* (del distrito)
dab [dæb] **1** *n (small quantity)* toque *m*
  2 *vt* (a) *(apply)* aplicar (b) *(touch lightly)* tocar ligeramente
dabble ['dæbəl] *vi* to **d. in politics** meterse en política
dachshund ['dækshʊnd] *n* perro *m* salchicha
dad [dæd], **daddy** ['dædɪ] *n Fam* papá *m*, papi *m*
daddy-longlegs [dædɪ'lɒŋlegz] *n inv Fam* (a) *Br (cranefly)* típula *f* (b) *US (spider)* segador *m*
daffodil ['dæfədɪl] *n* narciso *m*
daft [dɑ:ft] *adj Br Fam* chalado(a); *(idea)* tonto(a)
dagger ['dægə(r)] *n* puñal *m*, daga *f*
dahlia ['deɪlɪə] *n* dalia *f*
daily ['deɪlɪ] **1** *adj* diario(a), cotidiano(a)
  2 *adv* diariamente; **three times d.** tres veces al día
  3 *n* (a) *(newspaper)* diario *m* (b) *Br Fam (cleaning lady)* asistenta *f*
dainty ['deɪntɪ] *adj* **(daintier, daintiest)** *(flower)* delicado(a); *(child)* precioso(a); *(food)* exquisito(a)
dairy ['deərɪ] *n (on farm)* vaquería *f*; *(shop)* lechería *f*; **d. farming** industria lechera; **d. produce** productos lácteos
dais ['deɪɪs] *n (in hall)* tarima *f*; *(in ceremony)* estrado *m*
daisy ['deɪzɪ] *n* margarita *f*
daisywheel ['deɪzɪwi:l] *n (printer)* margarita *f*
dale [deɪl] *n* valle *m*, hondonada *f*
Dalmatian [dæl'meɪʃən] *n* (perro *m*) dálmata *m*
dam [dæm] **1** *n (barrier)* dique *m*; *(lake)* presa *f*
  2 *vt (water)* represar
  ▸ **dam up** *vt sep Fig (emotion)* contener
damage ['dæmɪdʒ] **1** *n* (a) *daño m; (to health, reputation)* perjuicio *m*; *(to relationship)* deterioro *m* (b) *Jur* **damages** daños *mpl* y perjuicios *mpl*
  2 *vt (harm)* dañar, hacer daño a; *(spoil)* estropear; *(undermine)* perjudicar
damaging ['dæmɪdʒɪŋ] *adj* perjudicial
damn [dæm] **1** *vt* condenar
  2 *interj Fam* **d. (it)!** ¡maldito(a) sea!; **well, I'll be damned!** ¡vaya por Dios!

  3 *n Fam* **I don't give a d.** me importa un bledo
  4 *adj Fam* maldito(a)
  5 *adv Fam* muy, sumamente
damned [dæmd] *adj & adv* = **damn**
damnedest ['dæmdɪst] *n Fam* **to do one's d. to ...** hacer todo lo posible para ...
damning ['dæmɪŋ] *adj (evidence)* irrefutable; *(criticism)* mordaz
damp [dæmp] **1** *adj* húmedo(a); *(wet)* mojado(a)
  2 *n* humedad *f*
  3 *vt* (a) *(for ironing)* humedecer (b) **to d. (down)** *(fire)* sofocar; *Fig (violence)* frenar
dampen ['dæmpən] *vt* humedecer; *Fig* frenar
damper ['dæmpə(r)] *n Fig* **to put a d. on sth** poner freno a algo
damsel ['dæmzəl] *n Literary* doncella *f*
damson ['dæmzən] *n* ciruela damascena
dance [dɑ:ns] **1** *n* baile *m*; *(classical, tribal)* danza *f*; **d. band** orquesta *f* de baile; **d. floor** pista *f* de baile; **d. hall** salón *m* de baile
  2 *vi & vt* bailar
dancer ['dɑ:nsə(r)] *n (by profession)* bailarín(ina) *m,f*
dandelion ['dændɪlaɪən] *n* diente *m* de león
dandruff ['dændrəf] *n* caspa *f*
Dane [deɪn] *n* danés(esa) *m,f*
danger ['deɪndʒə(r)] *n* (a) *(risk)* riesgo *m; (of war etc)* amenaza *f* (b) *(peril)* peligro *m*; **d.** *(sign)* peligro; **out of d.** fuera de peligro
dangerous ['deɪndʒərəs] *adj* peligroso(a); *(risky)* arriesgado(a); *(harmful)* nocivo(a); *(illness)* grave
dangerously ['deɪndʒərəslɪ] *adv* peligrosamente
dangle ['dæŋgəl] **1** *vi (hang)* colgar; *(swing)* balancearse
  2 *vt (legs)* colgar; *(bait)* dejar colgado(a); *(swing)* balancear en el aire
Danish ['deɪnɪʃ] **1** *adj* danés(esa); **D. pastry** pastel *m* de hojaldre
  2 *n (language)* danés *m*
dapper ['dæpə(r)] *adj* pulcro(a)
dappled ['dæpəld] *adj (shade)* moteado(a)
dare [deə(r)] **1** *vi* atreverse, osar; **he doesn't d. be late** no se atreve a llegar tarde; **how d. you!** ¿cómo te atreves?; *esp Br* **I d. say** quizás, *Ironic* ya (lo creo)
  2 *vt (challenge)* desafiar
  3 *n* desafío *m*
daredevil ['deədevəl] *adj & n* atrevido(a)

(m,f), temerario(a) *(m,f)*

daring ['deərɪŋ] **1** *adj* (**a**) *(bold)* audaz, osado(a) (**b**) *(clothes)* atrevido(a)
2 *n* atrevimiento *m*, osadía *f*

dark [dɑːk] **1** *adj* (**a**) *(room, colour)* oscuro(a); *(hair, complexion)* moreno(a); *(eyes, future)* negro(a) (**b**) *Fig (gloomy)* triste (**c**) *Fig* **to be d. horse** ser una incógnita; *(discreet)* ser una caja de sorpresas (**d**) *Fig (sinister)* siniestro(a)
2 *n* (**a**) *(darkness)* oscuridad *f*, tinieblas *fpl*; **after d.** después del anochecer (**b**) *Fig* **to be in the d. (about)** estar a oscuras (sobre)

darken ['dɑːkən] **1** *vt (sky)* oscurecer; *(colour)* hacer más oscuro(a)
2 *vi* oscurecerse; *(sky)* nublarse; *Fig (face)* ensombrecerse

darkness ['dɑːknɪs] *n* oscuridad *f*, tinieblas *fpl*

darkroom ['dɑːkruːm] *n* cuarto oscuro

darling ['dɑːlɪŋ] *adj & n* querido(a) *(m,f)*

darn [dɑːn] **1** *vt* zurcir
2 *n* zurcido *m*

dart [dɑːt] **1** *n* (**a**) *(missile)* dardo *m* (**b**) **darts** *sing* dardos *mpl*
2 *vi (fly about)* revolotear; **to d. in/out** entrar/salir corriendo

dartboard ['dɑːtbɔːd] *n* diana *f*

dash [dæʃ] **1** *n* (**a**) *(rush)* carrera *f* (**b**) *esp US (race)* sprint *m* (**c**) *(small amount)* poquito *m*; *(of salt)* pizca *f*; *(of liquid)* gota *f* (**d**) *Typ* guión largo; *(hyphen)* guión (**e**) *(vitality)* brío *m*
2 *vt* (**a**) *(throw)* arrojar (**b**) *(smash)* estrellar; *Fig* **to d. sb's hopes** desvanecer las esperanzas de algn
3 *vi (rush)* correr; **to d. around** correr de un lado a otro; **to d. out** salir corriendo; *Fam* **I must d.!** ¡me voy pitando!
▸ **dash off** *vi* salir corriendo

dashboard ['dæʃbɔːd] *n Aut* salpicadero *m*

dashing ['dæʃɪŋ] *adj (appearance)* garboso(a)

data ['deɪtə, 'dɑːtə] *npl* datos *mpl*; **d. bank** *or* **base** banco *m* de datos; **d. processing** *(act)* proceso *m* de datos; *(science)* informática *f*; **d. protection act** ley *f* de informática

date¹ [deɪt] *n* (**a**) *(day)* fecha *f*; **what's the d. today?** ¿qué día es hoy?; **out of d.** *(ideas)* anticuado(a); *(expression)* desusado(a); *(invalid)* caducado(a); **to d.** hasta la fecha; *Fig* **to be up to d.** estar al día; **d. of birth** fecha de nacimiento (**b**) *(social event)* compromiso *m*; *Fam (with girl, boy)* cita *f* (**c**) *US Fam (person dated)* ligue *m*
2 *vt (ruins)* datar
3 *vi (ideas)* quedar anticuado(a)
▸ **date back to, date from** *vt insep* remontar a, datar de

date² [deɪt] *n (fruit)* dátil *m*; **d. palm** datilera *f*

dated ['deɪtɪd] *adj (idea)* anticuado(a); *(fashion)* pasado(a) de moda; *(expression)* desusado(a)

daub [dɔːb] *vt* embadurnar; *(with oil, grease)* untar

daughter ['dɔːtə(r)] *n* hija *f*

daughter-in-law ['dɔːtərɪnlɔː] *n* nuera *f*, hija política

daunting ['dɔːntɪŋ] *adj* desalentador(a)

dawdle ['dɔːdəl] *vi Fam (walk slowly)* andar despacio; *(waste time)* perder el tiempo

dawn [dɔːn] **1** *n* alba *f*, amanecer *m*
2 *vi* (**a**) *(day)* amanecer (**b**) *Fig (age, hope)* comenzar (**c**) *Fig* **suddenly it dawned on him that ...** de repente cayó en la cuenta de que ...

day [deɪ] *n* (**a**) día *m*; **d. in, d. out** día tras día; **d. by d.** diariamente; **good d.!** ¡buenos días!; **once a d.** una vez al día; **one of these days** un día de éstos; **(on) the next** *or* **following d.** el *or* al día siguiente; **the d. after tomorrow** pasado mañana; **the d. before yesterday** anteayer; **the other d.** el otro día; *Fig* **to live from d. to d.** vivir al día; *Fig* **to win the d.** llevarse la palma; **to call it a d.** *(finish)* dar por acabado un trabajo; *(give up)* darse por vencido(a); *Fam* **to make sb's d.** alegrarle a algn el día; *Br Rail* **d. return (ticket)** billete *m* de ida y vuelta para el mismo día; **d. trip** excursión *f* de un día
(**b**) *(daylight)* día *m*; **by d.** de día; **d. and night** de día y de noche; *Br* **d. shift** turno *m* de día
(**c**) *(period of work)* jornada *f*; **an eight-hour d.** una jornada de ocho horas; **paid by the d.** pagado(a) a jornal; **d. off** día de fiesta; **I'll take a d. off tomorrow** mañana me tomaré el día libre
(**d**) *(era)* época *f*; **in those days** en aquellos tiempos; **these days, in this d. and age** hoy (en) día

daybreak ['deɪbreɪk] *n* amanecer *m*

daydream ['deɪdriːm] **1** *n* ensueño *m*; *(vain hope)* fantasía *f*
2 *vi* soñar despierto(a); *(hope vainly)* hacerse ilusiones

daylight ['deɪlaɪt] *n* luz *f* del día; **in broad d.** en pleno día; **to scare the (living) daylights out of sb** pegarle a algn un susto de muerte

daytime ['deɪtaɪm] *n* día *m*; **in the d.** de día

day-to-day ['deɪtədeɪ] *adj* cotidiano(a), diario(a)

daze [deɪz] *n* aturdimiento *m*; **in a d.** aturdido(a)

dazed [deɪzd] *adj* aturdido(a), atontado(a)

dazzle ['dæzəl] *vt* deslumbrar

D-day ['diːdeɪ] *n* día *m* D

deacon ['diːkən] *n* diácono *m*

dead [ded] **1** *adj* (**a**) muerto(a); **he was shot d.** le mataron a tiros; **to be d.** estar muerto(a); *Fam* **Fig over my d. body!** ¡sobre mi cadáver!; **d. man** muerto *m*
(**b**) *(machine)* averiado(a); *(phone)* cortado(a)
(**c**) *(numb)* entumecido(a); *(limb)* adormecido(a); **my leg's gone d.** se me ha dormido la pierna

(**d**) *(silence, secrecy)* total; **d. end** callejón *m* sin salida; *Sport* **d. heat** empate *m*; *Fam* **d. loss** inútil *m*, birria *f*

2 *adv* (**a**) *(exactly)* justo; **d. on time** a la hora en punto

(**b**) **to stop d.** pararse en seco

(**c**) *(very)* muy; *Fam* **d. beat, d. tired** rendido(a); *Fam* **it's d. easy!** ¡está chupado(a)!; *Aut* **d. slow** *(sign)* al paso; *Fam* **you're d. right** tienes toda la razón

3 *n* (**a**) **the d.** *pl* los muertos

(**b**) **at d. of night** a altas horas de la noche

deaden ['dedən] *vt (impact, noise)* amortiguar; *Fig (pain, feeling)* calmar, aliviar

deadline ['dedlaɪn] *n (date)* fecha *f* tope; *(time)* hora *f* tope; **we have to meet the d.** tenemos que hacerlo dentro del plazo

deadlock ['dedlɒk] *n* punto muerto

deadly ['dedlɪ] **1** *adj* (**deadlier, deadliest**) mortal; *(weapon)* mortífero(a); *(aim)* certero(a)

2 *adv (extremely)* terriblemente, sumamente

deadpan ['dedpæn] *adj Fam (face)* sin expresión; *(humour)* guasón(ona)

deaf [def] **1** *adj* sordo(a); *Fig* **to turn a d. ear** hacerse el sordo; **d. mute** sordomudo(a) *m,f*

2 *npl* **the d.** los sordos; **the d. and dumb** los sordomudos

deafen ['defən] *vt* ensordecer

deafening ['defənɪŋ] *adj* ensordecedor(a)

deafness ['defnɪs] *n* sordera *f*

deal [di:l] **1** *n* (**a**) *Com & Pol* trato *m*, pacto *m*; **business d.** negocio *m*, transacción *f*; **to do a d. with sb** *(transaction)* cerrar un trato con algn; *(agreement)* pactar algo con algn; *Fam* **it's a d.!** ¡trato hecho! (**b**) *(amount)* cantidad *f*; **a good d. of criticism** muchas críticas; **a good d. slower** mucho más despacio (**c**) *Cards* reparto *m*

2 *vt (pt & pp* **dealt**) (**a**) *Cards* dar (**to** a) (**b**) **to d. sb a blow** asestarle un golpe a algn

▸ **deal in** *vt insep (goods)* comerciar en, tratar en; *(drugs)* traficar con

▸ **deal out** *vt sep* repartir

▸ **deal with** *vt insep (firm, person)* tratar con; *(subject, problem)* abordar, ocuparse de; *(in book etc)* tratar de

dealer ['di:lə(r)] *n* (**a**) *Com (in goods)* comerciante *mf*; *(in drugs)* traficante *mf* (**b**) *Cards* repartidor(a) *m,f*

dealings ['di:lɪŋz] *npl* (**a**) *(relations)* trato *m* (**b**) *Com* negocios *mpl*

dealt [delt] *pt & pp* of **deal**

dean [di:n] *n* (**a**) *Rel* deán *m* (**b**) *Univ* decano *m*

dear [dɪə(r)] **1** *adj* (**a**) *(loved)* querido(a); **to hold sth/sb d.** apreciar mucho algo/a algn (**b**) *(in letter)* Querido(a); *Fam* **D. Andrew** Querido Andrew; *Fml* **D. Madam** Estimada señora; *Fml* **D. Sir(s)** Muy señor(es) mío(s) (**c**) **it is very d. to me** *(precious)* le tengo un

gran cariño (**d**) *Br (expensive)* caro(a)

2 *n* querido(a) *m,f*; **my d.** mi vida

3 *interj* **oh d.!, d. me!** *(surprise)* ¡caramba!; *(disappointment)* ¡qué pena!

dearly ['dɪəlɪ] *adv* muchísimo; *Fig* **he paid d. for his mistake** su error le costó caro

dearth [dɜ:θ] *n Fml* escasez *f*

death [deθ] *n* (**a**) muerte *f*; *Fml* fallecimiento *m*; **to put sb to d.** dar muerte a algn; *Fam* **to be bored to d.** aburrirse como una ostra; *Fam* **to be scared to d.** estar muerto(a) de miedo; *Fam Fig* **to be sick to d. of** estar hasta la coronilla de; **d. certificate** certificado *m* de defunción; **d. penalty, d. sentence** pena *f* de muerte; **d. rate** índice *m* de mortalidad; **d. squad** escuadrón *m* de la muerte (**b**) *Fig (end)* fin *m*

deathbed ['deθbed] *n* **to be on one's d.** estar en el lecho de muerte

deathly ['deθlɪ] *adj* (**deathlier, deathliest**) *(silence)* sepulcral; **d. pale** pálido(a) como un muerto

debacle [deɪ'bɑːkəl] *n* debacle *f*

debar [dɪ'bɑ:(r)] *vt Fml* excluir, prohibir

debase [dɪ'beɪs] *vt* envilecer; **to d. oneself** humillarse

debatable [dɪ'beɪtəbəl] *adj* discutible

debate [dɪ'beɪt] **1** *n* debate *m*; **a heated d.** una discusión acalorada

2 *vt* (**a**) *(discuss)* discutir (**b**) *(wonder about)* dar vueltas a

3 *vi* discutir

debateable dɪ'beɪtəbəl] *adj* = **debatable**

debauchery [dɪ'bɔ:tʃərɪ] *n* libertinaje *m*

debilitating [dɪ'bɪlɪteɪtɪŋ] *adj* debilitante; *(heat, climate)* agotador(a)

debit ['debɪt] **1** *n* débito *m*; **d. balance** saldo negativo

2 *vt* **d. Mr Jones with £20** cargar la suma de 20 libras en la cuenta del Sr. Jones

debris ['debri:, 'deɪbri:] *n sing* escombros *mpl*

debt [det] *n* deuda *f*; **to be deeply in d.** estar cargado(a) de deudas; *Fig* **to be in sb's d.** estar en deuda con algn

debtor ['detə(r)] *n* deudor(a) *m,f*

debug [di:'bʌg] *vt Comput* eliminar fallos de

debunk [di:'bʌŋk] *vt Fam* desacreditar, desprestigiar

debut ['debju:, 'deɪbju:] *n* debut *m*; **to make one's d.** debutar

debutante ['debjʊtɑ:nt] *n* debutante *f*

decade [de'keɪd, 'dekeɪd] *n* decenio *m*, década *f*

decadence ['dekədəns] *n* decadencia *f*

decadent ['dekədənt] *adj* decadente

decaffeinated [dɪ'kæfɪneɪtɪd] *adj* descafeinado(a)

decanter [dɪ'kæntə(r)] *n* jarra *f*, jarro *m*

decapitate [dɪ'kæpɪteɪt] *vt* decapitar

decay [dɪ'keɪ] **1** *n (of food, body)* descomposición *f*; *(of teeth)* caries *f inv*; *(of buildings)* desmoronamiento m; *Fig* decadencia f

2 *vi* descomponerse; *(teeth)* cariarse; *(building)* deteriorarse; *Fig* corromperse

deceased [dɪˈsiːst] *adj Fml* difunto(a), fallecido(a)

deceit [dɪˈsiːt] *n* (**a**) *(dishonesty)* falta f de honradez, falsedad f (**b**) *(trick)* engaño m, mentira f

deceitful [dɪˈsiːtfʊl] *adj* falso(a)

deceive [dɪˈsiːv] *vt (mislead)* engañar; *(lie to)* mentir

December [dɪˈsembə(r)] *n* diciembre m

decency [ˈdiːsənsɪ] *n* decencia f; *(modesty)* pudor m; *(morality)* moralidad f

decent [ˈdiːsənt] *adj* decente; *(person)* honrado(a); *Fam (kind)* simpático(a)

decentralize [diːˈsentrəlaɪz] *vt* descentralizar

deception [dɪˈsepʃən] *n* engaño m

⚠ Note that the Spanish word **decepción** is a false friend and is never a translation for the English word **deception**. In Spanish, **decepción** means "disappointment".

deceptive [dɪˈseptɪv] *adj* engañoso(a)

deceptively [dɪˈseptɪvlɪ] *adv* it looks d. simple parece engañosamente sencillo(a)

decibel [ˈdesɪbel] *n* decibelio m

decide [dɪˈsaɪd] **1** *vt* (**a**) *(decide)*; **to d. to do sth** decidir hacer algo (**b**) *(matter, question)* resolver, determinar

2 *vi (reach decision)* decidirse; **to d. against sth** decidirse en contra de algo

▸ **decide on** *vt insep (choose)* optar por

decided [dɪˈsaɪdɪd] *adj* (**a**) *(noticeable)* marcado(a) (**b**) *(resolute)* decidido(a); *(views)* categórico(a)

decidedly [dɪˈsaɪdɪdlɪ] *adv Fml* (**a**) *(clearly)* indudablemente (**b**) *(resolutely)* decididamente

deciding [dɪˈsaɪdɪŋ] *adj* decisivo(a)

deciduous [dɪˈsɪdjʊəs] *adj* de hoja caduca

decimal [ˈdesɪməl] **1** *adj* decimal; **d. point** coma f (de fracción decimal)

2 *n* decimal m

decimate [ˈdesɪmeɪt] *vt* diezmar

decipher [dɪˈsaɪfə(r)] *vt* descifrar

decision [dɪˈsɪʒən] *n* (**a**) decisión f; *Jur* fallo m; **to come to a d.** llegar a una decisión; **to make a d.** tomar una decisión (**b**) *(resolution)* resolución f

decisive [dɪˈsaɪsɪv] *adj* (**a**) *(resolute)* decidido(a), resuelto(a) (**b**) *(conclusive)* decisivo(a)

deck [dek] **1** *n* (**a**) *(of ship)* cubierta f; **on/ below d.** en/bajo cubierta; **d. chair** tumbona f (**b**) *(of bus)* piso m; **top d.** piso de arriba (**c**) *esp US (of cards)* baraja f (**d**) *(of record player)* plato m

2 *vt* **to d. out** adornar

declaration [dekləˈreɪʃən] *n* declaración f

declare [dɪˈkleə(r)] *vt* declarar; *(winner, innocence)* proclamar; *(decision)* manifestar

declared [dɪˈkleəd] *adj (opponent)* declarado(a); *(intention)* manifiesto(a)

decline [dɪˈklaɪn] **1** *n* (**a**) *(decrease)* disminución f (**b**) *(deterioration)* deterioro m; *(of health)* empeoramiento m; **to fall into d.** empezar a decaer

2 *vi* (**a**) *(decrease)* disminuir; *(amount)* bajar; *(business)* decaer (**b**) *(deteriorate)* deteriorarse; *(health)* empeorar (**c**) *(refuse)* negarse

3 *vt* (**a**) *(refuse)* rechazar (**b**) *Ling* declinar

declutch [diːˈklʌtʃ] *vi* soltar el embrague

decode [diːˈkəʊd] *vt* descifrar

decompose [diːkəmˈpəʊz] *vi* descomponerse

décor [ˈdeɪkɔː(r)] *n* decoración f; *Th* decorado m

decorate [ˈdekəreɪt] *vt* (**a**) *(adorn)* decorar, adornar (**with** con) (**b**) *(paint)* pintar; *(wallpaper)* empapelar (**c**) *(honour)* condecorar

decoration [dekəˈreɪʃən] *n* (**a**) *(decor)* decoración f; **Christmas decorations** adornos navideños (**b**) *(medal)* condecoración f

decorative [ˈdekərətɪv] *adj* decorativo(a)

decorator [ˈdekəreɪtə(r)] *n* decorador(a) m,f; *(painter)* pintor(a) m,f; *(paperhanger)* empapelador(a) m,f

decorum [dɪˈkɔːrəm] *n* decoro m

decoy [ˈdiːkɔɪ] *n Fig* señuelo m

decrease 1 *n* [ˈdiːkriːs] disminución f; *(in speed, size, price)* reducción f

2 *vi* [dɪˈkriːs] disminuir; *(strength)* menguar; *(price, temperature)* bajar; *(speed, size)* reducir

3 *vt* disminuir, reducir; *(price, temperature)* bajar

decree [dɪˈkriː] **1** *n* (**a**) *Pol & Rel* decreto m (**b**) *esp US Jur* sentencia f; **d. absolute** sentencia definitiva de divorcio; **d. nisi** sentencia provisional de divorcio

2 *vt Pol & Rel* decretar, pronunciar

decrepit [dɪˈkrepɪt] *adj* decrépito(a)

dedicate [ˈdedɪkeɪt] *vt* consagrar, dedicar

dedicated [ˈdedɪkeɪtɪd] *adj* ardiente; **d. to** entregado(a) a

dedication [dedɪˈkeɪʃən] *n* (**a**) *(act)* dedicación f; *(commitment)* entrega f; *(in book)* dedicatoria f

deduce [dɪˈdjuːs] *vt* deducir (**from** de)

deduct [dɪˈdʌkt] *vt* descontar (**from** de)

deduction [dɪˈdʌkʃən] *n* (**a**) *(conclusion)* conclusión f (**b**) *(subtraction)* descuento m

deed [diːd] *n* (**a**) *(act)* acto m; *(feat)* hazaña f (**b**) *Jur* escritura f; **title deeds** título m de propiedad

deem [diːm] *vt Fml* estimar

deep [diːp] **1** *adj* (**a**) profundo(a); *(breath, sigh)* hondo(a); **it's 10 m d.** tiene 10 m de profundidad (**b**) *(voice)* grave; *(shame)* grande; *(interest)* vivo(a) (**c**) *(colour)* oscuro(a) (**d**) *(serious)* grave

2 *adv* **to dig d.** cavar hondo; **to be d. in thought** estar absorto(a); **to look d. into sb's eyes** penetrar a algn con la mirada; *Fig* **nine d.** de nueve en fondo

deepen ['diːpən] **1** *vt (well)* profundizar, ahondar; *Fig (knowledge)* aumentar

2 *vi (river etc)* hacerse más hondo *or* profundo; *Fig (knowledge)* aumentar; *(colour, emotion)* intensificarse; *(sound, voice)* hacerse más grave

deep-freeze [diːp'friːz] **1** *n* congelador *m*

2 *vt* congelar

deep-fry [diːp'fraɪ] *vt* freír en mucho aceite

deeply ['diːplɪ] *adv* profundamente; *(breathe)* hondo; **to be d. in debt** estar cargado(a) de deudas

deep-rooted [diːp'ruːtɪd] *adj Fig* arraigado(a)

deep-seated [diːp'siːtɪd] *adj Fig* arraigado(a)

deep-set [diːp'set] *adj (eyes)* hundido(a)

deer [dɪə(r)] *n inv* ciervo *m*

deface [dɪ'feɪs] *vt (book, poster)* garabatear

de facto [deɪ'fæktəʊ] *adj & adv Fml* de hecho

defamation [defə'meɪʃən] *n* difamación *f*

default [dɪ'fɔːlt] **1** *vi* (**a**) *(not act)* faltar a sus compromisos (**b**) *Jur* estar en rebeldía (**c**) *(not pay)* suspender pagos

2 *n* (**a**) *(failure to act)* omisión *f* (**b**) *(failure to pay)* incumplimiento *m* de pago (**c**) *Jur* rebeldía *f*; **in d. of** a falta de; **to win by d.** ganar por incomparecencia del adversario

defaulter [dɪ'fɔːltə(r)] *n (on loan)* moroso(a) *m,f*; *Jur & Mil* rebelde *mf*

defeat [dɪ'fiːt] **1** *vt* (**a**) derrotar, vencer; *(motion)* rechazar (**b**) *Fig* frustrar

2 *n* (**a**) *(of army, team)* derrota *f*; *(of motion)* rechazo *m* (**b**) *Fig* fracaso *m*

defeatist [dɪ'fiːtɪst] *adj & n* derrotista *(mf)*

defect 1 *n* ['diːfekt] defecto *m*; *(flaw)* desperfecto *m*

2 *vi* [dɪ'fekt] desertar (**from** de); *(from country)* huir

defective [dɪ'fektɪv] *adj (faulty)* defectuoso(a); *(flawed)* con desperfectos; *(lacking)* incompleto(a)

defector [dɪ'fektə(r)] *n Pol* tránsfuga *mf*, tránsfuga *mf*

defence [dɪ'fens] *n* (**a**) defensa *f*; **the Ministry of D.** el Ministerio de Defensa; **to come to sb's d.** salir en defensa de algn (**b**) *usu sing Jur* defensa *f* (**c**) *Sport* [*Br* 'diːfens, *US* 'diːfens] **the d.** la defensa

defenceless [dɪ'fenslɪs] *adj* indefenso(a)

defend [dɪ'fend] *vt* defender

defendant [dɪ'fendənt] *n Jur* acusado(a) *m,f*

defender [dɪ'fendə(r)] *n* defensor(a) *m,f*; *Sport* defensa *mf*

defending [dɪ'fendɪŋ] *adj Sport* defensor(a); **d. champion** campeón(ona) *m,f* titular

defense [dɪ'fens, 'diːfens] *n US* = **defence**

defensive [dɪ'fensɪv] **1** *adj* defensivo(a)

2 *n* **to be on the d.** estar a la defensiva

defer¹ [dɪ'fɜː(r)] *vt* aplazar, retrasar

defer² [dɪ'fɜː(r)] *vi* **to d. to** deferir a

deference ['defərəns] *n Fml* deferencia *f*, respeto *m*; **out of** *or* **in d. to** por respeto o por deferencia a

defiance [dɪ'faɪəns] *n* (**a**) *(challenge)* desafío *m*; **in d. of** a despecho de (**b**) *(resistance)* resistencia *f*

defiant [dɪ'faɪənt] *adj (challenging)* desafiante; *(bold)* insolente

deficiency [dɪ'fɪʃənsɪ] *n* (**a**) *(lack)* falta *f*, carencia *f* (**b**) *(shortcoming)* defecto *m*

deficient [dɪ'fɪʃənt] *adj* deficiente; **to be d. in sth** carecer de algo

deficit ['defɪsɪt] *n* déficit *m*

defile [dɪ'faɪl] *vt Fml* (**a**) *(mind)* corromper; *(honour)* manchar; *(woman)* deshonrar (**b**) *(desecrate)* profanar

define [dɪ'faɪn] *vt* definir; *(duties, powers)* delimitar

definite ['defɪnɪt] *adj* (**a**) *(clear)* claro(a) *(progress)* notable (**b**) *(date, place)* determinado(a); **is it d.?** ¿es seguro?

definitely ['defɪnɪtlɪ] **1** *adv* sin duda; **he was d. drunk** no cabe duda de que estaba borracho

2 *interj* ¡desde luego!

definition [defɪ'nɪʃən] *n* definición *f*; **by d.** por definición

definitive [dɪ'fɪnɪtɪv] *adj* definitivo(a)

deflate [dɪ'fleɪt] *vt* (**a**) *(tyre etc)* desinflar (**b**) *Fig* rebajar; **to d. sb** hacer bajar los humos a algn (**c**) **to d. the economy** tomar medidas deflacionistas

deflationary [dɪ'fleɪʃənərɪ] *adj Econ* deflacionista

deflect [dɪ'flekt] *vt* desviar

deflection [dɪ'flekʃən] *n* desviación *f*

deforestation [diːfɒrɪ'steɪʃən] *n* deforestación *f*

deformed [dɪ'fɔːmd] *adj* deforme

deformity [dɪ'fɔːmɪtɪ] *n* deformidad *f*

defraud [dɪ'frɔːd] *vt* estafar

defrost [diː'frɒst] *vt* (**a**) *(freezer, food)* descongelar (**b**) *US (windscreen)* desempañar

deft [deft] *adj* hábil, diestro(a)

defunct [dɪ'fʌŋkt] *adj (person)* difunto(a); *(thing)* en desuso

defuse [diː'fjuːz] *vt (bomb)* desactivar; *Fig* **to d. a situation** reducir la tensión de una situación

defy [dɪ'faɪ] *vt* (**a**) *(person)* desafiar; *(law, order)* contravenir (**b**) *(challenge)* retar, desafiar

degenerate 1 *vi* [dɪ'dʒenəreɪt] degenerar (**into** en)

2 *adj & n* [dɪ'dʒenərɪt] degenerado(a) *(m,f)*

degrading [dɪ'greɪdɪŋ] *adj* degradante

degree [dɪ'griː] *n* (**a**) grado *m*; **to some d.** hasta cierto punto (**b**) *(stage)* etapa *f*; **by**

degrees poco a poco (**c**) *(qualification)* título *m*; *(doctorate)* doctorado *m*; **to have a d. in science** ser licenciado(a) en ciencias

dehydrated [di:har'dreɪtɪd] *adj (person)* deshidratado(a); *(vegetables)* seco(a)

de-ice [di:'aɪs] *vt* quitar el hielo a, deshelar

de-icer [di:'aɪsə(r)] *n* anticongelante *m*

deign [deɪn] *vi* dignarse

deity ['deɪtɪ] *n* deidad *f*

dejected [dɪ'dʒektɪd] *adj* desalentado(a), abatido(a)

delay [dɪ'leɪ] **1** *vt* (**a**) *(flight, train)* retrasar; *(person)* entretener; **delayed action** acción retardada (**b**) *(postpone)* aplazar

  2 *vi* **don't d.** no lo deje para más tarde

  3 *n* retraso *m*

delectable [dɪ'lektəbəl] *adj* delicioso(a)

delegate 1 *n* ['delɪgɪt] delegado(a) *m,f*

  2 *vt* ['delɪgeɪt] delegar (**to** en); **to d. sb to do sth** encargar a algn que haga algo

delegation [delɪ'geɪʃən] *n* delegación *f*

delete [dɪ'li:t] *vt* tachar, suprimir

deliberate 1 *adj* [dɪ'lɪbərɪt] *(intentional)* deliberado(a), intencionado(a); *(studied)* premeditado(a); *(careful)* prudente; *(unhurried)* pausado(a)

  2 *vt* [dɪ'lɪbəreɪt] deliberar

  3 *vi* deliberar (**on** or **about** sobre)

deliberately [dɪ'lɪbərɪtlɪ] *adv (intentionally)* a propósito; *(unhurriedly)* pausadamente

deliberation [dɪlɪbə'reɪʃən] *n* (**a**) *esp pl (consideration)* deliberación *f* (**b**) *(care)* cuidado *m*; *(unhurriedness)* pausa *f*

delicacy ['delɪkəsɪ] *n* (**a**) delicadeza *f* (**b**) *(food)* manjar *m* (exquisito)

delicate ['delɪkɪt] *adj* delicado(a); *(handiwork)* fino(a); *(instrument)* sensible; *(flavour)* sutil

delicious [dɪ'lɪʃəs] *adj* delicioso(a)

delight [dɪ'laɪt] **1** *n* (**a**) *(pleasure)* placer *m*; **he took d. in it** le encantó (**b**) *(source of pleasure)* encanto *m*, delicia *f*

  2 *vt* encantar

delighted [dɪ'laɪtɪd] *adj* encantado(a); *(smile)* de alegría; **I'm d. to see you** me alegro mucho de verte

delightful [dɪ'laɪtfʊl] *adj* encantador(a); *(view, person)* muy agradable; *(meal, weather)* delicioso(a)

delinquency [dɪ'lɪŋkwənsɪ] *n* delincuencia *f*; **juvenile d.** delincuencia juvenil

delinquent [dɪ'lɪŋkwənt] *adj & n* delincuente *(mf)*

delirious [dɪ'lɪrɪəs] *adj* delirante

deliver [dɪ'lɪvə(r)] *vt* (**a**) *(goods)* repartir, entregar; *(message)* dar; *(order)* despachar; *Fig* **to d. the goods** cumplir con la obligación (**b**) *(blow)* asestar; *(speech, verdict)* pronunciar (**c**) *Med* ayudar en el nacimiento de (**d**) *Fml (rescue)* liberar

delivery [dɪ'lɪvərɪ] *n* (**a**) *(of goods)* reparto *m*, entrega *f*; **to take d. of an order** recibir un

pedido; **d. note** albarán *m* de entrega; *Br* **d. van** furgoneta *f* de reparto (**b**) *(of speech)* declamación *f* (**c**) *(of baby)* parto *m*

delta ['deltə] *n Geog* delta *m*

delude [dɪ'lu:d] *vt* engañar; **don't d. yourself** no te hagas ilusiones

deluge ['delju:dʒ] **1** *n (flood)* inundación *f*; *(rain)* diluvio *m*; *Fig (of letters etc)* avalancha *f*

  2 *vt Fml* inundar

delusion [dɪ'lu:ʒən] *n* (**a**) *(state, act)* engaño *m* (**b**) *(false belief)* ilusión *f* (vana); **delusions of grandeur** delirios *mpl* de grandeza

de luxe [də'lʌks, də'lʊks] *adj* de lujo *inv*

delve [delv] *vi* **to d. into** *(pocket)* hurgar en; *(subject)* profundizar en

demand [dɪ'mɑ:nd] **1** *n* (**a**) solicitud *f*; *(for pay rise, rights)* reclamación *f*; *(need)* necesidad *f*; **on d.** a petición (**b**) *(claim)* exigencia *f*; **to be in d.** ser solicitado(a) (**c**) *Econ* demanda *f*

  2 *vt* (**a**) exigir; *(rights)* reclamar; **to d. that ...** insistir en que ... (+ *subj*) (**b**) *(need)* requerir

demanding [dɪ'mɑ:ndɪŋ] *adj* (**a**) *(person)* exigente (**b**) *(job)* agotador(a)

demean [dɪ'mi:n] *vt Fml* **to d. oneself** rebajarse

demeaning [dɪ'mi:nɪŋ] *adj Fml* humillante

demeanour, *US* **demeanor** [dɪ'mi:nə(r)] *n Fml* (**a**) *(behaviour)* comportamiento *m*, conducta *f* (**b**) *(bearing)* porte *m*

demented [dɪ'mentɪd] *adj Med* demente; *Fam* loco(a)

demise [dɪ'maɪz] *n Fml (death)* fallecimiento *m*; *Fig (of institution)* desaparición *f*; *(of ambition etc)* fracaso *m*

demist [di:'mɪst] *vt Aut* desempañar

demo ['deməʊ] *n Fam* manifestación *f*; **d. tape** maqueta *f*

demobilize [di:'məʊbɪlaɪz] *vt* desmovilizar

democracy [dɪ'mɒkrəsɪ] *n* democracia *f*

democrat ['deməkræt] *n* demócrata *mf*; *Pol* **Christian D.** democratacristiano(a) *m,f*; **Social D.** socialdemócrata *mf*

democratic [demə'krætɪk] *adj* democrático(a); *US Pol* **D. party** partido *m* demócrata

demographic [demə'græfɪk] *adj* demográfico(a)

demolish [dɪ'mɒlɪʃ] *vt (building)* derribar, demoler; *Fig (theory, proposal)* echar por tierra

demolition [demə'lɪʃən] *n* demolición *f*

demon ['di:mən] *n* demonio *m*

demonstrate ['demənstreɪt] **1** *vt* demostrar

  2 *vi Pol* manifestarse

demonstration [demən'streɪʃən] *n* (**a**) *(proof)* demostración *f*, prueba *f* (**b**) *(explanation)* explicación *f* (**c**) *Pol* manifestación *f*

demonstrative [dɪ'mɒnstrətɪv] *adj* expresivo(a)

demonstrator ['demənstreɪtə(r)] *n* manifestante *mf*

demoralize [dɪ'mɒrəlaɪz] *vt* desmoralizar

demoralizing [dɪ'mɒrəlaɪzɪŋ] *adj* desmoralizador(a), desmoralizante

demote [dɪ'məʊt] *vt* rebajar de graduación a

demure [dɪ'mjʊə(r)] *adj (person)* recatado(a)

den [den] *n* (**a**) *(of animal)* guarida *f* (**b**) *Fam (study)* estudio *m*

denial [dɪ'naɪəl] *n* (**a**) *(of charge)* desmentido *m* (**b**) *(of rights)* denegación *f*; *(of request)* negativa *f*

denim ['denɪm] *n* dril *m*; **d. skirt** falda tejana; **denims** tejanos *mpl*, vaqueros *mpl*

Denmark ['denmɑːk] *n* Dinamarca

denomination [dɪnɒmɪ'neɪʃən] *n* (**a**) *Rel* confesión *f* (**b**) *Fin (of coins)* valor *m*

denominator [dɪ'nɒmɪneɪtə(r)] *n* denominador *m*

denote [dɪ'nəʊt] *vt (show)* indicar; *(mean)* significar

denounce [dɪ'naʊns] *vt* denunciar; *(criticize)* censurar

dense [dens] *adj* (**a**) denso(a); *(crowd)* numeroso(a) (**b**) *Fam (stupid)* torpe

densely ['densli] *adv* densamente

density ['densɪtɪ] *n* densidad *f*

dent [dent] **1** *n* abolladura *f*
2 *vt (car)* abollar

dental ['dentəl] *adj* dental; **d. floss** hilo *m* dental; **d. surgeon** odontólogo(a) *m,f*; **d. surgery** *(place)* clínica *f* dental; *(treatment)* cirugía *f* dental

dentist ['dentɪst] *n* dentista *mf*

dentistry ['dentɪstrɪ] *n* odontología *f*

denture ['dentʃə(r)] *n (usu pl)* dentadura postiza

denunciation [dɪnʌnsɪ'eɪʃən] *n* denuncia *f*, condena *f*

deny [dɪ'naɪ] *vt* (**a**) *(repudiate)* negar; *(rumour, report)* desmentir; *(charge)* rechazar (**b**) *(refuse)* negar

deodorant [diː'əʊdərənt] *n* desodorante *m*

depart [dɪ'pɑːt] *vi* marcharse, irse; *Fig (from subject)* desviarse (**from** de)

department [dɪ'pɑːtmənt] *n* sección *f*; *(in university)* departamento *m*; *(in government)* ministerio *m*; **d. store** grandes almacenes *mpl*; *US* **D. of the Interior** Ministerio *m* del Interior

departure [dɪ'pɑːtʃə(r)] *n* partida *f*; *Av & Rail* salida *f*; *Av* **d. lounge** sala *f* de embarque

depend [dɪ'pend] **1** *vi (rely)* fiarse (**on** or **upon** de)
2 *v impers (be determined by)* depender (**on** or **upon** de); **it depends on the weather** según el tiempo que haga; **that depends** según

dependable [dɪ'pendəbəl] *adj (person)* responsable, fiable; *(income)* seguro(a); *(machine)* fiable

dependant, *US* **dependent** [dɪ'pendənt] *n* dependiente *mf*

dependence [dɪ'pendəns] *n* dependencia *f*

dependent [dɪ'pendənt] **1** *adj* dependiente; **to be d. on sth** depender de algo
2 *n US* = **dependant**

depict [dɪ'pɪkt] *vt Art* representar; *Fig* describir

deplete [dɪ'pliːt] *vt* reducir

deplorable [dɪ'plɔːrəbəl] *adj* lamentable

deplore [dɪ'plɔː(r)] *vt* deplorar

deploy [dɪ'plɔɪ] *vt Mil* desplegar; *Fig* utilizar

depopulate [diː'pɒpjʊleɪt] *vt* despoblar

deport [dɪ'pɔːt] *vt* expulsar *(* **from** de; **to** a*)*

deportation [diːpɔː'teɪʃən] *n* expulsión *f*

deportment [dɪ'pɔːtmənt] *n Fml* porte *m*

depose [dɪ'pəʊz] *vt* deponer

deposit [dɪ'pɒzɪt] **1** *n* (**a**) sedimento *m*; *Min* yacimiento *m*; *(in wine)* poso *m* (**b**) *(in bank)* depósito *m*; **d. account** cuenta *f* de ahorros (**c**) *Com (on purchase)* señal *f*; *(on rented car, flat)* depósito *m*; *(on house)* entrada *f*
2 *vt* depositar; *(into account)* ingresar

deposition [depə'zɪʃən] *n* (**a**) *(of leader)* destitución *f* (**b**) *Jur (of witness)* declaración *f*

depositor [dɪ'pɒzɪtə(r)] *n* depositante *mf*

depot ['depəʊ] *n* almacén *m*; *Mil* depósito *m*; *(bus garage)* garaje *m* (de autobuses); *US (bus station)* estación *f* de autobuses

depraved [dɪ'preɪvd] *adj (person)* depravado(a)

deprecate ['deprɪkeɪt] *vt* desaprobar, censurar

depreciate [dɪ'priːʃɪeɪt] *vi* depreciarse

depreciation [dɪpriːʃɪ'eɪʃən] *n* depreciación *f*

depress [dɪ'pres] *vt* (**a**) *(person)* deprimir (**b**) *Econ (profits)* reducir; *(trade)* dificultar (**c**) *Fml (switch, lever etc)* presionar; *(clutch, piano pedal)* pisar

depressed [dɪ'prest] *adj* (**a**) *(person)* deprimido(a); **to get d.** deprimirse (**b**) *(market)* en crisis (**c**) *(surface)* hundido(a)

depressing [dɪ'presɪŋ] *adj* deprimente

depression [dɪ'preʃən] *n* depresión *f*

deprivation [deprɪ'veɪʃən] *n (hardship)* privación *f*; *(loss)* pérdida *f*

deprive [dɪ'praɪv] *vt* privar (**of** de)

deprived [dɪ'praɪvd] *adj* necesitado(a)

dept *(abbr* **department)** dpt, dpto

depth [depθ] *n* (**a**) profundidad *f* (**b**) *Fig (of emotion)* intensidad *f*; *(of thought)* complejidad *f*; **to be in the depths of despair** estar completamente desesperado(a); **in d.** a fondo

deputation [depjʊ'teɪʃən] *n* delegación *f*

deputy ['depjʊtɪ] *n* (**a**) *(substitute)* suplente *mf*; **d. chairman** vicepresidente *m*; **d. head** subdirector(a) *m,f* (**b**) *Pol* diputado(a) *m,f*

derail [dɪ'reɪl] *vt* hacer descarrilar

deranged [dɪ'reɪndʒd] *adj* trastornado(a)

derby *n* (**a**) ['dɑːbɪ] *Sport* prueba *f* (**b**) ['dɜːrbɪ] *US* sombrero hongo

derelict ['derɪlɪkt] *adj* abandonado(a), en ruinas

deride [dɪ'raɪd] *vt* ridiculizar, burlarse de
derisive [dɪ'raɪsɪv] *adj* burlón(ona)
derisory [dɪ'raɪsərɪ] *adj* irrisorio(a)
derivative [dɪ'rɪvətɪv] **1** *adj (art, writing)* sin originalidad
2 *n (of word, substance)* derivado *m*
derive [dɪ'raɪv] **1** *vt* sacar
2 *vi (word)* derivarse (**from** de); *(skill)* provenir (**from** de)
derogatory [dɪ'rɒgətərɪ] *adj (remark, article)* despectivo(a); *(meaning)* peyorativo(a)
derrick ['derɪk] *n* torre *f* de perforación
descend [dɪ'send] **1** *vi* descender; **to d. from** *(be related to)* descender de
2 *vt (stairs)* bajar
descendant [dɪ'sendənt] *n* descendiente *mf*
descent [dɪ'sent] *n* (**a**) descenso *m* (**b**) *Fig (into madness, poverty)* caída *f* (**c**) *(slope)* declive *m* (**d**) *(ancestry)* ascendencia *f*
describe [dɪ'skraɪb] *vt* (**a**) describir (**b**) *(circle)* trazar
description [dɪ'skrɪpʃən] *n* (**a**) descripción *f*; **to defy d.** superar la descripción (**b**) *(type)* clase *f*
desecrate ['desɪkreɪt] *vt* profanar
desert¹ ['dezət] *n* desierto *m*
desert² [dɪ'zɜ:t] **1** *vt (place, family)* abandonar
2 *vi Mil* desertar (**from** de)
deserter [dɪ'zɜ:tə(r)] *n* desertor(a) *m,f*
desertion [dɪ'zɜ:ʃən] *n* abandono *m*; *Pol* defección *f*; *Mil* deserción *f*
deserts [dɪ'zɜ:ts] *npl* **to get one's just d.** llevarse su merecido
deserve [dɪ'zɜ:v] *vt (rest, punishment)* merecer; *(prize, praise)* ser digno(a) de
deservedly [dɪ'zɜ:vɪdlɪ] *adv* con (toda) razón
deserving [dɪ'zɜ:vɪŋ] *adj (person)* de valía; *(cause)* meritorio(a)
design [dɪ'zaɪn] **1** *n* (**a**) diseño *m* (**b**) *(drawing, blueprint)* plano *m* (**c**) *(layout)* disposición *f* (**d**) *(pattern)* dibujo *m* (**e**) *Fig (scheme)* intención *f*; **by d.** a propósito; *Fam* **to have designs on** tener puestas las miras en
2 *vt* diseñar
designate 1 *vt* ['dezɪgneɪt] (**a**) *(appoint)* designar, nombrar (**b**) *Fml (boundary)* señalar
2 *adj* ['dezɪgnɪt] designado(a)
designer [dɪ'zaɪnə(r)] *n Art* diseñador(a) *m,f*; **d. jeans** pantalones *mpl* de marca
desirable [dɪ'zaɪərəbəl] *adj* deseable; *(asset, offer)* atractivo(a)
desire [dɪ'zaɪə(r)] **1** *n* deseo *m*; **I haven't the slightest d. to go** no me apetece nada ir
2 *vt* desear
desist [dɪ'zɪst] *vi Fml* desistir (**from** de)
desk [desk] *n (in school)* pupitre *m*; *(in office)* escritorio *m*; *US* **d. clerk** recepcionista *mf*; **d. job** trabajo *m* de oficina; **news d.** redacción *f*; **reception d.** recepción *f*
desktop ['desktɒp] *n Comput* escritorio *m*; **d. computer** ordenador *m* de sobremesa, *Am*

computadora *f* de mesa; **d. publishing** autoedición *f*
desolate ['desəlɪt] *adj* (**a**) *(uninhabited)* desierto(a); *(barren)* yermo(a) (**b**) *(person)* desconsolado(a)
desolation [desə'leɪʃən] *n* (**a**) *(of place)* desolación *f*; *(by destruction)* asolamiento *m* (**b**) *(of person)* desconsuelo *m*
despair [dɪ'speə(r)] **1** *n* desesperación *f*; **to drive sb to d.** desesperar a algn
2 *vi* desesperar(se) (**of** de)
despairing [dɪ'speərɪŋ] *adj* desesperado(a)
despatch [dɪ'spætʃ] *n* & *vt* = dispatch
desperate ['despərɪt] *adj* (**a**) desesperado(a); *(struggle)* encarnizado(a) (**b**) *(need)* apremiante
desperately ['despərɪtlɪ] *adv (recklessly)* desesperadamente; *(struggle)* encarnizadamente; *(ill)* gravemente; *(in love)* locamente; *(difficult)* sumamente
desperation [despə'reɪʃən] *n* desesperación *f*; **in d.** a la desesperada
despicable [dɪ'spɪkəbəl] *adj* despreciable; *(behaviour)* indigno(a)
despise [dɪ'spaɪz] *vt* despreciar, menospreciar
despite [dɪ'spaɪt] *prep Fml* a pesar de
despondent [dɪ'spɒndənt] *adj* abatido(a)
despot ['despɒt] *n* déspota *mf*
dessert [dɪ'zɜ:t] *n* postre *m*; **d. wine** vino *m* dulce
dessertspoon [dɪ'zɜ:tspu:n] *n* (**a**) cuchara *f* de postre (**b**) **dessertspoon(ful)** *(measure)* cucharada *f* de postre
destination [destɪ'neɪʃən] *n* destino *m*
destined ['destɪnd] *adj* (**a**) **d. to fail** condenado(a) al fracaso (**b**) *(bound)* con destino (**for** a)
destiny ['destɪnɪ] *n* destino *m*
destitute ['destɪtju:t] *adj* indigente
destroy [dɪ'strɔɪ] *vt* destruir; *(vehicle, old furniture)* destrozar
destroyer [dɪ'strɔɪə(r)] *n Naut* destructor *m*
destruction [dɪ'strʌkʃən] *n* destrucción *f*; *Fig* ruina *f*
destructive [dɪ'strʌktɪv] *adj (gale etc)* destructor(a); *(tendency, criticism)* destructivo(a)
detach [dɪ'tætʃ] *vt (remove)* separar
detachable [dɪ'tætʃəbəl] *adj* separable (**from** de)
detached [dɪ'tætʃt] *adj* (**a**) *(separated)* separado(a); **d. house** casa *f* independiente (**b**) *(impartial)* objetivo(a)
detachment [dɪ'tætʃmənt] *n* (**a**) *(impartiality)* objetividad *f*; *(aloofness)* desapego *m* (**b**) *Mil* destacamento *m*
detail ['di:teɪl] **1** *n* (**a**) detalle *m*, pormenor *m*; **without going into detail(s)** sin entrar en detalles; **details** *(information)* información *f* (**b**) *Mil* destacamento *m*
2 *vt* (**a**) *(list)* detallar, enumerar (**b**) *Mil (appoint)* destacar

detailed ['di:teɪld] *adj* detallado(a), minucioso(a)

detain [dɪ'teɪn] *vt* (**a**) *Jur* detener (**b**) *(delay)* retener

detainee [di:teɪ'ni:] *n Pol* preso(a) *m,f*

detect [dɪ'tekt] *vt* (**a**) *(error, movement)* advertir; *(difference)* notar; *(smell, sound)* percibir (**b**) *(discover)* descubrir; *(enemy ship)* detectar; *(position)* localizar

detection [dɪ'tekʃən] *n* (**a**) descubrimiento *m*; *(of smell, sound)* percepción *f* (**b**) *(discovery) (of enemy ship)* detección *f*

detective [dɪ'tektɪv] *n* detective *mf*; **d. story** novela policíaca

detector [dɪ'tektə(r)] *n* aparato *m* detector

detention [dɪ'tenʃən] *n (of suspect etc)* detención *f*, arresto *m*; *Educ* **to get d.** quedarse castigado(a)

deter [dɪ'tɜː(r)] *vt (dissuade)* disuadir (**from** de); *(stop)* impedir

detergent [dɪ'tɜːdʒənt] *n* detergente *m*

deteriorate [dɪ'tɪərɪəreɪt] *vi* deteriorarse

deterioration [dɪtɪərɪə'reɪʃən] *n* empeoramiento *m*; *(of substance, friendship)* deterioro *m*

determination [dɪtɜːmɪ'neɪʃən] *n (resolution)* resolución *f*

determine [dɪ'tɜːmɪn] *vt* determinar

determined [dɪ'tɜːmɪnd] *adj (person)* decidido(a); *(effort)* enérgico(a)

deterrent [dɪ'terənt] **1** *adj* disuasivo(a) **2** *n* fuerza disuasoria

detest [dɪ'test] *vt* detestar, odiar

detonate ['detəneɪt] *vt & vi* detonar

detonation [detə'neɪʃən] *n* detonación *f*

detour ['di:tʊə(r)] *n* desvío *m*

detract [dɪ'trækt] *vi* quitar mérito (**from** a)

detractor [dɪ'træktə(r)] *n* detractor(a) *m,f*

detriment ['detrɪmənt] *n* perjuicio *m* (**to** de)

detrimental [detrɪ'mentəl] *adj* perjudicial (**to** para)

deuce [dju:s] *n (in tennis)* cuarenta iguales *mpl*

devaluation [di:vælju:'eɪʃən] *n* devaluación *f*

devastate ['devəsteɪt] *vt (city, area)* asolar; *Fig (person)* desolar

devastating ['devəsteɪtɪŋ] *adj (fire)* devastador(a); *(wind, flood)* arrollador(a)

devastation [devə'steɪʃən] *n* asolación *f*

develop [dɪ'veləp] **1** *vt* (**a**) desarrollar; *(trade)* fomentar; *(skill)* perfeccionar; *(plan)* elaborar; *(habit)* contraer; *(interest)* mostrar (**b**) *(natural resources)* aprovechar; *Constr (site)* urbanizar (**c**) *Phot* revelar **2** *vi* (**a**) *(body, industry)* desarrollarse; *(system)* perfeccionarse; *(interest)* crecer (**b**) *(appear)* crearse; *(evolve)* evolucionar

developer [dɪ'veləpə(r)] *n* (**property**) **d.** inmobiliaria *f*

development [dɪ'veləpmənt] *n* (**a**) desarrollo *m*; *(of trade)* fomento *m*; *(of skill)* perfec-

ción *f*; *(of character)* formación *f*; **d. aid** ayuda *f* al desarrollo (**b**) *(advance)* avance *m* (**c**) *(exploitation)* explotación *f* (**e**) *Constr* urbanización *f*

deviate ['di:vɪeɪt] *vi* desviarse (**from** de)

deviation [di:vɪ'eɪʃən] *n (from norm, route)* desviación *f* (**from** de); *(from truth)* alejamiento *m*

device [dɪ'vaɪs] *n* (**a**) aparato *m*; *(mechanism)* mecanismo *m* (**b**) *(trick, scheme)* ardid *m*

devil ['devəl] *n* diablo *m*, demonio *m*; **d.'s advocate** abogado(a) *m,f* del diablo; *Fam* **where the d. did you put it?** ¿dónde demonios lo pusiste?; **you lucky d.!** ¡vaya suerte que tienes!

devious ['di:vɪəs] *adj* (**a**) *(winding)* tortuoso(a) (**b**) *esp Pej (person)* taimado(a)

devise [dɪ'vaɪz] *vt* idear, concebir

devoid [dɪ'vɔɪd] *adj* desprovisto(a) (**of** de)

devolution [di:və'lu:ʃən] *n Pol* = transmisión de poderes a las regiones

devote [dɪ'vəʊt] *vt* dedicar; **she devoted her life to helping the poor** consagró su vida a la ayuda de los pobres

devoted [dɪ'vəʊtɪd] *adj* fiel, leal (**to** a)

devotee [devə'ti:] *n (of religion)* devoto(a) *m,f*; *(of theatre, sport)* aficionado(a) *m,f*; *Pol* partidario(a) *m,f*

devotion [dɪ'vəʊʃən] *n* devoción *f*; *(to cause)* dedicación *f*

devour [dɪ'vaʊə(r)] *vt* devorar

devout [dɪ'vaʊt] *adj* devoto(a)

dew [dju:] *n* rocío *m*

dexterity [dek'sterɪtɪ] *n* destreza *f*

dext(e)rous ['dekstrəs] *adj* diestro(a)

diabetes [daɪə'bi:ti:z, daɪə'bi:tɪs] *n* diabetes *f*

diabetic [daɪə'betɪk] *adj & n* diabético(a) *(m,f)*

diabolical [daɪə'bɒlɪkəl] *adj* (**a**) *(evil)* diabólico(a) (**b**) *Fam (unbearable)* espantoso(a)

diagnose ['daɪəgnəʊz] *vt* diagnosticar

diagnosis [daɪəg'nəʊsɪs] *n (pl* **diagnoses** [daɪəg'nəʊsi:z]) diagnóstico *m*

diagonal [daɪ'ægənəl] *adj & n* diagonal *(f)*

diagonally [daɪ'ægənəlɪ] *adv* en diagonal, diagonalmente

diagram ['daɪəgræm] *n* diagrama *m*; *(of process, system)* esquema *m*; *(of workings)* gráfico *m*

dial ['daɪəl, daɪl] **1** *n (of clock)* esfera *f*; *(of radio)* cuadrante *m*; *(of telephone)* disco *m*; *(of machine)* botón *m* selector **2** *vt & vi Tel* marcar; *Br* **dialling** *or US* **d. code** prefijo *m*; *Br* **dialling** *or US* **d. tone** señal *f* de marcar

dialect ['daɪəlekt] *n* dialecto *m*

dialogue, *US* **dialog** ['daɪəlɒg] *n* diálogo *m*

diameter [daɪ'æmɪtə(r)] *n* diámetro *m*

diametrically [daɪə'metrɪkəlɪ] *adv* diametralmente

diamond ['daɪəmənd] n (a) diamante m (b) (shape) rombo m

diaper ['daɪəpə(r)] n US pañal m

diaphragm ['daɪəfræm] n diafragma m

diarrhoea, US **diarrhea** [daɪə'rɪə] n diarrea f

diary ['daɪərɪ] n (a) diario m; **to keep a d.** llevar un diario (b) Br (for appointments) agenda f

dice [daɪs] 1 n (pl **dice**) dado m
2 vt Culin cortar en cuadritos

dichotomy [daɪ'kɒtəmɪ] n dicotomía f

dictate 1 vt [dɪk'teɪt] (letter, order) dictar
2 vi **to d. to sb** dar órdenes a algn
3 n ['dɪkteɪt] Fig **the dictates of conscience** los dictados de la conciencia

dictation [dɪk'teɪʃən] n dictado m

dictator [dɪk'teɪtə(r)] n dictador(a) m,f

dictatorship [dɪk'teɪtəʃɪp] n dictadura f

diction ['dɪkʃən] n dicción f

dictionary ['dɪkʃənərɪ] n diccionario m

did [dɪd] pt of **do**

die [daɪ] vi (a) morir, morirse; Fam Fig **to be dying for sth/to do sth** morirse por algo/de ganas de hacer algo (b) Fig (flame) extinguirse; Fig **to d. hard** (habit) tardar en desaparecer (c) (engine) calarse; (battery) agotarse
▸ **die away** vi desvanecerse
▸ **die down** vi (fire) extinguirse; (wind) amainar; (noise, excitement) disminuir
▸ **die off** vi morir uno por uno
▸ **die out** vi extinguirse

die-hard ['daɪhɑːd] n reaccionario(a) m,f

diesel ['diːzəl] n (a) (oil) gasoil m; **d. engine** motor m diesel (b) Fam (vehicle) vehículo m diesel

diet ['daɪət] 1 n (normal food) dieta f; (selected food) régimen m; **to be on a d.** estar a régimen
2 vi estar a régimen

dietician [daɪə'tɪʃən] n especialista mf en dietética

differ ['dɪfə(r)] vi (be unlike) ser distinto(a); (disagree) discrepar

difference ['dɪfərəns] n (a) (dissimilarity) diferencia f; **it makes no d. (to me)** (me) da igual; **what d. does it make?** ¿qué más da? (b) (disagreement) desacuerdo m

different ['dɪfərənt] adj diferente, distinto(a); **you look d.** pareces otro(a)

differentiate [dɪfə'renʃɪeɪt] 1 vt distinguir, diferenciar (**from** de)
2 vi distinguir (**between** entre)

differently ['dɪfərəntlɪ] adv de otra manera

difficult ['dɪfɪkəlt] adj difícil

difficulty ['dɪfɪkəltɪ] n dificultad f; (problem) problema m; **to be in difficulties** estar en un apuro

diffident ['dɪfɪdənt] adj tímido(a)

diffuse 1 adj [dɪ'fjuːs] (light) difuso(a); Fig vago(a)
2 vt [dɪ'fjuːz] difundir; (heat) desprender

dig [dɪg] 1 n (a) (poke) codazo m (b) Fam (gibe) pulla f (c) (archaeological) excavación f (d) Br **digs** (lodgings) alojamiento m; (room) habitación f alquilada
2 vt (pt & pp **dug**) (a) (earth) cavar; (tunnel) excavar (b) Fam Fig **to d. one's heels in** mantenerse en sus trece
3 vi (person) cavar; (animal) escarbar; (excavate) excavar
▸ **dig in** vi Mil atrincherarse
▸ **dig out** vt sep Fig (old suit) sacar; (information) descubrir
▸ **dig up** vt sep (weeds) arrancar; (buried object) desenterrar; (road) levantar; Fig sacar a relucir

digest 1 n ['daɪdʒest] (summary) resumen m
2 vt [dɪ'dʒest] (food) digerir; Fig (facts) asimilar

digestion [dɪ'dʒestʃən] n digestión f

digestive [dɪ'dʒestɪv] adj digestivo(a); Br **d. biscuit** galleta f integral

digger ['dɪgə(r)] n excavadora f

digit ['dɪdʒɪt] n (a) Math dígito m (b) Fml Anat dedo m

digital ['dɪdʒɪtəl] adj digital; **d. television** televisión f digital

dignified ['dɪgnɪfaɪd] adj (manner) solemne, serio(a); (appearance) majestuoso(a)

dignitary ['dɪgnɪtərɪ] n dignatario m

dignity ['dɪgnɪtɪ] n dignidad f

digress [daɪ'gres] vi apartarse del tema

dike [daɪk] n US = **dyke**

dilapidated [dɪ'læpɪdeɪtɪd] adj en mal estado

dilemma [dɪ'lemə, daɪ'lemə] n dilema m

diligent ['dɪlɪdʒənt] adj (worker) diligente; (inquiries, search) esmerado(a)

dilute [daɪ'luːt] 1 vt diluir; (wine, milk) aguar; Fig (effect, influence) atenuar
2 vi diluirse

dim [dɪm] 1 adj (**dimmer, dimmest**) (a) (light) débil, tenue; (room) oscuro(a); (outline) borroso(a); (eyesight) defectuoso(a); Fig (memory) vago(a); Fig (future) sombrío(a) (b) Fam (stupid) torpe
2 vt (light) bajar
3 vi (light) bajarse; (sight) nublarse; Fig (joy) extinguirse

dime [daɪm] n US moneda f de 10 centavos

dimension [daɪ'menʃən] n dimensión f

diminish [dɪ'mɪnɪʃ] vt & vi disminuir

diminutive [dɪ'mɪnjʊtɪv] 1 adj diminuto(a)
2 n Ling diminutivo m

dimly ['dɪmlɪ] adv vagamente

dimmer ['dɪmə(r)] n **d. (switch)** regulador m de voltaje

dimple ['dɪmpəl] n hoyuelo m

din [dɪn] n (of crowd) alboroto m; (of machinery) estruendo m

dine [daɪn] vi Fml cenar; **to d. out** cenar fuera

diner ['daɪnə(r)] n (a) (person) comensal mf (b) US (restaurant) restaurante barato

dinghy ▸ discharge

dinghy ['dɪŋɪ] *n* bote *m*; **(rubber) d.** bote neumático

dingy ['dɪndʒɪ] *adj* (**dingier, dingiest**) (**a**) *(dark)* oscuro(a) (**b**) *(dirty)* sucio(a) (**c**) *(colour)* desteñido(a)

dining car ['daɪnɪŋkɑː(r)] *n* vagón *m* restaurante

dining room ['daɪnɪŋruːm] *n* comedor *m*

dinner ['dɪnə(r)] *n (at midday)* comida *f*; *(in evening)* cena *f*; **d. jacket** smoking *m*; **d. service** vajilla *f*; **d. table** mesa *f* de comedor

dinosaur ['daɪnəsɔː(r)] *n* dinosaurio *m*

dint [dɪnt] *n* **by d. of** a fuerza de

diocese ['daɪəsɪs] *n* diócesis *f inv*

dioxide [daɪ'ɒksaɪd] *n* bióxido *m*

dip [dɪp] **1** *n* (**a**) *Fam (bathe)* chapuzón *m* (**b**) *(of road)* pendiente *f*; *(in ground)* depresión *f* (**c**) *Culin* salsa *f*
2 *vt* (**a**) bañar; *(spoon, hand)* meter (**b**) *Br Aut* **to d. one's lights** poner luces de cruce
3 *vi (road)* bajar
▸ **dip into** *vt insep* (**a**) *(savings)* echar mano de (**b**) *(book)* hojear

diphthong ['dɪfθɒŋ] *n* diptongo *m*

diploma [dɪ'pləʊmə] *n* diploma *m*

diplomacy [dɪ'pləʊməsɪ] *n* diplomacia *f*

diplomat ['dɪpləmæt] *n* diplomático(a) *m,f*

diplomatic [dɪplə'mætɪk] *adj* diplomático(a)

dipstick ['dɪpstɪk] *n* indicador *m* de nivel del aceite

dire ['daɪə(r)] *adj (urgent)* extremo(a); *(serious)* grave

direct [dɪ'rekt, 'daɪrekt] **1** *adj* (**a**) directo(a); **d. current** corriente continua (**b**) **the d. opposite** todo lo contrario
2 *adv* directamente
3 *vt* (**a**) dirigir; **can you d. me to a bank?** ¿me puede indicar dónde hay un banco? (**b**) *Fml (order)* mandar

direction [dɪ'rekʃən, daɪ'rekʃən] *n* (**a**) dirección *f*; **sense of d.** sentido *m* de la orientación (**b**) **directions** *(to place)* señas *fpl*; **directions for use** modo *m* de empleo (**c**) *Th* puesta *f* en escena

directive [dɪ'rektɪv, daɪ'rektɪv] *n* directiva *f*

directly [dɪ'rektlɪ, daɪ'rektlɪ] **1** *adv* (**a**) *(above etc)* exactamente, justo (**b**) *(speak)* francamente (**c**) *(descend)* directamente (**d**) *(come)* en seguida
2 *conj Fam* en cuanto

director [dɪ'rektə(r), daɪ'rektə(r)] *n* director(a) *m,f*

directory [dɪ'rektərɪ, daɪ'rektərɪ] *n Tel* guía telefónica; **d. enquiries** (servicio *m* de) información *f*

dirt [dɜːt] *n* suciedad *f*

dirt-cheap [dɜːt'tʃiːp] *adv & adj Fam* tirado(a)

dirty ['dɜːtɪ] **1** *adj* (**dirtier, dirtiest**) (**a**) sucio(a) (**b**) **to give sb a d. look** fulminar a algn con la mirada (**c**) *(joke)* verde; *(mind)* pervertido(a); **d. word** palabrota *f*; **d. old man**

viejo *m* verde
2 *vt* ensuciar

disability [dɪsə'bɪlɪtɪ] *n* incapacidad *f*, discapacidad *f*; **d. pension** pensión *f* por invalidez

disabled [dɪ'seɪbəld] **1** *adj* minusválido(a)
2 *npl* **the d.** los minusválidos

disadvantage [dɪsəd'vɑːntɪdʒ] *n* desventaja *f*; *(obstacle)* inconveniente *m*

disaffection [dɪsə'fekʃən] *n* descontento *m*

disagree [dɪsə'griː] *vi* (**a**) *(differ)* no estar de acuerdo (**with** con); **to d. on** *or* **over sth** reñir por algo (**b**) *(not match)* discrepar (**with** de *or* con) (**c**) **garlic disagrees with me** el ajo no me sienta bien

disagreeable [dɪsə'griːəbəl] *adj* desagradable

disagreement [dɪsə'griːmənt] *n* (**a**) desacuerdo *m*; *(argument)* riña *f* (**b**) *(non-correspondence)* discrepancia *f*

disallow [dɪsə'laʊ] *vt (goal)* anular; *(objection)* rechazar

disappear [dɪsə'pɪə(r)] *vi* desaparecer

disappearance [dɪsə'pɪərəns] *n* desaparición *f*

disappoint [dɪsə'pɔɪnt] *vt (person)* decepcionar, defraudar; *(hope, ambition)* frustrar

disappointed [dɪsə'pɔɪntɪd] *adj* decepcionado(a)

disappointing [dɪsə'pɔɪntɪŋ] *adj* decepcionante

disappointment [dɪsə'pɔɪntmənt] *n* decepción *f*

disapproval [dɪsə'pruːvəl] *n* desaprobación *f*

disapprove [dɪsə'pruːv] *vi* **to d. of** desaprobar

disarm [dɪs'ɑːm] **1** *vt* desarmar
2 *vi* desarmarse

disarmament [dɪs'ɑːməmənt] *n* desarme *m*

disarray [dɪsə'reɪ] *n Fml* **in d.** *(room, papers)* en desorden; *(hair)* desarreglado(a); *(thoughts)* confuso(a)

disaster [dɪ'zɑːstə(r)] *n* desastre *m*

disastrous [dɪ'zɑːstrəs] *adj* desastroso(a)

disband [dɪs'bænd] **1** *vt* disolver
2 *vi* disolverse

disbelief [dɪsbɪ'liːf] *n* incredulidad *f*

disc [dɪsk] *n* disco *m*; *Comput* disquete *m*; **d. jockey** disc-jockey *mf*, pinchadiscos *mf inv*

discard [dɪs'kɑːd] *vt (old things)* deshacerse de; *(plan)* descartar

discern [dɪ'sɜːn] *vt (shape, difference)* percibir; *(truth)* darse cuenta de

discerning [dɪ'sɜːnɪŋ] *adj (person)* perspicaz; *(taste)* refinado(a)

discharge *Fml* **1** *vt* [dɪs'tʃɑːdʒ] (**a**) *(smoke)* emitir; *(liquid)* echar; *(cargo)* descargar (**b**) *(prisoner)* soltar; *(patient)* dar de alta a; *(soldier)* licenciar; *(employee)* despedir (**c**) *(debt)* saldar (**d**) *(fulfil)* cumplir
2 *n* ['dɪstʃɑːdʒ] (**a**) *(of current, load)* descarga *f*; *(of gases)* escape *m* (**b**) *(of prisoner)*

liberación f; *(of patient)* alta f; *(of soldier)* licencia f **(c)** *(of debt)* descargo m **(d)** *(of duty)* cumplimiento m

disciple [dɪ'saɪpəl] n discípulo(a) m,f

discipline ['dɪsɪplɪn] **1** n disciplina f
2 vt *(child)* castigar; *(worker)* sancionar; *(official)* expedientar

disclaim [dɪs'kleɪm] vt *Fml* negar tener

disclose [dɪs'kləʊz] vt revelar

disclosure [dɪs'kləʊʒə(r)] n revelación f

disco ['dɪskəʊ] n *Fam (abbr* **discotheque)** disco f

discolour, *US* **discolor** [dɪs'kʌlə(r)] vt descolorir

discomfort [dɪs'kʌmfət] n **(a)** *(lack of comfort)* incomodidad f **(b)** *(pain)* malestar m **(c)** *(unease)* inquietud f

disconcert [dɪskən'sɜːt] vt desconcertar

disconcerting [dɪskən'sɜːtɪŋ] adj desconcertante

disconnect [dɪskə'nekt] vt desconectar **(from** de); *(gas, electricity)* cortar

disconnected [dɪskə'nektɪd] adj inconexo(a)

disconsolate [dɪs'kɒnsəlɪt] adj desconsolado(a)

discontent [dɪskən'tent] n descontento m

discontented [dɪskən'tentɪd] adj descontento(a)

discontinue [dɪskən'tɪnjuː] vt *Fml* abandonar; *(work)* interrumpir

discord ['dɪskɔːd] n **(a)** *Fml* discordia f **(b)** *Mus* disonancia f

discordant [dɪs'kɔːdənt] adj discordante

discotheque ['dɪskətek] n discoteca f

discount 1 n ['dɪskaʊnt] descuento m
2 vt [dɪs'kaʊnt] **(a)** *(price)* rebajar **(b)** *(view, suggestion)* descartar

discourage [dɪs'kʌrɪdʒ] vt *(dishearten)* desanimar; *(advances)* rechazar

discouraging [dɪs'kʌrɪdʒɪŋ] adj desalentador(a)

discover [dɪ'skʌvə(r)] vt descubrir; *(missing person, object)* encontrar

discovery [dɪ'skʌvərɪ] n descubrimiento m

discredit [dɪs'kredɪt] **1** n descrédito m
2 vt *(person, régime)* desacreditar; *(theory)* poner en duda

discreet [dɪ'skriːt] adj discreto(a); *(distance, silence)* prudente; *(hat, house)* modesto(a)

discrepancy [dɪ'skrepənsɪ] n diferencia f

discretion [dɪs'kreʃən] n discreción f; *(prudence)* prudencia f; **at the d. of ...** a juicio de ...

discriminate [dɪ'skrɪmɪneɪt] vi discriminar **(between** entre); **to d. against sth/sb** discriminar algo/a algn

discriminating [dɪ'skrɪmɪneɪtɪŋ] adj *(person)* entendido(a); *(taste)* refinado(a)

discrimination [dɪskrɪmɪ'neɪʃən] n **(a)** *(bias)* discriminación f **(b)** *(distinction)* diferenciación f

discuss [dɪ'skʌs] vt discutir; *(in writing)* tratar de

discussion [dɪ'skʌʃən] n discusión f

disdain [dɪs'deɪn] *Fml* **1** n desdén m
2 vt desdeñar

disdainful [dɪs'deɪnfʊl] adj *Fml* desdeñoso(a)

disease [dɪ'ziːz] n enfermedad f; *Fig* mal m

disembark [dɪsɪm'bɑːk] vt & vi desembarcar

disenchanted [dɪsɪn'tʃɑːntɪd] adj desencantado(a), desilusionado(a)

disengage [dɪsɪn'geɪdʒ] vt soltar; *Aut* **to d. the clutch** soltar el embrague, desembragar

disentangle [dɪsɪn'tæŋgəl] vt desenredar

disfigure [dɪs'fɪgə(r)] vt desfigurar

disgrace [dɪs'greɪs] **1** n **(a)** *(disfavour)* desgracia f; **to be in d.** estar desacreditado(a); **to fall into d.** caer en desgracia **(b)** *(shame)* vergüenza f, escándalo m
2 vt deshonrar, desacreditar

disgraceful [dɪs'greɪsfʊl] adj vergonzoso(a)

disgruntled [dɪs'grʌntəld] adj contrariado(a), disgustado(a)

disguise [dɪs'gaɪz] **1** n disfraz m; **in d.** disfrazado(a)
2 vt **(a)** *(person)* disfrazar **(as** de) **(b)** *(feelings)* disimular

disgust [dɪs'gʌst] **1** n **(a)** *(loathing)* repugnancia f, asco m **(b)** *(strong disapproval)* indignación f
2 vt **(a)** *(revolt)* repugnar, dar asco a **(b)** *(offend)* indignar

> ♪ Note that the Spanish words **disgusto** and **disgustar** are false friends and are never a translation for the English word **disgust**. In Spanish, **disgusto** means "annoyance, trouble", and **disgustar** means "to upset".

disgusting [dɪs'gʌstɪŋ] adj asqueroso(a), repugnante; *(behaviour, state of affairs)* intolerable

dish [dɪʃ] n *(for serving)* fuente f; *(course)* plato m; **to wash** *or* **do the dishes** fregar los platos
▸ **dish out** vt sep *Fam (food)* servir; *(books, advice)* repartir; **to d. it out (to sb)** *(criticize)* criticar (a algn)
▸ **dish up** vt sep *(meal)* servir

dishcloth ['dɪʃklɒθ] n trapo m de fregar

dishearten [dɪs'hɑːtən] vt desanimar

dishevelled, *US* **disheveled** [dɪ'ʃevəld] adj *(hair)* despeinado(a); *(appearance)* desaliñado(a)

dishonest [dɪs'ɒnɪst] adj *(person)* poco honrado(a); *(means)* fraudulento(a)

dishonesty [dɪs'ɒnɪstɪ] n *(of person)* falta f de honradez

dishonour, *US* **dishonor** [dɪs'ɒnə(r)] **1** n *Fml* deshonra f
2 vt *(name)* deshonrar

dishonourable, *US* **dishonorable** [dɪs'ɒnərəbəl] adj deshonroso(a)

dishtowel ['dɪʃtaʊəl] *n US* trapo *m* de cocina

dishwasher ['dɪʃwɒʃə(r)] *n* lavaplatos *m inv*; *(person)* lavaplatos *mf inv*

disillusion [dɪsɪ'luːʒən] *vt* desilusionar

disincentive [dɪsɪn'sentɪv] *n* freno *m*

disinfect [dɪsɪn'fekt] *vt* desinfectar

disinfectant [dɪsɪn'fektənt] *n* desinfectante *m*

disinherit [dɪsɪn'herɪt] *vt* desheredar

disintegrate [dɪs'ɪntɪgreɪt] *vi* desintegrarse

disintegration [dɪsɪntɪ'greɪʃən] *n* desintegración *f*

disinterested [dɪs'ɪntrɪstɪd] *adj* desinteresado(a)

disjointed [dɪs'dʒɔɪntɪd] *adj* inconexo(a)

disk [dɪsk] *n US* disco *m*; *Comput* disquete *m*; **on d.** en disco; **d. drive** disquetera *f*, disketera *f*

diskette [dɪs'ket] *n Comput* disquete *m*

dislike [dɪs'laɪk] **1** *n* antipatía *f*, aversión *f* (**of** a *or* hacia)
2 *vt* tener antipatía *or* aversión a *or* hacia

dislocate ['dɪsləkeɪt] *vt (joint)* dislocar

dislodge [dɪs'lɒdʒ] *vt* sacar

disloyal [dɪs'lɔɪəl] *adj* desleal

dismal ['dɪzməl] *adj* (**a**) *(prospect)* sombrío(a); *(place, weather)* deprimente; *(person)* triste (**b**) *(failure)* lamentable

dismantle [dɪs'mæntəl] *vt* desmontar

dismay [dɪs'meɪ] **1** *n* consternación *f*
2 *vt* consternar

dismiss [dɪs'mɪs] *vt* (**a**) *(idea)* descartar (**b**) *(employee)* despedir; *(official)* destituir (**c**) **to d. sb** *(from room, presence)* dar permiso a algn para retirarse (**d**) *(reject)* rechazar; *Jur* desestimar; *(case)* sobreseer

dismissal [dɪs'mɪsəl] *n* (**a**) *(of employee)* despido *m*; *(of official)* destitución *f* (**b**) *(of claim)* rechazo *m*; *Jur* desestimación *f*

dismount [dɪs'maʊnt] *vi Fml* apearse (**from** de)

disobedience [dɪsə'biːdɪəns] *n* desobediencia *f*

disobedient [dɪsə'biːdɪənt] *adj* desobediente

disobey [dɪsə'beɪ] *vt & vi* desobedecer; *(law)* violar

disorder [dɪs'ɔːdə(r)] *n* (**a**) *(untidiness)* desorden *m* (**b**) *(riot)* disturbio *m* (**c**) *(of organ, mind)* trastorno *m*; *(of speech)* defecto *m*

disorderly [dɪs'ɔːdəlɪ] *adj* (**a**) *(untidy)* desordenado(a) (**b**) *(meeting)* alborotado(a); *(conduct)* escandaloso(a)

disorganized [dɪs'ɔːgənaɪzd] *adj* desorganizado(a)

disorient [dɪs'ɔːrɪənt], **disorientate** [dɪs'ɔːrɪənteɪt] *vt* desorientar

disown [dɪs'əʊn] *vt* desconocer

disparaging [dɪ'spærɪdʒɪŋ] *adj* despectivo(a)

disparity [dɪ'spærɪtɪ] *n Fml* disparidad *f*

dispassionate [dɪs'pæʃənɪt] *adj* desapasionado(a)

dispatch [dɪ'spætʃ] **1** *n* (**a**) *(official message)* despacho *m*; *(journalist's report)* reportaje *m*; *(military message)* parte *m* (**b**) *(of mail)* envío *m*; *(of goods)* consignación *f*
2 *vt* (**a**) *(mail)* enviar; *(goods)* expedir (**b**) *Fam (food)* zamparse; *(job)* despachar

dispel [dɪ'spel] *vt* disipar

dispensary [dɪ'spensərɪ] *n* dispensario *m*

dispense [dɪ'spens] *vt (supplies)* repartir; *(justice)* administrar
▸ **dispense with** *vt insep (do without)* prescindir de

dispenser [dɪ'spensə(r)] *n* máquina expendedora; **cash d.** cajero automático; **soap d.** dosificador *m* de jabón

dispensing chemist [dɪspensɪŋ'kemɪst] *n Br* farmacéutico(a) *m,f*

dispersal [dɪ'spɜːsəl] *n* dispersión *f*

disperse [dɪ'spɜːs] **1** *vt* dispersar
2 *vi* dispersarse; *(fog)* disiparse

dispirited [dɪ'spɪrɪtɪd] *adj* abatido(a)

displace [dɪs'pleɪs] *vt* (**a**) desplazar; **displaced person** desterrado(a) *m,f* (**b**) *(supplant)* sustituir

display [dɪ'spleɪ] **1** *n* *(exhibition)* exposición *f*; *Comput* visualización *f*; *(of feelings, skills)* demostración *f*; *(of force)* despliegue *m*; **d. window** escaparate *m*; **military d.** desfile *m* militar
2 *vt* (**a**) mostrar; *(goods)* exponer; *Comput* visualizar (**b**) *(feelings)* manifestar

displease [dɪs'pliːz] *vt* disgustar; *(offend)* ofender

displeasure [dɪs'pleʒə(r)] *n* disgusto *m*

disposable [dɪ'spəʊzəbəl] *adj* (**a**) *(throwaway)* desechable (**b**) *(available)* disponible

disposal [dɪ'spəʊzəl] *n* (**a**) *(removal)* eliminación *f* (**b**) *(availability)* disponibilidad *f*; **at my d.** a mi disposición (**c**) *Fml (arrangement)* disposición *f* (**d**) *(sale)* venta *f*; *(of property)* traspaso *m*

dispose [dɪ'spəʊz] **1** *vi* **to d. of** *(remove)* eliminar; *(rubbish)* tirar; *(unwanted object)* deshacerse de; *(matter)* resolver; *(sell)* vender; *(property)* traspasar
2 *vt Fml (arrange)* disponer

disposed [dɪ'spəʊzd] *adj (inclined)* dispuesto(a)

disposition [dɪspə'zɪʃən] *n* (**a**) *(temperament)* genio *m* (**b**) *Fml (arrangement)* disposición *f*

disproportionate [dɪsprə'pɔːʃənɪt] *adj* desproporcionado(a) (**to** a)

disprove [dɪs'pruːv] *vt* refutar

dispute **1** *n* ['dɪspjuːt] *(disagreement)* discusión *f*; *(quarrel)* disputa *f*; **industrial d.** conflicto *m* laboral
2 *vt* [dɪ'spjuːt] *(claim)* refutar; *(territory)* disputar; *(matter)* discutir
3 *vi* discutir (**about** *or* **over** de *or* sobre)

disqualify [dɪs'kwɒlɪfaɪ] *vt* (**a**) *Sport* descalificar (**b**) *(make ineligible)* incapacitar

disquiet [dɪs'kwaɪət] *n* preocupación *f*, inquietud *f*

disregard [dɪsrɪ'gɑːd] **1** *n* indiferencia *f*; *(for safety)* despreocupación *f*
2 *vt* descuidar; *(ignore)* ignorar

disrepair [dɪsrɪ'peə(r)] *n* mal estado *m*; **in (a state of) d.** en mal estado; **to fall into d.** deteriorarse

disreputable [dɪs'repjʊtəbəl] *adj (person, area)* de mala fama; *(behaviour)* vergonzoso(a)

disrepute [dɪsrɪ'pjuːt] *n* mala fama, oprobio *m*

disrespectful [dɪsrɪ'spektfʊl] *adj* irrespetuoso(a)

disrupt [dɪs'rʌpt] *vt (meeting, traffic)* interrumpir; *(schedule etc)* desbaratar

disruption [dɪs'rʌpʃən] *n (of meeting, traffic)* interrupción *f*; *(of schedule etc)* desbaratamiento *m*

dissatisfaction [dɪssætɪs'fækʃən] *n* descontento *m*, insatisfacción *f*

dissatisfied [dɪs'sætɪsfaɪd] *adj* descontento(a)

dissect [dɪ'sekt, daɪ'sekt] *vt* disecar

disseminate [dɪ'semɪneɪt] *vt Fml* diseminar, difundir

dissent [dɪ'sent] **1** *n* disentimiento *m*
2 *vi* disentir

dissertation [dɪsə'teɪʃən] *n* disertación *f*; *Univ* tesina *f* (**on** sobre)

disservice [dɪs'sɜːvɪs] *n* perjuicio *m*; **to do sth/sb a d.** perjudicar algo/a algn

dissident [dɪsɪdənt] *adj & n* disidente *(mf)*

dissimilar [dɪ'sɪmɪlə(r)] *adj* distinto(a)

dissipate ['dɪsɪpeɪt] **1** *vt* (**a**) disipar (**b**) *(waste)* derrochar
2 *vi* disiparse

dissociate [dɪ'səʊʃɪeɪt] *vt* **to d. oneself** distanciarse

dissolute ['dɪsəluːt] *adj* disoluto(a)

dissolution [dɪsə'luːʃən] *n* disolución *f*; *(of agreement)* rescisión *f*

dissolve [dɪ'zɒlv] **1** *vt* disolver
2 *vi* disolverse

dissuade [dɪ'sweɪd] *vt* disuadir (**from** de)

distance ['dɪstəns] **1** *n* distancia *f*; **in the d.** a lo lejos; *Fam* **to stay the d.** completar la prueba
2 *vt* **to d. oneself (from)** distanciarse (de)

distant ['dɪstənt] *adj* (**a**) *(place, time)* lejano(a); *(look)* distraído(a) (**b**) *(aloof)* distante, frío(a)

distaste [dɪs'teɪst] *n* aversión *f*

distasteful [dɪs'teɪstfʊl] *adj* desagradable

distend [dɪ'stend] *Fml* **1** *vt* dilatar
2 *vi* dilatarse

distil, *US* **distill** [dɪ'stɪl] *vt* destilar

distillery [dɪ'stɪlərɪ] *n* destilería *f*

distinct [dɪ'stɪŋkt] *adj* (**a**) *(different)* diferente; **as d. from** a diferencia de (**b**) *(smell, change)* marcado(a); *(idea, intention)* claro(a)

distinction [dɪ'stɪŋkʃən] *n* (**a**) *(difference)* diferencia *f* (**b**) *(excellence)* distinción *f* (**c**) *Educ* sobresaliente *m*

distinctive [dɪ'stɪŋktɪv] *adj* distintivo(a)

distinguish [dɪ'stɪŋgwɪʃ] *vt* distinguir

distinguished [dɪ'stɪŋgwɪʃt] *adj* distinguido(a)

distinguishing [dɪ'stɪŋgwɪʃɪŋ] *adj* distintivo(a), característico(a)

distort [dɪ'stɔːt] *vt (misrepresent)* deformar; *(words)* tergiversar

distortion [dɪ'stɔːʃən] *n* deformación *f*; *(of sound, image)* distorsión *f*

distract [dɪ'strækt] *vt* distraer

distracted [dɪ'stræktɪd] *adj* distraído(a)

distraction [dɪ'strækʃən] *n (interruption)* distracción *f*; *(confusion)* confusión *f*; **to drive sb to d.** sacar a algn de quicio

distraught [dɪ'strɔːt] *adj (anguished)* afligido(a)

distress [dɪ'stres] **1** *n (mental)* angustia *f*; *(physical)* dolor *m*; **d. signal** señal *f* de socorro
2 *vt (upset)* apenar

distressing [dɪ'stresɪŋ] *adj* penoso(a)

distribute [dɪ'strɪbjuːt] *vt* distribuir, repartir

distribution [dɪstrɪ'bjuːʃən] *n* distribución *f*

distributor [dɪ'strɪbjʊtə(r)] *n* (**a**) *Com* distribuidor(a) *m,f* (**b**) *Aut* delco *m*

district ['dɪstrɪkt] *n (of country)* región *f*; *(of town)* barrio *m*; *US* **d. attorney** fiscal *m*; **d. council** corporación *f* local; **d. nurse** practicante *mf*

distrust [dɪs'trʌst] **1** *n* recelo *m*
2 *vt* desconfiar de

disturb [dɪ'stɜːb] *vt* (**a**) *(inconvenience)* molestar (**b**) *(silence)* romper; *(sleep)* interrumpir (**c**) *(worry)* perturbar (**d**) *(papers)* desordenar

disturbance [dɪ'stɜːbəns] *n* (**a**) *(of routine)* alteración *f* (**b**) *(commotion)* disturbio *m*, alboroto *m*

disturbed [dɪ'stɜːbd] *adj (mentally)* inestable

disturbing [dɪ'stɜːbɪŋ] *adj* inquietante

disuse [dɪs'juːs] *n* desuso *m*

disused [dɪs'juːzd] *adj* abandonado(a)

ditch [dɪtʃ] **1** *n* zanja *f*; *(at roadside)* cuneta *f*; *(for irrigation)* acequia *f*
2 *vt Fam (plan, friend)* abandonar

dither ['dɪðə(r)] *vi Br Fam* vacilar, titubear

ditto ['dɪtəʊ] *adv* ídem, lo mismo

dive [daɪv] **1** *n* (**a**) *(into water)* salto *m* de cabeza; *(of submarine)* inmersión *f*; *(of plane)* picado *m*; *Sport* salto (**b**) *Fam (bar)* antro *m*
2 *vi* (**a**) *(from poolside, diving board)* tirarse de cabeza; *(submarine)* sumergirse; *(plane)* bajar en picado; *Sport* saltar (**b**) *(move quickly)* **he dived for the phone** se precipitó hacia el teléfono

diver ['daɪvə(r)] *n (person)* buceador(a) *m,f*; *(professional)* buzo *m*; *Sport* saltador(a) *m,f*

diverge [daɪ'vɜːdʒ] *vi* divergir

diverse [daɪ'vɜːs] *adj (varied)* diverso(a),

variado(a); (different) distinto(a), diferente
diversion [daɪ'vɜ:ʃən] n (a) (distraction) distracción f (b) Br (detour) desvío m
divert [daɪ'vɜ:t] vt desviar
divide [dɪ'vaɪd] 1 vt dividir
  2 vi (road, stream) bifurcarse
  3 n división f, diferencia f
dividend ['dɪvɪdend] n Com dividendo m; Fig beneficio m
divine [dɪ'vaɪn] adj divino(a)
diving board ['daɪvɪŋbɔ:d] n trampolín m
divinity [dɪ'vɪnɪtɪ] n (a) divinidad f (b) (subject) teología f
division [dɪ'vɪʒən] n (a) división f (b) (sharing) reparto m (c) (of organization) sección f
divorce [dɪ'vɔ:s] 1 n divorcio m
  2 vt she divorced him se divorció de él
  3 vi divorciarse
divorcé [dɪ'vɔ:seɪ], **divorcée** [dɪvɔ:'si:] n divorciado(a) m,f
divulge [daɪ'vʌldʒ] vt Fml divulgar, revelar
DIY [di:aɪ'waɪ] n Br (abbr do-it-yourself) bricolaje m
dizziness ['dɪzɪnɪs] n vértigo m
dizzy ['dɪzɪ] adj (dizzier, dizziest) (a) (person) (unwell) mareado(a) (b) (height, pace) vertiginoso(a)
DJ ['di:dʒeɪ] n Fam (abbr disc jockey) pinchadiscos mf inv, disc-jockey mf
DNA [di:en'eɪ] n (abbr deoxyribonucleic acid) ADN m
do [du:, unstressed dʊ, də] 1 v aux

En el inglés hablado, y en el escrito en estilo coloquial, las formas negativas **do not**, **does not** y **did not** se transforman en **don't**, **doesn't** y **didn't**.

(3rd person sing pres **does**; pt **did**; pp **done**) (a) (in negatives and questions) (not translated in Spanish) **do you want some coffee?** ¿quieres café?; **do you drive?** ¿tienes carnet de conducir?; **don't you want to come?** ¿no quieres venir?; **he doesn't smoke** no fuma
  (b) (emphatic) (not translated in Spanish) **DO come with us!** ¡ánimo, vente con nosotros!; **I DO like your bag** me encanta tu bolso
  (c) (substituting main verb in sentence) (not translated in Spanish) **I don't believe him – neither do I** no le creo – yo tampoco; **I'll go if you do** si vas tú, voy yo; **I think it's dear, but he doesn't** a mí me parece caro pero a él no; **who went? – I did** ¿quién asistió? – yo
  (d) (in question tags) **he refused, didn't he?** dijo que no, ¿verdad?; **I don't like it, do you?** a mí no me gusta, ¿y a ti?
  2 vt (a) hacer; (task) realizar; (duty) cumplir con; **to do one's best** hacer todo lo posible; **to do sth again** volver a hacer algo; **to do sth for sb** hacer algo por algn; **to do the cooking/ cleaning** cocinar/limpiar; **to do the dishes** lavar los platos; **what can I do for you?** ¿en qué puedo servirle?; **what do you do (for a**

living)? ¿a qué te dedicas?; **what's to be done?** ¿qué se puede hacer?; Fam **he's done it!** ¡lo ha conseguido!
  (b) **do you do sportswear?** (make, offer) ¿(aquí) tienen ropa de deporte?
  (c) (distance) recorrer; (speed) **we were doing 80** íbamos a 80; **this car can do 120** este coche puede alcanzar los 120

Do, unido a muchos nombres, expresa actividades, como **to do the gardening**, **to do the ironing**, etc. En este diccionario, estas estructuras se encuentran bajo los nombres respectivos.

  3 vi (a) (act) hacer; **do as I tell you** haz lo que te digo; **you did right** hiciste bien
  (b) **he did badly in the exams** los exámenes le salieron mal; **how are you doing?** ¿qué tal?; **how do you do?** (greeting) ¿cómo está usted?; (answer) mucho gusto; **to do well** (person) tener éxito; (business) ir bien
  (c) **£5 will do** (suffice) con 5 libras será suficiente; Fam **that will do!** ¡basta ya!
  (d) **this cushion will do as a pillow** (be suitable) esto como cojín servirá de almohada; **this won't do** esto no puede ser
  4 n Fam (a) Br (party) fiesta f; (event) ceremonia f
  (b) **do's and don'ts** reglas fpl de conducta
  ▸ **do away with** vt insep (a) (abolish) abolir; (discard) deshacerse de (b) (kill) asesinar
  ▸ **do down** vt sep Fam (humiliate) hacer quedar mal
  ▸ **do for** vt insep Fam (destroy, ruin) arruinar; Fig **I'm done for if I don't finish this** estoy perdido(a) si no acabo esto
  ▸ **do in** vt Fam (a) (kill) cargarse (b) **I'm done in** (exhausted) estoy hecho(a) polvo
  ▸ **do over** vt sep Fam (a) US (repeat) repetir (b) Br (thrash) dar una paliza a
  ▸ **do up** vt sep (a) (wrap) envolver (b) (belt etc) abrochar; (laces) atar (c) (dress up) arreglar (d) Fam (redecorate) renovar
  ▸ **do with** vt insep (a) **I could do with a rest** (need) un descanso no me vendría nada mal (b) **to have** or **be to do with** (concern) tener que ver con
  ▸ **do without** vt insep pasar sin, prescindir de

docile ['dəʊsaɪl] adj dócil; (animal) manso(a)
dock¹ [dɒk] 1 n Naut **the docks** el muelle
  2 vi (a) (ship) atracar (b) (spacecraft) acoplarse
dock² [dɒk] vt (reduce) descontar
dock³ [dɒk] n Jur banquillo m (de los acusados)
docker ['dɒkə(r)] n estibador m
dockland ['dɒklænd] n zona f del puerto
dockyard ['dɒkjɑ:d] n astillero m
doctor ['dɒktə(r)] 1 n (a) Med médico(a) m,f (b) Univ doctor(a) m,f; **D. of Law** doctor en derecho

2 *vt Pej (figures)* falsificar; *(text)* arreglar; *(drink etc)* adulterar

doctorate ['dɒktərɪt] *n* doctorado *m*

doctrine ['dɒktrɪn] *n* doctrina *f*

document ['dɒkjəmənt] **1** *n* documento *m*; **documents** documentación *f*

2 *vt* documentar

documentary [dɒkjʊ'mentərɪ] *adj & n* documental *(m)*

dodge [dɒdʒ] **1** *vt* (**a**) *(blow)* esquivar; *(pursuer)* despistar; *Fig* (**b**) *Fam* **to d. one's taxes** engañar a Hacienda

2 *vi (move aside)* echarse a un lado

3 *n* (**a**) *(movement)* regate *m* (**b**) *Fam (trick)* truco *m*

Dodgem® ['dɒdʒəm] *n Br* **D. (car)** coche *m* de choque

dodgy ['dɒdʒɪ] *adj* (**dodgier, dodgiest**) *Br Fam (risky)* arriesgado(a); *(tricky)* difícil; *(dishonest, not working properly)* chungo(a)

doe [dəʊ] *n (of deer)* gama *f*; *(of rabbit)* coneja *f*

does [dʌz] *3rd person sing pres of* **do**

doesn't ['dʌzənt] = **does not**

dog [dɒg] **1** *n* (**a**) perro(a) *m,f*; *Fam Fig* **a d.'s life** una vida de perros; **d. collar** *(of dog)* collar *m* de perro; *Fam Rel* alzacuello *m* (**b**) *(male canine)* macho *m*; *(fox)* zorro *m*; *(wolf)* lobo *m* (**c**) *Fam* **dirty d.** canalla *m* (**d**) *US Fam (disappointment)* desastre *m*

2 *vt* acosar; **to d. sb's footsteps** seguir los pasos de algn; *Fig* **dogged by bad luck** perseguido(a) por la mala suerte

dog-eared ['dɒgɪəd] *adj (book)* con los bordes de las páginas dobladas; *(shabby)* sobado(a)

dogged ['dɒgɪd] *adj* obstinado(a), tenaz

doghouse ['dɒghaʊs] *n US Fam* perrera *f*; *Fig* **to be in the d.** estar castigado(a)

dogma ['dɒgmə] *n* dogma *m*

dogmatic [dɒg'mætɪk] *adj* dogmático(a)

dogsbody ['dɒgzbɒdɪ] *n Br Fam (drudge)* burro *m* de carga

doh [dəʊ] *n Mus* do *m*

doing ['duːɪŋ] *n* (**a**) *(action)* obra *f*; **it was none of my d.** yo no tuve nada que ver; *Fig* **it took some d.** costó trabajo hacerlo (**b**) **doings** *(activities)* actividades *fpl*

do-it-yourself [duːɪtjə'self] *n* bricolaje *m*

doldrums ['dɒldrəmz] *npl Fam Fig* **to be in the d.** *(person)* estar abatido(a); *(trade)* estar estancado(a)

dole [dəʊl] *Fam* **1** *n Br* **the d.** el paro; **to be on the d.** cobrar el paro; **to go on the d.** apuntarse al paro; *Fig* **d. queue** los parados

2 *vt* **to d. (out)** repartir

doleful ['dəʊlfʊl] *adj* triste, afligido(a)

doll [dɒl] **1** *n* (**a**) *(toy)* muñeca *f* (**b**) *US Fam (girl)* muñeca *f*

2 *vt Fam* **to d. oneself up** ponerse guapa

dollar ['dɒlə(r)] *n* dólar *m*

dolphin ['dɒlfɪn] *n* delfín *m*

domain [də'meɪn] *n* (**a**) *(sphere)* campo *m*, esfera *f*; **that's not my d.** no es de mi competencia (**b**) *(territory)* dominio *m* (**c**) *Comput* dominio *m*; **d. name** nombre *m* de dominio

dome [dəʊm] *n (roof)* cúpula *f*; *(ceiling)* bóveda *f*

domestic [də'mestɪk] *adj* (**a**) *(appliance, pet)* doméstico(a); **d. science** economía doméstica (**b**) *(home-loving)* casero(a) (**c**) *(flight, news)* nacional; *(trade, policy)* interior

domesticate [də'mestɪkeɪt] *vt (make home-loving)* volver hogareño(a) *or* casero(a)

domicile ['dɒmɪsaɪl] *n* domicilio *m*

dominant ['dɒmɪnənt] *adj* dominante

dominate ['dɒmɪneɪt] *vt & vi* dominar

domineering [dɒmɪ'nɪərɪŋ] *adj* dominante

Dominican [də'mɪnɪkən] *adj & n (of Dominica)* dominicano(a) *(m,f)*; **D. Republic** República Dominicana

dominion [də'mɪnjən] *n* dominio *m*

domino ['dɒmɪnəʊ] *n (pl dominoes) (piece)* ficha *f* de dominó; **dominoes** *(game)* dominó *m*

don [dɒn] *n Br Univ* catedrático(a) *m,f*

donate [dəʊ'neɪt] *vt* donar

donation [dəʊ'neɪʃən] *n* donativo *m*

done [dʌn] **1** *adj* (**a**) *(finished)* terminado(a); **it's over and d. with** se acabó (**b**) *Fam (tired)* rendido(a) (**c**) *(meat)* hecho(a); *(vegetables)* cocido(a)

2 *pp of* **do**

donkey ['dɒŋkɪ] *n* burro(a) *m,f*

donor ['dəʊnə(r)] *n* donante *m*

don't [dəʊnt] = **do not**

donut ['dəʊnʌt] *n US* dónut® *m*

doodle ['duːdəl] *vi Fam (write)* garabatear; *(draw)* hacer dibujos

doom [duːm] **1** *n (fate)* destino *m* (funesto); *(ruin)* perdición *f*; *(death)* muerte *f*

2 *vt usu pass (destine)* destinar; **doomed to failure** condenado(a) al fracaso

doomsday ['duːmzdeɪ] *n* día *m* del juicio final

door [dɔː(r)] *n* puerta *f*; **front/back d.** puerta principal/trasera; *Fig* **behind closed doors** a puerta cerrada; **d. handle** manilla *f* (de la puerta); **d. knocker** picaporte *m*; **next d. (to)** (en) la casa de al lado (de)

doorbell ['dɔːbel] *n* timbre *m* (de la puerta)

doorknob ['dɔːnɒb] *n* pomo *m*

doorman ['dɔːmən] *n* portero *m*

doormat ['dɔːmæt] *n* felpudo *m*, esterilla *f*; *Fam Fig (person)* trapo *m*

doorstep ['dɔːstep] *n* peldaño *m*; *Fig* **on one's d.** a la vuelta de la esquina

door-to-door ['dɔːtə'dɔː(r)] *adj* a domicilio

doorway ['dɔːweɪ] *n* portal *m*, entrada *f*

dope [dəʊp] **1** *n* (**a**) *Fam (drug)* chocolate *m* (**b**) *Fam (person)* imbécil *mf*

2 *vt (food, drink)* adulterar con drogas; *Sport* dopar

dop(e)y ['dəʊpɪ] *adj* (**dopier, dopiest**) *Fam*

(**a**) *(sleepy)* medio dormido(a); *(fuddled)* atontado(a) (**b**) *Fam (silly)* torpe

dork [dɔ:k] *n US Fam* petardo(a) *m,f*

dormant ['dɔ:mənt] *adj* inactivo(a); *Fig (rivalry)* latente

dormitory ['dɔ:mɪtərɪ] *n* (**a**) *(in school)* dormitorio *m* (**b**) *US (in university)* colegio *m* mayor

dosage ['dəʊsɪdʒ] *n Fml (amount)* dosis *f inv*

dose [dəʊs] **1** *n* dosis *f inv*
   2 *vt (patient)* medicar

doss [dɒs] *vi Br Fam* sobar

dosshouse ['dɒshaʊs] *n Br Fam* pensión *f* de mala muerte

dossier ['dɒsɪeɪ] *n* expediente *m*

dot [dɒt] **1** *n* punto *m*; **on the d.** en punto; *Comput* **d. matrix printer** impresora *f* matricial *or* de agujas
   2 *vt* (**a**) *Fam* **to d. one's i's and cross one's t's** poner los puntos sobre las íes (**b**) *(scatter)* esparcir, salpicar

dote [dəʊt] *vi* **to d. on sb** chochear con algn

double ['dʌbəl] **1** *adj* doble; **it's d. the price** cuesta dos veces más; **d. bass** contrabajo *m*; **d. bed** cama *f* de matrimonio; **d. bill** programa *m* doble; *Br* **d. cream** nata *f* para montar; **d. glazing** ventana *f* doble
   2 *adv* doble; **folded d.** doblado(a) por la mitad
   3 *n* (**a**) vivo retrato *m*; *Cin & Th* doble *m* (**b**) **to earn d.** ganar el doble; *Fam* **at** *or* **on the d.** corriendo (**c**) **doubles** *(in chess)* (partido *m* de) dobles *mpl*
   4 *vt* doblar; *Fig (efforts)* redoblar
   5 *vi* (**a**) *(increase)* doblarse (**b**) **to d. as** *(serve)* hacer las veces de
   ▸**double back** *vi* **to d. back on one's tracks** volver sobre sus pasos
   ▸**double up** **1** *vt sep (bend)* doblar
   2 *vi* (**a**) *(bend)* doblarse (**b**) *(share room)* compartir la habitación (**with** con)

double-barrelled ['dʌbəlbærəld] *adj* (**a**) *(gun)* de dos cañones (**b**) *Br (surname)* compuesto(a)

double-breasted ['dʌbəlbrestɪd] *adj* cruzado(a)

double-check [dʌbəl'tʃek] *vt & vi* repasar dos veces

double-cross [dʌbəl'krɒs] *Fam* **1** *vt* engañar, traicionar
   2 *n* engaño *m*, traición *f*

double-decker [dʌbəl'dekə(r)] *n Br* **d. (bus)** autobús *m* de dos pisos

double-edged ['dʌbəledʒd] *adj* de doble filo

doubt [daʊt] **1** *n* duda *f*; **beyond (all) d.** sin duda alguna; **no d.** sin duda; **there's no d. about it** no cabe la menor duda; **to be in d. about sth** dudar algo; **to be open to d.** *(fact)* ser dudoso(a); *(outcome)* ser incierto(a)
   2 *vt* (**a**) *(distrust)* desconfiar de (**b**) *(not be sure of)* dudar; **I d. if** *or* **whether he'll come** dudo que venga

doubtful ['daʊtfʊl] *adj* (**a**) *(future)* dudoso(a), *(look)* dubitativo(a); **I'm a bit d. about it** no me convence del todo; **it's d. whether ..** no se sabe seguro si ... (**b**) *(questionable)* sospechoso(a)

doubtless ['daʊtlɪs] *adv* sin duda, seguramente

dough [dəʊ] *n* (**a**) *(for bread)* masa *f*; *(for pastries)* pasta *f* (**b**) *Fam (money)* pasta *f*

doughnut ['dəʊnʌt] *n* rosquilla *f*, dónut® *m*

douse [daʊs] *vt* (**a**) *(soak)* mojar (**b**) *(extinguish)* apagar

dove [dʌv] *n* paloma *f*

dovetail ['dʌvteɪl] *vt Fig (plans)* sincronizar

dowdy ['daʊdɪ] *adj* (**dowdier, dowdiest**) poco elegante

down¹ [daʊn] **1** *prep* (**a**) *(to or at a lower level)* **d. the river** río abajo; **to go d. the road** bajar la calle
   (**b**) *(along)* por
   2 *adv* (**a**) *(to lower level)* (hacia) abajo; *(to floor)* al suelo; *(to ground)* a tierra; **to fall d.** caerse; **to go d.** *(price, person)* bajar; *(sun)* ponerse
   (**b**) *(at lower level)* abajo; **d. there** allí abajo **face d.** boca abajo; *Fig* **to be d. with a cold** estar resfriado(a); *Fam Fig* **to feel d.** estar deprimido(a); *Fam Fig* **d. under** en/a Australia y Nueva Zelanda
   (**c**) **I'm d. to my last stamp** no me queda más que un solo sello; **sales are d. by 5 percent** las ventas han bajado un 5 por ciento
   (**d**) **to take sth d.** *(in writing)* apuntar algo
   (**e**) **d. through the ages** a través de los siglos
   3 *adj (payment)* al contado; *(on property)* de entrada
   4 *vt Fam (drink)* tomarse de un trago; *(food)* zamparse
   5 *n* **ups and downs** altibajos *mpl*
   6 *interj* **d. with taxes!** ¡abajo los impuestos!

down² [daʊn] *n* (**a**) *(on bird)* plumón *m* (**b**) *(on cheek, peach)* pelusa *f*; *(on body)* vello *m*

down-and-out ['daʊnən'aʊt] **1** *adj* en las últimas
   2 *n* vagabundo(a) *m,f*

downbeat ['daʊnbi:t] *adj Fam (gloomy)* deprimido(a)

downcast ['daʊnkɑ:st] *adj* abatido(a)

downfall ['daʊnfɔ:l] *n (of regime)* caída *f*; *(of person)* perdición *f*

downgrade ['daʊngreɪd] *vt* degradar

downhearted [daʊn'hɑ:tɪd] *adj* desalentado(a)

downhill [daʊn'hɪl] **1** *adj (skiing)* de descenso; *Fam* **after his first exam, the rest were all d.** después del primer examen, los demás le fueron sobre ruedas
   2 *adv* **to go d.** ir cuesta abajo; *Fig (standards)* deteriorarse

download ['daʊn'ləʊd] *vt Comput* bajar, descargar

down-market [daʊn'mɑːkɪt] **1** *adj* barato(a) **2** *adv* **to move d.** *(of company)* producir artículos más asequibles

downpour ['daʊnpɔː(r)] *n* chaparrón *m*

downright ['daʊnraɪt] *Fam* **1** *adj (blunt)* tajante; *(categorical)* categórico(a); **it's a d. lie** es una mentira y gorda **2** *adv (totally)* completamente

downsizing ['daʊnsaɪzɪŋ] *n* Com reajuste *m* de plantillas

downstairs 1 *adv* [daʊn'steəz] abajo; *(to ground floor)* a la planta baja; **to go d.** bajar la escalera **2** *adj* ['daʊnsteəz] *(on ground floor)* de la planta baja

downstream [daʊn'striːm] *adv* río abajo

down-to-earth [daʊntʊ'ɜːθ] *adj* realista

downtown [daʊn'taʊn] *adv US* en el centro (de la ciudad)

downturn ['daʊntɜːn] *n* baja *f*

downward ['daʊnwəd] **1** *adj (slope)* descendente; *(look)* hacia abajo; *Fin (tendency)* a la baja **2** *adv* = **downwards**

downwards ['daʊnwədz] *adv* hacia abajo

dowry ['daʊərɪ] *n* dote *f*

doz *(abbr* **dozen)** docena *f*

doze [dəʊz] **1** *vi* dormitar **2** *n* cabezada *f*; **to have a d.** echar una cabezada
▸ **doze off** *vi* quedarse dormido(a)

dozen ['dʌzən] *n* docena *f*; **half a d./a d. eggs** media docena/una docena de huevos; *Fam* **dozens of** un montón de

Dr *(abbr* **Doctor)** Dr., Dra.

drab [dræb] *adj* **(drabber, drabbest)** (a) *(ugly)* feo(a); *(dreary)* monótono(a), gris (b) *(colour)* pardo(a)

draft [drɑːft] **1** *n* (a) borrador *m* (b) *(bill of exchange)* giro *m* (c) *US* servicio militar obligatorio (d) *US* = **draught** **2** *vt* (a) hacer un borrador de (b) *US Mil* reclutar

draftsman ['drɑːftsmən] *n US* = **draughtsman**

drag [dræg] **1** *vt* (a) *(pull)* arrastrar; *Fig* **to d. one's heels (over sth)** dar largas (a algo) (b) *(lake)* rastrear **2** *vi* (a) *(trail)* arrastrarse (b) *(person)* rezagarse **3** *n* (a) *Tech* resistencia *f* (aerodinámica) (b) *Fam (nuisance)* lata *f* (c) *Fam (on cigarette)* calada *f* (d) *Fam* **to be in d.** ir vestido de mujer (e) *US Fam* **the main d.** la calle mayor *or* principal
▸ **drag off** *vt sep* llevarse arrastrando
▸ **drag on** *vi (war, strike)* hacerse interminable
▸ **drag out** *vt sep (speech etc)* alargar

dragon ['drægən] *n* dragón *m*

dragonfly ['drægənflaɪ] *n* libélula *f*

drain [dreɪn] **1** *n* (a) *(for water)* desagüe *m*; *(for sewage)* alcantarilla *f* (b) *(grating)* sumidero *m* (c) *Fig* **the boys are a d. on her strength** los niños la dejan agotada **2** *vt* (a) *(marsh etc)* avenar; *(reservoir)* desecar (b) *(crockery)* escurrir (c) *(empty) (glass)* apurar; *Fig (capital etc)* agotar **3** *vi* (a) *(crockery)* escurrirse (b) **to d. (away)** *(liquid)* irse

drainage ['dreɪnɪdʒ] *n (of marsh)* drenaje *m*; *(of reservoir, building)* desagüe *m*; *(of town)* alcantarillado *m*

drainpipe ['dreɪnpaɪp] *n* tubo *m* de desagüe

dram [dræm] *n Fam* trago *m (de whisky)*

drama ['drɑːmə] *n* (a) *(play)* obra *f* de teatro; *Fig* drama *m* (b) *(subject)* teatro *m*

dramatic [drə'mætɪk] *adj* (a) *(change)* impresionante; *(moment)* emocionante (b) *Th* dramático(a), teatral

dramatist ['dræmətɪst] *n* dramaturgo(a) *m,f*

dramatization [dræmətaɪ'zeɪʃən] *n* adaptación *f* teatral

dramatize ['dræmətaɪz] *vt* (a) *(adapt)* hacer una adaptación teatral de (b) *(exaggerate)* dramatizar

drank [dræŋk] *pt of* **drink**

drape [dreɪp] **1** *vt* **to d. sth over sth** colgar algo sobre algo; **draped with** cubierto(a) de **2** *n* (a) *(of fabric)* caída *f* (b) *US* cortina *f*

draper ['dreɪpə(r)] *n Br* pañero(a) *m,f*

drastic ['dræstɪk] *adj* (a) *(measures)* drástico(a), severo(a) (b) *(change)* radical

draught [drɑːft] **1** *n* (a) *(of cold air)* corriente *f* (de aire) (b) *(of liquid)* trago *m* (c) **d. (beer)** cerveza *f* de barril (d) *Br* **draughts** *(game)* damas *fpl* (e) *Naut* calado *m* **2** *adj (animal)* de tiro

draughtboard ['drɑːftbɔːd] *n Br* tablero *m* de damas

draughtsman ['drɑːftsmən] *n* delineante *mf*

draw [drɔː] **1** *vt* (*pt* **drew**; *pp* **drawn**) (a) *(picture)* dibujar; *(line)* trazar (b) *(pull)* tirar de; *(train, carriage)* arrastrar; *(curtains) (open)* descorrer; *(close)* correr; *(blinds)* bajar (c) *(remove)* sacar; *(salary)* cobrar; *(cheque)* librar (d) *(attract)* atraer; *(attention)* llamar (e) *Fig (strength)* sacar (f) **to d. breath** respirar (g) **to d. lots** echar a suertes (h) *(comparison)* hacer; *(conclusion)* sacar **2** *vi* (a) *(sketch)* dibujar (b) *(move)* **the train drew into/out of the station** el tren entró en/salió de la estación; **to d. apart (from)** separarse (de); **to d. to an end** acabarse (c) *Sport* **they drew two all** empataron a dos **3** *n* (a) *(raffle)* sorteo *m* (b) *Sport* empate *m* (c) *Fig (attraction)* atracción *f*
▸ **draw in** *vi (days)* acortarse
▸ **draw on** *vt insep (savings)* recurrir a;

(experience) aprovecharse de

▸ **draw out** *vt sep* (a) *(make long)* alargar (b) *(encourage to speak)* desatar la lengua a (c) *(from pocket, drawer etc)* sacar

▸ **draw up** *vt sep (contract)* preparar; *(plan)* esbozar

drawback ['drɔːbæk] *n* desventaja *f*, inconveniente *m*

drawbridge ['drɔːbrɪdʒ] *n* puente levadizo

drawer ['drɔːə(r)] *n* cajón *m*

drawing ['drɔːɪŋ] *n* dibujo *m*; *Fam Fig* **to go back to the d. board** volver a empezar; *Br* **d. pin** chincheta *f*; *Fml* **d. room** sala *f* de estar

drawl [drɔːl] **1** *vi* hablar arrastrando las palabras

2 *n* voz cansina; *US* **a Southern d.** un acento sureño

drawn [drɔːn] **1** *adj (tired)* ojeroso(a)

2 *pp of* **draw**

dread [dred] **1** *vt* temer a, tener pavor a

2 *n* temor *m*

dreadful ['dredfʊl] *adj* (a) *(shocking)* espantoso(a) (b) *Fam (awful)* fatal; **how d.!** ¡qué horror!

dreadfully ['dredfʊlɪ] *adv Fam (horribly)* terriblemente; *(very)* muy, sumamente

dream [driːm] **1** *n* (a) *(when asleep)* sueño *m* (b) *(daydream)* ensueño *m* (c) *Fam (marvel)* maravilla *f*

2 *vt (pt & pp* **dreamed** *or* **dreamt)** soñar

3 *vi* soñar (**of** *or* **about** con)

dreamer ['driːmə(r)] *n* soñador(a) *m,f*

dreamt [dremt] *pt & pp of* **dream**

dreamy ['driːmɪ] *adj* (**dreamier, dreamiest)** *(absent-minded)* distraído(a); *(wonderful)* de ensueño

dreary ['drɪərɪ] *adj* (**drearier, dreariest)** (a) *(gloomy)* triste (b) *Fam (boring)* aburrido(a), pesado(a)

dredge [dredʒ] *vt & vi* dragar, rastrear

▸ **dredge up** *vt sep* (a) *(body)* sacar del agua (b) *Fam Fig* sacar a relucir

dregs [dregz] *npl* poso *m*

drench [drentʃ] *vt* empapar

dress [dres] **1** *n* (a) *(frock)* vestido *m* (b) *(clothing)* ropa *f*; **d. rehearsal** ensayo *m* general; **d. shirt** camisa *f* de etiqueta

2 *vt* (a) *(person)* vestir; **he was dressed in a grey suit** llevaba (puesto) un traje gris (b) *(salad)* aliñar (c) *(wound)* vendar

3 *vi* vestirse

▸ **dress up 1** *vi* (a) *(in disguise)* disfrazarse (**as** de) (b) *(in best clothes)* vestirse elegante

2 *vt sep Fig* disfrazar

dresser ['dresə(r)] *n* (a) *Br (in kitchen)* aparador *m* (b) *US (in bedroom)* tocador *m* (c) *Th* ayudante *mf* de camerino

dressing ['dresɪŋ] *n* (a) *(bandage)* vendaje *m* (b) *(salad)* aliño *m* (c) **d.** **gown** bata *f*; **d. room** *Th* camerino *m*; *Sport* vestuario *m*; **d. table** tocador *m*

dressmaker ['dresmeɪkə(r)] *n* modista *mf*

dressy ['dresɪ] *adj* (**dressier, dressiest)** vistoso(a)

drew [druː] *pt of* **draw**

dribble ['drɪbəl] **1** *vi* (a) *(baby)* babear (b) *(liquid)* gotear

2 *vt Sport (ball)* driblar

3 *n (saliva)* saliva *f*; *(of water, blood)* gotas *fpl*

dried [draɪd] *adj (fruit)* seco(a); *(milk)* en polvo

drier ['draɪə(r)] *n* = **dryer**

drift [drɪft] **1** *vi* (a) *(boat)* ir a la deriva; *Fig (person)* ir sin rumbo, vagar; **they drifted away** se marcharon poco a poco (b) *(snow)* amontonarse

2 *n* (a) *(flow)* flujo *m* (b) *(of snow)* ventisquero *m; (of sand)* montón *m* (c) *Fig (meaning)* idea *f*

driftwood ['drɪftwʊd] *n* madera *f* flotante

drill [drɪl] **1** *n* (a) *(hand tool)* taladro *m; Min* barrena *f*; **dentist's d.** fresa *f*; **pneumatic d.** martillo neumático (b) *esp Mil* instrucción *f*

2 *vt* (a) *(wood etc)* taladrar (b) *(soldiers, children)* instruir

3 *vi (by hand)* taladrar; *(for oil, coal)* perforar, sondar

drink [drɪŋk] **1** *vt (pt* **drank**; *pp* **drunk)** beber

2 *vi* beber; **to have sth to d.** tomarse algo; **to d. to sth/sb** brindar por algo/algn

3 *n* bebida *f*; *(alcoholic)* copa *f*

drinker ['drɪŋkə(r)] *n* bebedor(a) *m,f*

drinking ['drɪŋkɪŋ] *n* **d. water** agua *f* potable

drip [drɪp] **1** *n* (a) *(action)* goteo *m* (b) *Med* gota a gota *m inv* (c) *Fam (person)* necio(a) *m,f*

2 *vi* gotear; **he was dripping with sweat** el sudor le caía a gotas

drip-dry ['drɪp'draɪ] *adj* que no necesita planchado

dripping ['drɪpɪŋ] *n Culin* pringue *f*

drive [draɪv] **1** *vt (pt* **drove**; *pp* **driven)** (a) *(vehicle)* conducir, *Am* manejar; *(person)* llevar

(b) *(power)* impulsar

(c) *(enemy)* acosar; *(ball)* mandar

(d) *(stake)* hincar; *(nail)* clavar

(e) *(compel)* forzar, obligar; **to d. sb mad** volver loco(a) a algn

(f) **to d. (off)** rechazar

2 *vi* Aut conducir, *Am* manejar

3 *n* (a) *(trip)* paseo *m* en coche; **to go for a d.** dar una vuelta en coche

(b) *(to house)* camino *m* de entrada

(c) *(transmission)* transmisión *f; Aut* tracción *f; Aut* **left-hand d.** conducción *f* por la izquierda

(d) *(in golf)* golpe *m* inicial

(e) *(campaign)* campaña *f*

(f) *(need)* necesidad *f*; *(energy)* energía *f*, vigor *m*; **sex d.** instinto *m* sexual

(g) *Comput* unidad *f* de disco

drive-in ['draɪvɪn] *n US (cinema)* autocine *m*

driven ['drɪvən] *pp of* **drive**

driver ['draɪvə(r)] *n (of car, bus)* conductor(a) *m,f; (of train)* maquinista *mf; (of lorry)* camionero(a) *m,f; (of racing car)* piloto *mf; US* **d.'s license** carnet *m* de conducir

driveway ['draɪvweɪ] *n (to house)* camino *m* de entrada

driving ['draɪvɪŋ] **1** *n Br* **d. licence** carnet *m* de conducir; **d. school** autoescuela *f*; **d. test** examen *m* de conducir

2 *adj* (**a**) *(rain)* intenso(a) (**b**) **d. force** fuerza *f* motriz

drizzle ['drɪzəl] **1** *n* llovizna *f*

2 *vi* lloviznar

droll [drəʊl] *adj* gracioso(a)

dromedary ['drɒmədərɪ] *n* dromedario *m*

drone [drəʊn] *vi (bee etc)* zumbar

droop [druːp] *vi (flower)* marchitarse; *(eyelids)* caerse

drop [drɒp] **1** *n* (**a**) *(of liquid)* gota *f*; **eye drops** colirio *m*

(**b**) *(sweet)* pastilla *f*

(**c**) *(descent)* desnivel *m*

(**d**) *(in price)* bajada *f; (in temperature)* descenso *m*

2 *vt* (**a**) *(let fall)* dejar caer; *(lower)* bajar; *(reduce)* disminuir; **to d. a hint** soltar una indirecta

(**b**) *(abandon) (subject, charge etc)* abandonar, dejar; *Sport* **he was dropped from the team** le echaron del equipo

(**c**) *(omit) (spoken syllable)* comerse

3 *vi (object)* caerse; *(person)* tirarse; *(voice, price, temperature)* bajar; *(wind)* amainar; *(speed)* disminuir

► **drop by, drop in** *vi Fam (visit)* pasarse (**at** por)

► **drop off** *vi Fam (fall asleep)* quedarse dormido(a)

2 *vt sep (deliver)* dejar

► **drop out** *vi (from college)* dejar los estudios; *(from society)* marginarse; *(from competition)* retirarse

► **drop round** *vi Fam* = **drop by**

dropout ['drɒpaʊt] *n Fam Pej* automarginado(a) *m,f*

dropper ['drɒpə(r)] *n* cuentagotas *m inv*

droppings ['drɒpɪŋz] *npl* excrementos *mpl*

drought [draʊt] *n* sequía *f*

drove [drəʊv] **1** *n (of cattle)* manada *f*

2 *pt of* **drive**

drown [draʊn] **1** *vt* (**a**) ahogar (**b**) *(place)* inundar

2 *vi* ahogarse; **he (was) drowned** murió ahogado

drowsy ['draʊzɪ] *adj* (**drowsier, drowsiest**) soñoliento(a); **to feel d.** tener sueño

drudgery ['drʌdʒərɪ] *n* trabajo duro y pesado

drug [drʌg] **1** *n* (**a**) *(medicine)* medicamento *m* (**b**) *(narcotic)* droga *f*, estupefaciente *m*; **to be on drugs** drogarse; **d. addict** drogadicto(a) *m,f*; **d. addiction** drogadicción *f*; **d.**

squad brigada *f* antidroga

2 *vt (person)* drogar; *(food, drink)* adulterar con drogas

druggist ['drʌgɪst] *n US* farmacéutico(a) *m,f*

drugstore ['drʌgstɔːr] *n US* = establecimiento donde se compran medicamentos, periódicos, etc.

drum [drʌm] **1** *n* (**a**) tambor *m*; **to play the drums** tocar la batería (**b**) *(container)* bidón *m*

2 *vi Fig (with fingers)* tabalear

3 *vt Fig* **to d. sth into sb** enseñar algo a algn a machamartillo

► **drum up** *vt sep Fam* solicitar

drummer ['drʌmə(r)] *n (in band)* tambor *mf; (in pop group)* batería *mf*

drumstick ['drʌmstɪk] *n* (**a**) *Mus* baqueta *f* (**b**) *(chicken leg)* muslo *m*

drunk [drʌŋk] **1** *adj* borracho(a); **to get d.** emborracharse

2 *n* borracho(a) *m,f*

3 *pp of* **drink**

drunkard ['drʌŋkəd] *n* borracho(a) *m,f*

dry [draɪ] **1** *adj* (**drier, driest** *or* **dryer, dryest**) (**a**) seco(a); *US* **d. goods store** mercería *f*, tienda *f* de confección (**b**) *(wry)* socarrón(ona)

2 *vt (pt & pp dried)* secar

3 *vi* **to d. (off)** secarse

dry-clean [draɪˈkliːn] *vt* limpiar *or* lavar en seco

dryer ['draɪə(r)] *n* secadora *f*

dub[1] [dʌb] *vt (subtitle)* doblar (**into** a)

dub[2] [dʌb] *vt* (**a**) *(give nickname to)* apodar (**b**) *(knight)* armar

dubious ['djuːbɪəs] *adj* (**a**) *(morals etc)* dudoso(a); *(compliment)* equívoco(a) (**b**) *(doubting)* indeciso(a)

Dublin ['dʌblɪn] *n* Dublín

duchess ['dʌtʃɪs] *n* duquesa *f*

duck[1] [dʌk] *n* pato(a) *m,f; Culin* pato *m*

duck[2] [dʌk] **1** *vt* (**a**) *(submerge)* dar una ahogadilla a (**b**) *(evade)* esquivar

2 *vi* (**a**) *(evade blow)* esquivar **to d. (out)** rajarse

duckling ['dʌklɪŋ] *n* patito *m*

duct [dʌkt] *n (for fuel etc)* conducto *m; Anat* canal *m*

dud [dʌd] *Fam* **1** *adj* (**a**) *(useless)* inútil; *(defective)* estropeado(a) (**b**) *(banknote)* falso(a); *(cheque)* sin fondos

2 *n (useless thing)* engañifa *f; (person)* desastre *m*

dude [duːd] *n US Fam (man)* tipo *m*, tío *m*

due [djuː] **1** *adj* (**a**) *(expected)* esperado(a); **the train is d. (to arrive) at ten** el tren debe llegar a las diez (**b**) *Fml (proper)* debido(a); **in d. course** a su debido tiempo (**c**) *(owing)* pagadero(a); **how much are you d.?** *(owed)* ¿cuánto te deben? (**d**) **to be d. to** *(caused by)* deberse a; **d. to** *(because of)* debido de

2 *adv (north etc)* derecho hacia

3 *n* (**a**) **to give sb their d.** dar a algn su merecido (**b**) **dues** *(fee)* cuota *f*
duel ['dju:əl] *n* duelo *m*
duet [dju:'et] *n* dúo *m*
duffel ['dʌfəl] *n* **d. bag** petate *m*; **d. coat** trenca *f*
dug [dʌg] *pt* & *pp of* **dig**
duke [dju:k] *n* duque *m*
dull [dʌl] **1** *adj* (**a**) *(boring)* pesado(a); *(place)* sin interés (**b**) *(light)* apagado(a); *(weather)* gris (**c**) *(sound, ache)* sordo(a) (**d**) *Fig (slow-witted)* torpe
2 *vt* (**a**) *(pain)* aliviar (**b**) *Fig (faculty)* embotar
duly ['dju:lɪ] *adv Fml (properly)* debidamente; *(as expected)* como era de esperar; *(in due course)* a su debido tiempo
dumb [dʌm] **1** *adj* (**a**) *Med* mudo(a) (**b**) *Fam (stupid)* tonto(a)
2 *npl* **the d.** los mudos
dumbbell ['dʌmbel] *n Sport* pesa *f*
dumbfounded [dʌm'faʊndɪd], **dumb-struck** ['dʌmstrʌk] *adj* pasmado(a)
dummy ['dʌmɪ] *n* (**a**) *(sham)* imitación *f* (**b**) *(in shop window)* maniquí *m*; *(of ventrilo-quist)* muñeco *m* (**c**) *Br (for baby)* chupete *m*
dump [dʌmp] **1** *n* (**a**) *(tip)* vertedero *m*; *(for old cars)* cementerio *m* (de coches) (**b**) *Fam Pej (place)* estercolero *m*; *(town)* poblacho *m*; *(dwelling)* tugurio *m* (**c**) *Mil* depósito *m*
2 *vt* (**a**) *(rubbish)* verter; *(truck contents)* descargar (**b**) *(person)* dejar; *Com* inundar el mercado con (**c**) *Comput (transfer)* copiar de memoria interna
dumping ['dʌmpɪŋ] *n* vertido *m*
dumpling ['dʌmplɪŋ] *n Culin* = bola de masa hervida
dumpy ['dʌmpɪ] *adj* (**dumpier, dumpiest**) *Fam* rechoncho(a)
dunce [dʌns] *n Fam* tonto(a) *m,f*
dune [dju:n] *n* (**sand**) **d.** duna *f*
dung [dʌŋ] *n* estiércol *m*
dungarees [dʌŋgə'ri:z] *npl* mono *m*
dungeon ['dʌndʒən] *n* calabozo *m*, mazmorra *f*
duo ['dju:əʊ] *n Mus* dúo *m*; *Fam* pareja *f*
dupe [dju:p] **1** *vt* engañar
2 *n* ingenuo(a) *m,f*
duplex ['dju:pleks] *n US (house)* casa adosada; **d. apartment** dúplex *m inv*
duplicate 1 *vt* ['dju:plɪkeɪt] (**a**) *(copy)* duplicar; *(film, tape)* reproducir (**b**) *(repeat)* repetir
2 *n* ['dju:plɪkɪt] duplicado *m*; **in d.** por duplicado
durable ['djʊərəbəl] *adj* duradero(a)
duration [djʊ'reɪʃən] *n Fml* duración *f*
duress [djʊ'res] *n Fml* coacción *f*

> 🖉 Note that the Spanish word **dureza** is a false friend and is never a translation for the English word **duress**. In Spanish, **dureza** means "hardness, harshness".

during ['djʊərɪŋ] *prep* durante
dusk [dʌsk] *n Fml* crepúsculo *m*; **at d.** al anochecer
dust [dʌst] **1** *n* polvo *m*; **d. cloud** polvareda *f*; **d. jacket** sobrecubierta *f*
2 *vt* (**a**) *(furniture)* quitar el polvo a (**b**) *(cake)* espolvorear
dustbin ['dʌstbɪn] *n Br* cubo *m* de la basura
dustcart ['dʌstkɑ:t] *n Br* camión *m* de la basura
duster ['dʌstə(r)] *n (for housework)* trapo *m* or paño *m* (del polvo); **feather d.** plumero *m*
dustman ['dʌstmən] *n Br* basurero *m*
dustpan ['dʌstpæn] *n* recogedor *m*
dusty ['dʌstɪ] *adj* (**dustier, dustiest**) polvoriento(a)
Dutch [dʌtʃ] **1** *adj* holandés(esa); *Fig* **D. cap** diafragma *m*
2 *n* (**a**) *pl* **the D.** los holandeses (**b**) *(lan-guage)* holandés *m*; **it's double D. to me** me suena a chino
3 *adv Fig* **to go D.** pagar cada uno lo suyo
Dutchman ['dʌtʃmən] *n* holandés *m*
Dutchwoman ['dʌtʃwʊmən] *n* holandesa *f*
duty ['dju:tɪ] *n* (**a**) deber *m*; **to do one's d.** cumplir con su deber (**b**) *(task)* función *f* (**c**) **to be on d.** estar de servicio; *Med Mil* estar de guardia; **d. chemist** farmacia *f* de guardia (**d**) *(tax)* impuesto *m*; **customs d.** derechos *mpl* de aduana
duty-free [dju:tɪ'fri:] **1** *adj* libre de impuestos
2 *adv* sin pagar impuestos
3 *n* duty-free *m*
duvet ['du:veɪ] *n* edredón *m*
DVD [di:vi:'di:] *n Comput (abbr Digital Versa-tile Disk, Digital Video Disk)* DVD *m*
dwarf [dwɔ:f] **1** *n* (*pl* **dwarves** [dwɔ:vz]) *(person)* enano(a) *m,f*
2 *vt* hacer parecer pequeño(a) a
dwell [dwel] *vi (pt* & *pp* **dwelt**) *Fml* morar
▶ **dwell on** *vt insep* hablar extensamente de; **let's not d. on it** olvidémoslo
dwelling ['dwelɪŋ] *n Fml* & *Hum* morada *f*, vivienda *f*
dwelt [dwelt] *pt* & *pp of* **dwell**
dwindle ['dwɪndəl] *vi* menguar, disminuir
dye [daɪ] **1** *n* tinte *m*
2 *vt (pres p* **dyeing**; *pt* & *pp* **dyed**) teñir; **to d. one's hair black** teñirse el pelo de negro
dying ['daɪɪŋ] *adj (person)* moribundo(a), agonizante; *Fig (custom)* en vías de desaparición
dyke [daɪk] *n* (**a**) *(bank)* dique *m*; *(causeway)* terraplén *m* (**b**) *very Fam Pej* tortillera *f*
dynamic [daɪ'næmɪk] *adj* dinámico(a)
dynamics [daɪ'næmɪks] *n sing* dinámica *f*
dynamism ['daɪnəmɪzəm] *n* dinamismo *m*
dynamite ['daɪnəmaɪt] *n* dinamita *f*
dynamo ['daɪnəməʊ] *n* dínamo *f*
dynasty ['dɪnəstɪ] *n* dinastía *f*
dysentery ['dɪsəntrɪ] *n* disentería *f*
dyslexia [dɪs'leksɪə] *n* dislexia *f*

E, e [iː] *n* (**a**) *(the letter)* E, e *f* (**b**) *Mus* **E** mi *m*

E [iː] *n* (**a**) *(abbr* **East**) E (**b**) *Fam (abbr* **ecstasy**) *(drug)* éxtasis *m inv*

each [iːtʃ] **1** *adj* cada; **e. day/month** todos los días/meses; **e. person** cada cual; **e. time I see him** cada vez que lo veo

2 *pron* (**a**) cada uno(a); **£2 e.** 2 libras cada uno; **we bought one e.** nos compramos uno cada uno (**b**) **e. other** el uno al otro; **they hate e. other** se odian

eager ['iːgə(r)] *adj (anxious)* impaciente; *(desirous)* deseoso(a); **e. to begin** impaciente por empezar; **to be e. for success** codiciar el éxito

eagerly ['iːgəlɪ] *adv (anxiously)* con impaciencia; *(keenly)* con ilusión

eagle ['iːgəl] *n* águila *f*

ear [ɪə(r)] *n* (**a**) oreja *f*; *(sense of hearing)* oído *m* (**b**) *(of corn etc)* espiga *f*

earache ['ɪəreɪk] *n* dolor *m* de oídos

eardrum ['ɪədrʌm] *n* tímpano *m*

earl [ɜːl] *n* conde *m*

earlobe ['ɪələʊb] *n* lóbulo *m*

early ['ɜːlɪ] (**earlier, earliest**) **1** *adj* (**a**) *(before the usual time)* temprano(a); **to have an e. night** acostarse pronto; **you're e.!** ¡qué pronto has venido!

(**b**) *(at first stage, period)* **at an e. age** siendo joven; **in e. July** a principios de julio; **e. work** obra de juventud; **in her e. forties** a los cuarenta y pocos; **it's still e. days** aún es pronto

(**c**) *(in the near future)* **an e. reply** una respuesta pronta; **at the earliest** cuanto antes

2 *adv* (**a**) *(before the expected time)* temprano, pronto; **earlier on** antes; **five minutes e.** con cinco minutos de adelanto; **to leave e.** irse pronto

(**b**) *(near the beginning)* **as e. as 1914** ya en 1914; **as e. as possible** tan pronto como sea posible; **to book e.** reservar con tiempo; **e. on** temprano

earmark ['ɪəmɑːk] *vt* destinar (**for** para or *a*)

earn [ɜːn] *vt* (**a**) *(money)* ganar; **to e. one's living** ganarse la vida (**b**) *(reputation)* ganarse (**c**) **to e. interest** cobrar interés *or* intereses

earnest ['ɜːnɪst] **1** *adj* serio(a), formal

2 *n* **in e.** de veras, en serio

earnings ['ɜːnɪŋz] *npl* ingresos *mpl*

earring ['ɪərɪŋ] *n* pendiente *m*

earshot ['ɪəʃɒt] *n* **out of e.** fuera del alcance del oído; **within e.** al alcance del oído

earth [ɜːθ] **1** *n* (**a**) tierra *f*; *Fig* **to be down to e.** ser práctico; *Fam* **where/why on e. ...?** ¿pero dónde/por qué demonios ...? (**b**) *Br Elec* toma *f* de tierra

2 *vt Br Elec* conectar a tierra

earthenware ['ɜːðənweə(r)] **1** *n* loza *f*

2 *adj* de barro

earthquake ['ɜːθkweɪk] *n* terremoto *m*

earthshattering ['ɜːθʃætərɪŋ] *adj* trascendental; **e. news** noticia bomba

earthworm ['ɜːθwɜːm] *n* lombriz *f* de tierra

earthy ['ɜːθɪ] *adj* (**earthier, earthiest**) (**a**) *(taste)* terroso(a) (**b**) *(bawdy)* tosco(a)

earwig ['ɪəwɪɡ] *n* tijereta *f*

ease [iːz] *n* (**a**) *(freedom from discomfort)* tranquilidad *f*; *Mil* posición *f* de descanso; **at e.** relajado(a) (**b**) *(lack of difficulty)* facilidad *f* (**c**) *(affluence)* comodidad *f* (**d**) **e. of manner** naturalidad *f*

2 *vt* (**a**) *(pain)* aliviar (**b**) *(move gently)* deslizar con cuidado

▸ **ease off, ease up** *vi* (**a**) *(decrease)* disminuir (**b**) *(slow down)* ir más despacio

easel ['iːzəl] *n* caballete *m*

easily ['iːzɪlɪ] *adv* fácilmente; **e. the best** con mucho el mejor

east [iːst] **1** *n* este *m*; **the Middle E.** el Oriente Medio

2 *adj* del este, oriental; **E. Germany** Alemania Oriental

3 *adv* al *or* hacia el este

Easter ['iːstə(r)] *n* Semana Santa, Pascua *f*; **E. egg** huevo *m* de Pascua; **E. Sunday** Domingo *m* de Resurrección

easterly ['iːstəlɪ] *adj (from the east)* del este; *(to the east)* hacia al este

eastern ['iːstən] *adj* oriental, del este

eastward(s) ['iːstwəd(z)] *adv* hacia el este

easy ['iːzɪ] (**easier, easiest**) **1** *adj* (**a**) *(simple)* fácil, sencillo(a) (**b**) *(unworried, comfortable)* cómodo(a), tranquilo(a); *Fam* **I'm e.!** ¡me da lo mismo!; **e. chair** butacón *m*

2 *adv* **go e. on the wine** no te pases con el vino; *Fam* **to take things e.** tomarse las cosas con calma; *Fam* **take it e.!** ¡tranquilo!

easy-going [iːzɪ'gəʊɪŋ] *adj (calm)* tranquilo(a); *(lax)* despreocupado(a); *(undemanding)* poco exigente

eat [iːt] *vt (pt* **ate** [et, eɪt]; *pp* **eaten**) comer

▸ **eat away** *vt sep* desgastar; *(metal)* corroer

▸ **eat into** vt insep (**a**) (wood) roer (**b**) Fig (savings) consumir
▸ **eat out** vi comer fuera
▸ **eat up** vt sep (**a**) (meal) terminar (**b**) Fig (petrol) consumir; (miles) recorrer rápidamente
eatable ['i:təbəl] adj comestible
eaten ['i:tən] pp of **eat**
eau de Cologne [əʊdəkə'ləʊn] n colonia f
eaves [i:vz] npl alero m
eavesdrop ['i:vzdrɒp] vi escuchar disimuladamente
ebb [eb] **1** n reflujo m; **e. and flow** flujo y reflujo; Fig **to be at a low e.** estar decaído
2 vi (**a**) (tide) bajar; **to e. and flow** subir y bajar (**b**) Fig **to e. away** decaer
ebony ['ebənɪ] **1** n ébano m
2 adj de ébano
eccentric [ɪk'sentrɪk] adj & n excéntrico(a) (m,f)
ecclesiastic [ɪkli:zɪ'æstɪk] adj & n eclesiástico(a) (m,f)
echelon ['eʃəlɒn] n escalafón m
echo ['ekəʊ] **1** n (pl echoes) eco m
2 vt (repeat) repetir
3 vi resonar, hacer eco
eclectic [ɪ'klektɪk] adj ecléctico(a)
eclipse [ɪ'klɪps] **1** n eclipse m
2 vt eclipsar
ecological [i:kə'lɒdʒɪkəl] adj ecológico(a)
ecology [ɪ'kɒlədʒɪ] n ecología f
e-commerce [i:'kɒmɜːs] n comercio electrónico
economic [i:kə'nɒmɪk] adj económico(a); (profitable) rentable
economical [i:kə'nɒmɪkəl] adj económico(a)
economics [i:kə'nɒmɪks] n sing (science) economía f; Educ (ciencias fpl) económicas fpl
economist [ɪ'kɒnəmɪst] n economista mf
economize [ɪ'kɒnəmaɪz] vi economizar
economy [ɪ'kɒnəmɪ] n (**a**) Pol **the e.** la economía (**b**) (saving) ahorro m; **e. class** clase f turista
ecosystem ['i:kəʊsɪstəm] n ecosistema m
ecotax ['i:kəʊtæks] n ecotasa f
ecotourism ['i:kəʊtɔ:rɪzəm] n ecoturismo m
ecstasy ['ekstəsɪ] n éxtasis m
ecstatic [ek'stætɪk] adj extático(a)
Ecuador ['ekwədɔ:(r)] n Ecuador
eczema ['eksɪmə] n eczema m
eddy ['edɪ] **1** n remolino m
2 vi arremolinarse
edge [edʒ] **1** n borde m; (of knife) filo m; (of coin) canto m; (of water) orilla f; **on the e. of town** en las afueras de la ciudad; **to have the e. on sb** llevar ventaja a algn; Fig **to be on e.** tener los nervios de punta
2 vt Sewing ribetear
3 vi **to e. closer** acercarse lentamente; **to e. forward** avanzar poco a poco

edgeways ['edʒweɪz], **edgewise** ['edʒwaɪz] adv de lado; Fig **I couldn't get a word in e.** no pude decir ni pío
edging ['edʒɪŋ] n borde m; Sewing ribete m
edgy ['edʒɪ] adj (**edgier, edgiest**) nervioso(a)
edible ['edɪbəl] adj comestible
edict ['i:dɪkt] n Hist edicto m; Jur decreto m
Edinburgh ['edɪnbrə] n Edimburgo
edit ['edɪt] vt (**a**) (prepare for printing) preparar para la imprenta (**b**) (rewrite) corregir **to e. sth out** suprimir algo (**c**) Press ser redactor(a) de (**d**) Cin, Rad TV montar; (cut) cortar
edition [ɪ'dɪʃən] n edición f
editor ['edɪtə(r)] n (of book) editor(a) m,f; Press redactor(a) m,f; Cin & TV montador(a) m,f
editorial [edɪ'tɔ:rɪəl] **1** adj editorial; **e. staff** redacción f
2 n editorial m
educate ['edjʊkeɪt] vt educar
educated ['edjʊkeɪtɪd] adj culto(a)
education [edjʊ'keɪʃən] n (**a**) (schooling) enseñanza f; **adult e.** educación f de adultos **Ministry of E.** Ministerio m de Educación (**b**) (training) formación f (**c**) (studies) estudios mpl (**d**) (culture) cultura f
educational [edjʊ'keɪʃənəl] adj educativo(a), educacional
eel [i:l] n anguila f
eerie ['ɪərɪ] adj (**eerier, eeriest**) siniestro(a)
efface [ɪ'feɪs] vt borrar
effect [ɪ'fekt] **1** n (**a**) efecto m; **in e.** efectivamente; **to come into e.** entrar en vigor; **to have an e. on** afectar a; **to no e.** sin resultado alguno; **to take e.** (drug) surtir efecto; (law) entrar en vigor (**b**) (impression) impresión f (**c**) effects (possessions) efectos mpl
2 vt Fml provocar
effective [ɪ'fektɪv] adj (**a**) (successful) eficaz (**b**) (real) efectivo(a) (**c**) (impressive) impresionante
effectively [ɪ'fektɪvlɪ] adv (**a**) (successfully) eficazmente (**b**) (in fact) en efecto
effeminate [ɪ'femɪnɪt] adj afeminado(a)
effervescent [efə'vesənt] adj efervescente
efficiency [ɪ'fɪʃənsɪ] n (of person) eficacia f (of machine) rendimiento m
efficient [ɪ'fɪʃənt] adj eficaz, eficiente; (machine) de buen rendimiento
effigy ['efɪdʒɪ] n efigie f
effluent ['efluənt] n vertidos mpl
effort ['efət] n (**a**) esfuerzo m; **to make an e.** hacer un esfuerzo, esforzarse (**b**) (attempt) intento m
effortless ['efətlɪs] adj sin esfuerzo
effrontery [ɪ'frʌntərɪ] n desfachatez f
effusive [ɪ'fju:sɪv] adj efusivo(a)
eg [i:'dʒi:] (abbr **exempli gratia**) p. ej.
egalitarian [ɪgælɪ'teərɪən] adj igualitario(a)
egg [eg] **1** n huevo m; Fam Fig **to put all one's**

eggs in one basket jugárselo todo a una carta; **e. cup** huevera *f*; **e. timer** reloj *m* de arena; **e. white** clara *f* de huevo
  2 *vt* **to e. sb on (to do sth)** empujar a algn (a hacer algo)

eggplant ['egplɑːnt] *n US* berenjena *f*

eggshell ['egʃel] *n* cáscara *f* de huevo

ego ['iːgəʊ,'egəʊ] *n* (**a**) ego *m*; *Fam* **e. trip** autobombo *m* (**b**) *Fam* amor propio

egocentric(al) [iːgəʊ'sentrɪk(əl)] *adj* egocéntrico(a)

egoism ['iːgəʊɪzəm] *n* egoísmo *m*

egoist ['iːgəʊɪst] *n* egoísta *mf*

egotistic(al) [iːgəʊ'tɪstɪk(əl)] *adj* egotista

Egypt ['iːdʒɪpt] *n* Egipto

Egyptian [ɪ'dʒɪpʃən] *adj & n* egipcio(a) *(m,f)*

eiderdown ['aɪdədaʊn] *n* edredón *m*

eight [eɪt] *adj & n* ocho *(m inv)*

eighteen [eɪ'tiːn] *adj & n* dieciocho *(m inv)*

eighteenth [eɪ'tiːnθ] **1** *adj & n* decimoctavo *(m,f)*
  2 *n (fraction)* decimoctavo *m*

eighth [eɪtθ] **1** *adj & n* octavo(a) *(m,f)*
  2 *n (fraction)* octavo *m*

eighty ['eɪtɪ] *adj & n* ochenta *(m inv)*

Eire ['eərə] *n* Eire

either ['aɪðə(r), 'iːðə(r)] **1** *pron* (**a**) *(affirmative)* cualquiera; **e. of them** cualquiera de los dos; **e. of us** cualquiera de nosotros dos (**b**) *(negative)* ninguno/ninguna, ni el uno ni el otro/ni la una ni la otra; **I don't want e. of them** no quiero ninguno de los dos
  2 *adj (both)* cada, los dos/las dos; **on e. side** en ambos lados; **in e. case** en cualquier de los dos casos
  3 *conj* o; **e. ... or ...** o ... o ...; **e. Friday or Saturday** o (bien) el viernes o el sábado
  4 *adv (after negative)* tampoco; **I don't want to do it e.** yo tampoco quiero hacerlo

ejaculate [ɪ'dʒækjʊleɪt] *vi (man)* eyacular

eject [ɪ'dʒekt] **1** *vt* expulsar
  2 *vi Av* eyectarse

eke [iːk] *vt* **to e. out a living** ganarse la vida a duras penas

elaborate 1 *vt* [ɪ'læbəreɪt] (**a**) *(devise)* elaborar (**b**) *(explain)* explicar detalladamente
  2 *vi* explicarse; **to e. on sth** explicar algo con más detalles
  3 *adj* [ɪ'læbərɪt] (**a**) *(complicated)* complicado(a) (**b**) *(detailed)* detallado(a); *(style)* esmerado(a)

elapse [ɪ'læps] *vi* transcurrir, pasar

elastic [ɪ'læstɪk] **1** *adj* elástico(a); *Fig* flexible; **e. band** goma elástica
  2 *n* elástico *m*

Elastoplast® [ɪ'lɑːstəplɑːst] *n* tirita *f*, *Am* curita *f*

elated [ɪ'leɪtɪd] *adj* eufórico(a)

elation [ɪ'leɪʃən] *n* regocijo *m*

elbow ['elbəʊ] **1** *n* (**a**) codo *m*; *Fig* **e. room** espacio *m* (**b**) *(bend)* recodo *m*
  2 *vt* **to e. sb** dar un codazo a algn

elder¹ ['eldə(r)] **1** *adj* mayor
  2 *n* **the elders** los ancianos

elder² ['eldə(r)] *n Bot* saúco *m*

elderly ['eldəlɪ] **1** *adj* anciano(a)
  2 *npl* **the e.** los ancianos

eldest ['eldɪst] **1** *adj* mayor
  2 *n* **the e.** el/la mayor

elect [ɪ'lekt] **1** *vt* (**a**) *Pol* elegir (**b**) **to e. to do sth** *(choose)* decidir hacer algo
  2 *adj* **the president e.** el presidente electo

election [ɪ'lekʃən] **1** *n* elección *f*; **general e.** elecciones *fpl* generales
  2 *adj* electoral

electioneering [ɪlekʃə'nɪərɪŋ] *n* electoralismo *m*

elector [ɪ'lektə(r)] *n* elector(a) *m,f*

electoral [ɪ'lektərəl] *adj* electoral

electorate [ɪ'lektərɪt] *n* electorado *m*

electric [ɪ'lektrɪk] *adj* (**a**) eléctrico(a); **e. blanket** manta eléctrica, *Am* frazada eléctrica; **e. chair** silla eléctrica; **e. shock** electrochoque *m* (**b**) *Fig* electrizante

electrical [ɪ'lektrɪkəl] *adj* eléctrico(a)

electrician [ɪlek'trɪʃən] *n* electricista *mf*

electricity [ɪlek'trɪsɪtɪ] *n* electricidad *f*; **e. bill** recibo *m* de la luz

electrify [ɪ'lektrɪfaɪ] *vt* (**a**) *(railway line)* electrificar (**b**) *Fig (excite)* electrizar

electrocute [ɪ'lektrəkjuːt] *vt* electrocutar

electron [ɪ'lektrɒn] *n* electrón *m*

electronic [ɪlek'trɒnɪk] *adj* electrónico(a); **e. banking** banca electrónica, telebanca *f*

electronics [ɪlek'trɒnɪks] **1** *n sing (science)* electrónica *f*
  2 *npl (of machine)* componentes *mpl* electrónicos

elegant ['elɪgənt] *adj* elegante

element ['elɪmənt] *n* (**a**) elemento *m* (**b**) *(part)* parte *f* (**c**) *(electrical)* resistencia *f* (**d**) *Fam Fig* **to be in one's e.** estar en su salsa

elementary [elɪ'mentərɪ] *adj (basic)* elemental; *(not developed)* rudimentario(a); *(easy)* fácil; *US* **e. school** escuela primaria

elephant ['elɪfənt] *n* elefante *m*

elevate ['elɪveɪt] *vt* elevar; *(in rank)* ascender

elevation [elɪ'veɪʃən] *n* (**a**) elevación *f* (**b**) *Archit* alzado *m* (**c**) *(above sea level)* altitud *f*

elevator ['elɪveɪtər] *n US* ascensor *m*

eleven [ɪ'levən] *adj & n* once *(m,f)*

elevenses [ɪ'levənzɪz] *npl Fam* bocadillo *m* de las once

eleventh [ɪ'levənθ] **1** *adj & n* undécimo(a) *(m,f)*
  2 *n (fraction)* undécimo *m*

elicit [ɪ'lɪsɪt] *vt* obtener

eligible ['elɪdʒəbəl] *adj* apto(a); **he isn't e. to vote** no tiene derecho al voto

eliminate [ɪ'lɪmɪneɪt] *vt* eliminar

elite [ɪ'liːt] *n* elite *f*

elitist [ɪ'liːtɪst] *adj* elitista

elm [elm] *n* olmo *m*

elocution [elə'kjuːʃən] *n* elocución *f*
elongate [iːlɒŋgeɪt] *vt* alargar
elope [ɪ'ləʊp] *vi* fugarse para casarse
eloquent ['eləkwənt] *adj* elocuente
else [els] *adv* (**a**) **anyone e.** alguien más; **anything e.?** ¿algo más?; **everything e.** todo lo demás; **no one e.** nadie más; **someone e.** otro(a); **something e.** otra cosa, algo más; **somewhere e.** en otra parte; **what e.?** ¿qué más?; **where e.?** ¿en qué otro sitio? (**b**) **or e.** *(otherwise)* si no
elsewhere [els'weə(r)] *adv* en otra parte
elucidate [ɪ'luːsɪdeɪt] *vt* aclarar
elude [ɪ'luːd] *vt* (**a**) *(escape)* eludir; **his name eludes me** no consigo acordarme de su nombre (**b**) *(avoid)* esquivar
elusive [ɪ'luːsɪv] *adj* esquivo(a); *(evasive)* evasivo(a)
emaciated [ɪ'meɪsɪeɪtɪd] *adj* demacrado(a)
e-mail ['iːmeɪl] *Comput* **1** *n (system)* correo *m* electrónico; *(message)* (mensaje *m* por) correo electrónico; **e. address** dirección *f* de correo electrónico
   2 *vt (person)* enviar un correo electrónico a; *(file)* enviar por correo electrónico
emanate ['eməneɪt] *vi* provenir (**from** de)
emancipate [ɪ'mænsɪpeɪt] *vt* emancipar
emancipation [ɪmænsɪ'peɪʃən] *n* emancipación *f*
embankment [ɪm'bæŋkmənt] *n* (**a**) *(made of earth)* terraplén *m* (**b**) *(of river)* dique *m*
embargo [em'bɑːgəʊ] *n (pl embargoes)* embargo *m*
embark [em'bɑːk] **1** *vt (merchandise)* embarcar
   2 *vi* embarcar, embarcarse; *Fig* **to e. upon** emprender; *(sth difficult)* embarcarse en
embarkation [embɑː'keɪʃən] *n* embarque *m*
embarrass [ɪm'bærəs] *vt* avergonzar, *Andes, CAm, Carib, Méx* apenar
embarrassed [ɪm'bærəst] *adj* avergonzado(a), *Andes, CAm, Carib, Méx* apenado(a)

> ℐ Note that the Spanish word **embarazado** is a false friend and is never a translation for the English word **embarrassed**. In Spanish, **embarazado** means "pregnant".

embarrassing [ɪm'bærəsɪŋ] *adj* embarazoso(a), *Andes, CAm, Carib, Méx* penoso(a)
embarrassment [ɪm'bærəsmənt] *n* vergüenza *f*, *Andes, CAm, Carib, Méx* pena *f*
embassy ['embəsɪ] *n* embajada *f*
embed [ɪm'bed] *vt (jewels)* incrustar; *Fig* grabar
embellish [ɪm'belɪʃ] *vt* embellecer; *(story)* exagerar
ember ['embə(r)] *n* ascua *f*, rescoldo *m*
embezzle [ɪm'bezəl] *vt* desfalcar, malversar
embezzlement [ɪm'bezəlmənt] *n* malversación *f*
embitter [ɪm'bɪtə(r)] *vt* amargar

embittered [ɪm'bɪtəd] *adj* amargado(a), re sentido(a)
emblem ['embləm] *n* emblema *m*
embody [ɪm'bɒdɪ] *vt* (**a**) *(include)* abarca (**b**) *(personify)* encarnar
embossed [ɪm'bɒst] *adj* en relieve
embrace [ɪm'breɪs] **1** *vt* (**a**) abrazar (**b**) *(accept)* adoptar (**c**) *(include)* abarcar
   2 *vi* abrazarse
   3 *n* abrazo *m*
embroider [ɪm'brɔɪdə(r)] *vt* (**a**) *Sewing* bor dar (**b**) *Fig (story, truth)* adornar, embellece
embroidery [ɪm'brɔɪdərɪ] *n* bordado *m*
embryo ['embrɪəʊ] *n* embrión *m*
emerald ['emərəld] *n* esmeralda *f*
emerge [ɪ'mɜːdʒ] *vi* salir; *(problem)* surgir; **emerged that ...** resultó que ...
emergence [ɪ'mɜːdʒəns] *n* aparición *f*
emergency [ɪ'mɜːdʒənsɪ] *n* emergencia *Med* urgencia *f*; **in an e.** en caso de emergen cia; **e. exit** salida *f* de emergencia; **e. landin** aterrizaje forzoso; **e. measures** medidas *f* de urgencia; *US* **e. room** sala *f* de urgencias *Aut* **e. stop** frenazo *m* en seco; *Pol* **state of e** estado *m* de excepción
emery ['emərɪ] *n* **e. board** lima *f* de uñas
emigrant ['emɪgrənt] *n* emigrante *mf*
emigrate ['emɪgreɪt] *vi* emigrar
emigration [emɪ'greɪʃən] *n* emigración *f*
eminent ['emɪnənt] *adj* eminente
emission [ɪ'mɪʃən] *n* emisión *f*
emit [ɪ'mɪt] *vt (signals)* emitir; *(smells)* des pedir; *(sound)* producir
emotion [ɪ'məʊʃən] *n* emoción *f*
emotional [ɪ'məʊʃənəl] *adj* (**a**) emociona (**b**) *(moving)* conmovedor(a)
emotive [ɪ'məʊtɪv] *adj* emotivo(a)
emperor ['empərə(r)] *n* emperador *m*
emphasis ['emfəsɪs] *n (pl emphases* ['emfə siːz])* énfasis *m*; **to place e. on sth** hace hincapié en algo
emphasize ['emfəsaɪz] *vt* subrayar, hace hincapié en; *(insist)* insistir; *(highlight)* hace resaltar
emphatic [em'fætɪk] *adj (forceful)* enfáti co(a); *(convinced)* categórico(a)
emphatically [em'fætɪklɪ] *adv* categórica mente
empire ['empaɪə(r)] *n* imperio *m*
employ [ɪm'plɔɪ] *vt* emplear; *(time)* ocupar
employee [em'plɔɪiː, emplɔɪ'iː] *n* emplea do(a) *m,f*
employer [ɪm'plɔɪə(r)] *n* patrón(ona) *m,f*
employment [ɪm'plɔɪmənt] *n* empleo *m*; **e. agency** agencia *f* de colocaciones; **full e.** pleno empleo
empower [ɪm'paʊə(r)] *vt* autorizar
empress ['emprɪs] *n* emperatriz *f*
emptiness ['emptɪnɪs] *n* vacío *m*
empty ['emptɪ] **1** *adj* (**emptier, emptiest** vacío(a); **an e. house** una casa deshabitada **e. promises** promesas *fpl* vanas

2 *vt* vaciar

3 *vi* (**a**) vaciarse (**b**) *(river)* desembocar (**into** en)

4 *npl* **empties** envases vacíos

empty-handed [emptɪˈhændɪd] *adj* con las manos vacías

EMU [iːemˈjuː] *n Fin (abbr* **Economic and Monetary Union**) UEM *f*

emulate [ˈemjʊleɪt] *vt* emular

emulsion [ɪˈmʌlʃən] *n* emulsión *f*; **e. paint** pintura *f* mate

enable [ɪnˈeɪbəl] *vt* permitir

enact [ɪˈnækt] *vt (play)* representar; *(law)* promulgar

enamel [ɪˈnæməl] *n* esmalte *m*

enamoured, *US* **enamored** [ɪˈnæməd] *adj* **to be e. of** estar enamorado(a) de; **I'm not greatly e. of the idea** no me entusiasma la idea

encase [ɪnˈkeɪs] *vt* **encased in** revestido de

enchant [ɪnˈtʃɑːnt] *vt* encantar

enchanting [ɪnˈtʃɑːntɪŋ] *adj* encantador(a)

encircle [ɪnˈsɜːkəl] *vt* rodear

enclave [ˈenkleɪv] *n* enclave *m*

enclose [ɪnˈkləʊz] *vt* (**a**) *(surround)* rodear (**b**) *(fence in)* cercar (**c**) *(in envelope)* adjuntar; **please find enclosed** le enviamos adjunto

enclosure [ɪnˈkləʊʒə(r)] *n* (**a**) *(fenced area)* cercado *m* (**b**) *(in envelope)* documento adjunto (**c**) *(of racecourse)* recinto *m*

encompass [ɪnˈkʌmpəs] *vt* abarcar

encore [ˈɒŋkɔː(r)] **1** *interj* ¡otra!, ¡bis!

2 *n* repetición *f*, bis *m*

encounter [ɪnˈkaʊntə(r)] **1** *n (meeting)* encuentro *m*

2 *vt* encontrar, encontrarse con; *(problems)* tropezar con

encourage [ɪnˈkʌrɪdʒ] *vt* (**a**) *(person)* animar (**b**) *(tourism, trade)* fomentar

encouragement [ɪnˈkʌrɪdʒmənt] *n* estímulo *m*

encroach [ɪnˈkrəʊtʃ] *vi* **to e. on** *(territory)* invadir; *(rights)* usurpar; *(time, freedom)* quitar

encrusted [ɪnˈkrʌstɪd] *adj* incrustado(a) (**with** de)

encumber [ɪnˈkʌmbə(r)] *vt* estorbar; *(with debts)* gravar

encyclop(a)edia [ensaɪkləʊˈpiːdɪə] *n* enciclopedia *f*

end [end] **1** *n* (**a**) *(of stick)* punta *f*; *(of street)* final *m*; *(of table)* extremo *m*; *Fig* **to make ends meet** llegar a final de mes; *Fig* **it makes my hair stand on e.** me pone el pelo de punta (**b**) *(conclusion)* fin *m*, final *m*; **in the e.** al final; **for hours on e.** hora tras hora; **no e. of** un sinfín de; **to bring an e. to sth** poner fin a algo; **to put an e. to** acabar con (**c**) *(aim)* objetivo *m*, fin *m*; **to no e.** en vano

2 *vt* acabar, terminar

3 *vi* acabarse, terminarse

▸ **end up** *vi* terminar; **it ended up in the dustbin** fue a parar al cubo de la basura; **to e. up doing sth** terminar por hacer algo

endanger [ɪnˈdeɪndʒə(r)] *vt* poner en peligro

endangered [ɪnˈdeɪndʒəd] *adj* en peligro

endearing [ɪnˈdɪərɪŋ] *adj* simpático(a)

endeavour, *US* **endeavor** [ɪnˈdevə(r)] **1** *n* esfuerzo *m*

2 *vt* intentar, procurar

ending [ˈendɪŋ] *n* final *m*

endive [ˈendaɪv] *n Bot* (**a**) *(curly)* escarola *f* (**b**) *esp US (chicory)* endibia *f*

endless [ˈendlɪs] *adj* interminable

endorse [ɪnˈdɔːs] *vt* (**a**) *Fin* endosar (**b**) *(approve)* aprobar; *(support)* apoyar

endorsement [ɪnˈdɔːsmənt] *n* (**a**) *Fin* endoso *m* (**b**) *Aut* nota *f* de sanción (**c**) *(approval)* aprobación *f*

endow [ɪnˈdaʊ] *vt* dotar; **to be endowed with** estar dotado(a) de

endurance [ɪnˈdjʊərəns] *n* resistencia *f*

endure [ɪnˈdjʊə(r)] **1** *vt (bear)* aguantar, soportar

2 *vi* perdurar

enemy [ˈenəmɪ] *adj & n* enemigo(a) *(m,f)*

energetic [enəˈdʒetɪk] *adj* enérgico(a)

energy [ˈenədʒɪ] *n* energía *f*

enforce [ɪnˈfɔːs] *vt (law)* hacer cumplir

enforcement [ɪnˈfɔːsmənt] *n* aplicación *f*

engage [ɪnˈgeɪdʒ] *vt* (**a**) *(hire)* contratar (**b**) *(attention)* llamar (**c**) *(in conversation)* entablar (**d**) *Tech* engranar; *Aut* **to e. the clutch** pisar el embrague

engaged [ɪnˈgeɪdʒd] *adj* (**a**) *(betrothed)* prometido(a); **to get e.** prometerse (**b**) *(busy)* ocupado(a); *Br Tel* **it's e.** está comunicando

engagement [ɪnˈgeɪdʒmənt] *n* (**a**) *(betrothal)* petición *f* de mano; *(period)* noviazgo *m*; **e. ring** anillo *m* de compromiso (**b**) *(appointment)* cita *f* (**c**) *Mil* combate *m*

engaging [ɪnˈgeɪdʒɪŋ] *adj* simpático(a), agradable

engender [ɪnˈdʒendə(r)] *vt* engendrar

engine [ˈendʒɪn] *n* motor *m*; *Rail* locomotora *f*; **e. room** sala *f* de máquinas; **e. driver** maquinista *mf*

engineer [endʒɪˈnɪə(r)] **1** *n* (**a**) ingeniero(a) *m,f*; **civil e.** ingeniero de caminos (**b**) *US Rail* maquinista *mf*

2 *vt Fig (contrive)* maquinar

engineering [endʒɪˈnɪərɪŋ] *n* ingeniería *f*; **electrical e.** electrotecnia *f*; **civil e.** ingeniería civil

England [ˈɪŋglənd] *n* Inglaterra *f*

English [ˈɪŋglɪʃ] **1** *adj* inglés(esa)

2 *n* (**a**) *(language)* inglés *m* (**b**) *pl* **the E.** los ingleses

Englishman [ˈɪŋglɪʃmən] *n* inglés *m*

English-speaking [ˈɪŋglɪˈspiːkɪŋ] *adj* de habla inglesa

Englishwoman [ˈɪŋglɪʃwʊmən] *n* inglesa *f*

engraving [ɪnˈgreɪvɪŋ] *n* grabado *m*

engrossed [ɪn'grəʊst] *adj* absorto(a) (**in** en)

engulf [ɪn'gʌlf] *vt* tragarse

enhance [ɪn'hɑːns] *vt (beauty)* realzar; *(power, chances)* aumentar

enigma [ɪ'nɪgmə] *n* enigma *m*

enjoy [ɪn'dʒɔɪ] *vt* (**a**) disfrutar de; **to e. one-self** pasarlo bien (**b**) *(benefit from)* gozar de

enjoyable [ɪn'dʒɔɪəbəl] *adj* agradable; *(amusing)* divertido(a)

enjoyment [ɪn'dʒɔɪmənt] *n* placer *m*, gusto *m*

enlarge [ɪn'lɑːdʒ] **1** *vt* extender, ampliar; *Phot* ampliar
  2 *vi* **to e. upon a subject** extenderse sobre un tema

enlargement [ɪn'lɑːdʒmənt] *n Phot* ampliación *f*

enlighten [ɪn'laɪtən] *vt* iluminar

enlightened [ɪn'laɪtənd] *adj* (**a**) *(learned)* culto(a); *(informed)* bien informado(a) (**b**) *Hist* ilustrado(a)

enlightenment [ɪn'laɪtənmənt] *n* **the Age of E.** el Siglo de las Luces

enlist [ɪn'lɪst] **1** *vt Mil* reclutar; **to e. sb's help** conseguir ayuda de algn
  2 *vi Mil* alistarse

enmity ['enmɪtɪ] *n* enemistad *f*, hostilidad *f*

enormous [ɪ'nɔːməs] *adj* enorme

enormously [ɪ'nɔːməslɪ] *adv* enormemente; **I enjoyed myself e.** lo pasé genial

enough [ɪ'nʌf] **1** *adj* bastante, suficiente; **e. books** bastantes libros; **e. money** bastante dinero; **have we got e. petrol?** ¿tenemos suficiente gasolina?
  2 *adv* bastante; **oddly e. ...** lo curioso es que ...; **sure e.** en efecto
  3 *pron* lo bastante, lo suficiente; **e. to live on** lo suficiente para vivir; **it isn't e.** no basta; **more than e.** más que suficiente; *Fam* **e. is e.!** ¡ya está!; *Fam* **I've had e.!** ¡estoy harto!

enquire [ɪn'kwaɪə(r)] *vt* preguntar

enquiry [ɪn'kwaɪərɪ] *n* (**a**) *(question)* pregunta *f*; **to make an e.** preguntar; **enquiries** información *f* (**b**) *(investigation)* investigación *f*

enrage [ɪn'reɪdʒ] *vt* enfurecer

enrich [ɪn'rɪtʃ] *vt* enriquecer

enrol, *US* **enroll** [ɪn'rəʊl] **1** *vt* matricular, inscribir
  2 *vi* matricularse, inscribirse

> *Note that the Spanish verb **enrollar** is a false friend and is never a translation for the English verb **to enrol**. In Spanish, **enrollar** means "to roll up".*

enrolment [ɪn'rəʊlmənt] *n* matrícula *f*

en route [ɒn'ruːt] *adv* en or por el camino

ensign ['ensaɪn] *n* (**a**) *(flag)* bandera *f*; *Naut* pabellón *m* (**b**) *US (naval officer)* alférez *m* de fragata

enslave [ɪn'sleɪv] *vt* esclavizar

ensue [ɪn'sjuː] *vi* (**a**) *(follow)* seguir (**b**) *(result)* resultar (**from** de)

ensure [ɪn'ʃʊə(r)] *vt* asegurar

entail [ɪn'teɪl] *vt (involve)* suponer

enter ['entə(r)] **1** *vt* (**a**) *(go into)* entrar en; *Fig (join)* ingresar en (**b**) *(write down)* apuntar anotar (**c**) **to e. one's name for a course** *(register)* matricularse en un curso (**d**) *Comput* dar entrada a
  2 *vi* entrar

▶ **enter into** *vt insep* (**a**) *(agreement)* firmar *(negotiations)* iniciar; *(bargain)* cerrar (**b**) *(relations)* establecer; *(conversation)* entablar

enterprise ['entəpraɪz] *n* empresa *f*; **free e.** libre empresa; **private e.** iniciativa privada *(as a whole)* el sector privado; **public e.** el sector público

enterprising ['entəpraɪzɪŋ] *adj* emprendedor(a)

entertain [entə'teɪn] **1** *vt* (**a**) *(amuse)* divertir (**b**) *(consider)* considerar; **to e. an idea** abrigar una idea
  2 *vi* tener invitados

entertainer [entə'teɪnə(r)] *n* artista *mf*

entertaining [entə'teɪnɪŋ] *adj* divertido(a)

entertainment [entə'teɪnmənt] *n* (**a**) diversión *f* (**b**) *Th* espectáculo *m*

enthralling [ɪn'θrɔːlɪŋ] *adj* fascinante

enthuse [ɪn'θjuːz] *vi* entusiasmarse (**over** por)

enthusiasm [ɪn'θjuːzɪæzəm] *n* entusiasmo *m*

enthusiast [ɪn'θjuːzɪæst] *n* entusiasta *mf*

enthusiastic [ɪnθjuːzɪ'æstɪk] *adj* entusiasta *(praise)* caluroso(a); **to be e. about sth** entusiasmarse por algo

entice [ɪn'taɪs] *vt* seducir, atraer

enticing [ɪn'taɪsɪŋ] *adj* atractivo(a), tentador(a)

entire [ɪn'taɪə(r)] *adj* entero(a), todo(a)

entirely [ɪn'taɪəlɪ] *adv* (**a**) *(completely)* totalmente (**b**) *(solely)* exclusivamente

entirety [ɪn'taɪərɪtɪ] *n* **in its e.** en su totalidad

entitle [ɪn'taɪtəl] *vt* (**a**) dar derecho a; **to be entitled to** tener derecho a (**b**) *(book etc)* titular

entity ['entɪtɪ] *n* entidad *f*

entourage [ɒntʊ'rɑːʒ] *n* séquito *m*

entrails ['entreɪlz] *npl* tripas *fpl*; *Fig* entrañas *fpl*

entrance¹ ['entrəns] *n* (**a**) entrada *f*; **e. fee** *(to museum etc)* entrada; *(to organization)* cuota *f* (**b**) *(admission)* ingreso *m*; **e. examination** examen *m* de ingreso

entrance² [ɪn'trɑːns] *vt* encantar

entrant ['entrənt] *n (in competition)* participante *mf*; *(applicant)* aspirante *mf*

entreat [ɪn'triːt] *vt Fml* suplicar, rogar

entrée ['ɒntreɪ] *n Br (first course)* entrada *f* primer plato *m*; *US (main course)* plato principal

entrenched [ɪn'trentʃt] *adj* firmemente enraizado(a)

entrepreneur [ɒntrəprə'nɜː(r)] *n* empresario(a) *m,f*

entrust [ɪn'trʌst] *vt* encargar (**with** de); **to e. sth to sb** dejar algo al cuidado de algn

entry ['entrɪ] *n* (**a**) *(entrance)* entrada *f*; **no e.** *(sign)* dirección prohibida (**b**) *(in competition)* participante *mf*

enumerate [ɪ'njuːməreɪt] *vt* enumerar

enunciate [ɪ'nʌnsɪeɪt] *vt (words)* articular; *(ideas)* formular

envelop [ɪn'veləp] *vt* envolver

envelope ['envələʊp] *n* sobre *m*

envious ['envɪəs] *adj* envidioso(a); **to feel e.** tener envidia

environment [ɪn'vaɪərənmənt] *n* medio *m* ambiente

environmental [ɪnvaɪərən'mentəl] *adj* medioambiental

environmentally [ɪnvaɪərən'mentəlɪ] *adv* ecológicamente; **e. friendly** ecológico(a), que no daña el medio ambiente

envisage [ɪn'vɪzɪdʒ] *vt (imagine)* imaginarse; *(foresee)* prever

envoy ['envɔɪ] *n* enviado(a) *m,f*

envy ['envɪ] **1** *n* envidia *f*

  2 *vt* envidiar, tener envidia de

enzyme ['enzaɪm] *n* enzima *m*

ephemeral [ɪ'femərəl] *adj* efímero(a)

epic ['epɪk] **1** *n* epopeya *f*

  2 *adj* épico(a)

epidemic [epɪ'demɪk] *n* epidemia *f*; *Fig (of crime etc)* ola *f*

epilepsy ['epɪlepsɪ] *n* epilepsia *f*

epilogue, *US* **epilog** ['epɪlɒg] *n* epílogo *m*

episode ['epɪsəʊd] *n* episodio *m*

epistle [ɪ'pɪsəl] *n* epístola *f*

epitaph ['epɪtɑːf] *n* epitafio *m*

epitome [ɪ'pɪtəmɪ] *n Fml* personificación *f*

epitomize [ɪ'pɪtəmaɪz] *vt Fml* personificar

epoch ['iːpɒk] *n* época *f*

equable ['ekwəbəl] *adj* (**a**) *(person)* ecuánime (**b**) *(climate)* uniforme

equal ['iːkwəl] **1** *adj* igual; **to be e. to the occasion** estar a la altura de las circunstancias; **e. pay** igualdad *f* de salarios

  2 *n* igual *mf*; **to treat sb as an e.** tratar a algn de igual a igual

  3 *vt* (**a**) *Math* equivaler (**b**) *(match)* igualar

equality [iː'kwɒlɪtɪ] *n* igualdad *f*

equalize ['iːkwəlaɪz] **1** *vi Ftb* empatar

  2 *vt* igualar

equalizer ['iːkwəlaɪzə(r)] *n Ftb* gol *m* del empate; *(of sound)* ecualizador *m*

equally ['iːkwəlɪ] *adv* igualmente; **e. pretty** igual de bonito; **to share sth e.** dividir algo en partes iguales

equanimity [ekwə'nɪmɪtɪ] *n* ecuanimidad *f*

equate [ɪ'kweɪt] *vt* equiparar, comparar (**to** con)

equation [ɪ'kweɪʒən, ɪ'kweɪʃən] *n Math* ecuación *f*

equator [ɪ'kweɪtə(r)] *n* ecuador *m*

equatorial [ekwə'tɔːrɪəl] *adj* ecuatorial

equestrian [ɪ'kwestrɪən] *adj* ecuestre

equilibrium [iːkwɪ'lɪbrɪəm] *n* equilibrio *m*

equinox ['iːkwɪnɒks] *n* equinoccio *m*

equip [ɪ'kwɪp] *vt (with tools, machines)* equipar; *(with food)* proveer

equipment [ɪ'kwɪpmənt] *n (materials)* equipo *m*; **office e.** material *m* de oficina

equipped [ɪ'kwɪpt] *adj (with tools, machines)* equipado(a); *(with skills)* dotado(a)

equitable ['ekwɪtəbəl] *adj* equitativo(a)

equities ['ekwɪtɪz] *npl* acciones ordinarias

equivalent [ɪ'kwɪvələnt] *adj & n* equivalente *(m)*; **to be e. to** equivaler a, ser equivalente a

equivocal [ɪ'kwɪvəkəl] *adj* equívoco(a)

era ['ɪərə] *n* era *f*

eradicate [ɪ'rædɪkeɪt] *vt* erradicar

erase [ɪ'reɪz] *vt* borrar

eraser [*Br* ɪ'reɪzə(r), *US* ɪ'reɪsər] *n* goma *f* de borrar

erect [ɪ'rekt] **1** *adj* (**a**) *(upright)* erguido(a) (**b**) *(penis)* erecto(a)

  2 *vt (monument)* levantar, erigir

erection [ɪ'rekʃən] *n* (**a**) *(of building)* construcción *f* (**b**) *(penis)* erección *f*

ermine ['ɜːmɪn] *n* armiño *m*

erode [ɪ'rəʊd] *vt* (**a**) *(rock, soil)* erosionar (**b**) *(metal)* corroer, desgastar; *Fig (power, confidence)* hacer perder

erosion [ɪ'rəʊʒən] *n Geol* erosión *f*

erotic [ɪ'rɒtɪk] *adj* erótico(a)

err [ɜː(r)] *vi* errar; **to e. on the side of caution** pecar de prudente

errand ['erənd] *n* recado *m*; **e. boy** recadero *m*

erratic [ɪ'rætɪk] *adj (performance, behaviour)* irregular; *(weather)* muy variable; *(person)* caprichoso(a)

erroneous [ɪ'rəʊnɪəs] *adj* erróneo(a)

error ['erə(r)] *n* error *m*, equivocación *f*

erupt [ɪ'rʌpt] *vi* (**a**) *(volcano)* entrar en erupción; *(violence)* estallar (**b**) **his skin erupted in a rash** le salió una erupción

eruption [ɪ'rʌpʃən] *n* erupción *f*

escalate ['eskəleɪt] *vi (war)* intensificarse; *(prices)* aumentar; *(change)* convertirse (**into** en)

escalation [eskə'leɪʃən] *n (of war)* intensificación *f*, escalada *f*; *(of prices)* subida *f*

escalator ['eskəleɪtə(r)] *n* escalera mecánica

> Note that the Spanish word **escalador** is a false friend and is never a translation for the English word **escalator**. In Spanish, **escalador** means "climber, mountaineer".

escalope ['eskəlɒp] *n* escalope *m*

escapade ['eskəpeɪd] *n* aventura *f*

 Note that the Spanish word **escapada** is a false friend and is never a translation for the English word **escapade**. In Spanish, **escapada** means both "escape" and "quick trip".

---

escape [ɪ'skeɪp] **1** n huída f, fuga f; (of gas) escape m; **e. route** vía f de escape
  2 vi escaparse
  3 vt (a) (avoid) evitar, huir de; **to e. punishment** librarse del castigo (b) Fig **his name escapes me** no recuerdo su nombre
escapism [ɪ'skeɪpɪzəm] n evasión f
escort 1 n ['eskɔːt] (a) (companion) acompañante mf (b) Mil escolta f
  2 vt [ɪ'skɔːt] (a) (accompany) acompañar (b) (protect) escoltar
Eskimo ['eskɪməʊ] adj & n esquimal (mf)
esoteric [esəʊ'terɪk] adj esotérico(a)
especial [ɪ'speʃəl] adj especial
especially [ɪ'speʃəlɪ] adv especialmente, sobre todo
espionage ['espɪənɑːʒ] n espionaje m
esplanade [esplə'neɪd] n paseo marítimo
espouse [ɪ'spaʊz] vt Fml (cause) abrazar, adoptar
espresso [e'spresəʊ] n **e. (coffee)** café m exprés
esquire [ɪ'skwaɪə(r)] n Br señor m; **Timothy Whiteman E.** Sr. Don Timothy Whiteman
essay ['eseɪ] n Educ redacción f
essence ['esəns] n esencia f; **in e.** esencialmente
essential [ɪ'senʃəl] **1** adj esencial, imprescindible
  2 n necesidad básica; **the essentials** lo fundamental
essentially [ɪ'senʃəlɪ] adv esencialmente
establish [ɪ'stæblɪʃ] vt (a) (found) establecer; (business) montar (b) Jur **to e. a fact** probar un hecho; **to e. the truth** demostrar la verdad
established [ɪ'stæblɪʃt] adj (person) establecido(a); (fact) conocido(a)
establishment [ɪ'stæblɪʃmənt] n establecimiento m; **the E.** el sistema
estate [ɪ'steɪt] n (a) (land) finca f; Br **e. agent** agente mf inmobiliario(a); Br **e. car** coche m modelo familiar (b) (housing) **e.** zona urbanizada (c) (property) bienes mpl (d) (inheritance) herencia f
esteem [ɪ'stiːm] **1** n **to hold sb in great e.** apreciar mucho a algn
  2 vt estimar
esthetic [es'θetɪk] adj US estético(a)
estimate 1 n ['estɪmɪt] (calculation) cálculo m; (likely cost of work) presupuesto m; **rough e.** cálculo aproximado
  2 vt ['estɪmeɪt] calcular; Fig pensar, creer
estimation [estɪ'meɪʃən] n (a) (opinion) juicio m, opinión f (b) (esteem) estima f
Estonia [e'stəʊnɪə] n Estonia

Estonian [e'stəʊnɪən] **1** adj estonio(a)
  2 n (a) (person) estonio(a) m,f (b) (language) estonio m
estrange [ɪ'streɪndʒ] vt **to become estranged (from)** alejarse (de)
Estremadura [estreɪmə'dʊrə] n Extremadura
estuary ['estjʊərɪ] n estuario m
etching ['etʃɪŋ] n aguafuerte m
eternal [ɪ'tɜːnəl] adj eterno(a), incesante; **e. triangle** triángulo amoroso
eternity [ɪ'tɜːnɪtɪ] n eternidad f
ether ['iːθə(r)] n éter m
ethereal [ɪ'θɪərɪəl] adj etéreo(a)
ethical ['eθɪkəl] adj ético(a)
ethics ['eθɪks] n ética f
Ethiopia [iːθɪ'əʊpɪə] n Etiopía
ethnic ['eθnɪk] adj étnico(a)
ethos ['iːθɒs] n carácter distintivo
etiquette ['etɪket] n protocolo m, etiqueta f
etymology [etɪ'mɒlədʒɪ] n etimología f
EU [iː'juː] n (abbr **European Union**) UE f
eucalyptus [juːkə'lɪptəs] n eucalipto m
euphemism ['juːfɪmɪzəm] n eufemismo m
euphoria [juː'fɔːrɪə] n euforia f
euro ['jʊərəʊ] n (pl **euros**) (European currency) euro m
Eurocheque ['jʊərəʊtʃek] n eurocheque m
Eurocrat ['jʊərəʊkræt] n eurócrata mf
Euro-MP ['jʊərəʊempiː] n eurodiputado(a) m,f
Europe ['jʊərəp] n Europa
European [jʊərə'piːən] adj & n europeo(a) (m,f); **E. Economic Community** Comunidad Económica Europea
Eurosceptic ['jʊərəʊskeptɪk] n Br euroescéptico(a) m,f
euthanasia [juːθə'neɪzɪə] n eutanasia f
evacuate [ɪ'vækjʊeɪt] vt evacuar
evacuation [ɪvækjʊ'eɪʃən] n evacuación f
evade [ɪ'veɪd] vt evadir
evaluate [ɪ'væljʊeɪt] vt evaluar
evaluation [ɪvæljʊ'eɪʃən] n evaluación f
evangelical [iːvæn'dʒelɪkəl] adj evangélico(a)
evangelist [ɪ'vændʒɪlɪst] n evangelista mf
evaporate [ɪ'væpəreɪt] **1** vt evaporar; **evaporated milk** leche condensada sin endulzar
  2 vi evaporarse; Fig desvanecerse
evasion [ɪ'veɪʒən] n (a) evasión f (b) (evasive answer) evasiva f
evasive [ɪ'veɪsɪv] adj evasivo(a)
eve [iːv] n víspera f; **on the e. of** en vísperas de
even ['iːvən] **1** adj (a) (smooth) liso(a); (level) llano(a)
  (b) (regular) uniforme
  (c) (equally balanced) igual; Sport **to be e. in** empatados(as); **to get e. with sb** desquitarse con algn
  (d) (number) par
  (e) (at the same level) a nivel

(**f**) *(quantity)* exacto(a)

2 *adv* (**a**) incluso, hasta, aun; **e. now** incluso ahora; **e. so** aun así; **e. the children knew** hasta los niños lo sabían

(**b**) *(negative)* ni siquiera; **she can't e. write her name** ni siquiera sabe escribir su nombre; **without e. speaking** sin hablar siquiera

(**c**) *(before comparative)* aun, todavía; **e. worse** aun peor

(**d**) **e. as** mientras; **e. if** incluso si; **e. though** aunque

3 *vt* igualar

evening ['iːvnɪŋ] *n* (**a**) *(early)* tarde *f*; *(late)* noche *f*; **in the e.** por la tarde; **tomorrow e.** mañana por la tarde; **e. class** clase nocturna; **e. dress** *(for man)* traje *m* de etiqueta; *(for woman)* traje de noche; **e. paper** periódico vespertino (**b**) *(greeting)* **good e.!** *(early)* ¡buenas tardes!; *(late)* ¡buenas noches!

event [ɪ'vent] *n* (**a**) *(happening)* suceso *m*, acontecimiento *m* (**b**) *(case)* caso *m*; **at all events** en todo caso; **in the e. of fire** en caso de incendio (**c**) *Sport* prueba *f*

eventful [ɪ'ventfʊl] *adj* **an e. day** *(busy)* un día agitado; *(memorable)* un día memorable

eventual [ɪ'ventʃʊəl] *adj (ultimate)* final; *(resulting)* consiguiente

> 🖉 Note that the Spanish word **eventual** is a false friend and is never a translation for the English word **eventual**. In Spanish, **eventual** means both "possible" and "temporary".

eventuality [ɪventʃʊ'ælɪtɪ] *n* eventualidad *f*

eventually [ɪ'ventʃʊəlɪ] *adv* finalmente

> 🖉 Note that the Spanish word **eventualmente** is a false friend and is never a translation for the English word **eventually**. In Spanish, **eventualmente** means both "by chance" and "possibly".

ever ['evə(r)] *adv* (**a**) nunca, jamás; **stronger than e.** más fuerte que nunca (**b**) *(interrogative)* alguna vez; **have you e. been there?** ¿has estado allí alguna vez? (**c**) *(always)* siempre; **for e.** para siempre; **for e. and e.** para siempre jamás (**d**) *(emphasis)* **how e. did you manage it?** ¿cómo diablos lo conseguiste?; **why e. not?** ¿por qué no?; *Fam* **e. so expensive** tan carísimo; **such a lot of money** tantísimo dinero; **thank you e. so much** muchísimas gracias

evergreen ['evəgriːn] **1** *adj* de hoja perenne **2** *n* árbol *m*/planta *f* de hoja perenne

everlasting [evə'lɑːstɪŋ] *adj* eterno(a)

evermore [evə'mɔː(r)] *adv* **for e.** para siempre jamás

every ['evrɪ] *adj* (**a**) *(each)* cada; **e. now and then** de vez en cuando; **e. day** todos los días; **e. other day** cada dos días; **e. one of you** todos(as) vosotros(as); **e. citizen** todo ciudadano (**b**) **you had e. right to be angry** tenías toda la razón para estar enfadado

everybody ['evrɪbɒdɪ] *pron* todo el mundo, todos(as)

everyday ['evrɪdeɪ] *adj* diario(a), de todos los días; **an e. occurrence** un suceso cotidiano

everyone ['evrɪwʌn] *pron* todo el mundo, todos(as)

everyplace ['evrɪpleɪs] *adv US* = **everywhere**

everything ['evrɪθɪŋ] *pron* todo; **he eats e.** come de todo; **she means e. to me** ella lo es todo para mí

everywhere ['evrɪweə(r)] *adv* en todas partes, por todas partes

evict [ɪ'vɪkt] *vt* desahuciar

evidence ['evɪdəns] *n* (**a**) *(proof)* evidencia *f* (**b**) *Jur* testimonio *m*; **to give e.** prestar declaración (**c**) *(sign)* indicio *m*, señal *f*; **to be in e.** dejarse notar

evident ['evɪdənt] *adj* evidente, manifiesto(a)

evidently ['evɪdəntlɪ] *adv* evidentemente, al parecer

evil ['iːvəl] **1** *adj (wicked)* malo(a), malvado(a); *(harmful)* nocivo(a); *(unfortunate)* aciago(a) **2** *n* mal *m*

evocative [ɪ'vɒkətɪv] *adj* evocador(a)

evoke [ɪ'vəʊk] *vt* evocar

evolution [iːvə'luːʃən] *n* evolución *f*; *Biol* desarrollo *m*

evolve [ɪ'vɒlv] **1** *vi (species)* evolucionar; *(ideas)* desarrollarse **2** *vt* desarrollar

ewe [juː] *n* oveja *f*

ex [eks] *n* **her ex** su ex marido; **his ex** su ex mujer

ex- [eks] *pref* ex, antiguo(a); **ex-minister** ex ministro *m*

exacerbate [ɪg'zæsəbeɪt] *vt* exacerbar

exact [ɪg'zækt] **1** *adj (accurate)* exacto(a); *(definition)* preciso(a); **this e. spot** ese mismo lugar **2** *vt* exigir

exacting [ɪg'zæktɪŋ] *adj* exigente

exactly [ɪg'zæktlɪ] *adv* exactamente; precisamente; **e.!** ¡exacto!

exaggerate [ɪg'zædʒəreɪt] *vi & vt* exagerar

exaggeration [ɪgzædʒə'reɪʃən] *n* exageración *f*

exalt [ɪg'zɔːlt] *vt Fml* exaltar

exam [ɪg'zæm] *n Fam* examen *m*

examination [ɪgzæmɪ'neɪʃən] *n* (**a**) *Educ* examen *m*; **to sit an e.** hacer un examen (**b**) *Med* reconocimiento *m* (**c**) *Jur* interrogatorio *m*

examine [ɪg'zæmɪn] *vt Educ* examinar; *(customs)* registrar; *Med* hacer un reconocimiento médico a; *Jur* interrogar

examiner [ɪg'zæmɪnə(r)] *n* examinador(a) *m,f*

example [ɪg'zɑːmpəl] *n* ejemplo *m*; *(specimen)* ejemplar *m*; **for e.** por ejemplo

exasperate [ɪg'zɑːspəreɪt] *vt* exasperar

exasperation [ɪgzɑːspəˈreɪʃən] n exasperación f

excavate [ˈekskəveɪt] vt excavar

excavation [ekskəˈveɪʃən] n excavación f

exceed [ekˈsiːd] vt exceder, sobrepasar

exceedingly [ekˈsiːdɪŋlɪ] adv extremadamente, sumamente

excel [ɪkˈsel] **1** vi sobresalir
  2 vt superar

excellency [ˈeksələnsɪ] n **His E.** Su Excelencia

excellent [ˈeksələnt] adj excelente

except [ɪkˈsept] **1** prep excepto, salvo; **e. for the little ones** excepto los pequeños; **e. that ...** salvo que ...
  2 vt exceptuar

exception [ɪkˈsepʃən] n (**a**) excepción f; **with the e. of** a excepción de; **without e.** sin excepción (**b**) (objection) objeción f; **to take e. to sth** ofenderse por algo

exceptional [ɪkˈsepʃənəl] adj excepcional

excerpt [ˈeksɜːpt] n extracto m

excess 1 n [ɪkˈses] exceso m
  2 adj [ˈekses] excedente; **e. baggage** exceso m de equipaje; **e. fare** suplemento m

excessive [ɪkˈsesɪv] adj excesivo(a)

excessively [ɪkˈsesɪvlɪ] adv excesivamente, en exceso

exchange [ɪksˈtʃeɪndʒ] **1** n (**a**) cambio m; **e. of ideas** intercambio m de ideas; **in e. for a** cambio de (**b**) Fin **e. rate** tipo m de cambio (**c**) (telephone) central telefónica
  2 vt (**a**) intercambiar; **to e. blows** golpearse (**b**) (prisoners) canjear

exchequer [ɪksˈtʃekə(r)] n Br **the E.** Hacienda f; **Chancellor of the E.** Ministro m de Hacienda

excise [ˈeksaɪz] n impuesto m sobre el consumo; **e. duty** derechos mpl de aduana

excitable [ɪkˈsaɪtəbəl] adj excitable

excite [ɪkˈsaɪt] vt (stimulate) excitar; (move) emocionar; (enthuse) entusiasmar; (arouse) provocar

excitement [ɪkˈsaɪtmənt] n (stimulation) excitación f; (emotion) emoción f; (commotion) agitación f

exciting [ɪkˈsaɪtɪŋ] adj apasionante, emocionante

exclaim [ɪkˈskleɪm] **1** vi exclamar
  2 vt gritar

exclamation [ekskləˈmeɪʃən] n exclamación f; **e.** Br **mark** or US **point** signo m de admiración

exclude [ɪkˈskluːd] vt excluir; (from club) no admitir

excluding [ɪkˈskluːdɪŋ] prep excepto

exclusion [ɪkˈskluːʒən] n exclusión f

exclusive [ɪkˈskluːsɪv] **1** adj exclusivo(a); (neighbourhood) selecto(a); (club) cerrado(a)
  2 n Press exclusiva f

exclusively [ɪkˈskluːsɪvlɪ] adv exclusivamente

excommunicate [ekskəˈmjuːnɪkeɪt] vt excomulgar

excrement [ˈekskrɪmənt] n excremento m

excruciating [ɪkˈskruːʃɪeɪtɪŋ] adj insoportable

excruciatingly [ɪkˈskruːʃɪeɪtɪŋlɪ] adv horriblemente

excursion [ɪkˈskɜːʃən] n excursión f

excusable [ɪkˈskjuːzəbəl] adj perdonable

excuse 1 vt [ɪkˈskjuːz] (**a**) perdonar, disculpar; **e. me!** (to attract attention) ¡perdón! ¡oiga (por favor)!; (when trying to get past) con permiso; **may I be excused for a moment?** ¿puedo salir un momento? (**b**) (exempt) dispensar (**c**) (justify) justificar
  2 n [ɪkˈskjuːs] excusa f; **to make an e.** dar excusas

ex-directory [eksdɪˈrektərɪ] adj Br Tel = que no se encuentra en la guía telefónica

execute [ˈeksɪkjuːt] vt (**a**) (order) cumplir (task) realizar (**b**) Jur cumplir (**c**) (person) ejecutar

execution [eksɪˈkjuːʃən] n (**a**) (of order) cumplimiento m; (of task) realización f (**b**) Jur cumplimiento m (**c**) (of person) ejecución f

executioner [eksɪˈkjuːʃənə(r)] n verdugo m

executive [ɪgˈzekjʊtɪv] **1** adj ejecutivo(a)
  2 n ejecutivo(a) m,f

executor [ɪgˈzekjʊtə(r)] n albacea m

exemplary [ɪgˈzemplərɪ] adj ejemplar

exemplify [ɪgˈzemplɪfaɪ] vt ejemplificar

exempt [ɪgˈzempt] **1** vt eximir (**from** de)
  2 adj exento(a); **e. from tax** libre de impuesto

exemption [ɪgˈzempʃən] n exención f

exercise [ˈeksəsaɪz] **1** n ejercicio m; **e. book** cuaderno m
  2 vt (**a**) (rights, duties) ejercer (**b**) (dog) sacar de paseo
  3 vi hacer ejercicio

exert [ɪgˈzɜːt] vt (influence) ejercer; **to e. oneself** esforzarse

exertion [ɪgˈzɜːʃən] n esfuerzo m

exhale [eksˈheɪl] **1** vt (breathe) exhalar
  2 vi espirar

exhaust [ɪgˈzɔːst] **1** vt agotar
  2 n (gas) gases mpl de combustión; **e. pipe** tubo m de escape

exhausted [ɪgˈzɔːstɪd] adj agotado(a)

exhaustion [ɪgˈzɔːstʃən] n agotamiento m

exhaustive [ɪgˈzɔːstɪv] adj exhaustivo(a)

exhibit [ɪgˈzɪbɪt] **1** n Art objeto expuesto; Jur prueba f instrumental
  2 vt Art exponer; (surprise etc) mostrar

exhibition [eksɪˈbɪʃən] n exposición f

exhibitionist [eksɪˈbɪʃənɪst] adj & n exhibicionista (mf)

exhilarating [ɪgˈzɪləreɪtɪŋ] adj estimulante

exhilaration [ɪgzɪləˈreɪʃən] n regocijo m

exhume [eksˈhjuːm] vt exhumar

exile [ˈeksaɪl] **1** n (**a**) (banishment) exilio m

(**b**) *(person)* exiliado(a) *m,f*
2 *vt* exiliar

exist [ɪg'zɪst] *vi* existir; *(have little money)* malvivir

existence [ɪg'zɪstəns] *n* existencia *f*

existing [ɪg'zɪstɪŋ] *adj* existente, actual

exit ['eksɪt] **1** *n* (**a**) salida *f* (**b**) *Th* mutis *m*
2 *vi Th* hacer mutis

> *Note that the Spanish word **éxito** is a false friend and is never a translation for the English word **exit**. In Spanish, **éxito** means "success".*

exodus ['eksədəs] *n* éxodo *m*

exonerate [ɪg'zɒnəreɪt] *vt Fml* exonerar (**from** de)

exorbitant [ɪg'zɔːbɪtənt] *adj* exorbitante, desorbitado(a)

exotic [ɪg'zɒtɪk] *adj* exótico(a)

expand [ɪk'spænd] **1** *vt (enlarge)* ampliar; *(gas, metal)* dilatar
2 *vi (grow)* ampliarse; *(metal)* dilatarse; *(become more friendly)* abrirse
▸ **expand on** *vt insep* ampliar

expanse [ɪk'spæns] *n* extensión *f*

expansion [ɪk'spænʃən] *n (in size)* expansión *f*; *(of gas, metal)* dilatación *f*

expatriate 1 *adj & n* [eks'pætrɪɪt] expatriado(a) *(m,f)*
2 *vt* [eks'pætrɪeɪt] expatriar

expect [ɪk'spekt] **1** *vt* (**a**) *(anticipate)* esperar; **I half-expected that to happen** suponía que iba a ocurrir (**b**) *(demand)* contar con (**c**) *(suppose)* suponer
2 *vi Fam* **to be expecting** estar embarazada

expectancy [ɪk'spektənsɪ] *n* expectación *f*

expectant [ɪk'spektənt] *adj* ilusionado(a); **e. mother** mujer embarazada

expectation [ekspek'teɪʃən] *n* esperanza *f*; **contrary to e.** contrariamente a lo que se esperaba

expedient [ɪk'spiːdɪənt] **1** *adj* conveniente, oportuno(a)
2 *n* expediente *m*, recurso *m*

expedition [ekspɪ'dɪʃən] *n* expedición *f*

expel [ɪk'spel] *vt* expulsar

expend [ɪk'spend] *vt* gastar

expendable [ɪk'spendəbəl] *adj* prescindible

expenditure [ɪk'spendɪtʃə(r)] *n* desembolso *m*

expense [ɪk'spens] *n* gasto *m*; **all expenses paid** con todos los gastos pagados; **to spare no e.** no escatimar gastos; *Fig* **at the e. of** a costa de; **e. account** cuenta *f* de gastos de representación

expensive [ɪk'spensɪv] *adj* caro(a), costoso(a)

experience [ɪk'spɪərɪəns] **1** *n* experiencia *f*
2 *vt (sensation)* experimentar; *(difficulty, loss)* sufrir

experienced [ɪk'spɪərɪənst] *adj* experimentado(a)

experiment [ɪk'sperɪmənt] **1** *n* experimento *m*
2 *vi* experimentar, hacer experimentos (**on** *or* **with** con)

experimental [ɪksperɪ'mentəl] *adj* experimental

expert ['ekspɜːt] **1** *adj* experto(a)
2 *n* experto(a) *m,f*, especialista *mf*

expertise [ekspɜː'tiːz] *n* pericia *f*

expire [ɪk'spaɪə(r)] *vi* (**a**) *(die)* expirar; *(mandate)* terminar (**b**) *Com & Ins* vencer; *(ticket)* caducar

expiry [ɪk'spaɪərɪ] *n* vencimiento *m*; **e. date** fecha *f* de caducidad

explain [ɪk'spleɪn] **1** *vt* explicar; *(clarify)* aclarar; **to e. oneself** justificarse
2 *vi* explicarse

explanation [eksplə'neɪʃən] *n* explicación *f*; *(clarification)* aclaración *f*

explanatory [ɪk'splænətərɪ] *adj* explicativo(a), aclaratorio(a)

explicit [ɪk'splɪsɪt] *adj* explícito(a)

explode [ɪk'spləʊd] **1** *vt* (**a**) *(bomb)* hacer explotar (**b**) *Fig (theory)* echar por tierra
2 *vi (bomb)* estallar, explotar; *Fig* **to e. with** *or* **in anger** montar en cólera

exploit 1 *n* ['eksplɔɪt] proeza *f*, hazaña *f*
2 *vt* [ek'splɔɪt] explotar

exploitation [eksplɔɪ'teɪʃən] *n* explotación *f*

exploratory [ek'splɒrətərɪ] *adj* exploratorio(a)

explore [ɪk'splɔː(r)] *vt* explorar

explorer [ɪk'splɔːrə(r)] *n* explorador(a) *m,f*

explosion [ɪk'spləʊʒən] *n* explosión *f*

explosive [ɪk'spləʊsɪv] **1** *adj* explosivo(a); **e. issue** asunto delicado
2 *n* explosivo *m*

exponent [ɪk'spəʊnənt] *n* exponente *m*; *(supporter)* defensor(a) *m,f*

export 1 *vt* [ɪk'spɔːt] exportar
2 *n* ['ekspɔːt] (**a**) *(trade)* exportación *f* (**b**) *(commodity)* artículo *m* de exportación

exporter [ek'spɔːtə(r)] *n* exportador(a) *m,f*

expose [ɪk'spəʊz] *vt (uncover)* exponer; *(secret)* revelar; *(plot)* descubrir; **to e. oneself** exhibirse desnudo

exposed [ɪk'spəʊzd] *adj* expuesto(a)

exposure [ɪk'spəʊʒə(r)] *n* (**a**) *(to light, cold, heat)* exposición *f*; **to die of e.** morir de frío (**b**) *Phot* fotografía *f*; **e. meter** fotómetro *m* (**c**) *(of criminal)* descubrimiento *m*

expound [ɪk'spaʊnd] *vt* exponer

express [ɪk'spres] **1** *adj* (**a**) *(explicit)* expreso(a) (**b**) *Br (letter)* urgente; **e. train** expreso *m*
2 *n Rail* expreso *m*
3 *vt* expresar
4 *adv* **send it e.** mándalo urgente

expression [ɪk'spreʃən] *n* expresión *f*

expressly [ɪk'spreslɪ] *adv Fml* expresamente

expressway [ɪk'spresweɪ] *n US* autopista *f*

expulsion [ɪk'spʌlʃən] *n* expulsión *f*

exquisite [ɪk'skwɪzɪt] *adj* exquisito(a)

extend [ɪk'stend] **1** *vt* (**a**) *(enlarge)* ampliar; *(lengthen)* alargar; *(increase)* aumentar; *Fig* **the prohibition was extended to cover cigarettes** extendieron la prohibición a los cigarrillos (**b**) *(give)* rendir, dar; **to e. a welcome to sb** recibir a algn (**c**) *(prolong)* prolongar

2 *vi* (**a**) *(stretch)* extenderse (**b**) *(last)* prolongarse

extension [ɪk'stenʃən] *n* (**a**) extensión *f*; *(of time)* prórroga *f* (**b**) *Constr* anexo *m*

extensive [ɪk'stensɪv] *adj* extenso(a)

extent [ɪk'stent] *n* (**a**) *(area)* extensión *f* (**b**) **to some e.** hasta cierto punto; **to a large e.** en gran parte; **to a lesser e.** en menor grado; **to such an e.** hasta tal punto

extenuating [ɪk'stenjʊeɪtɪŋ] *adj* atenuante

exterior [ɪk'stɪərɪə(r)] **1** *adj* exterior, externo(a)

2 *n* exterior *m*

exterminate [ɪk'stɜːmɪneɪt] *vt* exterminar

extermination [ɪkstɜːmɪ'neɪʃən] *n* exterminación *f*, exterminio *m*

external [ɪk'stɜːnəl] *adj* externo(a), exterior

extinct [ɪk'stɪŋkt] *adj* extinguido(a)

extinction [ɪk'stɪŋkʃən] *n* extinción *f*

extinguish [ɪk'stɪŋgwɪʃ] *vt* extinguir, apagar

extinguisher [ɪk'stɪŋgwɪʃə(r)] *n* extintor *m*

extol, *US* **extoll** [ɪk'stəʊl] *vt* ensalzar, alabar

extort [ɪk'stɔːt] *vt* arrancar; *(money)* sacar

extortion [ɪk'stɔːʃən] *n* extorsión *f*

extortionate [ɪk'stɔːʃənɪt] *adj* desorbitado(a)

extra ['ekstrə] **1** *adj* extra; *(spare)* de sobra; **e. time** *(in soccer match)* prórroga *f*

2 *adv* extra; **e. fine** extra fino

3 *n* (additional charge) suplemento *m*; *Cin* extra *mf*; *(newspaper)* edición *f* especial

extract *n* ['ekstrækt] extracto *m*

2 *vt* [ɪk'strækt] *(tooth, information)* extraer; *(confession)* arrancar

extraction [ɪk'strækʃən] *n* extracción *f*

extracurricular [ekstrəkə'rɪkjʊlə(r)] *adj* extracurricular

extradite ['ekstrədaɪt] *vt* extraditar

extramarital [ekstrə'mærɪtəl] *adj* extramatrimonial

extramural [ekstrə'mjʊərəl] *adj* **e. course** = curso para estudiantes libres

extraordinary [ɪk'strɔːdənərɪ] *adj* (meeting) extraordinario(a); *(behaviour etc)* extraño(a)

extravagance [ɪk'strævəgəns] *n* (with money)

derroche *m*; *(of behaviour)* extravagancia *f*

extravagant [ɪk'strævəgənt] *adj* (wasteful) derrochador(a); *(excessive)* exagerado(a); *(luxurious)* lujoso(a)

extreme [ɪk'striːm] **1** *adj* extremo(a); **an e. case** un caso excepcional; **to hold e. views** tener opiniones radicales

2 *n* extremo *m*; **in the e.** en sumo grado

extremely [ɪk'striːmlɪ] *adv* extremadamente; **I'm e. sorry** lo siento de veras

extremist [ɪk'striːmɪst] *n* extremista *mf*

extremity [ɪk'stremɪtɪ] *n* extremidad *f*

extricate ['ekstrɪkeɪt] *vt* sacar; **to e. oneself (from)** lograr salir (de)

extrovert ['ekstrəvɜːt] *adj & n* extrovertido(a) *(m,f)*

exuberant [ɪg'zjuːbərənt] *adj* exuberante

exude [ɪg'zjuːd] *vt & vi (moisture, sap)* exudar; *Fig* rebosar

exultant [ɪg'zʌltənt] *adj* jubiloso(a)

eye [aɪ] **1** *n* ojo *m*; *Fig* **I couldn't believe my eyes** no podía creerlo; *Fig* **in the eyes of** según; *Fig* **not to take one's eyes off sb/sth** no quitar la vista de encima a algn/algo; *Fig* **to catch sb's e.** llamar la atención a algn; *Fig* **to have an e. for** tener buen ojo para; *Fig* **to make eyes at sb** echar miraditas a algn; *Fig* **to see e. to e. with sb** estar de acuerdo con algn; *Fig* **to turn a blind e. (to)** hacer la vista gorda (a); *Fig* **with an e. to** con miras a; **to keep an e. on sb/sth** vigilar a algn/algo; **to keep an e. out for** estar pendiente de; **black e.** ojo morado; *US* **e. doctor** óptico(a) *m,f*

2 *vt* observar

eyeball ['aɪbɔːl] *n* globo *m* ocular

eyebrow ['aɪbraʊ] *n* ceja *f*

eyecatching ['aɪkætʃɪŋ] *adj* llamativo(a)

eye-drops ['aɪdrɒps] *npl (medicine)* colirio *m*

eyeglasses ['aɪglɑːsɪz] *npl US (spectacles)* gafas *fpl*, *Am* lentes *mpl*, anteojos *mpl*

eyelash ['aɪlæʃ] *n* pestaña *f*

eyelid ['aɪlɪd] *n* párpado *m*

eyeliner ['aɪlaɪnə(r)] *n* lápiz *m* de ojos

eye-opener ['aɪəʊpənə(r)] *n* revelación *f*, gran sorpresa *f*

eyeshadow ['aɪʃædəʊ] *n* sombra *f* de ojos

eyesight ['aɪsaɪt] *n* vista *f*

eyesore ['aɪsɔː(r)] *n* monstruosidad *f*

eyestrain ['aɪstreɪn] *n* vista cansada

eyewash ['aɪwɒʃ] *n* colirio *m*; *Fig* **it's all e.** eso son disparates

eyewitness ['aɪwɪtnɪs] *n* testigo *mf* ocular

F, f [ef] *n* (a) *(the letter)* F, f *f* (b) *Mus* F fa *m*

F [ef] *(abbr* **Fahrenheit)** F

fable ['feɪbəl] *n* fábula *f*

fabric ['fæbrɪk] *n* (a) *Tex* tejido *m* (b) *Constr* estructura *f*

> 🖉 Note that the Spanish word **fábrica** is a false friend and is never a translation for the English word **fabric**. In Spanish, **fábrica** means "factory".

fabricate ['fæbrɪkeɪt] *vt* fabricar

fabrication [fæbrɪ'keɪʃən] *n Fig* fabricación *f*

fabulous ['fæbjʊləs] *adj* fabuloso(a)

façade [fə'sɑ:d, fæ'sɑ:d] *n* fachada *f*

face [feɪs] **1** *n* (a) cara *f*, rostro *m*; **f. to f.** cara a cara; **I told him to his f.** se lo dije en la cara; **she slammed the door in my f.** me dió con la puerta en las narices; **to look sb in the f.** mirarle a algn a la cara; **f. cloth** paño *m*; **f. cream** crema *f* facial; **f. pack** mascarilla *f* facial

(b) *(expression)* cara *f*, expresión *f*; **to pull a long f.** poner cara larga; **to pull faces** hacer muecas

(c) *(surface)* superficie *f*; *(of card, coin)* cara *f*; *(of watch)* esfera *f*; **f. down/up** boca abajo/arriba; *Fig* **in the f. of danger** ante el peligro; **f. value** valor *m* nominal; **to take sth at f. value** entender algo sólo en su sentido literal

(d) *(appearance)* aspecto *m*; **on the f. of it a** primera vista; **to lose f.** desprestigiarse; **to save f.** salvar las apariencias

2 *vt* (a) *(look on to)* dar a; *(be opposite)* estar enfrente de

(b) **to f. the wall/window** *(of person)* estar de cara a la pared/ventana

(c) *(problem)* hacer frente a; **let's f. it** hay que reconocerlo; **to f. up to** hacer cara a

(d) *(tolerate)* soportar, aguantar

3 *vi* **to f. on to** dar a; **to f. towards** mirar hacia; **f. this way** vuélvase de este lado

facelift ['feɪslɪft] *n Med* lifting *m*; *Fig* renovación *f*

facet ['fæsɪt] *n* faceta *f*

facetious [fə'si:ʃəs] *adj* bromista

facial ['feɪʃəl] *adj* facial

facile ['fæsaɪl] *adj* superficial

facilitate [fə'sɪlɪteɪt] *vt* facilitar

facility [fə'sɪlɪtɪ] *n* (a) *(ease)* facilidad *f* (b) **facilities** *(means)* facilidades *fpl*; **credit facilities** facilidades de crédito (c) **facilities** *(rooms, equipment)* instalaciones *fpl*; **cooking facilities** derecho *m* a cocina

facing ['feɪsɪŋ] *adj* de enfrente

facsimile [fæk'sɪmɪlɪ] *n* (a) *(copy)* facsímil *m* (b) *(message)* telefax *m* (c) *(machine)* facsímil *m*

fact [fækt] *n* hecho *m*; **as a matter of f.** de hecho; **the f. that he confessed** el hecho de que confesara; **in f.** en realidad

fact-finding ['fæktfaɪndɪŋ] *adj* investigador(a)

faction ['fækʃən] *n (group)* facción *f*

factor ['fæktə(r)] *n* factor *m*

factory ['fæktərɪ] *n* fábrica *f*

factual ['fæktʃʊəl] *adj* **a f. error** un error de hecho

faculty ['fækəltɪ] *n* (a) facultad *f* (b) *US Univ* profesorado *m*, cuerpo *m* docente

fad [fæd] *n Fam (craze)* moda pasajera; *(whim)* capricho *m*

fade [feɪd] *vi (colour)* desteñirse; *(flower)* marchitarse; *(light)* apagarse

▸ **fade away** *vi* desvanecerse

▸ **fade in, fade out** *vt sep Cin & TV* fundir

faded ['feɪdɪd] *adj (colour)* desteñido(a); *(flower)* marchito(a)

fag [fæg] *n* (a) *Br Fam (cigarette)* pitillo *m* (b) *US very Fam (homosexual)* marica *m*

faggot ['fægət] *n* (a) *Br (meatball)* albóndiga *f* (b) *US very Fam (homosexual)* maricón *m*

fail [feɪl] **1** *n* (a) *Educ* suspenso *m* (b) **without f.** sin falta

2 *vt* (a) **don't f. me** no me falles; **words f. me** no encuentro palabras (b) *(exam)* suspender (c) *(to be unable)* no lograr; **he failed to score** no logró marcar (d) *(neglect)* dejar de; **don't f. to come** no deje de venir

3 *vi* (a) *(show, film)* fracasar; *(brakes)* fallar (b) *(business)* quebrar; *Educ* suspender (c) *(of health)* deteriorarse

failing ['feɪlɪŋ] **1** *n* (a) *(shortcoming)* defecto *m* (b) *(weakness)* punto *m* débil

2 *prep* a falta de

failure ['feɪljə(r)] *n* (a) *(person)* fracaso *m* (b) *Com* quiebra *f* (c) *Educ* suspenso *m* (d) *(person)* fracasado(a) *m,f* (e) *(breakdown)* avería *f*; **brake f.** fallo *m* de los frenos; **power f.** apagón *m*; *Med* **heart f.** paro cardíaco (f) **her f. to answer** *(neglect)* el hecho de que no contestara

faint [feɪnt] **1** *adj* (a) *(sound)* débil; *(colour)* pálido(a); *(outline)* borroso(a); *(recollection)* vago(a); **I haven't the faintest idea** no tengo

la más mínima idea (**b**) *(giddy)* mareado(a)
2 *n* desmayo *m*
3 *vi* desmayarse
faint-hearted [feɪnt'hɑːtɪd] *adj* temeroso(a)
fair¹ [feə(r)] **1** *adj* (**a**) *(impartial)* imparcial; *(just)* justo(a); **it's not f.** no hay derecho; *Fam* **f. enough!** ¡vale!; **f. trade** comercio justo (**b**) *(hair)* rubio(a) (**c**) *(weather)* bueno(a) (**d**) *(beautiful)* bello(a) (**e**) **a f. number** un buen número; **he has a f. chance** tiene bastantes probabilidades
2 *adv* **to play f.** jugar limpio
fair² [feə(r)] *n* feria *f*; **trade f.** feria de muestras
fairground ['feəgraʊnd] *n* real *m* de la feria
fairly ['feəlɪ] *adv* (**a**) *(justly)* justamente (**b**) *(moderately)* bastante
fairness ['feənɪs] *n* justicia *f*, equidad *f*; **in all f.** para ser justo(a)
fairy ['feərɪ] *n* (**a**) hada *f*; **f. godmother** hada madrina; **f. tale** cuento *m* de hadas (**b**) *Fam Pej* marica *m*
fait accompli [feɪtə'kɒmpliː] *n Fml* hecho consumado
faith [feɪθ] *n* (**a**) *Rel* fe *f* (**b**) *(trust)* confianza *f*; **in good f.** de buena fe
faithful ['feɪθfʊl] **1** *adj* fiel
2 *npl* **the f.** los fieles
faithfully ['feɪθfʊlɪ] *adv* fielmente; **yours f.** *(in letter)* le saluda atentamente
fake [feɪk] **1** *adj* falso(a)
2 *n* (**a**) *(object)* falsificación *f* (**b**) *(person)* impostor(a) *m,f*
3 *vt* (**a**) *(forge)* falsificar (**b**) *(feign)* fingir
4 *vi* *(pretend)* fingir
falcon ['fɔːlkən] *n* halcón *m*
Falklands ['fɔːlkləndz] *npl* **the F.** las (Islas) Malvinas
fall [fɔːl] **1** *n* (**a**) caída *f* (**b**) *(of rock)* desprendimiento *m*; **f. of snow** nevada *f* (**c**) *(decrease)* baja *f* (**d**) *US* otoño *m* (**e**) *(usu pl)* cascada *f*; **Niagara Falls** las cataratas del Niágara
2 *vi* (*pt* **fell**; *pp* **fallen**) (**a**) caer, caerse; **they f. into two categories** se dividen en dos categorías; *Fig* **night was falling** anochecía; *Fig* **to f. into line** aceptar las reglas; *Fig* **to f. short (of)** no alcanzar (**b**) *(in battle)* caer (**c**) *(temperature, prices)* bajar (**d**) **to f. asleep** dormirse; **to f. ill** caer enfermo(a); **to f. in love** enamorarse
▸ **fall back** *vi* replegarse
▸ **fall back on** *vt insep* echar mano a, recurrir a
▸ **fall behind** *vi (in race)* quedarse atrás; **to f. behind with one's work** retrasarse en el trabajo
▸ **fall down** *vi* (**a**) *(picture etc)* caerse (**b**) *(building)* derrumbarse (**c**) *(argument)* fallar
▸ **fall for** *vt insep* (**a**) *(person)* enamorarse de (**b**) *(trick)* dejarse engañar por
▸ **fall in** *vi* (**a**) *(roof)* desplomarse (**b**) *Mil* formar filas

▸ **fall off** *vi* (**a**) *(drop off)* caerse (**b**) *(part)* desprenderse (**c**) *(diminish)* disminuir
2 *vt insep* **to f. off sth** caerse de algo
▸ **fall out** *vi* (**a**) *(hair)* caerse (**b**) *Mil* rompe[r] filas (**c**) *(quarrel)* pelearse
▸ **fall over** *vi* caerse
▸ **fall through** *vi (plan)* fracasar
fallacy ['fæləsɪ] *n* falacia *f*
fallen ['fɔːlən] *pp of* **fall**
fallible ['fælɪbəl] *adj* falible
fall-out ['fɔːlaʊt] *n* (**radioactive**) **f.** lluvi[a] radioactiva; **f. shelter** refugio antiatómico
fallow ['fæləʊ] *adj Agr* en barbecho
false [fɔːls] *adj* falso(a); **f. step** paso *m* en falso; **f. start** salida nula; **f. teeth** dentadur[a] postiza; **f. alarm** falsa alarma
falsehood ['fɔːlshʊd] *n* falsedad *f*
falsify ['fɔːlsɪfaɪ] *vt (records, accounts)* falsi[fi]car; *(story)* falsear
falter ['fɔːltə(r)] *vi* vacilar; *(voice)* fallar
faltering ['fɔːltərɪŋ] *adj* vacilante
fame [feɪm] *n* fama *f*
familiar [fə'mɪlɪə(r)] *adj* (**a**) *(common)* fami[li]liar, conocido(a); **his face is f.** su cara m[e] suena (**b**) *(aware, knowledgeable)* entera[r]do(a), al corriente (**with** de) (**c**) **to be on f**[amiliar] **terms with sb** *(know well)* tener confianza con algu[ien]
familiarity [fəmɪlɪ'ærɪtɪ] *n* (**a**) *(awareness, knowledge)* familiaridad *f* (**with** con) (**b**) *(intimacy)* confianza *f*
familiarize [fə'mɪljəraɪz] *vt* (**a**) *(become acquainted)* familiarizar (**with** con); **to f. oneself with sth** familiarizarse con algo (**b**) *(make widely known)* popularizar
family ['fæmɪlɪ] *n* familia *f*; **f. allowance** subsidio *m* familiar; **f. doctor** médico *m* de cabecera; **f. man** hombre hogareño; **f. planning** planificación *f* familiar; **f. tree** árbo[l] genealógico
famine ['fæmɪn] *n* hambre *f*, escasez *f* d[e] alimentos
famished ['fæmɪʃt] *adj Fam* muerto(a) d[e] hambre
famous ['feɪməs] *adj* célebre, famoso(a) (**for** por)
famously ['feɪməslɪ] *adv Fam* estupenda[mente]
fan [fæn] **1** *n* (**a**) abanico *m*; *Elec* ventilador *n*[...] (**b**) *(person)* aficionado(a) *m,f*; *(of pop star etc)* fan *mf*; **f. club** club *m* de fans; **football [f.]** hincha *mf*
2 *vt* (**a**) abanicar (**b**) *(fire, passions)* avivar
▸ **fan out** *vi (troops)* desplegarse en abanico
fanatic [fə'nætɪk] *adj & n* fanático(a) *(m,f)*
fanatical [fə'nætɪkəl] *adj* fanático(a)
fanciful ['fænsɪfʊl] *adj* (**a**) *(person)* capri[...]choso(a) (**b**) *(idea)* fantástico(a)
fancy ['fænsɪ] **1** *adj* (**fancier**, **fanciest**) d[e] fantasía; **f. dress** disfraz *m*; **f. dress ball** bail[e] *m* de disfraces; **f. prices** precios *mpl* exorbi[...]tantes

2 *n* (**a**) *(imagination)* fantasía *f* (**b**) *(whim)* capricho *m*, antojo *m*; **to take a f. to sb** cogerle cariño a algn; **to take a f. to sth** encapricharse con algo; **what takes your f.?** ¿qué se le antoja?

3 *vt* (**a**) *(imagine)* imaginarse; *Fam* **f. that!** ¡fíjate!; *Fam* **f. seeing you here!** ¡qué casualidad verte por aquí! (**b**) *(like, want)* apetecer; **do you f. a drink?** ¿te apetece una copa?; *Fam* **I f. her** ella me gusta; *Fam* **to f. oneself** ser creído(a) *or* presumido(a)

fanfare ['fænfeə(r)] *n* fanfarria *f*

fang [fæŋ] *n* colmillo *m*

fanny ['fænɪ] *n* (**a**) *US Fam (buttocks)* culo *m*, *Am* cola *f* (**b**) *Br Vulg (vagina)* coño *m*, *Andes*, *RP* concha *f*

fantasize ['fæntəsaɪz] *vi* fantasear

fantastic [fæn'tæstɪk] *adj* fantástico(a)

fantasy ['fæntəsɪ] *n* fantasía *f*

far [fɑː(r)] (**farther** *or* **further, farthest** *or* **furthest**) **1** *adj* (**a**) *(distant)* lejano(a); **the F. East** el Lejano Oriente
(**b**) **at the f. end** en el otro extremo
(**c**) **the f. left** la extrema izquierda
2 *adv* (**a**) *(distant)* lejos; **f. and wide** por todas partes; **f. off** a lo lejos; **farther back** más atrás; **farther north** más al norte; **how f. is it to Cardiff?** ¿cuánto hay de aquí a Cardiff?; *Fig* **as f. as I can** en lo que puedo; **as f. as I know** que yo sepa; **as f. as possible** en lo posible; *Fig* **f. from complaining, he seemed pleased** lejos de quejarse, parecía contento; *Fig* **he went so f. as to swear** llegó a jurar; *Fig* **I'm f. from satisfied** no estoy satisfecho(a) ni mucho menos; *Fig* **in so f. as …** en la medida en que …; *Fam* **to go too f.** pasarse de la raya
(**b**) *(in time)* **as f. back as the fifties** ya en los años cincuenta; **f. into the night** hasta muy entrada la noche; **so f.** hasta ahora
(**c**) *(much)* mucho; **by f.** con mucho; **f. cleverer** mucho más listo(a); **f. too much** demasiado; **you're not f. wrong** casi aciertas

faraway ['fɑːrəweɪ] *adj* lejano(a), remoto(a)

farce [fɑːs] *n* farsa *f*

farcical ['fɑːsɪkəl] *adj* absurdo(a)

fare [feə(r)] **1** *n* (**a**) *(ticket price)* tarifa *f*, precio *m* del billete; *(for boat)* pasaje *m*; **half f.** media tarifa (**b**) *(passenger)* pasajero(a) *m,f*
(**c**) *(food)* comida *f*
2 *vi* **how did you f.?** ¿qué tal te fue?

farewell [feə'wel] **1** *interj Literary* ¡adiós!
2 *n* despedida *f*

far-fetched [fɑː'fetʃt] *adj* rebuscado(a)

farm [fɑːm] **1** *n* granja *f*, *Am* hacienda *f*
2 *vt* cultivar, labrar
▸ **farm out** *vt sep* encargar fuera

farmer ['fɑːmə(r)] *n* granjero(a) *m,f*, *Am* hacendado(a) *m,f*

farmhand ['fɑːmhænd] *n* peón *m*, labriego(a) *m,f*

farmhouse ['fɑːmhaʊs] *n* granja *f*, *Am* hacienda *f*

farming ['fɑːmɪŋ] **1** *n* (**a**) *(agriculture)* agricultura *f* (**b**) *(of land)* cultivo *m*, labranza *f*
2 *adj* agrícola

farmyard ['fɑːmjɑːd] *n* corral *m*

far-reaching [fɑː'riːtʃɪŋ] *adj* de gran alcance

far-sighted [fɑː'saɪtɪd] *adj* (**a**) *(person)* con visión de futuro (**b**) *(plan)* con miras al futuro

fart [fɑːt] *Fam* **1** *n* pedo *m*
2 *vi* echarse un pedo

farther ['fɑːðə(r)] *adj & adv comp of* **far**

farthest ['fɑːðɪst] *adj & adv superl of* **far**

fascinate ['fæsɪneɪt] *vt* fascinar

fascinating ['fæsɪneɪtɪŋ] *adj* fascinante

fascination [fæsɪ'neɪʃən] *n* fascinación *f*

fascism ['fæʃɪzəm] *n* fascismo *m*

fascist ['fæʃɪst] *adj & n* fascista (*mf*)

fashion ['fæʃən] **1** *n* (**a**) *(manner)* manera *f*, modo *m*; **after a f.** más o menos (**b**) *(latest style)* moda *f*; **to go/be out of f.** pasar/no estar de moda; **f. designer** diseñador(a) *m,f* de modas; **f. parade** desfile *m* de modelos
2 *vt* *(metal)* labrar; *(clay)* formar

fashionable ['fæʃənəbəl] *adj* (**a**) *de moda*
(**b**) *(area, hotel)* elegante

fast[1] [fɑːst] **1** *adj* (**a**) *(quick)* rápido(a) (**b**) **hard and f. rules** reglas estrictas (**c**) *(clock)* adelantado(a)
2 *adv* (**a**) rápidamente, deprisa; **how f.?** ¿a qué velocidad? (**b**) *(securely)* firmemente; **f. asleep** profundamente dormido(a)

fast[2] [fɑːst] **1** *n* ayuno *m*
2 *vi* ayunar

fasten ['fɑːsən] **1** *vt* (**a**) *(attach)* sujetar; *(fix)* fijar (**b**) *(belt)* abrochar; *(bag)* asegurar; *(shoelaces)* atar
2 *vi* *(dress)* abrocharse

fastener ['fɑːsənə(r)] *n* cierre *m*

fastidious [fæ'stɪdɪəs] *adj* quisquilloso(a)

fat [fæt] **1** *adj* (**fatter, fattest**) (**a**) gordo(a) (**b**) *(book, file)* grueso(a) (**c**) *(meat)* que tiene mucha grasa
2 *n* grasa *f*; **cooking f.** manteca *f* de cerdo

fatal ['feɪtəl] *adj* (**a**) *(accident, illness)* mortal (**b**) *(ill-fated)* fatal, funesto(a) (**c**) *(fateful)* fatídico(a)

fatalistic [feɪtə'lɪstɪk] *adj* fatalista

fatality [fə'tælɪtɪ] *n* víctima *f* mortal

> 🖉 Note that the Spanish word **fatalidad** is a false friend and is never a translation for the English word **fatality**. In Spanish, **fatalidad** means both "fate" and "misfortune".

fatally ['feɪtəlɪ] *adv* **f. wounded** mortalmente herido(a)

fate [feɪt] *n* destino *m*, suerte *f*

fateful ['feɪtfʊl] *adj* fatídico(a), aciago(a)

father ['fɑːðə(r)] *n* (**a**) padre *m*; **my f. and mother** mis padres; **F. Christmas** Papá *m* Noel (**b**) *Rel* padre *m*

father-in-law ['fɑːðərɪnlɔː] *n* suegro *m*

fatherland ['fɑːðəlænd] *n* patria *f*

fatherly ['fɑːðəlɪ] *adj* paternal
fathom ['fæðəm] **1** *n Naut* braza *f*
  2 *vt* comprender
  ▸ **fathom out** *vt sep* comprobar; **I can't f. it out** no me lo explico
fatigue [fə'tiːg] *n* (**a**) *(tiredness)* fatiga *f* (**b**) *Mil* faena *f*; **f. dress** traje *m* de faena
fatten ['fætən] *vt* engordar
fattening ['fætənɪŋ] *adj* que engorda
fatty ['fætɪ] **1** *adj (food)* graso(a); *Anat (tissue)* adiposo(a)
  2 *n Fam (person)* gordinflón(ona) *m,f*
fatuous ['fætjʊəs] *adj* necio(a)
faucet ['fɔːsɪt] *n US* grifo *m*, *Chile, Méx* llave *f*, *RP* canilla *f*
fault [fɔːlt] **1** *n* (**a**) *(defect)* defecto *m* (**b**) *(in merchandise)* desperfecto *m*; **to find f. with** poner reparos a (**c**) *(blame)* culpa *f*; **to be at f.** tener la culpa (**d**) *(mistake)* error *m* (**e**) *Geol* falla *f* (**f**) *(in tennis)* falta *f*
  2 *vt* criticar
faultless ['fɔːltlɪs] *adj* intachable
faulty ['fɔːltɪ] *adj* defectuoso(a)
fauna ['fɔːnə] *n* fauna *f*
faux pas [fəʊ'pɑː] *n* (*pl* **faux pas**) *Fml (mistake)* paso *m* en falso; *(blunder)* metedura *f* de pata
favour, *US* **favor** ['feɪvə(r)] **1** *n* (**a**) favor *m*; **in f. of** a favor de; **to be in f. with sb** gozar del favor de algn; **to ask sb a f.** pedirle un favor a algn (**b**) **1-0 in our f.** *(advantage)* 1-0 a favor nuestro
  2 *vt* (**a**) *(person)* favorecer a (**b**) *(approve)* estar a favor de
favourable ['feɪvərəbəl] *adj* favorable
favourite ['feɪvərɪt] *adj & n* favorito(a) *(m,f)*
favouritism ['feɪvərɪtɪzəm] *n* favoritismo *m*
fawn[1] [fɔːn] **1** *adj* (de) color café claro
  2 *n* (**a**) *Zool* cervato *m* (**b**) color *m* café claro
fawn[2] [fɔːn] *vi* adular (**on** a)
fax [fæks] **1** *n (machine, message)* fax *m*; **f. modem** modem *m* fax
  2 *vt* mandar por fax
fear [fɪə(r)] **1** *n* miedo *m*, temor *m*; **for f. of** por temor a; *Fam* **no f.!** ¡ni pensarlo!
  2 *vt* temer; **I f. it's too late** me temo que ya es tarde
  3 *vi* temer (**for** por)
fearful ['fɪəfʊl] *adj* (**a**) *(person)* temeroso(a) (**b**) *(frightening)* espantoso(a)
fearless ['fɪəlɪs] *adj* intrépido(a)
feasibility [fiːzə'bɪlɪt] *n* viabilidad *f*
feasible ['fiːzəbəl] *adj (practicable)* factible; *(possible)* viable
feast [fiːst] *n* (**a**) banquete *m*; *Fam* comilona *f* (**b**) *Rel* **f. day** fiesta *f* de guardar
feat [fiːt] *n* hazaña *f*
feather ['feðə(r)] **1** *n* pluma *f*; **f. duster** plumero *m*
  2 *vt Fam* **to f. one's nest** hacer su agosto
feature ['fiːtʃə(r)] **1** *n* (**a**) *(of face)* rasgo *m*, facción *f* (**b**) *(characteristic)* característica *f*

(**c**) **f. film** largometraje *m* (**d**) *Press* crónica especial
  2 *vt* (**a**) poner de relieve (**b**) *Cin* tener como protagonista a
  3 *vi* figurar
February ['febrʊərɪ] *n* febrero *m*
fed [fed] **1** *adj Fam* **f. up (with)** harto(a) (de)
  2 *pt & pp of* **feed**
federal ['fedərəl] *adj* federal
federation [fedə'reɪʃən] *n* federación *f*
fee [fiː] *n (of lawyer, doctor)* honorarios *mp*, *Ftb* **transfer f.** prima *f* de traslado; *Univ* **tuition fees** derechos *mpl* de matrícula
feeble ['fiːbəl] *adj* débil
feed [fiːd] **1** *vt (pt & pp fed)* (**a**) *(give food to)* dar de comer a; *Fig (fire)* alimentar; **to f. baby** *(breast-feed)* amamantar a un bebé, *(with bottle)* dar el biberón a un bebé (**b**) *Elec* alimentar (**c**) *(insert)* introducir
  2 *vi (cows, sheep)* pacer; **to f. on sth** *(person)* comer algo
  3 *n* (**a**) *(food)* comida *f*; **cattle f.** pienso *m* (**b**) *Tech* alimentación *f*
  ▸ **feed up** *vt sep* cebar
feedback ['fiːdbæk] *n* (**a**) *Tech* feedback *m* (**b**) *Fig* reacción *f*
feeder ['fiːdə(r)] *n Tech* alimentador *m*
feeding ['fiːdɪŋ] *n Tech* biberón *m*
feel [fiːl] **1** *vi (pt & pp felt)* (**a**) *(emotion, sensation)* sentir; **how do you f.?** ¿qué tal te encuentras?; **I bad about it** me da pena; **I (sorry) for him** le compadezco; **to f. happy/ uncomfortable** sentirse feliz/incómodo; **to cold/sleepy** tener frío/sueño; *Fam* **to f. up to (doing)** sth sentirse con ánimos para hacer algo
  (**b**) *(seem)* **your hand feels cold** tienes la mano fría; **it feels like summer** parece verano
  (**c**) *(opinion)* opinar; **I f. sure that ...** estoy seguro/a de que ...
  (**d**) **I f. like an ice cream** me apetece un helado; **to f. like doing sth** tener ganas de hacer algo
  2 *vt* (**a**) *(touch)* tocar
  (**b**) **she feels a failure** se siente inútil
  (**c**) *(notice, be aware of)* notar
  3 *n* (**a**) *(touch, sensation)* tacto *m*; *Fig* **to get the f. for sth** cogerle el truco a algo
  (**b**) *(atmosphere)* ambiente *m*
  ▸ **feel for** *vt insep* (**a**) *(search for)* buscar (**b**) *(have sympathy for)* compadecer
feeler ['fiːlə(r)] *n (of insect)* antena *f*; *Fig* **to put one's feelers out** tantear el terreno
feeling ['fiːlɪŋ] **1** *n* (**a**) *(emotion)* sentimiento *m*; **ill f.** rencor *m* (**b**) *(compassion)* compasión *f* (**c**) **I had the f. that ...** *(impression)* tuve la impresión de que ... (**d**) *(sensitivity)* sensibilidad *f* (**e**) *(opinion)* opinión *f*; **to express one's feelings** expresar sus opiniones
  2 *adj* sensible, compasivo(a)
feet [fiːt] *pl of* **foot**

feign [feɪn] *vt* fingir

feint [feɪnt] *Sport* 1 *n* finta *f*
  2 *vi* fintar

fell¹ [fel] *pt of* fall

fell² [fel] *vt (trees)* talar; *Fig (enemy)* derribar

fellow ['feləʊ] *n* (a) *(companion)* compañero(a) *m,f*; **f. citizen** conciudadano(a) *m,f*; **f. countryman/countrywoman** compatriota *mf*; **f. men** prójimos *mpl*; **f. passenger/student** compañero(a) *m,f* de viaje/estudios (b) *Fam (chap)* tipo *m*, tío *m* (c) *(of society)* socio(a) *m,f*

fellowship ['feləʊʃɪp] *n* (a) *(comradeship)* camaradería *f* (b) *Univ* beca *f* de investigación

felony ['felənɪ] *n* crimen *m*, delito *m* mayor

felt¹ [felt] *pt & pp of* feel

felt² [felt] *n Tex* fieltro *m*

felt-tip(ped) ['felttɪp(t)] *adj* **f. pen** rotulador *m*

female ['fiːmeɪl] 1 *adj* (a) *Zool* hembra (b) femenino(a)
  2 *n* (a) *Zool* hembra *f* (b) *(woman)* mujer *f*; *(girl)* chica *f*

feminine ['femɪnɪn] *adj* femenino(a)

feminism ['femɪnɪzəm] *n* feminismo *m*

feminist ['femɪnɪst] *adj & n* feminista *(mf)*

fence [fens] 1 *n* cerca *f*, valla *f*; *Fig* **to sit on the f.** ver los toros desde la barrera
  2 *vi Sport* practicar la esgrima
  ▸ **fence in** *vt sep* meter en un cercado

fencing ['fensɪŋ] *n Sport* esgrima *f*

fend [fend] *vi* **to f. for oneself** valerse por sí mismo
  ▸ **fend off** *vt sep (blow)* parar; *(question)* rehuir; *(attack)* rechazar

fender ['fendə(r)] *n* (a) *(fireplace)* pantalla *f* (b) *US Aut* guardabarros *mpl* (c) *Naut* defensa *f*

ferment 1 *n* ['fɜːment] *Fig* **in a state of f.** agitado(a)
  2 *vt & vi* [fə'ment] fermentar

fern [fɜːn] *n* helecho *m*

ferocious [fə'rəʊʃəs] *adj* feroz

ferocity [fə'rɒsɪtɪ] *n* ferocidad *f*

ferret ['ferɪt] 1 *n* hurón *m*
  2 *vi* huronear, husmear
  ▸ **ferret out** *vt sep* descubrir

ferry ['ferɪ] 1 *n* (a) *(small)* barca *f* de pasaje (b) *(large, for cars)* transbordador *m*, ferry *m*
  2 *vt* transportar

fertile ['fɜːtaɪl] *adj* fértil

fertility [fə'tɪlɪtɪ] *n (of soil)* fertilidad *f*

fertilize ['fɜːtɪlaɪz] *vt* (a) *(soil)* abonar (b) *(egg)* fecundar

fertilizer ['fɜːtɪlaɪzə(r)] *n* abono *m*

fervent ['fɜːvənt] *adj* ferviente

fervour, *US* **fervor** ['fɜːvə(r)] *n* fervor *m*

fester ['festə(r)] *vi* supurar

festival ['festɪvəl] *n (event)* festival *m*; *(celebration)* fiesta *f*

festive ['festɪv] *adj* festivo(a); **the f. season** las fiestas de Navidad

festivity [fe'stɪvɪtɪ] *n* **the festivities** las fiestas

festoon [fe'stuːn] *vt* adornar

fetch [fetʃ] *vt* (a) *(go for)* ir a buscar (b) *(bring)* traer (c) **how much did it f.?** *(sell for)* ¿por cuánto se vendió?

fetching ['fetʃɪŋ] *adj* atractivo(a)

fete [feɪt] 1 *n* fiesta *f*
  2 *vt* festejar

fetish ['fetɪʃ, 'fiːtɪʃ] *n* fetiche *m*

fetus ['fiːtəs] *n US* = **foetus**

feud [fjuːd] 1 *n* enemistad duradera
  2 *vi* pelear

feudal ['fjuːdəl] *adj* feudal

fever ['fiːvə(r)] *n* fiebre *f*

feverish ['fiːvərɪʃ] *adj* febril

few [fjuː] 1 *adj* (a) *(not many)* pocos(as); **as f. as** solamente (b) *(some)* algunos(as), unos(as) cuantos(as); **a f. books** unos *or* algunos libros; **she has fewer books than I thought** tiene menos libros de lo que pensaba; **for the past f. years** durante estos últimos años; **in the next f. days** dentro de unos días; **quite a f.** bastantes
  2 *pron* (a) *(not many)* pocos(as); **there are too f.** no hay suficientes; **the fewer the better** cuantos menos mejor (b) **a f.** *(some)* algunos(as), unos(as) cuantos(as); **the chosen f.** los elegidos; **who has the fewest?** ¿quién tiene menos?

fiancé [fɪ'ɒnseɪ] *n* prometido *m*

fiancée [fɪ'ɒnseɪ] *n* prometida *f*

fiasco [fɪ'æskəʊ] *n* fiasco *m*

fib [fɪb] *Fam* 1 *n* trola *f*
  2 *vi* contar trolas

fibre, *US* **fiber** ['faɪbə(r)] *n* fibra *f*

fibreglass, *US* **fiberglass** ['faɪbəglɑːs] *n* fibra *f* de vidrio

fickle ['fɪkəl] *adj* inconstante, voluble

fiction ['fɪkʃən] *n* ficción *f*

fictional ['fɪkʃənəl] *adj* (a) *Lit* novelesco(a) (b) *(imaginative)* ficticio(a)

fictitious [fɪk'tɪʃəs] *adj* ficticio(a)

fiddle ['fɪdəl] *Fam* 1 *n* (a) *Mus* violín *m* (b) *(shady deal)* trampa *f*
  2 *vt* estafar; *(accounts)* falsificar
  3 *vi* juguetear (**with** con)
  ▸ **fiddle about** *vi* perder tiempo

fiddly ['fɪdlɪ] *adj Fam* laborioso(a)

fidelity [fɪ'delɪtɪ] *n* fidelidad *f*

fidget ['fɪdʒɪt] *vi* (a) moverse; **stop fidgeting!** ¡estáte quieto! (b) jugar (**with** con)

field [fiːld] 1 *n* (a) campo *m*; **f. glasses** gemelos *mpl*; **f. marshal** mariscal *m* de campo (b) *Geol Min* yacimiento *m* (c) **f. trip** viaje *m* de estudios; **f. work** trabajo *m* de campo
  2 *vt Sport* (a) *(ball)* parar y devolver (b) *(team)* presentar

fiend [fiːnd] *n* demonio *m*; *Fam (fanatic)* fanático(a) *m,f*

fiendish ['fiːndɪʃ] *adj Fam* diabólico(a)

fierce [fɪəs] *adj (animal)* feroz; *(argument)* acalorado(a); *(heat, competition)* intenso(a); *(wind)* violento(a)

fiery ['faɪərɪ] *adj (temper)* fogoso(a); *(speech)* acalorado(a); *(colour)* encendido(a)

fifteen [fɪf'tiːn] *adj & n* quince *(m inv)*

fifteenth [fɪf'tiːnθ] **1** *adj & n* decimoquinto(a) *(m,f)*
2 *n (fraction)* quinzavo *m*

fifth [fɪfθ] **1** *adj & n* quinto(a) *(m,f)*
2 *n (fraction)* quinto *m*

fifty ['fɪftɪ] *adj & n* cincuenta *(m inv)*

fifty-fifty ['fɪftɪ'fɪftɪ] *Fam* **1** *adj* **a f. chance** una probabilidad del cincuenta por ciento
2 *adv* **to go f.** ir a medias

fig¹ [fɪg] *n (fruit)* higo *m*

fig² [fɪg] *(abbr* **figure)** fig

fight [faɪt] **1** *vt (pt & pp* **fought)** **(a)** pelear(se) con, luchar con; *(of boxer)* enfrentarse a, luchar con; *(of bullfighter)* lidiar; *Fig (corruption)* combatir **(b)** *(battle)* librar; *(war)* hacer **(c)** *(decision)* recurrir contra
2 *vi* **(a)** pelear(se), luchar **(b)** *(quarrel)* reñir; **to f. over sth** disputarse la posesión de algo *(c) Fig (struggle)* luchar **(for/against** por/contra)
3 *n* **(a)** pelea *f*, lucha *f*; *(in boxing)* combate *m* **(b)** *(quarrel)* riña *f* **(c)** *Fig (struggle)* lucha *f* **(d)** *(spirit)* combatividad *f*
▸ **fight back 1** *vt sep (tears)* contener
2 *vi* contraatacar
▸ **fight off** *vt sep* **(a)** *(attack)* rechazar **(b)** *(illness)* cortar
▸ **fight out** *vt sep* discutir

fighter ['faɪtə(r)] *n* **(a)** *(person)* combatiente *mf*; *(in boxing)* púgil *m* **(b)** *Fig* luchador(a) *m,f*; **f. (plane)** (avión *m* de) caza *m*; **f. bomber** cazabombardero *m*

fighting ['faɪtɪŋ] **1** *adj* **he's got a f. chance** tiene verdaderas posibilidades
2 *n* lucha *f*

figment ['fɪgmənt] *n* **it's a f. of your imagination** es un producto de tu imaginación

figurative ['fɪgərətɪv] *adj* figurado(a)

figure ['fɪgə(r), *US* 'fɪgjər] **1** *n* **(a)** *(form, outline)* forma *f*, silueta *f* **(b)** *(shape, statue, character)* figura *f*; **she has a good f.** tiene buen tipo; *Br* **f. of eight,** *US* **f. eight** ocho *m* **(c)** *(in book)* dibujo *m* **(d)** **f. of speech** figura retórica **(e)** *Math* cifra *f*
2 *vt US Fam* imaginarse
3 *vi* **(a)** *(appear)* figurar **(b)** *US Fam* **that figures** eso tiene sentido
▸ **figure out** *vt sep Fam* comprender; **I can't f. it out** no me lo explico

figurehead ['fɪgəhed] *n Fig* figura decorativa

filament ['fɪləmənt] *n* filamento *m*

filch [fɪltʃ] *vt Fam* mangar, birlar

file [faɪl] **1** *n* **(a)** *(tool)* lima *f* **(b)** *(folder)* carpeta *f* **(c)** *(archive, of computer)* archivo *m*; **on f.** archivado(a) **(d)** *(line)* fila *f*; **in single f. en fila india**
2 *vt* **(a)** *(smooth)* limar **(b)** *(put away)* archivar
3 *vi* **to f. past** desfilar

filing ['faɪlɪŋ] *n* clasificación *f*; **f. cabinet** archivador *m*; *(for cards)* fichero *m*

Filipino [fɪlɪ'piːnəʊ] *n* filipino(a) *m,f*

fill [fɪl] **1** *vt* **(a)** *(space, time)* llenar **(with** de) **(b)** *(post, requirements)* cubrir **(c)** *Culin* rellenar
2 *vi* llenarse **(with** de)
3 *n* **to eat one's f.** comer hasta hartarse
▸ **fill in** *vt sep* **(a)** *(space, form)* rellenar **(b)** *Fam (inform)* poner al corriente **(on** de) **(c)** *(time)* pasar
2 *vi* **to f. in for sb** sustituir a algn
▸ **fill out** *vt sep US (form)* llenar
2 *vi Fam* engordar
▸ **fill up** *vt sep* llenar hasta arriba; *Fam Aut* **f. her up!** ¡llénelo!
2 *vi* llenarse

fillet ['fɪlɪt] *n* filete *m*; **f. steak** filete *m*

filling ['fɪlɪŋ] **1** *adj* que llena mucho
2 *n* **(a)** *(stuffing)* relleno *m* **(b)** *(in tooth)* empaste *m* **(c)** *Br* **f. station** gasolinera *f*, estación *f* de servicio, *Andes, Ven* bomba *f*, *Méx* gasolinería *f*, *Perú* grifo *m*

fillip ['fɪlɪp] *n Fam* estímulo *m*

film [fɪlm] **1** *n* **(a)** *Cin & Phot* película *f*; **f. star** estrella *f* de cine **(b)** *(layer)* capa *f*
2 *vt Cin* filmar
3 *vi Cin* rodar

film-strip ['fɪlmstrɪp] *n* cortometraje *m*

filter ['fɪltə(r)] **1** *n* filtro *m*; *Aut* **f. lane** carril *m* de acceso
2 *vt* filtrar
3 *vi Aut* **to f. to the right** girar a la derecha
▸ **filter through** *vi Fig* filtrarse **(to** a)

filter-tip ['fɪltətɪp] *n (cigarette)* cigarrillo *m* con filtro

filth [fɪlθ] *n (dirt)* porquería *f*; *Fig* porquerías *fpl*

filthy ['fɪlθɪ] *adj* **(filthier, filthiest)** **(a)** *(dirty)* asqueroso(a) **(b)** *(obscene)* obsceno(a)

fin [fɪn] *n Zool & Av* aleta *f*

final ['faɪnəl] **1** *adj* **(a)** *(last)* último(a), final **(b)** *(definitive)* definitivo(a)
2 *n* **(a)** *Sport* final *f* **(b)** *Univ* **finals** exámenes *mpl* de fin de carrera

finale [fɪ'nɑːlɪ] *n* final *m*

finalist ['faɪnəlɪst] *n* finalista *mf*

finalize ['faɪnəlaɪz] *vt* ultimar; *(date)* fijar

finally ['faɪnəlɪ] *adv (lastly)* por último, *(at last)* por fin

finance ['faɪnæns, fɪ'næns] **1** *n* **(a)** finanza *fpl* **(b)** **finances** fondos *mpl*
2 *vt* financiar

financial [faɪ'nænʃəl, fɪ'nænʃəl] *adj* financiero(a); **f. crisis** crisis económica; **f. year** año económico

financier [faɪ'nænsɪə(r), fɪ'nænsɪə(r)] *n* financiero(a) *m,f*

finch [fɪntʃ] *n* pinzón *m*

find [faɪnd] **1** *vt* (*pt & pp* **found**) (**a**) *(locate)* encontrar (**b**) *(think)* encontrar (**c**) **this found its way into my bag** esto vino a parar a mi bolso (**d**) *(discover)* descubrir; **it has been found that ...** se ha comprobado que ... (**e**) *Jur* **to f. sb guilty/not guilty** declarar culpable/inocente a algn (**f**) **I can't f. the courage to tell him** no tengo valor para decírselo; **I found it impossible to get away** me resultó imposible irme

2 *n* hallazgo *m*

▸ **find out 1** *vt sep* (**a**) *(inquire)* averiguar (**b**) *(discover)* descubrir

2 *vi* (**a**) **to f. out about sth** informarse sobre algo (**b**) *(discover)* enterarse

findings ['faɪndɪŋz] *npl* conclusiones *fpl*

fine¹ [faɪn] **1** *n* multa *f*

2 *vt* multar

fine² [faɪn] **1** *adj* (**a**) *(delicate etc)* fino(a) (**b**) *(subtle)* sutil (**c**) *(excellent)* excelente (**d**) *(weather)* bueno(a); **it was f.** hacía buen tiempo (**e**) **the f. arts** las bellas artes (**f**) *(all right)* bien

2 *adv* Fam muy bien

3 *interj* ¡vale!

finely ['faɪnlɪ] *adv* (**a**) finamente; **f. chopped** picado fino (**b**) **f. tuned** a punto

finery ['faɪnərɪ] *n* galas *fpl*

finesse [fɪ'nes] *n* *(delicacy)* finura *f*; *(cunning)* astucia *f*; *(tact)* sutileza *f*

finger ['fɪŋgə(r)] **1** *n* dedo *m* (de la mano); *Fam* **to keep one's fingers crossed** esperar que todo salga bien; *Fam* **you've put your f. on it** has dado en el clavo; **middle f.** dedo corazón

2 *vt* tocar; *Pej* manosear

fingernail ['fɪŋgəneɪl] *n* uña *f*

fingerprint ['fɪŋgəprɪnt] *n* huella *f* dactilar

fingertip ['fɪŋgətɪp] *n* punta *f* or yema *f* del dedo

finicky ['fɪnɪkɪ] *adj* *(person)* quisquilloso(a)

finish ['fɪnɪʃ] **1** *n* (**a**) fin *m*; *(of race)* llegada *f* (**b**) *(surface)* acabado *m*

2 *vt* (**a**) *(complete)* acabar, terminar; **to f. doing sth** terminar de hacer algo (**b**) *(use up)* agotar

3 *vi* acabar, terminar; **to f. second** quedar el segundo

▸ **finish off** *vt sep* (**a**) *(complete)* terminar completamente (**b**) *Fam (kill)* rematar

▸ **finish up** **1** *vt sep* acabar, agotar

2 *vi* **f. up in jail** ir a parar a la cárcel

finished ['fɪnɪʃt] *adj* (**a**) *(product)* acabado(a) (**b**) *Fam (exhausted)* rendido(a)

finishing ['fɪnɪʃɪŋ] *adj* **to put the f. touch(es) to sth** darle los últimos toques a algo; **f. line** línea *f* de) meta *f*; **f. school** = escuela privada de modales para señoritas

finite ['faɪnaɪt] *adj* finito(a); *(verb)* conjugable

Finland ['fɪnlənd] *n* Finlandia

Finn [fɪn] *n* finlandés(esa) *m,f*

Finnish ['fɪnɪʃ] **1** *adj* finlandés(esa)

2 *n* *(language)* finlandés *m*

fir [fɜː(r)] *n* abeto *m*

fire ['faɪə(r)] **1** *n* (**a**) fuego *m* (**b**) *(accident etc)* incendio *m*; **to be on f.** estar en llamas; **to catch f.** incendiarse; **f. alarm** alarma *f* de incendios; *Br* **f. brigade**, *US* **f. department** (cuerpo *m* de) bomberos *mpl*; **f. engine** coche *m* de bomberos; **f. escape** escalera *f* de incendios; **f. exit** salida *f* de emergencia; **f. extinguisher** extintor *m*; **f. fighting** extinción *f* de incendios; **f. station** parque *m* de bomberos (**c**) *(heater)* estufa *f* (**d**) *Mil* fuego *m*; **to open f.** abrir fuego; *Fig* **to come under f.** ser el blanco de las críticas

2 *vt* (**a**) *(gun)* disparar (**at** a); *(rocket)* lanzar; *Fig* **to f. questions at sb** bombardear a algn a preguntas (**b**) *Fam (dismiss)* despedir

3 *vi* *(shoot)* disparar (**at** sobre)

firearm ['faɪərɑːm] *n* arma *f* de fuego

fire-fighter ['faɪəfaɪtə(r)] *n* *US* bombero *m*

fireman ['faɪəmən] *n* bombero *m*

fireplace ['faɪəpleɪs] *n* chimenea *f*; *(hearth)* hogar *m*

fireside ['faɪəsaɪd] *n* hogar *m*; **by the f.** al calor de la lumbre

firewood ['faɪəwʊd] *n* leña *f*

fireworks ['faɪəwɜːks] *npl* fuegos *mpl* artificiales

firing ['faɪərɪŋ] *n* *Mil* tiroteo *m*; **f. line** línea *f* de fuego; **f. squad** pelotón *m* de fusilamiento

firm [fɜːm] **1** *adj* firme; **to be f. with sb** *(strict)* tratar a algn con firmeza

2 *n* *Com* empresa *f*, firma *f*

firmly ['fɜːmlɪ] *adv* firmemente

firmness ['fɜːmnɪs] *n* firmeza *f*

first [fɜːst] **1** *adj* primero(a); *(before masculine singular noun)* primer; **Charles the F.** Carlos Primero; **for the f. time** por primera vez; **in the f. place** en primer lugar; **f. aid** primeros auxilios; **f. aid box** botiquín *m*; **f. floor** primer piso, *US* planta baja; **f. name** nombre *m* de pila

2 *adv (before anything else)* primero; **f. and foremost** ante todo; **f. of all** en primer lugar

3 *n* (**a**) **the f.** el primero/la primera; **the f. of April** el uno or el primero de abril (**b**) **at f.** al principio; **from the (very) f.** desde el principio (**c**) *Aut* primera *f* (**d**) *Univ* **to get a f.** sacar un sobresaliente

first-class ['fɜːst'klɑːs] **1** *adj* de primera clase

2 *adv* **to travel f.** viajar en primera

first-hand ['fɜːst'hænd] *adv & adj* de primera mano

firstly ['fɜːstlɪ] *adv* en primer lugar

first-rate ['fɜːstreɪt] *adj* de primera

fiscal ['fɪskəl] *adj* fiscal

fish [fɪʃ] **1** *n* (*pl* **fish**) (**a**) pez *m*; **f. shop** pescadería *f* (**b**) *Culin* pescado *m*; **f. and chips** = pescado frito con patatas or *Am* papas fritas; **f.** *Br* **finger** or *US* **stick** palito *m* de pescado

2 *vi* pescar; *Fig* **to f. in one's pocket for sth** buscar algo en el bolsillo

fishbone ['fɪʃbəʊn] *n* espina *f*, raspa *f*

fisherman ['fɪʃəmən] *n* pescador *m*

fishfinger [fɪʃ'fɪŋgə(r)] *n* palito *m* de pescado

fishing ['fɪʃɪŋ] *n* pesca *f*; **to go f.** ir de pesca; **f. net** red *f* de pesca; **f. rod** caña *f* de pescar; **f. tackle** aparejo *m* de pescar

fishmonger ['fɪʃmʌŋgə(r)] *n Br* pescadero(a) *m,f*; **fishmonger's (shop)** pescadería *f*

fishy ['fɪʃɪ] *adj* (**fishier, fishiest**) de pescado; *Fam Fig* **there's something f. going on** aquí hay gato encerrado

fist [fɪst] *n* puño *m*

fit¹ [fɪt] 1 *vt* **(a)** ir bien a; **that suit doesn't f. you** ese traje no te entalla

(**b**) *Sewing* probar

(**c**) **the key doesn't f. the lock** la llave no es de esta cerradura

(**d**) *(install)* colocar; **a car fitted with a radio** un coche provisto de radio

(**e**) *Fig* **she doesn't f. the description** no responde a la descripción

2 *vi* (**a**) *(be of right size)* caber

(**b**) *(facts etc)* cuadrar

3 *adj* (**a**) *(suitable)* apto(a), adecuado(a) (**for** para); **are you f. to drive?** ¿estás en condiciones de conducir?

(**b**) *(healthy)* en (plena) forma; **to keep f.** mantenerse en forma

4 *n* ajuste *m*; *Sewing* corte *m*; **to be a good f.** encajar bien

▸ **fit in 1** *vi* (**a**) he didn't f. in with his colleagues no encajó con sus compañeros de trabajo (**b**) *(tally)* cuadrar (**with** con)

2 *vt sep (find time for)* encontrar un hueco para

▸ **fit out** *vt sep* equipar

fit² [fɪt] *n* (**a**) *Med* ataque *m* (**b**) *Fig* arrebato *m*; **f. of anger** arranque *m* de cólera; *Fig* **by fits and starts** a trompicones

fitful ['fɪtfʊl] *adj* discontinuo(a)

fitness ['fɪtnɪs] *n* (**a**) *(aptitude)* aptitud *f*, capacidad *f* (**b**) *(health)* (buen) estado físico

fitted ['fɪtɪd] *adj* empotrado(a); **f. carpet** moqueta *f*, **f. cupboard** armario empotrado

fitter ['fɪtə(r)] *n* ajustador(a) *m,f*

fitting ['fɪtɪŋ] 1 *adj* apropiado(a)

2 *n* (**a**) *(of dress)* prueba *f*; **f. room** probador *m* (**b**) *(usu pl)* accesorio *m*; **light fittings** apliques eléctricos

five [faɪv] *adj & n* cinco (*m inv*)

fiver ['faɪvə(r)] *n Fam* billete *m* de 5 libras/dólares

fix [fɪks] 1 *n* (**a**) *Fam* **to be in a f.** estar en un apuro (**b**) *Fam (drugs)* chute *m*

2 *vt* (**a**) *(fasten)* fijar, asegurar (**b**) *(date, price)* fijar; *(limit)* señalar (**c**) **he'll f. it with the boss** *(arrange)* se las arreglará con el jefe (**d**) *(repair)* arreglar (**e**) *US (food, drink)* preparar

▸ **fix up** *vt sep (arrange)* arreglar; **to f. sb u** **with sth** proveer a algn de algo

fixation [fɪk'seɪʃən] *n* idea fija

fixed [fɪkst] *adj* (**a**) fijo(a) (**b**) *Fam (match et* amañado(a)

fixture ['fɪkstʃə(r)] *n* (**a**) *Sport* encuentro *(* (**b**) **fixtures** *(in building)* accesorios *mpl*

fizz [fɪz] 1 *n* burbujeo *m*

2 *vi* burbujear

▸ **fizzle out** ['fɪzəl] *vi* quedar en nada

fizzy ['fɪzɪ] *adj* (**fizzier, fizziest**) *(water)* cc gas

flabbergasted ['flæbəgɑːstɪd] *adj* pasma do(a)

flabby ['flæbɪ] *adj* (**flabbier, flabbiest**) f fo(a)

flag [flæg] 1 *n* bandera *f*; *Naut* pabellón *m*

2 *vt Fig* **to f. down a car** hacer señales a u coche para que pare

3 *vi (interest)* decaer; *(conversation)* langu decer

flagpole ['flægpəʊl] *n* asta *f* de bandera

flagrant ['fleɪgrənt] *adj* flagrante

flagship ['flægʃɪp] *n* buque *m* insignia

flagstone ['flægstəʊn] *n* losa *f*

flair [fleə(r)] *n* facilidad *f*

flak [flæk] *n* (**a**) *Mil* fuego antiaéreo (**b**) *Fa* críticas *fpl*

flake [fleɪk] 1 *n* *(of snow)* copo *m*; *(of ski soap)* escama *f*; *(of paint)* desconchón *m*

2 *vi (skin)* descamarse; *(paint)* desconcha se

flamboyant [flæm'bɔɪənt] *adj* extravagan

flame [fleɪm] *n* (**a**) *(of fire)* llama *f*; **to go up flames** incendiarse (**b**) *Comput* llamarada = mensaje ofensivo

flameproof ['fleɪmpruːf] *adj* ininflamable

flamingo [flə'mɪŋgəʊ] *n* flamenco *m*

flammable ['flæməbəl] *adj* inflamable

flan [flæn] *n* tarta *f*; **fruit f.** tarta de fruta

> *Note that the Spanish word* **flan** *is a fals* friend and is never a translation for the Englis word *flan*. In Spanish, **flan** means "crème cara mel".

flank [flæŋk] 1 *n* (**a**) *(of animal)* ijada *f* (**b**) *M* flanco *m*

2 *vt* flanquear

flannel ['flænəl] *n* (**a**) *Tex* franela *f* (**b**) *(face cloth)* toallita *f*

flap [flæp] 1 *vt (wings, arms)* batir

2 *vi (wings)* aletear; *(flag)* ondear

3 *n* (**a**) *(of envelope, pocket)* solapa *f*; *(of ten* faldón *m* (**b**) *(of wing)* aletazo *m* (**c**) *Fam* get into a f. ponerse nervioso(a)

flare [fleə(r)] 1 *n* (**a**) *(flame)* llamarada *f* (* Mil & Naut* bengala *f*

2 *vi* **to f. (up)** *(fire)* llamear; *Fig (perso* encolerizarse; *(trouble)* estallar

flared [fleəd] *adj (trousers etc)* acampan do(a)

flash [flæʃ] **1** n (a) (of light) destello m; (of lightning) relámpago m; Fig **in a f.** en un santiamén; Fig **a f. in the pan** un éxito fugaz (b) **news f.** noticia f de última hora (c) Phot flash m
2 adj Fam chulo(a)
3 vt (a) (torch) dirigir (b) Rad & TV transmitir (c) **he flashed his card** enseñó rápidamente su carnet
4 vi (a) (light) destellar (b) **a car flashed past** un coche pasó como un rayo
flashback ['flæʃbæk] n flashback m
flashcube ['flæʃkjuːb] n cubo m flash
flashlight ['flæʃlaɪt] n US linterna f
flashy ['flæʃɪ] adj (flashier, flashiest) Fam chillón(ona)
flask [flɑːsk, flæsk] n frasco m; (Thermos®) f. termo m
flat [flæt] **1** adj (flatter, flattest) (a) (surface) llano(a) (b) (beer) sin gas (c) (battery) descargado(a); (tyre) desinflado(a) (d) (rate) fijo(a) (e) (categorical) rotundo(a) (f) (dull) soso(a) (g) Mus **B f.** si m bemol
2 adv (a) **to fall f. on one's face** caerse de bruces (b) **in ten seconds f.** en diez segundos justos (c) Fam **to go f. out** ir a todo gas
3 n (a) (apartment) piso m (b) US Aut pinchazo m (c) **mud flats** marismas fpl
flatly ['flætlɪ] adv rotundamente
flatmate ['flætmeɪt] n Br compañero(a) m,f de piso
flatten ['flætən] vt (a) (make level) allanar (b) (crush) aplastar
flatter ['flætə(r)] vt (a) adular, halagar (b) (clothes, portrait) favorecer (c) **to f. oneself** hacerse ilusiones
flattering ['flætərɪŋ] adj (a) (words) halagador(a) (b) (dress, portrait) favorecedor(a)
flattery ['flætərɪ] n adulación f, halago m
flaunt [flɔːnt] vt hacer alarde de
flavour, US **flavor** ['fleɪvə(r)] **1** n sabor m
2 vt Culin sazonar (with con)
flavoured, US **flavored** ['fleɪvəd] adj **strawberry f.** con sabor a fresa, Bol, CSur, Ecuad frutilla
flavouring, US **flavoring** ['fleɪvərɪŋ] n condimento m; **artificial f.** aroma m artificial
flaw [flɔː] n (failing) defecto m; (fault) desperfecto m
flawless ['flɔːlɪs] adj perfecto(a)
flax [flæks] n lino m
flaxen ['flæksən] adj (hair) rubio pajizo
flea [fliː] n pulga f; **f. market** rastro m
fleck [flek] n (speck) mota f, punto m
fled [fled] pt & pp of **flee**
fledg(e)ling ['fledʒlɪŋ] adj Fig novato(a)
flee [fliː] **1** vt (pt & pp fled) huir de
2 vi huir (from de)
fleece [fliːs] **1** n (a) (sheep's coat) lana f (b) (sheared) vellón m
2 vt Fam (cheat) sangrar
fleet [fliːt] n flota f

fleeting ['fliːtɪŋ] adj fugaz
Flemish ['flemɪʃ] **1** adj flamenco(a)
2 n (language) flamenco m
flesh [fleʃ] n (a) carne f; Fig **in the f.** en persona; Fig **to be of f. and blood** ser de carne y hueso; **f. wound** herida f superficial (b) (of fruit) pulpa f
flew [fluː] pt of **fly**
flex [fleks] **1** n Br Elec cable m
2 vt (muscles) flexionar
flexibility [fleksɪ'bɪlɪtɪ] n flexibilidad f
flexible ['fleksɪbəl] adj flexible
flick [flɪk] **1** n movimiento rápido; (of finger) capirotazo m
2 vt (with finger) dar un capirotazo a
▸ **flick through** vt insep (book) hojear
flicker ['flɪkə(r)] **1** n (a) parpadeo m; (of light) titileo m (b) Fig **a f. of hope** un destello de esperanza
2 vi (eyes) parpadear; (flame) vacilar
flier ['flaɪə(r)] n aviador(a) m,f
flight [flaɪt] n (a) vuelo m; **f. path** trayectoria f de vuelo; **f. recorder** registrador m de vuelo (b) (of ball) trayectoria f (c) (escape) huida f, fuga f; **to take f.** darse a la fuga (d) (of stairs) tramo m
flight-deck ['flaɪtdek] n (cockpit) cabina f del piloto
flimsy ['flɪmzɪ] adj (flimsier, flimsiest) (cloth) ligero(a); (paper) fino(a); (structure) poco sólido(a); (excuse) poco convincente
flinch [flɪntʃ] vi (wince) estremecerse
fling [flɪŋ] **1** vt (pt & pp flung) arrojar
2 n Fam **to have a f.** echar una cana al aire
flint [flɪnt] n (a) (stone) pedernal m (b) (in lighter) piedra f de mechero
flip [flɪp] **1** n (flick) capirotazo m; **f. chart** flip chart m, pizarra f de conferencia (con bloc)
2 vt (toss) tirar (al aire); **to f. a coin** echar a cara o cruz
flip-flop ['flɪpflɒp] n (a) Comput báscula f biestable (b) Br (footwear) chancla f
flippant ['flɪpənt] adj frívolo(a)
flipper ['flɪpə(r)] n aleta f
flirt [flɜːt] **1** n coqueto(a) m,f
2 vi flirtear, coquetear; **to f. with death** jugar con la muerte
flirtation [flɜː'teɪʃən] n flirteo m, coqueteo m
flit [flɪt] vi revolotear
float [fləʊt] **1** n (a) flotador m (b) (money) cambio m (c) (in procession) carroza f
2 vt (a) poner a flote (b) (shares) emitir; (currency, business) hacer flotar
3 vi flotar
floating ['fləʊtɪŋ] adj flotante; (voter) indeciso(a)
flock [flɒk] **1** n Zool rebaño m; Orn bandada f; Rel grey f; (crowd) multitud f
2 vi acudir en masa
flog [flɒg] vt (a) azotar; Fam Fig **flogged to death** (idea) trillado(a) (b) Fam (sell) vender
flood [flʌd] **1** n inundación f; (of river)

riada f; Fig torrente m

2 vt inundar

3 vi (river) desbordarse; Fig **to f. in** entrar a raudales

flooding ['flʌdɪŋ] n inundaciones fpl

floodlight ['flʌdlaɪt] n foco m

floor [flɔː(r)] **1** n (**a**) (of room) suelo m; **dance f.** pista f de baile (**b**) (of ocean, forest) fondo m (**c**) (storey) piso m; **first f.** Br primer piso, US planta baja; Br **ground f.** planta baja

2 vt Fig dejar perplejo(a)

floorboard ['flɔːbɔːd] n tabla f (del suelo)

flop [flɒp] **1** n Fam fracaso m

2 vi (**a**) **to f. down on the bed** tumbarse en la cama (**b**) Fam fracasar

floppy ['flɒpɪ] adj (floppier, floppiest) flojo(a); Comput **f. disk** disco m flexible

flora ['flɔːrə] n flora f

florid ['flɒrɪd] adj (style) florido(a)

florist ['flɒrɪst] n florista mf; **f.'s shop** floristería f

flounce¹ [flaʊns] vi **to f. in/out** entrar/salir airadamente

flounce² [flaʊns] n Sewing volante m

flounder¹ ['flaʊndə(r)] n (fish) platija f

flounder² ['flaʊndə(r)] vi (**a**) (struggle) forcejear; Fig enredarse (**b**) (be at a loss) no saber que decir or hacer

flour ['flaʊə(r)] n harina f

flourish ['flʌrɪʃ] **1** n (**a**) (gesture) ademán m (teatral) (**b**) (under signature) rúbrica f

2 vt (brandish) agitar

3 vi (thrive) florecer; (plant) crecer

flourishing ['flʌrɪʃɪŋ] adj floreciente

flout [flaʊt] vt Jur desacatar

flow [fləʊ] **1** n flujo m; (of river) corriente f; (of traffic) circulación f; (of capital) movimiento m; (of people, goods) afluencia f; **f. chart** diagrama m de flujo; Comput organigrama m

2 vi (blood, river) fluir; (sea) subir; (traffic) circular

flower ['flaʊə(r)] **1** n flor f; **f. bed** arriate m

2 vi florecer

flowerpot ['flaʊəpɒt] n maceta f

flowery ['flaʊərɪ] adj Fig florido(a)

flowing ['fləʊɪŋ] adj (hair) suelto(a); (dress) de mucho vuelo; (style) fluido(a); (shape, movement) natural

flown [fləʊn] pp of **fly**

flu [fluː] n (abbr **influenza**) gripe f

fluctuate ['flʌktjʊeɪt] vi fluctuar

fluctuation [flʌktjʊ'eɪʃən] n fluctuación f

flue [fluː] n conducto m de humos; (chimney) cañón m

fluent ['fluːənt] adj (**a**) **he speaks f. German** habla el alemán con soltura (**b**) (eloquent) fluido(a)

fluff [flʌf] **1** n (down) pelusa f

2 vt Fam **to f. sth** hacer algo mal

fluffy ['flʌfɪ] adj (fluffier, fluffiest) (pillow) mullido(a); (toy) de peluche; (cake) esponjoso(a)

fluid ['fluːɪd] **1** adj (movement) natural; (style, prose) fluido(a); (situation) incierto(a)

2 n fluido m, líquido m

fluke [fluːk] n Fam chiripa f; **by a f.** por chiripa

flummox ['flʌməks] vt Fam desconcertar

flung [flʌŋ] pt & pp of **fling**

flunk [flʌŋk] vt & vi US Fam catear

fluorescent [flʊə'resənt] adj fluorescente

fluoride ['flʊəraɪd] n fluoruro m

flurry ['flʌrɪ] n (**a**) (of wind) ráfaga f; (of snow) nevasca f (**b**) Fig (bustle) agitación f

flush [flʌʃ] **1** adj **f. with** (level) a ras de

2 n (blush) rubor m

3 vt **to f. the lavatory** tirar de la cadena

4 vi (**a**) **the loo won't f.** la cisterna del wáter no funciona (**b**) (blush) ruborizarse

flushed [flʌʃt] adj (cheeks) rojo(a), encendido(a); Fig **f. with success** emocionado(a) ante el éxito

fluster ['flʌstə(r)] vt **to get flustered** ponerse nervioso(a)

flute [fluːt] n flauta f

flutist ['fluːtɪst] n US Mus flautista mf

flutter ['flʌtə(r)] **1** vi (leaves, birds) revolotear; (flag) ondear

2 n Fam (bet, gambling) apuesta pequeña

flux [flʌks] n (flow) flujo m; (instability) inestabilidad f; Fig **to be in a state of f.** estar cambiando constantemente

fly¹ [flaɪ] **1** vt (pt **flew**; pp **flown**) (**a**) Av pilotar (**b**) (merchandise, troops) transportar (**c**) (distance) recorrer (**d**) (kite) hacer volar

2 vi (**a**) (bird, plane) volar (**b**) (go by plane) ir en avión (**c**) (flag) ondear (**d**) **to f. into a rage** montar en cólera (**e**) **the train flew past** el tren pasó volando (**f**) Fam **to go flying** (fall) caerse

3 npl **flies** bragueta f

fly² [flaɪ] n (insect) mosca f; **f. spray** spray m matamoscas

flying ['flaɪɪŋ] **1** adj volador(a); (rapid) rápido(a); **a f. visit** una visita relámpago; Fig **to come out of an affair with f. colours** salir airoso(a) de un asunto; Fig **to get off to a f. start** empezar con buen pie; **f. picket** piquete m (informativo); **f. saucer** platillo m volante

2 n (**a**) (action) vuelo m (**b**) (aviation) aviación f

flyleaf ['flaɪliːf] n (of book) guarda f

flyover ['flaɪəʊvə(r)] n Br paso elevado

flypast ['flaɪpɑːst] n Br Av desfile aéreo

flyweight ['flaɪweɪt] n (in boxing) peso m mosca

foal [fəʊl] n potro(a) m,f

foam [fəʊm] **1** n espuma f; **f. bath** espuma de baño; **f. rubber** goma espuma

2 vi hacer espuma

fob [fɒb] n (chain) cadena f (de reloj)

▸ **fob off** vt sep Fam **he fobbed off his old radio on a stranger** le colocó su radio vieja a un desconocido; **to f. sb off with excuses** darle largas a algn

focus ['fəʊkəs] **1** *vi* centrarse (**on** en)
2 *vi* enfocar; **to f. on sth** *Phot* enfocar algo; *Fig* centrarse en algo
3 *n (pl* **focuses)** foco *m*; **to be in f./out of f.** estar enfocado(a)/desenfocado(a); *Com Pol* **f. group** grupo *m* muestra

fodder ['fɒdə(r)] *n* pienso *m*

foe [fəʊ] *n Fml* enemigo(a) *m,f*

foetus ['fiːtəs] *n* feto *m*

fog [fɒg] *n* niebla *f*; *(at sea)* bruma *f*

fogey ['fəʊgɪ] *n Fam* **old f.** cascarrabias *mf inv*

foggy ['fɒgɪ] *adj* (**foggier, foggiest**) **it is f.** hay niebla; *Fam* **I haven't the foggiest (idea)** no tengo la más mínima idea

foghorn ['fɒghɔːn] *n* sirena *f* (de niebla)

foglamp ['fɒglæmp], *US* **foglight** ['fɒglaɪt] *n* faro *m* antiniebla

foil [fɔɪl] **1** *n* (**a**) **aluminium f.** papel *m* de aluminio (**b**) *(in fencing)* florete *m*
2 *vt (plot)* desbaratar

fold [fəʊld] **1** *n (crease)* pliegue *m*
2 *vt* plegar, doblar; **to f. one's arms** cruzar los brazos
3 *vi* **to f. (up)** *(chair etc)* plegarse; *Com* quebrar

folder ['fəʊldə(r)] *n* carpeta *f*

folding ['fəʊldɪŋ] *adj (chair etc)* plegable

foliage ['fəʊlɪdʒ] *n* follaje *m*

folk [fəʊk] **1** *npl* (**a**) *(people)* gente *f* (**b**) *Fam* **folks** *(family)* padres *mpl*; **one's folks** la familia
2 *adj* popular; **f. music** música *f* folk; **f. song** canción *f* popular

folklore ['fəʊklɔː(r)] *n* folklore *m*

follow ['fɒləʊ] **1** *vt* seguir; *(pursue)* perseguir; *(understand)* comprender; *(way of life)* llevar
2 *vi* (**a**) *(come after)* seguir; **as follows** como sigue (**b**) *(result)* resultar; **that doesn't f.** eso no es lógico (**c**) *(understand)* entender
▸ **follow through, follow up** *vt sep (idea)* llevar a cabo; *(clue)* investigar

follower ['fɒləʊə(r)] *n* seguidor(a) *m,f*

following ['fɒləʊɪŋ] **1** *adj* siguiente
2 *n* seguidores *mpl*

folly ['fɒlɪ] *n* locura *f*, desatino *m*

fond [fɒnd] *adj (loving)* cariñoso(a); **to be f. of sb** tenerle mucho cariño a algn; **to be f. of doing sth** ser aficionado(a) a hacer algo

fondle ['fɒndəl] *vt* acariciar

fondness ['fɒndnɪs] *n (love)* cariño *m* (**for** a); *(liking)* afición *f* (**for** a)

font [fɒnt] *n Rel* pila *f*

food [fuːd] *n* comida *f*; **f. chain** cadena trófica; **f. poisoning** intoxicación alimenticia

foodstuffs ['fuːdstʌfs] *npl* productos alimenticios

fool [fuːl] **1** *n* (**a**) tonto(a) *m,f*, imbécil *mf*; **to make a f. of sb** poner a algn en ridículo; **to play the f.** hacer el tonto (**b**) *Culin* ≃ mousse *f* de fruta

2 *vt (deceive)* engañar
3 *vi (joke)* bromear; **to f. about** *or* **around** hacer el tonto

foolhardy ['fuːlhɑːdɪ] *adj* (**foolhardier, foolhardiest**) *(person)* intrépido(a)

foolish ['fuːlɪʃ] *adj* estúpido(a)

foolproof ['fuːlpruːf] *adj* infalible

foot [fʊt] **1** *n (pl* **feet**) pie *m*; *Zool* pata *f*; **on f.** a pie, andando; *Fig* **to find one's feet** acostumbrarse; *Fam Fig* **to put one's f. down** *(control)* imponerse; *(in car)* pisar a fondo; *Fam Fig* **to put one's f. in it** meter la pata; *Fam Fig* **to put one's feet up** descansar
2 *vt* **to f. the bill** *(pay)* pagar la cuenta

footage ['fʊtɪdʒ] *n Cin* metraje *m*

football ['fʊtbɔːl] *n* (**a**) *(soccer)* fútbol *m*; **bar f.** futbolín *m*; **f. ground** campo *m* de fútbol; **f. match** partido *m* de fútbol; **f. pools** quinielas *fpl* (**b**) *(ball)* balón *m*

footballer ['fʊtbɔːlə(r)] *n* futbolista *mf*

footbridge ['fʊtbrɪdʒ] *n* puente *m* para peatones

foothills ['fʊthɪlz] *npl* estribaciones *fpl*

foothold ['fʊthəʊld] *n Fig* **to gain a f.** afianzarse en una posición

footing ['fʊtɪŋ] *n* **to lose one's f.** perder el equilibrio; **on a friendly f.** en plan amistoso; **on an equal f.** en pie de igualdad

footlights ['fʊtlaɪts] *npl* candilejas *fpl*

footman ['fʊtmən] *n* lacayo *m*

footnote ['fʊtnəʊt] *n* nota *f* a pie de página

footpath ['fʊtpɑːθ] *n (track)* sendero *m*

footprint ['fʊtprɪnt] *n* pisada *f*

footsore ['fʊtsɔː(r)] *adj* con los pies doloridos

footstep ['fʊtstep] *n* paso *m*

footwear ['fʊtweə(r)] *n* calzado *m*

for [fɔː(r), *unstressed* fə(r)] **1** *prep* (**a**) *(intended)* para; **curtains f. the bedroom** cortinas para el dormitorio; **f. sale** en venta; **it's time f. bed** es hora de acostarse
(**b**) *(representing)* por; **a cheque f. £10** un cheque de 10 libras; **J f. John** J de Juan; **what's the Spanish f. "rivet"?** ¿cómo se dice "rivet" en español?
(**c**) *(purpose)* para; **it's good f. the digestion** es bueno para la digestión; **what's this f.?** ¿para qué sirve esto?
(**d**) *(because of)* por; **famous f. its cuisine** famoso(a) por su cocina; **to jump f. joy** saltar de alegría
(**e**) *(on behalf of)* por; **the campaign f. peace** la campaña por la paz; **will you do it f. me?** ¿lo harás por mí?
(**f**) *(during)* por, durante; **I lent it to her f. a year** se lo presté por un año; **I shall stay f. two weeks** me quedaré dos semanas; **I was ill f. a month** estuve enfermo(a) durante un mes; **I've been here f. three months** hace tres meses que estoy aquí
(**g**) *(distance)* **I walked f. 10 km** caminé 10 km

(**h**) *(at a point in time)* para; **I can do it f. next Monday** puedo hacerlo para el lunes que viene; **f. the last time** por última vez

(**i**) *(destination)* para

(**j**) *(amount of money)* por; **I got the car f. £500** conseguí el coche por 500 libras

(**k**) *(in favour of)* a favor de; **are you f. or against?** ¿estás a favor o en contra?; **to vote f. sb** votar a algn

(**l**) *(to obtain)* para; **to run f. the bus** correr para coger al autobús; **to send sb f. water** mandar a algn a por agua

(**m**) *(with respect to)* en cuanto a; **as f. him** en cuanto a él; **f. all I care** por mí; **f. all I know** que yo sepa; **f. one thing** para empezar

(**n**) *(despite)* a pesar de; **f. all that** aún así; **he's tall f. his age** está muy alto para su edad

(**o**) *(instead of)* por; **can you go f. me?** ¿puede ir por mí?

(**p**) *(towards)* hacia, por; **affection f. sb** cariño hacia algn; **his love f. you** su amor por ti

(**q**) *(as)* por; **to leave sb f. dead** dar a algn por muerto(a); **what do you use f. fuel?** ¿qué utilizan como combustible?

(**r**) *(in exchange)* por; **to exchange one thing f. another** cambiar una cosa por otra; **how much did you sell it f.?** ¿por cuánto lo vendiste?

(**s**) *(+ object + infin)* **there's no reason f. us to quarrel** no hay motivo para que riñamos; **it's time f. you to go** es hora de que os marchéis; **it's easy f. him to say that** le es fácil decir eso

2 *conj (since, as)* ya que, puesto que
forage ['fɒrɪdʒ] **1** *n* forraje *m*
  2 *vi* hurgar
foray ['fɒreɪ] *n* incursión *f*
forbade [fə'beɪd] *pt of* **forbid**
forbearance [fɔː'beərəns] *n* paciencia *f*
forbid [fə'bɪd] *vt* (*pt* **forbade**; *pp* **forbidden** [fə'bɪdən]) prohibir; **to f. sb to do sth** prohibirle a algn hacer algo
forbidding [fə'bɪdɪŋ] *adj (stern)* severo(a); *(bleak)* inhóspito(a)
force [fɔːs] **1** *n* (**a**) fuerza *f*; **by f.** por la fuerza; **to come into f.** entrar en vigor (**b**) *Mil* cuerpo *m*; **the (armed) forces** las fuerzas armadas; **the police f.** la policía
  2 *vt* forzar; **to f. sb to do sth** forzar a algn a hacer algo
forced [fɔːst] *adj* forzado(a); **f. landing** aterrizaje forzoso
force-feed ['fɔːsfiːd] *vt* alimentar a la fuerza
forceful ['fɔːsfʊl] *adj* (**a**) *(person)* enérgico(a) (**b**) *(argument)* convincente
forceps ['fɔːseps] *npl* fórceps *m*
forcible ['fɔːsəbəl] *adj* **f. entry** allanamiento *m* de morada
forcibly ['fɔːsəblɪ] *adv* a *or* por la fuerza
ford [fɔːd] **1** *n* vado *m*
  2 *vt* vadear

fore [fɔː(r)] *n Fig* **to come to the f.** empezar destacar
forearm ['fɔːrɑːm] *n* antebrazo *m*
foreboding [fɔː'bəʊdɪŋ] *n* presentimiento *r*
forecast ['fɔːkɑːst] **1** *n* pronóstico *m*
  2 *vt (pt & pp* **forecast** *or* **forecasted**) pronos ticar
forecourt ['fɔːkɔːt] *n (of garage)* área *f* d servicio
forefathers ['fɔːfɑːðəz] *npl* antepasados *m*
forefront ['fɔːfrʌnt] *n* **in the f.** a la vanguar dia
forego [fɔː'gəʊ] *vt (pt* **forewent**; *pp* **foregon** [fɔː'gɒn]) *Fml* sacrificar
foregone ['fɔːgɒn] *adj* **a f. conclusion** u resultado inevitable
foreground ['fɔːgraʊnd] *n* primer plano
forehead ['fɒrɪd, 'fɔːhed] *n* frente *f*
foreign ['fɒrɪn] *adj* extranjero(a); *(trade policy)* exterior; **f. exchange** divisas *fpl*; **th F. Office** el Ministerio de Asuntos Exteriores **f. body** cuerpo extraño
foreigner ['fɒrɪnə(r)] *n* extranjero(a) *m,f*
foreman ['fɔːmən] *n* (**a**) *Ind* capataz *m* (**b** *Jur* presidente *m* del jurado
foremost ['fɔːməʊst] *adj* principal; **first an f.** ante todo
forename ['fɔːneɪm] *n* nombre *m* de pila
forensic [fə'rensɪk] *adj* forense
forerunner ['fɔːrʌnə(r)] *n* precursor(a) *m,f*
foresee [fɔː'siː] *vt (pt* **foresaw** [fɔː'sɔː]; *p* **foreseen**) prever
foreseeable [fɔː'siːəbəl] *adj* previsible; **i the f. future** en un futuro próximo
foreseen [fɔː'siːn] *pp of* **foresee**
foreshadow [fɔː'ʃædəʊ] *vt* presagiar
foresight ['fɔːsaɪt] *n* previsión *f*
forest ['fɒrɪst] *n* bosque *m*
forestall [fɔː'stɔːl] *vt (plan)* anticiparse *(danger)* prevenir
forestry ['fɒrɪstrɪ] *n* silvicultura *f*
foretaste ['fɔːteɪst] *n* anticipo *m* (**of** de)
foretell [fɔː'tel] *vt (pt & pp* **foretold** [fɔ 'təʊld]) presagiar
forever [fə'revə(r)] *adv* (**a**) *(eternally)* siem pre (**b**) *(for good)* para siempre (**c**) *Far (ages)* siglos *mpl*
forewent [fɔː'went] *pt of* **forego**
foreword ['fɔːwɜːd] *n* prefacio *m*
forfeit ['fɔːfɪt] **1** *n (penalty)* pena *f*; *(in games* prenda *f*
  2 *vt* perder
forgave [fə'geɪv] *pt of* **forgive**
forge [fɔːdʒ] **1** *n* (**a**) *(furnace)* fragua *f* (**b** *(blacksmith's)* herrería *f*
  2 *vt* (**a**) *(counterfeit)* falsificar (**b**) *(meta* forjar
  3 *vi* **to f. ahead** hacer grandes progresos
forger ['fɔːdʒə(r)] *n* falsificador(a) *m,f*
forgery ['fɔːdʒərɪ] *n* falsificación *f*
forget [fə'get] **1** *vt (pt* **forgot**; *pp* **forgotten** olvidar, olvidarse de; **I forgot to close th**

window se me olvidó cerrar *or* me olvidé de cerrar la ventana; **I've forgotten my key** he olvidado la llave
　2 *vi* olvidarse

forgetful [fə'getfʊl] *adj* olvidadizo(a)

forget-me-not [fə'getmɪnɒt] *n* nomeolvides *f inv*

forgive [fə'gɪv] *vt* (*pt* **forgave**; *pp* **forgiven** [fə'gɪvən]) perdonar; **to f. sb for sth** perdonarle algo a algn

forgiveness [fə'gɪvnɪs] *n* perdón *m*

forgo [fɔː'gəʊ] *vt Fml* = **forego**

forgot [fə'gɒt] *pt of* **forget**

forgotten [fə'gɒtən] *pp of* **forget**

fork [fɔːk] **1** *n* (**a**) *Agr* horca *f* (**b**) *(cutlery)* tenedor *m* (**c**) *(in road)* bifurcación *f*
　2 *vi (roads)* bifurcarse
　▸ **fork out** *vt sep Fam (money)* soltar

fork-lift truck [fɔːklɪft'trʌk] *n* carretilla *f* elevadora de horquilla

forlorn [fə'lɔːn] *adj (forsaken)* abandonado(a); *(desolate)* triste; *(without hope)* desesperado(a)

form [fɔːm] **1** *n* (**a**) *(shape)* forma *f* (**b**) *(type)* clase *f* (**c**) **for f.'s sake** para guardar las formas (**d**) *(document)* formulario *m* (**e**) **on/ on top/off f.** en/en plena/en baja forma (**f**) *Br Educ* clase *f*; **the first f.** el primer curso
　2 *vt* formar; **to f. an impression** formarse una impresión
　3 *vi* formarse

formal ['fɔːməl] *adj* (**a**) *(official)* oficial; **a f. application** una solicitud en forma (**b**) *(party, dress)* de etiqueta (**c**) *(ordered)* formal (**d**) *(person)* formalista

formality [fɔː'mælɪtɪ] *n* formalidad *f*

formally ['fɔːməlɪ] *adv* oficialmente

format ['fɔːmæt] **1** *n* formato *m*
　2 *vt Comput* formatear

formation [fɔː'meɪʃən] *n* formación *f*

formative ['fɔːmətɪv] *adj* formativo(a)

former ['fɔːmə(r)] *adj* (**a**) *(time)* anterior (**b**) *(one-time)* antiguo(a); *(person)* ex; **the f. champion** el excampeón (**c**) *(first)* aquél/ aquélla; **Peter and Lisa came, the f. wearing a hat** vinieron Peter y Lisa, aquél llevaba sombrero

formerly ['fɔːməlɪ] *adv* antiguamente

formidable ['fɔːmɪdəbəl] *adj (prodigious)* formidable; *(daunting)* terrible

formula ['fɔːmjʊlə] *n* fórmula *f*

forsake [fə'seɪk] *vt* (*pt* **forsook** [fə'sʊk]; *pp* **forsaken** [fə'seɪkən]) *Literary (abandon, desert)* abandonar (**b**) *(give up)* renunciar a

fort [fɔːt] *n* fortaleza *f*

forte ['fɔːteɪ] *n* fuerte *m*

forth [fɔːθ] *adv Fml* **and so f.** y así sucesivamente; **to go back and f.** ir de acá para allá

forthcoming [fɔːθ'kʌmɪŋ] *adj* (**a**) *(event)* próximo(a) (**b**) **no money was f.** no hubo oferta de dinero (**c**) *(communicative)* comunicativo(a)

forthright ['fɔːθraɪt] *adj* franco(a)

fortify ['fɔːtɪfaɪ] *vt* fortificar

fortitude ['fɔːtɪtjuːd] *n* fortaleza *f*, fuerza *f*

fortnight ['fɔːtnaɪt] *n Br* quincena *f*

fortnightly ['fɔːtnaɪtlɪ] *Br* **1** *adj* quincenal
　2 *adv* cada quince días

fortress ['fɔːtrɪs] *n* fortaleza *f*

fortunate ['fɔːtʃənɪt] *adj* afortunado(a); **it was f. that he came** fue una suerte que viniera

fortunately ['fɔːtʃənɪtlɪ] *adv* afortunadamente

fortune ['fɔːtʃən] *n* (**a**) *(luck, fate)* suerte *f*; **to tell sb's f.** echar la buenaventura a algn (**b**) *(money)* fortuna *f*

fortune-teller ['fɔːtʃəntelə(r)] *n* adivino(a) *m,f*

forty ['fɔːtɪ] *adj & n* cuarenta *(m inv)*

forum ['fɔːrəm] *n* foro *m*

forward ['fɔːwəd] **1** *adv* (**a**) *(also* **forwards**) *(direction and movement)* hacia adelante (**b**) *Fig* **to come f.** ofrecerse (**c**) **from this day f.** de ahora en adelante
　2 *adj* (**a**) *(movement)* hacia adelante; *(position)* delantero(a) (**b**) *(person)* fresco(a)
　3 *n Sport* delantero(a) *m,f*
　4 *vt* (**a**) *(send on)* remitir (**b**) *Fml (send goods)* expedir (**c**) *Fml (further)* fomentar

fossil ['fɒsəl] *n* fósil *m*; **f. fuel** combustible *m* fósil

foster ['fɒstə(r)] **1** *vt* (**a**) *(child)* criar (**b**) *Fml (hopes)* abrigar; *(relations)* fomentar
　2 *adj* **f. child** hijo(a) adoptivo(a); **f. father** padre adoptivo; **f. mother** madre adoptiva; **f. parents** padres adoptivos

fought [fɔːt] *pt & pp of* **fight**

foul [faʊl] **1** *adj* (**a**) *(smell)* fétido(a); *(taste)* asqueroso(a) (**b**) *(deed)* atroz; *(weather)* de perros (**c**) *(language)* grosero(a) (**d**) **to fall f. of** tener problemas con; *Sport* **f. play** juego sucio; *Jur* **f. play is suspected** se sospecha que se haya cometido un acto criminal
　2 *n Sport* falta *f*
　3 *vt* (**a**) *(dirty)* ensuciar; *(air)* contaminar (**b**) *Sport* cometer una falta contra

found¹ [faʊnd] *pt & pp of* **find**

found² [faʊnd] *vt (establish)* fundar

foundation [faʊn'deɪʃən] *n* (**a**) *(establishment)* fundación *f* (**b**) *(basis)* fundamento *m* (**c**) **f. (cream)** maquillaje *m* de fondo (**d**) *Constr* **foundations** cimientos *mpl*

founder¹ ['faʊndə(r)] *n* fundador(a) *m,f*

founder² ['faʊndə(r)] *vi* (**a**) *Fml (sink)* hundirse (**b**) *Fig (plan, hopes)* fracasar

foundry ['faʊndrɪ] *n* fundición *f*

fountain ['faʊntɪn] *n (structure)* fuente *f*; *(jet)* surtidor *m*; **f. pen** pluma estilográfica, *CSur* lapicera *f* fuente, *Perú* lapicero *m*

four [fɔː(r)] *adj & n* cuatro *(m inv)*; **on all fours** a gatas

four-door ['fɔːdɔː(r)] *adj Aut* de cuatro puertas

four-poster [fɔː'pəʊstə(r)] adj & n **f. (bed)** cama f con dosel

foursome ['fɔːsəm] n grupo m de cuatro personas

fourteen [fɔː'tiːn] adj & n catorce (m inv)

fourteenth [fɔː'tiːnθ] **1** adj & n decimocuarto(a) (m,f)
2 n (fraction) catorceavo m

fourth [fɔːθ] **1** adj & n cuarto(a) (m,f)
2 n (a) (fraction) cuarto m (b) Aut cuarta f (velocidad)

fowl [faʊl] n (pl fowl) ave f de corral

fox [fɒks] **1** n zorro/a m,f
2 vt (a) (perplex) dejar perplejo(a) (b) (deceive) engañar

foyer ['fɔɪeɪ, 'fɔɪə(r)] n vestíbulo m

fracas ['frækɑː] n gresca f, refriega f

> 🖉 Note that the Spanish word **fracaso** is a false friend and is never a translation for the English word **fracas**. In Spanish, **fracaso** means "failure."

fraction ['frækʃən] n fracción f

fracture ['fræktʃə(r)] **1** n fractura f
2 vt fracturar

fragile ['frædʒaɪl] adj frágil

fragment ['frægmənt] n fragmento m

fragrance ['freɪgrəns] n fragancia f, perfume m

fragrant ['freɪgrənt] adj fragante, aromático(a)

frail [freɪl] adj frágil, delicado(a)

frame [freɪm] **1** n (a) (of window, door, picture) marco m; (of machine) armazón m; (of bicycle) cuadro m; (of spectacles) montura f; Fig f. **of mind** estado m de ánimo (b) Cin TV fotograma m
2 vt (a) (picture) enmarcar (b) (question) formular (c) Fam (innocent person) incriminar

framework ['freɪmwɜːk] n Fig within the f. of ... dentro del marco de ...

franc [fræŋk] n franco m

France [frɑːns] n Francia f

franchise ['fræntʃaɪz] n (a) Pol derecho m al voto (b) Com concesión f, licencia f

frank [fræŋk] **1** adj franco(a)
2 vt (mail) franquear

frankly ['fræŋklɪ] adv francamente

frankness ['fræŋknɪs] n franqueza f

frantic ['fræntɪk] adj (anxious) desesperado(a); (hectic) frenético(a)

fraternal [frə'tɜːnəl] adj fraterno(a)

fraternity [frə'tɜːnɪtɪ] n (society) asociación f; Rel cofradía f; US Univ club m de estudiantes

fraud [frɔːd] n (a) fraude m (b) (person) impostor(a) m,f

fraught [frɔːt] adj (a) (full) cargado(a) (with de) (b) (tense) nervioso(a)

fray¹ [freɪ] vi (a) (cloth) deshilacharse (b)

(nerves) crisparse; **his temper frequentl**
frayed se irritaba a menudo

fray² [freɪ] n combate m

freak [friːk] **1** n (a) (monster) monstruo m (b
Fam (eccentric) estrafalario(a) m,f (c) Fan
(fan) fanático(a) m,f
2 adj (a) (unexpected) inesperado(a) (b
(unusual) insólito(a)

freckle ['frekəl] n peca f

free [friː] **1** adj (a) libre; **to set sb f.** poner e
libertad a algn; **f. kick** tiro m libre; **f. speec**
libertad f de expresión; **f. will** libre albedrí
m; **f. trade** libre cambio m; **f. time** tiempo r
libre (b) **f. (of charge)** (gratis) gratuito(a);
gift obsequio m (c) (generous) generoso(a)
2 adv (a) **(for)** f. gratis (b) (loose) suelto(a̅
3 vt (a) (liberate) poner en libertad (b) (le
loose, work loose) soltar (c) (untie) desata
(d) (exempt) eximir (**from** de)

freedom ['friːdəm] n (a) (liberty) libertad f;
of the press libertad de prensa (b) (exemp
tion) exención f

free-for-all ['friːfərɔːl] n pelea f

freehold ['friːhəʊld] adj en propiedad abso
luta

freelance ['friːlɑːns] adj independiente

freely ['friːlɪ] adv (a) libremente (b) (openly̅
abiertamente

freemason ['friːmeɪsən] n francmasón m

free-range ['friːreɪndʒ] adj Br de granja

free-style ['friːstaɪl] n estilo m libre

freeway ['friːweɪ] n US autopista f

freewheel [friː'wiːl] vi ir en punto muerto

freeze [friːz] **1** vt (pt froze; pp frozen) conge
lar
2 n Met helada f; **price f.** congelación f d
precios; TV Cin f. **frame** imagen congelada
3 vi (liquid) helarse; (food) congelarse

freeze-dried ['friːzdraɪd] adj liofilizado(a)

freezer ['friːzə(r)] n congelador m

freezing ['friːzɪŋ] adj (a) glacial (b) f. poir
punto m de congelación; **above/below**
point sobre/bajo cero

freight [freɪt] n (a) (transport) transporte
(b) (goods, price) flete m; US f. **car** vagón n
US f. **elevator** montacargas m inv; f. **trai**
tren m de mercancías

French [frentʃ] **1** adj francés(esa); **F. bea**
judía f verde, Bol, RP chaucha f, CAm ejot
m, Col, Cuba habichuela f, Chile poroto n
verde, Ven vainita f; **F. dressing** vinagreta
US **F. fries** patatas fpl or Am papas fpl fritas;
window puerta f vidriera
2 n (a) (language) francés m (b) pl **the F.** lc
franceses

Frenchman ['frentʃmən] n francés m

Frenchwoman ['frentʃwʊmən] n francesa /

frenetic [frɪ'netɪk] adj frenético(a)

frenzy ['frenzɪ] n frenesí m

frequency ['friːkwənsɪ] n frecuencia f

frequent 1 adj ['friːkwənt] frecuente
2 vt [frɪ'kwent] frecuentar

frequently ['fri:kwəntlɪ] *adv* frecuentemente, a menudo

fresh [freʃ] *adj* (**a**) fresco(a); **f. water** agua *f* dulce; **f. bread** pan del día (**b**) *(new)* nuevo(a); **open a f. packet** abre otro paquete (**c**) *(air)* puro(a); **in the f. air** al aire libre (**d**) *US Fam (cheeky)* fresco(a)

freshen ['freʃən] *vi (wind)* refrescar
▸ **freshen up** *vi* asearse

fresher ['freʃə(r)] *n Univ* estudiante *mf* de primer año, novato(a) *m,f*

freshly ['freʃlɪ] *adv* recién, recientemente

freshman ['freʃmən] *n US* = **fresher**

freshness ['freʃnɪs] *n* frescura *f*

freshwater ['freʃwɔ:tə(r)] *adj* de agua dulce

fret [fret] *vi* preocuparse (**about** por)

FRG [efɑ:'dʒi:] *n Hist (abbr* **Federal Republic of Germany)** RFA *f*

friar ['fraɪə(r)] *n* fraile *m*

friction ['frɪkʃən] *n* fricción *f*

Friday ['fraɪdɪ] *n* viernes *m*

fridge [frɪdʒ] *n* nevera *f*, frigorífico *m*, *Andes* frigider *m*, *RP* heladera *f*

friend [frend] *n* amigo(a) *m,f*; **a f. of mine** un(a) amigo(a) mío(a); **to make friends with sb** hacerse amigo(a) de algn; **to make friends again** hacer las paces

friendliness ['frendlɪnɪs] *n* amabilidad *f*, simpatía *f*

friendly ['frendlɪ] *adj* (**friendlier, friendliest**) *(person)* simpático(a); *(atmosphere)* acogedor(a); **f. advice** consejo de amigo; **f. nation** nación amiga

friendship ['frendʃɪp] *n* amistad *f*

frieze [fri:z] *n* friso *m*

frigate ['frɪgɪt] *n* fragata *f*

fright [fraɪt] *n* (**a**) *(fear)* miedo *m*; **to take f.** asustarse (**b**) *(shock)* susto *m*; **to get a f.** pegarse un susto

frighten ['fraɪtən] *vt* asustar
▸ **frighten away, frighten off** *vt sep* ahuyentar

frightened ['fraɪtənd] *adj* asustado(a); **to be f. of sb** tenerle miedo a algn

frightening ['fraɪtənɪŋ] *adj* espantoso(a)

frightful ['fraɪtfʊl] *adj* espantoso(a), horroroso(a)

frightfully ['fraɪtfʊlɪ] *adv* tremendamente, terriblemente

frigid ['frɪdʒɪd] *adj* frígido(a)

frill [frɪl] *n (on dress)* volante *m*; *Fig* **frills** *(decorations)* adornos *mpl*

fringe [frɪndʒ] *n* (**a**) *Br (of hair)* flequillo *m*, *Am* cerquillo *m* (**b**) *(edge)* borde *m*; *Fig* **on the f. of society** al margen de la sociedad; **f. theatre** teatro *m* experimental; **f. benefits** extras *mpl*

Frisbee® ['frɪzbɪ] *n* platillo *m*

frisk [frɪsk] *vt Fam (search)* registrar

frisky ['frɪskɪ] *adj* (**friskier, friskiest**) (**a**) *(children, animals)* juguetón(ona) (**b**) *(adult)* vivo(a)

fritter ['frɪtə(r)] *n* buñuelo *m*
▸ **fritter away** *vt sep* malgastar

frivolous ['frɪvələs] *adj* frívolo(a)

frizzy ['frɪzɪ] *adj* (**frizzier, frizziest**) crespo(a)

frock [frɒk] *n* vestido *m*; **f. coat** levita *f*

frog [frɒg] *n* rana *f*; **frogs' legs** ancas *fpl* de rana; *Fig* **to have a f. in one's throat** tener carraspera

frogman ['frɒgmən] *n* hombre *m* rana

frolic ['frɒlɪk] *vi* retozar, juguetear

from [frɒm, *unstressed* frəm] *prep* (**a**) *(time)* desde, a partir de; **f. now on** a partir de ahora; **f. Monday to Friday** de lunes a viernes; **f. the 8th to the 17th** desde el 8 hasta el 17; **f. time to time** de vez en cuando

(**b**) *(price, number)* desde, de; **dresses f. £5** vestidos desde 5 libras; **a number f. one to ten** un número del uno a diez

(**c**) *(origin)* de; **a letter f. her father** una carta de su padre; **f. English into Spanish** del inglés al español; **he's f. Malaga** es de Málaga; **the train f. Bilbao** el tren procedente de Bilbao; **to go f. door to door** ir de puerta en puerta; **her eyes were red f. crying** tenía los ojos rojos de llorar

(**d**) *(distance)* de; **the town is 4 miles f. the coast** el pueblo está a 4 millas de la costa

(**e**) *(out of)* de; **bread is made f. flour** el pan se hace con harina

(**f**) *(remove, subtract)* a; **he took the book f. the child** le quitó el libro al niño; **take three f. five** restar tres a cinco

(**g**) *(according to)* según, por; **f. what the author said** según lo que dijo el autor; **speaking f. my own experience** hablando por experiencia propia

(**h**) *(position)* desde, de; **f. here** desde aquí

(**i**) **can you tell margarine f. butter?** ¿puedes distinguir entre la margarina y la mantequilla?

front [frʌnt] **1** *n* (**a**) parte delantera; **in f. (of)** delante (de) (**b**) *(of building)* fachada *f* (**c**) *Mil, Pol Met* frente *m* (**d**) *(seaside)* paseo marítimo (**e**) *Fig* **she put on a brave f.** hizo de tripas corazón

2 *adj* delantero(a), de delante; *Pol* **f. bench** = primera fila de escaños donde se sientan los ministros del Gobierno o de la Oposición; **f. door** puerta *f* principal; **f. room** salón *m*; **f. seat** asiento *m* de delante

frontier ['frʌntɪə(r)] *n* frontera *f*

front-page ['frʌntpeɪdʒ] *adj* de primera página

frost [frɒst] **1** *n* (**a**) *(covering)* escarcha *f* (**b**) *(freezing)* helada *f*
2 *vt US Culin* recubrir con azúcar glas
▸ **frost over** *vi* escarchar

frostbite ['frɒstbaɪt] *n* congelación *f*

frosted ['frɒstɪd] *adj* (**a**) *(glass)* esmerilado(a) (**b**) *US Culin* recubierto(a) de azúcar glas

frosty ['frɒstɪ] *adj* (**frostier, frostiest**) (**a**) it will be a f. night tonight esta noche habrá helada (**b**) *Fig* glacial

froth [frɒθ] **1** *n* espuma *f*; *(from mouth)* espumarajos *mpl*
2 *vi* espumar

frothy ['frɒθɪ] *adj* (**frothier, frothiest**) espumoso(a)

frown [fraʊn] *vi* fruncir el ceño
▸ **frown upon** *vt insep* desaprobar

froze [frəʊz] *pt of* **freeze**

frozen ['frəʊzən] **1** *adj (liquid, feet etc)* helado(a); *(food)* congelado(a)
2 *pp of* **freeze**

frugal ['fruːgəl] *adj* frugal

fruit [fruːt] *n* (**a**) *Bot* fruto *m* (**b**) *(apple, orange etc)* fruta *f*; **f. cake** pastel *m* con fruto seco; **f. machine** máquina *f* tragaperras; **f. salad** macedonia *f* de frutas (**c**) **fruits** *(rewards)* frutos *mpl*

fruitful ['fruːtfʊl] *adj Fig* provechoso(a)

fruition [fruː'ɪʃən] *n Fml* **to come to f.** realizarse

frustrate [frʌ'streɪt] *vt* frustrar

frustrated [frʌ'streɪtɪd] *adj* frustrado(a)

frustration [frʌ'streɪʃən] *n* frustración *f*

fry¹ [fraɪ] **1** *vt (pt & pp fried)* freír
2 *vi Fig* asarse

fry² [fraɪ] *npl* **small f.** gente *f* de poca monta

frying pan ['fraɪŋpæn], *US* **fry-pan** ['fraɪpæn] *n* sartén *f*

ft *(abbr foot)* pie *m*; *(abbr feet)* pies *mpl*

fuck [fʌk] *vt & vi Vulg* joder; **f. (it)!** ¡joder!
▸ **fuck off** *vi Vulg* **f. off!** ¡vete a la mierda!
▸ **fuck up** *vt sep Vulg* joder

fucking ['fʌkɪŋ] *Vulg* **1** *adj* **f. idiot!** ¡gilipollas!; **where are my f. keys?** ¿dónde coño están las llaves?
2 *adv* **a f. good film** una película de puta madre

fuddy-duddy ['fʌdɪdʌdɪ] *n Fam* **an old f.** un carcamal *or Am* carcamán

fudge [fʌdʒ] **1** *n Culin* = dulce hecho con azúcar, leche y mantequilla
2 *vt (figures)* amañar

fuel ['fjʊəl] **1** *n* combustible *m*; *(for engines)* carburante *m*; **f. tank** depósito *m* de combustible
2 *vt Fig (ambition)* estimular; *(difficult situation)* empeorar

fugitive ['fjuːdʒɪtɪv] *n Fml* fugitivo(a) *m,f*

fulfil, *US* **fulfill** [fʊl'fɪl] *vt* (**a**) *(task, ambition) (promise)* realizar; *(promise)* cumplir; *(role)* desempeñar (**b**) *(wishes)* satisfacer

fulfilment, *US* **fulfillment** [fʊl'fɪlmənt] *n* (**a**) *(of ambition)* realización *f* (**b**) *(of duty, promise)* cumplimiento *m*

full [fʊl] **1** *adj* (**a**) lleno(a); **f. of** lleno(a) de; **I'm f. (up)** no puedo más (**b**) *(complete)* completo(a); **at f. speed** a toda velocidad; **f. text** texto íntegro; *Fam* **in f. swing** en plena marcha; **f. board** pensión completa; **f.**

employment pleno empleo; **f. house** lleno total; **f. moon** luna llena; **f. stop** punto *m*
2 *n* **in f.** en su totalidad; **name in f.** nombre y apellidos completos
3 *adv* **f. well** perfectamente

full-blown ['fʊlbləʊn] *adj* auténtico(a)

full-fledged ['fʊlfledʒd] *adj US* = **fully-fledged**

fullness ['fʊlnɪs] *n* **in the f. of time** con el tiempo

full-scale ['fʊlskeɪl] *adj* (**a**) *(model)* de tamaño natural (**b**) **f. search** registro *m* a fondo; **f. war** guerra generalizada *or* total

full-time ['fʊl'taɪm] **1** *adj* de jornada completa
2 *adv* **to work f.** trabajar a tiempo completo

fully ['fʊlɪ] *adv* completamente

fully-fledged ['fʊlɪfledʒd] *adj* hecho(a) y derecho(a)

fulsome ['fʊlsəm] *adj* excesivo(a), exagerado(a)

fumble ['fʌmbəl] *vi* hurgar; **to f. for sth** buscar algo a tientas; **to f. with sth** manejar algo con torpeza

fume [fjuːm] **1** *n (usu pl)* humo *m*
2 *vi* despedir humo

⚠ Note that the Spanish verb **fumar** is a false friend and is never a translation for the English verb **to fume**. In Spanish, **fumar** means "to smoke".

---

fun [fʌn] **1** *n (amusement)* diversión *f*; **in** *or* **for f.** en broma; **to have f.** divertirse, pasarlo bien; **to make f. of sb** reírse de algn
2 *adj* divertido(a)

function ['fʌŋkʃən] **1** *n* (**a**) función *f* (**b**) *(ceremony)* acto *m*; *(party)* recepción *f*
2 *vi* funcionar

functional ['fʌŋkʃənəl] *adj* funcional

fund [fʌnd] **1** *n* (**a**) *Com* fondo *m* (**b**) **funds** fondos *mpl*
2 *vt (finance)* financiar

⚠ Note that the Spanish verb **fundar** is a false friend and is never a translation for the English verb **to fund**. In Spanish, **fundar** means "to found".

---

fundamental [fʌndə'mentəl] **1** *adj* fundamental
2 *npl* **fundamentals** los fundamentos

funeral ['fjuːnərəl] *n* funeral *m*; *US* **f. home** funeraria *f*; **f. march** marcha *f* fúnebre; *Br* **f. parlour** funeraria *f*; **f. service** misa *f* de cuerpo presente

funfair ['fʌnfeə(r)] *n Br* parque *m* de atracciones

fungus ['fʌŋgəs] *n (pl fungi* ['fʌŋgaɪ]*)* (**a**) *Bot* hongo *m* (**b**) *Med* fungo *m*

funnel ['fʌnəl] **1** *n* (**a**) *(for liquids)* embudo *m* (**b**) *Naut* chimenea *f*
2 *vt Fig (funds, energy)* encauzar

funnily ['fʌnɪlɪ] *adv Fam* f. enough aunque parezca extraño

funny ['fʌnɪ] *adj* (**funnier, funniest**) (**a**) *(peculiar)* raro(a), extraño(a); **that's f.!** ¡qué raro! (**b**) *(amusing)* divertido(a), gracioso(a); **I found it very f.** me hizo mucha gracia (**c**) *Fam (ill)* mal (**d**) *Fam (dishonest)* dudoso(a)

fur [fɜː(r)] **1** *n* (**a**) *(of living animal)* pelo *m* (**b**) *(of dead animal)* piel *f* (**c**) *(in kettle, on tongue)* sarro *m*
  2 *adj* de piel; **f. coat** abrigo *m* de pieles

furious ['fjʊərɪəs] *adj* (**a**) *(angry)* furioso(a) (**b**) *(vigorous)* violento(a)

furlong ['fɜːlɒŋ] *n (measurement)* = aprox 201 m

furnace ['fɜːnɪs] *n* horno *m*

furnish ['fɜːnɪʃ] *vt* (**a**) *(house)* amueblar (**b**) *Fml (food)* suministrar; *(details)* facilitar

furnishings ['fɜːnɪʃɪŋz] *npl* (**a**) muebles *mpl* (**b**) *(fittings)* accesorios *mpl*

furniture ['fɜːnɪtʃə(r)] *n* muebles *mpl*; **a piece of f.** un mueble

furrow ['fʌrəʊ] *n Agr* surco *m*; *(on forehead)* arruga *f*

furry ['fɜːrɪ] *adj* (**furrier, furriest**) (**a**) *(hairy)* peludo(a) (**b**) *(tongue, kettle)* sarroso(a)

further ['fɜːðə(r)] **1** *adj (comp of* **far**) (**a**) *(new)* nuevo(a); **until f. notice** hasta nuevo aviso (**b**) *(additional)* otro(a), adicional (**c**) *(later)* posterior; **f. education** estudios *mpl* superiores
  2 *adv* (**a**) *(more)* más; **f. back** más atrás; **f. along** más adelante; **she heard nothing f.** no volvió a saber nada más (**b**) *Fml* **f. to your**

letter of the **9th** con referencia a su carta del 9 del corriente (**c**) *Fml (besides)* además
  3 *vt* fomentar

furthermore [fɜːðə'mɔː(r)] *adv Fml* además

furthest ['fɜːðɪst] *adj (superl of* **far**) más lejano(a)

furtive ['fɜːtɪv] *adj* furtivo(a)

fury ['fjʊərɪ] *n* furia *f*, furor *m*

fuse [fjuːz] **1** *n* (**a**) *Elec* fusible *m*; **f. box** caja *f* de fusibles (**b**) *(of bomb)* mecha *f*
  2 *vi* (**a**) *Elec* **the lights fused** se fundieron los plomos (**b**) *Fig (merge)* fusionarse (**c**) *(melt)* fundirse
  3 *vt* (**a**) *Elec* fundir los plomos de (**b**) *Fig (merge)* fusionar (**c**) *(melt)* fundir

fuselage ['fjuːzɪlɑːʒ] *n* fuselaje *m*

fuss [fʌs] **1** *n (commotion)* jaleo *m*; **to kick up a f.** armar un escándalo; **stop making a f.** *(complaining)* deja ya de quejarte; **to make a f. of** *(pay attention to)* mimar a
  2 *vi* preocuparse (**about** por)

fussy ['fʌsɪ] *adj* (**fussier, fussiest**) exigente; *(nitpicking)* quisquilloso(a)

futile ['fjuːtaɪl] *adj* inútil, vano(a)

futility [fjuː'tɪlɪtɪ] *n* inutilidad *f*

future ['fjuːtʃə(r)] **1** *n* futuro *m*, porvenir *m*; **in the near f.** en un futuro próximo; **in f.** de aquí en adelante
  2 *adj* futuro(a)

futuristic [fjuːtʃə'rɪstɪk] *adj* futurista

fuze [fjuːz] *n*, *vi* & *vt US* = **fuse**

fuzzy ['fʌzɪ] *adj* (**fuzzier, fuzziest**) (**a**) *(hair)* muy rizado(a) (**b**) *(blurred)* borroso(a)

G, g [dʒiː] *n* (**a**) *(the letter)* G, g f (**b**) *Mus* **G** sol *m*

G [dʒiː] *adj US Cin* ≃ (apta) para todos los públicos

g *(abbr* **gramme***)* g

gabble ['gæbəl] **1** *n* chapurreo *m*
2 *vi* hablar atropelladamente

gable ['geɪbəl] *n* aguilón *m*

gadget ['gædʒɪt] *n* artilugio *m*, aparato *m*

Gaelic ['geɪlɪk] **1** *adj* gaélico(a)
2 *n (language)* gaélico *m*

gaffe [gæf] *n* metedura f de pata, desliz *m*; **to make a g.** meter la pata, patinar

> Note that the Spanish word **gafe** is a false friend and is never a translation for the English word **gaffe**. In Spanish, **gafe** means "jinxed person".

gag [gæg] **1** *n* (**a**) mordaza f (**b**) *Fam (joke)* chiste *m*
2 *vt* amordazar

gage [geɪdʒ] *n & vt US =* **gauge**

gaiety ['geɪətɪ] *n* regocijo *m*

gaily ['geɪlɪ] *adv* alegremente

gain [geɪn] **1** *n* ganancia f, beneficio *m*; *(increase)* aumento *m*
2 *vt* ganar; *Fig* **to g. ground** ganar terreno; **to g. speed** ganar velocidad, acelerar; **to g. weight** aumentar de peso

gait [geɪt] *n* (manera f de) andar *m*

gal *(pl* **gal** *or* **gals***) (abbr* **gallon***)* galón *m*

gala ['gɑːlə, 'geɪlə] *n* gala f, fiesta f

galaxy ['gæləksɪ] *n* galaxia f

gale [geɪl] *n* vendaval *m*

Galicia [gə'lɪʃə] *n* Galicia f

Galician [gə'lɪʃɪən, gə'lɪʃən] **1** *adj* gallego(a)
2 *n* (**a**) *(person)* gallego(a) *m,f* (**b**) *(language)* gallego *m*

gall [gɔːl] **1** *n Fam* descaro *m*
2 *vt* molestar, irritar

gallant ['gælənt] *adj (brave)* valiente; *(also* [gə'lænt]) *(chivalrous)* galante

gallantry ['gæləntrɪ] *n (bravery)* gallardía f; *(politeness)* galantería f

galleon ['gælɪən] *n* galeón *m*

gallery ['gælərɪ] *n* (**a**) galería f (**b**) *Th* gallinero *m* (**c**) *(court)* tribuna f

galley ['gælɪ] *n* (**a**) *(ship)* galera f; **g. slave** galeote *m* (**b**) *(kitchen)* cocina f

Gallicism ['gælɪsɪzəm] *n* galicismo *m*

gallivant ['gælɪvænt] *vi Fam* callejear

gallon ['gælən] *n* galón *m (Br = 4,55 l;*

US = 3,79 l)

gallop ['gæləp] **1** *n* galope *m*
2 *vi* galopar

gallows ['gæləʊz] *n sing* horca f, patíbulo *m*

gallstone ['gɔːlstəʊn] *n* cálculo *m* biliar

galore [gə'lɔː(r)] *adv Fam* en cantidad, en abundancia

galvanize ['gælvənaɪz] *vt (metal)* galvanizar; *Fig* **to g. sb into action** galvanizar a algn

galvanized ['gælvənaɪzd] *adj* galvanizado(a)

gambit ['gæmbɪt] *n (in chess)* gambito *m*; *Fig* táctica f

gamble ['gæmbəl] **1** *n (risk)* riesgo *m*; *(risky undertaking)* empresa arriesgada; *(bet)* apuesta f
2 *vi (bet)* jugar; *(take a risk)* arriesgarse

gambler ['gæmblə(r)] *n* jugador(a) *m,f*

gambling ['gæmblɪŋ] *n* juego *m*

gambol ['gæmbəl] *vi* brincar

game [geɪm] **1** *n* (**a**) juego *m*; **g. of chance** juego de azar (**b**) *(match)* partido *m*; *(of bridge)* partida f (**c**) **games** *Sport* juegos *mpl*; *Br Educ* educación física (**d**) *(hunting)* caza f; *Fig* presa f; **g. reserve** coto *m* de caza
2 *adj* **g. for anything** dispuesto(a) a todo

gamekeeper ['geɪmkiːpə(r)] *n* guardabosque *mf*

gamely ['geɪmlɪ] *adv* resueltamente

gammon ['gæmən] *n Br* jamón ahumado *or* curado

gamut ['gæmət] *n* gama f; **to run the g. of ...** experimentar todas las posibilidades de ...

gang [gæŋ] *n (of criminals)* banda f; *(of youths)* pandilla f; *(of workers)* cuadrilla f
▸ **gang up** *vi Fam* confabularse **(on** contra)

gangplank ['gæŋplæŋk] *n* plancha f

gangrene ['gæŋgriːn] *n* gangrena f

gangster ['gæŋstə(r)] *n* gángster *m*

gangway ['gæŋweɪ] *n Naut* pasarela f; *Th* pasillo *m*

gantry ['gæntrɪ] *n* puente *m* transversal

gaol [dʒeɪl] *n & vt Br =* **jail**

gap [gæp] *n* (**a**) abertura f, hueco *m*; *(blank space)* blanco *m*; *(in traffic)* claro *m*; **to bridge a g.** rellenar un hueco (**b**) *(in time)* intervalo *m*; *(emptiness)* vacío *m* (**c**) *(gulf)* diferencia f (**d**) *(deficiency)* laguna f

gape [geɪp] *vi (person)* quedarse boquiabierto(a), mirar boquiabierto(a); *(thing)* estar abierto(a)

gaping ['geɪpɪŋ] *adj Fig* profundo(a)

garage ['gæraːʒ, 'gærɪdʒ] *n* garaje *m*; *(for repairs)* taller mecánico; *(filling station)* gasolinera *f*, estación *f* de servicio, *Andes, Ven* bomba *f*, *Méx* gasolinera *f*, *Perú* grifo *m*

garbage ['gɑːbɪdʒ] *n US* basura *f*; **g. can** cubo *m* de la basura; **g. dump** vertedero *m*; **g. man** basurero *m*; **g. truck** camión *m* de la basura

garbled ['gɑːbəld] *adj* embrollado(a); **g. account** relato confuso

garden ['gɑːdən] *n* jardín *m*; **g. centre** centro *m* de jardinería; **g. party** recepción *f* al aire libre

gardener ['gɑːdənə(r)] *n* jardinero(a) *m,f*

gardenia [gɑː'diːnɪə] *n* gardenia *f*

gardening ['gɑːdənɪŋ] *n* jardinería *f*; **his mother does the g.** su madre es la que cuida el jardín

gargle ['gɑːgəl] *vi* hacer gárgaras

gargoyle ['gɑːgɔɪl] *n* gárgola *f*

garish ['geərɪʃ] *adj* chillón(ona)

garland ['gɑːlənd] *n* guirnalda *f*

garlic ['gɑːlɪk] *n* ajo *m*

garment ['gɑːmənt] *n* prenda *f*

garnish ['gɑːnɪʃ] *vt* guarnecer

garrison ['gærɪsən] *n* guarnición *f*

garrulous ['gærʊləs] *adj* locuaz

garter ['gɑːtə(r)] *n* liga *f*

gas [gæs] **1** *n* (**a**) gas *m*; **g. chamber** cámara *f* de gas; **g. cooker** cocina *f* de gas; **g. fire** estufa *f* de gas; **g. mask** careta *f* antigás; **g. ring** hornillo *m* de gas (**b**) *US* gasolina *f*, *RP* nafta *f*; **g. pump** surtidor *m* de gasolina; **g. station** gasolinera *f*, estación *f* de servicio, *Andes, Ven* bomba *f*, *Méx* gasolinería *f*, *Perú* grifo *m*; **g. tank** depósito *m* de la gasolina

2 *vt (asphyxiate)* asfixiar con gas

3 *vi Fam (talk)* charlotear

gash [gæʃ] **1** *n* herida profunda

2 *vt* hacer un corte en; **he gashed his forehead** se hizo una herida en la frente

gasket ['gæskɪt] *n* junta *f*

gasoline ['gæsəliːn] *n US* gasolina *f*

gasp [gɑːsp] **1** *n (cry)* grito sordo; *(breath)* bocanada *f*; *Fig* **to be at one's last g.** estar en las últimas

2 *vi (in surprise)* quedar boquiabierto(a); *(breathe)* jadear

gassy ['gæsɪ] *adj* (**gassier, gassiest**) gaseoso(a)

gastric ['gæstrɪk] *adj* gástrico(a)

gastronomic [gæstrə'nɒmɪk] *adj* gastronómico(a)

gate [geɪt] *n* (**a**) puerta *f* (**b**) *(at football ground)* entrada *f*; **g. (money)** taquilla *f* (**c**) *(attendance)* entrada *f*

gateau ['gætəʊ] *n (pl* **gateaux** ['gætəʊz]*)* pastel *m* con nata

gatecrash ['geɪtkræʃ] **1** *vt* colarse en

2 *vi* colarse

gateway ['geɪtweɪ] *n* puerta *f*; *Fig* pasaporte *m*

gather ['gæðə(r)] **1** *vt* (**a**) *(collect)* juntar; *(pick)* coger; *(pick up)* recoger (**b**) *(bring together)* reunir (**c**) *(harvest)* cosechar (**d**) **to g. speed** ir ganando velocidad; **to g. strength** cobrar fuerzas (**e**) *(understand)* suponer; **I g. that ...** tengo entendido que ... (**f**) *Sewing* fruncir

2 *vi* (**a**) *(come together)* reunirse (**b**) *(form)* formarse

▸ **gather round** *vi* agruparse

gathering ['gæðərɪŋ] **1** *adj* creciente

2 *n* reunión *f*

gauche [gəʊʃ] *adj (clumsy)* torpe; *(tactless)* sin tacto

gaudy ['gɔːdɪ] *adj* (**gaudier, gaudiest**) chillón(ona)

gauge [geɪdʒ] **1** *n* (**a**) medida *f* estándar; *(of gun, wire)* calibre *m* (**b**) *Rail* ancho *m* de vía (**c**) *(calibrator)* indicador *m* (**d**) *Fig (indication)* indicación *f*

2 *vt* (**a**) *(measure)* medir, calibrar (**b**) *Fig (judge)* juzgar

gaunt [gɔːnt] *adj (lean)* demacrado(a); *(desolate)* lúgubre

gauntlet ['gɔːntlɪt] *n* guantelete *m*; *Fig* **to run the g. of ...** estar sometido(a) a ...; *Fig* **to throw down the g.** arrojar el guante

gauze [gɔːz] *n* gasa *f*

gave [geɪv] *pt of* give

gawky ['gɔːkɪ] *adj* (**gawkier, gawkiest**) desgarbado(a)

gay [geɪ] *adj* (**a**) *(homosexual)* gay (**b**) *(happy)* alegre

gaze [geɪz] **1** *n* mirada fija

2 *vi* mirar fijamente

gazelle [gə'zel] *n* gacela *f*

gazette [gə'zet] *n* gaceta *f*; *US* periódico *m*

gazump [gə'zʌmp] *vi Br Fam* = romper un compromiso de venta para vender a un precio más alto

GB [dʒiː'biː] *(abbr* **Great Britain***)* GB

GCE [dʒiːsiː'iː] *n Br Formerly (abbr* **General Certificate of Education (A-Level)***)* = certificado de enseñanza secundaria

GCSE [dʒiːsiːes'iː] *n Br (abbr* **General Certificate of Secondary Education***)* = certificado de enseñanza secundaria

GDP [dʒiːdiː'piː] *n (abbr* **gross domestic product***)* PIB *m*

GDR [dʒiːdiː'ɑː(r)] *n Hist (abbr* **German Democratic Republic***)* RDA *f*

gear [gɪə(r)] **1** *n* (**a**) *(equipment)* equipo *m* (**b**) *Fam (belongings)* bártulos *mpl* (**c**) *Fam (clothing)* ropa *f* (**d**) *Tech* engranaje *m* (**e**) *Aut* velocidad *f*, marcha *f*; **first g.** primera *f* *(velocidad f)*; **g. lever** *or US* **shift** palanca *f* de cambio

2 *vt* ajustar, adaptar

gearbox ['gɪəbɒks] *n* caja *f* de cambios

gearstick ['gɪəstɪk], *US* **gearshift** ['gɪəʃɪft] *n* palanca *f* de cambio

gee [dʒiː] *interj US* ¡caramba!

geese [giːs] *pl of* **goose**

gel [dʒel] **1** *n* gel *m; (for hair)* gomina *f*

2 *vi Fig (ideas etc)* cuajar

3 *vt (hair)* engominar

gelatin ['dʒelətɪn] *n* gelatina *f*

gelignite ['dʒelɪgnaɪt] *n* gelignita *f*

gem [dʒem] *n* piedra preciosa; *Fig (person)* joya *f*

Gemini ['dʒemɪnaɪ] *n* Géminis *m*

gen [dʒen] *n Fam* **to get the g. on sth** informarse sobre algo

gender ['dʒendə(r)] *n* género *m*

gene [dʒiːn] *n* gene *m*, gen *m*

general ['dʒenərəl] **1** *adj* general; **g. knowledge** conocimientos *mpl* generales; **in g.** en general; **the g. public** el público; **g. practitioner** médico *m* de cabecera

2 *n Mil* general *m; US* **g. of the army** mariscal *m* de campo

generalization [dʒenərəlaɪˈzeɪʃən] *n* generalización *f*

generalize ['dʒenərəlaɪz] *vt & vi* generalizar

generally ['dʒenərəlɪ] *adv* generalmente, en general

generate ['dʒenəreɪt] *vt* generar

generation [dʒenəˈreɪʃən] *n* generación *f;* **g. gap** abismo *m* or conflicto *m* generacional

generator ['dʒenəreɪtə(r)] *n* generador *m*

generosity [dʒenəˈrɒsɪtɪ] *n* generosidad *f*

generous ['dʒenərəs] *adj* generoso(a); *(plentiful)* copioso(a)

genetic [dʒɪˈnetɪk] *adj* genético(a); **g. engineering** ingeniería genética

genetically [dʒɪˈnetɪklɪ] *adv* **g. modified** *(plant, food)* modificado(a) genéticamente

genetics [dʒɪˈnetɪks] *n sing* genética *f*

Geneva [dʒɪˈniːvə] *n* Ginebra *f*

genial ['dʒiːnɪəl, 'dʒiːnjəl] *adj* cordial, amable

> 🖉 Note that the Spanish word **genial** is a false friend and is never a translation for the English word **genial**. In Spanish, **genial** means both "brilliant" and "terrific".

genie ['dʒiːnɪ] *n* duende *m*, genio *m*

genitals ['dʒenɪtəlz] *npl* órganos *mpl* genitales

genius ['dʒiːnjəs, 'dʒiːnɪəs] *n* (**a**) *(person)* genio *m* (**b**) *(gift)* don *m*

genre ['ʒɒːnrə] *n* género *m*

gent [dʒent] *n Fam (abbr* **gentleman**) señor *m*, caballero *m;* **the gents** los servicios (de caballeros)

genteel [dʒenˈtiːl] *adj* fino(a), distinguido(a)

> 🖉 Note that the Spanish word **gentil** is a false friend and is never a translation for the English word **genteel**. In Spanish, **gentil** means "kind" and "pagan".

gentle ['dʒentəl] *adj* dulce, tierno(a); *(breeze)* suave

gentleman ['dʒentəlmən] *n* caballero *m;* **g.'s agreement** pacto *m* de caballeros

gently ['dʒentlɪ] *adv* con cuidado

gentry ['dʒentrɪ] *n* pequeña nobleza, alta burguesía

genuine ['dʒenjʊɪn] *adj* auténtico(a), genuino(a); *(sincere)* sincero(a)

genuinely ['dʒenjʊɪnlɪ] *adv* auténticamente

geographic(al) [dʒɪəˈgræfɪk(əl)] *adj* geográfico(a)

geography [dʒɪˈɒgrəfɪ, 'dʒɒgrəfɪ] *n* geografía *f*

geologic(al) [dʒɪəˈlɒdʒɪk(əl)] *adj* geológico(a)

geology [dʒɪˈɒlədʒɪ] *n* geología *f*

geometric(al) [dʒɪəˈmetrɪk(əl)] *adj* geométrico(a)

geometry [dʒɪˈɒmɪtrɪ] *n* geometría *f*

geopolitical [dʒiːəʊpəˈlɪtɪkəl] *adj* geopolítico(a)

geranium [dʒɪˈreɪnɪəm] *n* geranio *m*

geriatric [dʒerɪˈætrɪk] *adj* geriátrico(a)

germ [dʒɜːm] *n* (**a**) *Biol & Fig* germen *m* (**b**) *Med* microbio *m*

German ['dʒɜːmən] **1** *adj* alemán(ana); **G. measles** rubeola *f*

2 *n* (**a**) *(person)* alemán(ana) *m,f* (**b**) *(language)* alemán *m*

Germany ['dʒɜːmənɪ] *n* Alemania

germinate ['dʒɜːmɪneɪt] *vi* germinar

gestation [dʒeˈsteɪʃən] *n* gestación *f*

gesticulate [dʒeˈstɪkjʊleɪt] *vi* gesticular

gesture ['dʒestʃə(r)] **1** *n* gesto *m*, ademán *m;* **it's an empty g.** es pura formalidad

2 *vi* gesticular, hacer gestos

get [get] **1** *vt (pt & pp* **got**; *pp US also* **gotten**) (**a**) *(obtain)* obtener, conseguir; **to g. one's own way** salirse con la suya

(**b**) *(earn)* ganar

(**c**) *(fetch) (something)* traer; *(somebody)* ir a por; **g. the police!** ¡llama a la policía!; *Tel* **g. me Mr Brown** póngame con el Sr. Brown

(**d**) *(receive)* recibir; *Fam* **he got the sack** le despidieron

(**e**) *(bus, train, thief etc)* coger; *Am* agarrar

(**f**) *(prepare)* preparar; **can I g. you something to eat?** ¿quieres comer algo?

(**g**) *(ask)* pedir; **g. him to call me** dile que me llame

(**h**) **to g. sb to agree to sth** conseguir que algn acepte algo

(**i**) **when did you g. the house painted?** ¿cuándo os pintaron la casa?; **to g. one's hair cut** cortarse el pelo

(**j**) **they got him in the chest** le dieron en el pecho

(**k**) **have got, have got to** *see* **have**

(**l**) *Fam (understand)* entender

(**m**) *(record) (in writing)* apuntar; *(on tape)* grabar

2 *vi* (**a**) *(become)* ponerse; **to g. dark** anochecer; **to g. dressed** vestirse; **to g. drunk**

emborracharse; **to g. late** hacerse tarde; **to g. married** casarse; **to g. used to doing sth** acostumbrarse a hacer algo; **to g. paid** cobrar

(**b**) *Fig* **we are not getting anywhere** así no vamos a ninguna parte

(**c**) *(arrive)* llegar

(**d**) **to g. to** *(come to)* llegar a; **to g. to know sb** llegar a conocer a algn

▸ **get about** *vi (person)* salir; *(news)* difundirse
▸ **get across** *vt sep (idea etc)* hacer comprender
▸ **get ahead** *vi* progresar
▸ **get along** *vi* (**a**) *(leave)* marcharse (**b**) *(manage)* arreglárselas (**c**) *(two people)* llevarse bien
▸ **get around** *vi (person)* salir; *(travel)* viajar; *(news)* difundirse
▸ **get at** *vt insep* (**a**) *(reach)* alcanzar (**b**) *(ascertain)* descubrir (**c**) *(insinuate)* insinuar; **what are you getting at?** ¿a dónde quieres llegar? (**d**) *(criticize)* criticar
▸ **get away** *vi* escaparse
▸ **get away with** *vt insep* salir impune de
▸ **get back 1** *vi* (**a**) *(return)* regresar, volver (**b**) **g. back!** *(move backwards)* ¡atrás!
   2 *vt sep (recover)* recuperar; *Fam* **to g. one's own back on sb** vengarse de algn
▸ **get by** *vi* (**a**) *(manage)* arreglárselas; **she can g. by in French** sabe defenderse en francés (**b**) *(pass)* pasar
▸ **get down 1** *vt sep (depress)* deprimir
   2 *vi (descend)* bajar
▸ **get down to** *vt insep* ponerse a; **to g. down to the facts** ir al grano
▸ **get in 1** *vi* (**a**) *(arrive)* llegar (**b**) *Pol* ser elegido(a)
   2 *vt sep* (**a**) *(buy)* comprar (**b**) *(collect)* recoger; *Fam* **he couldn't g. a word in edgeways** no pudo decir ni pío
▸ **get into** *vt insep Fig* **to g. into bad habits** adquirir malas costumbres; **to g. into trouble** meterse en un lío
▸ **get off 1** *vt insep (bus etc)* bajarse de
   2 *vt sep (remove)* quitarse
   3 *vi* (**a**) bajarse; *Fam* **g. off!** ¡fuera! (**b**) **to g. off to a good start** *(begin)* empezar bien (**c**) *(escape)* escaparse; **to g. off lightly** salir bien librado(a)
▸ **get off with** *vt insep Fam* ligar
▸ **get on 1** *vt insep (board)* subir a
   2 *vi* (**a**) *(board)* subirse (**b**) *(make progress)* hacer progresos; **how are you getting on?** ¿cómo te van las cosas? (**c**) **to g. on (well) (with sb)** llevarse bien (con algn) (**d**) *(continue)* seguir; **to g. on with one's work** seguir trabajando (**e**) **it's getting on for eleven** son casi las once; **time's getting on** se está haciendo tarde
▸ **get on to** *vt insep* (**a**) *(find a person)* localizar; *(find out)* descubrir (**b**) *(continue)* pasar a
▸ **get out 1** *vt sep (object)* sacar
   2 *vi* (**a**) *(room etc)* salir (**of** de); *(train)* bajar

(**of** de) (**b**) *(escape)* escaparse (**of** de); **to g. out of an obligation** librarse de un compromiso (**c**) *(news)* difundirse; *(secret)* hacerse público
▸ **get over 1** *vt insep* (**a**) *(illness)* recuperarse de; **I can't g. over him** no le puedo olvidar (**b**) *(difficulty)* vencer
   2 *vt sep (convey)* hacer comprender
▸ **get round** *vt insep* (**a**) *(problem)* salvar; *(difficulty)* vencer (**b**) *(rule)* soslayar (**c**) *(win over)* persuadir
▸ **get round to** *vt insep* **if I g. round to it** si tengo tiempo
▸ **get through 1** *vi* (**a**) *(message)* llegar (**b**) *Educ* aprobar (**c**) *Tel* **to g. through to sb** conseguir comunicar con algn
   2 *vt insep* (**a**) **to g. through a lot of work** trabajar mucho (**b**) *(consume)* consumir (**c**) *Educ* aprobar
▸ **get together 1** *vi (people)* juntarse, reunirse
   2 *vt sep (people)* juntar, reunir
▸ **get up 1** *vi (rise)* levantarse
   2 *vt sep* (**a**) *(wake)* despertar (**b**) *(disguise)* **to g. oneself up as ...** disfrazarse de ...
▸ **get up to** *vt insep* hacer; **to g. up to mischief** hacer de las suyas

getaway [ˈgetəweɪ] *n* fuga *f*; **to make one's g.** fugarse

get-together [ˈgettəgeðə(r)] *n* reunión *f*

geyser [ˈgiːzə(r), *US* ˈgaɪzər] *n* (**a**) *Geog* géiser *m* (**b**) *(water heater)* calentador *m* de agua

ghastly [ˈgɑːstlɪ] *adj* (**ghastlier, ghastliest**) horrible, espantoso(a)

gherkin [ˈgɜːkɪn] *n* pepinillo *m*

ghetto [ˈgetəʊ] *n* gueto *m*

ghost [gəʊst] *n* fantasma *m*; **g. story** cuento *m* de fantasmas; **g. town** pueblo *m* fantasma

ghost-writer [ˈgəʊstraɪtə(r)] *n* negro(a) *m,f*

ghoulish [ˈguːlɪʃ] *adj* macabro(a)

giant [ˈdʒaɪənt] *adj & n* gigante (*m*)

gibberish [ˈdʒɪbərɪʃ] *n* galimatías *m inv*

gibe [dʒaɪb] **1** *n* mofa *f*
   2 *vi* mofarse (**at** de)

giblets [ˈdʒɪblɪts] *npl* menudillos *mpl*

Gibraltar [dʒɪˈbrɔːltə(r)] *n* Gibraltar

Gibraltarian [dʒɪbrɔːlˈteərɪən] *adj & n* gibraltareño(a) *(m,f)*

giddiness [ˈgɪdɪnɪs] *n* mareo *m*; *(vertigo)* vértigo *m*

giddy [ˈgɪdɪ] *adj* (**giddier, giddiest**) mareado(a); **it makes me g.** me da vértigo; **to feel g.** sentirse mareado(a)

gift [gɪft] *n* (**a**) regalo *m*; *Com* obsequio *m*; **g. token** vale *m* (**b**) *(talent)* don *m*; **to have a g. for music** estar muy dotado(a) para la música

gifted [ˈgɪftɪd] *adj* dotado(a)

gig [gɪg] *n Fam Mus* actuación *f*

gigantic [dʒaɪˈgæntɪk] *adj* gigantesco(a)

giggle [ˈgɪgəl] **1** *n* (**a**) risita *f* (**b**) *(lark)* broma *f*, diversión *f*
   2 *vi* reírse tontamente

gild [gɪld] *vt* dorar

gill¹ [dʒɪl] *n (liquid measure)* = 0,142 l

gill² [gɪl] *n (of fish)* branquia *f*, agalla *f*

gilt [gɪlt] **1** *adj* dorado(a)

  2 *n (colour)* dorado *m*

gilt-edged ['gɪltedʒd] *adj* **g. securities** valores *mpl* de máxima garantía

gimmick ['gɪmɪk] *n* truco *m*; *(in advertising)* reclamo *m*

gin [dʒɪn] *n* ginebra *f*; **g. and tonic** gin tonic *m*

ginger ['dʒɪndʒə(r)] **1** *n* jengibre *m*; **g. ale** ginger ale *m*

  2 *adj* **(a)** de jengibre **(b)** *(hair)* pelirrojo(a)

gingerbread ['dʒɪndʒəbred] *n* pan *m* de jengibre

gingerly ['dʒɪndʒəlɪ] *adv* cautelosamente

gipsy ['dʒɪpsɪ] *adj & n* gitano(a) *(m,f)*

giraffe [dʒɪ'rɑːf] *n* jirafa *f*

girder ['gɜːdə(r)] *n* viga *f*

girdle ['gɜːdəl] *n* faja *f*

girl [gɜːl] *n* **(a)** chica *f*, joven *f*; *(child)* niña *f*; **g. guide**, *US* **g. scout** exploradora *f* **(b)** *(daughter)* hija *f* **(c)** *(sweetheart)* novia *f*

girlfriend ['gɜːlfrend] *n* **(a)** *(lover)* novia *f* **(b)** *(female friend)* amiga *f*

girlhood ['gɜːlhʊd] *n* niñez *f*

girlish ['gɜːlɪʃ] *adj* **(a)** de niña **(b)** *(effeminate)* afeminado(a)

giro ['dʒaɪrəʊ] *n Br* giro *m* (postal); **g. (cheque)** cheque *m* de giros postales

gist [dʒɪst] *n* esencia *f*; **did you get the g. of what he was saying?** ¿cogiste la idea de lo que decía?

give [gɪv] **1** *n (elasticity)* elasticidad *f*

  2 *vt (pt* **gave**; *pp* **given) (a)** dar; **to g. sth to sb** dar algo a algn; **to g. a start** pegar un salto; **to g. sb a present** regalar algo a algn

  (b) *(provide)* suministrar; **to g. sb sth to eat** dar de comer a algn

  (c) *(pay)* pagar

  (d) *(concert)* dar; *(speech)* pronunciar

  (e) *(dedicate)* dedicar

  (f) *(grant)* otorgar; **to g. sb one's attention** prestar atención a algn

  (g) to g. sb to understand that ... dar a entender a algn que ...

  (h) *(yield)* ceder; **to g. way** *Aut* ceder el paso; *Fig* ceder; *(of legs)* flaquear

  3 *vi* **(a) to g. as good as one gets** devolver golpe por golpe

  (b) *(yield)* ceder; *(fabric)* dar de sí

 ▸ **give away** *vt sep* **(a)** repartir; *(present)* regalar **(b)** *(disclose)* revelar; **to g. the game away** descubrir el pastel **(c)** *(betray)* traicionar

 ▸ **give back** *vt sep* devolver

 ▸ **give in 1** *vi* **(a)** *(admit defeat)* darse por vencido(a); *(surrender)* rendirse **(b) to g. in to** ceder ante

  2 *vt sep (hand in)* entregar

 ▸ **give off** *vt sep (smell etc)* despedir

 ▸ **give out** *vt sep* distribuir, repartir

 ▸ **give over 1** *vt sep (hand over)* entregar; *(devote)* dedicar

  2 *vi Fam* **g. over!** ¡basta ya!

 ▸ **give up 1** *vt sep* **(a)** *(idea)* abandonar; **to g. up smoking** dejar de fumar **(b)** *(betray)* traicionar **(c)** *(hand over)* entregar; **to g. oneself up** entregarse

  2 *vi (admit defeat)* darse por vencido(a), rendirse

 ▸ **give up on** *vt insep* darse por vencido con

given ['gɪvən] **1** *adj* **(a)** *(particular)* dado(a); **at a g. time** en un momento dado **(b) g. to** dado(a) a

  2 *conj* **(a)** *(considering)* dado(a) **(b)** *(if)* si

  3 *pp of* **give**

glacial ['gleɪsɪəl] *adj* **(a)** *Geol* glaciar **(b)** *(icy)* glacial; *Fig* **g. look** mirada *f* glacial

glacier ['glæsɪə(r)] *n* glaciar *m*

glad [glæd] *adj* **(gladder, gladdest)** contento(a); *(happy)* alegre; **he'll be only too g. to help you** tendrá mucho gusto en ayudarle; **to be g.** alegrarse

gladiator ['glædɪeɪtə(r)] *n Hist* gladiador *m*

gladly ['glædlɪ] *adv* con mucho gusto

glamor ['glæmər] *n US* = **glamour**

glamorous ['glæmərəs] *adj* atractivo(a), encantador(a)

glamour ['glæmə(r)] *n* atractivo *m*; *(charm)* encanto *m*; **a g. girl** una belleza

glance [glɑːns] **1** *n* mirada *f*, vistazo *m*; **at a g.** de un vistazo; **at first g.** a primera vista

  2 *vi* echar un vistazo **(at a)**

 ▸ **glance off** *vt insep (of ball etc)* rebotar de

glancing ['glɑːnsɪŋ] *adj (blow)* oblicuo(a)

gland [glænd] *n* glándula *f*

glandular ['glændjʊlə(r)] *adj* glandular; **g. fever** mononucleosis infecciosa

glare [gleə(r)] **1** *n (light)* luz *f* deslumbrante; *(dazzle)* deslumbramiento *m*; *(look)* mirada *f* feroz

  2 *vi (dazzle)* deslumbrar; *(look)* lanzar una mirada furiosa **(at a)**

glaring ['gleərɪŋ] *adj (light)* deslumbrante; *(colour)* chillón(ona); *(obvious)* evidente

glass [glɑːs] *n* **(a)** *(material)* vidrio *m*; **pane of g.** cristal *m* **(b)** *(drinking vessel)* vaso *m*; **wine g.** copa *f* (para vino) **(c) glasses** gafas *fpl*, *Am* lentes *mpl*, anteojos *mpl*; **to wear glasses** llevar gafas *or Am* lentes *or* anteojos

glasshouse ['glɑːshaʊs] *n* invernadero *m*

glassware ['glɑːsweə(r)] *n* cristalería *f*

glassy ['glɑːsɪ] *adj* **(glassier, glassiest)** *(water)* cristalino(a); *(eyes)* vidrioso(a)

glaze [gleɪz] **1** *n (varnish)* barniz *m*; *(for pottery)* vidriado *m*

  2 *vt (windows)* acristalar; **(b)** *(varnish)* barnizar; *(ceramics)* vidriar **(c)** *Culin* glasear

glazed [gleɪzd] *adj (eyes)* de mirada ausente

glazier ['gleɪzɪə(r)] *n* vidriero(a) *m,f*

gleam [gliːm] **1** *n* **(a)** destello *m* **(b)** *Fig (glimmer)* rayo *m*

  2 *vi* brillar, relucir

gleaming ['gliːmɪŋ] *adj* brillante, reluciente

glean [gliːn] *vt Fig* recoger, cosechar

glee [gliː] *n* gozo *m*

gleeful ['gliːfʊl] *adj* gozoso(a)

glen [glen] *n* cañada *f*

glib [glɪb] *adj* (**glibber, glibbest**) *Pej* de mucha labia

glide [glaɪd] *vi* (**a**) *(slip, slide)* deslizarse (**b**) *Av* planear

glider ['glaɪdə(r)] *n* planeador *m*

gliding ['glaɪdɪŋ] *n* vuelo *m* sin motor

glimmer ['glɪmə(r)] *n* (**a**) *(light)* luz *f* tenue (**b**) *Fig (trace)* destello *m*

glimpse [glɪmps] **1** *n* atisbo *m*
   2 *vt* atisbar

glint [glɪnt] **1** *n* destello *m*, centelleo *m*; **he had a g. in his eye** le brillaban los ojos
   2 *vi* destellar, centellear

glisten ['glɪsən] *vi* relucir, brillar

glitter ['glɪtə(r)] **1** *n* brillo *m*
   2 *vi* relucir

gloat [gləʊt] *vi* jactarse; **to g. over another's misfortune** recrearse con la desgracia de otro

global ['gləʊbəl] *adj* (**a**) *(of the world)* mundial (**b**) *(overall)* global

globe [gləʊb] *n* globo *m*, esfera *f*

gloom [gluːm] *n* (*obscurity*) penumbra *f*; (*melancholy*) melancolía *f*; (*despair*) desolación *f*

gloomy ['gluːmɪ] *adj* (**gloomier, gloomiest**) *(dark)* oscuro(a); *(weather)* gris; *(dismal)* deprimente; *(despairing)* pesimista; *(sad)* triste

glorify ['glɔːrɪfaɪ] *vt* glorificar

glorious ['glɔːrɪəs] *adj* *(momentous)* glorioso(a); *(splendid)* magnífico(a), espléndido(a)

glory ['glɔːrɪ] *n* gloria *f*, *Fig (splendour)* esplendor *m*; *Fig (triumph)* triunfo *m*

gloss [glɒs] **1** *n* (**a**) *(explanation)* glosa *f* (**b**) *(sheen)* brillo *m*; **g. (paint)** pintura *f* brillante
   2 *vi* glosar
   ▸ **gloss over** *vt insep Fig* encubrir

glossary ['glɒsərɪ] *n* glosario *m*

glossy ['glɒsɪ] *adj* (**glossier, glossiest**) lustroso(a); **g. magazine** revista *f* de lujo

glove [glʌv] *n* guante *m*; *Aut* **g. compartment** guantera *f*

glow [gləʊ] **1** *n* brillo *m*; *(of fire)* incandescencia *f*, *(of sun)* arrebol *m*; *(heat)* calor *m*; *(light)* luz *f*; *(in cheeks)* rubor *m*
   2 *vi* brillar; *(fire)* arder; *Fig* rebosar de

glower ['glaʊə(r)] *vi* poner cara de enfadado(a)

glowing ['gləʊɪŋ] *adj* (**a**) *(fire)* incandescente; *(colour)* vivo(a); *(light)* brillante (**b**) *(cheeks)* encendido(a) (**c**) *Fig (report)* entusiasta

glucose ['gluːkəʊz] *n* glucosa *f*

glue [gluː] **1** *n* pegamento *m*, cola *f*
   2 *vt* pegar (**to** a)

glum [glʌm] *adj* (**glummer, glummest**) alicaído(a)

glut [glʌt] *n* superabundancia *f*, exceso *m*

glutton ['glʌtən] *n* glotón(ona) *m,f*, *Fam Fig* **you're a g. for punishment** eres masoquista

GM [dʒiːˈem] *adj* (*abbr* **genetically modified**) transgénico(a), modificado(a) genéticamente; **GM food** (alimentos) transgénicos

GMO [dʒiːˈemˈəʊ] *n* (*abbr* **genetically modified organism**) OMG *m*

GMT [dʒiːˈemˈtiː] *n* (*abbr* **Greenwich Mean Time**) hora *f* del meridiano de Greenwich

gnarled [nɑːld] *adj* nudoso(a)

gnash [næʃ] *vt* rechinar

gnat [næt] *n* mosquito *m*

gnaw [nɔː] *vt & vi* *(chew)* roer

gnome [nəʊm] *n* gnomo *m*

GNP [dʒiːenˈpiː] *n* (*abbr* **gross national product**) PNB *m*

go [gəʊ] **1** *vi* (*3rd person sing pres* **goes**; *pt* **went**; *pp* **gone**) (**a**) ir; **to go by car/on foot** ir en coche/a pie; **to go for a walk** (ir a) dar un paseo; **to go on a journey** ir de viaje; **to go shopping** ir de compras; *Fig* **to go too far** pasarse (de la raya)
   (**b**) *(depart)* irse, marcharse; *(bus)* salir
   (**c**) *(disappear)* desaparecer
   (**d**) *(function)* funcionar; *Fig* **to get things going** poner las cosas en marcha
   (**e**) *(sell)* venderse; **shoes going cheap** zapatos a precios de rebaja
   (**f**) *(become)* quedarse, volverse; **to go blind** quedarse ciego(a); **to go mad** volverse loco(a)
   (**g**) *(progress)* ir, marchar; **everything went well** todo salió bien; **how's it going?** ¿qué tal (te van las cosas)?
   (**h**) **to be going to** *(in the future)* ir a; *(on the point of)* estar a punto de
   (**i**) *(fit)* caber
   (**j**) *(be kept)* guardarse
   (**k**) *(be available)* quedar; **I'll take whatever's going** me conformo con lo que hay
   (**l**) *(be acceptable)* valer; **anything goes** todo vale
   (**m**) *(break)* romperse; *(yield)* ceder
   (**n**) **how does that song go?** ¿cómo es aquella canción?
   (**o**) *(time)* pasar; **there are only two weeks to go** sólo quedan dos semanas
   (**p**) *(be inherited)* pasar (**to** a)
   (**q**) *(say)* decir; **as the saying goes** según el dicho
   (**r**) **to let sth go** soltar algo
   2 *vt* (**a**) *(travel)* hacer, recorrer
   (**b**) **to go it alone** apañárselas solo
   3 *n* (**a**) *(energy)* energía *f*, dinamismo *m*
   (**b**) *(try)* intento *m*; **to have a go at sth** probar suerte con algo
   (**c**) *(turn)* turno *m*; **it's your go** te toca a ti
   (**d**) **to make a go of sth** tener éxito en algo
   (**e**) **I knew from the word go** lo sabía desde el principio
   (**f**) **to have a go at sb** criticar a algn

▸ **go about 1** *vt insep* (**a**) *(task)* emprender; **how do you go about it?** ¿cómo hay que hacerlo? (**b**) **to go about one's business** ocuparse de sus asuntos

2 *vi (rumour)* correr

▸ **go after** *vt insep (pursue)* andar tras

▸ **go against** *vt insep (oppose)* ir en contra de; *(verdict)* ser desfavorable a

▸ **go ahead** *vi* (**a**) *(proceed)* proceder (**b**) **we'll go on ahead** iremos delante

▸ **go along 1** *vt insep (street)* pasar por

2 *vi (progress)* progresar

▸ **go along with** *vt insep* (**a**) *(agree with)* estar de acuerdo con (**b**) *(accompany)* acompañar

▸ **go around** *vi* (**a**) *(rumour)* correr (**b**) **there's enough to go around** hay para todos

▸ **go away** *vi* marcharse

▸ **go back** *vi* (**a**) *(return)* volver, regresar (**b**) *Fig* **to go back to** *(date from)* datar de

▸ **go back on** *vt insep* **to go back on one's word** faltar a su palabra

▸ **go back to** *vt insep* volver a

▸ **go by** *vi* pasar; **as time goes by** con el tiempo

▸ **go down** *vi* (**a**) *(descend)* bajar; *(sun)* ponerse; *(ship)* hundirse (**b**) *(diminish)* disminuir; *(temperature)* bajar (**c**) *(be received)* ser acogido(a)

▸ **go down with** *vt insep (contract)* coger

▸ **go for** *vt insep* (**a**) *(attack)* lanzarse sobre; *Fam Fig* **go for it!** ¡a por ello! (**b**) *(fetch)* ir por (**c**) *Fam (like)* gustar

▸ **go in** *vi* entrar

▸ **go in for** *vt insep (exam)* presentarse a; *(hobby)* dedicarse a

▸ **go into** *vt insep* (**a**) *(enter)* entrar en; **to go into journalism** dedicarse al periodismo (**b**) *(study)* examinar; *(matter)* investigar (**c**) *(energy, money)* invertir en

▸ **go off 1** *vi* (**a**) *(leave)* irse, marcharse (**b**) *(bomb)* explotar; *(gun)* dispararse; *(alarm)* sonar (**c**) *(food)* pasarse (**d**) *(event)* resultar

2 *vt insep Fam* **to go off sth** perder el gusto *or* el interés por algo

▸ **go on** *vi* (**a**) *(continue)* seguir, continuar; **to go on talking** seguir hablando; *Fam* **to go on and on about sth** no parar de hablar sobre algo; *(complain)* quejarse constantemente de algo (**b**) *(happen)* pasar, ocurrir (**c**) *(time)* transcurrir, pasar (**d**) *(light)* encenderse

▸ **go out** *vi* (**a**) *(leave)* salir; **to go out for a meal** comer *or* cenar fuera (**b**) *(boy and girl)* salir juntos (**c**) *(fire, light)* apagarse (**d**) *(tide)* bajar (**e**) *TV Rad* transmitirse (**f**) **to go (all) out** ir a por todas (**g**) *(in competition)* perder la eliminatoria

▸ **go over** *vt insep (revise)* repasar

▸ **go over to** *vt insep* (**a**) acercarse; **to go over to the enemy** pasarse al enemigo (**b**) *(switch to)* pasar a

▸ **go round** *vi* (**a**) *(revolve)* dar vueltas (**b**) **to go round to sb's house** pasar por casa de algn

▸ **go through 1** *vi (bill)* ser aprobado(a)

2 *vt insep* (**a**) *(examine)* examinar; *(search)* registrar (**b**) *(rehearse)* ensayar (**c**) *(spend)* gastar (**d**) *(list etc)* explicar (**e**) *(endure)* sufrir

▸ **go through with** *vt insep* llevar a cabo

▸ **go under** *vi* (**a**) *(ship)* hundirse (**b**) *(business)* fracasar

▸ **go up** *vi* (**a**) *(price etc)* subir (**b**) **to go up to sb** acercarse a algn (**c**) *(in a lift)* subir (**d**) **to go up in flames** quemarse (**e**) *Sport (be promoted)* subir

▸ **go with** *vt insep* (**a**) *(accompany)* ir con (**b**) *(colours)* hacer juego con

▸ **go without 1** *vt insep* (**a**) pasarse sin, prescindir de (**b**) *Fam* **that goes without saying** eso es evidente

2 *vi (not have)* aguantarse sin nada

goad [gəʊd] *vt* aguijonear

go-ahead ['gəʊəhed] *n Fam* **to give sb the g.** dar luz verde a algn

goal [gəʊl] *n* (**a**) *Sport* gol *m*; **g. kick** saque *m* de puerta; **g. post** poste *m*; **g. scorer** goleador(a) *m,f* (**b**) *(aim, objective)* meta *f*, objetivo *m*

goalkeeper ['gəʊlkiːpə(r)] *n* portero(a) *m,f*

goat [gəʊt] *n (female)* cabra *f*; *(male)* macho cabrío

gob [gɒb] *n Br Fam* boca *f*

gobble ['gɒbəl] *vt* engullir

go-between ['gəʊbɪtwiːn] *n* intermediario(a) *m,f*

goblet ['gɒblɪt] *n* copa *f*

god [gɒd] *n* dios *m*; **for G.'s sake!** ¡por Dios!; **G. Dios; (my) G.!** ¡Dios mío!; **G. forbid!** ¡Dios no lo quiera!; **G. only knows** sabe Dios

godchild ['gɒdtʃaɪld] *n* ahijado(a) *m,f*

goddam(n) ['gɒdæm] *US Fam* **1** *adj* maldito(a), dichoso(a), *Méx* pinche

2 *adv* **that was g. stupid!** ¡eso fue una auténtica estupidez!

goddaughter ['gɒdɔːtə(r)] *n* ahijada *f*

goddess ['gɒdɪs] *n* diosa *f*

godfather ['gɒdfɑːðə(r)] *n* padrino *m*

godforsaken ['gɒdfəseɪkən] *adj (place)* remoto(a)

godmother ['gɒdmʌðə(r)] *n* madrina *f*

godparents ['gɒdpeərənts] *npl* padrinos *mpl*

godsend ['gɒdsend] *n* regalo inesperado

godson ['gɒdsʌn] *n* ahijado *m*

goggles ['gɒgəlz] *npl* gafas *fpl* protectoras, *CSur* antiparras *fpl*

going ['gəʊɪŋ] **1** *adj* (**a**) *(price)* corriente; **the g. rate** el precio medio (**b**) **a g. concern** un negocio que marcha bien (**c**) **to get** *or* **be g.** marcharse (**d**) **to keep g.** resistir

2 *n* (**a**) **that was good g.!** ¡qué rápido! (**b**) *Fig* **to get out while the g. is good** retirarse antes que sea demasiado tarde

goings-on [gəʊɪŋz'ɒn] *npl Fam* tejemanejes *mpl*

go-kart ['gəʊkɑːt] *n Sport* kart *m*

gold [gəʊld] **1** *n* oro *m*; **g. leaf** pan *m* de oro; **g.**

medal medalla *f* de oro; **g. mine** mina *f* de oro
  2 *adj* de oro; *(colour)* dorado(a)
golden ['gəʊldən] *adj* de oro; *(colour)* dora-
do(a); *Fig* **a g. opportunity** una excelente
oportunidad; *Orn* **g. eagle** águila *f* real; *Fig*
g. handshake indemnización *f* por despido;
g. wedding bodas *fpl* de oro
goldfish ['gəʊldfɪʃ] *n* pez *m* de colores
gold-plated [gəʊld'pleɪtɪd] *adj* chapado(a)
en oro
goldsmith ['gəʊldsmɪθ] *n* orfebre *m*
golf [gɒlf] *n* golf *m*; **g. ball** pelota *f* de golf; **g.
club** *(stick)* palo *m* de golf; *(place)* club *m* de
golf; **g. course** campo *m* de golf
golfer ['gɒlfə(r)] *n* golfista *mf*
golly ['gɒlɪ] *interj* ¡vaya!
gone [gɒn] **1** *adj* desaparecido(a)
  2 *pp of* **go**
gong [gɒŋ] *n* gong *m*
good [gʊd] **1** *adj* (**better, best**) (**a**) *(before
noun)* buen(a); *(after noun)* bueno(a); **a g.
book** un buen libro; **g. afternoon/evening**
buenas tardes; **g. morning** buenos días; **g.
night** buenas noches; **it looks g.** tiene buena
pinta; **to be as g. as new** estar como nue-
vo(a); **to feel g.** sentirse bien; **to have a g.
time** pasarlo bien; **to smell g.** oler bien; **G.
Friday** Viernes *m* Santo
  (**b**) *(kind)* amable; *(generous)* generoso(a)
  (**c**) *(healthy)* sano(a)
  (**d**) *(morally correct)* correcto(a); **be g.!** ¡pórtate bien!
  (**e**) **he's g. at languages** tiene facilidad para
los idiomas
  (**f**) *(attractive)* bonito(a); **red looks g. on you**
el rojo te favorece mucho; **g. looks** atractivo
m, belleza *f*
  (**g**) **it's as g. as an offer** equivale a una
oferta; **it's as g. a way as any** es una manera
como otra cualquiera
  (**h**) *(at least)* como mínimo
  (**i**) *(sufficient)* bastante
  (**j**) **to make g.** *(injustice)* reparar; *(loss)*
compensar; *(succeed in life)* triunfar
  (**k**) *(reliable)* de confianza
  (**l**) *(propitious)* propicio(a)
  (**m**) **she comes from a g. family** es de buena
familia
  (**n**) *(character)* agradable; **he's in a g. mood**
está de buen humor
  2 *n* (**a**) bien *m*; **g. and evil** el bien y el mal; **to
do g.** hacer el bien
  (**b**) *(advantage)* bien *m*, provecho *m*; **for
your own g.** para tu propio bien; **it's no g.
waiting** no sirve de nada esperar; **it will do
you g.** te hará bien
  (**c**) **goods** *(possessions)* bienes *mpl*
  (**d**) *Com* **goods** artículos *mpl*, géneros *mpl*;
goods train tren *m* de mercancías
  3 *adv* **she's gone for g.** se ha ido para
siempre
  4 *interj* ¡muy bien!

goodbye [gʊd'baɪ] **1** *interj* ¡adiós!
  2 *n* adiós *m*, despedida *f*; **to say g. to sb**
despedirse de algn
good-for-nothing ['gʊdfənʌθɪŋ] *adj & n*
inútil *(mf)*
good-hearted [gʊd'hɑːtɪd] *adj* de buen corazón
good-looking [gʊd'lʊkɪŋ] *adj* guapo(a)
good-natured [gʊd'neɪtʃəd] *adj* amable,
bondadoso(a)
goodness ['gʊdnɪs] *n* bondad *f*; **my g.!** ¡Dios
mío!; **thank g.!** ¡gracias a Dios!; **for g. sake!**
¡por Dios!
good-tempered [gʊd'tempəd] *adj* apacible
goodwill [gʊd'wɪl] *n* (**a**) buena voluntad *f*
(**b**) *Com (reputation)* buen nombre *m*
goof [guːf] *US Fam* **1** *n* metedura *f* or *Am*
metida *f* de pata
  2 *vi* meter la pata
goose [guːs] *n (pl* **geese**) ganso *m*, oca *f*
gooseberry ['gʊzbərɪ, 'guːsbərɪ] *n* uva espina, grosella espinosa; *Fam* **to play g.** hacer
de carabina
gooseflesh ['guːsfleʃ] *n*, **goosepimples**
['guːspɪmpəlz] *npl* carne *f* de gallina
goose-step ['guːsstep] *vi* ir a paso de la oca
gore¹ [gɔː(r)] *n* sangre derramada
gore² [gɔː(r)] *vt (of bull)* cornear, dar corna-
das a
gorge [gɔːdʒ] **1** *n* desfiladero *m*
  2 *vt & vi* **to g. (oneself) (on)** atiborrarse
(de)
gorgeous ['gɔːdʒəs] *adj* magnífico(a), estu-
pendo(a); *(person)* atractivo(a), guapo(a)
gorilla [gə'rɪlə] *n* gorila *m*
gorse [gɔːs] *n* aulaga *f*
gory ['gɔːrɪ] *adj* (**gorier, goriest**) sangrien-
to(a)
gosh [gɒʃ] *interj Fam* ¡cielos!, ¡caray!
go-slow [gəʊ'sləʊ] *n* huelga *f* de celo
gospel ['gɒspəl] *n* the **G.** el Evangelio; *Fam*
it's the g. truth es la pura verdad
gossip ['gɒsɪp] **1** *n* (**a**) *(rumour)* cotilleo *m*; **g.
column** ecos *mpl* de sociedad (**b**) *(person)*
chismoso(a) *m,f*, cotilla *mf*
  2 *vi (natter)* cotillear, chismorrear
got [gɒt] *pt & pp of* **get**
Gothic ['gɒθɪk] *adj* gótico(a)
gotten ['gɒtən] *US pp of* **get**
gourmet ['gʊəmeɪ] *n* gourmet *mf*
gout [gaʊt] *n* gota *f*
govern ['gʌvən] *vt* (**a**) gobernar (**b**) *(determine)* determinar
governess ['gʌvənɪs] *n* institutriz *f*
governing ['gʌvənɪŋ] *adj* gobernante; **g.
body** consejo *m* de administración
government ['gʌvənmənt] *n* gobierno *m*
governmental [gʌvən'mentəl] *adj* gubernamental
governor ['gʌvənə(r)] *n (ruler)* goberna-
dor(a) *m,f*; *(of prison)* director(a) *m,f*; *(of
school)* administrador(a) *m,f*

gown [gaʊn] *n (dress)* vestido largo; *Jur & Univ* toga *f*

GP [dʒiː'piː] *n (abbr* **general practitioner**) médico(a) *m,f* de familia *or* de cabecera

GPO [dʒiːpiː'əʊ] *n Br Formerly (abbr* **General Post Office**) ≃ (Administración *f* Central de) Correos *mpl*

grab [græb] **1** *n* agarrón *m*; *Fam* **to be up for grabs** estar disponible
2 *vt* (a) agarrar; **to g. hold of sb** agarrarse a algn (b) *Fig* **g. a bottle of wine** píllate una botella de vino (c) *Fig* **how does that g. you?** ¿qué te parece?

grace [greɪs] **1** *n* (a) gracia *f*; *Fig* **to fall from g.** caer en desgracia (b) **to say g.** bendecir la mesa (c) **to do sth with good g.** hacer algo de buena gana (d) **five days' g.** *(reprieve)* un plazo de cinco días (e) *(elegance)* elegancia *f* (f) **Your G.** (Su) Excelencia
2 *vt* (a) *(adorn)* adornar (b) *(honour)* honrar

graceful ['greɪsfʊl] *adj* elegante; *(movement)* garboso(a)

gracefully ['greɪsfʊlɪ] *adv* (a) *(beautifully)* con gracia, con elegancia (b) *(accept)* con cortesía

gracious ['greɪʃəs] **1** *adj* (a) *(elegant)* elegante (b) *(courteous)* cortés (c) *(kind)* amable
2 *interj* **good g. (me)!**, **goodness g.!** ¡santo cielo!

grade [greɪd] **1** *n* (a) *(quality)* grado *m*; *(rank)* categoría *f*; *Mil* rango *m* (b) *US Educ (mark)* nota *f* (c) *US Educ (class)* clase *f*; **g. school** escuela primaria (d) *(level)* nivel *m*; **to make the g.** llegar al nivel deseado (e) *US (slope)* pendiente *f* (f) *US* **g. crossing** paso *m* a nivel
2 *vt* clasificar

gradient ['greɪdɪənt] *n (graph)* declive *m*; *(hill)* cuesta *f*, pendiente *f*

gradual ['grædjʊəl] *adj* gradual, progresivo(a)

gradually ['grædjʊəlɪ] *adv* poco a poco

graduate 1 *n* ['grædjʊɪt] *Educ* titulado(a) *m,f*; *Univ* licenciado(a) *m,f*; *US* **g. school** escuela *f* para graduados
2 *vi* ['grædjʊeɪt] (a) *Educ* sacarse el título; *Univ* licenciarse (**in** en) (b) **to g. to** pasar a (c) *US (from high school)* ≃ sacar el bachillerato

graduation [grædjʊ'eɪʃən] *n* graduación *f*; *Univ* **g. ceremony** ceremonia *f* de entrega de los títulos

graffiti [grə'fiːtiː] *npl* grafiti *mpl*

graft [grɑːft] **1** *n* (a) *Med* injerto *m* (b) *Fam (work)* trabajo *m* (c) *US (bribery)* soborno *m*
2 *vt Med* injertar (**on to** en)
3 *vi Fam* trabajar duro

grain [greɪn] *n* (a) *(cereals)* cereales *mpl* (b) *(particle)* grano *m*; *Fig* **there's not a g. of truth in it** no tiene ni pizca de verdad (c) *(in wood)* fibra *f*; *(in stone)* veta *f*; *(in leather)* flor *f*; *Fig* **to go against the g.** ir a contrapelo

gram [græm] *n* gramo *m*

grammar ['græmə(r)] *n* gramática *f*; **g. (book)** libro *m* de gramática; *Br* **g. school** = instituto estatal de segunda enseñanza al que se ingresa por examen selectivo

grammatical [grə'mætɪkəl] *adj* gramatical

gramme [græm] *n* gramo *m*

gramophone ['græməfəʊn] *n* gramófono *m*

granary ['grænərɪ] *n* granero *m*

grand [grænd] **1** *adj* (a) *grande*; *(before singular noun)* gran; **g. piano** piano *m* de cola; **G. Prix** Gran Premio *m* (b) *(splendid)* grandioso(a), magnífico(a); *(impressive)* impresionante (c) **g. total** total *m* (d) *Fam (wonderful)* estupendo(a)
2 *n Fam* mil libras *fpl*; *US* mil dólares *mpl*

grandchild ['græntʃaɪld] *n* nieto(a) *m,f*

granddad ['grændæd] *n Fam* abuelo *m*

granddaughter ['grændɔːtə(r)] *n* nieta *f*

grandeur ['grændʒə(r)] *n* grandeza *f*, grandiosidad *f*

grandfather ['grænfɑːðə(r)] *n* abuelo *m*; **g. clock** reloj *m* de caja

grandiose ['grændɪəʊs] *adj* grandioso(a)

grandma ['grænmɑː] *n Fam* abuelita *f*

grandmother ['grænmʌðə(r)] *n* abuela *f*

grandpa ['grænpɑː] *n Fam* abuelito *m*

grandparents ['grænpeərənts] *npl* abuelos *mpl*

grandson ['grænsʌn] *n* nieto *m*

grandstand ['grænstænd] *n* tribuna *f*

granite ['grænɪt] *n* granito *m*

granny ['grænɪ] *n Fam* abuelita *f*

grant [grɑːnt] **1** *vt* (a) *(allow)* conceder, otorgar (b) *(admit)* admitir; **to take sb for granted** no apreciar a algn en lo que vale; **to take sth for granted** dar algo por sentado
2 *n Educ* beca *f*; *(subsidy)* subvención *f*

granulated ['grænjʊleɪtɪd] *adj* granulado(a)

granule ['grænjuːl] *n* gránulo *m*

grape [greɪp] *n* uva *f*; **g. juice** mosto *m*

grapefruit ['greɪpfruːt] *n* pomelo *m*

grapevine ['greɪpvaɪn] *n Bot* vid *f*; *(against wall)* parra *f*; *Fam* **I heard it on** or **through the g.** me enteré por ahí

graph [grɑːf, græf] *n* gráfica *f*

graphic ['græfɪk] *adj* gráfico(a); **g. arts** artes gráficas; **g. designer** grafista *mf*

graphics ['græfɪks] *n* (a) *(study)* grafismo *m* (b) *pl Comput* gráficas *fpl*

grapple ['græpəl] **1** *vi (struggle)* luchar cuerpo a cuerpo (**with** con); *Fig* **to g. with a problem** intentar resolver un problema
2 *n (hook)* garfio *m*

grasp [grɑːsp] **1** *vt* (a) agarrar (b) *(understand)* comprender
2 *n* (a) *(grip)* agarrón *m* (b) *(understanding)* comprensión *f*; **within sb's g.** al alcance de algn

grasping ['grɑːspɪŋ] *adj* avaro(a)

grass [grɑːs] **1** *n* (a) hierba *f*; *(lawn)* césped *m*; *(pasture)* pasto *m*; **keep off the g.** *(sign)* prohibido pisar el césped; **g. court** pista *f* de

hierba; **g. roots** base *f*; **g. snake** culebra *f* (**b**) *Fam (drug)* hierba *f* (**c**) *Br Fam (informer)* soplón(ona) *m,f*, chivato(a) *m,f*
2 *vi Br Fam* chivarse (**on** a)
▸ **grass over** *vi* cubrirse de hierba

grasshopper ['grɑːʃhɒpə(r)] *n* saltamontes *m inv*

grassland ['grɑːslænd] *n* pradera *f*

grass-roots ['grɑːsruːts] *adj* de base; **at g. level** a nivel popular

grassy ['grɑːsɪ] *adj* (**grassier, grassiest**) cubierto(a) de hierba

grate¹ [greɪt] **1** *vt Culin* rallar
2 *vi* chirriar

grate² [greɪt] *n* (**a**) *(in fireplace)* rejilla *f* (**b**) *(fireplace)* chimenea *f* (**c**) *Constr* rejilla *f*, reja *f*

grateful ['greɪtfʊl] *adj* agradecido(a); **to be g. for** agradecer

grater ['greɪtə(r)] *n Culin* rallador *m*

gratification [grætɪfɪ'keɪʃən] *n (pleasure)* placer *m*, satisfacción *f*

gratify ['grætɪfaɪ] *vt* (**a**) *(please)* complacer (**b**) *(yield to)* sucumbir a

gratifying ['grætɪfaɪɪŋ] *adj* grato(a)

grating¹ ['greɪtɪŋ] *n* rejilla *f*, reja *f*

grating² ['greɪtɪŋ] *adj* chirriante; *(tone)* áspero(a)

gratis ['greɪtɪs, 'grætɪs] *adv* gratis

gratitude ['grætɪtjuːd] *n* agradecimiento *m*

gratuitous [grə'tjuːɪtəs] *adj* gratuito(a)

gratuity [grə'tjuːɪt] *n* gratificación *f*

grave¹ [greɪv] *n* sepultura *f*, tumba *f*

grave² [greɪv] *adj (look etc)* serio(a); *(situation)* grave

gravel ['grævəl] *n* grava *f*, gravilla *f*

gravestone ['greɪvstəʊn] *n* lápida *f* sepulcral

graveyard ['greɪvjɑːd] *n* cementerio *m*

gravity ['grævɪtɪ] *n* gravedad *f*

gravy ['greɪvɪ] *n* salsa *f*, jugo *m* (de la carne)

gray [greɪ] *adj & n US* = **grey**

graze¹ [greɪz] *vi* pacer, pastar

graze² [greɪz] **1** *vt (scratch)* rasguñar; *(brush against)* rozar
2 *n* rasguño *m*

grease [griːs, griːz] **1** *n* grasa *f*
2 *vt* engrasar

greaseproof ['griːspruːf] *adj* **g. paper** papel graso

greasy ['griːsɪ, 'griːzɪ] *adj* (**greasier, greasiest**) (**a**) *(oily)* grasiento(a); *(hair, food)* graso(a) (**b**) *(slippery)* resbaladizo(a) (**c**) *Fam (ingratiating)* pelotillero(a)

great [greɪt] **1** *adj* (**a**) *(large)* grande; *(before singular noun)* gran; *(pain, heat)* fuerte; **a g. many** muchos(as); **G. Britain** Gran Bretaña; *Br* **G. Bear** Osa *f* Mayor (**b**) *Fam (excellent)* estupendo(a), magnífico(a); **to have a g. time** pasarlo en grande
2 *adv Fam* muy bien, estupendamente

great-aunt [greɪt'ɑːnt] *n* tía abuela

great-grandchild [greɪt'græntʃaɪld] *n* bisnieto(a) *m,f*

great-grandfather [greɪt'grænfɑːðə(r)] *n* bisabuelo *m*

great-grandmother [greɪt'grænmʌðə(r)] *n* bisabuela *f*

greatly ['greɪtlɪ] *adv* muy, mucho

greatness ['greɪtnɪs] *n* grandeza *f*

great-uncle [greɪt'ʌŋkəl] *n* tío abuelo

Greece [griːs] *n* Grecia

greed [griːd], **greediness** ['griːdɪnɪs] *n (for food)* gula *f*; *(for money)* codicia *f*, avaricia *f*

greedy ['griːdɪ] *adj* (**greedier, greediest**) *(for food)* glotón(ona); *(for money)* codicioso(a) (**for** de)

Greek [griːk] **1** *adj* griego(a)
2 *n* (**a**) *(person)* griego(a) *m,f* (**b**) *(language)* griego *m*

green [griːn] **1** *n* (**a**) *(colour)* verde *m* (**b**) *(in golf)* campo *m*; **village g.** plaza *f* (del pueblo) (**c**) **greens** verdura *f*, verduras *fpl*
2 *adj* (**a**) verde; **g. bean** judía *f* verde, *Bol, RP* chaucha *f*, *CAm* ejote *m*, *Col, Cuba* habichuela *f*, *Chile* poroto *m* verde, *Ven* vainita *f*; **g. belt** zona *f* verde; *US* **g. card** *(work permit)* permiso *m* de trabajo; **g. pepper** pimiento *m* verde; **she was g. with envy** se la comía la envidia (**b**) *(inexperienced)* verde, novato(a); *(gullible)* crédulo(a) (**c**) *Pol* **G. Party** Partido *m* Verde

greenery ['griːnərɪ] *n* follaje *m*

greenfly ['griːnflaɪ] *n* pulgón *m*

greengage ['griːngeɪdʒ] *n* ciruela claudia

greengrocer ['griːngrəʊsə(r)] *n Br* verdulero(a) *m,f*

greenhouse ['griːnhaʊs] *n* invernadero *m*; **g. effect** efecto invernadero

greenish ['griːnɪʃ] *adj* verdoso(a)

Greenland ['griːnlənd] *n* Groenlandia

greet [griːt] *vt (wave at)* saludar; *(receive)* recibir; *(welcome)* dar la bienvenida a

greeting ['griːtɪŋ] *n* (**a**) *(wave)* saludo *m*; **greetings card** tarjeta *f* de felicitación (**b**) *(reception)* recibimiento *m*; *(welcome)* bienvenida *f*

gregarious [grɪ'geərɪəs] *adj* gregario(a), sociable

Grenada [grə'neɪdə] *n* Granada

grenade [grɪ'neɪd] *n* granada *f*

grew [gruː] *pt of* **grow**

grey [greɪ] **1** *adj (colour)* gris; *(hair)* cano(a); *(sky)* nublado(a); **g. matter** materia *f* gris
2 *n* (**a**) *(colour)* gris *m* (**b**) *(horse)* caballo *m* tordo

grey-haired ['greɪheəd] *adj* canoso(a)

greyhound ['greɪhaʊnd] *n* galgo *m*

greyish ['greɪɪʃ] *adj* grisáceo(a)

grid [grɪd] *n* (**a**) *(on map)* cuadrícula *f* (**b**) *(of electricity etc)* red *f* nacional (**c**) = **gridiron**

gridiron ['grɪdaɪən] *n Culin* parrilla *f*

grief [griːf] *n* dolor *m*, pena *f*; *Fam* **to come to g.** *(car, driver)* sufrir un accidente; *(plans)* irse al traste

grievance ['griːvəns] *n (wrong)* agravio *m*; *(resentment)* queja *f*

grieve [griːv] **1** *vt* apenar, dar pena a
2 *vi* apenarse, afligirse; **to g. for sb** llorar la muerte de algn

grievous ['griːvəs] *adj* (*offence*) grave; **g. bodily harm** lesiones *fpl* corporales graves

grill [grɪl] **1** *vt* (**a**) *Culin* asar a la parrilla (**b**) *Fam* (*interrogate*) interrogar duramente
2 *n* parrilla *f*; (*dish*) parrillada *f*

grill(e) [grɪl] *n* (*grating*) reja *f*

grim [grɪm] *adj* (**grimmer, grimmest**) (**a**) (*sinister*) macabro(a); (*landscape*) lúgubre; (*smile*) sardónico(a) (**b**) (*manner*) severo(a); (*person*) ceñudo(a) (**c**) (*resolute*) inexorable (**d**) *Fam* (*unpleasant*) desagradable; **g. reality** la dura realidad

grimace [grɪ'meɪs] **1** *n* mueca *f*
2 *vi* hacer una mueca

grimy ['graɪmɪ] *adj* (**grimier, grimiest**) mugriento(a)

grin [grɪn] **1** *vi* sonreír abiertamente
2 *n* sonrisa abierta

grind [graɪnd] **1** *vt* (*pt & pp* **ground**) (*mill*) moler; (*crush*) triturar; (*sharpen*) afilar; *US* (*meat*) picar; **to g. one's teeth** hacer rechinar los dientes
2 *vi* (**a**) rechinar; *Fig* **to g. to a halt** (*vehicle*) pararse lentamente; (*production etc*) pararse poco a poco (**b**) *US Fam* empollar
3 *n* (**a**) *Fam* **the daily g.** la rutina cotidiana; **what a g.!** ¡qué rollo! (**b**) *US Fam* (*studious pupil*) empollón(ona) *m,f*
▸ **grind down** *vt sep Fig* **to g. down the opposition** acabar con la oposición

grip [grɪp] **1** *n* (**a**) (*hold*) agarrón *m*; (*handshake*) apretón *m*; (*of tyre*) adherencia *f*; **get a g. on yourself!** ¡tranquilízate!; **to get to grips with a problem** superar un problema (**b**) (*handle*) asidero *m* (**c**) (*travel bag*) maletín *m* (**d**) (*hairgrip*) pasador *m*
2 *vt* (**a**) agarrar, asir; (*hand*) apretar (**b**) *Fig* (*of film, story*) captar la atención de; **to be gripped by fear** ser presa del miedo

gripe [graɪp] **1** *vi Fam* (*complain*) quejarse
2 *n* (**a**) *Med* (*pain*) retortijón *m* (**b**) *Fam* (*complaint*) queja *f*

gripping ['grɪpɪŋ] *adj* (*film, story*) apasionante

grisly ['grɪzlɪ] *adj* (**grislier, grisliest**) espeluznante

gristle ['grɪsəl] *n* cartílago *m*, ternilla *f*

grit [grɪt] **1** *n* (**a**) (*gravel*) grava *f* (**b**) *Fam* (*courage*) valor *m*
2 *vt Fig* **to g. one's teeth** apretar los dientes

gritty ['grɪtɪ] *adj* (**grittier, grittiest**) valiente

grizzly ['grɪzlɪ] *adj* **g. bear** oso pardo

groan [grəʊn] **1** *n* (**a**) (*of pain*) gemido *m* (**b**) *Fam* (*of disapproval*) gruñido *m*
2 *vi* (**a**) (*in pain*) gemir (**b**) *Fam* (*complain*) quejarse **(about** de)

grocer ['grəʊsə(r)] *n* tendero(a) *m,f*; **g.'s (shop)** tienda *f* de comestibles, *CSur* almacén *m*, *Andes, CAm, Méx* tienda *f* de abarrotes

groceries ['grəʊsərɪz] *npl* comestibles *mpl*

grocery ['grəʊsərɪ] *n* (*shop*) tienda *f* de ultramarinos; *US* **g. store** supermercado *m*

groggy ['grɒgɪ] *adj* (**groggier, groggiest**) *Fam* (*boxer*) grogui; *Fig* (*unsteady*) atontado(a); (*weak*) débil

groin [grɔɪn] *n* ingle *f*

groom [gruːm] **1** *n* (**a**) *mozo m* de cuadra (**b**) (*bridegroom*) novio *m*
2 *vt* (*horse*) almohazar; (*clothes, appearance*) cuidar

groove [gruːv] *n* (*furrow etc*) ranura *f*; (*of record*) surco *m*

grope [grəʊp] *vi* (**a**) (*search about*) andar a tientas; **to g. for sth** buscar algo a tientas (**b**) *Fam* (*fondle*) meter mano

gross [grəʊs] **1** *adj* (**a**) grosero(a); (*joke*) verde (**b**) (*fat*) obeso(a) (**c**) (*flagrant*) flagrante; (*ignorance*) craso(a) (**d**) *Com & Econ* bruto(a); **g. national product** producto nacional bruto
2 *vt Com* recaudar (en bruto)

grossly ['grəʊslɪ] *adv* enormemente

grotesque [grəʊ'tesk] *adj* grotesco(a)

grotto ['grɒtəʊ] *n* gruta *f*

ground¹ [graʊnd] **1** *n* (**a**) suelo *m*, tierra *f*; **at g. level** al nivel del suelo; *Av* **to get off the g.** despegar; *Av* **g. control** control *m* de tierra; **g. floor** planta baja; *Av* **g. staff** personal *m* de tierra; *Fig* **g. swell** marejada *f* (**b**) (*terrain*) terreno *m*; **to gain/lose g.** ganar/perder terreno; *Fig* **to stand one's g.** mantenerse firme; **football g.** campo *m* de fútbol (**c**) *US Elec* toma *f* de tierra (**d**) **grounds** (*gardens*) jardines *mpl* (**e**) **grounds** (*reason*) motivo *m* (**f**) **grounds** (*sediment*) poso *m*
2 *vt* (**a**) *Av* obligar a quedarse en tierra; *Naut* varar (**b**) *US Elec* conectar con tierra

ground² [graʊnd] **1** *adj* (*coffee*) molido(a); *US* (*meat*) picado(a)
2 *pt & pp of* **grind**

grounding ['graʊndɪŋ] *n* base *f*; **to have a good g. in** tener buenos conocimientos de

groundless ['graʊndlɪs] *adj* infundado(a)

groundsheet ['graʊndʃiːt] *n* tela *f* impermeable

groundsman ['graʊndzmən] *n* encargado *m* de campo

groundwork ['graʊndwɜːk] *n* trabajo preparatorio

group [gruːp] **1** *n* grupo *m*, conjunto *m*
2 *vt* agrupar, juntar (**into** en)
3 *vi* **to g. (together)** agruparse, juntarse

grouse¹ [graʊs] *n Orn* urogallo *m*

grouse² [graʊs] *Fam* **1** *vi* quejarse (**about** de)
2 *n* queja *f*

grove [grəʊv] *n* arboleda *f*

grovel ['grɒvəl] *vi* humillarse (**to** ante); (*crawl*) arrastrarse (**to** ante)

grow [grəʊ] **1** *vt* (*pt* **grew**; *pp* **grown**) (*cultivate*) cultivar; **to g. a beard** dejarse (crecer) la barba

2 *vi* (**a**) crecer; *(increase)* aumentar (**b**) *(become)* hacerse, volverse; **to g. accustomed to** acostumbrarse a; **to g. dark** oscurecer; **to g. old** envejecer

▸ **grow out of** *vt insep* (**a**) **he's grown out of his shirt** se le ha quedado pequeña la camisa (**b**) *Fig (phase etc)* superar

▸ **grow up** *vi* crecer, hacerse mayor

grower ['grəʊə(r)] *n* cultivador(a) *m,f*

growing ['grəʊɪŋ] *adj (child)* que crece; *(problem etc)* creciente; **he's a g. boy** está dando el estirón

growl [graʊl] **1** *vi* gruñir

2 *n* gruñido *m*

grown [grəʊn] **1** *adj* crecido(a), adulto(a)

2 *pp of* **grow**

grown-up ['grəʊnʌp] *adj & n* adulto(a) *(m,f)*; **the grown-ups** los mayores

growth [grəʊθ] *n* (**a**) crecimiento *m*; *(increase)* aumento *m*; *(development)* desarrollo *m* (**b**) *Med* bulto *m*

grub [grʌb] *n* (**a**) *(larva)* gusano *m* (**b**) *Fam (food)* papeo *m*

grubby ['grʌbɪ] *adj* (**grubbier, grubbiest**) sucio(a)

grudge [grʌdʒ] **1** *n* rencor *m*; **to bear sb a g.** guardar rencor a algn

2 *vt (give unwillingly)* dar a regañadientes; **he grudges me my success** me envidia el éxito

grudgingly ['grʌdʒɪŋlɪ] *adv* a regañadientes

gruelling, *US* **grueling** ['gruːəlɪŋ] *adj* penoso(a)

gruesome ['gruːsəm] *adj* espantoso(a), horrible

gruff [grʌf] *adj (manner)* brusco(a); *(voice)* áspero(a)

grumble ['grʌmbəl] **1** *vi* refunfuñar

2 *n* queja *f*

grumpy ['grʌmpɪ] *adj* (**grumpier, grumpiest**) gruñón(ona)

grunt [grʌnt] **1** *vi* gruñir

2 *n* gruñido *m*

guarantee [gærən'tiː] **1** *n* garantía *f*; *(certificate)* certificado *m* de garantía

2 *vt* garantizar; *(assure)* asegurar

guard [gɑːd] **1** *vt* (**a**) *(protect)* defender, proteger; *(keep watch over)* vigilar (**b**) *(control)* guardar

2 *vi* protegerse (**against** de *or* contra)

3 *n* (**a**) **to be on one's g.** estar en guardia; **to catch sb off his g.** coger desprevenido a algn (**b**) *(sentry)* guardia *mf*; **g. of honour** guardia de honor; **to stand g.** montar la guardia; **g. dog** perro *m* guardián (**c**) *Br Rail* jefe *m* de tren; **g.'s van** furgón *m* de cola (**d**) *(on machine)* dispositivo *m* de seguridad; **fire g.** pantalla *f*

guarded ['gɑːdɪd] *adj* cauteloso(a), precavido(a)

guardhouse ['gɑːdhaʊs] *n Mil* (**a**) *(headquarters)* cuerpo *m* de guardia (**b**) *(prison)*

prisión *f* militar

guardian ['gɑːdɪən] *n* (**a**) guardián(ana) *m,f*; **g. angel** ángel *m* de la guarda (**b**) *Jur (of minor)* tutor(a) *m,f*

Guatemala [gwɑːtə'mɑːlə] *n* Guatemala

Guatemalan [gwɑːtə'mɑːlən] *adj & n* guatemalteco(a) *(m,f)*

guava ['gwɑːvə] *n Bot* guayaba *f*; **g. tree** guayabo *m*

guer(r)illa [gə'rɪlə] *n* guerrillero(a) *m,f*; **g. warfare** guerra *f* de guerrillas

guess [ges] **1** *vt & vi* (**a**) adivinar; **I guessed as much** me lo imaginaba; **to g. right/wrong** acertar/no acertar (**b**) *US Fam* pensar, suponer; **I g. so** supongo que sí

2 *n* conjetura *f*; *(estimate)* cálculo *m*; **at a rough g.** a ojo de buen cubero; **to have** *or* **make a g.** intentar adivinar

guesswork ['geswɜːk] *n* conjetura *f*

guest [gest] *n (at home)* invitado(a) *m,f*; *(in hotel)* cliente(a) *m,f*, huésped(a) *m,f*; **g. artist** artista *mf* invitado(a); **g. room** cuarto *m* de los invitados

guesthouse ['gesthaʊs] *n* casa *f* de huéspedes

guffaw [gʌ'fɔː] *vi* reírse a carcajadas

guidance ['gaɪdəns] *n* orientación *f*, consejos *mpl*; **for your g.** a título de información

guide [gaɪd] **1** *vt* guiar, dirigir

2 *n* (**a**) *(person)* guía *mf*; *Br* **girl g.** exploradora *f*; **g. dog** perro lazarillo (**b**) *(guidebook)* guía *f*

guidebook ['gaɪdbʊk] *n* guía *f*

guided ['gaɪdɪd] *adj* dirigido(a); **g. tour** visita con guía; **g. missile** misil teledirigido

guideline ['gaɪdlaɪn] *n* pauta *f*

guild [gɪld] *n* gremio *m*

guile [gaɪl] *n* astucia *f*

guillotine ['gɪlətiːn] *n* guillotina *f*

guilt [gɪlt] *n* (**a**) culpa *f* (**b**) *Jur* culpabilidad *f*

guilty ['gɪltɪ] *adj* (**guiltier, guiltiest**) culpable (**of** de); **to have a g. conscience** remorderle a uno la conciencia

guinea¹ ['gɪnɪ] *n* **g. pig** conejillo *m* de Indias, cobayo *m*; *Fig* **to act as a g. pig** servir de conejillo de Indias

guinea² ['gɪnɪ] *n (coin)* guinea *f* (= 21 chelines)

guise [gaɪz] *n* **under the g. of** so pretexto de

guitar [gɪ'tɑː(r)] *n* guitarra *f*

guitarist [gɪ'tɑːrɪst] *n* guitarrista *mf*

gulf [gʌlf] *n* (**a**) golfo *m*; **G. of Mexico** Golfo de Méjico; **G. Stream** corriente *f* del Golfo de Méjico; **the G. War** la guerra del Golfo (**b**) *Fig* abismo *m*

gull [gʌl] *n* gaviota *f*

gulley ['gʌlɪ] *n* = **gully**

gullible ['gʌləbəl] *adj* crédulo(a)

gully ['gʌlɪ] *n* barranco *m*, hondonada *f*

gulp [gʌlp] **1** *n* trago *m*

2 *vt* tragar; **to g. sth down** *(drink)* tomarse algo de un trago; *(food)* engullir algo

3 *vi* (**a**) *(swallow air)* tragar aire (**b**) *Fig (with fear)* tragar saliva
gum¹ [gʌm] **1** *n* goma *f*
2 *vt* pegar con goma
gum² [gʌm] *n Anat* encía *f*
gumboots ['gʌmbuːts] *npl* botas *fpl* de agua
gun [gʌn] *n* arma *f* de fuego; *(handgun)* pistola *f*, revólver *m*; *(rifle)* fusil *m*, escopeta *f*; *(cannon)* cañón *m*; *Fam* **the big guns** los peces gordos
▸ **gun down** *vt sep* matar a tiros
gunboat ['gʌnbəʊt] *n* cañonero *m*
gunfire ['gʌnfaɪə(r)] *n* tiros *mpl*
gunman ['gʌnmən] *n* pistolero *m*, gángster *m*
gunpoint ['gʌnpɔɪnt] *n* **at g.** a punta de pistola
gunpowder ['gʌnpaʊdə(r)] *n* pólvora *f*
gunrunner ['gʌnrʌnə(r)] *n* traficante *mf* de armas
gunshot ['gʌnʃɒt] *n* disparo *m*, tiro *m*
gunsmith ['gʌnsmɪθ] *n* armero *m*
gurgle ['gɜːgəl] *vi (baby)* gorjear; *(liquid)* gorgotear; *(stream)* murmurar
guru ['gʊruː, 'guːruː] *n* gurú *m*
gush [gʌʃ] **1** *vi* (**a**) brotar (**b**) *Fig* **to g. over sb** enjabonar a algn
2 *n (of water)* chorro *m*; *(of words)* torrente *m*

gushing ['gʌʃɪŋ] *adj Fig (person)* efusivo(a)
gusset ['gʌsɪt] *n* escudete *m*
gust [gʌst] *n (of wind)* ráfaga *f*, racha *f*
gusto ['gʌstəʊ] *n* entusiasmo *m*
gut [gʌt] **1** *n* (**a**) *Anat* intestino *m* (**b**) *(catgut)* cuerda *f* de tripa (**c**) **guts** *(entrails)* tripas *fpl* *Fam* **to have guts** tener agallas
2 *vt* (**a**) *(fish)* destripar (**b**) *(destroy)* destrui por dentro
3 *adj Fam* **g. reaction** reacción *f* visceral
gutter ['gʌtə(r)] *n (in street)* arroyo *m*; *(or roof)* canalón *m*; *Fig* **g. press** prensa amarilla
guttural ['gʌtərəl] *adj* gutural
guy¹ [gaɪ] *n Fam* tipo *m*, tío *m*
guy² [gaɪ] *n (rope)* viento *m*, cuerda *f*
guzzle ['gʌzəl] *vt & vi Fam (food etc)* zam parse; *(car)* tragar mucho
gym [dʒɪm] *Fam* (**a**) *(gymnasium)* gimnasic *m* (**b**) *(gymnastics)* gimnasia *f*; **g. shoes** zapa tillas *fpl* de deporte
gymnasium [dʒɪm'neɪzɪəm] *n* gimnasio *m*
gymnast ['dʒɪmnæst] *n* gimnasta *mf*
gymnastics [dʒɪm'næstɪks] *n sing* gimnasia *f*
gynaecologist, *US* **gynecologist** [gaɪnɪ-'kɒlədʒɪst] *n* ginecólogo(a) *m,f*
gypsy ['dʒɪpsɪ] *adj & n* gitano(a) *(m,f)*
gyrate [dʒaɪ'reɪt] *vi* girar

H, h [eɪtʃ] *n (the letter)* H, h *f*
haberdashery [hæbə'dæʃərɪ] *n* (**a**) *Br* artículos *mpl* de mercería (**b**) *US* ropa masculina
habit ['hæbɪt] *n* (**a**) costumbre *f* (**b**) *(garment)* hábito *m*
habitable ['hæbɪtəbəl] *adj* habitable
habitat ['hæbɪtæt] *n* hábitat *m*
habitual [hə'bɪtjʊəl] *adj* habitual; *(drinker, liar)* empedernido(a)
habitually [hə'bɪtjʊəlɪ] *adv* por costumbre
hack¹ [hæk] **1** *n (cut)* corte *m*; *(with an axe)* hachazo *m*
 2 *vt (with knife, axe)* cortar; *(kick)* dar un puntapié a
hack² [hæk] *n Fam (writer)* escritorzuelo(a) *m,f*; *(journalist)* gacetillero(a) *m,f*
hackneyed ['hæknɪd] *adj* trillado(a)
hacksaw ['hæksɔː] *n* sierra *f* para metales
had [hæd] *pt & pp of* **have**
haddock ['hædək] *n* abadejo *m*
haemophilia [hiːmə'fɪlɪə] *n* hemofilia *f*
haemophiliac [hiːmə'fɪlɪæk] *adj & n* hemofílico(a) *(m,f)*
haemorrhage ['hemərɪdʒ] *n* hemorragia *f*
haemorrhoids ['hemərɔɪdz] *npl* hemorroides *fpl*
hag [hæg] *n Pej* bruja *f*, arpía *f*
haggard ['hægəd] *adj* ojeroso(a)
haggle ['hægəl] *vi* regatear
Hague [heɪg] *n* **The H.** La Haya
hail¹ [heɪl] **1** *n* granizo *m*; *Fig* **a h. of bullets/insults** una lluvia de balas/insultos
 2 *vi* granizar
hail² [heɪl] **1** *vt* (**a**) *(taxi etc)* parar (**b**) *(acclaim)* aclamar
 2 *vi* **to h. from** *(originate)* ser nativo(a) de
hailstone ['heɪlstəʊn] *n* granizo *m*
hailstorm ['heɪlstɔːm] *n* granizada *f*
hair [heə(r)] *n (strand)* pelo *m*, cabello *m*; *(mass)* pelo, cabellos *mpl*; *(on arm, leg)* vello *m*; **to have long h.** tener el pelo largo
hairbrush ['heəbrʌʃ] *n* cepillo *m* (para el pelo)
haircut ['heəkʌt] *n* corte *m* de pelo; **to have a h.** cortarse el pelo
hairdo ['heəduː] *n Fam* peinado *m*
hairdresser ['heədresə(r)] *n* peluquero(a) *m,f*; **h.'s (shop)** peluquería *f*
hairdryer, hairdrier ['heədraɪə(r)] *n* secador *m* (de pelo)
hairgrip ['heəgrɪp] *n Br* horquilla *f*

hairline ['heəlaɪn] **1** *adj* muy fino(a)
 2 *n* nacimiento *m* del pelo; **receding h.** entradas *fpl*
hairnet ['heənet] *n* redecilla *f*
hairpiece ['heəpiːs] *n* postizo *m*
hairpin ['heəpɪn] *n* horquilla *f*; **h. bend** curva muy cerrada
hair-raising ['heəreɪzɪŋ] *adj* espeluznante
hair-remover ['heərɪmuːvə(r)] *n* depilatorio *m*
hairspray ['heəspreɪ] *n* laca *f* (para el pelo)
hairstyle ['heəstaɪl] *n* peinado *m*, corte *m* de pelo
hairy ['heərɪ] *adj* (**hairier, hairiest**) (**a**) *(with hair)* peludo(a) (**b**) *Fig (frightening)* enervante, espantoso(a)
hake [heɪk] *n* merluza *f*; *(young)* pescadilla *f*
half [hɑːf] **1** *n (pl* **halves**) mitad *f*; *Sport (period)* tiempo *m*; **he's four and a h.** tiene cuatro años y medio; **to cut in h.** cortar por la mitad
 2 *adj* medio(a); **h. a dozen/an hour** media docena/hora; **h. board** media pensión; **h. fare** media tarifa; **h. term** medio trimestre; **h. year** semestre *m*
 3 *adv* medio, a medias; **h. asleep** medio dormido(a)
half-caste ['hɑːfkɑːst] *adj & n* mestizo(a) *(m,f)*
half-day [hɑːf'deɪ] *n* media jornada
half-hearted [hɑːf'hɑːtɪd] *adj* poco entusiasta
half-hour [hɑːf'aʊə(r)] *n* media hora
half-life ['hɑːflaɪf] *n* media vida
half-mast [hɑːf'mɑːst] *n* **at h.** a media asta
half-price [hɑːf'praɪs] *adv* a mitad de precio
half-time [hɑːf'taɪm] *n* descanso *m*
half-way ['hɑːfweɪ] **1** *adj* intermedio(a)
 2 **halfway** [hɑːf'weɪ] *adv* a medio camino, a mitad de camino
half-yearly ['hɑːfjɪəlɪ] *adj* semestral
halibut ['hælɪbət] *n* mero *m*
hall [hɔːl] *n* (**a**) *(lobby)* vestíbulo *m* (**b**) *(building)* sala *f*; *Univ* **h. of residence** colegio *m* mayor
hallmark ['hɔːlmɑːk] *n* (**a**) *(on gold, silver)* contraste *m* (**b**) *Fig* sello *m*
hallo [hə'ləʊ] *interj* ¡hola!
hallowed ['hæləʊd] *adj* santificado(a)
Hallowe(')en [hæləʊ'iːn] *n* víspera *f* de Todos los Santos
hallucinate [hə'luːsɪneɪt] *vi* alucinar

hallucination [həluːsɪˈneɪʃən] *n* alucinación *f*

hallucinogenic [həluːsɪnəʊˈdʒenɪk] *adj* alucinógeno(a)

hallway [ˈhɔːlweɪ] *n* vestíbulo *m*

halo [ˈheɪləʊ] *n* (**a**) *Rel* aureola *f* (**b**) *Astron* halo *m*

halt [hɔːlt] **1** *n* (*stop*) alto *m*, parada *f*; **to call a h. to sth** poner fin a algo
2 *vt* parar
3 *vi* pararse

halting [ˈhɔːltɪŋ] *adj* vacilante

halve [hɑːv] *vt* (**a**) partir por la mitad; (*reduce by half*) reducir a la mitad (**b**) (*share*) compartir

halves [hɑːvz] *pl of* **half**

ham [hæm] *n* jamón *m*; **boiled h.** jamón de York; **Parma** *or* **cured h.** jamón serrano

hamburger [ˈhæmbɜːgə(r)] *n* hamburguesa *f*

hamlet [ˈhæmlɪt] *n* aldea *f*

hammer [ˈhæmə(r)] **1** *n* (**a**) martillo *m*; **the h. and sickle** la hoz y el martillo (**b**) (*of gun*) percursor *m* (**c**) *Sport* lanzamiento *m* de martillo
2 *vt* (**a**) martillar; (*nail*) clavar; *Fig* **to h. home** insistir sobre (**b**) *Fam* (*defeat*) dar una paliza a
3 *vi* martillar, dar golpes

hammering [ˈhæmərɪŋ] *n Fam* paliza *f*

hammock [ˈhæmək] *n* hamaca *f*; *Naut* coy *m*

hamper¹ [ˈhæmpə(r)] *n* cesta *f*

hamper² [ˈhæmpə(r)] *vt* estorbar, dificultar

hamster [ˈhæmstə(r)] *n* hámster *m*

hamstring [ˈhæmstrɪŋ] *n* tendón *m* de la corva

hand [hænd] **1** *n* (**a**) mano *f*; **by h.** a mano; (**close**) **at h.** a mano; **hands up!** ¡manos arriba!; **on the one/other h.** por una/otra parte; *Fig* **to get out of h.** descontrolarse; *Fig* **to be on h.** estar a mano; *Fig* **to have a h. in** intervenir en; *Fig* **to have time in h.** sobrarle a uno tiempo; *Fig* **to wash one's hands of sth** lavarse las manos de algo; *Fig* **to give sb a h.** echarle una mano a algn; **h. grenade** granada *f* de mano
(**b**) (*worker*) trabajador(a) *m,f*; *Naut* tripulante *m*
(**c**) (*of clock*) aguja *f*
(**d**) **to give sb a big h.** (*applause*) dedicar a algn una gran ovación
(**e**) (*handwriting*) letra *f*
2 *vt* (*give*) dar, entregar; *Fam Fig* **I have to h. it to you** tengo que reconocerlo
▸ **hand back** *vt sep* devolver
▸ **hand down** *vt sep* dejar en herencia
▸ **hand in** *vt sep* (*homework*) entregar; (*resignation*) presentar
▸ **hand out** *vt sep* repartir
▸ **hand over** *vt sep* entregar
▸ **hand round** *vt sep* repartir

handbag [ˈhændbæg] *n Br* bolso *m*, cartera *f*, *Méx* bolsa *f*

handball [ˈhændbɔːl] *n Sport* balonmano *m*

handbook [ˈhændbʊk] *n* manual *m*

handbrake [ˈhændbreɪk] *n* freno *m* de mano

handcuff [ˈhændkʌf] **1** *vt* esposar
2 *npl* **handcuffs** esposas *fpl*

handful [ˈhændfʊl] *n* puñado *m*

handicap [ˈhændɪkæp] **1** *n* (**a**) *Med* minusvalía *f* (**b**) *Sport* hándicap *m*, desventaja *f*
2 *vt* impedir

handicapped [ˈhændɪkæpt] *adj* (**a**) (*physically*) minusválido(a); (*mentally*) retrasado(a) (**b**) *Sport* en desventaja (**c**) *Fig* desfavorecido(a)

handicraft [ˈhændɪkrɑːft] *n* artesanía *f*

handiwork [ˈhændɪwɜːk] *n* (*work*) obra *f*, (*craft*) artesanía *f*

handkerchief [ˈhæŋkətʃiːf] *n* pañuelo *m*

handle [ˈhændəl] **1** *n* (*of knife*) mango *m*; (*of cup*) asa *f*; (*of door*) pomo *m*; (*of lever*) palanca *f*; (*of drawer*) tirador *m*
2 *vt* (**a**) manejar; **h. with care** (*sign*) frágil (**b**) (*problem*) encargarse de; (*people*) tratar; *Fam* (*put up with*) soportar
3 *vi* (*car*) comportarse

handlebar [ˈhændəlbɑː(r)] *n* manillar *m*

handmade [hændˈmeɪd] *adj* hecho(a) a mano

hand-out [ˈhændaʊt] *n* (**a**) (*leaflet*) folleto *m* *Press* nota *f* de prensa (**b**) (*charity*) limosna *f*

hand-picked [hændˈpɪkt] *adj* selecto(a)

handrail [ˈhændreɪl] *n* pasamanos *m inv*

handshake [ˈhændʃeɪk] *n* apretón *m* de manos

handsome [ˈhænsəm] *adj* (**a**) (*person*) guapo(a) (**b**) (*substantial*) considerable

handwriting [ˈhændraɪtɪŋ] *n* letra *f*

handy [ˈhændɪ] *adj* (**handier, handiest**) (**a**) (*useful*) útil, práctico(a); (*nearby*) a mano (**b**) (*dextrous*) diestro(a)

hang [hæŋ] **1** *vt* (*pt & pp* **hung**) (**a**) colgar (**b**) (*head*) bajar (**c**) (*pt* **hanged**) ahorcar
2 *vi* (**a**) colgar (**from** de); (*in air*) flotar (**b**) (*criminal*) ser ahorcado(a); **to h. oneself** ahorcarse
▸ **hang about** *vi Fam* (**a**) perder el tiempo (**b**) (*wait*) esperar
▸ **hang around** *vi Fam* (**a**) esperar (**b**) frecuentar; **where does he h. around?** ¿a que lugares suele ir?
▸ **hang on** *vi* (**a**) agarrarse (**b**) (*wait*) esperar
▸ **hang out 1** *vt sep* (*washing*) tender
2 *vi Fam* (*frequent*) frecuentar
▸ **hang round** *vi Fam* = **hang about**
▸ **hang together** *vi* (*ideas*) ser coherente
▸ **hang up** *vt sep* (*picture, telephone*) colgar

hangar [ˈhæŋə(r)] *n* hangar *m*

hanger [ˈhæŋə(r)] *n* percha *f*

hang-glider [ˈhæŋglaɪdə(r)] *n* ala delta

hang-gliding [ˈhæŋglaɪdɪŋ] *n* vuelo *m* libre

hangman [ˈhæŋmən] *n* verdugo *m*

hangover [ˈhæŋəʊvə(r)] *n* resaca *f*

hang-up [ˈhæŋʌp] *n Fam* (*complex*) complejo *m*

hanker [ˈhæŋkə(r)] *vi* **to h. after** sth anhelar algo

hankie, hanky [ˈhæŋkɪ] *n Fam* pañuelo *m*

haphazard [hæpˈhæzəd] *adj* caótico(a), desordenado(a)

happen [ˈhæpən] *vi* suceder, ocurrir; **it so happens that** lo que pasa es que; **if you h. to see my friend** si por casualidad ves a mi amigo

happening [ˈhæpənɪŋ] *n* acontecimiento *m*

happily [ˈhæpɪlɪ] *adv* (*with pleasure*) felizmente; (*fortunately*) afortunadamente

happiness [ˈhæpɪnɪs] *n* felicidad *f*

happy [ˈhæpɪ] *adj* (*happier, happiest*) (*cheerful*) feliz, contento(a); (*fortunate*) afortunado(a); **h. birthday!** ¡feliz cumpleaños!

happy-go-lucky [hæpɪgəʊˈlʌkɪ] *adj* despreocupado(a); **a h. fellow** un viva la virgen

harangue [həˈræŋ] **1** *vt* arengar
2 *n* arenga *f*

harass [ˈhærəs] *vt* acosar

harassment [ˈhærəsmənt, həˈræsmənt] *n* hostigamiento *m*, acoso *m*

harbour, *US* **harbor** [ˈhɑːbə(r)] **1** *n* puerto *m*
2 *vt* (**a**) (*criminal*) encubrir (**b**) (*doubts*) abrigar

hard [hɑːd] **1** *adj* (**a**) duro(a); (*solid*) sólido(a), **h. court** pista (de tenis) rápida; *Comput* **h. disk** disco duro; *Br Aut* **h. shoulder** arcén *m, Andes* berma *f, Méx* acotamiento *m, RP* banquina *f, Ven* hombrillo *m*
(**b**) (*difficult*) difícil; **h. of hearing** duro(a) de oído; *Fam Fig* **to be h. up** estar sin blanca
(**c**) (*harsh*) severo(a); (*strict*) estricto(a); **to take a h. line** tomar medidas severas; **h. drugs** droga dura; *Pol* **h. left** extrema izquierda; **h. porn** pornografía dura; **h. sell** promoción *f* de venta agresiva
(**d**) **a h. drinker** un bebedor inveterado; **a h. worker** un trabajador concienzudo
(**e**) **h. luck!** ¡mala suerte!
(**f**) **h. evidence** pruebas definitivas; *Com* **h. cash** dinero *m* en metálico; **h. currency** divisa *f* fuerte
2 *adv* (**a**) (*hit*) fuerte
(**b**) (*work*) mucho, concienzudamente; *Fig* **to be h. on sb's heels** pisar los talones a algn
(**c**) **to be h. done by** ser tratado(a) injustamente

hardback [ˈhɑːdbæk] *n* edición *f* de tapas duras

hard-boiled [ˈhɑːdbɔɪld] *adj* duro(a)

hard-core [ˈhɑːdkɔː(r)] *adj* irreductible

harden [ˈhɑːdən] **1** *vt* endurecer
2 *vi* endurecerse

hardened [ˈhɑːdənd] *adj Fig* habitual

hard-headed [hɑːdˈhedɪd] *adj* realista

hard-hearted [hɑːdˈhɑːtɪd] *adj* insensible

hardliner [hɑːdˈlaɪnə(r)] *n* duro(a) *m,f*

hardly [ˈhɑːdlɪ] *adv* apenas; **h. anyone/ever** casi nadie/nunca; **he had h. begun when ...** apenas había comenzado cuando ...; **I can h.**

believe it apenas lo puedo creer

hardship [ˈhɑːdʃɪp] *n* privación *f*, apuro *m*

hardware [ˈhɑːdweə(r)] *n* (**a**) (*goods*) ferretería *f*; **h. shop** ferretería (**b**) *Comput* hardware *m*

hardwearing [hɑːdˈweərɪŋ] *adj* duradero(a)

hardworking [ˈhɑːdwɜːkɪŋ] *adj* muy trabajador(a)

hardy [ˈhɑːdɪ] *adj* (*hardier, hardiest*) (*person*) robusto(a), fuerte; (*plant*) resistente

hare [heə(r)] **1** *n* liebre *f*
2 *vi* correr muy de prisa

haricot [ˈhærɪkəʊ] *n* **h. (bean)** alubia *f*

harm [hɑːm] **1** *n* daño *m*, perjuicio *m*; **to be out of h.'s way** estar a salvo
2 *vt* hacer daño a, perjudicar

harmful [ˈhɑːmfʊl] *adj* perjudicial (**to** para)

harmless [ˈhɑːmlɪs] *adj* inofensivo(a)

harmonica [hɑːˈmɒnɪkə] *n* armónica *f*

harmonize [ˈhɑːmənaɪz] *vt & vi* armonizar

harmony [ˈhɑːmənɪ] *n* armonía *f*

harness [ˈhɑːnɪs] **1** *n* (*for horse*) arreos *mpl*
2 *vt* (**a**) (*horse*) enjaezar (**b**) *Fig* (*resources etc*) aprovechar

harp [hɑːp] *n* arpa *f*
▸ **harp on** *vi Fam* hablar sin parar

harpoon [hɑːˈpuːn] **1** *n* arpón *m*
2 *vt* arponear

harrowing [ˈhærəʊɪŋ] *adj* angustioso(a)

harsh [hɑːʃ] *adj* severo(a); (*voice*) áspero(a); (*sound*) discordante

harvest [ˈhɑːvɪst] **1** *n* cosecha *f*; (*of grapes*) vendimia *f*
2 *vt* cosechar, recoger

harvester [ˈhɑːvɪstə(r)] *n* (**a**) (*person*) segador(a) *m,f* (**b**) (*machine*) cosechadora *f*

has [hæz] *3rd person sing pres of* **have**

hash[1] [hæʃ] *n Culin* sofrito *m* de carne; *Fam Fig* **to make a h. of sth** estropear algo

hash[2] [hæʃ] *n Fam* hachís *m*

hashish [ˈhæʃiːʃ] *n* hachís *m*

hassle [ˈhæsəl] *Fam* **1** *n* (**a**) (*nuisance*) rollo *m* (**b**) (*problem*) lío *m* (**c**) (*wrangle*) bronca *f*
2 *vt* fastidiar

haste [heɪst] *n Fml* prisa *f*; **to make h.** darse prisa

hasten [ˈheɪsən] *vi* apresurarse

hastily [ˈheɪstɪlɪ] *adv* (*quickly*) de prisa

hasty [ˈheɪstɪ] *adj* (*hastier, hastiest*) apresurado(a); (*rash*) precipitado(a)

hat [hæt] *n* sombrero *m*

hatch[1] [hætʃ] *n* escotilla *f*; **serving h.** ventanilla *f*

hatch[2] [hætʃ] *vt* (**a**) (*eggs*) empollar (**b**) *Fig* (*plan*) tramar
▸ **hatch out** *vi* salirse del huevo

hatchback [ˈhætʃbæk] *n* coche *m* de 3/5 puertas

hatchet [ˈhætʃɪt] *n* hacha *f*; *Fam* **h. man** matón *m*

hate [heɪt] **1** *n* odio *m*
2 *vt* odiar

hateful ['heɪtfʊl] *adj* odioso(a)

hatred ['heɪtrɪd] *n* odio *m*

haughty ['hɔːtɪ] *adj* (**haughtier, haughtiest**) altanero(a), arrogante

haul [hɔːl] **1** *n* (**a**) (*journey*) trayecto *m* (**b**) (*of fish*) redada *f* (**c**) (*loot*) botín *m*
2 *vt* (**a**) tirar; (*drag*) arrastrar (**b**) (*transport*) acarrear
▸ **haul up** *vt sep Fam* (*to court*) llevar

haulage ['hɔːlɪdʒ] *n* transporte *m*

haulier ['hɔːljə(r)] *n* transportista *mf*

haunch [hɔːntʃ] *n* cadera *f*; *Culin* pernil *m*

haunt [hɔːnt] **1** *n* guarida *f*
2 *vt* (**a**) (*of ghost*) aparecerse en (**b**) *Fig* atormentar (**c**) (*frequent*) frecuentar

haunted ['hɔːntɪd] *adj* encantado(a), embrujado(a)

Havana [hə'vænə] *n* La Habana; **H. cigar** habano *m*

have [hæv]

En el inglés hablado, y en el escrito en estilo coloquial, el verbo auxiliar **have** se contrae de forma que **I have** se transforma en **I've, he/ she/it has** se transforman en **he's/she's/it's** y **you/we/they have** se transforman en **you've/we've/they've**. Las formas de pasado **I/you/he** *etc* **had** se transforman en **I'd, you'd, he'd** *etc*. Las formas negativas **has not, have not** y **had not** se transforman en **hasn't, haven't** y **hadn't**.

1 *vt* (*3rd person sing pres* **has**; *pt & pp* **had**) (**a**) (*possess*) tener; **h. you got a car?** ¿tienes coche?
(**b**) (*get, experience, suffer*) tener; **to h. a holiday** tomarse unas vacaciones
(**c**) (*partake of*) tomar; **to h. a cigarette** fumarse un cigarrillo; **to h. breakfast/lunch/tea/dinner** desayunar/comer/merendar/cenar
(**d**) **to h. a bath/shave** bañarse/afeitarse; **to h. a nap** echar la siesta
(**e**) **to h. to** (*obligation*) tener que, deber
(**f**) (*make happen*) hacer que; **I'll h. someone come round** haré que venga alguien
(**g**) (*receive*) recibir; **to h. people round** invitar a gente
(**h**) **can I h. your pen a moment?** (*borrow*) ¿me dejas tu bolígrafo un momento?
(**i**) (*party, meeting*) hacer, celebrar
(**j**) **to h. a baby** tener un niño
(**k**) **we won't h. it** (*allow*) no lo consentiremos
(**l**) (*hold*) tener; *Fig* **to h. sth against sb** tener algo en contra de algn
(**m**) **legend has it that ...** según la leyenda ...
(**n**) *Fam* (*deceive*) engañar
(**o**) **you'd better stay** más vale que te quedes

2 *v aux* (**a**) (*compound*) haber; **I had been waiting for half an hour** hacía media hora que esperaba; **he hasn't eaten yet** no ha co-

mido aún; **she had broken the window** había roto el cristal; **we h. lived here for ten years** hace diez años que vivimos aquí; **so I h.!** (*emphatic*) ¡ay, sí!, es verdad; **yes I h.!** ¡que sí!
(**b**) (*tag questions*) **you haven't seen my book, h. you?** no has visto mi libro, ¿verdad? **he's been to France, hasn't he?** ha estado en Francia, ¿verdad? *or* ¿no?
(**c**) (*have + just*) acabar de
▸ **have on** *vt sep* (**a**) (*wear*) vestir (**b**) *Fam* **to h. sb on** tomarle el pelo a algn
▸ **have out** *vt sep Fam* **to h. it out with sb** ajustar cuentas con algn
▸ **have over** *vt sep* (*invite*) recibir

haven ['heɪvən] *n* puerto *m*; *Fig* refugio *m*

haversack ['hævəsæk] *n* mochila *f*

havoc ['hævək] *n* **to play h. with** hacer estragos en

hawk [hɔːk] *n Orn & Pol* halcón *m*

hawker ['hɔːkə(r)] *n* vendedor(a) *m,f* ambulante

hawthorn ['hɔːθɔːn] *n* espino *m* albar

hay [heɪ] *n* heno *m*; **h. fever** fiebre *f* del heno

haystack ['heɪstæk] *n* almiar *m*

haywire ['heɪwaɪə(r)] *adj Fam* en desorden; **to go h.** (*machine etc*) estropearse; (*person*) volverse loco(a)

hazard ['hæzəd] **1** *n* peligro *m*, riesgo *m*; (*in golf*) obstáculo *m*
2 *vt Fml* arriesgar; **to h. a guess** intentar adivinar

hazardous ['hæzədəs] *adj* arriesgado(a), peligroso(a)

haze [heɪz] *n* (*mist*) neblina *f*; *Fig* (*blur*) confusión *f*

hazel ['heɪzəl] *adj* (de color) avellana

hazelnut ['heɪzəlnʌt] *n* avellana *f*

hazy ['heɪzɪ] *adj* (**hazier, haziest**) nebuloso(a)

he [hiː] *pers pron* él (*usually omitted in Spanish, except for contrast*); **HE did it** ha sido él; **he who** el que

head [hed] **1** *n* (**a**) cabeza *f*; (*mind*) mente *f*; *Fig* **£3 a h.** 3 libras por cabeza; *Fig* **to be h. over heels in love** estar locamente enamorado(a); *Fig* **to keep one's h.** mantener la calma; *Fig* **to lose one's h.** perder la cabeza; **success went to his h.** se le subió el éxito a la cabeza; **h. start** ventaja *f*
(**b**) (*of nail*) cabeza *f*; (*of beer*) espuma *f*; (*of tape recorder*) cabezal *m*; (*of steam*) presión *f*; *Fig* **to come to a h.** llegar a un momento decisivo
(**c**) (*boss*) cabeza *m*; (*of company*) director(a) *m,f*; **h. teacher** director(a) *m,f*
(**d**) (*of coin*) cara *f*; **heads or tails** cara o cruz
2 *adj* principal; **h. office** oficina *f* central
3 *vt* (**a**) (*list etc*) encabezar
(**b**) *Ftb* cabecear
▸ **head for** *vt insep* dirigirse hacia
▸ **head off 1** *vi* irse
2 *vt sep* (*avert*) evitar

headache ['hedeɪk] n dolor m de cabeza; Fig quebradero m de cabeza

headcheese ['hedtʃiːz] n US queso m de cerdo

header ['hedə(r)] n Ftb cabezazo m

head-first [hed'fɜːst] adv de cabeza

head-hunter ['hedhʌntə(r)] n Fig cazatalentos mf inv

heading ['hedɪŋ] n título m; (of letter) membrete m

headlamp ['hedlæmp] n faro m

headland ['hedlənd] n punta f, cabo m

headlight ['hedlaɪt] n faro m

headline ['hedlaɪn] n titular m; **the headlines** (on radio, TV) los titulares

headlong ['hedlɒŋ] adj & adv de cabeza; **to rush h. into sth** lanzarse a hacer algo sin pensar

headmaster [hed'mɑːstə(r)] n director m

headmistress [hed'mɪstrɪs] n directora f

head-on ['hedɒn] adj **a h. collision** un choque frontal

headphones ['hedfəʊnz] npl auriculares mpl

headquarters ['hedkwɔːtəz] npl (a) oficina f central, sede f (b) Mil cuartel m general

headrest ['hedrest] n Aut apoyacabezas m

headroom ['hedruːm] n altura f libre

headscarf ['hedskɑːf] n pañuelo m

headstrong ['hedstrɒŋ] adj testarudo(a)

headway ['hedweɪ] n **to make h.** avanzar, progresar

headwind ['hedwɪnd] n viento m de proa

heady ['hedɪ] adj (**headier, headiest**) embriagador(a)

heal [hiːl] 1 vi cicatrizar
2 vt (wound) curar

health [helθ] n salud f; Fig prosperidad f; **to be in good/bad h.** estar bien/mal de salud; **your good h.!** ¡salud!; **h. foods** alimentos mpl naturales; **h. food shop** tienda f de alimentos naturales; Br **H. Service** ≃ Insalud m

healthy ['helθɪ] adj (**healthier, healthiest**) sano(a); (good for health) saludable; (thriving) próspero(a)

heap [hiːp] 1 n montón m
2 vt amontonar; Fig **to h. praise on sb** colmar a algn de alabanzas; **a heaped spoonful** una cucharada colmada

hear [hɪə(r)] 1 vt (pt & pp heard [hɜːd]) (a) oír (b) (listen to) escuchar (c) **I won't h. of it!** ¡ni hablar! (d) (find out) enterarse (e) Jur ver; (evidence) oír
2 vi **to h. from sb** tener noticias de algn

hearing ['hɪərɪŋ] n (a) oído m; **h. aid** audífono m (b) Jur audiencia f; Fig **to give sb a fair h.** escuchar a algn

hearsay ['hɪəseɪ] n rumores mpl

hearse [hɜːs] n coche m fúnebre

heart [hɑːt] n (a) corazón m; **h. attack** infarto m de miocardio; **h. transplant** trasplante m de corazón; **a broken h.** un corazón roto; **at h.**

en el fondo; **to take sth to h.** tomarse algo a pecho; **to have a good h.** (be kind) tener buen corazón (b) (courage) valor m; **his h. wasn't in it** no ponía interés en ello; **to lose h.** desanimarse (c) (core) meollo m; (of lettuce) cogollo m

heartbeat ['hɑːtbiːt] n latido m del corazón

heart-breaking ['hɑːtbreɪkɪŋ] adj desgarrador(a)

heart-broken ['hɑːtbrəʊkən] adj hundido(a); **he's h.** tiene el corazón destrozado

heartburn ['hɑːtbɜːn] n acedía f

heartening ['hɑːtənɪŋ] adj alentador(a)

heartfelt ['hɑːtfelt] adj sincero(a)

hearth [hɑːθ] n (a) (fireplace) chimenea f (b) Fml (home) hogar m

heartless ['hɑːtlɪs] adj cruel, insensible

heart-throb ['hɑːtθrɒb] n ídolo m

hearty ['hɑːtɪ] adj (**heartier, heartiest**) (person) francote; (meal) abundante; (welcome) cordial; **to have a h. appetite** ser de buen comer

heat [hiːt] 1 n (a) calor m (b) Sport eliminatoria f (c) Zool **on h.** en celo
2 vt calentar
▸ **heat up** vi (a) (warm up) calentarse (b) (increase excitement) acalorarse

heated ['hiːtɪd] adj Fig (argument) acalorado(a)

heater ['hiːtə(r)] n calentador m

heath [hiːθ] n (land) brezal m

heathen ['hiːðən] adj & n pagano(a) (m,f)

heather ['heðə(r)] n brezo m

heating ['hiːtɪŋ] n calefacción f

heatwave ['hiːtweɪv] n ola f de calor

heave [hiːv] 1 n (pull) tirón m; (push) empujón m
2 vt (a) (lift) levantar; (haul) tirar; (push) empujar (b) (throw) arrojar
3 vi subir y bajar

heaven ['hevən] 1 n (a) cielo m; **for h.'s sake!** ¡por Dios!; **h. on earth** un paraíso en la tierra (b) **heavens** cielo m
2 interj **good heavens!** ¡por Dios!

heavenly ['hevənlɪ] adj celestial

heavily ['hevɪlɪ] adv **it rained h.** llovió mucho; **to sleep h.** dormir profundamente

heavy ['hevɪ] 1 adj (**heavier, heaviest**) pesado(a); (rain, meal) fuerte; (traffic) denso(a); (loss) grande; **h. going** duro(a); **is it h.?** ¿pesa mucho?; **a h. drinker/smoker** un(a) bebedor(a)/fumador(a) empedernido(a); Mus **h. metal** heavy metal m
2 n Fam gorila m

heavyweight ['hevɪweɪt] n peso pesado

Hebrew ['hiːbruː] 1 adj hebreo(a)
2 n (language) hebreo m

Hebrides ['hebrɪdiːz] npl **the H.** las (Islas) Hébridas

heckle ['hekəl] vt interrumpir

heckler ['heklə(r)] n altercador(a) m,f

hectare ['hektɑː(r)] n hectárea f

hectic ['hektɪk] *adj* agitado(a)

hedge [hedʒ] **1** *n* seto *m*

2 *vt* cercar con un seto; *Fig* **to h. one's bets** cubrirse

hedgehog ['hedʒhɒg] *n* erizo *m*

hedgerow ['hedʒrəʊ] *n* seto vivo

heed [hi:d] *n* **to take h. of** hacer caso de

heedless ['hi:dlɪs] *adj* desatento(a)

heel [hi:l] *n* (*of foot*) talón *m*; (*of shoe*) tacón *m*; (*of palm*) pulpejo *m*; *Fig* **to be on sb's heels** pisarle los talones a algn; **high heels** zapatos *mpl* de tacón alto

heeled [hi:ld] *adj Fam Fig* **well-h.** adinerado(a)

hefty ['heftɪ] *adj* (*heftier, heftiest*) (**a**) (*person*) fornido(a); (*package*) pesado(a) (**b**) (*large*) grande

height [haɪt] *n* (**a**) altura *f*; (*of person*) estatura *f*; *Av* **to gain/lose h.** subir/bajar; **what h. are you?** ¿cuánto mides?; *Fig* **the h. of ignorance** el colmo de la ignorancia (**b**) *Geog* cumbre *f*

heighten ['haɪtən] *vt* (*intensify*) realzar; (*increase*) aumentar

heir [eə(r)] *n* heredero *m*

heiress ['eərɪs] *n* heredera *f*

heirloom ['eəlu:m] *n* reliquia *f*/joya *f* de familia

held [held] *pt & pp of* **hold**

helicopter ['helɪkɒptə(r)] *n* helicóptero *m*

helium ['hi:lɪəm] *n* helio *m*

hell [hel] *n* infierno *m*; *Fam* **what the h. are you doing?** ¿qué diablos estás haciendo?; *Fam Pej* **go to h.!** ¡vete a hacer puñetas!; *Fam* **a h. of a party** una fiesta estupenda; *Fam* **she's had a h. of a day** ha tenido un día fatal

hellish ['helɪʃ] *adj Fam* infernal

hello [hə'ləʊ, he'ləʊ] *interj* ¡hola!; *Tel* ¡diga!; (*showing surprise*) ¡hala!

helm [helm] *n* timón *m*; **to be at the h.** llevar el timón

helmet ['helmɪt] *n* casco *m*

help [help] **1** *n* (**a**) ayuda *f*; **h.!** ¡socorro! (**b**) (*daily*) **h.** asistenta *f*

2 *vt* (**a**) ayudar; **can I h. you?** (*in shop*) ¿qué desea? (**b**) (*alleviate*) aliviar (**c**) **h. yourself!** (*to food etc*) ¡sírvete! (**d**) (*avoid*) evitar; **I can't h. it** no lo puedo remediar

▸ **help out** *vt sep* **to h. sb out** echarle una mano a algn

helper ['helpə(r)] *n* ayudante(a) *m,f*

helpful ['helpfʊl] *adj* (*person*) amable; (*thing*) útil

helping ['helpɪŋ] *n* ración *f*; **who wants a second h.?** ¿quién quiere repetir?

helpless ['helplɪs] *adj* (*defenceless*) desamparado(a); (*powerless*) incapaz

helplessly ['helplɪslɪ] *adv* inútilmente, en vano

helter-skelter [heltə'skeltə(r)] **1** *n* tobogán *m*

2 *adj* atropellado(a)

3 *adv* atropelladamente

hem [hem] **1** *n Sewing* dobladillo *m*

2 *vt Sewing* hacer un dobladillo a

▸ **hem in** *vt sep* cercar, rodear

hemisphere ['hemɪsfɪə(r)] *n* hemisferio *m*

hemophilia [hi:məʊ'fɪlɪə] *n US* = **haemophilia**

hemophiliac [hi:məʊ'fɪlɪæk] *adj & n* = **haemophiliac**

hemorrhage ['hemərɪdʒ] *n US* = **haemorrhage**

hen [hen] *n* gallina *f*; *Fam* **h. party** reunión *f* de mujeres

hence [hens] *adv Fml* (**a**) **six months h.** (*from now*) de aquí a seis meses (**b**) (*consequently*) por lo tanto

henceforth [hens'fɔ:θ] *adv Fml* de ahora en adelante

henchman ['hentʃmən] *n Pej* secuaz *m*

henna ['henə] *n Bot* alheña *f*; (*dye*) henna *f*

henpecked ['henpekt] *adj Fam* **a h. husband** un calzonazos

hepatitis [hepə'taɪtɪs] *n* hepatitis *f*

her [hɜ:(r), *unstressed* hə(r)] **1** *poss adj* (*one thing*) su; (*more than one*) sus; (*to distinguish*) de ella; **she has cut h. finger** se ha cortado el dedo

2 *pron* (**a**) (*direct object*) la; **I saw h. recently** la vi hace poco (**b**) (*indirect object*) le; (*with other third person pronouns*) se; **he gave h. money** le dio dinero; **they handed it to h.** se lo entregaron (**c**) (*after prep*) ella; **for h.** para ella (**d**) (*as subject*) *Fam* ella; **look, it's h.!** ¡mira, es ella!

herald ['herəld] **1** *n* heraldo *m*

2 *vt* anunciar

heraldry ['herəldrɪ] *n* heráldica *f*

herb [hɜ:b, *US* ɜ:rb] *n* hierba *f*; **h. tea** infusión *f*

herbal ['hɜ:bəl] *adj* herbario(a); **h. remedies** curas *fpl* de hierbas

herd [hɜ:d] *n* (*of cattle*) manada *f*; (*of goats*) rebaño *m*; *Fig* (*large group*) multitud *f*

here [hɪə(r)] **1** *adv* aquí; **come h.** ven aquí; **h.!** ¡presente!; **h. goes!** ¡vamos a ver!; **here's to success!** ¡brindemos por el éxito!; **h. you are!** ¡toma!

2 *interj* **look h., you can't do that!** ¡oiga, que no se permite hacer eso!

hereafter [hɪər'ɑ:ftə(r)] *Fml* **1** *adv* de ahora en adelante

2 *n* **the h.** la otra vida, el más allá

hereby [hɪə'baɪ] *adv Fml* por la presente

hereditary [hɪ'redɪtərɪ] *adj* hereditario(a)

heresy ['herəsɪ] *n* herejía *f*

heretic ['herətɪk] *n* hereje *mf*

heritage ['herɪtɪdʒ] *n* patrimonio *m*; *Jur* herencia *f*

hermetically [hɜ:'metɪklɪ] *adv* **h. sealed** herméticamente cerrado(a)

hermit ['hɜ:mɪt] *n* ermitaño(a) *m,f*

🖉 Note that the Spanish word **ermita** is a false friend and is never a translation for the English word **hermit**. In Spanish, **ermita** means "hermitage".

hermitage ['hɜːmɪtɪdʒ] *n* ermita *f*

hernia ['hɜːnɪə] *n* hernia *f*

hero ['hɪərəʊ] *n (pl* **heroes**) héroe *m; (in novel)* protagonista *m;* **h. worship** idolatría *f*

heroic [hɪ'rəʊɪk] *adj* heroico(a)

heroin ['herəʊɪn] *n* heroína *f*

heroine ['herəʊɪn] *n* heroína *f; (in novel)* protagonista *f*

heron ['herən] *n* garza *f*

herring ['herɪŋ] *n* arenque *m*

hers [hɜːz] *poss pron* (a) *(attribute) (one thing)* suyo(a); *(more than one)* suyos(as); *(to distinguish)* de ella; **they are h., not his** son de ella, no de él (b) *(noun reference) (one thing)* el suyo/la suya; *(more than one)* los suyos/las suyas; **my car is blue and h. is red** mi coche es azul y el suyo es rojo

herself [hɜː'self] *pers pron* (a) *(reflexive)* se; **she dressed h.** se vistió (b) *(alone)* ella misma; **she was by h.** estaba sola (c) *(emphatic)* **she told me so h.** eso dijo ella

hesitant ['hezɪtənt] *adj* vacilante

hesitate ['hezɪteɪt] *vi* vacilar

hesitation [hezɪ'teɪʃən] *n* indecisión *f*

heterogeneous [hetərəʊ'dʒiːnɪəs] *adj* heterogéneo(a)

heterosexual [hetərəʊ'seksjʊəl] *adj & n* heterosexual *(mf)*

hey [heɪ] *interj* ¡oye!, ¡oiga!

heyday ['heɪdeɪ] *n* auge *m*, apogeo *m*

HGV [eɪtʃdʒiː'viː] *n Br (abbr* **heavy goods vehicle)** vehículo *m* de carga pesada

hi [haɪ] *interj Fam* ¡hola!

hiatus [haɪ'eɪtəs] *n Fml* laguna *f*

hibernate ['haɪbəneɪt] *vi* hibernar

hibernation [haɪbə'neɪʃən] *n* hibernación *f*

hibiscus [haɪ'bɪskəs] *n* hibisco *m*

hiccup, hiccough ['hɪkʌp] *n* hipo *m; Fam (minor problem)* problemilla *m;* **to have hiccups** tener hipo

hide¹ [haɪd] 1 *vt (pt* **hid** [hɪd]; *pp* **hidden** ['hɪdən]) *(conceal)* esconder; *(obscure)* ocultar

2 *vi* esconderse, ocultarse

3 *n* puesto *m*

hide² [haɪd] *n (of animal)* piel *f*

hide-and-seek [haɪdən'siːk] *n* escondite *m*

hideous ['hɪdɪəs] *adj (horrific)* horroroso(a); *(extremely ugly)* espantoso(a)

hide-out ['haɪdaʊt] *n* escondrijo *m*, guarida *f*

hiding¹ ['haɪdɪŋ] *n* **to go into h.** esconderse

hiding² ['haɪdɪŋ] *n Fam* paliza *f*

hierarchy ['haɪərɑːkɪ] *n* jerarquía *f*

hi-fi ['haɪfaɪ] *n* hifi *m;* **h. equipment** equipo *m* de alta fidelidad

high [haɪ] 1 *adj* (a) alto(a); **how h. is that wall?** ¿qué altura tiene esa pared?; **it's 3 feet h.** tiene 3 pies de alto; **h. chair** silla alta para niños; **h. jump** salto *m* de altura

(b) *(elevated)* elevado(a); **h. blood pressure** tensión alta; **h. prices** precios elevados; **to be in h. spirits** estar de buen humor

(c) *(important)* importante; **h. wind** viento *m* fuerte; **to have a h. opinion of sb** tener muy buena opinión de algn; **H. Court** Tribunal Supremo; **h. fidelity** alta fidelidad; **h. road** carretera *f* principal; **h. school** instituto *m* de enseñanza media; **the H. Street** la Calle Mayor

(d) *Fam (drugged)* colocado(a)

2 *adv* alto; **to fly h.** volar a gran altura

3 *n (high point)* punto máximo

highbrow ['haɪbraʊ] *adj & n* intelectual *(mf)*

high-class ['haɪklɑːs] *adj* de alta categoría

higher ['haɪə(r)] 1 *adj* superior; **h. education** enseñanza *f* superior

2 *n Scot Educ* **H.** = examen final de los estudios preuniversitarios

high-five ['haɪ'faɪv] *n US Fam* palmada *f* en el aire *(saludo entre dos)*

high-flier, high-flyer [haɪ'flaɪə(r)] *n Fig* = persona dotada y ambiciosa

high-handed [haɪ'hændɪd] *adj* despótico(a)

high-heeled ['haɪhiːld] *adj* de tacón alto

highlands ['haɪləndz] *npl* tierras altas

highlight ['haɪlaɪt] 1 *n* (a) *(in hair)* reflejo *m* (b) *(of event)* atracción *f* principal

2 *vt* (a) hacer resaltar (b) *(text)* marcar con un rotulador fosforescente

highly ['haɪlɪ] *adv (very)* sumamente; **to speak h. of sb** hablar muy bien de algn

highly-strung [haɪlɪ'strʌŋ] *adj* muy nervioso(a)

Highness ['haɪnɪs] *n* alteza *mf;* **Your H.** Su Alteza

high-pitched ['haɪpɪtʃt] *adj* estridente

high-powered ['haɪpaʊəd] *adj (person)* dinámico(a)

high-ranking ['haɪræŋkɪŋ] *adj* **h. official** alto funcionario

high-rise ['haɪraɪz] *adj* **h. building** rascacielos *m inv*

high-speed ['haɪspiːd] *adj* **h. lens** objetivo ultrarrápido; **h. train** tren *m* de alta velocidad

highway ['haɪweɪ] *n US* carretera *f*, autopista *f; Br* **H. Code** código *m* de la circulación

highwayman ['haɪweɪmən] *n* salteador *m* de caminos

hijack ['haɪdʒæk] 1 *vt* secuestrar

2 *n* secuestro *m*

hijacker ['haɪdʒækə(r)] *n* secuestrador(a) *m,f; (of planes)* pirata *mf* del aire

hike [haɪk] 1 *n* (a) *(walk)* excursión *f* (b) *price* **h.** aumento *m* de precio

2 *vi* ir de excursión

hiker ['haɪkə(r)] *n* excursionista *mf*

hilarious [hɪ'leərɪəs] *adj* graciosísimo(a)

hill [hɪl] *n* colina *f; (slope)* cuesta *f*

hillside ['hɪlsaɪd] n ladera f
hilltop ['hɪltɒp] n cima f de una colina
hilly ['hɪlɪ] adj (**hillier, hilliest**) accidentado(a)
hilt [hɪlt] n puño m, empuñadura f; **I'll support you up to the h.** te daré mi apoyo total
him [hɪm] pron (**a**) (direct object) lo, le; **hit h.!** ¡pégale!; **she loves h.** lo quiere (**b**) (indirect object) le; (with other third person pronouns) se; **give h. the money** dale el dinero; **give it to h.** dáselo (**c**) (after prep) él; **it's not like h. to say that** no es propio de él decir eso (**d**) Fam (as subject) él; **it's h.** es él
himself [hɪm'self] pers pron (**a**) (reflexive) se; **he hurt h.** se hizo daño (**b**) (alone) solo, por sí mismo; **by h.** solo (**c**) (emphatic) él mismo
hind¹ [haɪnd] adj trasero(a); **h. legs** patas traseras
hind² [haɪnd] n Zool cierva f
hinder ['hɪndə(r)] vt dificultar, estorbar; **to h. sb from doing sth** impedir a algn hacer algo
hindrance ['hɪndrəns] n estorbo m
hindsight ['haɪndsaɪt] n retrospectiva f
Hindu [hɪn'duː, 'hɪnduː] adj & n hindú (mf)
Hinduism ['hɪnduːɪzəm] n hinduismo m
hinge [hɪndʒ] **1** n bisagra f; Fig eje m
2 vt engoznar
► **hinge on** vt insep depender de
hint [hɪnt] **1** n (**a**) indirecta f; **to take the h.** coger la indirecta (**b**) (clue) pista f (**c**) (trace) pizca f (**d**) (advice) consejo m
2 vi (**a**) lanzar indirectas (**b**) (imply) insinuar algo
hip¹ [hɪp] n cadera f; **h. flask** petaca f
hip² [hɪp] adj Fam en la onda
hippie ['hɪpɪ] adj & n Fam hippy (mf)
hippopotamus [hɪpə'pɒtəməs] n hipopótamo m
hire ['haɪə(r)] **1** n alquiler m; **bicycles for h.** se alquilan bicicletas; **taxi for h.** taxi m libre; **h. purchase** compra f a plazos
2 vt (**a**) (rent) alquilar, Méx rentar (**b**) (employ) contratar
► **hire out** vt sep (car) alquilar, Méx rentar; (people) contratar
his [hɪz] **1** poss adj (one thing) su; (more than one) sus; (to distinguish) de él; **he washed h. face** se lavó la cara; **is it h. dog or hers?** ¿el perro es de él o de ella?
2 poss pron (attribute) (one thing) suyo(a); (more than one) suyos(as); (to distinguish) de él (**b**) (noun reference) (one thing) el suyo/la suya; (more than one) los suyos/las suyas; **my car is blue and h. is red** mi coche es azul y el suyo es rojo
Hispanic [hɪ'spænɪk] **1** adj hispánico(a)
2 n US hispano(a) m,f, latino(a) m,f
hiss [hɪs] **1** n siseo m; Th silbido m
2 vt & vi silbar
historian [hɪ'stɔːrɪən] n historiador(a) m,f
historic [hɪ'stɒrɪk] adj histórico(a)
historical [hɪ'stɒrɪkəl] adj histórico(a);

h. novel novela histórica
history ['hɪstərɪ] n historia f
hit [hɪt] **1** n (**a**) (blow) golpe m; **direct h.** impacto directo; Fam **h. list** lista negra; Fam **h. man** asesino m a sueldo (**b**) (success) éxito m; **h. parade** lista f de éxitos (**c**) Comput (visit to web site) acceso m, visita f
2 vt (pt & pp **hit**) (**a**) (strike) golpear, pegar; **he was h. in the leg** le dieron en la pierna; **the car h. the kerb** el coche chocó contra el bordillo; Fam Fig **to h. the roof** poner el grito en el cielo (**b**) (affect) afectar (**c**) **to h. the headlines** ser noticia
► **hit back** vi (reply to criticism) replicar
► **hit on** vt insep dar con; **we h. on the idea of ...** se nos ocurrió la idea de ...
► **hit out** vi **to h. out at sb** atacar a algn
► **hit upon** vt insep = **hit on**
hit-and-run [hɪtən'rʌn] adj **h. driver** = conductor que atropella a algn y no para
hitch [hɪtʃ] **1** n dificultad f
2 vt (fasten) atar
3 vi Fam (hitch-hike) hacer autostop
► **hitch up** vt sep remangarse
hitch-hike ['hɪtʃhaɪk] vi hacer autostop or dedo
hitch-hiker ['hɪtʃhaɪkə(r)] n autostopista mf
hitherto [hɪðə'tuː] adv Fml hasta la fecha
HIV [eɪtʃaɪ'viː] n (abbr human immunodeficiency virus) VIH m; **to be diagnosed HIV positive/negative** dar seropositivo(a)/seronegativo(a) en la prueba del SIDA
hive [haɪv] n colmena f; Fig lugar muy activo
HM (abbr His/Her Majesty) SM
hoard [hɔːd] **1** n (provisions) reservas fpl; (money etc) tesoro m
2 vt (objects) acumular; (money) atesorar
hoarding ['hɔːdɪŋ] n (temporary fence) valla f; Br (billboard) valla publicitaria
hoarfrost ['hɔːfrɒst] n escarcha f
hoarse [hɔːs] adj ronco(a); **to be h.** tener la voz ronca
hoax [həʊks] n (joke) broma pesada; (trick) engaño m
hob [hɒb] n (of cooker) encimera f
hobble ['hɒbəl] vi cojear
hobby ['hɒbɪ] n pasatiempo m, afición f
hobbyhorse ['hɒbɪhɔːs] n (toy) caballito m de juguete; Fig (fixed idea) idea fija, manía f
hobo ['həʊbəʊ] n US vagabundo(a) m,f
hockey ['hɒkɪ] n hockey m
hog [hɒg] **1** n cerdo m, puerco m; Fam **to go the whole h.** liarse la manta a la cabeza
2 vt Fam acaparar
hoist [hɔɪst] **1** n (crane) grúa f; (lift) montacargas m inv
2 vt levantar, subir; **to h. the flag** izar la bandera
hold [həʊld] **1** vt (pt & pp **held**) (**a**) (keep in hand) aguantar, tener (en la mano); (grip) agarrar; (support) (weight) soportar; (opinion) sostener; **to h. sb** abrazar a algn; **to h.**

sb's hand cogerle la mano a algn; *Fig* **she can h. her own in French** se defiende en francés
  (**b**) *(contain)* dar cabida a; **the jug holds a litre** en la jarra cabe un litro
  (**c**) *(meeting)* celebrar; *(conversation)* mantener
  (**d**) *(reserve)* guardar
  (**e**) **to h. office** ocupar un puesto
  (**f**) *(consider)* considerar
  (**g**) **he was held for two hours at the police station** estuvo detenido durante dos horas en la comisaría; **to h. one's breath** contener la respiración; **to h. sb hostage** retener a algn como rehén
  (**h**) *Tel* **to h. the line** no colgar
  2 *vi* (**a**) *(rope)* aguantar
  (**b**) *Fig (offer)* ser válido(a)
  3 *n* (**a**) **to get h. of** *(grip)* coger, agarrar; *Fig* localizar; **can you get h. of a newspaper?** ¿puedes conseguir un periódico?
  (**b**) *(control)* control *m*
  (**c**) *Naut* bodega *f*
  (**d**) *(in wrestling)* llave *f*
  ▸ **hold back 1** *vt sep (crowd)* contener; *(feelings)* reprimir; *(truth)* ocultar; **I don't want to h. you back** *(delay)* no quiero entretenerte
  2 *vi (hesitate)* vacilar
  ▸ **hold down** *vt sep* (**a**) *(control)* dominar (**b**) *Fam (job)* desempeñar
  ▸ **hold off** *vt sep* mantener a distancia
  ▸ **hold on** *vi* (**a**) *(keep a firm grasp)* agarrarse bien (**b**) *(wait)* esperar; *Tel* **h. on!** ¡no cuelgue!
  ▸ **hold out 1** *vt sep (hand)* tender
  2 *vi* (**a**) *(last) (things)* durar; *(person)* resistir
  (**b**) **to h. out for** insistir en
  ▸ **hold up** *vt sep* (**a**) *(hold) (rob) (train)* asaltar; *(bank)* atracar (**b**) *(delay)* retrasar; **we were held up for half an hour** sufrimos media hora de retraso (**c**) *(raise)* levantar (**d**) *(support)* apuntalar

holdall ['həʊldɔːl] *n Br* bolsa *f* de viaje
holder ['həʊldə(r)] *n* (**a**) *(receptacle)* recipiente *m* (**b**) *(owner)* poseedor(a) *m,f*; *(bearer)* portador(a) *m,f*; *(of passport)* titular *mf*; **record h.** plusmarquista *mf*
holding ['həʊldɪŋ] *n* (**a**) *(property)* propiedad *f* (**b**) *Fin* valor *m* en cartera; **h. company** holding *m*
hold-up ['həʊldʌp] *n* (**a**) *(robbery)* atraco *m* (**b**) *(delay)* retraso *m*; *(in traffic)* atasco *m*
hole [həʊl] *n* (**a**) *(agujero m*; *(large)* hoyo *m*; *(in the road)* bache *m* (**b**) *(in golf)* hoyo *m* (**c**) *Fam (of place)* antro *m*
holiday ['hɒlɪdeɪ] **1** *n (one day)* día *m* de fiesta; *Br (several days)* vacaciones *fpl*; **to be/go on h.** estar/ir de vacaciones; **h. resort** lugar turístico
  2 *vi* (**a**) *Br* pasar las vacaciones; *(in summer)* veranear
holiday-maker ['hɒlɪdeɪmeɪkə(r)] *n Br* turista *mf*; *(in summer)* veraneante *mf*

holiness ['həʊlɪnɪs] *n* santidad *f*
Holland ['hɒlənd] *n* Holanda
hollow ['hɒləʊ] **1** *adj* (**a**) hueco(a) (**b**) *(cheeks, eyes)* hundido(a) (**c**) *Fig (insincere)* falso(a); *(empty)* vacío(a)
  2 *n* hueco *m*; *Geog* hondonada *f*
  3 *vt* **to h. (out)** hacer un hueco en
holly ['hɒlɪ] *n* acebo *m*
holocaust ['hɒləkɔːst] *n* holocausto *m*
holster ['həʊlstə(r)] *n* pistolera *f*
holy ['həʊlɪ] *adj* sagrado(a), santo(a); *(blessed)* bendito(a); **H. Ghost** Espíritu Santo; **H. Land** Tierra Santa; **H. See** Santa Sede
homage ['hɒmɪdʒ] *n* homenaje *m*; **to pay h. to sb** rendir homenaje a algn
home [həʊm] **1** *n* (**a**) casa *f*, hogar *m*; **at h.** en casa; *Fig* **make yourself at h.!** ¡estás en tu casa!; *Fig* **to feel at h.** estar a gusto; **h. banking** telebanco *m*; *Comput* **h. page** *(initial page)* portada *f*, página *f* inicial *or* de inicio; *(personal page)* página personal; **h. shopping** telecompra *f*; **h. shopping channel** teletienda *f*
  (**b**) *(institution)* asilo *m*; **old people's h.** asilo de ancianos
  (**c**) *(country)* patria *f*
  (**d**) *Sport* **to play at h.** jugar en casa; *US* **h. base** *(in baseball)* base *f* del bateador; **h. run** carrera completa
  2 *adj* (**a**) *(domestic)* del hogar; *Br* **h. help** asistenta *f*
  (**b**) *Pol* interior; **h. affairs** asuntos *mpl* interiores; *Br* **H. Office** Ministerio *m* del Interior; *Br* **H. Secretary** Ministro(a) *m,f* del Interior
  (**c**) *(native)* natal
  3 *adv* en casa; **to go h.** irse a casa; **to leave h.** irse de casa
homeland ['həʊmlænd] *n* patria *f*; *(birthplace)* tierra *f* natal
homeless ['həʊmlɪs] **1** *adj* sin techo
  2 *npl* **the h.** los sin techo
homely ['həʊmlɪ] *adj* (**homelier, homeliest**) (**a**) *Br (person)* casero(a); *(atmosphere)* familiar (**b**) *US (unattractive)* sin atractivo
home-made ['həʊmmeɪd] *adj* casero(a)
homeopathy [həʊmɪ'ɒpəθɪ] *n US* = **homoeopathy**
homesick ['həʊmsɪk] *adj* **to be h.** tener morriña
homeward(s) ['həʊmwəd(z)] *adv* hacia casa
homework ['həʊmwɜːk] *n* deberes *mpl*
homey ['həʊmɪ] *adj US Fam* hogareño(a)
homicide ['hɒmɪsaɪd] *n* homicidio *m*
homing ['həʊmɪŋ] *adj* (**a**) **h. device** cabeza buscadora *f* (**b**) **h. pigeon** paloma mensajera
homoeopathy [həʊmɪ'ɒpəθɪ] *n* homeopatía *f*
homogeneous [hɒmə'dʒiːnɪəs] *adj* homogéneo(a)
homosexual [həʊməʊ'seksjʊəl] *adj & n* homosexual *(mf)*

Honduran [hɒnˈdjʊərən] *adj & n* hondure-ño(a) *(m,f)*

Honduras [hɒnˈdjʊərəs] *n* Honduras

honest [ˈɒnɪst] *adj* honrado(a); *(sincere)* sincero(a), franco(a); *(fair)* justo(a); **the h. truth** la pura verdad

honestly [ˈɒnɪstlɪ] *adv* honradamente; *(question)* ¿de verdad?; *(exclamation)* ¡hay que ver!; **h., it doesn't matter** de verdad, no tiene importancia

honesty [ˈɒnɪstɪ] *n* honradez *f*

honey [ˈhʌnɪ] *n* miel *f*; *US Fam (endearment)* cariño *m*

honeycomb [ˈhʌnɪkəʊm] *n* panal *m*

honeymoon [ˈhʌnɪmuːn] *n* luna *f* de miel

honeysuckle [ˈhʌnɪsʌkəl] *n* madreselva *f*

honk [hɒŋk] *vi Aut* tocar la bocina

honor [ˈɒnər] *n & vt US =* **honour**

honorary [ˈɒnərərɪ] *adj (member)* honorario(a); *(duties)* honorífico(a)

honour [ˈɒnər] **1** *n* (a) honor *m* (b) *US Jur* **Her H./His H./Your H.** Su Señoría *f* (c) *Mil* **honours** honores *mpl* (d) **Honours degree** licenciatura *f* superior

2 *vt* (a) *(respect)* honrar (b) *(obligation)* cumplir con

honourable [ˈɒnərəbəl] *adj (person)* honrado(a); *(action)* honroso(a)

hood [hʊd] *n* (a) *(of garment)* capucha *f* (b) *(of car)* capota *f*; *US (bonnet)* capó *m* (c) *US Fam (gangster)* matón(ona) *m,f*

hoodlum [ˈhuːdləm] *n* matón *m*

hoodwink [ˈhʊdwɪŋk] *vt* engañar

hoof [huːf] *n (pl* **hoofs** *or* **hooves)** *(of horse)* casco *m*; *(of cow, sheep)* pezuña *f*

hook [hʊk] **1** *n* (a) gancho *m*; *(in fishing)* anzuelo *m*; *Sewing* **hooks and eyes** corchetes *mpl*; **to take the phone off the h.** descolgar el teléfono (b) *(in boxing)* gancho *m*

2 *vt* enganchar

▸ **hook up** *vt sep & vi Rad, TV & Comput* conectar (**with** con)

hooked [hʊkt] *adj* (a) *(nose)* aguileño(a) (b) *Fam (addicted)* enganchado(a) (**on** a); **to get h.** engancharse

hooker [ˈhʊkər] *n US Fam (prostitute)* fulana *f*, puta *f*

hookey [ˈhʊkɪ] *n US Fam* **to play h.** hacer novillos

hook-up [ˈhʊkʌp] *n* (a) *Comput* conexión *f* (b) *Rad & TV* emisión *f* múltiple

hooky [ˈhʊkɪ] *n US Fam =* **hookey**

hooligan [ˈhuːlɪgən] *n Fam* gamberro(a) *m,f*

hoop [huːp] *n* aro *m*; *(of barrel)* fleje *m*

hooray [huːˈreɪ] *interj* ¡hurra!

hoot [huːt] **1** *n* (a) ululato *m*; *Fam* **hoots of laughter** carcajadas *fpl*; *Fam* **I don't care a h.** me importa un pepino (b) *(of car horn)* bocinazo *m*

2 *vi* (a) *(owl)* ulular (b) *(car)* dar un bocinazo; *(train)* silbar; *(siren)* pitar

hooter [ˈhuːtər] *n esp Br (of car)* bocina *f*;

(siren) sirena *f*

Hoover® [ˈhuːvər] *Br* **1** *n* aspiradora *f*

2 *vt* **to h.** pasar la aspiradora por

hooves [huːvz] *pl of* **hoof**

hop¹ [hɒp] **1** *vi* saltar; **to h. on one leg** andar a la pata coja

2 *n (small jump)* brinco *m*

hop² [hɒp] *n Bot* lúpulo *m*

hope [həʊp] **1** *n* esperanza *f*; *(false)* ilusión *f*; **to have little h. of doing sth** tener pocas posibilidades de hacer algo

2 *vt & vi* esperar; **I h. so/not** espero que sí/no; **we h. you're well** esperamos que estés bien

hopeful [ˈhəʊpfʊl] *adj (confident)* optimista; *(promising)* prometedor(a)

hopefully [ˈhəʊpfʊlɪ] *adv* (a) *(confidently)* con optimismo (b) **h. the weather will be fine** *(it is hoped)* esperemos que haga buen tiempo

hopeless [ˈhəʊplɪs] *adj* desesperado(a); *Fam* **to be h. at sports** ser negado(a) para los deportes

hopelessly [ˈhəʊplɪslɪ] *adv* desesperadamente; **h. lost** completamente perdido(a)

horde [hɔːd] *n* multitud *f*

horizon [həˈraɪzən] *n* horizonte *m*

horizontal [hɒrɪˈzɒntəl] *adj* horizontal

hormone [ˈhɔːməʊn] *n* hormona *f*

horn [hɔːn] *n* (a) cuerno *m* (b) *Fam Mus* trompeta *f*; *French* **h.** trompa *f*; **hunting h.** cuerno *m* de caza (c) *Aut* bocina *f*

hornet [ˈhɔːnɪt] *n* avispón *m*

horny [ˈhɔːnɪ] *adj* (**hornier, horniest**) (a) *(hands)* calloso(a) (b) *very Fam (sexually aroused)* caliente, cachondo(a)

horoscope [ˈhɒrəskəʊp] *n* horóscopo *m*

horrendous [hɒˈrendəs] *adj* horrendo(a)

horrible [ˈhɒrəbəl] *adj* horrible

horrid [ˈhɒrɪd] *adj* horrible

horrific [həˈrɪfɪk] *adj* horrendo(a)

horrify [ˈhɒrɪfaɪ] *vt* horrorizar

horror [ˈhɒrə(r)] *n* horror *m*; *Fam* **a little h.** un diablillo; **h. film** película *f* de miedo *or* de terror

hors d'oeuvre [ɔːˈdɜːvr] *n (pl* **hors d'oeuvres)** entremés *m*

horse [hɔːs] *n* (a) caballo *m*; **h. race** carrera de caballos (b) *(in gymnastics)* potro *m* (c) *Tech* caballete *m* (d) **h. chestnut** *(tree)* castaño *m* de Indias

horseback [ˈhɔːsbæk] *n* **on h.** a caballo; *US* **h. riding** equitación *f*

horseman [ˈhɔːsmən] *n* jinete *m*

horseplay [ˈhɔːspleɪ] *n* payasadas *fpl*

horsepower [ˈhɔːspaʊə(r)] *n* caballo *m* (de vapor)

horseradish [ˈhɔːsrædɪʃ] *n* rábano rusticano

horseshoe [ˈhɔːsʃuː] *n* herradura *f*

horsewoman [ˈhɔːswʊmən] *n* amazona *f*

horticulture [ˈhɔːtɪkʌltʃə(r)] *n* horticultura

hose [həʊz] *n (pipe)* manguera *f*

hosiery ['həʊzɪərɪ] n medias fpl y calcetines mpl

hospice ['hɒspɪs] n residencia f para enfermos terminales

hospitable ['hɒspɪtəbəl, hɒ'spɪtəbəl] adj hospitalario(a); **h. atmosphere** ambiente acogedor

hospital ['hɒspɪtəl] n hospital m

hospitality [hɒspɪ'tælɪtɪ] n hospitalidad f

Host [həʊst] n Rel hostia f

host¹ [həʊst] **1** n (a) (at home) anfitrión m (b) Th & TV presentador m (c) Biol huésped m
2 vt Th & TV presentar

host² [həʊst] n (large number) montón m

hostage ['hɒstɪdʒ] n rehén m

hostel ['hɒstəl] n hostal m

hostess ['həʊstɪs] n (a) (at home etc) anfitriona f (b) Th & TV presentadora f (c) (air) **h. azafata** f

hostile ['hɒstaɪl] adj hostil

hostility [hɒ'stɪlɪtɪ] n hostilidad f

hot [hɒt] adj (hotter, hottest) (a) caliente; Fig **h. line** teléfono rojo; **h. spot** (nightclub) club nocturno (b) (weather) caluroso(a); **it's very h.** hace mucho calor; **to feel h.** tener calor (c) (spicy) picante; **h. dog** perrito m caliente (d) (temper) fuerte (e) Fam (fresh) de última hora (f) Fam (good) bueno(a); **it's not so h.** no es nada del otro mundo (g) (popular) popular (h) (dangerous) peligroso(a); Fig **to get oneself into h. water** meterse en un lío; Fam **h. seat** primera fila
▸ **hot up** vi Fam **things are hotting up** la cosa se está poniendo al rojo vivo

hotbed ['hɒtbed] n Fig hervidero m

hotel [həʊ'tel] n hotel m

hotelier [həʊ'teljeɪ] n hotelero(a) m,f

hot-headed [hɒt'hedɪd] adj impetuoso(a)

hothouse ['hɒthaʊs] n invernadero m

hotplate ['hɒtpleɪt] n (cooker) placa f de cocina; (to keep food warm) calientaplatos m inv

hotshot ['hɒtʃɒt] n Fam as m

hot-water [hɒt'wɔːtə(r)] adj **h. bottle** bolsa f de agua caliente

hound [haʊnd] **1** n perro m de caza
2 vt acosar

hour ['aʊə(r)] n hora f; **60 miles an h.** 60 millas por hora; **by the h.** por horas; **h. hand** manecilla f

hourly ['aʊəlɪ] **1** adj cada hora
2 adv por horas

house n ['haʊs] (a) casa f; **at my h.** en mi casa; Fig **on the h.** cortesía de la casa; **h. arrest** arresto domiciliario; **h. plant** planta f de interior (b) Pol **H. of Commons** Cámara f de los Comunes; **H. of Lords** Cámara de los Lores; US **H. of Representatives** Cámara de Representantes; **Houses of Parliament** Parlamento m (c) (company) empresa f; **publishing h.** editorial f (d) Th sala f
2 vt [haʊz] alojar; (store) guardar

houseboat ['haʊsbəʊt] n casa f flotante

housebreaking ['haʊsbreɪkɪŋ] n allanamiento m de morada

housebroken ['haʊsbrəʊkən] adj US (pet) = que ya ha aprendido a no hacer sus necesidades en casa

housecoat ['haʊskəʊt] n bata f

household ['haʊshəʊld] n hogar m; **h. products** productos domésticos

housekeeper ['haʊskiːpə(r)] n ama f de llaves

housekeeping ['haʊskiːpɪŋ] n administración doméstica; **h. money** dinero m para los gastos domésticos

house-train ['haʊstreɪn] vt (pet) educar

house-warming ['haʊswɔːmɪŋ] n **h. (party)** = fiesta que se da al estrenar casa

housewife ['haʊswaɪf] n ama f de casa

housework ['haʊswɜːk] n trabajo doméstico

housing ['haʊzɪŋ] n vivienda f; **h. estate** urbanización f

hovel ['hʌvəl, 'hɒvəl] n casucha f

hover ['hɒvə(r)] vi (bird) cernerse; (aircraft) permanecer inmóvil (en el aire)

hovercraft ['hɒvəkrɑːft] n aerodeslizador m

how [haʊ] adv (a) (direct question) ¿cómo?; **h. are you?** ¿cómo estás?; Fam **h. come?** ¿por qué? (b) (indirect question) cómo; **I don't know h. to tell you** no sé cómo decírtelo (c) (very) qué; **h. funny!** ¡qué divertido! (d) (suggestion) **h. about going to the cinema?** ¿te apetece ir al cine?; **h. about a stroll?** ¿qué te parece un paseo? (e) (quantity) cuánto; **h. old is she?** ¿cuántos años tiene?; **h. tall are you?** ¿cuánto mides? (f) **h. many?** ¿cuántos(as)?; **h. much?** ¿cuánto(a)?; **I don't know h. many people there were** no sé cuánta gente había

however [haʊ'evə(r)] adv (a) (nevertheless) no obstante, sin embargo (b) (with adjective) **h. difficult it may be** por difícil que sea; **h. much** por mucho que (+ subj)

howl [haʊl] **1** n aullido m
2 vi aullar

howler ['haʊlə(r)] n Fam despiste m

HP, hp [eɪtʃ'piː] n (a) Br (abbr **hire purchase**) compra f a plazos (b) (abbr **horsepower**) cv mpl

HQ [eɪtʃ'kjuː] n (abbr **headquarters**) sede f, central f

hub [hʌb] n Aut cubo m; Fig eje m

hubbub ['hʌbʌb] n alboroto m

hubcap ['hʌbkæp] n Aut tapacubos m inv

huddle ['hʌdəl] **1** n grupo m
2 vi **to h. (up** or **together)** acurrucarse

hue¹ [hjuː] n (colour) tinte m; (shade) matiz m

hue² [hjuː] n **h. and cry** fuerte protesta f

huff [hʌf] n **to be in a h.** estar de mala uva

hug [hʌg] **1** vt abrazar
2 n abrazo m

huge [hjuːdʒ] adj enorme

hugely ['hjuːdʒlɪ] adv enormemente

hulk [hʌlk] n (a) Naut casco m (b) (thing, person) armatoste m

hull [hʌl] n Naut casco m

hullabal(l)oo [hʌləbə'luː] n Fam follón m

hullo [hʌ'ləʊ] interj Br ¡hola!

hum [hʌm] **1** vt (tune) tararear
  2 vi (bees, engine) zumbar; (sing) tararear
  3 n (of bees) zumbido m

human ['hjuːmən] **1** adj humano(a); **h. race** raza humana; **h. being** ser humano
  2 n ser humano

humane [hjuː'meɪn] adj humano(a)

humanitarian [hjuːmænɪ'teərɪən] adj humanitario(a)

humanity [hjuː'mænɪtɪ] n (a) humanidad f (b) Univ **the humanities** las humanidades

humble ['hʌmbəl] **1** adj humilde
  2 vt humillar

humbug ['hʌmbʌg] n (a) Fam tonterías fpl (b) Br (mint) **h.** caramelo m de menta

humdrum ['hʌmdrʌm] adj monótono(a), aburrido(a)

humid ['hjuːmɪd] adj húmedo(a)

humidity [hjuː'mɪdɪtɪ] n humedad f

humiliate [hjuː'mɪlɪeɪt] vt humillar

humiliation [hjuːmɪlɪ'eɪʃən] n humillación f

humility [hjuː'mɪlɪtɪ] n humildad f

humor ['hjuːmə(r)] n US = **humour**

humorous ['hjuːmərəs] adj (writer) humorístico(a); (person, story) gracioso(a), divertido(a)

humour ['hjuːmə(r)] **1** n humor m
  2 vt seguir la corriente a

hump [hʌmp] **1** n (a) (on back) joroba f (b) (small hill) montículo m
  2 vt Br Fam (carry) cargar (a la espalda)

humus ['hjuːməs] n mantillo m, humus m

hunch [hʌntʃ] n Fam corazonada f

hunchback ['hʌntʃbæk] n jorobado(a) m,f

hundred ['hʌndrəd] **1** n cien m, ciento m; (rough number) centenar m; **a h. and twenty-five** ciento veinticinco; **five h.** quinientos
  2 adj cien; **a h. people** cien personas; **a h. percent** cien por cien; **two h. chairs** doscientas sillas

hundredth ['hʌndrədθ] adj & n centésimo(a) (m,f)

hundredweight ['hʌndrədweɪt] n Br = 50,8 kg; US = 45,36 kg

hung [hʌŋ] **1** adj Fam (a) **h. over** con resaca (b) **h. up** acomplejado(a)
  2 pt & pp of **hang**

Hungarian [hʌŋ'geərɪən] adj & n húngaro(a) (m,f)

Hungary ['hʌŋgərɪ] n Hungría

hunger ['hʌŋgə(r)] **1** n hambre f; **h. strike** huelga f de hambre
  2 vi Fig tener hambre (**for** de)

hungry ['hʌŋgrɪ] adj (hungrier, hungriest) hambriento(a); **to be h.** tener hambre; **to go h.** pasar hambre

hunk [hʌŋk] n (a) (piece) buen pedazo m (b) Fam (man) machote m

hunt [hʌnt] **1** vt cazar
  2 vi (for game) cazar; (search) buscar
  3 n caza f; (search) búsqueda f
  ▸ **hunt down** vt sep perseguir

hunter ['hʌntə(r)] n cazador(a) m,f

hunting ['hʌntɪŋ] n caza f; (expedition) cacería f

hurdle ['hɜːdəl] n Sport valla f; Fig obstáculo m

hurl [hɜːl] vt arrojar, lanzar

hurrah [hʊ'rɑː], **hurray** [hʊ'reɪ] interj ¡hurra!; **h. for John!** ¡viva John!

hurricane ['hʌrɪkən, 'hʌrɪkeɪn] n huracán m

hurried ['hʌrɪd] adj apresurado(a); (action etc) hecho(a) de prisa

hurriedly ['hʌrɪdlɪ] adv deprisa, apresuradamente

hurry ['hʌrɪ] **1** vi darse prisa
  2 vt meter prisa a
  3 n **to be in a h.** tener prisa

hurt [hɜːt] **1** vt (pt & pp hurt) hacer daño a; (wound) herir; (feelings) ofender
  2 vi doler; **my arm hurts** me duele el brazo; Fam **it doesn't h. to go out once in a while** no viene mal salir de vez en cuando
  3 adj (physically) herido(a); (mentally) dolido(a)

hurtful ['hɜːtfʊl] adj hiriente

hurtle ['hɜːtəl] vi lanzarse; **to h. down** desplomarse

husband ['hʌzbənd] n marido m, esposo m

hush [hʌʃ] **1** vt callar; **to h. sth up** echar tierra a un asunto
  2 n silencio m
  3 interj ¡silencio!

hush-hush [hʌʃ'hʌʃ] adj Fam confidencial

husky[1] ['hʌskɪ] adj (huskier, huskiest) ronco(a)

husky[2] ['hʌskɪ] n (dog) perro m esquimal

hustings ['hʌstɪŋz] npl Pol (a) (platform) tribuna f electoral (b) (election) elecciones fpl

hustle ['hʌsəl] **1** vt (a) (jostle) empujar (b) Fam meter prisa a
  2 n bullicio m; **h. and bustle** ajetreo m

hut [hʌt] n cabaña f; (shed) cobertizo m; Mil barraca f

hutch [hʌtʃ] n jaula f; **rabbit h.** conejera f

hyacinth ['haɪəsɪnθ] n jacinto m

hybrid ['haɪbrɪd] adj & n híbrido(a) (m,f)

hydrant ['haɪdrənt] n **fire h.** boca f de incendio

hydraulic [haɪ'drɒlɪk] adj hidráulico(a)

hydrocarbon [haɪdrəʊ'kɑːbən] n hidrocarburo m

hydrochloric [haɪdrəʊ'klɒrɪk] adj **h. acid** ácido clorhídrico

hydroelectric [haɪdrəʊɪ'lektrɪk] adj hidroeléctrico(a)

hydrofoil ['haɪdrəfɔɪl] n hidroala f

hydrogen ['haɪdrədʒən] n hidrógeno m

hydroplane ['haɪdrəpleɪn] *n US (seaplane)* hidroavión *m*

hyena [haɪ'iːnə] *n* hiena *f*

hygiene ['haɪdʒiːn] *n* higiene *f*

hygienic [haɪ'dʒiːnɪk] *adj* higiénico(a)

hymn [hɪm] *n* himno *m*; **h. book** cantoral *m*

hype [haɪp] *n Fam* campaña publicitaria, movida *f*

hyper- ['haɪpə(r)] *pref* hiper-; **hyperactive** hiperactivo(a)

hypermarket ['haɪpəmɑːkɪt] *n Br* hipermercado *m*

hypersensitive [haɪpə'sensɪtɪv] *adj* hipersensible

hyphen ['haɪfən] *n* guión *m*

hypnosis [hɪp'nəʊsɪs] *n* hipnosis *f*

hypnotist ['hɪpnətɪst] *n* hipnotizador(a) *m,f*

hypnotize ['hɪpnətaɪz] *vt* hipnotizar

hypochondriac [haɪpə'kɒndrɪæk] *adj & n* hipocondríaco(a) *(m,f)*

hypocrisy [hɪ'pɒkrəsɪ] *n* hipocresía *f*

hypocrite ['hɪpəkrɪt] *n* hipócrita *mf*

hypocritical [hɪpə'krɪtɪkəl] *adj* hipócrita

hypodermic [haɪpə'dɜːmɪk] *adj Med* hipodérmico(a); **h. needle** aguja hipodérmica

hypothesis [haɪ'pɒθɪsɪs] *n (pl* **hypotheses** [haɪ'pɒθɪsiːz]) hipótesis *f*

hypothetic(al) [haɪpə'θetɪk(əl)] *adj* hipotético(a)

hysteria [hɪ'stɪərɪə] *n* histeria *f*

hysterical [hɪ'sterɪkəl] *adj* histérico(a)

hysterics [hɪ'sterɪks] *npl* (**a**) ataque *m* de histeria (**b**) *Fam (of laughter)* ataque *m* de risa

I, i [aɪ] *n (the letter)* I, i *f*

I [aɪ] *pers pron* yo *(usually omitted in Spanish, except for contrast)*; **I know her** (yo) la conozco

ICBM [aɪsiːbiː'em] *n (abbr* **intercontinental ballistic missile)** misil *m* balístico intercontinental

ice [aɪs] **1** *n* hielo *m*; **i. axe** pico *m* (de alpinista); **i. cream** helado *m*; **i. cube** cubito *m* de hielo; **i. hockey** hockey *m* sobre hielo; *Br* **i. lolly** polo *m*; **i. rink** pista *f* de patinaje; **i. skate** patín *m* de cuchilla
2 *vt (cake)* alcorzar
▸ **ice over, ice up** *vi (pond etc)* helarse; *(windscreen, plane wings)* cubrirse de hielo

iceberg ['aɪsbɜːg] *n* iceberg *m*

icebox ['aɪsbɒks] *n* (**a**) *(compartment of fridge)* congelador *m* (**b**) *US (fridge)* nevera *f*, frigorífico *m*, *Andes* frigider *m*, *RP* heladera *f*

icecap ['aɪskæp] *n* casquete *m* glaciar

Iceland ['aɪslənd] *n* Islandia *f*

ice-skating ['aɪsskeɪtɪŋ] *n* patinaje *m* sobre hielo

icicle ['aɪsɪkəl] *n* carámbano *m*

icing ['aɪsɪŋ] *n* alcorza *f*; **i. sugar** azúcar *m* glas

icon ['aɪkɒn] *n* icono *m*

icy ['aɪsɪ] *adj* (**icier, iciest**) *(road etc)* helado(a); *Fig (smile)* glacial

ID [aɪ'diː] *n US* documentación *f*; **ID card** DNI *m*

I'd [aɪd] = **I would**; **I had**

idea [aɪ'dɪə] *n* (**a**) idea *f* (**b**) *(aim)* intención *f* (**c**) *(impression)* impresión *f*

ideal [aɪ'dɪəl] *adj & n* ideal *(m)*

idealist [aɪ'dɪəlɪst] *n* idealista *mf*

idealistic [aɪdɪə'lɪstɪk] *adj* idealista

idealize [aɪ'dɪəlaɪz] *vt* idealizar

ideally [aɪ'dɪəlɪ] *adv* (**a**) *(perfectly)* perfectamente (**b**) *(in the best conditions)* de ser posible

identical [aɪ'dentɪkəl] *adj* idéntico(a)

identification [aɪdentɪfɪ'keɪʃən] *n* (**a**) identificación *f* (**b**) *(papers)* documentación *f*

identify [aɪ'dentɪfaɪ] **1** *vt (body)* identificar; *(cause)* descubrir
2 *vi* identificarse (**with** con)

Identikit® [aɪ'dentɪkɪt] *n* **I. picture** retrato *m* robot

identity [aɪ'dentɪtɪ] *n* identidad *f*; **i. card** carné *m* de identidad; **proof of i.** prueba *f* de identidad

ideological [aɪdɪə'lɒdʒɪkəl] *adj* ideológico(a)

ideology [aɪdɪ'ɒlədʒɪ] *n* ideología *f*

idiom ['ɪdɪəm] *n* modismo *m*; *Fig (style)* lenguaje *m*

idiomatic [ɪdɪə'mætɪk] *adj* idiomático(a)

idiosyncrasy [ɪdɪəʊ'sɪŋkrəsɪ] *n* idiosincrasia *f*

idiot ['ɪdɪət] *n* idiota *mf*, tonto(a) *m,f*

idiotic [ɪdɪ'ɒtɪk] *adj (behaviour)* idiota, tonto(a); *(joke, plan)* estúpido(a)

idle ['aɪdəl] **1** *adj* holgazán(ana); *(not working) (person)* desempleado(a); *(machinery)* parado(a); *(gossip)* frívolo(a); *(threat)* vano(a)
2 *vi (engine)* funcionar en vacío
▸ **idle away** *vt sep (time)* desperdiciar

idleness ['aɪdəlnɪs] *n (laziness)* holgazanería *f*; *(unemployment)* desempleo *m*; *(stoppage)* paro *m*

idol ['aɪdəl] *n* ídolo *m*

idolize ['aɪdəlaɪz] *vt* idolatrar

idyllic [ɪ'dɪlɪk] *adj* idílico(a)

i.e. *(abbr* **id est)** i.e.

if [ɪf] **1** *conj* (**a**) si; **if at all** si acaso; **rarely, if ever** raras veces; **if I were rich** si fuera rico(a); **if necessary** en caso de que sea necesario; **if not** si no; **if so** de ser así; **if I were you** yo en tu lugar (**b**) *(whenever)* si; **if you need help, ask** siempre que necesites ayuda, pídela (**c**) *(although)* aunque, si bien (**d**) *(exclamations)* **if only I'd known!** ¡de haberlo sabido!; **if only she were here!** ¡ojalá estuviera aquí!
2 *n* **ifs and buts** pegas *fpl*

igloo ['ɪgluː] *n* iglú *m*

ignite [ɪg'naɪt] **1** *vt* encender
2 *vi* encenderse

ignition [ɪg'nɪʃən] *n* ignición *f*; *Aut* encendido *m*; **i. key** llave *f* de contacto

ignorance ['ɪgnərəns] *n* ignorancia *f*

ignorant ['ɪgnərənt] *adj* ignorante (**of** de); **to be i. of the facts** ignorar *or* desconocer los hechos

ignore [ɪg'nɔː(r)] *vt (warning, remark)* no hacer caso de; *(behaviour, fact)* pasar por alto

ill [ɪl] **1** *adj* (**a**) enfermo(a); **to be taken i.** caer enfermo(a); **to feel i.** encontrarse mal (**b**) *(bad)* malo(a); **i. feeling** resentimiento *m*; **i. will** mala voluntad
2 *n* mal *m*
3 *adv* difícilmente

I'll [aɪl] = **I shall; I will**
ill-advised [ɪləd'vaɪzd] *adj (person)* imprudente; *(act)* desatinado(a); **you'd be i. to go**
harías mal en ir
ill-disposed [ɪldɪ'spəʊzd] *adj* poco dispues-
to(a)
illegal [ɪ'liːgəl] *adj* ilegal
illegible [ɪ'ledʒɪbəl] *adj* ilegible
illegitimate [ɪlɪ'dʒɪtɪmɪt] *adj* ilegítimo(a)
ill-fated [ɪl'feɪtɪd] *adj* abocado(a) al fracaso
ill-founded [ɪl'faʊndɪd] *adj* infundado(a)
illicit [ɪ'lɪsɪt] *adj* ilícito(a)
illiteracy [ɪ'lɪtərəsɪ] *n* analfabetismo *m*
illiterate [ɪ'lɪtərɪt] *adj (person)* analfabe-
to(a); *Fam (uneducated)* inculto(a)
illness ['ɪlnɪs] *n* enfermedad *f*
illogical [ɪ'lɒdʒɪkəl] *adj* ilógico(a)
ill-treat [ɪl'triːt] *vt* maltratar
illuminate [ɪ'luːmɪneɪt] *vt* (**a**) *(light up)* iluminar, alumbrar; *Fig (clarify)* aclarar (**b**) *(manuscript)* iluminar
illuminating [ɪ'luːmɪneɪtɪŋ] *adj (experience,
book)* instructivo(a); *(remark)* revelador(a)
illumination [ɪluːmɪ'neɪʃən] *n* (**a**) *(light)* iluminación *f*; *Fig (clarification)* aclaración *f* (**b**) *Br*
illuminations iluminación *f*
illusion [i'luːʒən] *n* ilusión *f*; **to be under the
i. that ...** me trae sin cuidado si ...
illusory [ɪ'luːsərɪ] *adj* ilusorio(a)
illustrate ['ɪləstreɪt] *vt* ilustrar
illustration [ɪlə'streɪʃən] *n* ilustración *f*;
(example) ejemplo *m*
illustrious [ɪ'lʌstrɪəs] *adj* ilustre
I'm [aɪm] = **I am**
image ['ɪmɪdʒ] *n* imagen *f*
imagery ['ɪmɪdʒərɪ] *n Lit* imágenes *fpl*
imaginary [ɪ'mædʒɪnərɪ] *adj* imaginario(a)
imagination [ɪmædʒɪ'neɪʃən] *n* imaginación *f*; *(inventiveness)* inventiva *f*
imaginative [ɪ'mædʒɪnətɪv] *adj* imaginati-
vo(a)
imagine [ɪ'mædʒɪn] *vt (visualize)* imaginar;
(think) suponer, imaginarse; **just i.!** ¡imagínate!
imbalance [ɪm'bæləns] *n* desequilibrio *m*
imbecile ['ɪmbɪsiːl] *n* imbécil *mf*
imitate ['ɪmɪteɪt] *vt* imitar
imitation [ɪmɪ'teɪʃən] **1** *n* imitación *f*, copia *f*;
Pej remedo *m*
  2 *adj* de imitación
immaculate [ɪ'mækjʊlɪt] *adj (clean)* inmacu-
lado(a); *(tidy)* perfectamente ordenado(a);
(clothes) impecable; *(work)* perfecto(a); **the
I. Conception** la Inmaculada Concepción
immaterial [ɪmə'tɪərɪəl] *adj* irrelevante; **it's i.
to me whether ...** me trae sin cuidado si ...
immature [ɪmə'tjʊə(r)] *adj* inmaduro(a)
immediate [ɪ'miːdɪət] *adj* (**a**) inmediato(a);
(urgent) urgente (**b**) *(close)* cercano(a); *(danger)* inminente (**c**) *(cause)* primero(a)
immediately [ɪ'miːdɪətlɪ] **1** *adv* (**a**) inmediatamente (**b**) *(directly)* directamente

  2 *conj* en cuanto
immense [ɪ'mens] *adj* inmenso(a), enorme
immensely [ɪ'menslɪ] *adv (rich)* enormemente; *(interesting, difficult)* sumamente
immerse [ɪ'mɜːs] *vt* sumergir (**in** en); *Fig* **to
be immersed in sth** estar absorto(a) en algo
immersion [ɪ'mɜːʃən] *n* inmersión *f*; *Br* **i.
heater** calentador *m* de inmersión; **i. course**
cursillo intensivo
immigrant ['ɪmɪgrənt] *adj & n* inmigrante
(mf)
immigration [ɪmɪ'greɪʃən] *n* inmigración *f*
imminent ['ɪmɪnənt] *adj* inminente
immobile [ɪ'məʊbaɪl] *adj* inmóvil
immobilize [ɪ'məʊbɪlaɪz] *vt* inmovilizar
immodest [ɪ'mɒdɪst] *adj* indecente
immoral [ɪ'mɒrəl] *adj* inmoral
immortal [ɪ'mɔːtəl] *adj* inmortal
immortality [ɪmɔː'tælɪtɪ] *n* inmortalidad *f*
immortalize [ɪ'mɔːtəlaɪz] *vt* inmortalizar
immune [ɪ'mjuːn] *adj* inmune; *(exempt)*
exento(a)
immunity [ɪ'mjuːnɪtɪ] *n* inmunidad *f*
immunize ['ɪmjʊnaɪz] *vt* inmunizar (**against**
contra)
impact ['ɪmpækt] *n* impacto *m*; *(crash)* choque *m*
impair [ɪm'peə(r)] *vt* perjudicar; *(sight etc)*
dañar
impart [ɪm'pɑːt] *vt Fml (news)* comunicar;
(knowledge) transmitir
impartial [ɪm'pɑːʃəl] *adj* imparcial
impassable [ɪm'pɑːsəbəl] *adj (road, ground)*
intransitable; *(barrier)* infranqueable
impasse [æm'pɑːs] *n* punto muerto
impassive [ɪm'pæsɪv] *adj* impasible
impatience [ɪm'peɪʃəns] *n* impaciencia *f*
impatient [ɪm'peɪʃənt] *adj* impaciente; *(fret-
ful)* irritable; **to get i.** perder la paciencia
impeccable [ɪm'pekəbəl] *adj* impecable
impede [ɪm'piːd] *vt (prevent)* impedir; *(hinder)* estorbar; *(obstruct)* poner trabas a
impediment [ɪm'pedɪmənt] *n* impedimento
m; *(obstacle)* estorbo *m*; **speech i.** defecto *m*
del habla
impending [ɪm'pendɪŋ] *adj Fml* inminente
impenetrable [ɪm'penɪtrəbəl] *adj* impenetrable; *Fig (mystery, thoughts)* insondable
imperative [ɪm'perətɪv] **1** *adj Fml* imperati-
vo(a); *(tone)* imperioso(a); *(urgent)* urgente
  2 *n Ling* imperativo *m*
imperceptible [ɪmpə'septəbəl] *adj* imperceptible
imperfect [ɪm'pɜːfɪkt] **1** *adj* imperfecto(a);
(goods) defectuoso(a)
  2 *n Ling* imperfecto *m*
imperfection [ɪmpə'fekʃən] *n* defecto *m*
imperial [ɪm'pɪərɪəl] *adj* (**a**) imperial (**b**)
(measure) **i. gallon** galón británico *(aprox
4,546 l)*
imperialism [ɪm'pɪərɪəlɪzəm] *n* imperialismo *m*

imperialist [ɪm'pɪərɪəlɪst] *adj & n* imperialis-
ta *(mf)*

imperious [ɪm'pɪərɪəs] *adj* imperioso(a)

impersonal [ɪm'pɜːsənəl] *adj* impersonal

impersonate [ɪm'pɜːsəneɪt] *vt* hacerse pasar
por; *(famous people)* imitar

impersonation [ɪmpɜːsə'neɪʃən] *n* imitación *f*

impertinent [ɪm'pɜːtɪnənt] *adj* impertinente

impervious [ɪm'pɜːvɪəs] *adj (rock)* impermeable; *Fig* **to be i. to reason** no atender a
razones

impetuous [ɪm'petjʊəs] *adj* impetuoso(a)

impetus ['ɪmpɪtəs] *n* ímpetu *m*; *Fig* impulso
m

impinge [ɪm'pɪndʒ] *vi Fml* afectar (**on** a)

implant *Med* **1** *vt* [ɪm'plɑːnt] implantar
  2 *n* ['ɪmplɑːnt] implantación *f*

implement **1** *n* ['ɪmplɪmənt] *(tool)* herramienta *f*; *(instrument)* instrumento *m*; *farm*
implements aperos *mpl* de labranza
  2 *vt* ['ɪmplɪment] *(decision, plan)* llevar a
cabo; *(law, policy)* aplicar

implicate ['ɪmplɪkeɪt] *vt* implicar (**in** en)

implication [ɪmplɪ'keɪʃən] *n* implicación *f*;
(consequence) consecuencia *f*

implicit [ɪm'plɪsɪt] *adj (implied)* implícito(a);
(trust) absoluto(a); *(faith)* incondicional

implore [ɪm'plɔː(r)] *vt* implorar, suplicar

imply [ɪm'plaɪ] *vt* (**a**) *(involve)* implicar (**b**)
(hint) dar a entender; *(mean)* significar

impolite [ɪmpə'laɪt] *adj* maleducado(a)

import 1 *n* ['ɪmpɔːt] (**a**) *Com (usu pl)* importación *f*; **i. duty** derechos *mpl* de importación
(**b**) *Fml (meaning)* sentido *m*
  2 *vt* [ɪm'pɔːt] *Com* importar

importance [ɪm'pɔːtəns] *n* importancia *f*;
(standing) envergadura *f*; **of little i.** de poca
monta

important [ɪm'pɔːtənt] *adj* importante; **it's
not i.** no importa

importer [ɪm'pɔːtə(r)] *n Com* importador(a)
m,f

impose [ɪm'pəʊz] **1** *vt* imponer (**on** *or* **upon**
a)
  2 *vi* **to i. on** *or* **upon** *(take advantage of)*
abusar de

imposing [ɪm'pəʊzɪŋ] *adj* imponente, impresionante

imposition [ɪmpə'zɪʃən] *n (of tax etc)* imposición *f*; *(unfair demand)* abuso *m*; **would it
be an i. if ...?** ¿le molestaría si ...?

impossibility [ɪmpɒsə'bɪlɪtɪ] *n* imposibilidad *f*

impossible [ɪm'pɒsəbəl] **1** *adj* imposible;
(person) insoportable
  2 *n* **to do the i.** hacer lo imposible

impossibly [ɪm'pɒsəblɪ] *adv* de manera insoportable; **i. difficult** de una dificultad insuperable

impostor [ɪm'pɒstə(r)] *n* impostor(a) *m,f*

impotent ['ɪmpətənt] *adj* impotente

impound [ɪm'paʊnd] *vt* incautarse de

impoverished [ɪm'pɒvərɪʃt] *adj (person,
country)* empobrecido(a); *(soil)* agotado(a)

impracticable [ɪm'præktɪkəbəl] *adj* impracticable, irrealizable

impractical [ɪm'præktɪkəl] *adj (person)* poco
práctico(a); *(project, solution etc)* poco viable

imprecise [ɪmprɪ'saɪs] *adj* impreciso(a)

impregnable [ɪm'pregnəbəl] *adj* inexpugnable

impregnate ['ɪmpregneɪt] *vt* (**a**) *(soak)* impregnar (**with** de) (**b**) *Fml (fertilize)* fecundar

impress [ɪm'pres] *vt* (**a**) impresionar; **to i. sb
favourably/unfavourably** dar a algn buena/
mala impresión (**b**) *(mark)* imprimir (**on** en);
(pattern) estampar (**on** en); *Fig* **to i. sth on
sb** convencer a algn de la importancia de
algo

impression [ɪm'preʃən] *n* (**a**) impresión *f*; **to
be under the i. that ...** tener la impresión de
que ...; **to give the i. of ...** dar la impresión
de ... (**b**) *(imprint)* marca *f*; *(in snow)* huella *f*
(**c**) *(imitation)* imitación *f*

impressionist [ɪm'preʃənɪst] *adj & n* impresionista *(mf)*

impressive [ɪm'presɪv] *adj* impresionante

imprint 1 *vt* [ɪm'prɪnt] *(mark)* dejar huella (**on**
en)
  2 *n* ['ɪmprɪnt] (**a**) *(mark)* marca *f*; *(left by foot
etc)* huella *f* (**b**) *(publisher's name)* pie *m* de
imprenta

imprison [ɪm'prɪzən] *vt* encarcelar

imprisonment [ɪm'prɪzənmənt] *n* encarcelamiento *m*

improbable [ɪm'prɒbəbəl] *adj (event)* improbable; *(story)* inverosímil

impromptu [ɪm'prɒmptjuː] **1** *adj (speech)*
improvisado(a); *(visit)* imprevisto(a)
  2 *adv* de improviso

improper [ɪm'prɒpə(r)] *adj* (**a**) impropio(a);
(method) inadecuado(a) (**b**) *(indecent)* indecente; *(behaviour)* deshonesto(a) (**c**)
(wrong) incorrecto(a)

improve [ɪm'pruːv] **1** *vt* mejorar; *(knowledge)* perfeccionar; *(mind)* cultivar; *(increase)* aumentar
  2 *vi* mejorarse; *(increase)* aumentar
  ▸ **improve on** *vt insep* superar; *(offer, bid)*
sobrepujar

improvement [ɪm'pruːvmənt] *n* mejora *f*;
(in skill) perfeccionamiento *m*; *(increase)*
aumento *m*

improvise ['ɪmprəvaɪz] *vt & vi* improvisar

imprudent [ɪm'pruːdənt] *adj* imprudente

impudence ['ɪmpjʊdəns] *n* insolencia *f*

impudent ['ɪmpjʊdənt] *adj* insolente

impulse ['ɪmpʌls] *n* impulso *m*; **to act on (an)
i.** dejarse llevar por un impulso

impulsive [ɪm'pʌlsɪv] *adj* irreflexivo(a)

impunity [ɪm'pjuːnɪtɪ] *n* impunidad *f*

impure [ɪm'pjʊə(r)] *adj* (**a**) *(act)* impuro(a);

(thought) impúdico(a) (**b**) *(air)* contaminado(a)

impurity [ɪmˈpjʊərɪtɪ] *n* (**a**) *(of act)* deshonestidad *f* (**b**) *(usu pl) (in air, substance)* impureza *f*

in [ɪn] **1** *prep* (**a**) *(place)* en; *(within)* dentro de; **in bed** en la cama; **in England/Brazil/China** en Inglaterra/Brasil/China; **in prison** en la cárcel; **in the distance** a lo lejos

(**b**) *(motion)* en; **I threw it in the fire** lo eché al fuego; **she arrived in Paris** llegó a París

(**c**) *(time) (during)* en, durante; **I haven't seen her in years** hace años que no la veo; **in May/1945** en mayo/1945; **in spring** en primavera; **in the daytime** durante el día; **in the morning** por la mañana; **at ten in the morning** a las diez de la mañana

(**d**) *(time) (within)* dentro de; **I arrived in time** llegué a tiempo

(**e**) *(time) (after)* al cabo de

(**f**) *(manner)* en; **in alphabetical order** en orden alfabético; **in a loud/quiet voice** en voz alta/baja; **in fashion** de moda; **in French** en francés; **in an odd way** de una manera rara; **in writing** por escrito; **write in pencil** escribe con lápiz

(**g**) *(wearing)* en; **dressed in blue** vestido(a) de azul; **in uniform** de uniforme

(**h**) *(weather etc)* a, en; **in the rain** bajo la lluvia; **in the sun** al sol; **in darkness** en la oscuridad; **in daylight** a la luz del día; **in the shade** a la sombra

(**i**) *(state, emotion)* en; **carved in wood** tallado(a) en madera; **in bloom/danger/public/silence** en flor/peligro/público/silencio; **in love** enamorado(a); **in tears** llorando

(**j**) *(ratio, numbers)* de; **cut in half** cortado(a) por la mitad; **in threes** de tres en tres; **one in six** uno de cada seis; **2 m in length** 2 m de largo

(**k**) *(profession)* en; **to be in insurance** trabajar en seguros

(**l**) *(person)* en; **he has it in him to win** es capaz de ganar

(**m**) *(after superlative)* de; **the smallest car in the world** el coche más pequeño del mundo

(**n**) *(before present participle)* en; **in behaving this way** con su comportamiento; **in so doing** con ello

(**o**) *(phrases)* **in all** en total; **in itself/himself/herself** en sí; **in that ...** dado que ...

2 *adv* **in here/there** aquí/allí dentro; **let's go in** vamos adentro; **to be in** *(at home)* estar (en casa); *(at work)* estar; *(tide)* estar alta; *Fam (in fashion)* estar de moda; **the bus is in** el autobús ha llegado; **to invite sb in** invitar a algn a entrar; *Fam* **to be in on sth** estar enterado(a) de algo; *Fam* **we're in for a storm** vamos a tener tormenta

3 *adj Fam* (**a**) *(fashionable) (place)* de moda; *(clothes)* del último grito

(**b**) **an in joke** una broma privada

4 *n Fam* **ins and outs** detalles *mpl*

inability [ɪnəˈbɪlɪtɪ] *n* incapacidad *f*

inaccessible [ɪnækˈsesəbəl] *adj* inaccesible

inaccurate [ɪnˈækjʊrɪt] *adj* inexacto(a); *(statement)* erróneo(a); *(figures, total)* incorrecto(a)

inactivity [ɪnækˈtɪvɪtɪ] *n* inactividad *f*

inadequate [ɪnˈædɪkwɪt] *adj* (**a**) *(lacking)* insuficiente (**b**) *(not capable)* incapaz; *(unsuitable)* inadecuado(a) (**c**) *(defective)* defectuoso(a)

inadvertent [ɪnədˈvɜːtənt] *adj* involuntario(a)

inadvertently [ɪnədˈvɜːtəntlɪ] *adv* involuntariamente

inadvisable [ɪnədˈvaɪzəbəl] *adj* imprudente

inane [ɪˈneɪn] *adj* necio(a), fatuo(a)

inanimate [ɪnˈænɪmɪt] *adj* inanimado(a)

inappropriate [ɪnəˈprəʊprɪɪt] *adj* inoportuno(a); *(behaviour)* poco apropiado(a)

inarticulate [ɪnɑːˈtɪkjʊlɪt] *adj (cry, sound)* inarticulado(a); *(words)* mal pronunciado(a)

inasmuch as [ɪnəzˈmʌtʃəz] *conj Fml* (**a**) *(since)* puesto que, ya que (**b**) *(in so far as)* en la medida en que

inattentive [ɪnəˈtentɪv] *adj* desatento(a)

inaudible [ɪnˈɔːdəbəl] *adj* inaudible

inaugural [ɪnˈɔːgjʊrəl] *adj* inaugural

inaugurate [ɪnˈɔːgjʊreɪt] *vt (building)* inaugurar; *(president)* investir

inauguration [ɪnɔːgjʊˈreɪʃən] *n (of building)* inauguración *f*; *(of president)* investidura *f*

inauspicious [ɪnɔːˈspɪʃəs] *adj (start)* poco prometedor(a); *(circumstances)* desfavorable

inborn [ˈɪnbɔːn] *adj* innato(a)

inbred [ˈɪnbred] *adj* (**a**) *(quality)* innato(a) (**b**) *(family)* endogámico(a)

Inc, inc *US Com (abbr* **Incorporated**) ≃ S.A.

incalculable [ɪnˈkælkjʊləbəl] *adj* incalculable

incapable [ɪnˈkeɪpəbəl] *adj* incapaz

incapacitate [ɪnkəˈpæsɪteɪt] *vt Fml* incapacitar

incapacity [ɪnkəˈpæsɪtɪ] *n* incapacidad *f*

incarcerate [ɪnˈkɑːsəreɪt] *vt Fml* encarcelar

incarnation [ɪnkɑːˈneɪʃən] *n* encarnación *f*

incendiary [ɪnˈsendɪərɪ] **1** *adj* incendiario(a) **2** *n* bomba incendiaria

incense¹ [ˈɪnsens] *n* incienso *m*

incense² [ɪnˈsens] *vt* enfurecer, sacar de quicio

incentive [ɪnˈsentɪv] *n* incentivo *m*

incessant [ɪnˈsesənt] *adj* incesante; *(demands)* constante

incessantly [ɪnˈsesəntlɪ] *adv* sin cesar

incest [ˈɪnsest] *n* incesto *m*

inch [ɪntʃ] *n* pulgada *f (aprox 2,54 cm)*; *Fig* **i. by i.** poco a poco; *Fig* **she wouldn't give an i.** no quería ceder ni un ápice

▶ **inch forward** *vt sep & vi* avanzar poco a poco

incidence [ˈɪnsɪdəns] *n* frecuencia *f*

incident ['ɪnsɪdənt] *n* incidente *m*
incidental [ɪnsɪ'dentəl] *adj (accessory)* incidental, accesorio(a); *(risk)* inherente (**to** a); **i. music** música *f* de fondo
incidentally [ɪnsɪ'dentəlɪ] *adv* a propósito
incinerator [ɪn'sɪnəreɪtə(r)] *n* incinerador *m*
incipient [ɪn'sɪpɪənt] *adj Fml* incipiente
incision [ɪn'sɪʒən] *n* incisión *f*
incisive [ɪn'saɪsɪv] *adj (comment)* incisivo(a); *(reply)* tajante; *(mind)* penetrante
incite [ɪn'saɪt] *vt* incitar; **to i. sb to do sth** incitar a algn a hacer algo
inclination [ɪnklɪ'neɪʃən] *n* inclinación *f*; **my i. is to stay** yo prefiero quedarme
incline [ɪn'klaɪn] **1** *vt* (a) **I'm inclined to believe him** me inclino a creerlo; **if you feel so inclined** si quieres; **she's inclined to be aggressive** tiende a ser agresiva (b) *(head etc)* inclinar
2 *vi (slope)* inclinarse
3 *n* ['ɪnklaɪn] *(slope)* pendiente *f*; **steep i.** cuesta empinada
include [ɪn'kluːd] *vt* incluir (**in** en); *(in price)* comprender (**in** en); *(in list)* figurar (**in** en)
including [ɪn'kluːdɪŋ] *prep* incluso, inclusive
inclusion [ɪn'kluːʒən] *n* inclusión *f*
inclusive [ɪn'kluːsɪv] *adj* inclusivo(a); **pages 6 to 10 i.** de la página 6 a la 10, ambas inclusive; **the rent is i. of bills** el alquiler incluye las facturas
incognito [ɪnkɒg'niːtəʊ] *adv* de incógnito
incoherent [ɪnkəʊ'hɪərənt] *adj* incoherente
income ['ɪnkʌm] *n* ingresos *mpl*; *(from investment)* réditos *mpl*; **i. tax** impuesto *m* sobre la renta; **i. tax return** declaración *f* de la renta
incoming ['ɪnkʌmɪŋ] *adj (flight, train)* de llegada; *(tide)* ascendente; *(mail, message, call)* recibido(a)
incomparable [ɪn'kɒmpərəbəl] *adj* incomparable, sin par
incompatible [ɪnkəm'pætəbəl] *adj* incompatible (**with** con)
incompetence [ɪn'kɒmpɪtəns] *n* incompetencia *f*
incompetent [ɪn'kɒmpɪtənt] *adj* incompetente
incomplete [ɪnkəm'pliːt] *adj* incompleto(a)
incomprehensible [ɪnkɒmprɪ'hensəbəl] *adj* incomprensible
inconceivable [ɪnkən'siːvəbəl] *adj* inconcebible
inconclusive [ɪnkən'kluːsɪv] *adj (vote)* no decisivo(a); *(proof)* no concluyente
incongruous [ɪn'kɒŋgrʊəs] *adj* incongruente
inconsiderate [ɪnkən'sɪdərɪt] *adj* desconsiderado(a); **how i. of you!** ¡qué falta de consideración por tu parte!
inconsistency [ɪnkən'sɪstənsɪ] *n* inconsecuencia *f*; *(contradiction)* contradicción *f*
inconsistent [ɪnkən'sɪstənt] *adj* inconse-

cuente; *(contradictory)* contradictorio(a); **your evidence is i. with the facts** su testimonio no concuerda con los hechos
inconspicuous [ɪnkən'spɪkjʊəs] *adj* que pasa desapercibido(a); *(discreet)* discreto(a)
incontrovertible [ɪnkɒntrə'vɜːtəbəl] *adj Fml* incontrovertible
inconvenience [ɪnkən'viːnɪəns] **1** *n* inconveniente *f*; *(annoyance)* molestia *f*
2 *vt (annoy)* molestar; *(cause difficulty to)* incomodar
inconvenient [ɪnkən'viːnɪənt] *adj* molesto(a); *(time)* inoportuno(a); *(design)* poco práctico(a)
incorporate [ɪn'kɔːpəreɪt] *vt* incorporar (**in** or **into** a); *(include)* incluir; *(contain)* contener
incorporated [ɪn'kɔːpəreɪtɪd] *adj US Com* **i. company** sociedad anónima
incorrect [ɪnkə'rekt] *adj* incorrecto(a)
incorrigible [ɪn'kɒrɪdʒəbəl] *adj* incorregible
increase 1 *n* ['ɪnkriːs] aumento *m*; *(in number)* incremento *m*; *(in price etc)* subida *f*
2 *vt* [ɪn'kriːs] aumentar; *(price etc)* subir
3 *vi* aumentar
increasing [ɪn'kriːsɪŋ] *adj* creciente
increasingly [ɪn'kriːsɪŋlɪ] *adv* cada vez más
incredible [ɪn'kredəbəl] *adj* increíble
incredulous [ɪn'kredjʊləs] *adj* incrédulo(a)
increment ['ɪnkrɪmənt] *n* incremento *m*
incriminate [ɪn'krɪmɪneɪt] *vt* incriminar
incriminating [ɪn'krɪmɪneɪtɪŋ] *adj* incriminatorio(a)
incubation [ɪnkjʊ'beɪʃən] *n* incubación *f*
incubator ['ɪnkjʊbeɪtə(r)] *n* incubadora *f*
incumbent [ɪn'kʌmbənt] **1** *n* titular *mf*
2 *adj Fml* **to be i. on sb to do sth** ser la obligación de algn hacer algo
incur [ɪn'kɜː(r)] *vt (blame)* incurrir en; *(risk)* correr; *(debt)* contraer; *(loss)* sufrir
incurable [ɪn'kjʊərəbəl] *adj* incurable
indebted [ɪn'detɪd] *adj* endeudado(a); *Fig (grateful)* agradecido(a); *Fig* **to be i. to sb** estar en deuda con algn
indecent [ɪn'diːsənt] *adj* indecente; **i. assault** atentado *m* contra el pudor; **i. exposure** exhibicionismo *m*
indecision [ɪndɪ'sɪʒən] *n* indecisión *f*
indecisive [ɪndɪ'saɪsɪv] *adj (person)* indeciso(a); *(evidence)* poco concluyente; *(victory)* no decisivo(a)
indeed [ɪn'diːd] *adv* (a) *Fml (in fact)* efectivamente, en realidad (b) **I'm very sorry i.** lo siento de veras; **it's very hard i.** es verdaderamente difícil; **thank you very much i.** muchísimas gracias
indefinite [ɪn'defɪnɪt] *adj* indefinido(a)
indelible [ɪn'deləbəl] *adj* indeleble
indemnify [ɪn'demnɪfaɪ] *vt* indemnizar (**for** por)
indemnity [ɪn'demnɪtɪ] *n* (a) *(insurance)* indemnidad *f* (b) *(compensation)* indemnización *f*

indentation [ɪnden'teɪʃən] n (**a**) Typ sangría f (**b**) (of edge) muesca f; (of surface) depresión f

independence [ɪndɪ'pendəns] n independencia f; US **I. Day** día m de la Independencia (4 julio)

independent [ɪndɪ'pendənt] adj independiente; Br **i. school** = colegio no subvencionado por el estado; **to become i.** independizarse

in-depth ['ɪndepθ] adj minucioso(a), exhaustivo(a)

indestructible [ɪndɪ'strʌktəbəl] adj indestructible

indeterminate [ɪndɪ'tɜːmɪnɪt] adj indeterminado(a)

index ['ɪndeks] 1 n (pl **indexes** or **indices**) (**a**) (in book) índice m; (in library) catálogo m; **i. card** ficha f (**b**) Math exponente m; Econ índice m (**c**) **i. finger** dedo m índice
2 vt catalogar

index-linked ['ɪndekslɪŋkt] adj sujeto(a) al aumento de la inflación

India ['ɪndɪə] n (la) India

Indian ['ɪndɪən] adj & n (of America) indio(a) (m,f); (of India) hindú (mf); **I. Ocean** Océano Índico; **I. Summer** veranillo m de San Martín

indicate ['ɪndɪkeɪt] 1 vt indicar
2 vi Aut poner el intermitente

indication [ɪndɪ'keɪʃən] n indicio m

indicative [ɪn'dɪkətɪv] 1 adj indicativo(a)
2 n Ling indicativo m

indicator ['ɪndɪkeɪtə(r)] n indicador m; Br Aut intermitente m

indices ['ɪndɪsiːz] pl of **index**

indict [ɪn'daɪt] vt acusar (**for** de)

indictment [ɪn'daɪtmənt] n Jur acusación f; Fig **a damning i. of his books** una crítica feroz de sus libros

indifference [ɪn'dɪfərəns] n indiferencia f

indifferent [ɪn'dɪfərənt] adj (**a**) (uninterested) indiferente (**b**) (mediocre) regular

indigenous [ɪn'dɪdʒɪnəs] adj indígena

indigestion [ɪndɪ'dʒestʃən] n indigestión f; **to suffer from i.** tener un empacho

indignant [ɪn'dɪgnənt] adj indignado(a); (look) de indignación; **to get i. about sth** indignarse por algo

indignity [ɪn'dɪgnɪtɪ] n indignidad f

indigo ['ɪndɪgəʊ] 1 n añil m
2 adj (de color) añil

indirect [ɪndɪ'rekt, ɪndaɪ'rekt] adj indirecto(a)

indiscreet [ɪndɪ'skriːt] adj indiscreto(a)

indiscretion [ɪndɪ'skreʃən] n indiscreción f

indiscriminate [ɪndɪ'skrɪmɪnɪt] adj (punishment, shooting) indiscriminado(a); (praise, reading) sin criterio

indispensable [ɪndɪ'spensəbəl] adj indispensable, imprescindible

indisposed [ɪndɪ'spəʊzd] adj Fml indispuesto(a)

indisputable [ɪndɪ'spjuːtəbəl] adj indiscutible, incontestable

indistinct [ɪndɪ'stɪŋkt] adj indistinto(a); (memory) confuso(a), vago(a); (shape etc) borroso(a)

indistinguishable [ɪndɪ'stɪŋgwɪʃəbəl] adj indistinguible

individual [ɪndɪ'vɪdjʊəl] 1 adj (**a**) (separate) individual; (for one) particular; (personal) personal (**b**) (characteristic) particular; (original) original
2 n (person) individuo m; **private i.** particular m

individualist [ɪndɪ'vɪdjʊəlɪst] n individualista mf

indoctrinate [ɪn'dɒktrɪneɪt] vt adoctrinar

indoctrination [ɪndɒktrɪ'neɪʃən] n adoctrinamiento m

indolent ['ɪndələnt] adj Fml indolente

Indonesia [ɪndəʊ'niːzɪə] n Indonesia

Indonesian [ɪndəʊ'niːzɪən] 1 adj indonesio(a)
2 n (**a**) (person) indonesio(a) m,f (**b**) (language) indonesio m

indoor ['ɪndɔː(r)] adj (plant) de interior; **i. football** fútbol m sala; **i. pool** piscina cubierta

indoors [ɪn'dɔːz] adv (inside) dentro (de casa); (at home) en casa; **let's go i.** vamos adentro

induce [ɪn'djuːs] vt (**a**) (persuade) inducir, persuadir (**b**) (cause) producir; Med (labour) provocar

inducement [ɪn'djuːsmənt] n incentivo m, aliciente m

induction [ɪn'dʌkʃən] n (**a**) Med (of labour) provocación f (**b**) Elec inducción f (**c**) Educ introducción f

indulge [ɪn'dʌldʒ] 1 vt (**a**) (child) consentir; (person) complacer; **to i. oneself** darse gusto (**b**) (whim) ceder a, satisfacer
2 vi darse el gusto (**in** de)

indulgence [ɪn'dʌldʒəns] n (**a**) (of child) mimo m; (of attitude) indulgencia f (**b**) (of whim) satisfacción f

indulgent [ɪn'dʌldʒənt] adj indulgente

industrial [ɪn'dʌstrɪəl] adj industrial; (accident) laboral; (disease) profesional; Br **to take i. action** declararse en huelga; Br **i. dispute** conflicto m laboral; **i.** Br **estate** or US **park** polígono m industrial; **i. relations** relaciones fpl laborales

industrialist [ɪn'dʌstrɪəlɪst] n industrial mf

industrialize [ɪn'dʌstrɪəlaɪz] vt industrializar; **to become industrialized** industrializarse

industrious [ɪn'dʌstrɪəs] adj trabajador(a)

industry ['ɪndəstrɪ] n (**a**) industria f (**b**) (diligence) aplicación f

inebriated [ɪn'iːbrɪeɪtɪd] adj embriagado(a)

inedible [ɪn'edəbəl] adj incomible

ineffective [ɪnɪ'fektɪv] adj ineficaz

ineffectual [ɪnɪ'fektʃʊəl] *adj (aim, protest)* ineficaz; *(person)* incompetente

inefficiency [ɪnɪ'fɪʃənsɪ] *n* ineficacia *f; (of person)* incompetencia *f*

inefficient [ɪnɪ'fɪʃənt] *adj* ineficaz; *(person)* inepto(a)

ineligible [ɪn'elɪdʒəbəl] *adj* no apto(a) (**for** para)

inept [ɪn'ept] *adj (person)* inepto(a); *(remark)* estúpido(a)

inequality [ɪnɪ'kwɒlɪtɪ] *n* desigualdad *f*

inert [ɪn'ɜːt] *adj* inerte

inertia [ɪn'ɜːʃə] *n* inercia *f*

inescapable [ɪnɪ'skeɪpəbəl] *adj* ineludible

inevitability [ɪnevɪtə'bɪlɪtɪ] *n* inevitabilidad *f*

inevitable [ɪn'evɪtəbəl] *adj* inevitable

inexcusable [ɪnɪk'skjuːzəbəl] *adj* inexcusable, imperdonable

inexhaustible [ɪnɪg'zɔːstəbəl] *adj* inagotable

inexorable [ɪn'eksərəbəl] *adj Fml* inexorable

inexpensive [ɪnɪk'spensɪv] *adj* económico(a)

inexperience [ɪnɪk'spɪərɪəns] *n* inexperiencia *f*

inexperienced [ɪnɪk'spɪərɪənst] *adj* inexperto(a)

inexplicable [ɪnɪk'splɪkəbəl] *adj* inexplicable

infallible [ɪn'fæləbəl] *adj* infalible

infamous ['ɪnfəməs] *adj* infame

infancy ['ɪnfənsɪ] *n* infancia *f*

infant ['ɪnfənt] *n* niño(a) *m,f; Br* **i. school** parvulario *m*

infantile ['ɪnfəntaɪl] *adj* infantil

infantry ['ɪnfəntrɪ] *n* infantería *f*

infatuated [ɪn'fætjʊeɪtɪd] *adj* encaprichado(a)

infatuation [ɪnfætjʊ'eɪʃən] *n* encaprichamiento *m*

infect [ɪn'fekt] *vt (cut)* infectar; *(water)* contaminar; *(person)* contagiar

infection [ɪn'fekʃən] *n (of cut)* infección *f; (of water)* contaminación *f; (with illness)* contagio *m*

infectious [ɪn'fekʃəs] *adj (disease)* infeccioso(a); *Fig* contagioso(a)

infer [ɪn'fɜː(r)] *vt* inferir (**from** de)

inference ['ɪnfərəns] *n* inferencia *f*

inferior [ɪn'fɪərɪə(r)] **1** *adj* inferior (**to** a)
2 *n Pej* inferior *mf*

inferiority [ɪnfɪərɪ'ɒrɪtɪ] *n* inferioridad *f*

inferno [ɪn'fɜːnəʊ] *n Literary* infierno *m; Fig* **the house was a raging i.** la casa ardía en llamas

infertile [ɪn'fɜːtaɪl] *adj* estéril

infertility [ɪnfə'tɪlɪtɪ] *n* esterilidad *f*

infest [ɪn'fest] *vt* infestar, plagar (**with** de)

infighting ['ɪnfaɪtɪŋ] *n Fig* luchas *fpl* internas

infiltrate ['ɪnfɪltreɪt] *vt* infiltrarse (**into** en)

infinite ['ɪnfɪnɪt] *adj* infinito(a)

infinitive [ɪn'fɪnɪtɪv] *n* infinitivo *m*

infinity [ɪn'fɪnɪtɪ] *n* infinidad *f; Math* infinito *m*

infirm [ɪn'fɜːm] **1** *adj (ailing)* enfermizo(a); *(weak)* débil
2 *npl* **the i.** los inválidos

infirmary [ɪn'fɜːmərɪ] *n* hospital *m*

infirmity [ɪn'fɜːmɪtɪ] *n Fml (ailment)* enfermedad *f; (weakness)* debilidad *f*

inflame [ɪn'fleɪm] *vt (passion)* encender; *(curiosity)* avivar; *(crowd)* excitar; **to be inflamed with rage** rabiar

inflamed [ɪn'fleɪmd] *adj* inflamado(a); **to become i.** inflamarse

inflammable [ɪn'flæməbəl] *adj (material)* inflamable; *Fig (situation)* explosivo(a)

inflammation [ɪnflə'meɪʃən] *n* inflamación *f*

inflatable [ɪn'fleɪtəbəl] *adj* inflable

inflate [ɪn'fleɪt] **1** *vt* inflar
2 *vi* inflarse

inflated [ɪn'fleɪtɪd] *adj* (**a**) *Fig (prices)* inflacionista (**b**) *Pej (view, idea)* exagerado(a)

inflation [ɪn'fleɪʃən] *n* inflación *f*

inflexible [ɪn'fleksəbəl] *adj* inflexible

inflict [ɪn'flɪkt] *vt (blow)* asestar (**on** a); *(damage)* causar (**on** a); *(defeat)* infligir (**on** a)

in-flight ['ɪnflaɪt] *adj* durante el vuelo

influence ['ɪnflʊəns] **1** *n* influencia *f; Fam* **to be under the i.** llevar una copa de más
2 *vt* influir en

influential [ɪnflʊ'enʃəl] *adj* influyente

influenza [ɪnflʊ'enzə] *n* gripe *f*

influx ['ɪnflʌks] *n* afluencia *f*

inform [ɪn'fɔːm] **1** *vt* informar (**of** *or* **about** de *or* sobre); *(police)* avisar (**of** *or* **about** de)
2 *vi* **to i. against** *or* **on** denunciar

informal [ɪn'fɔːməl] *adj* (**a**) *(occasion, behaviour)* informal; *(language, treatment)* familiar (**b**) *(unofficial)* no oficial

informality [ɪnfɔː'mælɪtɪ] *n (of occasion, behaviour)* sencillez *f; (of treatment)* familiaridad *f*

informant [ɪn'fɔːmənt] *n* informante *mf*

information [ɪnfə'meɪʃən] *n* información *f; (details)* detalles *mpl; (facts)* datos *mpl; (knowledge)* conocimientos *mpl; (news)* noticias *fpl;* **a piece of i.** un dato; **i. bureau** centro *m* de información; **i. technology** informática *f*

informative [ɪn'fɔːmətɪv] *adj* informativo(a)

informed [ɪn'fɔːmd] *adj* enterado(a); **keep me i.** téngame al corriente

informer [ɪn'fɔːmə(r)] *n* delator(a) *m,f; (to the police)* soplón(ona) *m,f*

infrared [ɪnfrə'red] *adj* infrarrojo(a)

infrastructure ['ɪnfrəstrʌktʃə(r)] *n* infraestructura *f*

infringe [ɪn'frɪndʒ] **1** *vt (law, rule)* infringir; *(copyright)* no respetar

2 *vi* **to i. on** or **upon** *(rights)* violar; *(privacy)* invadir

infringement [ɪnˈfrɪndʒmənt] *n (of law, rule)* infracción *f; (of rights)* violación *f*

infuriate [ɪnˈfjʊərɪeɪt] *vt* poner furioso(a)

infuriating [ɪnˈfjʊərɪeɪtɪŋ] *adj* exasperante

infusion [ɪnˈfjuːʒən] *n* infusión *f*

ingenious [ɪnˈdʒiːnɪəs] *adj* ingenioso(a)

ingenuity [ɪndʒɪˈnjuːɪtɪ] *n* ingenio *m*

ingenuous [ɪnˈdʒenjʊəs] *adj* ingenuo(a)

ingot [ˈɪŋgət] *n* lingote *m*

ingrained [ɪnˈgreɪnd] *adj Fig* arraigado(a)

ingratiate [ɪnˈgreɪʃɪeɪt] *vt Pej* **to i. oneself with sb** congraciarse con algn

ingratiating [ɪnˈgreɪʃɪeɪtɪŋ] *adj* zalamero(a)

ingratitude [ɪnˈgrætɪtjuːd] *n* ingratitud *f*

ingredient [ɪnˈgriːdɪənt] *n* ingrediente *m*

inhabit [ɪnˈhæbɪt] *vt* vivir en, ocupar

inhabitable [ɪnˈhæbɪtəbəl] *adj* habitable

🖉 Note that the Spanish word inhabitable is a false friend and is never a translation for the English word inhabitable. In Spanish, inhabitable means "uninhabitable".

---

inhabitant [ɪnˈhæbɪtənt] *n* habitante *mf*

inhale [ɪnˈheɪl] **1** *vt (gas)* inhalar; *(air)* aspirar

2 *vi* aspirar; *(smoker)* tragar el humo

inherent [ɪnˈhɪərənt] *adj* inherente

inherit [ɪnˈherɪt] *vt* heredar *(from* de)

inheritance [ɪnˈherɪtəns] *n* herencia *f*

inhibit [ɪnˈhɪbɪt] *vt (freedom)* limitar; *(person)* cohibir; **to i. sb from doing sth** impedir a algn hacer algo

inhibited [ɪnˈhɪbɪtɪd] *adj* cohibido(a)

inhibition [ɪnhɪˈbɪʃən] *n* cohibición *f*

inhospitable [ɪnhɒˈspɪtəbəl] *adj* inhospitalario(a); *(climate, place)* inhóspito(a)

inhuman [ɪnˈhjuːmən] *adj* inhumano(a)

iniquity [ɪˈnɪkwɪtɪ] *n Fml* iniquidad *f*

initial [ɪˈnɪʃəl] **1** *adj* inicial, primero(a)

2 *n* (**a**) inicial *f* (**b**) **initials** *(of name)* iniciales *fpl; (of abbreviation)* siglas *fpl*

3 *vt* firmar con las iniciales

initially [ɪˈnɪʃəlɪ] *adv* al principio

initiate [ɪˈnɪʃɪeɪt] *vt* (**a**) iniciar; *(reform)* promover; *(lawsuit)* entablar (**b**) *(into society)* admitir (**into** en); *(into knowledge)* iniciar (**into** en)

initiation [ɪnɪʃɪˈeɪʃən] *n* (**a**) *(start)* principio *m* (**b**) *(admission)* iniciación *f*

initiative [ɪˈnɪʃɪətɪv] *n* iniciativa *f*

inject [ɪnˈdʒekt] *vt* (**a**) *(drug etc)* inyectar (**b**) *Fig (capital)* invertir; *(life, hope)* infundir

injection [ɪnˈdʒekʃən] *n* (**a**) inyección *f* (**b**) *Fig (of capital)* inversión *f*

injunction [ɪnˈdʒʌŋkʃən] *n* interdicto *m*

injure [ˈɪndʒə(r)] *vt* herir; **to i. oneself** hacerse daño; *Fig (health, reputation)* perjudicar

injured [ˈɪndʒəd] **1** *adj* herido(a); *Fig (look, tone)* ofendido(a)

2 *npl* **the i.** los heridos

injury [ˈɪndʒərɪ] *n (hurt)* herida *f; Fig (harm)* daño *m; Sport* **i. time** (tiempo *m* de) descuento *m*

injustice [ɪnˈdʒʌstɪs] *n* injusticia *f*

ink [ɪŋk] *n* tinta *f;* **invisible i.** tinta simpática

inkjet printer [ˈɪŋkdʒetˈprɪntə(r)] *n Comput* impresora *f* de chorro de tinta

inkling [ˈɪŋklɪŋ] *n (idea)* idea *f; (suspicion)* sospecha *f; (sign)* señal *f*

inkwell [ˈɪŋkwel] *n* tintero *m*

inlaid [ɪnˈleɪd] *adj (wood)* taraceado(a); *(ivory, gems)* incrustado(a)

inland 1 *adj* [ˈɪnlənd] (del) interior; *Br* **I. Revenue** Hacienda *f*

2 *adv* [ɪnˈlænd] *(travel)* tierra adentro

in-laws [ˈɪnlɔːz] *npl Fam* familia *f* política

inlet [ˈɪnlet] *n* (**a**) *(in coastline)* ensenada *f*, cala *f* (**b**) *(in pipe, machine)* entrada *f*, admisión *f*

inline [ˈɪnlaɪn] *adj* **i. skates** patines *mpl* en línea

inmate [ˈɪnmeɪt] *n (of prison)* preso(a) *m,f; (of hospital)* enfermo(a) *m,f; (of asylum, camp)* internado(a) *m,f*

inn [ɪn] *n (with lodging)* posada *f*, mesón *m*

innate [ɪˈneɪt] *adj* innato(a)

inner [ˈɪnə(r)] *adj (a) (region)* interior; *(structure)* interno(a); **i. city** zona urbana desfavorecida; **i. tube** cámara *f* de aire (**b**) *Fig (thoughts)* íntimo(a); *(peace etc)* interior

innermost [ˈɪnəməʊst] *adj (room)* más interior; *Fig (thoughts)* más íntimo(a)

innings [ˈɪnɪŋz] *npl (in cricket)* entrada *f*, turno *m*

innocence [ˈɪnəsəns] *n* inocencia *f*

innocent [ˈɪnəsənt] *adj & n* inocente *(mf)*

innocuous [ɪˈnɒkjʊəs] *adj* inocuo(a)

innovation [ɪnəˈveɪʃən] *n* novedad *f*

innuendo [ɪnjʊˈendəʊ] *n* indirecta *f*

inoculate [ɪˈnɒkjʊleɪt] *vt* inocular

inoculation [ɪnɒkjʊˈleɪʃən] *n* inoculación *f*

inoffensive [ɪnəˈfensɪv] *adj* inofensivo(a)

inopportune [ɪnˈɒpətjuːn, ɪnɒpəˈtjuːn] *adj* inoportuno(a)

inordinate [ɪˈnɔːdɪnɪt] *adj* desmesurado(a)

inpatient [ˈɪnpeɪʃənt] *n* interno(a) *m,f*

input [ˈɪnpʊt] *n (of resources)* inversión *f; (of power)* entrada *f; Comput (of data)* input *m*, entrada

inquest [ˈɪnkwest] *n* investigación *f* judicial

inquire [ɪnˈkwaɪə(r)] **1** *vt* preguntar; *(find out)* averiguar

2 *vi* preguntar (**about** por); *(find out)* informarse (**about** de)

▸ **inquire after** *vt insep* preguntar por

▸ **inquire into** *vt insep* investigar, indagar

inquiry [ɪnˈkwaɪərɪ] *n* (**a**) pregunta *f;* **inquiries** *(sign)* información (**b**) *(investigation)* investigación *f*

inquisitive [ɪnˈkwɪzɪtɪv] *adj (curious)* curioso(a); *(questioning)* preguntón(ona)

inroads [ˈɪnrəʊdz] *npl* **the firm is making i.**

into the market la empresa está ganando terreno en el mercado; **to make i. into one's capital** reducir su capital

insane [ɪn'seɪn] *adj* loco(a); *(act)* insensato(a); *Fig* **to drive sb i.** volver loco(a) a algn

insanity [ɪn'sænɪtɪ] *n* demencia *f*, locura *f*

insatiable [ɪn'seɪʃəbəl] *adj* insaciable

inscribe [ɪn'skraɪb] *vt Fml* inscribir; *(book)* dedicar

inscription [ɪn'skrɪpʃən] *n (on stone, coin)* inscripción *f*; *(in book, on photo)* dedicatoria *f*

inscrutable [ɪn'skruːtəbəl] *adj* inescrutable, insondable

insect ['ɪnsekt] *n* insecto *m*; **i. bite** picadura *f*

insecticide [ɪn'sektɪsaɪd] *n* insecticida *m*

insecure [ɪnsɪ'kjʊə(r)] *adj* inseguro(a)

insecurity [ɪnsɪ'kjʊərɪtɪ] *n* inseguridad *f*

insemination [ɪnsemɪ'neɪʃən] *n* inseminación *f*

insensible [ɪn'sensəbəl] *adj Fml* inconsciente

insensitive [ɪn'sensɪtɪv] *adj* insensible

inseparable [ɪn'sepərəbəl] *adj* inseparable

insert 1 *n* ['ɪnsɜːt] encarte *m*
2 *vt* [ɪn'sɜːt] introducir

insertion [ɪn'sɜːʃən] *n* introducción *f*; *(of clause, text)* inserción *f*

inshore 1 *adj* ['ɪnʃɔː(r)] *(fishing)* de bajura
2 *adv* [ɪn'ʃɔː(r)] cerca de la costa

inside [ɪn'saɪd] **1** *n* (a) interior *m*; **on the i.** por dentro; **to turn sth i. out** volver algo al revés (b) *Fam* **insides** tripas *fpl*
2 ['ɪnsaɪd] *adj* interior; *Sport* **i. forward** interior *mf*; *Aut* **i. lane** carril *m* interior
3 *adv* (be) dentro, adentro; *(run etc)* (hacia) adentro; **to come i.** entrar; *Br Fam* **he spent a year i.** pasó un año en chirona
4 *prep* (a) *(place)* dentro de (b) *Fam* **i. (of)** *(time)* en menos de

insider [ɪn'saɪdə(r)] *n* **i. dealing** = uso indebido de información privilegiada y confidencial para operaciones comerciales

insidious [ɪn'sɪdɪəs] *adj* insidioso(a)

insight ['ɪnsaɪt] *n* perspicacia *f*

insignia [ɪn'sɪgnɪə] *n inv* insignia *f*

insignificant [ɪnsɪg'nɪfɪkənt] *adj* insignificante

insincere [ɪnsɪn'sɪə(r)] *adj* poco sincero(a)

insinuate [ɪn'sɪnjʊeɪt] *vt* insinuar

insipid [ɪn'sɪpɪd] *adj* soso(a), insulso(a)

insist [ɪn'sɪst] **1** *vi* insistir (**on** en); *(argue)* obstinarse (**on** en)
2 *vt* **to i. that ...** insistir en que ...

insistence [ɪn'sɪstəns] *n* insistencia *f*

insistent [ɪn'sɪstənt] *adj* insistente

in so far as [ɪnsəʊ'fɑːrəz] *adv* en tanto que

insole ['ɪnsəʊl] *n (of shoe)* plantilla *f*

insolent ['ɪnsələnt] *adj* insolente

insoluble [ɪn'sɒljʊbəl] *adj* insoluble

insomnia [ɪn'sɒmnɪə] *n* insomnio *m*

insomniac [ɪn'sɒmnɪæk] *n* insomne *mf*

inspect [ɪn'spekt] *vt* inspeccionar, examinar; *(troops)* pasar revista a

inspection [ɪn'spekʃən] *n* inspección *f*; *(of troops)* revista *f*

inspector [ɪn'spektə(r)] *n* inspector(a) *m,f*; *(on bus, train)* revisor(a) *m,f*

inspiration [ɪnspɪ'reɪʃən] *n* inspiración *f*; **to get i. from sb/sth** inspirarse en algn/algo

inspire [ɪn'spaɪə(r)] *vt* (a) inspirar; **to i. respect in sb** infundir respeto a algn (b) **to i. sb to do sth** animar a algn a hacer algo

inspired [ɪn'spaɪəd] *adj* inspirado(a)

instability [ɪnstə'bɪlɪtɪ] *n* inestabilidad *f*

install, *US* **instal** [ɪn'stɔːl] *vt* instalar

installation [ɪnstə'leɪʃən] *n* instalación *f*

instalment, *US* **installment** [ɪn'stɔːlmənt] *n* (a) *(of payment)* plazo *m*; **to pay by instalments** pagar a plazos; *US* **i. plan** venta *f*/ compra *f* a plazos (b) *(of novel, programme)* entrega *f*; *(of journal)* fascículo *m*

instance ['ɪnstəns] *n* caso *m*, ejemplo *m*; **for i.** por ejemplo; **in the first i.** en primer lugar

> *📖* Note that the Spanish word **instancia** is a false friend and is never a translation for the English word **instance**. In Spanish, **instancia** means "request".

instant ['ɪnstənt] **1** *n (moment)* instante *m*, momento *m*; **in an i.** en un instante
2 *adj* inmediato(a); *(coffee, meal)* instantáneo(a)

instantly ['ɪnstəntlɪ] *adv* inmediatamente

instead [ɪn'sted] **1** *adv* en cambio
2 *prep* **i. of** en vez de, en lugar de

instep ['ɪnstep] *n* empeine *m*

instigation [ɪnstɪ'geɪʃən] *n* instigación *f*

instil, *US* **instill** [ɪn'stɪl] *vt (idea, habit)* inculcar (**in** a or en); *(courage, respect)* infundir (**in** a)

instinct ['ɪnstɪŋkt] *n* instinto *m*

instinctive [ɪn'stɪŋktɪv] *adj* instintivo(a)

institute ['ɪnstɪtjuːt] **1** *n (centre)* centro *m*; *(professional body)* colegio *m*
2 *vt Fml* (a) *(system)* establecer (b) *(start)* iniciar; *(proceedings)* entablar

institution [ɪnstɪ'tjuːʃən] *n* (a) institución *f* (b) *(home)* asilo *m*; *(asylum)* manicomio *m*

instruct [ɪn'strʌkt] *vt* instruir; *(order)* mandar; **I am instructed to say that ...** me han encargado decir que ...

instruction [ɪn'strʌkʃən] *n* (a) instrucción *f* (b) **instructions** instrucciones *fpl*; **instructions for use** modo de empleo

instructive [ɪn'strʌktɪv] *adj* instructivo(a)

instructor [ɪn'strʌktə(r)] *n* instructor(a) *m,f*; *(of driving)* profesor(a) *m,f*

instrument ['ɪnstrəmənt] *n* instrumento *m*; **i. panel** tablero *m* de mandos

instrumental [ɪnstrə'mentəl] *adj* (a) *Mus* instrumental (b) **to be i. in sth** contribuir decisivamente a algo

insubordinate [ɪnsə'bɔːdɪnɪt] *adj* insubordinado(a)

insubstantial [ɪnsəb'stænʃəl] *adj* insubstancial; *(structure)* poco sólido(a)

insufferable [ɪn'sʌfərəbəl] *adj* insoportable

insufficient [ɪnsə'fɪʃənt] *adj* insuficiente

insular ['ɪnsjʊlə(r)] *adj* (a) *Geog* insular (b) *Fig Pej* estrecho(a) de miras

insulate ['ɪnsjʊleɪt] *vt* aislar (**against** *or* **from** de)

insulating tape ['ɪnsjʊleɪtɪŋteɪp] *n* cinta *f* aislante

insulation [ɪnsjʊ'leɪʃən] *n* aislamiento *m*

insulin ['ɪnsjʊlɪn] *n* insulina *f*

insult **1** *n* ['ɪnsʌlt] *(words)* insulto *m*; *(action)* afrenta *f*, ofensa *f*
2 *vt* [ɪn'sʌlt] insultar, ofender

insulting [ɪn'sʌltɪŋ] *adj* insultante, ofensivo(a)

insuperable [ɪn'suːpərəbəl] *adj* insuperable

insurance [ɪn'ʃʊərəns] *n* seguro *m*; **fire i.** seguro contra incendios; **i. broker** agente *mf* de seguros; **i. company** compañía *f* de seguros; **i. policy** póliza *f* (de seguros); **private health i.** seguro médico privado

insure [ɪn'ʃʊə(r)] *vt* asegurar (**against** contra)

insurgent [ɪn'sɜːdʒənt] *adj & n* insurrecto(a) *(m,f)*

insurmountable [ɪnsə'maʊntəbəl] *adj* *(problem etc)* insuperable; *(barrier)* infranqueable

intact [ɪn'tækt] *adj* intacto(a)

intake ['ɪnteɪk] *n* (a) *(of air, water)* entrada *f*; *(of electricity etc)* toma *f* (b) *(of food, calories)* consumo *m* (c) *(of students, recruits)* número *m* de admitidos

integral ['ɪntɪɡrəl] **1** *adj* (a) *(intrinsic)* integrante (b) *(whole)* íntegro(a) (c) *Math* integral
2 *n Math* integral *f*

integrate ['ɪntɪɡreɪt] **1** *vt* integrar
2 *vi* integrarse

integration [ɪntɪ'ɡreɪʃən] *n* integración *f*

integrity [ɪn'teɡrɪtɪ] *n* integridad *f*, honradez *f*

intellect ['ɪntɪlekt] *n* intelecto *m*

intellectual [ɪntɪ'lektʃʊəl] *adj & n* intelectual *(mf)*

intelligence [ɪn'telɪdʒəns] *n* (a) inteligencia *f* (b) *(information)* información *f*

intelligent [ɪn'telɪdʒənt] *adj* inteligente

intelligentsia [ɪntelɪ'dʒentsɪə] *n* intelectualidad *f*

intelligible [ɪn'telɪdʒəbəl] *adj* inteligible

intend [ɪn'tend] *vt* (a) *(mean)* tener la intención de (b) **to i. sth for sb** destinar algo a algn

intended [ɪn'tendɪd] *adj (planned)* previsto(a)

intense [ɪn'tens] *adj* intenso(a); *(person)* muy serio(a)

intensely [ɪn'tenslɪ] *adv (extremely)* enormemente, sumamente

intensify [ɪn'tensɪfaɪ] *vt (search)* intensificar; *(effort)* redoblar; *(production, pollution)* aumentar

intensity [ɪn'tensɪtɪ] *n* intensidad *f*

intensive [ɪn'tensɪv] *adj* intensivo(a); *Med* **i. care unit** unidad *f* de vigilancia intensiva

intent [ɪn'tent] **1** *adj (absorbed)* absorto(a); *(gaze etc)* atento(a); **to be i. on doing sth** estar resuelto(a) a hacer algo
2 *n Fml* intención *f*, propósito *m*; **to all intents and purposes** a todos los efectos

intention [ɪn'tenʃən] *n* intención *f*

intentional [ɪn'tenʃənəl] *adj* deliberado(a)

intentionally [ɪn'tenʃənəlɪ] *adv* a propósito

interact [ɪntər'ækt] *vi (people)* interrelacionarse

interaction [ɪntər'ækʃən] *n* interacción *f*

interactive [ɪntər'æktɪv] *adj* interactivo(a)

intercede [ɪntə'siːd] *vi* interceder (**with** ante)

intercept [ɪntə'sept] *vt* interceptar

interchange **1** *n* ['ɪntətʃeɪndʒ] (a) *(exchange)* intercambio *m* (b) *(on motorway)* cruce *m*
2 *vt* [ɪntə'tʃeɪndʒ] intercambiar (**with** con)

interchangeable [ɪntə'tʃeɪndʒəbəl] *adj* intercambiable

intercity [ɪntə'sɪtɪ] *adj Rail* de largo recorrido

intercom ['ɪntəkɒm] *n* portero automático

intercontinental [ɪntəkɒntɪ'nentəl] *adj* **i. ballistic missile** misil balístico intercontinental

intercourse ['ɪntəkɔːs] *n* (a) *(dealings)* trato *m* (b) *(sexual)* relaciones *fpl* sexuales

interest ['ɪntrɪst] **1** *n* (a) interés *m* (b) *(advantage)* provecho *m*; **in the i. of** en pro de (c) *Com (share)* participación *f* (d) *Fin* interés *m*; **i. rate** tipo *m* de interés
2 *vt* interesar; **he's interested in politics** le interesa la política

interesting ['ɪntrɪstɪŋ] *adj* interesante

interface ['ɪntəfeɪs] *n* interface *f*

interfere [ɪntə'fɪə(r)] *vi* (a) *(meddle)* entrometerse (**in** en); **to i. with** *(hinder)* dificultar; *(spoil)* estropear; *(prevent)* impedir (b) *Rad & TV* interferir (**with** con)

interference [ɪntə'fɪərəns] *n (meddling)* intromisión *f*; *(hindrance)* estorbo *m*; *Rad & TV* interferencia *f*

interim ['ɪntərɪm] **1** *n Fml* **in the i.** en el ínterin
2 *adj* interino(a), provisional

interior [ɪn'tɪərɪə(r)] **1** *adj* interior
2 *n* interior *m*; **i. design** diseño *m* de interiores

interlock [ɪntə'lɒk] *vi* encajarse; *(fingers)* entrelazarse; *(cogs)* engranarse

interloper ['ɪntələʊpə(r)] *n* intruso(a) *m,f*

interlude ['ɪntəluːd] *n (break)* intervalo *m*; *Cin & Th* intermedio *m*; *Mus* interludio *m*

intermediary [ɪntə'miːdɪərɪ] *n* intermediario(a) *m,f*

intermediate [ɪntə'miːdɪɪt] *adj* intermedio(a)
interminable [ɪn'tɜːmɪnəbəl] *adj* interminable
intermission [ɪntə'mɪʃən] *n Cin & Th* intermedio *m*
intermittent [ɪntə'mɪtənt] *adj* intermitente
intern 1 *vt* [ɪn'tɜːn] internar
  2 *n* ['ɪntɜːn] *US Med* interno(a) *m,f*
internal [ɪn'tɜːnəl] *adj* interior; *(dispute, injury)* interno(a); *US* **I. Revenue Service** ≃ Hacienda *f*
internally [ɪn'tɜːnəlɪ] *adv* interiormente; **not to be taken i.** *(on medicine)* uso externo
international [ɪntə'næʃənəl] **1** *adj* internacional
  2 *n Sport (player)* internacional *mf*; *(match)* partido *m* internacional
Internet ['ɪntənet] *n Comput* **the I.** Internet; **it's on the I.** está en Internet; **I. access provider** proveedor *m* de acceso a Internet; **I. service provider** proveedor *m* de (acceso a) Internet
interplay ['ɪntəpleɪ] *n* interacción *f*
interpret [ɪn'tɜːprɪt] **1** *vt* interpretar
  2 *vi* actuar de intérprete
interpretation [ɪntɜːprɪ'teɪʃən] *n* interpretación *f*
interpreter [ɪn'tɜːprɪtə(r)] *n* intérprete *mf*
interrelated [ɪntərɪ'leɪtɪd] *adj* estrechamente relacionado(a)
interrogate [ɪn'terəgeɪt] *vt* interrogar
interrogation [ɪntərə'geɪʃən] *n* interrogatorio *m*
interrogative [ɪntə'rɒgətɪv] *Ling* **1** *adj* interrogativo(a)
  2 *n (word)* palabra interrogativa
interrupt [ɪntə'rʌpt] *vt & vi* interrumpir
interruption [ɪntə'rʌpʃən] *n* interrupción *f*
intersect [ɪntə'sekt] **1** *vt* cruzar
  2 *vi* cruzarse
intersection [ɪntə'sekʃən] *n* (**a**) *(crossroads)* cruce *m* (**b**) *(of two lines)* intersección *f*
intersperse [ɪntə'spɜːs] *vt* esparcir
intertwine [ɪntə'twaɪn] **1** *vt* entrelazar (**with** con)
  2 *vi* entrelazarse (**with** con)
interval ['ɪntəvəl] *n* (**a**) *(of time, space)* intervalo *m*; **at intervals** *(time, space)* a intervalos; *(time)* de vez en cuando (**b**) *Br Cin Th* intermedio *m*
intervene [ɪntə'viːn] *vi* (**a**) *(person)* intervenir (**in** en) (**b**) *(event)* sobrevenir (**c**) *(time)* transcurrir
intervention [ɪntə'venʃən] *n* intervención *f*
interview ['ɪntəvjuː] **1** *n* entrevista *f*; **to give an i.** conceder una entrevista
  2 *vt* entrevistar
interviewer ['ɪntəvjuːə(r)] *n* entrevistador(a) *m,f*
intestine [ɪn'testɪn] *n (usu pl)* intestino *m*; **large/small i.** intestino grueso/delgado

intimacy ['ɪntɪməsɪ] *n (closeness)* intimidad *f*; *Euph (sex)* relación íntima; **intimacies** intimidades *fpl*
intimate¹ ['ɪntɪmɪt] *adj* íntimo(a); *(knowledge)* profundo(a)
intimate² ['ɪntɪmeɪt] *vt Fml* dar a entender
intimidate [ɪn'tɪmɪdeɪt] *vt* intimidar
intimidating [ɪn'tɪmɪdeɪtɪŋ] *adj* atemorizante
into ['ɪntuː, *unstressed* 'ɪntə] *prep* (**a**) *(motion)* en, a, con; **he fell i. the water** se cayó al agua; **I bumped i. a friend** me topé con un amigo; **to get i. a car** subir a un coche; **to go i. a house** entrar en una casa (**b**) *(state)* en, a; **he grew i. a man** se hizo un hombre; **to burst i. tears** echarse a llorar; **to change pounds i. pesetas** cambiar libras en *or* por pesetas; **to translate sth i. French** traducir algo al francés (**c**) *(at work)* **i. the night** trabajar hasta muy avanzada la noche (**d**) **to divide sth i. three** dividir algo en tres (**e**) *Fam* **to be i. sth** ser aficionado(a) a algo
intolerable [ɪn'tɒlərəbəl] *adj* intolerable
intolerant [ɪn'tɒlərənt] *adj* intolerante
intonation [ɪntə'neɪʃən] *n* entonación *f*
intoxicated [ɪn'tɒksɪkeɪtɪd] *adj* borracho(a)

> 🖋 Note that the Spanish word **intoxicado** is a false friend and is never a translation for the English word **intoxicated**. In Spanish, **intoxicado** means "poisoned".

intoxicating [ɪn'tɒksɪkeɪtɪŋ] *adj* embriagador(a); **i. liquor** bebida alcohólica
intoxication [ɪntɒksɪ'keɪʃən] *n* embriaguez *f*

> 🖋 Note that the Spanish word **intoxicación** is a false friend and is never a translation for the English word **intoxication**. In Spanish, **intoxicación** means "poisoning".

intractable [ɪn'træktəbəl] *adj Fml (person)* intratable; *(problem)* insoluble
intranet ['ɪntrənet] *n Comput* intranet *f*
intransigent [ɪn'trænsɪdʒənt] *adj Fml* intransigente, intolerante
intransitive [ɪn'trænsɪtɪv] *adj* intransitivo(a)
intravenous [ɪntrə'viːnəs] *adj* intravenoso(a)
in-tray ['ɪntreɪ] *n* bandeja *f* de asuntos pendientes
intrepid [ɪn'trepɪd] *adj* intrépido(a), audaz
intricate ['ɪntrɪkɪt] *adj* intrincado(a)
intrigue 1 *n* [ɪn'triːg, 'ɪntriːg] intriga *f*
  2 *vt* [ɪn'triːg] intrigar
  3 *vi* intrigar, conspirar
intriguing [ɪn'triːgɪŋ] *adj* intrigante
intrinsic [ɪn'trɪnsɪk] *adj Fml* intrínseco(a)
introduce [ɪntrə'djuːs] *vt* (**a**) *(person, programme)* presentar (**to** a) (**b**) *(bring in)* introducir (**into** *or* **to** en); *Com* lanzar (**into** *or* **to** a); *(topic)* proponer
introduction [ɪntrə'dʌkʃən] *n* (**a**) *(of person,*

programme) presentación *f*; *(in book)* introducción *f* (**b**) *(bringing in)* introducción *f*; Com *(of product)* lanzamiento *m*

introductory [ɪntrə'dʌktərɪ] *adj* introductorio(a); *(remarks)* preliminar; Com de lanzamiento

introspective [ɪntrə'spektɪv] *adj* introspectivo(a)

introvert ['ɪntrəvɜːt] *n* introvertido(a) *m,f*

intrude [ɪn'truːd] *vi* entrometerse (**into** *or* **on** en); *(disturb)* molestar

intruder [ɪn'truːdə(r)] *n* intruso(a) *m,f*

intrusion [ɪn'truːʒən] *n* incursión *f*

intuition [ɪntjʊ'ɪʃən] *n* intuición *f*

inundate ['ɪnʌndeɪt] *vt* inundar (**with** de)

invade [ɪn'veɪd] *vt* invadir

invader [ɪn'veɪdə(r)] *n* invasor(a) *m,f*

invalid¹ ['ɪnvəlɪd] *n (disabled person)* minusválido(a) *m,f*; *(sick person)* enfermo(a) *m,f*

invalid² [ɪn'vælɪd] *adj* inválido(a), nulo(a)

invalidate [ɪn'vælɪdeɪt] *vt* invalidar

invaluable [ɪn'væljəbəl] *adj* inestimable

invariable [ɪn'veərɪəbəl] *adj* invariable

invasion [ɪn'veɪʒən] *n* invasión *f*

invent [ɪn'vent] *vt* inventar

invention [ɪn'venʃən] *n* invento *m*; *(creativity)* inventiva *f*; *(lie)* mentira *f*

inventive [ɪn'ventɪv] *adj* inventivo(a)

inventor [ɪn'ventə(r)] *n* inventor(a) *m,f*

inventory ['ɪnvəntərɪ] *n* inventario *m*

invert [ɪn'vɜːt] *vt* invertir

invertebrate [ɪn'vɜːtɪbrɪt] **1** *adj* invertebrado(a)

    2 *n* invertebrado *m*

inverted [ɪn'vɜːtɪd] *adj* **(in) i. commas** (entre) comillas *fpl*

invest [ɪn'vest] **1** *vt* invertir (**in** en); **to i. sb with sth** conferir algo a algn

    2 *vi* invertir (**in** en)

investigate [ɪn'vestɪgeɪt] *vt (crime, subject)* investigar; *(cause, possibility)* estudiar

investigation [ɪnvestɪ'geɪʃən] *n (of crime)* investigación *f*; *(of cause)* examen *m*

investigator [ɪn'vestɪgeɪtə(r)] *n* investigador(a) *m,f*; **private i.** detective privado

investment [ɪn'vestmənt] *n* inversión *f*

investor [ɪn'vestə(r)] *n* inversor(a) *m,f*

inveterate [ɪn'vetərɪt] *adj* empedernido(a)

invidious [ɪn'vɪdɪəs] *adj (task)* ingrato(a); *(comparison)* injusto(a)

📝 Note that the Spanish word **envidioso** is a false friend and is never a translation for the English word **invidious**. In Spanish, **envidioso** means "envious".

invigilator [ɪn'vɪdʒɪleɪtə(r)] *n* Br vigilante *mf*

invigorating [ɪn'vɪgəreɪtɪŋ] *adj* vigorizante

invincible [ɪn'vɪnsəbəl] *adj* invencible

invisible [ɪn'vɪzəbəl] *adj* invisible

invitation [ɪnvɪ'teɪʃən] *n* invitación *f*

invite [ɪn'vaɪt] *vt* (**a**) invitar (**to** a) (**b**) *(comments etc)* solicitar; *(criticism)* provocar; **to i. trouble** buscarse problemas

inviting [ɪn'vaɪtɪŋ] *adj (attractive)* atractivo(a); *(food)* apetitoso(a)

invoice ['ɪnvɔɪs] **1** *n* factura *f*

    2 *vt* facturar

invoke [ɪn'vəʊk] *vt* Fml invocar

involuntary [ɪn'vɒləntərɪ] *adj* involuntario(a)

involve [ɪn'vɒlv] *vt* (**a**) *(concern)* implicar (**in** en); **the issues involved** las cuestiones en juego; **to be involved in an accident** sufrir un accidente (**b**) *(entail)* suponer, implicar; *(trouble, risk)* acarrear

involved [ɪn'vɒlvd] *adj (complicated)* complicado(a); Fam *(romantically attached)* enredado(a), liado(a)

involvement [ɪn'vɒlvmənt] *n (participation)* participación *f*; *(in crime)* implicación *f*

inward ['ɪnwəd] **1** *adj* interior

    2 *adv* = **inwards**

inwardly ['ɪnwədlɪ] *adv* interiormente, por dentro

inwards ['ɪnwədz] *adv* hacia dentro

in-your-face ['ɪnjə'feɪs] *adj* Fam *(style)* descarado(a); *(movie, advert)* impactante, fuerte

iodine ['aɪədiːn] *n* yodo *m*

iota [aɪ'əʊtə] *n* pizca *f*, ápice *m*

IOU [aɪəʊ'juː] *n (abbr* **I owe you***)* pagaré *m*

IQ [aɪ'kjuː] *n (abbr* **intelligence quotient***)* CI *m*

IRA [aɪɑː'reɪ] *n (abbr* **Irish Republican Army***)* IRA *m*

Iran [ɪ'rɑːn] *n* Irán *m*

Iranian [ɪ'reɪnɪən] *adj & n* iraní *(mf)*

Iraq [ɪ'rɑːk] *n* Irak *m*

Iraqi [ɪ'rɑːkɪ] *adj & n* iraquí *(mf)*

irascible [ɪ'ræsɪbəl] *adj* Fml irascible

irate [aɪ'reɪt] *adj* airado(a), furioso(a)

Ireland ['aɪələnd] *n* Irlanda *f*; **Republic of I.** República de Irlanda

iris ['aɪərɪs] *n* (**a**) Anat iris *m inv* (**b**) Bot lirio *m*

Irish ['aɪrɪʃ] **1** *adj* irlandés(esa); **I. coffee** café *m* irlandés; **I. Sea** Mar *m* de Irlanda

    2 *n* (**a**) *(language)* irlandés *m* (**b**) *pl* **the I.** los irlandeses

Irishman ['aɪrɪʃmən] *n* irlandés *m*

Irishwoman ['aɪrɪʃwʊmən] *n* irlandesa *f*

irksome ['ɜːksəm] *adj* fastidioso(a)

iron ['aɪən] **1** *n* (**a**) hierro *m*; **the i. and steel industry** la industria siderúrgica; **I. Curtain** Telón *m* de Acero; **i. ore** mineral *m* de hierro (**b**) *(for clothes)* plancha *f* (**c**) *(for golf)* hierro *m* (**d**) **irons** *(chains)* grillos *mpl*

    2 *vt (clothes)* planchar

▸ **iron out** *vt sep* (**a**) *(crease)* planchar (**b**) Fam Fig *(problem)* resolver

ironic(al) [aɪ'rɒnɪk(əl)] *adj* irónico(a)

ironing ['aɪənɪŋ] *n* (**a**) **to do the i.** planchar; **i. board** mesa *f* de la plancha (**b**) *(clothes to be ironed)* ropa *f* para planchar; *(clothes ironed)* ropa planchada

ironmonger ['aɪənmʌŋgə(r)] *n* Br ferretero(a) *m,f*; **i.'s (shop)** ferretería *f*

irony ['aɪrənɪ] n ironía f
irrational [ɪ'ræʃənəl] adj irracional
irreconcilable [ɪrekən'saɪləbəl] adj irreconciliable
irrefutable [ɪrɪ'fjuːtəbəl] adj Fml irrefutable
irregular [ɪ'regjʊlə(r)] adj (a) irregular; (abnormal) anormal (b) (uneven) desigual
irrelevant [ɪ'reləvənt] adj no pertinente
irreparable [ɪ'repərəbəl] adj irreparable
irreplaceable [ɪrɪ'pleɪsəbəl] adj irremplazable
irrepressible [ɪrɪ'presəbəl] adj incontenible
irresistible [ɪrɪ'zɪstəbəl] adj irresistible
irresolute [ɪ'rezəluːt] adj Fml indeciso(a)
irrespective [ɪrɪ'spektɪv] adj i. of sin tener en cuenta
irresponsible [ɪrɪ'spɒnsəbəl] adj irresponsable
irreverent [ɪ'revərənt] adj irreverente
irrevocable [ɪ'revəkəbəl] adj irrevocable
irrigate ['ɪrɪgeɪt] vt regar
irrigation [ɪrɪ'geɪʃən] n riego m; **i. channel** acequia f; **i. system** sistema m de regadío
irritable ['ɪrɪtəbəl] adj irritable
irritate ['ɪrɪteɪt] vt (annoy) fastidiar; Med irritar
irritating ['ɪrɪteɪtɪŋ] adj irritante
irritation [ɪrɪ'teɪʃən] n (a) (annoyance) fastidio m; (ill humour) mal humor m (b) Med irritación f
is [ɪz] 3rd person sing pres of **be**
Islam ['ɪzlɑːm] n Islam m
Islamic [ɪz'læmɪk] adj islámico(a)
island ['aɪlənd] n isla f; **(traffic) i.** isleta f
islander ['aɪləndə(r)] n isleño(a) m,f
isle [aɪl] n isla f
isn't ['ɪzənt] = **is not**
isolate ['aɪsəleɪt] vt aislar (**from** de)
isolated ['aɪsəleɪtɪd] adj aislado(a)
isolation [aɪsə'leɪʃən] n aislamiento m
ISP [aɪes'piː] n Comput (abbr **Internet Service Provider**) PSI m
Israel ['ɪzreɪəl] n Israel
Israeli [ɪz'reɪlɪ] adj & n israelí (mf)
issue ['ɪʃuː] **1** n (a) (matter) cuestión f; **to take i. with sb (over sth)** manifestar su desacuerdo con algn (en algo) (b) (of banknotes etc) emisión f; (of passport) expedición f (c) (of journal etc) ejemplar m (d) (of supplies) reparto m (e) Fml (outcome) resultado m (f) Jur (offspring) descendencia f
2 vt (a) (book) publicar; (banknotes etc) emitir; (passport) expedir (b) (supplies) repartir (c) (order, instructions) dar; (warrant) dictar
3 vi Fml (blood) brotar (**from** de); (smoke)

salir (**from** de)
isthmus ['ɪsməs] n istmo m
it [ɪt] pers pron (a) (subject) él/ella/ello (usually omitted in Spanish, except for contrast); **it's here** está aquí
(b) (direct object) lo/la; **I don't believe it** no me lo creo; **I liked the house and bought it** me gustó la casa y la compré
(c) (indirect object) le; **give it a kick** dale una patada
(d) (after prep) él/ella/ello; **I saw the beach and ran towards it** vi la playa y fui corriendo hacia ella; **we'll talk about it later** ya hablaremos de ello
(e) (abstract) ello; **let's get down to it!** ¡vamos a ello!
(f) (impersonal) **it's late** es tarde; **it's me** soy yo; **it's raining** está lloviendo; **it's said that ...** se dice que ...; **it's 2 miles to town** hay 2 millas de aquí al pueblo; **that's it!** (agreeing) ¡precisamente!; (finishing) ¡se acabó!; **this is it!** ¡ha llegado la hora!; **who is it?** ¿quién es?
Italian [ɪ'tæljən] **1** adj italiano(a)
2 n (a) (person) italiano(a) m,f (b) (language) italiano m
italic [ɪ'tælɪk] n cursiva f
Italy ['ɪtəlɪ] n Italia
itch [ɪtʃ] **1** n picor m; Fig **an i. to travel** unas ganas locas de viajar
2 vi (a) (skin) picar (b) Fig anhelar; Fam **to be itching to do sth** tener muchas ganas de hacer algo
itchy ['ɪtʃɪ] adj (**itchier, itchiest**) que pica
item ['aɪtəm] n (a) (in list) artículo m; (in collection) pieza f; **i. of clothing** prenda f de vestir (b) (on agenda) asunto m; (in show) número m; **news i.** noticia f
itemize ['aɪtəmaɪz] vt detallar
itinerant [ɪ'tɪnərənt] adj Fml itinerante
itinerary [aɪ'tɪnərərɪ] n itinerario m
it'll ['ɪtəl] = **it will**
its [ɪts] poss adj (one thing) su; (more than one) sus
itself [ɪt'self] pers pron (a) (reflexive) se; **the cat scratched i.** el gato se arañó (b) (emphatic) él mismo/ella misma/ello mismo; (after prep) sí (mismo(a)); **in i.** en sí
ITV [aɪtiː'viː] n Br (abbr **Independent Television**) = canal privado de televisión británico
IUD [aɪjuː'diː] n (abbr **intrauterine (contraceptive) device**) DIU m
IVF [aɪviː'ef] n Med (abbr **in vitro fertilization**) fertilización f in vitro
ivory ['aɪvərɪ] n marfil m
ivy ['aɪvɪ] n hiedra f

J, j [dʒeɪ] *n (the letter)* J, j *f*

jab [dʒæb] **1** *n* pinchazo *m; (poke)* golpe seco
2 *vt* pinchar; *(with fist)* dar un puñetazo a

jabber ['dʒæbə(r)] *vi Fam (chatter)* charlotear; *(speak quickly)* hablar atropelladamente

jack [dʒæk] *n* (**a**) *Aut* gato *m* (**b**) *Cards* sota *f* (**c**) *(bowls)* boliche *m*
▸ **jack in** *vt sep Br Fam* dejar
▸ **jack up** *vt sep Aut* levantar (con el gato); *Fig (prices)* aumentar

jackal ['dʒækɔːl] *n* chacal *m*

jackdaw ['dʒækdɔː] *n Orn* grajilla *f*

jacket ['dʒækɪt] *n* (**a**) chaqueta *f; (of suit)* americana *f; (bomber jacket)* cazadora *f* (**b**) *(of book)* sobrecubierta *f; US (of record)* funda *f* (**c**) **j. potatoes** patatas *fpl or Am* papas *fpl* al horno

jack-knife ['dʒæknaɪf] **1** *n* navaja *f*
2 *vi* colear

jack-of-all-trades [dʒækəvˈɔːltreɪdz] *n* persona *f* mañosa *or* de muchos oficios

jackpot ['dʒækpɒt] *n (premio m)* gordo *m*

Jacuzzi® [dʒəˈkuːzɪ] *n* jacuzzi® *m*

jade [dʒeɪd] *n* jade *m*

jaded ['dʒeɪdɪd] *adj (tired)* agotado(a); *(palate)* hastiado(a)

jagged ['dʒægɪd] *adj* dentado(a)

jaguar ['dʒægjʊə(r)] *n* jaguar *m*

jail [dʒeɪl] **1** *n* cárcel *f*, prisión *f*
2 *vt* encarcelar

jailbreak ['dʒeɪlbreɪk] *n* fuga *f*, evasión *f*

jailer ['dʒeɪlə(r)] *n* carcelero(a) *m,f*

jam¹ [dʒæm] *n Culin* mermelada *f*

jam² [dʒæm] **1** *n* (**a**) *(blockage)* atasco *m; Fam (fix)* apuro *m* (**b**) *Mus* improvisación *f*
2 *vt* (**a**) *(cram)* meter a la fuerza (**b**) *(block)* atascar; *Rad* interferir
3 *vi (door)* atrancarse; *(brakes)* agarrotarse

Jamaica [dʒəˈmeɪkə] *n* Jamaica *f*

jam-packed [dʒæmˈpækt] *adj Fam (with people)* atestado(a); *(with things)* atiborrado(a)

jangle ['dʒæŋgəl] *vi* tintinear

janitor ['dʒænɪtə(r)] *n* portero *m*, conserje *m*

January ['dʒænjʊərɪ] *n* enero *m*

Japan [dʒəˈpæn] *n* (el) Japón *m*

Japanese [dʒæpəˈniːz] **1** *adj* japonés(esa)
2 *n (person)* japonés(esa) *m,f; (language)* japonés *m*

jar¹ [dʒɑː(r)] *n (glass)* tarro *m; (earthenware)* tinaja *f; (jug)* jarra *f; Br Fam* **to have a j.** tomar una copa

jar² [dʒɑː(r)] *vi (sounds)* chirriar; *(appearance)* chocar; *(colours)* desentonar; *Fig* **to j. on one's nerves** ponerle a uno los nervios de punta

jargon ['dʒɑːgən] *n* jerga *f*, argot *m*

jasmin(e) ['dʒæzmɪn] *n* jazmín *m*

jaundice ['dʒɔːndɪs] *n* ictericia *f*

jaundiced ['dʒɔːndɪst] *adj Med* ictérico(a); *Fig (bitter)* amargado(a)

jaunt [dʒɔːnt] *n (walk)* paseo *m; (trip)* excursión *f*

jaunty ['dʒɔːntɪ] *adj* (**jauntier, jauntiest**) *(sprightly)* garboso(a); *(lively)* vivaz

javelin ['dʒævəlɪn] *n* jabalina *f*

jaw [dʒɔː] **1** *n* mandíbula *f*
2 *vi Fam* estar de palique

jay [dʒeɪ] *n Orn* arrendajo *m (común)*

jaywalker ['dʒeɪwɔːkə(r)] *n* peatón *m* imprudente

jazz [dʒæz] *n* jazz *m*
▸ **jazz up** *vt sep* alegrar; *(premises)* arreglar

jazzy ['dʒæzɪ] *adj* (**jazzier, jazziest**) *Fam (showy)* llamativo(a); *(brightly coloured)* de colores chillones

jealous ['dʒeləs] *adj* celoso(a); *(envious)* envidioso(a); **to be j. of ...** tener celos de ...

jealousy ['dʒeləsɪ] *n* celos *mpl; (envy)* envidia *f*

jeans [dʒiːnz] *npl* vaqueros *mpl*, tejanos *mpl*

Jeep® [dʒiːp] *n* jeep *m*, todo terreno *m inv*

jeer [dʒɪə(r)] **1** *n (boo)* abucheo *m; (mocking)* mofa *f*
2 *vi (boo)* abuchear; *(mock)* burlarse

jeering ['dʒɪərɪŋ] *adj* burlón(ona)

Jehovah [dʒɪˈhəʊvə] *n* **J.'s Witness** testigo *mf* de Jehová

Jell-O®, jello ['dʒeləʊ] *n US* gelatina *f*

jelly ['dʒelɪ] *n* gelatina *f*

jellyfish ['dʒelɪfɪʃ] *n* medusa *f*

jeopardize ['dʒepədaɪz] *vt* poner en peligro; *(agreement etc)* comprometer

jeopardy ['dʒepədɪ] *n* riesgo *m*, peligro *m*

jerk [dʒɜːk] **1** *n* (**a**) *(jolt)* sacudida *f; (pull)* tirón *m* (**b**) *Pej (idiot)* imbécil *mf*
2 *vt (shake)* sacudir; *(pull)* dar un tirón a
3 *vi (move suddenly)* dar una sacudida; **the car jerked forward** el coche avanzaba a tirones

jerkin ['dʒɜːkɪn] *n* chaleco *m*

jersey ['dʒɜːzɪ] *n* jersey *m*, suéter *m*, pulóver *m*, *Andes* chompa *f*, *Urug* buzo *m*

jest [dʒest] **1** *n* broma *f*
  2 *vi* bromear
Jesuit ['dʒezjʊɪt] *adj & n* jesuita *(m)*
Jesus ['dʒiːzəs] *n* Jesús *m*; **J. Christ** Jesucristo *m*
jet¹ [dʒet] **1** *n* (a) *(stream of water)* chorro *m* (b) *(spout)* surtidor *m* (c) *Av* reactor *m*; **j. engine** reactor; **j. lag** = cansancio debido al desfase horario; **j. ski** moto náutica *or* acuática
  2 *vi Fam* volar
jet² [dʒet] *n* **j. black** negro(a) como el azabache
jet-set ['dʒetset] *n* **the j.** la alta sociedad, la jet
jettison ['dʒetɪsən] *vt* echar al mar; *Fig* deshacerse de; *(project etc)* abandonar
jetty ['dʒetɪ] *n* muelle *m*, malecón *m*
Jew [dʒuː] *n* judío(a) *m,f*
jewel ['dʒuːəl] *n* joya *f*; *(stone)* piedra preciosa; *(in watch)* rubí *m*; *Fig (person)* joya
jeweller, jeweler ['dʒuːələ(r)] *n* joyero(a) *m,f*; **j.'s (shop)** joyería *f*
jewellery, jewelry ['dʒuːəlrɪ] *n* joyas *fpl*, alhajas *fpl*
Jewess ['dʒuːɪs] *n* judía *f*
Jewish ['dʒuːɪʃ] *adj* judío(a)
jibe [dʒaɪb] *n & vi* = **gibe**
jiffy ['dʒɪfɪ] *n Fam* momento *m*; **in a j.** en un santiamén; **just a j.!** ¡un momento!
jig [dʒɪg] *n Mus* giga *f*
jigsaw ['dʒɪgsɔː] *n (puzzle)* rompecabezas *m inv*
jilt [dʒɪlt] *vt Fam* dejar plantado(a)
jingle ['dʒɪŋgəl] **1** *n Rad & TV* = canción que acompaña un anuncio
  2 *vi* tintinear
jingoistic [dʒɪŋgəʊˈɪstɪk] *adj* patriotero(a)
jinx [dʒɪŋks] **1** *n (person)* gafe *mf*
  2 *vt* gafar
jitters ['dʒɪtəz] *npl Fam* **to get the j.** tener canguelo
jive [dʒaɪv] **1** *n* swing *m*
  2 *vi* bailar el swing
job [dʒɒb] *n* (a) trabajo *m*; *(task)* tarea *f*; **to give sth up as a bad j.** darse por vencido(a); *Fam* **just the j.!** ¡me viene de perlas! (b) *(occupation)* (puesto *m* de) trabajo *m*, empleo *m*; *(trade)* oficio *m*; *Br Fam* **jobs for the boys** enchufismo *m*; *US* **j. office** oficina *f* de empleo; **j. hunting** búsqueda *f* de empleo; **j. sharing** trabajo compartido a tiempo parcial (c) *Fam* **we had a j. to ...** nos costó (trabajo) ... (d) *(duty)* deber *m* (e) *Fam* **it's a good j. that ...** menos mal que ...
Jobcentre ['dʒɒbsentə(r)] *n Br* oficina *f* de empleo
jobless ['dʒɒblɪs] *adj* parado(a)
jockey ['dʒɒkɪ] **1** *n* jinete *m*, jockey *m*
  2 *vi* **to j. for position** luchar para conseguir una posición aventajada
jocular ['dʒɒkjʊlə(r)] *adj* jocoso(a)

jog [dʒɒg] **1** *n* trote *m*
  2 *vt* empujar; *Fig (memory)* refrescar
  3 *vi Sport* hacer footing; *Fig* **to j. along** *(progress slowly)* avanzar poco a poco; *(manage)* ir tirando
jogging ['dʒɒgɪŋ] *n* footing *m*
john [dʒɒn] *n US Fam* **the j.** *(lavatory)* el váter
join [dʒɔɪn] **1** *vt* (a) juntar; **to j. forces with s** unir fuerzas con algn (b) *(road)* empalma con; *(river)* desembocar en (c) *(meet)* reuni se con (d) *(group)* unirse a; *(institution)* en trar; *(army)* alistarse a (e) *(party)* afiliarse *a* *(club)* hacerse socio(a) de
  2 *vi* (a) unirse a (b) *(roads)* empalmar; *(rivers* confluir (c) *(become member of politica party)* afiliarse; *(become member of club)* ha cerse socio(a)
  3 *n* juntura *f*
  ► **join in 1** *vi* participar, tomar parte; *(debate* intervenir
  2 *vt insep* participar en, tomar parte en
  ► **join up 1** *vt sep* juntar
  2 *vi (of roads)* unirse; *Mil* alistarse
joiner ['dʒɔɪnə(r)] *n Br* carpintero(a) *m,f*
joinery ['dʒɔɪnərɪ] *n* carpintería *f*
joint [dʒɔɪnt] **1** *n* (a) juntura *f*, unión *f*; *Tech é Anat* articulación *f*; **out of j.** dislocado(a) (b Culin* = corte de carne para asar; *(once roas ted)* asado *m* (c) *Fam (nightclub etc)* garito *n* (d) *Fam (drug)* porro *m*
  2 *adj* colectivo(a); **j. (bank) account** cuent conjunta; **j. venture** empresa conjunta
jointly ['dʒɔɪntlɪ] *adv* conjuntamente, e común
joist [dʒɔɪst] *n* vigueta *f*
joke [dʒəʊk] **1** *n* (a) chiste *m*; *(prank)* broma *f* **to play a j. on sb** gastarle una broma a algr **to tell a j.** contar un chiste (b) *Fam (persona* hazmerreír *m*, payaso(a) *m,f*; **to be a j.** *(c thing)* ser de chiste
  2 *vi* estar de broma; **you must be joking!** ¡n hablarás en serio!
joker ['dʒəʊkə(r)] *n* (a) bromista *mf* (b Cards* comodín *m*
jolly ['dʒɒlɪ] **1** *adj* (jollier, jolliest) alegre
  2 *adv Fam (very)* muy; **she played j. well** jugó muy bien
jolt [dʒəʊlt] **1** *n* (a) sacudida *f*; *(pull)* tirón *n* (b) *Fig (fright)* susto *m*
  2 *vi* moverse a sacudidas
  3 *vt* sacudir
Jordan ['dʒɔːdən] *n* (a) *(river)* Jordán *m* (b *(country)* Jordania
joss-stick ['dʒɒsstɪk] *n* varita *f* de incienso
jostle ['dʒɒsəl] **1** *vi* dar empujones
  2 *vt* dar empujones a
jot [dʒɒt] *n* jota *f*, pizca *f*; **not a j.** ni jota
  ► **jot down** *vt sep* apuntar
jotter ['dʒɒtə(r)] *n Br* bloc *m*
journal ['dʒɜːnəl] *n* (a) revista *f* (b) *(diary* diario *m* (c) *(newspaper)* periódico *m*

📖 Note that the Spanish word **jornal** is a false friend and is never a translation for the English word **journal**. In Spanish, **jornal** means "day's wage".

journalism ['dʒɜːnəlɪzəm] n periodismo m
journalist ['dʒɜːnəlɪst] n periodista mf
journey ['dʒɜːnɪ] **1** n viaje m; (distance) trayecto m
 2 vi Fml viajar
jovial ['dʒəʊvɪəl] adj jovial
jowl [dʒaʊl] n quijada f
joy [dʒɔɪ] n alegría f, (pleasure) placer m
joyful ['dʒɔɪfʊl] adj alegre, contento(a)
joyous ['dʒɔɪəs] adj Literary alegre
joyride ['dʒɔɪraɪd] n Fam = paseo en un coche robado
joystick ['dʒɔɪstɪk] n Av palanca f de mando; (of video game) joystick m
JP [dʒeɪ'piː] n Br Law (abbr **Justice of the Peace**) juez mf de paz
Jr (abbr **Junior**) **Neil Smith, Jr** Neil Smith, hijo
jubilant ['dʒuːbɪlənt] adj jubiloso(a)
jubilation [dʒuːbɪ'leɪʃən] n júbilo m
jubilee ['dʒuːbɪliː] n festejos mpl; **golden j.** quincuagésimo aniversario
judge [dʒʌdʒ] **1** n juez mf, jueza f; (in competition) jurado m
 2 vt (a) Jur juzgar (b) (estimate) considerar (c) (competition) actuar de juez de (d) (assess) juzgar
 3 vi juzgar; **judging from what you say** a juzgar por lo que dices
judg(e)ment ['dʒʌdʒmənt] n (a) Jur sentencia f, fallo m; **to pass j.** dictar sentencia (b) (opinion) juicio m; **to pass j. (on)** opinar (sobre); **to reserve j. (on)** no opinar (sobre) (c) (ability) buen juicio m (d) (trial) juicio m
judicial [dʒuː'dɪʃəl] adj judicial
judiciary [dʒuː'dɪʃərɪ] n magistratura f
judicious [dʒuː'dɪʃəs] adj Fml juicioso(a)
judo ['dʒuːdəʊ] n judo m
jug [dʒʌg] n Br jarra f; **milk j.** jarra de leche
juggernaut ['dʒʌgənɔːt] n Br camión pesado
juggle ['dʒʌgəl] vi (perform) hacer juegos malabares (**with** con); Fig (responsibilities) ajustar
juggler ['dʒʌglə(r)] n malabarista mf
juice [dʒuːs] n jugo m; (of citrus fruits) zumo m
juicy ['dʒuːsɪ] adj (**juicier, juiciest**) (a) jugoso(a) (b) Fam Fig picante
jukebox ['dʒuːkbɒks] n rocola f
July [dʒuː'laɪ, dʒə'laɪ] n julio m
jumble ['dʒʌmbəl] **1** n revoltijo m; **j. sale** mercadillo m de caridad
 2 vt revolver
jumbo ['dʒʌmbəʊ] n **j. (jet)** jumbo m
jump [dʒʌmp] **1** n salto m; (sudden increase) subida repentina; **j. leads** cables mpl de emergencia; **j. suit** mono m

 2 vi (a) saltar, dar un salto; Fig **to j. to conclusions** sacar conclusiones precipitadas (b) Fig (start) sobresaltarse (c) (increase) aumentar de golpe
 3 vt saltar; Fam Fig **to j. the gun** precipitarse; **to j. the lights** saltarse el semáforo; Br **to j. the queue** colarse; US **to j. rope** saltar a la comba
 ▸ **jump at** vt insep aceptar sin pensarlo
jumper ['dʒʌmpə(r)] n (a) Br (sweater) jersey m, suéter m, pulóver m, Andes chompa f, Urug buzo m (b) US (dress) pichi m, falda f con peto (c) US Aut **j. cables** cables mpl de emergencia
jumpy ['dʒʌmpɪ] adj (**jumpier, jumpiest**) Fam nervioso(a)
junction ['dʒʌŋkʃən] n (of roads) cruce m; Rail & Elec empalme m
juncture ['dʒʌŋktʃə(r)] n Fml **at this j.** en esta coyuntura
June [dʒuːn] n junio m
jungle ['dʒʌŋgəl] n jungla f, selva f; Fig laberinto m; **the concrete j.** la jungla de asfalto
junior ['dʒuːnjə(r)] **1** adj (a) (son of) hijo; **David Hughes J.** David Hughes hijo (b) US **j. high (school)** (between 11 and 15) escuela secundaria; Br **j. school** (between 7 and 11) escuela primaria; **j. team** equipo m juvenil (c) (lower in rank) subalterno(a)
 2 n (a) (person of lower rank) subalterno(a) m,f (b) (younger person) menor mf
junk [dʒʌŋk] n (a) Fam trastos mpl; **j. food** comida basura; **j. mail** propaganda f (por correo); **j. shop** tienda f de segunda mano (b) (boat) junco m
junkie ['dʒʌŋkɪ] n Fam yonqui mf
junkman ['dʒʌŋkmæn] n US trapero(a) m,f
junta ['dʒʌntə, US 'hʊntə] n junta f militar
jurisdiction [dʒʊərɪs'dɪkʃən] n Fml jurisdicción f
juror ['dʒʊərə(r)] n jurado(a) m,f
jury ['dʒʊərɪ] n jurado m
just [dʒʌst] **1** adj (fair) justo(a); Fml (well-founded) justificado(a)
 2 adv (a) **he had j. arrived** acababa de llegar (b) (at this very moment) ahora mismo, en este momento; **he was j. leaving when Rosa arrived** estaba a punto de salir cuando llegó Rosa; **I'm j. coming!** ¡ya voy!; **j. as ...** cuando..., justo al...; **j. as I thought** me lo figuraba (c) (only) solamente; **j. in case** por si acaso; **j. a minute!** ¡un momento! (d) (barely) por poco; **I only j. caught the bus** cogí el autobús por los pelos; **j. about** casi; **j. enough** justo lo suficiente (e) (emphatic) **it's j. fantastic!** ¡es sencillamente fantástico!; **you'll j. have to wait** tendrás que esperar (f) (exactly) exactamente, justo; **that's j. it!** ¡precisamente! (g) (equally) **j. as fast as** tan rápido como

justice ['dʒʌstɪs] *n* (**a**) justicia *f*; **he was brought to j.** lo llevaron ante los tribunales; **you didn't do yourself j.** no diste lo mejor de ti (**b**) *US (judge)* juez *mf*; *Br* **J. of the Peace** juez de paz

justifiable ['dʒʌstɪfaɪəbəl] *adj* justificable

justification [dʒʌstɪfɪ'keɪʃən] *n* justificación *f*

justified ['dʒʌstɪfaɪd] *adj* **to be j. in doing sth** tener razón en hacer algo

justify ['dʒʌstɪfaɪ] *vt* justificar

jut [dʒʌt] *vi* sobresalir; **to j. out over** proyectarse sobre

juvenile ['dʒuːvənaɪl] **1** *adj* (**a**) juvenil; **j. court** tribunal *m* de menores; **j. delinquent** delincuente *mf* juvenil (**b**) *(immature)* infantil **2** *n* menor *mf*, joven *mf*

juxtapose [dʒʌkstə'pəʊz] *vt* yuxtaponer

K, k [keɪ] *n (the letter)* K, k *f*
kaleidoscope [kə'laɪdəskəʊp] *n* caleidoscopio *m*
Kampuchea [kæmpʊ'tʃɪə] *n* Kampuchea
kangaroo [kæŋgə'ruː] *n* canguro *m*
karat ['kærət] *n US* quilate *m*
karate [kə'rɑːtɪ] *n* kárate *m*
kebab [kə'bæb] *n Culin* pincho moruno, brocheta *f*
keel [kiːl] *n* quilla *f; Fig* **to be on an even k.** estar en calma
▸ **keel over** *vi Fam* desmayarse
keen [kiːn] *adj* (a) *(eager)* entusiasta (b) *(intense)* profundo(a) (c) *(mind, senses)* agudo(a); *(look)* penetrante; *(blade)* afilado(a); *(competition)* fuerte
keep [kiːp] **1** *n* (a) **to earn one's k.** ganarse el pan
  (b) *(tower)* torreón *m*
  (c) *Fam* **for keeps** para siempre
  2 *vt (pt & pp* **kept**) (a) guardar; **to k. one's room tidy** mantener su cuarto limpio; **to k. sb informed** tener a algn al corriente; **to k. sth in mind** tener algo en cuenta
  (b) *(not give back)* quedarse con
  (c) *(detain)* detener; **to k. sb waiting** hacer esperar a algn
  (d) *(maintain)* mantener; *(animals)* criar
  (e) *(the law)* observar; *(a promise)* cumplir
  (f) *(a secret)* guardar
  (g) *(diary, accounts)* llevar
  (h) *(prevent)* **to k. sb from doing sth** impedir a algn hacer algo
  (i) *(own, manage)* tener; *(shop, hotel)* llevar
  (j) *(stock)* tener
  3 *vi* (a) *(remain)* seguir; **k. still!** ¡estáte quieto(a)!; **to k. fit** mantenerse en forma; **to k. going** seguir adelante; **to k. in touch** no perder el contacto
  (b) *(do frequently)* no dejar de; **she keeps forgetting her keys** siempre se olvida las llaves
  (c) *(food)* conservarse
▸ **keep at** *vt insep* perseverar en
▸ **keep away** **1** *vt sep* mantener a distancia
  2 *vi* mantenerse a distancia
▸ **keep back** *vt sep (information)* ocultar, callar; *(money etc)* retener
▸ **keep down** *vt sep* **to k. prices down** mantener los precios bajos
▸ **keep off** *vt insep* **k. off the grass** *(sign)* prohibido pisar la hierba

▸ **keep on** *vt sep* (a) *(clothes etc)* no quitarse; **to k. an eye on sth/sb** vigilar algo/a algn (b) *(continue to employ)* no despedir a
  2 *vi (continue to do)* seguir
▸ **keep out 1** *vt sep* no dejar pasar
  2 *vi* no entrar; **k. out!** *(sign)* ¡prohibida la entrada!
▸ **keep to** *vt insep (subject)* limitarse a; **to k. to one's room** quedarse en el cuatro; **k. to the point!** ¡cíñete a la cuestión!; **to k. to the left** circular por la izquierda
▸ **keep up** *vt sep* (a) mantener; **to k. up appearances** guardar las apariencias (b) **k. it up!** ¡sigue así! (c) *(prevent from sleeping)* mantener despierto(a)
▸ **keep up with** *vt insep* **to k. up with the times** estar al día
keeper ['kiːpə(r)] *n (in zoo)* guarda *mf; (in record office)* archivero(a) *m,f; (in museum)* conservador(a) *m,f*
keeping ['kiːpɪŋ] *n* (a) *(care)* cuidado *m* (b) **in k. with** en armonía con; **out of k. with** en desacuerdo con
keepsake ['kiːpseɪk] *n* recuerdo *m*
keg [keg] *n* barril *m*
kennel ['kenəl] *n* caseta *f* para perros; **kennels** hotel *m* de perros
Kenya ['kenjə, 'kiːnjə] *n* Kenia
Kenyan ['kenjən, 'kiːnjən] *adj & n* keniano(a) *(m,f)*
kept [kept] *pt & pp of* **keep**
kerb [kɜːb] *n Br* bordillo *m*
kernel ['kɜːnəl] *n (of fruit, nut)* pepita *f; (of wheat)* grano *m; Fig* meollo *m*
kerosene, kerosine ['kerəsiːn] *n US* queroseno *m*
ketchup ['ketʃəp] *n* ketchup *m*, salsa *f* de tomate
kettle ['ketəl] *n* hervidor *m;* **that's a different k. of fish** eso es harina de otro costal
key [kiː] **1** *n* (a) *(for lock)* llave *f;* **k. ring** llavero *m* (b) *(to code)* clave *f* (c) *(of piano, typewriter)* tecla *f* (d) *Mus* tono *m*
  2 *adj* clave; *Br Educ* **k. stage** etapa educativa
  3 *vt Comput* teclear
▸ **key in** *vt sep Comput* introducir
keyboard ['kiːbɔːd] *n* teclado *m*
keyed up [kiːd'ʌp] *adj* nervioso(a)
keyhole ['kiːhəʊl] *n* ojo *m* de la cerradura
keynote ['kiːnəʊt] *n Mus* tónica *f; Fig* nota *f* dominante
kg *(abbr* **kilogram(s))** kg

khaki ['kɑːkɪ] *adj & n* caqui *(m)*
kick [kɪk] **1** *n* (**a**) *(from person)* patada *f*, puntapié *m*; *(from horse etc)* coz *f*; *(from gun)* culatazo *m* (**b**) *Fam* **I get a k. out of it** eso me encanta; **to do sth for kicks** hacer algo por gusto
  2 *vi (animal)* cocear; *(person)* dar patadas; *(gun)* dar un culatazo
  3 *vt* dar un puntapié a
▸ **kick off** *vi Fam* empezar; *Ftb* sacar
▸ **kick out** *vt sep* echar a patadas
▸ **kick up** *vt insep Fam (fuss)* armar
kick-off ['kɪkɒf] *n Ftb* saque *m* inicial
kid¹ [kɪd] *n* (**a**) *Zool* cabrito *m*; *Fig* **to handle sb with k. gloves** tratar a algn con guante blanco (**b**) *Fam* niño(a) *m,f*, chiquillo(a) *m,f*; **the kids** los críos
kid² [kɪd] **1** *vi Fam* tomar el pelo; **no kidding!** ¡va en serio!
  2 *vt* tomar el pelo a; **to k. oneself** *(fool)* hacerse ilusiones
kidnap ['kɪdnæp] *vt* secuestrar
kidnapper ['kɪdnæpə(r)] *n* secuestrador(a) *m,f*
kidnapping ['kɪdnæpɪŋ] *n* secuestro *m*
kidney ['kɪdnɪ] *n* riñón *m*
kill [kɪl] *vt* matar; *Fig* **to k. time** pasar el rato; *Fam* **my feet are killing me!** ¡cómo me duelen los pies!
▸ **kill off** *vt sep* exterminar
killer ['kɪlə(r)] *n* asesino(a) *m,f*; **k. whale** orca *f*
killing ['kɪlɪŋ] *n* asesinato *m*; *Fig* **to make a k.** forrarse de dinero
killjoy ['kɪldʒɔɪ] *n* aguafiestas *mf inv*
kiln [kɪln] *n* horno *m*
kilo ['kiːləʊ] *n* kilo *m*
kilogram(me) ['kɪləʊgræm] *n* kilogramo *m*
kilometre, *US* **kilometer** [kɪ'lɒmɪtə(r)] *n* kilómetro *m*
kilowatt ['kɪləʊwɒt] *n* kilovatio *m*
kilt [kɪlt] *n* falda escocesa, kilt *m*
kin [kɪn] *n* familiares *mpl*, parientes *mpl*
kind¹ [kaɪnd] **1** *n* tipo *m*, clase *f*; **they are two of a k.** son tal para cual; **in k.** (*payment)* en especie; *(treatment)* con la misma moneda
  2 *adv Fam* **k. of** en cierta manera
kind² ['kaɪnd] *adj* amable, simpático(a); *Fml* **would you be so k. as to …?** ¿me haría usted el favor de …?
kindergarten ['kɪndəgɑːtən] *n* jardín *m* de infancia
kind-hearted [kaɪnd'hɑːtɪd] *adj* bondadoso(a)
kindle ['kɪndəl] *vt* encender
kindly ['kaɪndlɪ] **1** *adj* (**kindlier, kindliest**) amable, bondadoso(a)
  2 *adv Fml (please)* por favor; **k. remit a cheque** sírvase enviar cheque; **to look k. on** aprobar
kindness ['kaɪndnɪs] *n* bondad *f*, amabilidad *f*
kindred ['kɪndrɪd] *adj* **k. spirits** almas gemelas

kinetic [kɪ'netɪk] *adj* cinético(a)
king [kɪŋ] *n* rey *m*; *(draughts)* dama *f*
kingdom ['kɪŋdəm] *n* reino *m*
kingfisher ['kɪŋfɪʃə(r)] *n Orn* martín *m* pescador
king-size ['kɪŋsaɪz] *adj* extralargo(a)
kink [kɪŋk] *n (in rope)* coca *f*; *(in hair)* rizo *m*
kinky ['kɪŋkɪ] *adj* (**kinkier, kinkiest**) *Fam* raro(a); *(sexually)* pervertido(a)
kiosk ['kiːɒsk] *n* quiosco *m*
kiss [kɪs] **1** *n* beso *m*
  2 *vt* besar
  3 *vi* besarse
kit [kɪt] *n* (**a**) *(gear)* equipo *m*; *Mil* avíos *mpl* (**b**) *(clothing)* ropa *f* (**c**) *(toy model)* maqueta
▸ **kit out** *vt sep* equipar
kitchen ['kɪtʃɪn] *n* cocina *f*; **k. sink** fregadero *m*
kite [kaɪt] *n* (**a**) *(toy)* cometa *f* (**b**) *Orn* milano *m*
kitten ['kɪtən] *n* gatito(a) *m,f*
kitty ['kɪtɪ] *n (money)* fondo *m* común; *Cards* bote *m*
kiwi ['kiːwiː] *n Bot & Orn* kiwi *m*
km *(pl* **km** *or* **kms)** *(abbr* **kilometre(s))** km
knack [næk] *n* **to get the k. of doing sth** cogerle el truquillo a algo
knapsack ['næpsæk] *n* mochila *f*
knead [niːd] *vt* dar masaje a; *(bread etc)* amasar
knee [niː] **1** *n* rodilla *f*
  2 *vt* dar un rodillazo a
kneecap ['niːkæp] **1** *n* rótula *f*
  2 *vt* romper la rótula a
kneel [niːl] *vi (pt & pp* **knelt)** **to k. (down)** arrodillarse
knell [nel] *n Literary* toque *m* de difuntos
knelt [nelt] *pt & pp of* **kneel**
knew [njuː] *pt of* **know**
knickers ['nɪkəz] *npl Br* bragas *fpl*
knife [naɪf] **1** *n (pl* **knives)** cuchillo *m*
  2 *vt* apuñalar, dar una puñalada a
knight [naɪt] **1** *n Hist* caballero *m*; *(in chess)* caballo *m*
  2 *vt* armar caballero
knighthood ['naɪthʊd] *n (rank)* título *m* de caballero
knit [nɪt] **1** *vt (pt & pp* **knitted** *or* **knit)** (**a**) tejer (**b**) **to k. (together)** *(join)* juntar; *Fig* **to k. one's brow** fruncir el ceño
  2 *vi* (**a**) tejer, hacer punto (**b**) *(bone)* soldarse
knitting ['nɪtɪŋ] *n* punto *m*; **k. machine** máquina *f* de tejer; **k. needle** aguja *f* de tejer
knitwear ['nɪtweə(r)] *n* géneros *mpl* de punto
knives [naɪvz] *pl of* **knife**
knob [nɒb] *n* (**a**) *(of stick)* puño *m*; *(of drawer)* tirador *m*; *(button)* botón *m* (**b**) *(small portion)* trozo *m*
knock [nɒk] **1** *n* golpe *m*; *Fig* revés *m*
  2 *vt* (**a**) golpear (**b**) *Fam (criticize)* criticar

3 *vi* chocar (**against** *or* **into** contra); *(at door)* llamar (**at** a)

▸ **knock down** *vt sep* (**a**) *(demolish)* derribar (**b**) *Aut* atropellar (**c**) *(price)* rebajar

▸ **knock off 1** *vt sep* (**a**) tirar (**b**) *Fam (steal)* birlar (**c**) *Fam (kill)* liquidar

2 *vi Fam* **they k. off at five** se piran a las cinco

▸ **knock out** *vt sep* (**a**) *(make unconscious)* dejar sin conocimiento; *(in boxing)* poner fuera de combate, derrotar por K.O. (**b**) *(surprise)* dejar pasmado(a)

▸ **knock over** *vt sep (cup)* volcar; *(with car)* atropellar

knocker ['nɒkə(r)] *n (on door)* aldaba *f*

knock-kneed [nɒk'niːd] *adj* patizambo(a)

knockout ['nɒkaʊt] *n* (**a**) *(in boxing)* K.O. *m*, knock-out *m* (**b**) *Fam* maravilla *f*

knot [nɒt] **1** *n* nudo *m*; *(group)* grupo *m*

2 *vt* anudar

knotty ['nɒtɪ] *adj* (**knottier, knottiest**) nudoso(a); *Fig* **a k. problem** un problema espinoso

know [nəʊ] *vt & vi (pt* **knew***; pp* **known**) (**a**) saber; **as far as I k.** que yo sepa; **she knows how to ski** sabe esquiar; **to get to k. sth** enterarse de algo; **to let sb k.** avisar al algn (**b**) *(be acquainted with)* conocer; **we got to k. each other at the party** nos conocimos en la fiesta

know-all ['nəʊɔːl] *n Fam* sabelotodo *mf*

know-how ['nəʊhaʊ] *n Fam* conocimiento práctico

knowing ['nəʊɪŋ] *adj (deliberate)* delibera-do(a); **a k. smile** una sonrisa de complicidad

knowingly ['nəʊɪŋlɪ] *adv (shrewdly)* a sabiendas; *(deliberately)* deliberadamente

knowledge ['nɒlɪdʒ] *n* (**a**) conocimiento *m*; **without my k.** sin saberlo yo (**b**) *(learning)* conocimientos *mpl*

knowledgeable ['nɒlɪdʒəbəl] *adj* erudi-to(a); **k. about** muy entendido(a) en

known [nəʊn] **1** *adj* conocido(a)

2 *pp of* **know**

knuckle ['nʌkəl] *n Anat* nudillo *m*; *Culin* hueso *m*

▸ **knuckle down** *vi Fam* ponerse a trabajar en serio

KO [keɪ'əʊ] *n Fam (abbr* **knockout***)* K.O. *m*

Koran [kɔː'rɑːn] *n* Corán *m*

Korea [kə'riːə] *n* Corea

Korean [kə'riːən] *adj & n* coreano(a) *(m,f)*

Kurd [kɜːd] *n* curdo(a) *m,f*

Kuwait [kʊ'weɪt] *n* Kuwait

L, l [el] *n (the letter)* L, l *f*

lab [læb] *n Fam (abbr* **laboratory**) laboratorio *m*

label ['leɪbəl] **1** *n* etiqueta *f*; **record l.** ≃ casa discográfica

2 *vt* poner etiqueta a

labor ['leɪbər] *n, adj, vt & vi US* = **labour**

laboratory [lə'bɒrətərɪ, *US* 'læbrətɔːrɪ] *n* laboratorio *m*

laborious [lə'bɔːrɪəs] *adj* penoso(a)

labour ['leɪbə(r)] **1** *n* (a) *(work)* trabajo *m*; *(task)* tarea *f* (b) *(workforce)* mano *f* de obra (c) **labours** esfuerzos *mpl* (d) **the L. Party** el Partido Laborista (e) *(childbirth)* parto *m*; **to be in l.** estar de parto

2 *adj* laboral

3 *vt (stress, linger on)* machacar; *(a point)* insistir en

4 *vi* (a) *(work)* trabajar (duro) (b) *(move with difficulty)* avanzar penosamente

laboured ['leɪbəd] *adj (breathing)* fatigoso(a); *(style)* forzado(a)

labourer ['leɪbərə(r)] *n* peón *m*; **farm l.** peón *m* agrícola

labour-saving ['leɪbəseɪvɪŋ] *adj* **l. devices** electrodomésticos *mpl*

labyrinth ['læbərɪnθ] *n* laberinto *m*

lace [leɪs] **1** *n* (a) *(fabric)* encaje *m* (b) **laces** cordones *mpl*

2 *vt* (a) *(shoes)* atar (los cordones de) (b) *(add spirits to)* echar licor a

▸ **lace up** *vt sep* atar con cordones

lacerate ['læsəreɪt] *vt* lacerar

lack [læk] **1** *n* falta *f*, escasez *f*; **for l. of** por falta de

2 *vt* carecer de

3 *vi* carecer (**in** de)

lackadaisical [lækə'deɪzɪkəl] *adj (lazy)* perezoso(a); *(indifferent)* indiferente

lacklustre, *US* **lackluster** ['læklʌstə(r)] *adj (eyes)* apagado(a); *(performance)* anodino(a)

laconic [lə'kɒnɪk] *adj* lacónico(a)

lacquer ['lækə(r)] **1** *n* laca *f*

2 *vt (hair)* poner laca en

lad [læd] *n Fam* chaval *m*, muchacho *m*; *Fam* **the lads** los amigotes; **(stable) l.** mozo *m* de cuadra

ladder ['lædə(r)] **1** *n* (a) escalera *f* (de mano); *Fig* escala *f* (b) *(in stocking)* carrera *f*

2 *vt* **I've laddered my stocking** me he hecho una carrera en las medias

laden ['leɪdən] *adj* cargado(a) (**with** de)

ladle ['leɪdəl] *n* cucharón *m*

lady ['leɪdɪ] *n* señora *f*; *Pol* **First L.** primera dama; **Ladies** *(sign on WC)* Señoras; **ladies and gentlemen!** ¡señoras y señores!; **L. Brown** Lady Brown

ladybird ['leɪdɪbɜːd], *US* **ladybug** ['leɪdɪbʌg] *n* mariquita *f*

lady-in-waiting [leɪdɪɪn'weɪtɪŋ] *n* dama *f* de honor

ladylike ['leɪdɪlaɪk] *adj* elegante

ladyship ['leɪdɪʃɪp] *n* **her l./your l.** su señoría

lag [læg] **1** *n* **time l.** demora *f*

2 *vi* **to l. (behind)** quedarse atrás, retrasarse

3 *vt Tech* revestir

lager ['lɑːgə(r)] *n* cerveza rubia

lagoon [lə'guːn] *n* laguna *f*

laid [leɪd] *pt & pp of* **lay**

laid-back [leɪd'bæk] *adj Fam* tranquilo(a)

lain [leɪn] *pp of* **lie²**

lair [leə(r)] *n* guarida *f*

lake [leɪk] *n* lago *m*

lamb [læm] *n* cordero *m*; *(meat)* carne *f* de cordero; **l. chop** chuleta *f* de cordero; **l.'s wool** lana *f* de cordero

lame [leɪm] *adj* (a) cojo(a) (b) *Fig (excuse)* poco convincente; *(argument)* flojo(a)

lament [lə'ment] **1** *n Mus* elegia *f*

2 *vt (death)* llorar, lamentar

3 *vi* llorar (**for** a), lamentarse (**over** de)

lamentable ['læməntəbəl] *adj* lamentable

laminated ['læmɪneɪtɪd] *adj (metal)* laminado(a); *(glass)* inastillable; *(paper)* plastificado(a)

lamp [læmp] *n* lámpara *f*; *Aut* faro *m*

lampoon [læm'puːn] **1** *n* sátira *f*

2 *vt* satirizar

lamp-post ['læmppəʊst] *n* farola *f*

lampshade ['læmpʃeɪd] *n* pantalla *f*

lance [lɑːns] **1** *n* lanza *f*; *Br Mil* **l. corporal** cabo interino; *Med* lanceta *f*

2 *vt Med* abrir con lanceta

> *Note that the Spanish word* **lance** *is a false friend and is never a translation for the English word* **lance**. *In Spanish,* **lance** *means "event, incident".*

land [lænd] **1** *n* (a) tierra *f*; *(soil)* suelo *m*; **by l.** por tierra; **farm l.** tierras *fpl* de cultivo (b) *(country)* país *m* (c) *(property)* tierras *fpl*; *(estate)* finca *f*; **piece of l.** terreno *m*

2 *vt* (a) *(plane)* hacer aterrizar (b) *(disembark)* desembarcar (c) *(fish)* pescar (d) *Fam* *(obtain)* conseguir; *(contract)* ganar (**e**) *Fam* **she got landed with the responsibility** tuvo que cargar con la responsabilidad (**f**) *Fam (blow)* asestar

3 *vi* (**a**) *(plane)* aterrizar (**b**) *(disembark)* desembarcar (**c**) *(after falling)* caer (**in** sobre)

▸ **land up** *vi Fam* ir a parar

landing ['lændɪŋ] *n* (**a**) *(of staircase)* rellano *m* (**b**) *(of plane)* aterrizaje *m*; **l. strip** pista *f* de aterrizaje (**c**) *(of passengers)* desembarco *m*; **l. stage** desembarcadero *m*

landlady ['lændleɪdɪ] *n* *(of flat)* dueña *f*, propietaria *f*; *(of boarding house)* patrona *f*; *(of pub)* dueña

landlord ['lændlɔːd] *n* *(of flat)* dueño *m*, propietario *m*; *(of pub)* patrón *m*, dueño

landmark ['lændmɑːk] *n* (**a**) señal *f*, marca *f*; *(well-known place)* lugar muy conocido (**b**) *Fig* hito *m*

landowner ['lændəʊnə(r)] *n* terrateniente *mf*

landscape ['lændskeɪp] **1** *n* paisaje *m*

2 *vt* ajardinar

landslide ['lændslaɪd] *n* desprendimiento *m* de tierras; **l. victory** victoria arrolladora

lane [leɪn] *n* *(in country)* camino *m*; *(in town)* callejón *m*; *(of motorway)* carril *m*; *Sport* calle *f*; *Naut* ruta *f*

language ['læŋgwɪdʒ] *n* (**a**) lenguaje *m*; **bad l.** palabrotas *fpl* (**b**) *(of a country)* idioma *m*, lengua *f*; **l. laboratory** laboratorio *m* de idiomas; **l. school** academia *f* de idiomas

languid ['læŋgwɪd] *adj* lánguido(a)

languish ['læŋgwɪʃ] *vi* languidecer; *(project, plan etc)* quedar abandonado(a); *(in prison)* pudrirse

lank [læŋk] *adj (hair)* lacio(a)

lanky ['læŋkɪ] *adj* (**lankier, lankiest**) larguirucho(a)

lantern ['læntən] *n* farol *m*

lap¹ [læp] *n Anat* regazo *m*

lap² [læp] *n (circuit)* vuelta *f*; *Fig* etapa *f*

2 *vt (overtake)* doblar

lap³ [læp] **1** *vt (pt & pp* **lapped**) *(of cat)* beber a lengüetadas

2 *vi (waves)* lamer, besar

▸ **lap up** *vt sep* (**a**) *(of cat)* beber a lengüetadas (**b**) *Fig (wallow in)* disfrutar con; *(flattery)* recibir con estusiasmo (**c**) *Fig (believe)* tragar

lapel [lə'pel] *n* solapa *f*

Lapland ['læplænd] *n* Laponia *f*

lapse [læps] **1** *n* (**a**) *(of time)* lapso *m* (**b**) *(error)* error *m*, desliz *m*; *(of memory)* fallo *m*

2 *vi* (**a**) *(time)* pasar, transcurrir (**b**) *(expire)* caducar (**c**) *(err)* cometer un error; *(fall back)* caer (**into** en) (**d**) *Rel* perder la fe

larceny ['lɑːsənɪ] *n Br* latrocinio *m*; *US* hurto *m*

larch [lɑːtʃ] *n* alerce *m*

lard [lɑːd] *n* manteca *f* de cerdo

larder ['lɑːdə(r)] *n* despensa *f*

large [lɑːdʒ] **1** *adj* grande; *(amount)* importante; *(extensive)* amplio(a); **by and l.** por lo general

2 *n* **to be at l.** andar suelto(a); **the public at l.** el público en general

> 🔏 Note that the Spanish word **largo** is a false friend and is never a translation for the English word **large**. In Spanish, **largo** means "long".

largely ['lɑːdʒlɪ] *adv (mainly)* en gran parte; *(chiefly)* principalmente

large-scale ['lɑːdʒskeɪl] *adj (project, problem etc)* de gran envergadura; *(map)* a gran escala

lark¹ [lɑːk] *n Orn* alondra *f*

lark² [lɑːk] *n Fam (joke)* broma *f*; **what a l.!** ¡qué risa!

▸ **lark about, lark around** *vi Fam* hacer el tonto

larva ['lɑːvə] *n* larva *f*

laryngitis [lærɪn'dʒaɪtɪs] *n* laringitis *f*

larynx ['lærɪŋks] *n Anat* laringe *f*

laser ['leɪzə(r)] *n* láser *m*; **l. printer** impresora *f* láser

lash [læʃ] **1** *n* (**a**) *(eyelash)* pestaña *f* (**b**) *(blow with whip)* latigazo *m*

2 *vt* (**a**) *(beat)* azotar (**b**) *(rain)* azotar (**c**) *(tie)* atar

▸ **lash out** *vi* (**a**) *(with fists)* repartir golpes a diestro y siniestro; *(verbally)* criticar (**at** a) (**b**) *Fam (spend money)* tirar la casa por la ventana

lass [læs] *n Fam* chavala *f*, muchacha *f*

lasso [læ'suː] **1** *n* lazo *m*

2 *vt* coger con el lazo

last [lɑːst] **1** *adj* (**a**) *(final)* último(a), final; *Fam* **the l. straw** el colmo (**b**) *(most recent)* último(a) (**c**) *(past)* pasado(a); *(previous)* anterior; **l. but one** penúltimo(a); **l. month** el mes pasado; **l. night** anoche; **the night before l.** anteanoche

2 *adv* (**a**) **when I l. saw her** la última vez que la vi (**b**) *(at the end)* en último lugar; *(in race etc)* último; **at (long) l.** por fin; **l. but not least** el último en orden pero no en importancia

3 *n* **the l.** el último/la última

4 *vi* (**a**) *(time)* durar; *(hold out)* aguantar (**b**) *(be enough for)* llegar, alcanzar

last-ditch ['lɑːstdɪtʃ] *adj (effort, attempt)* último(a) y desesperado(a)

lasting ['lɑːstɪŋ] *adj* duradero(a)

lastly ['lɑːstlɪ] *adv* por último, finalmente

last-minute ['lɑːstmɪnɪt] *adj* de última hora

latch [lætʃ] *n* picaporte *m*, pestillo *m*

late [leɪt] **1** *adj* (**a**) *(not on time)* tardío(a); *(hour)* avanzado(a); **to be five minutes l.** llegar con cinco minutos de retraso (**b**) *(far on in time)* tarde; **in l. autumn** a finales del otoño; **in the l. afternoon** a última hora de la tarde; **she's in her l. twenties** ronda los treinta (**c**) *(dead)* difunto(a)

2 *adv* (**a**) *(not on time)* tarde; **to arrive l.** llegar tarde (**b**) *(far on in time)* tarde; **l. at night** a altas horas de la noche; **l. in life** a una edad avanzada (**c**) **as l. as 1950** todavía en 1950; **of l.** últimamente

latecomer ['leɪtkʌmə(r)] *n* tardón(ona) *m,f*

lately ['leɪtlɪ] *adv* últimamente, recientemente

latent ['leɪtənt] *adj* (**a**) latente (**b**) *(desire)* oculto(a)

later ['leɪtə(r)] **1** *adj* (**a**) *(subsequent)* más tarde; **in her l. novels** en sus novelas posteriores (**b**) *(more recent)* más reciente

2 *adv* más tarde, después; **l. on** más adelante, más tarde

lateral ['lætərəl] *adj* lateral

latest ['leɪtɪst] **1** *adj* *(superl of* **late***)* *(most recent)* último(a), más reciente

2 *n* the **l.** lo último; **have you heard the l.?** ¿te enteraste de lo último?; **Friday at the l.** el viernes a más tardar

lathe [leɪð] *n Tech* torno *m*

lather ['lɑːðə(r)] **1** *n* *(of soap)* espuma *f*; *(horse's sweat)* sudor *m*

2 *vt* *(with soap)* enjabonar

Latin ['lætɪn] **1** *adj & n* latino(a) *(m,f)*; **L. America** América Latina, Latinoamérica; **L. American** latinoamericano(a) *(m,f)*

2 *n* *(language)* latín *m*

latitude ['lætɪtjuːd] *n* latitud *f*

latrine [lə'triːn] *n* letrina *f*

latter ['lætə(r)] **1** *adj* (**a**) *(last)* último(a) (**b**) *(second of two)* segundo(a)

2 *pron* éste(a); **the former ... the l.** aquél ... éste/aquélla ... ésta

lattice ['lætɪs] *n* enrejado *m*, rejilla *f*

laudable ['lɔːdəbəl] *adj* loable

laugh [lɑːf] **1** *n* risa *f*, *(guffaw)* carcajada *f*; **for a l.** para divertirse

2 *vi* reír, reírse

▶ **laugh at** *vt insep* **to l. at sb/sth** reírse de algn/algo

▶ **laugh about** *vt insep* **to l. about sb/sth** reírse de algn/algo

▶ **laugh off** *vt sep* tomar a risa

laughable ['lɑːfəbəl] *adj* *(situation, suggestion)* ridículo(a); *(amount, offer)* irrisorio(a)

laughing-stock ['lɑːfɪŋstɒk] *n* hazmerreír *m inv*

laughter ['lɑːftə(r)] *n* risa *f*

launch [lɔːntʃ] **1** *n* (**a**) *(vessel)* lancha *f* (**b**) = launching

2 *vt* (**a**) *(attack, rocket, new product)* lanzar (**b**) *(ship)* botar (**c**) *(film, play)* estrenar (**d**) *(company)* fundar (**e**) *Fig (scheme)* iniciar

launching ['lɔːntʃɪŋ] *n* (**a**) *(of rocket, new product)* lanzamiento *m* (**b**) *(of ship)* botadura *f* (**c**) *(of film, play)* estreno *m* (**d**) *(of new company)* fundación *f*

launchpad ['lɔːntʃpæd] *n* plataforma *f* de lanzamiento

launder ['lɔːndə(r)] *vt* lavar y planchar; *Fig*

(money) blanquear

launderette [lɔːndə'ret], *US* **Laundromat®** ['lɔːndrəmæt] *n* lavandería automática

laundry ['lɔːndrɪ] *n* (**a**) *(place)* lavandería *f* (**b**) *(dirty clothes)* ropa sucia; **to do the l.** lavar la ropa

laurel ['lɒrəl] *n* laurel *m*; *Fam Fig* **to rest on one's laurels** dormirse en los laureles

lava ['lɑːvə] *n* lava *f*

lavatory ['lævətərɪ] *n* (**a**) *(excusado m, retrete m* (**b**) *(room)* baño *m*; **public l.** servicios *mpl*, aseos *mpl*

lavender ['lævəndə(r)] *n* lavanda *f*

lavish ['lævɪʃ] **1** *adj* (**a**) *(generous)* pródigo(a) (**b**) *(abundant)* abundante (**c**) *(luxurious)* lujoso(a)

2 *vt* **to l. praise on sb** colmar de alabanzas a alguien; **to l. attention on sb** prodigarse en atenciones con alguien

law [lɔː] *n* (**a**) *(ley f;* **by l.** según la ley; **l. and order** el orden público; **to lay down the l.** dictar la ley (**b**) *(as subject)* derecho *m*; **l. court** tribunal *m* de justicia (**c**) *Fam* **the l.** los maderos

law-abiding ['lɔːəbaɪdɪŋ] *adj* respetuoso(a) de la ley

lawful ['lɔːfʊl] *adj* legal; *(permitted by law)* lícito(a), *(legitimate)* legítimo(a)

lawn [lɔːn] *n* césped *m*; **l. tennis** tenis *m* sobre hierba

lawnmower ['lɔːnmɔʊə(r)] *n* cortacésped *m*

lawsuit ['lɔːsjuːt] *n* pleito *m*

lawyer ['lɔːjə(r)] *n* abogado(a) *m,f*; **l.'s office** bufete *m* de abogados

lax [læks] *adj* *(not strict)* relajado(a); *(not demanding)* poco exigente; *(careless)* descuidado(a)

laxative ['læksətɪv] *adj & n* laxante *(m)*

laxity ['læksɪtɪ] *n* relajamiento *m*; *(carelessness)* descuido *m*; *(negligence)* negligencia *f*

lay¹ [leɪ] *adj* (**a**) *Rel* laico(a) (**b**) *(non-specialist)* lego(a)

lay² [leɪ] *vt* *(pt & pp* laid*)* (**a**) *(place)* poner, colocar; *(cable, trap)* tender; *(foundations)* echar (**b**) *(fire)* preparar; *(table)* poner (**c**) *(leave)* dejar (**d**) *(eggs)* poner (**e**) *very Fam (have sex with)* follar (**f**) *(set down)* asentar; *(blame)* echar

▶ **lay aside** *vt sep* dejar a un lado

▶ **lay by** *vt sep* *(save)* guardar; *(money)* ahorrar

▶ **lay down** *vt sep* (**a**) *(put down)* poner; *(let go)* dejar; **to l. down one's arms** rendir las armas (**b**) *(plan)* formular; *(establish)* fijar, imponer; *(principles)* sentar

▶ **lay into** *vt insep Fam (physically)* dar una paliza a; *(verbally)* arremeter contra

▶ **lay off 1** *vt sep (dismiss)* despedir

2 *vt insep Fam* dejar en paz

3 *vi* **l. off!** ¡para ya!

▶ **lay on** *vt sep* (**a**) *(provide)* proveer de; *(food)* preparar (**b**) *(spread)* aplicar; *Fam* **to l. it on (thick)** cargar las tintas

► **lay out** *vt sep* (**a**) *(open out)* extender (**b**) *(arrange)* disponer (**c**) *(ideas)* exponer (**d**) *(plan)* trazar (**e**) *Fam (spend)* gastar (**f**) *Fam (knock out)* derribar

► **lay up** *vt sep* (**a**) *(store)* guardar (**b**) *(accumulate)* almacenar (**c**) *Fam* **to be laid up** tener que guardar cama

lay³ [leɪ] *pt of* **lie²**

layabout ['leɪəbaʊt] *n Fam* vago(a) *m,f*

lay-by ['leɪbaɪ] *n* área *f* de descanso

layer ['leɪə(r)] *n* capa *f*

layman ['leɪmən] *n* lego *m,f*

layout ['leɪaʊt] *n (arrangement)* disposición *f*; *(presentation)* presentación *f*; *Typ* composición *f*; *(plan)* diseño *m*, trazado *m*

laze [leɪz] *vi* holgazanear, gandulear

laziness ['leɪzɪnɪs] *n* pereza *f*, holgazanería *f*

lazy ['leɪzɪ] *adj* (**lazier, laziest**) perezoso(a), holgazán(ana); **at a l. pace** a paso lento

lb *(abbr pound)* libra *f*

lead¹ [led] *n* (**a**) *(metal)* plomo *m* (**b**) *(in pencil)* mina *f*

lead² [liːd] **1** *n* (**a**) *(front position)* delantera *f*; *(advantage)* ventaja *f*; **to take the l.** *(in race)* tomar la delantera; *(score)* adelantarse

(**b**) *(clue)* pista *f*

(**c**) *Th* primer papel *m*; **l. singer** cantante *mf* principal

(**d**) *(leash)* correa *f*

(**e**) *Elec* cable *m*

2 *vt* (*pt & pp* **led**) (**a**) *(conduct)* llevar, conducir

(**b**) *(be the leader of)* dirigir, encabezar

(**c**) *(influence)* llevar a; **this leads me to believe that** esto me lleva a creer que; **she's easily led** se deja llevar fácilmente

(**d**) *(life)* llevar

3 *vi* (**a**) *(road)* llevar, conducir (**to** a)

(**b**) *(go first)* ir delante; *(in race)* llevar la delantera

(**c**) **to l. to** llevar a

► **lead away** *vt sep* llevar

► **lead on 1** *vi (go ahead)* ir adelante

2 *vt sep (deceive)* engañar, timar

► **lead up to** *vt insep* llevar a

leaden ['ledən] *adj (sky)* plomizo(a); *(food)* pesado(a)

leader ['liːdə(r)] *n* (**a**) *(chief)* jefe(a) *m,f*, líder *mf*; *(in race)* líder (**b**) *Press* editorial *m*, artículo *m* de fondo

leadership ['liːdəʃɪp] *n* (**a**) *(command)* dirección *f*, mando *m*; *Pol* liderazgo *m* (**b**) *(leaders)* dirigentes *mpl*, cúpula *f*

lead-free ['ledfriː] *adj* sin plomo

leading ['liːdɪŋ] *adj* (**a**) *(main)* principal (**b**) *(outstanding)* destacado(a)

leaf [liːf] *n (pl* **leaves**) hoja *f*; **to turn over a new l.** hacer borrón y cuenta nueva

► **leaf through** *vt insep* hojear

leaflet ['liːflɪt] *n* folleto *m*

league [liːg] *n* (**a**) *(alliance)* alianza *f*; *(association)* sociedad *f*; *Fam* **to be in l. with sb**

estar conchabado(a) con algn (**b**) *Sport* liga *f*

leak [liːk] **1** *n* (**a**) *(hole)* agujero *m*; *(in roof)* gotera *f* (**b**) *(of gas, liquid)* fuga *f*, escape *m*; *(of information)* filtración *f*

2 *vt* (**a**) *(container)* tener un agujero; *(pipe)* tener un escape; *(roof)* gotear; *(boat)* hacer agua (**b**) *(gas, liquid)* escaparse; *(information)* filtrarse; *(news)* trascender

3 *vt (information)* filtrar (**to** a)

leaky ['liːkɪ] *adj* (**leakier, leakiest**) *(container)* agujereado(a); *(roof)* que tiene goteras; *(ship)* que hace agua

lean¹ [liːn] *adj (meat)* magro(a); *(person)* flaco(a); *(harvest)* escaso(a)

lean² [liːn] **1** *vi* (*pt & pp* **leaned** *or* **leant**) (**a**) inclinarse (**b**) **to l. on/against** apoyarse en/contra; *Fig* **to l. on sb** *(pressurize)* presionar a algn; *(depend)* depender de algn

2 *vt* apoyar (**on** en)

► **lean back** *vi* reclinarse

► **lean forward** *vi* inclinarse hacia delante

► **lean out** *vi* asomarse

► **lean over** *vi* inclinarse

leaning ['liːnɪŋ] **1** *adj* inclinado(a)

2 *n Fig (tendency)* inclinación *f*, tendencia *f*

leant [lent] *pt & pp of* **lean**

lean-to ['liːntuː] *n (hut)* cobertizo *m*

leap [liːp] **1** *n (jump)* salto *m*; *Fig* paso *m*; **l. year** año bisiesto

2 *vi* (*pt & pp* **leaped** *or* **leapt**) saltar; *Fig* **her heart leapt** su corazón dio un vuelco

► **leap at** *vt insep Fig (chance)* no dejar escapar

leapfrog ['liːpfrɒg] *n* pídola *f*

leapt [lept] *pt & pp of* **leap**

learn [lɜːn] **1** *vt* (*pt & pp* **learned** *or* **learnt**) (**a**) aprender; **to l. to ski** aprender a esquiar (**b**) **to l. that** enterarse de que

2 *vi* (**a**) aprender (**b**) **to l. about** *or* **of** *(find out)* enterarse de

learned ['lɜːnɪd] *adj* erudito(a)

learner ['lɜːnə(r)] *n (beginner)* principiante *mf*; **l. driver** aprendiz(a) *m,f* de conductor

learning ['lɜːnɪŋ] *n (knowledge)* conocimientos *mpl*; *(erudition)* saber *m*

learnt [lɜːnt] *pt & pp of* **learn**

lease [liːs] **1** *n* contrato *m* de arrendamiento; *Fig* **to give sb a new l.** *Br* **of** *or US* **on life** dar nueva vida a algn

2 *vt* arrendar

leasehold ['liːshəʊld] **1** *n* derechos *mpl* de arrendamiento

2 *adj (property)* arrendado(a)

leash [liːʃ] *n* correa *f*

least [liːst] *(superl of* **little**) **1** *adj* menor, mínimo(a); **he has the l. time** él es quien menos tiempo tiene

2 *adv* menos; **l. of all him** él menos que nadie

3 *n* **the l.** lo menos; **at l.** por lo menos, al menos; **not in the l.!** ¡en absoluto!; **to say the l.** por no decir más

leather ['leðə(r)] **1** n piel f, cuero m
2 adj de piel
leave¹ [liːv] **1** vt (pt & pp left) (a) dejar; (go away from) abandonar; (go out of) salir de (b) **l. him alone!** ¡déjale en paz!; Fam **l. it to me** yo me encargo (c) (bequeath) legar (d) (forget) dejarse, olvidarse (e) **I have two biscuits left** me quedan dos galletas (f) **to be left over** sobrar
2 vi (go away) irse, marcharse; (go out) salir; **the train leaves in five minutes** el tren sale dentro de cinco minutos
▶ **leave behind** vt sep (a) dejar atrás (b) (forget) olvidarse
▶ **leave on** vt sep (a) (clothes) dejar puesto(a) (b) (lights, radio) dejar encendido(a)
▶ **leave out** vt sep (omit) omitir; Fig **to feel left out** sentirse excluido(a)
leave² [liːv] n (a) (permission) permiso m (b) (time off) vacaciones fpl; Mil **on l. de permiso**; **l. of absence** excedencia f (c) **to take one's l. of sb** despedirse de algn
leaves [liːvz] pl of **leaf**
Lebanon ['lebənən] n **(the) L.** (el) Líbano
lecherous ['letʃərəs] adj lascivo(a)
lecture ['lektʃə(r)] **1** n (a) conferencia f; Univ clase f; **to give a l.** dar una conferencia (sobre); **l. hall, l. room, l. theatre** sala f de conferencias; Univ aula f (b) (rebuke) sermón m
2 vi dar una conferencia; Univ dar clases
3 vt (reproach) sermonear
lecturer ['lektʃərə(r)] n conferenciante mf; Univ profesor(a) m,f
led [led] pt & pp of **lead**
ledge [ledʒ] n (a) (shelf) repisa f; (of window) alféizar m (b) (on mountain) saliente m
ledger ['ledʒə(r)] n libro m mayor
lee [liː] n (a) Naut sotavento m (b) Fig abrigo m
leech [liːtʃ] n sanguijuela f
leek [liːk] n puerro m
leer [lɪə(r)] vi mirar con lascivia
leeway ['liːweɪ] n libertad f; **this gives me a certain amount of l.** esto me da cierto margen de libertad
left¹ [left] **1** adj izquierdo(a); Pol **l. wing** izquierda f
2 adv a la izquierda
3 n (a) izquierda f; **on the l.** a mano izquierda (b) Pol **to be on the l.** ser de izquierdas
left² [left] pt & pp of **leave**
left-hand ['lefthænd] adj **l. drive** con el volante a la izquierda; **on the l. side** a mano izquierda
left-handed [left'hændɪd] adj zurdo(a)
left-luggage [left'lʌgɪdʒ] n Br **l. office** consigna f
leftovers ['leftəʊvəz] npl sobras fpl
left-wing ['leftwɪŋ] adj de izquierdas, izquierdista
leg [leg] n (a) (of person) pierna f; (of animal,

table) pata f; Culin (of lamb) pierna; (of trousers) pernera f (b) (stage) etapa f
legacy ['legəsɪ] n herencia f, legado m
legal ['liːgəl] adj (a) legal; (permitted by law) lícito(a); **l. tender** moneda f de curso legal (b) (relating to the law) jurídico(a); **l. aid** asesoramiento jurídico gratuito; **l. dispute** contencioso m; **l. holiday** fiesta f nacional
legalize ['liːgəlaɪz] vt legalizar
legally ['liːgəlɪ] adv legalmente
legend ['ledʒənd] n leyenda f
legendary ['ledʒəndərɪ] adj legendario(a)
leggings ['legɪŋz] npl polainas fpl
legible ['ledʒəbəl] adj legible
legion ['liːdʒən] n legión f
legislation [ledʒɪs'leɪʃən] n legislación f
legislative ['ledʒɪslətɪv] adj legislativo(a)
legislator ['ledʒɪsleɪtə(r)] n legislador(a) m,f
legislature ['ledʒɪsleɪtʃə(r)] n asamblea legislativa
legitimate [lɪ'dʒɪtɪmɪt] adj legítimo(a)
legroom ['legruːm] n espacio m para las piernas
leisure ['leʒə(r), US 'liːʒər] n ocio m, tiempo m libre; **at l.** con calma; **do it at your l.** hazlo cuando tengas tiempo; **l. activities** pasatiempos mpl; **l. centre** centro recreativo
leisurely ['leʒəlɪ, US 'liːʒərlɪ] adj (unhurried) tranquilo(a); (slow) lento(a)
lemon ['lemən] n limón m; **l. curd** crema f de limón; **l. juice** zumo m de limón; **l. tea** té m con limón
lemonade [lemə'neɪd] n limonada f
lend [lend] vt (pt & pp lent) prestar; **to l. oneself/itself to sth** prestarse a or para algo
lending ['lendɪŋ] n **l. library** biblioteca pública
length [leŋkθ, leŋθ] n (a) longitud f, largo m; **it is 5 m in l.** tiene 5 m de largo (b) (duration) duración f (c) (of string) trozo m; (of cloth) retal m (d) (of swimming pool) largo m; Fig **to go to any lengths to achieve sth** hacer lo que sea para conseguir algo (e) **at l.** (finally) finalmente; (in depth) a fondo
lengthen ['leŋkθən, 'leŋθən] **1** vt alargar; (lifetime) prolongar
2 vi alargarse; (lifetime) prolongarse
lengthways ['leŋθweɪz] adv a lo largo
lengthy ['leŋkθɪ, 'leŋθɪ] adj (lengthier, lengthiest) largo(a); (film, illness) de larga duración; (meeting, discussion) prolongado(a)
lenient ['liːnɪənt] adj indulgente
lens [lenz] n (of eye) cristalino m; (of spectacles) lente f; Phot objetivo m
Lent [lent] n Cuaresma f
lent [lent] pt & pp of **lend**
lentil ['lentɪl] n lenteja f
Leo ['liːəʊ] n Leo m
leopard ['lepəd] n leopardo m
leotard ['liːətɑːd] n leotardo m
leper ['lepə(r)] n leproso(a) m,f

leprosy ['leprəsɪ] *n* lepra *f*

lesbian ['lezbɪən] *adj & n* lesbiana *(f)*

less [les] **1** *adj* (*comp of* **little**) menos

2 *pron* menos; **the l. said about it, the better** cuanto menos se hable de eso mejor

3 *adv* menos; **l. and l.** cada vez menos; **still l.** menos aún

4 *prep* menos; **a year l. two days** un año menos dos días

lessen ['lesən] *vt & vi* disminuir

lesser ['lesə(r)] *adj* menor; **to a l. extent** en menor grado

lesson ['lesən] *n* (**a**) clase *f*; (*in book*) lección *f*; **Spanish lessons** clases de español (**b**) *Rel* lectura *f*

lest [lest] *conj Fml* (**a**) para (que) no; **l. we forget** para que no lo olvidemos (**b**) (*for fear that*) por miedo a que

let [let] **1** *vt* (*pt & pp* **let**) (**a**) dejar, permitir; **to l. go of sth** soltar algo; **to l. sb know** avisar a algn; *Fig* **to l. oneself go** dejarse ir (**b**) (*rent out*) alquilar, *Méx* rentar; **to l.** (*sign*) se alquila (**c**) **l. alone** ni mucho menos

2 *v aux* **l. him wait** que espere; **l. me go!** ¡suéltame!; **l.'s go!** ¡vamos!, ¡vámonos!; **l.'s see** a ver

► **let down** *vt sep* (**a**) (*lower*) bajar; (*lengthen*) alargar; *Fam Fig* **to l. one's hair down** desmelenarse (**b**) (*deflate*) desinflar (**c**) (*fail*) fallar, defraudar

► **let in** *vt sep* (**a**) (*admit*) dejar entrar (**b**) **to l. oneself in for** meterse en

► **let off** *vt sep* (**a**) (*bomb*) hacer explotar; (*fireworks*) hacer estallar (**b**) (*liquid, air*) soltar (**c**) *Fam* **to l. sb off** (*pardon*) perdonar

► **let on** *vi Fam* **don't l. on** (*reveal information*) no se lo digas

► **let out** *vt sep* (**a**) (*release*) soltar; (*news*) divulgar; (*secret*) revelar (**b**) (*air, water*) dejar salir (**c**) (*cry*) soltar (**d**) *Sewing* ensanchar

► **let up** *vi* cesar, parar

letdown ['letdaʊn] *n* decepción *f*

lethal ['liːθəl] *adj* letal

lethargic [lɪ'θɑːdʒɪk] *adj* aletargado(a)

letter ['letə(r)] *n* (**a**) (*of alphabet*) letra *f*; *Fig* **to the l.** al pie de la letra (**b**) (*written message*) carta *f*; *Br* **l. box** buzón *m*; *Com* **l. of credit** carta de crédito

letterhead ['letəhed] *n* membrete *m*

lettering ['letərɪŋ] *n* rótulo *m*

lettuce ['letɪs] *n* lechuga *f*

let-up ['letʌp] *n Fam* descanso *m*, respiro *m*

leukaemia, *US* **leukemia** [luːˈkiːmɪə] *n* leucemia *f*

level ['levəl] **1** *adj* (**a**) (*flat*) llano(a); (*even*) nivelado(a); (*equal*) igual, parejo(a); **a l. spoonful of** una cucharada rasa de; **to be l. with** estar a nivel de; *Br* **l. crossing** paso *m* a nivel (**b**) (*steady*) estable; (*tone*) uniforme

2 *vt* (**a**) nivelar, allanar (**b**) (*building*) arrasar (**c**) (*stare, criticism*) dirigir

3 *n* nivel *m*; **to be on a l. with** estar al mismo

nivel que; *Fam* **to be on the l.** (*be honest*) ser de fiar; (*be truthful*) decir la verdad

► **level off, level out** *vi* estabilizarse

► **level with** *vt insep Fam* ser franco(a) con

level-headed [levəl'hedɪd] *adj* sensato(a)

lever ['liːvə(r)] **1** *n* palanca *f*

2 *vt* apalancar; **to l. sth out** sacar algo con palanca

leverage ['liːvərɪdʒ] *n Fig* influencia *f*

levy ['levɪ] **1** *vt* (*tax*) recaudar; (*fine*) imponer

2 *n* (*of tax*) recaudación *f*; (*of fine*) imposición *f*

lewd [luːd] *adj* (*person*) lascivo(a); (*story*) obsceno(a)

liability [laɪə'bɪlɪtɪ] *n* (**a**) *Jur* responsabilidad *f* (**b**) (*handicap*) estorbo *m* (**c**) *Fin* **liabilities** pasivo *m*

liable ['laɪəbəl] *adj* (**a**) *Jur* responsable; (*susceptible*) sujeto(a); **to be l. for** ser responsable de (**b**) **to be l. to do sth** ser propenso(a) a hacer algo; **it's l. to happen** es muy probable que (así) suceda

liaise [liː'eɪz] *vi* comunicarse (**with** con)

liaison [liː'eɪzɒn] *n* (**a**) enlace *m*; **l. officer** oficial *mf* de enlace (**b**) (*love affair*) amorío *m*

liar ['laɪə(r)] *n* mentiroso(a) *m,f*, embustero(a) *m,f*

libel ['laɪbəl] **1** *n* libelo *m*

2 *vt* difamar, calumniar

liberal ['lɪbərəl] **1** *adj* (**a**) liberal; **L. Party** Partido *m* Liberal (**b**) (*abundant*) abundante

2 *n Pol* **L.** liberal *mf*

liberate ['lɪbəreɪt] *vt* liberar; (*prisoner etc*) poner en libertad; **liberated woman** mujer liberada

liberation [lɪbə'reɪʃən] *n* liberación *f*

liberty ['lɪbətɪ] *n* libertad *f*; **to be at l. to say sth** ser libre de decir algo; **to take liberties** tomarse libertades

Libra ['liːbrə] *n* Libra *f*

librarian [laɪ'breərɪən] *n* bibliotecario(a) *m,f*

> 🖉 Note that the Spanish word **librero** is a false friend and is never a translation for the English word **librarian**. In Spanish, **librero** means "bookseller".

library ['laɪbrərɪ] *n* biblioteca *f*

> 🖉 Note that the Spanish word **librería** is a false friend and is never a translation for the English word **library**. In Spanish, **librería** means "bookshop".

Libya ['lɪbɪə] *n* Libia *f*

Libyan ['lɪbɪən] *adj & n* libio(a) *(m,f)*

lice [laɪs] *pl of* **louse**

licence ['laɪsəns] *n* (**a**) (*permit*) licencia *f*, permiso *m*; *Aut* **l. number** matrícula *f*; *US* **l. plate** (placa *f* de la) matrícula (**b**) (*freedom*) libertad *f*; (*excessive freedom*) libertinaje *m*

license ['laɪsəns] **1** *vt* dar licencia a, autorizar

2 *n US* = **licence**

licensed ['laɪsənst] *adj* autorizado(a); **l. premises** = local autorizado para la venta de bebidas alcohólicas

licentious [laɪ'senʃəs] *adj* licencioso(a)

lichen ['laɪkən, 'lɪtʃən] *n* liquen *m*

lick [lɪk] **1** *vt* lamer; **to l. one's lips** relamerse
2 *n* lamedura *f*; *Fam* **a l. of paint** una mano de pintura

licorice ['lɪkərɪs, 'lɪkərɪʃ] *n US* = **liquorice**

lid [lɪd] *n* (**a**) *(cover)* tapa *f* (**b**) *(of eye)* párpado *m*

lie¹ [laɪ] **1** *vi* mentir
2 *n* mentira *f*

lie² [laɪ] **1** *vi (pt* **lay***; pp* **lain**) (**a**) *(act)* echarse, acostarse; *(state)* estar echado(a), estar acostado(a); *(be buried)* yacer (**b**) *(be situated)* encontrarse, hallarse; **the valley lay before us** el valle se extendía ante nosotros (**c**) *(remain)* quedarse
2 *n (position)* situación *f*; *(direction)* orientación *f*
▸ **lie about, lie around** *vi (person)* estar tumbado(a); *(things)* estar tirado(a)
▸ **lie down** *vi* acostarse, echarse

lie-in ['laɪɪn] *n Fam* **to have a l.** levantarse tarde

lieu [ljuː, luː] *n* **in l. of** en lugar de

lieutenant [lef'tenənt, *US* luː'tenənt] *n* (**a**) *Mil* teniente *m* (**b**) *(non-military)* lugarteniente *m*

life [laɪf] *n (pl* **lives**) (**a**) vida *f*; **to come to l.** cobrar vida; **to take one's own l.** suicidarse; *Fam* **how's l.?** ¿qué tal?; **l. belt** cinturón *m* salvavidas; **l. imprisonment** cadena perpetua; **l. insurance** seguro *m* de vida; **l. jacket** chaleco *m* salvavidas; **l. style** estilo *m* de vida; **l. story** biografía *f* (**b**) *(liveliness)* vitalidad *f*; *Fam Fig* **to be the l. and soul of the party** ser el alma de la fiesta

lifeboat ['laɪfbəʊt] *n (on ship)* bote *m* salvavidas; *(on shore)* lancha *f* de socorro

lifeguard ['laɪfgɑːd] *n* socorrista *mf*

lifeless ['laɪflɪs] *adj* sin vida

lifelike ['laɪflaɪk] *adj* natural; *(portrait)* fiel

lifeline ['laɪflaɪn] *n Fig* cordón *m* umbilical

lifelong ['laɪflɒŋ] *adj* de toda la vida

life-size(d) ['laɪfsaɪz(d)] *adj* (de) tamaño natural

lifetime ['laɪftaɪm] *n* vida *f*; **in his l.** durante su vida; **it's the chance of a l.** es una ocasión única

lift [lɪft] **1** *vt* (**a**) levantar; *(head etc)* alzar; *(pick up)* coger (**b**) *(troops)* transportar (**c**) *Fam (steal)* birlar; *(plagiarize)* plagiar
2 *vi (clouds, mist)* disiparse
3 *n* (**a**) *Br (elevator)* ascensor *m* (**b**) **to give sb a l.** llevar a algn en coche (**c**) *Fig (boost)* estímulo *m*
▸ **lift up** *vt sep* levantar, alzar

lift-off ['lɪftɒf] *n* despegue *m*

light¹ [laɪt] **1** *n* (**a**) luz *f*; *Fig* **in the l. of** en vista de; *Fig* **to bring sth to l.** sacar algo a la luz; *Fig* **to come to l.** salir a la luz; **l. bulb** bombilla *f*; **l. meter** fotómetro *m*; **l. pen** lápiz óptico; **l. switch** interruptor *m* de la luz; **l. year** año *m* luz (**b**) *(lamp)* luz *f*, lámpara *f*; *(traffic light)* semáforo *m*; *(headlight)* faro *m* (**c**) *(flame)* lumbre *f*; **to set l. to sth** prender fuego a algo; *Fam* **have you got a l.?** ¿tiene fuego?
2 *vt (pt & pp* **lighted** *or* **lit**) (**a**) *(illuminate)* iluminar, alumbrar (**b**) *(ignite)* encender
3 *adj* claro(a); *(hair)* rubio(a)
▸ **light up 1** *vt sep* iluminar, alumbrar
2 *vi* (**a**) iluminarse (**b**) *Fam* encender un cigarrillo

light² [laɪt] **1** *adj* ligero(a); *(rain)* fino(a); *(breeze)* suave; *Fig (sentence etc)* leve; *Fig* **to make l. of sth** dar poca importancia a algo
2 *adv* **to travel l.** ir ligero(a) de equipaje

lighten¹ ['laɪtən] **1** *vt* (**a**) *(colour)* aclarar (**b**) *(illuminate)* iluminar
2 *vi* aclararse

lighten² ['laɪtən] *vt* (**a**) *(weight)* aligerar (**b**) *Fig (mitigate)* aliviar; *(heart)* alegrar

lighter¹ ['laɪtə(r)] *n (cigarette)* **l.** encendedor *m*, mechero *m*

light-headed [laɪt'hedɪd] *adj* (**a**) *(dizzy)* mareado(a) (**b**) *(frivolous)* frívolo(a)

light-hearted ['laɪthɑːtɪd] *adj* alegre

lighthouse ['laɪthaʊs] *n* faro *m*

lighting ['laɪtɪŋ] *n* (**a**) *(act)* iluminación *f* (**b**) *(system)* alumbrado *m*

lightly ['laɪtlɪ] *adv* (**a**) ligeramente (**b**) **to get off l.** salir casi indemne

lightness¹ ['laɪtnɪs] *n* luminosidad *f*, claridad *f*

lightness² ['laɪtnɪs] *n (of weight)* ligereza *f*

lightning ['laɪtnɪŋ] *n (flash)* relámpago *m*; *(stroke)* rayo *m*; **l. conductor** *or* **rod** pararrayos *m inv*; **l. strike** huelga *f* relámpago

lightweight ['laɪtweɪt] *adj (suit etc)* ligero(a); *(boxer)* de peso ligero; *Fig (person)* light

like¹ [laɪk] **1** *adj* (**a**) parecido(a), semejante (**b**) *(equal)* igual
2 *adv* **(as) l. as not** a lo mejor
3 *prep* (**a**) *(similar to)* como, parecido(a) a; *(the same as)* igual que; **it's not l. her to do that** no es propio de ella hacer eso; **I've never seen anything l. it** nunca he visto cosa igual; **l. that** así; **people l. that** ese tipo de gente; **what's he l.?** ¿cómo es?; *Fam* **that's more l. it!** ¡así se hace! (**b**) **to feel l.** *(want)* tener ganas de; **I feel l. a change** me apetece un cambio
4 *n* **brushes, combs and the l.** cepillos, peines y cosas por el estilo

like² [laɪk] **1** *vt* (**a**) **do you l. chocolate?** ¿te gusta el chocolate?; **he likes dancing** le gusta bailar; **she likes children** le gustan los niños (**b**) *(want)* querer; **whether you l. it or not** quieras o no (quieras); **would you l. a drink?** ¿te apetece tomar algo?
2 *vi* querer, gustar; **as you l.** como quieras; **whenever you l.** cuando quieras
3 *n* gusto *m*

likeable ['laɪkəbəl] *adj* simpático(a)

likelihood ['laɪklɪhʊd] *n* probabilidad *f*

likely ['laɪklɪ] **1** *adj* (**likelier, likeliest**) probable; **he's l. to cause trouble** es probable que cause problemas; **where are you l. to be this afternoon?** ¿dónde piensas estar esta tarde? **2** *adv* probablemente; **not l.!** ¡ni hablar!

likeness ['laɪknɪs] *n* (**a**) semejanza *f*, parecido *m* (**b**) *(portrait)* retrato *m*

likewise ['laɪkwaɪz] *adv* (**a**) *(also)* también, asimismo (**b**) *(the same)* lo mismo, igual

liking ['laɪkɪŋ] *n* (*for thing*) afición *f*; (*for person*) simpatía *f*; (*for friend*) cariño *m*; **to take a l. to sth** cogerle el gusto a algo; **to take a l. to sb** coger cariño a algn

lilac ['laɪlək] **1** *n* (**a**) *Bot* lila *f* (**b**) *(colour)* lila *m* **2** *adj* lila, de color lila

lilt [lɪlt] *n* melodía *f*

lily ['lɪlɪ] *n* lirio *m*, azucena *f*; **l. of the valley** lirio de los valles

limb [lɪm] *n* miembro *m*; *Fig* **to be out on a l.** *(in danger)* estar en peligro; *Br (isolated)* estar aislado(a)

▸ limber up ['lɪmbə(r)] *vi Sport* entrar en calor; *Fig* prepararse (**for** para)

limbo ['lɪmbəʊ] *n* limbo *m*; *Fig* olvido *m*; **to be in l.** caer en el olvido

lime¹ [laɪm] *n Chem* cal *f*

lime² [laɪm] *n (fruit)* lima *f*; *(tree)* limero *m*

limelight ['laɪmlaɪt] *n Fig* **to be in the l.** estar en el candelero

limerick ['lɪmərɪk] *n* quintilla humorística

limestone ['laɪmstəʊn] *n* piedra caliza

limit ['lɪmɪt] **1** *n* límite *m*; *(maximum)* máximo *m*; *(minimum)* mínimo *m* **2** *vt (restrict)* limitar

limitation [lɪmɪ'teɪʃən] *n* limitación *f*

limited ['lɪmɪtɪd] *adj* limitado(a); **l. edition** edición limitada; *Br* **l. (liability) company** sociedad anónima

limitless ['lɪmɪtlɪs] *adj* ilimitado(a)

limousine ['lɪməziːn, lɪmə'ziːn] *n* limusina *f*

limp¹ [lɪmp] **1** *vi* cojear **2** *n* cojera *f*

limp² [lɪmp] *adj* (**a**) *(floppy)* flojo(a) (**b**) *(weak)* débil

limpet ['lɪmpɪt] *n* lapa *f*

linchpin ['lɪntʃpɪn] *n Tech* pezonera *f*; *Fig* eje *m*

line¹ [laɪn] *n* (**a**) línea *f*; *(straight)* raya *f*; **to be on the right lines** ir por buen camino; *US* **State l.** límite *m* de un Estado

(**b**) *(of writing)* renglón *m*; *(of poetry)* verso *m*; *Th* **to learn one's lines** aprenderse el papel (**c**) *(row)* fila *f*; *(of trees)* hilera *f*; *US (queue)* cola *f*; *Mil* **l. of fire** línea *f* de fuego; *Mil* **to be in the front l.** estar en primera línea; *Fig* **to be in l. (with)** coincidir (con); *Fam* **to bring sb into l.** pararle los pies a algn; *US* **to stand in l.** *(queue)* hacer cola; *Fam* **to step out of l.** salirse de las reglas; *Fig* **sth along these lines** algo por el estilo; **l. dancing** = baile al ritmo de música country en el que los participantes se colocan en hileras y se mueven todos al mismo tiempo dando los mismos pasos

(**d**) *(rope)* cuerda *f*; *(wire)* cable *m*; **fishing l.** sedal *m*

(**e**) *Tel* línea *f*; **hold the l.!** ¡no cuelgue!

(**f**) *Br Rail* vía *f*

(**g**) *(range of goods)* surtido *m*; **a new l.** una nueva línea

(**h**) *(of descent)* linaje *m*

line² [laɪn] *vt (pipe etc)* revestir; *Sewing* forrar; *Fam* **to l. one's pockets** forrarse

▸ line up 1 *vt sep* (**a**) *(arrange in rows)* poner en fila (**b**) **he has something lined up for this evening** tiene algo organizado para esta noche

2 *vi (people)* ponerse en fila; *(troops)* formar; *(in queue)* hacer cola

linear ['lɪnɪə(r)] *adj* lineal

lined [laɪnd] *adj* (**a**) *(paper)* rayado(a); *(face)* arrugado(a) (**b**) *(garment)* forrado(a)

linen ['lɪnɪn] *n* (**a**) *(cloth)* lino *m* (**b**) *(clothes)* ropa *f*; *(sheets etc)* ropa blanca

liner ['laɪnə(r)] *n* transatlántico *m*

linesman ['laɪnzmən] *n Sport* juez *m* de línea

line-up ['laɪnʌp] *n Sport* alineación *f*

linger ['lɪŋgə(r)] *vi* tardar; *(dawdle)* rezagarse; *(smell, doubt)* persistir; *Fig (memory)* perdurar

lingerie ['lænʒəriː] *n Fml* ropa *f* interior (de mujer)

lingering ['lɪŋgərɪŋ] *adj (doubt)* persistente; *(look)* fijo(a)

lingo ['lɪŋgəʊ] *n (pl* **lingoes**) *Fam* (**a**) *(language)* lengua *f*, idioma *m* (**b**) *(jargon)* jerga *f*

linguist ['lɪŋgwɪst] *n* lingüista *mf*; **he's a good l.** se le dan bien los idiomas

linguistic [lɪŋ'gwɪstɪk] *adj* lingüístico(a)

linguistics [lɪŋ'gwɪstɪks] *n sing* lingüística *f*

lining ['laɪnɪŋ] *n* forro *m*

link [lɪŋk] **1** *n* (**a**) *(of chain)* eslabón *m* (**b**) *(connection)* conexión *f*; *Fig* vínculo *m*; **rail l.** enlace ferroviario (**c**) **links** campo *m* de golf **2** *vt* unir

▸ link up *vi* unirse; *(meet)* encontrarse; *(spaceships)* acoplarse

link-up ['lɪŋkʌp] *n Tel & TV* conexión *f*; *(meeting)* encuentro *m*; *(of spaceships)* acoplamiento *m*

lino ['laɪnəʊ] *n Fam* linóleo *m*

linoleum [lɪ'nəʊlɪəm] *n* linóleo *m*, linóleum *m*

lion ['laɪən] *n* león *m*

lioness ['laɪənɪs] *n* leona *f*

lip [lɪp] *n* (**a**) labio *m* (**b**) *(of jug)* pico *m*

lip-read ['lɪpriːd] *vt & vi* leer en los labios

lip-service ['lɪpsɜːvɪs] *n* palabrería *f*

lipstick ['lɪpstɪk] *n* lápiz *m* de labios

liqueur [lɪ'kjʊə(r)] *n* licor *m*

liquid ['lɪkwɪd] *adj & n* líquido(a) *(m)*

liquidate ['lɪkwɪdeɪt] *vt* liquidar

liquidation [lɪkwɪ'deɪʃən] *n* liquidación *f*; **to**

go into l. entrar en liquidación
liquidize ['lɪkwɪdaɪz] *vt* licuar
liquidizer ['lɪkwɪdaɪzə(r)] *n* licuadora *f*
liquor ['lɪkər] *n US* alcohol *m*, bebidas alcohólicas; **l. store** tienda *f* de bebidas alcohólicas
liquorice ['lɪkərɪs,'lɪkərɪʃ] *n* regaliz *m*
Lisbon ['lɪzbən] *n* Lisboa
lisp [lɪsp] **1** *n* ceceo *m*
  2 *vi* cecear
list¹ [lɪst] **1** *n* lista *f*; *(catalogue)* catálogo *m*
  2 *vt (make a list of)* hacer una lista de; *(put on a list)* poner en una lista; **it is not listed** no figura en la lista
list² [lɪst] *Naut* **1** *n* escora *f*
  2 *vi* escorar
listen ['lɪsən] *vi* escuchar; *(pay attention)* prestar atención
  ▸ **listen out for** *vt insep* estar atento(a) a
listener ['lɪsənə(r)] *n* oyente *mf*
listless ['lɪstlɪs] *adj* apático(a)
lit [lɪt] *pt & pp of* **light**
liter ['liːtər] *n US* = **litre**
literacy ['lɪtərəsɪ] *n* alfabetización *f*
literal ['lɪtərəl] *adj* literal
literally ['lɪtərəlɪ] *adv* literalmente
literary ['lɪtərərɪ] *adj* literario(a)
literate ['lɪtərɪt] *adj* alfabetizado(a)

> 🖉 Note that the Spanish word **literato** is a false friend and is never a translation for the English word **literate**. In Spanish, **literato** means "writer, author".

literature ['lɪtərətʃə(r)] *n* (a) literatura *f* (b) *Fam (documentation)* folleto informativo
lithe [laɪð] *adj Fml* ágil
Lithuania [lɪθjʊ'eɪnɪə] *n* Lituania
Lithuanian [lɪθjʊ'eɪnɪən] **1** *adj* lituano(a)
  2 *n (person)* lituano(a) *m,f*; *(language)* lituano *m*
litigation [lɪtɪ'geɪʃən] *n* litigio *m*
litmus ['lɪtməs] *n Fig* **l. test** prueba *f* contundente
litre ['liːtə(r)] *n* litro *m*
litter ['lɪtə(r)] **1** *n* (a) *(rubbish)* basura *f*; *(papers)* papeles *mpl*; **l. bin** papelera *f* (b) *(offspring)* camada *f*
  2 *vt* ensuciar
littered ['lɪtəd] *adj* cubierto(a) (**with** de)
little ['lɪtəl] **1** *adj* (a) pequeño(a); **a l. dog** un perrito; **a l. house** una casita; **l. finger** dedo *m* meñique; **L.** *Br* **Bear** *or US* **Dipper** Osa *f* Menor (b) *(not much)* poco(a); **a l. cheese** un poco de queso
  2 *pron* poco *m*; **save me a l.** guárdame un poco
  3 *adv* poco; **l. by l.** poco a poco; **as l. as possible** lo menos posible; **they were a l. surprised** se quedaron algo sorprendidos
live¹ [lɪv] **1** *vi* vivir; **long l. the King!** ¡viva el Rey!

  2 *vt* vivir; **to l. an interesting life** vivir una vida interesante
  ▸ **live down** *vt sep* conseguir que se olvide
  ▸ **live for** *vt insep* vivir para
  ▸ **live off** *vt insep* vivir de
  ▸ **live on 1** *vt insep (food, money)* vivir de
    2 *vi (memory)* persistir
  ▸ **live through** *vt insep* vivir durante
  ▸ **live together** *vi* vivir juntos
  ▸ **live up** *vt sep Fam* **to l. it up** pegarse la gran vida
  ▸ **live up to** *vt insep (promises)* cumplir con; **i didn't l. up to expectations** no fue lo que se esperaba
  ▸ **live with** *vt insep* (a) vivir con (b) *Fig (accept)* aceptar
live² [laɪv] *adj* (a) *(living)* vivo(a) (b) *TV &* *Rad* en directo, en vivo (c) *(ammunition)* real; *(bomb)* sin explotar; *Elec* con corriente; *Fam* **he's a real l. wire!** ¡éste no para nunca!
livelihood ['laɪvlɪhʊd] *n* sustento *m*
lively ['laɪvlɪ] *adj* (**livelier, liveliest**) *(person)* vivo(a); *(place)* animado(a); *Fig (interest)* entusiástico(a)
liven ['laɪvən] *vt* **to l. (up)** animar
liver ['lɪvə(r)] *n* hígado *m*
livery ['lɪvərɪ] *n* librea *f*
lives [laɪvz] *pl of* **life**
livestock ['laɪvstɒk] *n* ganado *m*
livid ['lɪvɪd] *adj* lívido(a); *Fam (angry)* furioso(a)
living ['lɪvɪŋ] **1** *adj* vivo(a)
  2 *n* vida *f*; **l. conditions** condiciones *fpl* de vida; **l. expenses** dietas *fpl*; **to earn** *or* **make one's l.** ganarse la vida; **l. room** sala *f* de estar; **l. standards** nivel *m* de vida; **l. wage** sueldo mínimo
lizard ['lɪzəd] *n (large)* lagarto *m*; *(small)* lagartija *f*
llama ['lɑːmə] *n* llama *f*
load [ləʊd] **1** *n (cargo)* carga *f*; *(weight)* peso *m*; *Elec & Tech* carga; *Fam* **loads (of)** montones de; *Fam* **that's a l. of rubbish!** ¡no son más que tonterías!
  2 *vt* cargar
  ▸ **load up** *vi & vt sep* cargar
loaded ['ləʊdɪd] *adj* (a) cargado(a) (**with** de); *Fig* **a l. question** una pregunta intencionada (b) *Fam* **to be l.** *(rich)* estar forrado(a) (c) *(dice)* trucado(a)
loading ['ləʊdɪŋ] *n* carga *f*; **l. bay** cargadero *m*
loaf¹ [ləʊf] *n (pl loaves)* pan *m*; *(French stick)* barra *f* de pan; *(sliced)* pan de molde
loaf² [ləʊf] *vi* **to l. (about** *or* **around)** holgazanear
loan [ləʊn] **1** *n* préstamo *m*; *Fin* empréstito *m*; **on l.** prestado(a); *(footballer)* cedido(a)
  2 *vt* prestar
loath [ləʊθ] *adj* **to be l. to do sth** ser reacio(a) a hacer algo
loathe [ləʊð] *vt* aborrecer, odiar

loathing ['ləʊðɪŋ] n aborrecimiento m, odio m

loathsome ['ləʊðsəm] adj odioso(a), repugnante

loaves [ləʊvz] pl of **loaf**

lobby ['lɒbɪ] **1** n (**a**) (hall) vestíbulo m (**b**) (pressure group) grupo m de presión, lobby m
2 vt presionar
3 vi ejercer presiones

lobe [ləʊb] n lóbulo m

lobster ['lɒbstə(r)] n langosta f

local ['ləʊkəl] **1** adj local; (person) del pueblo; Med **l. anaesthetic** anestesia f local; Tel **l. call** llamada urbana; **l. government** gobierno m municipal
2 n Fam (**a**) **the locals** los vecinos (**b**) Br (pub) bar m del barrio

locality [ləʊˈkælɪtɪ] n localidad f

locally ['ləʊkəlɪ] adv en or de la localidad

locate [ləʊˈkeɪt] vt (situate) situar, ubicar; (find) localizar

location [ləʊˈkeɪʃən] n (**a**) lugar m, situación f (**b**) Cin **l. shots** exteriores mpl; **they're on l. in Australia** están rodando en Australia

loch [lɒx, lɒk] n Scot lago m

lock¹ [lɒk] **1** n (**a**) (on door etc) cerradura f; (bolt) cerrojo m; (padlock) candado m (**b**) (on canal) esclusa f
2 vt cerrar con llave/cerrojo/candado
3 vi (door etc) cerrarse; (wheels) trabarse
▸ **lock up** vt sep (house) cerrar; (jail) meter en la cárcel

lock² [lɒk] n Literary (of hair) mechón m

locker ['lɒkə(r)] n (cupboard) armario ropero; US **l. room** vestuario m con armarios roperos

locket ['lɒkɪt] n medallón m

lockout ['lɒkaʊt] n cierre m patronal

locksmith ['lɒksmɪθ] n cerrajero m

lockup ['lɒkʌp] n (garage) garaje alejado de la casa; US (prison) cárcel f

loco ['ləʊkəʊ] adj US Fam pirado(a)

locomotive [ləʊkəˈməʊtɪv] n locomotora f

locust ['ləʊkəst] n langosta f

lodge [lɒdʒ] **1** n (**a**) (gamekeeper's) casa f del guarda; (porter's) portería f; (hunter's) refugio m (**b**) (masonic) logia f (**c**) (beaver's den) madriguera f
2 vt (**a**) (accommodate) alojar (**b**) (complaint) presentar
3 vi (**a**) (live) alojarse (**b**) (get stuck) meterse (**in** en)

lodger ['lɒdʒə(r)] n huésped(a) m,f

lodging ['lɒdʒɪŋ] n alojamiento m; **l. house** casa f de huéspedes

loft [lɒft] n desván m

lofty ['lɒftɪ] adj (**loftier, loftiest**) Literary (high) alto(a); Pej (haughty) altivo(a)

log [lɒg] **1** n (**a**) (of tree) tronco m; (for fuel) leño m; **l. cabin** cabaña f de troncos (**b**) Naut diario m de a bordo
2 vt (record) registrar

▸ **log in, log on** vi Comput entrar (en sistema)
▸ **log out, log off** vi Comput salir (del sistema)

logarithm ['lɒgərɪðəm] n logaritmo m

log-book ['lɒgbʊk] n Naut diario m de a bordo; Av diario de vuelo; Aut documentación f (del coche)

loggerheads ['lɒgəhedz] npl **to be at l. with sb** estar a mal con algn

logic ['lɒdʒɪk] n lógica f

logical ['lɒdʒɪkəl] adj lógico(a)

logistics [ləˈdʒɪstɪks] npl logística f

logo ['ləʊgəʊ] n logotipo m

loin [lɔɪn] n (of animal) ijada f; Culin (of pork) lomo m; (of beef) solomillo m

loiter ['lɔɪtə(r)] vi (hang about) holgazanear; (lag behind) rezagarse; (prowl) merodear

loll [lɒl] vi (tongue, head) colgar
▸ **loll about, loll around** vi repantigarse

lollipop ['lɒlɪpɒp] n pirulí m, chupachup® m; **ice(d) l.** polo m; Br Fam **l. lady/man** = guardia que para el tráfico para que crucen los colegiales

lolly ['lɒlɪ] n Fam (**a**) (sweet) pirulí m, chupachup® m; **ice(d) l.** polo m (**b**) Fam (money) pasta f

London ['lʌndən] n Londres

Londoner ['lʌndənə(r)] n londinense mf

lone [ləʊn] adj (solitary) solitario(a); (single) solo(a)

loneliness ['ləʊnlɪnɪs] n soledad f

lonely ['ləʊnlɪ] adj (**lonelier, loneliest**) solo(a), solitario(a)

long¹ [lɒŋ] **1** adj (**a**) (size) largo(a); **how l. is the table?** ¿cuánto tiene de largo la mesa?; **it's 3 m l.** tiene 3 m de largo; **l. jump** salto m de longitud (**b**) (time) mucho(a); **at l. last** por fin; **how l. is the film?** ¿cuánto tiempo dura la película?
2 adv mucho, mucho tiempo; **all day l.** todo el día; **as l. as the exhibition lasts** mientras dure la exposición; **as l. as** or **so l. as you don't mind** con tal de que no te importe; **before l.** dentro de poco; **how l. have you been here?** ¿cuánto tiempo llevas aquí?

long² [lɒŋ] vi añorar; **to l. for** anhelar

long-distance ['lɒŋdɪstəns] adj de larga distancia; **l. call** conferencia interurbana; **l. runner** corredor(a) m,f de fondo

longhand ['lɒŋhænd] n escritura f a mano

longing ['lɒŋɪŋ] n (desire) anhelo m; (nostalgia) nostalgia f

longitude ['lɒndʒɪtjuːd] n longitud f

long-playing ['lɒŋpleɪɪŋ] adj de larga duración; **l. record** elepé m

long-range ['lɒŋreɪndʒ] adj (missile etc) de largo alcance; (weather forecast) de largo plazo

long-sighted [lɒŋˈsaɪtɪd] adj (**a**) Med présbita (**b**) Fig previsor(a)

long-standing ['lɒŋstændɪŋ] adj antiguo(a), de mucho tiempo

long-suffering ['lɒŋsʌfərɪŋ] adj sufrido(a)

long-term ['lɒŋtɜːm] *adj* a largo plazo

long-winded [lɒŋ'wɪndɪd] *adj* prolijo(a)

loo [luː] *n Br Fam* wáter *m*

look [lʊk] **1** *n* (a) *(glance)* mirada *f*; **to take a l. at** *(peep)* echar un vistazo a; *(examine)* examinar (b) *(appearance)* aspecto *m*, apariencia *f*; **I don't like the l. of it** me da mala espina (c) *(fashion)* moda *f* (d) **(good) looks** belleza *f*

2 *vi* (a) mirar (b) *(seem)* parecer; **he looks well** tiene buena cara; **it looks delicious** tiene un aspecto buenísimo; **she looks like her father** *(resembles)* se parece a su padre

3 *vt* mirar

▸ **look after** *vt insep* cuidar a, ocuparse de

▸ **look at** *vt insep* mirar; *Fig* **whichever way you l. at it** desde cualquier punto de vista

▸ **look away** *vi* apartar la mirada

▸ **look back** *vi* (a) mirar hacia atrás; *Fig* **since then he has never looked back** desde entonces ha ido prosperando (b) *(remember)* recordar

▸ **look down** *vi Fig* **to l. down on sth/sb** despreciar algo/a algn

▸ **look for** *vt insep* buscar

▸ **look forward to** *vt insep* esperar con ansia; **I l. forward to hearing from you** *(in letter)* espero noticias suyas

▸ **look into** *vt insep* examinar, investigar

▸ **look on 1** *vt insep (consider)* considerar

2 *vi* quedarse mirando

▸ **look onto** *vt insep* dar a

▸ **look out** *vi* (a) **the bedroom looks out onto the garden** el dormitorio da al jardín (b) **l. out!** *(take care)* ¡cuidado!, ¡ojo!

▸ **look over** *vt sep (examine)* revisar; *(place)* inspeccionar

▸ **look round 1** *vi* mirar alrededor; *(turn head)* volver la cabeza

2 *vt insep (house, shop)* ver

▸ **look through** *vt insep* (a) *(window)* mirar por (b) *(leaf through)* hojear; *(examine)* revisar; *(check)* registrar

▸ **look to** *vt insep* (a) *(take care of)* velar por (b) *(turn to)* recurrir a

▸ **look up 1** *vi* (a) *(glance upwards)* alzar la vista (b) *Fam (improve)* mejorar

2 *vt sep* (a) *(look for)* buscar (b) *(visit)* ir a visitar

▸ **look upon** *vt insep* considerar

▸ **look up to** *vt insep (person)* respetar

lookout ['lʊkaʊt] *n (person)* centinela *mf*; *(place)* mirador *m*; **to be on the l. for** estar al acecho de; *Fam* **that's his l.!** ¡eso es asunto suyo!

loom¹ [luːm] *n* telar *m*

loom² [luːm] *vi* alzarse; *Fig (threaten)* amenazar

loony ['luːnɪ] *adj* **(loonier, looniest)** *Fam* loco(a)

loop [luːp] **1** *n* (a) lazo *m* (b) *Comput* bucle *m*

2 *vt* (a) encordar (b) *Av* **to l. the loop** rizar el rizo

loophole ['luːphəʊl] *n Fig* escapatoria *f*

loose [luːs] *adj* (a) *(not secure)* flojo(a); *(papers, hair, clothes)* suelto(a); *(tongue)* desatado(a); *(baggy)* holgado(a); **to set sb l.** soltar a algn; *Fam* **to be at a l. end** no saber qué hacer (b) *(not packaged)* a granel; **l. tobacco** tabaco *m* en hebras; **l. change** suelto *m* (c) *(not exact)* vago(a); *(translation)* libre (d) *(lax)* relajado(a); **a l. woman** una mujer fácil

loosely ['luːslɪ] *adv* (a) *(approximately)* aproximadamente (b) *(vaguely)* vagamente

loosen ['luːsən] **1** *vt* aflojar; *(belt)* desabrochar; *Fig (restrictions)* flexibilizar

2 *vi (slacken)* aflojarse

loot [luːt] **1** *n* botín *m*

2 *vt* saquear

lop [lɒp] *vt* podar

▸ **lop off** *vt sep* cortar

lope [ləʊp] *vi* andar a zancadas

lopsided [lɒp'saɪdɪd] *adj* ladeado(a)

lord [lɔːd] *n* (a) señor *m*; *(British peer)* lord *m*; **the House of Lords** la Cámara de los Lores; **the L. Mayor** el señor alcalde (b) *Rel* **the L.** El Señor; **good L.!** ¡Dios mío!; **the L.'s Prayer** el Padrenuestro (c) *(judge)* señoría *mf*

lordship ['lɔːdʃɪp] *n Br* **his l./your l.** su señoría

lorry ['lɒrɪ] *n Br* camión *m*; **l. driver** camionero(a) *m,f*; **l. load** carga *f*

lose [luːz] **1** *vt* (*pt & pp* **lost**) perder; **to l. time** *(of clock)* atrasarse

2 *vi* perder; **to l. to sb** perder contra algn; **to l. out** salir perdiendo

loser ['luːzə(r)] *n* perdedor(a) *m,f*

loss [lɒs] *n* pérdida *f*; **to make a l.** perder; *Fig* **to be at a l. for words** quedarse de una pieza; **to be at a l.** what to do no saber qué hacer

lost [lɒst] **1** *adj* (a) perdido(a); **to get l.** perderse; *Fam* **get l.!** ¡vete a la porra!; **l. property office,** *US* **l. and found department** oficina *f* de objetos perdidos (b) *(disoriented)* desorientado(a); *(distracted)* distraído(a); **l. in thought** ensimismado(a)

2 *pt & pp* de **lose**

lot [lɒt] *n* (a) *(fate)* suerte *f* (b) **to cast lots for sth** echar algo a suertes (c) *US (plot of land)* parcela *f* (d) *(in an auction)* lote *m* (e) *(everything)* todo *m*; **he ate the l.** se lo comió todo (f) **a l. of** *(much)* mucho(a); *(many)* muchos(as); **he feels a l. better** se encuentra mucho mejor; **she reads a l.** lee mucho; *Fam* **lots of** montones de, cantidad de

lotion ['ləʊʃən] *n* loción *f*

lottery ['lɒtərɪ] *n* lotería *f*; **l. ticket** ≃ décimo *m* de lotería

loud [laʊd] **1** *adj* (a) *(voice)* alto(a); *(noise)* fuerte; *(laugh)* estrepitoso(a); *(applause)* clamoroso(a); *(protests, party)* ruidoso(a) (b) *(flashy)* chillón(ona) (c) *(vulgar)* hortera

2 *adv* **to read/think out l.** leer/pensar en voz alta

loud-hailer [laʊd'heɪlə(r)] *n* megáfono *m*

loudspeaker [laʊd'spiːkə(r)] *n* altavoz *m*
lounge [laʊndʒ] **1** *n Br* salón *m*, sala *f* de estar
  2 *vi* hacer el vago
louse [laʊs] *n* (*pl* **lice**) piojo *m*
lousy ['laʊzɪ] *adj* (**lousier, lousiest**) *Fam* fatal;
  a l. trick una cochinada
lout [laʊt] *n* gamberro *m*
lovable ['lʌvəbəl] *adj* adorable
love [lʌv] **1** *n* (**a**) amor *m* (**for** por); (*passion*)
pasión *f* (**for** por); **to be in l. with sb** estar
enamorado(a) de algn; **to fall in l.** enamorarse; **to make l.** hacer el amor; (**with**) **l. (from**)
Mary (*in letter*) un abrazo, Mary; **l. affair**
amorío *m*; **l. letter/story** carta *f*/historia *f* de
amor; **l. life** vida *f* sentimental (**b**) (*person*)
amor *m*, cariño *m*; *Fam* chato(a) *m,f*; **my l.** mi
amor (**c**) (*in tennis*) **forty l.** cuarenta a cero
  2 *vt* (*person*) querer a, amar a; **he loves**
cooking/football le encanta cocinar/el fútbol
lovely ['lʌvlɪ] *adj* (**lovelier, loveliest**) (*charming*) encantador(a); (*beautiful*) hermoso(a),
precioso(a); (*delicious*) riquísimo(a)
lover ['lʌvə(r)] *n* (**a**) (*sexual partner*) amante
mf (**b**) (*enthusiast*) aficionado(a) *m,f*, ami-
go(a) *m,f*
loving ['lʌvɪŋ] *adj* cariñoso(a)
low¹ [ləʊ] **1** *adj* (**a**) bajo(a); (*neckline*) esco-
tado(a); **the L. Countries** los Países Bajos (**b**)
(*in quantity*) bajo(a) (**c**) (*poor*) pobre (**d**)
(*battery*) gastado(a); **l. frequency** baja frecuencia (**e**) **to feel l.** sentirse deprimido(a)
(**f**) (*reprehensible*) malo(a)
  2 *adv* bajo
  3 *n* (**a**) *Met* área *f* de baja presión (**b**) (*low
point*) punto más bajo; **to reach an all-time l.**
tocar fondo
low² [ləʊ] *vi* (*cow*) mugir
lowdown ['ləʊdaʊn] *n Fam* pormenores *mpl*
lower ['ləʊə(r)] **1** *adj* (*comp of* **low**) inferior;
Typ **l. case** minúscula *f*; **l. class** clase baja
  2 *adv comp of* **low**
  3 *vt* bajar; (*flag*) arriar; (*reduce*) reducir;
(*price*) rebajar
lower-class ['ləʊəklɑːs] *adj* de clase baja
lowest ['ləʊɪst] **1** *adj* (*superl of* **low**) más
bajo(a); (*price, speed*) mínimo(a)
  2 *n* **at the l.** como mínimo
low-key [ləʊ'kiː] *adj* sin ceremonia
lowlands ['ləʊləndz] *npl* tierras bajas
lowly ['ləʊlɪ] *adj* (**lowlier, lowliest**) humilde
low-necked ['ləʊnekt] *adj* escotado(a)
loyal ['lɔɪəl] *adj* leal, fiel
loyalty ['lɔɪəltɪ] *n* lealtad *f*, fidelidad *f*
lozenge ['lɒzɪndʒ] *n* pastilla *f*
LP [el'piː] *n* (*abbr* **long-playing record**) LP *m*
L-plate ['elpleɪt] *n Br* placa *f* de la "L"
LSD [eles'diː] *n* (*abbr* **lysergic acid diethyl-
amide**) LSD *m*
Ltd *Br Com* (*abbr* **Limited (Liability)**) ≃ S.A.
lubricant ['luːbrɪkənt] *n* lubricante *m*
lubricate ['luːbrɪkeɪt] *vt* lubricar; (*engine*)
engrasar

lubrication [luːbrɪ'keɪʃən] *n* engrase *m*
lucid ['luːsɪd] *adj* lúcido(a)
luck [lʌk] *n* suerte *f*; **bad l.!** ¡mala suerte!;
good l.! ¡(buena) suerte!; **to be in l.** estar de
suerte; **to be out of l.** no tener suerte; *Fig* **to
push one's l.** tentar la suerte; *Fig* **to try one's l.**
probar fortuna
luckily ['lʌkɪlɪ] *adv* por suerte, afortunadamente
lucky ['lʌkɪ] *adj* (**luckier, luckiest**) (*person*)
afortunado(a); (*day*) de suerte; (*move*) opor-
tuno(a); (*charm*) de la suerte; **a l. break** una
oportunidad
lucrative ['luːkrətɪv] *adj* lucrativo(a)
ludicrous ['luːdɪkrəs] *adj* absurdo(a), ridícu-
lo(a)
lug [lʌg] *vt Fam* arrastrar
luggage ['lʌgɪdʒ] *n* equipaje *m*; **l. rack** *Aut*
baca *f*; *Rail* portaequipajes *m inv*
lukewarm ['luːkwɔːm] *adj* (*water etc*) ti-
bio(a); *Fig* (*reception etc*) poco entusiasta
lull [lʌl] **1** *n* (*in storm*) calma chicha; (*in
fighting*) tregua *f*
  2 *vt* (*cause to sleep*) adormecer; **to l. sb into a
false sense of security** infundir una falsa
seguridad a algn
lullaby ['lʌləbaɪ] *n* canción *f* de cuna, nana *f*
lumbago [lʌm'beɪgəʊ] *n* lumbago *m*
lumber ['lʌmbə(r)] **1** *n* (**a**) *Br* (*junk*) trastos
viejos (**b**) *US* (*timber*) maderos *mpl*
  2 *vt Fam* cargar (**with** de)
lumberjack ['lʌmbədʒæk] *n* leñador *m*
luminous ['luːmɪnəs] *adj* luminoso(a)
lump [lʌmp] **1** *n* (*of coal etc*) trozo *m*; (*of
sugar, earth*) terrón *m*; (*in sauce*) grumo *m*;
(*swelling*) bulto *m*; *Fam Fig* (*in throat*) nudo
m; **l. sum** cantidad *f* global
  2 *vt Fam* (*endure*) aguantar
► **lump together** *vt sep* apelotonar
lumpy ['lʌmpɪ] *adj* (**lumpier, lumpiest**) (*bed*)
lleno(a) de bultos; (*sauce*) grumoso(a)
lunacy ['luːnəsɪ] *n* locura *f*
lunar ['luːnə(r)] *adj* lunar
lunatic ['luːnətɪk] *adj & n* loco(a) (*m,f*); **l.
asylum** manicomio *m*
lunch [lʌntʃ] **1** *n* comida *f*, almuerzo *m*; **l.
hour** hora *f* de comer
  2 *vi* comer, almorzar
luncheon ['lʌntʃən] *n Old-fashioned Fml* almuerzo *m*; **l. voucher** vale *m* de comida;
(pork) l. meat carne *f* de cerdo troceada,
chopped *m*
lunchtime ['lʌntʃtaɪm] *n* hora *f* de comer
lung [lʌŋ] *n* pulmón *m*
lunge [lʌndʒ] **1** *n* arremetida *f*
  2 *vi* **to l. (forward)** arremeter; **to l. (out) at
sb** arremeter contra algn
lurch [lɜːtʃ] **1** *n* (**a**) (*of vehicle*) sacudida *f*; (*of
person*) tambaleo *m* (**b**) *Fam* **to leave sb in
the l.** dejar a algn en la cuneta
  2 *vi* (*vehicle*) dar sacudidas; (*person*) tambalearse

lure [lʊə(r)] **1** n (decoy) señuelo m; (bait) cebo m; Fig (charm) aliciente m
  2 vt atraer con engaños
lurid ['lʊərɪd] adj (**a**) (gruesome) espeluznante; (sensational) sensacionalista (**b**) (gaudy) chillón(ona)
lurk [lɜːk] vi (lie in wait) estar al acecho; (hide) esconderse
luscious ['lʌʃəs] adj (food) delicioso(a)
lush [lʌʃ] adj (vegetation) exuberante
lust [lʌst] **1** n (sexual desire) lujuria f; (craving) ansia f; (greed) codicia f
  2 vi **to l. after sth/sb** codiciar algo/desear a algn
lustre, US **luster** ['lʌstə(r)] n lustre m
lusty ['lʌstɪ] adj (**lustier, lustiest**) robusto(a)
lute [luːt] n laúd m
Luxembourg ['lʌksəmbɜːg] n Luxemburgo

luxuriant [lʌgˈzjʊərɪənt] adj (plants) exuberante; (hair etc) abundante
luxurious [lʌgˈzjʊərɪəs] adj lujoso(a)
luxury ['lʌkʃərɪ] n lujo m; **l. flat** piso m de lujo

> 🖉 Note that the Spanish word **lujuria** is a false friend and is never a translation for the English word **luxury**. In Spanish, **lujuria** means "lust".

lychee ['laɪtʃiː] n lichi m
lying ['laɪɪŋ] **1** adj mentiroso(a)
  2 n mentiras fpl
lynch [lɪntʃ] vt linchar
lyre [laɪə(r)] n Mus lira f
lyric ['lɪrɪk] **1** adj lírico(a)
  2 n (**a**) (poem) poema lírico (**b**) **lyrics** (words of song) letra f
lyrical ['lɪrɪkəl] adj lírico(a)

M, m [em] *n (the letter)* M, m *f*

m (a) *(abbr* **metre(s))** m (b) *(abbr* **million(s))** m

mac [mæk] *n Br Fam (raincoat)* impermeable *m,* gabardina *f*

macabre [mə'kɑːbrə] *adj* macabro(a)

mac(c)aroni [mækə'rəʊnɪ] *n* macarrones *mpl*

mace¹ [meɪs] *n (club, ceremonial staff)* maza *f*

mace² [meɪs] *n (spice)* macis *f inv*

machine [mə'ʃiːn] **1** *n* máquina *f;* **m. gun** ametralladora *f;* **m. language** lenguaje *m* máquina
2 *vt* trabajar a máquina

machine-gun [mə'ʃiːngʌn] *vt* ametrallar

machine-readable [mə'ʃiːn'riːdəbəl] *adj Comput* para ser leído(a) por ordenador *or Am* computadora

machinery [mə'ʃiːnərɪ] *n (machines)* maquinaria *f; (workings of machine)* mecanismo *m; Fig* **the bureaucratic m.** la maquinaria burocrática

macintosh 'mækɪntɒʃ] *n* = **mackintosh**

mackerel ['mækrəl] *n (pl* **mackerel)** caballa *f*

mackintosh ['mækɪntɒʃ] *n* impermeable *m*

macroeconomics [mækrəʊiːkə'nɒmɪks] *n sing* macroeconomía *f*

mad [mæd] *adj* **(madder, maddest)** (a) loco(a); *(animal)* furioso(a); *(dog)* rabioso(a); **to be m.** estar loco(a); **to drive sb m.** volver loco(a) a algn; **to go m.** volverse loco(a); **you must be m.!** ¿estás loco?; *Fam* **m. cow disease** el mal de las vacas locas (b) *(idea, plan)* disparatado(a) (c) *Fam* **to be m. about sth/sb** estar loco(a) por algo/algn (d) *esp US Fam* **to be m. at sb** estar enfadado(a) con algn (e) *(gallop, race etc)* desenfrenado(a)

madam ['mædəm] *n* (a) señora *f;* **Dear M.** *(in letter)* Muy señora mía, Estimada señora (b) *(of brothel)* madam *f*

madden ['mædən] *vt* volver loco(a)

maddening ['mædənɪŋ] *adj* exasperante

made [meɪd] *pt & pp of* **make**

Madeira [mə'dɪərə] *n* (a) *(island)* Madeira (b) *(wine)* madeira *m;* **M. cake** bizcocho *m*

made-to-measure ['meɪdtə'meʒə(r)] *adj* hecho(a) a (la) medida

made-up ['meɪdʌp] *adj* (a) *(face, person)* maquillado(a); *(eyes, lips)* pintado(a) (b) *(story, excuse)* inventado(a)

madly ['mædlɪ] *adv Fam (extremely)* terriblemente; **to be m. in love with sb** estar loca-

mente enamorado(a) de algn

madman ['mædmən] *n* loco *m*

madness ['mædnɪs] *n* locura *f*

Madrid [mə'drɪd] *n* Madrid

Mafia ['mæfɪə] *n* mafia *f*

magazine [mægə'ziːn] *n* (a) *(periodical)* revista *f* (b) *(in rifle)* recámara *f* (c) *Mil (storehouse)* almacén *m; (for explosives)* polvorín *m*

maggot ['mægət] *n* larva *f,* gusano *m*

magic ['mædʒɪk] **1** *n* magia *f*
2 *adj* (a) mágico(a); **m. wand** varita mágica (b) *Fam (wonderful)* estupendo(a)

magical ['mædʒɪkəl] *adj* mágico(a)

magician [mə'dʒɪʃən] *n* (a) *(wizard)* mago(a) *m,f* (b) *(conjurer)* prestidigitador(a) *m,f*

magistrate ['mædʒɪstreɪt] *n* juez *mf* de primera instancia; **magistrates' court** juzgado *m* de primera instancia

magnanimous [mæg'nænɪməs] *adj* magnánimo(a)

magnet ['mægnɪt] *n* imán *m*

magnetic [mæg'netɪk] *adj* magnético(a); *Fig (personality)* carismático(a); **m. tape** cinta magnetofónica

magnetism ['mægnɪtɪzəm] *n* magnetismo *m*

magnificence [mæg'nɪfɪsəns] *n* magnificencia *f*

magnificent [mæg'nɪfɪsənt] *adj* magnífico(a)

magnify ['mægnɪfaɪ] *vt* (a) *(enlarge)* aumentar (b) *Fig (exaggerate)* exagerar

magnifying glass ['mægnɪfaɪɪŋglɑːs] *n* lupa *f*

magnitude ['mægnɪtjuːd] *n* magnitud *f*

magpie ['mægpaɪ] *n* urraca *f*

mahogany [mə'hɒgənɪ] **1** *n* caoba *f*
2 *adj* de caoba

maid [meɪd] *n* (a) criada *f, Andes, RP* mucama *f* (b) *Pej* **old m.** solterona *f*

maiden ['meɪdən] **1** *n Literary* doncella *f*
2 *adj* (a) *(unmarried)* soltera; **m. aunt** tía soltera; **m. name** apellido *m* de soltera (b) *(voyage, flight)* inaugural

mail [meɪl] **1** *n* correo *m;* **by m.** por correo; **m. order** venta *f* por correo; **m. train** tren *m* correo
2 *vt (post)* echar al buzón; *(send)* enviar por correo

mailbox ['meɪlbɒks] *n US* buzón *m*

mailing list ['meɪlɪŋlɪst] *n* lista *f* de direcciones

mailman ['meɪlmæn] *n US* cartero *m*

maim [meɪm] *vt* lisiar

main [meɪn] **1** *adj (problem, door etc)* principal; *(square, mast, sail)* mayor; *(office)* central; **the m. thing is to keep calm** lo esencial es mantener la calma; *Culin* **m. course** plato *m* principal; **m. road** carretera *f* principal; *US* **M. Street** la Calle Mayor

2 *n* (**a**) *(pipe, wire)* conducto *m* principal; **the mains** *(water or gas system)* la cañería maestra; *Elec* la red eléctrica; **a radio that works on battery or mains** una radio que funciona con pilas o con corriente (**b**) **in the m.** por regla general

mainframe ['meɪnfreɪm] *n* **m. computer** computer *or Am* ordenadora *f* central

mainland ['meɪnlənd] *n* continente *m*

mainly ['meɪnlɪ] *adv* principalmente, sobre todo; *(for the most part)* en su mayoría

mainstay ['meɪnsteɪ] *n Fig* sustento *m*, sostén *m*

mainstream ['meɪnstriːm] *n* corriente *f* principal

maintain [meɪn'teɪn] *vt* mantener; *(conversation)* sostener; *(silence, appearances)* guardar; *(road, machine)* conservar en buen estado

maintenance ['meɪntənəns] *n* (**a**) mantenimiento *m* (**b**) *(divorce allowance)* pensión *f*

maisonette [meɪzə'net] *n Br* dúplex *m*

maître d' ['meɪtrə'diː] *n US* maître *mf*

maize [meɪz] *n* maíz *m*

majestic [mə'dʒestɪk] *adj* majestuoso(a)

majesty ['mædʒɪstɪ] *n* majestad *f*

major ['meɪdʒə(r)] **1** *adj* (**a**) principal, mayor; *(contribution, operation)* importante (**b**) *Mus* mayor

2 *n* (**a**) *Mil* comandante *m* (**b**) *US Univ* especialidad *f*

3 *vi US Univ* **to m. in** especializarse en

Majorca [mə'jɔːkə] *n* Mallorca

Majorcan [mə'jɔːkən] *adj & n* mallorquín(ina) *(m,f)*

majority [mə'dʒɒrɪtɪ] *n* mayoría *f*; **to be in the m.** ser (la) mayoría

make [meɪk] *(pt & pp* **made**) **1** *vt* (**a**) hacer; *(manufacture)* fabricar; *(create)* crear; *(clothes, curtains)* confeccionar; *(meal)* preparar; *(payment)* efectuar; *(speech)* pronunciar; *(decision)* tomar; *(mistake)* cometer; **to be made of** ser de; **to m. a noise** hacer ruido

(**b**) *(render)* poner, volver; *(convert)* convertir (**into** en); *(appoint)* nombrar; **he made it clear that ...** dejó claro que ...

(**c**) *(force, compel)* obligar; *(cause)* causar; **to m. do with sth** arreglárselas con algo

(**d**) *(earn)* ganar; **to m. a living** ganarse la vida; **to m. a name for oneself** hacerse famoso(a); *Fig* **to m. the best of sth** sacar partido de algo

(**e**) **7 and 5 m. 12** 7 y 5 son 12

(**f**) *(calculate, reckon)* calcular; **what time do you m. it?** ¿qué hora tienes?

(**g**) *(think)* opinar; **I don't know what to m. of it** no sé qué pensar de eso; **it doesn't m. sense** no tiene sentido

(**h**) *(achieve)* alcanzar, conseguir

(**i**) **it will m. or break her** será su consagración o su ruina

(**j**) **to m. a fresh start** volver a empezar

2 *vi* (**a**) hacer; **to m. sure of sth** asegurarse de algo

(**b**) **she made as if to leave** hizo como si quisiera marcharse

3 *n* (**a**) *(brand)* marca *f*

(**b**) *Fam* **to be on the m.** andar tras el dinero

► **make for** *vt insep* (**a**) *(move towards)* dirigirse hacia; *(attack)* atacar a (**b**) **this makes for less work** esto ahorra trabajo

► **make out 1** *vt sep* (**a**) *(list, receipt)* hacer; *(cheque)* extender (**b**) *(perceive)* distinguir; *(writing)* descifrar (**c**) *(understand)* entender (**d**) *(claim)* pretender (**e**) **to m. out a case for doing sth** exponer los argumentos para hacer algo

2 *vi* **how did you m. out?** ¿qué tal te fue?

► **make up 1** *vt sep* (**a**) *(parcel, list)* hacer; *(prescription)* preparar; *(assemble)* montar (**b**) *(story)* inventar (**c**) *(apply cosmetics to)* maquillar; *(one's face)* maquillarse (**d**) *(loss)* compensar; *(lost time)* recuperar (**e**) *(constitute)* componer (**f**) **to m. it up (with sb)** hacer las paces (con algn) (**g**) **to m. up one's mind** decidirse

2 *vi* maquillarse

► **make up to 1** *vt insep Br Fam* **to m. up to sb** congraciarse con algn

2 *vt sep* **to m. it up to sb for sth** compensar a algn por algo

make-believe ['meɪkbɪliːv] *n (fantasy)* fantasía *f*; *(pretence)* fingimiento *m*; **to live in a world of m.** vivir en un mundo de ensueño

maker ['meɪkə(r)] *n* fabricante *mf*

makeshift ['meɪkʃɪft] *adj (improvised)* improvisado(a); *(temporary)* provisional

make-up ['meɪkʌp] *n* (**a**) *(cosmetics)* maquillaje *m*; **m. remover** desmaquillador *m* (**b**) *(composition)* composición *f*; *(character)* carácter *m*

making ['meɪkɪŋ] *n* (**a**) *(manufacture)* fabricación *f*; *(preparation)* preparación *f* (**b**) **he has the makings of a politician** tiene madera de político

malaise [mæ'leɪz] *n* malestar *m*

malaria [mə'leərɪə] *n* malaria *f*

Malay [mə'leɪ] **1** *adj* malayo(a)

2 *n* (**a**) *(person)* malayo(a) *m,f* (**b**) *(language)* malayo *m*

Malaysia [mə'leɪzɪə] *n* Malasia

male [meɪl] **1** *adj (animal, plant)* macho; *(person)* varón; *(sex)* masculino; *Pej* **m. chauvinism** machismo *m*

2 *n (person)* varón *m*; *(animal, plant)* macho *m*

malevolent [mə'levələnt] *adj* malévolo(a)

malfunction [mæl'fʌŋkʃən] **1** n mal funcionamiento m
2 vi funcionar mal

malice ['mælɪs] n malicia f; Jur **with m. aforethought** con premeditación

malicious [mə'lɪʃəs] adj malévolo(a)

malign [mə'laɪn] **1** adj maligno(a); (influence) perjudicial
2 vt calumniar, difamar

malignant [mə'lɪgnənt] adj (a) (person) malvado(a) (b) Med maligno(a)

mall [mɔːl] n US centro m comercial

malleable ['mælɪəbəl] adj maleable

mallet ['mælɪt] n mazo m

malnutrition [mælnju:'trɪʃən] n desnutrición f

malpractice [mæl'præktɪs] n procedimiento m ilegal; Med negligencia f

malt [mɔːlt] n malta f

Malta ['mɔːltə] n Malta

mammal ['mæməl] n mamífero m

mammary ['mæmərɪ] adj m. gland mama f

mammoth ['mæməθ] **1** n Zool mamut m
2 adj gigantesco(a)

man [mæn] **1** n (pl men) (a) hombre m; **old m.** viejo m; **young m.** joven m; Fig **he's a m. of his word** es hombre de palabra; Fig **the m. in the street** el hombre de la calle; **m. Friday** factótum m; Fam **dirty old m.** viejo verde (b) (humanity) el hombre (c) (husband) marido m; (partner) pareja f (d) **our m. in Madrid** nuestro representante en Madrid (e) (in chess) pieza f
2 vt (boat, plane) tripular; (post) servir; **manned flight** vuelo tripulado

manage ['mænɪdʒ] **1** vt (a) (company, household) llevar; (money, affairs, person) manejar (b) (succeed) conseguir; **to m. to do sth** lograr hacer algo
2 vi (cope physically) poder; (esp financially) arreglárselas; **we're managing** vamos tirando

manageable ['mænɪdʒəbəl] adj manejable

management ['mænɪdʒmənt] n dirección f

manager ['mænɪdʒə(r)] n (a) (of company, bank) director(a) m,f; (head of department) jefe(a) m,f (b) (of pop group etc) mánager m (c) Sport entrenador m

manageress [mænɪdʒə'res] n (of shop, restaurant) encargada f; (of company) directora f

managerial [mænɪ'dʒɪərɪəl] adj directivo(a)

managing ['mænɪdʒɪŋ] adj directivo(a); **m. director** director(a) m,f gerente

mandarin ['mændərɪn] n **m. (orange)** mandarina f

mandate ['mændeɪt] n mandato m

mandatory ['mændətərɪ] adj Fml obligatorio(a)

mane [meɪn] n (of horse) crin f; (of lion) melena f

maneuver [mə'nuːvər] n, vt & vi US = manoeuvre

manfully ['mænfʊlɪ] adv valientemente

manger ['meɪndʒə(r)] n pesebre m

mangle¹ ['mæŋgəl] n (for wringing) rodillo m

mangle² ['mæŋgəl] vt (crush) aplastar; (destroy by cutting) despedazar

mango ['mæŋgəʊ] n (pl mangoes) mango m

mangy ['meɪndʒɪ] adj (mangier, mangiest) (animal) sarnoso(a); Fam (carpet) raído(a)

manhandle ['mænhændəl] vt maltratar

manhole ['mænhəʊl] n boca f de acceso

manhood ['mænhʊd] n (a) (age) mayoría f de edad; **to reach m.** llegar a la edad viril (b) (manly qualities) virilidad f

mania ['meɪnɪə] n manía f

maniac ['meɪnɪæk] n maníaco(a) m,f; Fam loco(a) m,f

manic ['mænɪk] adj maníaco(a)

manic-depressive ['mænɪkdɪ'presɪv] adj & n maníaco(a) (m,f) depresivo(a)

manicure ['mænɪkjʊə(r)] **1** n manicura f
2 vt **to m. one's nails** hacerse la manicura

manifest ['mænɪfest] Fml **1** adj manifiesto(a)
2 vt manifestar

manifesto [mænɪ'festəʊ] n programa m electoral

manifold ['mænɪfəʊld] adj Fml (many) múltiples; (varied) diversos(as)

manipulate [mə'nɪpjʊleɪt] vt (a) manipular (b) Fig (accounts etc) falsificar

mankind [mæn'kaɪnd] n la humanidad, el género humano

manly ['mænlɪ] adj (manlier, manliest) varonil, viril

man-made ['mænmeɪd] adj (lake) artificial; (fibres, fabric) sintético(a)

manner ['mænə(r)] n (a) (way, method) manera f, modo m; **in this m.** de esta manera (b) (way of behaving) forma f de ser (c) Fml (type, class) clase f (d) (etiquette) **(good) manners** buenos modales; **bad manners** falta f de educación

mannerism ['mænərɪzəm] n (gesture) gesto m; (affectation) amaneramiento m

manoeuvre [mə'nuːvə(r)] **1** n maniobra f
2 vt maniobrar; (person) manejar
3 vi maniobrar

manor ['mænə(r)] n **m. house** casa solariega

manpower ['mænpaʊə(r)] n mano f de obra

mansion ['mænʃən] n casa f grande; (in country) casa solariega

manslaughter ['mænslɔːtə(r)] n homicidio involuntario

mantelpiece ['mæntəlpiːs] n (shelf) repisa f de chimenea; (fireplace) chimenea f

mantle ['mæntəl] n Fig (of snow) manto m, capa f

> 🖉 Note that the Spanish word **mantel** is a false friend and is never a translation for the English word **mantle**. In Spanish, **mantel** means "table-cloth".

manual ['mænjʊəl] *adj & n* manual *(m)*
manufacture [mænjʊ'fæktʃə(r)] 1 *vt* fabricar
2 *n* fabricación *f*
manufacturer [mænjʊ'fæktʃərə(r)] *n* fabricante *mf*
manure [mə'njʊə(r)] *n* abono *m*, estiércol *m*
manuscript ['mænjʊskrɪpt] *n* manuscrito *m*
many ['menɪ] 1 *adj* (**more, most**) mucho(a)/muchos(as); **a great m.** muchísimos(as); **as m. ... as ...** tantos(as) ... como ...; **how m. days?** ¿cuántos días?; **m. a time** muchas veces; **so m. flowers!** ¡cuántas flores!; **too m.** demasiados(as)
2 *pron* muchos(as)
map [mæp] 1 *n* (*of country*) mapa *m*; (*of town, bus route*) plano *m*
2 *vt* trazar un mapa de
▸ **map out** *vt sep* (*route*) trazar en un mapa; *Fig* (*future etc*) planear
maple ['meɪpəl] *n* arce *m*
mar [mɑː(r)] *vt* estropear; **to m. sb's enjoyment** aguarle la fiesta a algn
marathon ['mærəθən] *n* maratón *m*
marble ['mɑːbəl] 1 *n* (**a**) (*stone*) mármol *m* (**b**) (*glass ball*) canica *f*
2 *adj* de mármol
March [mɑːtʃ] *n* marzo *m*
march [mɑːtʃ] 1 *n* (**a**) *Mil* marcha *f*; *Fig* **to steal a m. on sb** tomar la delantera a algn; **m. past** desfile *m* (**b**) (*demonstration*) manifestación *f*
2 *vi* (**a**) marchar (**b**) (*demonstrate*) manifestarse
3 *vt Mil* hacer marchar
mare [meə(r)] *n* yegua *f*
margarine [mɑːdʒə'riːn] *n* margarina *f*
margin ['mɑːdʒɪn] *n* margen *m*; *Fig* **to win by a narrow m.** ganar por escaso margen; **m. of error** (*in statistics*) margen de error
marginal ['mɑːdʒɪnəl] *adj* marginal; *Pol* **m. seat** escaño *m* pendiente
marginally ['mɑːdʒɪnəlɪ] *adv* ligeramente
marigold ['mærɪɡəʊld] *n* caléndula *f*
marijuana, marihuana [mærɪ'hwɑːnə] *n* marihuana *f*, marijuana *f*
marinate ['mærɪneɪt] *vt* adobar
marine [mə'riːn] 1 *adj* marino(a)
2 *n* soldado *m* de infantería de marina; *Br* **the Marines**, *US* **the M. Corps** la infantería de marina
marital ['mærɪtəl] *adj* matrimonial; **m. status** estado *m* civil
maritime ['mærɪtaɪm] *adj* marítimo(a)
marjoram ['mɑːdʒərəm] *n* mejorana *f*
mark¹ [mɑːk] 1 *n* (**a**) (*left by blow etc*) señal *f*; (*stain*) mancha *f*; *Fig* **to make one's m.** distinguirse (**b**) (*sign, token*) señal *f*; (*indication*) indicio *m* (**c**) *Br* (*in exam etc*) nota *f*; **to get high marks** sacar buenas notas (**d**) *Fig* **to hit the m.** dar en el clavo; *Fig* **to be wide of the m.** estar lejos de la verdad
2 *vt* (**a**) (*stain*) manchar (**b**) (*with tick, cross*)

señalar (**c**) (*exam*) corregir; (*student*) dar notas a (**d**) **10 percent off marked price** (*sign*) descuento del 10 por ciento sobre el precio indicado (**e**) **m. my words** fíjate en lo que te digo (**f**) *Sport* marcar (**g**) hacer; **m. time** *Mil* marcar el paso; *Fig* hacer tiempo
▸ **mark out** *vt sep* (**a**) (*area*) delimitar (**b**) **to m. sb out for** destinar a algn a
mark² [mɑːk] *n* (*unit of currency*) marco *m*
marked [mɑːkt] *adj* (*noticeable*) marcado(a), acusado(a)
marker ['mɑːkə(r)] *n* (**a**) (*bookmark*) registro *m* (**b**) *Sport* marcador(a) *m,f* (**c**) (*pen*) rotulador *m* fluorescente
market ['mɑːkɪt] 1 *n* mercado *m*; **on the m.** en venta; **m. forces** tendencias *fpl* del mercado; *Br* **m. garden** (*small*) huerto *m*; (*large*) huerta *f*; *Br* **m. gardener** hortelano(a) *m,f*; **m. price** precio *m* de mercado; **m. research** estudio *m* de mercado
2 *vt* (*sell*) poner en venta; (*promote*) promocionar
marketable ['mɑːkɪtəbəl] *adj* comerciable
marketing ['mɑːkɪtɪŋ] *n* marketing *m*, mercadotecnia *f*
marketplace ['mɑːkɪtpleɪs] *n* mercado *m*
marksman ['mɑːksmən] *n* tirador *m*
marmalade ['mɑːməleɪd] *n* mermelada *f* (*de cítricos*)
maroon [mə'ruːn] *adj* (de color) granate
marooned [mə'ruːnd] *adj* bloqueado(a)
marquee [mɑː'kiː] *n* (**a**) *Br* (*tent*) carpa *f* (**b**) *US* (*of building*) marquesina *f*
marquess, marquis ['mɑːkwɪs] *n* marqués *m*
marriage ['mærɪdʒ] *n* (*state*) matrimonio *m*; (*wedding*) boda *f*; **m. bureau** agencia *f* matrimonial; **m. certificate** certificado *m* de matrimonio
married ['mærɪd] *adj* casado(a); **m. life** vida *f* conyugal
marrow ['mærəʊ] *n* (**a**) (**bone**) **m.** médula *f* (**b**) (*vegetable*) **m.** calabacín *m*
marry ['mærɪ] *vt* (*take in marriage*) casarse con; (*give in marriage*) casar (**to** con); (*unite in marriage*) casar; **to get married** casarse
Mars [mɑːz] *n* Marte *m*
marsh [mɑːʃ] *n* pantano *m*; **salt m.** marisma *f*
marshal ['mɑːʃəl] 1 *n* (**a**) *Mil* mariscal *m* (**b**) *Br* (*at sports event etc*) oficial *mf* (**c**) *US* (*sheriff*) alguacil *m* (**d**) *US* (*of police or fire department*) jefe *m*
2 *vt* (**a**) *Mil* formar (**b**) (*facts etc*) ordenar
marshy ['mɑːʃɪ] *adj* (**marshier, marshiest**) pantanoso(a)
martial ['mɑːʃəl] *adj* marcial; **m. arts** artes *fpl* marciales; **m. law** ley *f* marcial
Martian ['mɑːʃən] *adj & n* marciano(a) *(m,f)*
martyr ['mɑːtə(r)] 1 *n* mártir *mf*
2 *vt* martirizar
martyrdom ['mɑːtədəm] *n* martirio *m*
marvel ['mɑːvəl] 1 *n* maravilla *f*

2 *vi* **to m. at** maravillarse de
marvellous, *US* **marvelous** ['mɑːvələs] *adj* maravilloso(a)
Marxism ['mɑːksɪzəm] *n* marxismo *m*
Marxist ['mɑːksɪst] *adj & n* marxista *(mf)*
marzipan ['mɑːzɪpæn] *n* mazapán *m*
mascara [mæ'skɑːrə] *n* rímel *m*

> 🖉 Note that the Spanish word **máscara** is a false friend and is never a translation for the English word **mascara**. In Spanish, **máscara** means "mask".

mascot ['mæskət] *n* mascota *f*
masculine ['mæskjʊlɪn] *adj* masculino(a); *(woman)* hombruna
mash [mæʃ] **1** *n (for animals)* afrecho *m*
  2 *vt* **to m. (up)** machacar; **mashed potatoes** puré *m* de patatas *or Am* papas
mask [mɑːsk] **1** *n* máscara *f; (of doctor, dentist etc)* mascarilla *f*
  2 *vt* enmascarar; *Fig (conceal)* ocultar (**from** de)
masochist ['mæsəkɪst] *adj & n* masoquista *(mf)*
mason ['meɪsən] *n* (**a**) *(builder)* albañil *m* (**b**) *(freemason)* masón *m*, francmasón *m*
masonic [mə'sɒnɪk] *adj* masónico(a)
masonry ['meɪsənrɪ] *n (stonework)* albañilería *f*
masquerade [mæskə'reɪd] **1** *n (pretence)* farsa *f*
  2 *vi* **to m. as** hacerse pasar por
mass¹ [mæs] *n Rel* misa *f;* **to say m.** decir misa
mass² [mæs] **1** *n* (**a**) masa *f* (**b**) *(large quantity)* montón *m; (of people)* multitud *f* (**c**) **the masses** las masas
  2 *adj* masivo(a); **m. media** medios *mpl* de comunicación (de masas); **m. production** fabricación *f* en serie
  3 *vi (people)* congregarse; *Mil* concentrarse
massacre ['mæsəkə(r)] **1** *n* masacre *f*
  2 *vt* masacrar
massage ['mæsɑːʒ, mə'sɑːdʒ] **1** *n* masaje *m*
  2 *vt* (**a**) dar masajes a (**b**) *Fig (figures)* amañar
masseur [mæ'sɜː(r)] *n* masajista *m*
masseuse [mæ'sɜːz] *n* masajista *f*
massive ['mæsɪv] *adj* enorme; *(heart attack)* grave
mast [mɑːst] *n* (**a**) *Naut* mástil *m* (**b**) *Rad & TV* torre *f*
master ['mɑːstə(r)] **1** *n* (**a**) *(of dog, servant)* amo *m; (of household)* señor *m* (**b**) *Br (teacher)* profesor *m* (**c**) *Univ* **m.'s degree** ≃ máster *m* (**d**) *(expert)* maestro *m* (**e**) *(boy)* **M. James Brown** el señor James Brown
  2 *adj* (**a**) **m. copy** original *m;* **m. key** llave *f* maestra (**b**) *(expert)* maestro(a)
  3 *vt* (**a**) *(person, situation)* dominar (**b**) *(subject, skill)* llegar a dominar
masterful ['mɑːstəfʊl] *adj* autoritario(a);

(imperious) imperioso(a); *(personality)* dominante
masterly ['mɑːstəlɪ] *adj* magistral
mastermind ['mɑːstəmaɪnd] **1** *n (person)* cerebro *m*
  2 *vt* ser el cerebro de
masterpiece ['mɑːstəpiːs] *n* obra *f* maestra
mastery ['mɑːstərɪ] *n* (**a**) *(control)* dominio *m* (**of** de) (**b**) *(skill, expertise)* maestría *f*
masturbate ['mæstəbeɪt] *vi* masturbarse
mat¹ [mæt] *n (rug)* alfombrilla *f; (doormat)* felpudo *m; (rush mat)* estera *f; Sport* colchoneta *f*
mat² [mæt] *adj* mate
match¹ [mætʃ] *n* cerilla *f*, fósforo *m*
match² [mætʃ] **1** *n* (**a**) *Sport* partido *m; (in boxing)* combate *m* (**b**) *Fig* **to meet one's m.** *(equal)* encontrar uno la horma de su zapato
  2 *vt* (**a**) *(equal, be the equal of)* igualar (**b**) *(be in harmony with)* armonizar; **they are well matched** *(teams)* van iguales; *(couple)* hacen buena pareja (**c**) *(colours, clothes)* hacer juego con; *(pair of socks, gloves)* ser el compañero de
  3 *vi (harmonize)* hacer juego
matchbox ['mætʃbɒks] *n* caja *f* de cerillas
matching ['mætʃɪŋ] *adj* que hace juego
mate [meɪt] **1** *n* (**a**) *(at school, work)* compañero(a) *m,f*, colega *mf; Br Fam (friend)* amigo(a) *m,f* (**b**) *Zool (male)* macho *m; (female)* hembra *f* (**c**) *(assistant)* ayudante *mf* (**d**) *Naut* **first/second m.** primer/segundo oficial
  2 *vt Zool* aparear
  3 *vi Zool* aparearse
material [mə'tɪərɪəl] **1** *n* (**a**) *(substance)* materia *f* (**b**) *(cloth)* tejido *m*, tela *f* (**c**) *(information)* material *m* (**d**) **materials** *(ingredients, equipment)* materiales *mpl*
  2 *adj* (**a**) substancial (**b**) *(not spiritual)* material
materialistic [mətɪərɪə'lɪstɪk] *adj* materialista
materialize [mə'tɪərɪəlaɪz] *vi* (**a**) *(hopes)* realizarse; *(plan, idea)* concretarse (**b**) *(show up)* presentarse
maternal [mə'tɜːnəl] *adj* maternal; *(uncle etc)* materno(a)
maternity [mə'tɜːnɪtɪ] *n* maternidad *f;* **m. dress** vestido *m* premamá; **m. hospital** maternidad
math [mæθ] *n US =* **maths**
mathematical [mæθə'mætɪkəl] *adj* matemático(a)
mathematician [mæθəmə'tɪʃən] *n* matemático(a) *m,f*
mathematics [mæθə'mætɪks] *n sing* matemáticas *fpl*
maths [mæθs] *n sing Fam* matemáticas *fpl*
matinée ['mætɪneɪ] *n Cin* sesión *f* de tarde; *Th* función *f* de tarde
mating ['meɪtɪŋ] *n* apareamiento *m;* **m. call** reclamo *m;* **m. season** época *f* de celo

matrices [ˈmeɪtrɪsiːz] *pl of* **matrix**
matriculation [mətrɪkjʊˈleɪʃən] *n Univ* matriculación *f*
matrimonial [mætrɪˈməʊnɪəl] *adj* matrimonial
matrimony [ˈmætrɪmənɪ] *n* matrimonio *m*; *(married life)* vida *f* conyugal
matrix [ˈmeɪtrɪks] *n (pl* **matrices**) matriz *f*
matron [ˈmeɪtrən] *n (in hospital)* enfermera *f* jefe
matronly [ˈmeɪtrənlɪ] *adj* madura y recia
matt [mæt] *adj* mate
matted [ˈmætɪd] *adj* enmarañado(a)
matter [ˈmætə(r)] **1** *n* (**a**) *(affair, question)* asunto *m*; **as a m. of course** por rutina; **as a m. of fact** en realidad; **that's another m.** eso es otra cosa (**b**) *(problem)* **what's the m.?** ¿qué pasa? (**c**) **no m. what he does** haga lo que haga; **no m. when** no importa cuando; **no m. where you go** dondequiera que vayas; **no m. how clever he is** por muy inteligente que sea; **no m. how** como sea (**d**) *(substance)* materia *f*, sustancia *f* (**e**) *(content)* contenido *m*; *(subject)* tema *m* (**f**) *Med (pus)* pus en
2 *vi* importar; **it doesn't m.** no importa, da igual
matter-of-fact [ˈmætərəvˈfækt] *adj (person)* práctico(a); *(account)* realista; *(style)* prosaico(a)
mattress [ˈmætrɪs] *n* colchón *f*
mature [məˈtʃʊə(r)] **1** *adj* maduro(a); *Fin* vencido(a)
2 *vi* madurar; *Fin* vencer
3 *vt* madurar
maturity [məˈtʃʊərɪtɪ] *n* madurez *f*
maul [mɔːl] *vt* (**a**) *(wound)* agredir (**b**) *(handle roughly)* maltratar (**c**) *(touch in unpleasant way)* sobar
mauve [məʊv] *adj & n* malva *(m)*
max [mæks] *n (abbr* **maximum**) máx
maxim [ˈmæksɪm] *n* máxima *f*
maxima [ˈmæksɪmə] *pl of* **maximum**
maximize [ˈmæksɪmaɪz] *vt* maximizar
maximum [ˈmæksɪməm] **1** *n (pl* **maxima**) máximo *m*
2 *adj* máximo(a)
May [meɪ] *n* mayo *m*; **M. Day** el Primero *or* el Uno de Mayo
may [meɪ] *v aux (pt* **might**)

En el inglés hablado, y en el escrito en estilo coloquial, la forma negativa **might not** se transforma en **mightn't**. La forma **might have** se transforma en **might've**.

(**a**) *(expressing possibility)* poder, ser posible; **be that as it m.** sea como sea; **come what m.** pase lo que pase; **he m.** *or* **might come** puede que venga; **you m.** *or* **might as well stay** más vale que te quedes (**b**) *(permission)* poder; **m. I?** ¿me permite?; **you m. smoke** pueden fumar (**c**) *(wish)* ojalá (+ *subj*); **m. you always be happy!** ¡ojalá seas siempre feliz!

maybe [ˈmeɪbiː] *adv* quizá(s), tal vez
mayhem [ˈmeɪhem] *n (disturbance)* alboroto *m*; *(havoc)* estragos *mpl*
mayonnaise [meɪəˈneɪz] *n* mayonesa *f*, mahonesa *f*
mayor [meə(r)] *n (man)* alcalde *m*; *(woman)* alcaldesa *f*
mayoress [ˈmeəres] *n* alcaldesa *f*
maze [meɪz] *n* laberinto *m*
MD [emˈdiː] *n* (**a**) *(abbr* **Doctor of Medicine**) Dr. en Medicina (**b**) *Fam (abbr* **Managing Director**) director(a) *m,f* gerente
me [miː, *unstressed* mɪ] *pron* (**a**) *(as object)* me; **he gave it to me** me lo dio; **listen to me** escúchame; **she knows me** me conoce (**b**) *(after prep)* mí; **it's for me** es para mí; **with me** conmigo (**c**) *(emphatic)* yo; **it's me** soy yo; **what about ME?** ¿y yo, qué?
meadow [ˈmedəʊ] *n* prado *m*, pradera *f*
meagre, *US* **meager** [ˈmiːgə(r)] *adj* exiguo(a)
meal¹ [miːl] *n (flour)* harina *f*
meal² [miːl] *n (food)* comida *f*
mealtime [ˈmiːltaɪm] *n* hora *f* de comer
mean¹ [miːn] *vt (pt & pp* **meant**) (**a**) *(signify)* significar, querer decir; **what do you m. by that?** ¿qué quieres decir con eso? (**b**) *(intend)* pensar, tener la intención de; **I m. it** (te) lo digo en serio; **she was meant to arrive on the 7th** tenía que *or* debía llegar el día 7; **they m. well** tienen buenas intenciones; **she didn't m. to do it** lo hizo sin querer (**c**) *(entail)* suponer (**d**) *(refer to)* referirse a (**e**) *(destine)* destinar (**for** a *or* para)
mean² [miːn] *adj* (**meaner, meanest**) (**a**) *(miserly)* tacaño(a) (**b**) *(unkind)* malo(a); *(petty)* mezquino(a); *US (bad-tempered)* malhumorado(a); **to be m. to sb** tratar mal a algn (**c**) *(inferior)* mediocre; *(origins)* humilde (**d**) **it was no m. feat** fue toda una hazaña
mean³ [miːn] **1** *adj (average)* medio(a)
2 *n (average)* promedio *m*; *Math* media *f*
meander [mɪˈændə(r)] *vi (river)* serpentear; *(person)* vagar; *Fig (digress)* divagar
meaning [ˈmiːnɪŋ] *n* sentido *m*, significado *m*
meaningful [ˈmiːnɪŋfʊl] *adj* significativo(a)
meaningless [ˈmiːnɪŋlɪs] *adj* sin sentido
meanness [ˈmiːnnɪs] *n* (**a**) *(miserliness)* tacañería *f* (**b**) *(nastiness)* maldad *f*
means [miːnz] *n* (**a**) *sing or pl (method)* medio *m*, manera *f*; **by m. of** por medio de, mediante (**b**) *pl (resources, wealth)* medios *mpl* (de vida), recursos *mpl* (económicos); **to live beyond one's m.** vivir por encima de sus posibilidades (**c**) **by all m.!** ¡por supuesto!; **by no m.** de ninguna manera
meant [ment] *pt & pp of* **mean**
meantime [ˈmiːntaɪm] **1** *adv* mientras tanto
2 **in the m.** mientras tanto
meanwhile [ˈmiːnwaɪl] *adv* mientras tanto
measles [ˈmiːzəlz] *n sing* sarampión *m*
measure [ˈmeʒə(r)] **1** *n* (**a**) *(action, step)*

medida f (**b**) *(ruler)* regla f (**c**) **in some m. hasta cierto punto** (**d**) *Mus* compás m

2 *vt (object, area)* medir; *(person)* tomar las medidas de

🔊 Note that the Spanish word **mesura** is a false friend and is never a translation for the English word **measure**. In Spanish, **mesura** means "moderation, restraint".

▸ **measure up** *vi* **to m. up (to sth)** estar a la altura (de algo)

measurement ['meʒəmənt] *n* medida f

meat [miːt] *n* carne f; *Culin* **m. pie** empanada f de carne

meatball ['miːtbɔːl] *n* albóndiga f

meaty ['miːtɪ] *adj* (**meatier, meatiest**) (**a**) carnoso(a) (**b**) *Fig (story)* jugoso(a)

Mecca ['mekə] *n* la Meca

mechanic [mɪˈkænɪk] *n (person)* mecánico(a) m,f

mechanical [mɪˈkænɪkəl] *adj* mecánico(a)

mechanics [mɪˈkænɪks] **1** *n sing (science)* mecánica f

2 *npl (technical aspects)* mecanismo m

mechanism ['mekənɪzəm] *n* mecanismo m

medal ['medəl] *n* medalla f

medallion [mɪˈdæljən] *n* medallón m

medallist, *US* **medalist** ['medəlɪst] *n* medalla f

meddle ['medəl] *vi* entrometerse (**in** en); **to m. with sth** manosear algo

media ['miːdɪə] *npl* medios *mpl* de comunicación; **m. coverage** cobertura periodística

🔊 Note that the Spanish word **media** is a false friend and is never a translation for the English word **media**. In Spanish, **media** means both "stocking, sock" and "average".

median ['miːdɪən] **1** *adj* mediano(a); *US Aut* **m. (strip)** mediana f, *Col, Méx* camellón m

2 *n Geom* mediana f; *Math* valor mediano m

mediate ['miːdɪeɪt] *vi* mediar

mediator ['miːdɪeɪtə(r)] *n* mediador(a) m,f

Medicaid ['medɪkeɪd] *n (in US)* = seguro médico estatal para personas con renta baja

medical ['medɪkəl] **1** *adj (treatment)* médico(a); *(book)* de medicina

2 *n Fam* reconocimiento médico

Medicare ['medɪkeə(r)] *n (in US)* = seguro médico para ancianos y algunos discapacitados

medicated ['medɪkeɪtɪd] *adj* medicinal

medicine ['medɪsɪn] *n (science)* medicina f; *(drugs etc)* medicamento m

medieval [medɪˈiːvəl] *adj* medieval

mediocre [miːdɪˈəʊkə(r)] *adj* mediocre

meditate ['medɪteɪt] *vi* meditar (**on** sobre)

meditation [medɪˈteɪʃən] *n* meditación f

Mediterranean [medɪtəˈreɪnɪən] **1** *adj* mediterráneo(a)

2 *n* **the M.** el Mediterráneo

medium ['miːdɪəm] **1** *adj (average)* mediano(a); *Rad* **m. wave** onda media

2 *n* (**a**) *(pl* **media**) *(means)* medio m (**b**) *(pl* **mediums**) *(spiritualist)* médium mf

medley ['medlɪ] *n (mixture)* mezcla f; *Mus* popurrí m

meek [miːk] *adj* manso(a), sumiso(a); *(humble)* humilde

meet [miːt] **1** *vt (pt & pp* **met**) (**a**) *(by chance)* encontrar, encontrarse con; *(by arrangement)* reunirse con; *(in formal meeting)* entrevistarse con

(**b**) *(get to know)* conocer; **I'd like you to m. my mother** quiero presentarte a mi madre; **the first time I met him** cuando lo conocí; **pleased to m. you!** ¡mucho gusto!

(**c**) *(await arrival of)* esperar; *(collect)* ir a buscar

(**d**) *(danger)* encontrar; *(opponent)* enfrentarse con

(**e**) *(satisfy)* satisfacer; *(obligations)* cumplir con; *(expenses)* hacer frente a

2 *vi (by chance)* encontrarse; *(by arrangement)* reunirse; *(formal meeting)* entrevistarse; *(get to know each other)* conocerse; *Sport* enfrentarse; *(join)* unirse; *(rivers)* confluir; **their eyes met** cruzaron las miradas

3 *n (sports event)* encuentro m; *(in athletics)* reunión f atlética

▸ **meet with** *vt insep (difficulty)* tropezar con; *(loss)* sufrir; *(success)* tener; *esp US (person)* reunirse con

meeting ['miːtɪŋ] *n (chance encounter)* encuentro m; *(prearranged)* cita f; *(formal)* entrevista f; *(of committee etc)* reunión f; *(of assembly)* sesión f; *(of shareholders)* junta f; *(rally)* mitin m; *Sport* encuentro m; *(of rivers)* confluencia f

mega ['megə] *adj Fam (excellent)* genial, guay, *Andes, CAm, Carib, Méx* chévere, *RP* bárbaro

megabyte ['megəbaɪt] *n Comput* megabyte m

megaphone ['megəfəʊn] *n* megáfono m

melancholy ['melənkəlɪ] **1** *n* melancolía f

2 *adj* melancólico(a)

Melilla [meˈliːjə] *n* Melilla

mellow ['meləʊ] **1** *adj* maduro(a); *(wine)* añejo(a); *(colour, voice)* suave; *(person)* apacible

2 *vi (fruit)* madurar; *(colour, voice)* suavizarse

melodramatic [melədrəˈmætɪk] *adj* melodramático(a)

melody ['melədɪ] *n* melodía f

melon ['melən] *n* melón m

melt [melt] **1** *vt (metal)* fundir; *Fig (sb's heart)* ablandar

2 *vi (snow)* derretirse; *(metal)* fundirse; *Fig* ablandarse

▸ **melt away** *vi (snow)* derretirse; *Fig (money)* desaparecer; *Fig (confidence)* desvanecerse

▸ **melt down** *vt sep (metal)* fundir

melting ['meltɪŋ] *n* fundición *f*; **m. point** punto *m* de fusión; **m. pot** crisol *m*

member ['membə(r)] *n* miembro *mf*; *(of a society)* socio(a) *m,f*; *(of party, union)* afiliado(a) *m,f*; *US* **M. of Congress** congresista *mf*; *Br* **M. of Parliament** diputado(a) *m,f*

membership ['membəʃɪp] *n (state)* calidad *f* de socio; *(entry)* ingreso *m*; *Pol* afiliación *f*; *(number of members)* número *m* de socios; **m. card** carnet *m* de socio

memento [mə'mentəʊ] *n* recuerdo *m*

memo ['meməʊ] *n (official note)* memorándum *m*; *(personal note)* nota *f*, apunte *m*

memoirs ['memwɑ:z] *npl* memorias *fpl*

memorable ['memərəbəl] *adj* memorable

memorandum [memə'rændəm] *n (pl* **memoranda)** *(official note)* memorándum *m*; *(personal note)* nota *f*, apunte *m*

memorial [mɪ'mɔ:rɪəl] **1** *adj (plaque etc)* conmemorativo(a)
2 *n* monumento conmemorativo

memorize ['meməraɪz] *vt* memorizar, aprender de memoria

memory ['memərɪ] *n* memoria *f*; *(recollection)* recuerdo *m*

men [men] *pl of* **man**

menace ['menɪs] **1** *n (threat)* amenaza *f*; *(danger)* peligro *m*; *Fam (person)* pesado(a) *m,f*
2 *vt* amenazar

menacing ['menɪsɪŋ] *adj* amenazador(a)

menagerie [mɪ'nædʒərɪ] *n* casa *f* de fieras

mend [mend] **1** *vt* reparar, arreglar; *(clothes)* remendar; *(socks etc)* zurcir
2 *vi (ill person)* reponerse
3 *n (patch)* remiendo *m*; *(darn)* zurcido *m*; *Fig* **to be on the m.** ir mejorando

mending ['mendɪŋ] *n (repair)* reparación *f*; *(darning)* zurcido *m*; *(clothes for mending)* ropa *f* para remendar

menial ['mi:nɪəl] *adj (task)* servil, bajo(a)

menopause ['menəpɔ:z] *n* menopausia *f*

menstrual ['menstrʊəl] *adj* menstrual

menstruation [menstrʊ'eɪʃən] *n* menstruación *f*

mental ['mentəl] *adj* (a) mental; **m. home, m. hospital** hospital psiquiátrico; **m. illness** enfermedad *f* mental (b) *Fam (crazy)* chalado(a)

mentality [men'tælɪtɪ] *n* mentalidad *f*

mentally ['mentəlɪ] *adv* **m. ill** enfermo(a) mental; **to be m. handicapped** ser un(a) disminuido(a) psíquico(a)

mention ['menʃən] **1** *n* mención *f*
2 *vt* mencionar; **don't m. it!** ¡de nada!

mentor ['mentɔ:(r)] *n* mentor *m*

menu ['menju:] *n* (a) *(card)* carta *f*; *(fixed meal)* menú *m*; **today's m.** menú del día (b) *Comput* menú *m*

MEP [emi:'pi:] *n (abbr* **Member of the European Parliament)** eurodiputado(a) *m,f*

mercenary ['mɜ:sɪnərɪ] *adj & n* mercenario(a) *(m,f)*

merchandise ['mɜ:tʃəndaɪz] *n* mercancías *fpl*, géneros *mpl*

merchant ['mɜ:tʃənt] *n Com & Fin* comerciante *mf*; *(retailer)* detallista *mf*; **m. bank** banco *m* comercial; **m. navy** marina *f* mercante

merciful ['mɜ:sɪfʊl] *adj* clemente, compasivo(a) (**towards** con)

merciless ['mɜ:sɪlɪs] *adj* despiadado(a)

Mercury ['mɜ:kjʊrɪ] *n* Mercurio *m*

mercury ['mɜ:kjʊrɪ] *n* mercurio *m*

mercy ['mɜ:sɪ] *n* misericordia *f*, compasión *f*; **at the m. of** a la merced de; **to have m. on** tener compasión de

mere [mɪə(r)] *adj* mero(a), simple

merely ['mɪəlɪ] *adv* simplemente

merge [mɜ:dʒ] **1** *vt (blend)* unir (**with** con) *Com* fusionar
2 *vi* unirse; *(roads)* empalmar; *Com* fusionarse

merger ['mɜ:dʒə(r)] *n Com* fusión *f*

meringue [mə'ræŋ] *n* merengue *m*

merit ['merɪt] **1** *n (of person)* mérito *m*; *(of plan etc)* ventaja *f*
2 *vt* merecer

mermaid ['mɜ:meɪd] *n* sirena *f*

merry ['merɪ] *adj* (**merrier, merriest)** alegre; *Fam (tipsy)* achispado(a); **m. Christmas!** ¡felices Navidades!

merry-go-round ['merɪɡəʊraʊnd] *n* tiovivo *m*

mesh [meʃ] **1** *n Tex* malla *f*; *Tech* engranaje *m*; *Fig* red *f*
2 *vt Tech* engranar

mesmerize ['mezməraɪz] *vt* hipnotizar

mess [mes] **1** *n* (a) *(confusion)* confusión *f*; *(disorder)* desorden *m*; **to be in a m.** *(of room etc)* estar desordenado(a) (b) *(in life, affairs)* lío *m*; **to get into a m.** meterse en un lío (c) *(dirt)* suciedad *f* (d) *Mil (food)* rancho *m* (e) *Mil (room)* comedor *m*
▸ **mess about, mess around** *Fam* **1** *vt sep* fastidiar
2 *vi (act the fool)* hacer el primo; *(idle)* gandulear; *(kill time)* pasar el rato
▸ **mess about with** *vt insep Fam (fiddle with)* manosear; **to m. about with sb** tener un lío con algn
▸ **mess up** *vt sep Fam (make untidy)* desordenar; *(dirty)* ensuciar; *(spoil)* estropear

message ['mesɪdʒ] *n (communication)* recado *m*; *(of story etc)* mensaje *m*; *Fam* **to get the m.** comprender

messenger ['mesɪndʒə(r)] *n* mensajero(a) *m,f*

Messrs ['mesəz] *npl (abbr* **Messieurs)** Sres.

messy ['mesɪ] *adj* (**messier, messiest)** *(untidy)* desordenado(a); *(confused)* enredado(a); *(dirty)* sucio(a)

met [met] *pt & pp of* **meet**

metabolism [me'tæbəlɪzəm] n metabolismo m

metal ['metəl] **1** n metal m
2 adj metálico(a)

metallic [mɪ'tælɪk] adj metálico(a); **m. blue** azul metalizado

metallurgy [me'tælədʒɪ] n metalurgia f

metalwork ['metəlwɜːk] n (craft) metalistería f; (objects) objetos mpl de metal

metaphor ['metəfə(r)] n metáfora f

mete [miːt] vt **to m. out** imponer

meteor ['miːtɪə(r)] n bólido m

meteoric [miːtɪ'ɒrɪk] adj meteórico(a)

meteorite ['miːtɪəraɪt] n meteorito m

meteorology [miːtɪə'rɒlədʒɪ] n meteorología f

meter¹ ['miːtə(r)] n contador m

meter² ['miːtər] n US = **metre**

method ['meθəd] n método m

methodical [mɪ'θɒdɪkəl] adj metódico(a)

Methodist ['meθədɪst] adj & n metodista (mf)

meths [meθs] n sing Br Fam alcohol m de quemar

methylated spirits ['meθɪleɪtɪd'spɪrɪts] n alcohol metilado or desnaturalizado

meticulous [mə'tɪkjʊləs] adj meticuloso(a)

metre ['miːtə(r)] n metro m

metric ['metrɪk] adj métrico(a)

metropolis [mɪ'trɒpəlɪs] n metrópoli f

metropolitan [metrə'pɒlɪtən] adj metropolitano(a)

mettle ['metəl] n valor m

mew [mjuː] vi (cat) maullar

mews [mjuːz] n sing (street) callejuela f; **m. flat** = apartamento de lujo en unas caballerizas reconvertidas

Mexican ['meksɪkən] adj & n mejicano(a) (m,f), mexicano(a) (m,f)

Mexico ['meksɪkəʊ] n Méjico, México

miaow [miː'aʊ] **1** vi maullar
2 n maullido m

mice [maɪs] pl of **mouse**

mickey ['mɪkɪ] n Fam **to take the m. (out of sb)** tomar el pelo (a algn)

microbe ['maɪkrəʊb] n microbio m

microchip ['maɪkrəʊtʃɪp] n microplaqueta f, microchip m

microcomputer ['maɪkrəʊkəm'pjuːtə(r)] n microordenador m

microcosm ['maɪkrəʊkɒzəm] n microcosmo m

microfilm ['maɪkrəʊfɪlm] n microfilm m

microphone ['maɪkrəfəʊn] n micrófono m

microprocessor [maɪkrəʊ'prəʊsesə(r)] n microprocesador m

microscope ['maɪkrəskəʊp] n microscopio m

microwave ['maɪkrəʊweɪv] n microonda f; **m. (oven)** (horno m) microondas m inv

mid [mɪd] adj **(in) m. afternoon** a media tarde; **(in) m. April** a mediados de abril; **to**

be in one's m. thirties tener unos treinta y cinco años

midair 1 adj ['mɪdeə(r)] (collision, explosion) en el aire
2 n [mɪd'eə(r)] Fig **to leave sth in m.** dejar algo en el aire

midday 1 n [mɪd'deɪ] mediodía m
2 adj ['mɪddeɪ] de mediodía

middle ['mɪdəl] **1** adj de en medio; **m. age** mediana edad; **the M. Ages** la Edad Media; **the m. class** la clase media
2 n (a) centro m, medio m; **in the m. of** en medio de; **in the m. of winter** en pleno invierno; Fam **in the m. of nowhere** en el quinto pino (b) Fam (waist) cintura f

middle-aged [mɪdəl'eɪdʒd] adj de mediana edad

middle-class [mɪdəl'klɑːs] adj de clase media

middleman ['mɪdəlmæn] n intermediario m

middleweight ['mɪdəlweɪt] n peso medio

middling ['mɪdlɪŋ] adj mediano(a)

midfielder [mɪd'fiːldə(r)] n Sport centrocampista mf

midge [mɪdʒ] n mosca enana

midget ['mɪdʒɪt] n enano(a) m,f

Midlands ['mɪdləndz] npl **the M.** = la región central de Inglaterra

midnight ['mɪdnaɪt] n medianoche f

midst [mɪdst] n **in the m. of** en medio de

midsummer [mɪd'sʌmə(r)] n pleno verano; **M.'s Day** Día m de San Juan (24 de junio)

midway ['mɪdweɪ] adv a medio camino

midweek 1 adv [mɪd'wiːk] entre semana
2 adj ['mɪdwiːk] de entre semana

midwife ['mɪdwaɪf] n comadrona f, partera f

midwifery ['mɪdwɪfərɪ] n obstetricia f

midwinter [mɪd'wɪntə(r)] n pleno invierno m

might¹ [maɪt] v aux see **may**

might² [maɪt] n Fml fuerza f, poder m

mighty ['maɪtɪ] **1** adj (mightier, mightiest) (strong) fuerte; (powerful) poderoso(a); (great) enorme
2 adv US Fam cantidad de, muy

migraine ['miːgreɪn, 'maɪgreɪn] n jaqueca f

migrant ['maɪgrənt] **1** adj migratorio(a)
2 n (person) emigrante mf; (bird) ave migratoria

migrate [maɪ'greɪt] vi emigrar

migration [maɪ'greɪʃən] n migración f

mike [maɪk] n Fam micro m

mild [maɪld] adj (person, character) apacible; (climate) templado(a); (punishment) leve; (tobacco, taste) suave

mildew ['mɪldjuː] n moho m; (on plants) añublo m

mildly ['maɪldlɪ] adv (softly, gently) suavemente; (slightly) ligeramente; **and that's putting it m.** y esto es decir poco

mildness ['maɪldnɪs] n (of character) apacibilidad f; (of climate, taste) suavidad f; (of punishment) levedad f

mile [maɪl] n milla f; Fam **miles better** muchísimo mejor

mileage ['maɪlɪdʒ] n kilometraje m

milestone ['maɪlstəʊn] n hito m

milieu ['miːljɜː] n medio m ambiente

militant ['mɪlɪtənt] adj & n militante (mf)

military ['mɪlɪtərɪ] adj militar; **to do one's m.** service hacer el servicio militar

militia [mɪ'lɪʃə] n milicia f

milk [mɪlk] **1** n leche f; **m. chocolate** chocolate m con leche; **m. shake** batido m
 2 vt (**a**) (cow, goat) ordeñar (**b**) Fam **they milked him of all his money** le sangraron hasta la última peseta

milkman ['mɪlkmən] n lechero m

milky ['mɪlkɪ] adj (**milkier, milkiest**) lechoso(a); (colour) pálido(a); **M. Way** Vía Láctea

mill [mɪl] **1** n (grinder) molino m; (for coffee) molinillo m; (factory) fábrica f; **cotton m.** hilandería f
 2 vt moler
 ▸ **mill about, mill around** vi arremolinarse

millennium [mɪ'lenɪəm] n (pl **millenniums** or **millennia** [mɪ'lenɪə]) milenio m

miller ['mɪlə(r)] n molinero(a) m,f

millet ['mɪlɪt] n mijo m

milligram(me) ['mɪlɪgræm] n miligramo m

millilitre, US milliliter ['mɪlɪliːtə(r)] n mililitro m

millimetre, US millimeter ['mɪlɪmiːtə(r)] n milímetro m

milliner ['mɪlɪnə(r)] n sombrerero(a) m,f

millinery ['mɪlɪnərɪ] n sombreros mpl de señora

million ['mɪljən] n millón m

millionaire [mɪljə'neə(r)] n millonario(a) m,f

millstone ['mɪlstəʊn] n muela f; Fig carga f

mime [maɪm] **1** n (art) mímica f; (play) pantomima f
 2 vt representar con gestos

> Note that the Spanish verb **mimar** is a false friend and is never a translation for the English verb **to mime**. In Spanish, **mimar** means "to spoil, to pamper".

mimic ['mɪmɪk] **1** adj & n mímico(a) (m,f)
 2 vt imitar

mimicry ['mɪmɪkrɪ] n imitación f

minaret ['mɪnəret] n alminar m, minarete m

mince [mɪns] **1** n Br (meat) carne picada; **m. pie** (containing meat) = especie de empanada de carne picada; (containing fruit) pastel m de picadillo de fruta
 2 vt picar; Fig **he doesn't m. his words** no tiene pelos en la lengua
 3 vi (walk) **to m. (along)** andar con pasos menuditos

mincemeat ['mɪnsmiːt] n (dried fruit) conserva f de picadillo de fruta; (meat) carne picada

mincer ['mɪnsə(r)] n picadora f de carne

mind [maɪnd] **1** n (**a**) (intellect) mente f; (brain) cabeza f; **what kind of car do you have in m.?** ¿en qué clase de coche estás pensando?; **to lose one's m.** perder el juicio; **it slipped my m.** lo olvidé por completo; **to call sth to m.** recordar algo
 (**b**) (opinion) **to be in two minds (about sth)** estar indeciso(a) (acerca de algo); **to my m.** a mi parecer
 2 vt (**a**) (child) cuidar; (house) vigilar; (be careful of) tener cuidado con; **m. the step!** ¡ojo con el escalón!; **m. your own business!** ¡no te metas donde no te llaman!
 (**b**) (object to) tener inconveniente en; **I wouldn't m. a cup of coffee** me vendría bien un café; **never m.** no importa
 3 vi (**a**) **m. you, he is fifty** ten en cuenta que tiene cincuenta años
 (**b**) (object) importar; **do you m. if I open the window?** ¿le importa que abra la ventana?

minder ['maɪndə(r)] n Fam (bodyguard) guardaespaldas m inv; (for child) niñera f; (babysitter) canguro mf

mindful ['maɪndfʊl] adj consciente

mindless ['maɪndlɪs] adj (task) de autómata; (violence) injustificable

mine¹ [maɪn] poss pron (el) mío/(la) mía/(los) míos, (las) mías, lo mío; **a friend of m.** un amigo mío; **these gloves are m.** estos guantes son míos; **which is m.?** ¿cuál es el mío?

mine² [maɪn] **1** n mina f; Fig **a m. of information** un pozo de información
 2 vt (coal etc) extraer; Mil minar

minefield ['maɪnfiːld] n campo m de minas

miner ['maɪnə(r)] n minero(a) m,f

mineral ['mɪnərəl] **1** adj mineral; **m. water** agua f mineral
 2 n mineral m

minesweeper ['maɪnswiːpə(r)] n dragaminas m inv

mingle ['mɪŋgəl] vi mezclarse

miniature ['mɪnɪtʃə(r)] **1** n miniatura f
 2 adj (railway) en miniatura; (camera, garden) diminuto(a)

minibus ['mɪnɪbʌs] n microbús m

minim ['mɪnɪm] n Mus blanca f

minimal ['mɪnɪməl] adj mínimo(a)

minimum ['mɪnɪməm] **1** adj mínimo(a); **m. wage** salario mínimo
 2 n mínimo m

mining ['maɪnɪŋ] **1** n minería f, explotación f de minas; Mil & Naut minado m
 2 adj minero(a)

miniskirt ['mɪnɪskɜːt] n minifalda f

minister ['mɪnɪstə(r)] **1** n ministro(a) m,f; Rel pastor(a) m,f
 2 vi **to m. to sb** atender a algn

ministerial [mɪnɪ'stɪərɪəl] adj Pol ministerial

ministry ['mɪnɪstrɪ] n Pol ministerio m; Rel sacerdocio m

mink [mɪŋk] *n* visón *m*; **m. coat** abrigo *m* de visón

minnow ['mɪnəʊ] *n* piscardo *m*

minor ['maɪnə(r)] **1** *adj (lesser)* menor; *(unimportant)* sin importancia; *(role)* secundario(a); *Mus* menor
2 *n Jur* menor *mf* de edad

Minorca [mɪ'nɔːkə] *n* Menorca

minority [maɪ'nɒrɪtɪ] *n* minoría *f*; **to be in the m.** ser (la) minoría; *Pol* **m. party** partido minoritario

mint¹ [mɪnt] **1** *n Fin* **the M.** la Casa de la Moneda; **in m. condition** en perfecto estado
2 *vt (coin, words)* acuñar

mint² [mɪnt] *n Bot* menta *f*; *(sweet)* pastilla *f* de menta

minus ['maɪnəs] **1** *prep* **5 m. 3** 5 menos 3; **m. 10 degrees** 10 grados bajo cero
2 *adj* negativo(a)
3 *n* **m. (sign)** signo *m* (de) menos

minute¹ ['mɪnɪt] *n* (**a**) minuto *m*; **at the last m.** a última hora; **just a m.** (espera) un momento; **this very m.** ahora mismo (**b**) **minutes** *(notes)* el acta

minute² [maɪ'njuːt] *adj (tiny)* diminuto(a); *(examination)* minucioso(a)

miracle ['mɪrəkəl] *n* milagro *m*

miraculous [mɪ'rækjʊləs] *adj* milagroso(a)

mirage [mɪ'rɑːʒ] *n* espejismo *m*

mire [maɪə(r)] *n* fango *m*, lodo *m*; *(muddy place)* lodazal *m*

mirror ['mɪrə(r)] **1** *n* espejo *m*; *Fig* reflejo *m*; **rear-view m.** retrovisor *m*; **m. image** réplica *f*
2 *vt* reflejar

mirth [mɜːθ] *n* alegría *f*; *(laughter)* risas *fpl*

misadventure [mɪsəd'ventʃə(r)] *n* desgracia *f*; **death by m.** muerte *f* accidental

misanthropist [mɪ'zænθrəpɪst] *n* misántropo(a) *m,f*

misapprehension [mɪsæprɪ'henʃən] *n* malentendido *m*

misbehave [mɪsbɪ'heɪv] *vi* portarse mal

miscalculate [mɪs'kælkjʊleɪt] *vt & vi* calcular mal

miscarriage ['mɪskærɪdʒ] *n Med* aborto *m* (espontáneo); **m. of justice** error *m* judicial

miscellaneous [mɪsɪ'leɪnɪəs] *adj* variado(a); **m. expenses** gastos diversos

mischief ['mɪstʃɪf] *n (naughtiness)* travesura *f*; *Fml (evil)* malicia *f*; *Fam (harm)* daño *m*; **to get up to m.** hacer travesuras

mischievous ['mɪstʃɪvəs] *adj (naughty)* travieso(a); *(playful)* juguetón(ona); *Fml (wicked)* malicioso(a)

misconception [mɪskən'sepʃən] *n* concepto erróneo

misconduct [mɪs'kɒndʌkt] *n* mala conducta; **professional m.** error *m* profesional

misconstrue [mɪskən'struː] *vt* interpretar mal

miscount [mɪs'kaʊnt] *vt (votes etc)* contar mal

misdeed [mɪs'diːd] *n* fechoría *f*

misdemeanour, *US* **misdemeanor** [mɪsdɪ'miːnə(r)] *n (misdeed)* fechoría *f*; *Jur* delito *m* menor

miser ['maɪzə(r)] *n* avaro(a) *m,f*

miserable ['mɪzərəbəl] *adj (sad)* triste; *(unfortunate)* desgraciado(a); *(wretched)* miserable

miserly ['maɪzəlɪ] *adj* avaro(a), tacaño(a)

misery ['mɪzərɪ] *n (sadness)* tristeza *f*; *(wretchedness)* desgracia *f*; *(suffering)* sufrimiento *m*; *(poverty)* miseria *f*; *Fam (person)* aguafiestas *mf*

misfire [mɪs'faɪə(r)] *vi (engine, plan etc)* fallar

misfit ['mɪsfɪt] *n (person)* inadaptado(a) *m,f*

misfortune [mɪs'fɔːtʃən] *n* desgracia *f*

misgiving [mɪs'gɪvɪŋ] *n (doubt)* recelo *m*; *(fear)* temor *m*

misguided [mɪs'gaɪdɪd] *adj* equivocado(a)

mishandle [mɪs'hændəl] *vt* llevar *or* manejar mal

mishap ['mɪshæp] *n* contratiempo *m*

misinform [mɪsɪn'fɔːm] *vt* informar mal

misinterpret [mɪsɪn'tɜːprɪt] *vt* interpretar mal

misjudge [mɪs'dʒʌdʒ] *vt* juzgar mal

mislay [mɪs'leɪ] *vt* extraviar

mislead [mɪs'liːd] *vt* despistar; *(deliberately)* engañar

misleading [mɪs'liːdɪŋ] *adj (erroneous)* erróneo(a); *(deliberately)* engañoso(a)

mismanagement [mɪs'mænɪdʒmənt] *n* mala administración *f*

misnomer [mɪs'nəʊmə(r)] *n* nombre equivocado

misogynist [mɪ'sɒdʒɪnɪst] *n* misógino(a) *m,f*

misplace [mɪs'pleɪs] *vt (trust)* encauzar mal; *(book, spectacles etc)* extraviar

misprint ['mɪsprɪnt] *n* errata *f*, error *m* de imprenta

misrepresent [mɪsreprɪ'zent] *vt (facts)* desvirtuar; *(words)* tergiversar

miss¹ [mɪs] *n* señorita *f*

miss² [mɪs] **1** *n (throw etc)* fallo *m*; *Fam* **to give sth a m.** pasar de algo
2 *vt* (**a**) *(when throwing)* fallar; *(when shooting)* errar (**b**) *(train etc)* perder; *(opportunity)* dejar pasar; **you have missed the point** no has captado la idea; *Fig* **to m. the boat** perder el tren (**c**) *(omit)* saltarse (**d**) **I m. you** te echo de menos
3 *vi (when throwing)* fallar; *(when shooting)* errar; **is anything missing?** ¿falta algo?
▸ **miss out 1** *vt sep (omit)* saltarse; *(on purpose)* pasar por alto
2 *vt insep* **to m. out on** perderse

misshapen [mɪs'ʃeɪpən] *adj* deforme

missile ['mɪsaɪl, *US* 'mɪsəl] *n Mil* misil *m*; *(object thrown)* proyectil *m*

missing ['mɪsɪŋ] *adj (object)* perdido(a); *(person)* desaparecido(a); *(from meeting etc)* ausente; **m. person** desaparecido(a) *m,f*;

three cups are m. faltan tres tazas

mission ['mɪʃən] *n* misión *f*

missionary ['mɪʃənərɪ] *n* misionero(a) *m,f*

misspent ['mɪsspent] *adj (youth)* malgastado(a)

mist [mɪst] **1** *n* neblina *f; (thick)* niebla *f; (at sea)* bruma *f*
2 *vi* **to m. over** or **up** *(countryside)* cubrirse de neblina; *(window etc)* empañarse

mistake [mɪ'steɪk] **1** *n* error *m;* **by m.** por equivocación; **I hurt him by m.** le golpeé sin querer; **to make a m.** equivocarse, cometer un error
2 *vt (pt* **mistook;** *pp* **mistaken)** *(meaning)* malentender; **to m. Jack for Bill** confundir a Jack con Bill

mistaken [mɪ'steɪkən] *adj* equivocado(a), erróneo(a); **you are m.** estás equivocado(a)

mister ['mɪstə(r)] *n* señor *m*

mistletoe ['mɪsəltəʊ] *n* muérdago *m*

mistook [mɪ'stʊk] *pt of* **mistake**

mistreat [mɪs'triːt] *vt* tratar mal

mistress ['mɪstrɪs] *n (of house)* señora *f,* ama *f; (lover)* amante *f; Educ (primary school)* maestra *f; (secondary school)* profesora *f*

mistrust [mɪs'trʌst] **1** *n* recelo *m*
2 *vt* desconfiar de

misty ['mɪstɪ] *adj* (**mistier, mistiest**) *(day)* de niebla; *(window etc)* empañado(a)

misunderstand [mɪsʌndə'stænd] *vt & vi* malentender

misunderstanding [mɪsʌndə'stændɪŋ] *n* malentendido *m; (disagreement)* desavenencia *f*

misuse 1 *n* [mɪs'juːs] mal uso *m; (of funds)* malversación *f; (of power)* abuso *m*
2 *vt* [mɪs'juːz] emplear mal; *(funds)* malversar; *(power)* abusar de

miter ['maɪtər] *n US* = **mitre**

mitigate ['mɪtɪgeɪt] *vt* atenuar

mitigating ['mɪtɪgeɪtɪŋ] *adj* **m. circumstances** circunstancias *fpl* atenuantes

mitre ['maɪtə(r)] *n* mitra *f*

mitten ['mɪtən] *n* manopla *f; (fingerless)* mitón *m*

mix [mɪks] **1** *n* mezcla *f*
2 *vt* mezclar
3 *vi (blend)* mezclarse (**with** con); *(go well together)* ir bien juntos
▶ **mix up** *vt sep (confuse)* confundir (**with** con); *(papers)* revolver; **to be mixed up in sth** estar involucrado(a) en algo

mixed [mɪkst] *adj (assorted)* surtido(a); *(varied)* variado(a); *(school)* mixto(a); *(feelings)* contradictorio(a)

mixed-up [mɪkst'ʌp] *adj (objects, papers etc)* revuelto(a); *(person)* confuso(a)

mixer ['mɪksə(r)] *n* (**a**) *Culin* batidora *f* (**b**) **to be a good m.** tener don de gentes

mixture ['mɪkstʃə(r)] *n* mezcla *f*

mix-up ['mɪksʌp] *n Fam* confusión *f,* lío *m*

mm *(abbr* **millimetre(s))** mm

moan [məʊn] **1** *n (groan)* gemido *m,* quejido *m*
2 *vi (groan)* gemir; *(complain)* quejarse *(about* de)

moat [məʊt] *n* foso *m*

mob [mɒb] **1** *n* multitud *f; (riff-raff)* gentuza *f;* **the m.** el populacho
2 *vt* acosar

mobile ['məʊbaɪl, *US* 'məʊbəl] **1** *adj* móvil; **m. home** caravana *f;* **m. phone** teléfono *r* móvil, *Am* teléfono *m* celular
2 *n* (**a**) *(hanging ornament)* móvil *m* (**b**) *Fam (mobile phone)* móvil *m, Am* celular *m*

mobility [məʊ'bɪlɪtɪ] *n* movilidad *f*

mobilize ['məʊbɪlaɪz] *vt* movilizar

mock [mɒk] **1** *adj (sympathy etc)* fingido(a, *(objects)* de imitación
2 *vt (make fun of)* burlarse de
3 *vi* burlarse (**at** de)

mockery ['mɒkərɪ] *n* burla *f*

mode [məʊd] *n (manner)* modo *m,* estilo *m (fashion)* moda *f*

model ['mɒdəl] **1** *n* modelo *m; (fashio model)* modelo *mf; (scale)* **m.** maqueta *f*
2 *adj (railway)* en miniatura; *(pupil)* ejemplar; *(school)* modelo
3 *vt (clay etc)* modelar; *(clothes)* presentar
4 *vi (make models)* modelar; *(work as mode* trabajar de modelo

modem ['məʊdem] *n Comput* modem *m*

moderate¹ ['mɒdərɪt] **1** *adj* moderado(a *(reasonable)* razonable; *(average)* regula *(ability)* mediocre
2 *n Pol* moderado(a) *m,f*

moderate² ['mɒdəreɪt] **1** *vt* moderar
2 *vi* moderarse; *(wind)* calmarse; *(in debate* arbitrar

moderately ['mɒdərɪtlɪ] *adv* medianamente

moderation [mɒdə'reɪʃən] *n* moderación **in m.** con moderación

modern ['mɒdən] *adj* moderno(a); *(history* contemporáneo(a); **m. languages** lengua modernas

modernize ['mɒdənaɪz] *vt* modernizar

modest ['mɒdɪst] *adj* modesto(a); *(chaste* púdico(a); *(price)* módico(a); *(success)* discreto(a)

modesty ['mɒdɪstɪ] *n (humility)* modestia *(chastity)* pudor *m*

modification [mɒdɪfɪ'keɪʃən] *n* modifica ción *f*

modify ['mɒdɪfaɪ] *vt* modificar

module ['mɒdjuːl] *n* módulo *m*

mogul ['məʊɡʌl] *n* magnate *m*

mohair ['məʊheə(r)] **1** *n* mohair *m*
2 *adj* de mohair

moist [mɔɪst] *adj* húmedo(a)

moisten ['mɔɪsən] *vt* humedecer

moisture ['mɔɪstʃə(r)] *n* humedad *f*

moisturizer ['mɔɪstʃəraɪzə(r)] *n* crema *f* o leche *f* hidratante

molar ['məʊlə(r)] *n* muela *f*

molasses [məˈlæsɪz] n sing melaza f
mold¹ [məʊld] n US = **mould¹**
mold² [məʊld] n & vt US = **mould²**
molder [ˈməʊldər] vi US = **moulder**
molding [ˈməʊldɪŋ] n US = **moulding**
moldy [ˈməʊldɪ] adj US = **mouldy**
mole¹ [məʊl] n (beauty spot) lunar m
mole² [məʊl] n (animal) topo m
molecule [ˈmɒlɪkjuːl] n molécula f
molest [məˈlest] vt importunar; (sexually assault) acosar (sexualmente)
mollycoddle [ˈmɒlɪkɒdəl] vt Fam mimar, consentir
molt [məʊlt] vi US = **moult**
molten [ˈməʊltən] adj fundido(a); (lava) líquido(a)
mom [mɒm] n US Fam mamá f
moment [ˈməʊmənt] n momento m; **at the m.** en este momento; **for the m.** de momento; **in a m.** dentro de un momento; **at any m.** de un momento a otro
momentarily [ˈməʊməntərɪlɪ] adv momentáneamente; US (soon) dentro de poco
momentary [ˈməʊməntərɪ] adj momentáneo(a)
momentous [məʊˈmentəs] adj trascendental
momentum [məʊˈmentəm] n Phys momento m; (speed) velocidad f; Fig **to gather m.** cobrar velocidad
mommy [ˈmɒmɪ] n US Fam mamá f
Monaco [ˈmɒnəkəʊ] n Mónaco
monarch [ˈmɒnək] n monarca m
monarchy [ˈmɒnəkɪ] n monarquía f
monastery [ˈmɒnəstərɪ] n monasterio m
Monday [ˈmʌndɪ] n lunes m
monetarism [ˈmʌnɪtərɪzəm] n monetarismo m
monetary [ˈmʌnɪtərɪ] adj monetario(a)
money [ˈmʌnɪ] n dinero m; (currency) moneda f; **to make m.** ganar dinero; **to put m. on** apostar por
moneylender [ˈmʌnɪlendə(r)] n prestamista mf
money-spinner [ˈmʌnɪspɪnə(r)] n Fam negocio m rentable
Mongolia [mɒŋˈɡəʊlɪə] n Mongolia
mongolism [ˈmɒŋɡəlɪzəm] n mongolismo m
mongrel [ˈmʌŋɡrəl] n perro mestizo
monitor [ˈmɒnɪtə(r)] **1** n (screen) monitor m; Educ delegado(a) m,f
　2 vt (check) controlar; (progress, events) seguir de cerca
monk [mʌŋk] n monje m
monkey [ˈmʌŋkɪ] n mono m; **m. nut** cacahuete m, maní m, Méx cacahuate m; **m. wrench** llave inglesa
monochrome [ˈmɒnəkrəʊm] adj monocromo(a); (television, photo) en blanco y negro
monocle [ˈmɒnəkəl] n monóculo m
monologue, US **monolog** [ˈmɒnəlɒɡ] n monólogo m

monopolize [məˈnɒpəlaɪz] vt Fin monopolizar; (attention etc) acaparar
monopoly [məˈnɒpəlɪ] n monopolio m
monotone [ˈmɒnətəʊn] n **in a m.** con una voz monótona
monotonous [məˈnɒtənəs] adj monótono(a)
monotony [məˈnɒtənɪ] n monotonía f
monsoon [mɒnˈsuːn] n monzón m
monster [ˈmɒnstə(r)] n monstruo m
monstrosity [mɒnˈstrɒsɪtɪ] n monstruosidad f
monstrous [ˈmɒnstrəs] adj (huge) enorme; (hideous) monstruoso(a); (outrageous) escandaloso(a)
montage [ˈmɒntɑːʒ] n montaje m
month [mʌnθ] n mes m
monthly [ˈmʌnθlɪ] **1** adj mensual; **m. installment** mensualidad f
　2 n (periodical) revista f mensual
　3 adv mensualmente, cada mes
monument [ˈmɒnjʊmənt] n monumento m
monumental [mɒnjʊˈmentəl] adj monumental; Fam (huge) enorme
moo [muː] **1** n mugido m
　2 vi mugir
mooch [muːtʃ] Fam **1** vi **to m. around** vagar, dar vueltas
　2 vt **to m. sth off sb** (cadge) gorronearle algo a algn
mood [muːd] n humor m; **to be in a good/bad m.** estar de buen/mal humor; **to be in the m. for (doing) sth** estar de humor para (hacer) algo
moody [ˈmuːdɪ] adj (moodier, moodiest) (changeable) de humor variable; (bad-tempered) malhumorado(a)
moon [muːn] n luna f; Fam **over the m.** en el séptimo cielo
moonlight [ˈmuːnlaɪt] n luz f de la luna
moonlighting [ˈmuːnlaɪtɪŋ] n Fam pluriempleo m
moonlit [ˈmuːnlɪt] adj (night) de luna
Moor [mʊə(r)] n moro(a) m,f
moor¹ [mʊə(r)] n (heath) páramo m
moor² [mʊə(r)] vt Naut amarrar
Moorish [ˈmʊərɪʃ] adj moro(a)
moorland [ˈmʊələnd] n páramo m
moose [ˈmuːs] n (pl moose) alce m
moot [muːt] adj **it's a m. point** es discutible
mop [mɒp] **1** n (for floor) fregona f; Fam **m. of hair** melena f
　2 vt fregar
　▸**mop up** vt sep (liquids) enjugar; (enemy forces) acabar con
mope [məʊp] vi estar alicaído(a)
　▸**mope about, mope around** vi andar abatido(a)
moped [ˈməʊped] n ciclomotor m, vespa f
moral [ˈmɒrəl] **1** adj moral
　2 n moraleja f; **morals** moral f, moralidad f
morale [məˈrɑːl] n moral f, estado m de ánimo

morality [məˈrælɪtɪ] n moralidad f
morass [məˈræs] n pantano m; Fig lío m
moratorium [mɒrəˈtɔːrɪəm] n moratoria f
(on en)
morbid [ˈmɔːbɪd] adj Med mórbido(a);
(mind) morboso(a)
more [mɔː(r)] 1 adj más; **is there any m. tea?**
¿queda más té?; **I've no m. money** no me
queda más dinero; **m. tourists** más turistas
  2 pron más; **how many m.?** ¿cuántos más?; **I
need some m.** necesito más; **it's m. than
enough** es más que suficiente; **many/much
m.** muchos(as)/mucho más; **m. than a hundred** más de cien; **the m. he has, the m. he
wants** cuanto más tiene más quiere; **and
what is m.** y lo que es más
  3 adv más; **I won't do it any m.** no lo volveré
a hacer; **she doesn't live here any m.** ya no
vive aquí; **m. and m. difficult** cada vez más
difícil; **m. or less** más o menos; **once m.** una
vez más
moreover [mɔːˈrəʊvə(r)] adv además
morgue [mɔːg] n depósito m de cadáveres
morning [ˈmɔːnɪŋ] 1 n mañana f; (before
dawn) madrugada f; **in the m.** por la mañana;
on Monday mornings los lunes por la mañana; **tomorrow m.** mañana por la mañana
  2 adj matutino(a)
Moroccan [məˈrɒkən] adj & n marroquí (mf)
Morocco [məˈrɒkəʊ] n Marruecos
moron [ˈmɔːrɒn] n Fam imbécil mf
morose [məˈrəʊs] adj hosco(a), huraño(a)

  𝄎 Note that the Spanish word **moroso** is a false
friend and is never a translation for the English
word **morose**. In Spanish, **moroso** means "bad
debtor".

morphine [ˈmɔːfiːn] n morfina f
Morse [mɔːs] n **M. (code)** (alfabeto m) Morse
m
morsel [ˈmɔːsəl] n (of food) bocado m; Fig
trozo m
mortal [ˈmɔːtəl] 1 adj mortal
  2 n mortal mf
mortality [mɔːˈtælɪtɪ] n mortalidad f
mortally [ˈmɔːtəlɪ] adv mortalmente; **m.
wounded** herido(a) de muerte
mortar [ˈmɔːtə(r)] n mortero m
mortgage [ˈmɔːgɪdʒ] 1 n hipoteca f
  2 vt hipotecar
mortician [mɔːˈtɪʃən] n US (undertaker) en-
cargado(a) m,f de funeraria
mortify [ˈmɔːtɪfaɪ] vt mortificar; Fam **I was
mortified** me sentí avergonzado(a)
mortuary [ˈmɔːtʃʊərɪ] n depósito m de cadáveres
mosaic [məˈzeɪɪk] n mosaico m
Moscow [ˈmɒskəʊ, US ˈmɒskaʊ] n Moscú
Moslem [ˈmɒzləm] adj & n musulmán(ana)
(m,f)
mosque [mɒsk] n mezquita f

mosquito [mɒsˈkiːtəʊ] n (pl **mosquitoes**)
mosquito m; **m. net** mosquitero m
moss [mɒs] n musgo m
most [məʊst] 1 adj (superl of **much, many**) (a)
(greatest in quantity etc) más; **this house
suffered (the) m. damage** esta casa fue la
más afectada; **who made (the) m. mistakes?**
¿quién cometió más errores?
  (b) (the majority of) la mayoría de, la mayor
parte de; **for the m. part** por lo general; **m. of
the time** la mayor parte del tiempo; **m. people**
la mayoría de la gente
  2 pron (greatest part) la mayor parte; (greatest number) lo máximo, lo más; (the majority
of people) la mayoría; **at the (very) m.** como
máximo; **to make the m. of sth** aprovechar
algo al máximo
  3 adv (superl of **much**) (a) más; **the m. intelligent student** el estudiante más inteligente;
what I like m. lo que más me gusta
  (b) (very) muy; **m. likely** muy probablemente; **m. of all** sobre todo
mostly [ˈməʊstlɪ] adv (chiefly) en su mayor
parte; (generally) generalmente; (usually)
normalmente
MOT [eməʊˈtiː] n Br (abbr **Ministry of Transport**) **M. test** inspección técnica de ve-
hículos, ≃ ITV
motel [məʊˈtel] n motel m
moth [mɒθ] n mariposa nocturna; **clothes m.**
polilla f
mother [ˈmʌðə(r)] 1 n madre f; **unmarried m.**
madre soltera; **M.'s Day** Día m de la Madre; **m.
tongue** lengua materna
  2 vt cuidar maternalmente
motherhood [ˈmʌðəhʊd] n maternidad f
mother-in-law [ˈmʌðərɪnlɔː] n suegra f
motherly [ˈmʌðəlɪ] adj maternal
mother-of-pearl [mʌðərəvˈpɜːl] n madreperla f, nácar m
mother-to-be [mʌðətəˈbiː] n futura madre
motif [məʊˈtiːf] n Art & Mus motivo m; (embroidered etc) adorno m; Fig (main subject)
tema m
motion [ˈməʊʃən] 1 n (movement) movimiento m; (gesture) ademán m; (proposal)
moción f
  2 vt & vi hacer señas; **to m. (to) sb to do sth**
hacer señas a algn para que haga algo
motionless [ˈməʊʃənlɪs] adj inmóvil
motivate [ˈməʊtɪveɪt] vt motivar
motivation [məʊtɪˈveɪʃən] n motivación f
motive [ˈməʊtɪv] 1 adj (force) motriz
  2 n (reason) motivo m; Jur móvil m; **with the
best of motives** con la mejor intención
motley [ˈmɒtlɪ] adj (motlier, motliest) (multicoloured) abigarrado(a); (varied) variado(a)
motor [ˈməʊtə(r)] n (engine) motor m; Fam
(car) máquina f; **m. racing** carreras fpl de
coches
motorbike [ˈməʊtəbaɪk] n Fam motocicleta
f, moto f

motorboat [ˈməʊtəbəʊt] n (lancha) motora f

motorcar [ˈməʊtəkɑː(r)] n coche m, automóvil m

motorcycle [ˈməʊtəsaɪkəl] n motocicleta f

motorcyclist [ˈməʊtəsaɪklɪst] n motociclista mf

motoring [ˈməʊtərɪŋ] n automovilismo m

motorist [ˈməʊtərɪst] n automovilista mf

motorway [ˈməʊtəweɪ] n Br autopista f

mottled [ˈmɒtəld] adj (skin, animal) con manchas; (surface) moteado(a)

motto [ˈmɒtəʊ] n lema m

mould¹ [məʊld] n (fungus) moho m

mould² [məʊld] 1 n molde m

 2 vt moldear; (clay) modelar

moulder [ˈməʊldə(r)] vi to m. (away) desmoronarse

moulding [ˈməʊldɪŋ] n moldura f

mouldy [ˈməʊldɪ] adj (mouldier, mouldiest) mohoso(a); to go m. enmohecerse

moult [məʊlt] vi mudar

mound [maʊnd] n montón m; (small hill) montículo m

mount¹ [maʊnt] n monte m; **M. Everest** (Monte) Everest m

mount² [maʊnt] 1 n (horse) montura f; (support) soporte m, base f; (for photograph) marco m; (for jewel) engaste m

 2 vt (horse) subirse or montar a; (campaign) organizar; (photograph) enmarcar; (jewel) engastar

 3 vi (go up) subir; (get on horse, bike) montar; (increase) subir

 ▸ **mount up** vi (accumulate) acumularse

mountain [ˈmaʊntɪn] 1 n montaña f; Fig (pile) montón m

 2 adj de montaña, montañés(esa); **m. bike** bicicleta f de montaña; **m. range** sierra f, cordillera f

mountaineer [maʊntɪˈnɪə(r)] n alpinista mf, Am andinista mf

mountaineering [maʊntɪˈnɪərɪŋ] n alpinismo m, Am andinismo m

mountainous [ˈmaʊntɪnəs] adj montañoso(a)

mourn [mɔːn] vt & vi to m. (for) sb llorar la muerte de algn

mourner [ˈmɔːnə(r)] n doliente mf

mournful [ˈmɔːnfʊl] adj triste; (voice) lúgubre

mourning [ˈmɔːnɪŋ] n luto m; in m. de luto

mouse [maʊs] n (pl mice) also Comput ratón m

mousetrap [ˈmaʊstræp] n ratonera f

mousse [muːs] n Culin mousse f; (for hair) (styling) m. espuma f (moldeadora)

moustache [məˈstɑːʃ] n bigote m

mousy [ˈmaʊsɪ] adj (mousier, mousiest) (colour) pardusco(a); (hair) castaño claro; (shy) tímido(a)

mouth [maʊθ] 1 n (pl mouths [maʊðz]) (a) boca f; Fam down in the m. deprimido(a) (b)

(of cave etc) entrada f; (of river) desembocadura f

 2 vt [maʊð] pronunciar; (insults) proferir

mouthful [ˈmaʊθfʊl] n (of food) bocado m; (of drink) sorbo m; to be a bit of a m. ser difícil de pronunciar

mouth organ [ˈmaʊθɔːgən] n armónica f

mouthpiece [ˈmaʊθpiːs] n Mus boquilla f; (of telephone) micrófono m; Fig (spokesman) portavoz m

mouthwash [ˈmaʊθwɒʃ] n elixir m, enjuague m bucal

mouthwatering [ˈmaʊθwɔːtərɪŋ] adj muy apetitoso(a), que le hace a uno la boca agua

movable [ˈmuːvəbəl] adj movible, móvil

move [muːv] 1 n (a) (movement) movimiento m; to be on the m. estar en marcha; we must make a m. debemos irnos ya; Fam get a m. on! ¡date prisa!

 (b) (in game) jugada f; (turn) turno m

 (c) (course of action) medida f; to make the first m. dar el primer paso

 (d) (to new home) mudanza f; (to new job) traslado m

 2 vt (a) mover; (furniture etc) cambiar de sitio; (transfer) trasladar; to m. house mudarse (de casa)

 (b) (in game) mover

 (c) (motivate) inducir; (persuade) persuadir; I won't be moved no me harán cambiar de parecer

 (d) (affect emotionally) conmover

 (e) (resolution etc) proponer

 3 vi (a) (change position) moverse, desplazarse; (change house) mudarse (de casa); (change post) trasladarse; m. out of the way! ¡quítate de en medio!

 (b) (train etc) estar en marcha; to start moving ponerse en marcha

 (c) (travel) ir

 (d) (leave) irse, marcharse

 (e) (in game) hacer una jugada

 (f) (take action) tomar medidas

 ▸ **move about 1** vt sep cambiar de sitio

 2 vi (be restless) ir y venir; (travel) viajar de un lugar a otro

 ▸ **move along 1** vt sep (move forward) hacer avanzar; (keep moving) hacer circular

 2 vi (move forward) avanzar; (keep moving) circular; **m. along!** (to person on bench) ¡haz sitio!

 ▸ **move around** vt sep & vi = move about

 ▸ **move away 1** vt sep alejar, apartar (**from** de)

 2 vi (move aside) alejarse, apartarse; (leave) irse; (change house) mudarse (de casa)

 ▸ **move back 1** vt sep (to original place) volver

 2 vi (withdraw) retirarse; (to original place) volver

 ▸ **move forward 1** vt sep avanzar; (clock) adelantar

 2 vi avanzar, adelantarse

 ▸ **move in** vi (into new home) instalarse

▸ **move off** *vi* *(go away)* irse, marcharse; *(train)* salir

▸ **move on** *vi* *(keep moving)* circular; *(go forward)* avanzar; *(time)* transcurrir

▸ **move out** *vi* *(leave)* irse, marcharse; *(leave house)* mudarse

▸ **move over** *vi* correrse

▸ **move up** *vi* *(go up)* subir; *Fig* *(be promoted)* ser ascendido(a), ascender; *(move along)* correrse, hacer sitio

movement ['muːvmənt] *n* (**a**) movimiento *m*; *(gesture)* gesto *m*, ademán *m* (**b**) *(of goods)* transporte *m*; *(of employees)* traslado *m* (**c**) *(trend)* corriente *f* (**d**) *(of machine)* mecanismo *m* (**e**) *(of goods, capital)* circulación *f*

movie ['muːvi] *n* película *f*; **to go to the movies** ir al cine; **m. star** estrella *f* de cine; *US* **m. theater** cine *m*

moving ['muːvɪŋ] *adj* *(that moves)* móvil; *(car etc)* en marcha; *Fig* *(touching)* conmovedor(a)

mow [məʊ] *vt* *(pt* **mowed***; pp* **mown** *or* **mowed)** *(lawn)* cortar; *(corn, wheat)* segar; *Fig* **to m. down** segar

mower ['məʊə(r)] *n* cortacésped *m*

mown [məʊn] *pp of* **mow**

MP [em'piː] *n Br Pol (abbr* **Member of Parliament)** diputado(a) *m,f*

mph [empiː'eɪtʃ] *(abbr* **miles per hour)** millas *fpl* por hora

MPhil [em'fɪl] *n* *(abbr* **Master of Philosophy)** = curso de posgrado de dos años de duración, superior a un máster e inferior a un doctorado

Mr ['mɪstə(r)] *(abbr* **Mister)** Sr

Mrs ['mɪsɪz] *(abbr* **Missus)** Sra

Ms [məz] *n* Sra/Srta

Ms es el equivalente femenino de **Mr**, y se utiliza para dirigirse a una mujer sin precisar su estado civil.

MSc [emes'siː] *n* *(abbr* **Master of Science)** máster *m* en Ciencias

much [mʌtʃ] **1** *adj* mucho(a); **as m. ... as** tanto(a) ... como; **how m. chocolate?** ¿cuánto chocolate?; **m. admiration** mucha admiración; **so m.** tanto(a)

2 *adv* mucho; **as m. as** tanto como; **as m. as possible** todo lo posible; **how m.?** ¿cuánto?; **how m. is it?** ¿cuánto es?, ¿cuánto vale?; **m. better** mucho mejor; **m. more** mucho más; **so m. the better!** ¡tanto mejor!; **thank you very m.** muchísimas gracias; **they are m. the same** son más o menos iguales; **too m.** demasiado; **without so m. as** sin siquiera

3 *pron* mucho; **I thought as m.** lo suponía; **m. of the town was destroyed** gran parte de la ciudad quedó destruida; **m. remains to be done** queda mucho por hacer

muck [mʌk] *n* *(dirt)* suciedad *f*; *(mud)* lodo *m*; *Fig* porquería *f*

▸ **muck about, muck around** *Fam* **1** *vi* *(idle)*

perder el tiempo; *(play the fool)* hacer e tonto

2 *vt sep* **to m. sb about** fastidiar a algn

▸ **muck up** *vt sep* *(dirty)* ensuciar; *Fig (spoi* echar a perder

mucky ['mʌki] *adj* (**muckier, muckiest**) su cio(a)

mucus ['mjuːkəs] *n* moco *m*, mucosidad *f*

mud [mʌd] *n* lodo *m*, barro *m*; *(thick)* fango *m Fig* **to sling m. at sb** poner a algn por lo suelos; **m. flat** marisma *f*

muddle ['mʌdəl] **1** *n* desorden *m*; *Fig (mix up)* embrollo *m*, lío *m*; **to get into a m** hacerse un lío

2 *vt* confundir

▸ **muddle through** *vi* arreglárselas, ingeniá selas

▸ **muddle up** *vt sep* confundir

muddy ['mʌdi] *adj* (**muddier, muddiest** *(lane)* fangoso(a); *(hands)* cubierto(a) de lo do; *(liquid)* turbio(a)

mudguard ['mʌdɡɑːd] *n Br* guardabarros *n inv*

muff¹ [mʌf] *n* manguito *m*; **ear muffs** oreje ras *fpl*

muff² [mʌf] *vt Fam* pifiar; **to m. it (up** estropearlo

muffin ['mʌfɪn] *n* panecillo *m*

muffle ['mʌfəl] *vt (sound)* amortiguar; **to m (up)** *(person)* abrigar

muffler ['mʌflə(r)] *n US Aut* silenciador *m*

mug¹ [mʌɡ] *n* *(large cup)* tazón *m*; *(bee tankard)* jarra *f*

mug² [mʌɡ] **1** *n Fam (fool)* tonto(a) *m,f*; *(face* jeta *f*

2 *vt* atracar, asaltar

mugging ['mʌɡɪŋ] *n* asalto *m*

muggy ['mʌɡi] *adj* (**muggier, muggiest**) bo chornoso(a)

mule [mjuːl] *n* mulo(a) *m,f*

mull [mʌl] *vt* **mulled wine** = vino calient con especias

▸ **mull over** *vt sep* **to m. over sth** reflexiona sobre algo

multicoloured, *US* **multicolored** ['mʌl tɪkʌləd] *adj* multicolor

multinational [mʌltɪ'næʃənəl] *adj & n* mu tinacional *(f)*

multiple ['mʌltɪpəl] **1** *adj* múltiple; **m. scler osis** esclerosis *f* múltiple

2 *n* múltiplo *m*

multiplication [mʌltɪplɪ'keɪʃən] *n* multipl cación *f*; **m. sign** signo *m* de multiplicar

multiply ['mʌltɪplaɪ] **1** *vt* multiplicar (**by** por

2 *vi* multiplicarse

multipurpose [mʌltɪ'pɜːpəs] *adj* multiuse inv

multistorey [mʌltɪ'stɔːri] *adj (building)* d varios pisos; **m. car park** parking *m* de varia plantas

multitude ['mʌltɪtjuːd] *n* multitud *f*, muche dumbre *f*

mum¹ [mʌm] *n Fam* mamá *f*

mum² [mʌm] *adj* **to keep m.** no decir ni pío

mumble ['mʌmbəl] **1** *vi* hablar entre dientes
2 *vt* decir entre dientes

mumbo-jumbo ['mʌmbəʊ'dʒʌmbəʊ] *n
(nonsense)* palabrería *f*, monsergas *fpl*

mummy¹ ['mʌmɪ] *n Fam (mother)* mamá *f*,
mami *f*

mummy² ['mʌmɪ] *n (body)* momia *f*

mumps [mʌmps] *n sing* paperas *fpl*

munch [mʌntʃ] *vt & vi* mascar

mundane [mʌn'deɪn] *adj Pej (ordinary)* pro-
saico(a); *(job, life)* rutinario(a)

⏀ Note that the Spanish word **mundano** is a
false friend and is never a translation for the
English word **mundane**. In Spanish, **mundano**
means "worldly".

municipal [mju:'nɪsɪpəl] *adj* municipal

municipality [mju:nɪsɪ'pælɪtɪ] *n* municipio *m*

mural ['mjʊərəl] *adj & n* mural *(m)*

Murcia [mu:'si:ə] *n* Murcia

murder ['mɜ:də(r)] **1** *n* asesinato *m*, homicidio *m*
2 *vt* asesinar

murderer ['mɜ:dərə(r)] *n* asesino(a) *m,f*

murderess ['mɜ:dərɪs] *n* asesina *f*

murderous ['mɜ:dərəs] *adj* homicida

murky ['mɜ:kɪ] *adj* (**murkier, murkiest**) os-
curo(a); *(water)* turbio(a)

murmur ['mɜ:mə(r)] **1** *n* murmullo *m*; *(of
traffic)* ruido *m*; *(complaint)* queja *f*
2 *vt & vi* murmurar

muscle ['mʌsəl] **1** *n* músculo *m*
2 *vi Fam* **to m. in on sth** entrometerse en
asuntos ajenos

muscular ['mʌskjʊlə(r)] *adj (pain, tissue)*
muscular; *(person)* musculoso(a)

Muse [mju:z] *n (in mythology)* musa *f*

muse [mju:z] *vi* **to m. on** *or* **about sth** meditar
algo

museum [mju:'zɪəm] *n* museo *m*

mushroom ['mʌʃru:m] **1** *n* seta *f*, hongo *m*;
Culin champiñón *m*
2 *vi Fig* crecer de la noche a la mañana

music ['mju:zɪk] *n* música *f*; **m. hall** teatro *m*
de variedades; **m. library** fonoteca *f*; *Psy* **m.
therapy** musicoterapia *f*

musical ['mju:zɪkəl] **1** *adj* musical; **to be m.**
estar dotado(a) para la música
2 *n* musical *m*

musician [mju:'zɪʃən] *n* músico(a) *m,f*

Muslim ['mʊzlɪm] *adj & n* musulmán(ana)
(m,f)

muslin ['mʌzlɪn] *n* muselina *f*

mussel ['mʌsəl] *n* mejillón *m*

must [mʌst] **1** *v aux* **(a)** *(obligation)* deber,
tener que; **you m. arrive on time** tienes que *or*
debes llegar a la hora **(b)** *(probability)* deber
de; **he m. be ill** debe de estar enfermo
2 *n Fam* **to be a m.** ser imprescindible

mustache ['mʌstæʃ] *n US* bigote *m*

mustard ['mʌstəd] *n* mostaza *f*

muster ['mʌstə(r)] **1** *vt Fig* **to m. (up) courage**
cobrar fuerzas
2 *vi* reunirse, juntarse

mustn't ['mʌsənt] = **must not**

musty ['mʌstɪ] *adj* (**mustier, mustiest**) que
huele a cerrado *or* a humedad

mute ['mju:t] **1** *adj* mudo(a)
2 *n (person)* mudo(a) *m,f*; *Mus* sordina *f*

muted ['mju:tɪd] *adj (sound)* sordo(a); *(colour)* suave

mutilate ['mju:tɪleɪt] *vt* mutilar

mutiny ['mju:tɪnɪ] **1** *n* motín *m*
2 *vi* amotinarse

mutter ['mʌtə(r)] **1** *n (mumble)* murmullo *m*
2 *vt* murmurar, decir entre dientes
3 *vi (angrily)* refunfuñar

mutton ['mʌtən] *n (carne f de) cordero m*

mutual ['mju:tʃʊəl] *adj* mutuo(a); *(shared)*
común

Muzak® ['mju:zæk] *n* música *f* de supermercado

muzzle ['mʌzəl] **1** *n (snout)* hocico *m*; *(for
dog)* bozal *m*; *(of gun)* boca *f*
2 *vt (dog)* abozalar; *Fig* amordazar

my [maɪ] *poss adj* mi; **my cousins** mis primos;
my father mi padre; **one of my friends** un
amigo mío; **I washed my hair** me lavé el pelo;
I twisted my ankle me torcí el tobillo

myriad ['mɪrɪəd] *n Literary* miríada *f*

myself [maɪ'self] *pers pron* **(a)** *(emphatic)* yo
mismo(a); **my husband and m.** mi marido y
yo **(b)** *(reflexive)* me; **I hurt m.** me hice daño
(c) *(after prep)* mí *(mismo(a))*

mysterious [mɪ'stɪərɪəs] *adj* misterioso(a)

mystery ['mɪstərɪ] *n* misterio *m*

mystical ['mɪstɪkəl] *adj* místico(a)

mystify ['mɪstɪfaɪ] *vt* dejar perplejo(a)

mystique [mɪ'sti:k] *n* mística *f*

myth [mɪθ] *n* mito *m*; **it's a complete m.** es
pura fantasía

mythology [mɪ'θɒlədʒɪ] *n* mitología *f*

N, n [en] *n (the letter)* N, n *f*

N (*abbr* **North**) N

nab [næb] *vt Fam* pillar

naff [næf] *adj Br Fam* (**a**) *(tasteless)* hortera, cutre (**b**) *(for emphasis)* **n. all** nada de nada

NAFTA ['næftə] *n* (*abbr* **North American Free Trade Agreement**) NAFTA *f*, TLC *m*

nag [næg] **1** *vt* dar la tabarra a; **to n. sb to do sth** dar la tabarra a algn para que haga algo
2 *vi* quejarse

nagging ['nægɪŋ] *adj (persistent)* continuo(a)

nail [neɪl] **1** *n* (**a**) *(of finger, toe)* uña *f*; **n. clippers** cortaúñas *m inv*; **n. polish** *or* **varnish** esmalte *m or* laca *f* de uñas (**b**) *(metal)* clavo *m*; *Fig* **to hit the n. on the head** dar en el clavo
2 *vt* (**a**) clavar (**b**) *Fam (catch, trap)* pillar, coger

nailbrush ['neɪlbrʌʃ] *n* cepillo *m* de uñas

nailfile ['neɪlfaɪl] *n* lima *f* de uñas

nail-scissors ['neɪlsɪzəz] *npl* tijeras *fpl* de uñas

naïve [naɪ'iːv] *adj* ingenuo(a)

naked ['neɪkɪd] *adj* desnudo(a); *(flame)* sin protección; **the n. truth** la pura verdad

name [neɪm] **1** *n* (**a**) nombre *m*; *(surname)* apellido *m*; **what's your n.?** ¿cómo te llamas?; **to call sb names** poner verde a algn (**b**) *(reputation)* reputación *f*; **to have a bad/good n.** tener mala/buena reputación; **to make a n. for oneself** hacerse famoso(a)
2 *vt* (**a**) llamar; **to n. sb after** *or US* **for sb** poner a algn el nombre de algn (**b**) *(appoint)* nombrar (**c**) *(refer to)* mencionar

nameless ['neɪmlɪs] *adj* anónimo(a); **to remain n.** permanecer en el anonimato

namely ['neɪmlɪ] *adv* a saber

namesake ['neɪmseɪk] *n* tocayo(a) *m,f*

nanny ['nænɪ] *n* niñera *f*

nap [næp] **1** *n (sleep)* siesta *f*; **to have a n.** echar la *or* una siesta
2 *vi Fig* **to catch sb napping** coger a algn desprevenido(a)

napalm ['neɪpɑːm] *n* napalm *m*

nape [neɪp] *n* nuca *f*, cogote *m*

napkin ['næpkɪn] *n* (**table**) **n.** servilleta *f*

Naples ['neɪpəlz] *n* Nápoles

nappy ['næpɪ] *n Br* pañal *m*

narcissus [nɑː'sɪsəs] *n Bot* narciso *m*

narcotic [nɑː'kɒtɪk] **1** *adj* narcótico(a)
2 *n (usu pl)* narcótico *m*, estupefaciente *m*

narrate [nə'reɪt] *vt* narrar, relatar

narration [nə'reɪʃən] *n* narración *f*, relato *r*

narrative ['nærətɪv] **1** *n Lit* narrativa *f*; *(story* narración *f*
2 *adj* narrativo(a)

narrator [nə'reɪtə(r)] *n* narrador(a) *m,f*

narrow ['nærəʊ] **1** *adj* (**a**) *(passage, road ete* estrecho(a), angosto(a) (**b**) *(restricted)* redu cido(a); *(sense)* estricto(a); **to have a n. e** **cape** librarse por los pelos
2 *vi* estrecharse

narrowly ['nærəʊlɪ] *adv* (**a**) *(closely)* de ce ca (**b**) *(by a small margin)* por poco
▸ **narrow down 1** *vt sep* reducir, limitar
2 *vi* **to n. down to** reducirse a

narrow-minded ['nærəʊ'maɪndɪd] *adj* d miras estrechas

nasal ['neɪzəl] *adj* nasal; *(voice)* gangoso(a)

nastiness ['nɑːstɪnɪs] *n* (**a**) *(unpleasantnes.* carácter *m* desagradable (**b**) *(maliciousnes.* mala intención

nasty ['nɑːstɪ] *adj* (**nastier, nastiest**) (**a**) *(pe son)* desagradable; **a n. business** un asunt feo; **a n. trick** una mala jugada *or* pasad cheap and n. hortera; **to turn n.** *(of weathe situation)* ponerse feo(a) (**b**) *(unfriendl* antipático(a); *(malicious)* mal intenciona do(a); *Fam* **he's a n. piece of work** es un asc de tío (**c**) *(dirty)* sucio(a), asqueroso(a) (**d** *(illness, accident)* grave

nation ['neɪʃən] *n* nación *f*

national ['næʃnəl] **1** *adj* nacional; **n. anthe** himno *m* nacional; **n. insurance** seguridad social; *Br Mil* **n. service** servicio *m* militar
2 *n* súbdito(a) *m,f*

nationalism ['næʃnəlɪzəm] *n* nacionalism *m*

nationalist ['næʃnəlɪst] *adj & n* nacionalist *(mf)*

nationality [næʃə'nælɪtɪ] *n* nacionalidad *f*

nationalization [næʃnəlaɪ'zeɪʃən] *n* nacio nalización *f*

nationalize ['næʃnəlaɪz] *vt* nacionalizar

nationwide ['neɪʃənwaɪd] *adj* de ámbit nacional

native ['neɪtɪv] **1** *adj* (**a**) *(place)* natal; **n. lan** patria *f*; **n. language** lengua materna (**b** *(innate)* innato(a) (**c**) *(plant, animal)* origina rio(a) (**to** de)
2 *n* nativo(a) *m,f*, natural *mf*; *(original i* *habitant)* indígena *mf*

NATO, Nato ['neɪtəʊ] *n* (*abbr* **North Atlanti Treaty Organization**) OTAN *f*

natter ['nætə(r)] *Fam* **1** *vi* charlar
2 *n* charla *f*

natural ['nætʃərəl] **1** *adj* (**a**) natural (**b**) *(normal)* normal; **it's only n. that …** es lógico que … (**c**) *(born)* nato(a)
2 *n* (**a**) **she's a n. for the job** es la persona ideal para el trabajo (**b**) *Mus* becuadro *m*

naturalize ['nætʃərəlaɪz] *vt* **to become naturalized** naturalizarse

naturally ['nætʃərəlɪ] *adv* (**a**) *(of course)* naturalmente (**b**) *(by nature)* por naturaleza (**c**) *(in a relaxed manner)* con naturalidad

nature ['neɪtʃə(r)] *n* (**a**) naturaleza *f* (**b**) *(character)* naturaleza *f*, carácter *m*; **by n.** por naturaleza; **human n.** la naturaleza humana (**c**) *(sort, kind)* índole *f*, clase *f*

naught [nɔːt] *n Literary* nada *f*; **to come to n.** fracasar

naughtily ['nɔːtɪlɪ] *adv* **to behave n.** portarse mal

naughty ['nɔːtɪ] *adj* (**naughtier, naughtiest**) (**a**) *(child)* travieso(a) (**b**) *(joke, story)* atrevido(a), picante

nausea ['nɔːzɪə] *n Med (sickness)* náusea *f*

nauseate ['nɔːzɪeɪt] *vt (disgust)* dar asco a

nauseating ['nɔːzɪeɪtɪŋ] *adj* nauseabundo(a)

nautical ['nɔːtɪkəl] *adj* náutico(a); **n. mile** milla marítima

naval ['neɪvəl] *adj* naval; **n. officer** oficial *mf* de marina; **n. power** potencia marítima *or* naval

Navarre [nə'vɑː(r)] *n* Navarra

nave [neɪv] *n Archit* nave *f*

navel ['neɪvəl] *n Anat* ombligo *m*

navigate ['nævɪgeɪt] **1** *vt (river)* navegar por; *Naut (ship)* gobernar
2 *vi* navegar; *(in driving)* indicar la dirección

navigation [nævɪ'geɪʃən] *n Naut* navegación *f*

navigator ['nævɪgeɪtə(r)] *n* (**a**) *Naut* navegante *mf*, oficial *mf* de derrota (**b**) *Aut & Av* copiloto *mf*

navvy ['nævɪ] *n Br Fam* peón *m*

navy ['neɪvɪ] *n* marina *f*; **n. blue** azul marino

Nazi ['nɑːtsɪ] *adj & n* nazi (*mf*)

Nazism ['nɑːtsɪzəm] *n* nazismo *m*

NB, nb [en'biː] *(abbr* **nota bene)** N.B.

neap [niːp] *n* **n. (tide)** marea muerta

near [nɪə(r)] **1** *adj (in space)* cercano(a); *(in time)* próximo(a); **in the n. future** en un futuro próximo; **it was a n. thing** poco faltó
2 *adv (in space)* cerca; **n. and far** por todas partes; **that's n. enough** (ya) vale, está bien
3 *prep* cerca de; **n. the end of the film** hacia el final de la película
4 *vt* acercarse a

nearby [nɪə'baɪ] **1** *adj* cercano(a)
2 *adv* cerca

nearly ['nɪəlɪ] *adv* casi; **very n.** casi, casi; **we haven't n. enough** no alcanza ni con mucho

nearside ['nɪəsaɪd] *n Aut (with left-hand drive)* lado izquierdo; *(with right-hand drive)* lado derecho

near-sighted [nɪə'saɪtɪd] *adj* miope

neat [niːt] *adj* (**a**) *(room, habits etc)* ordenado(a); *(handwriting)* claro(a); *(appearance)* pulcro(a) (**b**) *(idea)* ingenioso(a) (**c**) *(whisky etc)* solo(a) (**d**) *US Fam (fine)* chulísimo(a)

neatly ['niːtlɪ] *adv* (**a**) *(carefully)* cuidadosamente (**b**) *(cleverly)* hábilmente

necessarily [nesɪ'serəlɪ] *adv* necesariamente, por fuerza

necessary ['nesɪsərɪ] **1** *adj* (**a**) *(essential)* necesario(a); **to do what is n.** hacer lo que haga falta; **if n.** si es preciso (**b**) *(unavoidable)* inevitable
2 *n* **the n.** lo necesario

necessitate [nɪ'sesɪteɪt] *vt* necesitar, exigir

necessity [nɪ'sesɪtɪ] *n* (**a**) necesidad *f*; **out of n.** por necesidad (**b**) *(article)* requisito *m* indispensable; **necessities** artículos *mpl* de primera necesidad

neck [nek] *n* (**a**) cuello *m*; *(of animal)* pescuezo *m*; **to be n. and n.** ir parejos; **to be up to one's n. in debt** estar hasta el cuello de deudas; **to risk one's n.** jugarse el tipo; **to stick one's n. out** arriesgarse; **to win/lose by a n.** *(in horse racing)* ganar/perder por una cabeza; **low n.** escote bajo
2 *vi Fam* magrearse

necklace ['neklɪs] *n* collar *m*

neckline ['neklaɪn] *n (of dress)* escote *m*

necktie ['nektaɪ] *n US* corbata *f*

nectar ['nektə(r)] *n* néctar *m*

nectarine ['nektəriːn] *n* nectarina *f*

née [neɪ] *adj* **n. Brown** de soltera Brown

need [niːd] **1** *n* (**a**) necesidad *f*; **if n. be** si fuera necesario; **there's no n. for you to do that** no hace falta que hagas eso (**b**) *(poverty)* indigencia *f*; **to be in n.** estar necesitado; **to help a friend in n.** sacar a un amigo de un apuro
2 *vt* (**a**) necesitar; **I n. to see him** tengo que verle; *Ironic* **that's all I n.** sólo me faltaba eso (**b**) *(action, solution etc)* requerir, exigir
3 *v aux* tener que, deber; **n. he go?** ¿tiene que ir?; **you needn't wait** no hace falta que esperes

> Cuando se emplea como verbo modal sólo existe una forma, y los auxiliares **do/does** no se usan: **he need only worry about himself**; **need she go?**; **it needn't matter**.

needle ['niːdəl] **1** *n* (**a**) *(for sewing, knitting)* aguja *f* (**b**) *Bot* hoja *f* (**c**) *Br Fam* **to get the n.** picarse
2 *vt Fam* pinchar

needless ['niːdlɪs] *adj* innecesario(a); **n. to say** huelga decir

needlessly ['niːdlɪslɪ] *adv* innecesariamente

needlework ['niːdəlwɜːk] *n (sewing)* costura *f*; *(embroidery)* bordado *m*

needy ['niːdɪ] *adj* (**needier, neediest**) necesitado(a)

negate [nɪ'geɪt] *vt* (**a**) (*deny*) negar (**b**) (*nullify*) anular

negative ['negətɪv] **1** *adj* negativo(a)
  2 *n* (**a**) *Ling* negación *f* (**b**) *Phot* negativo *m*

neglect [nɪ'glekt] **1** *vt* (**a**) (*child, duty etc*) descuidar, desatender (**b**) **to n. to do sth** (*omit to do*) no hacer algo
  2 *n* dejadez *f*; **n. of duty** incumplimiento *m* del deber

neglectful [nɪ'glektfʊl] *adj* descuidado(a), negligente

negligée ['neglɪʒeɪ] *n* salto *m* de cama

negligence ['neglɪdʒəns] *n* negligencia *f*, descuido *m*

negligent ['neglɪdʒənt] *adj* negligente, descuidado(a)

negligible ['neglɪdʒɪbəl] *adj* insignificante

negotiate [nɪ'gəʊʃɪeɪt] **1** *vt* (**a**) (*contract*) negociar (**b**) *Fig* (*obstacle*) salvar, franquear
  2 *vi* negociar

negotiation [nɪgəʊʃɪ'eɪʃən] *n* negociación *f*

negro ['niːgrəʊ] *n* (*pl* **negroes**) negro(a) *m,f*

neigh [neɪ] **1** *n* relincho *m*
  2 *vi* relinchar

neighbour, *US* **neighbor** ['neɪbə(r)] *n* vecino(a) *m,f*; *Rel* prójimo *m*

neighbourhood, *US* **neighborhood** ['neɪbəhʊd] *n* (*district*) vecindad *f*, barrio *m*; (*people*) vecindario *m*

neighbouring, *US* **neighboring** ['neɪbərɪŋ] *adj* vecino(a)

neither ['naɪðə(r), 'niːðə(r)] **1** *adj & pron* ninguno de los dos/ninguna de las dos
  2 *adv & conj* (**a**) ni; **n. ... nor** ni ... ni; *Fig* **it's n. here nor there** no viene al caso (**b**) tampoco; **she was not there and n. was her sister** ella no estaba, ni su hermana tampoco

neon ['niːɒn] *n* neón *m*; **n. light** luz *f* de neón

nephew ['nefjuː] *n* sobrino *m*

nerd [nɜːd] *n Fam* (**a**) (*boring person*) petardo(a) *m,f*, plasta *mf*, *Méx* sangrón(ona) *m,f*, *RP* nerd *mf* (**b**) (*as insult*) bobo(a) *m,f*, memo(a) *m,f*

nerve [nɜːv] *n* (**a**) *Anat* nervio *m*; **to get on sb's nerves** poner los nervios de punta a algn; **n. gas** gas nervioso (**b**) (*courage*) valor *m* (**c**) *Fam* (*cheek*) cara *f*, descaro *m*; **what a n.!** ¡qué cara!

nerve-racking ['nɜːvrækɪŋ] *adj* crispante, exasperante

nervous ['nɜːvəs] *adj* (**a**) nervioso(a); **n. breakdown** depresión nerviosa (**b**) (*afraid*) miedoso(a) (**c**) (*timid*) tímido(a)

nest [nest] **1** *n Orn* nido *m*; (*hen's*) nidal *m*; (*animal's*) madriguera *f*; *Fig* **n. egg** ahorros *mpl*
  2 *vi* (*birds*) anidar

nestle ['nesəl] **1** *vt* recostar
  2 *vi* (*settle comfortably*) acomodarse

Net [net] *n Fam Comput* **the N.** (*Internet*) la Red; **N. user** internauta *mf*

net¹ [net] *n* red *f*; *Br* **n. curtains** visillos *mpl*

net² [net] **1** *adj* neto(a); **n. weight** peso neto
  2 *vt* (*earn*) ganar neto

netball ['netbɔːl] *n Sport* baloncesto femenino

Netherlands ['neðələndz] *npl* **the N.** los Países Bajos

netting ['netɪŋ] *n* redes *fpl*, malla *f*

nettle ['netəl] **1** *n Bot* ortiga *f*
  2 *vt Fam* irritar

network ['netwɜːk] **1** *n* red *f*
  2 *vi* (*establish contacts*) establecer contactos

neurosis [njʊˈrəʊsɪs] *n* neurosis *f*

neurotic [njʊ'rɒtɪk] *adj & n* neurótico(a) (*m,f*)

neuter ['njuːtə(r)] **1** *adj* neutro(a)
  2 *n Ling* neutro *m*
  3 *vt* (*geld*) castrar

neutral ['njuːtrəl] **1** *adj* neutro(a); *Pol* **to remain n.** permanecer neutral
  2 *n Aut* punto muerto

neutrality [njuːˈtrælɪtɪ] *n* neutralidad *f*

neutralize ['njuːtrəlaɪz] *vt* neutralizar

neutron ['njuːtrɒn] *n Phys* neutrón *m*; **n. bomb** bomba *f* de neutrones

never ['nevə(r)] *adv* nunca, jamás; **he n. complains** nunca se queja, no se queja nunca; **n. again** nunca (ja)más; **n. in all my life** jamás en la vida; *Fam* **n. mind** da igual, no importa; *Fam* **well, I n. (did)!** ¡no me digas!

never-ending ['nevər'endɪŋ] *adj* sin fin, interminable

nevertheless [nevəðə'les] *adv* sin embargo, no obstante

new [njuː] *adj* nuevo(a); **as good as n.** como nuevo; **n. baby** recién nacido *m*; **n. moon** luna nueva; **N. Year** Año nuevo; **N. Year's Eve** Nochevieja *f*; **N. York** Nueva York; **N. Zealand** Nueva Zelanda

newborn ['njuːbɔːn] *adj* recién nacido(a)

newcomer ['njuːkʌmə(r)] *n* recién llegado(a) *m,f*; (*to job etc*) nuevo(a) *m,f*

newfangled ['njuːfæŋgəld] *adj* novedoso(a)

newly ['njuːlɪ] *adv* recién, recientemente

newlywed ['njuːlɪwed] *n* recién casado(a) *m,f*

news [njuːz] *n sing* noticias *fpl*; **a piece of n.** una noticia; **it's n. to me** ahora me entero; **n. agency** agencia *f* de información; *US* **n. in brief** avance informativo; **n. bulletin** boletín informativo; **n. clipping** recorte *m* de periódico; **n. summary** avance informativo;

newsagent ['njuːzeɪdʒənt] *n* vendedor(a) *m,f* de periódicos

newsflash ['njuːzflæʃ] *n* noticia *f* de última hora

newsgroup ['njuːzgruːp] *n Comput* grupo *m* de noticias

newsletter ['njuːzletə(r)] *n* hoja informativa

newspaper ['njuːzpeɪpə(r)] *n* periódico *m*, diario *m*

newsprint ['njuːzprɪnt] *n* papel *m* de periódico

newsreader ['njuːzriːdə(r)] *n TV & Rad* presentador(a) *m,f* de los informativos

newsreel ['njuːzriːl] *n* noticiario *m*

news-stand ['njuːzstænd] *n* quiosco *m* de periódicos

newt [njuːt] *n Zool* tritón *m*

next [nekst] **1** *adj* (**a**) *(in place)* de al lado (**b**) *(in time)* próximo(a); **the n. day** el día siguiente; **n. Friday** el viernes que viene; **n. time** la próxima vez; **the week after n.** dentro de dos semanas (**c**) *(in order)* siguiente, próximo(a); **n. of kin** pariente *m* más cercano
2 *adv* después, luego; **what shall we do n.?** ¿qué hacemos ahora?
3 *prep* **n. to** al lado de, junto a; **n. to nothing** casi nada

next-door 1 *adj* ['nekstdɔː(r)] de al lado; **our n. neighbour** el vecino/la vecina de al lado
2 *adv* [neks'dɔː(r)] al lado

NHS [eneɪtʃ'es] *n Br (abbr* **National Health Service)** Seguridad *f* Social

nib [nɪb] *n* plumilla *f*

nibble ['nɪbəl] *vt & vi* mordisquear

nice [naɪs] *adj* (**a**) *(person)* simpático(a); *(thing)* agradable; **n. and cool** fresquito(a); **to smell/taste n.** oler/saber bien (**b**) *(nice-looking)* bonito(a), *Am* lindo(a) (**c**) *Ironic* menudo(a); **a n. mess you've made!** ¡menudo lío has hecho! (**d**) *Fml (subtle)* sutil

nicely ['naɪslɪ] *adv* muy bien

niche [niːʃ] *n* (**a**) hornacina *f*, nicho *m* (**b**) *Fig* hueco *m*

nick [nɪk] **1** *n* (**a**) *(notch)* muesca *f*; *(cut)* herida pequeña; **Fam in the n. of time** en el momento preciso (**b**) *Br Fam* **the n.** *(prison)* chirona *f*
2 *vt Br Fam* (**a**) *(steal)* birlar (**b**) *(arrest)* pillar

nickel ['nɪkəl] *n* (**a**) níquel *m*; **n. silver** alpaca *f* (**b**) *US* moneda *f* de 5 centavos

nickname ['nɪkneɪm] **1** *n* apodo *m*
2 *vt* apodar

nicotine ['nɪkətiːn] *n* nicotina *f*

niece [niːs] *n* sobrina *f*

nifty ['nɪftɪ] *adj (niftier, niftiest)* (**a**) *(quick)* rápido(a); *(agile)* ágil (**b**) *(ingenious)* ingenioso(a)

Nigeria [naɪ'dʒɪərɪə] *n* Nigeria

nigger ['nɪgə(r)] *n Fam Pej* negro(a) *m,f*

niggling ['nɪgəlɪŋ] *adj (trifling)* insignificante; *(irritating)* molesto(a)

night [naɪt] *n* noche *f*; **at n.** de noche; **at twelve o'clock at n.** a las doce de la noche; **last n.** anoche; **to have a n. out** salir por la noche; **n. life** vida nocturna; *Fam* **n. owl** trasnochador(a) *m,f*; **n. school** escuela nocturna; **n. shift** turno *m* de noche

nightclub ['naɪtklʌb] *n* sala *f* de fiestas; *(disco)* discoteca *f*

nightdress ['naɪtdres] *n* camisón *m*

nightfall ['naɪtfɔːl] *n* anochecer *m*

nightgown ['naɪtgaʊn] *n* camisón *m*

nightingale ['naɪtɪŋgeɪl] *n* ruiseñor *m*

nightly ['naɪtlɪ] **1** *adj* de cada noche
2 *adv* todas las noches

nightmare ['naɪtmeə(r)] *n* pesadilla *f*

nightshade ['naɪtʃeɪd] *n Bot* **deadly n.** belladona *f*

night-time ['naɪttaɪm] *n* noche *f*; **at n.** por la noche

nil [nɪl] *n* nada *f*; *Sport* cero *m*; **two n.** dos a cero

Nile [naɪl] *n* **the N.** el Nilo

nimble ['nɪmbəl] *adj* ágil, rápido(a)

nine [naɪn] *adj & n* nueve *(m inv)*; *Fam* **dressed up to the nines** de punta en blanco

nineteen [naɪn'tiːn] *adj & n* diecinueve *(m inv)*

nineteenth [naɪn'tiːnθ] *adj* decimonoveno(a)

ninety ['naɪntɪ] *adj & n* noventa *(m inv)*

ninth [naɪnθ] **1** *adj & n* noveno(a) *(m,f)*
2 *n (fraction)* noveno *m*

nip [nɪp] **1** *vt* (**a**) *(pinch)* pellizcar (**b**) *(bite)* morder; **to n. sth in the bud** cortar algo de raíz
2 *n* (**a**) *(pinch)* pellizco *m* (**b**) *(bite)* mordisco *m*

nipple ['nɪpəl] *n* (**a**) *Anat (female)* pezón *m*; *(male)* tetilla *f* (**b**) *US (on baby's bottle)* tetilla *f*, tetina *f*

nippy ['nɪpɪ] *adj (nippier, nippiest) Fam* (**a**) *Br (quick)* rápido(a) (**b**) *(cold)* fresquito(a)

nit [nɪt] *n* liendre *f*

nitrogen ['naɪtrədʒən] *n Chem* nitrógeno *m*

nitroglycerin(e) [naɪtrəʊ'glɪsəriːn] *n Chem* nitroglicerina *f*

nitty-gritty [nɪtɪ'grɪtɪ] *n Fam* **to get down to the n.** ir al grano

nitwit ['nɪtwɪt] *n Fam* imbécil *mf*

no [nəʊ] **1** *adv* no; **come here! – no!** ¡ven aquí! – ¡no!; **no longer** ya no; **no less than** no menos de
2 *adj* ninguno(a); **she has no children** no tiene hijos; **I have no idea** no tengo (ni) idea; **it's no good** *or* **use** no vale la pena; *Aut* **no parking** *(sign)* prohibido aparcar; **no sensible person** ninguna persona razonable; *Fam* **no way!** ¡ni hablar!
3 *n* no *m*; **she won't take no for an answer** no para hasta salirse con la suya; **to say no** decir que no

no. *(pl* **nos.)** *(abbr* **number)** nº, núm.

nobility [nəʊ'bɪlɪtɪ] *n* nobleza *f*

noble ['nəʊbəl] *adj* noble

nobleman ['nəʊbəlmən] *n* noble *m*

noblewoman ['nəʊbəlwʊmən] *n* noble *f*

nobody ['nəʊbədɪ] **1** *pron* nadie; **there was n. there** no había nadie; **n. else** nadie más
2 *n* nadie *m*; **he's a n.** es un don nadie

nocturnal [nɒk'tɜːnəl] *adj* nocturno(a)

nod [nɒd] **1** *n* (**a**) *(of greeting)* saludo *m* (con la cabeza); *(of agreement)* señal *f* de asentimiento

2 *vi (greet)* saludar con la cabeza; *(agree)* asentir con la cabeza

3 *vt* **to n. one's head** inclinar la cabeza

▸ **nod off** *vi* dormirse

no-go ['nəʊ'gəʊ] *adj* **n. area** zona prohibida

noise [nɔɪz] *n* ruido *m*; **to make a n.** hacer ruido

noiseless ['nɔɪzlɪs] *adj* silencioso(a), sin ruido

noisy ['nɔɪzɪ] *adj* (**noisier, noisiest**) ruidoso(a)

nomad ['nəʊmæd] *n* nómada *mf*

no-man's-land ['nəʊmænzlænd] *n* tierra *f* de nadie

nominal ['nɒmɪnəl] *adj* nominal; *(payment, rent)* simbólico(a)

nominate ['nɒmɪneɪt] *vt* (**a**) *(propose)* designar, proponer (**b**) *(appoint)* nombrar

nomination [nɒmɪ'neɪʃən] *n* (**a**) *(proposal)* propuesta *f* (**b**) *(appointment)* nombramiento *m*

nominative ['nɒmɪnətɪv] *n* nominativo *m*

nominee [nɒmɪ'niː] *n* persona propuesta

non- [nɒn] *pref* no

non-aggression [nɒnə'greʃən] *n* Pol no agresión *f*; **n. pact** pacto *m* de no agresión

non-alcoholic [nɒnælkə'hɒlɪk] *adj* sin alcohol

non-aligned [nɒnə'laɪnd] *adj* Pol no alineado(a)

nonchalant ['nɒnʃələnt] *adj (indifferent)* indiferente; *(calm)* imperturbable, impasible

noncommittal ['nɒnkəmɪtəl] *adj (person)* evasivo(a); *(answer)* no compromete (a nada)

nonconformist [nɒnkən'fɔːmɪst] *n* inconformista *mf*

nondescript ['nɒndɪskrɪpt] *adj* indescriptible; *(uninteresting)* soso(a)

none [nʌn] **1** *pron* ninguno(a); **I know n. of them** no conozco a ninguno de ellos; **n. at all** nada en absoluto; **n. other than ...** nada menos que ...

2 *adv* de ningún modo; **she's n. the worse for it** no se ha visto afectada *or* perjudicada por ello; **n. too soon** a buena hora

nonentity [nɒ'nentɪtɪ] *n (person)* cero *m* a la izquierda

nonetheless [nʌnðə'les] *adv* no obstante, sin embargo

nonevent [nɒnɪ'vent] *n* fracaso *m*

nonexistent [nɒnɪg'zɪstənt] *adj* inexistente

nonfiction [nɒn'fɪkʃən] *n* no ficción *f*

no-nonsense ['nəʊ'nɒnsəns] *adj (person)* recto(a), serio(a)

nonplussed [nɒn'plʌst] *adj* perplejo(a)

non-profit(-making) [nɒn'prɒfɪt(meɪkɪŋ)] *adj* sin fin lucrativo

nonreturnable [nɒnrɪ'tɜːnəbəl] *adj* no retornable

nonsense ['nɒnsəns] *n* tonterías *fpl*, disparates *mpl*; **that's n.** eso es absurdo

nonsmoker [nɒn'sməʊkə(r)] *n* no fumador(a) *m,f*, persona *f* que no fuma

nonstarter [nɒn'stɑːtə(r)] *n* Fig **to be a n.** *(person)* estar destinado a fracasar; *(plan)* ser irrealizable

nonstick [nɒn'stɪk] *adj* antiadherente

nonstop [nɒn'stɒp] **1** *adj* sin parar; *(train)* directo(a)

2 *adv* sin parar

noodles ['nuːdəlz] *npl* Culin fideos *mpl*

nook [nʊk] *n* recoveco *m*, rincón *m*

noon [nuːn] *n* mediodía *m*; **at n.** a mediodía

no one ['nəʊwʌn] *pron* nadie; **n. came** no vino nadie

noose [nuːs] *n* lazo *m*; *(hangman's)* soga *f*

nor [nɔː(r)] *conj* ni, ni tampoco; **neither ... n.** ni ... ni; **neither you n. I** ni tú ni yo; **n. do I** (ni) yo tampoco

norm [nɔːm] *n* norma *f*

normal ['nɔːməl] *adj* normal

normality [nɔː'mælɪtɪ] *n* normalidad *f*

normally ['nɔːməlɪ] *adv* normalmente

Normandy ['nɔːməndɪ] *n* Normandía

north [nɔːθ] **1** *n* norte *m*; **the N.** el norte; **N. America** América del Norte, Norteamérica; **N. Korea** Corea del Norte; **N. Pole** Polo *m* Norte; **N. Sea** Mar *m* del Norte

2 *adv* hacia el norte, al norte

3 *adj* del norte; **n. wind** viento *m* del norte

northeast [nɔːθ'iːst] *n* nor(d)este *m*

northerly ['nɔːðəlɪ] *adj* del norte

northern ['nɔːðən] *adj* del norte, septentrional; **n. hemisphere** hemisferio *m* norte; **N. Ireland** Irlanda del Norte

northerner ['nɔːðənə(r)] *n* norteño(a) *m,f*

northward ['nɔːθwəd] *adj & adv* hacia el norte

northwest [nɔːθ'west] *n* noroeste *m*

Norway ['nɔːweɪ] *n* Noruega

Norwegian [nɔː'wiːdʒən] **1** *adj* noruego(a)

2 *n* (**a**) *(person)* noruego(a) *m,f* (**b**) *(language)* noruego *m*

nose [nəʊz] *n* (**a**) nariz *f*; *Fig* **(right) under sb's n.** delante de las propias narices de algn; *Br Fam* **to get up sb's n.** hincharle a algn las narices (**b**) *(sense of smell)* olfato *m* (**c**) *(of car, plane)* morro *m*

▸ **nose about, nose around** *vi* curiosear

nosebleed ['nəʊzbliːd] *n* hemorragia *f* nasal

nosedive ['nəʊzdaɪv] *Av* **1** *n* picado *m*

2 *vi* descender en picado

nostalgia [nɒ'stældʒɪə] *n* nostalgia *f*

nostalgic [nɒ'stældʒɪk] *adj* nostálgico(a)

nostril ['nɒstrɪl] *n* Anat orificio *m* nasal

nosy ['nəʊzɪ] *adj* (**nosier, nosiest**) *Fam* entrometido(a)

not [nɒt] *adv* no; **he's n. in today** hoy no está; **I'm n. sorry to leave** no siento nada irme; **n. at all** en absoluto; **thank you — n. at all** gracias — no hay de qué; **n. one (of them) thanked me** nadie me dio las gracias; **n. that I don't want to come** no es que no quiera ir; **n. too well**

bastante mal; **n. without reason** no sin razón; *Fam* **likely!** ¡ni hablar!

En el inglés hablado, y en el escrito en estilo coloquial, **not** se contrae después de verbos modales y auxiliares.

notable ['nəʊtəbəl] *adj* notable
notably ['nəʊtəblɪ] *adv* notablemente
notary ['nəʊtərɪ] *n* notario *m*
notch [nɒtʃ] *n* muesca *f*; *(cut)* corte *m*
▸**notch up** *vt sep Fig* **to n. up a victory** apuntarse una victoria
note [nəʊt] **1** *n* (**a**) *Mus* nota *f*; *Fig* **to strike the right n.** acertar (**b**) *(on paper)* nota *f* (**c**) **to take n. of** *(notice)* prestar atención a (**d**) *(banknote)* billete *m* (de banco) (**e**) **notes** apuntes *mpl*; **to take n.** tomar apuntes
2 *vt* (**a**) *(write down)* apuntar, anotar (**b**) *(notice)* notar, fijarse en
notebook ['nəʊtbʊk] *n* cuaderno *m*, libreta *f*
noted ['nəʊtɪd] *adj* notable, célebre
notepad ['nəʊtpæd] *n* bloc *m* de notas
notepaper ['nəʊtpeɪpə(r)] *n* papel *m* de carta
noteworthy ['nəʊtwɜːðɪ] *adj* digno(a) de mención
nothing ['nʌθɪŋ] **1** *n* nada; **I saw n.** no vi nada; **for n.** *(free of charge)* gratis; **it's n.** no es nada; **it's n. to do with you** no tiene nada que ver contigo; **n. else** nada más; **there's n. in it** no es cierto; *Fam* **n. much** poca cosa; *Fam* **there's n. to it** es facilísimo
2 *adv* **she looks n. like her sister** no se parece en nada a su hermana
notice ['nəʊtɪs] **1** *n* (**a**) *(warning)* aviso *m*; **he gave a month's n.** presentó la dimisión con un mes de antelación; **at short n.** con poca antelación; **until further n.** hasta nuevo aviso; **without n.** sin previo aviso (**b**) *(attention)* atención *f*; **to take no n. of sth** no hacer caso de algo; **to take n. of sth** prestar atención a algo; **it escaped my n.** se me escapó; **to come to one's n.** llegar al conocimiento de uno (**c**) *(in newspaper etc)* anuncio *m* (**d**) *(sign)* letrero *m*, aviso *m*
2 *vt* darse cuenta de, notar

⚠ Note that the Spanish word **noticia** is a false friend and is never a translation for the English word **notice**. In Spanish, **noticia** means "(piece of) news".

noticeable ['nəʊtɪsəbəl] *adj* que se nota, evidente
noticeboard ['nəʊtɪsbɔːd] *n Br* tablón *m* de anuncios
notification [nəʊtɪfɪ'keɪʃən] *n* aviso *m*
notify ['nəʊtɪfaɪ] *vt* avisar
notion ['nəʊʃən] *n* (**a**) idea *f*, concepto *m* (**b**) *(whim)* capricho *m* (**c**) *US Sewing* **notions** artículos *mpl* de mercería
notorious [nəʊ'tɔːrɪəs] *adj Pej* tristemente célebre

⚠ Note that the Spanish word **notorio** is a false friend and is never a translation for the English word **notorious**. In Spanish, **notorio** means both "obvious" and "famous, well-known".

notwithstanding [nɒtwɪθ'stændɪŋ] **1** *prep* a pesar de
2 *adv* sin embargo, no obstante
nougat ['nuːgɑː] *n* turrón blando
nought [nɔːt] *n* cero *m*; *Br* **noughts and crosses** *(game)* tres en raya *m*
noun [naʊn] *n* nombre *m*, sustantivo *m*
nourish ['nʌrɪʃ] *vt* nutrir; *Fig (hopes)* abrigar
nourishing ['nʌrɪʃɪŋ] *adj* nutritivo(a)
nourishment ['nʌrɪʃmənt] *n* alimentación *f*, nutrición *f*
novel[1] ['nɒvəl] *n* novela *f*
novel[2] ['nɒvəl] *adj* original, novedoso(a)
novelist ['nɒvəlɪst] *n* novelista *mf*
novelty ['nɒvəltɪ] *n* novedad *f*
November [nəʊ'vembə(r)] *n* noviembre *m*
novice ['nɒvɪs] *n* (**a**) *(beginner)* novato(a) *m,f*, principiante *mf* (**b**) *Rel* novicio(a) *m,f*
now [naʊ] **1** *adv* (**a**) *(at this moment)* ahora; **just n., right n.** ahora mismo; **from n. on** de ahora en adelante; **n. and then, n. and again** de vez en cuando (**b**) *(for events in past)* entonces (**c**) *(at present, these days)* actualmente, hoy (en) día (**d**) *(not related to time)* **n.** *(then)* ahora bien; **n., n.!** ¡vamos!, ¡ya está bien!
2 *conj* **n. (that)** ahora que, ya que
3 *n* **until n.** hasta ahora; **he'll be home by n.** ya habrá llegado a casa
nowadays ['naʊədeɪz] *adv* hoy (en) día, actualmente
nowhere ['nəʊweə(r)] *adv* en ninguna parte; **that will get you n.** eso no te servirá de nada; **it's n. near ready** no está preparado, ni mucho menos
noxious ['nɒkʃəs] *adj* nocivo(a)
nozzle ['nɒzəl] *n* boca *f*, boquilla *f*
nuance ['njuːɑːns] *n* matiz *m*
nub [nʌb] *n* **the n. of the matter** el quid de la cuestión
nuclear ['njuːklɪə(r)] *adj* nuclear; **n. arms** armas *fpl* nucleares; **n. disarmament** desarme *m* nuclear; **n. power** energía *f* nuclear; **n. power station** central *f* nuclear
nucleus ['njuːklɪəs] *n* núcleo *m*
nude [njuːd] **1** *adj* desnudo(a)
2 *n Art & Phot* desnudo *m*; **in the n.** al desnudo
nudge [nʌdʒ] **1** *vt* dar un codazo a
2 *n* codazo *m*
nudist ['njuːdɪst] *adj & n* nudista *(mf)*
nudity ['njuːdɪtɪ] *n* desnudez *f*
nugget ['nʌgɪt] *n Min* pepita *f*; **gold n.** pepita de oro
nuisance ['njuːsəns] *n* (**a**) molestia *f*, pesadez *f*; **what a n.!** ¡qué lata! (**b**) *(person)*

pesado(a) *m,f*

nuke [njuːk] *Fam* **1** *n (bomb)* bomba *f* nuclear *or* atómica

2 *vt* atacar con armas nucleares

null [nʌl] *adj* nulo(a); **n. and void** nulo y sin valor

nullify ['nʌlɪfaɪ] *vt* anular

numb [nʌm] **1** *adj (without feeling)* entumecido(a); *Fig* paralizado(a); **n. with fear** paralizado de miedo

2 *vt (with cold)* entumecer (de frío); *(with anaesthetic)* adormecer

number ['nʌmbə(r)] **1** *n* **(a)** número *m*; *Tel* **have you got my n.?** ¿tienes mi (número de) teléfono?; *Fam* **to look after n. one** barrer para adentro **(b)** *(quantity)* **a n. of people** varias personas **(c)** *Br (of car)* matrícula *f*; **n. plate** (placa *f* de la) matrícula *f*

2 *vt* **(a)** *(put a number on)* numerar **(b)** *(count)* contar; **his days are numbered** tiene los días contados

numeral ['njuːmərəl] *n* número *m*, cifra *f*

numerate ['njuːmərət] *adj* **to be n.** tener un conocimiento básico de matemáticas

numerical [njuːˈmerɪkəl] *adj* numérico(a)

numerically [njuːˈmerɪkəlɪ] *adv* numéricamente

numerous ['njuːmərəs] *adj* numeroso(a)

numismatics [njuːmɪzˈmætɪks] *n sing* numismática *f*

nun [nʌn] *n* monja *f*

nuptial ['nʌpʃəl] *adj* nupcial

nurse [nɜːs] **1** *n* enfermera *f*; *(male)* enfermero *m*; **children's n.** niñera *f*

2 *vt* **(a)** *(look after)* cuidar, atender **(b)** *(baby)* acunar **(c)** *(suckle)* amamantar **(d)** *Fig (grudge etc)* guardar

nursery ['nɜːsərɪ] *n* **(a)** *(institution)* guardería *f*; **n. school** jardín *m* de infancia **(b)** *(in house)* cuarto *m* de los niños; **n. rhyme** poema *m* infantil **(c)** *(garden centre)* vivero *m*

nursing ['nɜːsɪŋ] *n* **n. home** clínica *f*

nurture ['nɜːtʃə(r)] *vt (animal)* alimentar; *(feelings)* abrigar

nut [nʌt] *n* **(a)** *(fruit)* fruto seco; *Fig* **a tough n. to crack** un hueso duro de roer **(b)** *Fam (head)* coco *m* **(c)** *Fam (mad person)* loco(a) *m,f* **(d)** *Tech* tuerca *f*

nutcracker ['nʌtkrækə(r)] *n* cascanueces *m inv*

nutmeg ['nʌtmeg] *n* nuez moscada

nutrition [njuːˈtrɪʃən] *n* nutrición *f*

nutritious [njuːˈtrɪʃəs] *adj* nutritivo(a), alimenticio(a)

nuts [nʌts] *adj Fam* chalado(a); **to go n.** volverse loco; **he's n. about motorbikes** las motos le chiflan

nutshell ['nʌtʃel] *n* cáscara *f*; *Fig* **in a n.** en pocas palabras

nylon ['naɪlɒn] **1** *n* **(a)** nilón *m*, nailon *m* **(b)** **nylons** medias *fpl* de nilón

2 *adj* de nilón

nymph [nɪmf] *n* ninfa *f*

nymphomaniac [nɪmfəˈmeɪnɪæk] *n* ninfómana *f*

O, o [əʊ] *n* (**a**) *(the letter)* O, o *f* (**b**) *Math & Tel* cero *m*

oak [əʊk] *n* roble *m*

OAP [əʊei'pi:] *n Br (abbr old-age pensioner)* pensionista *mf*, jubilado(a) *m,f*

oar [ɔ:(r)] *n* remo *m*

oarsman ['ɔ:zmən] *n* remero *m*

oasis [əʊ'eisis] *n (pl oases* [əʊ'eisi:z]) oasis *m inv*

oat [əʊt] *n* avena *f*; **rolled oats** copos *mpl* de avena

oath [əʊθ] *n (pl oaths* [əʊðz]) (**a**) *Jur* juramento *m*; **to take an o.** prestar juramento; *Fam* **on my o.** palabra de honor (**b**) *(swearword)* palabrota *f*

oatmeal ['əʊtmi:l] *n* harina *f* de avena

obedience [ə'bi:diəns] *n* obediencia *f*

obedient [ə'bi:diənt] *adj* obediente

obese [əʊ'bi:s] *adj* obeso(a)

obey [ə'bei] *vt* obedecer; *(law)* cumplir con

obituary [ə'bitjʊəri] *n* necrología *f*

object¹ ['ɒbdʒikt] *n* (**a**) *(thing)* objeto *m* (**b**) *(aim, purpose)* fin *m*, objetivo *m* (**c**) **the o. of criticism** el blanco de las críticas (**d**) *(obstacle)* inconveniente *m* (**e**) *Ling* complemento *m*

object² [əb'dʒekt] *vi* oponerse (**to** a); **do you o. to my smoking?** ¿le molesta que fume?

objection [əb'dʒekʃən] *n* (**a**) objeción *f* (**b**) *(drawback)* inconveniente *m*; **provided there's no o.** si no hay inconveniente

objectionable [əb'dʒekʃənəbəl] *adj (unacceptable)* inaceptable; *(unpleasant)* ofensivo(a)

objective [əb'dʒektiv] **1** *adj* objetivo(a)

2 *n* objetivo *m*

objector [əb'dʒektə(r)] *n* objetor(a) *m,f*

obligation [ɒbli'geiʃən] *n* obligación *f*; **to be under an o. to sb** estarle muy agradecido(a) a algn

obligatory [ɒ'bligətəri] *adj* obligatorio(a)

oblige [ə'blaidʒ] *vt* (**a**) *(compel)* obligar; **I'm obliged to do it** me veo obligado(a) a hacerlo (**b**) *(do a favour for)* hacer un favor a (**c**) **to be obliged** *(grateful)* estar agradecido(a)

obliging [ə'blaidʒiŋ] *adj* solícito(a)

oblique [ə'bli:k] *adj* oblicuo(a), inclinado(a); *Fig* **an o. reference** una alusión indirecta

obliterate [ə'blitəreit] *vt* (**a**) *(memory)* borrar (**b**) *(species, race)* eliminar; *(village)* arrasar

oblivion [ə'bliviən] *n* olvido *m*; **to sink into o.** caer en el olvido

oblivious [ə'bliviəs] *adj* inconsciente

oblong ['ɒblɒŋ] **1** *adj* oblongo(a)

2 *n* rectángulo *m*

obnoxious [əb'nɒkʃəs] *adj* repugnante

oboe ['əʊbəʊ] *n* oboe *m*

obscene [əb'si:n] *adj* obsceno(a)

obscure [əb'skjʊə(r)] **1** *adj* (**a**) oscuro(a); *(vague)* vago(a) (**b**) *(author, poet etc)* desconocido(a)

2 *vt (truth)* ocultar

obsequious [əb'si:kwiəs] *adj* servil

observance [əb'zɜ:vəns] *n* (**a**) observancia *f* (**b**) *Rel* **observances** prácticas religiosas

observant [əb'zɜ:vənt] *adj* observador(a)

observation [ɒbzə'veiʃən] *n* observación *f*; *(surveillance)* vigilancia *f*

observatory [əb'zɜ:vətəri] *n* observatorio *m*

observe [əb'sɜ:v] *vt* (**a**) observar; *(in surveillance)* vigilar (**b**) *(remark)* advertir (**c**) *(obey)* respetar

observer [əb'zɜ:və(r)] *n* observador(a) *m,f*

obsess [əb'ses] *vt* obsesionar; **to be obsessed (with** or **by)** estar obsesionado(a) (con)

obsession [əb'seʃən] *n* obsesión *f*

obsessive [əb'sesiv] *adj* obsesivo(a)

obsolete ['ɒbsəli:t, ɒbsə'li:t] *adj* obsoleto(a)

obstacle ['ɒbstəkəl] *n* obstáculo *m*; *Fig* impedimento *m*; **o. race** carrera *f* de obstáculos

obstinate ['ɒbstinit] *adj* (**a**) *(person)* obstinado(a), terco(a) (**b**) *(pain)* persistente

obstruct [əb'strʌkt] *vt* (**a**) obstruir; *(pipe etc)* atascar; *(view)* tapar (**b**) *(hinder)* estorbar; *(progress)* dificultar

obstruction [əb'strʌkʃən] *n* (**a**) obstrucción *f* (**b**) *(hindrance)* obstáculo *m*

obtain [əb'tein] *vt* obtener, conseguir

obtainable [əb'teinəbəl] *adj* obtenible

obtrusive [əb'tru:siv] *adj* (**a**) *(interfering)* entrometido(a) (**b**) *(noticeable)* llamativo(a)

obtuse [əb'tju:s] *adj* obtuso(a)

obviate ['ɒbvieit] *vt Fml* obviar

obvious ['ɒbviəs] *adj* obvio(a), evidente

obviously ['ɒbviəsli] *adv* evidentemente; **o.!** ¡claro!, ¡por supuesto!

occasion [ə'keiʒən] **1** *n* (**a**) ocasión *f*; **on o.** de vez en cuando; **on the o. of** con motivo de (**b**) *(event)* acontecimiento *m* (**c**) *(cause)* motivo *m*

2 *vt Fml* ocasionar

occasional [ə'keiʒənəl] *adj* esporádico(a), eventual

occasionally [əˈkeɪʒənəlɪ] *adv* de vez en cuando

occupant [ˈɒkjʊpənt] *n* ocupante *mf*; *(tenant)* inquilino(a) *m,f*

occupation [ɒkjʊˈpeɪʃən] *n* (a) *(job, profession)* profesión *f*, ocupación *f* (b) *(pastime)* pasatiempo *m* (c) *(of building, house, country)* ocupación *f*

occupational [ɒkjʊˈpeɪʃənəl] *adj* profesional, laboral; **o. hazards** gajes *mpl* del oficio

occupied [ˈɒkjʊpaɪd] *adj* ocupado(a)

occupier [ˈɒkjʊpaɪə(r)] *n Br* ocupante *mf*; *(tenant)* inquilino(a) *m,f*

occupy [ˈɒkjʊpaɪ] *vt* (a) *(live in)* ocupar, habitar (b) *(time)* pasar; **to o. one's time in doing sth** dedicar su tiempo a hacer algo (c) *(building, factory etc in protest)* tomar posesión de

occur [əˈkɜː(r)] *vi* (a) *(event)* suceder, acaecer; *(change)* producirse (b) *(be found)* encontrarse (c) **it occurred to me that ...** se me ocurrió que ...

occurrence [əˈkʌrəns] *n* suceso *m*, incidencia *f*

> Note that the Spanish word **ocurrencia** is a false friend and is never a translation for the English word **occurrence**. In Spanish, **ocurrencia** means "witty remark" and "bright idea".

ocean [ˈəʊʃən] *n* océano *m*

ocean-going [ˈəʊʃəngəʊɪŋ] *adj* de alta mar

ochre, *US* **ocher** [ˈəʊkə(r)] 1 *n* ocre *m*; **red o.** almagre *m*; **yellow o.** ocre amarillo

2 *adj* (de color) ocre

o'clock [əˈklɒk] *adv* **(it's) one o.** (es) la una; **(it's) two o.** (son) las dos

octave [ˈɒktɪv] *n* octava *f*

October [ɒkˈtəʊbə(r)] *n* octubre *m*

octogenarian [ɒktəʊdʒɪˈneərɪən] *adj & n* octogenario(a) *(m,f)*

octopus [ˈɒktəpəs] *n* pulpo *m*

OD [əʊˈdiː] *(pt & pp* **OD'd** *or* **OD'ed)** *vi Fam* meterse una sobredosis

odd [ɒd] 1 *adj* (a) *(strange)* raro(a), extraño(a) (b) *(occasional)* esporádico(a); **at o. times** de vez en cuando; **the o. customer** algún que otro cliente; **o. job** trabajillo *m* (c) **an o. number** *(not even)* un impar (c) *(unpaired)* desparejado(a); **an o. sock** un calcetín suelto; *Fig* **to be the o. man out** estar de más

2 *adv* y pico; **twenty o. people** veinte y pico *or* y tantas personas

oddity [ˈɒdɪtɪ] *n* (a) *(thing)* curiosidad *f*; *(person)* estrafalario(a) *m,f* (b) *(quality)* rareza *f*

oddly [ˈɒdlɪ] *adv* extrañamente; **o. enough** por extraño que parezca

odds [ɒdz] *npl* (a) *(chances)* probabilidades *fpl*; **he's fighting against the o.** lleva las de perder; **the o. are that ...** lo más probable es

que ... (+ *subj*) (b) *(in betting)* puntos *mpl* de ventaja; **the o. are five to one** las apuestas están cinco a uno (c) *Br* **it makes no o.** da lo mismo; *Fig* **at o. with sb** reñido(a) con algn (d) **o. and ends** *(small things)* cositas *fpl*; *(trinkets)* chucherías *fpl*

odds-on [ˈɒdzɒn] *adj* seguro(a); **o. favourite** *(horse)* caballo favorito

ode [əʊd] *n* oda *f*

odious [ˈəʊdɪəs] *adj* repugnante

odour, *US* **odor** [ˈəʊdə(r)] *n* olor *m*; *(fragrance)* perfume *m*

OECD [əʊiːsiːˈdiː] *n (abbr* **Organization for Economic Co-operation and Development)** OCDE *f*

of [ɒv, *unstressed* əv] *prep* (a) *(belonging to, part of)* de; **a friend of mine** un amigo mío; **the end of the novel** el final de la novela

(b) *(containing)* de; **a bottle of wine** una botella de vino

(c) *(origin)* de; **of good family** de buena familia

(d) *(by)* de, por; **beloved of all** amado(a) por todos

(e) *(quantity)* de; **there are four of us** somos cuatro; **two of them** dos de ellos

(f) *(from)* de; **free of** libre de; **south of** al sur de

(g) *(material)* de; **a dress (made) of silk** un vestido de seda

(h) *(apposition)* de; **the city of Lisbon** la ciudad de Lisboa

(i) *(characteristic)* de; **that's typical of her** es muy propio de ella; **that's very kind of you** es usted muy amable

(j) *(with adj)* de; **hard of hearing** duro(a) de oído

(k) *(after superlative)* de; **the thing she wanted most of all** lo que más quería

(l) *(cause)* por, de; **because of** a causa de; **of necessity** por necesidad

(m) *(concerning, about)* de, sobre; **to dream of sth/sb** soñar con algo/algn; **to think of sb** pensar en algn

(n) *(with dates)* de; **the 7th of November** el 7 de noviembre

off [ɒf] 1 *prep* (a) *(movement)* de; **she fell o. her horse** se cayó del caballo

(b) *(removal)* de; **I'll take sth o. the price for you** se lo rebajaré un poco

(c) *(distance, situation)* de; **a few kilometres o. the coast** a unos kilómetros de la costa; **a house o. the road** una casa apartada de la carretera

(d) **the ship went o. course** el barco se desvió; **to be o. form** no estar en forma

(e) **I'm o. wine** he perdido el gusto al vino

2 *adv* (a) **he turned o. the radio** apagó la radio

(b) *(absent)* fuera; **I have a day o.** tengo un día libre; **to be o. sick** estar de baja por enfermedad (**c**) *(completely)* **this will kill o. any germs** esto rematará cualquier germen

(**d**) **his arrival is three days o.** faltan tres días para su llegada; **6 miles o.** a 6 millas

(**e**) **I'm o. to London** me voy a Londres; **she ran o.** se fue corriendo

(**f**) **10 percent o.** un descuento del 10 por ciento; **to take one's shoes o.** quitarse los zapatos

(**g**) **o. and on** de vez en cuando

3 *adj* (**a**) *(gas etc)* apagado(a); *(water)* cortado(a)

(**b**) *(cancelled)* cancelado(a)

(**c**) *(low)* bajo(a); *(unsatisfactory)* malo(a); **on the o. chance** por si acaso; **the o. season** la temporada baja

(**d**) **you're better o. like that** así estás mejor

(**e**) *(gone bad) (meat, fish)* malo(a), pasado(a); *(milk)* agrio(a)

offal ['ɒfəl] *n (of chicken etc)* menudillos *mpl*; *(of cattle, pigs)* asaduras *fpl*

off-colour, *US* **off-color** ['ɒf'kʌlə(r)] *adj* (**a**) *Br (ill)* indispuesto(a) (**b**) *(joke, story)* indecente

offence [ə'fens] *n* (**a**) *Jur* delito *m* (**b**) *(insult)* ofensa *f*; **to give o.** ofender; **to take o. at sth** ofenderse por algo (**c**) *Mil (attack)* ofensiva *f*

offend [ə'fend] *vt* ofender

offender [ə'fendə(r)] *n (criminal)* delincuente *mf*

offense [ə'fens] *n US* = **offence**

offensive [ə'fensɪv] **1** *adj* (**a**) *(insulting)* ofensivo(a) (**b**) *(repulsive)* repugnante

2 *n Mil* ofensiva *f*; **to be on the o.** estar a la ofensiva

offer ['ɒfə(r)] **1** *vt* (**a**) ofrecer; **to o. to do a job** ofrecerse para hacer un trabajo (**b**) *(propose)* proponer

2 *n* (**a**) oferta *f*; *(proposal)* propuesta *f*; **o. of marriage** proposición *f* de matrimonio (**b**) *Com* **on o.** de oferta

offering ['ɒfərɪŋ] *n* (**a**) ofrecimiento *m* (**b**) *Rel* ofrenda *f*

offhand **1** *adj* ['ɒfhænd] *(abrupt)* brusco(a); *(inconsiderate)* descortés

2 *adv* [ɒf'hænd] **I don't know o.** así sin pensarlo, no lo sé

office ['ɒfɪs] *n* (**a**) *(room)* despacho *m*; *(building)* oficina *f*; *(of lawyer)* despacho, bufete *m*; *US (of doctor, dentist)* consulta *f*; **o. hours** horas *fpl* de oficina (**b**) *Br Pol* ministerio *m* (**c**) *US (federal agency)* agencia *f* gubernamental (**d**) *(position)* cargo *m*; **to hold o.** ocupar un cargo (**e**) *Pol* **to be in o.** estar en el poder

officer ['ɒfɪsə(r)] *n* (**a**) *Mil* oficial *mf* (**b**) **(police) o.** agente *mf* de policía (**c**) *(government official)* funcionario(a) *m,f* (**d**) *(of company, society)* director(a) *m,f*

official [ə'fɪʃəl] **1** *adj* oficial

2 *n* funcionario(a) *m,f*

officiate [ə'fɪʃɪeɪt] *vi* (**a**) ejercer; **to o. as** ejercer de (**b**) *Rel* oficiar

officious [ə'fɪʃəs] *adj Pej* excesivamente celoso(a) *or* diligente

🖉 Note that the Spanish word **oficioso** is a false friend and is never a translation for the English word **officious**. In Spanish, **oficioso** means "unofficial".

off-licence ['ɒflaɪsəns] *n Br* tienda *f* de bebidas alcohólicas

off-line ['ɒflaɪn] *adj Comput* desconectado(a)

off-peak [ɒf'piːk] *adj (flight)* de temporada baja; *(rate)* de fuera de las horas punta

off-putting ['ɒfpʊtɪŋ] *adj Br Fam* desconcertante

offset [ɒf'set] *vt (pt & pp offset) (balance out)* compensar

offshoot ['ɒfʃuːt] *n* (**a**) *Bot* renuevo *m* (**b**) *Fig (of organization)* ramificación *f*

offshore [ɒf'ʃɔː(r)] *adj* (**a**) *(breeze etc)* terral (**b**) *(oil rig)* costa afuera (**c**) *(overseas)* en el extranjero; **o. investment** inversión *f* en el extranjero

offside 1 *adv* [ɒf'saɪd] *Ftb* fuera de juego

2 *n* ['ɒfsaɪd] *Aut (with left-hand drive)* lado derecho; *(with right-hand drive)* lado izquierdo

offspring ['ɒfsprɪŋ] *n (pl offspring) (child)* vástago *m*; *(children)* progenitura *f*

offstage [ɒf'steɪdʒ] *adj & adv* entre bastidores

often ['ɒfən, 'ɒftən] *adv* a menudo, con frecuencia; **every so o.** de vez en cuando

ogle ['əʊgəl] *vt & vi* **to o. (at) sb** comerse a algn con los ojos

oh [əʊ] *interj* ¡oh!, ¡ay!; **oh, my God!** ¡Dios mío!

oil [ɔɪl] **1** *n* (**a**) aceite *m*; **o. lamp** lámpara *f* de aceite, quinqué *m*; **o. slick** mancha *f* de aceite; **olive o.** aceite de oliva (**b**) *(petroleum)* petróleo *m*; **o. rig** plataforma petrolera; **o. tanker** petrolero *m* (**c**) *(painting)* pintura *f* al óleo; **o. paint** óleo *m*

2 *vt* engrasar

oilcan ['ɔɪlkæn] *n* aceitera *f*

oilfield ['ɔɪlfiːld] *n* yacimiento petrolífero

oilskin ['ɔɪlskɪn] *n* (**a**) hule *m* (**b**) **oilskins** chubasquero *m*, impermeable *m* de hule

oily ['ɔɪlɪ] *adj (oilier, oiliest)* aceitoso(a), grasiento(a); *(hair, skin)* graso(a)

ointment ['ɔɪntmənt] *n* ungüento *m*, pomada *f*

O.K., okay [əʊ'keɪ] *Fam* **1** *interj* ¡vale!, ¡de acuerdo!

2 *adj* bien; **is it O.K. if ...?** ¿está bien si ...?

3 *vt* dar el visto bueno a

old [əʊld] **1** *adj* (**a**) viejo(a); **an o. man** un anciano; **o. age** vejez *f*; **o.-age pensioner** pensionista *mf*; *Br* **o. boy** antiguo alumno; **o. hand** veterano(a) *m,f*; **good o. John!** ¡el bueno de John! (**b**) **how o. are you?** ¿cuántos años tienes?; **she's five years o.** tiene cinco años (**c**) *(previous)* antiguo(a)

2 *n* **of o.** de antaño

old-fashioned [əʊld'fæʃənd] *adj (outdated)* a la antigua; *(unfashionable)* anticuado(a), pasado(a) de moda

olive ['ɒlɪv] *n* (**a**) *(tree)* olivo *m*; **o. grove** olivar *m* (**b**) *(fruit)* aceituna *f*, oliva *f* (**c**) *(wood)* olivo *m* (**d**) **o. (green)** *(colour)* verde *m* oliva

Olympic [ə'lɪmpɪk] **1** *adj* olímpico(a); **O. Games** Juegos Olímpicos

2 *npl* **the Olympics** las Olimpiadas

omelette [US **omelet** ['ɒmlɪt] *n* tortilla *f*; **Spanish o.** tortilla española *or* de patatas *or Am* papas

omen ['əʊmen] *n* presagio *m*

ominous ['ɒmɪnəs] *adj* de mal agüero

omission [əʊ'mɪʃən] *n* omisión *f*, *Fig* olvido *m*

omit [əʊ'mɪt] *vt* omitir; *(accidentally)* pasar por alto; *(forget)* olvidarse (**to** de)

omnipotent [ɒm'nɪpətənt] **1** *adj* omnipotente

2 *n* **the O.** el Todopoderoso

on [ɒn] **1** *prep* (**a**) *(location)* sobre, encima de, en; **I hit him on the head** le di un golpe en la cabeza; **it's on the desk** está encima de *or* sobre el escritorio; **hanging on the wall** colgado de la pared; **on page 4** en la página 4; **have you got any money on you?** ¿llevas dinero?; **the drinks are on me/the house** invito yo/invita la casa

(**b**) *(alongside)* en; **a town on the coast** un pueblo en la costa

(**c**) *(direction)* en, a; **on the right** a la derecha; **on the way** en el camino

(**d**) *(time)* **on 3 April** el 3 de abril; **on a sunny day** un día de sol; **on Monday** el lunes; **on Mondays** los lunes; **on that occasion** en aquella ocasión; **on the following day** al día siguiente; **on time** a tiempo

(**e**) en; **on TV/the radio** en la tele/radio; **to play sth on the piano** tocar algo al piano; **on the phone** al teléfono

(**f**) *(at the time of)* a; **on his arrival** a su llegada; **on second thoughts** pensándolo bien; **on learning of this** al conocer esto

(**g**) **she lives on bread** vive de pan; **to depend on** depender de

(**h**) *(transport)* en/a; **on foot** a pie; **on the train/plane/bus** en el tren/avión/autobús; *(travel by)* en tren/avión/autobús

(**i**) *(state, process)* en/de; **on holiday** de vacaciones; **she is here on business** está aquí de negocios

(**j**) *(regarding)* sobre; **a lecture on numismatics** una conferencia sobre numismática; **they congratulated him on his success** le felicitaron por su éxito

(**k**) **on condition that** *(subject to)* bajo la condición de que

(**l**) *(against)* contra; **an attack on** un ataque contra

(**m**) **he's on the Times** *(working for)* trabaja para el Times

2 *adv* (**a**) *(covering)* encima, puesto; **she had a coat on** llevaba puesto un abrigo

(**b**) *Fam* **have you anything on tonight?** ¿tienes algún plan para esta noche?

(**c**) **and so on** y así sucesivamente; **go on!** ¡sigue!; **he talks on and on** habla sin parar; **to work on** seguir trabajando

(**d**) **from that day on** a partir de aquel día; **later on** más tarde

3 *adj Fam* (**a**) **to be on** *(TV, radio, light)* estar encendido(a); *(engine)* estar en marcha; *(film, play)* estar en cartelera; **that film was on last week** pusieron esa película la semana pasada

(**b**) *Th TV* **you're on!** ¡a escena!

(**c**) *(definitely planned)* previsto(a); **you're on!** ¡trato hecho!

(**d**) **that isn't on** eso no vale

once [wʌns] **1** *adv* (**a**) *(one time)* una vez; **o. a week** una vez por semana; **o. in a while** de vez en cuando; **o. more** una vez más; **o. or twice** un par de veces; *Fig* **o. and for all** de una vez por todas (**b**) *(formerly)* en otro tiempo; **o. (upon a time) there was ...** érase una vez ... (**c**) **at o.** en seguida, inmediatamente; **don't all speak at o.** no habléis todos a la vez

2 *conj* una vez que (+ *subj*), en cuanto (+ *subj*)

oncoming ['ɒnkʌmɪŋ] *adj (car, traffic)* que viene en dirección contraria

one [wʌn] **1** *adj* (**a**) un/una; **for o. thing** primero; **you're the o. person who knows** tú eres el único que lo sabe; **the o. and only** el único/la única; **o. and the same** el mismo/la misma

(**b**) *(indefinite)* un/una; **he'll come back o. day** un día volverá

2 *dem pron* **any o.** cualquiera; **that o.** ése/ésa; **this o.** éste/ésta; *(distant)* aquél/aquélla; **the blue ones** los azules/las azules; **the o. on the table** el/la que está encima de la mesa; **the ones that, the ones who** los/las que

3 *indef pron* (**a**) uno(a) *m,f*; **I, for o., am against it** yo, por lo menos, estoy en contra; **I'm not o. to complain** no soy de los que se quejan; **o. at a time** de uno en uno; **o. by o.** uno tras otro; *Fig* **o. and all** todo el mundo

(**b**) *(indefinite person)* uno(a) *m,f*; **o. has to fight** hay que luchar; **o. hopes that will never happen** esperemos que no ocurra; **to break o.'s leg/arm** romperse la pierna/el brazo

(**c**) **o. another** el uno al otro; **they love o. another** se aman

4 *n (digit)* uno *m*; **o. hundred/thousand** cien/mil

one-armed ['wʌnɑːmd] *adj Fig* **o. bandit** máquina *f* tragaperras

one-man ['wʌnmæn] *adj* **a o. show** un espectáculo con un solo artista

one-man band [wʌnmæn'bænd] *n* hombre *m* orquesta

one-off ['wʌnɒf] *adj Br Fam* único(a), fuera de serie

oneself [wʌn'self] *pron* (**a**) *(reflexive)* uno(a) mismo(a) *m,f*, sí mismo(a) *m,f*; **to talk to o.** hablar para sí (**b**) *(alone)* uno(a) mismo(a) *m,f*; **by o.** solo(a) (**c**) *(one's usual self)* el/la de siempre

one-sided [wʌn'saɪdɪd] *adj (bargain)* desigual; *(judgement)* parcial; *(decision)* unilateral

one-to-one ['wʌntə'wʌn] *adj* **o. tuition** clase *f* individual

one-way ['wʌnweɪ] *adj* (**a**) *US (ticket)* de ida (**b**) *(street)* de dirección única

ongoing ['ɒngəʊɪŋ] *adj* (**a**) *(in progress)* en curso, actual (**b**) *(developing)* en desarrollo

onion ['ʌnjən] *n* cebolla *f*

on-line ['ɒnlaɪn] *adj Comput* conectado(a)

onlooker ['ɒnlʊkə(r)] *n* espectador(a) *m,f*

only ['əʊnlɪ] **1** *adj* único(a); **o. son** hijo único

2 *adv* (**a**) solamente, sólo; **staff o.** *(sign)* reservado al personal (**b**) *(not earlier than)* apenas; **he has o. just left** acaba de marcharse hace un momento; **o. yesterday** ayer mismo (**c**) **o. too glad!** ¡con mucho gusto!

3 *conj* pero

onset ['ɒnset] *n (start)* comienzo *m*

onslaught ['ɒnslɔːt] *n* embestida *f*

onto ['ɒntʊ, *unstressed* 'ɒntə] *prep* = **on to**

onus ['əʊnəs] *n* responsabilidad *f*

onward ['ɒnwəd] *adj* hacia adelante

onward(s) ['ɒnwəd(z)] *adv* a partir de, en adelante; **from this time o.** de ahora en adelante

ooze [uːz] **1** *vi* rezumar

2 *vt* rebosar

opaque [əʊ'peɪk] *adj* opaco(a)

OPEC ['əʊpek] *n (abbr* **Organization of Petroleum-Exporting Countries)** OPEP *f*

open ['əʊpən] **1** *adj* (**a**) abierto(a); **half o.** entreabierto; **wide o.** abierto de par en par; **in the o. air** al aire libre; **to be o. with sb** ser sincero(a) con algn; *Fig* **with o. arms** con los brazos abiertos; **to keep an o. mind** no tener prejuicios; **I am o. to suggestions** acepto cualquier sugerencia; **o. to criticism** susceptible a la crítica; **o. admiration** franca admiración; *US* **o. house** fiesta *f* de inauguración de residencia; **an o. question** una cuestión sin resolver; **o. season** *(in hunting)* temporada *f* de caza; *Av Rail* **o. ticket** billete abierto; *Br* **O. University** Universidad *f* a Distancia; **o. verdict** veredicto inconcluso

(**b**) *(car etc)* descubierto(a)

(**c**) *(opposition)* manifiesto(a)

2 *vt* (**a**) abrir; **to o. fire** abrir fuego; *Fig* **to o. one's heart to sb** sincerarse con algn

(**b**) *(exhibition etc)* inaugurar; *(negotiations,*

conversation) entablar

3 *vi* (**a**) abrir, abrirse; **to o. onto** *(of door, window)* dar a

(**b**) *(start)* empezar; *Th Cin* estrenarse

4 *n* (**a**) **in the o.** al aire libre; *Fig* **to bring into the o.** hacer público

(**b**) *Sport* open *m*

▸ **open out 1** *vt sep* abrir, desplegar

2 *vi (flowers)* abrirse; *(view)* extenderse

▸ **open up 1** *vt sep (market etc)* abrir; *(possibilities)* crear

2 *vi* (**a**) abrirse; *Fam* **o. up!** ¡abre la puerta! (**b**) *(start)* empezar

opener ['əʊpənə(r)] *n* **tin** *or US* **can o.** abrelatas *m inv*

opening ['əʊpənɪŋ] *n* (**a**) *(act)* apertura *f*; **o. night** noche *f* de estreno; *Br* **o. time** hora *f* de apertura de los bares (**b**) *(beginning)* comienzo *m* (**c**) *(aperture)* abertura *f*; *(gap)* brecha *f* (**d**) *Com* oportunidad *f* (**e**) *(vacancy)* vacante *f*

openly ['əʊpənlɪ] *adv* abiertamente

open-minded [əʊpən'maɪndɪd] *adj* sin prejuicios

openness ['əʊpənnɪs] *n* franqueza *f*

open-plan ['əʊpənplæn] *adj (office)* abierto(a)

opera ['ɒpərə] *n* ópera *f*; **o. house** ópera, teatro *m* de la ópera

operate ['ɒpəreɪt] **1** *vi* (**a**) *(function)* funcionar (**b**) *Med* operar; **to o. on sb for appendicitis** operar a algn de apendicitis

2 *vt* (**a**) *(control)* manejar (**b**) *(business)* dirigir

operatic [ɒpə'rætɪk] *adj* de ópera

operating ['ɒpəreɪtɪŋ] *n* (**a**) **o. costs** gastos *mpl* de funcionamiento (**b**) *Med* **o. table** mesa *f* de operaciones; **o. theatre** *or US* **room** quirófano *m*

operation [ɒpə'reɪʃən] *n* (**a**) *(of machine)* funcionamiento *m*; *(by person)* manejo *m* (**b**) *Mil* maniobra *f* (**c**) *Med* operación *f*, intervención quirúrgica; **to undergo an o. for** ser operado(a) de

operational [ɒpə'reɪʃənəl] *adj* (**a**) *(ready for use)* operativo(a) (**b**) *Mil* operacional

operative ['ɒpərətɪv] *adj Jur (in force)* vigente; **to become o.** entrar en vigor (**b**) *(significant)* clave, significativo(a); **the o. word** la palabra clave

operator ['ɒpəreɪtə(r)] *n* (**a**) *Ind* operario(a) *m,f* (**b**) *Tel* operador(a) *m,f* (**c**) *(dealer)* negociante *mf*, agente *mf*; **tour o.** agente de viajes

opinion [ə'pɪnjən] *n* opinión *f*; **in my o.** en mi opinión, a mi juicio; **it's a matter of o.** es cuestión de opiniones; **to have a high o. of sb** tener buen concepto de algn; **o. poll** encuesta *f*, sondeo *m*

opinionated [ə'pɪnjəneɪtɪd] *adj* dogmático(a)

opium ['əʊpɪəm] *n* opio *m*

opponent [ə'pəʊnənt] *n* adversario(a) *m,f*

opportune [ˈɒpətjuːn] *adj* oportuno(a)

opportunist [ɒpəˈtjuːnɪst] *adj & n* oportunista *(mf)*

opportunity [ɒpəˈtjuːnɪtɪ] *n* (**a**) oportunidad *f*, ocasión *f* (**b**) *(prospect)* perspectiva *f*

oppose [əˈpəʊz] *vt* oponerse a

opposed [əˈpəʊzd] *adj* opuesto(a); **to be o. to sth** estar en contra de algo; **as o. to** comparado(a) con

opposing [əˈpəʊzɪŋ] *adj* adversario(a)

opposite [ˈɒpəzɪt] **1** *adj* (**a**) *(facing)* de enfrente; *(page)* contiguo(a) (**b**) *(contrary)* opuesto(a), contrario(a); **in the o. direction** en dirección contraria
2 *n* **the o.** lo contrario; **quite the o.!** ¡al contrario!
3 *prep* enfrente de, frente a
4 *adv* enfrente

opposition [ɒpəˈzɪʃən] *n* (**a**) oposición *f*; **in o. to** en contra de (**b**) *Pol* **the o.** la oposición

oppress [əˈpres] *vt* oprimir

oppression [əˈpreʃən] *n* opresión *f*

oppressive [əˈpresɪv] *adj* opresivo(a); *(atmosphere)* agobiante; *(heat)* sofocante

opt [ɒpt] *vi* optar; **to o. for** optar por; **to o. to do sth** optar por hacer algo
▸ **opt out** *vi* retirarse; **to o. out of doing sth** decidir no hacer algo

optical [ˈɒptɪkəl] *adj* óptico(a)

optician [ɒpˈtɪʃən] *n* óptico(a) *m,f*

optics [ˈɒptɪks] *n sing* óptica *f*

optimist [ˈɒptɪmɪst] *n* optimista *mf*

optimistic [ɒptɪˈmɪstɪk] *adj* optimista

optimistically [ɒptɪˈmɪstɪkəlɪ] *adv* con optimismo

optimum [ˈɒptɪməm] **1** *n* grado óptimo
2 *adj* óptimo(a)

option [ˈɒpʃən] *n* opción *f*; **I have no o.** no tengo más remedio; **to keep one's options open** no comprometerse; **with the o. of** con opción a

optional [ˈɒpʃənəl] *adj* optativo(a), facultativo(a); *Educ* **o. subject** (asignatura *f*) optativa *f*

opulence [ˈɒpjʊləns] *n* opulencia *f*

or [ɔː(r), *unstressed* ə(r)] *conj* (**a**) o; *(before a word beginning with* **o** *or* **ho**) u; **or else** si no, o bien; **whether you like it or not** tanto si te gusta como si no; **either a bun or a piece of cake** (o) una magdalena o un trozo de pastel (**b**) *(with negative)* ni; **he can't read or write** no sabe leer ni escribir; *see* **nor**

oral [ˈɔːrəl, ˈɒrəl] **1** *adj* oral
2 *n* examen *m* oral

orally [ˈɔːrəlɪ, ˈɒrəlɪ] *adv* **to be taken o.** *(on medicine)* por vía oral

orange [ˈɒrɪndʒ] **1** *n* naranja *f*; **o. juice** zumo *m or Am* jugo *m* de naranja
2 *adj* de color naranja

orator [ˈɒrətə(r)] *n* orador(a) *m,f*

oratory [ˈɒrətərɪ] *n* oratoria *f*

orbit [ˈɔːbɪt] **1** *n Astron* órbita *f*

2 *vt* girar alrededor de
3 *vi* girar

orchard [ˈɔːtʃəd] *n* huerto *m*

orchestra [ˈɔːkɪstrə] *n* orquesta *f*; *US (in theatre)* platea *f*

orchestral [ɔːˈkestrəl] *adj* orquestal

orchid [ˈɔːkɪd] *n* orquídea *f*

ordain [ɔːˈdeɪn] *vt* (**a**) *Rel* ordenar; **to be ordained** ordenarse (**b**) *(decree)* decretar

ordeal [ɔːˈdiːl] *n* mala experiencia *f*

order [ˈɔːdə(r)] **1** *n* (**a**) *(sequence)* orden *m*; **in alphabetical o.** por orden alfabético; **to put in o.** ordenar
(**b**) *(condition)* estado *m*; **is your passport in o.?** ¿tienes el pasaporte en regla?; **out of o.** *(sign)* averiado(a)
(**c**) *(peace)* orden *m*; **to restore o.** reestablecer el orden publico
(**d**) *(command)* orden *f*
(**e**) *Com* pedido *m*, encargo *m*; **to be on o.** estar pedido; **to o.** a la medida; **o. form** hoja *f* de pedido
(**f**) *Rel* orden *f*
(**g**) **of the highest o.** *(quality)* de primera calidad
(**h**) *(kind)* índole *f*, tipo *m*; *Biol* orden *m*
(**i**) **in the o. of** del orden de
(**j**) **in o. that** para que *(+ subj)*, a fin de que *(+ subj)*; **in o. to** *(+ infin)* para *(+ infin)*, a fin de *(+ infin)*
2 *vt* (**a**) *(command)* ordenar, mandar; **to o. sb to do sth** mandar a algn hacer algo
(**b**) *Com* pedir, encargar; **to o. a dish** pedir un plato

orderly [ˈɔːdəlɪ] **1** *adj* *(tidy etc)* ordenado(a)
2 *n* (**a**) *Med* enfermero *m* (**b**) *Mil* ordenanza *m*

ordinary [ˈɔːdənrɪ] **1** *adj* usual, normal; *(average)* corriente, común; **the o. citizen** el ciudadano de a pie
2 *n* **the o.** lo corriente, lo normal; **out of the o.** fuera de lo común

ordnance [ˈɔːdnəns] *n Br* **O. Survey** = instituto británico de cartografía

ore [ɔː(r)] *n* mineral *m*

organ [ˈɔːɡən] *n Mus & Anat etc* órgano *m*

organic [ɔːˈɡænɪk] *adj* orgánico(a); *(farming, food)* biológico(a), ecológico(a)

organism [ˈɔːɡənɪzəm] *n* organismo *m*

organization [ɔːɡənaɪˈzeɪʃən] *n* organización *f*

organize [ˈɔːɡənaɪz] *vt* organizar

organizer [ˈɔːɡənaɪzə(r)] *n* organizador(a) *m,f*

orgasm [ˈɔːɡæzəm] *n* orgasmo *m*

orgy [ˈɔːdʒɪ] *n* orgía *f*

Orient [ˈɔːrɪənt] *n* **the O.** el Oriente

Oriental [ɔːrɪˈentəl] *adj & n* oriental *(mf)*

origin [ˈɒrɪdʒɪn] *n* origen *m*; **country of o.** país *m* natal *or* de origen

original [əˈrɪdʒɪnəl] **1** *adj* (**a**) original; *(first)* primero(a) (**b**) *(imaginative)* original
2 *n* original *m*

originality [ərɪdʒɪˈnælɪtɪ] n originalidad f
originally [əˈrɪdʒɪnəlɪ] adv (a) (at first) en un principio (b) (with imagination) con originalidad
originate [əˈrɪdʒɪneɪt] 1 vt originar
  2 vi to o. from or in tener su origen en
Orkneys [ˈɔːknɪz] npl the O. las (Islas) Orcadas
ornament [ˈɔːnəmənt] n ornamento m, adorno m
ornamental [ɔːnəˈmentəl] adj decorativo(a)
ornate [ɔːˈneɪt] adj vistoso(a)
ornithology [ɔːnɪˈθɒlədʒɪ] n ornitología f
orphan [ˈɔːfən] 1 n huérfano(a) m,f
  2 vt she was orphaned quedó huérfana
orphanage [ˈɔːfənɪdʒ] n orfanato m
orthodox [ˈɔːθədɒks] adj ortodoxo(a)
orthodoxy [ˈɔːθədɒksɪ] n ortodoxia f
orthopaedic, US **orthopedic** [ɔːθəʊˈpiːdɪk] adj ortopédico(a)
Oscar [ˈɒskə(r)] n Óscar m
oscillate [ˈɒsɪleɪt] vi oscilar
ostensible [ɒˈstensɪbəl] adj (a) (apparent) ostensible (b) (pretended) aparente
ostentatious [ɒstenˈteɪʃəs] adj ostentoso(a)
osteopath [ˈɒstɪəpæθ] n osteópata mf
ostracize [ˈɒstrəsaɪz] vt (from society) condenar al ostracismo; (from group) aislar, excluir
ostrich [ˈɒstrɪtʃ] n avestruz f
other [ˈʌðə(r)] 1 adj (a) otro(a); every o. day cada dos días; on the o. hand por otra parte; o. people have seen it otros lo han visto; the o. four los otros cuatro; the o. one el otro/la otra; the o. thing lo otro (b) he must be somewhere or o. debe de estar en alguna parte
  2 pron otro(a) m,f; many others otros muchos; the others los otros, los demás; we see each o. quite often nos vemos con bastante frecuencia
otherwise [ˈʌðəwaɪz] 1 adv (a) (if not) si no (b) (differently) de otra manera (c) (in other respects) por lo demás
  2 adj distinto(a)
OTT [əʊtiːˈtiː] adj Br Fam (abbr over the top) exagerado(a)
otter [ˈɒtə(r)] n nutria f
ought [ɔːt] v aux

En el inglés hablado, y en el escrito en estilo coloquial, la forma negativa **ought not** se transforma en **oughtn't**.

(a) (obligation) deber; I thought I o. to tell you creí que debía decírtelo; she o. to do it debería hacerlo (b) (vague desirability) tener que, deber; you o. to see the exhibition deberías ver la exposición (c) (expectation) he o. to pass the exam seguramente aprobará el examen; that o. to do con eso bastará
ounce [aʊns] n onza f
our [aʊə(r)] poss adj nuestro(a)
ours [aʊəz] poss pron (a) (el) nuestro/(la)

nuestra (b) of o. nuestro(a); a friend of o. un amigo nuestro
ourselves [aʊəˈselvz] pers pron pl (a) (reflexive) nos (b) (emphatic) nosotros mismos/ nosotras mismas (c) by o. a solas
oust [aʊst] vt (a) (from a post) desbancar (b) (from property etc) desalojar
out [aʊt] 1 adv (a) (outside, away) fuera; o. there ahí fuera; to go o. salir
  (b) I told him straight o. se lo dije muy claramente; o. loud en voz alta
  (c) hear me o. escúchame hasta el final
  (d) o. of (place) fuera de; move o. of the way! ¡quítate de en medio!; o. of danger fuera de peligro; to go o. of the room salir de la habitación; o. of control fuera de control; o. of date (expired) caducado(a); (old-fashioned) pasado(a) de moda
  (e) o. of (cause, motive) por
  (f) o. of (made from) de
  (g) o. of (short of, without) sin; I'm o. of money se me ha acabado el dinero; o. of breath sin aliento
  (h) o. of (among) entre; forty o. of fifty cuarenta de cada cincuenta; (in exam etc) cuarenta sobre cincuenta
  2 adj (a) the sun is o. ha salido el sol
  (b) (unfashionable) pasado(a) de moda
  (c) (fire) apagado(a)
  (d) (not working) estropeado(a)
  (e) she's o. (not in) ha salido, no está
  (f) to be o. for sth buscar algo; to be o. to do sth pretender hacer algo
  (g) the book is just o. el libro acaba de salir
  (h) (inaccurate) equivocado(a); to be o. in one's calculations equivocarse en los cálculos
  (i) before the week is o. antes de que acabe la semana
  3 prep (out of) por; he jumped o. of the window saltó por la ventana
out-and-out [ˈaʊtənaʊt] adj redomado(a)
outboard [ˈaʊtbɔːd] adj o. motor fueraborda m
outbreak [ˈaʊtbreɪk] n (of war) comienzo m; (of spots) erupción f; (of disease) brote m; (of violence) ola f; (of anger) arrebato m; at the o. of war cuando estalló la guerra
outbuilding [ˈaʊtbɪldɪŋ] n dependencia f
outburst [ˈaʊtbɜːst] n (of anger) arrebato m; (of generosity) arranque m
outcast [ˈaʊtkɑːst] n marginado(a) m,f
outcome [ˈaʊtkʌm] n resultado m
outcrop [ˈaʊtkrɒp] n Geol afloramiento m
outcry [ˈaʊtkraɪ] n there was an o. hubo fuertes protestas
outdated [aʊtˈdeɪtɪd] adj anticuado(a), obsoleto(a)
outdo [aʊtˈduː] vt (pt outdid [aʊtˈdɪd]; pp outdone [aʊtˈdʌn]) to o. sb superar a algn
outdoor [ˈaʊtdɔː(r)] adj (a) al aire libre (b) (clothes) de calle

outdoors [aʊt'dɔːz] *adv* fuera, al aire libre
outer ['aʊtə(r)] *adj* exterior, externo(a)
outfit ['aʊtfɪt] *n* (**a**) *(kit, equipment)* equipo *m* (**b**) *(set of clothes)* conjunto *m* (**c**) *Fam (group)* grupo *m*
outgoing [aʊt'gəʊɪŋ] **1** *adj* (**a**) *(departing)* saliente (**b**) *(sociable)* extrovertido(a)
 2 *npl* **outgoings** gastos *mpl*
outgrow [aʊt'grəʊ] *vt* (*pt* **outgrew** [aʊt'gruː]; *pp* **outgrown** [aʊt'grəʊn]) **he's outgrowing all his clothes** toda la ropa se le está quedando pequeña; **she'll o. it** se le pasará con la edad
outhouse ['aʊthaʊs] *n* = **outbuilding**
outing ['aʊtɪŋ] *n* excursión *f*
outlandish [aʊt'lændɪʃ] *adj* estrafalario(a)
outlast [aʊt'lɑːst] *vt* durar más que
outlaw ['aʊtlɔː] **1** *n* proscrito(a) *m,f*
 2 *vt* prohibir
outlet ['aʊtlet] *n* (**a**) *(opening)* salida *f* (**b**) *(for emotions)* válvula *f* de escape (**c**) *Com* mercado *m* (**d**) *(for water)* desagüe *m*
outline ['aʊtlaɪn] **1** *n* (**a**) *(draft)* bosquejo *m* (**b**) *(outer line)* contorno *m*; *(silhouette)* perfil *m*
 2 *vt* (**a**) *(draw lines of)* perfilar (**b**) *(summarize)* resumir (**c**) *(describe roughly)* trazar las líneas generales de
outlive [aʊt'lɪv] *vt* sobrevivir a
outlook ['aʊtlʊk] *n* (**a**) *(point of view)* punto *m* de vista (**b**) *(prospect)* perspectiva *f*; *Met* previsión *f*
outlying ['aʊtlaɪɪŋ] *adj* (remote) aislado(a)
outmoded [aʊt'məʊdɪd] *adj* anticuado(a)
outnumber [aʊt'nʌmbə(r)] *vt* exceder en número
out-of-the-way [aʊtəvðə'weɪ] *adj* (**a**) *(distant)* apartado(a), aislado(a) (**b**) *(uncommon)* poco corriente
outpatient ['aʊtpeɪʃənt] *n* paciente externo(a); **outpatients' department** clínica ambulatoria
outpost ['aʊtpəʊst] *n* avanzada *f*
output ['aʊtpʊt] *n* (**a**) producción *f* (**b**) *Elec* potencia *f* (**c**) *Comput* salida *f*
outrage ['aʊtreɪdʒ] **1** *n* ultraje *m*; **it's an o.!** ¡es un escándalo!
 2 *vt* **to be outraged by sth** indignarse por algo
outrageous [aʊt'reɪdʒəs] *adj* (behaviour) escandaloso(a); *(clothes)* extravagante; *(price)* exorbitante
outright 1 *adj* ['aʊtraɪt] *(absolute)* absoluto(a)
 2 *adv* [aʊt'raɪt] (**a**) *(completely)* por completo (**b**) *(directly)* directamente, sin reserva (**c**) *(immediately)* en el acto
outset ['aʊtset] *n* comienzo *m*, principio *m*
outside 1 *prep* ['aʊt'saɪd, 'aʊtsaɪd] (**a**) fuera de (**b**) *(beyond)* más allá de (**c**) *(other than)* aparte de
 2 *adj* ['aʊtsaɪd] (**a**) *(exterior)* exterior, exter-

no(a) (**b**) *(remote)* remoto(a)
 3 *adv* [aʊt'saɪd] fuera, afuera
 4 *n* [aʊt'saɪd, 'aʊtsaɪd] exterior *m*; **on the o.** por fuera; *Fam* **at the o.** como mucho
outsider [aʊt'saɪdə(r)] *n* (**a**) *(stranger)* extraño(a) *m,f*, forastero(a) *m,f* (**b**) *Pol* = candidato(a) con pocas posibilidades de ganar
outsize(d) ['aʊtsaɪz(d)] *adj* (clothes) de talla muy grande
outskirts ['aʊtskɜːts] *npl* afueras *fpl*
outsourcing ['aʊtsɔːsɪŋ] *n Com* externalización *f*, subcontratación *f*, *Am* tercerización *f*
outspoken [aʊt'spəʊkən] *adj* directo(a), abierto(a)
outstanding [aʊt'stændɪŋ] *adj* (**a**) *(exceptional)* destacado(a) (**b**) *(unpaid, unresolved)* pendiente
outstretched [aʊt'stretʃt] *adj* extendido(a)
outward ['aʊtwəd] **1** *adj* (**a**) *(external)* exterior, externo(a) (**b**) **the o. journey** el viaje de ida
 2 *adv* = **outwards**
outwardly ['aʊtwədlɪ] *adv* aparentemente
outwards ['aʊtwədz] *adv* hacia (a)fuera
outweigh [aʊt'weɪ] *vt* (**a**) *(prevail over)* prevalecer sobre (**b**) *(weigh more than)* pesar más que
oval ['əʊvəl] **1** *adj* oval, ovalado(a)
 2 *n* óvalo *m*
ovary ['əʊvərɪ] *n* ovario *m*
ovation [əʊ'veɪʃən] *n* ovación *f*
oven ['ʌvən] *n* horno *m*
ovenproof ['ʌvənpruːf] *adj* refractario(a)
over ['əʊvə(r)] **1** *prep* (**a**) *(above)* encima de (**b**) *(on top of)* sobre, encima de (**c**) *(across)* al otro lado de; **the bridge o. the river** el puente que cruza el río (**d**) *(during)* durante (**e**) *(throughout)* por (**f**) **all o.** por todo(a); **famous all o. the world** famoso en el mundo entero (**g**) *(by the agency of)* por; **o. the phone** por teléfono (**h**) *(more than)* más de; **men o. twenty-five** hombres mayores de veinticinco años; **o. and above** además de (**i**) *(recovered from)* recuperado(a) de
 2 *adv* (**a**) **o. there** allá; **why don't you come o. tomorrow?** ¿por qué no vienes a casa mañana? (**b**) *(throughout)* por; **all o.** por todas partes (**c**) *(more)* más (**d**) *(again)* otra vez; **o. and o. (again)** una y otra vez; **twice o.** dos veces seguidas (**e**) *(in excess)* de más
 3 *adj* *(finished)* acabado(a); **it's (all) o.** se acabó; **the danger is o.** ha pasado el peligro
overall ['əʊvərɔːl] **1** *adj* total, global
 2 *n* (**a**) *Br* guardapolvo *m* (**b**) **overalls** mono *m*
 3 *adv* [əʊvər'ɔːl] *(on the whole)* por lo general, en conjunto

overawe [əʊvər'ɔː] *vt* **to be overawed** sobrecogerse

overbearing [əʊvə'beərɪŋ] *adj (domineering)* dominante; *(important)* significativo(a)

overboard [əʊvəbɔːd] *adv* por la borda; **man o.!** ¡hombre al agua!; *Fam* **to go o.** pasarse

overcast ['əʊvəkɑːst] *adj* nublado(a)

overcharge [əʊvə'tʃɑːdʒ] *vt* **(a)** *(charge too much)* cobrar demasiado **(b)** *(overload)* sobrecargar

overcoat ['əʊvəkəʊt] *n* abrigo *m*

overcome [əʊvə'kʌm] *vt* **(a)** *(conquer)* vencer; **o. by grief** deshecho por el dolor **(b)** *(obstacle)* superar

overconfident [əʊvə'kɒnfɪdənt] *adj* presumido(a), creído(a)

overcrowded [əʊvə'kraʊdɪd] *adj (room)* atestado(a) (de gente); *(country)* superpoblado(a)

overcrowding [əʊvə'kraʊdɪŋ] *n (of prisons etc)* hacinamiento *m*; *(of country)* superpoblación *f*

overdo [əʊvə'duː] *vt (pt overdid* [əʊvə'dɪd]; *pp overdone* [əʊvə'dʌn]*) (a) (carry too far)* exagerar; **don't o. it** no te pases **(b)** *Culin* cocer or asar demasiado

overdose ['əʊvədəʊs] *n* sobredosis *f*

overdraft ['əʊvədrɑːft] *n* giro *m* en descubierto; *(amount)* saldo *m* deudor

overdraw [əʊvə'drɔː] *vt* **to be overdrawn** tener la cuenta en descubierto

overdue [əʊvə'djuː] *adj (rent, train etc)* atrasado(a); *(reform)* largamente esperado(a)

overestimate [əʊvər'estɪmeɪt] *vt* sobreestimar

overflow 1 *vi* [əʊvə'fləʊ] *(river)* desbordarse; *(cup etc)* derramarse
2 *n* ['əʊvəfləʊ] *(of river etc)* desbordamiento *m*; **o. pipe** cañería *f* de desagüe

overgrown [əʊvə'grəʊn] *adj* **(a)** *(with grass)* cubierto(a) (de hierba) **(b)** *(in size)* demasiado grande

overhaul 1 *vt* [əʊvə'hɔːl] revisar
2 *n* ['əʊvəhɔːl] revisión *f* y reparación *f*

overhead 1 *adj* ['əʊvəhed] (por) encima de la cabeza; **o. cable** cable aéreo
2 *adv* [əʊvə'hed] arriba, por encima de la cabeza
3 *n* ['əʊvəhed] *US* = **overheads**

overheads ['əʊvəhedz] *npl Br* gastos *mpl* generales

overhear [əʊvə'hɪə(r)] *vt (pt & pp overheard* [əʊvə'hɜːd]*)* oír por casualidad

overheat [əʊvə'hiːt] *vi* recalentarse

overjoyed [əʊvə'dʒɔɪd] *adj* rebosante de alegría

overlap [əʊvə'læp] *vi* superponerse; *Fig* **our plans o.** nuestros planes coinciden parcialmente

overleaf [əʊvə'liːf] *adv* al dorso

overload 1 *vt* [əʊvə'ləʊd] sobrecargar
2 *n* ['əʊvələʊd] sobrecarga *f*

overlook [əʊvə'lʊk] *vt* **(a)** *(fail to notice)* saltarse **(b)** *(ignore)* no hacer caso de; **we'll o. it this time** esta vez haremos la vista gorda **(c)** *(have a view of)* dar a, tener vista a

overmanning [əʊvə'mænɪŋ] *n Ind* exceso *m* de empleados

overnight 1 *adv* [əʊvə'naɪt] **(a)** *(during the night)* por la noche; **we stayed there o.** pasamos la noche allí **(b)** *(suddenly)* de la noche a la mañana
2 *adj* ['əʊvənaɪt] *(sudden)* repentino(a)

overpass ['əʊvəpɑːs] *n Br* paso *m* elevado

overpay [əʊvə'peɪ] *vt (pt & pp overpaid* [əʊvə'peɪd]*)* pagar demasiado

overpower [əʊvə'paʊə(r)] *vt* **(a)** *(subdue)* dominar **(b)** *(affect strongly)* abrumar

overrate [əʊvə'reɪt] *vt* sobreestimar, supervalorar

override [əʊvə'raɪd] *vt (pt overrode; pp overridden* [əʊvə'rɪdən]*) (a) (disregard)* hacer caso omiso de **(b)** *(annul, cancel out)* anular **(c)** *(be more important than)* contar más que

overriding [əʊvə'raɪdɪŋ] *adj* principal; *(importance)* primordial; *(need)* imperioso(a)

overrode [əʊvə'rəʊd] *pt of* **override**

overrule [əʊvə'ruːl] *vt* invalidar; *Jur* denegar

overrun [əʊvə'rʌn] *vt* **(a)** *(country)* invadir **(b)** *(allotted time)* excederse de

oversaw [əʊvə'sɔː] *pt of* **oversee**

overseas 1 *adv* [əʊvə'siːz] en ultramar; **to live o.** vivir en el extranjero
2 *adj* ['əʊvəsiːz] *de* ultramar; *(person)* extranjero(a); *(trade)* exterior

oversee [əʊvə'siː] *vt (pt oversaw; pp overseen* [əʊvə'siːn]*)* supervisar

overseer ['əʊvəsiːə(r)] *n* supervisor(a) *m,f*; *(foreman)* capataz *m*

overshadow [əʊvə'ʃædəʊ] *vt Fig* eclipsar

overshoot [əʊvə'ʃuːt] *vt (pt & pp overshot* [əʊvə'ʃɒt]*)* **to o. a turning** pasarse un cruce; *Fig* **to o. the mark** pasarse de la raya

oversight ['əʊvəsaɪt] *n* descuido *m*

oversleep [əʊvə'sliːp] *vi (pt & pp overslept* [əʊvə'slept]*)* quedarse dormido(a)

overspill ['əʊvəspɪl] *n* exceso *m* de población

overstate [əʊvə'steɪt] *vt* exagerar

overstep [əʊvə'step] *vt Fig* **to o. the mark** pasarse de la raya

overt [əʊ'vɜːt] *adj* patente

overtake [əʊvə'teɪk] *vt (pt overtook; pp overtaken* [əʊvə'teɪkən]*) (a) Br Aut* adelantar **(b)** *(surpass)* superar a **(c)** *(of night)* sorprender

overthrow [əʊvə'θrəʊ] *vt (pt overthrew* [əʊvə'θruː]; *pp overthrown* [əʊvə'θrəʊn]*) (government)* derribar

overtime ['əʊvətaɪm] *n* **(a)** *(work)* horas *fpl* extra **(b)** *US* prórroga *f*

overtone ['əʊvətəʊn] *n* matiz *m*

overtook [əʊvə'tʊk] *pt of* **overtake**

overture ['əʊvətjʊə(r)] *n* (**a**) *Mus* obertura *f*; *Fig (introduction)* introducción *f* (**b**) *(proposal)* propuesta *f*

overturn [əʊvə'tɜːn] *vt & vi* volcar

overweight [əʊvə'weɪt] *adj* demasiado pesado(a)

overwhelm [əʊvə'welm] *vt* (**a**) *(defeat)* aplastar; *(overpower)* abrumar; **I'm overwhelmed** estoy abrumado (**b**) *(with letters, work etc)* inundar

overwhelming [əʊvə'welmɪŋ] *adj (defeat)* aplastante; *(desire etc)* irresistible

overwork [əʊvə'wɜːk] **1** *vi* trabajar demasiado

2 *vt (person)* forzar; *(excuse etc)* abusar de

overwrought [əʊvə'rɔːt] *adj* (**a**) *(tense)* muy nervioso(a) (**b**) *Literary (too elaborate)* forzado(a)

owe [əʊ] *vt* deber

owing ['əʊɪŋ] *adj* **o. to** debido a, a causa de

owl [aʊl] *n* lechuza *f*, búho *m*

own [əʊn] **1** *adj* propio(a); **it's his o. fault** es culpa suya

2 *pron* (**a**) **my o./your o./his o.***etc* lo mío/lo tuyo/lo suyo/*etc*; *Fig* **to come into one's o.** realizarse; *Fam* **to get one's o. back** tomarse la revancha (**b**) **on one's o.** *(without help)* uno(a) mismo(a); *(alone)* solo(a)

3 *vt* poseer, ser dueño(a) de

▸ **own up** *vi* **to o. up (to sth)** confesar (algo)

owner ['əʊnə(r)] *n* propietario(a) *m,f*, dueño(a) *m,f*

ownership ['əʊnəʃɪp] *n* propiedad *f*, posesión *f*

ox [ɒks] *n (pl* **oxen** ['ɒksən]) buey *m*

oxide ['ɒksaɪd] *n Chem* óxido *m*

oxtail ['ɒksteɪl] *n* rabo *m* de buey

oxygen ['ɒksɪdʒən] *n* oxígeno *m*; **o. mask** máscara *f* de oxígeno

oyster ['ɔɪstə(r)] *n* ostra *f*

ozone ['əʊzəʊn] *n* ozono *m*; **o. layer** capa *f* de ozono

P

P, p [pi:] *n (the letter)* P, p *f*

p (**a**) *(pl* **pp**) *(abbr* **page**) pág., p (**b**) [pi:] *Br Fam (abbr* **penny, pence**) penique(s) *m(pl)*

PA [pi:'eɪ] *n Fam* (**a**) *(abbr* **personal assistant**) ayudante *mf* personal (**b**) *(abbr* **public-address (system)**) megafonía *f*

p.a. *(abbr* **per annum**) al año

pace [peɪs] **1** *n (step)* paso *m; (speed)* ritmo *m*; **to keep p. with** seguir a; *Fig* avanzar al mismo ritmo que; **to set the p.** marcar el paso; *Fig* marcar la pauta

  2 *vi* **to p. up and down** ir de un lado a otro

pacemaker ['peɪsmeɪkə(r)] *n Sport* liebre *f; Med* marcapasos *m inv*

Pacific [pə'sɪfɪk] *adj* **the P. (Ocean)** el (océano) Pacífico

pacifier ['pæsɪfaɪə(r)] *n US (for baby)* chupete *m*

pacifist ['pæsɪfɪst] *adj & n* pacifista *(mf)*

pacify ['pæsɪfaɪ] *vt (person)* calmar; *(country)* pacificar

pack¹ [pæk] **1** *n (parcel)* paquete *m; (bundle)* bulto *m; (of cigarettes)* paquete; *Br (of cards)* baraja *f; (of hounds)* jauría *f*

  2 *vt* (**a**) *(goods)* embalar, envasar; *(in suitcase)* poner; **to p. one's bags** hacer las maletas; *Fig* marcharse (**b**) *(fill)* atestar (**c**) *(press down) (snow)* apretar

  3 *vi* (**a**) hacer las maletas; *Fam* **to send sb packing** mandar a paseo a algn (**b**) *(of people)* apiñarse (**into** en)

  ▸ **pack in** *vt sep Br Fam (give up)* dejar

  ▸ **pack off** *vt sep Fam* mandar

  ▸ **pack up** *Fam* **1** *vt sep (give up)* dejar

  2 *vi (stop working)* terminar; *(machine etc)* estropearse

pack² [pæk] *vt (meeting)* llenar de partidarios

package ['pækɪdʒ] **1** *n* (**a**) *(parcel)* paquete *m; (bundle)* bulto *m* (**b**) *(of proposals etc)* paquete *m; (agreement)* acuerdo *m*; **p. deal** convenio *m* general; **p. tour** viaje *m* todo incluido

  2 *vt (goods)* envasar, embalar

packet ['pækɪt] *n* paquete *m; Fam (fortune)* dineral *m*

packing ['pækɪŋ] *n* embalaje *m*; **p. case** caja *f* de embalar; **to do one's p.** hacer las maletas

pact [pækt] *n* pacto *m*

pad¹ [pæd] **1** *n* (**a**) almohadilla *f; (of paper)* bloc *m*, taco *m* (**b**) **launch p.** plataforma *f* de lanzamiento (**c**) *Fam (flat)* piso *m*

  2 *vt (chair)* acolchar

  ▸ **pad out** *vt sep Fig* meter paja en

pad² [pæd] *vi* **to p. about** *or* **around** andar silenciosamente

padding ['pædɪŋ] *n (material)* relleno *m; Fig (in speech etc)* paja *f*

paddle¹ ['pædəl] **1** *n* (**a**) *(oar)* pala *f*; **p. boat** *or* **steamer** vapor *m* de ruedas (**b**) *US (for table tennis)* pala *f*

  2 *vt (boat)* remar con pala en

  3 *vi (in boat)* remar con pala

paddle² ['pædəl] *vi* chapotear

paddling pool ['pædlɪŋpu:l] *n Br* piscina *f* para niños

paddock ['pædək] *n* potrero *m; (in race course)* paddock *m*

paddy ['pædɪ] *n* arrozal *m*

padlock ['pædlɒk] **1** *n* candado *m*

  2 *vt* cerrar con candado

paediatrician [pi:dɪə'trɪʃən] *n* pediatra *mf*

pagan ['peɪgən] *adj & n* pagano(a) *(m,f)*

page¹ [peɪdʒ] *n* página *f*

page² [peɪdʒ] **1** *n (servant)* paje *m; (of knight)* escudero *m; (at club)* botones *m inv*

  2 *vt (call)* llamar por altavoz

pageant ['pædʒənt] *n (show)* espectáculo *m; (procession)* desfile *m; (on horses)* cabalgata *f*

pageantry ['pædʒəntrɪ] *n* pompa *f*, boato *m*

paid [peɪd] **1** *adj* pagado(a); *Fig* **to put p. to sth** acabar con algo

  2 *pt & pp of* **pay**

pail [peɪl] *n* cubo *m; (child's)* cubito *m*

pain [peɪn] **1** *n* (**a**) dolor *m; (grief)* sufrimiento *m; Fam* **he's a p. (in the neck)** es un pelmazo; **on p. of death** so pena de muerte (**b**) **to take pains over sth** esmerarse en algo

  2 *vt (grieve)* dar pena a

pained [peɪnd] *adj* de reproche

painful ['peɪnfəl] *adj* doloroso(a); *Fam (very bad)* malísimo(a)

painfully ['peɪnfəlɪ] *adv* (**a**) **p. shy** lastimosamente tímido(a) (**b**) *Fam* terriblemente

painkiller ['peɪnkɪlə(r)] *n* analgésico *m*

painless ['peɪnlɪs] *adj* sin dolor; *Fig* sin dificultades

painstaking ['peɪnzteɪkɪŋ] *adj (person)* concienzudo(a); *(care, research)* esmerado(a)

paint [peɪnt] **1** *n* pintura *f*

  2 *vt* pintar; **to p. sth white** pintar algo de blanco

  3 *vi* pintar

paintbrush ['peɪntbrʌʃ] *n Art* pincel *m; (for walls)* brocha *f*

painter ['peɪntə(r)] *n* pintor(a) *m,f*

painting ['peɪntɪŋ] *n* cuadro *m; (activity)* pintura *f*

paintwork ['peɪntwɜːk] *n* pintura *f*

pair [peə(r)] *n (of gloves, shoes)* par *m; (of people, cards)* pareja *f*; **a p. of scissors** unas tijeras; **a p. of trousers** un pantalón, unos pantalones

pajamas [pə'dʒæməz] *npl US* = **pyjamas**

Pakistan [pɑːkɪ'stɑːn] *n* Paquistán

Pakistani [pɑːkɪ'stɑːnɪ] *adj & n* paquistaní *(mf)*

pal [pæl] *n Fam* amigo(a) *m,f*, colega *mf*

palace ['pælɪs] *n* palacio *m*

palatable ['pælətəbəl] *adj (tasty)* sabroso(a); *Fig* aceptable

palate ['pælɪt] *n* paladar *m*

palatial [pə'leɪʃəl] *adj* suntuoso(a), señorial

palaver [pə'lɑːvə(r)] *n Fam* lío *m*, follón *m*

pale¹ [peɪl] **1** *adj (skin)* pálido(a); *(colour)* claro(a); *(light)* tenue; **to turn p.** palidecer
2 *vi* palidecer

pale² [peɪl] *n Fig* **to be beyond the p.** ser inaceptable

Palestine ['pælɪstaɪn] *n* Palestina

Palestinian [pælɪ'stɪnɪən] *adj & n* palestino(a) *(m,f)*

palette ['pælɪt] *n* paleta *f*; **p. knife** espátula *f*

paling ['peɪlɪŋ] *n* valla *f*

palisade [pælɪ'seɪd] *n* palizada *f*, estacada *f*

pall¹ [pɔːl] *n Fig* manto *m; (of smoke)* cortina *f*

pall² [pɔːl] *vi* aburrir; **it never palls** nunca cansa

pallet ['pælɪt] *n* plataforma *f* de carga

pallid ['pælɪd] *adj* pálido(a)

pallor ['pælə(r)] *n* palidez *f*

palm¹ [pɑːm] *n (tree)* palmera *f; (leaf)* palma *f*; **date p.** palma datilera; **P. Sunday** domingo *m* de Ramos

palm² [pɑːm] *n Anat* palma *f*
▸ **palm off** *vt sep* **to p. sth off on sb** colocar *or* endosar algo a algn

palmistry ['pɑːmɪstrɪ] *n* quiromancia *f*

palpable ['pælpəbəl] *adj* palpable

palpitate ['pælpɪteɪt] *vi* palpitar

palpitation [pælpɪ'teɪʃən] *n* palpitación *f*

paltry ['pɔːltrɪ] *adj (paltrier, paltriest)* insignificante

pamper ['pæmpə(r)] *vt* mimar, consentir

pamphlet ['pæmflɪt] *n* folleto *m*

pan¹ [pæn] **1** *n* (a) *(saucepan)* cazuela *f*, cacerola *f* (b) *(of scales)* platillo *m* (c) *(of lavatory)* taza *f*
2 *vt Fam (criticize)* dejar por los suelos

pan² [pæn] *vi Cin* tomar vistas panorámicas

panacea [pænə'sɪə] *n* panacea *f*

panache [pə'næʃ] *n* garbo *m*, salero *m*

Panama ['pænəmɑː] *n* Panamá; **P. Canal** Canal *m* de Panamá

pancake ['pænkeɪk] *n* crepe *f*

panda ['pændə] *n* panda *m; Br* **p. car** coche *m* patrulla

pandemonium [pændɪ'məʊnɪəm] *n* alboroto *m*

pander ['pændə(r)] *vi* **to p. to** *(person)* complacer a; *(wishes)* acceder a

pane [peɪn] *n* cristal *m*, vidrio *m*

panel ['pænəl] *n* (a) *(of wall)* panel *m; (flat surface)* tabla *f; (of instruments)* tablero *m; (of ceiling)* artesón *m* (b) *(jury)* jurado *m; Rad & TV* concursantes *mpl*

panelling, *US* **paneling** ['pænəlɪŋ] *n* paneles *mpl*

pang [pæŋ] *n (of pain, hunger)* punzada *f; (of childbirth)* dolores *mpl; Fig (of conscience)* remordimiento *m*

panic ['pænɪk] **1** *n* pánico *m*; **to get into a p.** ponerse histérico(a)
2 *vi* aterrarse

panicky ['pænɪkɪ] *adj* asustadizo(a)

panic-stricken ['pænɪkstrɪkən] *adj* aterrado(a)

panorama [pænə'rɑːmə] *n* panorama *m*

pansy ['pænzɪ] *n Bot* pensamiento *m; Fam Pej* mariquita *m*

pant [pænt] **1** *n* jadeo *m*
2 *vi* jadear

panther ['pænθə(r)] *n* pantera *f*

panties ['pæntɪz] *npl* bragas *fpl*

🖉 Note that the Spanish word **panty** is a false friend and is never a translation for the English word **panties**. In Spanish, **panty** means "(pair of) tights".

---

pantomime ['pæntəmaɪm] *n Th (play)* función *f* musical navideña; *(mime)* pantomima *f*

pantry ['pæntrɪ] *n* despensa *f*

pants [pænts] *npl Br (underpants) (ladies')* bragas *fpl; (men's)* calzoncillos *mpl; US (trousers)* pantalones *mpl*, pantalón *m*

pantyhose ['pæntɪhəʊz] *n US* medias *fpl*, pantis *mpl*

papal ['peɪpəl] *adj* papal

paper ['peɪpə(r)] **1** *n* (a) papel *m; Fig* **on p.** en teoría; **p. money** papel moneda; **writing p.** papel de escribir (b) *(exam)* examen *m; (essay)* trabajo *m* (escrito) (c) *Pol* libro *m* (d) *(newspaper)* periódico *m*; **the papers** la prensa (e) **papers** *(documents)* documentos *mpl*
2 *vt* empapelar

paperback ['peɪpəbæk] *n* libro *m* en rústica

paperclip ['peɪpəklɪp] *n* clip *m*, sujetapapeles *m inv*

paperweight ['peɪpəweɪt] *n* pisapapeles *m inv*

paperwork ['peɪpəwɜːk] *n* papeleo *m*

papier-mâché [pæpjeɪ'mæʃeɪ] *n* cartón *m* piedra

paprika ['pæprɪkə] *n* pimentón molido

par [pɑː(r)] *n (parity)* igualdad *f; (in golf)* par *m; Fig* **it's p. for the course** es lo normal en estos casos; *Fig* **to feel below p.** estar en baja forma

parable ['pærəbəl] *n* parábola *f*

paracetamol [ˌpærə'siːtəmɒl] *n* paracetamol *m*

parachute ['pærəʃuːt] **1** *n* paracaídas *m inv*
   2 *vi* **to p. (down)** saltar *or* lanzarse en paracaídas

parade [pə'reɪd] **1** *n* desfile *m*; *Mil* **to be on p.** pasar revista
   2 *vt Mil* hacer desfilar; *Fig (flaunt)* hacer alarde de
   3 *vi (troops)* pasar revista; *(procession)* desfilar

paradise ['pærədaɪs] *n* paraíso *m*

paradox ['pærədɒks] *n* paradoja *f*

paradoxical [ˌpærə'dɒksɪkəl] *adj* paradójico(a)

paraffin ['pærəfɪn] *n* parafina *f*; **liquid p.** aceite *m* de parafina; **p. lamp** lámpara *f* de petróleo

paragliding ['pærəglaɪdɪŋ] *n* parapente *m*

paragon ['pærəgən] *n* modelo *m*

paragraph ['pærəgrɑːf] *n* párrafo *m*

Paraguay ['pærəgwaɪ] *n* Paraguay

Paraguayan [ˌpærə'gwaɪən] *adj & n* paraguayo(a) *(m,f)*

parallel ['pærəlel] **1** *adj* paralelo(a) (**to** *or* **with** a); *Fig* comparable (**to** *or* **with** a)
   2 *n Geog* paralelo *m*; *Geom* paralela *f*; *Fig* paralelo
   3 *vt Fig* ser paralelo(a) a

paralyse ['pærəlaɪz] *vt* paralizar

paralysis [pə'rælɪsɪs] *n* parálisis *f*

paralyze ['pærəlaɪz] *vt US* = **paralyse**

paramedic [ˌpærə'medɪk] *n* auxiliar *mf* sanitario(a)

parameter [pə'ræmɪtə(r)] *n* parámetro *m*

paramilitary [ˌpærə'mɪlɪtərɪ] *adj* paramilitar

paramount ['pærəmaʊnt] *adj* **of p. importance** de suma importancia

paranoid ['pærənɔɪd] *adj & n* paranoico(a) *(m,f)*

paraphernalia [ˌpærəfə'neɪlɪə] *n* parafernalia *f*

paraphrase ['pærəfreɪz] *vt* parafrasear

parasite ['pærəsaɪt] *n* parásito *m*

parasol ['pærəsɒl] *n* sombrilla *f*

paratrooper ['pærətruːpə(r)] *n* paracaidista *mf*

parcel ['pɑːsəl] **1** *n* paquete *m*; **p. bomb** paquete bomba
   2 *vt* **to p. up** envolver, empaquetar

parched [pɑːtʃt] *adj (land)* reseco(a); *(lips, mouth)* seco(a); *Fig* **to be p.** estar muerto(a) de sed

parchment ['pɑːtʃmənt] *n* pergamino *m*

pardon ['pɑːdən] **1** *n* perdón *m*; *Jur* indulto *m*; **I beg your p.** (Usted) perdone; **(I beg your) p.?** ¿cómo (dice)?
   2 *vt* perdonar; *Jur* indultar; **p. me!** ¡Usted perdone!

parent ['peərənt] *n* **parents** padres *mpl*

> 🖉 Note that the Spanish word **pariente** is a false friend and is never a translation for the English word **parent**. In Spanish, **pariente** means "relative, relation".

parental [pə'rentəl] *adj* paternal; **p. guidance** consejos *mpl* paternales

parenthesis [pə'renθɪsɪs] *n* (*pl* **parentheses** [pə'renθɪsiːz]) paréntesis *m inv*; **in p.** entre paréntesis

pariah [pə'raɪə] *n* paria *mf*

Paris ['pærɪs] *n* París

parish ['pærɪʃ] *n* parroquia *f*

Parisian [pə'rɪzɪən] *adj & n* parisino(a) *(m,f)*

parity ['pærɪtɪ] *n* igualdad *f*; *(of shares)* paridad *f*

park [pɑːk] **1** *n* parque *m*
   2 *vt (car)* aparcar, *Carib, Col, Pan* parquear

parking ['pɑːkɪŋ] *n* aparcamiento *m*, estacionamiento *m*; **no p.** *(sign)* prohibido aparcar; *US* **p. lot** parking *m*, aparcamiento *m*; **p. meter** parquímetro *m*; **p. space** aparcamiento

parliament ['pɑːləmənt] *n* parlamento *m*

parliamentary [pɑːlə'mentərɪ] *adj* parlamentario(a)

parlour, *US* **parlor** ['pɑːlə(r)] *n* salón *m*

parochial [pə'rəʊkɪəl] *adj* parroquial; *Pej (narrow-minded)* de miras estrechas

parody ['pærədɪ] *n* parodia *f*

parole [pə'rəʊl] *n Jur* libertad *f* condicional; **on p.** en libertad bajo palabra

parquet ['pɑːkeɪ] *n* **p. floor** suelo *m* de parqué

parrot ['pærət] *n* loro *m*, papagayo *m*

parry ['pærɪ] *vt* parar

parsimonious [ˌpɑːsɪ'məʊnɪəs] *adj* tacaño(a)

parsley ['pɑːslɪ] *n* perejil *m*

parsnip ['pɑːsnɪp] *n* chirivía *f*

parson ['pɑːsən] *n* cura *m*

part [pɑːt] **1** *n* (**a**) parte *f*; *(piece)* trozo *m*; *(episode)* capítulo *m*; *Tech* pieza *f*; **for the most p.** en la mayor parte (**b**) *Cin Th* papel *m*; **to play a p. in sth** desempeñar un papel en algo; **to take p. in sth** participar en algo (**c**) *(place)* lugar *m*; **in these parts** por estos lugares (**d**) **for my p.** por mi parte; **to take sb's p.** tomar partido por algn; **to take sth in good p.** tomarse bien algo (**e**) *US (in hair)* raya *f*
   2 *adj (partial)* parcial; **in p. exchange** como parte del pago
   3 *adv (partly)* en parte
   4 *vt (separate)* separar; **to p. company with sb** separarse de algn; **to p. one's hair** hacerse la raya (en el pelo)
   ▸ *vi* separarse; *(say goodbye)* despedirse
   ▸ **part with** *vt insep* separarse de

partial ['pɑːʃəl] *adj* parcial; **to be p. to sth** ser aficionado(a) a algo

participant [pɑː'tɪsɪpənt] *n* participante *mf*; *(in competition)* concursante *mf*

participate [pɑː'tɪsɪpeɪt] *vi* participar (**in** en)

participation [pɑːtɪsɪ'peɪʃən] *n* participación *f*

participle ['pɑːtɪsɪpəl] *n* participio *m*

particle ['pɑːtɪkəl] *n* partícula *f*

particular [pə'tɪkjʊlə(r)] **1** *adj* (**a**) *(special)* particular, especial; **in this p. case** en este caso concreto; **that p. person** esa persona en particular (**b**) *(fussy)* exigente

2 *npl* **particulars** pormenores *mpl*; **to take down sb's particulars** anotar los datos personales de algn

particularly [pə'tɪkjʊləlɪ] *adv* particularmente, especialmente

parting ['pɑːtɪŋ] **1** *n* *(separation)* separación *f*; *(farewell)* despedida *f*; *Br (in hair)* raya *f*

2 *adj* de despedida

partisan [pɑːtɪ'zæn, 'pɑːtɪzæn] **1** *n* *Mil* guerrillero(a) *m,f*; *(supporter)* partidario(a) *m,f*

2 *adj* *(supporter)* a ultranza; *(of party)* partidista

partition [pɑː'tɪʃən] **1** *n* *(wall)* tabique *m*; *(of country)* partición *f*

2 *vt* dividir

partly ['pɑːtlɪ] *adv* en parte

partner ['pɑːtnə(r)] **1** *n* compañero(a) *m,f*; *(in dancing, tennis)* pareja *f*; *(husband)* marido *m*; *(wife)* mujer *f*; *Com* socio(a) *m,f*

2 *vt* acompañar

partnership ['pɑːtnəʃɪp] *n* *(relationship)* vida *f* en común; *Com* sociedad *f*

partridge ['pɑːtrɪdʒ] *n* perdiz pardilla

part-time ['pɑːt'taɪm] **1** *adj* *(work etc)* de tiempo parcial

2 *adv* a tiempo parcial

party ['pɑːtɪ] **1** *n* (**a**) *(celebration)* fiesta *f* (**b**) *(group)* grupo *m* (**c**) *Pol* partido *m*; **p. political broadcast** espacio *m* electoral (**d**) *Jur* parte *f*

2 *adj* de fiesta; *Tel* **p. line** línea compartida

pass [pɑːs] **1** *n* (**a**) *(of mountain)* desfiladero *m* (**b**) *(permit)* permiso *m*; **bus p.** abono *m* de autobús

(**c**) *Sport* pase *m*

(**d**) *Fam* **to make a p. at sb** intentar ligar con algn

2 *vt* (**a**) pasar; *(overtake)* adelantar

(**b**) *(exam, law)* aprobar; *Jur* **to p. sentence** dictar sentencia

3 *vi* (**a**) pasar; *(procession)* desfilar; *(car)* adelantar; *(people)* cruzarse; *Sport* hacer un pase; **we passed on the stairs** nos cruzamos en la escalera

(**b**) *(pain)* remitir; *(opportunity)* perderse; *(time)* pasar

(**c**) *(happen)* ocurrir, pasar

(**d**) *(in exam)* aprobar

▸ **pass away** *vi Euph* pasar a mejor vida

▸ **pass by 1** *vt sep* pasar de largo

2 *vi* pasar

▸ **pass for** *vt insep* pasar por

▸ **pass off** *vt sep* hacer pasar; **to p. oneself off as sth** hacerse pasar por algo

2 *vi (happen)* transcurrir

▸ **pass on 1** *vt sep (hand on)* transmitir

2 *vi Euph* pasar a mejor vida

▸ **pass out** *vi (faint)* desmayarse; *Mil* graduarse

▸ **pass over** *vt insep* (**a**) *(aircraft)* volar por (**b**) *(disregard)* pasar por alto

▸ **pass up** *vt sep Fam (opportunity)* renunciar; *(offer)* rechazar

passable ['pɑːsəbəl] *adj (road)* transitable; *(acceptable)* pasable

passage ['pæsɪdʒ] *n* (**a**) *(alleyway)* callejón *m*; *(hallway)* pasillo *m* (**b**) *(movement)* tránsito *m*; *Naut* travesía *f* (**c**) *Mus & Lit* pasaje *m*

passageway ['pæsɪdʒweɪ] *n* *(interior)* pasillo *m*; *(exterior)* pasaje *m*

passbook ['pɑːsbʊk] *n* libreta *f* de banco

passenger ['pæsɪndʒə(r)] *n* pasajero(a) *m,f*

passer-by [pɑːsə'baɪ] *n* transeúnte *mf*

passing ['pɑːsɪŋ] **1** *n* (**a**) *(of time)* transcurso *m*; **in p.** de pasada (**b**) *(of law)* aprobación *f*

2 *adj* que pasa; *(glance)* rápido(a); *(thought)* pasajero(a)

passion ['pæʃən] *n* pasión *f*; **p. fruit** granadilla *f*

passionate ['pæʃənɪt] *adj* apasionado(a)

passive ['pæsɪv] *adj* pasivo(a)

Passover ['pɑːsəʊvə(r)] *n* Pascua *f* de los judíos

passport ['pɑːspɔːt] *n* pasaporte *m*

password ['pɑːswɜːd] *n* contraseña *f*

past [pɑːst] **1** *n* pasado *m*; **in the p.** en el pasado; **to have a p.** tener antecedentes

2 *adj* pasado(a); *(former)* anterior; **in the p. weeks** en las últimas semanas

3 *adv* por delante; **to run p.** pasar corriendo

4 *prep (beyond)* más allá de; *(more than)* más de; **he's p. forty** pasa de los cuarenta (años); **it's five p. ten** son las diez y cinco; *Fam* **to be p. it** estar muy carroza

pasta ['pæstə] *n* pasta *f*, pastas *fpl*

paste [peɪst] **1** *n* pasta *f*; *(glue)* engrudo *m*

2 *vt (stick)* pegar; *(put paste on)* engomar

pastel ['pæstəl] *adj & n* pastel *(m)*

pasteurized ['pæstjəraɪzd] *adj* pasteurizado(a)

pastille ['pæstɪl] *n* pastilla *f*

pastime ['pɑːstaɪm] *n* pasatiempo *m*

pastor ['pɑːstə(r)] *n* pastor *m*

pastoral ['pɑːstərəl] *adj* pastoral

pastry ['peɪstrɪ] *n* *(dough)* pasta *f*; *(cake)* pastel *m*

pasture ['pɑːstʃə(r)] *n* pasto *m*

pasty¹ ['pæstɪ] *n Culin* empanada *f*, pastel *m* de carne

pasty² ['peɪstɪ] *adj* (**pastier, pastiest**) *(complexion)* pálido(a)

pat [pæt] **1** *n (caress)* caricia *f*; *(tap)* palmadita *f*; *Fig* **to give sb a p. on the back** felicitar a algn

2 *vt* acariciar; **to p. sb on the back** dar a algn una palmadita en la espalda
patch [pætʃ] *n* (of material) parche *m*; (of land) terreno *m*; (of colour) mancha *f*; *Fig* **to go through a bad p.** pasar por una mala racha
▸ **patch up** *vt sep* (garment) poner un parche en; **to p. things up** (after argument) limar asperezas
patchwork ['pætʃwɜːk] **1** *n* labor *f* de retales
2 *adj* (quilt etc) hecho(a) con retales distintos
patchy ['pætʃɪ] *adj* (**patchier, patchiest**) (colour, performance) desigual; (knowledge) incompleto(a)
pâté ['pæteɪ] *n* paté *m*
patent¹ ['peɪtənt] **1** *n* *Com* patente *f*
2 *adj* (obvious) patente, evidente; **p. medicine** específico *m*
3 *vt* *Com* patentar
patent² ['peɪtənt] *n* **p. (leather)** charol *m*
patently ['peɪtəntlɪ] *adv* **it is p. obvious** está clarísimo
paternal [pə'tɜːnəl] *adj* paternal; (grandmother etc) paterno(a)
paternity [pə'tɜːnɪtɪ] *n* paternidad *f*
path [pɑːθ] *n* camino *m*, sendero *m*; (route) ruta *f*; (of missile) trayectoria *f*
pathetic [pə'θetɪk] *adj* (pitiful) patético(a); *Fam* (hopeless) malísimo(a); **she was a p. sight** daba lástima verla
pathological [pæθə'lɒdʒɪkəl] *adj* patológico(a)
pathologist [pə'θɒlədʒɪst] *n* patólogo(a) *m,f*
pathology [pə'θɒlədʒɪ] *n* patología *f*
pathos ['peɪθɒs] *n* patetismo *m*
pathway ['pɑːθweɪ] *n* camino *m*, sendero *m*
patience ['peɪʃəns] *n* (a) paciencia *f*; **to lose one's p. with sb** perder la paciencia con algn (b) *Br Cards* solitario *m*
patient ['peɪʃənt] **1** *adj* paciente; **to be p. with sb** tener paciencia con algn
2 *n* *Med* paciente *mf*
patio ['pætɪəʊ] *n* patio *m*
patriotic [pætrɪ'ɒtɪk] *adj* (person) patriota; (speech, act) patriótico(a)
patrol [pə'trəʊl] **1** *n* patrulla *f*; **p. car** coche *m* patrulla
2 *vt* patrullar por
patrolman [pə'trəʊlmən] *n* *US* policía *m*
patron ['peɪtrən] *n* (a) (of charity) patrocinador(a) *m,f*; (of arts) mecenas *m inv*; **p. saint** (santo(a) *m,f*) patrón(ona) *m,f* (b) (customer) cliente(a) *m,f* habitual
patronize ['pætrənaɪz] *vt* (a) (arts) fomentar; (shop) ser cliente(a) de; (club etc) frecuentar (b) *Pej* (person) tratar con condescendencia
patronizing ['pætrənaɪzɪŋ] *adj* *Pej* condescendiente
patter¹ ['pætə(r)] **1** *n* (of rain) repiqueteo *m*; (of feet) pasito *m*

2 *vi* (rain) repiquetear; (feet) hacer ruido sordo
patter² ['pætə(r)] *n* *Fam* labia *f*; (of salesman) discursillo preparado
pattern ['pætən] *n* *Sewing* patrón *m*; (design) dibujo *m*; (on material) estampado *m*; *Fig* (of behaviour) modelo *m*
paunch [pɔːntʃ] *n* panza *f*
pauper ['pɔːpə(r)] *n* pobre *mf*
pause [pɔːz] **1** *n* pausa *f*; (silence) silencio *m*
2 *vi* hacer una pausa; (be silent) callarse
pave [peɪv] *vt* pavimentar; (with stones) empedrar; *Fig* **to p. the way for sb/sth** preparar el terreno para algn/algo
pavement ['peɪvmənt] *n* (a) *Br* (beside road) acera *f*, *CSur, Perú* vereda *f*, *CAm, Méx* banqueta *f* (b) *US* (roadway) calzada *f*, pavimento *m*
pavilion [pə'vɪljən] *n* pabellón *m*; *Br Sport* (changing rooms) vestuarios *mpl*
paving ['peɪvɪŋ] *n* (on road) pavimento *m*; (on floor) enlosado *m*; (with stones) empedrado *m*; **p. stone** losa *f*
paw [pɔː] **1** *n* (of foot) pata *f*; (of cat) garra *f*; (of lion) zarpa *f*
2 *vt* (of lion) dar zarpazos a; *Pej* (of person) manosear, sobar
pawn¹ [pɔːn] *n* (in chess) peón *m*; *Fig* **to be sb's p.** ser el juguete de algn
pawn² [pɔːn] *vt* empeñar
pawnbroker ['pɔːnbrəʊkə(r)] *n* prestamista *mf*
pawnshop ['pɔːnʃɒp] *n* casa *f* de empeños
pay [peɪ] **1** *n* (wages) paga *f*, sueldo *m*; **p.** *Br* **packet** *or US* **envelope** sobre *m* de la paga; **p. rise** aumento *m* del sueldo; **p. slip** nómina *f*
2 *vt* (*pt & pp* **paid**) (a) pagar; **to be** *or* **get paid** cobrar (b) (attention) prestar; (homage) rendir; (visit) hacer; **to p. sb a compliment** halagar a algn (c) (be profitable for) compensar
3 *vi* (a) pagar; **to p. for sth** pagar (por) algo (b) (be profitable) ser rentable
▸ **pay back** *vt sep* reembolsar; *Fig* **to p. sb back** vengarse de algn
▸ **pay in** *vt sep* (money) ingresar
▸ **pay off 1** *vt sep* (debt) liquidar; (mortgage) cancelar
2 *vi* (be successful) dar resultado
▸ **pay out** *vt sep* (spend) gastar (**on** en)
▸ **pay up** *vi* pagar
payable ['peɪəbəl] *adj* pagadero(a)
payday ['peɪdeɪ] *n* día *m* de pago
payee [peɪ'iː] *n* portador(a) *m,f*
payment ['peɪmənt] *n* pago *m*; (of cheque) cobro *m*; **advance p.** anticipo *m*; **down p.** entrada *f*; **monthly p.** mensualidad *f*
payoff ['peɪɒf] *n* (reward) recompensa *f*; *Fam* (bribe) soborno *m*
pay-per-view ['peɪpə'vjuː] *n* pago *m* por visión
payroll ['peɪrəʊl] *n* nómina *f*

PC ['piː'siː] **1** *n* (**a**) *Br* (*abbr* **Police Constable**) agente *mf* de policía (**b**) (*abbr* **personal computer**) PC *m*
2 *adj* (*abbr* **politically correct**) políticamente correcto(a)

pc (*abbr* **per cent**) p.c.

PE ['piː'iː] *n Sch* (*abbr* **physical education**) educación *f* física

pea [piː] *n* guisante *m*, *Andes, Carib, RP* arveja *f*, *CAm, Méx* chícharo *m*

peace [piːs] *n* paz *f*; (*calm*) tranquilidad *f*; **at** *or* **in p.** en paz; **p. and quiet** tranquilidad; **to make p.** hacer las paces; (*of countries*) firmar la paz

peaceable ['piːsəbəl] *adj* pacífico(a)

peaceful ['piːsfʊl] *adj* (*demonstration*) pacífico(a); (*place*) tranquilo(a)

peace-keeping ['piːskiːpɪŋ] *adj* pacificador(a); **p. forces** fuerzas *fpl* de pacificación

peach [piːtʃ] *n* melocotón *m*, *Am* durazno *m*

peacock ['piːkɒk] *n* pavo *m* real

peak [piːk] *n* (*of cap*) visera *f*; (*of mountain*) pico *m*; (*summit*) cima *f*; *Fig* cumbre *f*; **p. hours** horas *fpl* punta; **p. period** horas de mayor consumo; **p. season** temporada alta

peal [piːl] *n* (*of bells*) repique *m*; **p. of thunder** trueno *m*; **peals of laughter** carcajadas *fpl*

peanut ['piːnʌt] *n* cacahuete *m*, maní *m*, *Méx* cacahuate *m*; **p. butter** mantequilla *f or* manteca *f* de cacahuete, maní, *Méx* cacahuate

pear [peə(r)] *n* pera *f*

pearl [pɜːl] *n* perla *f*

peasant ['pezənt] *adj & n* campesino(a) (*m,f*)

peat [piːt] *n* turba *f*; **p. bog** turbera *f*

pebble ['pebəl] *n* guijarro *m*; (*small*) china *f*

pecan [pɪˈkæn] *n* (*nut*) pacana *f*

peck [pek] **1** *n* (*of bird*) picotazo *m*; *Fam* (*kiss*) besito *m*
2 *vt* (*bird*) picotear; *Fam* (*kiss*) dar un besito a
3 *vi* **to p. at one's food** picar la comida

pecking order ['pekɪŋɔːdə(r)] *n Fig* jerarquía *f*

peckish ['pekɪʃ] *adj Fam* **to feel p.** empezar a tener hambre

peculiar [pɪˈkjuːlɪə(r)] *adj* (*odd*) extraño(a); (*particular*) característico(a)

peculiarity [pɪkjuːlɪˈærɪtɪ] *n* (*oddity*) rareza *f*; (*characteristic*) característica *f*, peculiaridad *f*

pedal ['pedəl] **1** *n* pedal *m*
2 *vi* pedalear

pedantic [pɪˈdæntɪk] *adj* pedante

peddle ['pedəl] *vt & vi Com* vender de puerta en puerta; **to p. drugs** traficar con drogas

peddler ['pedlə(r)] *n* (*of drugs*) traficante *mf*

pedestal ['pedɪstəl] *n* pedestal *m*; *Fig* **to put sb on a p.** poner a algn sobre un pedestal

pedestrian [pɪˈdestrɪən] **1** *n* peatón(ona) *m,f*; **p. crossing** paso *m* de peatones
2 *adj Pej* prosaico(a)

pediatrician [piːdɪəˈtrɪʃən] *n US* = **paediatrician**

pedigree ['pedɪgriː] **1** *n* linaje *m*; (*family tree*) árbol genealógico; (*of animal*) pedigrí *m*
2 *adj* (*animal*) de raza

pee [piː] *Fam* **1** *n* pis *m*
2 *vi* hacer pis

peek [piːk] **1** *n* ojeada *f*
2 *vi* **to p. at sth** mirar algo a hurtadillas

peel [piːl] **1** *n* piel *f*; (*of orange, lemon*) cáscara *f*
2 *vt* (*fruit*) pelar
3 *vi* (*paint*) desconcharse; (*wallpaper*) despegarse; (*skin*) pelarse

peeler ['piːlə(r)] *n* **potato p.** pelapatatas *m inv*

peelings ['piːlɪŋz] *npl* peladuras *fpl*, mondaduras *fpl*

peep¹ [piːp] *n* (*sound*) pío *m*

peep² [piːp] **1** *n* (*glance*) ojeada *f*; (*furtive look*) mirada furtiva
2 *vi* **to p. at sth** echar una ojeada a algo; **to p. out from behind sth** dejarse ver detrás de algo

peephole ['piːphəʊl] *n* mirilla *f*

peer¹ [pɪə(r)] *n* (*noble*) par *m*; (*equal*) igual *mf*; **p. group** grupo *m* paritario

peer² [pɪə(r)] *vi* mirar detenidamente; (*shortsightedly*) mirar con ojos de miope

peerage ['pɪərɪdʒ] *n* título *m* de nobleza

peeved [piːvd] *adj Fam* fastidiado(a), de mal humor

peevish ['piːvɪʃ] *adj* malhumorado(a)

peg [peg] **1** *n* clavija *f*; (*for coat, hat*) percha *f*
2 *vt* (*clothes*) tender; (*prices*) fijar

pejorative [pɪˈdʒɒrətɪv] *adj* peyorativo(a)

Pekinese [piːkəˈniːz] *adj & n* pequinés(esa) (*m,f*)

Peking [piːˈkɪŋ] *n* Pekín

pelican ['pelɪkən] *n* pelícano *m*; *Br* **p. crossing** paso *m* de peatones

pellet ['pelɪt] *n* bolita *f*; (*for gun*) perdigón *m*

pelt¹ [pelt] *n* (*skin*) pellejo *m*

pelt² [pelt] **1** *vt* **to p. sb with sth** tirar algo a algn
2 *vi Fam* (**a**) **it's pelting (down)** (*raining*) llueve a cántaros (**b**) **to p. along** (*rush*) correr a toda prisa

pelvis ['pelvɪs] *n* pelvis *f*

pen¹ [pen] **1** *n* pluma *f*, *RP* birome *f*
2 *vt* escribir

pen² [pen] **1** *n* (*enclosure*) corral *m*; (*for sheep*) redil *m*; (*for children*) corralito *m*
2 *vt* **to p. in** acorralar

penal ['piːnəl] *adj* penal

penalize ['piːnəlaɪz] *vt* castigar; *Sport* penalizar

penalty ['penəltɪ] *n* (*punishment*) pena *f*; *Sport* castigo *m*; *Ftb* penalti *m*; **to pay the p. for sth** cargar con las consecuencias de algo; **p. area** área *f* de castigo

penance ['penəns] *n* penitencia *f*

pence [pens] *pl of* **penny**

pencil ['pensəl] *n* lápiz *m*; **p. case** estuche *m* de lápices; **p. sharpener** sacapuntas *m inv*

pendant ['pendənt] n colgante m

pending ['pendɪŋ] **1** adj pendiente
  2 prep a la espera de; **p. a decision** (until) hasta que se tome una decisión

pendulum ['pendjʊləm] n péndulo m

penetrate ['penɪtreɪt] **1** vt penetrar; Fig adentrarse en
  2 vi atravesar; (get inside) penetrar

penetrating ['penɪtreɪtɪŋ] adj (look) penetrante; (mind) perspicaz; (sound) agudo(a)

penfriend ['penfrend] n amigo(a) m,f por carta

penguin ['peŋgwɪn] n pingüino m

penicillin [penɪ'sɪlɪn] n penicilina f

peninsula [pɪ'nɪnsjʊlə] n península f

penis ['piːnɪs] n pene m

penitent ['penɪtənt] adj Rel penitente; (repentant) arrepentido(a)

penitentiary [penɪ'tenʃərɪ] n US cárcel f, penal m

penknife ['pennaɪf] n navaja f, cortaplumas m inv

penniless ['penɪlɪs] adj sin dinero

penny ['penɪ] n (pl pennies, pence) Br penique m; US centavo m

penpal ['penpæl] n US = penfriend

pension ['penʃən] n pensión f; **retirement p.** jubilación f

pensioner ['penʃənə(r)] n jubilado(a) m,f

pensive ['pensɪv] adj pensativo(a)

pentagon ['pentəgɒn] n US Pol **the P.** el Pentágono

Pentecost ['pentɪkɒst] n Pentecostés m

penthouse ['penthaʊs] n ático m

pent-up ['pentʌp] adj reprimido(a)

penultimate [pɪ'nʌltɪmɪt] adj penúltimo(a)

people ['piːpəl] npl (a) gente f, (individuals) personas fpl; **many p.** mucha gente; **old p.'s home** asilo m de ancianos; **p. say that ...** se dice que ...; **some p.** algunas personas (b) (citizens) ciudadanos mpl; (inhabitants) habitantes mpl; **the p.** el pueblo (c) (nation) pueblo m, nación f

pep [pep] n Fam ánimo m, energía f; **p. talk** discurso m enardecedor
  ▸ **pep up** vt sep Fam animar

pepper ['pepə(r)] **1** n (spice) pimienta f; (fruit) pimiento m; **black p.** pimienta negra; **p. pot** pimentero m; **red/green p.** pimiento rojo/verde; **p. mill** molinillo m de pimienta
  2 vt Fig peppered with salpicado(a) de

peppermint ['pepəmɪnt] n menta f; (sweet) pastilla f de menta

per [pɜː(r)] prep por; **five times p. week** cinco veces a la semana; **p. cent** por ciento; **p. day/annum** al or por día/año; **p. capita** per cápita

perceive [pə'siːv] vt (see) percibir

percentage [pə'sentɪdʒ] n porcentaje m

perceptible [pə'septəbəl] adj (visible) perceptible; (sound) audible; (improvement) sensible

perception [pə'sepʃən] n percepción f

perceptive [pə'septɪv] adj perspicaz

perch¹ [pɜːtʃ] n (fish) perca f

perch² [pɜːtʃ] **1** n (for bird) percha f
  2 vi (bird) posarse (**on** en)

percolate ['pɜːkəleɪt] **1** vt filtrar; **percolated coffee** café m de cafetera
  2 vi filtrarse

percolator ['pɜːkəleɪtə(r)] n cafetera f

percussion [pə'kʌʃən] n percusión f

perennial [pə'renɪəl] adj Bot perenne

perfect 1 adj ['pɜːfɪkt] perfecto(a); **he's a p. stranger to us** nos es totalmente desconocido; **p. tense** tiempo perfecto
  2 vt [pə'fekt] perfeccionar

perfection [pə'fekʃən] n perfección f

perfectly ['pɜːfɪktlɪ] adv perfectamente; (absolutely) completamente

perforate ['pɜːfəreɪt] vt perforar

perforation [pɜːfə'reɪʃən] n perforación f; (on stamps etc) perforado m

perform [pə'fɔːm] **1** vt (task) ejecutar, realizar; (piece of music) interpretar; Th representar
  2 vi (machine) funcionar; Mus interpretar; Th actuar

performance [pə'fɔːməns] n (of task) ejecución f, realización f; Mus interpretación f; Th representación f; Sport actuación f; (of machine etc) rendimiento m

performer [pə'fɔːmə(r)] n Mus intérprete mf; Th actor m, actriz f

perfume ['pɜːfjuːm] n perfume m

perfunctory [pə'fʌŋktərɪ] adj superficial

perhaps [pə'hæps, præps] adv tal vez, quizá(s)

peril ['perɪl] n (risk) riesgo m; (danger) peligro m

perilous ['perɪləs] adj (risky) arriesgado(a); (dangerous) peligroso(a)

perilously ['perɪləslɪ] adv peligrosamente

perimeter [pə'rɪmɪtə(r)] n perímetro m

period ['pɪərɪəd] **1** n (a) período m; (stage) etapa f (b) Educ clase f (c) US (full stop) punto m (d) (menstruation) regla f
  2 adj (dress, furniture) de época

periodic [pɪərɪ'ɒdɪk] adj periódico(a)

periodical [pɪərɪ'ɒdɪkəl] **1** adj periódico(a)
  2 n revista f

periodically [pɪərɪ'ɒdɪklɪ] adv de vez en cuando

peripheral [pə'rɪfərəl] **1** adj periférico(a)
  2 n Comput unidad periférica

perish ['perɪʃ] vi perecer; (material) echarse a perder

perishable ['perɪʃəbəl] adj perecedero(a)

perjury ['pɜːdʒərɪ] n perjurio m

perk [pɜːk] n Fam extra m
  ▸ **perk up** vi (person) animarse; (after illness) reponerse

perky ['pɜːkɪ] adj (perkier, perkiest) animado(a), alegre

perm [pɜːm] **1** *n* permanente *f*
2 *vt* **to have one's hair permed** hacerse la permanente
permanent ['pɜːmənənt] *adj* permanente; *(address, job)* fijo(a)
permeate ['pɜːmɪeɪt] *vt & vi* penetrar; *Fig* extenderse por
permissible [pə'mɪsəbəl] *adj* admisible
permission [pə'mɪʃən] *n* permiso *m*
permissive [pə'mɪsɪv] *adj* permisivo(a)
permit 1 *n* [pɜːmɪt] permiso *m*; *Com* licencia *f*
2 *vt* [pə'mɪt] **to p. sb to do sth** permitir a algn hacer algo
pernicious [pə'nɪʃəs] *adj* pernicioso(a)
perpendicular [pɜːpən'dɪkjʊlə(r)] **1** *adj* perpendicular; *(cliff)* vertical
2 *n* perpendicular *f*
perpetrate ['pɜːpɪtreɪt] *vt* cometer
perpetual [pə'petʃʊəl] *adj (noise)* continuo(a); *(arguing)* interminable; *(snow)* perpetuo(a)
perplex [pə'pleks] *vt* dejar perplejo(a)
perplexing [pə'pleksɪŋ] *adj* desconcertante
persecute ['pɜːsɪkjuːt] *vt* perseguir; *(harass)* acosar
persecution [pɜːsɪ'kjuːʃən] *n* persecución *f*; *(harassment)* acoso *m*
perseverance [pɜːsɪ'vɪərəns] *n* perseverancia *f*
persevere [pɜːsɪ'vɪə(r)] *vi* perseverar
Persian ['pɜːʒən] *adj* persa; **P. Gulf** golfo Pérsico
persist [pə'sɪst] *vi* empeñarse (**in** en)
persistence [pə'sɪstəns] *n* empeño *m*
persistent [pə'sɪstənt] *adj (person)* perseverante; *(smell etc)* persistente; *(continual)* constante
person ['pɜːsən] *n (pl people)* persona *f*; *(individual)* individuo *m*; **in p.** en persona
personable ['pɜːsənəbəl] *adj (handsome)* bien parecido(a); *(pleasant)* amable
personal ['pɜːsənəl] **(a)** *adj (private)* personal; *(friend)* íntimo(a); **p. computer** ordenador *m* personal, *Am* computadora *f* personal; **p. column** anuncios *mpl* personales; **p. pronoun** pronombre *m* personal **(b)** *(in person)* en persona; **he will make a p. appearance** estará aquí en persona **(c)** *Pej (comment etc)* indiscreto(a)
personality [pɜːsə'nælɪtɪ] *n* personalidad *f*
personally ['pɜːsənəlɪ] *adv (for my part)* personalmente; *(in person)* en persona
personify [pɜː'sɒnɪfaɪ] *vt* personificar, encarnar
personnel [pɜːsə'nel] *n* personal *m*
perspective [pə'spektɪv] *n* perspectiva *f*
Perspex® ['pɜːspeks] *n* plexiglás® *m*
perspiration [pɜːspə'reɪʃən] *n* transpiración *f*
perspire [pə'spaɪə(r)] *vi* transpirar
persuade [pə'sweɪd] *vt* persuadir; **to p. sb to do sth** persuadir a algn para que haga algo

persuasion [pə'sweɪʒən] *n* persuasión *f*; *(opinion, belief)* credo *m*
persuasive [pə'sweɪsɪv] *adj* persuasivo(a)
pert [pɜːt] *adj* pizpireta, coqueto(a)
pertain [pə'teɪn] *vi* estar relacionado(a) (**to** con)
pertinent ['pɜːtɪnənt] *adj (relevant)* pertinente; **p. to** relacionado(a) con, a propósito de
perturbing [pə'tɜːbɪŋ] *adj* inquietante
Peru [pə'ruː] *n* Perú
peruse [pə'ruːz] *vt Fml* leer
Peruvian [pə'ruːvɪən] *adj & n* peruano(a) *(m,f)*
pervade [pɜː'veɪd] *vt (of smell)* penetrar; *(of light)* difundirse por; *Fig (of influence)* extenderse por
pervasive [pɜː'veɪsɪv] *adj (smell)* penetrante; *(influence)* extendido(a)
perverse [pə'vɜːs] *adj (wicked)* perverso(a); *(contrary)* contrario(a) a todo
perversion [pə'vɜːʃən] *n Med & Psy* perversión *f*; *(of justice, truth)* desvirtuación *f*
pervert 1 *n* ['pɜːvɜːt] *Med* pervertido(a) *m,f (sexual)*
2 *vt* [pə'vɜːt] pervertir; *(justice, truth)* desvirtuar
pessimist ['pesɪmɪst] *n* pesimista *mf*
pessimistic [pesɪ'mɪstɪk] *adj* pesimista
pest [pest] *n* **(a)** *Zool* animal nocivo; *Bot* planta nociva **(b)** *Fam (person)* pelma *mf*; *(thing)* lata *f*
pester ['pestə(r)] *vt* molestar, fastidiar
pet [pet] **1** *n* **(a)** animal doméstico **(b)** *(favourite)* preferido(a) *m,f*; *Fam* cariño *m*
2 *adj (favourite)* preferido(a)
3 *vt* acariciar
4 *vi (sexually)* besuquearse
petal ['petəl] *n* pétalo *m*
peter ['piːtə(r)] *vi* **to p. out** agotarse
petite [pə'tiːt] *adj* menuda, chiquita
petition [pɪ'tɪʃən] *n* petición *f*
petrify ['petrɪfaɪ] *vt Literary* petrificar; *Fig* **they were petrified** se quedaron de piedra
petrol ['petrəl] *n Br* gasolina *f*, *RP* nafta *f*; **p. can** bidón *m* de gasolina; **p. pump** surtidor *m* de gasolina; **p. station** gasolinera *f*, estación *f* de servicio, *Andes, Ven* bomba *f*, *Méx* gasolinería *f*, *Perú* grifo *m*; **p. tank** depósito *m* de gasolina

♪ Note that the Spanish word **petróleo** is a false friend and is never a translation for the English word **petrol**. In Spanish, **petróleo** means "oil, petroleum".

petroleum [pə'trəʊlɪəm] *n* petróleo *m*
petticoat ['petɪkəʊt] *n* enaguas *fpl*
petty ['petɪ] *adj* (**pettier, pettiest**) *(trivial)* insignificante; *(small-minded)* mezquino(a); **p. cash** dinero *m* para gastos pequeños; *Naut* **p. officer** sargento *m* de marina

petulant ['petjʊlənt] adj malhumorado(a)

🖉 Note that the Spanish word **petulante** is a false friend and is never a translation for the English word **petulant**. In Spanish, **petulante** means "opinionated, arrogant".

pew [pjuː] n banco m de iglesia; *Fam* take a **p.!** ¡siéntate!

pewter ['pjuːtə(r)] n peltre m

phantom ['fæntəm] adj & n fantasma (m)

pharmaceutical [fɑːməˈsjuːtɪkəl] adj farmacéutico(a)

pharmacist ['fɑːməsɪst] n farmacéutico(a) m,f

pharmacy ['fɑːməsɪ] n farmacia f

phase [feɪz] **1** n fase f
2 vt to p. sth in/out introducir/retirar algo progresivamente

PhD [piːeɪtʃˈdiː] n (abbr **Doctor of Philosophy**) (person) Doctor(a) m,f en Filosofía

pheasant ['fezənt] n faisán m (vulgar)

phenomena [fɪˈnɒmɪnə] pl of **phenomenon**

phenomenal [fɪˈnɒmɪnəl] adj fenomenal

phenomenon [fɪˈnɒmɪnən] n (pl **phenomena**) fenómeno m

phial [faɪəl] n frasco m

philanthropist [fɪˈlænθrəpɪst] n filántropo(a) m,f

philately [fɪˈlætəlɪ] n filatelia f

Philippines ['fɪlɪpiːnz] npl the P. las (Islas) Filipinas

philosopher [fɪˈlɒsəfə(r)] n filósofo(a) m,f

philosophical [fɪləˈsɒfɪkəl] adj filosófico(a)

philosophy [fɪˈlɒsəfɪ] n filosofía f

phlegm [flem] n flema f

phlegmatic [flegˈmætɪk] adj flemático(a)

phobia ['fəʊbɪə] n fobia f

phone [fəʊn] n = **telephone**

phone-in ['fəʊnɪn] n Fam = programa de radio o televisión con línea telefónica abierta

phonetic [fəˈnetɪk] **1** adj fonético(a)
2 n **phonetics** fonética f

phoney ['fəʊnɪ] **1** adj (**phonier, phoniest**) (thing) falso(a); (person) farsante
2 n (person) farsante mf

phonograph ['fəʊnəgrɑːf] n US tocadiscos m inv

phosphate ['fɒsfeɪt] n fosfato m

photo ['fəʊtəʊ] n foto f

photocopier ['fəʊtəʊkɒpɪə(r)] n fotocopiadora f

photocopy ['fəʊtəʊkɒpɪ] **1** n fotocopia f
2 vt fotocopiar

photogenic [fəʊtəʊˈdʒenɪk] adj fotogénico(a)

photograph ['fəʊtəgræf, 'fəʊtəgrɑːf] **1** n fotografía f; **black and white/colour p.** fotografía en blanco y negro/en color
2 vt fotografiar

photographer [fəˈtɒgrəfə(r)] n fotógrafo(a) m,f

photography [fəˈtɒgrəfɪ] n fotografía f

phrase [freɪz] **1** n frase f; **p. book** libro m de frases
2 vt expresar

physical ['fɪzɪkəl] adj físico(a); **p. education** educación física

physically ['fɪzɪkəlɪ] adv físicamente; **p. handicapped** minusválido(a); **to be p. fit** estar en forma

physician [fɪˈzɪʃən] n médico(a) m,f

physicist ['fɪzɪsɪst] n físico(a) m,f

physics ['fɪzɪks] n sing física f

physiological [fɪzɪəˈlɒdʒɪkəl] adj fisiológico(a)

physiotherapist [fɪzɪəʊˈθerəpɪst] n fisioterapeuta mf

physique [fɪˈziːk] n físico m

pianist ['pɪənɪst] n pianista mf

piano [pɪˈænəʊ] n piano m

piccolo ['pɪkələʊ] n flautín m

pick [pɪk] **1** n (a) (tool) pico m, piqueta f (b) **take your p.** (choice) elige el que quieras
2 vt (a) (choose) escoger; (team) seleccionar (b) (flowers, fruit) coger, recoger (c) (scratch) hurgar; **to p. one's nose** hurgarse la nariz; **to p. one's teeth** mondarse los dientes (d) **to p. sb's pocket** robar algo del bolsillo de algn (e) (lock) forzar
3 vi **to p. at one's food** comer sin ganas
▸ **pick off** vt sep (a) (remove) quitar (b) (shoot) matar uno a uno
▸ **pick on** vt insep (persecute) meterse con
▸ **pick out** vt sep (choose) elegir; (distinguish) distinguir; (identify) identificar
▸ **pick up 1** vt sep (a) (object on floor) recoger; (telephone) descolgar; **to p. oneself up** levantarse; Fig reponerse (b) (collect) recoger; (shopping, person) buscar; **to p. up speed** ganar velocidad (c) (acquire) conseguir; (learn) aprender
2 vi (improve) mejorarse, ir mejorando; (prices) subir

pickaxe, US **pickax** ['pɪkæks] n piqueta f

picket ['pɪkɪt] **1** n piquete m; **p. line** piquete m
2 vt piquetear
3 vi hacer piquete

pickle ['pɪkəl] **1** n (a) Br Culin salsa f picante (b) Fam (mess) lío m, apuro m
2 vt Culin conservar en adobo or escabeche; **pickled onions** cebollas fpl en vinagre

pick-me-up ['pɪkmiʌp] n Fam reconstituyente m, tónico m

pickpocket ['pɪkpɒkɪt] n carterista mf

pick-up ['pɪkʌp] n **p. (arm)** (on record player) brazo m; **p. (truck)** furgoneta f

picnic ['pɪknɪk] **1** n comida f de campo, picnic m
2 vi hacer una comida de campo

pictorial [pɪkˈtɔːrɪəl] adj ilustrado(a)

picture ['pɪktʃə(r)] **1** n (a) (painting) cuadro m; (drawing) dibujo m; (portrait) retrato m;

(photo) foto *f*; *(illustration)* ilustración *f*; **p. book** libro ilustrado; **p. postcard** tarjeta *f* postal (**b**) *TV* imagen *f*; *Cin* película *f*; **to go to the pictures** ir al cine

2 *vt (imagine)* imaginarse

picturesque [pɪktʃəˈresk] *adj* pintoresco(a)

pie [paɪ] *n (of fruit)* tarta *f*, pastel *m*; *(of meat etc)* pastel, empanada *f*; *(pasty)* empanadilla *f*

piece [piːs] *n* (**a**) *(of food)* pedazo *m*, trozo *m*; *(of paper)* trozo; *(part)* pieza *f*; **a p. of advice** un consejo; **a p. of furniture** un mueble; **a p. of land** una parcela; **a p. of news** una noticia; **to break sth into pieces** hacer algo pedazos; *Fig* **to go to pieces** perder el control (de sí mismo) (**b**) *Lit Mus* obra *f*, pieza *f* (**c**) *(coin)* moneda *f* (**d**) *(in chess)* pieza *f*; *(in draughts)* ficha *f*

▸ **piece together** *vt sep (facts)* reconstruir; *(jigsaw)* hacer

piecemeal [ˈpiːsmiːl] *adv (by degrees)* poco a poco, a etapas; *(unsystematically)* desordenadamente

piecework [ˈpiːswɜːk] *n* trabajo *m* a destajo; **to be on p.** trabajar a destajo

pier [pɪə(r)] *n* embarcadero *m*, muelle *m*; *(promenade)* = paseo de madera que entra en el mar

pierce [pɪəs] *vt* perforar; *(penetrate)* penetrar en

piercing [ˈpɪəsɪŋ] *adj (sound etc)* penetrante

piety [ˈpaɪtɪ] *n* piedad *f*

pig [pɪg] *n* (**a**) cerdo *m* (**b**) *Fam (person)* cochino *m*; *(glutton)* tragón(ona) *m,f* (**c**) *Fam Pej (policeman)* madero *m*

pigeon [ˈpɪdʒɪn] *n* paloma *f*; *Culin & Sport* pichón *m*

pigeonhole [ˈpɪdʒɪnhəʊl] *n* casilla *f*

piggy [ˈpɪgɪ] *n* **p. bank** = hucha en forma de cerdito

pigheaded [pɪgˈhedɪd] *adj* terco(a), cabezota

piglet [ˈpɪglɪt] *n* cerdito *m*, lechón *m*

pigment [ˈpɪgmənt] *n* pigmento *m*

pigskin [ˈpɪgskɪn] *n* piel *f* de cerdo

pigsty [ˈpɪgstaɪ] *n* pocilga *f*

pigtail [ˈpɪgteɪl] *n* trenza *f*; *(bullfighter's)* coleta *f*

pike [paɪk] *n (fish)* lucio *m*

pilchard [ˈpɪltʃəd] *n* sardina *f*

pile¹ [paɪl] **1** *n* montón *m*

2 *vt* amontonar

3 *vi* **to p. into** apiñarse en; **to p. on/off a bus** subir a/bajar de un autobús en tropel

▸ **pile up 1** *vt sep (things)* amontonar; *(riches, debts)* acumular

2 *vi* amontonarse

pile² [paɪl] *n (on carpet)* pelo *m*; **thick p.** pelo largo

piles [paɪlz] *npl Med* almorranas *fpl*, hemorroides *fpl*

pile-up [ˈpaɪlʌp] *n Aut* choque *m* en cadena

pilfer [ˈpɪlfə(r)] *vt & vi* hurtar

pilgrim [ˈpɪlgrɪm] *n* peregrino(a) *m,f*

pilgrimage [ˈpɪlgrɪmɪdʒ] *n* peregrinación *f*

pill [pɪl] *n* píldora *f*, pastilla *f*; **to be on the p.** estar tomando la píldora (anticonceptiva)

pillage [ˈpɪlɪdʒ] *vt & vi* pillar, saquear

pillar [ˈpɪlə(r)] *n* pilar *m*, columna *f*; *Br* **p. box** buzón *m*

pillion [ˈpɪljən] *n* asiento trasero *(de una moto)*

pillow [ˈpɪləʊ] *n* almohada *f*

pillowcase [ˈpɪləʊkeɪs] *n* funda *f* de almohada

pilot [ˈpaɪlət] **1** *n* piloto *m*

2 *adj (trial)* piloto *inv*; **p. light** piloto *m*; **p. scheme** proyecto piloto

3 *vt* pilotar

pimp [pɪmp] *n* chulo *m*

pimple [ˈpɪmpəl] *n* grano *m*, espinilla *f*

PIN [pɪn] *n (abbr personal identification number)* **P. (number)** PIN *m*

pin [pɪn] **1** *n* alfiler *m*; *Tech* clavija *f*; *(wooden)* espiga *f*; *(in plug)* polo *m*; *(in bowling)* bolo *m*; *US (brooch)* broche *m*; **pins and needles** hormigueo *m*

2 *vt (on board)* clavar con chinchetas; *(garment etc)* sujetar con alfileres; **to p. sb against a wall** tener a algn contra una pared; *Fig* **to p. one's hopes on sth** poner sus esperanzas en algo; *Fam* **to p. a crime on sb** endosar un delito a algn

▸ **pin down** *vt sep Fig* **to p. sb down** hacer que algn se comprometa

pinafore [ˈpɪnəfɔː(r)] *n (apron)* delantal *m*; **p. dress** pichi *m*

pinball [ˈpɪnbɔːl] *n* flipper *m*, máquina *f* de petacos

pincers [ˈpɪnsəz] *npl (on crab)* pinzas *fpl*; *(tool)* tenazas *fpl*

pinch [pɪntʃ] **1** *n (nip)* pellizco *m*; *Fig Br* **at** or *US* **in a p.** en caso de apuro; **a p. of salt** una pizca de sal

2 *vt* pellizcar; *Fam (steal)* birlar

3 *vi (shoes)* apretar

🖋 Note that the Spanish verb **pinchar** is a false friend and is never a translation for the English verb **to pinch**. In Spanish, **pinchar** means "to prick, to puncture".

---

pincushion [ˈpɪnkʊʃən] *n* acerico *m*

pine¹ [paɪn] *n (tree)* pino *m*; **p. cone** piña *f*

pine² [paɪn] *vi* **to p. (away)** consumirse, morirse de pena; **to p. for sth/sb** añorar algo/a algn

pineapple [ˈpaɪnæpəl] *n* piña *f*

ping [pɪŋ] *n* sonido metálico; *(of bullet)* silbido *m*

Ping-Pong® [ˈpɪŋpɒŋ] *n* ping-pong® *m*

pink [pɪŋk] **1** *n (colour)* rosa *m*; *Bot* clavel *m*

2 *adj (colour)* rosa *inv*; *Pol Fam* rojillo(a)

pinnacle [ˈpɪnəkəl] *n (of building)* pináculo *m*; *(of mountain)* cima *f*, pico *m*; *Fig (of success)* cumbre *f*

pinpoint ['pɪnpɔɪnt] *vt* señalar
pinstripe ['pɪnstraɪp] *adj* a rayas
pint [paɪnt] *n* pinta *f*; *Br Fam* **a p. (of beer)** una pinta (de cerveza)
pioneer [paɪə'nɪə(r)] **1** *n* (*settler*) pionero(a) *m,f*; (*forerunner*) precursor(a) *m,f*
   2 *vt* ser pionero(a) en
pious ['paɪəs] *adj* piadoso(a), devoto(a); *Pej* beato(a)
pip¹ [pɪp] *n* (*seed*) pepita *f*
pip² [pɪp] *n* (*sound*) señal *f* (corta); (*on dice*) punto *m*
pipe [paɪp] **1** *n* (a) conducto *m*, tubería *f*; (*of organ*) caramillo *m*; *Fam* **the pipes** (*bagpipes*) la gaita (b) (*for smoking*) pipa *f*; **p. cleaner** limpiapipas *m inv*; *Fig* **p. dream** sueño *m* imposible
   2 *vt* (*water*) llevar por tubería; (*oil*) transportar por oleoducto; **piped music** hilo *m* musical
   ▸ **pipe down** *vi Fam* callarse
   ▸ **pipe up** *vi Fam* hacerse oír
pipeline ['paɪplaɪn] *n* tubería *f*, cañería *f*; (*for gas*) gasoducto *m*; (*for oil*) oleoducto *m*
piper ['paɪpə(r)] *n* gaitero(a) *m,f*
piping ['paɪpɪŋ] **1** *n* (*for water, gas etc*) tubería *f*, cañería *f*
   2 *adj* **p. hot** bien caliente
piquant ['piːkənt] *adj* picante; (*fig*) intrigante
pique [piːk] **1** *n* enojo *m*
   2 *vt* herir
pirate ['paɪrɪt] *n* pirata *m*; **p. edition** edición *f* pirata; **p. radio** emisora *f* pirata; **p. ship** barco *m* pirata
pirouette [pɪrʊ'et] **1** *n* pirueta *f*
   2 *vi* hacer piruetas
Pisces ['paɪsiːz] *n* Piscis *m*
piss [pɪs] *very Fam* **1** *vi* mear
   2 *n* meada *f*
pissed [pɪst] *adj very Fam* (a) *Br* (*drunk*) borracho(a) (b) *US* (*angry*) cabreado(a)
pistachio [pɪs'tɑːʃɪəʊ] *n* (*nut*) pistacho *m*
pistol ['pɪstəl] *n* pistola *f*
piston ['pɪstən] *n* pistón *m*
pit¹ [pɪt] **1** *n* hoyo *m*; (*large*) hoya *f*; (*coal mine*) mina *f* de carbón; *Th* platea *f*; (*in motor racing*) foso *m*, box *m*
   2 *vt* **to p. one's wits against sb** medirse con algn
pit² [pɪt] *n* (*of cherry*) hueso *m*, pipo *m*; *US* (*of peach, plum*) hueso *m*
pitch¹ [pɪtʃ] **1** *vt* (a) *Mus* (*sound*) entonar (b) (*throw*) lanzar, arrojar (c) (*tent*) armar
   2 *vi* (*ship*) cabecear; **to p. forward** caerse hacia adelante
   3 *n* (a) *Mus* (*of sound*) tono *m* (b) *Sport* campo *m*, cancha *f* (c) (*in market etc*) puesto *m* (d) (*throw*) lanzamiento *m*
pitch² [pɪtʃ] *n* (*tar*) brea *f*, pez *f*
pitch-black [pɪtʃ'blæk], **pitch-dark** [pɪtʃ'dɑːk] *adj* negro(a) como la boca del lobo
pitched [pɪtʃt] *adj* **p. battle** batalla *f* campal

pitcher ['pɪtʃə(r)] *n* (*container*) cántaro *m*, jarro *m*
pitchfork ['pɪtʃfɔːk] *n* horca *f*
piteous ['pɪtɪəs] *adj* lastimoso(a)
pitfall ['pɪtfɔːl] *n* dificultad *f*, obstáculo *m*
pith [pɪθ] *n* (*of orange*) piel blanca; *Fig* meollo *m*
pithy ['pɪθɪ] *adj* (**pithier, pithiest**) *Fig* contundente
pitiful ['pɪtɪfʊl] *adj* (*producing pity*) lastimoso(a), (*terrible*) lamentable
pitiless ['pɪtɪlɪs] *adj* despiadado(a), implacable
pittance ['pɪtəns] *n* miseria *f*
pity ['pɪtɪ] **1** *n* (a) (*compassion*) compasión *f*, piedad *f*; **to take p. on sb** compadecerse de algn (b) (*shame*) lástima *f*, pena *f*; **what a p.!** ¡qué pena!, ¡qué lástima!
   2 *vt* compadecerse de; **I p. them** me dan pena
pivot ['pɪvət] **1** *n* pivote *m*
   2 *vi* girar sobre su eje
pizza ['piːtsə] *n* pizza *f*; **p. parlour** pizzería *f*
placard ['plækɑːd] *n* pancarta *f*
placate [plə'keɪt] *vt* aplacar, apaciguar
place [pleɪs] **1** *n* (a) sitio *m*, lugar *m*; **to be in/out of p.** estar en/fuera de su sitio; **to take p.** tener lugar
   (b) (*seat*) sitio *m*; (*on bus*) asiento *m*; (*at university*) plaza *m*; **to change places with sb** intercambiar el sitio con algn; **to feel out of p.** encontrarse fuera de lugar; **to take sb's p.** sustituir a algn
   (c) (*position on scale*) posición *f*; (*social position*) rango *m*; **in the first p.** en primer lugar; **to take first p.** ganar el primer lugar
   (d) (*house*) casa *f*; (*building*) lugar *m*; **we're going to his p.** vamos a su casa
   2 *vt* (a) poner, colocar; **to p. a bet** hacer una apuesta; **to p. an order with sb** hacer un pedido a algn
   (b) (*face, person*) recordar; (*in job*) colocar en un empleo
placid ['plæsɪd] *adj* apacible
plagiarize ['pleɪdʒəraɪz] *vt* plagiar
plague [pleɪg] **1** *n* (*of insects*) plaga *f*; *Med* peste *f*
   2 *vt* **to p. sb with requests** acosar a algn a peticiones
plaice [pleɪs] *n* (*pl* **plaice**) (*fish*) platija *f*
plaid [plæd, pleɪd] *n* (*cloth*) tejido *m* escocés
plain [pleɪn] **1** *adj* (a) (*clear*) claro(a), evidente; *Fig* **he likes p. speaking** le gusta hablar con franqueza (b) (*simple*) sencillo(a); (*chocolate*) amargo(a); (*flour*) sin levadura; **in p. clothes** vestido(a) de paisano; **the p. truth** la verdad lisa y llana (c) (*unattractive*) poco atractivo(a)
   2 *n Geog* llanura *f*, llano *m*
plainly ['pleɪnlɪ] *adv* claramente; (*simply*) sencillamente; **to speak p.** hablar con franqueza

plaintiff ['pleɪntɪf] n demandante mf
plaintive ['pleɪntɪv] adj lastimero(a)
plait [plæt] 1 n trenza f
  2 vt trenzar
plan [plæn] 1 n (scheme) plan m, proyecto m; (drawing) plano m
  2 vt (a) (for future) planear, proyectar; (economy) planificar (b) (intend) pensar, tener la intención de; **it wasn't planned** no estaba previsto
  3 vi hacer planes; **to p. on doing sth** tener la intención de hacer algo
plane¹ [pleɪn] 1 n (a) Math plano m; Fig nivel m (b) Fam Av avión m
  2 adj Geom plano(a)
  3 vi (glide) planear
plane² [pleɪn] 1 n (tool) cepillo m
  2 vt cepillar
plane³ [pleɪn] n Bot **p. (tree)** plátano m
planet ['plænɪt] n planeta m
plank [plæŋk] n tabla f, tablón m
planner ['plænə(r)] n planificador(a) m,f
planning ['plænɪŋ] n planificación f; **family p.** planificación familiar; **p. permission** permiso m de obras
plant¹ [plɑːnt] 1 n planta f
  2 vt (flowers) plantar; (seeds) sembrar; (bomb) colocar
plant² [plɑːnt] n (factory) planta f, fábrica f; (machinery) maquinaria f
plantation [plæn'teɪʃən] n plantación f
plaque [plæk] n placa f; (on teeth) sarro m
plaster ['plɑːstə(r)] 1 n Constr yeso m; Med escayola f; Br **sticking p.** esparadrapo m, tirita® f, Am curita f; **p. of Paris** yeso mate
  2 vt Constr enyesar; Fig (cover) cubrir (**with** de)
plastered ['plɑːstəd] adj Fam borracho(a), trompa
plasterer ['plɑːstərə(r)] n yesero(a) m,f
plastic ['plæstɪk] 1 n plástico m
  2 adj (cup, bag) de plástico; **p. surgery** cirugía plástica
Plasticine® ['plæstɪsiːn] n plastilina® f
plate [pleɪt] 1 n (a) plato m (b) (sheet) placa f; **gold p.** chapa f de oro; **p. glass** vidrio cilindrado (c) (in book) grabado m, lámina f
  2 vt chapar
plateau ['plætəʊ] n meseta f
platform ['plætfɔːm] n (a) plataforma f; (stage) estrado m; (at meeting) tribuna f (b) Rail andén m; **p. ticket** billete m de andén (c) Pol (programme) programa m
platinum ['plætɪnəm] n platino m
platitude ['plætɪtjuːd] n lugar m común, tópico m
platoon [plə'tuːn] n Mil pelotón m
platter ['plætə(r)] n fuente f
plausible ['plɔːzəbəl] adj plausible
play [pleɪ] 1 vt (a) (game) jugar a
  (b) Sport (position) jugar de; (team) jugar contra; **to p. a shot** (in golf, tennis) golpear

  (c) (instrument, tune) tocar; **to p. a record** poner un disco
  (d) Th (part) hacer (el papel) de; (play) representar; Fig **to p. a part in sth** participar en algo; Fig **to p. the fool** hacer el tonto
  2 vi (a) (children) jugar (**with** con); (animals) juguetear
  (b) Sport jugar; **to p. fair** jugar limpio; Fig **to p. for time** tratar de ganar tiempo
  (c) (joke) bromear
  (d) Mus tocar; (instrument) sonar
  3 n (a) Th obra f de teatro
  (b) Sport juego m; **fair/foul p.** juego limpio/sucio
  (c) Tech Fig (movement) juego m; Fig **to bring sth into p.** poner algo en juego; **a p. on words** un juego de palabras
  ▸ **play around** vi (waste time) gandulear; (be unfaithful) tener líos
  ▸ **play down** vt sep minimizar, quitar importancia a
  ▸ **play on** vt insep (take advantage of) aprovecharse de; (nerves etc) exacerbar
  ▸ **play up** 1 vt sep (annoy) dar la lata a, fastidiar
  2 vi (child etc) dar guerra
playboy ['pleɪbɔɪ] n playboy m
player ['pleɪə(r)] n Sport jugador(a) m,f; Mus músico(a) m,f; Th (man) actor m; (woman) actriz f
playful ['pleɪfʊl] adj juguetón(ona)
playground ['pleɪgraʊnd] n patio m de recreo
playgroup ['pleɪgruːp] n jardín m de infancia
playing ['pleɪɪŋ] n juego m; **p. card** carta f, naipe m; **p. field** campo m de deportes
playmate ['pleɪmeɪt] n compañero(a) m,f de juego
play-off ['pleɪɒf] n Sport partido m de desempate
playpen ['pleɪpen] n corralito m or parque m (de niños)
playschool ['pleɪskuːl] n jardín m de infancia
plaything ['pleɪθɪŋ] n juguete m
playwright ['pleɪraɪt] n dramaturgo(a) m,f
PLC, plc [piːel'siː] n Br (abbr **public limited company**) ≃ S.A.
plea [pliː] n (a) (request) petición f, súplica f; (excuse) pretexto m, disculpa f (b) Jur alegato m
plead [pliːd] 1 vt (a) Jur & Fig **to p. sb's cause** defender la causa de algn (b) **to p. ignorance** (give as excuse) alegar ignorancia
  2 vi (a) (beg) rogar, suplicar; **to p. with sb to do sth** suplicar a algn que haga algo (b) Jur **to p. guilty/not guilty** declararse culpable/inocente
pleasant ['plezənt] adj agradable
pleasantry ['plezəntrɪ] n cumplido m
please [pliːz] 1 vt (give pleasure to) agradar, complacer; (satisfy) satisfacer; Fam **p. yourself** como quieras
  2 vi complacer; (give satisfaction) satisfacer;

easy/hard to p. poco/muy exigente

3 *adv* por favor; **may I? – p. do** ¿me permite? – desde luego; **p. do not smoke** *(sign)* se ruega no fumar; **yes, p.** sí, por favor

pleased [pliːzd] *adj (happy)* contento(a); *(satisfied)* satisfecho(a); **p. to meet you!** ¡encantado(a)!, ¡mucho gusto!; **to be p. about sth** alegrarse de algo

pleasing ['pliːzɪŋ] *adj (pleasant)* agradable, grato(a); *(satisfactory)* satisfactorio(a)

pleasure ['pleʒə(r)] *n* placer *m*; **it's a p. to talk to him** da gusto hablar con él; **to take great p. in doing sth** disfrutar mucho haciendo algo; **with p.** con mucho gusto

pleat [pliːt] **1** *n* pliegue *m*

2 *vt* hacer pliegues en

pledge [pledʒ] **1** *n* promesa *f*; *(token of love etc)* señal *f*; *(guarantee)* prenda *f*

2 *vt (promise)* prometer; *(pawn)* empeñar

plentiful ['plentɪfʊl] *adj* abundante

plenty ['plentɪ] *n* abundancia *f*; **p. of books** muchos libros; **p. of time** tiempo de sobra; **we've got p.** tenemos de sobra

Plexiglas® ['pleksɪɡlɑːs] *n US* plexiglás® *m*

pliable ['plaɪəbəl] *adj* flexible

pliers ['plaɪəz] *npl* alicates *mpl*, tenazas *fpl*

plight [plaɪt] *n* situación *f* grave

plimsolls ['plɪmsəlz] *npl Br* zapatos *mpl* de tenis

plinth [plɪnθ] *n* plinto *m*

plod [plɒd] *vi* andar con paso pesado; *Fig* **to p. on** perseverar; *Fig* **to p. through a report** estudiar laboriosamente un informe

plodder ['plɒdə(r)] *n* trabajador(a) *m,f*/estudiante *mf* tenaz

plonk¹ [plɒŋk] *vt Fam* dejar caer

plonk² [plɒŋk] *n Br Fam (wine)* vinazo *m*

plot¹ [plɒt] **1** *n* **(a)** *(conspiracy)* complot *m* **(b)** *Th & Lit (story)* argumento *m*, trama *f*

2 *vt* **(a)** *(course, route)* trazar **(b)** *(scheme)* fraguar

3 *vi* conspirar, tramar

plot² [plɒt] *n Agr* terreno *m*; *(for building)* solar *m*; **vegetable p.** campo *m* de hortalizas

plough [plaʊ] **1** *n* arado *m*

2 *vt* arar

3 *vi Fig* **the car ploughed through the fencing** el coche atravesó la valla; **to p. into sth** chocar contra algo; *Fig* **to p. through a book** leer un libro con dificultad

▸ **plough back** *vt sep (profits)* reinvertir

plow [plaʊ] *n*, *vt & vi US* = **plough**

ploy [plɔɪ] *n* estratagema *f*

pluck [plʌk] **1** *vt* **(a)** arrancar (**out of** de) **(b)** *(flowers)* coger **(c)** *(chicken)* desplumar **(d)** *(guitar)* puntear

2 *n (courage)* valor *m*, ánimo *m*

▸ **pluck up** *vt sep* **to p. up courage** armarse de valor

plucky ['plʌkɪ] *adj* (**pluckier, pluckiest**) valiente

plug [plʌg] **1** *n* **(a)** *(in bath etc)* tapón *m* **(b)**

Elec enchufe *m*, clavija *f*; **two-/three-pin p.** clavija bipolar/tripolar

2 *vt* **(a)** *(hole)* tapar **(b)** *Fam (publicize)* dar publicidad a; *(idea etc)* hacer hincapié en

▸ **plug in** *vt sep & vi* enchufar

plum [plʌm] *n (fruit)* ciruela *f*; *Fig* **a p. job** un chollo

plumage ['pluːmɪdʒ] *n* plumaje *m*

plumb [plʌm] **1** *n* plomo *m*; **p. line** plomada *f*

2 *adj* vertical

3 *adv Fam* **p. in the middle** justo en medio; *US* **he's p. crazy** está completamente loco

4 *vt Fig* **to p. the depths** tocar fondo

plumber ['plʌmə(r)] *n* fontanero(a) *m,f*

plumbing ['plʌmɪŋ] *n (occupation)* fontanería *f*; *(system)* tuberías *fpl*, cañerías *fpl*

plume [pluːm] *n* penacho *m*

plummet ['plʌmɪt] *vi (bird, plane)* caer en picado; *Fig (prices)* bajar vertiginosamente; *(morale)* caer a plomo

plump¹ [plʌmp] *adj (person)* relleno(a); *(baby)* rechoncho(a)

plump² [plʌmp] *vi* **to p. for sth** optar por algo

▸ **plump down** *vt sep* dejar caer

▸ **plump up** *vt sep (cushions)* ahuecar

plunder ['plʌndə(r)] **1** *vt* saquear

2 *n (action)* saqueo *m*, pillaje *m*; *(loot)* botín *m*

plunge [plʌndʒ] **1** *vt (immerse)* sumergir; *(thrust)* arrojar

2 *vi (dive)* lanzarse, zambullirse; *Fig (fall)* caer, hundirse; *(prices)* desplomarse

3 *n (dive)* zambullida *f*; *Fig (fall)* desplome *m*; **to take the p.** dar el paso decisivo

plunger ['plʌndʒə(r)] *n Tech* émbolo *m*; *(for pipes)* desatascador *m*

pluperfect [pluːˈpɜːfɪkt] *n* pluscuamperfecto *m*

plural ['plʊərəl] *adj & n* plural *(m)*

plus [plʌs] *prep* más; **three p. four makes seven** tres más cuatro hacen siete

2 *n Math* signo *m* más; *Fig (advantage)* ventaja *f*

plush [plʌʃ] **1** *n* felpa *f*

2 *adj Fam* lujoso(a)

plutonium [pluːˈtəʊnɪəm] *n* plutonio *m*

ply [plaɪ] **1** *vt* **to p. one's trade** ejercer su oficio; **to p. sb with drinks** no parar de ofrecer copas a algn

2 *vi (ship)* ir y venir; **to p. for hire** ir en busca de clientes

plywood ['plaɪwʊd] *n* madera contrachapada

PM [piːˈem] *n Br (abbr* **Prime Minister**) primer(a) ministro(a) *m,f*

p.m. [piːˈem] *(abbr* **post meridiem**) después del mediodía; **at 2 p.m.** a las dos de la tarde

PMT [piːemˈtiː] *n (abbr* **premenstrual tension**) tensión *f* premenstrual

pneumatic [njuːˈmætɪk] *adj* neumático(a)

pneumonia [njuːˈməʊnɪə] *n* pulmonía *f*

PO [piːˈəʊ] *n (abbr* **Post Office**) oficina *f* de

correos; **PO Box** apartado *m* de correos, *CAm, Carib, Méx* casilla *f* postal, *Andes, RP* casilla de correos

poach¹ [pəʊtʃ] *vt* (**a**) *to* p. fish/game pescar/ cazar furtivamente (**b**) *Fam Fig (steal)* birlar

poach² [pəʊtʃ] *vt Culin (egg)* escalfar; *(fish)* hervir

poacher [ˈpəʊtʃə(r)] *n* pescador/cazador furtivo

pocket [ˈpɒkɪt] **1** *n* (**a**) bolsillo *m*; *Fig* **to be £10 in/out of p.** salir ganando/perdiendo 10 libras; **p. money** dinero *m* de bolsillo (**b**) *(of air)* bolsa *f* (**c**) *(of resistance)* foco *m*
2 *vt (money)* embolsar

pocketbook [ˈpɒkɪtbʊk] *n US* bolso *m*

pocketknife [ˈpɒkɪtnaɪf] *n* navaja *f*

pod [pɒd] *n* vaina *f*

podgy [ˈpɒdʒɪ] *adj* (**podgier, podgiest**) gordinflón(ona), regordete

podiatrist [pəˈdaɪətrɪst] *n US* pedicuro(a) *m,f*

podium [ˈpəʊdɪəm] *n* podio *m*

poem [ˈpəʊɪm] *n* poema *m*

poet [ˈpəʊɪt] *n* poeta *mf*

poetic [pəʊˈetɪk] *adj* poético(a)

poetry [ˈpəʊɪtrɪ] *n* poesía *f*

poignant [ˈpɔɪnjənt] *adj* conmovedor(a)

point [pɔɪnt] **1** *n* (**a**) *(sharp end)* punta *f*
(**b**) *(place)* punto *m*; *Fig* **p. of no return** punto sin retorno
(**c**) *(quality)* **good/bad p.** cualidad buena/ mala; **weak/strong p.** punto débil/fuerte
(**d**) *(moment)* **at that p.** en aquel momento; **from that p. onwards** desde entonces; **to be on the p. of doing sth** estar a punto de hacer algo
(**e**) *(score)* punto *m*, tanto *m*; **to win on points** ganar por puntos; **match p.** *(in tennis)* pelota *f* de match
(**f**) *(in argument)* punto *m*; **to make one's p.** insistir en el argumento; **I take your p.** entiendo lo que quieres decir
(**g**) *(purpose)* propósito *m*; **I don't see the p.** no veo el sentido; **that isn't the p., it's beside the p.** eso no viene al caso; **there's no p. in going** no merece la pena ir; **to come to the p.** llegar al meollo de la cuestión
(**h**) *(on scale)* punto *m*; *(in share index)* entero *m*; **six p. three** seis coma tres; *Fig* **up to a p.** hasta cierto punto
(**i**) *Geog* punta *f*
(**j**) *power* **p.** toma *f* de corriente
(**k**) **points** *Aut* platinos *mpl*; *Rail* agujas *fpl*
2 *vt (way etc)* señalar, indicar; **to p. a gun at sb** apuntar a algn con una pistola
3 *vi* señalar, indicar; **to p. at sth/sb** señalar algo/a algn con el dedo
▸ **point out** *vt sep* indicar, señalar; *(mention)* hacer resaltar

point-blank [ˈpɔɪntˈblæŋk] **1** *adj* a quemarropa; *(refusal)* rotundo(a)
2 *adv (shoot)* a quemarropa; *(refuse)* rotundamente

pointed [ˈpɔɪntɪd] *adj (sharp)* puntiagudo(a); *Fig (comment)* intencionado(a); *(cutting)* mordaz

pointedly [ˈpɔɪntɪdlɪ] *adv Fig (significantly)* con intención; *(cuttingly)* con mordacidad

pointer [ˈpɔɪntə(r)] *n* (**a**) *(indicator)* indicador *m*, aguja *f*; *(for map)* puntero *m* (**b**) *(dog)* perro *m* de muestra

pointless [ˈpɔɪntlɪs] *adj* sin sentido

poise [pɔɪz] **1** *n (bearing)* porte *m*; *(self-assurance)* aplomo *m*
2 *vt Fig* **to be poised to do sth** estar listo(a) para hacer algo

poison [ˈpɔɪzən] **1** *n* veneno *m*
2 *vt* envenenar

poisoning [ˈpɔɪzənɪŋ] *n* envenenamiento *m*; *(by food etc)* intoxicación *f*

poisonous [ˈpɔɪzənəs] *adj (plant, snake)* venenoso(a); *(gas)* tóxico(a); *Fig (rumour)* pernicioso(a)

poke [pəʊk] *vt (with finger or stick)* dar con la punta del dedo/del bastón a; **to p. one's head out** asomar la cabeza; **to p. the fire** atizar el fuego
▸ **poke about, poke around** *vi* fisgonear, hurgar
▸ **poke out** *vt sep (eye)* sacar

poker¹ [ˈpəʊkə(r)] *n (for fire)* atizador *m*

poker² [ˈpəʊkə(r)] *n Cards* póquer *m*

poker-faced [ˈpəʊkəfeɪst] *adj Fam* de cara impasible

poky [ˈpəʊkɪ] *adj* (**pokier, pokiest**) *Fam Pej* minúsculo(a); **a p. little room** un cuartucho

Poland [ˈpəʊlənd] *n* Polonia

polar [ˈpəʊlə(r)] *adj* polar; **p. bear** oso *m* polar

Pole [pəʊl] *n* polaco(a) *m,f*

pole¹ [pəʊl] *n* palo *m*; **p. vault** salto *m* con pértiga

pole² [pəʊl] *n Geog* polo *m*; *Fig* **to be poles apart** ser polos opuestos

police [pəˈliːs] **1** *npl* policía *f*; **p. car** coche *m* patrulla; **p. constable** policía *m*; **p. force** cuerpo *m* de policía; **p. record** antecedentes *mpl* penales; **p. state** estado *m* policial; **p. station** comisaría *f*
2 *vt* vigilar

policeman [pəˈliːsmən] *n* policía *m*

policewoman [pəˈliːswʊmən] *n* (mujer *f*) policía *f*

policy [ˈpɒlɪsɪ] *n Pol* política *f*; *(of company)* norma *f*, principio *m*; *Ins* póliza *f* (de seguros)

polio [ˈpəʊlɪəʊ] *n* poliomielitis *f*

Polish [ˈpəʊlɪʃ] **1** *adj* polaco(a)
2 *n* (**a**) **the P.** los polacos (**b**) *(language)* polaco *m*

polish [ˈpɒlɪʃ] **1** *vt* pulir; *(furniture)* encerar; *(shoes)* limpiar; *(silver)* sacar brillo a
2 *n* (**a**) *(for furniture)* cera *f*; *(for shoes)* betún *m*; *(for nails)* esmalte *m* (**b**) *(shine)* brillo *m*; *Fig (refinement)* refinamiento *m*
▸ **polish off** *vt sep Fam (work)* despachar;

(food) zamparse
▸ **polish up** *vt sep Fig* perfeccionar
polished ['pɒlɪʃt] *adj Fig (manners)* refinado(a); *(style)* pulido(a); *(performance)* impecable
polite [pə'laɪt] *adj* educado(a)
politeness [pə'laɪtnɪs] *n* educación *f*
politic ['pɒlɪtɪk] *adj* prudente
political [pə'lɪtɪkəl] *adj* político(a)
politically [pə'lɪtɪklɪ] *adv* políticamente; **p. correct** políticamente correcto(a)
politician [pɒlɪ'tɪʃən] *n* político(a) *m,f*
politics ['pɒlɪtɪks] *n sing* política *f*
polka ['pɒlkə] *n (dance)* polca *f*; **p. dot** lunar *m*
poll [pəʊl] **1** *n* (a) *(vote)* votación *f*; **the polls** las elecciones; **to go to the polls** acudir a las urnas (b) *(survey)* encuesta *f*
2 *vt (votes)* obtener
pollen ['pɒlən] *n* polen *m*
polling ['pəʊlɪŋ] *n* votación *f*; **p. booth** cabina *f* electoral; **p. station** colegio *m* electoral
pollute [pə'luːt] *vt* contaminar
pollution [pə'luːʃən] *n* contaminación *f*, polución *f*; **environmental p.** contaminación ambiental
polo ['pəʊləʊ] *n Sport* polo *m*; **p. neck (sweater)** jersey *m* de cuello vuelto
polyester [pɒlɪ'estə(r)] *n* poliéster *m*
polyethylene [pɒlɪ'eθəliːn] *n US* polietileno *m*
polymer ['pɒlɪmə(r)] *n Chem* polímero *m*
Polynesia [pɒlɪ'niːʒɪə] *n* Polinesia
polystyrene [pɒlɪ'staɪriːn] *n* poliestireno *m*
polytechnic [pɒlɪ'teknɪk] *n* escuela politécnica, politécnico *m*
polythene ['pɒlɪθiːn] *n Br* polietileno *m*
pomegranate ['pɒmɪgrænɪt] *n* granada *f*
pomp [pɒmp] *n* pompa *f*
pompom ['pɒmpɒm], **pompon** ['pɒmpɒn] *n* borla *f*, pompón *m*
pompous ['pɒmpəs] *adj (person)* presumido(a); *(speech)* rimbombante
pond [pɒnd] *n* estanque *m*
ponder ['pɒndə(r)] **1** *vt* considerar
2 *vi* **to p. over sth** meditar sobre algo
ponderous ['pɒndərəs] *adj* pesado(a)
pong [pɒŋ] *n Br Fam* hedor *m*
pontoon[1] [pɒn'tuːn] *n Constr* pontón *m*
pontoon[2] [pɒn'tuːn] *n Cards* veintiuna *f*
pony ['pəʊnɪ] *n* poney *m*
ponytail ['pəʊnɪteɪl] *n* cola *f* de caballo
poodle ['puːdəl] *n* caniche *m*
poof [pʊf] *n Br Fam Pej* marica *m*
pool[1] [puːl] *n (of water, oil etc)* charco *m*; *(pond)* estanque *m*; *(in river)* pozo *m*; **swimming p.** piscina *f*
pool[2] [puːl] **1** *n* (a) *(common fund)* fondo *m* común (b) **typing p.** servicio *m* de mecanografía (c) *US (snooker)* billar americano (d) *Br* **football pools** quinielas *fpl*
2 *vt (funds)* reunir; *(ideas, resources)* juntar
poor [pʊə(r)] **1** *adj* pobre; *(quality)* malo(a);

Fam **you p. thing!** ¡pobrecito!
2 *npl* **the p.** los pobres
poorly ['pʊəlɪ] **1** *adv (badly)* mal
2 *adj* **(poorlier, poorliest)** *(ill)* mal, malo(a)
pop [pɒp] **1** *vt (burst)* hacer reventar; *(cork)* hacer saltar
2 *vi (burst)* reventar; *(cork)* saltar; *Fam* **I'm just popping over to Ian's** voy un momento a casa de Ian
3 *n* (a) *(noise)* pequeña explosión (b) *Fam (drink)* gaseosa *f* (c) *US Fam (father)* papá *m* (d) *Fam Mus* música *f* pop; **p. singer** cantante *mf* pop
▸ **pop in** *vi Fam* entrar un momento, pasar
popcorn ['pɒpkɔːn] *n* palomitas *fpl*
Pope [pəʊp] *n* **the P.** el Papa
poplar ['pɒplə(r)] *n* álamo *m*
poppy ['pɒpɪ] *n* amapola *f*
Popsicle® ['pɒpsɪkəl] *n US* polo *m*
populace ['pɒpjʊləs] *n (people)* pueblo *m*
popular ['pɒpjʊlə(r)] *adj* popular; *(fashionable)* de moda; *(common)* corriente
popularity [pɒpjʊ'lærɪtɪ] *n* popularidad *f*
popularize ['pɒpjʊləraɪz] *vt* popularizar
populate ['pɒpjʊleɪt] *vt* poblar
population [pɒpjʊ'leɪʃən] *n* población *f*; **the p. explosion** la explosión demográfica
porcelain ['pɔːsəlɪn] *n* porcelana *f*
porch [pɔːtʃ] *n (of church)* pórtico *m*; *(of house)* porche *m*, entrada *f*; *US (veranda)* terraza *f*
porcupine ['pɔːkjʊpaɪn] *n* puerco *m* espín
pore[1] [pɔː(r)] *vi* **to p. over sth** leer *or* estudiar algo detenidamente
pore[2] [pɔː(r)] *n Anat* poro *m*
pork [pɔːk] *n* carne *f* de cerdo
pornography [pɔː'nɒgrəfɪ] *n* pornografía *f*
porous ['pɔːrəs] *adj* poroso(a)
porpoise ['pɔːpəs] *n* marsopa *f*
porridge ['pɒrɪdʒ] *n* gachas *fpl* de avena
port[1] [pɔːt] *n (harbour)* puerto *m*; **p. of call** puerto de escala
port[2] [pɔːt] *n Naut & Av* babor *m*
port[3] [pɔːt] *n (wine)* vino *m* de Oporto, oporto *m*
portable ['pɔːtəbəl] *adj* portátil
portal ['pɔːtəl] *n Comput (web page)* portal *m*
portent ['pɔːtent] *n Fml* augurio *m*
porter ['pɔːtə(r)] *n (in hotel etc)* portero(a) *m,f*; *Rail* mozo *m* de estación; *US* mozo de los coches-cama
portfolio [pɔːt'fəʊlɪəʊ] *n (file)* carpeta *f*; *(of artist, politician)* cartera *f*
porthole ['pɔːthəʊl] *n* portilla *f*
portion ['pɔːʃən] *n (part, piece)* parte *f*, porción *f*; *(of food)* ración *f*
▸ **portion out** *vt sep* repartir
portly ['pɔːtlɪ] *adj* **(portlier, portliest)** corpulento(a)
portrait ['pɔːtreɪt] *n* retrato *m*
portray [pɔː'treɪ] *vt (paint portrait of)* retratar; *(describe)* describir; *Th* representar

Portugal ['pɔːtjʊɡəl] *n* Portugal

Portuguese [pɔːtjʊˈgiːz] **1** *adj* portugués(esa)
2 *n (person)* portugués(esa) *m,f; (language)* portugués *m*

pose [pəʊz] **1** *vt (problem)* plantear; *(threat)* representar
2 *vi (for painting)* posar; *Pej (behave affectedly)* hacer pose; **to p. as** hacerse pasar por
3 *n (stance)* postura *f; Pej (affectation)* pose *f*

posh [pɒʃ] *adj Br Fam* elegante, de lujo; *(person)* presumido(a); *(accent)* de clase alta

position [pəˈzɪʃən] **1** *n* (**a**) posición *f; (location)* situación *f; (rank)* rango *m;* **to be in a p. to do sth** estar en condiciones de hacer algo (**b**) *(opinion)* postura *f* (**c**) *(job)* puesto *m*
2 *vt* colocar

positive ['pɒzɪtɪv] *adj* positivo(a); *(sign)* favorable; *(proof)* incontrovertible; *(sure)* seguro(a); *Fam (absolute)* auténtico(a)

possess [pəˈzes] *vt* poseer; *(of fear)* apoderarse de

possessed [pəˈzest] *adj* poseído(a)

possession [pəˈzeʃən] *n* posesión *f;* **possessions** bienes *mpl*

possessive [pəˈzesɪv] *adj* posesivo(a)

possibility [pɒsɪˈbɪlɪtɪ] *n* posibilidad *f;* **possibilities** *(potential)* potencial *m*

possible ['pɒsɪbəl] *adj* posible; **as much as p.** todo lo posible; **as often as p.** cuanto más mejor; **as soon as p.** cuanto antes

possibly ['pɒsɪblɪ] *adv* posiblemente; *(perhaps)* tal vez, quizás; **I can't p. come** no puedo venir de ninguna manera

post¹ [pəʊst] **1** *n (of wood)* poste *m*
2 *vt (fix)* fijar

post² [pəʊst] **1** *n (job)* puesto *m; US* **trading p.** factoría *f*
2 *vt* enviar

post³ [pəʊst] *Br* **1** *n (mail)* correo *m;* **by p.** por correo; **p. office** oficina *f* de correos; **P. Office Box** apartado *m* de correos
2 *vt (letter)* echar al correo; **to p. sth to sb** mandar algo por correo a algn

postage ['pəʊstɪdʒ] *n* franqueo *m*

postal ['pəʊstəl] *adj* postal, de correos; *Br* **p. code** código *m* postal **p. order** giro *m* postal; **p. vote** voto *m* por correo

postbox ['pəʊstbɒks] *n Br* buzón *m*

postcard ['pəʊstkɑːd] *n* (tarjeta *f*) postal *f*

postcode ['pəʊstkəʊd] *n Br* código *m* postal

postdate [pəʊstˈdeɪt] *vt (cheque)* extender con fecha posterior

poster ['pəʊstə(r)] *n* póster *m; (advertising)* cartel *m*

posterior [pɒˈstɪərɪə(r)] **1** *n Hum* trasero *m,* pompis *m*
2 *adj* posterior

posterity [pɒˈsterɪtɪ] *n* posteridad *f*

postgraduate [pəʊstˈgrædjʊɪt] **1** *n* posgraduado(a) *m,f*
2 *adj* de posgraduado

posthumous ['pɒstjʊməs] *adj* póstumo(a)

postman ['pəʊstmən] *n Br* cartero *m*

postmark ['pəʊstmɑːk] *n* matasellos *m inv*

postmaster ['pəʊstmɑːstə(r)] *n* administrador *m* de correos; **p. general** director *m* general de correos

postmortem [pəʊstˈmɔːtəm] *n* autopsia *f*

postpone [pəsˈpəʊn] *vt* aplazar

postscript ['pəʊsskrɪpt] *n* posdata *f*

posture ['pɒstʃə(r)] **1** *n* postura *f; (affected)* pose *f*
2 *vi* adoptar una pose

postwar ['pəʊstwɔː(r)] *adj* de la posguerra

posy ['pəʊzɪ] *n* ramillete *m*

pot [pɒt] **1** *n (container)* tarro *m,* pote *m; (for cooking)* olla *f; (for flowers)* maceta *f; Fam* **to go to p.** irse al traste; **p. shot** tiro *m* al azar
2 *vt (plant)* poner en una maceta

potassium [pəˈtæsɪəm] *n* potasio *m*

potato [pəˈteɪtəʊ] *n (pl* potatoes) patata *f, Am* papa *f*

potent ['pəʊtənt] *adj* potente

potential [pəˈtenʃəl] **1** *adj* potencial, posible
2 *n* potencial *m*

potentially [pəˈtenʃəlɪ] *adv* en potencia

pothole ['pɒthəʊl] *n Geol* cueva *f; (in road)* bache *m*

potholing ['pɒthəʊlɪŋ] *n Br* espeleología *f*

potion ['pəʊʃən] *n* poción *f,* pócima *f*

potluck [pɒtˈlʌk] *n Fam* **to take p.** conformarse con lo que haya

potted ['pɒtɪd] *adj (food)* en conserva; *(plant)* en maceta *or* tiesto

potter¹ ['pɒtə(r)] *n* alfarero(a) *m,f*

potter² ['pɒtə(r)] *vi Br* **to p. about** *or* **around** entretenerse

pottery ['pɒtərɪ] *n (craft, place)* alfarería *f; (objects)* cerámica *f*

potty¹ ['pɒtɪ] *adj* (pottier, pottiest) *Br Fam* chiflado(a)

potty² ['pɒtɪ] *n Fam* orinal *m*

pouch [paʊtʃ] *n* (**a**) bolsa pequeña; *(for ammunition)* morral *m; (for tobacco)* petaca *f* (**b**) *Zool* bolsa *f* abdominal

poultry ['pəʊltrɪ] *n (live)* aves *fpl* de corral; *(food)* pollos *mpl*

pounce [paʊns] *vi* **to p. on** abalanzarse encima de

pound¹ [paʊnd] **1** *vt (strike)* aporrear
2 *vi (heart)* palpitar; *(walk heavily)* andar con paso pesado

pound² [paʊnd] *n (money, weight)* libra *f*

pound³ [paʊnd] *n (for dogs)* perrera *f; (for cars)* depósito *m* de coches

pour [pɔː(r)] **1** *vt* echar, verter; **to p. sb a drink** servirle una copa a algn
2 *vi* correr, fluir; **it's pouring with rain** está lloviendo a cántaros
▸ **pour out** *vt sep* echar, verter; *Fig* **to p. one's heart out to sb** desahogarse con algn

pouring ['pɔːrɪŋ] *adj (rain)* torrencial

pout [paʊt] **1** *vi* hacer pucheros
2 *n* puchero *m*

poverty ['pɒvətɪ] n pobreza f
poverty-stricken ['pɒvətɪstrɪkən] adj necesitado(a); **to be p.** vivir en la miseria
powder ['paʊdə(r)] **1** n polvo m; **p. compact** polvera f; **p. keg** polvorín m; **p. puff** borla f; **p. room** servicios mpl de señoras
2 vt **to p. one's nose** ponerse polvos en la cara; Euph ir a los servicios or al tocador
powdered ['paʊdəd] adj (milk) en polvo
power ['paʊə(r)] **1** n (**a**) fuerza f, (energy) energía f; Elec **to cut off the p.** cortar la corriente; **p. point** enchufe m; **p. station** central eléctrica (**b**) (ability) poder m (**c**) (authority) poder m; (nation) potencia f; (influence) influencia f; **to be in p.** estar en el poder; Pol **to come into p.** subir al poder; **the p. of veto** el derecho de veto (**d**) Tech potencia f; (output) rendimiento m
2 vt propulsar, impulsar
powerboat ['paʊəbəʊt] n lancha f (motora)
powerful ['paʊəfʊl] adj (strong) fuerte; (influential) poderoso(a); (remedy) eficaz; (engine, machine) potente; (emotion) fuerte; (speech) conmovedor(a)
powerless ['paʊəlɪs] adj impotente, ineficaz
pp (abbr pages) págs., pp
PR [piː'ɑː(r)] (abbr public relations) relaciones fpl públicas
practicable ['præktɪkəbəl] adj factible
practical ['præktɪkəl] adj práctico(a); (useful) útil; (sensible) adecuado(a)
practicality [præktɪ'kælɪtɪ] n (of suggestion, plan) factibilidad f; **practicalities** detalles prácticos
practically ['præktɪkəlɪ] adv (almost) casi
practice ['præktɪs] **1** n (**a**) (habit) costumbre f (**b**) (exercise) práctica f; Sport entrenamiento m; Mus ensayo m; **to be out of p.** no estar en forma (**c**) (way of doing sth) práctica f; **in p.** en la práctica; **to put sth into p.** poner algo en práctica (**d**) (of profession) ejercicio m (**e**) (place) (of doctors) consultorio m; (of lawyers) bufete m (**f**) (clients) (of doctors) pacientes mpl; (of lawyers) clientela f
2 vt & vi US = **practise**
practicing ['præktɪsɪŋ] adj US = **practising**
practise ['præktɪs] **1** vt practicar; (method) seguir; (principle) poner en práctica; Mus ensayar; (profession) ejercer
2 vi practicar; Sport entrenar; Mus ensayar; (doctor) practicar; (lawyer) ejercer
practising ['præktɪsɪŋ] adj (doctor etc) en ejercicio; (Christian etc) practicante
practitioner [præk'tɪʃənə(r)] n Br Med general p. médico(a) m,f de cabecera; **medical p.** médico(a) m,f
pragmatic [præg'mætɪk] adj pragmático(a)
prairie ['preərɪ] n pradera f; US llanura f
praise [preɪz] **1** n alabanza f
2 vt alabar, elogiar
praiseworthy ['preɪzwɜːðɪ] adj loable
pram [præm] n Br cochecito m de niño

prance [prɑːns] vi (horse) encabritarse; **to p. about** (person) pegar brincos
prank [præŋk] n broma f; (of child) travesura f
prat [præt] n Br Fam soplagaitas mf inv, Am pendejo(a) m,f
prawn [prɔːn] n gamba f
pray [preɪ] vi rezar, orar
prayer [preə(r)] n rezo m, oración f; (entreaty) súplica f; **p. book** misal m
preach [priːtʃ] vi predicar
preacher ['priːtʃə(r)] n predicador(a) m,f
precarious [prɪ'keərɪəs] adj precario(a)
precaution [prɪ'kɔːʃən] n precaución f
precede [prɪ'siːd] vt preceder
precedence ['presɪdəns] n preferencia f, prioridad f; **to take p. over sth/sb** tener prioridad sobre algo/algn
precedent ['presɪdənt] n precedente m
preceding [prɪ'siːdɪŋ] adj precedente
precinct ['priːsɪŋkt] n (**a**) (area) recinto m; **pedestrian/shopping p.** zona f peatonal/comercial (**b**) US (administrative, police division) distrito m; (police station) comisaría f (de policía)

     Note that the Spanish word **precinto** is a false friend and is never a translation for the English word **precinct**. In Spanish, **precinto** means "seal".

precious ['preʃəs] **1** adj precioso(a); **p. stones** piedras preciosas
2 adv Fam **p. little/few** muy poco/pocos
precipice ['presɪpɪs] n precipicio m
precipitate 1 vt [prɪ'sɪpɪteɪt] precipitar; Fig arrojar
2 adj [prɪ'sɪpɪtət] precipitado(a)
precise [prɪ'saɪs] adj preciso(a), exacto(a); (meticulous) meticuloso(a)
precisely [prɪ'saɪslɪ] adv (exactly) precisamente, exactamente; **p.!** ¡eso es!, ¡exacto!
precision [prɪ'sɪʒən] n precisión f
preclude [prɪ'kluːd] vt excluir; (misunderstanding) evitar
precocious [prɪ'kəʊʃəs] adj precoz
preconceived [priːkən'siːvd] adj preconcebido(a)
precondition [priːkən'dɪʃən] n condición previa
precursor [prɪ'kɜːsə(r)] n precursor(a) m,f
predator ['predətə(r)] n depredador m
predecessor ['priːdɪsesə(r)] n antecesor(a) m,f
predetermine [priːdɪ'tɜːmɪn] vt predeterminar
predicament [prɪ'dɪkəmənt] n apuro m, aprieto m
predict [prɪ'dɪkt] vt predecir, pronosticar
predictable [prɪ'dɪktəbəl] adj previsible
prediction [prɪ'dɪkʃən] n pronóstico m
predispose [priːdɪ'spəʊz] vt **to be predis-**

posed to doing sth estar predispuesto(a) a hacer algo

predominant [prɪ'dɒmɪnənt] *adj* predominante

predominantly [prɪ'dɒmɪnəntlɪ] *adv* en su mayoría

predominate [prɪ'dɒmɪneɪt] *vi* predominar

pre-empt [prɪ'empt] *vt* adelantarse a

preen [priːn] *vt* **to p. oneself** *(of bird)* arreglarse las plumas; *Fig (of person)* pavonearse

prefab ['priːfæb] *n Br Fam (house)* casa prefabricada

prefabricated [priː'fæbrɪkeɪtɪd] *adj* prefabricado(a)

preface ['prefɪs] **1** *n* prefacio *m*
2 *vt* prologar

prefect ['priːfekt] *n Br Educ* monitor(a) *m,f*

prefer [prɪ'fɜː(r)] *vt* preferir; **I p. coffee to tea** prefiero el café al té

preferable ['prefərəbəl] *adj* preferible (**to** a)

preferably ['prefərəblɪ] *adv* preferentemente

preference ['prefərəns] *n* preferencia *f*; *(priority)* prioridad *f*; **to give p. to sth** dar prioridad a algo

preferential [prefə'renʃəl] *adj* preferente

prefix ['priːfɪks] *n* prefijo *m*

pregnancy ['pregnənsɪ] *n* embarazo *m*

pregnant ['pregnənt] *adj (woman)* embarazada; *(animal)* preñada; *Fig* **a p. pause** una pausa cargada de significado

prehistoric(al) [priːhɪ'stɒrɪk(əl)] *adj* prehistórico(a)

prejudice ['predʒʊdɪs] **1** *n (bias)* prejuicio *m*; *(harm)* perjuicio *m*
2 *vt (bias)* predisponer; *(harm)* perjudicar

prejudiced ['predʒʊdɪst] *adj* parcial; **to be p. against/in favour of** estar predispuesto(a) en contra/a favor de

preliminary [prɪ'lɪmɪnərɪ] **1** *adj* preliminar; *Sport (round)* eliminatorio(a)
2 *n* **preliminaries** preliminares *mpl*

prelude ['prelju:d] *n* preludio *m*

premarital [priː'mærɪtəl] *adj* prematrimonial

premature [premə'tjʊə(r), 'premətjʊə(r)] *adj* prematuro(a)

prematurely [premə'tjʊəlɪ, 'premətjʊəlɪ] *adv* antes de tiempo

premeditate [prɪ'medɪteɪt] *vt (crime)* premeditar

premenstrual [priː'menstrʊəl] *adj* **p. tension** tensión *f* premenstrual

premier ['premjə(r)] **1** *n Pol* primer(a) ministro(a) *m,f*
2 *adj* primer, primero(a)

premiere ['premɪeə(r)] *n Cin* estreno *m*

premise ['premɪs] *n* premisa *f*

premises ['premɪsɪz] *npl* local *m*; **on the p.** en el local

premium ['priːmɪəm] *n Com, Fin & Ind* prima *f*; **to be at a p.** tener sobreprecio; *Fig* estar muy solicitado(a); *Br* **p. bonds** = bonos nu-

merados emitidos por el Gobierno británico, cuyo comprador entra en un sorteo mensual de premios en metálico

premonition [premə'nɪʃən] *n* presentimiento *m*

preoccupied [priː'ɒkjʊpaɪd] *adj* preocupado(a); **to be p. with sth** preocuparse por algo

prep [prep] *n Br Fam* deberes *mpl*; **p. school** = colegio privado para alumnos de entre 7 y 13 años

prepacked [priː'pækt] *adj* empaquetado(a)

prepaid [priː'peɪd] *adj* con el porte pagado

preparation [prepə'reɪʃən] *n* preparación *f*; *(plan)* preparativo *m*

preparatory [prɪ'pærətərɪ] *adj* preparatorio(a), preliminar; **p. school** *Br* = colegio privado para alumnos de entre 7 y 13 años; *US* = escuela secundaria privada

prepare [prɪ'peə(r)] **1** *vt* preparar; **to p. to do sth** prepararse para hacer algo
2 *vi* prepararse (**for** para)

prepared [prɪ'peəd] *adj (ready)* preparado(a); **to be p. to do sth** *(willing)* estar dispuesto(a) a hacer algo

preponderance [prɪ'pɒndərəns] *n* preponderancia *f*

preposition [prepə'zɪʃən] *n* preposición *f*

preposterous [prɪ'pɒstərəs] *adj* absurdo(a), ridículo(a)

prerequisite [priː'rekwɪzɪt] *n* condición *f* previa

prerogative [prɪ'rɒgətɪv] *n* prerrogativa *f*

preschool [priː'skuːl] *adj* preescolar

prescribe [prɪ'skraɪb] *vt (set down)* prescribir; *Med* recetar; *Fig (recommend)* recomendar

prescription [prɪ'skrɪpʃən] *n Med* receta *f*

presence ['prezəns] *n* presencia *f*; *(attendance)* asistencia *f*; *Fig* **p. of mind** presencia de ánimo

present¹ ['prezənt] **1** *adj* (**a**) *(in attendance)* presente; *Ling* **p. tense** (tiempo *m*) presente *m*; **to be p. at** estar presente en (**b**) *(current)* actual
2 *n (time)* presente *m*, actualidad *f*; **at p.** actualmente; **for the p.** de momento; **up to the p.** hasta ahora

present² **1** *vt* [prɪ'zent] (**a**) *(give as gift)* regalar; *(medals, prizes etc)* entregar; **to p. sb with sth** obsequiar a algn con algo (**b**) *(report etc)* presentar; *(opportunity)* ofrecer; *(problems)* plantear (**c**) *(introduce) (person, programme)* presentar
2 *n* ['prezənt] *(gift)* regalo *m*; *(formal)* obsequio *m*

presentable [prɪ'zentəbəl] *adj* presentable; **to make oneself p.** arreglarse

presentation [prezən'teɪʃən] *n* (**a**) presentación *f*; **p. ceremony** ceremonia *f* de entrega (**b**) *Rad TV* representación *f*

present-day ['prezəntdeɪ] *adj* actual, de hoy en día

presenter [prɪ'zentə(r)] n Rad locutor(a) m,f; TV presentador(a) m,f

presently ['prezəntlɪ] adv (soon) dentro de poco; US (now) ahora

preservation [prezə'veɪʃən] n conservación f

preservative [prɪ'zɜːvətɪv] n conservante m

preserve [prɪ'zɜːv] **1** vt (a) (keep) mantener (b) Culin conservar
2 n (a) (hunting) coto m (b) Culin conserva f

preside [prɪ'zaɪd] vi presidir

president ['prezɪdənt] n Pol presidente(a) m,f; US Com director(a) m,f, gerente mf

presidential [prezɪ'denʃəl] adj presidencial

press [pres] **1** vt (a) (squeeze) apretar; (button) pulsar; (grapes) pisar; (trousers etc) planchar
(b) (urge) presionar; **to p. sb to do sth** acosar a algn para que haga algo
2 vi (a) (push) apretar; **to p. against sb/sth** apretarse contra algn/algo; **to p. (down) on sth** hacer presión sobre algo
(b) (urge) apremiar; **time presses** el tiempo apremia
3 n (a) **p. stud** botón m de presión
(b) (machine) prensa f; **to go to p.** (of newspaper) entrar en prensa
(c) Press prensa f; **the p.** la prensa; **to get a good/bad p.** tener buena/mala prensa; **p. agency** agencia f de prensa; **p. conference** rueda f de prensa; **p. cutting** recorte m de prensa
▸ **press on** vi seguir adelante

pressed [prest] adj **to be (hard) p. for** andar escaso(a) de; **I'd be hard p. to do it** me costaría mucho hacerlo

pressing ['presɪŋ] adj apremiante, urgente

press-up ['presʌp] n Br flexión f (de brazos)

pressure ['preʃə(r)] n presión f; Med & Met **high/low p.** altas/bajas presiones; **p. cooker** olla f a presión; **p. gauge** manómetro m; Fig **to bring p. (to bear) on sb** ejercer presión sobre algn

pressurize ['preʃəraɪz] vt Fig presionar; **pressurized cabin** cabina presurizada

prestige [pre'stiːʒ] n prestigio m

presumably [prɪ'zjuːməblɪ] adv es de suponer que

presume [prɪ'zjuːm] **1** vt suponer, presumir
2 vi (suppose) suponer; **we p. so/not** suponemos que sí/no

presumption [prɪ'zʌmpʃən] n (a) (supposition) suposición f (b) (boldness) osadía f; (conceit) presunción f

presumptuous [prɪ'zʌmptjʊəs] adj impertinente

🖉 Note that the Spanish word **presuntuoso** is a false friend and is never a translation for the English word **presumptuous**. In Spanish, **presuntuoso** means "vain" and "pretentious".

presuppose [priːsə'pəʊz] vt presuponer

pretence [prɪ'tens] n (a) (deception) fingimiento m; **false pretences** estafa f; **under the p. of** so pretexto de (b) (claim) pretensión f

pretend [prɪ'tend] **1** vt (feign) fingir, aparentar; (claim) pretender
2 vi (feign) fingir

pretense [prɪ'tens] n US = **pretence**

pretention [prɪ'tenʃən] n pretensión f

pretentious [prɪ'tenʃəs] adj presuntuoso(a), pretencioso(a)

pretext ['priːtekst] n pretexto m; **on the p. of** so pretexto de

pretty ['prɪtɪ] **1** adj (prettier, prettiest) bonito(a), guapo(a)
2 adv Fam bastante; **p. much the same** más o menos lo mismo

prevail [prɪ'veɪl] vi (a) (predominate) predominar (b) (win through) prevalecer (c) **to p. upon** or **on sb to do sth** (persuade) persuadir or convencer a algn para que haga algo

prevailing [prɪ'veɪlɪŋ] adj (wind) predominante; (opinion) general; (condition, fashion) actual

prevalent ['prevələnt] adj predominante; (illness) extendido(a)

prevaricate [prɪ'værɪkeɪt] vi andar con ambages

prevent [prɪ'vent] vt impedir; (accident) evitar; (illness) prevenir; **to p. sb from doing sth** impedir a algn hacer algo; **to p. sth from happening** evitar que pase algo

prevention [prɪ'venʃən] n prevención f

preventive [prɪ'ventɪv] adj preventivo(a)

preview ['priːvjuː] n (of film etc) preestreno m

previous ['priːvɪəs] **1** adj anterior, previo(a); **p. conviction** antecedente m penal
2 adv **p. to going** antes de ir

previously ['priːvɪəslɪ] adv anteriormente, previamente

prewar ['priːwɔː(r)] adj de antes de la guerra

prey [preɪ] **1** n presa f; Fig víctima f
2 vi **to p. on** alimentarse de

price [praɪs] **1** n precio m; **what p. is that coat?** ¿cuánto cuesta el abrigo?; **p. list** lista f de precios; **p. tag** etiqueta f
2 vt (put price on) poner un precio a; (value) valorar

priceless ['praɪslɪs] adj que no tiene precio

prick [prɪk] **1** vt picar; **to p. one's finger** pincharse el dedo; Fig **to p. up one's ears** aguzar el oído
2 n (a) (with pin) pinchazo m (b) very Fam (penis) polla f (c) very Fam Pej (person) gilipollas mf inv

prickle ['prɪkəl] **1** n espina f; (spike) pincho m; (sensation) picor m
2 vt & vi pinchar, picar

prickly ['prɪklɪ] adj (pricklier, prickliest) espinoso(a); Fig (touchy) enojadizo(a); **p. heat** = sarpullido por causa del calor; **p. pear** higo chumbo

pride [praɪd] **1** n orgullo m; (arrogance) so-

berbia f; **to take p. in sth** enorgullecerse de
algo
  2 vt **to p. oneself on** enorgullecerse de
priest [priːst] n sacerdote m, cura m
priestess [ˈpriːstɪs] n sacerdotisa f
priesthood [ˈpriːsthʊd] n (clergy) clero m;
  (office) sacerdocio m
prig [prɪg] n gazmoño(a) m,f, mojigato(a) m,f
prim [prɪm] adj (**primmer, primmest**) **p. (and
  proper)** remilgado(a)
primaeval [praɪˈmiːvəl] adj primitivo(a)
primarily [ˈpraɪmərɪlɪ] adv ante todo
primary [ˈpraɪmərɪ] **1** adj fundamental, principal; **of p. importance** primordial; **p. colour**
  color primario; **p. education/school** ense-
  ñanza/escuela primaria
  2 n US Pol (elección f) primaria f
primate¹ [ˈpraɪmeɪt] n Rel primado m
primate² [ˈpraɪmeɪt] n Zool primate m
prime [praɪm] **1** adj (**a**) (chief, major)
  primordial; **P. Minister** primer(a) ministro(a)
  m,f (**b**) (first-rate) de primera; **p. number**
  número primo
  2 n **in the p. of life** en la flor de la vida
  3 vt (pump, engine) cebar; (surface) impri-
  mar; Fig (prepare) preparar
primer¹ [ˈpraɪmə(r)] n (textbook) cartilla f
primer² [ˈpraɪmə(r)] n (paint) imprimación f
primeval [praɪˈmiːvəl] adj = **primaeval**
primitive [ˈprɪmɪtɪv] adj primitivo(a);
  (method, tool) rudimentario(a)
primrose [ˈprɪmrəʊz] n primavera f
Primus® [ˈpraɪməs] n hornillo m de camping
prince [prɪns] n príncipe m; **P. Charming**
  Príncipe Azul
princess [prɪnˈses] n princesa f
principal [ˈprɪnsɪpəl] **1** adj principal
  2 n Educ director(a) m,f; Th (in play) protagonista mf principal
principle [ˈprɪnsɪpəl] n principio m; **in p.** en
  principio; **on p.** por principio
print [prɪnt] **1** vt (**a**) (publish) publicar; Fig grabar; **printed matter** impresos
  mpl (**b**) (write) escribir con letra de imprenta
  2 n (**a**) (of hand, foot) huella f (**b**) (written
  text) letra f; **out of p.** agotado(a) (**c**) Tex
  estampado m; **p. skirt** falda estampada (**d**)
  Art grabado m; Phot copia f
  ▸ **print out** vt sep Comput imprimir
printer [ˈprɪntə(r)] n (person) impresor(a)
  m,f; (machine) impresora f
printing [ˈprɪntɪŋ] n (industry) imprenta f;
  (process) impresión f; (print run) tirada f; **p.
  press** prensa f
print-out [ˈprɪntaʊt] n Comput impresión f;
  (copy) copia impresa
prior [ˈpraɪə(r)] adj previo(a), anterior; **p. to
  leaving** antes de salir
priority [praɪˈɒrɪtɪ] n prioridad f
prise [praɪz] vt **to p. sth open** abrir algo con
  palanca; **to p. sth off** arrancar algo
prism [ˈprɪzəm] n prisma f

prison [ˈprɪzən] n cárcel f, prisión f
prisoner [ˈprɪzənə(r)] n preso(a) m,f; **to hold
  sb p.** detener a algn; **p. of war** prisionero(a)
  m,f de guerra
privacy [ˈpraɪvəsɪ, ˈprɪvəsɪ] n intimidad f
private [ˈpraɪvɪt] **1** adj privado(a); (secretary)
  particular; (matter) personal; (letter) confidencial; **one's p. life** la vida privada de uno;
  p. (notice) (on road) carretera privada; (on
  gate) propiedad privada; (on envelope) confidencial; **p. detective, Fam p. eye** detective mf
  privado(a); **p. school** escuela privada
  2 n Mil soldado raso
privately [ˈpraɪvɪtlɪ] adv en privado; (personally) personalmente
privet [ˈprɪvɪt] n alheña f
privilege [ˈprɪvɪlɪdʒ] n privilegio m
privileged [ˈprɪvɪlɪdʒd] adj privilegiado(a)
privy [ˈprɪvɪ] **1** adj Br **P. Council** Consejo
  Privado; **to be p. to sth** estar enterado(a) de
  algo
  2 n (lavatory) retrete m
prize [praɪz] **1** n premio m
  2 adj (first-class) de primera (categoría or
  clase)
  3 vt (value) apreciar, valorar
prize-giving [ˈpraɪzgɪvɪŋ] n distribución f de
  premios
prizewinner [ˈpraɪzwɪnə(r)] n premiado(a)
  m,f
pro¹ [prəʊ] n pro m; **the pros and cons of an
  issue** los pros y los contras de una cuestión
pro² [prəʊ] n Fam profesional mf
pro- [prəʊ] pref (in favour of) pro-
probability [prɒbəˈbɪlɪtɪ] n probabilidad f
probable [ˈprɒbəbəl] adj probable
probably [ˈprɒbəblɪ] adv probablemente
probation [prəˈbeɪʃən] n Jur **to be on p.**
  estar en libertad condicional; **to be on two
  months' p.** (at work) trabajar dos meses de
  prueba
probe [prəʊb] **1** n Med & (in outer space)
  sonda f; (investigation) sondeo m
  2 vt Med sondar; (investigate) investigar
  ▸ **probe into** vt insep investigar
problem [ˈprɒbləm] n problema m
problematic(al) [prɒbləˈmætɪk(əl)] adj pro-
  blemático(a); **it's p.** tiene sus problemas
procedure [prəˈsiːdʒə(r)] n procedimiento
  m; (legal, business) gestión f, trámite m
proceed [prəˈsiːd] vi seguir, proceder; **to p.
  to do sth** ponerse a hacer algo; **to p. to the
  next matter** pasar a la siguiente cuestión
proceedings [prəˈsiːdɪŋz] npl (of meeting)
  actas fpl; (measures) medidas fpl; Jur proceso
  m
proceeds [ˈprəʊsiːdz] npl ganancias fpl
process [ˈprəʊses] **1** n proceso m; (method)
  método m, sistema m; **in the p. of** en vías de
  2 vt (information) tramitar; (food) tratar;
  Comput procesar
processing [ˈprəʊsesɪŋ] n (of information)

evaluación f; *Comput* tratamiento m

procession [prəˈseʃən] n desfile m; *Rel* procesión f

proclaim [prəˈkleɪm] vt proclamar, declarar

proclamation [prɒkləˈmeɪʃən] n proclamación f

procrastinate [prəʊˈkræstɪneɪt] vi dejar las cosas para después

procure [prəˈkjʊə(r)] vt conseguir, procurarse

prod [prɒd] vt *(with stick etc)* golpear; *(push)* empujar

prodigal [ˈprɒdɪgəl] adj pródigo(a)

prodigious [prəˈdɪdʒəs] adj prodigioso(a)

prodigy [ˈprɒdɪdʒɪ] n prodigio m

produce 1 vt [prəˈdjuːs] **(a)** producir; *Ind* fabricar **(b)** *Th* dirigir; *Rad & TV* realizar; *Cin* producir **(c)** *(give birth to)* dar a luz a **(d)** *(document)* enseñar; *(bring out)* sacar
2 n [ˈprɒdjuːs] productos mpl; **p. of Spain** producto m de España

producer [prəˈdjuːsə(r)] n **(a)** productor(a) m,f; *Ind* fabricante mf **(b)** *Th* director(a) m,f de escena; *Rad & TV* realizador(a) m,f; *Cin* productor(a) m,f

product [ˈprɒdʌkt] n producto m

production [prəˈdʌkʃən] n **(a)** producción f; *Ind* fabricación f **(b)** *Th* representación f; *Rad & TV* realización f; *Cin* producción f; **p. line** cadena f de montaje

productive [prəˈdʌktɪv] adj productivo(a)

productivity [prɒdʌkˈtɪvɪtɪ] n productividad f

profane [prəˈfeɪn] adj *(secular)* profano(a); *(language)* blasfemo(a)

profess [prəˈfes] vt *(faith)* profesar; *(opinion)* expresar; *(claim)* pretender

profession [prəˈfeʃən] n profesión f

professional [prəˈfeʃənəl] **1** adj profesional; *(soldier)* de profesión; *(polished)* de gran calidad
2 n profesional mf

professor [prəˈfesə(r)] n *Univ Br* catedrático(a) m,f; *US* profesor(a) m,f

proficiency [prəˈfɪʃənsɪ] n *(in language)* capacidad f; *(in skill)* pericia f

proficient [prəˈfɪʃənt] adj *(in language)* experto(a); *(in skill)* hábil

profile [ˈprəʊfaɪl] n perfil m; **in p.** de perfil

profit [ˈprɒfɪt] **1** n **(a)** beneficio m, ganancia f; **to make a p. on** sacar beneficios de **(b)** *Fml (benefit)* provecho m
2 vi *Fig* sacar provecho; **to p. from** aprovecharse de

profitability [prɒfɪtəˈbɪlɪtɪ] n rentabilidad f

profitable [ˈprɒfɪtəbəl] adj *Com* rentable; *Fig (worthwhile)* provechoso(a)

profiteer [prɒfɪˈtɪə(r)] **1** n especulador(a) m,f
2 vi obtener beneficios excesivos

profound [prəˈfaʊnd] adj profundo(a)

profuse [prəˈfjuːs] adj profuso(a), abundante

profusely [prəˈfjuːslɪ] adv con profusión; **to sweat p.** sudar mucho

profusion [prəˈfjuːʒən] n profusión f, abundancia f

prognosis [prɒgˈnəʊsɪs] n *Med* pronóstico m; *Fig (prediction)* augurio m

program [ˈprəʊgræm] *Comput* **1** n programa m
2 vi & vt programar
3 *US* = **programme**

programer [ˈprəʊgræmər] n *US* = **programmer**

programme [ˈprəʊgræm] **1** n programa m; *(plan)* plan m
2 vt **(a)** *(plan)* planear, planificar **(b)** *(computer)* programar

programmer [ˈprəʊgræmə(r)] n programador(a) m,f

progress 1 n [ˈprəʊgres] progreso m; *(development)* desarrollo m; *Med* mejora f; **to make p.** hacer progresos; **in p.** en curso
2 vi [prəʊˈgres] avanzar; *(develop)* desarrollar; *(improve)* hacer progresos; *Med* mejorar

progressive [prəˈgresɪv] adj *(increasing)* progresivo(a); *Pol* progresista

progressively [prəˈgresɪvlɪ] adv progresivamente

prohibit [prəˈhɪbɪt] vt prohibir; **to p. sb from doing sth** prohibir a algn hacer algo

prohibitive [prəˈhɪbɪtɪv] adj prohibitivo(a)

project 1 n [ˈprɒdʒekt] proyecto m; *(plan)* plan m; *Educ* trabajo m; *US* **(housing) p.** = urbanización con viviendas de protección oficial
2 vt [prəˈdʒekt] proyectar, planear
3 vi *(stick out)* sobresalir

projectile [prəˈdʒektaɪl] n *Fml* proyectil m

projection [prəˈdʒekʃən] n **(a)** *(overhang)* saliente m **(b)** *Cin* proyección f **(c)** *(forecast)* proyección f

projector [prəˈdʒektə(r)] n *Cin* proyector m

proletariat [prəʊlɪˈeərɪət] n proletariado m

prolific [prəˈlɪfɪk] adj prolífico(a)

prologue [ˈprəʊlɒg] n prólogo m

prolong [prəˈlɒŋ] vt prolongar

prom [prɒm] n *Br Fam (seafront)* paseo marítimo; *Br (concert)* = concierto sinfónico en que parte del público está de pie; *US (school dance)* = baile de fin de curso

promenade [prɒməˈnɑːd] **1** n *(at seaside)* paseo marítimo
2 vi pasearse

prominence [ˈprɒmɪnəns] n prominencia f; *Fig (importance)* importancia f

prominent [ˈprɒmɪnənt] adj *(standing out)* saliente; *Fig (important)* importante; *(famous)* eminente

promiscuous [prəˈmɪskjʊəs] adj promiscuo(a)

promise [ˈprɒmɪs] **1** n promesa f; **to show p.** ser prometedor(a)
2 vt & vi prometer

promising ['prɒmɪsɪŋ] *adj* prometedor(a)

promontory ['prɒməntərɪ] *n* promontorio *m*

promote [prə'məʊt] *vt* ascender; *(product)* promocionar; *(ideas)* fomentar; *Ftb* **they've been promoted** han subido

promoter [prə'məʊtə(r)] *n* promotor(a) *m,f*

promotion [prə'məʊʃən] *n (in rank)* promoción *f*, ascenso *m*; *(of product)* promoción *f*; *(of arts etc)* fomento *m*

prompt ['prɒmpt] **1** *adj (quick)* rápido(a); *(punctual)* puntual

2 *adv* **at two o'clock p.** a las dos en punto

3 *vt* (**a**) *(motivate)* incitar; **to p. sb to do sth** instar a algn a hacer algo (**b**) *(actor)* apuntar

promptly [prɒmptlɪ] *adv (quickly)* rápidamente; *(punctually)* puntualmente

prone [prəʊn] *adj* (**a**) **to be p. to do sth** ser propenso(a) a hacer algo (**b**) *Fml (face down)* boca abajo

prong [prɒŋ] *n* punta *f*, diente *m*

pronoun ['prəʊnaʊn] *n* pronombre *m*

pronounce [prə'naʊns] **1** *vt* pronunciar; *Fml (declare)* declarar

2 *vi Fml* **to p. on sth** opinar sobre algo

pronounced [prə'naʊnst] *adj* pronunciado(a)

pronouncement [prə'naʊnsmənt] *n Fml* declaración *f*

pronunciation [prənʌnsɪ'eɪʃən] *n* pronunciación *f*

proof [pruːf] **1** *n* prueba *f*

2 *adj* (**a**) *(secure)* a prueba de (**b**) **this rum is 70 percent p.** este ron tiene 70 grados

3 *vt* impermeabilizar

prop¹ [prɒp] **1** *n (support)* puntal *m*; *Fig* sostén *m*

2 *vt (support)* apoyar; *Fig* sostener

▸ **prop up** *vt sep* apoyar

prop² [prɒp] *n Fam Th* accesorio *m*

propaganda [prɒpə'gændə] *n* propaganda *f*

propel [prə'pel] *vt* propulsar

propeller [prə'pelə(r)] *n* hélice *f*

propelling pencil [prə'pelɪŋ'pensəl] *n* portaminas *m inv*

propensity [prə'pensɪtɪ] *n Fml* propensión *f*

proper ['prɒpə(r)] *adj* (**a**) adecuado(a), correcto(a); **the p. time** el momento oportuno (**b**) *(real)* real, auténtico(a); *(actual, exact)* propiamente dicho(a) (**c**) *(characteristic)* propio(a); *Ling* **p. noun** nombre propio

properly ['prɒpəlɪ] *adv (suitably, correctly, decently)* correctamente; **it wasn't p. closed** no estaba bien cerrado(a); **she refused, quite p.** se negó, y con razón

property ['prɒpətɪ] *n* (**a**) *(quality)* propiedad *f* (**b**) *(possession)* propiedad *f*, posesión *f*; **personal p.** bienes *mpl*; **public p.** dominio público (**c**) *(estate)* finca *f*

prophecy ['prɒfɪsɪ] *n* profecía *f*

prophesy ['prɒfɪsaɪ] *vt (predict)* predecir; *Rel* profetizar

prophet ['prɒfɪt] *n* profeta *mf*

proportion [prə'pɔːʃən] *n* proporción *f*; *(part, quantity)* parte *f*; **in p. to** *or* **with** en proporción a

proportional [prə'pɔːʃənəl] *adj* proporcional (**to** a); *Pol* **p. representation** representación *f* proporcional

proportionate [prə'pɔːʃənɪt] *adj* proporcional

proposal [prə'pəʊzəl] *n* propuesta *f*; *(suggestion)* sugerencia *f*; **p. of marriage** propuesta de matrimonio

propose [prə'pəʊz] **1** *vt* proponer; *(suggest)* sugerir; *Fml (intend)* tener la intención de

2 *vi* declararse

proposition [prɒpə'zɪʃən] *n* propuesta *f*; *Math* proposición *f*

proprietor [prə'praɪətə(r)] *n* propietario(a) *m,f*

propriety [prə'praɪətɪ] *n (decency)* decoro *m*

propulsion [prə'pʌlʃən] *n* propulsión *f*

prosaic [prəʊ'zeɪk] *adj* prosaico(a)

prose [prəʊz] *n Lit* prosa *f*; *Educ* texto *m* para traducir

prosecute ['prɒsɪkjuːt] *vt* procesar

prosecution [prɒsɪ'kjuːʃən] *n (action)* proceso *m*, juicio *m*; **the p.** la acusación

prosecutor ['prɒsɪkjuːtə(r)] *n* acusador(a) *m,f*

prospect 1 *n* ['prɒspekt] *(outlook)* perspectiva *f*; *(hope)* esperanza *f*; **the job has prospects** es un trabajo con porvenir

2 *vt* [prə'spekt] explorar

3 *vi* **to p. for gold/oil** buscar oro/petróleo

prospective [prə'spektɪv] *adj (future)* futuro(a); *(possible)* eventual, probable

prospector [prə'spektə(r)] *n* **gold p.** buscador(a) *m,f* del oro

prospectus [prə'spektəs] *n* prospecto *m*

prosper ['prɒspə(r)] *vi* prosperar

prosperity [prɒ'sperɪtɪ] *n* prosperidad *f*

prosperous ['prɒspərəs] *adj* próspero(a)

prostitute ['prɒstɪtjuːt] *n* prostituta *f*

prostitution [prɒstɪ'tjuːʃən] *n* prostitución *f*

prostrate ['prɒstreɪt] *adj (face down)* boca abajo; **p. with grief** deshecho(a) de dolor

protagonist [prəʊ'tægənɪst] *n* protagonista *mf*

protect [prə'tekt] *vt* proteger; *(interests etc)* salvaguardar; **to p. sb from sth** proteger a algn de algo

protection [prə'tekʃən] *n* protección *f*

protective [prə'tektɪv] *adj* protector(a)

protégé ['prɒtəʒeɪ] *n* protegido *m*

protégée ['prɒtəʒeɪ] *n* protegida *f*

protein ['prəʊtiːn] *n* proteína *f*

protest 1 *n* ['prəʊtest] protesta *f*; *(complaint)* queja *f*

2 *vt* [prə'test] *US* protestar en contra de

3 *vi* protestar

Protestant ['prɒtɪstənt] *adj & n* protestante *(mf)*

protester [prə'testə(r)] *n* manifestante *mf*

protocol ['prəʊtəkɒl] n protocolo m
prototype ['prəʊtətaɪp] n prototipo m
protracted [prə'træktɪd] adj prolongado(a)
protrude [prə'truːd] vi Fml sobresalir
protuberance [prə'tjuːbərəns] n Fml protuberancia f
proud [praʊd] adj orgulloso(a); (arrogant) soberbio(a)
prove [pruːv] vt (a) probar, demostrar; Math comprobar; **to p. oneself** dar pruebas de valor (b) it proved to be disastrous (turned out) resultó ser desastroso(a)
proverb ['prɒvɜːb] n refrán m, proverbio m
provide [prə'vaɪd] 1 vt proporcionar; (supplies) suministrar, proveer
2 vi proveer; **to p. for sb** mantener a algn
provided [prə'vaɪdɪd] conj **p. (that)** con tal de que
providing [prə'vaɪdɪŋ] conj = **provided**
province ['prɒvɪns] n provincia f; Fig (field of knowledge) campo m
provincial [prə'vɪnʃəl] 1 adj provincial; Pej provinciano(a)
2 n Pej (person) provinciano(a) m,f
provision [prə'vɪʒən] n provisión f; (supply) suministro m; **provisions** (food) provisiones fpl, víveres mpl
provisional [prə'vɪʒənəl] adj provisional
proviso [prə'vaɪzəʊ] n **with the p. that** a condición de que
provocation [prɒvə'keɪʃən] n provocación f
provocative [prə'vɒkətɪv] adj provocador(a); (flirtatious) provocativo(a)
provoke [prə'vəʊk] vt provocar
prow [praʊ] n proa f
prowess ['praʊɪs] n destreza f
prowl [praʊl] 1 n merodeo m; **to be on the p.** merodear, rondar
2 vi merodear; Fam **to p. about** or **around** rondar
prowler ['praʊlə(r)] n Fam merodeador m
proximity [prɒk'sɪmɪtɪ] n proximidad f; **in p. to, in the p. of** cerca de
proxy ['prɒksɪ] n Jur (power) poderes mpl; (person) apoderado(a) m,f; **by p.** por poderes
prudence ['pruːdəns] n prudencia f
prudent ['pruːdənt] adj prudente
prudish ['pruːdɪʃ] adj remilgado(a)
prune¹ [pruːn] n ciruela pasa
prune² [pruːn] vt (roses etc) podar; Fig acortar
pry [praɪ] vi curiosear, husmear; **to p. into sb's affairs** meterse en asuntos ajenos
PS, ps [piː'es] (abbr **postscript**) P.S., P.D.
psalm [sɑːm] n salmo m
pseudo- ['sjuːdəʊ] pref pseudo-, seudo-
pseudonym ['sjuːdənɪm] n (p)seudónimo m
psyche ['saɪkɪ] n psique f
psychiatric [saɪkɪ'ætrɪk] adj psiquiátrico(a)
psychiatrist [saɪ'kaɪətrɪst] n psiquiatra mf
psychiatry [saɪ'kaɪətrɪ] n psiquiatría f
psychic ['saɪkɪk] 1 adj psíquico(a)

2 n médium mf
psychoanalysis [saɪkəʊə'nælɪsɪs] n psicoanálisis f
psychoanalyst [saɪkəʊ'ænəlɪst] n psicoanalista mf
psychological [saɪkə'lɒdʒɪkəl] adj psicológico(a)
psychologist [saɪ'kɒlədʒɪst] n psicólogo(a) m,f
psychology [saɪ'kɒlədʒɪ] n psicología f
psychopath ['saɪkəʊpæθ] n psicópata mf
psychotherapist ['saɪkəʊ'θerəpɪst] n psicoterapeuta mf
psychotherapy ['saɪkəʊ'θerəpɪ] n psicoterapia f
psychotic [saɪ'kɒtɪk] adj & n psicótico(a) (m,f)
PT [piː'tiː] n (abbr **physical training**) educación f física
PTA [piːtiː'eɪ] n (abbr **Parent-Teacher Association**) = asociación de padres de alumnos y profesores, ≃ APA f
PTO, pto [piːtiː'əʊ] (abbr **please turn over**) sigue
pub [pʌb] n Br Fam bar m, pub m
puberty ['pjuːbətɪ] n pubertad f
pubic ['pjuːbɪk] adj púbico(a)
public ['pʌblɪk] 1 adj público(a); **to make sth p.** hacer público algo; Com **to go p.** (of company) pasar a cotizar en Bolsa; **p. company** empresa pública; **p. convenience** servicios mpl, aseos mpl; **p. holiday** fiesta f nacional; Br **p. house** pub m, taberna f; Br **p. limited company** sociedad anónima; **p. opinion** opinión pública; Br **p. prosecutor** fiscal m; **p. relations** relaciones públicas; **p. school** Br colegio privado; US colegio público; **p. transport** transporte público
2 **the p.** el público; **in p.** en público
public-address system ['pʌblɪkə'dressɪstəm] n megafonía f
publican ['pʌblɪkən] n tabernero(a) m,f
publication [pʌblɪ'keɪʃən] n publicación f
publicity [pʌ'blɪsɪtɪ] n publicidad f
publicize ['pʌblɪsaɪz] vt (make public) hacer público(a); (advertise) hacer publicidad a
public-spirited [pʌblɪk'spɪrɪtɪd] adj de espíritu cívico
publish ['pʌblɪʃ] vt publicar, editar
publisher ['pʌblɪʃə(r)] n (person) editor(a) m,f; (firm) (casa f) editorial f
publishing ['pʌblɪʃɪŋ] n (business) industria f editorial; **p. company** or **house** casa f editorial
pucker ['pʌkə(r)] vt (lips, brow) fruncir, arrugar
pudding ['pʊdɪŋ] n Culin pudín m; (dessert) postre m; **Christmas p.** = pudín a base de frutos secos típico de Navidad; **p. basin** cuenco m; **steamed p.** budín m
puddle ['pʌdəl] n charco m
Puerto Rican ['pweətəʊ'riːkən] adj & n por-

torriqueño(a) *(m,f)*, puertorriqueño(a) *(m,f)*

Puerto Rico ['pweətəʊ'riːkəʊ] *n* Puerto Rico

puff [pʌf] **1** *n (of wind)* racha *f; (of smoke)* bocanada *f;* **p. pastry** pasta *f* de hojaldre

2 *vi (person)* jadear, resoplar; *(train)* echar humo; **to p. on one's pipe** chupar la pipa

3 *vt (cigarette)* dar una calada a

▸ **puff up** *vi* hincharse

puffy ['pʌfɪ] *adj* (**puffier, puffiest**) hinchado(a)

pugnacious [pʌg'neɪʃəs] *adj* belicoso(a)

pull [pʊl] **1** *n* (a) **to give sth a p.** *(tug)* dar un tirón a algo (b) *(of engine)* tracción *f; Fig (attraction)* atracción *f; (influence)* enchufe *m*

2 *vt* (a) *(tug)* dar un tirón a; **to p. a muscle** sufrir un tirón en un músculo; **to p. the trigger** apretar el gatillo; **to p. to pieces** hacer pedazos; *Fig* poner algo por los suelos; *Fig* **to p. sb's leg** tomar el pelo a algn (b) *(draw)* tirar, arrastrar; *Fig* **to p. one's weight** hacer su parte del trabajo (c) *(draw out)* sacar (d) *Fam (people)* atraer

3 *vi (drag)* tirar; **to p. alongside sb** acercarse a algn

▸ **pull apart** *vt sep* desmontar; *Fig (criticize)* poner por los suelos

▸ **pull down** *vt sep (building)* derribar

▸ **pull in 1** *vt sep (crowds)* atraer

2 *vi (train)* entrar en la estación; *(stop)* parar

▸ **pull off 1** *vt sep Fam (carry out)* llevar a cabo

2 *vi (vehicle)* arrancar

▸ **pull out 1** *vt sep (withdraw)* retirar

2 *vi Aut* **to p. out to overtake** salir para adelantar

▸ **pull over** *vi* hacerse a un lado

▸ **pull through** *vi* reponerse, restablecerse

▸ **pull together** *vt sep* **to p. oneself together** calmarse

▸ **pull up 1** *vt sep* (a) *(uproot)* desarraigar; **to p. up one's socks** subirse los calcetines; *Fig* espabilarse (b) *(chair)* acercar

2 *vi (stop)* pararse

pulley ['pʊlɪ] *n* polea *f*

pullover ['pʊləʊvə(r)] *n* jersey *m*, suéter *m*, pulóver *m, Andes* chompa *f, Urug* buzo *m*

pulp [pʌlp] **1** *n (of paper, wood)* pasta *f; (of fruit)* pulpa *f; Fam Fig (book etc)* basura *f*

2 *vt* reducir a pulpa

pulpit ['pʊlpɪt] *n* púlpito *m*

pulsate [pʌl'seɪt] *vi* vibrar, palpitar

pulse¹ [pʌls] *n Anat* pulso *m*

pulse² [pʌls] *n Bot & Culin* legumbre *f*

pumice ['pʌmɪs] *n* **p. (stone)** piedra *f* pómez

pummel ['pʌməl] *vt* aporrear

pump¹ [pʌmp] **1** *n* bomba *f*

2 *vt* bombear; **to p. sth in/out** meter/sacar algo con una bomba; *Fam Fig* **to p. sb for information** sonsacar información a algn

▸ **pump out** *vt sep (empty)* vaciar

▸ **pump up** *vt sep (tyre)* inflar

pump² [pʌmp] *n (shoe)* zapatilla *f*

pumpkin ['pʌmpkɪn] *n* calabaza *f*

pun [pʌn] *n* juego *m* de palabras

punch¹ [pʌntʃ] **1** *n (for making holes)* perforadora *f; (for tickets)* taladradora *f; (for leather etc)* punzón *m*

2 *vt (make hole in)* perforar; *(ticket)* picar; *(leather)* punzar

punch² [pʌntʃ] **1** *n (blow)* puñetazo *m; (in boxing)* pegada *f; Fig* **it lacks p.** le falta fuerza; **p. line** remate *m (de un chiste)*

2 *vt (with fist)* dar un puñetazo a

punch³ [pʌntʃ] *n (drink)* ponche *m*

punch-up ['pʌntʃʌp] *n Fam* pelea *f*

punctual ['pʌŋktjʊəl] *adj* puntual

punctuate ['pʌŋktjʊeɪt] *vt* puntuar; *Fig* salpicar

punctuation [pʌŋktjʊ'eɪʃən] *n* puntuación *f*

puncture ['pʌŋktʃə(r)] **1** *n* pinchazo *m*

2 *vt (tyre)* pinchar

pundit ['pʌndɪt] *n Fam* experto(a) *m,f*

pungent ['pʌndʒənt] *adj (smell)* acre; *(taste)* fuerte

punish ['pʌnɪʃ] *vt* castigar

punishable ['pʌnɪʃəbəl] *adj* castigable, punible

punishment ['pʌnɪʃmənt] *n* castigo *m*

punk [pʌŋk] *n Fam* (a) *(music)* punk *mf;* **p. music** música *f* punk (b) *US* mamón *m*

punt [pʌnt] **1** *n (boat)* batea *f*

2 *vi* ir en batea

punter ['pʌntə(r)] *n Br (gambler)* jugador(a) *m,f; (customer)* cliente(a) *m,f*

puny ['pjuːnɪ] *adj* (**punier, puniest**) enclenque, endeble

pup [pʌp] *n* cachorro(a) *m,f*

pupil¹ ['pjuːpəl] *n Educ* alumno(a) *m,f*

pupil² ['pjuːpəl] *n Anat* pupila *f*

puppet ['pʌpɪt] *n* títere *m*

puppy ['pʌpɪ] *n* cachorro(a) *m,f*, perrito *m*

purchase ['pɜːtʃɪs] **1** *n* compra *f*

2 *vt* comprar; **purchasing power** poder adquisitivo

purchaser ['pɜːtʃɪsə(r)] *n* comprador(a) *m,f*

pure [pjʊə(r)] *adj* puro(a)

purée ['pjʊəreɪ] *n* puré *m*

purely [pjʊəlɪ] *adv* simplemente

purge [pɜːdʒ] **1** *n* purga *f*

2 *vt* purgar

purify ['pjʊərɪfaɪ] *vt* purificar

purl [pɜːl] *vt (in knitting)* hacer punto del revés

purple ['pɜːpəl] *adj* morado(a), purpúreo(a); **to go p. (in the face)** ponerse morado(a)

purport [pɜː'pɔːt] *vi Fml* pretender; **to p. to be sth** pretender ser algo

purpose ['pɜːpəs] *n* (a) propósito *m*, intención *f;* **on p.** a propósito (b) *(use)* utilidad *f*

purposeful ['pɜːpəsfʊl] *adj (resolute)* decidido(a), resoluto(a)

purr [pɜː(r)] *vi (cat)* ronronear; *(engine)* zumbar

purse [pɜːs] **1** *n Br* monedero *m; US (bag)* bolso *m*, cartera *f, Méx* bolsa *f; (prize money)* premio *m* en metálico

2 *vt* **to p. one's lips** apretarse los labios

purser ['pɜːsə(r)] *n* contador(a) *m,f*

pursue [pə'sjuː] *vt* *(criminal)* perseguir; *(person)* seguir; *(pleasure)* buscar; *(career)* ejercer

pursuer [pə'sjuːə(r)] *n Fml* perseguidor(a) *m,f*

pursuit [pə'sjuːt] *n (of criminal)* persecución *f*; *(of animal)* caza *f*; *(of pleasure)* búsqueda *f*; *(pastime)* pasatiempo *m*

purveyor [pə'veɪə(r)] *n Fml* proveedor(a) *m,f*

pus [pʌs] *n* pus *m*

push [pʊʃ] **1** *n* empujón *m*; *Fig (drive)* brío *m*, dinamismo *m*

2 *vt* (**a**) empujar; *(button)* pulsar, apretar; **to p. one's finger into a hole** meter el dedo en un agujero (**b**) *Fig (pressurize)* instar; *(harass)* acosar; *Fam* **to be (hard) pushed for time** andar justo(a) de tiempo (**c**) *Fam (product)* promover; **to p. drugs** pasar droga

3 *vi* empujar

▸ **push aside** *vt sep (object)* apartar

▸ **push in** *vi* colarse

▸ **push off** *vi (in boat)* desatracar; *Fam* **p. off!** ¡lárgate!

▸ **push on** *vi (continue)* seguir adelante

▸ **push through** *vt sep* abrirse paso entre

pushchair ['pʊʃtʃeə(r)] *n Br* sillita *f* (de ruedas)

pusher ['pʊʃə(r)] *n Fam (of drugs)* camello *m*

pushover ['pʊʃəʊvə(r)] *n Fam* **it's a p.** está chupado; **she's a p.** es un ligue fácil

push-up ['pʊʃʌp] *n* flexión *f* (de brazos)

pushy ['pʊʃɪ] *adj* (**pushier, pushiest**) *Fam* agresivo(a)

puss [pʊs], **pussy** ['pʊsɪ] *n Fam* minino *m*

put [pʊt] **1** *vt* (*pt & pp* **put**) (**a**) poner; *(place)* colocar; *(insert)* meter; **to p. to bed** acostar a; **to p. a picture up on the wall** colgar un cuadro en la pared; **to p. a stop to sth** poner término a algo; *Fig* **to p. one's foot in it** meter la pata

(**b**) *(present)* presentar, exponer; **to p. a question to sb** hacer una pregunta a algn

(**c**) *(express)* expresar, decir; **to p. it mildly** y me quedo corto; **to p. sth simply** explicar algo de manera sencilla

(**d**) *(estimate)* calcular

(**e**) *(money)* ingresar; *(invest)* invertir

2 *vi Naut* **to p. to sea** zarpar

3 *adv* **to stay p.** quedarse quieto(a)

▸ **put about** *vt sep (rumour)* hacer correr

▸ **put across** *vt sep (idea etc)* comunicar

▸ **put aside** *vt sep (money)* ahorrar; *(time)* reservar

▸ **put away** *vt sep (tidy away)* recoger; *Fam (eat)* zamparse; *(save money)* ahorrar

▸ **put back** *vt sep (postpone)* aplazar; **to p. the clock back** retrasar la hora

▸ **put by** *vt sep (money)* ahorrar

▸ **put down** *vt sep (set down)* dejar; *(suppress)*

sofocar; *(humiliate)* humillar; *(criticize)* criticar; *(animal)* provocar la muerte de; *(write down)* apuntar

▸ **put down to** *vt sep* achacar a

▸ **put forward** *vt sep (theory)* exponer; *(proposal)* hacer; **to p. one's name forward for sth** presentarse como candidato(a) para algo

▸ **put in 1** *vt sep (install)* instalar; *(complaint, request)* presentar; *(time)* pasar

2 *vi Naut* hacer escala (**at** en)

▸ **put off** *vt sep (postpone)* aplazar; **to p. sb off (doing) sth** *(dissuade)* disuadir a algn de (hacer) algo

▸ **put on** *vt sep (clothes)* poner, ponerse; *(show)* montar; *(concert)* dar; *(switch on) (radio)* poner; *(light)* encender; *(water, gas)* abrir; **to p. on weight** aumentar de peso; **to p. on the brakes** frenar; *Fig* **to p. on a straight face** poner cara de serio(a)

▸ **put out** *vt sep (light, fire)* apagar; *(place outside)* sacar; *(extend) (arm)* extender; *(tongue)* sacar; *(hand)* tender; *(spread) (rumour)* hacer correr; *(annoy)* molestar; *(inconvenience)* incordiar; *(anger)* **to be p. out by sth** enojarse por algo

▸ **put through** *vt sep Tel* **p. me through to Pat, please** póngame con Pat, por favor

▸ **put together** *vt sep (join)* unir, reunir; *(assemble)* armar, montar

▸ **put up** *vt sep (raise)* levantar, subir; *(picture)* colocar; *(curtains)* colgar; *(building)* construir; *(tent)* armar; *(prices)* subir, aumentar; *(accommodate)* alojar, hospedar; **to p. up a fight** ofrecer resistencia

▸ **put up to** *vt sep* **to p. sb up to sth** incitar a algn a hacer algo

▸ **put up with** *vt insep* aguantar, soportar

putrid ['pjuːtrɪd] *adj Fml* putrefacto(a)

putt [pʌt] **1** *n* tiro *m* al hoyo

2 *vt & vi* tirar al hoyo

putting ['pʌtɪŋ] *n* **p. green** minigolf *m*

putty ['pʌtɪ] *n* masilla *f*

puzzle ['pʌzəl] **1** *n* rompecabezas *m inv*; *(crossword)* crucigrama *m*; *Fig (mystery)* misterio *m*

2 *vt* dejar perplejo(a); **to be puzzled about sth** no entender algo

▸ **puzzle over** *vt insep* **to p. over sth** dar vueltas a algo (en la cabeza)

puzzling ['pʌzlɪŋ] *adj* extraño(a), curioso(a)

PVC [piːviː'siː] *n (abbr* **polyvinyl chloride)** PVC *m*

pygmy ['pɪgmɪ] *n* pigmeo(a) *m,f*; *Fig* enano(a) *m,f*

pyjamas [pə'dʒɑːməz] *npl* pijama *m*

pylon ['paɪlən] *n* torre *f* (de conducción eléctrica)

pyramid ['pɪrəmɪd] *n* pirámide *f*

Pyrenees [pɪrə'niːz] *npl* **the P.** los Pirineos

Pyrex® ['paɪreks] *n* pírex® *m*

python ['paɪθən] *n* pitón *m*

Q, q [kjuː] *n (the letter)* Q, q *f*
quack [kwæk] **1** *n* (**a**) *(of duck)* graznido *m* (**b**) *Fam (doctor)* curandero(a) *m,f*
  2 *vi* graznar
quad [kwɒd] *n Fam* (**a**) *Br (of school, university)* patio *m* interior (**b**) *(quadruplet)* cuatrillizo(a) *m,f*
quadrangle ['kwɒdræŋɡəl] *n* (**a**) *Geom* cuadrángulo *m* (**b**) *(courtyard)* patio *m* interior
quadruple ['kwɒdrʊpəl, kwɒ'druːpəl] **1** *n* cuádruplo *m*
  2 *adj* cuádruple
  3 *vt* cuadruplicar
  4 *vi* cuadruplicarse
quadruplet ['kwɒdrʊplɪt, kwɒ'druːplɪt] *n* cuatrillizo(a) *m,f*
quagmire ['kwæɡmaɪə(r), 'kwɒɡmaɪə(r)] *n (land)* cenagal *m*
quail[1] [kweɪl] *n Orn* codorniz *f*
quail[2] [kweɪl] *vi Fig* encogerse
quaint [kweɪnt] *adj (picturesque)* pintoresco(a); *(original)* singular
quake [kweɪk] **1** *vi* temblar
  2 *n Fam* temblor *m* de tierra
Quaker ['kweɪkə(r)] *n* cuáquero(a) *m,f*
qualification [kwɒlɪfɪ'keɪʃən] *n* (**a**) *(ability)* aptitud *f* (**b**) *(requirement)* requisito *m* (**c**) *(diploma etc)* título *m* (**d**) *(reservation)* reserva *f*
qualified ['kwɒlɪfaɪd] *adj* (**a**) capacitado(a); **q. teacher** profesor titulado (**b**) **q. approval** *(modified)* aprobación *f* condicional
qualify ['kwɒlɪfaɪ] **1** *vt* (**a**) *(entitle)* capacitar (**b**) *(modify)* modificar; *(statement)* matizar; *Ling* calificar
  2 *vi* (**a**) **to q. as** *(doctor etc)* sacar el título de; **when did you q.?** ¿cúando terminaste la carrera? (**b**) *(in competition)* quedar clasificado(a)
qualifying ['kwɒlɪfaɪɪŋ] *adj (round, exam)* eliminatorio(a)
quality ['kwɒlɪtɪ] *n* (**a**) *(excellence)* calidad *f*; **q. control** control *m* de calidad; *Br* **q. newspapers** prensa *f* no sensacionalista (**b**) *(attribute)* cualidad *f*
qualm [kwɑːm] *n* (**a**) *(scruple)* escrúpulo *m* (**b**) *(doubt)* duda *f*
quandary ['kwɒndərɪ, 'kwɒndrɪ] *n* **to be in a q.** estar en un dilema
quango ['kwæŋɡəʊ] *n* = organización semiautónoma paralela
quantity ['kwɒntɪtɪ] *n* cantidad *f*

quarantine ['kwɒrəntiːn] *n* cuarentena *f*
quarrel ['kwɒrəl] **1** *n (argument)* riña *f*, pelea *f*; *(disagreement)* desacuerdo *m*
  2 *vi (argue)* pelearse, reñir; **to q. with sth** discrepar de algo
quarrelsome ['kwɒrəlsəm] *adj* camorrista
quarry[1] ['kwɒrɪ] *Min* **1** *n* cantera *f*
  2 *vt* extraer
quarry[2] ['kwɒrɪ] *n* presa *f*
quart [kwɔːt] *n (measurement)* = cuarto de galón *(Br = 1,13 l; US = 0,94 l)*
quarter ['kwɔːtə(r)] **1** *n* (**a**) cuarto *m*, cuarta parte; **a q. of an hour** un cuarto de hora; **a q. of a cake** la cuarta parte de un pastel (**b**) **it's a q.** *Br* **to** or *US* **of three** son las tres menos cuarto; **it's a q.** *Br* **past** or *US* **after six** son las seis y cuarto (**c**) *(three months)* trimestre *m* (**d**) *Br (weight)* cuarto *m* de libra (**e**) *US (coin)* cuarto *m* (de dólar) (**f**) *(district)* barrio *m* (**g**) **there was criticism from all quarters** *(areas, people)* todos lo criticaron (**h**) *(of moon)* cuarto *m* (**i**) *(lodgings)* alojamiento *m*; *Mil* **officers' quarters** residencia *f* de oficiales; **at close quarters** muy cerca (**j**) *US Mus* **q. note** negra *f*
  2 *vt* (**a**) *(cut into quarters)* dividir en cuartos (**b**) *(accommodate)* alojar
quarterfinal ['kwɔːtəfaɪnəl] *n Sport* cuarto *m* de final
quarterly ['kwɔːtəlɪ] **1** *adj* trimestral
  2 *n* publicación *f* trimestral
  3 *adv* trimestralmente
quartermaster ['kwɔːtəmɑːstə(r)] *n* (**a**) *Mil* oficial *m* de intendencia (**b**) *Naut* cabo *m* de la Marina
quartet(te) [kwɔː'tet] *n* cuarteto *m*
quartz [kwɔːts] *n* cuarzo *m*; **q. watch** reloj *m* de cuarzo
quash [kwɒʃ] *vt Jur* anular; *(uprising)* aplastar
quasi ['kwɑːzɪ, 'kweɪzaɪ, 'kweɪsaɪ] *pref* cuasi
quaver ['kweɪvə(r)] **1** *n* (**a**) *Mus* corchea *f* (**b**) *(in voice)* temblor *m*
  2 *vi (voice)* temblar
quay(side) ['kiː(saɪd)] *n* muelle *m*
queasy ['kwiːzɪ] *adj* (**queasier, queasiest**) **to feel q.** *(ill)* tener náuseas
queen [kwiːn] *n* (**a**) reina *f* (**b**) *Fam Pej* loca *f*, marica *m*

queer [kwɪə(r)] **1** *adj* (**a**) *(strange)* extraño(a), raro(a) (**b**) *Fam (mad)* loco(a) (**c**) *Fam (unwell)* mareado(a) (**d**) *Fam Pej* maricón
2 *n Fam Pej* marica *m*, maricón *m*

quell [kwel] *vt* reprimir

quench [kwentʃ] *vt* apagar

querulous ['kwerʊləs, 'kwerjʊləs] *adj Fml* quejumbroso(a)

query ['kwɪərɪ] **1** *n (question)* pregunta *f*
2 *vt (ask questions about)* preguntar acerca de; *(have doubts about)* poner en duda

quest [kwest] *n Literary* búsqueda *f*, busca *f*

question ['kwestʃən] **1** *n* (**a**) *(interrogative)* pregunta *f*; **to ask sb a q.** hacer una pregunta a algn; **he did it without q.** lo hizo sin rechistar; **q. mark** signo *m* de interrogación; *Fig* interrogante *m*
(**b**) *(problem, issue)* asunto *m*, cuestión *f*; **it's a q. of two hours** es cuestión de dos horas (**c**) *(doubt)* duda *f*; **beyond q.** fuera de duda; **in q.** en duda; **to call sth into q.** poner algo en duda
(**d**) **out of the q.** imposible; **that's out of the q.!** ¡ni hablar!
(**e**) *Educ* problema *m*
2 *vt (ask questions of)* hacer preguntas a; *(interrogate)* interrogar; *(query)* poner en duda

questionable ['kwestʃənəbəl] *adj (doubtful)* dudoso(a); *(debatable)* discutible

questionnaire [kwestʃə'neə(r)] *n* cuestionario *m*

queue [kjuː] *Br* **1** *n* cola *f*
2 *vi* **to q. (up)** hacer cola

quibble ['kwɪbəl] **1** *n* pega *f*
2 *vi* poner pegas (**with** a); *Fam* buscarle tres pies al gato

quiche [kiːʃ] *n* quiche *m* or *f*

quick [kwɪk] *adj (a) (fast)* rápido(a); **a q. look** un vistazo; **a q. snack** un bocado; **be q.!** ¡date prisa! (**b**) *(clever)* espabilado(a); *(wit)* agudo(a) (**c**) **she has a q. temper** se enfada con nada

quicken ['kwɪkən] **1** *vt* acelerar; **to q. one's pace** acelerar el paso
2 *vi (speed up)* acelerarse

quickly ['kwɪklɪ] *adv* rápidamente, de prisa

quickness ['kwɪknɪs] *n* (**a**) *(speed)* rapidez *f* (**b**) *(of wit)* agudeza *f*, viveza *f*

quicksand ['kwɪksænd] *n* arenas movedizas

quicksilver ['kwɪksɪlvə(r)] *n* mercurio *m*

quick-witted [kwɪk'wɪtɪd] *adj* agudo(a)

quid [kwɪd] *n (pl* quid) *Br Fam* libra *f* (esterlina)

quiet ['kwaɪət] **1** *n* (**a**) *(silence)* silencio *m* (**b**) *(calm)* tranquilidad *f*
2 *adj* (**a**) *(silent)* silencioso(a); *(street)* tranquilo(a); **a q. voice** una voz suave; **keep q.!** ¡silencio! (**b**) *(calm)* tranquilo(a) (**c**) *Com Fin* **business is q. today** hoy hay poco negocio (**d**) *(person)* reservado(a) (**e**) *(secret)* confidencial (**f**) *(not showy) (clothes)* sobrio(a);

(colours) apagado(a) (**g**) *(ceremony, dinner)* íntimo(a)
2 *vt US* calmar
3 *vi US* calmarse

quieten ['kwaɪətən] **1** *vt (silence)* callar; *(calm)* calmar
2 *vi (silence)* callarse; *(calm)* calmarse
▸ **quieten down** *Br* **1** *vt sep* calmar
2 *vi* calmarse

quietly ['kwaɪətlɪ] *adv* (**a**) *(silently)* silenciosamente; **he spoke q.** habló en voz baja (**b**) *(calmly)* tranquilamente (**c**) *(discreetly)* discretamente

quietness ['kwaɪətnɪs] *n* (**a**) *(silence)* silencio *m* (**b**) *(calm)* tranquilidad *f*

quill [kwɪl] *n (feather, pen)* pluma *f*; *(of porcupine)* púa *f*

quilt [kwɪlt] **1** *n* edredón *m*
2 *vt* acolchar

quin [kwɪn] *n Fam* quintillizo(a) *m,f*

quinine ['kwɪniːn, US 'kwaɪnaɪn] *n* quinina *f*

quint [kwɪnt] *n Fam US* = **quin**

quintessential [kwɪntɪ'senʃəl] *adj* fundamental

quintet(te) [kwɪn'tet] *n* quinteto *m*

quintuple ['kwɪntjʊpəl, kwɪn'tjuːpəl] **1** *adj* quíntuplo(a)
2 *n* quíntuplo *m*
3 *vt* quintuplicar

quintuplet ['kwɪntjʊplɪt, kwɪn'tjuːplɪt] *n* quintillizo(a) *m,f*

quip [kwɪp] **1** *n* salida *f*; *(joke)* chiste *m*
2 *vi* bromear

quirk [kwɜːk] *n* (**a**) *(peculiarity)* manía *f* (**b**) *(of fate)* arbitrariedad *f*

quit [kwɪt] **1** *vt (pt & pp* quitted *or* quit) (**a**) *(leave)* dejar, abandonar (**b**) **q. making that noise!** ¡deja de hacer ese ruido!
2 *vi* (**a**) *(go)* irse; *(give up)* dimitir (**b**) *(cease)* dejar de hacer algo
3 *adj* **let's call it quits** dejémoslo estar

> *Note that the Spanish verb* **quitar** *is a false friend and is never a translation for the English verb* **to quit**. *In Spanish,* **quitar** *means both "to remove" and "to take away".*

quite [kwaɪt] *adv* (**a**) *(entirely)* totalmente; **she's q. right** tiene toda la razón (**b**) *(rather)* bastante; **q. a few** bastantes; **q. a while** un buen rato; **q. often** con bastante frecuencia; **that's q. enough!** ¡ya está bien! (**c**) **he's q. a character** es un tipo original; **it's q. something** es increíble (**d**) *(exactly)* exactamente; **q. (so)!** ¡en efecto!, ¡exacto!

quiver¹ ['kwɪvə(r)] *vi* temblar

quiver² ['kwɪvə(r)] *n (for arrows)* aljaba *f*, carcaj *m*

quiz [kwɪz] *n Rad & TV* **q. show** concurso *m*
2 *vt* hacer preguntas a

quizzical ['kwɪzɪkəl] *adj* (**a**) *(bemused)* burlón(ona) (**b**) *(enquiring)* curioso(a)

quota ['kwəʊtə] *n* (**a**) *(proportional share)* cuota *f*, parte *f* (**b**) *(prescribed amount, number)* cupo *m*

quotation [kwəʊ'teɪʃən] *n* (**a**) *Lit* cita *f*; **q. marks** comillas *fpl* (**b**) *Fin* cotización *f*

quote [kwəʊt] **1** *vt* (**a**) *(cite)* citar (**b**) *Com* **to q. a price** dar un presupuesto (**c**) *Fin* cotizar

2 *n* (**a**) *Lit* cita *f* (**b**) *Com* presupuesto *m*

quotient ['kwəʊʃənt] *n* cociente *m*

R, r [ɑː(r)] *n (the letter)* R, r *f*
rabbi ['ræbaɪ] *n* rabí *m*, rabino *m*
rabbit ['ræbɪt] **1** *n* conejo(a) *m,f*; **r. hutch** conejera *f*
2 *vi Fam* **to r. (on)** enrollarse
rabble ['ræbəl] *n Pej* **the r.** el populacho
rabies ['reɪbiːz] *n* rabia *f*
RAC [ɑːreɪˈsiː] *n Br (abbr Royal Automobile Club)* = organización británica de ayuda al automovilista, ≃ RACE *m*
race¹ [reɪs] **1** *n* (a) *Sport* carrera *f* (b) *Br* **the races** las carreras (de caballos)
2 *vt* (a) **I'll r. you!** ¡te echo una carrera! (b) *(car, horse)* hacer correr (c) *(engine)* acelerar
3 *vi (go quickly)* correr; *(pulse)* acelerarse
race² [reɪs] *n (people)* raza *f*
racecourse ['reɪskɔːs] *n Br* hipódromo *m*
racehorse ['reɪshɔːs] *n* caballo *m* de carreras
racer ['reɪsə(r)] *n Sport* (a) *(person)* corredor(a) *m,f* (b) *(bicycle)* bicicleta *f* de carreras; *(car)* coche *m* de carreras
racetrack ['reɪstræk] *n (for cars, people, bikes)* pista *f*; *US (for horses)* hipódromo *m*
racial ['reɪʃəl] *adj* racial
racing ['reɪsɪŋ] **1** *n* carreras *fpl*
2 *adj* de carreras; **r. car/bike** coche *m*/moto *f* de carreras
racism ['reɪsɪzəm] *n* racismo *m*
racist ['reɪsɪst] *adj & n* racista *(mf)*
rack [ræk] **1** *n* (a) *(shelf)* estante *m*; *(for clothes)* percha *f*; **luggage r.** portaequipajes *m inv*; **roof r.** baca *f* (b) *(for torture)* potro *m*
2 *vt Literary (torment)* atormentar; *Fam Fig* **to r. one's brains** devanarse los sesos
racket¹ ['rækɪt] *n* (a) *(din)* ruido *m*, jaleo *m* (b) *(swindle)* timo *m*; *(shady business)* chanchullo *m*
racket² ['rækɪt] *n Sport* raqueta *f*
racquet ['rækɪt] *n* = **racket²**
racy ['reɪsɪ] *adj* (**racier, raciest**) *(lively)* vivo(a); *(risqué)* atrevido(a)
radar ['reɪdɑː(r)] *n* radar *m*
radiance ['reɪdɪəns] *n* resplandor *m*
radiant ['reɪdɪənt] *adj* radiante, resplandeciente
radiate ['reɪdɪeɪt] *vt* irradiar; *Fig* **she radiated happiness** rebosaba de alegría
radiation [reɪdɪˈeɪʃən] *n* radiación *f*
radiator ['reɪdɪeɪtə(r)] *n* radiador *m*
radical ['rædɪkəl] *adj* radical
radio ['reɪdɪəʊ] *n* radio *f*; **on the r.** en *or* por la radio; **r. station** emisora *f* (de radio)

radioactive [reɪdɪəʊˈæktɪv] *adj* radiactivo(a)
radio-controlled [reɪdɪəʊkənˈtrəʊld] *adj* teledirigido(a)
radiography [reɪdɪˈɒɡrəfɪ] *n* radiografía *f*
radiology [reɪdɪˈɒlədʒɪ] *n* radiología *f*
radiotherapy [reɪdɪəʊˈθerəpɪ] *n* radioterapia *f*
radish ['rædɪʃ] *n* rábano *m*
radius ['reɪdɪəs] *n* radio *m*; **within a r. of** en un radio de
RAF [ɑːreɪˈef] *n Br (abbr Royal Air Force)* = fuerzas aéreas británicas
raffle ['ræfəl] **1** *n* rifa *f*
2 *vt* rifar
raft [rɑːft] *n* balsa *f*
rafter ['rɑːftə(r)] *n* viga *f* de madera
rag¹ [ræɡ] *n* (a) *(torn piece)* harapo *m*; **r. doll** muñeca *f* de trapo (b) *(for cleaning)* trapo *m* (c) *Fam* **rags** *(clothes)* trapos *mpl* (d) *Pej Press* periodicucho *m*
rag² [ræɡ] **1** *n Br Univ* función benéfica
2 *vt* gastar bromas a
rag-and-bone ['ræɡənˈbəʊn] *adj Br* **r. man** trapero *m*
rage [reɪdʒ] **1** *n* (a) *(fury)* cólera *f* (b) *Fam* **it's all the r.** hace furor
2 *vi* (a) *(person)* rabiar, estar furioso(a) (b) *Fig (storm, sea)* rugir; *(wind)* bramar
ragged ['ræɡɪd] *adj* (a) *(clothes)* hecho(a) jirones (b) *(person)* harapiento(a) (c) *(edge)* mellado(a) (d) *Fig (uneven)* desigual
raging ['reɪdʒɪŋ] *adj* (a) *(angry)* furioso(a) (b) *Fig (sea)* embravecido(a) (c) *(intense)* feroz; *(storm)* violento(a)
raid [reɪd] **1** *n Mil* incursión *f*; *(by police)* redada *f*; *(robbery etc)* atraco *m*
2 *vt Mil* hacer una incursión en; *(police)* hacer una redada en; *(rob)* asaltar; *Fam* **to r. the larder** vaciar la despensa
raider ['reɪdə(r)] *n (invader)* invasor(a) *m,f*
rail [reɪl] *n* (a) barra *f* (b) *(railing)* barandilla *f* (c) *Rail* carril *m*; **by r.** *(send sth)* por ferrocarril; *(travel)* en tren
railcard ['reɪlkɑːd] *n Br* abono *m*
railing ['reɪlɪŋ] *n (usu pl)* verja *f*
railroad ['reɪlrəʊd] *n US* ferrocarril *m*
railway ['reɪlweɪ] *n Br* ferrocarril *m*; **r. line, r. track** vía férrea; **r. station** estación *f* de ferrocarril
railwayman ['reɪlweɪmən] *n Br* ferroviario *m*
rain [reɪn] **1** *n* lluvia *f*; **in the r.** bajo la lluvia
2 *vi* llover; **it's raining** llueve

rainbow ['reɪnbəʊ] n arco m iris
raincoat ['reɪnkəʊt] n impermeable m
raindrop ['reɪndrɒp] n gota f de lluvia
rainfall ['reɪnfɔːl] n (falling of rain) precipitación f; (amount) pluviosidad f
rainforest ['reɪnfɒrɪst] n selva f tropical
rainy ['reɪnɪ] adj (rainier, rainiest) lluvioso(a)
raise [reɪz] 1 n US aumento m (de sueldo)
2 vt (a) levantar; (glass) brindar; (voice) subir; (building) erigir (b) (prices) aumentar (c) (money, help) reunir (d) (issue) plantear (e) (crops, children) criar (f) Rad comunicar con (g) (standards) mejorar (h) (laugh) provocar
raisin ['reɪzən] n pasa f
rake¹ [reɪk] 1 n (garden tool) rastrillo m; (for fire) hurgón m
2 vt (leaves) rastrillar; (fire) hurgar; (with machine gun) barrer
rake² [reɪk] n (dissolute man) calavera m, libertino m
rally ['rælɪ] 1 n (a) (gathering) reunión f; Pol mitin m (b) Aut rallye m (c) (in tennis) jugada f
2 vt (support) reunir
3 vi recuperarse
▸ **rally round** vi formar una piña
RAM [ræm] n Comput (abbr **random access memory**) RAM f
ram [ræm] 1 n (a) Zool carnero m (b) Tech maza f
2 vt (a) (drive into place) hincar; (cram) embutir; Fam **to r. sth home** hacer algo patente (b) (crash into) chocar con
ramble ['ræmbəl] 1 n (walk) caminata f
2 vi (a) (walk) hacer una excursión a pie (b) Fig (digress) divagar
rambler ['ræmblə(r)] n (a) (person) excursionista mf (b) Bot rosal m trepador
rambling ['ræmblɪŋ] adj (a) (incoherent) incoherente (b) (house) laberíntico(a) (c) Bot trepador(a)
ramp [ræmp] n (a) rampa f (b) Av (movable stairway) escalerilla f
rampage 1 n ['ræmpeɪdʒ] **to be on the r.** desmandarse
2 vi [ræm'peɪdʒ] **to r. about** comportarse como un loco
rampant ['ræmpənt] adj incontrolado(a); **corruption is r.** la corrupción está muy extendida
rampart ['ræmpɑːt] n muralla f
ramshackle ['ræmʃækəl] adj destartalado(a)
ran [ræn] pt of **run**
ranch [rɑːntʃ] n US rancho m, hacienda f
rancher ['rɑːntʃə(r)] n US ranchero(a) m,f
rancid ['rænsɪd] adj rancio(a)
rancour, US **rancor** ['ræŋkə(r)] n Fml rencor m
R & D [ɑːrən'diː] n (abbr **Research and Development**) I+D
random ['rændəm] 1 n **at r.** al azar

2 adj fortuito(a); **r. selection** selección hecha al azar
randy ['rændɪ] adj (randier, randiest) Br Fam cachondo(a), caliente
rang [ræŋ] pt of **ring**
range [reɪndʒ] 1 n (a) (of mountains) cordillera f, sierra f (b) US (open land) pradera f (c) (choice) surtido m; (of products) gama f (d) Mus registro m (e) firing **r.** campo m de tiro (f) (of missile) alcance m; **at close r.** de cerca; **long-/short-r. missiles** mísiles mpl de largo/corto alcance (g) Culin cocina f de carbón
2 vi (extend) extenderse (**to** hasta); **prices r. from £5 to £20 pounds** los precios oscilan entre 5 y 20 libras
3 vt Literary (wander) vagar por
ranger ['reɪndʒə(r)] n (a) (forest) **r.** guardabosques mf inv (b) US (mounted policeman) policía montado
rank¹ [ræŋk] 1 n (a) Mil (row) fila f; **the ranks** los soldados rasos; **the r. and file** la base (b) (position in army) graduación f; (in society) rango m (c) (taxi) **r.** parada f de taxis
2 vt (classify) clasificar
3 vi (figure) figurar; **to r. above/below sb** figurar por encima/debajo de algn; **to r. with** estar al mismo nivel que
rank² [ræŋk] adj Fml (a) (vegetation) exuberante (b) (foul-smelling) fétido(a) (c) (thorough) total, absoluto(a)
ransack ['rænsæk] vt (plunder) saquear; (rummage in) registrar
ransom ['rænsəm] n rescate m; **to hold sb to r.** pedir rescate por algn; Fig poner a algn entre la espada y la pared
rant [rænt] vi vociferar; Fam **to r. and rave** pegar gritos
rap [ræp] 1 n (a) (blow) golpe m seco; (on door) golpecito m (b) Mus rap m
2 vt & vi (knock) golpear
rape¹ [reɪp] Jur 1 n violación f
2 vt violar
rape² [reɪp] n Bot colza f
rapeseed ['reɪpsiːd] n **r. oil** aceite m de colza
rapid ['ræpɪd] 1 adj rápido(a)
2 n **rapids** (in river) rápidos mpl
rapidity [rə'pɪdɪtɪ] n rapidez f
rapist ['reɪpɪst] n violador(a) m,f
rapport [ræ'pɔː(r)] n compenetración f
rapture ['ræptʃə(r)] n éxtasis m
rapturous ['ræptʃərəs] adj muy entusiasta
rare¹ [reə(r)] adj raro(a), poco común
rare² [reə(r)] adj (steak) poco hecho(a)
rarefied ['reərɪfaɪd] adj enrarecido(a)
rarely ['reəlɪ] adv raras veces
raring ['reərɪŋ] adj Fam **to be r. to do sth** morirse de ganas de hacer algo
rarity ['reərɪtɪ] n rareza f
rascal ['rɑːskəl] n granuja mf
rash¹ [ræʃ] n (a) Med erupción f, sarpullido m (b) Fig (of robberies etc) racha f
rash² [ræʃ] adj (reckless) impetuoso(a);

(words, actions) precipitado(a), imprudente

rasher ['ræʃə(r)] *n* loncha *f*

raspberry ['rɑːzbərɪ] *n* frambuesa *f*

rasping ['rɑːspɪŋ] *adj* áspero(a)

rat [ræt] *n* (**a**) *(animal)* rata *f*; **r. poison** raticida *m* (**b**) *US Fam (informer)* soplón(ona) *m,f*, chivato(a) *m,f*

rate [reɪt] **1** *n* (**a**) *(ratio)* índice *m*, tasa *f*; **at any r.** *(at least)* al menos; *(anyway)* en cualquier caso (**b**) *(cost)* precio *m*; *Fin (of interest, exchange)* tipo *m* (**c**) **at the r. of** *(speed)* a la velocidad de; *(quantity)* a razón de (**d**) **first r.** de primera categoría (**e**) *Br* **rates** impuestos *mpl* municipales
2 *vt* (**a**) *(estimate)* estimar (**b**) *(evaluate)* tasar (**c**) *(consider)* considerar

rateable ['reɪtəbəl] *adj Br* **r. value** valor *m* catastral

ratepayer ['reɪtpeɪə(r)] *n Br* contribuyente *mf*

rather ['rɑːðə(r)] *adv* (**a**) *(quite)* más bien, bastante; *(very much so)* muy (**b**) *(more accurately)* mejor dicho; **r. than** *(instead of)* en vez de; *(more than)* más que (**c**) **she would r. stay here** *(prefer to)* prefiere quedarse aquí

ratify ['rætɪfaɪ] *vt* ratificar

rating ['reɪtɪŋ] *n* (**a**) *(valuation)* tasación *f*; *(score)* valoración *f* (**b**) *TV* **(programme) ratings** índice *m* de audiencia (**c**) *Naut* marinero *m* sin graduación

ratio ['reɪʃɪəʊ] *n* razón *f*; **in the r. of** a razón de

ration ['ræʃən] **1** *n* (**a**) *(allowance)* ración *f* (**b**) **rations** víveres *mpl*
2 *vt* racionar

rational ['ræʃənəl] *adj* racional

rationale [ræʃə'nɑːl] *n* base *f*

rationalize ['ræʃənəlaɪz] *vt* racionalizar

rattle ['rætəl] **1** *n* (**a**) *(of train, cart)* traqueteo *m*; *(of metal)* repiqueteo *m*; *(of glass)* tintineo *m* (**b**) *(toy)* sonajero *m*; *(instrument)* carraca *f*
2 *vt* (**a**) *(keys etc)* hacer sonar (**b**) *Fam (unsettle)* poner nervioso(a)
3 *vi* sonar; *(metal)* repiquetear; *(glass)* tintinear

rattlesnake ['rætəlsneɪk] *n* serpiente *f* de cascabel

raucous ['rɔːkəs] *adj* estridente

ravage ['rævɪdʒ] *Fml* **1** *n* *(usu pl)* estragos *mpl*
2 *vt* asolar, devastar

rave [reɪv] **1** *vi* (**a**) *(be delirious)* delirar (**b**) *(be angry)* enfurecerse (**at** con) (**c**) *Fam (show enthusiasm)* entusiasmarse (**about** por)
2 *n Fam* **r. review** crítica *f* muy favorable

raven ['reɪvən] *n* cuervo *m*

ravenous ['rævənəs] *adj* **I'm r.** tengo un hambre que no veo

ravine [rə'viːn] *n* barranco *m*

raving ['reɪvɪŋ] *n Fam* **r. mad** loco(a) de atar

ravishing ['rævɪʃɪŋ] *adj (person)* encantador(a)

raw [rɔː] *adj* (**a**) *(uncooked)* crudo(a) (**b**) *(not processed)* bruto(a); *(alcohol)* puro(a); **r. ma-**

terial materia prima (**c**) *(emotion)* instintivo(a) (**d**) *(weather)* crudo(a) (**e**) **r. deal** trato injusto (**f**) *(wound)* abierto(a); **r. flesh** carne viva (**g**) *US (inexperienced)* novato(a) (**h**) *(frank)* franco(a)

ray¹ [reɪ] *n* rayo *m*; *Fig* **r. of hope** rayo de esperanza

ray² [reɪ] *n (fish)* raya *f*

rayon ['reɪɒn] *n* rayón *m*

raze [reɪz] *vt* arrasar

razor ['reɪzə(r)] *n (for shaving)* maquinilla *f* de afeitar; **r. blade** hoja *f* de afeitar

Rd *(abbr* **Road)** calle *f*, c/

re [riː] *prep* respecto a, con referencia a

reach [riːtʃ] **1** *vt* (**a**) *(arrive at)* llegar a (**b**) *(contact)* localizar
2 *vi* alcanzar; **to r. for sth** intentar coger algo; **to r. out** extender la mano
3 *n* (**a**) *(range)* alcance *m*; **out of r.** fuera del alcance; **within r.** al alcance (**b**) *(in boxing)* extensión *f* del brazo (**c**) **reaches** *(on a river)* recta *f*

react [rɪ'ækt] *vi* reaccionar

reaction [rɪ'ækʃən] *n* reacción *f*

reactor [rɪ'æktə(r)] *n* reactor *m*

read [riːd] **1** *vt* *(pt & pp* **read** [red]) (**a**) leer (**b**) *(decipher)* descifrar (**c**) *(understand)* entender; *(interpret)* interpretar (**d**) *Univ* estudiar (**e**) *(of dial)* marcar (**f**) *(of signpost, text)* decir
2 *vi* leer
► **read out** *vt sep* leer en voz alta

readable ['riːdəbəl] *adj* (**a**) *(interesting)* interesante (**b**) *(legible)* legible

reader ['riːdə(r)] *n* (**a**) lector(a) *m,f* (**b**) *(book)* libro *m* de lectura (**c**) *Br Univ* profesor(a) *m,f* adjunto(a)

readership ['riːdəʃɪp] *n Press* lectores *mpl*

readily ['redɪlɪ] *adv* (**a**) *(easily)* fácilmente; **r. available** disponible en el acto (**b**) *(willingly)* de buena gana

readiness ['redɪnɪs] *n* (**a**) *(preparedness)* preparación *f* (**b**) *(willingness)* buena disposición

reading ['riːdɪŋ] *n* (**a**) lectura *f* (**b**) *Fig* interpretación *f* (**c**) *(of laws, bill)* presentación *f*

readjust [riːə'dʒʌst] **1** *vt* reajustar
2 *vi (adapt oneself)* adaptarse

ready ['redɪ] *adj* (**a**) *(prepared)* listo(a), preparado(a); **r., steady, go!** ¡preparados, listos, ya! (**b**) **r. to** *(about to)* a punto de (**c**) *(to hand)* a mano; **r. cash** dinero *m* en efectivo (**d**) *(willing)* dispuesto(a)

ready-cooked ['redɪ'kʊkt] *adj* precocinado(a)

ready-made ['redɪ'meɪd] *adj* confeccionado(a); *(food)* preparado(a)

real [rɪəl] *adj* (**a**) real, verdadero(a); *Fam* **for r.** de veras (**b**) *(genuine)* auténtico(a); **r. leather** piel legítima (**c**) *US Com* **r. estate** bienes *mpl* inmuebles; **r. estate agent** agente inmobiliario

realism ['rɪəlɪzəm] n realismo m
realistic ['rɪəlɪstɪk] adj realista
reality [rɪ'ælɪtɪ] n realidad f; **in r.** en realidad
realization [rɪəlaɪ'zeɪʃən] n (a) (understanding) comprensión f (b) (of plan, assets) realización f
realize ['rɪəlaɪz] vt (a) (become aware of) darse cuenta de (b) (assets, plan) realizar
really ['rɪəlɪ] adv verdaderamente, realmente; **I r. don't know** no lo sé de verdad; **r.?** ¿de veras?
realm [relm] n (kingdom) reino m; Fig (field) terreno m
realtor ['rɪəltə(r)] n US agente mf inmobiliario(a)
ream [riːm] n (of paper) resma f
reap [riːp] vt Agr cosechar; Fig **to r. the benefits** llevarse los beneficios
reappear [riːə'pɪə(r)] vi reaparecer
reappraisal [riːə'preɪzəl] n revaluación f
rear¹ [rɪə(r)] **1** n (a) (back part) parte f de atrás (b) Fam (buttocks) trasero m
2 adj trasero(a); **r. entrance** puerta f de atrás
rear² [rɪə(r)] **1** vt (a) (breed, raise) criar (b) (lift up) levantar
2 vi **to r. up** (horse) encabritarse
rearguard ['rɪəɡɑːd] n retaguardia f
rearmament [riː'ɑːməmənt] n rearme m
rearrange [riːə'reɪndʒ] vt (a) (furniture) colocar de otra manera (b) (appointment) fijar otra fecha para
rear-view ['rɪəvjuː] adj **r. mirror** (espejo m) retrovisor m
reason ['riːzən] **1** n (a) motivo m, razón f; **for no r.** sin razón; **for some r.** por algún motivo (b) (good sense) razón f; **it stands to r.** es lógico; **to listen to r.** atender a razones
2 vi (a) **to r. with sb** convencer a algn (b) (argue, work out) razonar
reasonable ['riːzənəbəl] adj (a) (fair) razonable (b) (sensible) sensato(a) (c) (average) regular
reasonably ['riːzənəblɪ] adv (fairly) bastante
reasoning ['riːzənɪŋ] n razonamiento m
reassurance [riːə'ʃʊərəns] n consuelo m
reassure [riːə'ʃʊə(r)] vt (a) (comfort) tranquilizar (b) (restore confidence) dar confianza a
reassuring [riːə'ʃʊərɪŋ] adj consolador(a)
rebate ['riːbeɪt] n devolución f; **tax r.** devolución fiscal

---

*♪ Note that the Spanish verb **rebatir** is a false friend and is never a translation for the English verb **to rebate**. In Spanish, **rebatir** means "to refute".*

---

rebel 1 adj & n ['rebəl] rebelde (mf)
2 vi [rɪ'bel] rebelarse, sublevarse (**against** contra)
rebellion [rɪ'beljən] n rebelión f
rebellious [rɪ'beljəs] adj rebelde

rebound 1 n ['riːbaʊnd] (of ball) rebote m; Fig **on the r.** de rebote
2 vi [rɪ'baʊnd] (ball) rebotar
rebuff [rɪ'bʌf] **1** n desaire m
2 vt desairar
rebuild [riː'bɪld] vt reconstruir
rebuke [rɪ'bjuːk] **1** n reproche m
2 vt reprochar
rebut [rɪ'bʌt] vt refutar
recalcitrant [rɪ'kælsɪtrənt] adj Fml recalcitrante
recall [rɪ'kɔːl] vt (a) (soldiers, products) hacer volver; (ambassador) retirar (b) (remember) recordar
recant [rɪ'kænt] vi Fml retractarse
recap 1 vt & vi [riː'kæp] resumir; **to r.** en resumen
2 n ['riːkæp] recapitulación f
recapitulate [riːkə'pɪtjʊleɪt] vt & vi Fml recapitular
recapture [riː'kæptʃə(r)] vt Fig recuperar
recd Com (abbr **received**) recibido(a)
recede [rɪ'siːd] vi retroceder; (fade) desvanecerse
receipt [rɪ'siːt] n (a) (act) recepción f; **to acknowledge r. of sth** acusar recibo de algo (b) Com (paper) recibo m (c) **receipts** (takings) recaudación f
receive [rɪ'siːv] vt (a) recibir (b) Jur (stolen goods) ocultar (c) (welcome) acoger (d) TV & Rad captar
receiver [rɪ'siːvə(r)] n (a) (person) receptor(a) m,f (b) Jur (of stolen goods) perista mf (c) BrJur official **r.** síndico m (d) Tel auricular m (e) Rad receptor m
recent ['riːsənt] adj reciente; **in r. years** en los últimos años
recently ['riːsəntlɪ] adv hace poco, recientemente
receptacle [rɪ'septəkəl] n receptáculo m
reception [rɪ'sepʃən] n (a) (welcome) acogida f (b) (party) recepción f; **wedding r.** banquete m de bodas (c) **r. (desk)** recepción f (d) Rad TV recepción f
receptionist [rɪ'sepʃənɪst] n recepcionista mf
recess ['riːses, rɪ'ses] n (a) (in a wall) hueco m (b) (secret place) escondrijo m (c) US Educ recreo m; Pol período m de vacaciones
recession [rɪ'seʃən] n recesión f
recharge [riː'tʃɑːdʒ] vt (battery) recargar
rechargeable [riː'tʃɑːdʒəbəl] adj recargable
recipe ['resɪpɪ] n Culin receta f; Fig fórmula f
recipient [rɪ'sɪpɪənt] n receptor(a) m,f, (of letter) destinatario(a) m,f

---

*♪ Note that the Spanish word **recipiente** is a false friend and is never a translation for the English word **recipient**. In Spanish, **recipiente** means "receptacle, container".*

reciprocate [rɪˈsɪprəkeɪt] **1** *vt (favour etc)* devolver
2 *vi* hacer lo mismo
recital [rɪˈsaɪtəl] *n* recital *m*
recite [rɪˈsaɪt] *vt & vi* recitar
reckless [ˈreklɪs] *adj (unwise)* imprudente; *(fearless)* temerario(a)
reckon [ˈrekən] *vt & vi (calculate)* calcular; *(count)* contar (**b**) *Fam (think)* creer; *(consider)* considerar
  ▸ **reckon on** *vt insep* contar con
reckoner [ˈrekənə(r)] *n* **ready r.** tabla *f* de cálculo
reckoning [ˈrekənɪŋ] *n* cálculo *m*; **by my r. ...** según mis cálculos ...; *Fig* **day of r.** día *m* del juicio final
reclaim [rɪˈkleɪm] *vt* (**a**) *(recover)* recuperar; *(demand back)* reclamar (**b**) *(marshland etc)* convertir
recline [rɪˈklaɪn] *vi* recostarse, reclinarse
reclining [rɪˈklaɪnɪŋ] *adj* recostado(a); **r. seat** asiento *m* abatible
recluse [rɪˈkluːs] *n* solitario(a) *m,f*

> *Note that the Spanish word* **recluso** *is a false friend and is never a translation for the English word* **recluse**. *In Spanish,* **recluso** *means "prisoner".*

recognition [rekəɡˈnɪʃən] *n* reconocimiento *m*; *(appreciation)* apreciación *f*; **changed beyond all r.** irreconocible
recognizable [rekəɡˈnaɪzəbəl] *adj* reconocible
recognize [ˈrekəɡnaɪz] *vt* reconocer
recoil 1 *n* [ˈriːkɔɪl] *(of gun)* culatazo *m*; *(of spring)* aflojamiento *m*
  2 *vi* [rɪˈkɔɪl] (**a**) *(gun)* dar un culatazo; *(spring)* aflojarse (**b**) *(in fear)* espantarse
recollect [rekəˈlekt] *vt* recordar
recollection [rekəˈlekʃən] *n* recuerdo *m*

> *Note that the Spanish word* **recolección** *is a false friend and is never a translation for the English word* **recollection**. *In Spanish,* **recolección** *means "harvest, collection".*

recommend [rekəˈmend] *vt* recomendar
recommendation [rekəmenˈdeɪʃən] *n* recomendación *f*
recompense [ˈrekəmpens] **1** *n* recompensa *f*; *Jur* indemnización *f*
  2 *vt* recompensar; *Jur* indemnizar
reconcile [ˈrekənsaɪl] *vt (two people)* reconciliar; *(two ideas)* conciliar; **to r. oneself to** resignarse a
recondition [riːkənˈdɪʃən] *vt (engine)* revisar
reconnaissance [rɪˈkɒnɪsəns] *n Mil* reconocimiento *m*
reconnoitre, *US* **reconnoiter** [rekəˈnɔɪtə(r)] *vt Mil* reconocer
reconsider [riːkənˈsɪdə(r)] *vt* reconsiderar
reconstruct [riːkənˈstrʌkt] *vt* reconstruir

reconstruction [riːkənˈstrʌkʃən] *n* reconstrucción *f*
record 1 *n* [ˈrekɔːd] (**a**) *(account)* relación *f*; *(of meeting)* actas *fpl*; **off the r.** confidencialmente (**b**) *(document)* documento *m*; **r. of attendance** registro *m* de asistencia; **public records** archivos *mpl* (**c**) *Med* historial médico (**d**) *Mus* disco *m*; **r. player** tocadiscos *m inv* (**e**) *Sport* récord *m*
  2 *vt* [rɪˈkɔːd] (**a**) *(relate)* hacer constar; *(note down)* apuntar (**b**) *(record, voice)* grabar (**c**) *(of thermometer etc)* marcar
recorded [rɪˈkɔːdɪd] *adj* **r. delivery** correo certificado; **r. message** mensaje grabado
recorder [rɪˈkɔːdə(r)] *n* (**a**) *(person)* registrador(a) *m,f*; *Jur* magistrado(a) *m,f* (**b**) *Mus* flauta *f*
recording [rɪˈkɔːdɪŋ] *n (registering)* registro *m*; *(recorded music, message etc)* grabación *f*
recount [rɪˈkaʊnt] *vt (tell)* contar
re-count 1 *vi* [riːˈkaʊnt] *Pol* hacer un recuento
  2 *n* [ˈriːkaʊnt] *Pol* recuento *m*
recoup [rɪˈkuːp] *vt (losses etc)* recuperar
recourse [rɪˈkɔːs] *n* **to have r. to** recurrir a
recover [rɪˈkʌvə(r)] **1** *vt (items, lost time)* recuperar; *(consciousness)* recobrar
  2 *vi (from illness etc)* reponerse
recovery [rɪˈkʌvərɪ] *n* (**a**) *(retrieval)* recuperación *f* (**b**) *(from illness)* restablecimiento *m*
recreation [rekrɪˈeɪʃən] *n* (**a**) diversión *f* (**b**) *Educ (playtime)* recreo *m*; **r. ground** terreno *m* de juegos
recreational [rekrɪˈeɪʃənəl] *adj* recreativo(a)
recrimination [rɪkrɪmɪˈneɪʃən] *n* reproche *m*
recruit [rɪˈkruːt] **1** *n* recluta *m*
  2 *vt (soldiers)* reclutar; *(workers)* contratar
recruitment [rɪˈkruːtmənt] *n (of soldiers)* reclutamiento *m*; *(of employees)* contratación *f*
rectangle [ˈrektæŋɡəl] *n* rectángulo *m*
rectangular [rekˈtæŋɡjʊlə(r)] *adj* rectangular
rectify [ˈrektɪfaɪ] *vt* rectificar
rector [ˈrektə(r)] *n* (**a**) *Rel* párroco *m* (**b**) *Scot Educ* director(a) *m,f*
recuperate [rɪˈkuːpəreɪt] *vi* reponerse
recur [rɪˈkɜː(r)] *vi* repetirse

> *Note that the Spanish verb* **recurrir** *is a false friend and is never a translation for the English verb* **to recur**. *In Spanish,* **recurrir** *means "to appeal, to resort".*

recurrence [rɪˈkʌrəns] *n* repetición *f*, reaparición *f*
recurrent [rɪˈkʌrənt] *adj* constante; *Med* recurrente
recycle [riːˈsaɪkəl] *vt* reciclar
recycling [riːˈsaɪklɪŋ] *n* reciclaje *m*
red [red] **1** *adj* **(redder, reddest)** rojo(a); **r. light** semáforo *m* en rojo; **r. wine** vino tinto; **to go r.** ponerse colorado(a); **to have r. hair**

ser pelirrojo(a); *Fig* **r. herring** truco *m* para despistar; *Fam* **to roll out the r. carpet for sb** recibir a algn con todos los honores; **R. Cross** Cruz Roja; **R. Indian** piel roja *mf*; **R. Riding Hood** Caperucita Roja; **R. Sea** Mar Rojo; **r. tape** papeleo *m*

2 *n* (**a**) *(colour)* rojo *m* (**b**) *Fin* **to be in the r.** estar en números rojos

redcurrant ['redkʌrənt] *n* grosella roja

redden ['redən] **1** *vi (blush)* enrojecerse, ponerse colorado(a)

2 *vt (make red)* teñir de rojo

reddish ['redɪʃ] *adj* rojizo(a)

redeem [rɪ'diːm] *vt* (**a**) *(regain)* recobrar; *(from pawn)* desempeñar; *(voucher)* canjear (**b**) *(debt)* amortizar (**c**) *(film, novel etc)* salvar (**d**) *Rel* redimir; *Fig* **to r. oneself** redimirse

redeeming [rɪ'diːmɪŋ] *adj* compensatorio(a); **his only r. feature** lo único que le salva

redemption [rɪ'dempʃən] *n Fml* (**a**) *(of debt)* amortización *f* (**b**) *Rel* redención *f*; **beyond r.** sin remedio

redeploy [riːdɪ'plɔɪ] *vt* redistribuir

red-handed [red'hændɪd] *adj* **to catch sb r.** coger a algn con las manos en la masa

redhead ['redhed] *n* pelirrojo(a) *m,f*

red-hot [red'hɒt] *adj* (**a**) candente; **r. news** noticia(s) *f(pl)* de última hora (**b**) *Fam (passionate)* ardiente

redial [riː'daɪəl] *n Tel (facility)* rellamada *f*

redirect [riːdɪ'rekt] *vt* (**a**) *(funds)* redistribuir (**b**) *(letter)* remitir a la nueva dirección

red-light [red'laɪt] *adj Fam* **r. district** barrio chino

redouble [riː'dʌbəl] *vt* redoblar

redress [rɪ'dres] *Fml* **1** *n* reparación *f*

2 *vt* reparar

redskin ['redskɪn] *n* piel roja *mf*

reduce [rɪ'djuːs] *vt* (**a**) reducir (**b**) *(in rank)* degradar (**c**) *Culin (sauce)* espesar (**d**) *Med* recomponer

reduction [rɪ'dʌkʃən] *n* reducción *f*; *Com (in purchase price)* descuento *m*, rebaja *f*

redundancy [rɪ'dʌndənsɪ] *n* despido *m*

redundant [rɪ'dʌndənt] *adj* (**a**) *(superfluous)* redundante (**b**) *Ind* **to be made r.** perder el empleo; **to make sb r.** despedir a algn

reed [riːd] *n* (**a**) *Bot* caña *f* (**b**) *Mus* caramillo *m*

reef [riːf] *n* arrecife *m*

reek [riːk] **1** *n* tufo *m*

2 *vi* apestar

reel [riːl] **1** *n* (**a**) *(spool)* bobina *f*, carrete *m* (**b**) *Scot Mus* danza *f* tradicional

2 *vi (stagger)* tambalearse

re-elect [riːɪ'lekt] *vt* reelegir

ref [ref] *n* (**a**) *Fam Sport* árbitro *m* (**b**) *Com (abbr* **reference**) ref

refectory [rɪ'fektərɪ] *n* refectorio *m*

refer [rɪ'fɜː(r)] **1** *vt* mandar, enviar; **to r. a matter to a tribunal** remitir un asunto a un tribunal

2 *vi* (**a**) *(allude)* referirse, aludir (**to** a) (**b**) **to r. to** *(consult)* consultar

referee [refə'riː] **1** *n* (**a**) *Sport* árbitro(a) *m,f* (**b**) *(for job application)* garante *mf*

2 *vt Sport* arbitrar

reference ['refərəns] *n* (**a**) referencia *f*; **with r. to** referente a, con referencia a; **r. book** libro *m* de consulta; **r. library** biblioteca *f* de consulta (**b**) *(character report)* informe *m*, referencia *f*

referendum [refə'rendəm] *n* referéndum *m*

refill 1 *n* ['riːfɪl] (**a**) *(replacement)* recambio *m*, carga *f* (**b**) *Fam (drink)* otra copa

2 *vt* [riː'fɪl] rellenar

refine [rɪ'faɪn] *vt* refinar

refined [rɪ'faɪnd] *adj* refinado(a)

refinement [rɪ'faɪnmənt] *n* refinamiento *m*

refinery [rɪ'faɪnərɪ] *n* refinería *f*

reflect [rɪ'flekt] **1** *vt (light, attitude)* reflejar

2 *vi (think)* reflexionar; **to r. on sth** meditar sobre algo

reflection [rɪ'flekʃən] *n* (**a**) *(indication, mirror image)* reflejo *m* (**b**) *(thought)* reflexión *f*; **on r.** pensándolo bien (**c**) *(criticism)* crítica *f*

reflector [rɪ'flektə(r)] *n (of vehicle)* catafaro *m*

reflex ['riːfleks] *n* reflejo *m*

reflexive [rɪ'fleksɪv] *adj* reflexivo(a)

reform [rɪ'fɔːm] **1** *n* reforma *f*; **r. school** reformatorio *m*

2 *vt* reformar

reformation [refə'meɪʃən] *n* reforma *f*

reformatory [rɪ'fɔːmətərɪ] *n* reformatorio *m*

reformer [rɪ'fɔːmə(r)] *n* reformador(a) *m,f*

refrain [rɪ'freɪn] **1** *n Mus* estribillo *m*; *Fig* lema *m*

2 *vi* abstenerse (**from** de)

refresh [rɪ'freʃ] *vt* refrescar

refresher [rɪ'freʃə(r)] *n* **r. course** cursillo *m* de reciclaje

refreshing [rɪ'freʃɪŋ] *adj* refrescante; **a r. change** un cambio muy agradable

refreshment [rɪ'freʃmənt] *n* refresco *m*

refrigerator [rɪ'frɪdʒəreɪtə(r)] *n* nevera *f*, frigorífico *m*, *Andes* frigider *m*, *RP* heladera *f*

refuel [riː'fjuːəl] *vi* repostar combustible

refuge ['refjuːdʒ] *n* refugio *m*, cobijo *m*; **to take r.** refugiarse

refugee [refjʊ'dʒiː] *n* refugiado(a) *m,f*

refund 1 *n* ['riːfʌnd] reembolso *m*

2 *vt* [rɪ'fʌnd] reembolsar, devolver

refurbish [riː'fɜːbɪʃ] *vt* redecorar

refusal [rɪ'fjuːzəl] *n* negativa *f*; **to have first r. on sth** tener la primera opción en algo

refuse¹ [rɪ'fjuːz] **1** *vt* rechazar; **to r. sb sth** negar algo a algn

2 *vi* negarse

refuse² ['refjuːs] *n* basura *f*; **r. collector** basurero *m*

refute [rɪ'fjuːt] *vt* refutar, rebatir

regain [rɪ'geɪn] *vt* recuperar; *(consciousness)* recobrar

regal ['ri:gəl] *adj* regio(a)
regard [rɪ'gɑːd] **1** *n* (**a**) *(concern)* consideración *f*, respeto *m*; **with r. to** respecto a (**b**) *(esteem)* estima *f* (**c**) **regards** *(good wishes)* recuerdos *mpl*; **give him my regards** dale recuerdos de mi parte
2 *vt* (**a**) *(consider)* considerar (**b**) **as regards** *(regarding)* respecto a
regarding [rɪ'gɑːdɪŋ] *prep* respecto a
regardless [rɪ'gɑːdlɪs] **1** *prep* **r. of** sin tener en cuenta; **r. of the outcome** pase lo que pase
2 *adv* a toda costa
regime [reɪ'ʒiːm] *n* régimen *m*
regiment ['redʒɪmənt] **1** *n* regimiento *m*
2 *vt* regimentar
regimental [redʒɪ'mentəl] *adj* del regimiento
region ['riːdʒən] *n* (**a**) región *f* (**b**) **in the r. of** aproximadamente
regional ['riːdʒənəl] *adj* regional
regionalism ['riːdʒənəlɪzəm] *n* regionalismo *m*
register ['redʒɪstə(r)] **1** *n* registro *m*
2 *vt* (**a**) *(record)* registrar (**b**) *(letter)* certificar (**c**) *(show)* mostrar; **his face registered fear** en su rostro se reflejaba el miedo
3 *vi* *(for course)* inscribirse; *Univ* matricularse
registered ['redʒɪstəd] *adj* certificado(a); **r. letter** carta certificada; **r. trademark** marca registrada
registrar [redʒɪ'strɑː(r), 'redʒɪstrɑː(r)] *n* (**a**) *(record keeper)* registrador(a) *m,f* (**b**) *Br Med* interno(a) *m,f* (**c**) *Univ* secretario(a) *m,f* general
registration [redʒɪ'streɪʃən] *n* inscripción *f*; *Univ* matrícula *f*; *Br Aut* **r. number** matrícula *f*
registry ['redʒɪstrɪ] *n* registro *m*; **to get married in a r. office** casarse por lo civil; **r. office** registro civil
regret [rɪ'gret] **1** *n* *(remorse)* remordimiento *m*; *(sadness)* pesar *m*; **regrets** *(excuses)* excusas *fpl*; **to have no regrets** no arrepentirse de nada
2 *vt* arrepentirse de, lamentar
regretful [rɪ'gretfʊl] *adj* arrepentido(a)
regrettable [rɪ'gretəbəl] *adj* lamentable
regroup [riː'gruːp] **1** *vt* reagrupar
2 *vi* reagruparse
regular ['regjʊlə(r)] **1** *adj* (**a**) regular (**b**) *(usual)* normal (**c**) *(staff)* permanente (**d**) *(frequent)* frecuente (**e**) **r. army** tropas *fpl* regulares (**f**) *US Fam* **a r. guy** un tío legal, *Am* un tipo derecho
2 *n* (**a**) *(customer)* cliente *mf* habitual (**b**) *Mil* militar *m* de carrera
regularity [regjʊ'lærɪtɪ] *n* regularidad *f*
regularly ['regjʊləlɪ] *adv* con regularidad
regulate ['regjʊleɪt] *vt* regular
regulation [regjʊ'leɪʃən] **1** *n* (**a**) *(control)* regulación *f* (**b**) *(rule)* regla *f*

2 *adj* reglamentario(a)
rehabilitation [riːəbɪlɪ'teɪʃən] *n* rehabilitación *f*; **r. centre** centro *m* de reinserción
rehearsal [rɪ'hɜːsəl] *n* ensayo *m*
rehearse [rɪ'hɜːs] *vt & vi* ensayar
reign [reɪn] **1** *n* reinado *m*
2 *vi* reinar
reigning ['reɪnɪŋ] *adj* **r. champion** campeón *m* actual
reimburse [riːɪm'bɜːs] *vt* reembolsar
rein [reɪn] *n* *(for horse)* rienda *f*; *Fig* **he gave free r. to his emotions** dio rienda suelta a sus emociones
reindeer ['reɪndɪə(r)] *n* reno *m*
reinforce [riːɪn'fɔːs] *vt* *(strengthen)* reforzar; *(support)* apoyar; **reinforced concrete** hormigón armado
reinforcement [riːɪn'fɔːsmənt] *n* (**a**) refuerzo *m*; *Constr* armazón *m* (**b**) *Mil* **reinforcements** refuerzos *mpl*
reinstate [riːɪn'steɪt] *vt* *(to job)* reincorporar
reiterate [riː'ɪtəreɪt] *vt & vi* reiterar
reject 1 ['riːdʒekt] (**a**) desecho *m* (**b**) *Com* **rejects** artículos defectuosos
2 *vt* [rɪ'dʒekt] rechazar
rejection [rɪ'dʒekʃən] *n* rechazo *m*
rejoice [rɪ'dʒɔɪs] *vi* regocijarse (**at** *or* **over** de)
rejuvenate [rɪ'dʒuːvɪneɪt] *vt* rejuvenecer; *Fig* revitalizar
relapse [rɪ'læps] **1** *n* (**a**) *Med* recaída *f*; **to have a r.** sufrir una recaída (**b**) *(into crime, alcoholism)* reincidencia *f*
2 *vi* recaer
relate [rɪ'leɪt] **1** *vt* (**a**) *(connect)* relacionar (**b**) *(tell)* relatar
2 *vi* relacionarse
related [rɪ'leɪtɪd] *adj* (**a**) *(linked)* relacionado(a) (**to** con) (**b**) **to be r. to sb** ser pariente de algn
relation [rɪ'leɪʃən] *n* (**a**) *(link)* relación *f*; **in** *or* **with r. to** respecto a; **it bears no r. to what we said** no tiene nada que ver con lo que dijimos (**b**) *(member of family)* pariente(a) *m,f*
relationship [rɪ'leɪʃənʃɪp] *n* (**a**) *(link)* relación *f* (**b**) *(between people)* relaciones *fpl*; **to have a good/bad r. with sb** llevarse bien/mal con algn
relative ['relətɪv] **1** *n* pariente *mf*
2 *adj* relativo(a)
relatively ['relətɪvlɪ] *adv* relativamente
relax [rɪ'læks] **1** *vt* *(muscles, rules)* relajar
2 *vi* relajarse
relaxation [riːlæk'seɪʃən] *n* (**a**) *(rest)* descanso *m*, relajación *f* (**b**) *(of rules)* relajación *f* (**c**) *(pastime)* distracción *f*
relaxed [rɪ'lækst] *adj* relajado(a); *(peaceful)* tranquilo(a)
relaxing [rɪ'læksɪŋ] *adj* relajante
relay 1 *n* ['riːleɪ] (**a**) relevo *m*; **r. (race)** carrera *f* de relevos (**b**) *Rad TV* retransmisión *f*

2 vt [rɪ'leɪ] (**a**) (pass on) difundir (**b**) Rad & TV retransmitir

release [rɪ'liːs] **1** n (**a**) (of prisoner) liberación f, puesta f en libertad; (of gas) escape m (**b**) Com puesta f en venta (**c**) Cin estreno m (**d**) (record) disco m (**e**) Press comunicado m

2 vt (**a**) (let go) soltar; (prisoner) poner en libertad; (gas) despedir (**b**) Com poner en venta (**c**) Cin estrenar (**d**) (record) editar (**e**) (publish) publicar

relegate ['relɪgeɪt] vt (**a**) relegar (**b**) Ftb **to be relegated** bajar a una división inferior

relent [rɪ'lent] vi ceder; (storm) aplacarse

relentless [rɪ'lentlɪs] adj implacable

relevant ['reləvənt] adj pertinente (**to** a); **it is not r.** no viene al caso

> ⌀ Note that the Spanish word **relevante** is a false friend and is never a translation for the English word **relevant**. In Spanish, **relevante** means "outstanding, important".

reliability [rɪlaɪə'bɪlɪtɪ] n (**a**) (of person) formalidad f (**b**) (of car, machine) fiabilidad f

reliable [rɪ'laɪəbəl] adj (person) de fiar; **a r. car** un coche seguro; **a r. source** una fuente fidedigna

reliably [rɪ'laɪəblɪ] adv **to be r. informed that** saber de buena tinta que

reliant [rɪ'laɪənt] adj **to be r. on** depender de

relic ['relɪk] n (**a**) Rel reliquia f (**b**) (reminder of past) vestigio m

relief [rɪ'liːf] n (**a**) alivio m (**b**) (help) auxilio m, ayuda f; US **to be on r.** cobrar un subsidio (**c**) Art Geog relieve m

relieve [rɪ'liːv] vt (**a**) aliviar; (monotony) romper (**b**) (take over from) relevar (**c**) Euph **to r. oneself** hacer sus necesidades (**d**) **to r. sb of sth** coger algo a algn

relieved [rɪ'liːvd] adj aliviado(a), tranquilizado(a)

religion [rɪ'lɪdʒən] n religión f

religious [rɪ'lɪdʒəs] adj religioso(a)

relinquish [rɪ'lɪŋkwɪʃ] vt renunciar a; **to r. one's hold on sth** soltar algo

relish ['relɪʃ] **1** n (**a**) (enjoyment) deleite m (**b**) Culin condimento m

2 vt agradar

relocate [riːləʊ'keɪt] vt trasladar

reluctance [rɪ'lʌktəns] n desgana f

reluctant [rɪ'lʌktənt] adj reacio(a); **to be r. to do sth** estar poco dispuesto(a) a hacer algo

reluctantly [rɪ'lʌktəntlɪ] adv de mala gana, a regañadientes

rely [rɪ'laɪ] vi contar (**on** con), confiar (**on** en)

remain [rɪ'meɪn] **1** vi (**a**) (stay) permanecer, quedarse (**b**) (be left) quedar; **it remains to be seen** está por ver

2 npl **remains** restos mpl

remainder [rɪ'meɪndə(r)] n resto m

remaining [rɪ'meɪnɪŋ] adj restante

remand [rɪ'mɑːnd] Jur **1** vt remitir; **remanded**

in custody en prevención

2 n detención f; **on r.** detenido(a)

remark [rɪ'mɑːk] **1** n comentario m

2 vt comentar, observar

> ⌀ Note that the Spanish verb **remarcar** is a false friend and is never a translation for the English verb **to remark**. In Spanish, **remarcar** means "to stress, to underline".

remarkable [rɪ'mɑːkəbəl] adj extraordinario(a); (strange) curioso(a)

remedial [rɪ'miːdɪəl] adj reparador(a); **r. classes** clases fpl para niños atrasados en los estudios

remedy ['remɪdɪ] **1** n remedio m

2 vt remediar

remember [rɪ'membə(r)] **1** vt (**a**) acordarse de, recordar (**b**) **r. me to your mother** dale recuerdos a tu madre

2 vi acordarse, recordar; **I don't r.** no me acuerdo

remembrance [rɪ'membrəns] n **in r. of** en recuerdo de; Br **R. Day** or **Sunday** = día en que se conmemora el armisticio de 1918

remind [rɪ'maɪnd] vt recordar; **r. me to do it** recuérdame que lo haga; **she reminds me of your sister** me recuerda a tu hermana; **that reminds me** ahora que me acuerdo

reminder [rɪ'maɪndə(r)] n recordatorio m, aviso m

reminisce [remɪ'nɪs] vi rememorar

reminiscent [remɪ'nɪsənt] adj Fml nostálgico(a); **to be r. of** recordar

remiss [rɪ'mɪs] adj (negligent) descuidado(a)

remission [rɪ'mɪʃən] n (**a**) Med remisión f (**b**) Jur perdón m

remit [rɪ'mɪt] vt (**a**) (send) remitir (**b**) Jur referir a otro tribunal

remittance [rɪ'mɪtəns] n (**a**) (sending) envío m (**b**) (payment) giro m, pago m

remnant ['remnənt] n resto m; **remnants** (of cloth) retales mpl

remold ['riːməʊld] n US = **remould**

remorse [rɪ'mɔːs] n remordimiento m

remorseful [rɪ'mɔːsfʌl] adj lleno(a) de remordimiento

remorseless [rɪ'mɔːslɪs] adj despiadado(a)

remote [rɪ'məʊt] adj (**a**) (far away) remoto(a); **r. control** mando m a distancia (**b**) (isolated) aislado(a) (**c**) (possibility) remoto(a); **I haven't the remotest idea** no tengo la más mínima idea

remote-controlled [rɪ'məʊtkən'trəʊld] adj teledirigido(a)

remotely [rɪ'məʊtlɪ] adv (**a**) (vaguely) vagamente (**b**) (distantly) en lugar aislado

remould ['riːməʊld] n Aut neumático recauchutado

removable [rɪ'muːvəbəl] adj (detachable) que se puede quitar

removal [rɪ'muːvəl] n (**a**) (moving house)

mudanza *f*; **r. van** camión *m* de mudanzas (**b**) *(of stain etc)* eliminación *f*

remove [rɪˈmuːv] *vt* (**a**) *(move)* quitar; **to r. one's make-up** desmaquillarse; **to r. one's name from a list** tachar su nombre de una lista (**b**) *(from office)* despedir

*Note that the Spanish verb **remover** is a false friend and is never a translation for the English verb **to remove**. In Spanish, **remover** means "to move over, to turn over, to stir".*

removed [rɪˈmuːvd] *adj* **far r. from** muy diferente de

remover [rɪˈmuːvə(r)] *n* **make-up r.** desmaquillador *m*; **nail varnish r.** quitaesmalte *m*; **stain r.** quitamanchas *m inv*

remuneration [rɪmjuːnəˈreɪʃən] *n Fml* remuneración *f*

renaissance [rəˈneɪsəns] **1** *n* renacimiento *m*; **the R.** el Renacimiento
2 *adj* renacentista

rend [rend] *vt (pt & pp* **rent***) Fml* rasgar

render [ˈrendə(r)] *vt Fml* (**a**) *(give)* dar (**b**) *(make)* hacer (**c**) *Com* presentar (**d**) *(translate)* traducir

rendering [ˈrendərɪŋ] *n* (**a**) *(of song, piece of music)* interpretación *f* (**b**) *(translation)* traducción *f*

rendezvous [ˈrɒndɪvuː] **1** *n* (**a**) *(meeting)* cita *f* (**b**) *(place)* lugar *m* de reunión
2 *vi* reunirse

renegade [ˈrenɪgeɪd] *n* renegado(a) *m,f*

renew [rɪˈnjuː] *vt (contract etc)* renovar; **with renewed vigour** con renovadas fuerzas

renewal [rɪˈnjuːəl] *n (of contract etc)* renovación *f*; *(of talks etc)* reanudación *f*

renounce [rɪˈnaʊns] *vt Fml* renunciar

renovate [ˈrenəveɪt] *vt* renovar, hacer reformas en

renown [rɪˈnaʊn] *n* renombre *m*

renowned [rɪˈnaʊnd] *adj* renombrado(a)

rent [rent] **1** *n (for building, car, TV)* alquiler *m* (**b**) *(for land)* arriendo *m*
2 *vt* (**a**) *(building, car, TV)* alquilar, *Méx* rentar (**b**) *(land)* arrendar
3 *pt & pp of* **rend**

rental [ˈrentəl] *n (of house etc)* alquiler *m*

renunciation [rɪnʌnsɪˈeɪʃən] *n Fml* renuncia *f*

reorganize [riːˈɔːgənaɪz] *vt* reorganizar

rep [rep] *n Fam* (**a**) *Com* representante *mf* (**b**) *Th* teatro *m* de repertorio

repaid [riːˈpeɪd] *pt & pp of* **repay**

repair [rɪˈpeə(r)] **1** *n* reparación *f*, arreglo *m*; **in good/bad r.** en buen/mal estado
2 *vt* (**a**) *(car)* reparar; *(clothes)* remendar (**b**) *(make amends for)* reparar

repartee [repɑːˈtiː] *n* réplica aguda

repatriate [riːˈpætrɪeɪt] *vt* repatriar

repay [riːˈpeɪ] *vt (pt & pp* **repaid***)* devolver; **to r. a debt** liquidar una deuda; **to r. a kindness** devolver un favor

repayment [riːˈpeɪmənt] *n* pago *m*

repeal [rɪˈpiːl] *Jur* **1** *n* revocación *f*
2 *vt* revocar

repeat [rɪˈpiːt] **1** *vt* repetir; **to r. oneself** repetirse
2 *n (repetition)* repetición *f*; *TV* reposición *f*

repeated [rɪˈpiːtɪd] *adj* repetido(a)

repeatedly [rɪˈpiːtɪdlɪ] *adv* repetidas veces

repel [rɪˈpel] *vt* (**a**) *(fight off)* repeler (**b**) *(disgust)* repugnar

repellent [rɪˈpelənt] **1** *adj* repelente; **water-r.** impermeable
2 *n* **(insect) r.** loción *f or* spray *m* antiinsectos

repent [rɪˈpent] *vt & vi* arrepentirse (de)

repentance [rɪˈpentəns] *n* arrepentimiento *m*

repercussion [riːpəˈkʌʃən] *n (usu pl)* repercusión *f*

repertoire [ˈrepətwɑː(r)] *n* repertorio *m*

repertory [ˈrepətərɪ] *n Th* teatro *m* de repertorio

repetition [repɪˈtɪʃən] *n* repetición *f*

repetitive [rɪˈpetɪtɪv] *adj* repetitivo(a)

replace [rɪˈpleɪs] *vt* (**a**) *(put back)* volver a poner en su sitio (**b**) *(substitute for)* sustituir, reemplazar

replacement [rɪˈpleɪsmənt] *n* (**a**) *(returning)* reemplazo *m* (**b**) *(person)* sustituto(a) *m,f* (**c**) *(part)* pieza *f* de recambio

replay [ˈriːpleɪ] *n* repetición *f*

replenish [rɪˈplenɪʃ] *vt* (**a**) *(fill up)* rellenar (**b**) **to r. stocks** reponer las existencias

replete [rɪˈpliːt] *adj Fml* repleto(a)

replica [ˈreplɪkə] *n* réplica *f*

reply [rɪˈplaɪ] **1** *n* respuesta *f*, contestación *f*
2 *vi* responder, contestar

report [rɪˈpɔːt] **1** *n* (**a**) *(statement)* informe *m*; **medical r.** parte médico; *Br* **school r.** informe escolar (**b**) *(piece of news)* noticia *f* (**c**) *Press, Rad TV* reportaje *m* (**d**) *(rumour)* rumor *m* (**e**) *Fml (of gun)* estampido *m*
2 *vt* (**a**) **it is reported that ...** se dice que ... (**b**) *(tell authorities about)* denunciar (**c**) *Press* hacer un reportaje sobre
3 *vi* (**a**) *(of committee member etc)* hacer un informe (**b**) *Press* hacer un reportaje (**c**) *(for duty etc)* presentarse; *Mil* **to r. sick** coger la baja por enfermedad

reported [rɪˈpɔːtɪd] *adj* **r. speech** estilo indirecto

reportedly [rɪˈpɔːtɪdlɪ] *adv Fml* según se dice

reporter [rɪˈpɔːtə(r)] *n* periodista *mf*

repose [rɪˈpəʊz] *Fml* **1** *n* reposo *m*
2 *vt & vi* reposar

repossess [riːpəˈzes] *vt* **our house has been repossessed** el banco ha ejecutado la hipoteca de nuestra casa

reprehensible [reprɪˈhensəbəl] *adj* reprensible, censurable

represent [reprɪˈzent] *vt* representar

representation [reprɪzen'teɪʃən] n (a) representación f (b) Fml **representations** queja f
representative [reprɪ'zentətɪv] 1 adj representativo(a)
2 n (a) representante mf (b) US Pol diputado(a) m,f
repress [rɪ'pres] vt reprimir, contener
repressed [rɪ'prest] adj **to be r.** estar reprimido(a)
repression [rɪ'preʃən] n represión f
repressive [rɪ'presɪv] adj represivo(a)
reprieve [rɪ'priːv] 1 n (a) Jur indulto m (b) Fig alivio m
2 vt Jur indultar
reprimand ['reprɪmɑːnd] 1 n reprimenda f
2 vt reprender
reprisal [rɪ'praɪzəl] n represalia f
reproach [rɪ'prəʊtʃ] 1 n reproche m; **beyond r.** intachable
2 vt reprochar
reproachful [rɪ'prəʊtʃfʊl] adj reprobador(a)
reproduce [riːprə'djuːs] 1 vt reproducir
2 vi reproducirse
reproduction [riːprə'dʌkʃən] n reproducción f
reproof [rɪ'pruːf] n Fml reprobación f, censura f
reprove [rɪ'pruːv] vt Fml reprobar, censurar
reptile ['reptaɪl] n reptil m
republic [rɪ'pʌblɪk] n república f
republican [rɪ'pʌblɪkən] adj & n republicano(a) (m,f); US Pol **R. Party** Partido Republicano
repudiate [rɪ'pjuːdɪeɪt] vt Fml (a) (reject) rechazar (b) (not acknowledge) negarse a reconocer
repugnant [rɪ'pʌgnənt] adj repugnante
repulse [rɪ'pʌls] vt rechazar
repulsive [rɪ'pʌlsɪv] adj repulsivo(a)
reputable ['repjʊtəbəl] adj (company etc) acreditado(a); (person, products) de toda confianza
reputation [repjʊ'teɪʃən] n reputación f
repute [rɪ'pjuːt] n Fml reputación f
reputed [rɪ'pjuːtɪd] adj supuesto(a); **to be r. to be** ser considerado(a) como
reputedly [rɪ'pjuːtɪdlɪ] adv según se dice
request [rɪ'kwest] 1 n petición f, solicitud f; **available on r.** disponible a petición de los interesados; Br **r. stop** (for bus) parada f discrecional
2 vt pedir, solicitar
require [rɪ'kwaɪə(r)] vt (a) (need) necesitar, requerir (b) (demand) exigir
requirement [rɪ'kwaɪəmənt] n (a) (need) necesidad f (b) (demand) requisito m

🖉 Note that the Spanish word **requerimiento** is a false friend and is never a translation for the English word **requirement**. In Spanish, **requerimiento** means both "entreaty" and "writ, injunction".

requisite ['rekwɪzɪt] Fml 1 adj requerido(a)
2 n requisito m
requisition [rekwɪ'zɪʃən] 1 n requisición f
2 vt requisar
rescind [rɪ'sɪnd] vt Fml (contract) rescindir; (law) abrogar
rescue ['reskjuː] 1 n rescate m; **r. team** equipo m de rescate
2 vt rescatar
rescuer ['reskjʊə(r)] n rescatador(a) m,f
research [rɪ'sɜːtʃ] 1 n investigación f; **R. and Development** Investigación más Desarrollo
2 vt & vi investigar
researcher [rɪ'sɜːtʃə(r)] n investigador(a) m,f
resemblance [rɪ'zembləns] n semejanza f
resemble [rɪ'zembəl] vt parecerse a
resent [rɪ'zent] vt ofenderse por
resentful [rɪ'zentfʊl] adj ofendido(a)
resentment [rɪ'zentmənt] n resentimiento m
reservation [rezə'veɪʃən] n reserva f
reserve [rɪ'zɜːv] 1 n (a) reserva f; **to keep sth in r.** guardar algo de reserva (b) Sport suplente mf (c) Mil **reserves** reservas fpl
2 vt reservar
reserved [rɪ'zɜːvd] adj reservado(a)
reservoir ['rezəvwɑː(r)] n embalse m, pantano m; Fig reserva f
reshape [riː'ʃeɪp] vt rehacer; Fig reorganizar
reshuffle [riː'ʃʌfəl] n Pol remodelación f
reside [rɪ'zaɪd] vi Fml residir
residence ['rezɪdəns] n Fml (home) residencia f; (address) domicilio m; (period of time) permanencia f
resident ['rezɪdənt] adj & n residente (mf); US Med = médico que ha cumplido la residencia y prosigue con su especialización; **to be r. in** estar domiciliado(a) en
residential [rezɪ'denʃəl] adj residencial
residual [rɪ'zɪdjʊəl] adj residual
residue ['rezɪdjuː] n residuo m
resign [rɪ'zaɪn] 1 vt (a) (give up) dimitir (b) **to r. oneself to sth** resignarse a algo
2 vi (from job) dimitir
resignation [rezɪg'neɪʃən] n (a) (from a job) dimisión f (b) (acceptance) resignación f
resigned [rɪ'zaɪnd] adj resignado(a)
resilience [rɪ'zɪlɪəns] n resistencia f
resilient [rɪ'zɪlɪənt] adj (strong) resistente
resin ['rezɪn] n resina f
resist [rɪ'zɪst] 1 vt (a) (not yield to) resistir (b) (oppose) oponerse a
2 vi resistir
resistance [rɪ'zɪstəns] n resistencia f
resit [riː'sɪt] vt (exam) volver a presentarse a
resolute ['rezəluːt] adj resuelto(a), decidido(a)
resolution [rezə'luːʃən] n resolución f
resolve [rɪ'zɒlv] 1 n resolución f
2 vt resolver; **to r. to do** resolverse a hacer
3 vi resolverse
resonant ['rezənənt] adj resonante

resort [rɪˈzɔːt] **1** n (**a**) *(place)* lugar m de vacaciones; **tourist r.** centro turístico (**b**) *(recourse)* recurso m; **as a last r.** como último recurso

2 vi recurrir (**to** a)

> *Note that the Spanish word **resorte** is a false friend and is never a translation for the English word **resort**. In Spanish, **resorte** means both "spring" and "means".*

resound [rɪˈzaʊnd] vi resonar; *Fig* tener resonancia

resounding [rɪˈzaʊndɪŋ] adj **a r. failure** un fracaso total; **a r. success** un éxito rotundo

resource [rɪˈsɔːs] n recurso m

resourceful [rɪˈsɔːsfʊl] adj ingenioso(a)

respect [rɪˈspekt] **1** n (**a**) *(deference)* respeto m; **to pay one's respects to sb** presentar sus respetos a algn (**b**) *(relation, reference)* respecto m; **in that r.** a ese respecto; **with r. to** con referencia a

2 vt respetar

respectable [rɪˈspektəbəl] adj respetable; *(clothes)* decente

respectful [rɪˈspektfʊl] adj respetuoso(a)

respective [rɪˈspektɪv] adj respectivo(a)

respectively [rɪˈspektɪvlɪ] adv respectivamente

respite [ˈrespaɪt] n *Fml* respiro m

resplendent [rɪˈsplendənt] adj resplandeciente

respond [rɪˈspɒnd] vi responder

response [rɪˈspɒns] n (**a**) *(reply)* respuesta f (**b**) *(reaction)* reacción f

responsibility [rɪspɒnsəˈbɪlɪtɪ] n responsabilidad f

responsible [rɪˈspɒnsəbəl] adj responsable (**for** de); **to be r. to sb** tener que dar cuentas a algn

responsive [rɪˈspɒnsɪv] adj sensible

rest¹ [rest] **1** n (**a**) *(break)* descanso m; **r. cure** cura f de reposo; *US* **r. room** aseos mpl (**b**) *(peace)* tranquilidad f; **at r.** *(object)* inmóvil (**c**) *(support)* apoyo m (**d**) *Mus* pausa f

2 vt (**a**) descansar (**b**) *(lean)* apoyar; **to r. a ladder against a wall** apoyar una escalera contra una pared

3 vi (**a**) descansar (**b**) *(be calm)* quedarse tranquilo(a) (**c**) **it doesn't r. with me** no depende de mí; **we'll let the matter r.** dejémoslo estar

rest² [rest] n **the r.** (**a**) *(remainder)* el resto, lo demás; **the r. of the day** el resto del día; **the r. of the girls** las demás chicas; **the r. of us** los demás

restaurant [ˈrestərɒnt] n restaurante m; *Rail* **r. car** coche m restaurante

restful [ˈrestfʊl] adj relajante

restitution [restɪˈtjuːʃən] n *Fml* restitución f; **to make r.** restituir

restive [ˈrestɪv] adj inquieto(a), nervioso(a)

restless [ˈrestlɪs] adj agitado(a), inquieto(a)

restoration [restəˈreɪʃən] n (**a**) *(giving back)* devolución f (**b**) *Br Hist* **the R.** la Restauración (**c**) *(of building, piece of furniture)* restauración f

restore [rɪˈstɔː(r)] vt (**a**) *(give back)* devolver (**b**) *(re-establish)* restablecer (**c**) *(building etc)* restaurar

restrain [rɪˈstreɪn] vt contener; **to r. one's anger** reprimir la cólera; **to r. oneself** contenerse

restrained [rɪˈstreɪnd] adj *(person)* moderado(a); *(emotion)* contenido(a)

restraint [rɪˈstreɪnt] n (**a**) *(restriction)* restricción f; *(hindrance)* traba f (**b**) *(moderation)* moderación f

restrict [rɪˈstrɪkt] vt restringir, limitar

restriction [rɪˈstrɪkʃən] n restricción f, limitación f

restrictive [rɪˈstrɪktɪv] adj restrictivo(a)

result [rɪˈzʌlt] **1** n (**a**) resultado m (**b**) *(consequence)* consecuencia f; **as a r. of** como consecuencia de

2 vi (**a**) resultar; **to r. from** resultar de (**b**) **to r. in** causar

resume [rɪˈzjuːm] **1** vt *(journey, work, conversation)* reanudar; *(control)* reasumir

2 vi recomenzar

> *Note that the Spanish verb **resumir** is a false friend and is never a translation for the English verb **to resume**. In Spanish, **resumir** means "to sum up, to summarize".*

résumé [ˈrezjʊmeɪ] n (**a**) *(summary)* resumen m (**b**) *US (curriculum vitae)* currículum (vitae) m

resumption [rɪˈzʌmpʃən] n *(of journey, work, conversation)* reanudación f

resurface [riːˈsɜːfɪs] **1** vt *(road)* rehacer el firme de

2 vi *Fig* resurgir

resurgence [rɪˈsɜːdʒəns] n resurgimiento m

resurrection [rezəˈrekʃən] n resurrección f

resuscitate [rɪˈsʌsɪteɪt] vt *Med* reanimar

retail [ˈriːteɪl] **1** n venta f al por menor; **r. outlet** punto m de venta; **r. price** precio m de venta al público; **R. Price Index** Indice m de Precios al Consumo

2 vt vender al por menor

3 vi venderse al por menor

4 adv al por menor

retailer [ˈriːteɪlə(r)] n detallista mf

retain [rɪˈteɪn] vt (**a**) *(heat)* conservar; *(personal effects)* guardar (**b**) *(water)* retener (**c**) *(facts, information)* recordar (**d**) **to r. the services of a lawyer** contratar a un abogado

retainer [rɪˈteɪnə(r)] n (**a**) *(payment)* anticipo m sobre los honorarios (**b**) *(servant)* criado(a) m,f

retaliate [rɪˈtælieɪt] vi tomar represalias (**against** contra)

retaliation [rɪtælɪ'eɪʃən] n represalias fpl; **in r.** en represalia

retarded [rɪ'tɑːdɪd] adj retrasado(a)

retch [retʃ] vi tener náuseas

retentive [rɪ'tentɪv] adj retentivo(a)

rethink ['riːθɪŋk] n Fam **to have a r. about sth** volver a reflexionar sobre algo

reticent ['retɪsənt] adj reticente

retina ['retɪnə] n retina f

retinue ['retɪnjuː] n séquito m

retire [rɪ'taɪə(r)] 1 vt jubilar
2 vi (a) (stop working) jubilarse (b) (from race) retirarse; **to r. for the night** irse a la cama, acostarse

retired [rɪ'taɪəd] adj jubilado(a)

retiree [rɪtaɪə'riː] n US retirado(a) m,f

retirement [rɪ'taɪəmənt] n jubilación f

retiring [rɪ'taɪərɪŋ] adj (a) (reserved) reservado(a) (b) (official) saliente

retort [rɪ'tɔːt] 1 n réplica f
2 vi replicar

retrace [riː'treɪs] vt (recall) reconstruir; **to r. one's steps** volver sobre sus pasos

retract [rɪ'trækt] 1 vt (a) (claws) retraer; (landing gear) replegar (b) (statement) retirar
2 vi (a) (claws) retraerse; (landing gear) replegarse (b) Fml retractarse

retread ['riːtred] n Aut neumático recauchutado

retreat [rɪ'triːt] 1 n (a) Mil retirada f (b) (shelter) refugio m (c) Rel retiro m
2 vi retirarse (from de)

retrial ['riːtraɪəl] n Jur nuevo juicio

retribution [retrɪ'bjuːʃən] n represalias fpl

> 🔎 Note that the Spanish word **retribución** is a false friend and is never a translation for the English word **retribution**. In Spanish, **retribución** means "payment, reward".

retrieval [rɪ'triːvəl] n recuperación f; Comput **information r. system** sistema m de recuperación de datos

retrieve [rɪ'triːv] vt (a) (recover) recuperar; (of dog) cobrar; Comput recoger (b) (rescue) salvar

retriever [rɪ'triːvə(r)] n perro m cazador

retrograde ['retrəʊgreɪd] adj retrógrado(a)

retrospect ['retrəʊspekt] n **in r.** retrospectivamente

retrospective [retrəʊ'spektɪv] 1 adj retrospectivo(a)
2 n Art (exposición f) retrospectiva f

return [rɪ'tɜːn] 1 n (a) (of person) regreso m, vuelta f; **by r. of post** a vuelta de correo; **in r. for** a cambio de; **many happy returns!** ¡felicidades!; **r. match** partido m de vuelta; Br **r. (ticket)** billete m de ida y vuelta (b) (of sth borrowed, stolen) devolución f (c) (profit) beneficio m, ganancia f (d) (interest) interés m
2 vt (a) (give back) devolver; **r. to sender** (on envelope) devuélvase al remitente; **to r. a favour/sb's love** corresponder a un favor/al amor de algn (b) Br Pol elegir (c) Jur (verdict) pronunciar
3 vi (a) (come or go back) volver, regresar (b) (reappear) reaparecer

returnable [rɪ'tɜːnəbəl] adj (bottle) retornable

reunion [riː'juːnjən] n reunión f

reunite [riːju:'naɪt] vt **to be reunited with** (after separation) reunirse con

rev [rev] Fam Aut 1 n revolución f
2 vi **to r. (up)** acelerar el motor

revamp [riː'væmp] vt Fam modernizar, renovar

reveal [rɪ'viːl] vt (make known) revelar; (show) dejar ver

revealing [rɪ'viːlɪŋ] adj revelador(a)

reveille [rɪ'vælɪ] n diana f

revel ['revəl] vi disfrutar (in con); **to r. in doing sth** gozar muchísimo haciendo algo

revelation [revə'leɪʃən] n revelación f

revelry ['revəlrɪ] n jarana f, juerga f

revenge [rɪ'vendʒ] n venganza f; **to take r. on sb for sth** vengarse de algo en algn

revenue ['revɪnjuː] n renta f

reverberate [rɪ'vɜːbəreɪt] vi (a) (sound) reverberar (b) (ideas, news) resonar

reverberation [rɪvɜːbə'reɪʃən] n resonancia f

revere [rɪ'vɪə(r)] vt reverenciar

reverence ['revərəns] n reverencia f

reverend ['revərənd] Rel 1 adj reverendo(a); **R. Mother** reverenda madre
2 n (Protestant) pastor m; (Catholic) padre m

reverie ['revərɪ] n ensueño m

reversal [rɪ'vɜːsəl] n (a) (of order) inversión f (b) (of attitude, policy) cambio m total (c) Jur revocación f

reverse [rɪ'vɜːs] 1 adj inverso(a); Br **r.-charge call** llamada f or Am llamado m a cobro revertido
2 n (a) **quite the r.** todo lo contrario (b) (other side) (of cloth) revés m; (of coin) cruz f; (of page) dorso m (c) Aut **r. gear** marcha f atrás
3 vt (a) (order) invertir (b) (turn round) volver del revés (c) (change) cambiar totalmente (d) Jur revocar (e) Br Tel **to r. the charges** poner una conferencia a cobro revertido
4 vi Aut dar marcha atrás

revert [rɪ'vɜːt] vi volver (to a)

review [rɪ'vjuː] 1 n (a) (examination) examen m (b) Mil revista f (c) Press crítica f, reseña f (d) (magazine) revista f
2 vt (a) (examine) examinar (b) Mil **to r. the troops** pasar revista a las tropas (c) (book etc) hacer una crítica de

reviewer [rɪ'vjuːə(r)] n crítico(a) m,f

revile [rɪ'vaɪl] vt Fml injuriar

revise [rɪ'vaɪz] vt (a) (look over) revisar; (at

school) repasar (**b**) (change) modificar (**c**) (proofs) corregir

revision [rɪˈvɪʒən] n (**a**) revisión f; (at school) repaso m (**b**) (change) modificación f (**c**) (of proofs) corrección f

revitalize [riːˈvaɪtəlaɪz] vt revivificar

revival [rɪˈvaɪvəl] n (**a**) (of interest) renacimiento m; (of economy, industry) reactivación f; (of a country) resurgimiento m (**b**) Th reestreno m (**c**) Med reanimación f

revive [rɪˈvaɪv] 1 vt (**a**) (interest) renovar; (a law) restablecer; (economy, industry) reactivar; (hopes) despertar (**b**) Th reestrenar (**c**) Med reanimar
 2 vi (**a**) (interest, hopes) renacer (**b**) Med volver en sí

revoke [rɪˈvəʊk] vt revocar; (permission) suspender

revolt [rɪˈvəʊlt] 1 n rebelión f, sublevación f
 2 vi rebelarse, sublevarse
 3 vt repugnar, dar asco a

revolting [rɪˈvəʊltɪŋ] adj repugnante

revolution [revəˈluːʃən] n revolución f

revolutionary [revəˈluːʃənərɪ] adj & n revolucionario(a) (m,f)

revolve [rɪˈvɒlv] 1 vi girar; Fig to r. around girar en torno a
 2 vt hacer girar

⚠ Note that the Spanish verb **revolver** is a false friend and is never a translation for the English verb **to revolve**. In Spanish, **revolver** means "to stir, to mix" and "to mess up".

revolver [rɪˈvɒlvə(r)] n revólver m

revolving [rɪˈvɒlvɪŋ] adj giratorio(a)

revue [rɪˈvjuː] n revista f

revulsion [rɪˈvʌlʃən] n repulsión f

reward [rɪˈwɔːd] 1 n recompensa f
 2 vt recompensar

rewarding [rɪˈwɔːdɪŋ] adj provechoso(a)

rewire [riːˈwaɪə(r)] vt Elec to r. a house poner nueva instalación eléctrica a una casa

reword [riːˈwɜːd] vt expresar con otras palabras

rewrite [riːˈraɪt] vt (pt rewrote [riːˈrəʊt]; pp rewritten [riːˈrɪtən]) escribir de nuevo

rhapsody [ˈræpsədɪ] n Mus rapsodia f

rhetoric [ˈretərɪk] n retórica f

rhetorical [rɪˈtɒrɪkəl] adj retórico(a)

rheumatism [ˈruːmətɪzəm] n reuma m

rheumatoid [ˈruːmətɔɪd] adj r. arthritis reuma m articular

Rhine [raɪn] n the R. el Rin

rhinoceros [raɪˈnɒsərəs] n rinoceronte m

rhododendron [rəʊdəˈdendrən] n rododendro m

Rhone [rəʊn] n the R. el Ródano

rhubarb [ˈruːbɑːb] n ruibarbo m

rhyme [raɪm] 1 n rima f; (poem) poema m
 2 vi rimar

rhythm [ˈrɪðəm] n ritmo m

rib¹ [rɪb] n (**a**) Anat costilla f; r. cage caja torácica (**b**) (in knitting) canalé m (**c**) (of umbrella) varilla f (**d**) Bot (of leaf) nervio m

rib² [rɪb] vt Fam burlarse de

ribald [ˈrɪbəld] adj (humour) verde

ribbon [ˈrɪbən] n cinta f; (in hair etc) lazo m; torn to ribbons hecho(a) jirones

rice [raɪs] n arroz m; **brown r.** arroz integral; **r. paper** papel de arroz; **r. pudding** arroz con leche

rich [rɪtʃ] 1 adj (person, food) rico(a); (soil) fértil; (voice) sonoro(a); (colour) vivo(a)
 2 npl the r. los ricos

riches [ˈrɪtʃɪz] npl riquezas fpl

richly [ˈrɪtʃlɪ] adv ricamente; r. deserved bien merecido(a)

richness [ˈrɪtʃnɪs] n riqueza f; (of soil) fertilidad f; (of voice) sonoridad f; (of colour) viveza f

rickets [ˈrɪkɪts] n sing Med raquitismo m

rickety [ˈrɪkətɪ] adj (chair etc) cojo(a); (car) desvencijado(a)

ricochet [ˈrɪkəʃeɪ, ˈrɪkəʃet] 1 n rebote m
 2 vi rebotar

rid [rɪd] vt (pt & pp rid) librar; to get r. of sth deshacerse de algo; to r. oneself of librarse de

riddance [ˈrɪdəns] n Fam good r.! ¡ya era hora!

ridden [ˈrɪdən] pp of ride

riddle¹ [ˈrɪdəl] n (**a**) (puzzle) acertijo m, adivinanza f (**b**) (mystery) enigma m

riddle² [ˈrɪdəl] vt (with bullets) acribillar

ride [raɪd] 1 n paseo m, vuelta f; a short bus r. un corto trayecto en autobús; Fam to take sb for a r. tomar el pelo a algn; horse r. paseo a caballo
 2 vt (pt rode; pp ridden) (bicycle, horse) montar en; can you r. a bike? ¿sabes montar en bici?
 3 vi (**a**) (on horse) montar a caballo (**b**) (travel) (in bus, train etc) viajar (**c**) Naut to r. at anchor estar anclado(a)
 ▸ ride out vt sep sobrevivir; to r. out the storm capear el temporal

rider [ˈraɪdə(r)] n (of horse) (man) jinete m; (woman) amazona f; (of bicycle) ciclista mf; (of motorbike) motociclista mf

ridge [rɪdʒ] n (crest of a hill) cresta f; (hillock) loma f; (of roof) caballete m; Met área m

ridicule [ˈrɪdɪkjuːl] 1 n burla f
 2 vt burlarse de

ridiculous [rɪˈdɪkjʊləs] adj ridículo(a)

riding [ˈraɪdɪŋ] n equitación f; r. breeches pantalones mpl de montar; r. school escuela hípica

rife [raɪf] adj abundante; rumour is r. that ... corre la voz de que ...; to be r. with abundar en

riffraff [ˈrɪfræf] n Fam chusma f, gentuza f

rifle¹ [ˈraɪfəl] n fusil m, rifle m; r. range campo m de tiro

rifle² [ˈraɪfəl] vt desvalijar

rift [rɪft] n (a) Geol falla f (b) Fig (in friendship) ruptura f; Pol (in party) escisión f; (quarrel) desavenencia f
rig [rɪg] 1 n (a) Naut aparejo m (b) (oil) r. (onshore) torre f de perforación; (offshore) plataforma petrolífera
  2 vt Pej amañar
▸ **rig out** vt sep Fam ataviar
▸ **rig up** vt sep improvisar
rigging ['rɪgɪŋ] n aparejo m, jarcia f
right [raɪt] 1 adj (a) (not left) derecho(a); the r. hand la mano derecha
  (b) (correct) correcto(a); (time) exacto(a); to be r. tener razón; all r. de acuerdo; r.? ¿vale?; that's r. eso es; the r. word la palabra justa
  (c) (true) cierto(a)
  (d) (suitable) adecuado(a); the r. time el momento oportuno
  (e) (proper) apropiado(a)
  (f) Fam (healthy) bien
  (g) Fam (complete) auténtico(a)
  (h) (in order) en orden
  (i) r. angle ángulo recto
  2 n (a) (right side) derecha f
  (b) (right hand) mano derecha
  (c) Pol the R. la derecha
  (d) (lawful claim) derecho m; in one's own r. por derecho propio; r. of way (across land) derecho de paso; (on roads) prioridad f; civil rights derechos civiles
  (e) r. and wrong el bien y el mal
  3 adv (a) (correctly) bien; it's just r. es justo lo que hace falta
  (b) r. away (immediately) en seguida
  (c) (to the right) a la derecha; r. and left a diestro y siniestro; to turn r. girar a la derecha
  (d) (directly) directamente; go r. on sigue recto; r. at the top en todo lo alto; r. in the middle justo en medio; r. to the end hasta el final
  4 vt (a) (correct) corregir
  (b) (put straight) enderezar
righteous ['raɪtʃəs] adj (upright) recto(a)
rightful ['raɪtfʊl] adj legítimo(a)
right-hand ['raɪthænd] adj derecho(a); r. drive conducción f por la derecha; r. side lado derecho; Fam r. man brazo derecho
right-handed [raɪt'hændɪd] adj (person) que usa la mano derecha; (tool) para la mano derecha
rightly ['raɪtlɪ] adv debidamente; and r. so y con razón
right-wing ['raɪtwɪŋ] adj de derechas, derechista
right-winger [raɪt'wɪŋə(r)] n derechista mf
rigid ['rɪdʒɪd] adj rígido(a), inflexible
rigidity [rɪ'dʒɪdɪtɪ] n rigidez f, inflexibilidad f
rigmarole ['rɪgmərəʊl] n Fam galimatías m inv
rigor ['rɪgər] n US = rigour

rigorous ['rɪgərəs] adj riguroso(a)
rigour ['rɪgə(r)] n rigor m, severidad f
rile [raɪl] vt Fam irritar, sacar de quicio
rim [rɪm] n (edge) borde m; (of wheel) llanta f; (of spectacles) montura f
rind [raɪnd] n (of fruit, cheese) corteza f
ring¹ [rɪŋ] 1 n (a) (sound of bell) toque m; (of doorbell, alarm clock) timbre m (b) Tel llamada f
  2 vt (pt rang; pp rung) (a) (bell) tocar; Fig it rings a bell me suena (b) Br Tel llamar por teléfono
  3 vi (a) (bell, phone etc) sonar (b) my ears are ringing tengo un pitido en los oídos (c) Tel llamar
▸ **ring back** vt sep Br Tel volver a llamar
▸ **ring off** vi Br Tel colgar
▸ **ring out** vi resonar
▸ **ring up** vt sep Br Tel llamar por teléfono a
ring² [rɪŋ] 1 n (a) (metal hoop) aro m; (curtain r.) anilla f; r. binder carpeta f de anillas (b) (for finger) anillo m, sortija f; r. finger dedo m anular (c) (circle) círculo m; Br r. road carretera f de circunvalación (d) rings (in gymnastics) anillas fpl (e) (group of people) corro m; (of spies) red f; (of thieves) banda f (f) (arena) pista f; (for boxing) cuadrilátero m; (for bullfights) ruedo m; circus r. pista de circo
  2 vt (a) (bird, animal) anillar (b) (surround) rodear
ringing ['rɪŋɪŋ] n (of bell) toque m, repique m; (in ears) pitido m
ringleader ['rɪŋliːdə(r)] n cabecilla mf
ringlet ['rɪŋlɪt] n tirabuzón m
rink [rɪŋk] n pista f; ice r. pista de hielo
rinse [rɪns] 1 n (a) (of clothes, hair) aclarado m, enjuague m; (of dishes) enjuagado m (b) (tint for hair) reflejo m
  2 vt (a) aclarar; (the dishes) enjuagar (b) to r. one's hair (tint) darse reflejos en el pelo
riot ['raɪət] 1 n (a) disturbio m, motín m; to run r. desmandarse; r. police policía f antidisturbios (b) Fig (of colour) profusión f
  2 vi amotinarse
rioter ['raɪətə(r)] n amotinado(a) m,f
riotous ['raɪətəs] adj (a) amotinado(a) (b) (noisy) bullicioso(a) (c) (unrestrained) desenfrenado(a)
rip [rɪp] 1 n (tear) rasgón m
  2 vt rasgar, rajar; to r. one's trousers rajarse los pantalones
  3 vi rasgarse, rajarse
▸ **rip off** vt sep Fam to r. sb off timar a algn
▸ **rip up** vt sep hacer pedacitos
ripcord ['rɪpkɔːd] n cuerda f de apertura
ripe [raɪp] adj (a) maduro(a) (b) (ready) listo(a); the time is r. es el momento oportuno
ripen ['raɪpən] vt & vi madurar
rip-off ['rɪpɒf] n Fam timo m
ripple ['rɪpəl] 1 n (a) (on water, fabric) onda f

(**b**) *(sound)* murmullo *m*

2 *vt (water)* ondular

3 *vi* (**a**) *(water)* ondularse (**b**) *(applause)* extenderse

rise [raɪz] **1** *n* (**a**) *(of slope, hill)* cuesta *f*

(**b**) *(of waters)* crecida *f*

(**c**) *(in status)* ascenso *m*

(**d**) *(in prices, temperature)* subida *f*; *(in wages)* aumento *m*

(**e**) *(in sound)* aumento *m*

(**f**) **to give r. to** ocasionar

2 *vi (pt* **rose**; *pp* **risen** ['rɪzən]) (**a**) *(land etc)* elevarse

(**b**) *(waters)* crecer; *(river)* nacer; *(tide)* subir; *(wind)* levantarse

(**c**) *(sun, moon)* salir

(**d**) *(voice)* alzarse

(**e**) *(in rank)* ascender

(**f**) *(prices, temperature)* subir; *(wages)* aumentar

(**g**) *(curtain)* subir

(**h**) *(from bed)* levantarse

(**i**) *(stand up)* levantarse; *Fig (city, building)* erguirse

(**j**) **to r. to a challenge** aceptar un reto; **to r. to the occasion** ponerse a la altura de las circunstancias

▸ **rise above** *vt insep* estar por encima de

▸ **rise up** *vi (rebel)* sublevarse

rising ['raɪzɪŋ] **1** *adj (sun)* naciente; *(tide)* creciente; *(prices)* en aumento; **r. damp** humedad *f*

2 *n* (**a**) *(of sun)* salida *f* (**b**) *(rebellion)* levantamiento *m*

risk [rɪsk] **1** *n* riesgo *m*; **at r.** en peligro; **at your own r.** por su cuenta y riesgo; **to take risks** arriesgarse

2 *vt* arriesgar; **I'll r. it** correré el riesgo

risky ['rɪskɪ] *adj* (**riskier, riskiest**) arriesgado(a)

risqué ['rɪskeɪ] *adj* atrevido(a); *(joke)* picante

rite [raɪt] *n* rito *m*; **the last rites** la extremaunción

ritual ['rɪtjʊəl] *adj & n* ritual (*m*)

rival ['raɪvəl] **1** *adj & n* rival (*mf*)

2 *vt* rivalizar con

rivalry ['raɪvəlrɪ] *n* rivalidad *f*

river ['rɪvə(r)] *n* río *m*; **down/up r.** río abajo/arriba

river-bank ['rɪvəbæŋk] *n* orilla *f*, ribera *f*

river-bed ['rɪvəbed] *n* lecho *m*

rivet ['rɪvɪt] **1** *n Tech* remache *m*, roblón *m*

2 *vt Tech* remachar; *Fig* cautivar

riveting ['rɪvɪtɪŋ] *adj Fig* fascinante

roach [rəʊtʃ] *n US Fam (cockroach)* cucaracha *f*

road [rəʊd] *n* (**a**) carretera *f*; *Br* **A/B r.** carretera nacional/secundaria; **main r.** carretera principal; **r. accident** accidente *m* de tráfico; **r. safety** seguridad *f* vial; **r. sign** señal *f* de tráfico; **r.** *Br* **works** *or US* **work** obras *fpl*

(**b**) *(street)* calle *f* (**c**) *(way)* camino *m*

roadblock ['rəʊdblɒk] *n* control *m* policial

roadhog ['rəʊdhɒg] *n Fam* loco(a) *m,f* del volante, dominguero(a) *m,f*

roadside ['rəʊdsaɪd] *n* borde *m* de la carretera; **r. restaurant/café** restaurante *m*/cafetería *f* de carretera

roadway ['rəʊdweɪ] *n* calzada *f*

roadworthy ['rəʊdwɜːðɪ] *adj (vehicle)* en buen estado

roam [rəʊm] **1** *vt* vagar por, rondar

2 *vi* vagar

roar [rɔː(r)] **1** *n (of lion)* rugido *m*; *(of bull, sea, wind)* bramido *m*; *(of crowd)* clamor *m*

2 *vi (lion, crowd)* rugir; *(bull, sea, wind)* bramar; *(crowd)* clamar; *Fig* **to r. with laughter** reírse a carcajadas

roaring ['rɔːrɪŋ] *adj Fam Fig* **a r. success** un éxito clamoroso; **to do a r. trade** hacer un negocio redondo

roast [rəʊst] **1** *adj (meat)* asado(a); **r. beef** rosbif *m*

2 *n Culin* asado *m*

3 *vt (meat)* asar; *(coffee, nuts)* tostar

4 *vi* asarse; *Fam Fig* **I'm roasting** me aso de calor

rob [rɒb] *vt* robar; *(bank)* atracar

robber ['rɒbə(r)] *n* ladrón(ona) *m,f*; **bank r.** atracador(a) *m,f*

robbery ['rɒbərɪ] *n* robo *m*

robe [rəʊb] *n (ceremonial)* toga *f*; *(dressing gown)* bata *f*

robin ['rɒbɪn] *n* petirrojo *m*

robot ['rəʊbɒt] *n* robot *m*

robust [rəʊ'bʌst] *adj (sturdy)* robusto(a)

rock [rɒk] **1** *n* (**a**) roca *f*; *Fig* **to be on the rocks** *(of marriage)* estar a punto de fracasar; *Fig* **whisky on the rocks** whisky *m* con hielo (**b**) *US (stone)* piedra *f* (**c**) *Br (sweet)* **stick of r.** barra *f* de caramelo (**d**) *Mus* música *f* rock; **r. and roll** rock and roll *m*

2 *vt* (**a**) *(chair)* mecer; *(baby)* acunar (**b**) *(shake)* hacer temblar; *Fig (shock)* conmover

3 *vi* (**a**) *(move to and fro)* mecerse (**b**) *(shake)* vibrar

rock-bottom ['rɒk'bɒtəm] *adj* bajísimo(a); **r. prices** precios regalados

rockery ['rɒkərɪ] *n* jardín *m* de rocas

rocket ['rɒkɪt] **1** *n* cohete *m*; **r. launcher** lanzacohetes *m inv*

2 *vi Fam (prices)* dispararse

rocking-chair ['rɒkɪntʃeə(r)] *n* mecedora *f*

rocking-horse ['rɒkɪŋhɔːs] *n* caballito *m* de balancín

rocky ['rɒkɪ] *adj* (**rockier, rockiest**) rocoso(a); *Fam Fig (unsteady)* inseguro(a); **the R. Mountains** las Montañas Rocosas

rod [rɒd] *n (of metal)* barra *f*; *(stick)* vara *f*; **fishing r.** caña *f* de pescar

rode [rəʊd] *pt of* **ride**

rodent ['rəʊdənt] *n* roedor *m*

roe¹ [rəʊ] *n Zool* **r. (deer)** corzo(a) *m,f*

roe² [rəʊ] n (fish eggs) hueva f
rogue [rəʊg] n granuja m
role, rôle [rəʊl] n papel m; **to play a r.** desempeñar un papel
roll [rəʊl] **1** n (a) rollo m; **r. of banknotes** fajo m de billetes; Fam Fig **rolls of fat** micheline mpl (b) (bread) **r.** bollo m (c) (list of names) lista f, nómina f; **to call the r.** pasar lista (d) (movement of ship) balanceo m (e) (of drum) redoble m; (of thunder) fragor m
2 vt (a) (ball) hacer rodar (b) (cigarette) liar (c) (move) mover (d) (push) empujar (e) (lawn, road) allanar
3 vi (a) (ball) rodar; Fam **to be rolling in money** estar forrado(a) (b) (animal) revolcarse (c) (ship) balancearse (d) (drum) redoblar; (thunder) retumbar
▸ **roll about, roll around** vi rodar (de acá para allá)
▸ **roll by** vi (years) pasar
▸ **roll in** vi Fam (a) (arrive) llegar (b) (money) llegar a raudales
▸ **roll over** vi dar una vuelta
▸ **roll up 1** vt sep enrollar; (blinds) subir; **to r. up one's sleeves** (ar)remangarse
2 vi Fam (arrive) llegar
roll-call ['rəʊlkɔːl] n **to have a r.** pasar lista
roller ['rəʊlə(r)] n (a) Tech rodillo m; **r. blades** patines mpl en línea; **r. coaster** montaña rusa; **r. skates** patines mpl (de ruedas) (b) (large wave) ola f grande (c) (for hair) rulo m
rolling ['rəʊlɪŋ] **1** adj (a) Rail **r. stock** material m rodante (b) (countryside) ondulado(a)
2 n rodamiento m; (of ground) apisonamiento m; **r. pin** rodillo m (de cocina)
ROM [rɒm] n Comput (abbr **read-only memory**) ROM f
Roman ['rəʊmən] adj & n romano(a) (m,f); **R. Catholic** católico(a) m,f (romano(a)); **R. law** derecho romano; **R. numerals** números romanos
Romance [rəʊ'mæns] adj Ling románico(a), romance; **R. languages** lenguas románicas
romance [rəʊ'mæns] **1** n (a) (tale) novela romántica (b) (love affair) aventura amorosa (c) (romantic quality) lo romántico
2 vi fantasear
Romania [rə'meɪnɪə] n Rumanía
Romanian [rə'meɪnɪən] **1** adj rumano(a)
2 n (person) rumano(a) m,f; (language) rumano m
romantic [rəʊ'mæntɪk] adj & n romántico(a) (m,f)
Rome [rəʊm] n Roma
romp [rɒmp] **1** n jugueteo m
2 vi juguetear
rompers ['rɒmpəz] npl pelele m
roof [ruːf] n (pl **roofs** [ruːfs, ruːvz]) (a) tejado m; Fam Fig **to go through the r.** (of prices) estar por las nubes; (with anger) subirse por las paredes (b) Aut techo m; **r. rack**

baca f (c) (of mouth) cielo m
2 vt techar
roofing ['ruːfɪŋ] n materiales mpl usados para techar
rook [rʊk] n (a) Orn grajo m (b) (in chess) torre f
rookie ['rʊkɪ] n US Fam (novice) novato(a) m,f
room [ruːm] n (a) habitación f, cuarto m; **single r.** habitación individual; **r. service** servicio m de habitación (b) (space) espacio m; **make r. for me** hazme sitio
rooming-house ['ruːmɪŋhaʊs] n US pensión f
roommate ['ruːmmeɪt] n compañero(a) m,f de habitación
roomy ['ruːmɪ] adj (**roomier, roomiest**) amplio(a)
roost [ruːst] **1** n palo m, percha f; (hen) **r.** gallinero m; Fig **to rule the r.** llevar la batuta
2 vi posarse
rooster ['ruːstə(r)] n esp US gallo m
root¹ [ruːt] **1** n raíz f; **to take r.** echar raíces
2 vt arraigar
3 vi arraigar
▸ **root out, root up** vt sep arrancar de raíz
root² [ruːt] vi (search) buscar; **to r. about** or **around for sth** hurgar en busca de algo
root³ [ruːt] vi Fam **to r. for a team** animar a un equipo
rope [rəʊp] **1** n (a) (thin) cuerda f; (thick) soga f; Naut cabo m (b) Fig **to have sb on the ropes** tener a algn contra las cuerdas; Fam Fig **to know the ropes** estar al tanto
2 vt (package) atar; (climbers) encordar

> Note that the Spanish word **ropa** is a false friend and is never a translation for the English word **rope**. In Spanish, **ropa** means "clothes".

▸ **rope in** vt sep Fam enganchar
▸ **rope off** vt sep acordonar
rop(e)y ['rəʊpɪ] adj (**ropier, ropiest**) Br Fam chungo(a)
rosary ['rəʊzərɪ] n rosario m
rose¹ [rəʊz] pt of **rise**
rose² [rəʊz] n (a) Bot rosa f; **r. bed** rosaleda f; **r. bush** rosal m (b) (colour) rosa m (c) (of watering can) alcachofa f
rosé ['rəʊzeɪ] n (vino m) rosado m
rosebud ['rəʊzbʌd] n capullo m de rosa
rosemary ['rəʊzmərɪ] n romero m
rosette [rəʊ'zet] n (of ribbons) escarapela f
roster ['rɒstə(r)] n lista f
rostrum ['rɒstrəm] n estrado m

> Note that the Spanish word **rostro** is a false friend and is never a translation for the English word **rostrum**. In Spanish, **rostro** means "face".

rosy ['rəʊzɪ] adj (**rosier, rosiest**) (a) (complexion) sonrosado(a) (b) Fig (future) prometedor(a)
rot [rɒt] **1** n (a) (decay) putrefacción f; **dry r.**

putrefacción de la madera (**b**) *Fam (nonsense)* tonterías *fpl*
  2 *vt* pudrir
  ▸ **rot away** *vi* pudrirse
rota ['rəʊtə] *n esp Br* lista *f*
rotary ['rəʊtərɪ] **1** *n US (for traffic)* rotonda *f*
  2 *adj* rotatorio(a), giratorio(a)
rotate [rəʊ'teɪt] **1** *vt* (**a**) *(revolve)* hacer girar (**b**) *(jobs, crops)* alternar
  2 *vi (revolve)* girar
rotating [rəʊ'teɪtɪŋ] *adj* rotativo(a)
rotation [rəʊ'teɪʃən] *n* rotación *f*
rote [rəʊt] *n* **by r.** de memoria
rotten ['rɒtən] *adj* (**a**) *(decayed)* podrido(a); *(tooth)* picado(a) (**b**) *Fam (very bad)* malísimo(a); *Fam* **I feel r.** me encuentro fatal
rouble ['ruːbəl] *n* rublo *m*
rouge [ruːʒ] **1** *n* colorete *m*
  2 *vt* poner colorete a
rough [rʌf] **1** *adj* (**a**) *(surface, skin)* áspero(a); *(terrain)* accidentado(a); *(road)* desigual; *(sea)* agitado(a); *(weather)* tempestuoso(a)
  (**b**) *(rude)* grosero(a); *(violent)* violento(a)
  (**c**) *(voice)* bronco(a)
  (**d**) *(wine)* áspero(a)
  (**e**) *(bad)* malo(a); *Fam* **to feel r.** encontrarse fatal
  (**f**) *(approximate)* aproximado(a)
  (**g**) *(plan etc)* preliminar; **r. draft** borrador *m*; **r. sketch** esbozo *m*
  (**h**) *(harsh)* severo(a)
  2 *adv* duramente; *Fam Fig* **to sleep r.** dormir a la intemperie
  3 *n* (**a**) *Fam (person)* matón *m*
  (**b**) **the r.** *(in golf)* la hierba alta
  4 *vt Fam* **to r. it** vivir sin comodidades
roughage ['rʌfɪdʒ] *n (substance)* fibra *f*
rough-and-ready ['rʌfən'redɪ] *adj* improvisado(a)
roughen ['rʌfən] *vt* poner áspero(a)
roughly ['rʌflɪ] *adv* (**a**) *(crudely)* toscamente (**b**) *(clumsily)* torpemente (**c**) *(not gently)* bruscamente (**d**) *(approximately)* aproximadamente
roulette [ruː'let] *n* ruleta *f*
Roumania [ruː'meɪnɪə] *n* = **Romania**
round [raʊnd] **1** *adj* redondo(a); **in r. figures** en números redondos; **r. table** mesa redonda; **r. trip** viaje *m* de ida y vuelta
  2 *n* (**a**) *(circle)* círculo *m*
  (**b**) *(series)* serie *f*; **r. of talks** ronda *f* de negociaciones
  (**c**) *(of ammunition)* cartucho *m*; *(salvo)* salva *f*
  (**d**) **a r. of toast** una tostada
  (**e**) *(of drinks)* ronda *f*
  (**f**) **the daily r.** *(routine)* la rutina diaria
  (**g**) *(in golf)* partido *m*; *Cards* partida *f*
  (**h**) *(in boxing)* round *m*
  (**i**) *(in a competition)* eliminatoria *f*
  (**j**) **rounds** *(doctor's)* visita *f*; *(of salesman)* recorrido *m*

  3 *adv* **all year r.** durante todo el año; **to invite sb r.** invitar a algn a casa
  4 *prep* alrededor de; **r. here** por aquí; **r. the clock** día y noche; **r. the corner** a la vuelta de la esquina
  5 *vt (turn)* dar la vuelta a
  ▸ **round off** *vt sep* acabar, concluir
  ▸ **round on** *vt insep (attack)* atacar
  ▸ **round up** *vt sep (cattle)* acorralar, rodear; *(people)* reunir
roundabout ['raʊndəbaʊt] **1** *n* (**a**) *(merry-go-round)* tiovivo *m* (**b**) *Br Aut* rotonda *f*
  2 *adj* indirecto(a)
rounders ['raʊndəz] *n Br* = juego parecido al béisbol
roundly ['raʊndlɪ] *adv* completamente, totalmente
round-shouldered ['raʊnd'ʃəʊldəd] *adj* cargado(a) de espaldas
round-trip ['raʊnd'trɪp] *US* **1** *n* billete *m* de ida y vuelta
  2 *adj (ticket)* de ida y vuelta
round-up ['raʊndʌp] *n* (**a**) *(of cattle)* rodeo *m*; *(of suspects)* redada *f* (**b**) *(summary)* resumen *m*
rouse [raʊz] *vt* despertar; *(stir up)* suscitar
rousing ['raʊzɪŋ] *adj (cheer)* entusiasta; *(applause)* caluroso(a); *(speech, song)* conmovedor(a)
rout [raʊt] **1** *n* aniquilación *f*
  2 *vt* aniquilar
route [ruːt] **1** *n* (**a**) ruta *f*; *(of bus)* línea *f*; *Naut* derrota *f*; *Fig* camino *m*; **r. map** mapa *m* de carreteras (**b**) *US* **R.** ≃ carretera *f* nacional
  2 *vt* encaminar
routine [ruː'tiːn] **1** *n* (**a**) rutina *f* (**b**) *Th* número *m*
  2 *adj* rutinario(a)
roving ['rəʊvɪŋ] *adj* errante; **r. reporter** enviado(a) *m,f* especial
row¹ [rəʊ] *n* fila *f*, hilera *f*; *Fig* **three times in a r.** tres veces seguidas
row² [rəʊ] *vt & vi (in a boat)* remar
row³ [raʊ] **1** *n* (**a**) *(quarrel)* pelea *f*, bronca *f* (**b**) *(noise)* jaleo *m*; *(protest)* escándalo *m*
  2 *vi* pelearse
rowboat ['rəʊbəʊt] *n US* bote *m* de remos
rowdy ['raʊdɪ] **1** *adj* (**rowdier, rowdiest**) (**a**) *(noisy)* ruidoso(a); *(disorderly)* alborotador(a) (**b**) *(quarrelsome)* camorrista
  2 *n* camorrista *mf*
rowing ['rəʊɪŋ] *n* remo *m*; **r. boat** bote *m* de remos
royal ['rɔɪəl] **1** *adj* real; **r. blue** azul marino; **the R. Family** la Familia Real
  2 *npl* **the Royals** los miembros de la Familia Real
royally ['rɔɪəlɪ] *adv Fig* magníficamente
royalty ['rɔɪəltɪ] *n* (**a**) *(royal persons)* miembro(s) *m(pl)* de la Familia Real (**b**) **royalties** derechos *mpl* de autor
RPI [ɑːpiː'aɪ] *n (abbr Retail Price Index)* IPC *m*

rpm [ɑːpiːˈem] *n* (*abbr* **revolutions per minute**) r.p.m.

RSPCA [ɑːrespiːsiːˈeɪ] *n Br* (*abbr* **Royal Society for the Prevention of Cruelty to Animals**) ≃ Sociedad *f* Protectora de Animales

RSVP [ɑːresviːˈpiː] (*abbr* **répondez s'il vous plaît**) se ruega contestación, S.R.C.

Rt Hon *Br Pol* (*abbr* **(the) Right Honourable**) su Señoría

rub [rʌb] **1** *n* to give sth a r. frotar algo
2 *vt* frotar; (*hard*) restregar; (*massage*) friccionar
3 *vi* rozar (**against** contra)
▸ **rub down** *vt sep* rotar; (*horse*) almohazar; (*surface*) raspar
▸ **rub in** *vt sep* (**a**) (*cream etc*) frotar con (**b**) *Fam* **don't r. it in** no me lo refriegues
▸ **rub off** *vt sep* (*erase*) borrar
2 *vi Fig* **to r. off on sb** influir en algn
▸ **rub out** *vt sep* borrar
▸ **rub up** *vt sep Fam Fig* **to r. sb up the wrong way** fastidiar a algn

rubber¹ [ˈrʌbə(r)] *n* (**a**) (*substance*) caucho *m*, goma *f*; **r. band** goma; **r. plant** gomero *m*; **r. stamp** tampón *m* (**b**) *Br* (*eraser*) goma *f* (de borrar) (**c**) *Fam* (*condom*) goma *f*

rubber² [ˈrʌbə(r)] *n* (*in bridge*) rubber *m*

rubbery [ˈrʌbərɪ] *adj* (*elastic*) elástico(a)

rubbish [ˈrʌbɪʃ] *n* (**a**) *Br* (*refuse*) basura *f*; **r. bin** cubo *m* de la basura; **r. dump** *or* **tip** vertedero *m* (**b**) *Fam* (*worthless thing*) birria *f* (**c**) *Fam* (*nonsense*) tonterías *fpl*

rubble [ˈrʌbəl] *n* escombros *mpl*

rubric [ˈruːbrɪk] *n* rúbrica *f*

ruby [ˈruːbɪ] *n* rubí *m*

rucksack [ˈrʌksæk] *n* mochila *f*

ructions [ˈrʌkʃənz] *npl Fam* jaleo *m*

rudder [ˈrʌdə(r)] *n* timón *m*

ruddy [ˈrʌdɪ] *adj* (**ruddier, ruddiest**) (**a**) (*complexion*) rojizo(a), colorado(a) (**b**) *Br Fam* (*damned*) maldito(a)

rude [ruːd] *adj* (**a**) (*impolite*) maleducado(a); (*foul-mouthed*) grosero(a); **don't be r. to your mother** no le faltes al respeto a tu madre (**b**) (*abrupt*) **a r. awakening** un despertar repentino

rudimentary [ruːdɪˈmentərɪ] *adj* rudimentario(a)

rudiments [ˈruːdɪmənts] *npl* rudimentos *mpl*

rue [ruː] *vt* arrepentirse de

rueful [ˈruːfʊl] *adj* (*regretful*) arrepentido(a); (*sad*) triste

ruff [rʌf] *n* (*collar*) gorguera *f*

ruffian [ˈrʌfɪən] *n* canalla *m*

ruffle [ˈrʌfəl] *vt* (**a**) (*water*) agitar (**b**) (*feathers*) encrespar; (*hair*) despeinar (**c**) *Fig* (*annoy*) hacer perder la calma a

ruffled [ˈrʌfəld] *adj* (**a**) (*hair*) alborotado(a); (*clothes*) en desorden (**b**) (*perturbed*) perturbado(a)

rug [rʌg] *n* alfombra *f*, alfombrilla *f*

rugby [ˈrʌgbɪ] *n* rugby *m*; **r. league** rugby a trece; **r. union** rugby a quince

rugged [ˈrʌgɪd] *adj* (**a**) (*terrain*) accidentado(a) (**b**) (*features*) marcado(a) (**c**) (*character*) vigoroso(a)

rugger [ˈrʌgə(r)] *n Fam* rugby *m*

ruin [ˈruːɪn] **1** *n* (**a**) ruina *f* (**b**) **ruins** ruinas *fpl*, restos *mpl*; **in ruins** en ruinas
2 *vt* arruinar; (*spoil*) estropear

rule [ruːl] **1** *n* (**a**) regla *f*, norma *f*; **to work to r.** hacer una huelga de celo; **as a r.** por regla general (**b**) (*government*) dominio *m*; (*of monarch*) reinado *m*; **r. of law** imperio *m* de la ley
2 *vt & vi* (*govern*) gobernar; (*of monarch*) reinar (**b**) (*decide*) decidir; (*decree*) decretar (**c**) (*draw*) tirar
▸ **rule out** *vt sep* descartar

ruled [ruːld] *adj* rayado(a)

ruler [ˈruːlə(r)] *n* (**a**) dirigente *mf*; (*monarch*) soberano(a) *m,f* (**b**) (*for measuring*) regla *f*

ruling [ˈruːlɪŋ] **1** *adj* (*in charge*) dirigente; *Fig* (*predominant*) predominante; **the r. party** el partido en el poder
2 *n Jur* fallo *m*

rum [rʌm] *n* ron *m*

Rumania [ruːˈmeɪnɪə] *n* = **Romania**

Rumanian [ruːˈmeɪnɪən] *adj & n* = **Romanian**

rumble [ˈrʌmbəl] **1** *n* (**a**) ruido sordo; (*of thunder*) estruendo *m* (**b**) (*of stomach*) ruido *m*
2 *vi* (**a**) hacer un ruido sordo; (*thunder*) retumbar (**b**) (*stomach etc*) hacer ruidos

ruminate [ˈruːmɪneɪt] *vi* (*chew, ponder*) rumiar

rummage [ˈrʌmɪdʒ] *vi* revolver (**through** en); *US* **r. sale** (*in store*) = venta de productos discontinuados o sin salida en un almacén; (*for charity*) rastrillo benéfico

rumour, *US* **rumor** [ˈruːmə(r)] **1** *n* rumor *m*; **r. has it that ...** se dice que ...
2 *vt* **it is rumoured that** se rumorea que

rump [rʌmp] *n* (*of animal*) ancas *fpl*; *Fam Hum* (*of person*) trasero *m*; **r. steak** filete *m* de lomo

rumpus [ˈrʌmpəs] *n Fam* jaleo *m*

run [rʌn] **1** *n* (**a**) carrera *f*; **on the r.** fugado(a); **to go for a r.** hacer footing; *Fig* **in the long r.** a largo plazo
(**b**) (*trip*) paseo *m*, vuelta *f*
(**c**) (*sequence*) serie *f*
(**d**) **ski r.** pista *f* de esquí
(**e**) (*demand*) gran demanda *f*; **a r. on** una gran demanda de
(**f**) **to give sb the r. of a house** poner una casa a disposición de algn
(**g**) (*print run*) tirada *f*
(**h**) (*in stocking*) carrera *f*
2 *vt* (*pt* **ran**; *pp* **run**) (**a**) correr; **to r. a race** correr en una carrera; **to r. errands** hacer recados
(**b**) (*drive*) llevar
(**c**) (*house, business*) llevar; (*company*) dirigir; (*organize*) organizar

(**d**) *(fingers)* pasar

(**e**) **it's a cheap car to r.** *(operate)* es un coche económico; *Comput* **to r. a program** pasar un programa

(**f**) *Press* publicar

3 *vi* (**a**) correr

(**b**) *(colour)* desteñirse

(**c**) *(water, river)* correr; **to leave the tap running** dejar el grifo abierto; *Fam* **your nose is running** se te caen los mocos

(**d**) *(operate) (machine)* funcionar (**on** con); **trains r. every two hours** hay trenes cada dos horas

(**e**) *Naut* **to r. aground** encallar

(**f**) *Pol* **to r. for president** presentarse como candidato a la presidencia

(**g**) **so the story runs** según lo que se dice

(**h**) *(range)* oscilar (**between** entre)

(**i**) **we're running low on milk** nos queda poca leche

(**j**) **shyness runs in the family** la timidez le viene de familia

(**k**) *Cin Th* estar en cartel

(**l**) *(last)* durar

(**m**) *(stocking)* tener una carrera

▸ **run about** *vi* corretear

▸ **run across** *vt insep (meet)* tropezar con

▸ **run away** *vi* fugarse; *(horse)* desbocarse

▸ **run down 1** *vt insep (stairs)* bajar corriendo

2 *vt sep* (**a**) *(in car)* atropellar (**b**) *(criticize)* criticar

3 *vi (battery)* agotarse; *(clock)* pararse

▸ **run in** *vt sep Aut* rodar

▸ **run into** *vt insep* (**a**) *(room)* entrar corriendo en (**b**) *(people, problems)* tropezar con (**c**) *(crash into)* chocar contra

▸ **run off 1** *vt sep (print)* tirar

2 *vi* escaparse

▸ **run on 1** *vt sep Typ* enlazar

2 *vi (meeting)* continuar

▸ **run out** *vi* (**a**) *(exit)* salir corriendo (**b**) *(come to an end)* agotarse; *(of contract)* vencer; **to r. out of** quedarse sin

▸ **run over 1** *vt sep (in car)* atropellar

2 *vt insep (rehearse)* ensayar

3 *vi (overflow)* rebosar

▸ **run through** *vt insep* (**a**) *(of river)* pasar por (**b**) *(read quickly)* echar un vistazo a (**c**) *(rehearse)* ensayar

▸ **run up** *vt sep* (**a**) *(flag)* izar (**b**) *(debts)* acumular

▸ **run up against** *vt insep* tropezar con

runaway ['rʌnəweɪ] **1** *n* fugitivo(a) *m,f*

2 *adj (person)* huido(a); *(horse)* desbocado(a); *(vehicle)* incontrolado(a); *(inflation)* galopante; *(success)* clamoroso(a)

rundown ['rʌndaʊn] *n Fam* **to give sb a r.** poner a algn al corriente

run-down [rʌn'daʊn] *adj* (**a**) *(exhausted)* agotado(a) (**b**) *(dilapidated)* ruinoso(a)

rung¹ [rʌŋ] *pp of* ring

rung² [rʌŋ] *n (of ladder)* escalón *m*, peldaño *m*

runner ['rʌnə(r)] *n* (**a**) *(person)* corredor(a) *m,f* (**b**) *(horse)* caballo *m* de carreras (**c**) *(of skate)* cuchilla *f* (**d**) *(on table)* tapete *m* (**e**) **r. bean** judía escarlata

runner-up [rʌnər'ʌp] *n* subcampeón(ona) *m,f*

running ['rʌnɪŋ] **1** *n* (**a**) **he likes r.** le gusta correr; *Fig* **to be in the r. for sth** tener posibilidades de conseguir algo (**b**) *(of company)* dirección *f* (**c**) *(of machine)* funcionamiento *m*

2 *adj* (**a**) **r. commentary** comentario *m* en directo; **r. costs** gastos *mpl* de mantenimiento; *Pol* **r. mate** candidato *m* a la vicepresidencia; **r. water** agua *f* corriente (**b**) **three weeks r.** tres semanas seguidas

runny ['rʌnɪ] *adj* (**runnier, runniest**) blando(a); *(egg)* crudo(a); *(butter)* derretido(a); *(nose)* que moquea

run-of-the-mill ['rʌnəvðə'mɪl] *adj* corriente y moliente

runt [rʌnt] *n Fam* enano(a) *m,f*

run-up ['rʌnʌp] *n (to elections)* preliminares *mpl*

runway ['rʌnweɪ] *n Av* pista *f* (de aterrizaje y despegue)

rupee [ruː'piː] *n* rupia *f*

rupture ['rʌptʃə(r)] **1** *n* (**a**) *Med* hernia *f* (**b**) *Fig* ruptura *f*

2 *vt* (**a**) **to r. oneself** herniarse (**b**) *(break)* romper

rural ['rʊərəl] *adj* rural

ruse [ruːz] *n* ardid *m*, astucia *f*

rush¹ [rʌʃ] *n Bot* junco *m*

rush² [rʌʃ] **1** *n* (**a**) *(hurry)* prisa *f*; *(hustle and bustle)* ajetreo *m*; **there's no r.** no corre prisa; **r. hour** hora punta (**b**) *(demand)* demanda *f* (**c**) *(of wind)* ráfaga *f* (**d**) *(of water)* torrente *m* (**e**) *Mil* ataque *m*

2 *vt* (**a**) *(task)* hacer de prisa; *(person)* meter prisa a; **to r. sb to hospital** llevar a algn urgentemente al hospital (**b**) *(attack)* abalanzarse sobre; *Mil* tomar por asalto

3 *vi (go quickly)* precipitarse

▸ **rush about** *vi* correr de un lado a otro

▸ **rush into** *vt insep Fig* **to r. into sth** hacer algo sin pensarlo bien

▸ **rush off** *vi* irse corriendo

rusk [rʌsk] *n* = galleta dura para niños

Russia ['rʌʃə] *n* Rusia

Russian ['rʌʃən] **1** *adj* ruso(a)

2 *n* (**a**) *(person)* ruso(a) *m,f* (**b**) *(language)* ruso *m*

rust [rʌst] **1** *n* (**a**) *(substance)* herrumbre *f* (**b**) *(colour)* pardo rojizo

2 *vt* oxidar

3 *vi* oxidarse

rustic ['rʌstɪk] *adj* rústico(a)

rustle ['rʌsəl] **1** *n* crujido *m*

2 *vt (papers etc)* hacer crujir

3 *vi (steal cattle)* robar ganado

rustproof ['rʌstpruːf] *adj* inoxidable

rusty ['rʌstɪ] *adj* (**rustier, rustiest**) oxidado(a); *Fam Fig* **my French is a bit r.** tengo el francés un poco oxidado

rut [rʌt] *n* (**a**) *(furrow)* surco *m*; *(groove)* ranura *f* (**b**) *Fig* **to be in a r.** ser esclavo de la rutina (**c**) *Zool* celo *m*

ruthless ['ru:θlɪs] *adj* despiadado(a)

rye [raɪ] *n* centeno *m*; **r. bread** pan *m* de centeno; **r. grass** ballica *f*; *US* **r. (whiskey)** whisky *m* de centeno

S, s [es] *n (the letter)* S, s *f*
Sabbath ['sæbəθ] *n (Jewish)* sábado *m*; *(Christian)* domingo *m*
sabbatical [sə'bætɪkəl] *adj* sabático(a)
sabotage ['sæbətɑːʒ] **1** *n* sabotaje *m*
2 *vt* sabotear
saccharin ['sækərɪn] *n* sacarina *f*
sachet ['sæʃeɪ] *n* bolsita *f*, sobrecito *m*
sack [sæk] **1** *n* (a) *(bag)* saco *m* (b) *Br Fam* **to get the s.** ser despedido(a); *Fam* **to give sb the s.** despedir a algn
2 *vt* (a) *Br Fam* despedir (b) *Mil* saquear
sacking ['sækɪŋ] *n Tex* arpillera *f*
sacrament ['sækrəmənt] *n* sacramento *m*
sacred ['seɪkrɪd] *adj* sagrado(a)
sacrifice ['sækrɪfaɪs] **1** *n* sacrificio *m*
2 *vt* sacrificar
sacrificial [sækrɪ'fɪʃəl] *adj* **s. lamb** chivo expiatorio
sacrilege ['sækrɪlɪdʒ] *n* sacrilegio *m*
sacrosanct ['sækrəʊsæŋkt] *adj* sacrosanto(a)
sad [sæd] *adj* (**sadder, saddest**) triste; **how s.!** ¡qué pena!
sadden ['sædən] *vt* entristecer
saddle ['sædəl] **1** *n (for horse)* silla *f* (de montar); *(of bicycle etc)* sillín *m*
2 *vt (horse)* ensillar; *Fam* **to s. sb with sth** cargarle a algn con algo
saddlebag ['sædəlbæg] *n* alforja *f*
sadist ['seɪdɪst] *n* sádico(a) *m,f*
sadistic [sə'dɪstɪk] *adj* sádico(a)
sadness ['sædnɪs] *n* tristeza *f*
sadomasochism [seɪdəʊ'mæsəkɪzəm] *n* sadomasoquismo *m*
sae [eseɪ'iː] *n Br (abbr* **stamped addressed envelope)** = sobre franqueado con la dirección del remitente
safari [sə'fɑːrɪ] *n* safari *m*; **s. park** reserva *f*
safe [seɪf] **1** *adj* (a) *(unharmed)* ileso(a); *(out of danger)* a salvo; **s. and sound** sano(a) y salvo(a) (b) *(not dangerous)* inocuo(a) (c) *(secure, sure)* seguro(a); **to be on the s. side** para mayor seguridad; **s. house** *(for spies etc)* piso franco (d) *(driver)* prudente
2 *n (for money etc)* caja *f* fuerte
safe-conduct [seɪf'kɒndʌkt] *n* salvoconducto *m*
safe-deposit [seɪfdɪ'pɒzɪt] *n* **s. (box)** cámara blindada
safeguard ['seɪfɡɑːd] **1** *n (protection)* salvaguarda *f*; *(guarantee)* garantía *f*

2 *vt* proteger, salvaguardar
safekeeping [seɪf'kiːpɪŋ] *n* custodia *f*
safely ['seɪflɪ] *adv* (a) con toda seguridad (b) **to arrive s.** llegar sin incidentes
safety ['seɪftɪ] *n* seguridad *f*; **s. first!** ¡la seguridad ante todo!; **s. belt** cinturón *m* de seguridad; **s. net** red *f* de protección; **s. pin** imperdible *m*
saffron ['sæfrən] *n* azafrán *m*
sag [sæg] *vi* (a) *(roof)* hundirse; *(wall)* pandear; *(wood, iron)* combarse; *(flesh)* colgar (b) *Fig (spirits)* flaquear
sage¹ [seɪdʒ] **1** *adj (wise)* sabio(a)
2 *n (person)* sabio(a) *m,f*
sage² [seɪdʒ] *n* salvia *f*
Sagittarius [sædʒɪ'teərɪəs] *n* Sagitario *m*
Sahara [sə'hɑːrə] *n* **the S.** el Sahara
Saharan [sə'hɑːrən] *adj* saharaui, sahariano(a)
said [sed] **1** *adj* dicho(a)
2 *pt & pp of* **say**
sail [seɪl] **1** *n* (a) *(canvas)* vela *f*; **to set s.** zarpar (b) *(trip)* paseo *m* en barco
2 *vt (ship)* gobernar; *Literary* navegar
3 *vi* (a) ir en barco (b) *(set sail)* zarpar
▸ **sail through** *vt insep Fam* **he sailed through university** en la universidad todo le fue sobre ruedas
sailboat ['seɪlbəʊt] *n US* velero *m*
sailing ['seɪlɪŋ] *n* navegación *f*; *(yachting)* vela *f*; *Fam* **it's all plain s.** es todo coser y cantar; *Br* **s. boat** *or* **ship** velero *m*, barco *m* de vela
sailor ['seɪlə(r)] *n* marinero *m*
saint [seɪnt] *n* santo(a) *m,f*; *(before all masculine names except those beginning* **Do** *or* **To)** San; *(before feminine names)* Santa; **S. Dominic** Santo Domingo; **S. Helen** Santa Elena; **S. John** San Juan; **All Saints' Day** Día *m* de Todos los Santos
saintly ['seɪntlɪ] *adj* (**saintlier, saintliest**) santo(a)
sake [seɪk] *n* **for the s. of** por (el bien de); **for your own s.** por tu propio bien
salad ['sæləd] *n* ensalada *f*; **potato s.** ensalada de patatas *or Am* papas; **s. bowl** ensaladera *f*; **s. cream** salsa *f* tipo mahonesa; **s. dressing** vinagreta *f*, aliño *m*
salami [sə'lɑːmɪ] *n* salchichón *m*, salami *m*
salary ['sælərɪ] *n* salario *m*, sueldo *m*
sale [seɪl] *n* (a) *(venta f*; **for** *or* **on s.** en venta; **sales department** departamento *m* comer-

cial; **sales manager** jefe(a) *m,f* de ventas (**b**) *(at low prices)* rebajas *fpl*

salesclerk ['seɪlzklɑːk] *n US* dependiente(a) *m,f*

salesman ['seɪlzmən] *n* (**a**) vendedor *m*; *(in shop)* dependiente *m* (**b**) *(commercial traveller)* representante *m*

salesroom ['seɪlzruːm] *n* sala *f* de subastas

saleswoman ['seɪlzwʊmən] *n* (**a**) vendedora *f*; *(in shop)* dependienta *f* (**b**) *(commercial traveller)* representante *f*

salient ['seɪlɪənt] *adj Fig* sobresaliente

saliva [sə'laɪvə] *n* saliva *f*

sallow ['sæləʊ] *adj* cetrino(a)

salmon ['sæmən] **1** *n* salmón *m*

  2 *adj* (de color) salmón

salmonella [sælmə'nelə] *n Biol & Med (bacteria)* salmonela *f*; *(food poisoning)* salmonelosis *f*

salon ['sælɒn] *n* salón *m*

saloon [sə'luːn] *n* (**a**) *(on ship)* cámara *f* (**b**) *US (bar)* taberna *f*, bar *m*; *Br* **s. (bar)** bar de lujo (**c**) *(car)* turismo *m*

salt [sɔːlt] **1** *n* sal *f*; *Fig* **to take sth with a pinch of s.** creer algo con reservas; **bath salts** sales de baño; **smelling salts** sales aromáticas

  2 *adj* salado(a)

  3 *vt* (**a**) *(cure)* salar (**b**) *(add salt to)* echar sal a

saltcellar ['sɔːltselə(r)] *n* salero *m*

saltwater ['sɔːltwɔːtə(r)] *adj* de agua salada

salty ['sɔːltɪ] *adj* (**saltier, saltiest**) salado(a)

salubrious [sə'luːbrɪəs] *adj* salubre, sano(a)

salutary ['sæljʊtərɪ] *adj (experience)* beneficioso(a); *(warning)* útil

salute [sə'luːt] **1** *n (greeting)* saludo *m*

  2 *vt Mil* saludar (**b**) *Fig (achievement etc)* aplaudir

  3 *vi Mil* saludar

salvage ['sælvɪdʒ] **1** *n* (**a**) *(of ship etc)* salvamento *m*, rescate *m* (**b**) *(objects recovered)* objetos recuperados (**c**) *Jur* derecho *m* de salvamento

  2 *vt (from ship etc)* rescatar

salvation [sæl'veɪʃən] *n* salvación *f*; **S. Army** Ejército *m* de Salvación

Samaritan [sə'mærɪtən] *n* samaritano(a) *m,f*; **the Samaritans** ≃ el teléfono de la Esperanza

same [seɪm] **1** *adj* mismo(a); **at that very s. moment** en ese mismísimo momento; **at the s. time** *(simultaneously)* al mismo tiempo; *(however)* sin embargo; **in the s. way** del mismo modo; **the two cars are the s.** los dos coches son iguales

  2 *pron* **the s.** el mismo/la misma/lo mismo; *Fam* **the s. here** lo mismo digo yo; *Fam* **the s. to you!** ¡igualmente!

  3 *adv* del mismo modo, igual; **all the s., just the s.** sin embargo, aun así; **it's all the s. to me** (a mí) me da igual *or* lo mismo

sample ['sɑːmpəl] **1** *n* muestra *f*

  2 *vt (wines)* catar; *(dish)* probar

sanatorium [sænə'tɔːrɪəm] *n* sanatorio *m*

sanctimonious [sæŋktɪ'məʊnɪəs] *adj* beato(a)

sanction ['sæŋkʃən] **1** *n* (**a**) *(authorization)* permiso *m* (**b**) *(penalty)* sanción *f* (**c**) *Pol* **sanctions** sanciones *fpl*

  2 *vt* sancionar

sanctity ['sæŋktɪtɪ] *n (sacredness)* santidad *f*; *(of marriage)* indisolubilidad *f*

sanctuary ['sæŋktjʊərɪ] *n* (**a**) *Rel* santuario *m* (**b**) *Pol* asilo *m* (**c**) *(for birds, animals)* reserva *f*

sand [sænd] **1** *n* arena *f*; **s. castle** castillo *m* de arena; **s. dune** duna *f*

  2 *vt* **to s. (down)** lijar

sandal ['sændəl] *n* sandalia *f*

sandalwood ['sændəlwʊd] *n* sándalo *m*

sandbag ['sændbæg] *n* saco terrero

sandbox ['sændbɒks] *n US* arenal *m*

sandpaper ['sændpeɪpə(r)] *n* papel *m* de lija

sandpit ['sændpɪt] *n Br (in playground etc)* arenal *m*

sandshoe ['sændʃuː] *n Br* playera *f*

sandstone ['sændstəʊn] *n* arenisca *f*

sandwich ['sænwɪdʒ, 'sænwɪtʃ] **1** *n (bread roll)* bocadillo *m*; *(sliced bread)* sándwich *m*; *Educ* **s. course** curso teórico-práctico

  2 *vt* intercalar; **it was sandwiched between two lorries** quedó encajonado entre dos camiones

sandy ['sændɪ] *adj* (**sandier, sandiest**) (**a**) *(earth, beach)* arenoso(a) (**b**) *(hair)* rubio rojizo

sane [seɪn] *adj (not mad)* cuerdo(a); *(sensible)* sensato(a)

  ⚠ Note that the Spanish word **sano** is a false friend and is never a translation for the English word **sane**. In Spanish, **sano** means "healthy".

sang [sæŋ] *pt of* **sing**

sanitarium [sænɪ'teərɪəm] *n US* sanatorio *m*

sanitary ['sænɪtərɪ] *adj* sanitario(a); *(hygienic)* higiénico(a); **s.** *Br* **towel** *or US* **napkin** compresa *f*

sanitation [sænɪ'teɪʃən] *n* sanidad *f* (pública); *(plumbing)* sistema *m* de saneamiento

sanity ['sænɪtɪ] *n* cordura *f*, juicio *m*; *(good sense)* sensatez *f*

  ⚠ Note that the Spanish word **sanidad** is a false friend and is never a translation for the English word **sanity**. In Spanish, **sanidad** means "health".

sank [sæŋk] *pt of* **sink**

Santa Claus ['sæntə'klɔːz] *n* Papá Noel *m*, San Nicolás *m*

sap¹ [sæp] *n Bot* savia *f*

sap² [sæp] *vt (undermine)* minar; *Fig* agotar

sapling ['sæplɪŋ] *n Bot* árbol *m* joven

sapphire ['sæfaɪə(r)] *n* zafiro *m*

sarcasm ['sɑːkæzəm] *n* sarcasmo *m*

sarcastic [saːˈkæstɪk] *adj* sarcástico(a)
sardine [saːˈdiːn] *n* sardina *f*
Sardinia [saːˈdɪnɪə] *n* Cerdeña
sardonic [saːˈdɒnɪk] *adj* sardónico(a)
SASE [eseɪesˈiː] *n US (abbr* **self-addressed stamped envelope**) = sobre franqueado con la dirección del remitente
sash¹ [sæʃ] *n* faja *f*
sash² [sæʃ] *n* **s. window** ventana *f* de guillotina
sat [sæt] *pt & pp of* **sit**
Satan [ˈseɪtən] *n* Satán *m*, Satanás *m*
satanic [səˈtænɪk] *adj* satánico(a)
satchel [ˈsætʃəl] *n* cartera *f* de colegial
satellite [ˈsætəlaɪt] *n* satélite *m*; **s. dish (aerial)** antena parabólica
satin [ˈsætɪn] *n* satén *m*; **s. finish** (acabado *m*) satinado *m*
satire [ˈsætaɪə(r)] *n* sátira *f*
satirical [səˈtɪrɪkəl] *adj* satírico(a)
satisfaction [sætɪsˈfækʃən] *n* satisfacción *f*
satisfactory [sætɪsˈfæktərɪ] *adj* satisfactorio(a)
satisfied [ˈsætɪsfaɪd] *adj* satisfecho(a)
satisfy [ˈsætɪsfaɪ] *vt* (a) satisfacer (b) *(fulfil)* cumplir con (c) *(convince)* convencer
satisfying [ˈsætɪsfaɪɪŋ] *adj* satisfactorio(a); *(pleasing)* agradable; *(meal)* que llena
saturate [ˈsætʃəreɪt] *vt* saturar (**with** de)
Saturday [ˈsætədɪ] *n* sábado *m*
sauce [sɔːs] *n* (a) salsa *f* (b) *Fam (impudence)* descaro *m*
saucepan [ˈsɔːspən] *n* cacerola *f*; *(large)* olla *f*
saucer [ˈsɔːsə(r)] *n* platillo *m*
saucy [ˈsɔːsɪ] *adj* (**saucier, sauciest**) *Fam* fresco(a)
Saudi Arabia [saʊdɪəˈreɪbɪə] *n* Arabia *f* Saudita *or* Saudí
Saudi Arabian [saʊdɪəˈreɪbɪən] *adj & n* saudita *(mf)*, saudí *(mf)*
sauna [ˈsɔːnə] *n* sauna *f*
saunter [ˈsɔːntə(r)] **1** *n* paseo *m*
2 *vi* pasearse
sausage [ˈsɒsɪdʒ] *n (raw)* salchicha *f*; *(cured)* salchichón *m*; *(spicy)* chorizo *m*; *Fam* **s. dog** perro *m* salchicha; *Br* **s. roll** empanada *f* de carne
sauté [ˈsəʊteɪ] **1** *adj* salteado(a)
2 *vt* saltear
savage [ˈsævɪdʒ] **1** *adj* (a) *(ferocious)* feroz; *(cruel)* cruel; *(violent)* salvaje (b) *(primitive)* salvaje
2 *n* salvaje *mf*
3 *vt (attack)* embestir; *Fig (criticize)* criticar despiadadamente
save [seɪv] **1** *vt* (a) *(rescue)* salvar, rescatar; *Fig* **to s. face** salvar las apariencias (b) *(put by)* guardar; *(money, energy, time)* ahorrar; *(food)* almacenar; **it saved him a lot of trouble** le evitó muchos problemas
2 *vi* (a) **to s. (up)** ahorrar (b) **to s. on paper** *(economize)* ahorrar papel

3 *n Ftb* parada *f*
4 *prep Literary* salvo, excepto
saving [ˈseɪvɪŋ] **1** *n* (a) *(of time, money)* ahorro *m* (b) **savings** ahorros *mpl*; **savings account** cuenta *f* de ahorros; **savings bank** caja *f* de ahorros
2 *adj* **it's his only s. grace** es el único mérito que tiene
saviour, *US* **savior** [ˈseɪvjə(r)] *n* salvador(a) *m,f*
savour, *US* **savor** [ˈseɪvə(r)] **1** *n* sabor *m*, gusto *m*
2 *vi* saborear
savoury, *US* **savory** [ˈseɪvərɪ] *adj (tasty)* sabroso(a); *(salted)* salado(a); *(spicy)* picante
saw¹ [sɔː] **1** *n (tool)* sierra *f*
2 *vt & vi (pt* **sawed**; *pp* **sawed** *or* **sawn**) serrar
► **saw up** *vt sep* serrar (**into** en)
saw² [sɔː] *pt of* **see**
sawdust [ˈsɔːdʌst] *n* (a) serrín *m*
sawmill [ˈsɔːmɪl] *n* aserradero *m*, serrería *f*
sawn [sɔːn] *pp of* **saw**
sawn-off [ˈsɔːnɒf], *US* **sawed-off** [sɔːdˈɒf] *adj* recortado(a); **s. shotgun** escopeta *f* de cañones recortados
saxophone [ˈsæksəfəʊn] *n* saxofón *m*
say [seɪ] **1** *vt (pt & pp* **said**) (a) decir; **it goes without saying that ...** huelga decir que ...; **it is said that ...** se dice que ...; **not to s. ...** por no decir ...; **that is to s.** es decir; **to s. yes/no** decir que sí/no; *Fam* **I s.!** ¡oiga!; **what does the sign s.?** ¿qué pone en el letrero? (b) *(think)* pensar (c) **shall we s. Friday then?** ¿quedamos el viernes, pues?
2 *n* **I have no s. in the matter** no tengo ni voz ni voto en el asunto; **to have one's s.** dar su opinión
saying [ˈseɪɪŋ] *n* refrán *m*, dicho *m*
scab [skæb] *n* (a) *Med* costra *f* (b) *Fam Pej* esquirol *mf*
scaffold [ˈskæfəld] *n (for execution)* patíbulo *m*
scaffolding [ˈskæfəldɪŋ] *n Constr* andamio *n*
scald [skɔːld] **1** *n* escaldadura *f*
2 *vt* escaldar
scale¹ [skeɪl] *n (of fish, on skin)* escama *f*; *(in boiler)* incrustaciones *fpl*
scale² [skeɪl] *n* (a) escala *f*; **on a large s.** a gran escala; **to s.** a escala; **s. model** maqueta *f* (b) *(extent)* alcance *m* (c) *Mus* escala *f*
2 *vt (climb)* escalar
► **scale down** *vt sep (drawing)* reducir a escala; *(production)* reducir
scales [skeɪlz] *npl* **(pair of) s.** *(shop, kitchen)* balanza *f*; *(bathroom)* báscula *f*
scallop [ˈskɒləp] *n* (a) *(mollusc)* vieira *f* (b) *(shell)* venera *f*
scalp [skælp] **1** *n* cuero cabelludo
2 *vt* arrancar el cuero cabelludo a
scalpel [ˈskælpəl] *n* bisturí *m*
scamper [ˈskæmpə(r)] *vi* corretear

scampi ['skæmpɪ] *n* gambas empanadas

scan [skæn] **1** *vt* (**a**) *(scrutinize)* escrutar; *(horizon)* otear; *(glance at)* ojear (**c**) *(of radar)* explorar

2 *n Med* exploración ultrasónica; *(in gynaecology etc)* ecografía *f*

scandal ['skændəl] *n* (**a**) escándalo *m*; **what a s.!** ¡qué vergüenza! (**b**) *(gossip)* chismes *mpl*

Scandinavia [skændɪ'neɪvɪə] *n* Escandinavia

Scandinavian [skændɪ'neɪvɪən] *adj & n* escandinavo(a) *(m,f)*

scanner ['skænə(r)] *n Med & Comput* escáner *m*

scant [skænt] *adj* escaso(a)

scanty ['skæntɪ] *adj* (**scantier, scantiest**) escaso(a); *(meal)* insuficiente; *(clothes)* ligero(a)

scapegoat ['skeɪpɡəʊt] *n* chivo expiatorio

scar [skɑː(r)] *n* cicatriz *f*

scarce [skeəs] *adj* escaso(a); *Fig* **to make oneself s.** largarse

scarcely ['skeəslɪ] *adv* apenas

scarcity ['skeəsɪtɪ] *n* escasez *f*; *(rarity)* rareza *f*

scare [skeə(r)] **1** *n* *(fright)* susto *m*; *(widespread alarm)* pánico *m*; **bomb s.** amenaza *f* de bomba

2 *vt* asustar, espantar; *Fam* **to be scared stiff** estar muerto(a) de miedo

▶ **scare away, scare off** *vt sep* ahuyentar

scarecrow ['skeəkrəʊ] *n* espantapájaros *inv*

scarf [skɑːf] *n* (*pl* **scarfs** *or* **scarves**) *(long, woollen)* bufanda *f*; *(square)* pañuelo *m*; *(silk)* fular *m*

scarlet ['skɑːlɪt] **1** *adj* escarlata

2 *n* escarlata *f*; **s. fever** escarlatina *f*

scarves [skɑːvz] *pl of* **scarf**

scathing ['skeɪðɪŋ] *adj* mordaz, cáustico(a)

scatter ['skætə(r)] **1** *vt* (**a**) *(papers etc)* esparcir, desparramar (**b**) *(crowd)* dispersar

2 *vi* dispersarse

scatterbrained ['skætəbreɪnd] *adj Fam* ligero(a) de cascos; *(forgetful)* despistado(a)

scattered ['skætəd] *adj* **s. showers** chubascos aislados

scavenger ['skævɪndʒə(r)] *n* (**a**) *(person)* rebuscador(a) *m,f*, trapero *m* (**b**) *(animal)* (animal *m*) carroñero(a) *mf*

scenario [sɪ'nɑːrɪəʊ] *n* (**a**) *Cin* guión *m* (**b**) *(situation)* situación *f* hipotética

scene [siːn] *n* (**a**) *Th, Cin & TV* escena *f*; **behind the scenes** entre bastidores (**b**) *(place)* lugar *m*, escenario *m*; **a change of s.** un cambio de aires (**c**) *(view)* panorama *m* (**d**) *(fuss)* montar un espectáculo

scenery ['siːnərɪ] *n* (**a**) *(landscape)* paisaje *m* (**b**) *Th* decorado *m*

scenic ['siːnɪk] *adj* *(picturesque)* pintoresco(a)

scent [sent] **1** *n* (**a**) *(smell)* olor *m*; *(of food)*

aroma *m* (**b**) *(perfume)* perfume *m* (**c**) *(in hunting)* pista *f*

2 *vt* *(add perfume to)* perfumar; *(smell)* olfatear; *Fig* presentir

sceptic ['skeptɪk] *n* escéptico(a) *m,f*

sceptical ['skeptɪkəl] *adj* escéptico(a)

scepticism ['skeptɪsɪzəm] *n* escepticismo *m*

sceptre ['septə(r)] *n* cetro *m*

schedule ['ʃedjuːl, *US* 'skedʒʊəl] **1** *n* (**a**) *(plan, agenda)* programa *m*; *(timetable)* horario *m*; **on s.** a la hora (prevista); **to be behind s.** llevar retraso (**b**) *(list)* lista *f*; *(inventory)* inventario *m*

2 *vt* *(plan)* programar, fijar

scheduled ['ʃedjuːld, *US* 'skedʒʊəld] *adj* previsto(a), fijo(a); **s. flight** vuelo regular

scheme [skiːm] **1** *n* (**a**) *(plan)* plan *m*; *(project)* proyecto *m*; *(idea)* idea *f*; **colour s.** combinación *f* de colores (**b**) *(plot)* intriga *f*; *(trick)* ardid *m*

2 *vi* *(plot)* tramar, intrigar

scheming ['skiːmɪŋ] *adj* intrigante, maquinador(a)

schism ['sɪzəm] *n* cisma *m*

schizophrenic [skɪtsəʊ'frenɪk] *adj & n* esquizofrénico(a) *(m,f)*

scholar ['skɒlə(r)] *n* *(learned person)* erudito(a) *m,f*; *(pupil)* alumno(a) *m,f*

scholarship ['skɒləʃɪp] *n* (**a**) *(learning)* erudición *f* (**b**) *(grant)* beca *f*; **s. holder** becario(a) *m,f*

school [skuːl] **1** *n* (**a**) escuela *f*, colegio *m*; **drama s.** academia *f* de arte dramático; **of s. age** en edad escolar; **s. year** año *m* escolar (**b**) *US (university)* universidad *f* (**c**) *(university department)* facultad *f* (**d**) *(group of artists)* escuela *f*; **s. of thought** corriente *f* de opinión

2 *vt* *(teach)* enseñar; *(train)* formar

schoolbook ['skuːlbʊk] *n* libro *m* de texto

schoolboy ['skuːlbɔɪ] *n* alumno *m*

schoolchild ['skuːltʃaɪld] *n* alumno(a) *m,f*

schooldays ['skuːldeɪz] *npl* años *mpl* de colegio

schoolgirl ['skuːlɡɜːl] *n* alumna *f*

schooling ['skuːlɪŋ] *n* educación *f*, estudios *mpl*

schoolmaster ['skuːlmɑːstə(r)] *n* profesor *m*; *(primary school)* maestro *m*

schoolmistress ['skuːlmɪstrɪs] *n* profesora *f*; *(primary school)* maestra *f*

schoolteacher ['skuːltiːtʃə(r)] *n* profesor(a) *m,f*; *(primary school)* maestro(a) *m,f*

schooner ['skuːnə(r)] *n Naut* goleta *f*

sciatica [saɪ'ætɪkə] *n* ciática *f*

science ['saɪəns] *n* ciencia *f*; **s. fiction** ciencia-ficción *f*

scientific [saɪən'tɪfɪk] *adj* científico(a)

scientist ['saɪəntɪst] *n* científico(a) *m,f*

scintillating ['sɪntɪleɪtɪŋ] *adj* brillante

scissors ['sɪzəz] *npl* tijeras *fpl*; **a pair of s.** unas tijeras

scoff¹ [skɒf] *vi (mock)* mofarse (**at** de)
scoff² [skɒf] *vt Fam (eat)* zamparse
scold [skəʊld] *vt* regañar, reñir
scone [skəʊn, skɒn] *n* bollo *m*, pastelito *m*
scoop [sku:p] *n* (**a**) *(for flour)* pala *f*; *(for ice cream)* cucharón *m*; *(amount)* palada *f*, cucharada *f* (**b**) *Press* exclusiva *f*
▸ **scoop out** *vt sep (flour etc)* sacar con pala; *(water) (from boat)* achicar
▸ **scoop up** *vt sep* recoger
scooter ['sku:tə(r)] *n (child's)* patinete *m*; *(adult's)* Vespa® *f*
scope [skəʊp] *n* (**a**) *(range)* alcance *m*; *(of undertaking)* ámbito *m* (**b**) *(freedom)* libertad *f*
scorch [skɔ:tʃ] *vt (singe)* chamuscar
scorching ['skɔ:tʃɪŋ] *adj Fam* abrasador(a)
score [skɔ:(r)] **1** *n* (**a**) *Sport* tanteo *m*; *Cards & (in golf)* puntuación *f*; *(result)* resultado *m*
(**b**) *(notch)* muesca *f*
(**c**) **I have a s. to settle with you** tengo que ajustar las cuentas contigo
(**d**) **on that s.** a ese respecto
(**e**) *(twenty)* veintena *f*
(**f**) *Mus (of opera)* partitura *f*; *(of film)* música *f*
2 *vt* (**a**) *(goal)* marcar; *(points)* conseguir
(**b**) *(wood)* hacer una muesca en; *(paper)* rayar
3 *vi* (**a**) *Sport* marcar un tanto; *Ftb* marcar un gol; *(keep the score)* llevar el marcador
(**b**) *(have success)* tener éxito (**with** con); *Fam* ligar (**with** con)
▸ **score out** *vt sep (word etc)* tachar
scoreboard ['skɔ:bɔ:d] *n* marcador *m*
scorer ['skɔ:rə(r)] *n* (**a**) *(goal striker)* goleador *m* (**b**) *(scorekeeper)* encargado(a) *m,f* del marcador
scorn [skɔ:n] **1** *n* desprecio *m*
2 *vt* despreciar
scornful ['skɔ:nfʊl] *adj* desdeñoso(a)
Scorpio ['skɔ:pɪəʊ] *n* Escorpión *m*
scorpion ['skɔ:pɪən] *n* alacrán *m*, escorpión *m*
Scot [skɒt] *n* escocés(esa) *m,f*
Scotch [skɒtʃ] **1** *adj* escocés(esa); *US* **S. tape®** cinta adhesiva, celo® *m*
2 *n (whisky)* whisky *m* escocés
scotch [skɒtʃ] *vt (plot)* frustrar; *(rumour)* negar, desmentir
scot-free ['skɒt'fri:] *adj* impune
Scotland ['skɒtlənd] *n* Escocia
Scots [skɒts] **1** *adj* escocés(esa)
2 *n* (dialecto *m*) escocés *m*
Scotsman ['skɒtsmən] *n* escocés *m*
Scotswoman ['skɒtswʊmən] *n* escocesa *f*
Scottish ['skɒtɪʃ] *adj* escocés(esa)
scoundrel ['skaʊndrəl] *n* sinvergüenza *mf*, canalla *m*
scour¹ [skaʊə(r)] *vt (clean)* fregar, restregar
scour² [skaʊə(r)] *vt (search) (countryside)* rastrear; *(building)* registrar

scourge [skɜ:dʒ] *n Fig* azote *m*
scout [skaʊt] **1** *n Mil* explorador(a) *m,f*; *Sport & Cin* cazatalentos *m inv*; **boy s.** boy *m* scout
2 *vi Mil* reconocer el terreno; **to s. around for sth** andar en busca de algo
scowl [skaʊl] **1** *vi* fruncir el ceño; **to s. at sb** mirar a algn con ceño
2 *n* ceño *m*
scrabble ['skræbəl] *vi* escarbar; *Fig* **to s. around for sth** revolver todo para encontrar algo
scraggy ['skrægɪ] *adj* (**scraggier, scraggiest**) delgado(a), flacucho(a)
scramble ['skræmbəl] **1** *vi* trepar; **to s. for sth** pelearse por; **to s. up a tree** trepar a un árbol
2 *vt* (**a**) *Culin* **scrambled eggs** huevos revueltos (**b**) *Rad Tel (message)* codificar; *(broadcast)* interferir
3 *n (climb)* subida *f*; *Fig* **it's going to be a s.** *(rush)* va a ser muy apresurado
scrap¹ [skræp] **1** *n* (**a**) *(small piece)* pedazo *m*; **there isn't a s. of truth in it** no tiene ni un ápice de verdad; **s. (metal)** chatarra *f*; **s. dealer** *or* **merchant** chatarrero(a) *m,f*; **s. paper** papel *m* de borrador; **s. yard** *(for cars)* cementerio *m* de coches (**b**) **scraps** restos *mpl*; *(of food)* sobras *fpl*
2 *vt (discard)* desechar; *Fig (idea)* descartar
scrap² [skræp] *Fam* **1** *n (fight)* pelea *f*
2 *vi* pelearse (**with** con)
scrapbook ['skræpbʊk] *n* álbum *m* de recortes
scrape [skreɪp] **1** *vt (paint, wood)* raspar; *(knee)* arañarse, hacerse un rasguño en
2 *vi (make noise)* chirriar; *(rub)* rozar
3 *n Fam (trouble)* lío *m*
▸ **scrape through** *vi Fam (exam)* aprobar por los pelos
▸ **scrape together** *vt sep* reunir a duras penas
scraper ['skreɪpə(r)] *n* rasqueta *f*
scrapheap ['skræphi:p] *n (dump)* vertedero *m*
scratch [skrætʃ] **1** *n* (**a**) *(on skin, paintwork)* arañazo *m*; *(on record)* raya *f* (**b**) *(noise)* chirrido *m* (**c**) *Fig* **to be up to s.** dar la talla; *Fig* **to start from s.** empezar de cero
2 *adj* **s. team** equipo improvisado
3 *vt* (**a**) *(with nail, claw)* arañar, rasguñar; *(paintwork)* rayar (**b**) *(to relieve itching)* rascarse
scrawl [skrɔ:l] **1** *n* garabatos *mpl*
2 *vt (message etc)* garabatear
3 *vi* hacer garabatos
scrawny ['skrɔ:nɪ] *adj* (**scrawnier, scrawniest**) flaco(a)
scream [skri:m] **1** *n* chillido *m*; **screams of laughter** carcajadas *fpl*
2 *vt (insults etc)* gritar
3 *vi* chillar; **to s. at sb** chillar a algn
scree [skri:] *n* pedregal *m*
screech [skri:tʃ] **1** *n (of person)* chillido *m*; *(of tyres, brakes)* chirrido *m*

2 *vi (person)* chillar; *(tyres)* chirrar

screen [skriːn] **1** *n* (**a**) *(movable partition)* biombo *m* (**b**) *Fig* cortina *f* (**c**) *Cin, TV & Comput* pantalla *f*; **s. test** casting *m*

2 *vt* (**a**) *(protect)* proteger; *(conceal)* tapar (**b**) *(sieve) (coal etc)* tamizar; *Fig (candidates)* seleccionar (**c**) *(show) (film)* proyectar; *(for first time)* estrenar (**d**) *Med* examinar

screening [ˈskriːnɪŋ] *n* (**a**) *(of film)* proyección *f*; *(for first time)* estreno *m* (**b**) *Med* exploración *f*

screenplay [ˈskriːnpleɪ] *n* guión *m*

screw [skruː] **1** *n* (**a**) *(propeller)* tornillo *m* (**b**) *(propeller)* hélice *f*

2 *vt* (**a**) atornillar; **to s. sth down** *or* **in** *or* **on** fijar algo con tornillos (**b**) *Vulg* joder

▸ **screw up** *vt sep* (**a**) *(piece of paper)* arrugar; *(one's face)* torcer (**b**) *very Fam (ruin)* joder

screwdriver [ˈskruːdraɪvə(r)] *n* destornillador *m*

scribble [ˈskrɪbəl] **1** *n* garabatos *mpl*

2 *vt (message etc)* garabatear

3 *vi* hacer garabatos

script [skrɪpt] *n* (**a**) *(writing)* escritura *f*; *(handwriting)* letra *f*; *Typ* letra cursiva (**b**) *(in exam)* escrito *m* (**c**) *Cin* guión *m*

Scripture [ˈskrɪptʃə(r)] *n* **Holy S.** Sagrada Escritura

scroll [skrəʊl] *n* rollo *m* de pergamino

scrounge [skraʊndʒ] *Fam* **1** *vi* gorronear; **to s. (around) for** buscar; **to s. off sb** vivir a costa de algn

2 *vt* gorronear

scrounger [ˈskraʊndʒə(r)] *n Fam* gorrón(ona) *m,f*

scrub¹ [skrʌb] *n (undergrowth)* maleza *f*

scrub² [skrʌb] **1** *vt* (**a**) frotar (**b**) *Fam (cancel)* borrar

2 *n (cleaning)* fregado *m*

scruff [skrʌf] *n* pescuezo *m*, cogote *m*

scruffy [ˈskrʌfɪ] *adj* (**scruffier, scruffiest**) *Fam* desaliñado(a)

scrum [skrʌm] *n* melée *f*; **s. half** medio *m* melée

scruple [ˈskruːpəl] *n* escrúpulo *m*

scrupulous [ˈskruːpjʊləs] *adj* escrupuloso(a)

scrupulously [ˈskruːpjʊləslɪ] *adv* **s. honest** sumamente honrado(a)

scrutinize [ˈskruːtɪnaɪz] *vt* escudriñar

scrutiny [ˈskruːtɪnɪ] *n* escrutinio *m*

scuff [skʌf] *vt (the floor)* rayar; *(one's feet)* arrastrar

scuffle [ˈskʌfəl] **1** *n* pelea *f*

2 *vi* pelearse (**with** con)

scullery [ˈskʌlərɪ] *n* cuarto *m* de pila

sculptor [ˈskʌlptə(r)] *n* escultor(a) *m,f*

sculpture [ˈskʌlptʃə(r)] *n* escultura *f*

scum [skʌm] *n* (**a**) *(on liquid)* espuma *f* (**b**) *Fig* escoria *f*

scupper [ˈskʌpə(r)] *vt Br Fam (plan etc)* desbaratar

scurrilous [ˈskʌrɪləs] *adj (abusive)* difamatorio(a)

scurry [ˈskʌrɪ] *vi (run)* corretear; *(hurry)* apresurarse; **to s. away** *or* **off** escabullirse

scuttle¹ [ˈskʌtəl] *n* cubo *m*; **coal s.** cubo del carbón

scuttle² [ˈskʌtəl] *vt (ship)* barrenar

scuttle³ [ˈskʌtəl] *vi* **to s. away** *or* **off** escabullirse

scythe [saɪð] **1** *n* guadaña *f*

2 *vt* guadañar

SDI [esdiːˈaɪ] *n (abbr Strategic Defence Initiative)* Iniciativa *f* para la Defensa Estratégica

sea [siː] *n* mar *m or f*; **by the s.** a orillas del mar; **out at s.** en alta mar; **to go by s.** ir en barco; **to put to s.** zarpar; *Fig* **to be all at s.** estar desorientado(a); **s. breeze** brisa marina; *Fig* **s. change** metamorfosis *f*; **s. level** nivel *m* del mar; **s. lion** león marino; **s. water** agua *f* de mar

seabed [ˈsiːbed] *n* fondo *m* del mar

seaboard [ˈsiːbɔːd] *n US* costa *f*, litoral *m*

seafood [ˈsiːfuːd] *n* mariscos *mpl*

seafront [ˈsiːfrʌnt] *n* paseo marítimo

seagull [ˈsiːɡʌl] *n* gaviota *f*

seal¹ [siːl] *n Zool* foca *f*

seal² [siːl] **1** *n* (**a**) *(official stamp)* sello *m* (**b**) *(airtight closure)* cierre hermético; *(on bottle)* precinto *m*

2 *vt* (**a**) *(with official stamp)* sellar; *(with wax)* lacrar (**b**) *(close)* cerrar; *(make airtight)* cerrar herméticamente (**c**) *(determine)* **this sealed his fate** esto decidió su destino

▸ **seal off** *vt sep (pipe etc)* cerrar; *(area)* acordonar

seam [siːm] *n* (**a**) *Sewing* costura *f*; *Tech* juntura *f*; *Fam* **to be bursting at the seams** *(room)* rebosar de gente (**b**) *Geol Min* veta *f*, filón *m*

seaman [ˈsiːmən] *n* marinero *m*

seamy [ˈsiːmɪ] *adj* (**seamier, seamiest**) *Fig* sórdido(a)

séance [ˈseɪɑːns] *n* sesión *f* de espiritismo

seaplane [ˈsiːpleɪn] *n* hidroavión *m*

seaport [ˈsiːpɔːt] *n* puerto marítimo

search [sɜːtʃ] **1** *vt (files etc)* buscar en; *(building, suitcase)* registrar; *(person)* cachear; *(one's conscience)* examinar

2 *vi* buscar; **to s. through** registrar

3 *n* búsqueda *f*; *(of building etc)* registro *m*; *(of person)* cacheo *m*; **in s. of** en busca de; *Comput* **s. engine** motor *m* de búsqueda; **s. party** equipo *m* de salvamento; **s. warrant** orden *f* de registro

searching [ˈsɜːtʃɪŋ] *adj (look)* penetrante; *(question)* indagatorio(a)

searchlight [ˈsɜːtʃlaɪt] *n* reflector *m*

seashell [ˈsiːʃel] *n* concha marina

seashore [ˈsiːʃɔː(r)] *n (beach)* playa *f*

seasick [ˈsiːsɪk] *adj* mareado(a); **to get s.** marearse

seaside ['si:saɪd] *n* playa *f*, costa *f*; **s. resort** lugar turístico de veraneo; **s. town** pueblo costero

season¹ ['si:zən] *n* época *f*; *(of year)* estación *f*; *(for sport etc)* temporada *f*; **the busy s.** la temporada alta; **the rainy s.** la estación de lluvias; **in s.** *(fruit)* en sazón; *(animal)* en celo; *Br* **s. ticket** abono *m*

season² ['si:zən] *vt Culin* sazonar

seasonal ['si:zənəl] *adj* estacional

seasoned ['si:zənd] *adj* **(a)** *Culin* sazonado(a) **(b)** *Fig (campaigner)* curtido(a), avezado(a)

seasoning ['si:zənɪŋ] *n* condimento *m*, aderezo *m*

seat [si:t] **1** *n* **(a)** asiento *m*; *(place)* plaza *f*; *Cin & Th* localidad *f*; **to take a s.** sentarse; *Aut* **s. belt** cinturón *m* de seguridad **(b)** *(of cycle)* sillín *m*; *Fam (buttocks)* trasero *m* **(c)** *(of power, learning)* centro *m*, sede *f* **(d)** *Parl* escaño *m*
2 *vt* **(a)** *(guests etc)* sentar **(b)** *(accommodate)* tener cabida para

seating ['si:tɪŋ] *n* asientos *mpl*; **s. capacity** cabida *f*, aforo *m*

seaweed ['si:wi:d] *n* alga *f* (marina)

seaworthy ['si:wɜːðɪ] *adj* en condiciones de navegar

sec [sek] *n Fam (abbr* **second)** segundo *m*

secede [sɪ'si:d] *vi* separarse **(from** de)

secluded [sɪ'klu:dɪd] *adj* retirado(a), apartado(a)

second¹ ['sekənd] **1** *adj* segundo(a); **every s. day** cada dos días; **it's the s. highest mountain** es la segunda montaña más alta; **on s. thought(s)** ... pensándolo bien ...; **to have s. thoughts about sth** dudar de algo; **to settle for s. best** conformarse con lo que hay
2 *n* **(a)** *(in series)* segundo(a) *m,f*; **Charles the S.** Carlos Segundo; **the s. of October** el dos de octubre **(b)** *Aut (gear)* segunda *f* **(c)** *Com* **seconds** artículos defectuosos
3 *vt (motion)* apoyar
4 *adv* **to come s.** terminar en segundo lugar

second² ['sekənd] *n (time)* segundo *m*; *Fam* **in a s.** enseguida; *Fam* **just a s.!** ¡un momentito!; **s. hand** *(of watch, clock)* segundero *m*

secondary ['sekəndərɪ] *adj* secundario(a); *Br* **s. school** escuela secundaria

second-class ['sekənd'klɑːs] **1** *adj* de segunda clase
2 *adv* **to travel s.** viajar en segunda

second-hand ['sekənd'hænd] *adj & adv* de segunda mano

secondly ['sekəndlɪ] *adv* en segundo lugar

secondment [sɪ'kɒndmənt] *n Br* traslado *m* temporal

second-rate ['sekənd'reɪt] *adj* de segunda categoría

secrecy ['si:krəsɪ] *n* secreto *m*; **in s.** en secreto

secret ['si:krɪt] **1** *adj* secreto(a); **to keep sth s.** mantener algo en secreto; **s. ballot** votación secreta
2 *n* secreto *m*; *Fig* clave *f*; **in s.** en secreto; **to keep a s.** guardar un secreto

secretarial [sekrɪ'teərɪəl] *adj* de secretario(a)

secretary ['sekrətrɪ] *n* secretario(a) *m,f*; **S. of State** *Br* ministro(a) *m,f* sin cartera; *US* ministro(a) *m,f* de Asuntos Exteriores

secretion [sɪ'kri:ʃən] *n* secreción *f*

secretive ['si:krɪtɪv] *adj* reservado(a)

secretly ['si:krɪtlɪ] *adv* en secreto

sect [sekt] *n* secta *f*

sectarian [sek'teərɪən] *adj & n* sectario(a) *(m,f)*

section ['sekʃən] *n* **(a)** *(part)* sección *f*, parte *f*; *(of law)* artículo *m*; *(of community)* sector *m*; *(of orchestra, department)* sección *f* **(b)** *(cut)* corte *m*

sector ['sektə(r)] *n* sector *m*

secular ['sekjʊlə(r)] *adj (school, teaching)* laico(a); *(music, art)* profano(a); *(priest)* seglar, secular

secure [sɪ'kjʊə(r)] **1** *adj* seguro(a); *(window, door)* bien cerrado(a); *(ladder etc)* firme
2 *vt* **(a)** *(make safe)* asegurar **(b)** *(fix) (rope, knot)* sujetar, fijar; *(object to floor)* afianzar; *(window, door)* cerrar bien **(c)** *(obtain)* conseguir, obtener **(d)** *Fin (guarantee)* avalar

security [sɪ'kjʊərɪtɪ] *n* **(a)** seguridad *f*; **national s.** seguridad nacional; **S. Council** *(of United Nations)* Consejo *m* de Seguridad **(b)** *Fin (guarantee)* fianza *f*; *(guarantor)* fiador(a) *m,f* **(c)** *Fin* **securities** valores *mpl*

sedan [sɪ'dæn] *n* **(a)** *Hist* **s. chair** silla *f* de manos **(b)** *US Aut* turismo *m*

sedate [sɪ'deɪt] **1** *adj* sosegado(a)
2 *vt* sedar

sedation [sɪ'deɪʃən] *n* sedación *f*

sedative ['sedətɪv] *adj & n* sedante *(m)*

sediment ['sedɪmənt] *n* sedimento *m*; *(of wine)* poso *m*

seduce [sɪ'dju:s] *vt* seducir

seduction [sɪ'dʌkʃən] *n* seducción *f*

seductive [sɪ'dʌktɪv] *adj* seductor(a)

see¹ [si:] *vt & vi (pt* saw; *pp* seen) **(a)** ver; **I'll s. what can be done** veré lo que se puede hacer; **let's s.** a ver; **that remains to be seen** eso queda por ver; **s. page 10** véase la página 10; **s. you (later)/soon!** ¡hasta luego/pronto!
(b) *(meet with)* ver, tener cita con; **they are seeing each other** *(of couple)* salen juntos
(c) *(visit)* ver; **to s. the world** recorrer el mundo
(d) *(understand)* entender; **as far as I can s.** por lo visto; **I s.** ya veo; **you s., he hasn't got a car** es que no tiene coche, ¿sabes?
(e) **he sees himself as a second Caruso** se cree otro Caruso
(f) *(ensure)* asegurarse de **(g)** **to s. sb home** acompañar a algn a casa
► see about *vt insep (deal with)* ocuparse de

▸ **see off** *vt sep (say goodbye to)* despedirse de

▸ **see out** *vt sep* (a) *(show out)* acompañar hasta la puerta (b) *(survive)* sobrevivir

▸ **see through 1** *vt insep Fam* **to s. through sb** verle el plumero a algn

2 *vt sep* (a) **I'll s. you through** puedes contar con mi ayuda; **£20 should s. me through** con 20 libras me las apaño (b) **to s. sth through** *(carry out)* llevar algo a cabo

▸ **see to** *vt insep (deal with)* ocuparse de

see² [si:] *n Rel* sede *f*; **the Holy S.** la Santa Sede

seed [si:d] **1** *n* (a) *Bot* semilla *f*; *(of fruit)* pepita *f*; **to go to s.** *(of plant)* granar; *Fig (of person)* descuidarse (b) *(in tennis) (player)* cabeza *mf* de serie

2 *vt* (a) *(sow with seed)* sembrar (b) *(grapes)* despepitar (c) *(in tennis)* preseleccionar

seedling ['si:dlɪŋ] *n* plantón *m*

seedy ['si:dɪ] *adj* **(seedier, seediest)** *Fam (bar etc)* sórdido(a); *(clothes)* raído(a); *(appearance)* desaseado(a)

seeing ['si:ɪŋ] *conj* **s. that** visto que, dado que

seeing-eye dog ['si:ŋaɪ'dɒg] *n US* perro *m* lazarillo

seek [si:k] **1** *vt (pt & pp sought)* (a) *(look for)* buscar (b) *(advice, help)* solicitar

2 *vt* buscar; **to s. to do sth** procurar hacer algo

▸ **seek after** *vt insep* buscar; **much sought after** *(person)* muy solicitado(a); *(thing)* muy cotizado(a)

seem [si:m] *vi* parecer; **I s. to remember his name was Colin** creo recordar que su nombre era Colin; **it seems to me that** me parece que; **so it seems** eso parece

seeming ['si:mɪŋ] *adj* aparente

seemingly ['si:mɪŋlɪ] *adv* aparentemente, según parece

seen [si:n] *pp of* **see**

seep [si:p] *vi* **to s. through/into/out** filtrarse por/en/de

seesaw ['si:sɔ:] **1** *n* balancín *m*, subibaja *m*

2 *vi* (a) columpiarse, balancearse (b) *Fig* vacilar, oscilar

seethe [si:ð] *vi* bullir, hervir; *Fig* **to s. with anger** rabiar; **to s. with people** rebosar de gente

see-through ['si:θru:] *adj* transparente

segment ['segmənt] *n* segmento *m*; *(of orange)* gajo *m*

segregate ['segrɪgeɪt] *vt* segregar **(from** de)

segregation [segrɪ'geɪʃən] *n* segregación *f*

seize [si:z] *vt (grab)* agarrar, asir; *Jur (property, drugs)* incautar; *(assets)* secuestrar; *(territory)* tomar; *(arrest)* detener; **to s. an opportunity** aprovechar una ocasión; **to s. power** hacerse con el poder

▸ **seize on** *vt insep (chance)* agarrar; *(idea)* aferrarse a

▸ **seize up** *vi* agarrotarse

seizure ['si:ʒə(r)] *n* (a) *Jur (of property,*

drugs) incautación *f*; *(of newspaper)* secuestro *m*; *(arrest)* detención *f* (b) *Med* ataque *m* (de apoplejía)

seldom ['seldəm] *adv* rara vez, raramente

select [sɪ'lekt] **1** *vt (thing)* escoger, elegir; *(team)* seleccionar

2 *adj* selecto(a)

selected [sɪ'lektɪd] *adj* selecto(a), escogido(a); *(team, player)* seleccionado(a); *Lit* **s. works** obras escogidas

selection [sɪ'lekʃən] *n (choosing)* elección *f*; *(people or things chosen)* selección *f*; *(range)* surtido *m*

selective [sɪ'lektɪv] *adj* selectivo(a)

self [self] *n (pl* **selves)** uno(a) mismo(a), sí mismo(a); *Psy* **the s.** el yo

self- [self] *pref* auto-

self-adhesive [selfəd'hi:sɪv] *adj* autoadhesivo(a)

self-assured [selfə'ʃʊəd] *adj* seguro(a) de sí mismo(a)

self-catering [self'keɪtərɪŋ] *adj* sin servicio de comida

self-centred, *US* **self-centered** [self'sentəd] *adj* egocéntrico(a)

self-confessed [selfkən'fest] *adj* confeso(a)

self-confidence [self'kɒnfɪdəns] *n* confianza *f* en sí mismo(a)

self-confident [self'kɒnfɪdənt] *adj* seguro(a) de sí mismo(a)

self-conscious [self'kɒnʃəs] *adj* cohibido(a)

self-contained [selfkən'teɪnd] *adj (flat)* con entrada propia; *(person)* independiente

self-control [selfkən'trəʊl] *n* autocontrol *m*

self-defence, *US* **self-defense** [selfdɪ'fens] *n* autodefensa *f*

self-discipline [self'dɪsɪplɪn] *n* autodisciplina *f*

self-employed [selfɪm'plɔɪd] *adj (worker)* autónomo(a)

self-esteem [selfɪ'sti:m] *n* amor propio, autoestima *f*

self-evident [self'evɪdənt] *adj* evidente, patente

self-governing [self'gʌvənɪŋ] *adj* autónomo(a)

self-important [selfɪm'pɔ:tənt] *adj* engreído(a), presumido(a)

self-indulgent [selfɪn'dʌldʒənt] *adj* inmoderado(a)

self-interest [self'ɪntrɪst] *n* egoísmo *m*

selfish ['selfɪʃ] *adj* egoísta

selfishness ['selfɪʃnɪs] *n* egoísmo *m*

selfless ['selflɪs] *adj* desinteresado(a)

self-made ['selfmeɪd] *adj* **s. man** hombre *m* que se ha hecho a sí mismo

self-pity [self'pɪtɪ] *n* autocompasión *f*

self-portrait [self'pɔ:treɪt] *n* autorretrato *m*

self-possessed [selfpə'zest] *adj* sereno(a), dueño(a) de sí mismo(a)

self-preservation [selfprezə'veɪʃən] *n* **(instinct of) s.** instinto *m* de conservación

self-raising ['selfreɪzɪŋ] *adj* **s. flour** harina *f* con levadura
self-reliant [selfrɪ'laɪənt] *adj* autosuficiente
self-respect [selfrɪ'spekt] *n* amor propio, dignidad *f*
self-righteous [self'raɪtʃəs] *adj* santurrón(ona)
self-rising ['selfraɪzɪŋ] *adj US* = **self-raising**
self-satisfied [self'sætɪsfaɪd] *adj* satisfecho(a) de sí mismo(a)
self-service [self'sɜːvɪs] **1** *n* (*in shop etc*) autoservicio *m*
2 *adj* de autoservicio
self-sufficient [selfsə'fɪʃənt] *adj* autosuficiente
self-taught [self'tɔːt] *adj* autodidacta
sell [sel] **1** *vt* (*pt & pp* **sold**) vender
2 *vi* venderse; **this record is selling well** este disco se vende bien
3 *n* **hard/soft s.** (*in advertising*) publicidad *f* agresiva/discreta
▸ **sell off** *vt sep* vender; (*goods*) liquidar
▸ **sell out 1** *vi* **to s. out to the enemy** claudicar ante el enemigo
2 *vt sep Com* **we're sold out of sugar** se nos ha agotado el azúcar; *Th* **sold out** (*sign*) agotadas las localidades
seller ['selə(r)] *n* vendedor(a) *m,f*
selling ['selɪŋ] *n* venta *f*; **s. point** atractivo *m* comercial; **s. price** precio *m* de venta
Sellotape® ['seləteɪp] **1** *n* celo® *m*, cinta adhesiva
2 *vt* pegar *or* fijar con celo®
sell-out ['selaʊt] *n* (**a**) *Th* éxito *m* de taquilla (**b**) (*act of disloyalty*) claudicación *f*
selves [selvz] *pl of* **self**
semaphore ['seməfɔː(r)] *n* semáforo *m*
semblance ['sembləns] *n* apariencia *f*; **there was some s. of truth in it** había algo de verdad en ello
semen ['siːmen] *n* semen *m*
semester [sɪ'mestə(r)] *n* semestre *m*
semi- ['semɪ] *pref* semi-
semicircle ['semɪsɜːkəl] *n* semicírculo *m*
semicolon [semɪ'kəʊlən] *n* punto y coma *m*
semiconductor ['semɪkən'dʌktə(r)] *n* semiconductor *m*
semidetached [semɪdɪ'tætʃt] *Br* **1** *adj* adosado(a)
2 *n* chalé adosado, casa adosada
semifinal [semɪ'faɪnəl] *n* semifinal *f*
seminar ['semɪnɑː(r)] *n* seminario *m*
seminary ['semɪnərɪ] *n* seminario *m*
semitrailer ['semɪtreɪlə(r)] *n US* camión articulado
semolina [semə'liːnə] *n* sémola *f*
senate ['senɪt] *n* (**a**) *Pol* senado *m* (**b**) *Univ* claustro *m*
senator ['senətə(r)] *n* senador(a) *m,f*
send [send] **1** *vt* (*pt & pp* **sent**) (**a**) (*letter*) enviar, mandar; (*radio signal*) transmitir; (*rocket, ball*) lanzar; **he was sent to prison** lo

mandaron a la cárcel; **to s. sth flying** tirar algo (**b**) **to s. sb mad** (*cause to become*) volver loco(a) a algn
2 *vi* **to s. for sb** mandar llamar a algn; **to s. for sth** encargar algo
▸ **send away 1** *vt sep* (*dismiss*) despedir
2 *vi* **to s. away for sth** escribir pidiendo algo
▸ **send back** *vt sep* (*goods etc*) devolver; (*person*) hacer volver
▸ **send in** *vt sep* (*application etc*) mandar; (*troops*) enviar
▸ **send off** *vt sep* (**a**) (*letter etc*) enviar; (*goods*) despachar (**b**) *Ftb* (*player*) expulsar
▸ **send on** *vt sep* (*luggage*) (*ahead*) facturar; (*later*) mandar (más tarde)
▸ **send out** *vt sep* (**a**) (*person*) echar (**b**) (*invitations*) enviar (**c**) (*emit*) emitir
▸ **send up** *vt sep* (**a**) hacer subir; (*rocket*) lanzar; (*smoke*) echar (**b**) *Br Fam* (*make fun of*) (*person*) burlarse de; (*book etc*) satirizar
sender ['sendə(r)] *n* remitente *mf*
sendoff ['sendɒf] *n Fam* despedida *f*
senile ['siːnaɪl] *adj* senil
senior ['siːnjə(r)] **1** *adj* (**a**) (*in age*) mayor; **William Armstrong S.** William Armstrong padre; **s. citizen** jubilado(a) *m,f* (**b**) (*in rank*) superior; (*with longer service*) más antiguo(a); *Mil* **s. officer** oficial *mf* de alta graduación
2 *n* (**a**) **she's three years my s.** (*in age*) me lleva tres años (**b**) *US Educ* estudiante *mf* del último curso
seniority [siːnɪ'ɒrɪtɪ] *n* antigüedad *f*
sensation [sen'seɪʃən] *n* sensación *f*; **to be a s.** ser un éxito; **to cause a s.** causar sensación
sensational [sen'seɪʃənəl] *adj* (*marvellous*) sensacional; (*exaggerated*) sensacionalista
sense [sens] **1** *n* (**a**) (*faculty*) sentido *m*; (*feeling*) sensación *f*; **s. of direction/humour** sentido *m* de la orientación/del humor (**b**) (*wisdom*) sentido *m* común, juicio *m*; **common s.** sentido común (**c**) (*meaning*) sentido *m*; (*of word*) significado *m*; **in a s.** en cierto sentido; **it doesn't make s.** no tiene sentido (**d**) **to come to one's senses** recobrar el juicio
2 *vt* sentir, percatarse de
senseless ['senslɪs] *adj* (**a**) (*absurd*) insensato(a), absurdo(a) (**b**) (*unconscious*) sin conocimiento
sensibility [sensɪ'bɪlɪtɪ] *n* (**a**) (*sensitivity*) sensibilidad *f* (**b**) **sensibilities** susceptibilidad *f*
sensible ['sensɪbəl] *adj* (**a**) (*wise*) sensato(a) (**b**) (*choice*) acertado(a) (**c**) (*clothes, shoes*) práctico(a), cómodo(a)

> Note that the Spanish word **sensible** is a false friend and is never a translation for the English word **sensible**. In Spanish, **sensible** means both "sensitive" and "perceptible".

sensitive ['sensɪtɪv] *adj* (**a**) (*person*) sensible;

(touchy) susceptible (**b**) *(skin)* delicado(a); *(document)* confidencial

sensor ['sensə(r)] *n* sensor *m*

sensual ['sensjʊəl] *adj* sensual

sensuous ['sensjʊəs] *adj* sensual

sent [sent] *pt & pp of* **send**

sentence ['sentəns] **1** *n* (**a**) *(phrase)* frase *f; Ling* oración *f* (**b**) *Jur* sentencia *f;* **to pass s. on sb** imponer una pena a algn; **life s.** cadena perpetua
2 *vt Jur* condenar

sentiment ['sentɪmənt] *n* (**a**) *(sentimentality)* sensiblería *f* (**b**) *(feeling)* sentimiento *m* (**c**) *(opinion)* opinión *f*

sentimental [sentɪ'mentəl] *adj* sentimental

sentry ['sentrɪ] *n* centinela *m*

separate 1 *vt* ['sepəreɪt] separar (**from** de); *(divide)* dividir (**into** en); *(distinguish)* distinguir
2 *vi* separarse
3 *adj* ['sepərɪt] separado(a); *(different)* distinto(a); *(entrance)* particular
4 *npl* **separates** ['sepərɪts] *(clothes)* piezas *fpl*

separately ['sepərətlɪ] *adv* por separado

separation [sepə'reɪʃən] *n* separación *f*

separatist ['sepərətɪst] *n* separatista *mf*

September [sep'tembə(r)] *n* se(p)tiembre *m*

septic ['septɪk] *adj* séptico(a); **to become s.** *(of wound)* infectarse; **s. tank** fosa séptica

sequel ['siːkwəl] *n* secuela *f;* *(of film etc)* continuación *f*

sequence ['siːkwəns] *n* (**a**) *(order)* secuencia *f,* orden *m* (**b**) *(series)* serie *f,* sucesión *f; Cin* **film s.** secuencia *f*

serenade [serɪ'neɪd] *n* serenata *f*

serene [sɪ'riːn] *adj* sereno(a), tranquilo(a)

sergeant ['sɑːdʒənt] *n Mil* sargento *mf;* *(of police)* ≃ oficial *mf* de policía; **s. major** sargento *m* mayor

serial ['sɪərɪəl] *n* (**a**) *Rad & TV* serial *m;* *(soap opera)* radionovela *f,* telenovela *f* (**b**) **s. number** número *m* de serie

series ['sɪəriːz] *n* (*pl* **series**) serie *f;* *(of books)* colección *f;* *(of concerts, lectures)* ciclo *m*

serious ['sɪərɪəs] *adj* (**a**) *(solemn, earnest)* serio(a); **I am s.** hablo en serio (**b**) *(causing concern)* grave

seriously ['sɪərɪəslɪ] *adv* (**a**) *(in earnest)* en serio (**b**) *(dangerously, severely)* gravemente

seriousness ['sɪərɪəsnɪs] *n* gravedad *f,* seriedad *f;* **in all s.** hablando en serio

sermon ['sɜːmən] *n* sermón *m*

serpent ['sɜːpənt] *n* serpiente *f*

serrated [sɪ'reɪtɪd] *adj* dentado(a)

serum ['sɪərəm] *n* suero *m*

servant ['sɜːvənt] *n* *(domestic)* criado(a) *m,f; Fig* servidor(a) *m,f*

serve [sɜːv] **1** *vt* (**a**) servir (**b**) *(customer)* atender (**c**) *(in tennis)* servir (**d**) **if my memory serves me right** si mal no recuerdo; **it serves him right** bien merecido lo tiene (**e**)

Fam **to s. time** cumplir una condena; **to s. one's apprenticeship** hacer el aprendizaje
2 *vi* (**a**) servir; **to s. on a committee** ser miembro de una comisión (**b**) *(in tennis)* servir (**c**) *(be useful)* servir (**as** de)
3 *n* *(in tennis)* servicio *m*
▸ **serve out, serve up** *vt sep* servir

service ['sɜːvɪs] **1** *n* (**a**) servicio *m;* **at your s.!** ¡a sus órdenes!; **how can I be of s. to you?** ¿en qué puedo servirle?; **s. (charge) included** servicio incluido; **s. area** área *m* de servicio; **s. industry** sector *m* de servicios; *Br* **s. lift** montacargas *m inv;* **s. station** estación *f* de servicio (**b**) **medical s.** servicios médicos; *Mil* **the Services** las Fuerzas Armadas; **the train s. to Bristol** la línea de trenes a Bristol (**c**) *(maintenance)* revisión *f* (**d**) *Rel* oficio *m;* *(mass)* misa *f* (**e**) *(in tennis)* servicio *m;* **s. line** línea *f* de saque (**f**) *(set of dishes)* juego *m*
2 *vt (car, machine)* revisar

serviceable ['sɜːvɪsəbəl] *adj* (**a**) *(fit for use)* útil, servible (**b**) *(practical)* práctico(a)

serviceman ['sɜːvɪsmən] *n* militar *m*

serviette [sɜːvɪ'et] *n Br* servilleta *f*

sesame ['sesəmɪ] *n* sésamo *m*

session ['seʃən] *n* (**a**) sesión *f;* **to be in s.** estar reunido(a); *(of Parliament, court)* celebrar una sesión (**b**) *Educ (academic year)* año académico

set¹ [set] **1** *vt* (*pt & pp* **set**) (**a**) *(put, place)* poner, colocar; *(trap)* poner (**for** para); **the novel is s. in Moscow** la novela se desarrolla en Moscú; **to s. fire to sth** prender fuego a algo
(**b**) *(time, price)* fijar; *(record)* establecer; *(trend)* imponer
(**c**) *(mechanism etc)* ajustar; *(bone)* encajar; **to s. one's watch** poner el reloj en hora
(**d**) *(arrange)* arreglar; **he s. the words to music** puso música a la letra; **to s. the table** poner la mesa
(**e**) *(exam, homework)* poner; *(example)* dar; *(precedent)* sentar
(**f**) **to s. sail** zarpar; **to s. sb free** poner en libertad a algn; **to s. sth going** poner algo en marcha
(**g**) *(pearl, diamond etc)* engastar
(**h**) *Typ* componer
2 *vi* (**a**) *(sun, moon)* ponerse
(**b**) *(jelly, jam)* cuajar; *(cement)* fraguar; *(bone)* encajarse
(**c**) **to s. to** *(begin)* ponerse a
3 *n* (**a**) shampoo and **s.** lavar y marcar
(**b**) *(stage) Cin* plató *m; Th* escenario *m;* *(scenery)* decorado *m*
4 *adj* (**a**) *(task, idea)* fijo(a); *(date, time)* señalado(a); *(opinion)* inflexible; *(smile)* rígido(a); *(gaze)* fijo(a); **s. phrase** frase hecha; **to be s. on doing sth** estar empeñado(a) en hacer algo; **s. square** cartabón *m*
(**b**) *(ready)* listo(a)
▸ **set about** *vt insep* (**a**) *(begin)* empezar (**b**)

(attack) agredir
► **set aside** *vt sep (time, money)* reservar; *(differences)* dejar de lado
► **set back** *vt sep* (**a**) *(delay)* retrasar; *(hinder)* entorpecer (**b**) *Fam (cost)* costar
► **set down** *vt sep (luggage etc)* dejar (en el suelo); *Br (passengers)* dejar
► **set in** *vi (winter, rain)* comenzar; **panic s. in** cundió el pánico
► **set off 1** *vi (depart)* salir
2 *vt sep* (**a**) *(bomb)* hacer estallar; *(burglar alarm)* hacer sonar; *(reaction)* desencadenar (**b**) *(enhance)* hacer resaltar
► **set out 1** *vi* (**a**) *(depart)* salir; **to s. out for ...** partir hacia ... (**b**) **to s. out to do sth** proponerse hacer algo
2 *vt sep (arrange)* disponer; *(present)* presentar
► **set up 1** *vt sep* (**a**) *(position)* colocar; *(statue, camp)* levantar; *(tent, stall)* montar (**b**) *(business etc)* establecer; *Fam* montar; *(committee)* constituir; *Fam* **you've been s. up!** ¡te han timado!
2 *vi* establecerse
set² [set] *n* (**a**) *(series)* serie *f*; *(of golf clubs etc)* juego *m*; *(of tools)* estuche *m*; *(of turbines etc)* equipo *m*; *(of books, poems)* colección *f*; *(of teeth)* dentadura *f*; **chess s.** juego de ajedrez; **s. of cutlery** cubertería *f*; **s. of kitchen utensils** batería *f* de cocina (**b**) *(of people)* grupo *m*; *Pej (clique)* camarilla *f* (**c**) *Math* conjunto *m* (**d**) *(in tennis)* set *m* (**e**) **TV s.** televisor *m*
setback ['setbæk] *n* revés *m*, contratiempo *m*
settee [se'ti:] *n* sofá *m*
setting ['setɪŋ] *n* (**a**) *(background)* marco *m*; *(of novel, film)* escenario *m* (**b**) *(of jewel)* engaste *m*
settle ['setəl] **1** *vt* (**a**) *(put in position)* colocar (**b**) *(decide on)* acordar; *(date, price)* fijar; *(problem)* resolver; *(differences)* arreglar (**c**) *(debt)* pagar; *(account)* saldar (**d**) *(nerves)* calmar; *(stomach)* asentar (**e**) *Fam (put an end to)* acabar con (**f**) *(establish) (person)* instalar (**g**) *(colonize)* asentarse en
2 *vi* (**a**) *(bird, insect)* posarse; *(dust)* depositarse; *(snow)* cuajar; *(sediment)* precipitarse; *(liquid)* asentarse; **to s. into an armchair** acomodarse en un sillón (**b**) *(put down roots)* afincarse; *(in a colony)* asentarse (**c**) *(weather)* serenarse (**d**) *(child, nerves)* calmarse (**e**) *(pay)* pagar; **to s. out of court** llegar a un acuerdo amistoso
► **settle down** *vi* (**a**) *(put down roots)* instalarse; *(marry)* casarse (**b**) **to s. down to work** ponerse a trabajar (**c**) *(child)* calmarse; *(situation)* normalizarse
► **settle for** *vt insep* conformarse con
► **settle in** *vi (move in)* instalarse; *(become adapted)* adaptarse

► **settle with** *vt sep (pay debt to)* ajustar cuentas con
settlement ['setəlmənt] *n* (**a**) *(agreement)* acuerdo *m* (**b**) *(of debt)* pago *m*; *(of account)* liquidación *f* (**c**) *(dowry)* dote *f* (**d**) *(colonization)* colonización *f* (**e**) *(colony)* asentamiento *m*; *(village)* poblado *m*
settler ['setlə(r)] *n* colono *m*
setup ['setʌp] *n* (**system**) sistema *m*; *(situation)* situación *f*; *Fam* montaje *m*
seven ['sevən] *adj & n* siete *(m inv)*
seventeen [sevən'ti:n] *adj & n* diecisiete *(m inv)*, diez y siete *(m inv)*
seventeenth [sevən'ti:nθ] **1** *adj & n* decimoséptimo(a) *(m,f)*
2 *n (fraction)* decimoséptima parte
seventh ['sevənθ] **1** *adj & n* séptimo(a) *(m,f)*
2 *n* séptimo *m*
seventy ['sevəntɪ] *adj & n* setenta *(m inv)*
sever ['sevə(r)] *vt (cut)* cortar; *Fig (relations)* romper
several ['sevərəl] **1** *adj* (**a**) *(more than a few)* varios(as) (**b**) *(different)* distintos(as)
2 *pron* algunos(as)
severance ['sevərəns] *n (of relations etc)* ruptura *f*; **s. pay** indemnización *f* por despido
severe [sɪ'vɪə(r)] *adj (a) (climate, blow)* duro(a); *(illness, loss)* grave; *(pain)* intenso(a)
severity [sɪ'verɪtɪ] *n (of person, criticism, punishment)* severidad *f*; *(of climate)* rigor *m*; *(of illness)* gravedad *f*; *(of pain)* intensidad *f*; *(of style)* austeridad *f*
Seville [sə'vɪl] *n* Sevilla
sew [səʊ] *vt & vi (pt* **sewed**; *pp* **sewed** *or* **sewn**) coser
► **sew up** *vt sep (stitch together)* coser; *(mend)* remendar
sewage ['su:ɪdʒ] *n* aguas *fpl* residuales
sewer ['su:ə(r)] *n* alcantarilla *f*, cloaca *f*
sewerage ['su:ərɪdʒ] *n* alcantarillado *m*
sewing ['səʊɪŋ] *n* costura *f*; **s. machine** máquina *f* de coser
sewn [səʊn] *pp of* **sew**
sex [seks] *n* sexo *m*; **s. education** educación *f* sexual; **to have s. with sb** tener relaciones sexuales con algn; **s. appeal** sex-appeal *m*
sexist ['seksɪst] *adj & n* sexista *(mf)*
sexual ['seksjʊəl] *adj* sexual
sexuality [seksjʊ'ælɪtɪ] *n* sexualidad *f*
sexy ['seksɪ] *adj* (**sexier, sexiest**) *Fam* sexi, erótico(a)
shabby ['ʃæbɪ] *adj* (**shabbier, shabbiest**) (**a**) *(garment)* raído(a); *(house)* desvencijado(a); *(person) (in rags)* harapiento(a); *(unkempt)* desaseado(a) (**b**) *(treatment)* mezquino(a)
shack [ʃæk] *n* choza *f*
shackles ['ʃækəlz] *npl* grilletes *mpl*, grillos *mpl*; *Fig* trabas *fpl*
shade [ʃeɪd] **1** *n* (**a**) *(shadow)* sombra *f*; **in the s.** a la sombra (**b**) *(eyeshade)* visera *f*; *(lampshade)* pantalla *f*; *US (blind)* persiana *f* (**c**) *(of*

colour) tono m, matiz m; Fig (of meaning)
matiz (**d**) (small amount) poquito m (**e**) Fam
shades gafas fpl or Am anteojos mpl de sol

2 vt (from sun) proteger contra el sol

shadow ['ʃædəʊ] **1** n (**a**) (shade) sombra f;
(darkness) oscuridad f; Fig **without a s. of a
doubt** sin lugar a dudas (**b**) Br **the S. Cabinet**
el gabinete de la oposición

2 vt Fig seguir la pista a

shadowy ['ʃædəʊɪ] adj (dark) oscuro(a);
(hazy) vago(a)

shady ['ʃeɪdɪ] adj (**shadier, shadiest**) (place)
a la sombra; (suspicious) (person) sospecho-
so(a); (deal) turbio(a)

shaft [ʃɑːft] n (**a**) (of tool, golf club) mango m;
(of lance) asta f; (of arrow) astil m (**b**) Tech eje
m (**c**) (of mine) pozo m; (of lift, elevator)
hueco m (**d**) (beam of light) rayo m

shaggy ['ʃægɪ] adj (**shaggier, shaggiest**)
(hairy) peludo(a); (long-haired) melenu-
do(a); (beard) desgreñado(a)

shake [ʃeɪk] **1** n sacudida f

2 vt (pt **shook**; pp **shaken** ['ʃeɪkən]) (carpet
etc) sacudir; (bottle) agitar; (dice) mover;
(building) hacer temblar; **the news shook
him** la noticia le conmocionó; **to s. hands
with sb** estrechar la mano a algn; **to s. one's
head** negar con la cabeza

3 vi (person, building) temblar; **to s. with
cold** tiritar de frío

▸ **shake off** vt sep (**a**) (dust etc) sacudirse (**b**)
Fig (bad habit) librarse de; (cough, cold)
quitarse de encima; (pursuer) dar esquinazo
a

▸ **shake up** vt sep Fig (shock) trastornar; (reorganize) reorganizar

shake-up ['ʃeɪkʌp] n Fig reorganización f

shaky ['ʃeɪkɪ] adj (**shakier, shakiest**) (hand,
voice) tembloroso(a); (step) inseguro(a);
(handwriting) tembón(ona)

shall [ʃæl, unstressed ʃəl] v aux

> En el inglés hablado, y en el escrito en estilo co-
> loquial, el verbo **shall** se contrae de manera que
> **I/you/he** etc **shall** se transforman en **I'll/
> you'll/he'll** etc. La forma negativa **shall not**
> se transforma en **shan't**.

(**a**) (used to form future tense) (first person
only) **I s.** or **I'll buy it** lo compraré; **I s. not** or **I
shan't say anything** no diré nada (**b**) (used to
form questions) (usu first person) **s. I close the
door?** ¿cierro la puerta?; **s. I mend it for you?**
¿quieres que te lo repare?; **s. we go?** ¿nos vamos? (**c**) (emphatic, command, threat) (all
persons) **we s. overcome** venceremos; **you s.
leave immediately** te irás enseguida

shallow ['ʃæləʊ] adj poco profundo(a); Fig
superficial

sham [ʃæm] **1** adj falso(a); (illness etc) fingi-
do(a)

2 n (**a**) (pretence) engaño m, farsa f (**b**)
(person) fantoche m

3 vt fingir, simular

4 vi fingir

shambles ['ʃæmbəlz] n sing confusión f; **the
performance was a s.** la función fue un
desastre

shame [ʃeɪm] **1** n (**a**) vergüenza f; Andes,
CAm, Carib, Méx pena f; **to put to s.** (far
outdo) eclipsar, sobrepasar (**b**) (pity) pena f,
lástima f; **what a s.!** ¡qué pena!, ¡qué lástima!

2 vt avergonzar, Andes, CAm, Carib, Méx
apenar; (disgrace) deshonrar

shamefaced ['ʃeɪmfeɪst] adj avergonza-
do(a), Andes, CAm, Carib, Méx apenado(a)

shameful ['ʃeɪmfʊl] adj vergonzoso(a)

shameless ['ʃeɪmlɪs] adj descarado(a)

shampoo [ʃæm'puː] **1** n champú m

2 vt lavar con champú; **to s. one's hair**
lavarse el pelo

shamrock ['ʃæmrɒk] n trébol m

shandy ['ʃændɪ] n Br clara f, cerveza f con
gaseosa

shantytown ['ʃæntɪtaʊn] n barrio m de chabolas, Arg villa f miseria, Chile población f
callampa, Méx ciudad f perdida, Urug cantegril m, Ven rancho m

shape [ʃeɪp] **1** n (**a**) (shape) forma f; (shadow)
silueta m; **to take s.** tomar forma (**b**) in good/bad s.
(condition) en buen/mal estado; **to be in
good s.** (health) estar en forma

2 vt dar forma a; (clay) modelar; (stone)
tallar; (character) formar; (destiny) determinar; **star-shaped** con forma de estrella

3 vi (also **s. up**) tomar forma; **to s. up well**
(events) tomar buen cariz; (person) hacer
progresos

shapeless ['ʃeɪplɪs] adj amorfo(a), informe

shapely ['ʃeɪplɪ] adj (**shapelier, shapeliest**)
escultural

share ['ʃeə(r)] **1** n (**a**) (portion) parte f (**b**) Fin
acción f; **s. index** índice m de la Bolsa; **s.
prices** cotizaciones fpl

2 vt (**a**) (divide) dividir (**b**) (have in common)
compartir

3 vi compartir

▸ **share out** vt sep repartir

shareholder ['ʃeəhəʊldə(r)] n accionista mf

shark [ʃɑːk] n (**a**) (fish) tiburón m (**b**) Fam
(swindler) estafador(a) m,f; **loan s.** usurero(a)
m,f

sharp [ʃɑːp] **1** adj (**a**) (razor, knife) afilado(a);
(needle, pencil) puntiagudo(a)

(**b**) (angle) agudo(a); (features) angulo-
so(a); (bend) cerrado(a)

(**c**) (outline) definido(a); (contrast) marca-
do(a)

(**d**) (observant) perspicaz; (clever) listo(a);
(quick-witted) avispado(a); (cunning) astu-
to(a)

(**e**) (sudden) brusco(a)

(**f**) (pain, cry) agudo(a); (wind) penetrante

(**g**) (sour) acre

(**h**) (criticism) mordaz; (temper) arisco(a);

(tone) seco(a)

  (**i**) *Mus* sostenido(a); *(out of tune)* desafinado(a)

  2 *adv* **at two o'clock s.** *(exactly)* a las dos en punto

  3 *n Mus* sostenido *m*

sharpen ['ʃɑːpən] *vt* (**a**) *(knife)* afilar; *(pencil)* sacar punta a (**b**) *Fig (desire, intelligence)* agudizar

sharpener ['ʃɑːpənə(r)] *n (for knife)* afilador *m; (for pencil)* sacapuntas *m inv*

sharp-eyed ['ʃɑːpaɪd] *adj* con ojos de lince

sharply ['ʃɑːplɪ] *adv* (**a**) *(abruptly)* bruscamente (**b**) *(clearly)* marcadamente

shatter ['ʃætə(r)] **1** *vt* hacer añicos, *(nerves)* destrozar; *(hopes)* frustrar

  2 *vi* hacerse añicos

shave [ʃeɪv] **1** *n* afeitado *m;* **to have a s.** afeitarse; *Fig* **to have a close s.** escaparse por los pelos

  2 *vt* *(pt* **shaved***; pp* **shaved** *or* **shaven** ['ʃeɪvən]) *(person)* afeitar; *(wood)* cepillar

  3 *vi* afeitarse

shaver ['ʃeɪvə(r)] *n* (**electric) s.** máquina *f* de afeitar

shaving ['ʃeɪvɪŋ] *n* (**a**) *(of wood)* viruta *f* (**b**) **s. brush** brocha *f* de afeitar; **s. cream** crema *f* de afeitar; **s. foam** espuma *f* de afeitar

shawl [ʃɔːl] *n* chal *m*

she [ʃiː] *pers pron* ella *(usually omitted in Spanish, except for contrast)*

she- [ʃiː] *pref (of animal)* hembra; **s.-cat** gata *f*

sheaf [ʃiːf] *n (pl* **sheaves***) Agr* gavilla *f; (of arrows)* haz *m; (of papers, banknotes)* fajo *m*

shear [ʃɪə(r)] **1** *vt* *(pt* **sheared***; pp* **shorn** *or* **sheared***) (sheep)* esquilar; **to s. off** cortar

  2 *vi* esquilar ovejas

shears [ʃɪəz] *npl* tijeras *fpl* (grandes)

sheath [ʃiːθ] *n* (**a**) *(for sword)* vaina *f; (for knife, scissors)* funda *f* (**b**) *(contraceptive)* preservativo *m*

sheaves [ʃiːvz] *pl of* **sheaf**

shed¹ [ʃed] *n (in garden)* cobertizo *m; (workmen's hut)* barraca *f; (for cattle)* establo *m; (in factory)* nave *f*

shed² [ʃed] *vt* *(pt & pp* **shed***)* (**a**) *(clothes)* despojarse de; *(unwanted thing)* deshacerse de; **the snake s. its skin** la serpiente mudó de piel (**b**) *(blood, tears)* derramar

sheen [ʃiːn] *n* brillo *m*

sheep [ʃiːp] *n (pl* **sheep***)* oveja *f*

sheepdog ['ʃiːpdɒg] *n* perro *m* pastor

sheepish ['ʃiːpɪʃ] *adj* avergonzado(a)

sheepskin ['ʃiːpskɪn] *n* piel *f* de carnero

sheer [ʃɪə(r)] *adj* (**a**) *(utter)* total, puro(a) (**b**) *(cliff)* escarpado(a); *(drop)* vertical (**c**) *(stockings, cloth)* fino(a)

sheet [ʃiːt] *n* (**a**) *(on bed)* sábana *f* (**b**) *(of paper)* hoja *f; (of tin, glass, plastic)* lámina *f; (of ice)* capa *f*

sheik(h) [ʃeɪk] *n* jeque *m*

shelf [ʃelf] *n (pl* **shelves***) (on bookcase)* es-

tante *m; (in cupboard)* tabla *f;* **shelves** estantería *f*

shell [ʃel] **1** *n* (**a**) *(of egg, nut)* cáscara *f; (of pea)* vaina *f; (of tortoise etc)* caparazón *m; (of snail etc)* concha *f* (**b**) *(of building)* armazón *m* (**c**) *(mortar etc)* obús *m*, proyectil *m; (cartridge)* cartucho *m;* **s. shock** neurosis *f* de guerra

  2 *vt* (**a**) *(peas)* desvainar; *(nuts)* pelar (**b**) *Mil* bombardear

shellfish ['ʃelfɪʃ] *n (pl* **shellfish***)* marisco *m*, mariscos *mpl*

shelter ['ʃeltə(r)] **1** *n* (**a**) *(protection)* abrigo *m*, amparo *m;* **to take s. (from)** refugiarse (de) (**b**) *(place)* refugio *m; (for homeless)* asilo *m;* **bus s.** marquesina *f*

  2 *vt* (**a**) *(protect)* abrigar, proteger (**b**) *(take into one's home)* ocultar

  3 *vi* refugiarse

sheltered ['ʃeltəd] *adj (place)* abrigado(a); **to lead a s. life** vivir apartado(a) del mundo

shelve [ʃelv] *vt Fig (postpone)* dar carpetazo a

shelves [ʃelvz] *pl of* **shelf**

shepherd ['ʃepəd] **1** *n* pastor *m;* **s.'s pie** = pastel de carne picada con puré de patatas *or Am* papas

  2 *vt Fig* **to s. sb in** hacer entrar a algn

sheriff ['ʃerɪf] *n Br* gobernador *m* civil; *Scot* juez *m* presidente; *US* sheriff *m*

sherry ['ʃerɪ] *n* jerez *m*

Shetland ['ʃetlənd] *n* **the S. Isles, S.** las Islas Shetland; **S. wool** lana *f* Shetland

shield [ʃiːld] **1** *n* (**a**) escudo *m; (of policeman)* placa *f* (**b**) *(on machinery)* blindaje *m*

  2 *vt* proteger (**from** de)

shift [ʃɪft] **1** *n* (**a**) *(change)* cambio *m; US Aut* (**gear) s.** cambio de velocidad (**b**) *(period of work, group of workers)* turno *m;* **to be on the day s.** hacer el turno de día

  2 *vt (change)* cambiar; *(move)* cambiar de sitio, trasladar

  3 *vi (move)* moverse; *(change place)* cambiar de sitio; *(opinion)* cambiar; *(wind)* cambiar de dirección

shiftless ['ʃɪftlɪs] *n* perezoso(a), vago(a)

shiftwork ['ʃɪftwɜːk] *n* trabajo *m* por turnos

shifty ['ʃɪftɪ] *adj* (**shiftier, shiftiest**) *(look)* furtivo(a); *(person)* sospechoso(a)

shilling ['ʃɪlɪŋ] *n* chelín *m*

shimmer ['ʃɪmə(r)] **1** *vi* relucir; *(shine)* brillar

  2 *n* luz trémula, reflejo trémulo; *(shining)* brillo *m*

shin [ʃɪn] *n* espinilla *f;* **s. pad** espinillera *f*

shine [ʃaɪn] **1** *vi* *(pt & pp* **shone***)* (**a**) *(light)* brillar; *(metal)* relucir (**b**) *Fig (excel)* sobresalir (**at** en)

  2 *vt* (**a**) *(lamp)* dirigir (**b**) *(pt & pp* **shined***) (polish)* sacar brillo a; *(shoes)* limpiar

  3 *n* brillo *m*, lustre *m*

shingle ['ʃɪŋgəl] *n* (**a**) *(pebbles)* guijarros *mpl* (**b**) *(roof tile)* tablilla *f*

shingles ['ʃɪŋgəlz] *n sing Med* herpes *m*
shining ['ʃaɪnɪŋ] *adj Fig (outstanding)* ilustre
shiny ['ʃaɪnɪ] *adj* (**shinier, shiniest**) brillante
ship [ʃɪp] **1** *n* barco *m*, buque *m*
2 *vt* (**a**) *(take on board)* embarcar (**b**) *(transport)* transportar (en barco); *(send)* enviar, mandar
shipbuilding ['ʃɪpbɪldɪŋ] *n* construcción *f* naval
shipment ['ʃɪpmənt] *n* (**a**) *(act)* transporte *m* (**b**) *(load)* consignación *f*, envío *m*
shipper ['ʃɪpə(r)] *n (person)* cargador(a) *m,f*
shipping ['ʃɪpɪŋ] *n* (**a**) *(ships)* barcos *mpl*; **s. lane** vía *f* de navegación (**b**) *(loading)* embarque *m*; *(transporting)* transporte *m* (en barco); **s. company** compañía naviera
shipshape ['ʃɪpʃeɪp] *adj & adv* en perfecto orden
shipwreck ['ʃɪprek] **1** *n* naufragio *m*
2 *vt* **to be shipwrecked** naufragar
shipyard ['ʃɪpjɑːd] *n* astillero *m*
shire [ʃaɪə(r)] *n Br* condado *m*
shirk [ʃɜːk] **1** *vt (duty)* faltar a; *(problem)* eludir
2 *vi* gandulear
shirt [ʃɜːt] *n* camisa *f*; **in s. sleeves** en mangas de camisa; *Fam* **keep your s. on!** ¡no te sulfures!
shit [ʃɪt] *Vulg* **1** *n* mierda *f*; **in the s.** jodido(a)
2 *interj* ¡mierda!
3 *vi* cagar
shiver ['ʃɪvə(r)] **1** *vi (with cold)* tiritar; *(with fear)* temblar, estremecerse
2 *n (with cold, fear)* escalofrío *m*
shoal [ʃəʊl] *n (of fish)* banco *m*
shock [ʃɒk] **1** *n* (**a**) *(jolt)* choque *m*; **s. absorber** amortiguador *m*; **s. wave** onda expansiva (**b**) *(upset)* conmoción *f*; *(scare)* susto *m* (**c**) *Med* shock *m*
2 *vt (upset)* conmover; *(startle)* sobresaltar; *(scandalize)* escandalizar
shocking ['ʃɒkɪŋ] *adj* (**a**) *(causing horror)* espantoso(a); *Fam (very bad)* horroroso(a) (**b**) *(disgraceful)* escandaloso(a) (**c**) **s. pink** rosa chillón
shod [ʃɒd] *pt & pp of* **shoe**
shoddy ['ʃɒdɪ] *adj* (**shoddier, shoddiest**) *(goods)* de mala calidad; *(work)* chapucero(a)
shoe [ʃuː] **1** *n* (**a**) zapato *m*; *(for horse)* herradura *f*; **brake s.** zapata *f*; **s. polish** betún *m*; **s. repair (shop)** remiendo *m* de zapatos; **s. shop**, *US* **s. store** zapatería *f* (**b**) **shoes** calzado *m*
2 *vt (pt & pp shod) (horse)* herrar
shoebrush ['ʃuːbrʌʃ] *n* cepillo *m* para los zapatos
shoehorn ['ʃuːhɔːn] *n* calzador *m*
shoelace ['ʃuːleɪs] *n* cordón *m* (de zapatos)
shoestring ['ʃuːstrɪŋ] *n Fig* **to do sth on a s.** hacer algo con poquísimo dinero
shone [ʃɒn, *US* ʃəʊn] *pt & pp of* **shine**

shoo [ʃuː] **1** *interj* ¡fuera!
2 *vt* **to s. (away)** espantar
shook [ʃʊk] *pt of* **shake**
shoot [ʃuːt] **1** *n Bot* retoño *m*; *(of vine)* sarmiento *m*
2 *vt (pt & pp shot)* (**a**) pegar un tiro a; *(kill)* matar; *(execute)* fusilar; *(hunt)* cazar; **to s. dead** matar a tiros (**b**) *(missile, glance)* lanzar; *(bullet, ball)* disparar (**c**) *(film)* rodar, filmar; *Phot* fotografiar
3 *vi* (**a**) *(with gun)* disparar (**at sb** a algn); **to s. at a target** tirar al blanco; *Ftb* **to s. at the goal** chutar a puerta (**b**) **to s. past** *or* **by** pasar flechado(a)
▶ **shoot down** *vt sep (aircraft)* derribar
▶ **shoot out** *vi (person)* salir disparado(a); *(water)* brotar; *(flames)* salir
▶ **shoot up** *vi (flames)* salir, *(water)* brotar; *(prices)* dispararse (**b**) *Fam (inject drugs)* chutarse
shooting ['ʃuːtɪŋ] **1** *n* (**a**) *(shots)* tiros *mpl*; *(murder)* asesinato *m*; *(hunting)* caza *f*; **s. star** estrella *f* fugaz (**b**) *(of film)* rodaje *m*
2 *adj (pain)* punzante
shoot-out ['ʃuːtaʊt] *n* tiroteo *m*
shop [ʃɒp] **1** *n* (**a**) tienda *f*; *(large store)* almacén *m*; **s. assistant** dependiente(a) *m,f*; **s. window** escaparate *m* (**b**) *(workshop)* taller *m*; **s. floor** *(place)* planta *f*, *(workers)* obreros *mpl*; **s. steward** enlace *mf* sindical
2 *vi* hacer compras; **to go shopping** ir de compras
shopkeeper ['ʃɒpkiːpə(r)] *n* tendero(a) *m,f*
shoplifter ['ʃɒplɪftə(r)] *n* ladrón(ona) *m,f* (de tiendas)
shopper ['ʃɒpə(r)] *n* comprador(a) *m,f*
shopping ['ʃɒpɪŋ] *n (purchases)* compras *fpl*; **s. bag/basket** bolsa *f*/cesta *f* de la compra; **s. centre** *or* **precinct** centro *m* comercial
shopsoiled ['ʃɒpsɔɪld], *US* **shopworn** ['ʃɒpwɔːn] *adj* deteriorado(a)
shore [ʃɔː(r)] *n (of sea, lake)* orilla *f*; *US (beach)* playa *f*; *(coast)* costa *f*; **to go on s.** desembarcar
▶ **shore up** *vt sep* apuntalar
shorn [ʃɔːn] *pp of* **shear**
short [ʃɔːt] **1** *adj* (**a**) corto(a); *(not tall)* bajo(a); **in a s. while** dentro de un rato; **in the s. term** a corto plazo; **s. circuit** cortocircuito *m*; **s. cut** atajo *m*; *Br* **s. list** lista *f* de seleccionados; **s. story** relato corto, cuento *m*; **s. wave** onda corta
(**b**) *(brief)* corto(a), breve; **"Bob" is s. for "Robert"** "Bob" es el diminutivo de "Robert"; **for s.** para abreviar; **in s.** en pocas palabras
(**c**) **to be s. of breath** faltarle a uno la respiración; **to be s. of food** andar escaso(a) de comida
(**d**) *(curt)* brusco(a), seco(a)
2 *adv* (**a**) **to pull up s.** pararse en seco
(**b**) **to cut s.** *(holiday)* interrumpir; *(meeting)* suspender; **we're running s. of coffee** se nos

está acabando el café
  (**c**) **s. of** *(except)* excepto, menos
  3 *n* (**a**) *Cin* cortometraje *m*
  (**b**) *Fam (drink)* copa *f*
  4 *vi* **to s. (out)** tener un cortocircuito

shortage [ˈʃɔːtɪdʒ] *n* escasez *f*
shortbread [ˈʃɔːtbred] *n* mantecado *m*
short-change [ʃɔːtˈtʃeɪndʒ] *vt* **to s. sb** no devolver el cambio completo a algn; *Fig* timar a algn
short-circuit [ʃɔːtˈsɜːkɪt] **1** *vt* provocar un cortocircuito en
  2 *vi* tener un cortocircuito
shortcomings [ˈʃɔːtkʌmɪŋz] *npl* defectos *mpl*
shortcrust [ˈʃɔːtkrʌst] *n* **s. pastry** pasta brisa
shorten [ˈʃɔːtən] *vt (skirt, visit)* acortar; *(word)* abreviar; *(text)* resumir
shortfall [ˈʃɔːtfɔːl] *n* déficit *m*
shorthand [ˈʃɔːthænd] *n* taquigrafía *f*; *Br* **s. typist** taquimecanógrafo(a) *m,f*
short-list [ˈʃɔːtlɪst] *vt* poner en la lista de seleccionados
short-lived [ʃɔːtˈlɪvd] *adj* efímero(a)
shortly [ˈʃɔːtlɪ] *adv (soon)* dentro de poco; **s. after** poco después
short-range [ˈʃɔːtreɪndʒ] *adj* de corto alcance
shorts [ʃɔːts] *npl* (**a**) pantalones *mpl* cortos; **a pair of s.** un pantalón corto (**b**) *US (underpants)* calzoncillos *mpl*
short-sighted [ʃɔːtˈsaɪtɪd] *adj (person)* miope; *Fig (plan etc)* sin visión de futuro
short-staffed [ʃɔːtˈstɑːft] *adj* escaso(a) de personal
short-tempered [ʃɔːtˈtempəd] *adj* de mal genio
short-term [ˈʃɔːtɜːm] *adj* a corto plazo
shot¹ [ʃɒt] *n* (**a**) *(act, sound)* tiro *m*, disparo *m* (**b**) *(projectile)* bala *f*; *(pellets)* perdigones *mpl*; *Fig* **he was off like a s.** salió disparado; *Sport* **s. put** lanzamiento de peso (**c**) *(person)* tirador(a) *m,f* (**d**) *Ftb (kick)* tiro *m* (a puerta); *(in billiards, cricket, golf)* golpe *m* (**e**) *(attempt)* tentativa *f*; **to have a s. at sth** intentar hacer algo (**f**) *(injection)* inyección *f*; *Fam* pinchazo *m* (**g**) *(drink)* trago *m* (**h**) *Phot* foto *f*; *Cin* toma *f*
shot² [ʃɒt] *pt & pp of* **shoot**
shotgun [ˈʃɒtɡʌn] *n* escopeta *f*
should [ʃʊd, *unstressed* ʃəd] *v aux* (**a**) *(duty)* deber; **all employees s. wear helmets** todos los empleados deben llevar casco; **he s. have been an architect** debería haber sido arquitecto (**b**) *(probability)* deber de; **he s. have finished by now** ya debe de haber acabado; **this s. be interesting** esto promete ser interesante (**c**) *(conditional use)* **if anything strange s. happen** si pasara algo raro (**d**) **I s. like to ask a question** quisiera hacer una pregunta

---

La forma negativa **should not** se transforma en **shouldn't**.

---

shoulder [ˈʃəʊldə(r)] **1** *n* (**a**) hombro *m*; **s. blade** omóplato *m*; **s. strap** *(of garment)* tirante *m*; *(of bag)* correa *f*; *BrAut* **hard s.** arcén *m*, *Andes* berma *f*, *Méx* acotamiento *m*, *RP* banquina *f*, *Ven* hombrillo *m* (**b**) *Culin* paletilla *f* (**c**) *US Aut* arcén *m*, *Andes* berma *f*, *Méx* acotamiento *m*, *RP* banquina *f*, *Ven* hombrillo *m*
  2 *vt Fig (responsibilities)* cargar con
shout [ʃaʊt] **1** *n* grito *m*
  2 *vt* gritar
  3 *vi* gritar; **to s. at sb** gritar a algn
▸ **shout down** *vt sep* abuchear
shouting [ˈʃaʊtɪŋ] *n* gritos *mpl*, vocerío *m*
shove [ʃʌv] **1** *n* empujón *m*
  2 *vt* empujar; **to s. sth into one's pocket** meterse algo en el bolsillo a empellones
  3 *vi* empujar; *(jostle)* dar empellones
▸ **shove off** *vi Fam* largarse
▸ **shove up** *vi Fam (move along)* correrse
shovel [ˈʃʌvəl] **1** *n* pala *f*; **mechanical s.** excavadora *f*
  2 *vt* mover con pala *or* a paladas
show [ʃəʊ] **1** *vt* (*pt* **showed**; *pp* **shown** *or* **showed**) (**a**) *(ticket etc)* mostrar; *(painting etc)* exponer; *(film)* poner; *(latest plans etc)* presentar
  (**b**) *(display)* demostrar; **to s. oneself to be** comportarse como
  (**c**) *(teach)* enseñar; *(explain)* explicar
  (**d**) *(temperature, way etc)* indicar; *(profit etc)* registrar
  (**e**) *(prove)* demostrar
  (**f**) *(conduct)* llevar; **to s. sb in** hacer pasar a algn; **to s. sb to the door** acompañar a algn hasta la puerta
  2 *vi* (**a**) *(be visible)* notarse
  (**b**) *Fam (turn up)* aparecer
  (**c**) *Cin* **what's showing?** ¿qué ponen?
  3 *n* (**a**) *(display)* demostración *f*
  (**b**) *(outward appearance)* apariencia *f*
  (**c**) *(exhibition)* exposición *f*; **on s.** expuesto(a); **boat s.** salón náutico; **motor s.** salón del automóvil
  (**d**) *Th (entertainment)* espectáculo *m*; *(performance)* función *f*; *Rad TV* programa *m*; **s. business** *or Fam* **biz** el mundo del espectáculo
▸ **show off 1** *vt sep* (**a**) *(highlight)* hacer resaltar (**b**) *Fam (flaunt)* hacer alarde de
  2 *vi Fam* farolear
▸ **show up 1** *vt sep* (**a**) *(reveal)* sacar a luz; *(highlight)* hacer resaltar (**b**) *Fam (embarrass)* dejar en evidencia
  2 *vi* (**a**) *(stand out)* destacarse (**b**) *Fam (arrive)* aparecer
showdown [ˈʃəʊdaʊn] *n* enfrentamiento *m*
shower [ˈʃaʊə(r)] **1** *n* (**a**) *(rain)* chubasco *m*, chaparrón *m* (**b**) *Fig (of stones, blows etc)*

lluvia f (**c**) (*bath*) ducha f, *Col, Méx, Ven* regadera f; **to have a s.** ducharse
2 vt (**a**) (*spray*) rociar (**b**) *Fig* **to s. gifts/ praise on sb** colmar a algn de regalos/elogios
3 vi ducharse

showerproof ['ʃaʊəpruːf] *adj* impermeable
showing ['ʃəʊɪŋ] n (*of film*) proyección f
showjumping ['ʃəʊdʒʌmpɪŋ] n hípica f
shown [ʃəʊn] pp of **show**
show-off ['ʃəʊɒf] n Fam farolero(a) m,f
showpiece ['ʃəʊpiːs] n (*in exhibition etc*) obra maestra; *Fig* (*at school etc*) modelo m
showroom ['ʃəʊruːm] n Com exposición f; Art galería f

shrank [ʃræŋk] pt of **shrink**
shrapnel ['ʃræpnəl] n metralla f
shred [ʃred] **1** n triza f; (*of cloth*) jirón m; (*of paper*) tira f
2 vt (*paper*) hacer trizas; (*vegetables*) rallar
shredder ['ʃredə(r)] n (*for waste paper*) trituradora f; (*for vegetables*) rallador m
shrew [ʃruː] n (**a**) Zool musaraña f (**b**) Fig (*woman*) arpía f
shrewd [ʃruːd] adj astuto(a); (*clear-sighted*) perspicaz; (*wise*) sabio(a); (*decision*) acertado(a)
shriek [ʃriːk] **1** n chillido m; **shrieks of laughter** carcajadas fpl
2 vi chillar
shrill [ʃrɪl] adj agudo(a), estridente
shrimp [ʃrɪmp] **1** n camarón m
2 vi pescar camarones
shrine [ʃraɪn] n (*tomb*) sepulcro m; (*chapel*) capilla f; (*holy place*) lugar sagrado
shrink [ʃrɪŋk] **1** vt (pt **shrank**; pp **shrunk**) encoger
2 vi (**a**) (*clothes*) encoger(se) (**b**) (*savings*) disminuir (**c**) **to s. (back)** echarse atrás; **to s. from doing sth** no tener valor para hacer algo
2 n Fam (*psychiatrist*) psiquiatra mf
shrinkage ['ʃrɪŋkɪdʒ] n (**a**) (*of cloth*) encogimiento m; (*of metal*) contracción f (**b**) (*of savings etc*) disminución f
shrink-wrapped ['ʃrɪŋkræpt] adj envuelto(a) en plástico
shrivel ['ʃrɪvəl] **1** vt **to s. (up)** encoger; (*plant*) secar; (*skin*) arrugar
2 vi encogerse; (*plant*) secarse; (*skin*) arrugarse
shroud [ʃraʊd] **1** n Rel sudario m
2 vt Fig envolver
Shrove Tuesday ['ʃraʊv'tjuːzdɪ] n martes m de carnaval
shrub [ʃrʌb] n arbusto m
shrubbery ['ʃrʌbərɪ] n arbustos mpl
shrug [ʃrʌg] **1** vt **to s. one's shoulders** encogerse de hombros
2 vi encogerse de hombros
3 n encogimiento m de hombros
▸ **shrug off** vt sep no dejarse desanimar por
shrunk [ʃrʌŋk] pp of **shrink**

shudder ['ʃʌdə(r)] **1** n (**a**) escalofrío m, estremecimiento m (**b**) (*of machinery*) sacudida f
2 vi (**a**) (*person*) estremecerse (**b**) (*machinery*) dar sacudidas
shuffle ['ʃʌfəl] **1** vt (**a**) (*feet*) arrastrar (**b**) (*papers etc*) revolver; (*cards*) barajar
2 vi (**a**) (*walk*) andar arrastrando los pies (**b**) Cards barajar
shun [ʃʌn] vt (*person*) esquivar; (*responsibility*) rehuir
shunt [ʃʌnt] vt Rail cambiar de vía; Elec derivar
shut [ʃʌt] **1** vt (pt & pp **shut**) cerrar
2 vi cerrarse
3 adj cerrado(a)
▸ **shut down 1** vt sep (*factory*) cerrar
2 vi (*factory*) cerrar
▸ **shut off** vt sep (*gas, water etc*) cortar
▸ **shut out** vt sep (**a**) (*lock out*) dejar fuera a (**b**) (*exclude*) excluir
▸ **shut up 1** vt sep (**a**) (*close*) cerrar (**b**) (*imprison*) encerrar (**c**) Fam (*silence*) callar
2 vi Fam (*keep quiet*) callarse
shutdown ['ʃʌtdaʊn] n cierre m
shutter ['ʃʌtə(r)] n (**a**) (*on window*) contraventana f, postigo m (**b**) Phot obturador m
shuttle ['ʃʌtəl] **1** n (**a**) (*in weaving*) lanzadera f (**b**) Av puente aéreo; **(space) s.** transbordador m espacial
2 vi ir y venir
shuttlecock ['ʃʌtəlkɒk] n volante m
shy [ʃaɪ] **1** adj (**shyer, shyest** or **shier, shiest**) (*timid*) tímido(a), Andes, CAm, Carib, Méx penoso(a); (*reserved*) reservado(a)
2 vi (*horse*) espantarse (**at** de); Fig **to s. away from doing sth** negarse a hacer algo
shyness ['ʃaɪnɪs] n timidez f
Siberia [saɪ'bɪərɪə] n Siberia
sibling ['sɪblɪŋ] n Fml (*brother*) hermano m; (*sister*) hermana f; **siblings** hermanos
Sicily ['sɪsɪlɪ] n Sicilia
sick [sɪk] adj (**a**) (*ill*) enfermo(a); **s. leave** baja f por enfermedad; **s. pay** subsidio m de enfermedad (**b**) **to feel s.** (*about to vomit*) tener ganas de devolver; **to be s.** devolver (**c**) Fam (*fed up*) harto(a) (**d**) Fam (*mind, joke*) morboso(a); **s. humour** humor negro
sickbay ['sɪkbeɪ] n enfermería f
sicken ['sɪkən] **1** vt (*make ill*) poner enfermo; (*revolt*) dar asco a
2 vi (*fall ill*) enfermar
sickening ['sɪkənɪŋ] adj nauseabundo(a); (*revolting*) repugnante; (*horrifying*) escalofriante
sickle ['sɪkəl] n hoz f
sickly ['sɪklɪ] adj (**sicklier, sickliest**) (**a**) (*person*) enfermizo(a) (**b**) (*taste*) empalagoso(a) (**c**) (*smile*) forzado(a)
sickness ['sɪknɪs] n (**a**) (*illness*) enfermedad f (**b**) (*nausea*) náuseas fpl
side [saɪd] **1** n (**a**) lado m; (*of coin etc*) cara f;

(of hill) ladera *f*; **by the s. of** junto a

  (**b**) *(of body)* costado *m*; *(of animal)* ijar *m*; **a s. of bacon** una pieza de tocino; **by my s.** a mi lado; **s. by s.** juntos

  (**c**) *(edge)* borde *m*; *(of lake, river)* orilla *f*

  (**d**) *Fig (aspect)* aspecto *m*

  (**e**) *(team)* equipo *m*; *Pol* partido *m*; **she's on our s.** está de nuestro lado; **to take sides with sb** ponerse de parte de algn; **s. dish** plato *m* de guarnición; **s. effect** efecto secundario; **s. entrance** entrada *f* lateral; **s. street** calle *f* lateral

  2 *vi* **to s. with sb** ponerse de parte de algn
sideboard ['saɪdbɔːd] *n* aparador *m*
sideboards ['saɪdbɔːdz], **sideburns** ['saɪdbɜːnz] *npl* patillas *fpl*
sidelight ['saɪdlaɪt] *n Aut* luz *f* lateral, piloto *m*
sideline ['saɪdlaɪn] *n* (**a**) *Sport* línea *f* de banda (**b**) *Com (product)* línea suplementaria; *(job)* empleo suplementario
sidelong ['saɪdlɒŋ] *adj* de reojo
side-saddle ['saɪdsædəl] **1** *n* silla *f* de amazona

  2 *adv* **to ride s.** montar a la inglesa
sideshow ['saɪdʃəʊ] *n* atracción secundaria
sidestep ['saɪdstep] *vt (issue)* esquivar
sidetrack ['saɪdtræk] *vt Fig (person)* despistar
sidewalk ['saɪdwɔːk] *n US* acera *f*, *CSur, Perú* vereda *f*, *CAm, Méx* banqueta *f*
sideways ['saɪdweɪz] **1** *adj (movement)* lateral; *(look)* de reojo

  2 *adv* de lado
siding ['saɪdɪŋ] *n Rail* apartadero *m*, vía muerta
sidle ['saɪdəl] *vi* **to s. up to sb** acercarse furtivamente a algn
siege [siːdʒ] *n* sitio *m*, cerco *m*; **to lay s. to** sitiar
sieve [sɪv] **1** *n (fine)* tamiz *m*; *(coarse)* criba *f*

  2 *vt (fine)* tamizar; *(coarse)* cribar
sift [sɪft] *vt (sieve)* tamizar; *Fig* **to s. through** examinar cuidadosamente
sigh [saɪ] **1** *vi* suspirar

  2 *n* suspiro *m*
sight [saɪt] **1** *n* (**a**) *(faculty)* vista *f*; **at first s.** a primera vista; **to catch s. of** divisar; **to know by s.** conocer de vista; **to lose s. of sth/sb** perder algo/a algn de vista (**b**) *(range of vision)* vista *f*; **within s.** a la vista; **to come into s.** aparecer (**c**) *(spectacle)* espectáculo *m* (**d**) *(on gun)* mira *f*; *Fig* **to set one's sights on** tener la mira puesta en (**e**) **sights** monumentos *mpl*

  2 *vt ver; (land)* divisar
sightseeing ['saɪtsiːɪŋ] *n* turismo *m*; **to go s.** hacer turismo
sign [saɪn] **1** *n* (**a**) *(symbol)* signo *m* (**b**) *(gesture)* gesto *m*, seña *f*; *(signal)* señal *f* (**c**) *(indication)* señal *f*; *(trace)* rastro *m*, huella *f*; **as a s. of** como muestra de (**d**) *(notice)*

anuncio *m*; *(board)* letrero *m*

  2 *vt* (**a**) *(letter etc)* firmar (**b**) *Ftb* fichar

  3 *vi* firmar

▸ **sign on 1** *vt sep (worker)* contratar

  2 *vi (worker)* firmar un contrato; *Br Fam* apuntarse al paro; *(regularly)* firmar el paro

▸ **sign up 1** *vt sep (soldier)* reclutar; *(worker)* contratar

  2 *vi (soldier)* alistarse; *(worker)* firmar un contrato
signal ['sɪgnəl] **1** *n* señal *f*; *Rad & TV* sintonía *f*; *Rail* **s. box** garita *f* de señales

  2 *vt* (**a**) *(message)* transmitir por señales (**b**) *(direction etc)* indicar

  3 *vi (with hands)* hacer señales; *(in car)* señalar
signalman ['sɪgnəlmən] *n* guardavía *m*
signature ['sɪgnətʃə(r)] *n (name)* firma *f*; *Rad & TV* **s. tune** sintonía *f*
signet ['sɪgnɪt] *n* **s. ring** (anillo *m* de) sello *m*
significance [sɪg'nɪfɪkəns] *n (meaning)* significado *m*; *(importance)* importancia *f*
significant [sɪg'nɪfɪkənt] *adj (meaningful)* significativo(a); *(important)* importante
significantly [sɪg'nɪfɪkəntlɪ] *adv (markedly)* sensiblemente
signify ['sɪgnɪfaɪ] *vt* (**a**) *(mean)* significar (**b**) *(show, make known)* indicar
signpost ['saɪnpəʊst] *n* poste *m* indicador
silence ['saɪləns] **1** *n* silencio *m*

  2 *vt* acallar; *(engine)* silenciar
silencer ['saɪlənsə(r)] *n* (**a**) *(on gun)* silenciador *m* (**b**) *Br (on car)* silenciador *m*
silent ['saɪlənt] *adj* silencioso(a); *(not talkative)* callado(a); *(film)* mudo(a); **be s.!** ¡cállate!; **to remain s.** guardar silencio
silently ['saɪləntlɪ] *adv* silenciosamente
silhouette [sɪluː'et] *n* silueta *f*
silicon ['sɪlɪkən] *n* silicio *m*; **s. chip** chip *m* (de silicio)
silk [sɪlk] **1** *n* seda *f*

  2 *adj* de seda
silky ['sɪlkɪ] *adj* (**silkier, silkiest**) *(cloth)* sedoso(a); *(voice etc)* aterciopelado(a)
sill [sɪl] *n (of window)* alféizar *m*
silly ['sɪlɪ] *adj* (**sillier, silliest**) tonto(a)
silo ['saɪləʊ] *n* silo *m*
silt [sɪlt] *n* cieno *m*

▸ **silt up** *vi* obstruirse con cieno
silver ['sɪlvə(r)] **1** *n* (**a**) *(metal)* plata *f* (**b**) *(coins)* monedas *fpl* (de plata) (**c**) *(tableware)* vajilla *f* de plata

  2 *adj* de plata; **s. foil** *(tinfoil)* papel *m* de aluminio; **s. paper** papel de plata; **s. wedding** bodas *fpl* de plata
silver-plated [sɪlvə'pleɪtɪd] *adj* plateado(a)
silversmith ['sɪlvəsmɪθ] *n* platero(a) *m,f*
silverware ['sɪlvəweə(r)] *n* vajilla *f* de plata
silvery ['sɪlvərɪ] *adj* plateado(a)
similar ['sɪmɪlə(r)] *adj* parecido(a), semejante (**to** a); **to be s.** parecerse
similarity [sɪmɪ'lærɪtɪ] *n* semejanza *f*

similarly ['sımıləlı] *adv* (**a**) *(as well)* igualmente (**b**) *(likewise)* del mismo modo, asimismo

simile ['sımılı] *n* símil *m*

simmer ['sımə(r)] **1** *vt* cocer a fuego lento
2 *vi* cocerse a fuego lento
▸ **simmer down** *vi Fam* calmarse

simpering ['sımpərıŋ] *adj* melindroso(a)

simple ['sımpəl] *adj* (**a**) sencillo(a); **s. interest** interés *m* simple (**b**) *(natural)* natural (**c**) *(foolish)* simple; *(naïve)* ingenuo(a); *(dim)* de pocas luces

simplicity [sım'plısıtı] *n* (**a**) sencillez *f* (**b**) *(naïveté)* ingenuidad *f*

simplify ['sımplıfaı] *vt* simplificar

simply ['sımplı] *adv* (**a**) *(plainly)* sencillamente (**b**) *(only)* simplemente, sólo

simulate ['sımjʊleıt] *vt* simular

simulator ['sımjʊleıtə(r)] *n* **flight s.** simulador de vuelo

simultaneous [sıməl'teınıəs] *adj* simultáneo(a)

simultaneously [sıməl'teınıəslı] *adv* simultáneamente

sin [sın] **1** *n* pecado *m*
2 *vi* pecar

since [sıns] **1** *adv* (*ever*) **s.** desde entonces; **long s.** hace mucho tiempo; **it has s. come out that ...** desde entonces se ha sabido que ...
2 *prep* desde; **she has been living here s. 1975** vive aquí desde 1975
3 *conj* (**a**) *(time)* desde que; **how long is it s. you last saw him?** ¿cuánto tiempo hace que lo viste por última vez? (**b**) *(because, as)* ya que, puesto que

sincere [sın'sıə(r)] *adj* sincero(a)

sincerely [sın'sıəlı] *adv* sinceramente; **Yours s.** *(in letter)* (le saluda) atentamente

sincerity [sın'serıtı] *n* sinceridad *f*

sinew ['sınjuː] *n (tendon)* tendón *m*; *(in meat)* nervio *m*

sinful ['sınfʊl] *adj (person)* pecador(a); *(act, thought)* pecaminoso(a); *Fig (waste etc)* escandaloso(a)

sing [sıŋ] **1** *vt (pt* sang; *pp* sung) cantar
2 *vi (person, bird)* cantar; *(kettle, bullets)* silbar

singe [sındʒ] *vt* chamuscar

singer ['sıŋə(r)] *n* cantante *mf*

singing ['sıŋıŋ] *n (art)* canto *m*; *(songs)* canciones *fpl; (of kettle)* silbido *m*

single ['sıŋgəl] **1** *adj* (**a**) *(solitary)* solo(a) (**b**) *(only one)* único(a) (**c**) *(not double)* sencillo(a); **s. bed/room** cama *f*/habitación *f* individual (**d**) *(unmarried)* soltero(a)
2 *n* (**a**) *Br Rail* billete *m or Am* boleto *m or Am* pasaje *m* sencillo *or* de ida (**b**) *(record)* single *m* (**c**) *Sport* **singles** individuales *mpl*
▸ **single out** *vt sep (choose)* escoger; *(distinguish)* distinguir

single-breasted ['sıŋgəl'brestıd] *adj (suit, jacket)* recto(a)

single-handed ['sıŋgəl'hændıd] *adj & adv* sin ayuda

single-minded ['sıŋgəl'maındıd] *adj* resuelto(a)

singlet ['sıŋglıt] *n Br* camiseta *f*

singly ['sıŋglı] *adv (individually)* por separado; *(one by one)* uno por uno

singular ['sıŋgjʊlə(r)] **1** *adj* (**a**) *Ling* singular (**b**) *Fml (outstanding)* excepcional (**c**) *Fml (unique)* único(a)
2 *n Ling* singular *m*

singularly ['sıŋgjʊləlı] *adv* excepcionalmente

sinister ['sınıstə(r)] *adj* siniestro(a)

sink¹ [sıŋk] *n (in kitchen)* fregadero *m*

sink² [sıŋk] **1** *vt (pt* sank; *pp* sunk) (**a**) *(ship)* hundir, echar a pique; *Fig (hopes)* acabar con (**b**) *(hole, well)* cavar; *(post, knife, teeth)* hincar
2 *vi* (**a**) *(ship)* hundirse (**b**) *Fig* **my heart sank** se me cayó el alma a los pies (**c**) *(sun)* ponerse (**d**) **to s. to one's knees** hincarse de rodillas
▸ **sink in** *vi (penetrate)* penetrar; *Fig* **it hasn't sunk in yet** todavía no me he/se ha/*etc* hecho a la idea

sinner ['sınə(r)] *n* pecador(a) *m,f*

sinus ['saınəs] *n* seno *m* (nasal)

sip [sıp] **1** *n* sorbo *m*
2 *vt* sorber, beber a sorbos

siphon ['saıfən] *n* sifón *m*
▸ **siphon off** *vt sep (liquid)* sacar con sifón; *Fig (funds, traffic)* desviar

sir [sɜː(r)] *n Fml* (**a**) señor *m*; **yes, s.** sí, señor (**b**) *(title)* sir; **S. Walter Raleigh** Sir Walter Raleigh

siren ['saırən] *n* sirena *f*

sirloin ['sɜːlɔın] *n* solomillo *m*

sissy ['sısı] *n Fam (coward)* miedica *mf*

sister ['sıstə(r)] *n* (**a**) *(relation)* hermana *f* (**b**) *Br Med* enfermera *f* jefe (**c**) *Rel* hermana *f; (before name)* sor

sister-in-law ['sıstərınlɔː] *n* cuñada *f*

sit [sıt] **1** *vt (pt & pp* sat) (**a**) *(child etc)* sentar (**in/on** en) (**b**) *Br (exam)* presentarse a
2 *vi* (**a**) *(action)* sentarse (**b**) *(be seated)* estar sentado(a) (**c**) *(object)* estar; *(be situated)* hallarse; *(person)* quedarse (**d**) *(assembly)* reunirse
▸ **sit back** *vi* recostarse
▸ **sit down** *vi* sentarse
▸ **sit in** *vi insep* asistir sin participar a
▸ **sit in on** *vt insep* asistir a
▸ **sit out** *vt sep* aguantar hasta el final
▸ **sit through** *vt insep* aguantar
▸ **sit up** *vi* (**a**) incorporarse (**b**) *(stay up late)* quedarse levantado(a)

site [saıt] **1** *n* (**a**) *(area)* lugar *m*; **building s.** solar *m*; *(under construction)* obra *f* (**b**) *(location)* situación *f*; **nuclear testing s.** zona *f* de pruebas nucleares
2 *vt* situar

sit-in ['sıtın] *n Fam (demonstration)* sentada *f*;

(strike) huelga f de brazos caídos

sitting ['sɪtɪŋ] **1** n *(of committee)* sesión f; *(in canteen)* turno m

2 adj **s. room** sala f de estar

situated ['sɪtjʊeɪtɪd] adj situado(a), ubicado(a)

situation [sɪtjʊ'eɪʃən] n (**a**) situación f (**b**) *(job)* puesto m; Br **situations vacant** *(in newspaper)* ofertas de trabajo

six [sɪks] adj & n seis *(m inv)*

sixteen [sɪks'tiːn] adj & n dieciséis *(m inv)*, diez y seis *(m inv)*

sixteenth [sɪks'tiːnθ] **1** adj & n decimosexto(a) *(m,f)*

2 n *(fraction)* dieciseisavo m

sixth [sɪksθ] **1** adj sexto(a); Br Educ **s. form** ≃ COU; **s. former** ≃ estudiante de COU

2 n (**a**) *(in series)* sexto(a) m,f (**b**) *(fraction)* sexto m, sexta parte

sixty ['sɪkstɪ] adj & n sesenta *(m inv)*

sizable ['saɪzəbəl] adj = **sizeable**

size [saɪz] n tamaño m; *(of garment)* talla f; *(of shoes)* número m; *(of person)* estatura f; *(scope)* alcance m; **what s. do you take?** *(garment)* ¿qué talla tienes?; *(shoes)* ¿qué número calzas?

▸ **size up** vt sep *(person)* juzgar; *(situation, problem)* evaluar

sizeable ['saɪzəbəl] adj *(building etc)* bastante) grande; *(sum)* considerable; *(problem)* importante

sizzle ['sɪzəl] vi chisporrotear

skate¹ [skeɪt] **1** n patín m

2 vi patinar

skate² [skeɪt] n *(fish)* raya f

skateboard ['skeɪtbɔːd] n monopatín m

skater ['skeɪtə(r)] n patinador(a) m,f

skating ['skeɪtɪŋ] n patinaje m; **s. rink** pista f de patinaje

skeleton ['skelɪtən] **1** n (**a**) esqueleto m (**b**) *(of building)* armazón m (**c**) *(outline)* esquema m

2 adj *(staff, service)* reducido(a); **s. key** llave maestra

skeptic ['skeptɪk] n US = **sceptic**

sketch [sketʃ] **1** n (**a**) *(preliminary drawing)* bosquejo m, esbozo m; *(drawing)* dibujo m; *(outline)* esquema m; *(rough draft)* boceto m (**b**) Th & TV sketch m

2 vt *(draw)* dibujar; *(preliminary drawing)* bosquejar, esbozar

sketch-book ['sketʃbʊk], **sketch-pad** ['sketʃpæd] n bloc m de dibujo

sketchy ['sketʃɪ] adj *(sketchier, sketchiest)* *(incomplete)* incompleto(a); *(not detailed)* vago(a)

skewer ['skjʊə(r)] n pincho m, broqueta f

ski [skiː] **1** n esquí m

2 adj de esquí; **s. boots** botas fpl de esquiar; **s. jump** *(action)* salto m con esquís; **s. lift** telesquí m; *(with seats)* telesilla f; **s. pants** pantalón m de esquiar; **s. resort** estación f

de esquí; **s. stick** or **pole** bastón m de esquiar

3 vi esquiar; **to go skiing** ir a esquiar

skid [skɪd] **1** n patinazo m

2 vi patinar

skier ['skiːə(r)] n esquiador(a) m,f

skiing ['skiːɪŋ] n esquí m

skilful ['skɪlfʊl] adj hábil, diestro(a)

skill [skɪl] n (**a**) *(ability)* habilidad f, destreza f; *(talent)* don m (**b**) *(technique)* técnica f

skilled [skɪld] adj (**a**) *(dextrous)* hábil, diestro(a); *(expert)* experto(a) (**b**) *(worker)* cualificado(a)

skillet ['skɪlɪt] n US sartén f

skillful ['skɪlfʊl] adj US = **skilful**

skim [skɪm] **1** vt (**a**) *(milk)* desnatar; **skimmed milk** leche desnatada (**b**) *(brush against)* rozar; **to s. the ground** *(bird, plane)* volar a ras de suelo

2 vi Fig **to s. through a book** hojear un libro

skimp [skɪmp] vt & vi *(food, material)* escatimar; *(work)* chapucear

skimpy ['skɪmpɪ] adj *(skimpier, skimpiest)* *(shorts)* muy corto(a); *(meal)* escaso(a)

skin [skɪn] **1** n (**a**) *(of face)* cutis m; *(complexion)* tez f; **s. cream** crema f de belleza (**b**) *(of fruit)* piel f; *(of lemon)* cáscara f; *(peeling)* mondadura f (**c**) *(of sausage)* pellejo m (**d**) *(on milk etc)* nata f

2 vt (**a**) *(animal)* despellejar (**b**) *(graze)* arañar

skin-deep ['skɪn'diːp] adj superficial

skin-diving ['skɪndaɪvɪŋ] n buceo m, submarinismo m

skinhead ['skɪnhed] n Fam cabeza mf rapada

skinny ['skɪnɪ] adj *(skinnier, skinniest)* Fam flaco(a)

skin-tight ['skɪntaɪt] adj *(clothing)* muy ajustado(a)

skip¹ [skɪp] **1** n *(jump)* salto m, brinco m

2 vi *(jump)* saltar, brincar; *(with rope)* saltar a la comba; Fig **to s. over sth** saltarse algo

3 vt Fig saltarse

skip² [skɪp] n Br *(for rubbish)* contenedor m

skipper ['skɪpə(r)] n Naut & Sport Fam capitán(ana) m,f

skipping ['skɪpɪŋ] n comba f; **s. rope** comba f

skirmish ['skɜːmɪʃ] n escaramuza f

skirt [skɜːt] **1** n falda f

2 vt *(town etc)* rodear; *(coast)* bordear; Fig *(problem)* esquivar

skirting ['skɜːtɪŋ] n Br **s. (board)** zócalo m

skit [skɪt] n sátira f, parodia f

skittle ['skɪtəl] n (**a**) *(pin)* bolo m (**b**) **skittles** *(game)* (juego m de los) bolos mpl, boliche m

skive [skaɪv] vi Br Fam escaquearse

skulk [skʌlk] vi *(hide)* esconderse; *(prowl)* merodear; *(lie in wait)* estar al acecho

skull [skʌl] n Anat cráneo m; Fam calavera f

skunk [skʌŋk] n mofeta f

sky [skaɪ] n cielo m; **s. blue** azul m celeste

skylight ['skaɪlaɪt] n tragaluz m, claraboya f

skyline ['skaɪlaɪn] n *(of city)* perfil m

skyscraper ['skaɪskreɪpə(r)] *n* rascacielos *m inv*

slab [slæb] *n (of stone)* losa *f*; *(of chocolate)* tableta *f*; *(of cake)* trozo *m*

slack [slæk] **1** *adj* (a) *(not taut)* flojo(a) (b) *(lax)* descuidado(a); *(lazy)* vago(a) (c) *(market)* flojo(a); **business is s.** hay poco negocio
2 *n (in rope)* parte floja

slacken ['slækən] **1** *vt* (a) *(rope)* aflojar (b) *(speed)* reducir
2 *vi* (a) *(rope)* aflojarse; *(wind)* amainar (b) *(trade)* aflojar
▸ **slacken off** *vi* disminuirse

slacks [slæks] *npl* pantalones *mpl* ajustados

slag [slæg] *n* (a) *Min* escoria *f*; **s. heap** escorial *m* (b) *Br very Fam (woman)* puta *f*
▸ **slag off** *vt sep Br* poner verde a

slain [sleɪn] **1** *npl* **the s.** los caídos
2 *pp of* **slay**

slam [slæm] **1** *n (of door)* portazo *m*
2 *vt (bang)* cerrar de golpe; **to s. sth down on the table** soltar algo sobre la mesa de un palmetazo; **to s. the door** dar un portazo; **to s. on the brakes** dar un frenazo
3 *vi (door)* cerrarse de golpe

slander ['slɑːndə(r)] **1** *n* difamación *f*, calumnia *f*
2 *vt* difamar, calumniar

slang [slæŋ] *n* argot *m*, jerga *f*

slant [slɑːnt] **1** *n* (a) *(inclination f; (slope)* pendiente *f* (b) *Fig (point of view)* punto *m* de vista
2 *vt Fig (problem etc)* enfocar subjetivamente
3 *vi* inclinarse

slanting ['slɑːntɪŋ] *adj* inclinado(a)

slap [slæp] **1** *n* palmada *f*; *(in face)* bofetada *f*
2 *adv Fam* **he ran s. into the fence** se dio de lleno contra la valla; **s. in the middle of ...** justo en medio de ...
3 *vt* pegar con la mano; *(hit in face)* dar una bofetada a; **to s. sb on the back** dar a algn una palmada en la espalda

slapdash ['slæp'dæʃ] *adj Fam* descuidado(a); *(work)* chapucero(a)

slapstick ['slæpstɪk] *n* bufonadas *fpl*, payasadas *fpl*

slap-up ['slæpʌp] *adj Fam* **s. meal** comilona *f*

slash [slæʃ] **1** *n Fam Typ* barra oblicua
2 *vt* (a) *(with knife)* acuchillar; *(with sword)* dar un tajo a (b) *Fig (prices)* rebajar

slat [slæt] *n* tablilla *f*, listón *m*

slate [sleɪt] **1** *n* pizarra *f*, *Fig* **to wipe the s. clean** hacer borrón y cuenta nueva
2 *vt Br Fam* criticar duramente

slaughter ['slɔːtə(r)] **1** *n (of animals)* matanza *f*; *(of people)* carnicería *f*
2 *vt (animals)* matar; *(people)* matar brutalmente; *(in large numbers)* masacrar

slaughterhouse ['slɔːtəhaʊs] *n* matadero *m*

Slav [slɑːv] *adj & n* eslavo(a) *(m,f)*

slave [sleɪv] **1** *n* esclavo(a) *m,f*; **s. trade** trata *f* de esclavos
2 *vi* **to s. (away)** dar el callo

slavery ['sleɪvərɪ] *n* esclavitud *f*

Slavonic [slə'vɒnɪk] *adj* eslavo(a)

slay [sleɪ] *vt (pt slew; pp slain)* matar

sleazy ['sliːzɪ] *adj (sleazier, sleaziest)* sórdido(a)

sled [sled] **1** *n US* trineo *m*
2 *vi* ir en trineo

sledge [sledʒ] *n Br* trineo *m*

sledgehammer ['sledʒhæmə(r)] *n* almádena *f*

sleek [sliːk] *adj (hair)* lustroso(a); *(appearance)* impecable

sleep [sliːp] **1** *n* sueño *m*
2 *vi (pt & pp slept)* (a) dormir; **to go to s.** dormirse; **to send to s.** (hacer) dormir; *Fam* **s. like a log** dormir como un lirón (b) **my foot has gone to s.** se me ha dormido el pie
▸ **sleep in** *vi Br (oversleep)* quedarse dormido(a); *(have a lie-in)* quedarse en la cama
▸ **sleep with** *vt insep Fam* **to s. with sb** acostarse con algn

sleeper ['sliːpə(r)] *n* (a) *(person)* durmiente *mf*; **to be a heavy s.** tener el sueño pesado (b) *Br Rail (on track)* traviesa *f* (c) *Rail (coach)* coche-cama *m*; *(berth)* litera *f*

sleeping ['sliːpɪŋ] *adj* **s. bag** saco *m* de dormir; **S. Beauty** la Bella durmiente; **s. car** coche-cama *m*; *Br Com* **s. partner** socio(a) *m,f* comanditario(a); **s. pill** somnífero *m*

sleepless ['sliːpləs] *adj* **to have a s. night** pasar la noche en blanco

sleepwalker ['sliːpwɔːkə(r)] *n* sonámbulo(a) *m,f*

sleepy ['sliːpɪ] *adj (sleepier, sleepiest)* soñoliento(a); **to be** *or* **feel s.** tener sueño

sleet [sliːt] **1** *n* aguanieve *f*
2 *vi* **it's sleeting** cae aguanieve

sleeve [sliːv] *n (of garment)* manga *f*; *(of record)* funda *f*

sleigh [sleɪ] *n* trineo *m*; **s. bell** cascabel *m*

sleight [slaɪt] *n* **s. of hand** juego *m* de manos

slender ['slendə(r)] *adj* (a) *(thin)* delgado(a) (b) *Fig (hope, chance)* remoto(a)

slept [slept] *pt & pp of* **sleep**

slew [sluː] *pt of* **slay**

slice [slaɪs] **1** *n* (a) *(of bread)* rebanada *f*; *(of ham)* loncha *f*; *(of beef etc)* tajada *f*; *(of lemon etc)* rodaja *f*; *(of cake)* trozo *m* (b) *(utensil)* pala *f*
2 *vt (food)* cortar a rebanadas/tajos/rodajas; *(divide)* partir

slick [slɪk] *adj* (a) *(programme, show)* logrado(a) (b) *(skilful)* hábil, mañoso(a)
2 *n* **(oil) s.** marea negra

slide [slaɪd] **1** *n* (a) *(act)* resbalón *m* (b) *(in prices etc)* baja *f* (c) *(in playground)* tobogán *m* (d) *Phot* diapositiva *f*; **s. projector** proyector *m* de diapositivas (e) **s. rule** regla *f* de cálculo (f) *Br (for hair)* pasador *m*

2 *vt* (*pt & pp* **slid** [slɪd]) deslizar; (*furniture*) correr

3 *vi* (*on purpose*) deslizarse; (*slip*) resbalar

sliding ['slaɪdɪŋ] *adj* (*door, window*) corredizo(a); **Fin s. scale** escala *f* móvil

slight [slaɪt] **1** *adj* (**a**) (*small*) pequeño(a); **not in the slightest** en absoluto (**b**) (*build*) menudo(a); (*slim*) delgado(a); (*frail*) delicado(a) (**c**) (*trivial*) leve

2 *n* (*affront*) desaire *m*

3 *vt* (**a**) (*scorn*) despreciar (**b**) (*snub*) desairar

slightly ['slaɪtlɪ] *adv* (*a little*) ligeramente, algo

slim [slɪm] **1** *adj* (**slimmer, slimmest**) (**a**) (*person*) delgado(a) (**b**) *Fig* (*resources*) escaso(a); (*hope, chance*) remoto(a)

2 *vi* adelgazar

slime [slaɪm] *n* (*mud*) lodo *m*, cieno *m*; (*of snail*) baba *f*

slimming ['slɪmɪŋ] **1** *adj* (*diet, pills*) para adelgazar; (*food*) que no engorda

2 *n* (*process*) adelgazamiento *m*

slimy ['slaɪmɪ] *adj* (**slimier, slimiest**) (**a**) (*muddy*) lodoso(a); (*snail*) baboso(a) (**b**) *Fig* (*person*) zalamero(a)

sling [slɪŋ] **1** *n* (**a**) (*catapult*) honda *f*; (*child's*) tirador *m* (**b**) *Med* cabestrillo *m*

2 *vt* (*pt & pp* **slung**) (*throw*) tirar

slingshot ['slɪŋʃɒt] *n US* tirachinas *m inv*

slink [slɪŋk] *vi* (*pt & pp* **slunk**) **to s. off** escabullirse

slip [slɪp] **1** *n* (**a**) (*slide*) resbalón *m*; *Fam Fig* **to give sb the s.** dar esquinazo a algn (**b**) (*mistake*) error *m*; (*moral*) desliz *m*; **a s. of the tongue** un lapsus linguae (**c**) (*underskirt*) combinación *f* (**d**) (*of paper*) trocito *m*

2 *vi* (**a**) (*slide*) resbalar (**b**) *Med* dislocarse; **slipped disc** vértebra dislocada (**c**) (*move quickly*) ir de prisa (**d**) (*standards etc*) deteriorarse

3 *vt* (**a**) (*slide*) dar a escondidas (**b**) **it slipped my memory** se me fue de la cabeza

▸ **slip away** *vi* (*person*) escabullirse

▸ **slip off** *vt sep* (*clothes*) quitarse rápidamente

▸ **slip on** *vt sep* (*clothes*) ponerse rápidamente

▸ **slip out** *vi* (**a**) (*leave*) salir (**b**) *Fig* **the secret slipped out** se le escapó el secreto

▸ **slip up** *vi Fam* (*blunder*) cometer un desliz

slipper ['slɪpə(r)] *n* zapatilla *f*

slippery ['slɪpərɪ] *adj* resbaladizo(a)

slip-road ['slɪprəʊd] *n Br* vía *f* de acceso

slipshod ['slɪpʃɒd] *adj* descuidado(a); (*work*) chapucero(a)

slip-up ['slɪpʌp] *n Fam* (*blunder*) desliz *m*

slipway ['slɪpweɪ] *n* grada *f*

slit [slɪt] **1** *n* (*opening*) hendidura *f*; (*cut*) corte *m*, raja *f*

2 *vt* (*pt & pp* **slit**) cortar, rajar

slither ['slɪðə(r)] *vi* deslizarse

sliver ['slɪvə(r)] *n* (*of wood, glass*) astilla *f*; (*of ham*) loncha *f*

slob [slɒb] *n Fam* dejado(a) *m,f*

slog [slɒg] **1** *n Fam* **it was a hard s.** costó un montón

2 *vi* (**a**) *Fam* **to s. away** sudar tinta (**b**) (*walk*) caminar trabajosamente

3 *vt* (*hit*) golpear fuerte

slogan ['sləʊgən] *n* (e)slogan *m*, lema *m*

slop [slɒp] **1** *vi* **to s. (over)** derramarse; **to s. about** chapotear

2 *vt* derramar

slope [sləʊp] **1** *n* (*incline*) cuesta *f*, pendiente *f*; (*up*) subida *f*; (*down*) bajada *f*; (*of mountain*) ladera *f*; (*of roof*) vertiente *f*

2 *vi* inclinarse; **to s. up/down** subir/bajar en pendiente

▸ **slope off** *vi Fam* largarse

sloping ['sləʊpɪŋ] *adj* inclinado(a)

sloppy ['slɒpɪ] *adj* (**sloppier, sloppiest**) *Fam* descuidado(a); (*work*) chapucero(a); (*appearance*) desaliñado(a)

slot [slɒt] **1** *n* (**a**) (*for coin*) ranura *f*; (*opening*) rendija *f*; **s. machine** (*for gambling*) (máquina *f*) tragaperras *f inv*; (*vending machine*) distribuidor automático (**b**) *Rad TV* espacio *m*

2 *vt* (*place*) meter; (*put in*) introducir

3 *vi* **to s. in** *or* **together** encajar

sloth [sləʊθ] *n Fml* (*laziness*) pereza *f*

slouch [slaʊtʃ] *vi* andar *or* sentarse con los hombros caídos

Slovakia [sləʊ'vækɪə] *n* Eslovaquia

Slovakian [sləʊ'vækɪən] *adj & n* eslovaco(a) (*m,f*)

Slovene ['sləʊviːn] *n* (**a**) (*person*) esloveno(a) *m,f* (**b**) (*language*) esloveno *m*

2 *adj* esloveno(a)

Slovenia [sləʊ'viːnɪə] *n* Eslovenia

slovenly ['slʌvənlɪ] *adj* descuidado(a); (*appearance*) desaliñado(a); (*work*) chapucero(a)

slow [sləʊ] **1** *adj* (**a**) lento(a); **in s. motion** a cámara lenta; **to be s. to do sth** tardar en hacer algo (**b**) (*clock*) atrasado(a) (**c**) (*stupid*) lento(a), torpe

2 *adv* despacio, lentamente

3 *vt* (*car*) reducir la marcha de; (*progress*) retrasar

4 *vi* **to s. down** *or* **up** ir más despacio; (*in car*) reducir la velocidad

slowly ['sləʊlɪ] *adv* despacio, lentamente

sludge [slʌdʒ] *n* (*mud*) fango *m*, lodo *m*

slug [slʌg] **1** *n* (**a**) *Zool* babosa *f* (**b**) *US Fam* (*bullet*) posta *f* (**c**) *Fam* (*blow*) porrazo *m*

2 *vt Fam* (*hit*) aporrear

sluggish ['slʌgɪʃ] *adj* (**a**) (*river, engine*) lento(a); *Com* flojo(a) (**b**) (*lazy*) perezoso(a)

sluice [sluːs] *n* (*waterway*) canal *m*

sluicegate ['sluːsgeɪt] *n* esclusa *f*

slumber ['slʌmbə(r)] *Fml* **1** *n* (*sleep*) sueño *m*

2 *vi* dormir

slump [slʌmp] **1** *n* (**a**) (*drop in sales etc*) bajón *m* (**b**) (*economic depression*) crisis económica

2 *vi* (**a**) (*sales etc*) caer de repente; (*prices*)

desplomarse; *(the economy)* hundirse; *Fig (morale)* hundirse (**b**) *(fall)* caer
slums [slʌmz] *npl* barrios bajos
slung [slʌŋ] *pt & pp of* **sling**
slunk [slʌŋk] *pt & pp of* **slink**
slur [slɜː(r)] **1** *n (stigma)* mancha *f*; *(slanderous remark)* calumnia *f*
  2 *vt (word)* tragarse
slush [slʌʃ] *n* (**a**) *(melting snow)* nieve medio fundida (**b**) *Fam* sentimentalismo *m* (**c**) *US Fam* **s. fund** fondos *mpl* para sobornos
slut [slʌt] *n very Fam Pej* (**a**) *(untidy woman)* marrana *f* (**b**) *(whore)* fulana *f*
sly [slaɪ] *adj* (**slyer, slyest** *or* **slier, sliest**) (**a**) *(cunning)* astuto(a) (**b**) *(secretive)* furtivo(a) (**c**) *(mischievous)* travieso(a) (**d**) *(underhand)* malicioso(a)
smack¹ [smæk] **1** *n* (**a**) *(slap)* bofetada *f* (**b**) *(sharp sound)* ruido sonoro
  2 *vt* (**a**) *(slap)* dar una bofetada a (**b**) *(hit)* golpear; *Fig* **to s. one's lips** relamerse
smack² [smæk] *vi Fig* **to s. of** oler a
small [smɔːl] **1** *adj* (**a**) pequeño(a); **a s. table** una mesita; **in s. letters** en minúsculas; **in the s. hours** a altas horas de la noche; **s. ads** anuncios *mpl* por palabras; *Fig* **s. print** letra pequeña (**b**) *(in height)* bajo(a) (**c**) *(scant)* escaso(a); **s. change** cambio *m*, suelto *m* (**d**) *(minor)* insignificante; **s. businessmen** pequeños comerciantes; **s. talk** charloteo *m* (**e**) *(increase)* ligero(a)
  2 *n* (**a**) **s. of the back** región *f* lumbar (**b**) *Br Fam* **smalls** *(underwear)* paños *mpl* menores
smallholder ['smɔːlhəʊldə(r)] *n* minifundista *mf*
smallpox ['smɔːlpɒks] *n* viruela *f*
smarmy ['smɑːmɪ] *adj* (**smarmier, smarmiest**) *Fam* cobista, zalamero(a)
smart [smɑːt] **1** *adj* (**a**) *(elegant)* elegante (**b**) *(clever)* listo(a), inteligente; *Fam* **s. alec(k)** listillo (**c**) *(quick)* rápido(a); *(pace)* ligero(a)
  2 *vi* (**a**) *(sting)* picar, escocer (**b**) *Fig* sufrir
smarten ['smɑːtən] **1** *vt* **to s. (up)** arreglar
  2 *vi* **to s. (oneself) up** arreglarse
smash [smæʃ] **1** *n* (**a**) *(loud noise)* estrépito *m*; *(collision)* choque violento (**b**) *(in tennis)* smash *m*
  2 *vt* (**a**) *(break)* romper; *(shatter)* hacer pedazos; *(crush)* aplastar (**b**) *(destroy)* destrozar; *(defeat)* aplastar (**c**) *(record)* fulminar
  3 *vi* (**a**) *(break)* romperse; *(shatter)* hacerse pedazos; *(crash)* estrellarse; *(in tennis)* hacer un mate
  ▸ **smash up** *vt sep Fam (car)* hacer pedazos; *(place)* destrozar
smashing ['smæʃɪŋ] *adj Br Fam* estupendo(a)
smattering ['smætərɪŋ] *n* **he had a s. of** French hablaba un poquito de francés
smear [smɪə(r)] **1** *n* (**a**) *(smudge)* mancha *f*; **s. (test)** citología *f* (**b**) *Fig (defamation)* calumnia *f*

  2 *vt* (**a**) *(butter etc)* untar; *(grease)* embadurnar (**b**) *(make dirty)* manchar (**c**) *Fig (defame)* calumniar, difamar
smell [smel] **1** *n* (**a**) *(sense)* olfato *m* (**b**) *(odour)* olor *m*
  2 *vt* (*pt & pp* **smelled** *or* **smelt**) oler; *Fig* olfatear
  3 *vi* oler (**of** a); **it smells good/like lavender** huele bien/a lavanda; **he smelt of whisky** olía a whisky
smelly ['smelɪ] *adj* (**smellier, smelliest**) *Fam* maloliente, apestoso(a)
smelt¹ [smelt] *vt (ore)* fundir
smelt² [smelt] *pt & pp of* **smell**
smidgen ['smɪdʒən] *n Fam* pizca *f*
smile [smaɪl] **1** *n* sonrisa *f*
  2 *vi* sonreír; **to s. at sb** sonreír a algn; **to s. at sth** reírse de algo
smiling ['smaɪlɪŋ] *adj* sonriente, risueño(a)
smirk [smɜːk] **1** *n (conceited)* sonrisa satisfecha; *(foolish)* sonrisa boba
  2 *vi (conceitedly)* sonreír con satisfacción; *(foolishly)* sonreír bobamente
smith [smɪθ] *n* herrero *m*
smithereens [smɪðə'riːnz] *npl* **to smash/blow sth to s.** hacer algo añicos
smithy ['smɪðɪ] *n* herrería *f*
smitten ['smɪtən] *adj Fam* **to be s. with sb** estar enamorado(a) de algn
smock [smɒk] *n (blouse)* blusón *m*; *(worn in pregnancy)* blusón de premamá; *(overall)* bata *f*
smog [smɒg] *n* niebla tóxica, smog *m*
smoke [sməʊk] **1** *n* humo *m*; **s. bomb** bomba *f* de humo; **s. screen** cortina *f* de humo
  2 *vi* fumar; *(chimney etc)* echar humo
  3 *vt* (**a**) *(tobacco)* fumar; **to s. a pipe** fumar en pipa (**b**) *(fish, meat)* ahumar
smoked [sməʊkt] *adj* ahumado(a)
smokeless ['sməʊklɪs] *adj* **s. fuel** combustible sin humo; **s. zone** zona libre de humos
smoker ['sməʊkə(r)] *n* (**a**) *(person)* fumador(a) *m,f* (**b**) *Rail* vagón *m* de fumadores
smoking ['sməʊkɪŋ] *n* **no s.** *(sign)* prohibido fumar
smoky ['sməʊkɪ] *adj* (**smokier, smokiest**) (**a**) *(chimney)* humeante; *(room)* lleno(a) de humo; *(atmosphere)* cargado(a) (de humo); *(taste)* ahumado(a) (**b**) *(colour)* ahumado(a)
smolder ['sməʊldə(r)] *vi US* = **smoulder**
smooth [smuːð] **1** *adj* (**a**) *(surface)* liso(a); *(skin)* suave; *(road)* llano(a); *(sea)* tranquilo(a) (**b**) *(beer, wine)* suave (**c**) *(flowing)* fluido(a) (**d**) *(flight)* tranquilo(a); *(transition)* sin problemas (**e**) *Pej (slick)* zalamero(a)
  2 *vt* (**a**) *(hair etc)* alisar (**b**) *(plane down)* limar
  ▸ **smooth out** *vt sep (creases)* alisar; *Fig (difficulties)* allanar; *(problems)* resolver
  ▸ **smooth over** *vt sep Fig* **to s. things over** limar asperezas
smoothly ['smuːðlɪ] *adv* sobre ruedas

smother ['smʌðə(r)] vt (**a**) (asphyxiate) asfixiar; (suffocate) sofocar (**b**) Fig (cover) cubrir (**with** de)

smoulder ['sməʊldə(r)] vi (fire) arder sin llama; Fig (passions) arder; **smouldering hatred** odio latente

smudge [smʌdʒ] **1** n (stain) mancha f; (of ink) borrón m

   2 vt manchar; (piece of writing) emborronar

smug [smʌg] adj (**smugger, smuggest**) engreído(a)

smuggle ['smʌgəl] vt pasar de contrabando

smuggler ['smʌglə(r)] n contrabandista mf

smuggling ['smʌgəlɪŋ] n contrabando m

smutty ['smʌtɪ] adj (**smuttier, smuttiest**) Fam obsceno(a); (joke) verde; (book, film etc) pornográfico(a)

snack [snæk] n bocado m; **s. bar** cafetería f

snag [snæg] **1** n (difficulty) pega f, problemilla m

   2 vt (clothing) enganchar

snail [sneɪl] n caracol m

snake [sneɪk] n (big) serpiente f; (small) culebra f

snap [snæp] **1** n (**a**) (noise) ruido seco; (of branch, fingers) chasquido m (**b**) (bite) mordisco m (**c**) Phot (foto f) instantánea f

   2 adj (sudden) repentino(a)

   3 vt (**a**) (branch etc) partir (en dos) (**b**) (make noise) **to s. one's fingers** chasquear los dedos; **to s. sth shut** cerrar algo de golpe (**c**) Phot sacar una foto de

   4 vi (**a**) (break) romperse (**b**) (make noise) hacer un ruido seco (**c**) (whip) chasquear; **to s. shut** cerrarse de golpe (**d**) **to s. at sb** (dog) intentar morder a algn; Fam (person) regañar a algn

  ► **snap off 1** vt sep (branch etc) arrancar

   2 vi (branch etc) separarse

  ► **snap up** vt sep Fam **to s. up a bargain** llevarse una ganga

snappy ['snæpɪ] adj (**snappier, snappiest**) Fam (**a**) (quick) rápido(a); **look s.!, make it s.!** ¡date prisa! (**b**) (stylish) elegante (**c**) (short-tempered) irritable

snapshot ['snæpʃɒt] n (foto f) instantánea f

snare [sneə(r)] **1** n trampa f

   2 vt (animal) cazar con trampa; Fig (person) hacer caer en la trampa

snarl¹ [snɑːl] **1** n gruñido m

   2 vi gruñir

snarl² [snɑːl] **1** n (in wool) maraña f

   2 vt **to s. (up)** (wool) enmarañar; (traffic) atascar; (plans) enredar

snatch [snætʃ] **1** n (**a**) Fam (theft) robo m; **bag s.** tirón m (**b**) (fragment) fragmentos mpl

   2 vt (**a**) (grab) arrebatar (**b**) Fam (steal) robar; (kidnap) secuestrar

   3 vi **to s. at sth** intentar agarrar algo

sneak [sniːk] **1** n Fam chivato(a) m,f

   2 (pt & pp **sneaked** or US **snuck**) vt **to s. sth out of a place** sacar algo de un lugar a escondidas

   3 vi (**a**) **to s. off** escabullirse; **to s. in/out** entrar/salir a hurtadillas (**b**) Fam **to s. on sb** (tell tales) chivarse de algn

sneaker ['sniːkə(r)] n US playera f

sneaky ['sniːkɪ] adj (**sneakier, sneakiest**) solapado(a)

sneer [snɪə(r)] vi **to s. at** hacer un gesto de desprecio a

sneeze [sniːz] **1** n estornudo m

   2 vi estornudar

sniff [snɪf] **1** n (by person) aspiración f; (by dog) husmeo m

   2 vt (flower etc) oler; (suspiciously) husmear; (snuff etc) aspirar; (glue) esnifar

   3 vi aspirar por la nariz

snigger ['snɪgə(r)] **1** n risa disimulada

   2 vi reír disimuladamente; **to s. at sth** burlarse de algo

snip [snɪp] **1** n (**a**) (cut) tijeretada f; (small piece) recorte m (**b**) Br Fam (bargain) ganga f

   2 vt cortar a tijeretazos

sniper ['snaɪpə(r)] n francotirador(a) m,f

snippet ['snɪpɪt] n (of cloth, paper) recorte m; (of conversation) fragmento m

snivel ['snɪvəl] vi lloriquear

snivelling ['snɪvəlɪŋ] adj llorón(ona)

snob [snɒb] n (e)snob mf

snobbery ['snɒbərɪ] n (e)snobismo m

snobbish ['snɒbɪʃ] adj (e)snob

snooker ['snuːkə(r)] n snooker m, billar ruso

snoop [snuːp] vi fisgar, fisgonear

snooty ['snuːtɪ] adj (**snootier, snootiest**) Fam (e)snob

snooze [snuːz] Fam **1** n cabezada f

   2 vi echar una cabezada

snore [snɔː(r)] **1** n ronquido m

   2 vi roncar

snoring ['snɔːrɪŋ] n ronquidos mpl

snorkel ['snɔːkəl] n (of swimmer) tubo m de respiración; (of submarine) esnórquel m

snort [snɔːt] **1** n resoplido m

   2 vi resoplar

snout [snaʊt] n (of animal, gun etc) morro m

snow [snəʊ] **1** n nieve f; **s. shower** nevada f

   2 vi nevar; **it's snowing** está nevando

   3 vt Fig **to be snowed under with work** estar agobiado(a) de trabajo

snowball ['snəʊbɔːl] **1** n bola f de nieve

   2 vi Fig aumentar rápidamente

snowbound ['snəʊbaʊnd] adj aislado(a) por la nieve

snowdrift ['snəʊdrɪft] n ventisquero m

snowdrop ['snəʊdrɒp] n campanilla f de invierno

snowfall ['snəʊfɔːl] n nevada f

snowflake ['snəʊfleɪk] n copo m de nieve

snowman ['snəʊmæn] n hombre m de nieve

snowplough, US **snowplow** ['snəʊplaʊ] n quitanieves m inv

snowshoe ['snəʊʃuː] n raqueta f (de nieve)

snowstorm ['snəʊstɔːm] n nevasca f

snowy ['snəʊɪ] *adj* (**snowier, snowiest**) *(mountain)* nevado(a); *(climate)* nevoso(a); *(day)* de nieve

Snr *(abbr* **Senior**) Neil Smith S. Neil Smith padre

snub [snʌb] **1** *n (of person)* desaire *m; (of offer)* rechazo *m*

2 *vt (person)* desairar; *(offer)* rechazar

snub-nosed ['snʌbnəʊzd] *adj* de nariz respingona

snuck [snʌk] *US pt & pp of* **sneak**

snuff [snʌf] *n* rapé *m*

snug [snʌg] *adj* (**snugger, snuggest**) (**a**) *(cosy)* cómodo(a) (**b**) *(tightfitting)* ajustado(a)

snuggle ['snʌgəl] *vi* **to s. down in bed** acurrucarse en la cama; **to s. up to sb** arrimarse a algn

snugly ['snʌglɪ] *adv* **to fit s.** *(clothes)* quedar ajustado(a); *(object in box etc)* encajar

so [səʊ] **1** *adv* (**a**) *(to such an extent)* tanto; **he was so tired that ...** estaba tan cansado que ...; **it's so long since ...** hace tanto tiempo que ...; **he isn't so nice as his sister** no es tan agradable como su hermana; *Fam* **so long!** ¡hasta luego!

(**b**) *(degree)* tanto; **a week or so** una semana más o menos; **twenty or so** una veintena; **we loved her so (much)** la queríamos tanto; **so many books** tantos libros; *Fam* **he's ever so handsome!** ¡es tan guapo!; *Ironic* **so much for that** ¿qué le vamos a hacer?

(**c**) *(thus, in this way)* así; **and so on, and so forth** y así sucesivamente; **if so** en este caso; **I think/hope so** creo/espero que sí; **I told you so** ya te lo dije; **it so happens that ...** da la casualidad de que ...; **so be it!** ¡así sea!; **so far** hasta ahora *or* allí; **so it seems** eso parece; **so they say** eso dicen; **you're late! – so I am!** ¡llegas tarde! – ¡tienes razón!

(**d**) *(also)* **I'm going to Spain – so am I** voy a España – yo también

2 *conj* (**a**) *(expresses result)* así que; **so you like England, do you?** ¿así que te gusta Inglaterra, pues?; *Fam* **so what?** ¿y qué?

(**b**) *(expresses purpose)* para que; **I'll put the key here so (that) everyone can see it** pongo la llave aquí para que todos la vean

soak [səʊk] **1** *vt (washing, food)* remojar; *(cotton, wool)* empapar (**in** en)

2 *vi (washing, food)* estar en remojo

► **soak in** *vi* penetrar

► **soak up** *vt sep* absorber

soaking ['səʊkɪŋ] *adj (object)* empapado(a); *(person)* calado(a) hasta los huesos

so-and-so ['səʊənsəʊ] *n Fam* **Mr So-and-so** Don Fulano (de tal); *Pej* **an old so-and-so** un viejo imbécil

soap [səʊp] **1** *n* (**a**) jabón *m*; **s. flakes** jabón en escamas; **s. powder** jabón en polvo (**b**) *TV* **s. opera** culebrón *m*

2 *vt* enjabonar

soapy ['səʊpɪ] *adj* (**soapier, soapiest**) jabonoso(a); *(hands)* cubierto(a) de jabón

soar [sɔː(r)] *vi (bird, plane)* remontar el vuelo; *Fig (skyscraper)* elevarse; *(hopes, prices)* aumentar

sob [sɒb] **1** *n* sollozo *m*

2 *vi* sollozar

sober ['səʊbə(r)] *adj (not drunk, moderate)* sobrio(a); *(sensible)* sensato(a); *(serious)* serio(a); *(colour)* discreto(a)

► **sober up** *vi* **he sobered up** se le pasó la borrachera

so-called ['səʊkɔːld] *adj* supuesto(a), llamado(a)

soccer ['sɒkə(r)] *n* fútbol *m*

sociable ['səʊʃəbəl] *adj (gregarious)* sociable; *(friendly)* amistoso(a)

social ['səʊʃəl] *adj* social; **s. class** clase *f* social; **s. climber** arribista *mf*; **S. Democratic** socialdemócrata; *US* **s. insurance** seguro *m* social; **s. security** seguridad *f* social; **the s. services** los servicios sociales; **s. work** asistencia *f* social; **s. worker** asistente(a) *m,f* social

socialist ['səʊʃəlɪst] *adj & n* socialista *(mf)*

socialite ['səʊʃəlaɪt] *n* vividor(a) *m,f*

socialize ['səʊʃəlaɪz] **1** *vi* alternar, mezclarse con la gente

2 *vt* socializar

socially ['səʊʃəlɪ] *adv* socialmente

society [sə'saɪətɪ] **1** *n* (**a**) sociedad *f*; **the consumer s.** la sociedad de consumo; (**high**) **s.** la alta sociedad (**b**) *(club)* asociación *f* (**c**) *(companionship)* compañía *f*

2 *adj* de sociedad; **s. column** ecos *mpl* de sociedad

sociologist [səʊsɪ'ɒlədʒɪst] *n* sociólogo(a) *m,f*

sociology [səʊsɪ'ɒlədʒɪ] *n* sociología *f*

sock [sɒk] *n* calcetín *m*, *CSur* zoquete *m*

socket ['sɒkɪt] *n* (**a**) *(of eye)* cuenca *f* (**b**) *Elec* enchufe *m*

sod¹ [sɒd] *n Fml (piece of turf)* terrón *m*

sod² [sɒd] *very Fam* **1** *n* (**a**) *Pej (bastard)* cabrón(ona) *m,f*; **the lazy s.!** ¡qué tío más vago! (**b**) *(wretch)* desgraciado(a) *m,f*; **the poor s.** el pobrecito (**c**) **I've done s. all today** hoy no he pegado ni golpe

2 *vt* **s. it!** ¡maldita sea!

soda ['səʊdə] *n* (**a**) *Chem* sosa *f*; **baking s.** bicarbonato sódico (**b**) **s. water** soda *f* (**c**) *US (fizzy drink)* gaseosa *f*

sodden ['sɒdən] *adj* empapado(a)

sodium ['səʊdɪəm] *n* sodio *m*

sofa ['səʊfə] *n* sofá *m*; **s. bed** sofá cama

soft [sɒft] *adj* (**a**) *(not hard)* blando(a); **s. toy** muñeco *m* de peluche (**b**) *(skin, colour, hair, light, music)* suave; *(breeze, steps)* ligero(a) (**c**) *(lenient)* permisivo(a) (**d**) *(voice)* bajo(a) (**e**) *(foolish)* lelo(a); **to be a s. touch** ser fácil de engañar (**f**) **to have a s. spot for sb** tener debilidad por algn (**g**) *(easy)* fácil; **s. job** chollo *m* (**h**) *(drink)* no alcohólico(a); **s. drinks** refrescos *mpl* (**i**) **s. drugs** drogas blandas; **s. porn** pornografía blanda

soften ['sɒfən] **1** *vt (leather, heart)* ablandar; *(skin)* suavizar; *Fig (blow)* amortiguar
2 *vi (leather, heart)* ablandarse; *(skin)* suavizarse

softly ['sɒftlɪ] *adv (gently)* suavemente; *(quietly)* silenciosamente

softness ['sɒftnɪs] *n* (**a**) blandura *f* (**b**) *(of hair, skin)* suavidad *f* (**c**) *(foolishness)* estupidez *f*

software ['sɒftweə(r)] *n Comput* software *m*; **s. package** paquete *m*

soggy ['sɒgɪ] *adj* (**soggier, soggiest**) empapado(a); *(bread)* pastoso(a)

soil [sɔɪl] **1** *n (earth)* tierra *f*
2 *vt (dirty)* ensuciar; *Fig (reputation)* manchar

soiled [sɔɪld] *adj* sucio(a)

solace ['sɒlɪs] *n Fml* consuelo *m*

solar ['səʊlə(r)] *adj* solar

sold [səʊld] *pt & pp of* **sell**

solder ['sɒldə(r)] **1** *n* soldadura *f*
2 *vt* soldar

soldier ['səʊldʒə(r)] *n* soldado *m*; *(officer)* militar *m*; **toy s.** soldadito *m* de plomo
▸**soldier on** *vi Fig* continuar contra viento y marea

sole¹ [səʊl] *n (of foot)* planta *f*; *(of shoe, sock)* suela *f*

sole² [səʊl] *n (fish)* lenguado *m*

sole³ [səʊl] *adj (only)* único(a)

solemn ['sɒləm] *adj* solemne

solicit [sə'lɪsɪt] **1** *vt (request)* solicitar
2 *vi (prostitute)* abordar a los clientes

solicitor [sə'lɪsɪtə(r)] *n* abogado(a) *m,f*; *(for wills)* notario(a) *m,f*

solid ['sɒlɪd] **1** *adj* (**a**) *(not liquid)* sólido(a); *(firm)* firme (**b**) *(not hollow, pure) (metal)* macizo(a) (**c**) *(fog etc)* espeso(a); *(of strong material)* resistente; **a man of s. build** un hombre fornido (**d**) *(reliable)* formal (**e**) *(unanimous)* unánime
2 *n* sólido *m*

solidarity [sɒlɪ'dærɪtɪ] *n* solidaridad *f*

solidify [sə'lɪdɪfaɪ] *vi* solidificarse

solidly ['sɒlɪdlɪ] *adv* sólidamente; **s. built** *(house etc)* de construcción sólida; **to work s.** trabajar sin descanso

soliloquy [sə'lɪləkwɪ] *n* soliloquio *m*

solitaire [sɒlɪ'teə(r)] *n* solitario *m*

solitary ['sɒlɪtərɪ] *adj* (**a**) *(alone)* solitario(a); *(secluded)* apartado(a) (**b**) *(only)* solo(a)

solitude ['sɒlɪtjuːd] *n* soledad *f*

solo ['səʊləʊ] *n* solo *m*

soloist ['səʊləʊɪst] *n* solista *mf*

solstice ['sɒlstɪs] *n* solsticio *m*

solution [sə'luːʃən] *n* solución *f*

solve [sɒlv] *vt* resolver, solucionar

solvent ['sɒlvənt] *adj & n* solvente *(m)*

sombre, *US* **somber** ['sɒmbə(r)] *adj (dark)* sombrío(a); *(gloomy)* lúgubre; *(pessimistic)* pesimista

some [sʌm] **1** *adj* (**a**) *(with plural nouns)* unos(as), algunos(as); *(several)* varios(as); *(a few)* unos(as) cuantos(as); **did she bring s. flowers?** ¿trajo flores?; **there were s. roses** había unas rosas; **s. more peas** más guisantes
(**b**) *(with singular nouns)* algún/alguna; *(a little)* un poco de; **if you need s. help** si necesitas ayuda; **there's s. wine left** queda un poco de vino; **would you like s. coffee?** ¿quiere café?
(**c**) *(certain)* cierto(a), alguno(a); **in s. ways** en cierto modo; **to s. extent** hasta cierto punto; **s. people say that …** algunas personas dicen que …
(**d**) *(unspecified)* algún/alguna; **for s. reason or other** por una razón o por otra; **in s. book or other** en algún libro que otro; **s. day** algún día; **s. other time** otro día
(**e**) *(quite a lot of)* bastante; **it's s. distance away** queda bastante lejos; **s. years ago** hace algunos años
2 *pron* (**a**) *(people)* algunos(as), unos(as); **s. go by bus and s. by train** unos van en autobús y otros en tren
(**b**) *(objects)* algunos(as); *(a few)* unos(as) cuantos(as); *(a little)* algo, un poco; *(certain ones)* algunos(as)
3 *adv* **s. thirty cars** unos treinta coches

somebody ['sʌmbədɪ] *pron* alguien; **s. else** otro(a)

somehow ['sʌmhaʊ] *adv* (**a**) *(in some way)* de alguna forma (**b**) *(for some reason)* por alguna razón

someone ['sʌmwʌn] *pron* = **somebody**

someplace ['sʌmpleɪs] *adv US* = **somewhere**

somersault ['sʌməsɔːlt] **1** *n* voltereta *f*; *(by acrobat etc)* salto *m* mortal; *(by car)* vuelta *f* de campana
2 *vi* dar volteretas; *(acrobat etc)* dar un salto mortal; *(car)* dar una vuelta de campana

something ['sʌmθɪŋ] *pron & n* algo; **s. to eat/drink** algo de comer/beber; **are you drunk or s.?** ¿estás borracho o qué?; **s. must be done** hay que hacer algo; **she has a certain s.** tiene un no sé qué; **is s. the matter?** ¿le pasa algo?; **s. else** otra cosa; **s. of the kind** algo por el estilo

sometime ['sʌmtaɪm] *adv* algún día; **s. last week** un día de la semana pasada; **s. next year** durante el año que viene

sometimes ['sʌmtaɪmz] *adv* a veces, de vez en cuando

somewhat ['sʌmwɒt] *adv Fml* algo, un tanto

somewhere ['sʌmweə(r)] *adv* (**a**) *(in some place)* en alguna parte; *(to some place)* a alguna parte; **s. else** *(in some other place)* en otra parte; *(to some other place)* a otra parte; **s. or other** no sé dónde (**b**) **s. in the region of**

(approximately) más o menos

son [sʌn] *n* hijo *m*; **eldest/youngest s.** hijo mayor/menor

song [sɒŋ] *n* canción *f*; *(of bird)* canto *m*

songwriter ['sɒŋraɪtə(r)] *n* compositor(a) *m,f* (de canciones)

sonic ['sɒnɪk] *adj* sónico(a)

son-in-law ['sʌnɪnlɔː] *n* yerno *m*

sonnet ['sɒnɪt] *n* soneto *m*

sonny ['sʌnɪ] *n Fam* hijo *m*, hijito *m*

soon [suːn] *adv* **(a)** *(within a short time)* pronto, dentro de poco; *(quickly)* rápidamente; **see you s.!** ¡hasta pronto!; **s. after midnight** poco después de medianoche; **s. afterwards** poco después

(b) **as s. as I arrived** en cuanto llegué; **as s. as possible** cuanto antes

(c) *(early)* pronto; *Fig* **don't speak too s.** no cantes victoria

(d) *(preference)* **I would just as s. stay at home** prefiero quedarme en casa

(e) *(indifference)* **I would (just) as s. read as watch TV** tanto me da leer como ver la tele

sooner ['suːnə(r)] *adv* **(a)** *(earlier)* más temprano; **s. or later** tarde o temprano; **the s. the better** cuanto antes mejor **(b)** **no s. had he finished than he fainted** *(immediately after)* nada más acabar se desmayó **(c)** **I would s. do it alone** *(rather)* prefiero hacerlo yo solo

soot [sʊt] *n* hollín *m*

soothe [suːð] *vt (calm)* tranquilizar; *(pain)* aliviar

sop [sɒp] *n (concession)* favor *m*; *(bribe)* soborno *m*

▸ **sop up** *vt sep* empapar

sophisticated [sə'fɪstɪkeɪtɪd] *adj* sofisticado(a)

sophomore ['sɒfəmɔː(r)] *n US Univ* = estudiante de segundo curso

soporific [sɒpə'rɪfɪk] *adj* soporífero(a)

sopping ['sɒpɪŋ] *adj Fam* **s. (wet)** como una sopa

soppy ['sɒpɪ] *adj* **(soppier, soppiest)** *Fam* sentimentaloide

soprano [sə'prɑːnəʊ] *n* soprano *mf*

sorcerer ['sɔːsərə(r)] *n* brujo *m*

sorceress ['sɔːsərɪs] *n* bruja *f*

sordid ['sɔːdɪd] *adj* sórdido(a)

sore [sɔː(r)] **1** *adj* **(a)** *(painful)* dolorido(a); **to have a s. throat** tener dolor de garganta **(b)** *Fam (angry)* enfadado(a); **to feel s. about sth** estar resentido(a) por algo

2 *n* llaga *f*

sorely ['sɔːlɪ] *adv (very)* muy; *(a lot)* mucho; *(deeply)* profundamente

sorrow ['sɒrəʊ] *n* pena *f*, dolor *m*

sorrowful ['sɒrəʊfʊl] *adj* afligido(a)

sorry ['sɒrɪ] **1** *adj* **(sorrier, sorriest)** **(a)** **I feel very s. for her** me da mucha pena **(b)** *(pitiful)* triste **(c)** **to be s. (about sth)** sentir (algo); **I'm s. I'm late** siento llegar tarde

2 *interj* **(a)** *(apology)* ¡perdón! **(b)** *Br (for repetition)* ¿cómo?

sort [sɔːt] **1** *n* **(a)** *(kind)* clase *f*, tipo *m*; *(brand)* marca *f*; **it's a s. of teapot** es una especie de tetera **(b)** **he is a musician of sorts** tiene algo de músico; **there's an office of sorts** hay una especie de despacho **(c)** **s. of** en cierto modo

2 *vt (classify)* clasificar

▸ **sort out** *vt sep* **(a)** *(classify)* clasificar; *(put in order)* ordenar **(b)** *(problem)* arreglar, solucionar

sorting ['sɔːtɪŋ] *n* **s. office** sala *f* de batalla

SOS [esəʊ'es] *n (abbr* **save our souls***)* S.O.S. *m*

so-so ['səʊsəʊ] *adv Fam* así así, regular

soufflé ['suːfleɪ] *n* soufflé *m*, suflé *m*

sought [sɔːt] *pt & pp of* **seek**

soul [səʊl] *n* **(a)** alma *f* **(b)** **he's a good s.** *(person)* es muy buena persona **(c)** *Mus* (música *f*) soul *m*

soul-destroying ['səʊldɪstrɔɪɪŋ] *adj (boring)* monótono(a); *(demoralizing)* desmoralizador(a)

soulful ['səʊlfʊl] *adj* conmovedor(a)

sound¹ [saʊnd] **1** *n* sonido *m*; *(noise)* ruido *m*; *Fig* **I don't like the s. of it** no me gusta nada la idea; **s. barrier** barrera *f* del sonido; **s. effects** efectos sonoros

2 *vt (bell, trumpet)* tocar; **to s. the alarm** dar la señal de alarma

3 *vi* **(a)** *(trumpet, bell, alarm)* sonar **(b)** *(give an impression)* parecer; **how does it s. to you?** ¿qué te parece?; **it sounds interesting** parece interesante

sound² [saʊnd] **1** *adj* **(a)** *(healthy)* sano(a); *(in good condition)* en buen estado **(b)** *(safe, dependable)* seguro(a); *(correct)* acertado(a); *(logical)* lógico(a) **(c)** *(basis etc)* sólido(a) **(d)** *(defeat etc)* rotundo(a) **(e)** *(sleep)* profundo(a)

2 *adv* **to be s. asleep** estar profundamente dormido(a)

sound³ [saʊnd] *vt Naut & Med* sondar

▸ **sound out** *vt sep* sondear

sound⁴ [saʊnd] *n Geog* estrecho *m*

sounding ['saʊndɪŋ] *n Naut* sondeo *m*

soundproof ['saʊndpruːf] *adj* insonorizado(a)

soundtrack ['saʊndtræk] *n* banda sonora

soup [suːp] *n* sopa *f*; *(thin, clear)* caldo *m*; *Fam* **in the s.** en un apuro; **s. dish** plato hondo; **s. spoon** cuchara *f* sopera

sour [saʊə(r)] *adj* **(a)** *(fruit, wine)* agrio(a); *(milk)* cortado(a); **to go s.** *(milk)* cortarse; *(wine)* agriarse; *Fig (situation)* empeorar **(b)** *Fig (person)* amargado(a)

source [sɔːs] *n* fuente *f*; *(of infection)* foco *m*

south [saʊθ] **1** *n* sur *m*; **in the s. of England** en el sur de Inglaterra; **to the s. of York** al sur de York

2 *adj* del sur; **S. Africa** Sudáfrica; **S. African** sudafricano(a) *(m,f)*; **S. Korea** Corea del Sur; **S. Pole** Polo *m* Sur

3 *adv (location)* al sur; *(direction)* hacia el sur

southeast [sauθ'i:st] **1** *n* sudeste *m*

2 *adv (location)* al sudeste; *(direction)* hacia el sudeste

southeasterly [sauθ'i:stəlɪ] *adj* del sudeste

southerly ['sʌðəlɪ] *adj (direction)* hacia el sur; *(point)* al sur; *(wind)* del sur

southern ['sʌðən] *adj* del sur, meridional; **S. Europe** Europa del Sur; **the s. hemisphere** el hemisferio sur

southerner ['sʌðənə(r)] *n* sureño(a) *m,f*

southward ['sauθwəd] *adj & adv* hacia el sur

southwest [sauθ'west] **1** *n* suroeste *m*

2 *adj* suroeste

3 *adv (location)* al suroeste; *(direction)* hacia el suroeste

souvenir [su:və'nɪə(r)] *n* recuerdo *m*, souvenir *m*

sovereign ['sɒvrɪn] **1** *n* (**a**) *(monarch)* soberano(a) *m,f* (**b**) *Hist (coin)* soberano *m*

2 *adj* soberano(a)

soviet ['səuvɪət] **1** *n* (**a**) *(council)* soviet *m* (**b**) **the Soviets** los soviéticos

2 *adj* soviético(a); *Hist* **S. Union** Unión Soviética

sow¹ [səu] *vt (pt* sowed; *pp* sowed *or* sown*)* sembrar

sow² [sau] *n Zool* cerda *f*

sown [səun] *pp of* **sow**

soy [sɔɪ] *n* soja *f*; **s. sauce** salsa *f* de soja

soya ['sɔɪə] *n* soja *f*; **s. bean** semilla *f* de soja

spa [spɑ:] *n* balneario *m*

space [speɪs] **1** *n* (**a**) espacio *m*; **s. age** era *f* espacial; **s. shuttle** transbordador *m* espacial; **s. station** estación *f* espacial (**b**) *(room)* sitio *m*; **in a confined s.** en un espacio reducido

2 *vt (also* **s. out***)* espaciar, separar

spacecraft ['speɪskrɑ:ft] *n (pl* spacecraft*)* nave *f* espacial

spaceman ['speɪsmən] *n* astronauta *m*, cosmonauta *m*

spacing ['speɪsɪŋ] *n* **double s.** doble espacio

spacious ['speɪʃəs] *adj* espacioso(a), amplio(a)

spade¹ [speɪd] *n (for digging)* pala *f*

> 🖉 Note that the Spanish word **espada** is a false friend and is never a translation for the English word **spade**. In Spanish, **espada** means "sword".

spade² [speɪd] *n Cards* pica *f*

spaghetti [spə'getɪ] *n* espaguetis *mpl*

Spain [speɪn] *n* España

span [spæn] **1** *n* (*of wing)* envergadura *f*; *(of hand)* palmo *m*; *(of arch)* luz *f*; *(of road)* tramo *m*; *(of time)* lapso *m*; **life s.** vida *f*

2 *vt (river etc)* extenderse sobre, atravesar; *(period of time etc)* abarcar

3 *pt of* **spin**

Spaniard ['spænjəd] *n* español(a) *m,f*

spaniel ['spænjəl] *n* perro *m* de aguas

Spanish ['spænɪʃ] **1** *adj* español(a)

2 *n* (**a**) **the S.** los españoles (**b**) *(language)* español *m*, castellano *m*

Spanish-speaking ['spænɪ'spi:kɪŋ] *adj* de habla española, hispanohablante

spank [spæŋk] *vt* zurrar

spanner ['spænə(r)] *n* llave *f* (para tuercas); *Br Fam* **to throw a s. in the works** estropear los planes

spar¹ [spɑː(r)] *n Naut* palo *m*, verga *f*

spar² [spɑː(r)] *vi* (**a**) *(boxers)* entrenarse (**b**) *(argue)* discutir

spare [speə(r)] **1** *vt* (**a**) *(do without)* prescindir de; **can you s. me ten?** ¿me puedes dejar diez?; **I can't s. the time** no tengo tiempo; **there's none to s.** no sobra nada (**b**) *(begrudge)* escatimar (**c**) *(show mercy to)* perdonar (**d**) **s. me the details** ahórrate los detalles

2 *adj (left over)* sobrante; *(surplus)* de sobra, de más; **a s. moment** un momento libre; **s. part** (pieza *f* de) recambio *m*; **s. room** cuarto *m* de los invitados; **s. tyre** *Aut* neumático *m* de recambio; *Br Fam (on body)* michelines *mpl*; **s. wheel** rueda *f* de recambio (**b**) *(thin)* enjuto(a)

3 *n Aut* (pieza *f* de) recambio *m*

sparing ['speərɪŋ] *adj* **to be s. with praise** escatimar elogios; **to be s. with words** ser parco(a) en palabras

sparingly ['speərɪŋlɪ] *adv* en poca cantidad

spark [spɑːk] **1** *n* chispa *f*; *Aut* **s. plug** bujía *f*

2 *vi* echar chispas

▸ **spark off** *vt sep* desatar

sparking ['spɑːkɪŋ] *adj* **s. plug** bujía *f*

sparkle ['spɑːkəl] **1** *vi (diamond, glass)* centellear, destellar; *(eyes)* brillar

2 *n (of diamond, glass)* centelleo *m*, destello *m*; *(of eyes)* brillo *m*

sparkling ['spɑːklɪŋ] *adj* (**a**) *(diamond, glass)* centelleante; *(eyes)* brillante; **s. wine** vino espumoso (**b**) *Fig (person, conversation)* vivaz

sparrow ['spærəu] *n* gorrión *m*

sparse [spɑːs] *adj (thin)* escaso(a); *(scattered)* esparcido(a); *(hair)* ralo(a)

Spartan ['spɑːtən] *adj & n* espartano(a) *(m,f)*

spasm ['spæzəm] *n* (**a**) *Med* espasmo *m*; *(of coughing)* acceso *m* (**b**) *(of anger, activity)* arrebato *m*

spasmodic [spæz'mɒdɪk] *adj* (**a**) *Med* espasmódico(a) (**b**) *(irregular)* irregular

spastic ['spæstɪk] *adj & n Med* espástico(a) *(m,f)*

spat [spæt] *pt & pp of* **spit**

spate [speɪt] *n* (**a**) *(of letters)* avalancha *f*; *(of words)* torrente *m*; *(of accidents)* racha *f* (**b**) *Br (river)* desbordamiento *m*; **to be in full s.** estar crecido(a)

spatter ['spætə(r)] *vt* salpicar (**with** de)

spatula ['spætjʊlə] *n* espátula *f*

spawn [spɔːn] **1** n *(of fish, frogs)* huevas fpl
2 vi *(fish, frogs)* frezar
3 vt Fig Pej generar

speak [spiːk] **1** vt *(pt* **spoke**; *pp* **spoken**) (a) *(utter)* decir; **to s. the truth** decir la verdad (b) *(language)* hablar
2 vi (a) *(gen)* hablar; **roughly speaking** a grandes rasgos; **so to s.** por así decirlo; **speaking of ...** a propósito de ...; **to s. to sb** hablar con algn
(b) *(make a speech)* pronunciar un discurso; *(take the floor)* tomar la palabra
(c) Tel hablar; **speaking!** ¡al habla!; **who's speaking, please?** ¿de parte de quién?
▶ **speak for** vt insep *(person, group)* hablar en nombre de; **it speaks for itself** es evidente
▶ **speak out** vi **to s. out against sth** denunciar algo
▶ **speak up** vi hablar más fuerte; Fig **to s. up for sb** intervenir a favor de algn

speaker ['spiːkə(r)] n (a) *(in dialogue)* interlocutor(a) m,f; *(lecturer)* conferenciante mf; **(public) s.** orador(a) m,f (b) *(of language)* hablante mf (c) Br Pol **the S.** el Presidente de la Cámara de los Comunes; US **the S. of the House** el Presidente de la Cámara de los Representantes (d) *(loudspeaker)* altavoz m

spear [spɪə(r)] n lanza f; *(javelin)* jabalina f; *(harpoon)* arpón m

spearhead ['spɪəhed] vt encabezar

spec [spek] n Fam **on s.** sin garantías

special ['speʃəl] **1** adj especial; *(specific)* específico(a); *(exceptional)* extraordinario(a); **s. delivery** *(letter)* exprés; *(parcel)* de entrega inmediata; **s. edition** número m especial; **s. effects** efectos mpl especiales
2 n Rad & TV programa m especial

specialist ['speʃəlɪst] n especialista mf

speciality [speʃɪ'ælɪtɪ] n esp Br especialidad f

specialize ['speʃəlaɪz] vi especializarse (**in** en)

specially ['speʃəlɪ] adv *(specifically)* especialmente; *(on purpose)* a propósito

specialty ['speʃəltɪ] n US = **speciality**

species ['spiːʃiːz] n *(pl* **species**) especie f

specific [spɪ'sɪfɪk] adj específico(a); *(definite)* concreto(a); *(precise)* preciso(a); **to be s.** concretar

specifically [spɪ'sɪfɪklɪ] adv *(exactly)* específicamente; *(expressly)* expresamente; *(namely)* en concreto

specifications [spesɪfɪ'keɪʃənz] npl datos específicos

specify ['spesɪfaɪ] vt especificar, precisar

specimen ['spesɪmɪn] n *(sample)* muestra f; *(example)* ejemplar m; **urine/tissue s.** espécimen de orina/tejido

speck [spek] n *(of dust)* mota f; *(stain)* manchita f; *(small trace)* pizca f

speckled ['spekəld] adj moteado(a)

specs [speks] npl Fam *(spectacles)* gafas fpl

spectacle ['spektəkəl] n (a) *(display)* espectáculo m (b) **spectacles** *(glasses)* gafas fpl, Am lentes mpl, anteojos mpl

spectacular [spek'tækjʊlə(r)] **1** adj espectacular, impresionante
2 n Cin & TV *(gran)* espectáculo m

spectator [spek'teɪtə(r)] n espectador(a) m,f

spectre, US specter ['spektə(r)] n espectro m, fantasma m

spectrum ['spektrəm] n espectro m

speculate ['spekjʊleɪt] vi especular

speculation [spekjʊ'leɪʃən] n especulación f

sped [sped] pt & pp of **speed**

speech [spiːtʃ] n (a) *(faculty)* habla f; *(pronunciation)* pronunciación f; **freedom of s.** libertad f de expresión (b) *(address)* discurso m; **to give a s.** pronunciar un discurso (c) Ling **part of s.** parte f de la oración

speechless ['spiːtʃlɪs] adj mudo(a), boquiabierto(a)

speed [spiːd] **1** n velocidad f; *(rapidity)* rapidez f; **at top s.** a toda velocidad; **s. limit** límite m de velocidad
2 vi (a) *(pt & pp* **sped**) *(go fast)* ir corriendo; *(hurry)* apresurarse; **to s. along** *(car etc)* ir a toda velocidad; **to s. past** pasar volando (b) *(pt & pp* **speeded**) *(exceed speed limit)* conducir con exceso de velocidad
▶ **speed up** vt sep acelerar; *(person)* meter prisa a
2 vi *(person)* darse prisa

speedboat ['spiːdbəʊt] n lancha rápida

speeding ['spiːdɪŋ] n exceso m de velocidad

speedometer [spɪ'dɒmɪtə(r)] n velocímetro m

speedway ['spiːdweɪ] n (a) *(racing)* carreras fpl de motos (b) *(track)* pista f de carreras

speedy ['spiːdɪ] adj *(speedier, speediest)* veloz, rápido(a)

spell¹ [spel] **1** vt *(pt & pp* **spelt** or **spelled**) *(letter by letter)* deletrear; Fig *(denote)* significar; **how do you s. your name?** ¿cómo se escribe su nombre?
2 vi **she can't s.** comete faltas de ortografía
▶ **spell out** vt sep Fig explicar con detalle

spell² [spel] n *(magical)* hechizo m, encanto m

spell³ [spel] n (a) *(period)* período m; *(short period)* rato m; Met **cold s.** ola f de frío (b) *(shift)* turno m

spellbound ['spelbaʊnd] adj hechizado(a), embelesado(a)

spelling ['spelɪŋ] n ortografía f

spelt [spelt] pt & pp of **spell**

spend [spend] vt *(pt & pp* **spent**) (a) *(money)* gastar (**on** en) (b) *(time)* pasar; **to s. time on sth** dedicar tiempo a algo

spending ['spendɪŋ] n gastos mpl; **s. money** dinero m de bolsillo; **s. power** poder adquisitivo

spendthrift ['spendθrɪft] adj & n derrochador(a) (m,f)

spent [spent] **1** adj gastado(a)
2 pt & pp of **spend**

sperm [spɜ:m] *n* esperma *m*; **s. bank** banco *m* de esperma; **s. whale** cachalote *m*

spew [spju:] *vt* **to s. (up)** vomitar

sphere [sfɪə(r)] *n* esfera *f*

spice [spaɪs] **1** *n* (a) especia *f* (b) *Fig* sal *f*
2 *vt* (a) *Culin* sazonar (b) **to s. (up)** *(story etc)* salpimentar

spick-and-span [spɪkən'spæn] *adj (very clean)* limpísimo(a); *(well-groomed)* acicalado(a)

spicy ['spaɪsɪ] *adj* (**spicier, spiciest**) (a) *Culin* sazonado(a); *(hot)* picante (b) *Fig (story etc)* picante

spider ['spaɪdə(r)] *n* araña *f*; **s.'s web** telaraña *f*

spike¹ [spaɪk] *n (sharp point)* punta *f*; *(metal rod)* pincho *m*; *(on railing)* barrote *m*; *Sport (on shoes)* clavo *m*

spike² [spaɪk] *n Bot* espiga *f*

spiky ['spaɪkɪ] *adj* (**spikier, spikiest**) puntiagudo(a); *(hairstyle)* de punta

spill [spɪl] **1** *vt* (*pt & pp* **spilled** *or* **spilt** [spɪlt]) derramar
2 *vi (liquid)* derramarse
▸ **spill over** *vi* desbordarse

spin [spɪn] **1** *vt* (*pt* **span** *or* **spun**; *pp* **spun**) (a) *(wheel etc)* hacer girar; *(washing)* centrifugar (b) *(cotton, wool)* hilar; *(spider's web)* tejer
2 *vi (wheel etc)* girar; *Av* caer en barrena; *Aut* patinar
3 *n* (a) *(turn)* vuelta *f*, giro *m* (b) *Sport* efecto *m* (c) *Av* barrena *f*; *Aut* patinazo *m* (d) *Br* **to go for a s.** *(ride)* dar una vuelta (e) *Pol (on news story)* sesgo *m*; **s. doctor** asesor(a) *m,f* político(a) *(para dar buena prensa a un partido o político)*

spinach ['spɪnɪtʃ] *n* espinacas *fpl*

spinal ['spaɪnəl] *adj* espinal, vertebral; **s. column** columna *f* vertebral; **s. cord** médula *f* espinal

spindly ['spɪndlɪ] *adj* (**spindlier, spindliest**) *Fam (long-bodied)* larguirucho(a); *(long-legged)* zanquilargo(a)

spin-dryer [spɪn'draɪə(r)] *n* secador centrífugo

spine [spaɪn] *n* (a) *Anat* columna *f* vertebral, espinazo *m*; *(of book)* lomo *m* (b) *Zool* púa *f*; *Bot* espina *f*

spineless ['spaɪnlɪs] *adj Fig (weak)* sin carácter

spinning ['spɪnɪŋ] *n* (a) *(of cotton etc)* (act) hilado *m*; *(art)* hilandería *f*; **s. wheel** rueca *f* (b) **s. top** peonza *f*

spin-off ['spɪnɒf] *n (by-product)* derivado *m*; *Fig* efecto secundario

spinster ['spɪnstə(r)] *n* soltera *f*

spiral ['spaɪərəl] **1** *n* espiral *f*
2 *adj* en espiral; **s. staircase** escalera *f* de caracol

spirit¹ ['spɪrɪt] *n* (a) *(soul)* espíritu *m*, alma *f*; *(ghost)* fantasma *m* (b) *(attitude)* espíritu *m*; *(mood)* humor *m*; **to take sth in the right s.** tomar algo a bien; **community s.** civismo *m*

(c) *(courage)* valor *m*; *(liveliness)* ánimo *m*; *(vitality)* vigor *m*; **to break sb's s.** quebrar la voluntad de algn (d) **spirits** *(mood)* humor *m*; **to be in good spirits** estar de buen humor; **to be in high/low spirits** estar muy animado/desanimado

spirit² ['spɪrɪt] *n* (a) *Chem* alcohol *m*; **s. level** nivel *m* de aire (b) **spirits** *(alcoholic drinks)* licores *mpl*

spirited ['spɪrɪtɪd] *adj (person, attempt)* valiente; *(horse)* fogoso(a); *(attack)* enérgico(a)

spiritual ['spɪrɪtjʊəl] *adj* espiritual

spit¹ [spɪt] **1** *vt* (*pt & pp* **spat**) escupir
2 *vi* escupir; *Fam* **he's the spitting image of his father** es el vivo retrato de su padre
3 *n (saliva)* saliva *f*

spit² [spɪt] *n Culin* asador *m*

spite [spaɪt] **1** *n* (a) *(ill will)* rencor *m*, ojeriza *f* (b) **in s. of** a pesar de, pese a; **in s. of the fact that** a pesar de que, pese a que
2 *vt (annoy)* fastidiar

spiteful ['spaɪtfʊl] *adj (person)* rencoroso(a); *(remark)* malévolo(a); *(tongue)* viperino(a)

spittle ['spɪtəl] *n* saliva *f*

spittoon [spɪ'tu:n] *n* escupidera *f*

splash [splæʃ] **1** *vt* salpicar
2 *vi* (a) **to s. (about)** *(in water)* chapotear (b) *(water etc)* salpicar
3 *n* (a) *(noise)* chapoteo *m* (b) *(spray)* salpicadura *f*; *Fig (of colour)* mancha *f*
▸ **splash out** *vi Fam* tirar la casa por la ventana

spleen [spli:n] *n Anat* bazo *m*

splendid ['splendɪd] *adj* espléndido(a)

splendour, *US* **splendor** ['splendə(r)] *n* esplendor *m*

splint [splɪnt] *n* tablilla *f*

splinter ['splɪntə(r)] **1** *n (wood)* astilla *f*; *(bone, stone)* esquirla *f*; *(glass)* fragmento *m*; **s. group** grupo *m* disidente
2 *vi* (a) *(wood etc)* astillarse (b) *Pol* escindirse

split [splɪt] **1** *n* (a) *(crack)* grieta *f*, hendidura *f*; *(tear)* desgarrón *m*; *Fig (division)* cisma *m*; *Pol* escisión *f* (b) **to do the splits** abrir las piernas en cruz
2 *adj* partido(a); **in a s. second** en una fracción de segundo; **s. personality** desdoblamiento *m* de personalidad
3 *vt* (*pt & pp* **split**) (a) *(crack)* agrietar; *(cut)* partir; *(tear)* rajar; *(atom)* desintegrar; *Fig* **to s. hairs** buscarle tres pies al gato (b) *(divide)* dividir (c) *(share out)* repartir (d) *Pol* escindir
4 *vi* (a) *(crack)* agrietarse; *(into two parts)* partirse; *(garment)* rajarse (b) *(divide)* dividirse (c) *Pol* escindirse
▸ **split up** *vt sep (break up)* partir; *(divide up)* dividir; *(share out)* repartir
2 *vi (couple)* separarse

splutter ['splʌtə(r)] *vi (person)* balbucear; *(candle, fat)* chisporrotear; *(engine)* petardear

spoil [spɔɪl] **1** vt (pt & pp **spoiled** or **spoilt**) (**a**) (ruin) estropear, echar a perder (**b**) (child) mimar a; **to be spoilt for choice** tener demasiadas cosas para elegir
2 vi (food) estropearse

spoilsport ['spɔɪlspɔːt] n Fam aguafiestas mf inv

spoilt [spɔɪlt] **1** adj (**a**) (food, merchandise) estropeado(a) (**b**) (child) mimado(a)
2 pt & pp of **spoil**

spoke¹ [spəʊk] pt of **speak**

spoke² [spəʊk] n (of wheel) radio m, rayo m

spoken ['spəʊkən] pp of **speak**

spokesman ['spəʊksmən] n portavoz m

spokeswoman ['spəʊkswʊmən] n portavoz f

sponge [spʌndʒ] **1** n esponja f; Fig **to throw in the s.** arrojar la toalla; Br **s. cake** bizcocho m
2 vt (wash) lavar con esponja
3 vi Fam vivir de gorra
▸ **sponge off, sponge on** vt insep vivir a costa de

spongy ['spʌndʒɪ] adj (**spongier, spongiest**) esponjoso(a)

sponsor ['spɒnsə(r)] **1** vt patrocinar; Fin avalar; (support) respaldar
2 n patrocinador(a) m,f; Fin avalador(a) m,f

sponsorship ['spɒnsəʃɪp] n patrocinio m; Fin aval m; (support) respaldo m

spontaneous [spɒn'teɪnɪəs] adj espontáneo(a)

spoof [spuːf] n Fam (**a**) (parody) burla f (**b**) (hoax) engaño m

spooky ['spuːkɪ] adj (**spookier, spookiest**) Fam espeluznante

spool [spuːl] n bobina f, carrete m

spoon [spuːn] **1** n cuchara f; (small) cucharita f
2 vt sacar con cuchara; (serve) servir con cuchara

spoon-feed ['spuːnfiːd] vt (baby) dar de comer con cuchara a; Fig (spoil) mimar

spoonful ['spuːnfʊl] n cucharada f

sporadic [spə'rædɪk] adj esporádico(a)

sport [spɔːt] **1** n (**a**) (activity) deporte m (**b**) Fam **he's a good s.** es buena persona; **be a s.!** ¡sé amable!
2 vt (display) lucir

sporting ['spɔːtɪŋ] adj deportivo(a)

sports [spɔːts] **1** npl deportes mpl, deporte m
2 adj **s. car** coche deportivo; **s. jacket** chaqueta f (de) sport

sportsman ['spɔːtsmən] n deportista m

sportsmanlike ['spɔːtsmənlaɪk] adj deportivo(a)

sportsmanship ['spɔːtsmənʃɪp] n deportividad f

sportswear ['spɔːtsweə(r)] n (for sport) ropa f de deporte; (casual clothes) ropa (de) sport

sportswoman ['spɔːtswʊmən] n deportista f

sporty ['spɔːtɪ] adj (**sportier, sportiest**) Fam deportivo(a)

spot [spɒt] **1** n (**a**) (dot) punto m; (on fabric) lunar m (**b**) (stain) mancha f (**c**) (pimple) grano m (**d**) (place) sitio m, lugar m; **on the s.** (person) allí, presente; **to decide sth on the s.** decidir algo en el acto; **s. check** chequeo rápido; Fig **weak s.** punto débil; **to be in a tight s.** estar en un apuro; **to put sb on the s.** poner a algn en un aprieto
(**e**) Fam (small amount) poquito m; **a s. of bother** unos problemillas
(**f**) Rad, TV Th (in show) espacio m; (advertisement) spot m, anuncio m
2 vt (notice) darse cuenta de, notar; (see) ver

spotless ['spɒtlɪs] adj (very clean) impecable; Fig (reputation etc) intachable

spotlight ['spɒtlaɪt] n foco m; Aut faro m auxiliar; Fig **to be in the s.** ser objeto de la atención pública

spot-on [spɒt'ɒn] adj Fam exacto(a)

spotted ['spɒtɪd] adj (with dots) con puntos; (fabric) con lunares; (speckled) moteado(a)

spotty ['spɒtɪ] adj (**spottier, spottiest**) Pej con granos

spouse [spaʊs] n cónyuge mf

spout [spaʊt] **1** n (of jug) pico m; (of teapot) pitorro m
2 vt Fam (nonsense) soltar
3 vi **to s. out/up** (liquid) brotar

sprain [spreɪn] **1** n esguince m
2 vt torcer; **to s. one's ankle** torcerse el tobillo

sprang [spræŋ] pt of **spring**

sprawl [sprɔːl] **1** vi (**a**) (sit, lie) tumbarse (**b**) (city, plant) extenderse
2 n (of city) extensión f

spray¹ [spreɪ] **1** n (**a**) (of water) rociada f; (from sea) espuma f; (from aerosol) pulverización f (**b**) (aerosol) spray m; (for plants) pulverizador m; **s. can** aerosol m
2 vt (water) rociar; (insecticide, perfume) pulverizar

spray² [spreɪ] n (of flowers) ramita f

spread [spred] **1** n (**a**) (extension) extensión f; (of ideas) difusión f; (of disease, fire) propagación f; (of terrorism) generalización f
(**b**) (range) gama f
(**c**) (of wings) envergadura f
(**d**) (for bread) pasta f; **cheese s.** queso m para untar
(**e**) Fam (large meal) banquetazo m
(**f**) Press **full-page s.** plana entera; **two-page s.** doble página f
2 vt (pt & pp **spread**) (**a**) (unfold) desplegar; (lay out) extender; Fig **to s. one's wings** desplegar las alas
(**b**) (butter etc) untar
(**c**) (news) difundir; (rumour) hacer correr; (disease, fire) propagar; (panic) sembrar
3 vi (**a**) (stretch out) extenderse; (unfold) desplegarse
(**b**) (news) difundirse; (rumour) correr; (disease) propagarse

spread-eagled [spred'i:gəld] *adj* despatarrado(a)

spreadsheet ['spredʃiːt] *n Comput* hoja *f* de cálculo

spree [spriː] *n* juerga *f*; **to go on a s.** ir de juerga

sprig [sprɪg] *n* ramita *f*

sprightly ['spraɪtlɪ] *adj* (**sprightlier, sprightliest**) *(nimble)* ágil; *(energetic)* enérgico(a); *(lively)* animado(a)

spring¹ [sprɪŋ] **1** *n* (season) primavera *f*
2 *adj* primaveral; **s. onion** cebolleta *f*; **s. roll** rollo *m* de primavera

spring² [sprɪŋ] **1** *n* (**a**) *(of water)* manantial *m*, fuente *f* (**b**) *(of watch etc)* resorte *m*; *(of mattress)* muelle *m*; *Aut* ballesta *f*
2 *vi* (*pt* **sprang**; *pp* **sprung**) (**a**) *(jump)* saltar; **the lid sprang open** la tapa se abrió de golpe (**b**) *(appear)* aparecer (de repente)
3 *vt* (**a**) **to s. a leak** hacer agua (**b**) *Fig (news, surprise)* dar de golpe
▸ **spring up** *vi* aparecer; *(plants)* brotar; *(buildings)* elevarse; *(problems)* surgir

springboard ['sprɪŋbɔːd] *n* trampolín *m*

spring-clean [sprɪŋ'kliːn] *vt* limpiar a fondo

springtime ['sprɪŋtaɪm] *n* primavera *f*

springy ['sprɪŋɪ] *adj* (**springier, springiest**) *(bouncy)* elástico(a); *Fig (step)* saltarín

sprinkle ['sprɪŋkəl] *vt* (with water) rociar (**with** de); *(with sugar)* espolvorear (**with** de)

sprint [sprɪnt] **1** *n* esprint *m*
2 *vi* esprintar

sprinter ['sprɪntə(r)] *n* esprínter *mf*, velocista *mf*

sprout [spraʊt] **1** *vi* (bud) brotar; *Fig* crecer rápidamente
2 *n* (**Brussels**) **sprouts** coles *fpl* de Bruselas

spruce¹ [spruːs] *n Bot* picea *f*

spruce² [spruːs] *adj* (neat) pulcro(a); *(smart)* apuesto(a)
▸ **spruce up** *vt sep* acicalar

sprung [sprʌŋ] *pp* of **spring**

spry [spraɪ] *adj* (**sprier, spriest**) *(nimble)* ágil; *(active)* activo(a); *(lively)* vivaz

spun [spʌn] *pt & pp* of **spin**

spur [spɜː(r)] **1** *n* (**a**) *(of water)* espuela *f* (**b**) *Fig (stimulus)* acicate *m*; **on the s. of the moment** sin pensarlo
2 *vt* (**a**) *(horse)* espolear (**b**) *Fig* incitar

spurious ['spjʊərɪəs] *adj* falso(a), espurio(a)

spurn [spɜːn] *vt Fml* desdeñar, rechazar

spurt [spɜːt] **1** *n* (**a**) *(of liquid)* chorro *m* (**b**) *Fig (of activity etc)* racha *f*; *(effort)* esfuerzo *m*
2 *vi* (**a**) *(liquid)* chorrear (**b**) *(make an effort)* hacer un último esfuerzo; *(accelerate)* acelerar

spy [spaɪ] **1** *n* espía *mf*
2 *vt Fml (see)* divisar
3 *vi* espiar (**on** a)

spyhole ['spaɪhəʊl] *n* mirilla *f*

spying ['spaɪɪŋ] *n* espionaje *m*

squabble ['skwɒbəl] **1** *n* riña *f*, pelea *f*

2 *vi* reñir, pelearse (**over** or **about** por)

squad [skwɒd] *n Mil* pelotón *m*; *(of police)* brigada *f*; *Sport* equipo *m*; **drugs s.** brigada antidroga

squadron ['skwɒdrən] *n Mil* escuadrón *m*; *Av* escuadrilla *f*; *Naut* escuadra *f*

squalid ['skwɒlɪd] *adj* (very dirty) asqueroso(a); *(poor)* miserable; *(motive)* vil

squall¹ [skwɔːl] *n (wind)* ráfaga *f*

squall² [skwɔːl] *vi* chillar, berrear

squalor ['skwɒlə(r)] *n* (dirtiness) mugre *f*; *(poverty)* miseria *f*

squander ['skwɒndə(r)] *vt (money)* derrochar, despilfarrar; *(time)* desperdiciar

square [skweə(r)] **1** *n* (**a**) *(on chessboard, crossword)* casilla *f*; *Fig* **we're back to s. one!** ¡volvemos a partir desde cero! (**b**) *(in town)* plaza *f* (**c**) *Math* cuadrado *m*
2 *adj* (**a**) *(in shape)* cuadrado(a) (**b**) *Math* cuadrado(a); **s. metre** metro cuadrado; **s. root** raíz cuadrada (**c**) *Fam (fair)* justo(a); **to be s. with sb** *(honest)* ser franco(a) con algn (**d**) **a s. meal** una buena comida (**e**) *(old-fashioned)* carroza; *(conservative)* carca
3 *vt* (**a**) *(make square)* cuadrar; **to s. one's shoulders** sacar el pecho (**b**) *Math* elevar al cuadrado (**c**) *(settle)* arreglar
4 *vi* (agree) cuadrar (**with** con)

squarely ['skweəlɪ] *adv (directly)* directamente, de lleno

squash¹ [skwɒʃ] **1** *n Br (drink)* concentrado *m*
2 *vt* (**a**) *(crush)* aplastar (**b**) *Fig (objection)* echar por tierra
3 *vi* (crush) aplastarse

squash² [skwɒʃ] *n Sport* squash *m*

squash³ [skwɒʃ] *n US (vegetable)* calabacín *m*

squat [skwɒt] **1** *adj* (person) rechoncho(a)
2 *vi* (**a**) *(crouch)* agacharse, sentarse en cuclillas (**b**) *(in building)* ocupar ilegalmente
3 *n* (building) edificio *m* ocupado ilegalmente

squatter ['skwɒtə(r)] *n* ocupante *mf* ilegal, okupa *mf*

squawk [skwɔːk] **1** *n* graznido *m*
2 *vi* graznar

squeak [skwiːk] **1** *n* (of mouse) chillido *m*; *(of hinge, wheel)* chirrido *m*; *(of shoes)* crujido *m*
2 *vi* (mouse) chillar; *(hinge, wheel)* chirriar, rechinar; *(shoes)* crujir

squeaky ['skwiːkɪ] *adj* (**squeakier, squeakiest**) chirriante; *(voice)* chillón(ona); *(shoes)* que crujen

squeal [skwiːl] **1** *n* (of animal, person) chillido *m*
2 *vi* (**a**) *(animal, person)* chillar (**b**) *Fam (inform)* chivarse

squeamish ['skwiːmɪʃ] *adj* muy sensible

squeeze [skwiːz] **1** *vt* apretar; *(lemon etc)* exprimir; *(sponge)* estrujar; **to s. paste out of a tube** sacar pasta de un tubo apretando
2 *vi* **to s. in** apretujarse
3 *n* (a) *(pressure)* estrujón *m*; **a s. of lemon** unas gotas de limón (b) *(of hand)* apretón *m*; *(hug)* abrazo *m*; *(crush)* apiñamiento *m*; **credit s.** reducción *f* de créditos
squelch [skweltʃ] *vi* chapotear
squid [skwɪd] *n* calamar *m*; *(small)* chipirón *m*
squiggle ['skwɪgəl] *n* garabato *m*
squint [skwɪnt] **1** *n* (a) bizquera *f*; **to have a s.** ser bizco(a) (b) *Fig (quick look)* vistazo *m*
2 *vi* (a) ser bizco(a) (b) **to s. at sth** *(glance)* echar un vistazo a algo; *(with eyes half-closed)* mirar algo con los ojos entrecerrados
squirm [skwɜːm] *vi* retorcerse; *Fig (feel embarrassed)* sentirse incómodo(a)
squirrel ['skwɪrəl] *n* ardilla *f*
squirt [skwɜːt] **1** *n (of liquid)* chorro *m*
2 *vt* lanzar a chorro
3 *vi* **to s. out** salir a chorros
Sr *(abbr* **Senior)** **Thomas Smith, Sr** Thomas Smith, padre
Sri Lanka [sriː'læŋkə] *n* Sri Lanka
St (a) *(abbr* **Saint)** S./Sto./Sta. (b) *(abbr* **Street)** c/
st *Br (abbr* **stone)** = peso que equivale a 6,348 kg
stab [stæb] **1** *n (with knife)* puñalada *f*; *(of pain)* punzada *f*; *Fam Fig* **to have a s. at doing sth** intentar hacer algo
2 *vt* apuñalar
stabbing ['stæbɪŋ] *adj (pain)* punzante
stability [stə'bɪlɪti] *n* estabilidad *f*
stable¹ ['steɪbəl] *adj* estable
stable² ['steɪbəl] *n* cuadra *f*, caballeriza *f*
stack [stæk] **1** *n (pile)* montón *m*; *Fam* **he's got stacks of money** está forrado
2 *vt (pile up)* amontonar, apilar; *Fig* **the odds are stacked against us** todo está en contra nuestra
stadium ['steɪdɪəm] *n* estadio *m*
staff [stɑːf] **1** *n* (a) *(personnel)* personal *m*; *Mil* estado *m* mayor; **s. meeting** claustro *m*; *Br* **s. nurse** enfermera cualificada (b) *(stick)* bastón *m*; *(of shepherd)* cayado *m*
2 *vt* proveer de personal
staffroom ['stɑːfruːm] *n* sala *f* de profesores
stag [stæg] *n* ciervo *m*, venado *m*; *Fam* **s. party** despedida *f* de soltero
stage [steɪdʒ] **1** *n* (a) *(platform)* plataforma *f* (b) *(in theatre)* escenario *m*; **s. door** entrada *f* de artistas; **s. fright** miedo escénico; **s. manager** director(a) *m,f* de escena (c) *(phase) (of development, journey, rocket)* etapa *f*; *(of road, pipeline)* tramo *m*; **at this s. of the negotiations** a estas alturas de las negociaciones; **in stages** por etapas
2 *vt* (a) *(play)* poner en escena, montar (b) *(arrange)* organizar; *(carry out)* llevar a cabo

stagecoach ['steɪdʒkəʊtʃ] *n* diligencia *f*
stagger ['stægə(r)] **1** *vi* tambalearse
2 *vt* (a) *(amaze)* asombrar (b) *(hours, work)* escalonar
staggering ['stægərɪŋ] *adj* asombroso(a)
stagnant ['stægnənt] *adj* estancado(a)
stagnate [stæg'neɪt] *vi* estancarse
staid [steɪd] *adj (person)* conservador(a); *(manner, clothes)* serio(a), formal
stain [steɪn] **1** *n* (a) mancha *f*; **s. remover** quitamanchas *m inv* (b) *(dye)* tinte *m*
2 *vt* (a) manchar (b) *(dye)* teñir
3 *vi* mancharse
stained [steɪnd] *adj* **s. glass window** vidriera *f* de colores
stainless ['steɪnlɪs] *adj (steel)* inoxidable
stair [steə(r)] *n* escalón *m*, peldaño *m*; **stairs** escalera *f*
staircase ['steəkeɪs] *n* escalera *f*
stake¹ [steɪk] **1** *n (stick)* estaca *f*; *(for plant)* rodrigón *m*; *(post)* poste *m*
2 *vt* **to s. (out)** cercar con estacas
stake² [steɪk] **1** *n* (a) *(bet)* apuesta *f*; **the issue at s.** el tema en cuestión; **to be at s.** *(at risk)* estar en juego (b) *(investment)* interés *m*
2 *vt (bet)* apostar; *(invest)* invertir; **to s. a claim to sth** reivindicar algo
stale [steɪl] *adj (food)* pasado(a); *(bread)* duro(a)
stalemate ['steɪlmeɪt] *n (in chess)* tablas *fpl*; *Fig* **to reach s.** llegar a un punto muerto
stalk¹ [stɔːk] *n (of plant)* tallo *m*; *(of fruit)* rabo *m*
stalk² [stɔːk] **1** *vt (of hunter)* cazar al acecho; *(of animal)* acechar
2 *vi* **he stalked out** salió airado
stall¹ [stɔːl] **1** *n* (a) *(in market)* puesto *m*; *(at fair)* caseta *f* (b) *(stable)* establo *m*; *(stable compartment)* casilla *f* de establo (c) *Br Th* **stalls** platea *f*
2 *vt Aut* calar
3 *vi Aut* calarse; *Av* perder velocidad
stall² [stɔːl] *vi* **to s. (for time)** intentar ganar tiempo
stallion ['stæljən] *n* semental *m*
stalwart ['stɔːlwət] *n* incondicional *mf*
stamina ['stæmɪnə] *n* resistencia *f*
stammer ['stæmə(r)] **1** *n* tartamudeo *m*
2 *vi* tartamudear
stamp [stæmp] **1** *n* (a) *(postage stamp)* sello *m*; **s. album** álbum *m* de sellos; **s. collector** filatelista *mf*; *Br* **s. duty** póliza *f* (b) *(rubber stamp)* tampón *m*; *(for metals)* cuño *m* (c) *(with foot)* patada *f*
2 *vt* (a) *(with postage stamp)* poner el sello a; *Br* **stamped addressed envelope,** *US* **self-addressed stamped envelope** sobre franqueado con la dirección del remitente (b) *(with rubber stamp)* sellar (c) **to s. one's feet** patear; *(in dancing)* zapatear
3 *vi* patear

🔔 Note that the Spanish word **estampa** is a false friend and is never a translation for the English word **stamp**. In Spanish, **estampa** means "print, image".

▸ **stamp out** vt sep Fig (racism etc) acabar con; (rebellion) sofocar

stampede [stæm'pi:d] **1** n estampida f; Fig (rush) desbandada f
2 vi desbandarse; Fig (rush) precipitarse

stance [stæns] n postura f

stand [stænd] **1** n (a) (position) posición f, postura f; **to make a s.** resistir
(b) (of lamp, sculpture) pie m
(c) (market stall) puesto m; (at fair) caseta f; (at exhibition) stand m; **newspaper s.** quiosco m
(d) (platform) plataforma f; (in stadium) tribuna f; US (witness box) estrado m
2 vt (pt & pp **stood**) (a) (place) poner, colocar
(b) (tolerate) aguantar, soportar
(c) **to s. one's ground** mantenerse firme
3 vi (a) (be upright) estar de pie; (get up) levantarse; (remain upright) quedarse de pie; **s. still!** ¡estáte quieto(a)!
(b) (measure) medir
(c) (be situated) estar, encontrarse
(d) (remain unchanged) permanecer
(e) (remain valid) seguir vigente
(f) **as things s.** tal como están las cosas
(g) Pol presentarse
▸ **stand back** vi (allow sb to pass) abrir paso
▸ **stand by** **1** vi (a) (do nothing) quedarse sin hacer nada (b) (be ready) estar listo(a)
2 vt insep (person) apoyar a; (promise) cumplir con; (decision) atenerse a
▸ **stand down** vi Fig retirarse
▸ **stand for** vt insep (a) (mean) significar (b) (represent) representar (c) (tolerate) aguantar
▸ **stand in** vi sustituir
▸ **stand in for** vt insep sustituir
▸ **stand out** vi (mountain etc) destacarse (against contra); Fig (person) destacar
▸ **stand up** vi (get up) ponerse de pie; (be standing) estar de pie; Fig **it will s. up to wear and tear** es muy resistente; Fig **to s. up for sb** defender a algn; Fig **to s. up to sb** hacer frente a algn

standard ['stændəd] **1** n (a) (level) nivel m; **s. of living** nivel de vida (b) (criterion) criterio m (c) (norm) norma f, estándar m (d) (flag) estandarte m
2 adj normal, estándar; **s. lamp** lámpara f de pie

standardize ['stændədaɪz] vt normalizar

standby ['stændbaɪ] n (a) (thing) recurso m (b) (person) suplente mf; **to be on s.** Mil estar de retén; Av estar en la lista de espera; **s. ticket** billete m sin reserva

stand-in ['stændɪn] n suplente mf; Cin doble mf

standing ['stændɪŋ] **1** adj (a) (not sitting) de pie; (upright) recto(a); **to give sb a s. ovation** ovacionar a algn de pie; **there was s. room only** no quedaban asientos (b) (committee) permanente; (invitation) permanente; Br **s. order** pago fijo
2 n (a) (social position) rango m (b) (duration) duración f; (in job) antigüedad f

stand-offish [stænd'ɒfɪʃ] adj Fam distante

standpoint ['stændpɔɪnt] n punto m de vista

standstill ['stændstɪl] n **at a s.** (car, traffic) parado(a); (industry) paralizado(a); **to come to a s.** (car, traffic) pararse; (industry) paralizarse

stand-up ['stændʌp] adj **s. comic** or **comedian** = humorista que basa su actuación en contar chistes al público solo desde el escenario

stank [stæŋk] pt of **stink**

staple[1] ['steɪpəl] **1** n (fastener) grapa f
2 vt grapar

staple[2] ['steɪpəl] **1** adj (food) básico(a); (product) de primera necesidad
2 n (food) alimento básico

stapler ['steɪplə(r)] n grapadora f

star [stɑː(r)] **1** n estrella f
2 adj estelar
3 vt Cin tener como protagonista a
4 vi Cin **to s. in a film** protagonizar una película

starboard ['stɑːbəd] n estribor m

starch [stɑːtʃ] **1** n almidón m
2 vt almidonar

stardom ['stɑːdəm] n estrellato m

stare [steə(r)] **1** n mirada fija
2 vi mirar fijamente

starfish ['stɑːfɪʃ] n estrella f de mar

stark [stɑːk] adj (landscape) desolado(a); (décor) austero(a); **the s. truth** la dura realidad; **s. poverty** la miseria

stark-naked ['stɑːkneɪkɪd] adj Fam en cueros

starling ['stɑːlɪŋ] n estornino m

starry ['stɑːrɪ] adj (**starrier, starriest**) estrellado(a)

starry-eyed [stɑːrɪ'aɪd] adj (idealistic) idealista; (in love) enamorado(a)

start [stɑːt] **1** n (a) (beginning) principio m, comienzo m; (of race) salida f; **at the s.** al principio; **for a s.** para empezar; **from the s.** desde el principio; **to make a fresh s.** volver a empezar
(b) (advantage) ventaja f
(c) (jump) sobresalto m
2 vt (a) (begin) empezar, comenzar; **to s. doing sth** empezar a hacer algo
(b) (cause) causar, provocar
(c) (found) fundar; **to s. a business** montar un negocio
(d) (set in motion) arrancar

3 *vi* (**a**) *(begin)* empezar, comenzar; *(engine)* arrancar; **starting from Monday** a partir del lunes

(**b**) *(take fright)* asustarse, sobresaltarse

▸ **start off** *vi* (**a**) *(begin)* empezar, comenzar; **to s. off by/with** empezar por/con (**b**) *(leave)* salir, ponerse en camino

▸ **start up** *vt sep (engine)* arrancar

2 *vi* empezar; *(car)* arrancar

starter ['stɑːtə(r)] *n* (**a**) *Sport (official)* juez *mf* de salida; *(competitor)* competidor(a) *m,f* (**b**) *Aut* motor *m* de arranque (**c**) *Culin* entrada *f*

starting ['stɑːtɪŋ] *n* **s. block** taco *m* de salida; **s. point** punto *m* de partida; **s. post** línea *f* de salida

startle ['stɑːtəl] *vt* asustar

startling ['stɑːtlɪŋ] *adj* (**a**) *(frightening)* alarmante (**b**) *(news etc)* asombroso(a); *(coincidence)* extraordinario(a)

starvation [stɑː'veɪʃən] *n* hambre *f*

starve [stɑːv] **1** *vt* privar de comida; *Fig* **he was starved of affection** fue privado de cariño

2 *vi* pasar hambre; **to s. to death** morirse de hambre

starving ['stɑːvɪŋ] *adj* hambriento(a); *Fam* **I'm s.!** ¡estoy muerto(a) de hambre!

state [steɪt] **1** *n* (**a**) estado *m*; **s. of emergency** estado de emergencia; **s. of mind** estado de ánimo; **to be in no fit s. to do sth** no estar en condiciones de hacer algo (**b**) **the States** los Estados Unidos; *US* **s. highway** ≃ carretera *f* nacional; *US* **the S. Department** el Ministerio de Asuntos Exteriores

2 *adj* (**a**) *Pol* estatal; **s. education** enseñanza pública; **s. ownership** propiedad *f* del Estado (**b**) *(ceremonial)* de gala; **s. visit** visita *f* oficial

3 *vt* declarar, afirmar; *(case)* exponer; *(problem)* plantear

stated ['steɪtɪd] *adj* indicado(a)

stately ['steɪtlɪ] *adj* (**statelier, stateliest**) majestuoso(a); **s. home** casa solariega

statement ['steɪtmənt] *n* (**a**) declaración *f*; **official s.** comunicado *m* oficial; *Jur* **to make a s.** prestar declaración (**b**) *Fin* estado *m* de cuenta; **monthly s.** balance *m* mensual

statesman ['steɪtsmən] *n* estadista *m*

static ['stætɪk] **1** *adj* estático(a)

2 *n Rad* ruido *m*

station ['steɪʃən] **1** *n* (**a**) estación *f*; *US* **s. wagon** camioneta *f* (**b**) *(position)* puesto *m* (**c**) *(social standing)* rango *m*

2 *vt (place)* colocar; *Mil* apostar

stationary ['steɪʃənərɪ] *adj (not moving)* inmóvil; *(unchanging)* estacionario(a)

stationer ['steɪʃənə(r)] *n* papelero(a) *m,f*; **s.'s (shop)** papelería *f*

stationery ['steɪʃənərɪ] *n (paper)* papel *m* de escribir; *(pens, ink etc)* artículos *mpl* de escritorio

stationmaster ['steɪʃənmɑːstə(r)] *n* jefe *m* de estación

statistic [stə'tɪstɪk] *n* estadística *f*

statistical [stə'tɪstɪkəl] *adj* estadístico(a)

statistics [stə'tɪstɪks] **1** *n sing (science)* estadística *f*

2 *npl (data)* estadísticas *fpl*

statue ['stætjuː] *n* estatua *f*

status ['steɪtəs] *n* estado *m*; **social s.** estatus *m*; **s. symbol** signo *m* de prestigio; **s. quo** status quo *m*

statute ['stætjuːt] *n* estatuto *m*

statutory ['stætjʊtərɪ] *adj* reglamentario(a); *(offence)* contemplado(a) por la ley; *(right)* legal; *(holiday)* oficial

staunch [stɔːntʃ] *adj* incondicional, acérrimo

stave [steɪv] *n Mus* pentagrama *m*

▸ **stave off** *vt sep (repel)* rechazar; *(avoid)* evitar; *(delay)* aplazar

stay¹ [steɪ] **1** *n* estancia *f*

2 *vi* (**a**) *(remain)* quedarse, permanecer (**b**) *(reside temporarily)* alojarse; **she's staying with us for a few days** ha venido a pasar unos días con nosotros

3 *vt Fig* **to s. the course** aguantar hasta el final; **staying power** resistencia *f*

▸ **stay in** *vi* quedarse en casa

▸ **stay on** *vi* quedarse

▸ **stay out** *vi* **to s. out all night** no volver a casa en toda la noche

▸ **stay up** *vi* no acostarse

stay² [steɪ] *n (rope)* estay *m*, viento *m*

stead [sted] *n* **in sb's s.** en lugar de algn; **to stand sb in good s.** resultar muy útil a algn

steadfast ['stedfɑst, 'stedfɑːst] *adj* firme

steadily ['stedɪlɪ] *adv (improve)* constantemente; *(walk)* con paso seguro; *(gaze)* fijamente; *(rain, work)* sin parar

steady ['stedɪ] **1** *adj* (**steadier, steadiest**) firme, seguro(a); *(gaze)* fijo(a); *(prices)* estable; *(demand, speed)* constante; *(pace)* regular; *(worker)* aplicado(a); **s. job** empleo fijo

2 *vt (table etc)* estabilizar; *(nerves)* calmar

3 *vi (market)* estabilizarse

steak [steɪk] *n* bistec *m*

steal [stiːl] (*pt* **stole**; *pp* **stolen**) **1** *vt* robar; **to s. a glance at sth** echar una mirada furtiva a algo; **to s. the show** llevarse todos los aplausos

2 *vi* (**a**) *(rob)* robar (**b**) *(move quietly)* moverse con sigilo; **to s. away** escabullirse

stealth [stelθ] *n* sigilo *m*

stealthily ['stelθɪlɪ] *adv* a hurtadillas

stealthy ['stelθɪ] *adj* (**stealthier, stealthiest**) sigiloso(a), furtivo(a)

steam [stiːm] **1** *n* vapor *m*; *Fam* **to let off s.** desahogarse; **s. engine** máquina *f* de vapor

2 *vt Culin* cocer al vapor

3 *vi (give off steam)* echar vapor; *(bowl of soup etc)* humear

▸ **steam up** *vi (window etc)* empañarse

steamer ['stiːmə(r)] *n Naut* vapor *m*

steamroller ['stiːmrəʊlə(r)] *n* apisonadora *f*

steamship ['stiːmʃɪp] n vapor m
steamy ['stiːmɪ] adj (**steamier, steamiest**) lleno(a) de vapor
steel [stiːl] **1** n acero m; **s. industry** industria siderúrgica
  2 vt Fig **to s. oneself to do sth** armarse de valor para hacer algo
steelworks ['stiːlwɜːks] npl acería f
steep[1] [stiːp] adj (hill etc) empinado(a); Fig (price, increase) excesivo(a)
steep[2] [stiːp] vt (washing) remojar; (food) poner en remojo
steeple ['stiːpəl] n aguja f
steeplechase ['stiːpəltʃeɪs] n carrera f de obstáculos
steer [stɪə(r)] **1** vt dirigir; (car) conducir; (ship) gobernar
  2 vi (car) conducirse; Fig **to s. clear of sth** evitar algo
steering ['stɪərɪŋ] n dirección f; **assisted s.** dirección asistida; **s. wheel** volante m
stem [stem] **1** n (**a**) (of plant) tallo m; (of glass) pie m; (of pipe) tubo m (**b**) (of word) raíz f
  2 vi **to s. from** derivarse de
  3 vt (blood) restañar; (flood, attack) contener
stench [stentʃ] n hedor m
stencil ['stensəl] n (**a**) (for artwork etc) plantilla f (**b**) (for typing) cliché m
step [step] **1** n (**a**) (pace) paso m; (sound) paso, pisada f; **s. by s.** poco a poco (**b**) (measure) medida f; **a s. in the right direction** un paso acertado (**c**) (stair) peldaño m, escalón m (**d**) **steps** escalera f
  2 vi dar un paso; **s. this way, please** haga el favor de pasar por aquí; **to s. aside** apartarse
  ▸ **step down** vi dimitir
  ▸ **step forward** vi (volunteer) ofrecerse
  ▸ **step in** vi intervenir
  ▸ **step up** vt sep aumentar
stepbrother ['stepbrʌðə(r)] n hermanastro m
stepchild ['steptʃaɪld] n hijastro(a) m,f
stepdaughter ['stepdɔːtə(r)] n hijastra f
stepfather ['stepfɑːðə(r)] n padrastro m
stepladder ['steplædə(r)] n escalera f de tijera
stepmother ['stepmʌðə(r)] n madrastra f
stepping-stone ['stepɪŋstəʊn] n pasadera f; Fig trampolín m
stepsister ['stepsɪstə(r)] n hermanastra f
stepson ['stepsʌn] n hijastro m
stereo ['sterɪəʊ] **1** n estéreo m
  2 adj estereo(tónico(a))
stereotype ['sterɪətaɪp] n estereotipo m
sterile ['steraɪl] adj (barren) estéril
sterilize ['sterɪlaɪz] vt esterilizar
sterling ['stɜːlɪŋ] **1** n libras fpl esterlinas; **s. silver** plata f de ley; **the pound s.** la libra esterlina
  2 adj (person, quality) excelente
stern[1] [stɜːn] adj (severe) severo(a)
stern[2] [stɜːn] n Naut popa f

steroid ['sterɔɪd] n esteroide m
stethoscope ['steθəskəʊp] n estetoscopio m
stew [stjuː] **1** n estofado m, cocido m
  2 vt (meat) guisar, estofar; (fruit) cocer
steward ['stjʊəd] n (on estate) administrador m; (on ship) camarero m; (on plane) auxiliar m de vuelo
stewardess ['stjʊədɪs] n (on ship) camarera f; (on plane) azafata f
stick[1] [stɪk] n (**a**) palo m; (walking stick) bastón m; (of dynamite) cartucho m; Fam **to give sb s.** dar caña a algn (**b**) Fam **to live in the sticks** vivir en el quinto pino
stick[2] [stɪk] **1** vt (pt & pp **stuck**) (**a**) (push) meter; (knife) clavar; **he stuck his head out of the window** asomó la cabeza por la ventana (**b**) Fam (put) meter (**c**) (with glue etc) pegar (**d**) Fam (tolerate) soportar, aguantar
  2 vi (**a**) (become attached) pegarse (**b**) (window, drawer) atrancarse; (machine part) encasquillarse
  ▸ **stick at** vt insep perseverar en
  ▸ **stick by** vt insep (friend) ser fiel a; (promise) cumplir con
  ▸ **stick out 1** vi (project) sobresalir; (be noticeable) resaltar
  2 vt sep (tongue) sacar; Fig **to s. one's neck out** jugarse el tipo
  ▸ **stick to** vt insep (principles) atenerse a
  ▸ **stick up 1** vi (project) sobresalir; (hair) ponerse de punta
  2 vt sep (**a**) (poster) fijar (**b**) (hand etc) levantar
  ▸ **stick up for** vt insep defender
sticker ['stɪkə(r)] n (label) etiqueta adhesiva; (with slogan) pegatina f
sticking-plaster ['stɪkɪŋˌplɑːstə(r)] n Br tirita® f, Am curita f
stickler ['stɪklə(r)] n meticuloso(a) m,f; **to be a s. for detail** ser muy detallista
stick-up ['stɪkʌp] n US Fam atraco m, asalto m
sticky ['stɪkɪ] adj (**stickier, stickiest**) pegajoso(a); (label) engomado(a); (weather) bochornoso(a); Fam (situation) difícil
stiff [stɪf] **1** adj (**a**) rígido(a), tieso(a); (collar, lock) duro(a); (joint) entumecido(a); (machine part) atascado(a); **to have a s. neck** tener tortícolis (**b**) Fig (test) difícil; (punishment) severo(a); (price) excesivo(a); (drink) fuerte; (person) (unnatural) estirado(a)
  2 n Fam (corpse) fiambre m
stiffen ['stɪfən] **1** vt (fabric) reforzar; (collar) almidonar; Fig (resistance) fortalecer
  2 vi (person) ponerse tieso(a); (joints) entumecerse; Fig (resistance) fortalecerse
stiffness ['stɪfnɪs] n rigidez f
stifle ['staɪfəl] **1** vt sofocar; (yawn) reprimir
  2 vi ahogarse, sofocarse
stifling ['staɪflɪŋ] adj sofocante, agobiante
stigma ['stɪgmə] n estigma m
stile [staɪl] n = escalones para pasar por encima de una valla

stiletto [stɪˈletəʊ] *n* zapato *m* con tacón de aguja

still¹ [stɪl] **1** *adv* (a) *(up to this time)* todavía, aún

(b) *(with comp adj & adv)* *(even)* aún; **s. colder** aún más frío

(c) *(nonetheless)* no obstante, con todo

(d) *(however)* sin embargo

(e) *(motionless)* quieto; **to stand s.** no moverse

2 *adj (calm)* tranquilo(a); *(peaceful)* sosegado(a); *(silent)* silencioso(a); *(motionless)* inmóvil

3 *n Cin* fotograma *m*; *Art* **s. life** naturaleza muerta

4 *vt Fml (fears etc)* calmar

still² [stɪl] *n (apparatus)* alambique *m*

stillborn [ˈstɪlbɔːn] *adj* nacido(a) muerto(a)

stillness [ˈstɪlnɪs] *n* calma *f*; *(silence)* silencio *m*

stilt [stɪlt] *n* zanco *m*

stilted [ˈstɪltɪd] *adj* afectado(a)

stimulant [ˈstɪmjʊlənt] *n* estimulante *m*

stimulate [ˈstɪmjʊleɪt] *vt* estimular

stimulating [ˈstɪmjʊleɪtɪŋ] *adj* estimulante

stimulus [ˈstɪmjʊləs] *n* (*pl* **stimuli** [ˈstɪmjʊlaɪ]) estímulo *m*; *Fig* incentivo *m*

sting [stɪŋ] **1** *n (part of bee, wasp)* aguijón *m*; *(wound)* picadura *f*; *(burning)* escozor *m*; *Fig (of remorse)* punzada *f*; *Fig (of remark)* sarcasmo *m*

2 *vt (pt & pp* **stung)** picar; *Fig (conscience)* remorder; *Fig (remark)* herir en lo vivo

3 *vi* picar

stingy [ˈstɪndʒɪ] *adj* (**stingier, stingiest**) *Fam (person)* tacaño(a); *(amount)* escaso(a); **to be s. with** escatimar

stink [stɪŋk] **1** *n* peste *m*, hedor *m*

2 *vi (pt* **stank** *or* **stunk;** *pp* **stunk)** apestar, heder (**of** a)

stinking [ˈstɪŋkɪŋ] **1** *adj (smelly)* apestoso(a); *Fam* **to have a s. cold** tener un catarro bestial

2 *adv Fam* **he's s. rich** está podrido de dinero

stint [stɪnt] **1** *n (period)* período *m*, temporada *f*; *(shift)* turno *m*; **he did a two-year s. in the navy** sirvió durante dos años en la Marina

2 *vt* escatimar

stipulate [ˈstɪpjʊleɪt] *vt* estipular

stipulation [stɪpjʊˈleɪʃən] *n* estipulación *f*

stir [stɜː(r)] **1** *n Fig* revuelo *m*

2 *vt* (a) *(liquid)* remover (b) *(move)* agitar (c) *Fig (curiosity, interest)* despertar; *(anger)* provocar

3 *vi (move)* rebullirse

▸ **stir up** *vt sep Fig (memories, curiosity)* despertar; *(passions)* excitar; *(anger)* provocar; *(revolt)* fomentar

stirring [ˈstɜːrɪŋ] *adj* conmovedor(a)

stirrup [ˈstɪrəp] *n* estribo *m*

stitch [stɪtʃ] **1** *n* (a) *Sewing* puntada *f*; *(in knitting)* punto *m*; *Med* punto (de sutura); *Fam* **we were in stitches** nos tronchábamos

de risa (b) *(pain)* punzada *f*

2 *vt Sewing* coser; *Med* suturar, dar puntos a

stoat [stəʊt] *n* armiño *m*

stock [stɒk] **1** *n* (a) *(supply)* reserva *f*; *Com (goods)* existencias *fpl*, stock *m*; *(selection)* surtido *m*; **out of s.** agotado(a); **to have sth in s.** tener existencias de algo; *Fig* **to take s. of** evaluar

(b) *Fin* capital *m* social; **stocks and shares** acciones *fpl*, valores *mpl*; **S. Exchange** Bolsa *f* (de valores); **s. market** bolsa

(c) *Agr* ganado *m*; **s. farming** ganadería *f*

(d) *Culin* caldo *m*; **s. cube** cubito *m* de caldo

(e) *(descent)* estirpe *f*

2 *adj* (a) *(goods)* corriente

(b) *(excuse, response)* de siempre; *(phrase)* gastado(a)

3 *vt* (a) *(have in stock)* tener existencias de

(b) *(provide)* abastecer, surtir (**with** de); *(cupboard)* llenar (**with** de)

▸ **stock up** *vi* abastecerse (**on** *or* **with** de)

stockbroker [ˈstɒkbrəʊkə(r)] *n* corredor(a) *m,f* de Bolsa

stockholder [ˈstɒkhəʊldə(r)] *n US* accionista *mf*

stocking [ˈstɒkɪŋ] *n* media *f*; **a pair of stockings** unas medias

stockist [ˈstɒkɪst] *n* distribuidor(a) *m,f*

stockpile [ˈstɒkpaɪl] **1** *n* reservas *fpl*

2 *vt* almacenar; *(accumulate)* acumular

stocks [stɒks] *npl Hist* cepo *m*

stocktaking [ˈstɒkteɪkɪŋ] *n Com* inventario *m*

stocky [ˈstɒkɪ] *adj* (**stockier, stockiest**) *(squat)* rechoncho(a); *(heavily built)* fornido(a)

stodgy [ˈstɒdʒɪ] *adj* (**stodgier, stodgiest**) *(food)* indigesto(a); *Fig (book, person)* pesado(a)

stoical [ˈstəʊɪkəl] *adj* estoico(a)

stoke [stəʊk] *vt (poke)* atizar; **to s. (up)** *(feed)* alimentar

stole¹ [stəʊl] *pt of* **steal**

stole² [stəʊl] *n* estola *f*

stolen [ˈstəʊlən] *pp of* **steal**

stolid [ˈstɒlɪd] *adj* impasible

stomach [ˈstʌmək] **1** *n* estómago *m*; **s. ache** dolor *m* de estómago; **s. upset** trastorno gástrico

2 *vt Fig* aguantar

stone [stəʊn] **1** *n* (a) piedra *f*; *(on grave)* lápida *f*; *Fig* **at a s.'s throw** a tiro de piedra (b) *Med* cálculo *m* (c) *(of fruit)* hueso *m* (d) *(weight)* = 6,348 kg

2 *adj* de piedra; **the S. Age** la Edad de Piedra

3 *vt (kill)* lapidar

stone-cold [stəʊnˈkəʊld] *adj* helado(a)

stoned [stəʊnd] *adj Fam (drugged)* colocado(a); *(drunk)* como una cuba

stone-deaf [stəʊnˈdef] *adj* sordo(a) como una tapia

stonework [ˈstəʊnwɜːk] *n* mampostería *f*

stony [ˈstəʊnɪ] *adj* (**stonier, stoniest**)

(ground) pedregoso(a); *Fig (look, silence)* glacial

stood [stʊd] *pt & pp of* **stand**

stool [stuːl] *n* (**a**) *(seat)* taburete *m* (**b**) *Med* heces *fpl*

stoop [stuːp] *vi* (**a**) *(have a stoop)* andar encorvado(a) (**b**) *(bend)* **to s. down** inclinarse, agacharse (**c**) *Fig* **to s.** rebajarse a; **he wouldn't s. so low** no se rebajaría tanto

stop [stɒp] **1** *n* (**a**) *(halt)* parada *f*, alto *m*; **to come to a s.** pararse; **to put a s. to sth** poner fin a algo
　(**b**) *(break)* pausa *f*; *(for refuelling etc)* escala *f*
　(**c**) *(for bus, tram)* parada *f*
　(**d**) *(punctuation mark)* punto *m*
　2 *vt* (**a**) parar; *(conversation)* interrumpir; *(pain, abuse etc)* poner fin a
　(**b**) *(payments)* suspender; *(cheque)* anular
　(**c**) **to s. doing sth** dejar de hacer algo; **s. singing** deja de cantar; **s. it!** ¡basta ya!
　(**d**) *(prevent)* evitar; **to s. sb from doing sth** impedir a algn hacer algo
　(**e**) *(hole)* tapar; *(gap)* rellenar
　3 *vi* (**a**) *(person, moving vehicle)* pararse, detenerse; **my watch has stopped** se me ha parado el reloj; **to s. dead** pararse en seco
　(**b**) *(cease)* acabarse, terminar
　(**c**) *Fam (stay)* pararse
▸ **stop by** *vi Fam* visitar
▸ **stop off** *vi* pararse un rato
▸ **stop over** *vi (spend the night)* pasar la noche; *(for refuelling etc)* hacer escala
▸ **stop up** *vt sep (hole)* tapar

stopgap ['stɒpgæp] *n (thing)* medida *f* provisional; *(person)* sustituto(a) *m,f*

stopover ['stɒpəʊvə(r)] *n* parada *f*; *Av* escala *f*

stoppage ['stɒpɪdʒ] *n* (**a**) *(of game, payments)* suspensión *f*; *(of work)* paro *m*; *(strike)* huelga *f*; *(deduction)* deducción *f* (**b**) *(blockage)* obstrucción *f*

stopper ['stɒpə(r)] *n* tapón *m*

stop-press [stɒp'pres] *n* noticias *fpl* de última hora

stopwatch ['stɒpwɒtʃ] *n* cronómetro *m*

storage ['stɔːrɪdʒ] *n* almacenaje *m*, almacenamiento *m*; **s. battery** acumulador *m*; **s. heater** placa acumuladora

store [stɔː(r)] **1** *n* (**a**) *(stock)* provisión *f*; *Fig (of wisdom)* reserva *f* (**b**) *(warehouse)* almacén *m* (**c**) *esp US (shop)* tienda *f*; **department s.** gran almacén *m*
　2 *vt* (**a**) *(furniture, computer data)* almacenar; *(keep)* guardar (**b**) **to s. (up)** acumular

storekeeper ['stɔːkiːpə(r)] *n US* tendero(a) *m,f*

storeroom ['stɔːruːm] *n* despensa *f*

storey ['stɔːrɪ] *n* piso *m*

stork [stɔːk] *n* cigüeña *f*

storm [stɔːm] **1** *n* tormenta *f*; *(with wind)* vendaval *m*; *Fig (uproar)* revuelo *m*; *Fig* **she has taken New York by s.** ha cautivado a todo Nueva York
　2 *vt* tomar por asalto
　3 *vi (with rage)* echar pestes

stormy ['stɔːmɪ] *adj* (**stormier, stormiest**) *(weather)* tormentoso(a); *Fig (discussion)* acalorado(a); *(relationship)* tempestuoso(a)

story¹ ['stɔːrɪ] *n* historia *f*; *(tale, account)* relato *m*; *(article)* artículo *m*; *(plot)* trama *f*; *(joke)* chiste *m*; *(rumour)* rumor *m*; **it's a long s.** sería largo de contar; **tall s.** cuento chino

story² ['stɔːrɪ] *n US* = **storey**

storybook ['stɔːrɪbʊk] *n* libro *m* de cuentos

storyteller ['stɔːrɪtelə(r)] *n* cuentista *mf*

stout [staʊt] **1** *adj* (**a**) *(fat)* gordo(a), corpulento(a) (**b**) *(strong)* fuerte (**c**) *(brave)* valiente; *(determined)* firme
　2 *n (beer)* cerveza negra

stoutly ['staʊtlɪ] *adv* resueltamente

stove [stəʊv] *n* (**a**) *(for heating)* estufa *f* (**b**) *(cooker)* cocina *f*

stow [stəʊ] *vt* (**a**) *(cargo)* estibar (**b**) *(put away)* guardar
▸ **stow away** *vi (on ship, plane)* viajar de polizón

stowaway ['stəʊəweɪ] *n* polizón *mf*

straddle ['strædəl] *vt* (**a**) *(horse etc)* sentarse a horcajadas sobre (**b**) *Fig (embrace)* abarcar

straggle ['strægəl] *vi* (**a**) *(lag behind)* rezagarse (**b**) *(spread untidily)* desparramarse

straggler ['stræglə(r)] *n* rezagado(a) *m,f*

straight [streɪt] **1** *adj* (**a**) *(not bent)* recto(a), derecho(a); *(hair)* liso(a); **to keep a s. face** contener la risa
　(**b**) **I work eight hours s.** trabajo ocho horas seguidas
　(**c**) *(honest)* honrado(a); *(answer)* sincero(a); *(refusal)* rotundo(a); **let's get things s.** pongamos las cosas claras
　(**d**) *(drink)* solo(a), sin mezcla
　2 *adv* (**a**) *(in a straight line)* en línea recta
　(**b**) *(directly)* directamente, derecho; **keep s. ahead** sigue todo recto; **she walked s. in** entró sin llamar
　(**c**) **s. away** en seguida; **s. off** en el acto
　(**d**) *(frankly)* francamente
　3 *n Br Sport* **the home s.** la recta final

straighten ['streɪtən] *vt (sth bent)* enderezar, poner derecho(a); *(tie, picture)* poner bien; *(hair)* alisar
▸ **straighten out** *vt sep (problem)* resolver

straight-faced ['streɪt'feɪst] *adj* con la cara seria

straightforward [streɪt'fɔːwəd] *adj* (**a**) *(honest)* honrado(a) (**b**) *(sincere)* franco(a) (**b**) *Br (simple)* sencillo(a)

strain¹ [streɪn] **1** *vt* (**a**) *(rope etc)* estirar; *Fig* crear tensiones en (**b**) *Med* torcer(se); *(eyes, voice)* forzar; *(heart)* cansar (**c**) *(liquid)* filtrar; *(vegetables, tea)* colar
　2 *vi (pull)* tirar (**at** de); *Fig* **to s. to do sth** esforzarse por hacer algo
　3 *n* (**a**) *(tension)* tensión *f*; *(effort)* esfuerzo *m* (**b**) *(exhaustion)* agotamiento *m* (**c**) *Med*

torcedura f (**d**) *Mus* strains son m

strain² [strein] n (**a**) *(breed)* raza f (**b**) *(streak)* vena f

strained ['streind] adj (**a**) *(muscle)* torcido(a); *(eyes)* cansado(a); *(voice)* forzado(a) (**b**) *(atmosphere)* tenso(a)

strainer ['streinə(r)] n colador m

strait [streit] n (**a**) *(channel)* estrecho m (**b**) *(usu pl)* *(difficulty)* aprieto m; **in dire straits** en un gran aprieto

straitjacket ['streitdʒækit] n camisa f de fuerza

strait-laced [streit'leist] adj remilgado(a)

strand¹ [strænd] vt *Fig (person)* abandonar; **to leave stranded** dejar plantado(a)

strand² [strænd] n *(of thread)* hebra f; *(of hair)* pelo m

strange [streindʒ] adj (**a**) *(unknown)* desconocido(a); *(unfamiliar)* nuevo(a) (**b**) *(odd)* raro(a), extraño(a)

stranger ['streindʒə(r)] n *(unknown person)* desconocido(a) m,f; *(outsider)* forastero(a) m,f

strangle ['stræŋgəl] vt estrangular

stranglehold ['stræŋgəlhəʊld] n **to have a s. on sb** tener a algn agarrado(a) por el cuello

strangulation [stræŋgjʊ'leiʃən] n estrangulación f

strap [stræp] **1** n *(of leather)* correa f; *(on bag)* bandolera f; *(on dress)* tirante m
2 vt atar con correa

strapping ['stræpiŋ] adj *Fam* fornido(a), robusto(a)

strata ['strɑːtə] pl of **stratum**

strategic [strə'tiːdʒik] adj estratégico(a)

strategy ['strætidʒi] n estrategia f

stratosphere ['strætəsfiə(r)] n estratosfera f

stratum ['strɑːtəm] n *(pl* **strata***)* estrato m

straw [strɔː] n (**a**) *(straw)* paja f; *Fig* **to clutch at straws** agarrarse a un clavo ardiente; *Fam* **that's the last s.!** ¡eso ya es el colmo! (**b**) *(for drinking)* pajita f

strawberry ['strɔːbəri] n fresa f, *Bol, CSur, Ecuad* frutilla f; *(large)* fresón m

stray [strei] **1** vi *(from path)* desviarse; *(get lost)* extraviarse
2 n animal extraviado
3 adj *(bullet)* perdido(a); *(animal)* callejero(a)

streak [striːk] **1** n (**a**) *(line)* raya f; **s. of lightning** rayo m (**b**) *(in hair)* reflejo m (**c**) *Fig (of genius etc)* vena f; *Fig (of luck)* racha f
2 vt rayar (**with** de)
3 vi **to s. past** pasar como un rayo

stream [striːm] **1** n (**a**) *(brook)* arroyo m, riachuelo m (**b**) *(current)* corriente f (**c**) *(of water, air)* flujo m; *(of tears)* torrente m; *(of blood)* chorro m; *(of light)* raudal m (**d**) *Fig (of abuse)* sarta f; *(of people)* oleada f (**e**) *Br Educ* clase f
2 vt *Br Educ* poner en grupos
3 vi (**a**) *(liquid)* correr (**b**) *Fig* **to s. in/out/**

past *(people etc)* entrar/salir/pasar en tropel (**c**) *(hair, banner)* ondear

streamer ['striːmə(r)] n *(paper ribbon)* serpentina f

streamlined ['striːmlaind] adj (**a**) *(car)* aerodinámico(a) (**b**) *(system, method)* racionalizado(a)

street [striːt] n calle f; **the man in the s.** el hombre de la calle; **s. map, s. plan** *(plano m)* callejero m

streetcar ['striːtkɑː(r)] n *US* tranvía m

streetlamp ['striːtlæmp] n farol m

streetwise ['striːtwaiz] adj espabilado(a)

strength [streŋθ] n (**a**) *(of person)* fuerza f; *(of rope etc)* resistencia f; *(of emotion, colour)* intensidad f; *(of alcohol)* graduación f (**b**) *(power)* poder m; **on the s. of** a base de (**c**) *(ability)* punto m fuerte (**d**) **to be at full s./below s.** tener/no tener completo el cupo

strengthen ['streŋθən] **1** vt (**a**) reforzar; *(character)* fortalecer (**b**) *(intensify)* intensificar
2 vi (**a**) *(gen)* reforzarse (**b**) *(intensify)* intensificarse

strenuous ['strenjʊəs] adj (**a**) *(denial)* enérgico(a); *(effort, life)* intenso(a) (**b**) *(exhausting)* fatigoso(a), cansado(a)

stress [stres] **1** n (**a**) *Tech* tensión f (**b**) *Med* estrés m (**c**) *(emphasis)* hincapié m; *(on word)* acento m
2 vt *(emphasize)* subrayar; *(word)* acentuar

stretch [stretʃ] **1** vt *(elastic)* estirar; *(wings)* desplegar
2 vi *(elastic)* estirarse; *Fig* **my money won't s. to it** mi dinero no me llegará para eso
3 n (**a**) *(length)* trecho m, tramo m (**b**) *(of land)* extensión f; *(of time)* intervalo m

> 🖉 Note that the Spanish verb **estrechar** is a false friend and is never a translation for the English verb **to stretch**. In Spanish, **estrechar** means "to make narrow, to tighten".

▸ **stretch out 1** vt sep *(arm, hand)* alargar; *(legs)* estirar
2 vi (**a**) *(person)* estirarse (**b**) *(countryside, years etc)* extenderse

stretcher ['stretʃə(r)] n camilla f

strew [struː] vt *(pt* strewed*; pp* strewed *or* strewn [struːn]*)* esparcir

stricken ['strikən] adj *(with grief)* afligido(a); *(with illness)* aquejado(a); *(by disaster etc)* afectado(a); *(damaged)* dañado(a)

strict [strikt] adj (**a**) estricto(a) (**b**) *(absolute)* absoluto(a)

strictly ['striktli] adv (**a**) *(categorically)* terminantemente (**b**) *(precisely)* estrictamente; **s. speaking** en sentido estricto

stride [straid] **1** n zancada f, tranco m; *Fig (progress)* progresos mpl
2 vi *(pt* strode*; pp* stridden ['stridən]*)* **to s. (along)** andar a zancadas

strident ['straɪdənt] *adj (voice, sound)* estridente; *(protest etc)* enérgico(a)

strife [straɪf] *n* conflictos *mpl*

strike [straɪk] **1** *vt (pt & pp* **struck**) (**a**) *(hit)* pegar, golpear

(**b**) *(collide with)* chocar contra; *(of bullet, lightning)* alcanzar

(**c**) *(match)* encender

(**d**) *(pose)* adoptar

(**e**) *(bargain)* cerrar; *(balance)* encontrar

(**f**) **the clock struck three** el reloj dio las tres

(**g**) *(oil, gold)* descubrir; *Fam* **to s. it lucky/rich** tener suerte/hacerse rico(a)

(**h**) *(impress)* … impresionar; **it strikes me …** me parece …

2 *vi* (**a**) *(attack)* atacar; *(disaster)* sobrevenir

(**b**) *(clock)* dar la hora

(**c**) *(workers)* declararse en huelga

3 *n* (**a**) *(by workers)* huelga *f*; **on s.** en huelga; **to call a s.** convocar una huelga

(**b**) *(of oil, gold)* descubrimiento *m*

(**c**) *(blow)* golpe *m*

(**d**) *Mil* ataque *m*

▸ **strike back** *vi* devolver el golpe

▸ **strike down** *vt sep* fulminar, abatir

▸ **strike out 1** *vt sep (cross out)* tachar

2 *vi* **to s. out at sb** arremeter contra algn

▸ **strike up** *vt insep* (**a**) *(friendship)* trabar; *(conversation)* entablar (**b**) *(tune)* empezar a tocar

striker ['straɪkə(r)] *n* (**a**) *(worker)* huelguista *mf* (**b**) *Fam Ftb* marcador(a) *m,f*

striking ['straɪkɪŋ] *adj (eye-catching)* llamativo(a); *(noticeable)* notable; *(impressive)* impresionante

string [strɪŋ] **1** *n* (**a**) *(cord)* cuerda *f*; *Fig* **to pull strings for sb** enchufar a algn; **s. bean** judía *f* verde, *Bol, RP* chaucha *f*, *CAm* ejote *m*, *Col, Cuba* habichuela *f*, *Chile* poroto *m* verde, *Ven* vainita *f* (**b**) *(of events)* cadena *f*; *(of lies)* sarta *f* (**c**) *(of racket, guitar)* cuerda *f*; *Mus* **the strings** los instrumentos de cuerda

2 *vt (pt & pp* **strung**) (**a**) *(beads)* ensartar (**b**) *(racket etc)* encordar (**c**) *(beans)* quitar la hebra a

stringent ['strɪndʒənt] *adj* severo(a), estricto(a)

strip¹ [strɪp] **1** *vt* (**a**) *(person)* desnudar; *(bed)* quitar la ropa de; *(paint)* quitar (**b**) *Tech* **to s. (down)** desmontar

2 *vi (undress)* desnudarse; *(perform striptease)* hacer un striptease

▸ **strip off 1** *vt sep* quitar

2 *vi (undress)* desnudarse

strip² [strɪp] *n* tira *f*; *(of land)* franja *f*; *(of metal)* fleje *m*; **s. cartoon** historieta *f*; **s. lighting** alumbrado *m* fluorescente; **to tear sb off a s.** echar una bronca a algn

stripe [straɪp] *n* raya *f*; *Mil* galón *m*

striped [straɪpt] *adj* rayado(a), a rayas

stripper ['strɪpə(r)] *n* artista *mf* de striptease

strive [straɪv] *vi (pt* **strove**; *pp* **striven** ['strɪvən]) **to s. to do sth** esforzarse por hacer algo

strobe [strəʊb] *n* **s. lighting** luces estroboscópicas

strode [strəʊd] *pt of* **stride**

stroke [strəʊk] **1** *n* (**a**) **s. of luck** un golpe de suerte (**b**) *(in golf, cricket)* golpe *m*; *(in rowing)* remada *f*; *(in swimming)* brazada *f* (**c**) *(of pen)* trazo *m*; *(of brush)* pincelada *f* (**d**) *(caress)* caricia *f* (**e**) *Med* apoplejía *f*

2 *vt* acariciar

stroll [strəʊl] **1** *vi* dar un paseo

2 *n* paseo *m*

stroller ['strəʊlə(r)] *n US (for baby)* cochecito *m*

strong [strɒŋ] **1** *adj* (**a**) fuerte (**b**) *(durable)* sólido(a) (**c**) *(firm, resolute)* firme (**d**) *(colour)* intenso(a); *(light)* brillante (**e**) *(incontestable)* convincente (**f**) **to be twenty s.** contar con veinte miembros

2 *adv* fuerte; **to be going s.** *(business)* ir fuerte; *(elderly person)* conservarse bien

strongbox ['strɒŋbɒks] *n* caja *f* fuerte

stronghold ['strɒŋhəʊld] *n Mil* fortaleza *f*; *Fig* baluarte *m*

strongly ['strɒŋlɪ] *adv* fuertemente

strongroom ['strɒŋruːm] *n* cámara acorazada

stroppy ['strɒpɪ] *adj* (**stroppier, stroppiest**) *Br Fam* de mala uva

strove [strəʊv] *pt of* **strive**

struck [strʌk] *pt & pp of* **strike**

structural ['strʌktʃərəl] *adj* estructural

structure ['strʌktʃə(r)] *n* estructura *f*; *(constructed thing)* construcción *f*; *(building)* edificio *m*

struggle ['strʌgəl] **1** *vi* luchar

2 *n* lucha *f*; *(physical fight)* pelea *f*

strum [strʌm] *vt (guitar)* rasguear

strung [strʌŋ] *pt & pp of* **string**

strut [strʌt] *vi* pavonearse

stub [stʌb] **1** *n* (**a**) *(of cigarette)* colilla *f*; *(of pencil)* cabo *m*; *(of cheque)* matriz *f*

2 *vt* (**a**) *(strike)* golpear (**b**) **to s. (out)** apagar

stubble ['stʌbəl] *n* (**in field**) rastrojo *m*; *(on chin)* barba *f* de tres días

stubborn ['stʌbən] *adj* (**a**) terco(a), testarudo(a) (**b**) *(stain)* difícil (**c**) *(refusal)* rotundo(a)

stucco ['stʌkəʊ] *n* estuco *m*

stuck [stʌk] *pt & pp of* **stick**

stuck-up [stʌk'ʌp] *adj Fam* creído(a)

stud¹ [stʌd] **1** *n (on clothing)* tachón *m*; *(on football boots)* taco *m*; *(on shirt)* botonadura *f*

2 *vt (decorate)* tachonar (**with** de); *Fig (dot, cover)* salpicar (**with** de)

stud² [stʌd] *n (horse)* semental *m*

student ['stjuːdənt] *n* estudiante *mf*; **s. teacher** profesor(a) *m,f* en prácticas

studio ['stjuːdɪəʊ] *n TV & Cin* estudio *m*; *(artist's)* taller *m*; **s. (apartment** or *Br* **flat)** estudio

studious ['stjuːdɪəs] *adj* estudioso(a)
studiously ['stjuːdɪəslɪ] *adv* cuidadosamente
study ['stʌdɪ] **1** *vt* estudiar; *(facts etc)* examinar, investigar; *(behaviour)* observar
  2 *vi* estudiar; **to s. to be a doctor** estudiar para médico
  3 *n* (a) estudio *m*; **s. group** grupo *m* de trabajo (**b**) *(room)* despacho *m*, estudio *m*
stuff [stʌf] **1** *vt* (**a**) *(container)* llenar (**with** de); *Culin* rellenar (**with** con *or* de); *(animal)* disecar (**b**) *(cram)* atiborrar (**with** de)
  2 *n Fam* (**a**) *(substance)* cosa *f* (**b**) *(things)* cosas *fpl*
stuffing ['stʌfɪŋ] *n Culin* relleno *m*
stuffy ['stʌfɪ] *adj* (**stuffier, stuffiest**) (**a**) *(room)* mal ventilado(a); *(atmosphere)* cargado(a) (**b**) *(pompous)* estirado(a); *(narrow-minded)* de miras estrechas
stumble ['stʌmbəl] *vi* tropezar, dar un traspié; **to s. across** *or* **on** *or* **upon** tropezar *or* dar con
stumbling ['stʌmblɪŋ] *n* **s. block** escollo *m*
stump [stʌmp] **1** *n* (**a**) *(of pencil)* cabo *m*; *(of tree)* tocón *m*; *(of arm, leg)* muñón *m* (**b**) *(in cricket)* estaca *f*
  2 *vt (puzzle)* confundir; **to be stumped** estar perplejo(a)
stun [stʌn] *vt (of blow)* aturdir; *Fig (of news etc)* sorprender
stung [stʌŋ] *pt & pp of* **sting**
stunk [stʌŋk] *pt & pp of* **stink**
stunning ['stʌnɪŋ] *adj (blow)* duro(a); *(news)* sorprendente; *Fam (woman, outfit)* fenomenal
stunt¹ [stʌnt] *vt (growth)* atrofiar
stunt² [stʌnt] *n* (**a**) *Av* acrobacia *f* (**b**) **publicity s.** truco publicitario (**c**) *Cin* escena peligrosa; **s. man** doble *m*
stunted ['stʌntɪd] *adj* enano(a), mal desarrollado(a)
stupefy ['stjuːpɪfaɪ] *vt (alcohol, drugs)* aturdir; *Fig (news etc)* dejar pasmado(a)
stupendous [stjuːˈpendəs] *adj (wonderful)* estupendo(a)
stupid ['stjuːpɪd] *adj* estúpido(a), imbécil
stupidity [stjuːˈpɪdɪtɪ] *n* estupidez *f*
stupor ['stjuːpə(r)] *n* estupor *m*
sturdy ['stɜːdɪ] *adj* (**sturdier, sturdiest**) robusto(a), fuerte; *(resistance)* enérgico(a)
stutter ['stʌtə(r)] **1** *vi* tartamudear
  2 *n* tartamudeo *m*
sty [staɪ] *n (pen)* pocilga *f*
sty(e) [staɪ] *n Med* orzuelo *m*
style [staɪl] **1** *n* (**a**) estilo *m*; *(of dress)* modelo *m* (**b**) *(fashion)* moda *f* (**c**) **to live in s.** *(elegance)* vivir a lo grande
  2 *vt (hair)* marcar
stylish ['staɪlɪʃ] *adj* con estilo
stylist ['staɪlɪst] *n (hairdresser)* peluquero(a) *mf*
stylus ['staɪləs] *n (of record player)* aguja *f*

suave [swɑːv] *adj* amable, afable; *Pej* zalamero(a)

🖉 Note that the Spanish word **suave** is a false friend and is never a translation for the English word **suave**. In Spanish, **suave** means both "smooth" and "soft".

sub [sʌb] *n Fam* (**a**) *(to magazine)* suscripción *f*; *(to club)* cuota *f* (**b**) *(substitute)* suplente *mf*
sub- [sʌb] *pref* sub-
subconscious [sʌbˈkɒnʃəs] **1** *adj* subconsciente
  2 *n* **the s.** el subconsciente
subcontract [sʌbkənˈtrækt] *vt* subcontratar
subcontractor [sʌbkənˈtræktə(r)] *n* subcontratista *mf*
subdivide [sʌbdɪˈvaɪd] *vt* subdividir (**into** en)
subdue [səbˈdjuː] *vt* (**a**) *(nation, people)* sojuzgar (**b**) *(feelings)* dominar (**c**) *(colour, light)* atenuar
subdued [səbˈdjuːd] *adj* (**a**) *(person, emotion)* callado(a) (**b**) *(voice, tone)* bajo(a) (**c**) *(light)* tenue; *(colour)* apagado(a)
subject ['sʌbdʒɪkt] **1** *n* (**a**) *(citizen)* súbdito *m* (**b**) *(topic)* tema *m*; **s. matter** materia *f*; *(contents)* contenido *m* (**c**) *Educ* asignatura *f* (**d**) *Ling* sujeto *m*
  2 *adj* **s. to** *(law, tax)* sujeto(a) a; *(charge)* expuesto(a) a; *(changes, delays)* susceptible de; *(illness)* propenso(a) a; *(conditional upon)* previo(a)
  3 *vt* [səbˈdʒekt] someter
subjective [səbˈdʒektɪv] *adj* subjetivo(a)
subjunctive [səbˈdʒʌŋktɪv] **1** *adj* subjuntivo(a)
  2 *n* subjuntivo *m*
sublet [sʌbˈlet] *vt & vi* subarrendar
sublime [səˈblaɪm] *adj* sublime
submachine-gun [sʌbməˈʃiːngʌn] *n* metralleta *f*
submarine ['sʌbməriːn] *n* submarino *m*
submerge [səbˈmɜːdʒ] *vt* sumergir; *(flood)* inundar; *Fig* **submerged in ...** sumido(a) en ...
submission [səbˈmɪʃən] *n* (**a**) *(yielding)* sumisión *f* (**b**) *(of documents)* presentación *f* (**c**) *(report)* informe *m*
submissive [səbˈmɪsɪv] *adj* sumiso(a)
submit [səbˈmɪt] **1** *vt* (**a**) *(present)* presentar (**b**) *(subject)* someter (**to** a)
  2 *vi (surrender)* rendirse
subnormal [sʌbˈnɔːməl] *adj* subnormal
subordinate [səˈbɔːdɪnɪt] *adj & n* subordinado(a) *(m,f)*
subpoena [səbˈpiːnə] *Jur* **1** *n* citación *f*
  2 *vt* citar
subscribe [səbˈskraɪb] *vi (magazine)* suscribirse (**to** a); *(opinion, theory)* adherirse (**to** a)
subscriber [səbˈskraɪbə(r)] *n* abonado(a) *m,f*
subscription [səbˈskrɪpʃən] *n (to magazine)*

suscripción f; *(to club)* cuota f
subsequent ['sʌbsɪkwənt] *adj* subsiguiente
subsequently ['sʌbsɪkwəntlɪ] *adv* posteriormente
subside [səb'saɪd] *vi (land)* hundirse; *(floodwater)* bajar; *(wind, anger)* amainar
subsidence [səb'saɪdəns] *n (of land)* hundimiento m; *(of floodwater)* bajada f; *(of wind)* amaine f
subsidiary [sʌb'sɪdɪərɪ] **1** *adj (role)* secundario(a)
  2 *n Com* sucursal f, filial f
subsidize ['sʌbsɪdaɪz] *vt* subvencionar
subsidy ['sʌbsɪdɪ] *n* subvención f
subsistence [səb'sɪstəns] *n* subsistencia f
substance ['sʌbstəns] *n* **(a)** sustancia f **(b)** *(essence)* esencia f **(c) a woman of s.** *(wealth)* una mujer acaudalada
substantial [səb'stænʃəl] *adj* **(a)** *(solid)* sólido(a) **(b)** *(sum, loss)* importante; *(difference, improvement)* notable; *(meal)* abundante
substantiate [səb'stænʃɪeɪt] *vt* respaldar
substitute ['sʌbstɪtjuːt] **1** *vt* sustituir; **to s. X for Y** sustituir X por Y
  2 *n (person)* suplente mf; *(thing)* sucedáneo m
subtitle ['sʌbtaɪtəl] *n* subtítulo m
subtle ['sʌtəl] *adj* sutil; *(taste)* delicado(a); *(remark)* ingenioso(a); *(irony)* fino(a)
subtlety ['sʌtəltɪ] *n* sutileza f; *(of remark)* ingeniosidad f; *(of irony, joke)* finura f
subtract [səb'trækt] *vt* restar
subtraction [səb'trækʃən] *n* resta f
suburb ['sʌbɜːb] *n* barrio periférico; **the suburbs** las afueras
suburban [sə'bɜːbən] *adj* suburbano(a)
suburbia [sə'bɜːbɪə] *n* barrios residenciales periféricos
subversive [səb'vɜːsɪv] *adj & n* subversivo(a) (m,f)
subway ['sʌbweɪ] *n* **(a)** *Br (underpass)* paso subterráneo **(b)** *US (underground railway)* metro m
succeed [sək'siːd] **1** *vi* **(a)** *(person)* tener éxito; *(plan)* salir bien; **to s. in doing sth** conseguir hacer algo **(b)** *(follow after)* suceder; **to s. to** *(throne)* suceder a
  2 *vt (monarch)* suceder a
succeeding [sək'siːdɪŋ] *adj* sucesivo(a)
success [sək'ses] *n* éxito m

> ⚠ Note that the Spanish word **suceso** is a false friend and is never a translation for the English word **success**. In Spanish, **suceso** means both "event" and "incident".

successful [sək'sesfʊl] *adj* de éxito, exitoso(a); *(business)* próspero(a); *(marriage)* feliz; **to be s. in doing sth** lograr hacer algo
successfully [sək'sesfʊlɪ] *adv* con éxito
succession [sək'seʃən] *n* sucesión f, serie f;

in s. sucesivamente
successive [sək'sesɪv] *adj* sucesivo(a), consecutivo(a)
successor [sək'sesə(r)] *n* sucesor(a) m,f
succinct [sək'sɪŋkt] *adj* sucinto(a)
succumb [sə'kʌm] *vi* sucumbir (**to** a)
such [sʌtʃ] **1** *adj* **(a)** *(of that sort)* tal, semejante; **artists s. as Monet** artistas como Monet; **at s. and s. a time** a tal hora; **in s. a way that** de tal manera que **(b)** *(so much, so great)* tanto(a); **he's always in s. a hurry** siempre anda con tanta prisa; **she was in s. pain** sufría tanto
  2 *adv (so very)* tan; **it's s. a long time ago** hace tanto tiempo; **she's s. a clever woman** es una mujer tan inteligente; **s. a lot of books** tantos libros; **we had s. good weather** hizo un tiempo tan bueno
suchlike ['sʌtʃlaɪk] **1** *adj* tal
  2 *pron (things)* cosas fpl por el estilo; *(people)* gente f por el estilo
suck [sʌk] **1** *vt (by pump)* aspirar; *(liquid)* sorber; *(lollipop, blood)* chupar
  2 *vi (person)* chupar; *(baby)* mamar
  ▸ **suck in** *vt sep (of whirlpool)* tragar
sucker ['sʌkə(r)] *n* **(a)** *Fam* primo(a) m,f, bobo(a) m,f **(b)** *Zool* ventosa f; *Bot* chupón m
suckle ['sʌkəl] *vt (mother)* amamantar
suction ['sʌkʃən] *n* succión f
sudden ['sʌdən] *adj* **(a)** *(hurried)* súbito(a), repentino(a) **(b)** *(unexpected)* imprevisto(a) **(c)** *(abrupt)* brusco(a); **all of a s.** de repente
suddenly ['sʌdənlɪ] *adv* de repente
suds [sʌdz] *npl* espuma f de jabón, jabonaduras fpl
sue [suː, sjuː] *Jur* **1** *vt* demandar
  2 *vi* presentar una demanda; **to s. for divorce** solicitar el divorcio
suede [sweɪd] *n* ante m, gamuza f; *(for gloves)* cabritilla f
suet ['suːɪt] *n* sebo m
suffer ['sʌfə(r)] **1** *vt* **(a)** sufrir **(b)** *(tolerate)* aguantar, soportar
  2 *vi* sufrir; **to s. from** sufrir de
sufferer ['sʌfərə(r)] *n Med* enfermo(a) m,f
suffering ['sʌfərɪŋ] *n (affliction)* sufrimiento m; *(pain, torment)* dolor m
suffice [sə'faɪs] *vi Fml* bastar, ser suficiente
sufficient [sə'fɪʃənt] *adj* suficiente, bastante
sufficiently [sə'fɪʃəntlɪ] *adv* suficientemente, bastante
suffocate ['sʌfəkeɪt] **1** *vt* asfixiar
  2 *vi* asfixiarse
suffocating ['sʌfəkeɪtɪŋ] *adj (heat)* agobiante, sofocante
suffrage ['sʌfrɪdʒ] *n* sufragio m
suffuse [sə'fjuːz] *vt Literary* bañar, cubrir (**with** de)
sugar ['ʃʊɡə(r)] **1** *n* azúcar m or f; **s. beet** remolacha f (azucarera); **s. bowl** azucarero m; **s. cane** caña f de azúcar
  2 *vt* azucarar, echar azúcar a

sugary ['ʃʊgərɪ] *adj* (**a**) *(like sugar)* azucarado(a) (**b**) *Fig (insincere)* zalamero(a); *(oversentimental)* sentimentaloide

suggest [sə'dʒest] *vt* (**a**) *(propose)* sugerir (**b**) *(advise)* aconsejar (**c**) *(indicate, imply)* indicar

suggestion [sə'dʒestʃən] *n* (**a**) *(proposal)* sugerencia *f* (**b**) *(trace)* sombra *f*; *(small amount)* toque *m*

suggestive [sə'dʒestɪv] *adj* (**a**) *(reminiscent, thought-provoking)* sugerente (**b**) *(remark)* insinuante

suicidal [sjuːɪ'saɪdəl] *adj* suicida

suicide ['sjuːɪsaɪd] *n* suicidio *m*

suit [suːt, sjuːt] **1** *n* (**a**) *(clothes)* traje *m* de chaqueta (**b**) *Jur* pleito *m* (**c**) *Cards* palo *m*; *Fig* **to follow s.** seguir el ejemplo
2 *vt* (**a**) *(be convenient to)* convenir a, venir bien a (**b**) *(be right, appropriate for)* ir bien a; **red really suits you** el rojo te favorece mucho; **they are well suited** están hechos el uno para el otro (**c**) *(adapt)* adaptar a (**d**) *(please)* **s. yourself!** ¡como quieras!

suitable ['suːtəbəl] *adj (convenient)* conveniente; *(appropriate)* adecuado(a); **the most s. woman for the job** la mujer más indicada para el puesto

suitably ['sjuːtəblɪ] *adv (correctly)* correctamente; *(properly)* adecuadamente

suitcase ['suːtkeɪs] *n* maleta *f*, *Méx* petaca *f*, *RP* valija *f*

suite [swiːt] *n* (**a**) *(of furniture)* juego *m* (**b**) *(of hotel rooms, music)* suite *f*

suitor ['sjuːtə(r)] *n Literary (wooer)* pretendiente *m*

sulfur ['sʌlfə(r)] *n US* = **sulphur**

sulk [sʌlk] *vi* enfurruñarse

sulky ['sʌlkɪ] *adj* (**sulkier, sulkiest**) malhumorado(a), enfurruñado(a)

sullen ['sʌlən] *adj* hosco(a); *(sky)* plomizo(a)

sulphur ['sʌlfər] *n* azufre *m*

sulphuric [sʌl'fjʊərɪk] *adj* sulfúrico(a)

sultan ['sʌltən] *n* sultán *m*

sultana [sʌl'tɑːnə] *n (raisin)* pasa *f* de Esmirna

sultry ['sʌltrɪ] *adj* (**sultrier, sultriest**) (**a**) *(muggy)* bochornoso(a) (**b**) *(seductive)* sensual

sum [sʌm] *n* (**a**) *(arithmetic problem, amount)* suma *f* (**b**) *(total amount)* total *m*; *(of money)* importe *m*
▸ **sum up** *vt sep* resumir
2 *vi* resumir; **to s. up ...** en resumidas cuentas ...

summarize ['sʌməraɪz] *vt & vi* resumir

summary ['sʌmərɪ] **1** *n* resumen *m*
2 *adj* sumario(a)

summer ['sʌmə(r)] **1** *n* verano *m*
2 *adj (holiday etc)* de verano; *(weather)* veraniego(a); *(resort)* de veraneo

summerhouse ['sʌməhaʊs] *n* cenador *m*, glorieta *f*

summertime ['sʌmətaɪm] *n* verano *m*

summit ['sʌmɪt] *n* (**a**) *(of mountain)* cima *f*, cumbre *f* (**b**) *Pol* **s. (meeting)** cumbre *f*

summon ['sʌmən] *vt* (**a**) *(meeting, person)* convocar (**b**) *(aid)* pedir (**c**) *Jur* citar
▸ **summon up** *vt sep (resources)* reunir; **to s. up one's courage** armarse de valor

summons ['sʌmənz] **1** *n sing* (**a**) *(call)* llamada *f*, llamamiento *m* (**b**) *Jur* citación *f* judicial
2 *vt Jur* citar

sumptuous ['sʌmptjʊəs] *adj* suntuoso(a)

sun [sʌn] **1** *n* sol *m*
2 *vt* **to s. oneself** tomar el sol

sunbathe ['sʌnbeɪð] *vi* tomar el sol

sunbed ['sʌnbed] *n (in garden)* tumbona *f*; *(with sunlamp)* solario *m*

sunburn ['sʌnbɜːn] *n (burn)* quemadura *f* de sol

sunburnt ['sʌnbɜːnt] *adj (burnt)* quemado(a) por el sol; *(tanned)* bronceado(a)

Sunday ['sʌndɪ] *n* domingo *m inv*; **S. newspaper** periódico *m* del domingo; **S. school** catequesis *f*

sundial ['sʌndaɪəl] *n* reloj *m* de sol

sundown ['sʌndaʊn] *n US* anochecer *m*

sundry ['sʌndrɪ] **1** *adj* diversos(as), varios(as); *Fam* **all and s.** todos sin excepción
2 *npl Com* **sundries** artículos *mpl* diversos; *(expenses)* gastos diversos

sunflower ['sʌnflaʊə(r)] *n* girasol *m*

sung [sʌŋ] *pp of* **sing**

sunglasses ['sʌnglɑːsɪz] *npl* gafas *fpl* de sol, *Am* lentes *mpl* de sol, anteojos *mpl* de sol

sunk [sʌŋk] *pp of* **sink**

sunlamp ['sʌnlæmp] *n* lámpara *f* solar

sunlight ['sʌnlaɪt] *n* sol *m*, luz *f* del sol

sunlit ['sʌnlɪt] *adj* iluminado(a) por el sol

sunny ['sʌnɪ] *adj* (**sunnier, sunniest**) (**a**) *(day)* de sol; *(place)* soleado(a); **it is s.** hace sol (**b**) *Fig (smile, disposition)* alegre; *(future)* prometedor(a)

sunrise ['sʌnraɪz] *n* salida *f* del sol

sunroof ['sʌnruːf] *n Aut* techo corredizo

sunset ['sʌnset] *n* puesta *f* del sol

sunshade ['sʌnʃeɪd] *n* sombrilla *f*

sunshine ['sʌnʃaɪn] *n* sol *m*, luz *f* del sol

sunstroke ['sʌnstrəʊk] *n* insolación *f*

suntan ['sʌntæn] *n* bronceado *m*; **s. oil** crema protectora; **s. lotion** (aceite *m*) bronceador *m*

super ['suːpə(r)] *adj Fam* fenomenal

super- ['suːpə(r)] *pref* super-, sobre-

superannuation [suːpərænjʊ'eɪʃən] *n Br* jubilación *f*, pensión *f*

superb [sʊ'pɜːb] *adj* espléndido(a)

supercilious [suːpə'sɪlɪəs] *adj (condescending)* altanero(a); *(disdainful)* desdeñoso(a)

superficial [suːpə'fɪʃəl] *adj* superficial

superfluous [suː'pɜːflʊəs] *adj* sobrante, superfluo(a); **to be s.** sobrar

superglue ['suːpəgluː] *n* pegamento rápido

superhuman [suːpə'hjuːmən] *adj* sobrehumano(a)

superimpose [suːpərɪmˈpəʊz] *vt* sobreponer

superintendent [suːpərɪnˈtendənt] *n* director(a) *m,f*; **police s.** subjefe(a) *m,f* de policía

superior [suːˈpɪərɪə(r)] **1** *adj* (a) superior (b) *(haughty)* altivo(a)
2 *n* superior(a) *m,f*

superiority [suːpɪərɪˈɒrɪtɪ] *n* superioridad *f*

superlative [suːˈpɜːlətɪv] **1** *adj* superlativo(a)
2 *n Ling* superlativo *m*

superman [ˈsuːpəmæn] *n* superhombre *m*, supermán *m*

supermarket [ˈsuːpəmɑːkɪt] *n* supermercado *m*

supernatural [suːpəˈnætʃərəl] **1** *adj* sobrenatural
2 *n* **the s.** lo sobrenatural

superpower [ˈsuːpəpaʊə(r)] *n Pol* superpotencia *f*

supersede [suːpəˈsiːd] *vt Fml* suplantar

supersonic [suːpəˈsɒnɪk] *adj* supersónico(a)

superstitious [suːpəˈstɪʃəs] *adj* supersticioso(a)

supertanker [ˈsuːpətæŋkə(r)] *n* superpetrolero *m*

supervise [ˈsuːpəvaɪz] *vt* supervisar; *(watch over)* vigilar

supervision [suːpəˈvɪʒən] *n* supervisión *f*

supervisor [ˈsuːpəvaɪzə(r)] *n* supervisor(a) *m,f*

supper [ˈsʌpə(r)] *n* cena *f*; **to have s.** cenar

supplant [səˈplɑːnt] *vt* suplantar

supple [ˈsʌpəl] *adj* flexible

supplement 1 *n* [ˈsʌplɪmənt] suplemento *m*
2 *vt* [ˈsʌplɪment] complementar

supplementary [sʌplɪˈmentərɪ] *adj* adicional

supplier [səˈplaɪə(r)] *n* suministrador(a) *m,f*; *Com* proveedor(a) *m,f*

supply [səˈplaɪ] **1** *n* (a) suministro *m*; *Com* provisión *f*; *(stock)* surtido *m*; **s. and demand** oferta *f* y demanda (b) **supplies** *(food)* víveres *mpl*; *Mil* pertrechos *mpl*; **office supplies** material *m* para oficina
2 *vt* (a) *(provide)* suministrar (b) *(with provisions)* aprovisionar (c) *(information)* facilitar (d) *Com* surtir

support [səˈpɔːt] **1** *n* (a) *(moral)* apoyo *m* (b) *(funding)* ayuda económica
2 *vt* (a) *(weight etc)* sostener (b) *Fig (back)* apoyar; *(substantiate)* respaldar (c) *Sport* ser (hincha) de (d) *(sustain)* mantener; *(feed)* alimentar

supporter [səˈpɔːtə(r)] *n Pol* partidario(a) *m,f*; *Sport* hincha *mf*

suppose [səˈpəʊz] *vt* suponer; *(presume)* creer; **I s. not/so** supongo que no/sí; **you're not supposed to smoke in here** no está permitido fumar aquí dentro; **you're supposed to be in bed** deberías estar acostado(a) ya

supposed [səˈpəʊzd] *adj* supuesto(a)

supposedly [səˈpəʊzdlɪ] *adv* teóricamente

suppress [səˈpres] *vt* suprimir; *(feelings, laugh etc)* contener; *(news, truth)* callar; *(revolt)* sofocar

supremacy [sʊˈpreməsɪ] *n* supremacía *f*

supreme [sʊˈpriːm] *adj* supremo(a); **with s. indifference** con total indiferencia; *US Law* **S. Court** Tribunal *m* Supremo, *Am* Corte *f* Suprema

supremely [sʊˈpriːmlɪ] *adv* sumamente

surcharge [ˈsɜːtʃɑːdʒ] *n* recargo *m*

sure [ʃʊə(r)] **1** *adj* (a) seguro(a); **I'm s. (that) ...** estoy seguro(a) de que ...; **make s. that it's ready** asegúrate de que esté listo; **s. of oneself** seguro(a) de sí mismo(a) (b) *Fam* **s. thing!** ¡claro!; *US* **it s. is cold** qué frío que hace
2 *adv* (a) *(of course)* claro (b) *(certainly)* seguro (c) **s. enough** efectivamente

surely [ˈʃʊəlɪ] *adv (without a doubt)* sin duda; **s. not!** ¡no puede ser!

surety [ˈʃʊərɪtɪ] *n* (a) *(sum)* fianza *f* (b) *(person)* fiador(a) *m,f*; **to stand s. for sb** ser fiador de algn

surf [sɜːf] **1** *n (waves)* oleaje *m*; *(foam)* espuma *f*
2 *vt Comput* **to s. the Net** navegar por Internet
3 *vi Sport* hacer surf

surface [ˈsɜːfɪs] **1** *n* superficie *f*; *(of road)* firme *m*
2 *adj* superficial; **s. area** área *f* de la superficie; **by s. mail** por vía terrestre *or* marítima
3 *vt (road)* revestir
4 *vi (submarine etc)* salir a la superficie; *Fam (wake up)* levantarse

surface-to-air [ˈsɜːfɪstʊˈeə(r)] *adj* **s. missile** misil *m* tierra-aire

surfboard [ˈsɜːfbɔːd] *n* tabla *f* de surf

surfeit [ˈsɜːfɪt] *n Fml* exceso *m*

surfer [ˈsɜːfə(r)] *n* surfista *mf*

surfing [ˈsɜːfɪŋ] *n* surf *m*, surfing *m*

surge [sɜːdʒ] **1** *n* (a) *(growth)* alza *f* (b) *(of sea, sympathy)* oleada *f*; *Fig (of anger, energy)* arranque *m*
2 *vi* **to s. forward** *(people)* avanzar en tropel

surgeon [ˈsɜːdʒən] *n* cirujano(a) *m,f*

surgery [ˈsɜːdʒərɪ] *n* (a) *(operation)* cirugía *f* (b) *Br (consulting room)* consultorio *m*; **s. hours** horas *fpl* de consulta

surgical [ˈsɜːdʒɪkəl] *adj* quirúrgico(a); **s. spirit** alcohol *m* de 90°

surly [ˈsɜːlɪ] *adj* (**surlier**, **surliest**) *(bad-tempered)* hosco(a), malhumorado(a); *(rude)* maleducado(a)

surmount [sɜːˈmaʊnt] *vt* superar, vencer

surname [ˈsɜːneɪm] *n* apellido *m*

surpass [sɜːˈpɑːs] *vt* superar

surplus [ˈsɜːpləs] **1** *n (of goods)* excedente *m*; *(of budget)* superávit *m*
2 *adj* excedente

surprise [səˈpraɪz] **1** *n* sorpresa *f*; **to take sb**

by s. coger desprevenido(a) a algn
2 adj (visit) inesperado(a); **s. attack** ataque m sorpresa
3 vt sorprender

surprising [sə'praɪzɪŋ] adj sorprendente

surprisingly [sə'praɪzɪŋlɪ] adv sorprendentemente, de modo sorprendente

surrealist [sə'rɪəlɪst] adj & n surrealista (mf)

surrender [sə'rendə(r)] **1** n Mil rendición f; (of weapons) entrega f; Ins rescate m
2 vt Mil rendir; (right) renunciar a
3 vi (give in) rendirse

surreptitious [sʌrəp'tɪʃəs] adj subrepticio(a)

surrogate ['sʌrəgɪt] n Fml sustituto(a) m,f; **s. mother** madre f de alquiler

surround [sə'raʊnd] **1** n marco m, borde m
2 vt rodear

surrounding [sə'raʊndɪŋ] **1** adj circundante
2 npl **surroundings** (of place) alrededores mpl, cercanías fpl

surveillance [sɜː'veɪləns] n vigilancia f

survey 1 n ['sɜːveɪ] (a) (of building) inspección f; (of land) reconocimiento m (b) (of trends etc) encuesta f (c) (overall view) panorama m
2 vt [sə'veɪ] (a) (building) inspeccionar; (land) medir (b) (trends etc) hacer una encuesta sobre (c) (look at) contemplar

surveyor [sə'veɪə(r)] n agrimensor(a) m,f; **quantity s.** aparejador(a) m,f

survival [sə'vaɪvəl] n supervivencia f

survive [sə'vaɪv] **1** vi sobrevivir; (remain) perdurar
2 vt sobrevivir a

survivor [sə'vaɪvə(r)] n superviviente mf

susceptible [sə'septəbəl] adj (to attack) susceptible (**to** a); (to illness) propenso(a) (**to** a)

suspect ['sʌspekt] **1** adj (dubious) sospechoso(a)
2 n sospechoso(a) m,f
3 vt [sə'spekt] (a) (person) sospechar (**of** de); (plot, motives) recelar de (b) (think likely) imaginar, creer

suspend [sə'spend] vt suspender; (pupil) expulsar por un tiempo

suspended [sə'spendɪd] adj (a) suspendido(a); Jur **s. sentence** condena f condicional (b) Sport sancionado(a)

suspender [sə'spendə(r)] n (a) Br (for stocking) liga f; **s. belt** liguero m (b) US **suspenders** tirantes mpl

suspense [sə'spens] n incertidumbre f; Cin & Th suspense m; **to keep sb in s.** mantener a algn en la incertidumbre

suspension [sə'spenʃən] n (a) suspensión f (b) Sport sanción f (c) (of pupil, employee) expulsión f temporal (d) **s. bridge** puente m colgante

suspicion [sə'spɪʃən] n (a) sospecha f; (mistrust) recelo m; (doubt) duda f (b) (trace) pizca f

suspicious [sə'spɪʃəs] adj (a) (arousing suspicion) sospechoso(a) (b) (distrustful) receloso(a); **to be s. of sb** desconfiar de algn

▸ **suss out** [sʌs] vt sep Br Fam (person) calar; (system) coger or Am agarrar el truco a; **I haven't sussed out how it works yet** todavía no me he enterado de cómo funciona

sustain [sə'steɪn] vt (a) sostener (b) (nourish) sustentar (c) Jur (objection) admitir (d) (injury etc) sufrir

sustained [sə'steɪnd] adj sostenido(a)

sustenance ['sʌstənəns] n sustento m

swab [swɒb] **1** n (cotton wool) algodón m; (for specimen) frotis m
2 vt (wound) limpiar

swagger ['swægə(r)] **1** n pavoneo m
2 vi pavonearse

swallow¹ ['swɒləʊ] **1** n (of drink, food) trago m
2 vt (a) (drink, food) tragar (b) Fig (believe) tragarse
3 vi tragar
▸ **swallow up** vt sep Fig (a) (engulf) tragar (b) (eat up) consumir

swallow² ['swɒləʊ] n Orn golondrina f

swam [swæm] pt of **swim**

swamp [swɒmp] **1** n ciénaga f
2 vt (a) (boat) hundir (b) Fig inundar (**with** or **by** de)

swan [swɒn] **1** n cisne m
2 vi Fam **to s. around** pavonearse; **to s. around doing nothing** hacer el vago

swap [swɒp] **1** n Fam intercambio m
2 vt cambiar
▸ **swap round, swap over** vt sep (switch) cambiar

swarm [swɔːm] **1** n enjambre m
2 vi (bees) enjambrar; Fig **Neath was swarming with tourists** Neath estaba lleno de turistas

swarthy ['swɔːðɪ] adj (**swarthier, swarthiest**) moreno(a)

swastika ['swɒstɪkə] n esvástica f, cruz gamada

swat [swɒt] vt aplastar

swathe [sweɪð] vt (bind up) envolver

sway [sweɪ] **1** n (a) (movement) balanceo m (b) **to hold s. over sb** dominar a algn
2 vi (a) (swing) balancearse, mecerse (b) (totter) tambalearse
3 vt Fig (persuade) convencer

swear [sweə(r)] **1** vt (pt **swore**; pp **sworn**) (vow) jurar; **to s. an oath** prestar juramento
2 vi (a) (formally) jurar, prestar juramento (b) (curse) soltar tacos, decir palabrotas; (blaspheme) jurar; **to s. at sb** echar pestes contra algn

swear-word ['sweəwɜːd] n palabrota f

sweat [swet] **1** n (perspiration) sudor m; Fam (hard work) trabajo duro
2 vi (perspire) sudar; Fig (work hard) sudar la gota gorda

3 vt Fam **to s. it out** aguantar

sweater ['sweta(r)] n suéter m

sweatshirt ['swetʃɜːt] n sudadera f

sweaty ['swetɪ] adj (**sweatier, sweatiest**) sudoroso(a)

Swede [swiːd] n (person) sueco(a) m,f

swede [swiːd] n Bot nabo sueco

Sweden ['swiːdən] n Suecia

Swedish ['swiːdɪʃ] **1** adj sueco(a)

2 n (**a**) (language) sueco m (**b**) **the S.** los suecos

sweep [swiːp] **1** n (**a**) (with broom) barrido m; Fig **to make a clean s. of things** hacer tabla rasa (**b**) (of arm) gesto amplio (**c**) (of river, road) curva f (**d**) (**chimney**) **s.** deshollinador(a) m,f

2 vt (pt & pp **swept**) (**a**) (floor etc) barrer (**b**) (of searchlight) recorrer; (minefield) rastrear (**c**) (spread throughout) extenderse por

3 vi (**a**) (with broom) barrer (**b**) **to s. in/out/past** entrar/salir/pasar rápidamente

▸ **sweep aside** vt sep apartar bruscamente; Fig (objections) rechazar

▸ **sweep away** vt sep (**a**) (dust) barrer (**b**) (of storm) arrastrar

▸ **sweep up** vi barrer

sweeper ['swiːpə(r)] n (**a**) (machine) barredora f (**b**) Ftb líbero m

sweeping ['swiːpɪŋ] adj (**a**) (broad) amplio(a); **a s. statement** una declaración demasiado general (**b**) (victory) aplastante (**c**) (reforms, changes etc) radical

sweet [swiːt] **1** adj (**a**) dulce; (sugary) azucarado(a); **to have a s. tooth** ser goloso(a); **s. pea** guisante m de olor; **s. shop** confitería f (**b**) (pleasant) agradable; (smell) fragante; (sound) melodioso(a) (**c**) (person, animal) encantador(a)

2 n (**a**) Br (chocolate) bombón m; (**boiled**) **s.** caramelo m (**b**) (dessert) postre m

sweet-and-sour ['swiːtən'savə(r)] adj agridulce

sweetcorn ['swiːtkɔːn] n maíz tierno

sweeten ['swiːtən] vt (**a**) (tea etc) azucarar (**b**) Fig (temper) aplacar; **to s. the pill** suavizar el golpe

sweetener ['swiːtənə(r)] n (for tea, coffee) edulcorante m

sweetheart ['swiːthɑːt] n (**a**) (boyfriend) novio m; (girlfriend) novia f (**b**) (dear, love) cariño m, amor m

sweetness ['swiːtnɪs] n dulzura f; (of smell) fragancia f; (of sound) suavidad f

swell [swel] **1** n (of sea) marejada f, oleaje m

2 adj US Fam fenomenal

3 vi (pt **swelled**; pp **swollen**) (part of body) hincharse; (river) subir

▸ **swell up** vi hincharse

swelling ['swelɪŋ] n hinchazón f; Med tumefacción f

sweltering ['sweltərɪŋ] adj agobiante

swept [swept] pt & pp of **sweep**

swerve [swɜːv] **1** n (**a**) (by car) viraje m (**b**) Sport (by player) regate m

2 vi (**a**) (car) dar un viraje brusco (**b**) Sport (player) dar un regate

swift [swɪft] **1** adj rápido(a), veloz

2 n Orn vencejo m (común)

swiftly ['swɪftlɪ] adv rápidamente

swig [swɪg] Fam **1** n trago m

2 vt beber a tragos

swill [swɪl] **1** n (**a**) bazofia f (**b**) (rinse) enjuague m

2 vt (**a**) (rinse) enjuagar (**b**) Fam (drink) beber a grandes tragos

▸ **swill out** vt sep enjuagar

swim [swɪm] **1** vi (pt **swam**; pp **swum**) nadar; **to go swimming** ir a nadar; Fam **my head is swimming** la cabeza me da vueltas

2 vt (the Channel) pasar a nado

3 n baño m; **to go for a s.** ir a nadar or bañarse

swimmer ['swɪmə(r)] n nadador(a) m,f

swimming ['swɪmɪŋ] n natación f; **s. cap** gorro m de baño; **s. costume** traje m de baño, bañador m; **s. pool** piscina f; **s. trunks** bañador m

swimsuit ['swɪmsuːt] n traje m de baño, bañador m

swindle ['swɪndəl] **1** n estafa f

2 vt estafar

swindler ['swɪndlə(r)] n estafador(a) m,f

swine [swaɪn] n (**a**) (pl **swine**) (pig) cerdo m, puerco m (**b**) (pl **swines**) Fam (person) canalla mf, cochino(a) m,f

swing [swɪŋ] **1** n (**a**) balanceo m, vaivén m; Fig (in votes etc) viraje m; **s. bridge** puente giratorio; **s. door** puerta giratoria

(**b**) (in golf) swing m

(**c**) (plaything) columpio m

(**d**) (rhythm) ritmo m; (jazz style) swing m; **in full s.** en plena marcha

2 vi (pt & pp **swung**) (**a**) (move to and fro) balancearse; (arms, legs) menearse; (on swing) columpiarse; **to s. open/shut** abrirse/cerrarse de golpe

(**b**) (turn) girar; **he swung round** dio media vuelta

3 vt (**a**) (cause to move to and fro) balancear; (arms, legs) menear; (on swing) columpiar

(**b**) (turn) hacer girar; **she swung the sack onto her back** se echó el saco a los hombros

swingeing ['swɪndʒɪŋ] adj drástico(a)

swipe [swaɪp] **1** n golpe m

2 vt (**a**) (hit) dar un tortazo a (**b**) Fam (steal) birlar

swirl [swɜːl] **1** n remolino m; (of cream, smoke) voluta f

2 vi arremolinarse

swish [swɪʃ] **1** adj Fam (smart) elegante

2 vt (tail) menear

3 vi (whip) dar un chasquido; (skirt) crujir

Swiss [swɪs] **1** adj suizo(a)

2 n (pl **Swiss**) (person) suizo(a) m,f; **the S.** los suizos

switch [swɪtʃ] **1** n (**a**) Elec interruptor m (**b**) (changeover) cambio repentino; (exchange) intercambio m (**c**) (stick) vara f; (riding whip) fusta f (**d**) US Rail agujas fpl

2 vt (**a**) (jobs, direction) cambiar de (**b**) (allegiance) cambiar (**to** por); (attention) desviar (**to** hacia)
▸ **switch off** vt sep apagar
▸ **switch on** vt sep encender
▸ **switch over** vi cambiar (**to** a)

switchboard ['swɪtʃbɔːd] n centralita f

Switzerland ['swɪtsələnd] n Suiza

swivel ['swɪvəl] **1** n **s. chair** silla giratoria

2 vt & vi girar

swollen ['swəʊlən] **1** adj (ankle, face) hinchado(a); (river, lake) crecido(a)

2 pp of **swell**

swoon [swuːn] **1** n desmayo m

2 vi desmayarse

swoop [swuːp] **1** n (**a**) (of bird) calada f; (of plane) descenso m en picado (**b**) (by police) redada f

2 vi (**a**) to **s. down** (bird) abalanzarse (**on** sobre); (plane) bajar en picado (**b**) (police) hacer una redada

swop [swɒp] n & vt = **swap**

sword [sɔːd] n espada f

swordfish ['sɔːdfɪʃ] n pez m espada

swore [swɔː(r)] pt of **swear**

sworn [swɔːn] **1** adj jurado(a)

2 pp of **swear**

swot [swɒt] vi Br Fam empollar

swum [swʌm] pp of **swim**

swung [swʌŋ] pt & pp of **swing**

sycamore ['sɪkəmɔː(r)] n (**a**) Br sicomoro m (**b**) US (plane tree) plátano m

syllable ['sɪləbəl] n sílaba f

syllabus ['sɪləbəs] n programa m de estudios

symbol ['sɪmbəl] n símbolo m

symbolic [sɪm'bɒlɪk] adj simbólico(a)

symbolize ['sɪmbəlaɪz] vt simbolizar

symmetry ['sɪmɪtrɪ] n simetría f

sympathetic [sɪmpə'θetɪk] adj (**a**) (showing pity) compasivo(a) (**b**) (understanding) comprensivo(a); (kind) amable

> 🖊 Note that the Spanish word **simpático** is a false friend and is never a translation for the English word **sympathetic**. In Spanish, **simpático** means "nice, likeable".

sympathize ['sɪmpəθaɪz] vi (**a**) (show pity) compadecerse (**with** de) (**b**) (understand) comprender

sympathizer ['sɪmpəθaɪzə(r)] n simpatizante mf

sympathy ['sɪmpəθɪ] n (**a**) (pity) compasión f (**b**) (condolences) pésame m; **letter of s.** pésame; **to express one's s.** dar el pésame (**c**) (understanding) comprensión f

> 🖊 Note that the Spanish word **simpatía** is a false friend and is never a translation for the English word **sympathy**. In Spanish, **simpatía** means "liking, affection".

symphony ['sɪmfənɪ] n sinfonía f

symposium [sɪm'pəʊzɪəm] n simposio m

symptom ['sɪmptəm] n síntoma m

symptomatic [sɪmptə'mætɪk] adj sintomático(a)

synagogue ['sɪnəgɒg] n sinagoga f

synchronize ['sɪŋkrənaɪz] vt sincronizar

syndicate ['sɪndɪkɪt] n corporación f; **newspaper s.** sindicato periodístico

syndrome ['sɪndrəʊm] n síndrome m

synonym ['sɪnənɪm] n sinónimo m

synopsis [sɪ'nɒpsɪs] n sinopsis f inv

syntax ['sɪntæks] n sintaxis f inv

synthesis ['sɪnθɪsɪs] n (pl **syntheses** ['sɪnθɪsiːz]) síntesis f inv

synthesizer ['sɪnθɪsaɪzə(r)] n sintetizador m

synthetic [sɪn'θetɪk] adj sintético(a)

syphilis ['sɪfɪlɪs] n sífilis f

syphon ['saɪfən] n = **siphon**

Syria ['sɪrɪə] n Siria

Syrian ['sɪrɪən] adj & n sirio(a) (m,f)

syringe [sɪ'rɪndʒ] n jeringa f, jeringuilla f

syrup ['sɪrəp] n jarabe m, almíbar m

system ['sɪstəm] n sistema m; Fam **the s.** el orden establecido; Comput **systems analyst** analista mf de sistemas

systematic [sɪstɪ'mætɪk] adj sistemático(a)

T, t [tiː] *n (the letter)* T, t *f*

t *(abbr* **ton(s))** tonelada(s) *f(pl)*

ta [tɑː] *interj Br Fam* gracias

tab [tæb] *n (a) (flap)* lengüeta *f; (label)* etiqueta *f; Fam* **to keep tabs on sb** vigilar a algn **(b)** *US Fam (bill)* cuenta *f*

tabby ['tæbɪ] *n* **t. (cat)** gato(a) *m,f* romano(a)

table ['teɪbəl] **1** *n* **(a)** mesa *f;* **to lay** *or* **set the t.** poner la mesa; **t. lamp** lámpara *f* de mesa; **t. mat** salvamanteles *m inv;* **t. tennis** ping-pong® *m,* tenis *m* de mesa; **t. wine** vino *m* de mesa **(b)** *(of figures)* tabla *f,* cuadro *m;* **t. of contents** índice *m* de materias

2 *vt (motion, proposal) Br* presentar; *US* posponer

tablecloth ['teɪbəlklɒθ] *n* mantel *m*

tablespoon ['teɪbəlspuːn] *n* cucharón *m*

tablespoonful ['teɪbəlspuːnfʊl] *n* cucharada *f* grande

tablet ['tæblɪt] *n* **(a)** *Med* pastilla *f* **(b)** *(of stone)* lápida *f* **(c)** *(of soap)* pastilla *f; (of chocolate)* tableta *f* **(d)** *US (of writing paper)* bloc *m*

tableware ['teɪbəlweə(r)] *n* vajilla *f*

tabloid ['tæblɔɪd] *n* periódico *m* de pequeño formato; **t. press** prensa sensacionalista

taboo [tə'buː] *adj & n* tabú *(m)*

tabulate ['tæbjʊleɪt] *vt* disponer en listas

tacit ['tæsɪt] *adj* tácito(a)

taciturn ['tæsɪtɜːn] *adj* taciturno(a)

tack [tæk] **1** *n* **(a)** *(small nail)* tachuela *f* **(b)** *Sewing* hilván *m* **(c)** *Naut* amura *f; (distance)* bordada *f; Fig* **to change t.** cambiar de rumbo

2 *vt* **(a)** **t. sth down** clavar algo con tachuelas **(b)** *Sewing* hilvanar

3 *vi Naut* virar de bordo

▸ **tack on** *vt sep (add)* añadir

tackle ['tækəl] **1** *n* **(a)** *(equipment)* aparejos *mpl;* **fishing t.** aparejos de pescar **(b)** *Sport* placaje *m; Ftb* entrada *f*

2 *vt* agarrar; *(task)* emprender; *(problem)* abordar; *Sport* placar; *Ftb* entrar a

tacky¹ ['tækɪ] *adj* (**tackier, tackiest**) pegajoso(a)

tacky² ['tækɪ] *adj Fam (shoddy)* cutre

tact [tækt] *n* tacto *m,* diplomacia *f*

tactful ['tæktfʊl] *adj* diplomático(a)

tactic ['tæktɪk] *n* táctica *f;* **tactics** táctica *f*

tactical ['tæktɪkəl] *adj* táctico(a)

tactless ['tæktlɪs] *adj (person)* poco diplomático(a); *(question)* indiscreto(a)

tadpole ['tædpəʊl] *n* renacuajo *m*

taffy ['tæfɪ] *n US* caramelo *m* de melaza

tag [tæg] *n* **(a)** *(label)* etiqueta *f* **(b)** *(saying)* coletilla *f*

▸ **tag along** *vi Fam* pegarse

▸ **tag on** *vt sep (add to end)* añadir

tail [teɪl] **1** *n* **(a)** cola *f;* **t. end** cola *f* **(b)** *(of shirt)* faldón *m;* **to wear tails** ir de frac; **t. coat** frac *m* **(c)** **tails** *(of coin)* cruz *f*

2 *vt Fam (follow)* seguir de cerca

▸ **tail away, tail off** *vi* desvanecerse

tailback ['teɪlbæk] *n Br* caravana *f*

tail-gate ['teɪlgeɪt] **1** *n Aut* puerta trasera

2 *vt US* conducir *or Am* manejar pegado a, pisar los talones a

tailor ['teɪlə(r)] **1** *n* sastre *m;* **t.'s (shop)** sastrería *f*

2 *vt (suit)* confeccionar; *Fig* adaptar

tailor-made [teɪlə'meɪd] *adj* hecho(a) a la medida

tailwind ['teɪlwɪnd] *n* viento *m* de cola

taint [teɪnt] *vt* contaminar; *Fig* corromper

tainted ['teɪntɪd] *adj* contaminado(a); *(reputation)* manchado(a)

take [teɪk] **1** *vt (pt* **took***; pp* **taken**) **(a)** tomar, coger; **to t. an opportunity** aprovechar una oportunidad; **to t. hold of sth** agarrar algo; **to t. sth from one's pocket** sacarse algo del bolsillo; **t. your time!** ¡tómate el tiempo que quieras!; **to t. a bath** bañarse; **to t. care (of oneself)** cuidarse; **his car takes six people** caben seis personas en su coche; **is this seat taken?** ¿está ocupado este asiento?; **to t. a decision** tomar una decisión; **to t. a liking/dislike to sb** tomar cariño/antipatía a algn; **to t. a photograph** sacar una fotografía; **t. the first road on the left** coja la primera a la izquierda; **to t. the train** coger el tren **(b)** *(accept)* aceptar; *(earn)* **to t. so much per week** recaudar tanto por semana **(c)** *(win)* ganar; *(prize)* llevarse **(d)** *(eat, drink)* tomar; **to t. drugs** drogarse **(e)** **she's taking (a degree in) law** estudia derecho; **to t. an exam (in ...)** examinarse (de ...) **(f)** *(person to a place)* llevar **(g)** *(endure)* aguantar **(h)** *(consider)* considerar **(i)** **I t. it that ...** supongo que ...; **what do you t. me for?** ¿por quién me tomas? **(j)** *(require)* requerir; **it takes an hour to get there** se tarda una hora en llegar hasta allí **(k)** **to be taken ill** enfermar

2 *n Cin* toma *f*
▸ **take after** *vt insep* parecerse a
▸ **take apart** *vt sep (machine)* desmontar
▸ **take away** *vt sep* (**a**) *(carry off)* llevarse (**b**) **to t. sth away from sb** quitarle algo a algn (**c**) *Math* restar
▸ **take back** *vt sep* (**a**) *(give back)* devolver; *(receive back)* recuperar (**b**) *(withdraw)* retractarse
▸ **take down** *vt sep* (**a**) *(lower)* bajar (**b**) *(demolish)* derribar (**c**) *(write)* apuntar
▸ **take in** *vt sep* (**a**) *(shelter, lodge)* alojar, acoger (**b**) *Sewing* meter (**c**) *(include)* abarcar (**d**) *(understand)* entender (**e**) *(deceive)* engañar
▸ **take off 1** *vt sep* (**a**) quitar; **he took off his jacket** se quitó la chaqueta (**b**) *(lead or carry away)* llevarse (**c**) *(deduct)* descontar (**d**) *(imitate)* imitar burlonamente
2 *vi Av* despegar
▸ **take on** *vt sep* (**a**) *(undertake)* encargarse de (**b**) *(acquire)* tomar (**c**) *(employ)* contratar (**d**) *(compete with)* competir con
▸ **take out** *vt sep* sacar, quitar; **he's taking me out to dinner** me ha invitado a cenar fuera
▸ **take over 1** *vt sep Com & Pol* tomar posesión de; **the rebels took over the country** los rebeldes se apoderaron del país
2 *vi* **to t. over from sb** relevar a algn
▸ **take to** *vt insep (become fond of)* coger cariño a; **to t. to drink** darse a la bebida
▸ **take up** *vt sep Sewing* acortar (**b**) *(accept)* aceptar; *(adopt)* adoptar (**c**) **I've taken up the piano/French** he empezado a tocar el piano/a aprender francés (**d**) *(occupy)* ocupar

takeaway ['teɪkəweɪ] *Br* **1** *n (food)* comida *f* para llevar; *(restaurant)* restaurante *m* que vende comida para llevar
2 *adj (food)* para llevar

take-home pay ['teɪkhəʊm'peɪ] *n* sueldo neto

taken ['teɪkən] *pp of* **take**

takeoff ['teɪkɒf] *n* (**a**) *Av* despegue *m* (**b**) *(imitation)* imitación burlona

takeout ['teɪkaʊt] *US* **1** *n (food)* comida *f* para llevar
2 *adj (food)* para llevar

takeover ['teɪkəʊvə(r)] *n Com* absorción *f*; **military t.** golpe *m* de estado; **t. bid** oferta pública de adquisición, OPA *f*

takings ['teɪkɪŋz] *npl Com* recaudación *f*

talc [tælk] *n* talco *m*

talcum powder ['tælkəmpaʊdə(r)] *n* (polvos *mpl* de) talco *m*

tale [teɪl] *n* cuento *m*; **to tell tales** contar chismes

talent ['tælənt] *n* talento *m*

talented ['tæləntɪd] *adj* dotado(a)

talk [tɔːk] **1** *vi* hablar; *(chat)* charlar; *(gossip)* chismorrear; *Fam* **now you're talking!** ¡eso sí que me interesa!

2 *vt* **to t. nonsense** decir tonterías; **to t. sense** hablar con sentido común; **to t. shop** hablar del trabajo
3 *n* (**a**) *(conversation)* conversación *f* (**b**) *(words)* palabras *fpl*; **he's all t.** no hace más que hablar (**c**) *(rumour)* rumor *m*; *(gossip)* chismes *mpl* (**d**) *(lecture)* charla *f*
▸ **talk into** *vt sep* **to t. sb into sth** convencer a algn para que haga algo
▸ **talk out of** *vt sep* **to t. sb out of sth** disuadir a algn de que haga algo
▸ **talk over** *vt sep* discutir

talkative ['tɔːkətɪv] *adj* hablador(a)

talking ['tɔːkɪŋ] *n* **no t. please!** ¡silencio, por favor!; **t. point** tema *m* de conversación

talking-to ['tɔːkɪŋtuː] *n Fam* bronca *f*

tall [tɔːl] *adj* alto(a); **a tree 10 m t.** un árbol de 10 m (de alto); **how t. are you?** ¿cuánto mides?; *Fig* **that's a t. order** eso es mucho pedir

tally ['tælɪ] **1** *vi* **to t. with sth** corresponderse con algo
2 *n Com* apunte *m*; **to keep a t. of** llevar la cuenta de

talon ['tælən] *n* garra *f*

> 🔲 Note that the Spanish word **talón** is a false friend and is never a translation for the English word **talon**. In Spanish, **talón** means both "heel" and "cheque".

tambourine [tæmbə'riːn] *n* pandereta *f*

tame [teɪm] **1** *adj* (**a**) *(animal)* domado(a); *(by nature)* manso(a); *(person)* dócil (**b**) *(style)* soso(a)
2 *vt* domar

tamper ['tæmpə(r)] *vi* **to t. with** *(text)* adulterar; *(records, an entry)* falsificar; *(lock)* intentar forzar

tampon ['tæmpɒn] *n* tampón *m*

tan [tæn] **1** *n* (**a**) *(colour)* marrón rojizo (**b**) *(of skin)* bronceado *m*
2 *adj (colour)* marrón rojizo
3 *vt* (**a**) *(leather)* curtir (**b**) *(skin)* broncear
4 *vi* ponerse moreno(a)

tang [tæŋ] *n* sabor *m* fuerte

tangent ['tændʒənt] *n* tangente *f*; *Fig* **to go off at a t.** salirse por la tangente

tangerine [tændʒə'riːn] *n* clementina *f*

tangible ['tændʒəbəl] *adj* tangible

tangle ['tæŋgəl] *n (of thread)* maraña *f*; *Fig* lío *m*; *Fig* **to get into a t.** hacerse un lío

tank [tæŋk] *n* (**a**) *(container)* depósito *m* (**b**) *Mil* tanque *m*

tanker ['tæŋkə(r)] *n Naut* tanque *m*; *(for oil)* petrolero *m*; *Aut* camión *m* cisterna

Tannoy® ['tænɔɪ] *n* sistema *m* de megafonía

tantalize ['tæntəlaɪz] *vt* atormentar

tantalizing ['tæntəlaɪzɪŋ] *adj* atormentador(a)

tantamount ['tæntəmaʊnt] *adj* **t. to** equivalente a

tantrum ['tæntrəm] *n* rabieta *f*

tap¹ [tæp] **1** *vt* golpear suavemente; *(with hand)* dar una palmadita a

2 *vi* **to t. at the door** llamar suavemente a la puerta

3 *n* golpecito *m*; **t. dancing** claqué *m*

tap² [tæp] **1** *n Br (for water)* grifo *m*, *Chile, Méx* llave *f*, *RP* canilla *f*; *Fig* **funds on t.** fondos *mpl* disponibles

2 *vt* (a) *(tree)* sangrar; *Fig* **to t. new markets** explotar nuevos mercados (b) *(phone)* pinchar

tape [teɪp] **1** *n* (a) cinta *f*; **sticky t.** cinta adhesiva; **t. measure** cinta métrica (b) *(for recording)* cinta *f* (magnetofónica); **t. recorder** magnetófono *m*, cassette *m*; **t. recording** grabación *f*

2 *vt* (a) pegar (con cinta adhesiva) (b) *(record)* grabar (en cinta)

taper ['teɪpə(r)] **1** *vi* estrecharse; *(to a point)* afilarse

2 *n (candle)* vela *f*

▸ **taper off** *vi* ir disminuyendo

tapestry ['tæpɪstrɪ] *n* tapiz *m*

tapping ['tæpɪŋ] *n* (a) *(of tree)* sangría *f*; *(of resources)* explotación *f* (b) *Tel* intervención *f* ilegal de un teléfono

tar [tɑː(r)] *n* alquitrán *m*

target ['tɑːgɪt] *n* (a) *(object aimed at)* blanco *m*; **t. practice** tiro *m* al blanco (b) *(purpose)* meta *f*

tariff ['tærɪf] *n* tarifa *f*, arancel *m*

tarmac® ['tɑːmæk] **1** *n* (a) *(substance)* alquitrán *m* (b) *Av* pista *f* de aterrizaje

2 *vt* alquitranar

tarnish ['tɑːnɪʃ] *vt* deslustrar

tarpaulin [tɑː'pɔːlɪn] *n* lona *f*

tart¹ [tɑːt] *n Br Culin* tarta *f*

tart² [tɑːt] *adj (taste)* ácido(a), agrio(a)

tart³ [tɑːt] *Fam* **1** *n* puta *f*

2 *vt Br* **to t. oneself up** emperifollarse

tartan ['tɑːtən] *n* tartán *m*

tartar ['tɑːtə(r)] *n* (a) *Chem* tártaro *m* (b) *Culin* **t. sauce** salsa tártara

task [tɑːsk] *n* tarea *f*; **to take sb to t.** reprender a algn; *Mil* **t. force** destacamento *m* (de fuerzas)

tassel ['tæsəl] *n* borla *f*

taste [teɪst] **1** *n* (a) *(sense)* gusto *m*; *(flavour)* sabor *m*; **it has a burnt t.** sabe a quemado (b) *(sample) (of food)* bocado *m*; *(of drink)* trago *m*; **to give sb a t. of his own medicine** pagar a algn con la misma moneda (c) *(liking)* afición *f*; **to have a t. for sth** gustarle a uno algo (d) **in bad t.** de mal gusto; **to have (good) t.** tener (buen) gusto

2 *vt (sample)* probar

3 *vi* **to t. of sth** saber a algo

tasteful ['teɪstfʊl] *adj* de buen gusto

tasteless ['teɪstlɪs] *adj* (a) *(food)* soso(a) (b) *(in bad taste)* de mal gusto

tasty ['teɪstɪ] *adj* (**tastier, tastiest**) sabroso(a)

tattered ['tætəd] *adj* hecho(a) jirones

tatters ['tætəz] *npl* **in t.** hecho(a) jirones

tattoo¹ [tæ'tuː] *n Mil* retreta *f*

tattoo² [tæ'tuː] **1** *vt* tatuar

2 *n (mark)* tatuaje *m*

tatty ['tætɪ] *adj* (**tattier, tattiest**) *Br* en mal estado; *(material, clothing)* raído(a); *(décor)* deslustrado(a)

taught [tɔːt] *pt & pp of* **teach**

taunt [tɔːnt] **1** *vt* **to t. sb with sth** echar algo en cara a algn

2 *n* pulla *f*

Taurus ['tɔːrəs] *n* Tauro *m*

taut [tɔːt] *adj* tenso(a), tirante

tavern ['tævən] *n* taberna *f*

tawdry ['tɔːdrɪ] *adj* (**tawdrier, tawdriest**) hortera

tawn(e)y ['tɔːnɪ] *adj* leonado(a), rojizo(a)

tax [tæks] **1** *n* impuesto *m*; **t. free** exento(a) de impuestos; **t. collector** recaudador(a) *m,f* (de impuestos); **t. evasion** evasión *f* fiscal; **t. return** declaración *f* de renta

2 *vt* (a) gravar (b) *(patience etc)* poner a prueba

taxable ['tæksəbəl] *adj* imponible

taxation [tæk'seɪʃən] *n* impuestos *mpl*

taxi ['tæksɪ] **1** *n* taxi *m*; **t. driver** taxista *mf*; **t.** *Br* **rank** *or US* **stand** parada *f* de taxis

2 *vi (aircraft)* rodar por la pista

taxidermy ['tæksɪdɜːmɪ] *n* taxidermia *f*

taxing ['tæksɪŋ] *adj* exigente

taxpayer ['tækspeɪə(r)] *n* contribuyente *mf*

TB [tiː'biː] *n (tuberculosis)* tuberculosis *f inv*

tea [tiː] *n* (a) té *m*; **t. bag** bolsita *f* de té; **t. break** descanso *m*; **t. cosy** cubretetera *f*; **t. leaf** hoja *f* de té; **t. service** *or* **set** juego *m* de té; **t. towel** paño *m* (de cocina) (b) *(snack)* merienda *f*; **(high) t.** merienda-cena *f*

teach [tiːtʃ] **1** *vt* *(pt & pp* **taught**) enseñar; *(subject)* dar clases de; **to t. sb (how) to do sth** enseñar a algn a hacer algo; *US* **to t. school** ser profesor(a)

2 *vi* dar clases, ser profesor(a)

teacher ['tiːtʃə(r)] *n* profesor(a) *m,f*, *(in primary school)* maestro(a) *m,f*

teaching ['tiːtʃɪŋ] *n* enseñanza *f*

teacup ['tiːkʌp] *n* taza *f* de té

teak [tiːk] *n* teca *f*

team [tiːm] *n* equipo *m*; *(of oxen)* yunta *f*

team-mate ['tiːmmeɪt] *n* compañero(a) *m,f* de equipo

teamwork ['tiːmwɜːk] *n* trabajo *m* en equipo

teapot ['tiːpɒt] *n* tetera *f*

tear¹ [tɪə(r)] *n* lágrima *f*; **to be in tears** estar llorando; **t. gas** gas lacrimógeno

tear² [teə(r)] **1** *vt* (*pt* **tore**; *pp* **torn**) (a) rajar, desgarrar (b) **to t. sth out of sb's hands** arrancarle algo de las manos a algn

2 *vi* (a) *(cloth)* rajarse (b) **to t. along** ir a toda velocidad

3 *n* desgarrón *m*; *(in clothes)* rasgón *m*

▸ **tear down** *vt sep* derribar

▸ **tear off** *vt sep* arrancar

▸ **tear out** *vt sep* arrancar

▸ **tear up** *vt sep* (**a**) romper, hacer pedazos (**b**) *(uproot)* arrancar de raíz

tearful ['tɪəfʊl] *adj* lloroso(a)

tearoom ['tiːruːm] *n Br* = teashop

tease [tiːz] **1** *vt* tomar el pelo a
2 *n* bromista *mf*

teashop ['tiːʃɒp] *n Br* salón *m* de té

teaspoon ['tiːspuːn] *n* cucharilla *f*

teaspoonful ['tiːspuːnfʊl] *n* cucharadita *f*

teat [tiːt] *n (of animal)* teta *f*; *(of bottle)* tetina *f*

teatime ['tiːtaɪm] *n* hora *f* del té

technical ['teknɪkəl] *adj* técnico(a); **t. college** instituto *m* de formación profesional

technicality [teknɪ'kælɪtɪ] *n* detalle técnico

technically ['teknɪkəlɪ] *adv (theoretically)* en teoría

technician [tek'nɪʃən] *n* técnico(a) *m,f*

technique [tek'niːk] *n* técnica *f*

technological [teknə'lɒdʒɪkəl] *adj* tecnológico(a)

technology [tek'nɒlədʒɪ] *n* tecnología *f*

teddy bear ['tedɪbeə(r)] *n* oso *m* de felpa

tedious ['tiːdɪəs] *adj* tedioso(a), aburrido(a)

tee [tiː] *n (in golf)* tee *m*

teem [tiːm] *vi* **to t. with** rebosar de; *Fam* **it was teeming down** llovía a cántaros

teenage ['tiːneɪdʒ] *adj* adolescente

teenager ['tiːneɪdʒə(r)] *n* adolescente *mf*

teens [tiːnz] *npl* adolescencia *f*

tee-shirt ['tiː ʃɜːt] *n* camiseta *f*

teeter ['tiːtə(r)] *vi* balancearse

teeth [tiːθ] *pl of* tooth

teethe [tiːð] *vi* echar los dientes

teething ['tiːðɪŋ] *n* **t. ring** chupador *m*; *Fig* **t. troubles** dificultades *fpl* iniciales

teetotaller [tiː'təʊtələ(r)] *n* abstemio(a) *m,f*

telecommunications ['telɪkəmjuːnɪ'keɪʃənz] *n sing* telecomunicaciones *fpl*

telegram ['telɪgræm] *n* telegrama *m*

telegraph ['telɪgrɑːf] **1** *n* telégrafo *m*; **t. pole** poste telegráfico
2 *vt & vi* telegrafiar

telepathy [tɪ'lepəθɪ] *n* telepatía *f*

telephone ['telɪfəʊn] **1** *n* teléfono *m*; **t. banking** telebanca *f*; *Br* **t. booth** *or* **box** cabina *f* (telefónica); **t. call** llamada telefónica; **t. directory** guía telefónica; **t. number** número *m* de teléfono
2 *vt* telefonear, llamar por teléfono

telephonist [tɪ'lefənɪst] *n Br* telefonista *mf*

telephoto ['telɪfəʊtəʊ] *adj* **t. lens** teleobjetivo *m*

teleprinter ['telɪprɪntə(r)] *n* teletipo *m*

telescope ['telɪskəʊp] **1** *n* telescopio *m*
2 *vi* plegarse (como un catalejo)
3 *vt* plegar

telescopic [telɪ'skɒpɪk] *adj (umbrella)* plegable

televise ['telɪvaɪz] *vt* televisar

television ['telɪvɪʒən] *n* televisión *f*; **t.**

programme programa *m* de televisión; **t. (set)** televisor *m*

teleworker ['telɪwɜːkə(r)] *n* teletrabajador(a) *m,f*

teleworking ['telɪwɜːkɪŋ] *n* teletrabajo *m*

telex ['teleks] **1** *n* télex *m*
2 *vt* enviar por télex

tell [tel] **1** *vt (pt & pp* told) (**a**) *(say)* decir; *(relate)* contar; *(inform)* comunicar; **to t. lies** mentir; **to t. sb about sth** contarle algo a algn; **you're telling me!** ¡a mí me lo vas a contar! (**b**) *(order)* mandar; **to t. sb to do sth** decir a algn que haga algo (**c**) *(distinguish)* distinguir; **to know how to t. the time** saber decir la hora (**d**) **all told** en total
2 *vi* (**a**) *(reveal)* reflejar (**b**) **who can t.?** *(know)* ¿quién sabe? (**c**) *(have effect)* notarse; **the pressure is telling on her** está acusando la presión

▸ **tell off** *vt sep Fam* regañar, reñir

teller ['telə(r)] *n (in bank etc)* cajero(a) *m,f*

telling ['telɪŋ] *adj (action)* eficaz; *(blow, argument)* contundente

telltale ['telteɪl] *n* chivato(a) *m,f*; **t. signs** señales reveladoras

telly ['telɪ] *n Br Fam* **the t.** la tele

temp [temp] *n Fam* trabajador(a) *m,f* temporal

temper ['tempə(r)] **1** *n* (**a**) *(mood)* humor *m*; **to keep one's t.** no perder la calma; **to lose one's t.** perder los estribos (**b**) *(temperament)* **to have a bad t.** tener (mal) genio
2 *vt (in metallurgy)* templar; *Fig* suavizar

temperament ['tempərəmənt] *n* temperamento *m*

temperamental [tempərəmentəl] *adj* temperamental

temperate ['tempərɪt] *adj* (**a**) mesurado(a) (**b**) *(climate)* templado(a)

temperature ['temprɪtʃə(r)] *n* temperatura *f*; **to have a t.** tener fiebre

tempest ['tempɪst] *n* tempestad *f*

temple¹ ['templ] *n Archit* templo *m*

temple² ['templ] *n Anat* sien *f*

tempo ['tempəʊ] *n* tempo *m*

temporary ['tempərərɪ] *adj* provisional; *(setback, improvement)* momentáneo(a); *(staff)* temporal

tempt [tempt] *vt* tentar; **to t. providence** tentar la suerte; **to t. sb to do sth** incitar a algn a hacer algo

temptation [temp'teɪʃən] *n* tentación *f*

tempting ['temptɪŋ] *adj* tentador(a)

ten [ten] *adj & n* diez *(m inv)*

tenable ['tenəbəl] *adj (opinion)* sostenible

tenacious [tɪ'neɪʃəs] *adj* tenaz

tenancy ['tenənsɪ] *n (of house)* alquiler *m*; *(of land)* arrendamiento *m*

tenant ['tenənt] *n (of house)* inquilino(a) *m,f*; *(of farm)* arrendatario(a) *m,f*

tend¹ [tend] *vi (be inclined)* tender, tener tendencia (**to** a)

tend² [tend] *vt* (*care for*) cuidar
tendency ['tendənsɪ] *n* tendencia *f*
tender¹ ['tendə(r)] *adj* (*affectionate*) cariñoso(a); (*compassionate*) compasivo(a); (*meat*) tierno(a)
tender² ['tendə(r)] **1** *vt* ofrecer; **to t. one's resignation** presentar la dimisión
  2 *vi Com* **to t. for** sacar a concurso
  3 *n* (**a**) *Com* oferta *f* (**b**) **legal t.** moneda *f* de curso legal
tenderness ['tendənɪs] *n* ternura *f*
tendon ['tendən] *n* tendón *m*
tenement ['tenɪmənt] *n* casa *f* de vecindad
tenet ['tenɪt] *n* principio *m*
tennis ['tenɪs] *n* tenis *m*; **t. ball** pelota *f* de tenis; **t. court** pista *f* de tenis; **t. player** tenista *mf*; **t. racket** raqueta *f* de tenis; **t. shoe** zapatilla *f* de tenis
tenor ['tenə(r)] *n Mus* tenor *m*
tense¹ [tens] *adj* tenso(a)
tense² [tens] *n Gram* tiempo *m*
tension ['tenʃən] *n* tensión *f*
tent [tent] *n* tienda *f* de campaña; **t. peg** estaca *f*
tentacle ['tentəkəl] *n* tentáculo *m*
tentative ['tentətɪv] *adj* (**a**) (*not definite*) de prueba (**b**) (*hesitant*) indeciso(a)
tenterhooks ['tentəhʊks] *npl Fig* **on t.** sobre ascuas
tenth [tenθ] **1** *adj & n* décimo(a) (*m,f*)
  2 *n* (*fraction*) décimo *m*
tenuous ['tenjʊəs] *adj* (**a**) tenue (**b**) (*argument*) flojo(a)
tenure ['tenjʊə(r)] *n* (**a**) (*of office*) ocupación *f* (**b**) (*of property*) arrendamiento *m*
tepid ['tepɪd] *adj* tibio(a)
term [tɜːm] **1** *n* (**a**) (*period*) período *m*; *Educ* trimestre *m*; **t. of office** mandato *m*, legislatura *f*; **in the long/short t.** a largo/corto plazo (**b**) (*word*) término *m*; *Fig* **in terms of money** en cuanto al dinero (**c**) **terms** (*conditions*) condiciones *fpl*; **to come to terms with** hacerse a la idea de (**d**) **to be on good/bad terms with sb** tener buenas/malas relaciones con algn
  2 *vt* calificar de
terminal ['tɜːmɪnəl] **1** *adj* terminal; **t. cancer** cáncer incurable
  2 *n* terminal *f*
terminate ['tɜːmɪneɪt] **1** *vt* terminar; **to t. a pregnancy** abortar
  2 *vi* terminarse
termini ['tɜːmɪnaɪ] *pl of* **terminus**
terminology [tɜːmɪ'nɒlədʒɪ] *n* terminología *f*
terminus ['tɜːmɪnəs] *n* (*pl* **termini**) terminal *m*
terrace ['terəs] *n* (**a**) *Agr* bancal *m* (**b**) *Br* (*of houses*) hilera *f* de casas (**c**) (*patio*) terraza *f* (**d**) *Ftb* **the terraces** las gradas
terraced ['terəst] *adj Br* **t. houses** casas *fpl* (de estilo uniforme) en hilera

terrain [tə'reɪn] *n* terreno *m*
terrible ['terəbəl] *adj* terrible; *Fig* **I feel t.** (*ill*) me encuentro fatal
terribly ['terəblɪ] *adv* terriblemente
terrier ['terɪə(r)] *n* terrier *m*
terrific [tə'rɪfɪk] *adj* (**a**) *Fam* (*excellent*) fenomenal (**b**) (*extreme*) tremendo(a)
terrify ['terɪfaɪ] *vt* aterrorizar
terrifying ['terɪfaɪɪŋ] *adj* aterrador(a)
territory ['terɪtərɪ] *n* territorio *m*
terror ['terə(r)] *n* terror *m*
terrorism ['terərɪzəm] *n* terrorismo *m*
terrorist ['terərɪst] *adj & n* terrorista (*mf*)
terrorize ['terəraɪz] *vt* aterrorizar
terry ['terɪ] *n* **t. towel** toalla *f* de rizo
terse [tɜːs] *adj* (*curt*) lacónico(a)
test [test] **1** *vt* probar, someter a una prueba; (*analyse*) analizar; *Med* hacer un análisis de
  2 *n* prueba *f*, examen *m*; **to put to the t.** poner a prueba; **to stand the t.** pasar la prueba; **t. match** partido *m* internacional; **t. pilot** piloto *m* de pruebas; **t. tube** probeta *f*; **t.-tube baby** niño *m* probeta
testament ['testəmənt] *n* testamento *m*; **Old/ New T.** Antiguo/Nuevo Testamento
testicle ['testɪkəl] *n* testículo *m*
testify ['testɪfaɪ] **1** *vt* declarar
  2 *vi Fig* **to t. to sth** atestiguar algo
testimonial [testɪ'məʊnɪəl] *n* recomendación *f*
testimony ['testɪmənɪ] *n* testimonio *m*, declaración *f*
tetanus ['tetənəs] *n* tétano(s) *m inv*
tether ['teðə(r)] **1** *n* ronzal *m*; *Fig* **to be at the end of one's t.** estar hasta la coronilla
  2 *vt* (*animal*) atar
Texas ['teksəs] *n* Tejas
text [tekst] *n* texto *m*
textbook ['tekstbʊk] *n* libro *m* de texto
textile ['tekstaɪl] **1** *n* tejido *m*
  2 *adj* textil
texture ['tekstʃə(r)] *n* textura *f*
Thai [taɪ] *adj & n* tailandés(esa) (*m,f*)
Thailand ['taɪlænd] *n* Tailandia
Thames [temz] *n* **the T.** el Támesis
than [ðæn, *unstressed* ðən] *conj* que; (*with numbers*) de; **he's older t. me** es mayor que yo; **I have more/less t. you** tengo más/menos que tú; **more interesting t. we thought** más interesante de lo que creíamos; **more t. once** más de una vez; **more t. ten people** más de diez personas
thank [θæŋk] *vt* agradecer a; **t. you** gracias
thankful ['θæŋkfʊl] *adj* agradecido(a)
thankless ['θæŋklɪs] *adj* (*task*) ingrato(a)
thanks [θæŋks] *npl* gracias *fpl*; **no t.** no gracias; **many t.** muchas gracias; **t. for phoning** gracias por llamar; **t. to** gracias a
thanksgiving [θæŋks'gɪvɪŋ] *n US* **T. Day** Día *m* de Acción de Gracias
that [ðæt, *unstressed* ðət] **1** *dem pron* (*pl* **those**) (**a**) ése *m*, ésa *f*; (*further away*) aquél

m, aquélla *f*; **this one is new but t. is old** éste es nuevo pero ése es viejo

(**b**) *(indefinite)* eso; *(remote)* aquello; **after t.** después de eso; **like t.** así; **t.'s right** eso es; **t.'s where I live** allí vivo yo; **what's t.?** ¿qué es eso?; **who's t.?** ¿quién es?

(**c**) *(with relative)* el/la; **all those I saw** todos los que vi

2 *dem adj* (*pl* **those**) *(masculine)* ese; *(feminine)* esa; *(further away) (masculine)* aquel; *(feminine)* aquella; **at t. time** en aquella época; **t. book** ese/aquel libro; **t. one** ése/aquél

3 *rel pron* (**a**) *(subject, direct object)* que; **all (t.) you said** todo lo que dijiste; **the letter (t.) I sent you** la carta que te envié

(**b**) *(governed by preposition)* que, el/la que, los/las que, el/la cual, los/las cuales; **the car (t.) they came in** el coche en el que vinieron

(**c**) *(when)* que, en que; **the moment (t.) you arrived** el momento en que llegaste

> El pronombre relativo **that** puede omitirse salvo cuando es sujeto de la oración subordinada.

4 *conj* que; **come here so (t.) I can see you** ven aquí (para) que te vea; **he said (t.) he would come** dijo que vendría

> La conjunción **that** se puede omitir cuando introduce una oración subordinada.

5 *adv* así de, tanto, tan; **cut off t. much** córteme un trozo así de grande; **I don't think it can be t. old** no creo que sea tan viejo; **we haven't got t. much money** no tenemos tanto dinero

thatched [θætʃt] *adj* cubierto(a) con paja; **t. cottage** casita *f* con techo de paja; **t. roof** techo *m* de paja

thaw [θɔː] **1** *vt (snow)* derretir; *(food, freezer)* descongelar

2 *vi* descongelarse; *(snow)* derretirse

3 *n* deshielo *m*

the [ðə, *before vowel sound* ðɪ, *emphatic* ðiː] **1** *def art* (**a**) el/la; *pl* los/las; **at/to t.** al/a la; *pl* a los/a las; **of** *or* **from t.** del/de la; *pl* de los/de las; **t. Alps** los Alpes; **t. right time** la hora exacta; **t. voice of t. people** la voz del pueblo

(**b**) *(omitted)* **George t. Sixth** Jorge Sexto

(**c**) *(by)* **t. day** al día; **by t. dozen** a docenas

(**d**) *(with adjectives used as nouns)* **t. elderly** los ancianos

(**e**) *(indicating kind)* **he's not t. person to do that** no es de los que hacen tales cosas

(**f**) *(enough)* **he hasn't t. patience to wait** no tiene suficiente paciencia para esperar

2 *adv* **t. more t. merrier** cuantos más mejor; **t. sooner t. better** cuanto antes mejor

theatre, *US* **theater** ['θɪətə(r)] *n* teatro *m*

theatre-goer, *US* **theater-goer** ['θɪətəgəʊə(r)] *n* aficionado(a) *m,f* al teatro

theatrical [θɪ'ætrɪkəl] *adj* teatral

theft [θeft] *n* robo *m*; **petty t.** hurto *m*

their [ðeə(r)] *poss adj (one thing)* su; *(various things)* sus

theirs [ðeəz] *poss pron* (el) suyo/(la) suya; *pl* (los) suyos/(las) suyas

them [ðem, *unstressed* ðəm] *pers pron pl* (**a**) *(direct object)* los/las; *(indirect object)* les; **I know t.** los/las conozco; **I shall tell t. so** se lo diré (a ellos/ellas); **it's t.!** ¡son ellos!; **speak to t.** hábleles (**b**) *(with preposition)* ellos/ellas; **walk in front of t.** camine delante de ellos; **they took the keys away with t.** se llevaron las llaves; **both of t., the two of t.** los dos; **neither of t.** ninguno de los dos; **none of t.** ninguno de ellos

theme [θiːm] *n* tema *m*; **t. tune** sintonía *f*

themselves [ðəm'selvz] *pers pron pl (as subject)* ellos mismos/ellas mismas; *(as direct or indirect object)* se; *(after a preposition)* sí mismos/sí mismas; **they did it by t.** lo hicieron ellos solos

then [ðen] **1** *adv* (**a**) *(at that time)* entonces; **since t.** desde entonces; **there and t.** en el acto; **till t.** hasta entonces (**b**) *(next, afterwards)* luego (**c**) *(anyway)* de todas formas (**d**) *(in that case)* entonces; **go t.** pues vete

2 *conj* entonces

3 *adj* **the t. president** el entonces presidente

theology [θɪ'ɒlədʒɪ] *n* teología *f*

theoretic(al) [θɪə'retɪk(əl)] *adj* teórico(a)

theoretically [θɪə'retɪklɪ] *adv* teóricamente

theory ['θɪərɪ] *n* teoría *f*

therapist ['θerəpɪst] *n* terapeuta *mf*

therapy ['θerəpɪ] *n* terapia *f*

there [ðeə(r), *unstressed* ðə(r)] **1** *adv* (**a**) *(indicating place)* allí, allá; *(nearer speaker)* ahí; **here and t.** acá y allá; **in t.** ahí dentro; **is Peter t.?** ¿está Peter? (**b**) *(emphatic)* **that man t.** aquel hombre (**c**) *(unstressed)* **t. is …/t. are …** hay …; **t. were many cars** había muchos coches; **t. were six of us** éramos seis (**d**) *(in respect)* **t.'s the difficulty** ahí está la dificultad

2 *interj* **so t.!** ¡ea!; **t., t.** bien, bien

thereabouts ['ðeərəbaʊts], *US* **thereabout** ['ðeərəbaʊt] *adv* **in Cambridge or t.** en Cambridge o por allí cerca; **at four o'clock or t.** a las cuatro o así

thereafter [ðeər'ɑːftə(r)] *adv* a partir de entonces

thereby ['ðeəbaɪ] *adv* por eso *or* ello

therefore ['ðeəfɔː(r)] *adv* por lo tanto, por eso

thermal ['θɜːməl] **1** *adj (spring)* termal; *Phys* térmico(a)

2 *n Met* corriente térmica

thermometer [θə'mɒmɪtə(r)] *n* termómetro *m*

Thermos® ['θɜːməs] *n* **T. (flask)** termo *m*

thermostat ['θɜːməstæt] *n* termostato *m*

thesaurus [θɪ'sɔːrəs] *n* diccionario *m* de sinónimos

these [ðiːz] **1** *dem adj pl* estos(as)
2 *dem pron pl* éstos(as); *see* **this**
thesis ['θiːsɪs] *n* (*pl* **theses** ['θiːsiːz]) tesis *f inv*

they [ðeɪ] *pron pl* (**a**) ellos/ellas (*usually omitted in Spanish, except for contrast*); **t. are dancing** están bailando; **t. are rich** son ricos (**b**) (*stressed*) **t. alone** ellos solos; **t. themselves told me** me lo dijeron ellos mismos (**c**) (*with relative*) los/las (**d**) (*indefinite*) **that's what t. say** eso es lo que se dice; **t. say that ...** se dice que ...

thick [θɪk] **1** *adj* (**a**) (*book etc*) grueso(a); **a wall 2 m t.** un muro de 2 m de espesor (**b**) (*dense*) espeso(a) (**c**) *Fam* (*stupid*) tonto(a)
2 *adv* densamente
3 *n* **to be in the t. of it** estar metido(a) de lleno

thicken ['θɪkən] **1** *vt* espesar
2 *vi* espesarse; *Fig* (*plot*) complicarse
thickness ['θɪknɪs] *n* (*of wall etc*) espesor *m*; (*of wire, lips*) grueso *m*; (*of liquid, woodland*) espesura *f*
thickset [θɪk'set] *adj* (*person*) rechoncho(a)
thick-skinned [θɪk'skɪnd] *adj Fig* poco sensible
thief [θiːf] *n* (*pl* **thieves** [θiːvz]) ladrón(ona) *m,f*
thigh [θaɪ] *n* muslo *m*
thimble ['θɪmbəl] *n* dedal *m*
thin [θɪn] **1** *adj* (**thinner, thinnest**) (**a**) delgado(a); **a t. slice** una loncha fina (**b**) (*hair, vegetation*) ralo(a); (*liquid*) claro(a); (*population*) escaso(a) (**c**) *Fig* (*voice*) débil; **a t. excuse** un pobre pretexto
2 *vt* **to t.** (**down**) (*paint*) diluir
thing [θɪŋ] *n* (**a**) cosa *f*; **my things** (*clothing*) mi ropa *f*; (*possessions*) mis cosas *fpl*; **for one t.** en primer lugar; **the t. is ...** resulta que ...; **what with one t. and another** entre unas cosas y otras; **as things are** tal como están las cosas (**b**) **poor little t.!** ¡pobrecito(a)!
think [θɪŋk] **1** *vt* (*pt & pp* **thought**) (**a**) (*believe*) pensar, creer; **I t. so/not** creo que sí/no (**b**) **I thought as much** yo me lo imaginaba
2 *vi* (**a**) pensar (**of** *or* **about** en); **give me time to t.** dame tiempo para reflexionar; **to t. ahead** prevenir (**b**) (*have as opinion*) opinar, pensar; **to t. highly of sb** apreciar a algn; **what do you t.?** ¿a ti qué te parece? (**c**) **just t.!** ¡imagínate!
▸ **think out** *vt sep* meditar; **a carefully thought-out answer** una respuesta razonada
▸ **think over** *vt sep* reflexionar; **we'll have to think it over** lo tendremos que pensar
▸ **think up** *vt sep* imaginar, idear
thinking ['θɪŋkɪŋ] *adj* racional
think-tank ['θɪŋktæŋk] *n Fam* grupo *m* de expertos
thinly ['θɪnlɪ] *adv* poco, ligeramente

third [θɜːd] **1** *adj* tercero(a); (*before masculine singular noun*) tercer; (**on**) **the t. of March** el tres de marzo; **the T. World** el Tercer Mundo; **t. party insurance** seguro *m* a terceros
2 *n* (**a**) (*in series*) tercero(a) *m,f* (**b**) (*fraction*) tercio *m*, tercera parte
thirdly ['θɜːdlɪ] *adv* en tercer lugar
third-rate ['θɜːdreɪt] *adj* de calidad inferior
thirst [θɜːst] *n* sed *f*
thirsty ['θɜːstɪ] *adj* (**thirstier, thirstiest**) sediento(a); **to be t.** tener sed
thirteen [θɜː'tiːn] *adj & n* trece (*m inv*)
thirteenth [θɜː'tiːnθ] **1** *adj & n* decimotercero(a) *(m,f)*
2 *n* (*fraction*) decimotercera parte
thirtieth ['θɜːtɪɪθ] **1** *adj & n* trigésimo(a) *(m,f)*
2 *n* (*fraction*) trigésima parte
thirty ['θɜːtɪ] *adj & n* treinta (*m inv*)
this [ðɪs] **1** *dem adj* (*pl* **these**) (*masculine*) este; (*feminine*) esta; **t. book/these books** este libro/estos libros; **t. one** éste/ésta
2 *dem pron* (*pl* **these**) (**a**) (*indefinite*) esto; **it was like t.** fue así (**b**) (*place*) **t. is where we met** fue aquí donde nos conocimos (**c**) (*time*) **it should have come before t.** debería haber llegado ya (**d**) (*specific person or thing*) éste *m*, ésta *f*; **I prefer these to those** me gustan más éstos que aquéllos; (*introduction*) **t. is Mr Álvarez** le presento al Sr. Álvarez; *Tel* **t. is Julia** (*speaking*) soy Julia
3 *adv* **he got t. far** llegó hasta aquí; **t. small/big** así de pequeño/grande
thistle ['θɪsəl] *n* cardo *m*
thong [θɒŋ] *n* (**a**) (*for fastening*) correa *f* (**b**) *US & Austral* (*sandal*) chancla *f*
thorax ['θɔːræks] *n* tórax *m*
thorn [θɔːn] *n* espina *f*
thorough ['θʌrə] *adj* (*careful*) minucioso(a); (*work*) concienzudo(a); (*knowledge*) profundo(a); **to carry out a t. enquiry into a matter** investigar a fondo un asunto
thoroughbred ['θʌrəbred] **1** *adj* (*horse*) de pura sangre
2 *n* (*horse*) pura sangre *mf*
thoroughfare ['θʌrəfeə(r)] *n* (*road*) carretera *f*; (*street*) calle *f*
thoroughly ['θʌrəlɪ] *adv* (*carefully*) a fondo; (*wholly*) completamente
those [ðəʊz] **1** *dem pron pl* ésos(as); (*remote*) aquéllos(as); **t. who** los que/las que
2 *dem adj pl* esos(as); (*remote*) aquellos(as); *see* **that**
though [ðəʊ] **1** *conj* (**a**) aunque; **strange t. it may seem** por (muy) extraño que parezca (**b**) **as t.** como si; **it looks as t. he's gone** parece que se ha ido
2 *adv* sin embargo
thought [θɔːt] **1** *n* (**a**) (*act of thinking*) pensamiento *m*; **what a tempting t.!** ¡qué idea más tentadora! (**b**) (*reflection*) reflexión *f* (**c**) **it's the t. that counts** (*intention*) lo que

cuenta es la intención

2 pt & pp of **think**

thoughtful ['θɔːtfʊl] adj (pensive) pensativo(a); (considerate) atento(a)

thoughtless ['θɔːtlɪs] adj (person) desconsiderado(a); (action) irreflexivo(a)

thousand ['θaʊzənd] adj & n mil (m inv); **thousands of people** miles de personas

thousandth ['θaʊzənθ] **1** adj milésimo(a)

2 n (**a**) (in series) milésimo(a) m,f (**b**) (fraction) milésima parte

thrash [θræʃ] **1** vt dar una paliza a

2 vi to t. **about** or **around** agitarse

▶ **thrash out** vt sep discutir a fondo

thread [θred] **1** n (**a**) hilo m; **length of t.** hebra f (**b**) (of screw) rosca f

2 vt (**a**) (needle) enhebrar (**b**) **to t. one's way (through)** colarse (por)

threadbare ['θredbeə(r)] adj raído(a)

threat [θret] n amenaza f

threaten ['θretən] vt amenazar; **to t. to do sth** amenazar con hacer algo

threatening ['θretənɪŋ] adj amenazador(a)

threateningly ['θretənɪŋlɪ] adv de modo amenazador

three [θriː] adj & n tres (m inv)

three-dimensional ['θriːdɪ'menʃənəl] adj tridimensional

threefold ['θriːfəʊld] **1** adj triple

2 adv tres veces; **to increase t.** triplicarse

three-piece ['θriːpiːs] adj t. **suit** traje m de tres piezas; **t. suite** tresillo m

three-ply ['θriːplaɪ] adj de tres hebras

three-wheeler [θriː'wiːlə(r)] n Aut coche m de tres ruedas; (tricycle) triciclo m

thresh [θreʃ] vt trillar

threshold ['θreʃəʊld] n umbral m; Fig **to be on the t. of** estar a las puertas or en los umbrales de

threw [θruː] pt of **throw**

thrifty ['θrɪftɪ] adj (thriftier, thriftiest) económico(a), ahorrador(a)

thrill [θrɪl] **1** n (**a**) (excitement) emoción f (**b**) (quiver) estremecimiento m

2 vt (excite) emocionar; (audience) entusiasmar

thriller ['θrɪlə(r)] n novela f/película f de suspense

thrilling ['θrɪlɪŋ] adj emocionante

thrive [θraɪv] vi (pt thrived or throve; pp thrived or thriven ['θrɪvən]) (**a**) (person) rebosar de salud (**b**) Fig (business) prosperar; **he thrives on it** le viene de maravilla

thriving ['θraɪvɪŋ] adj Fig próspero(a)

throat [θrəʊt] n garganta f

throb [θrɒb] **1** n (of heart) latido m; (of machine) zumbido m

2 vi (heart) latir; (machine) zumbar; **my head is throbbing** me va a estallar la cabeza

throes [θrəʊz] npl **to be in one's death t.** estar agonizando; Fig **in the t. of ...** en pleno(a) ...

thrombosis [θrɒm'bəʊsɪs] n Med trombosis f inv

throne [θrəʊn] n trono m

throng [θrɒŋ] **1** n multitud f, gentío m

2 vi apiñarse

3 vt atestar

throttle ['θrɒtəl] **1** n t. **(valve)** (of engine) válvula reguladora

2 vt (person) estrangular

▶ **throttle back** vt sep (engine) desacelerar

through [θruː] **1** prep (**a**) (place) a través de, por; **to look t. the window** mirar por la ventana

(**b**) (time) a lo largo de; **all t. his life** durante toda su vida; US **Tuesday t. Thursday** desde el martes hasta el jueves inclusive

(**c**) (by means of) por, mediante; **I learnt of it t. Jack** me enteré por Jack

(**d**) (because of) a or por causa de; **t. ignorance** por ignorancia

2 adj **a t. train** un tren directo; **t. traffic** tránsito m

3 adv (**a**) (from one side to the other) de un lado a otro; **to let sb t.** dejar pasar a algn; **Fig socialist/French t. and t.** socialista/francés por los cuatro costados

(**b**) (from beginning to end) **I'm t. with him** he terminado con él

(**c**) Tel **to get t. to sb** comunicar con algn; **you're t.** ¡hablen!

throughout [θruː'aʊt] **1** prep por todo(a); **t. the year** durante todo el año

2 adv (place) en todas partes; (time) todo el tiempo

throve [θrəʊv] pt of **thrive**

throw [θrəʊ] **1** vt (pt threw; pp thrown) (**a**) tirar, arrojar; (to the ground) derribar; (rider) desmontar; Fig **he threw a fit** le dio un ataque; Fig **to t. a party** dar una fiesta (**b**) (disconcert) desconcertar

2 n tiro m, lanzamiento m; (in wrestling) derribo m

▶ **throw away** vt sep (rubbish) tirar; (money) malgastar; (opportunity) perder

▶ **throw in** vt sep (**a**) tirar; Sport sacar de banda; Fig **to t. in the towel** arrojar la toalla (**b**) (include) añadir; (in deal) incluir (gratis)

▶ **throw off** vt sep (person, thing) deshacerse de; (clothes) quitarse

▶ **throw out** vt sep (rubbish) tirar; (person) echar

▶ **throw up 1** vt sep (**a**) lanzar al aire (**b**) Constr construir rápidamente

2 vi Fam vomitar, devolver

throwaway ['θrəʊəweɪ] adj desechable

throw-in ['θrəʊɪn] n Sport saque m de banda

thrown [θrəʊn] pp of **throw**

thru [θruː] prep, adj & adv US Fam = **through**

thrush [θrʌʃ] n Orn tordo m, zorzal m

thrust [θrʌst] **1** vt (pt & pp thrust) empujar con fuerza; **he t. a letter into my hand** me puso una carta violentamente en la mano

2 n (push) empujón m; Av & Phys empuje m

thud [θʌd] *n* ruido sordo

thug [θʌg] *n* (*lout*) gamberro *m*; (*criminal*) criminal *m*

thumb [θʌm] **1** *n* pulgar *m*

  2 *vt* (**a**) manosear (**b**) **to t. a lift** hacer autostop

  ▸ **thumb through** *vt insep* (*book*) hojear

thumbtack ['θʌmtæk] *n US* chincheta *f*

thump [θʌmp] **1** *n* (**a**) (*sound*) ruido sordo (**b**) (*blow*) golpazo *m*; *Fam* torta *f*

  2 *vt* golpear

  3 *vi* (**a**) **to t. on the table** golpear la mesa (**b**) (*heart*) latir ruidosamente

thunder ['θʌndə(r)] **1** *n* trueno *m*; **t. of applause** estruendo *m* de aplausos

  2 *vi* tronar

thunderbolt ['θʌndəbəʊlt] *n* (*lighting*) rayo *m*; *Fig* (*news*) bomba *f*

thunderclap ['θʌndəklæp] *n* trueno *m*

thunderous ['θʌndərəs] *adj Fig* ensordecedor(a)

thunderstorm ['θʌndəstɔːm] *n* tormenta *f*

thundery ['θʌndərɪ] *adj* (*weather*) tormentoso(a)

Thursday ['θɜːzdɪ] *n* jueves *m*

thus [ðʌs] *adv* así, de esta manera; **and t. ...** así que ...

thwart [θwɔːt] *vt* frustrar, desbaratar

thyme [taɪm] *n* tomillo *m*

thyroid ['θaɪrɔɪd] *n* tiroides *f inv*

tiara [tɪ'ɑːrə] *n* diadema *f*; *Rel* tiara *f*

tic [tɪk] *n* tic *m*

tick[1] [tɪk] **1** *n* (**a**) (*sound*) tic-tac *m* (**b**) *Br Fam* **I'll do it in a t.** ahora mismo lo hago (**c**) (*mark*) marca *f* de visto bueno

  2 *vi* hacer tic-tac

  3 *vt* marcar

  ▸ **tick off** *vt sep* (**a**) (*mark*) marcar (**b**) *Br Fam* (*reprimand*) regañar

  ▸ **tick over** *vi Aut* funcionar al ralentí

tick[2] [tɪk] *n* (*insect*) garrapata *f*

ticket ['tɪkɪt] *n* (**a**) (*for bus etc*) billete *m*, *Am* boleto *m*; (*for theatre, cinema*) entrada *f*, *Méx* boleto; (*for lottery*) décimo *m*, *Am* boleto; **t. collector** revisor(a) *m,f*; **t. office** taquilla *f*; *Br* **tout** *or US* **scalper** revendedor *m* de entradas (**b**) (*receipt*) recibo *m* (**c**) (*label*) etiqueta *f* (**d**) *Aut* multa *f*

tickle ['tɪkəl] **1** *vt* hacer cosquillas a

  2 *vi* hacer cosquillas

  3 *n* cosquillas *fpl*

ticklish ['tɪklɪʃ] *adj* **to be t.** tener cosquillas

tick-tack-toe ['tɪktæk'təʊ] *n US* tres en raya *m*

tidal ['taɪdəl] *adj* de la marea; **t. wave** ola *f* gigante

tidbit ['tɪdbɪt] *n US* = **titbit**

tiddlywinks ['tɪdlɪwɪŋks] *n sing* (*game*) pulga *f*

tide [taɪd] *n* (**a**) marea *f*; **high/low t.** marea alta/baja (**b**) *Fig* (*of events*) curso *m*; **the t. has turned** han cambiado las cosas; **to go**

against the t. ir contra corriente

tidings ['taɪdɪŋz] *npl Fml* noticias *fpl*

tidy ['taɪdɪ] **1** *adj* (**tidier, tidiest**) (**a**) (*room, habits*) ordenado(a) (**b**) (*appearance*) arreglado(a)

  2 *vt* arreglar; **to t. away** poner en su sitio

  3 *vi* **to t. (up)** ordenar las cosas

tie [taɪ] **1** *vt* (*shoelaces etc*) atar; **to t. a knot** hacer un nudo

  2 *vi Sport* empatar (**with** con)

  3 *n* (**a**) (*bond*) lazo *m*, vínculo *m* (**b**) *Fig* (*hindrance*) atadura *f* (**c**) (*clothing*) corbata *f* (**d**) *Sport* (*match*) partido *m*; (*draw*) empate *m*

  ▸ **tie down** *vt sep* sujetar; *Fig* **to be tied down** estar atado(a); *Fig* **to t. sb down to a promise** obligar a algn a cumplir una promesa

  ▸ **tie up** *vt sep* (**a**) (*parcel, dog*) atar (**b**) (*deal*) concluir (**c**) (*capital*) inmovilizar; *Fig* **I'm tied up just now** de momento estoy muy ocupado(a)

tiebreaker ['taɪbreɪkə(r)] *n* tie-break *m*

tiepin ['taɪpɪn] *n* alfiler *m* de corbata

tier [tɪə(r)] *n* (*of seats*) fila *f*; (*in stadium*) grada *f*; **four-t. cake** pastel *m* de cuatro pisos

tiger ['taɪgə(r)] *n* tigre *m*

tight [taɪt] **1** *adj* (**a**) apretado(a); (*clothing*) ajustado(a); (*seal*) hermético(a); **my shoes are too t.** me aprietan los zapatos; *Fig* **to be in a t. corner** estar en un apuro (**b**) (*scarce*) escaso(a); **money's a bit t.** estamos escasos de dinero (**c**) (*mean*) agarrado(a) (**d**) *Fam* (*drunk*) borracho(a)

  2 *adv* estrechamente; (*seal*) herméticamente; **hold t.** agárrate fuerte; **shut t.** bien cerrado(a); **to sit t.** no moverse de su sitio

tighten ['taɪtən] **1** *vt* (*screw*) apretar, (*rope*) tensar; *Fig* **to t. (up) restrictions** intensificar las restricciones

  2 *vi* apretarse; (*cable*) tensarse

tightfisted [taɪt'fɪstɪd] *adj* tacaño(a)

tightrope ['taɪtrəʊp] *n* cuerda floja; **t. walker** funámbulo(a) *m,f*

tights [taɪts] *npl* (*thick*) leotardos *mpl*; (*of dancer*) mallas *fpl*; *Br* (*thin*) medias *fpl*, pantis *mpl*

tile [taɪl] **1** *n* (*of roof*) teja *f*; (*glazed*) azulejo *m*; (*for floor*) baldosa *f*

  2 *vt* (*roof*) tejar; (*wall*) azulejar; (*floor*) embaldosar

tiled [taɪld] *adj* (*roof*) de *or* con tejas; (*wall*) revestido(a) de azulejos; (*floor*) embaldosado(a)

till[1] [tɪl] *n* (*for cash*) caja *f*

till[2] [tɪl] *vt* (*field*) labrar, cultivar

till[3] [tɪl] **1** *prep* hasta; **from morning t. night** de la mañana a la noche; **t. then** hasta entonces

  2 *conj* hasta que

tiller ['tɪlə(r)] *n Naut* caña *f* del timón

tilt [tɪlt] **1** *n* (**a**) (*angle*) inclinación *f* (**b**) (**at**) **full t.** (*speed*) a toda velocidad

  2 *vi* **to t. over** volcarse; **to t. (up)** inclinarse

3 *vt* inclinar

timber ['tɪmbə(r)] *n* (*wood*) madera *f* (de construcción); (*trees*) árboles *mpl*; (**piece of**) **t.** viga *f*

time [taɪm] **1** *n* (**a**) *tiempo m*; **all the t.** todo el tiempo; **for some t.** (**past**) desde hace algún tiempo; **I haven't seen him for a long t.** hace mucho (tiempo) que no lo veo; **in a short t.** en poco tiempo; **in no t.** en un abrir y cerrar de ojos; **in t.** a tiempo; **in three weeks' t.** dentro de tres semanas; **to take one's t. over sth** hacer algo con calma; *Fam* **to do t.** cumplir una condena; **t. bomb** bomba *f* de relojería; **t. limit** límite *m* de tiempo; (*for payment etc*) plazo *m*; **t. switch** interruptor *m* electrónico automático; **t. zone** huso horario

(**b**) (*era*) época *f*, tiempos *mpl*; **a sign of the times** un signo de los tiempos; **to be behind the times** tener ideas anticuadas

(**c**) (*point in time*) momento *m*; (**at**) **any t.** (**you like**) cuando quiera; **at no t.** en ningún momento; **at that t.** (en aquel) entonces; **at the same t.** al mismo tiempo; **at times** a veces; **from t. to t.** de vez en cuando; **he may turn up at any t.** puede llegar en cualquier momento

(**d**) (*time of day*) hora *f*; **and about t. too!** ¡ya era hora!; **in good t.** con anticipación; **on t.** puntualmente; **what's the t.?** ¿qué hora es?

(**e**) **t. of year** época *f* del año

(**f**) **to have a good/bad t.** pasarlo bien/mal

(**g**) (*occasion*) vez *f*; **four at a t.** cuatro en una vez; **next t.** la próxima vez; **several times over** varias veces; **three times running** tres veces seguidas; **t. after t.** una y otra vez

(**h**) (*in multiplication*) **three times four** tres (multiplicado) por cuatro; **four times as big** cuatro veces más grande

(**i**) *Mus* compás *m*; **in t.** al compás

2 *vt* (**a**) (*speech*) calcular la duración de; *Sport* (*race*) cronometrar

(**b**) (*choose the time of*) escoger el momento oportuno para

time-consuming ['taɪmkənsjuːmɪŋ] *adj* que ocupa mucho tiempo

time-lag ['taɪmlæg] *n* intervalo *m*

timeless ['taɪmlɪs] *adj* eterno(a)

timely ['taɪmlɪ] *adj* (**timelier, timeliest**) oportuno(a)

timer ['taɪmə(r)] *n* (*device*) temporizador *m*

timetable ['taɪmteɪbəl] *n* horario *m*

timid ['tɪmɪd] *adj* tímido(a)

timing ['taɪmɪŋ] *n* (**a**) (*timeliness*) oportunidad *f*; (*coordination*) coordinación *f*; **your t. was wrong** no calculaste bien (**b**) *Sport* cronometraje *m*

tin [tɪn] **1** *n* (**a**) (*metal*) estaño *m*; **t. plate** hojalata *f* (**b**) (*container*) lata *f*

2 *vt* (*tins*) enlatar; **tinned food** conservas *fpl*

tinfoil ['tɪnfɔɪl] *n* papel *m* de estaño

tinge [tɪndʒ] **1** *n* tinte *m*, matiz *m*

2 *vt* teñir

tingle ['tɪŋgəl] *vi* **my feet are tingling** siento un hormigueo en los pies

tinker ['tɪŋkə(r)] **1** *n Pej* calderero(a) *mf*

2 *vi* **stop tinkering with the radio** deja de toquetear la radio

tinkle ['tɪŋkəl] *vi* tintinear

tin-opener ['tɪnəʊpənə(r)] *n* abrelatas *m inv*

tinsel ['tɪnsəl] *n* oropel *m*

tint [tɪnt] **1** *n* tinte *m*, matiz *m*

2 *vt* teñir; **to t. one's hair** teñirse el pelo

tiny ['taɪnɪ] *adj* (**tinier, tiniest**) pequeñito(a); **a t. bit** un poquitín

tip¹ [tɪp] **1** *n* (*end*) punta *f*; (*of cigarette*) colilla *f*; **it's on the t. of my tongue** lo tengo en la punta de la lengua

2 *vt* poner cantera a; **tipped with steel** con punta de acero

tip² [tɪp] **1** *n* (**a**) (*gratuity*) propina *f* (**b**) (*advice*) consejo *m* (**c**) *Sport* (*racing*) pronóstico *m*

2 *vt* (**a**) dar una propina a (**b**) *Sport* pronosticar

▸ **tip off** *vt sep* (*police*) dar el chivatazo a

tip³ [tɪp] **1** *n Br* (*rubbish*) **t.** vertedero *m*

2 *vt* inclinar; *Br* (*rubbish*) verter

3 *vi* **to t.** (**up**) ladearse; (*cart*) bascular

▸ **tip over** **1** *vt sep* volcar

2 *vi* volcarse

tipple ['tɪpəl] *Fam* **1** *vi* empinar el codo

2 *n* bebida alcohólica; **what's your t.?** ¿qué te gusta beber?

tipsy ['tɪpsɪ] *adj* (**tipsier, tipsiest**) contentillo(a)

tiptoe ['tɪptəʊ] **1** *vi* andar de puntillas; **to t. in/out** entrar/salir de puntillas

2 *n* **on t.** de puntillas

tiptop ['tɪptɒp] *adj Fam* de primera

tire¹ [taɪə(r)] *n US* = **tyre**

tire² [taɪə(r)] **1** *vt* cansar; **to t. sb out** agotar a algn

2 *vi* cansarse; **to t. of doing sth** cansarse de hacer algo

tired ['taɪəd] *adj* cansado(a); **t. out** rendido(a); **to be t.** estar cansado(a); **to be t. of sth** estar harto(a) de algo

tireless ['taɪəlɪs] *adj* incansable

tiresome ['taɪəsəm] *adj* pesado(a)

tiring ['taɪərɪŋ] *adj* agotador(a)

tissue ['tɪʃuː, 'tɪsjuː] *n* (**a**) *Biol* tejido *m* (**b**) *Tex* tisú *m*; **t. paper** papel *m* de seda (**c**) (*handkerchief*) pañuelo *m* de papel, kleenex® *m*

tit¹ [tɪt] *n* **to give t. for tat** devolver la pelota

tit² [tɪt] *n very Fam* (*breast*) teta *f*

titbit ['tɪtbɪt] *n* golosina *f*

titillate ['tɪtɪleɪt] *vt* excitar

title ['taɪtəl] *n* (**a**) título *m*; *Cin* **credit titles** ficha técnica; **t. page** portada *f*; **t. role** papel *m* principal (**b**) *Jur* título *m*

titter ['tɪtə(r)] **1** *vi* reírse nerviosamente; (*foolishly*) reírse tontamente

2 *n* risa ahogada; (*foolish*) risilla tonta

titular ['tɪtjʊlə(r)] *adj* titular

TM *n* (*abbr* **trademark**) marca registrada

to [tuː, *unstressed before vowels* tʊ, *before consonants* tə] **1** *prep* (**a**) (*with place*) a; (*expressing direction*) hacia; **from town to town** de ciudad en ciudad; **he went to France/Japan** fue a Francia/Japón; **I'm going to Mary's** voy a casa de Mary; **it is 30 miles to London** Londres está a 30 millas; **the train to Madrid** el tren de Madrid; **to the east** hacia el este; **to the right** a la derecha; **what school do you go to?** ¿a qué escuela vas?

(**b**) (*time*) a; **from day to day** de día en día; **from two to four** de dos a cuatro; **ten (minutes) to six** las seis menos diez

(**c**) (*as far as*) hasta; **accurate to a millimetre** exacto(a) hasta el milímetro

(**d**) (*with indirect object*) **he gave it to his cousin** se lo dio a su primo; **what's that to you?** ¿qué te importa a ti?

(**e**) (*towards a person*) **he was very kind to me** se portó muy bien conmigo

(**f**) (*of*) de; **heir to an estate** heredero *m* de una propiedad; **adviser to the president** consejero *m* del presidente

(**g**) **to come to sb's assistance** acudir en ayuda de algn; **to everyone's surprise** para sorpresa de todos; **to this end** con este fin

(**h**) (*to the best of my knowledge*) que yo sepa

(**i**) (*compared to*) **that's nothing to what I've seen** eso no es nada en comparación con lo que he visto yo

(**j**) (*in proportion*) **one house to the square kilometre** una casa por kilómetro cuadrado; **six votes to four** seis votos contra cuatro

(**k**) (*about*) **what did he say to my suggestion?** ¿qué contestó a mi sugerencia?

2 *with infin* (**a**) *with simple infinitives* **to** *is not translated but is shown by the verb endings;* **to buy** comprar; **to come** venir

(**b**) (*in order to*) para; (*with verbs of motion or purpose*) a, por; **he did it to help me** lo hizo para ayudarme; **he stopped to talk** se detuvo a hablar; **he fought to convince them** luchó por convencerlos

(**c**) *various verbs followed by dependent infinitives take particular prepositions* (a, de, en, por, con, para *etc*) *and others take no preposition; see the entry of the verb in question*

(**d**) (*with adj and infin*) a, de; **difficult to do** difícil de hacer; **ready to listen** dispuesto(a) a escuchar; **too hot to drink** demasiado caliente para bebérselo

(**e**) (*with noun and infin*) **the first to complain** el primero en quejarse; **this is the time to do it** éste es el momento de hacerlo; **to have a great deal to do** tener mucho que hacer

(**f**) (*expressing following action*) **he awoke to find the light still on** al despertarse encontró la lámpara todavía encendida

(**g**) (*with verbs of ordering, wishing etc*) **he asked me to do it** me pidió que lo hiciera

(**h**) (*expressing obligation*) **fifty employees are to go** cincuenta empleados deben ser despedidos; **to have to do sth** tener que hacer algo

(**i**) (*replacing infin*) **go if you want to** váyase si quiere

3 *adv* **to go to and fro** ir y venir; **to push the door to** encajar la puerta

toad [təʊd] *n* sapo *m*

toadstool ['təʊdstuːl] *n* hongo *m* (venenoso)

toast¹ [təʊst] *Culin* **1** *n* pan tostado; **a slice of t.** una tostada

2 *vt* tostar

toast² [təʊst] **1** *n* (*drink*) brindis *m inv*; **to drink a t. to** brindar por

2 *vt* brindar por

toaster ['təʊstə(r)] *n* tostador *m* (de pan)

tobacco [tə'bækəʊ] *n* tabaco *m*

tobacconist [tə'bækənɪst] *n Br* estanquero(a) *m,f*; *Br* **t.'s (shop)** estanco *m*

toboggan [tə'bɒgən] *n* tobogán *m*

today [tə'deɪ] **1** *n* hoy *m*

2 *adv* hoy; (*nowadays*) hoy en día; **a week t.** justo dentro de una semana

toddler ['tɒdlə(r)] *n* niño(a) *m,f* que empieza a andar; **the toddlers** los pequeñitos

toddy ['tɒdɪ] *n* (*drink*) ponche *m*

to-do [tə'duː] *n* lío *m*, jaleo *m*

toe [təʊ] **1** *n* dedo *m* del pie; **big t.** dedo gordo

2 *vt* **to t. the line** conformarse

toenail ['təʊneɪl] *n* uña *f* del dedo del pie

toffee ['tɒfɪ] *n* caramelo *m*

together [tə'geðə(r)] *adv* junto, juntos(as); **all t.** todos juntos; **t. with** junto con; **to bring t.** reunir

toil [tɔɪl] **1** *n* trabajo duro

2 *vi* afanarse, trabajar (duro); **to t. up a hill** subir penosamente una cuesta

toilet ['tɔɪlɪt] *n* (**a**) *water m*, retrete *m*; (*for public*) servicios *mpl*; **t. paper** *or* **tissue** papel higiénico; **t. roll** rollo *m* de papel higiénico (**b**) (*washing etc*) aseo *m* (*personal*); **t. bag** neceser *m*; **t. soap** jabón *m* de tocador

toiletries ['tɔɪlɪtrɪz] *npl* artículos *mpl* de aseo

token ['təʊkən] **1** *n* (**a**) (*sign*) señal *f*; **as a t. of respect** en señal de respeto (**b**) *Com* vale *m*; **book t.** vale para comprar libros

2 *adj* simbólico(a)

told [təʊld] *pt & pp of* **tell**

tolerable ['tɒlərəbəl] *adj* tolerable

tolerance ['tɒlərəns] *n* tolerancia *f*

tolerant ['tɒlərənt] *adj* tolerante

tolerate ['tɒləreɪt] *vt* tolerar

toll¹ [təʊl] **1** *vt* tocar

2 *vi* doblar

toll² [təʊl] *n* (**a**) *Aut* peaje *m* (**b**) (*loss*) pérdidas *fpl*; **the death t.** el número de víctimas mortales

toll-free [təʊl'friː] *US* **1** *adj* **t. number** (número *m* de) teléfono *m* gratuito

2 *adv* (*call*) gratuitamente

tomato [tə'mɑːtəʊ, US tə'meɪtəʊ] n (pl **tomatoes**) tomate m; **t. sauce** salsa f de tomate

tomb [tuːm] n tumba f, sepulcro m

tomboy ['tɒmbɔɪ] n marimacho f

tombstone ['tuːmstəʊn] n lápida f sepulcral

tomcat ['tɒmkæt] n gato m (macho)

tomorrow [tə'mɒrəʊ] **1** n mañana m; **the day after t.** pasado mañana; **t. night** mañana por la noche

2 adv mañana; **see you t.!** ¡hasta mañana!; **t. week** dentro de ocho días a partir de mañana

ton [tʌn] n tonelada f; Fam **tons of** montones de

tone [təʊn] **1** n tono m

2 vi to t. (in) with sth armonizar con algo

▸ **tone down** vt sep atenuar

tone-deaf ['təʊn'def] adj **to be t.** no tener oído

tongs [tɒŋz] npl (for sugar, hair) tenacillas fpl; (fire) tenazas fpl

tongue [tʌŋ] n (a) lengua f; Fig **to say sth t. in cheek** decir algo con la boca pequeña; Fig **t. twister** trabalenguas m inv (b) (of shoe) lengüeta f; (of bell) badajo m

tongue-tied ['tʌŋtaɪd] adj mudo(a) (por la timidez)

tonic ['tɒnɪk] **1** n (a) Med tónico m (b) (drink) tónica f

2 adj tónico(a)

tonight [tə'naɪt] adv & n esta noche

tonnage ['tʌnɪdʒ] n (of ship) tonelaje m

tonne [tʌn] n = **ton**

tonsil ['tɒnsəl] n amígdala f; **to have one's tonsils out** ser operado(a) de las amígdalas

tonsillitis [tɒnsɪ'laɪtɪs] n amigdalitis f

too [tuː] adv (a) (besides) además (b) (also) también (c) (excessively) demasiado; **t. much money** demasiado dinero; **£10 t. much** 10 libras de más; **t. frequently** con demasiada frecuencia; **t. old** demasiado viejo

took [tʊk] pt of **take**

tool [tuːl] n (utensil) herramienta f

toolbox ['tuːlbɒks] n caja f de herramientas

toot [tuːt] Aut **1** vt tocar

2 vi tocar la bocina

tooth [tuːθ] n (pl **teeth**) (a) diente m; (molar) muela f; Fig **to fight t. and nail** luchar a brazo partido (b) (of saw) diente m; (of comb) púa f

toothache ['tuːθeɪk] n dolor m de muelas

toothbrush ['tuːθbrʌʃ] n cepillo m de dientes

toothpaste ['tuːθpeɪst] n pasta dentífrica f

toothpick ['tuːθpɪk] n mondadientes m inv

top¹ [tɒp] **1** n (a) (upper part) parte f de arriba; (of hill) cumbre f, cima f; (of tree) copa f; **from t. to bottom** de arriba a abajo; **on t.** de encima de; Fig **on t. of it all** ... para colmo ...; **t. hat** sombrero m de copa

(b) (surface) superficie f

(c) (of list etc) cabeza f

(d) (of bottle etc) tapa f, tapón m

(e) (garment) camiseta f

(f) (best) lo mejor

(g) Fig **at the t. of one's voice** a voz en grito

2 adj (a) (part) superior, de arriba; **the t. floor** el último piso; **t. coat** (of paint) última mano

(b) (highest) más alto(a); Aut **t. gear** directa f

(c) (best) mejor

3 vt (a) (place on top of) coronar

(b) Th **to t. the bill** encabezar el reparto

▸ **top up** vt sep llenar hasta el tope; **to t. up the petrol tank** llenar el depósito; Fig **and to t. it all** y para colmo

top² [tɒp] n (toy) peonza f

topic ['tɒpɪk] n tema m

> ✎ Note that the Spanish word **tópico** is a false friend and is never a translation for the English word **topic**. In Spanish, **tópico** means "cliché".

topical ['tɒpɪkəl] adj de actualidad

top-level ['tɒplevəl] adj de alto nivel

topmost ['tɒpməʊst] adj (el) más alto/(la) más alta

topple ['tɒpəl] **1** vi (building) venirse abajo; **to t. (over)** volcarse

2 vt volcar; Fig (government) derrocar

top-secret ['tɒp'siːkrɪt] adj de alto secreto

topsy-turvy ['tɒpsɪ'tɜːvɪ] adj & adv al revés; (in confusion) en desorden, patas arriba

torch [tɔːtʃ] n (electric) linterna f

tore [tɔː(r)] pt of **tear**

torment 1 vt [tɔː'ment] atormentar

2 n ['tɔːment] tormento m, suplicio m

torn [tɔːn] pp of **tear**

tornado [tɔː'neɪdəʊ] n tornado m

torpedo [tɔː'piːdəʊ] n torpedo m

torrent ['tɒrənt] n torrente m

torrential [tɒ'renʃəl] adj torrencial

torrid ['tɒrɪd] adj tórrido(a)

torso ['tɔːsəʊ] n torso m

tortoise ['tɔːtəs] n tortuga f (de tierra)

tortoiseshell ['tɔːtəʃel] n carey m

torture ['tɔːtʃə(r)] **1** vt torturar; Fig atormentar

2 n tortura f; Fig tormento m

Tory ['tɔːrɪ] adj & n Br Pol conservador(a) (m,f)

toss [tɒs] **1** vt (a) (ball) tirar; **to t. a coin** echar a cara o cruz (b) (throw about) sacudir

2 vi (a) **to t. about** agitarse; **to t. and turn** dar vueltas en la cama (b) Sport **to t. (up)** sortear

3 n (a) (of ball) lanzamiento m; (of coin) sorteo m (a cara o cruz) (b) (of head) sacudida f

tot¹ [tɒt] n (a) (tiny) **t.** (child) nene(a) m,f (b) (of whisky etc) trago m

tot² [tɒt] vt Br **to t. up** sumar

total ['təʊtəl] **1** n total m; (in bill) importe m; **grand t.** suma f total

2 adj total

3 *vt* sumar

4 *vi* to t. up to ascender a

totalitarian [təʊtælɪ'teərɪən] *adj* totalitario(a)

totally ['təʊtəlɪ] *adv* totalmente

tote [təʊt] *n Fam Sport* totalizador *m*

tote bag ['təʊtbæg] *n US* petate *m*

totem ['təʊtəm] *n* tótem *m*

totter ['tɒtə(r)] *vi* tambalearse

touch [tʌtʃ] **1** *vt* (**a**) tocar; *Fig* to t. on a subject tocar un tema

(**b**) *(equal)* igualar

(**c**) *(move)* conmover

2 *vi* tocarse; *Fig* it was t. and go whether we caught the train estuvimos a punto de perder el tren

3 *n* (**a**) toque *m*

(**b**) *(sense of touch)* tacto *m*

(**c**) it was a nice t. of his fue un detalle de su parte; to put the finishing touches to sth dar los últimos toques a algo

(**d**) *(ability)* habilidad *f*

(**e**) *(contact)* contacto *m*; to be/get/keep in t. with sb estar/ponerse/mantenerse en contacto con algn; to be out of t. with sth no estar al tanto de algo

(**f**) *(small amount)* pizca *f*

(**g**) *Sport* in t. fuera de banda

▸ touch down *vi (plane)* aterrizar

▸ touch off *vt sep* desencadenar

▸ touch up *vt sep (picture)* retocar

touchdown ['tʌtʃdaʊn] *n* (**a**) *(of plane)* aterrizaje *m*; *(of space capsule)* amerizaje *m* (**b**) *(in American football)* ensayo *m*

touched [tʌtʃt] *adj* (**a**) *(moved)* emocionado(a) (**b**) *Fam (crazy)* tocado(a)

touching ['tʌtʃɪŋ] *adj* conmovedor(a)

touchline ['tʌtʃlaɪn] *n* línea *f* de banda

touchy ['tʌtʃɪ] *adj* (**touchier, touchiest**) *Fam (person)* susceptible; *(subject)* delicado(a)

tough [tʌf] **1** *adj (material, competitor etc)* fuerte, resistente; *(test, criminal, meat)* duro(a); *(punishment)* severo(a); *(problem)* difícil

2 *n (person)* matón *m*

toughen ['tʌfən] *vt* endurecer

toupee ['tuːpeɪ] *n* tupé *m*

tour [tʊə(r)] **1** *n* (**a**) *(journey)* viaje *m*; package t. viaje organizado (**b**) *(of monument etc)* visita *f*; *(of city)* recorrido turístico (**c**) *Sport Th* gira *f*; on t. de gira

2 *vt* (**a**) *(country)* viajar por (**b**) *(building)* visitar (**c**) *Th* estar de gira en

3 *vi* estar de viaje

tourism ['tʊərɪzəm] *n* turismo *m*

tourist ['tʊərɪst] *n* turista *mf*; t. centre centro *m* de información turística; *Av* t. class clase *f* turista

tournament ['tʊənəmənt] *n* torneo *m*

tousled ['taʊzəld] *adj (hair)* despeinado(a)

tout [taʊt] **1** *vt Com* tratar de vender; *(tickets)* revender

2 *vi* = salir a la caza y captura de compradores

3 *n Com* gancho *m*

tow [təʊ] **1** *n* to take a car in t. remolcar un coche; *US* t. truck grúa *f*

2 *vt* remolcar

towards [tə'wɔːdz, tɔːdz] *prep* (**a**) *(direction, time)* hacia (**b**) *(with regard to)* hacia, (para) con; our duty t. others nuestro deber para con los demás; what is your attitude t. religion? ¿cuál es su actitud respecto a la religión?

towel ['taʊəl] **1** *n* toalla *f*; hand t. toallita *f*; t. Br rail *or US* bar toallero *m*

2 *vt* to t. dry secar con una toalla

towelling ['taʊəlɪŋ] *n* felpa *f*

tower ['taʊə(r)] **1** *n* torre *f*

2 *vi* to t. over *or* above sth dominar algo

towering ['taʊərɪŋ] *adj* impresionante, enorme

town [taʊn] *n* ciudad *f*; *(small)* pueblo *m*; to go into t. ir al centro; *Fam* to go to t. tirar la casa por la ventana; t. council ayuntamiento *m*; t. councillor concejal(a) *m,f*; t. hall ayuntamiento *m*; t. planning urbanismo *m*

townspeople ['taʊnzpiːpəl] *npl* ciudadanos *mpl*

towpath ['təʊpɑːθ] *n* sendero *m* a lo largo de un canal

towrope ['təʊrəʊp] *n* cable *m* de remolque

toxic ['tɒksɪk] *adj* tóxico(a)

toy [tɔɪ] **1** *n* juguete *m*

2 *vi* to t. with an idea acariciar una idea; to t. with one's food comer sin gana

toyshop ['tɔɪʃɒp] *n* juguetería *f*

trace [treɪs] **1** *n* (**a**) *(sign)* indicio *m*, vestigio *m* (**b**) *(tracks)* huella(s) *f(pl)*

2 *vt* (**a**) *(drawing)* calcar (**b**) *(plan)* bosquejar (**c**) *(locate)* seguir la pista de

tracing ['treɪsɪŋ] *n* t. paper papel *m* de calco

track [træk] **1** *n* (**a**) *(trail)* huellas *fpl*, pista *f*; to keep/lose t. of sb no perder/perder de vista a algn

(**b**) *(pathway)* camino *m*; to be on the right / wrong t. ir por el buen/mal camino

(**c**) *Sport* pista *f*, *(for motor racing)* circuito *m*; *Fig* t. record historial *m*

(**d**) *Rail* vía *f*; *Fig* he has a one-t. mind tiene una única obsesión

(**e**) *(on record, CD)* canción *f*

(**f**) *US Educ* = cada una de las divisiones del alumnado en grupos por niveles de aptitud

2 *vt* seguir la pista de; *(with radar)* seguir la trayectoria de

▸ track down *vt sep (locate)* localizar

tracksuit ['træksuːt] *n* chándal *m*, *Arg* buzo *m*, *Méx* pants *m*, *Urug* jogging *m*, *Ven* mono *m*

tract¹ [trækt] *n (expanse)* extensión *f*

tract² [trækt] *n (treatise)* tratado *m*; *(pamphlet)* folleto *m*

traction ['trækʃən] *n* tracción *f*

tractor ['træktə(r)] *n* tractor *m*

trade [treɪd] **1** n (**a**) *(profession)* oficio m; **by t.** de oficio (**b**) *Com* comercio m; **it's good for t.** es bueno para los negocios; **the building t.** (la industria de) la construcción; **t. name** nombre m comercial; **t. union** sindicato m; **t. unionist** sindicalista mf

2 vi comerciar (**in** en)

3 vt **to t. sth for sth** trocar algo por algo
▸ **trade in** vt sep dar como entrada

trademark ['treɪdmɑːk] n marca f (de fábrica); **registered t.** marca registrada

trader ['treɪdə(r)] n comerciante mf

tradesman ['treɪdzmən] n *(shopkeeper)* tendero m

trading ['treɪdɪŋ] n comercio m; *Br* **t. estate** polígono m industrial

tradition [trə'dɪʃən] n tradición f

traditional [trə'dɪʃənəl] adj tradicional

traffic ['træfɪk] **1** n (**a**) tráfico m, circulación f; *US* **t. circle** rotonda f; **t. island** isleta f; **t. jam** atasco m; **t. lights** semáforo m; *Br* **t. warden** ≃ guardia mf urbano(a) (**b**) *(trade)* tráfico m

2 vi *(pt & pp* **trafficked)** **to t. in drugs** traficar con droga

trafficker ['træfɪkə(r)] n traficante mf

tragedy ['trædʒɪdɪ] n tragedia f

tragic ['trædʒɪk] adj trágico(a)

trail [treɪl] **1** vt (**a**) *(drag)* arrastrar (**b**) *(follow)* rastrear

2 vi (**a**) *(drag)* arrastrarse (**b**) **to t. behind** rezagarse

3 n (**a**) *(track)* pista f, rastro m (**b**) *(path)* senda f, camino m (**c**) *(of smoke)* estela f

trailer ['treɪlə(r)] n (**a**) *Aut* remolque m (**b**) *US Aut (caravan)* caravana f (**c**) *Cin* trailer m, avance m

train [treɪn] **1** n (**a**) *Rail* tren m (**b**) *(of vehicles)* convoy m; *(of followers)* séquito m; *(of events)* serie f (**c**) *(of dress)* cola f

2 vt (**a**) *(teach)* formar; *Sport* entrenar; *(animal)* amaestrar; *(voice etc)* educar (**b**) *(gun)* apuntar (**on** a); *(camera)* enfocar (**on** a)

3 vi prepararse; *Sport* entrenarse

trainee [treɪ'niː] n aprendiz(a) m,f

trainer ['treɪnə(r)] n (**a**) *Sport* entrenador(a) m,f; *(of dogs)* amaestrador(a) m,f; *(of lions)* domador(a) m,f (**b**) **trainers** *(shoes)* zapatillas fpl de deporte

training ['treɪnɪŋ] n *(instruction)* formación f; *Sport* entrenamiento m; *(of animals)* amaestramiento m; *(of lions)* doma f; **to go into t.** empezar el entrenamiento; **vocational t.** formación profesional

traipse [treɪps] vi *Fam* vagar

trait [treɪt] n rasgo m

traitor ['treɪtə(r)] n traidor(a) m,f

trajectory [trə'dʒektərɪ] n trayectoria f

tram [træm], **tramcar** ['træmkɑː(r)] n *Br* tranvía m

tramp [træmp] **1** vi (**a**) *(travel on foot)* caminar (**b**) *(walk heavily)* andar con pasos pesados

2 n *(person)* vagabundo(a) m,f; *Pej* **she's a t.** es una fulana

> 🖉 Note that the Spanish word **trampa** is a false friend and is never a translation for the English word **tramp**. In Spanish, **trampa** means both "trap" and "trick".

trample ['træmpəl] vt **to t. down the grass** pisotear la hierba; **to t. sth underfoot** pisotear algo

trampoline ['træmpəliːn] n cama elástica

> 🖉 Note that the Spanish word **trampolín** is a false friend and is never a translation for the English word **trampoline**. In Spanish, **trampolín** means both "diving board" and "ski jump".

trance [trɑːns] n trance m

tranquil ['træŋkwɪl] adj tranquilo(a)

tranquillity [træŋ'kwɪlɪtɪ] n tranquilidad f

tranquillizer ['træŋkwɪlaɪzə(r)] n tranquilizante m

transact [træn'zækt] vt negociar

transaction [træn'zækʃən] n *(procedure)* tramitación f; *(deal)* transacción f

transatlantic [trænzət'læntɪk] adj transatlántico(a)

transcend [træn'send] vt trascender

transcribe [træn'skraɪb] vt transcribir

transcript ['trænskrɪpt] n transcripción f

transcription [træn'skrɪpʃən] n transcripción f

transfer 1 vt [træns'fɜː(r)] trasladar; *(funds)* trasferir; *Jur* ceder; *Ftb* traspasar; *US Rail* hacer transbordo

2 n ['trænsfɜː(r)] (**a**) traslado m; *(of funds)* trasferencia f; *Jur* cesión f; *Ftb* traspaso m (**b**) *(picture, design)* calcomanía f (**c**) *US Rail* transbordo m

transform [træns'fɔːm] vt trasformar

transformation [trænsfə'meɪʃən] n trasformación f

transfusion [træns'fjuːʒən] n *Med* transfusión f (de sangre)

transgenic [trænz'dʒiːnɪk] adj transgénico(a)

transgress [trænz'gres] vi *Fml* transgredir

transient ['trænzɪənt] adj transitorio(a)

transistor [træn'zɪstə(r)] n transistor m

transit ['trænzɪt] n tránsito m; **in t.** de tránsito

transition [træn'zɪʃən] n transición f

transitive ['trænzɪtɪv] adj transitivo(a)

transitory ['trænzɪtərɪ] adj transitorio(a)

translate [træns'leɪt] vt traducir

translation [træns'leɪʃən] n traducción f

translator [træns'leɪtə(r)] n traductor(a) m,f

translucent [trænz'luːsənt] adj translúcido(a)

transmission [trænz'mɪʃən] n transmisión f

transmit [trænz'mɪt] vt transmitir

transmitter [trænz'mɪtə(r)] n *Rad (set)* transmisor m; *Rad & TV (station)* emisora f

transparency [træns'pærənsɪ] n Phot diapositiva f

transparent [træns'pærənt] adj transparente

transpire [træn'spaɪə(r)] vi (happen) ocurrir; **it transpired that ...** ocurrió que ...

transplant 1 vt [træns'plɑːnt] trasplantar
2 n ['trænsplɑːnt] trasplante m

transport 1 vt [træns'pɔːt] transportar
2 n ['trænspɔːt] transporte m; **t. aircraft/ship** avión m/buque m de transporte; Br **t. café** bar m de carretera

transportation [trænspɔː'teɪʃən] n transporte m

transvestite [trænz'vestaɪt] n Fam travestí mf

trap [træp] **1** n trampa f; **t. door** trampilla f; Th escotillón m
2 vt atrapar

trapeze [trə'piːz] n trapecio m

trappings ['træpɪŋz] npl parafernalia f

trash [træʃ] n (inferior goods) bazofia f; US (rubbish) basura f; Fig **to talk a lot of t.** decir tonterías; US **t. can** cubo m de la basura

trashy ['træʃɪ] adj (trashier, trashiest) de ínfima calidad

trauma ['trɔːmə] n trauma m

traumatic [trɔː'mætɪk] adj traumático(a)

travel ['trævəl] **1** vi (a) viajar; **to t. through** recorrer (b) (vehicle, electric current) ir; Fig (news) propagarse
2 vt recorrer
3 n viajar m; **t. agency** agencia f de viajes

traveller, US **traveler** ['trævələ(r)] n viajero(a) m,f; **t.'s** Br **cheque** or US **check** cheque m de viaje

travelling, US **traveling** ['trævəlɪŋ] **1** adj (salesman) ambulante
2 n viajes mpl, (el) viajar m; **I'm fond of t.** me gusta viajar; **t. expenses** gastos mpl de viaje

travel-sick ['trævəlsɪk] adj **to be t.** estar mareado(a)

travesty ['trævɪstɪ] n parodia f burda

> ℓ Note that the Spanish word **travesti** is a false friend and is never a translation for the English word **travesty**. In Spanish, **travesti** means "transvestite".

trawler ['trɔːlə(r)] n barco m de arrastre

tray [treɪ] n (for food) bandeja f; (for letters) cesta f (para la correspondencia)

treacherous ['tretʃərəs] adj (a) (person) traidor(a); (action) traicionero(a) (b) (dangerous) peligroso(a)

treachery ['tretʃərɪ] n traición f

treacle ['triːkəl] n Br melaza f

tread [tred] **1** vi (pt trod; pp trod or trodden) pisar; **to t. on** pisar
2 vt (a) (step on) pisar (b) **to t. water** mantenerse a flote verticalmente
3 n (a) (step) paso m; (sound) ruido m de pasos (b) (of tyre) banda f de rodadura

treadmill ['tredmɪl] n Fig rutina f

treason ['triːzən] n traición f

treasure ['treʒə(r)] **1** n tesoro m
2 vt (keep) guardar como oro en paño; (value) apreciar muchísimo

treasurer ['treʒərə(r)] n tesorero(a) m,f

treasury ['treʒərɪ] n Pol Br **the T.,** US **the Department of the T.** ≃ el Ministerio de Hacienda; **T. bill** bono m del Tesoro

treat [triːt] **1** n (a) (present) regalo m (b) (pleasure) placer m
2 vt (a) tratar; **to t. badly** maltratar (b) (regard) considerar (c) **he treated them to dinner** les invitó a cenar

treatise ['triːtɪz] n tratado m

treatment ['triːtmənt] n (a) (of person) trato m (b) (of subject, of patient) tratamiento m

treaty ['triːtɪ] n tratado m

treble ['trebəl] **1** adj (a) (triple) triple (b) Mus **t. clef** clave f de sol; **t. voice** voz f tiple
2 vt triplicar
3 vi triplicarse

tree [triː] n árbol m; **apple/cherry t.** manzano m/cerezo m

treetop ['triːtɒp] n copa f

trek [trek] **1** n (journey) viaje m (largo y difícil); Fam (walk) caminata f
2 vi (pt & pp trekked) hacer un viaje largo y difícil; Fam (walk) ir caminando

trellis ['trelɪs] n enrejado m

tremble ['trembəl] vi temblar, estremecerse

trembling ['tremblɪŋ] adj tembloroso(a)

tremendous [trɪ'mendəs] adj (huge) enorme; (success) arrollador(a); (shock etc) tremendo(a); Fam (marvellous) estupendo(a)

tremor ['tremə(r)] n temblor m

trench [trentʃ] n (a) (ditch) zanja f; Mil trinchera f (b) **t. coat** trinchera f

trend [trend] **1** n (tendency) tendencia f; (fashion) moda f
2 vi tender (**to** or **towards** hacia)

trendy ['trendɪ] adj (trendier, trendiest) Fam (person) moderno(a); (clothes) a la última

trepidation [trepɪ'deɪʃən] n turbación f

trespass ['trespəs] vi entrar sin autorización

> ℓ Note that the Spanish verb **traspasar** is a false friend and is never a translation for the English verb **to trespass**. In Spanish, **traspasar** means "to go through, to cross, to transfer" and "to exceed".

trespasser ['trespəsə(r)] n intruso(a) m,f

trestle ['tresəl] n caballete m

trial ['traɪəl] n (a) Jur proceso m, juicio m (b) (test) prueba f; **on t.** a prueba; **by t. and error** a fuerza de equivocarse (c) **trials** (competition) concurso m (d) **trials** (suffering) sufrimiento m; **trials and tribulations** tribulaciones fpl

triangle ['traɪæŋgəl] n triángulo m

tribe [traɪb] n tribu f

tribunal [traɪˈbjuːnəl] *n* tribunal *m*

tributary [ˈtrɪbjʊtərɪ] *n (river)* afluente *m*

tribute [ˈtrɪbjuːt] *n* (**a**) *(payment)* tributo *m* (**b**) *(mark of respect)* homenaje *m*; **to pay t. to** rendir homenaje a

trice [traɪs] *n Fam* **in a t.** en un abrir y cerrar de ojos

trick [trɪk] **1** *n* (**a**) *(ruse)* ardid *m*; *(dishonest)* engaño *m*; *(in question)* trampa *f* (**b**) *(practical joke)* broma *f*; **to play a t. on sb** gastarle una broma a algn; *(malicious)* jugar una mala pasada a algn (**c**) *(of magic, knack)* truco *m*; **that'll do the t.!** ¡eso es exactamente lo que hace falta! (**d**) *Cards* baza *f*

2 *vt* engañar; **to t. sb out of sth** estafar algo a algn

trickery [ˈtrɪkərɪ] *n* engaños *mpl*, trampas *fpl*

trickle [ˈtrɪkəl] **1** *vi* discurrir; *(water)* gotear

2 *n* hilo *m*

tricky [ˈtrɪkɪ] *adj* (**trickier, trickiest**) *(person)* astuto(a); *(situation, mechanism)* delicado(a)

tricycle [ˈtraɪsɪkəl] *n* triciclo *m*

tried [traɪd] *pt & pp of* **try**

trifle [ˈtraɪfəl] **1** *n* (**a**) *(insignificant thing)* bagatela *f*; **he's a t. optimistic** es ligeramente optimista (**b**) *Br Culin* = postre de bizcocho, gelatina, frutas y nata

2 *vi* **to t. with** tomar a la ligera

trifling [ˈtraɪflɪŋ] *adj* insignificante, trivial

trigger [ˈtrɪɡə(r)] **1** *n (of gun)* gatillo *m*; *(of mechanism)* disparador *m*

2 *vt* **to t. (off)** desencadenar

trill [trɪl] *n (of music, bird)* trino *m*; *Ling* vibración *f*

trilogy [ˈtrɪlədʒɪ] *n* trilogía *f*

trim [trɪm] **1** *adj* (**trimmer, trimmest**) *(neat)* aseado(a); **to have a t. figure** tener buen tipo

2 *vt* (**a**) *(cut)* recortar; *Fig (expenses)* disminuir (**b**) *(decorate)* adornar

3 *n* (**a**) *(condition)* estado *m*; *Naut* asiento *m* (**b**) *(cut)* recorte *m*

trimming [ˈtrɪmɪŋ] *n* (**a**) *(cut)* recorte *m* (**b**) *(on clothes)* adorno *m* (**c**) *Culin* **trimmings** guarnición *f*

trinket [ˈtrɪŋkɪt] *n* baratija *f*

trio [ˈtriːəʊ] *n* trío *m*

trip [trɪp] **1** *n* (**a**) *(journey)* viaje *m*; *(excursion)* excursión *f*; **to go on a t.** ir de excursión (**b**) *Fam* **to be on a t.** *(on drugs)* estar colocado(a)

2 *vi* (**a**) **to t. (up)** *(stumble)* tropezar (**over** con); *Fig (err)* equivocarse (**b**) **to t. along** ir con paso ligero

3 *vt* **to t. sb (up)** poner la zancadilla a algn; *Fig* coger *or* pillar a algn

tripe [traɪp] *n* (**a**) *Culin* callos *mpl* (**b**) *Fam* bobadas *fpl*

triple [ˈtrɪpəl] **1** *adj* triple

2 *vt* triplicar

3 *vi* triplicarse

triplet [ˈtrɪplɪt] *n* trillizo(a) *m,f*

triplicate [ˈtrɪplɪkɪt] *adj* **in t.** por triplicado

tripod [ˈtraɪpɒd] *n* trípode *m*

trite [traɪt] *adj (sentiment)* banal; *(subject)* trillado(a)

triumph [ˈtraɪəmf] **1** *n* triunfo *m*

2 *vi* triunfar

triumphant [traɪˈʌmfənt] *adj* triunfante

trivia [ˈtrɪvɪə] *npl* trivialidades *fpl*

trivial [ˈtrɪvɪəl] *adj* trivial, banal

trod [trɒd] *pt & pp of* **tread**

trodden [ˈtrɒdən] *pp of* **tread**

trolley [ˈtrɒlɪ] *n Br* carro *m*

trombone [trɒmˈbəʊn] *n* trombón *m*

troop [truːp] **1** *n* (**a**) *(of people)* grupo *m* (**b**) *Mil* **troops** tropas *fpl*

2 *vi* **to t. in/out/off** entrar/salir/marcharse en tropel

trooper [ˈtruːpə(r)] *n* (**a**) *(soldier)* soldado *m* de caballería (**b**) *US (policeman)* policía *mf*

trooping [ˈtruːpɪŋ] *n Br* **t. the colour** = ceremonia de homenaje a la bandera de un regimiento

trophy [ˈtrəʊfɪ] *n* trofeo *m*

tropic [ˈtrɒpɪk] *n* trópico *m*

tropical [ˈtrɒpɪkəl] *adj* tropical

trot [trɒt] **1** *vi* trotar

2 *n* trote *m*; **to go at a t.** ir al trote; *Fam* **on the t.** *(in succession)* seguidos(as)

trouble [ˈtrʌbəl] **1** *n* (**a**) *(misfortune)* desgracia *f*

(**b**) *(problems)* problemas *mpl*; **to be in t.** estar en un lío; **to cause sb t.** ocasionar problemas a algn; **to get sb out of t.** sacar a algn de un apuro; **the t. is that …** lo que pasa es que …

(**c**) *(effort)* esfuerzo *m*; **it's no t.** no es ninguna molestia; **it's not worth the t.** no merece la pena; **to take the t. to do sth** molestarse en hacer algo

(**d**) *(conflict)* conflicto *m*

(**e**) *Med* enfermedad *f*; **to have liver t.** tener problemas de hígado

2 *vt* (**a**) *(affect)* afligir; *(worry)* preocupar; **that doesn't t. him at all** eso le tiene sin cuidado

(**b**) *(bother)* molestar

3 *vi* molestarse

troubled [ˈtrʌbəld] *adj* agitado(a)

troublemaker [ˈtrʌbəlmeɪkə(r)] *n* alborotador(a) *m,f*

troubleshooter [ˈtrʌbəlʃuːtə(r)] *n Ind* = persona encargada de solucionar problemas

troublesome [ˈtrʌbəlsəm] *adj* molesto(a)

trough [trɒf] *n* (**a**) *(drinking)* **t.** abrevadero *m*; *(feeding)* pesebre *m* (**b**) *(of wave)* seno *m* (**c**) *Geog Met* depresión *f*

trounce [traʊns] *vt* dar una paliza a

troupe [truːp] *n Th* compañía *f*

trousers [ˈtraʊzəz] *npl* pantalón *m*, pantalones *mpl*

trousseau [ˈtruːsəʊ] *n* ajuar *m*

trout [traʊt] *n* trucha *f*

trowel [ˈtraʊəl] *n* (**a**) *(builder's)* palustre *m* (**b**) *(for gardening)* desplantador *m*

truant ['truːənt] *n Br* **to play t.** hacer novillos
truce [truːs] *n* tregua *f*
truck¹ [trʌk] *n* (**a**) *Br Rail* vagón *m* (**b**) *Aut* camión *m*; **t. driver** camionero(a) *m,f*; *US* **t. farm** huerta *f*; *US* **t. farmer** hortelano(a) *m,f*
truck² [trʌk] *n* (**a**) **to have no t. with** no estar dispuesto a tolerar (**b**) *US* verduras *fpl*; **t. farm** huerta *f*; **t. farming** cultivo *m* de hortalizas
truculent ['trʌkjʊlənt] *adj* agresivo(a), airado(a)

> 🖉 Note that the Spanish word **truculento** is a false friend and is never a translation for the English word **truculent**. In Spanish, **truculento** means "horrifying, terrifying".

trudge [trʌdʒ] *vi* caminar con dificultad
true [truː] *adj* (**truer, truest**) (**a**) verdadero(a); **it's t. that ...** es verdad que ...; **to come t.** cumplirse, hacerse realidad (**b**) *(faithful)* fiel (**c**) *(aim)* acertado(a)
truffle ['trʌfəl] *n* trufa *f*
truly ['truːlɪ] *adv* (**a**) de verdad; **really and t.?** ¿de veras? (**b**) *(faithfully)* fielmente; **yours t.** atentamente
trump [trʌmp] *Cards* **1** *n* triunfo *m*
   2 *vt* fallar
trumped-up ['trʌmptʌp] *adj* inventado(a)
trumpet ['trʌmpɪt] *n* trompeta *f*
trumpeting ['trʌmpɪtɪŋ] *n* (*of elephant*) berrido *m*
truncheon ['trʌntʃən] *n Br* porra *f (de policía)*
trundle ['trʌndəl] *vi* rodar
trunk [trʌŋk] *n* (**a**) *(of tree, body)* tronco *m* (**b**) *(of elephant)* trompa *f* (**c**) *(luggage)* baúl *m* (**d**) *Br Tel* **t. call** conferencia interurbana; *Br* **t. road** carretera *f* principal (**e**) *US (of car)* maletero *m, CAm, Méx* cajuela *f, RP* baúl *m*
trunks [trʌŋks] *npl (bathing)* **t.** bañador *m*
truss [trʌs] **1** *vt (tie)* atar
   2 *n* (**a**) *Constr* cuchillo *m* de armadura (**b**) *Med* braguero *m*
trust [trʌst] **1** *n* (**a**) confianza *f*; **breach of t.** abuso *m* de confianza (**b**) *Jur* fideicomiso *m* (**c**) *Fin* trust *m*
   2 *vt* (**a**) *(hope)* esperar (**b**) *(rely upon)* fiarse de; **to t. sb with sth** confiar algo a algn
   3 *vi* confiar (**in** en)
trusted ['trʌstɪd] *adj* de fiar
trustee [trʌs'tiː] *n Jur* fideicomisario(a) *m,f*, *(in bankruptcy)* síndico *m*
trustful ['trʌstfʊl], **trusting** ['trʌstɪŋ] *adj* confiado(a)
trustworthy ['trʌstwɜːðɪ] *adj (person)* de confianza; *(information)* fidedigno(a)
trusty ['trʌstɪ] *adj (trustier, trustiest)* fiel, leal
truth [truːθ] *n* verdad *f*; **to tell the t.** decir la verdad
truthful ['truːθfʊl] *adj (person)* veraz, sincero(a); *(testimony)* verídico(a)

truthfully ['truːθfʊlɪ] *adv* sinceramente
try [traɪ] **1** *vt (pt & pp tried)* (**a**) *(attempt)* intentar; **to t. to do sth** tratar de *or* intentar hacer algo (**b**) *(test)* probar, ensayar; **to t. sb's patience** poner a prueba la paciencia de algn (**c**) *Jur* juzgar
   2 *vi* intentar
   3 *n* (**a**) *(attempt)* tentativa *f*, intento *m* (**b**) *Sport* ensayo *m*
   ► **try on** *vt sep (dress)* probarse
   ► **try out** *vt sep* probar
trying ['traɪɪŋ] *adj (person)* molesto(a), pesado(a); **to have a t. time** pasar un mal rato
tsar [zɑː(r)] *n* zar *m*
T-shirt ['tiːʃɜːt] *n* camiseta *f*
tub [tʌb] *n* (**a**) *(container)* tina *f*, cuba *f* (**b**) *(bath)* bañera *f*
tuba ['tjuːbə] *n* tuba *f*
tubby ['tʌbɪ] *adj (tubbier, tubbiest)* rechoncho(a)
tube [tjuːb] *n* (**a**) *(container)* tubo *m*; *Anat* conducto *m*; *(of bicycle)* cámara *f* (de aire) (**b**) *Br Fam* **the t.** *(underground)* el metro
tuberculosis [tjʊbɜːkjʊ'ləʊsɪs] *n* tuberculosis *f*
tubing ['tjuːbɪŋ] *n* tubería *f*; **(piece of) t.** (trozo *m* de) tubo *m*
tubular ['tjuːbjʊlə(r)] *adj* tubular
tuck [tʌk] **1** *vt* **to t. in the bedclothes** remeter la ropa de la cama; **to t. sb in** arropar a algn; **to t. one's shirt into one's trousers** meterse la camisa por dentro (de los pantalones)
   2 *n Sewing* pliegue *m*
   ► **tuck in** *vi Fam* devorar
Tuesday ['tjuːzdɪ] *n* martes *m*
tuft [tʌft] *n (of hair)* mechón *m*
tug [tʌg] **1** *vt (pull at)* tirar de; *(haul along)* arrastrar; *Naut* remolcar
   2 *n* (**a**) *(pull)* tirón *m*; **t. of war** *(game)* lucha *f* de la cuerda; *Fig* lucha encarnizada (**b**) *Naut* remolcador *m*
tugboat ['tʌgbəʊt] *n* remolcador *m*
tuition [tjuː'ɪʃən] *n* instrucción *f*; **private t.** clases *fpl* particulares; **t. fees** honorarios *mpl*
tulip ['tjuːlɪp] *n* tulipán *m*
tumble ['tʌmbəl] **1** *vi (person)* caerse; *(acrobat)* dar volteretas; *(building)* venirse abajo
   2 *vt* volcar
   3 *n* (**a**) caída *f* (**b**) **t. dryer** secadora *f*
tumbledown ['tʌmbəldaʊn] *adj* en ruinas
tumbler ['tʌmblə(r)] *n* vaso *m*
tummy ['tʌmɪ] *n Fam* estómago *m*, barriga *f*
tumour, *US* **tumor** ['tjuːmə(r)] *n* tumor *m*
tumult ['tjuːmʌlt] *n* tumulto *m*
tuna ['tjuːnə] *n* atún *m*, bonito *m*

> 🖉 Note that the Spanish word **tuna** is a false friend and is never a translation for the English word **tuna**. In Spanish, **tuna** means "group of student minstrels".

tune [tjuːn] **1** *n* (**a**) *(melody)* melodía *f*; *Fig* **to**

change one's t. cambiar de tono (**b**) *Mus* tono *m*; **in/out of t.** afinado/desafinado; **to sing out of t.** desafinar

  2 *vt Mus* afinar

  3 *vi Rad & TV* **to t. in to a station** sintonizar una emisora

▸ **tune up** *vi* afinar los instrumentos

tuneful ['tjuːnfʊl] *adj* melodioso(a)

tuner ['tjuːnə(r)] (**a**) *(of pianos)* afinador(a) *m,f* (**b**) *Rad & TV (knob)* sintonizador *m*

tunic ['tjuːnɪk] *n* túnica *f*

tuning ['tjuːnɪŋ] *n* (**a**) *Mus* afinación *f*; **t. fork** diapasón *m* (**b**) *Rad TV* **t. in** sintonización *f*

Tunisia [tjuːˈnɪzɪə] *n* Túnez

Tunisian [tjuːˈnɪzɪən] *adj & n* tunecino(a) *(m,f)*

tunnel ['tʌnəl] **1** *n* túnel *m*; *Min* galería *f*

  2 *vt* **to t. through** abrir un túnel a través de

turban ['tɜːbən] *n* turbante *m*

turbine ['tɜːbaɪn] *n* turbina *f*

turbulent ['tɜːbjʊlənt] *adj* turbulento(a)

tureen [təˈriːn] *n* sopera *f*

turf [tɜːf] *n* (**a**) *(grass)* césped *m*; *(peat)* turba *f* (**b**) *Br* **t. accountant** *(in horse racing)* corredor(a) *m,f* de apuestas

▸ **turf out** *vt sep Br Fam* **to t. sb out** poner a algn de patitas en la calle

Turk [tɜːk] *n* turco(a) *m,f*

Turkey ['tɜːkɪ] *n* Turquía

turkey ['tɜːkɪ] *n* pavo *m*

Turkish ['tɜːkɪʃ] **1** *adj* turco(a)

  2 *n (language)* turco *m*

turmoil ['tɜːmɔɪl] *n* confusión *f*

turn [tɜːn] **1** *vt* (**a**) volver; *(rotate)* girar, hacer girar; **to t. sth inside out** volver algo del revés; **to t. a page** volver una hoja; **to t. one's head/ gaze** volver la cabeza/mirada (**towards** hacia); **to t. the corner** doblar la esquina; *Fig* **he's turned forty** ha cumplido los cuarenta

  (**b**) *(change)* transformar (**into** en)

  (**c**) *(on lathe)* tornear

  2 *vi* (**a**) *(rotate)* girar

  (**b**) *(turn round)* volverse, dar la vuelta; **to t. to sb** volverse hacia algn; *Fig (for help)* acudir a algn; **to t. upside down** volcarse; *Fig* **to t. on sb** volverse contra algn

  (**c**) *(become)* volverse; **the milk has turned sour** la leche se ha cortado

  3 *n* (**a**) *(of wheel)* vuelta *f*; **done to a t.** *(meat)* en su punto

  (**b**) *(change of direction)* cambio *m* de dirección; *(in road)* curva *f*; **to take a t. for the better** empezar a mejorar; **left/right t.** giro *m* al izquierdo/a la derecha; *US Aut* **t. signal** intermitente *m*

  (**c**) **to do sb a good t.** hacer un favor a algn

  (**d**) *Med* ataque *m*

  (**e**) *(in game, queue)* turno *m*, vez *f*; **it's your t. to** te toca a ti; **to take it in turns to do sth** turnarse para hacer algo

  (**f**) *Th* número *m*

  (**g**) **t. of phrase** giro *m*

▸ **turn aside 1** *vt sep* desviar

  2 *vi* desviarse

▸ **turn away 1** *vt sep (person)* rechazar

  2 *vi* volver la cabeza

▸ **turn back 1** *vt sep (person)* hacer retroceder; *(clock)* retrasar

  2 *vi* volverse

▸ **turn down** *vt sep* (**a**) *(gas, radio etc)* bajar (**b**) *(reject)* rechazar (**c**) *(fold)* doblar

▸ **turn in** *Fam* **1** *vt sep (person)* entregar a la policía

  2 *vi* acostarse

▸ **turn off 1** *vt sep (electricity)* desconectar; *(gas, light)* apagar; *(water)* cerrar

  2 *vi* desviarse

▸ **turn on** *vt sep (electricity)* encender; *(tap, gas)* abrir; *(machine)* poner en marcha; *Fam* **it turns me on** me encanta

▸ **turn out 1** *vt sep* (**a**) *(extinguish)* apagar (**b**) *(eject)* echar; *(empty)* vaciar (**c**) *(produce)* producir

  2 *vi* (**a**) *(attend)* asistir (**b**) **it turns out that ...** resulta que ...; **things have turned out well** las cosas han salido bien

▸ **turn over 1** *vt sep (turn upside down)* poner al revés; *(page)* dar la vuelta a

  2 *vi* volverse

▸ **turn round 1** *vt sep* volver

  2 *vi (rotate)* girar, dar vueltas

▸ **turn up 1** *vt sep* (**a**) *(collar)* levantar; **to t. up one's shirt sleeves** arremangarse; **turned-up nose** nariz respingona (**b**) *Rad TV* subir

  2 *vi* (**a**) *Fig* **something is sure to t. up** algo saldrá (**b**) *(arrive)* llegar, presentarse; **nobody turned up** nadie se presentó (**c**) *(attend)* asistir

turning ['tɜːnɪŋ] *n* (**a**) *Fig* **t. point** punto decisivo (**b**) *(in road)* salida *f*

turnip ['tɜːnɪp] *n* nabo *m*

turnout ['tɜːnaʊt] *n* asistencia *f*

turnover ['tɜːnəʊvə(r)] *n Com (sales)* facturación *f*; *(of goods)* movimiento *m*

turnpike ['tɜːnpaɪk] *n US* autopista *f* de peaje

turnstile ['tɜːnstaɪl] *n* torniquete *m*

turntable ['tɜːnteɪbəl] *n (for record)* plato *m* (giratorio)

turn-up ['tɜːnʌp] *n Br* (**a**) *(of trousers)* vuelta *f* (**b**) *Fam Fig* **what a t. for the books!** ¡vaya sorpresa!

turpentine ['tɜːpəntaɪn] *n* (esencia *f* de) trementina *f*

turquoise ['tɜːkwɔɪz] **1** *n (colour, stone)* turquesa *f*

  2 *adj* **t. (blue)** azul turquesa

turret ['tʌrɪt] *n* torrecilla *f*

turtle ['tɜːtəl] *n* tortuga *f*; *US (tortoise)* tortuga *f*

turtledove ['tɜːtəldʌv] *n* tórtola *f*

turtleneck ['tɜːtəlnek] *n* **a t. (sweater)** un jersey de cuello alto

tusk [tʌsk] *n* colmillo *m*

tussle ['tʌsəl] *n* pelea *f*, lucha *f*

tutor ['tjuːtə(r)] *n Univ* tutor(a) *m,f*; **private t.**

profesor(a) *m,f* particular

tutorial [tjuːˈtɔːrɪəl] *n Univ* tutoría *f*, seminario *m*

tuxedo [tʌkˈsiːdəʊ] *n US* smoking *m*

TV [tiːˈviː] *n* (*abbr* **television**) televisión *f*

twang [twæŋ] **1** *n* (**a**) (*of instrument*) sonido *m* vibrante (**b**) nasal **t.** gangueo *m*

   2 *vt* puntear

   3 *vi* (*string*) vibrar

tweak [twiːk] *vt* pellizcar

tweed [twiːd] *n* cheviot *m*

tweezers [ˈtwiːzəz] *npl* pinzas *fpl*

twelfth [twelfθ] **1** *adj & n* duodécimo(a) (*m,f*)

   2 *n* (*fraction*) duodécimo *m*

twelve [twelv] *adj & n* doce (*m inv*)

twentieth [ˈtwentɪθ] **1** *adj & n* vigésimo(a) (*m,f*)

   2 *n* (*fraction*) vigésimo *m*

twenty [ˈtwentɪ] *adj & n* veinte (*m inv*)

twice [twaɪs] *adv* dos veces; **he's t. as old as I am** tiene el doble de años que yo

twiddle [ˈtwɪdəl] **1** *vt* dar vueltas a; **to t. one's moustache** mesarse el bigote; **to t. one's thumbs** estar mano sobre mano

   2 *vi* **to t. with sth** juguetear con algo

twig¹ [twɪg] *n* ramilla *f*

twig² [twɪg] *vi Br Fam* caer en la cuenta

twilight [ˈtwaɪlaɪt] *n* crepúsculo *m*

twin [twɪn] **1** *n* mellizo(a) *m,f*; **identical twins** gemelos (idénticos); **t. brother/sister** hermano gemelo/hermana gemela; **t. beds** camas *fpl* gemelas

   2 *vt* hermanar

twine [twaɪn] **1** *n* bramante *m*

   2 *vt* entretejer

   3 *vi* **to t. round sth** enroscarse alrededor de algo

twinge [twɪndʒ] *n* (*of pain*) punzada *f*; *Fig* **t. of conscience** remordimiento *m*

twinkle [ˈtwɪŋkəl] *vi* (*stars*) centellear; (*eyes*) brillar

twinkling [ˈtwɪŋklɪŋ] *n* (*of stars*) centelleo *m*; *Fig* **in the t. of an eye** en un abrir y cerrar de ojos

twirl [twɜːl] **1** *vt* girar rápidamente

   2 *vi* (*spin*) girar rápidamente; (*dancer*) piruetear

   3 *n* (*movement*) giro rápido; (*of dancer*) pirueta *f*

twist [twɪst] **1** *vt* torcer; (*sense*) tergiversar; **to t. one's ankle** torcerse el tobillo

   2 *vi* (*smoke*) formar volutas; (*path*) serpentear

   3 *n* (**a**) (*of yarn*) torzal *m* (**b**) (*movement*)

torsión *f*; *Med* torcedura *f*; *Fig* **to give a new t. to sth** dar un nuevo enfoque a algo (**c**) (*in road*) vuelta *f* (**d**) (*dance*) twist *m*

twit [twɪt] *n Br Fam* memo(a) *m,f*

twitch [twɪtʃ] **1** *vt* dar un tirón a

   2 *vi* crisparse; **his face twitches** tiene un tic en la cara

twitter [ˈtwɪtə(r)] **1** *vi* gorjear

   2 *n* gorjeo *m*

two [tuː] **1** *adj* dos *inv*; *Fig* **to be in** or **of t. minds about sth** estar indeciso(a) respecto a algo

   2 *n* dos *m inv*; *Fig* **to put t. and t. together** atar cabos

two-faced [ˈtuːˈfeɪst] *adj* hipócrita

two-party [ˈtuːpɑːtɪ] *adj* **t. system** bipartidismo *m*

twopence [ˈtʌpəns] *n Br* dos peniques

two-piece [ˈtuːˈpiːs] **1** *adj* de dos piezas

   2 *n* (*suit*) traje *m* de dos piezas

two-seater [ˈtuːˈsiːtə(r)] *adj & n* biplaza (*f*)

twosome [ˈtuːsəm] *n* pareja *f*

two-time [ˈtuːtaɪm] *vt Fam* poner los cuernos a

two-way [ˈtuːweɪ] *adj* (**a**) (*street*) de dos direcciones (**b**) **t. radio** aparato *m* emisor y receptor

tycoon [taɪˈkuːn] *n* magnate *m*

type [taɪp] **1** *n* (**a**) (*kind*) tipo *m*, clase *f*; (*brand*) marca *f*; (*of car*) modelo *m* (**b**) *Typ* carácter *m*; (*print*) caracteres *mpl*

   2 *vt & vi* escribir a máquina

typecast [ˈtaɪpkɑːst] *vt* encasillar

typescript [ˈtaɪpskrɪpt] *n* texto *m* escrito a máquina

typeset [ˈtaɪpset] *vt* componer

typesetter [ˈtaɪpsetə(r)] *n* (**a**) (*person*) cajista *mf* (**b**) (*machine*) máquina *f* para componer tipos

typewriter [ˈtaɪpraɪtə(r)] *n* máquina *f* de escribir

typewritten [ˈtaɪprɪtən] *adj* escrito(a) a máquina

typhoid [ˈtaɪfɔɪd] *n* **t. (fever)** fiebre tifoidea

typhoon [taɪˈfuːn] *n* tifón *m*

typical [ˈtɪpɪkəl] *adj* típico(a)

typify [ˈtɪpɪfaɪ] *vt* tipificar

typing [ˈtaɪpɪŋ] *n* mecanografía *f*

typist [ˈtaɪpɪst] *n* mecanógrafo(a) *m,f*

tyrannical [tɪˈrænɪkəl] *adj* tiránico(a)

tyrannize [ˈtɪrənaɪz] *vt* tiranizar

tyranny [ˈtɪrənɪ] *n* tiranía *f*

tyrant [ˈtaɪrənt] *n* tirano(a) *m,f*

tyre [taɪə(r)] *n* neumático *m*; **t. pressure** presión *f* de los neumáticos

U, u [juː] *n (the letter)* U, u *f*
U [juː] *adj (film)* ≃ (apta) para todos los públicos
ubiquity [juːˈbɪkwɪtɪ] *n* ubicuidad *f*
udder [ˈʌdə(r)] *n* ubre *f*
UFO, ufo [ˈjuːefˈəʊ, ˈjuːfəʊ] *n (abbr* **unidentified flying object)** OVNI *m*
ugh [ʌx] *interj* ¡uf!, ¡puf!
ugly [ˈʌglɪ] *adj* (uglier, ugliest) feo(a); *(situation)* desagradable; *Fig* **u. duckling** patito feo
UK [juːˈkeɪ] *n (abbr* **United Kingdom)** R.U. *m*
Ukraine [juːˈkreɪn] *n* the **U.** Ucrania
ulcer [ˈʌlsə(r)] *n (sore)* llaga *f; (internal)* úlcera *f*
ulterior [ʌlˈtɪərɪə(r)] *adj (motive)* oculto(a)
ultimate [ˈʌltɪmɪt] *adj* (**a**) *(final)* último(a); *(aim)* final (**b**) *(basic)* esencial
ultimately [ˈʌltɪmɪtlɪ] *adv* (**a**) *(finally)* finalmente (**b**) *(basically)* en el fondo
ultimatum [ʌltɪˈmeɪtəm] *n* ultimátum *m*
ultrasound [ˈʌltrəsaʊnd] *n* ultrasonido *m*
ultraviolet [ʌltrəˈvaɪəlɪt] *adj* ultravioleta
umbilical [ʌmˈbɪlɪkəl] *adj* **u. cord** cordón *m* umbilical
umbrella [ʌmˈbrelə] *n* paraguas *m inv*
umpire [ˈʌmpaɪə(r)] **1** *n* árbitro *m*
 2 *vt* arbitrar
umpteen [ʌmpˈtiːn] *adj Fam* muchísimos(as), la tira de
umpteenth [ʌmpˈtiːnθ] *adj* enésimo(a)
UN [juːˈen] *n (abbr* **United Nations (Organization))** ONU *f*
unabashed [ʌnəˈbæʃt] *adj* (**a**) *(unperturbed)* inmutable, imperturbable (**b**) *(shameless)* desvergonzado(a), descarado(a)
unable [ʌnˈeɪbəl] *adj* incapaz; **to be u. to do sth/anything** no poder hacer algo/nada
unacceptable [ʌnəkˈseptəbəl] *adj* inaceptable
unaccompanied [ʌnəˈkʌmpənɪd] *adj* solo(a)
unaccountable [ʌnəˈkaʊntəbəl] *adj* inexplicable
unaccounted-for [ʌnəˈkaʊntɪdfɔː(r)] *adj* **to be u.** faltar
unaccustomed [ʌnəˈkʌstəmd] *adj* **he's u. to this climate** no está muy acostumbrado a este clima
unaffected [ʌnəˈfektɪd] *adj* (**a**) *no afectado(a) (by por)* (**b**) *(indifferent)* indiferente *(by a)* (**c**) *(natural) (person)* natural; *(style)* llano(a)

unaided [ʌnˈeɪdɪd] *adj* sin ayuda, solo(a)
unanimous [juːˈnænɪməs] *adj* unánime
unannounced [ʌnəˈnaʊnst] *adj* sin avisar
unanswered [ʌnˈɑːnsəd] *adj* sin contestar
unapproachable [ʌnəˈprəʊtʃəbəl] *adj* inabordable, inaccesible
unarmed [ʌnˈɑːmd] *adj* desarmado(a)
unashamed [ʌnəˈʃeɪmd] *adj* desvergonzado(a)
unasked [ʌnˈɑːskt] *adv* **u. (for)** *(unrequested)* no solicitado(a); *(spontaneous)* espontáneo(a)
unassuming [ʌnəˈsjuːmɪŋ] *adj* sin pretensiones
unattached [ʌnəˈtætʃt] *adj* (**a**) *(independent)* libre; *(loose)* suelto(a) (**b**) *(person)* soltero(a) y sin compromiso
unattended [ʌnəˈtendɪd] *adj (counter etc)* desatendido(a); **to leave a child u.** dejar a un niño solo
unauthorized [ʌnˈɔːθəraɪzd] *adj* (**a**) *(person)* no autorizado(a) (**b**) *(trade etc)* ilícito(a), ilegal
unavoidable [ʌnəˈvɔɪdəbəl] *adj* inevitable; *(accident)* imprevisible
unaware [ʌnəˈweə(r)] *adj* **to be u. of sth** ignorar algo
unawares [ʌnəˈweəz] *adv* (**a**) *(unexpectedly)* desprevenido(a) (**b**) *(without knowing)* inconscientemente
unbalanced [ʌnˈbælənst] *adj* desequilibrado(a)
unbearable [ʌnˈbeərəbəl] *adj* insoportable
unbeatable [ʌnˈbiːtəbəl] *adj (team)* invencible; *(price, quality)* inmejorable
unbelievable [ʌnbɪˈliːvəbəl] *adj* increíble
unbend [ʌnˈbend] *vi Fam Fig* relajarse
unbia(s)sed [ʌnˈbaɪəst] *adj* imparcial
unborn [ʌnˈbɔːn] *adj* sin nacer, nonato(a)
unbreakable [ʌnˈbreɪkəbəl] *adj* irrompible; *Fig* inquebrantable
unbroken [ʌnˈbrəʊkən] *adj* (**a**) *(whole)* intacto(a) (**b**) *(uninterrupted)* continuo(a) (**c**) *(record)* imbatido(a)
unbutton [ʌnˈbʌtən] *vt* desabrochar
uncalled-for [ʌnˈkɔːldfɔː(r)] *adj (inappropriate)* insensato(a); *(unjustified)* inmerecido(a)
uncanny [ʌnˈkænɪ] *adj* misterioso(a), extraño(a)
unceasing [ʌnˈsiːsɪŋ] *adj* incesante
uncertain [ʌnˈsɜːtən] *adj* (**a**) *(not certain)* incierto(a); *(doubtful)* dudoso(a); **in no u.**

terms claramente (**b**) *(hesitant)* indeciso(a)
uncertainty [ʌnˈsɜːtəntɪ] *n* incertidumbre *f*
unchanged [ʌnˈtʃeɪndʒd] *adj* igual
unchecked [ʌnˈtʃekt] *adj* (**a**) *(unrestrained)* desenfrenado(a) (**b**) *(not examined)* no comprobado(a)
uncivilized [ʌnˈsɪvɪlaɪzd] *adj (tribe)* incivilizado(a), salvaje; *(not cultured)* inculto(a)
uncle [ˈʌŋkəl] *n* tío *m*
uncomfortable [ʌnˈkʌmftəbəl] *adj* incómodo(a); **to make things u. for** complicarle la vida a
uncommon [ʌnˈkɒmən] *adj* (**a**) *(rare)* poco común; *(unusual)* extraordinario(a) (**b**) *(excessive)* excesivo(a)
uncommonly [ʌnˈkɒmənlɪ] *adv* **not u.** con cierta frecuencia
uncompromising [ʌnˈkɒmprəmaɪzɪŋ] *adj* intransigente; **u. honesty** sinceridad absoluta
unconcerned [ʌnkənˈsɜːnd] *adj* indiferente (**about** a)
unconditional [ʌnkənˈdɪʃənəl] *adj* incondicional; **u. refusal** negativa rotunda
unconnected [ʌnkəˈnektɪd] *adj* no relacionado(a)
unconscious [ʌnˈkɒnʃəs] **1** *adj* (**a**) inconsciente (**of** de) (**b**) *(unintentional)* involuntario(a)
  2 *n* **the u.** el inconsciente
unconsciousness [ʌnˈkɒnʃəsnɪs] *n Med* pérdida *f* del conocimiento
uncontested [ʌnkənˈtestɪd] *adj Pol* **u. seat** escaño *m* ganado sin oposición
uncontrollable [ʌnkənˈtrəʊləbəl] *adj* incontrolable; *(desire)* irresistible
unconventional [ʌnkənˈvenʃənəl] *adj* poco convencional, original
uncooperative [ʌnkəʊˈɒpərətɪv] *adj* poco cooperativo(a)
uncouth [ʌnˈkuːθ] *adj (rude)* grosero(a)
uncover [ʌnˈkʌvə(r)] *vt* destapar; *Fig* descubrir
undamaged [ʌnˈdæmɪdʒd] *adj (article etc)* sin desperfectos; *(person)* indemne; *(reputation)* intacto(a)
undaunted [ʌnˈdɔːntɪd] *adj* firme, impávido(a)
undecided [ʌndɪˈsaɪdɪd] *adj* (**a**) *(person)* indeciso(a) (**b**) *(issue)* pendiente; **it's still u.** está aún por decidir
undefeated [ʌndɪˈfiːtɪd] *adj* invicto(a)
undefined [ʌndɪˈfaɪnd] *adj* indeterminado(a)
undeniable [ʌndɪˈnaɪəbəl] *adj* innegable
under [ˈʌndə(r)] **1** *prep* (**a**) debajo de; **u. the sun** bajo el sol (**b**) *(less than)* menos de; **incomes u. £1,000** ingresos inferiores a 1.000 libras; **u. age** menor de edad (**c**) *(of rank)* de rango inferior a (**d**) **u. Caesar** bajo César (**e**) *(subject to)* bajo; **u. arrest** detenido(a); **u. cover** a cubierto; **u. obligation to** en la obligación de; **u. the circumstances** dadas las

circunstancias; *Fig* **I was u. the impression that ...** tenía la impresión de que ... (**f**) *(according to)* según, conforme a
  2 *adv* abajo, debajo
under- [ˈʌndə(r)] *pref (below)* sub-, infra-; *(insufficiently)* insuficientemente
underarm [ˈʌndərɑːm] **1** *adj* **u. deodorant** desodorante *m* para las axilas
  2 *adv Sport* por debajo del hombro
undercarriage [ˈʌndəkærɪdʒ] *n* tren *m* de aterrizaje
undercharge [ʌndəˈtʃɑːdʒ] *vt* cobrar menos de lo debido
underclothes [ˈʌndəkləʊðz] *npl* ropa *f* interior
undercoat [ˈʌndəkəʊt] *n (of paint)* primera mano
undercover [ʌndəˈkʌvə(r)] *adj* secreto(a)
undercurrent [ˈʌndəkʌrənt] *n* (**a**) *(in sea)* corriente submarina (**b**) *Fig* sentimiento *m* latente
undercut [ʌndəˈkʌt] *vt (pt & pp* **undercut**) *Com* vender más barato que
underdeveloped [ʌndədɪˈveləpt] *adj* subdesarrollado(a)
underdog [ˈʌndədɒg] *n* desvalido(a) *m,f*
underestimate [ʌndərˈestɪmeɪt] *vt* infravalorar
underexposure [ʌndərɪkˈspəʊʒə(r)] *n Phot* subexposición *f*
underfed [ʌndəˈfed] *adj* subalimentado(a)
underfoot [ʌndəˈfʊt] *adv* en el suelo
undergo [ʌndəˈgəʊ] *vt (pt* **underwent**; *pp* **undergone** [ʌndəˈgɒn]) experimentar; *(change)* sufrir; *(test etc)* pasar por
undergraduate [ʌndəˈgrædjʊɪt] *n* estudiante *mf* universitario(a)
underground [ˈʌndəgraʊnd] **1** *adj* subterráneo(a); *Fig* clandestino(a)
  2 *n* (**a**) *Pol* movimiento clandestino (**b**) *Br* **the u.** *(train)* el metro
  3 *adj* [ʌndəˈgraʊnd] *Fig* **to go u.** pasar a la clandestinidad
undergrowth [ˈʌndəgrəʊθ] *n* maleza *f*
underhand 1 *adj* [ˈʌndəhænd] *(method)* ilícito(a); *(person)* solapado(a)
  2 *adv* [ʌndəˈhænd] bajo cuerda
underline [ʌndəˈlaɪn] *vt* subrayar
underling [ˈʌndəlɪŋ] *n Pej* mandado(a) *m,f*
underlying [ʌndəˈlaɪŋ] *adj (basic)* fundamental
undermine [ʌndəˈmaɪn] *vt* socavar, minar
underneath [ʌndəˈniːθ] **1** *prep* debajo de, bajo
  2 *adv* abajo, debajo
  3 *adj* de abajo
  4 *n* parte *f* inferior
undernourished [ʌndəˈnʌrɪʃt] *adj* desnutrido(a)
underpaid [ʌndəˈpeɪd] *adj* mal pagado(a)
underpass [ˈʌndəpɑːs] *n* paso subterráneo
underprivileged [ʌndəˈprɪvɪlɪdʒd] **1** *adj*

desfavorecido(a)

2 *npl* **the u.** los menos favorecidos

under-secretary [ʌndə'sekrətərɪ] *n* subsecretario(a) *m,f*

undershirt ['ʌndəʃɜːt] *n US* camiseta *f*

underskirt ['ʌndəskɜːt] *n* combinación *f*

understand [ʌndə'stænd] *vt & vi* (*pt & pp* **understood**) (**a**) *(comprehend)* entender, comprender; **do I make myself understood?** ¿me explico? (**b**) *(assume, believe)* entender; **she gave me to u. that ...** me dio a entender que ... (**c**) *(hear)* tener entendido (**d**) **to u. one another** entenderse

understandable [ʌndə'stændəbəl] *adj* comprensible

understanding [ʌndə'stændɪŋ] **1** *n* (**a**) *(intellectual grasp)* entendimiento *m*, comprensión *f* (**b**) *(interpretation)* intepretación *f* (**c**) *(agreement)* acuerdo *m* (**d**) **on the u. that ...** a condición de que ...

2 *adj* comprensivo(a)

understatement [ʌndə'steɪtmənt] *n* **to make an u.** minimizar, subestimar; **to say that the boy is rather clever is an u.** decir que el chico es bastante listo es quedarse corto

understood [ʌndə'stʊd] **1** *adj* (**a**) **I wish it to be u. that ...** que conste que ... (**b**) *(agreed on)* convenido(a) (**c**) *(implied)* sobreentendido(a)

2 *pt & pp of* **understand**

understudy ['ʌndəstʌdɪ] *n* suplente *mf*

undertake [ʌndə'teɪk] *vt* (*pt* **undertook**; *pp* **undertaken** [ʌndə'teɪkən]) (**a**) *(responsibility)* asumir; *(task, job)* encargarse de (**b**) *(promise)* comprometerse a

undertaker ['ʌndəteɪkə(r)] *n* empresario(a) *m,f* de pompas fúnebres; **u.'s** funeraria *f*

undertaking [ʌndə'teɪkɪŋ] *n* (**a**) *(task)* empresa *f* (**b**) *(promise)* compromiso *m*

undertone ['ʌndətəʊn] *n* **in an u.** en voz baja

undertook [ʌndə'tʊk] *pt of* **undertake**

underwater [ʌndə'wɔːtə(r)] **1** *adj* submarino(a)

2 *adv* bajo el agua

underwear ['ʌndəweə(r)] *n* ropa *f* interior

underwent [ʌndə'went] *pt of* **undergo**

underworld ['ʌndəwɜːld] *n* *(criminals)* hampa *f*, bajos fondos

underwrite ['ʌndəraɪt] *vt* (*pt* **underwrote**; *pp* **underwritten**) (**a**) *(guarantee)* garantizar, avalar (**b**) *(insure)* asegurar

underwriter ['ʌndəraɪtə(r)] *n* (**a**) *Fin* suscriptor(a) *m,f* (**b**) *(insurer)* asegurador(a) *m,f*

underwritten [ʌndə'rɪtən] *pp of* **underwrite**

underwrote [ʌndə'rəʊt] *pt of* **underwrite**

undesirable [ʌndɪ'zaɪrəbəl] *adj & n* indeseable *(mf)*

undeterred [ʌndɪ'tɜːd] *adj* sin inmutarse; **u. by** sin arredrarse ante

undid [ʌn'dɪd] *pt of* **undo**

undies ['ʌndɪz] *npl Fam* bragas *fpl*

undignified [ʌn'dɪgnɪfaɪd] *adj (attitude etc)*

indecoroso(a)

undisciplined [ʌn'dɪsɪplɪnd] *adj* indisciplinado(a)

undisclosed [ʌndɪs'kləʊzd] *adj* sin revelar

undiscovered [ʌndɪ'skʌvəd] *adj* sin descubrir

undisguised [ʌndɪs'gaɪzd] *adj Fig* no disimulado(a)

undisputed [ʌndɪ'spjuːtɪd] *adj (unchallenged)* incontestable; *(unquestionable)* indiscutible

undivided [ʌndɪ'vaɪdɪd] *adj* **to give one's u. attention** prestar toda la atención

undo [ʌn'duː] *vt* (*pt* **undid**; *pp* **undone**) (**a**) deshacer; *(button)* desabrochar (**b**) *(put right)* enmendar

undone¹ [ʌn'dʌn] *adj (unfinished)* inacabado(a)

undone² [ʌn'dʌn] **1** *adj (knot etc)* deshecho(a); **to come u.** *(shoelace)* desatarse; *(button, blouse)* desabrocharse; *(necklace etc)* soltarse

2 *pp of* **undo**

undoubted [ʌn'daʊtɪd] *adj* indudable

undress [ʌn'dres] **1** *vt* desnudar

2 *vi* desnudarse

undressed [ʌn'drest] *adj (naked)* desnudo(a)

undue [ʌn'djuː] (**a**) *adj (excessive)* excesivo(a) (**b**) *(improper)* indebido(a)

undulate ['ʌndjʊleɪt] *vi* ondular, ondear

unearth [ʌn'ɜːθ] *vt* desenterrar

unearthly [ʌn'ɜːθlɪ] *adj* (**a**) *(being)* sobrenatural (**b**) *Fam (din)* espantoso(a); **at an u. hour** a una hora intempestiva

uneasy [ʌn'iːzɪ] *adj* (**a**) *(worried)* preocupado(a); *(disturbing)* inquietante (**b**) *(uncomfortable)* incómodo(a)

uneconomic(al) [ʌniːkə'nɒmɪk(əl)] *adj* poco económico(a)

uneducated [ʌn'edjʊkeɪtɪd] *adj* inculto(a)

unemployed [ʌnɪm'plɔɪd] **1** *adj* en paro, parado(a); **to be u.** estar en paro

2 *npl* **the u.** los parados

unemployment [ʌnɪm'plɔɪmənt] *n* paro *m*, desempleo *m*; **u. benefit**, *US* **u. compensation** subsidio *m* de desempleo

unending [ʌn'endɪŋ] *adj* interminable

unenviable [ʌn'envɪəbəl] *adj* poco envidiable

unequal [ʌn'iːkwəl] *adj* desigual

unequivocal [ʌnɪ'kwɪvəkəl] *adj* inequívoco(a)

uneven [ʌn'iːvən] *adj* (**a**) *(not level)* desigual; *(bumpy)* accidentado(a) (**b**) *(variable)* irregular

uneventful [ʌnɪ'ventfʊl] *adj* sin acontecimientos

unexceptional [ʌnɪk'sepʃənəl] *adj* ordinario(a)

unexpected [ʌnɪk'spektɪd] *adj (unhoped for)* inesperado(a); *(event)* imprevisto(a)

unfailing [ʌnˈfeɪlɪŋ] *adj* indefectible; *(incessant)* constante; *(patience)* inagotable

unfair [ʌnˈfeə(r)] *adj* injusto(a); *Sport* sucio(a)

unfaithful [ʌnˈfeɪθfʊl] *adj (friend)* desleal; *(husband, wife)* infiel

unfamiliar [ʌnfəˈmɪljə(r)] *adj (unknown)* desconocido(a); *(not conversant)* no familiarizado(a) (**with** con)

unfashionable [ʌnˈfæʃənəbəl] *adj* pasado(a) de moda; *(ideas etc)* poco popular

unfasten [ʌnˈfɑːsən] *vt (knot)* desatar; *(clothing, belt)* desabrochar

unfavourable, *US* **unfavorable** [ʌnˈfeɪvərəbəl] *adj* desfavorable; *(criticism)* adverso(a); *(winds)* contrario(a)

unfeeling [ʌnˈfiːlɪŋ] *adj* insensible

unfinished [ʌnˈfɪnɪʃt] *adj* inacabado(a); **u. business** un asunto pendiente

unfit [ʌnˈfɪt] *adj* (**a**) *(thing)* inadecuado(a); *(person)* no apto(a) (**for** para) (**b**) *(incompetent)* incompetente (**c**) *(physically)* incapacitado(a); **to be u.** no estar en forma

unflinching [ʌnˈflɪntʃɪŋ] *adj* (**a**) *(determined)* resuelto(a) (**b**) *(fearless)* impávido(a)

unfold [ʌnˈfəʊld] **1** *vt* (**a**) *(sheet)* desdoblar; *(newspaper)* abrir (**b**) *(plan, secret)* revelar
2 *vi* (**a**) *(open up)* abrirse; *(landscape)* extenderse (**b**) *(plot)* desarrollarse (**c**) *(secret)* descubrirse

unforeseen [ʌnfɔːˈsiːn] *adj* imprevisto(a)

unforgettable [ʌnfəˈgetəbəl] *adj* inolvidable

unforgivable [ʌnfəˈgɪvəbəl] *adj* imperdonable

unfortunate [ʌnˈfɔːtʃənɪt] *adj (person, event)* desgraciado(a); *(remark)* desafortunado(a); **how u.!** ¡qué mala suerte!

unfortunately [ʌnˈfɔːtʃənɪtlɪ] *adv* desgraciadamente, por desgracia

unfounded [ʌnˈfaʊndɪd] *adj* infundado(a)

unfriendly [ʌnˈfrendlɪ] *adj* (**unfriendlier, unfriendliest**) antipático(a), poco amistoso(a)

unfurl [ʌnˈfɜːl] *vi* desplegarse

unfurnished [ʌnˈfɜːnɪʃt] *adj* sin amueblar

ungainly [ʌnˈgeɪnlɪ] *adj (gait)* desgarbado(a)

ungodly [ʌnˈgɒdlɪ] *adj* (**ungodlier, ungodliest**) *(behaviour)* impío(a); *Fam Fig* **at an u. hour** a una hora intempestiva

ungrateful [ʌnˈgreɪtfʊl] *adj (person)* desagradecido(a); *(task)* ingrato(a)

unguarded [ʌnˈgɑːdɪd] *adj* (**a**) *(unprotected)* desatendido(a); *(imprudent)* desprevenido(a) (**b**) *(frank)* franco(a)

unhappiness [ʌnˈhæpɪnɪs] *n* (**a**) *(sadness)* tristeza *f* (**b**) *(wretchedness)* desdicha *f*

unhappy [ʌnˈhæpɪ] *adj* (**unhappier, unhappiest**) (**a**) *(sad)* triste (**b**) *(wretched)* desgraciado(a), infeliz; *(unfortunate)* desafortunado(a)

unharmed [ʌnˈhɑːmd] *adj* ileso(a), indemne

unhealthy [ʌnˈhelθɪ] *adj* (**unhealthier, unhealthiest**) (**a**) *(ill)* enfermizo(a) (**b**) *(unwholesome)* malsano(a)

unheard [ʌnˈhɜːd] *adj* (**a**) **her request went u.** su petición no fue atendida (**b**) **u. of** *(outrageous)* inaudito(a); *(without precedent)* sin precedente

unhesitating [ʌnˈhezɪteɪtɪŋ] *adj* resuelto(a)

unhook [ʌnˈhʊk] *vt (from hook)* descolgar; *(clothing)* desabrochar

unhurt [ʌnˈhɜːt] *adj* ileso(a), indemne

unhygienic [ʌnhaɪˈdʒiːnɪk] *adj* antihigiénico(a)

unidentified [ʌnaɪˈdentɪfaɪd] *adj* **u. flying object** objeto volador no identificado, ovni *m*

unification [juːnɪfɪˈkeɪʃən] *n* unificación *f*

uniform [ˈjuːnɪfɔːm] *adj & n* uniforme *(m)*

uniformity [juːnɪˈfɔːmɪtɪ] *n* uniformidad *f*

unify [ˈjuːnɪfaɪ] *vt* unificar

unilateral [juːnɪˈlætərəl] *adj* unilateral

unimportant [ʌnɪmˈpɔːtənt] *adj* poco importante

uninformed [ʌnɪnˈfɔːmd] *adj (opinion)* sin fundamento

uninhabited [ʌnɪnˈhæbɪtɪd] *adj* despoblado(a)

uninhibited [ʌnɪnˈhɪbɪtɪd] *adj* sin inhibición

uninspired [ʌnɪnˈspaɪəd] *adj (person)* falto(a) de inspiración; *(performance)* insulso(a)

uninspiring [ʌnɪnˈspaɪərɪŋ] *adj* que no inspira

unintelligible [ʌnɪnˈtelɪdʒəbəl] *adj* ininteligible, incomprensible

unintentional [ʌnɪnˈtenʃənəl] *adj* involuntario(a)

unintentionally [ʌnɪnˈtenʃənəlɪ] *adv* sin querer

uninteresting [ʌnˈɪntrɪstɪŋ] *adj* poco interesante

uninterrupted [ʌnɪntəˈrʌptɪd] *adj* ininterrumpido(a)

union [ˈjuːnjən] **1** *n* (**a**) *(sadness)* unión *f* (**b**) *(organization)* sindicato *m* (**c**) *US* **the U.** los Estados Unidos; *Br* **U. Jack** bandera *f* del Reino Unido
2 *adj* sindical

unique [juːˈniːk] *adj* único(a)

unison [ˈjuːnɪsən] *n Mus* unisonancia *f*; *Fig (harmony)* armonía *f*; **in u.** al unísono

unit [ˈjuːnɪt] *n* (**a**) *(unit)* unidad *f*; **monetary u.** unidad monetaria; *Br Fin* **u. trust** sociedad *f* de inversiones (**b**) *(piece of furniture)* módulo *m*; **kitchen u.** mueble *m* de cocina (**c**) *Tech* grupo *m*; *Comput* **central processing u.** procesador *m* central; **visual display u.** monitor *m* (**d**) *(department)* servicio *m* (**e**) *(team)* equipo *m*

unite [juːˈnaɪt] **1** *vt* unir
2 *vi* unirse

united [juːˈnaɪtɪd] *adj* unido(a); **U. Kingdom** Reino Unido; **U. States (of America)** Estados Unidos (de América); **U. Nations** Naciones Unidas

unity ['ju:nɪtɪ] *n* unidad *f*; *(harmony)* armonía *f*
universal [ju:nɪ'vɜ:səl] *adj* universal
universe ['ju:nɪvɜ:s] *n* universo *m*
university [ju:nɪ'vɜ:sɪtɪ] **1** *n* universidad *f*
2 *adj* universitario(a)
unjust [ʌn'dʒʌst] *adj* injusto(a)
unkempt [ʌn'kempt] *adj* descuidado(a); *(hair)* despeinado(a); *(appearance)* desaliñado(a)
unkind [ʌn'kaɪnd] *adj (not nice)* poco amable; *(cruel)* despiadado(a)
unknown [ʌn'nəʊn] **1** *adj* desconocido(a); **u. quantity** incógnita *f*
2 *n* **the u.** lo desconocido
unlawful [ʌn'lɔ:fʊl] *adj (not legal)* ilegal
unleash [ʌn'li:ʃ] *vt* **(a)** *(dog)* soltar **(b)** *Fig (release)* liberar; *(provoke)* desencadenar
unless [ʌn'les] *conj* a menos que, a no ser que
unlike [ʌn'laɪk] **1** *adj* diferente, distinto(a)
2 *prep* a diferencia de
unlikely [ʌn'laɪklɪ] *adj* **(a)** *(improbable)* poco probable **(b)** *(unusual)* raro(a)
unlimited [ʌn'lɪmɪtɪd] *adj* ilimitado(a)
unlisted [ʌn'lɪstɪd] *adj US Tel* que no se encuentra en la guía telefónica
unload [ʌn'ləʊd] *vt & vi* descargar
unlock [ʌn'lɒk] *vt* abrir (con llave)
unluckily [ʌn'lʌkɪlɪ] *adv* desafortunadamente, por desgracia
unlucky [ʌn'lʌkɪ] *adj* (**unluckier, unluckiest**) *(unfortunate)* desgraciado(a); **to be u.** *(person)* tener mala suerte; *(thing)* traer mala suerte
unmanageable [ʌn'mænɪdʒəbəl] *adj (people)* ingobernable; *(child, hair)* incontrolable
unmanned [ʌn'mænd] *adj (spacecraft etc)* no tripulado(a)
unmarried [ʌn'mærɪd] *adj* soltero(a)
unmask [ʌn'mɑ:sk] *vt Fig (plot)* descubrir
unmistak(e)able [ʌnmɪs'teɪkəbəl] *adj* inconfundible
unmistak(e)ably [ʌnmɪs'teɪkəblɪ] *adv* sin lugar a dudas
unmitigated [ʌn'mɪtɪgeɪtɪd] *adj* **(a)** *(absolute)* absoluto(a); *(liar)* rematado(a) **(b)** *(grief)* profundo(a)
unnamed [ʌn'neɪmd] *adj (anonymous)* anónimo(a)
unnatural [ʌn'nætʃərəl] *adj* **(a)** *(against nature)* antinatural; *(abnormal)* anormal **(b)** *(affected)* afectado(a)
unnecessary [ʌn'nesɪsərɪ] *adj* innecesario(a), inútil; **it's u. to add that ...** sobra añadir que ...
unnoticed [ʌn'nəʊtɪst] *adj* desapercibido(a); **to let sth pass u.** pasar algo por alto
unobserved [ʌnɒb'zɜ:vd] *adj* inadvertido(a)
unobtainable [ʌnəb'teɪnəbəl] *adj* inasequible, inalcanzable
unobtrusive [ʌnəb'tru:sɪv] *adj* discreto(a)
unoccupied [ʌn'ɒkjʊpaɪd] *adj (house)* desocupado(a); *(seat)* libre
unofficial [ʌnə'fɪʃəl] *adj* no oficial; *Ind* **u. strike** huelga *f* no apoyada por los sindicatos
unorthodox [ʌn'ɔ:θədɒks] *adj* **(a)** *(behaviour etc)* poco ortodoxo(a) **(b)** *Rel* heterodoxo(a)
unpack [ʌn'pæk] **1** *vt (boxes)* desembalar; *(suitcase)* deshacer
2 *vi* deshacer la(s) maleta(s)
unpalatable [ʌn'pælətəbəl] *adj* desagradable
unparalleled [ʌn'pærəleld] *adj* **(a)** *(in quality)* incomparable **(b)** *(without precedent)* sin precedente
unpardonable [ʌn'pɑ:dənəbəl] *adj* imperdonable
unperturbed [ʌnpə'tɜ:bd] *adj* impasible
unpleasant [ʌn'plezənt] *adj* desagradable *(to* con*)*
unpleasantness [ʌn'plezəntnɪs] *n* disgusto *m*
unplug [ʌn'plʌg] *vt* desenchufar
unpopular [ʌn'pɒpjʊlə(r)] *adj* impopular; **to make oneself u.** ganarse la antipatía de todos
unprecedented [ʌn'presɪdentɪd] *adj* sin precedente
unpredictable [ʌnprɪ'dɪktəbəl] *adj* imprevisible
unprepared [ʌnprɪ'peəd] *adj (speech etc)* improvisado(a); *(person)* desprevenido(a)
unprincipled [ʌn'prɪnsɪpəld] *adj* sin escrúpulos
unprintable [ʌn'prɪntəbəl] *adj (word, comment)* malsonante
unproductive [ʌnprə'dʌktɪv] *adj (inefficient)* improductivo(a); *(fruitless)* infructuoso(a)
unprofessional [ʌnprə'feʃənəl] *adj (unethical)* poco profesional; *(substandard)* de aficionado
unprotected [ʌnprə'tektɪd] *adj* indefenso(a)
unprovoked [ʌnprə'vəʊkt] *adj* gratuito(a)
unpunished [ʌn'pʌnɪʃt] *adj* impune
unqualified [ʌn'kwɒlɪfaɪd] *adj* **(a)** *(without qualification)* sin título; *(incompetent)* incompetente **(b)** *(unconditional)* incondicional; *(denial)* rotundo(a); *(endorsement)* sin reserva; *(success)* total
unquestionable [ʌn'kwestʃənəbəl] *adj* indiscutible
unquestioning [ʌn'kwestʃənɪŋ] *adj* incondicional; *(obedience)* ciego(a)
unravel [ʌn'rævəl] **1** *vt* desenmarañar
2 *vi* desenmarañarse
unreadable [ʌn'ri:dəbəl] *adj* **(a)** *(handwriting)* ilegible **(b)** *(book)* imposible de leer
unreal [ʌn'rɪəl] *adj* irreal
unrealistic [ʌnrɪə'lɪstɪk] *adj* poco realista
unreasonable [ʌn'ri:zənəbəl] *adj* poco razonable; *(demands)* desmedido(a); *(prices)* exorbitante; *(hour)* inoportuno(a)
unrefined [ʌnrɪ'faɪnd] *adj* **(a)** *(sugar, oil etc)*

sin refinar (**b**) *(person)* tosco(a), basto(a)

unrelated [ʌnrɪ'leɪtɪd] *adj (not connected)* no relacionado(a)

unrelenting [ʌnrɪ'lentɪŋ] *adj (behaviour)* implacable; *(struggle)* encarnizado(a)

unreliable [ʌnrɪ'laɪəbəl] *adj* (**a**) *(person)* de poca confianza (**b**) *(information)* que no es de fiar; *(machine)* poco fiable

unrelieved [ʌnrɪ'li:vd] *adj (boredom)* total

unremitting [ʌnrɪ'mɪtɪŋ] *adj* (**a**) *(efforts etc)* incesante (**b**) *(person)* incansable

unrepentant [ʌnrɪ'pentənt] *adj* impenitente

unreserved [ʌnrɪ'zɜ:vd] *adj (praise, support)* sin reserva

unreservedly [ʌnrɪ'zɜ:vɪdlɪ] *adv* sin reserva

unrest [ʌn'rest] *n (social etc)* malestar *m*; **political u.** agitación política

unrivalled, *US* **unrivaled** [ʌn'raɪvəld] *adj* sin par, sin rival

unroll [ʌn'rəʊl] *vt* desenrollar

unruffled [ʌn'rʌfəld] *adj Fig* tranquilo(a)

unruly [ʌn'ru:lɪ] *adj* (**unrulier, unruliest**) *adj* (**a**) *(child)* revoltoso(a) (**b**) *(hair)* rebelde

unsafe [ʌn'seɪf] *adj (dangerous)* peligroso(a); *(risky)* inseguro(a); **to feel u.** sentirse expuesto(a)

unsaid [ʌn'sed] *adj* **it's better left u.** más vale no decir nada; **much was left u.** quedó mucho por decir

unsatisfactory [ʌnsætɪs'fæktərɪ] *adj* insatisfactorio(a); **it's most u.** deja mucho que desear

unsavoury, *US* **unsavory** [ʌn'seɪvərɪ] *adj* desagradable

unscathed [ʌn'skeɪðd] *adj* ileso(a), indemne

unscrew [ʌn'skru:] *vt* destornillar

unscrupulous [ʌn'skru:pjʊləs] *adj* sin escrúpulos

unseemly [ʌn'si:mlɪ] *adj* impropio(a)

unseen [ʌn'si:n] **1** *adj* invisible; *(unnoticed)* inadvertido(a)

2 *n Br Educ* = texto no trabajado en clase

unselfish [ʌn'selfɪʃ] *adj* desinteresado(a)

unsettle [ʌn'setəl] *vt* perturbar

unsettled [ʌn'setəld] *adj* (**a**) *(person)* nervioso(a); *(situation)* inestable (**b**) *(weather)* inestable (**c**) *(matter, debt)* pendiente (**d**) *(land)* sin colonizar

unshaven [ʌn'ʃeɪvən] *adj* sin afeitar

unsightly [ʌn'saɪtlɪ] *adj* feo(a), desagradable

unskilled [ʌn'skɪld] *adj (worker)* no cualificado(a); *(work)* no especializado(a)

unsociable [ʌn'səʊʃəbəl] *adj* insociable, huraño(a)

unsophisticated [ʌnsə'fɪstɪkeɪtɪd] *adj* (**a**) *(naïve)* ingenuo(a) (**b**) *(simple)* poco sofisticado(a)

unsound [ʌn'saʊnd] *adj* (**a**) *(unstable)* inestable; **of u. mind** demente (**b**) *(fallacious)* falso(a)

unspeakable [ʌn'spi:kəbəl] *adj* (**a**) indecible

(**b**) *Fig (evil)* atroz

unspoken [ʌn'spəʊkən] *adj* (**a**) *(tacit)* tácito(a) (**b**) *(feeling)* interior, secreto(a)

unstable [ʌn'steɪbəl] *adj* inestable

unsteady [ʌn'stedɪ] *adj (not firm)* inestable; *(table, chair)* cojo(a); *(hand, voice)* tembloroso(a)

unstinting [ʌn'stɪntɪŋ] *adj* pródigo(a) (**in** en)

unstuck [ʌn'stʌk] *adj* **to come u.** despegarse; *Fig* venirse abajo

unsuccessful [ʌnsək'sesfʊl] *adj* (**a**) *(fruitless)* fracasado(a); *(useless)* vano(a) (**b**) *(businessman etc)* fracasado(a); *(candidate)* derrotado(a); **to be u. at sth** no tener éxito con algo

unsuccessfully [ʌnsək'sesfʊlɪ] *adv* sin éxito, en vano

unsuitable [ʌn'su:təbəl] *adj* (**a**) *(person)* no apto(a) (**b**) *(thing)* inadecuado(a); *(remark)* inoportuno(a); *(time)* inconveniente

unsuited [ʌn'su:tɪd] *adj* (**a**) *(person)* no apto(a); *(thing)* impropio(a) (**to** para) (**b**) *(incompatible)* incompatible

unsure [ʌn'ʃʊə(r)] *adj* poco seguro(a)

unsuspecting [ʌnsə'spektɪŋ] *adj* confiado(a); **he went in u.** entró sin sospechar nada

unswerving [ʌn'swɜ:vɪŋ] *adj* firme

unsympathetic [ʌnsɪmpə'θetɪk] *adj (unfeeling)* impasible; *(not understanding)* poco comprensivo(a)

untapped [ʌn'tæpt] *adj (resource)* sin explotar

untarnished [ʌn'tɑ:nɪʃt] *adj Fig* sin mancha

untenable [ʌn'tenəbəl] *adj* insostenible

unthinkable [ʌn'θɪŋkəbəl] *adj* impensable, inconcebible

untidy [ʌn'taɪdɪ] *adj* (**untidier, untidiest**) *(room, person)* desordenado(a); *(hair)* despeinado(a); *(appearance)* desaseado(a)

untie [ʌn'taɪ] *vt* desatar; *(free)* soltar

until [ʌn'tɪl] **1** *conj* hasta que; **she worked u. she collapsed** trabajó hasta desfallecer; **u. she gets back** hasta que vuelva

2 *prep* hasta; **u. now** hasta ahora; **u. ten o'clock** hasta las diez; **not u. Monday** hasta el lunes no

untimely [ʌn'taɪmlɪ] *adj* (**a**) *(premature)* prematuro(a) (**b**) *(inopportune)* inoportuno(a); *(hour)* intempestivo(a)

untold [ʌn'təʊld] *adj* (**a**) *(indescribable)* indecible (**b**) *Fig (loss, wealth)* incalculable (**c**) *(not told)* sin contar

untouchable [ʌn'tʌtʃəbəl] *adj & n* intocable (*mf*)

untoward [ʌntə'wɔːd] *adj* (**a**) *(unfortunate)* desafortunado(a) (**b**) *(adverse)* adverso(a)

untrained [ʌn'treɪnd] *adj* (**a**) *(unskilled)* sin preparación profesional (**b**) *(inexpert)* inexperto(a)

untrue [ʌn'truː] *adj* (**a**) *(false)* falso(a) (**b**) *(unfaithful)* infiel (**c**) *(inexact)* inexacto(a)

untrustworthy [ʌn'trʌstwɜ:ðɪ] *adj* (**a**) *(per-*

son) de poca confianza (**b**) (*source*) no fidedigno(a)

unused [ʌnˈjuːzd] *adj* (**a**) (*car*) sin usar; (*flat etc*) sin estrenar; (*stamp*) sin matar (**b**) (*not in use*) que ya no se utiliza (**c**) [ʌnˈjuːst] (*unaccustomed*) desacostumbrado(a) (**to** a)

unusual [ʌnˈjuːʒʊəl] *adj* (*rare*) insólito(a), poco común; (*original*) original; (*exceptional*) excepcional

unusually [ʌnˈjuːʒʊəlɪ] *adv* excepcionalmente

unveil [ʌnˈveɪl] *vt* descubrir

unwarranted [ʌnˈwɒrəntɪd] *adj* injustificado(a); (*remark*) gratuito(a)

unwavering [ʌnˈweɪvərɪŋ] *adj* (*loyalty*) constante, firme; (*courage*) inquebrantable

unwelcome [ʌnˈwelkəm] *adj* (*visitor*) molesto(a); (*visit*) inoportuno(a); *Fig* (*news etc*) desagradable

unwell [ʌnˈwel] *adj* malo(a), indispuesto(a)

unwieldy [ʌnˈwiːldɪ] *adj* (*difficult to handle*) poco manejable; (*clumsy*) torpe

unwilling [ʌnˈwɪlɪŋ] *adj* **to be u. to do sth** no estar dispuesto a hacer algo

unwillingly [ʌnˈwɪlɪŋlɪ] *adv* de mala gana

unwind [ʌnˈwaɪnd] **1** *vt* (*pt & pp* **unwound**) desenrollar

2 *vi* (**a**) desenrollarse (**b**) (*relax*) relajarse

unwise [ʌnˈwaɪz] *adj* imprudente, desaconsejable

unwitting [ʌnˈwɪtɪŋ] *adj* involuntario(a)

unworkable [ʌnˈwɜːkəbəl] *adj* (*not feasible*) impracticable; (*suggestion*) irrealizable

unworthy [ʌnˈwɜːðɪ] *adj* indigno(a)

unwound [ʌnˈwaʊnd] *pt & pp of* **unwind**

unwrap [ʌnˈræp] *vt* (*gift*) desenvolver; (*package*) deshacer

unwritten [ʌnˈrɪtən] *adj* no escrito(a); (*agreement*) verbal

unyielding [ʌnˈjiːldɪŋ] *adj* inflexible

up [ʌp] **1** *prep* (**a**) (*movement*) **to climb up the mountain** escalar la montaña; **to walk up the street** ir calle arriba

(**b**) (*position*) en lo alto de; **further up the street** más adelante (en la misma calle); **halfway up the ladder** a mitad de la escalera **2** *adv* (**a**) (*upwards*) arriba, hacia arriba; (*position*) arriba; **from £10 up** de 10 libras para arriba; **halfway up** a medio camino; **right up (to the top)** hasta arriba (del todo); **to go/come up** subir; **this side up** (*sign*) este lado hacia arriba

(**b**) **the moon is up** ha salido la luna

(**c**) (*towards*) hacia; **to come** *or* **go up to sb** acercarse a algn; **to walk up and down** ir de un lado a otro

(**d**) (*in, to*) **he's up in Yorkshire** está en Yorkshire

(**e**) (*increased*) **bread is up** el pan ha subido

(**f**) **it's up for discussion** se está discutiendo; **up for sale** en venta

(**g**) *Fam* **something's up** pasa algo; **what's up (with you)?** ¿qué pasa (contigo)?

(**h**) **to be up against sth** enfrentarse con algo

(**i**) **up to** (*as far as, until*) hasta; **I can spend up to £5** puedo gastar un máximo de 5 libras; **up to here** hasta aquí; **up to now** hasta ahora

(**j**) **to be up to** (*depend on*) depender de; (*be capable of*) estar a la altura de; **I don't feel up to doing it today** hoy no me encuentro con fuerzas para hacerlo; **it's not up to much** no vale gran cosa

(**k**) **he's up to sth** está tramando algo

3 *adj* (**a**) (*out of bed*) levantado(a)

(**b**) (*finished*) terminado(a); **time's up** (ya) es la hora

4 *vt Fam* aumentar

5 *n Fig* **ups and downs** altibajos *mpl*

up-and-coming [ˈʌpənˈkʌmɪŋ] *adj* prometedor(a)

upbringing [ˈʌpbrɪŋɪŋ] *n* educación *f*

update [ʌpˈdeɪt] *vt* actualizar, poner al día

upgrade **1** *vt* [ʌpˈgreɪd] (**a**) (*promote*) ascender (**b**) (*improve*) mejorar la calidad de (**c**) *Comput* (*software, hardware*) actualizar

2 *n* [ˈʌpgreɪd] *Comput* actualización *f*

upheaval [ʌpˈhiːvəl] *n* trastorno *m*

upheld [ʌpˈheld] *pt & pp of* **uphold**

uphill **1** *adj* [ˈʌphɪl] ascendente; *Fig* arduo(a)

2 *adv* [ʌpˈhɪl] cuesta arriba

uphold [ʌpˈhəʊld] *vt* (*pt & pp* **upheld**) sostener

upholstery [ʌpˈhəʊlstərɪ] *n* tapizado *m*, tapicería *f*

upkeep [ˈʌpkiːp] *n* mantenimiento *m*

up-market [ˈʌpmɑːkɪt] *adj* de categoría

upon [əˈpɒn] *prep Fml* en, sobre; **once u. a time ...** érase una vez ...; **u. my word** (mi) palabra de honor

upper [ˈʌpə(r)] **1** *adj* (**a**) (*position*) superior; **u. storey** piso de arriba; *Fig* **to have the u. hand** llevar la delantera (**b**) (*in rank*) alto(a); **the u. class** la clase alta; **the U. House** la Cámara Alta

2 *n* (*of shoe*) pala *f*

upper-class [ˈʌpəˈklæs] *adj* de la clase alta

uppermost [ˈʌpəməʊst] *adj* más alto(a); *Fig* **it was u. in my mind** era lo que me preocupaba más

upright [ˈʌpraɪt] **1** *adj* (**a**) (*vertical*) vertical (**b**) (*honest*) honrado(a)

2 *adv* derecho

3 *n Ftb* (*post*) poste *m*

uprising [ˈʌpraɪzɪŋ] *n* sublevación *f*

uproar [ˈʌprɔː(r)] *n* tumulto *m*, alboroto *m*

uproot [ʌpˈruːt] *vt* (*plant*) arrancar de raíz

upset [ʌpˈset] **1** *vt* (*pt & pp* **upset**) (**a**) (*overturn*) volcar; (*spill*) derramar (**b**) (*shock*) trastornar; (*worry*) preocupar; (*displease*) disgustar (**c**) (*spoil*) desbaratar (**d**) (*make ill*) sentar mal a

2 *adj* (*shocked*) alterado(a); (*displeased*) disgustado(a); **to have an u. stomach** sentirse mal del estómago

3 n ['ʌpset] (**a**) *(reversal)* revés m (**b**) *Sport* resultado inesperado

upshot ['ʌpʃɒt] n resultado m

upside ['ʌpsaɪd] n al revés

upstage [ʌp'steɪdʒ] vt Fam eclipsar

upstairs [ʌp'steəz] **1** adv al piso de arriba; **she lives u.** vive en el piso de arriba

2 n piso m de arriba

upstart ['ʌpstɑːt] n advenedizo(a) m,f

upstream [ʌp'striːm] adv río arriba

uptake ['ʌpteɪk] n Fam **to be quick on the u.** cogerlas al vuelo

uptight [ʌp'taɪt] adj Fam nervioso(a)

up-to-date [ʌptə'deɪt] adj (**a**) *(current)* al día (**b**) *(modern)* moderno(a)

upturn ['ʌptɜːn] n mejora f

upward ['ʌpwəd] adj ascendente

upward(s) ['ʌpwəd(z)] adv hacia arriba; **from ten (years) u.** a partir de los diez años; Fam **u. of** algo más de

uranium [jʊ'reɪnɪəm] n uranio m

urban ['ɜːbən] adj urbano(a)

urbane [ɜː'beɪn] adj urbano(a), cortés

urchin ['ɜːtʃɪn] n (**a**) *(child)* pilluelo(a) m,f (**b**) **sea u.** erizo m de mar

urge [ɜːdʒ] **1** vt (**a**) instar; *(plead)* exhortar (**b**) *(advocate)* preconizar; **to u. that sth should be done** insistir en que se haga algo

2 n impulso m

▸ **urge on** vt sep animar a

urgency ['ɜːdʒənsɪ] n urgencia f

urgent ['ɜːdʒənt] adj urgente; *(need, tone)* apremiante

urinal [jʊ'raɪnəl] n *(toilet)* urinario m; *(bowl)* orinal m

urinate ['jʊərɪneɪt] vi orinar

urine ['jʊərɪn] n orina f

URL [juːɑː'rel] n Comput *(abbr* **uniform resource locator)** URL m

urn [ɜːn] n (**a**) urna f (**b**) **tea u.** tetera f grande

Uruguay ['jʊərəgwaɪ] n Uruguay

Uruguayan [jʊərə'gwaɪən] adj & n uruguayo(a) (m,f)

US [juː'es] n *(abbr* **United States)** EE.UU. mpl

us [ʌs, *unstressed* əs] pers pron (**a**) *(as object)* nos; **let's forget it** olvidémoslo (**b**) *(after prep)* nosotros(as); **both of us** nosotros dos; **he's one of us** es de los nuestros (**c**) *(after v to be)* nosotros(as); **she wouldn't believe it was us** no creía que fuéramos nosotros (**d**) Fam me; **give us a kiss!** ¡dame un beso!

USA [juːes'eɪ] n *(abbr* **United States of America)** EE.UU. mpl

usage ['juːsɪdʒ] n (**a**) *(habit, custom)* costumbre f (**b**) Ling uso m

use [juːz] **1** vt (**a**) emplear, utilizar; **what is it used for?** ¿para qué sirve?; **to u. force** hacer uso de la fuerza

(**b**) *(consume)* consumir, gastar

(**c**) *(take unfair advantage of)* aprovecharse de

(**d**) Fam **I could u. a drink** no me vendría mal un trago

2 v aux **used to** ['juːstə] soler, acostumbrar; **where did you u. to live?** ¿dónde vivías (antes)?

> Como verbo auxiliar, aparece siempre en la forma **used to**. Se traduce al español por el verbo principal en pretérito imperfecto, o por el pretérito imperfecto de **soler** más infinitivo.

3 n [juːs] (**a**) uso m, empleo m; *(handling)* manejo m; **directions for u.** modo de empleo; **in u.** en uso; **not in u.** *(on lift)* no funciona; **ready for u.** listo para usar; **to make (good) u. of sth** aprovechar algo; **to put to good u.** sacar partido de

(**b**) *(application)* aplicación f

(**c**) *(usefulness)* utilidad f; **it's no u.** es inútil; **what's the u.?** ¿para qué?; Fam **it's no u. crying** no sirve de nada llorar; **of u.** útil; **to be of u.** servir

▸ **use up** vt sep acabar

used adj (**a**) [juːzd] *(second-hand)* usado(a) (**b**) [juːst] **to be u. to** estar acostumbrado(a) a

useful ['juːsfʊl] adj útil; *(practical)* práctico(a); **to come in u.** venir bien

usefulness ['juːsfʊlnɪs] n utilidad f

useless ['juːslɪs] adj inútil

user ['juːzə(r)] n (**a**) usuario(a) m,f (**b**) Fam *(of drugs)* drogadicto(a) m,f

usher ['ʌʃə(r)] **1** n (**a**) Cin & Th acomodador(a) m,f (**b**) *(in court etc)* ujier m

2 vt **to u. in** Cin Th acomodar; *(at home)* hacer pasar; **to u. out** acompañar hasta la puerta

USSR [juːeses'ɑː(r)] n Hist *(abbr* **Union of Soviet Socialist Republics)** URSS f

usual ['juːʒʊəl] **1** adj corriente, normal; **as u.** como siempre; **at the u. hour** a la hora habitual; **earlier than u.** más pronto que de costumbre; **the u. problems** los problemas de siempre

2 n lo habitual; **out of the u.** fuera de lo común

usually ['juːʒʊəlɪ] adv normalmente

usurp [juː'zɜːp] vt usurpar

utensil [juː'tensəl] n utensilio m; **kitchen utensils** batería f de cocina

uterus ['juːtərəs] n útero m

utilitarian [juːtɪlɪ'teərɪən] adj (**a**) *(in philosophy)* utilitarista (**b**) *(useful)* utilitario(a)

utility [juː'tɪlɪtɪ] n (**a**) utilidad f; **u. room** cuarto m de planchar; *(for storage)* trascocina f (**b**) *(public)* **u.** empresa f de servicio público

utilize ['juːtɪlaɪz] vt utilizar

utmost ['ʌtməʊst] **1** adj sumo(a); **of the u. importance** de suma importancia

2 n máximo m; **to do** *or* **try one's u.** hacer todo lo posible; **to the u.** al máximo, a más no poder

utopian [juː'təʊpɪən] adj utópico(a)

utter¹ ['ʌtə(r)] *vt (words)* pronunciar; *(sigh)* dar; *(cry, threat)* lanzar
utter² ['ʌtə(r)] *adj* total, completo(a)

utterance ['ʌtərəns] *n* declaración *f*
U-turn ['juːtɜːn] *n* cambio *m* de sentido; *Pol* giro *m* de 180 grados

V, v [viː] *n (the letter)* V, v *f*

V *(abbr* **volt(s))** V

v (**a**) *(abbr* **verse)** v (**b**) *(also* **vs)** *(abbr* **versus)** contra

vacancy ['veɪkənsɪ] *n* (**a**) *(job)* vacante *f* (**b**) *(room)* habitación *f* libre; **no vacancies** *(sign)* completo

vacant ['veɪkənt] *adj* (**a**) *(empty)* vacío(a) (**b**) *(job)* vacante; *Br* **situations v.** *(in newspaper)* ofertas de trabajo (**c**) *(free, not in use)* libre

vacate [və'keɪt] *vt (flat)* desalojar

vacation [və'keɪʃən] *US* **1** *n* vacaciones *fpl*; **on v.** de vacaciones

2 *vi* pasar las vacaciones (**in/at** en)

vacationer [və'keɪʃənə(r)], **vacationist** [və'keɪʃənɪst] *n US* **summer v.** veraneante *mf*

vaccinate ['væksɪneɪt] *vt* vacunar

vaccine ['væksiːn] *n* vacuna *f*

vacuum ['vækjʊəm] **1** *n* vacío *m*; **v. cleaner** aspiradora *f*; **v. flask** termo *m*

2 *vt (carpet, room)* pasar la aspiradora por

vacuum-packed ['vækjʊəm'pækt] *adj* envasado(a) al vacío

vagina [və'dʒaɪnə] *n* vagina *f*

vagrant ['veɪgrənt] *adj & n* vagabundo(a) (*m,f*)

vague [veɪg] *adj (imprecise)* vago(a), impreciso(a); *(indistinct)* borroso(a)

vain [veɪn] *adj* (**a**) *(proud)* vanidoso(a), presumido(a) (**b**) *(hopeless)* vano(a); **in v.** en vano

valentine ['væləntaɪn] *n* (**a**) *(card)* = tarjeta que se manda el Día de los Enamorados (**b**) *(sweetheart)* novio(a) *m,f*

valet ['vælɪt, 'væleɪ] *n* ayuda *m* de cámara

valiant ['væljənt] *adj* valiente

valid ['vælɪd] *adj* válido(a); **no longer v.** caducado(a)

valley ['vælɪ] *n* valle *m*

valour, *US* **valor** ['vælə(r)] *n* valor *m*, valentía *f*

valuable ['væljʊəbəl] **1** *adj* valioso(a), de valor

2 *npl* **valuables** objetos *mpl* de valor

valuation [vælju'eɪʃən] *n* (**a**) *(act)* valoración *f* (**b**) *(price)* valor *m*

value ['væljuː] **1** *n* valor *m*; **50 pence is good v.** 50 peniques es un buen precio; **to get good v. for money** sacarle jugo al dinero; **v.-added tax** impuesto *m* sobre el valor añadido

2 *vt* valorar

valve [vælv] *n* (**a**) *Anat & Tech* válvula *f* (**b**) *Rad* lámpara *f*

vampire ['væmpaɪə(r)] *n* vampiro *m*

van [væn] *n Br* (**a**) *Aut* furgoneta *f* (**b**) *Rail* furgón *m*

vandal ['vændəl] *n* vándalo(a) *m,f*

vandalism ['vændəlɪzəm] *n* vandalismo *m*

vandalize ['vændəlaɪz] *vt* destruir, destrozar

vanguard ['vænguːd] *n* vanguardia *f*

vanilla [və'nɪlə] *n* vainilla *f*

vanish ['vænɪʃ] *vi* desaparecer

vanity ['vænɪtɪ] *n* vanidad *f*; **v. bag** *or* **case** neceser *m*

vantage ['vɑːntɪdʒ] *n* ventaja *f*; **v. point** posición estratégica

vapor ['veɪpər] *n US =* **vapour**

vaporizer ['veɪpəraɪzə(r)] *n (device)* vaporizador *m*; *(spray)* pulverizador *m*

vapour ['veɪpə(r)] *n* vapor *m*; *(on windowpane)* vaho *m*; **v. trail** estela *f* de humo

variable ['veərɪəbəl] *adj & n* variable *(f)*

variance ['veərɪəns] *n Fml* **to be at v.** no concordar; **to be at v. with sb** estar en desacuerdo con algn

variation [veərɪ'eɪʃən] *n* variación *f*

varicose ['værɪkəʊs] *adj* **v. veins** varices *fpl*

varied ['veərɪd] *adj* variado(a), diverso(a)

variety [və'raɪɪtɪ] *n* (**a**) *(diversity)* variedad *f*; *(assortment)* surtido *m*; **for a v. of reasons** por razones diversas (**b**) **v. show** espectáculo *m* de variedades

various ['veərɪəs] *adj* diversos(as), varios(as)

varnish ['vɑːnɪʃ] **1** *n* barniz *m*; *Br* **nail v.** esmalte *m* de uñas

2 *vt* barnizar; *(nails)* esmaltar

vary ['veərɪ] *vi* variar; **prices v. from £2 to £4** los precios oscilan entre 2 y 4 libras; **to v. in size** variar de tamaño

varying ['veərɪŋ] *adj* **with v. degrees of success** con más o menos éxito

vase [*Br* vɑːz, *US* veɪs] *n* jarrón *m*

🖉 Note that the Spanish word **vaso** is a false friend and is never a translation for the English word **vase**. In Spanish, **vaso** means both "glass" and "vessel".

vasectomy [və'sektəmɪ] *n Med* vasectomía *f*

Vaseline® ['væsɪliːn] *n* vaselina *f*

vast [vɑːst] *adj* vasto(a); *(majority)* inmenso(a)

VAT [viːeɪ'tiː, væt] *n (abbr* **value-added tax)** IVA *m*

vat [væt] *n* cuba *f*, tina *f*

Vatican ['vætɪkən] n **the V.** el Vaticano

vault¹ [vɔ:lt] n bóveda f; (for wine) bodega f; (tomb) cripta f; (of bank) cámara acorazada

vault² [vɔ:lt] 1 vt & vi saltar

  2 n salto m

vaunt [vɔ:nt] vt Fml jactarse de, hacer alarde de

VCR [vi:si:'ɑ:(r)] n (abbr **video cassette recorder**) (aparato m de) vídeo m

VD [vi:'di:] n (abbr **venereal disease**) enfermedad venérea

VDU [vi:di:'ju:] n (abbr **visual display unit**) monitor m

veal [vi:l] n ternera f

veer [vɪə(r)] vi (ship) virar; (car) girar

vegan ['vi:gən] n vegetaliano(a) m,f, = vegetariano estricto que no come ningún producto de origen animal

vegeburger ['vedʒɪbɜːgə(r)] n hamburguesa vegetariana

vegetable ['vedʒtəbəl] n (food) verdura f, hortaliza f; **v. garden** huerta f, huerto m

vegetarian [vedʒɪ'teərɪən] adj & n vegetariano(a) (m,f)

vegetation [vedʒɪ'teɪʃən] n vegetación f

vehement ['vi:mənt] adj vehemente

vehicle ['vi:ɪkəl] n vehículo m

veil [veɪl] 1 n velo m

  2 vt velar

vein [veɪn] n vena f

velocity [vɪ'lɒsɪtɪ] n velocidad f

velvet ['velvɪt] n terciopelo m

velvety ['velvɪtɪ] adj aterciopelado(a)

vendetta [ven'detə] n vendetta f

vending ['vendɪŋ] n **v. machine** máquina expendedora

vendor ['vendɔ:(r)] n vendedor(a) m,f

veneer [vɪ'nɪə(r)] n (a) (covering) chapa f (b) Fig apariencia f

venerable ['venərəbəl] adj venerable

venereal [vɪ'nɪərɪəl] adj venéreo(a)

Venetian [vɪ'ni:ʃən] adj & n veneciano(a) (m,f); **v. blind** persiana f graduable

Venezuela [venɪ'zweɪlə] n Venezuela

Venezuelan [venɪ'zweɪlən] adj & n venezolano(a) (m,f)

vengeance ['vendʒəns] n venganza f; Fam **it was raining with a v.** llovía con ganas

Venice ['venɪs] n Venecia

venison ['venɪsən] n carne f de venado

venom ['venəm] n veneno m

venomous ['venəməs] adj venenoso(a); Fig **v. tongue** lengua viperina

vent [vent] 1 n (a) (opening) abertura f, orificio m; (grille) rejilla f de ventilación; **air v.** respiradero m (b) (of volcano) chimenea f

  2 vt Fig (feelings) descargar

ventilate ['ventɪleɪt] vt ventilar

ventilation [ventɪ'leɪʃən] n ventilación f

ventilator ['ventɪleɪtə(r)] n ventilador m

ventriloquist [ven'trɪləkwɪst] n ventrílocuo(a) m,f

venture ['ventʃə(r)] 1 vt arriesgar, aventurar; **he didn't v. to ask** no se atrevió a preguntarlo

  2 vi arriesgarse; **to v. out of doors** atreverse a salir

  3 n empresa arriesgada, aventura f; Com **business/joint v.** empresa comercial/colectiva

venue ['venju:] n (a) (meeting place) lugar m de reunión (b) (for concert etc) local m

Venus ['vi:nəs] n (goddess) Venus f; (planet) Venus m

veranda(h) [və'rændə] n porche m, terraza f

verb [vɜ:b] n verbo m

verbal ['vɜ:bəl] adj verbal

verbatim [və'beɪtɪm] 1 adj textual

  2 adv textualmente

verbose [vɜ:'bəʊs] adj prodigio(a) en palabras

verdict ['vɜ:dɪkt] n (a) Jur veredicto m, fallo m (b) (opinion) opinión f, juicio m

verge [vɜ:dʒ] 1 n (a) (margin) borde m; Fig **on the v. of** al borde de; Fig **to be on the v. of doing sth** estar a punto de hacer algo (b) Br (of road) arcén m, Andes berma f, Méx acotamiento m, RP banquina f, Ven hombrillo m

  2 vi rayar (**on** en)

verification [verɪfɪ'keɪʃən] n verificación f, comprobación f

verify ['verɪfaɪ] vt verificar, comprobar

veritable ['verɪtəbəl] adj auténtico(a)

vermicelli [vɜ:mɪ'tʃelɪ] n fideos mpl

vermin ['vɜ:mɪn] npl (a) (animals) bichos mpl, sabandijas fpl (b) Fig gentuza f

vermouth ['vɜ:məθ] n vermú m, vermut m

verruca [və'ru:kə] n verruga f

versatile ['vɜ:sətaɪl] adj (person) polifacético(a); (object) versátil

verse [vɜ:s] n (a) (stanza) estrofa f (b) (poetry) versos mpl, poesía f (c) (of song) copla f (d) (of Bible) versículo m

versed [vɜ:st] adj **to be (well) v. in** ser (muy) versado en

version ['vɜ:ʃən, 'vɜ:ʒən] n (a) versión f; **stage v.** adaptación f teatral (b) Aut modelo m

versus ['vɜ:səs] prep contra

vertebra ['vɜ:tɪbrə] n (pl **vertebras** or **vertebrae** ['vɜ:tɪbri:]) vértebra f

vertical ['vɜ:tɪkəl] adj & n vertical (f)

vertigo ['vɜ:tɪgəʊ] n vértigo m

verve [vɜ:v] n vigor m, brío m

very ['verɪ] 1 adv (a) (extremely) muy; **to be v. hungry** tener mucha hambre; **v. much** muchísimo; **v. well** muy bien (b) (emphatic) **at the v. latest** como máximo; **at the v. least** como mínimo; **the v. best** el mejor de todos; **the v. first/last** el primero/último de todos; **the v. same day** el mismo día

  2 adj (a) **at the v. end/beginning** al final/principio de todo (b) (precise) **at this v. moment** en este mismo momento; **her v. words** sus palabras exactas; **in the v. middle**

justo en medio (**c**) *(mere)* **the v. thought of it!** ¡sólo con pensarlo!

vespers ['vespəz] *npl* vísperas *fpl*

vessel ['vesəl] *n* (**a**) *(container)* vasija *f* (**b**) *Naut* buque *m*, nave *f* (**c**) *Anat & Bot* vaso *m*

vest [vest] **1** *n* (**a**) *Br (undershirt)* camiseta *f* de tirantes (**b**) *US* chaleco *m*
2 *vt Jur* **by the power vested in me ...** por los poderes que se me han conferido ...

vested ['vestɪd] *adj Jur & Fin* **v. interests** derechos adquiridos; *Fig* intereses *mpl* personales

vestibule ['vestɪbjuːl] *n* vestíbulo *m*

vestige ['vestɪdʒ] *n* vestigio *m*

vestry ['vestrɪ] *n* sacristía *f*

vet [vet] **1** *n* veterinario(a) *m,f*
2 *vt Br* someter a investigación, examinar

veteran ['vetərən] *n* (**a**) veterano(a) *m,f* (**b**) *US* **(war) v.** ex combatiente *mf*

veterinarian [vetərɪ'neərɪən] *n US* veterinario(a) *m,f*

veterinary ['vetərɪnərɪ] *adj* veterinario(a); **v. medicine** veterinaria *f*; *Br* **v. surgeon** veterinario(a) *m,f*

veto ['viːtəʊ] **1** *n* (*pl* **vetoes**) veto *m*
2 *vt Pol* vetar; *(suggestion etc)* descartar

vexed [vekst] *adj* (**a**) *(annoyed)* disgustado(a) (**b**) *(debated)* controvertido(a)

VHF [viːeɪtʃ'ef] (*abbr* **very high frequency**) VHF

via ['vaɪə] *prep* por, vía

viable ['vaɪəbəl] *adj* viable, factible

viaduct ['vaɪədʌkt] *n* viaducto *m*

vibrant ['vaɪbrənt] *adj* (**a**) *(sound)* vibrante (**b**) *Fig (personality)* vital; *(city)* animado(a)

vibrate [vaɪ'breɪt] *vi* vibrar (**with** de)

vibration [vaɪ'breɪʃən] *n* vibración *f*

vicar ['vɪkə(r)] *n* párroco *m*

vicarage ['vɪkərɪdʒ] *n* casa *f* del párroco

vicarious [vɪ'keərɪəs] *adj* experimentado(a) por otro; *(punishment)* sufrido(a) por otro

vice¹ [vaɪs] *n* vicio *m*

vice² [vaɪs] *n Br (tool)* torno *m* de banco

vice- [vaɪs] *pref* vice-; **v.-chancellor** rector(a) *m,f*; **v.-president** vicepresidente(a) *m,f*

vice-chairman [vaɪs'tʃeəmən] *n* vicepresidente *m*

vice versa [vaɪsɪ'vɜːsə] *adv* viceversa

vicinity [vɪ'sɪnɪtɪ] *n (area)* vecindad *f*; **in the v. of** *(geographic location)* cerca de, en las inmediaciones de; *(amount)* alrededor de

vicious ['vɪʃəs] *adj (violent)* violento(a); *(malicious)* malintencionado(a); *(cruel)* cruel; **v. circle** círculo vicioso

victim ['vɪktɪm] *n* víctima *f*

victimize ['vɪktɪmaɪz] *vt* perseguir, tratar injustamente

victor ['vɪktə(r)] *n* vencedor(a) *m,f*

victorious [vɪk'tɔːrɪəs] *adj* victorioso(a)

victory ['vɪktərɪ] *n* victoria *f*

video ['vɪdɪəʊ] *n* vídeo *m*; **v. camera** videocámara *f*; **v. cassette** videocasete *m*; **v. club** videoclub *m*; **v. game** videojuego *m*; **v. (cassette) recorder** vídeo *m*; **v. tape** cinta *f* de vídeo

video-tape ['vɪdɪəʊteɪp] *vt* grabar (en vídeo)

vie [vaɪ] *vi* competir (**against** *or* **with** con)

Vienna [vɪ'enə] *n* Viena

Viennese [vɪə'niːz] *adj & n* vienés(esa) *(m,f)*

Vietnam [vjet'næm] *n* Vietnam

view [vjuː] **1** *n* (**a**) *(sight)* vista *f*, panorama *m*; **in full v.** completamente visible; **on v.** a la vista; **to come into v.** aparecer; *Fig* **in v. of the fact that ...** dado que ... (**b**) *(opinion)* opinión *f*; **point of v.** punto *m* de vista; **to take a dim v. of** ver con malos ojos (**c**) *(aim)* fin *m*; **with a v. to** con la intención de
2 *vt* (**a**) *(look at)* mirar; *(house etc)* visitar (**b**) *(consider)* contemplar; *(topic, problem)* enfocar

viewer ['vjuːə(r)] *n* (**a**) *TV* televidente *mf* (**b**) *Phot* visionador *m*

viewfinder ['vjuːfaɪndə(r)] *n* visor *m*

viewpoint ['vjuːpɔɪnt] *n* punto *m* de vista

vigil ['vɪdʒɪl] *n* vigilia *f*

vigilante [vɪdʒɪ'læntɪ] *n* **v. group** patrulla ciudadana

vigorous ['vɪgərəs] *adj* vigoroso(a), enérgico(a)

vigour, *US* **vigor** ['vɪgə(r)] *n* vigor *m*

vile [vaɪl] *adj* (**a**) *(evil)* vil, infame (**b**) *(disgusting)* repugnante (**c**) *Fam (awful)* horrible

vilify ['vɪlɪfaɪ] *vt* denigrar

villa ['vɪlə] *n* (**a**) *(in country)* casa *f* de campo (**b**) *Br* chalet *m*

village ['vɪlɪdʒ] *n (small)* aldea *f*; *(larger)* pueblo *m*

villager ['vɪlɪdʒə(r)] *n* aldeano(a) *m,f*

villain ['vɪlən] *n* villano(a) *m,f*; *Cin & Th* malo(a) *m,f*

vinaigrette [vɪneɪ'gret] *n* vinagreta *f*

vindicate ['vɪndɪkeɪt] *vt* justificar, vindicar

vindictive [vɪn'dɪktɪv] *adj* vengativo(a)

vine [vaɪn] *n* vid *f*; *(climbing)* parra *f*

vinegar ['vɪnɪgə(r)] *n* vinagre *m*

vineyard ['vɪnjəd] *n* viña *f*, viñedo *m*

vintage ['vɪntɪdʒ] **1** *n* (**a**) *(crop, year)* cosecha *f* (**b**) *(season)* vendimia *f* (**c**) *(era)* era *f*
2 *adj* (**a**) *(wine)* añejo(a) (**b**) *(classic)* clásico(a); **v. car** coche *m* de época

vinyl ['vaɪnɪl] *n* vinilo *m*

viola [vɪ'əʊlə] *n* viola *f*

violate ['vaɪəleɪt] *vt* violar

violence ['vaɪələns] *n* violencia *f*

violent ['vaɪələnt] *adj* (**a**) violento(a) (**b**) *(intense)* intenso(a)

violet ['vaɪəlɪt] **1** *n* (**a**) *Bot* violeta *f* (**b**) *(colour)* violeta *m*
2 *adj* violeta

violin [vaɪə'lɪn] *n* violín *m*

violinist [vaɪə'lɪnɪst] *n* violinista *mf*

VIP [viːaɪ'piː] *n Fam* (*abbr* **very important person**) personaje *m* muy importante

viper ['vaɪpə(r)] *n* víbora *f*

virgin ['vɜːdʒɪn] **1** *n* virgen *f*; **the V. Mary** la Virgen María; **to be a v.** ser virgen
2 *adj* virgen

virginity [və'dʒɪnɪtɪ] *n* virginidad *f*

Virgo ['vɜːgəʊ] *n* Virgo *m*

virile ['vɪraɪl] *adj* viril

virtual ['vɜːtjʊəl] *adj* virtual; *Comput* **v. reality** realidad *f* virtual

virtually ['vɜːtjʊəlɪ] *adv (almost)* prácticamente

virtue ['vɜːtjuː] *n* virtud *f*; **by v. of** en virtud de

virtuous ['vɜːtjʊəs] *adj* virtuoso(a)

virulent ['vɪrʊlənt] *adj* virulento(a)

virus ['vaɪrəs] *n* virus *m inv*; *Comput* **v. check** detección *m* de virus

visa ['viːzə] *n* visado *m*, *Am* visa *f*

vis-à-vis [viːzɑː'viː] *prep* (**a**) *(regarding)* respecto a (**b**) *(opposite)* frente a

viscose ['vɪskəʊs] *n* viscosa *f*

viscount ['vaɪkaʊnt] *n* vizconde *m*

vise [vaɪs] *n US (tool)* torno *m* de banco

visibility [vɪzɪ'bɪlɪtɪ] *n* visibilidad *f*

visible ['vɪzɪbəl] *adj* visible

vision ['vɪʒən] *n* (**a**) visión *f* (**b**) *(eyesight)* vista *f*

visit ['vɪzɪt] **1** *vt* (**a**) *(person)* visitar, hacer una visita a (**b**) *(place)* visitar, ir a
2 *n* visita *f*; **to pay sb a v.** hacerle una visita a algn

visiting ['vɪzɪtɪŋ] *adj* **v. card** tarjeta *f* de visita; *Med* **v. hours** horas *fpl* de visita; *Sport* **v. team** equipo *m* visitante

visitor ['vɪzɪtə(r)] *n* (**a**) *(guest)* invitado(a) *m,f*; **we've got visitors** tenemos visita (**b**) *(in hotel)* cliente(a) *m,f* (**c**) *(tourist)* turista *mf*

visor ['vaɪzə(r)] *n* visera *f*

> ⚠ Note that the Spanish word **visor** is a false friend and is never a translation for the English word **visor**. In Spanish, **visor** means ; viewfinder".

vista ['vɪstə] *n* vista *f*, panorama *m*

visual ['vɪʒʊəl] *adj* visual; **v. aids** medios *mpl* visuales

visualize ['vɪʒʊəlaɪz] *vt* (**a**) *(imagine)* imaginar(se) (**b**) *(foresee)* prever

vital ['vaɪtəl] *adj* (**a**) *(lively)* enérgico(a) (**b**) *(essential)* fundamental (**c**) *(decisive)* decisivo(a); *Fam* **v. statistics** medidas *fpl* del cuerpo de la mujer (**d**) *Med (function, sign)* vital

vitality [vaɪ'tælɪtɪ] *n* vitalidad *f*

vitally ['vaɪtəlɪ] *adv* **it's v. important** es de vital importancia

vitamin ['vɪtəmɪn, *US* 'vaɪtəmɪn] *n* vitamina *f*

viva ['vaɪvə] *n Br* examen *m* oral

vivacious [vɪ'veɪʃəs] *adj* vivaz

vivacity [vɪ'væsɪtɪ] *n* viveza *f*, vivacidad *f*

vivid ['vɪvɪd] *adj* (**a**) *(bright, lively)* vivo(a), intenso(a) (**b**) *(graphic)* gráfico(a)

vixen ['vɪksən] *n* zorra *f*

V-neck(ed) ['viːnek(t)] *adj* con el cuello en pico

vocabulary [və'kæbjʊlərɪ] *n* vocabulario *m*

vocal ['vəʊkəl] *adj* vocal; **v. cords** cuerdas *fpl* vocales

vocalist ['vəʊkəlɪst] *n* cantante *mf*

vocation [vəʊ'keɪʃən] *n* vocación *f*

vocational [vəʊ'keɪʃənəl] *adj* profesional; **v. training** formación *f* profesional

vociferous [vəʊ'sɪfərəs] *adj* (**a**) *(protest)* enérgico(a) (**b**) *(noisy)* clamoroso(a)

vodka ['vɒdkə] *n* vodka *m*

vogue [vəʊg] *n* boga *f*, moda *f*; **in v.** de moda

voice [vɔɪs] **1** *n* voz *f*; **to lose one's v.** quedarse afónico; *Fig* **at the top of one's v.** a voz en grito; *Comput* **v. mail** buzon *m* de voz
2 *vt* (**a**) *(express)* manifestar (**b**) *Ling* sonorizar

void [vɔɪd] **1** *adj* (**a**) **v. of** sin (**b**) *Jur* nulo(a), inválido(a)
2 *n* vacío *m*

volatile ['vɒlətaɪl] *adj* volátil

volcanic [vɒl'kænɪk] *adj* volcánico(a)

volcano [vɒl'keɪnəʊ] *n (pl* **volcanoes)** volcán *m*

volition [və'lɪʃən] *n Fml* **of one's own v.** por voluntad propia

volley ['vɒlɪ] **1** *n* (**a**) *(of shots)* descarga *f* (**b**) *Fig (of stones, insults)* lluvia *f* (**c**) *(in tennis, football)* volea *f*
2 *vt (in tennis, football)* volear

volleyball ['vɒlɪbɔːl] *n* voleibol *m*

volt [vəʊlt] *n* voltio *m*

voltage ['vəʊltɪdʒ] *n* voltaje *m*

voluble ['vɒljʊbəl] *adj* locuaz

> ⚠ Note that the Spanish word **voluble** is a false friend and is never a translation for the English word **voluble**. In Spanish, **voluble** means "fickle, changeable".

volume ['vɒljuːm] *n* (**a**) volumen *m* (**b**) *(book)* volumen *m*, tomo *m*; *Fig* **to speak volumes** decirlo todo

voluntary ['vɒləntərɪ] *adj* voluntario(a); **v. organization** organización benéfica

volunteer [vɒlən'tɪə(r)] **1** *n* voluntario(a) *m,f*
2 *vt (help etc)* ofrecer
3 *vi* (**a**) ofrecerse (**for** para) (**b**) *Mil* alistarse como voluntario

voluptuous [və'lʌptjʊəs] *adj* voluptuoso(a)

vomit ['vɒmɪt] **1** *vt & vi* vomitar
2 *n* vómito *m*

voracious [vɒ'reɪʃəs] *adj* voraz

vortex ['vɔːteks] *n (pl* **vortices** ['vɔːtɪsiːz]) vórtice *m*; *Fig* vorágine *f*

vote [vəʊt] **1** *n* voto *m*; *(voting)* votación *f*; **v. of confidence** voto de confianza; **to take a v. on sth** someter algo a votacíon; **to have the v.** tener derecho al voto
2 *vt* (**a**) votar (**b**) *(elect)* elegir (**c**) *Fam* proponer

3 *vi* votar; **to v. for sb** votar a algn
voter ['vəʊtə(r)] *n* votante *mf*
voting ['vəʊtɪŋ] *n* votación *f*
vouch [vaʊtʃ] *vi* **to v. for sth/sb** responder de
algo/por algn
voucher ['vaʊtʃə(r)] *n Br* vale *m*
vow [vaʊ] **1** *n* voto *m*
  2 *vt* jurar
vowel ['vaʊəl] *n* vocal *f*

voyage ['vɔɪdʒ] *n* viaje *m*; *(crossing)* travesía *f*; **to go on a v.** hacer un viaje (en barco)
vulgar ['vʌlgə(r)] *adj (coarse)* vulgar, ordina-
rio(a); *(in poor taste)* de mal gusto
vulgarity [vʌl'gærɪtɪ] *n (coarseness)* vulgaridad *f*, ordinariez *f*; *(poor taste)* mal gusto *m*
vulnerable ['vʌlnərəbəl] *adj* vulnerable
vulture ['vʌltʃə(r)] *n* buitre *m*
vulva ['vʌlvə] *n* vulva *f*

W, w ['dʌbəlju:] *n (the letter)* W, w *f*

W (**a**) (*abbr* **West**) O (**b**) (*abbr* **Watt(s)**) W

wad [wɒd] *n (of paper)* taco *m*; *(of cotton wool)* bolita *f*; *(of banknotes)* fajo *m*

waddle ['wɒdəl] *vi* andar como los patos

wade [weɪd] *vi* caminar por el agua; **to w. across a river** vadear un río
▸ **wade through** *vt insep* hacer con dificultad; **I'm wading through the book** me cuesta mucho terminar el libro

wading pool ['weɪdɪŋpu:l] *n US* piscina *f* para niños

wafer ['weɪfə(r)] *n* barquillo *m*; *Rel* hostia *f*

waffle¹ ['wɒfəl] *n Culin* = tipo de barquillo

waffle² ['wɒfəl] *Br Fam* **1** *vi* meter mucha paja; **to w. on** parlotear
2 *n* paja *f*

waft [wɑːft, wɒft] **1** *vt* llevar por el aire
2 *vi* flotar (por *or* en el aire)

wag [wæg] **1** *vt* menear
2 *vi (tail)* menearse

wage [weɪdʒ] **1** *n (also* **wages**) salario *m*, sueldo *m*; **w. earner** asalariado(a) *m,f*; **w. freeze** congelación *f* salarial
2 *vt (campaign)* realizar (**against** contra); **to w. war (on)** hacer la guerra (a)

wage-packet ['weɪdʒpækɪt] *n* sueldo *m*

wager ['weɪdʒə(r)] **1** *n* apuesta *f*
2 *vt* apostar

waggle ['wægəl] **1** *vt* menear
2 *vi* menearse

wa(g)gon ['wægən] *n (horse-drawn)* carro *m*; *Br Rail* vagón *m*

wail [weɪl] **1** *n* lamento *m*, gemido *m*
2 *vi (person)* lamentar, gemir

waist [weɪst] *n Anat* cintura *f*; *Sewing* talle *m*

waistcoat ['weɪstkəʊt] *n Br* chaleco *m*

waistline ['weɪstlaɪn] *n Anat* cintura *f*; *Sewing* talle *m*

wait [weɪt] **1** *n* espera *f*; *(delay)* demora *f*; **to lie in w.** estar al acecho
2 *vi* (**a**) esperar, aguardar; **I can't w. to see her** me muero de ganas de verla; **while you w.** en el acto; **to keep sb waiting** hacer esperar a algn (**b**) **to w. at table** servir la mesa
▸ **wait about, wait around** *vi* esperar
▸ **wait on** *vt insep* servir

waiter ['weɪtə(r)] *n* camarero *m*, *CAm, Col, Méx* mesero *m*, *Chile, Ven* mesonero *m*, *Perú, RP* mozo *m*

waiting ['weɪtɪŋ] *n* **no w.** *(sign)* prohibido aparcar; **w. list** lista *f* de espera; **w. room** sala *f* de espera

waitress ['weɪtrɪs] *n* camarera *f*, *CAm, Col, Méx* mesera *f*, *Chile, Ven* mesonera *f*, *Perú, RP* moza *f*

waive [weɪv] *vt Fml (rule)* no aplicar

wake¹ [weɪk] **1** *vt (pt* **woke**; *pp* **woken) to w. sb (up)** despertar a algn
2 *vi* **to w. (up)** despertar(se)
3 *n (for dead)* velatorio *m*

wake² [weɪk] *n (in water)* estela *f*; *Fig* **in the w. of** tras

waken ['weɪkən] *vt Literary* despertar

Wales [weɪlz] *n* (el país de) Gales

walk [wɔːk] **1** *n* (**a**) *(long)* caminata *m*; *(short)* paseo *m*; **it's an hour's w.** está a una hora de camino; **to go for a w.** dar un paseo; **to take the dog for a w.** sacar a pasear al perro (**b**) *(gait)* modo *m* de andar (**c**) **people from all walks of life** gente *f* de toda condición
2 *vt* (**a**) **we walked her home** la acompañamos a casa (**b**) *(dog)* pasear
3 *vi* (**a**) andar (**b**) *(go on foot)* ir andando
▸ **walk away** *vi* alejarse; *Fig* **to w. away with a prize** llevarse un premio
▸ **walk into** *vt insep* (**a**) *(place)* entrar en; *Fig (trap)* caer en (**b**) *(bump into)* chocarse contra
▸ **walk out** *vi* salir; *Ind* declararse en huelga; **to w. out on sb** abandonar a algn
▸ **walk up** *vi* **to w. up to sb** abordar a algn

walkabout ['wɔːkəbaʊt] *n (by Queen etc)* = paseo informal entre la gente

walker ['wɔːkə(r)] *n* paseante *mf*; *Sport* marchador(a) *m,f*

walkie-talkie [wɔːkɪ'tɔːkɪ] *n* walkie-talkie *m*

walking ['wɔːkɪŋ] **1** *n* andar *m*; *(hiking)* excursionismo *m*
2 *adj* **at w. pace** a paso de marcha; **w. shoes** zapatos *mpl* de andar; **w. stick** bastón *m*

Walkman® ['wɔːkmən] *n (pl* **Walkmans)** walkman® *m*

walkout ['wɔːkaʊt] *n Ind* huelga *f*

walkover ['wɔːkəʊvə(r)] *n* **it was a w.** fue pan comido

walkway ['wɔːkweɪ] *n* paso *m* de peatones

wall [wɔːl] *n* (**a**) *(freestanding, exterior)* muro *m*; *Fig* **to have one's back to the w.** estar entre la espada y la pared; **city w.** muralla *f*; **garden w.** tapia *f* (**b**) *(interior)* pared *f*; **w. map** mapa *m* mural (**c**) *Ftb* barrera *f*
▸ **wall up** *vt sep (door, fireplace)* tabicar

walled [wɔːld] *adj (city)* amurallado(a); *(garden)* cercado(a) con tapia

wallet [ˈwɒlɪt] *n* cartera *f*

wallflower [ˈwɔːlflaʊə(r)] *n* (**a**) *Bot* alhelí *m* (**b**) *Fam* **to be a w.** ser un convidado de piedra

wallop [ˈwɒləp] *Fam* **1** *n* golpazo *m*
2 *vt* (**a**) *(hit)* pegar fuerte (**b**) *(defeat)* dar una paliza a

wallow [ˈwɒləʊ] *vi* revolcarse (**en** in); *Fig* **to w. in self-pity** sumirse en la autocompasión

wallpaper [ˈwɔːlpeɪpə(r)] **1** *n* papel pintado
2 *vt* empapelar

wally [ˈwɒlɪ] *n Fam* idiota *mf*

walnut [ˈwɔːlnʌt] *n* nuez *f*; *(tree, wood)* nogal *m*

walrus [ˈwɔːlrəs] *n* morsa *f*

waltz [wɔːls] **1** *n* vals *m*
2 *vi* bailar un vals

wan [wɒn] *adj* (**wanner, wannest**) pálido(a); *(look, smile)* apagado(a)

wand [wɒnd] *n* (**magic**) **w.** varita *f* (mágica)

wander [ˈwɒndə(r)] **1** *vt* **to w. the streets** vagar por las calles
2 *vi* (**a**) *(aimlessly)* vagar, errar; **to w. about** deambular; **to w. in/out** entrar/salir sin prisas (**b**) *(stray)* desviarse; *(mind)* divagar; **his glance wandered round the room** recorrió el cuarto con la mirada

wandering [ˈwɒndərɪŋ] *adj* errante; *(tribe)* nómada; *(speech)* divagador(a)

wane [weɪn] *vi* menguar; *(interest)* decaer

wangle [ˈwæŋgəl] *vt Fam* agenciarse

wank [wæŋk] *Br Vulg* **1** *n* paja *f*
2 *vi* hacerse una paja

wanker [ˈwæŋkə(r)] *n Br Vulg* mamón(ona) *m,f*

want [wɒnt] **1** *n* (**a**) *(lack)* falta *f*; **for w. of** por falta de (**b**) *(poverty)* miseria *f*
2 *vt* (**a**) *(desire)* querer, desear; **to w. to do sth** querer hacer algo (**b**) *Fam (need)* necesitar; **the grass wants cutting** hace falta cortar el césped (**c**) *(seek)* buscar; **you're wanted on the phone** te llaman al teléfono
▸ **want for** *vt insep* carecer de; **to w. for nothing** tenerlo todo

wanting [ˈwɒntɪŋ] *adj* (**a**) **she is w. in tact** le falta tacto (**b**) **he was found w.** no daba la talla

wanton [ˈwɒntən] *adj* (**a**) *(motiveless)* sin motivo; **w. cruelty** crueldad gratuita (**b**) *(unrestrained)* desenfrenado(a); *(licentious)* lascivo(a)

war [wɔː(r)] *n* guerra *f*; **to be at w. (with)** estar en guerra (con); *Fig* **to declare/wage w. on** declarar/hacer la guerra a; **w. crime** crimen *m* de guerra

warble [ˈwɔːbəl] *vi* gorjear

ward [wɔːd] *n* (**a**) *(of hospital)* sala *f* (**b**) *Jur* pupilo(a) *m,f*; **w. of court** pupilo(a) bajo tutela judicial (**c**) *Br Pol* distrito *m* electoral
▸ **ward off** *vt sep (blow)* parar, desviar;

(attack) rechazar; *(danger)* evitar; *(illness)* prevenir

warden [ˈwɔːdən] *n* *(of residence)* guardián(ana) *m,f*; **game w.** guardia *m* de coto

warder [ˈwɔːdə(r)] *n Br* carcelero(a) *m,f*

wardrobe [ˈwɔːdrəʊb] *n* (**a**) *(furniture)* armario *m*, ropero *m* (**b**) *(clothes)* guardarropa *m* (**c**) *Th* vestuario *m*

warehouse [ˈweəhaʊs] *n* almacén *m*

wares [weəz] *npl* mercancías *fpl*

warfare [ˈwɔːfeə(r)] *n* guerra *f*

warhead [ˈwɔːhed] *n* (**nuclear**) **w.** ojiva *f* nuclear

warm [wɔːm] **1** *adj* (**a**) *(water)* tibio(a); *(hands)* caliente; *(climate)* cálido(a); **a w. day** un día de calor; **I am w.** tengo calor; **it is (very) w. today** hoy hace (mucho) calor; **w. clothing** ropa *f* de abrigo (**b**) *(welcome, applause)* cálido(a)
2 *vt* calentar; *Fig* alegrar
3 *vi* calentarse; **to w. to sb** cogerle simpatía a algn
▸ **warm up 1** *vt sep* (**a**) calentar; *(soup)* (re)calentar (**b**) *(audience)* animar
2 *vi* (**a**) calentarse; *(food)* (re)calentarse; *(person)* entrar en calor (**b**) *(athlete)* hacer ejercicios de calentamiento (**c**) *Fig (audience, party)* animarse

warm-blooded [wɔːmˈblʌdɪd] *adj* de sangre caliente

warm-hearted [wɔːmˈhɑːtɪd] *adj* afectuoso(a)

warmly [ˈwɔːmlɪ] *adv Fig* calurosamente; *(thank)* con efusión

warmth [wɔːmθ] *n* *(heat)* calor *m*; *Fig* cordialidad *f*

warn [wɔːn] *vt* avisar (**of** de), advertir (**about/against** sobre/contra); **he warned me not to go** me advirtió que no fuera; **to w. sb that** advertir a algn que

warning [ˈwɔːnɪŋ] **1** *adj* **w. light** piloto *m*; **w. sign** señal *f* de aviso
2 *n* (**a**) *(of danger)* advertencia *f*, aviso *m* (**b**) *(replacing punishment)* amonestación *f* (**c**) *(notice)* aviso *m*; **without w.** sin previo aviso

warp [wɔːp] **1** *vt* (**a**) *(wood)* alabear, combar (**b**) *Fig (mind)* pervertir
2 *vi* alabearse, combarse

warrant [ˈwɒrənt] **1** *n Jur* orden *f* judicial; **death w.** sentencia *f* de muerte (**b**) *(authorization note)* cédula *f*; *Com* bono *m*
2 *vt* (**a**) *(justify)* justificar (**b**) *(guarantee)* garantizar

warranty [ˈwɒrəntɪ] *n Com* garantía *f*

warren [ˈwɒrən] *n* conejera *f*; *Fig* laberinto *m*

warrior [ˈwɒrɪə(r)] *n* guerrero(a) *m,f*

Warsaw [ˈwɔːsɔː] *n* Varsovia

warship [ˈwɔːʃɪp] *n* buque *m* or barco *m* de guerra

wart [wɔːt] *n* verruga *f*

wartime [ˈwɔːtaɪm] *n* tiempos *mpl* de guerra

wary ['weərɪ] *adj* (**warier, wariest**) cauteloso(a); **to be w. of doing sth** dudar en hacer algo; **to be w. of sb/sth** recelar de algn/algo

was [wɒz] *pt of* **be**

wash [wɒʃ] **1** *n* (**a**) lavado *m*; **to have a w.** lavarse (**b**) *(of ship)* estela *f*; *(sound)* chapoteo *m*

2 *vt* (**a**) lavar; *(dishes)* fregar; **to w. one's hair** lavarse el pelo (**b**) *(of sea, river)* arrastrar

3 *vi* (**a**) *(person)* lavarse; *(do the laundry)* hacer la colada (**b**) *(lap)* batir

▸ **wash away** *vt sep* *(of sea)* llevarse; *(traces)* borrar

▸ **wash off** *vi* quitarse lavando

▸ **wash out 1** *vt sep* (**a**) *(stain)* quitar lavando (**b**) *(bottle)* enjuagar

2 *vi* quitarse lavando

▸ **wash up 1** *vt sep Br (dishes)* fregar

2 *vi* (**a**) *Br* fregar los platos (**b**) *US* lavarse rápidamente

washable ['wɒʃəbəl] *adj* lavable

washbasin ['wɒʃbeɪsən], *US* **washbowl** ['wɒʃbəʊl] *n* palangana *f*

washcloth ['wɒʃklɒθ] *n US* manopla *f*

washer ['wɒʃə(r)] *n (on tap)* junta *f*

washing ['wɒʃɪŋ] *n (action)* lavado *m*; *(of clothes)* colada *f*; **(dirty) w.** ropa sucia; **to do the w.** hacer la colada; **w. line** tendedero *m*; **w. machine** lavadora *f*; **w. powder** detergente *m*

washing-up [wɒʃɪŋ'ʌp] *n Br* (**a**) *(action)* fregado *m*; **w. bowl** barreño *m*; **w. liquid** (detergente *m*) lavavajillas (**b**) *(dishes)* platos *mpl* (para fregar)

washout ['wɒʃaʊt] *n Fam* fracaso *m*

washroom ['wɒʃruːm] *n US* servicios *mpl*

wasp [wɒsp] *n* avispa *f*

wastage ['weɪstɪdʒ] *n* pérdidas *fpl*

waste [weɪst] **1** *adj* (**a**) *(unwanted)* desechado(a); **w. food** restos *mpl* de comida; **w. products** productos *mpl* de desecho (**b**) *(ground)* baldío(a)

2 *n* (**a**) *(unnecessary use)* desperdicio *m*; *(of resources, effort, money)* derroche *m*; *(of time)* pérdida *f*; **to go to w.** echarse a perder (**b**) *(leftovers)* desperdicios *mpl*; *(rubbish)* basura *f*; **radioactive w.** desechos radioactivos; **w. disposal unit** trituradora *f* (de desperdicios); **w. pipe** tubo *m* de desagüe

3 *vt* *(squander)* desperdiciar, malgastar; *(resources)* derrochar; *(money)* despilfarrar; *(time)* perder

▸ **waste away** *vi* consumirse

wasteful ['weɪstfʊl] *adj* derrochador(a)

wasteland ['weɪstlænd] *n* baldío *m*

wastepaper [weɪst'peɪpə(r)] *n* papeles usados; **w. basket** papelera *f*

watch [wɒtʃ] **1** *n* (**a**) *(look-out)* vigilancia *f*; **to keep a close w. on sth/sb** vigilar algo/a algn muy atentamente (**b**) *Mil (body)* guardia *f*; *(individual)* centinela *m*; **to be on w.** estar de guardia (**c**) *(timepiece)* reloj *m*

2 *vt* (**a**) *(observe)* mirar, observar (**b**) *(keep an eye on)* vigilar; *(with suspicion)* acechar (**c**) *(be careful of)* tener cuidado con; *Fig* **to w. one's step** ir con pies de plomo

3 *vi (look)* mirar, observar; **w. out!** ¡cuidado!

▸ **watch out for** *vt insep (be careful of)* tener cuidado con

watchband ['wɒtʃbænd] *n US* = **watchstrap**

watchdog ['wɒtʃdɒg] *n* perro *m* guardián; *Fig* guardián(ana) *m,f*

watchful ['wɒtʃfʊl] *adj* vigilante

watchmaker ['wɒtʃmeɪkə(r)] *n* relojero(a) *m,f*

watchman ['wɒtʃmən] *n* vigilante *m*; **night w.** *(of site)* vigilante nocturno

watchstrap ['wɒtʃstræp] *n* correa *f* (de reloj)

watchtower ['wɒtʃtaʊə(r)] *n* atalaya *f*

water ['wɔːtə(r)] **1** *n* (**a**) agua *f*; **w. bottle** cantimplora *f*; **w. lily** nenúfar *m*; **w. main** conducción *f* de aguas; **w. polo** water polo *m*; **w. sports** deportes acuáticos; **w. tank** depósito *m* de agua; **territorial waters** aguas jurisdiccionales; *Fig* **it's all w. under the bridge** ha llovido mucho desde entonces (**b**) **to pass w.** orinar

2 *vt (plants)* regar

3 *vi* **my eyes are watering** me lloran los ojos; **my mouth watered** se me hizo la boca agua

▸ **water down** *vt sep (drink)* aguar

watercolour, *US* **watercolor** ['wɔːtəkʌlə(r)] *n* acuarela *f*

watercress ['wɔːtəkres] *n* berro *m*

waterfall ['wɔːtəfɔːl] *n* cascada *f*; *(very big)* catarata *f*

waterfront ['wɔːtəfrʌnt] *n (shore)* orilla *f* del agua; *(harbour)* puerto *m*

watering ['wɔːtərɪŋ] *n (of plants)* riego *m*; **w. can** regadera *f*; **w. place** abrevadero *m*

waterline ['wɔːtəlaɪn] *n* línea *f* de flotación

waterlogged ['wɔːtəlɒgd] *adj* anegado(a)

watermark ['wɔːtəmɑːk] *n* filigrana *f*

watermelon ['wɔːtəmelən] *n* sandía *f*

waterproof ['wɔːtəpruːf] **1** *adj (material)* impermeable; *(watch)* sumergible

2 *n (coat)* impermeable *m*

watershed ['wɔːtəʃed] *n Geog* línea divisoria de aguas; *Fig* punto decisivo

water-skiing ['wɔːtəskiːɪŋ] *n* esquí acuático

watertight ['wɔːtətaɪt] *adj* hermético(a)

waterway ['wɔːtəweɪ] *n* vía *f* fluvial

waterworks ['wɔːtəwɜːks] *npl* central *f* de abastecimiento de agua; *Fig* **to turn on the w.** empezar a llorar

watery ['wɔːtərɪ] *adj* (**a**) *(soup)* aguado(a); *(coffee)* flojo(a) (**b**) *(eyes)* lacrimoso(a) (**c**) *(pale)* pálido(a)

watt [wɒt] *n* vatio *m*

wave [weɪv] **1** *n* (**a**) *(at sea)* ola *f* (**b**) *(in hair)* & *Rad* onda *f* (**c**) *Fig (of anger, strikes etc)* oleada *f* (**d**) *(gesture)* saludo *m* con la mano

2 *vt* (**a**) agitar; *(brandish)* blandir (**b**) *(hair)* ondular

3 *vi* (**a**) agitar el brazo; **she waved (to me)** *(greeting)* me saludó con la mano; *(goodbye)* se despidió (de mí) con la mano; *(signal)* me hizo señas con la mano (**b**) *(flag)* ondear; *(corn)* ondular

wavelength ['weɪvleŋθ] *n* longitud *f* de onda

waver ['weɪvə(r)] *vi* *(hesitate)* vacilar (**between** entre); *(voice)* temblar; *(courage)* flaquear

wavy ['weɪvɪ] *adj* (**wavier, waviest**) ondulado(a)

wax¹ [wæks] **1** *n* cera *f*
   2 *vt* encerar

wax² [wæks] *vi* (**a**) *(moon)* crecer (**b**) **to w. lyrical** exaltarse

waxworks ['wækswɜːks] *n sing* museo *m* de cera

way [weɪ] **1** *n* (**a**) *(route)* camino *m*; *(road)* vía *f*, camino; **a letter is on the w.** una carta está en camino; **on the w.** en el camino; **on the w. here** de camino para aquí; **out of the w.** apartado(a); **to ask the w.** preguntar el camino; **to go the wrong w.** ir por el camino equivocado; **to lose one's w.** perderse; **to make one's w. through the crowd** abrirse camino entre la multitud; **which is the w. to the station?** ¿por dónde se va a la estación?; *Fig* **she went out of her w. to help** se desvivió por ayudar; **w. in** entrada *f*; **w. out** salida *f*; *Fig* **the easy w. out** la solución fácil; **I can't find my w. out** no encuentro la salida; **on the w. back** en el viaje de regreso; **on the w. up/down** en la subida/bajada; **there's no w. through** el paso está cerrado; **you're in the w.** estás estorbando; **(get) out of the w.!** ¡quítate de en medio!; *Fig* **to get sb/sth out of the w.** desembarazarse de algn/algo; **I kept out of the w.** me mantuve a distancia; *Aut* **right of w.** prioridad *f*; **there's a wall in the w.** hay un muro en medio; **to give w.** ceder; *Aut* ceder el paso

   (**b**) *(direction)* dirección *f*; **come this w.** venga por aquí; **which w. did he go?** ¿por dónde se fue?; **that w.** por allá; **the other w. round** al revés

   (**c**) *(distance)* distancia *f*; **a long w. off** lejos; *Fig* **he'll go a long w.** llegará lejos; *Fig* **we've come a long w.** hemos hecho grandes progresos

   (**d**) **to get under w.** *(travellers, work)* ponerse en marcha; *(meeting, match)* empezar

   (**e**) *(means, method)* método *m*, manera *f*; **do it any w. you like** hazlo como quieras; **I'll do it my w.** lo haré a mi manera

   (**f**) *(manner)* modo *m*, manera *f*; **in a friendly w.** de modo amistoso; **one w. or another** de un modo o de otro; **the French w. of life** el estilo de vida francés; **the w. things are going** tal como van las cosas; **to my w. of thinking** a mi modo de ver; *Fam* **no w.!** ¡ni hablar!; **she has a w. with children** tiene un don para los niños; **by w. of** a modo de; **either w.** en

cualquier caso; **in a w.** en cierto sentido; **in many ways** desde muchos puntos de vista; **in some ways** en algunos aspectos; **in no w.** de ninguna manera

   (**g**) *(custom)* hábito *m*, costumbre *f*; **to be set in one's ways** tener costumbres arraigadas

   (**h**) *(state)* estado *m*; **leave it the w. it is** déjalo tal como está; **he is in a bad w.** está bastante mal

   (**i**) **by the w.** a propósito; **in the w. of business** en el curso de los negocios

   2 *adv Fam* mucho, muy; **it was w. off target** cayó muy desviado del blanco; **w. back in 1940** allá en 1940

waylay [weɪ'leɪ] *vt* (*pt & pp* **waylaid** [weɪ'leɪd]) (**a**) *(attack)* atacar por sorpresa (**b**) *Fig (intercept)* abordar, detener

wayside ['weɪsaɪd] *n Fig* **to fall by the w.** quedarse en el camino

wayward ['weɪwəd] *adj* rebelde; *(capricious)* caprichoso(a)

WC [dʌblju:'si:] *n* (*abbr* **water closet**) váter *m*, WC *m*

we [wiː] *pers pron* nosotros(as) *(usually omitted in Spanish, except for contrast)*

weak [wiːk] *adj* débil; *(argument, excuse)* pobre; *(team, piece of work, tea)* flojo(a)

weaken ['wiːkən] **1** *vt* debilitar; *(argument)* quitar fuerza a
   2 *vi* (**a**) debilitarse (**b**) *(concede ground)* ceder

weakling ['wiːklɪŋ] *n* enclenque *mf*

weakness ['wiːknɪs] *n* debilidad *f*; *(character flaw)* punto flaco

wealth [welθ] *n* riqueza *f*; *Fig* abundancia *f*

wealthy ['welθɪ] *adj* (**wealthier, wealthiest**) rico(a)

wean [wiːn] *vt (child)* destetar; *Fig* **to w. sb from a habit** desacostumbrar (gradualmente) a algn de un hábito

weapon ['wepən] *n* arma *f*

wear [weə(r)] **1** *vt* (*pt* **wore**; *pp* **worn**) (**a**) *(clothes)* llevar puesto, vestir; *(shoes)* llevar puestos, calzar; **he wears glasses** lleva gafas; **to w. black** vestirse de negro (**b**) *(erode)* desgastar
   2 *vi* **to w. (thin/smooth)** desgastarse (con el roce); *Fig* **my patience is wearing thin** se me está acabando la paciencia
   3 *n* (**a**) ropa *f*; **leisure w.** ropa de sport (**b**) *(use) (clothes)* uso *m* (**c**) *(deterioration)* desgaste *m*; **normal w. and tear** desgaste natural
   ▸ **wear away 1** *vt sep* erosionar
   2 *vi (stone etc)* erosionarse; *(inscription)* borrarse
   ▸ **wear down 1** *vt sep (heels)* desgastar; *Fig* **to w. sb down** vencer la resistencia de algn
   2 *vi* desgastarse
   ▸ **wear off** *vi (effect, pain)* pasar, desaparecer
   ▸ **wear out 1** *vt sep* gastar; *Fig* agotar
   2 *vi* gastarse

wearily ['wɪərɪlɪ] *adv* con cansancio
wearisome ['wɪərɪsəm] *adj* fatigoso(a)
weary ['wɪərɪ] **1** *adj* (**wearier, weariest**) (**a**) *(tired)* cansado(a) (**b**) *(fed up)* harto(a)
2 *vt* cansar
3 *vi* cansarse (**of** de)
weasel ['wi:zəl] *n* comadreja *f*
weather ['weðə(r)] **1** *n* tiempo *m*; **the w. is fine** hace buen tiempo; *Fig* **to feel under the w.** no encontrarse bien; **w. chart** mapa meteorológico; **w. forecast** parte meteorológico; **w. vane** veleta *f*
2 *vt Fig (crisis)* aguantar; *Fig* **to w. the storm** capear el temporal
weather-beaten ['weðəbi:tən] *adj* curtido(a)
weathercock ['weðəkɒk] *n* veleta *f*
weatherman ['weðəmæn] *n* hombre *m* del tiempo
weave [wi:v] **1** *n* tejido *m*
2 *vt* (*pt* **wove**; *pp* **woven**) (**a**) *Tex* tejer (**b**) *(intertwine)* entretejer (**c**) *(intrigues)* tramar
3 *vi (person, road)* zigzaguear
weaver ['wi:və(r)] *n* tejedor(a) *m,f*
web [web] *n* (**a**) *(of spider)* telaraña *f* (**b**) *(of lies)* sarta *f* (**c**) *Comput* **the W.** la Web; **w. page** página *f* web; **w. site** sitio *m* web
webbed [webd] *adj Orn* palmeado(a)
wed [wed] *vt Literary* (*pt & pp* **wed** or **wedded**) casarse con
wedding ['wedɪŋ] *n* boda *f*, casamiento *m*; **w. cake** tarta *f* nupcial; **w. day** día *m* de la boda; **w. dress** traje *m* de novia; **w. present** regalo *m* de boda; **w. ring** alianza *f*
wedge [wedʒ] **1** *n* (**a**) *(for table leg)* cuña *f*; *(for table leg)* calce *m* (**b**) *(of cake, cheese)* trozo *m* grande
2 *vt* calzar; **to be wedged tight** *(object)* estar completamente atrancado(a)
Wednesday ['wenzdɪ] *n* miércoles *m*
wee¹ [wi:] *adj esp Scot* pequeñito(a)
wee² [wi:] *Fam* **1** *n* pipí *m*
2 *vi* hacer pipí
weed [wi:d] **1** *n Bot* mala hierba
2 *vt* (**a**) *(garden)* escardar (**b**) *Fig* **to w. out** eliminar
3 *vi* escardar
weedkiller ['wi:dkɪlə(r)] *n* herbicida *m*
weedy ['wi:dɪ] *adj* (**weedier, weediest**) *Pej* debilucho(a)
week [wi:k] *n* semana *f*; **a w. (ago) today/ yesterday** hoy hace/ayer hizo una semana; **a w. today** justo dentro de una semana; **last/ next w.** la semana pasada/que viene; **once a w.** una vez por semana; **w. in, w. out** semana tras semana
weekday ['wi:kdeɪ] *n* día *m* laborable
weekend [wi:k'end] *n* fin *m* de semana
weekly ['wi:klɪ] **1** *adj* semanal
2 *adv* semanalmente; **twice w.** dos veces por semana
3 *n Press* semanario *m*
weep [wi:p] **1** *vi* (*pt & pp* **wept**) llorar; **to w.**

for sb llorar la muerte de algn
2 *vt (tears)* derramar
weeping ['wi:pɪŋ] *adj* **w. willow** sauce *m* llorón
weigh [weɪ] **1** *vt* (**a**) pesar (**b**) *Fig (consider)* ponderar (**c**) **to w. anchor** levar anclas
2 *vi* (**a**) pesar (**b**) *Fig (influence)* influir
▶ **weigh down** *vt sep* sobrecargar
▶ **weigh in** *vi* (**a**) *Sport* pesarse (**b**) *Fam (join in)* intervenir
▶ **weigh up** *vt sep (matter)* evaluar; *(person)* formar una opinión sobre; **to w. up the pros and cons** sopesar los pros y los contras
weight [weɪt] *n* (**a**) peso *m*; **to lose w.** adelgazar; **to put on w.** subir de peso; *Fam Fig* **to pull one's w.** poner de su parte (**b**) *(of clock, scales)* pesa *f* (**c**) *Fig* **that's a w. off my mind** eso me quita un peso de encima
weighting ['weɪtɪŋ] *n Br (on salary)* suplemento *m* de salario
weightlifter ['weɪtlɪftə(r)] *n* halterófilo(a) *m,f*
weighty ['weɪtɪ] *adj* (**weightier, weightiest**) pesado(a); *Fig (problem, matter)* importante, grave; *(argument)* de peso
weir [wɪə(r)] *n* presa *f*
weird [wɪəd] *adj* raro(a), extraño(a)
welcome ['welkəm] **1** *adj (person)* bienvenido(a); *(news)* grato(a); *(change)* oportuno(a); **to make sb w.** acoger a algn calurosamente; **you're w.!** ¡no hay de qué!
2 *n (greeting)* bienvenida *f*
3 *vt* acoger; *(more formally)* darle la bienvenida a; *(news)* acoger con agrado; *(decision)* aplaudir
welcoming ['welkəmɪŋ] *adj (person)* acogedor(a); *(smile)* de bienvenida
weld [weld] *vt* soldar
welfare ['welfeə(r)] *n* (**a**) *(well-being)* bienestar *m*; **animal/child w.** protección *f* de animales/de menores; **w. work** asistencia *f* social; **w. worker** asistente *mf* social (**b**) *US (social security)* seguridad *f* social
well¹ [wel] *n* (**a**) pozo *m* (**b**) *(of staircase, lift)* hueco *m* (**c**) *(of court, hall)* hemiciclo *m*
▶ **well up** *vi* brotar
well² [wel] **1** *adj* (**a**) *(healthy)* bien; **are you keeping w.?** ¿estás bien de salud?; **to get w.** reponerse (**b**) *(satisfactory)* bien; **all is w.** todo va bien; **it's just as w.** menos mal (**c**) **it is as w. to remember that** conviene recordar que
2 *adv* (**better, best**) (**a**) *(properly)* bien; **he has done w. (for himself)** ha prosperado; **the business is doing w.** el negocio marcha bien; **she did w. in the exam** el examen le fue bien; **w. done!** ¡muy bien!; **he took it w.** lo tomó a bien (**b**) *(thoroughly)* bien; **I know it only too w.** lo sé de sobra; *Culin* **w. done** muy hecho(a) (**c**) **he's w. over thirty** tiene treinta años bien cumplidos; **w. after six o'clock** mucho después de las seis (**d**) *(easily, with*

good reason) **he couldn't very w.** say no difícilmente podía decir que no; **I may w. do that** puede que haga eso (**e**) **as w.** también; **as w. as** así como; **children as w. as adults** tanto niños como adultos

3 *interj* (**a**) *(surprise)* ¡bueno!, ¡vaya!; **w. I never!** ¡no me digas! (**b**) *(agreement, interrogation, resignation)* bueno; **very w.** bueno; **w.?** ¿y bien? (**c**) *(doubt)* pues; **w., I don't know** pues no sé (**d**) *(resumption)* **w., as I was saying** pues (bien), como iba diciendo

well-behaved ['welbɪheɪvd] *adj (child)* formal, educado(a)

well-being ['welbiːɪŋ] *n* bienestar *m*

well-built ['welbɪlt] *adj (building etc)* de construcción sólida; *(person)* fornido(a)

well-earned ['welɜːnd] *adj* merecido(a)

well-educated [wel'edʊkeɪtɪd] *adj* culto(a)

well-heeled ['welhiːld] *adj Fam* adinerado(a)

well-informed ['welɪnfɔːmd] *adj* bien informado(a)

wellingtons ['welɪŋtənz] *npl* botas *fpl* de goma

well-known ['welnəʊn] *adj* (bien) conocido(a)

well-mannered ['welmænəd] *adj* educado(a)

well-meaning [wel'miːnɪŋ] *adj* bien intencionado(a)

well-off [wel'ɒf] *adj (rich)* acomodado(a)

well-read [wel'red] *adj* culto(a)

well-spoken [wel'spəʊkən] *adj* con acento culto

well-to-do [weltə'duː] *adj* acomodado(a)

well-wisher ['welwɪʃə(r)] *n* admirador(a) *m,f*

Welsh [welʃ] **1** *adj* galés(esa); **W. rarebit** = tostada con queso fundido

2 *n* (**a**) *(language)* galés *m* (**b**) **the W.** los galeses

Welshman ['welʃmən] *n* galés *m*

Welshwoman ['welʃwʊmən] *n* galesa *f*

welterweight ['weltəweɪt] *n* (peso *m*) wélter *m*

wench [wentʃ] *n Old-fashioned* moza *f*

went [went] *pt of* **go**

wept [wept] *pt & pp of* **weep**

were [wɜː(r), *unstressed* wə(r)] *pt of* **be**

west [west] **1** *n* oeste *m*, occidente *m*; **in/to the w.** al oeste; *Pol* **the W.** los países occidentales

2 *adj* del oeste, occidental; **the W. Indies** las Antillas; **W. Indian** antillano(a)

3 *adv* al oeste, hacia el oeste

westerly ['westəlɪ] *adj (wind)* del oeste

western ['westən] **1** *adj* del oeste, occidental; **W. Europe** Europa Occidental

2 *n Cin* western *m*, película *f* del oeste

westward ['westwəd] *adj* **in a w. direction** hacia el oeste

westwards ['westwədz] *adv* hacia el oeste

wet [wet] **1** *adj* (**wetter, wettest**) (**a**) mojado(a); *(slightly)* húmedo(a); **w. paint** *(sign)* recién pintado; **w. through** *(person)* calado(a) hasta los huesos; *(thing)* empapado(a); **w. suit** traje isotérmico (**b**) *(rainy)* lluvioso(a) (**c**) *Fam (person)* soso(a); **w. blanket** aguafiestas *mf inv*

2 *n Fam* apocado(a) *m,f*

3 *vt (pt & pp* **wet**) mojar; **to w. oneself** orinarse

whack [wæk] **1** *vt (hit hard)* golpear fuertemente

2 *n* (**a**) *(blow)* porrazo *m* (**b**) *Fam (share)* parte *f*, porción *f*

whale [weɪl] *n* ballena *f*

wharf [wɔːf] *n (pl* **wharves** [wɔːvz]) muelle *m*

what [wɒt, *unstressed* wət] **1** *adj* (**a**) *(direct question)* qué; **w. (sort of) bird is that?** ¿qué tipo de ave es ésa?; **w. good is that?** ¿para qué sirve eso?

(**b**) *(indirect question)* qué; **ask her w. colour she likes** pregúntale qué color le gusta

2 *pron* (**a**) *(direct question)* qué; **w. are you talking about?** ¿de qué estás hablando?; **w. about your father?** ¿y tu padre (qué)?; **w. about going tomorrow?** ¿qué te parece si vamos mañana?; **w. can I do for you?** ¿en qué puedo servirle?; **w. did it cost?** ¿cuánto costó?; **w. did you do that for?** ¿por qué hiciste eso?; **w. (did you say)?** ¿cómo?; **w. does it sound like?** ¿cómo suena?; **w. is happening?** ¿qué pasa?; **w. is it?** *(definition)* ¿qué es?; *(what's the matter)* ¿qué pasa?; **w.'s it called?** ¿cómo se llama?; **w.'s this for?** ¿para qué sirve esto?

(**b**) *(indirect question)* qué, lo que; **he asked me w. I thought** me preguntó lo que pensaba; **I didn't know w. to say** no sabía qué decir

(**c**) *(and)* **w.'s more** y además; **come w. may** pase lo que pase; **guess w.!** ¿sabes qué?; **it's just w. I need** es exactamente lo que necesito

(**d**) *(in exclamations)* **w. a goal!** ¡qué *or* vaya golazo!; **w. a lovely picture!** ¡qué cuadro más bonito!

3 *interj (surprise, indignation)* ¡cómo!; **w., no dessert!** ¿cómo, no hay postre?

whatever [wɒt'evə(r), *unstressed* wət'evə(r)] **1** *adj* (**a**) *(any)* cualquiera que; **at w. time you like** a la hora que quieras; **of w. colour** no importa de qué color (**b**) *(with negative)* **nothing w.** nada en absoluto; **with no interest w.** sin interés alguno

2 *pron* (**a**) *(what)* **w. happened?** ¿qué pasó? (**b**) *(anything, all that)* (todo) lo que; **do w. you like** haz lo que quieras (**c**) *(no matter what)* **don't tell him, w. you do** no se te ocurra decírselo; **w. (else) you find** cualquier (otra) cosa que encuentres; **he goes out w. the weather** sale haga el tiempo que haga

whatsoever [wɒtsəʊ'evə(r)] *adj* **anything w.** cualquier cosa; **nothing w.** nada en absoluto

wheat [wiːt] *n* trigo *m*; **w. germ** germen *m* de trigo

wheedle ['wiːdəl] *vt* **to w. sb into doing sth** engatusar a algn para que haga algo; **to w. sth out of sb** sonsacar algo a algn halagándole

wheel [wiːl] **1** *n* rueda *f*

  2 *vt (bicycle)* empujar

  3 *vi* (a) *(bird)* revolotear (b) **to w. round** girar sobre los talones

wheelbarrow ['wiːlbærəʊ] *n* carretilla *f*

wheelchair ['wiːltʃeə(r)] *n* silla *f* de ruedas

wheeze [wiːz] *vi* respirar con dificultad, resollar

when [wen] **1** *adv* (a) *(direct question)* cuándo; **since w.?** ¿desde cuándo?; **w. did he arrive?** ¿cuándo llegó? (b) *(indirect question)* cuándo; **tell me w. to go** dime cuándo debo irme (c) *(on which)* cuando, en que; **the days w. I work** los días en que trabajo

  2 *conj* (a) cuando; **I'll tell you w. she comes** se lo diré cuando llegue; **w. he was a boy ...** de niño ... (b) *(whenever)* cuando (c) *(given that, if)* si (d) *(although)* aunque

whence [wens] *adv Fml Literary (from where)* de dónde

whenever [wen'evə(r)] **1** *conj (when)* cuando; *(every time)* siempre que

  2 *adv* **w. that might be** sea cuando sea

where [weə(r)] *adv* (a) *(direct question)* dónde; *(direction)* adónde; **w. are you going?** ¿adónde vas?; **w. did we go wrong?** ¿en qué nos equivocamos?; **w. do you come from?** ¿de dónde es usted? (b) *(indirect question)* dónde; *(direction)* adónde; **tell me w. you went** dime adónde fuiste (c) *(at, in which)* donde; *(direction)* adonde, a donde (d) *(when)* cuando

whereabouts 1 *adv* [weərə'baʊts] **w. do you live?** ¿por dónde vives?

  2 *n* ['weərəbaʊts] paradero *m*

whereas [weər'æz] *conj* (a) *(but, while)* mientras que (b) *Jur* considerando que

whereby [weə'baɪ] *adv* por el/la/lo cual

whereupon [weərə'pɒn] *conj Fml* después de lo cual

wherever [weər'evə(r)] **1** *conj* dondequiera que; **I'll find him w. he is** le encontraré dondequiera que esté; **sit w. you like** siéntate donde quieras

  2 *adv (direct question)* adónde

wherewithal ['weəwɪðɔːl] *n Fam* pelas *fpl*

whet [wet] *vt* **to w. sb's appetite** abrir el apetito a algn

whether ['weðə(r)] *conj* (a) *(if)* si; **I don't know w. it is true** no sé si es verdad; **I doubt w. he'll win** dudo que gane (b) **w. he comes or not** venga o no

which [wɪtʃ] **1** *adj* (a) *(direct question)* qué; **w. colour do you prefer?** ¿qué color prefieres?; **w. one?** ¿cuál?; **w. way?** ¿por dónde? (b) *(indirect question)* qué; **tell me w. dress**

you like dime qué vestido te gusta

  (c) **by w. time** y para entonces; **in w. case** en cuyo caso

  2 *pron* (a) *(direct question)* cuál/cuáles; **w. of you did it?** ¿quién de vosotros lo hizo?

  (b) *(indirect question)* cuál/cuáles; **I don't know w.** I'd rather have no sé cuál prefiero

  (c) *(defining relative)* que; *(after preposition)* que, el/la cual, los/las cuales, el/la que, los/las que; **here are the books (w.) I have read** aquí están los libros que he leído; **the accident (w.) I told you about** el accidente del que te hablé; **the car in w. he was travelling** el coche en (el) que viajaba; **this is the one (w.)** I like éste es el que me gusta

  (d) *(non-defining relative)* el/la cual, los/las cuales; **I played three sets, all of w. I lost** jugué tres sets, todos los cuales perdí

  (e) *(referring to a clause)* lo cual, lo que; **he won, w. made me very happy** ganó, lo cual *or* lo que me alegró mucho

whichever [wɪtʃ'evə(r)] **1** *adj* el/la que, cualquiera que; **I'll take w. books you don't want** tomaré los libros que no quieras; **w. system you choose** cualquiera que sea el sistema que elijas

  2 *pron* el/la que

whiff [wɪf] *n* (a) *(quick smell)* ráfaga *f*; *(of air, smoke)* bocanada *f* (b) *Fam (bad smell)* tufo *m*

while [waɪl] **1** *n* (a) *(length of time)* rato *m*, tiempo *m*; **in a little w.** dentro de poco; **once in a w.** de vez en cuando (b) **it's not worth your w. staying** no merece la pena que te quedes

  2 *conj* (a) *(time)* mientras; **he fell asleep w. driving** se durmió mientras conducía (b) *(although)* aunque (c) *(whereas)* mientras que

  ▸ **while away** *vt sep* **to w. away the time** pasar el rato

whilst [waɪlst] *conj* = **while**

whim [wɪm] *n* capricho *m*, antojo *m*

whimper ['wɪmpə(r)] **1** *n* quejido *m*

  2 *vi* lloriquear

whine [waɪn] *vi* (a) *(child)* lloriquear; *(with pain)* dar quejidos (b) *(complain)* quejarse (c) *(engine)* chirriar

whip [wɪp] **1** *n* (a) *(for punishment)* látigo *m*; *(for riding)* fusta *f* (b) *Br Pol* = oficial encargado(a) de la disciplina de un partido

  2 *vt* (a) *(as punishment)* azotar; *(horse)* fustigar (b) *Culin* batir; **whipped cream** nata montada (c) *Fam (steal)* mangar

  ▸ **whip away** *vt sep* arrebatar

  ▸ **whip up** *vt sep (passions, enthusiasm)* avivar; *(support)* incrementar

whipping ['wɪpɪŋ] *n Fig* **w. boy** cabeza *f* de turco

whip-round ['wɪpraʊnd] *n Fam* colecta *f*

whir [wɜː(r)] *vi* = **whirr**

whirl [wɜːl] **1** *n* giro *m*; *Fig* torbellino *m*

2 *vt* **to w. sth round** dar vueltas a *or* hacer girar algo

3 *vi* **to w. round** girar con rapidez; *(leaves etc)* arremolinarse; **my head's whirling** me está dando vueltas la cabeza

whirlpool ['wɜːlpuːl] *n* remolino *m*

whirlwind ['wɜːlwɪnd] *n* torbellino *m*

whirr [wɜː(r)] *vi* zumbar, runrunear

whisk [wɪsk] **1** *n Culin* batidor *m*; *(electric)* batidora *f*

     2 *vt Culin* batir

▸ **whisk away, whisk off** *vt sep* quitar bruscamente, llevarse de repente

whisker ['wɪskə(r)] *n* **whiskers** *(of person)* patillas *fpl*; *(of cat)* bigotes *mpl*

whisky, *US* **whiskey** ['wɪskɪ] *n* whisky *m*

whisper ['wɪspə(r)] **1** *n* (**a**) *(sound)* susurro *m* (**b**) *(rumour)* rumor *m*

     2 *vt* decir en voz baja

     3 *vi* susurrar

whistle ['wɪsəl] **1** *n* (**a**) *(instrument)* pito *m* (**b**) *(sound)* silbido *m*, pitido *m*

     2 *vt (tune)* silbar

     3 *vi (person, kettle, wind)* silbar; *(train)* pitar

white [waɪt] **1** *adj* blanco(a); **to go w.** *(face)* palidecer; *(hair)* encanecer; **w. coffee** café *m* con leche; **w. hair** pelo cano; **a w. Christmas** una Navidad con nieve; *Fig* **a w. lie** una mentira piadosa; *US* **the W. House** la Casa Blanca; *Pol* **w. paper** libro blanco; **w. sauce** bechamel *f*

     2 *n* (**a**) *(colour, person, of eye)* blanco *m* (**b**) *(of egg)* clara *f* (**c**) **whites** ropa *f* blanca

white-collar ['waɪtkɒlə(r)] *adj* **w. worker** empleado *m* de oficina

whiteness ['waɪtnɪs] *n* blancura *f*

whitewash ['waɪtwɒʃ] **1** *n* (**a**) cal *f* (**b**) *Fig (cover-up)* encubrimiento *m* (**c**) *Fig (defeat)* paliza *f*

     2 *vt* (**a**) *(wall)* enjalbegar, blanquear (**b**) *Fig* encubrir

whiting ['waɪtɪŋ] *n (pl* **whiting**) *(fish)* pescadilla *f*

Whitsun(tide) ['wɪtsən(taɪd)] *n* pentecostés *m*

whittle ['wɪtəl] *vt* cortar en pedazos; **to w. away at** roer; *Fig* **to w. down** reducir poco a poco

whiz(z) [wɪz] *vi* (**a**) *(sound)* silbar (**b**) **to w. past** pasar volando; *Fam* **w. kid** joven *mf* dinámico(a) y emprendedor(a)

who [huː] *pron* (**a**) *(direct question)* quién/ quiénes; **w. are they?** ¿quiénes son?; **w. is it?** ¿quién es? (**b**) *(indirect question)* quién; **I don't know w. did it** no sé quién lo hizo (**c**) *rel (defining)* que; **those w. don't know** los que no saben (**d**) *rel (nondefining)* quien/ quienes, el/la cual, los/las cuales; **Elena's mother, w. is very rich ...** la madre de Elena, la cual es muy rica ...

whodun(n)it [huː'dʌnɪt] *n Fam* novela *f/*

obra *f* de teatro/película *f* de suspense

whoever [huː'evə(r)] *pron* (**a**) quienquiera que; **give it to w. you like** dáselo a quien quieras; **w. said that is a fool** el que dijo eso es un tonto; **w. you are** quienquiera que seas (**b**) *(direct question)* **w. told you that?** ¿quién te dijo eso?

whole [həʊl] **1** *adj* (**a**) *(entire)* entero(a), íntegro(a); **a w. week** una semana entera; **he took the w. lot** se los llevó todos (**b**) *(in one piece)* intacto(a)

     2 *n* (**a**) *(single unit)* todo *m*, conjunto *m*; **as a w.** en su totalidad (**b**) *(all)* totalidad *f*; **the w. of London** todo Londres (**c**) **on the w.** en general

wholefood ['həʊlfuːd] *n* alimentos *mpl* integrales

wholehearted [həʊl'hɑːtɪd] *adj (enthusiastic)* entusiasta; *(sincere)* sincero(a); *(unreserved)* incondicional

wholemeal ['həʊlmiːl] *adj Br* integral

wholesale ['həʊlseɪl] *Com* **1** *n* venta *f* al por mayor

     2 *adj* al por mayor; *Fig* total

     3 *adv* al por mayor; *Fig* en su totalidad

wholesaler ['həʊlseɪlə(r)] *n* mayorista *mf*

wholesome ['həʊlsəm] *adj* sano(a)

wholly ['həʊlɪ] *adv* enteramente, completamente

whom [huːm] *pron Fml* (**a**) *(direct question) (accusative)* a quién; **w. did you talk to?** ¿con quién hablaste?; *(after preposition)* **of/from w.?** ¿de quién?; **to w. are you referring?** ¿a quién te refieres? (**b**) *rel (accusative)* que, a quien/a quienes; **those w. I have seen** aquéllos a quien he visto (**c**) *rel (after preposition)* quien/quienes, el/la cual, los/las cuales; **my brothers, both of w. are miners** mis hermanos, que son mineros los dos

> En la actualidad, sólo aparece en contextos formales. **Whom** se puede sustituir por **who** en todos los casos salvo cuando va después de preposición.

whooping cough ['huːpɪŋkɒf] *n* tos ferina

whopping ['wɒpɪŋ] *adj Fam* enorme

whore [hɔː(r)] *n very Fam Pej* puta *f*

whose [huːz] **1** *pron* (**a**) *(direct question)* de quién/de quiénes; **w. are these gloves?** ¿de quién son estos guantes?; **w. is this?** ¿de quién es esto? (**b**) *(indirect question)* de quién/de quiénes; **I don't know w. these coats are** no sé de quién son estos abrigos (**c**) *rel* cuyo(s)/cuya(s); **the man w. children we saw** el hombre a cuyos hijos vimos

     2 *adj* **w. car/house is this?** ¿de quién es este coche/esta casa?

why [waɪ] **1** *adv* por qué; *(for what purpose)* para qué; **w. did you do that?** ¿por qué hiciste eso?; **w. not go to bed?** ¿por qué no te acuestas?; **I don't know w. he did it** no sé por qué lo hizo; **that is w. I didn't come** por eso no vine; **there's no reason w. you shouldn't go** no hay motivo para que no vayas

2 *interj* (**a**) *(fancy that!)* ¡toma!, ¡vaya!; **w., it's David!** ¡si es David! (**b**) *(protest, assertion)* sí, vamos

wick [wɪk] *n* mecha *f*

wicked ['wɪkɪd] *adj* (**a**) malvado(a) (**b**) *Fam* malísimo(a); *(temper)* de perros

wicker ['wɪkə(r)] **1** *n* mimbre *m*

2 *adj* de mimbre

wickerwork ['wɪkəwɜːk] *n (material)* mimbre *m*; *(articles)* artículos *mpl* de mimbre

wicket ['wɪkɪt] *n (in cricket) (stumps)* palos *mpl*

wide [waɪd] **1** *adj* (**a**) *(road, trousers)* ancho(a); *(gap, interval)* grande; **it is 10 m w.** tiene 10 m de ancho (**b**) *(area, knowledge, support, range)* amplio(a); **w. interests** intereses muy diversos (**c**) *(off target)* desviado(a)

2 *adv* **from far and w.** de todas partes; **to open one's eyes w.** abrir los ojos de par en par; **w. apart** muy separados(as); **w. awake** completamente despierto(a); **w. open** abierto(a) de par en par; **with mouth w. open** boquiabierto(a)

wide-angle ['waɪdæŋgəl] *adj Phot* **w. lens** objetivo *m* gran angular

widely ['waɪdlɪ] *adv (travel etc)* extensamente; *(believed)* generalmente; **he is w. known** es muy conocido

widen ['waɪdən] **1** *vt* ensanchar; *(interests)* ampliar

2 *vi* ensancharse

wide-ranging ['waɪd'reɪndʒɪŋ] *adj (interests)* muy diversos(as); *(discussion)* amplio(a); *(study)* de gran alcance

widespread ['waɪdspred] *adj (unrest, belief)* general; *(damage)* extenso(a); **to become w.** generalizarse

widow ['wɪdəʊ] *n* viuda *f*

widowed ['wɪdəʊd] *adj* enviudado(a)

widower ['wɪdəʊə(r)] *n* viudo *m*

width [wɪdθ] *n* (**a**) anchura *f* (**b**) *(of material, swimming pool)* ancho *m*

wield [wiːld] *vt (weapon)* blandir; *Fig (power)* ejercer

wife [waɪf] *n (pl wives)* mujer *f*, esposa *f*

wig [wɪg] *n* peluca *f*

wiggle ['wɪgəl] **1** *vt (finger etc)* menear; **to w. one's hips** contonearse

2 *vi* menearse

Wight [waɪt] *n* **Isle of W.** Isla *f* de Wight

wild [waɪld] **1** *adj* (**a**) *(animal, tribe)* salvaje; **w. beast** fiera *f*; *Fig* **w. goose chase** búsqueda *f* inútil

(**b**) *(plant)* silvestre

(**c**) *(landscape)* agreste; **the W. West** el Salvaje Oeste

(**d**) *(temperament, behaviour)* alocado(a); *(appearance)* desordenado(a); *(passions etc)* desenfrenado(a); *(laughter, thoughts)* loco(a); *(applause)* fervoroso(a); **to make a w. guess** adivinar al azar; *Fam Fig* **she is w. about him/about tennis** está loca por él/por el tenis

(**e**) *Br Fam Fig (angry)* furioso(a)

2 *adv Fig* **to run w.** *(children)* desmandarse

3 *n* **in the w.** en el estado salvaje; *Fig* **to live out in the wilds** vivir en el quinto pino

wildcat ['waɪldkæt] *n* **w. strike** huelga *f* salvaje

wilderness ['wɪldənɪs] *n* desierto *m*

wildfire ['waɪldfaɪə(r)] *n* **to spread like w.** correr como la pólvora

wildlife ['waɪldlaɪf] *n* fauna *f*; **w. park** parque *m* natural

wildly ['waɪldlɪ] *adv* (**a**) *(rush round etc)* como un(a) loco(a); *(shoot)* sin apuntar; *(hit out)* a tontas y a locas; **w. enthusiastic** loco(a) de entusiasmo; **w. inaccurate** totalmente erróneo(a)

wilful, *US* **wilfull** ['wɪlfʊl] *adj* (**a**) *(stubborn)* terco(a) (**b**) *Jur* premeditado(a)

will¹ [wɪl] **1** *n* (**a**) voluntad *f*, *(free will)* buena/mala voluntad; **of my own free w.** por mi propia voluntad (**b**) *Jur (testament)* testamento *m*; **to make one's w.** hacer testamento

2 *vt* fate willed that ... el destino quiso que ...

will² [wɪl] *v aux (pt would)*

En el inglés hablado, y en el escrito en estilo coloquial, el verbo **will** se contrae de manera que **I/you/he** *etc* **will** se transforman en **I'll, you'll, he'll** *etc* y el verbo **would** se contrae de manera que **I/you/he** *etc* **would** se transforman en **I'd, you'd, he'd** *etc*. Las formas negativas **will not** y **would not** se transforman en **won't** y **wouldn't**.

(**a**) *(future) (esp 2nd & 3rd person)* **they'll come** vendrán; **w. he be there? – yes, he w.** ¿estará allí? – sí(, estará); **you'll tell him, won't you?** se lo dirás, ¿verdad?; **don't forget, w. you!** ¡que no se te olvide, vale!; **she won't do it** no lo hará

(**b**) *(command)* **you w. be here at eleven!** ¡debes estar aquí a las once!

(**c**) *(future perfect)* **they'll have finished by tomorrow** habrán terminado para mañana

(**d**) *(willingness)* **be quiet, w. you! – no, I won't!** ¿quiere callarse? – no quiero; **I won't have it!** ¡no lo permito!; **w. you have a drink? – yes, I w.** ¿quiere tomar algo? – sí, por favor; **won't you sit down?** ¿quiere sentarse?

(**e**) *(custom)* **accidents w. happen** siempre habrá accidentes

(**f**) *(persistence)* **if you w. go out without a coat ...** si te empeñas en salir sin abrigo ...

(**g**) *(probability)* **he'll be on holiday now** ahora estará de vacaciones

(**h**) *(ability)* **the lift w. hold ten people** en el

ascensor caben diez personas

willing ['wɪlɪŋ] *adj (obliging)* complaciente; **I'm quite w. to do it** lo haré con mucho gusto; **to be w. to do sth** estar dispuesto(a) a hacer algo

willingly ['wɪlɪŋlɪ] *adv* de buena gana

willingness ['wɪlɪŋnɪs] *n* buena voluntad

willow ['wɪləʊ] *n* **w. (tree)** sauce *m*

willpower ['wɪlpaʊə(r)] *n* (fuerza *f* de) voluntad *f*

willy-nilly ['wɪlɪ'nɪlɪ] *adv* por gusto o por fuerza

wilt [wɪlt] *vi* marchitarse

wily ['waɪlɪ] *adj* (**wilier, wiliest**) astuto(a)

wimp [wɪmp] *n Fam (physically)* debilucho(a) *m,f*; *(lacking character)* blandengue *mf*

win [wɪn] **1** *n* victoria *f*
2 *vt (pt & pp won)* (**a**) ganar; *(prize)* llevarse; *(victory)* conseguir (**b**) *Fig (sympathy, friendship)* ganarse; *(praise)* cosechar; **to w. sb's love** conquistar a algn
3 *vi* ganar
▸ **win back** *vt sep* recuperar
▸ **win over** *vt sep (to cause, idea)* atraer (**to** a); *(voters, support)* ganarse
▸ **win through** *vi* conseguir triunfar

wince [wɪns] *vi* tener un rictus de dolor

winch [wɪntʃ] *n* cigüeña *f*, torno *m*

wind¹ [wɪnd] **1** *n* (**a**) viento *m*; *Fig* **to get w. of sth** olerse algo; **w. farm** parque eólico; **w. tunnel** túnel aerodinámico (**b**) *(breath)* aliento *m*; **to get one's second w.** recobrar el aliento (**c**) *Med* flato *m*, gases *mpl* (**d**) **w. instrument** instrumento *m* de viento
2 *vt* **to be winded** quedarse sin aliento

wind² [waɪnd] **1** *vt (pt & pp wound)* (**a**) *(on to a reel)* enrollar; **to w. a bandage round one's finger** vendarse el dedo (**b**) **to w. on/back** *(film, tape)* avanzar/rebobinar (**c**) *(clock)* dar cuerda a
2 *vi (road, river)* serpentear
▸ **wind down 1** *vt sep (window)* bajar
2 *vi Fam (person)* relajarse
▸ **wind up 1** *vt sep* (**a**) *(roll up)* enrollar (**b**) *(business etc)* cerrar; *(debate)* clausurar (**c**) *(clock)* dar cuerda a
2 *vi (meeting)* terminar

windfall ['wɪndfɔːl] *n Fig* ganancia inesperada

winding ['waɪndɪŋ] *adj (road, river)* sinuoso(a); *(staircase)* de caracol

windmill ['wɪndmɪl] *n* molino *m* (de viento)

window ['wɪndəʊ] *n* ventana *f*; *(of vehicle, ticket office etc)* ventanilla *f*; *(shop)* **w.** escaparate *m*; **to clean the windows** limpiar los cristales; **w. box** jardinera *f*; **w. cleaner** limpiacristales *mf inv*

windowpane ['wɪndəʊpeɪn] *n* cristal *m*

window-shopping ['wɪndəʊʃɒpɪŋ] *n* **to go w.** ir a mirar escaparates

windowsill ['wɪndəʊsɪl] *n* alféizar *m*

windpipe ['wɪndpaɪp] *n* tráquea *f*

windscreen ['wɪndskriːn], *US* **windshield** ['wɪndʃiːld] *n* parabrisas *m inv*; **w. washer** lavaparabrisas *m inv*; **w. wiper** limpiaparabrisas *m inv*

windswept ['wɪndswept] *adj (landscape)* expuesto(a) a los vientos; *(person, hair)* despeinado(a) (por el viento)

windy ['wɪndɪ] *adj* (**windier, windiest**) *(weather)* ventoso(a); *(place)* desprotegido(a) del viento; **it is very w. today** hoy hace mucho viento

wine [waɪn] *n* vino *m*; **w. cellar** bodega *f*; **w. list** lista *f* de vinos; **w. merchant** vinatero(a) *m,f*; **w. tasting** cata *f* de vinos; **w. vinegar** vinagre *m* de vino

wineglass ['waɪnglɑːs] *n* copa *f* (para vino)

wing [wɪŋ] *n* (**a**) *Orn & Av* ala *f* (**b**) *(of building)* ala *f* (**c**) *Aut* aleta *f*; **w. mirror** retrovisor *m* externo (**d**) *Th* (**in the**) **wings** (entre) bastidores *mpl* (**e**) *Ftb* banda *f* (**f**) *Pol* ala *f*; **the left w.** la izquierda

winger ['wɪŋə(r)] *n Ftb* extremo *m*

wink [wɪŋk] **1** *n* guiño *m*; *Fam Fig* **I didn't get a w. (of sleep)** no pegué ojo
2 *vi* (**a**) *(person)* guiñar (el ojo) (**b**) *(light)* parpadear

winner ['wɪnə(r)] *n* ganador(a) *m,f*

winning ['wɪnɪŋ] *adj (person, team)* ganador(a); *(number)* premiado(a); *(goal)* decisivo(a); **w. post** meta *f*

winnings ['wɪnɪŋz] *npl* ganancias *fpl*

winter ['wɪntə(r)] **1** *n* invierno *m*
2 *adj* de invierno; **w. sports** deportes *mpl* de invierno
3 *vi* invernar

wintry ['wɪntrɪ] *adj* (**wintrier, wintriest**) invernal

wipe [waɪp] *vt* limpiar; **to w. one's brow** enjugarse la frente; **to w. one's feet/nose** limpiarse los pies/las narices
▸ **wipe away** *vt sep (tear)* enjugar
▸ **wipe off** *vt sep* quitar frotando; **to w. sth off the blackboard/the tape** borrar algo de la pizarra/de la cinta
▸ **wipe out** *vt sep* (**a**) *(erase)* borrar (**b**) *(army)* aniquilar; *(species etc)* exterminar
▸ **wipe up** *vt sep* limpiar

wire [waɪə(r)] **1** *n* (**a**) alambre *m*; *Elec* cable *m*; *Tel* hilo; **w. cutters** cizalla *f* (**b**) *(telegram)* telegrama *m*
2 *vt* (**a**) **to w. (up) a house** poner la instalación eléctrica de una casa; **to w. (up) an appliance to the mains** conectar un aparato a la toma eléctrica (**b**) *(information)* enviar por telegrama

wireless ['waɪəlɪs] *n* radio *f*

wiring ['waɪərɪŋ] *n (network)* cableado *m*; *(action)* instalación *f* del cableado

wiry ['waɪərɪ] *adj* (**wirier, wiriest**) *(hair)* estropajoso(a); *(person)* nervudo(a)

wisdom ['wɪzdəm] *n* (**a**) *(learning)* sabiduría

f, saber m (**b**) (good sense) (of person) cordura f; (of action) sensatez f (**c**) **w. tooth** muela f del juicio

wise [waɪz] adj (**a**) sabio(a); **a w. man** un sabio; **the Three W. Men** los Reyes Magos (**b**) (remark) juicioso(a); (decision) acertado(a); **it would be w. to keep quiet** sería prudente callarse

wisecrack ['waɪzkræk] n Fam salida f, ocurrencia f

wisely ['waɪzlɪ] adv (with prudence) prudentemente

wish [wɪʃ] **1** n (**a**) (desire) deseo m (**for** de); **to make a w.** pedir un deseo

(**b**) best wishes felicitaciones fpl; **give your mother my best wishes** salude a su madre de mi parte; **with best wishes, Peter** (at end of letter) saludos cordiales, Peter

2 vt (**a**) (want) querer, desear; **I w. I could stay longer** me gustaría poder quedarme más tiempo; **I w. you had told me!** ¡ojalá me lo hubieras dicho!; **to w. to do sth** querer hacer algo

(**b**) **to w. sb goodnight** darle las buenas noches a algn; **to w. sb well** desearle a algn mucha suerte

3 vi (want) desear; **as you w.** como quieras; **do as you w.** haga lo que quiera; **to w. for sth** desear algo

wishful ['wɪʃfʊl] adj **it's w. thinking** es hacerse ilusiones

wishy-washy ['wɪʃɪ'wɒʃɪ] adj Fam (person) soso(a); (ideas) poco definido(a)

wisp [wɪsp] n (of wool, hair) mechón m; (of smoke) voluta f

wistful ['wɪstfʊl] adj melancólico(a)

wit [wɪt] n (**a**) (intelligence) (often pl) inteligencia f, Fig **to be at one's wits' end** estar para volverse loco(a); Fam Fig **to have one's wits about one** ser despabilado(a) (**b**) (humour) ingenio m (**c**) (person) ingenioso(a) m,f

witch [wɪtʃ] n bruja f, Fig **w. hunt** caza f de brujas

witchcraft ['wɪtʃkrɑːft] n brujería f

with [wɪð, wɪθ] prep con; **a room w. a bath** un cuarto con baño; **do you have any money w. you?** ¿traes dinero?; **the man w. the glasses** el hombre de las gafas; **he went w. me/you** fue conmigo/contigo; Fam **w. (sugar) or without (sugar)?** ¿con o sin azúcar?; **I have six w. this one** con éste tengo seis; **w. all his faults, I admire him** le admiro con todos sus defectos; **w. your permission** con su permiso; **we're all w. you** (support) todos estamos contigo; **you're not w. me, are you?** (understand) no me entiendes, ¿verdad?; **he's w. Lloyds** trabaja para Lloyds; **she is popular w. her colleagues** todos sus colegas la estiman mucho; **to fill a vase w. water** llenar un jarrón de agua; **it is made w. butter** está hecho con mantequilla; **she put on weight w. so much eating** engordó de tanto comer;

to be paralysed w. fear estar paralizado(a) de miedo; **w. experience** con la experiencia

withdraw [wɪð'drɔː] **1** vt (pt **withdrew**; pp **withdrawn**) (**a**) retirar, sacar; **to w. money from the bank** sacar dinero del banco (**b**) (go back on) retirar; (statement) retractarse de; (plan, claim) renunciar a

2 vi (**a**) retirarse (**b**) (drop out) renunciar

withdrawal [wɪð'drɔːəl] n retirada f; (of statement) retractación f; (of complaint, plan) renuncia f; **w. symptoms** síndrome m de abstinencia

withdrawn [wɪð'drɔːn] **1** adj (person) introvertido(a)

2 pp of **withdraw**

withdrew [wɪð'druː] pt of **withdraw**

wither ['wɪðə(r)] vi marchitarse

withering ['wɪðərɪŋ] adj (look) fulminante; (criticism) mordaz

withhold [wɪð'həʊld] vt (pt & pp **withheld** [wɪð'held]) (money) retener; (decision) aplazar; (consent) negar; (information) ocultar

within [wɪ'ðɪn] **1** prep (**a**) (inside) dentro de (**b**) (range) **the house is w. walking distance** se puede ir andando a la casa; **situated w. 5 km of the town** situado(a) a menos de 5 km de la ciudad; **w. sight of the sea** con vistas al mar; Fig **w. an inch of death** a dos dedos de la muerte (**c**) (time) **they arrived w. a few days of each other** llegaron con pocos días de diferencia; **w. the hour** dentro de una hora; **w. the next five years** durante los cinco próximos años

2 adv dentro; **from w.** desde dentro

with-it ['wɪðɪt] adj Fam **she is very w.** tiene ideas muy modernas; **to get w.** ponerse de moda

without [wɪ'ðaʊt] prep sin; **he did it w. my knowing** lo hizo sin que lo supiera yo; Fig **to do** or **go w. sth** (voluntarily) prescindir de algo; (forcibly) pasar(se) sin algo

withstand [wɪð'stænd] vt (pt & pp **withstood** [wɪð'stʊd]) resistir a; (pain) aguantar

witness ['wɪtnɪs] **1** n (**a**) (person) testigo mf; **w. box**, US **w. stand** barra f de los testigos (**b**) (evidence) **to bear w. to sth** dar fe de algo

2 vt (**a**) (see) presenciar, ser testigo de (**b**) Fig (notice) notar (**c**) Jur **to w. a document** firmar un documento como testigo

witticism ['wɪtɪsɪzəm] n ocurrencia f, salida f

witty ['wɪtɪ] adj (**wittier**, **wittiest**) ingenioso(a), agudo(a)

wives [waɪvz] pl of **wife**

wizard ['wɪzəd] n hechicero m, mago m

wizened ['wɪzənd] adj (face) arrugado(a)

wobble ['wɒbəl] vi (table, ladder etc) tambalearse; (jelly) temblar

woe [wəʊ] n Literary infortunio m; **w. betide you if I catch you!** ¡ay de ti si te cojo!

woeful ['wəʊfʊl] adj (**a**) (person) afligido(a) (**b**) (sight) penoso(a); **w. ignorance** una ignorancia lamentable

woke [wəʊk] *pt of* **wake**

woken ['wəʊkən] *pp of* **wake**

wolf [wʊlf] *n (pl* wolves [wʊlvz]) lobo *m; Fig* **a w. in sheep's clothing** un lobo con piel de cordero

woman ['wʊmən] *n (pl* women) mujer *f;* **old w.** vieja *f; Fam* **women's libber** feminista *mf; Fam* **women's lib** movimiento *m* feminista; **women's rights** derechos *mpl* de la mujer

womanhood ['wʊmənhʊd] *n (adult)* edad adulta de la mujer

womanizer ['wʊmənaɪzə(r)] *n* mujeriego *m*

womanly ['wʊmənlɪ] *adj* femenino(a)

womb [wuːm] *n* matriz *f,* útero *m*

women ['wɪmɪn] *pl of* **woman**

won [wʌn] *pt & pp of* **win**

wonder ['wʌndə(r)] **1** *n* (**a**) *(miracle)* milagro *m;* **no w. he hasn't come** no es de extrañar que no haya venido (**b**) *(amazement)* admiración *f,* asombro *m*

2 *vt* (**a**) *(be surprised)* sorprenderse (**b**) *(ask oneself)* preguntarse; **I w. why** ¿por qué será?

3 *vi* (**a**) *(marvel)* maravillarse; **to w. at sth** admirarse de algo (**b**) *(reflect)* te da qué pensar

wonderful ['wʌndəfʊl] *adj* maravilloso(a)

wonderfully ['wʌndəfʊlɪ] *adv* maravillosamente

wont [wəʊnt] *Fml* **1** *adj* **to be w. to** soler

2 *n* costumbre; **it is his w. to ...** tiene la costumbre de ...

woo [wuː] *vt Literary (court)* cortejar; *Fig* intentar congraciarse con

wood [wʊd] *n* (**a**) *(forest)* bosque *m* (**b**) *(material)* madera *f;* (*for fire*) leña *f; Fam Fig* **touch w.!** ¡toca madera! (**c**) *(in golf)* palo *m* de madera (**d**) *(bowling)* bola *f*

woodcarving ['wʊdkɑːvɪŋ] *n* (**a**) *(craft)* tallado *m* en madera (**b**) *(object)* talla *f* en madera

woodcutter ['wʊdkʌtə(r)] *n* leñador(a) *m,f*

wooded ['wʊdɪd] *adj* arbolado(a)

wooden ['wʊdən] *adj* (**a**) de madera; **w. spoon/leg** cuchara *f/*pata *f* de palo (**b**) *(acting)* sin expresión

woodlouse ['wʊdlaʊs] *n* cochinilla *f*

woodpecker ['wʊdpekə(r)] *n* pájaro carpintero

woodwind ['wʊdwɪnd] *n* **w. (instruments)** instrumentos *mpl* de viento de madera

woodwork ['wʊdwɜːk] *n* (**a**) *(craft)* carpintería *f* (**b**) *(of building)* maderaje *m*

woodworm ['wʊdwɜːm] *n* carcoma *f*

wool [wʊl] **1** *n* lana *f; Fig* **to pull the w. over sb's eyes** dar gato por liebre a algn

2 *adj* de lana

woollen, *US* **woolen** ['wʊlən] **1** *adj* (**a**) de lana (**b**) *(industry)* lanero(a)

2 *npl* **woollens** géneros *mpl* de lana o de punto

woolly, *US* **wooly** ['wʊlɪ] *adj* (**woollier, woolliest,** *US* **woolier, wooliest**) (**a**) *(made*

of wool) de lana (**b**) *Fig (unclear)* confuso(a)

word [wɜːd] **1** *n* (**a**) *(spoken, written)* palabra *f;* **in other words ...** es decir ..., o sea ...; **words failed me** me quedé sin habla; *Fig* **a w. of advice** un consejo; *Fig* **I'd like a w. with you** quiero hablar contigo un momento; *Fig* **she didn't say it in so many words** no lo dijo de modo tan explícito; **in the words of the poet ...** como dice el poeta ...; *Fig* **w. for w.** palabra por palabra; **w. processing** tratamiento *m* de textos; **w. processor** procesador *m* de textos

(**b**) *Fig (message)* mensaje *m;* **by w. of mouth** de palabra; **is there any w. from him?** ¿hay noticias de él?; **to send w.** mandar recado

(**c**) *Fig (rumour)* voz *f,* rumor *m*

(**d**) *Fig (promise)* palabra *f;* **he's a man of his w.** es hombre de palabra

2 *vt (express)* formular; **a badly worded letter** una carta mal redactada

wording ['wɜːdɪŋ] *n* expresión *f;* **I changed the w. slightly** cambié algunas palabras

word-perfect [wɜːd'pɜːfekt] *adj* **to be w.** saberse el papel perfectamente

wore [wɔː(r)] *pt of* **wear**

work [wɜːk] **1** *n* (**a**) trabajo *m;* **his w. in the field of physics** su labor en el campo de la física; **it's hard w.** cuesta trabajo

(**b**) *(employment)* trabajo *m,* empleo *m;* **out of w.** parado(a)

(**c**) *(action)* obra *f,* acción *f;* **keep up the good w.!** ¡que siga así!

(**d**) **a piece of w.** un trabajo; **a w. of art** una obra de arte

(**e**) **works** obras *fpl;* **public works** obras (públicas)

(**f**) **works** *(machinery)* mecanismo *m*

(**g**) *Br* **works** *(factory)* fábrica *f*

2 *vt* (**a**) *(drive)* hacer trabajar; **to w. one's way up/down** subir/bajar a duras penas; *Fig* **to w. one's way up in a firm** trabajarse el ascenso en una empresa

(**b**) *(machine)* manejar; *(mechanism)* accionar

(**c**) *(miracles, changes)* operar, hacer

(**d**) *(land)* cultivar; *(mine)* explotar

(**e**) *(wood, metal etc)* trabajar

3 *vi* (**a**) trabajar (**on** *or* **at** en); **to w. as a gardener** trabajar de jardinero

(**b**) *(machine)* funcionar; **it works on gas** funciona con gas

(**c**) *(drug)* surtir efecto; *(system)* funcionar bien; *(plan, trick)* salir bien

(**d**) *(operate)* obrar; **to w. loose** soltarse; **we have no data to w. on** no tenemos datos en que basarnos

▸ **work off** *vt sep (fat)* eliminar trabajando; *(anger)* desahogar

▸ **work out 1** *vt sep* (**a**) *(plan)* idear; *(itinerary)* planear; *(details)* desarrollar (**b**) *(problem)* solucionar; *(solution)* encontrar; *(amount)*

calcular; **I can't w. out how he did it** no me explico cómo lo hizo

2 *vi* (**a**) **things didn't w. out for her** las cosas no le salieron bien (**b**) **it works out at five each** sale a cinco cada uno (**c**) *Sport* hacer ejercicio

▸ **work through** *vi* penetrar (**to** hasta)

▸ **work up** *vt sep* (*excite*) acalorar; **to get worked up** excitarse; **to w. up enthusiasm (for)** entusiasmarse (con)

workable [ˈwɜːkəbəl] *adj* factible

workaholic [wɜːkəˈhɒlɪk] *n Fam* trabajadicto(a) *m,f*

workbench [ˈwɜːkbentʃ] *n* obrador *m*

worker [ˈwɜːkə(r)] *n* trabajador(a) *m,f*; (*manual*) obrero(a) *m,f*

workforce [ˈwɜːkfɔːs] *n* mano *f* de obra

working [ˈwɜːkɪŋ] **1** *adj* (**a**) (*population, capital*) activo(a); **w. class** clase obrera; **w. man** obrero *m* (**b**) (*clothes, conditions, hours*) de trabajo; **w. day** día *m* laborable; (*number of hours*) jornada *f* laboral (**c**) **it is in w. order** funciona (**d**) (*majority*) suficiente; **w. knowledge** conocimientos básicos

2 *n* **workings** (*mechanics*) funcionamiento *m*; *Min* explotación *f*

workman [ˈwɜːkmən] *n* (*manual*) obrero *m*

workmanship [ˈwɜːkmənʃɪp] *n* (*appearance*) acabado *m*; (*skill*) habilidad *f*, arte *m*; **a fine piece of w.** un trabajo excelente

workmate [ˈwɜːkmeɪt] *n* compañero(a) *m,f* de trabajo

work-out [ˈwɜːkaʊt] *n* entrenamiento *m*

worksheet [ˈwɜːkʃiːt] *n* plan *m* de trabajo

workshop [ˈwɜːkʃɒp] *n* taller *m*

worktop [ˈwɜːktɒp] *n* encimera *f*

work-to-rule [ˈwɜːktəˈruːl] *n* huelga *f* de celo

world [wɜːld] *n* mundo *m*; **all over the w.** en todo el mundo; **the best in the w.** el mejor del mundo; *Fig* **there is a w. of difference between A and B** hay un mundo de diferencia entre A y B; *Fig* **to feel on top of the w.** sentirse fenomenal; *Fig* **to think the w. of sb** adorar a algn; *Fam Fig* **it is out of this w.** es una maravilla; **the W. Bank** el Banco Mundial; *Ftb* **the W. Cup** los Mundiales; **w. record** récord *m* mundial; **w. war** guerra *f* mundial

world-class [ˈwɜːldˈklɑːs] *adj* de categoría mundial

world-famous [ˈwɜːldˈfeɪməs] *adj* de fama mundial

worldly [ˈwɜːldlɪ] *adj* mundano(a)

worldwide [ˈwɜːldwaɪd] *adj* mundial

worm [wɜːm] **1** *n* (**a**) (*earth*) gusano *m*; (**earth**) *m*; lombriz *f* (**b**) *Med* **worms** lombrices *fpl*

2 *vt* **to w. a secret out of sb** sonsacarle un secreto a algn

worn [wɔːn] **1** *adj* gastado(a), usado(a)

2 *pp* of **wear**

worn-out [ˈwɔːnaʊt] *adj* (*thing*) gastado(a); (*person*) rendido(a), agotado(a)

worried [ˈwʌrɪd] *adj* inquieto(a), preocupado(a)

worry [ˈwʌrɪ] **1** *vt* (**a**) preocupar, inquietar; **it doesn't w. me** me trae sin cuidado (**b**) (*pester*) molestar

2 *vi* preocuparse (**about** por); **don't w.** no te preocupes

3 *n* (*state*) inquietud *f*; (*cause*) preocupación *f*

worrying [ˈwʌrɪɪŋ] *adj* inquietante, preocupante

worse [wɜːs] **1** *adj* (*comp of* **bad**) peor; **he gets w. and w.** va de mal en peor; **to get w.** empeorar; *Fam* **w. luck!** ¡mala suerte!

2 *n* **a change for the w.** un empeoramiento; *Fig* **to take a turn for the w.** empeorar

3 *adv* (*comp of* **badly**) peor; **w. than ever** peor que nunca

worship [ˈwɜːʃɪp] **1** *vt* adorar

2 *n* (**a**) adoración *f* (**b**) (*ceremony*) culto *m* (**c**) *Br* **his W. the Mayor** el señor alcalde; *Jur* **your W.** señoría

worshipper [ˈwɜːʃɪpə(r)] *n* devoto(a) *m,f*

worst [wɜːst] **1** *adj* (*superl of* **bad**) peor; **the w. part about it is that ...** lo peor es que ...

2 *n* (**a**) (*person*) el/la peor, los/las peores (**b**) **the w. of the storm is over** ya ha pasado lo peor de la tormenta

3 *adv* (*superl of* **badly**) peor; *Fig* **to come off w.** salir perdiendo

worth [wɜːθ] **1** *adj* (**a**) **to be w. £3** valer 3 libras; **a house w. £50,000** una casa que vale 50.000 libras (**b**) (*deserving of*) merecedor(a) de; **a book w. reading** un libro que merece la pena leer; **for what it's w.** por si sirve de algo; **it's w. your while, it's w. it** vale *or* merece la pena; **it's w. mentioning** es digno de mención

2 *n* (**a**) (*in money*) valor *m*; **£5 w. of petrol** gasolina por valor de 5 libras (**b**) (*of person*) valía *f*

worthless [ˈwɜːθlɪs] *adj* sin valor; (*person*) despreciable

worthwhile [wɜːθˈwaɪl] *adj* valioso(a), que vale la pena

worthy [ˈwɜːðɪ] *adj* (**worthier, worthiest**) (**a**) (*deserving*) digno(a) (**of** de); (*winner, cause*) justo(a) (**b**) (*citizen*) respetable; (*effort, motives, action*) loable

would [wʊd, *unstressed* wəd] *v aux* (**a**) (*conditional*) **I w. go if I had time** iría si tuviera tiempo; **he w. have won but for that** habría ganado su no hubiera sido por eso; **we w. if we could** lo haríamos si pudieramos; **you w. have to choose me!** ¡tenías que elegirme precisamente a mí!

(**b**) (*reported speech*) **he said that he w. come** dijo que vendría

(**c**) (*willingness*) **the car wouldn't start** el coche no arrancaba; **they asked him to come but he wouldn't** le invitaron a venir pero no quiso; **w. you do me a favour?** ¿quiere hacerme un favor?

(**d**) *(wishing)* **he w. like to know why** quisiera saber por qué; **I'd rather go home** preferiría ir a casa; **w. you like a cigarette?** ¿quiere un cigarrillo?

(**e**) *(custom)* **we w. go for walks** solíamos dar un paseo

(**f**) **try as I w.** por mucho que lo intentara

(**g**) *(conjecture)* **it w. have been about three weeks ago** debe haber sido hace unas tres semanas; **w. this be your cousin?** ¿será éste tu primo?

(**h**) *(expectation)* **so it w. appear** según parece

would-be ['wʊdbiː] *adj* en potencia; **a w. politician** un aspirante a político; *Pej* **a w. poet** un supuesto poeta

wound¹ [waʊnd] *pt & pp of* **wind**²

wound² [wuːnd] **1** *n* herida *f*
2 *vt* herir

wove [wəʊv] *pt of* **weave**

woven ['wəʊvən] *pp of* **weave**

wow [waʊ] *Fam* **1** *vt* encandilar
2 *interj* ¡caramba!

WP *n* (**a**) *(abbr* **word processor)** procesador *m* de textos (**b**) *(abbr* **word processing)** tratamiento *m* de textos

wrangle ['ræŋɡəl] **1** *n* disputa *f*
2 *vi* disputar (**over** por)

wrap [ræp] **1** *vt* **to w. (up)** envolver; **he wrapped his arms around her** la estrechó entre sus brazos; *Fam* **we wrapped up the deal** concluimos el negocio
2 *vi Fam* **w. up well** abrígate
3 *n (shawl)* chal *m; (cape)* capa *f*

wrapper ['ræpə(r)] *n (of sweet)* envoltorio *m; (of book)* sobrecubierta *f*

wrapping ['ræpɪŋ] *n* **w. paper** papel *m* de envolver

wreath [riːθ] *n (pl* **wreaths** [riːðz, riːθs]) *(of flowers)* corona *f;* **laurel w.** corona de laurel

wreck [rek] **1** *n* (**a**) *Naut* naufragio *m; (ship)* barco naufragado (**b**) *(of car, plane)* restos *mpl; (of building)* ruinas *fpl* (**c**) *Fig (person)* ruina *f*
2 *vt* (**a**) *(ship)* hacer naufragar (**b**) *(car, machine)* destrozar (**c**) *Fig (health, life)* arruinar; *(plans, hopes)* desbaratar; *(chances)* echar a perder

wreckage ['rekɪdʒ] *n (of ship, car, plane)* restos *mpl; (of building)* ruinas *fpl*

wren [ren] *n* chochín *m*

wrench [rentʃ] **1** *n* (**a**) *(pull)* tirón *m* (**b**) *Med* torcedura *f* (**c**) *(tool) Br* llave inglesa; *US* llave f
2 *vt* **to w. oneself free** soltarse de un tirón; **to w. sth off sb** arrebatarle algo a algn; **to w. sth off/open** quitar/abrir algo de un tirón

wrestle ['resəl] *vi* luchar

wrestler ['reslə(r)] *n* luchador(a) *m,f*

wrestling ['reslɪŋ] *n* lucha *f*

wretch [retʃ] *n (poor)* **w.** desgraciado(a) *m,f*

wretched ['retʃɪd] *adj* (**a**) desdichado(a); *(conditions)* deplorable; *Fam (bad, poor)*

horrible (**b**) **I feel w.** *(ill)* me siento fatal (**c**) *(contemptible)* despreciable (**d**) *Fam (damned)* maldito(a), condenado(a)

wriggle ['rɪɡəl] **1** *vt* menear
2 *vi* **to w. (about)** *(worm)* serpentear; *(restless child)* moverse nerviosamente; **to w. free** escapar deslizándose

wring [rɪŋ] *vt (pt & pp* **wrung)** (**a**) *(clothes)* escurrir; *(hands)* retorcer (**b**) *Fig (extract)* arrancar, sacar

wringing ['rɪŋɪŋ] *adj* **to be w. wet** estar empapado(a)

wrinkle ['rɪŋkəl] **1** *n* arruga *f*
2 *vt* arrugar
3 *vi* arrugarse

wrist [rɪst] *n* muñeca *f*

wristwatch ['rɪstwɒtʃ] *n* reloj *m* de pulsera

writ [rɪt] *n* orden *f* judicial

write [raɪt] **1** *vt (pt* **wrote;** *pp* **written)** escribir; *(article)* redactar; *(cheque)* extender
2 *vi* escribir (**about** sobre); **to w. for a paper** colaborar en un periódico
▸ **write back** *vi* contestar
▸ **write down** *vt sep* poner por escrito; *(note)* apuntar
▸ **write in** *vi* escribir
▸ **write off** **1** *vt sep (debt)* condonar; *(car)* destrozar
2 *vi* **to w. off for sth** pedir algo por escrito
▸ **write out** *vt sep (cheque, recipe)* extender
▸ **write up** *vt sep (notes)* redactar; *(diary, journal)* poner al día

write-off ['raɪtɒf] *n* **the car's a w.** el coche está hecho una ruina

writer ['raɪtə(r)] *n (by profession)* escritor(a) *m,f; (of book, letter)* autor(a) *m,f*

writhe [raɪð] *vi* retorcerse

writing ['raɪtɪŋ] *n* (**a**) *(script)* escritura *f; (handwriting)* letra *f;* **in w.** por escrito (**b**) **writings** *mpl* (**c**) *(action)* escritura *f;* **w. desk** escritorio *m*

written ['rɪtən] *pp of* **write**

wrong [rɒŋ] **1** *adj* (**a**) *(person)* equivocado(a); **I was w. about that boy** me equivoqué con ese chico; **to be w.** no tener razón; **you're w. in thinking that ...** te equivocas si piensas que ...
(**b**) *(answer, way)* incorrecto(a), equivocado(a); **my watch is w.** mi reloj anda mal; **to drive on the w. side of the road** conducir por el lado contrario de la carretera; **to go the w. way** equivocarse de camino; *Tel* **I've got the w. number** me he confundido de número
(**c**) *(unsuitable)* impropio(a), inadecuado(a); *(time)* inoportuno(a); **to say the w. thing** decir algo inoportuno
(**d**) *(immoral etc)* malo(a); **there's nothing w. in that** no hay nada malo en ello; **what's w. with smoking?** ¿qué tiene de malo fumar?
(**e**) **is anything w.?** ¿pasa algo?; **something's w.** hay algo que no está bien; **what's w.?** ¿qué pasa?; **what's w. with you?**

¿qué te pasa?

2 *adv* mal, incorrectamente; **to get it w.** equivocarse; *Fam* **to go w.** *(plan)* fallar, salir mal

3 *n* (**a**) *(evil, bad action)* mal *m*; **you did w. to hit him** hiciste mal en pegarle

(**b**) *(injustice)* injusticia *f*; *(offence)* agravio *m*; **the rights and wrongs of a matter** lo justo y lo injusto de un asunto

(**c**) **to be in the w.** *(be to blame)* tener la culpa

4 *vt (treat unfairly)* ser injusto(a) con; *(offend)* agraviar

wrongdoing ['rɒŋduːɪŋ] *n* maldad *f*

wrongful ['rɒŋfʊl] *adj* injusto(a)

wrongly ['rɒŋlɪ] *adv* (**a**) *(incorrectly)* incorrectamente (**b**) *(mistakenly)* equivocadamente (**c**) *(unjustly)* injustamente

wrote [rəʊt] *pt of* **write**

wrung [rʌŋ] *pt & pp of* **wring**

wry [raɪ] *adj* (**wrier, wriest** *or* **wryer, wryest**) sardónico(a)

(**e**) *(object) (polite use) (singular) (before verb)* le; *(after preposition)* usted; *(pl) (before verb)* les; *(after preposition)* ustedes; **I saw y.** le vi/les vi; **it's for y.** es para usted/es para ustedes; **with y.** con usted/con ustedes
(**f**) *(object) (impers use)* **alcohol makes y. drunk** el alcohol emborracha

> In Spanish, the formal form **usted** takes a third person singular verb, and **ustedes** takes a third person plural verb. In many Latin American countries, **ustedes** is the standard form of the second person plural *(vosotros)* and is not considered formal. Note also that in some of those countries **usted** is used in the second person singular **(tú)**, and is likewise not considered formal.

young [jʌŋ] **1** *adj (age)* joven; *(brother etc)* pequeño(a); **y. lady** señorita *f*; **y. man** joven *m*
2 *npl* (**a**) *(people)* **the y.** los jóvenes, la juventud (**b**) *(animals)* crías *fpl*
youngster [ˈjʌŋstə(r)] *n* muchacho(a) *m,f*
your [jɔː(r), *unstressed* jə(r)] *poss adj* (**a**) *(familiar use) (singular)* tu/tus; *(pl)* vuestro(a)/vuestros (**b**) *(polite use)* su/sus (**c**) *(impers use)* **the house is on y. right** la casa queda a la derecha; **they clean y. shoes for you** te limpian los zapatos (**d**) *(formal address)* Su; **Y. Majesty** Su Majestad
yours [jɔːz] *poss pron* (**a**) *(familiar use) (singular)* el tuyo/la tuya/los tuyos/las tuyas; *(pl)* el vuestro/la vuestra/los vuestros/las vuestras; **the house is y.** la casa es tuya (**b**) *(polite use) (singular)* el suyo/la suya; *(pl)* los suyos/las suyas; **the house is y.** la casa es suya (**c**) *(in letters)* **y. faithfully** le(s) saluda atentamente; **y. sincerely** reciba un cordial saludo de

> In Spanish, the forms **tuyo(a)**, **suyo(a)** and **vuestro(a)** require a definite article in the singular and in the plural when they are the subject of the phrase.

yourself [jɔːˈself, *unstressed* jəˈself] *(pl* **yourselves** [jɔːˈselvz]) **1** *pers pron* (**a**) *(familiar use) (singular)* tú mismo(a); *(pl)* vosotros(as) mismos(as); **by y.** (tú) solo; **by yourselves** vosotros(as) solos(as) (**b**) *(polite use) (singular)* usted mismo(a); *(pl)* ustedes mismos(as); **by y.** (usted) solo(a); **by yourselves** (ustedes) solos(as)
2 *reflexive pron* (**a**) *(familiar use) (singular)* te; *(pl) (familiar use)* os; **enjoy y.!** ¡diviértete!; **enjoy yourselves!** ¡divertíos! (**b**) *(polite use)* se; **enjoy y.!** ¡diviértase!; **enjoy yourselves!** ¡diviértanse!

> In many Latin American countries, **se/ustedes** is the standard form of the second person plural and is not considered formal.

youth [juːθ] *n* (**a**) juventud *f* (**b**) *(young man)* joven *m*; **y. club** club *m* juvenil; **y. hostel** albergue *m* juvenil
youthful [ˈjuːθful] *adj* juvenil, joven
Yugoslav [ˈjuːgəʊslɑːv] *adj & n* yugoslavo(a) *(m,f)*
Yugoslavia [juːgəʊˈslɑːvɪə] *n* Yugoslavia
Yugoslavian [juːgəʊˈslɑːvɪən] *adj & n* yugoslavo(a) *(m,f)*
YWCA [ˈwaɪdʌbəljuːsiːˈeɪ] *n (abbr* **Young Women's Christian Association**) ACJ *f*, Asociación *f* Cristiana de Jóvenes *(que regenta hostales económicos)*

Z, z [zed, *US* ziː] *n (the letter)* Z, z *f*
zany [ˈzeɪnɪ] *adj* (**zanier, zaniest**) *Fam* (**a**) *(mad)* chiflado(a) (**b**) *(eccentric)* estrafalario(a)
zap [zæp] **1** *interj* ¡zas!
2 *vt Fam* (**a**) *(hit)* pegar a (**b**) *(kill)* cargarse a
3 *vi TV* hacer zapping
zeal [ziːl] *n (enthusiasm)* entusiasmo *m*
zealous [ˈzeləs] *adj (enthusiastic)* entusiasta
zebra [ˈziːbrə, ˈzebrə] *n* cebra *f*; *Br* **z. crossing** paso *m* de cebra
zenith [ˈzenɪθ] *n Astron* cenit *m*; *Fig* apogeo *m*
zero [ˈzɪərəʊ] *n* cero *m*; **z. hour** hora *f* cero
zest [zest] *n (eagerness)* entusiasmo *m*
zigzag [ˈzɪgzæg] **1** *n* zigzag *m*
2 *vi* zigzaguear
Zimbabwe [zɪmˈbɑːbweɪ] *n* Zimbabue
zinc [zɪŋk] *n* cinc *m*, zinc *m*
zip [zɪp] **1** *n* (**a**) *Br* **z. (fastener)** cremallera *f* (**b**) *Fam* brío *m*; *US* **z. code** código *m* postal
2 *vi* cerrarse con cremallera
▸ **zip by** *vi* pasar como un rayo
▸ **zip up** *vt sep* cerrar con cremallera; **to z. sb up** cerrar la cremallera a algn
zipper [ˈzɪpə(r)] *n US* cremallera *f*
zodiac [ˈzəʊdɪæk] *n* zodiaco *m*, zodíaco *m*
zombie [ˈzɒmbɪ] *n* zombie *mf*
zone [zəʊn] **1** *n* zona *f*
2 *vt* dividir en zonas
zoo [zuː] *n* zoo *m*
zoological [zuːəˈlɒdʒɪkəl] *adj* zoológico(a)
zoologist [zuːˈɒlədʒɪst] *n* zoólogo(a) *m,f*
zoology [zuːˈɒlədʒɪ] *n* zoología *f*
zoom [zuːm] **1** *n* (**a**) *(buzz)* zumbido *m* (**b**) **z. lens** zoom *m*, teleobjetivo *m*
2 *vi* (**a**) *(buzz)* zumbar (**b**) **to z. past** pasar volando
▸ **zoom in** *vi (camera)* acercarse rápidamente
zucchini [zuːˈkiːnɪ] *n US* calabacín *m*, *CSur* zapallito *m*
Zulu [ˈzuːluː] *adj & n* zulú *(mf)*

XYZ

xenophobia [zenə'fəʊbɪə] *n* xenofobia *f*

Xerox® ['zɪərɒks] **1** *n* fotocopia *f*, xerocopia *f*
2 *vt* fotocopiar

Xmas ['krɪsməs, 'eksməs] *n* (*abbr* **Christmas**) Navidad *f*

X-ray ['eksreɪ] **1** *n* (*radiation*) rayo *m* X; (*picture*) radiografía *f*; **to have an X.** hacerse una radiografía
2 *vt* radiografiar

Y, y [waɪ] *n* (*the letter*) Y, y *f*

yacht [jɒt] *n* yate *m*; **y. club** club náutico

yachting ['jɒtɪŋ] *n Sport* navegación *f* a vela; (*competition*) regatas *fpl*

yachtsman ['jɒtsmən] *n* balandrista *m*

yachtswoman ['jɒtswʊmən] *n* balandrista *f*

yam [jæm] *n* (**a**) ñame *m* (**b**) *US* (*sweet potato*) boniato *m*, batata *f*, *Andes, CAm, Carib, Méx* camote *m*

Yank [jæŋk] *n Br Pej* yanqui *mf*

yank [jæŋk] *vt Fam* tirar; (*tooth*) arrancar

Yankee ['jæŋkɪ] *adj & n Pej* yanqui (*mf*)

yap [jæp] *vi* (*dog*) aullar; *Fam* (*person*) darle al pico

yard¹ [jɑːd] *n* (*measure*) yarda *f* (aprox 0,914 *m*)

yard² [jɑːd] *n* patio *m*; *US* jardín *m*

yardstick ['jɑːdstɪk] *n Fig* criterio *m*, norma *f*

yarn [jɑːn] *n* (**a**) *Sewing* hilo *m* (**b**) (*story*) historia *f*, cuento *m*; **to spin a y.** (*lie*) inventarse una historia

yawn [jɔːn] **1** *vi* bostezar
2 *n* bostezo *m*

yawning ['jɔːnɪŋ] *adj* (*gap*) profundo(a)

yd (*pl* **yds**) (*abbr* **yard**) yarda *f*

yeah [jeə] *adv Fam* sí

year [jɪə(r)] *n* (**a**) año *m*; **all y. round** durante todo el año; **last y.** el año pasado; **next y.** el año que viene; **y. in, y. out** año tras año; **I'm ten years old** tengo diez años (**b**) *Educ* curso *m*; **first-y. student** estudiante *mf* de primero

yearly ['jɪəlɪ] **1** *adj* anual
2 *adv* anualmente, cada año

yearn [jɜːn] *vi* **to y. for sth** anhelar algo

yearning ['jɜːnɪŋ] *n* anhelo *m* (**for** de)

yeast [jiːst] *n* levadura *f*

yell [jel] **1** *vi* gritar
2 *n* grito *m*, alarido *m*

yellow ['jeləʊ] **1** *adj* amarillo(a); *Fam Fig* (*cowardly*) cobarde; *Tel* **Y. Pages**® páginas amarillas
2 *n* amarillo *m*

yelp [jelp] **1** *vi* aullar
2 *n* aullido *m*

yen [jen] *n* (**a**) (*currency*) yen *m* (**b**) **to have a y. for sth** tener ganas de algo

yeoman ['jəʊmən] *n Br* **Y. of the Guard** = alabardero de la Casa Real británica

yes [jes] **1** *adv* sí; **you said y.** dijiste que sí
2 *n* sí *m*

yesterday ['jestədeɪ] *adv & n* ayer *m*; **the day before y.** anteayer; **y. morning** ayer por la mañana

yet [jet] **1** *adv* (**a**) **not y.** aún no, todavía no; **as y.** hasta ahora; **I haven't eaten y.** no he comido todavía (**b**) (*in questions*) ya; **has he arrived y.?** ¿ha venido ya? (**c**) (*even*) más; **y. again** otra vez; **y. more** todavía más (**d**) (*eventually*) todavía, aún; **he'll win y.** todavía puede ganar
2 *conj* sin embargo

yew [juː] *n* tejo *m*

yield [jiːld] **1** *n* (**a**) rendimiento *m* (**b**) *Agr* cosecha *f* (**c**) *Fin* beneficio *m*
2 *vt* producir; *Agr* dar; (*money*) producir
3 *vi* (**a**) (*surrender, break*) ceder (**b**) *US Aut* ceder el paso

YMCA [waɪemsiː'eɪ] *n* (*abbr* **Young Men's Christian Association**) ACJ *f*, Asociación *f* Cristiana de Jóvenes (*que regenta hostales económicos*)

yob(bo) ['jɒb(əʊ)] *n Fam* gamberro(a) *m,f*

yoga ['jəʊgə] *n* yoga *m*

yog(h)urt ['jɒgət] *n* yogur *m*

yoke [jəʊk] **1** *n* yugo *m*
2 *vt* (*oxen*) uncir; *Fig* unir

yokel ['jəʊkəl] *n Pej* paleto(a) *m,f*

yolk [jəʊk] *n* yema *f*

yonder ['jɒndə(r)] *adv* más allá

you [juː, *unstressed* jʊ] *pers pron* (**a**) (*subject*) (*usually omitted in Spanish, except for contrast*) (*familiar use*) (*singular*) tú; (*pl*) vosotros(as); **how are y.?** ¿cómo estás?, ¿cómo estáis?
(**b**) (*subject*) (*polite use*) (*singular*) usted; (*pl*) ustedes; **how are y.?** ¿cómo está?, ¿cómo están?
(**c**) (*subject*) (*impers use*) **y. never know** nunca se sabe
(**d**) (*object*) (*familiar use*) (*singular*) (*before verb*) te; (*after preposition*) ti; (*pl*) (*before verb*) os; (*after preposition*) vosotros(as); **I saw y.** te vi/os vi; **it's for y.** es para ti/es para vosotros(as); **with y.** contigo/con vosotros(as)